RADIOLOGY OF THE CHEST
AND
RELATED CONDITIONS

Saint Ansanus (Patron Saint of Siena and **Chest Diseases**) holding his **trachea, lungs, heart and liver in his right hand** – in allusion to his martyrdom – after Tiberio di Diotallevi, also called Tiberio d'Assisi (c. 1470-1524).

This fresco is reproduced by kind permission of The Barber Institute of Fine Arts, The University of Birmingham, where it has been since 1944.

Further details of Saint Ansanus and pictures of his life and death are given on the INFO SHEET with Illus. **ANSANUS** (see Illus. **Ansanus** a-g) in the main illustration collection.

[Regarding other saints in medicine:-
St. Luke is usually regarded as the patron saint of medicine – see Oxford Picts, **LINCOLN COLLEGE, St. Luke.**
St. Thomas should be regarded as the patron saint of radiology – **'seeing is believing'**.
St. Jude is often regarded as the patron saint of lost causes - ? of most patients with lung cancer, and many patients in the UK have worn the brand-label of St. Michael on their clothing!]

RADIOLOGY OF THE CHEST
AND
RELATED CONDITIONS

Together with an extensive illustrative collection of radiographs, conventional and computed tomograms, isotope studies, MRs, etc.on CD-ROM.
(Cross-platform for Mac and Windows version 3.1 or later)

Fred W Wright, MA, DM, FRCP, FRCR

Honorary Consulting Radiologist, Oxfordshire Health Authority (now Oxford Radcliffe Hospitals NHS Trust) and retired Clinical Lecturer, University of Oxford.
(Formerly Consultant Radiologist, United Oxford Hospitals)

London and New York

First published 2002
by Taylor and Francis
11 New Fetter Lane, London EC4P 4EE

Simultaneously published in the USA and Canada
by Taylor and Francis
29 West 35th Street, New York, NY 10001

Taylor and Francis is an imprint of the Taylor & Francis Group

Publisher's note
This book has been prepared from camera-ready copy provided by the author.

Printed and bound in Great Britain by TJ International Ltd, Padstow, Cornwall

British Library Cataloguing in Publication Data
A catalogue record for this book is available from the British Library

Library of Congress Cataloging in Publication Data
A catalog record has been requested.

ISBN 0-415-28141-5

Radiology of the Chest and Related Conditions - Fred. W. Wright.

Frontispiece.

Contents.

Preface and Introduction.

Collection information re main picture collection - (also included in Image AXS - Collection Information on CD-ROM).

KEYWORDS to illustrations in main picture collection on CD-ROM - **Dr FW Illus**.

Oxford Picture Collection + KEYWORDS (see also note below).

CD-ROM Licence Agreement and Information

Subject Index to Text pages.

References to the text and Illustrations of over 8,660 x ray etc. picture files are on the accompanying **CD-ROM**, together with browsers for Image AXS (in Mac & Windows versions) and Acrobat for the references (over 10,000 listed alphabetically) and a copy of the text .

For added interest and in response to colleagues in the USA 202 pictures of Oxford etc. are included as a second smaller Image AXS collection - **OXFORD Picts** (also with **Keywords** to colleges etc.) - further details are given in the Collection Info (with this collection) and in the **INFO sheets** with each illustration.

Acknowledgements are given with the main and Oxford Picts collection information notes, with Figures etc. in the text, or in the Info Sheets with the individual illustrations.

Instructions for using the CD-ROM are on the disc and after KEYWORDS in the book.

PREFACE and INTRODUCTION.

This volume and its accompanying CD-ROM have been produced as an individual and group teaching aid on the radiology of chest diseases for all who may be interested in the subject - viz. radiologists and chest physicians (especially those in training), medical students, technologists and radiographers. The CD-ROM is particularly valuable as a very compact source of over 8,660 teaching film files (about 12,000 images allowing for composites) which can easily be accessed through **KEYWORDS** - either in the special 'keywords' dictionary or given in the text in the **BOOK MANUAL** and then selecting images from those shown in the illustration collection, as large **'thumbnails'** on the monitor or via the list mode ('fields'). Each image has a description in its accompanying **INFO SHEET**. Image AXS browsers are provided for accessing the collection in both Macintosh & Windows (3.1 & '95 + later versions), and Acrobat 3.1 for accessing the copy of the text on the CD-ROM and the references.

The illustration collection is essentially the best of the teaching films which the author acquired over a 30 year period, supplemented by others which have been donated or lent by others to the author (see acknowledgements).

The images have mainly been scanned into an Apple-Mac computer via a high quality transparency scanner, edited in Photoshop 2.5, then compressed in JPEG, before being placed into the Image AXS authoring programme. The images have then had the titles, descriptions (on Info Sheets) etc. added, before being placed onto the Master CD-ROM in a format allowing the source files to be read in Mac or Windows. In these they can be viewed as large 'thumbnails' or larger images - with the option of a slide-show.

Thus all that is needed to view the CD-ROM is a disc drive (a 24X drive or faster will give quicker access) and either a Mac or Windows compatible viewer. 10 MB of RAM is advised, but the size of viewing monitor is not critical - however the larger the size of the monitor the more thumbnails can be seen at a time (e.g. 24 with a 17 inch monitor), and 'full images', larger enlargements, and Info Sheet displays are readily made.

The CD-ROM can be used with most desk-top or lap-top colour computers and via the latter with liquid crystal projectors (which are becoming increasingly popular for medical meetings) - these are best used in a small meeting room where good quality projections are readily made - in a large lecture theatre there may be a poorer quality of projection of chest radiographs, unless very powerful projection lamps are available.

The CD-ROM should prove invaluable to most radiology and chest departments (especially those that do not have the space for large teaching collections), post-graduate centres, and individuals. A large room housed the original radiographs, which progressively reduced in size to 20 optical discs, and finally with compression and the use of a Jazz disc to a single CD-ROM.

A few colour images of paintings, patients, specimens, etc. are included for interest. Most of the images have been made from the original radiographs, but a few images have been made from copy-films, 35mm slides or photographic prints. Whilst most of the images were digitised using a Hewlett Packard transparency scanner, a few initially were acquired via Kodak PhotoCD.

In 1956 when the author started in radiology, the only radiological methods of examining the chest were plain radiographs, direct fluoroscopy (with dark adaptation on a fluorescent screen) and conventional tomography. In 1961 he obtained a Transverse Axial Tomograph (essentially a radiographic precursor of CT, but which also allowed "inclined frontal tomography" of the trachea and larger bronchi, etc.). TV image intensification arrived 1966, and 'A' scan ultra-sound in 1968 (followed by compound 'B' scanning and later 'real-time'). CT came to the Churchill Hospital, Oxford in 1981, following local generosity in a public appeal. Following retirement in 1992 the author has tried to keep as 'up to date as possible', and has been very glad to receive further images for the collection from colleagues (see acknowledgements following collection notes and with some images). The CD-ROM has taken about five years to produce, and the book about ten years.

Regarding **the book**, its object is to review the appearances produced by thoracic disease processes. A thorough knowledge of the way these cause their radiographic appearances is of paramount importance in interpreting radiographs, as is a knowledge of the relevant anatomy, lung functions and alterations produced by physiological and pathological processes. Historical points of interest are also included.

References in the text are given in the following form:
(a) for single or two author(s) - the surnames followed by the year of publication and either the title of the article or book (often abbreviated) or a note giving the salient point(s) from it;
(b) for three or more authors - the first surname + 'et al.' and as in (a) above.
[The rationale for this is that the author prefers names to numbers, as used in the Harvard system]. In some cases an initial is added to the surname for clarity and in others 'a', 'b', etc. are placed after the year.

The alphabetical **reference list is on the CD-ROM,** and has not been printed as this would require very many pages adding considerably to the bulk and price of the work.

For convenience a **second copy of the text has been placed on the CD-ROM** - both this and the references can be viewed using the **ACROBAT browser.**

Image viewing - noting an abnormality is the first important step in chest radiological diagnosis. Not only does a radiologist have to be able to see these himself, but he has also to demonstrate them to others. Then follows the determination of the cause, probable pathology and diagnosis. Only a clear understanding of disease processes and their appearances is likely to ensure that the best is done for the patients. Many problems may be solved quickly, by plain radiographs, ultra-sound and e.g. the aspiration of a little pleural fluid, or a little tissue for cytology (if possible at a single out-patient visit). Not all patients need CT or MR examinations! Many just need more simple techniques applied, as a result of what is seen on plain radiographs + a judicious amount of good clinical expertise and judgement on the part of the radiologist.

Regarding **lung tumours**, the author published a volume entitled 'The Radiological Diagnosis of Lung and Mediastinal Tumours' in 1973, which was based on a historical review of the radiological literature and a personal experience of about 5,000 patients with lung and mediastinal tumours, who had been examined with plain films, tomography and bronchography. Since then he has seen about a further 12,000 cases, many of whom have been examined with CT, which has greatly helped in the understanding of disease processes affecting the thorax. It is at the present time superior to MR for examining the lungs, but the latter is overtaking it for the mediastinum. Other techniques which have improved immensely have been ultra-sound and isotopic studies.

We have come a long way since William Conrad Roentgen's discovery of X rays in Nov. 1895 (see Illus. **FAMOUS PEOPLE**, Roentgen - for a review of Roentgen's life, his discovery of x-rays and for early developments see Brailsford, 1946); he is reported to have given demonstrations in London and Birmingham a few weeks later. In April 1896 Sydney Rowland included a chest radiograph of a child in his Archives of Clinical Skiagraphy, commissioned by the British Medical Journal. Two chest radiographs, taken on Eastman paper and also published in Great Britain, appeared in '**Archives of the Roentgen Ray**' in July 1897; these were of a patient aged 68 years with presumptive cancer of the oesophagus and a child aged 5 with tuberculosis. Walsham and Orton (1906) from St Bartholomew's and the National Heart Hospitals published a book '**The Roentgen Rays in the Diagnosis of Diseases of the Chest**' with eighteen illustrations.

In the USA, Williams in Boston, Mass. began looking at the chest with **fluoroscopy** in the spring of 1896 and used the method for studying the heart and for the detection of tuberculosis or other life-threatening disorders, and by the summer of that year had collected 100 volumes of tracings from his observations. In April 1896, he noted an 'air bronchogram' in a patient with pneumonia (See Greene, 1992 and Nath, 1993). At that time it could take an exposure time of several minutes even for a child's chest (Jupe, 1961 quoted 30 minutes). Hickey (from Detroit, 1905) gave a paper to the American Roentgen Ray Society in 1904 - 'The interpretation of radiographs of the chest', in which he advocated 'short exposures' of 1 to 2 seconds, especially for the diagnosis of tuberculosis. He noted that the right side of the diaphragm was l to 2 ins higher than the left, and that its outline was lost with effusions, etc. He determined that the radiating shadows from the hila were mainly vascular (and not bronchial) by filling the vessels in cadavers with bismuth and glycerine or lead solutions or paste prior to radiography. He concluded that chest radiography "is destined through future study and experiment to yield conclusions which will be still more valuable!"

Diagnostic radiology now provides the "eyes of medicine" in detecting lesions in the chest, particularly if serious disease is present or suspected. Miniature radiographs taken by photofluorography have almost ceased to be used, because of their relatively high radiation dose. Fast radiographic screens, image intensification and digital radiography are now becoming more developed and increasingly used.

The standard of plain chest radiography and its interpretation has undoubtedly improved over the past 20 to 30 years. Its limitations are now better understood, but greater attention to detail can still improve its diagnostic accuracy, however it is surprising that some chest radiographs and conventional tomograms continue to be poorly taken. Digital chest radiography e.g. with Amber or Thoravision is greatly helping in the detection of disease. However even with these techniques some fine lesions are still not seen except with HRCT, so a good index of suspicion is still of paramount importance.

Radiology departments now are generally well equipped to further investigate patients with chest abnormalities, with ultrasound for the detection of pleural or pericardial fluid, masses adjacent to the chest wall, enlarged nodes in certain situations etc., liver abnormalities, adrenal masses, etc. Many patients can have simple biopsies done as out patients, under such guidance. Larger departments may have CT, MR and/or facilities for isotope studies particularly for studying the skeleton. A few radiologists carry out fibre-optic bronchoscopy, but in the UK most are done by chest physicians; similarly mediastinoscopy is usually only done by thoracic surgeons. Diagnostic or exploratory thoracotomies for patients with tumours should no longer be routine, as only about 5-10% of lung cancer patients will prove to be operable, and an exploratory thoracotomy not only costs a great deal of money but also causes the patient considerable disability. Thoracoscopy and 'VATS' have some advantages for studying the pleura and the surface of the lungs and are starting to be done by radiologists.

High Resolution Computed Tomography (HRCT) has shown pathology that may not be visible on plain radiographs, and has greatly improved our understanding of the finer anatomy of chest disease. In interstitial lung disease HRCT may obviate the necessity for biopsy. However in assessing nodal involvement by tumours, HRCT can be relatively insensitive as even small nodes may contain tumour deposits and large nodes may be entirely reactive. Also some early lung changes may be invisible even on HRCT sections. **Spiral CT** is making 3D reconstructions of the tracheo-bronchial tree, and vessels readily available; it is also making examinations quicker and less likely to 'miss' lesions in between sections, by its ability to achieve all the basic data in a single breath-hold (e.g. 10 secs). Spiral CT is also becoming a popular and easy way of diagnosing most pulmonary emboli, and may become be the best method of excluding embolism in the future. **Multislice** apparatus and **CT fluoroscopy** are also becoming available.

However the effect of CT on patient management should always be considered, including its radiation dosage as it has become one of the largest contributors to that received by the population in some countries. CT examinations should also be regarded as part of the diagnostic armamentarium and not "stand-alone-tests". Their value is greatest where they affect clinical decisions, particular treatment regimens, and in resolving uncertainty about diagnosis, the extent of disease or the prognosis.

Conventional tomography of the chest still has a place for showing if inflammatory disease, or even a tumour, are present. Often a conventional tomogram will show calcification within an old TB lesion, or a typical air bronchogram with consolidation, the patency of major bronchi, etc. Conventional (and inclined frontal) tomograms were better than sequential axial CT sections for showing the longitudinal anatomy of the airways, but as noted above '3D' reconstructions with **spiral CT** can now show this. Conventional tomograms are also available most of the time in radiology departments, and do not tend to be as 'fully booked' as CT, so a quick answer to a simple question may still be obtained using them.

Very few positive contrast **bronchograms** are now carried out, but the author has included examples of them (as well as inclined frontal tomograms and a set of '3D' reconstructions) on the CD-ROM for comparison and for reference, which seem relevant now that CT '3D bronchography' has produced considerable interest.

Magnetic resonance imaging (MRI) is not available yet in all centres for examining the chest, but the number of machines has greatly increased over the past few years. It has the advantage of not causing any radiation hazard and of portraying images in several planes. It is good for showing the mediastinum, heart and major vessels, but generally gives poorer lung detail. However with increased speed and newer sequences it is portraying some features of lung disease. Nodal enlargements may be seen as with CT. With the use of some sequences, such as STIR, some tissue characterisation is becoming possible in the differentiation of tumour from benign disease. Time of flight and other sequences are showing vascular anatomy and physiological processes more clearly, and even pulmonary emboli are beginning to be shown directly using their methaemoglobin content.

Some historical quotations.

In 1898 William Osler (then Regius Professor of Medicine in Oxford - see OXFORD Picts - **Osler**) wrote "in the majority of cases, the x-rays tell us no more than a careful clinical examination." (See also under OXFORD Picts - **Nuffield 1** for Oxford's former regard for radiology).

In 1918 F. Barjon wrote "Radiological examination shows on the screen or plate only lines and shadows - black and white. It shows the forms, extent, location, degree of opacity.... It gives no information of their nature, their anatomical value or development... The physician ought to become interested in radiology. If the radiologist ought to be a physician, it would be well also for the physician to be, in a less degree, a radiologist."

Radiological interpretaion and images have clearly come a long way in the past 105 years since Roentgen's discovery!

A note re radiological reports.
Göthlin (1999) from Gothenburg, Sweden called for more responsible reporting and quoted Olle Olsson of Lund that radiological reports should be short and end with a definite diagnosis; only in special cases should a differential diagnosis be offered, unclear reports causing confusion, repeat examinations and new investigations. Göthlin pointed out that indecisiveness can be more of a threat than a missed diagnosis, common findings being too much information re old TB scars, age related changes, technical details and overdoing the differential diagnosis. He also quoted from Brendan Francis in Roget's International Thesaurus that "Some persons are very decisive when it comes to avoiding decisions."

If this volume and CD-ROM helps to achieve some improvement in diagnostic accuracy the author will be very pleased.

Some further references (see also p. 1.59).
Bergonie (1896) : New fluoroscopic findings of intrathoracic lesions.
Bouchard (1896) : Radioscopy in the diagnosis of heart disease.
Wright (1973) : Radiology of Lung and Mediastinal Tumours (showed many illustrations of inclined frontal tomograms).
Hansell (1997) : Thoracic imaging - then and now.
Stender et al. (1997) : Evolution of x-ray applications 1895 - 1995.

SOME NOTES ABOUT THE MAIN IMAGE COLLECTION - FWW Illus - in IMAGE AXS (Mac - 2.0d & Windows - 2.5) + ACKNOWLEDGEMENTS.

These notes also appear in the 'collection info' in the main illustration collection (book images) on the CD-ROM, entitled FWW Illus.

The main illustration collection comprises over 12,000 images which are contained in 8,666 picture files. Many of the files are composites (particularly CTs, some PA and lateral views, MRs, etc.). Most are thoracic or related radiological images, but some clinical colour illustrations are included, as well as a few art reproductions to illustrate certain points.

The main collection of images has been largely made from radiographs etc., collected by the author since he started radiology in 1956. He worked nearly all the time in Oxford (mainly at the Churchill Hospital and in close collaboration with the Chest Physicians, Thoracic Surgeons and Radiotherapists). He kept some original films, copies, slides, etc. of interesting cases that he saw, which were used for teaching purposes with medical students and postgraduates. A few images came from Sweden, and from the Henry Ford Hospital in Detroit (where he worked for a short period in the mid 1960s, and which he again visited in early 1999). A few images have come from Worthing, where the author held locum appointments, following his retirement in Oxford in 1992.

Other images have been kindly loaned for reproduction by colleagues, former registrars or friends. The author is particularly indebted to all those who have helped in many ways - especially the radiographers, the secretaries and other staff at the Churchill Hospital, and to the Local Public who subscribed to purchase the first CT scanner at the Churchill in 1980. See also further acknowledgements below and with many of the relevant images.

Most of the images have been scanned in from original radiographs or copy films, but some have been made from prints or slides (see also Preface and Introduction).

The illustrations are in two types of file:

(i) **Image AXS** files in both MAC and Windows formats - these give access to the source files, and those to be viewed should first be selected using a **KEYWORD** selection (under heading **BROWSE** - Mac) - for Windows use **BROWSE or the binoculars+key button** (3rd from right).

Full images of each of these can then be accessed as in (a), (b) or (c) - below - or after making a selection using **FULL IMAGE** under the heading **WINDOW** [Mac] or **SOURCE IMAGE** under the heading **VIEW** or the 6th button from the left [Windows].

The author advises viewing both **FULL IMAGES** and the **thumbnails** with a **light grey background** - black is too harsh for most people (see **preferences** under **EDIT** in both Mac & Windows if a change is desired).

(ii) **Source files** in Mac version of Photoshop 2.5 (compressed with JPEG) - these are mainly at 100 pixels per inch, which is the resolution of most computer monitor display screens and this resolution and file sizes allow nearly 8,900 images to be accommodated on this single CD-ROM disc. These are named according to the Windows (3.1) notation - i.e. 8 characters, including letters giving an abbreviated subject followed by a number indicating a patient and finally a letter to indicate the views included of each individual patient. - e.g. ABNDS10a - d (+ suffix .JPG).

[To determine where a source file is stored: - click and hold on the miniature CD player to the left of the image title under each image (Mac) or double-click on the similar CD player or last button on the right (Windows)]

The **Image AXS files** can be accessed in **three ways**:
(a) By the large size "**thumbnails**" - compressed preview images - (each about 5.5 cm^2 or 128 pixels^2) - these are 24-bit compressed images which can be accessed in either the MAC or Windows modes.
 [In Windows use the large format for "**thumbnails**" or the titles may be incomplete.]

Double clicking on a thumbnail image will access the **SOURCE FILE** image, which itself can be magnified or minified.

Single clicking will make a thumbnail active, and multiple images can be made active if the pointer is passed across the desired images, whilst holding down the **command key** (MAC) or clicking on individual images whilst holding down the **control key** (**Ctrl** with some PCs using Windows). The active state is indicated by a red box around the image(s).

(b) From the "**list view**" (to the right of the thumbnails button and above the numbers - Mac) or **"Text list"** (Windows - 3rd button from left) mode which gives file names, image titles, and the main + other features of each of the images. Single or multiple image files can be made active in a similar manner as with thumbnails. In this mode also clicking on an image file and then clicking on a later file whilst holding down the shift key will select those in between as well. Further images can also be selected by holding down the command key (MAC) or control key (**Ctrl** with Windows as above) and clicking on the desired files.

The **list view** can be a quicker way of selecting items (via the title names or features listed in the columns) than by using thumbnails from some fairly large selections made using the keywords.

(c) From "**Info sheets**" for each image - '**Info**' button (Mac) or 4th button from L (Windows) - these give some clinical history and relevant clinical details plus a **short description** of the image displayed. Each sheet also contains a "**thumbnail**", which can be used (by clicking on it) to access the **FULL IMAGE** (MAC) or double-clicking (Windows).

The author strongly advises viewing the images via the info sheets, as in this way the information about them can be noted and the FULL IMAGE can then be viewed by clicking (or double-clicking) on the small image or thumbnail on each info sheet. Thus after making a selection via a KEYWORD and sorting (if required) the information with each image is readily seen.

(Avoid routinely using other search parameters except perhaps of the items in the active window as these will usually waste much time - see below)

KEYWORDS

The **KEYWORD list** is given in the following section (or under Keywords on the disc).

Each **KEYWORD** includes **selections** across the whole collection .

The relevant **KEYWORDS** are indicated with each relevant part of the book text (each reference to them being preceded by Illus. in the text).

Thus using **KEYWORDS** it is then an easy matter to select the appropriate **images corresponding to the section of the book text being studied.**

Sorting - the images have already been sorted by file names, not titles per se, so the need for sorting should not be great after selecting images via a **KEYWORD**.

However to sort the images in the active window first **SELECT ALL** (under **EDIT -** both Mac & Windows) then use the **SORT** button (Mac) or 2nd button from right (Windows) - alternatively

Sort under **BROWSE** (Mac & Windows) - to place the **selected   images** in order in both list and 'thumbnail' modes.

[**SHOW ALL** will place the whole collection into the active window].

Providing that the column titles in the list mode have not been altered by the reader, sorting will then be made from the **TITLES** placed under each image (as also shown in the **List   Mode**). These **TITLES** largely correspond to the Source File names (with Windows 3.1 notations - see above). To help these appear in numerical order, the numbers with each title have been arranged with single figure numbers slightly staggered in relation to double figure numbers - to avoid the computer sorting them into an alpha-numeric sequence.

Slide-shows of multiple full-sized images - obtained via Keywords - or by individual selections can be made: -
Mac - under the Browse Command - select e.g. Whorled Nodules from Keywords, then **SELECT ALL** (under **EDIT**) and then Slide Show under **BROWSE**. In Slide-show only the file names (in Windows 3.1 notation) will be seen with each image. The number of images selected and images shown also appears.

Windows - Slide-show is under **BROWSE**, and adjustments may be made in the dialogue box. In Windows it is important to select thumbnails or full images (6th button from left) as the slide show option can be used with both.

The file names (not titles) can be seen with both MAC and Windows versions in the full image slide-show mode.

Searches can also be made of every word in the descriptions, titles and features under Search in **BROWSE** Command (or with the button showing **binoculars**   - 4th from right), but this can be slow and quite time-consuming even with a fast computer.
Because of this the use of Keywords is recommended and is to be preferred for routine use.

COMPUTER - either a Mac or Windows compatible computer with over 15 MB (or better 32 MB) of RAM is advised.

CD-ROM DRIVE - one with a high access speed is recommended to facilitate the computer sorting through the data base. With slower speed drives, access and sorting may be slower.

In PCs using Windows the CD-ROM drive will frequently be labelled C, D, E or F.
(A few computers connected to server systems with the CD-ROM disc drive labelled Z may have problems with the source files appearing "off line" as indicated by red 'Xs' at the bases of the thumbnails - this may be corrected by relabelling the CD-ROM drive server to the slave viewer stations, and reconfiguring the 'neighbourhood drive' in the controlling computer.)
The CD-ROM should work with all letters up to Y.

MONITOR - the size of viewing monitor is not critical but the larger its size the more thumbnails can be seen at a time (e.g. 24 with a 17 inch monitor), and 'full images', larger enlargements, and Info-sheet displays are readily made. With small monitors only six thumbnails may be seen at a time. A 17 inch (or larger) monitor is ideal because the text can then be displayed simultaneously on the left side of the monitor, and the illustrations on the right side.

The CD-ROM can also be used with most **lap-top colour computers** and also with **liquid crystal projectors** (which are becoming increasingly popular for medical meetings) - these are best used with a relatively short projection distance when good quality projections are readily made - with longer projection distances there may be a poorer quality of projection of chest radiographs, unless very powerful projection lamps are available.

The CD-ROM should prove invaluable to most radiology and chest departments, post-graduate centres, and individuals. Many departments do not have the space for large teaching collections.

A large room housed the original radiographs, which progressive reduced in size to 20 optical discs, and finally with compression and editing to a single CD-ROM.

Nearly all of the images were digitised using a HP transparency scanner directly from the radiographs, CT hard-copy images, etc. a few earlier ones being obtained via 35mm film and Kodak PhotoCD. The text has been prepared over a period of about ten years, and the illustration collection has taken five years to complete, nearly all of this at home. The computer work has been done using an Apple Mac computer with System 7 and using Photoshop 2.5 + the Mac version of Image AXS 2. Transmission to the PC version of Image AXS and the making of the master CD-ROM was done by Mr. M. Laye (see below under Acknowledgements).

The scanning, editing, combination of images, and the annotations have taken a very great deal of time. The author hopes that by doing this himself he has been able to get the images to show their relevant points to the best advantage. In doing this himself he has had to work the images into the 650 MB of a standard CD-ROM. Trial and error suggested that if 200 to 800K images were compressed to 40 to 100K acceptable images could be reproduced which would allow 2 to 4 times magnification. To obtain higher magnification would have required much larger files - this might have been possible with a super CD-ROM, or DVD but these were not then available. It also seemed to be most appropriate if all the illustrations etc. could be placed on a single CD-ROM disc.

In the collection, it will be noted that as well as CTs, MRs etc., the author has included many images made with IFTs (inclined frontal tomograms) and bronchograms, although these last techniques are now not commonly employed. He makes no apology for this, as these are still invaluable for showing and understanding pathological anatomy. Such images are very useful in helping to understand similar anatomical displays made from spiral CT - viz. 3D virtual bronchographic displays etc. which are being produced in some centres.

Copying of images and description of images in the main and the Oxford Picture Collections.

The images on this CD-ROM are copyright to Taylor and Francis Publishers, 11 New Fetter Lane, London EC4P 4EE, UK, and 29 West 35th Street, New York, NY 10001, USA, and the author (Dr F W Wright, Eynsham, Oxford, OX29 4LH), or to those acknowledged who have given permission for their images to be included.

None may be copied without permission for commercial or publishing use, i.e. without consent in writing from the above.

To make copies of images* (for personal use only) this can be done by copying the individual source files into an authoring programme, either from the FULL IMAGES or directly from the individual source files (found within each of the source folders).

(* By special arrangement with the author some individual images may be supplied at higher resolution.)

Similarly the descriptions of the images may be copied for personal use but not for commercial or publishing use without consent in writing from the above.

BRIEF NOTES RE TEXT & REFERENCES ON THE CD-ROM.

The text and references (completed over a period of about 10 years) have been produced using Microsoft Word (version 5.0), converted to Acrobat 3.01 for the CD ROM.

Access to the **text** and **reference** files is made via the folders on the CD-ROM in both MAC and Windows.

When reading the text on the CD-ROM please only use the **Acrobat browser provided - version 3.1 - or higher reader**, as the 2.1 version tends to break-up the line drawings into dots and dashes. Most of the drawings have been made by the author, edited and converted first to Word 5.0. Others have been copied or adapted with permission which is gratefully acknowledged with each of the relevant drawings, etc.

The references are given in full and in alphabetical order in the reference list, but are only in abbreviated form in the text, with a note of the relevant or salient point(s) from each and not necessarily the titles - see also p. ii of Preface.

Note also Acrobat Reader copyright statement:

The license agreement for Image AXS is to be found under Read Me.

ACKNOWLEDGEMENTS for advice or help given, and for loans of radiographs, etc.:

Barber Institute, University of Birmingham for photographing the fresco of St. Ansanus - Patron Saint of Chest Diseases, who holds his trachea, lungs, heart and liver in his right hand.
Dr. Laurie B. Brock, Liverpool (now deceased) for help with photography.
Prof. J. Carmichael, formerly Consultant Oncologist, Oxford, now in Nottingham.
Dr. Mark. Charig, Wexham Park. Hospital, Slough (formerly in Oxford).
Dr. M.D. Crane, Llandough, S. Wales.
Dr. T. Creasey, Bournemouth (formerly in Oxford).
Dr. Anne Davies, Barnet General Hospital, London.
Dr. M. Dunnill, formerly Pathologist, John Radcliffe Hospital, Oxford.
Dr. W.R. Eyler, Henry Ford Hospital, Detroit, Michigan, USA for giving the author a film-reel of interesting cases and for other advice and help.
Dr. T. Faulkner (formerly in Oxford) and now in Norway for supplying pictures of Prof. Frimann-Dahl.
Dr. Charles Fletcher of ASH for help with Chapter 24a.
Dr. Joy Fowler, formerly at Frenchay Hospital, Bristol.
Prof. Paul. Goddard, formerly at Bristol Royal Infirmary and now Professor of Radiology at University of West of England (for providing several of the MRs and advice).
Dr. D. Hall, Worthing for allowing me to copy some of the radiographs.
Dr. Anne Hubbard, Consultant Radiologist, formerly in Worthing, now at Kingston upon Hull.
Dr. A.W.L Leung, formerly at Paul Strickland Scanner Centre, Mount Vernon Hospital, Northwood, Middx, now in Penrith, NSW, Australia,. for some of the MR images.
Sir Thomas Lodge, Brighton and formerly in Sheffield (now deceased).
Dr. G. Mayall, Exeter (formerly in Oxford).
Prof. E.N.C. Milne (now in Scotland) for help with Chapter 8.
Dr. D. Nag, Kingston-upon-Hull, (formerly in Oxford).
Prof. Martine Rémy-Jardin, Lille, France for providing spiral CTs.
Prof. L.G. Rigler (now deceased) of Minneapolis and Los Angeles.

Dr. H. Westbury, formerly at Harefield Hospital, Uxbridge, Middx.
Prof. A. G. Wilson, St. George's, Hospital, London
Mr. A. Gunning and Mr. S. Westaby, Cardio-Thoracic Surgeons, Oxford.
Dr. M. Benson, Chest Physician, Churchill Hospital, Oxford.
Dr. W.S. Hamilton, Chest Physician, Churchill Hospital, Oxford (now deceased).
Prof. J. Hopkin, formerly Chest Physician, Churchill Hospital, Oxford and now in Swansea.
Dr. D. Lane, formerly Chest Physician, Churchill Hospital, Oxford.
Dr. J. Stradling, Chest Physician, Churchill Hospital, Oxford.
Dr. A. Laing, Oncologist and Radiotherapist, Churchill Hospital, Oxford.
Prof. P. Sleight, formerly Cardiologist, John Radcliffe Hospital, Oxford.
Dr. D. Oliver, Renal Unit, Churchill Hospital, Oxford (now deceased).
Dr. F. Gleeson, Dr. N. Cowan, Dr. Zoe Traill and Dr. C. Woodham, Radiologists, Churchill and John Radcliffe Hospitals, Oxford.

Mrs. Pat. Moran (my Secretary for over 20 years) for typing an early version of the manuscript.

Mrs. Sue Poulter, Secretary, Chest Clinic, Churchill Hospital for help with clinical records (to check the information given with several of the descriptions).

Eastman Kodak Company, Kodak Pathé and Mr. Bruce Brown, Kodak Ltd. for permission to reproduce or adapt diagrams and for early help with PhotoCD and other advice.

Mr. Terry Cooke, formerly of IGE Ltd. for arranging the purchase of the original 8800 CT apparatus and radiotherapy planner.

Oxford Medical Illustration at the John Radcliffe Hospital, for help with some drawings, reproductions and advice.

The radiographers at the Churchill Hospital, Oxford for producing most of the medical images.

The author is also greatly indebted to the generosity of local people in raising money for the first body type CT scanner in Oxford - installed at the Churchill Hospital in 1981- see also Preface and **Illus. APPARATUS, IGE 8800** in main picture collection and **OXFORD PICTS, scanner appeal**. Following its installation many very interesting patients were referred by colleagues in other hospitals in the Oxford Region and beyond, and some of these are illustrated on the CD-ROM disc.

Many other people and colleagues have also helped with advice and loans of radiographs, photographs etc. and permissions to reproduce or adapt drawings, etc. - see further acknowledgements included within the Text and in the Info-sheets with the illustrations.

Acknowledgements re the Oxford pictures appear with the Oxford Picture Collection and notes.

Mr. Mike Laye, image-access.net, 9 - 12, Middle Street, Brighton BN1 1AL (Email: mail@image-access.net) for most invaluable help with making the CD-ROM (+ prototypes for demonstration purposes) - see also file 'Read me too'.

Finally I have to thank my wife Lilian Wright for her forbearance during the long preparation of this work.

Fred. W. Wright.

COLLECTION OF 203 OXFORD PICTURES.

When the author visited the USA in March 1999, he showed Dr. Bill Eyler and his colleagues at the Henry Ford Hospital in Detroit, a prototype of this CD-ROM + some slides of Oxford.

The author is greatly indebted to them for helpful suggestions, including one that a smaller collection of views of Oxford be included on this CD-ROM for added interest and to give some flavour of Oxford to those who have not visited the city, its environs or university. [The author went up to Lincoln College in 1948, and later became a member of the Senior Common Room.]

202 images (+ an explanatory diagram of Green College sundial) are so included in this further collection. Many have been taken over several years by the author, and have been scanned-in from slides or prints. Others have been kindly loaned by friends and former members of the staff of the Radiology Dept. of the Churchill Hospital.

Acknowledgement is also made to the following for help or for permission to reproduce pictures:

Oxford University - Bodleian Library - Summer Eights - 1; Ashmolean Library - Watercolour of Dodo, University Museum of Natural History - Dinosaur.

Rev. Vivian H.H. Green, D.D. (formerly Rector of Lincoln College) and Thomas-Photos, Oxford (J.W. Thomas, MA, ARPS - Obiit Jan. 2000 and Paul Lucas) - illustrations from booklets on Lincoln College and John Wesley in Oxford and from other photographs in their collection.

Norman Hayes - watercolour of Eynsham.

Oxford Medical School Gazette - wall plaque of Osler and Osler Medal.

Oxford Picture Library and Chris Andrews - three pictures of Oxford Spires including two from the 'Oxford Scene' and some pictures of Blenheim.

Oxford Photo Library and Chris Donoghue - Summer Eights 2 and Oriel College.

Oxford Mail - aerial view of John Radcliffe Hospital & front of hospital; Plaque to Lord Nuffield (William Morris); Sir Richard Doll - photograph; Magdalen College Choir on Magdalen Tower.

As with the main collection, the Oxford pictures are grouped under KEYWORDS as follows:

AERIAL VIEWS	GARGOYLES	QUEEN'S COLLEGE
ALL SOULS	GREEN COLLEGE	RADCLIFFE CAMERA
ASHMOLEAN MUSEUM	HERTFORD	RADCLIFFE INFIRMARY
BALLIOL	HIGH STREET	RADCLIFFE JOHN
BLENHEIM & CHURCHILL	JAMES 1	RADCLIFFE OBSERVATORY
BODLEIAN LIBRARY	JESUS COLLEGE	RANDOLPH HOTEL
BOTANIC GARDEN	JOHN RADCLIFFE HOSP	RHODES HOUSE
BRASENOSE	KEBLE	RIVER CHERWELL
BROAD STREET	LIBRARIES	RIVER THAMES
CARFAX	LINCOLN COLLEGE	SCANNER APPEAL
CHRIST CHURCH	MAGDALEN	SHELDONIAN
CHURCHILL HOSPITAL	MAGNET FACTORY	ST EDMUND HALL
CITY WALL	MARTYRS MEMORIAL	ST MARY'S
CLARENDON BUILDING	MERTON	TOWER OF WINDS
CORNMARKET	NEW COLLEGE	TURL STREET
CORPUS CHRISTI	NUFFIELD	UNIV MUSEUM
ENCAENIA+HON DEGREESOLD OXFORD		UNIV PARKS
EXETER	ORIEL	UNIVERSITY COLLEGE
EYNSHAM	OXFORD CRESTS	WADHAM
FAMOUS PEOPLE	PUBS	WORCESTER

ABD SWELLING CA LUNG	AORTA PSEUDOCOARCTATION	BLASTOMA
ABDOMINAL NODES	AORTA R DESC	BLASTOMYCOSIS
ABSCESS	AORTA RING	BLEOMYCIN
ACANTHOSIS NIGRICANS	AORTA RUPTURE	BLOCKED BRONCHUS
ACCESSORY FISSURE	AORTA SPURIOUS DISSECT	BLOOD ETC
ACHALASIA	AORTA SYPHILIS	BN&MAL CAL NODS/NDS
ACHALASIA+ NEO	AORTA TORTUOUS	BOCHDALEK HERNIA
ACHONDROPLASIA	AORTA TRAUMA	BOERHAAVE'S SYNDROME
ACROMIO-CLAV JOINTS	AORTIC ARCH ANEURYSM	BOILER-SCALER
ACTINOMYCOSIS	AORTIC BODY TUMOUR	BONE DEPOSITS 1
ACUTE BRONCHIOLITIS	AORTIC NIPPLE	BONE DEPOSITS 2
ADDISON'S DISEASE	AORTIC VALVE	BONE DEPS CT
ADENOCA	AORTOGRAM	BONE DEPS LIMBS
ADENOMAS	AP WINDOW	BONE DEPS SCLEROTIC
ADRENAL CALCIFICATION	AP WINDOW NODES	BONE INFECTION NOT TB
ADRENAL DEPOSIT	APICAL CA	BONE ISLAND
ADRENAL FALSE TUMOUR	APICAL FAT PADS	BONE MISC
ADRENAL TUMOUR	APICAL HAEMATOMA	BONE SARCOMA
ADRENALS	APICAL MASS VASCULITIS	BONE SCAN 1
AIDS	APICAL PL THICKNG	BONE SCAN 2
AIR BRON IN CA	APLASIA/HYPOPLASIA	BONE SCAN-GROSS DEPS
AIR BRONCHOGRAM	APPARATUS/TECHNIQUE	BONE SCAN-NEG DEFECT
AIR CRESCENT SIGN	ARDS	BONE SCAN-SUPERSCAN
AIR TRAPPING	ARM & FOREARM	BONE SCAN-TUM UPTAKE
ALBERT EXHIBITION	ARM LYMPHOGRAM	BONE SCLEROSIS
ALCAPTONURIA	ARM STUMP	BOOP/COP
ALCOHOL	ARTEFACT	BOWEL DISPLACEMENT
ALLERGIC ALVEOLITIS	ASB LUNG FIBROSIS	BOWEL OBSTRUCTION
ALV ADENOMA	ASB PLEURAL PLQS	BOXER
ALV CELL CA	ASB PLEURISY+PL THICKNG	BRACHIAL PLEXUS
ALV CELL CA SURVIVAL	ASB WHITE LINE	BRAIN & SKULL
ALV CELL CA+CAVITATION	ASB WHORLED NODS	BRAIN DEPS
ALV CELL CA+SARCOID	ASBESTOS	BRANCHIAL CYST
ALVEOLAR PROTEINOSIS	ASCARIS	BREAST
ALVEOLAR ROSETTE	ASCITES	BREAST CA
AMBER	ASKIN TUMOUR	BREAST RT
AMIODARONE	ASPERGILLOSIS	BREAST SARCOMA
AMOEBIC ABSCESS	ASTHMA	BREAST- IMPLANT
AMYLOID	ATYP MYCOBACT	BREAST- NIPPPLE
ANATOMY	AV ANEURYSM/FISTULAE	BREAST- NIPPPLE SPURIOUS
ANGEL WINGS	AVIUM-INTRACELLULARE	BREASTS - ELEVATED
ANGIOMA	AXILLA	BRON&INTERCOST ARTERIES
ANGIOMA OF RIB	AXILLA HAEMATOMA	BRON&MED CYSTS
ANKYLOSING SPONDYLITIS	AXILLARY ARTERY	BRON-PL FISTULA
ANOREXIA NERVOSA	AXILLARY NODES	BRONCH-MIMOSA
ANSANUS	AZ LB+VN	BRONCHI COMPRESSED
ANT MED MASS	AZ PTR NODES	BRONCHI MISC
ANT MED NODES	AZATHIOPRINE	BRONCHIAL ARTERIOGRAM
ANTHRACITE	AZYGOS NODES	BRONCHIAL BUD
AORTA	AZYGOS VEIN	BRONCHIAL CALC
AORTA 'DOUBLE ARCH'		BRONCHIAL EMBOLUS
AORTA ANEURYSM		BRONCHIAL FB
AORTA ANGIO ISOTOPE	B COLI	BRONCHIAL LAVAGE
AORTA ARCH RIGHT	BAT'S WING	BRONCHIAL PAPILLOMA
AORTA ASCENDING	BCG-OSIS	BRONCHIAL RINGS
AORTA ATHEROMA	BENIGN NODULE	BRONCHIAL TEAR
AORTA CALCIFICATION	BERYLLIUM	BRONCHIECTASIS
AORTA COARCTATION	BILHARZIA	BRONCHIECT. FOLLICULARIS
AORTA DISSECTION	BIOPSY/ASPIRATION	BRONCHIECTASIS REVERSIBLE
AORTA DOUBLE LUMEN	BIRD ALLERGY	BRONCHIECTASIS+MYCET
AORTA FALSE LUMEN	BISMUTH ETC. DEPOSITS	BRONCHIOLITIS
AORTA INTIMAL FLAP	BLADDER CA	BRONCHITIS
AORTA MARFAN	BLALOCK OPERATION	BRONCHOGENIC CYST

BRONCHOGRAM
BRONCHOGRAM NORMAL
BRONCHOGRAM-BRCTSIS
BRONCHOGRAM-CARCINOID
BRONCHOLITH
BRONCHOPNEUMONIA
BRONCHOSCOPY
BRONCHUS BLOCKED
BRONCHUS DEV ABN
BRONCHUS NARROWED
BRONCHUS SIGN
BRONCHUS STRETCHED
BRONCHUS STRICTURE
BRUCELLOSIS
BULLAE/CYSTS
BUSULPHAN

CA ADENO
CA ADJ AORTA
CA ADJ CX WALL
CA ADJ FISSURE
CA ADJ PULM VEIN
CA ADJ SPINE
CA ADJ SVC/AZY VEIN
CA ANAPLASTIC
CA APEX LLL
CA APEX RLL
CA BILAT & MULT
CA CARDIA
CA CARINA
CA CAVITATION
CA COLON
CA DEP IN THYROID
CA ENDOBRONCHIAL
CA EXT CX WALL
CA EXT HILUM
CA EXT MEDIAST
CA HILUM
CA INT BRONCHUS
CA KIDNEY AND DEPOSITS
CA L HILUM
CA L LUNG
CA LARYNX
CA LINGULA
CA LLL
CA LMB
CA LOBULATED
CA LUL
CA LUNG INV PLEURA
CA LUNG MISC
CA LUNG MISC EFFECTS
CA LUNG MISSED
CA LUNG SNOWSTORM DEPS
CA LUNG YOUNG PT
CA LUNG+ASBESTOS
CA LUNG+OES INVOLVEMENT
CA MILIARY
CA MIMICKING INFECTION
CA MULT
CA OAT-LUNG
CA OVARY
CA PANCOAST

CA POORLY DIFFERENTIATED
CA R HILUM
CA R LUNG
CA RECURRENT
CA RLL
CA RMB
CA RML
CA RUL
CA SCAR
CA SHAPES
CA SPOUSES
CA SQUAMOUS
CA SURVIVAL&PROGRESSION
CA T1&TX
CA TRACH/CARINA
CA&AORTA ETC.
CA+AIR BRONCHOGRAM
CA+BRONCHIECTASIS
CA+BRONCHOGRAM
CA+BULLAE, CYSTS ETC
CA+CALC
CA+CONGESTION
CA+CONSOLIDATION
CA+FUNGUS
CA+PULM VESSELS
CA+RECURRENT PN
CA+SARCOID
CA+TB
CAFFEY'S DISEASE
CALC IN ADENOMA
CALC IN BRONCHI
CALC IN LUNG DEPOSIT
CALC IN MUSCLES
CALC IN NODES
CALC IN TUMOURS/DEPS
CALC LG NODULES
CALC LUNG FOCI/SCARS
CALC MILIARY
CALC MYOCARDIUM
CALCIFICATION
CAPLAN'S SYNDROME
CARCINOID SMALL BOWEL
CARCINOIDS ETC
CARCINOSARCOMA
CARDIAC HERNIA
CARDIO-PHRENIC ANGLE
CARINA
CARNEY SYNDROME
CASTLEMAN DISEASE
CAVITATION
CAVITATION AIDS&PCP
CAVITATION ALV CA/AD
CAVITATION DEPOSITS
CAVITATION FUNGUS
CAVITATION GRANULOMA
CAVITATION HONEYCOMBING
CAVITATION INFARCT
CAVITATION LAM/TUB SCL
CAVITATION LYMPHOMA
CAVITATION NODULES
CAVITATION PNEUMOCONIOS
CAVITATION PNEUMONIA
CAVITATION RAD LUNGS

CAVITATION RHEUMATOID
CAVITATION SARCOID
CAVITATION SKIN DISEASE
CAVITATION TB+ATYP MYCO
CAVITATION TRAUMA
CAVITATION TUMOURS
CAVITATION VASCULITIS
CERVICAL NODES
CERVICAL RIB
CERVICAL SPINE
CHEMODECTOMA
CHEMOTHERAPY
CHEST DRAIN
CHEST WALL
CHEST WALL ABSCESS
CHEST WALL ANGIOMA
CHEST WALL DEPOSIT
CHEST WALL HAEMATOMA
CHEST WALL INVASION
CHEST WALL TUMOUR
CHILAIDITI'S SYNDROME
CHILDREN
CHONDROMA
CHRONIC INFECTION
CHYLOTHORAX/ASCITES
CIRRHOSIS
CISTERNA CHYLI
CLAVICLE
CLAVICLE ABSENT
CLAVICLE DEPOSIT
CLAVICLE FRACTURE
CLAVICLE OSTEOMA
CLAVICLE PAGET'S
CLAVICLE SARCOMA
CLEAR CELL CA
CLOTHING ARTEFACTS
CLUBBING
CMV PNEUMONIA
COAL-MINER
COCCIDIOIDOMYCOSIS
COELIAC NODES
COIFFE SIGN
COLLAPSE BASES
COLLAPSE L LUNG
COLLAPSE LLL
COLLAPSE LOBES
COLLAPSE LUL
COLLAPSE R LUNG
COLLAPSE RLL
COLLAPSE RM&LLS
COLLAPSE RML
COLLAPSE RU&MLS
COLLAPSE RUL
COLON
COLON CA
COLON PERFORATION
COMET TAIL SIGN
CONGEST NODULAR
CONGEST RE-EXPANSION
CONGEST SEPTAL LINES
CONGEST UNILAT
CONGESTION
CONGESTION RUL

CONNOISSEUR SIGN
CONSOL APEX LLL
CONSOL APEX RLL
CONSOL AZ LOBE
CONSOL BASAL
CONSOL CA
CONSOL L LUNG
CONSOL LINGULA
CONSOL LLL
CONSOL LUL
CONSOL MIM CA
CONSOL NODULAR
CONSOL R LUNG
CONSOL RLL
CONSOL RML
CONSOL ROUND
CONSOL ROUND+PREV CA
CONSOL RUL
CONSOL SPREAD HILUM
CONSOL+BREAKDOWN
CONSOLIDATION 1
CONSOLIDATION 2
CONTRACTED L LUNG
CONTRACTED LLL
CONTRACTED LUL
CONTRACTED R LUNG
CONTRACTED UPPER LBS
CONTRALATERAL NODES
CONTRAST ENHANCEMENT
CONTUSED LUNG
COP/BOOP
COR PULMONALE
CORONA MALIGNA
CORONARY ARTERY
CORONARY SINUS
COSTAL CART INFECTION
COSTAL CARTILAGES
COUGH FRACTURE
CRAZY PAVING
CROHN'S DISEASE
CROSSED NODES
CRURA
CRYPTOCOCCUS
CT-SPIRAL
CUSHING'S SYNDROME
CV LINE
CYCLOPHOSPHAMIDE
CYLINDROMA
CYSTIC FIBROSIS
CYSTICERCI
CYSTS/BULLAE

DEGEN IN LUNG TUMOUR
DEP IN BUTTOCK
DEP IN SOFT TISSUE
DEP IN THYROID
DERMOID
DERMOID-MALIGNANT
DESMOID
DESTROYED LUNG
DEVELOP ABN
DEWBERRY SIGN

DIABETES & TB ETC
DIABETES INSIPIDUS
DIAPHRAGM
DIAPHRAGM-CRURA
DIAPHRAGM-ELEVATED
DIAPHRAGM-EVENTRATED
DIAPHRAGM-HERNIA
DIAPHRAGM-HERNIA CHILD
DIAPHRAGM-HIATUS HERNIA
DIAPHRAGM-INVERTED
DIAPHRAGM-PLAQUES
DIAPHRAGM-TRAUMA
DIAPHRAGM-TUMOUR
DIAPHRAGM-WHITE LINE
DISTAL SOFT TISSUE DEP
DIVER
DIVERTICULITIS
DORSAL KYPHOSIS
DROWNED LOBE
DRUG REACTION
DRY PLEURISY
DUODENUM
DYSTROPHIA MYOTONICA

EATON LAMBERT
ELONGATED TUMOUR
EMBOLUS/INFARCT
EMPHYSEMA
EMPHYSEMA ETC.
EMPYEMA
END STAGE LUNG
ENDOBRON DEPOSITS
ENDOBRON HAMARTOMA
ENDOBRON LIPOMA
ENDOBRON SPREAD CA
ENDOBRON TUMOUR
ENDOMETRIOSIS
ENDOTRACHEAL TUBE
ENDOVASCULAR TUMOUR
ENHANCEMENT/BLUSH
ENL PUL ARTERIES
ENLARGED HILUM
EOSINOPHIL
EOSINOPHIL EFFUSION
EOSINOPHIL GRANULOMA
EOSINOPHIL PNEUMONIA
EPIPHRENIC DIVERTIC
ERYTHEMA NODOSUM
EWART'S SIGN
EWING'S SARCOMA
EXOPHTHALMOS
EXPIRATION
EXTRAMED HAEMOPOIESIS
EXTRAPLEURAL SPACE

FACE
FALLEN LUNG
FALLOT
FAMOUS PEOPLE ETC.
FARMERS LUNG
FAT

FAT PADS
FAT WIDE MEDIAST
FAT/OIL EMBOLISM
FEET&ANKLES
FEMORA
FIBROSING ALV+ NEO
FIBROSING ALVEOLITIS
FIBROTHORAX LOCALISED
FILARIASIS
FILM FOGGING - ISOTOPES
FINGER CLUBBING
FLEISCHNER SIGN
FOREARM
FOREIGN BODY BRONCHUS
FOREIGN BODY NOT BRON
FREE SPINE SIGN
FREIDLANDER'S PN
FUNGUS
FUNGUS-HIL/MED ENL

GALAXY SIGN
GANGLIONEUROMA
GAS FORMING INFECTION
GAS GANGRENE
GAS IN BREAST
GAS IN JOINTS/DISCS
GAS INTERSTITIAL
GAS INTRAVASC
GERM CELL TUMOUR
GHON FOCUS
GLANDULAR FEVER
GOITRE
GOITRE ECTOPIC
GOLD
GOLDEN'S SIGN
GOODPASTURE
GOUT
GRANULOMAS
GROUND-GLASS
GUINEA WORMS
GYNAECOMASTIA

HAEM THYROID CYST
HAEMANGIOMA
HAEMANGIOPERICYTOMA
HAEMATOMA
HAEMATOMA ABD WALL
HAEMATOMA CHEST WALL
HAEMOCHROMATOSIS
HAEMOPHILIA
HAEMOPHILUS
HAEMOSIDEROSIS
HAEMOTHORAX
HAIR LOCK
HALO SIGN
HALOES
HAMARTOMA MALIGNANT
HAMARTOMAS
HAMPTON'S HUMP
HANDS &WRISTS
HARRISON'S SULCUS

HEALING RIB DEPOSIT
HEART
HEART ALCOHOL
HEART AORTIC VALVE
HEART ASD
HEART CALCIFICATION
HEART DEXTROROTATION
HEART EBSTEIN ANOMALY
HEART FAILURE
HEART FALLOT
HEART FALLOT+BLALOCK
HEART HOCM
HEART L ATRIUM
HEART L VENT
HEART L VENT ANEURYSM
HEART MITRAL STENOSIS
HEART MITRAL VALVE
HEART SMALL
HEART TRANSPOSITION
HEART TRICUSPID VALVE
HEART TRUNCUS
HEART TUMOUR
HEART VALVE CALC
HEART VALVE PROSTHESIS
HEART VSD
HEMAZ LB + VN
HEMIAZYGOS VEIN
HEPATIC DEPOSITS
HEPATOMA
HERXHEIMER REACT
HIATUS HERNIA
HICKMAN LINE
HIGH & LOW KV
HILAR ELEVATION
HILAR ENL - INFLAM
HILAR ENLARGEMENT
HILAR INVASION
HILAR NODES
HILAR TUMOUR
HIPS/PELVIS
HISTIOCYTOMA
HISTIOCYTOSIS
HISTOPLASMOSIS
HODG/MYELO-LUNG INFIL
HODGKIN EXTENSIVE
HODGKIN'S DISEASE
HONEYCOMBING
HORMONES/PARANEO
HORNER'S SYNDROME
HPOA
HRCT
HUMERUS
HUMERUS FRACTURE
HYDATID CYSTS
HYDROPNEUMOTHORAX
HYPERPARATHYROIDISM
HYPERTHYROIDISM
HYPOGLOBULIN
HYPOPLASIA/APLASIA

ICEBERG SIGN
IDIOT TUMOUR

ILEUM
INCL FRONT TOMO
INFARCT
INFARCT CAVITATING
INFARCT CHRONIC
INFARCT INFECTED
INFARCT/EMBOLUS
INFILTRATING TUMOUR
INFILTRATION TO HILUM
INFLUENZA
INHALATION LUNG CHANGES
INHALATION PNEUMONIA
INHALED BA
INHALED FB
INNOMINATE ARTERY
INNOMINATE VEINS
INT MAMMARY ARTERIES
INT MAMMARY NODES
INTERCOSTAL ARTERIOGRAM
INTERCOSTAL TUBE
INTERMEDIATE BRONCHUS
INTERSTITIAL GAS
INTERVERT DISCS
INTRA PULM NODES
INTRAVASC GAS
INTRAVASC TUMOUR
IRREGULAR TUMOUR
IVC ANATOMY
IVC AZYGOS CONTINUATION
IVC FILTER
IVC THROMBOSIS
IVC/PELV VEINS
IVORY VERTEBRA

JEWISH NOSE SIGN
JUXTAPHRENIC PEAK

KANSASII INF
KAPOSI SARCOMA
KARTAGENER'S SYNDROME
KIDNEYS
KIDNEYS POLYCYSTIC
KIDNEYS SWOLLEN
KLEBSIELLA PNEUMONIA
KNEES
KNOBBLY PLEURA
KYMOGRAM
KYPHOSCOLIOSIS
KYPHOSIS

L ATRIUM
L SUP INTERCOSTAL VEIN
L VENT ANEURYSM
L VENTRICLE
LACUNAE
LAM
LARGE CELL TUMOUR
LARYNX
LAVAGE
LEAD

LEGIONELLA PNEUMONIA
LEGS
LEIOMYOMAS
LESSER SAC
LEUKAEMIA
LINGULAR VEINS
LIPIODOL
LIPOID PNEUMONIA
LIPOMA
LIPOMA CHEST WALL
LIPOSARCOMA
LIVER
LIVER ABSCESS
LIVER ARTEFACT
LIVER CALCIFICATION
LIVER CIRRHOSIS
LIVER COLLOID SCAN
LIVER CYSTS
LIVER DEPOSITS
LIVER FATTY
LIVER HAEMANGIOMA
LIVER TRAUMA
LOBECTOMY
LOBULATED TUMOUR
LOEFFLER'S SYNDROME
LOOFA LUNG
LOSS OF SILHOUETTE
LOWER LIMB SWELLING
LOWER THORACIC NODES
LUFTSICHEL SIGN
LUNG ABSCESS
LUNG CA CAUSES
LUNG CA MISC EFFECTS
LUNG CA RT
LUNG CA/RENAL DEP
LUNG CAVITIES
LUNG CYSTS/BULLAE
LUNG DEPOSITS 1
LUNG DEPOSITS 2
LUNG DEPS-CA KIDNEY
LUNG DEPS-CAVITATING
LUNG DEPS-MILIARY
LUNG FALLEN
LUNG FIBROSIS
LUNG GRANULOMA
LUNG HAEMATOMA
LUNG HERNIA
LUNG INFIL-HODG/MYELO
LUNG MASS VASCULITIS
LUNG NODULES
LUNG NODULES-FINE
LUNG PEEL SIGN
LUNG SARCOMA
LUNG SCAN
LUNG SCARS
LYMPHANGIOGRAM
LYMPHANGITIS
LYMPHATIC SPREAD
LYMPHOCYST
LYMPHOGRANULOMA
LYMPHOMA ETC
LYMPHOMA+RENAL FAIL
LYMPHOMA-ABD+RENAL

LYMPHOMA-ANT MED
LYMPHOMA-CAVIT
LYMPHOMA-ENGULF
LYMPHOMA-LYMPH
LYMPHOMA-MIM CA LUNG
LUNGLYMPHOMA-R LUNG
LYMPHOMA-RT COMPS
LYMPHOSARCOMA

MACLEOD SYN
MAIN BRONCHI
MALARIA
MALLORY WEISS SYNDROME
MALMOENSE
MARBLE BONE DISEASE
MARFAN SYNDROME
MASCAGNI
MASS VESSEL SIGN
MASTECTOMY
MECONIUM ILEUS-ADULT
MEDIAST ABSCESS
MEDIAST ENL-FUNGUS
MEDIAST GAS
MEDIAST HAEMATOMA
MEDIAST HERNIATION
MEDIAST INFILTRATION
MEDIAST INVASION
MEDIAST LINES
MEDIAST MYELO+MESO
MEDIAST NODE OPACIFIED
MEDIAST NODES
MEDIAST SYPHILIS
MEDIAST TAIL
MEDIAST VARICES
MEDIAST VEINS+GOITRE
MEDIAST WIDE-FAT
MEDIAST&BRON CYSTS
MEDULLOBLASTOMA
MEIGS' SYNDROME
MELANOMA
MENINGOCOELE LAT THOR
MERCURY IV
MESENCHYMOMA
MESOTHEL-PERICARDIUM
MESOTHEL-PERITOMEUM
MESOTHELIOMA
METALS
METHOTREXATE
MICROANEURYSMS
MICROLITHIASIS
MILIARY CALCIFICATION
MILIARY DEPOSITS/CA
MILIARY NODULES
MILIARY TB
MILLERI PNEUMONIA
MISC TUMOURS
MISSED LUNG TUMOUR
MITRAL STENOSIS
MITRAL VALVE
MORGAGNI HERNIA
MOSAIC PATTERN
MOUNIER-KUHN

MR
MUCOCOELES
MUCORMYCOSIS
MUCUS IN BRONCHUS
MUCUS IN TRACHEA
MUCUS PLUG
MULTIFOCAL TUMOUR
MULTIPLE TUMOURS
MUMMY
MUSCLE CALCIFICATION
MYASTHENIA GRAVIS
MYCETOMA
MYCOBACT ATYPICAL
MYCOPLASMA PN
MYCOSIS FUNGOIDES
MYELOFIBROSIS
MYELOGRAM
MYELOMA

NARROWED BRONCHUS
NASOGASTRIC TUBE
NASOPHARYNGEAL TUMOUR
NECK-ABSCESS
NECK-GAS
NECK-HAEMATOMA
NECK-NODES/DEPS
NECK/LARYNX
NECROBACILLOSIS
NEUROBLAS+WILMS TUM
NEUROBLASTOMA
NEUROFIB-ENDOBRON
NEUROFIB-MALIG
NEUROFIB-VAGI
NEUROFIBROMA
NOCARDIA
NODES-ABDOMINAL
NODES-ANT MEDIAST
NODES-AP WINDOW
NODES-AXILLA
NODES-AZPRETR
NODES-AZYGOS
NODES-CALCIFICATION
NODES-CERVICAL
NODES-COELIAC
NODES-CROSSED DRAINAGE
NODES-HILAR
NODES-INTMAMM
NODES-INTRAPULMONARY
NODES-MEDIAST
NODES-PARA-AORTIC
NODES-PARACARDIAC
NODES-PARASPINAL
NODES-PARATRACHEAL
NODES-PELVIC
NODES-PRETRACHEAL
NODES-R UPPER MEDIAST
NODES-RETROCRURAL
NODES-SENTINEL
NODES-SUBAORTIC
NODES-SUBCARINAL
NODES-THYMIC
NODES-UPPER MEDIAST

NODULAR CONSOLIDATION
NORMAL
NOSE
NOT ASBESTOS

OAT CELL CA LUNG
OBSTRUCTIVE EMPHYSEMA
OCHRONOSIS
OES-ABER SUB ART
OES-ACHAL+NEOPLASM
OES-ACHALASIA
OES-AORTA
OES-ATONIC
OES-CA LUNG
OES-CARDIA MUCOSA
OES-CAUSTIC SODA
OES-CORKSCREW
OES-DILATATION
OES-DIVERTICULA
OES-FOREIGN BODY
OES-GAS
OES-LEIOMYOMA
OES-MELANOMA
OES-MONILIA
OES-OAT CELL CA
OES-PARKINSON
OES-PERFORATION
OES-POLYP
OES-POST OP
OES-PRESSURE
OES-PSEUDODIVERTICULA
OES-REFLUX
OES-SCHATZKI RING
OES-SCLERODERMA
OES-SPASM
OES-STENT/TUBE
OES-STRICTURE
OES-SWALLOWING
OES-TUMOUR
OES-TUMOUR+RT
OES-ULCER
OES-VARICES
OES-VOMITING
OES-WEBS
OESER SIGN
OESOPHAGUS
OIL/FAT EMBOLI
OPACIFIED NODES
ORBIT
OSLER WEBER
OSTEOCHONDROMA
OSTEOCHONDROSARCOMA
OSTEOGENESIS IMPERFECTA
OSTEOGENIC SARCOMA
OSTEOMA
OSTEOPHYTES
OSTEOPOROSIS
OVARIAN CA/TUM

PACEMAKER
PAGET'S DISEASE
PANCOAST TUMOUR
PANCREAS
PANCREAS CA
PANCREAS DEP FROM LUNG
PANCREATATITIS
PAPILLOMA-SKIN
PARA-AORTIC NODES
PARACARDIAC NODES
PARANEO SYNDS/HORMS
PARAQUAT
PARASITES
PARASITES CHEST WALL
PARASPINAL LINES
PARASPINAL MASS
PARASPINAL NODES
PARATHYROID
PARATHYROID TUMOUR
PARATRACHEAL NODES
PARAVERTEBRAL SPREAD
PARAVERTEBRAL WIDENING
PARENCHYMAL BANDS
PATENT DUCTUS
PELVIC NODES
PELVIC VEIN THROMBOSIS
PELVIS/HIPS
PEMPHIGUS
PENDRED'S SYNDROME
PERICARDIAL CALCIFICATION
PERICARDIAL CONSTRICTION
PERICARDIAL CYST
PERICARDIAL DEPOSITS
PERICARDIAL EFFUSION
PERICARDIAL GAS
PERICARDIAL RECESSES
PERICARDIAL TUMOUR
PERICARDIUM
PERITONEOGRAM
PHAEOCHROMOCYTOMA
PHARYNGEAL POUCH
PHARYNGEAL POUCH+CA
PHARYNGEAL WEB
PHRENIC N & PALSY
PITUITARY SNUFF
PL-CALCIFICATION
PL-COIFFE
PL-DEPOSITS
PL-DRAINAGE
PL-EFFUS CHYLOUS
PL-EFFUS EOS
PL-EFFUS FISS
PL-EFFUS MYX
PL-EFFUS SPURIOUS
PL-EFFUS SUBPULM
PL-EFFUS YELLOW NL
PL-EFFUSION 1
PL-EFFUSION 2
PL-FIBROMA
PL-FISSURES
PL-GAS/AIR POST OP
PL-IRREGULAR
PL-KNOBBLY

PL-LIPOMA
PL-MASS FOLL ASP
PL-MOUSE
PL-MUSHROOMS
PL-NODULE
PL-PLAQUE HAIRY
PL-PLAQUES ASB
PL-PLQ FISS ASB
PL-PLQ NOT ASBESTOS
PL-REACTION
PL-RIND
PL-TAG/TAIL
PL-THICKENING
PL-WHITE LINE ON US
PLAGUE
PLASMACYTOMA
PLEURISY ASB
PLEURISY MALIG BONE SC
PLOMBAGE
PLUMBER'S JOINT SIGN
PMF
PMF+CAVITY
PNEUMATOCOELES
PNEUMATOSIS
PNEUMOCOCCUS
PNEUMOCON+CA LUNG
PNEUMOCONIOSIS
PNEUMOCYSTIS PN
PNEUMOMEDIASTINUM
PNEUMONECTOMY
PNEUMONIA
PNEUMONIA BACT&VIRAL
PNEUMONIA ROUND
PNEUMONIA SPURIOUS
PNEUMOTHORAX
PNEUMOTHORAX BILATERAL
PNEUMOTHORAX CENTRAL
PNMO/CONTPERITONEUM
PNX & TUMOUR
PNX LUNG PEEL SIGN
POLYART NODOSA
POLYCYTHAEMIA
POLYMYALGRHEUM
POST-CRICOID CA
POST-OPERATIVE
POST-RAD BONES
POST-RAD CHS MEDIAST
POST-RAD HYPOPLASIA
POST-RAD LUNGS
POST-RAD TUMOUR
PREGNANCY
PRETRACHEAL NODES
PREV CA LARYNX
PREV LOBECTOMY
PREV PNEUMONECTOMY
PREVERTEBRAL ABSCESS
PRODROMAL EFFECTS NEO
PROGERIA
PROSTATE
PROSTATE CA
PROSTATITIS
PSEUDARTHROSIS-SPINE
PSEUDOCAVITATION

PSEUDOCYST-PANCREAS
PSEUDOMONAS
PSEUDOMYXOMA
PSITTACOSIS
PSOAS
PSOAS ABSCESS
PSOAS CALCIFICATION
PSOAS DEPOSIT
PSOAS HAEMATOMA
PSOAS MASS
PSORIASIS
PULM ANGIOGRAM
PULM ART ANEURYSM
PULM ART APLASIA
PULM ART BODY TUM
PULM ART ELEVATION
PULM ART RED CIRC-CA LG
PULM ART TRAUMA
PULM ART TUMOUR
PULM ARTERIES
PULM ARTS ENLARGED
PULM ARTS SMALL
PULM CONGESTION
PULM EMB/INFARCT
PULM FIBROSIS
PULM OLIGAEMIA
PULM PLETHORA
PULM STENOSIS
PULM VARIX
PULM VEIN-ANOMALOUS
PULM VEINS
PULM VESSELS
PYO/PURP GANGRENOSUM

Q FEVER
QUARRY WORKER
QUEEN OF SCOTS VIEW

R ATRIUM
R ATRIUM TUMOUR
R UPPER MED NODES
RADIATION OTHER
RADIATION SARCOMA
RADIOTHERAPY
RADON
RADON/THORIUM
RECTAL CA
RECURRENT NERVE PALSY
RECURRENT TUMOUR
RENAL ANGIO
RENAL BONE DISEASE
RENAL CA&DEPOSITS
RENAL CALCULI
RENAL CYSTS
RENAL FAILURE
RENAL VEIN
RETICULOSARCOMA
RETROCRURAL NODES
RETROPERITONEAL GAS
RETROPERITONEAL TUMOUR
RETROPHARYNGEAL ABSCESS

RHEUMATOID
RHEUMATOID+CA
RHOMBOID FOSSA
RIB ANGIOMA/HAEMANGIOMA
RIB BENIGN TUMOUR
RIB CAFFEY
RIB CERVICAL
RIB CHONDROMA
RIB DEPOSITS
RIB DEPOSITS SCLEROTIC
RIB EROSION
RIB FIBROMA
RIB FIBROUS DYSPLASIA
RIB FIRST
RIB FORKED
RIB FRACTURES
RIB IDIOT TUMOURS
RIB INFECTION
RIB INTRAPULM
RIB NODULES
RIB NOTCHING
RIB OSTEOMA
RIB SARCOMA
RIB SPOT VIEW
RIB STRESS FRACTS
RIB TONGUE
RIB TRAUMA
RIB TUMOURS
RIBS 1
RIBS 2
RICKETS
RIGLER'S SIGN
ROTTER'S NODE
ROUND PNEU/CONS
RUBELLA

SACRUM
SALMONELLA
SARCOID
SARCOID&TB
SARCOID+CA
SARCOID+MYCET
SARCOID+ULC COLITIS
SARCOID-ENDOBRON
SARCOID-HANDS+LIMBS
SARCOID-LG NODULES
SARCOID-LUNGS
SARCOID-MISC
SARCOID-MR
SARCOID-NODES
SARCOID-NODES CALC
SARCOID-NODES+CONT CT
SARCOID-STOMACH
SARCOID-UNILAT
SARCOMA
SARCOMA LUNG
SATELLITE NODULE
SCALENUS ANT SYND
SCAPULA
SCAR CANCER
SCHISTOSOMIASIS
SCIMITAR VEIN

SCL BONE DEPS
SCL BONE ISLAND
SCLERODERMA
SCLERODERMA+CA LG
SCOLIOSIS
SCURVY
SEMINOMA
SENTINEL NODES
SEPTAL LINES
SEPTAL THICKENING
SEQUESTRATION
SHOULDER
SHOULDER OA
SHOULDER POST RT
SICKLE CELL DISEASE
SIGNET-RING SIGN BRCT
SILHOUETTE SIGN
SILICOSIS
SILICOSIS+CA LUNG
SILO-FILLERS DISEASE
SINUSES
SITUS INVERSUS
SKIN
SKULL
SKULL DEP-HALO SIGN
SLE
SLEEP APNOEA
SLOW-K-TABLET
SMALL BOWEL
SMOOTH MASS-CA LUNG
SOFT TISSUE DEPOSIT
SPINE
SPINE CERVICAL
SPINE DEPOSITS
SPINE DEPS SCLEROTIC
SPINE EROSION
SPINE INFECTION
SPINE LIPPING
SPINE PSEUDARTHROSIS
SPINE TB
SPINE TRAUMA
SPIRAL CT
SPL+COEL ART AN+CALC
SPLEEN
SPLEEN SCAN
SPLENIC CALC
SPLENIC CYST
SPLENIC DEPOSIT
SPLENIC HAEMANGIOMA
SPLENIC HAEMATOMA
SPLENIC LYMPHOMA
SPLENIC TRAUMA
SPLENUNCULUS
SPRENGEL'S SHOULDER
SPURIOUS PNEUMONIA
SPURIOUS TB
SPURIOUS TUMOURS
SQUAMOUS CA
STAPH PNEUM+SPINE INF
STENT
STERILISED DEPOSIT
STERNAL DEPOSIT/EROSION
STERNO-CLAV JOINTS

STERNUM
STERNUM CARRINATUM
STERNUM CT
STERNUM EXCAVATUM
STERNUM IFT
STERNUM TRAUMA
STERNUM TUMOUR
STEROID HIP/SHOULDER
STOMACH CA
STOMACH GAS
STOMACH&DUOD
STONY LUNG DISEASE
STRESS FRACTURE
STRETCHED BRONCHUS
SUBAORTIC NODES
SUBCARINAL NODES
SUBCLAV ART ABERRANT
SUBCLAV STEAL
SUBCLAV&INNOM VESSELS
SUBCLAVIAN ARTERY
SUBCLAVIAN VEIN
SUBCUT CALC
SUBDURAL HAEMATOMA
SUBMUCOSAL TUM SPREAD
SUBPHRENIC ABSCESS
SUBPHRENIC CALC
SUBPLEURAL WHITE LINE
SUBPULM GAS
SUPRASTERNAL FOSSA
SURGICAL EMPHYSEMA
SVC
SVC GRAM
SVC LEFT
SVC OBSTRUCTION
SVC STENT
SWOLLEN LEGS
SWOLLEN LOBE
SWYER JAMES SYN
SYPHILIS
SYPHILIS-AORTA
SYPHILIS-BISMUTH
SYPHILIS-BONE
SYPHILIS-MEDIASTINITIS
SYPHILIS-VARICES

TAIL-PL&MEDIAST
TB&BREAST
TB&CROHNS
TB&MYCETOMA/FUNGUS
TB&SARCOID
TB+CA LUNG
TB-ADRENAL
TB-ASIAN
TB-BONE
TB-CALC
TB-CALC NODES
TB-CAVITATION
TB-CHEST
TB-CHILD
TB-CLAVICLE
TB-CONGENITAL
TB-FIBROSIS

TB-FOOT
TB-GENERAL
TB-GHON FOCUS
TB-HANDS & WRISTS
TB-HILAR NODES
TB-HIP
TB-KIDNEY
TB-KNEE
TB-MANTOUX
TB-MEDIAST NODES
TB-MILIARY
TB-MIM CA LUNG
TB-NODES ADJ SVC
TB-NODES ADULT
TB-NODES CHILD
TB-OLD
TB-OMA
TB-PERICARD EFFUSION
TB-PLEURAL
TB-REN/AD
TB-RIB
TB-SACRO-ILIAC JOINT
TB-SHOULDER
TB-SKIN
TB-SPINE
TB-SPURIOUS
TB-THYMIC
TB-TUBE/OVARY
TEETH & JAW
TERATOMA
TESTES DEPS
THALASSAEMIA
THERMOGRAM
THORACIC DUCT
THORACIC INJURY
THORACOPLASTY
THORAVISION
THOROTRAST
THYMIC CALC
THYMIC CYST
THYMIC DEPOSIT
THYMIC LYMPHOMA
THYMIC NODES
THYMIC TB
THYMOMA
THYMUS
THYROID
THYROID CA
THYROID DEP FROM CA-LG
THYROID ECTOPIC
THYROID LINGUAL
THYROID MED CYST
THYROID SCAN
TIETZE SYNDROME
TOMOS 55^0 POST OBL
TOOL-MAKER
TRAC&BRON NARROWING
TRACH/BRON STENT
TRACH/CARINA CA
TRACHEA
TRACHEA INV BY CA LUNG
TRACHEA-CHONDRITIS
TRACHEA-COMPRESSION

TRACHEA-DEFORMITY
TRACHEA-MUCUS PLUG
TRACHEA-PAPILLOMA
TRACHEA-SCABBARD
TRACHEA-STRICTURE
TRACHEAL BRONCHUS
TRACHEO-OES FISTULA
TRACHEOMEGALY
TRACHEOPATH-OSTEOPLAS
TRACHEOSTOMY
TRANS AXIAL TOMO
TRAUMA
TRAUMA BRONCHUS
TRAUMA LUNG
TREE IN BUD SIGN
TUBE COMPLICATION
TUBEROSE SCLEROSIS
TUM ENHANCEMENT
TUM ONLY SEEN ON LAT
TUMORAL CALCIFICATION
TUMOUR CALCIFICATION
TUMOUR ENHANCEMENT
TUMOUR MISSED
TUMOUR SPURIOUS
TX TUMOUR

ULTRASOUND
UPPER LOBE FIBROSIS
UPPER MEDIAST NODES
UTERUS CA

VALSALVA& MULLER
VARICELLA
VARICES
VASCULITIS
VENOGRAM
VENOUS CONFLUENCE
VENOUS SAMPLING
VENOUS THROMBOSIS
VESSELS - REDUCED LG TUM
VIRAL PNEUMONIA

WALDENSTROM
WANDERING PNEUMONIA
WEGENER'S GRANULOMA
WEIL'S DISEASE
WEINBERG OPERATION
WELDER
WESTERMARK SIGN
WHITE LINE
WHORLED NODULES
WILM'S TUMOUR

XENOPII

YELLOW NAIL SYNDROME
YOUNG'S SYNDROME

CD-ROM LICENCE AGGREEMENT AND INFORMATION

Please read this Agreement carefully before loading the CD-ROM

By loading the CD-ROM, you acknowledge that you have read and understand the following terms and conditions and agree to be bound thereby. If you do not agree with these terms and conditions, return the entire package to the following address and any payment that you have made for it will be returned to you:

Editorial Dept – Life Sciences
Taylor & Francis
11 New Fetter Lane
London EC4P 4EE
UK

LICENCE AGREEMENT

1. Grant of Licence. This Licence Agreement ("Licence") permits you to use one copy of the RADIOLOGY OF THE CHEST AND RELATED CONDITIONS software product acquired with this Licence ("Software") in accordance with the terms of this Licence on any single computer but only if the Software is in use on only one computer at any time. This Licence permits you: a) to make one copy of the Software solely for backup or archival purposes; or b) to transfer the Software to a single hard disk provided you keep the original solely for backup or archival purposes. You shall not sublicence, assign or transfer the Licence or the Software.

2. Copyright. Copyright © 2001 Taylor & Francis. All rights reserved. You shall not republish, copy, modify, transfer, translate, decompile, disassemble or create derivative works of the Software, or any part thereof.

LIMITED WARRANTY AND DISCLAIMER

The publishers of the Software, Taylor & Francis ("Publishers"), warrant that, for a period of ninety (90) days from the date of delivery to you, as evidenced by a copy of your receipt, the CD-ROM containing the Software will be free from defects in materials and workmanship, and the Software, under normal use, will perform without significant errors that make it unusable. Publishers' entire liability and your exclusive remedy under this warranty will be, at Publishers' option, to attempt to correct or help you around errors, or to give you a functionally equivalent Software or, upon you returning the Software to the Publishers, to refund the purchase price and terminate this Agreement.

EXCEPT FOR THE ABOVE EXPRESS LIMITED WARRANTIES, PUBLISHERS MAKE AND YOU RECEIVE NO WARRANTIES OR CONDITIONS, EXPRESS, IMPLIED, STATUTORY OR IN ANY COMMUNICATION WITH YOU, AND SPECIFICALLY DISCLAIMS ANY IMPLIED WARRANTY OF MERCHANTABILITY OR FITNESS FOR A PARTICULAR PURPOSE. PUBLISHERS DO NOT WARRANT THAT THE OPERATION OF THE SOFTWARE WILL BE UNINTERRUPTED OR ERROR FREE.

This CD-ROM has been designed to complement the book *Radiology of the Chest and Related Conditions* and is supplied in a pocket within its front cover. Its main purpose is to provide the medical illustrations that are referred to within the book. These are held in source files and are accessed via ImageAXS (version 2.5) using Windows 3.1 or later Windows versions, or using ImageAXS (version 2.0) on Macintosh computers.

In addition the disc holds the reference files for the book, a copy of the text and 202 pictures of Oxford for added interest.

The references and text are accessed via Acrobat 3 (or 4), and a browser is provided for those who do not already have copies of this programme.

The ImageAXS programmes (in both Windows and Mac versions) will run from the CD-ROM (provided that the CD-ROM disc remains in the drive). ImageAXS allows the source images to be accessed as thumbnails or full images. The latter can be accessed from the thumbnails, the Info sheets or the list mode ("text list" on PC).

If the whole of the collection is selected - 8,666 image files - these can be scanned through using the scroll bar on the far right of the display, but it is much easier to use the KEYWORDS which appear within the text of the book. Further details are given in the Main Collection info.

Opening the main collection -
A. MACINTOSH COMPUTERS:
1. Open the disc icon with a double click and a folder containing the following items should appear: - FWW ILLUS, Book Text, Refs, Oxford Picts, Read me, Read me too, Disc Info, Source FL, Oxford SF, and Utilities (containing Quick Time, Simple Text, Adobe Acrobat Reader 3.01 and ImageAXS-CD). In addition an HTML file - entitled HTMLlink is provided as an alternative means of access to the book and reference files for those users who have web browsers on their computers. (See also note under Windows below).

2. Double click on FWW ILLUS and the main collection will open, ImageAXS-CD running directly from the CD-ROM - thus you will later need to 'quit' to remove the CD-ROM disc when finishing viewing.

3. The Oxford picture collection may be opened in a similar way by double clicking on the ImageAXS - Mac file - Oxford Picts.

To open the text and reference files it may be necessary to install the Acrobat Reader (and Quick Time) programmes in the Extensions folder if not already on the hard-disc. Use only Acrobat Reader 3.01 (as supplied) or higher, or the line diagrams within the text files may be discontinuous.

If you have to install Acrobat Reader (by opening the Acrobat Reader folder and using the installer), please check that Adobe Type Manager 4 has been installed in the Control Panels, as unless this has been done the Acrobat files cannot be viewed - If not so installed please do this manually.

The text and reference, etc. files and the picture collections are then ready to be opened by double clicking on the appropriate icons.

B. COMPUTERS USING WINDOWS (All versions):
To install ImageAXS-CD browser –

1. Ensure that all programmes currently running on your machine are closed, particularly large programmes such as Microsoft Office, etc.

2. Place the CD-ROM disc in the disc drive.

3. From the toolbar, click on START, then RUN (or open MY COMPUTER and select CD DRIVE).

4. Click on BROWSE option and select your CD drive (e.g. D, E or F) and a window will appear, showing a list of items on the CD-ROM.(If the CD DRIVE is shown as drive Z:, as may occur with some server systems, ImageAXS may be unable to locate the source files and red 'X's may be shown against each selection - in this instance a non-server system should be used).

5. Select SETUP or SETUP.EXE from this, then click OPEN to return to the RUN option.

6. Click OK, and the ImageAXS programme will then be installed on your computer follow the instructions shown. After installation a window may appear showing a FWWILLUS Icon and the READ_ME instructions; the main picture collection can be opened via the icon.

7. Following installation, and on subsequent occasions after reinserting the CD-ROM, both the main and Oxford picture collections can be accessed via START, PROGRAMMES, (or from CD DRIVE as before) then choosing FWWILLUS (the main picture collection) or OXFORD (the Oxford picture collection).

The CD-ROM also contains further files or folders:
DISCINFO (this file), READ_ME (license agreement for ImageAXS), READ_ME2 (about ImageAXS and image-access net), the BOOKTEXT (a copy of the text files on the disc), the REFS (references referred to in the text) and UTILITIES (containing the ImageAXS-CD and Acrobat browsers, and QuickTime).

To access the Text Files and References, etc. (with Windows) it may be necessary to install the Acrobat Reader (as for MACINTOSH COMPUTERS - above) - i.e. if you do not have Acrobat 3 (or a higher version) on your computer please install the Acrobat Reader in a similar manner to the instructions given above.

Note that if a computer with a server system is being used and the Windows programme is on the server network and not fully on the 'C drive' it may be necessary to consult the local IT service as local 'locking' may cause problems with the installation of new software!

The HTMLlink file may also be used to access the book and reference files - see above under Macintosh Computers paragraph one.

The text or reference files may be viewed alongside the illustrations with Macintosh computers and also with many Windows machines. With some Windows machines it may be more convenient to alternate text (or references) and illustrations using the ImageAXS and Acrobat boxes at the base of the display. In most instances however it is anticipated that viewers will use the printed text + the illustrations and references on the computer.

CD-ROM information ii
Further information is given in the Collection notes in the book and on the CD-ROM (both with the book-text and the collection-info in ImageAXS main image collection - FWWIllus).

The total size of all the files on the CD-ROM (including both MAC and Windows) is approximately 600 MB.

Chapter 1 : **Reading of Chest Radiographs**
Some basic Anatomy and Physiology; including Pleural Fissures,
Mediastinal Lines, The Bronchi and Para-Tracheal Lines,
Hilar Anatomy, the Pulmonary Lobules, Acini and Lung Cortex,
Distribution of Lung Disease in Relation to Anatomy and Physiology,
Basic CT and Pathological Anatomy.

Reading of chest radiographs.

In reading chest radiographs it is important to understand their limitations, basic anatomy and some physiology, and to have a systematic system of scrutiny. In this chapter the author goes into most of the points in some detail, as they have a profound influence on what can be seen. High KV (or similar digital) views are considered as essential by the author as the standard for most purposes, as many low KV examinations can fail to display 30% or more of the lungs, particularly the retrocardiac, and retro-diaphragmatic areas and areas hidden by the ribs.

Value of high KV technique - It is essential to have a good technique for chest radiography, as abnormalities which should be noted may otherwise be missed. In many centres chest radiographs are still taken even now with low or inadequate KV (e.g. 50 to 70), and with a 6 ft (approx. 2 metre) focus-film distance (f.f.d.). Such techniques may easily miss or inadequately demonstrate lesions in the lungs, fail to show the larger air passages and may completely miss gross mediastinal abnormalities, such as enlarged nodes, etc. Quite often the descending aorta and the various mediastinal lines are invisible within the 'white area' covered by the heart, or the domes of the diaphragm. The subcarinal area is not displayed, and masses or nodal enlargements here may be entirely missed - this probably accounts for the usual text-book statement that nodal enlargement in sarcoidosis is typically hilar, whereas the largest nodes are often in the subcarinal and azygos regions (see also p. 19.67).

Mediastinal visibility is an essential part of chest radiography, since it is only by noting the presence, displacement or absence of the normal lines, that many abnormalities will be detected. Loss of a mediastinal line or organ outline will usually indicate adjacent disease (see 'loss of silhouette sign' - p. 2.25). Air may often be seen in the oesophagus, and may be a good indicator of normality, dilatation or displacement. Two references emphasise these points:

Evans et al. (1968) : Only about 25% of the lungs are unobscured on most conventional chest radiographs.
Chotas and Ravin (1995) : 26.4 % of lung volumes and 43 % of lung areas are obscured by the heart, mediastinum and diaphragm on many frontal chest radiographs.

Viewers used to studying fairly contrasty low KV radiographs may have some initial difficulty in interpretation of high KV or digital radiographs, but will usually soon prefer the latter (and especially digital high KV radiographs) that **contain so much more information.**

Because calcification may be less readily seen, a low KV radiograph may be taken as well in a few cases (Illus. **HIGH & LOW KV**). However for the initial detection of disease or anatomical abnormality, the high KV has so many advantages that the author is greatly surprised that it is not universally used in the UK, despite the slightly increased initial cost of such an installation. **It seems quite wrong to regard as the standard chest radiograph, one which displays only about two-thirds of the lungs, and almost totally neglects the mediastinum and the larger air passages.**

Fig. 1.1 Graph showing relationship between radiographic contrast and increasing KV for the various contrast agents and the body tissues. Numbers in brackets refer to atomic weights.

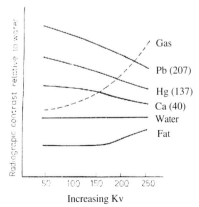

The high KV and digital techniques are further considered in Chapter 20.

Table 1.1 - **Rapid check list - PA Chest Views.**

1. Soft tissue abnormality - breasts (absence, gynaecomastia, etc.).
2. Symmetry of two sides of the chest (a) lung disease.
                                                                                                     (b) skeletal.
3. Real or apparent increased translucency.
4. Symmetry in **number** of blood vessels in either lung:
   - a 50 % loss in one (or both) = loss of expansion of a major lobe,
   - note loss of upper or lower lobe vessels (note deviation from normal pattern).
5. Alteration in size of vessels
     (a) bilateral - congestion
                                  plethora (e.g. with intra-cardiac shunt)
                                  oligaemia
     (b) unilateral - Swyer James/Macleod syndrome
                                  Oeser sign (spasm from hypoxia due to endobronchial obstruction).
     (c) proximal dilatation with peripheral pruning -
                                  pulmonary hypertension
                                  pulmonary embolism.
6. Position, patency or distortion of the trachea, carina and larger bronchi.
7. Diminished volume of a lung or lobe, altered position of fissures, bronchi or pulmonary vessels.
8. Obstructive emphysema (especially on expiration views).
9. Intra-pulmonary consolidation, masses, nodules or other shadows, e.g. septal line engorgement, fibrosis, etc.
10. Loss of part of the cardiac, aortic, SVC or diaphragmatic outline - 'loss of outline' or 'loss of silhouette sign' - see p.2.25.
11. Pleural abnormality - fluid, air, thickening, mass, etc.
12a. Diaphragmatic elevation caused by: - phrenic nerve palsy, eventration, secondary to lung collapse or hepatic enlargement, or mimicked by fluid or trans-diaphragmatic hernia.
12b. Diaphragmatic depression caused by lung distension.
     Note that the right side is more commonly higher than the left (see also p. 15.6).
13. Presence of mediastinal and/or hilar masses - nodes, other tumours or cysts, dilated aorta, oesophagus, hiatal hernia, etc. - **always study the mediastinal lines.**
14. Bone lesions - ribs, spine, sternum, scapulae, etc.
15. Other abnormalities of the chest wall.
16. Position or absence of fundal gas bubble, size of liver, site of gas in the transverse colon, etc.

Comment : It seems a great pity that many clinicians and radiologists as well, do not really look for the signs of incomplete chest expansion (reduced volume and vessel changes), when a visual inspection of chest movement and its expansion is one of the first observations that is made in every clinical examination of the chest. This lack of appreciation of the findings in partial collapse, together with low radiographs, and the poor demonstration of the mediastinum, has been a major problem in chest radiography. CT (particularly HRCT) has greatly helped in the investigation of the mediastinum and with diffuse lung disease.

On Lateral Views (details on ps. 1.26 to 1.32).
1. Similar points as on frontal views i.e. soft tissue abnormalities, symmetry, altered position of fissures, pleural fluid, visible lung (or lobe) outline indicating a pneumothorax, presence of lung, hilar or mediastinal masses, consolidation, signs of congestion, loss of silhouette - heart, diaphragm etc., elevated or 'humped' hemidiaphragm, abnormalities of visceral gas shadows, bony abnormalities, etc.
2. Particular attention to :
     (i) Tracheal gas column, and stripes, carina, ring shadows of main bronchi.
     (ii) Vascular patterns in the two lungs, especially the pulmonary arteries, which have different patterns on each side (Figs. 1.33 - 1.35 and Chapter 7).
     (iii) The normally transradiant upper anterior mediastinum above the heart.
     (iv) The normally transradiant retrocardiac area.

(v) The subcarinal area.

(vi) Differences between the two lungs - volume, partial collapse, or over-expansion, absence of normal vascular shadows, etc.

Pleural fissures.

Oblique (or major) and horizontal (minor or lesser) fissures

The normal position of these is well known. The oblique fissures normally run from about the level of the D6 vertebral body posteriorly to the anterior costophrenic angles at about the level of the ninth costo-chondral-junction, with the left slightly more vertical and posterior in its lower part (Fig. 1.4). This difference in orientation is probably related to the presence of the heart on the left.

The oblique fissures do not run completely in the same plane and are somewhat obliquely orientated and undulating. Below the lower lobe bronchial levels, the central (and lateral, on the left) parts of each oblique fissure are located more anteriorly than the medial parts, whilst above this level the relationship is reversed, with the lateral parts more posterior. The parts which are seen on lateral radiographs are those which lie tangential to the X-ray beam. The relationships change with many disease processes which cause reorientation of the fissures.

Reorientation, adjacent consolidation, or air or fluid within major fissures may allow them to be seen on frontal views. This particularly happens if the fissures become rotated into a horizontal or vertical perpendicular plane due to over distension or partial or complete collapse of adjacent lobes. Fig. 1.3d shows a part of the left oblique fissure rotated horizontally, as a result of obstructive emphysema of the left upper lobe. When rotated in the vertical axis the oblique fissures may give rise to linear vertical - shadows (sometimes termed the '**vertical fissure lines**' - Fig. 1.3c). These extend upwards from the lateral part of the diaphragm, roughly parallel to the chest wall. These are particularly seen if the patient is slightly oblique and may be more commonly seen on AP views. Usually they are seen on one side but may occasionally be seen on both. These lines are more readily seen if bounded by fluid (as with cardiac failure), consolidation or a localised pneumothorax, but may also be seen on normal radiographs. This latter is particularly evident if the fissures are not straight but undulate, and occasionally both superiorly and inferiorly they may assume a position nearly perpendicular to the horizontal plane. With a lower lobe collapse an oblique fissure may even be visible right up to the hilum.

The horizontal fissure normally lies at the level of the right fourth costo-chondral junction. It is seen on about 80% of normal frontal radiographs, but is commonly not quite horizontal. Alterations in its position are commonly indications of adjacent collapse, overdistension, etc. When not parallel to the plane of the incident x-ray beam, it will not be visualised, except on a lateral view.

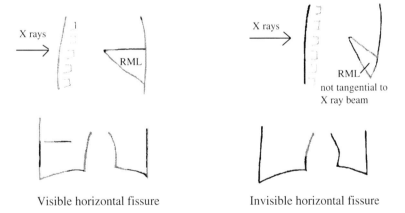

Visible horizontal fissure   Invisible horizontal fissure

Fig. 1.2 The visibility of the horizontal (or lesser) fissure on frontal radiographs depends on how tangential the fissure is to the x-ray beam.

(a)
Variant position of horizontal fissure.

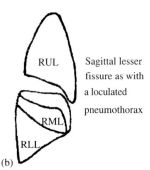

RUL

Sagittal lesser fissure as with a loculated pneumothorax

RML

RLL

(b)
The medial part of the horizontal fissure may turn downwards and be sagittally orientated. (It may then be seen on CT sections, lying anteriorly in the cardio-phrenic angle).

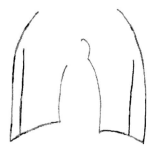

(c) Vertical fissure lines, due to rotation of part of a major fissure orientating it into an AP plane. These may be accentuated or thickened by pleural fluid and congestion.

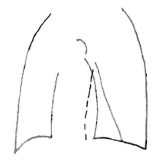

(d) Rotated and visible major or oblique fissure on frontal chest radiographs due to a collapsed lower lobe.

Fig. 1.3   Some appearances of the pleural fissures as seen on frontal radiographs.

The right oblique fissure usually has a more oblique course than that of the left, probably due to the mass of the heart being on the left.
        right ------------
        left - - - - - - -

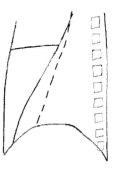

Fig. 1.4 Normal fissures on lateral radiographs.

Undulation may occur in the horizontal fissure, and this coupled with undulation of the right major fissure may sometimes cause the horizontal fissure to appear to extend posterior to the major fissure. This should not be confused with an accessory fissure between the anterior and apical segments of an upper lobe or a superior accessory fissure in a lower lobe - these are usually a little higher in position. The minor fissure may, in its more medial part, turn downwards and be sagittally orientated - see Fig. 1.3(b).

The **azygos fissure** is a developmental abnormality (present in about 1% of the population) is caused by the right posterior cardinal vein (one of the precursors of the azygos vein) failing to migrate over the right lung apex, and instead penetrating and grooving it. When present, the upper part of the right upper lobe tucks medially behind the azygos arch, and the azygos vein and arch lie at the bottom of the azygos fissure (Fig. 1.6 - see also p. 9.11).

The **azygos lobe** (when present) lies above and medial to the azygos fissure. Occasionally a left sided azygos or **hemiazygos lobe** may be seen together with a hemiazygos fissure.

Various accessory fissures may occur between neighbouring lung segments, some complete, and others incomplete. Superficial clefts or short fissures - often only 1 to 2 cm deep - are quite common, and may give rise to peripheral linear shadows, especially when they contain fluid - they resemble pleural tags (or tails) and pleural thorns, but when present are usually multiple.

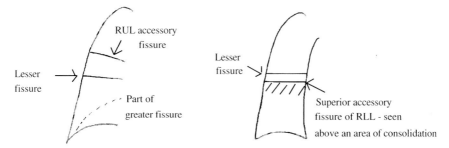

Fig. 1.5. An apparent '**double horizontal fissure**' may be produced by:
(a) an accessory fissure in the right upper lobe, between the anterior and apical segments (continuous line).
(b) part of the greater fissure being 'caught' in the horizontal plane by the x-ray beam (dotted line),
(c) a lower lobe superior accessory fissure, separating the apex of a lower lobe from the rest of the lobe (occurs in about 2% of people). When there is consolidation below such an accessory fissure on the right, it will mimic middle lobe consolidation.
(d) motion artefact on CT (see Fig. 1.12).

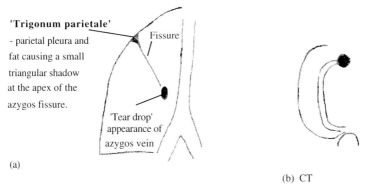

Fig. 1.6 **Azygos fissure** (a) with azygos vein at its base (rarely a similar **hemiazygos fissure** may be seen on the left), esp. in the presence of a left sided SVC). (b) An azygos vein in an azygos fissure is encircled by the '**mesoazygos**' - a double layer of pleura.

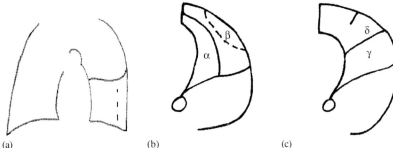

(a) (b) (c)

Fig. 1.7 (a) A ' **left sided horizontal fissure**' may be: straight, curved or incomplete, and may be produced by: (i) 'situs inversus', 'mirror image' or Kartagener's syndrome ' (ps. 3.15-16 & 15.6), (ii) a rotated oblique fissure - with obstruction or emphysema of the LUL or (iii) a '**lingular accessory fissure**' (between the lingula and the anterior segment of the LUL) which occurs in about 4% of people - this fissure is usually higher than a right-sided transverse fissure and often its lateral part inclines upwards it may also mimic a vertical major fissure line (dotted) (b & c). On CT a **LUL accessory fissure** may have a concave, convex, or straight line (complete or incomplete) appearance (α, β, γ & δ).

Fig. 1.8 A lower lobe '**inferior accessory fissure**' is best seen on CT sections, where it may form a ' **retro-cardiac lobe** '. This is more common on the right, where it separates the medial basic segment from the rest of the lower lobe but may also be present on the left or even bilaterally. On PA views it may mimic a 'juxta-phrenic peak' (p. 2.35). Sometimes these fissures may pass posteriorly or have a branch passing posteriorly (dotted line).

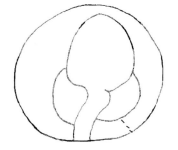

See ps. 2.35-36 for inferior accessory fissures causing the juxta-phrenic peak appearance.

CT of pleural fissures.

The appearance of pleural fissures on CT sections largely depends on their relationship to the plane of a fissure to a section and the thickness of the latter. When a fissure is perpendicular (or nearly so) to the plane of a thick (10 mm) section, it will appear as a line shadow, as on plain radiographs or conventional tomograms. With increasing obliquity, a fissure will tend to become wider and less well-defined, and may be shown as a dense band-like shadow, or as a hypovascular band area (representing the peripheral areas of the adjacent lobes, which contain only the smallest vessels). Fissures are more readily seen when they are thickened by fluid or pleural reaction, and are also **much better portrayed on thin CT sections (e.g. 2 mm thick)**.

The horizontal (or lesser) fissure is well seen on 'scout' views, but as its plane usually lies parallel to transverse CT sections, it may be invisible on thicker sections, except as a hypovascular area - '**the right mid-lung window**'. However, as the middle lobe tends to dome somewhat into the base of the upper lobe, it may be seen in most cases as a thin line shadow on thin sections. It will also be seen if it is thickened, if its orientation is altered by collapse, or if its medial tip turns downwards (Fig. 1.3b). If a thin section passes along the plane of the lesser fissure, it may be seen as a broad band or opaque sheet lying above the middle lobe - spreading antero-laterally from the region of the origin of its bronchus. If the section passes just below a small bulge of the fissure upwards, a ring shadow may be produced. (Similar considerations apply to a left-sided lesser fissure and to accessory fissures).

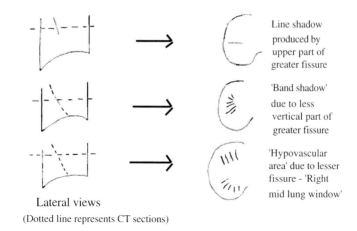

Line shadow produced by upper part of greater fissure

'Band shadow' due to less vertical part of greater fissure

'Hypovascular area' due to lesser fissure - 'Right mid lung window'

Lateral views

(Dotted line represents CT sections)

Fig. 1.9   Varying appearances of interlobar fissures on standard thickness CT sections.

Fig. 1 10   Varying positions of the lesser fissure and uppermost part of the RML on CT.

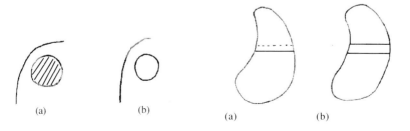

(a)   (b)

(a)   (b)

Fig. 1.11   On thin CT sections the lesser fissure may appear as :
(a) a broad band or opaque sheet or
(b) a ring shadow.

Fig. 1.12 The '**Double fissure sign**'
- an HRCT artefact produced by cardiac movement during a 'long' CT exposure.

Incomplete inter-lobar fissures.
    It is not commonly realised that inter-lobar fissures are often incomplete, particularly in relation to the middle lobe. When incomplete, collateral air-drift may take place into the adjoining lobe (p. 2.8). This is illustrated with regard to the middle lobe on p. 2.10 (Fig. 2.8).
    Incomplete fissures may also alter the expected patterns of inter-lobar fluid or air. Dandy (1978) noted that when an incomplete fissure is present, a pleural effusion may fill part of the inter-lobar fissure only. He wrote "clear areas of peri-hilar lucency are bordered laterally by a sharp concave line, peripheral to which is opacification consistent with fluid rising into the major fissure. Peri-hilar lucency, curvi-linear demarcation and lateral opacity indicate fluid extending into the major

pulmonary fissure. The fissure is incomplete medial to the line" i.e. fluid may fill part of the inter-lobar fissure only.

Further references.

Maylord (1886) : Post-mortem series - increased pleural fissuring was common.

Rigler and Ericksen(1933): The inferior accessory lobe of the lung.

Foster-Carter (1946) : Despite anomalous fissuring, the bronchial branching is rarely disturbed.

Medlar (1947): Variations in the inter-lobar fissures - in 570 cases - classical complete fissures in only 35% of right and 83% of left lungs.

Boyden (1952): The distribution of bronchi in gross anomalies of the right upper lobe, particularly lobes subdivided by the azygos vein and those containing pre-eparterial bronchi.

Davis (1960) : Described the vertical fissure line, but only noted it on the right.

Wier (1960) : Additional or deficient pleural fissuring - the most common congenital abnormalities.

Webber and O'Loughlin (1964) : Discussed variations of the vertical fissure line.

Friedman (1966): Further observations on the vertical fissure line.

Dandy (1978): Incomplete pulmonary interlobar fissure sign.

Yamashita (1978): Found varying degrees of fusion of the major and minor fissures. He studied 140 specimens, and found varying degrees of incompleteness of the major fissures (especially in their upper two thirds in about 70 %). The lesser fissure was complete in only about 1. 5 %, the remainder showing varying degrees of incompleteness.

Proto and Speckman (1979 & 1980) : Fissures on lateral chest radiographs.

Yiu et al. (1979): Showed the positions of the fissures using a lung model.

Langolis and Henderson (1980) : Variant pulmonary lobation - post-mortem study of 100 fixed and air-inflated lungs (40 right and 60 left) with radiography and retrospective study of pre-mortem radiographs - incidence of fissural variants was 45%, single anomalies in 33% and double anomalies in 6%.
Right lung complete or partial **absence of lesser fissure** 10 (25%), complete or partial **presence of   superior accessory fissure** 7 (17.5%), **inferior accessory (medial basal) fissure** 4 (10%),other anomalies 4 (10%) Left lung **lingular   fissure** 9 (15%), **superior   accessory   fissure** 1 (2%), **inferior   accessory   (medial basal) fissure** 11 (18%).
They pointed out that the **presence of accessory fissures could affect the extent of consolidation within a lobe**, etc. and its radiological appearance (e.g. **pneumonia sparing the apex of a lower lobe -** present author's comment).They concluded that a heightened awareness of the incidence of accessory fissures should permit their increased recognition, and thus avoid misinterpretation of the roentgen findings in pulmonary disease.

Fisher (1981) : Significance of a visible major fissure on frontal chest radiographs.-

Raasch et al. (1982): Radiographic anatomy of the interlobar fissures - a study of 100 specimens.

Frija et al. (1982) : CT of the pulmonary fissures - normal anatomy.

Marks and Kuhns (1982) : Identification of pleural fissures with CT.

Goodman et al. (1982): The right mid-lung window - a potential source of error at CT - hypovascular area in the position of the lesser fissure.

Proto and Ball (1983a): The supero-lateral major fissures.(b): CT of the major and minor fissures.

Rosenbloom et al. (1983): Incomplete fissures in relation to the RML.

Godwin and Tarver (1985) : Accessory fissures of the lung.

Austin (1986) : The left minor fissure.

Gross et al. (1988): Sagittal orientation of the medial part of the lesser fissure.

Mayo et al. (1987): The double-fissure sign: a motion artefact on thin-section CT scans.

Otsuji et al. (1989): Right upper lobe versus right middle lobe differentiation with thin-section CT.

Berkmen et al. (1989): Anatomy of the minor fissure - evaluation with thin section CT in 40 patients. It was seen in 32 - complete in 7, but absent in 8, incomplete in 23 and indeterminate in 2. The upper part of the RML could be situated medially or laterally.

Frija et al. (1988 & 1989): Incompleteness of the minor fissure is common - in 76 of their cases varying from 0 to 100 %. They wrote ' generally, when the minor fissure is incomplete, it is the inner part that is absent, this is also true for the major fissure. We have never found the absence of the outer part of a normal fissure without its inner part.' They noted its appearance as a band or ring shadow.

Hourihane and Owens (1989) Superior accessory fissure - a pitfall in the diagnosis of lobar collapse.

Glazer et al. (1991) : Anatomy of the major fissure - evaluation with standard and thin-section CT - studied 50 patients and found that on standard CT sections the fissures usually appeared as hypoattenuating bands and less often as lines or hyperattenuating bands. On HRCT in most cases the major fissure was shown as a line, esp. in the upper part of the left major fissure. A '**double-fissure**' sign was most frequently seen at the base of the left lung. Incomplete fissures were seen in about 50% of cases.

Otsuji et al. (1993) : Incomplete interlobar fissures - bronchovascular analysis with CT - some bronchovascular structures crossed or passed through two adjacent lobes in the fused area, the most common being a pulmonary vein.

Berkmen et al. (1994) : Accessory fissures of the LUL can separate any two contiguous segments and are frequently incomplete.

Davis et al. (2000) : A superior accessory fissure of the lower lobe, more common on the right than the left, can be identified on transverse CT sections. It may be orientated obliquely, and contain fluid with an effusion. On frontal radiographs such orientation corresponds with a curvilinear band , coursing from its intersection with the lateral aspect of the major fissure towards the infrahilar region on the right (or heart border on the left).

Note also: Cameron (1993) - a juxta-phrenic peak may be produced by rotation of an inferior accessory fissure - see also p. 2.36.

Sakai et al. (1993) : Visualisation of the major fissure may be improved when **tilted CT** rather than conventional axial scans are used.

Azygos and hemiazygos lobes.
Stibbe (1919) : The accessory pulmonary lobe of the vena azygos.

Weston (l954) : Left-sided lobe of the azygos vein.

Lesser (1964) : Left azygos lobe - case report.

Hanke (1967) : Die vena hemiazygos accessoria mit Röntgenbild - are most apparent left azygos fissures due to left apical bullae?

Neufang and Buelo (1981) : Pleural effusion and azygos lobe.

Postmus et al. (1986) : A family with lobus venae azygos.

Takasugi and Godwin (1989) : Left azygos lobe (CT demonstration of pleural septum).

Felson (1989): The azygos lobe - its variation in health and disease. - look for the **absent   crotch** of the normal azygos in the upper right hilum.

Speckman et al (1981) : Alterations in CT mediastinal anatomy produced by an azygos lobe.

Mata et al. (1990) : CT of intrapulmonary right brachiocephalic vein with an azygos lobe.

Mata et al. (1991) : Normal anatomy and variations of the azygos lobe - the fissure may undulate.

Cáceres et al. (1993) : Increased density of the azygos lobe on frontal chest radiographs **simulating**   disease and due to overlapping tortuous supra-aortic vessels or the thymus.

Mata et al. (1996) : Azygos continuation of IVC associated with an azygos lobe.

For illustrations of pleural fissures see   Illus. **PL-FISSURES**
                                              Illus. **ACCESSORY FISSURE**
                                              Illus. **AZ LB + VN.**

For consolidation in an azygos lobe see Illus. **CONSOL AZYGOS LOBE.**

See also ps. 9.11 - 9.15 re azygos and hemiazygos veins.

Mediastinal lines

Over the past twenty years there has been an increasing awareness of the importance of the mediastinal lines in the recognition of thoracic disease. Effacement and displacement are often a good indication of the presence of disease. Their make-up is well shown on CT axial views. A good knowledge of them is essential for reading plain radiographs and tomograms, including CTs.

If one looks at a plain PA film one can see pleural reflections where the lungs virtually meet, both anteriorly in front of the plane of the trachea and also posteriorly behind the trachea, hila and heart. These are the anterior and posterior junction lines, the posterior being higher. The anterior junction line overlies the lower trachea and carinal area. Para-tracheal, para-aortic, para-oesophageal and para-spinal lines are also present. These are all produced by soft -tissue /air-filled lung interfaces (Fig. 1.13). The upper part of the para-oesophageal line continues upwards into the azygo-oesophageal recess, and the para-azygos and para-tracheal lines. There is some variation between different subjects due to the individual shape of the chest, the depth of the anterior or posterior mediastinum, distortion from old scarring or disease processes, etc.

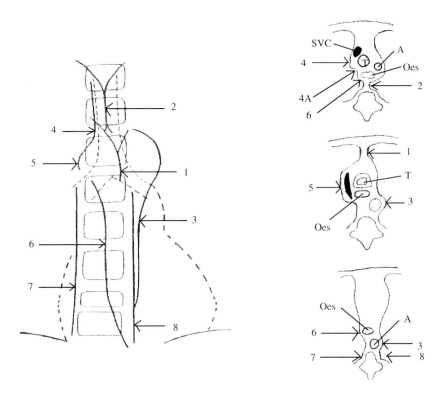

Fig. 1.13 **Mediastinal lines** (formed by tangential surfaces in the mediastinum - after Rémy et al., 1981, Le Poumon Pathologique, by permission).

1 - Anterior mediastinal or Junction line   2 - Posterior Mediastinal or Junction line
3 - Para-aortic line   4 - Right para-tracheal line   4A - Posterior tracheal stripe
5 - Para-azygos line   6 - Para-oesophageal line   7 & 8 - Left & right para-spinal lines.
(The anterior mediastinal line is often obliquely orientated - see p.1.11 and Fig. 1.14c).

The Anterior Junction Line: (Septum or Stripe).
   The anterior pleural reflections give rise to the **anterior junction line**, together with the superior and inferior recesses. The **superior recesses** are produced by the anterior aspects of the lungs contacting the mediastinum behind the manubrium sterni. The line itself is formed by the apposition of the two lungs, together with their respective pleural coverings and the thin layer of mediastinum in this area. It lies retrosternally, and is usually inclined downwards and to the left (rarely to the right). Inferiorly the diverging lungs form the inferior recesses.

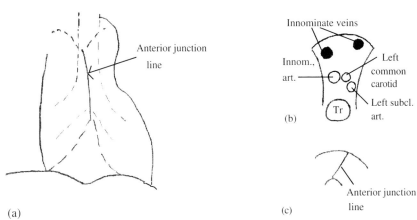

(a)   (c)

Fig. 1.14   Anterior Junction Line.
(a) The anterior mediastinal or junction line, running obliquely downwards, with its superior and inferior recesses (dotted lines).
CT - shows that :   (b) superiorly there is considerable tissue between the recesses, but
(c) inferiorly there is just a thin membrane - when this is directed straight forward a clearly defined anterior mid line will be seen, but when it is obliquely orientated it may not be so readily seen.

   The anterior junction line may be widened by mediastinal fat or an anterior mediastinal mass, such as a goitre, a tumour arising within the thymus or an enlarged aortic arch. The size of the thymus in young children accounts for them not having a visible line (see also ps. 18.17 - 18.18). Obliteration or opacity on one side of the line may occur with adjacent lung consolidation or collapse, or from adjacent pleural fluid. Conversely a pneumothorax may accentuate the line. Movement of the line commonly occurs with lung or lobar collapse. Movement with left or right upper lobe collapse is described on ps. 2.2 - 2.28. Movement may also occur with right lower lobe collapse - '**the upper triangle sign**' - see p. 2.29.
   '**Anterior lung herniation**' may be seen with collapse or reduced volume of the left lung or upper lobe and is due to compensatory hyperexpansion of the right upper lobe and the movement of the anterior junction anatomy to the left (see Fig. 2.24 and ps. 2.28 - 2.29) - also lung and pulmonary artery hypoplasia (ps. 7.8 - 9). When there is a deep anterior mediastinum, as with emphysema, an anterior mediastinal mass may only occupy part of the anterior mediastinum, and then a normal line may not exclude the presence of a small mass.
   The **superior   recesses**, which reflect off the great vessels, commonly project lateral to the manubrium sterni, but the lower parts of these usually lie behind it. The superior recesses are best shown on tomograms, but may also be seen on oblique views of the upper mediastinum or sternum. Normally the superior recesses bound mediastinal fat, but goitres or dilatations of the innominate veins etc. may displace them laterally. The superior recesses may be further apart on supine radiographs or those taken in expiration.
   Unlike the posterior junction line (ps. 1.14 - 1.16) the anterior junction line does not extend above the level of the supra-sternal notch.
   The **inferior recesses** are somewhat variable in appearance, although they are usually oblique and straight. With much mediastinal fat or ' fat pads ' they may become convex. Similarly they may be displaced by pericardial cysts, very large internal mammary nodes, etc. A good example of

fatty displacement is shown in Illus. **FAT Pt. 8a-c.** Differentiation from the shadow of the inferior vena cava is usually made by the more medial extension of the recess.

Fig. 1.15   Inferior recesses and IVC.

Anterior junction anatomy should also be considered in relation to the retro-sternal line and space (see ps. 1.27 - 1.29). 'The latter is essentially the lateral projection of the same structures.

References.
Gray (1936) wrote: "In the front of the chest, where the parietal pleura is reflected backwards to the pericardium, the two pleural sacs are in contact for a short distance".
Knuttson (1955) : The mediastinal pleura.
Cimmino (1964) : Proved the nature of the anterior junction line by taking a tomographic cut just deep to the sternum, with the patient- lying transversely across the table to avoid 'parasitic' or 'ghost' shadows.
Blank and Castellino (1972) : Patterns of pleural reflections of left upper mediastinum.
Proto and Tocino (1980) : Lobar collapse patterns and the line.
Rémy et al. (1981) : The pathological lung.
Proto et al. (1983c) : Anterior junction anatomy.
Coussement (1984) : The Normal Lung, its Variants and Traps.

The Supra-Azygos Recess.
    This space lies behind the superior vena cava. Air filled lung within it outlines the right upper mediastinum - the trachea, oesophagus and para-spinal line. The **anterior junction line** may be seen depending on the amount of fat present, the depth of the anterior mediastinum, or the position of the cross section (i.e. higher or lower across this space).

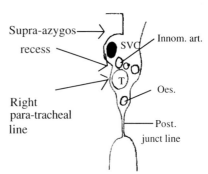

Fig. 1.16   The supra-azygos recess.

    The superior vena cava pushes into this space to a variable degree, more in the elderly and in those with heart failure. Tortuous innominate or subclavian arteries or a high aortic arch may all bulge into it and simulate a tumour.

The lung/right tracheal interface produces the right para-tracheal line which is present in 80-90% of people and is not present when the superior vena cava and fat, etc. overlie the trachea.

The left superior mediastinal reflections and the aorto-pulmonary line or stripe.

The upper anterior mediastinum lies at a varying depth from the upper sternum, and in those who have the anterior mediastinum more closely abutting the anterior chest wall, a less marked or poor anterior junction line is formed, and para-tracheal, para-subclavian and aorto-pulmonary lines may be formed.

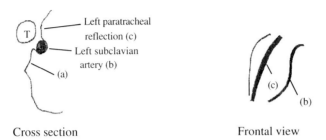

Cross section   Frontal view

Fig. 1.17 Left superior mediastinal reflections - these are due to air-filled lung contacting the mediastinum in front of the subclavian artery (a), alongside the left subclavian artery (b), and (c) behind the artery. However when much fat is present, the individual lines will not be formed as the subclavian artery will not stand-out from the mediastinum.

Keats (1972) noted an **aorto-pulmonary mediastinal stripe** extending obliquely downwards to the left; it arises supero-medially, crosses the aortic knuckle and merges inferiorly with the pulmonary artery and/ or the heart. This stripe represents the pleural-lung reflection over the left supero-anterior part of the mediastinum.

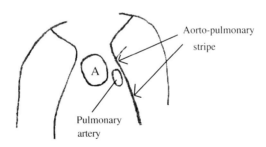

Fig. 1.18 The aorto-pulmonary stripe (coronal section).

The stripe is seen particularly in subjects who do not have a well marked anterior junction line, i.e. having the anterior mediastinum more abutting the chest wall. It is produced by tangential x-rays striking the mediastinum a little further posteriorly than the position of the normal anterior junction, and lies a little anterior to the aorto-pulmonary window (ps. 13.24 - 13.26). It has some variability in its appearance as is shown below.
This line was further studied by Blank and Castellino (1972 and 1977 - the latter paper dealing mainly with mediastinal lymphadenopathy), by Cimmino (1975) and by Heitzman (1988).
It may be displaced laterally by adjacent mediastinal masses, enlarged lymph nodes or a left sided SVC (see ps. 9.16 - 9.17).

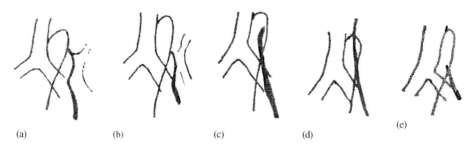

(a)   (b)   (c)   (d)   (e)

Fig. 1.19 Patterns of pleural reflection between the aortic arch, the left pulmonary artery, the left heart border and the left main bronchus - (after Blank and Castellino, 1972, Radiology, **102**, 585 - 789, by permission).

Further reference.

Proto et al. (1989) - The left paratracheal reflection - a reflection present in 30% of patients - it extends vertically from the aortic knuckle and lies medial to the reflection produced by the left subclavian artery. It is most readily seen on tomograms, 1 to 2 cm anterior to the coronal plane which shows the left subclavian artery.

The interface between the right lung and the mediastinum.

On the right, the interface between the right lung (the right middle and upper lobes) and the pleura overlying the right side of the pericardium, the ascending aorta and SVC have also been studied by Blank (1989). The lower part is usually complete (unless a depressed sternum is present - see ps. 2.25 and 12.35), but the upper part is variably complete or absent.

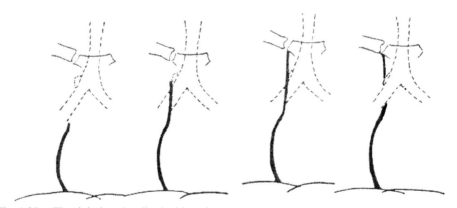

Fig. 1.20   The right lung/mediastinal interface - note that the upper part may be complete or incomplete. (after Blank, 1989, Chest Radiographic Analysis, Fig. 7.5 with permission from Churchill Livingstone).

The Posterior Junction Line. (or stripe).

The posterior junction anatomy, like the anterior, comprises the **posterior   junction   line,** together with its **superior   and   inferior   recesses** (see Figs. 1.21 to 1.23). It lies higher than the anterior junction line (Fig. 1.14). The superior recesses are formed by the two lungs approaching the mediastinum in front of Dl and D2 vertebral bodies. The line is due to the double layer of left and right parietal pleura overlying D3 to D5 vertebrae, and lying behind the oesophagus. The inferior recesses are formed by the lungs diverging from the midline, due to the forward arching of the right and left superior intercostal vein, the posterior parts of the azygos vein and the aortic arch. The right inferior recess lies lower than the left. The depth of the space between the spine and the oesophagus is variable in different subjects and is also affected by the degree of expansion of the lungs and the amount of fat present. When widened by fat, or the oesophagus itself, the line may appear as a stripe. It may also be widened when the two sides are deviated by a mediastinal abscess or haematoma. It usually overlies the tracheal air column, and is often slightly concave to the right.

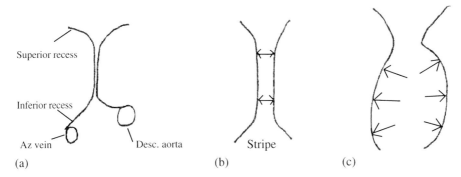

(a) (b) (c)

Fig. 1.21   (a & b) Normal anatomy of the posterior junction line - note its vertical course. It is also higher in position as compared with the anterior junction line and may rise as high as the lung apices and above the supra-sternal notch. (c) Grossly widened line or stripe due to an abscess or haematoma.

The position of the line in relation to the midline may be variable.

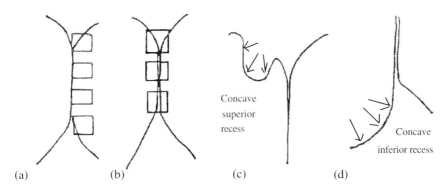

(a)   (b)   (c)   (d)

Fig. 1.22 (a & b) Variant positions of the posterior junction line. (c & d) Deformed superior and inferior recesses - a convex superior recess usually indicates pressure from a superior mediastinal mass. Similarly a concave inferior recess may indicate an overlying mass.

The oesophagus may affect the posterior junction line, but this is variable and depends on the local anatomy. In most people the oesophagus lies in front of the line, so that when the oesophagus is well visualised and dilated with air (or fluid) it will be superimposed on the line (Fig. 1.27a). However it may lie within the line or stripe and when it does and is dilated it will then spread the two sides of the line (Fig. 1.27b) - in the latter instance the oesophagus lies immediately in front of the spine and/may be considered as having a 'mesentery', in reality the inferior posterior junction line.

The posterior inferior junction line and left pleurooesophageal stripe are more clearly seen in patients with emphysema - see Curtis and Fisher (1998) and Fig. 1.16.

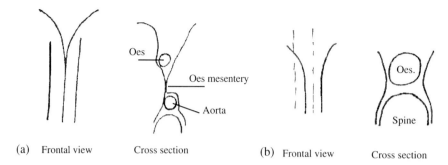

(a) Frontal view   Cross section   (b) Frontal view   Cross section

Fig. 1.23   (a) Air-filled oesophagus superimposed on a normal posterior junction line. The **'oesophageal mesentery'** is produced when there is virtual contact of the two lungs behind the oesophagus.   (b) If the oesophagus lies immediately in front of the spine it may widen the posterior mediastinal stripe particularly if it is distended with air or fluid.

Sometimes the oesophagus and the trachea may be side by side. When this happens a normal air-filled oesophagus may mimic mediastinal emphysema or a dilated trachea. On barium swallow examinations and CT the oesophagus is the seen to lie more to the left than usual. On both sides 'stripes' may be seen, but most commonly only the right is visible.

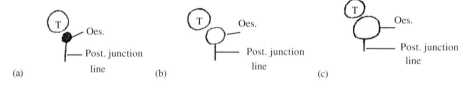

(a)   (b)   (c)

(a) No air in oesophagus   (b) Normal air-filled oesophagus   (c) Dilated air-filled oesophagus
    T = trachea   and posterior junction line.   with virtual obliteration of the
                                                                                 posterior junction line (see also
                                                                                 Fig. 1.23b above).

Fig. 1.24   Almost ' side-by- side ' trachea and oesophagus.

References.
Cimmino : (1981) : 'The esophago-pleural tripe - an update'.
Proto (1983d) : Review of anatomy.

The Para-oesophageal line (also known as the pleuro-oesophageal or azygo-oesophageal lines) is seen on high KV frontal views and tomograms lying behind the heart and mediastinum. It is formed by the interface between the air-filled right lung and the posterior mediastinum, often adjacent to the mid and lower oesophagus, but as shown in Fig. 1.26, it may be separated from the oesophagus by a varying amount of fat. It curves upwards and a little laterally to the right behind the trachea, and joins the para-azygos and para-tracheal lines above the azygo-oesophageal recess. It is a **very important landmark, for the localisation and detection of disease in this area of the chest.** A clearly defined and normally situated line is usually a good indication of normality in this part of the mediastinum.
   The line may be displaced to either side by collapse or loss of volume in a lung, particularly a lower lobe. It may also be displaced by a dilated oesophagus or an oesophageal mass, Loss of the line is produced by consolidation or total collapse of the right lower lobe, a posteriorly situated right sided pleural effusion, a leaking aortic aneurysm or an abscess in the posterior mediastinum, etc. The line is usually preserved with sub-carinal node enlargement, as these nodes lie mainly

anterior to it, but very large sub-carinal nodes may obliterate the upper part of the line or displace it to the right. It may also be displaced to the right by enlarged aorto-pulmonary nodes (see ps. 13.24 - 26) or a large neurinoma arising from the left sympathetic chain.

Sometimes the para-oesophageal line may appear thickened or double, due to fluid or air in the oesophagus. A double stripe may also be seen if the left lower lobe extends considerably in front of the descending aorta, even beyond the position of the pre-aortic line (see next section).

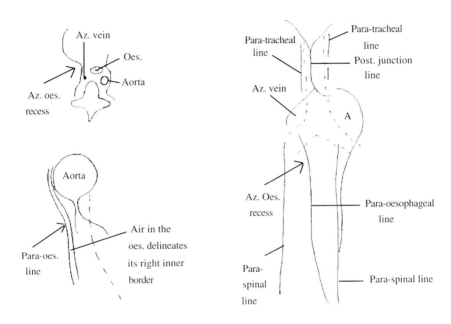

Fig. 1.25   Lines in the posterior mediastinum, including the para-oesophageal line.

References.
Lachman (1942), Gladnikoff (1948), Knuttson (1955) : The mediastinal pleura.
Cimmino (1956, 1961, 1964, 1965, 1981), Cimmino and Snead (1965)
Ormond et al. (1963), Palayew (1971) - the 'tracheo-oesophageal stripe',
Rémy et al. (1981)
Généreux (1983a), Coussement et al. (1984), Heitzman (1984).

The Azygo-oesophageal Recesses.
There are in fact two recesses, one above and one below the level of the azygos vein, but the lower is usually more developed and is most commonly referred to as the '**azygo-oesophageal recess**'. It is usually well seen in adults and in children, particularly those with asthma, and is best seen on high KV radiographs and tomograms displaying the lower chest in front of the dorsal spine. Its medial boundary is seen as a smooth arc, convex to the left and extending inferiorly from the azygos vein (Fig. 1.26). It becomes larger with full inspiration and is accentuated by a marked dorsal kyphosis and with severe emphysema. The space is filled by the apex of the right lower lobe. It has a close but somewhat variable relationship to the oesophagus, depending on the amount of fat etc. in the mediastinum (see previous section).

When the recess is fully developed, the right lung will lie behind the carina and the main bronchi, and this will. make the posterior aspects of these clearer on tomograms etc. When the mediastinal pleura meets that of the other side behind the oesophagus it forms the inferior posterior junction line (see Fig. 1.27).

The inferior posterior junction line is produced when the posterior aspect of the azygo-oesophageal recess contacts the left mediastinal pleura behind the oesophagus. This occurs because the oesophagus variably contacts the air-filled right lung both above and below the level of the azygos vein. When present, the para-oesophageal line lies more posteriorly and the oesophagus appears to have a mesentery.

The **azygo-oesophageal recess** may he shallow or deep if the recess extends in front of the spine. It tends to be larger with emphysema, left lower lobe collapse or in older people. The lung tucking into the azygo-oesophageal recess is sometimes known as the '**crista   pulmonis**'.

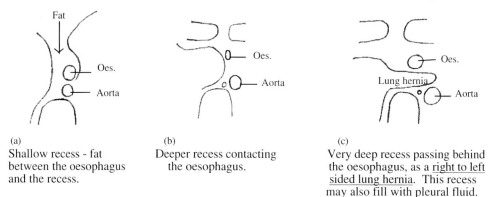

(a)	(b)	(c)
Shallow recess - fat between the oesophagus and the recess.	Deeper recess contacting the oesophagus.	Very deep recess passing behind the oesophagus, as a <u>right to left sided lung hernia</u>. This recess may also fill with pleural fluid.

Fig. 1.26 Variable size of the azygo-oesophageal recess.

Pathological conditions which may obliterate the recess are:
   anteriorly and medially - right tracheo-bronchial and/or subcarinal node enlargement a sub-carinal bronchogenic cyst (see also p. 3.13) and left atrial enlargement or a pericardial effusion;
   posteriorly - oesophageal dilatation or tumour, para-oesophageal lymph nodes (enlarged from lung or oesophageal tumours, reticulosis, etc.) para- or pre-vertebral masses; a large hiatus hernia will extend up into it medially and inferiorly (Fig. 1.27 b).

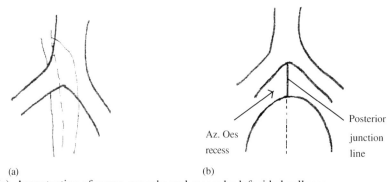

(a)   (b)

Fig. 1.27 (a) Accentuation of azygo-oesophageal recess by left sided collapse.
(b) Large hiatal hernia pressing into the azygo-oesophageal recess from in front. If the lungs do not appear to be displaced laterally this may be due to them passing behind the hernia, with an inferior posterior junction line.

   Herniation of the right lung, with left sided collapse or following a left pneumonectomy will markedly accentuate the space, sometimes with actual lung herniation to the left (see p. 2.40). Similarly with some large pleural effusions, an apparent medially situated mass may be due to fluid distending and herniating the recess to the left. An air/fluid level may been seen within the recess with a hydropneumothorax, and drainage tubes may pass to the left of the midline in the recess.

Dilatation of, or masses arising from the oesophagus may displace the recess to the right. The line should always be looked for on high KV radiographs. In achalasia ballooning out of the oesophagus may occur both above the level of the azygos arch and/or below it.

References
Heitzman et al. (1971 a) : Azygos vein and pleural reflections.
Heitzman (1977 and 1988) : The mediastinum.
Onitsuka and Kuhns (1980) : Dextroconcavity of the mediastinum in the azygo-oesophageal recess - a normal variant in young adults.
Lund and Lien (1982 and 1983) : Abnormalities of the azygo-oesophageal recess at CT.
Pecorari and Weisbrod (1989) : Pseudotumoral pleural fluid collections in the azygo-oesophageal recess.

The Pre-aortic line
In many subjects the left lower lobe extends in front of the descending aorta to produce the pre-aortic line. This is often seen on high KV radiographs and is due to the left lower lobe tucking into the aorto-pulmonary window, behind the left lower lobe bronchus and behind the heart. It is often seen to extend down as far as Dl0. The left lower lobe tends to extend into this space more commonly with emphysema, when the aorta is tortuous, or with a dorsal kyphosis.

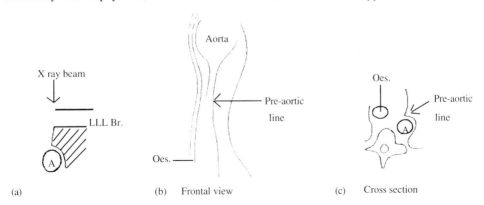

Fig. 1.28   The 'pre-aortic line'.

The para-aortic line.
This follows the line of the descending aorta on its left side. Its presence depends on aerated left lung and particularly an aerated left lower lobe being adjacent to it. Like the para-oesophageal line, it is a very important landmark in the chest, and is well seen on high KV radiographs.

Displacement of the line may be seen with aortic abnormalities, masses arising in the spine and creeping around the descending aorta, or other masses such as a sympathetic chain neurinoma, etc.

Loss of the line is usually due to consolidation or collapse in the adjacent lung, usually the left lower lobe. It may also be lost with a posteriorly situated pleural effusion, an adjacent tumour, a leaking aneurysm or an abscess e.g. resulting from oesophageal perforation, etc. It is also lost when the mediastinum is squashed, particularly by the left inferior pulmonary vein, as with pectus excavatum (see also p.12.34). It is also partially lost in thin people, in whom the aorta tends to be 'buried' in the mediastinum (see also references below, especially the study by Okawada et al. on Japanese people, many of whom are thin and have a narrow AP diameter of the chest). Partial loss also may occur with adjacent tumour or due to contact of part of the aorta with normal structures (see ref. to Takahashi et al., below).

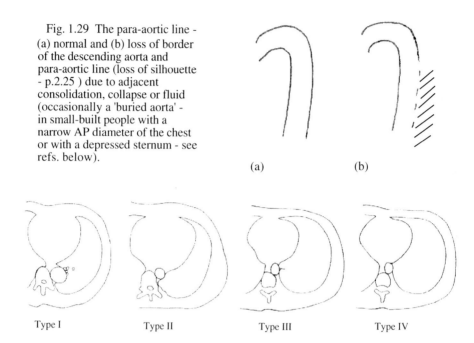

Fig. 1.29 The para-aortic line - (a) normal and (b) loss of border of the descending aorta and para-aortic line (loss of silhouette - p.2.25) due to adjacent consolidation, collapse or fluid (occasionally a 'buried aorta' - in small-built people with a narrow AP diameter of the chest or with a depressed sternum - see refs. below).

(a)   (b)

Type I   Type II   Type III   Type IV

(c) Four types of mediastinum/lung interface - type I - the descending aorta is in contact with the left hilar and lower lobe vessels, - types II - IV the aorta tends to be 'buried' in the mediastinum, with an obliquely or AP orientated interface, and with a 'beak' (? due to the pulmonary ligament) in type III (after Okawada et al., 1993, with permission from Clinical Radiology).

References.
Berne et al. (1969) : Implicated **pulmonary ligament nodes in its loss**.
Figley (1969) : Loss with **consolidation, pleural fluid, mediastinal haematoma or neoplasm**.
Takahashi et al. (1992) : Obliteration of the descending aortic interface in **pectus   excavatum** - correlation with clockwise rotation of the heart.
van Gelderen (1992) : Reviewed 45,000 chest radiographs over a 12 year period and found a localised loss of the infrabronchial descending aorta interface as a normal variant in 18 cases. CT in one showed this to be due to the **overlapping left inferior pulmonary vein**.
Okawada et al. (1993) : Showed that the para-aortic line could be partially obliterated in about 25% of subjects by (a) an **elongated aorta making contact with the left lower lobe or hila vessels** and (b) if there was an obliquely-orientated mediastinum /lung interface lateral to the descending aorta. This occurred particularly in patients with a narrow AP diameter of the chest.
Takahashi et al. (1994) : **Partial aortic interface obliteration ('buried aorta')** can be seen on some normal frontal chest radiographs due to direct contact with or proximity to the aortic margin by pulmonary arteries in the suprahilar and upper hilar area, superior segment vessels in the lower hilar region and various structures including L inferior pulmonary vein, mediastinal fat and L ventricle more inferiorly.

Dee (1974) : Deviation of the descending thoracic aorta as a sign of left atrial enlargement (it may push it laterally).

For illustrations showing mediastinal lines see Illus. **MEDIAST LINES**.

The bronchi and bronchial segments.

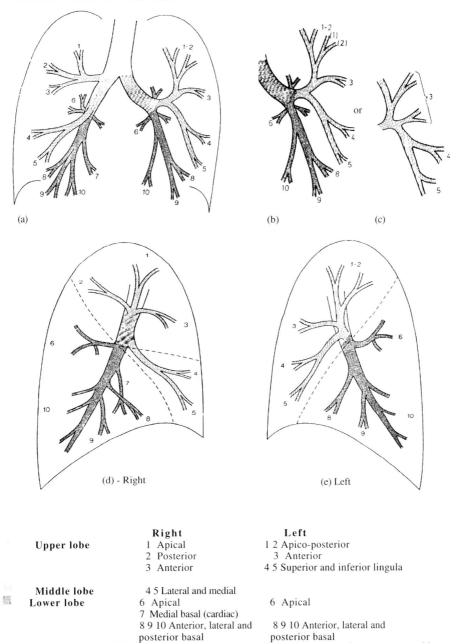

	Right	**Left**
Upper lobe	1 Apical	1 2 Apico-posterior
	2 Posterior	3 Anterior
	3 Anterior	4 5 Superior and inferior lingula
Middle lobe	4 5 Lateral and medial	
Lower lobe	6 Apical	6 Apical
	7 Medial basal (cardiac)	
	8 9 10 Anterior, lateral and posterior basal	8 9 10 Anterior, lateral and posterior basal

Fig. 1.30   Diagrams of the broncho-pulmonary segments, with nomenclature approved by an International Committee (1949) and by the Thoracic Society. (a) Anterior view, (b-c) left oblique views and (d-e) lateral views (after Pallardy and Rémy, 1970, with permission from Kodak Ltd.).

[Some American authors renumber segments 2 and 3, as 3 and 2 respectively. Bronchi and arteries to the various segments may be given similar numbers, prefixed by 'B' or 'A' as appropriate.]

The **intermediate bronchus** is the continuation of the R main bronchus from the origin of the RUL bronchus to its division into middle and lower lobe bronchi.

For bronchograms showing normal anatomy - see Illus. **BRONCHOGRAM NORMAL**.

The tracheo-bronchial tree and some congenital abnormalities (See also p. 3.8).

   A detailed knowledge of bronchial anatomy and its common variations is essential. The first good description was given by Professor Aeby in 1880. He noted that the right main bronchus was wider than the left and descended more vertically from the trachea. He also attached considerable importance to the so-called eparterial bronchus. Brock (1946 & 1954) published a well illustrated monograph on the anatomy of the bronchial tree in particular relation to his theory that 'bronchial emboli' are the cause of many lung abscesses (see p.19.2). At an International Congress in London, in 1949, a **nomenclature for the bronchial tree was agreed** (see Brock, 1950 and Sealy et al., 1993)**, and this should always be used to avoid confusion** (Fig. 1.30).

   Common anatomical variations include -

   (i) anterior segmental bronchus of the left upper lobe arising with the apico-posterior segment instead of with the lingula;

   (ii) segmental bronchi or groups of bronchi of an upper lobe arising from the trachea or from a main bronchus; - may be missed at bronchoscopy, but **not** usually at bronchography - may be supernumerary or part of an otherwise normal right upper lobe.

(iii) Localised bronchial atresia (see p. 3.8).

(iv) A sub-apical bronchus in either or both lower lobes.

(v) Occasionally the bronchial anatomy of the two lungs is reversed, as in '**situs   inversus**' (ps. 3.15 & 15.6), or two 'left lungs' are present - '**situs ambiguus**' (Landay et al., 1982).

| (a) supplying all of the RUL. | (b) supernumerary RUL. | (c) supernumerary segment. | (d) supplying a segment. | (e) CT - small round translucency postero-lateral to the trachea. |

Fig. 1.31 Appearances of tracheal bronchus (a to d after Davidson, 1956, with permission from Clinical Radiology).
For illustrations of tracheal bronchus see Illus. **TRACHEAL BRONCHUS**.

Further references.

Boyden (1949) : Cleft left upper lobes and the split anterior bronchus. (1955a) : Segmental anatomy of the lungs.
Gans and Potts (1951) : Anomalous lobe of lung arising from the oesophagus.
Davidson (1956) : Described three cases and reviewed the literature.
Harris (1958) : Clinical significance of the tracheal bronchus.
Atwell (1967) : Major and minor anomalies of the tracheobronchial tree.
Béquery et al. (1980) : Accessory cardiac bronchus.
Iannaccone et al. (1983) : Double right tracheal bronchus.
Maesen (1983) : Supernumerary bronchus of right upper lobe.
Ritsema et al., (1983) : 8 pts. with 'ectopic' apical bronchi of the RUL (one with bronchiectasis in this segment).
Gubbawy (1984) : Left tracheal bronchus with situs inversus.
Shipley et al. (1985) : CT of the tracheal bronchus.
Morrison (1988) : Demonstration of tracheal bronchus by CT.
Sotile et al. (1988) : Accessory cardiac bronchus demonstrated by CT.
Lee et al. (1991) : CT anatomy of the lingular segmental bronchi.
McGuinness et al. (1993) : Accessory cardiac bronchus (arising from the medial wall of the intermediate bronchus) shown by CT, with vestigial enhancing lung tissue.
Wu et al. (1999) : Variant bronchial anatomy - CT appearance and classification.

The tracheal and bronchial lines and stripes.

   The right para-tracheal line or stripe - normally this is from 1 to 4 mm thick (average 2 mm). It extends from the thoracic inlet to the right tracheo-bronchial angle, and it is formed by the tracheal wall, interstitial mediastinal tissue and adjacent pleura. Thickening may be due to adjacent fat, but is often good evidence of local adjacent disease such as lymphadenopathy, infection or haemorrhage, pleural thickening or thickening of the tracheal wall. It should always be looked for on frontal radiographs, and is a particularly valuable sign following severe trauma, since a normal right para-tracheal stripe usually implies that there is no adjacent haematoma, and therefore that a serious vascular injury is unlikely.

Loss of the line occurs with opacification of the adjacent lung i.e. consolidation or collapse of the right upper lobe, or from adjacent pleural fluid.

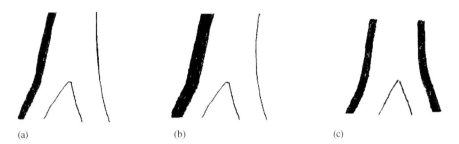

(a)   (b)   (c)

Fig. 1.32 Para-tracheal lines or stripes (a) Normal right para-tracheal stripe. (b) Thickened right para-tracheal stripe. (c) Left and right para-tracheal stripes.

Left para-tracheal line - in some subjects the left lung may lie adjacent to the left side of the trachea, medial to the left subclavian artery and give rise to a similar stripe to that on the right side.

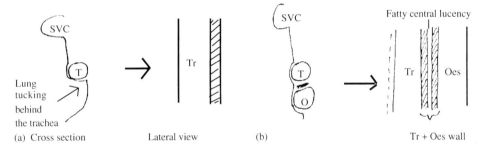

Fig. 1.33 (a) Retro-tracheal and (b) tracheo-oesophageal stripes - the less common anterior tracheal line is shown in (b) as a dotted line.

The '**retro-tracheal**' or '**posterior tracheal stripe**' is due to air in the trachea, outlining its posterior inner border and air filled lung tucking behind the trachea (Fig. 1.33). It is normally 2 to 3 mm thick, but may sometimes appear thicker when the oesophagus lies behind it and is air-filled. It is then really a 'tracheo-oesophageal stripe'. It extends from the thoracic inlet to the tracheal bifurcation.

The presence of one or the other stripes (sometimes one, and then the other in the same individual on serial studies) probably accounts for a rather wide range in thickness, and its variability on some serial radiographs. True thickening may be caused by mediastinal thickening, oesophageal wall thickening or by fat in the mediastinum between the oesophagus and the trachea giving rise to a lucent thin vertical line within the '**tracheo-oesophageal   stripe**'. This stripe may extend down lower than the position of the azygos vein where it would be obliterated by this adjacent arch if retrotracheal, thus demonstrating that the posterior aspect of the stripe is endo-oesophageal. Apparent thickening may also be due to an empty oesophagus, outlined posteriorly by the contacting lungs at the posterior mediastinal, junction lines.

Occasionally 'anterior tracheal stripes' are seen, due to air-filled lung tucking in, in front of the trachea, or it lying medial to the azygos vein, when an azygos lobe is present.

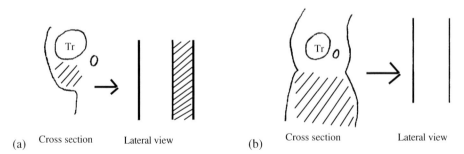

(a)   Cross section   Lateral view   (b)   Cross section   Lateral view

Fig. 1.34 (a) Tumour, nodes or oesophageal mass thickening the retro-tracheal stripe.
(b) When there are very large nodes or a tumour which obliterates the retro-tracheal space, the stripe will be completely lost, as no air filled lung will project behind the trachea.

When there is free fluid (as opposed to loculated fluid, soft tissue thickening or tumour), an upright lateral radiograph may show a normal posterior tracheal stripe, even though a corresponding CT section taken with the patient lying down may show fluid in the recess.

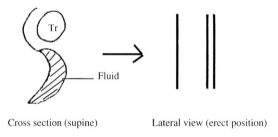

Cross section (supine)   Lateral view (erect position)

Fig. 1.35 Effect of masses or fluid on the retro-tracheal stripe.

Lung in the azygo-oesophageal excess outlines the posterior wall of the right main and intermediate bronchi, forming the 'stripe of the intermediate bronchus'.

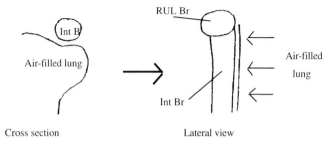

Cross section   Lateral view

Fig. 1.36 Stripe of intermediate bronchus - this may be thickened posteriorly or obliterated by disease processes, e.g. nodes, tumours, consolidation, or congestive heart failure.

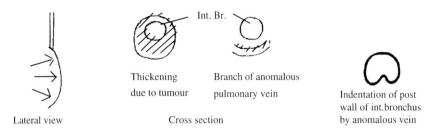

Lateral view | Thickening due to tumour | Cross section | Branch of anomalous pulmonary vein | Indentation of post wall of int.bronchus by anomalous vein

Fig. 1.37 An anomalous pulmonary vein may sometimes pass behind the intermediate bronchus to simulate a hilar mass (see also p.13.13). This vein can sometimes produce a small indentation or nodule in the posterior wall of the intermediate bronchus as seen on CT sections.

Air-filled lung in the azygo-oesophageal and pre-aortic recesses may give rise to '**retro-bronchial stripes**' behind the main bronchi (see also p.13.12). Air filled lung may pass behind the right lower and middle lobe bronchi, accounting for stripes being seen with these. On the left side, air-filled lung may give rise to stripes of the lingular and lower lobe bronchi. A thicker stripe due to gas in the oesophagus may sometimes be seen.

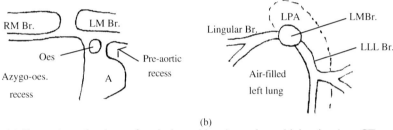

(a)　　　　　　　　　　　　　　　　　　　　(b)

Fig. 1 38　(a) Formation of stripes of main bronchi or 'retro-bronchial stripes' on CT sections - see also p. 13.12. (b)Formation of stripes of lingula and LLL bronchi (lateral view).

　　With enlarged nodes, a localised tumour, or air-less lung due to consolidation or collapse, part of the stripe may be thickened or lost on the lateral view. Also a poorly developed recess will not allow a normal stripe to be seen.

　　Fat may also aid in the visualisation of the larger bronchi, especially outlining the anterior aspect of the intermediate bronchus. When this occurs air-less adjacent lung may not render the stripe invisible.

Further references.

Para-tracheal line:
Savoca et al. (1977) : Right para-tracheal stripe.
Kittredge (1979) : Right postero-lateral tracheal band.
Neufang and Beyer (1982) : Right para-tracheal stripe.
Woodring et al. (1982 b and 1984) : Trauma.

Left sided stripes :
Webb and Gamsu (1983) : CT of the left retrobronchial stripe.
Fraser et al. (1988).

Posterior tracheal stripe:
Bachman and Teixidor (1975) : Loss of the posterior tracheal line may be due to tumour, nodes, fluid or consolidation displacing the normally air-filled right lung tucking behind the trachea. It is **not** usually produced by lesions in the **left lung** unless there is gross mediastinal shift or marked lymphadenopathy and usually means inoperability. Loss of the line may also be produced by an oesophageal tumour or a fluid filled dilated oesophagus. A dilated air-filled oesophagus may produce a double stripe.

Putman et al. (1976) : Thickening of the stripe due to oesophageal tumour. 20 patients had stripes > 4.5 mm on lateral views - a sign of perioesophageal involvement which may be found 6 months before symptoms start in up to 50% of cases on previous radiographs.
Shields and Holtz (1976) : The retrosternal space.
Kormano and Yrjanä (1980) : Correlation of CT and plain films.
Yrjanä (1980): Recurrent oesophageal tumours.
Proto and Speckman (1979 & 1980) : Lateral chest radiographs and discussion of the lines.
Palayew (1979) : The tracheo-oesophageal stripe and the posterior tracheal band.
Saks et al. (1983) : Deformities due to varices may be accentuated following endoscopic sclerosant therapy.

Intermediate bronchus - posterior stripe:
Schnur et al. (1981) : Thickening of the posterior wall of the intermediate bronchus - a sign on
lateral radiographs of congestive heart failure, lymph node enlargement and neoplastic infiltration.
Webb et al. (1984d) : Neoplastic infiltration - noted that an anomalous vein may pass behind the intermediate bronchus to simulate a hilar mass.
Martinez and Esserman (1984) : Right lung pneumonia.
Kim et al. (1995) : Nodule in posterior wall of intermediate bronchus caused by an anomalous pulmonary vein branch in 14/280 pts. - it originated in the posterior segment of the RUL or apical segment of the RLL and drained into the superior or inferior pulmonary vein.

Left lower lobe bronchus - anterior wall stripe on lateral radiographs:
Lang and Friedman (1990) : Noted considerable variation in the thickness of this stripe and concluded that thickening or effacement of this stripe is an **unreliable** sign of disease.

Visualisation of major bronchi by air within them:
Gladnikoff (1948).

(See also p. 13. 19 - CT of the hila).

The lateral chest radiograph.
    The technique is discussed on ps 1.1. and 20.9. Sometimes the question is posed - should a lateral radiograph be taken in addition to a frontal view (usually PA)? The author's practice is always to have this done if disease is seen on the frontal view, or if there is a good index of suspicion of disease on clinical grounds. With low KV PA examinations, so much of the thorax and lungs is omitted or poorly displayed, that lateral views are then even more important.
    On high KV lateral views, using the air-gap technique and an 11 ft f.f.d., there is little difference between a right and left lateral view, and for practical purposes it really does not matter which lateral is taken. However with low KV and a 6 ft f.f.d., and because of beam divergence, magnification will be apparent on the side further from the cassette. Thus with a left lateral (i.e. the left side adjacent to the cassette), the right hemi-thorax will be slightly magnified. The right side will also tend to project more anteriorly, posteriorly, superiorly and inferiorly, than the corresponding areas on the left. The right breast will tend to project more anteriorly, sometimes suggesting an anterior mediastinal pseudomass. The dome of the left hemidiaphragm will tend to project below that of the right. (The reverse will happen with the right side closer to the cassette).

Middle lobe collapse or disease, may sometimes be **completely   missed** on frontal views, if the disease or lesser fissure is not tangential to the x-ray beam (Figs. 1.12 & 2.16). Tumours adjacent to the spine, or in the costo-phrenic angles, behind or anterior to the dome of the diaphragm may also not be seen. The same is true regarding some nodules lying anteriorly, overlying the heart or great vessels.

Special points to note on lateral views:
    (i) technical: (a) well positioned lung apex, shoulders and scapulae out of the way,
                (b) good lateral position (usually easily obtained, except in patients with gross scoliosis or similar spinal deformity and maximal lung expansion.
    (ii) reading the lateral radiograph: most students and clinicians (and even some radiologists) have considerable difficulty, so some points need emphasis
                (a) The scapulae and axillary folds (also arm stumps etc. - Illus. **ARM   STUMPS** - see p. 6.28) must be distinguished from vascular structures, the tracheal air-column, etc.

(b) One should learn to recognise the different appearances of the left and right lungs - not only the differing fissures (see Fig. 1.4), but also their bronchi and differing pulmonary arteries (see Fig. 1.47 and ps. 1.33 - 35), particularly by studying the occasional 'selective left or right laterals' in patients who have had a pneumonectomy. Illus. **PNEUMONECTOMY, Pts. 11 & 12.**

(c) Recognising the normal anatomy in the various areas and any added shadows.

1. Air-filled anterior area above the heart, in front of the anterior mediastinum, the height of the two leaves of the diaphragm, and the position of the gastric fundal gas bubble.

2. Well inflated lower lobes overlying the lower dorsal spine, with a 'whiter area' over the upper dorsal spine due to the shoulder girdle muscles. Reversal of this will occur with lower lobe collapse, consolidation or - a pleural effusion (see also Fig. 2.18 & p. 2.21).

3. Position and size of the tracheal column, defects within it, and its posterior stripe.

4. The ring shadows of the upper (or other large) bronchi (see also ps. 2.29 - 2.30 and Illus. **BRONCHIAL RINGS**).
Normally the ring shadows in the hilar region are due to the right upper lobe and left upper lobe bronchi, being seen end-on, with the right being uppermost and a little more anterior (Fig. 2.25a). However reorientation may occur with collapse, fibrosis, etc., and a main bronchus may become horizontally orientated, and give rise to a ring shadow. Sometimes even a lower lobe bronchus may lie horizontally, but mostly they are displaced backwards or forwards (Fig. 2.25 b, c & d).

When one or both ring shadows are very well outlined on a lateral view, one should always consider the possible presence of surrounding solid or air-less tissue, such as consolidation, tumour, nodes, etc.

5. The pulmonary arteries are discussed on ps. 1.33 to 1.38. However it must be emphasised that on lateral views, both must always be studied with the rounded right pulmonary artery lying anterior to the carina, and the 'crook-like' left lying posterior and a little higher (Fig. 1.47). Noting only one pulmonary artery usually implies a major collapse, fluid or absence of lung on the contra-lateral side.

6. The inferior pulmonary veins make a nodular shadow in the lower hilum (see also Illus. **VENOUS CONFLUENCE**), roughly overlain by the intermediate bronchus, and their recognition is of considerable importance in differentiation from tumour or other masses - one should look for joining veins - Fig. 1.51). Varices may also be noted in the same position.

7. The typical concave posterior margin of the IVC is usually well seen on lateral views (particularly with a major collapse or pleural fluid on the contra-lateral side - Fig. 9.5a), as is its variants- the straight or convex borders (Figs. 9.5 b & c). As this part may be normal with azygos continuation of the IVC, visualisation of the IVC on a lateral view does not preclude this anomaly.

The '**interface of caval continuity**' may be seen where the SVC and IVC enter the right atrium in 10 to 20% of subjects. This interface follows a near vertical course through the posterior part of the heart shadow. Its visualisation depends on good inspiration. A small break in continuity may be found at the position of the intervening right atrium.

Fig. 1.39   Interface of caval continuity.

8. **The retrosternal space.**
Between the sternum anteriorly and mediastinum proper is a radiolucent area on lateral radiographs which is equal in density to the retro-cardiac area. Anterior to the parietal pleura is the retrosternal soft tissue which produces the 'retro-sternal stripe'. It consists mainly of fat and varies in thickness from about 2 to 4.5 mm. This space also contains the internal mammary arteries, veins and lymphatics, and the intercostal nerves, etc. Tumour masses or vessel dilatations may arise from these e.g. nodes in secondary breast carcinoma or reticulosis, dilated arteries, which may be aneurysmal (Illus. **AORTA COARCTATION, Pt. 8a-c**) in coarctation - these may even be calcified (Stern et al., 1970), or neuromas in neurofibromatosis.

This radiolucent area may be larger in emphysema and is also exaggerated in elderly osteoporotic females with a kyphosis and the '**dowager chest deformity**'.

Fatty masses, haematomas (secondary to sternal fractures), and secondary deposits or primary tumours of the sternum may extend into this space. Tumours of the anterior mediastinum may also extend forwards into this area. Probably the most common indentation of the space arises from osteophytes of the manubriosternal junction.

This vertical retro-sternal shadow has been ascribed to various causes. Several authors, including Scheff and Laforet (1966), Shopfner et al. (1968) and Pfister et al. (1970) considered that it was due to the '**transverse thoracic muscle**', and pointed out that the shadow was accentuated if the radiograph was slightly 'off lateral'. Whalen et al. (1973 and 1975) studied this area on sections of frozen adult cadavers and found that the somewhat undulating interface was a composite shadow of the pre-mediastinal fat and the interface of the adjacent pleura and lungs. Keats (1974) agreed with this and noted the parasternal line in frontal projection, and also noted a right parasternal stripe in like manner to that caused by fat in corresponding frontal projections i.e. small fat pads (see also p. 6.15). As Coussement et al. (1984) wrote: "Il existe une grande confusion dans la littérature entre les interfaces rétrosternaux et para-sternaux" and termed these (i) '**L'Interface retosternaux**' and (ii) '**Les interfaces parasternaux**', noting that the first is produced by retrosternal fat, and the latter by the pleural reflections of the lungs, the left being posterior to the right.

Whalen et al. (1975) studying the upper part of the retrosternal space noted three notches, the upper due to the innominate artery, the second the innominate veins and the third due to hypertrophic first costo-chondral junctions. They emphasised enlargement within the space from enlarged nodes in Hodgkin's disease, and pointed out that tumours arising in the vagal nerves (see p. 18.36) lie between the innominate veins and the trachea and do not displace the retrosternal line.

When a hemithorax is reduced in volume, a 'retrosternal band' may be produced on lateral radiographs as a result of the retrosternal mediastinal fat being seen en face (see Illus. **HYPOPLASIA/APLASIA - lateral views**).

Retrosternal soft tissues were further studied by Jamelin and Candardjis (1973) and the retrosternal line by Jarlot et al. (1976).

Further references.

Simon (1964): Used the aorto-sternal distance as a guide to the presence of emphysema (if > 3cm).

Keats (1973) : Spurious anterior mediastinal masses due to increased opacity from the breasts (see also ps. 6.26-7).

Raider (1973) : The retro-sternal triangle.

Thurlbeck and Simon (1978) : Whilst an increased retrosternal space correlated with marked emphysema, it should not be the sole criterion.

Proto and Speckman (1980) : The left lateral radiograph of the chest.

Pratt (1987) : Normal distance from sternum to anterior border of the aorta = 2.5 cms.

Landay (1994) : "Anterior clear space - how clear? How often?" - in many patients in whom radiographs are otherwise normal, the retrosternal area may have an opacity greater than that of the retro-cardiac area. Furthermore the anterior aspect of the aorta cannot be seen on many normal lateral radiographs (due to residual thymic tissue or fat abutting the aorta) and thus the sternal-aortic distance cannot then be measured, **it is also often** > **2.5cm**. The importance is that if retrosternal opacity is the only remarkable finding on PA & Lat. views, further examination is usually unnecessary.

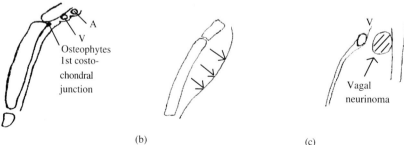

(a)	(b)	(c)
Normal anatomy (lateral view)	Mass in retrosternal space displacing the retrosternal line posteriorly.	Neurinoma of a vagal nerve.

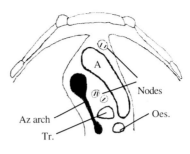

Cross section - the normal width of the retrosternal space is from 2 to 4.5 mm. It is larger in obese subjects, but is thinner in those with emphysema.

Fig. 1.40   The retrosternal space, and retrosternal line or stripe.

(d)

The parasternal lines (anterior extrapleural lines) are formed by the air-filled lung and its pleural coverings, abutting the lateral borders of the sternum and the posterior aspects of the coastal cartilages. Depending on the prominence of the sternum, these lines (especially the right) may overlie the sternum on the lateral view, or be projected posteriorly. With marked sternal depression, they may lie anterior to the sternum. They are also affected by minor or greater degrees of obliquity. The retrosternal line often lies between the two lines, but its precise position follows that of the posterior aspect of the sternum. The parasternal line may be obliterated by a depressed sternum - see ps. 12.34 - 12.35.

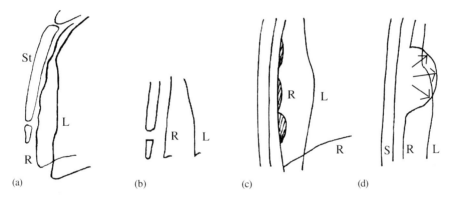

(a)   (b)   (c)   (d)

(a) Lateral view (**inspiration**). (b) In **expiration** the lower part of the left parasternal line (the 'cardiac incisura') moves considerably posterior - such movement may aid in differentiating the cardiac border from a possible adjacent mass.
Enlargements (c) showing costal cartilage impressions on the right, & (d) a mass displacing the right retrosternal line posteriorly (arrowed).

(e)   Cross section upper thorax

(f)   Cross section lower thorax

Fig. 1.41   The parasternal lines.

9. **The retrotracheal area.**

This is a radiolucent area produced by the air-filled upper parts of the lungs lying behind the trachea and above the aortic arch. Lymph node masses, aortic arch anomalies, a posteriorly lying goitre, and oesophageal or neurogenic masses may press into it.

References.
Shields and Holtz (1976) : The retrotracheal space.
Parkinson and Bedford (1936) : The aortic triangle.

10. **The great arteries and veins** produce anatomical landmarks, which should always be studied.

Air-filled lung outlines the right ventricular outflow tract and the ascending aorta anteriorly. The right ventricular outflow tract lies more anteriorly, with the medial portion of the right lung outlining the ascending margins of the innominate veins and the left subclavian artery may also be noted, particularly when air-filled lung extends behind them and the mediastinum is not obese. The innominate artery usually lies within the mediastinal fat and so is not readily visualised, whilst the left subclavian artery frequently protrudes into the lung and is then seen as an oblique shadow passing upwards and backwards and backwards. The right innominate vein often has a sigmoid shape, and lies posterior and inferior to the shadow of the left innominate vein - when buckled the latter may produce a spurious tumour (Fig. 1.42 below).

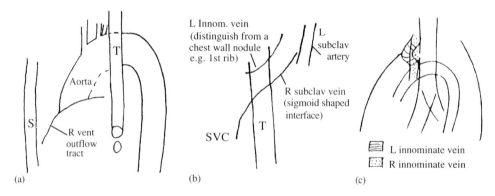

(a) Outflow tracts of the right and left ventricles. (Note that the arch and ascending parts of the aorta may have enhanced outlines with a collapsed left upper lobe, due to the air-filled apex of the left lower lobe being adjacent to and overlain by the dense left upper lobe - the **lateral equivalent of the 'Luftsichel sign'** - see p. 2.26).

(b) At the apex the aerated lung outlines the left subclavian artery. The SVC /right innominate vein (+ the innominate artery) form a sigmoid shaped curve, below and behind that of the left side. The SVC may also be seen on lateral views if the lung tucks behind it (Fig. 1.33) - it then appears as a shadow continuous with that of the innominate veins.

(c) The left innominate vein may have a marked anterior bow, which may give an elongated or 'double' appearance on CT (after Coussement et al., 1984, with permission).

Fig. 1.42   The great arteries and veins on lateral views.

Marked bowing or buckling of the subclavian artery may give rise to a spurious tumour - see also ps. 6.28 and 12.7 - 12.8. This may be further elucidated by ultrasound or CT.

Note the proximity of the pulmonary trunk and the ascending aorta to the posterior aspect of the sternum - it is important not to damage these when performing a sternal biopsy - see p. 21.17.

Sometimes the left subclavian artery may project deeply into the lung as seen on CT, and when this happens an apparent nodule may be seen projecting over the tracheal air column or lying just behind it on lateral radiographs.

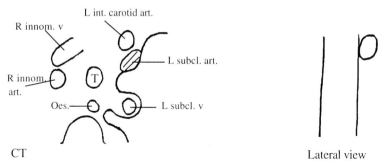

CT   Lateral view

Fig. 1.43   Left subclavian artery indenting the left upper lobe.

References.
Cáceres et al. (1988) : Pulmonary nodule simulated on lateral chest radiograph by branches of the aortic arch.
Subramanyam and Horii (1984) : Use of ultra-sound for demonstrating tortuous innominate vessels.
Paling and Pope (1987) : Variable nature of the mediastinal contour lines - noted that all cases in which the innominate veins failed to produce a visible interface with the right lung occurred in thin young people with a narrow AP diameter of the chest.

11. The aorto-pulmonary area on lateral radiographs.
The left pulmonary artery may lie close to the descending aorta and obscure the anterior aspect of the latter. This is where a ductus, or more commonly its relic, the ligamentum arteriosum may he present. Occasionally this may be seen on lateral views or tomograms, particularly with a pseudo-coarctation, with tethering of this part of the aorta by the ligament (see also p. 10.3).

Masses in this area are commonly due to enlarged nodes (especially with a left recurrent nerve palsy), but neurofibromas etc. should also be considered - see p. 13.24-25 and Illus. **AP WINDOW, Neurofibroma 46a-b**).

The azygos vein (see ps. 9.11 - 13) may produce a nodule on lateral views, overlying the lower part of the aortic arch and just behind the trachea, due to the posterior turn of the azygos arch. This should be distinguished from other structures such as azygos nodes which are more anterior.

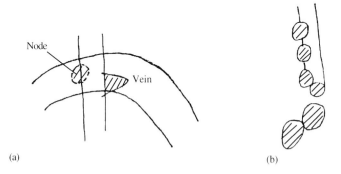

(a)   (b)

Fig. 1.44   (a) Azygos node lying anteriorly - compare with more posteriorly pointing arrowhead type of shadow overlying the lower posterior part of the aortic arch due to the azygos arch.
(b) Nodal enlargement may be noted superimposed on that of the normal vessels, the trachea, the sub-carinal areas, overlying the aortic arch or in the anterior mediastinum (see also ps. 13. 24 - 13.25).

12. The lower mediastinum and leaves of the diaphragm.

One should note the presence of a possible hiatus hernia, a dilated oesophagus, fatty masses in relation to the pericardium, calcification in this, within, the coronary arteries, heart valves, etc, or on the diaphragm. Both sides of the diaphragm should be studied, the position of the liver and stomach gas (or other bowel gas) or absent fundal stomach gas, as with achalasia, noted. Morgagni or Bochdalek herniae may be suggested by recognisable bowel loops or the liver, omentum, or other structures passing through the diaphragm anteriorly or posteriorly.

It is important to study the diaphragm on lateral views, noting the two sides and gas shadows beneath. Loss of the silhouette will usually indicate a disease process above it. On the left the heart tends to obliterate the anterior part of the outline of the left dome. Loss of the silhouette of one dome may also be due to disease in the lung above it - usually a lower lobe, or from an overlying pleural effusion e. g. subpulmonary (see p. 14.4).

Loss of a pulmonary artery, bronchi on one side, or one side of the diaphragm may indicate opaque lung - either lobar or whole lung, or complete loss of normal anatomy on this on one side (e.g. due to previous pneumonectomy).

Lower internal mammary node enlargement (in breast cancer, mesothelioma or with reticulosis) may cause a partial loss of the diaphragmatic silhouette; similarly it may be bulged upwards by lower para-aortic node enlargement with testicular tumours, or from other tumours which have spread up from the abdomen.

Fat and vascularised tissue may make this area more dense, even in normal individuals, causing a small loss in diaphragmatic outline.

A juxta-phrenic peak, causing a local 'sharp tenting' of part of the diaphragm may be due to traction from an inferior pulmonary ligament or partial lung rotation - see ps. 2.35-36.

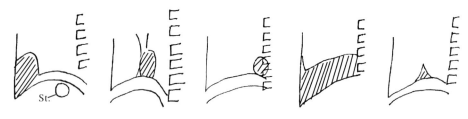

| Morgagni hernia cont. fat or liver | Hiatal hernia cont. stomach, colon etc. | Bochdalek hernia cont. bowel, kidney, spleen | Subpulmonary effusion | Peak due to pulm. ligt. or rotated acc. fissure |

Fig. 1.45   Some abnormalities adjacent to the diaphragm seen on lateral views - see also Chapter 15 (Morgagni and Bochdalek herniae on ps. 15.16 - 15.17).

Note: **The paraspinal and prespinal lines** are discussed with the posterior mediastinum - see ps.18.28 - 29.

Further references re lateral chest radiographs are given on p. 20.12.

The hilar regions.
  The hila contain the larger bronchi, the pulmonary vessels and lymph nodes. Primary tumour masses may arise from the bronchi. Nodes and vessels may enlarge, and a detailed knowledge of anatomy is required. Nodes are discussed in Chapter 13, as well as some detailed anatomy of the hilar structures.

The pulmonary trunk and pulmonary arteries.
  The pulmonary trunk, lies a little to the left, below and anterior to the ascending aorta. The pulmonary trunk and the left and right pulmonary arteries are well demonstrated by CT, and have an **'inclined wishbone' appearance** on frontal views.

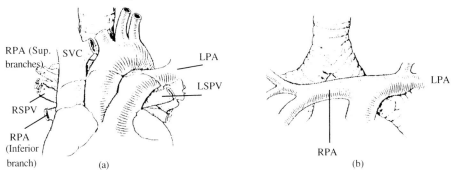

Fig. 1.46 (a) The pulmonary trunk, aorta, SVC and pulmonary veins.
          (b) Relationships of the left and right pulmonary arteries to the main bronchi.
  (After Hollinshead, Anatomy for Surgeons, vol. 2, p. 46, 1956 and McLeod et al., 1976, with permission from Lippincott - Raven).

  The right pulmonary artery inclines slightly posteriorly in front of the main and intermediate bronchi and behind the SVC. Within the mediastinum it divides into its two main branches, the upper and lower (or descending) trunks giving rise to a **'horizontal V'** or 'Harvey Smith sign'*
  The upper trunk passes in front of and above the right upper lobe bronchus (hence the term 'eparterial bronchus' which is sometimes used), whilst the lower and larger trunk (note the **'elephant head and trunk appearance'** - Fig. 1.50) passes downwards in front of and lateral to the intermediate bronchus.

  *Actually an ' intact finger' sign of archers, showing that these had not been amputated following capture during the 100 years War with France (1337 to 1453). English archers, if captured by the French, had their index and middle fingers and part of the thumb amputated before release making them unable to shoot arrows, and those who took no notice of this sign were lucky not to be killed.

  The left pulmonary artery has a shorter course within the pericardium and **'shepherd's   crook'** appearance, caused by the larger branch (or trunk) to the lingula and lower lobe curving at first upwards, and then sweeping downwards and a little laterally.
  Most often the left pulmonary artery lies a little higher than the right. Altered positions may be due to collapse, fibrosis, etc.
  The proximal parts of the pulmonary veins lie inferior to the arteries (Fig. 1.47a) and their entrances into the left atrium are usually well seen on high KV radiographs. The inferior pulmonary veins run more horizontally than the arteries, and with practice should always be recognised on plain radiographs. After the segmental veins join, the superior veins run a more vertical course, the right crossing the inferior or descending part of the right pulmonary artery in the middle part of the right hilum. Both superior and inferior pulmonary veins may give rise to pseudo-tumours, particularly where they enter the back of the left atrium via the venous confluences - see p. 6.29 & Fig. 6.11. Abnormalities of the pulmonary veins are discussed on ps. 7.16-19.
  The azygos vein is usually visible just above the origin of the right main bronchus.

Nodes will not be seen unless enlarged or calcified.

On P.A. views, spurious hilar enlargement must always be excluded. It may be caused by rotation, scoliosis, enlargement of the ascending aorta or by a <u>mass lying anteriorly or posteriorly to the hilum.</u> One should not only note the overlying mass (the 'hilum overlay sign' but also the underlying normal anatomy, tracing the vessels and bronchi back into the hilum from the lung (the **'hilum convergence sign'**).

A lateral view will also be helpful supplemented by tomograms as required.

Any deviation from the normal pattern should always promote further scrutiny and study in order to determine the nature of the abnormality and the possible presence of added shadows, especially in the apex of either lower lobe.

The hila are commonly displaced and elevated as a result of collapse or fibrosis due to past tuberculosis or sarcoidosis, fungus disease, radiotherapy or previous surgery (see Illus. **HILAR ELEVATION**). This may happen on one or both sides, and with tracheal buckling, etc., particularly if the fibrosis is bilateral - see also alteration in bronchial ring shadows on lateral views (p. 2.29).

<u>Further references.</u>
Hearnheiser (1962) : The anatomic Roentgenologic analysis of the normal hilar shadow.

Homer (1978) : The hilar height ratio - a numerical expression of the fact that normally the left hilum lies in the upper part of its hemithorax and the right in the lower part.

Rémy et al. (1981) : Le Poumon Pathologique .

Généreux (1983): Conventional tomographic hilar anatomy emphasising the pulmonary veins.

Müller and Webb (1985) and Webb (1986) : Radiographic imaging of the pulmonary hila.

Don and Hammond (1986) : Vascular converging points of the right pulmonary hilum and their diagnostic importance.

Heitzman (1988) : The Mediastinum.

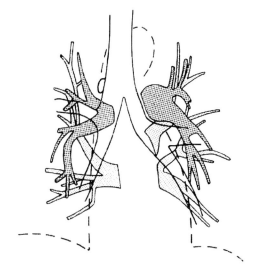

(a) Diagram of hilar anatomy (frontal view). In assessing normality on plain radiographs, shadows additional to those of normal vessels should always provoke further study since they are likely to represent pathological conditions. Collapse will also alter the anatomy of the vascular pattern.

In the upper lobes the veins lie anterior and lateral to the arteries and almost run vertically downwards. In the lower lobes the reverse happens - the veins lie posterior to the arteries, and run more horizontally, the lower lobe arteries being almost vertically orientated.

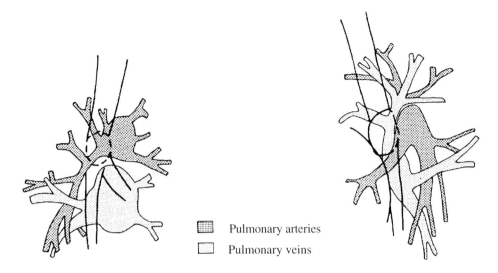

(b) and (c) Anatomy of the hilar regions as seen on lateral chest radiographs or tomograms. (Anterior aspects of hila regions face the centre of the diagram.)

Note that the **right pulmonary artery lies anterior to the carina**, whilst the **left lies posterior** - in many cases this knowledge will show that a mass cannot be the pulmonary artery. (Although the intrapericardial part of the left pulmonary artery, like the right, lies anterior to the carina, what is seen on lateral radiographs or tomograms lies posterior, as the artery curves around the left main bronchus.)

Fig. 1.47 Anatomy of the hilar regions as seen on frontal and lateral radiographs and tomograms.

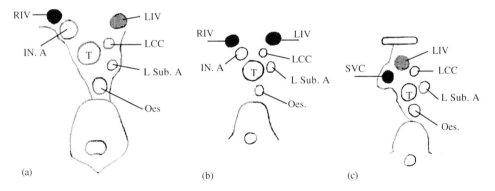

(a - c) Superior mediastinum showing positions of the main vessels (sections 1.5 cm apart). In (c) the left innominate vein crosses in front of the arteries joining the right innominate vein to form the SVC.

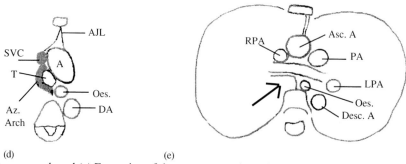

(d)   (e)

(d) Azygos arch and (e) Formation of the azygo-oesophageal recess (arrowed) by the posterior part of the right lung. (This also produces the paraoesophageal line - see p. 1.16 - 1.17.)

Notes : (i) There is no soft tissue density behind the airway and in front of the spine, except the oesophagus, and (ii) No soft tissue density lies in front of the aorta, except possibly a low left innominate vein.

Fig. 1.48   Diagrams of the larger mediastinal vessels and azygo-oesophageal recess in cross section.

AJL - Pleural boundary between the lungs producing the anterior junction line.
LPA and RPA - Left and right pulmonary arteries.
IN. A - Innominate artery LCC - Left common carotid artery   L Sub. A - Left subclavian artery.
LIV and RIV - Left and right innominate veins.

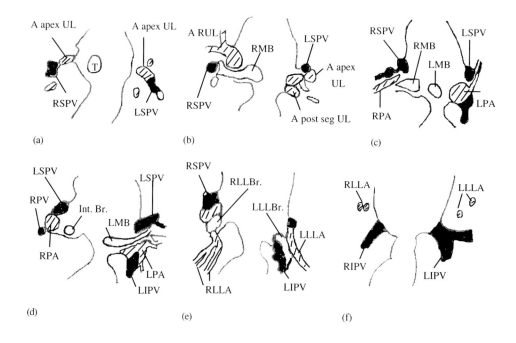

(a)   (b)   (c)

(d)   (e)   (f)

Fig. 1.49 Diagrams of larger pulmonary
vessels as seen on cross sections.
(g = Section through main bronchi).

Notes (i) The right pulmonary and vein are
in contact in the right hilum, whereas the
left pulmonary and vein are separated by the
left main bronchus.
  (ii) The left superior pulmonary vein
crosses in front of the left upper lobe
bronchus and may be seen in this position
on plain radiographs or tomograms below
the left pulmonary artery.
  (iii) The left superior pulmonary vein
often has an 'irregular' or 'knobbly' outline.

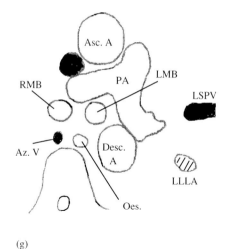

(g)

(a)   (b)   (c)

(a) The right pulmonary artery passes between the right
main bronchus and the SVC.
(b) The left pulmonary artery, especially its lower part
(which gives rise to the 'crook') swings **behind** the left
main and lower lobe bronchi.
(c) At the level of the origin of the RML bronchus, the
RSPV and the descending branch of the RPA give rise to the
'**elephant head and trunk**' or '**claw hammer**' appearance
(see also p. 13.13). (d) At the level of the RML bronchus,
the RSPV turns medially before entering the venous confluence.
(e) Sometimes with severe emphysema, the lower part of the
right pulmonary artery may appear 'aneurysmal' behind the
plane of the intermediate bronchus.

Fig. 1.50 Some points of detail of anatomy in the hilar regions.

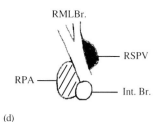

(d)

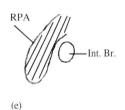

(e)

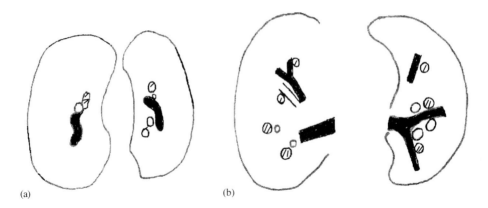

(a)   (b)

Notes : (i) The lower lobe veins tend to lie more horizontally, and thus have a longer course than their corresponding arteries on a single CT section. (ii) 'Greineder's Law' (see p. 7.2) - the arteries, bronchi and veins in the upper lobes are arranged in this order - clockwise in the left upper lobe, and anticlockwise in the right upper lobe. (iii) In understanding the anatomy of the vessels and bronchi of the lung segments, it is essential to have a good understanding of them in cross section as well as frontal and lateral planes.

⊘ = Artery

▰ = Vein

◯ = Bronchus

Fig. 1.51 Diagram showing positions of the larger pulmonary arteries and veins in (a) the upper lobes and (b) the lower lobes.

Some references.

Yamashita et al. (1978) : The anterior subsegmental artery of the left upper lobe usually runs medial to its accompanying bronchus.

Otsuji et al. (1989) : The anterior subsegmental artery of the anterior segment of the right upper lobe is always medial to the accompanying bronchus, unless the segmental artery of the right middle lobe is lateral to the accompanying bronchus.

Lee, K. et al. (1991a) : CT anatomy of the lingular segmental bronchi - study of 40 pts. - the lingular bronchi were seen in all pts. The lower branch of the ant. seg. vein of the LUL which runs horizontally between the ant. seg. and the lingula is a good landmark.

Lee, K. et al. (1991b) : Bronchovascular anatomy of the upper lobes - evaluation with thin section CT. The right upper lobe anterior segmental artery was seen medial to its accompanying branches in 90% of cases, the posterior segmental artery of the right upper lobe lay posterior to its bronchus as did mostly the similar artery in the left upper lobe.

CT of the bronchi and bronchopulmonary segments.

When looking for tumours, 'key areas' include the carina, the main bronchi, lobar bronchi and the bronchial bifurcations. Tumours both within and adjacent to these are usually well demonstrated, as well as tumour infiltration or spread along their outer borders. Endobronchial secondary masses (see ps. 4.26 & 13.8) may also be seen, though these are usually better recognised at bronchoscopy.

Incomplete bronchial obstruction may allow some air to pass into the distal bronchi, giving rise to a **partial 'air bronchogram'** - see ps. 2.1 - 2.2. When segmental or subsegmental bronchi are blocked mucocoeles may be seen. Complete lobar bronchial occlusions usually give rise to collapse of the lobe, but even with this mucocoeles may been seen within part of the lobe, due to collateral air drift (ps. 2.8 - 2.9).

The CT appearance of bronchopulmonary segmental and subsegmental structures depends on their orientation to the tomographic slice. Bronchopulmonary segmental structures (bronchi, arteries and veins) all radiate from the hilum. Thus segments whose axes are largely oriented in the long axis of the body (e.g. apex of upper lobe, basic segments of lower lobes etc.) are seen in transverse section, whilst those running transversely (e.g. anterior segment of upper lobe and apex of lower lobe) are seen in longitudinal section. Those obliquely oriented appear in oblique sections. The most difficult bronchi to identify on CT are those of the lingula. Disease processes naturally alter the anatomy with collapse, fibrosis, etc. so that different orientations are produced.

See also ps. 20.22 - 20.23 re spiral CT & 3D reconstructions.

References.
Jackson & Huber (1943) : Correlated applied anatomy of the bronchial tree and lung with a system of nomenclature.
Boyden (1945) : Intra-hilar and related segmental anatomy of the lung.
Boyden (l955a) : Developmental anomalies of the lungs. (1955b) : Segmental anatomy of the lungs.
Brock (1946 & l954) : The anatomy or the bronchial tree.
Foster-Carter (1946) : Broncho-pulmonary abnormalities.
Cordier and Cabrol (1952): The segments of the lung.
Bo et al. (I980) : Basic cross sectional anatomy.
Naidich et al. (1980 a and b) : CT of the bronchi - normal and abnormal.
Naidich et al. (l981a and b) : CT of the pulmonary, hila, normal and abnormal.
Rémy et al.(1981) : Tomodensitometric (CT) anatomy.
Webb el el. (1981a and b) : CT of the normal. and abnormal pulmonary hilum.
Osborne et al. (1984) : Studied 50 patients with normal chest radiographs with reference to the bronchopulmonary segments, and found that they could identify 70% of the segmental bronchi and about 75% of the segmental arteries up to their 6th or 7th branchings.
Bechai and Wise (1985) : Segmental anatomy of the lung in cross section.
Généreux (1985) : Central arteries and veins can be distinguished on CT sections by following their course on sequential scans; by -identifying their relationship to the bronchi, or by their vertical or horizontal orientation in the upper or lower lobes.
Jardin and Rémy (1986) : Studied the segmental bronchovascular anatomy of the lower lobes by CT. They noted that although there is some variation (in up to 20%) there is considerable constancy in the anatomy of lower lobe segments, with the **arteries generally lying towards the lung periphery** (anterior, lateral or posterior) relative to their corresponding bronchi. The veins, by comparison, generally lie **centrally** to their corresponding bronchi. Common variations were that the segmental arteries may be single, duplicate or triplicate as they accompany the segmental bronchi. (They used the nomenclature of Jackson and Huber, 1943).
Gladnikoff (1948) : Visualisation of major bronchi by air within them.
Lodin (1953) : The value of tomography in the examination of the intra-pulmonary bronchi.
Henschke (1987) : Comparison of CT and bronchoscopy in the detection of bronchial abnormalities.
Khan et al. (1985) : Oblique hilar tomography, CT and mediastinoscopy for staging of bronchial carcinoma.
Naidich et al. (1988) : Demonstrated basal bronchi by thin section CT.
Mayr et al. (1989): Over 90 % of endobronchial tumours could be detected using 8 mm thick CT sections.

Otsuji et al. (1989) : Because the horizontal fissure is not always visible on CT sections, it is often difficult to distinguish the RML from the anterior segment of the RUL. A method of differentiation is to note that in the RUL, a medial sub-segmental bronchus in the anterior segment always lies **lateral** to its corresponding artery, whereas in the RML, the medial sub-segmental bronchus of the lateral segment, and the superior and inferior sub-segmental bronchi are always located medial to the corresponding artery.

Ant. seg.
RUL

RML

Anatomy of the pulmonary airways and lobules.

The gross anatomy of the tracheo-bronchial tree is illustrated in Fig. 1.30, and the anatomy of the cartilages is discussed on p. 3.2. Cell types in the mucosa are described on ps. 24.13 - 24.14.

Within each lobe and segment; the airways divide by asymmetric dichotomy (i.e. usually into two at each division, but often into unequal parts. Cartilage is continued in the bronchial walls, but stops in the bronchioles. The smaller bronchi divide at almost 1 cm intervals until the terminal bronchioles are reached, when branching occurs at 1 - 2 mm intervals, i. e. with branches passing into the secondary lobules, which are partially separated from one another by the inter-lobular septa - these secondary lobules appear to be the most important radiological sub-units of the lung. Within the secondary lobules, each terminal bronchiole gives rise to between two and seven respiratory bronchioles which take part in gas exchange and also give rise to the alveolar ducts and alveoli. The primary lobules are much smaller, and consist of a group of alveoli arising from a respiratory bronchiole, via an alveolar duct. An acinus is produced by the branchings of a terminal bronchiole, and may be seen on bronchograms as a 'rosette' if 'bronchiolar filling' occurs. Disease processes may give rise to similar 'alveolar patterns', especially the 'acino-nodose' (or 'tree in bud') pattern seen in some cases of tuberculosis.

Miller (1947) defined the micro-anatomy of the lung as : - (a) **secondary lobule** arising from a **bronchiole** with polyhedral shape - 1 - 2.5 (sometimes up to 4) cm in size; (b) **acinus** arising from a **terminal bronchiole** - round in shape - 6 - 8 mm in size; (c) **primary lobule** arising from a **respiratory bronchiole** - variable in shape and size.

In summary : a primary lobule is a component of an acinus, which in turn is part of a secondary lobule, the latter being largely bounded by interlobular septa, giving them their typical polyhedral shape. Those at the periphery of the lung are like truncated cones, with their bases on the pleural surface of the lung and their apices pointing centrally. A secondary lobule contains a variable number of acini (usually 3 - 5, but up to 20 sometimes). The **bronchioles and arteries lie in the centre of the secondary lobule**, whilst the **veins and main lymphatics lie in the intervening septa** (see also ps. 1.45 & 13.3 - 13.4). The central arteries (1 mm in diameter) may be seen on thin CT sections as tiny dots, or branching densities within secondary lobules, but the accompanying bronchiole is not commonly visualised (normally 0.6 mm in diameter).

Fig. 1.52 Central arteries (adjacent to small bronchi) within polyhedral secondary lobules, which are bounded by interlobular septa - normally 0.1 mm thick and 1 to 2. 5 cm long. (Arteries & bronchi are usually of equal size.)

Air space disease (e.g. pneumonic consolidation) occurs within the components of the secondary lobule, and theoretically should give rise to indistinct shadows as the disease process spreads via the alveoli, the pores of Kohn and the canals of Lambert. By contrast **nodules** occurring within the interstitial tissue or septa should give rise to clearly demarcated shadows as they will tend to push into and deform the air spaces. However in practice the differentiation is not easy due to superimposition of nodules or coalescence. Capillary permeability **oedema** involves the alveoli, as does lobar or segmental pneumonia, and both of these spread via the alveoli, the pores and canals. Interstitial oedema occurs in the septa, which become thickened (see p.8.13).

Note also that some **secondary lobules** may be shown to be filled with exudate, whilst others are clear in alveolar proteinosis (see ps. 19.63-64). In **honeycombing** (see p.6.6) the polygonal shape of the secondary lobules is changed by the formation of dilated air spaces filling them, as also occurs in lymphangioleiomyomatosis (see p. 5.18). In **panbronchiolitis** (see p.3.29), the inflammatory process occurs mainly in the walls of the respiratory bronchioles, leading to a disease process mainly involving the primary lobules.

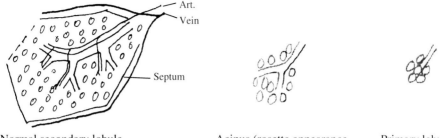

Normal secondary lobule
(surrounded by septa or a 'gap').

Acinus (rosette appearance
on a bronchogram).

Primary lobule.

Fig. 1.53   Diagrams of a secondary lobule, an acinus and a primary lobule.

Fig. 1.54   Component parts of the acinus
(according to Thurlbeck, 1968)
TB = terminal bronchiole;
RB = respiratory bronchiole,
AD = alveolar duct, AS = alveolar sac.

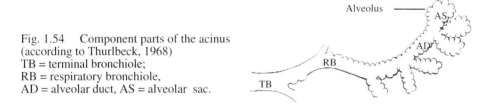

Lynne Reid and Rubino (1959) wrote that the connective tissue septa in the adult human lung are most marked in the outer parts of the lung - about twice as frequent as in the deeper parts of the lung - thus **collateral ventilation is less easy in the subpleural zone of the lung** (where bullae and emphysema seem to start to develop).

Generally septa are frequent over the sharp edges and angles of the lung (such as the anterior edge of the upper and middle lobes, the costo-phrenic edge of the lower lobe, and the costo-vertebral margins), relatively scarce over the lateral and costal aspects, and absent over the fissural surfaces.

The **incompleteness of septa is essential to the operation of collateral ventilation**, a phenomenon whose effectiveness is relatively impaired in regions where septa are numerous and which influences the functioning of the lung and its appearance in disease. The irregular operation of collateral ventilation in the subpleural zone is seen in chronic bronchitis with peripheral fibrosis and collapse.

Some studies.

Greenspan (1967) considered 'chronic disseminated diseases of the lung' and wrote "it should be borne in mind that the diseases...producing the Roentgen image of **acinar density** or alveolar consolidation, generally demonstrate pathologically involvement of both the airways **and** the interstitial tissues. In addition, as the disease progresses, thickening of the alveolar septa occurs, along with fibrosis and alveolar distribution, altering the Roentgenographic image from one of primarily alveolar distribution to one of mixed airway and interstitial involvement. Indeed the end result of many of the 'alveolar diseases' ....is interstitial pulmonary fibrosis, therefore, the stage of disease has a great bearing on its Roentgen appearance".

Raskin (1982) reviewed radiological appearances and concluded that part of the controversy surrounding the term 'acinus' is because processes other than those due to alveolar-filling can mimic it, and because alveolar-filling processes can produce non-acinar shadows. A diseased alveolus may be partially aerated by collateral air-drift, and the disease process can spread to neighbouring alveoli. Thus a typical acinar pattern with 6 to 8 mm shadows of consolidation is not often found, and when it does, it rapidly changes with spread or clearing of the condition.

Murata et al. (1986 - from Japan) used 1.5 mm (thin) sections to study the secondary lobules and acini in autopsy specimens, in which the lung was inflated, the arteries having been injected with 15 % gelatin solution. They could distinguish the smaller arteries and veins (the latter tending to be fuller and more peripheral). They suggested that diseases, in which the pathogen enters via the bronchial tree, cause inflammatory changes in the centrilobular area, whereas metastases showed no constant relation to bronchioles. The thin sections were also able to show whether emphysema was centri- or para-lobular.

Bergin et al. (1988) studied the secondary pulmonary lobule by CT. They also noted that is supplied by 3 - 5 terminal bronchioles, and is bounded by fibrous septa. Fine section CT was able to show the inter-lobular septa, terminal bronchioles and pulmonary artery branches within the broncho-vascular bundle. In lymphangitis carcinomatosa the broncho-vascular bundles and inter-lobular septa were thickened. These were also thickened in sarcoidosis, but fibrosis caused distortion of the normal polygonal shape of the secondary lobule. In lymphangioleiomyomatosis there were often multiple cysts within the secondary lobules, distorting the polygonal appearance.

Webb et al. (1988) studied air-inflated excised lungs by high resolution CT and found that they could show interlobular septa, and arteries in the central areas of secondary lobules. Oedema fluid produced thickening of the septa. Emphysema appeared as focal areas of decreased density and suggested a centri-lobular distribution. Honeycombing gave rise to cystic spaces surrounded by a fibrotic wall, but microcysts (< 1 mm in size) could not be seen.

Fraser et al. (1988) pointed out that the distribution of secondary lobules within the lungs is not uniform. Septa are most numerous in the lateral and anterior aspects of the lower lobes and close to their pleural surfaces, but are virtually non-existent along the inter-lobar fissures and in the posterior and mediastinal aspects of the lungs. They are also poorly developed centrally. Besides being non-uniform in distribution, they are also non-uniform in size. They preferred to use the acinus as the basic anatomical unit, and felt that in conditions such as pulmonary oedema, acute alveolar pneumonia and idiopathic pulmonary haemorrhage, recognition of the ' distinctive acinar pattern ' enables the radiologist to narrow the differential diagnosis to the relatively few diseases capable of consolidating pulmonary air spaces. These also include alveolar cell carcinoma.

They felt that an acinar distribution of air-space pathology would give rise to poorly marginated nodules, whether caused by consolidation (including tuberculosis) oedema or local spread of tumour (as with alveolar cell carcinoma).

Spread of disease would occur through the collateral pathways (pores of Kohn, etc.) giving rise to coalescent disease in neighbouring acini. The tangential x-ray projection of an opacified acinus probably accounts for the **'spoke wheel nodule'** containing a lucent centre. They hold that thickening of septa or alveolar, etc. walls would cause nodular or reticulo-nodular patterns, as small nodules within them would press into the air-spaces, which being air-filled would outline the nodules.

Fig. 1.55
Spokewheeled nodule.

As noted in Appendices p.2, the repetitive nature of miliary etc. shadows may enhance their visibility. It may also slightly alter their appearance due to superimposition etc, making larger and smaller nodules, as well as tiny ellipsoid patterns. Such is seen with miliary tuberculosis, miliary carcinomatosis, silicosis and pneumoconiosis. It may also be seen in some cases of sarcoidosis.
A fine or coarser fibrotic pattern with small cystic spaces (and honeycombing) may result in a network appearance plus fine nodules - sometimes termed a reticulo-nodular pattern and especially seen with sarcoidosis and pneumoconiosis.
Cystic spaces may also be accompanied by linear shadows.

Further references.

Malpighi (1661) : Described the vesicular nature of the lung with pyramidal, almost crystalline shaped units.
Willis (1679): Using mercury casts of the bronchi, identified the lobules.
Aschoff (1924) : First suggested that nodules resulting from air space disease represented involvement of the pulmonary acinus.
Twining (1938) : Noted on some bronchograms a 'rosette' pattern (0.5 to 1.0 cm in size) which resembled petals around a lucent centre.
Ziskind et al. (1963 and 1964) : Nodules sometimes filled the 'acinar' space.
          (1967) : An acinal nodule = 'alveolar rosette' seen on bronchography.
Recarvarren et al.. (1967) : Air space disease causing peribronchiolar nodules.
Reid (1958) & Reid and Simon (1958) : Peripheral pulmonary anatomy and secondary lobules - centimetre/millimetre pattern.
Pump (1964) : The morphology of the finer branches of the bronchial tree.
     (1969) : Morphology of the acinus of the human lung.
Heitzman et al. (1969) : I - Roentgen anatomy of the normal secondary pulmonary lobule.
          (1969) : II - Application of the anatomic concept to an understanding of Roentgen pattern in disease states.

Gamsu et al. (1971) : Roentgenographic appearance of the pulmonary acinus.

Itoh et al. (1978) : Correlated the radiological and pathological findings in 66 patients, and found an 'acinar pattern' in some cases of bronchopneumonia, including tuberculosis.

Osborne et al. (1983) : Postnatal growth and size of the pulmonary acinus and the secondary lobule in man.

Weibel and Taylor (1988) : Morphology and Structure of the Human Lung.

Berend et al. (1991) : Structure of a human pulmonary acinus. They **defined an acinus functionally as the lung unit in which all airways participate in gas exchange.**

They studied the branching pattern of respiratory bronchioles and alveolar ducts in an acinus from the peripheral part of the lung of an 18 year old man. The acinus was bounded on two sides by pleura, and on the remaining sides by connective tissue septa. The terminal bronchi divided into two respiratory bronchioles, each of which gave rise to four systems of alveolar ducts.

Giovagnorio and Cavallo (1995) : HRCT evaluation of secondary lobules and acini using a limited reconstruction field of 4 - 10 cm with a narrow window to increase the visibility of small structures.

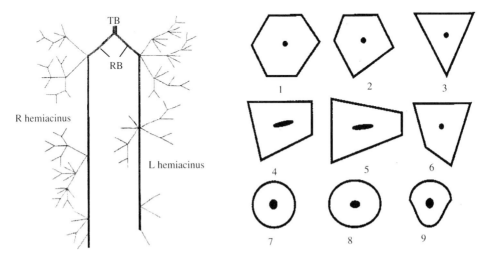

Fig. 1.56a Schematic representation of the overall structure of an acinus.
(after Berend et al., 1991 - Thorax, **46**, 117 - 121 with permission from the BMJ Publishing Group).

TB = terminal bronchiole, RB = respiratory bronchiole,
___ = alveolar duct.

Fig. 1.56b Varying shapes of secondary lobules (1 - 6) and acini (7 - 9) as seen with HRCT.
(After Giovagnorio & Cavallo, 1995 - HRCT evaluation of secondary lobules & acini of the lung. J. Thoracic Imaging, **10**, 129 - 133 with permission).

The lung cortex.

Barden (1960 and 1966) showed that there is a difference between the perfusion of the outermost rim of the lung - the 'cortex' - compared with the rest of the lung - the **'medulla'**. He noted an abrupt change in the number of visible small vessels between the medulla and cortex (see Illus. **ANATOMY 29**) and pointed out that "there are **many more** 'respiratory' capillaries in the medulla, but these are too small to be seen." Such a difference between the cortex and the medulla has also been noted by others.

Fleischner (1969) noted well defined layered lobules in the cortex, and a less well defined medulla. Généreux (1985) noted that veins and arteries could not be differentiated radiographically in the cortex, and after carrying out exhaustive density measurements, concluded that the **'cortex'** may be a reservoir zone capable of accommodating increased blood flow under appropriate conditions. The cortical circulation also differs by having vessels and lymphatics largely running at right angles to the pleural surfaces, with the lymphatics from the outermost lobules draining subpleurally (p. 13.3). As noted on p. 1.44, secondary lobules and septa are best developed over the surface of the lung, where they are generally arranged in irregular layers, two or three lobules deep.

Gurney (1991) studied the cross sectional physiology of the lung and noted that the **cortex** or outermost 3 - 4 cm of lung is composed of well organised and developed secondary pulmonary lobules. The outer secondary lobules are the largest - 1 cm wide and 2.5 cm high, and are shaped like truncated cones pointed towards the hilum, whilst the inner secondary lobules have a similar shape but are smaller. Other differences in structure and physiology are listed in the following table.

Table 1.1

	cortex	medulla
Bronchi	< 1.5 mm	larger vessels and bronchi with cilia
Blood vessels		which branch disproportionately
Blood flow	high flow with high resistance	high flow with low resistance
Lymph flow	centrifugal	centripetal
Size	3 - 4 cm	smaller and less regular in shape
Interlobular septa	thicker	thinner and less well defined.

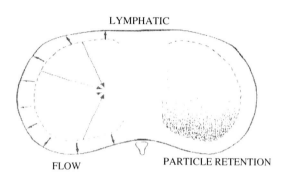

LYMPHATIC

Fig. 1. 57 Lymph flows centripetally in the centre of the lung, and centrifugally in the periphery - see also p. 13.3.

Clearance of particles is poorer posteriorly, especially in the upper zones, because of regional differences in lymphatic function.
(Reproduced from Gurney, 1991 - Radiology, **178**, 1 - 10 with permission).

FLOW   PARTICLE RETENTION

Webb et al. (1992) stated " the lung cortex is composed of one or two rows, or tiers of well-defined secondary pulmonary lobules, which together form a layer about 3 - 4 cm in thickness" and are "similar to the stones of a Roman arch - all of similar size and shape". They also noted that "the lung cortex is not limited to the periphery of the lung, but surrounds the entirety of each lobe, under the pleural surface". However the typical appearance is not always seen on HRCT because the plane of the scan typically traverses different parts of adjacent lobules.

Fig. 1.58 Cortico-medullary differentiation in the lung.

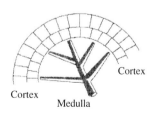

Medullary lobules are smaller and less well-defined than those in the cortex, which have an appearance similar to a **Roman arch**. (After Webb et al., 1992 - HRCT of the Chest - Fig. 3.14, Raven Press, with permission).

Cortex

Cortex   Medulla

See also arches (and inner or soffit stones) of **Swinford Bridge** 1767 in Oxford Picts collection.

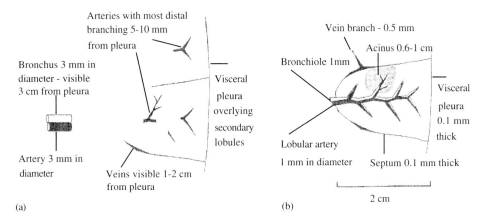

(a)   (b)

Fig. 1.59 (a) Normal lobular dimensions.   (b) HRCT anatomy of the normal secondary lobule.
(Adapted from Webb et al., 1992, HRCT of the Chest - Fig. 3.6. Raven Press, with permission).
Usually only the smaller arteries can be seen (as sharply defined round or linear branching
opacities) in the centrilobular regions on HRCT. With disease processes the bronchioles are more
readily seen, as a result of dilatation, mucus plugging, etc.

Exactly how the lung cortex functions is uncertain, but it does show some differences which
can be demonstrated by CT, particularly if the outermost rim is well displayed by the use of an
'extended scale' and considerable magnification.

In some normal people, localised collapse or oedema may be shown in the dependent part of this
zone of the lung (see p. 8.7); conversely in mild congestive failure this area may be spared, when
the medulla appears congested. Emphysema also may cause the vessels in the cortex to dilate.

The cortex often shows a different pattern to the medulla in several disease processes. Small
bullae may form in the cortex, particularly in young people, and these may give rise to spontaneous
pneumothoraces; the underlying lung being spared from any emphysematous change. Cortical
bullae may more easily form, because the more complete cortical inter-lobular septa make collateral
ventilation in the lung cortex more difficult (see also ps. 2.8-9). Small cortical bullae may also be
present in patients with asthma or emphysema. Others develop superficial 'blebs' in relation to
underlying tuberculosis, adjacent lung consolidation (staphylococcal pneumonia, etc. - see ps. 6.4
& 19.3-4), or primary or secondary tumours (e.g. scar cancers, some adenocarcinomas and
tumours giving rise to spontaneous pneumothoraces). Apical bullae affecting both medulla and
cortex are common (mainly as a result of our erect posture most of the day and this resulting in
reduced blood perfusion of the lung apices) but are most marked in the medulla. Some toxic and
drug reactions (e.g. bleomycin and paraquat - see ps. 19.111 - 19.112), also infections (e.g.
pneumocystis) cause lung changes to extend up to the transition zone between cortex and medulla,
whilst the cortex remains clear. A 'white line' may be produced at the junction zone in asbestosis
(see p.14.33 - 14.34), in interstitial pneumonia (Kubota et al., 1983), in interstitial lung disease
(Naidich et al., 1984, who considered it to be due to thickened secondary interlobular septa) and in
some cases of idiopathic pulmonary fibrosis (Nakata et al., 1985).

The distribution of lung metastases, as seen on CT (see also p. 5.36), appears often to be related
to the cortico-medullary junction - since it is in this zone that many deposits are found i.e. very
peripherally - presumably because of the richness of the circulation in the area. Also microfilariae
of filariasis which cause tropical eosinophilic lung (see ps. 19.55 & 19.59) cause a reaction in the
same region, with a 'white line ' similar to the chronic white line seen in asbestosis (see above).

A good differentiation of the lung cortex and its distinction from the medulla may be seen in
fibrosing alveolitis, with emphysema of the outer cortical ring of pulmonary acini (see also ps.
19.116 - 19.119 and Strickland and Strickland, 1988).

Opacity of the cortico-medullary junction may sometimes he seen in normal lungs on CT
sections - it is probably a normal gravitational effect (see also p. 8.7). The lung cortex may be
spared in some patients with pulmonary oedema, particularly if sub-acute (see ps. 8.3 & 8.17).

Note (i) pulmonary oedema peripheral to a lung tumour (Illus. **CONGESTION, Pt. 17**).
(ii) Table 1.2 listing the various conditions which may affect the different zones of the lungs (p.1.48).
(iii) Illus. **ANATOMY, 27 & 28** show reproductions of radiographs of thin sections of lungs which have had the arterial branches injected with barium, and which show (a) the lobular vessels and (b) the abrupt change in the number of visible small vessels, between "medulla" and "cortex."

The distribution of pulmonary disease in relation to anatomy and physiology
A - General points (including some effects of noxious gases).

1. In our normal upright position, blood flow and ventilation predominate at the lung bases, yet in many adults the greatest alteration occurs in the upper zones.

2. Although the basal predominance increases in a linear fashion from apex to base, the rate of increase is unequal, with blood flow increasing faster than ventilation. **Thus the apices are underperfused compared with ventilation by a ratio of about 1:3** and the bases are a little overperfused.

3. Inhaled noxious gases such as cigarette smoke trigger a neutrophil or macrophage reaction, with release of proteases and elastases which (like some bacterial products) destroy lung parenchyma. Protection is afforded by antitrypsin.

4. The balance between destruction and protection may be triggered by the normal mismatch between ventilation and perfusion in our normal upright position.

5. There is a paradox, in that whilst more smoke, etc. passes to the lung bases, because of their greater ventilation, the concentration may be higher in the upper zones due to the greater ratio of ventilation to perfusion there, and thus leading to the protective proteases being overwhelmed. This also helps to explain why centri-lobular emphysema, caused by cigarette smoking, particularly involves the upper zones. It also explains why oedema may sometimes be seen more predominantly in the upper lobes from the inhalation of other noxious gases.

6. **Upper lobe oedema** may also be seen secondary to regurgitated jets of blood if they shoot back into a superior pulmonary vein. This particularly happens in the right upper lobe following an acutely developing mitral incompetence caused by a ruptured chorda or valve cusp. It may also be seen following artificial shunts for treating Fallot's tetralogy, or with some intra-cardiac shunts, but is then secondary to arterial hypertension. The author has seen it in some patients who have had cardiac failure secondary to renal failure (Illus. **CONGESTION, Pts. 5, 18 & 20a-b**).
Upper lobe oedema may also be seen in cases of neurogenic shock and may in part be due to alterations from the normal blood distribution, secondary to sympathetic activity.

7. To preserve **gas exchange**, the alveolar capillary membrane must be kept dry. Lymph flow can increase up to about 120 times to remove excess water. Although most particles are removed by the 'mucociliary escalator' (see p. 3.17), a few are removed via the lymphatics, with a half-life possibly as long as 1 - 2 years, to finally clear from the hilar, etc. nodes. There is greater lymphatic clearance at the lung bases. Approximately one-third of the lymphatic fluid drains centrifugally via the sub-pleural plexus and about two-thirds centrally via the peri-bronchial plexus.
Disorders of **lymphatic clearance** (see impaired mucociliary clearance) or retained toxic agents may explain the distribution of granulomatous disease (tuberculosis, sarcoid, eosinophilic granuloma), pneumoconiosis, farmer's lung or even pulmonary - lipogranulomatosis (due to 'apple gluttony' - see p. 6.14).

8. The lung has to support its own weight and with the pumping action of the diaphragm and the changes discussed above, the greatest changes are often found at the apices. In Marfan's syndrome, where elastic tissue is poorly developed, apical bullous disease is very common leading in many cases to pneumothoraces (see also ps. 10.15 - 10.16).

9. **Age** - Edge et al. (1964) studied the radiographic appearances of the chest in persons of advanced age but could **not recognise a senile lung pattern**, the only consistent findings being in the bony skeleton viz. - decalcification of the ribs, and degenerative spinal changes. Diminution in the lung volumes was due to shrinkage of the thoracic cage. Lungs removed from aged patients showed a mild degree of panacinar emphysema only, without air-trapping.

B. Special points in some conditions

1. In **cystic fibrosis** (see ps. 3.22 - 3.24) there is an abnormal mucus which cannot easily be expectorated. One would expect, because of the greater ventilation of the lower zones that clearing of mucus from the lower lobe bronchi with coughing would be easier and that those in the upper lobes would be more affected. This is often found in practice. A similar finding is often found with allergic aspergillosis (see ps. 19.38 - 19.43).

2. In **pulmonary tuberculosis** and other mycobacterial infections, the disease is often most marked in the upper zones and particularly in the apices of the upper and lower zones. This appears to be related to the high pH and -HCO_3; spread into surrounding lung also occurs more readily from miliary disease in the upper zones (Illus. **TB MILIARY**).

When the upper zones, are as well as, or better perfused than the lung bases (as occurs in mitral stenosis - see p. 8.2) this appears to produce an environment in which tuberculosis will not easily develop. In the days when tuberculosis and rheumatic carditis were common, one almost never saw a patient with mitral stenosis, except for perhaps a healed **Ghon focus**.

Similar observations, may be seen with pulmonary valvular stenosis. Tuberculosis may complicate the condition in children. However when marked collaterals are present from the arteries and other systemic collaterals (from the intercostals etc. - see p.7.14), tuberculosis is again almost unknown.. These multiple systemic collaterals are sometimes termed 'pseudo-fibrosis', because the fine vessels may mimic fibrosis on PA chest views.

3. **Fixity of the ribs.**

(a) In **ankylosing spondylitis** some patients develop apical (sometimes leading to more generalised) fibrosis and bullous formation. This is probably due to increased stress at the lung apices caused by the pumping action of the diaphragm superimposed, through a rigid thorax, on the normal decreased upper lobe perfusion (p. 19.90 - see also West and Matthews, 1972: Stresses. strains and surface pressures in the lung caused by its weight.).

Similar findings may be seen in some patients with **rheumatoid arthritis** (see ps. 19.81 - 19.85) and Marfan's syndrome (ps. 10.15 - 10.16).

(b) Poorer movement of the posterior aspects of the ribs, compared with the anterior ends may have a bearing on:

(i) the usual posterior position of tuberculosis in the apices of the upper and lower lobes, where there is both reduced perfusion and poor ventilation, with reduced lymphatic clearance posteriorly;

(ii) bullae being more commonly anterior than posterior.

4. **Cross sectional physiology of the lung.**

In silicosis the upper lobes are more severely affected, and in asbestosis the lower lobes. The upper or lower tendency is evident with many disease processes and is thought to be due to the effects of gravity on the erect lung.

Particles 10 μ are mostly removed from inhaled air in the nasopharynx, intermediate-sized particles (5 - 10 μ) are removed by impaction in mucus and then by the ciliary escalator and only the smallest particles (5 μ) tend to reach the terminal air spaces. Clearance from the alveoli is much slower than from the airways (where most particles are removed within about 30 minutes), the half time being in weeks or months. Thus pollens and spores tend to be removed via the airways and make their pathological effects there e.g. bronchospasm and aspergillus infection, whilst silica and minute microbacteria tend to affect the peripheral lung. A paradox occurs with asbestos, with its needle shaped particles (se p. 14.34), which although being larger, may be carried peripherally, due to their aerodynamic shape, and deeply penetrate the lung. (See also reference to Graham et al., 1990 - p.1.57).

5. Interstitial and air-space disease, especially related to chronic infiltration.
Often the radiographic appearance has been divided into 'interstitial' (septal) and 'air-space' (alveolar). Felson (1979b) felt that this was often unreliable, and that it is usually better to discern the **predominant** pattern in order to attempt to determine the underlying cause. The author agrees with this and feels that some descriptive terms such as e.g. 'reticular' do not help in differential diagnosis, and feels that it is better to try to discern the underlying pathological anatomy.

C. The position and distribution of lung lesions in differential diagnosis.
The position of lung disease as noted on plain radiographs, tomograms and CT sections may be of considerable diagnostic importance. The apical preponderance of tuberculosis and bullous disease is well known, also sarcoidosis in the mid zones and bronchiectasis at the bases. These and other conditions are illustrated in the scheme below. This however is only a rough guide, as there is a considerable overlap in the appearances of several conditions.

The shapes and patterns of distribution and spread of small multiple lung nodules are considered in Chapter 4, and the causes of solitary and multiple lung nodules are listed in Tables 4.2 & 5.6.

Table 1.2   The position of lung lesions may be considered in relation to:
(a) the lung 'zones' as commonly noted on frontal and lateral radiographs, and (b) the central, intermediate and peripheral (and especially 'cortical' positions), as seen on CT sections.

(a) Frontal and lateral views

(b) CT sections

Apical or upper zone.
Bullae
Tuberculosis (esp. if posterior)
Neoplasm - esp. Pancoast tumours
Aspergillosis
Pneumoconiosis

Central area.
Lymphoma

Intermediate area.
Silicosis (upper and mid zone esp.) -
External allergic alveolitis

Mid zone (often upper as well).
Pneumonic consolidation
Sarcoidosis
Rheumatoid nodules
Pneumoconiosis

Peripheral and cortical areas.
Secondary deposits (usually rounded)
Fibrosing alveolitis/Idiopathic fibrosis
COP (BOOP) / eosinophilic pneumonia
Rheumatoid nodules and fibrosis
Fibrosing alv. and systemic sclerosis
Honeycomb lung

Bases.
Pneumonic consolidation/ post. op collapse
Embolism
Inhaled foreign body
Bronchiectasis
Pulmonary oedema

Parasites/Eosinophilia
Some drug reactions
Asbestosis
Pneumoconiosis

All areas or one area.
Neoplasm
Secondary deposits
Lymphangitis carcinomatosa
Idiopathic or allergic alveolitis, etc.,
Fibrosing alveolitis (often with lower
zone preponderance).

All areas.
Sarcoidosis (esp. alongside broncho-
vascular bundles & in subpleural areas).
Lymphangitis carcinomatosa.
Bronchiolitis
Pneumonia - may be peripheral, central,
or spreading diffusely e.g. pneumocystis

General comment and 'caveat'.
Considerable **overlap** occurs, as also occurs between interstitial and air-apace disease. Although nodular shadows tend to occur in the lung interstitium - interlobular septa and alveolar walls, etc., whilst consolidation largely affects the alveoli, the two are often combined.

In fibrosing alveolitis, nodular shadows not only occur in the interstitium, but macrophages appear in the alveoli, causing air-space obliteration. As degeneration proceeds, cystic spaces develop due to dilated alveoli and more proximal bronchioles, leading to honeycomb lung and eventually 'end stage lung'.

D. CT and HRCT.

Over the last ten years, our understanding of the fine radiological anatomy (both normal and pathological) has greatly increased, particularly as a result of fast and fine section CT (HRCT). CT has the advantage of removing many superimposed structures or diseased areas from a given displayed area, and thus allows a better assessment of the pattern and severity of parenchymal disease, than can be gauged from plain radiographs. Of particular importance are the lobular anatomy, and the interlobular septa, as diseases may affect these in different ways.

Centilobular emphysema, pulmonary oedema, bronchopneumonia, sarcoidosis, hypersensitivity pneumonitis, panbronchiolitis and simple pneumoconiosis all involve the **core structures**.
Lymphatic metastases, sarcoid, asbestos, drug toxicity and fat embolism primarily the **septal structures**.
However sarcoidosis may affect either the core structures or the septa, largely depending on the acute or chronic stage of the condition.

Many patients will need a lung biopsy for definitive diagnosis, and this may be carried out either by open lung biopsy or the trans-bronchial route (see Chapter 21). The latter is simpler, but tends to be limited in diffuse infiltrative disease to the diagnosis of sarcoidosis or lymphangitis carcinomatosa.

Brief notes on some **HRCT lung appearances** are given in the following diagrams and the notes below, others appear with the discussions of various disease processes particularly in Chapters 4 to 8, 18 & 19 - see also Chapter 20 re techniques.

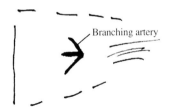

Perivascular lymphatic shadowing - neoplasm or infection spreading towards hilum.

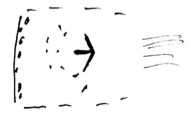

+ nodular shadows alongside pleura & in septa (sarcoid, silicosis, lymphangitis carcinomatosa).

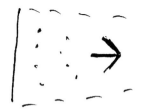

Random distribution of tiny nodules - not related to vessels (miliary ca, miliary TB, miliary fungus infection).

Centrilobular distribution - bronchiolitis/bronchopneumonia, histiocytosis x, pneumoconiosis, hypersensitivity pneumonitis.

Small rings - atypical pneumonia, mycoplasma bronchiolitis, hypersensitivity, BOOP, asbestos, bronchogenic ca., oedema, vasculitis.

Fig. 1.60 Diagram showing how some disease processes affect the secondary lobules.

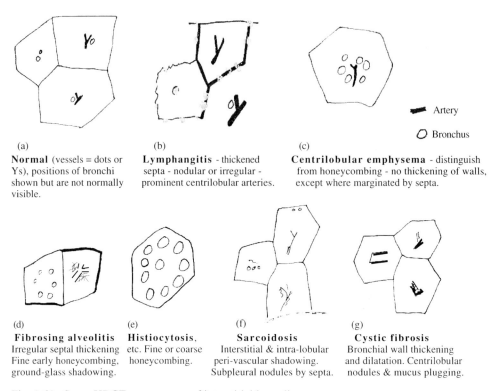

(a)

Normal (vessels = dots or Ys), positions of bronchi shown but are not normally visible.

(b)

Lymphangitis - thickened septa - nodular or irregular - prominent centrilobular arteries.

(c)

Centrilobular emphysema - distinguish from honeycombing - no thickening of walls, except where marginated by septa.

━ Artery

○ Bronchus

(d)

Fibrosing alveolitis
Irregular septal thickening
Fine early honeycombing, ground-glass shadowing.

(e)

Histiocytosis,
etc. Fine or coarse honeycombing.

(f)

Sarcoidosis
Interstitial & intra-lobular peri-vascular shadowing.
Subpleural nodules by septa.

(g)

Cystic fibrosis
Bronchial wall thickening and dilatation. Centrilobular nodules & mucus plugging.

Fig. 1.61 Some HRCT appearances of interstitial lung disease.

(i) **Signs** and pathology associated with CT and HRCT appearances of lung disease.

Diffuse **alveolar damage** - a common histological pattern of injury in inflammatory lung disease, hypersensitivity pneumonitis, toxic gases, drugs, collagen diseases, post-radiation, ARDS, alveolar haemorrhage (Goodpasture, DLE, etc.), and immunocompromised patients. Early phases - oedema, epithelial necrosis and sloughing, fibrinous exudate in air spaces and hyaline membrane formation. With organisation and repair alveolar type II cells proliferate, hyaline membranes resorb and fibroblastic proliferation occurs in the interstitium and air spaces.

Bronchiolar and peribronchiolar disease - increased prominence or irregularity of centrilobular branching structures may represent bronchiolar dilatation and intraluminal mucus, fluid or pus ('**tree in bud**' appearance - esp. seen in panbronchiolitis - see also p. 3.29), but this may also be a feature of cystic fibrosis, infective conditions - bronchopneumonia, mycoplasma, acute TB, hypogammaglobulinaemia and yellow nail syndrome.

Nodules in the lungs.
Fine nodules may be seen in bronchiolitis, pneumoconiosis, eosinophilic lung, talcosis, the effects of smoking, etc. These dots may be centrilobular, perilymphatic or random (as with haematogenous disease) - giving rise to well defined **dot-like** or **Y shaped opacities** - these may be overlooked unless attention is directed to normal pulmonary arterial branches.
Examples: -
Hypersensitivity pneumonia - diffuse ground-glass nodules
Peribronchiolar disease - e.g. due to BOOP - the nodules are separated from lobular borders and do not reach the fissural or pleural surfaces.

Eosinophilic granuloma (in nodular phase) - peri-bronchiolar interstitium - centrilobular nodules - vessels obscured by ground-glass shadowing.
Adult onset papillomatosis (some nodules may be cavitated) - separated from pleural surface.
Talcosis - perivascular inflammatory response.

Randomly distributed nodules are often part of miliary infections such as TB, fungal or viral infections. In histiocytosis x and silicosis they may appear randomly distributed late in their course, although early on they develop in a bronchocentric or lymphatic distribution respectively. Many nodular processes (e.g. sarcoid & some neoplasms) are not randomly distributed, but show a lymphatic pattern at scanning magnification.

Centrilobular nodules - bronchiolitis/bronchopneumonia, histiocytosis x, pneumoconiosis, hypersensitivity pneumonia - see Fig. 1.60 - note also '**tree in bud**' appearance or '**jacks**' - due to mucus or pus-filled bronchioles (distinguish from perilymphatic disease - see below).
Examples: -
Bacterial bronchopneumonia plus impaction of small airways - mycoplasma, TB.
Bronchiolectasis with areas of small airway impaction.
(Distinguish from : focal branching patterns of vessels; **sarcoidosis** with beading of arterial branches and irregularity - no 'jacks' present [esp. in central lung] - perilymphatic distribution of the nodules may be more widespread reaching to the **pleural surface of the lung** see below.)

Perilymphatic nodules - (a) around **bronchovascular bundles** (axial interstitium), (b) in **interlobular septa** (peripheral interstitium) and (c) in **subpleural spaces along pleural surfaces and fissures** are typically seen in **sarcoidosis** (with beading of the arterial branches or broncho-vascular bundles and adjacent to the subpleural spaces due to perilymphatic granules and nodules affecting the subpleural lymphatic plexus - see p. 13.3.)
Perilymphatic nodules are also seen with **Kaposi's sarcoma.**

Fibrosis is particularly seen with asbestosis, silicosis, fibrosing alveolitis and chronic hypersensitivity conditions and may give rise to a **reticular pattern** of intralobular linear opacities and architectural distortion.
Cellular **interstitial infiltrates of lymphocytes and plasma cells** with but little fibrosis and preservation of lung architecture are common but are rarely useful in differential diagnosis.
Interstitial fibrosis - is often accompanied by permanent and irreversible alteration of lung architecture, commonly termed **honeycombing** - with metaplastic epithelial lining, mucostasis and fibrotic walls. There is often a variegated pathological appearance with areas of normal lung tissue, others of honeycombing or of active fibrosis with a still recognisable architecture. (Causes - CFA, LIP, collagen vascular diseases, drug reactions, pneumoconioses, sarcoid, histiocytosis X, chronic granulomatous or aspiration infections, chronic hypersensitivity pneumonitis, organised chronic eosinophilic pneumonia, organising (or organised) diffuse alveolar damage, chronic interstitial oedema, chronic post-radiation change, healed infectious pneumonia.

Ground-glass shadowing (see also p. 2.3) - vessel calibre uniform throughout the affected lung - is due to oedema or inflammatory reaction in the lung tissue within the lobule and may occur with pulmonary oedema, acute injury or sensitivity, or as a feature of the more active phase of fibrosing alveolitis. It may also be seen with PCP, alveolar proteinosis (+ some crazy paving), and should be differentiated from the:
Mosaic pattern (p. 2.4) i.e. patchy attenuation differences (with vessels in the **denser normal areas** of the lung larger than vessels in the more lucent lung parenchyma) - secondary to:
(a) airways disease with air trapping and reflex vasoconstriction of arteries supplying diseased segments (e.g. bronchiolitis obliterans), or
(b) pulmonary vascular disease with inhomogeneous perfusion.
Expiratory scans are often useful for confirming the mosaic pattern by showing **air trapping in the lucent abnormal areas**. (Air-trapping also occurs in emphysema and smokers, but note that some normal people may show air trapping in some lung segments - see p. 3.27).

Septal thickening is particularly seen in lymphangitis carcinomatosa, but may also occur with fibrosis, pulmonary oedema, PAP, etc. It tends to be **irregular in carcinomatosis**.

Holes in the lung - note :
thickness of walls - imperceptible in emphysema.
- thin - cysts, bullae or honeycombing.
- thick - bronchiectasis, cavitation or honeycombing.
Examples:
Bronchiectasis - note '**signet rings**' - with aspergillosis the dilated bronchi may appear cystic and may be bizarre in shape with fairly thin walls.
Eosinophilic granuloma and **histiocytosis** - cyst walls thinner than in bronchiectasis and may coalesce to form bizarre shapes (relationship to arterial branches is not common).
Honeycombing - thin or thick walls but size is fairly uniform - tend to be peripheral and often appear as '**stacks of coins**' (+ associated signs of fibrosis).
Emphysema (often better shown with narrower window settings) - normal parenchyma becomes lighter (more grey) whilst air remains black - coalescent holes without perceptible walls, giving a '**moth-eaten**' appearance. **Vessels also run through 'emphysematous cysts'**.
Paraseptal emphysema - holes with very thin walls.
Lymphangiomyomatosis - uniform monotonous cysts (in **histiocytosis** focal areas may be more severely affected).
Thick-walled cavities may be seen with primary or secondary tumours, lymphomas, Wegener's granuloma. etc. - see Chapter 6.

(ii). Brief notes on CT and HRCT appearances in various conditions.

Alveolar proteinosis - Ground-glass opacity or consolidation, smooth septal thickening in abnormal areas, 'crazy-paving' (some areas being well-marked, whilst others are clearing), or 'mosaic' pattern of air-space filling (see also p. 2.3) & geographic distribution (see also p. 19.64).

Asbestos - Postero-lateral ground-glass shadowing, curvi-linear subpleural lines esp. posterolaterally in both lower lobes, parenchymal bands, thickened inter- and intra-lobular lines, honeycombing particularly in lung cortex, traction bronchiectasis, pseudo-tumours or whorled-nodules plus surrounding fibrosis, localised pleural plaques and areas of pleural thickening and reaction or transient effusions; persistent effusions and/or irregular thickening in mesothelioma.
     Well defined nodules + early conglomeration (like early PMF) in the middle third of the lung).

Aspergillosis - acute - infiltration $\rightarrow$ consolidation, cavitation + mycetoma, pl. thickening, 'haloes; also localised bronchitis + mucocoeles - see also under bronchiectasis below & p. 19.38.

Bronchiolitis (obliterans) - Centrilobular small nodular and branched opacities - due to filling or obliteration of the centrilobular bronchioles or peribronchiolar inflammation; mucous plugs may cause air-trapping with areas of patchy **decreased** lung opacity (mosaic pattern), lung overexpansion and poor expiration. Minor linear and reticular interstitial abnormalities may also be present. Small areas of ground-glass shadowing may have a centrilobular distribution.
Scarring may lead to narrowing of intra-pulmonary vessels and large main pulmonary arteries, fine nodular shadows, bronchiolectasis and bronchiectasis.

Bronchiectasis - The enlarged bronchi are usually well shown, as well as the lobar distribution, peribronchial thickening, etc. Proximal and distal dilatations can mostly be recognised.
Signs : 'signet-ring' (vertically oriented bronchi).
          'tram-tracks' (horizontally oriented bronchi).
          'string of pearls' or fluid filled tubular or branching shadows due to mucoid impaction or
          fluid-filled dilated bronchi.
          'cluster of cysts' within collapsed lung.
Post-infective bronchiectasis is usually more marked in the bases of the lower lobes, the lingula and RML - soon after an acute infection it may be reversible -'**pseudobronchiectasis**'.
Traction bronchiectasis occurs with scarring particularly post-radiation fibrosis and CFA.
In **aspergillosis** the bronchial dilatation tends to be proximal, and the bronchi may be large and oval in shape, with the more distal bronchi being normal, the upper lobes are especially affected.

In **cystic fibrosis** both proximal and distal parts of the bronchi are dilated, and there is much peribronchial thickening; all lobes are often affected, often the upper being worse (ps. 3.22 - 24).
Air-trapping may occur with aspergillosis and cystic fibrosis, but is uncommon in post-infective types.
Bronchography is now rarely carried out, and surgical resection is rarely indicated, unless the patient has intractable haemoptyses. However in some patients with such haemoptyses, HRCT may sometimes show 'thin walled bronchiectasis' with no apparent abnormality on chest radiographs.

Congestive failure - smooth thickening of interlobular septa + ground-glass opacity - bronchiolocentric distribution - lumen ± wall thickening e.g. (i) **mycoplasma** with subpleural sparing, (ii) preferential bronchiolar infiltrate + interstitial infiltrate in extrinsic allergic alveolitis.

Consolidation - either diffuse or patchy is very common in many interstitial or infiltrative lung diseases, including acute and organising infections, lung haemorrhage, alveolar proteinosis, chronic eosinophilic pneumonia, DIP, bronchiolitis, etc.
Infection - localised or more widespread air space disease, often with a lobar, segmental or lobular distribution, usually with poor definition of its borders (except at pleural surfaces) because of spread into neighbouring acini via the **pores of Kohn**. Air-bronchograms are common.
Bronchopneumonia may give rise to a 'rosette' or 'patchwork quilt' appearance.
TB. - Patchy uni- or bilateral consolidation of bronchopneumonic distribution, with one or more cavitating areas where the consolidation is more dense, and from where the disseminated infection has spread transbronchially. Pleural reaction or effusion, miliary nodules, hilar or mediastinal node enlargement (often of low density), abscess formation (from ribs, spine, clavicle or nodes) - ps. 19.16 - 19.24.
PCP - Patchy bilateral foci of ground-glass opacification, central or more peripheral. May be accompanied by thin-walled cysts (and pneumothoraces) or dense conglomerate nodules (ps. 19. 10 - 19.13).

COP (BOOP) - Patchy unilateral or bilateral multifocal areas of consolidation (or ground-glass shadowing), often with a peripheral distribution; also multiple small, poorly circumscribed peribronchiolar nodular opacities, and bronchial wall thickening in abnormal areas.

DIP - HRCT - multifocal areas of ground-glass opacification. Pathology - increased numbers of alveolar macrophages + inflammatory changes in alveolar walls (also seen with bronchiolitis + interstitial lung disease, histiocytosis X, drug reactions [esp. amiodarone], chronic haemorrhage, eosinophilic pneumonia, pneumoconioses [esp. talc, hard metal, asbestos], obstructive pneumonias [with foamy macrophages], lipoid pneumonia and lipid-storage, infection in immunocompromised, and focally in many others.

Drugs - in general - widespread parenchymal changes, often in some central areas.
Amiodarone - basal, peripheral, high-density, pleuro-parenchymal linear opacities.
Bleomycin - pleuro-parenchymal linear and nodular opacities with a coarse reticular shadowing extending centrally as the pneumonitis progresses.
Methotrexate - acute patchy widespread alveolar shadowing (see also p. 19.111-112).

Eosinophilic pneumonia - patchy uni- or bilateral consolidation , esp. of upper lobes and often with a peripheral or subpleural predominance and crescentic subcortical shadowing on CT. There is often a sharp demarcation between consolidated and air-filled lung, esp. at septa. There may also be areas of ground-glass opacity. It may be difficult to distinguish radiologically from BOOP.

Emphysema - HRCT is the method of choice for assessing the size, shape and number of bullae present, and the involvement of the various lobes. Sections in both inspiration and expiration will show whether deflation (and hence useful ventilation) takes place via the bullae - in most no appreciable change occurs. **Bullae often have septa or vessels traversing them**.
Centrilobular emphysema (may not be visible on plain radiographs) but is well shown by HRCT. It may also occur with other diffuse disease, and so alter the pattern of this to make it almost

unrecognisable. When diffuse, with no recognisable bullae, areas of low density may be seen without any identifiable walls.

Cicatricial emphysema gives rise to air-space enlargement - irregular areas of decreased opacity in regions of fibrosis or scarring.

Panlobular emphysema results in a uniform destruction of lobules particularly in the lower lobes (especially seen with α_1 antitrypsin deficiency).

Paraseptal emphysema - subpleural bullae and cysts.

Extrinsic allergic alveolitis - (e.g. bird-fancier's lung and farmer's lung) - pathologically - increased 'juicy' lymphocytes and inflammation of tiny bronchioles.

acute - non-specific air-space opacification - diffuse bilateral small poorly circumscribed infiltrates and multifocal regions of ground-glass opacity - the **bronchocentricity of diffuse small poorly circumscribed nodular opacities** may be difficult to appreciate on HRCT. There are often multilobular regions of hyperinflated lung with air-trapping (**mosaic pattern**).

sub-acute - small rounded opacities and patchy air-space opacification particularly affecting the mid zones; sparing of lung apices.

chronic - superimposition of fibrosis and reticulation.

Fibrosing alveolitis (Cryptogenic FA or UIP - predominance of fibroblastic cells) - The earliest change is ground-glass shadowing progressing to a diffuse subpleural reticular infiltrative process with fibrosis and honeycombing - typically most severe at lung bases and peripherally (regions affected radiologically correlate with the peripheral acinar scarring - **more acini being affected in the peripheral or subpleural regions** of the lung than in the central or perihilar regions). In the mid zones CT may cut the pleural interfaces at the periphery of a lobe - at an inter-lobar fissure to give a spurious central appearance of disease (see diagrams below).

In less advanced cases a sub-pleural crescent of increased density (as well as peripheral honeycombing) may be present posteriorly in the lower lobes, and will persist if the patient is turned prone. In more advanced cases, anteriorly situated crescents and honeycombing may be present in the upper lobes. **Traction bronchiectasis** is not uncommon and there is often 'saw toothed irregularity' of the visceral pleura, especially where it overlies the mediastinum.

Ground-glass shadowing (without architecture change) may indicate a partially reversible process, but **honeycombing is irreversible**.

Where interlobar septa are sectioned on CT cuts, e.g. in the RMZ, odd appearances may occur due to abnormal subpleural areas adjacent to the inter-lobar fissures apparently lying within the lung.

The diagram shows this in relation to the lesser fissure.

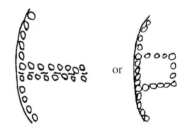

Histiocytosis X (eosinophilic granuloma) - In the early stages, only a background pattern of tiny nodules may be seen. Later small nodules or cavitated nodules (tending to be stellate or centrally cystic) are commonly present. These lead to thin-walled cysts, usually with an upper lung predominance and appearing as true hexagons or a reticular pattern, but some cysts may be confluent with bizarre shapes. The lung volumes may be increased (giving rise to a **'vanishing lung syndrome'**, similar to that seen with gross bullous disease and emphysema - see p. 6.7); pneumothoraces are common. Many of the lung changes may be related to smoking.

Diffuse pulmonary **lymphangiomatosis** - abnormal proliferation of lymphatics along normal sites in the lung - HRCT shows diffuse involvement of the lymphatic system - mild thickening of septa, subpleural and bronchovascular bundles + ground glass shadowing; pleural effusions, thickening and hilar prominence are common.

Lymphangiomyomatosis (**'LAM'**) **and tuberose sclerosis** - Diffuse random distribution in the interstitium of thin-walled cysts (some confluent) pushing the vessels to one side + minimal or no detectable abnormality of non-cystic lung - i.e. **the intervening lung looks relatively normal**. A few cysts may coalesce, but most are similar in size. There is also a more generalised form (see also ps. 5.18 & 13.6). Lung nodules are not a prominent feature as in histiocytosis.

Lymphangitis carcinomatosa - non-uniform or **nodular thickening of interlobular septa, pleura & bronchovascular bundles**, the generalised increase in the thickness of the interlobular septa, often causing a coarse honeycomb appearance. The septa commonly have a **beaded or 'knotted' appearance** caused by tumour deposits within the lobular interstitium. Centrally in the lobules, the **broncho-vascular bundles** (which are also enveloped by interstitium) become **thickened and nodular, giving rise to a larger centri-lobular 'dot'**. There is usually very little increased opacity within the lobules. The adjacent pleural surfaces (including fissures) may also become irregular from tumour infiltration.
   The appearances may be unilateral (esp. with lung cancer). They remain fixed in a non-dependent position.

Lymphoma - may mimic pneumonia as bilateral multifocal nodules or areas of consolidation, or involvement of peribronchovascular and interlobular septal regions with nodularity.

Pneumoconiosis - nonspecific fine nodules throughout the lungs; PMF may occur especially in mid thirds of lungs - may be non-spherical with a larger lateral diameter, and may parallel the major fissure.

Pulmonary embolism - clot defects in central and segmental pulmonary arteries, reduced peripheral areas of lung perfusion, peripheral bronchial arterial arcades, linear or larger areas of collapse, Hampton's hump, small pleural effusions, acute right-sided heart failure and ventricular dilatation.

Rheumatoid - fibrosis spreading into the lungs from the periphery (similar to fibrosing alveolitis), nodules and Caplan's type nodules. Honeycombing ± pleural effusion or reaction.

Sarcoidosis - predominantly due to **granulomas** and not fibrosis in the acute stage - infiltration tends to follow the distribution of the broncho-vascular bundles, with peri-bronchial wall thickening, 'cuffing', 'beading' or nodularity. **Small well-defined nodules** are mostly found in the upper and mid-zones in relation to septa, bronchioles or in the **sub-pleural areas** (i.e. peripheral subpleural aggregates) where they **may mimic metastases** - these last are **characteristic**. Coalescence of nodules may occur. Fibrosis may lead to septal thickening, traction bronchiectasis, hilar elevation and cor pulmonale. Intrapulmonary as well as hilar and mediastinal enlargement may be seen.
HRCT findings - characteristic: central perihilar, peribronchovascular, nodular infiltrates; also common: interlobular septal and subpleural nodularity.
HRCT may also detect infiltration and nodules in most patients with sarcoidosis whose plain radiographs appear clear.
Lung contraction and fibrosis towards the hila are present in end-stage disease.

Scleroderma - sub-pleural crescents, traction bronchiectasis & basal fibrosis - also air-space opacification leading to a more generalised pulmonary fibrosis.

Silicosis and coal-miners pneumoconiosis - (infiltrates of dust-laden histiocytes and nodules form along the lymphatic routes, the sites of dust clearance). HRCT - diffuse distribution, with upper and posterior predominance - nodules (2 - 5 mm in diameter and centrilobular or subpleural), may coalesce to PMF with conglomerate masses which may contain areas of necrosis - may be complicated by centrilobular and subpleural focal or irregular cicatricial emphysema.

GIP (hard metal disease) - non-specific diffuse interstitial infiltrates + small ill-defined nodules' often mid + lower predominance.

SLE (or DLE) - pleural thickening and/or effusions. Peripheral and basal linear, band-like opacities. Small areas of consolidation.

Veno-occlusive   disease - (primarily manifesting as pulmonary hypertension but often associated with passive congestion and prominence of septal veins and septa) - smooth thickening of intralobular septa + ground-glass opacity - may be due to concomitant pulmonary haemorrhage.

Further references:

Kempner (1939) : Oxygen tension and the tubercle bacillus.

Bahl et al. (1971) : Localised unilateral pulmonary oedema.
Mutchler et al. (1974) : Localised RUL oedema following surgically corrected left to right shunts.
Gamsu et al. (1981) : Isolated right upper lobe pulmonary oedema.
Gurney and Goodman (1989) : Pulmonary oedema localised to the RUL and accompanying mitral incompetence - four cases - may mimic RUL consolidation.
Alarcón et al. (1995) : Localised RUL (± RML) oedema should suggest mitral incompetence.

West (1971) : Distribution of mechanical stress in the lung- possible factor in the localisation of pulmonary disease.
Haroutunian et al. (1972) : Pulmonary 'pseudofibrosis' in cyanotic heart disease.
West and Matthews (1972) : Stresses, strains and. surface pressures in the lung caused by its weight.
Vawter et al. (1975) : Effect of shape and size of lung and chest wall on chest wall on stresses in the lung.
Davis (1985) : Pathophysiology of pulmonary disease in cystic fibrosis.
McLoud et al. (1984) : Chronic diffuse infiltrative lung disease.
Nakata et al. (1985) : Diffuse peripheral lung disease - evaluation by high resolution CT.
Murata et al. (1986) : Centrilobular lesions of the lung using high resolution CT.
Bergin and Müller (1985 & 1987) : CT of interstitial lung disease.
Gurney and Schroeder (1988) : Upper lobe lung disease- physiologic correlates.

Bergin et al. (1989) : Chronic lung diseases - **specific   diagnosis   by   using   CT** in 48 patients plus 8 normal controls - looked for specific parenchymal features - **disease   distribution, lung   distortion, thickening   of broncho-vascular   bundles   (carcinoma   and   sarcoid),   bronchiectasis,   cysts, nodules.** Accuracy was found in fibrosing alveolitis (20 pts. - peripheral distribution of disease with lung parenchymal distortion), sarcoidosis (16 pts. - tending to affect central and middle areas), lymphangitis (lobular walls were thickened and their central dots were increased in size, bronchovascular bundles were thickened, nodules and /or polygons in 5 of 7 pts.), lymphangioleiomyomatosis (2 pts.- cysts with thin walls), eosinophilic granuloma (1 patient - diffuse cysts in upper zones plus nodules) , drug toxicity (patchy air-space disease).

Naidich et al. (1989) : (i) About **10% of patients with infiltrative lung disease had normal pre-biopsy   chest   radiographs** (ii) **CT**, by eliminating superimposition and by enhancing contrast differences, improved the 'visual window' within the lungs. (iii) **HRCT** should be used to examine patients with equivocal chest radiographs, to give rise to a more accurate assessment of the extent and severity of the disease, as well as its probable type. (iv) **Standardisation of nomenclature** is required, related to the secondary pulmonary nodule.

Mathieson et al. (1989) : Assessed the accuracy of plain radiographs and CT in the diagnosis of 118 consecutive patients with chronic diffuse infiltrative lung disease. Three observers listed the three most likely diagnoses in order of probability. CT was about twice as accurate as plain radiography, and the most accurate interpretations were made with silicosis, fibrosing alveolitis, lymphangitis carcinomatosa and sarcoidosis, CT also indicated whether a trans-bronchial or open lung biopsy was likely to give a representative portion of lung for histological study.

Strickland (1989) : In assessing parenchymal disease by CT, it is important to note its distribution, and then to assess the pattern of abnormal areas: - **fibrosing alveolitis** (bilateral, peripheral, crescentic and maximal in lower zones), **sarcoidosis** (following distribution of bronchovascular bundles, with peribronchial wall thickening, widely distributed nodules) and **drugs** (widespread parenchymal changes, often in more central areas - mixture of air-space and mediastinal disease).

Webb et al.(1989) : HRCT optimises the spatial resolution of the lung parenchyma by using thin-collimation, image reconstruction with a high-spatial frequency algorithm, targeting and sometimes increased KV and MA settings. He found alterations in secondary lobule anatomy can be diagnostic in certain situations.
Webb et al. (1992, 1996 & 2000) : **High-Resolution CT of the Lung.**
Stern and Swensen (2000) : **High-Resolution CT of the Chest: Comprehensive Atlas.**

Graham et al. (1990) : Studied the distribution of particles < 1μ in diameter with SPECT and found increased deposition in the periphery of the lung compared with more central regions. (See also p. 1.47).

Zerhouni (1991) : Thick sections have some advantages because they demonstrate blood vessels as branching structures allowing easy recognition.
  Lack of calcification in nodules is a good indicator of malignant disease.
  In carcinomas the calcification is usually stippled and eccentric. Most calcified lesions are > 3 cms.
  Deposits are predominantly distributed in outer third of the lower lobes, & within 3 cm of the pleural surface.
  Deposits may show a connection to the pulmonary artery, when the vessel runs parallel to the scanned plane.
  Carcinoids are most commonly found at bifurcations of lobar and segmental bronchi.
  Current resolution of current scanners is about 300μm. The airways have 23 generations of branching, but
    only the 7th to the 9th can be visualised by HRCT. The arteries have 28 generations of branching, and the
    16th to 17th may be shown by HRCT.
  Septic emboli or infarcts are typically subpleural in location, have a triangular shape with their apices towards
    the hilum; cavitation is common and the rim may enhance with contrast agents.

1a   Normal visceral pleura.
1b   A slightly serrated visceral pleura is typical
      of early interstitial disease.
2a   Normal bronchus (only visible into the
      middle part of the lung).
2b   A bronchus with a thickened and irregular wall
      (as a result of interstitial disease) may be seen in
      the outer part of the lung.
3a   Normal pulmonary arteries.
3b   Irregularly marginated arteries as a result of
      interstitial lung disease.
4a-d Interstitial nodules.
5a-c Reticular shadows.
6a-c Ground glass shadowing.

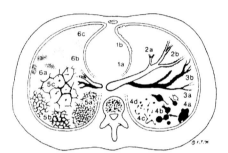

Fig. 1.62 HRCT signs of diffuse parenchymal disease (reproduced from Zerhouni, 1991, CT of parenchymal lung disease in Higgins, CB & Pattersson, H, Chest & Cardiac Radiology, with permission from Merit Publications).

Wood et al. (1992) : HRCT of the chest - an integrated approach - should consider the following:
(i) the lobar distribution of the disease process,
(ii) its distribution within the individual lobes,
(iii) is the primary abnormality bronchiectatic change, parenchymal disease or fibrosis?,
(iv) abnormalities seen in the secondary pulmonary lobule,
(v) the physiology of the vascular response to the lung disease.

Rémy-Jardin et al. (1993) : Importance of ground-glass attenuation in chronic diffuse infiltrative lung disease - CT correlation with pathology - in the absence of concomitant signs of lung fibrosis. ground-glass attenuation is a reliable indicator of lung inflammation.
Schnyder et al. (1993) : Prevalence of predominant involvement of the right upper lobe in pulmonary oedema associated with pulmonary regurgitation.
Gruden et al. (1994) : Centrilobular opacities in the lung on HRCT.

Gurney (1995) : The pathophysiology of airways disease - normally there is little resistance to airflow in the small airways (<2mm diameter); thus extensive disease may be present before it becomes clinically evident. **Centrilobular** **emphysema** is characterised by dilation and destruction of small airways, compared with **bronchiolitis obliterans** - concentric fibrous obliteration of small airways. HRCT, particularly with inspiration and expiration studies, is the most sensitive method of imaging small airways disease.

Grenier (1996) : HRCT patterns of lung disease - air space abnormalities tend to be ill-defined, less dense than vessels, small nodules with peri-lymphatic, random or centrilobular distribution, may be difficult to recognise.

Colby and Swensen (1996) : HRCT correlation with anatomy and histological patterns of diffuse lung disease.
Some interstitial lung diseases affect certain anatomical compartments of the lung and are appreciated by low power microscopy - these show the best correlation with radiology; in other cases an anatomical distribution is more difficult to appreciate and radiology usually manifests as airspace or ground glass shadowing.
Lymphatic distribution - sarcoid & some lymphoreticular infiltrates - nodular infiltrates along lymphatic routes in the pleura, septa, along bronchovascular bundles and around larger veins.
Only a few diffuse interstitial pneumonias are dominated by **sarcoid-like granulomas** (± necrosis) - sarcoid (inc. necrotising sarcoid), ext. allergic alveolitis, drug reactions, granulomatous infections, IV talc, pneumoconiosis, pneumoconioses (inhaled talc, beryllium), Sjögren's syndrome (LIP + granulomas), aspiration pneumonia, tumours (esp. lymphomas), Wegener's granuloma, bronchocentric or allergic granuloma.

See also chapter 20 re further HRCT references.

Some basic principles in the diagnosis of lung diseases.
  It is interesting to note that before the advent of CT and particularly HRCT, the characteristics of disease processes as portrayed on plain radiographs was less certain.
  Felson et al. (1959) in an article entitled '**Some basic principles of clinical diseases**' discussed :
(a) calcification in a 'coin lesion' due to histoplasmosis,
(b) cavitation within 'coin lesions' due to neoplasm - these had thick walls,
(c) Kerley's 'B' lines due to interstitial oedema, dusts (tin oxide, iron ores, haematite, fluorides and other inert dusts), and lymphangitis, (also seen with some lung infections - see p. 8.11),
(d) intrapulmonary vessels - veins v arteries, and arterial loss in pulmonary embolism,
(e) pleural fluid which may arrange itself around an individual lobe, and
(f) honeycomb lung due to eosinophilic lung and congenital adenomatoid malformation.

  Felson (1967) continued this discussion in '**The Roentgen diagnosis of disseminated pulmonary alveolar diseases**'. He wrote : 'The margins of alveolar infiltrates are fluffy and ill-defined, fading imperceptibly except where they abut upon a pleural surface. The edges of the infiltrates are wispy and ill-defined, a bit like cotton candy. The fluffiness is due to the irregular interdigitation of groups of completely involved alveoli with adjacent groups of less involved or normal alveoli." By comparison "most **metastases** originate in the interstitial tissue and enlarge concentrically" - they are "nearly always sharply outlined, since they **compress** rather than infiltrate the marginal alveoli". However "certain tumours, particularly metastatic may incite **hemorrhage** into the surrounding lung, the alveolar blood then being responsible for the fluffy outline"; bleeding may also occur from direct chest trauma, blast injury, aspirated blood, anticoagulants, leukaemia, haemosiderosis, Goodpasture's syndrome, etc.

  Felson* (1979b) in a paper entitled '**A new look at pattern recognition of diffuse pulmonary disease**' wrote "A variety of patterns is recognisable on chest films...these include miliary, honeycomb, vascular, bronchial, Kerley line, destructive, alveolar, and small irregular patterns. The clinical diagnosis is easier to predict than the histologic distribution of the disease. It is extremely important that pattern ... approach (should) **not be used unless one is certain a pattern can be identified.**" The 'alveolar pattern' includes the air bronchogram or alveologram, alveolar nodules (e.g. in varicella pneumonia), the butterfly shadow, fluffy margins and segmental or lobar distribution; early appearance, after onset of symptoms, and early coalescence are characteristic. The 'alveolar' disease is not uncommonly not confined to the alveoli and may affect the interstitium as in alveolar sarcoidosis, the early form of reversible disease.

  Blank (1989) in his book '**Chest Radiographic Analysis**' considered the **clinical utility of pattern analysis** and wrote "My impression, unsupported by any data, is that too many lesions characterised by inhomogeneity are considered 'interstitial' when they are not. Much less commonly, lesions characterised by homogeneous opacity are considered 'air space' or 'acinar' lesions when they are not." He continued "However, I cannot think of any pattern that is specific for any single cause, nor do most avid proponents of pattern analysis make such claims. Therefore, careful correlation with clinical and laboratory data is required, and frequently lung biopsy is necessary to reach a definite diagnosis. Moreover, there are times when even histopathologic analysis and all the special tests that can be performed on a generous lung biopsy specimen yield non-specific abnormalities that do not permit a precise diagnosis."

Milne and Pistolesi (1993) produced a book 'Reading the Chest Radiograph - A Physiologic Approach' which is well recommended as showing how to deduce physiology as well as anatomy and pathology from plain chest radiographs. Their main interests were pulmonary blood flow and pulmonary oedema - see also ps. 8.3-4.

Milne and Pistolesi completed this book with a 'Compendium of Pathophysiologic Patterns' illustrated with 26 figures - line drawings made by Prof. Milne to show in pictorial and textual summary form the various abnormal plain chest radiographic patterns associated with pulmonary oedema, overhydration, dehydration, cardiac failure, renal failure (including the less common nodular form), pericardial tamponade, emphysema, chronic bronchitis + pulmonary hypertension pulmonary plethora, pulmonary hypertension, injury oedema, etc. - these also included indications of chest wall swelling, which might be considerable with severe burns. These drawings are also copied into a small pocket book (located in a pocket in the inside of the back cover) for easy carrying and reference - a valuable guide for doctors concerned particularly with acutely ill or injured patients, especially in intensive care units, when incorrect interpretation of plain chest radiographs may sometimes lead to unnecessary and rapid catastrophic results.

Further references (see also references in Preface p. iv).
Recavarren et al. (1967) : The pathology of acute alveolar diseases of the lung.
Greenspan (1967) : Chronic disseminated alveolar diseases of the lung.
Posner (1971) : The early years of chest radiology in Britain.
Tuddenham (1956) : Fifty years of progress in chest Roentgenology.
Rigler (1977a) : An overview of cancer of the lung.
Trapnell (1982) : Chest radiology - guesswork or science.
Burrows (1986) : Pioneers and Early Years - A History of British Radiology.
Szamosi (1995) : Lung Cancer - The Art of Detection by Conventional Radiography - a reminder to radiologists and how to detect subtle changes on chest radiographs which may lead to the possible diagnosis of tumour.
Heitzman (2000) : Thoracic radiology - the past 50 years - a review including conventional radiography, film processing, chest fluoroscopy, kymography, bronchography, CT & MR. [A surprise is that with one exception - a reference to iodised oil for bronchography - all the others are from the US literature!]

* For Obituary to Felson - see Felson (1989) - Memorial to Dr. Benjamin Felson (Editor of Seminars in Roentgenology).

Some notes on visibility of lung structures on HRCT.

Secondary lobule = 1 - 2.5 (sometimes up to 4) cm in size (see also p. 1.40).

Septa = 0.1 mm thick (see also p. 1.45).

Lobular veins in septa = 0.5 mm in diameter (see also p. 1.45).

Lobular bronchiole = 1 mm in diameter (see also p. 1.45).

Lobular (central) artery = 1 mm in diameter (see also p. 1.45).

Terminal bronchiole = 0.6 mm in diameter.

A dilated small bronchus may be larger than its adjacent pulmonary artery branch and then may be seen more peripherally than normal, both towards the chest wall and medial branches towards the mediastinum.

(Normal clear limit of visibility on HRCT = 1 mm).

SOME NOTES RE TERMINOLOGY

In this book and illustration comments, the author has used English spellings and has mainly used terms that are generally accepted.

He mainly uses the term radiograph to refer to a plain film, rather than the clinical colloquial 'chest x-ray', but strictly it should be a radiogram, like tomogram etc. Technically a radiograph is really the apparatus used to take a radiogram!

Some other points:

atelectasis - the author feels that if Classical Greek terms are used, then they should be used correctly. The simple English term is **collapse (usually short for absorption collapse),** and the author feels this should always be used for clarity. An alternative would be to use the term **'reduced volume'**. In this volume the author almost always uses 'collapse'.

The term 'atelectasis' ('ατελης = imperfect, 'εκτασις = expansion) **really refers to collapse which has been present since birth i.e. the lung has never expanded.**
According to Mayne and Mayne, 1881, Dr. Jorg of Leipzig first described the circumstances and gave the name 'atelectasis' to a condition in new-born children which may last for days or weeks.
To a purist therefore the apparently more learned term thus refers to a congenital condition i.e. neonatal collapsed lung!

Fraser et al. (1988-9) rather awkwardly tried to get over this problem by terming failure of lung expansion in the neonate 'anectasis'- see p. xv of their glossary. They also stated that 'collapse' connotes 'total ateleactasis' in which lung tissue has been reduced to its smallest volume, but what is wrong with partial, total, lung, lobar, segmental, subsegmental or linear, cicatricial, absorption, etc. collapse? (Their statement appears illogical to the present author.)
Others including Woodring and Reed (1996a & b) and the Fleischner Society (apparently erroneously) equate atelectasis with collapse.

coin lesions - are essentially misnomers - they are really spherical - other than perhaps pebbles used by umpires for counting the number of balls played in an 'over' of cricket (the umpires move them one at a time from one pocket to another as balls are bowled) - are any coins spherical? - see also p. 4.5 & 4.7.

loss of silhouette sign - is a much more logical term than 'silhouette sign' as it is only positive when lost - see p. 2.25 - 26.

pseudoplaque - this to the author really should equal a non-pulmonary opacity that is just extrapleural i.e. (like true plaques, excepting those that are intrafissural) - that described by the Fleischner Society is a subpulmonary opacity due to small micronodules - and should be termed subpleural lung micro-nodules (as described by Rémy-Jardin et al., 1990). The author uses the term pseudoplaque to refer to fat, old haematomas or rib bulges (especially in boxers - see p. 14. 39), which seems more logical.

signet ring sign - the author does not believe there is any real differential diagnosis from a dilated bronchus (usually with bronchiectasis) + an accompanying vessel (usually a pulmonary artery branch).

Some references:
1. Dept. of Health definitions of lung positions (1947 - see Fletcher, 1949):
upper zone - the area above a straight line running through the lower borders of the anterior ends of the 2nd ribs.
middle zone - the area between the above line & one through the lower borders of the anterior ends of the 4th ribs.
lower zone - the area below the middle zone.
Names of the bronchi - approved by International Committee and the Thoracic Society in 1949 (see p. 1.21).
2. The Fleischner Society recommendations re terminology (Tuddenham , 1984).
3. Webb et al. (1991) HRCT of the Lung (glossary).and Webb et al. (1993) : Standardised terms for lung HRCT.
4. Austin et al. (1996) : Glossary of terms for CT of the lungs - recommendations of the Fleischner Society.

Chapter 2 : **Lung Consolidation, Ground Glass Shadowing, Obstructive Emphysema, Collateral Air-drift, Mucocoeles, patterns of Collapse, Lung Torsion and Herniation**.

Radiological Signs of Consolidation

As well as occurring in pneumonia (see Chapter 19) the signs of consolidation must also be considered in relation to lung tumours, as there is considerable overlap in the appearances (adenocarcinomas, alveolar cell carcinomas and lymphomas may per se produce consolidation) and by the fact that infection commonly complicates tumours.

Infection may also give rise to bronchitis, a broncho-pneumonia, segmental or lobar consolidation, local infiltration, nodules, etc. These in turn may be complicated by pleural or nodal disease, cavitation, etc. The lung pattern is broadly determined by the type of infection and the local pathology - nodules with granulomas, bronchopneumonic spread with tuberculosis, spread through segments or a lobe with many pneumonias.

As noted on p. 1.40 the individual lung acinus measures about 7-8 μ in diameter, thus disease occupying it will tend to form a nodule of this size on radiographs provided that the surrounding acini are air filled. As spread occurs to neighbouring acini, coalescence will occur filling the secondary lobules and the individual acini will no longer be seen.

Since chest radiographs are normally taken in full inspiration, and consolidated lung cannot expand with respiration, there will often appear to be **some loss of volume** - hence the common radiological description '**consolidation and some collapse**' but this is **not** really true since there is often little loss of volume - just a portrayal of the normal mid-respiration volume of the affected part of the lung.

With infection occurring distal to an endobronchial block, this will tend to block the inter-alveolar and other intra-pulmonary connections and stop collateral air drift so the lung opacity will increase, with further loss of volume retained secretions and lung consolidation. Occasionally with a virulent infection (e.g. staphylococcal, Klebsiella, or influenza infection - see Chapter 19) a consolidated lobe will be larger than normal with bulging fissures to give a '**drowned lung**' appearance. This may be due to severe local infection and may also be seen with an endo-bronchial block secondary to a tumour (ps. 4.20-21) or marked lymphatic or venous obstruction.

Other signs are the air bronchogram, cavitation, abscess, syn- or post-pneumonic pleural effusion, empyema, etc.

When nodules in the lung are too small to be individually seen as with early miliary tuberculosis or diffuse fine areas of infection (i.e. before coalescence) etc., a '**ground-glass**' appearance may be seen (see p. 2.3).

The Air Bronchogram and Bronchial Wall Thickening.

On high KV radiographs one should normally be able to see the air-filled trachea, the carina, the main, lobar and intermediate bronchi. In addition the proximal parts of the air-filled segmental bronchi may just be made out. The more distal bronchi have relatively thin walls, and are not usually seen, unless their walls are thickened, or the surrounding lung is opaque. Any process which makes the surrounding alveoli and peri-bronchial tissues denser (consolidation, oedema, etc.), whilst at the same time leaving the bronchi patent, will render the bronchi more readily visible - the '**air bronchogram**'. The sign usually implies a patent bronchial tree in the diseased area and is most commonly seen in lobar pneumonia, but also be seen with ground-glass shadowing.

Fig. 2.1   The '**air bronchogram**'
within consolidated lung (see also
Illus. **AIR BRONCHOGRAM**).

Air bronchograms may also be seen on plain radiographs, conventional tomograms and CT sections with congestion, infarction, intrapulmonary bleeding (such as occurs with Goodpasture's syndrome), bronchiolo-alveolar carcinomas, pulmonary lymphomas, Wegener's granuloma, some florid sarcoid infiltrations, etc. With collapse, air bronchograms will be present if this is secondary to extrinsic pressure (from a pleural effusion or mass), but not when the supplying bronchus has become completely occluded, either by tumour or mucous, etc. Some consolidating-type tumours (adenocarcinomas, bronchiolo-alveolar cell tumours or anaplastic rapidly spreading tumours) may also show air bronchograms (Illus. **AIR BRON IN CA**).

Crowding of air bronchograms also denotes loss of lung volume in a similar way to crowding of vessels (see also p. 2.14). End-on air bronchograms may be seen on lateral views or tomograms in some cases of RLL collapse (the '**Gatling gun**' sign - see also ps. 2.29 - 2.31).

With tumours completely blocking a bronchus, no 'air-bronchogram' will be present, but with those incompletely doing this, and with those which have ceased to completely block the bronchus (either through spontaneous necrosis, or following radiotherapy or chemotherapy), enough air may pass through the partial blockage to produce a **partial 'air-bronchogram'**. This may outline the tumour (see Illus. **ENDOBRON TUMOUR, Ca RUL Pt. 22c**). Some of the bronchi distal to such a partial obstruction may be larger than normal, as they may be drained 'mucocoeles' (see p. 2.10 and Illus. **ENDOBRON TUMOUR, esp. Ca RUL Pt. 22c**).

The point of obstruction of a bronchus may often be inferred from an inspection of the 'air-bronchogram' and noting where the air column stops. One may, particularly on tomograms, be able to see the shape of the obstruction: - round filling defect, conical narrowing, a partly outlined mucus plug, etc. Sometimes the outline of a foreign body may be visible. Mucus plugs are particularly important in post-operative patients and in those in intensive care, as physiotherapy may cause their expectoration with re-expansion of the distal partially collapsed lung. In resistant cases, and with foreign bodies, bronchoscopy made be needed for their removal.

Fig. 2.2   (a) Collapsed and airless RUL   (b) Incomplete obstruction with
due to complete bronchial obstruction.   partial air bronchogram.

Bronchial wall thickening may be seen acutely with pulmonary oedema (see ps. 8.3 - 8.4) and in lymphangitis carcinomatosa (see p.8.11). More chronic thickening is seen in bronchiectasis or cystic fibrosis and to a lesser extent in chronic bronchitis and asthma. The thickening of less affected and less dilated bronchi may be '**tram line**' like, and in the grosser cases the bronchi will be dilated and frankly bronchiectatic as well as thickened (see p. 3.19).

When seen 'end on', bronchial wall thickening has been termed '**bronchial   cuffing**' or the '**bronchial cuff sign**'. It may be noted in the anterior segment of either lower lobe, the apex of a lower lobe, the main bronchi on lateral views, the intermediate bronchus on CT sections, etc. The '**anterior bronchus sign**' is one example. Other similar signs may be seen with other segmental bronchi.

The **anterior segmental bronchus** of an upper lobe is commonly well seen in the upper hilar region (in 50% or more of high KV radiographs or on tomograms), as a small air-filled circular structure. Its wall is normally about 2 - 3 mm thick, but an accompanying vessel may occasionally make it appear thicker. When thickened, especially on its lateral aspect, then adjacent disease, e.g. neoplasm, consolidation, etc. is likely to be present.

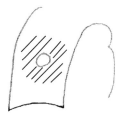

Fig. 2.3 'Air bronchogram' with consolidation of apex of LLL. (Bronchus seen 'end on'.)

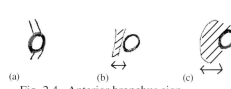

Fig. 2.4 Anterior bronchus sign.
(a) normal ant. seg. bron. (b) + vessel (c) + tumour
(Wall = 2-3 mm) (4 mm) (> 5 mm)

Thickening of the walls of the intermediate and lower lobe bronchi may be seen on lateral radiographs. The right side is usually better portrayed, because of the air-filled lung in the azygo-oesophageal recess (see Fig. 1.36). The stripe of the intermediate bronchus (normally 1 to 2mm thick - see Fig. 1.36, p.1.24) can be thickened posteriorly by congestion, consolidation, tumours or enlarged nodes. Schnur et al. (1981) found this sign in 23 patients with congestive heart failure, 9 with neoplasm (including lymphoma and secondary deposits from extra-thoracic primary neoplasms), and two cases of sarcoidosis. Lobulation was particularly suggestive of enlarged nodes. They made the point that this sign may be the only 'clue' to abnormalities on plain radiographs.

Ground-Glass Shadowing (increased lung density or haziness, **not** obscuring underlying bronchi or vessels) - sometimes termed 'grey lung' - Illus. **GROUND-GLASS.**

This is best shown by HRCT and may be **due to any process which decreases the air content of the lung parenchyma without totally obliterating it.** Causes include **pulmonary oedema, alveolar proteinosis, alveolitis** and **allergic** or **interstitial pneumonitis, sarcoidosis, bronchiolitis, cryptogenic organising pneumonia**, some **infections** (e.g. Pneumocystis pneumonia) and acute **post-radiation pneumonitis**. It is commonly seen in **fibrosing alveolitis** (both idiopathic and due to systemic sclerosis, etc.) and is often (but sometimes erroneously) regarded as an **indicator of active disease** - with increased cellularity of the alveolar walls. However a fine fibrosis may also be present in the affected areas, or grosser fibrosis elsewhere in the lungs. The presence of ground-glass shadowing has been suggested by some protagonists as a 'sine qua non' for the treatment of fibrosing alveolitis with steroids, but not all clinicians agree. Acute changes in fibrosing alveolitis are usually reversible, but fibrosis, honeycombing and end-stage lung are not reversible (see ps. 19.116 - 9).

The early appearance may be partly physiological in the dependent lung cortex (p. 8.6). It may also be simulated by normal lung which appears denser than hyperaerated lung, as with emphysema, bronchiolitis, and cryptogenic organising pneumonia, etc. (see also ps. 3.31 - 3.33). An air bronchogram may be present. Localised ground-glass shadowing may be seen with some adenocarcinomas and with bronchioloadenocarcinomas or bronchial adenomas in association with air bronchograms (see Illus. **AIR BRON IN CA**).

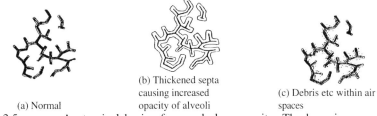

(a) Normal

(b) Thickened septa causing increased opacity of alveoli

(c) Debris etc within air spaces

Fig. 2.5 Anatomical basis of ground-glass opacity. The hazy increase in lung opacity corresponds to morphological changes at alveolar level that cannot be resolved by HRCT.
The alveolar walls may be thickened or the air spaces partially filled with fluid, cells or debris (after Engeler et al., 1993, AJR, **160**, 249 - 251, with permission).

Spurious ground-glass shadowing can sometimes be seen with narrow CT window settings, and also after recent broncho-alveolar lavage (especially seen in RML or lingula - see Illus. **BRONCHIAL LAVAGE**).

Mosaic pattern of lung attenuation on CT

With obstruction of the small airways as occurs in bronchiolitis, thin CT sections taken in expiration may show hyperinflation of parts of the lung (i.e. some secondary lobules remain air-filled in expiration, the normally deflating lobules losing their air and becoming more vascular and more opaque (see also ps. 3.25-28). This may also happen with acute extrinsic allergic alveolitis (ps. 19.101-102 & Illus. **MOSAIC PATTERN**) and in sarcoidosis (ps. 19.68 & 71).

This pattern may also be mimicked by vascular impairment in some cases of pulmonary embolism or pulmonary vascular disease. See also discussions on pulmonary embolism ps. 7.26 and bronchiolitis ps. 3.25-30.

Very often even in normal subjects, some normal lobules remain hyperinflated in expiration as shown on HRCT sections taken in expiration (see p. 2.6).

Crazy-paving pattern of lung attenuation.

This pattern - often 'geographic' and patchy with well-defined areas of **ground-glass** attenuation within lobules + **superimposed septal thickening** - see Fig. 19.9 - was first described with alveolar proteinosis, but may also be seen with lipoid pneumonia, bronchioloavleolar carcinoma lymphangitis carcinomatosa and non-specific interstitial pneumonia, etc. (see ps. 5.1-3, 6.16, 8.11-12, 19.63-64 & 19.122 and Illus. **CRAZY PAVING**).

References.

Air bronchogram.
Williams (1886) : The air bronchogram (quoted by Greene, 1992).
Fleischner (1937) : 'Air bronchogram' in pneumonia.
(1948) : Visible air filled bronchial tree in pneumonia and other consolidations.
Bachynski (1971) : **Absence of air bronchogram sign** - a reliable finding in pulmonary embolism with infarction or haemorrhage.
Felson (1973) : The air bronchogram.
Reed and Madewell (1975) : The 'air bronchogram' in interstitial disease of the lungs.
Reed (1977) : Pathologic correlations of the 'air bronchogram' - a reliable sign in chest radiology.
ZuWallack et al. (1977) : Air bronchograms in metastatic melanoma.
Fraser and Paré (1979) : The air bronchogram.
Friedman (1982) : Consolidation in the apical segment of the lower lobe - the '**B6 bronchus sign**'.
Harris (1985) : The importance of proximal and distal air bronchograms in the management of collapse - esp. valuable in post-operative collapse, compression collapse or poor muco-ciliary clearance.: (a) **proximal** - air visible only down to level of main, intermediate or lobar bronchi; (b) **intermediate** - air down to level of segmental bronchi; and (c) **distal** - air visible down to level of subsegmental bronchi or beyond.
Kuriyama et al. (1991) : **Air bronchograms in peripheral adenocarcinomas** on thin section CT (rare in benign nodules).
O'Donovan and Stoller (1992) : Air bronchograms in lung metastases from adenoca of colon.

Bronchial wall thickening.
Simon (1976) : Noted in children small (3 - 5 mm) ring shadows lying laterally near the upper part of the hilum, due to the anterior bronchus seen end-on.
Don and Johnson (1977) : Peribronchial cuffing in pulmonary oedema.
Genereux (1977) : Noted the '**bronchial cuff**' as an unusual manifestation of bronchogenic carcinoma.
Littleton and Durizch (1983) : Noted the sign with a tumour in the wall of the apical bronchus of the RLL.
Foster et al. (1985) : Reported it as a CT finding with a squamous tumour of the RLL (invisible on plain films).
Fraser et al. (1989) : Illustrated a case with thickening around the anterior segment of the RUL due to tumour, together with a normal radiograph from 6 years before.
Spizarny and Cavanaugh (1985) : Stated that the '**anterior bronchus sign**' was a ' new clue ' to hilar anatomy. They studied 100 normal radiographs re the anterior segment bronchus - it was visible on the right in 45 and on the left in 50. Four cases with tumours were reported.

Ground-glass shadowing.
Webb et al. (1992) : HRCT of the Lung.
Engeler et al. (1993) : Ground glass opacity of the lung parenchyma - guide to analysis with HRCT.

Müller and Miller (1993) : Ground-glass attenuation, nodules, alveolitis and sarcoid granulomas.

Rémy-Jardin et al. (1993) : CT assessment of ground-glass opacity. The ground-glass appearance is defined as an increase in lung density which does not obscure surrounding lung anatomy. It is the most difficult sign of parenchymal lung disease to diagnose, and is most influenced by CT technique, being only confidently seen on HRCT sections. It may result from changes in the air spaces or interstitial tissues in acute or chronic inflammatory lung disease, or as a result of increased capillary blood volume in redistribution of blood flow due to airway disease, emphysema or thromboembolism. An air bronchogram may be seen.

Primack et al. (1994) : MR of infiltrative lung disease - MR of parenchymal opacification usually indicates a potentially reversible disease, whereas reticulation generally indicated irreversible disease.

Gross, B.H. (1995 Year Book of Radiology p.41) : commented "I am not yet on the HRCT bandwaggon...I'm always interested in the added value provided by a diagnostic test. In my experience, most patients who undergo HRCT get no added value. Detection by HRCT of ground-glass attenuation in patients with pulmonary fibrosis would provide added value if it separated patients with active inflammation, in whom steroid therapy would be helpful, from those with burned-out fibrosis, in whom steroid therapy would be of no help (and, given its side effects, might hurt).

Mosaic pattern of lung attenuation

Martin et al. (1986) : A mosaic pattern of lung attenuation similar to that with air trapping can be seen with pulmonary emboli.

Eber et al. (1993) : BO on HRCT - a pattern of mosaic oligaemia.

Stern et al. (1995) : **CT mosaic pattern of lung attenuation** can reflect vascular disease, airway abnormalities, ground glass interstitial or air-space infiltrates. **Typically in small airways disease and pulmonary vascular disease, the pulmonary vessels within the lucent regions of lung are small relative to the vessels in the more opaque lung.** Whereas with **infiltrative diseases, the lung vessels are more uniform in size.** Differentiation of small airways disease from pulmonary vascular disease requires paired inspiratory/expiratory sections.

Müller (1996) : Two main manifestations - nodules - clumps/rosettes, loss of attenuation - in one or several lobes.

Sherrick et al. (1997) : A mosaic pattern of lung attenuation can be seen in pts. with pulmonary arterial hypertension due to cardiac or lung disease.

Gückel et al. (1998) : Mosaic pattern in obstructive airways disease as seen on inspiratory HRCT sections is caused by hypoxic pulmonary vasoconstriction, rather than raised intra-alveolar pressure.

Worthy et al. (1998) : Mosaic lung attenuation on HRCT - differentiation between parenchymal, airway and vascular aetiologies - infiltrative lung disease and airway disease were usually correctly identified as the cause but vascular disease was often misinterpreted as infiltrative lung or airway disease.

Crazy paving pattern of lung attenuation

Godwin et al. (1988), Noma et al. (1990), Murch & Carr (1989), Hansell & Kerr (1991) and Usui et al. (1992) : Crazy-paving pattern in pulmonary alveolar proteinosis.

Tan and Kuzo (1997) : Crazy-paving pattern with alveolar cell carcinoma.

Franquet et al. (1998) : Exogenous lipoid pneumonia giving rise to a crazy-paving CT pattern.

Johkoh et al. (1999) : Crazy-paving - a non-specific HRCT finding in various interstitial & air space lung diseases - including ARDS, bacterial pneumonia, mycoplasma pn., PCP, TB, drug & radiation induced pn., pulm. haemorrhage, cardiogenic oedema, obstructive pneumonitis, acceleration of UIP & BOOP.

Coche et al. (2001) : Non specific interstitial pneumonia. showing crazy paving pattern on HRCT.

Obstructive emphysema.

Now that it has ceased to be a routine matter to 'screen the chest' by fluoroscopy in the investigation, detection or exclusion of chest disease, obstructive emphysema and associated abnormal mediastinal movements are rarely recognised despite being noted by Golden 1925, see also p. 4.1). In some ways this is to be regretted because such phenomena often accompany incomplete bronchial obstructions including foreign bodies, and some otherwise invisible tumours (which may be resectable) on plain radiographs. Obstructive emphysema has often been looked for in young children who may have inhaled a foreign body, by taking radiographs in **expiration** as well as **inspiration** (Illus. **INHALED FB, Pt. 6a-b**). This is only usually done if turning upside down, or use of the Heimlich manoeuvre* has failed to dislodge a foreign body and the child has travelled to hospital, with the possibility of a residual one being present. Note also that in children the origins of the main bronchi are asymmetrical, thus giving in them the **roughly equal incidence of left and right sided foreign bodies.**

* Arms wrapped around the upper abdomen from behind and the upper abdomen and lower ribs squeezed.

It should be noted that a film in full inspiration is usually normal, **the expiratory one showing that the lung or lobe with the obstructed bronchus does not deflate as much as the other lobes or lung**. This is because the bronchi are not rigid tubes, but have larger diameters in inspiration, and smaller ones in expiration.

Sometimes air trapping is so great that the affected portion of lung can become larger than normal. Obstructive emphysema may then be noted in **normal inspiratory views. This** probably happens after coughing when air if forced at a greater than normal pressure into the affected lung, or lobe. Indeed many cases that the author picked up were initially detected on the normal inspiratory PA view, then proceeding to an expiratory view as well.

The reasons for the neglect of the sign are the attention which has been given to maximum inspiration for almost all chest radiographs (except for instance when a pneumothorax might be expected - see below); the decline in the use of chest fluoroscopy over the past 15-20 years, largely in the interest of reducing the radiation dosage to the patient; and the awareness that a radiograph provides a much better record of disease processes than a visual memory, particularly in the follow -up of chest diseases.

When obstructive emphysema is produced by obstruction of a main bronchus, the whole of one lung will **remain distended in expiration** and the chest wall and diaphragm on the affected side will have a greatly reduced range of movement. Lesser degrees of obstructive emphysema may be demonstrated in a lobe or segment if its bronchus is occluded.

If an adult patient presents with blood-stained sputum and an audible wheeze, then the author feels that an expiratory film should always be taken in addition to the one in inspiration. Brief fluoroscopy (with image amplification and TV) may also be useful. The author has also found localised obstructive emphysema to be present with some small endobronchial tumours on CT sections (especially taken in expiration), and this may be a valuable sign (Illus. **OBSTRUCTIVE EMPHYSEMA, Ca+obst emp Pt. 3b**).

Expiratory CT views are also being used to show the effects of small bronchial disease in extrinsic allergic alveolitis, sarcoid etc. (see Chapter 19). Obstructive emphysema may also be seen with the Swyer-James/Macleod syndrome (ps. 7.9 - 7.10) and in smokers (ps. 3.29 - 30) and some healthy volunteers (see p. 20.26).

See also Fig. 4.7, p. 4.22 re obstructive emphysema and tumours.

Note: the use of a radiograph taken in expiration for the demonstration of air-trapping appears to be **much** more useful than taking one for a pneumothorax - the author has **never** seen one in erect views in adults that was not visible on an inspiratory view (see also p. 14.21).

Further references

Manges (1922, 1926) : Showed that an inhaled foreign body might cause (i) an increased transparency of the affected lung, (ii) depression and limitation of movement of the diaphragm on the affected side, (iii) displacement of the heart and mediastinum away from the affected side, and (iv) increased excursion of the diaphragm on the contralateral side.

Korol and Scott (1934) : Stressed the value of expiration radiographs in detecting obstructive emphysema due to a tumour.

Morlock (1934), Rigler and Kelby (1947), Møller (1950) and Sherman and Phillips (1968). Greenspan et al. (1973) used timed expiratory chest radiographs for the detection of air-trapping. Wesenberg and Blumhagen (1979) : Discussed assisted expiratory chest radiography for the diagnosis of foreign body aspiration.

Capitanio and Kirkpatrick (1972) : Lateral decubitus view to show the lack of normal elevation of the dependent side of the diaphragm as a sign of air trapping by a foreign body (see ps. 15.6 - 15.7).

Fraser (1984) : Felt that obstructive emphysema could only be shown with expiratory views.

Shure (1991) : About 40% of (77) patients, with almost complete bronchial obstruction as seen at bronchoscopy, had no volume loss on routine PA inspiratory radiographs. Over half had hilar enlargement, pulmonary infiltration, etc. He felt that segmental bronchial obstruction was more likely to be undetectable than of more proximal airways (presumably due to collateral air drift).

Mediastinal and Diaphragmatic Movement and Mediastinal Fixation.

The following signs may be seen with fluoroscopy or on inspiration/expiration views.

(a) Lung collapse

With unilateral lung or lobar collapse, the mediastinum usually moves towards the affected side on inspiration. This was first noted by Holzknecht (1899, four years after Roentgen's discovery of x-rays) who found inspiratory retraction of the mediastinum and heart into the **affected** side of the chest in a patient with a simple stenosis of a main bronchus, the '**Holzknecht Sign**'.

This phenomenon was termed '**mediastinal jerking**' by Lenk (1954). Kassay (1960) further analysed mediastinal movement seen at fluoroscopy and found that in some cases 'valvular emphysema' occurred on both sides at the same time, the mediastinum then moving during inspiration towards the side on which the greater part of the lung is affected (Fig. 2.7).

Kassay also pointed out that the movement of the mediastinum in inspiration with obstructive emphysema or pneumothorax is towards the abnormal side, whilst with a phrenic palsy there is both paradoxical movement of the affected hemidiaphragm and mediastinum.

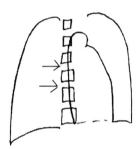

Free Spine Sign Mediastinal movement due to lobar collapse, besides causing tracheal shift, etc. with upper lobe collapse, also causes cardiac movement. With left lower lobe collapse the heart moves to the left and rotates, giving rise to the '**free spine sign**', i.e. the heart has moved to the left, sufficiently to prevent it overlapping part (or rarely all) of the lower dorsal spine. The sign may also be present with hypoplasia of the left lung (Illus. **FREE SPINE SIGN**).

Fig. 2.6 The 'free spine sign'.

(b) Phrenic palsy (see also chapter 15).

When a phrenic palsy occurs acutely, due to injury (e.g. due to stretching of the phrenic nerve in the neck) or virus infection (e.g. herpes zoster) the paradoxical mediastinal movement may make the patient even more breathless, than might otherwise be expected. This lessens usually after a few weeks, when the patient learns how to maintain each inspiration for a longer period to allow the lung on the contralateral side to fully inflate. He also appears to move the still active hemi-diaphragm less vigorously, thus tending to reduce movement and to 'fix it'.

With neoplastic infiltration of a phrenic nerve, which commonly occurs in the upper mediastinum (Fig. 15. 1) or where it runs under the pleural surface overlying the pericardium (in relation to the lingula or middle lobe) the adjacent mediastinum is usually involved with tumour and will often be partially fixed. Such a palsy tends to occur slowly and the effect on respiration is less dramatic, as the patient is able to partially compensate for it as it occurs.

A traumatic phrenic palsy may take from three up to 18 months to recover, and one caused by a viral infection may, or may not, do so.

The causes of a phrenic palsy, their effects, and differentiation from eventration are further discussed in Chapter 15.

(c) Fixation

Failure of the mediastinum to move with a major degree of collapse or with a large pneumothorax usually signifies **mediastinal fixation by infiltration with neoplasm or by mediastinitis** - see also ps. 2.27 - 28.

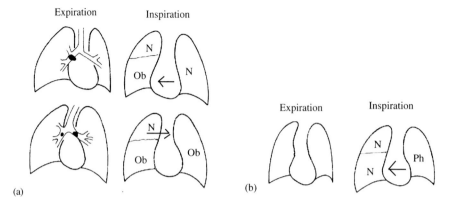

Fig. 2.7   Diagrams explaining the Holzknecht sign and mediastinal movements with (a) obstructive emphysema and (b) phrenic palsy. (N = normal, Ob = obstructed lung, Ph = side of phrenic palsy.)

   With obstructive emphysema or pneumothorax (a), the mediastinum moves towards the **abnormal (or more affected) side in inspiration**, whereas with a phrenic palsy (b) it moves towards the **normal or unaffected side**.
   In expiration the diameters of the trachea and bronchi are reduced, so that an obstruction produced by an endobronchial mass is accentuated in expiration.
   Although Holzknecht described the movement of the mediastinum in inspiration, it is more correct to think of the mediastinal movement towards the normal side in expiration as being caused by the failure of the lung to deflate properly.
(a) - after Kassay (1960) by courtesy of McGraw-Hill, New York.

Note : As with obstructive emphysema, these signs were commonly looked for with fluoroscopy, but may also be seen with inspiration/ expiration views.

Collateral Air Drift and Respiration.
     Kohn (1893) described the inter-alveolar pores ('Poren'), but noted that communicating 'holes' had been seen by Luschka in 1863. They were further studied by Loosli (1933), Macklin (1935), Culiner and Reich (1961), Reich and Abouav (1965) and Cordingly (1972). As Culiner and Reich pointed out: "in contra-distinction to the segments of the lobe, the total lobe is an isolated unit with essentially no collateral channel communications with adjacent lobes. Thus, total lobar bronchial obstruction is invariably followed by collapse of the lobe and absence of aeration", whereas "segmental bronchial occlusion may be followed by ventilation of that segment of lung tissue through collateral channels." Since the **'pores of Kohn'** are, like bronchi, larger in inspiration and smaller on expiration, there is a partial check valve mechanism in these pathways, and some obstructive emphysema may be present in the lung inflated by collateral air drift. However, the resistance through collateral channels appears to decrease with developing emphysema (Hogg et al., 1969), and may be a mechanism causing partial compensation (Terry et al., 1978).
     Collateral air-drift, i.e. with air passing from one lobule to another within a lobe, was first demonstrated by van Allen et al. (1930 - see also van Allen and Lindskog, 1931 and van Allen et al., 1931) in dogs - both in excised lungs and in vivo. Scanlon and Benumof (1979) also demonstrated inter-lobar collateral ventilation.
     As well as the pores of Kohn, there are other intra-pulmonary connections - the accessory bronchiole-alveolar connections described by Margaret Lambert (1955) and the inter-bronchiolar channels of Martin (1966) - between the respiratory bronchioles. With infection and/or fluid in the alveoli and respiratory bronchioles, all the collateral channels may become blocked, and the segment with an obstructed bronchus will then become collapsed.

Not all inter-lobar fissures are complete (see ps. 1.7 - 8). When incomplete, as often occurs with the middle lobe, collateral air drift may take place from one lobe to another. Thus the '**middle lobe syndrome**' (see below) may only be produced when there is no collateral air drift, i.e. when it has complete fissures bounding it.

In humans the pores of Kohn vary from about 3 to 13μ during respiration. Few are present in new-born infants, but they increase in number rapidly with increasing age. The channels of Lambert and Martin are larger and particles of over 60μ have been shown to pass through them. These collateral pathways also explain the pattern of spread of lobar pneumonia, with bacteria passing through them to adjacent alveoli and bronchioles, and between one secondary lobule and another (see p. 19.1). They also allow oedema fluid to spread to neighbouring alveoli and lobules.

Special notes.
(i) Parts of the lung, which have been aerated by collateral air drift do not easily deflate with expiration.
(ii) Collateral air drift explains the differing appearances of segmental and lobar bronchial obstruction - in the former the lung parenchyma may remain air filled despite the segmental bronchus being occluded.
(iii) The more complete cortical inter-lobular septa make collateral ventilation in the lung cortex more difficult and the **formation of bullae easier** (see also p. 1.45).
(iv) An obstructed RML bronchus may not result in RML collapse if the adjacent fissures are incomplete.
(v) Congenital atresia of the apico-posterior segmental bronchus of the LUL, does not usually lead to collapse of this segment, but to hypoplastic vessels and impaired decrease in size of the segment in expiration. Sometimes mucocoeles of the bronchi distal to the narrowed part are filled with fluid as mucocoeles (see Illus. **MUCOCOELES, Atresia Pt. 3a&b** and ps. 2.10 & 3.8).

Illus. **ANATOMY 27** shows a scanning electron micrograph of an alveolar duct with alveoli opening off it; small spaces of varying size between the capillaries in the alveolar walls are the pores of Kohn.

Further reference.
Macklem (1971) : Airway obstruction and collateral respiration.

Middle Lobe Syndrome.
This term was coined by Graham et al. (1948), who described twelve cases of middle lobe disease of non-tuberculous origin, secondary to pressure on the middle lobe bronchus by enlarged lymph nodes. However many patients with chronic middle lobe disease have patent bronchi, as shown by bronchoscopy, tomograms or bronchograms. The reason for poor clearance of inflammatory disease with a patent bronchus appears to be a lack of collateral air drift, when the surrounding pleural fissures are complete, resulting in a relative isolation of the middle lobe. The majority of people have incomplete fissures bordering the middle lobe - about 80% incomplete lesser and 70% incomplete oblique fissures - thus permitting air to pass into the middle lobe from the upper and/ or lower lobes via the pores of Kohn etc., and hence allowing the easier expectoration of secretions etc.

Hampton and King (1936) advised lateral radiographs for the demonstration of middle lobe disease. They noted the triangular shape of the lateral and rectangular shape of the medial segments as seen on lateral views, also that the shape and position of contracted middle lobes are influenced by pleural adhesions and surrounding structures.

Doig (1946) used the AP lordotic view to accentuate the opacity of a collapsed middle lobe - a point which now might almost be forgotten, except patients being examined AP in chairs, bed, etc.

Brock (1950, 1954) found that most of his cases of middle lobe disease were due to tuberculosis, and that related affected nodes often became calcified. Such nodes might also lead to broncholithiasis (ps. 3.24 - 3.25). Only eight out of 1,200 of Brock's cases had neoplasm in the middle lobe, but others noted a higher incidence of neoplasm (e.g. Locke, 1953-1954), and the author considers it to be not uncommon. Wagner and Johnston (1983) quote 22% of middle lobe collapses as being due to this cause.

Other causes include aspiration from the nasal sinuses, bronchiectasis, benign tumours, sarcoidosis of its bronchi, other infections, chronic inflammatory or fibrotic states. Cavitation is usually due to bullae or bronchiectasis, but tuberculosis with cavitation has also been noted by the author - even a solitary cavity in the middle lobe - others include infarcts, degenerating tumours, etc. The middle lobe syndrome was further studied by Rosenbloom et al. (1983) who also noted that incomplete fissures allow for collateral ventilation from adjacent lobes. They also noted a similar situation with the lingula.

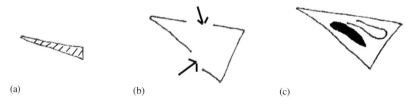

(a)   (b)   (c)

Fig. 2.8   Collapsed RML   Collateral air drift into RML   Mucocoeles and/or dilated
                                                                                           air-filled bronchi.

Further reference.

Dux et al. (1980) : Middle lobe syndrome as an unusual presentation of metastatic osteogenic sarcoma.

Mucocoeles (dilated fluid filled bronchi due to bronchial obstructions including atresia).

Although the tendency for tumours to produce secondary bronchiectasis and cause retention of secretions had been noted by Kirklin and Paterson (1928), Chandler (1932) and Kerley, (1962), Rees and Ruttley (1970) described the appearance of mucocoeles with bronchogenic tumours as a 'new' sign.

Following radiotherapy or chemotherapy it is not at all unusual to see air filled dilated and bronchiectatic bronchi in a re-expanded part of the lung which has been collapsed, even if mucocoeles were not seen in it before treatment. This is because they would be invisible radiographically, unless the surrounding lung was aerated. In gross cases or resected or autopsy specimens tumour can be seen to extend into the dilated bronchi. Most times the mucus within mucocoeles only contains inflammatory cells. However, Aronberg et al. (1979) noted that sometimes neoplastic cells may be found if the mucus is aspirated at bronchoscopy.

At bronchoscopy it is not uncommon to find retained secretions distal to an obstruction in a large bronchus. They are also frequently seen in surgical and autopsy specimens. Mucocoeles (often looking like 'gloved   fingers' - Fig. 2.9) are more likely to be seen in the dependent bronchi, but may develop anywhere and with tumour are more often present with slowly growing bronchial carcinomas and adenomas. On radiographs the affected bronchi appear as enlarged, dense shadows with the surrounding lung still aerated by collateral air drift, thus indicating that part of the affected lobe must still have a supplying patent, or largely patent, air transmitting bronchus. Such mucocoeles may be visible on plain films or tomograms, or occasionally on bronchograms as the continuation of patent bronchi (see Illus. **MUCOCOELE, Pt. 3**).

Fluid filled bronchi may also be shown by CT. They then show a branching pattern likened to a 'V', 'Y', or **'bundle of snakes'**   radiating from the hilum. Distally the bronchi may become air-filled again due to collateral air drift. When seen end on they may appear as a **'cottage   loaf'** (Illus. **CARCINOID, Pt. 19**), **'bunch of grapes'**   or **'pawnbroker's   brass   balls'** (Pugatch and Gale, 1983) - see Illus. **MUCOCOELE, Pts. 10a-b, 23, 28c**.

Tumours are a common cause of mucocoeles (Wright, 1971b) - a letter in response to a leading article, in the BMJ on 'mucocoeles' which totally omitted to note the malignant cause of many of them. They are not, however, a specific sign of bronchial neoplasm and can occur with bronchial obstruction from other causes - a huge mucocoele caused by a mesothelioma is shown in Illus. **MUCOCOELE, mesothelioma Pt. 22d**.

Benign causes of mucocoele include benign tumours (Illus. **CARCINOID, Pts. 2, 14a-d, 19**, **CYLINDROMA, Pt. 2a-c, LIPOMA, Pt. 4a-c**) inspissated mucus plugs, particularly found with aspergillosis (Illus. **FUNGUS, Pt. 45, MUCOCOELE, Pt. 24**). This may cause squamous metaplasia leading to keratinised plugs blocking a bronchus (Illus. **MUCOCOELE, Pts. 3, 5a-b**). Occasionally **mucocoeles may calcify** (see p.3.20 and Illus. **MUCOCOELE 12c**). Some moderate increased density in acute cases may be due to haemorrhage. Other causes include tuberculous scarring, cystic fibrosis (Illus. **CYSTIC FIBROSIS, Pts. 8d, 18c**), endo-bronchial infections, poorly draining bronchiectasis (Illus. **BRONCHIECTASIS 4, 16a, 20b, 24, 30, 33a-b, 36, 37a-b, 38**) and broncholithiasis.

A mucocoele may also be found in association with '**bronchial atresia**' (Illus. **AGENESIS, Pt. 3a-b**). This is mainly seen in the left upper lobe, particularly in the bronchi leading towards the apex. Lung distal to the obstruction may still remain aerated via collateral air drift. This condition may be associated with pulmonary sequestration and/or bronchogenic cysts.

As with blocked bronchi secondary to tumours, foreign bodies and mucous plugs may cause reflex vascular vasoconstriction. Bray et al. (1984) showed that: in two cases mucous plugs caused virtual absence of perfusion of a whole lung. Pham et al. (1987) found in eight cases a marked reduction in ventilation and a less marked loss of perfusion in the hypoxic areas on isotope studies.

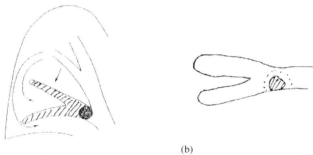

(a)   (b)

Fig. 2.9 (a) **Bronchial mucocoeles, bronchocoeles or 'Gloved Fingers'** - fluid filled bronchi - the surrounding lung remains filled with air, which continues to pass into it via collateral air drift, despite the fluid filled bronchi.
(b) Dilated air filled bronchi may occur if mucocoeles can drain e.g. following tumour necrosis or shrinkage following treatment. If the obstruction is short-lived the bronchi may return to normal diameter (see Illus. **BRONCHIECTASIS Pt. 44**).
For illustrations of mucocoeles see Illus. **MUCOCOELES**.

Further references to mucocoeles.

Shaw (1951) : First drew attention to bronchial mucoid impaction, not only in asthmatics but also in some chronic bronchitics, leading to mucocoeles.
Shaw et al. (1957) : Surveyed a further 36 cases and Greer (1957) reported a further eight cases.
Culiner and Grimes (1961) : Localised emphysema - association with bronchial cysts or mucocoeles.
Wilson (1964) : Literature survey & reported 3 cases and stated 'mucous plugs are greenish-grey in appearance and may enlarge to a size from 1 to 3 cm. in length and from 1 to 2.5 cm. in diameter. They may occur in any bronchi but often in second order branch bronchi distal to a bifurcation '. He also noted the association with aspergillosis.
Carlson et al. (1966) : Roentenographic features of mucoid impaction of the bronchi.
Shaw et al. (see Urschel, 1966) : Found an upper lobe predominance and that the plugs could be quite large. They were often putty like and were sometimes branched, or forked. If persistent they could lead to bronchial wall necrosis and replacement of bronchial wall respiratory epithelium by squamous cells.
Sheehan and Schonfeld (1963) : Mucoid impaction simulating tumour.
Simon and Reid (1963) : Atresia of apical bronchus of left upper lobe - three cases.
Waddell et al. (1965) : Bronchial atresia of left upper lobe.
Williams and Schuster (1985) : Congenital lobar emphysema of LUL secondary to LUL atresia + bronchogenic cyst.
Curry and Curry (1966) : Atresia of the apico-posterior segment bronchus of the LUL - two cases.
Lemine et al. (1970) : Six cases of mucocoeles (not due to neoplasm) which they termed 'bronchocoele or blocked bronchiectasis', appearing as rounded shadows on radiographs in asymptomatic patients and mimicked lung tumours. Tomograms showed them as oval or branching structures.

Talner et al. (1970) : Two new cases and review of 100 cases of benign mucocoeles in the literature. Noted the frequent association of regional lung hyperinflation which fails to deflate in expiration., presumably due to the collateral air drift and restricted expiration through the pores of Kohn. (see p.2.8).

Cohen et al. (1980) : CT in bronchial atresia.

Gullotta et al. (1980): Mucoid impaction and the mucoid bronchogram.

McCarthy (1970), Mintzer et al. (1978), Klein & Gamsu (1980) and Gefter et al. (1981a) : Aspergillosis and mucocoeles.

Starkey and Mark (1978) : Bronchial obstruction associated with calcification in a woman aged 55.

Woodring et al. (1985) : Thought that cases of 'mucoid impaction of the bronchi' could be placed in two main categories - (a) those associated with bronchial obstruction and (b) those which are not. Like Felson (1979a) they noted that unless destroyed by tumour or infection, the mucous glands continue to function in an obstructed bronchus until the intra-bronchial pressure is raised above the secretory pressure.

Dorne (1986) : Sonographic fluid bronchogram (see also p. 20.33).

Woodring (1988) : The CT mucous bronchogram sign.

Glazer et al. (1989) : Studied bronchial impaction in lobar collapse by CT, and found that the impacted bronchi were best seen on post-contrast studies. They appeared as branching structures, extending from the hilum peripherally into the more opaque and enhancing collapsed lung.

Shin and Ho (1991) : CT fluid bronchogram in post-obstructive pulmonary consolidation.

Goyal et al. (1992) : High attenuation mucous plugs at CT in allergic bronchopulmonary aspergillosis.

See also pulmonary and bronchial atresia - p. 3.8.

Lung collapse - may be due to:
(a) absorption of air behind a blocked bronchus, due to tumour, mucous plug or foreign body,
(b) fibrosis (bronchiectasis, chronic infection, TB, sarcoid, FA, post R/T, silicosis, asbestos, etc.)
(c) secondary to chronic infection (with patent bronchi), as with bronchiectasis,
(d) pressure - from pleural fluid, large pneumothorax, a large mass, raised diaphragm etc.,
(e) passive - with a small pneumothorax or effusion,
(f) surfactant deficiency (or 'adhesive collapse') when the alveolar walls tend to adhere making re-expansion difficult as in hyaline membrane disease, ARDS, smoke inhalation, acute pneumonia, embolism or acute post radiation reaction.

Collapse may be qualified as partial (incomplete) or complete, and besides being lobar may affect a whole lung, or both lungs (usually partially - or no respiration could occur). Segmental collapse is less common owing to collateral air drift, but may occur is this is deficient (with e.g. infection blocking the collateral pathways or an accessory fissure).

Table 2.1 - Summary of signs of lung collapse.

1. Loss of volume of lobe or lung, and compensatory emphysema of remainder of lung on the same and other side.
2. Crowding of ribs, elevation of hemi-diaphragm, movement of trachea and mediastinum towards the side of the collapse.
3. Movement of upper mediastinal triangle, herniation of RUL anteriorly with LUL collapse, etc.
4. Displacement of interlobar fissures:
     (a) Horizontal fissure with RUL or RML collapse.
     (b) Oblique fissure on lateral view.
5. Changes in pulmonary vessels and bronchi:
     (a) Reduction in number by approx. 50% in one lung with collapse of UL or LL. Loss of normal vascular architecture of collapsed lobe.
     (b) Crowding, of vascular markings in a partly collapsed lobe, and splaying out of vessels with compensatory emphysema. (Fig. 2.10).
     (c) Movement of larger bronchi and '**ring sign**' (ps. 2.29 - 2.30).
     (d) Crowding of 'air bronchograms'.
6. (a) Loss of outline of part of heart, diaphragm. aorta, IVC etc. ('**Loss of Silhouette Sign**').
     (b) Peri-aortic lucency or '**Luftsichel sign**' with LUL collapse.

(c) '**Conoisseur's sign**' (linear collapse in lingula or dilated and horizontally running lingula veins with LLL collapse.

7. Changes in hilar shadows:

(a) Due to an associated mass or hilar nodes ('**Golden's sign**' - collapse with mass).

(b) Due to alteration in pulmonary blood flow, reduced on the side of collapse or tumour, and increased on the opposite side ('**Paradoxical Hilus**' or '**Oeser's sign**' - p. 7.10 - 11).

(c) Hilar elevation with UL collapse, depression with LL, esp. L, which will widen the aorto-pulmonary window.

8. Traction of the inferior pulmonary ligament, producing the ' juxta-phrenic peak' etc.

9. On a lateral view, increased density over the lower dorsal spine with a LL collapse - the '**vertebral fade sign**'. (Normally the greater density is over the upper dorsal vertebrae, produced by the shoulder muscles).

10. The pattern of collapse with a segment or segments usually corresponds with the anatomy of the segments. However the signs within the affected segments are often modified by the effect of '**collateral air drift**', with aeration continuing, despite blockage of the supplying bronchus.

11. **Movement of lung granulomata** or scars on sequential radiographs (see next para.).

Some specific features relating to collapse

(i) **Alterations in position of fissures** (- minor and/or major), larger bronchi (see ps. 2.29 - 2.30), old scars or granulomata in the lung on sequential radiographs - note reference to Rohlfing (1977) p. 2.24 - the '**shifting granuloma' sign.**

(ii) **Difficulty of recognition and reduction in number of pulmonary vessels.**

A major lobar collapse can often be one of the more difficult abnormalities for trainee radiologists, and even some more experienced readers, to appreciate. This, the author believes is due to poor basic training in the reading of chest radiographs. Not all inspect the approximate symmetry of lung volumes (with the right being a little larger than the left) or the **number** of pulmonary vessels on each side. They should also note other signs of **loss of volume** - alterations in **position** of **the hila**, the mediastinum and heart or the diaphragm, and the **loss of various silhouettes** - heart outline, descending aorta, diaphragm, etc. (remembering that none of these structures are usually directly portrayed on radiographs and that they are only visualised by virtue of adjacent gas-filled lung - see p. 2.25).

In the author's view it is very **wrong** to only look for increased density shadows of the lobes per se as indicating collapse, particularly as these may only be noted with difficulty. Many observers and even some experienced radiologists do not seem to learn the normal pulmonary vascular patterns i.e. vessel patterns in the various lobes; this seems a great pity for noting their presence or absence is often of great help in the recognition of abnormality or otherwise. Failure to appreciate a vascular loss is, the author believes, the major cause of the not uncommon poor recognition of lobar collapse, and he teaches not only radiologists in training, but also medical students, to look for approximate symmetry in the number of pulmonary vessels, and to ascertain the cause if only half are seen. (It seems ridiculous that if a sparrow can note the loss of one egg out of two from her nest, that medical students, etc. often do not note a 50% loss of pulmonary vascularity !) Unfortunately many text-books **still** overlook this basic sign.

The same sign is also seen following a lobectomy. The 50% loss in number of pulmonary vessels in one lung is very different from **attenuation** or a reduction in size of pulmonary arterial branches due to embolism, scarring from previous pneumonia, radiotherapy, or from a developmental cause (e.g. Swyer James/Macleod syndrome - ps. 7.9 - 7.10). Note also that an endobronchial mass may itself cause a reduction in the size of the same side, with paradoxical dilatation on the contra-lateral side (Oeser Sign - see ps. 7.10 - 7.11).

(iii) **Compensatory emphysema, vascular re-orientation and the 'opened out' and 'closed fan signs'.**

As well as a loss in the number of vessels in a lung, with a major lobe collapsed, compensatory emphysema will usually be seen in the rest of the lung. The '**opened out fan sign**' with compensatory emphysema is illustrated in Fig. 2.10.

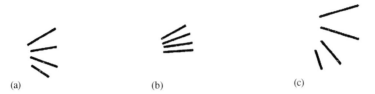

(a)   (b)   (c)

Fig. 2.10   The 'fan sign' - (a) Normal,   (b) Crowded vessels ('**closed fan sign**'), (c) Splayed vessels ('**opened out fan sign**').

     Splaying out of vessels in an over-expanded upper lobe, secondary to a left lower lobe collapse, may make the vessels more prominent along the left cardiac border - the '**vascular nodule**' sign, seen particularly in children and young people (Lacombe et al., 1982). One should also note the normal pattern of branching of vessels in the lung e.g. three sub-segments in the apex of a lower lobe, which will be seen at the apex of the thorax with an upper lobe collapse or fibrosis. These and other lower lobe vessels and their accompanying bronchi, with an upper lobe collapse, will then rotate and tend to run more vertically (and may be mistaken on CT sections for tiny nodules or abnormal branching structures).

     When there is lobar collapse, then the vessels in the remaining aerated lobes will rotate and change in position, and with experience an observent chest radiologist (etc.) should be able to recognise particular vessels as being in abnormal positions.

Some references.

Proto and Tocino (1980) : Noted crowding of vessels within a lobe if it had lost two-thirds or more of its volume - a point also noted by Robbins and Hale (1945a) - this is the '**closed fan sign**' (see above).

Proto and Moser (1987) : Illustrated divergent and parallel patterns of vascular **reorientation** with upper lobe volume loss.

(iv) **Crowding of air bronchograms** as a sign of volume loss (see also p. 2.1).

(v) **Collapse of a lobe will alter the positions of the main pulmonary artery branches and the larger bronchi.**

On the left with an upper lobe collapse the main trunk of the pulmonary artery can still be seen together with its lower lobe branches, and the main trunk, being more clearly outlined (and elevated) may simulate a mass (see ps. 2.18 - 2.19). With a lower lobe collapse, the left pulmonary artery will be depressed in position and the aorto-pulmonary window opened out.

On the right half of the horizontal V of the pulmonary artery will tend to be obliterated, as well as air in the corresponding larger bronchus (including the intermediate bronchus).

(vi) **CT features of lobar collapse.** These are discussed in some detail under the patterns of lobar collapse (ps. 2.18 - 2.24). In general, CT sections may show more clearly the loss of volume of a hemithorax, due to the cross-sectional display. It also assists in appreciating mediastinal movement, which may be more marked with a collapsed lower lobe. CT also assists in the differentiation of collapse due to a mass, a pleural effusion, or 'passively' from other causes. It will show the spread of fluid into adjacent pleural fissures. Intravenous contrast medium may also allow the collapsed lobe to be opacified and a degenerate tumour within it may then appear as a lower density area. Compensatory emphysema is commonly recognised (see also Flanagan et al., 1982).

     Khoury et al. (1985) studied the varied CT appearance of obstructive lobar collapse in 25 cases and concluded that the final shape of a collapsed lobe is dependent in the size and location of the obstructing tumour and on the amount of retained fluid. They also found out that focal bulging of the fissure (**Golden's 'S' sign** - see p. 2.31) was the most helpful sign in identifying the obstructing tumour. IV contrast enhancement did not differentiate the tumour from collapsed lung in six out of eight cases. The difficulty of evaluating mediastinal or pleural invasion with adjacent collapsed lung was stressed.

(vii) **Complete collapse and altered density of a collapsed lobe.**

Complete collapse of a segment, lobe, or lung may give rise to a shadow of increased density on chest radiographs, corresponding to the anatomical distribution of the collapsed portion of the lung. Typical patterns of lobar collapse are shown diagrammatically in Figs. 2.12 to 2.30. together with some notes about the pattern of collapse with each of the lobes. A summary of the signs of lung collapse is given in Table. 2.1 - see ps. 2.12 - 2.13 and radiographic illustrations of lobar collapse are shown in Illus. **COLLAPSE LLL, etc**. Lobar collapse in the absence of a pneumothorax or pleural effusion nearly always causes compensatory changes in the chest secondary to the loss of lung volume, namely compensatory emphysema of the remainder of the lung, crowding of the ribs, mediastinal movement and herniation of the contralateral lung, and raising of the homolateral hemidiaphragm.

The patterns of lobar collapse have been studied by several authors, including Robbins and Hale (1945a-g), Lubert and Krause (1951, 1956 &1963), Krause and Lubert (1958), Felson (1960) and Simon (1950, 1956 & 1971). Naidich et. al. (1983a & b and 1984) used CT to study lobar collapse (a) due to endo-bronchial obstruction or (b) passive collapse caused by air and/or fluid in the pleura, scarring or diffuse tumour infiltration of a lobe. They wrote: "Lobar collapse due to endobronchial obstruction should be viewed as a dynamic process accounting for a wide variability of radiographic and CT appearances. Usually, bronchial obstruction causes increased density within an affected lobe, secondary to the presence of intra-alveolar fluid combined with a decreased volume of lung. How much fluid is present and the degree of volume loss are generally functions of both the degree of bronchial obstruction and time. Occasionally, in the presence of endobronchial obstruction, the affected lobe may contain air and appear relatively normal in density.....(and) aerated....if there is sufficient collateral air drift, as may occur between various portions of a lobe or between lobes, presumably as a function of incompletely formed fissures. "

The density of a collapsed or reduced-volume-lobe is variable and seems to depend on its volume, fluid and/or solid tissue content. Thus in a patient with a collapsed lobe (or lobes) secondary to a large pneumothorax, and hence with a patent bronchus, the collapsed lobe(s) will only give a low density shadow. With bronchiectasis, the lobe may also be partly aerated and not very dense. When the supplying bronchus is occluded by a mucus plug a lobe may almost completely collapse and cast a low density shadow, but with tumour or consolidation distal to a bronchial obstruction loss of volume is not so marked and the density is much greater. Sometimes a lobe which has acutely collapsed does not become dense for some days, presumably not until it fills with fluid. It is the filling of the collapsed lobe with fluid which largely causes the density change - in extreme cases leading to the '**drowned lung**' appearance. Obstructive pneumonitis is a term applied to consolidation in the lung distal to a bronchial block - it is usually non-infective in origin. These conditions are discussed further on ps. 4.19 - 4.20.

(viii) **Partial collapse.**

Partial collapse is much more difficult to visualise on radiographs, and is frequently not recognised even when gross. This is because it does not always produce an area of increased density on radiographs in the absence of superadded consolidation. It often only gives rise to secondary signs, such as crowding of the ribs over the affected area, displacement of a fissure, elevation of a part of the hemidiaphragm, movement of the diaphragm towards the affected side, mediastinal herniation, or adjacent compensatory emphysema. The collapse may also be inferred from a crowding of the vessels in the affected lobe or segment, or from a lack of the particular segmental or lobar vascular shadows in the lung. Loss of some organ or other outlines (such as the right mediastinal border, the SVC, right paratracheal stripe, right or left borders of the heart, descending aorta, or dome of diaphragm) may occur. On fluoroscopy the affected area may not expand or inflate normally.

Some references.

Steiner (1958) : 'Satisfactory assessment of the radiographic pattern of the pulmonary artery, particularly its major branches, and to a lesser extent its minor branches, is possible on adequate chest radiographs'.

Simon (1962) : Noted the constancy of most lung vessels, and stressed that they changed in position when collapse was present.

Cranz and Pribram (1965) : The pulmonary vessels can be identified and the diagnosis of collapse made from them when other signs are absent.

(ix) **Segmental collapse.**

Segments may collapse in a similar fashion to lobes, particularly when accessory fissures are present, but more often the effects of blockage of a segmental bronchus are not as dramatic in their appearances as those affecting a lobe. This is due to the effect of collateral air drift (see ps. 2.8 - 2.9) allowing air to continue to allow aeration of the bronchioles and alveoli. Note also that with an incomplete fissure, collateral air drift may take place into an adjoining lobe (see discussion of middle lobe syndrome - ps. 2.9 - 2.10).

(x) **Basal collapse** - may be due to a distended abdomen with raised diaphragm, the effect of tight corsets in obese females (often with a hiatal hernia as well), chronic basal infection or small basal lung infarcts. It is common in association with heart failure in debilitated patients. It may appear as linear collapse (see below).

For illustrations of basal collapse see Illus. **COLLAPSE BASES**.

(xi) **Linear or 'subsegmental' collapse ('plate-like' or ' discoid collapse').**

Linear collapse is one of the most common, yet least understood appearances on chest radiographs. The lines have been ascribed to various causes, such as localised collapse, pneumonitis, 'inverted pleura', thrombosed vessels, infarcts or unknown factors. They were first described by Fleischner (1936) and are sometimes referred to as **"Fleischner's lines"**. Fleischner noted that they were commonly horizontal in orientation, and thought that they represented a conical portion of the lung, collapsed in a ' fan-like' fashion. Fleischner et al (1941) considered them to be due to interlobar pleuritis, collapse and healed infarction.

Baron (1972) studied the lines in relation to pulmonary emboli. He felt that the linear shadows are cast by focal areas of collapse seen on end, thought that when they are present bilaterally they are ' definitely suggestive ' of the diagnosis. He wrote that they usually measure 2 - 7 cm in length and between 2 - 7 mm in thickness. Other points he made are as follows. As the entire subsegment beyond the obstructed supplying bronchus is collapsed, a Fleischner line always reaches a pleural surface. Such a line also never crosses an interlobar fissure. Because of the varying orientation of the different pulmonary subsegments, Fleischner lines can course in almost any direction, although they are always perpendicular to a pleural surface. They can also occur in asthmatics or with chronic bronchial disease or with spillover of infection. Baron also noted that a small obstructed bronchus will not of itself cause collapse, because of collateral respiration.

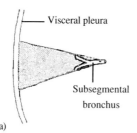

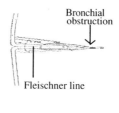

(a)

(a) Normal pulmonary subsegment

Fig. 2.11 Fleischner's lines (After Baron, 1972, Fleischner's lines & pulmonary emboli. Circulation, **45**, 171 - 178, with permission).

(b)

(b) Collapsed pulmonary subsegment - the lung has collapsed towards its bronchus drawing inwards a double layer of visceral pleura. (Note the similarity to transpulmonary bands seen in asbestosis - p. 14.35).

Westcott and Cole (1985) studied 15 cases passing to necropsy and found that these lines corresponded with "peripheral subpleural linear collapse, combined with invagination of the overlying pleura". They noted that they were frequently associated with prominent interlobular septa - the bronchi, supplying the lung in the areas of these lines, showed no obstruction and despite a frequent association with pulmonary emboli, there was no suggestion that thrombosed vessels and infarcts had a direct bearing on the appearance. They postulated that the process may often occur at sites of pre-existing pleural invagination.

The author's view is that the lines are most frequently seen with poor diaphragmatic movement, due to a variety of causes, such as splinting due to pleurisy, poor movement due to general debility or DLE, or the wearing of tight belts or corsets. In other cases, gross abdominal obesity, emphysema, or basal fibrosis may be the predisposing factors causing poor diaphragmatic movement, in turn leading to lobular collapse with localised pleural thickening.

Although usually orientated horizontally, these lines may sometimes run obliquely or vertically, particularly in the mid zones. They may be single and unilateral, or multiple and bilateral. They may vary in length and width, elderly ladies with tight corsets - in these breathing exercises repeated for 10 to 20 minutes may cause the lines to disappear, i.e. it would appear that the 'linear collapse' has re-expanded.

In sick patients the position of the lines may be related to diaphragmatic splinting, subdiaphragmatic disease, overlying pleural adhesions and/or thickening.

Further references.
Fleischner *(1958) : Linear shadows in the lung fields.   [* For obituary see Clinical Radiology (1969), **20**.464.]
Simon (1970) : Also thought that these lines may be related to pulmonary embolism - thrombosed veins surrounded by septal and adjacent alveolar oedema.
Trapnell (1973) : The differential diagnosis of linear shadows in chest radiographs.
Tudor et al. (1973) : Lung shadows after acute myocardial infarction - daily chest radiographs showed that 21% of patients develop abnormal shadows at the lung bases in the first few days. There is little correlation with the incidence of deep venous thrombosis in the legs, and it seems likely that the shadows are the result of a local pulmonary abnormality due to bronchial occlusion with collapse and consolidation, rather than embolic episodes.

(xii) Patterns of lobar collapse.

(a) **Right upper lobe collapse -** usually causes the horizontal fissure to be elevated obliquely upwards, with the collapsed lobe lying supero-medially to it. When there is an accompanying hilar or juxta-hilar mass, **Golden's sign** may be produced (see p. 2.31), with the collapsed lobe lying supero-medially to it, and on a lateral view an appearance similar to a wedge or an opened umbrella. A collapsed RUL commonly collapses towards and abuts the right upper mediastinum, with loss of the outline of the SVC and the azygos vein.

Sometimes due to adhesions, a collapsed RUL may swing laterally, with an almost normally situated horizontal fissure and the apex of the air-filled lower lobe may lie above it. It may also occasionally '**pancake**' medially adjacent to the mediastinum or lie across the apex of the right pleural cavity. It was thought that this appearance was due to adhesions, but it can also occur with a pneumothorax (Gurney, 1996).

In all instances the number of vessels in the right lung will be reduced by about 50% as only the RML & RLL will be aerated, the visible vessels will also be rotated and elevated as the RML & RLL expand to take up the space formerly occupied by the RUL.

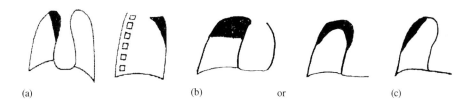

(a)   (b)   or   (c)

Fig. 2.12 RUL collapse - plain films   (a) typical appearance   (b) 'pancake'   (c) peripheral.

CT: The collapsed lobe retains its attachment with the hilum, as a wedge-shaped dense part of the lung, extending towards the apex of the right pleural cavity. This commonly lies anteriorly, but may extend from front to back adjacent to the right side of the superior mediastinum, be stretched over a hilar or intra-pulmonary mass (**Golden's   sign**) or lie centrally in the right pleural cavity, with the air-filled middle and lower lobes surrounding it. Although the right pulmonary artery normally lies at a lower plane than the left, with right upper lobe collapse the right hilum is often elevated, so that both right and left may be seen on the same section. Anterior lung herniation may be less marked than with left upper lobe collapse, due to the 'splinting effect' of the collapsed lobe adjacent to the upper mediastinum.

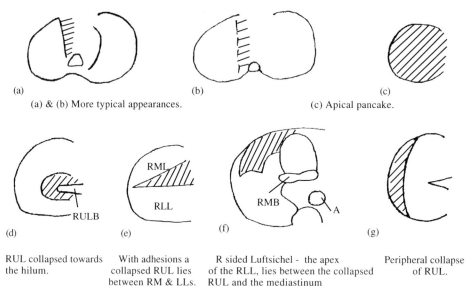

(a)   (b)   (c)

(a) & (b) More typical appearances.   (c) Apical pancake.

(d)   (e)   (f)   (g)

RUL collapsed towards   With adhesions a   R sided Luftsichel - the apex   Peripheral collapse
the hilum.   collapsed RUL lies   of the RLL, lies between the collapsed   of RUL.
                                          between RM & LLs.   RUL and the mediastinum

Fig. 2.13.   Patterns of RUL collapse as seen on CT sections.

In children a collapsed lobe (esp. the RUL) may be associated with a localised peripheral pneumothorax (**'pneumothorax ex vacuo'**) - see also p. 14.24.

For illustrations of right upper lobe collapse - see Illus. **COLLAPSE RUL.**

(b)   **Left upper lobe collapse** - with this the shadow of the collapsed lobe may not be well defined or readily visible on frontal views. However the collapse is usually obvious because of reduced volume of the left lung, only half of its normal number of vessels being visible and the loss of most or the upper part of the outline of the left border of the heart (**'loss   of silhouette sign'** - see below). When most of the left cardiac border has been lost due to an airless lingula, it may **almost appear that the patient's 'heart has vanished'** (Illus. **COLLAPSE   LUL, Pt.   31**). In addition the left main pulmonary artery is often elevated, giving a prominent hilar shadow. The aortic 'knob' is often obscured or its shadow absent, contrariwise it may also be better seen if peri-aortic lucency (the **'Luftsichel'   sign**) is present (see p. 2.26 and Illus. **LUFTSICHEL SIGN**). A chronically collapsed LUL may lie closely against the mediastinum so that little of it is seen on a frontal view - see Illus. **COLLAPSE LUL, Pts. 11, 26 & 31**. Collapse or fibrosis of the LUL may also occasionally give rise to a raised left pulmonary artery (see Fig. 7.3, p. 7.5 and Illus. **PULM ART ELEVATED**).

On lateral views there is often a transradiant zone behind the sternum, due to the air-filled anteriorly situated part of the right upper lobe lying in front of the upper mediastinum (see CT illustration - Fig. 2.15).

Note also lower lobe vessel and bronchial reorientations (see ps. 2.29 - 2.31).

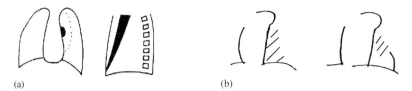

(a) Plain radiographic appearances. (b) The amount or loss of the cardiac silhouette depends on the amount of collapse of the lingula, or its position, or to the volume of the opaque LUL (i.e. the amount of 'obstructive pneumonitis' present, and its contact with the pericardium).

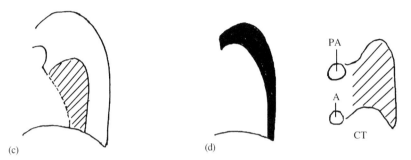

(c) A collapsed LUL may lie in the lower two-thirds of the left pleural cavity due to basal adhesions holding it down.

(d) It may lie peripherally if lateral adhesions hold the collapsed upper lobe to the chest wall.

Fig. 2.14.   Collapsed LUL

CT : With LUL collapse, more volume is lost than with a collapsed RUL, due to the lingula being part of the LUL. Mediastinal shift is also more marked. The collapsed lobe usually appears as a sharply defined triangular density extending anteriorly and upwards. from the left hilum. It tends to remain in contact antero-laterally with the chest wall, but as collapse becomes more complete, its contact with the lateral chest wall decreases and the lobe swings in as a thin sheet against the mediastinum to become a sharply defined triangular shadow with its apex at the pulmonary hilum (Fig. 2.15a). The tongue of aerated right upper lobe projecting anteriorly to the left in front of the heart and behind the upper sternum is equivalent to the air-filled vertical lung stripe seen in front of the collapsed left upper lobe on lateral radiographs (Fig. 2.14a). A collapsed LUL due to simple bronchial blockage, will tend to taper smoothly from the hilum and widening of this tends to signify the presence of a mass, within the collapsed lobe or hilum.

Peri-aortic   lucency (the **CT   equivalent   of   the   Luftsichel   sign** - p. 2.26) is due to compensatory hyper-expansion of the apex of the adjacent lower lobe (Fig. 2.15b). Because of the collapse, the left hilum, with the left main bronchus, will tend to be elevated and the aorto-pulmonary window foreshortened. When the hilum lies lateral to the aortic arch it must he distinguished from nodal enlargement - this position may also occur as a variant of normal (Mencini and Proto, 1982).

 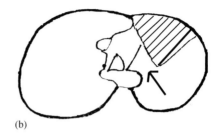

(a) (b)

Fig. 2.15 (a) CT of collapsed LUL.   (b) CT equivalent of left Luftsichel sign.
(The arrow points to the RUL,   (The arrow points to the hyper- extended
'tucking in front of the heart).   apex of the LLL, which slips between the
                                             descending aorta and the collapsed LUL.)

For illustrations of left upper lobe collapse see Illus. **COLLAPSE LUL**.

(c) **Right middle lobe collapse** may not always be obvious on a PA view. This depends on the orientation of the collapsed lobe to the x-ray beam. If not fully tangential to it there may be insufficient density for an opaque shadow to be cast.

Often the horizontal fissure will he depressed in position and the right lower cardiac outline obscured. The collapsed lobe is usually well shown on lateral views. It was also sometimes well shown on lordotic views (see p. 20.10), but the lateral view is preferable.

(a)   (b)   (c)

Fig. 2.16.   RML collapse (a) and (b) Plain   (c) The '**lower position**'- contact
radiographs - a collapsed RML often becomes   with the diaphragm is maintained.
elevated in position and loses its contact with   in both positions the right side of the
the diaphragm - the '**raised position**'.   cardiac silhouette is often obliterated.

CT : A collapsed middle lobe tends to give rise to a triangular mass. It may point anteriorly, laterally or collapse against the mediastinum or the right hemidiaphragm. Medial widening (**Golden's sign**) may signify a mass within the collapsed lobe.

When only a single segment is involved, the other segment will tend to remain inflated, as may also happen with incomplete fissures, and such may mimic a mass per se With the considerable rotation and variability of position that may occur, the collapsed RML or its segments may be found in various positions.

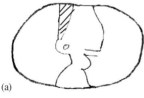      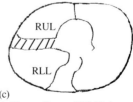

(a)   (b)   (c)

(a) The RML is   (b) The RML is collapsed   (c) The collapsed RML is
collapsed anteriorly.   medially against the   tethered to the lateral chest wall by
                         mediastinum.   adhesions and the aerated RUL
                                                     has filled the space in front of it.

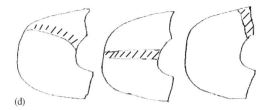

(d) Partial collapse of the RML.

(d)

Fig. 2.17 CT appearances of RML collapse.

For illustrations of right middle lobe collapse see Illus. **COLLAPSE RML** - [Illus. **TB, Pt. 24a** shows RML collapse causing a small triangular opacity adjacent to the diaphragm.]

(d) **Lower lobe collapse** is also manifested by loss of volume on the same side and about 50 % of the lung vessels, and the lower half of the appropriate pulmonary artery. The heart outline is preserved, as the adjacent upper and/or middle lobes will still be inflated. The collapsed lower lobe will be 'hidden' behind the heart, and may be visible only on penetrated or high KV films. With a LLL collapse, the aorto-pulmonary window (see ps. 13.24 - 13.26) may be opened up, and the outline of the descending aorta will be lost (see Fig. 1.29). Similarly with a RLL collapse, the outline of the IVC (seen through the cardiac shadow) will be absent (it may be accentuated on lateral views with a LLL collapse - see also p. 9.2). Much of the silhouette of the diaphragm will be lost on the affected side, and it is often elevated. **In such cases the collapsed and dense lower lobe may be mistaken for a pleural effusion on plain films, but the true nature is easily distinguished with ultrasound.**
  On lateral views, collapsed lower lobes tend to lie posteriorly, or against the posterior mediastinum (allowing much or all of the homolateral hemi-diaphragm to be normally silhouetted) - this is because they are tethered to it by the inferior pulmonary ligament - **'fully opened door'** sign of LL collapse (ps. 2.22 & 2.36). As on PA views, where the collapsed lobe abuts the diaphragm, the outline of the latter will be lost. The density of the collapsed lobe alters the density over the lower dorsal vertebrae, reversing the normal superior-inferior density change from white over the upper dorsal vertebrae, to black over the lower vertebrae - i.e. the increased density apparently making the lower dorsal vertebrae white. (This sign can also be produced with posteriorly placed pleural fluid).

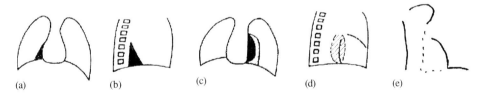

(a)   (b)   (c)   (d)   (e)

Fig. 2.18 Lower lobe collapse as seen on plain radiographs.
(a) & (b) RLL. (c) and (d) LLL. (e) The descending aorta and the medial aspect of the diaphragm are obliterated.

  An end-on air bronchogram seen on a lateral view or tomogram with right lower lobe collapse may give rise to the '**Gatling gun sign**' and bronchial '**ring shadows**' - see also ps. 2.2 and 2.29 - 2.31.

CT : A collapsed lower lobe usually gives rise to a wedge shaped soft tissue density adjacent to the lower dorsal spine. Its size will depend on the degree of collapse, the presence or absence of a hilar mass, and the completeness of the (inferior) pulmonary ligament which anchors the lower lobe to the mediastinum and diaphragm. If this is incomplete, a collapsed lower lobe may collapse completely towards the lower hilum and simulate a mass (see Fig. 2.36, p. 2.36).

 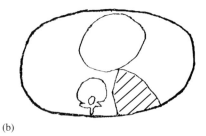

(a)   (b)

Fig. 2.19   (a) Collapsed right lower lobe   (b) Collapsed left lower lobe

The collapsed lower lobe swings posteriorly as it is tethered to the lower mediastinum. If it swings upwards, with an incomplete inferior pulmonary ligament, it may simulate a lung mass (see p. 2.2.).

For further signs of left & right lower collapse see ps. 2.25 - 2.29.
For illustrations of lower lobe collapse see Illus. **COLLAPSE LLL** and **COLLAPSE RLL.**

On **lateral   views** depression of the left hilum will often allow both left and right pulmonary arteries to be seen at the same level. The larger bronchi tend to be more posterior on the affected side (see p. 2.30, Fig. 2.26 and Illus. **ANATOMY 4**).

(e) '**Sentinel lines**' or '**Connoisseur's sign**' of left lower lobe collapse.
     With a collapsed left lower lobe, it is not uncommon to see a few fairly thin horizontal lines in the lingula. Nordenström and Novek (1960) ascribed these to linear collapse, but they look far more like dilated and partly obstructed lingula veins (or possibly lymphatics) - see Illus. **CONOISSEUR SIGN.**

     Strickland (1976) termed them '**sentinel lines**', but the author (like the late Dr. Benje Pierce, from St Thomas Hospital) terms them the '**Connoisseur's sign**', although they are in fact quite common.
     Pajewski (1970) using lateral oblique tomograms showed the close relationship of the lingula veins to the origin of the lower lobe bronchus and venous confluence.

     See also Price (1991) linear collapse in lingula as a feature of LLL collapse - '**Nordenström's sign'.**

     Rarely dilated lingula veins may be found without any concomitant lower lobe collapse or be seen on the right - Illus. **CONOISSEUR   SIGN, Conoisseur sign Pt. 3 & collapse RM&LLs, Pt. 1**.

(f) A **right middle lobe plus right lower lobe collapse** follows **blockage of the intermediate bronchus**, and is not uncommon. It causes a marked loss in the number of vessels in the right lung (Fig. 2.20), and compensatory emphysema of the right upper lobe. An opacity is often seen behind the right side of the heart, due to the collapsed lower lobe (which also obliterates the shadow of the IVC), and the lower right heart border will be obliterated due to the collapsed middle lobe, which tends to lie more horizontally as well as anteriorly. Superficially the appearance may be mistaken for a raised side of the diaphragm or a subpulmonary effusion (easily distinguished by ultrasound if not obvious on the plain radiographs).

(a)   (b)   (c)

Fig. 2.20.   Collapse of the right middle and lower lobes.
    (a) and (b) Plain radiographs.   (c) Cross section.

For illustrations of combined right middle and lower lobe collapse see Illus. **COLLAPSE RM&LLS.**

(g) **Collapse of the right upper lobe and right middle lobe** may give a similar appearance on a lateral view, to that seen with a left upper lobe collapse, i.e. an anteriorly situated band of collapse (extending from the apex to the diaphragm), together with anterior herniation of the contra-lateral upper lobe. On frontal views the two collapsed lobes are separate.

  The cause cannot easily be single, as there is no common bronchus. Causes include : tumours of both upper and middle lobe bronchi, a tumour of the upper lobe bronchus with enlarged nodes compressing the middle lobe bronchus; tumour of the upper lobe bronchus and bronchiectasis of the middle lobe; mucous plugs blocking upper and middle lobe bronchi, etc.

(h) **Combined RML plus RLL collapse** is difficult to explain on the lines of a single anatomical cause, but a tumour may extend through one lobe, cross a fissure and involve the second, or one endobronchial lesion may spread submucosally to involve the second or two endobronchial lesions may be present e.g. mucus plugs. Felson (1973) termed it the '**double lesion sign**'. See also references below.

Fig. 2.21 Right upper and middle lobe collapse.

For illustrations of combined right upper and middle lobe collapse see Illus. **COLLAPSE RU&MLS.**

(i) **Collapse of an entire lung** is common with advanced neoplasm, plugging of a main bronchus by a benign tumour, FB (foreign body), etc., or as a result of pressure on a main bronchus by large nodes, or the lung by a large pleural effusion or pneumothorax.

For illustrations of a collapsed left or right lung see Illus. **COLLAPSE L LUNG** and **COLLAPSE R LUNG.**

Conclusions:
Patterns of single lobar collapse are shown in Figs. 2.12 to 2.19, and patterns of complicated lobar collapse in Figs. 2.20 & 2.21.

Note that adhesions tethering the lung to the chest wall may alter the position of a collapsed lobe.

Further references.

Fleischner (1937) : The meaning of collapse in lung pathology and its related radiology.

Dornhurst and Pierce (1954) : Pulmonary collapse and consolidation. The role of collapse in the production of lung field shadows and the significance of segments in inflammatory lung disease.

Felson (1960) : Lesions in widely separated lobes or segments in inflammatory lung disease.

Rohlfing (1977) : The **shifting granuloma** - an internal marker for collapse.

Berger et al. (1980) : CT of the occult tracheo-bronchial foreign body.

Naidich et al. (1983) : CT of lobar collapse   (1) - endobronchial obstruction. (2) - collapse in the absence of endobronchial obstruction.   Naidich et al. (1984) : CT of lobar collapse.

Raasch et al (1984) : CT study of broncho-pulmonary collapse.

Godwin (1984) : CT of the Chest (Chapter on lobar collapse).

Paling and Griffin (1985) : Lower lobe collapse due to pleural effusion - CT analysis.

Henschke et al. (1987) : Comparison of CT and bronchoscopy in the detection of bronchial abnormalities.

Herold et al. (1991) : Pulmonary collapse - signal patterns with MR imaging.

Woodring (1988) : Compared plain radiography with CT in determining the cause of lung collapse in fifty patients. 27 had an obstructing tumour and in 24 of these the chest radiograph identified the tumour because of a hilar mass or bronchial abnormality. CT demonstrated all 27 by a central bronchial abnormality or hilar mass. Absence of air bronchograms or the presence of mucus-filled bronchi were secondary CT findings suggesting tumour, but four patients with obstructing tumours still had **'air   bronchograms'.** CT failed to miss any tumours but produced about 10% of false positive diagnoses of tumour due to bronchial narrowing or occlusion due to bronchial stricture, mucous plugging or bronchial compression from effusions, etc. Although the demonstration of 'air bronchograms' on CT was not considered to have diagnostic significance, their **absence on CT   sections** was thought to favour an obstructing tumour.

Woodring and Reed (1996a) : Types and mechanisms of pulmonary collapse (atelectasis).

Woodring and Reed (1996b) : Radiographic manifestations of lobar collapse (atelectasis).

Ashizawa et al. (2001) : Lobar collapse (atelectasis) - diagnostic pitfalls on chest radiography.

Franken and Klatte (1977) : Atypical 'peripheral' upper lobe collapse in 10 children mimicking apical pleural fluid.

Kattan (1983) : Angiographic confirmation of normal pleural thickness in right upper lobe collapse.

Kattan (1991) : The various faces of RUL collapse.

Johnson et al. (1984) : Peripheral RUL collapse in the newborn.

Adler and Cameron (1988) : CT correlation in peripheral right upper lobe collapse.

Don and Desmarais (1989) : **Peripheral   upper   lobe   collapse** in adults, simulating apical pleural effusion or other localised pleural disease - occurs when the collapsed lobe maintains its adherence to the lateral chest wall - the inferior border of the collapsed lobe giving the sharply marginated border.

Hourihane and Owens (1989) : In patients who have a superior accessory fissure, a collapse of the upper and middle lobes may be mistaken for the horizontal fissure (5 cases).

Chong et al. (1990) : Atypical collapse of right upper lobe simulated combined right upper and middle lobe collapse.

Davies and Turner (1990) : In typical RUL collapse the right hilum will be elevated with upward displacement of the horizontal fissure (an accessory fissure intersects the right hilum at a lower point than the horizontal fissure - usually at the right mid hilar point - the point of overlap of the upper lobe vessels and the lower lobe artery).

Park and Bahk (1991) : Peripheral upper lobe collapse simulating pleural effusion - segmental collapse of apical or apico-posterior segments may give rise to an identical appearance.

Teel and Engeler (1996) : CT in peripheral RUL collapse.

Le Roux (1971) : Studied 17 examples of 'shrinkage and opacification of the right upper and middle lobes in combination' and found that nine were caused by inflammatory disease, whilst eight were due to neoplasm.

Harrison et al. (1978) : Pattern of combined collapse of RU & MLs.

Saterfiel et al. (1988) : CT of combined RU & ML collapse.

Lee et al. (1994) : Combined lobar collapse of the right lung - three combinations -

(i) RM+LLs - due to blockage of intermediate bronchus by tumour, FB, mucous plug or inflammatory stricture.

(ii) RU+MLs - bronchi of both lobes must be occluded or stenosed by a single or two separate lesions, whilst the LL bronchus (**not** IB as stated) remains patent - can be due to Ca. bronchus, mucous plug and inflammatory disease. With bronchial ca., one is often blocked, whilst the other is secondarily affected by tumour extension via the lung, the bronchial sheath or by enlarged nodes.

(iii) RU+LLs - rare - causes include mucous plugs, alveolar cell ca. - often the RML becomes hyperinflated.

Gurney (1996) : Atypical manifestations of pulmonary collapse - **'elephant's   right   ear   appearance'** of RU + ML collapse - two cases (i) lymphoma, (ii) bronchial ca.

Saida et al. (1997) : Showed on CT sections that the normal broncho-arterial relationships were preserved in combined RML + RLL collapse despite the caudal extension of the RUL.

For mucocoeles associated with collapse see ps. 2.10 - 11.

How long does it take for a lobe to collapse after its bronchus becomes obstructed?

Assuming the absence of collateral ventilation, gas in alveoli distal to a bronchial obstruction is approx. 4% O_2, 6% CO_2 and 90% N_2. This mixture tends to remain stable, nitrogen being the least diffusible. It has been estimated that a lobe will usually take about six hours to collapse. Thus a chest radiograph can still show an aerated lobe for several hours after its bronchus becomes occluded, if the patient has been breathing air, but if the patient has been breathing 100% O_2, it can happen in a few minutes.

The volume of a collapsed lobe also depends on whether the bronchus is obstructed or not. Thus a collapsed lobe or lung due to a large pneumothorax can often be very small, but if secretions can not be expectorated or there is accompanying infection it is often much larger.

Some references.

Dale and Rahn (1952) : Rate of gas absorbtion during collapse.
Pierce et al. (1980) : Radiographic, scintigraphic and gas-dilution estimates of lung and lobar volumes in man.
Stein et al. (1976) : Experimentally induced lobar collapse in canine lungs - found that collapsed lobes reached a volume 15% below residual volume.
Felson (1986) : With chronic fibrosis a collapsed lobe may be so small that it is not visible radiographically.
Gurney (1996) : Atypical appearances of pulmonary collapse.

'Loss of silhouette' sign or 'Loss of outline' sign

This sign reflects the point that most anatomical structures bordering the lungs, are not themselves seen, but depend on adjacent air-filled lung for their recognition. This is true for the heart, aorta, diaphragm, IVC or SVC, etc. Thus when the outline of these is obliterated or absent, the sign shows that air-less lung (fluid or solid tumour) is adjacent to the lost anatomical border. This will allow in many instances, the anatomical localisation of the disease process from a single view. On PA views collapse or consolidation of the **left upper lobe** will obliterate the left cardiac border - the **left lower lobe**, the left border of the descending aorta, the **right middle lobe**, the lower right cardiac border , the **right lower lobe**, the inferior vena cava, the **right upper lobe**, the ascending aorta and azygos vein, etc. The posterior parts of either side of the diaphragm are also obscured with a non-aerated lower lobe. The normal IVC and the loss of its silhouette are best seen on the lateral view. On a lateral view, a collapsed left lower lobe will often obliterate the posterior margin of the heart and the posterior part of the diaphragm as well as obscure the descending aorta. These points are further shown in Illus. **LOSS OF SILHOUETTE** or **SILHOUETTE SIGN**.

Loss of the paratracheal, para-oesophageal etc. lines or stripes is essentially a similar phenomenon and may be noted on both PA and lateral views. Even a small mass, area of collapse or consolidation which makes a part of the lung airless, will similarly mask part of a normal structure, e.g. left pulmonary artery, etc.

Caveat : **A false 'loss of silhouette' sign** simulating RML collapse or consolidation may be seen on the lower right cardiac border with a **pectus excavatum** (see p. 12.34); this (and a 'buried aorta' - see p.1.20) may also give rise to a false loss of silhouette to the descending aorta.

References:

Felson and Felson (1950) : Termed the sign - '**the silhouette sign**' but as it is the loss of the silhouette which is abnormal it is illogical to imply its presence when the opposite happens with disease processes.
Hodson (1956) : The localisation of pulmonary collapse-consolidation - termed it the 'outline sign' and noted that the various segments or lobes which abut the trachea, mediastinum, diaphragm and chest wall or fissures will obliterate these boundaries if consolidated. He also noted that on a normal lateral view, 'the shadows of the vertebral bodies decrease gradually and evenly in density from above downwards (i.e. in negative film appear gradually darker until the diaphragm is reached', and that and a loss of aeration of overlying lung will interfere with this.
Felson (1960 &1973) : In 1973 he stated that he was shown the sign by H.K. Dunham in 1935,
the sign was also noted by Robbins and Hale (1945g).
Foote and Meredith (1974) : Silhouette and the IVC.

Grainger and Pierce (1980) : Pointed out that in order to show the sign, the x-ray beam has to be tangential to a border and parallel to a plane surface.

Webber and Davies (1981) : Loss of the proximal part of the right pulmonary artery may occur with RUL collapse, so that the lower lobe vessels appear to commence away from the cardiac shadow (in Luftsichel paper - see p. 2.27).

Kattan et al. (1984) : The silhouette sign revisited experimentally.

Davies, P. (1991) : Experiments may be performed to show how the eye tends to join and complete objects which are incomplete (see also discussion on Mach bands - App. p.5). He also noted the fibrous wax experiment (as follows).

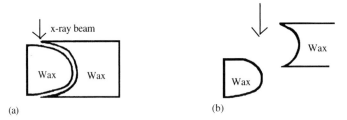

Fig. 2.22   The eye tends to join objects which are neighbouring.
(a) No clear border between the two objects.
(b) Borders between the two objects are easily observed with their greater separation.

'Luftsichel' or 'air crescent' sign of upper lobe collapse, (with **'Peri-Aortic Lucency'** on the left) and **mediastinal herniation.**

With collapse of an upper lobe, particularly the left upper lobe, the apex of the lower lobe, tends to fill the apex and upper part of the affected pleural cavity. Aerated lung may be seen on the medial side of the opaque and collapsed upper lobe, (due to the apex of the lower lobe tucking itself between the collapsed lobe and the mediastinum. This occurs much more commonly on the left than the right. On the left the translucency due to medially lying air-filled lower lobe tissue has been termed **'peri-aortic lucency'** or the **'Luftsichel sign'** (Fig. 2.23). This is not an uncommon appearance on the left and is almost always seen with left upper lobe collapse on high KV views (or inclined frontal tomograms). The author has also seen it with a partially opaque left upper lobe due to lymphangitis carcinomatosa.

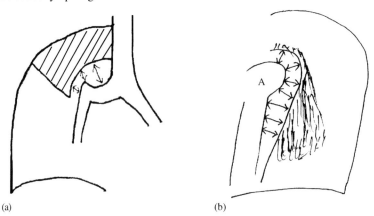

Fig 2.23   Luftsichel sign - diagrams.
(a) Right side - the collapsed RUL is separated from the hilum by the aerated apex of the RUL.
(b) Left side - the hyper-expanded apex of the LLL tucks in between the collapsed LUL and the mediastinum, producing **'peri-aortic lucency'** (arrowed).
For the corresponding CT appearances - see p.2.20 and Fig. 2.15.

For illustrations of Luftsichel sign - see Illus. **LUFTSICHEL SIGN.**

References.
Dahm (1942) : Left side.
Bürgel and Oleck (1960) : Right side.
Franken and Klatte (1977)
Proto and Tocino (1980)
Webber and Davies (1981) : 5 right sided and 19 left sided.
Heitzman (1984) : Right side.

Mediastinal Movement (see also p. 2.7 - 'free spine sign' and p. 2.8).

   With a lobar collapse mediastinal movement normally takes place unless the mediastinum has become fixed by fibrosis or tumour. Medical students are taught to look for tracheal movement, but that of the heart, larger bronchi, para-oesophageal lines, azygo-oesophageal recess and junction lines etc. should also be noted. The upper mediastinum may be deviated with both upper or lower lobe collapse. With upper lobe collapse the anterior junction line will tend to move across ipsilaterally and due to hyper-expansion, of the contra-lateral upper lobe, a clearer silhouette of the ascending aorta may be seen with left upper lobe collapse, and a clearer outline of the pulmonary trunk with right upper lobe collapse, not to be confused with right upper lobe collapse per se.

   Because a lower lobe collapse, also pulls the respective air filled upper lobe down with it, the upper mediastinum may be deviated as well as the lower. Thus an '**anterior triangle sign**' may be present with a right lower lobe collapse, the triangle comprising the normal mediastinal soft tissues - thymus, fat, etc.

   With a l**eft lower lobe collapse**, not only may the heart move to the left but it will also often rotate, so that on frontal views it appears as it normally does in the right anterior oblique position, i.e.. with lose of the normal concavity of the left heart border at the level of the pulmonary artery - the '**flat waist sign**'. As noted on ps. 2.25 & 2.26 - loss of the silhouette sign - a collapsed LLL caused this, the descending aorta outline is obliterated and sometimes the aortic knuckle, the latter caused by displacement of the upper left anterior mediastinal structures.

   Noting the mobility of apparent paraspinal, anterior mediastinal or some central mediastinal masses on CT sections taken in more than one position, e.g. supine + prone, may show that what appeared to be a fixed mass in one of these positions (e.g. paraspinal, when surgery may be very difficult) is in fact a mobile and non-fixed mass.

   Considerable mediastinal movement is also seen following surgery, sometimes with marked contralateral lung herniation. Similar findings may also be seen with the scimitar syndrome (see p. 7.7).

References.
Kattan et a1. (1975) : Upper triangle sign.
Kattan and Wiot (l976) : Flat waist sign.
Kattan (1980) : Obliteration of the top of the aortic knob in lower lobe collapse.
Proto (1992) : Anatomic understanding of newer observations.

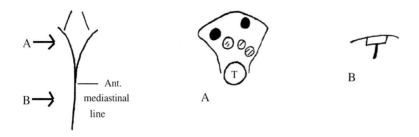

(a) Anterior mediastinal line -normal.

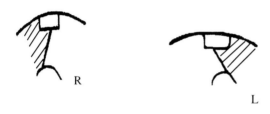

(b) Line displaced to right or left with upper lobe collapse.

(c) RUL collapse - the main
pulmonary artery is better seen.

(d) LUL collapse - the ascending aorta is better seen,
especially on lateral view.

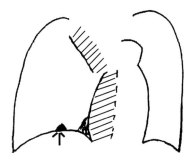 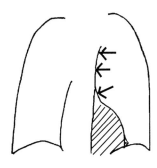

(e) **Upper triangle sign** with RLL collapse, due to shift of the upper mediastinum. Note also the '**juxta-phrenic peak sign**' (see also p. 2.35).

(f) **Flat waist sign** and obscured aortic knuckle in association with LLL collapse.

Fig. 2.24   Effects of upper anterior mediastinal movement with lobar collapse.

Movement of other structures especially larger airways with a major lobar collapse.

With a major degree of collapse, there will be considerable displacement of the other thoracic structures to compensate for the loss of volume. Thus not only will the mediastinum and its structures move, but also the affected hilum will be elevated or depressed or rotated. Thus vessels and bronchi may move and be reorientated. It is important, both on PA and lateral radiographs, to consider the positions of the larger bronchi, as well as their patency. Displacement may be caused by collapse, pleural effusions or masses. Whilst these may be obvious on frontal views, some experience is necessary to appreciate them on lateral views, but this may be even more important in the recognition of underlying disease.

When an upper lobe is collapsed, the ipsilateral main bronchus is commonly elevated, and with a collapsed left upper lobe the main bronchus will tend to lie horizontally, thus giving rise to a larger '**ring shadow**'. Similarly a lower lobe collapse will tend to lower the position of the 'ring shadow' or efface it if the main bronchus becomes too oblique to the radiographic beam; with a left lower lobe collapse the 'ring' of the left lower lobe moves posteriorly. With a major lobar collapse there is thus an up or downwards change in position of the '**rings**', with possible superimposition of them or a widening of their normal positions. These changes are seen on lateral views or tomograms (Illus. **BRONCHIAL RINGS**).

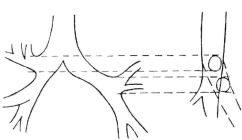 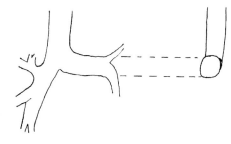

Fig. 2.25 (a) Diagram showing the formation of ring shadows on lateral views due to the larger bronchi (after Coussement et al., Le Poumon Normal, 1984, with permission).

(b) Collapsed left upper lobe causing elevation of the left main bronchus and a larger than normal ring shadow on the lateral view. The two 'rings' are also superimposed.

Movement may also occur in the AP plane, with the affected main bronchus moving backwards in relation to the other.

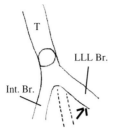

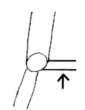

(c) Posterior displacement of the left main bronchus by a collapsed LLL - the 'open legs' sign.

(d) The LLL bronchus is very elevated and passes directly posteriorly when the collapse takes place towards a tethered apex of the lower lobe.

[Similar displacements may also occur in relation to large pleural effusions, cardiac enlargements or pericardial effusions.]

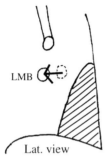

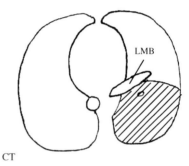

Fig. 2.26   Anterior displacement of the left main bronchus by a fairly large pleural effusion, a large mass or a 'drowned lobe'.

Further references.

Lane and Whalen (1969) : Posterior displacement of the left bronchial tree - a new sign of left atrial enlargement.
Whalen and Lane (1969) : Bronchial rearrangements in pulmonary collapse, as seen on the lateral radiograph.
Vix and Klatte (1970) : The lateral chest radiograph in the diagnosis of hilar and mediastinal masses.
Austin (1984) : The lateral chest radiograph.
Proto and Merhar (1984) : Value of noting the position of the main bronchi on lateral radiographs and on tomograms, including CTs - pointed out than when there is a large opacity posteriorly, anterior displacement of the larger homolateral bronchi is often a good indication that the opacity is likely to be a pleural effusion.
Alexander et al. (1988 and 1989) : Left lower lobe ventilation and its relation to cardiomegaly and posture.

Milne (1986) : End-on air bronchograms in some cases of RLL collapse may be seen on lateral radiographs - the 'Gatling gun' sign of RLL collapse.

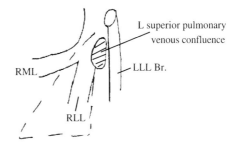

Fig. 2.27 **Ewart 's sign**- an enlarged heart, left atrium or pericardial effusion may cause pressure on the left lower lobe bronchus and displace it posteriorly, sometimes causing actual collapse of the lower lobe (Illus. **EWART'S SIGN**).

Fig. 2.28 'Inferior hilar window'.

Filling-in of the 'inferior hilar window'.

A normally avascular region on lateral chest radiographs situated below the right pulmonary artery and anterior to both lower lobe bronchi has been termed the '**inferior hilar window**' by Park et al. (1991). They could identify the anterior walls of the right and left lower lobe bronchi in 36 % and 84 % of 50 normal patients respectively. In 25 others they were able to note unilateral or bilateral masses over 1 cm in size, but only eight had the laterality correctly diagnosed.

Bowing of a fissure by a hilar or juxta-hilar mass. (**Golden's sign**). See also p. 4.1.

Golden (1925) noted that when the lesser fissure has a convex instead of a straight or concave lower border in association with right upper lobe collapse, this usually indicates the presence of a tumour mass - in the author's experience most often a large tumour with markedly enlarged right hilar lymph nodes. A similar 'hump' may also be seen on lateral views, with convexity of an oblique fissure and caused by a mass or nodes. Likewise large masses at the origin of the left upper lobe may bulge out the left oblique fissure at hilar level.

Such bulges are usually a good sign of advanced and inoperable neoplasm but one should note that with lobar consolidation and a larger than normal lobe, slight but smooth contoured bulging may occur. However in most cases one should also consider a '**drowned   lobe**' due to consolidation distal to a neoplastic obstruction of the supplying bronchus.

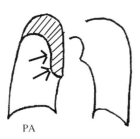

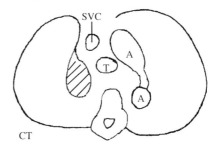

Fig. 2.29   (a) Convex lesser fissure with neoplasm (reversed S-shaped curve).

(b) The 'S-sign' of Golden, as shown by CT - the lesser fissure is stretched posteriorly over a mass of nodes.(T = trachea: A = aorta).

 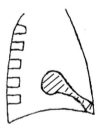 

Fig. 2.30 Masses at the origins of the RUL, RML and LUL causing bulging of the adjacent fissures. (Wedge or 'open umbrella' appearance on lateral view).

Further reference.
Reinig and Ross (1984) : CT appearance of Golden's sign.

For illustrations of Golden's sign - see Illus. **GOLDEN'S SIGN**.

The (Inferior) Pulmonary Ligaments (pulmono-diaphragmatic ligaments).
 These thin structures consist of double layers of parietal pleura and some intervening connective tissue, including sometimes small lymph nodes. They arise from the lower pulmonary hila, at the level of the inferior pulmonary veins passing into the mediastinum from the adjacent lower lobes. They extend downwards from this position to end, either (a) in a free border (the 'incomplete' form) or (b) by reflecting onto the superior surface of the diaphragm ('complete' form). Medially the ligaments reflect from the mediastinum exterior to the plane of the oesophagus and laterally fuse with the visceral pleura over the lower lobes. Thus each ligament 'binds' the lower lobe towards the hilum and helps prevent torsion or lateral displacement with a pleural effusion or pneumothorax. It also divides the mediastinal pleura below the lung hilum into anterior and posterior compartments. The small lymph nodes which may be found within the ligaments are known as the inferior pulmonary ligament nodes.

Complete or incomplete (inferior) pulmonary ligament -

  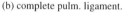 

(a) Position of pulm.
ligament - lat.view.   (b) complete pulm. ligament.   (c) incomplete pulm. ligament.

Fig. 2.31   (a) Diagram of lateral view of (inferior) pulmonary ligament - this is formed by two pleural layers, one in front of and the other behind the hilum passing down to the diaphragm, where they reach it to form the small bare area on its upper surface - after Godwin et al. (1983).
(b) & (c) The ligaments may sometimes be demonstrated on tomograms as thin lines extending from the inferior pulmonary veins to the diaphragm.

Normal plain film findings - the ligaments are not normally visible on P.A. and lateral views although they may have tenting effects on the pleura overlying the diaphragm which may obscure a portion of the latter.

Appearances on CT - on viewing CT sections, from the hilum caudally the pulmonary ligaments appear as soft tissue 'beaks' passing postero-laterally from just below the position of the inferior pulmonary veins - often they can be seen extending well into the adjacent lower lobe. They are not visualised in all subjects - about 50'%. of adults - the left being seen more readily than the right. The right ligament is shorter and runs in a more transverse plane, owing to the higher right dome of the diaphragm - its smaller size may account for its less frequent visualisation.

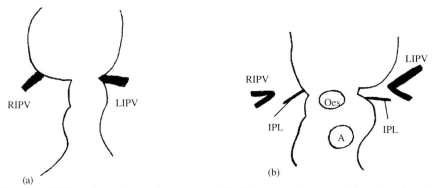

(a) Diagram of CT section at level of inferior pulmonary veins.
(IPV = inferior pulmonary vein,

(b) Diagram of more caudal section showing inferior pulmonary ligaments.
IPL = inferior pulmonary ligament)

Fig. 2.32   The inferior pulmonary veins and pulmonary ligaments as seen on CT sections.

Other appearances within the pulmonary ligaments (Figs. 2.33a-e).
   The pulmonary ligaments can be thickened with pleural disease, particularly that due to exposure to asbestos, and are more readily seen with over-distended and emphysematous lungs. Small pleural effusions, may collect either in front of, or behind, the ligaments in the supine patient. The medial position of the ligament may also cause sub-pulmonary fluid collections to he larger laterally than medially. A pneumothorax may allow one to be outlined with air on both sides. With hiatal hernias the ligaments will be effaced by the distorted lower mediastinum. Nodal enlargements within the ligaments may produce nodules within them.

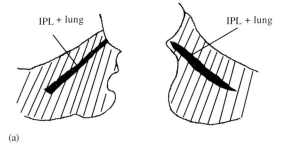

The pulmonary ligaments may cause tethering of the lung- thin areas of collapsed lung - passing medially through pleural effusions - see also ps. 14.14 & 15.12-13. This sign can be seen both with CT and US.

(a)

Subpulmonary pleural effusions may also cause a ligament to be seen especially on the right as a triangular shadow - tethering of the lower lobe by the ligament will also prevent medial elevation of the lobe and the lung will be more elevated laterally.

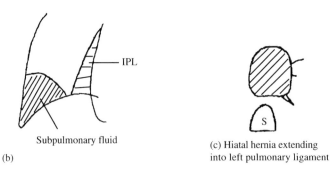

Subpulmonary fluid

(b)

(c) Hiatal hernia extending
into left pulmonary ligament

Huge hiatal hernias may pass into the ligament and separate its two layers, incorporating them into the mediastinum. Tumours may also invade the ligament and simulate mediastinal or inferior pulmonary vein involvement - producing a triangular shadow on the medial aspect of the lung base. Masses within the pulmonary ligament may also be due to varices (see p. 18.31).

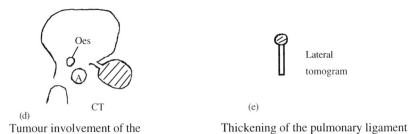

(d)

Tumour involvement of the
inferior pulmonary ligament.

(e)

Thickening of the pulmonary ligament
secondary to nodal enlargement.

NB - The systemic blood supply to a sequestrated segment or the primitive persistent blood supply to the lung also passes through the pulmonary ligament (see ps. 3.11 - 3.12).

Aerocoeles within or adjacent to the ligaments (Fig. 2.34) have been reported following trauma and noted on plain radiographs or tomograms by several authors (see references). Such aerocoeles presumably follow lung laceration adjacent to the ligaments, and air may pass between the two layers. Such an air collection does not alter with the patient's position, as might be expected with a pneumothorax and is not uncommonly accompanied by a pneumomediastinum. Ravin et al. (1976) felt that these were pneumatocoeles within the inferior pulmonary ligaments. Others have questioned this theory. Friedman (1985a) suggested that most reported adult cases may have been neighbouring loculated pneumothoraces as the air collections lay very posteriorly. A similar view was held by Godwin et al. (1985), who studied four cases, and wondered if the gas collections in this position were in the postero-medial parts of the pleural cavities, the posterior mediastinum or within bullae ('para-mediastinal pneumatocoeles') - the pulmonary ligaments in these cases being intact. Thomas et al. (1990) described two cases and wrote "Traumatic paramediastinal air cysts are uncommon; when they do occur they are seen usually in the young, in whom the elasticity of the thoracic cage allows the applied force to be transmitted directly to the lung." In the reported cases, "chest pain, breathlessness and haemoptysis, often severe, are common presenting symptoms. Occasionally radiological signs are present on arrival in hospital but more commonly, symptoms and radiological changes are delayed. In all the cases so far described **spontaneous   resolution has occurred...If the typical appearance of a traumatic para-mediastinal air cyst is present, no further investigation is necessary.**"

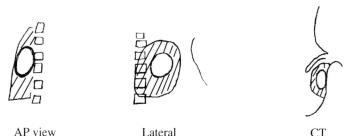

AP view   Lateral   CT
Fig. 2.34 "Aerocoeles" in the pulmonary ligament (? adjacent pulmonary bullae).

Apparent 'aerocoeles within the pulmonary ligament' may in fact be loculated pneumothoraces, para-vertebral air-collections, or more likely post-traumatic bullae in the adjacent lung (perhaps caused by tethering of the lung by the ligament). Thin walls of adjacent lung bullae, accessory fissures, scars and medial extension of the central tendon of the diaphragm, can all be mistaken for the pulmonary ligament.

Diaphragmatic or ' Juxta-Phrenic' Peaks (see also ps. 1.6, 1.32, 2.29 & 11.20).

Kattan et al. (1980a & b) noted that a 'peak-like' shadow is often seen on the upper border of the diaphragm with an upper lobe collapse. They ascribed this to traction on the pleura overlying the diaphragm caused by a complete form of the pulmonary ligament. Collapse or fibrosis of an upper lobe will elevate the ipsilateral pulmonary hilum, in turn transmitting traction to the diaphragm via the ligament. Such peaks are commonly found with pulmonary fibrosis following radiotherapy for carcinoma of the breast, sometimes there being two or even three peaks, which may be seen on both frontal and lateral views. Peaks may also be seen occasionally with loss of volume of a hemithorax with lower lobe collapse, basal pleural adhesions, in some patients with severe emphysema, generalised fibrosis, following pleurisy, etc. There appear to be several mechanisms in their production.

Heitzman (1984) noted that peaks often lie anteriorly, in the position of the anterior inferior end of the major fissure and may contain fat, where they arise from the diaphragm. He postulated that they are due to supradiaphragmatic fat being pulled up into the fissure, due to basal adhesions.

Davis et al. (1996) using CT studies in 32 patients with upper or middle volume loss concluded that juxta-phrenic peaks are most commonly due to inferior accessory or other fissures and are uncommonly attributable to the inferior pulmomary ligament.   See also refs. below.

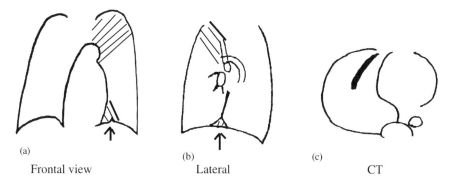

(a)   (b)   (c)
Frontal view   Lateral   CT

Fig. 2.35 (a) and (b) Juxta-phrenic peak with left upper lobe collapse or fibrosis - less commonly. seen with RUL collapse.(see also Fig. 2.24e). (Arrow = peak).
(c) CT section showing supra-diaphragmatic fat being pulled up into the lower part of a greater fissure.
For illustrations of juxta-phrenic peaks - see Illus. **JUXTAPHRENIC PEAK**.

The pulmonary ligament and lower lobe collapse.
    As already noted on p. 2.21, with collapse of a lower lobe, the pulmonary ligament tends to pull the collapsed lobe medially and posteriorly, thus accounting for its usual very posterior position on lateral radiographs - it swings back rather like a **'fully opened door'**.
    When the ligament is incomplete, the lobe may rise up from its contact with the diaphragm, to form an elongated oval shaped para-vertebral density, with a lower extension formed by the ligament. On the left, such may easily be hidden behind the heart. Such collapsed lobes may also simulate a lung mass, especially to those observers who do not study the pulmonary vessels.

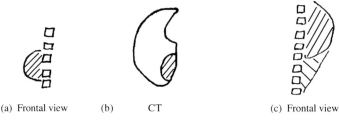

(a) Frontal view   (b)   CT   (c) Frontal view

Fig. 2.36 (a) & (b) Ball shaped mass due to a   (c) Oval shaped para-vertebral
collapsed RLL and an incomplete pulmonary   collapsed LLL, associated with an
ligament.   incomplete pulmonary ligament,
                                                         which gives it an inferior extension.

Further references.
Rabinowitz and Wolf (1966)
Hanke (1978) : The (inferior) pulmonary ligaments.
Mintzer et al. (1979)
Rudikoff (1981) : The inferior pulmonary ligaments and sub-pulmonary effusions.
Friedman (1985b) : CT demonstration of tethering of the lung by the pulmonary ligaments.
Cooper et al. (1983)
Godwin et al. (1983) : CT of the pulmonary ligaments.
Rost and Proto (1983)

    Pneumatocoeles in or adjacent to pulmonary ligaments
Hyde (1971)   (two cases on left).
Ravin et al. (1976)   (two on left and one on right).
Fagan and Swischuk (1976)   (one on right).
Elyaderani and Gabriele (1979)   (two cases on left).

Stulz et al. (1984) : Traumatic pulmonary pseudocysts and mediastinal air cysts.
Volberg et al. (1979) : Inferior pulmonary ligament air collections in neonates with respiratory distress - noted that they pass posteriorly as they descend, as well as incline posteriorly.
Moskowitz and Griscom (1976) : Pointed out that a pneumothorax lying medially on supine radiographs may be mistaken for air in a pulmonary ligament.

Kattan, Eyler and Felson (1980 a& b) : Juxta-phrenic peaks.
Glay and Palayew (1981) : Incomplete pulmonary ligament, allowing a lower lobe to collapse upwards towards the hilum and mediastinum - thus simulating a lung mass.
Thomas et al. (1990) : Traumatic para-mediastinal air cysts (two cases).

Berkmen et al.(1989) : Right phrenic nerve anatomy - CT appearance and differentiation from pulmonary ligament with which it has often been confused.
Berkmen et al. (1992) : Intersegmental (intersublobar) septum of the lower lobe in relation to the pulmonary ligament: anatomical, histological, and CT correlations - the thin linear area of increased density seen on CT is a connective tissue septum separating the medial from the posterior basic segment of the LL. A 'beak-like' structure represents the pulmonary ligament.
Cameron (1993) : The juxta-phrenic peak - Kattan's sign - is produced by **rotation of an inferior accessory fissure**.

Lobar and lung collapse due to endotracheal tubes.

Endotracheal tubes used during general anaesthesia may sometimes be too long, and their lower ends may pass into the main, intermediate or lower lobe bronchi, and lead to collapse of the non-ventilated lung e.g. right upper lobe and/or left lung. The anaesthetist may note, following intubation with the neck extended, that there is good equal lung expansion on both sides, but when the head is elevated the tube tip may be pushed further down and cause obstruction to the non-ventilated bronchi.(see also p.19.2).

For illustrations - see Illus. **ENDOTRACHEAL TUBE, Tube comp (TUBAN) 5 & 6a-c.**

Lobar rearrangements, lung torsion and hernias.

Lobar rearrangements often occur following lobar resections. Following a **right upper lobectomy** the upper part of the right pleural cavity is filled by the middle and lower lobes - the lower lobe in a similar way as with upper lobe collapse. The middle lobe may over-expand and fill most of the front of the right pleural cavity with a largely coronal and obliquely situated fissure (sometimes termed the **'neo-fissure'**).

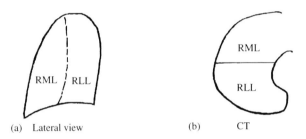

(a)   Lateral view   (b)   CT

Fig. 2.37   **'Neo-fissure'** after right upper lobectomy.

With collapse of such a middle lobe, this may mimic a right upper lobe collapse, as it may lie adjacent to the right upper mediastinum. Such a lobe may also undergo torsion, especially in the post-operative period.

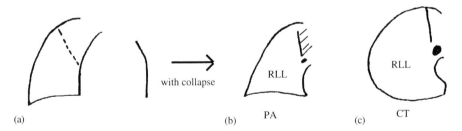

(a)   (b)   PA   (c)   CT

Fig. 2.38   Occasionally part of the fissure may be obliterated on a PA view.

Some references.
Ettinger et al. (1952) : Bronchial rearrangement and bronchiectasis following lung resection.
Shipley and Mahoney (1988) : Right middle lobe collapse following right upper lobectomy (also quote further cases of lung torsion from the literature).
Mahoney and Shipley (1988) : Neo-fissure after right upper lobectomy.

Lung or lobar torsion.
This can occur under three sets of circumstances :
    (i) spontaneously, but usually with some other pulmonary abnormality, infections, etc.
    (ii) following traumatic or spontaneous pneumothorax or effusion.
    (iii) as a complication of thoracic surgery.
   Two reviews by Felson (1987) and Moser and Proto (1987) drew attention to over 20 cases. Serious torsion can cause interruption to the venous drainage, arterial supply and/or bronchus of an affected lobe or lung, and if missed and untreated can cause serious morbidity or mortality. The reported cases have included, twisting of the lingula to occupy the left lung apex in a newborn infant, twisting of an accessory LUL, 180% torsion of a RML in association with a large congenital diaphragmatic hernia, the RUL with pneumonia, collapse secondary to an endobronchial adenoma, or occurring with a spontaneous pneumothorax. Three of Felson's cases had torsion of a lobe secondary to a tumour mass in two of these tumour masses had moved on subsequent radiographs and thus suggested the condition. In another, old calcified scars moved and demonstrated the twist.
   Several cases have followed trauma or surgery. A case reported by Moser and Proto (1987) showed a LUL collapse with twisting vessels, seven weeks after a high fall. Others have occurred following lung resection or other injuries. A survey of US thoracic surgeons (Carr, 1980) revealed 82 further cases. Sometimes these were due to residual lung after resection being more mobile, within a post-operative effusion or pneumothorax or because adhesions or the inferior phrenic ligament had been divided. A collapsed lobe post-operatively, one enlarging through oedema, twisting its vessels or bronchi should make one consider the possibility. Neglect may allow the twisted lobe to become gangrenous.
   In veterinary work, particularly with dogs, lung torsion is not that uncommon. Stein et al. (1976) reported it in racing greyhound dogs and Felson quoted five further references to veterinary papers.

Comment. Lobar rearrangements and torsions are obviously more common than many imagine. When patients were admitted to sanatoria for artificial pneumothorax treatment of tuberculosis (30 or so years ago), twisting of the diseased lung was not uncommonly seen, as was pointed out to me in my training by my former chief, W.S. Holden. These usually caused no trouble. Lobar rearrangements also occur with infection and adhesions. Acute collapse sometimes produces unusual patterns, due to excessive mobility of a lobe(s) e.g. the '**Luftsichel** sign' (see ps. 2.26 -27). Lobes may also partially twist producing '**whorled** nodules' presumably initially at the time of a transient pleural effusion, not uncommonly stimulated by asbestos inhalation (see ps. 14.42 - 14.44).
   Twisted lobes may be demonstrated by bronchography, CT or angiography. Persisting torsion may lead to severe anoxia, infection and gangrene in the affected lobe if not corrected surgically.

Further references.
Fadhli and Derrick (1965) : Twisted lingula - a cause of a solitary pulmonary nodule.
Hislop and Reid (1971) : Child aged two presented with acute bronchiolitis. CXRs showed increased translucency of left lung & displacement of the mediastinum to R. It was thought that he had congenital emphysema, but at surgery the LUL was three to four times larger than normal, and had rotated through 180°. It appeared that the lobe in twisting had caused narrowing of the bronchus with obstructive emphysema.
Huang and Cho (1979) : 44 year old man had pneumococcal RUL pneumonia which cleared. A week later there was consolidation in the position of the RML, adjacent to the right heart border. On subsequent radiographs the right hilum remained elevated and a right bronchogram showed that the RML bronchus was constricted and pointed towards the lung apex. At thoracotomy the RML was partially collapsed and lay behind the RUL, and had undergone a 180° torsion. It had a long pedicle and there was no parenchymal bridging to the adjacent lobes. The torsion was corrected and the lobe fixed. A later repeat bronchogram was normal.
Meisell (1980) : Torsion of the RUL with collapse and a spontaneous pneumothorax.
Berkmen (1985) : RUL torsion with collapse and a pneumothorax.
Berkmen et al. (1989) : Torsions of the upper lobe in association with a pneumothorax. With a large pneumothorax, a rounded density is occasionally seen overlapping the superior portion of a lower lobe, and hangs from the hilum when the patient is erect. This is due to a twisted collapsed upper lobe. This mechanism was confirmed by inducing a large (75 - 80%) right pneumothorax in a baboon, when the RUL twisted.
Pinstein et al. (1985) : Middle lobe torsion - wedge shaped opacity with a characteristically positioned oblique fissure, following right upper lobectomy in a baboon.

Munk et al. (1991) : Torsion of LUL following repair of aortic rupture after car deceleration injury. It became consolidated. Pulmonary angiography showed a very slowed circulation.

Graham et al. (1992) : Lung torsion after percutaneous lung needle biopsy of the lung - also had a pneumothorax.

Grillo et al. (1992) : 11 cases of post-pneumonectomy syndrome - air-way obstruction after R pneumonectomy with extreme mediastinal shift (7 cases) and after L pneumonectomy with R aortic arch (4 cases) - delay in presentation following surgery varied from 5 months to 17 years.

Spizarny et al. (1998) : Torsion of the RUL following clearing of ARDS infiltration subsequent to upper GI bleeding in a man aged 42 with cirrhosis and varices. A pulm. angio. showed the RUL artery to be narrowed, displaced inferiorly & feeding consol. lung at R base. The RUL bronchus was occluded at bronchoscopy with no endobronchial lesion. A 90° RUL torsion was found at surgery, the specimen showing haemorrhagic infarction.

Gilkeson et al. (2000) : Helical CT of lung torsion after lung transplantation.

Lung herniation.

A true lung hernia is a protrusion of the lung, covered by parietal and visceral pleura, outside the normal boundaries of the pleural cavity. Such may occur in the neck, in the chest wall, through the diaphragm or into the pericardium.

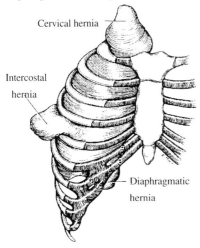
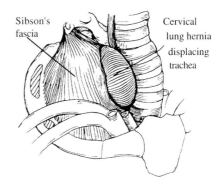

Fig. 2.39 (a) Diagram showing cervical, intercostal and diaphragmatic lung herniae
(Reproduced from Moncada et al., 1996, Congenital and acquired lung hernias. Journal of Thoracic Imaging, **11**, 75 - 82, with permission).

(b) Cervical lung hernia through or alongside Sibson's fascia and displacing the trachea to the left.
(Reproduced from McAdams et al., 1996, Apical lung hernia: radiologic findings in six cases. AJR, **167**, 927 - 930, with permission).

Cervical herniae are usually right sided and when large may (like a goitre) pass through a defect in the deep cervical or Sibson's fascia, which covers the pleural apex (Fig. 2.39). A gap may be present between the sternomastoid and anterior scalene muscles, through which the hernia protrudes. The hernia is essentially an exaggeration of the not uncommon extension of the lungs into the base of the neck. They are most easily seen on lateral radiographs producing '**air goitres**' when the patient coughs, strains or forcibly exhales (Illus. **LUNG HERNIA, Pts. 2, 3a-c &4**). These herniae, like laryngocoeles, may be accentuated in people who have a chronic cough, play wind instruments or lift heavy weights. One memorable case that the author investigated (using a series of lateral lower neck views taken during straining and coughing on 100 mm film under fluoroscopic control) had his mother laugh whilst watching the procedure and reveal that she had the same anomaly!

Other causes of '**air goitres**' include tracheocoeles (see p. 3.6), laryngocoeles (see p. 12.4) or large posterior pharyngeal ('Zenker's') diverticula (p. 16.8). They may be mimicked by fatty lumps (Illus. **LUNG HERNIA, Pt. 6a-b**).

Lung herniae extending into the chest wall are rare. They are usually caused by trauma, and are associated often with rib fractures, but may also follow chest wall abscesses or surgery, particularly the drainage of an empyema treated by rib resection or tube drainage. They largely depend on adhesions for their continuance, as otherwise lung which has passed into the chest wall would be sucked back into the chest with the negative pressure of inspiration, and without the affected part of lung being trapped in a false or herniated pleural sac they would be expected to spontaneously reduce and become obliterated. However an emphysematous lung may poorly deflate in expiration, and this may be a factor in their persistence.

Resections of adjacent ribs (e.g. for lung cancer spreading into the chest wall or for a chest wall tumour) or a chest wall defect in Poland's syndrome (p. 12.17) may also lead to lung herniae. In postoperative cases a hernia may be more likely after assisted respiration or with emphysema.

Clinically lung herniae in the chest wall give rise to crepitant masses, which alter in size with respiration, coughing, straining, or on palpation. They may occasionally cause mild discomfort.

Radiographically lung will be demonstrated outside the normal confines of the pleural cavity, and this may be noted at fluoroscopy, on 'spot views' or tomograms, including CT.

Trans-diaphragmatic lung herniae are very rare, but small tongues of lung may be found tucking into the retro-crural areas on CT sections in about 1% of adults as small Bochdalek herniae (see also ps. 15.16 - 15.17 & Fig. 15.10).

Lung herniation across the mediastinum may follow collapse of a lung or lobe, a lobectomy or pneumonectomy. It occurs much more commonly from right to left than the reverse. This may be because the aorta lying to the left of the spine tends to prevent the left lung herniating posteriorly into the azygo-oesophageal recess, and with a right sided collapse, or following a right pneumonectomy, the space is mainly filled by cross movement of the mediastinum towards the right.

A left pneumonectomy or collapse of the left lung or upper lobe commonly produces anterior herniation, as well as rotation and posterior displacement of the heart into the left hemithorax. Alternatively herniation may occur posteriorly through the pleural recesses above and below the azygos arch (the 'azygo-oesophageal recesses') between the aorta and spine posteriorly and the rest of the mediastinum, including the oesophagus anteriorly. Masses or large pleural effusions may also cross the mediastinum and fill the azygos recesses behind the heart, and extend across the mediastinum to the left (Illus. **LUNG HERNIA, Pl fibroma Pt. 1c**). Similar extension may be seen with a tension pneumothorax, and this may occasionally make left-sided retro-cardiac abnormalities more obvious.

Occasionally following a long standing right pneumonectomy, the left lung may herniate anteriorly into the right pleural cavity, causing counter-clockwise rotation of the heart and great vessels and with compression of the lower trachea or left main bronchus between the aorta and pulmonary arteries.

Lung herniation into the pericardium may occur when a small portion of the lung passes through a congenital or surgical defect into the pericardial sac (Fig. 15.21).

For illustrations of lung herniae see Illus. **LUNG HERNIA.**

References
General :
Roland (1499), Morel-Lavallee (1845 - 1847), Goodman (1933),
Hartung and Grossman (1941) : Case report and brief review.
Maurer and Blades (1946), Hurwich (1949)
Lodin (1957) : Herniation of the mediastinum and contralateral lung studied by transverse axial tomography.
Donato et al. (1973) : Spontaneous lung hernia.
Prasad et al. (1990)
Moncada et al. (1996) : Congenital and acquired lung hernias.

Cervical or apical lung hernia :
Graham (1922) : Hernia of lung and adenoma of the thyroid.
Palazzo and Garnett (1951), Reinhart and Hermel (1951), Fenichel and Epstein (1955) - 20 cases, Bidstrup et al. (1966) 22 cases - they felt that acquired cervical lung herniae were common in elderly people with a chronic cough and emphysema, in whom the deep cervical fascia becomes weakened and strained.
Cunningham and Peter (1969) : Cervical hernia of the lung associated with '**cri du chat**' syndrome.
Jones (1970) : Cervical hernia of the lung.
Lightwood and Cleland (1974) : Cervical lung hernia.
Grunebaum and Griscom (1978) : Protrusion of the lung apex through Sibson's fascia in infancy.
Bhalla et al. (1990) : see below.
Li and Miller (1990) : Air in the neck.
McAdams et al. (1996) : Apical lung hernia in 6 cases.

Post-traumatic and thoracic wall herniae :
Taylor and Jacobson (1962), Munnell (1968).
Seibel et al. (1987) : Mammographic and CT detection of extra-thoracic lung hernia.
Bhalla et al. (1990) : Radiographic features of lung herniae - described five cases - two congenital cervical herniae in infants, one post-traumatic intercostal hernia seen on a plain chest radiograph and confirmed by CT, and two acquired intercostal herniae at the site of previous intercostal tube drainage of tuberculous empyemas.
Scullion et al. (1994) : Herniation of tongue of RLL into postero-lateral chest wall in a 60 year old man with chronic airways disease and old adjacent healed rib fractures (Plain films and CT).

Diaphragmatic hernia (see also Chapter 15) :
Beale (1882) : On a case of hernia of the lung through the diaphragm.

Post-pneumonectomy:
Fisch et al. (1968) : Right to left., Shephard et al. (1986) : Left to right.
Sukumaran and Berger (1979) : Mediastinal herniation of pleural sac in massive pleural effusion.
Hipona and Crummy (1964) : Lung hernia into pericardium.
Heitzman (1977 and 1988).

Chapter 3 : **Tracheal and Bronchial Developmental Abnormalities, and Inflammatory Diseases including Bronchiectasis, Cystic Fibrosis and Bronchiolitis.**

Tracheal and carinal abnormalities (including narrowing).
Radiological inspection of the trachea is often limited to noting displacement by goitres or other large masses. Intraluminal masses are often not seen, and this is partly due to the poor demonstration of the trachea, carina and larger bronchi on low KV radiographs. On high KV or well exposed radiographs they are usually shown quite well, and can be even better demonstrated on tomograms, particularly inclined frontal radiographs. As well as being deformed by intra-luminal masses, these larger airways may be compressed, or invaded by tumours outside them - either extension of bronchial tumours into the hilum or mediastinum, or by secondary tumours e.g. from breast, kidney, etc. Secondary tumours may also 'creep along' the larger air passages, and severely narrow them. Any adjacent mass, whether malignant or benign, may also cause deformity of these by compression - such masses include aneurysms, goitres, oesophageal tumours or diverticula, enlarged nodes, abscesses, bronchogenic or other cysts etc. (Soft nodes with sarcoidosis however rarely cause compression).

Stark (1982 c) wrote: "the trachea should be visible on every film of the thorax and should always be inspected - in particular, a stridor should direct particular attention to the trachea. " The author agrees with this and feels that **in patients with a stridor, the larger airways should always be closely inspected for narrowings or endobronchial masses, and when there is doubt tomograms should be taken.**

Berkmen (1984) termed the trachea the '**blind spot in the chest**' and noted that 'inadvertent overlooking of obvious findings can occur despite proper exposure, perhaps owing to radiologists tendency to examine the trachea less carefully than other structures on the chest Roentgenogram'.

Displacement and narrowing may occur both in the coronal and sagittal planes. Goitres may slip behind it, and cause anterior bowing, as may altered posture with kyphosis. Tortuosity is common with raised hila and upper lobe fibrosis. As well as the normal aortic arch impression, the trachea may be slightly indented by the innominate artery, azygos vein or a dilated ascending aorta.

Spurious narrowing may be simulated by superimposition of other lines or structures e.g. junction lines (see p.1.10 - 17). Students commonly mistake the 'space' between the two borders of the scapulae as seen on lateral radiographs for the trachea, but this is unlikely to he done by the experienced observer. A dilated air filled oesophagus (as with achalasia) may simulate tracheomegaly (see Illus. **OES-GAS**).

The trachea normally moves independently from the aorta on swallowing, but when fixed by fibrosis or tumour, the upward movement of the trachea on swallowing may be transmitted to the aorta, and both may be seen to move together on TV fluoroscopy.

The trachea - **normal appearances**-
The trachea forms the axis of the mediastinum. Its intra-thoracic part varies from 6 to about 9 cms in length. It deviates slightly to the right in the upper mediastinum. The aortic arch commonly imprints it. On the right, the pleura contacts it to form the '**para-tracheal line**' or 'stripe', which is a good sign of normality in this area. 'The apparent thickness of its wall does not normally exceed 0.5 cm. The SVC lies in front of this line, but usually takes no part in its formation. A '**posterior tracheal line**' (or retro-tracheal band) is similarly seen on lateral radiographs. This may be effaced with oesophageal tumours, enlarged adjacent nodes or inflammatory lung changes. (For further details see p. 1.23).

The tracheal walls are parallel, except for the slight aortic impression; the azygos vein lies on its right side, just above the right main bronchus.

Normally the trachea is somewhat horse-shoe shaped in cross section, with the 'open part' lying posteriorly. It alters in calibre with respiration and coughing. This is particularly well seen in the neck, where the posterior part is more mobile and may flap anteriorly. The flap may be more mobile in females (Griscom and Wohl, 1983), but is less marked in the intra-thoracic portion.*

*NB Tumours mostly compress the trachea from side-to-side, or push in its posterior aspect.

Inspiration   Expiration   Forced expiration against a closed glottis

Fig. 3.1   Shape of the trachea in cross section with respiration.

The 'horse-shoe' shape of tracheal cartilages extends down to the lower trachea, but progressively changes to the more bronchial type comma shaped overlapping cartilages.

The normal trachea varies in diameter in men from about 1.3 to 2.5 cm, and in women from about 1 to 2.1 cm. The sagittal diameters may be about 2 mm longer than the coronal. (These diameters have been studied by several writers including: Brown et al, 1983, Breatnach et al., 1984 in adults, and by Griscom, 1982 and 1983 in children and adolescents).

Further references.
Effman et al. (1983) and Vock et al. (1984) : Used CT to assess the cross-sectional area of the trachea in children and adults respectively.
Stern et al. (1993) : Dynamic CT measurements of normal trachea during forced expiration - the mean cross-sectional area decreased from 280 mm^2 at the end of inspiration to 178 mm^2 at the end of expiration.

Table 3.1   Causes of tracheo-bronchial obstruction/ compression.
Thyroid hypertrophy, cysts or tumours.
Mediastinal cysts, tumours, etc.
Air-way tumours - benign - adenoma, papilloma, lipoma, neurofibroma, etc.
               malignant - carcinoma, cylindroma, etc.
               secondary endo-bronchial tumour - lung, breast, melanoma, neural tumours, reticulosis, etc.
Blood clot, mucus plugs, inhaled foreign bodies, injury, etc.
Broncho- or tracheo- or broncho-stenosis - congenital, tuberculosis, sarcoid, broncholithiasis or tumour.
Nodal pressure - neoplasm from lung or elsewhere, reticulosis - also TB, amyloid, rheumatoid, etc.

Techniques for examining the trachea.
These include plain radiography, spot views under TV fluoroscopic control, xerograms (now rarely done as the equipment is not often available, and the radiation dose is high) or tomography. Longitudinal tomograms will show its length and lumen, inclined frontal tomograms (see Illus. **INCL FRONTAL TOMO**) have been ideal for showing the walls, lumen and adjacent normal structures or masses.

CT will also show coronal narrowing (e.g. compression by a goitre, scabbard trachea, etc.), invasion of the tracheal wall, and occasionally intra-luminal extension of a tumour. 3D CT is also now able to give longitudinal reconstructions of the trachea (Illus. **CT-SPIRAL,   Trachea polychond Pt. 1**).

Positive contrast tracheograms (like bronchograms) are now rarely carried out.

Further references.
Harle et al. (1975) : Xerotomography of the tracheo-bronchial tree.
Muhm and Crowe (1976) : Tomography or tracheal abnormalities.
Kittredge (1981) : CT of the trachea - there is considerable variability in the shape, position and relationship of the trachea to other structures - it may also be round, oval. or concave posteriorly.
Gamsu and Webb (1982) : Normal and abnormal appearances of the trachea on CT.
               (1983) : CT of the trachea and main stem bronchi.
Kwong et al. (1993) : CT is superior to chest radiography in diagnosing diseases of the trachea and main bronchi.
Webb et al. (2000) : CT to diagnose non-neoplastic tracheal and tracheal wall abnormalities.

Tracheal bifurcation, carinal or sub-carinal angle.

The usual sub-carinal angle is about 70%, but varies from about 40% to 75% with respiration. It may he increased by enlarged sub-carinal nodes, left atrial enlargement or a pericardial effusion. It may also be widened by the elevation of a main bronchus associated with an upper lobe collapse. Malignant sub-carinal nodes tend to cause much more deformity of the carina and larger bronchi, than softer nodes due to sarcoidosis, lymphoma or leukaemia.

References.
Avali et al. (1970) : The angle of tracheal bifurcation.
Haskin and Goodman (1982) : A re-assessment of the normal tracheal bifurcation angle.
Chen et al. (1982) : Widening of the sub-carinal angle by pericardial effusion.
Cleveland (1979) : Symmetry of bronchial angles in children.
Murray et al. (1995) : Widening of the tracheal bifurcation on chest radiographs is an insensitive and non-specific sign of left atrial enlargement and is of little value in its diagnosis.

Buckling of the trachea.

In old age the trachea tends to elongate. It then becomes too long and tends to buckle. Buckling may also be produced by upper lobe fibrosis or collapse, particularly when this is bilateral.

Scabbard trachea.

A 'scabbard' or 'sabre-sheath' shaped trachea may be found in some patients with emphysema and obstructive air-ways disease, and in a few normals also. When present, the trachea is usually of normal shape above the thoracic inlet, though narrowed below it. Its shape is presumably due to chronic pressure on the trachea secondary to forced expiration. It is best seen on CT sections.

Fig. 3.2   The scabbard trachea
See also Illus. **TRACHEA-SCABBARD**.

References.
Greene and Lechner (1975), Greene (1978), Rubinstein et al. (1978).
Pilate et al. (1978) : CT of 'sabre-sheath' trachea.
Hoskins et al. (1991) : 'Sabre-sheath' trachea with mediastinal lipomatosis mimicking a mediastinal tumour - 2 cases shown by CT.

Tracheal stenosis (diffuse).

This may be accompanied by tracheal softening (see above) or occur per se.
Some patients may have a very narrow trachea from a developmental cause (Illus. **TRAC&BRON NARROWING 3**) whilst others develop it as a result of inflammatory disease, fibrous mediastinitis or diffusely spreading neoplasm (e.g. metastasis from breast carcinoma).

References.

Wolman (1941) : 11 cases in literature
 - 2 types -
(a) short narrowing of the trachea,
with a normal calibre below the stricture and
(b) funnelling of the trachea down to the carina.
(Drawings reproduced from Sidaway, 1963,
with permission from Brit. J. Radiol.)

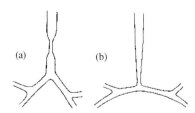

(a)   (b)

Sidaway (1963) : Congenital tracheal stenosis - 2 cases.
Hemmingson and Lindgren (1978) : Tracheal stenosis - 55 cases - high KV ? better than tomography - also used positive contrast tracheography.
James et al. (1980) : Tracheal stenosis as the presenting feature of fibrosing mediastinitis.
Choplin et al. (1983) : Diffuse lesions of the trachea.
Lui and Daneman (1984) : Used CT for demonstrating laryngeal and tracheal abnormalities in children - mainly cases of stenosis and one case each of congenital and acquired tracheo-oesophageal fistula.

Tracheomalacia.

Softening of the trachea may be caused by external pressure from long-standing external masses such as enlarged nodes in lymphoma, or from tumour masses such as goitres. It may also be secondary to damage from polychondritis (p. 3.7) or following long-standing intubation (see below). The danger is that following anaesthesia, the trachea may collapse when the endotracheal tube is withdrawn, and this may lead to respiratory obstruction, particularly in the recovery period. In such cases, local anaesthesia for biopsy, or an awareness of the possibility developing, should promote later extubation, or a silicon rubber (Westaby et al., 1982) or expandable metal stent may be inserted. Even in children, considerable tracheal compression may be produced by mediastinal masses (see Kirks et al., 1983).

Complications of tracheostomy, and long standing endo-tracheal tubes.

These include stenosis, granulation tissue and tracheomalacia, which allows dilatation in inspiration and collapse in expiration. They mostly occur at or close to the position where a cuff has been inflated. Pressure from this, particularly with head and neck movement, may cause damage, with local tissue necrosis - it may also occur at the tip of a long-standing metal tube. Lesions are usually short, and thin 'webs' may be difficult to demonstrate by radiography, except on high quality tomograms (Illus. **ENDOTRACHEAL TUBE, Tracheal stricture 1 - 11**). Rarely the cuff of an inflatable tube may cause perforation if inflated too hard and lead to abscess formation, etc. This may be suspected on radiographs by the tube-balloon size, gas in the mediastinum, the tube being deviated to the right, or migration of the inflated cuff towards the tube-tip. A long standing tracheo-oesophageal, fistula due to this cause is described on p. 16.11.

Fig. 3.3 Mechanism of stomal stenosis, granuloma formation, tracheomalacia (at the site of the inflatable cuff) and stricturing following tracheostomy (after Weber, AL and Grillo, HC, 1978, Tracheal stenosis. An analysis of 151 cases. Radiologic Clinics of North America, **16**, 291 - 308, by permission from WB Saunders Company).

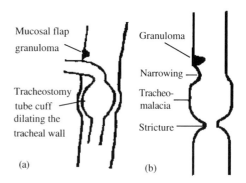

References.

James et al. (1970) : Radiology of tracheal stenosis resulting from cuffed endo-tracheal tubes.
Pearson and Andrews (1971) : 60 pts. with symptomatic post-tracheostomy stricture - 20 stomal & 20 cuff-strictures were treated surgically.
MacMillan et al. (1973) : Radiological evaluation of post-tracheostomy lesions - stenosis, granulation tissue, tracheomalacia and perforation.
Grillo (1979) : Surgical treatment of post-intubation tracheal injuries. Weber and Grillo (1978b) : 151 cases.
Rollins and Tocino (1987) : Early radiographic signs of tracheal rupture.
Newman and Oh (1994) : Iatrogenic tracheobronchial perforation of endotracheal tubes in infants (4 cases).
Spittle and McCluskey (2000) : 3cm tracheal stenosis from thyroid isthmus to manubrium sterni presenting as 'severe asthma' in a 16 yr old youth following intubation after mechanical ventilation 7 wks after RTA head injury.
Dikkers (2001) : Tracheal stenosis can occur 20 yrs after intubation - case due to 60 mins intubation.

Tracheo- and tracheo-bronchomegaly.
(a) The Mounier-Kuhn syndrome.

This disorder which produces a marked dilatation of the trachea and larger bronchi has often been considered to be rare, but is becoming increasingly recognised in association with lower (and often recurrent) respiratory tract infections and bronchiectasis. Some patients have no symptoms, whilst others have repeated respiratory infections, often with a loud rasping and ineffective cough. They may go down-hill rapidly when cor pulmonale supervenes. Most cases occur in middle aged men, but the presentation can be at all ages. Some cases appear to be familial. The cause appears to be a congenital defect or atrophy of the elastic and smooth muscle of the trachea and larger bronchi. CT is very useful for showing the tracheo-bronchial abnormalites. The walls are often thinned as well as dilated, and tend to pout between atrophied and stretched tracheal rings giving rise to an irregularly corrugated appearance, and/or small posteriorly situated diverticula. In addition many cases show bronchiectasis, which is often saccular in type. The condition may progress onto tracheo-bronchomalacia.
For illustrations - see Illus. **MOUNIER-KUHN**.

References.
Mounier-Kuhn (1932), Katz et al. (1962), Zismor et al. (1965), Aaby and Blake (1966), Bateson and Woo-Ming (1973), Gay and Dee (1984), Midenberger and Schild (1988), Shin et al. (1988), Van Schoor et al. (1991) : two cases, Woodring et al. (1991) : 10 cases, Schraufnagel and Boomsma (1992)
Johnston and Green (1964) : Five cases and demonstration of familial occurrence.
Rindsberg et al. (1987) : MRI appearances.
Dunne and Reiner (1988), Shin et al. (1988), Doyle (1989) : CT appearances.
Messahel (1989) : Tracheal dilatation followed by stenosis in Mounier-Kuhn syndrome.
Roditi and Weir (1994) : The association of tracheomegaly and bronchiectasis - felt that enlarged major airways are a potentiating factor for the development of bronchiectasis due to impaired clearance used measurements of AP and transverse diameters of the trachea at aortic arch level for comparison between individuals.
Smith et al. (1994) : 56 year old man with severe life-threatening pneumonia, and no CT evidence of bronchiectasis.
Collard et al. (1996) : Respiratory failure due to tracheo-bronchomalacia secondary to tracheo-bronchomegaly and treated by a Y shaped tracheobronchial stent.

(b) The Williams-Campbell syndrome (congenital bronchiectasis due to bronchial cartilage deficiency).

In this condition there is a deficiency of cartilage in the bronchial walls, which leads to generalised bronchiectasis and spontaneous haemoptyses which may be severe.

References.
Williams, H. and Campbell (1960), Williams et al. (1972), Al-Mallah and Quantock (1986), Rahbar and Tabatabai (1971), Mitchell and Bury (1975)
Wayne and Taussig (1976) : Probable familial congenital bronchiectasis due to cartilage deficiency (Williams-Campbell syndrome).
Watanabe et al. (1987) : CT.

(c) Other conditions causing a large trachea.
(i) Cystic fibrosis or chronic fibrotic lung disease.

In the former the trachea may be abnormally flaccid and irregular in shape, probably caused by years of frequent vigorous coughing. In the latter the enlargement may be partly due to hilar elevation and buckling of the trachea.
(ii) **Ehlers-Danlos syndrome**, with poor or absent elastic tissue - see also ps. 10.15 - 10.17.
(iii) **Ankylosing spondylitis** - see also ps. 12.29 & 19.90 - 19.91.

References.
Wonderer et al. (1969) : Tracheobronchomegaly and acquired cutis laxa in a child.
Ayres et al. (1981) : Haemoptysis and non-organic upper airways obstruction in a patient with previously undiagnosed Ehlers-Danlos syndrome.
Ayres et al. (1985) : Abnormalities of the lungs and thoracic cage in the Ehlers-Danlos syndrome.
Griscom et al. (1987) : The trachea in older patients with cystic fibrosis.
Woodring et al. (1989) : Acquired tracheomegaly in adults as a complication of diffuse pulmonary fibrosis.
Padley et al. (1991) : Ankylosing spondylitis - single case report.

(d) **Idiopathic** (see Illus. **TRACHEOMEGALY, Pts. 3a-c & 4**).

Often no cause is found for a large trachea, which may be a normal variant and of no clinical importance. Some older people have larger tracheas. Johnston and Green (1964) reported a familial group and suggested a possible autosomal dominant mode of inheritance.

Tracheocoeles and tracheal diverticula.

Tracheocoeles are rare and are a cause of an '**air goitre**' - a swelling that appears with straining and disappears when this is relaxed (see also p. 2.39). **Diverticula** are also very uncommon and may represent blind aberrant bronchial buds or occur in association with severe lung or bronchial scarring.

References.
Gronner and Trevino (1971) : Reported a tracheocoele and quoted two others from the literature.
Ettman and Keel (1962) : Tracheal diverticulosis.
Suprenant and O'Loughlin (1966) : Tracheal diverticula and tracheobronchomegaly.
Goo et al. (1999) : R paratracheal cysts in the thoracic inlet in a patient with tracheomegaly.

Tracheal and bronchial calcification.

Tracheal ring and bronchial cartilage calcification is relatively common over the age of 40 and is usually of no clinical importance, but may be more common with hypercalcaemia and hyperphosphataemia. It occasionally occurs in children and adolescents, and may then be due to the condition known as '**tracheo- and broncho-pathia osteoplastica**', in which small submucosal cartilage particles become calcified, as well as the tracheal and bronchial cartilages. This calcification may be demonstrated by tomography, including CT, and the tiny polypoid 'knobs' may also be visualised at bronchoscopy. An isotope bone scan may show increased uptake of isotope labelled phosphate compounds in the ectopic bone and calcified areas. In the majority of cases no symptoms are produced, but if the small bronchi are affected, obstruction and complicating infection may supervene. The author has seen a few cases, including twin sisters aged six (Illus. **TRACHEOPATH-OSTEOPLAS**).

Fig. 3.4   Triangular thickened
trachea in tracheopathia osteoplastica
as shown by CT.

Tracheo-bronchial calcification may also be seen in children who have been on long term treatment with **Warfarin**, or who were subjected to this during development in pregnancy.

References.
Lloyd and Taylor (1990) : Studied tracheal calcification by CT in 96 males and 96 females and found an increased incidence of calcification with increasing age. 65 % of males over 60 showed it and 40 % of females. About 25 % of males and females showed it over 40 years of age.

Tracheo-broncho-pathia osteoplastica.
Wilks (1857) : Ossific deposits on the larynx, trachea and bronchi.
Aschoff (1910), Howland and Good (1958), Secrest et al. (1964), Way (1967), Young et al. (1980), Lundgren & Lundgren and Sternberg (1981), Clee (1983), Spencer (1985)
Whitehouse (1968) : Tracheopathia   Gautam (1968) : review.
Rifkin and Pritzker (1984) : Tracheobronchial calcification in children.
Alroy et al. (1972) : ? end stage of primary lung amyloidosis.

CT of tracheo-broncho-pathia osteoplastica
Bottles et al. (1983), Onitsuka et al (1983), Hirsch et al. (1985), Manning et al. (1988), Akyol et al. (1993).
Hodges and Israel (1988) : Presentation with RML collapse - diagnosis by bronchoscopy and CT.

Mariotta et al. (1997) : Spiral CT and endoscopic findings in a case of tracheo-bronchopathia osteochondroplastica.

Abbott et al. (1977) : Chondrodysplasia punctata and maternal Warfarin.
Struwe et al. (1977) : Coumarin embryopathie.
Taybi and Capitanio (1990) : Tracheo-bronchial calcification in three children following mitral valve replacement and Warfarin treatment.

Relapsing polychondritis.
    This is a rare inflammatory disorder, sometimes associated with rheumatoid arthritis, but mostly of unknown cause, which affects the cartilage in the nose, causing a 'saddle-nose' deformity (also seen with congenital syphilis), ears, larynx, trachea, larger bronchi, costal cartilages, and joints. Narrowing of the trachea and bronchi may occur. Steroids and broncho-dilators may be helpful. Young patients with laryngo-tracheal involvement may have a worse prognosis than those with tracheo-bronchial disease. During relapses acid mucopolysaccharides may be recovered from the urine, and sometimes the patients develop glomerulo-nephritis and renal failure. A case is shown in Illus. **TRACHEA-CHONDRITIS.**

References.
Kaye and Soner (1964) : Relapsing polychondritis - 14 cases.
Gibson and Davis (1974) : Respiratory complications of relapsing polychondritis.
McAdam et al. (1976) : Prospective study of 25 patients with relapsing polychondritis and literature review.
Neild et al. (1978) : Relapsing polychondritis with crescentic glomerulonephritis.
Kilman (1979) : Narrowing of the airway in relapsing polychondritis.
Mendelson et al. (1985) : CT studies.
Rogerson et al. (1987) : Tracheal stenosis due to relapsing polychondritis in rheumatoid arthritis.
Crockford and Kerr (1988) : Four cases - plain films and tomograms.
Im et al. (1988) : CT of two patients with tracheal stenosis showed diffuse smooth tracheo-bronchial calcium deposition, especially within the thickened tracheal cartilage. Following steroid treatment the tracheo-bronchial wall thickening was decreased, and the tracheal lumina became normal.
Doherty et al. (1998) : Relapsing polychondritis presenting as tracheomalacia and causing air-flow flutter and a vibrating trachea in expiration in a 55 yr. old woman who died 10 yrs after initial presentation from acute broncho-pneumonia - at post-mortem much of the tracheo-broncho cartilage had been replaced by fibrous tissue.

Tracheal infection.
    Acute tracheitis is usually associated with the common upper respiratory tract infections and rarely merits further study, other than perhaps a plain chest radiograph to exclude a concomitant pneumonia.
    Some infections may give rise to tracheal abnormalities. In past times syphilis and tuberculosis gave rise to tracheitis and laryngitis. Fungal infections, particularly due to candida or aspergillosis, may give rise to tracheal ulceration, and partial obstruction from mucus plugs or fungal balls.
The author not long ago saw such a case, when the patient collapsed in the department, and after thumping his chest he coughed up a mucus plug over 6 ins long and about 1 cm in diameter. These may sometimes be seen in the trachea on plain radiographs. Such masses are sometimes termed '**mucoid pseudo-tumours**' (Illus. **TRACHEA-MUCUS PLUG**). When present they may cause considerable respiratory obstruction and lead to syncope and death. They often occur post-operatively, particularly after thoracic operations, and may be removed by coughing, physiotherapy or at bronchoscopy. They may complicate an asthmatic bronchitis or pneumonia, or be caused by fungus infections such as aspergillosis, candida, etc. Occasionally tomograms are needed for their confirmation, but often their presence may be inferred by the abrupt ending of the normal '**air tracheogram**', perhaps with the loss of air from a main bronchus. Lobar or lung collapse may also be present. A '**post-tussive**' study may show clearing. Recurrence may occur. Tracheal and/or main bronchial wall damage, metaplasia or keratinisation may predispose to their formation.
    Tracheal infection may be complicated by **acute epiglottitis**, a condition found more commonly in children than adults. It may cause severe sudden stridor and death. On lateral views a large epiglottis may be seen. It is usually enlarged by oedema.

Foreign bodies. (Illus. **FOREIGN BODY** and **FOREIGN BODY BRONCHUS**).

These are rarely seen in the trachea, most passing on into the bronchi. The author has seen a plastic tooth brush in the trachea, in a prisoner from Oxford Prison - it was causing only moderate stridor'! - he had also swallowed cutlery.

Tomography may be used to demonstrate endo-tracheal foreign bodies (e.g. meat bones). If the foreign body moves around the tracheo-bronchial tree (e.g. a pheasant's vertebra) it may give rise to a '**wandering type of pneumonia**' (see also ps. 19.1 & 19.59). Bronchiectasis is also a common feature with a chronic foreign body - Illus. **INHALED FB Pt. 12**. MR may demonstrate the fat within a peanut.

References.
Silverman (1945) : TB of the trachea and larger bronchi.
Boyden et al. (1970) : Adult epiglottitis presenting as a possible foreign body.
Spear et al.(1976) : Tracheal obstruction caused by a candida fungus ball.
Gerrish et al. (1987) : Adult epiglottitis (three cases).
Kaufman (1988) : Tracheal blastomycosis.

Mucoid pseudo-tumours of the trachea (and larger bronchi).
Karasich et al. (1979) : Two cases.
Shortsleeve and Foster (1979) , Keats (1973), Stark (1982d) : Post-tussive study.

Foreign bodies.
Berger et al. (1980) : Used CT to locate an occult tracheo-bronchial foreign body.
Adler et al. (1982) : CT localisation of FBs in the chest.
Newton et al. (1987) : CT detection of radiolucent denture base material.
O'Uchi et al. (1992) : MR imaging to detect peanut causing bronchial obstruction.
Imiazumi et al. (1994) : Diagnosis and localisation of peanuts in the airways using MR.
Kavanagh et al. (1999) : Most thoracic FBs are shown on plain CXRs. CT will show their location even if radiolucent - illustrations included a man aged 39 with retained secretions and secretions in the LUL due to an inhaled plastic whistle - c.f. Illus. **INHALED FB Pt. 12.**

Developmental abnormalities of the lungs and bronchi.

These are of many types, ranging from accessory or incomplete fissures (ps. 1.3 to 1.9), accessory bronchi, the scimitar, etc. syndrome to pulmonary hypoplasia or atresia of a lung, lobe or segmental bronchus. When only a segment is affected, collateral air-drift may allow that part of the lung to be aerated (see ps. 2.8 - 2.9), and it may even be hyperinflated (see below).

Most anomalies arise through some developmental failure of division of the primitive bronchial bud (which arises from the foregut) or its union with the primitive mesenchyme through which it grows. With some anomalies, the affected part of the lung retains its primitive blood supply from the aorta, and primitive veins may drain into the systemic veins.

In the following paragraphs the following are considered: agenesis, cystic adenomatoid malformation, 'loofa lung' lymphangiectasis, sequestrated lung segments and broncho-pulmonary foregut duplication cysts. Other developmental abnormalities are considered as follows: - immotile cilia syndrome (ps. 3.15 - 16), Swyer-James (or Macleod) syndrome (ps. 7.9 - 10), dysmorphic, hypoplastic or hypogenetic lung, and congenital veno-lobar and 'scimitar' syndromes (ps. 7.6 - 7).

Pulmonary and bronchial agenesis.

The tracheo-bronchial bud may fail to develop at any level. Blockage of the trachea is incompatible with extra-uterine life, but connections of it or the main bronchi to the oesophagus may produce a congenital fistula (ps. 16.10 - 11), and an abortive fistula may lead to a mid oesophageal diverticulum.

Blockage or failure of development of a main, lobar or segmental bronchus may occur, the major defects tending to present in infancy or childhood, whilst the more minor defects may be found only incidentally in adult life.

Agenesis usually refers to a complete absence of a lung and its bronchus. It may occur on either side, and this occurs in about equal numbers. Sometimes a small bronchial stump is present. Agenesis on the right tends to carry a poorer prognosis, probably due to the consequent mediastinal distortion. It may also result in the trachea being compressed by a stretched aorta. Herniation of the normal-sided lung may occur anteriorly and/or posteriorly (see also Fig. 7.5).

Atresia of a lobar, segmental or subsegmental bronchus often produces a mucus plug or bronchocoele, with the affected portion of lung aerated from collateral air-drift and giving rise to hyperinflation best seen **in expiration**. The most commonly affected segments are those of the apico-posterior segment of the left upper lobe and the apical segments of the lower lobes. Conventional tomograms and CT can readily show these abnormalities (see also Illus. **APLASIA-agenesis 3a-b**). The anomaly may be associated with air-filled cysts and may mimic sequestration with a large systemic vessel to the affected area.

CT is particularly useful for differentiation. In many patients with agenesis, the pulmonary artery on the affected side remains as large (or even larger) than on the opposite normal side. **Hypoplasia** is commonly associated with the scimitar syndrome (p.7.7) - often there is an absence of lobes, especially the RM & ULs, with an anomalous arterial supply and scimitar veins.

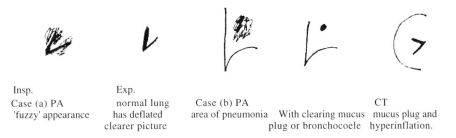

Insp.	Exp.			
Case (a) PA	normal lung	Case (b) PA		CT
'fuzzy' appearance	has deflated	area of pneumonia	With clearing mucus	mucus plug and
	clearer picture		plug or bronchocoele	hyperinflation.

Fig. 3.5   Some presentations of bronchial atresia - see also Illus. **APLASIA/HYPOPLASIA**.

References.

Falor and Kyriakides (1949) : Ectopia bronchi.
Ramsay (1953) : Mucocoele of the lung due to congenital obstruction of a segmental bronchus.
Schaffer and Rider (1957) : Note on prognosis of pulmonary agenesis and hypoplasia according to the side affected.
Sidaway (1963) : Congenital tracheal stenosis.
Simon and Reid (1963) : Atresia of apical bronchus of the left upper lobe - 3 cases.
Waddell et al. (1965) : Bronchial atresia of the left upper lobe.
Curry and Curry (1966) : Atresia of apico-posterior segment of the left upper lobe.
Généreux (1971) : Bronchial atresia.
Lacquet et al. (1971) : Bronchial atresia with corresponding segmental pulmonary emphysema.
Felson (1972) : Pulmonary agenesis and related abnormalities.
Harrison and Hendren (1975) : Agenesis of the lung complicated by vascular compression and bronchomalacia.
Meng et al. (1978) : Bronchial atresia.
Schuster et al. (1978) : Bronchial atresia - recognisable entity in the paediatric age group.
McCormick and Kuhns (1979) : Tracheal compression by a normal aorta associated with right lung agenesis.
Cohen et al. (1980) : CT in bronchial atresia.
Benson et al. (1985) : Broncho-pulmonary anomalies associated with tracheo-oesophageal malformations.
Jederlinic et al. (1986) : Congenital bronchial atresia - report of 4 cases & literature review.
Lau et al. (1987) : Bronchial atresia - radiographic, CT and bronchographic correlation.
Finck and Milne (1988) : Segmental bronchial atresia - CT and MRI.
Rémy-Jardin et al. (1989) : Bronchial atresia - diagnostic criteria and embryological considerations.
Dohlermann et al. (1990) : Deviated trachea in hypoplasia and aplasia of the right lung - airway obstruction and its release by aortopexy.
Argent and Cremin (1992) : CT in agenesis of the lung in infants - 3 cases (2 R and 1 L).
Kinsella et al. (1992) : 3 cases of bronchial atresia - boy of 14 with hyperinflation of the posterior basal segment of the LLL and air trapping in expiration; man aged 55 with atresia of the apical segmental bronchus of the right lower lobe causing gross hyperinflation and making it almost fill the chest; and male aged 25 with an ovoid density above the left hilum and increased radiolucency in the left upper zone with branching mucocoeles.
Kuln and Kuln (1992) : Co-existence of bronchial atresia and bronchogenic cyst.
Rappaport et al. (1994) : Congenital bronchopulmonary diseases in adults - CT findings - agenesis, atresia & hypoplasia, anomalous bronchial branches, foregut cysts, sequestration and AV malformations.
Rossoff and Steinberg (1994) : Bronchial atresia and mucocoele - a report of two cases.
Caceres (1996) : Congenital anomalies of the bronchial tree.

Wu et al. (1996) : Agenesis of the right lung, diagnosed by 3D reconstruction of helical CT - 2 girls aged 16 days and 14 yrs - individuals with L lung agenesis have a longer life expectancy than those with R lung agenesis, who have a greater incidence of heart and mediastinal shift with corresponding distortion of blood vessels and bronchi.
Ko et al. (1998) : Bronchial atresia associated with epibronchial right pulmonary artery and aberrant RML artery.
Ward and Morcos (1999) : Congenital bronchial atresia - three cases & pictorial review.

Bronchial tree anomalies are also discussed on p. 1.22 and mucocoeles + atresia on ps. 2.10 - 11.

Cystic adenomatoid malformation of the lung.

This rare anomaly is caused by proliferation of the bronchial structures at the expense of the alveoli, and produces a multicystic mass of pulmonary tissue. In many cases it is associated with bronchial atresia or occlusion. Like sequestration this condition may sometimes have a systemic blood supply and/or an associated scimitar vein (see ps. 7.7 - 8). The condition usually presents in babies and young children as basal masses, containing a disorganised overgrowth of cysts, often with a more solid component of bronchiolar or adenomatoid structures, containing smooth muscle, which has suggested a hamartomatous origin to some authors. Neighbouring bronchi may be grouped around it. Many patients with it have repeated chest infections.

Ultrasound may reveal the cystic nature of the fluid-filled masses, especially in children (Hartenberg and Brewer, 1983, and Cave and Adam, 1984).

If the cysts fill with air, this may produce a variety of the 'loofa lung'.

References.
Craig et al. (1956) : 4 cases - surgical resection in first two weeks of life.
Belanger et al. (1964) : Case report and literature review.
Moncrieff et al. (1969) : Congenital cystic adenomatoid malformation.
Madewell et al. (1975) : Morphologic analysis.
Tucker et al. (1977) : Fluid filled cystic adenomatoid malformation.
Uleda et al. (1977) : Rhabdomyosarcoma of the lung arising in a congenital cystic adenomatoid malformation.
Wexler and Valdes Dapena (1978) : Three cases - one showed a very large perfusion defect on an isotope perfusion scan which involved most of the left lung.
Miller et al. (1980) : Reported 17 cases and reviewed 142 from the literature.
Blane et al. (1981) : CT appearance., Hulnick et al. (1984) : Adults., Pulpeiro et al. (1987) : Young adult.
Shackelford and Siegel (1989)
Deacon et al. (1990) : The antenatal diagnosis of congenital cystic adenomatoid malformation of the lung.

'Loofa lung'

This produces diffuse cystic disease in a lobe, or lobes of one or both lungs. Recurrent infections may lead to surrounding consolidation and fluid levels with the cysts, which communicate with the bronchi. These are usually acute episodes which clear with antibiotics and physiotherapy. In severe cases a narrowed pulmonary artery to the affected lobe or lung, may show the greatly reduced blood supply to that part. An example with an acute exacerbation is illustrated in Illus. **LOOFA-LUNG**.

This condition may be related to adenomatoid malformation. It may manifest as '**congenital lobar emphysema**', if one or more lobes in a lung become 'overdistended' - this latter may be related to a deficiency in bronchial cartilage. Such a lobe usually presents in young children as a large hyperlucent lobe with decreased 'splayed out' vessels. In some cases it may show increased density, due to oedema or other fluid filling the cysts.

Other similar cases, may be caused by childhood infections of the adeno-virus type, and be related to the Swyer-James (Macleod) syndrome or the 'destroyed lung' condition (ps. 7.9 - 10 & 19.122 - 123). Some patients may have frank cystic bronchiectasis.

Pulmonary lymphangiectasis.

This may also produce cystic lung masses, or a mottled linear pattern in the lungs of children - see also section on lymphangioleiomyomatosis - ps. 5.18 - 19.

Congenital lobar emphysema may be associated with lymphatic abnormalities.

References.
Laurence (1959), Li et al. (1985)
Allen et al. (1966) : Congenital lobar emphysema with dilated lymphatics.
Leonidas et al. (1979) : Persistent localised pulmonary interstitial emphysema and lymphangiectasis.

Sequestrated lung segments (Illus. SEQUESTRATION).

Sequestration is essentially the isolation from the bronchial tree of a portion of lung tissue. The affected segments may be **intra**- or **extra**-lobar in type depending on whether they are separated from the rest of the lobe by an accessory fissure. They are usually basal in position, and although having no direct communication with the bronchi, may be aerated by collateral air drift (see p. 2.8 - 9) from adjacent segments (particularly in the intra-lobar type). As fissures separate the extra-lobar type from adjacent aerated lung, these mostly give rise to airless solid densities, but occasionally an incomplete fissure will allow some air to cross into the sequestrated segment. Both types may be confused with tumours, or mimic bronchiectasis if 'cavities' are present. These 'cavities' may be bullae or abscesses, and one area of the affected segment may be relatively airless, whilst the remainder is overdistended by such bullae. With infection fluid-levels may be seen, and repeated episodes of infection within such segments are common, as the contents cannot easily be coughed up, unless a secondary bronchial connection occurs. A bronchogram will show no bronchus passing to the segment in question (Illus. **SEQUESTRATION, Pts. 1c, d & e, 3cd, 6b & 7cd**).

These segments often have an abnormal blood supply with systemic arteries and veins. The artery may be very large and arise above or below the diaphragm (Illus. **SEQUESTRATION, Pts. 1f & 5b**). It is important to consider the condition before surgery, to make the surgeon aware of it, so that he may look for abnormal vessels before putting his hand under the lung to elevate and deflate it and thereby avoid damage to the vessels. Although pre-operative demonstration is not essential and only an awareness of the possibility, ultra-sound and CT have been to demonstrate the abnormal circulation. Ultra-sound was used by Kaude and Laurin (1984) and by Thind and Pilling (1985) in infants, CT identification of the supplying vessel was reported by Miller et al. (1982). Rarely the supplying artery may spontaneously rupture to form a haemothorax (Zumbro et al., 1974, & Zapatero et al., 1983) and the condition may be present in association with bronchial and pulmonary isomerism (Mohan et al., 1983). The condition may be bilateral (Karp, 1977 and Wimbish et al., 1983). Occasionally double or bilateral systemic vessels may be found with a sequestrated segment (McDowell et al., 1955 and Ennis et al., 1972). Collateral ventilation has been noted by Culiner and Wall (1965) and has been demonstrated by nuclear medicine ventilation studies (Hopkins et al., 1982). In the inter-lobar type, venous drainage is usually via the pulmonary veins, but in the extra-lobar type it may be to systemic veins.

The condition is interesting embryologically, as its occurrence indicates that the statement sometimes seen that the lung develops entirely from terminal budding of the primitive 'bronchial bud' is probably incorrect. As Davidson (1956) described, the lung develops in part from mesenchyme as well as the 'endodermal lung buds' (see Fig. 3.6), which form the bronchi and their branches and grow down into the mesenchyme (the development of the kidneys and ureters is similar!). If bronchial development fails in an area of the lung, then neither the bronchi, nor the pulmonary artery branches which grow in with it, will be present, and that part of the lung consisting of alveoli (and no bronchial elements) will retain its primitive and systemic blood supply. The veins which develop separately, are usually less affected and commonly pass to the pulmonary veins.

Fig. 3.6 Stages in the development of the endodermal lung buds (after Davidson, 1956, with permission from Clinical Radiology).

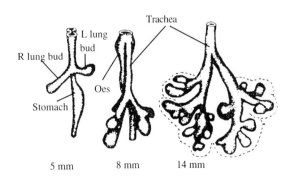

CT and angiography.

Paul and Mueller (1982) studied pulmonary sequestration by CT and demonstrated the supplying vessels as well as the air/or fluid filled spaces, usually at the left base. They found that 85% of sequestrations had no separate pleural investment and were therefore intra-lobar. Three-quarters of these had the arterial blood supply arising from the thoracic aorta, a blood supply from the abdominal aorta arising in only 20%, with the venous drainage being via the pulmonary veins; 13% of the sequestrations were extra-lobar, with systemic arterial and venous connections, and 2% were of mixed types. Radionucleide angiography and/or digital subtraction angiograms may also show the vessel connections, The aberrant vessel has also been shown by MR (Cohen et al., 1987, Oliphant et al., 1987, Naidich et al., 1988, and Doyle, 1992). These vessels run through the pulmonary ligaments - ps. 2.32 - 2.35.

The anomaly has also been found in horses and cows (Davidson, 1956) and a rabbit (Hansen and Olin, 1972).

Cysts and sequestration.

Sequestration may also be associated with bronchopulmonary reduplication cysts (bronchogenic and enteric cysts - see p. 3.12), also other developmental abnormalities such as ectopic pancreas, diaphragmatic herniae, etc. (Thornhill et al., 1982). Occasionally sequestrated segments may arise from the oesophagus (Gans and Potts, 1951). Both sequestration and developmental cysts may be variants of a similar malformation, and sequestrated segments may occasionally be found at the base of the thorax close to the diaphragm.

Diverticulosis of the main bronchi.

Barbato et al. (1993) from Padua described this anomaly in a boy of 12 associated with recurrent bronchopneumonia. It was demonstrated by bronchoscopy and Hytrast bronchography. Diverticulosis may also be seen with polychondritis and tracheo-bronchomegaly.

Tracheal and Oesophageal bronchi are discussed on p. 1.22.

Horse-shoe lung, accessory diaphragm & scimitar syndrome - see ps. 7.6 - 8.

Further references.
Pryce (1946) : Lower accessory pulmonary artery with intralobar sequestration - report of 7 cases.
Wyman and Eyler (1952) : Anomalous pulmonary artery from the aorta + intralobar sequestration.
Boyden (1955a) : Developmental anomalies of the lungs., (1958) : Bronchogenic cysts and sequestration.
McDowell et al. (1955) : Two cases of intralobar sequestration of the lung.
Abbey Smith (1956) : Suggested that the primary lesion in intralobar sequestration was failure of the pulmonary artery in foetal life to supply the segment of the lung involved.
Lynch et al. (1957) : Intralobar bronchopulmonary sequestration of the lung.
Beskin and Rouge (1961) : Intralobar enteric sequestration of the lung containing aberrant pancreas.
Turk and Lindskog (1961) : The importance of angiographic diagnosis in intralobar pulmonary sequestration.
Nielsen (1964) : Intralobar sequestration.
Ranniger and Valvassori (1964) : Angiographic diagnosis of intralobar sequestration.
Culiner and Wall (1965) : Collateral ventilation in 'intralobar pulmonary sequestration'.
Blesovsky (1967) : Pulmonary sequestration - unusual case and literature review.
Bates (1968) : Total sequestration of right lung in a boy aged 7 months - right main bronchus communicating with lower oesophagus - had a pneumonectomy.
Williams and Enumah (1968) : Extralobar pulmonary sequestration.
Köhler (1969) : Two-thirds of cases in LLL, one-third in RLL.
Felson (1972) : The many faces of pulmonary sequestration.
Zumbro et al. (1974) : Pulmonary sequestration with spontaneous intrapleural haemorrhage.
          (1975) : Pulmonary sequestration - a broad spectrum of bronchopulmonary foregut cysts.
Sade et al. (1974) : The spectrum of pulmonary sequestration.
Takahashi et al. (1975) : Intralobar sequestration.
Gooneratne and Conway (1976) : Radionucleide angiographic diagnosis of bronchopulmonary sequestration.
Kirks et al. (1976) : Systemic arterial supply to normal basal segments of the left lower lobe.
Karp (1977) : Bilateral sequestrations., Roe et al. (1980) : Bilateral sequestrations.
Turner and Hayward (1977) : Sequestrations may occasionally contain calcification.

Savic et al. (1979) : Lung sequestration - seven cases and review of **540 published cases - in the majority the arterial blood supply was from the descending thoracic or upper abdominal aorta.**
Choplin and Siegel (1980) : Pulmonary sequestration shown by CT.
Baker et al. (1982) : Retroperitoneal pulmonary sequestration shown by CT.
Miller et al. (1982) : Pulmonary sequestration - visualisation of the feeding artery by CT.
Mortiz et al. (1982) : Intralobar sequestration.   Paul and Mueller (1982) : Pulmonary sequestration.
Thornhill et al. (1982) : Gastric duplication associated with pulmonary sequestration CT findings.
Mohan et al. (1983) : Intralobar sequestration with bronchial isomerism.
Wimbish et al. (1983) : Bilateral sequestration - CT appearance.
Stocker and Malczak (1984) : A study of pulmonary ligament arteries - relationship to intralobar sequestration.
Zapatero et al. (1983) : Haemothorax as rare presentation of intralobar pulmonary sequestration.
Wojtowycz et al. (1984) : Calcified bronchopulmonary sequestration.
Kobayashi et al. (1985) : Radionucleide angiography in pulmonary sequestration,
Van Dyke and Sagel (1985) : Densely calcified sequestrated segment in LLL in patient with renal failure.
Buckwalter et al. (1987) : Bolus dynamic CT in the evaluation of sequestration.
Clements and Warner (1987) : Pulmonary sequestration and related bronchopulmonary vascular malformations.
Naidich et al. (1987) : MR evaluation.   Coblentz et al. (1988) : Calcified intralobar pulmonary sequestration.
Pedersen et al. (1988): CT of intralobar pulmonary sequestration in RLL with blood supply from right renal artery.
Creagh et al.(1989) : Radio-opaque hemithorax in a neonate due to right lung sequestration.
Felker and Tonkin (1990) : Imaging of pulmonary sequestration - case of bilateral **'oesophageal lung'** i.e. bronchi in the affected segments arising from lower oesophagus in an infant.
Ikezoe et al. (1990) : CT assessment of bronchopulmonary sequestration - characteristic manifestations -
(a) complex lesion containing solid or fluid components combined with emphysematous lung, or (b) any basal lesion supplied by a systemic artery.
Smart and Hendry (1991) : Imaging of neonatal pulmonary sequestration including Doppler ultrasound.
Stern et al. (1991) : Dynamic, ultrafast, HRCT evidence of air trapping and multicystic component of broncho-pulmonary sequestration.
Cerruti et al. (1993) : Bilateral intralobar pulmonary sequestration with **horseshoe lung** in a woman aged 20.
Kim et al. (1993) : Coexistent intralobar and extralobar sequestration on either side of the thorax in a child.
Schlesinger et al. (1994) : Sonography in the diagnosis of bronchopulmonary sequestration.
Amitai et al. (1996), Frush et al. (1997) : Helical CT angiography of pulmonary sequestration.
Herman-Schulman (1997) : Retroperitoneal pulmonary sequestration (about 2% of cases may be found in the new born) - report of 4 cases found as left juxta-adrenal cystic masses by ultra-sound + review of 15 from the literature.
Franco et al. (1998) : Diagnosis of pulmonary sequestration by spiral CT angiography.
Au et al. (1999) : 3D MR diagnosis of pulmonary sequestration.
Kopecky et al. (2000) : Subdiaphragmatic pulm. sequestration simulating metastatic testicular cancer.
Ko et al. (2000) : Noninvasive imaging of bronchopulmonary sequestration.
Arenas et al. (2001) : Systemic supply to normal RLL arising from the coeliac axis - CXR & spiral CT.

Broncho-pulmonary foregut duplication or bronchogenic cysts (also termed 'bronchial' or 'neurenteric' cysts).

These arise developmentally from abnormal budding of the tracheo-bronchial tree and foregut. They account for about 10% of primary mediastinal masses. They most commonly occur adjacent to the larger bronchi or the carina, and in the latter position they may press into the subcarinal area, where they may mimic nodal enlargement . They may also occur in other parts of the mediastinum (where they may be termed **'para-oesophageal'** or **'neurenteric'** cysts) or at the base of the neck. Their walls are most commonly formed by columnar type respiratory or oesophageal epithelium, with cartilage, muscle and mucous glands producing mucin. Their fluid content varies from clear and serous (hence the older term 'sweetwater cyst') to turbid or viscid mucus. The latter types may contain calcium (as 'calcospherites') in suspension or as a dependent density. Cornell et al. (1965) found a thin layer in the dependent parts. This has since been confirmed with CT, which has also shown that CT numbers of 40 HU or more within the cysts are not uncommon, and a few have shown fairly dense generalised calcium containing contents.

Radiologically they usually appear as solid or fluid-filled rounded or ovoid well-defined structures, a few contain **calcium within the fluid or in the wall of the cyst**. About 10% press into the lungs and appear to be intra-pulmonary, and these may develop a bronchial communication and contain air or air and fluid, with a fluid level on erect views. The thin walls of air filled cysts may become thickened with repeated infections, and this may lead to haemoptysis. Pressure on neighbouring bronchi may cause distortion, peripheral bronchiectasis or mucocoeles. Lobar collapse may also occur, especially in children, but also in adults (see Delarue et al., 1981 and other references below). When lying centrally they may press on the SVC, the pulmonary artery or other vessels, and SVC obstruction may occur if the cyst is distended following infection.

Most of the cysts are asymptomatic, and are found by chance. Symptoms mainly occur following infection (Haller et al., 1972). It is often possible to aspirate these cysts percutaneously under CT, fluoroscopic or ultrasound control. The last is particularly valuable when the cysts lie anteriorly or adjacent to the pericardium. More posteriorly lying cysts may be aspirated by a trans-bronchial, trans-oesophageal or para-spinal extra-pleural approach. Sclerosant fluid (e.g. alcohol) may be instilled into the cyst to try to prevent it refilling.

Cysts in the posterior mediastinum may be associated with vertebral anomalies, which are not always at the same vertebral level as the cysts. These anomalies may appear at a higher level, if the cyst has descended in the mediastinum, and may resemble neurofibromas or lateral thoracic meningocoeles (p. 18.35). Occasionally these cysts may have a connection with the spinal canal. Rarely bronchogenic cysts may occur in the diaphragm or diaphragmatic crura; these last may mimic adrenal masses. Rarely also, like Meckle's diverticula of the ileum, enteric cysts may contain gastric type mucosa, and develop peptic ulcers in their walls, leading to haemoptysis or haematemesis (Kirwan et al., 1973). They may also contain mural pancreatic tissue, and Carr et al. (1977) found a large left anterior mediastinal cyst containing acinar type pancreatic tissue and islets. Malignancy in such cysts is extremely rare, and the author has only been able to find a single report of such a case (Chuang et al., 1981). Such change is however more common in abdominal cysts (Rice et al., 1986). These cysts may be associated with **lung sequestration** (Mahour et al., 1971), McClelland et al., 1977 and Thornhill et al., 1982 - the last showed one case with CT). They may extend both above and below the diaphragm to give rise to a 'dumb-bell' type of bronchial cyst, with a raised right side of the diaphragm, double contour and basal collapse. (Amendola et al., 1982, described one case and referred to nine others from the literature). The small vessels passing to their walls may be of systemic origin.

Bronchial cysts containing fluid and/or air or mimicking nodal enlargements or tumours are shown in Illus. **BRONCHOGENIC CYST** and **BRONCH & MEDIAST CYSTS.**

Further references.

Wilson (1969) : Neurenteric cyst of the mediastinum. Doub (1950-51) : Mediastinal cysts of embryological origin.
Miller et al. (1953) : Bronchogenic cyst anomalies resulting from maldevelopment of primitive foregut and midgut.
Stoner and Kiragus (1957) : Bronchogenic cyst causing lung collapse in a child.
Neuhauser et al. (1958) : Roentgenographic features of neurenteric cysts.
Rogers and Osmer (1964) : Bronchogenic cysts - review of 48 cases.
Cornell (1965) : Calcium in the fluid of mediastinal bronchogenic cyst - a new Roentgenographic finding.
Baum et al. (1966) : Bronchial cysts are more common in males and Yemenite Jews.
Boyden (1968) : Bronchogenic cysts and theory of inter-lobar sequestration.
Ziter et al. (1969) : Calcified mediastinal bronchogenic cysts.
Berg (1970) : Giant bronchogenic cyst causing a 'pseudopneumothorax'.
BMJ, Editorial (1973) : Even a small bronchial cyst may cause pressure on adjacent structures.
Cubillo and Rockoff (1971) : Milk of calcium in intra-pulmonary bronchogenic cyst.
Ikard (1972) : Bronchogenic cyst causing repeated left lower lobe collapse in an adult.
Bergström et al. (1973) : Unusual Roentgen findings in bronchogenic cysts.
Kirwan et al. (1973) : Cystic intra-thoracic derivatives of foregut cysts and their complications, including leakage into the pericardium with tamponade.
Reed and Reeder (1974) : Retrocardiac position of these cysts is not uncommon.
Reed and Sobonya (1974) : Foregut cysts of the thorax - reviewed 77 bronchial (or respiratory) and 9 enteric cysts and found the former to be more common inferiorly, the latter tending to be more superior and posterior. Bronchial cysts tended to be juxtaposed about the carina and most were middle mediastinal.
Mahajan et al. (1975), Rammohan et al. (1975) : SVC compression caused by bronchogenic cyst.
Miller et al. (1978) : SVC and bronchial obstruction caused by recurrent bronchogenic cyst.
Marvasti et al. (1981) : Misleading density of mediastinal cysts on CT.
Bargallo et al. (1982) : Fluid-fluid level in bronchogenic cysts.
Nakata et al. (1982) : CT of mediastinal bronchogenic cysts.
Ries et al. (1982) : Real time ultrasound of subcarinal bronchial cysts in two children.
Mendelson et al. (1983) : Bronchial cysts with high CT numbers.
Weiss et al. (1983) : CT demonstration of oesophageal duplication cyst.
Godwin (1984) : Retro-crural cyst resembling a neurofibroma.
Watts et al. (1984) : Pulm. artery compression by a bronchogenic cyst simulating congenital pulm. artery stenosis.

duMontier et al. (1985) : 33 cases in children - mainly 2 - 3 cm cysts with sharply demarcated borders near to the carina or in the right para-tracheal area.
Bankoff et al. (1985) : Bronchial cyst causing SVC obstruction - CT appearances.
Kuhlman et al. (1985) : Oesophageal duplication cyst - CT and transoesophageal aspiration.
Williams and Schuster (1985) : Bronchial atresia associated with a bronchial cyst.
Nakata et al. (1986) : Analysed the contents of a bronchial cyst and found calcium present.
Yernault et al. (1986) : 'Solid' mediastinal bronchial cyst with mineralogical analysis.
Coselli et al. (1987) : Bronchogenic cysts above and below the diaphragm - report of eight cases.
Kuhlman et al. (1988) : Five adults with mediastinal cysts who had transbronchial or transoesophageal aspiration of serous or mucoid fluid following CT examinations.
Van Beers et al. (1989) : Fluid reaccumulation after transbronchial aspiration.
Adam et al. (1989) : CT guided extrapleural drainage of a bronchial cyst - a posterior paraspinal approach to a centrally positioned mediastinal cyst. (see also Whyte et al., 1989.)
Page et al. (1989) : Value of transoesophageal ultrasound in the management of a mediastinal foregut cyst. It showed layering of 'sludge' in the dependent part of the cyst which was aspirated percutaneously under fluoroscopic control.

Woodring et al. (1989) : Air-filled, multiloculated bronchopulmonary foregut duplication cyst of the mediastinum - unusual CT appearance - 2cm diameter cyst to the right of the trachea and the oesophagus and communicating with the trachea (35 year old woman).
Palmer et al. (1991) : Bilateral paraspinal bronchial cysts - bright signals in both cysts on MR.
Kuln and Kuln (1992) : Coexistence of bronchial atresia and a bronchogenic cyst.
Matzinger et al. (1992) : Spontaneous pneumothorax as the presenting sign of an intrapulmonary bronchogenic cyst.
Padovani et al. (1992) : CT & MR demonstration of intrapericardial bronchogenic cyst.
Lyon and McAdams (1993) : Fluid-fluid level in mediastinal bronchogenic cyst shown by MR.
De Nunzio and Evans (1994) : CT of mediastinal subcarinal bronchogenic cyst containing air-fluid level.
Fischbach et al. (1994) : Infradiaphragmatic bronchogenic cyst with high CT numbers in a boy with primitive neuroectoderm tumour.
LeBlanc et al. (1994) : MR of foregut cysts - two patterns (i) long T_1 (bright) and short T_2 values (typical of serous fluid collections) and (ii) short T_1 values (due to proteinaceous or haemorrhagic contents) and long T_2 (bright) - their six cysts were all round or oval and lay in the middle or posterior mediastinum.
Eustace et al. (1995) : Chest pain due to haemorrhage (dense on CT) into a bronchogenic cyst on R of mid dorsal spine and related to carina and RMB - was aspirated percutaneously.
Aydingöz et al. (1997) : Calcium within a bronchogenic cyst with a fluid level.
Cioffi et al. (1998) : Presentation & surgical management of bronchogenic & oes. duplication cysts in adults.

Aaron (1965) : Intradiaphragmatic cyst - a rare entity. Rozenblit et al. (1998) : Intradiaphragmatic bronchogenic cyst.
Gourlay and Aspinall (1966) : Bronchogenic cyst of the diaphragm.
Foerster et al. (1991) : Retroperitoneal bronchogenic cyst presenting as an adrenal mass.
Swanson et al. (1991) : Pseudoadrenal mass - unusual presentation of bronchogenic cyst.
Dagenais et al. (1995) : Bronchogenic cyst of the right hemidiaphragm.
McAdams et al. (2000) : Bronchogenic cyst imaging in 68 cases - MR can be useful in showing cystic nature.

Immotile-cilia syndrome.
    This condition also predisposes to chronic chest infections and bronchiectasis. Afzelius (1976) and Afzelius and Mossberg (1980) found that in men with immotile sperms, the cilia in the respiratory tract and elsewhere showed a similar defect. It may be the cause of some cases of chronic bronchitis (Trapnell, 1982). The abnormality is found in about half of the patients with **Kartagener's syndrome** (situs inversus, chronic sinusitis and bronchiectasis). This usually presents in childhood with a history of excessive nasal discharge, infections and the finding of nasal polyps. Nadel et al. (1985) studied its radiological appearances and found them to be non-specific; early changes including bronchial wall thickening, with or without hyperinflation. They illustrated their cases with electron micrographs showing - (i) complete dynein defect, (ii) radial spoke defect, and (iii) microtubular transposition. Greenstone et al. (1988) re-termed it the

'**primary ciliary dyskinesia**' syndrome, with a clinical picture of life-long sinusitis and recurrent bronchial infection, but much broader than Kartagener's syndrome (14 out of 30 of their patients having a normal cardiac position).

Cilia beat one after the other at up to 25 times/sec., and to be effective have to beat in a fluid medium of correct pH, salt concentration and temperature (Dunnill, 1982).

Bronchiectasis due to this cause tends to have a lower lobe predominance.

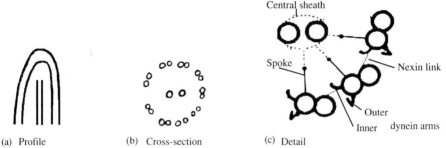

(a) Profile   (b) Cross-section   (c) Detail

Fig. 3.7   On electron microscopy cilia are seen to contain paired peripheral and central structures (normally 9 peripheral pairs + a central pair) with arms and spokes - (c) after Dunnill (1982) with permission from Churchill Livingstone.

Abnormalities   7 peripheral pairs + central pair
                          dynein defect
                          radial spoke defect
                          micro-tubular transposition.

Illustrations of Kartagener's syndrome are shown in Illus. **KARTAGENER'S   SYNDROME** and **SITUS INVERSUS.**

Further references.
Kartagener (1933) : A triad of bronchiectasis, sinusitis and situs inversus.
Kartagener and Stucki (1962) : Bronchiectasis with situs inversus.
Bergström et al. (1950) : 6 siblings - 2 with the triad & 2 others with bronchiectasis.
Miller and Divertie (1972) : Kartagener's syndrome.
Rott (1979) : Kartagener's syndrome and the syndrome of immotile cilia.
Whitelaw et al. (1981) : Immotile cilia syndrome - a new cause of neonatal respiratory distress.
Pedersen and Mygind (1982) : Rhinitis, sinusitis and otitis media in Kartagener's syndrome (primary ciliary dyskinesia).
Shebab and Pearman (1996) : Kartagener's syndrome - a triad of symptoms in an Asian girl aged 11 - nasal sinusitis + polyps and dextrocardia.
Schwarzenberg et al. (1997) : **Haemoptysis** requiring lobectomy in an 11 yr. old girl with Kartagener's syndrome.
Afzelius (1998) : Review of immotile cilia syndrome - past, present and future - not all affected men are infertile!

Young's syndrome.
This syndrome refers to obstructive azoospermia secondary to obstruction of the epididymis by inspissated secretions and chronic sinopulmonary infections. It differs from the immotile-cilia syndrome by the absence of ultrastructural cilial disorders, and from cystic fibrosis by the presence of normal sweat and pancreatic functions. It probably has a genetic origin, most likely of autosomal type. Men with this condition may be diagnosed as a result of their chronic sinus and chest infections, or from their infertility. Most have normal motile sperms, and the epididymal obstruction may be only partial at puberty, so that some have fathered children. Chest symptoms (as with cystic fibrosis) usually start in childhood, but tend to be less severe in adult life.
A case is shown in Illus. **YOUNG'S   SYNDROME.**

References.
Young (1970) : Surgical treatment of male infertility - probably did not distinguish such infertile men from CF.
Hendry et al. (1978): Obstructive azoospermia, respiratory function tests, electron microscopy & surgical results.

Handelsman et al. (1984) : Review of 29 men with Young's syndrome. The pattern of sinopulmonary infections is characterised by early onset, amelioration in adult life, and less severity than in either CF or the immotile-cilia syndrome. Hospitalisation or surgical drainage (as for empyema) is rarely required, effort tolerance and pulmonary function are well preserved and most pts. have minimal symptoms. Some are diagnosed following investigations for infertility. Progression of chest symptoms is not a feature. They wondered if it was a sub-type of CF, but found no causative blood or biochemical abnormalities - pts. were also typically above normal weight and were not malnourished.
Currie et al. (1998) : Efficacy of "mucoregulatory" agents in Young's syndrome.

Impaired mucociliary transport.

The mucociliary 'escalator' is a very important mechanism in removing noxious substances from the lungs and bronchi. The ciliary action wafts these from the smaller bronchi to the larger, from where they may be expectorated. As noted in ps. 24.13 - 14, impairment of this mechanism may occur in relation to infection (particularly viral), or cigarette smoking. It may also be impaired post-operatively. Its action has been studied following bronchography, when if a patient lies still the contrast medium will be slowly transported (over a period of 20 to 30 mins) into the larger bronchi, prior to expectoration. Radio-isotope labelled and inhaled particles (sometimes used for ventilation studies) are similarly transported, and can be followed with a gamma-camera.

Impairment is also seen with chronic bronchitis, mucus plugs, bronchiectasis, CF, chronic pneumonia, etc. Pyocyanin (the green pigment produced in pseudomonas infection) causes ciliary paralysis (see also under cystic fibrosis ps. 3.22 - 3.24).

Reference.

Gamsu et al. (1976) : Postoperative impairment of mucus transport in the lung. When mucociliary transport was impaired, tantalum labelled mucus migrated in a retrograde fashion into the peripheral airways and was retained there for up to six days - esp. seen in gravity dependent parts, and did not clear until the lung became re-expanded.
Seen with - thoracic and abdominal pain, surgery or trauma, CNS depression, morphine, codeine, anticholinergic drugs, general anaesthesia or endotracheal tubes, dry-gas ventilation, and oxygen in high concentration.

The effects of polymorph WBC's on the lungs.

Polymorph WBCs appear to have a considerable effect on chest disease, not only in combating infections, but also in the **development** of some disease processes.

It has long been recognised that where infection continues locally in the bronchi for a protracted period, that the bronchi become deformed, with the production of bronchiectasis. This happens not only in relation to childhood infections, such as measles and pertussis, but also with some adult persisting infections e.g. localised aspergillosis, eosinophilic pneumonia, etc. WBC, labelled with isotopes, have been shown to be abundant in such areas, and to persist in a similar way to that seen in inflammatory bowel disease. It is assumed that such cells in addition to engulfing and phagocytosing harmful bacteria, probably also harm the host tissues they should be protecting. This they appear to do through the release of proteolytic enzymes and the production of free radicals, particularly of oxygen (see also note re free oxygen radicals re bronchopulmonary dysplasia in young infants - ps. 19.106 - 107 and with asbestos induced lung injury - p. 14.33).

As well as contributing to the development of bronchiectasis, such cells also appear to play a part in the development of emphysema (through activation by tobacco smoke), bronchiolitis, and some forms of pulmonary fibrosis, particularly that occurring in ARDS (ps. 8.13 - 8.16).

It has been shown that WBCs pass much more slowly through capillaries than RBCs (60 to 100 times longer through the pulmonary capillary bed) because of their larger size, and their inability to fold. They also pass more slowly through the upper parts of the lungs, than the lower, where the vessels tend to be more dilated. This slowing in the upper parts of the lungs may have a considerable bearing on the production of apical emphysema in smokers, allowing a greater time for the cigarette smoke to trigger its response. It is thought that cigarette smoke causes activation of the polymorph WBCs to release proteolytic enzymes and **free radicals of oxygen**, the latter oxidising the plasma proteolytic inhibitor, and reducing the ability to inactivate proteolytic enzymes, which then damage the lung tissues. Emphysema is further discussed on ps. 6.7 - 8.

In infection, more polymorphs migrate out of the capillaries, into the alveoli and bronchi, where they may be activated and damage the lung tissues and bronchi. For the use of radioactive labelled leucocytes - see ps. 22.11 - 12.

Some references.
Senior et al. (1977) : Induction of pulmonary emphysema with leukocyte elastase.
Klut et al. (1993) : Activation of neutrophils within pulmonary microvessels of rabbits exposed to cigarette smoke.
Hogg (1994) : Traffic of polymorphs through pulmonary microvessels in health and disease.

Bronchitis

Acute bronchitis is commonly initiated by a viral infection, which in turn is often complicated by a bacterial infection, of multiple organisms. The chronic condition is particularly common in smokers (in whom nicotine may inhibit polymorphs and proteases). Damage to the ciliary epithelium in smokers is discussed on ps. 24.13 - 14. This allows the ingress of pathogens such as Rhinophyllia cattharalis, Pneumococcus (esp. type 3) and Haemophilus influenzae into the normally protective mucus layer, and excessive mucus production. Chronic bronchitis may also lead to bronchial wall thickening, enlarged bronchial mucous glands and epithelial metaplasia. Spasm of smooth muscle in the smaller bronchial and bronchiolar walls may lead to air trapping and emphysema. Damage and emphysema may also result from proteolytic enzymes (overwhelming anti-proteases e.g. $\alpha 1$ antitrypsin) and the release of free oxygen radicals (see above).

Bronchiolitis, interstitial lung changes and fine lung nodules associated with cigarette smoking are discussed on p. 3.29 - 30.

See also ps. 6.7 - 6.12 for notes on emphysema.

Illus. **BRONCHITIS** show enlarged mucous glands arising from the bronchial walls and enlarged main pulmonary artery shadows.

Bronchiectasis.

Well marked bronchiectasis, is often readily recognised on plain radiographs, with saccular dilated air-filled or partly fluid-filled bronchi in the basic segments of the lower lobes, lingula and middle lobe. It is often associated with some loss of volume in the affected areas. The dilated bronchi may be surrounded by varying amounts of inflammatory change, in association with repeated infections. Thickening of adjacent supplying bronchi may also be noted.

In cystic fibrosis and in some other patients with immune deficiency (e.g. case with thymoma - see Illus. **THYMUS Pt. 29a-g**), the changes may be rapidly progressive, widely distributed and affect all segments of both lungs. More localised disease may be seen in a middle lobe or lingula, or within an upper lobe per se following persistent pneumonia, TB or aspergillosis.

Twenty to thirty years ago when bronchiectasis was more common, mainly as a result of childhood measles or whooping-cough, bronchograms were frequently carried out to determine the amount of disease for assessment prior to possible surgical resection of the worst affected areas. Various forms were noted, i.e. saccular, tubular or no actual sacs (but loss of smaller side branches, as following bronchiolitis).

Conventional tomograms were also often used to demonstrate the condition, if well marked. The author used to carry out up to 20 bronchographic examinations per week, and performed about 8,000 in toto (see also Chapter 24). In most cases we took 'spot views' (under TV fluoroscopy control) and larger PA, lateral (for RML), oblique (esp. for lingula) views in inspiration, and extra oblique views in expiration (as affected bronchi often did **not** collapse in expiration). Most patients also had their sinuses radiographed since persisting antral infection was common and was often a cause of continuing bronchial infection and its eradication often alleviated this.

We also used to find that in most patients **bronchiectasis was stationary** (as shown by serial bronchographic studies) **unless another episode of severe infection and persisting consolidation occurred** e.g. postoperatively after lung resection. Some authors e.g. Munro et al., 1992 and Smith, I. and Flower (1996 from Cambridge in their review on 'imaging in bronchiectasis') say they have seen some patients with progression. However this author believes that without a continuing 'on-going' condition (e.g. immunodeficiency, CF or recurrent damaging pneumonia) most patients with bronchiectasis do have a static pattern.

As very few cases now pass on to surgery, the necessity for bronchography to provide a good surgical 'road-map' no longer applies and CT and HRCT are now mainly used to diagnose the condition in patients with **recurrent infections, haemoptyses** or **chronic sputum production**. Relatively thick-walled bronchi down to about the 6th generation can usually be visualised by CT but those with a diameter < 1.5 to 2 mm and a wall thickness < 0.3 mm are too small to be visualised by HRCT when air filled, but may be seen as small 'dots' if fluid-filled (see diagram on HRCT appearances - Fig. 1.52).

CT signs of bronchiectasis include the demonstration of the **dilated bronchi, bronchial wall and peri-bronchial thickening, loss of the normal vascular pattern and lung volume with crowded bronchi and vessels** - other signs:

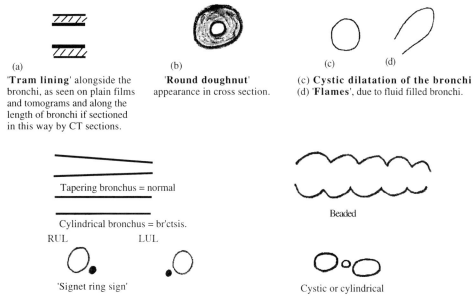

(a)

'**Tram lining**' alongside the bronchi, as seen on plain films and tomograms and along the length of bronchi if sectioned in this way by CT sections.

(b)

'**Round doughnut**' appearance in cross section.

(c) **Cystic dilatation of the bronchi**
(d) '**Flames**', due to fluid filled bronchi.

Tapering bronchus = normal

Cylindrical bronchus = br'ctsis.

RUL   LUL

'Signet ring sign'

Beaded

Cystic or cylindrical

(e) **Cylindrical bronchiectasis** - when the bronchi are parallel to the tomographic plane their walls may appear slightly irregular and fail to taper. When the section plane cuts the bronchi obliquely or transversely a 'signet ring' appearance is produced - the bronchial lumen should be compared in size with that of the adjacent pulmonary arterial branch.

(f) **Varicose bronchiectasis** gives rise to a 'beaded' or 'string of pearls' appearance when the bronchi are cut longitudinally by tomography (including CT), but gives a cystic or cylindrical appearance if the tomographic section cuts the bronchi obliquely or transversely.
(g) Areas of decreased lung attenuation may also be seen on CT sections taken in expiration.

Fig. 3.8   Radiological signs of bronchiectasis.

Because **post-inflammatory bronchial dilatation** (often with viscid secretions) may resolve ('**reversible bronchiectasis**') it is probably better to wait for three months before doing CT after an acute infection, unless underlying neoplasm is suspected.

Long standing bronchiectasis may be surrounded by peribronchial air-space densities - particularly when there is an acute exacerbation of infection. Lung segments involved by bronchiectasis may be considerably scarred with localised reduced volume, honeycombing or reduced pulmonary vascularity. (Bronchial wall thickening is itself a non-specific sign as it may also occur with chronic bronchitis, cigarette smoking and asthma).

Cylindrical bronchiectasis is the most common type. Often the affected bronchi are thick-walled and extend to the periphery of the lung, without their normal tapering. In cross section, such bronchi when having a relatively vertical course may appear as larger than normal rings, and with the accompanying pulmonary artery branches may give a 'signet ring' appearance. The cause may be idiopathic or due to past infection.

Varicose   bronchiectasis may be typical of broncho-pulmonary aspergillosis but has other causes as well.

Traction   bronchiectasis is usually associated with severe pulmonary fibrosis or honeycombing. The affected bronchi often show a '**corkscrew**' appearance and **do not taper**.

Gross unilateral cystic bronchiectasis may be seen with destroyed or end-stage lung.

Mucoid impaction or fluid-filled bronchi - 'mucocoeles' - cause opaque tubular or branching structures within the lung. This may be of varying density and **may   even   calcify**. Being avascular these fluid or mucus collections do nor enhance with IV contrast agents. They may be due to benign or malignant causes - see ps. 2.10 - 12. As noted above tiny fluid-filled bronchi or bronchioles when sectioned tangentially may give rise to small 'dots'.

   Causes : As noted above bronchiectasis often followed **slowly   resolving   childhood pneumonia** associated with measles, pertussis or adenovirus, etc. infection sometimes leading to the Swyer-James (Macleod) syndrome (ps. 7.9 - 10). **Tuberculosis** (ps. 19.16 - 24) was also a common cause from infection per se or from bronchial obstruction caused by enlarged nodes or the effects of bronchial strictures. It may also occur as a result of **aspiration of nasal emboli** (see p.19.2) or **inhaled   food** with reflux, **oesophageal   fistulae** or as a result of **neurological disease** affecting swallowing or oesophageal obstruction. Other causes include **slowly growing   endobronchial   tumours** (esp. adenomas but also some malignant tumours), a persisting **endobronchial foreign body**, **aspergillosis** (p. 19.38), **atypical   mycobacteria** (esp. Kansasii and avium-intracellulare, particularly in AIDS patients) - p. 19.25 - 26, **cystic fibrosis** (p. 3.22 - 24), **Young's syndrome** (p. 3.16), **chronic   sarcoid** (p. 19.65), **ARDS** (p. 8.13), **hypogammaglobulinaemia** (or other immmunodeficiency syndromes including AIDS - ps. 5.47 & 19.32), **immotile   cilia** and **Kartagener's   syndromes** (p. 3.15), **thymoma** (with which it may be rapidly progressive - p. 18.22), **end-stage   lung** (p.19.122), **post-transplant patients with infection or graft v host disease**, **radiotherapy** (p. 11.16), **COP and BO** (see ps. 3.31) and some congenital syndromes such as the **Mounier-Kuhn** and **Williams-Campbell   syndromes** in adults (ps. 3.5) and Wiscott-Aldrich and Chediak-Higashi syndromes in children. Many of these cause persistent secondary infection and the persistent consolidation appears to damage the bronchial walls - see also polymorphs and the lung (p. 3.17), however in other cases e.g. post R/T, sarcoid, ARDS etc. it is really just a feature of the lung scarring (seen with HRCT) and is of little practical clinical importance.
   Spurious or '**pseudobronchiectasis**' may be produced by inappropriate CT windowing, with blurring of edges (no 'best window' exists - see p. 20.18), poor collimation, motion artefacts on CT sections esp. in the lingula and LLL, or vessels and bronchi running obliquely to the CT plane.
   Bronchiectasis may also sometimes be simulated by cavitary conditions such as cavitating metastases, histiocytosis X, lymphangioleiomyomatosis, etc. and the cavities seen in sequestration (p. 3.11).

Note on radiation dosage and protection - as bronchiectasis is now only treated rarely by surgery, one should question the necessity of taking very many fine sections of the chest for its diagnosis, or for follow-up examinations. The author found that 5mm sections at 10mm spacing usually sufficed. He also strongly feels that a view of the **nasal antra** is still an important additional radiological investigation, as this not uncommonly is the site of continuing infection (even without a nasal history) - see also above and note on bronchial emboli p. 19.1.

Illustrations   of   bronchiectasis   are   shown   under   Illus.   **BRONCHIECTASIS, BRONCHIECTASIS REVERSIBLE** - also **BRONCHIECTASIS   FOLLICULARIS** and **BRONCHIECTASIS + MYCET** - both associated with fungus infection and especially aspergillosis.

References.
Laennec (1819) : First clinical recognition of bronchiectasis.
Fleischner (1941) : Reversible bronchiectasis.   (1949) : The pathogenesis of bronchiectasis.
Reid (1950) : Reduction in bronchial sub-divisions in bronchiectasis.

Cureton and Hill (1955) : Malignant change in bronchiectasis.

Gudjberg (1955) : 114 pts. with bronchiectasis - only 8 had a normal chest radiograph.

Nelson and Christoforidis (1958) : Reversible bronchiectasis.

Scarrow (1964) : The radiology of chronic bronchitis.

Kurklu et al. (1973) : Bronchiectasis consequent upon foreign body retention.

Spencer (1977) : Pathology of the Lung.

Ellis et al. (1981) : Outlook in bronchiectasis - clinical and social study and review of factors influencing prognosis.

Naidich et al. (1982) : CT of bronchiectasis - used 10 mm sections.

Müller et al. (1984) : Role of CT in the recognition of bronchiectasis.

Whyte and Williams (1984) : Bronchiectasis after mycoplasma pneumonia.

Breatnach et al. (1985) : Preoperative evaluation of bronchiectasis by CT.

Kelsey Fry (1985) : CT of the lung.

Mootsamay et al. (1985) : Assessment of bronchiectasis by CT.

Grenier et al. (1986) : Assessment of bronchiectasis by thin section CT - defined 'bronchial dilatation' if it had an internal diameter greater than that of the accompanying pulmonary artery branch..

Phillips et al. (1986) : Compared the value of CT with bronchography in the diagnosis and assessment of cylindrical and varicose bronchiectasis. In a study of 15 patients, they found an approximate 80 % sensitivity and almost 100 % specificity in the CT diagnosis of bronchiectasis.

Westcott and Cole (1986) : Traction bronchiectasis in end-stage pulmonary fibrosis.

Cooke et al. (1987) : Role of CT in the diagnosis of bronchiectasis.

Currie et al. (1987) : Abnormalities due to bronchiectasis were only seen in 9/19 pts. on chest radiograph compared with bronchography.

Joharjy et al. (1987) : Medium thickness CT in the diagnosis of bronchiectasis.

Silverman et al. (1987) : CT/bronchographic correlations in bronchiectasis in 14 pts. with bronchiectasis - the chest radiograph was diagnostic in none.

Ashford et al. (1988) : Used 99mDTPA aerosol to demonstrate ventilation defects, complicating bronchiectasis in 22 gross cases.

Barker and Bardana (1988) : Bronchiectasis - update on an orphan disease.

Hansell (1988) : Narrow section CT may show cylindrical, varicose and cystic patterns of bronchiectasis.

Rémy-Jardin and Rémy (1988) : Comparison of vertical and oblique CT in evaluation of bronchial tree. **20⁰ cranially oblique CT scans considerably improve the CT analysis** of segmental and subsegmental bronchi and allow bronchi to be analysed along their lengths (particularly in the RML and lingula).

Tarver et al. (1988) : Motion artefacts on CT sections may simulate bronchiectasis.

Pang et al. (1989) : Value of CT in the diagnosis and management of bronchiectasis.

Strickland (1989) : Noted three types of bronchiectasis as seen on HRCT studies.

(i) with aspergillosis, the bronchial dilatation tended to be proximal, and the affected bronchi were often large and oval in shape, the distal bronchi usually being normal;

(ii) cystic fibrosis caused a moderate fairly uniform dilatation of segmental and subsegmental bronchi, with marked thickening of the bronchial walls;

(iii) with infective bronchiectasis, the proximal bronchi were frequently normal, with dilated terminal sacs.

A (iv)th group had bronchial wall thickening, without bronchial wall dilatation. Aspergillosis and cystic fibrosis particularly affected the upper lobes, and both could cause air-trapping.

Grenier et al. (1990) : CT assessment of bronchiectasis - used 1.5 mm thick sections - the vessels and bronchial walls were better delineated because of reduced partial volume effect on oblique bronchi. Used 10 mm spacing of sections from lung apices to diaphragm. Diameter of smallest bronchi seen by CT was 2 mm (terminal bronchioles being 0.5 mm in diameter).

Munroe et al. (1990) : Comparison of HRCT with bronchography in identifying bronchiectatic segments with chronic sputum production - concluded that the sensitivity and specificity of 3 mm section HRCT permits serial examinations without recourse to repeat bronchography. Bronchography may still be needed before surgery, but CT will avert the need for bronchography in many pts. with diffuse disease.

Westcott (1991) : Bronchiectasis.

Wong-You-Cheong (1992) : Airways obstruction and bronchiectasis - correlation with duration of symptoms and extent of bronchiectasis on CT.

McGuinness et al. (1993a) : CT evaluation of bronchiectasis - reviewed the whole range of CT appearances and problems in diagnosis.

McGuinness et al. (1993b) : CT features of AIDS with bronchiectasis.

Rémy-Jardin et al. (1993) : Traction bronchiectasis with lung scarring.

Desai et al. (1994) : Reproducibility of bronchial circumference measurements using CT - useful in demonstrating the progression of bronchiectasis.

Hansell et al. (1994) : Areas of decreased attenuation on expiratory CT (due to air trapping) are common in severe bronchiectasis. ? small airways disease may precede bronchiectasis.

Gleeson (1995) : Review - advocated 1-2 mm CT sections at 10 mm spacing.

Herman et al. (1993) : HRCT of bronchiectasis in children (2mm slices with 10 mm interslice spacing).

Kang et al. (1995) : Bronchiectasis - comparison of pre-operative HRCT and pathology in resected specimens.

Lee et al. (1995) : The causes of bronchiectasis cannot be reliably diagnosed on the basis of CT alone.

McGuinness and Naidich (1995) : Bronchiectasis - CT clinical correlations.

Reiff et al. (1995a) : Pattern and distribution of bronchiectasis as a predictor of aetiology.

Reiff et al. (1995b) : CT in bronchiectasis - limited value in distinguishing between idiopathic and specific types.

Roberts et al. (1996) : Observer variation in the interpretation of CT features of bronchiectasis - HRCT (insp. & limited exp. sections) of 100 consecutive pts. Each lobe (including the lingula) was scored independently for (i) bronchiectasis, (ii) bronchial dilatation, (iii) bronchial wall thickening, (iv) bronchial collapse on expiration, (v) predominant pattern of ectasia, + presence of (vi) centrilobular or (vii) larger mucus plugs and (viii) evidence of air-trapping on expiratory images.

Smith and Flower (1996) : Review of imaging in bronchiectasis - the radiological investigation has advanced considerably in the last decade with HRCT emerging as the investigation of choice. Airway diameter is well demonstrated, but thickening of the bronchial wall still awaits an accepted definition. Air trapping (on expiratory scans) correlates with the degree of airflow limitation and may offer new insights into the natural history.

Miszkiel et al. (1997) : HRCT showed more extensive bronchiectasis and thicker bronchial walls when Pseudomonas aeruginosa infection was present.

Kim et al. (1997) : In most cases thin-section CT allows reliable distinction of pts. with cylindrical bronchiectasis from healthy subjects.

Morehead (1997) : Bronchiectasis in bone marrow transplantation - ? manifestation of graft v host disease of lung.

Cartier et al. (1999) : HRCT differentiation of causes - bilat. esp. CF & ABPA, unilat. UL - TB, LL after childhood viral infection.

Hansell (1999) : Prediction of causes - ABPA = varicose & proximal, CF = ULs & cylindrical, hypogammaglob. = mildly cylindrical in LLs, post pertussis = cystic in LLs. No pattern truly pathognomic - considerable overlap.

Jones et al. (1985) : 6 of 40 pts. examined by combined bronchoscopy and bronchography in the assessment of **haemoptysis** had underlying bronchiectasis.

Naidich et al. (1990) : 10 out of 58 pts. with haemoptysis were found to have bronchiectasis by CT and bronchoscopy.

Millar et al. (1992) : CT showed bronchiectasis in 7 out of 40 pts. with haemoptysis and a normal bronchoscopy.

Set et al. (1993) : 15% of pts. with haemoptysis had bronchiectasis shown by CT and fibreoptic bronchoscopy.

Cystic fibrosis.

 The cystic fibrosis (CF) gene is on the long arm of chromosome 7, the condition being recessive (with an estimated incidence of one per 2,000 births among Caucasians). Patients produce mucus which is thicker and contains less water than normal. Its high viscosity makes it difficult for it to be expectorated, and it can look like strands of 'spaghetti'. The retained secretions tend to become infected with Pseudomonas aeruginosa (the green pigment - pyocyanin causing ciliary paralysis), Staph. aureus, H. influenzae, etc. As a result the bronchi lose their cilia and cartilage, and become dilated and unstable. The trachea also becomes larger and unduly collapsible. The bronchi of the upper lobes are usually most affected, perhaps related to the slower circulation in the upper lobes allowing the leucocytes a longer time to be activated or migrate out of the vessels (see p. 3.17), and because mucus in the lower lobe bronchi may be thinned due to the greater blood circulation there; the thickened mucus tending to persist in the upper lobes, and the dilatation being made worse by repeated bouts of coughing. Patients with cystic fibrosis now live much longer than 20 years ago (as a result of better nutrition, oral pancreatic enzymes and control of infection, including physiotherapy) and most centres now see many adult cases. The present median age of survival is 31 years, this is rising and it is expected that those now being born will survive to age 40 or greater. Some patients may also present as a 'forme fruste' as young adults, but most are found in childhood using a sweat test for elevated Na & Cl. Some may be detected as 'salty tasting babies'!, others presenting with new-born meconium ileus.

 Most patients have widespread areas of bronchiectasis, which may be of various types - cylindrical with thickened bronchial walls, cystic or varicose. Some have thin-walled 'cystic spaces' adjacent to these. Surrounding inflammatory shadowing, with small or larger areas of collapse or consolidation are not uncommon, particularly when the patients have an acute exacerbation. Some may have enlarged hilar shadows due to adenopathy and/or cor pulmonale. A recent study has shown that the likelihood of acquiring antibiotic resistant flora is increased by attending a large national centre and by having repeat bronchoscopies - they appear to 'pick up' resistant hospital flora. Pseudomonas (or Burkholderia) cepacia (with long tentacles - previously recognised as a plant pathogen which causes onion rot - cepia = onion), which first presented in Toronto, has a particular predisposition to infect patients with CF, causing accelerated lung disease, and in some overwhelming septicaemia and necrotising pneumonia. Although the numbers infected with P. cepacia are relatively small, the organism often shows resistance to most available antibiotics.

Some CF patients are being treated with indwelling central venous catheters to give IV antibiotics. A lobectomy may occasionally be carried out to remove a single destroyed lobe. A few in the later stages have heart plus bilateral (or sequential single) lung transplants (single lung transplants per se are mostly unsuccessful as they become infected from the contralateral lung, particularly with the use of anti-rejection drugs). In those with hepatomegaly, liver transplantation may also be carried out. Gene therapy has also being tried, but the viral carrier causes a significant pulmonary inflammatory response as shown by CT, and it is being replaced with a liposomal carrier. DNA loss in the sputum is high and about a third of cases may benefit from a (very expensive) human DNase - an enzyme which breaks down the long strands of DNA and hence reduces the viscosity of purulent sputum.

Other complications include pneumothorax and haemoptysis, which may be life-threatening. A scoring system for assessing chest disease has been used by some workers (Brasfield et al., 1979 & 1980 - from Birmingham, Alabama, and O'Laoide et al, 1991) - assessing air trapping (more common in children), linear markings, nodular cystic lesions, general severity and large lesions also collapse/consolidation, cardiac enlargement or pneumothorax. Other scoring systems (Crispin Norman and Northern) are used more commonly in the UK.

Another abnormality which the radiologist should be aware of with this condition is 'meconium ileus of the adult' - i.e. inspissated distal small bowel content - Illus. MECONIUM ILEUS-ADULT. A dose of Gastrografin plus Maxalon (as used for a follow-through examination of the small intestine) will usually relieve it; similarly a Gastrografin enema if the colon is involved. In some cases a local inflammatory bowel reaction to drugs (e.g. pancreatin may lead to ulceration leading to stricture formation in the small bowel or ascending colon). Children may also develop an intussuception.

Hepatic fatty infiltration and cirrhosis is being found in about 20% of the cystic fibrosis population, and may lead to biliary obstruction and infection. Liver ultra-sound in now a part of the annual review of children with cystic fibrosis in Oxford.

Illustrations of cystic fibrosis are shown in Illus. CYSTIC FIBROSIS.

Further references.
Dunnill (1959) : Small lung abscesses in CF may extend into the pleural space.
Hodson and France (1962) : Pulmonary changes in cystic fibrosis of the pancreas.
Mack et al. (1965) The bronchial arteries in CF in eight cases were dilated and tortuous as shown by angiography.
Crispin and Norman (1974) : The systematic evaluation of chest radiograph in cystic fibrosis.
Schwartz and Holsclaw (1974) : Pulmonary involvement in adults with CF. (55 pts. > age 15 - 24 F & 31 M).
Wood et al. (1976) : Cystic fibrosis.
Stern et al. (1977) : CF diagnosed after age 13 - 25 teenage & adult pts. including 3 asymptomatic men.
Stern et al. (1978) : Treatment and prognosis of massive haemoptysis with CF.
Friedman et al. (1981) : Pulmonary cystic fibrosis in the adult.
Davis (1985) : Pathophysiology of pulmonary disease in cystic fibrosis.
Friedman (1987) : Chest radiographic findings in the adult with cystic fibrosis.
Jacobson et al. (1986) : Studied 12 patients with cystic fibrosis by CT and showed hilar adenopathy, enlarged pulmonary arteries, bronchiectasis and mucocoeles.
Currie et al. (1987) : Interpretation of bronchograms and chest radiographs with chronic sputum production.
Griscom et al. (1987) : Radiologic and pathologic abnormality of the trachea in older patients with cystic fibrosis.
Hansell and Strickland (1989) : HRCT on 21 pts. (age range 15 - 43) in addition to plain films - CT better showed the bronchiectasis - often more extensive than expected. Both proximal and distal parts of the bronchi were affected, mostly cylindrical disease, others were cystic or varicose. Twelve of these had cystic spaces; some probably dilated

bronchi, because of continuity or signet ring appearance. Overinflation was seen in some as well as localised consolidation. One had a pneumothorax and 12 showed pleural thickening posteriorly in the upper zones.

Sweezey and Fellows (1990) : Bronchial artery embolisation for severe haemoptysis in cystic fibrosis.

Bhalla et al. (1991) : Cystic fibrosis - scoring system with thin-section CT - taking account of bronchiectasis, peribronchial thickening, mucus plugging, abscesses or bronchiectatic sacculations, bullae, emphysema and collapse or consolidation. Such a system may be of value in patients being considered for surgery.

Elborn et al. (1991) : Presently there are 5,200 patients with CF, including 3,300 under 16 yrs. - expected increase by AD 2,000 is to 6 000 & 3,400 respectively. Median life expectancy is now 40 years (double that of 20 yrs ago).

Kinsella et al. (1991) : MR imaging in CF - studied eight patients and showed greater extent of disease than predicted by chest radiographs alone - clearly showed peribronchial thickening and mucoid impacted bronchi - also distinguished between enlarged nodes and enlarged proximal pulmonary vessels as the cause of hilar enlargement.

Santis et al. (1991) : HRCT in adult cystic fibrosis - studied 38 patients with unusually mild lung disease, out of 500 adults attending the hospital. Three had normal chest radiographs and HRCT studies. Thickening of the wall of proximal right upper lobe bronchi was the earliest abnormal feature with HRCT. The commonest abnormal feature was mild uniform dilatation of proximal bronchi - the lumen dilatation was less marked than the degree of thickening. Ten cases were first diagnosed in adult life.

Stiglbauer et al. (1992) : HRCT in children with cystic fibrosis - 24 patients.

Elborn (1994) : Prospects for gene therapy - the object is to replace the defective CFTR gene, thus allowing normal chloride ion transport to take place, so that Na and Cl may pass into the bronchial lumina, and the bronchial mucus glycoproteins be salinated rather than sulphated. An adenovirus has been used as a gene carrier.

Greene et al. (1994) : Radiographic changes in acute exacerbations of CF in adults showed worsening of mucus plugging, fluid levels in bronchiectatic cavities etc. or rare complications such as pneumothorax or pneumonia.

King et al. (1994) : Five children with CF developed colonic strictures secondary to high dose pancreatic enzymes.

Carr et al.(1995) : CT & MR of 17 pts. concluded "the resolution of MR does not, at present, compare with CT".

Helbich et al. (1996) : Evolution of CT findings at follow-up in cystic fibrosis - pulmonary changes in CF progress slowly and continuously - a reasonable time between studies is 30 months. Features studied were bronchiectasis, bronchial wall thickening, mucus plugging, bullae, air-trapping, emphysema and consolidation.

Maffessanti et al. (1996) : HRCT in CF - the ULs were more heavily involved than the lower, esp. on the right.

Thompson (1996 - Oxford) : Cystic fibrosis - current status and future prospects.

Hayllar et al. (1997 - London) : A new prognostic index for predicting survival and the need for transplantation (see also comment by Shale, 1997).

Walter et al. (1997) : Results show that there is no change in the P. aeruginosa population before and after lung transplantation and it is assumed that reinfection is caused by the bacterial reservoir in the sinuses and the trachea.

Webb and Egan (1997) : Pts. infected with B. cepacia should have equal access to transplantation as other CF pts.

Littlewood (1998) : Report on the value of centralised treatment service in CF pts. in Denmark, with prevention and early treatment of P. aeruginosa.

Torrens et al. (1998) : Occasionally pts with CF may have infection with non-tuberculous mycobacteria.

Wilson and Dowling (1998) : P. aeruginosa and other related species.

Wittram and Rappaport (1998) : Expiratory helical CT minimum intensity projection imaging in cystic fibrosis.

Mason and Nakielna (1999) : Bronchiectasis in newly diagnosed CF in adults is predominantly cylindrical and ULs.

Brown et al. (2000) : Colon cancer may mimic meconium ileus of the adult (distal intestinal obstruction syndrome).

Broncholithiasis.

A broncholith is a calcified mass within a bronchus. In the UK it is usually caused by an old tuberculous lymph node eroding into a bronchus (most often the intermediate bronchus or the right middle or lower lobe bronchi), but occasionally may be caused by calcification within inspissated secretions within mucocoeles (see ps. 2.10 - 12), or within chronic cavities. Endobronchial obstruction may lead to collapse and distal infection. When a calcified node erodes into a neighbouring bronchus, it may precipitate a brisk haemoptysis. Erosion may also indicate reactivation of the dormant tuberculosis. 'Stones' may be expectorated (as noted by ancient authors such as Aristotle and Galen). Prior to expectoration, broncholiths may move around in the bronchial tree, and like other foreign bodies (or aspergillosis) cause a '**wandering   pneumonia**' (see also p. 19.59).

Plain radiographs may show that a calcified mass is in a bronchus, has changed in shape due to the expectoration of a part of it, that it has changed in position or that it has disappeared, if fully coughed up. Tomograms are often required to confirm the endobronchial position, but care should be taken to avoid 'ghost' shadows due to neighbouring calcification being confused with true endobronchial calcification. This may require tomography in two planes or CT.

Other causes besides past tuberculosis include past histoplasmosis (see p. 19.45), other fungal disease and sarcoidosis. A chronic tracheo-oesophageal fistula is another rare cause (see p. 16.10).

The condition may be mimicked by a calcifying endobronchial hamartoma (ps. 5.14 - 15) or an endobronchial carcinoid (ps. 5.5 - 5.9).

Intrapulmonary micronodules due to **pulmonary microlithiasis** are discussed on p. 6.23.

(a)
(b)

Fig. 3.9 Calcified node eroding into a bronchus and   Calcified mucocoele in RUL.
leading to a broncholith, bronchial obstruction + a mucocoele.

Clinical examples are shown in Illus. **BRONCHOLITH**.

References.

Freedman and Billings (1949) : Active bronchopulmonary lithiasis.
Davis et al. (1956) : Broncholithiasis - a neglected cause of broncho-oesophageal fistula.
Weed and Andersen (1960) : Aetiology of broncholithiasis.
Arrigoni et al. (1971) : Broncholithiasis.
McLeod et al. (1976) : Tomography of hila - broncholiths.
Vix (1978), Kelly (1979), Pinet et al. (1982) : Radiographic manifestations.
Kowal et al. (1983), Shin and Ho (1983a), Adler and Peleg (1987) : CT of broncholithiasis.
Dixon et al. (1984) : Advances in the diagnosis of broncholithiasis.
Trastek et al. (1985) : Surgical management of broncholithiasis.
Hirshfield et al. (1989) : Broncholithiasis due to Histoplasma capsulatum & subsequently infected by actinomycetes.
Morris et al. (1989) : Lithoptysis in a marathon runner.
Conces et al. (1991) : CT features in 15 patients (5 patients had peribronchial nodes + bronchial distortion).

See also endobronchial hamartomas simulating broncholithiasis.
Dovenbarger and Elstun (1961) : Endobronchial hamartoma with calcification.
Shin et al. (1989) : CT demonstration of an ossifying bronchial carcinoid simulating broncholithiasis - one should consider both calcifying adenomas and hamartomas in the differential diagnosis.

SMALL AIRWAYS DISEASE (bronchi under 2 mm in diameter and non-cartilaginous - note later development of emphysema - may also be associated with bronchitis and asthma).

Bronchiolitis, bronchiolectasis and bronchiolitis obliterans.

These conditions may be caused by a number of pathogens, both bacterial and viral (including adeno-virus, influenza, pneumocystis, mycoplasma, aspergillosis and other lung infections), drugs (e.g. penicillamine and sulphasalazine - see p. 19. 112), toxic fumes or chemicals, some interstitial lung diseases, including connective tissue disorders and sarcoidosis, acute inhalation of organic allergens and mineral dust exposure. They may also occur post-transplantation (heart-lung and bone marrow), with bronchiectasis and in relation to tumourlets (p. 24.18). A few cases may be 'cryptogenic' or idiopathic.

Bronchiolitis is not uncommon in children with viral infections. In the acute stage in adults (particularly with mycoplasma) bronchiolitis may produce a **miliary type of pattern** on plain chest radiographs (Illus. **MYCOPLASMA PN, Pt. 7**). Clinically there is often an unexplained irreversible air flow limitation leading to **air trapping**. Non-specific symptoms (dyspnoea and cough) and signs (mid inspiratory squeaks) may be present. The severity of symptoms and rate of progression of the condition is highly variable. The bronchiolar walls may exude mucus or become thickened by inflammation (with some spread into the peri-bronchiolar tissues) and causing dilatation of the terminal bronchioles. In severe or chronic cases small cystic air-filled spaces may occur, especially at the lung bases. Ground glass shadowing and small granular nodules may be seen acutely on HRCT.

(a) Mucus exudate into lumen
   (proliferative type of reaction).

(b) Bronchiolar wall thickening
   (constrictive reaction with submucosal collagenisation).

Fig. 3.10 Diagrams showing the mechanisms of small airways damage in bronchiolitis; (a) may lead to centrilobular nodules (in cross section) or branching opacities ('jacks' - in long axis) on CT and (b) reflex vasoconstriction and air trapping with a vascular redistribution mosaic pattern.

In 1835 Raynaud (Mémoire sur l'obliteration des bronches.) gave the first anatomical description of small airways obstruction and Lange (1901) noted plugging of small airways by tissue. Until recently and with the increasing use of HRCT the condition has not received much attention in radiological journals. Whilst many patients recover fully, in others the condition may lead to lung damage. Scarring follows adenovirus and other virus infections in children (see Swyer James /Macleod syndrome - p. 7.9 CMV, p. 19.29) and this is one manifestation of bronchiolitis obliterans. It may also follow influenza and some bacterial broncho-pneumonias. Granulomatous plugs appear to damage the terminal and respiratory bronchioles and lead to **diffuse   scarring**, or cause **air-trapping   leading   to   emphysema**. It appears to be one cause of 'small airways disease' as is present on chronic obstructive airways disease (COAD) - a condition which in Oxford in the 1950s was often termed "**Thames   Valley   Chest**" - so many local inhabitants being affected by the prevalent winter 'smogs', before smokeless zones came in and coal fires were the norm for household heating (see also '**air pollution and health**' - ps 19.109 & 24.2).

   Geddes et al. (1977) noted the association of BO with **rheumatoid   arthritis**. They studied six patients who rapidly developed obstructive lung disease, manifested pathologically by bronchiolitis and fibrotic bronchiolar obliteration. Patients with the condition have dyspnoea which worsens rapidly, and they often have a mid-inspiratory 'squeak'. Others (see below) have noted a similar association and findings, but many of the patients have been receiving penicillamine or gold therapy. In the affected parts of the lung, there is an intense inflammatory infiltrate of lymphocytes and plasma cells, in and around the bronchioles, sometimes with small nodules. The patients may go on to develop apical bullae, diffuse fibrosis and emphysema.

   Radiologically the appearances vary with the severity of the lung changes. In many the chest radiograph may appear normal in inspiration. In others there may be some hyperinflation, but **the main sign is a failure of deflation in expiration** - seen on plain radiographs or CT.

   Breatnach and Kerr (1982) noted subtle peripheral vascular attenuation confined to the mid and lower zones and/or mild hyperinflation. They performed bronchograms in some patients and found generalised '**pruning**' of the smaller bronchial branches, abrupt termination of the smaller bronchi and incomplete distal filling of them.

   HRCT examinations have shown that many patients have nodular opacities, which vary in size from granular to several mm in size. Larger nodules may appear as patchy foci of consolidation, which may mimic pulmonary oedema if they become confluent. Some have fine linear shadows as well and the appearance may then mimic that seen in fibrosing alveolitis. Indeed these two conditions may overlap, and bronchiolitis may be a precursor of 'interstitial pneumonia' and fibrosing alveolitis (see ps. 19. 115 et seq.).

   HRCT examinations have also shown diffuse para-vascular areas of increased shadowing in some cases, or areas of decreased density with patchy attenuation of small vessels - apparent 'vascular loss' - (**the normal lung then   appearing   denser**, and sometimes confused by inexperienced observers as abnormal areas - further sections in **expiration** will show that these normal areas deflate whilst those that are hypovascular secondary to small airways disease or thrombo-embolic lung disease secondary to pulmonary hypertension do not! - see also 'mosaic pattern of lung attenuation' p. 2.4). A mosaic pattern may also be seen as a result of vascular impairment as with pulmonary emboli - see p. 7.26. Areas of lung with vascular shut-down will appear black on CT - 'black lung'.

These studies clearly relate to the air-trapping and hyper-expansion that may be clinically observed, especially in some cases of influenza (Illus. INFLUENZA) - similar findings occurring in acute toxic states e.g. with toxic fumes or smoke, or in acute allergic alveolitis including drug reactions. The condition may progress to COP or BOOP. Chronic changes may lead to emphysema, Swyer-James syndrome or interstitial lung disease. (Diagrams of some changes which may be seen in the secondary lobules are shown in Figs. 1.60 & 1.61.)

Small areas of air trapping may be found in normal people, and in some with **bronchiectasis**, the 'floppy' airways closing down in expiration - see also ps. 2.4 & 2.6.

'Slab sections' made with spiral CT (see p. 20.28) may also show differences between contiguous sections.

NB The clinical FEV_1 lung function test is also a reflection of small airways disease.

Further references.

Culiner (1963) : Obstructive bronchitis and bronchiolitis with bronchiectasis.
Hogg et al. (1968) : Site and nature of airway obstruction in chronic obstructive lung disease.
Becroft (1971) : BO, bronchiectasis and other sequelae of adenovirus type 21 infection in young children.
Macklem et al. (1971) : Chronic obstructive disease of the small airways.
Gosink et al. (1973) : Bronchiolitis obliterans - radiological and pathological association.
Geddes et al. (1977) : Progressive airway obliteration in adults and its association with **rheumatoid arthritis**.
Lyle (1977) : **D-penicillamine** and fatal obliterative bronchiolitis.
Wohl and Chernik (1978) : Bronchiolitis.
Epler et al. (1979) : Bronchiolitis and bronchiolitis in connective tissue disease, ? related to **penicillamine**.
Turton et al. (1981) : Cryptogenic obliterative bronchiolitis in adults (areas of reduced vascularity).
Halla et al. (1982) : Sequential **gold** and **penicillamine** therapy in **rheumatoid arthritis**.
Nikki et al. (1982) : Severe bronchiolitis probably caused by **varicella-zoster virus**.
Cooke and Bamji (1983) : **Gold** and pulmonary function in **rheumatoid arthritis**.
Epler and Colby (1983) : Spectrum of bronchiolitis obliterans.
McCann et al. (1983) : Obliterative bronchiolitis and upper zone pulm. consolidation in **rheumatoid arthritis**.
Seggev et al. (1983) : 3 cases of BO with physiological studies.
Jacobs et al. (1984) : Rapidly fatal bronchiolitis obliterans with circulating antinuclear and **rheumatoid** factors.
Sato et al. (1985) : Bronchiolitis obliterans caused by **Legionella** pneumophilia.
Hakala et al. (1986) : Association of bronchiolitis with connective tissue disorders.
McLoud et al. (1986) : Bronchiolitis obliterans.   Miki et al. (1988) : CT of bronchiolitis obliterans.
Myers et al. (1987) : Respiratory bronchiolitis causing interstitial lung disease - 6 cases.
Blank (1989) : Radiological appearances.
Kindt et al. (1989) : Bronchiolitis in adults - a reversible cause of airway obstruction associated with airway neutrophils and neutrophil products.
Yousem et al. (1989) : Respiratory bronchiolitis-associated interstitial lung disease and its relationship to DIP.
Sweatman et al. (1990) : Examined 15 cases with CT (both in inspiration and expiration and in prone and supine positions) and found abnormalities (both para-vascular areas of increased density and areas of reduced density) in 13. The changes were not gravity dependent, and were **more marked in expiration**.
Coblentz et al. (1991) : Observer variation in detecting the radiological features associated with bronchiolitis.
Padley et al. (1992, 1993) : Examined 18 cases with HRCT, and stressed the importance of areas of **decreased attenuation**. They also noted some bronchial dilatation, small airway occlusion and vascular shunting from the affected areas. Correlation with pulmonary function tests was poor, the latter showing more severe changes; the radiographic changes were mainly subtle, indicating small vessel and small airway disease.
Holt et al. (1993) : HRCT in respiratory bronchiolitis - associated interstitial lung disease.
Penn and Liu (1993) : Bronchiolitis following infection in adults and children.
Wells and du Bois (1993) : Bronchiolitis in association with connective tissue disease.
Aquino et al. (1994) : BO associated with **rheumatoid arthritis**, findings on HRCT and dynamic expiratory CT.
Douglas and Colby (1994) : Fume-related bronchiolitis obliterans.
Epler (1994) : Diseases of the Bronchioles.
Ezri et al. (1994) : BO - current concepts.

Garg et al. (1994) : **Histological classification** - divided bronchiolitis into **proliferative** and **constrictive** types which frequently correlate with the radiographic appearances - the former with air-space opacification and the latter with lobular areas of decreased density and airway dilatation. They also noted: -
(i) **BOOP** is the most common cause of the proliferative form, with patchy bilateral air-space consolidation, often with sub-pleural patchy consolidation, ground-glass density or nodules.
(ii) **Secondary proliferative bronchiolitis** is associated with collagen vascular disease, hypersensitivity pneumonitis, ARDS, aspiration and eosinophilic pneumonia. Focal organising pneumonia appears as a localised mass on radiographs.
(iii) Cryptogenic BO is the prototype of **constrictive bronchiolitis**, a rare condition mainly affecting women (40 - 60 years of age) and causing severe progressive airway obstruction with lobular segmental areas of decreased lung attenuation and narrowed pulmonary vessels at CT and between them areas of normal or increased attenuation. Peripheral or central bronchiolitis may be present. Secondary constrictive bronchiolitis may complicate collagen diseases, post-viral or mycoplasma infection, toxic-fume exposure, chronic hypersensitivity pneumonitis, drugs, transplantation and the Swyer-James syndrome.
(iv) **Respiratory bronchiolitis** principally affects the respiratory bronchioles with filling of the bronchiolar lumen - esp. in cigarette smokers - on HRCT a hazy opacity or sometimes tiny centri-lobular nodules.
Landau (1994) : Bronchiolitis and asthma - are they related? Viral infections are the most important triggers of asthma attacks and it has long been considered that respiratory tract infections, particularly during early childhood, could contribute in a causal way to the development of airway hyper-responsiveness and asthma.
Stern and Frank (1994) : CT in suspended full expiration may show air-trapping in pts. with small air-ways disease.
Müller and Miller (1995) : Diseases of the bronchioles - CT and histopathological findings.
Hansell (1996) : Also divided bronchiolar pathology broadly into constrictive and proliferative bronchiolitis, but regarded BOOP/COP as a distinctive clinico-pathological condition affecting the air spaces. He noted 'skip' lesions on pathology, normal volume lungs, bronchial wall thickening, bronchiolar pruning and areas of reduced vascularity with mosaic perfusion.
Müller (1996) : HRCT pathological correlation of bronchiolitis - hypoxic vasoconstriction → hypoxic dilatation, presence of mucoplugs etc.
Vershakekelen (1996) : HRCT - 3 groups - acute cellular bronchiolitis (fine nodules + centrilobular consolidation), BO with intraluminal polyps, & submucosal collagenisation and fibrosis. Direct signs - centri-lobular branching structures (uncommon); indirect signs - wall thickening/bronchiolitis, mosaic perfusion, air trapping (early collapse of narrowed bronchioles during expiration).
Desai and Hansell (1997) : **Expiratory CT** accentuates the changes caused by small airways disease.
Hansell (1997) : Extrinsic allergic alveolitis is really an allergic bronchiolitis - the nodules are organising pneumonia in and cellular reaction around small airways - often lymphocytic and leading to ground-glass shadowing, faint nodules and areas of decreased attenuation on CT in expiration.
   In sarcoidosis there is infiltration alongside the small bronchi as well as nodules causing air trapping in expiration in early disease, at pulmonary lobule level. Thus a reticular pattern is the major determinant of airflow obstruction.
Hansell et al. (1997) : BO - CT signs of small airways disease - decreased attenuation of lung parenchyma (**mosaic perfusion** - within areas of decreased perfusion the vessels are of decreased calibre, compared with areas of increased attenuation, where the vessels are of increased calibre), end-expiration CT signs of air-trapping, bronchial dilatation, wall thickening and mucus plugging.
Vershakekalen (1998) : Acute or cellular bronchiolitis (A) may lead to polyp formation and proliferative bronchiolitis and BOOP reaction (B) or to submucosal collagenisation with the development of constrictive or obliterative bronchiolitis (C). A & B are reversible, but not C.
Zhang et al. (1999) : HRCT in children with postinfectious BO - bronchial wall thickening, bronchiectasis, etc.

Follicular bronchiolitis.

   This may occur in relation to suppurative bronchial disease i.e. bronchiectasis - the 'secondary type' or as the 'primary type' in association with connective tissue disorders (rheumatoid, Sjögren's syndrome or immune deficiency states) or hypersensitivity reactions (e.g. pulmonary eosinophilia). such patients tend to present in early or mid adult life with dyspnoea. the disease may be progressive. Its response to steroids is variable. On CT nodular enlargement of intrapulmonary lymphoid tissue may be seen (see also p. 13.4 and quoted Illus.).

References.

Fortoul et al. (1985) : Follicular bronchiolitis in association with connective tissue disease.
Yousem et al. (1985) : Follicular bronchiolitis/bronchitis.
Nicholson et al. (1995) : Reactive pulmonary lymphoid disorders.
Gibson and Hansell (1998) : Lymphocytic disorders of the chest.
Howling et al. (1999) : HRCT in 12 cases showed small centrilobular nodules ± peribronchial nodules & ground-glass shadowing.

Bronchiolar obstruction may also be a feature of some rare conditions.

Aguayo et al. (1992) : Idiopathic diffuse hyperplasia of pulmonary neuroendocrine cells and airway disease.

Miller and Müller (1995) : Neuroendocrine cell hyperplasia and obliterative bronchiolitis in pts. with peripheral carcinoid tumours.

Sherrin et al. (1995) : Obliterative bronchiolitis caused by multiple tumourlets and microcarcinoids successfully treated by single lung transplantation.

Brown, M. et al. (1997) : Neuroendocrine BO due to neuroendocrine hyperplasia in a female aged 65.

Lai et al. (1996), Higgenbottam (1997) & Yang et al. (1997) : Bronchiolitis obliterans following the ingestion of an Asian shrub leaf used as an appetite suppressant - Sauropus androgynus.

Janoski et al. (2000) : Psyllium (derived from fleawort seeds - used as a laxative) aspiration causing bronchiolitis - HRCT showed small well-defined centrilobular nodules & branching linear opacities like a tree in bud.

Diffuse (Asian) panbronchiolitis.

This form of bronchiolitis is a chronic inflammatory lung disease of unknown aetiology, but with a proliferation of foamy macrophages in distended bronchioles, which occurs mainly in Asian peoples (Chinese, Japanese and Koreans); it has been studied by several authors (see below), but may be becoming less common. Affected patients often have repeated or worsening attacks of lower respiratory infection and sinusitis leading to respiratory failure and cor pulmonale. Plain radiographs show miliary nodules and in the later stages, especially basal 'cystic changes'. HRCT may give an appearance like a '**tree in bud**'* in the earlier stages, the later stages showing the cysts and due to exudate in small bronchi + air trapping.

* a sign also seen in some other forms of bronchiolitis e.g. **mycoplasma   and   tuberculosis, following aspiration and in some HIV patients and post transplantation.**

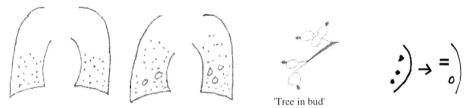

'Tree in bud'

a - Basal miliary shadows   b - More generalised miliary   c - Tiny nodules + small cysts   d - CT-small nodules
shadows + basal cystic changes. due to dilated bronchioles.   → bronchiolectasis &
peribronchiolar thickening.

Fig. 3.11   Diagrams - lung changes due to panbronchiolitis (c after Akira et al., 1988, Radiology, **168**, 437 - 438 with permission).

References.

Nakata and Tanimoto (1981).   Todo et al. (1982) : 'Tree in bud' appearance.

Homma et al. (1983) : A disease of the transitional zone of the lung.   Akira et al. (1988) : Evaluation with HRCT.

Murata et al. (1989) : Demonstrated, using positron emission tomography with radioactive nitrogen and CT in 7 cases, that lung hyperinflation occurred in this condition mainly around the periphery of the lung, and was characteristic of diffuse bronchiolar narrowing.

Nishimura et al. (1992) : Diffuse panbronchiolitis - correlation of CT and pathology - CT showed small rounded nodules of increased density associated with dilated airways (see c above).

Akira et al. (1993) : Serial CT of patients treated with long term low dose erythromycin showed some regression, whilst in those given no such treatment rounded centrilobular dense areas progressed to dilatation of the airways.

Ichikawa et al. (1995) : Reversible airway lesions in pts. with diffuse bronchiolitis with erythromycin therapy.

Tsang et al. (1998) : Clinical profiles of Chinese pts. with diffuse bronchiolitis.

Gujjar lung - due to the inhalation of smoke from fire-wood and cow dung is seen in Northern India. Anthracotic type micronodules containing carbon correspond to fine nodules on chest radiographs. Raison et al. (2000) demonstrated centrilobular nodules on HRCT.

Bronchiolitis, interstitial lung changes and fine lung nodules associated with cigarette smoking.
    As well as mucosal changes and dilatation of bronchial mucous glands in the larger bronchi (see ps. 24.5 & 24.14), cigarette smoking also causes changes in the smaller bronchi, bronchioles and alveoli. Each puff produces over 10^{10} particles and many smokers will deposit over 5kg of tar and other material in their lungs during their life-time. Much of this is engulfed by macrophages.

Respiratory bronchiolitis is often found in the lungs of smokers, and is characterised by the presence of PAS positive brown pigmented macrophages in the lungs of smokers; this is usually asymptomatic. In a few cases (usually 20 to 40 year old smokers) a symptomatic bronchiolitis may be found with denuded bronchiolar epithelium and mural inflammatory cells. This may be associated with ground-glass shadowing on CT (due to less air and more cells particularly in the upper lobes, and may lead on to a fine fibrotic nodular pattern. This is more pronounced posteriorly, with tiny micro-nodules at the bases of the inter-lobular septa.

Tiny micronodules on CT at the bases of the inter-lobular septa.

    These changes are similar to those seen in DIP (see also ps. 19.119 & 122), but in the latter the pathological findings are more pronounced in the alveolar ducts and alveoli. Bronchiolar wall fibrosis and thickening may reduce the diameter of bronchioles and be a precursor to the development of 'chronic obstructive pulmonary disease' (COPD or COAD = airways disease), and emphysema, particularly centri-lobular emphysema (p. 6.8)
    There may be a synergistic effect with asbestos and other agents producing diffuse fibrosis.

References.
Rémy-Jardin et al. (1993a&b) : Studied CT abnormalities of cigarette smoking on the lung in adults and noted parenchymal micro-nodules, areas of ground-glass attenuation and emphysema, esp. in the upper zones. Emphysema and bronchial wall thickening were the only HRCT signs associated with reduced functional parameters.
Gruden and Webb (1993) : CT findings in a proven case of respiratory bronchiolitis - a 29 year old female smoker had bilateral, patchy ground-glass opacities, most prominent in the upper lobes, which tended to have a centrilobular predominance - there was also mild paraseptal emphysema at the lung apices. An open lung biopsy showed evidence of respiratory bronchiolitis with mild ectasia and inflammation of terminal airways; numerous pigment-laden macrophages filled the respiratory bronchioles and extended into alveolar ducts and sacs. The patients condition improved with reducing her smoking and treatment with oral steroids.
Gückel and Hansell (1998) : Imaging the 'dirty lung' - has HRCT cleared the smoke?
Rémy-Jardin (1998) : HRCT of normal lung and normal variations.- pointed out that the ground-glass shadowing is due to less air and more cells i.e. a **macrophage alveolitis.**

Weiss (1984 and 1988) : Nodule formation in cigarette smokers may be associated with interstitial lung fibrosis, or bronchial wall thickening, particularly in association with asbestos inhalation, & probably due to interference with fibre clearance through impaired ciliary action, thus increasing the number of fibres retained in the lungs.
Blanc et al. (1988) : Studied 294 shipyard workers to evaluate asbestos exposure and cigarette smoking interactions in non-malignant disease and found synergism only for parenchymal lung opacities. The affected subjects had decreased air flow at low lung volumes, on function studies.
Hnizdo and Sluis-Cremer (1988) : Effect of tobacco smoking on the presence of asbestosis at post-mortem and on the presence of irregular chest x-ray opacities in asbestos exposed workers.
Rosenstock et al. (1988) : Chest Roentgenographic abnormalities and smoking status in an asbestos-exposed cohort - suggested that pleural abnormalities may be associated with physiological impairment in such persons.
(See also Garg et al, 1994 - p. 3.28, and p. 3.18).

Micro-carcinoid tumourlets (neuroendocrine hyperplasia) may mimic bronchiolitis, by scarring and narrowing the small airways, leading to overinflated lungs and tiny nodules. HRCT may show **black lungs** and thinned vessels, tiny nodules and air trapping.

Organising pneumonia (including cryptogenic organising pneumonia ['COP'] and bronchiolitis obliterans organising pneumonia ['BOOP'] - Illus. **COP/BOOP**).

Organising pneumonia is a relatively uncommon condition which represents one of the ways in which the lung may respond to an inflammatory stimulus or injury caused by infection, drugs, radiation or rejection as with a transplanted lung. It may also be a feature of the organising stage of ARDS or vasculitis such as Wegener's granuloma. It also includes 'COP' or 'BOOP' which are essentially different terms for organising pneumonia of undetermined cause. The term COP is preferable to BOOP which can easily be confused with bronchiolitis, mainly characterised by airflow obstruction (see below and ps. 3.25 - 28).

The clinical and radiological features often suggest a pneumonic illness that does not respond to antibiotic treatment, but shows an often rapid response to steroids. A diffuse form may however be resistant to therapy (Illus. **COP/BOOP, Pt. 1a-e**). Patients usually have fever, malaise, dyspnoea, a non-productive cough, peripheral lung infiltrates on chest radiographs and intra-luminal pneumonitis on biopsy. Certain diagnosis is only made by open lung biopsy, but trans-bronchial lavage and biopsy may be helpful.

The typical histological picture is of a '**boot-like**' fibrotic or granulomatous mass extending from the alveoli into alveolar ducts and bronchioles, causing plugging of the smaller airways and leading to their destruction with obliterative scarring (Fig. 3.12a). Interstitial inflammation is usually minimal. The granulomatous masses may also extend into adjacent alveoli through the pores of Kohn.

As noted above the pathological features are not specific as to aetiology, as this type of response may be found with viral and other infections (e.g. mycoplasma), infarction, allergic alveolitis, collagen disease (e.g. rheumatoid), drug reactions (e.g. acebutolol, amiodarone, bleomycin, cocaine, gold salts, paraquat and penicillamine), ARDS and **post-radiation pneumonitis**. It may also be seen in the graft vs host disease following lung transplantation and as a reaction to toxic fumes e.g. methyl isocyanate (see p. 19.108).

Post-radiation pneumonitis may occur as a **COP/BOOP** type of consolidation starting in the irradiated area (e.g. upper lobe in patients with ca breast) and later spreading as nodular type consolidation to other parts of the same and/or the contralateral lung. Some of these lesions may resolve spontaneously, but most clear more quickly with steroids, and relapses may occur on stopping treatment.

Overlap may also occur with Wegener's granuloma, eosinophilic lung, etc. A distinction from fibrosing alveolitis is that finger clubbing is common in that condition, but rare with BOOP/ COP. The condition is rare in SLE or systemic sclerosis, but occasionally occurs in polyarteritis nodosa.

The condition affects men and women equally, and most patients are aged 50 to 60, but a few are adolescents. Onset is usually subacute, with a viral like illness, and dyspnoea may be mild to severe in more acute cases.

Radiologically the condition may be characteristic, particularly on CT - there are usually multiple patchy alveolar opacities (either **unilateral** or **bilateral**) varying from **ground-glass shadowing to frank consolidation** with air-bronchograms, with most commonly a sub-pleural or peribronchovascular distribution on CT. Some patients have more diffuse bilateral infiltration and about a third of cases show nodules (particularly seen in those who are immunocompromised); these may have a broad pleural tag. The CT findings may mimic chronic bacterial, fungal or viral infection (especially '**round pneumonia**'), chronic eosinophilic pneumonia (p. 19.55 - with curvilinear opacities of consolidation around the bronchi), alveolar cell carcinoma, lymphoproliferative disorders, low grade lymphomas, sarcoidosis, fibrosing alveolitis or occasionally a cavitating lung tumour (see references). Pleural effusions and pneumatocoeles are rare. The areas of consolidation have a tendency to migrate or 'wander', thus confirmation of the position of lesions is important before a biopsy (usually surgical) is taken and now often taken at video-assisted thoracoscopy.

Sometimes as well as giving steroids, cytotoxic drugs especially cyclophosphamide and azathioprine have been given as well, particularly to those patients who have been severely ill (see Illus. **COP/BOOP, Pt. 2a-d**). Some also give antibiotics as the condition can be triggered by infections.

Unusual triggers for COP/BOOP include parasites such as malaria - see Illus. **MALARIA**.

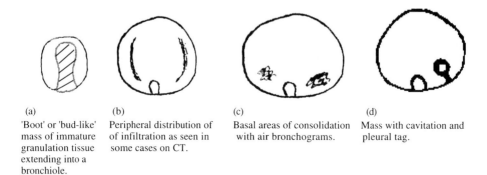

(a)
'Boot' or 'bud-like'
mass of immature
granulation tissue
extending into a
bronchiole.

(b)
Peripheral distribution of
of infiltration as seen in
some cases on CT.

(c)
Basal areas of consolidation
with air bronchograms.

(d)
Mass with cavitation and
pleural tag.

Fig. 3.12   Some pathological and radiological appearances in organising pneumonia.

Bronchiolitis obliterans (BO - p. 3.25) should not be confused with COP/BOOP. Bronchiolitis obliterans causes narrowing of the bronchioles due to deposition of submucosal collagen but does not produce an intraluminal exudate, whereas COP produces streams of granulation tissue within the small air spaces. OB also produces little if any abnormal shadowing on plain chest radiographs which are often unremarkable in inspiration, but tend to show marked air-trapping in expiration (see also p. 3.26).

References and historical review.
    Although sporadic cases of chronic organising pneumonia have been described by various authors from the beginning of the century and the condition has been included in some monographs, most interest in the condition dates from the early 1980s.

Davison et al. (1982) : Steroid responsive relapsing cryptogenic organising pneumonitis.
Davison et al. (1983 - from the Brompton Hospital) : Described a series of 8 patients with an alveolar disease and a poorly defined chest radiographic pattern and termed it 'cryptogenic organising pneumonitis'. This description emphasised the buds of connective tissue in the air spaces, indicating the organisation of persistent exudate by fibroblasts and other cells, the connective tissue extending the alveolar ducts and occasionally into the respiratory bronchioles. They assumed the cells were largely derived from type 2 pneumocytes.
Epler et al. (1985 - from Boston, Mass., USA) : Reviewed 2,000 reports of open lung biopsies taken over a period of 30 years, and found 94 which described 'bronchiolitis obliterans', with plugs of granulation tissue involving bronchioles and alveolar ducts, together with extension of the organisation into the alveoli, with varying degrees of infiltration by monoclonal cells. Fifty had no apparent cause, and as the changes were those of organising pneumonia, they were termed 'bronchiolitis obliterans- organising pneumonia'.
Chandler et al. (1986) : Radiographic manifestations of BOOP versus UIP.
Allen and Wevers (1989) : HIV-associated BOOP.
Bartter et al. (1989) : Idiopathic BOOP with peripheral infiltrates on chest radiographs.
Camus et al. (1989) : BOOP in patients taking acebutolol or amiodarone.
Cordier et al. (1989) : Reviewed 16 patients and confirmed the predominantly alveolar distribution of the abnormalities. They grouped the radiographic abnormalities as follows :
 (i) Multiple migrating patches of pneumonia having a sub-acute course. CT showed multiple peripheral alveolar opacities.
 (ii) A solitary area of pneumonia simulating a mass - most common in the left upper lobe.

(iii) Diffuse interstitial lung disease (with severe dyspnoea - only half responded to steroids).

Dunnill (1989 in Oxford) : Found that in several cases the appearance has been associated with or caused by diffuse disseminated small pulmonary emboli, the fibrosis apparently being stimulated by the anoxia.

Sulavik (1989) : The concept of 'organising pneumonia'.

Müller et al. (1987): Differential diagnosis of BOOP and UIP (fibrosing alveolitis).

Swinburn et al. (1988) : BOOP in a patient with ulcerative colitis.

Müller et al. (1990) : BOOP - CT features in 14 patients. The findings included unilateral or bilateral air-space consolidation, small nodular opacities, irregular linear opacities, bronchial wall thickening and dilatation, and small pleural effusions.

Sweatman et al. (1990) : Chronic airflow obstruction seldom occurs.

Bellomo et al. (1991 from Australia) : 6 patients with COP - 2 had diffuse infiltrates, 2 peripheral infiltrates and 2 localised involvement. They suggested the term 'cryptogenic intraluminal fibrosis of distal air-spaces'. They also noted three main radiographic patterns of disease viz. (i) patchy peripheral infiltration, (ii) localised lobar infiltration and (iii) diffuse widespread parenchymal infiltration.

du Bois and Geddes (1991) : OB, COP and BOOP - three names for two different conditions.

Geddes (1991) : 'Bronchiolitis obliterans' is very different from 'COP' and 'BOOP'. In the former, patients have small airway disease with normal alveoli and hypertransradiant lung fields without infiltrates and show little (if any) response to treatment, whereas those with 'COP' or 'BOOP' have alveolar disease with granulomatous tissue that extends variably into the airways. These patients have radiographic lung infiltrates and are steroid responsive.

Hogg (1991) : Reviewed 910 biopsy samples of interstitial lung disease collected at the Brompton Hospital over a ten year period, and previously published by Corrin et al. (1989), and proposed a new classification based on pathogenesis. This gave three major categories: - (i) Chronic **non-granulomatous inflammatory process** (most common) - fibrosing alveolitis, (ii) Chronic **granulomatous inflammatory process**, (iii) **Infiltration of the interstitial** space by benign, borderline or frankly neoplastic cells (e.g. eosinophilic granuloma, lymphangioleiomyomatosis, lymphoid hyperplasia, pseudolymphoma, Sjögren's syndrome, lymphangitis, etc.). He regarded **COP or BOOP** (with organisation of the inflammatory exudate within the distal airways) as a variant of (i) and **DIP** (a cellular form of fibrosing alveolitis) as a variant of (ii). He also felt that the cells in the exudate were alveolar macrophages and not desquamating pneumocytes, and that when the inflammatory exudate fills the alveolar spaces completely, rather than being limited to the surface of the alveolar ducts, the air spaces can be obliterated as the exudate is organised by connective tissue. Both fibrosing alveolitis and BOOP may progress to **end-stage lung** (p. 19.122), as may some granulomas and neoplastic processes.

Perämäki et al. (1991) : Unilateral BOOP and broncho-alveolar lavage neutrophilia in a patient with parainfluenza 3 virus infection.

Epler (1992) : BOOP - definition and clinical features.

Epstein and Bennett (1992) : BOOP with migratory pulmonary infiltrates in a 67 year old woman.

Flowers et al. (1992) : BOOP - report of seven cases - predominantly lower zone and peripheral consolidation.

Gammon et al. (1992) : BOOP associated with SLE (see also p. 19.103).

Haddock and Hansell (1992) : Reviewed nine cases from the Royal Brompton Hospital. The patients had a cough with mucus, fever and weight loss. Multifocal consolidation was present in five, two had a poorly defined nodular pattern tending to be confluent and two others dense consolidation. CT was carried out in five and mainly showed a peripheral distribution of infiltration.

Hansell (1992a) : What are BOOP and COP?

Hansell (1992b) : BO, BOOP and COP. BO affects the small airways, and mostly occurs following viral chest infections - its radiological appearances are often unremarkable, but include bronchial wall thickening and overinflation of the lungs. COP gives rise to granulation tissue identical to that found in the air spaces in cases of slowly resolving bacterial pneumonia. They usually have predominantly lower zone areas of consolidation and show a prompt response to steroid treatment. There may be a seasonal variation with more cases occurring in the spring.

Nishimura and Itoh (1992) : HRCT features of BOOP.

Kohno et al. (1993) : CT appearances in focal organising pneumonia.

Lee et al. (1994) : COP - CT findings in 43 patients - in immunocompetent patients the findings most commonly consist of bilateral areas of consolidation mainly involving the subpleural and/or peribronchovascular regions. In those immunocompromised the appearances are variable, most commonly ground-glass shadowing or nodules.

Preidler et al. (1996) : Distribution pattern of CT changes in patients with BOOP.

Voloudaki et al. (1996) : Two cases of BOOP with crescentic and ring-shaped opacities - **pseudocavities** due to ground-glass shadowing within denser granulomatous tissue.

Murphy et al. (1998) : 5 cases of BOOP presenting as **lung nodules up to 3.5 cm in diameter** - 4 showed **cavitation**, 3 had haemoptysis, 2 were smokers - one of whom had a false diagnosis of lung ca on biopsy. Resection in all cases was curative.

Akira et al. (1998) : BOOP manifesting as **multiple large nodules or masses** - 12 pts. with 60 lesions - features included: air bronchograms, irregular margins, relatively broad pleural tags in contact with the pleura, parenchymal bands or subpleural lines or are associated with focal thickening of interlobar pleura.

Cordier (2000) : Organising pneumonia - review - **"Taken together, the clinical, pathological and biopathological data suggest that COP reflects the response to an initial injury of unknown** cause(s) which causes pulmonary inflammation, which is further self-perpetuated in some patients to produce the characteristic buds of intra-alveolar granulation tissue associating (myo)fibroblasts and connective matrix. The most intriguing feature of COP is its rapid resolution with corticosteroids, the mechanism of which is currently unknown."

BOOP due to nitrofurantoin - this may cause pulmonary oedema and diffuse pulmonary interstitial thickening with mosaic perfusion pattern and ground-glass opacification. It usually clears on withholding the drug and giving steroids - references are given on p. 19.112.

Chapter 4 : **Lung and Tracheo-Bronchial Tumours - main types.**
a **Historical Review and some General Points,**
b **Peripheral Lung Tumours, infection complicating tumours,**
c **Central Bronchial Tumours,**
d **Tracheal Tumours, Papillomas and Endobronchial Deposits.**

(a) HISTORICAL REVIEW AND SOME GENERAL POINTS.

The early history of chest radiography is given in the Preface.

In 1909 Robert Knox published two cases, one a sarcoma of the chest wall, and the other pneumonia in a patient aged 20 which was very slow to clear. The same author presented a paper entitled 'The x-ray diagnosis of malignant disease of the lungs' at the 17th International Congress of Medicine, London, 1913. Knox (1917) published a textbook '**Radiography and Radio-therapeutics**', and in discussing the differential diagnosis of diseases in the lungs, noted the gross appearances of some lung and mediastinal tumours and their not uncommon association with tuberculosis.
Adler (1912) published a monograph, in which he not only briefly summarised each of the 374 cases of malignant lung tumour which were all that he could collect from the world literature, but also gave a concise and accurate description of the pathological and clinical aspects of the disease. Adami and Nicholls (1909) and Kaufman (1911), noted that lung tumours may cavitate and may arise either within a large bronchus or peripherally within a lobe.

Irregular peripheral tumours.
Professor Wenckebach (1913) from Strasbourg also at the 17th International Congress of Medicine discussed the radiology of the chest and stated that 'tumours generally throw uniform deep shadows and are usually easy to distinguish from infiltrations by their sharp boundaries. In the case of rapidly growing malignant tumours, the edges are not sharp but **frayed,** yet still distinguishable from the surrounding pneumonic shadow'. He also noted that 'primary tumours of the lungs, such as bronchial carcinoma, may produce fantastic x-ray pictures'.

Effects of bronchostenosis.
Golden (1925) found that similar appearances to those seen with endobronchial foreign bodies might occur with some bronchogenic tumours, and also described the effect of bronchostenosis in producing collapse. He stated that with complete obstruction there is collapse of the corresponding part of the lung because the air remaining in the alveoli is quickly absorbed by the circulating blood, whereas with incomplete obstruction, the bronchi distal to it became dilated. He wrote "Hence in the gradually developing stenosis of a bronchial carcinoma, the condition is first that of incomplete obstruction, and bronchiectasis follows with infection in train".
Woodburn Morrison (1923) reported **phrenic palsy secondary to lung neoplasm**.
In 1928, Ralston Paterson discussed the Roentgen ray treatment of primary carcinoma of the lung (and references in his paper related largely to single case reports or to small series of patients).

In the same year, Kirklin and Paterson, published two excellent papers based on a review of the literature at this time, and on the early manifestations of the disease in 55 patients who presented at the Mayo Clinic during the period 1923 -1927. They divided primary malignant lung tumours into two main groups, **parenchymal** and **bronchial**, the 'pathological, clinical and Roentgenological features' differing considerably.

(a) **Parenchymal tumours.**
Most of the parenchymal tumours were adenocarcinomas, with an extraordinarily latent progress, pain of an indefinable but persistent nature and loss of weight without apparent cause. Later, invasion of the pleura, erosion of a bronchus or infection produced the usual triad of cough, dyspnoea and pain in the chest.
Early cases fell into three groups, **nodular, lobar** and **hilar** or **infiltrating**. A **cancerous nodule** was often irregular with its edges infiltrating into the surrounding lung tissue. The **lobar tumour** was much less clear-cut and appeared as a more or less complete consolidation of the whole of a lobe, without the varied texture seen in most cases of pneumonia and it had an irregularly infiltrating edge. The **hilar** or **infiltrating** group was difficult to relate to typical Roentgenological characteristics, although it was the most common type.

(b) **Bronchial tumours**.
The three features of early bronchial malignant disease (adenocarcinoma and 'epithelioma' in about equal numbers) were given as **hilar density** (or enlargement), **atelectasis*** (or collapse) and **bronchiectasis. Pseudo-bronchiectasis** (earlier in this book termed **mucocoeles** - see p. 2.10 -12) was defined as a collection of fluid collected by gravity and aspiration distal to the lesion, the fluid-filled bronchial tree thus causing a density. "If the lesion were really an early bronchial carcinoma, there should be no other characters present, the unaffected lung must be perfectly clear, the upper portion of the mediastinum unthickened and there should never be an appearance as of metastasis distal to the lesion: at this early stage pleurisy is a rare manifestation." They noted that metastasis to the

supraclavicular nodes might occur quite early and that "the Roentgen-ray picture may be altered by extension of the lesion to the mediastinal lymph nodes." The lungs were also a common site for metastases, and the authors observed that "the picture of a primary carcinoma of the lung might easily be obscured by multiple metastases in the other lung or a small bronchial carcinoma may be overlooked in the picture which gives an impression of true miliary carcinosis."

In differentiating a breaking-down tumour from an infective abscess they noted that "abscesses often extended to involve the periphery of the lung" - also a distinguishing feature of encysted fluid or empyema.
* See note on p. 1.60.

In 1950 Lodge (later Sir Thomas - see note on p. 7.2) in Sheffield, and Møller, in Copenhagen both emphasised the important role of diagnostic radiology in the diagnosis of bronchogenic tumours, Møller emphasising the importance of collapse and the value of expiration and lateral views and tomograms. Lodge found that the most common tumours, as shown radiographically in 130 cases, were those producing collapse, a hilar or a peripheral mass; less common were those producing consolidation, infiltration or cavitation. In 1960 he ascribed the **bad prognosis in many peripheral carcinomas to their being positioned in a bed of numerous small veins, so that an invasive growth might produce early distant metastases**. He reviewed the literature and supplied further evidence regarding the distinction between central and peripheral tumours.

Rigler, working in Minneapolis and later in Los Angeles, became very interested in the presentation of lung tumours. He published extensively on this subject, including a book (1946), an article on the early diagnosis of lung cancer (1947), the significance of unilateral hilar enlargement, which could be mimicked by overlying lesions, etc. (Rigler et al., 1952).**

Rigler et al. (1953) found that in many cases, the duration of lung cancer was much longer than had been considered likely, and when previous radiographs were available, these often showed that tiny tumours had been present many months or years before. They advocated 'excision biopsy' of suspicious lesions.

Rigler's further papers are summarised in Tables 4.1 a & b. Observations on what was later known as '**Rigler's   notch**' were first published in 1955 (Rigler, 1955b) as 'a new Roentgen sign of malignancy in the solitary pulmonary nodule' - it was best seen on tomograms (but see Frimann-Dahl below).

Table 4.1 a   Appearances Suggesting a Bronchial Carcinoma (Rigler - see also Illus. **FAMOUS PEOPLE, Rigler**).
Solitary pulmonary shadow, especially if the patient is past middle age.
Increase in size of nodule or mass.
Absence of calcification.
Notching, umbilication or an irregular edge.
Hilar enlargement, especially with the space between the pulmonary artery and the mediastinum being obliterated.
Increasing infiltration of a beaded or nodular type.
Pneumonic lesions :   failing to resolve,
                        having a nodular appearance, or
                        segmental consolidation.
Thick-walled cavities with irregular nodular inner walls.
Segmental, lobar or unilateral obstructive emphysema.
Collapse.
Changes in the lumina of bronchi.

Table 4.1 b   Roentgen Findings in the Evolution of Lung Cancer Found by Retrospective Analysis (Rigler).
Half the cases show some evidence of carcinoma more than two years before symptoms appear.
Two-thirds appear to originate centrally - tend to have symptoms earlier.
One-third originate peripherally - better for surgical resection - symptoms occur later.
Bronchial obstruction may precede the onset of symptoms.
Obstructive emphysema of a lobe or lung may be concomitant with segmental collapse.
Cavitation may occur early in peripheral or central lesions and may disappear as the tumour becomes larger.
Inflammatory changes may appear and disappear during the time of the tumour.
The growth rate of a tumour may show varying rapidity at different times.

(Summarised and adapted from Rigler, 1955a, 1957b and 1960) **For Rigler's Obituary see Radiology (1980), **135**, 247 - 248. See also Dr. Rigler's prophecies Radiology (1997) **204**, 32A - 33A.

Professor Frimann-Dahl (1946 - see Illus. **FAMOUS PEOPLE, Frimann-Dahl 1&2**) and Drevattne and Frimann-Dahl (1961) from Oslo, analysed the appearances of peripheral bronchial neoplasms on tomograms. They took tomograms in three planes (AP, lateral and transverse axial) and found that umbilication of a 'round lesion' occurred not only in 27 out of 31 peripheral neoplasms, but also in 16 out of 22 tuberculomas. They also found similar notchings in metastases of various origins, but did not encounter these with benign masses such as hamartomas or neurinomas. They also described other signs of malignancy such as **scalloping**, **umbilication** with '**apple stalk**' (the growth of a tumour to be very similar to the growth of an apple around its stalk.), and **radiating vessels**. The hilum or notch of a tumour was thought to correspond with the entrance of its vascular supply. Often there was only one notch, but occasionally two or three were present, depending upon the number of vessels in the area of the lung in which the neoplasm originated. Such notching was seen in tumours from 1 to 10 cm^2 in area and was most marked when the diameter exceeded 2.5 cm. They also pointed out that the **bad prognosis with central tumours occurred despite the earlier symptoms; they were also more difficult to demonstrate because they were hidden by the heart and the pulmonary vessels.**

Scalloping, many "Umbilication" Smaller indentations Many shallow   Radiating vessels   Necrotic centre-
small indentations with"apple-stalk" plus larger concavity   indentations   irregular contour.

Fig. 4.1 Schematic representation of tomographic appearance of different peripheral bronchial carcinomas (After Drevattne and Frimann-Dahl, 1961, with permission from Brit. J. Radiology).

Møller (1950) thought that a small area of collapse, or less commonly, obstructive emphysema was the earliest sign of a bronchial tumour, and pointed out the necessity of lateral views.

Schinz et al. (1953 - in their text book), classified malignant primary tumours of the lung into pulmonary sarcoma, bronchial carcinoma and cancer of the alveolar epithelium. They noted that Roentgenograms could be negative, also that in early cases, 'stenotic' or 'obstructive emphysema' might be seen, whereas with progressive bronchial stenosis, segmental collapse occurred and there was often hilar enlargement.

The site of origin of tumours in the lungs.

It was commonly thought that the majority of tumours arose in the larger bronchi, and close to the hila. This was largely because tumours are mostly found at this site at post-mortem and also because tumours are often seen within the larger bronchi at bronchoscopy.

Fried (1938) wrote ' the tumour always originates in the main-stem bronchus or in some of its smaller branches but not in those whose diameter is about 10 mm or less'. Boyd (1950) stated 'the hilus tumour is by far the commonest variety. Over 90% of the cases fall into this group.' Willis (1948) wrote 'at least three-quarters of the tumours demonstrably arise in the larger bronchi, either the main bronchi or in the lobar bronchi or near the hilar region.' Schinz et al. (1953) stated that bronchial or hilar carcinoma was most common in the upper lobes, whilst Kerley (1954), pointed out that tuberculomas are seldom seen in the anterior parts of the lungs or in the basic segments of the lower lobes, whereas a **tumour may originate anywhere in the lungs**.

Raeburn (1951) had put forward the view that most lung cancers had a peripheral origin. Having previously failed to find small tumours in the large bronchi in a series of patients dying from other causes, he sliced up the whole of both lungs in a series of 400 patients, and found four small tumours of peripheral type and none in the large bronchi. Raeburn and Spencer (1953) added another six cases, making ten in all, nine of which were peripheral and one central. However four were minute 'oat-cell' lesions or tumourlets.

Walter and Price (1955b) noted "the view that the majority of lung cancers arise in the main bronchi is based mainly on post-mortem studies of the disease in its terminal stages when the tumour has in most instances, attained a large size: direct spread and lymphatic metastasis have combined to produce the familiar hilar mass involving lung, bronchi, vessels and mediastinal structures alike. Gross involvement of the large hilar bronchi is usually present and this has been assumed to be the origin; it is doubtful whether this assumption is often justified." The appearances may be mimicked by metastatic tumour or Hodgkin's disease; they may also be produced by peripheral lung tumours involving the large bronchi secondarily, either by direct extension or by lymphatic metastasis. "From examination of large tumours it is impossible to estimate the frequency of this occurrence, and it is only in the small or early cases that the site of origin is likely to be recognisable." In a careful study of operative specimens, these authors found 47% to be central tumours (arising in a main or segmental bronchus), 3% indeterminate and 50% peripheral (arising in the smaller bronchi or bronchioles). They also found that central tumours tended to be squamous and adenocarcinomas were more often peripheral, whilst oat-cell tumours were equally divided between central and peripheral positions.

Garland et al. (1961) found that not only were peripheral tumours twice as common as those arising centrally, but that in the group of peripheral tumours in the upper lobes, there was a preponderance of tumours originating in the apical and posterior segments. Dunnill (1982) gave a rather different view, based on resection and post-mortem studies, that the majority of bronchial carcinomas arose centrally, but in 1987 wrote that "they arise from bronchi".

As also discussed on p. 13.7, the author believes that some tumours, which appear to have a central origin, may in fact have arisen peripherally, with central spread via lymphatics to the larger bronchial walls. The author's previously published series (1973) gave a slight upper lobe preponderance - about 10%, and a 3 : 1 peripheral to central distribution for the origins of all types of tumour. These figures may be because he had gone to considerable lengths to demonstrate peripheral masses by tomography in doubtful cases. He also believes that all segments and lobes of both lungs are subject to the development of tumours. The frequency with which tumours arise in any segment or lobe, being roughly proportional to its volume, but with some upper lobe preponderance, and possibly also a slight posterior preponderance.

[Right middle lobe tumours are discussed on p. 4.19]

(b) PERIPHERAL LUNG TUMOURS.

It would be of great benefit if one could distinguish tumours from benign lesions by radiological methods with any degree of certainty. As pointed out in the preceding historical survey, a great deal of effort has been put into this by several authors, and further surveys and papers are quoted in this section. In many cases (perhaps the majority) an informed 'guess' after perusing the radiographs and tomograms, together with a knowledge of the patient's age and history (including smoking habit) may well be correct. However certainty can only be achieved with positive cytology or histology, obtained by sputum cytology, needle biopsy or '**excision biopsy**'.

When a patient presents with a lung nodule, one should always try to obtain previous radiographs. Some tumours are slow growing, and an unrecognised tiny abnormality some two, three or even four years earlier may have become larger. In other cases, an old scar will be noted to be entirely similar. Enlargement usually implies a sinister cause, whilst an abnormality, that has remained unchanged for two or more years is nearly always benign.

If the shape of a lesion cannot be readily assessed on plain radiographs, it should be studied by conventional tomograms and /or CT. This will determine if it is smooth or irregular in outline, its precise position in the lung, and the presence of calcification, fat or degeneration within it. Fat or calcification usually signify a benign lesion, but as discussed on p.6.20 calcification may occasionally be seen in some lung tumours. Degeneration usually implies a tumour, abscess or infarct.

Many authors feel that a small tumour is less likely to give rise to metastases than a larger one, and that in smokers below the age the age of 70 they should be removed as soon as possible after being found. Illus. **CA RUL, Pt. 47** illustrates such a small nodule found by chance on a 'routine radiograph' in the right upper lobe of a man of 50. A lobectomy was carried out, the nodule being a small squamous tumour. He lived for twelve years, without any sign of recurrence, and died from ischaemic heart disease.

In other cases, small peripheral neoplasms may he associated with gross metastatic disease at the time of presentation. Examples of this are shown in Illus. **AZYGOS NODES, Pt. 5a-b** - small well marginated tumour in right upper lobe, but tomograms showed azygos node enlargement; Illus. **BRAIN DEPS, Brain Pt. 6a-c**, where there was a small (1cm) left upper lobe tumour + hilar node enlargement at the time of presentation, as well as a large cerebral secondary deposit; and in Illus. **CA CAVITATION, Ca cavitary Pt. 54a-b**, where a small cavitating right upper lobe tumour was associated with widespread bony metastases.

(Similar findings are often found with primary tumours in other sites, e.g. the breast, and very often it is the spread and degree of malignancy of a tumour which is of paramount importance, rather than the actual size of the primary mass. One also has to remember that no radiological method will demonstrate microscopic or tiny metastases).

Small round **(spherical)** foci or 'coin' lesions (solitary lung lesions).
The term 'coin lesion' was defined by Thornton et al. (1944) as a solitary lesion, 1 to 5 cm in size, round or oval in shape, with well-defined margins and surrounded by normal lung. Most are homogeneous in texture, but may contain calcification. The term 'coin' is somewhat unfortunate since when studied in more than one plane such nodules are seen to be **'spherical'**. (See also - Storey et al., 1953, 'Coin lesions of the lung' and author's note on p. 1.59).

Such foci are usually discovered fortuitously. There are many possible causes including bronchial tumours, adenomas, tuberculomas, hamartomas, secondary deposits, rheumatoid nodules, collagen disease nodules, pulmonary infarcts, pneumoconiotic or other fibrotic nodules, A/V malformations or aneurysms, intrapulmonary lymph node enlargements, etc.

Multiple spherical lesions.
These may be due to infection in patients with bronchopneumonia, or to secondary deposits in patients with cancer. In the latter they are usually well defined, and are sometimes referred to as 'cannon balls'. They may be the presenting feature of renal, testicular and some bowel tumours. Occasionally they may be due to a lung tumour which has metastasised to the lungs, or to multiple primary lung tumours (see p.4.18). Rarely multiple pulmonary nodules may be due benign tumours - multiple adenomas or hamartomas. They may also be due to more than one cause, e.g. tuberculomas and secondary deposits or a primary lung tumour, etc.

Single and multiple lesions.
With both single and multiple lesions, the likelihood of a particular cause will depend on the patient's age, smoking habit, prior medical and occupational history, history of contact with tuberculosis, race or country of origin (tuberculosis is far more common than lung cancer in those who have come from the Indian sub-continent), hydatids may he found in some people in Wales, the north of Scotland, coming from the Middle East or Orient, fungal infections causing granulomas in people from, or who have visited, some parts of the USA, etc.

Occasionally, as shown by tomography, a lung nodule may contain unusual or foreign material, such as the portions of ribs demonstrated in Illus. **TRAUMA, Pts. 11 & 13a-e**, or a bullet (see also Illus. **FOREIGN BODIES**).

During the past three decades, the number of tuberculomas seen in the UK, has markedly declined, whilst the incidence of bronchial tumours has risen. Black and Poole (1955, from the Churchill Hospital, Oxford) studied 124 solitary round foci, none of which was shown to be neoplastic in origin. Garland (1958) found 25% of round foci to be caused by carcinoma. Paulson (1957) found 50% were malignant. Toomes et al. (1983 from Heidelberg in West Germany) reported a series of 955 peripheral 'coin' lesions, resected between 1970 & 1980 - male to female ratio - 4 : 1 and right to left lung - 5 : 4 (roughly reflecting the relative sizes of the two lungs) and found 49 % to be malignant; the proportion of malignant cases (mainly bronchial neoplasms) increased sharply with increasing age, so that so that over age 50 - 65 % were malignant, whilst under age 50 the figure was 33 %.

In Oxford we have found a similar distribution.

Further causes of single and multiple nodules are shown in Table 4.2 (p. 4.11).

Pulmonary Nodules - benign or malignant? - calcification - change in size over time.
Several points should be considered in attempting to distinguish benign from malignant nodules.
(i) **Size** - by chance alone single lesions > 2cm in diameter are likely to be neoplasms.
Usually a nodule which has remained unchanged in size for two to three years may be considered as benign - see also reference to Good (below) and to Siegelman et al. (1986a - p. 4.7 who felt that benign hamartomas should not increase by > 1mm/yr.) and Geddes & Elliott (1989 - p. 4.8). When ascertaining a change in size, previous radiographs are essential, and should always be sought! Whilst the '**two year rule**' may generally be true (Illus. **BENIGN NODULE, Pt. 2a-d**), one still has to consider possible exceptions, and changes that may take place in the degree of malignancy and growth rates in tumours. A memorable case is shown in Illus. **CA SURVIVAL, Pt. 6a-e** - an elderly lady in whom a small lung nodule slowly increased in size over several years, and then suddenly enlarged with the production of multiple pulmonary and other deposits.
(ii) **Calcification** - when calcified, lung nodules are most likely to be benign, but see also ps. 6.19 - 22 re other benign causes and calcification in primary and secondary tumours.

Abeles and Chaves (1952), Flavell (1954) and Good (1963) stressed the importance of calcification as indicating non-malignant disease. O'Keefe, Good and McDonald (1957) at the Mayo Clinic radiographed 207 pulmonary nodules after resection and found calcification in 77 (3.7%). It occurred most frequently in the granulomas, where it was largely laminated, and was next commonest in the hamartomas. Small punctate areas of calcification, similar to those seen in some primary breast tumours at mammography, were visible in 16% of primary lung tumours, in 10% of pulmonary metastases and in some bronchial adenomas.

Good (1963) listed four types of calcification in peripheral nodules as seen on plain films or tomograms (Fig. 4.2): (a) a small central nidus, (b) multiple punctate foci, (c) an appearance of lamination, sometimes resembling a rifle target with a bulls-eye and (d) conglomerate or interconnected foci giving a 'popcorn' appearance.

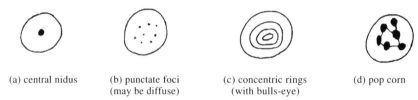

| (a) central nidus | (b) punctate foci (may be diffuse) | (c) concentric rings (with bulls-eye) | (d) pop corn |

Fig. 4.2   Types of calcification in peripheral lung nodules - see also Fig. 5.2.

The first two types were found in granulomas or hamartomas, the third only in granulomas and the fourth in hamartomas. Good considered that the finding of calcification was a very favourable sign that the lesion was benign. He did, however, encounter a case in which a neoplasm engulfed an old Ghon focus, giving an appearance of eccentric calcification (Good and McDonald, 1956). (See also Davis et al., 1956 - calcification within the solitary pulmonary nodule).

Illustrations of benign nodules are shown in Illus. **BENIGN NODULE** and **CALC LG NODULES.**   Eccentric calcification in some larger granulomas is shown in Illus. **BENIGN NODULE 1a-b & 9a-b**.
Good and Wilson (1958) and Good (1963) from the Mayo Clinic recommended that all patients with recently discovered **uncalcified solitary nodules should have them removed and examined microscopically. However, should scrutiny of past radiographs show that such a nodule had been present for two or more years and had not enlarged during this time, the nodule may be kept under periodic review. Good felt that it would be a very unusual cancer that would not grow, albeit slowly, in a period of two years and that further investigation of such a peripheral nodule, other than by tomography, is unlikely to provide any useful information.** This advice was repeated by Theresa McLoud (1983) - see also p. 24.38. However Yankelevitz and Henschke (1997) reviewed this 'rule' and expressed caution, particularly when a patient has smaller nodules. Illus. **CA SURVIVAL Pt. 6a-e** shows the films of an elderly woman who had a static small nodule (an adenoca) for 7 years before it enlarged and metastasised.

(iii) **Tumour edges** - Bateson (1963 & 1964) analysed 100 cases of circumscribed bronchogenic carcinoma: 38 patients had no symptoms, and in only 9 could the diagnosis be confirmed by bronchoscopy; 47 of the shadows were under 5 cm. in diameter, 36 were between 5 and 7 cm., and 17 had diameters of 7 cm. or over. Bateson's findings were that lung tumours may show ill-defined borders, infiltration, a spreading edge, or a combination of these features. Shadows with well-defined outlines - 29/100 showed lobulations. The prognosis was better with well-defined lesions and worse with very large tumours, which were most commonly squamous cell tumours. **Cavitation occurred in all three histological types**. A year later he studied 155 solitary lung masses and found that only 22 of 80 primary carcinomas had well defined and lobulated margins, six of 15 solitary metastases had well defined margins, of 20 inflammatory lesions five had well defined margins and of 40 hamartomatous lesions and other benign processes - all but one had sharply defined margins. **Thus a well defined margin tended to indicate a more benign type of mass and an ill-defined lesion an infiltrating type of process   which could be either malignant or inflammatory**. However, neither sign was absolute. He also found that an ill-defined solitary shadow containing calcification is probably tuberculous and a well defined shadow containing calcification is probably a "mixed tumour" (or hamartoma). He noted three types of tumour edges:

'**Spreading**'   - fine linear shadows
'**Infiltration**'   - coarser lines of variable length extending into the surrounding lung, and
'**Irregularity**'   - a coarse ill defined border which merges imperceptibly into surrounding lung.

In his series 5-6% of masses were hamartomas. Adenomas were more frequent in larger than in smaller bronchi and therefore did not often present as 'coin lesions' but when they did they were circular, oval, or elongated, and perhaps slightly lobulated. The **coin   shadow** ' could be due to the mass per se or due to a blocked bronchus filled with mucus, i.e. a mucocoele (see p. 2.10).

(iv) **Further studies**

Dunlop and Harvey (1982) considered what further investigation should be carried out following the detection of a solitary pulmonary nodule and confirming its presence. In many cases they performed percutaneous or transbronchial biopsy. If these were negative and the patient remained asymptomatic, they reviewed the site, etc. of the nodule with repeated radiographs after a few months, but if the diagnosis remained in doubt they recommended early thoracotomy.

Shin and Ho (1982) studied 24 solitary pulmonary nodules by CT and found that intra-pulmonary malignant tumours tended to have irregular 'fuzzy' borders, finger like projections or fine spiculations, CT numbers of 45 to 65 HU, and an absence of calcification. Non-calcified granulomas had an irregular shape and borders and were usually small, well demarcated and had lower CT numbers of 25 to 55 HU, compared with calcified granulomas 80 HU. However, they did not distinguish between a neoplasm and a non-calcified granuloma on the CT number alone.

Siegelman et al. (1986a) studied 720 patients with solitary pulmonary nodules, including 283 primary lung tumours (119 adeno-, 48 squamous, 43 large cell, 26 alveolar, 17 small cell, 15 undifferentiated, l0 carcinoid, 2 lymphoma and 3 miscellaneous) by CT between 1978 and l982. They analysed: (a) the edges of lesions -

(i) sharp and smooth (or   (ii) moderately smooth or   (iii) irregular undulations   (iv) grossly irregular
spherical 'coin' lesions -   lobulated (35% benign, 45%   or slight spiculation   with spiculation.
70% benign, 20% malignant: malignant - primary or
& 10% indeterminate).   secondary & 20% indeterminate).   (in iii & iv 90% were malignant).
(Reproduced from Radiology, (1968), **160**, 307 - 312 with permission.)

(b) density values : diffuse calcification throughout a nodule (> 164 HU) indicated a benign lesion as did fat (minus 40 to minus 120 HU) within a 2.5 cm hamartoma, or in lipoid pneumonia (due to inhaled medicinal paraffin). However malignant lesions could contain focal areas of calcification (this was found in 38). One carcinoid contained dense bony fibrous looking septa. Calcified granulomas tended to be peripheral.

(c) lesions > 2 cm in size were more likely to be malignant. Bilobed or complex masses could be partly an old scar and partly a neoplasm ('scar cancer').
Lesions with definite criteria were diagnosed as benign. Others which were considered 'indeterminate' were removed or biopsied.
Even benign hamartomas were followed - should not increase in size by > 1 mm/year.
Cavitating nodules which increased in size warranted further investigation.
Other criteria included the vessels entering and leaving A/V malformations, and water density within a bronchogenic cyst.
72 patients had metastatic disease.
They found that CT assessment was most effective with nodules 2 cm or less in diameter. With larger lesions the chance of malignancy was increased.

Fraser et al. (1989) suggested that dual energy digital chest radiography (see p.20.5) is better than both conventional chest radiography and CT (with 10 mm collimation), and is equal to thin section CT in the recognition of **calcification** in lung nodules. (Dual energy chest radiography is also capable of detecting metastatic calcification in the lungs and heart in dialysis patients).

Geddes and Elliott (1989, from London) considered the management of asymptomatic solitary pulmonary nodules and stated :
  (i) benign nodules are apt to be smaller than malignant ones,
  (ii) benign nodules are usually smooth in outline, whereas malignant ones tend to be irregular in outline, lobulated or spiculated,
  (iii) no growth should have taken place over two years, if previous radiographs are available,
  (iv) a central calcified nidus, laminated or diffuse calcification usually indicates a granuloma,
  (v) malignancy under the age of 35 is rare,
  (vi) a negative biopsy does not exclude malignancy.
They tried to assess various management stratagems (continued observation, biopsy, or resection) with life expectancy, but found surprisingly small differences between them.

(v) **Contrast enhancement of lung tumours at CT** (Illus. TUMOUR ENHANCEMENT).
As lung tumours have a dual blood supply, from both pulmonary and bronchial vessels, they might be expected to show **contrast enhancement.** However, as noted in Table 18.4, p. 18.3, benign tumours such as carcinoids and Castleman's tumours have a greater vascularity, and hence would be expected to show the greatest contrast enhancement.

Rubin and Casarett (1966a & b) studied the microcirculation of tumours. Major branches from the host vessels supply the tumour via a hilum (not unlike that in the kidney). Two main patterns of vascularisation were described - (a) peripheral (with and without penetrating vessels), and (b) central vascularisation. The first type is more prone to central necrosis:

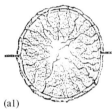
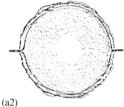

(a1)
Peripheral vascularisation with penetrating vessels.

(a2)
Peripheral vascularisation without penetrating vessels.

(b)
Central vascularisation with no necrosis.

(Reproduced with permission from Clinical Radiology.)

(a1) and (a2)   May undergo central necrosis; the peripheral vascularisation may also allow enhancement with IV contrast agents at CT and positive colour Doppler detection in some cases (see also p. 20.34) - this may also be accentuated by neovascularity (see ps. 24.43 - 44).

Littleton et al. (1990) used trispiral tomography before and after IV contrast injection and found that tumours tended showed 22% increased enhancement compared with 7% for benign lesions.

Other studies using CT are summarised in the references below (e.g. Swensen et al., 1992) but the generally held overall view in the UK is that **enhancement or unenhancement alone is in itself an insufficiently accurate sign for differential diagnosis**.

MR may also be used to study the vascularity or enhancement of lung nodules - see ref. to Bull et al. p. 4.10.

In summary

Unless there is good reason to suspect some non-malignant condition in an otherwise fit person over 40 years of age, a new single peripheral rounded lesion (i.e. not seen or noted on previous radiographs) is probably best removed as soon as possible. The same is true for an enlarging lesion (unless this be due to recent infection or acute enlargement following biopsy etc. i.e. local haemorrhage). Reasons for delay might be other serious disease or disability, suspected malignancy elsewhere in the body, recent contact with open tuberculosis, adjacent soft areas of infiltration\, old scarring, or the presence of calcification. However, when considering tuberculosis in the differential diagnosis one needs to be aware of the possibility of satellite shadows or other signs of local spread of lung tumours which may mimic tuberculosis or other inflammatory disease (Illus. **SATELLITE NODULE** and Fig. 4.3g).

Further references.
Steele (1964) : The Solitary Pulmonary Nodule.
Higgins et al. (1975) : The solitary pulmonary nodule.
Godwin et al. (1982a) : Distinguishing benign from malignant nodules by CT.
Godwin (1983) : The solitary pulmonary nodule.
Siegelman et al. (1984) : CT of the solitary pulmonary nodule.
Kuriyama et al. (1987) : CT - pathological correlation in small peripheral lung cancers - spiculation, lobulation, pleural reaction and convergence of peripheral vessels.

Meziane et al. (1988) : HRCT of the lung parenchyma with pathologic correlation - CT sign showing connection of a nodule to pulmonary arterial branch with secondary deposits and emboli.
Mayr et al. (1989) : Tumours of the bronchi - evaluation with CT should be considered a complementary method to bronchoscopy - it is invaluable in guiding bronchoscopy and in resolving equivocal results of bronchoscopy.
Kuriyama et al. (1991):**Air bronchograms** in small peripheral lung carcinomas (see also p. 2.2).

Naidich et al. (1987) : Comparison of CT and fibreoptic bronchoscopy in the evaluation of bronchial disease (**'bronchus sign'**).

Mori et al. (1990): Used axial and multiplanar CT reconstruction to give a '3D' display of the relationships between vessels, bronchi and peripheral lung nodules (< 3 cm. in diameter) in 26 patients. Involvement of pulmonary veins was seen with all tumours, but only in one (of eight) benign lesions.
(Reproduced from Radiology, **177**, 843 - 849 with permission).

[Note also mass-vessel sign ps. 5.38 & 20.24.]

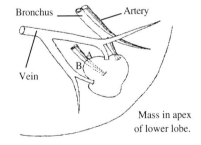

(For diagrams illustrating the 'bronchus sign' see Fig. 21.1, p. 21.2).

Gaeta et al. (1991) : '**Bronchus   sign**' on CT in peripheral carcinoma of the lung - **the   presence   of   a bronchus leading directly to a peripheral pulmonary lesion**.

Gaeta et al. (1993) : HRCT evaluation of tumour-bronchial relationships with carcinomatous solitary pulmonary nodules. Five basic types of tumour-bronchus relationships were seen with CT - (a) bronchus cut off by the tumour, (b) bronchus contained within the tumour, (c) bronchus compressed by the tumour, (d) thickening and smooth narrowing of the bronchus leading to the tumour, and (e) thickening and irregular narrowing of the bronchus leading to the tumour. (The diagnostic yield of transbronchial forceps biopsy and bronchial brushing was significantly higher in nodules characterised by a cut-off or contained bronchus).

Zwirewich et al. (1991a) : Studied HRCT and pathological correlation in 93 patients with solitary pulmonary nodules and found:

(i) **Spiculation** (irregular fibrosis, localised lymphatic tumour spread or infiltrative tumour growth) was seen with six (of 11) benign and 74 (of 85) malignant nodules.

(ii) **Pleural tags** (with three benign and 49 malignant nodules) usually represented fibrotic bands associated with cicatricial pleural retraction.

(iii) **Bubble like areas of low   attenuation** within the nodule (in one benign and 21 malignant lesions) was most common in bronchioloalveolar carcinoma (seven out of 14 cases) - due to patent small bronchi or small cystic spaces within neoplastic areas.

(iv) **Malignant   tumours** as a group were **larger** than benign, and more commonly showed **spiculation, lobulation and inhomogeneous attenuation.**

Gurney (1993) and Gurney et al. (1993) : Determining the likelihood of malignancy in solitary pulmonary nodules with Bayesian analysis (the 'odds-likelihood ratio'). For **malignant   nodules**, the most important radiographic characteristics were **thickness   of   the   cavity   wall**, a **spicular   edge**, and a **diameter > 3 cm.**, and for **benign   nodules**, the most important features were a **benign   growth   rate** and a **benign   pattern   of calcification**.

Harris et al. (1993) : The effect of apparent size of simulated pulmonary nodules by using different window settings - the size must be measured with the lungs properly displayed (i.e. on lung windows or extended scale); if the lungs are 'blacked out' the nodules will appear smaller.

Rémy-Jardin et al. (1993) : Detection of pulmonary nodules with **thick-section   spiral   CT   compared   with conventional CT** (see also Chapter 20).

Kido et al. (1995) : Single-exposure dual energy subtraction chest radiography + iterative noise-reduced bone-subtracted images improved detection of pulmonary nodules.

Swensen et al. (1992) : Solitary pulmonary nodule - CT evaluation of enhancement - **malignant   nodules usually enhanced   a   little   more   than   benign   nodules** (20 to 60 HU) in the first two mins. after IV injection of contrast media, but some granulomas enhanced by 20 to 40 HU.

Swensen et al. (1995) : Malignant neoplasms enhanced (20 - 108 HU) with dynamic CT more than granulomas and benign tumours (111 malignant, 43 granulomas & 9 benign tumours studied). A problem was that in 10% of pts. nodules could not be assessed because of variability in respiration (spiral CT was not used). A problem was that in 10% of pts. nodules could not be assessed because of variability in respiration (spiral CT not used). They also suggested that CT guided biopsy should be reserved for unresectable lesions and for highly suspicious nodules in pts. with severe physiological impairment.

Swensen (1995) wrote "As enhancement techniques with CT, MRI and PET are refined, I believe it is possible that the rate of benign nodule resection could drop into single digits...(presently about 50%)...Realistically, one cannot expect that any single technique will, in practice, approach 100% accuracy in diagnosis of lung nodules."

Bull et al. (1995 & 1996 from Sheffield) : Evaluation of solitary pulmonary nodule with Gd enhanced MR (19 pts.- lesions 1-3 cms in size in coronal plane at 4 & 10 mins) - malignant lesions tend to be more vascular, but can be mimicked by inflammation or A/V malformations. Large cell tumours only showed a slight enhancement. They found the technique difficult to do because of movement in and out of the scan plane (close to the heart and with respiration), and because cavitating lesions only cover a few pixel elements. **Overall it was unreliable**.

Murayama et al. (1995) : CT enhancement in noncalcified tuberculomas - ring or curvilinear enhancement was present in 9 of 12 tuberculomas.

Yamashita et al. (1995) : Incremental dynamic CT in the evaluation of solitary pulmonary nodules - examined before and 30s, 2 & 5m after contrast - 18 lung cancers (< 3 cm), 10 tuberculomas and 4 hamartomas - all cancers + 1 hamartoma showed complete enhancement & 3 hamartomas + 8 tuberculomas showed peripheral enhancement.

Potente et al. (1996) : 32 pts. with solitary pulmonary nodules (SPNs) were examined by 1mm HRCT before and after contrast enhancement - CT numbers of nodules were calculated before, 30 sec., 1 & 3-5 mins after non-ionic contrast IV agent. 1 of 2 TBomas was surrounded by a low infiltration infiltrate ('halo sign'). 211 malignant SPNs enhanced significantly, whilst benign nodules did not show such enhancement. All lung cancers showed a complete enhancement, 2/5 hamartomas and 2/8 TBomas showed a capsular enhancement. A carcinoid also enhanced.

[Noted pulm. vessel involvement, 1 adeno. dep. with calc., and capsular enhancement in fungal masses.]

Molina et al. (1996) : Contrast enhanced CT or MR may distinguish an obstruction in a bronchus from collapsed lung or adjacent mediastinal structures.

Zhang and Kono (1997) : Evaluation of blood flow patterns at dynamic CT with solitary pulmonary nodules - malignant and inflammatory nodules showed higher perfusion than benign ones, & benign nodules tended to have lower precontrast attenuation.

Sone et al. (1997) : Reviewed the radiological & pathological correlations of primary lung cancers & found (a) an irregular or indistinct tumour margin may be caused by tumour infiltration, an irregular desmoplastic response to tumour growth or irregular contraction in the central portion of the tumour whilst (b) solid tumour growth may be associated with a well-defined tumour margin, with or without displacement of adjacent anatomical structures.

Szamosi (1995) : A chest physician from the Karolinska Sjukhuset, Stockholm wrote a monograph 'Lung Cancer - the Art of Detection by Conventional Radiography' - for further details see p. 24.34.

Swensen et al. (2000) : Multicentre study of 356 lung nodules with final diagnosis (out of a total of 550 nodules) - absence of significant nodule enhancement (≤15 HU) at CT is strongly predictive of benignity.

The discussion on calcification, especially within tumours is continued on ps. 6.19.

Table 4.2 Some causes of Solitary and Multiple Pulmonary Nodules.

Inflammatory
(a) Bronchopneumonia (bacterial, fungus or viral), segmental pneumonia, lung abscess, etc.
(b) Round area of consolidation,
(c) Fluid filled bronchi distal to mucoid impaction (mucocoeles - see also below,
(d) Inflammatory pseudo-tumour or histiocytoma - see below.   (e) Lipoid pneumonia.

Granuloma
(a) Viral - varicella   (b) Bacterial - tuberculosis, brucellosis, etc.
(c) Fungal - histoplasmosis, blastomycosis, etc.   (d) Parasitic - schistosomiasis, other worms, etc.
(e) Sarcoidosis.

Tumours
(a) Benign - hamartomas, adenomas, etc.
(b) Malignant - bronchial carcinomas, alveolar cell tumours, lymphomas, etc.
(c) Secondary deposits from various primary tumours, including bronchial.

Other metastases
(a) Abscesses, septic emboli, etc.   (b) Myomas.
(c) Endometriosis, placental deciduous tissue (deciduosis), etc.

Mucocoeles - fluid filled bronchi distal to a blocked bronchus or in a sequestrated or atretic segment.
Broncholith - calcified node entering a bronchus, or calcified mucocoele.

Cysts
(a) Fluid filled bulla   (b) Bronchogenic cyst
(c) Hydatid cyst   (d) Thin-walled fluid-filled neoplasm.

Haematomas and Infarcts.
Haematomas usually clear rapidly, but may cavitate and become cystic.
Infarcts may also produce nodules which usually clear rapidly.
Sometimes they may apparently enlarge for a few months before becoming fibrotic or cavitating. They may be rounded, or have a 'tennis racquet handle' when they become fibrotic.

Vasculitis
(a) Wegener's granuloma and
(b) Polyarteritis nodosa (may also have renal or mesenteric micro- aneurysms on angiography).

Lymphomas
(a) Hodgkin's disease, non-Hodgkin lymphoma, etc.
(b) Pseudolymphoma, lymphoid granuloma, Castleman's tumour, etc.

Fibrotic or necrobiotic nodules
(a) Pneumoconioses   (b) Asbestos, lung nodules or rounded (or whorled) nodules
(c) Rheumatoid, Caplan's syndrome, etc.   (d) Fibrotic lung nodules in association with retroperitoneal fibrosis, etc.
(e) 'Sterilised' metastases, scars following lung abscesses, infarcts, etc.   (f) Post-radiation nodules, etc.

Intrapulmonary lymphoid tissue and nodes
Nodules with lymphoproliferative diseases in AIDS, etc.; nodes with sarcoid or reticulosis.

Nodular pulmonary oedema
(a) Allergy to drugs or parasites (Loeffler's syndrome).   (b) Occasionally due to shock or hypoxia, etc.
(c) Following inhalation of toxic materials.

Vascular
(a) Pulmonary artery aneurysm (occurring per se, in Behçet's disease, or after the use of a Swan Ganz catheter, etc.)
(b) Arterio-venous malformation.   (c) Pulmonary varix.

Infiltration
Histiocytosis-X, eosinophilic granuloma, Gaucher's disease, etc.   Amyloid.
Skin lesions - Pemphigus, pyoderma, etc.
Inhalation
(a) metal - barium, lead, iron, tin, silver, mercury, etc.   (b) oil - paraffin, iodised oil, etc.
(c) protein - bird droppings, spores, pituitary snuff, etc.
Embolism
Infarcts, iodised oil following lymphangiography, hysterosalpingography, etc., barium or mercury after intravasation
Spurious lung masses
(a) Clothing - buttons, starch or barium in hospital gowns, etc.
(b) Nodules on chest wall - accessory nipples, skin tags, warts, neurofibromata, lipomas, etc.
(c) Healing rib fractures, arm stump, etc.
(d)Transient pleural fluid collections in inter-lobar fissure ('vanishing tumours'), etc.
(e) Vascular - subclavian artery.
(f) A calcified first costo-chondral junction (the common 'idiot's tumour') etc.

See also: Table 5.6 - Miliary small lung nodules and references to miliary shadows ps. 5.41-42.

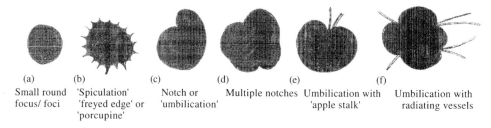

(a)	(b)	(c)	(d)	(e)	(f)
Small round focus/ foci	'Spiculation' 'freyed edge' or 'porcupine'	Notch or 'umbilication'	Multiple notches	Umbilication with 'apple stalk'	Umbilication with radiating vessels

(a) Carcinoma, tuberculoma, adenoma, hamartoma, fungus, rheumatoid nodule, polyarteritis, etc.; metastasis, esp. if multiple; infarct, lung contusion - usually clears, but some persist.
(b) Carcinoma, secondary deposit (unusual), tuberculoma (rare).
(c) & (d) Carcinoma, adenoma, hamartoma, metastasis (rarely).
(e) & (f) Carcinoma, metastasis - distinguish from A/V malformation.

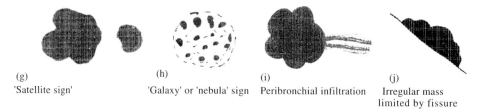

(g)	(h)	(i)	(j)
'Satellite sign'	'Galaxy' or 'nebula' sign	Peribronchial infiltration	Irregular mass limited by fissure

(g) Carcinoma - (distinguish from tuberculosis). (h) Carcinoma, esp. of bronchioloalveolar type.
(i) Carcinoma or infection.   (j) Carcinoma

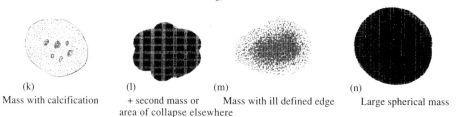

(k)	(l)	(m)	(n)
Mass with calcification	+ second mass or area of collapse elsewhere	Mass with ill defined edge	Large spherical mass

(k) Tubercoloma, fungus granuloma , adenoma/ hamartoma, secondary tumour (bone, bowel, etc. - primary), carcinoma engulfing old TB (dystrophic calcification is usually eccentric).
(l) Two tumours - primary or secondary or primary plus secondary tumour.
(m) Carcinoma, metastasis (unusual), infection/ fibrosis.
(n) Carcinoma, carcinosarcoma or sarcoma, adenoma, hydatid or bronchogenic cyst, secondary deposit (unusual).

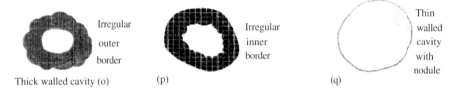

Thick walled cavity (o)   (p)   (q)

Irregular outer border

Irregular inner border

Thin walled cavity with nodule

(o) & (p) Carcinoma - (o) often has a much worse prognosis than (p).
(q) Infection in a bulla, carcinoma (note that a carcinoma may rarely appear as a thin walled cavity without any visible nodule); sequestrated segment with infection.

Fig. 4.3 Diagrammatic differential diagnosis of peripheral lung masses.

NB: Lung abscesses, infarcts, primary tumours and benign masses may be multiple, as well as metastases. There may be more than one type in any patient. A mass or masses may be present in one or more areas and the effects of bronchostenosis in another. Small tumours may be scar-like or too small to show a typical appearance.

Spiculation and 'Corona maligna' (Corona radiata or Corona complex).

Spiculation, which is usually a sign suggestive of a peripheral bronchial neoplasm, was first noted by Wenckebach (1913 - see also p 4.1). He described it as the '**frayed edge**' of a rapidly growing tumour. It has also been likened to a brush ('brushed border), and also resembles the spines of a hedgehog or porcupine (Illus. **CA SHAPES** and **CORONA MALIGNA**). It is mostly seen with primary malignant lung tumours, but may also occasionally be seen with secondary lung tumours. Rarely it may be found with benign lung nodules such as tuberculomas or adenomas, scars from peripheral pulmonary infarcts, or around the edge of pneumoconiotic fibrous masses (Illus. **PNEUMOCONIOSIS**). The radiating lines appear to be due to oedema in the interlobular septa, neoplastic cellular invasions of the surrounding lung tissue, distended lymphatics, tiny bronchi filled with secretions and distended small vessels.

This sign, has also been termed '**radiating line shadows**' by Simon (1971)and the '**corona maligna**' by Nordenström (1969a) - see Fig. 4.4b. According to the latter author, "this reliable sign of malignancy is characterised by an uneven borderline of the tumour", zone of surrounding increased transradiancy, and beyond this a zone of decreased transradiancy. Through these zones, 'multiple radiating thread-like structures' extend from the tumour into the lung parenchyma, often for a distance of several centimetres.

                    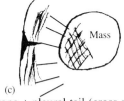

Mass

          (a)   (b)   (c)
Fig. 4.4 Spiculation, 'hedgehog',   Corona maligna.   Corona + pleural tail (cross section).
or 'porcupine' sign.

Nordenström (1984 & 1987) preferred the term '**corona complex**' and noted several features. He termed the transradiant zone the '**A** zone ' which is traversed by radiating strands. The denser outer rim of tissue or '**B** zone' appears to be due to oedema fluid; it may disappear with a localised pneumothorax. He considered that a tumour may behave like an electric cell or battery - due to necrosis in the tumour - and the resultant electro-osmosis may be responsible for the development of the corona, in the same way that injured muscle sets up an injury potential via lactic acid. Conductivity occurs in part by the adjacent small vessels and also via 'electron transferring steps' into connecting cellular membranes. Sometimes the current is electro-positive and at others electro-negative, and the polarity may change over days or weeks. Leukocytes become attached to the electro-positive tissue. The electro-osmosis will tend to repel fluid and the outer or 'B zone' may extend to the pleura. The radiating structures do not necessarily contain malignant cells and most are fibrotic only. Spasm of vessels may also contribute to the transradiant zone in relation to the osmosis. (See also ps. 21.3 & 24.46 re Nordenström's results re biopsy and electro-coagulation of tumours and Illus. **FAMOUS PEOPLE, Nordenström**).

Electro-osmosis may also induce the deposition of calcification. The electric potential and fields may be measured by an electrode inserted into the tumour or surrounding area, as first noted by Nordenström (1971).

In the author's experience tumours showing the corona sign are not uncommonly accompanied by HPOA (see Illus. **CORONA MALIGNA, HPOA Pt. 4a-d**).

Heitzman et al. (1982) used the term '**corona radiata**', as they have seen it with some benign fibrotic conditions. Nordenström (1987) also noted its occurrence with some benign tumours and granulomas.

The **pleural tail** may be partly due to dehydration producing contraction and is essentially a 'retraction pocket' on the surface of the lung (see also p. 4.17).

Scalloping, notching or umbilication and radiating vessels

Although Rigler, 1955a (see p. 4.2) and Rigler, 1957b, and Rigler and Heitzman, 1955, considered notching as a reliable sign of a peripheral bronchial tumour, my own experience (like that of Drevvatne and Frimann-Dahl, 1961) is that single notches or umbilications may be seen not only with bronchogenic tumours but also with hamartomas, adenomas and occasionally with pulmonary metastases. Others, e.g. Felson (1973) and Eisenberg (1984) also pointed out that notching may be seen with some granulomas. However, this last is uncommon and multiple notchings seem to be most commonly associated with malignancy, and usually a primary tumour (see also reference to Siegelman et al., 1986a, p. 4.7) Examples are shown in Illus. **CA LOBULATED**.

The notching may also be associated with radiating vessels or 'apple stalks', where vessels appear to enter and/or leave the tumour at the point of indentation. The tumour appears to expand outward into the lung parenchyma between the groups of vessels presumably as a result of the pattern of the blood supply. Sometimes notching is seen together with spiculation, but this is more unusual. All these features are best demonstrated by tomography including CT. This sign has to be distinguished from the radiating vessels of pulmonary arterio-venous malformations; such produce smoother rounded 'mass lesions' with vessels passing into and out of them, as seen on plain films, tomograms or angiograms (Illus. **AV ANEURYSM/FISTULAE**) - see also ps. 7.12 - 7.16.

On its own notching like spiculation does not determine with certainty the presence of a neoplasm, but it should serve to direct particular attention to the hilum, and mediastinum, bones, etc. for signs of secondary neoplasm. It has also been discussed by Marmorshtain (1956), Theros (1977), Fraser and Paré (1979) and Sone et al. (1997) who felt that lobulation is caused by contraction in a tumour or differential growth due to the local blood supply.

Bluth (1966) studied vessels adjacent to lung nodules, particularly those which were circumscribed, and on tomograms showed displacement of such vessels, which often appeared 'taut'. Sone et al. (1997) also felt that with many tumours pulmonary vessels tend to converge towards a tumour. The present author however notes that the relationship of vessels to tumours is variable, sometimes converging, and at other times the vessels apparently being unaffected by the tumour.

Mass with ill-defined edge

An ill-defined edge may be due to local macroscopic spread of the tumour into the surrounding lung, to local venous or lymphatic stasis due to involvement of these channels by the tumour, or to surrounding infection. This last cause is not uncommon even with peripheral tumours and explains the apparent partial regression of some growths following antibiotic chemotherapy. Secondary infection is, (as discussed on ps. 4.18) much more frequent with central tumours causing bronchial obstruction, and where infection is present in relation to peripheral tumours, some degree of partial obstruction due to enlarged hilar or mediastinal nodes must always be considered.

'Satellite' sign

Local spread of a tumour into the surrounding lung may be suggested by the presence of small nodules or satellites, probably small tumours developing secondarily to interstitial permeation (Illus. **SATELLITE NODULE**). These nodules are often hidden by associated congestion or infection.

'Galaxy' or 'nebula' sign

This is an important sign caused by local spread of tumour. Such a soft-looking multifocal lesion (see Fig. 4.3h & Illus. **GALAXY SIGN**) may easily be mistaken for pulmonary tuberculosis, but usually indicates a rapidly progressive and invasive peripheral tumour, e.g. of bronchiolo-alveolar type (see also ps. 4.12, 5.1 & 13.7).

Very large round (spherical) or lobulated masses.

Primary bronchial tumours may sometimes become very large - even 10 cm or more in diameter. Some may have a smooth or lobulated outer border, whilst others are irregular. Such masses may occur with all types, but seem to be more common with squamous tumours, particularly those that are slowly growing. Those with a regular outer border seem to have a better prognosis than those with an irregular edge, presumably due to less permeation by the tumour. Both types may degenerate and cavitate. Sometimes the degenerate tumour material may be retained within the tumour 'capsule' and when aspirated appear identical to pus. It may indeed be full of pus cells, but be sterile and contain tumour cells. Large tumours may also be carcinosarcomas (see p. 24.18) with a very bad prognosis (Illus. **CARCINOSARCOMA**).

Differential diagnosis of large smooth walled masses includes a bronchogenic or hydatid cyst, a hamartoma or an adenoma. Masses pushing into the lung (e.g. the huge neurofibromas illustrated in Illus. **NEUROFIBROMA, Pts. 18 & 25**) may mimic intrapulmonary masses - in this case distinguished by a pneumothorax, which was induced after the aspiration of a concomitant pleural effusion.

Mass bounded by an inter-lobar fissure.

Inter-lobar fissures often provide a temporary barrier to the spread of a tumour, presumably because of the movement which occurs between the two lobes. Freely moving pleural surfaces appear to have this property, which is lost if the fissure becomes obliterated. Because of this a mass in the lung with an otherwise irregular outline may have an almost straight edge at an inter-lobar fissure. By contrast an encysted collection of fluid in an inter-lobar fissure is typically biconcave in shape. A middle lobe collapse may also have a similar biconvex appearance, and Illus. **CA RML, Pt. 20 a-b** illustrates how a bronchogram differentiated this by showing a blocked bronchus to the middle lobe.

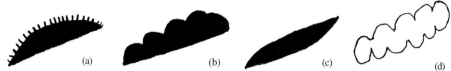

Fig. 4.5 Diagrams of spiculated or lobulated tumours limited by an interlobar fissure (a & b). For comparison - (c) - loculated interlobar effusion, and (d) - lobulated 'knobbly' mass on both upper and lower aspects, suggesting primary or secondary pleural malignancy (including reticulosis).

Other lung masses.

Round   consolidation : This is more commonly seen in children than in adults. When present the mass may mimic a tumour, but it usually clears rapidly, either spontaneously or in response to antibiotics - see also p. 19.1 and Illus. **ROUND PNEU/CONS**.

Other **'vanishing   tumours'** include haematomas, loculated pleural fluid (p.14.6) or a lung mass becoming obscured by increasing lobar or lung collapse, or resolving infarcts.

References.

Greenfield and Gyepes (1964) : Oval-shaped consolidation simulating new growth of the lung.
Rose and Ward (1973) : Spherical pneumonias in children simulating lung & mediastinal masses.
Kirkpatrick (1980) : Pneumonia in children as it differs from adult pneumonia.
Cohen et al. (1981 & 1982) :Unusual non-metastatic nodules in the lungs of children with cancer.
Kohno et al. (1993) : 'Focal organising pneumonia' - CT appearance - 18 cases - round or oval masses ± satellite shadows and pleural tags and mimicking neoplasm even with CT.
Wagner et al.(1998) : Radiological manifestations of round pneumonia in adults.

Histiocytoma or Inflammatory pseudo-tumours: These are yellowish nodules consisting of histiocytes, plasma cells and fibroblasts. They are usually well circumscribed spherical or oval peripheral pulmonary masses of one to a few cms in diameter. Associated nodal enlargement is rare. Most are asymptomatic; for further details see p. 5.33 and Illus. **HISTIOCYTOMA**.

Nodular pulmonary oedema: May occasionally be seen in relation to 'broncho-pneumonia', drugs including antibiotics, following surgery or parasites. The author has seen it with AHG treatment for haemophilia (about five cases), with anti-hypertensive treatment (one case), in schistosomiasis and in Loeffler's syndrome (due to ascaris larvae) - see also ps. 8.6 & 19.59. The patients may have eosinophilia. Illustrations are shown in Illus. **CONGEST   NODULAR** & **LOEFFLER'S SYNDROME**.

Reference.
Kernoff et al. (1972).

Nodular post-radiation 'pneumonia'.

Post-radiation 'pneumonia' is common in an upper lobe, following treatment e.g. of a breast tumour and/or nodal areas (see p. 11.19 et seq.), where this is discussed in some detail). Radiation treatment may also occasionally give rise to small nodular shadows in the lungs, which may mimic metastases. These usually resolve spontaneously or following steroid therapy - see Illus. **POST-RAD LUNGS**.

References.
Talerman (1973),   Cohen et al. (1982).

Intra-pulmonary nodes may be enlarged in sarcoidosis and reticulosis, but are rarely enlarged by tumours. For further details see p. 13.4 and Illus. **NODES-INTRAPULMONARY.**

Vasculitis

Nodules due to vasculitis are discussed on ps. 19.76 et seq. They usually enlarge much faster than those caused by tumours - Illus. **VASCULITIS.**

General references.
Kalifa et al. (1976) : Differential diagnosis of multiple chronic benign pulmonary nodules.
Lillington (1982) : Differential diagnosis of solitary and multiple pulmonary nodules.

The 'Pleuro-Pulmonary Tail', 'Pleural Tag' (or 'Retraction Line').

Simon (1956) regarded this sign as almost diagnostic of a tuberculoma. Bryk (1969) also felt that the sign indicated a granuloma. Simon (1970 with Lynne Reid) noted a similar line (or pleural scar) with infarcts - see p.7.29 and in 1971 found that the sign could also be found with circular looking neoplasms. Shapiro et al. (1972) also found the sign with alveolar cell tumours, and Schraufnagel et al. (1985) termed it the **'pleural tag'** when found with bronchiolo-alveolar cell carcinomas. Webb (1978) had noted that pleural tails occurred both with benign and malignant lesions and were no more common with malignant lesions than benign; with malignant lesions their association with bronchiolo-alveolar carcinoma appeared to be most common. Heitzman (1981) wrote that the 'tail' may indicate extension of disease along a septal plane within the lung to the pleura, and often with pleural puckering as seen an the surface of a resected specimen.

Hill (1982) made a critical reappraisal of this sign, and agreed that it could occur with both benign and malignant lesions. The present author (1973) noted it as a linear area of collapse passing towards the periphery of the lung from a tumour, either primary or secondary. It is especially seen in an upper lobe, when the line of collapse passes towards the axilla. The sign appears to be largely non-specific, and may be found with several types of lung nodule, including primary (especially bronchiolo-alveolar cell neoplasm - see p. 5.1) and secondary neoplasm, a reticulosis mass, granuloma or infarct. In most cases it appears to be a **local pleural reaction to the spread of the disease process or to fibrosis related to it, with a fibrous band or strand passing down to the tumour.** The value of noting the sign is that it may draw attention to an otherwise obscure nodule. Sometimes it will disappear, if related to an inflammatory nodule or infarct. The sign is usually well seen on plain radiographs or conventional tomograms. It may also be seen on CT sections. Occasionally two lines may be present when the epithets of **'tails'** * or **'rabbit's ears'** have been applied.

(*a type of white tie worn ceremonially by senior officers of Oxford University, barristers and some clergymen.)

The **'pleural thorn'** (see p. 14.6) is a somewhat similar sign due to a localised pleural reaction or a trace of fluid in the outer part of the horizontal fissure. **Multiple 'thorns'** or a **'saw- tooth'** appearance may be seen in some cases of fibrosing alveolitis - (see Fig. 19.15f, p. 19.117).

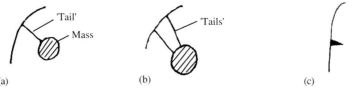

(a)   (b)   (c)

Fig. 4.6   (a) 'Pleuro-pulmonary tail'.   (b) 'Tails' or 'rabbit's ears'.   (c) 'Pleural thorn' - local thickening laterally in the lesser fissure.

Illustrations of pleural tails or tags are shown in Illus. **PL-TAG/TAIL.**

Further references.
Fraser and Paré (1979)
Sone et al. (1997) : Factors affecting the radiologic appearance of peripheral bronchogenic tumours - the pleural tail is "a linear density extending from the tumor margin to the pleural surface, represents retraction of the pleura toward the tumor and consists of a fibrous strand, rarely accompanied by tumor invasion".

Presence of more than one primary lung tumour

With metaplasia of the bronchial epithelium, secondary to cigarette smoking etc., it is not surprising that multiple tumours may develop in the bronchial tree. Many such cases have been reported in the literature and more are being recognised with accurate tomography and fibre-optic tomography. Such tumours may be synchronous (i.e. present at the same time as the main or first noted tumour) or metachronous (occurring months or years later). One may give rise to a mass lesion in the lung and the second to bronchial obstruction (see Illus. **CA MULT or MULTIPLE TUMOURS**), or may also appear as a mass.

It is quite possible for multiple tumours to be of the same or differing types. Chaudhuri (1971) considered the criteria needed for the diagnosis of a second primary tumour and said that both should be malignant and neither should be a metastasis of the other.

It is, of course, difficult to prove that a second tumour is not a metastasis from the first or from another tumour the patient has had, unless biopsies are carried out and give different histology, but even then some are indistinguishable. However, many primary tumours have fairly characteristic radiological or endobronchial appearances, whereas pulmonary secondary deposits are usually multiple in number and spherical in shape. With metachronous tumours, a long interval, sometimes of several years, may favour the diagnosis of a second tumour, but with slow doubling times it may take a long time for metastases to become apparent (see p. 24.35). In some cases the demonstration of differing histological types also supports the development of more than one tumour, but even this is not absolute proof, since tumours may contain considerable heterogenicity, with several cell types within a given tumour (see p. 24.19). Willis (1973) found a heterogeneous or variable microscopic structure in 23% of necropsy specimens.

Abbey Smith (1966) followed up 269 patients who had undergone previous lobectomy; 19 appeared to develop second pulmonary tumours. In 1976, he reported ten synchronous primary tumours and 45 metachronous tumours. Stark (1982a) found five synchronous tumours in approximately, 1,400 patients at the Massachusetts General Hospital between 1976 and 1981. The author, however, puts the incidence rather higher at approximately 5 to 10%.

Further references.

Beyreuther (1924) : First drew attention to multiple primary malignancy of the lungs.
Warren and Gates (1932), Newman and Adkins (1958 - three different primary tumours in a left lower lobe), Robinson and Jackson (1958), Britt et al. (1960), Hughes and Blades (1961), Le Gal and Bauer (1961), Langston and Sherrick (1962), Payne et al. (1962), Peterson et al. (1963), Cliffton et al. (1964), Glennie et al. (1964), Shields et al. (1964), Watson et al. (1964), Lehman and Cross (1966), Auerbach et al. (1967), Leafstedt et al. (1968), Mobley and Martinez (1968 - reviewed 33 cases from the literature plus one of their own, and noted that although tumours were often of similar type, that squamous, oat-cell or adenocarcinomas may exist together), Ott and Titscher (1969), Cáceres and Felson (1972), Razzuk et al.(1974), Salerno et al. (1979), Shields (1979), Jesnik (1981 - reported a 36 % cumulative survival at five years with 'aggressive surgery' for the second primary tumour, but with a 9 % operative mortality), Stark (1982 - out of 1,381 patients, 5 had synchronous and 5 metachronous). Bower et al. (1983) : Multiple primary carcinomas of the lung.
Shankar (1981) : Laryngeal carcinoma with synchronous or metachronous bronchial carcinoma
Mann (1985) : Wrote: 'Among the entire lung cancer population one half percent will. develop a second primary before death. Two per cent of those who undergo resection, and ten per cent of long-term survivors will also develop a second primary lung cancer. Most of these occur within the first five years after diagnosis.'
Shepherd (1985) : Multiple primary pulmonary malignancy - 750 cases have been reported in the Western literature - resection remains the treatment of choice.

Fleisher et al. (1991) : Over a 16 year period, 19 of approx. 1,700 patients surgically treated for bronchogenic carcinoma developed a second primary lung cancer.

Pulmonary secondary deposits from lung tumours

Pulmonary secondary deposits are not uncommon from primary lung and bronchial tumours (as well as other tumours - see Table 5.6, p. 5.41). They may vary in size from multiple small miliary shadows (like '**ball bearings**') to single or multiple rounded nodules. Like primary tumours, they may also cavitate, particularly squamous tumours. Lung deposits may at times be so numerous, as to mimic consolidation due to pneumonia on clinical examination at presentation and a '**snow-storm**' appearance radiologically (Illus. **CA LUNG SNOWSTORM DEPS**). Such deposits may occur on their own, or together with other distant metastases. Their presence is explained by tumour emboli passing into the bronchial veins, thence to the right side of the heart and pulmonary arteries. Such deposits are probably more common with adenocarcinomas - see also p. 5.37.

More than one type of lung mass or nodule.

One also has to consider that more than one type of mass or nodule can be present at any given time. Old (or active tuberculosis) or other inflammatory lesion, sarcoid, silicosis, rheumatoid nodule, etc. may be present at the time a neoplasm is seen. Also deposits from another primary neoplasm, e.g. prostate, breast, colon, renal, etc. may be present at the same time as a primary lung tumour. Differentiation of a second primary tumour from a secondary deposit from a known (e.g. breast, renal, bowel, bladder, etc.) or unknown primary tumour is a frequent clinical problem. In many cases a needle biopsy may solve the problem, but in others even a pathologist may not be able to distinguish the two.

Some references.

Zwirewich et al. (1990) and Kushihashi et al. (1994) : Drew attention to multicentric adenocarcinomas and bronchioloalveolar adenoma of the lung giving rise to second nodules or areas of ground-glass shadowing seen on CT in pts. with lung tumours especially adenocarcinomas or bronchiolo-alveolar cell carcinomas.
Marom et al. (1999) : Bronchogenic carcinoma with pulmonary metastases at presentation.

Middle lobe tumours

These probably account for about 5 % of bronchial tumours, and represent about the expected number one would expect from the volume of this lobe. Tumours originating within it have a rather poor prognosis (whatever the cell type), because of the greater propensity for contra-lateral metastasis via the lymphatic system. Lymphatics draining the middle lobe also tend to by-pass the more proximal nodes, thus making lymphatic borne metastases more easy - see also ps. 13.8 - 9. Illustrations of middle lobe tumours are shown in Illus. **CA RML**.

References

Palva et al. (1973) : Mediastinoscopic observation of metastatic spread in pulmonary carcinoma.
Freise et al. (1978) : Bronchial carcinoma and long term survival.
Huhti et al. (1983) : Does the location of lung carcinoma affect its prognosis?
Peleg et al. (1987) : Prognosis after resection of non-small cell cancer of the RML.
Bedini et al. (1989) : Surgical prognosis in stage 1 bronchogenic carcinoma of the RML. They studied 31 pts. and found a 5 year disease free survival in 30% of operated cases, compared with almost 60% in non-middle lobe cases.

Carcinomatous consolidation

Local spread may become so dense as to lead to carcinomatous consolidation (Illus. **CA CONSOL**) and may go on to produce the 'drowned lung' appearance (see next section). This latter is often largely due to retained secretions distal to a blocked bronchus. Consolidation may also be produced by infection complicating a tumour. Ill-defined masses mimicking areas of consolidation are also seen with reticulosis or with some secondary neoplasms; they are also a feature in many cases of bronchiolo-alveolar cell carcinoma (p. 5.1 and Illus. **ALV CELL CA**).

Infection complicating a lung tumour. 'Obstructive pneumonitis' and 'Drowned lung').

This may be minor or gross. Frequently patients with tumours present due to superadded inflammatory disease, particularly if there is an area of bronchostenosis, causing difficulty with the expectoration of secretions. Not uncommonly they present with a clinical pneumonia, and this may be confirmed radiologically. Follow up for complete resolution is essential in all smokers over the age of 40 presenting in this way, and in those in whom resolution does not occur tomography (including CT) may be required and/or bronchoscopy. This is particularly important in those who have had **haemoptyses**.

The lung consolidation may break down to give rise to a lung abscess, and possibly an empyema, which will often make the condition inoperable, if it was not already (see also p. 24.22 et seq.). Infection may also cause a lung tumour mass to break down. If the bronchial obstruction is incomplete, the patient may aspirate some of the infected material he is trying to cough up into the contra-lateral lung, or the remainder on the same side, producing widespread broncho-pneumonic changes. Infection distal to an endo-bronchial obstruction may prevent collateral air drift taking place from neighbouring patent bronchi (see ps. 2.8 - 9) and make the collapse more marked.

Consolidation distal to an endo-bronchial obstruction was termed **'obstructive pneumonitis'** by Fraser and Paré (1983), but not all cases are infected. Burke and Fraser (1988) studied the pathological findings and compared them with the radiological appearances. They thought that the cause was more likely the effect of retained secretions than due to infection. The pathological features of foamy alveolar macrophages containing lipid and interstitial thickening by mononuclear inflammatory cells and collagen are not commonly associated with bacterial pneumonia. Mucus is retained distal to the bronchial obstruction and cannot be expectorated. Others have termed this **'golden pneumonia'**. When infection occurs, it is mainly intra-bronchial.

In gross cases a **'drowned lung'** or lobe is produced, i.e. a lung or lobe that is larger than normal (see also p. 2.1) - this sign is caused by oedema within the lobe or lung, and may be caused by toxic and some inflammatory processes, bronchial and venous and/or lymphatic obstruction.

When infection and obstruction have been present for some time, and some reaeration of the lung occurs, an appearance resembling 'honeycomb lung' may be produced. This is largely due to air-filling of previously very dilated fluid filled bronchi or mucocoeles.

Yang et al. (1990) from Taiwan, used ultra-sound to study lung tumours causing obstructive pneumonitis, and were able to use the 'window' provided by the consolidated lung and showed fluid bronchograms and the obstructing tumour mass. In several cases they performed ultra-sound guided biopsies of the tumour.

Illustrations are shown under Illus. **DROWNED LOBE** or **SWOLLEN LOBE**.

Scar cancer.(see also p. 6.2)

There appears to be a much greater chance for tumours to develop in the site of an old scar, especially a tuberculous one. These are not uncommonly found at a lung apex and may be surrounded by multiple bullae - giving an appearance resembling a **'spider within its web'**. Most are adenocarcinomas, less commonly squamous or other types. They also occur with other chronic lung disease e.g. scleroderma, fibrosing alveolitis, lipoid pneumonia, etc. The surrounding bullae may make them difficult to biopsy. Whilst some are detected before symptoms occur, others present with metastases or pain due to local spread into the chest wall, etc. Increasing size of an apparent old TB focus brought the case illustrated in Illus. **CA SURVIVAL & PROGRESSION, Pt. 6a-e** to attention. These tumours may readily engulf old calcification - see Illus. **CA+CALC Calc in tum Pt. 1a-c**. Further illustrations of scar cancer as shown under Illus. **SCAR CANCER**.

References .
Raeburn and Spencer (1957), Wofford et al. (1962), Ripstein et al. (1968), Limas et al. (1971), Freant et al. (1974), Bakris et al . (1983)
Yakoo and Suckow (1961) : Peripheral lung cancers arising in scars.
Auerbach et al . (1979) : The number of these tumours appears to be increasing.
Madri and Carter (1984) : Scar cancers of the lung - origin and significance.
Barsky et al. (1986) : The extracellular matrix of pulmonary scar cancer is suggestive of a desmoplastic origin.

Natural history of some bronchial tumours and their apparent response to antibiotic chemotherapy.

Some tumours are mimicked by tuberculosis in their radiological appearance, whilst in others a patient may be thought to have tuberculosis, but really has a tumour. In some cases, even an apparent response to chemotherapy may ' clinically confirm' the presence of TB, but later the tumour enlarges. This is either because the chemotherapy will help to resolve some surrounding inflammation or because the tumour naturally changes in size, particularly if much of it undergoes spontaneous ischaemic degeneration.

The filling in of a cavitated lesion should not necessarily be regarded as a direct response to antibiotics in tuberculous and other infections, or even as an indication that such an infection was the cause of the disease process, if a trial of treatment has been undertaken without positive bacteriology. A tumour may break down to form a necrotic cavity which may later appear solid again. Such breakdown and filling up of a cavity in a tumour may occur several times during its growth (Illus. CA **CAVITATION, Pt. 55a-c**).

The Association of Bronchial Neoplasm with Tuberculosis .

Tuberculosis has always to be considered in relation to neoplasm. An old tuberculous focus may be engulfed by a tumour and become incorporated into it - Illus. **CA+CALC, Calc in tum Pt. 1a-c.**

The tumour, either from its own invasion, or because of secondary infection, may allow a dormant tuberculous focus to become reactivated, and the author has encountered a number of patients, often with fairly extensive tuberculosis, who had tumours in the supplying bronchus, or at a different site. It is not that unusual with someone becoming debilitated from a tumour to develop secondary infection, including tuberculosis elsewhere in the lungs. Illus. **CA+TB, Pancoast tum Pt. 2a-b** illustrates a patient with sputum positive tuberculosis at one apex, and cancer at the other. Illus. **CA+TB, Pt. 2a-c** shows a RUL tumour and tuberculosis

This association of neoplasm with tuberculosis has also been noted by: Fried (1935, 1948), Hauser and Glazer (1955), Greenberg et al. (1964), Holden et al. (1965), Kaplan et al. (1973), Ting et al. (1976) and Mok et al.(1978).

Other cases of TB and neoplasm are shown in Illus. **CA+TB**.

Table 4.3 - The association of lung and bronchial tumours with other lung diseases.

Lung neoplasms may also complicate:

asbestos (ps. 14.33 and 24.2).

broncho--pulmonary- sequestration (Bell-Thomson et al ., 1979), ps. 3.11 - 13.

hamartoma (Cavin et al, 1958, Karpas and Blackman (1967) - ps. 5.14 - 18.

lipoid pneumonia - with alveolar cell or squamous neoplasm (Felson and Ralaisomay, 1983) ps. 6.14.

rheumatoid - ps. 19.81 - 85, ankylosing spondylitis ps. 19.90 - 91, scleroderma - ps. 19.85 - 86, fibrosing alveolitis - ps. 19.120, lung scarring & scar cancer (below), end-stage lung - p.19.122, lung cysts & bullae - ps. 6.2 - 3, AIDS - p. 19.33, honeycomb lung - ps. 6.6, or hypoglobulinaemia - p. 5.47.

A neoplasm may be difficult to detect when there is severe lung scarring (e.g. with sarcoidosis) or nodularity as with pneumoconiosis, especially when massive fibrosis is present. Cavitating disease can also cause great difficulty. Fungal disease, particularly aspergillosis, may colonise a chronic slow-growing cavitating squamous carcinoma (see also p. 19.39).

Alveolar call carcinoma may be provoked by previous infection, lipoid pneumonia. DIP or scleroderma (see p. 5.1).

See also Chapter 24 (ps. 24.1- 4) for further discussion on the causes of lung cancer (including radon).

(c) CENTRAL BRONCHIAL TUMOURS

Although, as Rigler (1957b) and Walter and Pryce (1955b) pointed out the symptoms caused by central bronchial tumours may commence earlier than those caused by peripheral tumours, nevertheless, by the time most central tumours present clinically they are unresectable and have spread into the mediastinum. Also many peripheral tumours, by virtue of their metastases to hilar and mediastinal nodes, may give rise to central symptoms, and many apparent central tumours may in fact be bronchial wall metastases, which have occurred via the peri-bronchial lymphatics (see Fig. 13.2 and ps. 13.7 - 10).

If lesions are to be discovered at a resectable stage, it is important that the effects of a central lesion should be fully understood, so that radiographic changes can be correctly interpreted at the earliest possible time and suspicion of neoplasm aroused in order that other investigations including tomography, bronchography, bronchoscopy and sputum examination may be instituted.

The early radiological presentation of a central tumour depends on the effects of partial or complete bronchial obstruction as shown in the following diagrams - Fig. 4.7.

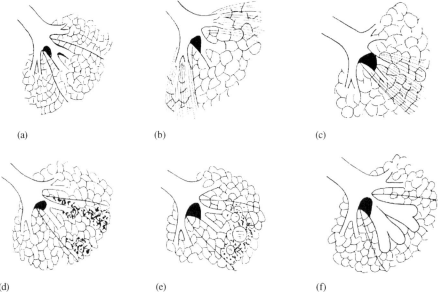

(a)   (b)   (c)

(d)   (e)   (f)

Fig. 4.7 Effects of central tumours on the underlying lung (a) No effect, (b) Obstructive emphysema (in expiration), (c) Collapse, (d) Pneumonia, (e) Abscess formation, (f) Mucocoeles and bronchiectasis. (Expanded from Sherman and Phillips, 1968, and reproduced from Wright, F.W., 1973).

Central tumours are often undiagnosed for the following reasons:
(1) The obstruction has not become sufficient to cause secondary phenomena.
(2) Obstructive emphysema is not demonstrated.
(3) The partial collapse of a segment, lobe or lung is not recognised.
(4) A 'mass' lesion is unrecognised or invisible within the mediastinum or the hilar region
- often due to poor radiographic technique.

All too frequently little attention is paid radiologically to the central air passages, the trachea, the carina and the larger bronchi. As noted in Chapter 24 (p. 24.22) it is unfortunate that many patients do not have their first radiograph until disease is far advanced, the condition often remaining undiagnosed because the effects of central tumours are not recognised.

Probably the most important clinical indication of a central tumour is a wheeze over one area of the bronchial tree, noticed by the patient or heard with the stethoscope. In more advanced cases, a central stridor may be heard with the unaided ear when the patient walks in or performs minimal exercise.

Wheezes due to obstruction or partial obstruction of the trachea or the main bronchi may be relatively early signs of tumour occurring in these air passages, but are more often late phenomena due to compression of these structures by grossly enlarged mediastinal nodes or from severe luminal stenosis. Other early clinical signs and symptoms depend upon the development of secondary infection, with pneumonia or the expectoration of sputum. Frank haemoptysis is often a late symptom but slight blood staining of the sputum may occur relatively early. Occasionally a slight pleurisy produced by the effects of the secondary infection may give an early presentation.

The various effects of central lesions are summarised in Table 4.4

Table 4.4   Effects of central lesions
> Obstructive emphysema.
> Collapse.
> Mucocoeles in bronchi.
> Infection - pneumonia.
> > lung abscess.
> > pleurisy and empyema.
> > reactivation of TB.
> Hilar and/or mediastinal mass or nodes (including contralateral node enlargement).
> Paradoxical hilar enlargement due to enlarged contralateral pulmonary artery (Oeser's sign).
> Lymphatic or pulmonary venous obstruction.
> Pleural nodules or effusion.
> Pericardial involvement or effusion.
> Nerve palsy - recurrent laryngeal or phrenic.

(d) TRACHEAL TUMOURS, PAPILLOMAS & ENDOBRONCHIAL DEPOSITS

<u>Tracheal tumours.</u>
Primary tracheal neoplasms are relatively rare tumours, only one being found for every 500 to 1,000 bronchial tumours. Malignant types include adeno-carcinomas, squamous tumours, cylindromas and endo-tracheal lymphoma masses.   Examples   are   shown   in   Illus.
TRACH/CARINA CA.
Benign types include pedunculated **lipomas,** which may alter in shape and move with respiration. (Illus. **ENDOBRON LIPOMA** illustrates such a mass which altered in shape and position, and which projected down into the left main bronchus). Leiomyomas, chondromas and neurofibromas (sometimes termed granular cell myoblastomas) may also be found. Neurofibromas occur in branches of the vagus (see also p. 18.36). Mucus plugs (pseudo-tumours) and blood clots may also be found.
Tracheal tumours project into the tracheal lumen, causing a defect in the tracheal 'air-column '. Malignant types may 'seed' down the trachea and into the main bronchi, presumably via the sub-mucosal lymphatic plexus. They may also spread outwards into the mediastinum.

Fig. 4.8 Tracheal tumour seeding down the trachea and into the main bronchi. also into the bronchial walls - see also p. 13.7.

Most tracheal tumours present with marked stridor and are not infrequently misdiagnosed as 'asthma' by their G.P.s or other clinicians. The stridor may not be present at rest, and only be found with exercise which may be minimal. It may be present in both inspiration or expiration. It is often possible to suspect these tumours from the grossly audible stridor the patients have, when walking into the x-ray department. The obstruction may sometimes be worse in inspiration if the tumour is mobile, and becomes sucked downwards plugging the trachea when he breathes in. In such cases there may be marked retraction of the soft tissues of the lower neck, and exaggerated use of the accessory muscles of respiration (Illus. **TRACH/CARINA CA, Trach ca, Pt. 17a**).

Conventional tomograms (or inclined frontal tomograms) may be taken to confirm the endotracheal mass. CT sections will show the cross-sectional shape of the trachea at various levels and any mediastinal extension which may be present. Further cases are shown in Illus. **CA TRACH/CARINA** or **TRACH/CARINA CA**.

Spizarny et al. (1986) analysed the CT features of six cases of adenoid cystic carcinoma of the trachea in relation to bronchoscopic, surgical and pathological findings. They found that CT accurately demonstrated extra-tracheal extension of the tumours, which occurred in all their six cases. However it **underestimated the longitudinal extent** of the tumours and was a poor predictor of mediastinal organ invasion. The tumour tends to spread beneath the tracheal mucosa and infiltrates into adjacent structures e.g. the oesophagus, pericardium, etc. The tumour may also give rise to lymph node or distant metastases.

Treatment policy in the Oxford Thoracic Surgical Unit has been to attempt to carry out a sleeve resection of the affected part of the trachea. In those in whom this appears impossible, the patient is first fully oxygenated, and then the tumour is rapidly 'cored-out' using the distal end of a rigid bronchoscope as a cutting tool, the debris being rapidly sucked out. If necessary an intra-luminal splinting tube can be inserted. Post-operative radiotherapy can be used to treat residual or surrounding tumour, which has been demonstrated by CT. Unfortunately local and tracheal recurrence is not uncommon.

Further references.

Fleming et al. (1962) : Tracheal tumours - Roentgen aspects.
McCafferty et al. (1964) : Primary cancers of the trachea.
Dines et al. (1965) : Solitary plasmacytoma of the trachea.
Perelman and Koroleva (1968) : Surgery of tumours in the thoracic portion of the trachea - end to end anastomosis if possible (report of 9 patients) - see also (1980) & (1987).
Houston et al. (1969) : Primary cancers of the trachea.
Janower et al. (1970) : Radiological appearance of carcinoma of the trachea.
Pradham et al. (1975) : Primary solitary lymphoma of the trachea.
Fleetham (1977) : Tracheal leiomyosarcoma.
Grillo (1978) : Surgical management of tracheal tumours.
Weber and Grillo (1978a) : Tracheal tumours (84 cases).
Weber et al. (1978c) : Cartilaginous tumours of the larynx and trachea.
Ho and Rassekh (1980) : Rhabdomyosarcoma of the trachea.
Le-Tian et al.(1982) from Peking, China : 27 patients were seen with tumours of the trachea or larger bronchi (excluding tumours of the lungs themselves) over an 18 year period, & out of a local population of 100,000 around the teaching hospital and with referrals from other parts of the city. 20 had surgery. The tumours included 10 squamous, 5 adeno-cystic, two carcinoids, two neurofibromas, two papillomas, a leiomyoma, haemangioma and a teratoma. Their patients presented mainly with 'asthma', stridor or haemoptysis.
Stark (1982c) : Cylindroma of the trachea (9 cases).
Allen et al. (1983) : Tracheal leiomyoma.
Felson (1983) : Neoplasms of the trachea and main stem bronchi.
Pearson et al. (1984) : Experience with primary neoplasm of the trachea and carina.
Slasky et al. (1985) : Tracheal chondrosarcoma with overview of other tracheal tumours.
Larsson et al. (1987) : Surgical management of tracheal tumours (5 patients).
Swain and Coblentz (1988) : CT of tracheal chondroma.
Wiggins et al. (1988) : Primary B cell malignant lymphoma of the trachea.
Larsson et al. (1989) : Primary tracheal rhabdomyosarcoma (most common soft tissue sarcoma in children).
Grillo and Mathiesen (1990) : Primary tracheal tumours in treatment and results.
Gelder and Hetzel (1993) : Survey of primary tracheal tumours in UK over a ten year period.
Grillo (1993) : Primary tracheal tumours - current approach is surgery combined with irradiation.
Naka et al. (1993) : Solitary squamous cell papilloma of the trachea.
Cleasby et al. (1998) from Birmingham, UK. : CT of tracheal tumours - 10 cases - endoluminal tracheal mass in 2, tracheal wall thickening in 6, tracheal narrowing in 6, pre-tracheal soft tissue mass in 2 & subcarinal soft tissue in 1. There was also invasion of adjacent lung structures in 3, but no oesophageal involvement was seen. 1 had no ventilation of a lung on a ventilation scan.
Kittinger (1961) : **Neurofibroma of the trachea**.
Meredith and Valicenti (1978) : Neurofibroma of the trachea.

Coleman et al. (1984) : About 50 examples of endobronchial myeloblastoma in literature.
Fishman et al.(1984) : Endobronchial blood clot shown by CT.

Upper airway obstruction may also be caused by a laryngeal chondroma
(see Stafford Johnson et al., 1995 : an unusual cause of upper airway obstruction.)

Polyps in the trachea and bronchi.
Both single and multiple polyps may be found in the trachea and bronchi - Illus.
BRONCHIAL PAPILLOMA or TRACHEA-PAPILLOMA.

(a) **Solitary   polyps** are uncommon, but may be found in patients with asthma, or may follow various forms of injury. Many are very small and are found fortuitously at bronchoscopy. Larger polyps may cause lobar collapse or lead to pneumonia.
Hamartomatous or lipomatous polyps (**endobronchial   lipomas**) may also be found (see p. 6.13). Rarely malignant tumours may develop within or adjacent to polyps.

(b) **Papillomatosis** (or multiple polyposis) occurs mainly in children or juveniles, but may also be seen in adults. It appears to be caused by the human papilloma virus, and the infection is probably contracted during birth from a mother affected with genital warts. Papillomas tend to seed down from the larynx to the bronchi, or even into the lungs where nodules may occur which may later cavitate or produce severe cystic bronchiectasis. The cavities are usually thick-walled and may contain papillomatous fronds resembling mycetomas. Such spread may follow repeated endoscopy or surgery, but can also happen fortuitously. Whether the spread occurs via air-borne metastasis, as has often been thought, or from multiple areas affected by viral infection, or via spread through the sub-mucosal lymphatics (see ps. 13.7-10) is uncertain. It has also been thought that prolonged nursing in the supine position may favour involvement of the posterior parts of the lungs.

Antibiotics may cause some amelioration, but interferon has no effect.

References.
(a) Solitary polyps
Ashley et al. (1963) : Bronchial polyps.
Spencer et al. (1980) : Non-invasive bronchial epithelial papillary tumours.
Shale et al. (1983) : Endobronchial polyp in an asthmatic subject (female aged 51).
Berman et al. (1984) : Endobronchial inflammatory polyp associated with a foreign body.
Maxwell et al. (1985) : Solitary squamous papilloma of the bronchus.

(b) multiple polyps or papillomatosis
Hitz and Oesterlin (1932) : Autopsy on a patient with papillomatosis of the larynx and trachea - many small cavities in the lung lined by similar tumour - ? aerial metastases.
Buffmire et al. (1950) : Male aged 25 with papillomata of the larynx, removed annually from age 16. He later developed a rounded thin-walled air-filled cyst in the apex of the left lower lobe which slowly enlarged with partial malignant transformation into a papillary squamous epithelioma.
Kircher (1952) : Child aged 28 with papillomatosis of the entire respiratory tree, with multiple large rounded cystic areas of 'bronchial expansion by papillomatosis' in all lung lobes.
Castleman (1957) : Man aged 28 - multi-centric cystic bronchial papillomatosis + larynx papillomas from age 3.
Moore and Lattes (1959) : Recurrent laryngeal papillomatosis between ages of 7 and 19. At age 32 had cystic bronchial papillomatosis of the left lower lobe resected, and further resections of lesions in the right upper and middle lobes and apex of right lower lobe at age 38.
Stein and Volk (1959) : Papillomatosis of the trachea and lung in a girl of 8 who died of intractable asthma - at autopsy a large tracheal polyp was present and the lung parenchyma was filled with papillomas.
Elliott et al. (1962) : Cavitating lesion in LLL due to cystic bronchial papillomatosis in a 52 year old male.
Greenfield and Herman (1963) : Papillomatosis of the trachea and bronchi.
Kaufman and Klopscock (1963) : Male aged 47 when the condition presented - he died 8 years later-when malignant change was seen in the lung.
Singer (1966) : Papillomatosis of the lung - report of a case and review of the condition.
Rosenbaum et al. (1968) : Pulmonary parenchymal spread of juvenile laryngeal papillomatosis.
Smith and Gooding (1974) : Pulmonary involvement.
Adams et al. (1979): Polyposis secondary to thermal injury.
Glazer and Webb (1979) : Laryngeal papillomatosis with pulmonary spread in a 69 year old man.

Williams et al. (1983) : Endobronchial polyposis following smoke inhalation.
Mounts and Kashima (1984): Papilloma virus ? the cause.
Kramer et al. (1985) : Pulmonary manifestations.
Singer et al. (1985) : Papilloma-virus.
Clements and Gravelle (1986) : Laryngeal papillomatosis.
Oleszczuk-Raszke and Cremin (1988) : Computed tomography of pulmonary lesions.
Goddard (1998) : Teenage girl with tracheal polyps + lung cavities (became smaller with antibiotics) shown by MR.

Endobronchial metastases (Secondary tumours occurring within the trachea and bronchi).
    Besides submucosal spread of bronchial and tracheal tumours (see above and ps. 13.7 - 10), other tumours may spread into the bronchi walls. These include those arising in the breast, thyroid, kidney, colon and skin (melanomas). These metastases appear to occur from blood-stream or lymphatic spread to the submucosa. As they enlarge, these tumours may produce sub-mucosal nodules pushing onto the bronchial lumen, rather like an adenoma. If the bronchial lining is breached, then ulcerating lesions may occur. Local spread may produce bronchostenosis, which may 'creep' along the bronchial walls ('creeping bronchostenosis') - an appearance rather like that sometimes seen with sarcoidosis (see p. 19.68). They may also lead to 'lymphangitis carcinomatosa'. An endobronchial deposit may also lead to a large surrounding mass, if the tumour spreads through the bronchial wall.

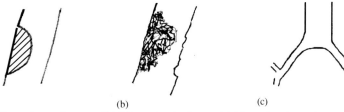

(a)   (b)   (c)

Fig. 4.9 (a) Smooth meniscus   (b) Ulcerating lesion.   (c) 'Creeping bronchostenosis' causing
caused by a submucosal tumour.   marked narrowing of the main bronchi.

Examples are shown in Illus. **ENDOBRON DEPOSITS**.

References.
King and Castleman (1943) : Bronchial involvement in metastatic pulmonary malignancy.
Caplan (1959) : Renal cell carcinomas.
Trinidad et al. (1963) : Bronchogenic carcinoma simulated by metastatic tumour.
Schoenbaum and Viamonte (1971) : Subepithelial endobronchial metastasis from breast, thyroid & skin melanomas.
Braman and Whitcomb (1975) : Endobronchial metastasis.
Webb and Gamsu (1977) : Thoracic metastasis in malignant melanoma (65 pts.- spread to bronchi, lungs and nodes).
Albertini and Ekberg (1980) : Endobronchial metastasis in breast cancer.
Baumgartner and Mark (1980) : Metastatic malignancies from distant sites to the tracheobronchial tree.
Dux et al. (1980) : Middle lobe syndrome as an unusual presentation of metastatic osteogenic sarcoma.
Chen et al. (1981) : Metastatic melanoma to the thorax (130 patients).
Shepherd (1982) : Endobronchial metastatic disease.
Lalli et al. (1983) : Multiple endobronchial metastases from carcinoma of the prostate.
Amin (1984) : Endobronchial metastasis from a malignant Schwannoma arising in a leg.
Chernoff et al. (1984) : Endobronchial lymphocytic infiltration - in chronic lymphatic leukaemia.
Coppage et al. (1987) : Metastatic disease to the chest in patients with extrathoracic malignancy.
Bourke et al. (1989) : Endobronchial metastases simulating primary carcinoma of the lung - 10 cases (6 breast, 2 renal, 1 pancreas and 1 cervix).
Coulden and Flower (1989) : Endobronchial metastasis from the breast causing RLL collapse.
Taylor and Braude (1990) : LUL collapse due to endobronchial metastatic prostatic carcinoma - re-expansion with antiandrogen treatment.
Plavsic et al. (1994) : Melanoma metastatic to the bronchus - two cases.
Gollub and Castellino (1995) : CT demonstration of diffuse endobronchial non-Hodgkin's lymphoma.
Walker (1995) : Endobronchial metastasis from unsuspected renal primary diagnosed by cytological examination of expectorated small bronchial cast.

Chapter 5 : **Less Common Lung and Bronchial Tumours; Bronchiolo-Alveolar Ca., Carcinoids, Hamartomas, Reticuloses, Protein Disorders, Lung Deposits and Leukaemia.**

Bronchiolo-alveolar carcinoma.

The first description of this tumour was by Melassey (1876), with a multiple nodular form found at autopsy. Musser (1903), also on autopsy material, described a diffuse or pneumonic form. The first in vivo diagnosis was probably by Skorpil (1941), the patient having hilar metastases at autopsy. Post-mortem examinations often suggested a multicentric origin, but in some cases it was more localised, and was often associated with lung scarring from previous disease. Lipoid pneumonia (see also p. 6.14) was suggested as a precursor by Felson and Ralaisomay (1983) and Maesen et al. (1985). Others, e.g. Woodring and Stelling (1983a) incriminated tobacco smoking. It may follow desquamative interstitial pneumonia (DIP - p. 19.119) or scleroderma (see ps. 19.85 - 87).

Liebow (1960) described the condition as "a generally well differentiated adenocarcinoma, primary in the periphery of the lung beyond a grossly recognisable bronchus." Because its origin is uncertain as between an alveolus and a terminal bronchiole, it is often referred to as 'bronchiolo-alveolar carcinoma'. According to Berkmen (1977), electron microscopy suggests either origin; he wrote "as both alveolar and bronchiolar cells arise from the same parent cells, it is likely that similar tumours may arise from either type of daughter cell". Some will be type II pneumocytes (or cuboidal cells), which produce surfactant, and respond to alveolar injury by proliferation and replacement of sloughed type I cells (see also p. 24.14). As Berkmen also pointed out, the naturally occurring sheep adenomatosis (see below) and tumours produced experimentally by oral urethran, etc. are composed of type II cells. Manning (1984) felt that type II (the mucus producing cells) gave rise to multifocal tumours, and type I cells (no mucus) unifocal tumours.

Adenomatous hyperplasia of alveolar cells, may be a precursor of tumour formation. Electron microscopy studies have indicated a bronchiolar origin from mucus secreting goblet cells, non-ciliated Clara cells or ciliated cells. Although some recent authors still consider this tumour to be a variant of adenocarcinoma (primary or secondary in the lung, e.g. Woodring and Stelling, 1983a) most consider it to be a distinct entity (e.g. Schraufungel, 1982 and 1985, and Hill, 1984).

The disease gives rise to a variety of clinical and radiological appearances. It accounts for about 1% to 5% of malignant lung tumours, the variation in the estimated incidence depending on the strictness of the diagnostic criteria. The sex incidence is about equal. It presents with three main forms (i) a peripheral lung tumour or tumours (which may be diagnosed by needle biopsy), (ii) as areas of consolidation affecting one or more areas of the lungs, and (iii) as lymphangitis carcinomatosa or diffuse miliary nodules (both with breathlessness). In some the disease may be invisible radiologically when symptoms start. Nodal **disease tends to occur late** and **rarely gives to any significant enlargement**. Chest wall invasion, collapse and pleural effusions are uncommon when the disease is not in an advanced stage.

Kittredge and Sherman (1962) studied 36 patients with bronchiolo-alveolar carcinoma and found that in half the disease presented as a localised nodule, in a quarter as a local infiltrate and in the rest as segmental consolidations or a variable pattern.

Although the main clinical presentations are with cough, chest pain, dyspnoea, haemoptysis or weight loss, other have peripheral thrombophlebitis, vague symptoms, secondary lung infection, or little or no symptoms. The often described '**bronchorrhoea**' i.e. copious frothy or gelatinous sputum is an uncommon manifestation, occurring in 10% or less of patients. The clinical course of the disease is also very variable, from weeks after presentation to several years. The latter tends to occur when there is one or more localised areas of consolidation. The author has seen some patients survive three to four years, and one for eight. Another (a man of 77) presented with gross nodules throughout both lungs, but these remained almost static for about ten years. A biopsy proven case, treated with radiotherapy, has shown no suggestion of recurrence over five years. Arany (1958) reported one patient surviving 12 years with no symptoms from the disease.

Spread of the disease may be local or generalised. Localised spread may cause satellite nodules or infiltrates, giving rise to the '**galaxy' 'star' or 'nebula'** signs (a **multi-nodulated appearance** also likened to a '**dewberry**'). Ill-defined borders or radiating spicules, suggested the '**cocklebur sign**' (like cornfield burrs) as described by Ludington et al. (1972) - they reviewed 41 cases and termed the condition '**another great imitator**', as it may mimic other acute or chronic pulmonary diseases. Cavitation is uncommon, and may more often be mimicked by normal areas of aerated lung (or '**pseudocavitation**') lying between areas of patchy tumour dissemination.

Disseminated spread may take place through one or both lungs, with multiple nodules, **chronic patchy areas of consolidation**, up to lobar in size, or with very diffuse spread. This last is thought to take place via the bronchi (i.e. a '**broncho-pneumonic carcinomatosis**'), or via the lymphatics to give a '**lymphangitis carcinomatosa**' type of picture, with small nodules, distended septal spaces (septal lines - see ps. 8.9 - 10), etc. This disseminated form may mimic other diffuse secondary tumour deposits (breast, ovary, pancreas, lung, bronchus, etc.); it also has a morphological resemblance to '**Jaagsiekte**' or pulmonary adenomatosis (an epizootic disease of sheep, particularly the Texel type, a black-coated breed - Bonne, 1939, Wood and Pierson, 1945 and Delarue and Graham, 1949).

Other radiological signs include the pleural '**pleural tail sign**' or '**pleural retraction**' (see ps. 4.17 - 18), pleural effusions, or presentation with a pneumothorax. Tomography (including CT) will show the diffuse nature of the nodule(s), or infiltration more clearly, areas of consolidation with 'air bronchograms' and loss of the smaller side branches giving rise to the '**leafless tree**' type of appearance (also seen with some lymphomas).

Examples are shown in Illus. **ALV CELL CA** and **ALV CELL CA+SARCOID**.

Table 5.1 - <u>Summary of possible findings in bronchiolo-alveolar carcinoma.</u>
Nodule or disseminated nodules, especially irregular peripheral nodules - local spread with
'**nebula**' or '**galaxy**' sign.
Single or multiple areas of consolidation (sometimes mimicking lobar or broncho-pneumonia),
with '**air bronchograms**' on plain films or tomograms. The bronchi may also be stretched or
displaced. ('**Leafless tree**' appearance on tomograms and bronchograms, due to the smaller
bronchial branches not filling with air or contrast medium).
The **CT angiogram sign**, originally considered to be specific (Im et al., 1990), has been shown
to occur with other conditions e.g. pneumonia and primary pulmonary lymphoma (p. 5.27).
Disseminated nodular and widespread areas of consolidation due to airborne spread of tumour.
Pleural tags or 'tails'.
Septal lines may be present in patients with 'lymphangitis' or 'bronchorrhoea'.
Nodule(s) with cavitation.
Miliary nodules may represent acinar rosettes.
Pleural effusion (uncommon).
Spontaneous pneumothorax.
Normal perfusion scan or angiogram.
Spread to chest wall.
Osteoblastic as well as osteolytic bony metastases may be present.

Fig. 5.1   Airway or broncho-pneumonic
type of spread of bronchiolo-alveolar
carcinoma.

Notes.
(i) Airway spread or **local** lymphatic permeation may give rise to the 'nebula' (or 'galaxy') sign (Illus. **GALAXY SIGN**), or the 'dewberry' (or 'cocklebur') sign (Illus. **DEWBERRY SIGN**).

(ii) **Pseudocavitation** - normal intervening air-filled alveoli and lobules may simulate cavitation (see Illus. **PSEUDOCAVITATION**).

(iii) **True cavitation** - may also occur in rapidly growing nodules, but is uncommon. The author has seen it in a few cases especially with tumour recurrence after surgery. Illus. **ALV CELL CA+CAVIT** includes cavitation in one case at presentation, and others with recurrence.

(iv) For long surviving cases of alveolar carcinoma see Illus. **ALV CELL CA SURVIVAL**.

Further references.

Fried (1948)

Abrahamson et al. (1950) : Bilateral alveolar lung cancer associated with Thorotrast.

Storey et al. (1953) : Studied 145 cases and noted - (i) **solitary   peripheral   nodules** (26%), (ii) **bilateral nodules** (20%), (iii) **consolidation** (16%), (iv) **ill-defined   shadowing** (12%), (v) **consolidation + nodules** (8%), (vi) **pleural effusion ± nodules** (8%), (vii) **para-hilar mass** (3%).

Zheutlin et al. (1954) : Ciné and TV fluoroscopic studies after bronchography showed that the affected bronchi did not alter in calibre with respiration.

Woodruff et al. (1958) : 16 cases - **two radiological stages** - (a) **localised lesions** (small or larger), (b) **disseminated lesions** (early or late).

Belgrad et al. (1962) : Surgically excised tumours, esp. localised lesions.

Kittredge and Sherman (1962) : 36 cases - 18 had nodules, 9 single infiltrations, 5 segmental consolidations and 4 were unclassable. **Some cases progressed slowly over several years.**

Howells (1964) : 18 cases - solitary lesions in 5, single area of consolidation in 3 (one with cavitation), more extensive consolidation (patchy, nodular or confluent and usually bilateral) in 9, pleural effusions in 2.

Rigler (1965b) : New Roentgen sign - '**pleural tail**'.

Montes et al. (1966) : Bronchiolar apocrine tumour.

Munnell et al. (1966) : **Seven** cases of solitary bronchiolar carcinoma in females (aged 51 to 76) - all were alive and well 18 months to 6 years following resection.

Watson and Farpour (1966) : Clinical review of 265 cases.

Berkmen (1969) : The many facets of alveolar-cell carcinoma of the lung.

McNamara et al. (1969) : Surgery of bronchiolo-alveolar carcinoma.

Wolinsky et al. (1969) : Lung perfusion in bronchiolo-alveolar carcinoma.

Wormer (1969) : **Cavitating bronchiolar cell carcinoma.**

Theros and Highman (1970) : **Architecture sparing behaviour of this neoplasm.**

Williams, H. and Kinder (1971) : Alveolar cell carcinoma presenting with a **pneumothorax.**

Delarue et al. (1972) : 24 years reappraisal.

Shapiro et al. (1972) : Useful Roentgen sign - '**rabbits ears**' or '**tail sign**'.

Généreux and Merriman (1973) : **Desquamative interstitial pneumonia** leading to alveolar cell carcinoma.

Marcq and Galy (1973) : 29 cases - natural history, prognosis and clinicopathological relationships.

Wright (1973) : **Galaxy sign.**

Joshi et al. (1977) : Alv. cell ca in male identical twins both aged 58 at presentation, one in RLL and second in LUL - both developed brain secondary deposits - suggested genetic disposition to this tumour (both were heavy smokers).

Miller et al. (1978) : **Two clinical entities with one pathologic diagnosis**.

Ravel et al. (1979) : Value of **air bronchogram sign** on CT in alveolar cell carcinoma.

Metzger et al. (1981) : **CT differentiation of solitary from diffuse type.**

Epstein et al. (1982) : **Lobar** bronchiolo-alveolar carcinoma.

Schraufnagel et al. (1982) : Differentiating bronchiolo-alveolar carcinoma from adenocarcinoma.

Schraufnagel et al. (1985) : Radiographic differences between two subtypes.

Spriggs et al. (1982) : Noted the difficulty with **sputum cytology** of distinguishing benign bronchial cell clusters seen in asthma, from clumps of alveolar carcinoma cells.

Edwards (1984), and Marzano et al. (1984) : Reviews.

Hill (1984) : Review of 136 patients. The varied radiographic manifestations were due to the characteristic peripheral location of the tumour, its tendency to infiltrate the local airways (with mucin production) and desmoplasia, and its variable aggressiveness causing a wide variation in rate of intrathoracic and extrathoracic spread. Without surgical intervention, **localised lesions progressed to diffuse in all patients.**

Manning et al. (1984) : The significance of **two histological types** have a bearing on the **prognosis**. Type I is associated with gross and microscopic mucus production and is likely to be multicentric, whilst type II has lesser amounts of mucus and is likely to be solitary. Five year survival in type I was 26% and in type II 72%.

Pritchard et al. (1984) :Bronchiolo-alveolar carcinoma arising in **long-standing air cysts**.

Steinbacher et al. (1985) : CT and radiological findings.

Thomas et al. (1985) : 21 year retrospective review at Western Infirmary, Glasgow.

Clayton (1986) : Cell types, patterns of growth and prognostic correlations.

Greco et al. (1986) : Broncho-alveolar carcinoma of the lung.

Huang et al. (1986) : Unusual radiological findings.

Im et al. (1986) : CT in a man of 75 (with 5 months history) showed **stretching, spreading and uniform narrowing of bronchi** (without blockage) in consolidated right middle and lower lobes.

Mallens et al. (1986) : **Calcified lymph node metastases** in bronchiolo-alveolar cell carcinoma.

Tao et al. (1986) : 181 (of 275) patients had the diagnosis made by **fine needle aspiration**. Three types were seen - **non-secretory, secretory and poorly differentiated**.

Geddes (1987) : Bronchiolo-alveolar cell carcinoma.

Harpole et al. (1988) : Studied 205 patients. Presentation as a peripheral mass in 121(approx. 60%), infiltrate in 84 (40%). Many had anorexia, weight loss, weakness and dyspnoea. 80 with localised disease had resections with a **55% five year survival.**

Kuhlman et al. (1988) : Studied 30 patients with solitary bronchiolo-alveolar carcinoma by **CT** and noted some common features : (a) **peripheral or sub-pleural** location of a pulmonary mass in 25
(b) **pseudo-cavitation** in 18   (c) **heterogenous attenuation** with denser and less dense areas in 17
(d) irregular margins forming a 'star pattern' in 22   (e) **pleural tags** in 21.
These were the counter-parts of plain radiographic signs and there was some overlap with signs of large cell undifferentiated carcinomas and adenocarcinomas.

Menzies et al. (1988) : **Acanthosis nigricans** associated with alveolar cell carcinoma.

DeJong et al. (1989) : Presentation as a thin-walled cavity in a young man.

Sutton et al. (1987 &1989) : 20 patients in Leeds - 15 male and 5 female (17 to 80 years of age). Half had focal disease, of which 60% The prominent features at presentation were lung nodules (either single or multiple), focal consolidations (usually with air bronchograms), volume loss or interstitial lines. **Survival following surgery** (seven cases) **was generally better with those with a mass or nodule**, but one case with focal consolidation remained alive 10.5 years after surgery, compared with 4.5 years for the longest survivor with a mass. The mean survival in unoperated cases was 102 days (8 to 224).
They also noted that the Yorkshire Cancer Organisation recorded 91 cases of bronchiolo-alveolar carcinoma as well as 29,641 cases of other lung carcinomas between 1975 and 1985 i.e. 3% (3.6 million population).

Clark et al. (1990) : Bronchiolo-alveolar carcinoma in a 37 year old drug addict **mimicking PCP.**

Epstein (1990) : Review - female preponderance of 30 - 50%.

Im et al. (1990) : **CT** appearances of **lobar** bronchiolo-alveolar cell carcinoma and '**CT angiogram sign**'. Following IV contrast medium, the consolidated lung typically appeared as an area of homogeneous low attenuation, within which were enhanced branching pulmonary vessels. The sign was produced by the intact framework within the low-attenuating consolidation, caused by the production of mucin or other fluid. (See also reference to Shah & Friedman, 1998 - below).

Sider (1990) : Radiographic manifestations.

Zwirewich et al. (1991a) : Solitary pulmonary nodule - HRCT - **pseudocavitation** in alveolar cell carcinoma.

Adler et al. (1992) : **HRCT** of bronchiolo-alveolar carcinoma - three patterns - **solitary nodule, consolidation and multicentric or diffuse disease** (in 27%). The spiculated appearance is probably due to infiltrative tumour. A characteristic finding in 50% was the presence of '**bubble-like' lucencies** or '**pseudo-cavitation**' which corresponded to patent small bronchi or air containing spaces within papillary tumours (was found in 50%). Overt cavitation occurred in 7%. The combination of growth along the alveolar wall and secretion of **mucin** may cause features of **air-space consolidation with air bronchograms** (segmental or lobar). Production of mucin can cause **swelling of the affected lobe**, leading to bulging of the interlobar fissures. The tumour may also **cross a fissure** and spread into the adjacent lobe. **Mucin is of lower radiographic density than tumour**, causing heterogeneous attenuation in small masses or uniform low attenuation in more confluent consolidation allows vessels to be visualised esp. after IV contrast - the '**CT angiogram sign'**.

Trotman-Dickenson and Wright (1992) : Bronchiolo-alveolar carcinoma - review of 28 cases.

Weisbrod et al. (1992) : Thin-walled cystic lesions in bronchiolo-alveolar cell carcinoma - tumour necrosis or emphysematous cysts. 4 cases (plus literature review).

Barsky et al. (1994 from California) : Rising incidence of bronchoalveolar lung carcinoma (5%-1955, 24%-1990) - mucinous types had diffuse pulmonary involvement; sclerotic type was associated with multifocal involvement; 20% showed dedifferentiation into patterns of poorly differentiated adenoca.

Schultze et al. (1994) : Man aged 77 with bilateral diffuse consolidation, worse on R
- noted **three types of consolidation may occur:**
(i) non-mucinous - most common.
(ii) diffuse mucinous type - associated with flooding of alveoli and bronchorrhoea.
(iii) sclerosing type associated with desmoplastic reaction and cicatrization.

Singh et al. (1994) : Bronchiolo-alveolar carcinoma causing pulmonary hypertension in a 57 year old man - large main pulmonary arteries and diffuse shadowing (esp. at bases) on CXR & HRCT.

Wong et al. (1994) : Bronchiolar carcinoma the '**air bronchogram sign**' - caused by mucus secretion into alveoli, tumour cell ingrowth or desquamation into the alveoli, or septal thickening by tumour compressing the alveoli.

Akata et al. (1995) : CT of bronchoalveolar carcinoma - specific appearances.

Mikaye et al. (1995) : Mucin-producing tumour of the lung (bronchioloalveolar carcinoma and ca colon deposit) - CT - low attenuation, irregular margins & slight enhancement with IV contrast.

Weisbrod et al. (1995) : Cystic change (pseudocavitation) associated with bronchioloalveolar carcinoma - report of four patients - ca + paracicatrical emphysema, 2 + localised honeycombing, and one with segmental bronchiectasis.
Tan and Kuzo (1997) : Mucinous bronchiolo-alveolar carcinoma mimicking alveolar proteinosis on HRCT with an asymmetrical and **crazy-paving** pattern.
Shah and Friedman (1998) : The **'CT angiogram sign'** is commonly found with lobar consolidations and is not specific in radiological diagnosis - it may be seen with postobstructive consolidation, lobar pneumonia, passive collapse, lymphoma, bronchio-alveolar carcinoma and lipoid pneumonia.
Kim, B. et al. (1998) : Lower uptake of FDG/PET in localised bronchiolo-alveolar cell ca than other lung cancers.
Akira et al. (1999) : HRCT in 38 pts. - consolidation & nodules esp. centrilobular nodules + remote ground glass.
Mihara et al. (1999) : Subtypes of bronchiolo-alveolar cell ca - CT & pathological correlation in 18 cases.
Aquino et al. (2000) : Do CT criteria work in distinguishing bronchioloalveolar alveolar ca from pneumonia?

Haemangioendotheliomas and 'intravascular bronchiolo-alveolar tumours'.

   These are rare tumours which arise from vascular endothelial cells. They should be differentiated from haemangiopericytomas (ps. 5.10 - 11). Haemangioendotheliomas have been considered as more benign and intravascular bronchiolo-alveolar tumours as malignant. About 50 cases have been recognised, mainly in women. Most present with asymptomatic multiple pulmonary nodules, resembling widespread secondary deposits.
   Histologically they also have a similar appearance to epithelioid haemangioma of the liver. However Dail et al. (1983) who described 20 cases felt that they are a form of bronchiolo-alveolar carcinoma which had invaded alveoli, bronchioles and blood vessels. Several cases have run an indolent course (5 to 10 years), whilst others have progressed fairly rapidly. The diagnosis is usually made by open biopsy. Deposits in lymph nodes and the liver have been reported. Possible simulators are multiple pulmonary hamartomas, leiomyomas or pulmonary endometriosis.

Further references.
Dail and Liebow (1974) , Sherman et al. (1981), Marsh et al. (1982)
Corrin et al. (1979) : Histogenesis of so-called intravascular bronchial and alveolar tumour.
Weiss and Enzinger (1982) : Epithelioid haemangioendothelioma - a vascular tumour often mistaken for a carcinoma - clinical and histological features similar to intravascular bronchiolo-alveolar tumour.
Weiss et al. (1986) : Epithelioid hemangioendothelioma and related lesions.
Gledhill and Kay (1984) : Hepatic metastases.
Verbeken et al. (1985) : Woman aged 40 with multiple nodules in both lungs and a small tumoral mass at the level of the left brachial artery. The nodules appeared to be metastases of a haemangioendothelioma.
Sweeney et al. (1987) : A distinctive surgical and pathological entity.
Blank (1989) : Case report., Ross et al. (1989) : CT appearance.
Shirakusa et al. (1989) : Advanced intravasvcular bronchiolo-alveolar tumour - two cases (men aged 31 & 32) and review of seven other cases from Japan.
Carter et al. (1990) : Alveolar haemorrhage with epithelioid haemangioendothelioma.
Ledson et al. (1999) : Female aged 24 with **HPOA and miliary lung nodules** - the HPOA responded to indomethacin, & with azathioprine the lung lesions calcified & became smaller - 16 yrs later she was alive and well with no deterioration in lung function, although CT showed showed some diffuse fibrosis and calcified liver deposits.

Bronchial Adenomas and Carcinoids.
   These may be classified into three types :
(i) **cylindroid type** (more commonly termed an '**adenoma**') - Illus. **CARCINOIDS**,
(ii) **cylindromas** or adeno-cystic carcinomas - Illus. **CYLINDROMA**, and
(iii) **mucoepidermoid** tumours.

   The first tends to protrude into a bronchial lumen, producing obstruction or haemoptysis, whilst the other two types tend to occur more proximally and are more likely to extend along the bronchial walls. Carcinoids occurring in the chest have a close histological resemblance to those arising in the intestine (Illus. **CARCINOID SMALL BOWEL**). They account for about 5% of endobronchial tumours, and are generally slow growing, locally invasive tumours, which occasionally show evidence of regional (15%) and distant metastases (5%). Their overall prognosis is good - Lawson et al. (1976) from the Royal Brompton Hospital, reported a 75% survival at 15 years in patients who had had adenomas removed surgically.
   Eighty to 90% occur in the major bronchi, close to the bronchial bifurcations. As bronchial cartilage elements extend down to the smallest bronchi (1 mm in diameter), adenomas may occur

down as far as this level. The 20%, which occur peripherally, are usually well-demarcated, round, or slightly lobulated nodules, which may occasionally be calcified (see below). They have an abundant vascular supply arising from the bronchial arteries, wand this together with ulceration of the normal covering of epithelium, is responsible for frequent bleeding and haemoptysis. Not uncommonly, only a small part is endo-bronchial, and the rest may form a lung mass, which may become quite large (Illus. **CARCINOIDS, Pt. 16a-b**). These tumours may be multiple (Illus. **CARCINOIDS, Pt. 11**).

Historical review.

The term 'Karcinoide' was first used by Oberndorfer (1907) to describe a small-intestine tumour, which was less aggressive than a carcinoma. The first diagnosis of a bronchial adenoma during life, appears to have been made by Kramer (1930), although the condition had been identified in autopsy specimens by Müller (1882), Heine (1927) and Reisner (1928). Kramer recognised that an adenoma might undergo malignant change, and that the patient might give a long history of his illness - a fact he correlated with its slow growth. A similar view was held by Goldman (1949), and by Clerf and Crawford (1936). Fried (1947) described an adenoma as a benign mass arising from the mucous glands of the bronchi. Hamperl (1937) distinguished two types - the **cylindroid** and the **carcinoid**, and thought that the latter (unlike carcinoids arising in the appendix) did not contain argentaffin cells. Holley (1946), Feyrter (1959) and Williams, E. and Azzopardi (1960) showed that this view was incorrect, and that the carcinoid type of bronchial adenoma is little different from carcinoid tumours elsewhere in the body, and capable of giving rise to the carcinoid syndrome. Holley divided his 38 cases into polypoid and carcinoid types and several showed features of malignancy, with local invasion and nodal or hepatic metastases.

Clinical effects.

Patients commonly present with haemoptysis, due to the vascular nature of the tumours. Others have repeated attacks of infection, sometimes leading to haemoptysis, lung collapse, mucocoeles, etc. Others are found by chance. Dyspnoea may result from bronchial obstruction, and patients may be able to localise the site of the tumour from their wheeze. Peripherally situated adenomas (which are less common than central) usually cause no symptoms. Bronchoscopy is helpful for assessing central lesions.

The male / female sex ratio is about one to four.

Hormonal syndromes, associated with carcinoid lung tumours, are rare, except with large tumours, or following extensive metastasis. The **carcinoid syndrome** is the most important. Their hormone producing ability is because (like oat cell tumours) they are derived from the 'paracrine' or APUD system of cells (see p. 24.16). These contain neuro-secretory type granules, which stain 'black' with silver. They may produce 5 hydroxy-tryptamine, serotonin, bradykinin, SH 4 (a gastrin-like substance), ACTH, anti-diuretic hormone, etc. (as listed on p. 23.1). The carcinoid syndrome is much less common with bronchial carcinoids, than those arising in the intestine, and most patients with it have widespread metastases or liver involvement. Smith, R. (1969) felt that no single feature, either histological or clinical, could be the basis for reaching a reliable prognosis. Isawa et al. (1973) reported a patient who survived for twelve years with this and reviewed 17 others. The present author has only seen a few patients with bronchial carcinoids, who developed the carcinoid syndrome. One had hepatic metastases, 24 years after a lung resection. Another had a tumour arising from the intermediate bronchus and involving mediastinal nodes (Illus. **CARCINOIDS, Pt. 22a-e**). At exploratory thoracotomy, she had an acute carcinoid reaction, when the tumour was palpated, presumably due to release of hormone products. The tumour was extending into the posterior aspect of the left atrium (Illus. **CARCINOIDS, Pt. 22d**). Resection had to be deferred to a later date, when it was successfully removed, using pump by-pass (see also Darby et al., 1990). No reaction had been induced by previous and bronchoscopy. Somatostatin (which inhibits peptide hormone release) was used to treat the carcinoid crisis; this is a product of hypothalamic neurones and δ cells of the pancreatic islets - (it is also used to treat diarrhoea, flushing and palpitations caused by intestinal carcinoids and glucagonomas - Bloom and Polak, 1987). Streptozotocin (a polypeptide toxin) may be used together with 5-fluorouracil to produce a one in five chance of regression of carcinoid deposits (Grahaeme-Smith, 1987), but with considerable toxicity. A long-acting analogue of somatostatin is becoming available. Serotonin antagonists and tumour embolisation (especially of hepatic metastases) may also be employed (Hodgson, 1988).

Radioactive labelled somatostatin analogues are now being used in some centres for the imaging of carcinoid tumours (see p. 22.13).

The carcinoid syndrome may also produce endocardial fibrosis on the right side of the heart leading to contracture of the pulmonary and tricuspid valves, with stenosis of the former and incompetence of the latter, due to it being unusually fixed in an open position. This may lead to early opacification of the IVC on contrast enhanced spiral CT studies (see also p. 9.3).

See also:
Greminger et al. (1991) : Carcinoid tumour causing left sided valvular heart disease (as opposed to the more common right sided disease).

Radiological appearances.

These may be due to the mass per se - central (esp. in the middle third of the lung adjacent to pulmonary vessels and bronchi), endo- or exo-bronchial mass, or a peripheral pulmonary tumour, or to secondary effects - collapse, bronchiectasis, bronchocoeles (see ps. 2.10 - 12) with the surrounding lung remaining air filled due to collateral air-drift (ps. 2.8 - 9).

Bronchiectasis, e.g. of an upper lobe with a smooth endo-bronchial tumour is very suggestive, but the tumour may occur in any of the bronchi. The tumour may be almost entirely endo-bronchial, or only part of it, with a much larger mass extending into the lung, so that only the 'tip of the "iceberg" ' may be seen bronchoscopically. As with other endo-bronchial neoplasms, **reduced air flow and hypoxia may result in reflex vasoconstriction**, simulating on plain radiographs the Swyer-James (Macleod) syndrome (ps. 7.9 - 10), and give rise to Oeser's sign of contra-lateral pulmonary artery enlargement and hyperaemia (see ps. 7.10 - 12 and Illus. **CARCINOIDS 27**). Such cases due to an adenoma have been reported by McGuinness and Lull (1976), Spitzer et al. (1979), and Paré and Fraser (1983). Nodal enlargement due to deposits and distant metastases are uncommon, but a sarcoid type of reaction may occur (see ps. 19.74 - 75).

Calcification within carcinoids may occasionally be seen (Illus. **CARCINOIDS, Pt. 26**), due to bone in fibrous septa traversing the tumour - such cases have been reported by: Thomas, C. and Morgan (1958) , Markel et al. (1964), Troupin (1968), Salyer et al. (1975a) and Siegelman et al. (1986a). Rarely they may produce well calcified lesions on plain radiographs or tomograms. Bateson et al. (1970) reported one in a 25 year old man, with both radial and circumferential arrangement of bony trabeculae. Calcification and bone formation is however more commonly noted in resected specimens.

Cavitation is rare.

Pleural fibrosis may be a complication of metastatic carcinoid disease (Moss et al., 1993).

Metastasising carcinoids may give rise to nodal, hepatic and bony deposits (Illus. **CARCINOIDS, Pts. 22, 25 & Sclerotic deps., Pt. 2**) + skin petechial haemangiomas & Campbell de Morgan spots and also cause the **carcinoid syndrome** (see above).

Bony deposits are rare but if present may be osteoblastic. Such cases have been reported by Pollard et al. (1962), Thomas, B. (1968 - who reviewed 24 cases - 23 osteoblastic and one mixed osteoblastic and lytic), and by Ashraf (1977). (Other sclerosing deposits are discussed on ps. 22.1 & 22.5).

CT appearances.

Adenomas are usually well-defined, smooth-surfaced nodules, which tend to be centrally placed in the thorax, close to or lying wholly or partially within a bronchus (see Illus. **CARCINOIDS, Pts. 1, 2, 7, 14 & 29**).

A large lobulated adenoma is shown in Illus. **CARCINOIDS, Pt. 16a-b**. Occasionally multiple adenomas may be shown (Illus. **CARCINOIDS, Pt. 11**). Being very vascular they will often enhance with IV contrast agents. Confusion with other vascular lesions may be experienced, and in difficult cases, differentiation may be aided by dynamic scanning, using a time-density curve. Calcification may be demonstrated.

The cylindromas (or adenocystic tumours).

These arise in the trachea and larger bronchi, especially the main bronchi, from mucous cells and mucous glands. Radiologically they cause narrowing of the airway within these structures, often with a smooth outline of the swelling within them. Bronchoscopy shows a pale tumour with an intact mucosa. For the latter reason bleeding and haemoptysis are uncommon. The cut surface of an excised specimen looks waxy or gelatinous. Occasionally these tumours are multiple. Surgical removal may be difficult because of their position, but a sleeve resection may be possible. Local recurrence is not uncommon. Regional and distal metastases may appear late. Death is usually due to bronchial obstruction. Examples are shown in Illus. **CYLINDROMA**.

Mucoepidermoid tumours (cystadenomas or bronchial gland tumours) arise from bronchial mucous glands and are usually small (< 1.5 cm in diameter), polypoid nodules which project into the bronchial lumen and may cause obstruction (Illus. **CARCINOID Pt. 2**). Very occasionally large cystic adenomas or tumours resembling salivary gland tumours may be found.

Variants
(i) **Atypical carcinoid** - some recognise this as a tumour intermediate in type between carcinoid and small cell tumours - all three may show neuro-endocrine features. They may present with lobulated or rounded lung nodules, or from the effects of bronchial obstruction. Occasionally they may produce lymphangitis, nodal spread and metastases. (See Arrigoni et al., 1972, Mills et al., 1982, and Choplin et al, 1986 - 32 cases).

(ii) **Onchocytomas** are tumours with cells containing small nuclei and abundant eosinophilic cytoplasm, due to mitochondrial hyperplasia, and are similar radiologically to carcinoids -see Dunnill, 1982.

(iii) **Acinic cell tumours - t**hese arise from serous cells and have vesicular nuclei, and a vacuolated or granular cytoplasm. They are arranged around small glandular spaces, similar to salivary gland tumours.
They may be locally invasive but are not known to metastasise. They are similar to the mucoepidermoid tumours (see above).

(iv) **'Clear cell' (or 'sugar') tumours of the lung** - benign types are sharply-defined pulmonary masses, which are usually discovered by chance. Pathologically they are reddish-brown in colour, are not encapsulated, and do not appear to arise from the bronchi. They grow very slowly and do not metastasise. They may be a variety of carcinoid, but have an intra-cytoplasmic excess of glycogen (hence their name). It is uncertain whether they arise from K cells, smooth cells or pericytes.
Malignant types may mimic deposits from renal tubular cell tumours ('hypernephromas').
Cases have been described by Liebow and Castleman (1971), Spencer (1984) and Gaffey, et al. (1990). A further case is illustrated in Illus. **CLEAR CELL CA.**

(v) **Alveolar adenoma** (the benign form of alveolar carcinoma) may produce nodules or cavitating lesions with thickened walls - see Yousem and Hochholzer (1986) & Fraser et al. (1988). Miller (1990) described their pathology. Kushihashi et al. (1994) reported 7 small BAA nodules shown by CT in association with ground-glass shadowing in patients with lung cancer and wondered if these were precursors of multifocal carcinomas. Charig (1999) showed a solitary cavitating case (see diagram and Illus. **ALV ADENOMA**).

Diagram of cavitating broncho-alveolar adenoma (BAA).

Further references.
Carcinoids
Naclerio and Langer (1948) : 8% of lung tumours. Thomas (1954) : 2% of lung tumours.
McBurney et al. (1952) : Obstructive pneumonitis secondary to bronchial adenoma.
Good and Harrington (1953) : 100 cases of asymptomatic bronchial adenoma. 77 caused obstructive signs, and 23 sharply circumscribed, round or roughly oval mass lesions, usually at some distance from the hilum.
Walderström and Ljungberg (1955) : Functional circulatory influence from metastasising carcinoid tumours.
Zellos (1962) : 40 cases - 26 endobronchial tumours with secondary lung collapse, and 14 rounded peripheral lung masses. 13 had spread to mediastinal nodes, and 2 hepatic metastases. One showed the carcinoid syndrome. (They represented 1.3% of lung tumours seen over a 12 year period).

O'Keefe et al. (1957) : Calcification in resected adenomas.

Warner and Southern (1958) : Carcinoid syndrome produced by metastasising bronchial adenoma.

Toomey and Felson (1960) : Osteoblastic bone metastasis in gastrointestinal and bronchial carcinoids.

Thomas (1968) : Three unusual carcinoid tumours, with particular reference to osteoblastic bone metastases.

Guistra and Stassa (1969) : Multiple presentations of bronchial adenomas - review of 99 cases.

Templeton et al. (1971) : Bronchography and bronchial adenomas.

Burcharth and Axelsson (1972) : 26 cases of adenomas - should be regarded as malignant tumours with a slower rate of growth and slower development of metastases than bronchogenic carcinomas.

Turnbull et al. (1972) : Malignant potential of bronchial adenomas.

Altman et al. (1973) : Radiographic appearance of bronchial carcinoid.

Mojab et al. (1974) : Angiographic findings in bronchial adenoma.

Godwin (1975) : Analysis of 2837 carcinoid tumours.

Salyer et al. (1975a) : Bronchial carcinoid tumours. Bonikos et al. (1976) : Peripheral pulmonary carcinoid tumours.

Goldstraw et al. (1976) : The malignancy of bronchial adenoma.

Skinner and Ewen (1976) : Multifocal bronchial carcinoid tumour in a young man with flushing, diarrhoea, and weight loss - died 10 years later ? from same cause.

Kennedy (1979) : Carcinoids are not uncommonly misdiagnosed as bronchial carcinomas, particularly oat cell tumours - pointed out that the possibility of carcinoid should be considered in any patient who is unusually young, is a non-smoker or where bone or calcification is present in the tumour.

Lima (1980) : 53 patients - none developed the carcinoid syndrome.

Godwin et al. (1981) : Dynamic CT of vascular lung lesions.

Naidich et al. (1982) : CT of bronchial adenoma.　　Aronchick et al. (1986) : CT of bronchial carcinoid.

Webb et al. (1983b) : CT of bronchial carcinoid with recurrent pneumonia and hyperplastic hilar adenopathy.

Bertelsen et al. (1985) : Bronchial carcinoid tumours. A clinicopathological study of 82 cases (65 benign carcinoids ; two patients later developed fatal carcinoid syndrome with regional and distal metastases. Metastases were also found in another 10 patients, but three had long term survival).

Magid et al. (1989) : CT of pulmonary carcinoid tumours - 12 cases out of 634 surgically proven solitary nodules - 5 central and 7 peripheral, 4 showed focal calcification, particularly in the periphery of the nodule.

Shin et al. (1989) : CT of ossifying bronchial carcinoid simulating broncholithiasis.

Davis, S. et al. (1990) : Peripheral carcinoid of lung - endobronchial component shown on HRCT - this plus contrast enhancement suggested the correct diagnosis.

Clague et al. (1991) : Medullary carcinoma of thyroid presenting as multifocal bronchial tumour, with carcinoid type syndrome in a man aged 21.

Doppman et al. (1991) : Detection of ACTH producing bronchial carcinoid tumours - MR vs CT. On MR they may be shown best by T_2 and STIR sequences.

Zwibel et al. (1991) : CT assessment of location and intratumoral assessment in 31 cases - 18 central and 13 peripherally located, 8 showed calcification (non-central and smoothly rounded in 5 and irregularly chunky in three). In three further cases calcification was seen on pathological examination.

Bennett and Chew (1994) : Pulmonary carcinoid tumourlets in a 69 year old non-smoking woman with incidental finding of multiple small bilateral lung nodules on CT.

Douek et al. (1994) : Diagnosis of bronchial carcinoid by ultrafast contrast-enhanced MR.

Mahadeva et al. (1998) : Radiolabelled octreotide scanning as guide to management of an occult carcinoid tumour.

MacDonald and Robbins (1957) : Pathology of the heart in the carcinoid syndrome.

Cosh et al. (1959), Roberts and Sjoerderma (1964) : Carcinoid heart disease.

O'Byrne et al. (1994) : Imaging of bronchial carcinoid tumours with In[111] pentreotide.

Erasmus et al. (1998) : Lower uptake of FDG/PET in pulmonary carcinoid tumours than in malignant tumours.

Reid (1952) : Adenoid cystic carcinoma (cylindroma) and mucoepidermoid carcinoma of the bronchial tree.

Payne et al. (1959) : Surgical treatment of cylindroma and mucoepidermoid tumours of the bronchi.

Dowling et al. (1962) : Mucoepidermoid tumours of the bronchi.

Axelsson (1973) : Mucoepidermoid lung tumours.

Conlan et al. (1978) : Adenoid cystic carcinoma (cylindroma) and mucoepidermoid carcinoma of the bronchus.

Yousem and Hochholzer (1978) : Mucoepidermoid tumours of the lung.

Spencer (1979) : Bronchial mucous gland tumour.

Breyer et al. (1980) : Mucoepidermoid tumours of the trachea & bronchus - case for conservative surgery.

Mills et al. (1982) : Atypical carcinoid tumour of the lung.

Barsky et al. (1983) : 'Low grade' mucoepidermoid in the bronchus with 'high grade' biological behaviour.

Gale et al. (1986) : Benign mixed tumour of salivary gland origin presenting as a mediastinal mass.

Wolf et al. (1988) : Mucoepidermoid carcinoma of the lung with intracranial metastases.

Green et al. (1991) : Peripheral RML mucoepidermoid tumour of the lung.

Inoue et al. (1991) : Peripheral pulm. adenocystic ca. with submucosal extension to the proximal bronchus.

Moran et al. (1994) : Clinicopath. & immumohistochemical study of 16 cases of primary adenoid cystic lung ca.

Wright, C. et al. (1996) : Adenoid cystic carcinoma simulating Macleod's syndrome (see also ps. 7.9 - 10).
Kim et al. (1999) : Mucoepidermoid ca. of the tracheo-bronchial tree - CT in 12 cases showed smoothly oval or lobulated airway masses.
Smidley et al. (2000) : Endobronchial mucoepidermoid ca in childhood.

Malignant melanoma

Both secondary and primary melanomas may occur in the trachea and bronchi, but the latter is rare and much less common than in the oesophagus. As with melanomas occurring elsewhere, metastases in the lungs, nodes, pleura, liver and skeleton are common. (Illus. **MELANOMA**).

References. (for deposits see p. 4.26).
Reid and Mehta (1966) : Melanoma of the lower respiratory tract.
Jensen and Egedorf (1967) : Primary malignant melanoma of the lung.
Taboada et al. (1972) : Primary melanoma of the lung.
Webb and Gamsu (1977) : Thoracic metastasis in malignant melanoma - a radiographic survey of 65 patients.
Robertson et al. (1980) : Primary melanocarcinoma of the lower respiratory tract.
Cagle et al. (1984) : Primary melanomas of the lung vs metastatic disease.
Carstens et al. (1984) : Primary malignant melanoma of the lung.
Santos et al. (1987) : Primary bronchopulmonary malignant melanoma.
Farrell et al. (1996) : Primary malignant melanoma of the bronchus.

Endobronchial teratoma.

Several adults have been reported in the literature, occurring in children and young adults, and like teratomas occurring in the mediastinum (or abdomen) may exhibit calcification.

References.
Lafitte (1937) : Patient coughed up hair.
Bateson et al. (1968) : Also had bronchiectasis.
Gawtam (1969) : Intrapulmonary malignant teratoma.
Pound and Willis (1969)   Day and Taylor (1978)
Holt et al. (1978) : Teratoma of the lung containing thymic tissue.

Other endobronchial tumours.
Endobronchial deposits   -   see also p. 4.26
Endobronchial lipoma   -   see also p. 6.13
Endobronchial neurofibroma   -   see also p. 18.37
Endobronchial reticulosis -   see also p. 5.27

Haemangiopericytomas (spindle cell mesenchymal neoplasms).

The term 'haemangiopericytoma' was introduced in 1942 by Stout and Murray to describe a vascular tumour characterised by the presence of numerous capillary blood-vessels around which are grouped masses of spindle-shaped or rounded cells believed to be pericytes. Pericytes (described by Zimmerman, 1923) are separated by a fibrous sheath from the normal endothelial cells lining the capillaries. Haemangiopericytomas consist of spindle and round shaped (?modified muscle) cells lying outside the endothelial lining of the capillaries and probably have the function of altering their calibres. The tumours contain dilated radiating vessels and a dense radiating reticulum network around the tumour cells. Their origin from pericytes and immunopathological stains helps to distinguish them from haemangioendotheliomas and other vascular tumours.

These tumours are unpredictable in behaviour; some are benign, whilst others are highly malignant and metastasise, and histology may be an unreliable predictor of the degree of malignancy. Their surrounding false capsules are often infiltrated by tumour. Bony deposits may be sclerotic.

Chemodectomas or glomus tumours (see ps. 18.37 - 38) are related, but contain many nerve fibres as well as pericytes.

Haemangiopericytomas may arise in most tissues of the body, and in the thorax may arise in the lung, pleura or chest wall. Within the lung most arise centrally and present as well defined solid masses. They later spread in all directions towards the lung periphery. Some arise in previously irradiated tissue. Both the primary tumours and secondary nodal deposits may exhibit speckled calcification. Most are very vascular and give rise to a 'blush' on angiography or enhance with IV contrast agents on CT examinations. A biopsy may give rise to considerable pain. Those arising outside the lungs not uncommonly give rise to lung deposits. A case in a young woman arose bilaterally from the subclavian arteries and caused bilateral Pancoast-like masses, with bilateral Pancoast syndromes. Two cases occurring in the external temporal fossae have lasted 10 and 30 years, both with metastases.

Illustrations of haemangiopericytomas are shown in Illus. **HAEMANGIOPERICYTOMA**.

References.

Murray and Stout (1942) : Glomus tumour.
Stout and Murray (1942) : Haemangiopericytoma (9 cases).
Ackerman and Warren (1943) : Haemangiopericytoma - esp. of retroperitoneum.
Stout and Cassell (1943) : Haemangiopericytoma of the omentum lasting 60 years.
Stout (1949 & 1956) : Reviewed a large series and found haemangiopericytomas to be equally divided between external soft tissues, internal soft tissues and bone. The mediastinum and retroperitoneum were common sites.
Kent (1957) : Spicules of calcification within the tumour mass; case treated with radiotherapy.
Mujahed et al. (1959) : Four cases and literature review - may contain whorled calcification.
Feldman and Seaman (1964) : Primary thoracic haemangiopericytoma.
Wheeler and Baker (1964) : Two cases of blushing orbital haemangiopericytomas.
Joffe (1966) : Angiographic findings - vascular blush in leg.
De Villiers et al. (1967) : Angiography in pelvic tumour.
Sutton and Pratt (1967) : Angiography of two cases - one in aortic wall did not blush.
Meade et al. (1974) : Pulmonary haemangiopericytomas - four cases - also quoted 24 cases from literature - patients may have hypoglycaemia and hypertension. Prognosis better in asymptomatic females with small tumours than in males with large tumours.
Enzinger and Smith (1976) : Analysis of 106 cases.
Dietz et al. (1979) : Diagnosis and treatment of malignant haemangiopericytoma.
Saw and Prathrap (1979) : Problems in diagnosis and treatment.
Shin and Ho (1979) : Two cases and review of 34.
Ouimette and Schwab (1982), Spencer (1984) : Pulmonary haemangiopericytoma.
Alpern et al. (1986) : CT appearance in 7 cases, speckled calcification in 5. Felt that 'the CT presentation of solid areas or septations, and speckled calcifications is suggestive of, although not specific for, malignant haemangiopericytoma.'
Nakamura et al. (1987) : Pseudoaneurysm in association with a haemangiopericytoma of pulmonary outflow tract.
Lorigan et al. (1989) : Clinical and radiological manifestations of haemangiopericytoma.
Hansen et al. (1990) : Primary pulmonary haemangiopericytoma - three cases.
Smith, R.T. et al. (1995) : Haemangiopericytoma of the oesophagus (see also p. 16.24).

Chorioncarcinoma.

As well as appearing as a gestational trophoblastic tumour in females, it may occur in the testis, in midline situations such as the mediastinum or retroperitoneum and in the lung. As Durieu et al. (1994), who reported a case in a 51 year old man, noted 'the course of primary choriocarcinoma of the lung is not well established. Some patients have no recurrence of tumour after surgical resection, while others develop pulmonary metastases which may be single or multiple as occurred in their case. These tumours can give rise to the '**chorioncarcinoma** syndrome', due to the secretion of β-chorionic gonadotropin. (See also ps. 5.40, 7.19 & 20, and 18.15 - 16).

Note: chorioncarcinoma tumours typically cause an increased blood ß human chorion gonadotropin (normal = < 5U/100ml); this can be assessed by blood assay - they may also be imaged by PET using FDG (see p. 22.11).

Further references.

Bagshawe and Brooks (1959) : Subacute pulmonary hypertension due to chorionepithelioma - first suggested that pulmonary embolism and hypertension could be caused by chorioncarcinoma of the pulmonary arteries.
Green et al. (1973) : Angiography of A/V shunts in pulmonary metastatic chorioncarcinoma.
Seckl et al. (1991) : Pulmonary embolism, pulmonary hypertension and chorioncarcinoma.
Gangadhaaran et al. (1993) : Pulmonary hypertension - a rare presentation of chorioncarcinoma.
Trübenbach et al. (1997) : Primary chorioncarcinoma of the pulmonary artery mimicking pulmonary embolus - woman aged 33 - 5/12 history of recurrent episodes of exertional dyspnoea - CT showed complete occlusion of LPA

by an enhancing mass - also confirmed by pulm. angio. which also showed defects in R inf. pulm. art. She had a very elevated serum ß-hCG (human chorionic gonadotrophin). Methotrexate treatment was started but she died.

Primitive lung tumours and sarcomas.
Embryomas and pulmonary blastomas (foetal type of lung tumour). are rare tumours which may occur at any age, either de novo or possibly on the basis of a pre-existing hamartomatous malformation. However, Spencer (1968) considered that they should be differentiated from hamartomas, which also are derived from a single germ layer, by their differential growth characteristics. Hamartomas grow by expansion and are usually non-invasive, whereas pulmonary blastomas infiltrate lung tissue locally may cavitate and eventually metastasise. Some consider them to be a benign form of carcinosarcoma.

   Wright (1973) illustrated a pulmonary mesenchymoma (or embryoma) in a woman of 42. This started as a mass in the left upper lobe (Illus. **BLASTOMA 1**); she later developed masses in the right lung, which may have been metastases or multiple primary tumours. She remained well for many years.

   The author has more recently seen a girl aged 19 who presented with a partially calcified left apical mass (Illus. **BLASTOMA, Calc in tum. Pt. 10a-c**) in association with an ovarian mass. Despite resections of both and chemotherapy, tumour recurred in the chest and abdomen with fairly rapid deterioration. It was uncertain whether this **blastoma** arose in the lung or ovary.

Granulocytic sarcomas (Chloromas) are rare extra-medullary tumours which were originally termed chloromas because of their green colour due to the high levels of the enzyme myeloperoxidase within about 70% of them. They usually arise in relation to acute or chronic myeloid leukaemia, but may occur in relationship to other myeloid proliferative disorders such as polycythaemia, myelofibrosis and eosinophilia or precede the clinical presentations of these. They can occur at any age, but are more common in the young, usually associated with leukaemia. They may be found in many tissues, including the skeleton (esp. skull, & spine), skin, soft tissues, lymph nodes, dura, the pleura and pericardium, where mesothelioma or other secondary carcinoma may be mimicked. This may give rise to fluid and circumferential or 'knobbly' thickening, and in some cases mediastinal lymph node enlargement. The tumours are often multifocal.

Other lung sarcomas
   Carcinosarcomas are discussed on ps. 4.15 & 24.18,
   Lymphosarcomas on p. 5.23 and **Kaposi's sarcoma** on ps. 19.33 - 34.

   Leiomyosarcomas and fibrosarcomas - both of these are occasionally found. They tend to produce large irregular infiltrating tumours (often with pulmonary deposits), and are usually rapidly progressive. Fleetham et al. (1977) referred to 73 cases, one in the anterior mediastinum and one in the pleura, also one in the trachea in a 26 year old student.

   Rhabdomyosarcomas of the trachea - see p. 4.24.

   Pulmonary artery and vein tumours - see ps. 7.19 - 20.

Lung tumours in children are uncommon, and one tends to see them rarely. Adenomas, metastases and reticuloses are the most common, but primary tumours are occasionally seen.

References.
Greene et al. (1977) : Other malignant tumours of the lung.

Hartman and Shochat (1983) : Primary pulmonary neoplasms of childhood - reviewed 230 cases - adenomas were the largest group (8% being malignant). They collected 47 bronchial carcinomas <16 yrs (12% squamous). Inflammatory pseudotumours accounted for 56% of benign masses. Leiomyosarcoma and mucoepidermoid carcinoma among the malignant types had a more favourable prognosis.
Shelley and Lorezno (1983) : Primary squamous cell carcinoma of the lung in a child.
McDermott et al. (1993) : Primary intrathoracic malignancy - a rare childhood malignancy.

Barnard (1952) : **Blastoma** - resembled bronchial buds growing into undifferentiated mesoderm in the developing lung of an embryo.

Spencer (1961) : Pulmonary blastomas.

Stackhouse et al. (1969) : Primary mixed lung malignancies - carcinosarcoma and blastoma.

Thompson et al. (1972) : Roentgen manifestations of pulmonary blastoma.

Herzog and Putman (1974) : Embryoma lung or pulmonary blastoma causing a RLL mass (female aged 63).

Kennedy and Prior (1976) : Two cases of blastoma and literature review.

Han et al. (1976) : Pulmonary blastoma - case report and literature review.

Peacock and Whitwell (1976) : Pulmonary blastoma.

Ashworth (1983) : One case of blastoma.

Koss et al. (1991) : Pulmonary blastomas - review of 52 cases. Prognosis is poor and the clinical course is not readily predicted from the histological appearance. Most often appear as peripheral or mid-lung masses.

Senac et al. (1991) : 7 cases of pulmonary blastoma - rare childhood malignancy.

Chin et al. (1994) : Pulmonary blastoma in an adult presenting as a chronic loculated effusion.

Katz et al. (1995) : Pleuropulmonary blastoma simulating an empyema in a young child.

Teplick et al. (1975) : Granular cell **myoblastoma** of the lung.

Butchart et al. (1976) : Granular cell myoblastoma of the bronchus.

Valenstein and Thurer (1978) : Granular cell myoblastoma of the bronchus.

Pind and Willis (1969) : Malignant teratoma of the lung in an infant.

McDermott et al. (1992) : Primary **rhabdomyosarcoma** in children - four cases - one with bilateral chylothoraces and three with large masses, one associated with a congenital cyst.

Uleda et al. (1977) : Rhabdomyosarcoma of lung in congenital cystic adenomatoid formation.

King (1953) : A case of **chloroma**.

Liu et al. (1973) : Autopsy study in Japan - Hiroshima - Nagasaki.

Krause (1979) : Granulocytic sarcoma preceding acute leukaemia.

Neiman et al. (1981) : Chloromas - 61 cases.

Pomeranz et al. (1985) : CT manifestations of granulocytic sarcoma.

Eshghabadi et al. (1986) : Case report of chloroma (granulocytic sarcoma) and literature review.

Callahan et al. (1987) : Granulocytic sarcoma presenting as pulmonary nodules and lymphadenopathy.

Hicklin and Devyanko (1988) : Primary granulocytic sarcoma presenting with pleural and pulmonary involvement - female aged 36 with LLL collapse and left pleural effusion.

Lee et al. (1991) : Pleural granulocytic sarcoma.

Dingerkus et al. (1994) : Mediastinal chloroma affecting the right heart with superior vena cava syndrome.

Pui et al. (1994) : Granulocytic sarcoma in childhood leukaemia.

Takasugi et al. (1996) : Intrathoracic granulocytic sarcomas - 9 cases - 6 involved the mediastinum, & 2 each the lungs, pleura, pericardium and hila.

Sajjad et al. (1997) : Dorsal spine deposits causing cord compression in a 22 yr old man - 4 weeks before myeloid leukaemia became apparent.

Wide & Curtis (1997) : 32 yr old man with known myeloid leukaemia. Two yrs later he had a R apical pleural mass + R 3 & 4 th rib destruction and soon afterwards skull & spinal deposit with cord compression.

Randall and Blades (1946) : Primary bronchogenic **leiomyosarcoma**.

Ochsner and Ochsner (1958) : Pneumonectomy for leiomyosarcoma.

Rosen et al. (1964) : Primary leiomyosarcoma of the lung.

Caves and Jacques (1971) : Primary intrapulmonary neurogenic sarcoma with HPOA and asbestosis.

Guccion and Rosen (1972) : Bronchopulmonary leiomyosarcoma (19 cases) & fibrosarcoma (13 cases) + lit. review.

Chaudhuri (1973) : Primary leiomyosarcoma of the lung.

Dowell (1974) : Primary pulmonary leiomyosarcoma - report of cases and review of the literature.

Ramanathan (1974) : Primary leiomyosarcoma of the lung.

Wang et al. (1974) : Pulmonary leiomyosarcoma associated with an A-V fistula.

Gil-Zunicaldy et al. (1982) : Primary pedunculated leiomyosarcoma of the right lung in a woman of 59 - may have a good prognosis.

Pedersen et al. (1984) : Primary pulmonary leiomyosarcoma - review of 38 cases from the literature and case report. Median age 57 (range 4 - 79).

Akamatsu et al. (1992) : Pulmonary rupture with primary pulmonary leiomyosarcoma.

Berney et al. (1992) : Leiomyosarcoma of the pulmonary hilar vessel.

Stark,P. et al. (1994): Primary intrathoracic malignant mesenchymal tumours (leiomyosarcoma, rhabdomyosarcoma, fibrosarcoma, malignant fibrous histiocytoma, haemangiopericytoma, liposarcoma, and **intrathoracic extraosseous osteogenic sarcoma**).

Ablett et al. (1998) : Pulmonary leiomyosarcoma presenting as a pseudoaneurysm.

Hamartomas, chondromas and chondromatous hamartomas (Illus. **HAMARTOMAS**).

The term **hamartoma** (derived from the Greek words 'αμαρτανειν - to 'go wrong' or 'err' and the suffix 'ωμα − a 'mass') was used by Albrecht (1904) to describe masses formed by mixed mesenchymal rests, which may enlarge to form tumour-like masses in various soft tissue organs, including the lungs. These may appear both as solitary or multiple masses, or occasionally as more diffuse processes. In the lungs they usually are present without being part of a more widespread condition, such as tuberose sclerosis. Willis (1953) and Bateson (1965) termed them 'mixed tumours' and the latter found that of approximately 3,800 lung masses, they comprised about 6%. Bateson (1967) considered them as chondromas occurring in the lungs, and reported an instance of such multiple masses. He thought that chondromas were of two types (a) those arising from the cartilage of the trachea or major bronchi, which might present with obstruction and/ or collapse - these tumours being small and only visible on tomograms or at bronchoscopy, and (b) those arising in the lung parenchyma, which were only partly cartilaginous and contained a mixture of tissues and were really hamartomas. Perhaps a few of the latter arise from the smaller bronchi.

Pulmonary hamartomas are typically solitary, sharply delineated masses, without any demonstrable change in the surrounding lung. They may be spherical or ovoid, and are occasionally notched (Rigler's sign - see ps. 4.2 & 4.14 - 15). Like hamartomas elsewhere, they contain a mixture of tissue elements - cartilage, smooth muscle, fat, fibrous and other connective tissues, and blood vessels. The cartilage may calcify and become bony. It gives rise to the typical 'pop corn' or 'ring' types of calcification, seen in these masses, and when present usually signifies that no active treatment is required. A more diffuse type (difficult to detect, even with CT) may also be found.

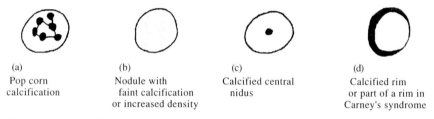

(a)   (b)   (c)   (d)
Pop corn   Nodule with   Calcified central   Calcified rim
calcification   faint calcification   nidus   or part of a rim in
                      or increased density   Carney's syndrome

Fig. 5.2   Radiographic patterns of hamartomas (see also Fig. 4.2).

Hickey and Simpson (1926) stated that when 'pop corn' calcification was present in a lung nodule, it is usually diagnostic of a hamartoma.

The incidence of calcification has varied in reported series of these masses. Lemon and Good (1950) at the Mayo Clinic found calcification in 11 out of 17 hamartomas removed surgically, though only two showed 'pop corn' calcification, and only six showed calcification on plain films. In a further study at the Mayo Clinic (O'Keefe et al., 1957), 11 out of 32 hamartomas showed calcification on plain films, four of 'pop corn' type and seven others with scattered areas of calcification. Bleyer and Marks (1957) found calcification in 15% of their cases. These authors also noted that four of the hamartomas occurred in patients with malignant disease elsewhere in the thorax. Freundlich (1981) gave an incidence of 25% showing calcification.

Calcification of the 'pop corn' type should be readily recognised on plain films or tomograms (Illus. **HAMARTOMAS, Pts. 3, 4, 5, 10, 12, 14**). CT may also show increased density in nodules which do not show overt calcification (see Illus. **HAMARTOMAS, Pt. 8**). As with renal hamartomas (**HAMARTOMAS, Pts. 20, 21, 22**), fat may also be demonstrated in some hamartomas (Illus. **HAMARTOMAS, Pt. 11**). Many however are only diagnosed after excision. About a third show neither calcification nor fat at CT (Siegelman et al., 1986a).

Only rarely have lung hamartomas been studied by angiography, but when this has been done (e.g. Botenga, 1970) a well marked vascular blush was seen on bronchial arteriography. Darke et al. (1972) described a giant hamartoma which grew in size over 20 years; it showed an area of perfusion deficit on a pulmonary perfusion scan corresponding to the mass and at operation it was supplied by the bronchial arteries.

Multiple hamartomas, diffuse forms and tuberose sclerosis.

Multiple hamartomas may be present in the same or both lungs - see note under leiomyomas below. Other cases have been reported by Bateson (1967) and by Ramchand and Baskerville (1969) who reported multiple hamartomas in the same lung. Other multiple hamartomas occur in the Carney syndrome (see p. 5.17 and Illus. **HAMARTOMAS, Pts. 9 & 16**).

Diffuse hamartomatous malformations may also be found in pulmonary lymphangioleiomyomatosis (see p. 5.18), and in tuberose sclerosis. In the latter, multiple small hamartomas may produce a coarse miliary pattern in about 5% of patients with this condition, or give rise to diffuse fibrosis and a fine 'honeycomb lung' or cystic appearance, similar to that seen with histiocytosis X. HRCT has shown that in both conditions the honeycombs and reticular pattern as seen on plain radiographs are essentially small thin-walled cysts, scattered randomly throughout the lungs. The cysts appear to be caused by muscular hyperplasia obstructing bronchioles and giving rise to secondary air-trapping.

In **tuberose sclerosis**, the underlying condition is essentially one of diffuse hamartomatous malformations involving not only the lungs, but also the skin (adenoma sebaceum and café au lait spots), eyes (retinal phakomata), brain (multiple tubers causing hydrocephalus and epilepsy - Illus. **HAMARTOMAS, Pt. 17c**), renal and hepatic masses (often containing considerable fat and are very vascular with nodular or beaded aneurysmal vessels - Illus. **HAMARTOMAS, Pts. 18b, 22**), bony erosions (tiny cystic areas in hands and feet and small sclerotic lesions in the axial skeleton - Illus. **HAMARTOMAS, Pt. 18c**), etc. The lung lesions (Illus. **HAMARTOMAS, Pts. 16, 17a-b, 18a**), when they appear, usually carry a grave prognosis. See also p. 12.29.

Chondromas (or hamartomas) occurring in the bronchi, cavities or cysts.

Chondromas may occur in the air passages, and look similar to hamartomas. It has also been suggested that up to 10% of hamartomas may originate within the bronchi. They may show calcification, and be a 'trigger' to asthma. Hickey and Simpson (1926) reported two cases and reviewed 40 from the literature. Davidson (1941) noted their presence in the trachea and bronchi. Darke (1960) described a case in which a hamartoma compressed the anterior basic bronchus of the right lower lobe which was shown by bronchography. The author has seen a small densely calcified chondroma arising from a right lower lobe bronchial cartilage, causing partial chronic collapse of the lower lobe. In another case an upper lobe chondroma turned into a chondrosarcoma, producing the Pancoast syndrome, and was unresectable.

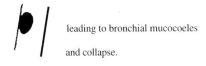

leading to bronchial mucocoeles

and collapse.

Fig. 5.3   (a) Endobronchial hamartoma.   (b) Fatty hamartoma in a cyst (? dilated bronchus).

An endobronchial case is shown in Illus. **HAMARTOMAS, Pt. 6b.**

Other endobronchial cases have been reported by Dovenbarger and Elstun (1961 - endobronchial hamartoma with calcification), Allen et al.(1963), and Borro et al. (1989 - 7 cases). Kallquist and Carlens (1962) felt that a chondroma could act as a 'trigger mechanism' for asthma. Davis, W. et al. (1988) described the CT findings of an endobronchial hamartoma; three other cases were reported by Ahn et al. (1994) - (i) Coll. RM+LLs with low density mass blocking Int. Br - tumour mainly fatty tissue & similar to endobronchial lipoma (see p. 6.12), (ii) Coll. LUL with a higher density central core - tumour contained connective tissue, fat, lymphoid tissue, smooth muscle and cartilage with calcification, (iii) endobronchial mass with density similar to muscle.

Chondromas of the chest wall or mediastinum.

Chondromas may arise from the ribs, costal cartilages, sternum or spine (see also Chapter 12). A rare case of a large intra-thoracic soft tissue chondroma arising in the posterior mediastinum and presenting as a heavily calcified mass above the right kidney in a girl of 19 was reported by Widdowson and Lewis Jones (1988).

Cardiac hamartomas.(see also p. 15.30).

Hamartomas may also occur in the heart. Heart tumours are very uncommon and (with the exception of atrial myxomas) most appear to occur in patients with tuberose sclerosis, or in relation to a pre-existing hamartoma. They may cause an obstructive cardiomyopathy, fatal pericardial haemorrhage, or even give rise to metastases, and one recorded case presented with multiple cavitating pulmonary secondary deposits.

Mesenchymal hamartomas.

These may be of a diffuse soft tissue and vascular type, and be associated with serious malformations of the lymphatic trunks. They may be found in the chest or abdominal wall, as well as the limbs. They may mimic locally malignant tumours by causing erosion of the ribs, producing soft tissue mass, spread into the chest and/or abdomen, and induce exudation of lymph into the pleura, peritoneum or externally. On CT sections, the malformations may appear more extensive than is suggested by the clinical appearance.

CT of hamartomas -Siegelman et al. (1986b) studied 47 patients with proven or presumed hamartomas by fine section CT. Their criteria for diagnosis were a diameter of 2.5 cm or less, a smooth edge, and focal collections of fat or fat alternating with areas of calcification. They also pointed out that fat must not be mistaken for air included in the measured area because of partial volume effect. Degenerate tissue may also mimic fat in large neoplasms (i.e. over 3 cm in diameter - see Illus. **HAMARTOMA, Pt. 11a-c** and compare with Illus. **CA+CALC, calc in tum 1a-b**). Slow growth is usually found on serial studies (though one rapidly growing hamartoma was reported by Sagel and Ablow, 1968).

MR of hamartomas - Sakai et al. (1994) found Gd enhancement of septa that separated the nodules into less marked nodules in 6 cases, corresponding to cleft-like branching mesenchymal connective tissue that dipped into the cartilaginous mass.

Malignant change - the question of malignant change in hamartomas has provoked considerable discussion. Albrecht (1904) did not specifically exclude this possibility, though some recent authors have suggested that hamartomas never become malignant. However if this were so, then they would be one of the very few (if any) tissues which cannot undergo malignant change. Malignant changes may be present in lung masses, even with calcification, in the Carney syndrome (see also p. 5.17 and Illus. **Carney syndrome**).

Karpas and Blackman (1967) reported an adenocarcinoma arising with a bronchial hamartoma and associated with multiple benign nodules elsewhere in the lungs. Poulsen (1979) also reported probable malignant transformation of a pulmonary hamartoma. The author has also seen bilateral malignant change in association with renal hamartomas (see also **HAMARTOMA MALIGNANT, Hamartoma Pt. 22**).

Biopsy of hamartomas can be quite difficult, because many hamartomas are small and like mammary fibro-adenomas, contain a great deal of cartilage, which is resistant to being punctured, particularly in a mobile structure such as the lung. They are much more resistant to this than lung tumours. Occasionally the masses can be quite large, and then a biopsy is much easier.

Sinner (1982) from the Karolinska Sjukhuset, Stockholm, described his experience in trying to puncture hamartomas percutaneously, and found this difficult with a false negative rate for biopsy of 29%. He concluded that suspected hamartomas should be considered as neoplasms and that hamartomas are the most common benign tumour among solitary pulmonary nodules. He described the nodules as typically well circumscribed usually under 4 cm, and without a significant lobar predominance; cavitation was rare, but in his series only 5% were calcified.

Hamper et al. (1985) also used trans-thoracic needle biopsy to establish the diagnosis in 12 of 14 cases, cytology being positive in five, and tissue specimens in 11. Eight were positive at the first biopsy.

Surgery - hamartomas usually 'shell out' of false capsules, with but little effort, as soon as these are incised. Little or no lung resection is usually necessary for their removal.

Cases examined by the author are shown in Illus. **HAMARTOMAS.**

Further references.

Von Recklinghausen (1863) : Tuberous sclerosis.
Bourneville (1880) : Tuberose sclerosis (Concentration á l'étude de l'idiote).
McDonald et al. (1945), Bragg and Levene (1950) : Hamartoma of the lung.
Rubin and Berkman (1952) : Malignant hamartoma of the lung.
Stein and Poppel (1955) Hamartomas have also been termed 'papillomas', 'fibroadenoma', 'mixed tumours', 'adenochondromas' and 'lipochondromas'.
Cavin et al. (1958) : Malignant hamartoma of the lung in an infant.
Jensen and Schmidt (1958) : Growth considerations of hamartoma of the lung.
Whitaker (1959) : Radiological manifestations of tuberose sclerosis.
Logan et al. (1964) : Excision of 2 fibrous hamartomas from R and 2 from L lung - female aged 46.
Bateson and Abbott (1960) : Mixed lung tumours or hamarto-chondromas - studied 200 cases.
Bateson (1965) : Intrapulmonary and endobronchial cartilage containing tumours; so called hamartomata.
Bateson (1967) : Cartilage-containing tumours of the lung. Relationship between purely cartilaginous type (chondroma) and mixed type (hamartoma) - unusual case of multiple tumours.
Blair and McElvein (1963) : Hamartoma of the lung - clinical study of 25 cases.
Christoforidis et al. (1964) : Diffuse fibro-muscular hamartomatosis + diffuse bronchiolectasis and polycystic lung.
Doppman and Wilson (1965) : Cystic pulmonary hamartoma.
Milledge at al. (1966) : Pulmonary manifestations of tuberose sclerosis - honeycombed cystic appearance which may be complicated by spontaneous pneumothorax.
Sargent et al. (1970) : Multiple pulmonary fibroleiomyomatous hamartomas.
Poirier and van Orstrand (1971) : Chrondromatous hamartoma - 17 cases and literature review.
Poulsen et al. (1979) : Probable malignant transformation of a pulmonary hamartoma.
Karasik et al. (1980) : Increased risk of lung cancer in patients with chondromatous hamartoma.
Ledor et al. (1981) : CT of pulmonary hamartomas.
Demos et al. (1983) : Cystic hamartoma of the lung.
Bennett et al. (1985) : Multiple calcified chondrohamartomas of the lung at CT.
Potente et al. (1999) : CT of 30 noncalcified hamartomas - contrast-enhancing septa were present in 24 corresponding to loose connective tissue; a rare finding was an **air bronchogram** related to bronchial epithelium.
Burke and Rubens (1993) : Uptake of Tc^{99m}MDP by a pulmonary hamartoma/ mesenchymoma.

Green (1968) : The radiology of tuberose sclerosis - 13 patients - four had lung changes with honeycombing or a fine nodular pattern. (He also noted bone changes - sclerosis and /or cysts in the hands and feet, sclerosis in the skull, spine, pelvis and long bones, basal ganglia calcification and hamartomas in the kidneys).
Liberman et al. (1984) : Tuberous sclerosis with pulmonary involvement.
Chew et al. (1980), Biondetti et al. (1982a) : Infiltrative angiolipoma of the thoraco-abdominal wall.
Hauser et al. (1980) : Multiple hamartoma syndrome (**Cowden disease**).
Wright et al. (1974) , Meisel and Apitszch (1978) : Renal hamartomas.
Wright (1983, 1987) : General review.   Cheung et al. (1993) : Liver hamartomas in tuberose sclerosis.
Castro et al. (1995, Mayo Clinic) : Pulmonary tuberous sclerosis - review of 9 cases (all female) - 5 had hormone therapy (as with LAM ? same underlying disease) - 3 clinically responded & 2 who had no treatment died of progressive respiratory failure. HRCT showed cystic spaces with thin walls.
Evans and Curtis (2000) : Pictorial review - radiological appearances of tuberous sclerosis.

Hamartomatous like lesions in the thorax.
    There are a number of conditions, particularly occurring in females, which resemble hamartomas - (for cystic adenomatoid malformations and Castleman tumours and see ps. 3.10 & 5.30 - 33).

The Carney syndrome (or 'triad') was so named following the description of four cases by Carney and Hayles (1977) and Carney et al. (1977), followed by 14 other cases in a review of the world literature (Carney, 1979). The author encountered one case in the early 1970's; this was a young woman who had calcifying lung and liver 'deposits' - she had had a previous partial gastrectomy (Illus. **CARNEY SYNDROME, Hamartoma Pt. 19a-d**). Gastric lesions are part of the triad and some have been termed leiomyoblastomas or leiomyosarcomas. The patients may also have functioning extra-adrenal paragangliomas (see also ps. 18.37 - 38). The pulmonary lesions may be true metastases, hamartomas or chondromas.
Mazas-Artasona et al. (1988) reported a girl aged 12 with gastric and oesophageal leiomyomas and pulmonary chondromas, in which no paraganglioma had appeared in a six year follow-up, and termed this the '**incomplete triad**'.

Further references.
Müller et al. (1974) : Bilateral multiple pulmonary hamartomas in a female aged 24 who had a gastric leiomyoma.
Appelman and Helwig (1976) : Gastric epithelioid leiomyoma and leiomyosarcoma.
Dajee et al. (1982) : Pulmonary chondroma, extra-adrenals paraganglioma and gastric leiomyosarcoma.
Carney (1983) : The triad of gastric epithelioid leiomyosarcoma, pulmonary chondroma and functioning extra-adrenal paraganglioma - five year review.
Mishkin et al. (1985) : Carney's triad - radiographic diagnosis, natural history and pulmonary chondromas.
Rufenacht et al. (1985) : Gastric epithelioid leiomyomas, pulmonary chondroma, non-functioning extra-adrenal paraganglioma and myxoma - a variant of Carney's triad.
Tortella et al. (1985) : Gastric autonomic nerve tumour and extra-adrenal paraganglioma in Carney's triad - a common origin.
Raafat et al. (1986) : Carney's triad - gastric leiomyosarcoma, pulmonary chondroma and extra-adrenal paraganglioma in young females.
Margulies and Sheps (1988) : Carney's triad - guidelines for management.
Evans et al. (1990) : Indolent gastric epithelioid leiomyosarcoma in Carney's triad.

Pulmonary lymphangiomyomatosis ('muscular hyperplasia of the lungs' - see also p. 1.55).
   This is the localised form of thoracic lymphangiomyomatosis (see also p. 13.6). It is a rare and aggressive condition affecting women, principally of child bearing age (17 to 50 years). Radiologically the manifestations include a fine irregular and apparently nodular pattern in the lungs, **cyst-like honeycombed spaces randomly distributed throughout the lungs**, with **normal intervening lung**, lung overinflation, recurrent pneumothoraces and chylous pleural effusions. The CT changes (Illus. **LAM, Pleural effusions, Hamartoma, Pt. 24**) may be similar to those seen with histiocytosis (see ps. 19.61 - 63), but focal areas may be more severely affected.
   Histology shows hyperplasia of atypical smooth muscle fibres particularly alongside the pulmonary lymphatics. Haemiosiderin-laden macrophages may be found in broncho-alveolar washings. The condition may be a 'forme fruste' of tuberose sclerosis (see above). An infantile type with a large mass filling a lobe or lung may be found.
   The author has seen a girl aged 15 with the more generalised type. She had recurrent chylous pleural effusions over an eight year period until her death. At post-mortem the RLL showed fibrotic nodular scarring and the right pleural cavity was obliterated by pink/grey fibrous tissue which extended into the mediastinum and pericardium - Illus. **LAM, Pleural effusions**.
   A further pleural case is shown in Illus. **LAM, Lymphatics, Pt. 14a-k**.
   Hormonal treatment using progesterone or tamoxifen may be helpful, a Leveen shunt for intractable effusions or single lung transplantation for respiratory failure.

References (see also p. 13.6).
Silverstein et al. (1974) : Death from respiratory failure usually occurs in 4.5 years.
Corrin et al. (1975) : Review.
Carrington (1977) : Physiology, pathology & radiology - 6 cases, 4 with pneumothorax (2 recurrent), 4 with progressive dyspnoea, haemoptysis in 3, & 1 each with chylothorax or retroperitoneal haemorrhage.
Bradley et al. (1980), McCarty et al. (1980)
Ovenfors et al. (1980) : Muscular hyperplasia of the lung., Berger and Shaff (1981)
Capron et al. (1983) : Pulmonary LAM and tuberose sclerosis with pulm. involvement ? the same disease.
Merchant et al. (1985) : CT in the diagnosis of lymphangioleiomyomatosis - patient with chylothorax - involvement of lungs, lymphatics and kidneys - they illustrated contrast medium passing into the pleural cavity following lymphangiography, from a leaking thoracic duct.
Luna et al. (1985) : Pulmonary LAM + tuberose sclerosis - treated with tamoxifen and tetracycline pleurodesis.
Shen et al. (1987) : Exacerbation of pulmonary lymphangiomyomatosis by exogenous oestrogens.
Sherrier et al. (1989) : CT findings - multiple thin-walled lung cysts, pleural effusions and pneumothorax - also enlarged mediastinal and retrocrural nodes.
Templeton et al. (1989) : HRCT in two cases showed numerous thin-walled cystic air spaces of varying sizes which were distributed diffusely throughout the lungs. Most of the lung parenchyma surrounding the air-spaces was normal.
Rappaport et al. (1989) : HRCT findings in four cases of pulmonary lymphangioleiomyomatosis.
Aberle et al. (1990) : CT of 8 women (aged 29 to 63) - cystic air spaces in lung parenchyma - comparison with histiocytosis and emphysema.
Hansell et al. (1990) : HRCT of 10 patients with pathologically proven disease - replacement of the lung by very thin-walled cysts of varying size from 2 to 30 mm in diameter, distributed throughout all lobes and with no central or peripheral predominance.

Lenoir et al. (1990) from France : Comparison of radiographic and HRCT findings in 9 women with pulmonary lymphangiomyomatosis and two with tuberose sclerosis. In all cases there were small cysts distributed randomly throughout the lungs. They considered that bronchiolar obstruction, secondary to muscular proliferation, leads to a valve-like obstruction with bronchiolectasis, dilatation and disruption of alveolar walls. Rupture of subpleural cysts leads to pneumothoraces. One patient showed septal lines and dependent alveolar oedema.
Müller et al. (1990) from Canada : Compared the chest and CT radiographic findings and pulmonary function tests in 14 patients with lymphangiomyomatosis and found CT to be greatly superior, although one patient appeared to have an abnormal chest radiograph and normal CT.
Burger et al. (1991) : Pulmonary mechanics in lymphangioleiomyomatosis - study of eight patients. In seven there was some respiratory obstruction due to airway narrowing rather than the loss of elastic recoil forces.
Taylor et al. (1990) : Clinical course of lymphangioleiomyomatosis in 32 patients - infiltration of lymphatics, and also around the small airways and blood vessels - the conducting airways being compressed and causing airflow obstruction, alveolar disruption and distal cystic changes. Hormone manipulation may lead to longer survival and improvement in some cases. 25 /32 of their patients were still alive 8.5 years after clinical presentation.
Stern et al. (1992) : Cystic lung disease associated with eosinophilic granuloma and tuberous sclerosis - air trapping at dynamic ultrafast HRCT.
Worthy et al. (1998) : The majority of lung cysts (including in LAM) decrease in size in expiration suggesting that they communicate with the airways. Avila et al. (2000) : Trapping of Tc99mDTPA aerosol in the cysts.
Boehler et al. (1996) : Lung transplantation for LAM.   Oh et al. (1999) : 23 cases in Korea.
Johnson, E. (1999) : LAM - review - clinical features, management & basic mechanisms - rate of progression is variable between pts. - a few years to 2 to 3 decades.

Pulmonary leiomyomas.

These may be part of the Carney syndrome or occur per se. They present with multiple nodules throughout both lungs, looking like metastases, but only slowly progress, and the patients have no symptoms from them. They almost invariably occur in women, and the author has collected three such cases, one of which is illustrated in Illus. **LEIOMYOMA, Pt. 1**, another had very slowly enlarging nodules over a period of 30 years. Lung nodules vary in size from miliary to 1- 2 cm (or occasionally more) in size. Other cases have been reported by Sherman and Malone (1950) and Robbins (1954) who described patients presenting with multiple asymptomatic round leiomyomatous masses throughout the lungs. Sargent (1970) found other cases in the literature, and reported another. They all occurred in women aged 35 to 60.

Some of these cases occur as '**metastasising benign uterine myomata**'. Such cases have been reported by Harper and Scully (1961), Idelson and Davids (1963) and Horstman et al. (1977). Spencer (1985) pointed out that cells may occasionally be seen entering the pelvic veins draining uterine myomata on surgical specimens. Kaszar-Seibert et al. (1988) reported intracardiac extension of intravenous leiomyomatosis.

Some pulmonary leiomyomas, etc. in females may regress with hormonal changes following hysterectomy, myomectomy, the ending of pregnancy or following progesterone, etc. treatment (Horstman et al., 1977). As with hamartomas, myomas may be very vascular, as they are often in the alimentary tract (Uflacker et al., 1981).

Further references.
Williams and Daniel (1950) : Leiomyoma of the lung. Freireich et al. (1951) : Primary bronchogenic leiomyoma.
Orlowski et al. (1978) : Leiomyoma of the lung. Martin (1982) : Leiomatous lung lesions - proposed classification.
Vera-Román et al. (1983) : Leiomyoma of the lung - review of 65 cases.
Charig (1999) : Miliary lung shadows during pregnancy, reduced following Caesarean section, later hysterectomy for large fibroids and progesterone treatment - MR had shown the fibroids + extension into the IVC.
Koh et al. (2000) : Benign metastasising leiomyoma with intracaval leiomyomatosis (+ further refs.).

Thoracic endometriosis (pulmonary deciduosis - Illus ENDOMETRIOSIS).

This may spread to the thorax, as well as to the peritoneum, kidneys and peritoneal areas. A number of women with the condition have catamenial haemoptysis, and a few have small peripheral lung or endo-bronchial nodules found, but in the majority no abnormality is discovered at bronchoscopy or on tomograms (including CTs) or on bronchograms or at bronchoscopy. Others may have catamenial pneumothoraces, a pneumediastinum, pleural nodules or effusions. Pleural disease is more commonly seen on the right.

Two methods of spread occur to the thorax: (i) embolisation via the uterine vessels and thence embolisation to the lungs, and (ii) via pores in the diaphragm (see thoracic ascites - ps. 14.9 - 10).

According to Foster et al. (1981) lung parenchymal disease is more common in older women and pleural in younger, the latter being more commonly associated with pleural endometriosis and a pneumothorax.

Regarding embolisation it is a common observation during hysterosalpingography (if this is accidentally carried out whilst a woman is at or close to menstruation) that intravasation of contrast medium readily occurs into the uterine vessels, and this is one reason why the oily medium was abandoned (see also under oil embolism - p. 6.14). Hobbs and Bortneck (1940) showed experimentally that endometrial tissue injected intravenously can survive and proliferate within the pulmonary vessels and the adjacent lung parenchyma. Park (1954) and Hartz (1956) noted that fragments of decidua may occasionally be found in the lungs of post-partum women. Cases with pulmonary masses have been reported by Sturzenegger (1960), Jelihovsky and Grant (1968), Foster et al. (1981) and Karpel et al. (1985), whilst endobronchial endometriosis was reported by Rodman and Jones (1962).

Pleural disease is usually clinically manifested by right shoulder pain and dyspnoea due to pneumothoraces, which are probably related to leaking from small blebs or bullae lying beneath visceral pleural nodules. Surgically and pathologically pleural disease appears as bluish-purple single or multiple nodules scattered throughout one or both pleural cavities (usually the right), and these may be found on both the parietal and visceral pleura. Commonly the adjacent diaphragm is involved as well, and 'chocolate' cysts as are found with abdominal endometriosis are not uncommon. Plaques of fibrosis may represent healed lesions. Pneumothoraces have been reported by Wilhelm and Scrommenga (1979) and by Furman et al. (1980). The first described a nulliparous woman with bilateral recurrent pneumothoraces, due to pleural involvement. The second report described a woman of 30 who had chest pains with the menses, pneumothoraces and a pneumoperitoneum. (Other cases are noted in the references below.) Defects in the diaphragm were seen at pleuroscopy before using sclerosants. 32 such cases were described in the 1980 Year book of Radiology. Im et al. (1987) used CT and ultra-sound to demonstrate numerous small defects in the diaphragm and masses in the pleural and peritoneal cavities; he also quoted 87 cases in toto. Flower from Cambridge (1988) demonstrated increased vascularity over the surface of the diaphragm by bronchial arteriography, with retrograde flow into pulmonary artery branches and a negative area on a lung perfusion scan in such a case.

Further references.
Hart (1912) : Multiple pulmonary lesions with endometrial glands and stroma - interpreted as hamartomatous.
Schwarz (1938) : Recurrent haemoptysis during menstrual cycle - associated with endometriosis of inguinal nodes.
Buengeler (1939) : Pleural endometriosis.
Lattes et al. (1956) : Clinical and pathologic study of endometriosis of the lung.
Maurer et al. (1958) : Chronic recurring pneumothorax due to endometriosis of the diaphragm.
Mobbs and Pfranner (1963) : Endometriosis of the lung.
Kovarik and Toll (1966) : Thoracic endometriosis and recurrent spontaneous pneumothorax.
Yeh (1966) : Reviewed 19 cases of thoracic endometriosis, involving the pleura in 6, the diaphragm in 6, the lung parenchyma in 6, the bronchus (one case) and the myocardium (one case).
Crutcher et al. (1967) : Recurring spontaneous pneumothorax associated with menstruation.
Davies (1968) : Recurring spontaneous pneumothorax concomitant with menstruation.
Jelihovsky and Grant (1968) : Endometriosis of lung - case report and review.
Weldon and Tumulty (1968) : Recurrent pneumothorax associated with menstruation.
Lillington et al. (1972) : Catamenial pneumothorax.
Farinacci et al. (1973) : Multifocal pulmonary lesions of possible decidual origin.
Rossi and Goplerund (1974) : Recurrent catamenial pneumothorax (8 cases who had had hysterectomies thus proving that the air could not have passed via the uterus and fallopian tubes to the peritoneal cavity and chest).
Soderberg and Dahlquist (1990) : Catamenial pneumothorax.
Yamazaki et al. (1980) : Catamenial pneumothorax associated with endometriosis of the diaphragm.
Foster et al. (1981) : 54 cases of thoracic endometriosis - 54 pleural and 11 parenchymal.
Hibbard et al. (1981) : Thoracic endometriosis - review and report of two cases.
Ronnberg and Ylostalo (1981) : Treatment of pulmonary endometriosis with Danazol.
Rosenberg and Riddick (1981) : Successful treatment of catamenial haemoptysis with Danazol.
Slasky et al. (1982) : Catamenial pneumothorax - the roles of diaphragmatic defects and endometriosis.
Elliot et al. (1985) : Catamenial haemoptysis - new methods of diagnosis and therapy.
Müller and Nelems (1986) : Postcoital catamenial pneumothorax not due to endometriosis and cured by laparoscopic sterilisation - ? due to air passing through the uterus and fallopian tubes to the peritoneal cavity and thence through lacunae in the diaphragm.

Shahar and Angellillo (1986) : Catamenial pneumediastinum.
Gray et al. (1987) : CT of pulmonary endometriosis.
Herzanu et al. (1987) : CT of pulmonary endometriosis.
Di Palo et al. (1989) : Endometriosis of the lung with endobronchial mass occluding left main bronchus + review.
Downey et al. (1990) : Pneumothoraces with catamenial pneumothorax - wondered if gas passed through the uterus and fallopian tubes.

Other rare endo-bronchial tumours include lipomas (ps. 6.12 - 13), fibromas (Kovarik and Prather Ashe, 1963) meningeomas (Moran et al., 1996 - review of 10 cases) and neural tumours (pulmonary neurofibromas and Schwannomas are essentially tumours of vagal nerve fibres - see p. 18.37).

Reviews of benign lung and bronchial tumours have been made by Hochberg and Schachter (1955), Peleg and Pauzner (1965), Arrigoni et al. (1970), Madewell and Feigin (1977), and Miller, J. (1992). (see also references under trachea - ps. 4.24 - 25).

RETICULOSES

Table 5.2 - Reticuloses affecting the thorax.
(a) **Malignant lymphomas or reticuloses** including:
      Hodgkin's disease
      Non-Hodgkin's lymphoma (B or T cell)
      Lymphosarcoma
      Kaposi sarcoma (see ps. 19.33 - 34)
      Malignant histiocytosis
      Lymphomatoid (lymphoid) granuloma (overlaps with angiitis - see ps. 19.76 et seq.).

(b) **Non-malignant lymphoid disorders** including :
      Castleman's tumour (angiofollicular lymphoid hyperplasia)
      Histiocytoma (plasma cell granuloma or inflammatory pseudo-tumour), including
      fibroxanthoma and xanthogranuloma (may have **malignant** forms).
      Sinus histiocytosis with lymphadenopathy
      Pseudolymphoma
      Lymphoid interstitial pneumonia (see also p. 19.119)
      Angio-immunoblastic lymphadenopathy
      Pulmonary hyalinising lymphadenopathy (Engelman's disease)
      Cyclosporin induced lymphoproliferative disease.

Some of the **non-malignant types may progress to frank lymphomas** e.g.
      Lymphoid granuloma
      Pseudolymphoma
      Histiocytoma
      Castleman's disease
      (Hypoglobulinaemia), LIP, etc.

Thoracic reticuloses - see Illus. **HODGKIN'S DISEASE, LYMPHOMA, LYMPHOMA, ETC. and HODG/MYELO LUNG INFIL.**
The intrathoracic effects of these are **protean and may affect many organs.** Lymph nodes are commonly involved and are often considerably enlarged, especially in non-Hodgkin's lymphomas. Any node groups may be involved, but particularly those in the anterior mediastinum at first presentation - thymic Hodgkin's (see ps. 13.22 & 18.16 - 17) - see Illus. **THYMIC LYMPHOMA.** This enlargement may cause a choking feeling and discomfort on leaning forwards. It may also cause pressure on the trachea, and cause severe respiratory embarrassment particularly following anaesthesia. (An endotracheal tube usually prevents problems during anaesthesia, but when removed the **air-way may collapse**, sometimes with a fatal result, as

reintubation may be impossible - Illus. **HODGKIN'S DISEASE, Pt. 15a-d**). Other commonly enlarged nodes occur in the para-tracheal areas, in relation to the aortic arch (sub-aortic fossa, etc.), the internal mammary chain, subcarinal nodes, etc. Posterior mediastinal and cardio-phrenic node enlargement more often occurs at a later stage of the disease. Lung nodules may be seen at presentation, but are more common with recurrence, and in general the **findings of recurrence are often different from those at initial presentation.**

Lung lesions may be mass-like or infiltrative, and be single or multiple, the latter simulating metastases. Solitary lesions, particularly with non-Hodgkin's lymphomas, tend to be wedge shaped areas of consolidation or infiltration, with rigid though patent bronchi running through them and showing '**air bronchograms**' (sometimes with a **leafless-tree** appearance as with alveolar cell carcinoma - see ps. 5.1 - 5) on tomograms or bronchograms. Lymphoma nodules may cavitate and give rise to pneumothoraces (Illus. **LYMPHOMA-CAVIT**). Pleural effusions are not uncommon, particularly with recurrent disease, and nodules may be present in the pleura. Occasionally a nodular 'dry' pleurisy is produced. Similarly, pericardial effusions and masses may occur. SVC obstruction may be present with large masses or with a fibrosing mediastinitis following treatment. Endobronchial lesions may mimic bronchial tumours and lead to lobar or lung collapse. Like primary bronchial tumours, the endobronchial deposits may spread sub-mucosally up and down the larger bronchi (see ps. 13.7 - 9). Lung disease may be accompanied by HPOA (see ps. 23.1 - 5). Thoracic disease is commonly associated by disease in other areas, cervical nodes, the abdomen (retrocrural and other nodes, liver, spleen, kidneys, stomach, etc.) or bones, where lesions are often surrounded by soft tissue masses. A well known but rare presentation is the sclerotic '**ivory**' vertebra (Illus. **HODGKIN'S DISEASE, Pt. 7b**), with adjacent soft tissue swelling and cord compression.

Lymphomas often '**envelop**' or '**engulf**' organs, with the structure and function of the organs being preserved. This is best seen with the kidneys but also occurs in the mediastinum, and other parts of the abdomen. (A similar appearance may also occasionally be seen with lung tumours - see Illus. **LYMPHOMA ENGULF**).

CT has greatly improved the demonstration of the extent of the spread of all types of lymphoma. Thus it helps with initial assessment, determining the best place for biopsy, staging and the planning of treatment particularly radiotherapy. It is very good for showing the extent of disease in the thorax, and for differentiating anterior mediastinal disease from other abnormalities - vascular, fat, etc. Masses in the anterior mediastinum, or thymic area, may become very large (Illus. **LYMPHOMA-ANT MED**), and extend almost across the front of the chest from side to side. Some of these may show a 'peripheral blush' with IV contrast media, and a central degenerate area (Illus. **HODGKIN'S DISEASE, Pt. 58a-c**), this appearance not being uncommon in nodular sclerosing Hodgkin's disease. CT has greatly reduced and almost obliterated the need for lymphangiograms and staging laparotomies with splenectomy.

ß cell lymphomas of the lung.

These may arise in extra-nodal lymphoid tissue in the lungs giving rise to dense focal areas of consolidation, containing air bronchograms, which do not clear with conventional antibiotic therapy and tend to run an indolent course. They resemble lung lesions in Wegener's granuloma but these are usually more rapidly progressive. Many in the past have been termed pseudo-lymphomas (see p. 5.33). Others give rise to a miliary or cavitating miliary appearance (Illus. **LYMPHOMA-CAVIT, Pt. 4a-c**). The presence of enlarged nodes suggests more aggressive disease.

Appearances on lymphography.

The author carried out many hundreds of lymphangiograms for the assessment of lymphomas, in the days before CT was available. Affected para-aortic nodes were typically enlarged, and many had a 'lace work' appearance (Illus. **LYMPHOMA-LYMPH**). Only those nodes on the pathway from the feet were usually opacified, other enlargements being inferred by displaced ureters, renal tract obstruction or by soft tissue masses in the abdomen and lower chest (note especially the '**ice-berg sign**' - p. 18.31 and Illus. **ICEBERG SIGN**). Occasionally, nodes in the mediastinum were opacified, and those which were enlarged sometimes also showed a 'lace work' like appearance. Nodes which took up the oil could remain opacified for 12 to 18 months.

Recurrence of disease and second neoplasms.

Although most lymphomas usually rapidly regress in size, and commonly chest radiographs return to normal following treatment with chemotherapy or radiotherapy, it is important to review patients for evidence of recurrence of disease. A big problem is that affected nodes may not be significantly enlarged, in the same way that small deposits in the liver, spleen and bone marrow may be invisible. Another problem is that following treatment affected nodes and other masses, particularly in the anterior mediastinum, may not fully regress, and residual masses may be present in the hilar and mediastinal areas, which may not be malignant. A special problem is the recurrence or persistence of thymic swelling - is it recurrence, a rebound change or hyperplasia? (see also p. 18.20 & seq. refs.). Fibrous masses often persist after radiotherapy (post-radiation changes are discussed on p. 11.19 et seq.). Recurrence in these areas may be difficult to detect, and MR, especially with STIR (or similar sequences, see ps. 20.29 et seq.) or PET scanning may assist in differentiation. (For a review of the value of FDG PET in lymphoma see Shah et al, 2000).

Sometimes the degree of malignancy changes, and it may become more anaplastic, or other complicating neoplasms occur (see refs. below) Opportunistic infections may also complicate the disease.

Calcification.

Occasionally nodes in areas treated by radiotherapy calcify. This may also rarely be seen following chemotherapy or rarely occur in untreated cases.

Lymphomas complicating other conditions.

Lymphomas may complicate other diseases affecting the immune system; these include hypogammaglobulinaemia, AIDS, etc. They may also occur in those having immunosuppressive treatment, e.g. following renal or other organ transplantations, or in those having long-term treatment with some forms of chronic renal failure. In these, nodal enlargements in the mediastinum, etc., pleural effusions or lung masses may be found. The lung masses may appear as wedge-shaped areas of consolidation, with patent bronchi running through them. These wedge-shaped masses may be localised, but may be fairly widespread and disseminated. They often have a poor prognosis. Examples are shown in Illus. **LYMPHOMA+RENAL FAIL & AIDS.**

Similarly a form of reticulosis - Kaposi's sarcoma - is being seen more frequently, particularly in patients with AIDS (ps. 19. 33 - 34). This may cause lung nodules, pleural effusions and massive enlargements (Illus. **KAPOSI SARCOMA**). It too usually carries a very poor prognosis. This appears to be triggered by genital herpes, but other viruses may also stimulate the development of a reticulosis - EB virus or even monkey virus accidentally given with older types of antipoliomyelitis vaccine.

Incidence and staging.

Lymphomas account for about 5 - 10% of tumours in adults. In Hodgkin's disease, the staging far outweighs the importance of the histological subtype, but in non-Hodgkin's lymphoma the subtype has a more profound effect on the prognosis than the anatomical staging. **Hodgkin's disease tends to spread to neighbouring nodes or tissue, whilst non-Hodgkin's lymphoma tends to involve multiple sites simultaneously.** CT should always be carried out at presentation, even with disease apparently confined to the neck, because nodal enlargement and lung changes may be found in about 20% of those with apparently normal chest radiographs. Those who have large masses, lung nodules accompanied by pleural and/or pericardial effusions, tend to have more aggressive disease - see also tables below.

Lymphosarcomas have a similar morphology to other lymphomas, but are usually more rapidly progressive, producing lung and other metastases. Cyto-histology is essential for differentiation. Examples are shown under Illus. **LYMPHOSARCOMA**.

Table 5.3 - <u>Ann Arbor staging classification.</u>

Stage I	Involvement of a single lymph node region,
IE	or of a single extralymphatic organ or site.
Stage II	Involvement of two or more lymph node regions on the same side of the diaphragm.
IIE	or localised involvement of an extralymphatic organ or site and of one or more lymph node regions on the same side of the diaphragm.
Stage III	Involvement of lymph node regions on both sides of the diaphragm,
IIIS	with involvement of the spleen,
IIIE	or a localised extralymphatic organ or site.
Stage IV	Diffuse or disseminated involvement of one or more extralymphatic organs or tissues (e.g. liver, bone marrow, lung, bone and skin).
Suffix A	No systemic symptoms.
B	Systemic symptoms - unexplained weight loss over previous six months, and/or unexplained fever > 38°C, and/or night sweating.
	S, H, M, P and O may be used to denote splenic, hepatic, marrow, pulmonary or osseous involvement.

Table 5.4 - <u>Some differences between Hodgkin's* and non-Hodgkin's lymphomas, at presentation.</u>

	Hodgkin's disease	**Non-Hodgkin's**
	Most are now curable	
age	Most common in young adults or teenagers	40 to 70 years
	More aggressive in older patients	
extent of disease at presentation	Most commonly a single node group is involved predominantly in the longitudinal axis of the body with largely contiguous spread and mediastinal involvement in about 50%.	Multiple node groups are usually involved with centrifugal, non-contiguous spread and the mediastinum is only involved in about 20%.
bone marrow, GI tract & abdominal nodes, etc.	uncommon	common
brain	uncommon	Primary brain disease in 20-30%

Table 5.5 - <u>Summary of radiological signs.</u>
Lung mass or masses - wedge shaped or rounded, typically with an 'air bronchogram' passing through it - like a segmental or lobar consolidation - especially in Hodgkin's disease.
In other cases of primary lung disease the picture may mimic chronic lung infection with peribronchial shadowing, bronchiectasis and fluid bronchograms - and may show a positive CT angiogram sign on contrast enhanced CT. Such disease may be multifocal and bilateral.
Multiple nodules - larger or miliary (metastases) may be present and may cavitate.
Nodal enlargement - any node groups, but massive enlargement is most common in the anterior mediastinum and particularly 'thymic nodes'. Enlarged internal mammary nodes may be present.
Pleural effusion - may be accompanied by nodular thickening - rarely a 'dry' nodular pleurisy or 'cancer en cuirasse' like a mesothelioma.
Para-spinal masses.
Bony lesions - especially in the spine - may be lytic, sclerotic (with **'ivory vertebra'**) or mixed.
Bone marrow involvement.
Para-aortic nodes - 'lace-work' like appearance on lymphograms - note also **'ice-berg' sign**.
Omental masses and GI involvement - stomach, ileum, etc.
Liver and spleen enlargement and deposits (liver more commonly involved with follicular lymphomas). Spleen more commonly involved, than other abdominal organs - may be diffuse.
Renal lesions and encasement.

*Thomas Hodgkin (1798-1866) - morbid anatomist at Guy's Hosp. wrote about 'some marked appearances of lymph nodes and spleen' - not TB - which caused death in young people. Also philanthropist and traveller - statue in Jaffa.
See also: Kass and Kass (1989) Perfecting the World: The Life and Times of Dr. Thomas Hodgkin 1798 - 1866.

Further references.

General

Vieta and Craver (1941) : Intrathoracic manifestations of lymphomatoid disease.

Baron and Whitehouse (1961) : **Lymphosarcoma** appearing as an area of consolidation or infiltration with rigid though patent bronchi passing through it.

Fisher et al. (1962) : Hodgkin's disease - a radiological survey.

Kreel and Mackay (1962) : **Pericardial effusion** in mediastinal lymphoma.

Simon (1967) : Lung consolidation in Hodgkin's disease may produce a variety of shadows - an ill-defined area, a well defined mass resembling carcinoma, an 'air-bronchogram' or a cavitating lesion which may have a thin wall with a fluid level or be thick walled with endo-mural nodules.

Strickland (1967) : Reviewed 200 cases of intra-thoracic Hodgkin's disease and termed it the '**great deceiver**' in radiological diagnosis. He found that nodules in the lungs tended to be more irregular in shape than with carcinoma deposits and mostly these appeared after nodal enlargement. Pressure on a pulmonary artery could cause narrowing of the distal vessels. A large rapidly growing peripheral lesion might suggest Hodgkin's sarcoma. Calcification, often punctate in type, may be seen in nodes or lung lesions following radiotherapy.
Sternal involvement was common and was suggested by retro-sternal soft tissue enlargement like a truncated wigwam.

Sternum

Wigwam sign of retrosternal soft-tissue swelling (also can be produced by a post-sternotomy haematoma see - also p. 12.34).

Fayos (1968) : Extra-pulmonary intra-thoracic manifestations of Hodgkin's disease.

Dahlgren and Overfors (1969) : Primary malignant lymphoma of the lung with a ten year course at first a rounded, poorly delineated infiltration which later broke down to give a cystic appearance.

Wyman and Weber (1969) and Bertrand et al. (1977) : Nodal calcification following RT and/or chemotherapy.

Parker et al. (1974) : Lymphographic appearance of benign conditions simulating lymphoma.

Balikian and Herman (1976) : Non-Hodgkin's lymphoma of the lungs.

Dunnick et al. (1976) : Rapid onset pulmonary infiltration due to histiocytic lymphoma.

Filly et al. (1976) : Radiographic distribution of intra-thoracic disease in previously untreated patients.

Feigin et al. (1977) : Non-malignant lymphoid disorders of the chest.

Bragg (1978) : Clinical, pathological and radiographic spectrum of intra-thoracic lymphomas.

Pilepich et al. (1978) : Contribution of CT to lymphomas.

Costello and Mauch (1979) : Recurrent intra-thoracic Hodgkin's disease following radiotherapy : 21 patients had intra-thoracic relapses out of 254 who had surgery and mantle radiotherapy - superior mediastinal nodes, pulmonary disease including nodules and/or unilateral effusion.

Jelliffe (1979) : 'Hodgkin's disease - the pendulum swings' noted that Hodgkin's disease used to be thought of as inevitably fatal and is now constantly curable, but it has never been inevitably fatal nor uniformly curable.

Blank and Castellino (1980) : Intrathoracic manifestations of malignant lymphomas and **leukaemias**.

Shields et al. (1980) : Pulmonary artery constriction by mediastinal lymphoma simulating pulmonary embolus.

Best and Blackledge (1981) : Studied 60 patients - none with a negative CT had abnormal lymphograms.

Blackledge et al. (1981) : Role of abdominal CT in lymphoma following treatment.

Burgener and Hamlin (1981) : Intrathoracic histiocytic lymphoma.

North et al. (1982) : Importance of initial mediastinal adenopathy in Hodgkin's disease.

Jochelson et al. (1983) : **Peri and paracardial involvement** in lymphoma.

Angelini and Butchart (1984) : Lymphoma mimicking cardiomegaly.

Bethancourt et al. (1984) : Mediastinal **haematoma** simulating recurrent Hodgkin's disease during chemotherapy.

Cho et al. (1984) : CT evaluation of **cardiophrenic angle nodes** in patients with malignant lymphoma.

Gallagher et al. (1984) : Role of CT in the detection of intrathoracic lymphoma.

Meyer et al. (1984) : Impact of thoracic CT on radiotherapy planning in Hodgkin's disease.

Shields (1984) : Studied 34 patients with Hodgkin's disease, by chest radiography, lymphography and CT. CT altered management in only two, by indicating that radiotherapy fields should be enlarged. Lymphography changed five from stage II to III. They felt that CT and lymphography were complimentary, but performed CT first. CT showed more extensive disease but this did not usually alter management. Mediastinal disease was shown in two cases with 'normal' chest radiographs. Rib lesions were better shown by isotope bone scans and conventional tomography.

Shuman and Libshitz (1984) : Solid pleural manifestations of lymphoma.

Jochelson et al. (1985) : Significance of residual mass in treated Hodgkin's disease.

Meyer et al. (1985) : CT demonstration of **cardiophrenic lymphadenopathy** in Hodgkin's disease - 11 patients - 4 at initial staging and remainder with relapse after therapy.

Weaver et al. (1985) : Spontaneous regression of a mediastinal lymphoma in a 69 year old woman following small bowel obstruction presumably due to endogenous steroids.

Amin and Anthony (1986) : Non-Hodgkin lymphoma following successful treatment of Hodgkin's disease.

Bragg et al. (1986) : Only about 20-25% of low grade Non-Hodgkin lymphomas remain localised.

Castellino et al. (1986a) : Hodgkin's disease - practical concept for the diagnostic radiologist - studied chest radiographs and CT examinations in 203 patients with newly diagnosed Hodgkin's disease. Superior mediastinal enlargement was present in 170 (about 85%), and was mostly shown by plain radiographs. CT better demonstrated hilar nodes (especially in the presence of a mediastinal mass). 20% had enlarged subcarinal nodes, 8% cardiophrenic angle nodes and 5% posterior mediastinal or internal mammary nodes. CT showed more extensive lung, pleural, mediastinal (including pericardial) and chest wall disease. However **in most cases the additional knowledge did not affect treatment.**

Castellino et al. (1986b) : CT in initial staging - enlarged cardiophrenic angle nodes modified treatment in 18% - particularly affected the planning of radiotherapy fields.

Glickstein et al. (1986) : 22 cases., (1988) : Non-lymphomatous disorders of the lung

Khoury et al. (1986) : Role of chest CT in non-Hodgkin lymphoma.

Seltzer et al. (1986) : Noted that lymphomas may envelop or engulf organs.

Rose et al. (1986) : Endobronchial involvement with non-Hodgkin's lymphoma.

Chen et al. (1987) : Residual fibrous masses in treated Hodgkin's disease.

Heron et al. (1987), from the Royal Marsden Hospital : Reviewed 90 examinations following treatment for Hodgkin's disease. Chest radiography and CT agreed in 26. CT gave additional information in 7, and helped to distinguish post-radiation change from recurrence. Lung disease was seen in 9.

　　　(1988a) : Reviewed 44 patients with 50 separate episodes of suspected recurrent disease., and found recurrent disease in 18 episodes. In two cases the recurrence was only shown by CT.

　　　(1988b) : Noted **thymic enlargement** in about 30% of cases at presentation, and in almost 40% at the time of relapse. Also found a thymic cyst develop following radiotherapy.

Greco et al. (1988) : Impact on therapy of MR imaging of patients with lymphomas, using STIR (see p. 20.30) or phase contrast LATE images. With STIR the signal from the fat is suppressed and the increase in T_2 is dominant, inducing a marked increase in signal intensity in involved tissue. The examinations often showed additional lesions below the diaphragm. After treatment residual hypointense soft tissue masses at the site of the prior disease did not always imply viable tumour, and both low signal intensity and stability over a period of time were considered evidence of tumour control.

Hopper at al. (1988) : Hodgkin's disease - utility of CT in initial staging and treatment - studied 107 new cases of Hodgkin's disease and found that the CT examination was normal in 30 out of 31 cases, who had normal chest radiography, but in the other 76 it showed 194 new sites of disease and disproved 25 others. It changed the staging in 20 patients. 36 also had extra-nodal extension of the disease.

Prakash et al. (1988) : Mediastinal mass due to Hodgkin's disease and tracheal obstruction during general anaesthesia.

Epstein and Glickstein (1989) : Pulmonary lymphoproliferative disorders.

Goddard and Cobby (1989) and **Cobby** et al. (1989 & 1990) : Recurrent lymphoma may show the following signs -

(i) Centrally placed masses with thickening of the broncho-vascular bundles producing 'stalks' (like drumsticks or mushrooms), sometimes with cavitation. These mainly occurred at bronchial bifurcations, i.e. **within small intra-pulmonary nodes.**

(ii) Peripheral lung nodules (which may cavitate) adjacent to the pleura, giving rise to **pleuro-pulmonary 'tails'** (see p. 4.17).

(iii) areas of lymphoid lung consolidation, some with cavitation,

(iv) extension of mediastinal disease into adjacent lung tissue, and

(v) chest wall involvement.

Some patients also had pleural effusions or pericardial involvement.

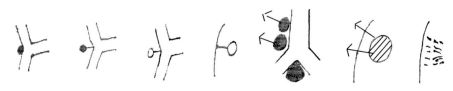

Node at bronchial bifurcation	Thickening alongside broncho-vascular bundle with mushroom or drumstick like nodule which may cavitate	Cavitating peripheral nodule with pleural tail	Azygos and R hilar node enlargement with spread into adjacent lung	Spread into chest wall	Lymphoid type of lung consolidation

Nyman et al. (1989) : Residual mediastinal masses in Hodgkin disease - prediction of size with MR imaging.
Uematsu et al. (1989) : Residual masses on follow-up CT in patients with mediastinal non-Hodgkin's lymphoma.
Bergin et al. (1990) : MR evaluation of chest wall involvement in malignant lymphoma - appeared to be superior to CT by showing more sites and involvement.
Charles et al. (1990) : The use of ^{31}P MR spectroscopy in differentiating radiation fibrosis from recurrent tumour.
Reznek and Husband (1990) : The radiology of lymphomas (review article).
Castellino (1991) : The non-Hodgkin lymphomas - practical concepts for the diagnostic radiologist.
Goerg and Schwerk (1991) : Ultra-sound of extranodal abdominal lymphoma - a review.
Lewis et al. (1991) : Lymphoma of the lung - CT findings in 31 patients - most common was a mass or mass-like consolidation >1 cm (in 68%). Second most common was nodules < 1 cm. Many had three or more abnormalities - others included alveolar or interstitial infiltrates, masses of pleural origin, peribronchial or perivascular thickening with or without collapse, pleural effusions and hilar or mediastinal lymphadenopathy.
Wernecke et al. (1991) : Sonography is superior to chest radiography and comparable to CT for monitoring patients with mediastinal lymphomas.
Yellin et al. (1992) : SVC syndrome associated with lymphoma in 11 children.
Carlsen et al. (1993) : MR imaging may show extension of lymphoma into the chest wall and along pleural surfaces more commonly than previously recognised - careful attention to parasternal areas on CT and MR is recommended.
Carty and Martin (1993) : Staging of lymphoma in childhood.
Cordier et al. (1993) : Primary pulmonary lymphomas - study of 70 cases in nonimmunocompromised pts.
North et al. (1993) : Lymphography for staging lymphomas no longer needed with CT + increased chemotherapy.
Sandrasegaran et al. (1994) : Staging of lymphoma in adults.
Gollub and Castellino (1995) : CT demonstration of diffuse endobronchial non-Hodgkin's lymphoma.
Parnell and Frew (1995) : Non-Hodgkin's lymphoma presenting as an encasing pleural mass.
Winer-Muram et al. (1995) : Accuracy of CXRs for severe pulmonary complications of childhood lymphoma.
Lazar et al. (1996) : Lymphoma of bronchus - associated lymphoid tissue.
Au and Leung (1997) : Radiological manifestations of lymphoma in the thorax.
Vinnicombe and Reznek (1999) : Imaging the lymphomas - **mini-symposium** - esp. extranodal manifestations.

Yousem et al. (1986) : Primary pulmonary Hodgkin's disease - study of 15 patients.
Handsmann et al. (1990), Radin (1990) : Primary pulmonary Hodgkin's disease.
Tredaniel et al. (1994) : Endobronchial Hodgkin's disease - 9 cases + literature review.
Lee et al. (1997) : Imaging of the pulmonary lymphomas.
Cartier et al. (1999) : CT in three patients with primary pulmonary Hodgkin's disease - 2 with cavitating upper lobe masses and one with lower lobe nodules.
Kim et al. (1999) : Polypoid endobronchial Hodgkin's disease with pneumomediastinum + mediastinal lymph nodes.
Ooi et al. (1999) : CT features of primary pulm. non-Hodgkin's lymphoma in 6 pts. - ill-defined alveolar opacities, usually multifocal + peribronchial disease, proximal bronchiectasis & positive **CT angiogram sign** (p.5.4).

Wotherspoon et al. (1990) : Low-grade primary **B-cell lymphoma of the lung.**
Canver et al (1993) : Primary B-cell malignant lymphoma of the lung.
Jackson et al. (1994) : Multiple cavitating pulmonary lesions in non-Hodgkin's lymphoma.
O'Donnell et al. (1998) : Radiological appearances of lymphomas arising from mucosa-associated lymphoid tissue (MALT) in the lung - review of 13 pts. - age range 44 - 75 yrs, 11 females & 2 males - 16 had low-grade disease - 4 later progressing to intermediate grade disease.

Ditchfield and Tung (1998) : 2 cases of primary **cardiac   lymphoma** presenting with pericardial effusions and containing lymphoma cells + 3rd case with relapse of NHL involving the heart, pericardium and mediastinal nodes.

Granger and Whitaker (1967) : **Bone manifestations -** marrow is first involved and spread to the periosteum may cause periosteal reaction, and through it an adjacent soft-tissue mass. Bones may also be invaded from adjacent soft tissue disease. Bony involvement may be lytic, sclerotic or of a mixed appearance. The dorsal spine is commonly involved and may produce an 'ivory   vertebra' and para-vertebral swelling (Illus. **IVORY VERTEBRA**). The ribs, sternum and clavicles may also be affected.
Borg et al. (1993) : Bone involvement in Hodgkin's disease - studied 147 pts. - 7 had bone involvement, but only one at presentation.

Calcification
Bertrand et al. (1977) : Lymph node calcification in Hodgkin's disease after chemotherapy.
Riviero et al. (1984) : Calcified mediastinal nodes in Hodgkin's disease.
Shuman and Libshitz (1984) : Solid pleural manifestations of lymphoma.
Shin et al. (1985) : Massive mediastinal Hodgkin's disease with calcification mimicking teratocarcinoma.
Struck (1985) : Lymph node calcification in malignant lymphoma - nine cases and literature review.

Panicek et al. (1988) : Calcification in untreated mediastinal lymphoma - two cases, one with dense calcification in the thymus due to nodular sclerosing Hodgkin's disease. They also noted three others from the literature.
Lautin et al. (1990) : Calcification in non-Hodgkin's lymphoma, occurring before therapy - identification on plain films and CT.

Thymic Hodgkin's (see also general references above and refs. on p. 18.22)
Keller and Castleman (1974) : Hodgkin's disease of the thymus gland.
Federle and Callen (1979) : CT of cystic Hodgkin's lymphoma of the thymus.
Baron et al. (1981c) : Thymic cysts following radiotherapy for Hodgkin's disease.
Lindfors et al. (1985) : Thymic cysts in mediastinal Hodgkin's disease.
Heron et al. (1988) : CT of the thymus in Hodgkin's disease.
Wernecke et al. (1991) : Thymic involvement in Hodgkin's disease - CT and US.
Wong-You-Chong and Radford (1995) : Enlargement of a mediastinal mass during treatment for Hodgkin's disease may be due to accumulation of fluid within thymic cysts.
Husband et al. (1997) : Successfully treated thymic lymphoma usually has a low signal intensity on MR irrespective of the size of the residual mass. High intensity cysts may be seen. Most relapses occurred in pts. with large masses and/or a high heterogeneous signal intensity.

Renal and abdominal involvement (see Illus. **LYMPHOMA-ABD+RENAL**)
Heiken et al. (1983) : CT of renal lymphoma with ultra-sound correlation.
Cohan et al. (1990) : CT of renal lymphoma - involving kidneys or retroperitoneal space.
Reznek et al. (1990) : CT in renal and peri-renal lymphoma. A further look.
Dodd et al. (1992) : Thoracic & abdominal manifestations of lymphoma occurring in the immunocompromised pt. - see also below
Stomper et al.(1993) : Abdominal staging of thoracic Hodgkin disease: CT-lymphangiography-Ga-67 scanning correlation - CT is of little value in showing splenic involvement. In early cases both the lymphogram and Ga add little to CT for showing disease in abdominal nodes.
Görg et al. (1995) : 'Swelling' around kidney on US due to peri-renal involvement.

Lymphoma of the spleen (see p.17.12).

Lymphoma in immunocompromised patients (see also under AIDS refs. + neoplasm ps. 19.36 - 37).
Tester et al. (1984) : Second malignant neoplasms complicating Hodgkin's disease.
Chechani et al. (1990) : Pulmonary non-Hodgkin's lymphoma mimicking infection - rapidly progressive lung shadows in three patients (two with AIDS) mimicking rapidly spreading bronchopneumonia.
Kaldor (1990) : Leukaemia following Hodgkin's disease.
Dodd (1992) : Thoracic and abdominal manifestations of lymphoma occurring in immunocompromised patients - those who are iatrogenically immune suppressed, as with organ transplantation, have the same strikingly increased incidence and peculiar manifestations of lymphoma as patients with AIDS.
Radin et al. (1993) : AIDS-related non-Hodgkin's lymphoma-abdominal CT findings in 112 patients - lymphoma was the initial AIDS defining illness in about 80% of these patients. CT demonstration was seen in almost all pts. with abdominal. signs and symptoms.
Blunt and Padley (1995) : Thoracic manifestations of AIDS related lymphomas (review of 116 pts.) - pleural or lung masses, frequently peripheral and sometimes with cavitation, also pleural effusions and nodal enlargement.
Carignan et al. (1995) : Intrathoracic lymphoproliferative disorders in the immunocompromised patient : CT findings - these conditions are seen more commonly in pts. with AIDS and those without AIDS than in the normal host. Pts. with AIDS more often have LIP and non-Hodgkin B-cell lymphoma. Lymphoma is also seen more frequently in such pts. without AIDS. Organ transplant recipients are predisposed to post-transplant lymphoproliferative disorders, ranging from benign lymphoid hyperplasia to poorly differentiated non-Hodgkin's lymphoma. In those with AIDS, and the recipients of organ transplants the disorders are commonly associated with the Epstein-Barr virus. They concluded that the intrathoracic CT findings of lymphoproliferative disorders appear to be similar in immunocompromised pts. with and without AIDS and are usually extranodal with ground-glass shadowing and lung nodules, some of which had a halo of ground-glass shadowing.

Lymphoma and second tumour etc.
Tucker et al. (1988) : Risk of second cancers after treatment for Hodgkin's disease.
Van Leeuwen et al. (1989) : Increased risk of lung cancer, non-Hodgkin lymphoma & leukaemia following Hodgkin's disease.
Swerdlow et al. (1992) : Risk of second primary cancers after Hodgkin's disease by type of treatment - study of 2846 pts. in British national lymphoma investigation.
Sont et al. (1992) : Increased risk of second cancers in managing Hodgkin's disease - 20 year Leiden experience.
Abrahamsen et al. (1993) : Second malignancies after treatment of Hodgkin's disease.

Unger et al. (1994) : Man age 46 with Hodgkin's disease developed miliary nodules due to eosinophilic granuloma whilst in remission. Noted the association of the two conditions in 18 patients quoted in the literature (six with lung involvement) - ? association related to T-cell deficits resulting in uncontrolled proliferation of Langerhan's cells.

Lambert et al. (1998) : Pancreatic cancer as a second tumour 9 yrs after R/T treatment of Hodgkin's disease.

Pseudolymphoma and maltoma.

In this condition lung lesions may be single or multiple, and usually range in size from 2 to 5 cm in diameter. Their margins are mainly ill-defined and patent bronchi run through the lesions i.e. with an '**air bronchogram**'. There is usually no lymphadenopathy, collapse or pleural involvement. It may progress to true lymphoma. Most cases are asymptomatic or have a cough.

References.
Salzstein (1963) : Pulmonary malignant lymphoma and pseudolymphoma: classification, therapy and prognosis.
Hutchinson et al. (1964) : Primary pulmonary pseudolymphoma.
Gibbs and Seal (1978) : Primary lymphoproliferative conditions of the lung.
Fisher, C. et al. (1980) : Pseudolymphoma of the lung - a rare case of a solitary nodule.
Holland et al. (1991) : Evolution of pulmonary pseudolymphomas - clinical and radiological manifestations - review of 45 cases - plain radiographs show ill-defined masses or areas of consolidation.
Bolton-Maggs et al. (1993) : Mucosa associated lymphoma of the lung ('**MALTOMA**') - see also p. 13.5.
Brown et al. (2000) : Low grade gastric MALT lymphoma.

Mycosis fungoides and lymphoma with skin involvement - Illus. **MYCOSIS FUNGOIDES.**

Mycosis fungoides is a cutaneous manifestation or type of T-cell lymphoma, which not infrequently involves the lungs, lymph nodes and other viscera. The skin lesions start as pruritic, erythematous, scaly plaques which may ulcerate. The lung lesions may be nodular, resemble pneumonic consolidation or appear as reticulo-nodular infiltrates. Hilar and/or mediastinal lymphadenopathy and pleural effusions may be present. In most patients skin or superficial lymph node biopsies may confirm the diagnosis, and spread to the chest may be fairly confidently surmised from the radiological appearances. In some the lung lesions may progress rapidly suggesting pneumonia, and in these lung biopsy may be necessary to confirm the diagnosis; this is important as aggressive chemotherapy may produce a remission.

References.
Long and Mihm (1974) : Mycosis fungoides.
Israel (1977) : Mycosis fungoides with rapidly progressive pulmonary infiltration.
Stein (1978) : Mycosis fungoides with pulmonary involvement and complete remission.
Marglin et al. (1979) : Mycosis fungoides - radiographic manifestations of extracutaneous intrathoracic involvement.
Wolfe (1980) : Pulmonary manifestations of mycosis fungoides.
Rubin and Blank (1985) : Pulmonary dissemination in mycosis fungoides simulating pneumonia - case report and review of the literature.
Bunn (1994) : Cutaneous T cell lymphomas.
Giovagnorio (1997) : Sonography of cutaneous non-Hodgkin's lymphomas.

Lymphocytic interstitial pneumonia - see p. 19.119.

Lymphomatoid (lymphoid) granuloma - Illus. **LYMPHOGRANULOMA.**

This multi-system disease (also known as polymorphic granulomatosis or lethal mid-line granuloma) almost always involves the lungs. Lung infiltration is usually present and nodules may cavitate and change rapidly in number and size (Illus. **LYMPHOGRANULOMA, Pt. 1**).

When untreated lymphoid granuloma tends to have a fairly rapid course, but some patients may have a remission, particularly after steroid therapy and remain well. Cytotoxic drugs and radiotherapy may also help. In addition to the lungs, the skin, eyes, heart and abdominal organs (including the kidneys) may be affected, but clinical renal disease is rare. CNS involvement and peripheral neuritis is common. Hilar and mediastinal nodal enlargement and pleural effusions also occur, but nodal enlargement often signifies progression to frank lymphoma. Bone marrow involvement is uncommon.

Rarely a generalised lymphoid hyperplasia may precede the onset of pulmonary lesions, sometimes by several years. It may also progress to a typical lymphoma. The disease is most common in patients beyond middle age, but the age range is from childhood to old age. Patients may have a cough, fever or dyspnoea and haemoptysis when cavitation is present.

Liebow et al. (1972) studied the first 40 described cases and defined the condition as an angiocentric and angio-destructive lymphoreticular disease primarily involving the lungs. Liebow (1973) considered it to be a form of pulmonary angiitis, similar to Wegener's granuloma (p. 19.76). It may thus be classified either as a lymphoma, a type of angiitis, or possibly a form of hypersensitivity reaction, but most pathologists now feel that it is a form of lymphoma presenting primarily in the lungs, with a tendency for the affected cells to involve vessels and with metastases more commonly found in the skin and nervous system, than in lymph nodes. However it differs from a typical lymphoma by not involving most of the reticulo-endothelial system, and like an angiitis it has some vasodestructive features.

Although lymphomatoid granuloma tends to involve the lower part of the respiratory tract, a histologically similar lesion 'polymorphic reticulosis' can affect the upper airways (Eichel, 1966).

Lung lesions not uncommonly look like metastases as is shown in the following figure:

Bilateral nodules in 14 Unilateral nodules in 5 Ill defined opacities in 4 Unilateral mass in 1

Fig. 5.4 Diagram of chest radiographs in 24 patients (after Hicken et al., 1979 - reproduced with permission from Clinical Radiology).

Further references.

Hammar et al. (1977) : Lymphomatoid granulomatosis in a man of 51, associated with retroperitoneal fibrosis.
McCall and WooMing (1978) : Radiological appearances of plasma cell granuloma of the lung.
Shank et al. (1978) : Radiation therapy in lymphomatoid granulomatosis.
Cohen et al. (1979) : Pulm. lymphomatoid granulomatosis & immunodeficiency ending as malignant lymphoma.
DeRemee et al. (1979) : Radiology of lymphomatoid granulomatosis in the lung.
Hicken et al. (1979) : Unilateral or bilateral nodules or opacities - may be small or large.
Katzenstein et al. (1979) : A clinicopathological study of 152 cases.
Lipper et al. (1980) : A variant - 'malignant pulmonary angiitis' (a monoclonal neoplasm) - nodular infiltrates and no enlarged lymph nodes, with a fatal progression.
Dee et al. (1982) : Pulmonary manifestations of lymphomatoid granulomatosis.
Fauci et al. (1982) : Lymphomatoid granulomatosis, prospective clinical and therapeutic experience over ten years.
Patton and Lynch (1982) : Lymphomatoid granulomatosis.
Wechsler et al. (1984) : Comparison with Wegener's granuloma (p. 19.76).
Prénovault et al. (1988) : Review of 12 cases -10 had bilateral disease with middle and lower lobe predominance of ill-defined nodular densities being the most common radiographic presentation. CT showed these to be mainly peripheral and sub-pleural in distribution. Three patients had cavitating nodules, and two had mixed alveolar and interstitial disease. Three had hilar adenopathy, five pleural effusions and one a spontaneous pneumothorax.
Weisbrod (1989) : Pulmonary angiitis and granulomatosis - a review.
Abeln et al. (1988) : CT of renal lymphomatoid granulomatosis - small nodules in kidneys (predominantly peripheral in distribution) regressed with treatment (male aged 63).
Isaacson (1990) and Troussard et al. (1990) : A form of malignant lymphoma of peripheral T-cell type.
Lee et al. (2000) : CT - peri-bronchovascular nodules, coarse irregular opacities & small thin walled cysts.

Castleman tumour (angiofollicular or benign **giant lymph node hyperplasia**; angiomyomatous lymphoid hamartoma or lymphoid hamartoma).

This has been considered as a low grade lymphoma, or possibly a hamartomatous condition, but recent studies have suggested that it may be a group of conditions with similar clinical and histological features. In some patients there appears to be an antigenic or immune cause. Patients with the plasma cell subtype have a raised I_gG, titres to Epstein-Barr capsid antigen and dysregulation of interleukin-6.

Symmers (1921) termed it 'primary haemangiolymphoma of the nodes'. Castleman and Towne (1954) and Castleman et al. (1956) described a series of thirteen patients with benign mediastinal lymphoid masses resembling a thymoma on radiographs.

About 350 cases have been reported. The condition largely affects lymph nodes in the thorax, abdomen, neck and axillae, but may also produce nodules in the lungs (possibly in intra-pulmonary nodes - Sumerling, 1987), larynx, parotid glands, pancreas and muscle. Castleman and his colleagues (Keller et al., 1972) later studied 81 cases (70 involving the mediastinum, especially the anterior superior mediastinum) and also reviewed another 102 cases from the literature - 71% of the combined series involved the thorax (85% being mediastinal). They noted that the condition may be localised or more widespread, the localised cases being of **two types**: (a) **hyaline-vascular** (in 90%), with hyaline follicles and intra-follicular capillary proliferation and (b) the **plasma cell type** (in 10%) with larger follicles and many plasma cells.

Those with the **hyaline-vascular type** are usually teenagers or young adults of either sex. They are mostly asymptomatic, and have the nodes discovered by chance on chest radiographs, though in a few cases symptoms may result from pressure on adjacent structures e.g. the larger bronchi. They commonly exhibit well marginated hilar or mediastinal masses, often overlapping the right and left cardiac borders, which may mimic lymphoma or a thymoma. As noted below this type is often very vascular. Complete surgical removal usually cures the condition.

The **plasma cell type** is less vascular and patients may have minor symptoms - fever, night sweats, mild anaemia, a raised ESR and hypoglobulinaemia. Nodes in these cases particularly occur in the abdomen. Surgical removal and/or radiotherapy + steroids is usually curative.

In a rarer and more disseminated form - **the generalised (or multicentric) sub-type** - the patients may have peripheral lymphadenopathy, hepatic and splenomegaly, as well as anaemia. Some may also have a neuropathy - **the neuropathic sub-type** - which sometimes occurs with the POEMS syndrome - polyneuropathy, organomegaly, endocrinopathy, monoclonal protein abnormality and skin abnormalities. The generalised type may progress to malignant lymphoma or other malignancy including Kaposi's sarcoma. Steroids and anti-neoplastic drugs, such as cyclophosphamide, melphalan and nitrogen mustard may produce a remission (Lisbon et al., 1988 - see below). Radiotherapy may induce remission of symptoms and disappearance of the mass (Nordenström et al., 1978, Weisburger, 1979, Sethi et al., 1990) but Keller et al.(1972) felt that it had little effect.

In most cases the condition has to be differentiated from lymphoma, or other mediastinal masses, including neurofibromatosis. Histology (usually obtained at thoracotomy) is required for diagnosis, but in some cases the condition may be suggested preoperatively because the nodes in the hyaline-vascular type may show a marked vascular blush at angiography or enhance with contrast on CT (unlike lymphomas or most thymomas, but similar to that seen with goitres, chemodectomas or some adenomas). In a few cases (see Illus. **CASTLEMAN'S DISEASE, Pt. 1a - f), calcification may be found within the enlarged nodes**, but this does not necessarily indicate a benign course of the disease, as in this case rapid spread occurred following surgery. It is typically central and dense, with an arborising pattern within the affected node. Studying calcified nodes within the pelvis, Goodman et al. (1983) considered the pattern to be 'characteristic enough to be diagnostic of this unusual condition'. Other cases showing the chest have been reported by Inada and Hamazaki (1958) and by Walter et al. (1978). Keller et al. (1972) noted that nodal calcification was unusual, occurring in fibrotic areas, surrounding large central vessels.

Some cases occurring in patients with AIDS (like some lymphomas) have also suggested an immune or viral basis.

Further references

Pemberton et al. (1950) : Giant haemolymph node - report of two cases.
Inada and Hamazaki (1958) : Localised lymph node hyperplasia resembling lymphoma.
Katz and Dziadiw (1960) : Localised mediastinal lymph node hyperplasia.
Jamplis et al. (1961) : Benign interlobar hyperplastic lymph node resembling thymoma.
Harrison and Bernatz (1963) : Angiofollicular mediastinal lymph node hyperplasia resembling thymoma.
Veneziale et al. (1964) : Angiofollicular lymph node hyperplasia of the mediastinum.
Tung and McCormack (1967) : Angiomatous lymphoid hamartoma.
Abell (1968) : Lymphoid hamartoma.
Anagnostou et al. (1972) : Angiofollicular lymph node hyperplasia (Castleman).

Keller, Hochholzer and Castleman (1972) : Hyaline-vascular and plasma cell types of giant lymph node hyperplasia.
Emson (1973) : Intrathoracic angiofollicular lymphoid hyperplasia resembling thymoma.
Tanaka et al. (1976) : Castleman's lymphoma among Japanese population.
Gaba et al. (1978) : A case of multicentric lymph node hyperplasia.
Walter et al. (1978) : Castleman's disease - angiographic and clinical features - two cases involving the mediastinum (i) an asymptomatic man aged 27 with a mediastinal mass present for seven years and containing dense flocculent calcification - could not be resected owing to its great vascularity - it was embolised and (ii) an asymptomatic female aged 19 with a large para-cardiac mass which was resected. Both cases showed hypervascularity on angiography.
Riba (1979) : Vascular nature of Castleman tumour.
Tuttle and Shier (1979) : Castleman tumour - vascular mass at angiography.
Bartoli et al. (1980) : Multicentric giant lymph node hyperplasia - a hyperimmune syndrome with a rapidly progressive course.
Olscamp et al. (1980) : Unusual manifestations of an unusual disorder.
Gibbons et al. (1981) : Castleman tumour resembling a pericardial cyst - CT differentiation.
Phelan (1982) : Castleman 'giant lymph node hyperplasia'.
Schlosnagle et al. (1982) : **Plasmacytoma** arising in giant lymph node hyperplasia.
Fiore et al. (1983) : CT demonstration of bilateral Castleman tumours of the mediastinum.
Frizzera et al. (1983) : A systemic lymphoproliferative disorder with morphological features of Castleman's disease.
Iida et al. (1983) : Mesenteric Castleman tumour demonstrated by CT.
Kessler and Beer (1983) : Multicentric type with associated Kaposi's sarcoma - one of three cases.
Onik and Goodman (1983) : CT of Castleman disease.
Chen (1984) : Multicentric Castleman's disease and Kaposi's sarcoma.
Dickson et al. (1985) : Multicentric giant lymph node hyperplasia, Kaposi sarcoma and lymphoma.
Frizzera, G. (1985) : Castleman's disease : more questions than answers.
McAloon (1985) : Hodgkin's disease in a patient with Castleman's disease.
Mohamedani and Bennett (1985) : Lung nodule and enlarged subcarinal nodes due to angiofollicular lymphoid hyperplasia in a female aged 19.
Stokes et al. (1985) : Castleman's disease associated with vertebral destruction.
Btreatnach et al. (1985) : Calcified anterior mass.
Weisenburger et al. (1985) : Multicentric Castleman's disease - 16 cases.
Koslin et al. (1986) : Cervical Castleman disease - CT study with angiographic correlation.
Libson et al. (1988) : Widespread Castleman disease - CT and US findings.
Ferreiros et al. (1988) : CT in abdominal Castleman's disease.
Frizzera et al. (1988) : Castleman's disease and related disorders.
Meissel et al. (1988) : Uncommon CT features.
Serour et al. (1989) : Castleman's disease of the mediastinum - misleading clinical and radiological characteristics - three cases of hyaline vascular type - (i) left hilar and right mediastinal enlargement in a man of 54 - (ii) right hilar enlargement in a man of 28, and - (iii) right paratracheal mass in a woman of 53.
Awotedu et al. (1990) : Castleman's disease with recurrent pleural effusion.
Charig (1990) : Mediastinal Castleman's disease.
Gould et al. (1990) : Multicentric Castleman's disease in association with a solitary plasmacytoma.
Samuels et al. (1990) : Mediastinal Castleman's disease - demonstration with CT and angiography.
Buckley and Sundaram (1991) : Skeletal lymphoma in a patient with Castleman disease.
Garber and Shaw (1991) : US and CT appearance of mesenteric Castleman's disease.
Stansby et al. (1991) : Gallium uptake in multifocal plasma cell type of Castleman's disease.
Hsieh et al. (1993) : Enhancing mediastinal mass at MR in Castleman's disease.
Mandel et al. (1993) : Fatal pulmonary **Kaposi's sarcoma** and Castleman's disease in a renal transplant recipient.
Peterson and Frizzera (1993) : Multicentric Castleman's disease.
Ecklund and Hartnell (1994) : Mediastinal Castleman disease - MR showed a very vascular mass in the lower posterior mediastinum with prominent feeding vessels, displacing the posterior wall of the left atrium and the inferior pulmonary vein.
Freeman et al. (1994) : Cervical Castleman's disease shown by CT and MR.
Moon et al. (1994) : MR of two cases of hyaline vascular type. T_1 - rounded hilar masses of indeterminate or high signal intensity with areas of low signal due to linear and serpiginous vessels and calcification; T_2 - masses were of high signal intensity.
Moon et al. (1994) : CT findings in Castleman's disease.
Moon et al. (1995) : Castleman disease with renal amyloidosis.
Shahadi et al. (1995) : The multicentric type is a systemic illness, sometimes with the POEMS syndrome.
Barrie et al. (1996) : HRCT and pathologic findings in Castleman's disease of the lung.
McCarty et al. (1996) : Angiofollicular lymph node hyperplasia (Castleman's disease).
Bradley et al. (1997) : 22 yr old Asian woman with a left upper anterior mediastinal & hilar mass - highly vascular and intimately related to thymus & left main bronchus on CT - surgical biopsy confirmation.
Johkoh et al. (1998) : Intrathoracic multicentric Castleman disease - CT findings in 12 pts.

Kirsch et al. (1997) : Multicentric Castleman's disease and POEMS syndrome (extensive mediastinal node enlargement + calcification, splenomegaly, pleural effusion, & skin thickening typical of scleroderma) in a woman aged 53.
McAdams et al. (1998) : 30 pts. with thoracic disease - 24 localised & 6 disseminated.
Bui-Mansfield et al. (2000) : Castleman disease of the axilla.

Histiocytoma (Plasma cell granuloma/ inflammatory pseudo-tumour) - Illus. **HISTIOCYTOMA.**
   This is an uncommon chest lesion. When present it usually appears as a well circumscribed solitary peripheral lung mass. It ranges in size from 1 cm up to an entire lobe. It may occasionally be intra-bronchial. Tissues within them consist of several cell types - fibroblasts, histiocytes, primitive mesenchymal stem cells and giant cells. Degenerative foamy cells may also be present, with histiocytic features developing within a chronic granuloma. Histiocytomas may also occur as plasma cell granulomas containing many plasma cells and lymphocytes. When mononuclear cells in the mass are laden with lipid, the terms **fibroxanthoma** and **xanthogranuloma** have been applied. Some may be related to β cell lymphomas.
   Most of these tumours cause no symptoms, and most are found fortuitously. They are usually spherical in shape and lack a true capsule. They may contain areas of haemorrhage or necrosis, which may calcify. Most are soft and friable, whilst others are fibrotic. Slow enlargement occurs. Local recurrence may follow surgery, but only a limited wedge resection is usually needed. Associated nodal enlargement is rare.
   The differential diagnosis includes true plasmacytomas (p. 5.43) and plasma cell reactions to secondary tumour deposits. Some may arise in the pleura and be related to pleural fibromas (p. 14.28).
   Whilst most histiocytomas are benign, malignant forms also occur; these are not uncommon in soft tissues generally within the body, but are rare within the lung.

Malignant histiocytosis.
   This condition was first described by Scott and Robb-Smith (1939) from the Radcliffe Infirmary, Oxford, as an uncommon malignancy characterised by the proliferation of atypical histiocytes, predominantly in the liver, spleen, lymph nodes and bone marrow. Almost half of the cases affect the thorax, and chest symptoms may be the presenting feature. The patients may have enlarged hilar and mediastinal nodes, a reticulo-nodular interstitial lung pattern and pleural effusions. Primary lung tumours often have a non-specific appearance with a peripheral non-cavitating mass. They may invade the chest and mediastinum.

Further references.
(a) **Benign histiocytomas**.
Baum et al. (1960) : Enlarging pulmonary histoplasmoma.
Kilburn and Schmidt (1960) : Intrathoracic plasmacytoma and literature review.
Mason et al. (1963) : Inflammatory pseudotumour of the lung.
Kinare et al. (1965) : Extensive ossification in a pulmonary plasmacytoma and literature review.
Taraska (1966) : Fatal post-inflammatory pseudo-tumour of the trachea in a Negro boy of 14.
Carter et al. (1968) : Intrathoracic fibroxanthomatous pseudotumours - 10 cases.
Wentworth et al. (1968) : Girl aged 5 with 10 cm scalloped mass in RLL.
Pearl (1972) : Masses in children.
Bahadori and Liebow (1973), Strutynsky et al. (1974)
Armstrong et al. (1975) : Endobronchial histiocytomas.
Cox (1975), Kalifa et al. (1976), McCall and Woo-Ming (1978)
Sandström et al. (1978) : Fibrous histiocytoma of the trachea.
Yu et al. (1979) from Peking : 41 cases.
Schwartz et al. (1980) : Post-inflammatory pseudotumours of the lung - fibrous histiocytomas and related lesions.
Mandelbaum et al. (1981): Surgical course and treatment of pulmonary pseudotumour.
Monzon et al. (1982) : Plasma cell granuloma of the lung in children.
Spencer (1984) : The pulmonary plasma cell/histiocytoma complex.
Wells and Sty (1986) : Lung mass in a 5 year old girl.
Shapiro et al. (1987) : Variable CT appearance of plasma cell granuloma of the lung.
Kaufman (1988) : Densely calcified 5 cm mass in the RLL of a girl aged 8 resembling a hamartoma - CT features.

Matsubara et al. (1988) : Inflammatory pseudotumours of the lung - progression from organising pneumonia to fibrous histiocytoma or plasma cell granuloma in 32 cases.

Ishida et al. (1989) : Radiology of seven adult patients with inflammatory pseudo-tumours of the lung - showed radiating spicules, pleural indentation, vascular convergence or a combination of these. In 5 the signs had suggested possible lung cancer, and even at surgery pleural changes resembled lung cancer in 6. In two frozen sections revealed a benign mass and in 5 (who did not have frozen sections) a lobectomy was carried out.

Urschel et al. (1992) : Plasma cell granuloma of the lung.

Brown, G. and Shaw (1995) : Inflammatory pseudotumours in children: CT and US + histology - 5 cases - 1 in lung with white polypoid endobronchial lesion, 1 oesophageal, 2 abdominal & 2 lower limb.

Snyder et al. (1995) : Clonal changes in inflammatory pseudotumour of the lung.

(b) Malignant histiocytoma.

Weiss and Enzinger (1978) : 200 cases (all sites).

Burgener and Landman (1976) : Angiographic features of malignant fibrous histiocytoma.

Kern et al. (1979) : Malignant fibrous histiocytoma of the lung.

Enjoli et al. (1980) : Malignant fibrous histiocytoma - 130 cases.

Paulsen et al. (1981) : Malignant fibrous histiocytoma of the lung.

Chen et al. (1982) : Malignant fibrous histiocytoma of the mediastinum.

Mills et al. (1982) : Malignant fibrous histiocytoma of the mediastinum and lung.

Larsen et al. (1984) : Primary malignant fibrous histiocytoma of the lung.

Lee et al. (1984) : Primary malignant fibrous histiocytoma of the lung - 5 cases.

Ros et al. (1984) : Mesenchymal tumour of ubiquitous origin.

Venn et al. (1986) : Malignant fibrous histiocytoma in thoracic surgical practice.

Ismalier et al. (1987) : CT of primary malignant fibrous histiocytoma of the lung.

Schmall et al. (1987) : Imaging malignant fibrous histiocytomata using C^{11} aminoisobutyric acid.

Yousem and Hochholzer (1987) : Malignant fibrous histiocytoma of the lung.

McDonnell et al. (1988) : Malignant fibrous histiocytoma of the lung.

Reifsnyder et al. (1989) : Partially calcified mass at the right lung base (in a patient with a history of asbestos exposure) which showed increased uptake on an isotope bone scan.

White et al. (1989) : Malignant fibrous histiocytoma of the lung.

Yellin et al. (1989) : Malignant fibrous histiocytoma of the ant. mediastinum - a rare case with 19 years survival.

Amin and Ling (1995) : Malignant fibrous histiocytoma of the lung following R/T of fibrous dysplasia.

Ferrozzi and Bova (1998) : CT of malignant hepatic fibrous histiocytoma.

(c) Malignant histiocytosis.

Dunnick et al. (1976) : Radiographic manifestations.

Colby et al. (1981) : Pulmonary involvement.

Wongshaowart et al. (1981) : Respiratory failure in malignant histiocytosis.

Stempel et al. (1982) : Malignant histiocytosis presenting as interstitial pulmonary disease.

Sinus histiocytosis with lymphadenopathy.

This condition is a pseudolymphomatous benign disorder which mainly affects the mucosa of the trachea and the larger bronchi, often causing severe narrowing. It is often accompanied by nodal enlargement in the mediastinum, hila, neck and axillae. The tracheal cartilages are unaffected (in contrast to relapsing polychondritis (see p. 3.7).

References.

Rosai and Dorfman (1972) : Analysis of 34 cases.

Okada et al. (1988) : CT and MR of a case with the trachea almost completely occluded by a tumour mass, the condition having been present for 5 years.

Sclerosing haemangioma of the lung.
It is uncertain whether this is a vascular tumour or a variety of histiocytoma with alveolar epithelial hyperplasia. It has been given little prominence in the radiological literature and is rather uncommon, though more common than other vascular tumours such as pulmonary haemangiopericytomas or haemangioendotheliomas. The WHO describe it as a well-defined but non-encapsulated, round tumour-like lesion characterised by progressive proliferation and gradual replacement of alveolar structures by sclerotic fibrous tissue.
Radiologically the tumour tends to appear as a round or oval mass, and may be lobulated. When cavitation is present a 'halo' or 'meniscus' may be produced (Bakk et al., 1978) - as with aspergillus lesions - see ps. 19.39 - 40.
Haemoptysis is relatively common, but no bronchial involvement or vascular enhancement has been shown.

References.
Liebow et al. (1956) : Lesion characterised by proliferation and sclerosis of small vessels, with projections of vascular tissue extending into the alveoli, areas of haemorrhage and infiltration of fibrous supporting tissues by fat and haemosiderin-laden histiocytes.
Webb and Gamsu (1977) : Review and a case with a 2 cm slightly lobulated mass in RLL.
Katzenstein et al. (1980) : Sclerosing haemangioma of the lung - a clinicopathological study of 51 cases.

Angio-immunoblastic lymphadenopathy.
This condition affects elderly patients and usually presents with an acute febrile illness, weight loss, pruritis, skin rash and generalised lymphadenopathy. The liver and spleen may also be enlarged. There may be multiple immuno-globulin abnormalities or a haemolytic anaemia. Radiologically there are basal lung infiltrates, lung consolidation, enlarged hilar and mediastinal nodes and pleural effusions. Some patients have indolent disease, whilst others deteriorate rapidly, often with superimposed infection. The condition may progress to frank lymphoma.

References.
Frizzera et al. (1975) : Angio-immunoblastic lymphadenopathy.
Libshitz et al. (1997) : Radiographic findings.
Nathwani et al. (1978) : Malignant lymphoma arising in angio-immunoblastic lymphadenopathy.
Kuijpers et al. (1983) : Reviewed the literature and described lung changes.
Limpert et al. (1984) : Clinical and radiological features.
Watanabe et al. (1986) : A spectrum of T cell neoplasm.
Anagnostopoulos et al. (1992) : Epstein-Barr virus infection patterns in peripheral T cell lymphoma of angio-immunoblastic lymphadenopathy type.
Locksmith et al. (1991) : CT contrast enhancement of cervical lymph nodes in angio-immunoblastic lymphadenopathy.
Weiss et al. (1992) : Epstein-Barr virus genome in angio-immunoblastic lymphadenopathy.

Pulmonary hyalinising granuloma (Engelman's disease).
This rather rare condition produces lung nodules and sometimes lung infiltrates. The nodules are usually multiple and are frequently bilateral. They are usually well circumscribed and solid. Only rarely do they cavitate, and calcification within them is uncommon, but may be shown centrally on CT sections. The nodules may enlarge, stay static or become smaller. Patients are usually well and the nodules are often an incidental finding. They seem to be more common in young females, but they may be found in men as well. Lesions near a lung hilum may progress to hilar and/or mediastinal fibrosis.
Pathologically the nodules resemble pulmonary amyloid, but staining reactions with Congo red, etc., are not as intense, and the 'apple green' colour of amyloid with polarised light is absent. The nodules are demarcated and greyish-white in appearance. They may shell-out easily from the lung parenchyma. Histologically they consist of numerous interconnecting lamellae of hyaline material. The condition appears to be a chronic localised response to some sensitising agent (like rheumatoid nodules). Some consider it to be a form of pulmonary histiocytoma.
A diagram of an example from a case the author has seen with several nodules showing central calcification is shown in the following figure:

Fig. 5.5   Diagram of nodules in a case of Engelman's disease.

References.
Engelman et al. (1977) : 20 cases.
Drasin et al. (1979) : Pulmonary hyalinising granulomas in a patient with malignant lymphoma - nine years later developed multiple myeloma and systemic amyloid.
Dent et al. (1983) : Pulmonary hyalinising granuloma in association with retroperitoneal fibrosis.
Macedo and Adolph (1985) : Pulmonary hyalinising granulomas.
Yousem and Hochholzer (1987) : Pulmonary hyalinising granuloma (24 cases).
Fraser et al. (1989).

Cyclosporine induced lymphoproliferative disorders.
    Cyclosporine is a fungal metabolite which is used as an immunosuppressive agent in conjunction with steroids in post-transplant (renal, liver, heart or lung) patients. It inhibits T cells and may stimulate a lymphoproliferative disorder in about 3% of those receiving this treatment. The condition may involve the chest (with a solitary lung mass, **multiple small nodules** or hilar node enlargement), the GI tract and other lymph nodes. In many cases the reaction appears to be linked to Epstein-Barr virus (p. 19.30) due to the T cells being unable to prevent the B cell proliferation caused by the virus. This disorder usually regresses with reduction of the cyclosporine dose. (See also ps. 11.16 - 17).

LUNG DEPOSITS.

For illustrations see:

Illus. **LUNG DEPOSITS**
Illus. **LUNG DEPS-CAVITATING**
Illus. **LUNG DEPS-CA KIDNEY**
Illus. **LUNG DEPS-MILIARY**

Distribution of secondary tumour deposits in the lungs.
    Scholten and Kreel (1977) and Crow et al. (1981) studied the distribution of secondary deposits in the lung by CT and on autopsy specimens. They found that the **majority of these occur peripherally in the lungs, and especially subpleurally**. The author wonders if this is due to the increased vessels in the sub-cortical part of the lung (see ps. 1.43 - 45) They also occur sub-cortically at the lung bases, where they are obscured on PA radiographs by the dome of the diaphragm. About 60 % are under 5 mm in size. Small deposits, particularly '**micro-metastases**', those lying sub-pleurally, para-spinally, retro-sternally, or below the dome of the diaphragm, are particularly well demonstrated by CT.

    Such '**micrometastases**' (like small '**ball-bearings**' - see above and Illus. **LUNG DEPS-MILIARY**) are often otherwise invisible on plain chest radiographs unless there is a '**snow-storm**' pattern (as with miliary tuberculosis) causing optical enhancement and make them more visible (see Appendices ps. 2 - 4).

Detection of secondary deposits in the lungs and differential diagnosis,
    Whilst plain chest radiographs are sufficient for the detection of many pulmonary secondary deposits, conventional and particularly computed tomograms are invaluable for showing 'hidden' or smaller deposits. CT is also more accurate for detecting deposits than conventional whole lung

tomography (best carried out with the patient in the erect position). Such detection is particularly important in planning curative surgery, in deciding on chemotherapy, etc., e.g. with osteogenic sarcomas, teratomas, seminomas, etc. However, with patients in whom their discovery is **not** going to affect treatment, one has always to weigh up the advantages or disadvantages of knowing on not knowing about the presence of such lesions, and with many untreatable deposits, it may be kinder **not t**o find out!

Not all nodules that are found in the lungs of patients with cancer at the time of presentation or subsequently are due to tumour metastasis. As noted above some are due to past tuberculosis, fungus, other inflammatory disease, infarcts, etc. In others post-irradiation nodules, 'sterilised' metastases (especially in children) may be seen. Benign 'tumours' due to hamartomas, etc., or second primary tumours may be found. The author has seen many examples of all of these.

Onuigbo et al. (1974) found that metastases from lung cancer to the contralateral lung are relatively infrequent at presentation, occurring in about 20% of autopsies; they are typically small and have a predilection for damaged lung.

Peuchot and Libshitz (1987) studied pulmonary metastatic disease by CT in 84 patients and found that a 'solitary' pulmonary metastasis as seen on chest radiographs was truly 'solitary' in only half of the cases. In the other half other nodules were found and 80% appeared to be secondary deposits. In addition further small lesions were probably missed.

Libshitz and North (1982) in a previous article on pulmonary metastases noted that "in general both lungs are affected equally by metastases, and multiple metastases are usually bilateral. The bases are more frequently involved than apices". They agreed with Willis (1973) that the earliest and most numerous metastases are peripheral or sub-pleural in position. They also pointed out that Spencer (1977) had noted that deposits tend to be spherical in shape and range in size from miliary to 5 cm or larger, Willis had also noted that most pulmonary metastases are spherical and well circumscribed. but when situated subpleurally they may be plaque-like or have a stellate shape.

Not all pulmonary deposits are shown by CT. Problems may occur with (a) partial volume averaging, when a tiny nodule may not be differentiated from air-filled lung, (b) the sections being too far apart, (c) a patient not taking the same depth of inspiration with each breath, during which the sections are taken, and (d) confusion with scars or vessels.

Problems (c) & (d) are now being largely overcome by the use of spiral CT (see ps. 20.22 - 24).

Other problems: Movement of vessels or pulsation have given rise to the **'twinkling star (or seagull) sign'** when longer CT exposures were formerly employed, but in most cases the arborising vessels can usually be traced into neighbouring sections, and deposits may thus be distinguished.

Robertson et al. (1988) studied pulmonary nodules in children with cancer by plain chest radiographs and CT, and compared the findings with those found at thoracotomy and on histology. Most children with positive CT findings had abnormal plain radiograph. CT missed some lesions due to uneven respiration i.e. a given area was omitted on all sections taken, and they later examined children under general anaesthesia to try to obviate this problem. They also found that nodules under 0.5 cm in diameter were no more likely to be benign than larger ones. On serial CT examinations nodules that increased in size contained tumour cells, and in those that regressed, some still contained tumour.

Keogan et al. (1993) found that small soft tissue density nodules are often found on CT staging of lung cancer - 85 of 551 patients (16%) had small non-calcified nodules. Adequate follow-up was possible in 25 patients who had 36 nodules - 25 of these proved benign, 4 were malignant and the nature of 7 could not be determined.

Bonomo et al. (1996) studied contralateral pulmonary nodules in patients with lung neoplasm by spiral CT in combination with video-assisted thoracoscopy (VATS). Of 165 patients, 14 had nodules - 9 were metastases from a contralateral lung tumour (4 adenocarcinomas, 4 squamous and 1 small cell) - the remaining 5 were chronic inflammatory (**reference to a vessel on CT was more often seen with a metastasis**).

The differential diagnosis of nodules includes granulomata, benign tumours (such as carcinoids), intra-pulmonary lymph nodes, fibrotic nodules, metastases or second primary tumours, metastasising uterine fibroids (p. 5.19).

See also Table 4.2, ps. 4.11 - 12, ps. 4.18 - 19 re **pulmonary deposits from primary lung tumours** and Table 5.6, ps. 5.41 - 42.

Shapes of secondary deposits in the lungs.

The **majority** of pulmonary secondary deposits are **spherical** or near spherical in shape and have **well defined** or **slightly fuzzy edges**. A few are **lobulated,** star-shaped or **spiculated** or have **ill-defined borders** like primary peripheral bronchial neoplasms. Others may **cavitate** (especially eccentrically), exhibit a 'halo' due to oedema or may mimic areas of broncho-pneumonia. Poorly defined edges may be due to tumour permeation, localised oedema, adjacent, haemorrhage or infection. Rarely they may produce a wedge shaped area of collapse, perhaps as a result of an initial endobronchial metastasis (see p 4.26) or later endobronchial extension and bronchial blockage. Illus. **LUNG DEPOSITS, Pt. 54a-b** show unusual lobulated deposits.

Several authors have studied the shapes of pulmonary deposits, particularly since HRCT became available.

Willis (1973) - two types of tumour growth - (i) intra-alveolar growth where the alveolar wall provides a framework or stroma (infiltrative type) and (ii) interstitial (expansile type).

Both Milne and Zerhouni (1987) and Meziane et al. (1988) found a correlation between a metastatic nodule and a pulmonary vessel (the '**mass-vessel sign**') in about 75% of cases, and considered that it was a sign of tumour embolic disease. (This sign is however also seen with infarcts, whorled nodules and vasculitis) - see also p. 20.24 & Illus. **MASS VESSEL SIGN.**

Spencer (1985) described growth factors of metastatic pulmonary nodules as **hilic** (in which a solid mass fills the surrounding intra-alveolar space), and **lepidic** in which tumour proliferates to cover the alveolar wall (see also ps. 13.7 & 13.9).

Shirakusa et al. (1988) compared the histological findings of resected nodules with prognosis and found the latter to be poorer with irregular nodules.

Zwirewich et al. (1991a) found that poorly defined margins can be due to a lepidic growth of tumour, and irregular margins to an infiltrative tumour or irregular tumour growth.

Murata et al. (1992) studied the position of tiny deposits (< 3 mm) in relation to the secondary lobules and found that about 10% were central, 20% were peripheral or perilobular, whilst 70% were between these. Tumour emboli were seen mainly in capillaries or arterioles, running alongside respiratory bronchioles. The deposits often spread into adjacent lymphatics and along peribronchial and perivascular connective tissue; however this appearance could also be mimicked by secondary thrombosis.

Hirakata et al. (1993) studied autopsy excised lungs from 14 patients with pulmonary metastases (87 nodules) with HRCT and found well-defined smooth or irregular margins, and poorly-defined smooth or irregular margins. The well-defined smooth margins corresponded histologically to expanding or alveolar space-filling types, the poorly-defined margins to an alveolar cell type and the irregular margins to an interstitial proliferative type. About 12% of small nodules were connected with the central broncho-vascular bundle, 28% were on the perilobular structures and 60% were indeterminate.

Both Murata et al. and Hirakata et al. (1993) found that minute tumour emboli and early lymphangitic spread could not be seen on HRCT studies.

Lymphangitic metastases are discussed on ps. 8.11 - 13.

Sterilised metastases: After chemotherapy and/or radiotherapy, some secondary lung tumours may become fibrotic and nodular, instead of disappearing. When excised, no viable cancer cells can be found. This is particularly seen in deposits e.g. of Wilm's tumour in children, but may also be seen in some adults, particularly with testicular deposits, etc. Even deposit nodules which cavitate may be fibrotic and no longer active (see also p. 6.4 esp. lacunae - Illus. **LACUNAE**).

Slowly growing and late metastases, regressing and calcifying deposits.

Some pulmonary metastases enlarge very slowly. The author has noted this with some renal tumours, some thyroid tumours and with some carcinoids, metastasising myomas and with one or two haemangiopericytomas. In one case metastases from a renal tumour occurred in the lungs, three years before the renal tumour (in a papilla) became apparent. The patient was followed for 14 years, during which time the deposits gradually enlarged to fill the lungs. In other cases metastases from a temporal fossa haemangiopericytoma have doubled in size over about 25 years and deposits from a uterine tumour have been present in the lungs for 30 years.

Thyroid deposits sometimes occur late, sometimes are very slow growing and may calcify (causing calcified miliary nodules - the author has seen two such cases), or producing larger calcifying masses (see p. 18.9) or spontaneously regress; one case with calcified lung deposits later had a large uncalcified renal deposit - see also Illus. **CALC IN TUMOUR, Pt. 7a-c**. In another case of thyroid cancer (Illus. **LUNG DEPOSITS, Pt. 16a-c**) spontaneous resolution occurred.

Other secondary deposits in the lungs which may **calcify** include those from osteogenic sarcomas, synoviomas, chorioncarcinomas, testicular, nasal, ovarian and renal tumours.

Late pulmonary deposits are occasionally seen with breast, renal etc. carcinomas, or some slow growing sarcomas or chondro-angiomas - some 15-20 yrs later - Illus. **RENAL CA DEPS, Pt. 4a-c** shows renal tumour deposits appearing in the lung and brain after 18 years.

Note also:
1. Lung nodules in association with pulmonary oedema may appear to decrease in size with clearing of the oedema (Lams and Williams, 1976) .
2. Haemorrhage may occur in relation to lung nodules especially after biopsy and this may initially cause an increase in size and subsequently clear.
3. Pulmonary infarcts in patients with malignant disease may be mistaken for metastases that spontaneously resolve - the author has seen several examples.
4. Chorioncarcinoma deposits are sometimes very vascular and may mimic A/V fistulae.
5. Several cases of spontaneous resolution of pulmonary deposits have been recorded, particularly after intercurrent infection and especially pneumonia - see also ca lung - p. 24.41.
6. Pulmonary deposits from renal tract tumours may also occasionally spontaneously resolve, resolve following chemotherapy e.g. with Provera (see ps. 24.43 - 44), or after nephrectomy, but nephrectomy may also upset the 'hormonal balance' of a renal tumour so that some deposits which have been stationary or regressed then rapidly increase in size.

References.
Detection of pulmonary secondary deposits.
Lams and Williams (1976) : Primary malignant nodule variation in size with pulmonary venous pressure - surrounding oedema appeared to make it larger.
Polga and Watnick (1976) : Whole lung tomography of 100 pts. with metastatic disease. 28 appeared to have solitary metastases on plain radiographs, but 8 of these had more than one shown on tomograms. Two out of 72 with apparently normal plain radiographs had metastases shown on tomograms.
Muhm et al. (1977 & 1981) : CT for the detection of pulmonary nodules.
Schaner et al. (1978) : Comparison of whole lung tomograms and CT for detecting pulmonary nodules - suggested that CT is more sensitive for the detection of deposits than conventional tomography.
Curtis et al. (1980) : Breast carcinoma - limited value of full lung tomography.
         (1982) : Efficacy of lung tomography in the detection of early metastatic disease from melanoma.
Crow et al. (1981) : Pulmonary metastases - a pathologic and radiologic study.
Cohen et al. (1982) : If insufficient volume of a small nodule is included in a CT scan slice, it may be invisible.
Krudy et al. (1982) : Failure to detect a 1.5 cm lung nodule by CT - a secondary deposit from an osteogenic sarcoma in a girl aged 6.
Heaston et al. (1983) : Studied 42 patients with melanoma. 11 were positive on plain radiographs, 16 on tomograms and 20 on CT, 22 were negative on all studies.
Amene et al. (1984): studied 27 patients with hepatomas and found coin lesions and found coin lesions, nodular, lymphangitic or nodal deposits in 50%.
Fry (1985) : Small metastases may appear like '**ball bearings**' in the lungs, but beware of small benign calcified nodules - TB, previous chicken pox pneumonia, etc.
Gross et al. (1985 - from Ann Arbor, Michigan): Reviewed CT exams showing three or more focal lung densities, and were able to establish the cause in 114 out of 137 cases. Metastases accounted for 73 %, with primary colon, lung, renal tract neoplasms and lymphoma being the most common cause . Benign scars tended to be linear, and some showed calcification, whilst malignant lesions tended to be more numerous, more rounded and larger.
Kagan and Steckel (1986) : Found that **plain films, conventional tomograms and CT gave sensitivities in the detection of metastases of 30%, 60% and 80% respectively**.
Mitchell et al. (1986) : CT was better than plain radiographs for detecting nodules in patients with bronchial. ca.
Vanel et al. (1984) : Pulmonary evaluation of patients with osteosarcoma, roles of standard radiography, CT, scintigraphy and tomoscintigraphy.
Steckel and Kagan (1990) : Pitfalls in the diagnosis of metastatic disease or local tumour extension with modern imaging techniques.
Davis (1991) : CT evaluation for pulmonary metastases with patients with extra-thoracic malignancy.

Daly et al. (1993) : Nasopharyngeal carcinoma may give rise to pulmonary deposits (which may cavitate) but also commonly causes hilar and mediastinal node enlargement.

Mostbeck et al. (1996) : Is every lung nodule a metastasis? At least 12% of children with solid malignant tumours present with probably benign, predominantly solitary pulmonary nodules on spiral-CT. Although not specific, small size (<5mm), subpleural location (7/10 = benign) and unsharp demarcation may help to differentiate these nodules from metastases.

Unusual pulmonary deposits.
Hughes (1973) : Metastatic basal cell carcinoma - two cases to lungs and literature review (mostly to lymph nodes).
Jha et al. (1991) : Intracranial meningeoma with pulmonary metastases.
Mackay and Holloway (1991) : Late onset pulmonary metastases from 'benign' ovarian cystadenomata (four cases).
McGrath et al. (1992) : Pulmonary and hepatic deposits from cerebellar and spinal haemangioblastomas in Hippel - Lindau disease.

'Sterilised deposits'.
Swett and Westcott (1974) : Residual non-malignant pulmonary nodules in **chorioncarcinoma**.
Wright (1976) : Sterilised cavitating deposits in Wilm's tumour.
Lewis et al. (1982) : Lymphoma patients.
Libshitz et al. (1983) : Sterilised metastases - a diagnostic and therapeutic dilemma .
Hidalgo et al. (1983) : The problem of benign pulmonary nodules in children receiving cyto-toxic chemotherapy.
Vogelzang and Steinlund (1983) : Residual pulmonary nodules after combination chemotherapy of testicular cancer.

Late, regressing and calcified deposits (see also testicular deposits below & ps. 24.41-42)**.**
Semple and West (1955) : Calcified pulmonary metastases from testicular and ovarian tumours .
McGee and Warren (1966) : 24 year radiographic follow up of thyroid deposits to lungs.
Casciato et al. (1982) : Prolonged survival with unresected pulmonary metastases.
Going et al. (1986) : Late deposits from sarcoma - two cases after 15 years.
Zollinkhofer et al. (1980) : Lung deposits from synovial sarcoma simulating granulomata (due to calcification).
Bumpus (1928) : The apparent disappearance of pulmonary metastases from a renal tumour following nephrectomy.
Freed et al. (1977) : Idiopathic regression of metastases of renal cell carcinoma.
Fairlamb (1981) : Spontaneous regression of renal cancer - 2 cases + review of 60.
Davis et al. (1989) : Spontaneous regression of pulmonary deposits from renal cell carcinoma.
Ogihara et al. (1994) : Spontaneous regression of lung deposits from osteosarcoma.
Wadsworth et al. (1999) : Two cases of spontaneous regression of pulmonary metastases - one in a man aged 63 with poorly differentiated adenocarcinoma of unknown origin (? a response to Aloe extract) and the second, a 67 yr. old man with previous ca rectum, had a RUL nodule positive for adenocarcinoma on fine needle aspiration - this resolved following pulmonary reaction attributed to BOOP.

Secondary deposits from testicular tumours (see also ps. 6.4-5, 17.11 & 18.15 & 31).
Rostom and Morgan (1977) : Unusual isolated seminoma metastases to the lung .
Franklin (1977)., Hassenstein (1977) : **Spon. regression** of pulmonary testicular deposits - quoted 10 other cases.
Dixon et al. (1986) : Distribution of abdominal lymphadenopathy as shown by CT of testicular tumours.
Williams, M. et al. (1987) : CXR & CT manifestations of metastatic testicular seminoma.
MacVicar (1993) : Staging of testicular germ cell tumours.
Wood et al. (1996) : Relative importance of **haematogenous spread with teratomas** and **lymphatic spread with seminomas.** The contiguous spread from the abdomen to the chest and neck of seminomas was confirmed. In non-seminomatous germ-cell tumours, supradiaphragmatic spread is more random, but tends to occur in the para-oesophageal and sub-carinal node groups.

Deposits from chorioncarcinoma (more common in Nigeria and West Africa, and parts of the Far East).
Bagshawe and Brooks (1959) : Subacute pulmonary hypertension due to chorionepithelioma.
Bagshawe and Garnett (1963) : Three principal forms - (i) discrete with well-defined rounded opacities, (ii) 'snowstorm' pattern of multiple soft tissues, and (iii) confined to pulmonary arteries, so that the clinical and radiological picture closely mimics pulmonary thrombo-embolism with pulmonary infarction and cor pulmonale.
Evans and Hendrickse (1965) : Pulmonary changes in malignant trophoblastic disease.
Cockshott and Hendrickse (1969): Pulmonary calcification at the site of trophoblastic metastases.
Swett and Westcott (1974) : Residual non-malignant pulmonary nodules in chorioncarcinoma.
Libshitz et al. (1977) : The pulmonary metastases of chorioncarcinoma.
Evans et al. (1983) : Malignant trophoblastic disease - studied 66 cases in Nigeria and found secondary deposits and embolic phenomena - pulmonary infarction and cor pulmonale - deposits were single or multiple, discrete or ill-defined, evolving or progressing and may be accompanied by pleural effusions.
(See also ps. 5.11, 7.19 - pulmonary hypertension & p. 7.20 - primary pulmonary choriocarcinoma, and p. 18.16).

Note: chorioncarcinoma tumours typically cause an increased blood ß human chorion gonadotropin (normal = < 5U/100ml); this can be assessed by blood assay - they may also be imaged by PET using FDG (see p. 22.11).

Follow up studies for the detection of secondary deposits for consideration of metastectectomy.
Robinson et al. (1994) : Following surgery for soft tissue sarcomata, chest radiographs were taken at all clinical visits and chest CT 3 monthly in first year, 4 monthly in second, 6 monthly in third and yearly thereafter. (Study in Sheffield, Brompton and Royal Marsden Hospitals).

See also section on 'Spiral CT' - p. 20.22.

<u>The shapes and patterns of distribution and speed of appearance of multiple small lung nodules.</u>
The shape and distribution of multiple small lung nodules may give an indication of their likely pathology.
(a) **Shape** - Very small nodules may occur in the alveoli and enlarge to involve an acinus or the whole of a secondary lobule. If well defined, they may be chronic or be slowly enlarging e.g. TB miliary foci or metastases. Most pneumonic, or rapidly infiltrative conditions will tend to spread within the secondary alveolus and give rise to 'fuzzy' outlines, whilst disease within the interstitial septa will tend to produce a network (or reticular) pattern. Bronchopneumonic lesions tend to have poorly shaped borders, (whilst **peripheral tumours tend to show spiculation, lobulation, pleural tags, localised thickening or retraction and convergence of peripheral vessels, particularly veins**).
(b) **Distribution** - whilst there are no 'golden rules' the following guide is often useful:
tuberculosis tends to affect the upper two-thirds of both lungs,
sarcoidosis the middle two-thirds and lesions tend to follow the broncho-vascular bundles .
pneumoconiosis will often spare the apices, because of bullae there,
and when all parts of the lungs are affected one should think of miliary carcinomatosis - on **CT sections secondary deposits usually lie very peripherally.**
(c) **Speed of appearance** - very rapidly appearing nodules are unlikely to be due to neoplasm - inflammatory disease or angiitis is more likely (see also Churg-Strauss syndrome - p. 19.79).
(d) **'Snow-storm' pulmonary deposits** are not uncommonly due to secondary deposits from tumours of the breast, ovary, prostate, pancreas, kidney, thyroid, lung (including alveolar cell carcinoma), testis, colon, liver (hepatoma), chorioncarcinoma, etc.
(e) **Reinforcement of shadows** i.e. superimposition may make miliary shadows more visible. This and the importance of sharp or bevelled edges in rendering nodules visible is discussed in Appendix 3.

Honeycomb and oedema patterns are discussed on p. 6.6 and in Chapter 8 respectively.

Causes of single and multiple lung nodules are considered in table 4.2. ps. 4.11-12 and the following table - Table 5.6.

Table 5.6   <u>Multiple tiny nodules on plain chest radiographs</u> - causes include:
Micronodules (under 1 mm).
       Pneumoconiosis - stage 1 to 2 : coal miners, fettlers, quarry workers, etc .*
       kaolin, talc, etc.
       metals (inhaled, etc.)
       haemosiderosis
         (a) Inhaled iron : haematite miners and other ore workers, knife and lens polishers
           using rouge (ferric oxide), knife grinders, welders, etc.
         (b) Mitral stenosis
         (c) Idiopathic (see also p. 19.97).
       berylliosis, stannosis (tin - mining in Cornwall, etc., silver,
       mercury - inhaled amalgam, ruptured Negus bag or thermometer, accidental IV injection.

Miliary nodules (1 to 2 mm)
TB*
sarcoid
miliary carcinoma * - secondary deposits from various primary tumours including lung, breast, prostate, kidney, pancreas, thyroid, etc.; alveolar cell carcinoma* - "**snow-storm**" deposits.
lymphoma* esp. B cell
endometriosis (pulmonary deciduosis)*,   metastasising fibroids
amyloid/ rheumatoid arthritis*
acute alveolitis or bronchiolitis - infective or allergic, including viral infections, mycoplasma pneumonia
septic emboli*
acute chicken pox pneumonia (see ps. 19.29 - 30), measles
allergy - bird fancier's lung, farmer's lung, etc.
fungus disease - aspergillosis, blastomycosis, histoplasmosis*
lipid infiltration - histiocytosis, Gaucher's disease, apple gluttony, etc.*
chronic inhalation including mineral oil inhalation*
smoking plus asbestosis
parasites - toxoplasmosis, schistosomiasis, filariasis, etc.
embolised fat or iodised oil, following injury, lymphangiography (or salpingography)
previous bronchogram using iodised oil
fibrosing alveolitis, LIP, etc.
honeycomb lung (early form - 'subliminal honeycombing')/ tuberose sclerosis, histiocytosis, etc.*
dilated bronchial vessels

Larger nodules (3 to 4 mm)
TB/ sarcoid/ fungus disease, etc.*
rheumatoid/ amyloid/ scleroderma/ Sjögren's syndrome, etc. *
fibrotic nodules (pneumoconiotic nodules, retroperitoneal fibrosis, organised infarcts, etc.)*
secondary tumour deposits*
adenomas/ carcinoids/ hamartomas
bronchopneumonia - bacterial (including TB)*, mycoplasma, viral
cystic fibrosis
drug reactions
polyarteritis nodosa*
lymphomatoid granuloma
Wegener's granuloma*
hamartomas/ leiomyomas and metastasising uterine fibroids
A/V aneurysms
septic infarcts*,   pyoderma gangrenosum (see also p. 23.7-8)*

If calcified (see also Table 6.5 - p. 6.19)
Previous chicken pox pneumonia (see p. 19.29 - 30), previous smallpox, previous rubella
Past TB, toxoplasmosis, blastomycosis, coccidiodomycosis, histoplasmosis   Microlithiasis - mitral stenosis (microlithiasis pulmonale)
Alveolar microlithiasis or 'stony lung disease'
Healed secondary deposits - thyroid, renal, chorioncarcinoma, etc.

Spurious lung nodules (see also chapter 6).
Neurofibromatosis (subcutaneous)
Clothing artefact
Dirty cassette, etc.
Double x-ray exposure

                                    * May cavitate

References.
Buechner (1959) : The differential diagnosis of miliary diseases of the lung.
Scadding (1952) : Listed 83 causes of miliary shadows on chest radiography.
Felson (1952) : Miliary lung diseases., (1973) : Chest Roentgenology.
Reeder and Felson (1975, 1993) : Gamuts in Radiology.
McGuinness et al. (1992) : HRCT in miliary lung disease.
Goddard (1993) : More than '57 varieties' - about 300 causes!

For endobronchial deposits - see p. 4.26.

PROTEIN DISORDERS

Including plasmacytoma, myeloma, myelomatosis, amyloid, macroglobulinaemia and hypo- or agammaglobulinaemia.

(a) **Plasmacytoma** (Illus. **PLASMACYTOMA**) - these tumours are essentially the 'solitary' forms of myelomatosis, but the condition may be multifocal and also lead on to myelomatosis. Plasmacytomas may arise in soft tissues, but most occur within the bone marrow, expanding within it to give rise to a honeycombed or soap-bubble appearance, with thinned rather sparse bone trabeculae. Pressure on the bone cortex causes it to be thinned, and ballooned out, with the affected bone becoming larger than normal. The cortex may be breached with the tumour extending into adjacent soft tissues. A good example of the progression of such lesions is shown in Illus. **PLASMACYTOMA, Myeloma Pt. 22a - d**. Such tumours may occur in any bones including the ribs, scapulae, spine, etc. - see also p. 12.23.

Some plasmacytomas may stimulate amyloid production within them (Willis, 1960) - see amyloid tumours below.

(b) **Myelomatosis** (see also plasmacytomas of chest wall - p. 12.23) - Illus. **MYELOMA**.

Thoracic complications include :

Osteolytic lesions of ribs, spine, etc, with '**soap bubble**' or '**rain drop**' appearance of bony lesions - rib lesions may not uncommonly cause bone expansion with nodules and extraosseous soft tissue swellings pressing into the pleura and underlying lung (Illus. **MYELOMA, Pt. 6**). The ribs and spine may fracture, with considerable vertebral collapse, and may be mistaken for osteoporosis, particularly when the ribs become considerably deformed as with a Harrison's sulcus (Illus. **MYELOMA, Pt. 7**) - see also ps. 12.24 & 18.30.

Isotope bone scans are commonly negative unless there are concomitant fractures, because (a) myeloma cells are largely in the bone marrow and (b) they produce an osteoclast activating factor leading to multiple bone erosions. Thus by contrast with metastatic carcinoma, little osteoblastic activity occurs.

Recurrent chest infections.

Pulmonary plasma cell infiltrates and nodules (i.e. **lung deposits**).

In a few cases enlarged lymph nodes - some may progress to or be complicated by amyloid (see below).

Diffuse alveolar septal **pulmonary amyloidosis** or pulmonary amyloidoma(s).

Pleural effusions.

References.

Gilroy and Adams (1959) : Extraosseous infiltration in multiple myeloma.
Willis (1960) : "Are the multiple tumours in bone marrow and the deposits in soft tissues produced by metastasis or by multifocal origin? Probably both processes participate. There is no doubt that the tumours in bones arise multifocally as a 'system' disaese of the bone marrow..."
Yentis (1961) : Myelomatosis - three main groupings -
      (i) Bone marrow - solitary or multiple myeloma.
      (ii) Extramedullary - upper respiratory tract, lymph nodes, other sites.
      (iii) Plasma cell leukaemia.
  Radiology - multiple bony lytic lesions - clear cut, internal scalloping of cortex, soft tissue extension from ribs, scapulae, vertebrae, etc.
          - myelomatous osteoporosis - honeycombed pattern of bone destruction, coarse bony spiculation of cortex of some bones into soft tissue mass - sternum, femur, etc. He noted a spectrum of malignancy from the more benign apparently localised tumours to the most malignant, the frequent infiltration of soft tissues, and the **threat of frank dissemination which hangs over every patient with a "solitary" lesion.**
Hamilton Fairley et al. (1964) : Osteosclerosis in myelomatosis.
Gompels et al. (1972) : Correlation of radiological manifestations of multiple myeloma with immunoglobulin abnormalities and prognosis.
Meszaros (1974) : The many facets of multiple myeloma.
Alexanian (1977) : Plasma cell neoplasms - about 80% of pts. have skeletal involvement at presentation.
Kyle (1975) : Multiple myeloma - review of 869 cases.
Kaplan et al. (1980) : Mediastinal adenopathy in myeloma.

Leonard et al. (1981) : Multiple myeloma - radiology or bone scanning.
Wilson et al. (1979) & Brenner et al. (1984) : Pancoast's syndrome in **multiple myeloma.**
Chea and Chea (1984) : Myeloma with primary pleural involvement.
Kravis and Hutton (1993) : Solitary plasma cell tumour of the pleura presenting with a massive haemothorax.
Curtis et al. (1995) : Multiple myeloma presenting with hepatomegaly and multiple hypoechoic lesions on US.
Tirovola et al. (1996) : The use of Tc^{99m}MIBG scanning in multiple myeloma.
Geetha et al. (1999) : Plasma cell neoplasms in the young - rare under age 30 - report of 2 cases + review.

(c) **Thoracic amyloidosis** - Illus. **AMYLOID.**

Amyloid is a waxy, firm amorphous substance, with a green birefringence with congo-red. Amyloidosis was described by Rokitansky in 1842 and may be primary, or occur secondary to suppurative disease or tumours (particularly myeloma). Both forms may occur in the thorax.

The condition may affect the tracheo-bronchial tree (with submucosal amyloid plaques), the lung parenchyma, lymph nodes and the heart. Pulmonary disease may appear as localised or multiple diffuse bronchial deposits, as fine or larger lung nodules, which may later coalesce (Illus. **AMYLOID, Pt. 2**), or in pulmonary vessels. Endo-bronchial masses may become quite large, and cause bronchial obstruction with secondary lung collapse, mucocoeles, bronchiectasis, fibrosis, etc. The condition may develop fairly rapidly, or have an insidious course. Treatment by endoscopic resection has been effective in maintaining the patency of the airways in several cases, and recently laser beam coagulation has also been helpful. Hilar and other lymph node enlargements may also occur and be **massive** - then **resembling advanced bronchial neoplasm** (Illus. **AMYLOID, Pt. 3a-e**). The affected nodes may also calcify. Diffuse involvement of intra-thoracic and/or abdominal lymph nodes may simulate lymphoma and such may produce inhomogeneously enhancing masses on CT and trans-sonic nodes on ultrasound.

Lung nodules may be single or closely aggregated nodules, with cavitation or calcification. There may also be a miliary pattern, a segmental or lobar fine nodular and fibrotic pattern or a diffuse pulmonary form, with diffuse infiltrates which may lead to respiratory insufficiency and honeycombing (Zundel and Prior, 1971, Crosbie et al., 1972, Dunnill, 1982). Gibney and Connolly (1984) reported a pulmonary amyloidoma simulating a Pancoast tumour which showed annular calcification on tomography.

Amyloid tumours may also produce masses in the ribs and other bones, resembling or complicating plasmacytomas (see above), but differing in that some calcification may be present in the absence of treatment (Illus. **AMYLOID, Pt. 1a-d**).

Pleural effusions, or cardiac enlargement may also be present.

A **recent new form** of the condition is **amyloidosis complicating long-term haemodialysis** (usually over five years, due to the deposition of circulating β 2 microglobulin (MW 12,000) that is not filtered by standard dialysis membranes (110 mg, normally being excreted by the kidneys per day). It particularly affects the joints, the retained globulin 'creeping' along cartilage and synovium. It not only affects the wrists (with carpal tunnel compression), hips (with arthritis and cysts in the femoral necks and acetabula - Illus. **AMYLOID. Pt. 8**), shoulders, the intervertebral discs in the cervical spine (with subluxation and compression fractures - Illus. **AMYLOID, Pts. 5a-b & 7a-b**), but also the **heart, lungs, kidneys, blood vessel walls and connective tissues** - Illus. **AMYLOID, Pt. 4a-e.** The condition may be recognised by plain radiography, isotope studies or MR. Following renal transplantation it may reverse.

Amyloidosis may also be associated with bronchial carcinoids (see ps. 5.5 - 5.9) and medullary carcinoma of the thyroid (see p. 18.9).

Further references.

(i) **General**
Pear et al. (1971) : The radiological manifestations of amyloidosis.
Wright, J. and Calkins (1981) : Clinical-pathological differentiation of common amyloid syndromes.
Suzuki et al. (1986) : CT in hepatic and splenic amyloidosis - large low density lesions in right lobe of liver.
Scott, P. et al. (1986) : Overview of amyloidosis.
Mikaye et al. (1988) : CT of amyloid goitre
Kennan and Evans (1991) : Hepatic and splenic calcification due to amyloid.

(ii) **Pulmonary amyloidosis.**
Whitwell (1953) : Localised amyloid infiltration of the lower respiratory tract.
Wang and Robbins (1956).
Prowse (1958) : Amyloid of the lower respiratory tract - three types: -
  (i) **Multiple nodules** confined to lung parenchyma,
  (ii) A **solitary tumour-like mass** affecting one or both major bronchi and the trachea,
  (iii) **Diffuse tracheo-bronchial amyloidosis** of the mucosa and submucosa of the major air passages
Dodd and Mahan (1959) : Primary diffuse amyloidosis of the respiratory tract.
Schüller et al. (1962) : Tumour forming amyloidosis of the lower respiratory tract.
Cotton and Jackson (1964) : Localised amyloid tumours of the lung simulating malignant neoplasms - RUL bronchus mass presenting with haemoptysis.
Brown, J. (1964) : Primary amyloidosis - included four thoracic cases - three with nodal involvement, two also having lung nodules (one being miliary in type).
Craver (1965) : Solitary amyloid tumour of the lung.
Firestone and Joison (1966) : Cause of primary lung tumours.
McGurk (1968) : Primary bronchial amyloid (female with nodular tumour almost blocking both main bronchi).
Thomsen (1968) : Primary amyloidosis in lung and heart.
Chaudhuri and Parker (1970), Teixidor and Bachman (1971) : A solitary amyloid nodule in the lung.
Fenoglio and Pascal (1970) : Nodular amyloidosis of the lungs.
Zundel and Prior (1971) : An amyloid lung.
Attwood et al. (1972) : Primary diffuse tracheobronchial amyloidosis.
Gordonson et al. (1972) : Roentgenographic manifestations of pulmonary amyloidosis.
Gottlieb and Gold (1972) : Primary tracheobronchial amyloidosis.
Cook et al. (1973) : Diffuse amyloid of tracheo-bronchial tree.
Dyke et al. (1974) : Pulmonary amyloidoma.
Saab et al. (1974) : Primary pulmonary amyloidosis.
Lee, S. and Johnson (1975) : Multiple nodular form.
Wilson et al. (1976) : 9 cases - calcific lymph node enlargement and aggregated nodules were particular features,
Himmelfarb et al. (1977) : The radiologic spectrum of cardiopulmonary amyloidosis.
Bierny (1978) : Multinodular primary amyloidosis of the lung - diagnosis by needle biopsy.
Celli et al. (1978) : Patterns of pulmonary involvement in systemic amyloidosis.
Rubenow et al. (1978) : Localised amyloidosis of the lower respiratory tract.
Kyle and Byrd (1975) : Amyloidosis - review of 236 cases.
Kyle and Griepp (1983) : Amyloidosis - clinical and laboratory features in 229 cases.
Desai et al. (1979) : 3 cases, 2 with localised pulmonary amyloid and extrapulmonary involvement.
Fleming et al. (1980) : Treatment of endobronchial amyloidosis by intermittent bronchoscopic resection.
Thompson et al. (1983) : Primary bronchopulmonary amyloid tumour with massive lymphadenopathy.
Thompson and Citron (1983) : Amyloid and the lower respiratory tract.
Laden et al. (1984) : Nodular pulmonary amyloid with extra-pulmonary involvement.
Shaw et al. (1984) : Nodular mediastinal amyloid.
Spencer, H. (1984) : Pathology of the Lung.
Breuer (1985) : Tracheobronchial amyloid - treatment by CO_2 resection.
Cordier et al. (1986) : Amyloidosis of the lower respiratory tract in 21 patients.
Gross et al. (1986) : The respiratory tract in amyloidosis and the plasma cell dyscrasias.
Graham, C. (1992) : HRCT appearance of diffuse alveolar septal amyloidosis.
Schima et al. (1994) : Sicca syndrome (dry eyes and dry mouth) due to primary amyloidosis.
Slanetz et al. (1994) : Nodular pulmonary amyloid with central calcification.
Desai and Hansell (1996) : Thin-walled cysts (20-50mm), non-cavitating nodules with calcification, and mosaic attenuation and air-trapping in two patients with Sjögren's syndrome and amyloid infiltration.
Pickford et al. (1997) : Thoracic cross-sectional imaging of amyloidosis - 19 cases - localised amyloid can occur in pts. as lung nodules or as laryngotracheobronchial involvement. Nodules are typically solitary with a smooth or lobular contour and are frequently subpleural or peripheral. Pts may also have adenopathy, diffuse irregular lines and interlobular septal thickening.
Kircher et al. (1998) : CT findings in extensive tracheobronchial amyloidosis.

(iii) **Nodal enlargement.**
Bottomley et al. (1974) : Waldenström's macroglobulinaemia and amyloidosis.
Gallego and Canelas (1974) : Hilar enlargement in amyloidosis.
Gross (1981) : Radiographic manifestations of lymph nodes in a patient with multiple myeloma.
Melato et al. (1983) : Massive amyloidosis of mediastinal nodes in a patient with multiple myeloma.
Thompson et al. (1983) : Primary bronchopulmonary amyloid tumour with massive hilar enlargement.
Takebayashi et al. (1983) : Nodal enlargement may resemble lymphoma.

Sharma and Guleria (1985) : Cervical nodes.

(iv) **Bone amyloid.**
Gardner (1961) : Bone lesions in primary systemic amyloidosis - case report with soft tissue swelling and dusky atrophic skin of fingers and thumbs, associated with a coarse trabecular pattern of the phalanges and osteoporosis of the femoral heads and necks.
Hawkins et al. (1988) : Diagnostic radionucleide imaging of amyloid (esp. of bones) using the specific affinity of plasma protein for amyloid fibrils.
Rosetto et al. (1988) : Bone scan in systemic amyloidosis - studied 30 patients with $Tc^{99m}MDP$ and found extraosseous uptake in 9 (5 /6 with primary amyloidosis and 4/24 with secondary).
Daly and Moore (1989) : Reported a slowly enlarging amyloid tumour mass in the left clavicle, present for several years before the onset of clinical myeloma. It contained multiple punctate areas of calcification, and showedincreased activity on a bone scan.
Sargent et al. (1989) : Bone cysts and haemodialysis-related amyloidosis in patients with chronic renal failure.
Ross et al. (1991) : Haemodialysis-related amyloidosis amyloidomas of bone - four cases with multiple well-defined, juxta-articular lytic lesions without matrix calcification.
Cobby et al. (1991) : MR imaging in dialysis related amyloid.

(v) **Nerve amyloid.**
Conaghan et al. (2000) : Recurrent laryngeal nerve palsy associated with mediastinal amyloid masses and lung nodules both of which contained calcification.

(d) **Waldenström's macroglobulinaemia.**
   Waldenström (1944) described the syndrome of macroglobulinaemia, which is an uncommon low grade B-cell lymphoproliferative malignancy of the elderly (especially males). It is characterised by infiltration of the bone marrow by plasmacytoid lymphocytes and high serum concentrations of IgM paraprotein, causing **blood   hyperviscosity** which may be as high as 30 times normal. Affected patients may have retinal and other haemorrhages and infarcts, also splenomegaly and lymphadenopathy. The condition is allied to myeloma, and may progress to it or other lymphoid types of malignancy.
   Thoracic manifestations include inflammatory lesions, mediastinal and hilar lymphadenopathy, dilated pulmonary vessels and congestion. Treatment in acute cases is with plasma exchange followed by chlorambucil.

Illus. **WALDENSTROM, Pt. 1a-f** shows a cavitating infarct in the RUL and calcification in muscles.
Illus. **WALDENSTROM, Pt. 2a-b** shows large main pulmonary arteries from pulmonary hypertension and increased blood viscosity.

References.
Waldenström (1944) : Incipient myelomatosis or 'essential' hyperglobulinaemia with fibrinogenopaenia - a new syndrome. Patients had symptoms of fatigue, weight loss, epistaxis and decreased visual acuity - findings associated with anaemia, hepatosplenomegaly, lymphadenopathy and retinal haemorrhage.
                (1962) : Monoclonal and polyclonal gammopathies and the biological system of gamma globulins.
                (1986) : Macroglobulinaemia - a review.
Smith and James (1992) : Waldendström's syndromes revisited.
Furgerson et al. (1963) : Waldenström's macroglobulinaemia with diffuse pulmonary infiltration - lung biopsy and response to chlorambucil.
Renner et al. (1971) : Radiological manifestations.
Major et al. (1973) : Presentation as a pulmonary mass.
Nieman et al. (1973) : Reticular lung changes with progressively enlarging rounded densities.
Bottomley et al. (1974) : Waldenström's macroglobulinaemia and amyloidosis.
Winterbauer et al. (1974) : Pleuro-peritoneal manifestations.
Blattner et al. (1980) : Waldenström's macroglobulinaemia in a family.
Rizzo and Campagnoli (1984) : Chylothorax as a complication.
Kobayashi et al. (1985) : Two cases.
Williamson (1989) : Waldenström's macroglobulinaemia - three cases in shoe repairers (? in relation to inhaled vapours from adhesives).
Clifton and Baily (1991) : Renal lymphoma in a patient with Waldenström's macroglobulinaemia.

(e) **Hypoglobulinaemia** (Good's syndrome, etc.).

Several syndromes may cause hypoglobulinaemia. Some are congenital in origin and present in childhood or as adults. Others are linked to blood dyscrasias, immune system disorders, etc. or are associated with **thymomas** (see p. 18.22 & Illus. **THYMOMA, Pt. 29a-g**). Some cases are familial. Many have a genetic background.

The congenital type was first described by Bruton (1952) in a boy with recurrent infections. His patient lacked gamma-globulin on blood electrophoresis and he failed to form antibody in response to antigenic stimulation.

Many cases are however much milder and some children (especially boys) who have repeated pneumonia in their first two years of life, tend to correct their hypogammaglobulinaemia by the age of three.

Chest manifestations are often persistent or recurrent, and may lead to lung scarring, bronchiectasis and permanent loss of volume. One lung may be more affected. The reduced immune response and immunodeficiency may lead to disorders of the lymphatic system - benign lymphoid hyperplasia, LIP, or lymphoma, when nodal enlargement may be seen. These complications are probably in considerable part stimulated by complicating viral infection - especially by the EB virus (see p. 19.30).

HRCT studies may show small lung nodules (due to enlargement of the pulmonary lymphoid aggregates, see also ps. 13.3 - 4), scarring, bronchiectasis, areas of collapse, air trapping, etc.

Two further cases are illustrated:

Illus. **HYPOGLOBULIN, Pt. 1a-d** - a 65 yr old woman with long-standing immune deficiency disease. Her lungs showed fine nodules and septal thickening. She also had a large liver and spleen.

Illus. **HYPOGLOBULIN, Pt. 2a-i** - a teen-age girl with multiple lung nodules, more marked in the right lung, moderately enlarged nodes in the fat of the anterior mediastinum, left basal bronchiectasis, and an enlarged liver and spleen.

Further references.

Good (1954) : Agammaglobulinaemia - a provocative experiment of nature.
Margulis et al. (1957) : The radiological appearances in nine children - found that they usually present with a history of having suffered for several years from recurrent episodes of life-threatening infections - pneumonia, meningitis, septicaemia, middle ear and para-nasal infections.
Waldenström (1962) : Gammopathies - also termed agammaglobulinaemia occurring with lymphopenia - the 'Swiss type', in recogniition of Swiss workers who defined the condition.
Renner et al. (1971) : Radiological manifestations.
Liebow and Carrington (1973) : Diffuse pulmonary lymphoreticular infiltrations associated with dysproteinaemia.
Major et al. (1973) : Mass lesion with infection.
Dukes et al. (1978) : Pulmonary manifestations of hypogammaglobulinaemia.
Asherson and Webster (1980) : Diagnosis and Treatment of Immunodeficiency Disease.
Pruzanski (1980) : Lymphadenopathy associated with dysgammaglobulinaemia.
Buckley (1987) : Immunodeficiency diseases.
Rubin (1988) : Radiology of immunological diseases of the lung.
Buckley and Schiff (1991) : Uses of IV immune globulin in immunodeficiency diseases.
Curtin et al. (1991) : Bronchiectasis in hypogammaglobulinaemia - CT assessment in 38 patients - 22 had bronchiectasis, 7 bronchial wall thickening and 9 were normal. They also noted that patients with X-linked hypogammmaglobulinaemia develop bronchiectasis at an earlier age.
Chapel (1993) : IV immunoglobulin as a therapeutic tool.
Cohen, A. et al. (1994) : Localised pulmonary resection for bronchiectasis in hypogammaglobulinaemic patients.
Obregon et al. (1994) : Contribution of CT in adult primary immunodeficiency.
Curtin et al. (1995) : Primary hypogammaglobulinaemia occurs in two main forms (a) an x-linked agammaglobulinaemia affecting boys in early childhood and (b) a more heterogenous syndrome ('common variable immunodeficiency'). Enlarged nodes and/or splenomegaly are frequently found in the latter group and are usually due to a benign, non-neoplastic process.
Rosen et al. (1995) : The primary immunodeficiency.
Feydy et al. (1996) : Chest HRCT in adults with primary humoral immunodeficiency - study of 19 pts. - findings included bronchial wall thickening, bronchiolectasis, lobar or segmental collapse and air trapping.

(f) Hyperimmunoglobulin E (Job's) Syndrome.

This syndrome is characterised by extremely high levels of serum immunoglobulin (I_g) E, recurrent infections (esp. with Staphylococcus aureus and fungi), a chronic dermatitis with eczema, boils and coarse facies. The lungs are prone to recurrent consolidation leading to thin-walled cystic lung lesions and bronchiectasis.

References.

Davis et al. (1966) : Job's syndrome - recurrent 'cold' staphylococcal abscesses.
Merten et al. (1979) : Hyperimmunoglobulinaemia E syndrome - radiographic observations.
Lui et al. (1990) : Job's syndrome - a rare cause of recurrent lung abscess in children.
Shamberger et al. (1992) : Pneumatocoele complicating hyperimmunoglobulin E syndrome.

(g) Protein C deficiency.

Protein C deficiency leads to a hypercoagulable state by reducing the inactivation of factors Va and VIIIa. Protein C is a vitamin K-dependent plasma protein synthesised in the liver, which is activated by thrombin, and then stimulates fibrinolysis. It may be familial.

Reference.

Warren and Cook (1993) : **IVC thrombosis** and L sided empyema in a boy aged 13 with protein C deficiency.

Leukaemia.

Leukaemia may produce lung changes due to the presence of tumour nodules, haemorrhage, the effects of coincident secondary infection, or due to the effects of drugs, e.g. busulphan (see p. 19.111). Enlarged mediastinal and hilar lymph nodes may be found particularly with chronic lymphatic leukaemia. Chronic myeloid leukaemia may lead to leukaemic alveolar infiltration or leukostasis, giving rise to lung consolidation or alveolar infiltrates, which may mimic pneumocystis infection (ps. 19.10 - 13). Leukaemic nodules may also be found in other soft tissues such as the liver, spleen, bowel, para-spinal tissues, the spinal canal, etc.

Illus. **LEUKAEMIA** show enlarged subcarinal nodes, a lung nodule, abdominal nodes and monilia infection of the oesophagus.

Eosinophilic leukaemia is a 'malignant' form of eosinophilia, which especially in men may lead to myocardial infarction, heart failure and death. It may also be accompanied by eosinophilic pneumonia and pleurisy.

References.

Green and Nichols (1959) : Pulmonary involvement in leukaemia.
Klatte et al. (1963) : The pulmonary manifestations and complications of leukaemia.
Blank and Castellino (1980) : The intrathoracic manifestations of the leukaemias.
Knowles et al. (1980) : Bronchiectasis complicating chronic lymphocytic leukaemia and hypogammaglobulinaemia.
Maile et al. (1983) : Chest radiographic-pathologic correlation in adult leukaemia patients.
Chernoff et al. (1984) : Endobronchial lymphocytic infiltration in chronic lymphocytic leukaemia.
Heiberg et al. (1984) : CT findings in leukaemia.
Gefter et al. (1985) : Invasive pulmonary aspergillosis and acute leukaemia - limitations and diagnostic utility of the **'air crescent sign'**.
Palosaari and Colby (1986) : Bronchiolocentric lymphocytic leukaemia.
van Buchem et al. (1987) : Pulmonary leukostasis.
Liu et al. (1988) : **SVC syndrome** - a rare presenting feature of acute myeloid leukaemia.
Desjardins et al. (1990) : Recurrent localised pneumonia due to bronchial infiltration in a patient with chronic lymphocytic leukaemia.
Kovalski et al. (1990) : Localised leukaemic pulmonary infiltrates - three patients - resolution with chemotherapy.
Seynaeve et al. (1992) : The **'air crescent sign'** in pulmonary leukaemic infiltrate.
Kim and Fennessy (1994) : Pleural thickening caused by leukaemic infiltration - CT findings.
Heyneman et al. (2000) : HRCT of pulm. leukaemic infiltrations in 10 pts. esp. involved perilymphatic pulm. interstitium.

For chloromas (granulocytic sarcomas) and leukaemia see p. 5.12.

Chapter 6 : **Cavitation, Thin-walled Cysts and Bullae, their Association with Tumours. Emphysema. Fat and Calcification. Spurious Tumours. Intravascular, Pulmonary Interstitial & Mediastinal Gas, and Pneumoperitoneum.**

Cavitation.
The causes of lung cavitation are protean. Properly a cavity is a solid focus, the centre of which has been replaced by air. Many causes are listed in **Table 6.1**, which also includes cysts and 'apparent cavities' due to intrathoracic loops of bowel, etc.

When studying cavities, one should note - their size and shape (round or irregular), thickness of the wall, any irregularity of the inner or outer wall, detachment of the lining, contents in addition to air, disease in the adjacent lung, and lesions elsewhere.

When tuberculosis was more common, a cavitating apical lesion, especially if lying posteriorly, was nearly always due to this cause. Nowadays an infected bulla (see **Table 6.2**), a lung abscess, an acute bulla due to PCP or other infection, or a cavitating carcinoma may be more common.

Table 6.1 - Causes of lung cavities, cysts or apparent cavitation.
1. Congenital or developmental - bronchogenic cysts, sequestrated segment, cystic adenomatoid malformation.
2. Bullous emphysema, lung cysts, loofa-lung, etc. (small cysts may inter-communicate and due to air-trapping become larger).
3. Cystic bronchiectasis.
4. Pneumonia due to bacteria or fungi -
    (a) cavities with TB, atypical mycobacteria, Staph. aureus, Strep. faecalis, milleri, Klebsiella, Pseudomonas, haemophilus, Pneumocystis, aspergillosis, other fungus disease, etc.
    (b) acute pneumatocoeles with Staph. aureus, some Gram. negative organisms, PCP, bronchiolitis, etc.
    (c) inhalation pneumonia - septic bronchial embolism, inhaled hydrocarbons (paraffin), etc.
    (d) pneumonia secondary to bronchial obstruction - endobronchial tumour, bronchostenosis, pressure from nodes, fibrosis, etc.
    (e) infected haematoma.
5. Septic emboli or ischaemic necrosis in infarcts - in drug addicts, those secondary to osteomyelitis or thrombosis around IV catheters or shunts, the picture can change rapidly, and new lesions appear as others resolve. Thick walled lesions may later give rise to thin-walled cavities.
6. Cavitating primary or secondary tumours - especially squamous tumours (but any type may cavitate including alveolar cell ca.), anaplastic deposits from many types of tumour (including lymphomas). Thin-walled 'cystic' neoplasms (esp. in young women). 'Lacunae' following the resolution of some pulmonary secondary deposits after chemotherapy.
7. Infection distal to a bronchial tumour.
8. Papillomatosis.
9. Auto-immune disease or necrobiotic nodules -
    (a) Rheumatoid, etc.
    (b) Angiitis - Wegener's granuloma, Behçet's disease, skin disease, etc.
    (c) Pneumoconiosis.
    (d) Lymphomatoid granuloma, etc.
    (e) Macroglobulinaemia and hypoglobulinaemia.
10. Sarcoidosis
    (a) Breakdown of lung nodules (rare).
    (b) Fibrosis, bronchiectasis and bullae (more common).
11. Lymphangioleiomyomatosis and tuberose sclerosis.
12. Histiocytosis X, Gaucher's disease, amyloid, myeloma, leukaemia.
13. Fibrosing alveolitis and scleroderma.
14. Extrinsic allergic alveolitis - Farmer's lung, etc.
15. Trauma - lung cysts, haematoma, ARDS, etc.
16. Parasites - Hydatid disease.
17. Trans-diaphragmatic herniae with intrathoracic loops of bowel mimicking lung cavities.
18. Plombage, Lucite balls or sponges communicating (after many years) with the lungs.

Table 6.2 - <u>Causes of apical and upper lobe bullae.</u>
Physiological - due to upright posture.
Smoking.
Emphysema.
Congenital or developmental cysts (including 'loofa lung').
Scarring from - pneumonia - TB, fungus, etc.
       sarcoidosis
External allergic alveolitis - chemical and drug reactions, Farmer's lung, etc.
Ankylosing spondylitis, neurofibromatosis and rheumatoid.
Marfan's syndrome.
Infarction.
Pneumoconioses.

<u>Notes on some cavitating conditions.</u>
 Tuberculosis tends to cause single or multiple cavities, often with evidence of surrounding disease and bronchopneumonic spread elsewhere in the lungs. Anterior cavities at the lung apices are nearly always accompanied by others posteriorly, and in their absence, one should think of mycobacteria. Most TB cavities are rounded, but cavities due to atypical mycobacteria may be multiloculated, diamond or lozenge shaped (see also ps. 19.24 - 25).

 A **breaking down carcinoma** typically gives rise to eccentric cavitation, an irregular wall and a necrotic mass (see below and Fig. 4.3, p. 4.13). Sometimes the tumour may be small with a serrated edge. Thick-walled irregular malignant tumours are mostly squamous tumours, and those with irregular outer walls tend to be more aggressive and more often appear to accompanying HPOA. However adenocarcinomas, sarcomas, bronchiolo-alveolar tumours and even oat cell tumours may also cavitate. A tumour occurring within a bullous or scarred area of lung is often termed a **'scar cancer'** (Illus. **SCAR CANCER**) and often gives the appearance of a **'spider in the centre of its web'** see also p. 4.20 - (they are often adenocarcinomas). An endobronchial tumour may also give rise to a more peripheral lung abscess. Other benign and malignant tumour masses (including reticuloses and secondary tumours) may also cavitate, as described in the various sections of this book.

(a) Eccentric cavity (b) Irregular inner wall (c) Tiny cavitating (d) Nodule on
within a loculated mass   squamous tumour inner border

Fig. 6.1 Some patterns of malignant cavitation

 Strang and Simpson (1952) studied carcinomatous abscesses of the lung and found several mechanisms :
(i) Infection distal to a bronchial obstruction.
(ii) Necrosis of the tumour may establish free drainage, and the destroyed tissue be coughed up,
(iii) Necrosis may be accompanied by infection and infarction.
Sometimes so much of the tumour tissue is coughed up that only a thin carcinomatous wall is left. In many cases tumour necrosis is a terminal event. At autopsy more cases of cavitation are seen than can be shown radiologically.

<u>Thickness of the wall of a cavitating lesion </u>and **lung cysts + cancer**.
 Most thin-walled air filled cystic looking spaces in the lungs are bullae or pneumatocoeles, and even those that become infected usually have thin walls. By contrast, thick walled cavities are more commonly seen with lung abscess, breaking down infarcts, granulomas (TB, Wegener's granuloma, etc) and neoplasms. Most cavitating neoplasms have thick or thickened walls, which

are often irregular on their inner and/or outer aspects. Some are misdiagnosed, and the author has a case (from another hospital) where a slowly growing squamous tumour was misdiagnosed as a bulla, but serial radiographs showed that it increased in size slowly over 12 years until it filled the whole lung!

Woodring et al. (1980) found that all lesions in which the thickest part of the wall was 1 mm thick were benign. In contrast 95% of those > 15 mm thick were malignant, and between 5 and 15 mm, 50% were benign and 15% malignant. In a further study Woodring and Fried (1983) found that the vast majority of cavities with a maximum wall thickness of 4 mm or less were benign, and > 16 mm most were malignant.

Even so, a few thin walled 'cysts' may be malignant - a 'thin-walled' adenocarcinoma in a young woman is shown in Illus. **CA+BULLAE, CYSTS ETC., Pt. 4a-d.**

Illus. **CA+BULLAE, CYSTS ETC., Pt. 9a-d** shows the coexistence of lung cysts with bilateral lung cancer in a young man.

Cancers + apical bullae or cysts are common with '**scar cancers**' - see - Illus. **SCAR CANCER.**

Some references.
Cancers associated with cysts and bullae

Lodge (1950) : Review of 130 cases of lung cancer.
Farinas et al. (1955) : Co-existence of a neoplasm with a lung cyst in 4 out of 133 patients.
Larkin and Phillips (1955) : Tumour within a lung cyst which enlarged over a period of 2 years.
Peabody et al. (1957b) : Observed a cyst over a period of 33 months and watched a nodule in its lumen increase in size until it reached a diameter of 5.5 cm, when it was removed and shown to be an undifferentiated carcinoma with a long-standing cyst.
West and Van Schoonhoven (1957) : Chance finding of a carcinoma in the wall of a lung cyst which had been present for 16 years in a woman of 34.
Goldstein et al. (1968) : Bronchogenic carcinoma and giant bullous disease.
Stoloff et al. (1971) : The risk of lung cancer in males with bullous disease of the lung.
Aronberg et al. (1980) : Three cases of lung carcinoma associated with bullous lung disease in young men (out of 940 cases of ca. bronchus at Mallinkrodt, 1973-1978).
Scannell (1980) : 'Bleb' carcinoma of the lung.
Gross et al. (1984) : Two cases presenting with air/ fluid levels within bullae.
Pritchard (1984) : Broncho-alveolar carcinoma arising in long standing air cysts.
Guerin et al. (1986) : Distrophie bulleuse et cancers bronchopulmonaires chez des sujets jeunes.
DeJong et al. (1989) : Presentation of **bronchioloalveolar carcinoma** as a thin-walled cavity in a young man.
Nickoladze (1993) : Bullae and lung cancer.
Pigula et al. (1996) : Unsuspected lung cancer found in work-up for lung reduction operation (for emphysematous bullae).
Venuta et al. (1997) : Occult lung cancer in patients with bullous emphysema.

Other thin-walled tumours have been reported by Møller (1950), Peabody et al. (1957a), Grainger and Pierce (1969), Simon (1971), Wright (1973), Godwin et al. (1980) and Woodring et al. (1980).

Meniscus or air-crescent sign.
This is discussed in detail in relation to leukaemia (p. 5.48), pulmonary gangrene (p. 19.6) and aspergillosis (ps. 19.39 - 40). It may also be seen with TB, hydatid disease, septic pulmonary embolism, lung abscess, pulmonary haematoma, Rasmussen aneurysm, cavitating squamous carcinoma, reticulosis, leukaemia, macroglobulinaemia or a sclerosing haemangioma.

References.
Cubillo-Herguera and McAlister (1969) : Meniscus sign in bronchial carcinoma.
Zelfesky and Lutzker (1977) : Septic pulmonary embolism.
Bakk et al. (1978) : Meniscus sign in sclerosing haemangioma.
Seyneave et al. (1992) : The air-crescent sign in pulmonary leukaemic infiltrate.
Gaeta et al. (1999) : A CT halo sign is nonspecific, but suggests invasive aspergillosis, Kaposi's sarcoma & LIP in immunocompromised pts. & bronchioloalveolar carcinoma in immunocompetent pts.

Secondary lung tumours and cavitation.
　　Secondary lung deposits may cavitate, even in the absence of chemotherapy. These may be of almost any type, but best known are deposits from squamous primary tumours occurring in various sites (including lung, cervix, ENT areas, etc) or from tumours that are rapidly growing and reach a large size (often outgrowing their blood supply) such as those from reticuloses, sarcomas, embryonic tumours, teratomas, or rapidly growing colonic or renal tumours. Such cavitating deposits (like peripheral cavitating primary tumours) may give rise to severe or recurrent pneumothoraces, which may be unilateral or bilateral (see also ps. 14.24 - 25).

　　Secondary deposits may also cavitate following treatment by radiotherapy and/or chemotherapy, and occasionally a persisting cavitating area may be found in a fibrotic residue remaining after all detectable tumour cells have gone. Such thin-walled spaces demonstrated by CT and in the position of former secondary deposits have been termed '**lacunae**' by Charig and Williams (1990 - see refs. below). The sequence of events would appear to be: central cavitation → thick walled cavity → thin walled cavity → resolution and fibrous scar. Such a process particularly appears to occur in deposits that are responsive to treatment, and such a continuing thin-walled cavity should not be taken as necessarily indicating continuing disease.

　　Earlier Papavasiliou and Constantes (1975) studied cavitating metastases and noted that
(i) they are unstable lesions but are prone to respond to anti-cancer treatment,
(ii) as many arose from primary sites in the upper air-ways they may have arisen from the inoculation of inhaled cancer cells and have a poor blood supply,
(iii) complete spontaneous resolution of one case (ca. thyroid) took place,
(iv) radiotherapy or other treatment accelerated cavity formation,
(v) a ball-valve mechanism may contribute to the increasing size of cyst-like lesions,
(vi) tumour regrowth may occur from new cell clones lining the cavity,
(vii) following radiotherapy the usual sequence is central cavitation, a thick-walled cavity, a thin-walled cavity, enlargement of the cavity with a ball-valve mechanism and eventual resolution.

For illustrations of secondary lung tumours and cavitation: - see
Illus. **LUNG　DEPS-CAVITATING**　(NB - squamous ca deposits most commonly cavitate) and　Illus. **LACUNAE.**

Cavitating nodules due to non-malignant causes.
　　Many benign nodules may cavitate. Some have already been noted above. Others include cavitating granulomas -TB, fungus, and bacterial infections [e.g. Staph., Pneumococcus, Milleri, Haemophilus, Klebsiella, PCP], amyloid, Wegener's granuloma, pneumoconiosis, rheumatoid, parasites, etc. - see Tables 6.1 & 6.2 & Chap. 19.

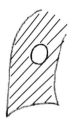　　

Lung consolidation with breakdown　　　　**Silicosis** may give an 'angel wing' appearance - p. 19.92.
Fig. 6.2　　Cavitation in pneumonia and silicosis.

　　Staphylococcal pneumonia may produce a lung cavity due to tissue necrosis or a lung abscess, but more commonly produces pneumatocoeles. They develop acutely but often take two to three weeks to clear (see also ps. 19.3 - 4). Pneumatocoeles may also be seen with other infections e.g. Haemophilus. They are sometimes multiple, in one or both lungs.

Rheumatoid and Caplan nodules, other granulomas, embolic infarcts and even some tumour deposits (particularly after chemotherapy) may cavitate before disappearance or leaving a scar.

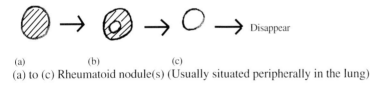

(a)   (b)   (c)

(a) to (c) Rheumatoid nodule(s) (Usually situated peripherally in the lung)

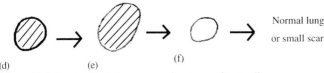

(d)   (e)   (f)

(d) to (f) Infarct - Nodule progressing to cavity to disappearance. (The nodule may enlarge, for several weeks after its first appearance - spuriously suggesting neoplasm.)

Fig. 6.3   Cavitating rheumatoid nodules and infarcts.

Further references.

Brock (1948) : Bronchial carcinoma was the cause of 56 out of 405 cases of lung abscess.
Crow and Brogdon (1959) : Cystic lung lesions from metastatic sarcoma.
Deck and Sherman (1959) : Excavation of metastatic nodules in the lung.
Dodd and Boyle (1961) : Cavitating pulmonary metastases.
Don and Gray (1967) : Cavitating secondary carcinoma of the lung.
Chaudhuri (1970) : Cavitating pulmonary metastases.
        (1973) : Primary pulmonary cavitating carcinomas.
Kassner et al. (1976) : Cavitating lung nodules and pneumothorax in children with metastatic lung nodules.
Wright (1976) : Cavitating metastases from osteogenic sarcoma, haemangiopericytoma, leiomyosarcoma of psoas, kidney (three cases including Wilm's tumour treated by adriamycin), teratoma of testis, parotid carcinoma and squamous carcinoma of bronchus and cervix - literature review included ; sarcomas of various types, squamous tumours originating in various sites, Hodgkin's disease, carcinoma of breast, bladder, pharynx, larynx, oesophagus, colon, mediastinal teratoma, etc.
Barker and Smith (1979) : Rapidly developing pulmonary metastases.
Kier and Godwin (1986) : Residual cavities from lung metastases following chemotherapy.
Carey et al. (1989) : CT appearances of metastatic testicular tumours.
Alexander et al. (1990) : Cavitary pulmonary metastases from transitional cell carcinoma of the urinary bladder.
Charig and Williams (1990) : **Pulmonary lacunae** - sequelae of metastases following chemotherapy.
Lawton et al. (1990) : Bilateral pneumothorax as a presenting feature of metastatic angiosarcoma of the scalp.
Beigelman et al. (1994) : Cystic degeneration of lung deposits from a pineal teratoma.

Differentiation from infection.

    With an acute pneumonic process, there is usually adjacent consolidation, but one has to beware that such is not mimicked by secondary collapse or tumour invasion. A 'shaggy' outline is more suggestive of tumour, but this may also be a feature of fungus infection.

    Occasionally what appears to be a lung abscess on radiological grounds, i.e. it has a thin wall, and what looks like pus to the naked eye on aspiration, will on microscopy prove to be tumour - Illus. **CA SQUAMOUS, Pt. 4a-d** shows such a case where the macroscopic pus was found to be composed of degenerate squamous tumour cells. Similarly a case referred to Oxford with what was considered to be multiple lung abscesses, was due to multiple tumour deposits from squamous lung cancer.

    Contrariwise Illus. **EMBOLUS/INFARCT,   Pt.   22a-e** shows multiple lung abscesses secondary to an infected dialysis shunt.

    Congenital and developmental abnormalities producing cavities include bullae, cystic congenital bronchiectasis, 'loofa lung', cystic adenomatoid malformation, etc. All of these may become infected and show 'cavities' within surrounding consolidation and/or fluid levels within the cavities.

Plombages (see p. 14.2) may become aerated years after insertion, and show a sponge, rounded 'table tennis balls' or plastic small 'billiard like' balls, with central lucencies.

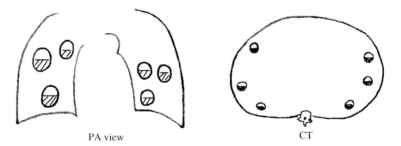

PA view   CT

Fig. 6.4. Multiple cavities with infected infarcts, e.g. in drug addicts, patients with infected AV shunts for dialysis, etc. These tend to be peripherally situated on CT sections.

<u>Honeycombing</u>. (See also 'holes in lung' - p. 1.52).

Fig. 6.5 Honeycombed cavities
(NB 'honeycombs' are properly true hexagons
but pathologically and radiologically are often
not so regularly or accurately shaped).

Honeycomb shadows in the lungs are multiple rounded or polygonal tiny cavities about 0.5 to 1 cm (or a little more) in diameter, some of which probably represent totally disorganised secondary lobules (with septal thickening). They are more often basal in distribution, but in gross cases can occur throughout the lungs. They occur as a result of chronic lung scarring, with loss of alveoli from the secondary lobules, and some of the causes are listed in **Table 6.3** below:

Table 6.3 <u>Causes of honeycombing</u>.
  Pulmonary fibrosis - fibrosing alveolitis, ARDS
         sarcoidosis
         pneumoconiosis, haemosiderosis.
  Histiocytosis (often + diabetes insipidus), Gaucher's disease, amyloid,
  Neurocutaneous diseases neurofibromatosis
         tuberose sclerosis
         lymphangioleiomyomatosis (LAM)
  Collagen diseases - rheumatoid
         Sjögren's syndrome
         scleroderma (fibrosing alveolitis of scleroderma -sometimes in this
         condition the honeycombs have been termed 'sclerocystic disease').
  Inhalation   - chronic paraffin oil inhalation, farmer's lung, allergic alveolitis
  Other conditions - alveolar proteinosis
         mucinous bronchioloalveolar carcinoma
  Infection   - pneumonia, esp. mycoplasma.
  Acutely following reexpansion of a lobar collapse with necrosis of an endobronchial tumour.

For illustrations see Illus. **HONEYCOMBING** and **KEYWORD** selections under the causes listed above.

Note : **In histiocytosis the typical HRCT appearance is of small nodules + cysts** (+ pneumothoraces, an upper lobe predominance & may be more focal than with LAM), compared with **LAM - thin walled cysts with no nodules**.

Table 6.4 Multiple cystic appearances may also be seen in:
>Emphysema
>End stage lung (see below)
>Drug reactions
>Bronchiectasis
>Cystic fibrosis
>Lymphangitis carcinomatosa

Sometimes honeycombing is equated to '**end stage lung**' (see also ps. 19.122 - 123), when the affected areas of lung become replaced by diffuse cystic spaces - a sign of irreversible damage. Pathologically such lungs may be firm, shrunken and non-compliant, with an irregular 'hob-nailed' pleura.

Occasionally the condition is complicated by neoplasm - a form of '**scar cancer**', or by osseous metaplasia with multiple small calcified shadows throughout the lung (Illus. **MICROLITHIASIS, Pt. 6a-b**).

References.

Oswald and Parkinson (1949) : First emphasised that honeycomb lung occurs in various diseases, in which there is diffuse interstitial pulmonary infiltration - in six cases there was an associated disorder such as tuberose sclerosis or heart disease, but in 10 others they found none.

Heppleston (1956) : Defined honeycomb lung as cystic translucencies in association with interstitial granulomata or fibrosis - in most cases the result of patchy interstitial fibrosis - showed pathologically that the essential abnormality was an obliteration of the respiratory or non-respiratory bronchioles - suggested that neighbouring unaffected bronchioles underwent compensatory enlargement to form the cystic spaces.

Dixon and Ball (1948) : Honeycomb lung and chronic rheumatoid arthritis.

Meyer and Liebow (1965) : The relationship of interstitial pneumonia, honeycombing and atypical epithelial proliferation to cancer of the lung.

Heitzman (1984) : The condition indicates interstitial lung disease. One should be able to identify a full circle of 360° to be certain of honeycombs - replacement of normal lung architecture by small rounded cyst-like spaces within areas of extensive fibrosis.

Stern et al. (1992) : Thin-walled cystic lung disease (honeycombing) has been shown by dynamic ultra-fast HRCT in patients with eosinophilic granuloma and lymphangioleiomyomatosis to be associated with focal or more diffuse air-trapping.

Emphysema.

The term 'emphysema' derives from the Greek word "Εμφυσαω = to inflate", and has been defined as "A collection of air in the cellular texture under the skin, or beneath the pleural and interlobicular cellular tissue of the lungs" (Mayne and Mayne, 1881). Its gross radiological appearances have been studied by several authors including Lodge (1946) who wrote: "Emphysema besides giving rise to increased lung density, causes widened intercostal spaces, a flattened depressed diaphragm and widened costo-phrenic angles. There is a greater residual air in the lung." Others have noted that it is often accompanied by a considerable loss of pulmonary vessels, as in the '**vanishing lung syndrome**' with gross emphysema (p. 6.8) . The word is also included in the terms 'compensatory emphysema' and 'obstructive emphysema'.

With the development of CT, radiologists, have become more interested in the smaller pathological anatomy studied by pathologists, and emphysema has more recently been defined as an anatomical alteration of lung characterised by permanent enlargement of air spaces distal to the terminal bronchioles, accompanied by destructive changes in the alveolar walls and without obvious fibrosis (Heitzman, 1973, Sanders, 1991). It may follow bronchiolitis - see discussion (p. 3.25 et seq.) re air trapping leading to emphysema. It is subtyped according to the position of the airway dilatation within the secondary lobule - **centrilobular** (or **proximal** which may lead to **bullous formation**), **diffuse (panacinar** or **panlobular**), and **paraseptal** (or **distal**

lobular). There is also **cicatricial emphysema**, which occurs alongside areas of lung scarring; and a similar process may be seen with some tumours (e.g. Illus. **CA ADENO, Pt. 1**).

Centrilobular emphysema is the most common form and is due to the destruction of alveoli around the proximal respiratory bronchiole (see Fig. 1.61c, p. 1.50). It is commonly linked with cigarette smoking, and particularly affects the upper segments of the upper and lower lobes. Coalescence of the destroyed alveoli results in the formation of bullae, through which strands of residual lung tissue (mainly bronchi and vessels) may pass. The walls of the bullae are not usually visible and the distribution tends to be non-uniform.

Diffuse or **panlobular** emphysema by contrast principally affects the lower lobes, and is caused by α_1 anti-trypsin deficiency, and the Swyer-James syndrome. It is also found in the elderly and also appears to be potentiated by cigarette smoking. It tends to show uniformly decreased parenchymal attenuation and a paucity of vessels. Severe panlobular emphysema may be indistinguishable from severe centrilobular emphysema, except on the basis of zonal distribution.

Paraseptal or **distal lobular** emphysema occurs in relation to the interlobular septa, particularly in the cortical parts of the lung (including the parts adjacent to the interlobar fissures). It may also lead to the formation of bullae and blebs, and is often associated with spontaneous pneumothoraces. The interlobular septa remain intact.

A '**black lung**' appearance besides being present in emphysema, may also be seen with vascular shut-down in mosaic pattern changes in bronchiolitis etc. (see ps. 2.4, 3.27, 19.68 & 101-102).

Cysts and bullae.

A **cyst** is typically an air-containing space in otherwise normal lung. Some appear to be congenital in origin, and others acquired. They characteristically have a respiratory epithelial lining and may or may not communicate with a bronchus. **They usually displace vessels, in contrast to bullae, which often have vessels running through them.**

The term cysts is also applied to air-filled spaces occurring in damaged lung - with fibrosis, scarring from pneumonia (including pneumocystis), sarcoid, histiocytosis, LAM, amyloid, medicinal paraffin, trauma, etc. Occasionally cysts or bullae may be associated with a tumour, especially an adenocarcinoma - see also ps. 6.3 & 24.16 & Illus. **CA+BULLAE/CYSTS ETC.**

In children cysts may be simple, follow infection, or be due to congenital malformations such as ademomatoid or sequestration, or be caused by tumours such as mesenchymoma.

A **bulla** refers to a localised area of destruction of lung tissue with dilatation, usually involving several adjacent secondary lobules. Bullae may be single or multiple and uni- or multi-locular (with an epithelialised or 'fibrous wall' and internal trabeculations made up of portions of alveolar septa, small bronchi or vessels). They are clearly demarcated from surrounding lung. Frequently the base of a bulla is composed of a mesh of fibrous strands with multiple bronchiolar communications. They may occur both in the periphery of the lung (types 1 and 2 due to paraseptal and centrilobular emphysema respectively) and within the lung (type 3 -associated with generalised emphysema).

Honeycombing (see ps. 6.6 & 19.61 - 62) is caused by clustered small cystic air-spaces, etc.

Giant bullous emphysema or ('**vanishing lung syndrome**') may give rise to severe disability with precocious, often asymmetrical giant bullous emphysema, particularly in the upper lobes. The condition is seen most commonly in **male smokers, but also occurs in non-smokers**. HRCT shows extensive paraseptal and centrilobular emphysema coalescing into giant bullae (see also p. 6.10).

Sub-groups of bullae: Pneumatocoeles - are due to air trapping (check valve obstruction), emphysema, staphylococcal, PCP etc. pneumonia, post traumatic, barotrauma, etc. Some clearly follow severe lung damage, and represent a part of end-stage-lung. Their development may be followed in patients with ARDS (ps. 8.13 - 14).   **Blebs** - are sub-pleural (arising within the cortical secondary lobules). According to Reid (1967) they develop outside the internal elastic layer of the lung - thus differentiating them from bullae. They may be a reflection of the different morphology of the these lobules.

Peripheral bullae should be distinguished from honeycombing by the thickness of the walls - bullae are thin (< 1mm thick), whereas honeycombs are usually thicker.

Causation of emphysema, cysts and bullae.

Several writers have considered the reasons for the formation of emphysema, cysts and bullae. Clearly lung damage occurs with infection especially viral or chronic. Chronic bronchitis or bronchiolitis may damage the smaller bronchi and bronchioles. Macrophages also may release proteolytic enzymes, damaging the alveolar walls, particularly if the antiproteases are reduced by a genetic defect (as with α_1 anti-trypsin deficiency) or neutralised by tobacco smoke or other factors. Mechanical factors also occur, perhaps related to collateral air drift, loss of elasticity with a failure to deflate in expiration, etc.

One problem relates to the '**Law of Laplace**' i.e. that the tension in the wall of a container necessary to contain a given pressure on its contents is **inversely** proportional to the radius of curvature of any part. This is more often quoted in relation to the urinary bladder and the formation of bladder diverticula, but equally applies to the emptying of bullae and cysts. It implies that once they occur they are more likely to enlarge. They also tend to enlarge with obstructive and hyperexpansion conditions (like the ears of an inflatable Mickey Mouse balloon only blow up when Mickey is himself well inflated!). Ting et al (1963) felt that these structures did not easily deflate, because their main openings and also their pores of Kohn (see ps. 2.8 - 9) become compressed when they become inflated, and radiographs taken in expiration demonstrate 'air-trapping'. Some also appear to have wider bronchial connections, so that they are more readily inflated.

CT of emphysema.

CT and HRCT are very useful for the visualisation and assessment of bullous disease in the lungs, as part of our understanding of what occurs and in the differentiation of the various types - see diagrams below.

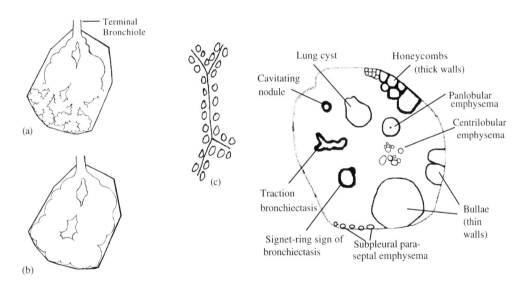

Fig. 6.6   Diagrams showing alveolar destruction in : (a) centrilobular, (b) panlobular and (c) paraseptal emphysema. (a & b after Netter, 1979, Ciba Labs   &   c after Stern and Frank, 1994, AJR, **162**, 791 - 798, by permission).

Fig. 6.7 Diagram of air-filled abnormal spaces in the lung. (adapted from Webb et al., 1992, HRCT of the Chest, Fig. 4.31, Raven Press - by permission).

Surgical treatment of emphysema and bullous disease.

In patients with severe emphysema, and the development of large bullae, CT has been used to try to assess the possible selection for surgical removal of some of the worst cysts (but often the problem is that the disease process is diffuse, though often worse in the upper lobes, and even removing large bullae is not uncommonly followed by the enlargement of others).

Resection of large bullae or cysts has been practised to attempt to improve lung function for many years. Mostly this has been carried out at formal thoracotomy, but unless a lobectomy was done, complications from persistent air leakage from the lung were common. More recently some resections of bullae have been carried out through mini-thoracotomy with VATS, using laser surgery and stapling to 'seal' the lung.

Whatever surgical method is used, preoperative CT is needed to portray the giant bullae (UL predominance + mild LL disease appears best) and to exclude small complicating tumours.

Further references

Golden (1940) : Abnormally wide resp. movement of lower lungs - Roentgen evidence of obstructive emphysema.
Belsey (1958) : Tension cysts of the lung in infancy and childhood.
Laws and Heard (1962) : A reduction in the calibre and number of the peripheral pulmonary arteries, plus a background increased transradiancy due to a reduction in the vascular bed were the most reliable radiological signs of emphysema. Large lungs may be emphysematous or normal, and normal sized lungs may be emphysematous. Local severity of emphysema was the most important feature.
Simon (1964) : Radiology and emphysema.
Reid and Millard (1964) : Correlation between radiological diagnosis and structural lung changes in emphysema.
Baum et al. (1966) : Cystic disease of the lung (80 cases).
Scarrow (1966) : The pulmonary angiogram in chronic bronchitis and emphysema - three groups -
(i) '**Pink puffers**' - primary disease both clinically and radiologically in emphysema - show a progressive symmetrical diminution in the pulmonary vascular bed.
(ii) '**Blue puffers**' or winter bronchitics - non-specific lung disease - tortuous and irregular or enlarged mid pulmonary arteries with distal occlusions and loss of smaller vessels.
(iii) '**Blue bloaters**' - cor pulmonale - peripheral oedema with CO_2 retention - more normal branching with enlarged vessels and early filling of pulmonary veins.
Scarpelli (1968) : Surfactant system of the lung - also changes in alveolar diameters occurring with respiration.
Bell (1970) : Grossly reduced lower lung perfusion in α_1 anti-trypsin deficiency shown by lung perfusion scan.
Ziskind et al. (1970) : Incomplete consolidation in pneumococcal pneumonia complicating emphysema.
Hislop and Reid (1971) : Emphysema of childhood - overinflation of a normal lobe,
Roghair (1972) : Non-operative management of emphysema - long term follow-up.
Stilwell (1973) : **Law of Laplace.**, Fraser (1974) : The radiologist and obstructive airways disease.
Thurlbeck (1976) : Morphology of emphysema and emphysema-like conditions.
Hepper et al. (1978) : Radiological study of chronic obstructive pulmonary disease by a_1 antitrypsin phenotype.
Thurlbeck and Simon (1978) : Radiographic appearance of the chest in emphysema.
Godwin et al. (1980c) : Thin walled cystic lesions of the lung.
Semple et al.(1980) : Widespread panacinar emphysema with α_1 antitrypsin deficiency. Assessed the radiographic diagnosis of emphysema compared with necropsy lung sections in almost 700 patients and found that two-thirds of those with severe emphysema correlated well.
Freundlich (1981) : Pulmonary masses, cysts and cavities.
Gishen et al. (1982) : Radiological features of α_1 antitrypsin deficiency in 165 patients - emphysema predominantly affected the lower zones and was more common in smokers.
Robb et al. (1982) : Dynamic volume imaging of moving organs.
Robb et al. (1983) : Non-invasive quantitative imaging of the volume of the lungs.
Pugatch (1983) : The radiology of emphysema.
Trapnell (1983) : Design, dynamics and deduction - a radiologist looks at the human lung - in obstructive lung disease - the areas which are poorly ventilated are also poorly perfused.
Jones et al. (1985) : α_1 antitrypsin deficiency presenting as bronchiectasis.
Gaensler et al. (1986) : Patient work-up for bullectomy.
Burki (1989) : Radiological diagnosis of emphysema - accurate or not ?
Buckley et al. (1991) : Detection of bullous lung disease with conventional radiography and digital storage phosphor radiography - any differences were likely to be insignificant.
Takasugi et al. (1998) : Changes in thoracic dimensions after lung-volume reduction surgery for diffuse emphysema.
Cleverley and Hansell (1999) : Imaging of pts. with severe emphysema considered for lung reduction surgery.
Cleverley et al. (2000) : The strong correlation between lung perfusion assessed by HRCT and scintigraphy suggests that latter is superfluous in assessing pts. for lung reduction surgery.

CT

Fiore et al. (1982) : Role of CT in the evaluation of emphysema.

Goddardet al. (1980, 1982) : CT in pulmonary emphysema - found that it gave a good demonstration of the distribution of emphysema and had a good correlation with angiography. They also found that the normal lung density gradient may be abolished or reversed.

Pardes et al. (1983) : CT of congenital lobar emphysema.

Gross et al. (1984) : CT of solitary cavitary infiltrates - causes:

TB cavities in 10% of primary cases, 75% reactivated - usually well seen with conventional films - CT may be misleading as it shows adenopathy, perhaps suggesting neoplasm.

Aspergillosis complicating TB.

Lung abscess - Strep. viridans, Staph. aureus, pyogenes, pneumococcus.

Empyema tends to be more ovoid or oblong in shape - extends to chest wall and as obtuse angle.

'Split pleura sign' - smooth thin wall.

Malignant cavitary infiltrate most often results from lymphoma or squamous carcinoma.

Contusion or penetrating trauma - pneumatocoele.

Irradiated lung with ectatic bronchi.

Morgan and Strickland (1984) : CT assessment of bullous lung disease.

Putman et al. (1984) : CT of localised lucent lung lesions - intrapulmonary air sacs - bullae, pneumatocoele, etc (occult neoplasm in a bulla), squamous etc. carcinoma, TB, fungus, embolism, PMF.

Foster et al. (1986) : CT - pathological correlation in centrilobular emphysema.

Bergin et al. (1986a) : CT in the qualitative assessment of emphysema.

(1986b) : The diagnosis of emphysema - compared with pulmonary function tests, CT was a better predictor of emphysema - it also distinguished patients with moderate emphysema from patients with normal lungs.

Hruban et al. (1987) : HRCT of inflation-fixed lungs, pathological - radiological correlation of centrilobular emphysema.

Gould et al. (1988) : CT measurements of lung density in life can quantify distal air space enlargement.

Müller et al. (1988) : 'Density mask' is an objective method of quantifying emphysema using CT.

Kinsella et al. (1990) : CT quantification of emphysema using a 'density mask' - correlation with pulmonary function testing.

Kuwano et al. (1990) : Correlation of CT and pathology scores in the diagnosis of mild emphysema.

Miller, R. et al. (1989) : Limitations of CT in the assessment of emphysema - even fine section CT underestimated the earliest lesions of emphysema, most lesions <5 mm in diameter were missed.

Adams et al. (1991) : Appraisal of CT pulmonary density mapping may help to locate and quantify pulmonary emphysema. "Enlargement of the distal air spaces in emphysema produces a fall in mean CT lung density, and the normal gravity-dependent lung density may be abolished or reversed...It is against this background that the use of lung density mapping in the investigation of emphysema has been described. Good correlation between highlighted lung and areas of emphysema at subsequent pathological examination have been demonstrated. Highlighted pixels in dependent areas of lung may correspond to areas of emphysema as assessed visually....On CT scanning, pulmonary emphysema can be assessed visually or by using densitometric techniques....Lung density mapping is relatively quick and simple and provides a rapid assessment of the gravity-dependent pulmonary density gradient. However in common with other densitometric methods, there is considerable variability amongst normal subjects and the method is dependent on technical factors. These limitations should be considered when using lung density mapping in the assessment of pulmonary disease." (see also note on p. 7.37 under pulmonary densitometry).

Knudson et al. (1991) : Expiratory CT for assessment of suspected pulmonary emphysema.

Guest and Hansell (1992) : HRCT in emphysema associated with α_1 antitrypsin deficiency - areas of low density and reduced perfusion and attenuation of the pulmonary parenchyma were present in all of 17 cases studied. Frank bulla formation occurred in 7 but was not a major feature. A striking CT finding was bronchial wall thickening or dilatation in 7 and gross cystic bronchiectasis in one. Although upper zones may appear normal on chest radiographs, they were also affected as shown on fine CT sections. CT findings correlated well with abnormal lung function tests.

Klein et al. (1992) : HRCT diagnosis of emphysema in symptomatic patients with normal chest radiographs and isolated low diffusing capacity.

Gurney et al. (1992) : Regional distribution of emphysema - correlation of HRCT with pulmonary function tests in unselected smokers. Found that 'even though the upper lung zones were more severely affected by emphysema, the degree of emphysema in the lower zones had a stronger correlation with pulmonary function abnormalities. The upper long zones are a relatively silent region where extensive distribution may occur before functional abnormalities become known.'

Spouge et al. (1993) : CT & pathologic findings in panacinar emphysema.

Snider et al. (1985) : Definition of emphysema.

Snider (1994) : Pathogenesis and terminology of emphysema.
Stern et al. (1994) : Idiopathic giant bullous emphysema (vanishing lung syndrome) - HRCT in 9 cases - extensive paraseptal emphysema coalescing into giant bullae.
Stern and Frank (1994) : CT of the lung in patients with pulmonary emphysema.
Thurlbeck and Müller (1994) : Emphysema - definition, imaging and quantification.
Shteyngart et al. (1998) : Damage to elastic fibres increases lysozyme binding to them which may enhance the progression of pulmonary emphysema.
Marti-Bonmati et al. (1991) : Cysts associated with bronchiectasis decrease in size on expiratory CT, but not bullae.
Stern et al. (1992) : Cystic lung disease associated with eosinophilic granuloma and tuberous sclerosis - air trapping at dynamic ultrafast HRCT.
Aquino et al. (1994) : Cysts (> 1cm in diameter) associated with honeycombing are often lined with bronchiolar type epithelium and have fibrous walls, they may decrease in size with expiration.
Tanaka et al. (1997) : Paratracheal air cysts communicating with the trachea.
Carr and Pride (1984) : CT in pre-operative assessment of bullous emphysema.
Little et al. (1995) : Unilateral laser reduction pneumoplasty is giving encouraging results.
Mino et al. (1995) : Serial changes of cystic air spaces in fibrosing alveolitis - a CT-pathological study.
Wakabayashi (1995) : Thoracoscopic laser pneumoplasty - 500 procedures in 443 pts. with improvement in respiratory function - 4.8% deaths. Main postoperative problem is with air leakage. (See also p. 24.47).
Gierada et al. (1997) : Pseudomasses due to areas of lung collapse in patients with severe bullous emphysema.
Gierada and Slone (1997) : Lung volume reduction surgery - radiographic findings in the early postoperative period - noted **pleural tents** - parietal pleura lifted from the chest wall (esp. in the upper part of the chest) to contact the visceral pleura, and thereby minimise the upper pleural space if the reduced lung size does not initially fill it.
Gierada et al. (1998) : MR analysis of lung volume and thoracic dimensions in pts. with emphysema before & after lung volume reduction surgery - comparable to CT.
Worthy et al. (1998) : The majority of lung cysts decrease in size on expiratory CT lung scans suggesting that they communicate with the airways (study of 23 cases).
Bradshaw and Murray (1996) : Spontaneous regression of a giant pulmonary bulla.
Orton and Gurney (1999) : Spontaneous reduction in size of bullae (autobullectomy).
Johnson et al. (2000) : **Large lung bullae in marijuana (cannabis) smokers**.
Smit et al. (2000) : CT was not routinely advised for showing bullae in pts. with spontaneous pneumothoraces.

Fatty masses in the thorax.

Fat is common in many parts of the thorax, adjacent to the aortic arch, in the anterior mediastinum, adjacent to the pericardium and above the diaphragm. The well known supra-diaphragmatic 'fat pads' are frequently found adjacent to the lower parts of the pericardium, particularly in obese subjects (see below). Sometimes other parts of the mediastinum may be widened by fat (lipomatosis) and this may mimic a tumour (Illus. **FAT, Pts. 2-8**).

There are two types of adipose tissue (i) **white fat**, which is more common, and is widely distributed throughout the human body, and (ii) **brown fat,** which is more commonly found in hibernating animals, but which may also be found in man and especially in infants. The former tends to form **lipomas**, and the latter '**hibernomas**', which are much less common. A 'hibernoma' may show IV contrast enhancement similar to that seen with a liposarcoma (Illus. **LIPOSARCOMA, Pt. 2a**).

Extra-pleural costal fat, immediately outside the parietal pleura, and overlying the medial aspect of the intercostal muscles, is often seen as a linear thickening on the inner aspect of the ribs. It is most abundant over the 4th to 8th ribs postero-laterally, and is best demonstrated on posterior-oblique views. It may mimic pleural plaques, but is more generalised and does not calcify. Lipomas may arise from it, and have smooth tapering or rounded borders overlying the pleura, and may extend through the chest as '**dumb-bell**' **tumours** - passing through a rib space, widening it and possibly causing rib erosion or notching and/or hyperostosis. These lipomas may occur anywhere from the lung apex down to the base, and may extend up into the neck or down into the abdomen. The intrathoracic part is usually seen as a well-defined sub-pleural mass, and the fatty nature may often be recognised on conventional tomograms or CT (see Illus. **LIPOMA CHEST WALL, Lipoma Pt. 1**) because of the lower density as compared with adjacent other soft tissue. The '**dumb-bell**' appearance may be due to the negative pressure within the chest 'sucking-in' a portion of the semi-fluid fatty mass in the outer part of the chest wall. Lipomas may also occur in the mediastinum, the pericardium and bronchi (see below).

Fat may also be found in the extrapleural space adjacent to pleural plaques (see p. 14.37), pseudoplaques (ps. 14.2 & 14.39), apical pleural caps (p. 12.4), and old calcified empyemata. It may extend into pleural fissures, especially the greater fissures - '**intra-fissural fat**'. Omental fat may extend into the chest through hiatal or other trans-diaphragmatic herniae (Chapter 15).

Because of their semi-fluid nature, fatty masses tend not to deform and only minimally displace other tissues or organs. They may alter in shape with posture or respiration, and may 'wobble' with an undulating motion. They usually have smooth outlines, and tend to smoothly cover adjacent organs, the diaphragm or chest-wall. Their pliant nature resembles that of female breasts, and **thymolipomas** (p. 18.23) or those lying on the diaphragm may have a breast-like appearance.

Fatty masses may be more translucent on plain films or conventional tomograms, than other soft tissues. However this is more readily appreciated on CT sections, when the density may also be measured (fat usually gives - 80 to 140 HU). MR will also demonstrate fat, but old haematomas may give a similar appearance by this method.

When fat is infiltrated by tumour, it may have an increased density on CT sections - '**dirty fat**' - see also p. 12.20 & 14.31.

Excessive fat may be a feature of steroid treatment e.g. in renal failure patients or Cushing's syndrome.

Oil or fatty collections within plombages are discussed on p. 14.2.

Fat in intra-pulmonary masses.

Fat may be found within intra-pulmonary hamartomas (p. 5.14 & Illus. **HAMARTOMAS, Pt. 11**), and occasionally within degenerating tumours (Illus. **DEGEN IN LUNG TUMOUR**). Such fat within degenerating tumours sometimes produces a 'pseudo-cavity' on tomograms (Illus. **BREAST, Pt. 22d**).

Endobronchial lipomas.

These are uncommon, but Vine et al. (1981) reviewed 40 cases. The author has also seen a few cases. The case shown in Illus. **ENDOBRON LIPOMA** had an ever changing shape on TV fluoroscopy with respiration, which was well seen following bronchography, and this correctly suggested its nature (see also references below).

Endovascular lipomata - see p. 9.9.

Benign lipoblastomas may occur in infancy (see references).

Liposarcomas.

Fortunately these are rare and the author has only seen a few cases. One lay just above the diaphragm in a young policeman and was seen well before the arrival of CT (Illus. **DIAPHRAGM-TUMOUR**. Two have been in the thymic region. Both of these showed some enhancement of the tumour with IV contrast, in comparison with the normal mediastinal fat which did not enhance (Illus. **LIPOSARCOMA, Pts. 1 & 2**). Secondary tumours in the chest are not unusual with primary tumours elsewhere. Liposarcomas of the oesophagus are noted on p. 16.24 and of the thymus on p. 18.23 - see also refs. on p. 18.27.

The breasts.

In older females, these are largely formed by fat (unless they are having HRCT) which allows tumours to be readily displayed in many cases by mammography. Sometimes when performing CT of the chest, unexpected breast tumours may be detected (Illus. **BREAST, Pts. 1a-d, 3, 26, 38**), and checked that they are not cysts with ultrasound and biopsied.

Some females have injected paraffin oil or jelly into the breasts to try to augment their 'figures'. This may give rise to local transradiant areas in the breasts, or the oil may track and induce calcification at more dependent sites. Silicone gel, not within implants (where it is innocuous, unless it leaks) has also been employed for this purpose, and may stimulate fibrosis within the breasts, sinus formations and microcalcifications simulating neoplasm - the author has seen one or two such patients who have been former 'bunny girls'. The gel may also stimulate a mild generalised auto-immune reaction or pneumonia (see also p. 12.18).

Lipoid pneumonia.

(a) **Exogenous lipoid pneumonia** - (Illus. **LIPOID PNEUMONIA, Pt. 1 & 2**) mineral oil, usually taken as 'medicinal paraffin' as an aperient, may be inhaled; inhalation most often occurring without much coughing or vomiting, as it is bland and virtually non-irritating. However it may occasionally cause an inhalation pneumonia, particularly in patients with swallowing disorders. When taken 'last-thing' at night, it may be aspirated after reflux during sleep. Occasionally an acute 'pneumonia' is produced, and sometimes it is rounded or spherical in type. Repeated long-term inhalation (or absorption from the intestine together with lymphatic permeation may) give rise to lower and mid zone infiltrates ('chronic consolidation with air-bronchograms') throughout both lungs, with a '**ground-glass**' appearance or '**crazy-paving**' and/or nodules. CT in such cases may demonstrate that the infiltrates contain material of fatty density, but many areas of 'consolidation' due to this cause are fibrotic, without any radiological fatty density. When rounded such nodules may mimic PMF, primary lung neoplasm or secondary deposits. In children inhaled hydrocarbons may lead to the formation of **pneumatocoeles**.

Lipoid pneumonia can also occur from nasal medications containing mineral oil (even pure olive oil), smoking tobacco containing 'black fat', cleaning aircraft undercarriages with an oil mist, inhaling oil from oil lubricated air compressors, the inhalation of burning animal fat, and the spraying of car bodies with waxy-oils, prior to transportation (Illus. **EMPHYSEMA, Pt. 37a-b**). The inhaled oil is emulsified by lung lipase, resulting in a foreign body reaction.

(b) **Endogenous** (or degenerative) **lipoid pneumonia** may be produced within obstructed bronchi or lobes, and fatty degeneration is often seen within large degenerating lung tumours (see below).

Some cases of neoplasm, particularly **alveolar cell tumours**, have been reported complicating lipoid pneumonia (see p. 5.1).

Hereditary lipocytosis.

In this condition the bone marrow is replaced by fat, and there may be an almost identical radiological picture to that seen with thalassaemia - see p. 18.32-33. Following splenectomy these people do not need so large a red cell production.

Pulmonary lipogranulomatosis.

It is often said that 'an apple a day will keep the doctor away'. However even excessive apple ingestion may apparently produce disease. Duboucher et al. (1986) from Toulouse in Southern France reported the case of a 55 year old farmer, who ate 1 Kg. of apples between meals each day for 18 years (six tons in all). He developed angina, had a chest radiograph which showed multiple tiny nodules throughout both lungs and soon after died of coronary insufficiency. At autopsy the lungs contained multiple small nodules, composed of aliphatic hydro-carbons similar to those found in apple peel. The pleura, liver and spleen were also involved. The radiographic appearance was similar to that seen with chronic mineral oil ingestion (see above), and the authors made the point that lung deposition of mineral oil (as in this condition) may occur via absorption into the lymphatics.

Fat and oil embolism (see also Chapter 11).

This may be seen after severe trauma (fractured femoral shaft, etc.), following accidental IV infusion of lymphangiographic contrast medium, oil hysterosalpingography, etc., and also in acutely ill patients with acute pancreatitis, severe liver disease, burns, prolonged steroid treatment, etc., when it may give rise to a similar clinical picture as with ARDS (p. 8.13 - 14).

About 5 to 20% of patients with multiple severe injuries probably have some degree of this condition, almost certainly as a result of liquid bone marrow fat passing into torn veins within the marrow. Most develop signs of respiratory distress, cerebral irritation, sometimes leading to coma and skin petechiae within 12 to 48 hours. The petechiae are usually more marked in the upper half of the body, and lipuria is common. This embolisation causes release of serotonin and histamine, and haemorrhage into the alveoli, so that the patient tends to develop ARDS. Better management has improved the prognosis.

Following lymphography many patients cough up a few oil droplets, and may also taste it. One always tries to keep the amount of Lipiodol injected as low as possible. 40 to 60% reaches the lungs by 24 hours, as shown by transient miliary shadows on chest radiographs - and also when we tried using I^{131} labelled Lipiodol to treat pelvic and abdominal node metastases from melanoma, and found that most had reached the lungs at 24 hours; we then abandoned this method of treatment!

Illustrations are shown under Illus. **FAT/OIL EMBOLISM.**

Fat pads.

Fat pads adjacent to the base of the heart are common, especially in obese subjects, but may also occur in others, and particularly those having long term steroids. Pathologically they may be more common on the left, but they are usually more obvious on the right on PA chest radiographs. They may be seen as rounded or triangular shadows (on both views) and may sometimes be quite large and extend into the lower parts of the oblique fissures. Fluoroscopy may show that they change in shape with respiration and cardiac movement - i.e. they are semi-fluid at body temperature. They also mould and dampen cardiac pulsations, a point which can also be checked with ultrasound. They are also well demonstrated by CT. Differential diagnosis includes pericardial cysts, Morgagni herniae, pericardial or lung masses, right middle lobe collapse, thymolipomas (p. 18.23 - 24), teratomas, chemodectomas or loculated pleural effusions. A huge right-sided fat-pad which had been referred to the author as a possible bronchial tumour is shown in Illus. **FAT PADS, Fatty mass Pt. 3a-c**.

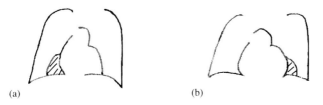

(a)   (b)

Fig. 6.8   Common appearance of 'fat pads' (a) right side, (b) left side.

After studying left sided fat-pads by CT, Paling and Williamson (1987) pointed out that although epicardial fat frequently causes a well-marginated opacity in the anterior cardiophrenic angle on lateral chest radiographs, a similar appearance may be produced by cardiomegaly alone. Varying geometry of the anterior aspect of the left lung may also alter the appearance of a fat-pad. (The retro-sternal stripe and retrosternal lines are discussed on ps. 1.27 to 1.29).

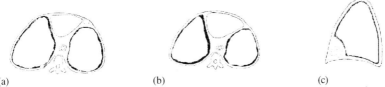

(a)   (b)   (c)

(a) A small fat pad (but with a sharp fat /lung interface), and (b) an enlarged heart (and no significant fat pad) may give rise to an identical lateral picture(c) suggesting a well-marginated fat pad, because of the similar pericardial /lung interface.

(d)   (e)   (f)   (g)

(d) A large fat pad may produce a poorly defined opacity on the lateral view (e) due to a non-tangential air /fat interface.

(f) A sharp anterior angle, with the left lung extending forwards alongside the heart, will not give rise to any fat pad on the lateral view (g).

Fig. 6.9   The formation of the 'fat pad shadow' on lateral radiographs. (adapted from Paling and Williamson, 1987, Radiology, **165**, 335 - 339, by permission.).

Illustrations are shown under Illus. **FAT PADS.**

Further references.
Lipoid pneumonia
Wagner et al. (1955) : Foreign body granuloma of the lungs due to liquid paraffin.
Brody and Levin (1962) : Interlobular septal thickening in lipid pneumonia.
Baghdassarian and Weiner (1965) : Pneumatocoele formation complicating hydrocarbon pneumonitis.
Wren and Crosbie (1968) : The radiological features of paraffinomata.
Généreux (1970) : Lipids in the lungs.
Bergeson et al. (1975) : Pneumatocoeles following hydrocarbon ingestion.
Harris and Brown (1975) : Pneumatocoeles as a complication of chemical pneumonia after hydrocarbon ingestion.
Kennedy et al. (1981) : Exogenous lipoid pneumonia.
Wheeler et al.(1981) : CT demonstration and needle biopsy confirmation.
Subramanian et al. (1982) : Lipoid pneumonia with Cryptococcus neoformans colonisation. The lipoid pneumonia occurred following the nasal installation of 'Vick's Vaporub' (a mixture of oils) for five years.
Felson and Ralaisomay (1983) : Carcinoma of the lung complicating lipoid pneumonia.
Beermann et al. (1984) : Severe case of aspiration pneumonia, following the inhalation of a mouthful of ignition fluid (80% paraffin) by a trainee fire-eater. This produced consolidation in the LLL followed by its collapse with some basal fluid- recovery after penicillin and steroids.
De Olivera et al.(1985) : Four children with lipoid pneumonia taken to relieve small bowel obstruction caused by ascaris worms.
Joshi and Cholankeril (1985) : CT in lipoid pneumonia.
Carrillon et al. (1988), Carette et al. (1989) : MR gives a high signal intensity in lipoid pneumonia similar to subcutaneous fat.
Fraser et al. (1988) : CT appearance of chronic lipoid pneumonia.
Lauque et al. (1990) : Bronchoalveolar lavage in liquid paraffin pneumonitis.
Brèchot et al. (1991) : CT and MR findings in lipoid pneumonia - considered CT to be superior - segmental collapse within the RUL containing fatty densities (-68 to -110 HU).
Lee, K. et al. (1995) : Lipoid pneumonia - CT findings - low density mass like lesion with lipid deposits.
Franquet et al. (1998) : '**Crazy-paving**' pattern on CT sections in chronic lipoid pneumonia - 3 cases - all had used nasal drops for chronic sinusitis - 2 only pure olive oil - stopping the nasal drops produced clinical and radiological improvement.

Fat embolism
Scott et al. (1942) : Areas of consolidation from this cause were predominantly basal (four cases).
Grossman (1946) : Two cases of severe pulmonary oil embolism following hysterosalpingography particularly affected the basal vessels.
Glas et al. (1953), Sevitt (1962) : Fat embolism.
Bron et al. (1963) : Oil embolism in lymphangiography.
Berrigan et al. (1966) : Diffuse bilateral alveolar consolidation resembling pulmonary oedema.
Brueck et al. (1971) : Oil embolism in lymphangiography.
Weisz and Steiner (1971) : Cause of death in fat embolism.

Wright and Stallworthy (1973) : Oil embolism and female sterility produced by oil salpingography.

Feldman et al. (1975) : The fat embolism syndrome. Guenter and Braun (1981) : Fat embolism syndrome.

Riska and Myllynen (1982) : Fat embolism syndrome in patients with multiple injuries.

Chan et al. (1984) : Post-traumatic fat embolism, its clinical and subclinical presentations.

Park et al. (1986) : Pulmonary imaging in fat embolism.

Rosen et al. (1986) : Nontraumatic fat embolism - rare cause of pulmonary infiltrates in immunocompromised pt.

Williams, A. et al. (1986), Batra (1987) : Fat embolism syndrome.

Chrysikopoulos et al. (1996) : CT & MR of 2 cases of post traumatic cerebral fat embolism + literature review.

Kutzner et al. (2000) : Fatal fat embolism following intraarterial angiography.

Lipomas and hibernomas

Heuer (1933) : Thoracic lipomas - three types (I) **limited to thoracic cavity**, (ii) **extend into the** neck, (iii) **'dumb-bell' type** with intrathoracic and extrathoracic portions connected by an isthmus through an intercostal space - generally cause peripheral radiolucency in a large mediastinal mass.

Dollery and Brewer (1943) : Mediastinal lipomas may transmit the cardiac impulse with a characteristic undulating motion or 'wobble'.

Wiper and Miller (1944) : Changing shape of lipomas between erect and head-down positions.

Watson, W. and Urban (1944) : Huge mediastinal lipoma filling left side of chest - removed successfully.

Keeley and Vana (1956) : Flattening of a lipoma lying in contact with the diaphragm - like an intrathoracic breast.

Ten Eyck (1960) : Subpleural lipoma - three cases - one splayed the adjacent ribs like a neurofibroma.

Faer et al. (1978) : Transmural thoracic lipoma shown by CT.

Trigaux et al. (1990) : Hour-glass lipoma of the chest wall.

Buxton et al. (1988) : CT in two cases of transmural thoracic lipoma with pressure erosion of adjacent ribs.

Staub et al. (1965) : Intrathoracic fatty tumours.

Gramiak and Koerner (1966) : Pliability or change of shape of lipomas with respiration.

Chahlaoui et al. (1981) : Inspiration + expiration films for diagnosing fatty tumours - change in shape with respiration.

Vix (1974) : Extrapleural costal fat and lipomas arising from this (six cases).

Koerner and Sun (1966), Taetes (1970) : Steroid induced fatty mediastinal widening.

Bodman and Condemi (1967) : Mediastinal widening in iatrogenic Cushing's disease.

Drasin et al. (1978) : Ectopic ACTH production and mediastinal lipomatosis.

Reed and Morgan (1988) : Mediastinal widening following radiotherapy and dexamethasone.

Ahn and Harvey (1990) : Mediastinal hibernoma - a rare tumour.

Balestreri and Canzonieri (1998) : Axillary hibernoma with enhancement on CT and angiography.

Whyte and Powell (1990) : Mediastinal lipoblastoma of infancy.

Wang et al. (1998) : Lipoblastomatosis of the shoulder in a child - low signal on MR T1 (more usually high signal).

Crutcher et al. (1968), Politis et al. (1979- 3 cases), Vine et al. (1981) : Endobronchial lipoma.

Jensen and Peterson (1970) : Bronchial lipoma - three cases and a review of the literature.

MacArthur et al. (1977) : Endobronchial lipoma - review plus four cases.

Schraufnagel et al. (1979) : Endobronchial lipoma - ? form of hamartoma.

Mendelsohn et al. (1983) : Endobronchial lipoma demonstrated by CT.

Spinelli et al. (1982) : Resection of obstructive bronchial fibrolipoma through the flexible fibreoptic bronchoscope.

Box et al. (1991) : Endobronchial lipoma associated with lobar bronchiectasis.

Price and Rigler (1970) : Mediastinal widening due to fat.

Razzuk et al. (1971) : Liposarcoma of the mediastinum - two cases and literature review.

Lee and Fattal (1976) : Mediastinal lipomatosis in simple obesity.

Cohen et al. (1977), Homer et al. (1978), Mendez et al. (1979), Coulomb (1980) : CT of thoracic fatty masses.

Bein et al. (1978) : CT in the evaluation of mediastinal lipomatosis.

Schwitzer and Aguam (1977) : Liposarcoma of the mediastinum.

Rohlfing et al. (1977) : CT of intrathoracic omental herniation and other fatty masses.

Prohm et al. (1981) : Liposarcoma of the mediastinum - case report and review of the literature.

Viamonte and Vaimonte (1981) : Radiology and pathology of fat.

Rao and Woodlief (1981) : Excessive right subdiaphragmatic fat.

Streiter et al. (1982) : Glickstein et al. (1987) : Paraspinal lipomatosis.

Pantoja et al. (1984) : Some uncommon lower mediastinal densities.

Sargent et al. (1984) : Extrapleural fat - subpleural fat pads in patients exposed to asbestos - distinction from non-calcified pleural plaques.

Dimock et al. (1985) : Lipoma of the chest wall.

Evans et al. (1985) : Primary pleural liposarcoma.

Dooms et al. (1985) : MR of fatty masses.

Black et al. (1986) : CT appearance of cervical lipoblastoma.

Coblentz et al. (1986), Rossi et al. (1988), Ward and Hornsby (1990) : Hibernoma.

Epler et al. (1986) : Pleural lipoma - diagnosis by CT.

Gale and Grief (1986) : Intrafissural fat.

Geis et al. (1988) : CT of a symptomatic infarcted huge thoracic lipoma filling most of left pleural cavity in a young woman - pedunculated, inhomogeneous and of low attenuation - some herniation to right behind heart and oesophagus.

Munk and Müller (1988) : CT diagnosis of pleural liopsarcoma.

Williamson and Paling (1988) : CT of low peri-oesophageal focal fat collections which may mimic a hiatus hernia.

London et al. (1989) : MR imaging of liposarcomas.

Kleine et al.(1990) : Non-infiltrating angiolipoma of the mediastinum (to the right of the lower oesophagus) - an encapsulated mass with fatty and soft tissue components on CT.

Krieghauser et al. (1990) : MR imaging of fat in and around the heart.

Lionarons et al. (1990) : Constrictive pericarditis caused by liposarcomas.

Adler et al. (1990) : Grading liposarcomas using PET by uptake of F^{18} 2-deoxy-2-fluoroglucose.

Martin et al. (1990) : Fatty transformation of thoracic haemopoiesis following splenectomy.

Coode et al. (1991) : Diffuse lipomatosis involving the thoracic and abdominal wall.

Hoskins et al. (1991) : Sabre-sheath trachea with mediastinal lipomatosis mimicking a mediastinal tumour.

Meis and Enzinger (1991) : Myolipoma of soft tissue.

Carroll et al. (1992) : Huge liposarcoma filling L pleural cavity in a 33wk pregnant woman aged 23 who presented with respiratory distress + a suspected recurrent L diaphragmatic hernia.

Glazer, H. et al. (1992) : CT of fatty thoracic masses.

Weis and Rao (1992) : 92 cases of well differentiated liposarcoma.

Fisher and Godwin (1993) : Extrapleural fat collections lie in the chest wall or mediastinum. Lung or pleural scarring can pull on the mediastinal pleura and mediastinal fat to simulate a tumour. If the mediastinum is moved to one side, due to loss of volume in a hemithorax, a retrosternal band may be produced by the edge of the mediastinal fat. It may also extend into fissures, the pulmonary ligament or alongside the phrenic nerves.

Liang et al. (1996) : Myolipoma or liposarcoma of the retroperitoneum.

Jung et al. (1998) : Radiological findings in myxoid liposarcoma of the anterior mediastinum - frond-like peripheral enhancement on CT and on MR T1 relatively well-defined inhomogeneous mass and on T2 high signal intensity.

Munden et al. (2000) : Liposarcoma of mediastinum - large -70HU mass surrounding & displacing trachea & aorta.

Birnholz and Macmillan (1973) : Laryngeal compression due to diffuse, symmetric lipomatosis (Madelung's disease).

Enzi et al. (1982) : CT of deep fat masses in **multiple symmetrical lipomatosis**.

Enzi (1984) : Multiple symmetric lipomatosis: an updated clinical report.

Loke et al. (1998) : Multiple symmetric lipomatosis in the Chinese - Ultrasound, CT and MR imaging.

Watt and McMillan (1999) : MR appearances of multiple symmetric lipomatosis.

Fat pads and pericardial fat - for Breast (see p. 12.18).

Evander (1948) : Pleural fat pads. Cohen (1953) : The right pericardial fat pad.

Torrance (1955) : Subepicardial fat mimicking pericardial effusion on plain radiographs.

Fayos and Lampre (1971) : Fat pad over apex of heart mimicked by Hodgkin's disease.

Pond and Bjelland (1980) : Enlarging pericardial fat pad mimicking tumour.

Krieghauser et al. (1990) : MR imaging of fat in and around the heart.

Harjola et al. (1985) : Epicardial lipoma.   King et al. (1993) : Epicardial lipoma - usefulness of MR for showing the site of origin of the tumour and its relationships to underlying cardiac chambers, valves and coronary vessels.

Obstructive sleep dyspnoea (Illus. **SLEEP APNOEA**).

In this condition excessive fat combined with flabby neck musculature tends to allow the cervical pharyngeal and upper tracheal air-way to collapse in **inspiration,** instead of being held open by muscle power. Patients with this condition (particularly men) have repeated attacks of apnoea during sleep, and wake or almost wake in order to breathe again. They suffer from excessive tiredness and loss of concentration which is particularly important in drivers of heavy goods vehicles. The physiology may be shown by ciné MR studies, and the disturbed sleep by EEGs. Breathing air at a slightly elevated pressure e.g. from a small fan with air piped to a nose piece may relieve the problem.

A similar muscle weakness + fat may be the cause of infant cot-deaths, as apnoeic infants who close off their upper air-ways in sleep, may have immature brains which do not wake them up.

Reference - Jenkinson et al. (1999) - from Churchill Hospital, Oxford.

CALCIFICATION

Causes of calcification.

Calcification within a pulmonary nodule.
    The value of detecting calcification in lung nodules has already been partially considered on ps. 4.6 to 4.11, together with diagrams of the main types of calcification seen within them. Causes of lung calcification are also given in Tables 5.6 and 6.5.
    The most common cause of calcification in the thorax is still past TB (Illus. **TB-CALC** and **TB-CALC NODES**), even though fewer people are now being infected. When present in an old Ghon focus, in hilar or mediastinal nodes, or in the pleura, it usually presents little of a diagnostic problem in the UK, but particularly in the USA fungi may give rise to a similar appearance.
    Although most nodules containing calcification are benign, some tumours may contain calcification. This is particularly seen in adenocarcinomas. Calcification may also be seen in some secondary deposits (p. 6.20). An old calcified focus may become incorporated within a tumour (Illus. **CALC IN TUMOUR, Pt. 1**) or chondromas. Vascular anomalies only **rarely** calcify in the lungs. Scarring from an infarct may eventually calcify.

On **CT of nodules** one should particularly note:
(i) Nodules are more readily identified in the peripheral or sub-pleural parts of the lungs, and are less readily seen in the perihilar regions.
(ii) Partial volume artefacts are a considerable problem with determining the attenuation values of lung nodules - in general their diameters should be **twice** the slice thickness.
(iii) Spiral or rapid scanning (see ps. 20.22-23) during a single breath-hold may help in both nodule detection, and edge and density determinations.
(iv) The degree of inspiration at the time of CT is very important, as partial expiration may simulate dependent increased density.

The discussion on the use of phantoms for CT densitometry is continued on ps. 6.21- 22.

Table 6.5 - Causes of pulmonary calcification (see also Table 5.6, p. 5.41-42).
Calcification may be present in the lungs in :
        Chondromas and hamartomas (p 5.14)
        Carcinoids or adenomas (see p. 5.5) - this may be central or diffuse.
        Some adenocarcinomas and other tumours(see p 6.20)
        Pulmonary blastomas (see p. 5.12)
        Histiocytoma or pseudotumour (see p. 5.33)
        Reticuloses, especially following treatment (see p. 5.23)
        Castleman and Engelman tumours (see ps. 5.30 and 5.35)
        Granulomas - TB, (see above and p. 19.18)
        Fungal diseases (see ps. 19.44 - 45)
        Worms and other parasites (see p. 19.50 - 57)
        Healed infarcts (p. 7.29)
        Broncholithiasis (p. 3.24)
        Some metastatic tumour deposits
                    - osteogenic sarcoma (Tsuji, 1988, using Tc^{99m} MDP to study lung metastases
                    from osteogenic sarcomas found that only about one third of such deposits took
                    up the bone scanning agent. This appeared to depend on the amount of osteoid
                    present. Brady and Ennis, 1990, however found the technique superior to CT for
                    showing pulmonary and mediastinal metastases from osteosarcoma. Goddard and
                    Davis, 1991, found that CT showed deposits in one case better and scintigraphy in another).
                    - healing or sterilised metastases (see ps. 5.38, 6.20) - thyroid, renal, chorioncarcinoma, etc.)
                    - metastasising hamartomas (Carney's syndrome - see p. 5.17).
        Metastatic calcification in renal disease and hypercalcaemia.
        Rheumatoid and pneumoconiotic nodules (ps. 19. 81 & 19.91)
        Pulmonary sequestration (p. 3.11).
        Destroyed or end-stage lung (p. 19.123).

Chapter 6

Calcification in tumours is most readily found if they are examined by micro-radiography following surgical removal. In vivo a few exhibit calcification on plain films, but mostly this is shown by CT. It is most commonly seen with adenocarcinomas but can be seen within all tumour types, a point also noted by Mahoney et al. (1990).

A tumour, showing extensive osseous stromal metaplasia, had calcification demonstrated by conventional tomography, CT and on histology (McLendon et al., 1985). Fraser et al. (1989, see below and p. 20.6) found calcification in one case by digital radiography. Two adenocarcinomas showing diffuse stippled (dystrophic) calcification were reported by Stewart et al. (1987).

Eight bronchial tumours - six adenocarcinomas, one squamous and one oat - containing calcification especially within degenerate tumours have been seen by the author (Illus. **CALC IN TUMOUR**), and it seems clear that its presence **does not always signify a benign lesion.**

Siegelman et al. (1986a - see p. 4.7) also studied calcification in tumours, but noted different findings - diffuse calcification in benign lesions and focal calcium deposits in cancers, with no significant overlap. They had only one doubtful case - a 1.9 cm bilobed adenocarcinoma with eccentric calcification in one pole, the larger half of the lesion being calcified.

Calcification due to ossification may also be seen in some metastases, particularly those of bone and joint tumours (osteogenic sarcomas and chondrosarcomas, osteoclastoma and synovioma - see p. 5.38) and occasionally with those from other organs e.g. rectal villous papilloma, thyroid, breast and ovarian neoplasms. The author has seen deposits from carcinoma of the thyroid occasionally calcify in the lungs - two cases mimicked varicella calcification - the deposits had regressed and calcified. The third had nodular deposits in the lungs for 18 years which progressively calcified (Illus. **CALC IN TUMOUR, Pt. 7a-d**); she then developed a large non-calcified mass in the right kidney which resembled a primary renal tumour, but on histology following removal was shown to be a further thyroid metastasis. Calcified deposits may also occur after treatment of chorioncarcinoma (Cockshott and Hendrickse, 1969) and rarely in lung infarcts caused by renal tumour thromboembolism. A rare cause of calcifying deposits is seen in the Carney syndrome (the malignant hamartoma - see p. 5.17 and Illus. **CARNEY SYNDROME**).

A tumour containing dense calcification at the left lung apex, mimicking a neurofibroma (or an ectopic phaeochromocytoma) but due to a blastoma or an ovarian tumour deposit is shown in Illus. **CALC IN TUMOUR, Pt. 10a-c** (see also p. 5.12). Illus. **CALC IN TUMOUR, Pt. 2a-b** shows two small foci of central calcification in an oval-shaped solitary secondary deposit from a squamous antral carcinoma which contained speckled calcification.

NB: Calcification in adenocarcinomas probably occurs mainly in psammoma bodies (πσαμμος = sand) - these are also found in thyroid, ovarian and bronchiolo-alveolar carcinomas and their secondary deposits.

Further references.
Loudon and Winter (1954) : Calcification within a carcinoma of the lung.
Unterman and Reingold (1972) : Psammoma bodies in papillary adenocarcinoma of the lung.
Scataridge et al. (1983) : Calcification in liver deposits from lung adenocarcinoma.
Goldstein et al. (1984) : A calcified adenocarcinoma of the lung with very high CT numbers.
Darras and Collette (1985) : Malignant pulmonary nodule with central calcification.
McLendon et al. (1985) : Carcinoma of the lung with osseous stromal metaplasia.
Kyser et al. (1986) : Calcification within a small cell carcinoma of the lung.
Mallens et al. (1986) : Calcified lymph node metastases due to bronchiolo-alveolar carcinoma.
Kelly et al. (1987) : A calcified carcinoma of the lung and calcified intracerebral metastasis.
Austin et al. (1988) : Adenocarcinoma of the RML (in a non-smoking female aged 61) which contained laminated and amorphous calcific deposits on microscopy; these were not visible on plain radiographs or CT, whereas nodal deposits showed calcification on CT sections.
Fraser et al. (1989) : Illustrated calcification within a necrotic small cell lung cancer, & within lung metastases from a mucinous granulomatous nodule.
Jones, F. et al. (1989) : Calcified adenocarcinoma classified as benign on densitometry.
Mahoney et al. (1990) : CT demonstration of calcification in carcinoma of the in 20 patients. The pattern was punctate in 10. amorphous in 8 and reticular in two; cell types small in 8, squamous in 7, adeno in 4 and undifferentiated in 1. (They also studied pathological specimens of the tumours and nodes).
Charig et al. (1990) : Calcification in a large stellate metastasis in the RUL and a right hilar node from an osteogenic sarcoma of the thigh in a boy aged 15 - also positive bone scan).

Stark et al. (1990) : Calcification in primary intrathoracic extraosseous osteogenic sarcoma - three cases originating in (i) the left pulmonary artery (also multiple lung deposits containing calcification) aged 30, (ii) in LLL of a man aged 59 and (iii) in the pleura of a 14 year old boy (within a previous radiation field for treatment of Wilm's tumour).
Grevel and Austin (1994) : CT demonstration of calcification in lung cancer - 39 (out of 500) cases seen over 5 yrs - 80% were non-small-cell tumours and the calcification was punctate, chunky or amorphous and tended to occur in large tumours.
Guest and Husband (1994) : Disseminated osteogenic sarcoma in a 46 year old man, with pulmonary deposits containing calcification, and multiple bony deposits, including the hyoid bone which was expanded; the dominant lesion appeared to be in the right humeral head. Such spread is often termed 'osteosarcomatosis'.

Maile et al. (1982) : Reported three cases with calcification in pulmonary metastases (i) a malignant mesenchymoma of the thigh two years after resection, (ii) a fibrosarcoma of the breast and (iii) a medullary carcinoma of the thyroid which presented with calcified nodules in the lungs, liver and neck and four years later had osteolytic bone deposits.
Semple and West (1955) : Found calcification in testicular and ovarian tumour deposits.
Ferenczy et al (1977) : Ultrastructural studies on the morphogenesis of psammo bodies in ovarian serous neoplasia.
Mitchell, D. et al. (1986) : CT identification of calcified metastasis from serous ca of ovary.
Ferretti et al. (1997) : CT demonstration of supra-diaphragmatic calcified metastatic nodes from ovarian carcinoma.

Radiographic methods and use of phantoms for detecting calcification.

The determination of CT density of pulmonary nodules can be a considerable problem, since calcification may not be distributed evenly throughout the nodule e.g. nodulated within the mass or around its rim. There is also the 'partial volume effect', by which air filled lung may be partly included in the 'pixels' (see p. 20.17). Fullness of respiration, the exact positioning of the slice, differences between machines and various techniques, electronic drift, etc. can all produce variations. Levi et al. (1982) also noted the unreliability of CT numbers as absolute values.

Studies have been made using perspex models both in the USA (Godwin et al., 1982b, Tarver et al., 1983, Zerhouni et al., 1982, 1983), and in the UK in Manchester (Checkley et al., 1984). The main problem is that these are unlike patients who move! High numbers (> 150 HU) may be reliable, but low ones are often artificially low due to air. Readings also vary on different apparatus, and in some there is considerable overshoot. Checkley et al. concluded 'Area measurements made over a period of time may more reliably discriminate between benign and malignant nodules'. Some like Cann (1982) have used dual energy CT to detect minute calcium content, e.g. 20 mg /cm^3, but for routine use this is not very practicable.

Further references.
Collins et al. (1972) : Investigated the minimum detectable calcification - nodules containing 1 mg of calcium and measuring 1 x 2 mm could be seen on linear tomograms.
Chasen and McCarthy (1985) : Found linear was superior to pleuri-directional tomographic movement in showing calcification in lung nodules.
Godwin et al. (1982a) : Distinguished benign from malignant nodules (22 benign and 14 malignant) by high CT numbers, but all but one of those with high CT numbers also had calcification shown on plain radiographs or conventional tomograms.
Siegelman et al. (1980) and Aronberg and Sagel (1981) : Showed the value of CT values in benign pulmonary nodules. (Whilst in some cases small size made determination difficult, high values (>60) appeared to indicate incipient calcification, some calcified later).
Tarver et al. (1983) : Developed an experimental lung nodule to study the effect of nodule size, nodule environment and calcium content on the attenuation values of CT scans - showed that calcium was mostly responsible for the CT number, but that small nodules may have falsely low CT numbers and that numbers may vary from scanner to scanner. They also found that higher CT numbers were found when experimental nodules were scanned in air rather than in water.
Proto and Thomas (1985) : Analysed pulmonary nodules using thin-section CT and determined a representative CT number from a computer print-out - concluded that CT could separate some nodules having high values from malignant ones having lower figures. All their malignant nodules gave figures of 150 HU or below. About half of the benign nodules gave figures > 200 HU, and when calcified > 750 HU, the other half showing lower numbers, and minus figures when fat was present in hamartomas. They have also made a standard model nodule, to be able to check the CT value at each examination and prevent false numbers due to drift, etc.
Fraser et al. (1986) : Found dual energy digital radiography to be highly accurate in determining the presence of calcification within lung nodules.
Niklason et al. (1986) : Compared a dual-energy digital chest radiography unit (with 145 KV and 3 m air gap) with a conventional system for detecting calcified and non-calcified nodules, using simulated nodules superimposed over the

lungs of a frozen unembalmed corpse. They found that the dual-energy digital unit was far superior and attributed this to the removal of structured noise and superior control of scatter. They concluded that whilst high KV chest radiographs have had the effect of decreasing bone contrast, relative to pulmonary opacities (thereby allowing radiologists to 'see through the ribs') with **dual-energy digital radiography, it is possible to remove the ribs from the soft-tissue image and conversely remove soft-tissue structures from the bone image.**

Sagel (1986) : Discussed solitary pulmonary nodules and the role of CT and noted that most do not need CT to sort them out. With only a few cases is a phantom of any value, most being sorted out by comparison with previous radiographs, spot views under fluoroscopic control or by conventional tomograms. Such usually determine whether the mass is circumscribed, or contains internal benign looking calcification. If no calcification was seen on these, they had CT, and about 10% showed calcification and very occasionally fat. In the remainder densities were compared with the phantom developed by Zerhouni (1983) and its reference nodules or rods. About one case per month had values equal to or above that of the reference nodule, and was considered as benign.

de Geer et al. (1986) : Studied the characteristics of a chest phantom using two KVs and found considerable variation in the density of phantom rods (1 and 2.5 cm in diameter) placed in different parts of the phantom. This was more marked with the 1 cm rods. They also found that they could not detect any calcium within them.

Zerhouni et al. (1986) : Studied 384 nodules < 6 cm by CT which had not been considered to be calcified by conventional methods. 118 (30%) proved to be benign, and in 65 (55%) unsuspected calcification was demonstrated, being shown by simple inspection of CT sections in 28, and by comparison with the phantoms in 37. They considered it **useful in showing benign nodules < 3 cm in diameter, but it rarely gave a confident diagnosis in larger nodules and those with irregular and spiculated borders.**

Im et al. (1988) : Performed CT densitometry of pulmonary nodules in a frozen human thorax and felt that nodules < 2 cm and overtly calcified (150 HU) could be considered as benign.

Huston and Muhm (1989) : CT reference phantom was a useful adjuvant to plain tomography in patients whose nodules were uncalcified and had an indeterminate shape.

Jones, F. et al. (1989) : Studied 31 pulmonary nodules by CT densitometry in 29 patients using a nodule phantom. 11 were classified as benign, and 20 as indeterminate (of which 11 were benign and 9 malignant at thoracotomy). One classified as benign because of calcification, proved to be an adenocarcinoma.

Ward et al. (1989) : Used phantom CT scanning on 40 patients with solitary pulmonary nodules - 20 were regarded as benign. 30 patients had densities lower than the reference nodules and were removed, 17 being malignant. They regarded eccentrically placed calcification as 'intermediate'.

Swensen et al. (1991) : Studied 296 cases by reference to a phantom - 85 nodules were diagnosed as 'benign', but 10 were subsequently shown to be malignant tumours.

Khan et al. (1991) : Studied 75 patients - two classified as 'benign' with both HRCT and phantom reference proved to be malignant - a peripheral ossified carcinoid, and a 3.5 cm carcinoma.

Author's conclusions re the use of phantoms

(i) He questions the value of spending £5,000 on such phantoms because of (a) the questionable reliability and (b) problems associated with partial volume artefacts rendering even calcified nodules less dense.

(ii) Present evidence suggests that calcification in small lung nodules (< 2.5 cm) usually indicates a benign process, especially if it is central, laminated or 'pop corn' in type. Larger nodules containing calcification, especially those with irregular borders, may be tumours. Tumours may also engulf an old calcified scar.

(iii) Calcification besides occurring in some lung carcinomas also occurs in other tumours including some secondary deposits (from ovarian ca., osteogenic sarcoma, etc.), adenomas, carcinoids, hamartomas, reticuloses, Castleman's and Engelman's diseases - see above and Illus. **CA+CALC, CALC IN ADENOMA, CALC IN TUMOUR & CALC LG NODULES.**

Other causes of pulmonary calcification -

Dystrophic calcification occurs in damaged lung (infarction, previous prolonged infection, intra-uterine rubella, pulmonary fibrosis, end-stage lung, etc.).

Metabolic calcification may be seen in normal lung exposed to an abnormal metabolic environment - renal failure (see above), secondary hyperparathyroidism, extensive bone metastases, hypervitaminosis D, myelomatosis, the milk-alkali syndrome, following heart surgery with prolonged ITU therapy, liver or lung transplantion, prolonged coumarin treatment, etc.

Miliary calcification is most often caused by past varicella pneumonia (ps. 19.29 - 30) - other causes are listed in Tables 5.5 (p. 5.42) & 6.5. Healed tuberculosis may give rise to multiple small calcified foci, but these usually result from previous bronchopneumonic tuberculosis, miliary disease usually clearing completely. Similarly some fungus infections (e.g. histoplasmosis - p. 19.45) may also give rise to calcified miliary shadows. Other calcified miliary shadows may result from miliary secondary deposits (e.g. carcinoma of thyroid - the author has seen three such cases; chorioncarcinoma, etc.). When mitral stenosis was more common, **microlithiasis   pulmonale** was sometimes seen (ossification from tiny chronic haematomas in the lung). Dystrophic calcification may be seen with hyperparathyroidism. A further rare cause is described below.

Illustrations are shown in Illus. **MILIARY CALCIFICATION**.

Pulmonary alveolar microlithiasis.

This is a rare condition in which there are numerous calcospherites in the lung parenchyma. These may eventually fill the lungs to cause 'stony lung disease', with a 'sand-storm' appearance on chest radiographs. The nodules may have lucent centres. Coincident subpleural bullae may lead to spontaneous pneumothoraces which may be so numerous as to produce a '**black   peripheral pleural   line**' outlining the lungs on chest radiographs ('**black   pleura   sign**') or give rise to a '**black peripheral rim**' on CT, **overlying a sub-pleural 'white   line'**, probably caused by an accumulation of subpleural calcospherites. The condition may also be complicated by severe pulmonary fibrosis. The lung shadowing is often so extensive as to cause the heart and diaphragmatic borders to become obscured. (Similar pleural lines may also be seen in some patients with hyperparathyroidism). The condition is sometimes familial. Illus. **MICROLITHIASIS, Stony lung disease 1** shows a chest radiograph of a patient from a local family the author has examined.

As with microlithiasis pulmonale, the calcified nodules may show increased uptake of an isotopic bone scanning agent - see Illus. **MICROLITHIASIS, Stony lung disease Pt. 6a-b**.

When patients develop respiratory failure (usually in middle age, but sometimes even in childhood) the prognosis is often very limited. Cortocosteroids, chelating agents and bronchial lavage have been used to treat the condition, but with no apparent success. At autopsy the lungs are extremely hard, and have to be sawn, rather than cut up with a knife. Histology is only possible after decalcification with nitric acid (Dunnill, 1982).

Idiopathic pulmonary calcification   has been described by several authors and may show typical branching or ossified lesions particularly at the lung bases. It is probably a form of dystrophic pulmonary calcification - about 100 cases have been described in the literature.

Further references.
Galloway et al. (1961) : Pulmonary ossified nodules in mitral valve disease.
Epstein et al. (1963) : Pulmonary ossified nodule formation without mitral valve disease ? due to pulmonary venous hypertension - 4 cases.
Ventura (1966), Mendeloff (1971) : Disseminated nodular pulmonary ossification with Hamman-Rich syndrome.

Freidrich (1856) : Corpora amylacea in der Lungen.
Harbitz (1918) : Extensive calcification of the lungs as a distinct disease.
Puhr (1933) : 'Microlithiasis alveolaris pulmonum'.
Sosman et al. (1957) : Familial incidence - 50% of cases reported come from 13 families.
Cole (1959), Viswanathan (1962), Barr and Ferguson (1963), Sears et al. (1971) : Pulmonary alveolar microlithiasis.
Gomez et al. (1959) : Familial incidence - four cases ? an environmental disease.
Caffrey and Altman (1965) : Occurrence in premature twins,   O'Neill et al. (1967) : Family study.
Balikian et al. (1968) : Report of five cases with special emphasis on radiological findings.
Coetzee (1970) : PAM with involvement of the sympathetic nervous system and gonads.
Kino et al (1972) : Pulmonary alveolar microlithiasis in two young sisters.
Thurairajasingham et al. (1975), ThInd and Batia (1978), Cheong et al. (1988) : Pulmonary alveolar microlithiasis.
Palombini et al. (1981) : Bronchopulmonary lavage in alveolar microlithiasis.
Miro et al. (1982) : Pulmonary alveolar microlithiasis with an unusual radiological pattern.
Cale et al. (1983) : Transbronchial biopsy of pulmonary alveolar microlithiasis.
Prakash et al (1987): Review including ultrastructural and pulmonary function studies.

Volle and Kaufmann (1987) : Pulmonary alveolar microlithiasis in children - literature review.
Brown et al. (1978), Shigeno et al. (1982) : Positive diphosphonate scan.
Garty et al. (1985) : Positive bone scan in two siblings.
Türktas et al. (1988) : Negative bone scan.
Winzelberg et al. (1984), Chalmers et al. (1986),Cluzel et al. (1991), Korn et al. (1992) : CT & HRCTfindings.
Emri et al. (1991) : HPOA in a patient with pulmonary alveolar microlithiasis.
Ratjen et al. (1992) : Pulmonary alveolar microlithiasis and LIP in a ten year old girl.
Ritchie et al. (1992) : Pulmonary alveolar microlithiasis & diaphyseal aclasia - unusual combination.
Ucan et al. (1993) : PAM - review of 52 cases from Turkey (one had bilateral apical pneumothoraces).
Melamed et al. (1994) : Interstitial thickening in pulmonary alveolar microlithiasis - under-appreciated finding.

Nouh (1989) : Is the **desert lung syndrome** (non-occupational dust pneumoconiosis - p. 19.95).
a variant of alveolar microlithiasis?
Salzman (1969) : Lung Calcification in X-ray Diagnosis.
Reingold and Mizunoue (1961), Pear (1968), Felson et al. (1984) : Idiopathic pulmonary ossification.

Lymph node calcification (Illus. **CALC IN NODES**).
   This is common following TB and fungus infections; it is also seen occasionally with **sarcoidosis, rheumatoid disease and silicosis**. It may rarely be seen in patients with AIDS and **pneumocystis** infection. It is rare with **secondary   carcinoma,** but more common with **treated lymphoma** (see p. 5.23), and may be a pointer to **Castleman's disease**.

   Calcification within nodes is usually of a diffuse **amorphous** or random type pattern, but lace-work or flocculent pattern may be seen with **reticulosis, sarcoid** or some **fungal   infections**. **Dense calcification is most commonly due to past tuberculosis**. Diffuse nodal calcification throughout the mediastinum, abdomen (also in the spleen and kidneys) may be an indication of past sarcoid (some used to be treated with high dosage of vitamin D), or of amyloidosis. Rare causes of **centrally   arising** and **arborising   calcification** include **Castleman's disease** (p. 5.30), and **phaeochromocytoma** (p. 18.37 - 38).

   'Rim' or 'egg shell' calcification (either complete or broken) may be seen in broncho-pulmonary and other intra-thoracic nodes as a result of -
   Silicosis (esp. coal miner's pneumoconiosis)
   Sarcoidosis
   Fungus disease (blastomycosis, histoplasmosis, etc.
   Scleroderma
   Amyloidosis and **Rheumatoid.**

Note also
(i)   Nodes showing rim calcification often exhibit central calcification as well.
(ii) Beware of a past lymphogram mimicking calcification - (not so often carried out in the 1990s).
(iii) Acute nodal calcification may occur with **pneumocystis** infection with mixed ring and amorphous calcification.

Mediastinum
   The most common calcification is in the thoracic aorta, particularly the arch; it usually has no pathological significance in people over 40, but if widened or extensive may draw attention to an aneurysm, long-standing granulomatous disease, past injury, etc.
   Calcification may also be seen in goitres, neurogenic tumours (esp. neurofibromas), phaeochromocytomas, bronchogenic cysts, dermoids and other germ-cell tumours, thymic cysts and tumours, tumours arising from cartilage of bony elements, and within or around foreign bodies.

Pleura and pericardium.
   Calcification in these serous spaces may be caused by past infection (particularly TB), previous trauma or surgery, haemorrhage or infarction, collagen disease, rheumatoid, foreign material (asbestos, talc, etc.) - see also Chapters 14 and 15.
   Apical pleural calcification may be caused by scarring from degenerative apical lung bullous disease, etc. and may be bilateral (see also ps. 12.4 - 5).

Examples of pleural, heart and pericardial calcification are shown in Illus. **PL-CALCIFICATION, HEART CALCIFICATION, PERICARDIAL CALCIFICATION**.

Metabolic thoracic calcification in renal failure.

In patients with chronic renal failure, vascular calcification is common; it may be also be seen in subcutaneous tissues (e.g. of the limbs, chest wall etc., where it may occasionally be fulminant and simulate tumoral calcinosis - see below) and in many internal organs, including the kidneys, liver, spleen, lungs and pleura. Pulmonary and /or pleural and chest wall calcification may be diffuse, localised or extensive. An isotope bone scan in such patients may show increased uptake in these areas. Damaged lung in such patients e.g. following pneumonia or infarction may show focal calcification.

Tumoral calcinosis.

This occurs as a result of a genetic abnormality (with hyperphosphataemia and elevated serum 1,25-didihydroxy vitamin D levels) leading to the deposition of masses of hydroxyapatite in relation to joints or extra-articular bursae e.g. in relation to the shoulders, scapulae or ribs, also pelvis and limbs. It may also be seen in patients with Waldenström's macroglobulinaemia.

Examples of tumoral type calcification are shown in Illus. **TUMORAL CALCIFICATION**.

References.
Pulmonary nodules.
Bloch (1948) : Tuberculous calcification - a clinical and experimental study.
Davis et al. (1956) : Calcification within the solitary pulmonary nodule.
Hickey et al. (1987) and Sherrier et al. (1987) : Used digitisation to demonstrate calcification in an attempt to distinguish between benign and malignant nodules.
Khouri et al. (1987) : The solitary pulmonary nodule - assessment, diagnosis and management.
Webb (1990) : Radiological evaluation of the solitary pulmonary nodule.
Chai and Patz (1994) : Lung CT - patterns of calcification and other high attenuation abnormalities.

Lymph node calcification (see also under sarcoid - p. 19.71, TB - p. 19.16 & pneumoconiosis p. 19.91).
Grayson and Bluemenfeld (1949) : "Egg shell" calcifications in silicosis.
Jacobson et al. (1967) : Egg shell calcification in coal and metal workers.
Wyman and Weber (1969) : Calcification in intrathoracic nodes in Hodgkin's disease.
Scadding (1970) : Late stages in pulmonary sarcoid.
Whitfield and Jones (1970) : Lymph node calcification in Hodgkin's disease (after radiotherapy for cervico-thoracic disease).
Carasso et al. (1973) : Egg-shell silicotic calcification causing broncho-oesophageal fistula.
McLoud et al. (1974) : Egg shell calcification in sarcoidosis.
Bertrand et al. (1977) : Lymph node calcification in the anterior mediastinum in **Hodgkin's   disease** after chemotherapy in two cases.
Gross et al. (1980) : General review of egg shell calcification (plus histoplasmosis and amyloid) - noted it in two cases of sarcoidosis.
Riviero et al. (1984) : Calcification in **Hodgkin's nodes** (especially in children) following radiotherapy.
Strijk (1985) : Nine cases of malignant lymphoma causing lymph node calcification.
Panicek et al. (1988) : Calcification in untreated mediastinal lymphoma.
Im et al. (1993) : Eggshell calcification on lateral chest radiograph in TB on treatment.
Gawne-Cain and Hansell (1996) : CT study of the pattern of calcified mediastinal lymph nodes in sarcoid and TB - concluded that there are differences, which can largely be explained by differences in pathogenesis - the route of lymphatic drainage in pulmonary TB and the caseating nature of TB granulomas. "Where hilar node calcification is present, it is more likely to be unilateral in TB and bilateral in sarcoidosis. A focal pattern of calcification is commoner in sarcoidosis pts. and complete nodal calcification is commoner following TB. However "the pattern and type of calcification should not be used in isolation to decide between sarcoidosis and TB."
Ferretti et al. (1997) : CT demonstration of supra-diaphragmatic calcified nodes from ovarian carcinoma.
Patel (1998) : CT demonstration of calcified R cervical & mediastinal metastatic lymph nodes from ovarian ca.

Renal failure
Firooznia et al. (1977) : Diffuse interstitial lung calcification in chronic renal failure mimicking pulmonary oedema.
Bein et al. (1979), Gilman et al. (1980) : Pulmonary calcification in renal transplant patients.
Jost and Sagel (1979) : Metastatic calcification at the lung apex.
Schnyder et al. (1979) : Accelerated arteriosclerosis in patients having haemodialysis.

Watanabe and Kobayashi et al. (1983) : Pleural calcification - a type of 'metastatic calcification' in chronic renal failure.
Van Dyke and Sagel (1985) : Calcified pulmonary **sequestration** in a patient with renal failure.
McLachlan et al. (1986) : Pulmonary calcification in renal failure - three cases.
Sanders et al. (1987) : Metastatic calcification of the heart and lungs in end-stage renal disease.
Kuhlman et al. (1989) : Fulminant pulmonary calcification complicating renal transplantation.
Gross (1991, Year Book p. 241) : Altered 'tissue resistance to calcification' due to previous azotaemia, steroids & vitamin D.
Hartman et al. (1994) : Metastatic pulmonary calcification in patients with hypercalcaemia - findings on CXR (often normal) and CT (diffuse, nodular or confluent nodular).

Pleura
Shapir et al. (1981), Schmitt et al. (1983).

Miscellaneous
Felson (1969) : Thoracic calcification.
Feuerstein et al, (1990b) : Widespread visceral calcification in disseminated Pneumocystis carinii infection - CT appearances.
Radin et al. (1990) : Visceral and nodal calcification in patients with AIDS related Pneumocystis carinii infection.
Glazer et al. (1991) : High attenuation mediastinal masses on unenhanced CT.
Hamrick-Turner et al. (1994) : Diffuse lung calcifications on CT following fat emboli and ARDS.
Libson et al. (1993) : Pulmonary calcinosis following orthoptic liver transplantation.
Winter et al. (1995) : Pulmonary calcification after liver transplantation in children.
Avery and Chippindale (1995) : Hypervitaminosis D secondary to miliary tuberculosis in an infant.
Rook et al. (1988) : Role of vitamin D in tuberculosis.

Tumoral calcinosis
Duret (1889) : Single and multiple tumours of serous bursae.
Hug et al. (1974) : Tumoral calcinosis with the sedimentation sign.
Balchandaran and Prince (1980) : Tumoral calcinosis - scintigraphic study of an affected family.
Lyles et al. (1985) : Genetic transmission of tumoral calcinosis.
Martinex et al. (1990) : Imaging of tumoral calcinosis.
McGuinness (1995) : Hyperphosphataemic tumoral calcinosis in Bedouin Arabs.

SPURIOUS LESIONS

Spurious shadows or lesions mimicking tumours may be caused by film or processing artefacts, by clothing worn by the patient, abnormal postures (e.g. with the chin over the upper thorax in severe kyphosis or patients with severe ankylosing spondylitis) or various anatomical structures (Illus. **CLOTHING ARTEFACT**; **FILM FOGGING**; **ANKYLOSING SPONDYLITIS Pt. 1b**; **KYPHOSIS**; **KYPHOSCOLIOSIS**).

The best known spurious lung nodules are due to **male nipples**, which when prominent and project well out, may produce small rounded densities on PA chest radiographs. They usually have well-defined outer margins due to the air/ soft tissue interface and a poorly defined inner margin (also noted by Ferris and White, 1976). They are usually symmetrical in position. Some mark them in doubtful cases with an opaque marker and take further views, but TV fluoroscopy is quicker and more definite, if the patient is turned slightly oblique whilst observing the relative movement. In difficult cases tomography (including CT) may be carried out to show that no lung nodule is present.
The nipples of adult females are more variable in position. In women with large and pendulous breasts, the nipples do not cause any difficulty since they will hang below the level of the dome of the diaphragm, when the patient is in the erect position, but females with tiny breasts may present the same problem as in males. Another method of differentiation is to get the lady to lift up her breasts with her fingers (Illus. **BREAST-NIPPLE, Artefact Pt. 16a-b**) when the apparent mass will usually disappear!

Breast   prostheses, following mastectomy (which contain many types of filling including home-made ones with padding, foam, bird-seed, etc.) are normally removed before chest radiography, but implants may sometimes be confusing, especially when calcified (Illus. **BREAST-IMPLANT, Breast Pts. 36 & 37a-b**).

Other   problems - some manual workers have hypertrophied pectoral muscles on their 'handed' side - the author remembers being asked to perform bronchography on a left-handed labourer who was branded as having 'bronchiectasis', solely because of a hypertrophied left pectoralis major! Others have poorly developed pectoral muscles, or an absent muscle on one side - **Poland's   syndrome** (p. 12.17), but a mastectomy is the most common cause of hypertranslucency due to chest wall thinning (Illus. **MASTECTOMY**).

Gynaecomastia should be noted in men having steroid treatment for prostatic neoplasm, with cirrhosis, etc. (Illus. **GYNAECOMASTIA**). It may be 'normal' in fat men.

Illus. **BREAST-NIPPLE   SPURIOUS, ARTEFACT, Pt. 2a-b** shows pleural plaques which mimic nipple shadows or lung nodules.

Illus. **ARTEFACT, Pts. 18** and **15a-b** show skin papillomas and Illus. **ARTEFACT,   Pt. 22** a large lipoma on a patient's back.

Small dense nodules arising from the inner aspects of the ribs are shown in Illus. **ARTEFACT, Pt. 24** and forked ribs producing a spurious mass in the right upper chest in Illus. **ARTEFACT, Pt. 25a-b.**

Other spurious nodules - skin and chest wall nodules, etc.

Accessory nipples, lipomas, or papillomas, skin folds or warts, lipomas on the back, subcutaneous neurofibromas, dressings or clothing (buttons, residual barium in hospital gowns, etc.), may also give rise to spurious round shadows. Long hair locks or plaits have not uncommonly been diagnosed as 'tuberculosis', and should be pinned or tied out of the way. Long hair may also simulate mediastinal emphysema, when hanging over the medial part of the chest (Illus. **HAIR LOCK**).

Confusing shadows may be produced by **rib fractures with callus** (Illus. **ARTEFACT, Pts. 3a-b** and **15a-b**, see also p. 12.22), or an organising chest-wall haematoma; both are not uncommonly mistaken for intra-pulmonary pathology. Other confusing shadows include **sclerotic bone islands or sclerotic rib deposits** and masses in or overlying the chest wall, e.g. lipomas, abscesses, etc. The common upper thoracic **'idiot tumour'** is due to a considerably **calcified first costo-chondral junction** which is not uncommonly mistaken by students and others for a small lung mass - the converse can also happen in that a lung nodule may be labelled as a calcified first costo-chondral junction. The first costo-chondral junction can also give rise to apparent intra-pulmonary nodules on CT, unless one examines adjacent sections (Illus. **IDIOT TUMOUR** - see also Paling and Dwyer, 1980). A truly intra-thoracic rib may also be shown (Stark and Lawrence, 1984, showed such an example in a patient with a bronchial carcinoma). Such depression, or true intra-pulmonary position may be secondary to a past penetrating (including gun-shot) injury - Illus. **RIB INTRAPULM, Trauma lung Pt. 13a-e**.

Rib companion shadows, intercostal or serratus anterior muscles, extra-pleural fat, or intercostal bulging of the lungs in thin or emaciated patients may also cause problems, as may **pleural plaques or pseudoplaques** (see ps. 14.35 - 39).

Sometimes the structures at the base of the neck, e.g. a deep supra-sternal notch, or prominent or absent sternomastoid muscles may cause confusion, particularly after a laryngectomy or radical neck dissection (see also ps. 12.1 - 2). Axillary soft tissue swellings (nodes, tumours or excessive fat) may also simulate mediastinal tumours on lateral chest radiographs. These usually have a well-defined anterior curvi-linear anterior margin overlying the antero-superior of middle mediastinum (see also Bonté and Schonfeld, 1962). The author has encountered a Sprengel's shoulder misdiagnosed as an upper lobe consolidation (Illus. **SHOULDER   SPRENGEL**, or **Shoulder Pt. 7**). The rhomboid fossa of the clavicle (Pendergrass and Hodes, 1937) can also be mistaken for a bony erosion - see also ps. 12.10, 12.40 and Illus. **RHOMBOID FOSSA**. A **scapular 'companion shadow'** on its medial aspect may be seen in patients who are cachectic or who have lost weight, and in whom the scapula is partially rotated (Lams and Jolles, 1981).

Other confusing structures.

Fig. 6.9 Diagram of spurious mediastinal mass on lateral radiograph due to enlarged axillary nodes or fat. (N.B. 'Fold lines' are usually straighter). See also next para re a spurious tumour due to an arm stump.

The **stump of an amputated arm** may cause confusion on a lateral view (Illus. **ARM STUMP**), as the patient may not elevate it out of the way, as one does with a normal arm in this projection. Often the proximal humeral bone stump is visible, and the ipsilateral clavicle is often elevated on frontal views, because of the reduced arm weight on this side. A similar 'mass' may be produced by a huge fatty arm (Illus. **ARTEFACT, Pt. 1a-b**).

Trouble may occur with spinal osteophytes, especially with large **spinal osteophytes**, in the lower dorsal region, which particularly on under-exposed radiographs may be mistaken for an intra-pulmonary mass. Spinal (Bucky) views will usually sort this out, if it is not readily apparent on chest radiographs, but occasionally tomograms may be required (including CT), as the appearances can sometimes be very bizarre. Shortsleeve and Foster (1979) pointed out that slight thickening of bone in the lower dorsal region, where the two laminae join to form the spinous processes, may give rise to an apparent lung nodule overlying the lower dorsal spine.

Malformations of the aorta, such as a right-sided descending aorta, or a double aortic arch, have been mistaken for tuberculous nodes, and one Indian woman (treated at 'St. Elsewhere's') had had anti-tuberculous treatment for two years! - see Illus. **AORTA ARCH R, Pt. 2.** The aorta in the lateral view, especially if tortuous, folded or notched from pseudo-coarctation, has also been mistaken for a mediastinal tumour (Stark et al., 1985) - see also Illus. **AORTA PSEUDOCOARCTATION & AORTA TORTUOUS.** A spurious tumour due to a transversely running aorta in a patient with severe kyphoscoliosis is shown in Illus. **ARTEFACT, Pt. 20.**

The **subclavian arteries** may cause curvi-linear shadows at the lung apices, which may simulate tumour masses (see also Figs. 12.3 - 5, ps. 12.7 - 8) - Illus. **ARTEFACT, Pt. 19a-b.**

Upper mediastinal veins (e.g. a larger than normal innominate vein), tortuous or even normal sized veins with a narrow thoracic inlet may cause spurious masses; similarly a **left superior vena cava** or a left-sided azygos vein may cause confusion. Even a **tortuous azygos arch** or a normal azygos 'knob' with its 'V' or 'tail-like' arch, extending behind the trachea to the left (Fig. 9.8d), have been mistaken for a pulmonary lesion (Rockoff and Drury, 1982, Kattan, 1984). Flow phenomena, after bolus injections of contrast media and due to uncalcified blood, may simulate apparent filling defects within the SVC or other large veins. Arrested respiration may cause their tributaries to fill retrogradely. Contrast medium may also 'layer' within the descending aorta and mimic dissection. In difficult cases dynamic scans may help resolve these problems (Godwin et al., 1982).

A **dilated oesophagus** may cause confusion, whether air or fluid-filled, or a combination of the two. Many observers may note the latter with its fluid-level, but in error consider the oesophagus to be a dilated trachea, or the lower fluid-filled part as an enlarged left atrium, etc. Similarly an air or partly air-filled pharyngeal or oesophageal diverticulum, may cause problems in diagnosis relative to the airway. A good diagnostic point is the 'fluid trap' causing a gas-less gastric fundus.

A **humped diaphragm** may simulate a basal lung tumour. Similarly on CT the dome of the diaphragm, particularly on the right, and especially if 'humped' or 'eventrated', will need to be diferentiated from intrathoracic structures by studying adjacent sections, plain radiographs or the 'scout view'. Contraction of muscle fibres may produce nodules in the crura, etc. (see Fig. 15.8, ps. 15.9 - 10), and in the periphery of the dome, mimicking enlarged lymph nodes, or mural nodules apparently within the stomach or colon (see also Rosen et al., 1983). Chilaiditidi's syndrome, diaphragmatic herniae and para-cardiac fat pads and cysts may also cause problems in diagnosis. Upper intrathoracic fatty masses (Illus. **FAT & FATTY MASS Pts. 2 - 8**), a narrow chest with straight back ('Twiggy syndrome') or a **pectus   excavatum** (Illus. **STERNUM   EXCAVATUM**) may cause confusion if not recognised. These may cause simulated cardiomegaly, a simulated mass due to the confluence of the left pulmonary veins, simulated basal congestion or **middle lobe consolidation**.

Accessory fissures may also give rise to confusion. That of the azygos vein is well known, but others may be seen such as the lingular fissure, superior and inferior accessory fissures of the lower lobes, the vertical fissure line, etc. (see ps. 1.5 - 6).

The **pulmonary   vessels** may be mistaken for pulmonary masses and give rise to pseudotumours. This may occur with both arteries and veins, particularly where they cross one another. A common problem is due to a dilated pulmonary artery mimicking enlarged nodes and vice versa. Usually tracing the outline of the artery and noting possible added structures due to nodes, etc. will distinguish the two, but in other cases tomography (including CT) and in a few instances angiography may be required to differentiate.

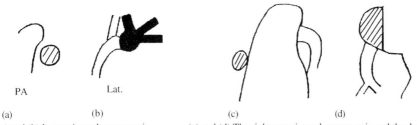

PA

Lat.

(a)   (b)   (c)   (d)

(a) and (b) L superior pulmonary vein.   (c) and (d) The right superior pulmonary vein and the descending
                                                 pulm. artery forming the 'Elephant head + trunk' appearance on CT.

Fig. 6.10   Pseudotumours due to pulmonary vessels.

Other   pseudotumours occur where the upper lobe artery crosses the aortic arch as seen on a lateral view, or with the **lobar pulmonary veins or venous confluences**, particularly if they are enlarged. Idiopathic enlargement of an inferior pulmonary vein is not uncommon.

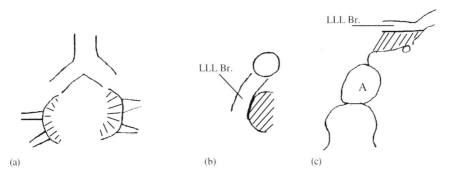

LLL Br.

LLL Br.

A

(a)   (b)   (c)

(a) High KV view or tomogram - inferior pulm.   (b) Lateral view and (c) CT - with a well defined posterior
veins passing to venous confluences and L atrium.   border adjacent to the LLL bronchus

Fig. 6.11   Pseudotumours due to the venous confluences and left inferior pulmonary vein.

(Abnormalities of the **pulmonary veins** are discussed on ps. 7.16 - 19).

Areas of consolidation. especially if rounded, may simulate lung tumours, only to clear spontaneously on follow-up radiographs. **'Vanishing'** or **'pseudotumours'** due to inter-lobar effusions are discussed on p. 14.6 (Illus. **PL-EFFUS FISS**). **'Pseudocavitation'** within an intra-pulmonary mass may be produced by high lipid content in a degenerating area of a tumour, or a still aerated area with a bronchiolar-alveolar carcinoma. **Illusory consolidation of the left lower lobe** may be seen in two ways ; (i) in patients with emphysema and a deeply posteriorly curving left side of the diaphragm, and (ii) on portable radiographs there may be a loss of definition of the left side of the diaphragm produced by loss of tangential imaging of it due to cranial angulation of the x-ray beam and projection of extra-pleural fat onto the base of the right lung (Zylak et al., 1988).

Some apparent pulmonary nodules, in cancer patients, may not be due to metastases. Drug reactions, emboli and subcutaneous nodules may simulate these.

Indwelling catheters (Hickman lines) may produce para-sternal nodules on CT sections (see also p. 11.13 & Fig. 11.4), which may mimic deposits from e.g. a melanoma (see also Fernandez et al., 1989).

Catheter or nodule

First rib

Fig. 6.12   Spurious tumour nodule due to a Hickman line (see also p. 11.11).

Postoperative nodules may be due to bleeding, other fluid collections, infection, fibrosis or foreign material (see also p. 11.15).

Pseumomasses of the liver are discussed on ps. 17.3-4.

Further references.

Smith, M. (1965) : Errors in diagnostic radiology.
Rawlings (1960), Mayall (1974) : 'Straight back' or 'twiggy' syndrome causing pseudo-heart disease.
Fisher (1968) : The simulation of pneumoperitoneum by basal atelectasis.
Keats (1973) : Atlas of Normal Roentgen Variants that may Simulate Disease (3rd Edn., 1984, 5th Edn., 1992, 6th Edn., 1996).
        (1976) : Small breasts mimicking anterior mediastinal tumour on lateral radiographs.
Ferris and White (1976) : The round nipple shadow.
Ellis (1977) : Incomplete border sign of extra-pleural masses.
Collins and Pagani (1978) : Extrathoracic musculature mimicking pleural lesions.
Shin and Bradley (1978) : Chest wall lesions mimicking pleural lesions.
Godwin and Webb (1982) : Contrast-related flow phenomena mimicking pathology on CT.
Généreux (1983b) : Conventional tomographic anatomy emphasising the pulmonary veins.
Kuhns and Seegar (1983) : Atlas of Computed Tomography Variants.
Gallagher and Dixon (1984) : Streak artefacts of thoracic aorta - pseudodissection.
Kattan (1984) : Some telltales and pitfalls in chest radiology.
Miller et al. (1985) : The troublesome nipple shadow.
Proto and Rost (1985) : CT of the thorax - pitfalls in interpretation.
Stark, P. et al. (1985) : Pseudolesion of the chest - a conglomerate shadow on the lateral radiograph.
Jardin et al. (1986) : Narrow thoracic inlets causing apparent mediastinal widening and pseudomasses.
Cáceres et al. (1988) : Pulmonary nodule simulated on lateral chest radiograph by branches of the aortic arch.
Fernandez et al. (1989) : Hickman nodule - a mimic of metastatic disease.
Edwards et al. (1989) : Offset ECG electrode simulating a pulmonary nodule.
Kim et al. (1989) : Pulmonary nodule mimicked by ECG lead artefact.
Cáceres et al. (1993) : Increased density of the azygos lobe on frontal chest radiographs **simulating**   disease and due to overlapping tortuous supra-aortic vessels or the thymus.
Fisher and Godwin (1993) : Extrapleural fat collections & pseudotumours (see also ps. 14.1- 2).

Gronner and Ominsky (1994) : Findings that simulate disease on plain film radiography of the chest :
nipples, supernumary or accessory nipples (males + females).
skin lesions - moles, pedunculated lesions, lipomata,

superimposed   bone - bone islands, exostoses, bone hypertrophy at costo-vertebral joints (esp. on R at T5-7 levels - shielded by aorta on L), healing rib fractures and pseudo-arthroses, rhomboid fossa of clavicle, extra-thoracic soft-tissue calcification,
chest wall deformity, depressed sternum, etc., calcified costal cartilage, myositis ossificans,
loculated pleural fluid, drainage tubes and tube tracks, ECG leads,
breast tumours, gas in breast cysts after aspiration, padded bra, etc.

Raymond et al. (1997) : Congenital thoracic lesions that mimic neoplastic disease on chest radiographs of adults:
Vascular anomalies - R aortic arch, coarctation, aberrant R subclavian artery, scimitar syndrome, pulmonary a/v malformation.
Foregut duplication cysts.
Congenital diaphragmatic anomalies.
Pulmonary sequestration.
Cystic ademomatoid malformation.
Lateral thoracic meningocoele or neurofibroma.

INTRAVASCULAR AND INTERSTITIAL GAS.

Intravascular gas.
   Gas, particularly carbon dioxide, used to be injected deliberately to aid in the detection of a pericardial effusion. If the patient lay on his left side in the head-down position, then with a horizontal x-ray beam, gas which had collected in the right atrium would show the thickness of its wall (usually 2 mm) plus that of the pericardium (Illus. **GAS IV**). However, since real-time ultrasound became available intravascular gas is no longer used.
   Accidental injection of gas (usually air) may occasionally occur with contrast media. Small bubbles are sometimes recognised at venography, and may occasionally be seen in the thoracic veins etc. at CT.
   The author has only seen a few cases of **serious   air   embolism**. These have followed nasal-antral wash-outs, an air-filled (instead of contrast filled) syringe used for angiocardiography, small amounts of gas accidentally injected at cerebral angiography (with gas bubbles visible on the angiograms), but none after retroperitoneal or GI gas insufflation. Only the antral cases proved fatal, and only one of the others had any demonstrable morbidity - the angiocardiography patient who had cerebellar signs, until she was placed in an hyperbaric oxygen chamber, which induced an immediate complete recovery, even though the incident had occurred some 5 or 6 hours earlier. In the 1950's when opaque rubber tubing was used in IV infusion sets, it was not uncommon for several ml of air to be intravasated. Many patients having haemodialysis treatment also had small amounts of air intravasated, but with no harmful sequelae. It has been estimated that up to 50-100 ml of IV air is usually of no consequence, provided that there is no patent foramen ovale, and one famous physiology teacher used to inject himself with 50 ml of air IV in front of his class, to show that this amount was usually harmless - see also note re central venous and other catheters (p. 11.10).
    Air embolism in association with percutaneous lung biopsies is discussed on p. 21.8. It may also occur rarely with assisted respiration, and with trauma.

Some references.
Dickey and Haaga (1984) : Venography with bubbles of gas being trapped in the left innominate vein in association with an obstructed SVC.
Faer and Messerschmidt (1978) : Radiographic demonstration of non-fatal pulmonary air embolism (also reviewed nine other cases).
Kizer and Goodman (1982) : Three men with venous air embolism. One tripped whilst convalescing from pancreatitis and inadvertently disconnected his CVP line. The second (a mentally deranged patient) deliberately blew several breaths down a CV line. The third, a policeman, had been shot in the chest and neck. The first and third showed intravascular gas on radiographs, and in the second diffuse bilateral interstitial and air-space consolidation.
McHugh and Brunton (1990) : Post-mortem chest radiograph in a young woman who had been exsanguinated and had gross venous air embolism, as a result of suicide with a shot-gun blast to her brain - the lung vessels were almost invisible. There was also considerable gas in the right side of the heart - see also note on p. 7.3.
Lau and Lam (1991) : Systemic air embolism - a complication of ventilatory therapy in hyaline membrane disease.

Cholankeril et al. (1992) : Massive air embolism of the pulmonary artery in a 14 year old mentally retarded boy having intermittent positive pressure respiration - after severe haemoptysis - embolism occurred from the superior branch of the LLL bronchus.

Decompression sickness, the 'bends', etc.

J.S. Haldane, the famous Oxford physiologist, in 1907 developed a method of staged decompression, which made it possible for a deep-sea diver to ascend to the surface safely. He found that gas-bubble formation occurs whenever the ambient pressure falls below half the total pressure of unit gas in solution. **Thus a person can ascend from 10 m. water depth without stopping, but if ascending from deeper depths, he must take a controlled stepped ascent (e.g. at 30 & 10m) if he has been down for more than a few minutes.** Gas within lung cavities or emphysematous areas expands according to Boyle's law*, so that the pressure in them may double during ascent between 30 m and 15 m depth and be four times as great at the surface.

*A plaque to Boyle is on the wall of University College in High Street, Oxford - this reads: 'In a house on this site between 1655 and 1668 lived ROBERT BOYLE. Here he discovered BOYLE'S LAW and made experiments with an air pump designed by his assistant ROBERT HOOKE, Inventor, Scientist and Architect who made a microscope and thereby first identified the living cell.'

During descent Henry's law applies - as pressure increases, more gas (nitrogen and oxygen) dissolves in body fluids, fat and soft organs. Conversely during ascent gas is released. At 60 m a diver has six times the normal amount of gas in solution, so that if he suddenly ascends, the effect is similar to taking the cap off a bottle of fizzy liquid (e.g. champagne) - i.e. there is almost an explosive release of gas. If this happens he may die from the **'chokes'** - see Illus. **DIVER, Intravasc gas Pt. 1** - in which a post-mortem chest radiograph shows gross gaseous filling of all vessels, heart chambers, the theca, biliary ducts, etc, due to release of gas from solution. This diver had been in a diving bell at the bottom of the North Sea at high pressure for over 48 hours. He panicked and left the bell, after the chain from the ship fractured; his companion stayed in the bell, and was later rescued unharmed and decompressed. The post-mortem radiograph (the standard method of examination in such circumstances) produces an interesting anatomical study, well delineating the thickness of the diaphragm, the right atrial wall, the left ventricle, chordae tendinae, etc. (Courtesy of Dr. Michael Allen, formerly of Aberdeen, and Medical Officer to the Jockey Club).

In most divers non-fatal amounts of gas are released into the circulation during decompression after diving, following escapes from submarines (the escaper has to be compressed in the escape chamber to allow the hatch to open, although the air pressure in the submarines may be near normal), in tunnelling (when high atmospheric pressures may be used to keep out water), or even in pilots of military aircraft who suddenly climb to high altitudes.

Placing ultrasound probes on the front of divers chests to record sounds emanating from the heart, suggests that all divers get bubbles in the heart and pulmonary vessels when they ascend. Probably most bubbles are filtered from the blood by the pulmonary capillaries and later reabsorbed, though some pass through the pulmonary capillaries, other a/v communications in the lungs or a patent foramen ovale to cause insidious damage to the brain, spinal cord and certain bones, particularly the upper femora and humeri, and the knee regions. Acute brain and spinal cord damage may lead to the **'staggers'**. The **'bends'** occur as a result of joint pain, when the limbs are held semi-bent for relief. Even diving in relatively shallow waters can cause insidious damage to the brain and spinal cord. It has been suggested that dives below 30 m should only be carried out with an oxygen helium mixture, or in a diving bell which can be attached to a decompression chamber. The practice of diving and breathing air, being quickly hauled to the surface, then being recompressed in a chamber and slowly decompressed seems dangerous, as gas bubbles will pass through the pulmonary capillaries to the brain and spinal cord.

SCUBA (self contained underwater breathing apparatus) was developed by de Cousteau in Southern France in 1944 and has become very popular especially with young people. Using this divers automatically receive the correct amount of air to breathe, related to depth. They however sometimes rely too much on computers strapped to their wrists with too little a safety margin, especially with repeated dives; they are also particularly at risk if they dive and return home by air the same day (the pressure in an aircraft cabin usually corresponding to about 8,000 feet i.e. half normal atmospheric pressure).

Divers may also be subject to nitrogen narcosis with an alcohol-like effect (at 30m for 30 mins = one Martini etc.). They may also be liable to panic.

As well as the release of gas from solution, when saturation has occurred, ascent from the sea bed may cause simple over-expansion within the lungs, due to air-trapping in bullae, or from lung damage due to a failure to **exhale all the way to the surface** during a 'free ascent'. If this happens, **barotrauma** may occur with gas escaping from the alveoli (causing interstitial and mediastinal emphysema and pneumothoraces, and passing intravascularly if the vessel walls tear). A pneumothorax at depth is a particular problem, due to expansion during ascent.

Gas in vessel wall sheaths in the lungs and the formation of a pneumediastinum and pneumothorax with trauma is discussed on ps. 6.34 - 5 - see also diagrams Figs. 6.14 & 6.15 - if these sheaths rupture, then gas can be forced into the thin-walled pulmonary veins giving rise to gas embolism.

Two cases of barotrauma were reported in SCUBA divers by Foote et al. (1977). One had a large bulla in the right upper lobe. The second became unconscious for three weeks after ascending from his first dive; he had air-trapping in expiration, with unilateral interstitial pulmonary emphysema - presumably air embolism followed overexpansion and rupture of the alveolar walls, due to the Swyer-James (Macleod) syndrome (see also ps. 7.9 - 10).

Thus radiological examination of the lungs of potential divers is essential to try to exclude those with bullae from diving. If there is any doubt on plain radiographs, a PA view in **expiration**, and **CT sections of suspicious areas in expiration should be taken** (see Illus. **DIVER, Emphysema Pt. 22a-c**).

Other effects of compression and decompression in the nasal sinuses (particularly when complicated by inflammatory disease - colds, allergy, etc.) and in the ears due to a failure of the Eustachian tubes to equalise pressure. The cartilaginous medial part of the tubes may collapse with early increasing pressure - in severe cases leading to a haemotympanum, oval or round window rupture, etc. Swallowing or a Valsalva manoeuvre with the nares pinched may keep the Eustachian tubes open - a trick many people use in aircraft. Even teeth may become painful with pressure changes, particularly when diseased.

Further references.
Liebow et al. (1959) : Two cases with air trapping in the lungs - thought to be the cause of air embolism in men learning to escape from submarines.
Campbell Golding et al. (1960) : 2 pts. with lung cysts & decompression sickness constructing the Dartford tunnel. and two had ill defined linear or nodular densities in the lungs (probably from air embolism) and recovered.
Davidson (1964) : Pulmonary changes in decompression sickness in 3 compressed air workers at the Clyde Tunnel - one died with lung, mediastinal and subcutaneous emphysema (had a large subpleural bulla in the right lower lobe).
Krantz and Holtas (1983) : Post-mortem CT in a diving fatality.
MacLeod et al. (1988) : Demonstrated ischaemic areas in the brains of three divers using Tc99mHMPAO and SPETS tomography. Two were young naval ratings undergoing submarine escape training from depths of 18 and 28 m., and the third a 47 year old recreational diver, who had repeatedly dived to about 30 m with inadequate decompression. All needed recompression treatment, and slow decompression.
Carvalho and Denison (1989) : Pulmonary barotrauma and secondary gas embolism are serious hazards in diving and submarine escape, which result from rapid ascent when an air space does not empty fast enough and ruptures. It is more likely to occur in 'disordered' than healthy lungs. They performed CT studies in **expiration** in 48 divers (or submariners) and 16 potential divers, following suspected barotrauma, chest injury or with a history of lung disease. Bullae, or areas of lung which did not deflate properly, were found in 8 of 11 divers with previous barotrauma, 1 diver without barotrauma and in 2 potential divers.
Horizon programme, 'Perils of the Deep' - BBC 2, 23 Jan. 1989.
Saywell (1989) : Reported the case of a 21 year old rating undergoing submarine escape training. After his first ascent from 9m, he had transient right sided chest pain, but seemed clinically normal. He then made another similar ascent, after which he was pale and unsteady, with dizziness and diplopia. He was immediately recompressed to 50 m pressure, and slowly decompressed, but developed a right pneumothorax. Despite tube drainage, this persisted with a broncho-pleural fistula. At thoracotomy multiple cysts were found in the right lung; these were also shown by subsequent CT. Although routine inspiration and expiration PA radiographs, taken before training, had been regarded as normal, the expiratory one on review showed gross air trapping in the RUL, indicating the presence of the cysts.
Edmonds et al. (1992) : Investigation of diving fatalities.
Roobottom et al. (1994) : Diagnosis of fatal gas embolism with plain film radiography - two young male divers - intracardiac and intracerebral gas.

Pearson (1994) : The lungs and diving.
Harris et al. (1995) : Scuba diving accident with near drowning and decompression sickness.
Colman (1996) : Scuba diving, medical and other aspects - in 1995 there were 15 fatal diving accidents in the UK (75,000 divers with 3 million dives) compared with 21 fatalities due to sailing.
Reuter et al. (1996 & 1997) : CT of the chest in diving related pulmonary barotrauma - 11 pts. - 5 showed subpleural emphysematous blebs or cysts (not detected by conventional radiography) - recommended spiral CT in all pts. who have suspected barotrauma to predict future fitness to dive.

Mediastinal gas and pulmonary interstitial emphysema.

(a) **A spontaneous pneumomediastinum and pulmonary interstitial emphysema** are often accompanied by surgical emphysema of the neck or chest wall. In about half of the severe cases there is also a pneumothorax.

There are many causes: including **trauma** (including surgical trauma to the chest, endoscopy, oesophageal or bronchial rupture - see p. 11.3), **asthma** (see mechanism below & p. 19.58), **straining** with parturition, belching, vomiting, hiccuping, prolonged Valsalva manoeuvres (p. 13.19), violent coughing, straining at stool, strong exercise, **mountain or decompression sickness** (p. 8.6), some **infections** (e.g. cytomegalus virus - p. 19.29), and **drug abuse** (heroin, cannabis, etc.). It may even be a presenting feature in some patients with **anorexia nervosa**, and occur with **starvation**. About 5 - 15% of patients having mechanical respiration develop subcutaneous emphysema and pneumothoraces and some have pulmonary interstitial emphysema and a pneumomediastinum - these may also occasionally be present with bronchial obstruction caused by tumours, pressure from nodes, etc.

In **asthma** gas escapes from the smaller bronchi or alveoli as a result of bronchospasm, mucosal oedema and inspissation of secretions, causing air to be trapped with stretching of the alveolar walls. This stretching and gaseous distension induces rupture of the alveolar walls, the escaping air passing along the peri-vascular and broncho-vascular sheaths to the hila, and thence into the mediastinum. It may then pass upwards into the neck or decompress through the parietal pleura covering the mediastinum, to produce a pneumothorax.

Rupture of the alveolar walls also occurs with trauma, and with the other causes, as a result of air-trapping, etc.

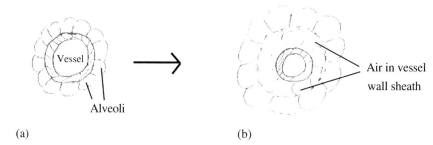

(a)   (b)

Fig. 6.13   Escape of air from alveoli - (a) Normal.   (b) Air in vessel wall sheath.
[See also Macklin (1935 & 1937) and Macklin and Macklin (1944)].
Note: gas in perivascular and peribronchial spaces can be shown by CT - see refs. below.

Many signs of a pneumomediastinum have been described: -
(i) a sharply defined radiolucent line framing the heart and pericardium on frontal chest radiographs, and between the heart and sternum on lateral views, where it may outline the thymus giving rise in young children) to the '**thymic main-sail**' and the '**spinnaker-sail**' signs (see Fig. 18.5, p. 18.18).
(ii) gas outlining the aortic arch and great vessels,
(iii) gas around the pulmonary trunk and right pulmonary artery ('**ring around the artery sign**' seen on a lateral view - Hammond, 1984, Landay et al., 1985, Piscitelli et al., 1988).

Fig. 6.14 - 'Ring around the artery sign' on lateral radiograph.

(iv) gas outlining the SVC, azygos and innominate veins, sometimes with a 'V' between them (Cyrlak et al., 1984),

(v) a sharply angulated 'V' shaped gas collection where the left side of the diaphragm meets the para-spinal tissues, especially seen with rupture of the oesophagus (Naclerio, 1957),

(vi) ? gas separating the two layers of the inferior phrenic ligaments (p. 2.35 & Fig. 2.34) - (distinguish from localised and loculated posterior mediastinal or extra-pleural pneumothoraces).

(vii) gas extending medially across the extra-pleural space below the right and left lungs (the '**continuous diaphragm sign**' especially in children - normally the central part is invisible - Levin, 1973),

(viii) sometimes gas may also be seen outlining the upper and lower surfaces of the diaphragm, or its sternal origins on a lateral radiograph (Kleinman et al., 1978),

(ix) interstitial emphysema of the lungs outlining the trachea, main bronchi (esp. left) and bronchovascular bundles, (note that the right main bronchus is often normally outlined by air-filled lung or fat - see Figs. 1.36 & 1.38),

(x) emphysema of the chest wall and subcutaneous tissues,

(xi) an accompanying pneumothorax in 50% (Lillard and Allen, 1965).

For illustrations of pneumomediatinum see Illus. **PNEUMOMEDIASTINUM.**   An example of interstitial gas in the lungs is shown in Illus.**GAS   INTERSTITIAL,   Fibrosing   alveolitis Pt. 25.**

(b) **Gas mediastinography** was used in some centres, prior to the advent of CT, for the better demonstration of mediastinal tissues both on plain radiographs and tomograms. The gas was injected via the neck (trans-tracheally or via a catheter inserted into the wound following scalene node biopsy), trans-sternally, behind the xiphisternum, or pre-sacrally (the route mainly used for the retroperitoneum). It was particularly used for assessing the spread of tumours, including bronchogenic tumours, and for the thymus. A knowledge of how gas spreads throughout the mediastinum, helps in understanding the spread of tumours, haematomas, and abscesses in the chest. Injected gas widens the mediastinum, by displacing the mediastinal pleura laterally; it fills the anterior mediastinum, especially the thymic area, and tracks around the trachea and oesophagus as well as the aorta and pericardium. It has also been injected prior to CT to better delineate the mediastinum.

Besides air, oxygen, nitrous oxide and carbon dioxide have been used, but the last two are really only of value for the first check injection (i.e. ensuring that the gas is not being injected intravascularly) as they are too quickly soluble in tissue fluids.

Illus. **PNEUMOMEDIASTINUM, Thymus Pts. 2, 3, 4, 5** & **27** show (a) the thymus demonstrated by a spontaneous pneumomediastinum. Illus. **RETROPERITONEAL   GAS, Bone deposit Pt. 18 & Adrenals Pts. 17 and 18** - a soft tissue mass around a spinal deposit in a patient with lung cancer (which was not causing any demonstrable bone erosion on plain radiographs or tomograms), a large phaeochromocytoma and normal adrenal glands - the last also clearly shows the origins of the psoas muscles.

Further references.
Lillard and Allen (1965) : The extrapleural air sign in pneumomediastinum.
Ruttley and Mills (1971) : Subcutaneous emphysema and pneumomediastinum in diabetic ketoacidosis.
Toomey and Chinnock (1975) : Spontaneous emphysema, pneumomediastinum and pneumothorax in diabetic ketoacidosis.
Schulman et al. (1982) : Some air in unusual places - some causes and ramifications of pneumomediastinum in five cases. Three were probably caused by straining against a closed glottis during violent exercise, criminal assault or competitive sport. They pointed out that as well as tracking into the mediastinum, chest wall and neck, it can also track downwards through the diaphragmatic openings producing extraperitoneal emphysema, outlining the under aspect of the diaphragm, etc.
Aldridge et al. (1986) : Reported the occurrence of spontaneous pneumomediastinum in two young men who stowed away in the cold hold of a ship and had very little to eat or drink during the 17 day voyage.
Beyers and Melonas (1987) : The visible wall of a main bronchus - a radiological sign of pneumomediastinum, especially on the left.

Varkey and Kory (1973) : Mediastinal and subcutaneous emphysema following pulmonary function tests.
Westcott and Cole (1974) : Interstitial pulmonary emphysema in children and adults.
Maunder et al. (1984) : Subcutaneous and mediastinal emphysema.
Woodring (1985) : Pulmonary interstitial emphysema in the adult.
Goldberg et al. (1987) : Pneumomediastinum associated with cocaine abuse.
Boothroyd and Barson (1988) : Pulmonary interstitial emphysema.
Unger et al. (1989) : Interstitial emphysema in adults.
Agia and Hurst (1990) : Pneumomediastinum following Heimlich manoeuvre - male aged 8 choked on a fishbone.
Cunningham et al. (1992) : Pulmonary interstitial emphysema - review.
Parker et al. (1993) : Mechanisms of ventilator-induced lung injury.
Janz and Pierson (1994) : Pneumothorax and barotrauma.
Mumford et al. (1996) : Clinically significant pulmonary barotrauma in a 24 yr old non-smoking male 24 hrs after inflating 20 party balloons in one hour.
Satoh et al. (1996) : CT of interstitial pulmonary emphysema.
Kim et al. (1999) : Polypoid endobronchial **Hodgkin's** disease with pneumomediastinum + mediastinal lymph nodes.
Wintermark et al. (1999) : Blunt traumatic pneumomediastinum in a 19 year old woman - CT revealed the Macklin effect, which probably occurs in up to 10% of blunt chest trauma cases.

Condorelli (1936) : First reported the use of gas mediastinography.
Simécek and Holub (1961), Hughes et al. (1962), Ikins et al. (1962) and Sumerling and Irvine (1966) : Gas mediastinography for assessing the spread of bronchial carcinoma.
Condorelli et al. (1951) and Pohlenz et al. (1966) : Trans-tracheal introduction of gas.
Hughes et al. (1962) : Retro-xiphisternal insufflation of gas.
Ikins et al. (1962) : CO_2 Insufflation via a catheter in the scalene area.
Baccaglini (1951) : Gas mediastinography via the presacral route.
Bariety et al. (1965) and Pohlenz et al. (1966) : Gas mediastinography for the thymus.
Nordenström (1967a & 1969a) : Injected Lipiodol as well as gas to outline enlarged mediastinal lymph nodes.
Kreel et al. (1964) : Trans-sternal route.
Mitsuoka et al. (1981) and Sone et al. (1980 & 1982) : Gas pneumomediastinum prior to CT.

Examples of:

Gas forming infection are shown in   Illus. **GAS FORMING INFECTION** and **GAS GANGRENE.**

Gas in joints - having been pulled out of solution - are shown in Illus. **GAS IN JOINTS/DISCS.**

Pneumoperitoneum.

This may be mimicked by Chilaiditi's syndrome (see ps. 15.8-9) and if present usually allows the underside of the diaphragm to be visualised, unless the gas is trapped by adhesions or limited to the lesser sac. A spontaneous pneumoperitoneum most commonly implies an intestinal perforation, which occasionally may be asymptomatic e.g. in patients with small bowel diverticula (Illus. **PNEUMOPERITONEUM Pt. 5a - b**; other cases are quoted below) and in some elderly or long-stay patients (esp. in mental hospitals) with gross constipation and stercoral ulceration.

Text books often quote as an asymptomatic cause pneumatosis intestinalis, but this appears to be very unusual, as none of the cysts (if they should rupture) contain sufficient gas - Illus. **PNEUMATOSIS**. However some cases have been reported, and some have both small bowel diverticula and pneumatosis. Pneumatosis intestinalis appears not to be related to asthma per se, but to nitrogen accumulation as a result of decreased pressure in the abdominal cavity (like gas pulled out of solution in 'vacuum discs' or stressed joints - see Illus. **GAS IN JOINTS/DISCS**) and can be 'cured' by breathing a greater concentration of oxygen or the use of a hyperbaric oxygen chamber (the treatment lasting long enough for the residual nitrogen in the cysts to be adsorbed). Peritoneal gas can occur in females following vaginal douches with a bulb syringe or effervescent fluid; it may occur when a mobile uterus can pump air through the Fallopian tubes - such has been reported in charladies who scrubbed floors on their hands and knees, and in a post-partum woman carrying out knee-chest position exercises. The presence of gas below the diaphragm has also been used to confirm the patency of Fallopian tubes after gas insufflation into them.

An artificial pneumoperitoneum used to be used to demonstrate the external surfaces of the liver and spleen (see p. 17.2) and the author has used it to show the under aspect of the diaphragm in a patient with a liposarcoma of the diaphragm (Illus. **DIAPHRAGM TUMOUR Pt. 1a-b**) and also in obese females to demonstrate the ovaries before ultrasound was available.

Catheter drainage of a large uncomfortable pneumoperitoneum in a dying patient in a hospice is shown in Illus. **PNEUMOPERITONEUM Pt. 6a-b**.

References.

Rigler (1941) : Sign of spontaneous pneumoperitoneum - gas outside of bowel loops, as well as the inside.

Dodek and Friedman (1953) : Spontaneous pneumoperitoneum.

Spensley et al. (1956) : Unusual causes of free intraperitoneal air in acute conditions of the abdomen.

Herrington (1962 & 1967) : Spontaneous asymptomatic pneumoperitoneum in jejunal diverticulosis 'apparently results gross faecal contamination, entering the peritoneal cavity through minute perforations in the wall of the thin-walled diverticula as a result of hyperactive peristaltic activity.'

Wright and Lumsdan (1975) : Recurrent pneumoperitoneum due to jejunal diverticulosis + review of causes of spontaneous pneumoperitoneum.

Wright, P.H. (1975) : Oxygen therapy for pneumatosis coli.

Craft and Ellis (1967) : Pneumoperitoneum due to pneumatosis intestinalis associated with jejunal diverticula.

Chapter 7 : **The Pulmonary and Bronchial Vessels, Pulmonary Vascular Abnormalities including Embolism, Pulmonary and Bronchial Angiography, and A/V Malformations.**

The pulmonary vessels and hilar regions - distinguishing nodes or tumour masses from hilar vessels.

The gross anatomy of the pulmonary trunk and vessels has already been discussed on ps. 1.33 - 35.

When reading chest radiographs, it is always essential to study the pulmonary vessels, to note the normal anatomy and any deviations from this. The vessels are roughly symmetrical in number on the two sides, and the pulmonary veins are situated lower in the hilar regions than the arteries - they also cross the arteries in passing towards the rear of the left atrium In viewing radiographs one should note the **'horizontal V-shaped' right pulmonary artery,** and the **'crook-shaped' left pulmonary artery** and follow the branches into the respective lobes of the two lungs. The pulmonary arteries follow the major bronchi from the hilum, and the smaller bronchi to the periphery of the lung, small branches usually being visible up to 1.5 cm from the lung periphery.

In recognising the normal vascular pattern one should note apparent additions to this or dilatations, etc. Such apparent additions may be due to anterior or posterior structures (e.g. masses in the apex of a lower lobe) or to tumours or nodes in the hilum itself. In the differentiation of hilar masses it is important to remember that the **right pulmonary artery and its branches lie in front of the carinal plane,** whilst the **left pulmonary artery and its branches lie mainly superiorly, and posteriorly to the carina** (Fig. 1.47 a - c); thus if a mass or enlarged nodes lie anteriorly on the left, or posteriorly on the right, they are very unlikely to be mimicked by enlarged vascular structures. The **pulmonary veins** pass to the back of the left atrium and should also be distinguished from nodal enlargement which may occur in this lower position (pulmonary ligament and paraoesophageal nodes - groups 9 and 8 respectively on lymph node mapping system - Fig. 13.9, p. 13.16).

Besides lying behind the carinal plane, the left pulmonary artery lies superior and posterior to the left upper lobe bronchus (a point also made by Vix and Klatte, 1970) and is well delineated in most cases by surrounding air filled lung. The right pulmonary artery lies in the mid part of the hilum and is surrounded by structures which might be expected to make it less distinct. However, as it initially has a straighter lateral course, it is usually clearly seen on lateral radiographs and tomograms.

Vessels always have to be distinguished from nodes. Often this differentiation is obvious on plain radiographs or conventional tomograms, or with using Valsalva/ Müller manoeuvres. In more difficult cases, CT, contrast enhanced CT, pulmonary angiography (including DVI or MR) may be required for differentiation.

Chang and Zinn (1976): Felt that with conventional tomography, nodes were best demonstrated on lateral sections. They found most lymph node masses to be somewhat lobulated and often encircled the orifices of the corresponding lobar, intermediate or segmental bronchi. They are also separate from the arterial and venous branchings.

Illustrations of the pulmonary arteries are shown under Illus. **PULMONARY ARTERIES** etc.

Historical review.

Aeby (1880) in his book 'The Bronchial Tree in Mammals and in Man' thought that branching only took place from the dorsal or ventral aspects of a larger bronchus or artery.

Ewart (1889) challenged this and showed that the bronchial and arterial branches may arise from any part of the circumference as seen in the 'tripod arrangement' of the true relationship between the pulmonary artery. or bronchus. He also showed the true relationship between the pulmonary artery, bronchus and vein, i.e. that the artery usually lay above, lateral and close to the corresponding bronchus, whilst the vein was situated below and to the medial side. He also could not accept Aeby's conception of an 'eparterial' bronchus in the right upper lobe.

Hickey (1905 - see also p. ii) noted that shadows radiating from the hilar areas were mainly vascular and in 1922 Sergent et al. 'proved' that these were vascular and not bronchial shadows.

Brenner (1935) found that the pulmonary artery branches > 1,000μ were elastic and between 100 and 1,000 μ were muscular.

Greineder (1935) took tomograms in posterior, anterior, lateral and oblique positions and was able to demonstrate not only lobar arteries, but also lobar veins and other main tributaries. He found that arteries, bronchi, and veins occur in that order (i.e. alphabetical - A, B & V) proceeding anticlockwise in the right lung, and clockwise in the left. Lodge (see below) termed this observation **'Greineder's Law'** (see diagrams Fig. 1.51, p. 1.38 - where this largely holds for the upper lobes but not in the lower).

Miller (1937) in his book 'The Lung' stated that in the pig and dog the pulmonary artery follows the subdivisions of the bronchial tree and each main branch comes to occupy a position posterior and slightly lateral to the bronchus, whilst the venous trunks lie anterior and slightly medial to the corresponding bronchi.

Twining (1938) in the radiological text-book 'British Authors' gave a general account of the main pulmonary vessels.

Lodge* (1946 from Sheffield) studied the radiological anatomy of the pulmonary vessels and found after allowing for some upper lobe variations (where two thinner vessels may replace one thick trunk) that "on the whole the arterial system follows the branching and distribution of the bronchial tree", whereas "the veins tend to be distant from the bronchi and to lie in their interspaces" (i.e. inter-lobular connective tissue). He also found that veins "cross the bronchi at an angle and are never parallel with them". Lodge also quoted Fishberg (1937) - pulmonary changes of cardiac failure : (i) Increased visibility of the vessels which appear dilated, (ii) whole vascular tree becomes ill-defined and (iii) lung fields are obscured by areas of oedema and pleural transudates. He also pointed out that Berthwhistle (1942) was incorrect in ascribing the branching pulmonary shadows to bronchi!

* Obiit 16 Feb. 1997 - Sir Thomas ("Tommy") Lodge (knighted in 1974) - Illus. **FAMOUS PEOPLE** - was awarded the Twining Medal of the Faculty of Radiologists for this Thesis. He was later President of the Faculty of Radiologists - precursor of the Royal College of Radiologists, and was awarded the College's Gold Medal in 1986. He also gave the author early help with this book, checking some points with his Thesis. Obituaries in Clinical Radiology, 1997, **52**, 637 - 638 & BIR Annual Report, 1997, 65-66.   (see also note on p. 4.2).

Elliott and Reid (1965) studied the branching of the pulmonary artery using a barium-gelatine suspension and cutting serial sections and noted:

(i) A **great disparity between the branching patterns** of the **pulmonary artery and the bronchial tree** due to the presence of **numerous supernumerary arterial branches, most of which are muscular**.

(ii) If the whole branching pattern of the artery is considered it is clear that the pulmonary artery is dominantly a **'muscular organ'**.

(iii) Muscular arteries also arise directly from the elastic part of the axial artery and be interspersed among the elastic arteries.

(iv) The **diameter of succeeding side-branches** does **not decrease in a regular fashion**; one branch may be much larger or smaller than its predecessor.

(v) It is the **diameter of an artery which determines its structure rather than its proximity to the hilum**.

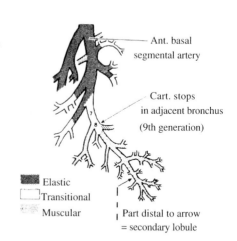

Reproduced with permission from Clinical Radiology.

Heitzman (1984): like Elliott and Reid (see above) also noted that besides the pulmonary artery branches following the bronchi down to the secondary lobules, there are others not so clearly related - the **'supernumerary arteries'**.

NB The muscular branches, as shown above, are often blocked by small pulmonary emboli, and the final branching pattern may account for the peripheral lodgement of tumour emboli (with their peripheral distribution) and also parasites (also giving rise to a peripheral pattern on CT with eosinophilia - see p. 19.59).

Simon and Rona (1976): standard of the descending (basal) pulmonary artery in children from the routine chest radiograph.

Moore et al. (1988): studied the relationship between pulmonary pressure and pulmonary artery diameter in pulmonary hypertension and found : (a) in patients with primary hypertension and chronic thrombo-embolic pulmonary hypertension, dilatation correlated with raised pulmonary vascular resistance and reduced cardiac output, but not with mean arterial pressure, and
(b) In those with chronic lung disease, no correlations were shown, although a trend between raised pressure and size was seen. They speculated that pulmonary artery compliance was an important factor in determining the degree of dilatation in response to raised pressure. They concluded that estimations of pressure cannot be made from measurements of pulmonary artery size, without a knowledge of the underlying disease.

Sanders, C. et al. (1988): reviewed the appearances of atrial septal defects on chest radiographs in older adults (70 patients over age 50). A typical ASD showed shunt vascularity without left atrial enlargement. Atypical features included : left atrial enlargement, pulmonary venous hypertension, interstitial pulmonary oedema and absence of shunt vascularity - these were common.

McHugh and Brunton (1990): reported a post-mortem chest radiograph in a young woman who had been exsanguinated and had gross venous air embolism, as a result of suicide with a shot-gun blast to her brain, and noted that the lung vessels were almost invisible showing that **blood within them normally shows them up** (see also p.6.31 for further note on this case).

Lavender et al. (1962) and Lavender and Doppman (1962) studied the vascular anatomy of the hilar regions by tomography (in the supine position) in patients with mitral valve disease and left ventricular failure, and also in normal individuals. They found that arteries could usually be differentiated from veins. There was a certain amount of anatomical variation between different subjects, but the main vascular pattern was fairly constant. (In the erect position there is usually a greater separation of hilar vessels). The pulmonary artery was shown to be enlarged in patients with mitral stenosis, having pulmonary arterial hypertension, and a similar enlargement was found in over 50% of cases of left ventricular failure. In both groups the lateral border of the hilum was straightened or convex, a change shown to be due to enlarged upper lobe veins (a useful sign in pulmonary hypertension).

Raphael and Newman (1966) studied variations in calibre of the lower zone pulmonary veins with changes in posture. They found a reduction in the calibre of the lower lobe veins in normal subjects in changing from the supine to the erect position.

Pulmonary arteries and veins may often be **differentiated by their different branching patterns**. The segmental arteries tend to continually bifurcate with axial notching and follow the bronchi, whilst the veins (which contain no valves) have branches joining from the side, and roughly maintain their original direction, the inferior veins running almost horizontally. Coussement et al. (1984) termed the arterial pattern '**division dichotomique**'.

In the lung periphery the smaller veins may also show a dichotomous combination pattern, in between that of the arterial branches. Peripheral pulmonary veins may also take a curved subpleural course.

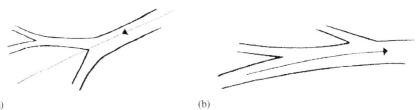

(a)   (b)

Fig. 7.1 Branching patterns of (a) pulmonary arteries and (b) pulmonary veins (after Coussement, 1984, Le Poumon Normal, by permission.).

Size of pulmonary arteries.
    The size of the pulmonary arteries is important - are they generally enlarged and plethoric i.e. contain too much blood, as with intra-cardiac left to right shunting or in polycythaemia? **Proximal enlargement** occurs with pulmonary hypertension, cor pulmonale, etc. and **peripheral pruning** with pulmonary hypertension, emphysema or severe lung scarring. Thinning of vessels in an area may occur acutely with pulmonary embolism. Vessels may be displaced by large emphysematous bullae, etc. As shown in Figs. 1.47 (a, b & c) - ps. 1.34 - 35 - the lower lobe vessels tend to be larger than those in the upper lobes, on radiographs taken in the erect position.

Fig. 7.2   Normal measurements of pulmonary arteries on an erect radiograph (after Elliott and Reid, 1965, with permission from Clinical Radiology).

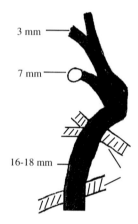

3 mm

7 mm

16-18 mm

A change in size, or reversal of the normal upper lobe/lower lobe ratio occurs with raised pulmonary venous pressure, lower lobe pulmonary or lung disease; the resultant upper lobe 'blood diversion' being best seen in mitral stenosis. Enlargement of upper lobe vessels is also best seen with intra-cardiac left to right shunts and with a hyperdynamic circulation, as with severe anaemia. The pulmonary arteries may also be enlarged in those who live at high altitudes (Ghio et al., 1996).

Several authors have attempted to measure the maximum normal diameters of the main pulmonary arteries by CT. Kuriyama et al. (1984) on Japanese subjects and using contrast enhancement suggested a figure of 2.86cm, whilst Edwards et al. (1998 from Cambridge) studied 100 normal subjects and 12 patients with pulmonary artery hypertension with unenhanced CT examinations and determined the upper limit of normal to be 3.32cm.

Causes of small or large hila.
(a) **Unilateral small hilum** - usually associated with contralateral hilar enlargement.
Causes : include lower lobe collapse, reflex vaso-constriction secondary to hypoxia, involvement of hilar vessels by tumour (**Oeser's sign** - see p. 7.10 - 12), poor development of a pulmonary artery per se or due to Swyer-James /Macleod syndrome (ps. 7. 9 - 10), severe emphysema of one lung, pulmonary thrombo-embolism. old TB scarring, chronic mediastinitis (see p. 18.4).
    Chronic cases may be associated with systemic-pulmonary vascular anastomoses (see p. 7.14). A lung perfusion scan may show reduced or absent pulmonary vascular perfusion.

(b) **Bilateral small hila** are usually due to smaller vessels than normal.
Causes : include asthma, idiopathic pulmonary hypertension, diffuse pulmonary arteries with attenuated distal branches), congenital heart disease, including pulmonary atresia, tricuspid atresia, Eisenmenger's syndrome (pulmonary hypertension with a reversed shunt due to ASD, VSD or PDA), Ebstein's anomaly (deformed tricuspid valve), etc. (For reviews of Eisenmenger's syndrome see Spitz 1968a, Fallot's tetralogy - Johnson, 1965 and Ebstein's anomaly - Spitz,

1968b, Mu-Sheng et al., 1986, Link et al., 1988, MR imaging in four cases, Garrett et al., 1986 - ciné CT, and Choi et al, 1994 and Eustace et al., 1994 - ciné MR of Ebstein anomaly).

(c) **Unilateral hilar enlargement** - this may be due to tumour per se, enlarged nodes, or vessels, or be simulated by overlying masses e.g. in the apex of a lower lobe or lying anteriorly. Common causes: include bronchial tumour masses, bronchogenic cysts, adenomas, nodal enlargements secondary to tumours, reticulosis, tuberculosis or fungus infection (usually aspergillosis in the UK), etc. Unilateral enlargement in sarcoidosis in uncommon. True or apparent vascular enlargements include pulmonary artery aneurysm, pulmonary embolism (due to altered blood flow), contralateral pulmonary dilatation secondary to a reduction on the other side (embolism, hypoxia, hypoplasia, Swyer-James /Macleod syndrome, etc. Apparent enlargement may be due to upper lobe collapse (see Illus. **COLLAPSE LUL** esp. **Pts. 24a-b, 26, 27, 28 31 & PULM ARTERY Pt. 10a-c).**

(d) **Bilateral hilar enlargement** may be due to enlarged vessels (Illus. **PULM ARTS ENLARGED**) or nodes (Illus. **HILAR NODES**). Enlarged vessels may be seen with left to right shunts (with an ASD these may be aneurysmal and may even be found in symptomless old ladies!), obstructive airways disease and 'cor pulmonale'. Nodal enlargements may be due to sarcoid (but note that paratracheal and subcarinal node enlargement is usually present as well), lymphoma (but unilateral enlargement is more common), leukaemia, metastases (often in association with lymphangitis carcinomatosa), infection (acute tuberculosis - now most commonly seen in Asians, glandular fever, fungus diseases, amyloid, myelomatosis, etc.).

(e) **Enlarged pulmonary artery** - post-stenotic dilatation in pulmonary stenosis.

High pulmonary arteries.
    Occasionally the pulmonary trunk or the left pulmonary artery may be found at a higher level than normal, at the level of the aortic arch, where it may simulate a left-sided mediastinal mass, lateral to the aortic arch or a left upper lobe collapse which can give rise to a similar appearance.

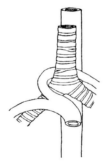

Fig. 7. 3   High left pulmonary artery.
(Note - a similar elevation may be
    produced by LUL collapse).

Fig. 7. 4   Aberrant left pulmonary artery
(After Philp et al., 1972, with permission
    from Clinical Radiology).

See also - collapsed LUL (Fig. 2.14, p. 2.19) and Illus. **PULM ART ELEVATION**.

Reference.
Mencini and Proto (1982) : High main pulmonary arteries.

Anomalous (or aberrant) left pulmonary artery - also known as 'pulmonary artery vascular sling'
    In this condition, the main pulmonary artery fails to bifurcate normally; it becomes elongated and follows the course of the right pulmonary artery, the left arising from it extra-pericardially and from its posterior part. It then sweeps around the junction of the trachea and the right main

bronchus to pass between the trachea, the right main bronchus or the oesophagus, causing unilateral emphysema, dyspnoea, stridor, wheezing or dysphagia. In some the anomaly causes no symptoms. Sometimes cardiac and/or bronchial abnormalities are associated, e.g. the intermediate bronchus arising from the left main bronchus. The oesophagus is usually indented anteriorly and displaced to the left by the aberrant left pulmonary artery. Both infantile and adult cases have been found.

References.
Wittenborg et al. (1956) : Anomalous course of left pulmonary artery with respiratory obstruction.
Jue et al. (1965) : Anomalous origin of the left pulmonary artery from the right pulmonary artery - two cases and literature review.
Kale et al. (1970) : Aberrant left pulmonary artery presenting as a mediastinal mass in an adult.
Philp et al. (1972) : Aberrant left pulmonary artery - three cases in children - diagnosis from plain radiographs and barium swallow.
Stone et al. (1980) : Anomalous left pulmonary artery - two adult cases.
Moncada et al. (1983) : Chronic stridor and tracheal narrowing by an anomalous left pulmonary artery, causing a 'vascular sling'.
Wells et al. (1988) : Reconsideration of the anatomy of sling left pulmonary artery - **type I** with normal bronchial anatomy and **type II** with narrowing or a rudimentary RMB or bridging bronchus from the LMB.
Cobby et al. (1989) : Jekyll and Hyde chest radiographs (unilateral lobar emphysema due to anomalous left pulmonary artery).
Hendry et al. (1991) : Sling left pulmonary artery with congenital airway stenosis - non-invasive investigation and conservative management? (Child aged 3 months - rudimentary RMB and narrowed LMB).
Vogi et al. (1993) : MRI in pre- and postoperative assessment of tracheal stenosis due to pulmonary artery sling.

Other causes of pulmonary artery disease.
   These include poor development, intrinsic disease, pulmonary embolism, arterial wall disease as in Takayasu's arteritis (see p. 10.17), pulmonary hypertension or secondary compression by fibrosis from sarcoid, TB, fungus infection, idiopathic fibrosis, etc. or nodes enlarged by tumour, amyloid or rheumatoid. Occasionally a tumour may develop in a pulmonary artery (see p. 7.19).

Some references
Watts et al. (1984) : Pulm. artery compression by a bronchogenic cyst simulating congenital pulm. artery stenosis.
Cramer et al. (1985) : Pulmonary artery compression by aortic aneurysm.
Drake et al (1997) : Pulmonary artery occlusion in two pts. caused by tuberculous mediastinal nodes.
Beaconsfield et al. (1998) : Pulmonary artery stenosis due to tuberculous pulmonary arteritis.

For references to sarcoidosis causing pulmonary compression - see p. 19.73.
For references to histoplasmosis causing pulmonary compression - see ps. 18.4 & 19.45 & 19.47.

Dysmorphic, hypoplastic or hypogenetic lung, congenital veno-lobar and 'scimitar' syndromes.
   These are more common in females, and on the right side. They may be found in children and adults. Many are asymptomatic or have only minor symptoms. More marked cases may have dyspnoea, fatigue and repeated infections. The syndromes describe a collection of thoracic abnormalities, which include 'mirror image lung', hypogenetic lung, and 'scimitar syndrome' (with a primitive foetal and arcuate shaped large vein, lying peripherally and crossing the inter-lobar fissures, draining into the IVC, azygos, hepatic, portal, or occasionally inferior pulmonary veins) - For Illus. see **HYPOPLASIA/APLASIA, PUL VEIN ANOMALOUS** or **DEVELOP ABN**.
   Compared with the Swyer-James (Macleod) syndrome (ps. 7.9 - 10), the volume of a hypoplastic lung is usually much smaller than normal. Its blood supply is often reduced, and may be via a hypoplastic pulmonary artery or from bronchial type vessels from the aorta. As with a sequestrated segment, these may arise from the abdominal aorta. Sometimes the vascular abnormalities are complicated - e.g. with a **proximally interrupted main pulmonary artery**, reversed blood flow to this from bronchial vessel anastomoses and drainage via a scimitar vein.
   The anomaly is often associated with diaphragmatic abnormalities, duplication, a hernia, reduplication cysts or other congenital abnormalities such as cystic adenomatoid malformation. Absence of right middle and upper lobes is common and lung agenesis may an extreme example of

the condition. This hypoplasia may give rise to the spurious appearance of an anterior mediastinal mass on plain lateral radiographs, due to rotation of the heart and mediastinum; though Felson (1986) thought that excessive fat or areolar tissue may be responsible in some cases. Agenesis may also be associated with other anomalies such as patent ductus, etc.

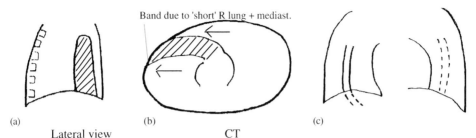

(a)   (b)   (c)

Lateral view   CT

Fig. 7. 5   (a) and (b) Mediastinal deformity and shift, giving a similar appearance to that seen following lobectomy (short R lung in AP direction); it also makes the heart outline indistinct. (c) Position of scimitar veins.

'**Scimitar veins**' **may be mimicked by systemic arteries** (both of which appear to traverse the normal fissure lines) or '**meandering pulmonary veins**' (which connect to the left atrium and may be associated with hypogenesis of the right lung and cardiac dextroposition). Rarely scimitar veins are bilateral. (See also p. 7.16).

The presence of systemic arteries to the lung with the scimitar syndrome, is explained by embryology. The circulation to the primitive lung bud arises from the splanchnic plexus and in early foetal life there are numerous anastomoses between the postbranchial pulmonary plexus and the primitive ventral and dorsal aortae. When the pulmonary artery develops from the sixth branchial arch and spreads into the developing lung with the bronchial bud, anastomoses occur and the primitive vessels mainly atrophy, the bronchial vessels only remaining. These abdominal vessels commonly pass into the chest via the inferior pulmonary ligaments (ps. 2.32 - 35).

Fig. 7. 6 (a) **Scimitar vein** passing to IVC +   (b) **Horse-shoe** segment of right lung passing systemic artery to dysmorphic lung - CT view.   to left in front of the spine - CT view.

A **horse-shoe lung** is an uncommon anomaly in which there is partial fusion of the two lungs, usually of the postero-basal segments, in the mid-line behind the heart. It is usually accompanied by anomalies of the pulmonary vessels, with e.g. the right pulmonary artery supplying part of the left lung, and anomalous veins of the scimitar type. A fissure may be parallel to the left heart border. Because of repeated infections these cases are often symptomatic.

Iatrogenic **buffalo chest** - both pleural cavities may communicate after surgery, when the chest has been opened by sternotomy. In such cases a pneumothorax may pass into both pleural cavities. A common pleural cavity is normal in some animals (buffalo, sheep, horses, cats, etc.) and a bilateral pneumothorax may be recognised if such animals are radiographed in veterinary practice. Examples may be found in veterinary text-books (e.g. Douglas and Williamson, 1970). Engeler et al. (1992b) noted that a pneumothorax may move from one side to the other after heart lung transplantation. This leaves an open communication between the two sides of the chest that may allow air or fluid to shift from one side to the other (see also p. 14.23).

An **accessory   diaphragm** is a rare congenital anomaly which may be present alone or in association with cardio-pulmonary malformations, including the scimitar syndrome. It occurs most frequently on the right, and is composed of connective and muscular tissue. It extends above the normal hemidiaphragm anteriorly and extends upwards and posteriorly to join the posterior chest wall at the level of the 5th to 7th rib. An accessory diaphragm is usually deficient medially where it crosses the broncho-vascular structures. The affected hemithorax tends to be smaller. It is manifest radiologically as a haziness or blurring of the hemidiaphragm on frontal views and a homogeneous density or abnormal pressure on lateral views. A CT may show upturned distal bronchi and radiating vessels. Most cases have been found in infants.

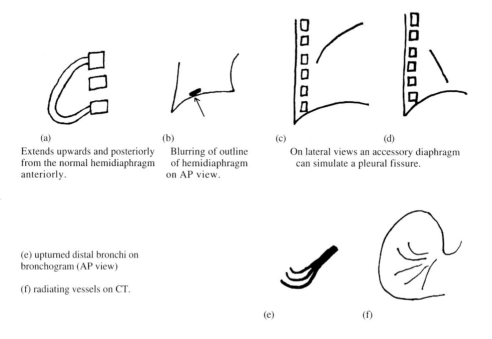

(a)	(b)	(c)	(d)
Extends upwards and posteriorly from the normal hemidiaphragm anteriorly.	Blurring of outline of hemidiaphragm on AP view.	On lateral views an accessory diaphragm can simulate a pleural fissure.	

(e) upturned distal bronchi on bronchogram (AP view)

(f) radiating vessels on CT.

(e)   (f)

Fig. 7.7   Diagrams showing some of the features associated with an 'accessory diaphragm'.

References.

Roehm et al. (1966) : Scimitar syndrome.
Fulsonie and Molnar (1966) : Anomalous pulmonary venous return, pulmonary sequestration, bronchial atresia, aplastic right upper lobe, pericardial defect and intra-thoracic kidney.
Kiely et al. (1967) : Anomalous venous drainage of the right lung to the IVC (review of 70 cases).
Bessolo and Maddison (1968) : Scimitar syndrome.
Morgan and Forker (1971) : Hypoplasia of the right lung, scimitar sign and normal pulmonary venous drainage.
Goodman et al. (1972) : Meandering right pulmonary vein simulating the scimitar syndrome.
Felson (1972 & 1973) : **Pulmonary   agenesis** and related anomalies - these are all facets and part of the same entity; also raised the question - does the abnormal vein look more like a Turkish scimitar or a woman's leg.
Folger (1976) : Scimitar syndrome (anatomy, physiology, development and therapy).
Beizke et al. (1982) : Scimitar syndrome with horse-shoe lung.
Ang and Proto (1984) : CT of congenital venolobar syndrome - a collection of thoracic abnormalities.
Schorlemmer et al. (1984) : Bilateral pneumothoraces secondary to iatrogenic buffalo chest - an unusual complication of mediastinotomy and subclavian vein catheterisation.
Dische et al. (1974) : Horse-shoe lung associated with a variant of the 'scimitar syndrome'.
Freedom et al. (1986) : Horse-shoe lung - five cases.
Frank et al. (1986) : Horse-shoe lung - new plain film finding.
Godwin and Tarver (1986) : Scimitar syndrome - four new cases examined with CT.
Olson and Becker (1986) : CT findings in scimitar syndrome.

Pennes and Ellis (1986) : CT of anomalous pulmonary venous drainage of the LUL.
Schatz et al. (1986) : Partial anomalous venous drainage of the RLL shown by CT.
Clements and Warner (1987) : The 'crossover lung segment' - a variant of scimitar syndrome.
Heron et al. (1988) : Anomalous venous drainage in association with hypogenetic lung. Hypoplastic right lung containing a shadow like a scimitar vein on plain film, but was a large anomalous pulmonary vein. A large right scimitar vein was demonstrated by angiography.
Partridge et al. (1988) : Scimitar, etc. - dysmorphic right lung.
Ersoz et al. (1992) : Horseshoe lung with left lung hypoplasia.
Cerruti et al. (1993) : Bilateral intralobar pulmonary sequestration with horseshoe lung in a woman aged 20.
Figa et al. (1993) : Horseshoe lung - infant with unusual bronchial and pleural anomalies.
Cloutier et al. (1993) : Lung hypoplasia with congenital diaphragmatic hernia in infants.
Gao et al. (1993) : Scimitar syndrome in infancy is usually severe and is associated with a poor prognosis - 13 cases - many had pulmonary hypertension + other cardiovascular anomalies.
Dupuis et al. (1994) : The "horseshoe" lung: six new cases.
Partridge (1995) : The scimitar syndrome - 4 types - 'classical', concealed, partial, + related abnormalities (agenesis with absent pulmonary artery excluded). Pulmonary angiography and aortography are often needed to show the abnormal systemic vessels arising from the abdomen - the area supplied by these usually have a pulmonary artery deficit. An associated ASD may be present. Increased blood flow through the contralateral lung may cause pulmonary hypertension. The scimitar vein most often drains to the right atrium, sometimes the left.
Kriss et al. (1995) : 'Meandering' pulmonary veins (connecting to the left atrium) - asymptomatic 12 year old girl.
Caceres (1996) : Congenital anomalies of the bronchial tree, etc.
Chen et al. (1997) : Crossed ectopic left lung with fusion to the right lung - a variant of 'horseshoe lung'?
Takahashi et al. (1997) : Demonstration of horseshoe lung by electron-beam CT.

Anderson, R. et al. (1958) : **Absence of a pulmonary artery**.
Pool et al. (1962) : Absence of a pulmonary artery - importance of flow in pulmonary hypertension.
Kieffer et al. (1965) : Proximal interruption of a pulmonary artery may be asymptomatic in the absence of pulmonary hypertension or associated vascular abnormalities. Roentgen features and surgical correction.
Ellis et al. (1967) : Some congenital abnormalities of the pulmonary arteries.
Bahler et al. (1969) : Absent right pulmonary artery - problems with diagnosis and treatment.
Felson (1972) : Pulmonary agenesis and related anomalies.
Hoeffel et al. (1974) : Congenital stenoses of the pulmonary artery and its branches are not uncommon.
Hackett et al. (1980) : **High altitude pulmonary oedema** in persons with no right pulmonary artery.
Moser et al. (1989) : Chronic thromboembolic occlusion in the adult can mimic pulmonary artery agenesis.
Lynch and Higgins (1990) : MR imaging of unilateral pulmonary artery anomalies - 7 children - 5 with congenital absence or interruption of a pulmonary artery (2 had narrowing or thrombosis following banding).
Morgan et al. (1991), Catala et al. (1993) : CT and MR of absence of right pulmonary artery in the adult.
Davis et al. (2000) : Proximal interruption of a main pulmonary artery in a man aged 67 who had R lung hypoplasia, R **rib notching** & an **anterior junction line** bowed to the R on a PA film.

Nigogosyan and Osarda (1961), Davis, W. and Allen (1968) : Duplication of the diaphragm (accessory diaphragm).
Nazarian et al. (1971) : Accessory diaphragm - case report with physiological evaluation & surgical correlation.
Kenanaghi and Sherman (1978) : Left sided accessory diaphragm.
Hopkins and Davis (1988) : Haziness of the right hemithorax in a newborn.
Mata et al. (1990) : CT of congenital malformations of the lung.

The Swyer-James or Macleod syndrome (Illus. **SWYER-JAMES SYN**).
    In this condition, as well as the abnormal 'translucency' of a lung or lobe, which is usually a little smaller than normal, the vessels are markedly reduced in calibre within it, and the bronchi distally are poorly formed and ectatic.
    The affected lung also alters but little in size with respiration, and may show air-trapping in expiration (see also under CT below). Lung ventilation and perfusion scans show poor ventilation and very little perfusion (Illus. **SWYER-JAMES SYN, Pts. 1d, 9b & 10c**). Adeno-virus infections have been considered to be the cause (Macpherson et al., 1969). Others may have been due to tuberculosis, etc. Reid and Simon (1962) wrote - "we believe the condition is the result of infective damage to the airways in childhood, to which the small artery and hypoplasia of the lung are secondary". Probably bronchiolitis obliterans occurs with granulomatous tissue plugs leading to severe damage to the terminal and respiratory bronchioles, preventing the normal development of their alveolar buds (see also ps. 3.25-27). In conditions producing pulmonary congestion, only the unaffected lung may show congestive changes (Saleh et al., 1974, Vanker, 1987, and see p.

8.6). Surgical treatment is best avoided unless the patient has a gross and intractable haemoptysis from the bronchiectasis. Repeated minor inflammatory changes may occur within the affected lung.

Studying mediastinal and mediastinal movement by TV fluoroscopy in such patients may be interesting and give some insight into the breathlessness some of these patients get with exercise. A recent case studied by the author (a woman of 45) on inspiration showed paradoxical movement of the mediastinum towards the normal side, and initial elevation of the hemidiaphragm on the same side, as though she had difficulty with **inflation,** as well as the greater known difficulty with **expiration and 'air trapping'** seen in such patients. Perhaps one should consider '**difficult air movement both in inspiration and in expiration**' - difficult due to the impaired distal bronchial ventilation as a result of the poor development.

Foote et al. (1977) reported a case in a scuba diver which resulted in severe air embolism due to the inability to expire air during ascent from the sea bed (see also ps. 6.32 - 33).

A lobar Macleod's syndrome may be more frequent than total lung involvement (Grainger, 1985) and may manifest as loss of volume of a lower lobe, coupled with Macleod involvement of the upper lobe, and appearing more radiolucent than the corresponding contralateral tissue. More severe damage may result in 'Loofa lung' (p. 3.10 & 6.5) or 'destroyed lung' (p. 19.123).

References.
Swyer and James (1953) : Working in Coventry and Warwick described a single case.
Macleod (1954) : Working in Southampton studied nine cases.
Katz and Wagner (1959) : Termed the condition '**unilateral pulmonary emphysema**'.
Felson et al. (1959) : Termed it the '**lazy lung**'.
Margolin et al. (1959) : '**Unilateral hyperlucent lung**'.
Darke et al. (1960) : Unilateral lung transradiancy - physiological study.
Rakower and Moran (1962) : Unilateral hyperlucent lung ('Swyer-James syndrome').
Weg et al. (1965) : Unilateral hyperlucent lung - a physiologic syndrome.
Culiner (1966) : The hyperlucent lung, a problem in differential diagnosis.
MacPherson et al. (1969) : Unilateral hyperlucent lung - a complication of viral pneumonia.
Steinberg and Lyons (1967) : Ipsilateral hypoplasia of the pulmonary artery in advanced bronchiectasis.
Lang et al. (1969) : Bronchopneumonia with serious sequelae in children - evidence of adenovirus type 21 infection.
Kogutt et al. (1973) : Swyer-James syndrome (unilateral hyperlucent lung).
O'Dell et al. (1976) : Ventilation - perfusion studies in the Swyer-James syndrome.
Stokes et al. (1978) : Unilateral hyperlucent lung (Swyer-James syndrome) after severe Mycoplasma pneumonia.
Hekali et al. (1982) : Analysed 40 consecutive patients with chronic unilateral hyperlucent lung and found 18 to have the Swyer-James (Macleod) syndrome (8 localised emphysema, 4 previous massive embolism, 2 previous radiotherapy, and 4 lung tumours - 3 malignant and one benign). The most marked changes were seen with the Swyer-James syndrome and the least with neoplasm.
Peters et al. (1982) : Swyer-James-Macleod syndrome - case with baseline normal chest x-ray.
McLoud et al. (1986) : Considered that the Swyer-James (Macleod) syndrome is part of the larger condition sometimes termed bronchiolitis obliterans (see ps. 3.25 - 28), but **should be differentiated from an endobronchial lesion causing incomplete obstruction of the supplying bronchus and from pulmonary artery agenesis**.
Marti-Bonmati et al. (1989) : Studied nine patients with the Swyer-James syndrome by CT and were able to confirm bronchial patency in all cases, as well as study the peripheral pulmonary arteries and the degree of bronchiectasis. CT sections taken in inspiration and expiration showed little change in the size of the affected lung, but air trapping produced mediastinal shift in expiration towards the normal lung which always deflated during expiration.
Moore et al. (1992) : CT findings in eight patients - air trapping in hyperlucent regions was confirmed by a lack of change in volume on expiratory CT scans in five cases. Bronchiectasis was found in only three patients.

Small hilum and reduced homolateral pulmonary vascularity secondary to a tumour, and contralateral PA enlargement ('Oeser's sign') - Illus. - **OESER SIGN**.
Reduction in the blood supply to a lobe or a lung containing a tumour is very common. This often occurs with considerable hilar and/or mediastinal involvement. It may also occur with relatively small endobronchial masses (even benign ones or foreign bodies) which cause partial obstruction and a reduced oxygen tension in the affected lung. Oeser et al. (1969) described unilateral reduction in the size of the hilum on the side of the tumour as the '**paradoxical hilus sign**' and pointed out that this may occur relatively early with tumour due to an '**alveolar-vascular reflex**' which reduces the calibre of the pulmonary arterial branches on the side of the

tumour (Fig. 7.8). This reduction in vascularity may resemble the Swyer-James (Macleod) syndrome and the affected lung will also show air trapping in expiration, as well as being a little smaller than normal in inspiration.

Apau (1972) found that a foreign body in a right main bronchus caused virtual absence of perfusion to the entire lung, as shown by a perfusion scan. A lowered oxygen tension in the affected lung has been studied experimentally in dogs by Allison and Stanbrook (1980). Its occurrence with adenomas has been noted by McGuinnis and Lull (1976), Spitzer et al. (1979), Fraser and Paré (1983) and by Grainger (1985) who illustrated a case due to a carcinoid of the left main bronchus with return to normal vascularity after resection.

This reflex shutdown, in the presence of anoxia, does not always take place, and collapsed or poorly aerated lung may sometimes maintain its normal perfusion. When this happens blood passing through the anoxic part of the lung will fail to be oxygenated, and will tend to accentuate a patient's hypoxia and breathlessness, This has been shown by scintigraphic studies (Lavender et al., 1981), Sostman et al, 1983, Goddard et al., 1986) and by CT (Bell et al., 1987 who found perfusion of a collapsed left lower lobe which had an 'air bronchogram' but no alveolar aeration and was well perfused as shown by marked enhancement with contrast medium, the lobe being compressed by pleural fluid secondary to an aortic dissection).

A reduction in size of the pulmonary artery on the side of a tumour may also be produced by tumour invasion or constriction by tumour or fibrosis.

Several authors including Held and Siegelman (1974) have illustrated cases of severe constriction of the pulmonary artery secondary to bronchial carcinoma, which have been investigated by pulmonary angiography and isotope lung scans. Tomography will often also show this. Pulmonary artery invasion is difficult to diagnose with CT, but ciné MR may be helpful in showing this. Pulmonary artery invasion is difficult to diagnose with CT but ciné MR may be helpful in showing this.

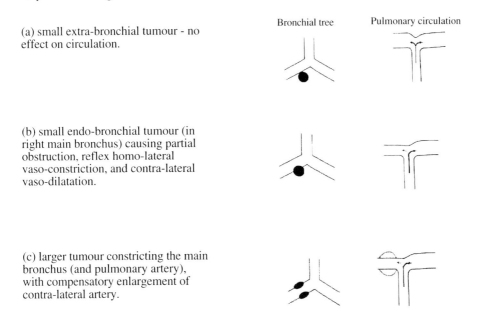

(a) small extra-bronchial tumour - no effect on circulation.

(b) small endo-bronchial tumour (in right main bronchus) causing partial obstruction, reflex homo-lateral vaso-constriction, and contra-lateral vaso-dilatation.

(c) larger tumour constricting the main bronchus (and pulmonary artery), with compensatory enlargement of contra-lateral artery.

Bronchial tree   Pulmonary circulation

Fig. 7.8 Diagram explaining the **paradoxical hilar** (or **Oeser's**) **sign** - enlargement of the contra-lateral pulmonary artery, and homolateral vaso-constriction of the pulmonary vessels.

Note that this sign may be seen with other obstructions to a main bronchus, including foreign bodies, mucous plugs, etc. It is also a feature of the Swyer-James (Macleod) syndrome - ps. 7.9-10. (Reproduced from Oeser and Gerstenberg, 1969, Fortschr. Röntgenstr., **110**, 205-8, with permission from Georg Thieme Verlag Stuttgart & New York).

Further references.

White et al. (1971) : The significance of unilateral absence of pulmonary artery perfusion of lung scanning.

Moncada et al. (1973) : Reversible unilateral pulmonary hypoperfusion secondary to acute check-valve obstruction to main bronchus.

Marshall and Trump (1982) : Acquired pulmonary stenoses caused by mediastinal tumours.

Fox, R. et al (1984) : Detection by Doppler echocardiography of acquired pulmonary stenosis due to extrinsic tumour compression.

Giovagnoni et al. (1992) : Evaluation of the pulmonary artery by ciné MRI.

Uberoi et al. (1996) : A pulmonary embolus, or what? - man aged 36 - nodal enlargement L hilum causing pulm. art. compression - due to non-Hodgkin B cell lymphoma.

Wright, W. et al. (1996) : Adenoid cystic carcinoma of LMB mimicking Macleod's syndrome - 23 yr. old woman with hyperlucent L lung, first diagnosed as Macleod's syndrome at age 15 - absent vent. & perf. to L lung - vascular tumour seen on bronchoscopy & CT showed a 3cm mass compressing the LMB. 2 wks after a L pneumonectomy, she had back pain and was found to have vertebral and pelvic metastases.

Drake et al (1997) : Pulmonary artery occlusion in two pts. caused by tuberculous mediastinal nodes.

Loukides et al. (1997) : Unilateral hypertranslucency of the L hemithorax due to compression of the LMB by a chronic traumatic aneurysm of the desc. aorta in a man aged 19 shown by CT.

Beaconsfield et al. (1998) : TB pulmonary arteritis - an unusual cause of R pulmonary stenosis.

Arterio-venous malformations, shunts and pulmonary arterio-venous aneurysms - Illus. **AV ANEURYSM/FISTULAE.**

These may be found per se, in the Osler-Weber-Rendu syndrome (haemorrhagic telangiectasia - Illus. **OSLER WEBER**) or in association with hepatic cirrhosis. They are more common in the lower lobes and in females. Sometimes the condition is diffuse and 'fine' but when larger vessels are involved A/V aneurysms are often present. Many A/V aneurysms are seen on chest radiographs and the feeding artery and draining vein may be shown by tomography including CT. 'Fine' lesions may be barely visible even at angiography, but the larger nodular lesions are usually well demonstrated. With multiple lesions, shunting may give rise to haemodynamic problems (e.g. patients being breathless in the upright posture and normal lying down) and polcythaemia (to compensate for unoxygenated blood). Rupture may occur into the pleura or a bronchus, the former because many are subpleural in position. **Paradoxical embolism** may occur with larger shunts, leading to transient ischaemic attacks, cerebral infarction or brain abscesses. Some patients may develop finger clubbing (see p. 23.1). Some lesions are undoubtedly congenital, but others arise later. Most are found by chance after the second or third decade, and outside pregnancy enlargement during adult life.

About half of the patients with A/V malformations have effort dyspnoea and/or cyanosis. Spencer (1984) estimated that cyanosis may result if 30% of the right ventricular output passes through the fistula, in turn leading to polycythaemia and increased blood volume.

The term 'angiodysplasia' was used by Oh et al. (1983) to describe cases in association with liver disease in children.

Idiopathic aneurysms are most commonly familial and are linked to autosomal dominant genes. It is thus important to study other members of the family since they, although largely asymptomatic, may be liable to have paradoxical emboli, with cerebral infarction and/or abscess, or suffer from fatigue and dyspnoea.

Pulmonary artery aneurysms may also develop in relation to infection such as tuberculosis, schistosomiasis, syphilis, or fungus disease (particularly aspergillosis and mucormycosis), etc - these have been termed '**Rasmussen aneurysms**' (Rasmussen, 1868). Others may follow an infected embolus (mycotic aneurysms), or occur following trauma, especially penetrating trauma from knife or bullet wounds, or occur with secondary deposits (e.g. thyroid), or with Behçet's syndrome (p. 19.87 - 88). An increasing number have been reported following the use of **Swan-Ganz** (balloon type) catheters for monitoring pulmonary artery pressure or after right heart catheterisation; some acute ones may resolve spontaneously after removing the catheter, but others may need resection to prevent massive haemorrhage (see also p. 11.10).

Many aneurysms will be recognised on plain films or tomograms. CT (especially dynamic CT) will often demonstrate the vascular nature of the nodule(s), but in some cases angiography (including DVI) will be required. MR has also been employed. Examples are shown in Illus. **PULM ART ANEURYSM**.

'**Contrast echocardiography**' may also be used; after a rapid IV injection of normal saline or indocyanine green, bubbles of these may produce an ultra-sonic signal as they pass through the heart. With a large right to left shunt, this may be seen in both right and left cardiac chambers simultaneously.

A word of caution must be expressed in diagnosing vascular lesions by CT, since some lung tumours can appear hypervascular - the author has seen this a few times. A case of scar cancer with hypervascularity simulating an A/V malformation (in a patient with mouth and genital naevi) was reported by Halbsguth et al. (1983). Oliver et al. (1997) reported a case of a large pulmonary artery pseudoaneurysm associated with a squamous carcinoma in the right lower lobe, which presented with repeated haemoptyses needing transfusion. As he had mediastinal lymphadenopathy and an adrenal deposit, the aneurysm was embolised, with no recurrence of haemoptysis. Geddes and Kerr (1976) reported pulmonary arterial aneurysms in association with a right ventricular myxoma, and Nakamura et al. (1987) a pseudoaneurysm in association with a haemangiopericytoma of the pulmonary outflow tract.

Larger aneurysms may be surgically clipped, removed or embolised, the last now being the treatment of choice. Castaneda-Zuniga et al. (1980), Kaufman et al. (1980) and White et al. (1983) - see also other refs. below - embolised such aneurysms with rings, balloons or plugs, via a percutaneous approach. The last authors also pointed out that AV aneurysms may have more than one supplying artery and that it is important to study their vascular architecture first. Rodan et al. (1981) found that pulmonary hypertension may be made worse by surgical resection and that ethanol embolisation may occasionally result in a fatal haemorrhage. Mostly silicone coated stainless steel coils (or small foam particles) are now used for such embolisation. An example of embolism treatment is shown in Illus. **A-V ANEURYSM/FISTULA, Pt. 7a-b.**

Diffuse cases of AV shunting may also occur. Faber et al. (1989) reported three cases of **pulmonary capillary haemangiomas** which had been referred for heart-lung transplantation; they had pulmonary hypertension, haemoptysis and a reticulo-nodular infiltrate on chest radiographs, inhomogeneously enhanced perfusion on a lung scan and increased peripheral pulmonary vascularity on angiography. The author saw a case several years ago who had diffuse cutaneous angiomas, then developed severe pulmonary shunting (proved angiographically) lead to breathlessness even in bed. A physician colleague treated him empirically with large dosage of oestrogens, when the patient markedly improved, this being maintained until he died in 1995 (see Illus. **OSLER WEBER, Pt. 1a-c.**

Other arterio-venous shunts - vascular shunting may also occur between the bronchial arteries and the pulmonary circulation in chronic pulmonary inflammatory or ischaemic conditions, e.g. congenital heart disease, bronchiectasis, fungus infections, etc, and between bronchial and pulmonary veins in severe emphysema. Other anastomoses may occur with the intercostal vessels, inferior phrenic artery, etc. and may occur with tumours involving the chest wall.
Tadavarthy et al. (1982) felt that three basic mechanisms could lead to shunting:
(i) with obstruction of the pulmonary veins, multiple pre-existing anastomoses open up due to change in pressure gradients;
(ii) with chronic inflammation, newly formed vessels in granulation tissue lead to shunting;
(iii) with occlusion of the pulmonary artery, shunting may be secondary to PE or surgical ligation.
Trans-pleural anastomoses depend on adhesions or tumour spread, for the transmission of vessels across this space. These vessels can sometimes become quite large and give rise to 'apparent negative defects' on isotope lung perfusion scans or pulmonary angiograms, as a result of the systemic blood supply. (For references see under bronchial artery references below).

Fig. 7.9   The bronchial (1), intercostal (2) and left phrenic arteries (3) all originate from the aorta and may give rise to systemic collaterals to the left pulmonary artery (Reproduced from Tadavarthy et al., 1982, Radiology, **144**, 55 - 59 with permission).

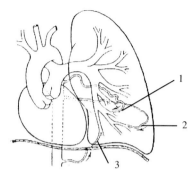

Further references.

Fearn (1841)
Osler (1885) : First description of mycotic aneurysm.
Auerbach (1939) : Pathology and pathogenesis of pulmonary arterial aneurysm in TB cavities.
Lindren (1946) : Roentgen diagnosis of A/V aneurysm of the lungs (used Valsalva manoeuvre to show an alteration in size).
Hodgson et al. (1959) : Survey of a large family with haemorrhagic telangiectasia - 15% had A/V fistulae.
Viamonte (1967) : Intrathoracic extracardiac shunts.
Weintraub and Abrams (1968) : Mycotic aneurysm.
Gomes (1970) : Ten year experience at Mayo Clinic.
Stevenson et al. (1971) : Use of isotope angiography to demonstrate A/V malformations.
Dines et al. (1974) & (1983) : Pulmonary A/V fistulae.
Hoffman and Rabens (1974) : Multiple pulmonary A/V fistulae as evolving pulmonary nodules.
Jaffe and Condon (1975) : Mycotic aneurysms of the aorta and pulmonary artery - six cases - they are potentially fatal lesions, which tend to grow rapidly and eventually rupture. They may be associated with a patent ductus or coarctation, or may follow lung infection or endocarditis.
Kirks et al. (1976) : Systemic arterial supply to normal basal segments of the left lower lobe.
Castanega-Zuniga et al. (1980) : Embolism of multiple pulmonary artery fistulae in a girl of 6.
Rémy et al. (1980) : Treatment of massive haemoptysis by occlusion of a Rasmussen aneurysm.
Hatfield and Fried (1981) : Therapeutic embolisation of diffuse pulmonary A/V aneurysms.
Godwin and Webb (1981) : Dynamic CT in the evaluation of vascular lung lesions.
Pezzella et al. (1981) : Stapling of lesions at surgery, with the aid of a Doppler ultrasound for localisation.
Rodan et al. (1981) : Worsening pulmonary hypertension after resection of A/V fistulae.
Dillon et al. (1982) : Traumatic pulmonary artery pseudoaneurysm simulating pulmonary embolism.
Rankin et al. (1982) : CT diagnosis of pulmonary arteriovenous malformations.
Kilgore and Chasen (1983) : A/V fistulae simulating a vanishing tumour.
Shin et al. (1983) : CT diagnosis of false aneurysm of pulmonary artery not shown by angiography.
White, R. et al. (1983) : Angioarchitecture of pulm. A/V malformations - an important consideration before therapy.
Gutierrez et al. (1984) : MR of A/V fistulae.
Webb (1984) : Dynamic CT of solitary pulmonary vascular lesions (A/V fistulae, varix, sequestration) including use of time-density curve (patient must hold his breath or the lesion may move in and out of the plane of the scan).
Webb et al. (1984 f) : MR of pulmonary A/V fistulae.
Hunter and Ayers (1985) : Digital subtraction angiography.
Mootoosamy et al. (1985) : CT of mycotic aneurysms of intra-pulmonary arteries of the right lung.
Burke et al. (1986) : Pulmonary A/V malformations - a critical update.
Salimi et al. (1985) : Detection of right to left shunt with radionucleide angiography in refractory hypoxaemia.
Davis et al. (1987) : False pulmonary artery aneurysm induced by a Swan-Ganz catheter.
Dieden (1987) : Pulmonary artery false aneurysms secondary to balloon tips of Swan-Ganz catheters - 10 cases in 9 years - 6 presented radiologically and 4 with haemoptysis. These were well defined persistent pulmonary nodules, with or without calcification or cavitation. Two ruptured fatally.
Flower (1987) : Review of A/V fistulae.

Chilvers et al. (1988) : Quantified A/V malformations using Tc^{99m} albumen microspheres, by comparing the uptake in the lungs with that in the right kidney. Assuming a 10% blood flow through the kidney, and multiplying this by ten, will allow one to make a rough estimate of the relative blood flow through the lung capillaries and via the shunt.

Brown et al (1988) : MR - pulmonary A/V malformation and a chronic pulmonary haematoma had similar appearances with spin echo techniques, giving a central absence of signal. However phase images discriminated flowing blood in the A/V malformation from stationary lung tissues., whereas the haematoma was not distinguished from lung parenchyma.

White et al. (1988) : Pulmonary A/V malformations - techniques and long-term outcome of embolotherapy (276 malformations in 76 patients - 65% in lower lobes, which corresponded with greater hypoxaemia in the upright position). They felt that the families of patients should be screened to prevent paradoxical emboli, with strokes, etc).

Pinet et al. (1989) : Therapeutic embolisation in the chest - three types of lesion can be embolised :

(i) A/V fistulae of the thoracic wall. These are rare and usually are congenital. More than one embolisation may be necessary to reduce the large volumes of the lesions.

(ii) Isolated or multiple pulmonary A/V fistulae. Embolisation is performed after selective and bilateral pulmonary angiography.

(iii) Haemoptysis related to hypervascularisation of the systemic circulation with various acquired diseases.

Dinsmore et al. (1990) : Pulmonary arteriovenous malformations - diagnosis by gradient-refocussed MR imaging - study of 4 pts. with 6 AVMs.

Hughes and Allison (1990) : Pulmonary A/V malformations - the radiologist replaces the surgeon.

Jackson et al. (1990) : The effect of various physiological parameters of embolisation of pulmonary A/V formations - no long term complications and safe, with no loss of lung volume after embolisation. Some residual shunting is usual. >20% of untreated patients may have paradoxical emboli (TIAs, cerebral embolism or abscess). Most have arterial desaturation and polycythaemia.

Rémy-Jardin et al. (1991) : Transcatheter occlusion of pulmonary arterial circulation and collateral supply - failures, incidents and complications.

Rémy et al. (1992) : Pulmonary arteriovenous malformations - evaluation with CT of the chest before and after treatment - 40 patients with 109 AVM's - progressive aneurysmal retraction associated with successful occlusion.

Ference et al. (1994) : Life threatening pulmonary haemorrhage associated with pulmonary A/V malformations and hereditary haemorrhagic telangiectasia.

Stark et al. (1994) : Aneurysms of the pulmonary artery - usually arise in association with an underlying cardiovascular cause.

White et al. (1994) : MR angiographic diagnosis of recanalisation in a thrombosed pulmonary AVM, initially diagnosed on angiography as a pulmonary embolus.

Allison (1995) : It is important to **study other members of the family of patients with AVMs** because of the increased risk of **paradoxical   emboli** (with cerebral infarction, etc.). Most AVMs lie in the LLs, thus when a patient with these stands up, more blood will flow through the AVMs, giving rise to effort syncope, etc. (but being normal whilst lying down). Uses Chilvers method (see above) as main-stay of detection, prior to pulmonary angiography and embolisation with coils or balloons in such patients. He stresses that as lung vessels behave as end-arteries, one must preserve as much of the lung circulation as possible. Often 5 or 6 sessions may be necessary to cure the lung lesions and give a normal result. Some with microscopic lesions may have larger anastomoses as well.

Dutton et al. (1995) : Pulmonary A/V malformations - results of treatment with coil embolisation in 53 pts.

Jackson (1996) : Interventional radiology of pulmonary AVMs - coils must be of the correct size, otherwise they may pass through the aneurysm; uses balloons for large sacs, follow-up is mandatory as small anastomoses may open up - in one case used 104 coils! Reserves balloons for large sacs.

Vernhet et al. (1996) : Detachable balloons are more efficient than non-detachable coils in the treatment of PAMs.

Coley and Jackson (1998) : Pulmonary A/V malformations - radiological techniques represent the primary treatment of choice with surgical treatment rarely being required.

Sagara et al. (1998) : Recanalisation after coil embolotherapy of pulmonary arteriovenous malformations - study of long-term outcome and mechanism for recanalisation in 8/14 pts. Coils should be as close as possible to the AVM to avoid future bronchial artery to pulmonary artery recanalisation.

Inflammatory A/V aneurysms (see also refs. under TB, fungus diseases and schistosomiasis).

Choyke et al. (1982) : Mycotic pulmonary artery aneurysm following aspergillus endocarditis after cardiac surgery.

Lundell and Finck (1983) : A/V fistulae resulting from Rasmussen aneurysms.

Loevner et al. (1992) : Multiple mycotic pulmonary artery aneurysms - a complication of invasive mucormycosis.

Jackson (1998) : Peripheral pulmonary artery pseudoaneurysms in chronic TB - angiography and embolisation.

Patankar et al. (2000) : Fatal haemoptysis caused by a ruptured giant Rasmussen's aneurysm secondary to TB.

Trauma to pulmonary artery and traumatic A/V aneurysms.

Crivello et al. (1986) : Traumatic left pulmonary artery aneurysm due to knife wound shown by CT.

Daykin et al. (1986) : CT demonstration of a traumatic aneurysm of the pulmonary artery - false aneurysm in right lower lobe - mimicking an enlarging haematoma.
Collins and Robinson (1989), Katz et al. (1993) : Pulmonary artery trauma.
Clements et al. (1997) : Survival after blunt intrapericardial rupture of the pulmonary artery.
Weltman et al. (2000) : CT diagnosis of laceration of the main pulm. artery after blunt trauma.

Ruptured AVM simulating pulmonary embolism.
Poon and Chalmers (1995) : Ruptured pulmonary AVM - **danger of misdiagnosis as pulmonary embolism** - pregnant female collapsed - L bloody pleural effusion with matched V/P defect. AVM shown by pulmonary angiogram, and treated by embolisation.

Vascular lung lesions simulating A/V malformations.
Green et al. (1973) : Angiographic demonstration of A/V shunts in pulmonary metastatic chorioncarcinoma.
Cirimelli et al. (1988) : Metastatic chorioncarcinoma simulating an A/V malformation on chest radiography and dynamic CT (highly vascular nodule in RLL).

Note also **Behçet's syndrome aneurysms** - ps. 19.87 - 88.

Abnormalities of the pulmonary veins - Illus. **PUL VEINS** - these include:
Localised dilatation or a large, but otherwise normal vein.
Pseudotumours of the pulmonary veins are discussed on p. 6.29.
The venous part of an A/V fistula.
A pulmonary varix (p. 7.17 - 18).
Obstruction and/or thrombosis (esp. of an inferior pulmonary vein) may occur secondary to a left atrial myxoma, a primary endovascular tumour), lung or other tumours extending along the veins to the left atrium, chronic or fibrosing mediastinitis (p. 18.4), or from primary pulmonary veno-occlusive disease.
Hypoplasia of an intrapulmonary portion (obstruction in infants).
Anomalous pulmonary venous drainage (total or partial from one or both lungs - see below).
Scimitar veins (see also p. 7.7 and ref. below).
Cor triatrium with a common venous confluence, often with partial obstruction into left atrium.
Trauma - blunt or penetrating (see also Appx. p. 10).

Invasion by bronchogenic tumour - microscopic invasion of vein radicles is common. Sometimes gross invasion is present, causing a pulmonary vein to be enlarged; this is most commonly seen radiologically with an inferior pulmonary vein (Illus. **CA ADJ PULM VEIN**) - its recognition often implies extension of tumour into the heart or pericardium, and may be a sign suggesting inoperability. Surgical manipulation of such a vein at thoracotomy may cause a tumour/thrombus to be released and cause **systemic embolism**.

Some references. (see also p.19.101).
Hinson and Nohl (1965) : Involvement of the pulmonary veins by bronchogenic carcinoma - may be macroscopic in one third of cases.
Heitmiller (1992) : Prognostic significance of massive bronchogenic tumour embolus - saddle embolus removed from aortic bifurcation (also quotes other cases of bronchial tumour embolism from literature).
Spencer et al. (1993) : Multiple tumour emboli (of brain and both femoral arteries) after pneumonectomy - femoral arteries explored and tumour emboli removed.
Pitman et al. (2000) : IV extension of lung ca to the L atrium shown by PET and CT.
Yoshida et al. (2000) : **Scimitar type vein** occurring secondary to pulmonary venous stenosis.
Nelson and Klein (2000) : Osteogenic sarcoma lung metastases with infarction and pulmonary venous thrombosis.

Anomalous pulmonary venous drainage.
This is an uncommon congenital abnormality and may be partial or total. When total (about 50% present in infancy) all the pulmonary veins may drain into a persistent left SVC (see p. 9.16) giving rise to the 'figure of eight' sign (Fig. 7.10). In order to survive there has to be an intra-cardiac communication and these cases usually have to be corrected urgently by surgery. Partial cases have a variation of insertion of the pulmonary veins into the coronary sinus, the right atrium, a right SVC or into veins below the diaphragm.

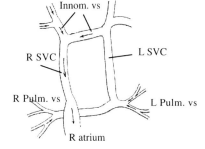

Fig. 7.10   Diagram showing the anatomy
of total anomalous venous drainage (after
Owen, 1962, with permission from Clinical
Radiology. - See also Fig. 9.16, p. 9.17).

For illustrations see Illus. **PULM**

VEIN-ANOMALOUS.

References.
Friedlowski (1868) : Total anomalous pulmonary venous drainage unassociated with any other serious cardiac defect.
Brody (1942) : Drainage of veins into the right side of the heart.
Healey (1952) : Clinical significance of anomalous pulmonary venous drainage.
Snellen and Albers (1952) : The clinical diagnosis of anomalous pulmonary venous drainage.
Owen (1962) : Total anomalous pulmonary venous drainage with persistent left SVC (9 cases).
Fulsonie and Molnar (1966) : Anomalous pulmonary venous return, pulmonary sequestration, bronchial atresia,
aplastic right upper lobe, pericardial defect and intrathoracic kidney.
Adler and Silverman (1973) : Anomalous LUL venous drainage.
Brenner et al. (1983) : Extrapulmonary drainage of one lung to the other + total anomalous venous return.
Green and Miller (1986) : Anomalous pulmonary venous drainage from the left lower lobe shown by CT.
Pennes and Ellis (1986) : Anomalous pulmonary venous drainage of the RLL shown by CT.
Schatz et al. (1986) : Partial anomalous venous drainage of the right lower lobe shown by CT.
Thorsen et al. (1990) : CT and MR of pulmonary venous return to the azygos vein.
Masui et al. (1991) : Abnormalities of the pulmonary veins - evaluation with MR and comparison with cardiac
angiography and echocardiography.
Black et al. (1992) : Pulmonary resection & contralateral anomalous venous drainage - a lethal combination which
gives rise to a large L to R shunt, requiring surgical correction of the anomalous drainage.
Dillon et al. (1993) : Partial anomalous venous drainage of LUL vs duplication of SVC - distinction with CT.
Hale and Padhani (1997) & Padhani and Hale (1998) : Mediastinal venous anomalies - **potential   pitfalls   in
cancer diagnosis** - 11 pts. - 8 had anomalous pulmonary venous drainage (see also p. 9.17).
Orme et al. (1998) : CVP line in anomalous pulm. vein of LUL.

Pulmonary varix.
A pulmonary varix is a localised enlargement of a segment of a pulmonary vein which enters the
left atrium normally. On plain films pulmonary varices may mimic rounded lung nodules or hilar
nodes. Tomograms, particularly CT or in the lateral plane, may show them to be smooth, lobulated
or elongated worm-like or sausage shaped masses in the position of the pulmonary veins. They
may change in shape or size with Valsalva and Müller manoeuvres. Calcification within them has
not been reported.
The most common site is in the right lower lobe, followed by the left upper lobe. They may be
associated with anomalous pulmonary venous drainage i.e. into the right atrium or the scimitar
syndrome. This is because part of the foetal splanchnic venous system may persist with
connections to the cardinal and vitelline systems.
Angiography or dynamic CT may show opacification of varices but this may not be dense as the
supplying vessels i.e. the arteries and capillaries may be normal and considerable dilution of
contrast may occur. Retrograde shunting may take place from the abdomen via a scimitar vein,
from the systemic or portal systems, giving rise to a 'stagnant pool of blood'. Reflux from the
main pulmonary veins may also occur.
The condition may be more common than is generally recognised. The vast majority of patients
are completely asymptomatic and are best left untreated.
A few patients may have associated pulmonary venous hypertension. Haemoptysis probably
warrants surgical resection, since a massive bleed may occur if they rupture. Thrombosis may also

lead to cerebral or peripheral embolism. Embolisation should **never** be attempted, since without the 'protection' of the pulmonary capillaries, emboli are almost certain to be produced.

Fig. 7.11   Sausage or worm-like masses due to pulmonary varices. A clinical case is shown in Illus. **PULM VARIX**

References.
Bartram and Strickland (1971) : Reviewed 31 cases and reported 6 further cases.
Papamichael et al. (1972) : Pulmonary varicosities and other congenital abnormalities.
Ben-Menachen et al. (1975) : Various forms of pulmonary varices + 3 cases & review.
Borkowski et al.(1981) : CT findings.
Chaise et al. (1983) : Demonstration by dynamic CT.
Généreux (1983b) : Conventional tomographic hilar anatomy emphasising the pulmonary veins.

Pulmonary hypertension.
    This occurs most commonly secondary to pulmonary fibrotic conditions (including severe emphysema, chronic bronchitis, fibrosing alveolitis, sarcoidosis, rheumatoid lung disease, etc.), cardiac disease (mitral valve disease, L to R shunts, etc.), multiple pulmonary embolism, Takayasu's disease (p. 10.17), portal hypertension, HIV infection etc. In many cases the main pulmonary artery branches are enlarged with peripheral pruning.
    Primary pulmonary hypertension is less common and is often caused by **pulmonary veno-occlusive disease** which is an uncommon but serious disease affecting infants or adults, especially young females. It may occur as part of a generalised debilitating condition, in relation to lung infection or infarction, secondary to drugs (e.g. Aminorex used for slimming) or be a manifestation of neoplasm, either from venous obstruction (caused by some lung or mediastinal tumours or a myxoma) or as a para-neoplastic manifestation. It may occur in infants in association with hypoplastic pulmonary veins or in relation to slowed or obstructive pulmonary venous return caused by various cardiac malformations. In some cases it is familial, but the majority are idiopathic and present with dyspnoea and signs of pulmonary hypertension. There may be a 'flu-like illness before the onset of symptoms and radiographically there is often peripheral interstitial shadowing due to inflammatory interstitial pneumonitis or interstitial pulmonary oedema. Pathologically there is a fibrous intimal proliferation within the pulmonary veins (and sometimes the arteries as well) suggesting a pan-pulmonary vascular occlusive condition.

References.
Stovin and Mitchinson (1965) : Pulmonary hypertension due to obstruction of the pulmonary veins.
Carrington and Liebow (1970)
Heath et al. (1971) : Epidemic ? due to Aminorex.
Rosenthal et al. (1973) : Diagnosis from radiological and haemodynamic findings.
Corrin et al. (1974) : An auto-immune complex disease?
Thanadi et al. (1975),   Chawla et al. (1976) : Pulmonary veno-occlusive diseases.
Wagenvoort et al. (1971) : Of presumably intrauterine origin.   Wagenvoort (1976) : Entity or syndrome.
Wagenvoort et al. (1985) : Pulm. veno-occlusive disease - involvement of pulmonary arteries & literature review.
Sanderson et al. (1977) : Case responding to treatment with azathioprine - immune complexes were found in the alveolar walls.
Voordees et al. (1977) : Familial cause.   Dail et al. (1978) : 43 cases.
Rambihar et al. (1979) : Antemortem diagnosis from radiological and haemodynamic findings.
Swischuk and L'Heureux (1980) : Unilateral pulmonary vein atresia.
Capewell et al. (1984) : Association with **Hodgkin's disease.**
Troussard et al. (1984) : Following bone marrow transplantation.
Hasleton et al. (1986) : Four cases.

Lombard et al. (1987) : Following therapy for malignant neoplasms.

Salzman and Rosa (1989) : Prolonged survival in pulmonary veno-occlusive disease treated by nifedipine.

Matthews and Buchanan (1990) : New bronchoscopic sign - intense hyperaemia and vascular engorgement in the form of bright red longitudinal streaks.

Gilroy et al. (1991) : Fatal progression despite steroid induced remission of interstitial pneumonitis.

Murch and Taylor (1991) : 16 year old boy with gross pulmonary oedema - increasing shortness for four months following a sore throat.

Cassart et al. (1993) : Pulmonary veno-occlusive disease - CT findings before and after single-lung transplantation. Before transplantation - interstitial pattern associated with patchy air-space consolidation. Following transplantation on the left the right lung changes resolved probably as a result of reduced blood flow through it.

Kim et al. (1993) : Congenital obstruction of the pulmonary veins - 2 cases examined by MR.

Peacock (1999) : Primary pulmonary hypertension and classification of causes of pulmonary hypertension.

Selvedge and Gevant (1999) : Idiopathic pulmonary vein thrombosis shown by CT and MR imaging.

Au et al. (2001) : Pulm. hypertension secondary to L heart disease causing V/P mismatch mimicking embolism.

Pulmonary venous impressions on the oesophagus (see also p. 16.1 and Fig. 16.1).

Nash et al. (1961) : Aberrant insertion of a pulmonary vein into the left atrium simulating an intrinsic lesion of the oesophagus.

Jacobs et al. (1972) : Dysphagia associated with a distended pulmonary vein.

Yeh and Wolf (1975) : A pulmonary venous indentation on the oesophagus - normal variant.

Chorioncarcinoma causing pulmonary hypertension - see ps. 5.11, 5.40 & the following section.

Pulmonary artery and vein tumours.

Tumours of the pulmonary artery (like tumours of the other great vessels or endocardium) are rare. Most are sarcomas of various types, but others may be chorioncarcinomas arising in the vessel wall (see refs.), occasionally benign tumours such as a chemodectoma may be seen (see below and also ps. 18.35 - 36). Most of the benign tumours arise in a main pulmonary artery and spread peripherally, retrograde spread into the right ventricle being less common. Secondary deposits in the brain, abdomen and lungs may occur. Occlusion of the pulmonary circulation with right ventricular outflow obstruction usually causes the clinical presentation.

Radiologically there may be a hilar mass (Illus. **CA+PULM ARTERY**), enlargement of the main pulmonary arteries, deficient perfusion of part or the whole of a lung or lungs as seen on plain radiographs, on isotope lung scan or pulmonary angiogram, giving a similar appearance to pulmonary emboli, a lobulated mass within the pulmonary artery on contrast enhanced CT, or a mass moving with the cardiac cycle as seen with ultrasound or a ciné angiogram. Prognosis is usually poor - a few months in most cases despite attempted surgery, but in the case of the illustrated chemodectoma, recurrence did not occur (Illus. **CHEMODECTOMA, Pt. 4a-c**).

Most tumour involvement of pulmonary arteries is due to constriction by, or reflex anoxia caused by bronchial carcinomas (Oeser's sign - see ps. 7.10 - 12). It may also be mimicked by aggressive fibromatosis (see p. 18.4).

Primary tumours of the pulmonary veins are also rare, most venous tumour involvement being due to lung cancer (Illus. **PULM VEINS, Ca lg&pul vein Pt. 1 - 9**). Tumour thrombosis of a pulmonary vein may also occur secondary to obstruction by a left atrial myxoma.

Intravascular bronchiolo-alveolar tumours are discussed on p. 5.5. Haemangiopericytomas may occur in the lungs - see p. 5.10 - 11. See also pulmonary leiomyosarcomas p. 5.12.

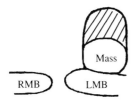

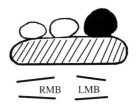

Fig. 7. 12   (a) Tumour in pulmonary artery (defect in contrast enhanced blood).

(b) Mass extending backwards from the pulmonary trunk in front of the main bronchi.

References.

Munk et al. (1965) : Primary mesenchymoma of the pulmonary artery - first report in radiological literature - quoted 18 cases - largely from pathological papers.

Moffat et al. (1972) : Roentgen considerations in primary pulmonary artery sarcoma.

Bleisch and Kraus (1980) : Polypoid sarcoma of the pulmonary trunk.

Wright, E. et al. (1983) : Pulmonary artery sarcoma diagnosed by two-dimensional echocardiography.

Fitzgerald (1983) : Found 60 cases in the literature and reported a case shown by CT (see diagram above).

de Smet et al. (1986) : Pulmonary artery leiomyosarcoma treated surgically.

Schermoly et al. (1987) : Smooth tapering of the pulm. artery due to plaque like tumour spreading along the lumen.

Promiskoff et al. (1988) : Sarcoma of the pulmonary artery.

Britton (1990) : Primary pulmonary artery sarcoma - two cases - plain film, scintigraphic, angiographic and CT demonstration (found 105 cases in the literature).

Wightman (1990) : Two cases of primary pulmonary artery sarcoma (i) presenting with haemoptysis, and (ii) as a result of pulmonary emboli. Both caused masses within the right pulmonary artery as seen on contrast enhanced CT, and both had absent perfusion of the right lung on isotope perfusion lung scans.

In a third case (Shannon et al., 1994) the diagnosis was made with transoesophageal echocardiography (showing a tumour in the main and right pulmonary artery with characteristic "to-and-fro" motion) and spiral CT (showing the precise extent and nature of the primary intraluminal mass and pulmonary nodules).

Stark et al. (1990) : Osteogenic sarcoma arising in the left pulmonary artery.

Berney et al. (1992) : Leiomyosarcoma of the pulmonary hilar vessel.

Burke and Virmani (1993) : Sarcomas of the great vessels.

Delany et al. (1993) : Pulmonary artery sarcoma mimicking pulmonary embolism.

Kauczor et al. (1994) : Pulmonary artery sarcoma mimicking chronic thromboembolic disease - CT & MR findings.

Okano et al. (1999) : Pulmonary artery sarcoma diagnosed using intravascular ultrasound images.

Bagshawe and Brooks (1959) : Suggested that pulmonary embolism and hypertension could be caused by **chorioncarcinoma** of the pulmonary arteries.

Trübenbach et al. (1997) : Primary chorioncarcinoma of the pulmonary artery mimicking pulmonary embolus - woman aged 33 - 5/12 history of recurrent episodes of exertional dyspnoea - CT showed complete occlusion of LPA by an enhancing mass - also confirmed by pulm. angio. which also showed defects in R inf. pulm. art. She had a very elevated serum ß-hCG (human chorionic gonadotrophin). Methotrexate treatment was started but she died. (Chorioncarcinoma is also discussed on ps. 5.11, 5.40, 7.19 & 18.15 - 16).

Note: chorioncarcinoma tumours typically cause an increased blood ß human chorion-gonadotropin - normal = < 5U/100ml - this can be assessed by blood assay - they may also be imaged by PET using FDG (see p. 22.11).

The bronchial arteries.

The normal bronchial arteries are small vessels (up to 2 mm in diameter), which are somewhat variable in their anatomy, but usually arise from the descending aorta (just distal to the left subclavian artery) and supply the bronchi, the oesophagus and mediastinal lymph nodes.

The right bronchial artery frequently arises as a common trunk with an intercostal artery, dorsally or medially from the aorta at D5 or D6 level. Initially it commonly runs vertically, then makes a 'hairpin bend' at the level of the aortic arch, before running caudally towards the right hilar area, closely applied to the wall of the right main bronchus. It then divides into tortuous branches which are distributed within the medial third of the lung.

The left bronchial artery most often arises anteriorly, but in older people, with elongation and twisting of the aorta, its origin may become antero-lateral. This artery may also be double (in about two-thirds of patients in some series) or arise as a common trunk with the right. It may pass behind the oesophagus, and a branch from it commonly passes through the medial part of the aorto-pulmonary window, to supply lymph nodes and the bronchi.

Normally the bronchial arteries supply only about 50 to 100 ml of blood/minute to the bronchial walls, compared with about five litres to the alveolar capillaries via the pulmonary arteries. They may become enlarged with congenital interruption, or severe narrowing of a pulmonary artery, the Swyer-James (Macleod) syndrome, bronchiectasis, cystic fibrosis, aspergillosis, emphysema, severe scarring from past TB, sarcoid or radiotherapy, or lung and bronchial tumours, including carcinoids and hamartomas. When enlarged they may be seen as vessels which are more irregular than the pulmonary artery branches - ill-defined, linear and sometimes nodular, and more apparent in the lungs above the hila.

Other 'bronchial type vessels' from the aorta (or its main intrathoracic branches - e.g. the innominate and subclavian arteries) may give rise to 'abnormal branches', sometimes as large as the main bronchial arteries, entering the hila of the lungs, then tending to branch like pulmonary vessels, particularly when grossly enlarged as with congenital heart disease. Grainger (1985) wrote "these **must** be formed during intrauterine life, to compensate for the poor pulmonary circulation". Some are present with sequestration and other similar anomalies.

Other anastomoses may occur from other vessels in the mediastinum or the chest wall (intercostal and internal mammary arteries, etc), particularly after pleural adhesions have formed - see also refs. below and p. 7.14.

CT of bronchial vessels - when enlarged, bronchial arteries may be seen on CT sections as soft tissue nodules in the retro-oesophageal or retro-bronchial spaces, particularly when dilatation has occurred following damage to the pulmonary circulation (see above). Exceptionally they may dilate up to about 1 cm in diameter, and such dilatation can be shown by dynamic CT, and is best shown with a few sections taken at or just above the carina. Distinction should be made from the azygos and hemi-azygos veins, and the vascular blushing which may be seen in some lymph nodes, supplied by the bronchial vessels.

Bronchial artery embolisation - (using Gelfoam, alcohol or coils) has been used for the treatment of **severe haemoptysis**, particularly in benign conditions (aspergillosis, bronchiectasis or cavitating sarcoidosis). A preliminary angiogram is necessary to ensure that the blood supply to the spinal cord does not arise from the same vessel - see Illus. **BRONCHIAL ARTERIOGRAM.**

Problems are (i) that collateral channels may open up after embolisation, (ii) the vessels may be too small to insert coils, and (iii) that emboli, caused by gel flakes or alcohol, may become relatively **quickly recanalised - often within a few days**.

Bronchial artery embolisation will **not** stop haemoptysis due to **erosion of a pulmonary artery branch into a bronchus or lung cavity** (Rémy et al, 1984; and Rasmussen aneurysms - p. 7.12), or in some cases with gross bronchiectasis. As pointed out by Patel et al. (1994) - see below - surgical removal of the cause, still often offers the best chance of cure. Other methods of treating severe haemoptysis have been by laser photocoagulation (Edmonstone et al., 1983) and radiotherapy (Schneerson et al., 1980 - from an aspergilloma).

Bronchial artery embolisation has also been used to control haemoptysis in some cases of bronchial neoplasm. A problem is that entering a tiny vessel with a minute catheter may provoke arterial spasm, and more than one attempt may be required.

Keller et al. (1987) pointed out that anastomoses to the lung circulation from the axillary, subclavian or phrenic vessels may give rise to a bronchial type collateral circulation. Jardin and Rémy (1988) showed similar anastomoses from the internal mammary arteries. Jackson and Allison (1989) reported a case with anastomoses from the lateral thoracic artery and intercostals to the pulmonary artery branches and quoted several other cases from the literature. All these authors noted the importance of the collateral vessels in the control of haemoptysis.

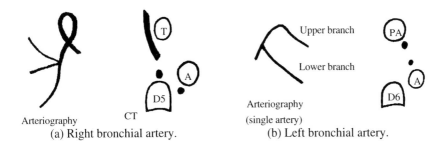

(a) Right bronchial artery. (b) Left bronchial artery.

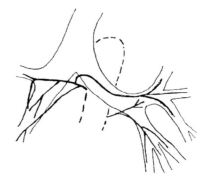

(c) The upper part of the
left bronchial artery may
arise from a common trunk
with the right bronchial artery.

Fig. 7.13   Diagrams of
the bronchial arteries.

Further references.

Galen (1562) : First noted that the aorta sent small branches to the lung.
Ruysch (1721) : Showed the bronchial vessels to be separate from, but anastomosed with the pulmonary circulation.
Von Haller (1761): Described their origin and course.
Virchow (1856) : A lobe of the lung could be kept viable by the bronchial arteries after pulmonary artery occlusion.
Miller (1906) : Anatomy of the bronchial arteries.
Cauldwell et al. (1948) : Anatomical study of bronchial arteries in 150 cadavers.
Cudkowicz and Armstrong (1951) : Normal anatomy of bronchial arteries.
Pump (1963) : Bronchial arteries and their anastomoses in the human lung.
Pump (1972) : Distribution of bronchial arteries in the human lung.
Liebow (1965) : Patterns of origin and distribution of the major bronchial arteries.
Liebow et al. (1949) : Bronchial artery enlargement and pulmonary circulation anastomosis in bronchiectasis.
Viamonte (1964) : Selective bronchial arteriography in man.
        (1965) : Angiographic evaluation of lung neoplasms.
Boijsen and Zsigmond (1965) : Selective angiography of the bronchial and intercostal arteries.
Mack et al. (1965) : Bronchial arteries in cystic fibrosis.
Newton and Preyer (1965) : Selective bronchial arteriography.
Viamonte (1964) : Selective bronchial arteriography in man.
        (1965) : Angiographic evaluation of lung neoplasms.
Nordenström (1967c) : Catheterisation and angiography of bronchial and mediastinal arteries.
        (1969b) : Bronchial arteriography.
Darke and Lewtas (1968) : Selective bronchial arteriography to show abnormal pulmonary systemic circulation.
North et al. (1969) : Bronchial and intercostal arteriography in non-neoplastic pulmonary disease.
Botenga (1968) : Selective angiography for showing bronchopulmonary anastomoses in chronic pulmonary inflammatory processes.
        (1970) : Selective bronchial and intercostal angiography.
Kardjiev et al. (1974) : Aetiology, pathogenesis and prevention of spinal cord lesions in selective angiography of the bronchial and intercostal arteries.
Ishikawa (1977) : Systemic - pulmonary artery communication in Takayasu's arteritis.
Rémy et al. (1977) : Treatment of haemoptysis by embolising bronchial arteries.
Webb and Jacobs (1977) : Transpleural abdominal systemic and pulmonary anastomosis with chronic pulmonary infection.
Tadavarthy et al. (1982) : Systemic to pulmonary collaterals.
Grenier et al. (1983) : Use of isobutyl-2cyanoacrylate for bronchial artery occlusion for severe haemoptysis (14 cases - 9 TB, 2 bronchiectasis, 2 neoplasm and 1 carcinoid).
Ivanick et al. (1983) : Infarction of LMB resulting from bronchial artery embolisation.
Nohara et al. (1983) : Giant coronary-to-bronchial artery anastomosis complicated by myocardial infarction.
Uflacker et al. (1985) : Bronchial artery embolisation to control haemoptysis.
O'Halpin et al. (1984) : Five years experience of therapeutic arterial embolisation.
Cadotte et al. (1986) : Bronchial angiography (21 cases including 5 with embolisation).
Furlonger (1987) Used CT to show active bleeding from the left bronchial artery into the pleura in a patient with a bronchial carcinoma, adjacent to the descending aorta, and mimicking a dissecting aneurysm on plain radiographs.
Furuse et al. (1987) : CT demonstration of bronchial arteries with arteriographic correlation.
Jardin and Rémy (1988) : Control of haemoptysis - systemic angiography & anastomoses of int. mammary artery.

Jackson et al. (1989) : Coils are a safe alternative to balloons for the embolisation of A/V malformations.

Lois et al. (1989) : Systemic to pulmonary collateral vessels and shunts - treatment with embolisation (16 procedures in 15 patients).

Girard et al. (1990) : Stenosis of left main bronchus complicating bronchial artery embolisation.

Prendergast et al. (1990) : Value of bronchial artery embolisation in acute major haemoptysis - 40 embolisations in 26 patients - emphasised the value of bronchoscopy in localising the site of bleeding prior to embolisation and the very poor outcome for patients with aspergillomas.

Ruttley (1990) : Bronchial arteriography and embolisation by a simple catheter technique - using Judkins left coronary catheter.

Roberts (1990) : Bronchial artery embolisation therapy.

Tan et al. (1991) : Bronchial artery embolisation in management of haemoptysis.

Hayakawa et al. (1992) : Bronchial artery embolisation for haemoptysis using gelatin sponge in 80 pts. Pts with bronchiectasis had best results, followed by idiopathic and inflammatory disease. Those with neoplasm fared worst.

John and Procter (1992) : Life threatening haemoptysis from an iatrogenic chronic pulmonary abscess (due to a retained surgical swab, managed initially by bronchial artery embolisation).

Patel et al. (1994) : Management of **massive   haemoptysis** - the source of bleeding is almost always the high-pressure pulmonary systemic circulation (i.e. the **bronchial   arteries**). On rare occasions (<2%) when the pulmonary arteries are the source, haemoptysis usually occurs secondary to a structural defect such as an aneurysm or arteriovenous fistula. They listed three '**key points**' :

(i) Massive haemoptysis has a high mortality rate and patients can relapse rapidly. **Surgical   removal   of   the cause offers the best chance of cure.**

(ii) The bleeding point is most successfully located by **rigid bronchoscopy** and this should be undertaken as soon as the patient's clinical state allows.

(iii) All endobronchial and arteriographic measures should be considered **temporary solutions**.

Rémy-Jardin (1994) : If cessation of bleeding after arterial embolisation is used to identify the responsible blood vessel, our experience indicates that bronchial arteries are the immediate cause of bleeding in approx. 90% of cases. The majority of bronchial bleeding relates to bronchial hypervascularisation, which in itself is a nonspecific response to several stimuli.

The aim of bronchial artery embolisation is to occlude the most peripheral part of the artery with a particulate material about 300 μ in diameter. In more than 300 patients haemoptysis was immediately stopped in 70%. Delayed recurrence occurs occasionally, the lowest rate with the sequelae of TB, and the highest with intracavitary aspergillomas.

Santelli et al. (1994) : Although most patients with haemoptysis and active TB may bleed from the bronchial circulation, Rasmussen aneurysms may occur from the pulmonary artery branches and may be embolised with coils (see also p. 7.12).

Cowling and Belli (1995) : Point out that the bronchial arteries may communicate with the phrenic, intercostal, internal mammary, thyrocervical and other branches of the axillary and subclavian arteries, with the possible danger of particulate emboli passing into the thyro-cervical, vertebral and spinal arteries.

Allison (1995) : Felt that CT was the best 'tool' for preliminary study before considering embolisation. **Ionic contrast media should never be used for bronchial angiography because of the danger of paraplegia.** He also felt that alcohol or other **liquid embolisation agents should never be employed** because of the danger that these may pass down to capillary level in the spinal cord, the oesophagus, heart or coronary vessels (via collaterals not seen on a preliminary angiogram). He also pointed out that a greatly increased blood-flow through dilated bronchial arteries to part of a lung (e.g. RUL) may 'displace' blood from the PA supply or cause this part of the PA to shut down and hence give rise to an area of reduced or apparently absent perfusion, on a perfusion lung scan (i.e. the part perfused by the dilated bronchial vessels 'appears' underperfused').

Jackson et al. (1996) : Massive haemoptysis = > 300 ml - 50% will die if untreated. Bronchial artery embolism will give immediate control in 75 to 90%, but about 20% will rebleed. Illustrated a case of PMF causing severe haemoptysis.

Marshall et al. (1996) : Role of radiology in the investigation and management of pts. with haemoptysis. Immediate control of haemoptysis is achieved in 75 to 90% of pts. by bronchial artery embolisation but up to 20% will re-bleed within six months and 50% will have further significant haemoptyses on longer term follow-up.

Van den Berg et al. (1996) : Bronchial to coronary artery anastomosis - a potential hazard in bronchial artery embolisation.

Vujic et al. (1980) : Reported a case where intercostal artery embolisation caused spinal cord infarction, even though no blood supply to the spinal cord was seen on angiography prior to embolisation.

Moteki et al. (1998) : Evaluation of intradural and oesophageal enhancement by bronchial arterial angio-CT before bronchial artery infusion - this is much more sensitive than DSA in showing such circulation and in preventing oesophageal ulceration and spinal cord damage with bronchial artery infusions or embolisation.

Phillips and Ruttley (2000) : A branch from the inferior phrenic artery may supply the medial lung base in about 8% of individuals.

Isotope lung scans (Illus. **LUNG SCAN**) are a more convenient method for demonstrating pulmonary perfusion than carrying out pulmonary angiography, even though the anatomical detail obtained is much less. Lung perfusion and ventilation scans are commonly carried out (as for suspected pulmonary embolism). If both are to be carried out seriatim, the ventilation study is usually carried out first, as the isotope used for this will be exhaled and not interfere with the perfusion study. If the perfusion is done first, then Compton scatter from the injected colloid may degrade the following ventilation study.

Technique - In pulmonary scintiscanning, particular aggregates, e.g. of albumen of the order of 20 to 100μ in diameter, and labelled with a suitable radioactive isotope such as Tc^{99m}, are injected IV and lodge temporarily in the pulmonary capillaries. The injection is made with the patient lying down to try to avoid postural perfusion artefacts. Usually 500,000 to 1 M or more particles are injected and the safety factor is large, as the normal lung-bed contains about 350 M pre-capillary arterioles, with diameters of 10 to 30μ. However in patients with poor respiratory reserve, it may be prudent to reduce the number of particles used to 200,000 or less. (The author had one patient die 30 mins. following the injection of 2M particles several years ago - he was having syncopal attacks of breathlessness, and at autopsy all muscular pulmonary artery branches were filled by small emboli. As these were distributed **evenly** throughout the lungs, the **lung scan appeared normal**. His plain chest radiograph showed enlarged main pulmonary arteries - see Wright, 1974b).

Several views (PA., AP, oblique and lateral) are taken with a gamma camera. SPECT (see p. 22.8) tomograms may also be taken if the camera is capable of rotation and is fitted with a dedicated computer. For the ventilation study, an inhaled gas such as Kr^{81m} or Xe^{133} may be used, or labelled inhaled micro-particles which may be inhaled in aerosol form.

Clinical usage - Besides being useful for demonstrating reduced pulmonary perfusion due to larger pulmonary emboli, with a mismatched, normal ventilation and reduced perfusion pattern, in the affected areas, the technique will also demonstrate other perfusion defects due to bullae, poor development (as in the Swyer-James or Macleod syndrome - see ps. 7.9 - 10), aerated lung squashed by a fluid collection or a peripheral mass, etc. With consolidation there is often normal perfusion, but a reduced area(s) of ventilation. After a few days the distribution may become blurred, with unclear differentiation. Asthma and emphysema may also show patchy defects in perfusion like lace-work often accompanied by similar ventilation defects.

The effects of tumours are variable. Peripheral masses give rise to defects in ventilation and perfusion and ventilation corresponding to the mass. Central lesions may cause a reduction in the blood supply to the affected lung in a variety of ways (a) due to hilar involvement of vessels, (b) by causing lobar or lung collapse or consolidation and (c) by stimulating reflex vasoconstriction in response to anoxia - particularly caused by a tumour in a main bronchus (see Fig. 7.8). This is further discussed as **Oeser's sign** - see ps. 7.10 - 12. Tumour spreading in the hilum or mediastinum may like fibrosis (p. 18.4) also constrict a pulmonary artery. For these reasons lung scans have often been used to study the amount of properly perfused lung in patients for possible lung surgery, including transplantation.

Following radiotherapy, there is often a marked reduction in perfusion of the irradiated lobe or lung, particularly if the hilum has been included in the irradiated area (see also ps. 11.19 - 20). Scarring due to past TB, surgery (e.g. thoracoplasty), fungus disease, mediastinitis, etc. may have a similar effect.

Bizarre effects may sometimes be encountered, such as the diffuse para-vascular loss of perfusion and ventilation with lymphangitis carcinomatosa (see Illus. **LYMPHANGITIS, Pt. 37a-c**); the 'stripe sign' with centrilobular emphysema (see ref. to Sostman & Gottschalk. 1982, p. 7.31), a defect corresponding to an interlobar or subpulmonary pleural effusion, or 'bright areas' of greatly increased activity due to a labelled thrombus being injected if there is difficulty in cannulating a patient's vein with the needle, and blood clots in the syringe.

A number of authors have used the method for trying to assess the operability of bronchial tumours, but the author has not used the method routinely for this purpose - only to answer specific clinical questions.

Maynard et al. (1969) noted that the vascular impairment of a lung containing a tumour was often of greater magnitude than plain chest radiographs suggested. They found that hilar lesions produced greater changes than peripheral lesions on the scan and thought that except in isolated cases, lung scans were likely to be of little value in the early diagnosis of carcinoma. They did not think that scans determine resectability, but suggested that they might be of some use as an indication of response to radiotherapy.

Garnett (1969) noted such a good correlation of lung scanning compared with differential bronchospirometry, that they were able to abandon the latter.

Secker Walker and Goodwin (1971) suggested that pulmonary scintiscanning might be more accurate in determining **inoperability of lung tumours** than plain chest radiographs, and pointed out that as a **tumour approached the main bronchus as judged by bronchoscopy**, or the **hilum as indicated by radiography, the relative perfusion of the affected lung was diminished**. Secker Walker and Provan (1969) and Secker Walker et al. (1971) found that when perfusion of the affected lung was less than one-third of the total, the tumour was unlikely to be resectable.

Katz et al. (1981) studied 114 patients with early lung cancer by both ventilation and perfusion studies and found no pattern that was diagnostic for cancer. Occasionally the investigation might help with localising an occult tumour, but often the co-existence of other abnormalities, especially emphysema made this difficult.

A ventilation scan may also demonstrate **air-trapping** behind a bronchial block, or in an emphysematous cyst or bulla. Ackery (1971) felt that he could demonstrate air-trapping in up to 80% of patients with central bronchial tumours i.e. due to obstructive emphysema. He also found this with some peripherally situated tumours (presumably due to secondary central spread of the tumour). Hicks et al. (1990) compared changes of ventilation with CT in middle aged smokers, and found a non-uniform ventilation was often present, but this was not always associated with anatomical changes shown by CT, suggesting that temporary airway narrowing occurred. Cunningham and Mitchell (1991) showed that some bullae could be well ventilated, with absent perfusion. (Some bullae showed delayed emptying of Kr^{81m}, as well as slow or almost absent filling).

Pulmonary embolism and infarction - Illus. **EMBOLUS/INFARCT**.

The two terms are not synonymous for embolism may not lead to infarction (from infarciri = to stuff), if sufficient circulation persists, either through the pulmonary or bronchial arteries. Embolism is common with lower limb or pelvic vein thrombosis and may follow injury, prolonged bed-rest, long air-line flights, the encasement of a lower limb or the abdomen in a plaster cast (see below), complicate carcinoma (especially the pancreas) or the use of a high oestrogen contraceptive pill (more common ten or more years ago), follow surgery or disseminated intravascular coagulation. In some patients there may be a metabolic cause such as antibodies to phospholipids or some other condition producing hypercoagulability, such as occurs following myocardial infarction.

Emboli are usually removed fairly rapidly from the pulmonary vessels, by a combination of fibrinolysis, breaking up and organisation. The time scale for this is variable from days to weeks, and depends on the size of the embolus and the well-being of the patient. Incomplete resolution, leading to infarction, scarring or permanent pulmonary hypertension occurs in a few cases. One should also note that in discussing BOOP (ps. 3.31 - 33) the point is made that ischaemic lung may respond by producing fibrotic reactions.

Acute embolism causes a sudden reduction in the pulmonary circulation to the affected part(s) of the lung. This may be accentuated by vascular spasm, perhaps due to sudden **hypoxia** in the affected lobe or lung. Reduced perfusion may lead to reduced fluid within the lung producing increased translucency, narrowing of the arteries on the affected side and contralateral dilatation. If the condition is bilateral, then the changes may be reflected in the vessels of the affected lobes. With major blockages, it is untrue to state, as often appears in text-books that the chest radiograph is likely to be normal. Westermark (1938), Shapiro and Rigler (1948) and Chang (1967) described the 'characteristic appearance of ischaemic lung' as the 'Westermark sign' i.e. - a marked increased radio-lucency of the involved lung, with elevation of the hemidiaphragm (from decreased lung volume), the hilar shadow being small, the descending pulmonary artery (and its branches) small and spastic - often accompanied by compensatory dilatation of the pulmonary vessels in the contra-lateral lung.

Sometimes the **main pulmonary artery in the hilum is enlarged**, with **oligaemia in the lung**; this sign may be bilateral with gross blockage of both pulmonary arteries. (Clinically such patients will often be shocked, with a ashen or cyanosed appearance, chest pain , sometimes referred to the diaphragm, a right ventricular strain on an ECG and a split second heart sound). In less marked cases, with segmental or sub-segmental lesions, greater difficulty is experienced in recognising the subtle minor vascular changes, but if a previous radiograph is available for comparison, it may often be of great help.

In patients with distal or smaller or symmetrical emboli there may no plain film signs, but in chronic cases, the bronchial vessels may become hypertrophied. HRCT studies show that vascular impairment may result in a **mosaic pattern** of lung attenuation similar to that seen with air-trapping in bronchiolitis etc. (see ps. 3.25 - 28).

The majority of emboli and infarcts occur in the lower lobes, presumably due to the normally greater amount of blood passing through them. Basal lesions may produce collapse, consolidation or nodules (see below), and are often associated with blood-stained pleural fluid. Even congestive changes with septal line engorgement may be seen with an established infarct.

Diagnosis is important as there is a mortality of 30% untreated, compared with 6% in treated patients.

Pulmonary blood flow is markedly impaired when emboli obstruct central arteries, but infarction appears to be uncommon although frequent when distal arteries are occluded. This is probably partly explained by the collateral blood flow from the bronchial arteries entering the pulmonary circulation, distal to the site of the central obstruction. Also emboli may not fill the whole of the lumina of embolised pulmonary vessels, thus allowing some blood to pass around the emboli and retain a degree of perfusion.

Lung ventilation and perfusion scans are commonly used for the diagnosis of embolism, and when this is acute and gross, they can be quite reliable. However when carried out late and when infarction has occurred with the alveoli filling with fluid and cellular reaction, then the picture becomes confused - ventilation reduced and revascularisation occurring due to the lysis of the emboli. Small emboli are not well demonstrated and may be confused with scars, inflammatory disease, pleural exudates pressing on the lung, etc. Larger defects may also be confused with scars, emphysema, etc.

When embolism in the lungs is diffuse and small (in the smaller conducting arteries) then a lung scan may appear normal, as the overall pattern of perfusion in the lungs will appear symmetrical and even - it is only the larger emboli which can be detected. Such patients have a very precarious pulmonary circulation, and can easily be tipped into complete circulatory failure and die (as occurred in the patient described two sections above). This case was not unique, and diffuse emboli are not uncommonly seen at post-mortem examinations (about 30% of patients dying in hospital have evidence of embolism) - it is thus still very common.

Pulmonary angiography, particularly with DVI, is used in some centres to confirm pulmonary embolism suggested by lung scans. It is however not a perfect 'gold standard', as difficulties are still experienced due to overlapping vessels, reduced lung volume or collapse. Quinn et al. (1987) studied 60 cases in this way and found that different observers **agreed** when segmental or larger pulmonary arteries were occluded, but often **disagreed** if only subsegmental vessels were involved. **MR angiography** is also starting to be used for diagnosing pulmonary embolism (Schiebler et al., 1993); **spiral CT** is very impressive (see below - p. 7.33 - 34 and p. 20.22 - 23), but the dose of IV contrast medium needed can be rather high for a severely ill patient. Central emboli may also be shown by **transoesophageal echocardiography** and this method may be particularly valuable for follow-up during thrombolytic or anticoagulant therapy (Chan et al., 1994).

Many studies have been made to try to assess the value and accuracy of lung scans. Reports are often written as **'high'**, **'intermediate'** or **'low probability'** for emboli, or **'normal'**. In many patients the study may be 'indeterminate' particularly when the patients have marked emphysema, congestive cardiac failure, bullae or lung cysts. In the differentiation of pneumonia, one has to remember that ventilation is characteristically reduced first with the pulmonary circulation being maintained, but after a few days the picture may become blurred (as noted above).

In many clinical situations there may be obvious venous problems in the lower limbs and attention is often paid to them by carrying out venograms, or US (including Doppler) studies.

In other cases e.g. with renal or pelvic tumours, post renal transplant, abdominal trauma, etc., there may be an IVC or pelvic vein thrombosis leading to pulmonary embolism. Others at particular risk are those having orthopaedic or gynaecological surgery. The author has studied many with embolism complicating these and knows of many deaths complicating plaster-cast treatment for lower limb severe sprains or fractures or surgery and feels that these patients should take soluble aspirin to try to prevent such complications. Anecdotal cases have included a young woman with a severely sprained ankle (who died five days later from PE), a hotel manager who fractured his tibia (the same day the author sustained a similar injury) who died five days later, and a senior medical colleague who had a plaster jacket for a back problem (the latter correctly diagnosing himself shortly before he died) and including gross cases, successfully diagnosed, who had thrombolytic therapy or emergency Trendelenberg operations.

In order to study the value of V/Q scans, various multicentre studies have been carried out in the UK, the USA and other countries. The largest has been in the USA (PIOPED - Prospective Investigation of Pulmonary Embolism Diagnosis), which demonstrated that normal scans were most valuable in largely excluding pulmonary embolism. A real problem exists with 'blind' reporting, particularly by 'experts' who do not actually see the patients, check the complementary chest radiographs or study the leg veins of doubtful cases with US or venography. In cases which appear gross most 'sensible' clinicians will start anticoagulant treatment immediately and check that **improvement is occurring with a follow-up study, thus proving the diagnosis!**

Pulmonary angiography is less frequently considered necessary in the UK (even in centres with access to DSA) than in the USA, unless thrombectomy is being considered (e.g. in cases of diffuse intravascular coagulation, or with a **'saddle embolus'**). Note also that 'apparent pulmonary emboli' (ventilation/perfusion mismatches) may be caused by abnormal lung perfusion - i.e. shunting into the lung from a bronchial, or other systemic, pulmonary anastomotic circulation.

Opaque lung shadows due to infarction.

Pulmonary emboli do not produce opaque lung shadows unless infarction supervenes. When this happens and the alveoli become filled with blood (from the bronchial circulation or collateral circulation), the affected area of lung may become dense, the 'classical' appearance being a dense wedge-shaped area, with its base adjacent to the pleura (reflecting the perfusion loss in the lung). This may sometimes be seen on plain radiographs, or better on tomograms, including CT sections (see Illus. **EMBOLUS/INFARCT, Pt. 3a-c**). Such areas of consolidation may also be demonstrable by **ultrasound**, where they abut the pleura. Gordon, G.A.Douglas (1909 - 97, from the Willesden Hospital, London) used to demonstrate the use of A scan ultra-sound, via the intercostal spaces esp. posteriorly, for the diagnosis of peripheral pulmonary emboli in the 1960's. The present author saw one of these demonstrations and tried the method but found it rather unreliable as one could not differentiate infarction from other causes of consolidation, particularly pneumonia. (He published the method in two monographs in 1962 & 1964 - for Gordon's obituary - see British Institute of Radiology, BIRthday News - Nov. 1997, p. 4). **Transoesophageal ultrasonography** has also been used for detecting pulmonary emboli - see p. 16.22.

Fig. 7.14 '**Hampton's hump**' - lung mass caused by infarction.

Hampton and Castleman (1940) studied the radiographic appearance of emboli by radiographing corpses in the erect position and by correlating their findings with post-mortem appearances. They noted the difference between embolism, with and without infarction, and found that granulation tissue at the edge of an infarct may produce a sharp margin, such that with an infarct at the bases or in the mid zones, a sharp upper border or 'hump' may be seen. This is often referred to as

'Hampton's hump' and is a useful sign in the differentiation of infarction from pleural thickening or fluid, in a costo-phrenic angle or horizontal fissure (Fig. 7.14 and Illus. **HAMPTON'S HUMP, Embolus/Infarct Pt. 35a-d**).

The author has encountered a few cases where peripheral rounded, notched or tennis racquet-shaped nodules were due to pulmonary infarction. Some had a tail; others were similar radiologically and at surgery to peripheral lung tumours, their true nature only being revealed at histology. In one patient a peripheral nodule increased to nearly double its original size over a period of 14 months, and others have increased a little in size, presumably due to increased peripheral fibrosis. Some have also cavitated (see below). A good number, however, have been recognised by their shapes, and diminishing size.

One memorable case warns that the 'obvious' may not be the cause. A young man had a testicular teratoma removed. A few weeks later he became jaundiced, had a large liver and rapidly increasing spherical lung nodules. This was before ultrasound became available to examine the liver. It was thought that he was going to die, but he recovered spontaneously. It was found that the liver enlargement was due to an incompatible blood transfusion, and the lung nodules to pulmonary infarcts, secondary to a leg vein thrombosis. They all regressed and he recovered.

Other cases of infarcts mimicking 'disappearing deposits' or tumours have been seen in patients with bladder tumours, the pulmonary nodules occurring first, and then resolving before the primary tumours became apparent. They were probably due to emboli from pelvic vein thrombosis.

Fibrinolysis and organisation often resolve smaller emboli within 48 hours. Organisation and resolution of infarcts may take weeks or months, whether or not anticoagulants have been given. Most end with complete clearing, but linear scars (Simon, 1970 described two cases), nodules, cavitation (Fig. 7.15) or calcification may occur. Infarction may also cause progressive fibrosis or shrinkage of a lobe, much as is seen with infarction secondary to staphylococcal pneumonia. Infarcts may also become secondarily infected, e.g. the case shown in Illus. **GAS GANGRENE Pt. 1a-e**, in this case with Clostridium perfringens (or welchii - see also p. 19.14).

Walker and Wilson (1967) reported four cases where lobar or segmental lesions due to infarcts mimicked lung tumours radiologically and were only diagnosed after excision and a further case where infarction and a lung tumour co-existed. They also reviewed 19 cases from the literature. They noted that the majority of the patients were males and in the cancer age group. Pain of pleuritic character was present in many, haemoptysis was variable. Some of the patients had weight loss. Cavitation was a common feature. The lower lobes were involved in most cases and multiple lesions were sometimes present. Increase in the size of the lesion whilst under observation and persistence of the changes for weeks or months was not uncommon. Hilar enlargement could occur from enlargement of a main pulmonary artery. Bronchography showed non-filling of the affected segmental bronchi, and bronchial stenosis was often found at bronchoscopy.

Heitzman (1984) noted than infarcts may involve a secondary lobule or a larger area of lung. In some cases the embolism is diffuse and widespread, and may only be noted clinically because of pulmonary hypertension. Each secondary lobule appears to have separated vascularity from its neighbours, the only collaterals being via the bronchial arteries, or possibly via retrograde blood flow in the branches of the pulmonary veins. Anastomoses between the branches of the pulmonary and bronchial arteries appear to take place at capillary level.

CT was used by several authors (e.g. Godwin et al., 1980b, Cholankeril et al., 1982 and Sinner, 1978 and 1982) to study infarction, either deliberately or fortuitously when e.g. neoplasm has been suspected. The CT findings were reviewed by Chintapalli et al. (1988) and grouped into two categories :
(a) Vascular - intraluminal filling defect(s) in pulmonary arteries on contrast enhanced dynamic studies; together with oligaemia, dilatation of main pulmonary arteries, a decrease in the calibre of small branches and irregularity of the vessels.
(b) Parenchymal - wedge-shaped, pleural-based lesions, nodules or masses, linear (mainly horizontal) shadows, cavitary lesions and pleural effusion.
(See also references to Kereiakes et al., 1983, Balakarishnan et al, 1989, Huang et al., 1989 and Kuhlman et al., 1990, below).
Spiral CT is being used more and more for the diagnosis of pulmonary embolism, and also to **check patients with doubtful isotope scans**. It is particularly

valuable for showing emboli in the more central vessels, but not all segmental vessel emboli are demonstrated. Embolism distal to segmental vessels is beyond the capability of spiral CT for diagnosis, but is clinically not so acutely important, although this reduced peripheral circulation due to pulmonary embolism may result in areas of lung fibrosis.

Further discussion and references to spiral CT are given in the references below (see esp. Louvegny et al., 1996, Rémy-Jardin, 1992, 1996 & 1997, Vernhet et al., 1996, and Hansell 1997, etc. and on p. 20.27 - 28).

Cavitation, scar or bullous formation following infarction - Illus. **INFARCT CAVITATING.**

Infarcts may become infected or be septic in origin, and both may undergo cavitation (Fig. 7.15). However, **cavitation within infarcts appears to be uncommon**. McGoldrick et al. (1979) followed 58 angiographically proven pulmonary infarcts by serial chest radiography for over three months but did not find a single case. Besides aseptic or degenerative cavitation (as described in the next section), cavitation may be caused by **septic emboli** or by secondary infection of infarcted areas - Zelefsky and Lutzker (1977) - 'target sign' of septic emboli.

Septic infarcts may be seen in drug addicts, in patients with osteomyelitis, an infected A/V shunt (for haemodialysis), etc. Other infarcts, may become secondarily infected (Illus. **INFARCT INFECTED**). Especially in the upper half of the chest, infarcts may undergo **aseptic or degenerative cavitation**, and this is not very rare. Wilson et al. (1986) reported eight cases - six with single and two with multiple cavities. These occurred in areas of infarct consolidation (> 4 cm.) after about two weeks. The outer margins of the lesions tended to be well-defined, rounded or oval and some were lobulated. Cavities tended to first increase and later decrease in size. Initially after the appearance of a cavity, its wall thickness was thick (up to 1 cm.) and uneven, but after weeks or months become thinner (2 to 3 mm.). Some cavities had scalloped margins and/or band like shadows or strands crossing them and dividing them into more than one compartment. If a patient survived, the cavities tended to heal leaving a scar. Secondary infection may produce fluid within the cavity, and possibly an aspergilloma.

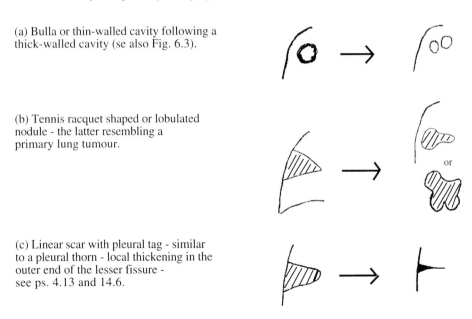

(a) Bulla or thin-walled cavity following a thick-walled cavity (se also Fig. 6.3).

(b) Tennis racquet shaped or lobulated nodule - the latter resembling a primary lung tumour.

or

(c) Linear scar with pleural tag - similar to a pleural thorn - local thickening in the outer end of the lesser fissure - see ps. 4.13 and 14.6.

Fig. 7.15   Types of scar which may follow pulmonary infarction - see also 'whorled nodule' - Fig. 14.23 (p. 14.43) & Illus. **INFARCT CHRONIC** & **WHORLED NODULE 24 & 27.** N.B. Some scars due to infarction may become calcified.

Further references.

Coke and Dundee (1955) : Cavitation in bland infarcts of the lung.
Grieco and Ryan (1968) : Aseptic cavitary pulmonary infarction.
Scharf et al.(1971) : Aseptic cavitation in pulmonary infarction.
Hall et al. (1977) : Pneumothorax complicating aseptic cavitating pulmonary infarction.

Fleischner (1959) : Unilateral pulmonary embolism with **increased 'compensatory' circulation** in unoccluded lung - **'Fleischner "plump hilar" sign'**.
(1962) : Pulmonary embolism.
(1967a) : Recurrent pulmonary embolism and cor pulmonale.
(1967b) : Roentgenology of the plain infarct - suggested that an enlarging pulmonary infarct may be due to failure of the collateral circulation with cardiac failure. Healed infarcts may be linear or rounded and contiguous with pleural scars.
Chrispin et al. (1963) : Radiology of obliterative pulmonary hypertension and thrombo-embolism. Multiple small clot emboli may impact in the small pulmonary arteries occluding them. Proximal to the site of occlusion, the arterial wall thickens as pulmonary hypertension develops. Two groups are seen at arteriography - (a) patent major arteries and tortuosity in small peripheral arteries with some random pruning and (b) occlusion of major arteries and leashes of patent abnormal vessels which may produce ill-defined, rounded shadows on chest radiographs.
Scarrow and Galloway (1966) : Non-traumatic pulmonary haematoma - man aged 48 with recurrent thrombophlebitis developed a spherical RUL mass. It decreased in size over 8 to 10 weeks, becoming elliptical and containing a crescentic air shadow with an irregular thick wall. He died following haemoptysis, and at autopsy there were multiple pulmonary infarcts, with an organising cavitating haematoma in the RUL.
Fred et al. (1966) : Rapid resolution of pulmonary-emboli in man.
Chat et al. (1967) : Observations on the fate of large pulmonary emboli.
Change (1967) : Classified emboli into acute or chronic, with proximal, intermediate or distal embolism. Also noted that occlusion of the pulmonary artery does not always result in haemorrhagic infarction, since collateral circulation from bronchial vessels will prevent alveolar damage, and allow complete resolution. An acute occlusion of **major branch** of a pulmonary artery may cause an **'amputated appearance'** of the **descending pulmonary artery** with **dilatation above it from pulmonary hypertension**.
Figley et al. (1967) : Radiographic aspects of pulmonary embolism.
Kerr et al. (1971) : The value of the plain radiograph in acute massive pulmonary embolism.
Woesner et al. (1971) : The **'melting sign'** "is that of a gradual reduction in size and shrinkage of the pathological shadow, with the same general configuration seen on the initial Roentgenogram being maintained".
Anderson et al. (1973) : Radiographic appearances in primary and thrombotic pulmonary hypertesnsion primary pulmonary hypertension was often associated with enlargement of the main and hilar pulmonary arteries without evidence of pulmonary infarction; it was less common in those with thrombo-embolic disease.
Dalen and Alpert (1975) : Natural history of pulmonary embolism.
Dalen et al. (1977) : Pulmonary embolism, pulmonary haemorrhage and pulmonary infarction.
Bookstein et al. (1980) : Diagnosis of pulmonary embolism.
Li et al. (1978) : V/Q mismatches unassociated with pulmonary embolism.
Lavender et al. (1981) : Kr^{81m} ventilation scanning in acute respiratory disease.
(1988) : Ventilation and perfusion imaging - a review.
(1990) : Ventilation and perfusion imaging has a high accuracy where the perfusion defects are large or multiple, but when subsegmental lesions are poorly imaged compared with angiography. (An alternative approach is to localise venous thrombosis by ultrasound or by using a radioactive labelled monoclonal antibody with a high affinity for platelets (see Lavender et al. 1988 and Stuttle et al, 1989, below).
Lavender (1991) : Ventilation/perfusion in respiratory disease - both pneumonia and collapse are associated with perfused non-ventilated lung. Hypoxia is due to R to L shunting through the non-ventilated lung - also happens post-operatively, and in chronic lung disease in response to airway obstruction. Note also (a) that a large heart can cause pressure on the left lung, and reduce ventilation and (b) pulmonary vasculitis may be due to large or small vessel disease and some patients may have multiple non-segmental defects.
Cholankeril et al. (1982) : Pulmonary embolism diagnosed by CT.
Greenspan et al. (1982) : Accuracy of the chest radiograph in diagnosis of pulmonary embolism.

Sinner (1978) : CT patterns of pulmonary thrombo-embolism and infarction.
(1982) : Studied 21 consecutive cases of clinically suspected pulmonary embolism with chest radiographs - peripheral changes with **wedge-shaped densities, with their bases adjacent to the periphery of the lung and their apices pointing towards the hila**.

Sostman et al. (1982 & 1983) : Ventilation and perfusion scans produce too many indeterminate readings and are not sufficiently specific.

Sostman and Gottschalk (1982) : The '**stripe sign**' - defects which do not quite extend to the lung edge - leaving a peripheral parenchymal stripe, may be seen in non-embolic lung disease. The presence of the 'stripe sign' was accurately predictive of the absence of pulmonary embolism in the specific area of the sign.
Sostman and Gottschalk (1992) : Concluded that the 'stripe' is a useful indication that a perfusion defect is **not due** to pulmonary embolism. However they showed at least one example of a 'false stripe sign'; they also noted that the sign may be seen in lungs that contain emboli.

Wedge - embolus

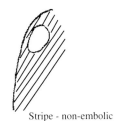

Stripe - non-embolic

Murata et al. (1986) : '**Stripe sign**' - central pattern defect of pulmonary emphysema.

Kereiakes et al. (1983) : CT in acute and chronic thrombo-embolic pulmonary hypertension.
Palla et al. (1983) : Studied **enlargement of the descending branch of the right pulmonary artery** in cases of pulmonary embolism. They measured this in 73 patients with embolism at four points starting from the superior venous angle. The **artery was larger in acute embolism - 25% having a 'sausage' shaped appearance**, and with resolution the arterial size decreased.
Hull et al. (1985) : In patients with matched small lesions, who should have a low probability of pulmonary emboli, a quarter were regarded as having pulmonary emboli on angiography.
Lisbona et al. (1985) : Lung scans in primary pulmonary hypertension were associated with non-segmental patchy defects of perfusion (i.e. emphysema), whilst in thrombo-embolic hypertensives, they were characterised by segmental and/or lobar defects of perfusion, with or without subsegmental defects.
Sostman et al. (1986) : Imaging of pulmonary embolism.
Wellman (1986) : Current status report on the role of nuclear medicine in pulmonary embolism.
Dorfman et al. (1987) : Occult pulmonary embolism is a common occurrence with deep vein thrombosis.
Matsumoto et al. (1987) : CT demonstration of pulmonary venous and arterial occlusive disease.
Strauss et al. (1987) : Noted that no patient had a radiographic lung parenchymal opacity, a matching perfusion defect and normal ventilation, without having pulmonary embolism.
Balakrishnan et al. (1989) : CT of 12 patients with pulmonary infarcts showed wedge-shaped peripheral densities that extended to the pleura. The extent of the pleural margin showed considerable variation. In more than half low density areas were seen within the lesion. Those without a broad pleural base may be older lesions which have lost volume and become partly organised.
Huang et al. (1989) : CT of septic pulmonary emboli in 15 patients - the signs included -
(i) peripheral nodules with clearly identifiable feeding vessels associated with metastatic lung abscesses (10 cases),
(ii) subpleural wedge-shaped densities with or without necrosis caused by septic infarcts (11 cases).
Moser et al. (1989) : Chronic thrombo-embolic occlusion in the adult can mimic pulmonary artery agenesis.
Robinson (1989) from Leeds : Lung scintigraphy - doubt and certainty in the diagnosis of pulmonary embolism - **a normal lung scan excludes embolism as well as a normal arteriogram**. No problem occurs with patients with high clinical probabilities of embolism and a highly probable lung scan. Difficult groups include those with pre-existing lung disease and patients with contraindications to anticoagulant treatment.
Stuttle et al. (1989) : Sequential imaging of post-operative thrombosis with labelled platelet-specific monoclonal antibody.
Goddard et al. (1990) : Factors contributing to an indeterminate lung scan - most common was congestive cardiac failure, others were due to infection, but COAD was a less important factor than is usually expected. **Delay in scanning should be avoided, as this contributed to the uncertainty in many cases**.
Hayward et al. (1990) and Cooper et al. (1991) : Surveyed 360 acute hospitals in the UK to assess the usage of lung scanning and pulmonary angiography in pulmonary embolism. Lung scanning was available at 199 hospitals and angiography at 120, with 99 providing both. About 20 V/Q scans (on average) were performed in each centre per month (total 47,000 per year), but only about four angiograms per year (total 490 per year). Several hospitals which could perform angiograms had not done them for more than 3 years. They concluded 'thus pulmonary angiography is used in the UK in no more than a tiny percentage of patients with suspected thrombo-embolism, in contrast with the widespread and frequent use of lung scanning.'
Kuhlman et al. (1990) : Diagnosis of **septic pulmonary emboli** with CT in 18 cases - signs :
    multiple peripheral nodules (0.5 to 3.5 cm)

feeding vessel sign
cavitation, wedge-shaped peripheral lesions abutting the pleura, air bronchograms within nodules and extension into the pleural space.

Whitehouse (1990) : Venous thrombosis and thrombo-embolism.

James et al. (1991) : Tc^{99m} technegas ventilation scintigraphy in the diagnosis of pulmonary embolism.

Auger et al. (1992) : Chronic major-vessel thrombo-embolic pulmonary artery obstruction -angiographic appearance.

Kester and Hassien (1992) : Pulmonary embolism caused by a surgical sponge.

Morrell and Seed (1992) : Diagnosing pulmonary embolism. If the lung scan is non-diagnostic attention should turn to the proximal leg veins. "Patients with a non-diagnostic lung scan, which most doctors currently regard as a negative result, therefore require phlebography, Doppler ultrasonography or impedance plethysmography".

Go et al. (1993) : **Increased ventilation** in areas of decreased perfusion due to pulmonary embolism - the 'enhanced V-P mismatch sign' - seen in 15 of 700 scans.

Gottschalk et al. (1993a&b) : **PIOPED** study of V/Q scans, pulmonary angiograms and clinical outcomes (731 in randomised group had pulmonary angiograms). Recommended adjustments to usual criteria - (i) incorrect to consider a single mismatch as low probability, (ii) & (iii) V/Q defects in a clear area of the lung and two areas of segmental mismatch should be considered as intermediate.

Gray et al. (1993, UK) : Lung scan reporting language - what does it mean? (Gross in the 1995 Year Book comments on this study and **agrees with the present author that it is the radiologist's duty to report exactly what he thinks, without the equivocation often used i.e. pseudo-science of degree of probability!**).

Grist et al. (1993) : Pulmonary angiography with MR imaging.

Kaboli et al. (1993) : V/P lung scintigraphy - analysed 244 patients - concluded it was a safe and effective non-invasive method for diagnosing PE and has a significant effect on pt. management.

Teigen et al. (1993) : Contrast-enhanced CT for the diagnosis of PE in 86 pts. out of 25 with angiographic or pathological proof of PE, 19 proven positive CT scans.

Tourassi et al. (1993) : Artificial neural network for diagnosis of acute pulmonary embolism.

Worsley et al. (1993a) : Chest radiographic findings with acute PE in **PIOPED** study - were normal in only 12% - most common abnormalities were collapse or areas of increased opacity (in lower zones 'intermediate probability', compared with 'low probability' in upper and mid zones) - also occurred with equal prevalence in those without PE - 1063 pts. had pulm. angios., 383 having PE.

Worsley et al. (1993b) : Detailed analysis of pts. with matched V/P defects and chest radiographic opacities.

Wattie and Marshall (1993) : V/P scans and pulm. angios. (within 48 hrs) commonly disagreed.

Alderson (1994) : MR and US can diagnose deep venous thrombosis. MR can detect PE in the central pulmonary vasculature and high-speed CT seems capable of visualising PE in 2nd to 4th division pulm. vessels. Perfusion scintigraphy as a road map for these methods is attractive.

Goldberg et al. (1994) : The results of V/P scanning are not useful with focal consolidation.

Matsumoto and Tegtmeyer (1995) : Contemporary diagnostic approaches to acute pulmonary embolism.

Worsley and Alavi (1995) : Comprehensive analysis of the results of the **PIOPED** study.
(a) **High probability of PE** - 2 or more large (>75% of a segment) segmental perfusion defects; one large segmental perfusion defect and more than two moderate (26% of a segment) segmental perfusion defects; or four or more moderate segmental perfusion defects - in each group without corresponding abnormalities in ventilation or on chest radiograph.
(b) **Intermediate probability of PE** - one moderate or less than two large segmental perfusion defects without corresponding abnormalities in ventilation or chest radiograph; corresponding V/P defects and radiographic parenchymal opacity in lower lung zone; single moderate matched V/P defects with normal chest radiograph; corresponding V/P defects and small pleural effusion; difficulty in categorising scan as normal, low or high probability of PE.
(c) **Low probability of PE** - multiple matched V/P defects, regardless of size, with normal chest radiograph; corresponding V/P defects and radiographic parenchymal opacity in upper or middle lung zone; corresponding V/P defects and large pleural effusion; any perfusion defects with substantially larger abnormality on chest radiography; defects surrounded by normally perfused lung (stripe sign); more than three small (<25% of a segment) segmental perfusion defects with normal results on chest radiography; non-segmental perfusion defects (cardiomegaly, aortic impression, enlarged hila).
(d) **Very low probability of PE** - up to three small (<25% of a segment) segmental perfusion defects with a normal chest radiograph.
(e) **Normal findings** - no perfusion defects, perfusion outlining the shape of the lung in a chest radiograph.

Kember et al. (1996) : How do clinicians interpret the indeterminate V/Q scan report? Often wrongly as 30 - 40% of pts. with such reports may have had PE -necessity for better descriptions!

Fennerty (1997) : Diagnosis of PE - pts. with a non-diagnostic scan and negative results on non-invasive investigation of the leg veins have <5% risk of a further clinically detectable thrombo-embolic event. The mortality associated with a suspected but untreated PE in pts. with reduced cardio-resp. reserve is high (8.5%), even in those with a low probability scan - therefore these have a low threshold for initiating anti-coagulant therapy. **The mortality associated with anti-coagulant treatment for thrombo-embolic disease is 0.1%.**

Michaelis et al. (1997) : **Percutaneous removal of pulmonary artery thrombus** in a pt. with massive pulmonary embolism using the hydrolyser catheter.

Miller (1993) : Differentiation of slow flow from thrombus in thoracic MR imaging, emphasising phase images.
Loubeyre et al. (1994) : Compared **dynamic contrast enhanced MR angiography** with pulmonary angiography and found the former to be an accurate method for detecting emboli in the proximal portions of the pulmonary arteries, but was of little value for peripheral emboli.
Oser et al. (1996) : Anatomic distribution of PEs at pulmonary angiography - implications for cross-sectional images - those situated peripherally are likely to be detected by spiral CT.

Miszkiel and Shaw (1995) : **Helical CT contrast studies** (from aortic arch level downwards) showed pulm. arterial defects due to emboli (complete obstruction or **'rail track'** signs, including **'saddle emboli'**) particularly in the segmental vessels in the lower 2/3 of the R lung. False positives could be due to enlarged nodes; the method would also show unsuspected chest tumours.
Goodman et al. (1995) : In 20 patients with unresolved clinical and scintigraphic diagnosis, helical CT was only 63% sensitive compared with pulmonary angiography.
Gefter et al. (1995) : Well-designed clinical trials are warranted before CT (helical & electron beam) and MR can be used routinely in the diagnosis of acute PE.
Louvegny et al. (1996) : Spiral CT angiographic follow-up of acute central pulmonary embolism - 62 pts. - 30 had complete resolution - in remainder 21 had persistence of emboli in lobar and/or segmental arteries (90% asymptomatic) - pts. with persisting changes, including webs or diaphragms in vessels, received prolonged anticoagulation treatment.
Rémy-Jardin et al. (1992) : Used spiral volumetric CT in 42 patients to show complete or partial filling defects, 'railway track' signs and mural defects - (some false positive cases were due to 'intersegmental' lymph nodes or asymmetrical lung perfusion).
Rémy-Jardin et al. (1995) : Diagnosis of central pulmonary embolism with helical CT - role of 2D reconstructions.
Rémy-Jardin (1996) : Spiral CT of pulmonary embolism - important factors are **optimal vascular opacification** (data acquisition, cont. media injection, reconstruction & interpretation). Examines from bottom of aortic arch to IPVs - 3mm section thickness, 5mm table feed & 20s data acquisition time (or 5mm section thickness and 10s data acquisition) Breath hold 10s.- 180° linear interpolation algorithm with overlapping sections. Segmental arteries with thrombi are usually well seen especially with zooming. **Problems - pseudo-emboli** - due to insufficient time allowed for contrast medium to opacify arteries (bolus must be equated to scan) - normal haemodynamic shunts, - artefacts around IVC, - low concentration of cont. medium and high flow rates. **Hilar lymph nodes** - ULs lat. to PA; ML, ling. & LLs lat. to bronchi, but medial and ant. to PA.
Rémy-Jardin et al. (1996) : Spiral CT can reliably detect central PE.
Vernhet et al. (1996a) : Value of spiral CT in prone position for pulmonary embolism - considered it superior for lower lobes - greater blood flow and more thrombi seen in segmental arteries.
Vernhet et al. (1996b) : Spiral CT detection of pulmonary embolism in pts. with acute haemoptysis - 3/22 pts. had PE 2 of these also bronchiectasis.
Oliver and Reid (1997) : PEs and paradoxical embolus (occluding L subclavian artery) shown by spiral CT - presented clinically as a dissecting aneurysm, with chest pain, cyanosis and acute ischaemia of L arm.
Rémy-Jardin et al. (1997a) : Optimisation of spiral CT acquisition protocol for peripheral pulm. arteries - 2mm collimation at 0.75 per revolution enables marked improvement in the analysis of segmental and subsegmental pulmonary arteries.
Rémy-Jardin et al. (1997b) : CT studies showed that chronic pulmonary embolism may lead to ipsilateral proximal bronchial dilatation.
Rémy-Jardin et al. (1997c) : Spiral CT is expected to simplify the most widely accepted guidelines.
Van Rossum et al. (1996) : Role of spiral volumetric CT in pts. with clinical suspicion of PE and abnormal V/P scan - 24/42 pts. with non-diagnostic V/P scans had non-embolic abnormalities.
Hansell (1997) : Review - spiral CT & pulmonary embolism.
Technical - contrast enhanced spiral CT is currently unable to identify emboli within pulm. arts. below segmental level, therefore the region to be scanned may be confined to the volume between the level of the aspect of the aortic arch and the inf. pulm veins - a dist. of about 10cms. This covers < 2/3 of the volume of the thorax, therefore the limited contrast enhanced spiral CT should be preceded by an unenhanced scan covering the thorax; this may show lung densities due to peripheral infarcts, or other disease explaining the cause of the clinical complaint (e.g. ca lung, dissecting aortic aneurysm, etc.). The contrast enhanced spiral CT views may be narrow and fairly widely spaced, contrast may be given as a high density bolus given quickly with careful timing, or may be given in a larger volume with lower density at a lower flow rate. High contrast can cause streak artefacts from the opacified SVC on the adjacent R pulm. artery. Vascular shunts or SVC obstruction may alter normal blood flow and cause poor

opacification of the pulmonary vessels. Some vessels e.g. of lingula & RML run obliquely and will not be seen easily on transverse CT images, but can be visualised by reformatting in an oblique or longitudinal axis.

Radiological signs - the cardinal sign of PE is a **filling-defect** in an opacified pulm. artery; when contrast can flow around this a **'railway track'** may be seen if the artery lies parallel to & within the plane of section, or a **'polo-mint'** if the artery runs perpendicular to the plane of section. With complete obstruction from an embolus, it may **prevent any opacification** of that vessel. False negative and positive exams. can be caused by flow problems, motion artefacts, adjacent enlarged nodes (mistaken for vessels), excess mediastinal fat etc.

Conclusion - he quotes that the present tendency to use US of lower limb veins + spiral CT in some north American hospitals may not be the final answer, as MR may be the method choice for diagnosing PEs in the future.

Delany and Peebles (1997, from Southampton) : Perform a whole chest spiral CT before doing a contrast enhanced study of the central portion. They are not able to replace V/Q scans with spiral CT because of numbers, and reserve spiral CT for the more problematic cases. They find that CT often shows more thrombus than anticipated (**'increased clot burden'**) and that it also images 'saddle emboli' better than pulmonary angiography.

Lee, K. and Guest (1998) : Since contrast enhanced spiral CT is currently unreliable in identifying PE beyond segmental level, the region to be scanned can be limited to an area between the aortic arch and the inferior aspect of the inferior pulmonary veins. They also quote Goodman and Lipchik (1996) who provided indirect evidence to suggest that peripheral PEs are probably of limited clinical significance and the PIOPED follow-up study (Stein et al., 1995) showed no significance at mortality and morbidity between the treated and untreated groups.

Herold (1999) from Vienna : Spiral CT pulmonary angiography for PE should be viewed both with static sections and on **ciné loops**; as well as looking for clot defects in larger pulmonary arteries and their branches, one should also note the presence of pl. effusion, linear or larger areas of collapse, Hampton's hump, localised oligaemia and peripheral arcades (bronchial vessels). He uses 2 or 3mm CT sections and a couch speed of 5mm/sec. 120 - 150 ml of IV contrast is injected via a catheter, and scans are started after 10 - 15sec delay. Problem areas were at the origins of the RML and lingula, and pressure from enlarged nodes. 10% of patients could have poor opacification due to heart failure, etc.; in others even a patent foramen ovale could cause early opacification of the aorta, if the patient performed a good Valsalva manoeuvre. He also advocated **venograms of both legs to help prevent later emboli following a sentinel embolus**.

Higginson et al. (1999) : CT pulmonary angiography is most sensitive at detecting central thrombus. Peripheral hypovascular areas can be identified in association with pulmonary emboli and may be a marker of subsegmental emboli in cases where no central thrombus is demonstrated.

Reid et al. (1999) : Spiral CT performed for possible pulmonary embolism also allows the **heart** to be studied - relative size of the ventricles and thickness of their walls; thus indicating R or L cardiac failure, acute infarction, intraventricular thrombus, etc. **Acute right ventricular failure is a principal cause of death in PE**.

Moody (1999) : MR is becoming much better at showing clot-embolic defects within pulmonary arteries using shorter T1 and short TR with rapid acquisition and 3D viewing. It also has the advantage of being able to demonstrate **methaemoglobin** within thrombi using the **bright clot technique**. Previously **Time of Flight sequences could give rise to stasis artefacts mimicking thrombi**.

Steiner et al. (1996) : In comparison with helical CT, transthoracic and transoesophageal endobronchial echocardiography had limited accuracy for detecting pulmonary embolism.

Traill and Gleeson (1998) : Venous thrombo-embolic disease.
Reid and Murchison (1998) : Acute right ventricular dilatation - a new helical CT sign of massive PE.
Oliver et al. (1998) : Interventricular septal shift due to massive pulmonary embolism shown by spiral CT angiography - an old sign revisited.

Müller (2000) : Concluded that 2/3 of V/Q scans in the pts. in the PIOPED study were not useful in establishing or excluding PE. Pulm. angiography is associated with a 6% morbidity & 0.5% mortality and is rarely used in most centres. Spiral CT allows the whole chest to be examined in a short time + analysis of the pulmonary arteries during the peak of contrast enhancement. This needs careful attention to technique. CT also has the advantage of showing other unsuspected pathology e.g. tumour or vascular spasm in association with infection. Difficulties may be associated with enlarged lymph nodes adjacent to pulm. art. branches mimicking vascular defects - a useful point in differentiation is that vessels cont. emboli are often larger than normal. Technical failures occur in 1 - 5% of scans and are largely due to motion artefacts or insufficient vascular opacification.

Present author's comments - a big problem appears to be that radiologists appear to have been striving almost too hard for a 'gold standard' for the diagnosis of PE in all patients. He feels that much of the problem stems from the current trend in not giving a diagnosis based on the clinical picture + chest radiograph(s) and lung scintigraphy, and appearing to be 'scientific' with a lung scan report (often seen separately) and noting **high, intermediate or poor probability of PE is often regarded by the clinicians as the "radiologist is sitting on the fence, and can't make up his mind" - the clinician having to make up his!** This particularly happens where the chest radiographs and lung scans are reported in vacuo, without seeing the patient and the investigations together. In the author's view it is best if the lung perfusion scan is done as quickly as possible after admission, etc., and ideally the same person should look at the **lower limb veins with US &/or venography**. Even if the lung/perfusion scan is equivocal but the leg venogram is positive, the clinical diagnosis is clear thrombo-embolism that needs anticoagulant treatment. It is also a great mistake to delay the perfusion scan, because the ventilation one cannot be done that day - in most cases the latter is superfluous and non-contributory (except with emphysema etc. which can usually be seen from the chest radiograph!) [In Italy PISAPED is used instead of PIOPED, and appears better in advising that isotope scans are reported as "high or low probability, or that further investigation is advised"].

If one considers the **natural history of pulmonary emboli, many are large and initially lodge in the larger pulmonary arteries, but then tend to break up and move peripherally**. When this happens, signs on a perfusion scan will **not** be so clear, and it would seem more logical in non-clear-cut cases to write "you have sat on this case for five days, which makes interpretation difficult, please send patients with suspected embolism earlier in future". Follow-up scans can also be educationally revealing, showing resolution with treatment and that one was correct in one's interpretation. Occasionally pulmonary embolectomy (Trendelenberg operation) is still carried out with good effect, if there is massive embolism, and particularly in those who have accompanying DIC (**diffuse intravascular coagulation**). A main reason for not performing pulmonary angiograms is that most clinicians regard these as too invasive for a sick patient, and most will recover with anticoagulant treatment (heparin acutely followed by coumarin type drugs for several weeks).

Some further points: A clinical review in the BMJ (Fennerty, 1997) concentrated only on V/Q and leg vein US for the diagnosis of PE. Hansell and Flower (1998) in a BMJ Editorial dealt with the challenge of diagnosing PE with spiral CT. However Van Beek from Amsterdam in a letter to the BMJ (1988) pointed out that **whilst central emboli are easily visualised by spiral CT, segmental emboli may be missed**; for this reason he advocated that further studies are required before the method is used routinely. He also felt that spiral CT compared unfavourably with lung scintigraphy + lower limb US or pulmonary angiography.

D-dimer - a degradation product of cross-linked fibrin - is usually raised in patients with thrombo-embolic but is **non-specific**.

It follows from the above that spiral CT is likely to be better (see Illus. **SPIRAL CT, Embolism Pt. 11a-c**) in specificity to acute lung perfusion scans, but that it cannot be done in all suspected cases because of logistics (i.e. numbers).

MR may also demonstrate **emboli within pulmonary vessels as defects** and also as **'bright areas' containing methaemoglobin**, but obviously not all patients with suspected emboli can have such examinations again on logistic grounds. MR may also show late changes due to continuing pulmonary ischaemia and infarction, which have not resolved either spontaneously of with anticoagulant treatment.

It is also interesting that if spiral CT or MR is positive for embolism, some also advise leg venograms or ultrasound!

Logically it thus follows that if leg vein thrombosis has been demonstrated by venography and/or ultra-sound, and the patient has an abnormal perfusion scan, then for practical purposes he should be anticoagulated, confirmation being made later by a second lung scan showing resolution! This is often easier to arrange on logistic grounds than either spiral CT or MR and may still be valuable.

Lung perfusion scans have a high sensitivity as shown in the following table, and the specificity for many patients is greatly increased by lower limb vein examinations and follow up scans.

	scan	angio	CT
sensitivity (any ?abnormality on scan)	95%	95%	90+%
specificity	30%	95%	90+%

Pulmonary tumour-thrombosis and embolism.

Pulmonary embolism may not only be produced by thrombi originating in the veins of the lower (or upper) limbs, pelvis, kidneys, etc., but also by fat and gas bubbles (see ps. 6.14-15, 6.31-33, 8.14 & 21.8) and by tumour emboli. The latter may be combined with thrombus to produce 'tumour thrombo-embolism', leading to dyspnoea, tumour spread within the lungs, multiple metastases, acute or chronic cor pulmonale and death. When enveloped in thrombus, such tumour emboli may not grow and may produce "**sterilised   deposits**", which sometimes calcify (Illus. **STERILISED   DEPOSITS**) - this in the author's experience mainly occurs with renal and thyroid tumours, which have a strong tendency to spread into the bronchi, sometimes into the great veins and even the heart (Illus. **THYROID CA, SVC obst Pt.   11a-g**). Calcification may also occur in response to chemotherapy.

Tumour embolism may sometimes be the presenting feature of a tumour, and lead to the death of the patient. It may also be unsuspected in patients with known tumours who develop breathlessness, until a perfusion lung scan is carried out. As with non-malignant emboli a ventilation study is usually normal. Tumour embolisation not only occurs with thyroid and renal tumours (which may extend into the SVC and IVC respectively) but also with tumours arising in the breast, pancreas, ovary, uterus, bladder, hepatomas, chorioncarcinoma, etc. A case studied by the author followed treatment of endometrial carcinoma with Provera (see Illus. **LUNG DEPOSITS, Pt. 47a-c** and Paine et al., 1970). Another case had a fatal lung haemorrhage after being treated with anticoagulants. A case is illustrated (Illus. **LYMPHANGITIS, Pt.   33a-c**) of diffuse lymphangitic spread with vascular looking deposits on a lung perfusion scan occurring from breast cancer.

The not uncommon metastasis of bronchial tumours to the lungs (see ps. 4.18-19) presumably occurs via the bronchial veins.

References.

Woo-Ming et al. (1966) : Calcified tumour-thrombus of the left pulmonary artery due to metastatic renal carcinoma.
Winterbauer et al. (1968) : Incidence and clinical significance of tumour embolisation to the lungs.
Kane et al. (1975) : Microscopic pulmonary tumour thrombi associated with dyspnoea.
Gonzalez-Vitale and Garcia-Bunnel (1976) : Pulmonary tumour emboli & cor pulmonale in primary lung carcinoma.
Graham et al. (1976) : Tumour emboli presenting as pulmonary hypertension.
Daughtry et al. (1977) : Pulmonary embolus presenting as the initial manifestation of renal cell carcinoma.
Fanta et al. (1980) : Microscopic pulm. tumour emboli - hidden cause of dyspnoea and pulmonary hypertension.
Chakeres and Spiegel (1982) : Fatal pulmonary hypertension secondary to intravascular metastatic tumour emboli.
Burchard and Carney (1984) : Tumour embolism as the first manifestation of cancer.
Crane et al. (1984) : Tumour micro-embolism appearance is given by numerous subsegmental defects evenly distributed throughout the lung fields (quoted 11 cases from the literature).
Chan et al. (1987) : Pulmonary tumour embolism - critical review of clinical, imaging and haemodynamic features.
Rawlinson and Ackery (1988) : Microscopic tumour embolism - an unusual cause of ventilation-perfusion mismatch - female patient aged 59 who did not respond to anti-coagulant therapy. Pancreatic neoplasm found at autopsy.
Shephard et al. (1993) : Pulm. intravascular tumour emboli - dilated & beaded peripheral pulmonary arteries on CT.
Kim et al. (1999) : CT of pulm. tumour embolism presenting as infarcts on CT - a rare cause of respiratory failure.
(see also lymphangitis carcinomatosa - p. 8.11 and pulmonary artery tumours causing pulmonary emboli p. 7.19).

Pulmonary densitometry.

This began with fluoro-densitometry, which itself started as an extension of the technique of electro-kymography - used to study cardiac pulsation (Henny and Boone, 1945, Bartley, 1960, Lissner, 1962). It was also used to study pulmonary vascular pulsations, in patients with bronchial carcinomas and in the assessment of pulmonary ventilation. Marchal and Marchal (1963) found that in over 80% of patients with bronchial neoplasms, the pulmonary vascular pattern was reduced or absent, whereas this did not happen with pulmonary metastases. Sutherland et al. (1968) studied 20 patients with bronchial carcinomas, and found a reduction not only in the vascularity, but also in the ventilation of the affected lung.

A radio-isotope method of estimating pulmonary density is to use a large flat container filled with the isotope (preferably in liquid form filling the vessel completely, so as to ensure uniformity in the source of radiation) and using the transmission of the gamma rays one may estimate the pulmonary density and hence vascularity. It is relatively easy to note a unilateral reduction in perfusion by noting increased transmission of the gamma rays on that side. For this purpose Tc^{99m} (with a gamma energy of 140 keV) is suitable.

Another method of measuring regional values of vascular and extra-vascular lung density uses positron and emission tomography. Quantitative values of lung density in the trans-axial plane have been obtained using transmission scans from a ring source of Ga^{68}, and values of blood density were obtained by labelling the subject's red cells with $C^{11}O$ (half-life = 20.4 mins), injected as a bolus (Rhodes et al., 1981).

CT has also been used to try to measure lung density, either by taking readings using the cursor, by using a colour monitor display or contours to denote density differences, or by using two kVs to estimate the density differences. Coarse readings of a large area of lung are relatively easy to make, but small areas are subject to considerable artefacts and errors arising from partial volume, overlying artefact ghosts from home, or the great density difference between air and vascular structures. As Kreel (1978) found, the lung is denser in its more dependent areas due to greater blood flow through these. This pattern is changed in position, but constant with gravity, as shown by turning the patient prone from the more normal supine position or by turning him on his side. It is also altered by respiration and disease processes which affect localised perfusion, or by inflammatory changes and calcification. Normally the right lung is a little denser than the left.

Reduced lung density may be seen with emphysema, acute pulmonary embolism, Swyer-James (Macleod) syndrome, etc. and similarly increased density with inflammation, fibrosis, congestion, etc. Allowance has to be made for apparent increased or decreased density due to obliquity of the patient, abnormalities of the chest wall, e.g. following mastectomy, pleural disease, etc.

Further references.

Laws and Steiner (1965) : X-ray densitometry in the study of pulmonary ventilation and the pulmonary circulation.
Kreel (1977b) : CT with tissue density measurements.
Wegener et al. (1978) : Measurement of lung density by CT.
Robinson and Kreel (1979) : Pulmonary tissue attenuation with CT - comparison of inspiration & expiration scans.
Rosenblum et al. (1980) : Density patterns in the normal lung as determined by CT - suggested that CT should have a place in assessing lung ventilation and perfusion.
Hedelund et al. (1982) : Two methods for isolating the lung area of a CT scan for dosimetric information.
Hedlund et al. (1983) : Evaluating lung density by CT.
McCullough and Morin (1983) : CT number variability in thoracic geometry - variation between scanners can be a problem in the measurement of absolute CT numbers within the thorax.
Vock and Salzmann (1986) : Comparison of CT lung density with haemodynamic data of the pulmonary circulation.
Kalender et al. (1990) : Measurement of pulmonary parenchymal attenuation : use of spirometric gating with quantitative CT.
Adams et al. (1991) : An appraisal of CT pulmonary density mapping in normal subjects - it has been suggested that highlighting areas of low CT density can locate and quantitate areas of pulmonary emphysema. However there is considerable variability in the lung density map of normal individuals and the method is also dependent on radiographic technique, factors which should be taken into account when considering the use of CT mapping for the assessment of lung disease. (See also p. 6.11).

Pulmonary angiography - Illus. **PULM ANGIOGRAPHY**.

This is now usually carried out with DSA (digital subtraction angiography), but formally was done using a film changer with fluorescent screens. A catheter is placed in the SVC or R atrium, or for more selective studies into the pulmonary arteries or other branches.

(a) **Historical and assessment of tumours.**

In 1950 Dotter et al. advocated venous angiocardiography, performed by the rapid injection of contrast medium into the veins of both arms, in the pre-operative assessment of patients with bronchial carcinoma. This was to assess possible mediastinal involvement as shown by complete or partial occlusion of the left pulmonary artery close to its origin, by complete or partial occlusion of the 'great mediastinal vessels' displaced or deformed by metastases and by pericardial thickening. They studied 53 patients with bronchial carcinoma and found that of 25, who had been considered inoperable although angiographically not inoperable. They emphasised that non-neoplastic conditions, either on their own or complicating a neoplasm, could simulate neoplastic conditions and wrote "No patient should be denied exploratory surgery on the basis of angiocardiographic changes alone."

Others (including Amundsen and Sorenson, 1956, Lyons and Vertova, 1958, Steinberg and Finby, 1959, Sanders et al., 1962 & 1970) also used angiocardiography for this purpose and the last claimed a 95% accuracy, when combined with mediastinoscopy.

(b) **Diagnosis and assessment of pulmonary artery aneurysms.**

Pulmonary angiography is still a very useful technique for demonstrating pulmonary artery anomalies which may be confused with neoplasm (Illus. **PULM ART ANEURYSM, Plum arteries Pt. 9**) shows a large hilar pulmonary artery aneurysm), artery-venous anomalies, or reduced vascularity secondary to tumour, mediastinitis or other disease. However, isotope studies may be more convenient for the latter. Also digital vascular imaging makes angiography easier to perform.

(c) **Pulmonary embolism.**

Although pulmonary angiography is used in some centres for the diagnosis of pulmonary embolism (see p. 7.26), many clinicians are reluctant to send their patients for this investigation. Many feel that it is too drastic a procedure in severely ill patients, and that lung scans, and ultrasound vein examinations suffice for clinical purposes. Indeed in a some cases there can be severe reactions to the contrast medium used, which can cause a sudden rise in pulmonary artery pressure, with both morbidity and mortality in patients with pulmonary hypertension. Many studies have been carried out to ascertain the cause of this and its mediation. Contrast media tend to produce a response i.e. a transient followed by a more sustained phase of vasoconstriction - "**rebound vasoconstriction**".

The subject has been studied and reviewed by Wang et al. (1997 & 1998) who found reduced effects in vitro with low contrast agents. The risk is very low.

Aortography

Before CT became available, the main indication for arteriography was with mediastinal masses to prove or exclude an aneurysm. Aortography not only could show this, but also a vascular blush in some adjacent tumours (e.g. goitres, parathyroid tumours or chemodectomas). It could also show displacement of vessels by a large goitre, or feeding vessels to sequestration. Selective angiography of the bronchial, intercostal and internal mammary arteries was sometimes carried out to help elucidate the nature of upper mediastinal masses (see also section on bronchial arteriography below), to show chest wall invasion (Illus. **INTERCOSTAL ARTERIOGRAM, Pts. 2 & 3**) or to differentiate neurofibromata from aneurysms.

Wood and Miller (1938) and Cudkowicz and Armstrong (1953) considered that bronchial tumours might receive their main blood supply from the bronchial arteries, whilst metastases might be mainly perfused by the pulmonary circulation, a view supported by Darke and Lewtas (1968). It was also suggested that **haemoptysis** with bronchial tumours might in some cases be related to the higher blood pressure in the systemic bronchial circulation, as compared with the lower pressure in the pulmonary circulation supplying the secondary deposits. Besides malignant bronchial tumours having an increased bronchial circulation, this may also be found with more benign masses e.g. adenomas, hamartomas, etc. A hamartoma with a very vascular bronchial circulation was illustrated by Darke et al. (1972). In some cases metastases may derive a bronchial artery supply as shown by Turner-Warwick (1963a), Boijsen and Zsigmond (1965) and Noonan et al. (1965).

Further references.

Greenspan and Capps (1963): Bronchiectasis & other benign disease often showed an extensive abnormal circulation.
Viamonte (1965): Segmental pulmonary angiography often revealed no abnormality when extensive malignant disease (either primary or secondary) was present.
Düx et al. (1969) : Angiographic diagnostic methods in bronchial carcinoma.
Raphael (1970): In a general review of the value of pulmonary angiography, discussed its use for assessing the operability of lung tumours, but pointed out that the technique had not found general acceptance in the UK. It had also proved unreliable in distinguishing benign from malignant disease; the most reliable sign of malignant involvement being the 'napkin ring' constriction of one or more pulmonary artery branches, often with obstructed distal vessels.
Mills et al. (1980) : Incidence, aetiologies and avoidance of complications of pulm. angiography in a large series.
Perlmutt et al. (1987) : Reviewed the reports on 1,434 pts. who underwent pulmonary arteriography. Major immediate complications related to contrast media injection (excluding obvious allergic reactions) occurred in 30 (3%) & included acute chest pain, arrhythmias, heart block or arrest & death secondary to acute cor pulmonale in 2; 6 (1.5%) occurred in 388 (27%) who had pulmonary hypertension.
Stein et al. (1992) : Complications and validity of pulmonary angiography in acute pulmonary embolism.

Chapter 8 : Pulmonary Oedema, Lymphangitis Carcinomatosa and ARDS.

Pulmonary oedema.

The radiological picture depends on a number of factors. These include the various causes :

(i) cardiac failure and fluid overload (including over-transfusion) - this is often complicated by anoxia or underlying lung disease.

(ii) renal failure - also gives rise to fluid overload, and through altered electrolytes, changes in capillary permeability.

(iii) increased blood volume (post-pregnancy, etc., oedema).

(iv) decreased blood volume and sudden loss of fluid into the lung in post-aspiration oedema.

(v) anoxia leading to vascular changes (see below) and changes in capillary permeability.

(vi) altered lung capillary permeability due to anoxia, inhalation, drug reactions, harmful gases, etc. - sometimes this type can give nodular shadows in the lungs.

(vii) infection, embolism or haemorrhage leading to localised areas of oedema.

(viii) inhalation injuries, shocked lung, 'pump lung' and the 'adult respiratory distress syndrome' may cause a mixture of effects, fluid overload, poor pulmonary circulation and changes in capillary permeability - often complicated by varying degrees of infection and/or infarction.

(ix) blocked lymphatics leading to lymphangitis carcinomatosa.

Often the picture is complicated by pulmonary fibrosis, localised or generalised emphysema, gross embolism, or generalised metabolic upsets e.g. hepatic failure, complicating renal failure, hypotension or gross neurological disease, etc.

Historical review.

Many authors have studied the patterns of oedema, particularly as they may have a bearing on treatment, but most have found considerable overlap in the types noted above.

Gleason and Steiner (1966, from the Hammersmith Hospital) studied the value of lateral, in addition to PA views, and noted that the accumulation of fluid in the apical segments of the lower lobes may be mistaken for 'central oedema', as may anteriorly situated oedema in the upper lobes. They also noted that:

(a) **intra-alveolar and interstitial oedema may accompany each other**,

(b) **peri-hilar haze may be confused with intra-alveolar oedema**, and

(c) **oedema may shift easily from one lobe to another**, as a result of changes in posture, etc. i.e. it is often more marked in dependent areas.

Heard et al. (1968, also from the Hammersmith Hospital) pointed out the basic differing features of (a) interstitial and (b) intra-alveolar oedema:

(a) **Interstitial oedema** causes peri-bronchial and peri-vascular cuffing, peri-hilar haze, together with 'peripheral' and 'long septal' lines (Kerley's A, B, and C lines - see ps. 8.11 - 12), whilst

(b) **intra-alveolar oedema** produces transient episodes of uncharacteristic shadowing, frequently changing in distribution. This may be of '**bat's wing**' or (more properly) '**butterfly wing**' shape (as only the butterfly wing is indented laterally), and this may occur with or without uraemia. Organisation of this type of oedema may lead to fine fibrosis and the presence of siderophages - points which could be seen on lung specimens and which were not apparent on radiographs.

The distribution of blood flow to the lungs also has to be considered:

Bjure and Laurell (1927) noted that patients had **narrower blood vessels in the upper parts of their lungs** (than at their bases) **when they were erect**, a difference that disappeared on lying down, which they termed '**orthostatic apical anaemia**'. This 'anaemia' was considered as probably responsible for the prevalence of tuberculosis at the lung apices (see also p. 1.47).

Barden (1952) and Barden and Comroe (1956) studied the correlation of radiological signs with pulmonary function and noted that in pulmonary arterial hypertension, the peripheral pulmonary vessels 'disappeared' while the more proximal ones dilated.

West and Dollery (1960) studied the distribution of blood flow and ventilation and measured lung perfusion ratios with radioactive CO_2. They confirmed that the blood flow to the upper parts of the lungs was determined by gravity, with blood flow mainly to the lower parts in the erect position, whilst the variation in ventilation was relatively slight.

In **mitral stenosis** '**diversion**' of blood flow from the lung bases to the upper lobes is often most pronounced; the effect being mainly in response to raised pulmonary venous pressure, and when it rises above about 25 mm Hg, pulmonary oedema tends to occur. Constriction of the basal vessels appears to be a protective mechanism in preventing pulmonary oedema. This mechanism was studied by plain films, conventional tomograms or post-mortem angiography by Saldanha (1944), De Bettencourt et al. (1953), Doyle et al. (1957, at Hammersmith Hospital, London), Kerley (1958), Simon, M. (1958), and Simon, G. (1964 & 1972). Friedman, W. and Braunwald (1966) used radioisotope scanning. Ormond and Poznanski (1960, from Henry Ford Hospital, Detroit) used plain films and tomograms in the upright position and noted dilatation of upper lobe veins in patients with mitral stenosis and raised atrial pressure.

Lavender et al. (1962, from Hammersmith Hospital) also using tomograms to study patients with **mitral stenosis** and **left ventricular failure**, wrote "**there appears to be considerable evidence to show a comparative decrease of lower lobe blood flow in cases of left ventricular failure. This response is similar to that previously demonstrated in mitral stenosis and is probably closely related to elevated left atrial pressure.**" They also felt it was a protective phenomenon against pulmonary hypertension to prevent pulmonary oedema and paroxysmal dyspnoea.

James et al. (1960) noted lower lobe vascular constriction in the lungs of patients dying in left ventricular failure, and Bishop (1961) demonstrated a diminished lower lobe arterial supply in post-mortem pulmonary angiograms in patients dying in LVF.

Dilatation affects arteries as well as veins, and is due to opening up of the normally partially shut-down upper lobe circulation resulting from our mainly upright stance (see also p. 1.47). Normally in the upright position, the alveolar pressure at the lung apices becomes higher than the capillary pressure, and lung capillaries there are only poorly developed (leading in some, and particularly smokers, to apical lung degeneration and bullous formation). The 'driving pressure' in the pulmonary circulation is greatly influenced by gravity, because the mean hydrostatic pressure in the pulmonary artery is only about 14 mm Hg., with a systolic peak of about 30 mm.

Jefferson and Rees (1973) in their book 'Clinical Cardiac Radiology' noted that in pulmonary venous hypertension, the earliest change on chest radiographs is **dilatation of the upper lobe vessels**, which roughly parallels the height of the pulmonary venous pressure, the lower vessels remaining dilated.

Bennett and Rees (1974) also studied related changes in the lungs in acute myocardial infarction, and compared the radiographic findings with pulmonary arterial pressures. They took:
(a) upper zone vessel **dilatation** as evidence of slight pulmonary venous hypertension, and
(b) interstitial or alveolar oedema as indicating severe pulmonary venous hypertension.
(The other signs of pulmonary oedema which they listed included - septal lines, hilar oedema, mottling, perivascular oedema, loss of translucency, pleural effusion and alveolar oedema).

Grainger (1985) considered that the pulmonary circulation may be likened to a household hot water system, with a tank-cylinder in the loft supplying taps on two floors. When all taps are open, flow through the ground floor taps is much greater, because of the greater hydrostatic pressure at ground level - this is similar to the flow in the pulmonary circulation in the erect posture. If the ground floor taps are closed, then flow through the taps on the upper floor is greatly increased - this reflects the situation in the pulmonary circulation with reduced basal flow, as occurs with pulmonary oedema, mitral stenosis, etc. (Also turning off the taps on one side of the house will increase the flow on the other side, as happens with unilateral embolism, obstructive emphysema or following a pneumonectomy).

Milne et al. (1985) differentiated cardiogenic oedema from non-cardiogenic by studying plain chest radiographs. They thought that these could usually be distinguished by noting :
(a) Three principal features - the **distribution of pulmonary blood flow**, the **oedema pattern** and the **width of the vascular pedicle**, and
(b) seven ancillary signs - **pulmonary blood volume, peri-bronchial cuffing, septal lines, pleural effusions, air bronchograms, lung volume** and **cardiac size**. They found that the highest accuracy was achieved in differentiating chronic cardiac oedema from the other types, and the lowest in differentiating chronic cardiac oedema from that caused by renal failure.

Aberle et al. (1988) studied the radiographic criteria for differentiating hydrostatic from increased permeability oedema in 45 critically ill patients, and found a patchy peripheral distribution of oedema was the single most discriminating criterion, and was relatively specific for increased permeability oedema, although there was considerable overlap. Some factors often considered more typical of hydrostatic oedema were commonly found in patients with increased pulmonary capillary permeability, viz. - **peribronchial cuffing** in 72%, a **widened vascular pedicle** in 56%, **septal lines** in 40% and **pleural effusions** in 36%. They considered that one can only distinguish between the different types radiologically in severe clear-cut cases. (See also NB 2 p.8.6).

Miniati et al. (1988) analysed 119 chest radiographs of patients with pulmonary oedema and achieved an accuracy in diagnosing the cause in 88%. 56 patients had left ventricular failure, 19 renal failure and 44 lung capillary damage.

Rocker et al (1989, in Nottingham), studied 51 patients with radiographic evidence of **pulmonary oedema** (renal 16, cardiac 13 and ARDS 22). A scoring method was used to assess the plain radiographs. Pulmonary capillary permeability was assessed with reference to transferrin permeability, using a double-isotope method (with Tc^{99m} labelled RBCs and In^{113m} labelled transferrin) to devise a protein accumulation index. Comparing the clinical diagnosis (used as the reference standard for each type) and the radiographic scoring system, they failed to distinguish between pulmonary oedema of renal and cardiac origin. They also found that radiographic appearances suggestive of capillary injury and increased capillary permeability to transferrin occurred in all groups and that such findings are not specific to ARDS.

Milne and Pistolesi (1993) in an extremely well presented book 'Reading the Chest Radiograph - A Physiologic Approach' (see also p. 1.59) further presented their reasons and radiographic signs for differentiating **increased pressure** from **injury pulmonary oedema.** In the former fluid accumulates initially in the interstitial spaces, but may pass on into the lymphatics, the pleural cavities and also into the alveoli, whereas in the latter there is damage to the alveolar walls causing filling of the alveoli with high protein content fluid and cellular debris. They noted that septal lines "virtually never occur in injury oedema" and that injury oedema clears much more slowly than increased pressure oedema.
    They felt that '**bat's-wing**' oedema occurs if cardiac (or renal) decompensation is **abrupt** and massive, and that the interstitial phase of oedema may then be short-lasting, with the alveolar flooding phase paramount. They also noted that it is uncommon to see perivascular cuffing in association with such a pattern, and gave some explanations. They illustrated an excellent PA view beautifully showing the typical bat's wing shadowing extending up into the apices of the lower lobes, but not any acute cases with CT sections (a problem being that these are not often done). They however showed several CT sections of a patient with chronic renal failure who developed extensive bilateral ossification of lobular distribution in the upper lobes and apices of the lower lobes (**with sparing of the lung cortex**). This was said to exactly duplicate the distribution of bat's-wing oedema shown in a lateral view one year earlier; and apparently he had no intercurrent infection, which may have played a part in such calcification that sometimes takes place in renal failure (see p. 6.22).   See also reference to Ketai and Godwin (1998) - p. 8.17.
    Milne and Pistolesi criticised Rocker et al. for some of their scoring and argued the case for 'central oedema with perivascular cuffing.' They also stated that if central ('bats-wing') oedema is present with a narrow vascular pedicle and normal sized pulmonary vessels the cause is left-sided heart failure, whereas if the vascular pedicle is widened and the pulmonary vessels dilated, the diagnosis is renal failure or overhydration.

The present author feels that whilst most cases of pulmonary oedema are studied from plain radiographs one should not lose sight of the fact that it may redistribute fairly rapidly with change in posture as shown by CT studies (see reference to Langer et al., 1988 - see p. 8.15). CT studies have shown that 'bat's wing' type oedema may often be mainly posterior (in the lower lobes and extending into their apical segments) and not central, which may account for the uncommonly associated peribronchial cuffing (see also the reference to Gleason and Steiner, 1966 - p. 8.1). However redistribution is less likely to occur when the protein content of the fluid is high, as in many cases of injury oedema (as in ARDS, inhalation of noxious gases, etc.), these last giving rise to ground-glass shadowing, consolidation and interstitial fluid. Thus both in renal and heart failure, oedema fluid can be redistributed relatively quickly with change in posture, but **not** with injury oedema, where it tends to persist at the site or sites of lung injury.

Hypoxia can also induce vascular spasm. This may be potentiated by the perivascular and peribronchial oedema in affected areas leading to local vascular spasm and compensatory dilatation in unaffected parts of the lung. Vascular spasm also accounts for the reduction in size of the pulmonary artery, sometimes seen on the side of partial obstruction of a main bronchus and compensatory contralateral pulmonary artery enlargement- **Oeser's sign** - see ps. 7.10 - 12 (which may be seen in both malignant and non-malignant conditions). See also footnote below.

Septic shock causes severe pulmonary oedema and has a high mortality. In this condition, bacteria and/or toxins entering the circulation cause rigors, fever, vascular spasm, thrombocytopaenia, micro-embolism, stagnant anoxia, diffuse intra-vascular coagulation, myocardial toxicity and pulmonary and peripheral oedema. Radiological manifestations occur later than clinical signs, and mainly consist of pulmonary oedema spreading upwards from the lung bases, usually without the concomitant signs of pulmonary hypertension, or redistribution of blood to the upper zones. It may occur in relation to several sites of infection e.g. renal tract (esp. following instrumentation), retained vaginal tampons (infected with Staphylococci or Streptococci) - see Sanderson, 1990.

Amniotic fluid embolism may cause sudden pulmonary oedema, breathlessness and collapse during labour and in recently delivered women. Coughed up foetal squamous cells prove the diagnosis - see Dooley and Leary, 1952, Peterson and Taylor (1970), and Mulder (1985).
(For **post-partum** and **post-operative** effusions, pulmonary oedema, etc. - see p. 14.13).

Young people with pulmonary oedema and apparent cardiac failure.
  The author has seen several such cases present with congestion and hypertensive cardiac failure secondary to acute nephritis. These may have a very poor prognosis if not correctly diagnosed - Illus. **CONGESTION, Pt. 7**.

Table 8.1 Increased pressure (or hydrostatic) pulmonary oedema etc. - summary of signs.
(a) Peri-bronchial and peri-bronchial cuffing.
(b) Kerley's lines (interstitial fluid).
(c) Patchy shadowing or occasionally nodules (see under nodular oedema).
(d) Increased lung density at bases, in peri-hilar regions or butterfly or bat's wing appearance.
(e) Basal pleural effusions, fluid in inter-lobar fissures, etc.
(f) With the onset of heart failure or overhydration, the pulmonary veins will tend to dilate, both in the lower parts of the lungs and in the upper zones as well (pulmonary venous dilatation). This is followed by dilatation of the upper zone arteries i.e. of the vessels which are normally shut down in the upright posture.
(g) With raised venous pressure (? also hypoxia*) the lower lobe vessels will tend to constrict - the best example is in mitral stenosis - see p. 8.2.
(h) When heart failure is superimposed on severe emphysema, particularly emphysema of the upper lobes, then upper lobe vessel dilatation will not easily occur, as the upper lobe vessels will be severely damaged or attenuated. Note also that in cor pulmonale, many of the peripheral vessels will be narrowed, with proximal dilatation of the main pulmonary arteries.

* Hypoxia certainly appears to play the major role in unilateral reflex vascular shut-down as in Oeser's syndrome - see above. It is also the most potent known stimulus for pulmonary vasoconstriction, which normally helps match

blood flow and ventilation, diverting blood flow away from poorly ventilated areas; it does this without increasing pulmonary arterial pressure - but with widespread alveolar hypoxia, this normally protective response may cause a large fraction of the pulmonary vasculature to constrict, thereby increasing pulmonary artery pressure (Armstrong, P. et al., 1990, see also Fishman, 1976 and Michael and Summer, 1985). However this response sometimes fails - see p. 7.11 and the reference to Sostman et al., 1983.

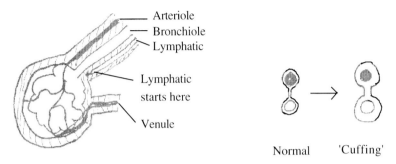

Fig. 8.1   Peri-Bronchial and Peri-Vascular Cuffing - with the onset of oedema, excess fluid leaves the capillaries and passes into the sheath around the arteriole and bronchiole, the alveolus and venule to cause 'cuffing'. Later as pressure increases, fluid passes into the alveoli.

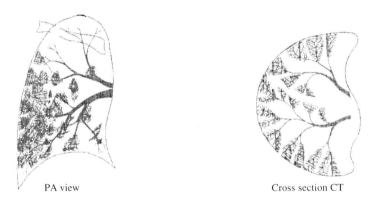

Fig. 8.2 Capillary permeability oedema causing peripheral patchy shadows (bronchi patent).

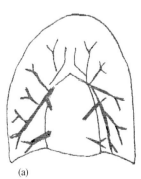

(a)

Normal pulmonary circulation - little upper upper lobe & more lower lobe perfusion.

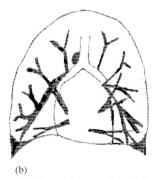

(b)

Opening up of upper lobe arteries and distension of pulmonary veins, esp. basal in cardiac or renal failure.

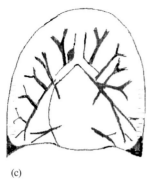

(c)

With raised pulm. venous pressure the lower lobe
vessels constrict whilst those in the upper lobes dilate.*

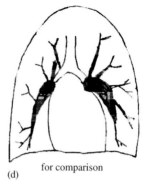

for comparison

(d)

Cor pulmonale - large main pulmonary
arteries and thin peripheral vessels.

Fig. 8.3 Radiological vascular patterns - High KV radiographs are very good for showing these -
also note distension of azygos vein (and SVC) and Kerley's B lines.

* N.B. 1 - Milne (1999) points out that the 'inversion' reflex does not occur after cardiac transplantation, even with
severe LVF, as the nerve connections have been lost. He also feels that hypoxia plays no part in its production.
        The inversion reflex is also not possible in patients with severe upper lobe emphysema.
N.B. 2 - Milne (1999) also feels that there is a great danger that patients with lung injury oedema (as in ARDS)
may have superimposed hydrostatic oedema (with waterlogged lungs) as a result of treatment.

N.B. 3 - Transient (or 'flash') pulmonary oedema may be caused by **renal   artery   stenosis**, and be relieved by
dilatation of the stenosis (Pickering et al., 1988, Missouris et al., 1993, Lye et al., 1996 & Rankin et al., 2000).

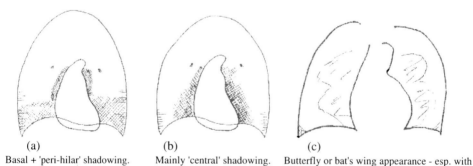

(a)   (b)   (c)

Basal + 'peri-hilar' shadowing.   Mainly 'central' shadowing.   Butterfly or bat's wing appearance - esp. with
                                                                    renal failure - also seen in some cases of heart
Note that this shadowing may be largely in the lower lobes or   failure - may be partly related to the patient's
adjacent pleura, if CT sections are taken - see also note on p. 8.1. posture i.e. lying on his back (see p. 8.4).

Fig. 8.4 Some patterns of pulmonary oedema.

(Figs. 8.1, 8.2, 8.3 & 8.4 a & b are reproduced or adapted from Milne et al., 1985, AJR, **144**, 879 - 894 with
permission from the American Roentgen Ray Society).

    The position of congestion (hyperaemia ± oedema) may alter with posture, as may be
demonstrated on plain radiographs - e.g. a patient is nursed on his left side and the left lung shows
increased density. He then is turned to the right for several minutes and a further radiograph may
show that the right lung becomes less transradiant, whilst the left clears. Gravity dependent
congestion may also be shown by CT, turning the patient from one side to the other, or by turning
him prone from supine (if clinically possible) - in both instances leaving him in the new position
for 5 to 10 minutes.

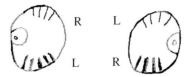

Fig. 8.5 Movement of congestion in lateral decubitus positions. i.e. - lying on left side leads to left sided congestion and left basal pleural effusion.
 - sitting up leads to basal congestion.
 - lying on back leads to a **'butterfly'** or **'bat's wing'** type appearance.

'Dependent opacity' or 'dependent increased attenuation'.
This may be seen in the dependent **corttico-medullary** part of the lung in normal people (i.e. without any evidence of cardiac decompensation, etc.) on CT sections. It is usually of no clinical importance, and should be differentiated from lung disease e.g. fibrosing alveolitis etc. This is gravity dependent and may be 'moved' from the back of the lung to the front, by turning the patient into the prone from the supine position (see also p. 1.45) - Illus. **CONGESTION, Pt. 19**. It was previously considered to be oedema (see Arni et al, 1990), but may represent localised collapse, due to the density gradient of the lung. It may also clear with a Valsalva manoeuvre.

Supine   Prone

Fig. 8.6 Dependent opacity at cortico-medullary junction in supine and prone positions.

Nodular oedema - (miliary or larger nodules) may occur in relation to several stimuli
(a) 'allergic' nodules in response to drugs, local infection, parasites or renal failure (especially with Goodpasture's syndrome - p. 19.98). The author has also seen some cases following plasma transfusion in haemophilic patients. (Drugs may also produce a more generalised type of pulmonary oedema e.g. cytotoxic agents, opiates, nitofurantoin, amphoteracin-B, aspirin, etc. - see also ps. 19.110 - 112).
(b) in response to inhaled gases with smoke, fires, fumes, etc. - see ps. 19. 59 & 107 - 110.

Illustrations of nodular oedema are shown in Illus. **CONGESTION NODULAR**.

High altitude pulmonary oedema.
This can occur at altitudes above 8,000 or more commonly 10,000 feet (approx. 3,000 m). The cardinal symptoms are increasing dyspnoea, retrosternal discomfort, frothy sputum, tachycardia, etc. Radiologically there may be patchy or generalised hazy alveolar shadowing, progressing to more widespread congestion or consolidation and resembling in some cases a bronchopneumonia. These tend to clear rapidly with breathing oxygen, but rapid removal to a lower altitude is advisable. The precise mechanism is uncertain - ?intrapulmonary shunting and hypoxia allowing transudation of fluid through alveolar walls, or reflex vasoconstriction.

Unilateral pulmonary oedema - this together with lymphangitis may be the presenting feature of a **lung tumour**, without any obvious mass on plain radiographs (Illus. **CONGESTION UNILAT**). It is not a very uncommon presentation and tomograms will often show associated hilar node enlargement. Unilateral oedema may also be seen with lymphangitis as a result of the spread of primary tumours outside the lungs, but this is more commonly bilateral. It may be found with infection, and in extreme forms with the **'drowned lung'** appearance - usually seen as lobar oedema; it may be also be caused by the spread of a central lung tumour (see also ps. 4.19 - 20 and 19.1 - 19.4). In cardiac or renal failure with the patient lying on his side, oedema may collect in the dependent lung.

Other causes of unilateral pulmonary oedema include -
(i) Acute infection - i.e. before frank consolidation has taken place,
(ii) Pulmonary contusion - crush injury - in association with a haematoma or bleeding,
(iii) Contralateral large pulmonary embolus, with proximal narrowing or interruption of a pulmonary artery, with marked shunting of blood to the contralateral lung,
(iv) Thrombosis of the pulmonary veins - veno-occlusive disease or secondary to a myxoma,
(v) Acute bronchostenosis of a main bronchus - bronchial plug due to mucus or a misplaced endotracheal tube.
(vi) Damaged contralateral lung (recent surgery, severe bullous disease or fibrosis, Swyer-James /Macleod syndrome - see p. 7.9 - 10).
(vii) Following rapid aspiration of a pleural effusion or pneumothorax,
(viii) With certain flow patterns within the heart, especially surgically created left to right shunts.

Re-expansion and re-perfusion pulmonary oedema, after rapid removal of a large pleural effusion or a pneumothorax, may be life-threatening. It probably occurs secondary to anoxia in the underperfused collapsed lobe or lung, allowing rapid ingress of fluid into it and capillary leakage if re-expansion occurs quickly, but rapid re-expansion with a high intrapleural negative pressure may play a part. (Similarly, pulmonary oedema may also occur following gas embolism.) It may happen immediately, or up to two hours following aspiration, and usually involves a whole lung, but may occasionally only involve a lobe.

For this reason large pneumothoraces or pleural effusions should **not be fully aspirated rapidly if they have been present for several days or weeks** - the author always stopped when the patient started to cough (see also ps. 14.13 - 14 & 21.1). If oedema occurs diuretics must **not** be given - only fluids by mouth or IV (together with dextrans) to restore blood volume - in order to prevent a fatal outcome. This complication is **uncommon**, but **very dramatic** when it occurs. Mild cases may respond to oral fluid, in some cases a few cups of tea!

Patients symptoms include dyspnoea, tachycardia, cough with pink frothy sputum, collapse, nausea and vomiting. Unilateral crepitations may be heard with the stethoscope. Severe cases may progress to ARDS.   Illustrations are shown in Illus. **CONG RE-EXPANSION**.

Neurogenic pulmonary oedema may occur with many intracranial conditions including trauma, strokes, haemorrhage and tumours even in patients with no detectable lung or heart disease. It may occur very rapidly, and is probably caused by a gross sympathetic nervous stimulation.

Mechanical causes of pulmonary oedema (see also under ARDS p. 8.14-15; & ps. 1.46 & 11.14).
The way mechanical effects (particularly under anaesthesia or with assisted respiration) cause pulmonary oedema is uncertain, but is probably due to the marked negative intrathoracic pressures in association with upper airway obstruction, down to -50 or -100 cm of water (normal -2 to -5) on the lung. These, together with possible tissue anoxia, may cause a marked transudation of fluid into the pulmonary interstitium. Radiologically patients may have symmetrical bilateral central pulmonary shadowing with a wide vascular pedicle and a normal sized heart.

Further references.
Nessa and Rigler (1941) : Butterfly shadows with pulmonary oedema.
Hodson (1950) : Pulmonary oedema and **bat's-wing shadows**.
Hernheiser and Hinson (1954) : Anatomical explanation of the formation of **butterfly shadows***.
Gould and Torrance (1955) : Pulmonary oedema.
Heitzman and Zeiter (1966) : Acute interstitial pulmonary oedema.
Rigler and Suprenant (1967) : Pulmonary oedema.
Fleischner (1969) : Butterfly pattern of pulmonary oedema*.
Harrison, M. et al. (1971) : Radiological detection of clinically occult cardiac failure following myocardial infarction.
Milne (1973) : Correlation of physiological findings with chest radiology.
   (1977) : Pulmonary blood flow distribution., (1978) : Some new concepts of pulmonary blood flow and volume.
Milne et al. (1984) : Vascular pedicle of heart and vena azygos.
Milne et al. (1985) : Radiological distinction between cardiogenic and noncardiogenic oedema.

Steckel (1974) : The radiolucent kinetic border line in acute pulmonary oedema and pneumonia ('silent' or 'akinetic' heart border).

Bachofen et al. (1993) : Oedema formation in rabbit lungs showed considerable inhomogeneity in distribution

* Both Hernheiser and Hinson and Fleischner suggested that the better pumping action with respiration of the periphery of the lung forces fluid centrally, but this was before CT was available.

Adams and Ledingham (1977) : Septic shock.

Pistolesi and Giuntine (1978) : Assessment of extra-vascular lung water.

Westcott and Rudick (1978) : Cardiopulmonary effects of intravenous fluid overload - radiological manifestations.

Trapnell (1973) : The differential diagnosis of linear shadows in chest radiographs.

     (1983) : Design dynamics and deduction - a radiologist looks at the human lung.

Forster et al. (1992) : HRCT of experimental hydrostatic pulmonary oedema.

Herold et al. (1992) : Assessment by HRCT of the acute effects of increased intravascular volume and hypoxia on the pulmonary circulation.

Arai et al. (1990) : Transient subpleural linear shadow caused by pulmonary congestion.

Verschakelen et al. (1993) : Differences in CT density between dependent and nondependent portions of the lung, and the influence of lung volume - the largest changes occurred in the dependent regions, and were smallest for lung volumes near total lung capacity.

Storto et al. (1995) : HRCT findings in hydrostatic pulmonary oedema - areas of ground-glass opacity (increased lung attenuation not obscuring the underlying vessels), interlobular septal thickening, bronchovascular interstitial thickening, increased vascular calibre, pleural effusion and thickening of fissures.

Badouin (1997) : Oedema and cor pulmonale - oedema is rarely present if the arterial CO_2 tension is normal.

Virchis et al. (1997) : Acute non-cardiogenic lung oedema after platelet transfusion.

Bonbrest (1965) Pulmonary oedema following an epileptic seizure.

Felman (1971) : **Neurogenic** pulmonary oedema. Cohen & Abraham (1976) : After cerebro-vascular accidents.

Theodore and Robin ((1976) : Speculations on neurogenic pulmonary oedema - sudden burst of sympathetic activity leads to increased pulmonary blood volume and raised pulmonary venous pressure.

Colice et al. (1984) : Neurogenic pulmonary oedema.

Milne and Pistolesi (1993) : Neurogenic pulmonary oedema is due to a very high right ventricular pressure directly affecting the lung capillary bed. It may cause a 'whiteout' or have a patchy distribution. It is often accompanied by an abrupt increase in the size of the main pulmonary arteries.

Kernoff et al. (1972, author's case) : Severe (**nodular**) allergic type of pulmonary oedema following plasma transfusion in haemophilic patients.

Higgins and Niklasson (1990) : Nodular oedema due to trimethoprim.

Marticorena et al. (1964) : Pulmonary oedema by ascending to **high altitudes.**

Viswanathan et al. (1969), Maldanado (1978) : High altitude pulmonary oedema.

Hackett et al. (1980) : High altitude pulmonary oedema in persons without the right pulmonary artery - four cases with serious left sided pulmonary oedema in young men going mountain skiing with one death.

Lockhart and Saiag (1984) : Altitude and the human pulmonary circulation.

Hultgren et al. (1985) : Physiological studies of pulmonary oedema at high altitude.

Harvey et al. (1988) : Showed that adding CO_2 to O_2 can more quickly relieve mountain sickness.

Vock et al. (1989) : Examined 25 males who had had a few episodes of high altitude pulmonary oedema by chest radiography at 500m and 4,500 m air pressure and showed enlargement of the pulmonary arteries, fluid overload oedema and normal pulmonary venous pressure (six had had previous high altitude pressure episodes).

Reeves et al. (1994) : The heart and lungs at extreme altitude - Operation Everest II - 'although it has long been known that chronic hypoxia elevates pulmonary arterial pressure, the impaired vascular function and the suggestion of interstitial oedema indicate that the lung may be less tolerant of chronic alveolar hypoxia than has previously been thought'.

Grissom et al. (2000) : High altitude pulmonary oedema may be associated with alveolar haemorrhage.

Hartley (1905) : Albuminous expectoration following paracentesis of the chest (42 cases).

Schlaeffer (1924) : Capillary changes after aspiration of pneumothorax leading to pulmonary oedema.

Carlson et al. (1958) : Pulmonary oedema following the **rapid re-expansion of a totally collapsed lung due to a pneumothorax.**

Ziskind et al. (1965) : Acute pulmonary oedema following the treatment of spontaneous pneumothorax with excessive negative intra-pleural pressure (review).

Trapnell and Thurston (1970) : **Unilateral pulmonary oedema after pleural aspiration.**

Childness et al. (1971) : Unilateral pulmonary oedema resulting from treatment of spontaneous pneumothorax.

Sautter et al. (1971) : Fatal pulmonary oedema and pneumonitis after re-expansion of chronic pneumothorax.

Miller et al. (1973) : Experimental pulmonary oedema following re-expansion of pneumothorax.

Steckel (1973) : Unilateral pulmonary oedema following re-expansion of pneumothorax.

Saleh et al. (1974) : Unilateral pulmonary oedema in Swyer-James (Macleod) syndrome.

Calenoff et al. (1974) : Unilateral pulmonary oedema.

Waqaruddin and Bernstein (1975) : Re-expansion pulmonary oedema.

Youngberg (1977) : Study of 100 patients with unilateral diffuse lung opacity - 70 on right.

90% comprised lymphangitis carcinomatosa, pneumonia, pulmonary oedema per se, aspiration and radiation injury. Noted (i) that it is usually right sided, and the heart is not enlarged and (ii) unilateral lymphangitis is also usually right sided, and is most often due to a primary lesion in the involved lung.

Sewell et al. (1978) : Experimental evaluation of re-expansion pulmonary oedema.

Brennan and Fitzgerald (1979) : Localised re-expansion pulmonary oedema following pneumothorax drainage.

Mahajan et al. (1979) : Re-expansion pulmonary oedema.

Peatfield et al. (1979) : Two unexpected deaths from pneumothorax.

Pavlin and Cheney (1979) : Unilateral pulmonary oedema in rabbits after re-expansion of collapsed lung.

Pavlin et al. (1981) : Increased pulmonary vascular permeability as a cause of re-expansion oedema in rabbits.

Pavlin et al. (1987) : Haemodynamic effects of rapidly evacuating prolonged pneumothorax in rabbits.

Sherman and Ravikrisham (1980) : Unilateral pulmonary oedema after re-expansion of brief duration pneumothorax.

Buczko et al. (1981) : Re-expansion pulmonary oedema - evidence for increased capillary permeability.

Sprung et al. (1981) : Evidence of increased permeability in re-expansion pulmonary oedema.

Marland and Glauser (1982) : Haemodynamic pulmonary oedema - protein measurements in a case of re-expansion pulmonary oedema.

Shaw et al. (1984) : **Recurrent re-expansion pulmonary oedema** (pneumothoraces two months apart).

Henderson et at al. (1985) : Re-expansion pulmonary oedema - a potentially serious complication of delayed diagnosis of pneumothorax.

Jackson et al. (1988) : Re-expansion pulmonary oedema.

Mahfood et al. (1988) : Re-expansion pulmonary oedema - review of 51 cases from the literature.

Vuong et al. (1989) : Re-expansion pulmonary oedema localised to a lobe.

Matsuura et al. (1991) : Clinical analysis of re-expansion pulmonary oedema.

Tarver et al. (1966) : Re-expansion pulmonary oedema.

Jackson et al. (1980), Szucs and Floyd (1989) : Laryngospasm-induced pulmonary oedema.

Lorch and Sahn (1986) : Post-extubation pulmonary oedema following anaesthesia induced upper airway obstruction.

Willms and Shure (1988) : Pulmonary oedema due to upper airway obstruction in adults.

Miro et al. (1989) : Severe pulmonary **oedema** after laser relief of upper airway obstruction by a tracheal neoplasm.

Timby et al. (1990) : "Mechanical" causes of pulmonary oedema.

Cascade et al. (1993) : Negative pressure pulmonary oedema after endotracheal intubation should be suspected in young patients in the immediate post-operative period who have bilateral central type pulmonary oedema, a wide vascular pedicle, and no cardiac enlargement.

Oudjhane et al. (1992) : Pulmonary oedema complicating upper airway obstruction in infants and children.

Padley and Downes (1994) : Pulmonary oedema secondary to laryngospasm following general anaesthesia. A chest radiograph in the immediate post-operative period showed extensive 'bat's-wing' type of alveolar and interstitial oedema, which cleared completely at 36 hours.

Williams, E. et al. (1996) : Is one lung anaesthesia to blame for acute lung injury following lung resection? - "post-pneumonectomy pulmonary oedema" - leading to a rapidly rising progressive and refractory arterial hypoxaemia with a devastating clinical decline. Radiologically there is diffuse interstitial infiltration or florid alveolar oedema. In its extreme form it is indistinguishable from ARDS.

[Vogel et al. (1996) : Advocated 3D spiral CT for optimal placement of double-lumen-endotracheal tubes in order to minimise complications.]

Vanker (1987) : Asymmetrical pulmonary oedema due to **Swyer-James syndrome**.

Bahl et al. (1971) : Localised pulmonary oedema - unusual presentation of **left heart failure**.

Mutchler et al. (1974) : Localised pulmonary oedema following **surgically created left to right shunts.**

Gamsu et al. (1981) : Isolated RUL pulmonary oedema.

Gyves-Ray et al. (1987) : Unilateral pulmonary oedema due to post-lobectomy pulmonary vein thrombosis.

Gurney and Goodman (1989) : Pulmonary oedema localised to the **right upper lobe** and accompanying mitral incompetence (four cases) - may mimic RUL consolidation.

Turberg et al. (1990) : Unilateral pulmonary oedema in a patient with **hypertrophic cardiomyopathy and severe narrowing of the left pulmonary artery.**

Schnyder et al. (1993) : Prevalence of predominant involvement of the right upper lobe in pulmonary oedema associated with pulmonary regurgitation.

Greatrex and Fisher (1997) : Sparing of accessory lobes in diffuse pulmonary oedema ? due to reduced perfusion in these lobes and a fissure interfering with collateral spread of fluid from the rest of the lung.

Hyers et al. (1981) : Focal pulmonary oedema after **massive pulmonary embolism.**
Levinson et al. (1986) : Hyperperfusion pulmonary oedema after pulmonary artery thromboendarterectomy.
Ward and Pearse (1988) : Reperfusion pulmonary oedema after streptokinase thrombolytic therapy of massive pulmonary embolism.
Horgan et al. (1989) : Reperfusion pulmonary oedema after pulmonary artery occlusion.
Erasmus and Goodman (1995) : Focal pulmonary oedema - a complication of endovascular stent dilatation of pulmonary artery stenoses.
Bishop et al. (1987) : Lung reperfusion in dogs causes lung injury.
Miller et al. (1998) : Reperfusion oedema with peripheral alveolar infiltrates is common after thromoendarterectomy.

Wong et al. (1991) : **PEEP ventilation - the treatment for life threatening pulmonary oedema?**

Septal or "Kerley's" lines - Illus. **CONGEST SEPTAL LINES** or **SEPTAL LINES**.
   These lines may be seen in various types of pulmonary oedema, viral and atypical pneumonias (when there is no gross consolidation), but are most marked with lymphangitis carcinomatosa. They are common with over-hydration acute cardiac failure.
   Kerley (1933, 1951) described thickening of the interlobar fissures, miliary type shadows, and linear shadows, which he termed A and B lines, in patients with mitral stenosis, and with pulmonary oedema due to congestive heart failure and to other conditions (see **Table 8.1**, p. 8.3).
   The B lines (which are most common) are 1 to 2 cm long horizontal lines in the outermost part of either lung, and may be likened to the 'rungs of a ladder'.
   A lines are longer (2 to 4 cm) and often radiate from the hilar regions. They are present in the deeper parts of the lung, and are more often seen in the upper lobes, but rarely extend to the pleura peripherally.
   Kerley also described C lines, which are probably due to septal lines seen end-on or lying obliquely in the lungs. These are most commonly seen with dust diseases, and give rise to a fine network pattern, resulting from thickening of the interlobular tissue septa. Honeycombing due to pulmonary oedema is essentially thickening of the septa or fissures - these being seen 'end on' (see p. 6.6).

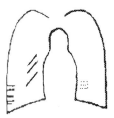

Fig. 8.7.   Kerley's A, B and C lines - these resemble honeycombs in cross section (see Fig. 6.5, p. 6.6).

   Although Kerley suggested that the lines may be due to dilated lymphatics, Grainger (1958) in a very clear account of their nature and causation, and Trapnell (1963, 1967, 1970) showed that both A and B lines are caused by dilated connective tissue septa, the B lines being due to dilated superficial interlobular septa. Both of these authors thought that the lines should be termed '**septal**' and not lymphatic lines. Gleason and Steiner (1966) termed the A lines - '**long septal lines**' and the B lines - '**peripheral septal lines**'. A further study was by Heitzman (1967 - see refs. below). D lines were described by Kreel et al. (1975) - these run obliquely at the lung bases, in the right middle lobe and lingula, and are best seen overlying the heart shadow on lateral views.
   Septal lines become visible when they are abnormally thick, as with pulmonary oedema, when they are usually accompanied by small or larger pleural effusions. Trapnell studied the lines in lymphangitis carcinomatosa (1964b), pneumoconiosis (1964c), and sarcoidosis (1964d). Fleischner and Reiner (1964) noted their presence with haemosiderosis. They may be noted with some infections, e.g. viral, pneumocystis and mycoplasma pneumonia and in pulmonary alveolar proteinosis (ps. 19.63 - 64).

Unilateral septal lines.

These are most common with lymphatic blockage due to tumours. When found in patients with lung cancer, their presence usually signifies hilar obstruction of veins and/or lymphatics. They may also be due to diffuse permeation of the lung by tumour. They may be accompanied by a fine nodularity in the lung due to multiple tumour deposits. The appearances are more commonly seen on one side of the chest (but may be bilateral) and **may be the presenting features of a lung tumour** (Illus. **LYMPHANGITIS Pts 1,2,3,4 & CONGESTION Pt. 17**). The appearance is also seen with many secondary tumours e.g. from breast, kidney, prostate, pancreas, etc. and with lymphoma.

With the Swyer-James (Macleod) syndrome or hypoplasia of a pulmonary artery, septal lines may also only be seen with congestion on the unaffected side, as the poor lung development may preclude their distension on the affected side.

Table 8.2   Causes of septal or "Kerley's" lines* - see Illus. **SEPTAL THICKENING**.

(a) Acute : Pneumonia - viral (e.g. varicella) or atypical (e.g. PCP, Mycoplasma, etc.)
   (N.B. dense consolidation often stops them being seen)
   Pulmonary oedema (overhydration, heart failure, etc.)
   Pulmonary haemorrhage
   Diffuse tumour spread in the lungs (see below).

(c) Chronic : Hilar node obstruction, etc. (lung cancer, reticulosis, etc.)
   Lymphangitis carcinomatosa
   Alveolar cell carcinoma
   Sarcoidosis (especially in acute exacerbations)
   Pneumoconiosis (including tin, iron ores and fluorides)
   Haemosiderosis of the lungs
   Pulmonary fibrosis - external allergic
                   fibrosing alveolitis
                   post radiation
                   post inflammatory
   Lymphatic obstruction / lymphangiectasia / lymphangiomyomatosis
   Alveolar proteinosis
   Veno-occlusive disease / left atrial tumour, etc.

Further references.
Reid   (1959) : Connective tissue septa in adult human lung.
Reid and Rubino (1959) : Connective tissue septa in foetal human lung.

Felson et al.(1959) - see p. 1.57.
Heitzman et al. (1967) : Kerley's interlobular septal lines - Roentgen - pathologic correlation - studied both radiographs and fixed lungs and found that A, B and C lines were all due to thickened interlobular septa, each pattern representing a different arrangement of the connective tissue septa in the various parts of the lung. In the lung periphery (the 'cortex' - p. 6.48), where the lobules are well developed, thickening of the septa produces B lines. In the upper and mid portions of the lung, the lobules are so arranged that long unbroken tissue septa are produced (especially in the apical and anterior parts of the upper lobes), giving rise to A lines. Where the peripheral pulmonary lobules are seen 'en face', the cortical septa are superposed on the more central parts of the lung, giving rise to C lines.
Youngberg (1977) : Also noted that unilateral septal line engorgement was often a sign of neoplasm.

*Note : Sir Peter James Kerley was knighted (KCVO) in 1972 for his help with investigating George VI's bronchial carcinoma in 1951 - see appx. 4. He was made a CVO and CBE at the time. He was President of the Faculty of Radiologists, 1952-1955 and Consultant Radiologist at the Westminster Hospital. London. He was awarded the RCR Gold Medal in 1976. (For his obituary see BJR, **52**, 604, 1979).

Lymphangitis carcinomatosa.

This is often a rapidly progressive lethal condition, leading to severe dyspnoea and anoxia, but a few patients may have more slowly progressive disease and live for a few or several months. In many cases little can be done except for the removal of an accompanying pleural effusion, but some amelioration may be produced by steroids and/or diuretics. Some cases, due to breast, ovarian or prostatic neoplasm may respond to chemotherapy or hormones. Diagnosis may be established by biopsy of the lung or accompanying enlarged nodes or from a knowledge of proven gradually spreading neoplasm. In some cases sputum cytology will be positive and in others fibre-optic bronchoscopy can be carried out to aspirate secretions, but this may be quite hazardous in view of the severe dyspnoea. Aspiration of **concomitant pleural fluid** (which is often present) is likely to produce positive cytology. In a few cases examined by the author with isotope lung scans, one has been able to observe linear branching perfusion defects running alongside the lines of the vessels (Illus. **LYMPHANGITIS, Pt. 37a-c**). In the case illustrated, the deposits were mainly perivenous, and the patient died about 24 hours later - she also had gross bony deposits from her breast carcinoma.

Illustrations of unilateral and bilateral lymphangitis are shown in Illus. **LYMPHANGITIS.**

Janower and Blenerhasset (1971) noted an interstitial linear pattern and parenchymal nodules in some patients with 'lymphangitic spread of metastatic cancer to the lung' from various tumours. Others had normal or near normal radiographs. Lymph node deposits were only present in about half the cases, while arterial tumour emboli were noted in nearly all of them. They postulated that lymphangitic spread may be due to **tumour vascular embolism** rather than the more commonly held view of retrograde spread from central lymph node involvement. Such emboli may spread through the vessel walls, thence into the septal spaces and the draining lymphatics and finally into the draining nodes. Spencer (1985) concurred with this view and felt that in most cases lymphangitis is caused by blood-borne metastases which extend from the capillaries to the lymphatics. In other cases retrograde tumour flow into the pulmonary lymphatics most probably occurs, especially when this occurs with abdominal tumours causing mediastinal and/or hilar node enlargement.

CT of lymphangitis - see also p. 1.55.

HRCT shows a generalised increase in the number and thickness of interlobar septa, with many lobules completely bordered by abnormal septa. Focal nodular opacities along the thickened interstitium, imparting a 'beaded' appearance and a central branching or enlarged 'arterial dot' are characteristic (Figs. 1.52 and 1.61). These nodules represent focal tumour deposits within the central and lobular interstitium. The changes remain fixed in non-dependent positions.

The author has seen lymphangitis with many tumours - lung, breast, prostate, kidney, ovary, bladder, pancreas, bowel, etc. One case the author has studied had marked radiographic changes of lymphangitis due to alveolar cell carcinoma for over ten years - Illus. **ALV CELL CA, Pt. 33a-d**. In another case of alveolar cell carcinoma - a rapidly progressive one - HRCT showed progression of miliary nodules to lymphangitis in one month - Illus. **ALV CELL CA, Pt. 45 a-f.**

The author has also studied other cases of lymphangitis by CT, and several examples are shown in Illus. **LYMPHANGITIS**. Both central and peripheral changes are illustrated but in order to demonstrate fine detail , thin sections are essential (see also Illus. **HRCT**).

Further references.

Mueller and Sniffen (1945) : Roentgenographic appearance and pathology of intrapulmonary lymphatic spread of metastatic spread.

Fichera and Hagerstrand (1965) : The small lymph vessels of the lungs in lymphangitis carcinomatosa.

Pendergrass et al. (1972) : Lung perfusion pattern associated with widespread occlusion of the pulmonary vessels and lymphatics.

Yang and Lin (1972) : Lymphatic carcinomatosis of the lungs.

Sadoff et al. (1975) : Lymphatic pulmonary metastases secondary to breast cancer with normal chest x-rays and abnormal perfusion lung scans.

Green et al. (1976) : Lymphangitic carcinomatosis - lung scan abnormalities.

Trapnell (1984) : Radiological appearance of lymphangitic carcinomatosis of the lung.

Sostman et al. (1981) : Perfusion scan in pulmonary vascular /lymphangitic carcinomatosis.

Bergin and Müller (1985) : Three cases with **thickened, lobulated or 'knotted' interlobular septa**.

Bergin and Müller (1987) : The condition affects the central, middle and peripheral parts of the lungs, with **thickening spreading along the broncho-vascular bundles radiating from the hila**, and being more prominent close to the hila, also **multiple linear densities, probably representing metastatic involvement of the inter-lobular septa.**

Naidich et al. (1984) : CT sections showed a **network of small 'knotted vessels' spreading out from the hila, as if surrounding pulmonary lobules.**

Weisbrod et al. (1985) : Diagnosis by percutaneous fine needle aspiration biopsy.

Stein et al. (1987) : **HRCT** appearances -
(a) thickening of the interlobular septa with 1 - 2 cm lines in the lung periphery, esp. anteriorly or posteriorly and extending to the pleural surface of the lung,
(b) thickened Y or U shaped 'peripheral arcades' (peripheral venules and lymphatics of the septa),
(c) central dots between these due to the central arterioles,
(d) peripheral wedge-shaped opacities due to avleolar oedema,
(e) sub-pleural bands,
(f) polygonal or multi-angulated structures,
(g) a central network pattern, and
(h) thickened fissure lines.

Munk et al. (1988) : Studied 21 cases by CT and found **uneven thickening of bronchovascular bundles, thickening of interstitial lines and the presence of polygonal lines**. These reflected the pathological findings of gross thickening of bronchovascular bundles and interlobar septa plus fine accentuation of the pleural lymphatic network.

Toye et al. (1990) : Lymphangitis of RML from renal cell carcinoma and resembling RML pneumonia.

Johkoh et al. (1992) : CT findings in 20 cases - correlation with histological features and pulmonary function tests. They found that CT gave a variable appearance depending on the involvement of the peripheral and/ or axial interstitium as shown in the following diagrams:

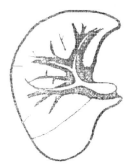 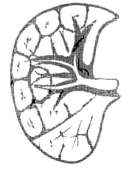 

(a) Uneven thickening of broncho   (b) Thickening of bronchovascular   (c) Thickened septa and
-vascular bundles also slight   bundles and septal lines.   polygonal lines are prominent.
thickening of septal lines.   (Reproduced from AJR, **158**, 1217 - 1222 with permission)

Ikezoe et al. (1995) : Pulmonary lymphatic carcinomatosis - chronicity of radiographic findings in long-term survivors.

Adult Respiratory Distress Syndrome - Illus. **ARDS**

This may follow several types of injury to the lung, including: severe trauma (including burns), shock and direct lung insults (including smoke inhalation), sepsis and septicaemia, extra-corporeal circulation ('pump lung'), oxygen therapy, fat embolism, fluid overload/blood transfusion, aspiration, thrombo-embolism, miliary tuberculosis and severe sensitivity reactions. Often there are **multiple factors**, leading to immune complexes with alveolar injury, platelet aggregation, the release of proteolytic enzymes from macrophages, diffuse intra-vascular coagulation ('DIC'), and necrosis. These lead to the **loss of capillary integrity in the lung, producing oedema within the alveoli and bronchioles, together with exudation of protein**, rather like that seen in alveolar proteinosis (see p. 19.63 - 64).

Chest radiographs tend to show a mixed pattern of ill-defined irregular nodules of varying size, together with patchy areas of consolidation. These lead on to pulmonary oedema and haemorrhagic consolidation - the **'exudative stage'** or 'soggy lung', with gross opacification of the lungs, but often with marked **'air bronchograms'** and other areas of **compression collapse** leading to only a relatively small proportion of normally inflatable lung. Reduced lung compliance may be present and intra-pulmonary shunting of blood may occur. The lung changes are usually symmetrical, and are most marked posteriorly as shown by CT sections. They involve the periphery as much as the peri-hilar regions. Repositioning may allow the opaque areas to clear, with opacification of the former clear areas. In some cases pneumothoraces may be seen on CT sections as well as a pneumomediastinum or interstitial pulmonary emphysema (see ps. 6.34 - 36).

Pleural effusions are relatively uncommon, and the heart is often of normal size. Some patients recover completely, whilst others develop diffuse fibrosis (sometimes within one to two weeks), and when this occurs only slowly recover after several weeks or months. About half of the cases are fatal, particularly if secondary infection, diffuse intra-vascular coagulation, coma or multi-system failure occur. Assisted ventilation is often used to maintain blood oxygenation, as well as general supportive therapy. The assisted ventilation may lead to bullous formation and pneumothoraces, the latter often being difficult to recognise on radiographs taken in supine or semi-recumbent positions (see ps. 14.22 - 23); 'shoot-through' lateral views and/or CT may be required to show them (see above).

The author has studied the lung changes in some cases with serial HRCT. In the acute stage there is a ventro-dorsal gradient of parenchymal shadowing, caused by congestion with diffuse ground-glass shadowing leading to localised areas of lung fibrosis, minute and larger lung cysts and later more diffuse ground-glass opacification. The follow-up examinations showed that whilst much ground-glass lung opacification may clear, the other changes tend to be irreversible. Some have suggested that a prone position of the patient for part of the time (if physically possible!) might help to relieve or prevent grosser changes. It has also been suggested that the most scarring (usually anterior) is caused by **barotrauma**, due to the mechanical respiration, the consolidated lung being "protected" and when the consolidation clears this part is more normal.

The relationship of ARDS to high concentrations of oxygen is discussed on ps. 19.106 - 107. See also Mendelson's syndrome (p. 19.2), thrombo-embolism (p.7.25 et seq.) , fat embolism (ps. 6.14 - 15), etc.

In patients with **miliary tuberculosis**, the miliary nodules may be masked by concomitant pulmonary congestion. Severe influenza (p.19.29), **chicken-pox** (ps. 19.29 - 30) and other lung infections (including fungi, hantavirus, etc.) may also lead to ARDS, and this and the necessary mechanical assisted respiration in turn may lead to scarring - with a persisting pattern of peripheral scarring ± small nodules on follow-up CT sections.

References.
Ashbaugh et al. (1967) : Acute respiratory distress in adults - 12 pts.
Martin et al. (1968) : Pathologic anatomy of lungs following shock and trauma.
Moore, J. et al. (1969) : Post-Traumatic Pulmonary Insufficiency.
Joffe (1970) : Roentgenographic findings in post-shock and post-operative pulmonary insufficiency.
Petty and Ashbaugh (1971) : Clinical features and factors influencing prognosis and principles of management.
Putman et al. (1972) : Roentgen appearance of disseminated intra-vascular coagulation.

Joffe (1974) : ARDS - used the term to 'describe a serious and often fatal condition, which may develop in any patient subjected to severe trauma, major surgery or critical illness.' Other conditions to be considered in the differential diagnosis include - pulmonary oedema, massive aspiration, primary pulmonary infection, pulmonary contusion and haemorrhage, pulmonary thrombo-embolism and fat embolism.

Tudor et al. (1976) : The value of radiology in ARDS - radiological and pathological study.
Adams and Ledingham (1977) : Septic shock.
Bachofen and Weibel (1982) : Structural alterations of the lung parenchyma in ARDS.
Murray et al. (1977) : Mechanism of acute respiratory failure.
Divertie (1982) : 156 cases.
Gobien et al. (1982) : Localised tension pneumothorax - unrecognised forms of barotrauma in ARDS.
Rinaldo and Rogers (1982) : ARDS - changing concepts of lung injury and repair.
Alberts et al. (1983) : The outlook for survivors of ARDS.
Balk and Bone (1983) : ARDS.
Martin, T. et al. (1983) : ARDS following thrombolytic therapy for pulmonary embolism.
Heitzman (1984)

Wardle (1984) : Shock lungs - the post traumatic respiration syndrome.
Wegenius et al. (1984) : Value of chest radiography in ARDS.
Petty (1985) : Indicators of risk, course and prognosis in ARDS.
Gattinoni et al. (1986) : ARDS profiles shown by CT.

Redline et al. (1985) : Five patients with ARDS were found at necropsy to have cavitated lung infarcts following bland (non-infected) pulmonary thrombo-embolism. They postulated that raised airway pressure as a result of positive pressure mechanical ventilation together with microvascular injury and bacterial pneumonia were important factors in causing lung necrosis, cavitation and broncho-pleural fistulae.
Iannuzzi and Petty (1986) : Diagnosis, pathogenesis and treatment of ARDS.

Greene (1987) : ARDS - **acute alveolar damage**.
Greene et al. (1987) : Pulmonary vascular obstruction in severe ARDS - lysis of thrombi by streptokinase.
Stark, D. et al. (1987) : CT findings in ARDS.
Langer et al.(1988) : CT showed a bilateral postero-basal distribution of densities is prevalent in nearly all patients with ARDS, undergoing mechanical ventilation with sedation and paralysis. They suggested that the **prone position improved oxygenation**. In two patients, CT in both supine and prone positions, showed **clearing of the posterobasal densities in the prone position**, with new ones appearing anteriorly.
Murray, J. et al. (1988) : An expanded definition of ARDS.
Rocker et al. (1989) : Time for reappraisal of diagnostic criteria for ARDS.
Tharratt et al. (1988) : Pressure controlled inverse ratio ventilation in severe adult respiratory failure.
Matthay (1989) : New modes of mechanical ventilation for ARDS.
Similowski et al. (1989) : AIDS related **cryptococcosis** causing ARDS.
Aberle and Brown (1990) : Radiological considerations in ARDS.
El Bayadi et al. (1990) : ARDS after limited resection of adenocarcinoma of the lung. They felt that the development of ARDS in various clinical settings has led to the idea that it represents a final common expression of diffuse lung injury, including inhaled or blood borne factors, chemotherapy, radiotherapy, etc.
Mishkin and Mason (1990) : Application of nuclear medicine techniques to the study of ARDS.
Turner et al. (1990) : ARDS - advances in diagnosis and ventilatory management. Estimated that 10,000 to 15,000 cases occur annually in Britain. The condition is characterised by refractory hypoxaemia and decreased lung compliance secondary to high permeability pulmonary oedema. They reported a 36 year old West Indian woman, who was 32 weeks pregnant, and who developed giant cell pneumonia secondary to herpetic infection. She died from multi-system failure despite the use of high pressure computer controlled assisted respiration. They felt that although high frequency ventilation may be effective in maintaining oxygenation, the patients may still die from other systems failure. Radiology showed consolidation with air bronchograms, 'ground-glass' appearance and pneumothoraces. At necropsy the lungs were solid and congested with large areas of fibrosis, and giant cell pneumonia.

Trotman-Dickenson et al. (1992 from Oxford - author's cases) : Do the lung changes of ARDS resolve? Four patients who developed chronic lung changes were studied with HRCT. The studies showed localised areas of lung fibrosis, minute and larger lung cysts and diffuse persistent ground glass opacification. Serial examinations showed that whilst the lung opacification may clear, the other changes appeared to be irreversible. Bronchiectasis was not a feature   As with other chronic lung diseases, HRCT clearly demonstrated abnormalities poorly shown by conventional radiography.

Owens et al. (1993) : Studied 8 cases by HRCT - ground-glass opacification is reversible, but patients may develop interstitial fibrosis, emphysema and bronchial dilatation.
Owens et al. (1994) : CT in established ARDS - correlation with lung injury score.
Hamrick-Turner et al. (1994) : Diffuse lung calcifications following fat emboli and ARDS shown by CT.
Hert and Albert (1994) : Sequelae of ARDS - many survivors have some dyspnoea. In the first year most physiological abnormalities will improve, but if deficits persist at one year further improvement is unlikely.
Beards et al. (1995) : Inter-observer variation in the chest radiograph component of the lung injury severity score.
Martin et al. (1995) : Pulmonary fibrosis diagnosed by trans-bronchial lung biopsy was closely related to fatality in established ARDS.
Meduri et al. (1994) : Causes of fever and pulmonary densities in patients with ventilator-associated pneumonia.
Winer-Muram et al. (1995) : Ventilator-associated Pseudomonas aeruginosa pneumonia (PAPn) was found by bronchoscopic sampling (in about 25% of such pts.) leading to diffuse or multifocal opacities, cavitation, pl. effusions and empyemas.
Hahn et al. (1996) : CT & HRCT of ARDS - 61 pts. - HRCT improved the diagnostic evaluation, esp. in early cases of ARDS in which appropriate therapeutic management is most appropriate - particularly those with peri-bronchial vascular thickening.
Howling et al. (1996) : HRCT in 16 pts. with ARDS - dilatation of the airways seen in areas of ground-glass opacification is likely to persist and is often accompanied by areas of parenchymal fibrosis.

Ryan and Pelosi (1996) : The prone position in ARDS - rapid improvement in oxygenation in at least 70% of pts. - CT showed redistribution of lung densities. However problems occur with fluid lines, endotracheal tubes and placing the pt. on pillows to allow free diaphragmatic excursion.

Anzueto et al. (1996) and Baudoin (1997) : The continuous administration of aerosolised synthetic surfactant to pts. with sepsis induced ARDS had no significant effect on 30 day survival, length of stay in ITU, duration of mechanical ventilation or physiological function.

Baudouin (1997) : Surfactant medication and improved survival in ARDS - chance, technology or experience? Noted that hypoxaemia is a relatively unusual cause of death in ARDS and most pts. who die do so of multi-organ failure and intractable sepsis.

Desai et al. (1997) : The functional significance of HRCT abnormalities in survivors of ARDS - study of 19 pts. - felt that **reticular changes with emphysema seen anteriorly might be caused by barotrauma**, the posterior parts of the lungs being "protected" by the more posterior consolidation. One also has to consider **oxygen toxicity**.

Nicholas et al. (1997) : A recent large trial showed that surfactant therapy in ARDS was unsuccessful - possibly due to inappropriate proteins in the exogenous product - concluded that ventilation regimens might be adjusted to minimise trauma and to conserve endogenous surfactant.

Desai et al. (1998) : A reticular pattern was a common finding on follow-up CT in 27 survivors. It has a striking anterior distribution and is strongly related to the duration of mechanical ventilation. The appearances on follow-up CT are very similar to those described in infant broncho-pulmonary dysplasia and may have a similar pathogenesis. Other findings were ground-glass shadowing, dense consolidation, parenchymal consolidation, emphysema & small airways disease.

Gattinoni et al. (1998) : Challenged the proposition that all causes of ARDS result in similar patterns of pulmonary involvement - with intrapulmonary causes such as pneumonia (in which there is a higher lung elastase) compared with extra-pulmonary causes (e.g. acute pancreatitis) - see also Hansell (1999).

Howling et al. (1998) : In pts. with ARDS, dilatation of the airways within areas of ground-glass pattern is a frequent observation in the acute phase and tends to persist at follow-up, usually with CT features of pulm. fibrosis.

Ketai and Godwin (1998) : New view of pulmonary oedema and ARDS needs at least four categories for classification - (i) hydrostatic oedema, (ii) ARDS (permeability oedema caused by acute alveolar damage), (iii) permeability oedema without alveolar damage, and (iv) mixed hydrostatic and permeability oedema. They emphasised the importance of the barriers provided by the capillary and alveolar endothelia. When the alveolar endothelium is intact the radiographic manifestations are those of interstitial (not air-space) oedema, this pattern predicting a mild clinical course and prompt resolution. These authors also illustrated a case of subacute or chronic pulmonary oedema, with a central ground-glass pattern, and sparing the lung cortex - similar to that described by Milne and Pistolesi (1993) - see p. 8.3.

Marshall et al. (1998) : **ARDS - 'fibrosis in the fast lane'** - despite advances in treatment, 40 - 70% of patients still die from this syndrome. Damage to the endothelial and epithelial surfaces leads to exudation and inflammation; fibroproliferation then ensues which, if excessive and unabated results in established fibrosis.

Spizarny et. al. (1998) : **ARDS and lung torsion** (see also p. 2.39).

Van der Werf et al. (1998) : Prone position in ARDS pts. increases ventilation to the dorsal lung areas, but the dependent parts of the lungs collapse, resulting in decreased sharpness of the cardiac silhouette.

Goodman et al. (1999) : ARDS due to a pulmonary cause tends to be asymmetric with consolidation & ground-glass shadowing, whereas that due to an extrapulmonary cause has symmetric ground-glass opafication. In both groups pleural effusions and air bronchograms are common, but Kerley B lines and pneumatocoeles are common.

Moss et al. (2000) : Clinical detoriation in ARDS - an unchanged CXR & functioning chest drains do **not** exclude Wegenius (2000) : Pointer out that pulmonary oedema may show a dependency pattern on CT within each lobe, especially in patients with ARDS and that posture may contribute to barotrauma of the still aerated lung with mechanical respiration, thus turning the patient is very important. Using oleic acid to produce pulmonary oedema, he showed that collapsed alveoli with oedema may rapidly re-expand and become aerated with mild positive respiration. Opaque and non-opaque groups of alveoli can occur in close proximity.

Miliary TB and ARDS.

Huseby and Hudson (1976). Vaz (1979) : Renal transplant recipient. Dee et al. (1980) : Surviving case.

Dyer et al. (1985) : Three cases and review of 26 from the literature, of whom 75% were black, 40% were alcoholics and three women in whom there was a relationship to pregnancy. and DIC were common as well as hepatic enlargement and deranged liver function. 60% died. Sputum and urine may be positive for AFB, but bronchial lavage and /or lung biopsy may be necessary for diagnosis.

Reider and Snider (1986), Roglan et al. (1987), Heap et al. (1989) : case reports.

Chon et al. (2000) : CT-guided catheter drainage of loculated thoracic air collections in mechanically ventilated pts. with ARDS.

Other infections.

Ketai et al. (1994) : Hantavirus respiratory syndrome (an influenza-like illness which may lead to the rapid onset of pulmonary oedema, renal disease and death) - 16 cases.

Chapter 9 : **Systemic Veins of the Thorax.**

The systemic veins of the thorax.

A knowledge of the anatomy of these, together with possible collateral pathways, is essential for interpreting pathological anatomy, and for understanding many disease processes. Veins which need particular study include the IVC, SVC, azygos and hemiazygos veins and their tributaries. The azygos vein, where it arches from posteriorly to anteriorly to join the SVC has considerable anatomical, as well as anastomotic importance. At this point it bounds the upper part of the azygo-oesophageal recess, and hence it can be used to mark a natural dividing line between the upper and lower parts of the mediastinum (see ps. 18.1 - 2).

The systemic veins are illustrated in the following diagrams:

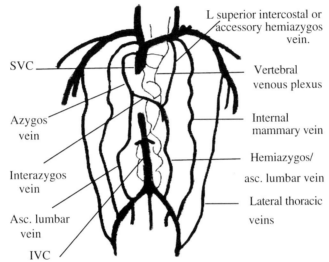

Fig. 9.1   Diagram of collateral venous circulation between the thorax and the abdomen.

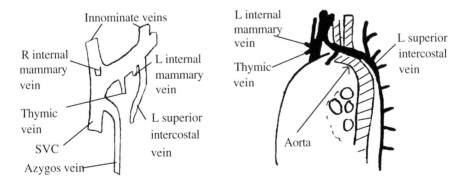

Fig. 9.2   (a) Major superior thoracic veins   (b) Left superior intercostal vein (oblique view).

Note that thoracic veins, particularly the larger veins, such as the SVC, innominate and azygos veins may be larger on radiographs in the supine position than the erect, and may alter in size with the Müller and Valsalva manoeuvres, which may help to distinguish them from enlarged nodes, arteries, etc.

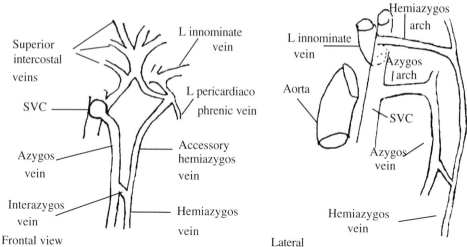

Fig. 9.3   Anatomy of the azygos and hemiazygos veins.

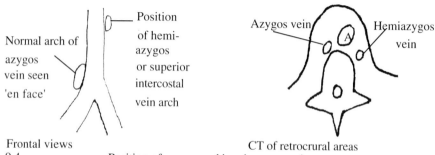

Fig. 9.4   Position of azygos and hemi-azygos veins.

The inferior vena cava - Illus. **IVC**, **IVC ANATOMY** and **IVC THROMBOSIS**.

The shadow of the inferior vena cava can usually be seen on lateral and some frontal radiographs, due to its contact with air-filled lung. It is often overlaid by the oblique fissure on lateral radiographs. Most times on lateral views its posterior border is concave with respect to the spine but it may occasionally be straight. When convex, the IVC is large; this may be normal, but is commonly due to fluid overload or cardiac failure. When fully outlined by air-filled lung, both anteriorly and posteriorly, it has been termed '**isolation of the IVC**'. The '**interface of caval continuity**' between the SVC and IVC on lateral radiographs is discussed on p. 1.27.

(a) Normal IVC with concave ant. +   (b) Straight posterior   (c) Convex post. border - occasionally
post. borders. Dotted line = fissure   border - may be normal.   normal but mostly secondary to cardiac
(a) - enlarged compared with (b & c).   failure or fluid overload.

Fig. 9.5 Diagrams showing the appearances of the IVC on lateral radiographs (b & c after Toombs and Miller, 1979, Radiology, **132**, 577 - 581, with permission).

The supra-diaphragmatic part of the IVC may also be enlarged due to congenital heart disease, or with right sided decompensation. Similarly it may be small or absent with venous anomalies such as **azygos and hemiazygos continuation of the IVC**, (due to agenesis of its pre-renal segment) when the IVC returns only hepatic blood to the right atrium. (Azygos continuation of the IVC may also be associated with **polysplenia** or **asplenia** - see ps. 17.12 - 13).

With **azygos continuation of the IVC** (Illus. **IVC AZYGOS CONTINUATION**), the azygos vein may be more prominent, particularly if its upper part lies within an azygos fissure, and the lower part may form a tubular structure behind the right side of the heart - seen also in some cases of SVC obstruction.

Occasionally the IVC may be double, and in such cases the left IVC typically crosses to join the right at renal vein level. Its recognition is of importance radiologically when staging abdominal or testicular tumours, etc. as a triple row of prespinal round nodules may all be vascular.

The IVC may rarely have a diaphragm across its supra-hepatic part - '**coarctation of the IVC**'. This may lead to the **Budd-Chiari syndrome** (see below).

Other anomalies include - **double IVC**, **left sided IVC**, etc. They may be accompanied by an '**aortic nipple**' on PA chest views - see ps. 9.11 - 12. Occasionally the supra-diaphragmatic part is longer than normal with '**high insertion into the right atrium**'.

Loss of the silhouette of the IVC occurs with consolidation or collapse of the middle or right lower lobe or adjacent pleural fluid. (see also p. 2.25). This is because the IVC (as it passes upwards from the level of the diaphragm to the right atrium) indents the medial basic segment of the right lower lobe (or the RML), and if this part of the lung is opaque, then the silhouette of the IVC will be lost. Similarly displacement of the lung from the IVC, with loss of its outline, may assist in the detection and localisation of a retro-sternal mass. Pleural fluid in the right medial sulcus will also obliterate the IVC silhouette - a point particularly to note with sub-pulmonary effusions, which often go unrecognised (see p. 14.4). A raised right hemi-diaphragm may also obscure the IVC shadow.

Asthma with overdistension of the right lower lobe and a low hemidiaphragm may make the IVC more readily visible on frontal views and CT sections (Illus. **IVC Pts. 9 & 10**), and collapse of a lower lobe may have a similar effect.

CT appearances - within the liver, the IVC appears as an oval low density on the right adjacent to the spine (Illus. **IVC ANATOMY, Liver Pts. 3a-b & 23**). With IV contrast medium it opacifies. It continues up through the diaphragm to the right atrium through the mediastinal fat - see Illus. **IVC ANATOMY, IVC Pts. 2 & 9**. **Intense opacification** of the IVC and the hepatic veins (exceeding that in the abdominal aorta) may be seen with tricuspid incompetence on contrast enhanced CT due to direct reflux of contrast of contrast from the right atrium to the IVC (the 'old-fashioned' sign was hepatic pulsation due hepatic vein reflux. **Early IVC opacification** may also be seen with (a) other causes of right sided heart failure, (b) carcinoid syndrome (when there is fibrosis affecting the pulmonary and tricuspid valves leading to pulmonary stenosis and tricuspid regurgitation - see p. 5.6), (c) SVC obstruction, (d) vascular compromise (e.g. iatrogenic) and (e) aorto-caval fistulae.

Pseodothrombosis may also be seen due to poor mixing of blood and contrast medium in the IVC - (see refs. below).

A varix of the IVC may cause a bulge in the position of the IVC on a lateral chest radiograph.

The **Budd-Chiari syndrome** is a rare disorder of the hepatic veins, or impaired hepatic venous drainage due to anomalies of the IVC. There are two types:

(i) **Primary** due to **congenital obstruction of the hepatic veins or hepatic portion of the IVC by webs or diaphragms**, and

(ii) **Secondary** due to **tumour** (especially a hepatoma), **thrombosis** or **trauma**.

In most cases the obstruction is partial - thus patients present with variable degrees of hepatic enlargement, pain, tenderness and ascites. Jaundice, portal hypertension and bleeding from varices may also be present. Rarely there may be a fulminating presentation with liver failure and shock. Other associations are with polycythaemia, leukaemia, oral contraceptives and pregnancy.

Methods of investigation

Real-time ultra-sound may show a thickened IVC wall, stenosis with irregularity, frank thrombus formation, and/or proximal dilatation. Webs and diaphragms may also be seen. In many cases tumour within the adjacent liver may be the cause of IVC compression and distortion.

An **isotope venogram** (using a small bolus of e.g. 15 mCi Tc^{99m} pertechnetate, or other soluble labelled compound, injected into a vein in either foot) may demonstrate compression of the IVC, a failure to fill the hepatic vein or show it arched over a swelling. (This is the least invasive method and often suffices for the demonstration of Budd-Chiari syndrome. Surgical relief will however need a more detailed study for its planning.)

An **IVC venogram** will usually show these findings more clearly. Contrast flowing up the IVC should reflux into the hepatic veins with a Valsalva manoeuvre. For finer details a catheter may be inserted into the hepatic veins via the IVC. In chronic cases there may be a **'spider-web'** pattern of collateral intra-hepatic veins, but these may need an injection into the hepatic artery for their demonstration.

An **isotope colloid scan** may demonstrate a large defect in the area of the hepatic veins. In gross cases, there may be defective perfusion and uptake in most of the liver, perhaps with sparing of the caudate lobe.

CT - hepatomegaly with ascites is readily apparent. With IV contrast media, the hepatic veins may fail to be visualised, and the part of the liver around the IVC may not enhance. Collaterals may be seen, as well as an 'infarcted' area of liver adjacent to the hepatic veins, or an adjacent tumour.

MR - a swollen liver and obstructed hepatic veins may be seen ± a hepatic tumour mass or infarct.

Collateral pathways with IVC occlusion include the ascending lumbar veins, the vertebral venous plexuses, the azygo-hemiazygos system, the ureteric, gonadal and left renal to azygos and hemiazygos systems and the portal system via the inferior mesenteric vein, superficial veins such as the inferior and superior epigastric and the circumflex iliac veins.

Prognosis and treatment - in cases secondary to tumour, the prognosis is very poor. With thrombosis per se, some patients may recover, particularly if the condition is secondary to a hepatic abscess. In cases complicating IVC malformations, the condition may be chronic. Surgical treatment of the latter may be possible. In a few cases transluminal angioplasty may be of value (e.g. from structural failure and migration to the lungs).

IVC filters for trapping venous emboli - their use is not without risk of complications e.g. from structural failure and migration to the lungs, and appear to have probably been overused in some centres. They should only be used in patients who continue to produce pulmonary emboli despite adequate anticoagulation, or if this is impracticable Illus. **IVC FILTER**.

References.

Ferris et al. (1969) : Venography of the IVC and its branches.
Oh et al. (1973) : IVC varix., Moncada et al. (1985a) : IVC varix.
Chuang et al. (1974) : Congenital anomalies of the IVC - review of embryology and classification.
Toombs and Miller (1979) : The convex supra-diaphragmatic IVC.
Tonkin et al. (1977) : Radiographic isolation of the IVC - i.e. air-filled lung in front of and behind the IVC.
Mayo et al. (1983) : Anomalies of the IVC.

Anderson et al. (1961) : Azygos and hemiazygos continuation of the IVC.
Berdon and Baker (1968) : Azygos continuation of the IVC - plain film findings.
Heller et al. (1971) : A useful sign in recognition of azygos continuation of the IVC - absence of IVC shadow on lateral view.
Floyd and Nelson (1976) : Azygos and hemiazygos continuation of the IVC.
Haswell and Berrigan (1976) : Anomalous IVC with accessory hemiazygos continuation.
Oreilly and Grollman (1976) : The lateral chest radiograph may be an unreliable indicator of azygos continuation of the IVC - the shadow may still be present as it may drain the hepatic vein.
Breckenridge and Kinlaw (1980) : Azygos continuation of the IVC - CT findings.
Schultz et al. (1984) : Azygos continuation of the IVC - MR findings.
Churchill et al. (1980) : CT of anomalous IVC with azygos continuation.
Ginaldi et al. (1980) : Absence of hepatic segment of IVC with azygos continuation.
Allen and Haney (1981) : Left IVC with hemiazygos continuation.

Cohen, M. et al. (1984) : Accessory hemiazygos continuation of IVC.

Barack (1986) : CT - persistence of abdominal cardinal venous system and absence of IVC in female aged 33 with recurrent lower limb DVTs.

Burkhalter and Gray (1985) : Transhepatic collaterals circumventing IVC obstruction due to hypernephroma.

Pomeranz and Proto (1986) : Azygos continuation of the IVC with azygos lobe, causing tubular shadow in the lung.

Arakawa et al. (1987) : Two continuation pathways in the interruption of the IVC -
(i) azygos and hemiazygos continuation, and (ii) unusual extrathoracic pathway - phrenic and pericardial veins draining through the highest intercostal vein into the left innominate vein.

Ghossain et al. (1988) : Portal and hemiazygos continuation of the IVC.

Shah (1989) : Azygos lobe and azygos continuation of the IVC.

Balkanci and Özman (1993) : Interruption of the IVC with anomalous intrahepatic continuation.

Evans (1993) : Azygos/accessory hemiazygos continuation of the IVC mimicking dissection of the aorta - correct diagnosis by contrast enhanced CT.

Mata et al. (1996) : Azygos continuation of IVC + azygos lobe - CT showed huge azygos vein in the fissure.

Hawkins and Metcalfe (1996) : A markedly enlarged azygos vein (above the level of the renal veins) continued into the thorax to a normal termination in the SVC.

Hunter et al. (1998) : Double IVC in a young man with a testicular tumour.

Lin et al. (1981) : Local colloid trapping in the IVC syndrome.

Edeburn et al. (1985) : Passage of lung scan macroaggregates (injected into a lower limb vein) to liver, kidneys and brain via collaterals with IVC occlusion.

Mitchell, M. et al. (1982) : Budd-Chiari syndrome - aetiology, diagnosis and management.

Murphy, P. et al. (1986) : The Budd-Chiari syndrome.

Vogelzang et al. (1987) : Budd-Chiari syndrome - CT observations.

Jayanthi et al. (1988) : Coarctation of IVC causing chronic Budd-Chiari syndrome - demonstration by US in 9 cases.

Kobayashi et al. (1988) : Calcification in membrane in IVC causing the Budd-Chiari syndrome.

Hayward (1990) : Portal venous collateral drainage in IVC obstruction (3 patients with testicular teratoma).

Menu et al. (1990) : MR evaluation of the Budd-Chiari syndrome.

Arora et al. (1991) : Unusual CT appearances in a case of Budd-Chiari syndrome - multiple space occupying lesions on CT due to areas of haemorrhagic necrosis which simulated tumour deposits.

Nishida and Okuda (1991) : Diagnosis of cavo-portal shunt in IVC obstruction - comparison between venography and dynamic scintigraphy.

Coulden et al. (1992) : Doppler ultrasound of the hepatic veins - normal appearances.

Lim et al. (1992) : Membranous obstruction of the IVC - comparison of sonography, CT and venography - noted that whereas in Western countries, the Budd-Chiari syndrome is most often due to thrombotic obstruction of the hepatic veins and IVC resulting from systemic diseases or malignant tumours, membranous or segmental obstruction of the IVC is a common cause of Budd-Chiari syndrome in Korea, Japan, India and S. Africa resulting in chronic liver disease and the formation of port-systemic collateral vessels.

Griffith et al. (1996) : Radiological intervention in Budd-Chiari syndrome.

Mitchell, A. and Jackson (1996) : Budd-Chiari syndrome.

Markert et al. (1997) : Budd-Chiari syndrome resulting from intrahepatic IVC compression secondary to blunt hepatic trauma - decompression by surgical or subcutaneous drainage of intrahepatic or subcapsular haematoma was curative in two of three patients.

Warren and Cook (1993) : Left empyema and IVC thrombosis in a 13 year old boy due to protein C deficiency - a vitamin K dependent plasma protein synthesised in the liver.

Glazer, G. et al. (1981) : CT diagnosis of tumour thrombus in the inferior vena cava.

Godwin and Webb (1982) : Contrast-related flow phenomena mimicking pathology on thoracic CT.

Vogelzang et al. (1985) : Inferior vena cava CT pseudothrombus produced by rapid arm-vein contrast injection.

McWilliams and Chalmers (1995) : Pseudothrombosis of the infra-renal inferior vena cava during helical CT.

Fox et al. (1996) : Pseudothrombosis of the intra-renal IVC during helical CT - what causes this pitfall?
(a) incomplete mixing of blood with contrast (b) local collapse of IVC near the diaphragm on deep inspiration.

Collins, M. et al. (1996) : CT manifestations of tricuspid regurgitation - 6 cases.

Hatrick et Al. (1997) : Poor opacification of IVC on helical CT caused by a congenital web in the IVC.

Naik and Chalmers (1997) : The differential diagnosis of early IVC opacification on dynamic CT.

Jones, A. et al. (1988) : IVC filter in the management of IVC thrombosis complicating acute pancreatitis.

Stringer et al. (1988) : IVC thrombosis complicating acute pancreatitis.

Peillon et al. (1991) : IVC thrombosis to chronic pancreatitis & pseudocyst.

Antony et al. (1994): IVC thrombosis associated with acute pancreatitis.

Goenka et al. (1994) : Acute pancreatitis complicated by pulmonary thromboembolism secondary to IVC thrombosis.

Treatment
Arnold et al. (1993) : Overuse of IVC filters in a community hospital.
Ferris et al. (1993, Arkansas) : Follow up of IVC filters in 320 patients - 120 died (8 from further pulmonary embolism). 40 had (proven or suspected) IVC thrombosis, 36 venous thrombosis at puncture site, 13 filter migration, 12 penetration of IVC wall and 4 suspected repeated pulmonary emboli.
Perry and Wells (1993) : Long term follow up of Günther vena cava filters.
Perry and Wells (1994) : Structural failure of a bird's nest IVC filter.
Vaislic et al. (1993) : Migration of an Antheor filter to the pulmonary artery.
Entwistle et al. (1995) : Use of wall-stent endovascular prosthesis in the treatment of malignant IVC obstruction.
Ritchie et al. (1995) : Migration of a vena caval filter to the main pulmonary artery.
Owen and Krarup (1997) : The successful use and removal of the Gunther Tulip IVC filter in pregnancy.
King and Dacie (1997) : Early structural failure of an Anthéor inferior cava filter.
Harries et al. (1998) : Long-term follow-up of the Antheor IVC filter in 20 cases - 3 became fractured, one containing thrombus & one IVC was occluded. One pt. died 6 weeks after insertion due to central migration to the main pulmonary artery.

The superior vena caval syndrome (thrombosis and/or compression) - Illus. **SVC** and **SVC OBSTRUCTION.**
   This may be produced by a number of conditions. Hunter (1757 - see p. 10.8) described it in relation to a luetic aneurysm. A review by McIntyre and Sykes (1949) gave roughly equal numbers due to (a) primary intrathoracic tumours, (b) pressure from aortic aneurysms, and (c) mediastinitis, etc. A further review by Parish et al. (1981) from the Mayo Clinic showed that there were roughly three malignant cases to each benign one. Malignant cases now account for over 90%.
   Virtually any intrathoracic tumour may lead to SVC obstruction and thrombosis. This mainly occurs with lung tumours, especially in relation to enlarged right upper mediastinal nodes. However it may also be seen with other tumours involving the mediastinal nodes (lymphoma, breast, testis, etc.), thymic and thyroid masses, or be part of a para-neoplastic syndrome, with secondary thrombosis (see Chapter 23). Rarely it may occur with tumour occurring in the right atrium, creeping down the great veins from a thyroid neoplasm (Illus. **SVC   OBSTRUCTION, Pt. 11a-g**) i.e. similar to IVC thrombosis with renal neoplasms, or be due to a primary tumour occurring in the SVC itself, e.g. an angiosarcoma (see p. 9.9).
   Benign causes of the SVC syndrome are largely due to mediastinitis, either acute infection, often with an abscess, chronic fibrosis (from tuberculosis or fungus disease), sarcoid (p. 19.73 - refs. 'm'), aggressive fibromatosis (p. 18.4), Behçet's disease (ps. 19.87 - 88) or mediastinal (and especially bronchogenic cysts - see ps. 3.13 - 14). It may follow axillary, subclavian (and innominate vein thrombosis and an increasing number are being found secondary to CVP lines, pacemakers, chemotherapy catheters, etc. (It is not uncommon to find thrombus around these at venography). Radiotherapy may be associated with SVC thrombosis, particularly with a severe mediastinal fibrotic reaction. The author has seen one case due to syphilitic mediastinitis in a clergyman, thought to be dying from lung carcinoma (see also ps. 19.49 - 50).
   Long-standing obstruction of the SVC e.g. with a benign cause or a slowly progressive tumour (e.g. a mesothelioma) may give rise to visible collateral veins in the axillae or anterior chest wall.
   Acute obstruction may also cause swelling of the head and neck, proptosis, swelling of the upper limb(s), chest wall and the breasts in women and some may even present with the last mentioned!
   SVC obstruction is most readily investigated by venography from the arms, but may also be carried out via the intra-osseous (bone marrow) route e.g. via the ribs or vertebral spinous processes, to fill the azygos and hemi-azygos systems (Viamonte, 1965, Wolfel et al., 1966, Janower et al., 1966 and Ranninger, 1968). Rinker et al. (1967) used the combined techniques of superior vena cavography and azygography to study 63 patients with suspected bronchial carcinoma, and found six signs of neoplastic involvement of these veins - (i) complete obstruction, (ii) a partial or segmental block, (iii) reflux of contrast medium from the azygos system up the SVC or into the IVC, (iv) displacement of part of the azygos or caval system, (v) delayed emptying of the arch of the azygos vein, and (vi) involvement of the SVC of the or the innominate veins with a normal azygos system.

As well as demonstrating thrombus within the SVC and/or great veins, extraluminal masses pressing upon them need also to be demonstrated, and for this CT is invaluable. When accompanied by a contrast infusion from an arm, intraluminal defects may usually be demonstrated as well. The 'scout view' may also give a useful 'venogram'. The contrast medium will help to show other vessels, tumour enhancement, etc.

CT is complementary to venography. Whilst both many demonstrate displacement, compression and obstruction, as well as defects due to thrombi (distinguish from flow defects, as seen in other veins), CT is better at demonstrating soft tissue tumour masses pressing on the veins, whilst venography shows more clearly the pattern of the thrombosis and the collateral venous drainage.

Technique for SVC venography - SVC GRAM.
For this the author has preferred to have the patient erect or semi-erect, standing, or lying on the x-ray table raised head up. Either one or both antecubital veins are cannulated and an assistant or assistants inject(s) 50 ml of contrast medium into one or both arms, which are elevated. The passage of contrast medium is monitored by TV fluoroscopy and is usually recorded on 100 mm (or digital) film, but larger 'spot films' or video-recording may also be used. 100 mm (or digital) films are preferred because fluoroscopic monitoring allows the films to be taken at the optimum time and avoids the necessity of taking numerous large films with a serial film-changer, many of which provide little information. DVI is preferable for this purpose when available. As with vascular studies elsewhere, venography of the cava may also be carried out using a small bolus of a radioactive isotope and a gamma camera. (Coltart and Wraight, 1985, used this method of venography for the SVC in 27 patients and 10 controls).

Most patients with SVC obstruction due to tumour and/ or tumour thrombosis have tumour masses pressing upon the SVC, and are usually treated urgently by radiotherapy, chemotherapy and/or steroids, in many cases with temporary or longer gratifying results. In some cases (and particularly those due to benign disease, e.g. the case shown in Illus. **SUBCLAV VEIN 6a-c** and caused by infectious mononucleosis) anticoagulants may help resolve an intra-venous thrombosis.

Another method of palliating SVC obstruction is to use self expanding metallic stents. Balloon dilatation is carried out first. It may be carried out following radiotherapy, but endo-vascular thrombus and/or tumour should be excluded by preliminary venography. Preliminary treatment with streptokinase may help 'unblock' a thrombus.

N.B. Neovascularity may sometimes be seen within a tumour thrombus (Leifer and Chan, 1994, reported this in the IVC secondary to a renal tumour - see Illus. **IVC THROMBOSIS 4a-c**).

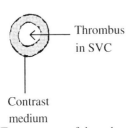

Thrombus
in SVC

Contrast
medium

Fig. 9.6 CT appearance of thrombus surrounded
by contrast medium. cf. endoluminal lipoma
with low density centre (see below).

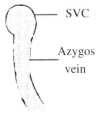

SVC

Azygos
vein

Fig. 9.7 Dilated azygos vein in
association with SVC obstruction.

Further references.
Guozdanovic and Oberhofer (1953) : Mediastinal phlebography.
Hudson (1957) : Venography in SVC obstruction.
Otto and Kurtzman (1964) : Oesophageal varices in SVC obstruction.
Steinberg (1966) : SVC syndrome with tuberculosis.
Okay and Bryk (1969) : Collateral veins in occlusion of the SVC and its tributaries.
Adams and de Weese (1971) : "Effort" thrombosis of the axillary and subclavian veins.
Bryk (1974) : Venous compression and obstruction by intrathoracic goitre.

Chamoord et al. (1978) : SVC syndrome complicating transvenous pacemaker implantation.

Linos et al. (1980) : Subclavian vein - a 'golden route'.

Martinez et al. (1981) : SVC obstruction as the presentation of AV fistula of the thoracic aorta.

Barek et al. (1982) : Role of CT in the assessment of SVC obstruction.

Godwin and Webb (1982) : Contrast-related flow phenomena mimicking pathology on thoracic CT.

Hidalgo et al. (1982) : Venous collaterals shown in subcutaneous tissues by CT. Intraluminal thrombus with enhancing rim.

Engel et al. (1983) : CT diagnosis of mediastinal and thoracic inlet venous obstruction.

Moncada et al. (1984) : Used CT and digital phlebography ('scout views' on the CT apparatus) to study nine patients with the SVC syndrome and demonstrated external compression, encasement or intraluminal thrombus, and collateral venous channels; the technique did not always fully opacify a patent SVC, due to rapid blood flow through it.

Bechtold et al. (1985) : CT detection of SVC obstruction.

Borts et al. (1985) : Intra-luminal bronchogenic cavo-atrial tumour thrombus shown by CT, using a concomitant injection of contrast medium.

Fourestie et al. (1985) : Left innominate vein stenosis as a late complication of central venous catheterisation.

Godwin and Chen (1986) : Thoracic venous anatomy.

Gooding et al. (1986) : Obstruction of SVC and subclavian veins - US diagnosis in 11 patients - non-collapsing with respiration if obstructed.

Holbert and Libshitz (1986) : SVC syndrome in primary germ cell tumours.

McMurdo et al. (1986) : Normal and occluded mediastinal veins shown by MR. In a study of over 50 patients (25 of whom were normal) noted that generally venous collaterals in the mediastinum and chest wall were better seen with contrast enhanced CT. MR showed marked contrast differences between the 'signal void' of normal vascular structures, the moderate signal intensity of tumours and the high signal intensity of a thrombus or slowly flowing blood. This latter allowed ready detection of venous occlusion and could also suggest its cause.

Stanford and Doty (1986) : Role of venography and surgery in management of SVC obstruction.

Stanford et al. (1987) : Collateral blood flow types in 27 patients with SVC obstruction:

(i) partial obstruction of SVC (up to 90%) with patent azygos vein,

(ii) near complete obstruction of SVC, with azygos vein keeping an antegrade flow to lower SVC (below block),

(iii) total obstruction of SVC with reversed azygos flow (azygos draining superior intercostal veins),

(iv) complete block of SVC and azygos veins with chest wall and internal mammary collaterals.

Andrews et al. (1987) : Digital subtraction venography of upper limb & mediastinum - abnormalities in 74 pts.

Benenati et al. (1986) : Digital subtraction venography in central venous obstruction.

Falk and Smith (1987) : Diagnosis of thrombosis of upper limb and thoracic inlet veins by duplex Doppler US.

Yedlicka et al. (1987) & (1989) : CT findings of and in SVC obstruction.

Wilson et al. (1987) : Subclavian and axillary vein thrombosis following radiotherapy for carcinoma of the breast.

Liu et al. (1988) : SVC syndrome - a rare presenting feature of acute **myeloid leukaemia**.

Mendelson et al. (1988) : CT of mediastinal collaterals in the SVC syndrome - the collateral veins may cause a fine nodular pattern in the mediastinal fat as seen on axial sections.

Hansen et al. (1990) : Value of MR for assessing the patency of mediastinal and thoracic inlet veins in 31 patients. It missed non-occlusive thrombus in two cases, but otherwise showed abnormalities shown by other methods.

Trigaux and van Beers (1990) : Thoracic collateral venous channels - normal and pathological CT findings - **opacification of an anterior channel should arouse suspicion of SVC obstruction** - posterior channels are sometimes normal.

Kirstler et al. (1991) : Demonstration of SVC obstruction **fibrosing mediastinitis** - venous collaterals with R to L shunt shown by Tc^{99m} albumen aggregates.

Yellin et al. (1992) : SVC syndrome associated with lymphoma in 11 children.

Brown, G. and Husband (1993) : Mediastinal widening - a valuable radiographic sign of SVC thrombosis - 9 patients related to Hickman catheter insertion - 5 showed lateral displacement of Hickman catheter with SVC thrombosis.

Escalante (1993) : Causes and management of SVC syndrome.

Kim et al. (1993) : CT diagnosis of SVC syndrome - importance of collateral vessels.

Tello et al. (1993) : Subclavian vein thrombosis detected with spiral CT and 3D reconstruction.

Cave et al. (1994) : SVC syndrome caused by an aneurysm of an aberrant right subclavian artery.

Dingerkus et al. (1994) : Mediastinal **chloroma** affecting the right heart with superior vena cava syndrome.

Royston and Corr (1995) : Hypoplastic left innominate vein - collateral pathway via hemiazygos system to L renal vein shown at IVU.

Bryant (1995) : Non-malignant cause of L innominate vein compression following L upper lobectomy and radiotherapy for lung cancer.

Maldjian et al. (1995) : **Focal enhancement of areas in the liver on CT** - a sign of SVC obstruction.

Holemans et al. (1997) : SVC obstruction can give rise on enhanced CT to (a) **dilated pericardial veins** and (b) **focal areas of hepatic enhancement** - due to contrast being trapped in narrow hepatic vascular channels - as may also be seen on radioisotope studies.

Belli and Hemingway (1990) : Treatment of SVC syndrome by percutaneous metal stent insertion.

Irving and Walker (1990) : Self expandable (Gianturco) stents for relief of SVC obstruction.

Edwards, R. et al. (1992) : SVC obstruction, secondary to large cell ca bronchus, complicated by central venous thrombosis - treated by thrombolysis and Gianturco- Z stents.

Rösch et al. (1992) : Gianturco-expandable Z stents in the treatment of SVC syndrome.

Edwards nd Jackson (1993) : SVC obstruction secondary to squamous cell lung cancer treated by thrombolysis, mechanical thrombectomy using the Amplatz Thrombectomy Device and metallic stenting.

Dyet et al. (1993) : Wallstent endovascular prosthesis in the treatment of malignant obstruction of the SVC.

Gaines et al. (1994) : SVC obstruction managed by the Gianturco Z stent (20 cases). These authors also pointed out the necessity of modification of the 'fixing hooks' to prevent stent migration.

Dondelinger (1996) : Interventional radiology of thoracic venous obstruction - 90% success rate with stenting IVC/SVC - low morbidity of 7% - no cases of migration of stent in SVC. Most cases of lining thrombus in SVC have been due to CV lines, esp. those used for dialysis - use urokinase for local thrombolysis.

Entwistle et al. (1996) : Migration and shortening of a self-expanding metallic stent complicating the treatment of malignant SVC stenosis.

Cleveland et al. (1997) : Stenting of the SVC without removal of a long-term central feeding line.

Loveday (1997) : Self expanding stents undergo a dynamic process of radial expansion and shortening. The shortening may take a too-short stent out of a narrowing or stricture, therefore it is important to ensure it is of sufficient length before insertion.

Ho et al. (1999) : Systemic to pulmonary venous shunting in SVC obstruction shown by spiral CT.

Old (1999) : SVC obstruction due to prostatic cancer.

Van Putten et al. (2000) : SVC obstruction caused by radiation induced venous fibrosis.

Venous endoluminal tumours including lipomata.

Several examples of lipomata have been reported within or closely related to the SVC or IVC. They cause no obstruction and typically have a low density of approx. -100 HU.

Other tumours include angiosarcomas, leiomyomas (see p. 5.19) leiomyosarcomas and reticuloses, as well as secondary tumours particularly from the thyroid or the kidney (see also p. 9.6). Those arising in the upper IVC may develop the Budd-Chiari syndrome (Illus. **IVC Pt. 16**). IVC tumours appear to be more common than those arising in the SVC.

References.

Mikaye et al. (1992) : Localised fat collection adjacent to the intrahepatic portion of IVC - normal variant on CT.

Mousseau et al. (1992) : MR tissue-characterisation of a right atrial lipoma.

Vinnicombe et al. (1994) : CT features of intravascular lipoma of SVC. (See also Wilson, 1994).

Perry et al. (1994) : Lipomata of IVC - normal variant ? - 7 pts. (6m & 1f) shown by CT, and one also with ultrasound as a hypoechoic density defect.

Thorogood and Maskell (1996) : Intravascular lipoma of the SVC - CT & MR appearances - suppression of the signal within the lesion on STIR sequence. Pt. also had multiple calcareous lipomata.

Perl (1871) : **Sarcoma of IVC**.   Abbatt et al. (1983) : Angiosarcoma of SVC.

Lok et al. (1986) : Radiological diagnosis of leiomyosarcoma of the IVC - reviewed 78 cases from the literature and reported another - mean age 56 - range 27 - 83 years with 5 females to one male.

Davis, G. et al. (1976) : Leiomyosarcoma of SVC.   Van-Rooij (1988) : Leiomyosarcoma of IVC - CT & MR.

Burke (1986) and Virmani (1993) : Sarcomas of the great vessels.

Monig et al. (1995) : Leiomyosarcoma of IVC - 3 cases + review.

Harrison et al. (1996) : SVC obstruction in a 64 yr. old man due to high grade B cell lymphoma of the right atrium.

Mingoli et al. (1996) : 218 pts. with IVC leiomyosarcoma.

Delany (1998) : Malignant SVC hamartoma with SVC obstruction.

Ferretti et al. (1998) : Epithelioid haemangioendothelioma of the SVC - CT demonstration and literature review.

Redla and Kantor (1999) : Woman aged 51 with leiomyosarcoma of IVC + hepatic deposits.

Thompson et al. (1978) : Follicular carcinoma of the **thyroid** with massive angio-invasion up to the heart.

Perez and Brown (1984) : Follicular carcinoma of the **thyroid** appearing as an intraluminal SVC tumour.

Thomas et al. (1991) : Bilateral massive internal jugular vein thrombosis in carcinoma of the **thyroid** - CT evaluation - the tumour thrombus enhanced as did the vein walls ? due to vasa vasorum.

Venous dilatations and varices - Illus. **VARICES**.

Dilatations of the thoracic veins are not uncommon in heart failure, with pericardial disease, following trauma, with portal hypertension, anomalous pulmonary venous return or A/V fistulae, high volume states such as pregnancy, with congenital abnormalities, especially cystic hygromas (see refs. below) or in relation to obstruction, due to tumour, fibrosis, etc. These may be coupled with thrombosis and the opening up of collateral pathways. Idiopathic dilatations may also be found, the most common being of the innominate veins at the base of the neck, and in the thoracic inlet - these are most readily examined with ultra-sound. Dilatations of the SVC or IVC may also be found. Most thoracic venous aneurysms are treated expectantly, as few give rise to any complications, and the blood-flow rate through them is rapid However, thrombosis may occur in a few. Surgical treatment is associated with high morbidity and mortality.

Posterior and lower mediastinal **varices** may be found with portal hypertension (see also ps. 18.31 - 32), and azygos continuation of the IVC (see above). Sometimes these become so large that they may be seen as soft tissue masses paravertebrally and mimic enlarged posterior mediastinal lymph nodes see Fig. 18.15 or produce masses in the retro-crural space. Such posterior mediastinal varices may be seen as soft tissue masses paravertebrally - on plain radiographs, conventional tomograms or CTs in patients with portal hypertension, etc. - Illus. **VARICES, Syph. varic Pt. 11a-h and Oes varices Pt. 6a-c.**

Anteriorly situated mediastinal varices, may be seen particularly on the right, and have been termed pericardial or cardio-phrenic varices.

As well as the more normal **'uphill varices'** produced by upper IVC and portal vein obstruction, dilated mediastinal veins may be produced by SVC obstruction. Felson and Lessure (1964) termed these **'downhill varices'**, and described cases due to various causes, including past-radiotherapy, thyroid masses and lung cancer. Those secondary to benign tumours may resolve following surgery.

References.

Abbot (1950) : Congenital aneurysm of SVC - 19 yr. old student - mass in R upper mediastinum - changed shape in deep inspiration and deep expiration - angiocardiogram showed fusiform dilatation of SVC - at surgery it was wrapped in cellophane and its size diminished.

Lawrence and Burford (1956) : Congenital aneurysm of SVC - was resected relieving symptoms.

Bell et al. (1970) : SVC aneurysm - angiography showed no change in its size after four years.

Okay et al. (1970) : Phlebectasia of the jugular and great mediastinal veins.

Ream and Giardina (1972) : Congenital SVC aneurysm with complications caused by infectious mononucleosis - thrombophlebitis, pulmonary emboli and infarcts leading to death - (see also p. 19.31).

Hidvegi et al. (1979), Modry et al. (1980) : Congenital saccular aneurysm of the SVC.

Mok et al. (1981) : Coexisting congenital primary superior vena caval aneurysm and rheumatic mitral stenosis.

Taira and Akita (1981) : Ruptured aneurysm of a persistent left SVC.

Train et al. (1981) : Fusiform aneurysm of the SVC.

Furakawa et al. (1984) : Aneurysm of jugular and mediastinal veins - radioisotope blood pool study.

Moncada et al (1985a) : Discussed CT of aneurysms of the thoracic systemic veins and reported

(a) an aneurysm of the SVC (man aged 70 - smooth mass in right upper mediastinum due to a large SVC)

(b) aneurysm of L innominate vein (man aged 23 - chance finding in CT examination of R sterno-clavicular joint),

(c) aneurysm of IVC (woman aged 58 with a renal tumour - bulge in position of IVC on lateral chest x-ray, i.e. retro-cardiac - enhanced on CT and venocavography. Surgery confirmed IVC aneurysm -no evidence of tumour in it).

They also gave references to 16 other cases of SVC aneurysm - both fusiform and saccular types.

Joseph et al. (1989) : 8 of 15 pts. with mediastinal cystic hygromas had enlargement of neck or thoracic veins - 5 children had aneurysmal dilatation of SVC and 3 mild enlargement.

Yokomise et al. (1990) : Systemic venous aneurysms.

Gorenstein et al. (1992) : Giant cystic **hygroma** associated with a venous aneurysm.

Rapaport et al. (1992) : Idiopathic dilatation of the thoracic venous system.

Kurihara et al. (1993) : Saccular aneurysm of azygos vein simulating a paratracheal tumour.

Calligaro et al. (1995) : Venous aneurysms - surgical indications and review of the literature.

Pasic et al. (1995) : Aneurysm of superior mediastinal veins - 18 yr. old woman with saccular dilatation of SVC and innominate veins had reconstruction on cardiac bypass surgery.

Burkill and Padley (1996) and Burkill et al. (1997) : Saccular aneurysm of left innominate vein (incidental finding on a supine chest radiograph in a woman aged 21 who fell off a bus causing a head injury - it was much smaller on a subsequent erect radiograph. A mass enhancing almost as much as the aorta was seen on CT, and a L arm venogram showed the saccular aneurysm draining into the SVC. Blood flow through the aneurysm was rapid with no evidence of aneurysm).

Davies and Roberts (1998) : Aneurysm R innominate vein & SVC causing mediastinal widening in woman of 50.

(See also under azygos vein refs. - p. 9.17 - for further reports of thoracic venous aneurysms.)

Doyle et al. (1961) : The mediastinum in portal hypertension.

Otto and Kurtzman (1964) : Oesophageal varices in SVC obstruction.

Castellino et al. (1968) : Dilated azygos and hemiazygos veins presenting as paravertebral intrathoracic masses.
Ishikawa et al. (1980) : Venous abnormalities in portal hypertension shown by CT.
Moult et al. (1975) : Posterior mediastinal masses in patients with portal hypertension.
Solokin et al. (1977) : Downhill varices - report of a case 29 years after resection of a **substernal thyroid**.
Johnson et al. (1978) : 'Downhill' oesophageal varices.
Clark et al. (1980) : CT of oesophageal and upper abdominal varices.
Fleig et al. (1982) : Upper gastro-intestinal haemorrhage from downhill oesophageal varices.
Saks et al. (1983) : Deformities produced by varices could be accentuated following endoscopic injection therapy with sclerosant compounds - a technique pioneered by Macbeth in Oxford.*
Balthazar et al. (1984) : CT recognition of gastric varices., (1987) : CT of 20 patients with varices demonstrating thickening in the oesophageal wall, scalloped contours and intraluminal protrusions enhancing with IV contrast.
Hirose et al. (1984) : 'Downhill' and pericardial varices shown by CT.
Ishikawa et al. (1985) : Detection of paraoesophageal varices by plain films.
Millward et al. (1985) : Pericardial varices shown by CT.
Shirakusa et al. (1988) : Downhill oesophageal varices secondary to increased blood drainage from a benign giant lymphoma, the SVC still being patent.
Kedar and Cosgrove (1994) : Retroperitoneal varices mimicking a mass - diagnosis on colour Doppler.
Wachsberg et al. (1995) : Cardiophrenic varices in portal hypertension - evaluation with CT.

*Ronald Graeme Macbeth (1933 - 1968) Director, Dept of Otolarynglogy, Radcliffe Infirmary, Oxford (Obiit, 1992).

The right and left **superior intercostal veins** are often seen on CT sections, and **these** should not be confused with lung, pleural or mediastinal pathology. These veins may become dilated in heart failure, with obstruction of the SVC, innominate veins or the IVC. With an azygos lobe, the right superior intercostal vein follows an anomalous course through the posterior aspect of the azygos fissure. The superior intercostal veins may also be dilated with azygos or hemiazygos continuation of the IVC, hypoplastic innominate veins, a persistent left SVC, and anomalous pulmonary venous return.

The azygos and hemi-azygos veins - Illus. **AZYGOS VEIN** and **HEMIAZYGOS VEIN**.
    These veins are formed by the cephalic continuation of the ascending lumbar veins, entering the thorax behind the crura of the diaphragm and passing through the aortic hiatus accompanied by the sympathetic chains.
    The **azygos vein** lies anterior to or just to the right of the vertebral bodies until it arches anteriorly over the right main bronchus to join the SVC. It is usually well seen on frontal chest radiographs or conventional tomograms in the right tracheo-bronchial angle, where it makes an oval or rounded shadow above the right main bronchus, unless it lies more laterally within the right upper lobe within an azygos fissure (see below). It often produces a slight indentation on the lower right aspect of the trachea, especially when dilated. Its diameter is variable, being smaller in inspiration, the erect position or during the Valsalva manoeuvre. On erect radiographs its diameter is between 0.6 and 1 cm., but it is larger in heart failure with pericardial disease, venous obstruction (SVC or IVC obstruction), portal hypertension, or in pregnancy (up to 1.5 cm.). In the recumbent position it is commonly 1 to 1.5 cm., but larger even up to 2 cm. with the above conditions. Its appearance also varies with the patterns of pleural reflection. Occasionally the azygos vein is aneurysmal.
    The retro-tracheal part of the azygos vein often appears as a 'tail', which should not be confused with pathology. This is commonly seen on high KV radiographs or tomograms. This part of the azygos vein was studied by Austin and Thorsen (1981) on supine tomograms (Fig. 9.8, a - c). They found several minor variants of a basic arch pattern coursing around the right border of the lower trachea or right main bronchus. The posterior part of the arch was also shown well by inclined frontal tomography (Illus. **INCL FRONTAL TOMO, IVC Az cont Pt. 1c** shows well the azygos vein ascending in the right side of the mediastinum). It may also sometimes be seen as a small round or triangular shaped nodule behind the lower trachea on lateral radiographs or tomograms (see Fig. 1.44, p. 1.31). The azygos lobe anomaly is discussed on p. 1.5.

    The **hemiazygos vein** ascends on the left to join the azygos vein in front of D8 or D9, its cranial extension being known as the accessory hemi-azygos vein, which joins the left superior intercostal vein to arch forwards to join the left innominate vein, where it forms the '**hemi-azygos arch**'. This arch sometimes produces a small 'bump' on the left side of the aortic knuckle - the '**aortic nipple**' (McDonald et al., 1970). It may also occasionally be seen as a tiny rounded density or as a small band shadow behind the aortic arch. It is usually visualised on contrast enhanced CT studies (Illus. **AORTIC NIPPLE**). It usually ranges in size from 1 to 4 mm. in diameter, but may be larger in congenital absence of the azygos vein (Hatfield et al., 1987) or SVC obstruction, when it may be considerably enlarged and be associated with '**downhill varices**' (see above). Carter et al. (1985) noted it as a sign of impending SVC syndrome.

A paracardiac or para-pulmonary artery nipple may be seen with a dilated pericardiophrenic vein - Chung et al. (1993) described four cases due to membranous obstruction of the IVC and left innominate - inferior phrenic vein anastomosis.

A right sided nipple is shown in Illus **AORTIC NIPPLE, R mediast nipple.**

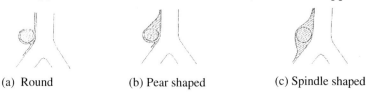

(a) Round   (b) Pear shaped   (c) Spindle shaped

(a), (b) & (c) Variations in the shape of the azygos vein on PA views or tomograms - the shape depending on the investment of the vein by the mediastinal pleura.

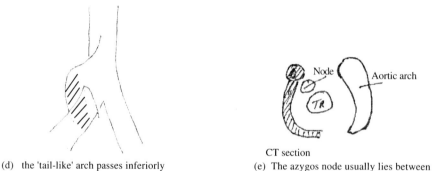

(d) the 'tail-like' arch passes inferiorly behind the right main bronchus.

CT section

(e) The azygos node usually lies between the SVC/azygos junction and the trachea.

Fig. 9.8   The azygos vein and arch ('αζυγὸs = unpaired).

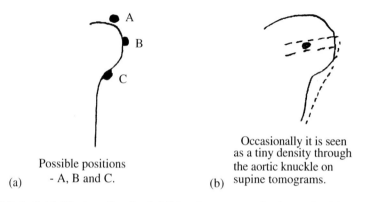

(a) Possible positions - A, B and C.

(b) Occasionally it is seen as a tiny density through the aortic knuckle on supine tomograms.

Fig. 9.9 (a & b). The '**aortic nipple**'. Like the azygos vein, it may be fuller when the patient is lying down. It may also be considerably enlarged with SVC obstruction, etc.

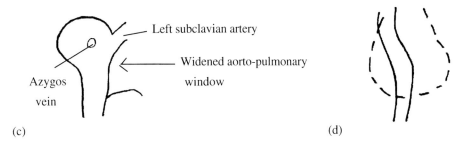

(c)   (d)

Fig. 9.9 (c) A well marked 'nipple' behind the aortic knuckle may also be produced by the azygos vein with a right sided arch and right sided descending aorta.

(d) With azygos continuation of the IVC, the azygos vein may be much more prominent than normal. particular if its upper part lies within an azygos fissure, and the lower part may form a tubular structure behind the right side of the heart - seen also in some cases of SVC obstruction.

The azygos and hemiazygos (or superior intercostal) arches : Normal and pathological CT appearances.

The azygos arch is a commonly identified landmark on contrast-enhanced chest CT sections. It forms the lateral boundary of the pre-tracheal-retrocaval space and with its pleural reflections, demarcates the mediastinum from the right lung. It also divides the mediastinum supero-inferiorly - see p. 18.1.

Malignant infiltration may obstruct it. Nodes lie close to it (Illus. **AZYGOS NODES**).

Lateral displacements are common from enlarged adjacent nodes, retrosternal goitres, abscesses, etc. and medial displacement or compression may be caused by lung masses. Contrast enhancement is invaluable in differentiation.

In patients with an azygos lobe, a right sided haemopneumothorax can mimic upper mediastinal widening because in the recumbent position fluid can collect in the azygos lobe recess (Neufang and Buelo, 1981). With mediastinal abscesses pus may collect above the azygos vein and then fail to track down to the lower mediastinum.

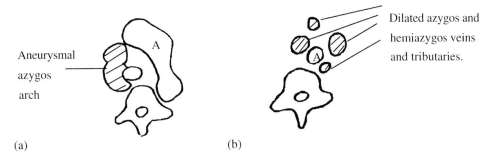

(a)   (b)

Fig. 9.10 (a and b) Dilatations of the azygos and hemiazygos venous systems. These may be present with or without oesophageal varices. They may displace the oesophagus or produce a mass on plain films or tomograms in the para-oesophageal area. Dilated azygos and hemiazygos veins should be distinguished from enlarged lymph nodes, especially in the retrocrural space.

The hemiazygos arch is seen on CT sections posteriorly and laterally to the aortic arch Fig. 9.11 (a and b). It is normally 1 to 4 mm in diameter. It should **always** be noted on CT examinations and be distinguished from nodal enlargement. Occasionally its entrance into the left innominate vein may be visualised Fig. 9.11 (c).

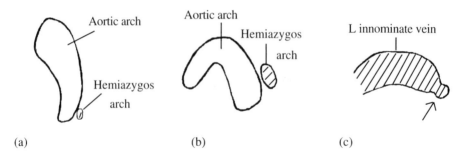

Fig. 9.11   The hemiazygos arch.

Both the azygos and hemiazygos arches may change in size with respiration, posture or the Valsalva /Müller manoeuvres (see also p. 13.19).

Anomalies

In about 1% of people the azygos lobe is a normal variant (Illus. **AZ LOBE+VN**). Sometimes the hemiazygos vein is predominant with a large left sided intercostal vein arch and a very small azygos arch.

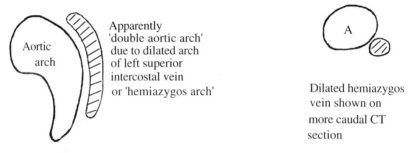

Fig. 9.12   **Apparently 'double aortic arch'** (or 'hemiazygos arch') due to arch of dilated left superior intercostal or 'hemiazygos' vein.

Occasionally the **inter-azygos vein** - i.e. the connection between the hemi-azygos and azygos veins crosses in a pre-aortic location, instead of the normal retro-aortic position, as may be noted on CT sections.

Fig. 9.13   The inter-azygos vein.

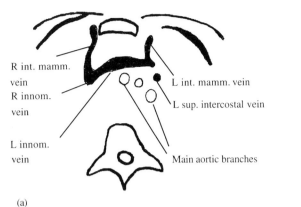

R int. mamm. vein

R innom. vein

L int. mamm. vein

L sup. intercostal vein

L innom. vein

Main aortic branches

(a)

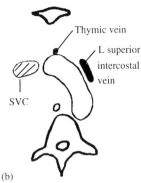

Thymic vein

L superior intercostal vein

SVC

(b)

Fig. 9.14   (a) Outflow of the internal mammary veins. Note that the left innominate vein passes to the right in front of the main branches of the aorta.

(b) Thymic and left superior intercostal veins.

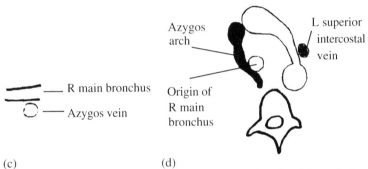

Azygos arch

L superior intercostal vein

R main bronchus

Azygos vein

Origin of R main bronchus

(c)

(d)

(c and d) The azygos vein passes around and postero-lateral to the right main bronchus, where it may mimic an intra-pulmonary mass, if it is 'cut' tangentially on a particular CT section or sections. (Rockoff and Druy, 1982 and Landay, 1983 pointed out that this anomaly should be considered in the differential diagnosis of a mass in this situation, particularly if the azygos vein is tortuous.)

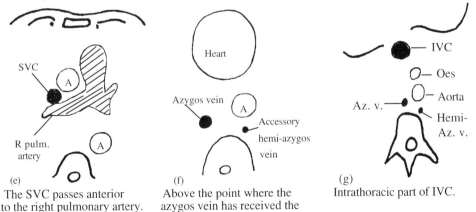

SVC

A

R pulm. artery

A

(e)

The SVC passes anterior to the right pulmonary artery.

Heart

Azygos vein

A

Accessory hemi-azygos vein

(f)

Above the point where the azygos vein has received the hemiazygos vein, the azygos vein is larger than on more caudal sections.

IVC

Oes

Aorta

Az. v.

Hemi-Az. v.

(g)

Intrathoracic part of IVC.

Left Superior Vena Cava and double venae cavae.

A left superior vena cava may persist if the embryonic left common cardinal vein fails to be obliterated. It is present in about 0.5 % of the population (Steinberg et al., 1953), and is more common in children with congenital heart disease - in up to 10% of these (see Buirski et al., 1986, below). When present it descends lateral to the aortic arch, where it may be seen with contrast enhanced CT (Fig. 9.15a), it then passes anterior to the left hilum to enter the right atrium, via the coronary sinus (Fig. 9.17). In most cases there is a right SVC as well, and there may also be an inter-communicating innominate vein. When no right SVC is present, this last will convey blood to the left SVC. Sometimes a large left hemiazygos arch is present as well (rarely with a left sided 'azygos' or 'hemiazygos' lobe - see also p. 1.5). Hemiazygos continuation may be secondary to a left IVC, which may also be associated with **polysplenia** (see also p. 17.13) and some amount of mirror imaging. (A recent Oxford case had bilateral SVCs, a large left hemiazygos arch and a left sided 'IVC' with polysplenia and partial mirror imaging).

A left SVC may give rise to a vertical, or a nearly vertically orientated shadow in the left upper mediastinum. It overlies both the aortic arch and the left pulmonary artery. A central venous line (or pacemaker) inserted on the left side may pass into it, and sometimes on into the coronary sinus. The author has seen a patient with renal failure, having successive central venous catheters put down both a left and right SVC.

On CT sections, a left SVC lies lateral to the left common carotid and anterior to the left subclavian arteries. It may be seen to the left of the aortic arch and the main pulmonary artery. It then passes in front of the left hilum and enters the coronary sinus, passing posteriorly to the left atrium and ventricle. In the upper mediastinum it mainly mirrors a right SVC, but more inferiorly it is more posterior in the mediastinum.

Sometimes, instead of draining into the right atrium, and most often via the coronary sinus, a left sided SVC drains into the left atrium (this happened in about 7% of Buirski's cases). When this happens, and a colloid lung scan is performed, injection of the colloid into a vein in the right arm will give a proper colloid lung scan, if a right SVC is present as well, but if the injection is given into a vein in the left arm, then the colloid will pass from the left SVC to the left ventricle and aorta and on into the systemic vessels. Such a case was reported by Morgan and Evans (1989), in a man of 44 with no known heart disease and a right pleural effusion. The left sided injection was carried out first and suggested the diagnosis.

A left sided SVC may also be suspected by echocardiography, if the coronary sinus appears large in the parasternal long axis plane (Huhta et al., 1982). It is rarely suspected as a cause of left upper mediastinal widening on plain radiographs.

A left SVC may be associated with anomalous pulmonary venous return - some however describe this as the '**vertical vein**' which may lie in a similar position. A gross example may be seen in infants with the '**figure of eight**' appearance of total anomalous venous return (Fig. 7.10, p. 7.17 & Fig. 9.16) but minor varieties are more common and may also be seen in adults.

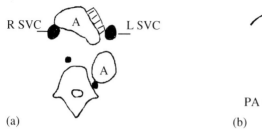
(a)

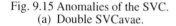
PA view
(b)

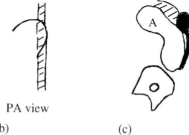
(c)

Fig. 9.15 Anomalies of the SVC.
  (a) Double SVCavae.

(b & c) Left SVC and dilated left superior
  intercostal (or hemiazygos) arch.

(When the right SVC is absent the azygos vein may be on the left as a hemiazygos arch).

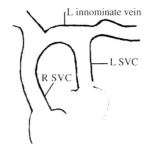

Fig. 9.16   Left and right SVCs, with a left innominate vein forming an intercommunicating vein (after Kjellberg, 1955). See also Fig. 7.10, p. 7.17.

Further references.

Stauffer et al (1951) : Normally situated arch of the azygos vein.
Fleischner et al. (1952) : Dilatation of the azygos vein - a Roentgen sign of venous engorgement.
Abrams (1957) : Vertebral and azygos venous systems.
Doyle et al. (1961) : The mediastinum in portal hypertension - studied the size of the azygos arch.
Janower et al. (1966) : Azygography and lung cancer.
Keats et al. (1968) : Mensuration of the azygos arch.
Preger et al. (1969) : Width of the azygos vein related to central venous pressure.
Heitzman et al. (1971 a & b) : The azygos vein and its pleural reflections - normal Roentgen anatomy and its applications in the diagnosis of mediastinal abnormality.
Milne et al. (1984) : The vascular pedicle of the heart and vena azygos.
Pistolesi et al. (1984) : The vascular pedicle of the heart in acquired heart disease.
Steinberg (1962) , Berk (1964) : Dilatation of the left superior intercostal vein in SVC obstruction.
McDonald et al. (1970) : Identified the aortic nipple on tomograms in two (out of 50) healthy adult volunteers and in seven (out of 100) adult patients with no suspected chest disease.
Lane et al. (1976) : Radiology of the superior intercostal veins.
Freidman et al. (1978) : Normal and abnormal left superior intercostal vein.
Kolbenstedt et al. (1979 a & b) : Veins of the chest and abdomen; also anomalous azygos vein as seen on CT.
Ball and Proto (1982) : Variable appearance of left superior intercostal vein, with good discussion on aortic nipple.
Foote (1982) & Foote and Wilkinson (1982b) : Mediastinal veins as seen on CT.
Speckman et al. (1982) : Altered CT mediastinal anatomy produced by an azygos lobe.
Smathers et al. (1982) : The azygos arch - normal and abnormal CT appearance.
                (1984) : Anomalous pre-aortic interazygos vein.
Webb et al. (1982b) : CT demonstration of mediastinal venous abnormalities.
Engel et al. (1983) : CT of mediastinal and thoracic inlet venous obstruction.
Bechtold et al. (1985) : CT of SVC and mediastinal venous obstruction.
Barack (1986) : CT demonstration of persistence of the cardinal veins and thrombosis.
Godwin and Chen (1986) : Thoracic venous anatomy.
Hatfield et al. (1987) : Congenital abnormalities of the azygos vein - a cause for 'aortic nipple' enlargement.
Woodring and Olson (1987) : CT of the superior intercostal veins.
Dudiak et al. (1989) : Abnormalities of the azygos system - CT evaluation.
Takasugi and Godwin (1990) : CT appearance of retroaortic anastomoses of the azygos system - distinguish from enlarged lymph nodes.

Shuford and Weens (1958) : Azygos vein dilatation simulating mediastinal tumour.
Campbell and Baruch (1960) : Aneurysm of hemiazygos vein associated with portal hypertension.
Magitang et al. (1960) : Dilated azygos vein simulating a mediastinal tumour.
Ramsey (1966) : Sacculated aneurysm of the azygos vein.
Rockoff and Druy (1982) : Tortuous azygos arch simulating a pulmonary lesion.
Moncada et al. (1985a) : CT of idiopathic aneurysms of thoracic systemic veins.
Kurihara et al. (1993) : Saccular aneurysm of the azygos vein simulating a paratracheal tumour in an asymptomatic 62 year old man - plain film, CT and MR appearances diagnosed preoperatively as a tumour.
Gallego et al. (1999) : Idiopathic azygos vein aneurysm in a woman aged 64 - mass behind trachea on lat. CXR, enlarging mass on exp. PA, venous aneurysm confirmed by CT & MR - quoted other cases.

Campbell and Deuchar (1954) : Left SVC.
Winter (1954) : Persistent left SVC - report of 30 cases.
Fleming and Gibson (1964) : Absent right SVC - the left SVC caused upper mediastinal widening (in a symptomless woman aged 28) and overlay the aorto-pulmonary window.
Cha and Khoury (1972) : Left SVC.
Baron et al. (1981a) : CT of anomalies of mediastinal vessels in 12 patients - included left SVC.
Huggins et al. (1982) : CT appearance of left SVC.

Buirski et al. (1986) : Bilateral SVCs are common in children with congenital heart disease or situs inversus.
Hale and Padhani (1997), & Padhani and Hale (1998) : Mediastinal venous anomalies - potential pitfalls in cancer diagnosis - 11 pts. - 2 had double SVCs, and one an isolated left SVC and others anomalous pulmonary venous drainage (see p. 7.18).
Minami et al. (1993) : Postaortic left innominate vein - a curved shadow behind the aortic knob is suggestive on PA film (c.f. left SVC). Well shown on venography and by CT. Is often associated with a high aortic arch, or other anomalies of it.

Reid and Murchison (1998) : Venous reflux in pulmonary embolism.
Harries et al. (1998) : Azygos reflux: a CT sign of cardiac tamponade.
Price et al. (1999) : Although azygos reflux may occur with cardiac tamponade, it occurs whenever the central venous pressure in greater or equal to the pressure within the azygos system and can occur with both cardiac and pulmonary disease; it also varies with the phase of respiration. They saw it in 16/100 helical chest CT exams.
Duddy (1999) : Venous reflux into IVC & hepatic veins at CT in association with bilateral tension pneumothoraces.

The coronary sinus (Illus. **CORONARY SINUS**).

   The coronary sinus needs also to be considered with the thoracic great veins. If there is a left sided SVC, this may drain into it and it will then be larger than normal and may be confused with enlarged nodes. In normal cases, a hazard at angiography and catheterisation is that a catheter may pass into it and if a pressure injection is made into it the sinus may be ruptured, with gross leakage of contrast and a contrast pericardium.

   CVP lines and pacemaker wires may also pass into the coronary sinus, and whilst some pacemaker wire tips in this position appear to work satisfactorily others fail to pace the heart properly. Usually this position occurs when junior doctors are inserting the pacemaker and think they have placed the tip in the right atrium - the fishhook type course to the left should suggest its true position, but relatively normal movement seen on fluoroscopy with cardiac contractions can be a trap for the unwary - such a position is usually easily corrected. A pacemaker wire passing down a left SVC (see p. 9.16) may also pass into the coronary sinus, which is then often enlarged.

   Anatomically, the coronary sinus lies in the left atrio-ventricular groove on the posterior aspect of the heart. Superiorly it begins as a continuation of the great cardiac vein, then descends vertically receiving blood from cardiac veins, turns horizontally and after passing anterior to the IVC empties into the right atrium.

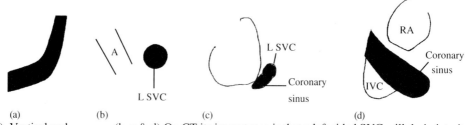

| (a) | (b) | (c) | (d) |

(a) Vertical and horizontal limbs of the coronary sinus.

(b, c & d) On CT its importance is that a left sided SVC will drain into it, and it will then be larger than normal (see previous section). It may then be confused with enlarged nodes.

Fig. 9.17   Diagrams showing the anatomy of the coronary sinus. As the vertical limb is orientated perpendicular to cross-section CT slices, it appears as a rounded density on CT sections. The horizontal limb may be seen as an elongated tubular density which empties into the R atrium.

Reference.
Micklos and Proto (1985) : CT demonstration of the coronary sinus.

Chapter 10 : **The Aorta and Related Disorders (except trauma).**

The aorta develops from the 4th branchial arches, the carotid arteries from the 3rd and the pulmonary arteries from the 6th. The aorta initially forms a vascular ring, with bilateral descending aortae. Normally the right descending aorta and the posterior right sided part of the ring atrophy. However either or both of these may persist (one side usually being dominant), and the ring may 'break' in an abnormal place to give rise to various anomalies. The atrophied part may persist as a 'ligament' which 'fixes' or 'pegs' the adjacent vessels. An aortic **vascular ring** (including an atretic part or an atretic ductus) may cause compression of the trachea and/or oesophagus; many cases presenting in infancy, but some only as adults. In the latter chronic tracheal compression may lead to tracheomalacia, so that surgical correction is usually more successful in children.

Aortic anomalies include :
'**Double arch**' - with a persisting ring and **bilateral descending aortae** - Illus. **AORTA 'DOUBLE ARCH'**,
'**Right sided arch and descending aorta**' - Illus. **AORTA ARCH RIGHT** - 10% of these have an **aberrant left subclavian artery**.
'**Aberrant right subclavian artery**' - the persisting posterior part of the ring (the 'break' then occurring between the ascending aorta and the right carotid) - see also below (p.10.3).
'**Coarctation**' - narrowing usually just distal to the ductus - often associated with post-stenotic dilatation, an abnormally high arch, a prominent proximal part of the left subclavian artery and collateral vessels producing 'rib notching', etc. - Illus. **AORTA COARCTATION**. (Rarely coarctation occurs at the level of the renal arteries with the "middle aortic syndrome" - p. 10.18).

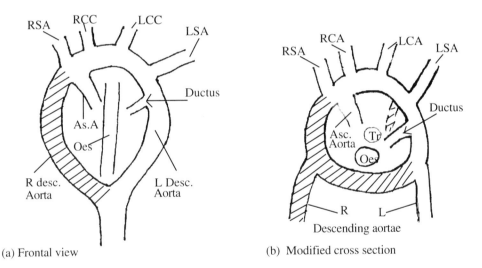

(a) Frontal view   (b) Modified cross section

Fig. 10.1   The aortic arch develops from the branchial arches as a vascular ring - see also Illus. **AORTA RING, R AORTIC ARCH, Pt. 1**. The shaded parts usually atrophy, but may persist and other parts atrophy, giving rise to anatomical abnormalities, but mostly with normal physiology.   (The author is indebted to Dr. Max Clarke, formerly of the Henry Ford Hospital, Detroit for showing him this diagram in 1965 - modified from Edwards, JE, 1948, 'Anomalies of the aortic arch system.' Medical Clinics of North America, **32**, 925 - 929 with permission from W.B. Saunders Company).

RSA - right subclavian artery (the innominate artery develops from the residual right anterior part of the 'ring').   LSA - left subclavian artery.
RCC and LCC - right and left common carotid arteries.   AA - ascending aorta.
DA - ductus arteriosus (its position may vary). RDA and LDA - right and left descending aortae.

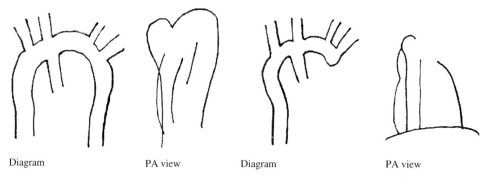

| Diagram | PA view | Diagram | PA view |

Double ascending aortae   -   On PA views
'double aortic knuckles' may be mistaken for
a tumour - but they are usually readily
identified on tomograms.

Right sided descending aortae are not uncommon.
On PA views, a right-sided descending aorta may be
mistaken for enlarged nodes. (The author found two Asians
who were treated for supposed TB because of this anomaly!
see - Illus. **Spurious TB, R aortic arch 4a-b**).

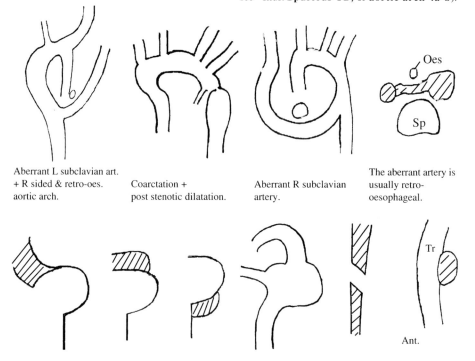

Aberrant L subclavian art.
+ R sided & retro-oes.
aortic arch.

Coarctation +
post stenotic dilatation.

Aberrant R subclavian
artery.

The aberrant artery is
usually retro-
oesophageal.

Various positions of the right aberrant subclavian artery
as seen on frontal views. It may partially obscure the
aortic arch.

Aneurysm of
a diverticulum
of Kommerell.*

Indentation of
barium filled oes.
by the artery.

On lateral views
the trachea may
be bowed forwards.

Fig. 10.2 Diagrams showing aortic arch anomalies.

*A Kommerell diverticulum (or aneurysm) usually develops in relationship to blood flow via the ductus during
foetal life (and persists with its remnant into adult life); it may be seen with both R & L aberrant subclavian arteries
(with L & R arches respectively) - see Fig. 10.1.

Other anomalies:

Cervical aortic arch - is an anomaly in which the arch lies cranial to its normal location; most commonly it is right sided. It may be an isolated anomaly or be associated with a cardiac (e.g. VSD, etc.) or other aortic lesion e.g. aneurysm or diverticulum of Kommerell.

'**Presbyaorta**' - as people grow older, the aorta tends to lose its elasticity, elongates, and may to some extent dilate. The lengthening causes it to 'fold' or become tortuous, an anomaly readily seen on high kV views (see also Fig. 18.11, p. 18.30).

'**Pseudo-coarctation**' - an elongated aorta, tethered by the fibrous remnant of the ductus - Illus. **PSEUDOCOARCTATION.**

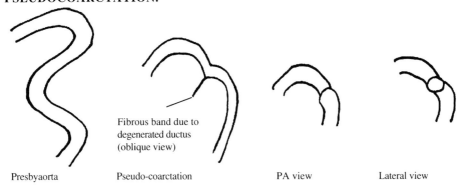

Presbyaorta   Pseudo-coarctation   PA view   Lateral view

Fig. 10.3   Presbyaorta and pseudo-coarctation.

Dysphagia from vascular causes.

Dysphagia   aortica is due to pressure on the oesophagus by the aorta or one of its major branches - see also Fig. 16.1.

(a) In elderly patients a **tortuous   and   somewhat   dilated   lower   thoracic   aorta** may press upon the lower oesophagus, and cause some obstruction, mainly at about diaphragmatic level, but frank dysphagia due to this cause is rare.

(b) **An aberrant right subclavian artery** (present in about 1 in 200 of the population - Comer et al., 1972) sometimes causes '**dysphagia lusoria**' ('lusus naturae' = a 'sport of nature', in this case caused by an abnormal R subclavian artery). In most cases the 'aberrant vessel' passes **behind   the   oesophagus**. Occasionally the anomaly may be noted on plain radiographs by the presence of a 'knob' lying just behind the plane of the trachea on lateral views. Mostly it is discovered on barium swallow examinations as an indentation angled upwards from left to right towards the right first rib (Fig. 10.2 and Illus. **SUBCLAV   ART   ABERRANT**). Occasionally its origin from the aorta may give rise to a '**diverticulum   of   Kommerell**' which is usually an incidental finding. Sometimes however it may be large, equalling the size of the aorta, or even larger if aneurysmal - see also note on p. 10.2 and reference to Kommerell p. 10.5.
   Despite the idea that an aberrant subclavian artery is a common cause of symptoms, nearly all patients are asymptomatic, but a Kommerell aneurysm may cause dysphagia, dyspnoea, or a Horner's syndrome. Such aneurysms may also be a source of emboli passing peripherally into the right arm. They can also erode into the oesophagus or the trachea leading to a gross fatal haematemesis or haemoptysis.

(c) **Venous   impression** on the oesophagus e.g. the left inferior pulmonary vein may cause an indentation on it about 4 to 5 cm below the level of the carina. It is of no consequence save in the recognition of its cause (Fig. 16.1).

(d) **A pulmonary arterial ring**, pseudo-vascular rings or slings with the left pulmonary artery arising from the right (see also ps. 7.5-6), persistent patent ductus, etc. may also occasionally cause pressure on the oesophagus and dysphagia, as well as dyspnoea. These are uncommon and are usually found in children. Pressure on the oesophagus from an anomalous left pulmonary artery is usually **anterior**.

References.

Congenital aortic malformations.

Neuhauser (1946) : Double aortic arch and other anomalies.
Neuhauser (1949) : Tracheo-oesophageal constriction produced by right aortic arch and ligamentum arteriosum.
Felson and Palayew (1963) : Two types of right aortic arch.
Stewart et al. (1964) Atlas of vascular rings and related malformations of the aortic arch.
D'Cruz et al. (1966) : Right aortic arch, right descending aorta and associated anomalies.
Hastreiter et al. (1966) : Right sided aorta - occurrence in various types of congenital heart disease.
Stewart et al. (1966) : Right aortic arch.
Grollman et al. (1968) : Right aortic arch with aberrant retro-oesophageal innominate artery.
Deutsch (1970) : Right aortic arch in the neonate - diagnosis by displacement of barium filled oesophagus to the left.
Shuford et al. (1970a) : Three types of right aortic arch. (1970b) + isolation of L subclavian artery.
Baron (1971) : Right aortic arch.
Shuford et al. (1972a) : Cervical aortic arch.
Shuford et al. (1972b) : Angiographic features of double aortic arch.
Shuford and Sybers (1974) : The aortic arch and its malformations.
Garti et al. (1973) : R aortic arch with mirror-image branching causing vascular ring.
Knight and Edwards (1974) : R aortic arch - types and associated cardiac abnormalities.
Haughton et al. (1975) The cervical aortic arches.
Domingues et al. (1978) : Left aortic arch with right descending aorta.
Taber et al. (1979b) : Diagnosis of retro-oesophageal right aortic arch by CT.
Baron et al. (1981a) : CT of anomalies of the mediastinal vessels.
McLoughlin et al. (1981) : CT of congenital anomalies of the aortic arch and subclavian arteries.
Wechsler (1981) : Left sided cervical aortic arch.
Webb, W. et al. (1982a) : CT demonstration of aortic arch anomalies.
Kennard et al. (1983) : Cervical aortic arch - CT correlation with conventional radiologic studies.
Coscina et al. (1986) : MR of double aortic arch.
Fletcher and Jacobstein (1986) : MR of congenital abnormalities of the great arteries.
Schiebler et al. (1986) : CT appearances of a right cervical aortic arch.
Shuford et al. (1986) : Circumflex retro-oesophageal right aortic arch simulating a tumour or dissecting aneurysm.
Gomes et al. (1987) : MR of congenital abnormalities of the aortic arch.
Kersting - Somerhoff et al. (1987) : MR imaging of congenital abnormalities of the aortic arch.
Felson (1989) : Aortic arch anomalies.
Felson and Strife (1989) : Cervical aortic arch (50 cases in literature).
Predey et al. (1989) : CT of congenital abnormalities of the aortic arch.
Chen (1990) : Plain radiographic evaluation of the aorta.
Jaffe (1990) : MR of vascular rings.
Glew and Hartnell (1991) : Right aortic arch may be associated with cardiac anomalies.
Holland and Fitzpatrick (1991) : MR of right-sided cervical aortic arch with a congenital aneurysm.
VanDyke et al. (1993) : 3D reconstruction in the diagnosis of cong. abns. of thoracic great vessels.
VanDyke and White (1994) : Congenital abnormalities of the thoracic aorta presenting in the adult.
Van Son et al. (1994) : Imaging strategies for vascular rings - MR is by far the best method for visualising rings and related strictures of the tracheo-bronchial tree.
Partridge (1995) : The radiology of vascular rings - review. He emphasised the importance of the **residual 'ligaments'** which fix or 'peg' the adjacent vessels, and may play a part in the formation of vascular diverticula or aneurysms esp. of aberrant subclavian vessels.
Kumar et al. (1997) : MR angiography of cervical aortic arch.

Coarctation.

Craigie (1841) : Coarctation of the aorta.
Figley et al. (1954) : Accessory Roentgen signs of coarctation.
Godwin et al. (1981) : CT for evaluation of coarctation.
Amparo et al. (1984) : MR demonstration of coarctation of the aorta.
von Schulthess et al. (1986a) : MR imaging of coarctation of the aorta.
Doyle, L. (1991) : Reviewed a case of coarctation of the aorta, dissecting aneurysm and haemopericardium, first recorded by Joseph Jordan of Manchester in 1830.

Greenberg et al. (1995) : Diagnostic imaging after corrective surgery for coarctation now largely with Doppler echocardiography and MR.
Watson, N. et al. (1998) : MR of 19 pts. (aged 23 to 57 yrs) with aortic coarctation ranging from localised webs and tubular narrowings to complete aortic interruption - one having a supra-diaphragmatic coarctation. MR also disclosed secondary features - poststenotic dilatation, etc., it was also used for follow-up studies after repair.

Pseudo-coarctation.
Stevens (1958) : Buckling of the aortic arch (pseudocoarctation, kinking).
Steinberg et al. (1969), Gaupp et al. (1981)
Hoeffel et al. (1974 & 1975) : Pseudocoarctation or congenital kinking of the aorta.
Mirowitz et al. (1990) : 'Pseudo-coarctation' due to MR imaging in some normal people.
Tsai et al. (1990) : Figure-eight kinking of the aorta coexistent with coarctation.
Briley (1993)
Munjal et al. (1994) : MR imaging of pseudocoarctation of aorta (+ L subclavian artery dilatation).

Aberrant right subclavian artery.
Kommerell (1936) : Pressure on the oesophagus by an abnormal course of the R subclavian artery ('arteria lusoria').
Mucklow and Smith (1954), Birnholtz et al. (1974) : Dysphagia aortica.
McCallen and Shaff (1956) : Aneurysm of an anomalous R subclavian artery.
Klinkhamer (1966) : Aberrant right subclavian artery.
Branscom and Austin (1973) : Aberrant right subclavian artery - plain film findings.
Scheldrup (1957) : Aberrant right subclavian or innominate arteries passing **anterior** to the trachea or the oesophagus and posing a hazard to tracheostomy (post-mortem study).
Hunter et al. (1970) : Anterior sclerotic aneurysm of anomalous right subclavian artery.
Maier (1981) : CT demonstration of anomalous origin of the right subclavian artery causing dysphagia lusoria.
Lupetin et al. (1984) : Aneurysmal dilatation of aberrant right subclavian artery shown by CT (lobulated asymptomatic R upper mediastinal mass on plain chest radiograph).
Salomonowitz et al. (1984) : The three types of aortic diverticula.
Austin and Wolfe (1985) : Review of 31 cases of diverticulum of Kommerell - many were successfully resected.
Hicks and Carr (1986) : Aberrant right subclavian artery causing pain in the hand and a mediastinal mass.
Walker and Geller (1987) : Aberrant right subclavian artery with large diverticulum of Kommerell.
Brown, K and Batra (1987) : MR of aneurysm of an aberrant right subclavian artery.
Proto et al. (1987) : Aberrant right subclavian artery - further observations.
Vega et al. (1987) : CT of ruptured aneurysm of aberrant R subclavian artery.
Poon and Stewart (1988) : Aneurysm of aberrant R subclavian artery - chest radiography, DVI and barium swallow.
Felson (1989) : **Ruptured anomalous R subclavian artery - aneurysm or diverticulum?**
Hartnell (1989) : Child with stridor - combined bronchogram and barium swallow showed posterior indentation of both the trachea and the oesophagus just below the level of the aortic arch. An aberrant right subclavian artery was confirmed by DVI.
Kullnig (1989) : Aneurysm of aberrant R subclavian artery with bleeding into oesophageal wall.
Cave et al. (1994) : Aneurysm of an aberrant right subclavian artery causing SVC syndrome.
Turkenburg et al. (1994) : Aneurysm of an aberrant right subclavian artery diagnosed by MR.
Haesemeyer and Gavant (1999) : Imaging of acute traumatic tear in pts. with an aberrant R subclavian artery.

Pulmonary venous impressions on the oesophagus.
Nash et al. (1961) : Aberrant insertion of a pulmonary vein into the left atrium simulating an intrinsic lesion of the oesophagus.
Jacobs et al. (1972) : Dysphagia associated with a distended pulmonary vein.
Yeh and Wolf (1975) : A pulmonary venous indentation on the oesophagus - normal variant.

<u>Methods of investigation of aortic abnormalities</u> - Illus. **AORTA.**
(a) **Plain radiographs**.
   High quality, adequately exposed radiographs, are required to demonstrate the thoracic aorta, including its ascending and descending parts and the arch. The descending part lies behind the heart and is often poorly visualised (or even not seen) on low KV radiographs. Its lateral border is often more readily seen than its medial border, which is adjacent to the medial border of the right pleural cavity, usually just to the left of the midline (Fig. 1.29). Mediastinal swellings, including haematomas arising from aneurysms may extend laterally and also forwards between the medial borders of the pleural cavities and displace them, especially where they overlie the spine and the descending aorta. Note also that the outline of the descending aorta may be obliterated by an adjacent opaque lower lobe or pleural effusion ('**Loss of silhouette sign**' - see p. 2.25 and Illus. **LOSS OF SILHOUETTE**).

(b) **Conventional tomograms** (including inclined frontal tomograms) have been used for demonstrating the size, shape and gross abnormalities of the thoracic aorta, as well as adjacent haematomas and/ or fluid collections, but this is now better done by CT and MR.

(c) **Aortography (including DVI)** - Illus. **AORTOGRAM** will show patency and deformities of the lumen, including aneurysmal dilatations, or narrowings, and intimal flaps with dissection, etc. However it will not show the thickness of the wall, unless this is calcified; indeed there may be a normal sized lumen even within a large aneurysm, the remainder being filled by thrombus. Aortography may be needed as well as tomography to demonstrate this latter, but is usually more easily recognised by CT.

(d) **CT** is now the usual method of choice for demonstrating thoracic aortic abnormalities, particularly when combined with the use of IV contrast agents., to show the lumen, and hence the wall thickness and adjacent thrombus. It will also demonstrate calcification, intimal flaps surrounding, tumour, etc. An occasional problem is when the aorta is very tortuous, and lies across, instead of at right angles to the cross-sectional CT display, this is particularly a problem with severe scoliosis (Illus. **AORTA TORTUOUS**, **Tortuous aorta, Pt. 1a & b**).

(e) **Ultrasound** may be used to visualise the subclavian and axillary vessels, but its use with external probes is not usually practicable for the thoracic aorta, unless there is a large left pleural effusion to give an acoustic window, or a large aneurysm of the arch which can be visualised from the neck or via the pericardium. This is contrary to the position in the abdomen where ultrasound is usually able to visualise the aorta quite well. However an intra-oesophageal probe may be able to show thoracic aneurysms quite well.

(f) **MR** is ideally suited to the examination of the thoracic aorta, as it will demonstrate mediastinal vessels, depict blood flow and produce direct oblique, sagittal and coronal, as well as transverse images. The other major advantage is that contrast media are usually unnecessary. It may also demonstrate intimal flaps and tears as well as true and false lumina.

(g) **Isotopes** - as well as the lumen being readily shown by an IV bolus of e.g. Tc^{99m} pertechnetate (Illus. **AORTA ANGIO ISOTOPE**) inflammatory conditions of the aorta may be examined with labelled leucocytes. Fink et al. (1994) found that among 1100 patients examined with In^{111} WBCs for occult sepsis, three had localised uptake in the aorta due to (i) periaortitis in Wegener's granulomatosis, (ii) aortic dissection in giant cell arteritis and (iii) streptococcal aortitis with impending rupture. They initially mistook the areas of increased uptake for bowel loops, but performed CT or MR for definitive diagnosis.

(h) When there is a thoracic aneurysm, the **abdominal aorta** should also be studied, as dissecting aneurysms may extend downwards, and with atheromatous aneurysms, a second aneurysm may be present lower down. The abdominal aorta may be studied as part of a general aortic study, but is most readily examined by ultrasound, which can readily show dissections, etc.

References.

Le Roux et al. (1971) : Plain film and aortographic appearances in 40 African patients with large aneurysms - some showed sternal, chest wall or vertebral erosion, tracheal and/or oesophageal compression, phrenic or recurrent laryngeal palsy, SVC and /or obstruction or a fistula into it. Many aneurysms produced a mediastinal mass and/or calcification. Some grew in size before rupture.
Cooley and Schriber (1980) : Radiology of heart and great vessels.
Machida and Tasaka (1980) : CT patterns of mural thrombus in aortic aneurysms.
Culliford et al. (1982) : Aneurysms of the ascending aorta and arch.
Grossman et al. (1984) : DVI of the thoracic aorta.
Mirvis et al. (1986) : DVI for demonstrating thoracic aortic rupture.
Amparo et al. (1985) : MR of aortic dissection.
Glazer et at. (1985) : MR of the thoracic aorta.
Dinsmore et al. (1986) : MR of thoracic aortic aneurysms and comparison with other methods - studied 15 patients including 10 with Marfan's syndrome.
Mulcahy et al. (1986) : Diagnosis of aortic root abscess by ultra-sound.

Barentsz et al. (1987) : MR of thoraco-abdominal dissection in a man of 58. Following CT and aortography the patient was treated conservatively, but MR subsequently well demonstrated the false lumen, the long intimal flap and slowly moving blood or thrombus in the lower part of the false lumen.

Taams et al. (1988) : Saccular aneurysm of the aortic arch detected by trans-oesophageal echocardiography.

Gomes (1989) : MR imaging of congenital abnormalities of the thoracic aorta and pulmonary arteries (including adult right aortic arch, aberrant L subclavian artery with retro-oesophageal diverticulum, coarctation of aorta, double aortic arch, transposition, Marfan's syndrome, etc.

Lewin et al. (1991) : Three-dimensional time of flight MR angiography : applications in the abdomen and thorax.

Link and Lesco (1992) : The role of MR imaging in the evaluation of acquired diseases of thoracic aorta.

Hartnell et al. (1994) : MR imaging of the thoracic aorta - comparison of spin echo, angiographic, and breath-hold techniques.

Kumar et al. (1996) : Three-dimensional time-of-flight MR angiography of the arch of aorta and its major branches : a comparative study with contrast angiography.

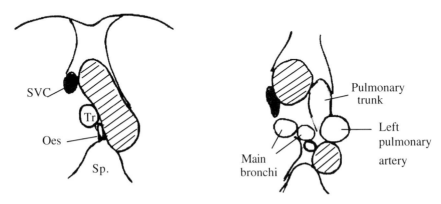

Fig. 10.4   Diagrams of (a) the aortic arch and (b) of the ascending and descending parts of the aorta, as shown by CT.

With increasing age the descending
aorta may become wider and equal,
or slightly exceed the diameter,
of the ascending aorta.

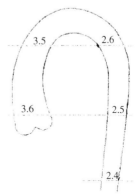

Fig. 10.5   Normal thoracic aortic diameters
as determined on CT sections (after Aronberg et al., 1984,
Normal aortic diameters by CT. JCAT, **8**, 247 - 250,
with permission from Lippincott - Raven).

Causes of thoracic aneurysms and some difficulties in recognition - Illus. **AORTA   ANEURYSM & AORTA ARCH ANEURYSM.**

   Aneurysms of the thoracic aorta, or its larger branches, may give rise to swellings which may be fusiform or saccular in shape. Some, on plain radiographs or conventional tomograms, closely resemble mediastinal tumours. Problems in diagnosis may occur anywhere. When luetic aneurysms were common, many occurred in the superior mediastinum, some being mistaken for intra-thoracic goitres, etc.; aneurysms of 'signs' were those arising in the ascending aorta, and those of 'symptoms' in the arch; the descending aorta was also often affected (Illus. **SYPHILIS-AORTA**). These aneurysms often showed considerable calcification in their walls, including the intima, which was often roughened at autopsy or surgery. (Care had to be employed in the use of iodine contrast media for aortography, until after treatment e.g. with initially small and later increasing doses of penicillin for fear of a Herxheimer sensitivity reaction - see also Wright, F. and Ardran, 1971). Large syphilitic aneurysms also caused SVC obstruction (p. 9.6) and pressure erosion of adjacent bones e.g. the sternum, ribs or spine - Illus. **SYPHILIS-AORTA, Pt. 2**).

 Most aneurysms are now dissecting, atheromatous or traumatic in origin. Fast or spiral CT or MR now usually differentiates vascular structures from other thoracic masses, without recourse to formal angiography (including DVI) particularly after the injection of intravenous contrast media. When aneurysms are present, the lumen size can readily be shown: in some it will be near normal, the outer parts of the aneurysmal sacs being filled with thrombus.
 Traumatic and dissecting aneurysms are considered in detail in the next section. The former should always be considered in younger people after severe injuries, particularly those involving sudden deceleration (road accidents, falling from heights, etc.).
 Aneurysms may also be secondary to collagen disease (particularly in the ascending aorta), aortitis, dilatation distal to a bicuspid or stenotic aortic valve, Marfan's syndrome, etc. Dilatation and tortuosity are common in the elderly, and these may lead to athero-sclerotic aneurysms.
 Bizarre appearances may be seen with some aneurysms e.g. those arising from a sinus of Valsalva, or with those arising from cannulation sites used for by-pass surgery. A pseudo-aneurysm as well as true aneurysms may be found in association with Takayasu's disease (Peterson and Guthaner, 1986).
Aneurysms may also occur at the site of a ductus diverticulum, both in children and adults and give rise to a swelling in the aorto-pulmonary window - for a recent review (including the use of DSA, CT & MR) see Taneja et al., 1997.
 '**Patch aneurysms**' may also occur at the site of Dacron patches used for repairing coarctation, but bovine pericardium is being used to obviate this problem. Bertaccini et al. (1996) used MR to detect such aneurysms.

Table 10.1   Complications of aortic aneurysms.

(a) Pressure on bronchi, trachea or pulmonary artery. Luetic aneurysms not uncommonly did this, but both dissecting and atheromatous aneurysms may also do it.
(b) Stretching of left recurrent laryngeal nerve (common with luetic aneurysms).
(c) Pressure on heart, etc.
(d) Bone erosion - anteriorly - sternum, - posteriorly spine and ribs (was not uncommon with large luetic aneurysms).
(e) Rupture - sometimes containment in a thin layer of adventitia or 'false capsule'.
(f) Pleural effusion or haemomediastinum - leakage or sympathetic pleural effusion.
(g) Intraluminal thrombus and embolism.
(h) Blockage of main channel, esp. with dissecting aneurysm.
(i) Aortic branch occlusion.
(j) Fistula to bronchus - may present with minor haemoptysis before a fatal bleed.
        (Coblentz et al., 1988, described four cases).
(k) Fistula to duodenum - more common with atheromatous aneurysms.

Further references.
Charrett et al. (1983) : Acute respiratory insufficiency caused by a descending aortic aneurysm.
Pattison et al. (1984) : Oesophageal obstruction due to saccular aneurysm of the distal thoracic aorta.
Duke et al. (1987) : Pressure on left main bronchus and left pulmonary artery by an arch aneurysm.

Historical note: The famous anatomist John Hunter (see Oxford Picts, **UNIV MUSEUM, John Hunter**) inoculated himself with pus from a patient to try to differentiate syphilis from gonorrhoea, and as a result developed a syphilitic aneurysm from which he died.

Table 10.2 <u>Problems in CT diagnosis and differentiation</u>.

These may be due to :
(a) Streak artefacts due to contrast-related flow phenomena mimicking pathology on CT sections (Godwin & Webb, 1982, Thorsen et al., 1983, Gallagher & Dixon, 1984 and Vasile et al., 1986).
(b) Failure to visualise an intimal flap (due to insufficient contrast, oblique angle, too slow a section speed, too wide a section gap, etc.) - problems no longer encountered with spiral CT.
(c) Absence of density difference between true and false lumina, due to a large tear and simultaneous enhancement (Vasile et al., 1986).
(d) Some fusiform aneurysms with thrombus may have this distributed atypically and be difficult to differentiate.
(e) Extra-aortic structures - such as mediastinal veins, pericardium, thickened pleura and lung may be mistaken for a false channel in the aorta. (Taber et al., 1979a, reported a **left innominate vein simulating dissection**).
Note : MR may also give rise to artefacts (see ps. 10.13 & 20.29 et seq.). It may also show continuing dissection after surgery, sometimes giving rise to later problems and re-dissection (e.g. Brown et al., 1996).

<u>Dissecting aortic aneurysm</u> - Illus. **AORTA DISSECTION**.
  The underlying causes of this include cystic medial necrosis, Marfan's syndrome, and coarctation of the aorta, with bleeding into the aortic wall, initially it is thought from the vasa vasorum or an intimal tear. In some cases bleeding may be confined to the aortic wall without any intimal rupture. In some cases an intimal ulcer may be present and may be seen with ultra-sound and/or MR. These cases may resolve spontaneously, in a similar fashion to those produced accidentally during angiography, either by the catheter tip or contrast jet during rapid injection. An interesting point is that the iatrogenic cases are mostly painless; they also usually clear quickly. This may be because little bleeding occurs from the vasa vasorum, and because pain is probably related to sudden adventitial distension. A similar appearance may also be caused by trauma.
  Plain radiographs may show mediastinal widening, increased soft tissue shadowing alongside the arch or descending aorta (which may be less dense than the aorta itself), or a sympathetic pleural effusion, particularly on the left side. The aorta may also be increased in size. Rarely a dissection may become chronic and calcify (Illus. **AORTA DISS ANEURYSM, Pt. 1a-b**). Plain radiographic findings are however unreliable of their own, since apparent aortic wall thickening may also be produced by fat, aortitis, or neoplasm spreading along the aortic wall. Blood, from a leaking abdominal aneurysm and inflammation (especially from pancreatitis) may spread up alongside the descending aorta, from the abdomen and mimic a dissecting thoracic aneurysm.
  Angiography (including DVI), CT and MR may be used to confirm the condition and show its extent. CT and angiography are complementary, but CT and MR are non-invasive and are probably best done first. When carried out with contrast, CT will show the aortic dilatation, the true and false lumina and whether they both communicate with the circulating blood, the translucent band of an intimal flap, and the extent of the aneurysm, downwards towards the aortic bifurcation or proximally towards the aortic valve. However angiography may still be required for determining the full length of the dissection, its spread up into the neck vessels and which arteries (if any) are blocked.
  Dissecting aneurysms often have asymmetric shapes, because **dissection within the aortic wall commonly spirals**, and often it may extend only around half to two-thirds of the lumen, whereas with an atheromatous aneurysm, the gradual formation of mural thrombus, as a result of stasis, will usually produce a circular and symmetrical mural thrombus. Dissections are often anteriorly situated on the right side in the ascending aorta, superiorly in the arch and posteriorly on the left in the descending and abdominal parts. Quite often the true lumen may be constricted differently in different planes at different levels, giving rise to a 'localised dissection', a circumferential dissection, '**three barrels**', or the '**twisted tape**' sign (Sutton, 1975). In addition the torn intima may **intussuscept further narrowing the lumen** (Hufnagel, 1962, Symbas et al, 1980, Kastan et al., 1988, Nelson et al., 1994).
  Depending on the pattern and the area sectioned by tomography the following broad patterns may be seen.

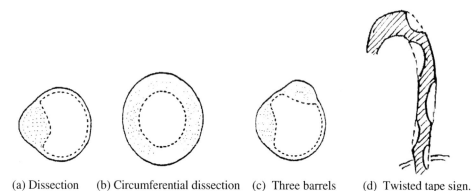

(a) Dissection   (b) Circumferential dissection   (c) Three barrels   (d) Twisted tape sign.

Fig. 10.6   Dissections in aortic wall (a to c after Hayashi et al. 1974, AJR, **122**, 769 -782 and d after Sutton, 1975, Textbook of Radiology, Churchill Livingstone with permissions).

With dissecting aneurysms, it is important to distinguish those involving the ascending aorta, from those involving the descending. The former are more likely to rupture into the pericardium or cause severe aortic incompetence, and need active surgical treatment for survival, whilst those involving the descending aorta often do well with conservative treatment (and will not run the risk of paraplegia from damage to the spinal arteries with descending aorta replacement). A few patients with ischaemia of the lower limbs and trunk have been treated by making a 're-entry' **hole** in the dissected intima during catheterisation.

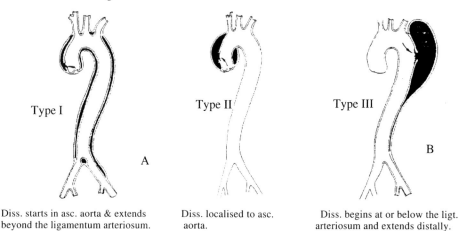

Type I   Type II   Type III   A   B

Diss. starts in asc. aorta & extends beyond the ligamentum arteriosum.

Diss. localised to asc. aorta.

Diss. begins at or below the ligt. arteriosum and extends distally.

Fig. 10.7 Types of aortic dissection based upon the classification of DeBakey (after Hayashi et al., 1974, AJR, **122**, 769 - 782 with permission).

The clinical classification commonly used is that of Daily et al. (1970), which separates those with an intimal tear proximal to origin of the left subclavian artery which is usually in the ascending aorta (type A), from those with a more distal tear (type B). One month survival for untreated type A is 8%, whereas with type B it is 50 to 75%. Typing is therefore regarded as an emergency procedure - **type A often receiving emergency surgery, whilst those with type B largely having expectant treatment, but some are now starting to be stented with good results in prevent progression of the dissection** - see also p. 10.15.

A dissecting aneurysm, like a traumatic aneurysm, can produce a false aneurysmal sac with a leak contained by adventitia, mediastinal tissues or the mediastinal pleura. In such cases the aortic wall may mimic an intimal flap (DeBakey - type III).

Heiberg et al. (1985) analysed 60 cases and noted that the differentiation of dissection from atherosclerotic aneurysm when a **septum is identified** or **differential opacification of two lumina** is seen. An aneurysm (without dissection) is diagnosed when it has a thin wall, is saccular or there is opacification of a single lumen. Central (i.e. intra-luminal) **calcification** is most often associated with dissection, and peripheral calcification is mainly seen with simple aneurysms, but neither sign is specific. Indeed calcification (which is most often present in intimal atheroma) can appear as central or peripheral, depending on which part of the circumference is affected by the dissection. With time, the false channel may be lined by endothelium, new atheroma forms, and this may eventually calcify leading to a 'healed dissection' (see above).

Central calcification may indicate an incipient rupture. However one has to beware of an illusion of central calcification, with an apparent septum between dual lumina, that may be produced by taking sections across a saccular aneurysm.

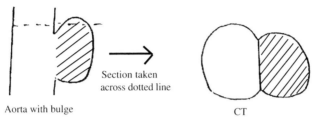

Aorta with bulge   CT

Fig. 10.8 Apparent septum due to a CT section being taken across the rim of a saccular aneurysm (shaded).

Increased density at CT, within a haematoma in the aortic wall, may be due to haemoconcentration in an area of recent haemorrhage; later liquefaction occurs and the density decreases. The normal aortic wall is 2 to 3 mm thick, but thickening alone will not distinguish between the two types of aneurysm, though thinning of the wall or dilatation of the ascending aorta may be the only signs of dissection in some cases. Occasionally a haemopericardium may enhance with contrast medium if active haemorrhage is taking place - Illus. **AORTA RUPTURE** (see also Meziane et al., 1984).

Kucich et al. (1986) pointed out that rupture of a thoracic aortic aneurysm may occasionally occur into the right side of the chest, leading to right sided pleural or extra-pleural haematomas, and wrote "rupture of a thoracic aneurysm can be diagnosed confidently using CT when **high density blood** is detected in the pleural or extra-pleural spaces" - also that "aortography is probably not necessary since CT can accurately differentiate between atherosclerotic rupture and dissection".

Vasile et al. (1986, from the Henri Mondor Hospital in Paris) examined 137 patients by CT (32 with angiography as well) over a five year period and found 54 dissections and 11 atheromatous aneurysms without dissection. Criteria for dissection were: a false channel, intimal flap or displaced intimal calcification. Aortic sizes were similar in both groups (4.6 up to about 8 cm) in both the ascending and descending aorta. Eight had a haemopericardium, but only one died.

Mathiew et al. (1986, also from Paris) used CT to study 52 patients who had had surgery up to 14 years previously, and found patent grafts in 45, persisting patency of the false lumen in 40, and an extension of the aneurysm in one. There were no ruptures or false aneurysms.

Geisinger et al. (1985) suggested that MR might obviate the need for angiography in dissections involving the descending aorta. However with dissections of the ascending aorta, early studies found it difficult to assess the competence of the aortic valve, the state of the coronary arteries, and could not distinguish slowly moving blood from thrombus in the false lumen. The presence or absence of blood flow within a false lumen is also of clinical importance, because flow in a large part of the lumen indicates the presence of a **'re-entry' hole** (Mitchell, L. et al., 1988). Forward, followed by reverse flow, may occur solely from the effects of systole and diastole.

Barentsz et al. (1987) used MR to study the dissected thoracic aorta and wrote: "MR is ideally suited to the examination of the thoracic aorta because of the ability of the technique to demonstrate mediastinal vessels, depict blood flow and produce direct, oblique and sagittal as well as coronal and transaxial images". They were also able to demonstrate thrombus within a false lumen.

MR ciné field-echo and velocity mapping studies may show not only the blood flow within the true and false lumina, but also the amount of any aortic incompetence (regurgitated blood being shown as a jet passing back into the left ventricle). Widening of the arch, the intimal flap and split, the false lumina, and adjacent haematoma, or pressure deformity of adjacent organs such as the trachea are clearly demonstrated with good technique - see also references below (esp. Underwood, 1987, Bogren et al., 1988 and Mitchell et al., 1988).

As shown in the references below MR is now becoming the method of choice in many centres for diagnosing and monitoring aortic dissection and some are providing a 24 hour service for this type of patient and views are made in both AP and LAO projections. It is also invaluable for the follow-up of surgery - particularly of type A dissections. However in others spiral or fast CT is similarly used and may show not only the intimal flap, but also its movement with cardiac pulsations. A mobile aorta (i.e. pulsating) is likely to be normal whereas a diseased one is most likely to be immobile.

Ultrasound may be carried out by transthoracic echocardiography or via the trans-oesophageal route and offers considerable advantages - it is non-invasive and the apparatus can be taken to e.g. ITU or the admission unit. Rapid diagnosis is usually achieved. Transthoracic US can image the proximal ascending aorta in most patients, and the demonstration of an intimal flap may obviate the need for further investigation. The left ventricular function, aortic regurgitation and the presence of pericardial fluid are readily assessed. Transoesophageal US can be used both pre- and intra-operatively to assess the size of an aortic wall haematoma. A dissecting aneurysm, like a traumatic aneurysm, can produce a false aneurysmal sac with a leak contained by adventitia, mediastinal tissues or the mediastinal pleura. In such cases the aortic wall may mimic an intimal flap (DeBakey - type III).

[Historical note: King George II died suddenly whilst straining at stool on a commode on 25 Oct. 1760 aged 78 - an autopsy showed haemopericardium & dissecting aneurysm - Nicholls, 1761, Hirst et al., 1958. Demos et al, 1989.]

Further references.
Hirst et al. (1958) : Review of 505 cases.
DeBakey et al. (1964) : Surgical management of dissecting aneurysm of the ascending aorta.
Eyler and Clark (1965) : Dissecting aneurysms compared with other aneurysms.
Daily et al. (1970) : Type A - proximal to left subclavian artery and B distal to left subclavian.
Price et al. (1971) : Aortic wall thickness as an unreliable sign in the diagnosis of dissecting aorta.
Dinsmore et al. (1972) : Dissecting aneurysm - angiographic features affecting prognosis.
Hayashi et al. (1974) : True lumen often compressed by false lumen, esp. in desc. and abd. parts.
McReynolds et al. (1978) : Three channelled thoracic aortic dissection demonstrated by angiography - second channel parallel to and overlying chronic dissection in descending aorta.
Ambas et al. (1979) : The chronic healed dissection and unsuspected dissection.
Guthaner et al. (1979) : Fate of false lumen following surgical repair of dissection.
Hedgcock et al. (1979) : Fate of false lumen following surgical repair of dissection.
Taber et al. (1979a) : The left innominate vein simulating aortic dissection on CT.
Egan et al. (1980) : CT in the diagnosis of dissection or traumatic aneurysm.
Gross et al. (1980) : CT in dissection - 11 pts. - leak esp. posteriorly and around lumen.
Godwin et al. (1980a & 1982c) : CT & dynamic CT - difficulty of distinguishing dissection from a simple aneurysm.
Godwin et al. (1981) : CT for the follow up of chronic aortic dissection.
Godwin et al. (1982) : Problems and pitfalls in the evaluation of thoracic aortic dissection by CT.
Suchato et al. (1980) : Dissecting aneurysm on non-contrast CT.
Lardé et al. (1980), Heiberg et al. (1981), Moncada et al. (1981 & 1983) : CT for diagnosis of dissecting aneurysm.
Godwin and Korobkin (1983) : CT and ultra-sound of acute aortic disease.
Thorsen et al. (1983) : Dissecting aortic aneurysms - accuracy of CT diagnosis.
Danza et al. (1984) : CT of dissecting aneurysms - widening of the ascending aorta as the only sign.

Miller, G. et al. (1984) : CT differentiation of thoracic aortic aneurysms from pulmonary masses adjacent to the mediastinum using bolus injections of contrast.
(a) Aneurysm with false lumen and aorto-pulmonary window.
(b) Mass adjacent to aortic arch filling the a right supra-hilar mass.

(a)   (b)

Amparo et al. (1985) : MR is not able to evaluate the competence of the aortic valve or status of the coronary arteries, so cardiac catheterisation may be necessary.

Geisinger et al. (1985) : MR of thoracic aortic dissections.

Smith, T. and Khoury (1985) : CT and angiography - aneurysm of proximal thoracic aorta.

Chiles et al. (1986) : Superior cardiac recess simulating aortic dissection on CT.

Demos et al. (1986) : Detection of intimal flap of aortic dissection on unenhanced images.

Dinsmore et al. (1986) : MR has the potential to provide additional information relating to blood flow patterns and velocity as well as morphological detail.

Nayler et al. (1986) : MR ciné phase shift mapping technique to demonstrate blood flow.

Underwood et al. (1987) : MR velocity mapping.

Bogren et al. (1988) : Studied three patients with dissecting aneurysms using velocity mapping techniques.

Kennedy and Hansell (1988) : Frequency of plain film findings in 21 cases - widening of (i) superior mediastinum in 16, (ii) ascending aorta in 15, (iii) descending aorta in 13, (iv) left para-vertebral stripe in 12, (v) apparent cardiac enlargement (due to haemopericardium) in 10, (vi) deviation of trachea to right in 9, (vii) left apical cap in 8, (viii) blurring of the aortic knuckle (due to dissection along the posterior and superior borders) in 8, (ix) left pleural effusion in 7, (x) displacement of intimal calcification (if a plaque is projected > 5 mm within the outer border of the aorta) in 2 - this sign is only really valid in the descending aorta as this is largely perpendicular to the x-ray beam - the arch is foreshortened in frontal views, and a calcified plaque that appears to be in apposition to the external contour may really be at a considerable distance.

Kersting-Somerhoff et al. (1988) : MR for diagnosing aortic dissection requires considerable experience because of the need to recognise flow artefacts.

Mitchell et al. (1988) : CT and MR to study morphology, but MR showed the velocity flow patterns within the true and false lumina.

Shin, H. et al. (1988) : Three-channelled dissection or 'Mercedes-Benz sign' - postulated that after the initial dissection in the upper descending aorta, this branched out and simultaneously created two parallel false channels of approximately equal size.
(a) Double lumen just below arch level
(b) Triple lumen at carinal level.

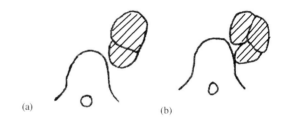

(a)   (b)

White et al. (1988) : MR for studying the residual false lumen after surgery.

Nicholson and Hayward (1988) : Dissecting aneurysm - intimal flap shown well by CT.

Demos et al. (1989) : CT of aortic dissection - most intimal tears occur close to relatively fixed aortic points (i) at the aortic valve & (ii) the isthmus between the L subclavian artery and the ligamentum arteriosum, whilst media degeneration probably plays a secondary role.

Pozniak et al. (1989) : CT of the normal aorta and thoracic aneurysms.

Spielman et al. (1989) : MR of ruptured aneurysm of the ascending aorta.

Godwin (1990) : **Conventional CT of the aorta** - CT's advantage over aortography is that it shows the wall and the mural thrombus, not just the contrast column. **With dissection, it will show blood in the false channel if it is clotted rather than free flowing, with high-attenuation in the aortic wall or periaortic tissues (if recent), and displaced intimal calcifications.** When emergency surgery is contemplated, aortography is often preferred because CT cannot provide information about aortic insufficiency or the condition of the aortic branches. MR may be used in patients who are stable, or cannot have IV contrast media.

For follow up CT, and MRI are preferred as they are non-invasive.

Morgan et al. (1990) : Surveyed CT and angiographic findings in acute dissection in relation to treatment and survival over a 10 year period - they found emergency repair of type A (ascending aortic) dissection improves prognosis, whereas immediate surgery with type B (the more distal type) in the absence of complications, offered no survival advantage. Both CT and angiography were reliable techniques for assessment. They advised carrying out both when the clinical suspicion is high, as this minimised errors of misdiagnosis, CT alone missing some type A dissections.

Solomon et al. (1990) : Pitfalls and artefacts in MR imaging of thoracic aortic dissection - many of these occur including motion artefacts - mostly grade 1 artefacts occurring mostly in the axial plane and the descending aorta. Others occurred with sagittal images of the ascending aorta or were due to fibrosing mediastinitis.

Stanford et al. (1990) : Ultrafast CT for diagnosing aortic aneurysms and dissections ? equal to aortography.

Raby et al. (1990) : Aortic dissection presenting as acute ischaemia.

Wakely et al. (1990) : The chest radiograph may contain important clues but is inaccurate and should not be used either to make or refute the diagnosis of dissection.

Burns et al. (1991) : Double-lumen circular motion artefact simulating dissection due to aortic wall movement on CT (other may be due to L innominate vein, thickened pleura, streak artefacts, pericardial fibrosis and atherosclerotic aneurysms with thrombus).

Wolff et al. (1991) : Aortic dissection - atypical patterns seen on MR - acutely some may only show aortic wall thickening and no flap, whilst others may only have a flap in the abdominal region - thus the whole of the aorta should be examined. Atypical appearances were seen in 29% of acute cases vs 7% in chronic dissections.

Costello (1992) : Spiral CT in the assessment of the thoracic aorta.

Posniak et al. (1993) : Aortic motion - a potential pitfall in CT imaging of dissection on CT scans - elimination with reconstructive segmental images.

Ogilvie and Delany (1994) : MR has emerged as the emergency method of choice in suspected aortic dissections - increasing experience has shown that many patients are being imaged at a stage when only a mural haematoma is present and there is no intimal flap. Ciné sequences can also be very helpful in assessing the aortic valve. Repeat examinations may reveal evolving dissection.

Williams, M. and Farrow (1994) : Eight cases of atypical CT appearance of aortic dissection - intramural haematoma, often crescentic in shape and not necessarily compressing the aortic lumen.

Delany et al. (1995) : Emergency MR is safe and accurate in the diagnosis of aortic dissection and when available can effectively replace all other methods.

Duvernoy et al. (1995) : Aortic motion - a potential pitfall in CT imaging of dissections in the ascending aorta.

Panting et al. (1995) : MR in acute aortic dissection - 26 of 50 pts. studied had dissection - 14 type A and 12 type B.

Brown et al. (1995) : MR is very valuable for follow up of surgery, esp. with type A dissections.

Zeman et al. (1995) : Value of helical CT with multiplanar reformation and 3D rendering to show aortic dissection and the extent of the intimal flap.

Small et al. (1996) : Fast CT for aortic dissection.

Kasper et al. (1978) : Diagnosis of dissecting aortic aneurysm with suprasternal echocardiography.

Erbel et al. (1989) : Echocardiography in the diagnosis of aortic dissection.

Tottle et al. (1992) : Diagnosis of acute thoracic aortic dissection using combined echocardiography and CT (23 cases - dissection diagnosed in 18, 15 in ascending and 3 in descending aorta).

Brooks et al. (1992) : Pointed out that the distal ascending, proximal aortic arch and the innominate artery cannot be seen by trans-oesophageal echocardiography because of the intervening trachea. Although cardiac contusion was diagnosed in some patients, none were haemodynamically compromised.

Pell and Sutherland (1993) : Transoesophageal echocardiography as a diagnostic tool - it may be used at the bedside, in intensive care units, etc. The cardiac chambers, walls, valves, the first part of the ascending aorta, much of the arch and the entire descending aorta may be examined. Intimal flaps, mural thrombi, dissections and swellings are easily recognised.

Laissy et al. (1994) : Diagnosis of thoracic aortic dissection with trans-oesophageal echocardiography vs MR - TOE should be used first for assessment, MR for evaluating surgical patients and for follow up. (NB - angiography can be negative with a thrombosed dissection).

Sakamoto et al. (1994) : Aortic dissection caused by angiographic procedures - course similar to other types of dissection - antegrade dissections persisted or enlarged, whilst retrograde ones resolved (as shown by CT). None needed surgery.

Lee, D. et al. (1997) : The dissected aorta - the differentiation of the true from the false lumen with intravascular ultrasound.

Williams, D. et al. (1997) : The dissected aorta - early anatomical changes in an in vitro model - depend on hydrostatic pressure and the percentage of the aortic wall involved in the dissection.

Brown (1998) : Aortic dissection - the case for MR.

Ettles (1998) : Aortic dissection - the case for US.

Gischen (1998) : Aortic dissection - the case for angiography - may again have an important place with stenting.

Nicholson (1998) : Aortic dissection - the case for CT.

Williams, G. et al. (1981) : Aortic mural thrombus - important frequently neglected cause of large peripheral thrombi.

Machleder et al. (1986) : Aortic mural thrombus - an occult source of arterial thrombo-embolism.

Seelos et al. (1991) : MR detection of aortic arch thrombi (not uncommonly overlooked) - on dissection or aortic plaques - no aneurysm - 3 cases shown by spin-echo and ciné sequences (echocardiography negative).

Qanadli et al. (2000) : Intraluminal thrombi of asc. aorta & arch diagnosed by spiral CT (also further refs.).

Posniak et al. (1994) : Coronary artery interposition graft simulating **pseudoaneurysm of asc. aorta** on CT.

Yamada et al. (1988) : Aortic dissection without intimal rupture - MR imaging.

Kazerooni et al. (1992) : Penetrating atherosclerotic ulcers of the descending thoracic aorta - evaluation with CT and distinction from aortic dissection.

Robbins et al. (1993) : Management of pts. with intramural haematoma of the thoracic aorta.

Weiss et al. (1995) : Bronchial obstruction caused by descending aorta **pseudoaneurysm** (**haematoma secondary to ulceration of media**) and treated by expandable metal stent.
Nienaber et al. (1995) : Intramural haemorrhage of the thoracic aorta.
Ide et al. (1996) : 27 cases of acute dissection with intramural haematoma - 11 developed a classic dissection or aneurysm during follow up.
Oliver et al. (1997) : Serial MR in the management of intramural haemorrhage of the thoracic aorta - man aged 66 - resolution occurred in 6 weeks.
Roidy (2000) : **Use of endovascular stents in treating dissections and aortic rupture with a combined surgical + radiological approach** (the cost of the stents is about £4,000 each).

For   aorto-bronchial fistulae see p. 14.27
        aorto-oesophageal fistulae see p. 16.12

Ascending aorta and aortic root aneurysms - Illus. **AORTA ASCENDING**.
    These may be due to various causes including dissection, syphilis, granulomatous disease, Takayasu's disease, etc. Some are associated with Marfan's disease or Ehler's-Danlos syndromes.
    Sinus of Valsalva aneurysms often remain undiagnosed until they rupture, usually into the right ventricle or atria, They may present with obstruction to the right ventricular outflow tract, cause aortic incompetence, coronary artery compression or tricuspid valve stenosis or incompetence. In other cases there may be conduction defects or sudden death. Occasionally they may be discovered on plain chest radiographs or CT sections, etc. Congenital sinus aneurysms usually involve a single cusp, whilst aneurysms of the aortic root extending through the annulus cause dilatation of all three sinuses. Because of the danger of rupture or severe aortic incompetence they should be diagnosed and if possible resected. Prospective studies are now being instituted in patients with Marfan's disease (see below).
    Calcified aneurysms of the ascending aorta were often syphilitic - examples are shown in Illus.
    A memorable case was an aneurysm which ruptured during CT examination, and Illus. **AORTA RUPTURE** shows the jet of contrast enhanced blood passing into the pericardium at the time of rupture.

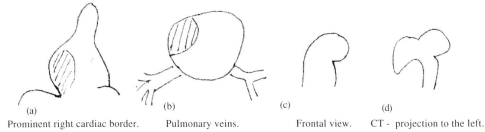

| (a) | (b) | (c) | (d) |
| Prominent right cardiac border. | Pulmonary veins. | Frontal view. | CT - projection to the left. |

Fig. 10.9   Diagrammatic appearances of aortic root aneurysms.

References.
Keene et al. (1971) : Radiographic and pathological features of aortic root aneurysm.
Reinke et al. (1974) : Two cases of calcified non-syphilitic aneurysm of the sinuses of Valsalva.
Magliner (1980) : When aneurysms affect the proximal part of the aortic arch they may project to the left of the spine and simulate tumours.
Henze et al. (1983) : Ruptured sinus of Valsalva aneurysms.
Smith, T. and Khoury (1985) : Aneurysm of the proximal thoracic aorta simulating neoplasm - role of CT and angiography - poorly opacified on CT and angiography due to it being largely filled with thrombus.
Reid et al. (1990) : Thrombosed saccular aneurysm of a sinus of Valsalva (33 yr. old man).

Marfan's and Ehlers-Danlos Syndromes - Illus. **MARFAN SYNDROME**.
    Marfan (1986) noted a skeletal anomaly with long slender extremities in a young girl. Archard (1902) termed the long 'spider-leg-like' fingers as 'arachnodactyly'; he also noted a laxity of joint ligaments and a familial tendency. McKusick (1955) felt the condition was a disorder of connective tissues, principally involving the skeletal, cardiovascular and ocular tissues. He and Pyeritz

subsequently have shown it to be a disorder of the fibrillin gene. Its prevalence is estimated at about 1 in 10,000.

Patients tend to have an asthenic build, with a funnel chest, or scoliosis, arachnodactyly, joint instability, high ('Gothic cathedral-arch like') palates and subluxated or dislocated ocular lenses with early cataract formation. (Possibly US President Abraham Lincoln suffered from Marfan's syndrome because of his long face, tall stature, long limbs and loose jointedness.) Cardiovascular complications include mitral and/or aortic incompetence and aortic root and dissecting aortic aneurysm. Aortic root and dissecting aneurysms are their most common cause of death, especially root aneurysms which are particularly prone to rupture. These may involve the coronary arteries and lead to myocardial ischaemia. Many such aortic root aneurysms are treated by replacement surgery, and annual measurement by trans-oesophageal echocardiography may be helpful in judging progressive enlargement and the need for surgery. (Note that plain chest radiographs may appear normal with aortic root aneurysms). Other associated heart disease includes bicuspid aortic valve, ASD, coarctation, Fallot and Wolff-Parkinson-White syndromes. Dissecting aneurysms in these patients may extend from the aortic arch down to the aortic bifurcation and into the iliac vessels - see Illus. **MARFAN SYNDROME Pt. 2**.

Sometimes patients present with **spontaneous pneumothoraces** (Illus. **MARFAN SYNDROME Pt. 3**), and many have apical bullae, due to the lack of normal elastic tissue in the lung and also possibly the pumping action of the diaphragm with a long thin chest, as in ankylosing spondylitis (see ps. 1.47 & 19.90). This apical disease may be complicated by aspergillus infection, cavitation and haemoptyses. The patients may also have tracheobronchomegaly (see p. 3.5).

Other similar thoracic changes and joint instability may be associated with the Ehlers-Danlos syndrome, which is transmitted by a dominant gene, whose location has not yet been identified.

Further References.

Dwyer and Troncale (1965) : Spontaneous pneumothorax and pulmonary disease in the Marfan syndrome.
Reye and Bale (1973) : Elastic tissue in pulmonary emphysema in Marfan's syndrome.
Hirst and Gore (1973) : Review of Marfan's syndrome.
Turner and Stanley (1976) : Fragile lung in the Marfan syndrome.
Teoh (1977) : Bronchiechiectasis and spontaneous pneumothorax in Marfan's syndrome.
Baumer and Hankey (1980) : Transient **pulmonary cysts** in an infant with the Ehlers-Danlos syndrome.
Cupo et al. (1981) : Ehlers-Danlos syndrome with abnormal collagen fibrils, sinus of Valsalva aneurysms, myocardial infarctions, panacinar emphysema or cerebral heterotopias.
O'Neill et al. (1981) : Pneumothorax in the Ehlers-Danlos syndrome.
Hall et al. (1984) : Pneumothorax in Marfan's syndrome.
Wood et al. (1984) : Pulmonary disease in patients with Marfan's syndrome.
Ayres et al. (1985) : Abnormalities of the lungs and thoracic cage in the Ehlers-Danlos syndrome.
Dinsmore et al. (1986) : MR of aneurysms.
Soulen et al. (1987) : Compared CT with MR in 25 pts. with Marfan's syndrome - both showed aortic, dural and hip abnormalities well, but MR was better in post-operative cases and in some clearly demonstrated residual dissection.
Kersting-Sommerhoff et al. (1987) : MR imaging of the thoracic aorta in Marfan patients.
Super (1988) : Diagnosing Marfan's syndrome and the value of surveys.
Hollister et al. (1990) : Immunohistological abnormalities of the microfibrillar fibre system in the Marfan system.
Fox and Wedzicha (1991) : Pulmonary complications in Marfan's syndrome - recurrent pneumothoraces, haemoptysis from apical fibrosis and cavities, and development of mycetoma.
Chong and Al-Katoubi (1991) : Retroperitoneal fibrosis in Marfan's syndrome.
Young (1991) : Understanding Marfan's syndrome.
Tanoue (1992) : Pulmonary manifestations of the Marfan syndrome, etc.
Francke and Furthmayr (1994) : Marfan's syndrome and other disorders of fibrillin.
Shores et al. (1994) : Progression of aortic dilatation and the benefit of long-term beta-adrenergic blockade in Marfan's syndrome.
Celleti et al. (1996) : MR study of alterations of the elastic properties of the thoracic aorta as an early expression of Marfan's syndrome (esp. in the ascending aorta).
Thomas et al.(1996) : The role of the metacarpal index is probably insignificant in the assessment of Marfan's syndrome and the best single test is echocardiography which will detect the most important abnormality - **aortic root dilatation.**
Price et al. (2000) : MR of intramural haematoma of the ascending aorta in Marfan's syndrome.

Ayres et al. (1981) : Haemoptysis and non-organic upper airways obstruction in a patient with previously undiagnosed Ehlers-Danlos syndrome.
Ayres et al. (1985) : Abnormalities of the lungs and thoracic cage in the Ehlers-Danlos syndrome.
Corrin (1990) : Fibrous pseudotumours and cyst formation in the lungs in Ehlers-Danlos syndrome.
Murray, R. (1995) : Rare pulmonary manifestation of Ehlers-Danlos syndrome - parenchymal cysts and fibrous and fibro-osseous nodules ? related to abnormal attempt of repair of parenchymal or vascular tears.

Aortoarteritis (Takayasu's disease) - may affect the pulmonary artery as well as the aorta.

In 1908 Migito Takayasu, a Tokyo ophthalmologist, described an advanced chronic ischaemic retinopathy in a young woman. Others noted similar appearances together with a loss of the radial pulse, and the findings soon became recognised as due to disease of the aortic arch. Subsequently it was found to involve the descending and abdominal parts of the aorta as well, and it became known as Takayasu's disease or 'pulseless disease'. Arch disease and aortitis of the ascending aorta with dilatation of the aortic valve ring, aortic incompetence and obliteration of the coronary arteries is not uncommon in Japan, South Africa and Thailand. In India the descending thoracic aorta is most commonly involved, and abdominal involvement is more common in Negroes in Africa. The disease is thought to be an auto-immune phenomenon, affected by genetic origin. It is more common in females under 40 years of age, and may also occur in children.

Branches of the aorta are not uncommonly narrowed or blocked, hence the loss of peripheral pulses, and with involvement of the renal arteries severe hypertension. narrowed vessels may respond to angioplasty. Aneurysms of the aorta or more peripheral vessels may occur.

The condition may also affect the **pulmonary arteries and their branches**, with the development of pulmonary infarcts and systemic-pulmonary anastomoses.

The thickened aortic or pulmonary artery walls may show contrast enhancement on CT or MR in the acute phases of the disease. Secondary intimal thrombosis in the aorta or pulmonary arteries is common, and may lead to renal (etc.) or pulmonary infarction.

Treatment with steroids may lead to reversal of acute disease.

References.
Grollman and Hanafee (1964) : Roentgen diagnosis.
Hachiya (1970) : Current concepts of Takayasu's diagnosis.
Deutsch et al. (1974) : Takayasu's arteritis - an angiographic study with remarks on ethnic distribution in Israel.
Lande and Rossi (1975) : The value of total aortography in the diagnosis of Takayasu's arteritis.
Lupi et al. (1975) : Pulmonary artery involvement in Takayasu's arteritis.
Lupi-Herrera et al. (1977) : Clinical study of 107 cases.
Ishikawa (1977) : Systemic-pulmonary artery association in Takayasu's arteritis.
Cook et al. (1986) : Renovascular hypertension in Takayasu's disease treated by angioplasty.
Haas and Steihm (1986) : Takayasu's arteritis presenting as pulmonary hypertension.
Hayashi et al. (1986) : Takayasu's arteritis - decrease in aortic wall thickening following steroids.
Peterson and Guthaner (1986) : Aortic pseudoaneurysm complicating Takayasu's disease - CT appearance.
Yamato et al. (1986) : Radiographic and angiographic findings in 59 patients.
Dong et al. (1987) : Percutaneous transluminal angioplasty for renovascular hypertension in arteritis - experience in China.
Park et al. (1989) : Takayasu's arteritis - angiographic findings and results of angioplasty.
Sharma et al. (1989) : Intravenous digital subtraction angiography in non-specific aorto-arteritis.
          (1990a) : The incidence and patterns of **pulmonary artery involvement** in Takayasu's arteritis - 6 of 42 patients showed pulmonary artery involvement which was not suspected clinically and chest radiographs were abnormal in only two patients.
          (1990b) : Association between aneurysm formation and systemic hypertension in Takayasu's arteritis.
          (1991a & b) : Non-specific aorto-arteritis (Takayasu's disease) in children - 32 cases - 5 with aneurysms of descending aorta - 5 had pulmonary artery involvement.
Sharma et al. (1992) : Study of 126 pts. from North India.
Sharma and Rajani (1993) : The detection and localisation of the aortic occlusion is important in management - IV digital angiography is usually sufficient for assessment.
Sharma et al. (1998) : Intravascular US imaging of mural aortic changes in Takayasu's arteritis.

Kumar et al. (1990) : Aneurysmal form - analysis of 30 cases.
Lopez et al. (1992) : Therapeutic bronchial artery immobilisation in a case of Takayasu's arteritis. Patient had bronchial artery hypertrophy secondary to occlusive pulmonary arterial disease. Estimated that **pulmonary arteries are involved in 40 to 100% of cases.**

Oneson et al. (1992) : MR angiography of Takayasu's arteritis.
Yamada et al. (1992) : **Pulmonary artery disease in Takayasu's arteritis** - angiographic findings in 98 patients - 30 had pulmonary arteriography, 21 showing pulmonary artery involvement - the upper lobe branches showing the most frequent abnormalities.
Mandalam et al. (1993) : Aorto-arteritis of abdominal aorta - angiographic profile in 110 patients.
Yamada et al. (1993) : Evaluation with MR imaging.
Mandalam et al. (1994) : Natural history of aortoarteritis - angiographic study in 26 survivors.
McConachie et al. (1995) : Takayasu's arteritis causing periosteal new bone formation of both clavicles and left scapula.
Park et al. (1995) : Takayasu arteritis - evaluation of mural changes in the aorta and pulmonary artery with CT angiography.
Hayashi et al. (1996) : Imaging of Takayasu arteritis in the acute stage - (i) initially suspected from a slightly wavy contour of the descending aorta, and (ii) thickening of the aortic and pulmonary arterial walls was demonstrated by CT and MR in the acute non-pulseless stage of the disease. (See also correspondence, 1997).
Sharma et al. (1999) : Results of treatment of aortic stenosis caused by non-specific aortitis by percutaneous stent placement.

The middle aorta syndrome and 'abdominal coarctation'.
   This term has been used to describe childhood or adolescent stenoses of the supra-diaphragmatic aorta and the upper abdominal aorta and the upper abdominal aorta often with involvement of the visceral and renal vessels (sometimes termed abdominal coarctation). Progression of the stenosis does not appear to progress after adolescence. Many present with renal failure or hypertension due to renal artery stenosis. Abdominal coarctation may lead to lower rib notching - see ps. 12.29 & 31.

References.
Bahnson et al. (1949) : Coarctation of the aorta at unusual sites.
Konar et al. (1955) : Coarctation of the aorta at an unusual site.
Sen (1963) : 16 pts. all under age 30 & hypertensive - over half had TB - ? an antigenic link.
Graham et al. (1979) : Abdominal aortic coarctation and segmental hypoplasia.
Lewis, V. et al. (1988) : The mid aortic syndrome.
Gupta et al. (1981) : Middle aortic syndrome as a cause of heart failure in children.
Watson, N. et al. (1998) : Supradiaphragmatic middle aorta syndrome - MR and angiographic imaging.

Tumours of the aorta and its wall.
   Theoretically these are of five types:
(a) Tumours secondarily involving the aorta from without.

(b) Metastatic tumour developing in the aortic wall from tumour embolisation.

(c) **Aortic body tumours or chemodectomas** are discussed on p. 18.37-38, see also Illus. **AORTIC BODY TUMOUR**.

(d) **Sarcomas, etc. developing in its wall.**
   Schipper et al. (1989) reported a leiomyosarcoma in a 74 year old woman, which caused a large left-sided para-ortic mass just above the diaphragm. It two-thirds surrounded the anterior, lateral and posterior aspects of the descending aorta, as shown by CT. Punctate calcifications were present in its periphery, and it contained several degenerate areas. The aortic lumen was only marginally involved. They reviewed 27 other reported cases of aortic wall tumour, most of which were fibro- or spindle cell sarcomas, myxomas or leiomyosarcomas. These were categorised into two main types :
   (i) Those primarily involving the intima, and
   (ii) Those arising in the media or adventitia.
   Their case had successful surgical resection and palliative radiotherapy.

(e) **Intraluminal tumours.**
   Silverman and Wexler (1972) described a myxoma developing within the aortic arch in a woman of 72. It extended into the right subclavian and left carotid arteries, and caused clinical features of headache, dizzy spells and hypertension.

Chapter 11 : **Chest Trauma, Iatrogenic Trauma including drainage tubes and some Post-surgical Conditions and Complications of Radiotherapy.**

Chest trauma.

This is the third commonest cause of death (after coronary heart disease and cancer) and is therefore an important subject for the radiologist as well as the accident surgeon, thoracic surgeon, etc. Chest trauma may be relatively trivial or life threatening, particularly when there are multiple concomitant injuries to the head, face, abdomen, or limbs, etc. Injuries may be penetrating, with knife or bullet wounds, but are more commonly due to blunt trauma. This may give rise to rib and/or sternal fractures, a flail anterior or lateral chest wall or damage to the diaphragm and/or heart or great vessels. The dorsal spine may be injured together with cord compression. Intra-thoracic nerves, such as the phrenics, may be stretched or divided.

Penetrating injuries are always more obvious from the front, but the great vessels and the heart, etc. may also be injured by a posteriorly entering object, and the possible track of a missile should always be considered. (**An object e.g. a knife penetrating the chest should not be removed, except at surgery, as removal may cause torrential internal bleeding**). Broken off knife blades or bullets may be difficult to see, and may be 'missed' on poorly exposed frontal radiographs, particularly when they are 'end on'.

Bullets may pass right through the chest, with both entry and exit wounds, and may carry rib fragments into the lung (Illus. **FOREIGN BODY, Trauma lung, Pts. 13a-d & 14**); they also cause 'tracks' which may fill with air and/or fluid or cause cavities with surrounding shadowing. The severity of such chest injuries will depend on whether vital tissues are injured (heart, great vessels, spinal cord, etc.) and on the amount of energy lost to the tissues by the bullet (or other metallic missile) and whether it fragments or ricochets e.g. on hitting the spine.

(High velocity bullets may travel at 1,800 m/sec, $m=v^2/r$, and may cause internal destruction & cavitation in the injured tissue, gas embolism, etc. Bullets may precess or nutate, causing a wider track; necrotic tissue may become infected. Vascular injury commonly leads to death.)

The trachea and larger bronchi may be injured by both penetrating and blunt trauma, and lead to a pneumomediastinum and/or pneumothorax.

Subcutaneous emphysema may occur from gas spreading from the mediastinum, or from pneumothoraces with rib fractures, particularly those penetrating into the lung (see Fig. 11.1).

Trauma may lead to complicating pleural or pericardial fluid, lung collapse and/or consolidation, pneumothorax, etc. The clinical reading of a hemi-thorax as a '**white-out' is to be totally deprecated** - as it does not even try to determine underlying pathology - whether pleural, collapse, etc. The signs of these are often apparent on the plain films, supplemented by ultrasound. **CT is being increasingly used in patients who have been severely injured, not only to show vascular injuries but also occult pneumothoraces, pneumediastinum (which may indicate a lung contusion or bronchial tear), sternal and rib fractures, etc. Indeed many now consider CT availability (particularly spiral CT) should be adjacent to a major trauma room. Many also examine the chest** (e.g. five to ten sections) **after taking cranial CT views for trauma** -particularly for the diagnosis of occult pneumothorax.

As about half of the cases of severe chest injury or chest complications of severe trauma who get to hospital still prove fatal (and often unnecessarily fatal), one should look carefully for key radiographic signs, particularly in cases of multiple injury. Speed in resuscitation and diagnosis are frequently of paramount importance and delay may well be fatal. If there are signs of haemorrhage on an immediate chest film after admission, control of blood pressure (to prevent hypertension, and further bleeding) may be life saving before angiography and/or surgery.

Some special points in acute chest trauma.

Commonly radiographs are taken in the supine position of patients who are severely injured, but erect or semi-erect views (if possible) are preferable for assessing (hydro-) pneumothoraces.

(a) **Chest wall, ribs, sternum, clavicles and spine** - each may be injured on its own or as part of multiple trauma, with steering wheel type injuries fracturing the anterior aspects of the ribs and sternum, and hyperflexion injuries of the spine, together with compression, etc. of the intervening soft tissues.

The first and second ribs are relatively protected, but when injured (and especially with bilateral injuries) this should make one consider damage to internal structures, particularly vascular injuries - with these fractures the morbidity and mortality is often high (see p. 12.11).

Shoulder injuries may also be associated with vascular and neural lesions. A fractured clavicle may penetrate the subclavian artery (see p. 12.40 and Illus. **CLAVICLE FRACTURE 2a-b**), and **an upper humeral fracture tear the axillary artery** (Illus. **CHEST WALL HAEMATOMA Pts. 2a-b & SUBCLAVIAN ARTERY Pt. 4**). Illus. **AORTA TRAUMA Pt. 2** shows a ruptured aorta and bilateral clavicular fractures.

(b) **Extra-pulmonary air** may be found in a pleural cavity (or cavities), in the mediastinum or chest wall. Gas may pass through the track of a penetrating wound, or escape from a lung or bronchus via a laceration or be due to pumping action from the damaged alveoli or bronchi (see also p. 6.31 et seq.). It may also arise from the oesophagus or a ruptured trachea. Mediastinal emphysema will often result and may track into the neck, supraclavicular fossae or chest wall. **Tension pneumothoraces** should be differentiated from large bullae or pneumatocoeles, since the tapping of these may cause a large air-leak and induce a tension pneumothorax. Pneumothoraces may also be bilateral. The diagnosis, particularly of pneumothoraces on supine radiographs may be very difficult - see ps. 14.22 - 23 and CT may be of considerable value and a **valuable early CT sign of air leakage is gas around the trachea**.

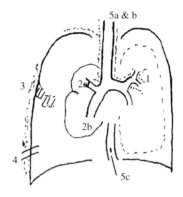

Fig. 11.1 Causes of mediastinal, interstitial pulmonary, chest wall and neck emphysema following injury.

1 - Macklin effect with gas tracking alongside
bronchi to mediastinum - may be accentuated
by resuscitation/assisted respiration,
2a - bronchial tear - 2b if severe may be fallen lung,
3 - injury to lung from penetration of rib
fracture, stab wound, etc.
4 - leakage of gas into chest wall alongside
an intercostal drain, and
5 - tracheal, laryngeal or oesophageal laceration.

(c) **Pleural fluid** presenting soon after an injury is nearly always due to blood oozing from the lung or from bleeding intercostal or mediastinal vessels. It is often associated with air as a pneumothorax. It may also be seen with major vessel or diaphragmatic injury (see e and g below), may be associated with a pneumothorax or complicate secondary collapse, infection, embolism, etc. A chylothorax, secondary to damage to the thoracic duct is uncommon (Illus. **CHYLOTHORAX, Pts. 12 - 14**). Blood may cause persisting pleural thickening (a 'fibrothorax') or rarely a 'mouse' or 'whorled nodule' (see p. 14. 3 & ps. 14.42 - 43).

(d) **Injury to the underlying lung**, besides causing a pneumothorax, surgical emphysema of the chest wall or a pneumomediastinum, may result in areas of lung contusion, traumatic pneumatocoeles or cavities containing air-fluid levels. As well as the nearest part of the lung to the area of impact being contused, **contra-coup** and more distant crush injuries may occur. Haemorrhage into the lung is the most common cause of an 'acute oedema pattern' or 'fuzzy' ground-glass shadowing occurring two to four hours after an injury. Most of this will clear in three to four hours, but in other cases, areas of consolidation may form - sometimes spherical or ellipsoid nodules (which may leave a dense scar); but most resolving completely in days or weeks. Diffusely spreading extravasated blood tends to clear more rapidly than a frank haematoma. Infection supervening within a haematoma may also give rise to cavity formation.

Lung shadowing may also be caused by secondary collapse, due to pleural air or fluid, chest wall splinting, mucous plugs in the bronchi, secondary infection or inhalation, etc. Fat embolism,

ARDS and 'pump lung' (if open heart surgery or repair of the aorta has been carried out) have to be considered in the causes of diffuse lung shadowing (see ps. 8.13 - 14).

Wagner et al. (1988) classified **pulmonary lacerations into four types on the basis of CT** findings and the mechanism of injury in 85 cases. They considered that pulmonary laceration is usually involved in the production of pulmonary contusions, haematomas, lung cysts or pneumatocoeles, or cavitation within an area of contusion. Mechanisms include:

(i) **compression rupture** producing air-filled or air/fluid levels within intra-parenchymal cavities - these result from sudden compression of a pliable chest wall, wherein the air-filled lung ruptures.

(ii) **compression shear** occurs when the more pliable lower chest wall is acutely and severely compressed, causing the lower lobe to shift suddenly across the vertebral bodies and producing a shearing type of injury.

(iii) **rib penetration** gives rise to a small peripheral cavity or peripheral linear radiolucency, that is close to the chest wall, where a rib has been fractured and has penetrated the lung. It is often associated with a pneumothorax.

(iv) **adhesion tears** of the lung occur when the overlying chest wall is violently pushed inwards or fractured.

The lung may occasionally herniate into an injured chest wall and produce a lung hernia (see ps. 2.39 - 40).

Explosions, inhaled gases, including smoke and hot gases, may also injure the lungs. These may lead to acute death, tears, haemorrhage, oedema, etc, and later be complicated by collapse or consolidation. The effect of noxious gases on the lungs is discussed more fully on ps. 19.108 - 110.

(e) **Injury to the trachea or a major bronchus** may cause leakage of air into the mediastinum or pleura, severe haemorrhage, an endobronchial plug leading to secondary lobar or lung collapse, etc. Such injuries (mainly due to vehicle crashes or by heavy machinery) may be life threatening, especially with a haemopneumothorax. Although any part of the tracheo-bronchial tree may be injured, most injuries occur within 2.5 cm of the carina. When there is a rupture of the intra-thoracic part of the trachea, or a proximal main bronchus, the dominant feature is often a pneumediastinum, with subcutaneous emphysema of the neck and anterior thoracic wall. When the rupture is more distal, and the injured bronchus communicates directly with the pleural cavity, the major findings are a pneumothorax with a large air leak and persistent collapse of the lung. The 'fallen lung' sign may be present (see diagram under refs.- Kumpe et al., 1970, below).

In many cases, the bronchi and the peribronchial tissues remain sufficiently patent and intact to permit ventilation of the affected lung. Intubation may be of help, especially during resuscitation, but tracheal tears (unless minor) may need very careful intubation to prevent a total loss of continuity.

The injury may lead to scarring (including **whorled nodule** formation - see Fig 14.23, p. 14.43 and Illus. **WHORLED NODULE, Pt. 23**) and in some cases the injury will only be discovered by later collapse and/or infection caused by granulomatous tissue at the injury site. Tracheal injuries caused by endotracheal tubes and instrumentation are discussed on p. 3.4 - see also references below.

(f) **Mediastinal injury** may produce widening due to bleeding with injury to the aorta, mediastinal veins or other vessels. It may also be seen with undiagnosed oesophageal tears - trauma to the aorta and adjacent great vessels as discussed below.

(g) **Pericardial and cardiac injuries** may give rise to fluid and/or gas in the pericardial sac, tamponade, etc. They are most commonly produced by direct anterior penetrating trauma, and rapid surgery is required to close the defect in most cases. The heart may also be contused by blunt trauma, with fractured ribs or sternum, and this may lead to true or simulated cardiac infarction, fibrosis or damage to the mitral or tricuspid valves, damaged papillary muscles, etc. which may require surgery.

Pericardiocentesis may give only temporary relief from tamponade, and if carried out this should be done under ultra-sound control. However the procedure may be dangerous if a coronary artery is transfixed, or of the removal of pericardial fluid leads to a sudden increase in cardiac output, which may cause a severe and fatal haemorrhage. Often patients with cardiac or pericardial injuries who survive the journey to hospital are in a fragile state of equilibrium, and if this is altered, except by surgery, the outcome may be rapidly fatal. On no account should a knife or other penetrating object be removed except during surgery as is may partially plug a hole in the heart or a great vessel and to some extent prevent further haemorrhage.

(h) **Diaphragmatic and upper abdominal injuries** are commonly associated with fractures of the lower ribs and occur in about 3 to 5% of trauma cases. Injury to the diaphragm is discussed further on ps. 15.17 - 18. Underlying hepatic, splenic and renal trauma per se may be more acutely life threatening. Diaphragmatic rupture occurs in about equal numbers on both sides, but often its presentation is delayed. On the right the liver may 'plug' the hole in the diaphragm, and the rupture may only become apparent weeks, months or even years later. Plugging may also occur on the left, largely by the omentum. In a case not long ago seen by the author, the patient had a successful diaphragmatic repair, but the avulsed hepatic veins caused his death (Illus. **LIVER TRAUMA, Liver Pt. 41**). Torn abdominal organs, e.g. the spleen, may be found in the chest with diaphragmatic ruptures.

(i) **Injuries to the skeleton are also common and may be shown by plain radiographs or CT.**
Spine - fractures, haematoma, paralysis due to cord damage etc.
Shoulder, clavicle, scapula, clavicle + scapula + brachial plexus injury, esp. with lateral displacement (= 'closed fore-quarter amputation')
Sternum (steering wheel or seat-belt injury) - may be associated with torn internal mammary arteries.
Ribs - fractures (single or multiple of involved ribs - multiple with flail area of chest wall) - penetrating lung or pleura.

(j) **The 'Golden Hour'.**
   The Report of the Royal College of Surgeons (1988) and a similar study carried out in Manchester on 1,000 patients referred to the **'Golden   Hour'**, i.e. the **first hour** after a severe injury, in which many (about 30%) of **potentially fatally injured patients may be resuscitated**, before blood loss, aortic tear, pneumothoraces, etc. have proved fatal. Although these occur only once or twice a week (or less often) in many areas, when they occur there are often several severely injured patients at the same time. Such particularly occurs with severe road, rail or aircraft accidents. It is always important to be aware of the various possible injuries and to diagnose them expeditiously. It is often safer for patients to 'by-pass' inadequately staffed hospitals, and to go to a major centre. The danger is that incompletely trained staff may miss or not be able to treat the injuries in the time available, and they may be referred on only when almost moribund. To obviate this some areas have organised a helicopter service to take the injured quickly to a major centre. Some feel that the provision of treatment for major injuries in the UK still requires major reform (e.g. Westaby, 1989).

(k) **Children, adolescents and young adults tend to have flexible chest walls.** In these severe trauma may rupture the vessels, larger airways, lung or diaphragm, often without any fractures of the bony thorax.

Further references.
Hollerman et al. (1990) : Bullets, ballistics and mechanisms of injury.
George and Goodman (1992) : Radiographic appearance of bullet tracks in the lung.

Kinsella and Johnsrud (1947) : Traumatic rupture of bronchus - review of 38 cases.
Dark and Dewsbury (1955) : Fracture of the trachea and bronchus in a boy of 6 with a fracture of the trachea and RUL bronchus. Crushing is the most common cause, esp. in vehicle crashes or by heavy machinery.
Bates and Beard (1956) : Traumatic rupture of the bronchus - six cases.
Hood and Sloan (1959) : Injuries of the trachea and major bronchi.
Burke et al. (1962) : Early diagnosis of traumatic rupture of the bronchus is required as there is a mortality of about 30%, half of those affected dying within an hour.

Williams, J. & Bonte (1962) : Roentgenological aspects of non-penetrating chest injuries - discussed car accidents, aircraft disasters, explosions and industrial accidents, including the exhaust of jet engines. They stressed the importance of radiological follow up, since many serious injuries only become apparent after an interval of weeks.
                    (1963) : Pulmonary damage in non-penetrating chest injuries.
Williams, J. and Stembridge (1964) : Pulmonary contusion secondary to non-penetrating chest injuries.
Sorsdahl and Powell (1965) : Cavitary pulmonary lesions following non-penetrating chest trauma in children.

Stevens and Templeton (1965) : Traumatic non-penetrating lung contusion.
Chestertman and Sastangi (1966) : Rupture of the trachea and bronchi caused by closed injury.
Ting (1966) : 14 out of 200 patients with blunt chest trauma developed a haematoma and/or a pneumatocoele.
Oh et al. (1969) : A characteristic finding with a traumatic complete transection of a main bronchus is a pneumothorax, which may or may not respond to chest tube drainage, plus a **pneumomediastinum,**   and the pathognomonic (or characteristic) finding of 'the **lung "falling" away from the hilum**'.
Eijgelaar and Van der Heide (1970) : A reliable early symptom of bronchial or tracheal rupture.
Kumpe et al. (1970) : In unilateral complete bronchial transection '**the affected lung, having lost the anchoring support normally provided by the main bronchus, falls away from the mediastinum rather than collapsing toward it as with a pneumothorax.**' Thus '**the affected portion of the lung will fall to the most dependent site, depending on the patient's position.**' (see below and Illus. **FALLEN LUNG, AORTA TRAUMA Pt. 2a**).

The lung has 'fallen away' or 'dropped below
the level of the RMB due to transections of the
right upper and intermediate bronchi.

Moghissi (1971) : Laceration of the lung following blunt chest trauma.
Bertelsen and Howitz (1972) : Injuries of the trachea and bronchi.
Wiot (1975) : Radiological manifestations of blunt chest trauma.
Cochlin and Shaw (1978) : Traumatic lung cysts may develop within hours of blunt chest trauma.
Grover et al. (1979) : Major tracheal or bronchial injury - 9 penetrating, 5 blunt. Subcutaneous emphysema was the most consistent sign. A pneumothorax was present in 50%. **Bronchoscopy was the most definitive study**. All cases recovered.
Lotz et al. (1979) : Mediastinal and deep cervical emphysema may indicate traumatic tracheo-bronchial laceration; in a patient who has not had positive pressure ventilation, its presence should prompt bronchoscopy.
Toombs et al. (1981) : CT of chest trauma.
Stanbridge (1982) : Tracheo-oesophageal fistula and bilateral recurrent laryngeal nerve palsies after blunt chest trauma.
Wiot (1983) : Tracheobronchial trauma.
Halttunen et al. (1984) : Bronchial rupture caused by blunt chest trauma.
Roxburgh (1987) from Norwich : 11 cases of rupture of the tracheo-bronchial tree. 9 were due to external non-penetrating trauma, 6 having other serious injuries. Three were in the neck, two requiring tracheostomy and the third recovering spontaneously. Three intrathoracic ruptures were recognised on admission - 1 died of uncontrollable haemorrhage, and 2 had an immediate repair. Three were not diagnosed until 3, 5 or 12 weeks later with the development of bronchial stenosis.
Rollins and Tocino (1987) : Early radiographic signs of tracheal rupture.
Weir et al. (1988) : CT diagnosis of bronchial rupture - total opacification of the left hemithorax - CT showed shift of the mediastinum towards the compromised lung, with retraction of the trachea towards the opposite direction, thus indicating the discontinuity. The patient died from sepsis after pneumonectomy.
Wagner et al. (1988) : Quantification & pattern of parenchymal lung injury in blunt chest trauma - CT assessment.
Unger et al. (1989) : With tears of the trachea and main bronchi, most signs are non-specific, and are due to leakage of air (**subcutaneous emphysema, pneumomediastinum, pneumothorax and air surrounding a bronchus**). Two reliable signs were (i) the 'fallen lung sign' (**collapse of the lung towards the lateral chest wall**) and (ii) endotracheal tube abnormalities (**overdistension of the cuff or extraluminal position of the tip**) - see also p. 3.4
Kerns and Gay (1990) : CT of blunt chest trauma revealed rib and sternal fractures not seen on plain radiographs, together with complications such as haemo- or pneumothorax, pulmonary (including pericardial) and spinal injuries. CT also aided the placement of drainage tubes.

Spencer. J. et al. (1991) from Oxford : Review of 17 cases of rupture of the major airways. 60% had laryngeal rupture with massive mediastinal and deep cervical emphysema without pneumothorax. 7 with bronchial rupture had an ipsilateral pneumothorax and in most cases a pneumomediastinum; two had tension pneumothoraces and two a **'fallen lung'**.

Tobias (1991) : Pointed out the sign of **hyoid bone elevation** (Polansky et al., 1984) indicating a crico-tracheal separation or a tracheal transection. This sign consists of elevation of the hyoid above a line projected along the body of the third cervical vertebra, provided that the patient's mouth is closed and that he is not swallowing at the time of the radiograph.

Hartley and Morritt (1993) : Bronchial rupture secondary to blunt chest trauma - rarity and two modes of presentation may considerably delay diagnosis. (i) The rupture may be intra-pleural with escape of air into the intra-pleural space. (ii) Rupture with early extra-pleural space leakage and with little communication with the pleural cavity - symptoms may be mild or absent initially but complications may occur later. 80% of bronchial ruptures occur within 2.5 cm of the carina, right and left being equally at risk.

Tack et al. (1996) : Two cases of unsuspected RMB tear (men aged 23 & 65 - latter died) detected by demonstration of the **"fallen lung sign"** by conventional CT - elongation of R main bronchus and a lowering of the anterior and posterior RUL segmental bronchi (by 2 to 3 cms).

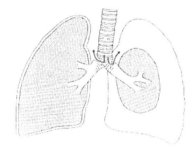

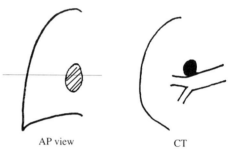

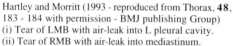

Hartley and Morritt (1993 - reproduced from Thorax, **48**, 183 - 184 with permission - BMJ publishing Group) (i) Tear of LMB with air-leak into L pleural cavity. (ii) Tear of RMB with air-leak into mediastinum.	AP view CT Tack et al (1996 - drawing of case presented) Elongation of RMB + lowering of ant. & post. RUL segmental bronchi + pneumothorax.

Trauma including traumatic aneurysms of the thoracic aorta and adjacent great vessels.

These injuries mainly follow blunt or closed trauma, such as rapid deceleration in vehicle crashes or falls from a height. A theory usually given is that with sudden deceleration, the relatively free descending aorta 'snaps forwards' in relation to its more fixed parts, i.e. the arch and descending aorta at diaphragm level (Fig. 11.2a & Illus. **AORTA TRAUMA, Pt. 2b**). A tear thus tends to occur at the 'isthmus', i.e. just below the origin of the left subclavian artery. An aircraft accident occurred at London Airport, Heathrow some years ago, when a RAF Viscount aircraft ran into a pile of drain pipes whilst taxiing, and many aortic ruptures occurred among the passengers. This prompted the RAF to seat passengers in its transport aircraft (including formerly VC 10s, facing backwards, a policy followed for some time in Trident airliners, and now being reconsidered for some civilian aircraft, following the 1989 crash on the M1 near Nottingham (where many died as a result of floor collapse freeing the seat anchorages). The main problems are not only that many people seem to only want to travel facing forwards, but that modern jets climb from take off at a very steep angle and if facing backwards, passengers would then almost be suspended from their seat belts!

Injuries of the upper aorta and adjacent great vessels may be associated with fractures of the upper dorsal spine or overlying upper chest wall, and this has suggested an 'osseous **pinch**;' mechanism between the anterior chest wall and the spine (Fig. 11.2b), to account for many traumatic aortic injuries, as well as injuries to the larger airways and heart. This may also happen with sudden vertical deceleration, possibly with greatly increased intra-luminal pressure. Stab wounds may also involve these vessels. In other cases trauma, including surgical or radiological (catheter) trauma, may precipitate a dissecting aneurysm - see references below.

Many serious aortic injuries are **'false aneurysms'**, with only the adventitia bridging the ruptured intima and media. This is often very stretched and continuity may only be made by the support of neighbouring tissues. Many of these ruptures are immediately fatal, others rupture hours or days later, whilst some may heal with calcification (Illus. **AORTA TRAUMA, Pt. 5a-e**), or '**blow out**' even years later, especially in the descending aorta (Illus. **AORTA TRAUMA, Pt. 4a-b**). Those with incomplete rupture are often difficult to diagnose, and even at surgical exploration e.g. for repair of another injury, the aorta and innominate vessels may appear normal. Diagnosis depends on the demonstration of a bulge in the wall plus a possible associated haematoma, which may be noted on plain radiographs or tomograms. A haematoma may also be seen with venous bleeding, and differentiation of the possible causes is very important. Clinical suspicion is aroused by associated injuries, upper limb hyper- or hypo-tension, a mid-scapular systolic murmur, anuria, dyspnoea, back pain, etc. (Hypertension is explained by poor blood-flow to the pressure receptors and/ or the kidneys).

The aortic wall and lumen may be demonstrated by CT (with IV contrast), or by angiography, including DVI. CT has the advantage of demonstrating surrounding swelling, but both may demonstrate a localised bulge in the wall. This latter may be quite subtle to recognise, with only a little swelling at the site of rupture, and only a minimal change in the outline of the wall. Intimal intussusception may also occur as with aortic dissections (Kim et al., 200 - see also Illus. **AORTA TRAUMA Pt. 2b**).

A haematoma, besides causing mediastinal widening and poor definition of the aorta and other thoracic structures, may also track over a lung apex or apices (especially on the left), to produce **an apical cap or caps** (Fig. 11.3 - see also ps. 12.4 - 5). A left apical cap may be produced by blood tracking cranially alongside the left subclavian artery, between the parietal pleura and the extra-pleural soft tissues (see Simeone et al., 1975 & 1981). It may in addition displace the trachea and / or the oesophagus to the right, the left main bronchus anteriorly, inferiorly and to the right, and cause a pleural effusion (more often on the left), either from blood per se, or by irritation ('sympathetic effusion' - see also p. 14.8). The para-spinal lines may be displaced laterally, the para-tracheal stripe thickened and the left main bronchus pushed downwards.

Woodring et al. (1982b &1984) studied the common signs of mediastinal haemorrhage in relation to aneurysms and found the most reliable to be (i) an **abnormal aortic contour**, (ii) a **widened mediastinum**, (iii) a **widened right para-tracheal stripe**, (iv) a **thickened apical pleural cap**, (v) **tracheal deviation**, and (vi) **deviation of the oesophagus to the right**, as shown by an indwelling naso-gastric tube. They also found that if after trauma, the **right para-tracheal stripe measured over 5 mm in width, a haematoma with arterial rupture was likely**, and unlikely if less.

Blunt trauma may also produce an **aneurysm of a main pulmonary artery** - which may be recognised on CT sections - see ps. 7.12 - 13 - or a **torn internal mammary artery** (which can lead to cardiac tamponade) - see reference to Braatz et al. p. 11.9 - four cases shown by CT.

Further references.

Cammack et al. (1959) : Deceleration injuries of the thoracic aorta.

Laforet (1965) : Acute hypertension in traumatic rupture of the thoracic aorta.

Greendyke (1966) : Traumatic rupture of the aorta - special reference to automobile accidents.

Molnar and Pace (1966), Lipchik and Robinson (1968) : Traumatic rupture of the thoracic aorta.

Bennett and Cherry (1967) : The natural history of traumatic aneurysms of the aorta.

Flaherty et al. (1969) : Non-penetrating injuries to the thoracic aorta.

Davies and Roylance (1970) : Aortography in the investigation of traumatic mediastinal haematoma - six cases - arterial lesions were present in five and multiple in three. Four had aortic isthmus injuries, but injuries to the right subclavian, innominate and left common carotid arteries were also seen.

Sandborn et al. (1970) : Traumatic rupture of the thoracic aorta - radiology and pathology.

Tisnado et al. (1977) : New radiographic sign of traumatic rupture of the thoracic aorta - displacement of the nasogastric tube to the right.

Gerlock et al. (1980) : Traumatic aortic aneurysm - validity of oesophageal tube displacement sign.

Fisher et al. (1981) : Laceration of the thoracic aorta and brachiocephalic vessels by blunt chest trauma.

Seltzer et al. (1981) : Plain film findings in traumatic aortic rupture.   Toombs et al. (1981) : CT of chest trauma.

Federle and Brant-Zawadzki (1982) : Chest injuries and complications may be fatal in 50% of patients with severe multiple injuries.

Woodring et al. (1982a) : Fractures of the 1st and 2nd ribs - predictive value for arterial and bronchial injury.

Barcia and Livoni (1983) : Indications for angiography in blunt chest trauma.

Heiberg et al. (1983) : CT in aortic trauma.   Shulman and Samuels (1983) : Radiology of blunt chest trauma.

Gundry et al. (1984) : Late traumatic aneurysms of the thoracic aorta.

Marnocha et al. (1984) : Mediastinal width / chest width ratio in blunt chest trauma.

Milne et al. (1984) : The "vanishing" azygos vein in trauma - obscured by oedema or haematoma.

Chew et al. (1985) : Late discovery of a post-traumatic right aortic arch aneurysm.

Marnocha and Maglinte (1985) : 86 patients - only two plain film signs were important -
(i) deviation of naso-gastric tube to right at D4 level, (ii) depression of left main bronchus - 40% below horizontal.

Daykin et al. (1986) : CT demonstration of a traumatic aneurysm of the pulmonary artery.

Haywood et al. (1986) : Chronic thin-walled 5cm post-traumatic upper desc. aorta aneurysm shown by CXRs, CT, MR & angio. in 27 yr old man thrown through windscreen of car 8 yrs previously - successful resection and repair.

Heystraten et al. (1986) : 11 patients with **chronic post-traumatic aneurysms - average time before diagnosis > 5 yrs.** Nine were resected - felt that although progressive enlargement and risk of rupture decreased with time, elective surgery was advisable because of their unpredictable course.

Heystraten et al. (1988) Reviewed 123 patients with blunt chest trauma including 61 with aortic rupture - most suggestive signs were - (i) a widened right paratracheal stripe, (ii) an opacified aorto-pulmonary window, (iii) lateral displacement of right paraspinal stripe and (iv) displaced naso-gastric tube.

Mirvis et al. (1986) : Digital subtraction angiography was 50% faster than conventional angiography in the diagnosis of aortic rupture.

Adler and Troupin (1987) : Trauma Imaging in the Thorax and Abdomen (many CT demonstrations).

Mirvis et al. (1987) : Value of chest radiography in excluding traumatic aortic rupture.

Morse et al. (1988) : Traumatic aortic rupture - false positive aortographic diagnosis due to atypical ductus diverticulum.

Brooks and Olson (1989) : Studied 36 patients with chest injuries by CT and found it useful in the diagnosis and management of post-traumatic infective complications (empyema, lung abscess, mediastinal fluid), sterno-clavicular joint dislocations and the position of foreign bodies and tubes) CT however missed manubrio-sternal and some spinal fractures.

Brooks et al. (1989) : Literature review - if CT failed to show a haematoma, aortography was not indicated, aortography was essential to show the tear, and in 47 cases was carried out without prior CT, being positive in 4. Haematomas also arose from the spine, sternum and other injured areas.

Miller, F. et al. (1989) : Role of CT in the diagnosis of major arterial injury after blunt thoracic trauma - in 104 haemodynamically stable patients, CT followed by angiography was carried out but with only a 55% sensitivity for CT, thus suggesting that it had no screening role in the evaluation of blunt chest trauma when there was possible major vascular injury.

Schwartz et al. (1989) : Traumatic false aneurysm of left common carotid artery presenting as an upper mediastinal mass - followed a stab injury 7 yrs. previously.

Westaby (1989) : Trauma - Pathogenesis and Treatment.

Woodson and Kendrick (1989) : **Laryngeal paralysis** as the presenting sign of aortic trauma - about 10% of patients who survive lung enough for a pseudoaneurysm to develop sustain left recurrent laryngeal nerve paralysis.

Davies (1991) : The mediastinal haematoma that accompanies blunt thoracic trauma is, for all practical purposes, due to injury of small arteries and veins in the mediastinum. The severity of aortic injury extends from 'intimal tear to tear of the full thickness of the wall...'

Richardson et al. (1991) : CT is valuable in detecting potential great vessel injury in patients with blunt decelerating thoracic trauma and equivocal abnormal mediastinal contours on chest radiography.

Morgan et al. (1992) : Does dynamic contrast-enhanced CT play a role in the evaluation of traumatic aortic injury? They concluded that it can help exclude injury, but in those at high risk aortography is preferred.

Williams et al. (1992) : Acute traumatic aortic rupture - intravascular US findings.

Fisher et al. (1994) : CT vs aortography in the diagnosis of injuries of the aorta and brachiocephalic arteries caused by blunt chest trauma - normal CT in 25% effectively excluded such injury - but most still needed aortography.

Hughes et al. (1994) : Traumatic aortic rupture demonstrated by MR imaging.

Ratcliff and Landay (1994) : Chronic pseudoaneurysm of the thoracic aorta - 2 cases following gunshot injury.

Schnyder et al. (1996) : Helical CT angiography for traumatic aortic rupture : Correlation with aortography and surgery in five cases.

Crass et al. (1990) : "The Osseous Pinch" - a proposed new mechanism of traumatic aortic injury.

Cohen, A. et al. (1992) : CT evidence for the **"osseous pinch"** mechanism of traumatic aortic injury.

Gordon et al. (1996) : The tensile strength of the aorta exceeds the decelerative forces developed in motor vehicles whilst the hydrostatic force required to rupture it (greater than 2000 mm Hg) would not be approached in a road traffic accident, thus supporting the 'osseous pinch' theory of aortic injury.

Gavant et al. (1995) : Helical CT demonstration of blunt traumatic aortic rupture.

Gavant (1996) : CT aortography of thoracic aortic rupture.

White and Mirvis (1995 from Baltimore) : Imaging of traumatic aortic injury.- pictorial review of 120 pts. who reached hospital. DVI is as accurate as conventional angiography - the typical appearance is an abnormal outpouching of the aorta just distal to the origin of the left subclavian artery - localised to one margin, circumferential or the appearance of a pseudoaneurysm - these should be differentiated from (i) the 'ductus bump', (ii) a 'ductus diverticulum' or (iii) an 'ulcerated aortic plaque'. In acute cases MR is often impracticable because of supportive treatment lines, wires, etc. CT in stable cases with equivocal plain chest radiographs, may obviate the necessity for angiography.

Loukides et al. (1997) : Unilateral hypertranslucency of the L hemithorax due to compression of the LMB by a chronic traumatic aneurysm of the desc. aorta in a man aged 19 shown by CT.

Beese et al. (1998) : Spiral CT in the management of blunt aortic trauma - a confident diagnosis of a tear may be made in most cases.

Reid, J. and Beggs (1998) : Paraplegia due to tracking of haematoma from ruptured thoracic aorta at D11 level due to trauma and demonstrated by MR - also wedge fracture D11.

Patel et al. (1998) : Review - imaging of acute thoracic aortic injury due to blunt trauma - timely diagnosis remains a challenge - several centres in the USA have used CT & transoesophageal US.

Braatz et al. (2001) : CT diagnosis of **internal mammary artery injury** caused by blunt chest trauma.

Heller and Fink (1997) : Radiology of Trauma - review by Banergee (BJR, 1998, **71**, 349) - he commented "Trauma radiology in Britain has long been a 'Cinderella subspecialty' generating little enthusiasm amongst clinical radiologists. This is a shame since trauma is extremely common and radiological expertise has a lot to contribute in the acute phase in the management of these patients."

Brown, B. et al. (1982) : Dynamic CT using reconstruction in spinal column trauma - 25 pts.

Sudhindran (1999) : Calcified and thrombosed large old traumatic left subclavian artery aneurysm compressing the trachea and brachial plexus.

Roidy (2000) : **Use of endovascular stents in aortic rupture** (see also p. 10.15).

Some useful diagrams

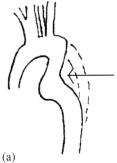

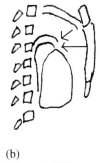

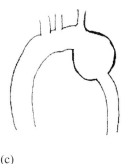

(a)

Fig. 11.2 'Aortic whipping' theory of mechanism of deceleration injury to aortic isthmus (after Keen, 1972 - by permission R. Coll. Surgeons).

(b)

'Osseous pinch' theory of mechanism of aortic injury (see also p. 11.6).

(c)

Diagram of a chronic post-traumatic aneurysm. Note: localised atheromatous aneurysms may give a similar appearance. 12 such cases were reported by Higgins et al. (1975) - see also Illus. **AORTA TRAUMA Pts. 4a-b & 5a-e**.

A - aortic or B - venous injury

A 1. Loss of sharp aortic outline.
  2. Abnormal aortic contour.
  3. Widening of the superior mediastinum.
  4. Lost aorto-pulmonary window.
  5. Downward displacement of LMB to 160^0 from trachea
  6. Displaced trachea or oesophagus - a nasogastric tube may be displaced to the right.
  7. L apical cap & haemothorax.
  8. R paratracheal stripe > 5mm thick.

B 1. Widened upper mediastinum esp. R.
  2. R apical cap & haemothorax.

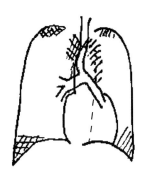

Fig. 11.3 Plain film signs suggesting aortic rupture or venous bleeding.

For injury to **chest wall** - see ps. 11.1, 11.4, 12.10 - 13, & 12.17.
For injury to **brachial plexus** and **thoracic outlet** - see p.12.12.
For injury to **diaphragm** - see p. 11.4 & 15.17 - 19.
For injury to **lung -** see ps. 11.2 - 3.   For **lung torsion** - see ps. 2.37 - 39.
For injury to **pulmonary arteries and veins -** see ps. 7.15 - 16.
For **FBs** in **oesophagus, perforations and fistulae** - see ps. 16.9 - 16.
For **blast injury, smoke, toxic fumes and gases** - see ps. 19.107 - 110.
For **endotracheal tubes and post-operative collapse** - see ps 2.37, 3.4 & 19.2.
For **fat embolism** - see ps. 6.14 - 15.
For **pulmonary and mediastinal emphysema** - see ps. 6.34 - 36.

Iatrogenic trauma (see also p. 15.32).
    This is an increasing cause of injury, with the greater use of instrumentation of various types, including endoscopy, resuscitation, IV tubes, etc.
    Complications from **CV lines, pacemaker insertions** etc. are prone to complications despite the large number that are inserted correctly. These include (a) **pneumothorax** - the most common if the lung and particularly an apical bulla is punctured - but usually insignificant unless large or bilateral (from bilateral punctures), (b) **haemorrhage** into the pleura, extra-pleural space or mediastinum from e.g. subclavian line insertion or biopsy (this can occasionally be massive with mediastinal widening - see Illus. **TUBE COMPLICATION, Pt. 2**), (c) damage to the brachial plexus, (d) air embolism, (e) AV fistulae and (f) cardiac tamponade.
    The tips of CV lines should lie in the SVC or in an innominate vein, but it is not uncommon to find them in the right atrium, or rarely in the right ventricle or coronary sinus, where they may provoke **arrhythmias**. If the tips lie within the jugular or axillary veins, this may stimulate **thrombosis**; in smaller veins fibrin masses seem particularly prone to develop adjacent to the tube tips or in their lumina. Occasionally a CV line may pass down a L SVC (Illus. **SVC 15b**).
    Occasionally **gas may enter the circulation through central venous or other catheters**, but large amounts of IV air are usually required to produce symptoms or death. Both the amount and speed of ingression are important factors and it is suggested that 70 to 100 ml of air per second or a total of 200 ml are required to kill. Prevention should be the watchword, but if air embolism occurs, turning the patient into the left lateral decubitus position will tend to trap the gas in the right atrium until it is absorbed in solution in the blood. (Intravascular gas is also discussed on ps. 6.31 - 34).
    Swan-Ganz type catheters (which are used for monitoring pulmonary artery pressures, should be placed between the main pulmonary and interlobar arteries on either side) may induce temporary or more chronic pulmonary artery aneurysm formation, if the balloon is inflated too much (see also p. 7.12). They may also induce intravascular thrombosis, and recent articles feel that their use probably needs re-evaluation (Soni et al., 1996).
    Naso-gastric and feeding tubes may be introduced into the tracheo-bronchial tree (Illus. **NASOGASTRIC TUBE, Inhaled FB Pt. 10**), and this may lead to flooding of the bronchi if fluids are injected through them in this position. Tips of small diameter tubes may pass through the lung to the pleural surface, leading to a pneumothorax and/or empyema. In difficult cases, fluoroscopic guidance or introduction over a guide-wire may be helpful.
    Endotracheal tubes are not uncommonly misplaced. Ideally their lower ends should lie about 5 to 8 cm above the carina (when the patient's head and neck are in neutral position) since head and neck flexion may result in the tube-tip passing into a main, lower lobe or the intermediate bronchus. This happens more commonly on the right side, so that only the right lung or middle and lower lobes are inflated; the left lung (and sometimes the RUL) may become collapsed. A higher position of the tip or inflatable cuff may cause tracheal scarring or perforation, leading to mediastinal emphysema. Positive pressure ventilation mat also cause mediastinal emphysema, by causing extra-alveolar and peri-bronchial escape of air (see also ps. 6.34 - 36).
    Pleural drainage tubes may cause problems by being placed in an inter-lobar fissure, being partly extra-pleural (with their outer holes in the chest wall) or fully extra-pleural, or even in the lung parenchyma. This last complication usually occurs when a drain is inserted for a supposed (but absent) large pneumothorax, often because of concomitant surgical emphysema in trauma patients. Such an insertion may severely damage the lung, particularly in the 1 to 2% of patients who have marked pleural adhesions.

Some references.

Page et al. (1990) : The **insertion of chronic indwelling central venous catheters (Hickman lines)** in interventional radiology - a subclavicular approach to the subclavian vein with prior digital subtraction angiography or video imaging of the vein is the technique of choice. Fluoroscopy also aided the correlation of malpositioning, etc.

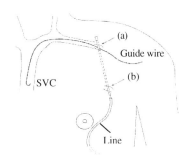

Fig. 11.4 Diagram showing subcutaneous tunnel creation for a Hickman line (between points a & b) - reproduced by permission from Gishen, P. - the diagram in Page et al. (in Clinical Radiology, 1990) was similar but also illustrated the use of a peel-away sheath around the catheter.

Chan et al. (1993) - recommended this as the **technique of choice** for introducing **long-term central venous catheters.**

Dilkes et al. (1991) : Intracerebral air embolism secondary to the insertion of a Hickman line.

Brown, P. et al. (1994) : Hickman catheter rescue.

Groskin and McCrohan (1994) : **Pseudometastasis of chest wall** due to Hickman catheter. (See also p. 6.30).

Adam (1995) : Advised Hickman line placement by radiologists using fine puncture needles.

Folb et al. (1998) : Misposition of a Hickman line into the ascending aorta via the L subclavian vein, piercing the wall of the innominate vein and entering the innominate artery and passing into the ascending aorta.

Murphy et al. (1999) : Hickman lines in unusual places.

Note that **thrombosis not infrequently occurs around CV catheters** (& especially their tips) - Illus. **VENOUS THROMBOSIS, Cystic fibrosis Pt. 5d & Subclav A+V 12**.

At the Churchill Hospital this was noted several years ago : -

Ratcliffe and Oliver (1982) : Massive thrombosis around subclavian catheters used for haemodialysis.

Other references

Horshal et al. (1971) : Fibrin sleeve formation on indwelling subclavian central venous catheters.

Brennan et al. (1972) : Venobronchial fistula - a rare complication of central venous catheterisation for parenteral hyperalimentation.

Faer and Messerschmidt et al. (1978) : Radiographic demonstration of non-fatal air embolism due to CVP lines.

Hewes et al. (1979) : Iatrogenic hydromediastinum due to CVP lines simulating aortic laceration (three patients).

Mitchell, S. and Clark (1979) : Complications of central venous catheterisation.

Iberti et al. (1983) : Hydrothorax as a late complication of central venous catheters (two cases).

Conces and Holden (1984) : Aberrant locations and complications in central placement of subclavian vein catheters.

Gibson, R. et al. (1985) : Complications of central venous catheters - pneumothorax, vascular injuries with haemomediastinum, haemothorax, A /V fistula, extravascular infusion, thrombosis, air or catheter embolism, brachial plexus injury, cardiac injuries or arrhythmias, local haematomas, subclavian artery puncture and malplaced catheter.

Cassidy et al. (1987) : Non-infectious complications of long-term central venous catheters found by radiological studies included deposition of fibrin (fibrin sheath) around the catheter tip, frank venous thrombosis, a constricting suture, abutment of the catheter tip against the vessel wall, passage outside the vein or malposition within branches of the SVC. Streptokinase dissolved about half of the fibrin sheaths.

Cobb and Mendelson (1987) : CT finding in mediastinal extravasation of hyperalimentation fluid.

Woodall et al. (1987), Gelfand and Ott (1988), Ghahremani (1988), McLean et al. (1988) : Complications of inadvertent tracheobronchial placement of feeding tubes.

Venta and Feldman (1991) : AV fistula following a subclavian line insertion.

Wechsler et al. (1988) : Monitoring the monitors - the radiology of thoracic catheters, wires and tubes.

Hinke et al. (1990) : 'Pinch-off' syndrome - complication of implantable subclavian venous catheters.

Krauss and Schmidt (1991) : Cardiac tamponade and contralateral haemothorax after subclavian vein catheterisation.

Lipton (1991) : Venobronchial fistula between SVC and right main bronchus due to malpositioned central venous line, causing a broncho-pneumonic type pattern in the right lung.

Mauro and Jaques (1993) : Review of radiological placement of long-term central venous catheters.

Trigaux et al. (1994) : Radiological findings of normal and compromised thoracic venous catheters - it is essential to determine that a catheter is in a vein rather than in an artery, the mediastinum or the pleural space. Ideally its tip should lie in the SVC (distal to the last valves of the innominate veins) and lie parallel to its walls (to avoid perforation or thrombosis). An innominate vein, the R atrium, or a L SVC are also acceptable positions. Perforation may occur hours or days after insertion and may result in mediastinal, pleural or pericardial effusions - the last particularly occurring with the tip in the pericardiophrenic vein. Kinking may predispose to thrombosis or breakage of the catheter (compression between the clavicle and the first rib - the 'pinch-off' sign esp. seen with long-term access catheters).

Main and Moss (1994) : Removal of intra-arterial subclavian catheter aided by occlusion balloon catheter and percutaneous tract embolisation.

Mansfield et al. (1994) : Complications and failures of subclavian vein catheterisation.

Winston et al. (1994) : Vertebral vein migration of a long-term central venous catheter causing brachial plexopathy.

Anderson et al. (1995) : Radiological appearances of implantable defibrillator systems.

de Kervilier (1995) : Additional technique for repositioning central venous catheters.

Hartnell and Roizental (1995) : Percutaneous repositioning of malpositioned central venous catheters.

Ramsden et al. (1995) : Fracture of CV catheter due to compression between the clavicle and first rib.

Robinson et al. (1995) : Perforation of the great vessels during central venous line insertion.

Köksoy et al. (1995) : Diagnostic value of colour Doppler in central venous catheter related thrombosis.

Fisher, K. and Leun (1996) : Radiographic appearance of central venous catheters.

Kreutchen et al. (1996) : The mechanism of positional dysfunction of subclavian venous catheters.

Bankier et al. (1997) : Azygos arch cannulation by central venous catheters.

Damascelli et al. (1997) : Placement of long-term CV catheters in out-patients - study of 134 pts. over 24,596 catheter days.

Fox, B. et al. (1997) : demonstration of a potentially fatal complication of **pacing** - the wire may fracture and part may migrate through the polyurethane coating.

Rockall et al. (1997) : Stripping of fibrin sheath around catheter tips.

Boardman and Hughes (1998) : Radiological evaluation & management of malfunctioning central venous catheters (pictorial review including catheter malfunction resulting from malposition, displacement, kinking and occlusion).

Graham et al. (1988) : US-guided jugular placement of CVP lines - comparison with blind technique of subclavian vein puncture, showed reduced complication rate, time and cost benefits.

Orme et al. (1998) : CVP line passing into anomalous pulmonary vein.

Parkinson et al. (1998) : Establishing an ultra-sound peripherally inserted central venous catheter service.

Egglin et al. (1995) : Retrieval of intravascular foreign bodies - experience in 32 cases.

Moore, E. et al. (1984) : CT in the diagnosis of iatrogenic false aneurysms of the ascending aorta.

Thorsen et al. (1986) : **Dissecting aneurysms and pseudoaneurysms of the ascending aorta** can occur after surgery - from clamping, incision or cannulation for cardio-pulmonary by-pass.)

Sakamoto et al. (1994) : Aortic dissection caused by retrograde angiographic procedures - six cases studied by CT - all resolved without surgery. (NB Present author has had a similar experience in a few cases).

Intercostal tubes and drains

Neff et al. (1984) : Serious complications following transgression of the pleural space in drainage procedures - needle drainage causes fewer complications than a catheter remaining in situ for several days.

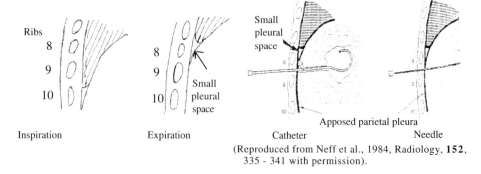

(Reproduced from Neff et al., 1984, Radiology, **152**, 335 - 341 with permission).

Fig. 11.5 Diagrams of the positions of lung bases & parietal pleura in inspiration & expiration.

(Note also that a small amount of pleural fluid collects in the small pleural space below the lung in the costophrenic angle in expiration, whence it may be readily aspirated under US control - see also ps. 14. 13 - 14).

Milliken et al. (1980) : Complications of tube thoracostomy for acute trauma.
Stark, D. et al. (1983) : CT and radiographic assessment of tube thoracostomy.
Webb, W. and La Berge (1983) : Trauma - major fissure tube placement.
Miller, K. and Sahn (1987) : Chest tubes - indications, technique, management and complications.
O'Moore et al. (1987) : Sonographic guidance in diagnostic and therapeutic intervention in the **pleural space**.
Glassberg and Sussman (1990) : Life-threatening haemorrhage due to percutaneous transthoracic intervention - importance of the **internal mammary artery**.
Lai et al. (1990) : Intercostal arterio-venous fistula due to **pleural biopsy**.

Westaby (from Oxford) and Brayley (1990) : Pointed out that less than 15% of patients with chest trauma need surgical intervention, pathology in the remainder being confined to the thoracic cage and underlying lung.

Multiple rib fractures with pulmonary contusion, haemothorax or pneumothorax can be treated simply and efficiently by a chest drain and supportive treatment. Only rarely is rib fixation needed.

Except in an **extreme emergency** with a **gross tension pneumothorax**, **drain insertion should always be preceded by chest radiography - this will avoid transfixing an already damaged lung by the drainage tube.** They noted that it is surprising how many patients have a drainage tube inserted inappropriately in peripheral casualty departments, and when the patients become, not surprisingly worse, and are transferred to a major centre, the most appropriate treatment is often to remove the tube. They also pointed out that a drain should be inserted **above the lower rib** to avoid the intercostal vessels.

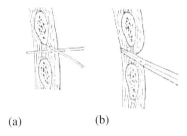

(a) (b) (c) (d)

(a) Penetration of the skin, muscle and pleura. (c) Exploration of the pleural cavities.
(b) Blunt dissection of the parietal pleura. (d) Tube directed posteriorly and superiorly.

Fig. 11.6   Chest drain insertion   (Reproduced from Westaby, S. and Brayley, N., 1990, Thoracic trauma, BMJ, **300**, 1639 - 1643 with permission from the BMJ).

(For diagram of the relationships of the intercostal nerves and vessels to the adjacent ribs - see Fig. 12.15, p. 12..29).

Curtin et al. (1994) : A large percentage (> 50%) of thoracostomy tubes inserted for acute chest trauma appear to lie within a pleural fissure - these, however, appear to function as effectively as those located elsewhere in the pleural space.
Baldt et al. (1995) : Assessment of complications of emergency tube thoracostomy with CT - about a third of tubes were inserted in extrathoracic, intrafissural, intraparenchymal or unclear positions.
Kurihara et al. (1996) : Utility of chest radiograph in the evaluation of chest drain placement (compared with lateral) - 56 CXRs in 45 pts. with 61 drains (18 anterior, 9 interlobar and 34 posterior). Most anterior drains had a curved appearance at the insertion site, whilst 50% of posterior drains and all interlobar drains were straight at this site. A curved intrapleural drain was common when positioned anteriorly and posteriorly. Interlobar drains were often straight throughout their course, and their tips were usually positioned at the hilum.
Gayer et al. (2000) : CT diagnosis of malpositioned chest tubes - pictorial review.
[NB in Oxford we usually took both frontal and lateral views with any tube problems.]

Neurological complications due to CV catheters
Vest et al. (1980) : Phrenic nerve injury associated with venipuncture of internal jugular vein.
Rigg et al. (1997) : R phrenic nerve palsy as a complication of indwelling central venous catheters.
Prokesch et al. (1999) : Transient elevation of R hemidiaphragm following CV catheter insertion (int. jug. vein).

Complications arising from tracheostomy tubes are discussed on p. 3.4 and endotracheal tubes on ps. 2.37 & 19.2.

The post-pneumonectomy space and some post-operative abnormalities.

The easiest method of examining the opaque **post-operative pleural space** is with ultra-sound. Commonly there is an outer layer of pleural thickening, a chronic collection of fluid and herniated mediastinum and contra-lateral lung. The pleural thickening usually gives a good acoustic window, and masses projecting into the fluid may be shown, giving an irregular appearance within the fluid or lying on the pericardium, etc. Such may indicate a recurrence of tumour, which may be confirmed by aspiration of fluid and cytology. An empyema within the space may be suggested by debris and diffuse acoustic shadowing within the fluid.

Fluid accumulates in this space from bleeding, leaking lymphatics and pressure transudation. There is a wide variation in the rate that this occurs and in the degree to which a fibrothorax occurs. It may take months until all the air is reabsorbed, and in some patients a little persists indefinitely. About two thirds of patients maintain a fluid-filled space, the remainder having a solid fibrothorax.

CT is also used to study this space (Illus. **PNEUMONECTOMY, Ca RML, Pt. 9b**). Biondetti et al. (1982b) studied 22 patients and found that 13 still contained fluid (or semi-fluid) many years after a pneumonectomy, and in the remaining nine it became obliterated.

Mediastinal shift depends on expansion of the residual lung. It rotates following a right pneumonectomy and tends to shift following a left pneumonectomy, nearly always with an anterior lung herniation; some also with a posterior herniation (see also lung herniation ps. 2.39 - 40). Reversal of the shift, with a more central mediastinum and a convex fluid interface, may suggest increased fluid in a pneumonectomy space, usually due to recurrence of tumour or infection.

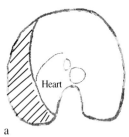 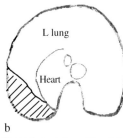 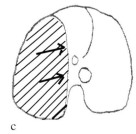

a

Herniation of the contra-lateral lung & shift of the mediastinum - usual appearance after pneumonectomy.

b

Excessive rotation of heart & mediastinum causing the post-pneumonectomy syndrome.

c

Fluid, gas, etc. displacing the mediastinum back towards the midline with **convexity** due to a recurrence of tumour or empyema.

Fig. 11.7 The post-pneumonectomy space (a) normal, (b) excessive herniation and rotation of heart and mediastinum, and (c) increase in fluid indicating recurrent disease. An empyema (often associated with a broncho-pleural fistula) or a chylothorax may also occur.

Illus. **PNEUMONECTOMY, Ca recurrent Pt. 6, & Pneumonectomy Pts. 6b, 8 & 9** show examples of recurrence. Other Illus. under this Keyword show examples of the post-pneumonectomy space.

The **pneumonectomy syndrome** occurs most commonly on the right and particularly in children or adolescents and is due to the mediastinal shift with marked herniation of the remaining lung anteriorly and contralaterally + cardiac rotation (Fig. 11.7b). The left main or left lower lobe bronchi may become stretched across the spine, between the aorta and the pulmonary artery. This syndrome may lead to severe dyspnoea and recurrent infection and may be relieved by injecting fluid into the residual pleural space, by inserting a plombage or by performing a pericardiectomy.

The **bronchial stump.** The integrity of bronchial closure depends on an adequate blood supply, and to help preserve this the bronchial vessels are usually ligated as close to the suture line as possible. Some cover the stump with fascial or other tissue. Stump leak and post-operative broncho-pleural fistula (see previous section) may be indicated by increasing gas in the post-pneumonectomy space, and surgical emphysema if the chest wall, or a reduction in the amount of fluid in the space (and an increase in air) together with broncho-pneumonic type changes in the opposite lung. The sudden appearance of an air-filled space which had previously been fluid-filled is particularly suggestive. [Parker et al. (2000) used Kr^{81m} ventilation to prove the diagnosis].

Pulmonary oedema of the contralateral lung may occur after pneumonectomy, and is often fatal unless treated immediately. Similarly a remaining lobe (or lung - should only an exploratory thoracotomy have been carried out) may become oedematous if its vein has been ligated or it becomes thrombosed.

Postoperative lung nodules may be of several types including :
(i) haemorrhage; (ii) infarcts (which may sometimes enlarge);
(iii) fibrotic nodules following the above; (iv) suture/ talc granulomata.

The **phrenic nerves** (particularly the left) may be damaged by pressure, stretching or the cryoprobe (see ps. 15.1 - 3).

The **pericardium** - cardiac herniation may occur soon after surgery and be accompanied by tachycardia, hypotension and elevated venous pressure, but this is usually prevented by closing the pericardium or by greatly enlarging the pericardial defect so that no constriction by its edges may occur (see also ps. 15.28 - 30).

Post-cardiac transplantation or heart-lung transplantation - the pericardium is usually removed and pacing wires are present. Rejection changes (as well as signs of failure, infection, etc.) may occur in the lungs, giving rise to small or larger nodules. Nodules may also occur as a result of immunosuppression (esp. with cyclosporine). Both pleural cavities may communicate, allowing air or pleural fluid to pass from one side to the other post-operatively and even later (Paranjpe et al., 1994 found six such cases who had bilateral simultaneous pneumothoraces following lung biopsy, etc. procedures up to two years later). Narrowing of the tracheal anastomosis is less common (about 2%) compared with that of bronchial with lung transplantation (10 to 20%) in some series. See also iatrogenic buffalo chest - p. 7.7 & 14.23.

Post-thoracotomy deformities may affect the chest wall muscles, as well as the rib-cage, pleura and lungs.
    Absence of part of a rib (often much of it) or its irregular re-growth and calcification follows a thoracotomy incision made through the bed of a rib (most often the 5th or 6th). This was the older approach, but many thoracic surgeons now enter a pleural cavity between the ribs, and only section the posterior end of a rib in order to gain access to the appropriate hemithorax.
    A thoracoplasty was often performed to reduce the volume of the upper part of a pleural cavity in the treatment of tuberculosis, and occasionally was done on both sides. This procedure is still occasionally carried out with a persistent empyema, or lung infection. Examples are shown under Illus. **THORACOPLASTY**.
    An intercostal incision which extends posteriorly may damage the long thoracic nerve leading to atrophy of the serratus anterior and a '**winged scapula**'. Similarly damage to the thoracodorsal nerve may lead to atrophy of the latissimus dorsi (see Goodman, P. et al., 1993 and Frola et al., 1995); this muscle may also be deformed after cardiomyoplasty, when it is 'wrapped around the heart' to increase vascularity. See also Bhalla et al. (1994) - Surgical flaps in the chest.

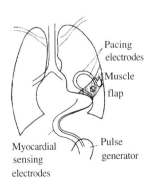

Fig. 11.8 Diagram of appearances after cardiomyoplasty (after Walker, J. 1996, with permission from Brit. J. Radiology).

Pacing electrodes

Muscle flap

Myocardial sensing electrodes

Pulse generator

Lung transplantation and some post-transplantation lung changes (see also p. 19.7).

Lung transplantation may be followed by several complications, including lung torsion (p. 2.38 - 39) and bronchiolitis obliterans. The latter is a late complication and is thought to be a form of chronic rejection and may be influenced by repeated infections. Morrish et al. (1991, from Toronto) stated that it may occur in up to 50% of cases of heart-lung transplantation, but is less common after lung transplantation.

(Technically it is often easier to replace both lungs and the heart, than both lungs, the removed heart then being used for a further recipient).

Plain radiographs may show decreased peripheral vessels, linear collapse and linear areas of increased opacity, whilst HRCT may show mild peripheral bronchiectasis as well as decreased peripheral vasculature.

Other complications include : (a) new infection, (b) recrudescence of old infection within the donor lung, and (c) the **'reimplantation response'** (non-cardiogenic pulmonary oedema due to ischaemia, trauma, denervation and lymphatic interruption). This last may be an early transient process, varying from a subtle perihilar haze to dense consolidation with air bronchograms; on clearing it may leave residual interstitial changes, and be a precursor of bronchiolitis obliterans.

(d) **Bronchial dehiscence** may be demonstrated by CT in showing extraluminal air adjacent to the bronchial anastomosis (an attempt is usually made to prevent this by wrapping omentum around the anastomosis - this also helps to revascularise the bronchial circulation and prevent bronchial ischaemia). (e) Narrowing of the bronchial anastomosis is more common after lung transplantation as compared with heart-lung transplantation. (f) Lung torsion - see p. 2.39. (g) Development of lymphomata, etc.

Cyclosporine and steroids are usually given to try to prevent the lung changes occurring, but cyclosporine may give rise to small lung nodules, especially at the lung bases (see p. 5.36).

Further references.

Allison and Johnstone (1950) : The chest after thoracic operations.
Suarez et al. (1969) : The post-pneumonectomy space - factors influencing its obliteration.
Twersky et al. (1972) : Post-traumatic broncho-pleural fistula - a complication of extra-pleural **oleothorax.**
O'Meara and Slade (1974) : Disappearance of fluid from the post-pneumonectomy space.
Friedman, P. and Hellekant (1977) : Radiological recognition of **broncho-pleural fistula**.
Kerr (1977) : Late-onset post-pneumonectomy syndrome.
Lams (1980) : Radiographic signs in post-pneumonectomy **broncho-pleural fistula**.
Carter et al. (1983) : Thoracic alterations after cardiac surgery.
Lautin et al. (1983) : Demonstration of pleural track tubularity.
Peters, J. and Desai (1983) : Post-pneumonectomy space and CT - 7 patients, 6 with recurrence, 5 shown by CT.
Peters, M. et al. (1983) : Broncho-pleural fistula shown by CT.
Stark, D. et al. (1983) : CT and radiographic assessment of tube thoracostomy.
Glazer, H. et al. (1984a) : CT for detecting post pneumonectomy tumour recurrence.
Heater et al. (1985) : CT of **empyema** in the post-pneumonectomy space.
Wechsler and Goodman (1985) : Mediastinal position and air-fluid height after pneumonectomy - the effect of the respiratory cycle.
Shepard et al. (1986) : Right pneumonectomy syndrome - radiological findings and CT correlation.
Karwande et al. (1986) : Post-pneumonectomy tension chylothorax.
Gyves-Ray et al. (1987) : Unilateral pulmonary oedema due to post-lobectomy pulmonary vein thrombosis.
Holbert et al. (1987) : The postlobectomy chest - anatomical considerations.
Spirn et al. (1988) : Radiology of the chest after thoracic surgery.
Laissy et al. (1989) : MR appearance of the normal chest after pneumonectomy. This showed a homogenous signal, both on T_1 and T_2 spin-echo sequences. Vascular and bronchial stumps were clearly delineated, and were surrounded by low signal areas, considered to be post-operative scars.
Shauffer and Sequecra (1977) : Suture granuloma simulating recurrent carcinoma.
Fink et al. (1993) : Suture granuloma simulating lung neoplasm occurring after segmentectomy.

Hopkins et al. (1985) : Modern use of **thoracoplasty** - reducing the pleural space with broncho-pleural fistula, etc.
Moore et al. (1986) : Pleural thickening and skeletal deformity following thoracoplasty, and their relationship with respiratory failure.
Phillips, M. et al. (1987) : Late sequelae of pulmonary TB treated by thoracoplasty.
Moore et al. (1988) : CT appearances following thoracoplasty for TB - bullae, bronchiectasis and pleural thickening (study of 32 patients).
Vilji et al. (1998) : Postpneumonectomy syndrome - 4 cases on R and 1 on left.

Trimble et al. (1966) : Changes in alveolar surfactant after lung reimplantation - reduced leading to excessive bronchial secretions, temporary oedema of lung tissues & reduced ventilatory capacity.

Burke et al. (1984) : Obliterative bronchiolitis and other late sequelae of heart-lung transplantation.

Herman et al. (1989a) : Chest x-ray findings after single & (1989b) bilateral lung transplantation.

Skeens et al. (1989) : Bronchiolitis obliterans following heart-lung transplant in 11 patients.

Bergin et al. (1990) : Acute lung rejection after heart-lung transplantation. The combination of septal lines and new or increasing pleural effusions, without concomitant increase in cardiac size or vascular pedicle width or vascular redistribution tended to indicate acute lung rejection.

Carlsen and Bergin (1990) : Reactivation of tuberculosis in a donor lung after transplantation.

Kramer et al. (1991) : Ulcerative tracheobronchitis - a new form of **invasive aspergillosis** (starting at the anastomosis) in six patients after lung or heart-lung transplantation.

Levine et al. (1990) : Single lung transplantation for primary pulmonary hypertension.

Emery et al. (1991) : Treatment of end-stage COAD with double lung transplantation.

Schafers et al. (1991) : Prevalence and management of bronchial anastomotic complications after lung transplantation - disruption of bronchial anastomoses and formation of broncho-pleural and broncho-vascular fistulae were the common causes of death in patients who survived the first two weeks after lung transplantation.

Glazer, H. et al. (1992) : Surgeons sometimes wrap the omental flap - producing a 'mass' on chest radiographs.

Lentz et al. (1992) : Diagnosis of BO in heart lung transplantation pts. - importance of bronchial dilatation on CT.

Levine, S. et al. (1993) : Graft position and pulmonary function after single lung transplantation for obstructive lung disease - compared R with L bypassing an emphysematous native lung - no functional difference found despite apparent compression of the L sided graft by a native R lung.

Haramati et al. (1993) : Lung nodules and masses after cardiac transplantation.

Kramer (1994) : Bronchiolitis obliterans following heart lung and lung transplantation.

Anderson, D. et al. (1995) : The spectrum of findings attributable to lung transplantation or reperfusion oedema is variable and diminishes the use of chest radiography as an early postoperative method for monitoring acute rejection.

Davis, R. and Pasque (1995) : Since 1983 the International Lung Transplant Registry has recorded over **2,700** lung transplants. **Single-lung transplantation** can be performed as treatment for most respiratory diseases. However, chronic conditions such as cystic fibrosis are a contraindication because there of the severe risk of infection from the native lung contaminating the graft and the effects of immunosuppression. In the absence of major pleural adhesions, the one that is replaced is the one in which scintigraphic results indicate that function is most diminished. **Double-lung transplantation** usually is indicated in patients in whom mechanical ventilation must be used for more than a few days. All patients (except those with pulmonary hypertension) should be weaned from mechanical ventilation as soon as possible. Most acute deaths occur from pneumonia. Later bronchial strictures and allograft dysfunction may occur, with obliterative bronchiolitis due to CMV, defective ciliary clearance or immunological mechanisms.

Kazerooni et al. (1994) : Sarcoidosis - recurrence after lung transplantation (see also p. 19. 74).

Kazerooni et al. (1995) : Nodules following transbronchial biopsy in transplanted lungs due to lung injury and haematoma.

Keller et al. (1995) : BO in recipients of single, double and heart lung transplants.

Loubeyre et al. (1995) : Bronchiectasis shown by HRCT as a predictor of lung transplant rejection (could also be seen with CMV infection).

Semenkovich et al. (1995) : CT evaluation of bronchial dehiscence following lung transplantation.

McAdams et al. (1997) : CT appearance of telescoping bronchial anastomoses after unilateral or bilateral linear or spherical air collections can be a normal feature and should not necessarily be interpreted as dehiscence.

Lau et al. (1998) : HRCT diagnosis of obstructive changes due to BO syndrome in infants and young children after lung transplantation - findings included mosaic perfusion pattern and dilatation of smaller bronchi.

Lok and Egan (1998) : FB - a green pea - in RUL bronchus of a transplanted lung - denervation associated with transplantation carries a risk of unrecognised aspiration.

Matar et al. (1999) : Respiratory viral infections in lung transplant recipients - infection with parainfluenza &/or respiratory syncytial virus is commonly asymptomatic & causes no radiographic abnormalities., whereas adenoviral infection is typically symptomatic, gives rise to new radiographic abnormalities and is rapidly lethal.

Ward and Müller (2000) : Review of pulmonary complications following lung transplantation - **immediately** (mechanical, pneumothorax, hyperacute rejection, diaphragmatic paralysis), early - **within 2 months** (reimplantation response, acute rejection, infection, bronchial dehiscence, pulmonary embolism), and late - **after 2 months** (chronic rejection/BO syndrome, post transplant lymphoproliferative disorder, bronchial stenosis, diaphragmatic hernia) - also **transbronchial biopsy complications**.

Collins et al. (2000) : CT findings of pneumonia after lung transplantation - mainly nonspecific re cause.

Lymphoproliferative conditions - (see also under EB virus ps. 19.30).

Starvl et al. (1984) : Reversibility of lymphomas & lymphoproliferative lesions under cyclosporin-steroid therapy.

Harris et al. (1987) : Clinical and radiological manifestations of post-transplant cyclosporin induced lymphoproliferative disorders.

Honda et al. (1990) : Clinical and radiological features of malignant neoplasms in organ transplant recipients - cyclosporin treated vs untreated patients.

Dodd et al. (1992) : Intrathoracic manifestations of post-transplant lymphoproliferative disorders.
Craig et al. (1993) : Post-transplantation lympho-proliferative disorders.
Tubman et al. (1983) : Lymphoma after organ transplantation - radiological findings in CNS, thorax & abdomen.
Randhawa et al. (1984) : The clinical spectrum, pathology and clonal analysis of EBV associated lymphoproliferative disorder in heart-lung transplant recipients.

Other transplants - references.
Wyatt et al. (1984) : Airways obstruction associated with graft v host disease after bone marrow transplantation.
Trotman-Dickenson et al. (1990) : Pulmonary graft versus host disease - is associated with obliterative bronchiolitis. Typically chest radiographs are normal, but V /P scans and CT are abnormal with diffuse patchy ground-glass shadowing.
Graham et al. (1991) : CT findings of intrathoracic complications after bone marrow transplantation. included :
    ground-glass pattern in early pneumonia, peripheral distribution in graft versus host disease, BOOP eosinophilic drug reaction, cavitating lesions in Pneumocystis pneumonia, haemorrhagic infarcts in aspergillosis mediastinal lymph node enlargement in recurrent reticulosis.
Crawford and Clark (1993) : Bronchiolitis associated with bone marrow transplantation.

Other post-operative abnormalities are discussed as follows:

Broncho-pleural fistula	- ps. 14.27 - 28
Buffalo chest	- p. 7.7
Extra-pleural space	- p. 14.1
Heart hernia	- p. 15.28 - 29
Lobar rearrangements & neofissure	- ps. 2.37 - 38
Lung hernia	- ps. 2.39 - 41
Lung rotation/torsion	- ps. 2.37 - 38
Mediastinal gas	- ps. 6.31 &18.24
Oleothorax and plombage	- p. 14.2
Post-thoracotomy deformities	- p. 11.15
Sternotomy	- ps. 5.25, 12.31 & 12.35
Tube problems	- p. 11.10 et seq.
Retained swabs	- **FOREIGN BODY, Trauma lung Pt. 16***

[*A patient with previous ruptured right hemidiaphragm who developed renal failure - calcified swab at right base - medially.
Another patient from the Churchill Hospital renal unit with a calcified retained swab within an abdominal abscess which indented the liver is reported by Boardman et al. (1999).]

See also ps. 12.17 - 19 re breast disease.

Radiation induced changes in the lungs, mediastinum and chest wall - (Illus. **RADIOTHERAPY**).

   These follow radiotherapy for various tumours (lung, breast, oesophagus, lymphoma, etc), but are most commonly seen in breast patients, partly because of their numbers, the fact that many survive the tumour, and from the overlapping fields.
   The affected area usually corresponds to the area and volume traversed by the radiation beams. It is usually more marked close to the site of entry. Such beams may have been AP or PA, or applied tangentially as 'glancing beams' to the breast, axillae, etc. Sometimes these may overlap over the upper chest with treatment to more than one nodal area. Affected areas of lung often have an unnatural anatomical shape, i.e. they do not conform to the normal borders of lobes, fissures, segments, etc. They commonly have rather **straight borders -** square, rectangular, 'Gothic cut-out' etc. corresponding to the areas treated. When the mediastinum has been treated the borders of the affected lung are often seen as vertical para-mediastinal lines.
   Pathological changes are initially similar to those following a severe thermal burn, with oedema, pneumonitis and vasculitis with an endothelial injury and loss of type II pneumocytes in the lung. This is followed by fibrosis, shrinking of the affected area, vascular thinning, bullous formation,

overlying pleural thickening, localised bronchial damage, etc. When the hilum has been irradiated, secondary changes may be seen in the remainder of the affected lung, due to vascular damage, at times appearing on isotope studies to be equivalent functionally to a pneumonectomy, with an almost total loss of perfusion and reduced ventilation. Less severe damage will show smaller defects. Sometimes the loss of vascularity is later made apparent in patients developing pulmonary oedema (when the affected lung is spared), or metastases (with the irradiated area of lung remaining free from these whilst the remainder show a 'snow-storm' pattern).

Chronic changes may mimic tuberculosis, lung tumours, etc. Distinction from recurrent tumour may at times be very difficult, and both may be present together.

Radiological changes.

LUNG CHANGES - see Illus. **POST-RAD LUNGS**.

(a) **Acute lung disease** ('Post-radiation pneumonitis' - usually within 4 to 12 weeks).
These include :
(i) A slight increase in lung density affecting the irradiated portion(s) of the lung(s) or a diffuse 'acute radiation pneumonitis' - really an acute burn. Occasionally Kerley's lines may be seen, which may mimic lymphangitis carcinomatosa.
(ii) Patchy or discrete areas of consolidation corresponding to the irradiated area tend to appear three to twelve weeks after treatment. Most occur after about four to six weeks, whilst others are delayed for two to three months or longer. Most appear if more than 4,000 rads (40 Gy) have been given, and a large volume of lung has been included in the irradiated area. The incidence appears to depend not only on the total dose of radiation given, but also on the dose rate. Some patients seem to have more sensitive tissues than others, and develop greater changes from a lower radiation dosage. Lung changes often parallel skin changes, but this is not always so, and the lung changes may be more severe. Commonly the affected area is close to the entry portals) - antero-laterally with breast treatment, etc.
(iii) In a few cases a **COP/ BOOP type of reaction** may occur, with consolidation occurring in the irradiated area, followed by consolidation elsewhere in the same or contralateral lung. In most cases steroid treatment will lead to clearing; relapse may also occur (see also p. 3.31).
(iv) Gross lung changes leading to death may occur if an overdose occurs from omitting radiation filters in the treatment apparatus, or through calculation errors. Fortunately such accidents are rare. The author has seen one or two cases when this happened several years ago, with some fatalities, including a young girl who had a huge neurofibroma containing a few mitoses, but no overt malignancy.
(v) CT and MR studies may often show acute or long standing post-radiation damage, when the chest radiograph is normal.
(vi Apparent widening of the mediastinum due to para-mediastinal lung changes.
(vii) A small pleural reaction or effusion may be present.

Asymptomatic patients are usually best left untreated. Those with dyspnoea or a marked reaction usually respond to steroids. Antibiotics are also often given, as many patients are mildly febrile, and may have secondary infection. In a few there may be a frank complicating pneumonia, sometimes with opportunistic bacteria (see p. 19.7). Steroids may sometimes have to be continued if the post-radiation changes become worse on their withdrawal.

Synergism with some drugs may occur, the radiation effect on the lungs being greater if they are given at the same time. These drugs include bleomycin, adriamycin and cyclophosphamide (see references). The incidence of serious cases is getting rarer as a result of better radiotherapy planning.

Notes on some studies.

Wiernik (1965): wrote 'when radical treatment is given to an intrathoracic lesion, a tumour dose of 4,500 rads can be delivered in five weeks and following such dosage, the clinical syndrome of radiation pneumonitis may develop within a few days of completion of treatment. There is no direct relationship between the total dose and the post-irradiation interval before onset of either acute radiation pneumonitis or subsequent radiation fibrosis. Doses greater than 6,000 rads given in five to six weeks almost invariably lead to severe radiation pneumonitis with a very early onset, whereas dosage of 2,000 to 5,000 rads over four to six weeks only occasionally gives rise to this syndrome and radiographic evidence of radiation fibrosis does not become manifest for at least six months in the majority of cases'.

Sir Stanford Cade (1966): noted that radiation damage to the lungs was first described by Groover et al. (1922) and that most cases followed treatment for breast cancer. Cade quoted Lacassagne (1928) - 'La façon de donner vaut mieux que ce qu'on donne' - may be the answer to the problem of radiation pneumonitis and the finest preventative. Cade continued - 'if I were to write a prescription for the production of post-radiation pulmonary fibrosis, I would suggest : low-voltage, opposing fields, high dose and short time; this would ensure radiation pneumonitis in a large percentage of patients, with fixation of the shoulder in some, fractured ribs in others and always the signature tune of this technique, the inevitable patch of telangiectasia over the scapula and the pectoral area'.

Libshitz et al. (1973): after studying chest radiographs in patients who had had radiotherapy for Hodgkin's disease, concluded that radiation pneumonitis was rarely seen with dosages below 3,000 rads (30 Gy), was variable between 3,000 and 4,000 and was almost invariable above 4,000 rads. At the higher dosage radiation pneumonitis was expected after eight weeks and for every 1,000 rads above this occurred a week earlier.

Ikezoe et al. (1988): from Osaka, Japan studied 17 patients (who had fractionated radiotherapy) repeatedly by CT at short intervals and found that in 13 CT abnormalities were evident within four weeks. In some the changes were invisible or misdiagnosed on chest radiographs. Homogeneous or patchy consolidation was seen, which in four cases extended beyond the treatment fields. It is suggested that these may in part be a sensitivity effect, but may also be a response to scattered radiation. In those not taking steroids, the changes tended to progress from homogeneously increased density or patchy consolidation to discrete consolidation, whilst in those given steroids, the changes tended to regress rapidly. This suggested that acute changes represented reversible early exudative pneumonitis. In a further paper Ikezoe et al. (1990) stated that HRCT gives a clearer demonstration of the post-radiation changes, especially those surrounding the bronchovascular bundle and alongside the chest wall or fissures.

Bell et al. (1988): studied post-irradiation changes in the chest by plain radiographs, CT and isotope lung scans. They found CT to be more sensitive than plain radiographs in detecting the changes. They also found SPECT (see p. 22.8) to be more sensitive than planar views on gamma camera studies. They considered that damage outside the radiation field was related to irradiation of the hilum or mediastinum, which should be avoided wherever possible.

(b) **Chronic lung disease** ('fibrosis' - usually after 6 to 12 months).
These include :
(i) Persisting consolidation within the irradiated area.
(ii) Persisting soft tissue density, fibrosis or fibrous bands blending into the pleural surfaces and/or adjacent mediastinal structures.
(iii) Fibrosis leading to volume loss, fibrotic traction on the mediastinum, hilum, etc. Traction on the inferior phrenic ligament, or partial lung rotation, may give rise to juxta-phrenic peaks (see ps. 2.35-36 & Illus. **JUXTAPHRENIC PEAK**).
(iv) Overlying pleural thickening may sometimes be nodular or appear nodular with a glancing field.
(v) Localised emphysema, bullous formation, bronchiectasis and distortion of the normal intra-thoracic anatomy.
(vi) Fibrotic mass or masses - these may break down and cavitate.
(vii) Loss of pulmonary vascularity - usually seen well on plain radiographs, but also demonstrated by tomography including CT and by lung perfusion studies.

The chronic picture often appears to bear little relation to the severity or duration of the acute radiation pneumonitis. Sometimes later chemotherapy can precipitate a radiation reaction within previously irradiated tissue - **'radiation recall'**. This can happen within hours to days after giving the chemotherapeutic drugs, and a few days to many years after the radiotherapy.

After post-radiation changes have become stable, an alteration in them may indicate complicating infection, or recurrent tumour including lymphangitis carcinomatosa. In the diagnosis of this comparison with previous radiographs is important, followed by CT and biopsy if necessary.

(c) **Other effects.**
(i) The mediastinum may become widened due to mediastinitis (Illus. **POST-RAD CHS MEDIAST**).

(ii) The heart may be pathologically affected, though usually the patients have no symptoms. This may be accompanied by a mild pericarditis. In a few cases valve cusp thickening may be produced and also coronary artery disease.

(iii) Oesophagitis may occur, either as a direct effect of the radiation or from complicating candida or other infection.

(iv) Venous obstruction in the mediastinum, secondary to the fibrosis, most commonly affects the SVC and azygos system and may result in the development of collaterals, including 'downhill oesophageal and para-oesophageal varices' (see p. 18.31). Such obstruction may also be due in part to tumour recurrence, which often does not become manifest until much later.

(vi) Hepatic failure or partial hepatic failure may occur if the liver or the upper part of it is included within a radiation field. With a high right side of the diaphragm, the whole of the liver may be so included and the patient become jaundiced. In the past an isotope colloid scan has show poor uptake of colloid in the affected part of the liver, with a horizontal cut-off border between the normal and irradiated parts - see also liver pseudomasses ps. 17.3 - 4, Fig. 19.3.

(d) **Changes in the chest wall and spine.**

In children who have been irradiated long before (e.g. for tumour within the spine, or at the apex of the chest or upper mediastinum) considerable growth distortion may take place, with the affected side or area remaining smaller - Illus. **POST-RAD HYPOPLASIA**. The patient may develop a severe scoliosis, etc. Modern practice avoids some of the deformities by always treating a whole vertebra, so that loss of height is equal on both sides.

In adults irradiated chest wall tissue may be thinner than on the contralateral side. Also the bones (ribs, scapula, clavicle, etc.) may become atrophic with areas of sclerosis, patchy porosis, a less well defined and thinner cortex and trabecular pattern, which may mimic rib notching (p. 12.29). Not uncommonly the affected bones become brittle and produce fractures which do not heal, leaving gaps between the bone ends, which become poorly defined. Occasionally necrotic pieces of bone may slough through chronic sinuses and be discharged. With severe post-radiation change, particularly in a shoulder, it is not uncommon for secondary atrophic arthritis to occur in the joint, and for secondary atrophic changes to occur distally in the limb - see Illus. **POST-RAD BONES**.

With low voltage radiotherapy the absorbed dose within the bone is much greater than with super voltage, etc. treatment. Also the tumour dose with low voltage may be lowered due to the shielding effect of the bone, sometimes even 3 :1 bone to tumour dose. (Note the analogy with high KV chest radiography - absorption depending more on air/water difference rather than atomic number as with lower KV - see Fig. 1.1, p. 1.1).

The spinal cord is very sensitive to radiation and entry portals are designed as much as possible to obviate damaging it. However, with tumour involving the spine, this may not be possible and radiation levels of direct beam are usually kept below about 3,000 rads (30 Gy), unless it is felt that the patient has little time to live, when increased dosage is sometimes given.

(Radiotherapy damage to the brachial plexus, and arm oedema are discussed on ps. 12.13 - 14).

(e) **Radiation induced tumours** - Illus. **POST-RAD TUMOUR.**

These take three to 20 or more years to develop, and may occur within the chest wall, neck or within the thorax. The best documented are bony tumours and tumours following childhood irradiation of the thymus (see below). Some breast tumours have been blamed on repeated chest radiography and fluoroscopy for monitoring artificial pneumothorax treatment of tuberculosis in the 1930's to 1950's. However the incidence in such cases has been about equal on the two sides and the association seems completely fortuitous. Such is also likely to be the case with lung cancers developing after radiation treatment for breast cancer, but 'scar cancers' (see p. 4.20) are a possibility. No group of cases is common, but the following have been noted:

(i) **Osteogenic sarcoma** - the author has seen three sarcomas of the clavicle in patients who have had radiotherapy for breast carcinoma or lymphoma - the whole bone may disappear or be replaced by a soft tissue mass (Illus. **POST-RAD TUMOUR, Rad Sarcoma Pt. 1a-b**).

(ii) Radiation induced **osteochondromas in young people** when an epiphyseal plate has been included in the treatment field (e.g.. in the upper humerus).

(iii) Haemangiopericytoma in an irradiated axilla (Illus. **POST-RAD TUMOUR, Haemangiopericytoma Pt. 2a-b**).

(iv) **Angiosarcoma** following treatment for lymphoma (Illus. **POST-RAD TUMOUR Rad Sarcoma Pt. 2a-b.**

(v) **Leukaemia** e.g. following previous treatment for ankylosing spondylitis (a memorable case affected a physician colleague) or pelvic disease with extensive bone marrow irradiation.

(vi) **Lymphoma**, especially non-Hodgkin's lymphoma or soft tissue sarcoma.

(vii) Radiation associated malignancies of the **oesophagus**.

(viii)**Tumours in young adults in the mediastinum, neck (particularly the thyroid) or lower face**, resulting from irradiation of a large but normal thymus in infancy (see also ps. 18.18 - 19). Several series have been reported from the USA (mainly New York State). The author has seen a few examples of such tumours in US servicemen. The irradiated field commonly included the neck and skull as well as the thorax!

Thyroid tumours are also being found in young people in the Ukraine and have been ascribed to radioactive fall-out after the Chernobyl accident in April 1986 - see also p. 18.11 and Mould (2000) Chernobyl Record. Brewin (1994 & 2000) however has pointed out the excessive media-driven health scares relating to this accident rather than the reality - 2 acute deaths from the initial steam explosion, 28 firemen etc. being killed by radiation burns, and the children with thyroid tumours have well differentiated papillary tumours, with only about three recorded deaths. The other reactors continued working after the accident - the last closing in late 2000.

Further references.

(a) **Radiation pneumonitis and fibrosis.**

Ross, W. (1956) : Radiation fibrosis of the lungs.

Cooper et al. (1961) : Some consequences of pulmonary irradiation.

Johnson et al. (1968) : Changes in pulmonary arterial perfusion due to intrathoracic neoplasia and lung irradiation.

Bennett et al. (1969) : Bilateral-radiation pneumonitis following treatment of lung cancer.

Talerman (1973) : Foci of atypical epithelial hyperplasia in irradiated human lungs.

Libshitz and Banner (1974) : Spontaneous pneumothorax as a complication of radiation therapy to the thorax.

Gross (1977) : Pulmonary effects of radiation injury.

Prato et al. (1977) : Physiological and radiographic assessment during the development of pulm. radiation fibrosis.

Roswit and White (1977) : Severe radiation injury of the lung.

Twiford et al. (1978) : Recurrent pneumothorax after radiation therapy to the thorax.

Do Pico et al. (1979) : Lung reaction to upper mantle radiation therapy in Hodgkin's disease.

Blane et al. (1981) : Radiation therapy and spontaneous pneumothorax.

Nabawi et al. (1981) : CT of radiation-induced lung injuries.

Pagani and Libshitz (1982) : CT manifestations of radiation induced changes in chest tissue.

Ward and Davies (1982) : Pulmonary aspergilloma after radiation therapy.

Libshitz and Shuman (1984) : CT of radiation-induced pulmonary change.

Harnsberger and Armstrong (1983) : Bilateral supero-medial hilar displacement.

Lever, H. et al. (1984) : Radiation fibrosis mimicking recurrence in small cell carcinoma.

Glazer et al. (1984) : MR may be better than CT for differentiating post-radiation fibrosis from recurrent neoplasm in the lung, by showing different signal characteristics for the two tissues.

Coscina et al. (1986) : CT demonstration of lung changes following tangential beam radiation.

Mah et al. (1986) : Assessment of acute radiation-induced pulmonary changes using CT.

Isaacs et al. (1987) : Massive **haemoptysis** as a late consequence of pulmonary irradiation.

Bell et al. (1988) : Imaging of post-irradiation changes in the chest.

Ikezoe et al. (1988) : CT appearance of acute radiation-induced injury in the lung.

Makker et al. (1989) : Post-irradiation pulmonary fibrosis complicated by aspergilloma and bronchocentric granulomatosis.

Ikezoe et al. (1990) : Acute radiation induced injury - CT evaluation.

Kaufman and Komorowski (1990) Bronchiolitis obliterans - a new complication of irradiation pneumonitis.

de Vuyst et al. (1990) : Lung fibrosis 40 years after Thorotrast thoracic fistulography following bilateral haemothoraces in 1940 - considerable Thorotrast in the lungs at autopsy.

(For lung cancer + other tumours and Thorotrast - see ps. 5.3 & 24.3).

Makker and Barnes (1991) : Fatal haemoptysis from the pulmonary artery - a late complication of lung irradiation.

Travis, S. (1991) : Lung morbidity of radiotherapy.

Davis et al. (1992) : Radiation effects in the lungs - clinical features, pathology and imaging findings - felt that bilateral changes might represent a hypersensitivity pneumonitis, perhaps arising from a radiation-induced release of lung antigens or imbalance among T lymphocyte subsets.

Libshitz (1993) : Radiation changes in the lung.

Lin (1994) : Radiation pneumonitis caused by Y^{80} microspheres used for intra-arterial treatment of a hepatoma - produced crescentic patchy shadowing, mainly peripheral in distribution, but sparing the lung cortex, and more posterior than anterior - similar to that seen in eosinophilia (Illus. **EOSINOPHIL PNEUMONIA**) and presumably due to embolisation of the smaller arteries in the lungs.
Fenlon et al. (1996) : HRCT study of acute and long-term effects of radiotherapy on pulmonary tissue - while the predominant CT pattern at 4 wks. was focal alveolitis, interstitial abnormalities were more common at 4 months.
Deladian (1998) : Striking regression of radiation-induced fibrosis by a combination of pentoxifylline and tocopherol (vitamin E).
Ooi et al. (2000) : Serial HRCT lung changes after 5-field radiation treatment of breast cancer.

(b) Drugs and post-radiation pneumonitis.

Rubin et al. (1958) : Response of radiation pneumonitis to adrenocorticoids.
Parris et al. (1970) : Severe radiation pneumonitis precipitated by withdrawal of steroids.
Castellino et al. (1974) : Latent radiation injury activated by steroid withdrawal.
Einhorn et al. (1976) : Enhanced pulmonary toxicity with bleomycin and radiotherapy in oat-cell lung cancer.
McInerney and Bullimore (1977) : Reactivation of radiation pneumonitis by adriamycin.
Trask et al. (1985) : Radiation induced lung fibrosis after treatment of small cell carcinoma of the lung with very high-dose cyclophosphamide.
Ma et al. (1993) : Recall pneumonitis caused by adriamycin in two children.
Soh et al. (1997) : Delayed radiation pneumonitis induced by chemotherapy (ifosamide and cisplatin) 6 weeks after radiotherapy in a young woman with a mediastinal carcinoma - it responded to IV steroids and antibiotics.
Patz et al. (1994) : Pulmonary drug toxicity following high-dose chemotherapy with autologous bone marrow transplantation.
Wilezynski et al. (1998) : Delayed pulmonary toxicity syndrome following high-dose chemotherapy and bone marrow transplantation for breast cancer.
Connolly et al. (1999) : Thoracic manifestations of breast carcinoma, metastatic disease and complications of treatment - including drug induced alveolitis.

(c) Other post-radiation effects.

Ellis and Stoll (1949) : Herpes zoster after irradiation - can potentiate its effect.
Ward (1965) : Disordered vertebral growth following irradiation.
Dawson (1968) : Growth impairment following radiotherapy in childhood.
Lyons et al. (1973) : Growth impairment following irradiation in one of a pair of monozygotic twins (treated for Wilm's tumour).
Bricout et al. (1985) : Necrosis of the humeral head following radiotherapy for breast neoplasm.
Perrault et al. (1985) : Echocardiographic abnormalities following cardiac radiation.
Wilson et al. (1987) : Subclavian and axillary vein thrombosis following radiotherapy for carcinoma of the breast.
Libshitz (1994) : Radiation changes in bone.
Okada et al. (1998) : Ipsilateral spontaneous pneumothorax after rapid development of large thin-walled cavities in two patients who had undergone radiation therapy for lung cancer.

(d) Radiation induced tumours.

Cahan et al. (1948) : Sarcoma arising in irradiated bone - report of 11 cases.
Court-Brown and Doll (1957) : **Leukaemia** and aplastic anaemia in patients irradiated for **ankylosing spondylitis**.
Court-Brown and Doll (1965) : Mortality from cancer and other causes after radiotherapy for ankylosing spondylitis - of 13,352 patients with ankylosing spondylitis treated by radiotherapy, 25 developed leukaemia (ten times the expected rate).
Darby et al. (1987) : Long term mortality after radiotherapy for **ankylosing spondyliti**s.
Lewis et al. (1988) : Estimated radiation doses to different organs among patients treated for ankylosing spondylitis with a single course of x-rays.
Stevens et al. (1990) : Leiomyosarcoma following irradiation for ankylosing spondylitis.

Berdon et al. (1965) : Unusual benign and malignant sequelae to childhood radiation therapy.
Pifer et al. (1963), Hempelman et al. (1975): Neoplasms following radiotherapy for large **thymus** in childhood.
Phillips and Sheline (1963) : Bone sarcoma following radiotherapy.
Boyer and Navin (1965) : Extraskeletal osteogenic sarcoma complicating radiotherapy.
Hatfield and Schulz (1970) : Post-irradiation sarcoma including 5 cases after x-ray therapy of breast cancer.
Steinfeld and Ross (1976) : Squamous cell lung cancer after post-mastectomy radiotherapy.
Tountas et al. (1979) : Post-irradiation bone sarcoma.

Ron and Modan (1980) : Benign and malignant thyroid neoplasms after childhood irradiation for tinea capitis.

Lynch and Herr (1981) : Sarcoma following radiotherapy for testicular tumours.

Libshitz, J. and Cohen (1982) : Radiation induced osteochondromas.

Smith (1982) : Review of 43 patients who had radiotherapy for various neoplasms (including lymphoma and carcinoma of breast) who developed sarcomas in the irradiated area. 27 were bone sarcomas, and the others soft tissue sarcomas. 14 of the bone sarcomas showed bone destruction, but in the others sclerosis or a mixed pattern was present. In some, peripheral sclerosis was not due to the new tumour, but to post-radiation osteitis. Typical thoracic sites were the clavicle, sternum or ribs. An angiogram may show increased vascularity. Prognosis is usually 'baleful'. Any tumour arising in a radiation field should be biopsied, particularly where there is radiation osteitis. Latent periods ranged from 4 to 27 years.

Ducatman and Scheithauser (1983) : Post-irradiation **neurofibrosarcoma**.

Hay et al. (1984) : Subsequent malignancies in patients irradiated for testicular malignancies.

Redman et al. (1984) : **Leukaemia** following treatment of **germ cell tumours** in men.

Sherrill et al. (1984) : Radiation associated malignancies of the oesophagus.

Stein et al. (1984) : Small cell lung carcinoma 24 years after radiotherapy for breast carcinoma.

(Discussion on possibility of carcinoma of the breast following repeated chest radiographs and fluoroscopy).

Anderson et al. (1985) : **Malignant mesothelioma** following radiotherapy in a 16 year old boy.

Leslie et al. (1986) : Hodgkin's disease during surveillance of stage I testicular teratomas.

Souba et al. (1986) : Radiation induced sarcomas of the chest wall.

Trenker et al. (1986) : Non-Hodgkin's lymphomas following R/T for Hodgkin's disease.

Bleehen (1987) : Insights from radiation treatment for benign disease.

Ironside (1987) : Three cases of osteogenic sarcoma following irradiation for childhood cancer.

Inbar et al. (1988) : Malignant **melanoma** developing in an irradiation field.

Laskin et al. (1988) : Post-radiation soft tissue sarcomas.

Stark et al. (1990) : Development of a pleural osteogenic sarcoma within the field of treatment ten years previously of a Wilm's tumour

Neugut et al. (1994) : Increased risk of lung cancer after breast radiation therapy in cigarette smokers.

Amin and Ling (1995) : Malignant fibrous **histiocytoma** following radiation therapy of fibrous dysplasia.

Shannon et al. (1995) : Malignant pleural **mesothelioma** after radiation therapy for breast cancer.

Rustmeyer et al. (1997) : Radiation induced malignant mesenchymoma of the left anterior chest wall 24 yrs. after treatment of breast cancer. CT showed a large mass containing areas of calcification. Review of chest radiographs taken 2 yrs. earlier showed patchy calcification best seen on the lateral view - it had previously been thought to have been in areas of fibrosis induced by the radiotherapy and in a silicon implant.

Connolly et al. (1999) : Thoracic manifestations of breast carcinoma, metastatic disease and complications of treatment - including radiation induced **osteosarcoma of sternum**.

Sheppard and Libshitz (2001) : Post-radiation sarcomas - 63 cases - including osteosarcoma of the scapula.

(e) **General references**.

Wang et al. (1988) : Cancer among medical diagnostic x-ray workers in China - 50% higher risk - leukaemia, breast, thyroid and skin, but **not** lung cancer.

Jochelson (1990) : Complications of treatment of cancer.

Ross, W. (1990) : Medicolegal aspects of medical radiation exposure - noted the concept of damages for psychological trauma. (Note that following the Moorgate tube station disaster in London on 28 Feb. 1975 in which 42 people died, the damages for psychological trauma (for a lawyer standing on the station platform)were greater than those for physical injury to the victims!).

The author has also seen a severe radiation burn to the hand following prolonged irradiation during fluoroscopic control for the removal of a foreign body - the hand was amputated 25 years later for fear of developing neoplasm (Wright, 1978) - see Illus. **RADIATION OTHER, Radiation hand Pt. 5a-b**.

Husband (1995) : Imaging of treated cancer - Mackenzie Davidson Memorial Lecture.

Malpas (1988) : Cancer - the consequences of cure.

Malpas (1996) : Long-term effects of childhood malignancy - late effects of chemotherapy and R/T may result in growth defects, organ dysfunction or associated second neoplasms - estimated that about 200,000 on USA and 12,000 in UK will have survived childhood malignancies by 2,000. Late cardiac and pulmonary effects - post irradiation pericarditis (53 to 124 months) may lead to constriction, heart failure, coronary heart disease, arrhythmias, etc., stenoses of major branches of aorta. Radiation pneumonitis (could be worse if deposits from Wilm's tumours were treated with Actinomycin D) - also toxic problems with drugs - methotrexate, bleomycin, busulphan, BCNU, etc. Bone changes - shortening of clavicles (following mantle treatment of lymphoma <13 yrs.), limbs, etc., scoliosis. 2nd malignancies - sarcoma, etc., leukaemia, thyroid ca., etc.

Chapter 12 : **The neck, Thoracic Inlet and Outlet, the Axilla and Chest Wall, the Ribs, Sternum and Clavicles.**

The neck and thoracic inlet.
Usually the base of the neck, and in some cases the neck up to the larynx, is displayed on chest radiographs. Several features should be noted -
(I) The larynx - symmetry of cords - ? one paralysed with asymmetry and adducted - (see also recurrent laryngeal nerve palsy - ps. 15.1 - 2) - mostly only the left cord is paralysed.
(ii) The trachea - shape and position - ? displaced or deformed by goitre, etc.
(iii) Calcification - nodes, goitre, etc.
(iv) A 'U' or 'V' shaped air shadow may be noted may be noted between the lower parts of the two sternomastoid muscles particularly in thin subjects, in those with severe emphysema, in patients who have had a laryngectomy, or in those with inspiratory obstruction, e.g. due to a tracheal neoplasm (Illus. **SUPRASTERNAL FOSSA, Trach Ca Pt. 17a**).

The innominate veins run in front of the respective arteries and meet behind the right side of the manubrium sterni to form the SVC.

The subclavian arteries lie behind the innominate and subclavian veins and are crossed by the scalenus anterior muscles (inserting into the scalene tubercle), which divide the arteries into three parts. The second part, behind the muscle, lies in front of Sibson's fascia, before making a groove on the upper aspect of the first rib. The common carotid arteries are related to the trachea. The subclavian and innominate vessels may cause soft tissue shadows on both PA and lateral views - see ps. 12.7 - 8. They may become dilated or tortuous, producing nodules, etc. - see Figs. 1.42 & 12.5.

The vagi and phrenic nerves lie in front of the subclavian arteries and behind the great veins, the phrenics being more lateral. Thus neuromas of these at the thoracic inlet will tend to separate the veins from the arteries (see also Figs. 1.40, 1.42 & 1.43).

On each side the cupola of the pleura covers the lung apex, which normally extends to the level of the posterior aspect of the first rib. It is reinforced by the supra-pleural membrane pressing from the transverse process of C7 to the first rib anteriorly. Deficiencies in these may allow a lung hernia to occur or an apical lipoma to slip upwards during respiration - see also p. 2.39.

On lateral views the pre-vertebral space may be widened with an abscess, (sometimes containing gas) or by a tumour. A goitre may slip behind the trachea and a malignant goitre may not only compress and distort it but also cause thickening of its wall and sometimes show tumour nodules within the tracheal air column.

Thyroid masses are readily investigated by ultra-sound, isotope scans or CT. They may be solid or cystic, more, less or normally active - occasionally secondary deposits (e.g. from oat cell tumours) may lie within the thyroid (see also p. 18.10).

The **'cervico-thoracic' sign** is useful in the differentiation of masses at a pleural apex, and allows viewers to judge from a PA view, whether the mass is anterior or posterior. Because the upper border of the anterior mediastinum ends at the level of the clavicle, whilst that of the posterior mediastinum extends much higher, any lesion with well defined lateral borders (i.e. it indents the lung) that lies above the clavicle must lie posteriorly on a standard PA vies, unless the patient is very kyphotic (see Fig. 12.1e). An anterior lesion adjacent to or within the soft tissues of the neck will not indent the lung and will not produce such a clear border. The trachea forms the dividing line between anterior and posterior parts. See also the use of lordotic views to differentiate cervical masses from those in the in the chest - Fig. 20.6, p. 20.10.

References.
Amory and Sieber (1953) : Supraclavicular shadows.
Simpson et al. (1956) : Changes following radical neck dissection.
Felson (1973) : General reference.
Kattan (1973) : Inspection of the lower cervical spine may allow one to determine whether a chest radiograph has been taken AP or PA, by looking at the lower cervical and upper thoracic vertebrae. On PA views the end plates are usually well seen, whereas on PA views the lateral apophyseal joints and the neural arches are well visualised. The differences are due to the obliquities of the structures to the horizontal plane.
Oliphant et al. (1976) : The cervico-thoracic continuum.
Ominsky and Bernison (1977) : The suprasternal fossa.

Rémy et al. (1981) : General reference.

Vock and Owens (1981) : CT of the normal and pathological thoracic inlet.

Jones, M. et al. (1984) : The cervico-thoracic junction.

Stark, D. et al. (1984) : MR imaging of the neck.

Weinreb et al. (1986) : MR evaluation of mediastinal and thoracic inlet obstruction.

Spring and Schiebler (1991) : Normal anatomy of the thoracic inlet as seen on transaxial MR images. High resolution MR (using anti-aliasing softwear suppresses artefacts from the shoulders) now allows greater detail to be shown at the thoracic inlet. Not only can the major vessels, trachea, etc, be well visualised, but also the lung apices, thoracic duct, and the vagus, phrenic and recurrent laryngeal nerves.

Peh et al. (1993) : Chest radiograph appearances after head and neck flap reconstructive surgery - abnormal axillary and supraclavicular folds, replacement of normal vertical neck fold by an oblique fold, soft tissue mass and loss of facial plane at base of neck.

Wittram and Kenny (1994b) : Radiographic appearances of the larynx on the chest radiograph - one should avoid misrepresentation of normal appearances as incidental disease.

Chong and Fan (2000) : Radiology of the retropharyngeal space.

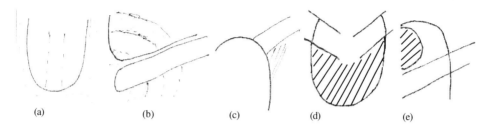

(a)	(b)	(c)	(d)	(e)
'U' shaped suprasternal fossa (Illus. **SUPRASTERNAL FOSSA**	Supra-clavicular fossa produced by the sterno-mastoid and skin overlying the clavicle	Anterior opacity anomalous SVC subclavian artery + coarctation	Middle opacity goitre in juxta-tracheal position	Posterior opacity neurogenic tumour

Fig. 12.1 Suprasternal and supraclavicular fossae and opacities at the thoracic inlet. (The suprasternal fossa may be accentuated following a laryngectomy, and the supra-clavicular fossa is accentuated in thin people and may then dip behind the clavicle.)

Lymph nodes in the neck - Illus. **NODES CERVICAL**.

These are frequently of great importance in studying thoracic disease, as they are often also involved by tumours or other disease spreading into them. Their involvement with tumours usually precludes surgery, and a simple needle biopsy is very easy to perform. It is certainly much easier than of most structures in the thorax, unless they extend into the chest wall or have a good acoustic window - see ps. 20.33 - 34, and should be the **first site to be biopsied if enlarged nodes are found**.

Many cervical nodes that are enlarged are readily palpated (esp. after smearing the neck with ultrasound coupling jelly). Lower cervical nodes are most frequently enlarged with intra-thoracic tumours, but higher ones may also be enlarged. Occasionally metastases spreading up from the thorax will miss the lower nodes, and produce enlargements in those higher up, e.g. below the mastoid processes.

Ultrasound, using a high frequency probe or the '**water bag technique**' (see p. 20.33) will detect many impalpable nodes and also be a good guide for biopsy. It may also show some of the internal structure of nodes, which typically have a cortex, medulla and hilum.

CT - nodes that are surrounded by fat are readily recognised but when covered by muscle layers may be more difficult to differentiate. Nodes < 15 mm and homogeneous in texture are usually considered normal, and > 15 mm probably abnormal, particularly when they have low density areas within them, or adjacent extension into fat. Some may have rim enhancement with contrast medium.

MR may also give good multiplanar demonstration of nodes, and some tissue characterisation with STIR, etc. sequences.

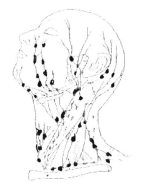

Fig. 12.2.   Lymph nodes of the neck
             (retropharyngeal nodes excluded)
             - reproduced from Som, 1987,
             Radiology, **165**, 593 - 600 with permission.

Cervical node enlargement*, besides being secondary to neoplasms arising in the head and neck, the thorax, abdomen (including pelvis and testes) or the limbs, may also be enlarged with reticuloses, sarcoidosis, or infections such as tuberculosis, chronic throat infections, AIDS, etc. They should always be distinguished from cysts, thyroid enlargements, etc.

Nodal enlargements from thoracic or abdominal malignancies particularly affect the supraclavicular (esp. left) and the internal jugular (or scalene) nodes. The latter, and sometimes other groups, may be affected bilaterally because of lymph vessel anastomoses.

References.

Phillips and Barker (1985) : Extrathoracic (esp. cervical) lymph node aspiration in bronchial carcinoma is an easy procedure. The diagnostic yield is high - about 90%.

Som (1987) : Out of 800 nodes in the body, about 300 are found in the neck. He advocated CT for the localisation of nodal tumour enlargements.

Carvalho et al. (1991) : Accuracy of CT in detecting squamous carcinoma metastasis in cervical lymph nodes - CT was sensitive and specific but missed 37% of cases of extra-nodal spread.

Evans, R. et al. (1993) : The 'linear echogenic hilus' seen within cervical nodes (?due to the converging sinuses within the medulla) may be found in both benign and malignant nodes (present in 46 cases - 7 TB, 12 benign and 27 malignant).

Ahuja et al. (1996) : US in differentiating cervical lymphomatous lymph nodes from cervical metastatic lymph nodes - study of 48 pts. Lymphomatous nodes most commonly occurred in submandibular, submental and deep cervical groups (similar to metastases from oral cavity tumours). Distal enhancement occurred most commonly in NHL. Necrosis (cystic or coagulative) was more common in metastatic nodes.

Na et al. (1997) : Colour Doppler US in the differential diagnosis of cervical lymphadenopathy - unlike nodes with benign reactive disease, 98% of nodes with malignant disease & 100% of TB nodes showed abnormal patterns of nodal vascularity.

Enlarged cervical nodes should always be examined with ultrasound, as they may contain abscesses, which sometimes may be very large (related to an infected tooth, tonsil, etc.). In such a case the abscess may be aspirated with considerable benefit to the patient. They should also be differentiated from **branchial cysts** (which are usually in the mid-line anteriorly) and typically show a coarse granular/fluid appearance, sometimes with layering on CT (Illus. **BRANCHIAL CYST**) or other cysts e.g. thyroid or thyroglossal. Like infected nodes, these are readily checked under ultrasound control by needle aspiration for pus or cellular content (the author has done this very many times, and feels that it is the **only** method of differentiating an infected from an uninfected cyst - unless there is overt inflammatory change around it - and even then feels that it should be aspirated to remove the pus - 'ubi pura, ibi evacua' as with empyemas). Differentiation should also be made from thyroid nodules (including cystic tumours), and rare masses e.g. carotid body tumours, or parathyroid tumours, etc. and neck abscesses (Illus. **NECK ABSCESS**).

*See also ps. 13.23, 15.10 - 11 & 17.10 for examples of other 'sentinel nodes'.

References.
Harnsberger et al. (1984) : Branchial cleft anomalies & their mimics - CT evaluation.
Muller, N. et al. (1984) : Needle aspiration biopsy in cystic papillary ca of the thyroid.
Reynolds and Wolinski (1993) : Sonographic (and CT) appearance of branchial cysts.
Ahuja et al. (1995) : Metastatic cervical lymph nodes in papillary ca thyroid - US + histology.
Ahuja et al. (1998) : Solitary cystic nodal metastases from occult papillary thyroid ca mimicking a branchial cyst.
Tahir et al. (1999) : MR may show fat or fluid contents in branchial cysts.
King et al. (1999) : Adult thyroglossal cysts typically have a high T1 signal due to their high protein content.

Laryngocoeles are dilatations of the laryngeal saccule - a narrow blind pouch arising from the anterior end of the laryngeal ventricle. They extend superiorly into the paralaryngeal space and are bounded laterally by the thyroid cartilage. Internal, external and mixed types occur - most are air-filled, but they can become fluid or pus filled if their necks become obstructed. The sac appears to be a developmental remnant of a larger sac in apes, which is used for rebreathing. Many people with laryngocoeles play wind instruments (esp. trumpets) or lift heavy weights (see also note on p. 2.39 re cervical lung herniae). In some cases dilatation of the sac is due to a concomitant laryngeal neoplasm.

References.
Negus (1929) : The mechanism of the larynx.
Trapnell (1962) : Radiological diagnosis.
Hubbard (1984) : Study of five cases.
Close et al. (1987) : Association with a laryngeal tumour.
Harvey et al. (1996) : Association with a laryngeal tumour.
Morgan and Emberton (1994) : CT.
Kumar et al. (1998) : CT.

The retropharyngeal space - Illus. **RETROPHARYNGEAL TUMOUR**.
    This extends up to the base of the skull and is a potential space for the spread of tumours, haemorrhage, infection and pus. Illus. **TB ASIAN, Pt. 1a-e** shows a huge TB abscess extending up from the posterior thorax.

References.
Davis et al. (1990) : Evaluation of the normal anatomy and diseases of the retropharyngeal space with CT & MR.
Chong and Fan (1998) : Retropharyngeal space - route of tumour spread.

Lung apex - anatomy.
    The lung apex is bounded superiorly by Sibson's fascia, the subclavian vessels, the lower part of the brachial plexus (postero-superiorly), D1 vertebral body, the first rib, costal cartilages and the manubrium sterni.
    Possible spurious tumours due to the **subclavian arteries** are discussed on ps. 12.7 - 8. The subclavian veins may similarly produce apical shadows if dilated and tortuous (see ps. 9.9 - 10). Tumours may occasionally arise from the vessel walls or more commonly from neighbouring structures e.g. sarcomas or haemangiopericytomas, primitive lung tumours and chondromas or chondrosarcomas.

Apical pleural thickening.
    When tuberculosis was more prevalent, it was often thought that nearly all cases of apparent apical pleural thickening (as well as nearly all instances of apical lung disease) were due to this cause. It is now however recognised that the majority of examples of apical 'scarring' are adjacent thickening are due to bullous formation, consequent upon our **upright posture** and **reduced apical perfusion whilst in the erect position**, perhaps in many cases accentuated by the effects of smoking (see also ps. 1.46, 3.29 - 30 & 10.16). The extrapleural apical fat may also thickened.
        Renner and Pernice (1977) termed thickening over the apex of the lung, the **'apical cap'**. They described it as an irregular, non-homogeneous density located at the extreme apex, its lower

border being usually sharply marginated, and frequently tented or undulating. It does not follow a rib and is denser than rib companion shadows (see p. 12.16). It may be unilateral, but is more commonly bilateral. It has a variable height - usually less than 5 mm., and may progress to **calcification** (see also p. 6.24 and Illus. **PL-CALCIFICATION, Pt. 8**) particularly in diabetics and patients with chronic renal failure. In many patients with apical caps in life, no serious abnormality is found at autopsy.

Apparent apical pleural thickening or 'apical caps' may also be seen with a pleural effusion which passes up over the lung apex, due to capillary attraction. Intra-pleural or extra-pleural blood or a haematoma may also be seen following neck injuries, aortic rupture (Fig. 11.3, p. 11.9), etc.

The following table lists some of the causes:

Table 12.1 - causes of true or simulated apical pleural opacity:

Degenerative - due to upright stance, smoking, etc.
Ankylosing spondylitis, Marfan's syndrome.
Inflammatory - TB, aspergillosis, abscess extending from the neck, mediastinum, etc.
Post-radiation fibrosis - esp. after R/T for breast ca. or Hodgkin's disease.
Neoplasm - Pancoast or other superior sulcus tumour, breast deposit - lymphoma, etc.
Trauma - fractured first ribs, leaking aorta or mediastinal veins (the latter not uncommonly occurring with CVP lines), leaking CSF after avulsion injury to upper brachial plexus ('closed fore-quarter amputation).
Fat - mediastinal lipomatosis.
Vascular - collateral vessels in coarctation (Illus. **AORTA COARCTATION, Pt. 8a-c**), normal or dilated subclavian artery, etc.
Neural - neurofibromatosis.
(See examples of the above under Illus. **APICAL PLEURAL THICKENING**).

Further references (see also ps. 12.12-13).
Zilka et al. (1970) : Traumatic subarachnoid - mediastinal fistula.
Cimmino (1974) : The apex pulmonis.
Epstein, B. and Epstein (1974) : Extra-pleural intrathoracic apical traumatic pseudomeningocoele.
Renner et al. (1974) : The apical cap.
Sturm et al. (1974) : Blunt trauma to subclavian artery.
McLoud et al. (1981) : Wrote - 'apical caps, either unilateral or bilateral), are a common feature of advancing age, and are usually the result of subpleural scarring unassociated with other diseases.'
Simeone et al. (1981) : Value of left apical cap in the diagnosis of aortic rupture.
Proto (1989) : The normal apical opacity.
Im et al. (1991) : Apical pleural thickening following TB is largely due to extrapleural fat.
Glazer, H. et al. (1992) : CT often shows fat overlying apical pleural thickening.
McKillop and Beggs (1995) : Apical pleural cap mimicked by post traumatic pseudomeningocoele.

Tumours at the apex of a pleural cavity (Illus. **PANCOAST TUMOUR**).
These may be primary or secondary (breast, mesothelioma, myeloma, thyroid, larynx, etc.), and arise in the lung (most commonly), the chest wall, or the soft tissues adjacent to the apical pleura. Those causing the Pancoast syndrome tend to lie posteriorly, whilst those that are anterior are often clinically 'silent'.

Teixeira (1983) posed the question "what is the superior pulmonary sulcus?", because Pancoast thought that the tumour arose from primitive embryonic material in the apex of a pleural cavity and not from the lung. Others e.g. Paulson (1975) and Fraser and Paré (1977) considered the pulmonary sulcus to be the depression in the lung caused by the subclavian artery. Such however is surely absurd, as there are several sulci of the apex of the lung, caused by the SVC, 1st ribs, oesophagus. etc. Pancoast's description "of a peculiar neoplastic entity found in the upper portion of the pulmonary sulcus of the thorax" clearly referred to the area of the lung apex and the covering structures.

The **Pancoast** (or '**superior sulcus**') **tumour** was first described by Pancoast in 1924, when he reported five cases. He gave details of another nine cases in 1932. Although Pancoast originally thought that these tumours were sarcomas arising in the pleural apex, they are essentially peripheral lung tumours which have spread into the apical chest wall. Their positions in the lung apex (anterior, posterior, medial or lateral) and the degree of spread, will determine the likelihood of nerve involvement. Tumours spreading posteriorly, and postero-medially tend to involve the brachial plexus most often, giving rise to a lower brachial plexus lesion (mainly T1) with severe pain, loss of sensation over the upper arm and chest, loss of power in the small muscles of the hand, involvement of the lower cervical sympathetic, leading to **Horner's syndrome*** and bony erosion of the posterior ribs and adjacent vertebral bodies. One presumes that as adhesions are common at the lung apex and as pleural movement during respiration is minimal at this site and the space is small, spread of tumour across the apical pleura can occur here more easily than in other places unless adhesions are present. Problems occur in the differentiation from tuberculosis (Illus. **TB+CA LUNG**), the demonstration of bone erosion or the peripherally situated tumour, particularly if it lies anteriorly. Pain or a neurological lesion should prompt careful radiography, tomography and CT if these appear negative. CT is a good method for showing these lesions, but MR is being used in some centres, as it can give clear coronal sections. A bone scintigram may be useful, but if there is little or no bone destruction it may be normal; also total destruction of a first rib may give rise to the rib being 'absent' on the bone scan.

Additional plain views are sometimes useful, but apical or lordotic views are frequently misleading. Tomograms and CT sections give the best demonstration of disease in the lung apex, and show the position of an apical tumour, whether it is situated medially (where it may affect the nerves, including the sympathetic chain and spine), posteriorly where it may extend into a rib, laterally where it may also affect the brachial plexus, or anteriorly when the top of the sternum or the anterior part of the first rib may be eroded.

Direct spinal column involvement, unless gross (Illus. **PANCOAST TUMOUR Pts. 13 & 23**) is often difficult to demonstrate without tomograms or CT. Localised views or tomograms, especially in the AP projection, may show erosion of the lateral border of a vertebral body, of a transverse process or the neck of a rib. Occasionally local spread will give rise to spinal cord compression and paraplegia (see Illus. **PANCOAST TUMOUR Pt. 23**).

The demonstration of chest wall involvement usually implies a poor prognosis, but the author has seen a few patients who have shown a very good response to radiotherapy, with recalcification of the eroded bone and long survival, in one case, over 30 years and a second over 15 years.

In considering the differential diagnosis, it is worth remembering that **tuberculous bone erosion is usually painless**, whereas **erosion due to tumour is commonly very painful. Bilateral disease** may be due to e.g. tuberculosis on one side and Pancoast on the other (Illus. **PANCOAST TUMOUR Pts. 21a-b & 34**). A case of bilateral Pancoast tumours (in association with asbestosis) was reported by Schabel et al. (1979) and 10 by Milleron et al. (1979). The author has also seen two cases of bilateral apical lung tumours, one synchronous and the other metachronous. A rare bilateral case in a young woman was due to bilateral haemangiopericytomas (see p. 5.10).

Non-neoplastic causes of Pancoast's syndrome are rare, but **include tuberculosis, fungal infection, hydatid cysts and trauma.**

* Other causes of a Horner's syndrome include damage to the cervical sympathetic from secondary breast cancer, radiotherapy, fibrosis, post-surgery, traction with the after-coming head in breech delivery, etc. - see also p. 12.6.

Use of pneumothorax in the assessment of apical tumours (see also p. 14.26).
Rockoff (1982) pointed out that an 'accidental pneumothorax' during biopsy of a supposed Pancoast tumour may show that the apical lung lesion is in fact separate from the chest wall and not a Pancoast tumour. This may happen even when the patient has experienced brachial plexus type pain - presumably as a result of nerve irritation, rather than actual infiltration (Illus. **PNX&TUMOUR, Pt. 6**). Wilson et al. (1985) reported that a spontaneous pneumothorax revealed an apical haematoma in a young man, which simulated an apical tumour mass on plain radiographs; it also gave a semi-solid appearance on ultrasound.

Further references.

(a) **Tumours**
Herbert and (1946) : Tumour of the thoracic inlet producing the Pancoast syndrome - report of 17 cases.
Hilarious et al. (1974) : The value of preoperative radiation therapy in apical cancer of the lung.
 et al. (1974) : Pulmonary **needle biopsy** in the diagnosis of Pancoast tumours - diagnosed 26 of 27 cases.
Paulson (1975) : Superior sulcus tumours - 92 patients.

Miller, J. et al. (1979) : Carcinoma of the superior pulmonary sulcus.

Wilson et al. (1979) : **Myeloma** presenting with left sided Pancoast's syndrome + weakness of left hand.

Webb et al. (1981c) : **CT** in superior sulcus tumours.

Johnson et al. (1982) : Pancoast's syndrome and **small cell lung cancer**.

O'Connell et al. (1983) : Review of 29 patients presenting with Pancoast tumours at Mass. General Hospital (1970 - 1980) PA & lateral films - apical cap in 15 and apical mass in 14.

Brenner et al. (1984) : Pancoast's syndrome in **multiple myeloma**.

Shaw (1984) : Pancoast's syndrome.

Anderson et al. (1986) : Factors affecting survival in superior sulcus tumours.

Aisner et al. (1988) : Bilateral apical masses due to **sympathetic chain granular cell tumours.**

Heelan et al. (1989) : **CT and MR** imaging in 31 cases of superior sulcus tumour. Coronal and sagittal MR more accurately showed their soft tissue extent.

McLoud et al. (1989) : **MR of superior sulcus carcinoma** in ten patients - chest wall invasion or extension into the base of the neck was shown in five, and into the mediastinum in three. There was good definition between tumour and other soft tissues (esp. between fat and tumour). It gave a good demonstration of subclavian artery encasement, but was poor for showing bone erosion.

Takasugi et al. (1989) : Superior sulcus tumours - the role of imaging.

Wang et al. (1989) : Pancoast syndrome in an elderly man with a left apical **malignant lymphoma.**

Rabano et al. (1991) : **Thyroid carcinoma** presenting as Pancoast's syndrome.

Freundlich et al. (1996) : MR imaging of apical tumours - illustrations included normal anatomy, carcinomas (confined to the lung or spreading into adjacent tissues), a Schwannoma and a granulomatous apical lung lesion.

Muscolino et al. (1997) : Stage III lung cancer classified as Pancoast tumour, is best treated by R/T, combined radio-surgical treatment being reserved for pts. with potentially resectable cancer without N_2 disease and/or malignant invasion of the first rib.

(b) **Other causes of Pancoast syndrome** (Aspergillosis, hydatid cysts, etc.)

Stathatos et al. (1969) : Pancoast's syndrome due to **hydatid cysts** of the thoracic outlet.

Aletras and Papaconstantinou (1982) : Pancoast's syndrome following an intra-pleural rupture of a hepatic **echinococcus cyst.**

Simpson et al. (1986) : Pancoast's syndrome associated with invasive **aspergillosis**.

Campbell et al. (1989) : Horner's syndrome caused by an **intercostal chest drain**.

Gottetrer et al. (1990) : Pancoast's syndrome caused by **pulmonary hydatid cyst** at left apex in a boy of 15.

The innominate and subclavian arteries (and veins).

The subclavian artery may be seen on plain chest radiographs at either apex, and on one or both sides, but more commonly on the left, in about 40% of patients. It is seen as a curved poorly defined homogeneous shadow - 3 to 4 cm in length crossing the upper intercostal spaces, and the left is seen where it passes over and indents the upper medial aspect of the left lung. It may in part be overlapped by the aortic arch, as this is more cranial than the origin of the subclavian artery. Its origin may also merge with the aorto-pulmonary stripe (see p. 1.13). The second part, which lies behind the scalenus anterior muscle, sometimes has calcification in its wall, giving rise to a curvi-linear shadow just behind the lung apex, and lying just above and overlying the first rib. This most commonly happens when the artery is somewhat dilated and/or tortuous in hypertensive patients, or is dilated with collaterals in association with coarctation. Occasionally such a shadow is due to a left innominate artery.

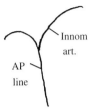

Fig. 12.3 Shadow of a left innominate artery merging into the aorto-pulmonary line.

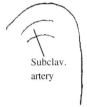

Calcification in the left subclavian artery, producing curvi-linear shadows just below the left lung apex.

On the right, the innominate artery is usually surrounded by mediastinal fat, and only occasionally forms a separate identifiable structure on plain radiographs. In hypertensive patients it may be buckled, and when this happens it may simulate a mediastinal mass.

Like the left, the right subclavian artery may produce a rather indistinct rounded nodule just below the right lung apex, where the artery passes behind the scalenus anterior muscle and where it indents the lung. Either subclavian artery may be visualised by a pneumothorax or pneumomediastinum. The subclavian veins do not normally 'groove' the lung apices as the arteries do, but may do this if they become dilated or tortuous.

Blockage of these vessels may occur in relation to tumours (especially veins - see SVC syndrome p. 9.6) or arteries affected by cervical ribs (ps. 12.9 -10), Takayasu's disease, etc.

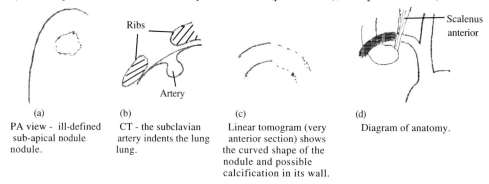

(a)	(b)	(c)	(d)
PA view - ill-defined sub-apical nodule nodule.	CT - the subclavian artery indents the lung lung.	Linear tomogram (very anterior section) shows the curved shape of the nodule and possible calcification in its wall.	Diagram of anatomy.

Fig. 12.4 The right subclavian artery at the right lung apex.

The subclavian arteries may also be visualised by real-time ultrasound, with a curvi-linear probe held over a water-bag placed just above the clavicle. This is a very convenient method, and using it the author has seen two cases of elderly women who had haematomas adjacent to (or false aneurysms) which had arisen from the left subclavian artery (or small adjacent vessels) as a result of their disabled husbands 'grabbing' them just medial to the left shoulder as they tried to help to pull them up. Presumably the husbands finger-tips caused the injuries. In both cases there was a spontaneous recovery. Illus. **SUBCLAVIAN ARTERY, Clavicle haemat, Pt. 1a-b)** shows one of these, the other lady's husband had had a severe stroke.

Fig. 12.5 Buckling of the innominate artery mimicking an upper mediastinal tumour. The position of these vessels on lateral views is discussed on ps. 1.30 - 31. Buckling of the left innominate vein, producing a spurious anterior mass is shown in Fig. 1.42c.

The subclavian veins are affected by disease processes which affect the SVC - see p. 9.6. Sometimes the left innominate vein has an anomalous course - descending laterally on the left side of the aorta and crossing the mediastinum at the level of the AP window, then passing behind the ascending aorta to the right to join the right innominate vein to form the SVC.

References.

Gondos (1961) : The Roentgen image of the subclavian artery in the pulmonary apex.
Schneider and Felson (1961) : Buckling of the innominate artery simulating a right apical lung tumour.

Sturm et al. (1974) : Blunt trauma to subclavian artery.
Christensen et al. (1978) : Buckling of the innominate artery simulating aneurysm and tumour.
Tamaki et al. (1978) : Buckling of the innominate artery simulating a right apical lung tumour.
Subramanyan and Horii (1984) : Sonographic demonstration of buckling of the great vessels of the neck.
Austin (1986) : Invagination of the left subclavian artery into the left upper lobe - a normal variant.
Proto and Chaliff (1986) : Apical opacity - a normal finding on PA chest radiographs.
Proto (1992) : Anatomic understanding of newer observations on conventional chest radiography.
Takada et al. (1992) : Anomalous L brachiocephalic vein - CT findings.
Sudhindran (1999) : Calcified and thrombosed large old traumatic left subclavian artery aneurysm compressing the trachea and brachial plexus.
Hughes et al. (1999) : Congenital arterio-venous malformations arising from the subclavian artery presenting in adult life.

The axillae and thoracic outlets.
    These important parts of the upper thorax include the nerves and vessels to the upper limbs, lymph nodes draining the breast, upper chest walls and upper limbs, etc. All of these may be affected by disease e.g. arteries by the scalenus anterior /cervical rib /band syndrome, the veins by thrombus or thrombosis, and the nodes by spread of breast tumour, melanoma, AIDS, etc. Nerve lesions are far more common than vascular - almost fifty to one. Trauma may be the cause in some cases - fractures of first ribs, avulsion injuries of the brachial plexus, etc.

Normal anatomy.
    The subclavian artery and the lower trunk of the brachial plexus run across the upper surface of the first rib, posterior to the scalene tubercle, whilst the vein lies anterior to it. The clavicle lies just above these. A cervical rib or band is present in about 1% of the population, but symptoms arise in under 10%. Up to half of the cases have the anomalies bilaterally.
    The brachial plexus is formed from the anterior rami of C5 to T1 nerve roots, which pass behind scalenus anterior, and unite to form the nerve trunks at the lateral border of the muscle. The trunks in turn give rise to the cords, which divide into the radial, median and ulnar nerves, as well as smaller branches. In the caudal aspect of the axilla, the three peripheral nerves have a similar relationship to the axillary artery as the cords from which they arise, with the exception of the medial root of the median nerve. The branches from the lateral cord lie lateral to the axillary artery, branches from the medial cord are medial and branches of the posterior cord lie posteriorly (Fig. 12.6). Unfortunately, due to their oblique downwards course, these relationships cannot all be visualised by CT, though they are more easily shown by MR.
    Asymmetry on CT sections is not uncommon, due to asymmetric positioning of the two shoulders or due to minor anatomical variations which are not uncommon. The anatomy is altered as a result of surgery, but very little by lymph node sampling.
    Scalene nodes are not easily differentiated from muscles and often look like enlarged muscles on CT.

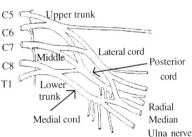

Fig. 12.6 The brachial plexus.
(Reproduced from Blair et al., 1987,
Radiology, **165**, 763 - 767 with permission).

Lesions caused by cervical ribs, vascular abnormalities and tumours.
    Aneurysms of the subclavian arteries may be caused by pressure from the scalenus anterior muscle or a cervical rib or band; others may be caused by whiplash injuries, injuries to the clavicle, etc., pressure from osteochondromas or follow intra-arterial manipulation or cannulation. The veins may suffer primary or secondary thrombosis from pressure, spreading thrombosis, etc.

Similarly a long 'drooping' C7 transverse process and scalene muscle spasm may narrow the scalene triangle causing pressure on the nerves and vessels.

Intra-thoracic tumours may also affect both nerves and vessels, particularly Pancoast tumours, secondary tumours involving the apex of a pleural cavity, masses arising from the lower cervical nodes, the upper parts of the brachial plexuses (esp. neurofibromas) or from vessels.

The **'subclavian steal' syndrome** is caused by thrombus blocking the first part of a subclavian artery, with a collateral blood supply to the arm partly via the circle of Willis, and retrograde flow down the vertebral artery. Exercising the arm may cause cerebral and cerebellar ischaemia - See Illus. **SUBCLAVIAN STEAL**.

Plain radiographs may reveal soft tissue masses, but tomography, including CT and MR , may also be required the last showing the patency of vessels without the need for formal angiography. Ultrasound is also invaluable for showing the size and patency of the vessels - see Illus. **RIB CERVICAL, Pt. 10d.**

Further illustrations of vascular problems associated with cervical ribs are shown in Illus. **RIB CERVICAL** and **SUBCLAVIAN ARTERY.**

Fig. 12.7   Post-stenotic dilatation of the right subclavian artery distal to a stricture caused by the scalenus anterior (band) syndrome. Such an aneurysm may thrombose or contain thrombus. This may cause emboli into the upper limb vessels, and thrombus may extend centrally to involve the vertebral artery.

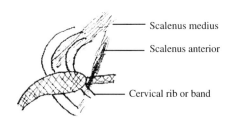

Scalenus medius

Scalenus anterior

Cervical rib or band

Injuries to the subclavian and axillary arteries from fractures of the clavicle or upper humerus are illustrated in Illus. **AXILLARY ARTERY** and **SUBCLAVIAN ARTERY** - see also Illus. **CLAVICLE FRACTURE** and p. 12.40 - clavicular fractures although commonly regarded as trivial can sometimes prove fatal!

References.
Telford and Stopford (1931) : Vascular complications of the cervical rib.
Hill (1939) : Vascular anomalies of the upper limb associated with cervical ribs.
Rob and Standeven (1958) : Arterial occlusion complicating thoracic outlet compression syndrome.
Fisher (1961) : A new vascular syndrome 'the subclavian steal'.
Lang (1965) : Arteriographic diagnosis of the thoracic outlet syndrome.
Weibel and Fields (1967) : Arteriographic studies of thoracic outlet syndrome - examinations with the affected upper limb in the positions in which symptoms were experienced.
Nelson and Davis (1969) : Thoracic outlet compression syndrome - arterial and venous disorders.
Adler and Hooshmand (1973) : Angiographic spectrum of the thoracic outlet syndrome, with emphasis on mural thrombosis and emboli and congenital vascular abnormalities, etc.
Kelly (1979) : Thoracic outlet syndrome.
Bilbey et al. (1989) : Evaluation of the thoracic outlet syndrome with CT.
Ohkawa et al. (1992) : MR angiography of the thoracic outlet syndrome.
Sidhu and Morarji (1995) : Variant of subclavian steal syndrome.

The first ribs are short, broad and relatively thick, and lie in a protected position at the base of the neck. Their heads articulate posteriorly with the upper part of either side of the first thoracic vertebra. Each first rib has two tubercles, one posterior and just lateral to the neck (which points upwards and backwards and which bears an articular facet for articulation with the transverse process of D1), and a second mores anteriorly (between the grooves for the subclavian artery and vein) where the scalenus anterior muscle is inserted - the **'scalene tubercle'**. The costo-clavicular ligament normally connects the first costal cartilage with the under surface of the medial end of the clavicle and in some individuals there may be a small articular joint where the first rib so articulates, producing the **'rhomboid fossa'** - see also p. 12.40 and Illus. **RHOMBOID FOSSA.**

The clavicles cross the first ribs, with the subclavian vessels lying between them, where they may be injured.

Arbuthnot Lane (1885), in an article extending to 118 pages, pointed out that the first ribs, enduring greater stress than any of the other ribs, are the first to show calcification and ossification of their cartilages (thus giving rise to the most common 'idiot tumours' - see ps. 6.27 & 12.22 and Illus. **IDIOT TUMOUR**).

Blair Hartley (1959) studied first rib stresses and noted that "the region of the first rib and its cartilage tends to be one of the diagnostic radiologist's 'blind spots'". He emphasised the necessity of considering these as a 'whole living unit', since the first ribs transmit more energy than any of the other ribs from the sternum to the spine and verse versa, and that this happens both with respiration and other applied strains or forces (see Fig. 12.9b).

In youth the first costal cartilage are pliant, and the spine and its ligaments are resilient, thus ensuring adequate 'give'. When the cartilages calcify, arthrodial joints may form within the ossifying cartilage, the sites being inconstant - sometimes adjacent to the sternum, and sometimes nearer the costo-chondral junction. When inadequate a second joint may form.

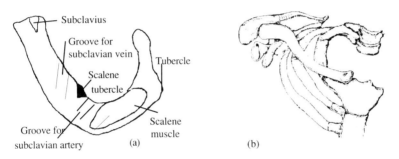

Fig. 12.8 (a) Anatomy of the left first rib (superior aspect). (b) Clavicle and first rib relationships.

First rib fractures.
(a) **Traumatic fractures.**
Fractures of the first ribs, when associated with trauma, are often indicators of potentially dangerous injuries to the adjacent major vessels and nerves. Whenever a complicating vascular lesion seems likely (as evidenced by a haematoma over the lung apex on plain chest radiographs, a reduced or absent radial pulse, distal emboli, pleural effusion, etc.), angiography should be carried out. Such injuries (which occur particularly in motor cyclists or car drivers) may be bilateral, and the affected ribs may show more than one fracture. The clavicle is often also fractured. The vessels and nerves may be crushed by a 'scissors type' mechanism between the clavicle and the first rib. If the posterior part of the rib is fractured, then the more anterior part may be levered upwards by the scalenus medius muscle, squashing the vessels and nerve between the rib and the clavicle. Less commonly the jagged edges of an anterior fracture of a first rib may do this directly, as may a fracture of the clavicle.

(b) **Spontaneous or stress fractures.**
As noted above considerable force is transmitted between the spine and the sternum by the first ribs, and both the scalenus anterior and medius muscles are attached to them. During violent muscle contractions, e.g. associated with sneezing, coughing or heavy lifting, especially if repetitive, stress fractures may occur. These were first studied in recruits to the British Army in the Second World War by Alderson (1944). Illus. **RIB FRACTURE, Pt. 7** illustrates bilateral stress fractures of the first ribs on a CT section.

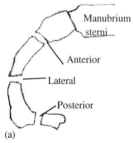

(a)

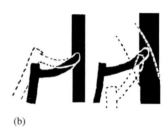

(b)

Fig. 12.9   Diagram showing the common positions of fractures of the first ribs.

Reproduction of Hartley's diagram (1959, with permission from Brit. J. Radiology) illustrating the 'link' function of the first rib and how it transmits force applied to the sternum or the vertebral column. (see also osseous pinch injury to the aorta - p. 11.6).

<u>Trauma to the thoracic outlet</u> may damage the brachial plexuses as well as the subclavian etc. vessels. Three patterns of injury are evident in closed traction lesions. The most common follows distraction of the head from the shoulder, when preganglionic injury is very likely. The clavicle may be depressed against the first rib crushing nerves, as well as vessels. In the third group the force is expended on the lower part of the plexus and is associated with fractures of the humerus or scapula. Many are associated with motor cycle injuries.

Other cases are caused by penetrating injuries - missiles, knives, glass, etc. A few follow surgery for tumours, cervical rib excision, node biopsy or sympathectomy.

In severe cases early repair or grafting is usually recommended i.e. before fibrosis may occur

Subdural tears and traumatic pseudo-meningocoeles may follow nerve root injuries. These may be shown as small or larger sacs or fistulae at myelography. They may be single or multiple and usually indicate fairly severe past trauma. Most acute leaks of CSF usually seal off, but in a few cases the leakage remains chronic (see Illus. **BRACHIAL PLEXUS, Pts. 4 & 5**).

<u>References.</u>
Breslin (1937) : Fractures of the first rib unassociated with fractures of other ribs.
Alderson (1944) : Fractures of the first ribs in army recruits, (1947) : Further observations on fracture of the first rib.
Jenkins (1952) : Spontaneous fractures of both first ribs.
Holmes and Netterville (1956) : Complications of first rib fracture, including one case each of tracheo-oesophageal fistula and aortic arch aneurysm.
Freiberger and Mayer (1964) : Ununited bilateral fatigue fractures of the first ribs.
Curran and Kelly (1966) : Stress fractures of the first rib.
Fisher and Reinhoff (1966) : Subclavian artery laceration resulting from fractured first rib.
Weiner and O'Dell (1969) : Fractures of the first rib associated with injuries to the clavicle.
Galbraith et al. (1973) : Fracture of the first rib associated with laceration of the subclavian artery.
Pierce et al. (1975) : Special hazards of first rib fractures - patient with haemothorax six days after the injury - an arteriogram showed a false aneurysm of the right subclavian artery with extravasation. A vein graft was carried out, but ten days later he had a recurrent haemothorax, as the graft had been torn by the jagged rib fracture.
Phillips et al. (1981) : First rib fractures - incidence of vascular injury and indications for arteriography. 45 patients with 49 fractures of the first ribs caused by trauma had angiography, and 7 had serious vascular injuries.
Fisher et al. (1981) : Arteriography and the fractured first rib.
Livoni and Barcia (1982) : Fractures of the first & second ribs - incidence of vascular injury relative to fracture type.

Mendelsohn et al. (1957) : Myelographic demonstration of brachial plexus avulsion.
Lester (1961) : Myelography in avulsion of the brachial plexus.
Varley (1961) : Importance of cervical myelography in cervical and upper thoracic nerve root avulsion.
Wilson and Jumer (1962) : Traumatic spinal-pleural fistula.
Davies et al. (1966) : Myelography in brachial plexus injury.
Epstein and Epstein (1974) : Extrapleural intrathoracic apical traumatic pseudomeningocoele.
Kaiser et al. (1983) : Thoracic inlet mass due to cervical root avulsion diagnosed by CT.
Birch (1984) : Traction lesions of the brachial plexus.

Ochi et al. (1994) : MR is as accurate as myelography in diagnosing nerve root avulsion at C5-C6 in traumatic brachial plexus injury (60 - 70%). However in the absence of a traumatic meningocoele a confident diagnosis of root diagnosis is difficult. Also found that because of their steep obliquity it was difficult to image C8 & T1 nerve roots.
Pender et al. (1997) : MR in brachial plexus injury - diagnosis depends on noting nodes & finding pseudomeningocoeles adjacent to the injured nerve roots.
Potterton et al. (1999) : MR of the axilla after treated breast cancer - a mass is likely to represent recurrent disease, but in 20% this may be fibrosis secondary to radiotherapy or surgery. An abnormal neurovascular bundle suggests recurrence but high-signal can be due to recurrence or fibrosis. Streaking or a 'dirty axilla' may also indicate recurrent disease or fibrosis.

The axillae - nodes, nerve lesions, fibrosis and tumour infiltration (Illus. **AXILLA** & **BRACHIAL PLEXUS**).

The axillae are usually fairly accurately examined by palpation, but great difficulty is experienced in obese subjects or in injured, oedematous or scarred axillae. In patients who have had tumours (especially **breast carcinomas**), both radiotherapy and surgery can injure the various tissues including the lymphatics and oedema may be due to this cause or recurrence. Radiotherapy can cause much fibrosis as well as tissue necrosis and endarteritis. Neuropathy may also follow radiotherapy or be due to recurrence of tumour. In these patients it may be impossible to feel whether nodules, enlarged lymph nodes or recurrent tumour are present. For this reason soft tissue radiography using mammographic film, lymphangiography, ultrasound, CT or MR or a combination of some of these techniques is also employed to try to elucidate the pathological anatomy. However, no non-invasive investigation will discern microscopic tumour recurrence, and even fairly advanced recurrence may be very difficult to recognise in the presence of severe scarring. The simplest method is ultrasound, using a high frequency probe, or a lower frequency one with a water bag. The subclavian and axillary vessels can usually be identified and most nodal enlargements. Conventional radiography will only show the grossest lesions, but soft tissue views of the axillae can demonstrate nodes of about 1 cm. in size if they are surrounded by fat.

Lymphography via the hand has also been useful for demonstrating axillary node metastases, especially when followed by CT. Occasionally this route may also show some mediastinal lymph nodes. When swelling is present in an upper limb, caution should be exercised in the amount of contrast medium oil that is injected, to avoid making the obstruction and oedema worse - usually 2 to 3 ml will suffice (with an infusion rate at half the normal speed for the lower limbs). Sometimes after radical axillary node removal as with a radical mastectomy, the number of remaining patent lymph trunks in the arm may be very small, and give rise to the oedema. (See Illus. **AXILLA, Pt. 2a-e** & **LYMPHATICS, Pt. 17, 18, 19a-b & 26**).

Using CT it is essential to examine not only the axillae but also the lower neck, the thoracic outlets and anterior chest wall as well as the axillae because abnormalities may be seen in all of these areas. Thin (2 - 5 mm) thick sections at 5 mm intervals are essential when only small sized abnormalities are expected, or much fibrosis is present (e.g. after radiotherapy for breast neoplasm, reticulosis or an apical lung tumour). The biggest problems are (a) understanding the anatomy and (b) distinguishing fibrosis from tumour recurrence, Large nodes may be recognised on CT sections e.g. the interpectoral (or **Rotter's**) node (p. 12.19 & Illus. **ROTTER'S NODE**), and smaller ones may be outlined by surrounding fat, or have faint contrast enhancement. When embedded in fibrous tissue their identification is very difficult with CT. A similar difficulty is with infiltrating tumour sheets. For these MR appears to have considerable advantage, particularly with STIR sequence on which tumour is often portrayed in white against the grey background of other tissues. PET scanning may also help.

For differentiating vessels from nerves and other tissues, IV contrast agents should be employed, preferably in large dosage just prior to and continuing by infusion during the examination. The vessels and nerves largely run obliquely downwards and laterally and on most sections only small parts of these are portrayed. Streak artefacts may be caused by too dense IV contrast , metallic foreign bodies or by bones, particularly the humeral heads.

In a few cases the author has performed HRCT following arm lymphography, particularly patients with melanoma or breast carcinoma (Illus. **LYMPHATICS, Pt. 19**). For illustrations of axillary nodes see Illus. **AXILLARY NODES**.

Brachial plexopathy - Illus. **BRACHIAL PLEXUS**.

Post radiation plexopathy tends to occur 12 to 18 months after radiotherapy treatment for breast tumours and is not entirely dose related, some patients having more severe changes with similar dosage. It is mainly seen in patients who have had the axillae and supraclavicular areas treated to -'sterilise' possible metastases there from cancer of the breast, but may also be seen in some patients who have had radiotherapy for reticulosis or apical lung cancer. Clinically it is almost impossible to distinguish it from pressure or nerve invasion due to tumour recurrence, which may occur even years later. Paresthesiae are common to both post-radiation and malignant groups, whilst pain is more characteristic of malignant involvement. With malignant disease, sensory symptoms tend to be more prominent than a motor deficit, but in some motor weakness may predominate.

Radiological differentiation, even on CT, is also difficult, in the absence of any large nodes or tumour masses. Both will give a 'streaky fibrotic' appearance in the axillary fat, and **both may be present together**. Radiotherapy may also cause considerable apical lung change, muscle and other tissue atrophy, including post-radiation changes in the underlying bones (ribs, clavicles, etc.).

Ultrasound has been used for a long time to assess breast 'lumps' (cystic or solid) and for the detection of enlarged axillary nodes. Walsh et al. (1994) used colour Doppler ultrasound studies of the axillae in 80 patients with breast carcinoma and showed axillary node metastases due to increased peripheral hypervascularity in 23 patients (nodes 4 - 13 mm in diameter) with 10 negatives (although nodes involved) and one false positive. False positives appeared to be associated with relatively avascular tumours.

Even secondary deposits elsewhere do not mean that brachial plexus disease is metastatic, nor does a negative surgical biopsy exclude it. Vertebral body metastases with collapse can produce a kyphosis leading to pressure on the nerve roots and causing brachial plexus damage.

The early stages of microscopic metastatic involvement of the brachial plexus will not be detected by CT and patients with this are likely to have no symptoms.

Concomitant Horner's syndrome.

Although an accompanying Horner's syndrome is usually regarded as diagnostic of malignant spread, and is not seen in patients with nerve damage secondary to irradiation (Kori et al., 1981. Cooke et al., 1988b), this is not always correct. A post-operative Horner's syndrome is often transient. An example caused by aggressive fibromatosis was described by Gebarski et al. (1982).

Other causes of plexopathy.

Vertebral body metastases with collapse can produce a kyphosis leading to pressure on the nerve roots causing brachial plexus damage.

Table 12.2 Lesions which may be found in the thoracic outlet, axillae and anterior chest wall.

Nodal enlargements	- bronchus neoplasm
	- breast etc. neoplasm
	- reticulosis
	- infections e.g. glandular fever, AIDS, infected hand, etc.

[Always examine the lower neck as well, as neck nodes are often more easily biopsied.]
Soft tissue spread of metastases   - breast, bronchus, etc.
Fibrosis, particularly after radiotherapy - may also cause nerve damage.

Nerve damage	- compression by tumour - note that a Horner's syndrome is nearly always caused by malignant disease (Pancoast lung tumour, secondary breast, etc. tumour)
	- avulsion injury
	- neuroma.
Artery	- thrombosis, pressure (cervical rib/band syndrome or tumour, e.g. haemangiopericytoma).
Vein	- thrombosis, pressure from enlarged nodes /trauma, etc.
Bone erosion	- spine, ribs and clavicles is most often due to malignant disease, either metastatic to, or from direct extension into bone, but tumours arising in bone (including myeloma) and abscesses also have to be considered.

Further references.

Thomas and Colby (1971) : Brachial plexopathy - radiation induced or metastatic.

Kalisher (1975) : Xeroradiography of axillary lymph nodes.

Gebarski et al. (1982) : CT of brachial plexus - studied 50 patients with no neurological disease, and compared the CT anatomy with cadaver cross sections. They also examined a further ten who had brachial plexopathy, seven of whom showed disease affecting the brachial plexus, due to localised pressure from tumour or fibrosis in the surrounding fat or from a localised adjacent mass.

Casiano et al. (1983) : CT of the brachial plexus in patients with cancer. They found that the most common brachial plexus pathology was caused by tumour involvement - usually localised or from nodal secondaries from breast or lung tumours. It was also seen with lymphoma, thyroid carcinomas and squamous cell carcinomas of the head and neck. They also noted reports of brachial plexus involvement by schwannomas and neurofibromas by Usselman et al. (1980).

Glazer et al. (1985c) : Radiation fibrosis, differentiation from tumour recurrence by MR.

Goldberg and Austin (1985) : CT of axillary and supraclavicular lymphadenopathy in the differentiation of normal axillary and supraclavicular structures from enlarged lymph nodes. They found that axillary structures - 1.4 cm or more in diameter were suggestive of lymphadenopathy. Between 1.0 and 1.3 cm suggested this. 'Crescent-shaped' structures with central hilar fat suggested normal nodes sectioned across their longitudinal axes, whilst spherical structures with homogeneous density and obliteration of the fatty hila more likely represented pathologically enlarged lymph nodes. One should be familiar with the appearance of the lower part of the scalenus anterior muscle to avoid mistaking it for an enlarged node.

Bruneton et al. (1986) : Preoperative detection of lymph node metastases in breast cancer by ultra-sound. They searched for adenopathy on transverse scans following the course of the axillary and subclavian vessels, and found the method good in cases where the axilla had not been scarred by surgery or radiotherapy.

Blair et al. (1987) : CT gives limited separation of vascular and other soft tissues, but is better following IV contrast agents. nerves could not be differentiated from vessels without careful timing of the injection of the contrast agent. They felt that MR gave a better differentiation.(This paper contains very useful anatomical diagrams).

Kneeland (1987) : Diagnosis of diseases of the supra-clavicular region by MR.

Cooke et al. (1988a) : The anatomy and pathology of the brachial plexus by CT.

(1988b) : CT diagnosis of brachial plexus lesions following radiotherapy for carcinoma of the breast. They used fine section CT (0.4 cm wide at 0.5 cm intervals) during a rapid hand injection of 150 ml. of contrast medium diluted to an iodine concentration of 275 mg/ml. via an antecubital vein in the unaffected upper limb, at a rate of 30 to 40 ml/min. They studied 62 patients (20 prior to radiotherapy, and 42 following it) and found varying grades of abnormality in nearly all the 28 patients who had neurological problems in the arm or hand on the affected side. Nearly all had abnormalities shown by CT. They felt that they could localise the site of maximum disease, and in most cases differentiate recurrence from fibrosis. Following chemotherapy masses regressed, whilst fibrosis was unchanged. Three of the patients had oedematous arms.

Rapoport et al. (1988) : CT and MR - MR showed more extensive disease in patients with breast cancer, schwannomas, post-traumatic neuromas (very good as it showed proximal avulsion injuries, etc.), meningocoele, oedema with a fractured clavicle, etc.

Oliff and Cherryman (1991) : CT of the axilla only appears to be of value when the axilla is impossible to palpate due to previous treatment, supplemented by aspiration cytology of any mass. When the mass is evident on clinical examination, CT is unlikely to demonstrate disease.

Moore, N. et al. (1990) : Axillary fibrosis or recurrent tumour - a MR study in breast cancer of 35 patients who had arm oedema or neurological symptoms, features compatible with fibrosis were shown in 21 and tumour recurrence in 10. Equivocal findings were made in four. The findings were opposite to the clinical opinion in ten (8 having recurrence and two radiation fibrosis).

Olson et al. (1990) : Radiation-induced brachial plexus neuropathy in breast cancer patients.

Svensson et al. (1991) : The use of colour Doppler to define venous abnormalities in the swollen arm following therapy for breast carcinoma.

Dixon et al. (1993) : CT or MR imaging for axillary symptoms following treatment for breast carcinoma - a randomised trial of 58 patients - both were efficacious. CT will usually provide adequate information on which to base adequate management and the choice of MR or CT does not appear to influence the patients quality of life.

Posniak et al. (1994) : MR imaging of the brachial plexus - difficult with CT but MR is superior with multiplanar imaging and soft-tissue resolution.

Yang et al. (1995 & 1996) : Normal axillary nodes on US are usually ovoid hypoechoic structures surrounded by a C-shaped hyperechoic rim, whilst breast cancer deposits are typically hypoechoic masses >5 mm in diameter, with eccentric cortical hypertrophy and/or obliteration of the fatty hilum.

Iyer and Libschitz (1997) : Late sequelae after radiation therapy for breast cancer.

Murray and Given-Wilson (1997) : Pts. with axillary lymphadenopathy as the sole finding on screening mammography - 50% had underlying malignancy.

Yang et al. (1997) : Mammographic, sonographic and histopathological correlation of benign axillary masses - 3 TB nodes, 3 accessory breast tissue, 1 lipoma, 1 chronic inflammation.

Yang and Metreweli (1998) : Colour Doppler flow in normal axillary lymph nodes.

Balestreri and Canzonieri (1998) : Axillary hibernoma with enhancement on CT and angiography.
Bradley et al. (2000) : Accuracy of axillary MR for distinguishing recurrent breast tumour and treatment effects.

The chest wall.
    The chest wall may be involved with disease processes, arising within it or extending from within the thorax, etc. - see **Table   12.3**. Conditions involving or originating in the skin, the breasts (including accessory nipples), axillae, etc. also have to be considered, in addition to normal structures and normal variants which may be evident on chest radiographs.
    Axillary folds are well shown on lateral radiographs. The shadows of the pectoral muscles may be prominent particularly in male manual workers or athletes. Not uncommonly these (particularly pectoralis major) are thicker on the 'handed' side of the patient. Similarly they may be asymmetrical in unilateral agenesis or Poland's syndrome. Following a radical mastectomy, the horizontal shadow of the lower border of pectoralis minor may be seen. Trapezius and serratus anterior may also be seen; the costal slips of the latter and external oblique muscles give a rhythmic series of wavy shadows between successive intercostal spaces, most common in relation to the 9th ribs, but extending from the 5th to the 9th. These muscle shadows have sharp medial margins which fade inferiorly and become **invisible** on slightly oblique views, which enhance the visibility of pleural plaques (p. 14.36).

Rib companion shadows (thin smooth lines running parallel to the ribs) are best seen just below the inferior aspects of the first and second ribs, and in relation to the axillary parts of the lower ribs. Zandowski (1936) noted that they are due to intercostal muscle and fat between the bone and the parietal pleura. Glucket et al. (1972) however felt that fat was the main cause and Vix (1974) noted that extra-pleural costal fat is thicker over the 4th to 8th ribs postero-laterally. They are commonly seen on most high kV radiographs. On CT extra-pleural fat appears as a smooth postero-lateral 'lining' to the chest wall (note also fat on the inner aspect of the ribs (Fig. 14.20a, p. 14.37).
    Bulging of the intercostal spaces, inwards in expiration and outwards in expiration, may be seen in patients with asthma, severe emphysema or occasionally in normal subjects.

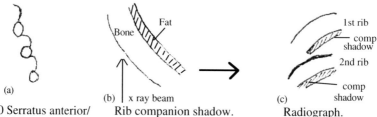

(a) Fig. 12.10 Serratus anterior/   external oblique muscle.
(b) x ray beam   Rib companion shadow.
(c) Radiograph.

    Callus from fractures, and metastases in ribs or soft tissues may cause problems in diagnosis, as may a 'scapula companion shadow' in a cachectic patient (see also p. 6.27).

Table 12.3   Chest wall lesions.
These are of many types and include :
    Fat - hypertrophy, lipoma or a relative absence (see ps. 6.12 - 13). Lipomas are common and
        may produce soft tissue densities on chest radiographs which may sometimes be very large
        or give rise to 'dumb-bell' tumours (Illus. **LIPOMA CHEST WALL**).
    Muscle lesions - haematoma, sarcoma, absence, calcification, etc.
    Breast disease - cyst, tumour, abscesses, absence, gynaecomastia, etc. (Illus. **BREAST**).
    Abscess - including infection arising in the ribs, sternum or costal cartilages, breasts, or tracking
        from the spine or pleura (pyogenic, TB or fungus - Illus. **CHEST WALL ABSCESS**).
    Parasites - cysticercosis, Guinea worm, hydatid disease - see ps. 19 50 - 57 & Illus.
        PARASITES CHEST WALL.
    Neural lesions - neurofibromatosis, etc. - see ps. 18.35 et seq.
    Vascular - aneurysms of intercostal and/or internal mammary arteries, with coarctation of the

aorta, angiomatous malformations (e.g. in Maffucci's syndrome) - may be localised or extend down to the abdomen - Illus. **CHEST WALL ANGIOMA, Pt. 1a-d**, venous collaterals, etc. - always look for phleboliths! - see Illus. **ANGIOMA NECK Pt. 1a-b.** Most arterio-venous fistulae or angiomatous malformations in the chest wall are congenital, but a few are caused by bullet or other penetrating injuries.

Desmoids (or fibromas - see ps. 18.4 - 5), elastofibroma, sarcoma, etc.

Haemangiopericytoma - see ps. 5.10 - 11 (Illus. **HAEMANGIOPERICYTOMA**).

Haematomas of the lower thoracic and upper abdominal wall may be due to rupture of the superior (or inferior) epigastric arteries, following trauma, occurring spontaneously, or in response to spasm of the abdominal muscles with stress (Illus. **CHEST WALL HAEMATOMA**).

Rib, sternal and other bony lesions - see below.

Tumours (Illus. **CHEST WALL TUMOUR**, see also Illus. **RIBS, RIB DEPOSITS, CHEST WALL INVASION**, etc.

Calcification (besides being due to haematomas and parasites - see above) may be due to dermatomyositis, chronic renal failure, myositis ossificans tumoral calcification (Illus. **TUMORAL CALCIFICATION**) or be mimicked by pleural calcification.

Elastofibroma of chest wall - this is a benign pseudotumour, probably caused by reactive hyperplasia of elastic fibres secondary to mechanical stimulation and is usually seen in the subscapular region between the tip of the scapula and the chest wall as an asymptomatic mass in elderly patients. It may also be found in the elbow below the olecranon, in relation to the ischial tuberosities, greater trochanters, etc. Negamine (1982) from Japan reviewed approximately 300 cases and Berthoty et al. (1986) reported one bilateral case examined by CT in which the subscapular mass was non-homogeneous, with irregular low-density streaking, but no calcification, as may be seen with desmoids and liposarcomas. Bilateral cases may occur but are typically asymmetrical - the author saw one case in a man who repeatedly lifted heavy TV sets.

References.
Kransdorf et al. (1992) : MR & CT appearances reflect entrapped fat within a predominantly fibrous mass.
Vande Berg et al. (1996) : Elastfibroma dorsi: a pseudomalignant lesion.
Brandser et al. (1998) : 2% prevalence in an elderly population as shown by CT.
Roche et al. (1998) : 3 cases - MR - mixed areas of high and low signal reflect fat interspersed in a fibrous matrix.
Bui-Mansfield et al. (2000) : Elastofibroma in right infrascapular area of a 51 yr old man.

Developmental lesions are not uncommon and may affect the ribs, muscles, breasts, sternum, etc. Particularly common are 'forked' or 'fused' ribs (Illus. **FORKED RIBS, Artefact Pt. 12a-b**), hemivertebrae, not uncommonly associated with other body malformations in the same, adjacent or other dermatomes. Sprengel's shoulder (i.e. the scapula lying higher and more medial than usual - **SPRENGEL'S SHOULDER, SHOULDER, Pt. 7**) may be mistaken for lung consolidation (the author's registrars have more than once done this! - see also p. 6.27). Such rib or shoulder anomalies may also be a feature of more complex congenital abnormality syndromes such as BCNS, costo-vertebral-renal and VATER syndromes (Ratcliffe et al., 1995).

Poland's syndrome comprises a group of congenital anomalies of the chest wall. It is usually unilateral but may be bilateral. Poland (1841) reported an autopsy on a 27 year old man with absence of most of the pectoralis major, the pectoralis minor and malformations of the ipsilateral hand. Over 400 cases have been reported in the literature. In addition to malformations of the pectoral muscles, other anomalies may be found including breast hypoplasia, absence of the nipple, Sprengel's shoulder and webbing of the axillae or fingers. The axilla may be anhidrotic. Sometimes there are rib anomalies or hypoplasia leading to intercostal herniae see ps. 2.39 - 40.

Further references.
Ashbury et al. (1942) and Etter (1944) : Radiographic chest survey of about 40,000 US Army recruits - about 1% had rib anomalies.
David (1972) : Nature and aetiology of the Poland syndrome.
Beals and Crawford (1976) : Congenital absence of the pectoral muscles - review of 25 patients.
Goldberg and Mazzel (1977) : Poland syndrome - a concept based on limb bud embryology.

Demos et al. (1985) : CT of partial agenesis of the pectoral muscles.

Partridge (1986) : Congenital absence of R pectoralis major causing apparent hypertranslucency of R lung on CXR in a male patient; also a female patient who had a R breast implant prosthesis to correct a similar deformity.

Seyfer et al. (1988) : Poland's anomaly - 33 cases (25 women and 8 men).

Cooper and Johnson (1990) : Mammographic depiction of Poland's syndrome.

Wright et al. (1992) : Studied seven cases of Poland's syndrome with CT and MR - absence of the sterno-costal head of pectoralis major was clearly shown, as were abnormalities of pectoralis minor, serratus anterior and latissimus dorsi. The last was important for surgical improvement of the 'absent breast' and if this muscle is hypoplastic, cosmetic surgery may well be impracticable.

The breasts must always be studied on chest radiographs, CT examinations, etc. Absence (uni- or bilateral), gynaecomastia (from obesity, steroid drugs, adrenal hypersecretion, paraneoplastic effect from lung tumour - see p. 23.1, liver failure, Kleinfelter's syndrome, etc.), the presence of prostheses, etc. should be noted. Occasionally intra-mammary calcification may be noted on chest radiographs, e.g. within a large fibroadenoma, but micro-calcifications as seen within breast carcinomas are usually only noted on mammograms taken at low kV (usually 24 to 30). Soft tissue masses may sometimes be seen or occasionally gas within fungating and necrotic tumours or abscesses. The underlying ribs should be scrutinised for evidence of destruction by tumour or osteomyelitis. An abscess may extend into the breast e.g. with TB (see Illus. **TB&BREAST**).

On CT sections the breasts are well shown, and skin thickening, masses or infiltration may be noted, and primary diagnosis of breast tumour may sometimes be made in this way (Illus. **BREAST, Pt. 1a-c, 3 & 26**). Most times this will already be known, the study being carried out to try to elucidate the axilla, chest wall, internal mammary area, the underlying lung, etc.

Prostheses, their potential or actual rupture may be shown by mammography, US, CT and/or MR. The importance of this is related to the possible stimulation of disease syndromes by leaking silicone-gel. It has long been known that women who had had silicone-gel injected into their breasts to improve their appearance in topless 'bunny clubs' in the 1960's often developed lumpiness, scarring and/or skin fistulae some months or years later, and some had mastectomies to deal with the complications. Some women, particularly in the USA, have complained of local aches and pains, hardening of the breasts, skin thickening and auto-immune conditions such as scleroderma, Sjögren's syndrome, arthritides, which may have resulted from the slow release of silicone from implants which have ruptured. The association has not yet been proved but the manufacturers have offered compensation, and implants have now been banned in the USA. They are still however used, particularly for reconstructive surgery, in the UK. Soya-bean-oil prostheses have also leaked and were withdrawn in the UK in 1999.

Internal mammary nodes are discussed on ps. 13.20 - 21, axillary nodes on p. 12.13 and Rotter's nodes below.

Occasionally mammography may be useful with disease in the male breast - the author showed several tumours in this way.

Spurious tumours may be due to, fat, an abnormality of the pectoralis major, injury, or a spontaneous haematoma in patients on anticoagulant treatment, or TB abscess.

Spurious chest masses due to the breasts are discussed on ps. 6.26 - 27. FBs in the breast include embedded old rubber or plastic drains, pins, sewing or surgical needle fragments - a memorable case was a seamstress of poor intelligence who used her large breasts as pin-cushions - she had over 100 symptomless pins (some rusting) in each breast as seen on a chest radiograph!

References.

McLeod et al. (1978) : CT of soft tissues and breast.

Munzenrider et al. (1979) : CT in breast cancer - internal mammary nodes and radiotherapy planning.

Doust et al. (1981) : CT of the breast.

Meyer and Munzenrider (1981) : CT of int. mammary node deposits in a patient with locally recurrent breast cancer.

Chang et al. (1982) : CT mammography.

Heywang et al. (1986) : MR, mammography and ultra-sound in 57 cases. MR was comparable to mammography, and superior to ultra-sound in fatty to medium dysplastic breasts, but inferior to combined mammography and ultrasound in dense breasts.

Crosbie and Kaufman (1967) : Self inflicted oleogranuloma of breast.

Minagi et al. (1968) : Roentgen appearance of injected silicone in the breast.

Symmers (1986) : Silicone mastitis in 'Topless' waitresses etc.

Taupmann and Adler (1993) : Silicone pleural effusion due to rupture of breast implant following chest drain inserted 1 yr. previously.
Gorzyca et al. (1994) : Silicone breast implant rupture : comparison between three-point Dixon and fast spin-echo MR imaging.
Lai et al. (1994) : 7 cases of acute pneumonitis following intra-mammary silicone injections. Bronchoalveolar lavage revealed alveolar macrophages containing silicone globules. They quoted other cases including trans-sexual men.
Monticciolo et al. (1994) : MR detection of leakage from silicone breast implants.
Conant et al. (1995) : US during surgery can help remove leaked silicone from ruptured breast implants.
Yang et al. (1995) : Paraffinomas of the breast with diffuse conglomerate calcification in chest wall and axillae on chest radiographs.
Chantra et al. (1995) : Mammography of the male breast.
Stewart et al. (1997) : The imaging features of male breast disease.
Gawne-Cain et al. (1993) : Radiographic patterns of intrathoracic disease in breast carcinoma.
Connolly et al. (1999) : Thoracic manifestations of breast carcinoma, metastatic disease and treatment complications.

Interpectoral lymph nodes.
    Nodes are present between the pectoralis major and minor muscles - **Rotter's nodes.** They may become enlarged due to secondary tumour particularly from breast neoplasm, and may also be enlarged with reticulosis (see Fig. 12.11 and Illus. **ROTTER'S NODE**).

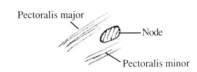

Fig. 12.11   Rotter's node.

References.
Rotter (1899) : Topography of mammary carcinomas.
Holbert et al. (1987) : CT of interpectoral lymph nodes.
Shea et al. (1987) : CT appearance of normal post-operative anatomy, post-irradiation changes and optimal scanning techniques.

Radiological examination of the chest wall.
    Although in many cases, tiny lesions of the chest wall are fairly well portrayed, or detected, on plain chest radiographs, supplementary views (e.g. oblique Bucky views of the ribs) and attention to detail is often required.
    A Bucky diaphragm view (to remove scattered radiation) and low KV should be used to give a clear definition of the ribs. In difficult cases, 'spot views' of the ribs taken under fluoroscopic TV control, at low KV and utilising fine focus (0.6 or 0.3 mm^2) as well as a moving grid, will frequently solve the problem of whether a rib lesion is present or not (Illus. **RIB SPOT VIEW**). In other cases and particularly with secondary metastatic disease, an isotope bone scan may be necessary to detect lesions (see also Chapter 22).
    Conventional tomograms may also be used to show the pattern of rib lesions and their internal structure, but one has to beware of false lesions due to a rib running out of the plane of the section.
    CT has the advantage of being able to demonstrate **both** soft tissue and bony pathology, and often makes the demonstration of these extremely clear, e.g. primary or secondary tumours in or adjacent to the spine or posterior ribs (including Pancoast tumours - see ps. 12.5 - 6). CT often also shows the structure pattern of rib disease - expansion through the periosteum, a broken cortex, internal 'soap bubble' appearance, etc. However, CT sections like conventional tomograms may give a spurious appearance of erosion or destruction if a rib due to its curvature runs out of the section of the tomographic cut.
    MR may also be used to assess lesions within bones or soft tissues by various sequences - see p. 20.29 et seq.
    Ultra-sound is invaluable for localising and diagnosing fluid collections, haematomas and for the control of biopsies or drainage procedures. It may also be used to assess the chest wall:
(a) Thickness - in planning treatment for carcinoma of the breast.

(b) Tumours of the pleural or lung extending into it.
(c) The presence of cysts or haematomas.
(d) Internal mammary lymph node enlargement.
(e) Bony deposits with soft tissue components - prior to needle biopsy.

Swellings due to callus around fractures, other rib and soft tissue masses may cause problems in their recognition or may mimic intrapulmonary lesions. This may be because of superimposition, or be due to the tendency of masses arising in the ribs to push more into the chest than outwards, presumably as a result of the negative intra-thoracic pressure and the lack of resistance in that direction. As noted on p. 14.1, masses arising in the chest wall and pleura, which push into the chest tend to have a clear-cut well demarcated outline (the '**pleural coiffe**') because the overlying intact parietal and/or visceral pleura tends to smooth out surface irregularities. Extra-pleural masses, also tend to have tapered superior and inferior edges and a horizontal diameter somewhat less than their vertical diameter. When seen **partially en face,** an extra-pleural mass may exhibit an incomplete outline where this merges with the chest wall, and an oblique view or lateral will show the typical appearance.

References.
Leitman et al. (1983) : Studied 49 patients and found that CT was indispensable for detecting and localising chest wall lesions. Bone destruction, lung, pleural and mediastinal involvement were demonstrated and invasion of the spinal canal if present. CT clearly showed the pathology in the axial plane, its relationship to surrounding structures and avoided problems due to superimposition.
Rosenberg (1983) : Ultrasound in the assessment of pleural densities.
Edelstein et al.(1985) : Reviewed 63 patients with rib abnormalities shown by CT and compared the findings with those on plain radiographs and isotope scans, and found that -
(i) Spread of tumour into or a metastasis in a rib showed subtle or segmental lytic rib destruction.
(ii) A secondary deposit (including a myeloma deposit) was often accompanied by an extra-pleural soft tissue mass.
(iii) CT often showed rib destruction that had been obscured by the heart, diaphragm, a lung mass or pleural effusion on plain radiographs. It also distinguished rib lesions from intrapulmonary disease.
(iv) CT helped to exclude structural bony disease, e.g. in Tietze's syndrome (see p. 12.36).
(v) A smoothly marginated homogeneous density within a rib may be caused by a 'dense bone island' (see also p. 12.28 and Illus. **SCL BONE ISLAND**).

Sharif et al. (1990) : MR imaging of thoracic and abdominal wall infections (S. aureus, TB, streptococcus, Klebsiella) - considered CT to be **superior** to MR for biopsy or drainage procedures.
Radin (1994) : Angiomatomasosis of the abdominal wall.
Morris and Adams (1995) : With intramuscular haemangiomas - don't overlook the phleboliths! - see also p. 12.17.

Spread of lung and other intrathoracic tumours into the chest wall.
The 'hall mark' of this is bone destruction, which may be shown on plain radiographs or CT, or be suggested by positive isotope bone scans. However tumours not uncommonly spread into the chest wall around the ribs, without eroding them. In most cases a soft tissue mass may be demonstrated within the chest wall by CT, or it may displace the adjacent pleura inwards, as seen on plain radiographs. The mass may be seen to invade fat in the chest wall ('**dirty fat**' appearance - see also ps. 6.13 & 14.31). This may be difficult to differentiate in thin or wasted patients. MR may have some advantage in visualising this. When tumour surrounds ribs, there will often be sufficient periosteal infiltration to give rise to a positive bone scan, though in other cases this will be negative.
Ultra-sound examination of the chest wall is easy to perform, particularly in areas overlying peripheral lung tumours which are invading or abutting it. Displacement or interruption of the parietal pleural '**white line**' interface by tumours is illustrated in Fig. 12.12 (below) and also discussed on p. 14.13. An **abutting tumour may also be readily imaged and biopsied using ultra-sound for localisation**, as may a mass extending into the chest wall.

Colour Doppler studies showing the presence of neovascularisation around tumours may also help to show involvement of the pleura and chest wall. In the future echo-enhancing agents may be able to show this more clearly (see also p. 20.34).

Ultrasound will also readily demonstrate pleural fluid adjacent to the chest wall, and even a thin layer of this may be aspirated for cytological examination (particularly if it is localised and aspirated in **expiration**).
Note the reference to Shirakawa et al., 1994 (below) to the use of inspiration/expiration views.

(see also ps. 14.13 - 14)

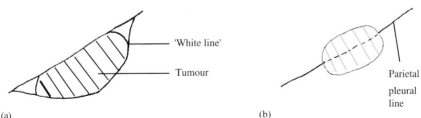

(a)
'**White line**' of lung/pleural interface - pushed inwards by a pleural mass.

(b)
Loss of parietal pleural line or its interruption, due to infiltration by tumour.

Fig. 12.12 The parietal pleural line - this line can also become thickened or irregular with fibrotic lung disease (e.g. scleroderma, CFA, chronic allergic alveolitis, sarcoid, asbestosis, etc.).

References (see also ps. 14.30 & 20.35).
Bradley (1989) : Ultra-sound in the diagnosis of peripheral lung masses - imaging and biopsy.
Mitchell (1990) : Colour Doppler imaging.
Carlsen et al. (1993) : MR detection of chest wall and pleural involvement in pts. with lymphoma.
Padovani et al. (1993) : Chest wall invasion by bronchogenic carcinoma - evaluation with MR.
Suzuki et al. (1993) : Tumour invasion of the chest wall in lung cancer - diagnosis with US.
Shirakawa et al. (1994) : Parietal pleural invasion of lung masses - evaluation with CT during deep inspiration and expiration - respiratory phase shift is a reliable indicator of the lack of parietal pleural invasion for tumours in the middle and lower lobes.

Thoracic skeletal deformities.
Thoracic skeletal deformities are common, but most are mild and are of no real medical importance. Some are developmental, and others due to past injury. Surgical deformities are not uncommon and may be due to past **thoracoplasty** (usually for TB), thoracotomy, sternotomy, etc. They should be noted, and may draw attention to a previous lobectomy, cardiac surgery, etc. A bilateral past thoracoplasty may cause confusion (Illus. **THORACOPLASTY, Pt. 16d & e**).
Marked deformities (such as severe scoliosis, kyphosis or kyphoscoliosis) may lead to cor pulmonale, but is uncommon. Respiratory failure may be due to stiffness of the chest wall, perhaps accompanied by obesity. An immobile rib cage may be present in ankylosing spondylitis with a fused dorsal spine (often with severe kyphosis) and fused costo-vertebral joints.
Flail ribs, sucked in with inspiration, may follow double rib fractures (i.e. anterior and posterior), and sometimes with fractures complicating severe and extensive secondary deposits until they become stabilised may cause severe dyspnoea. Also indrawing of the middle ribs may occur if they are 'softened' with hyperparathyroidism (e.g. with renal failure) and lead to Harrison's sulci (Illus. **HARRISON'S SULCUS**).
Outward intercostal bulging - of the intercostal spaces - may be seen in emaciated patients in expiration; in inspiration the intercostal spaces are sucked inwards.
Developmental rib abnormalities are common. Cervical ribs and bands may cause pressure on the subclavian vessels (see ps. 12.9 - 10). Forked or bifid ribs or the absence of an anterior part are of no clinical importance, but may be associated with hemivertebrae.

'**Intra-thoracic ribs**'
Supernumerary ribs, and sometimes other normally arising ribs, when fractured or with benign masses on them, may project into the pleura and rarely into the lung. On CT sections due to the

curvature of the upper chest from above downwards, the first rib may spuriously appear to project into the lung - Illus. **ARTEFACT, Pts. 9 - 12**. The author has also found true intrapulmonary rib fragments in patients who have had a penetrating injury due to a bullet or from a stab wound - Illus. **RIB INTRAPULM** shows an intrathoracic rib as a result of a bullet wound in World War II.

Other bone lesions are of many types, and may involve the ribs, sternum and /or spine. Erosion by tumours is common, either by metastases or from direct extension, and is usually painful, by comparison with some inflammatory lesions such as tuberculous 'cold' abscesses which are often painless. Pressure erosion of ribs by benign masses is considered separately under 'rib notching' (p. 12.29), but may also be seen on the spine due to nodules such as neurofibromata. A large aneurysm may also erode the spine or the sternum (Illus. **AORTA SYPHILIS, Pt. 2a-c**). Probably the **most common rib lesion is a fracture**, or **callus resulting from a fracture**, and one should always exclude this before diagnosing anything more sinister! It is surprising how many times one encounters patients with old fractures misdiagnosed as lung lesions or metastases!

Rib fractures are common in alcoholics, jockeys, and other horse riders, etc. - these people may have had multiple injuries at different times. Fractures in alcoholics and epileptics (often without a volunteered history of injury) may direct attention to the underlying condition. Rib fractures are often grouped together in neighbouring ribs, or on both sides of the chest - such may be secondary to osteoporosis, resuscitation or occur in areas affected by tumour deposits. (See Illus. **RIB DEPOSITS**).

Stress and pseudo-fractures may occur with brittle ribs and the various types of oeteomalacia, osteoporosis, in athletic individuals or those unused to certain stresses. They are particularly brittle following steroid treatment, or in Cushing's syndrome, and then may be more easily fractured after relatively minor trauma. They may also be more easily fractured after radiotherapy, e.g. the upper ribs in patients who have had irradiation for breast tumours, and these fractures may be chronic and not heal, with erosion of the fractured ends. Such ribs also are thinner and are often slightly more sclerotic than normal. Other post-radiation changes in the ribs and chest wall are discussed on ps. 11.19 et seq. Resuscitation e.g. after cardiac arrest may also produce multiple fractures. Surgical resection of a rib is usually obvious, but one should beware of the '**positive rib**' on a **post-operative bone scan**, which may be due to this cause, a simple fracture (see below) or to recurrence of tumour.

Well known are the **stress fractures** which occur in the **first ribs**, which may follow unaccustomed exertion (Rademaker et al., 1983). These give rise to lucent bands or nodules, especially posteriorly, and may be acutely or sometimes chronically painful - Illus. **RIB STRESS FRACTURE, Rib fracture Pt. 7**. Like the calcified first costo-chondral junctions these may give rise to spurious or '**idiot tumours**' of the lung (see p. 6.27 and Illus. **RIB IDIOT TUMOUR**). Even learning to play golf (or trying to play left handed after a right-sided thoracotomy - Illus. **RIB TRAUMA, Pt. 22**) may result in such fractures. Rasad (1974) from Indonesia, reported fractures of the ribs in three golfing beginners occurring in the left upper ribs posteriorly in right handed players!

The '**cough fracture**' is a special type of stress fracture, common with pneumonia or other chest infections. These may become chronic or be slow to heal, with the development of 'false-joints' at the fracture sites - Illus. **RIB FRACTURES, Rib trauma Pt. 15b-d**.

Large ribs ('**big rib**' sign) - Rib enlargement may be seen in a number of conditions. Generalised enlargement may be seen with bone marrow expansion (thalassaemia, myeloma, amyloid, etc.) hyperparathyroidism, fibrous dysplasia, neurofibromatosis, diffuse chronic metastatic deposits, etc. Localised enlargement may follow fractures, surgery or infection (bacterial, TB, fungus), occur with tumours - of various types - both primary and secondary (and particularly prostatic deposits see Illus. **PROSTATE CA, Pt. 3a-b**), Paget's disease, bone infarcts in sickle cell disease, with osteoid osteomas, adjacent to angiomatosis, with Klippel - Fiel syndrome, Caffey's disease in infants, etc. Eyler et al. (1997) noted rib enlargement adjacent to chronic pleural disease especially TB or empyema, presumably as a result of local hyperaemia from the adjacent inflammatory process (see also p. 14.19). Note also a second **'big rib' sign** from differential enlargement on a lateral view (see p. 20.12).

Osteogenesis imperfecta, as well as giving rise to true fractures or stress fractures, may lead to hypoplastic or 'ribbon-like' ribs. Incomplete or pseudo-fractures may also be seen in other conditions including Paget's disease, fibrous dysplasia, hyperparathyroidism and Gaucher's disease.

Osteoporotic bones are brittle bones, but the bone is normal in composition, although there is not enough bone present to provide its normal strength. Such bones therefore fracture readily, with crush fractures especially in vertebral bodies. Schmorl's nodes are often present. A caveat is that one should beware of myeloma mimicking osteoporosis. (Illus. **OSTEOPOROSIS**).

Osteomalacic bones, in contrast, are abnormal in composition, containing a great deal of uncalcified osteoid tissue, which lacks strength and tends to bend slowly rather than fracture; in particular vertebral bodies affected by osteomalacia do not fracture, but become equally deformed and assume a biconcave ('codfish vertebrae') appearance. Looser's zones or pseudo-fractures - ribbon-like radio-lucent zones of uncalcified osteoid are also a feature of osteomalacia. Both osteoporosis and osteomalacia may be present together.

Hyperparathyroidism may be primary or secondary. Illustrations of both are shown in Illus. **HYPERPARATHYROIDISM**. The hands show subperiosteal erosions of the middle phalanges of the fingers, cysts in carpal bones, etc. and small 'brown tumours' or osteoclastomata. The skull may be decalcified with a 'pepper and salt' appearance with mixed sclerosis and porosis, and may be thickened as well as osteoporotic. The spine typically shows osteoporotic changes with progression to 'cod fish vertebrae', and the pelvis may become triradiate, with a narrowed cavity. The ribs may be generally softened in patients with renal failure, leading to a Harrison's sulcus, whilst in those with a primary hyperparathyroidism only some of the ribs may be radiologically affected; these my become expanded and twisted as with fibrous dysplasia, show healing or healed fractures, and localised swellings due to brown tumours. See also Illus. **RENAL FAILURE.**

References.
Rose (1964) : The radiological diagnosis of osteoporosis, osteomalacia and hyperparathyroidism - loss of 30% and possibly 50 - 60% of bone calcium is necessary before decalcification becomes visible on most bone radiographs.
Doppman et al. (1979) : Differentiation of brown tumour from cystic osteitis by arteriography and CT.
Hayes and Conway (1991) : Hyperparathyroidism.
Chew and Huang-Hellinger (1993) : Brown tumour.

Macones et al. (1989) : Stress-related rib and vertebral changes. In a 4 yr. period, 80 asymptomatic pts. were found to have localised hyperostosis of the posterior ribs and articulating transverse processes. Records were reviewed in 50. Occupational histories, male-to-female ratio (5:1), right-to-left rib involvement (9:1) etc. suggested that this hyperostosis occurs at sites most stressed with bending and rotation of the thorax. It probably occurs due the pull of the iliocostalis muscle (most heavily stressed with flexion, lateral flexion and rotation - motions used in heavy lifting and other physical activities) and is of no clinical significance.

Swischuk (1991) : Radiographic manifestations of anomalies of the chest wall.
Cockshott (1992) : Rib infarcts in sickling disease.

Bone tumours in the chest wall.
   The most common tumours of the ribs, sternum, clavicle, scapulae and dorsal spine are **secondary deposits**, either haematogenous in origin or due to direct extension from the beast, pleural, chest wall or lung. Most are lytic in type but sclerotic or mixed deposits may also be found - for sclerotic deposits see p. 22.1.

   Sometimes deposits may appear to arise in areas affected by trauma - within old rib fractures, soft tissue haematomas, etc. Probably circulating metastatic cells find haematomas suitable 'soil' in which to develop. An example is shown in Illus. **RIB DEPOSITS, Pt. 5a-b**, in which it appeared that deposits occurred in fractured ribs; however 'grouped' or neighbouring rib lesions are more commonly due to trauma, in contrast to metastases which are usually of random distribution.

Myeloma and amyloid   (see also ps. 5.43 - 44) deposits occur commonly in the bone marrow. Enlarging within this they produce outward pressure on the cortex, thinning it from within and not infrequently widening bones such as the ribs. The bone structure within the deposit may be lost or give rise to a 'soap bubble' appearance, particularly within slowly growing deposits or solitary plasmacytomas. Lesions within the ribs, spine, etc. may cause enlargement inwards producing extra-pleural masses. In gross cases multiple concomitant fractures may be present and the ribs become softened, causing a marked Harrison's sulcus. Unless fractures are present, isotope bone scans tend to be negative or show negative defects. Fractures or active repair may give rise to positive outlining of the affected areas. The solitary myeloma is often responsive to radiotherapy, but multiple myeloma may supervene later.

Although amyloid deposits may calcify spontaneously (Illus. **AMYLOID, Pt. 1a-d**), myeloma deposits usually only calcify after radiotherapy - Illus. **MYELOMA, Pt. 24**, but occasionally lytic and sclerotic deposits may be present together (Illus. **MYELOMA, Sclerotic deposits Pt. 16**). A patient with a rib plasmacytoma and Paget's disease of a lumbar vertebra is shown in Illus. **MYELOMA, Pt. 23a-b**.

Primary rib tumours, apart from exostoses and osteochondromas are uncommon. **Exostoses** and other benign tumours may occur on any part of a rib, but are most common at the anterior ends, i.e. at the costo-chondral junctions. When these are present, the affected area of the rib is usually displaced inwards, so that the tumour is often barely palpable. These may also project into the pleura and give rise to a haemothorax (see also p. 14.8). Rarely they may even project into the pericardium or the heart.

Fig. 12.13   Exostosis of anterior end of rib projecting into the pleura, and leading to a haemothorax. It also projected into the pericardium, and caused anginal type pain in a young man.

Radiography   - high quality radiographs of rib etc. tumours is essential in order to try to determine their nature. In many the type of lesion will often be obvious, but there is often a good deal of overlap in the radiological appearances of malignant tumours and some benign ones, e.g. haemangioma, some cases of fibrous dysplasia or aneurysmal bone cyst. Differentiation of some lesions without excision or adequate biopsy may also be difficult for the pathologist. Without good views, i.e. with Bucky diaphragm, etc, attempted radiological differentiation may even be dangerous.

Table 12.4   - Primary bone tumours etc. arising in the chest wall - these are of many types.

Benign -   exostosis, osteoma (solitary or as part of diaphyseal aclasia, etc.),
            osteoid osteoma,
            chondroma, osteochondroma, osteoblastoma, osteoclastoma (giant cell tumour),
            haemangioma - widened localised area of rib with coarsened bone pattern, almost
                        radially arranged within it - see Illus. **RIB ANGIOMA/HAEMANGIOMA**.
            solitary or aneurysmal bone cyst (affected rib is dilated and honeycombed - contrast
            enhancement of soft tissues within bone - well demarcated from old areas of
            haemorrhage), mesenchymal hamartoma, fibrous dysplasia,
            fibroma, desmoid, chondromyxoid fibroma, histiocytoma, eosinophilic granuloma,
            haemangiopericytoma (may be malignant), extra-medullary haemopoiesis.
Malignant - osteogenic -)
            chondro -   ) sarcoma or combination of these (may follow previous radiotherapy),
            fibro -   )
            Ewing's sarcoma, Askin tumour,
            Plasmacytoma (affected area enlarged, cortex tends to be thinned and not to be

transgressed by soft tissue extension until late - see p. 5.43) / myeloma/ leukaemia.
Reticulosarcoma / Paget's sarcoma,
Clear cell sarcoma, angiosarcoma,
Giant cell tumour,
Lymphoma.

(Note : About 5% of primary bone tumours occur in the ribs or sternum.)

Bone sarcomas - both Ewing's sarcomas and osteogenic sarcomas may occur in the ribs, sternum, scapulae or dorsal spine of children or young adults, but osteogenic sarcomas may also occur in older adults, particularly those who have had radiotherapy (see ps. 11.21 - 22).

Osteogenic sarcomas (including chondro- and fibro-sarcomas and mixed types) - the precise type of cell from which these tumours is radiologically less important than the diagnosis of malignancy. Malignant cells are often pleomorphic, with cartilaginous, osteogenic or fibroblastic cells predominating. Osteochondrosarcomas and chondrosarcomas may arise on pre-existing chondromas, and often contain areas of calcification (Illus. **OSTEOCHONDROSARCOMA**), but when they arise from a costal cartilage this may be minimal (Illus. **OSTEOCHONDROSARCOMA, Costal cart sarcoma, Pt. 1a-b**). When an osteogenic sarcoma arises in a rib, it may spread from end to end and be surrounded by a soft tissue swelling (Illus. **OSTEOGENIC SARCOMA, Rib tumour, Pt. 3a-b**). A **mesenchymal sarcoma** is a rare subtype which may involve the ribs and tends to occur in the 2nd and 3rd decades of life.

Ewing's sarcoma was described by Ewing in 1926 and 1928, but its cell of origin is still uncertain. It may arise in many bones, and probably about 5% arise in the ribs, others in the dorsal spine, etc. (Illus. **EWING'S SARCOMA**). As the tumour often metastasises to other bones, an isotope scan may be invaluable for showing these as well as the extent of the primary tumour, which is often very vascular (Illus. **EWING'S SARCOMA, 1e, 2e & 5e**). Affected patients (usually aged 10 to 20 and 70% male) may give a history of trauma or present with signs suggesting osteomyelitis, reticulosis or eosinophilic granuloma. Radiographic signs are variable and include lytic lesions, mottled destruction of the medulla, cortical erosion and periosteal new bone formation. Rib lesions may show an increased width of the medullary cavity and coarseness, leading to cortical destruction and bone expansion, with new periosteal bone deposited in layers, like '**onion skin**'. The boundary between normal and abnormal bone is often poorly defined, and there is usually a surrounding or adjacent soft tissue mass, which may become very large (see Illus. **EWING'S SARCOMA, Pt. 2a-f**). Some lesions, including deposits in other bones, and the lung are sclerotic or calcified. Not all cases have a hopeless prognosis, and chemotherapy with multiple drugs is becoming more effective. A patient is illustrated in Illus. **EWING'S SARCOMA, Pt. 1a-g** who had a large Ewing's tumour which arose in the left lower ribs, she had the diagnosis confirmed by 'radiological biopsy, followed by radiotherapy, when the tumour shrunk down; it was then removed surgically - she has since had two successful pregnancies and remains well.

MR is being used increasingly for the assessment of operability (Illus. **EWING'S SARCOMA, Pt. 2f**), but periosteal new bone and reactive sclerosis are more difficult to show with this technique.

Two variants of Ewing's sarcoma are:
(i) '**Extraskeletal Ewing's sarcomas**' and (ii) '**Askin tumours**' (Illus. **ASKIN TUMOUR**).
The first tends to occur in a slightly older age group (4 to 50) years, and may arise in the limbs, abdomen, or chest, especially in the chest wall or para-vertebral regions. They often have a pseudo-capsule and thus appear to be well-circumscribed on CT, ultrasound or MR, being hypoechoic and of low density, although spontaneous haemorrhage may change their features. Askin (or small cell) tumours of the chest wall were first described by Askin (1979) and are primitive neuro-ectodermal tumours of children and young adults, which may produce a large chest wall or intrathoracic mass (especially paravertebrally), rib destruction or a pleural effusion. They

may be differentiated from Ewing's sarcomas and neuroblastomas by immunochemistry and electron microscopy. As with neuroblastomas, calcification may be present within the masses, and widespread metastases may occur in the liver, adrenals, retroperitoneum, other bones or the sympathetic chain.

Mesenchymoma (hamartoma) of the chest wall.

These are rare tumours which arise from the ribs most commonly in small infants. They consist of an overgrowth of normal chondral and primitive skeletal elements with features similar to those of an aneurysmal bone cyst, and produce a hard mass in the chest wall which may contain calcification. Sometimes they become very large and compress the underlying lung. They may be multiple and affect two or more ribs. Occasionally a malignant variety may be seen in adolescents or young adults.

Further references.

Osteogenic sarcoma
Green et al. (1996) : Imaging of primary osteosarcoma of the spine - differs from conventional appendicular osteosarcoma in several ways - a review of 52 cases showed no sig. sex difference (in contradistinction to appendicular osteosarcoma which has a 2 : 1 M to F ratio), it occurs in an older age group, 50% were partly lytic. CT is of value in characterisation and for guiding needle biopsy, but MR is the method of choice for local staging. Treatment is difficult and prognosis poor.

Ewing's sarcoma
Nouri and Hashemian (1975) : Ewing's tumour, a review of 73 cases - the tumour frequently involves young patients and seldom occurs after 40 years of age.
Vanel et al. (1982) : CT in the evaluation of 41 cases of Ewing's sarcoma.
Azouz (1983) : Ewing's sarcoma of the ribs - five cases.
Levine and Levine (1984) : Ewing's tumour of rib, radiology and CT (six cases).
Thomas (1983) : Reviewed 36 patients with primary Ewing's sarcoma of the ribs. Those who had surgical removal, radiotherapy and chemotherapy mostly remained well. Half of those with regional disease also remained well, but those with metastatic disease faired badly.
Boyco et al. (1987) : MR imaging of osteogenic and Ewing's sarcoma.
Brown et al. (1987) : 67 patients with Ewing's sarcoma - 18 had rib lesions, 4 being localised.
Lee (1989) : Pointed out that up to 30% of Ewing's tumours may show sclerotic changes. (They described a Ewing's sarcoma in an 18 year old woman with a sclerotic Ewing's sarcoma adjacent to the left sacro-iliac joint).

Extraskeletal Ewing's sarcoma
Tefft et al. (1969) : Paravertebral round cell chest tumours closely resembling Ewing's sarcoma of bone (4 cases).
Angervall and Enzinger (1975) : Extraskeletal neoplasm resembling Ewing's sarcoma - 35 cases,
Rose et al. (1983) : Extraskeletal Ewing's sarcoma - 3 cases.
Rud et al. (1989) : 42 cases.
O'Keefe et al. (1990) : Radiological features of extraskeletal Ewing's sarcoma - review of 22 cases, 5 in the chest.

Askin tumours
Askin et al. (1979) : A destructive clinico-pathological entity of uncertain histogenesis.
Gonzalez - Crussi et al. (1984) : Peripheral neuroectodermal tumour of the chest wall in childhood.
Fink et al. (1985) : Malignant thoraco-pulmonary small cell 'Askin' tumour - ten patients (10 - 33 years).
Shamberger et al. (1989) : Chest wall tumours in infancy and childhood.
Saifuddin et al. (1991) : Radiology of Askin tumours.
Winer-Muram et al. (1993) : CT and MR findings in Askin tumours - areas of haemorrhage and necrosis in the large tumours of the chest wall are responsible for their heterogeneous appearance.
Sabaté et al. (1994) : Malignant neuroectodermal tumour of the chest wall (Askin tumour) - CT & MR in 8 pts.

Mesenchymal tumour of chest wall
Stout (1948) : Mixed tumour of mesenchymal derivatives.
McLeod and Dahlin (1979) : Mesenchymal hamartoma of the chest wall in infancy.
Campbell et al. (1982) : Benign mesenchymoma of the chest wall in infancy.
Oakley et al. (1985) : Multiple benign mesenchymomata of the chest wall.
Odell and Benjamin (1986) : 2 cases.
Gwyther and Hall (1991) : 2 cases.
Jain et al. (1993) : 20 year-old man with huge right anterior chest wall mass, extending into the right side of the chest and mediastinum - it contained areas of focal degeneration and calcification.
There were also pulmonary, pleural and axillary lymph node metastases.

Other non-malignant conditions affecting the ribs, etc. include :

Paget's disease - coarsened bony architecture with widened ribs and thick cortices(occasionally complicated by Paget's sarcoma).

Rheumatoid (ribs eroded on superior aspects, sometimes thinned, distorted or pencilled upper ribs and clavicles and disease in shoulders, etc.) - similar appearances may be seen in other collagen diseases such as scleroderma, etc. - see also ps. 19.81 et seq.

Fibrous dysplasia (fibro-cystic disease) may be mono- or polyostotic and be part of the Albright syndrome. Medullary bone is replaced by fibrosing tissue in which osteoid may develop and calcify. The ribs may be widened and deformed with tubular expansion, thickening and coarsening of the normal bone and sometimes a 'twisted tape' appearance (Illus. **RIB FIBROUS DYSPLASIA, Pt. 4a**). Incomplete or pseudo-fractures may be present, as well as well-defined cystic looking areas (Illus. **RIB FIBROUS DYSPLASIA, Pt. 1 & 3**). The cortex is usually intact, but may be thinned or thickened like 'orange peel'. In gross cases a 'soap bubble' appearance may be produced. The lesions progress mostly in adolescence or young adults, but can enlarge in older patients. Localised expansion may mimic a tumour. Illus. **RIB FIBROUS DYSPLASIA, Pt. 2a-c** shows a localised lesion which had been present for 30 years, and then enlarged further - it also gave a positive isotope bone scan.

Achondroplasia - widened horizontal ribs with reduced intercostal spaces due to shortened height of vertebrae. In children swelling of the costo-chondral junctions produces a 'rosary' in rickets and scurvy. A Harrison's sulcus may also be present. (Illus. **ACHRONDROPLASIA** shows horizontal ribs, shortened clavicles and shoulder deformities.)

Past poliomyelitis, quadriplegia or other chronic paralysis may lead to thinned ribs, atrophy of the shoulder girdle and distortion, especially on the affected side.

Alcaptonuria - due to impaired metabolism of homogentisic acid, may give rise to porotic bones, thinning and calcification of intervertebral disc cartilages (Illus. **ALCAPTONURIA**).

Infection - osteomyelitis (both TB or pyogenic - Staph., fungus - especially actinomycosis, etc.) may occur within a rib. It commonly starts within the marrow, causing intra-medullary bone destruction, later periosteal reaction, some bone expansion, and an extra-osseous abscess. A 'favourite' place is close to the costochondral junction. Illustrations of rib and costal cartilage infection (see also costal cartilage - p. 12.37) are shown under Illus. **RIB INFECTION**.

Extramedullary haemopoiesis may occur with many conditions, including thalassaemia, sickle cell disease, pernicious anaemia, myeloid metaplasia and fibrosis, polycythaemia rubra vera, severe Paget's disease, and with some chronic neoplasms affecting the bone marrow such as lymphoma and leukaemia.
   The most common sites are the liver and spleen. It may also occur in lymph nodes, the kidneys, adrenals, pleura, mediastinum (mainly posteriorly and adjacent to the spine and within the spinal canal), the presacral area, etc.

   In **thalassaemia** the ribs become widened, with cortical thickening and narrowing of the intercostal spaces. Blood forming tissues proliferate within the marrow, and may perforate the cortex to form a localised bulge (or 'cortical osteoma'), thickening of the ribs under the periosteum giving rise to a '**rib within a rib**' appearance, sub-cortical lucencies and extra-medullary haemopoiesis (see also ps. 18.32 - 33 and Illus. **THALASSAEMIA**).

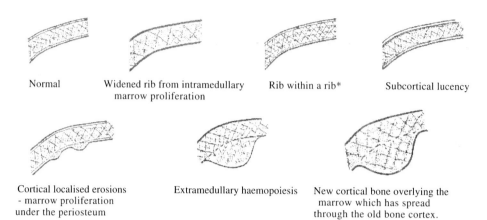

Normal Widened rib from intramedullary marrow proliferation Rib within a rib* Subcortical lucency

Cortical localised erosions - marrow proliferation under the periosteum Extramedullary haemopoiesis New cortical bone overlying the marrow which has spread through the old bone cortex.

Fig. 12.14 Rib appearances in thalassaemia (Reproduced from Lawson et al., 1981, Radiology, **140**, 663 - 672 & 673 - 679 with permission). *[Lawson (1999) writes " I have revised my idea about 'rib within a rib'. I had the chance to evaluate some skeletons and the appearance appears to be due to focal linear thickening of the outer cortex of the rib. This is an adaptation to provide maximal strength with minimal bone."]

Patients with thalassaemia may develop **haemosiderosis** as a result of repeated blood transfusions and this latter may lead to hepatic failure (see also ps. 19.97 - 98).

Sickle cell disease may produce similar bone changes to those seen in thalassaemia, as well as bone infarcts sickling crises and cardiomegaly - see also p. 19.100.

A 'bone within a bone' appearance is typically seen in **osteopetrosis**, but may also be seen with some secondary deposits e.g. some prostatic and breast deposits (Illus. **PROSTATE CA, Pts. 2 & 3a-b**). The occasional sclerotic bone deposit from a bronchial tumour may cause periosteal thickening, bone expansion and a '**bone within a bone**' appearance on CT (Illus. **PL-COIFFE, Pt. 3**). This sign may also be seen with secondary deposits from Ewing's sarcoma and childhood adrenal **medulloblastoma**.

Tubular expansion may also be seen in **familial metaphyseal dysplasia (Pyle's disease) and Gaucher's disease.**

Gaucher's disease - an infiltrative disorder of the bone marrow is due to a deficiency of the enzyme glucocerebroside, and gives rise to large histiocytes which engulf kerasin. The ribs and vertebrae may be porotic and expanded with fractures and extra-skeletal masses. Schmorl's nodes and cartilage necrosis and some bone sclerosis may occur as a result of infarction. Splenic and hepatic enlargement is usually marked. Children with severe disease may be treated with marrow transplantation.

Fluorosis - may affect the thoracic cage, giving rise to increased density of the ribs, etc. with roughening and thickening of the points of attachment of the intercostal muscles. Gross cases may follow ingestion of wine to which fluorine has been added as a preservative, industrial poisoning, or excessive fluoridation of the drinking water.

Sclerotic bone islands - are not uncommon in the various bones of the skeleton, and may be seen in the ribs and spine - Illus. **SCL BONE ISLAND**. They should not be confused with metastases or with nodules in the underlying lung. They are usually well-defined, evenly densely calcified endosteal nodules of compact bone, which slowly increase in size with time (Blank and Lieber, 1965, Ngan, 1972). Sclerotic bone islands are usually not seen on isotope bone scans.

'**Benign deposits**' include **histiocytosis, eosinophilic granuloma**, etc - these are more commonly seen in the lower ribs. Rib lesions in **histiocytosis** are often lucent small cysts (typically in the lower ribs - see also ps. 19.61 - 63).with a more sclerotic rim, but may be entirely lytic. (Illus. **HISTIOCYTOSIS, Pt. 10c**).

Tuberose sclerosis (see also p. 5.15) may also cause tiny sclerotic or cystic lesions in the hands and feet, but only rarely does this in the ribs or spine. However, the author has seen this in the 'forme fruste' - i.e. patients with normal intelligence, etc. When rib nodules are present they may produce 'pseudo-rib-notching' or sclerotic rib expansions (Nathanson and Avnet, 1966).

Multicentric reticulohistiocytosis is a rare systemic disorder which primarily affects the skin and synovium causing a severe erosive arthritis, but may also cause soft tissue masses in the chest wall. About 20 to 30% of affected patients have associated malignancy, including bronchial tumours. Kamel et al. (1996) described an 8 x 4 cm mass in the left serratus anterior muscle which gave rise to intense peripheral enhancement.

Mastocytosis - a disorder of histamine producing tissues and particularly mast cells, usually gives rise to sclerosing bony lesions (either diffuse or localised and mimicking deposits). They may initially be osteolytic. The author has only seen three such cases - all in the same year!

Some references. Schorr et al. (1964), Huang et al. (1987).

Myelosclerosis, myelofibrosis and renal osteodystrophy may also produce bone sclerosis (Illus. **MYELOSCLEROSIS, RENAL BONE DISEASE**).

Ankylosing spondylitis is discussed on p. 19.90.

Rib notching - (Illus. **RIB NOTCHING**).

   Rib notching may occur on either the inferior or superior borders of the ribs -

(a) **Inferior notching** is more common because the intercostal vessels and nerves lie directly below the ribs, and enlargement of these, particularly the arteries, most commonly cause notching.

Fig. 12.15   Position of the intercostal vessels and nerves.

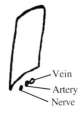

Vein
Artery
Nerve

   Arterial notching is usually secondary to enlarged intercostal arteries in association with coarctation of the thoracic aorta. This usually affects the **upper** ribs, but notching of the **lower** ribs may be found with 'abdominal coarctation' or '**middle aorta syndrome**' (see p. 10.18), which is rare, but occurs at the level of the renal arteries. Arterial notching may also follow occlusion of one of the larger branches of the thoracic aorta, and on the left side following a Blalock operation (subclavian-pulmonary artery anastomosis) for the treatment of Fallot's tetralogy. It may also be caused by a systemic to pulmonary artery anastomosis associated with pulmonary artery agenesis or hypoplasia, which occurs more commonly on the right side (see also ps. 7.6 - 8).
   Venous notching may be caused by dilated and/or tortuous intercostal veins, secondary to chronic obstruction of the SVC. It may also be seen with arterio-venous malformations of the chest wall. (See Felson - SVC: conventional projections, 1989).
   Solitary neurofibromas of the intercostal nerves may cause single notches, whilst more generalised neurofibomatosis usually causes multiple notchings.

(b) **Superior rib notching** is usually manifested by longer erosions than are seen inferiorly. Its most common causes are rheumatoid cystic bursae occurring between the ribs, other collagen diseases, radiation damage and hyperparathyroidism. Other causes include poliomyelitis and chronic palsies, including traumatic quadriplegia, the effects of localised pressure, restrictive lung disease and ? hypervitaminosis D.

(c) **Other rib notchings** may be produced by masses in the chest wall, which produce pressure erosions on the ribs. These include lipomas, especially transmural lipomas - see Illus. **LIPOMA CHEST WALL, Lipoma Pt. 1** and p. 6.12) and neurofibromas - see Illus. **NEUROFIBROMA, Pt. 30a - b**. Joffe (1959) reported notching caused by a synovioma, and Saksouk (1979) with peripherally located pulmonary hydatid cysts which had extended into the pleura (see also p. 19.53). Occasionally notching may be idiopathic or familial.

(d) **'Pseudo-notching'** may be caused by tuberose sclerosis or fibrous dysplasia.

Postoperative rib deformites are discussed on p. 11.15 et seq.

Further references.

General.
Kattan et al. (1971) : Intercostal bulging of the lung without emphysema.
Gilmartin (1979) : The serratus anterior muscle on chest radiographs.
Lams and Jolles (1981) : The scapular companion shadow.
Subbarao and Jacobson (1984) : Systemic disorders affecting the thoracic cage.
Weinstein and Mueller (1965) : Intrathoracic ribs.
Kollins (1977) : CT of chest wall.
Kelleher et al. (1979) : Two cases of intrathoracic ribs (one supernumerary) - also referred to 17 others..
Paling and Dwyer (1980) : First ribs as a cause of apparent intrapulmonary nodules on CT.
Stark and Lawrence (1984) : Intrathoracic rib shown by CT (incidental finding in patient with bronchial ca.).
Grusd (1978) : Pseudo and stress fractures.
Gouliamos et al. (1980) : CT of chest wall.
de Gauthard et al. (1981) : CT of thoracic bony lesions, including primary tumours.
Vock and Fuchs (1983) : CT of pleura and chest wall.
Schultz et al. (1989) : The chest and the skeleton - radiological considerations.

Kyphoscoliosis.
Bergofsky et al. (1959) : Cardio-respiratory failure in kyphoscoliosis.
Cremin (1970) : Infantile thoracic dystrophy - a familial asphyxiant with chondrodystrophic features.
Reckles et al. (1975) : The association of scoliosis and congenital heart disease.
Branthwaite (1986) : Cardiorespiratory consequences of unfused idiopathic scoliosis.
Simonds et al. (1989) : Kyphoscoliosis as a cause of cardio-respiratory failure - pitfalls of diagnosis - four cases (pulmonary emboli, ASD, severe emphysema) - felt that respiratory failure, pulmonary hypertension and right heart failure should not be attributed primarily to kyphoscoliosis unless the curve is severe (Cobb's angle 100° or more), is of early onset or demonstrable weakness of respiratory muscles.
Carvalho and Carr (1990) : Thoracic CT - value in respiratory failure secondary to kyphoscoliosis - CT of 10 patients with gross kyphoscoliosis - were able to confirm or exclude pulmonary consolidation, to determine pulmonary artery size and show pathology not easily visible on plain chest radiographs.

Rib notching
Bernstein et al. (1958) : Erosive rib lesions in paralytic poliomyelitis.
Wilson, W. (1960) : Review of the causes of rib notching, with a report of a case due to an A/V fistula from intercostal arteries to the lung.
Noetzli and Steinbach (1961) : Subperiosteal reabsorption along the upper cortical margins of the ribs posteriorly in patients with hyperparathyroidism.
Boone et al. (1964) : Many causes of rib notching.
Drexler et al. (1969) : Many causes of rib notching.
Gilmartin (1966) : Cartilage calcification and rib erosion in chronic respiratory poliomyelitis - 3rd to 9th ribs eroded - especially upper borders - when both surfaces were involved the ribs became 'waisted'.
Nathanson and Avnet (1966) : An unusual x-ray finding in tuberose sclerosis - thickening and sclerotic changes in the ribs with expansion in their superior - inferior diameters, with no evidence of periosteal new bone formation, periostitis or lytic defects.

Sargent et al. (1969) : Superior marginal rib defects - three classes (i) disturbed osteoblastic activity (polio, collagen diseases, localised pressure and radiation damage, (ii) disturbed osteoclastic activity (hyperparathyroidism and hyper-vitaminosis D) and (iii) idiopathic.

Keats (1975) : Superior marginal rib defects in restrictive lung disease.

Woodlief (1978) : Superior marginal rib defects in traumatic quadriplegia.

Bliznak and Barginer (1974) : **Coarctation of abdominal aorta** plus literature review - accounts for 2% of aortic coarctations.

Dernevik and Larsson (1990) : **Dumb-bell tumours** of the chest wall - seven cases - 4 neurilemmomas, a neuroblastoma, chondrosarcoma and a **hydatid cyst**.

Developmental, inflammatory and metabolic conditions.

Simon and Zorab (1961) : Radiographic changes in **alcaptonuric** arthritis - 3 cases - one in an Egyptian mummy.

Blank and Lieber (1965) : The significance of **growing bone islands.**

Ngan (1972) : **Growing bone islands.**

Nathanson and Avnet (1966) : Sclerotic rib expansions - unusual finding in **tuberose sclerosis.**

Lichtenstein (1938) and Lichtenstein and Jaffe (1942) : **Polyostotic fibrous dysplasia -** medullary cavities in the involved bones were replaced by fibrous tissue and contained primitive bone trabeculae. Rib lesions are often monostotic.

Warrick (1973) : Some aspects of **polyostotic fibrous dysplasia** - may be complicated by sarcoma.

Daffner et al. (1982) : **CT of fibrous dysplasia** - (mainly of femur, sacrum and skull) - lucent amorphous decalcified area surrounded by a sclerotic rim or expansile and ground-glass appearance. CT numbers 70 - 130 compared with low numbers in eosinophilic granuloma, pus or secondary neoplasm. In eosinophilic granuloma lesions are more lucent and have a denser edge or rim..

Wright, J. and Stoker (1988) : **Fibrous dysplasia** (especially of the spine) - expansion of bone, sometimes with thinning of the cortex - may have central lytic lesions with sclerotic margins or generalised mixed lytic and sclerotic changes, with or without soft tissue swelling. The condition may be confused with non-ossifying fibroma, Paget's disease, aneurysmal bone cyst, hyperparathyroidism and eosinophilic granuloma.

Li et al. (1988) : **Gaucher's disease** (gives good list of references).

Takahashi et al. (1966) : Variable appearance of idiopathic **histiocytosis.**

Schorr et al. (1964) : **Mastocytosis,** urticaria pigmentosa and occlusive panarteritis.

Huang et al. (1987) : Radiological features of **mast cell disease.**

Pyle (1931) and Shibuya et al. (1982) : **Familial metaphyseal dysplasia.**

Brown, T. (1980) : **TB of ribs** - 7 cases - bone destruction, extrapleural soft tissue opacities and fluctuant swellings.

Fitzgerald and Hutchinson (1992) : **TB of the ribs** - CT findings.

Lee, G. et al. (1993) : **TB of the ribs**: CT appearance.

Lawson et al. (1981) : The ribs in **thalassaemia**.

Singcharoen (1989) : Unusual long bone changes in **thalassaemia**, findings on plain radiography and CT (gives good illustration of intra-thoracic masses arising from the ribs).

A V malformations of the chest wall.

Bradley et al. (1991) : Diagnosis of **peripheral cavernous haemangioma** - comparison of US, CT and RBC scintigraphy - **RBC scintigraphy was the preferred technique.**

Tumours and cysts.

O'Neal and Ackerman (1951) : **Cartilaginous tumours of the ribs and sternum** - reviewed 85 cases and added 11 of their own.

Mendl and Evans (1958) : Cyst-like and cystic lesions of the ribs - radiological differential diagnosis in five cases - haemangioma (soap-bubble appearance in an expanded segment of rib), **plasmacytoma** (multi-locular appearances in an expanded segment of rib), hydatid cyst (large rounded opacity of soft tissue density extending out of a rib), eosinophilic granuloma (sharply defined, rounded, oval or scalloped translucency within the bone - may expand the cortex & extend into surrounding soft tissue), & a neuroblastoma deposit in a child.

Banna et al. (1970) : Bone deposits from **cerebellar medulloblastoma - sclerotic,** osteolytic or mixed.

Omell et al. (1973) : Chest wall tumours.

Franken et al. (1977) : Tumours of the chest wall in infants and children.

Klein et al. (1977), Dashiell et al. (1978) : Desmoid tumours of the chest wall. (see also p. 18.4).

Zeman and Hurley (1979) : **chondro-myxoid fibroma** (with a thin rim of calcification) arising from the 4th left costo-chondral junction. It had initially been mistaken for a lung lesion in a woman of 63.

Fogelman (1980) : Rib lesions detected by **isotope bone scanning** included **Ewing's sarcoma, tuberculosis, cough fractures, pseudo-fractures in osteomalacia and Paget's disease.**

Mayes et al. (1981) : CT of **chondrosarcoma.**

Norman and Sissons (1984) : Radiographic hallmarks of peripheral **chondrosarcoma.**

Sabanathan et al. (1985 - surgeons from Nottingham) : **Primary chest wall tumours** (after reviewing 53 cases) **thought that radiological differentiation of benign from malignant chest wall tumours was not possible** - such a statement overstates the case, but in many a good biopsy or, if possible, an 'excision biopsy" is essential when there is any doubt.

McAfee et al. (1985) : **Chondrosarcoma of the chest wall** - factors affecting survival.
Phillips and Choong (1991) : **Chondrosarcoma** arising from the left upper costal cartilages and presenting as an anterior mediastinal mass.
Biondetti et al. (1982a) : CT of **lipoma** or **angio-lipoma** of thoraco-abdominal wall.
Steiner et al. (1982) : **Rib destruction in malignant mesothelioma** - a neglected finding.
Collins and Eckert (1985) : **Bone deposits from seminoma** - report of three cases.
Cumming and Sabbah (1985) : Of 11 large **unilateral chest tumours in children**, 7 were **Ewing's sarcomas arising from the ribs**. The rib abnormalities were seen clearly on chest radiographs, and because of their site were readily assessed with ultrasound.
Shulman et al. (1977) : **Unicameral bone cyst** in a rib of a child.
Marsh et al. (1992) : **CT of a unicameral bone cyst in a rib.**
Pascuzzi et al. (1957) : **Primary tumours of the ribs and sternum** - 2,000 cases (of the sternal tumours only one was benign).
Pratt et al. (1958) : **Tumours of the scapula and clavicle.**
Ochsner et al. (1966) : Tumours of the thoracic skeleton - review of 134 cases (included one sternal case - an **eosinophilic granuloma**).
Smith, J. et al. (1975) : **Primary tumours of the clavicle and scapula.**
Friedman et al. (1989) : **Giant cell tumour of the clavicle** - two cases.
Stelzer and Gay (1980) : **Tumours of the chest wall.**
King, R. et al. (1986) : **Primary chest wall tumours** - factors affecting survival. Between 1955 and 1975 chest wall resection was carried out on 90 patients at the Mayo Clinic for primary chest wall tumours (71 malignant and 19 benign). 60% of malignant tumours were **malignant fibrous histiocytomas, chondrosarcomas and rhabdomyosarcomas**, the histiocytomas having the worst prognosis.
Ala-Kulju et al. (1988) : **Primary tumours of the ribs** - 34 primary rib tumours (24 benign and 10 malignant) were surgically treated at Helsinki University Hospital between 1966 and 1985. These comprise about 6% of primary bone tumours, soft tissue tumours of the chest wall being more common.
Waller and Newman (1990) : Leeds Regional Bone Tumour Registry - **primary bone tumours of the thoracic skeleton** accounted for 90 (out of 2004 tumours - 4.5%). 33 were in the ribs, 29 in the scapulae, 10 in thoracic vertebrae, 9 in the sternum (6 chondrosarcomas) and 8 in the clavicles. Malignant tumours were more common than benign and occurred in an older population. The scapulae were the most common site for malignant lesions and the ribs for benign tumours. In older patients chondrosarcomas were most common, in the middle age group - fibrous dysplasia and plasmacytoma, and in children - eosinophilic granuloma. They felt that early biopsy is necessary and only 7 had a correct preoperative diagnosis.

CT
Bhalla et al. (1990) : Counting ribs on chest CT - the method involves recognising the characteristic anatomical relationships of the medial end of the clavicle with the first rib, the vertebral pedicle and the transverse process with the corresponding rib and the arrangement of the ribs with respect to each other.

False aneurysms of the chest wall.
Martin et al. (1973) : False aneurysm of internal mammary artery following sternotomy.
Millner et al. (1991) : False aneurysm of the right internal mammary artery.
Callaway et al. (2000) : False aneurysm of intercostal artery following sternotomy and treated by using a covered intra-coronary stent graft.

THE STERNUM, COSTAL CARTILAGES AND MANUBRIO-STERNO AND STERNOCLAVICULAR JOINTS.

The Sternum - anatomy.

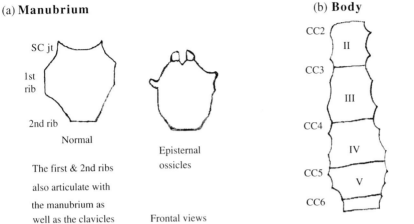

Fig. 12.16 Anatomy of the manubrium and body of the sternum.

Occasionally the body of the sternum may also be bifid (in the absence of surgery), due to its development from paired germinal centres; if partially so, with a '**bow tie**' appearance on CT.

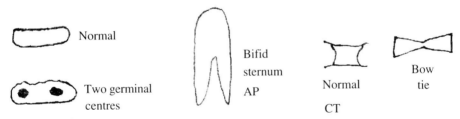

Fig. 12.17 Bifid sternum.

(c) **Xiphoid** - this is variable in shape - rhomboid, triangular or oval and its tail gives several appearances - see below.

(d) **Episternal ossicles** - small 'tooth-like ossicles' may be seen above the manubrium in 1 to 2% of people. They may be uni- or bilateral. On CT they may produce nodules which should be distinguished from fractures, osteophytes, etc.

Radiography.

The sternum is a difficult bone to examine clearly by plain radiography. Confusion is often compounded by the oblique view (so often taught to radiographers) as this is often of **little value**, except perhaps for showing osteoarthritic lipping of the sterno-clavicular or first or second costo-sternal joints.

A lateral view, particularly is the arms are extended behind the patient's back, and the sternum pushed forwards ('Mary Queen of Scots view' - see p. 20.9) - will often show fractures and secondary deposits (Illus. **QUEEN OF SCOTS VIEW**).

Plain **tomography** in the lateral erect position, or AP (with the patient slightly oblique to avoid ghost shadows from the spine), will often show larger deposits, or other disease. For most secondary deposits one tends to rely on isotope bone scans, supplemented by CT (Illus. **STERNAL DEPOSIT/EROSION**).

Historical.
'Inclined frontal tomograms' (see p. 20.14) were used by the author for many years to show disease in the sternum (Illus. **STERNUM IFT**).
Smith, R. (1968) described a transverse tomographic movement on a conventional tomographic table, with the patient standing and bending over across the table. CT is also very valuable for showing the sternum, as it will show it clear of any ghost shadows and also demonstrate adjacent soft tissues (Illus. **STERNUM CT**).

CT of the sternum.

The manubrium forms an angle of 10° to 30° to the horizontal in most patients, whilst the body tends to be more horizontal. Thus, if particular attention to the manubrium is desired, it may be advisable to tilt the gantry to obtain more perpendicular cross-sections. When this is done, the cortical margins may be clearer.

The manubrio-sternal joint often has a somewhat sclerotic appearance, and this should not be confused with disease.

The manubrium usually has a slightly curved shape, with the clavicles articulating with its upper part on both sides, via the sterno-clavicular joints. These have a fibro-cartilaginous disc in their centres and are normally about 2 to 4 mm wide.

Fig. 12.18 CT of the sternum and sterno-clavicular joints.

The **xiphoid   process** is variable in shape (rhomboid, triangular or oval) and its 'tail' may show a clumped, irregular nodular calcified appearance, or be bifid.

Table 12.5 - Causes of sternal disease.

Congenital anomalies - depressed sternum ('**pectus excavatum**' or '**funnel chest**').
Fracture - trauma - direct violence - steering wheel injury, crush injuries, etc.
　　　　　　- spontaneous - secondary to osteoporosis, & esp. with severe thoracic kyphosis.
　　　　　　- through secondary deposits - breast, prostate, myeloma, etc.

- note that a fracture, whether simple trauma
or through a secondary deposit can
produce a step-like line on an AP view,
the lateral showing the displacement.

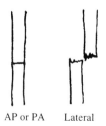

AP or PA　　Lateral

Neoplasm - primary - sarcoma (rare) - Illus. **STERNUM TUMOUR**.
- secondary - breast, bronchus, prostate, myeloma, etc.
- erosion by mesothelioma, etc. - see Illus. **STERNAL DEPOSIT/EROSION,**
    Mesothel 19j, 26a, 42c-d.

Pressure erosions - a syphilitic aortic aneurysm is now very rare - Illus. **STERNUM, Syph**
    ao an Pt. 2a-c.

Radiation - post radiotherapy necrosis /infection.

Surgery - sternotomy for cardiac, mediastinal, etc. surgery   (see p. 12.32 re false aneurysms).
    Wire sutures are commonly used to hold the two sides together in the post-operative
    period until bony union occurs. A sternotomy may also give rise to a 'click', localised
    osteomyelitis (stitch abscess), para-sternal and retro-sternal abscesses, mediastinitis,
    and surgical dehiscence with failure of the sternum to heal. (About 75% of
    asymptomatic patients have small air/fluid collections or haematomas following
    sternotomy, but most clear spontaneously). (See p. 5.25 for '**wigwam sign**').
    - a flap or a breast may be swung over the sternum following debridement for post-
    surgical infection, radio-necrosis, etc. (Leitman et al., 1988, termed such a '**pectoral
    flap**'). However a mid-line breast, although achieving a good surgical result, may
    cause an embarrassing appearance for the patient!
    (Coppage et al., 1994, reported CT findings in 10 patients who had pectoralis major or
    rectus abdominis muscle flap or omental transposition procedures top fill the bone gap
    after debridement, in the treatment of poststernotomy mediastinitis.)

Pectus excavatum and carinatum - both of these are due to overgrowth of the costal cartilages
and may be mixed with carinatum superiorly and excavatum inferiorly.
    In **pectus   excavatum** (Illus. **STERNUM   EXCAVATUM**) the anterior aspects of the ribs
descend more vertically than normal, and to the inexperienced the heart (which often appears to be
squashed) may appear to be enlarged; it is often displaced to the left and there may be spurious
right middle lobe disease, or a simulated mass in the right cardiophrenic angle.
    In **pectus carinatum** (Illus. **STERNUM CARINATUM** - carinatum = pertaining to keel or
spur - same meaning as carina) or '**pigeon chest deformity**' the ribs and costal cartilages curve
anteriorly more than normal, thus elevating the sternum, particularly its lower part.

    Neither condition usually causes much disability, and most deformities are cosmetic only, often
worrying parents or young juveniles. In some young females a depressed sternum may even be an
advantage by giving a 'greater depth of cleavage' ! Fred. Brunton of Southampton noted that in
females with a depressed sternum, the breasts may be more medially situated, with the nipples
pointing anteriorly, rather than antero-laterally (see Rawlinson, 1989 - who termed this
'**Brunton's sign**'.
    Occasional cases, particularly those that are familial, may cause marked cardiac compression
leading to cor pulmonale and death. Both conditions are usually well illustrated on plain chest
radiographs, but may also be shown in cross section by CT (e.g. prior to surgery - Illus.
STERNUM EXCAVATUM, Sternum deform Pt. 4a-b).

    A depressed sternum may give rise to spurious middle lobe consolidation (see ps. 2.25 & 6.29)
and to spurious mediastinal masses and pressure deformity on the oesophagus (see p. 16.1).

Hougaard and Arendrup (1983) warned of serious growth deformities of the female breasts, which
may occur if they are injured during corrective surgery for funnel chest in young girls.

Further references.
Magan (1949) : Fissura sterni congenita.
Chang and Davis (1961) : Congenital bifid sternum with partial ectopia cordis.
Larsen and Ibach (1962) : Complete congenital fissure of the sternum.
Jewett et al. (1962) : Congenital bifid sternum - benign form of ectopia cordis.
Murray (1966) : Bifid sternum.
Resnick and Brower (1979) : Midline circular defect in the sternum.
Destouet et al. (1981) : CT of sternoclavicular joints and sternum.
Goodman et al. (1983b) : CT of normal sternum.

Hatfield et al. (1984) : CT of sternum and its articulations.
Stark, P. (1985) : CT of middle sternal foramen.
Stark, P. and Jaramillo (1986) : CT of the sternum.
Brown (1960), Elster and Stark (1985), Stark et al. (1987) : Episternal ossicles.
Williams, C. (1872) : Great depression of the sternum.
Sweet (1944) : Pectus excavatum - two cases successfully operated on.
Soteropoulos et al. (1979) : Pectus excavatum simulating mediastinal masses (three cases).
Raithel et al. (1983) : CT of funnel chest.
Ward and Wilson (1987) : Studied 72 cases of sternal depression and noted the position of the heart, heart size and contour, the main pulmonary artery and right lower zone density. The degree of sternal depression was noted on lateral radiographs.
Ward et al. (1989) : Felt that an PA radiographs the most significant signs were - a straight left heart, border, displacement of the heart to the left and an indistinct left heart border.

Maier (1947) : Infections of the costal cartilages and sternum.
Biesecker et al. (1973) : Primary sternal osteomyelitis.
Culliford et al. (1976) : Sternal and chondral infection following open heart surgery.
Mandal et al. (1978) : Pseudomonas sternal osteomyelitis.
Kelly and Chetty (1985) : Primary sternal osteomyelitis - a rare condition.
Goodman, L. et al. (1983a), Kay (1983) : Complications after sternotomy.
Shafir et al. (1988) : Faulty sternotomy and complications after median sternotomy, esp. in a paramedian fashion.
Takahashi et al. (1992) : Obliteration of the descending aortic interface in pectus excavatum - correlation with clockwise rotation of the heart (see also p. 1.20) - also obliterates the para-sternal line (p. 1.29).
Templeton and Fishman (1992) : CT of post-sternotomy complications.
Vassallo (1969) : Spontaneous fracture of the sternum simulating pulmonary embolism
Watts et al. (1987) : Spontaneous fracture of the sternum and sternal tuberculosis.
Cooper (1988) : Insufficiency fractures of the sternum ? a consequence of thoracic kyphosis.
Sapherson and Mitchell (1990) : Atraumatic sternal fractures - secondary to osteoporosis are not uncommon with kyphosis in the elderly when the costal cartilages become ossified.
Maddern et al. (1993) : CT after reconstructive repair of the sternum and chest wall.
Jolles et al. (1996) : CT of mediastinitis following median sternotomy.
Hynes and Whitehouse (1997) : Haemoptysis due to aorto-bronchial fistula (with anterior segment bronchus RUL) caused by mycotic aneurysm of the ascending aorta associated with chronic osteomyelitis of the sternum two years after coronary by-pass and aortic valve replacement.

Sternal tumours.- (Illus. **STERNUM TUMOUR**).

The most common sternal tumours are metastatic from primary tumours such as the breast, bronchus, prostate, myeloma, etc. Soft tissue masses may extend out of these, especially with prostatic deposits, and these may ossify. Further deformities may occur due to pathological fractures.

Primary tumours include chondromas, osteochondromas and sarcomas. Other bony type tumours may occur and very vascular tumours such as a haemangioma may cause visible pulsation and may give rise to parasternal as well as sternal masses.

References.
O'Neal and Ackerman (1951) : Cartilaginous tumours of ribs and sternum.
Pygott and Hutton (1959) : A pulsating tumour of the sternum - ? a malignant haemangioma - angiographic study.
Rutledge (1962) : Spontaneous fracture of the sternum simulating myocardial infarction.
Vietta and Maier (1962) : Tumours of the sternum.
Katz (1966) : Sternal chondroma.
Peabody (1971) : Chondrosarcoma of sternum - six year survival.
Alonso - Sej and De Linera (1977) : Giant chondromyxoid fibroma of the sternum - replacement by acrylic resin prosthesis.
Urovitz et al. (1977) : Sternal metastases and associated pathological fractures.
Shin et al. (1986) : CT evaluation of primary and secondary sternal neoplasms.
Aoki et al. (1989) : CT of chondrosarcoma of the sternum - reviewed 11 cases - typically there was a large painless anterior chest wall mass in an elderly person, with stippled, flocculent or curvilinear calcification. The tumours were also scalloped or lobulated.
Eng et al. (1989) : Primary sternal tumours (9 cases - 4 benign).
Fink et al. (1990) : Giant chondroma of the sternum mimicking a mediastinal mass.
Obaro (1992) : Desmoplastic **fibroma** of the sternum.

The Costal Cartilages are normally symmetrical in size and shape at any one level, and commonly lie in a horizontal plane. They are thickened close to the sternum, and taper towards the costochondral junctions. For illustrations see Illus. **COSTAL CARTILAGES.**

Costo-chondritis of the costal cartilages (or **Tietze's syndrome**) is an 'inflammatory' condition of unknown cause, which was described by Tietze in 1921. It produces swelling of the affected cartilage(s) and overlying oedema in the acute phase. It usually occurs in those aged 20 to 40 and most commonly affects the 2nd to 6th cartilages, and particularly the 2nd. There may be decalcification in the affected cartilage, or adjacent rib-end or sternum. If bone is involved, a bone scan may be positive. Ultra-sound may show the peri-cartilaginous oedema in less marked cases. CT may show swelling of the cartilage in the acute phase, and some calcification within the cartilage after recovery. It may occasionally mimic and be mimicked by metastases. For illustrations see Illus. **TIETZE SYNDROME.**

References.
Edelstein et al. (1984) : Studied six patients by CT and found two with swelling of a costal cartilage, two with ventral angulation of the involved cartilage, whilst two were completely normal: isotope scans were negative.
Hamburg and Abdelwahab (1987) : Studied one case by CT, both acutely and following recovery. They found swelling of the affected costo-chondral junction with scattered calcifications within it.
Birnholz (1988) : Unilateral costochondral swelling shown by ultrasound.
Miro et al. (1988) : Costo-chondritis in 26 **heroin** addicts with systemic **candidiasis** shown by gallium scanning.
Honda et al. (1989) :: Gallium scan and CT in a patient with Tietze's syndrome.
Massie et al. (1993) : Bone scintigraphy and costochondritis.
Ikehira et al. (1999) : Acute pan-costochondritis probably caused by straining from severe coughing - gallium scan.

Infection of a costal cartilage may complicate trauma (including surgical trauma), be secondary to intra-thoracic disease or be metastatic from another site. Two memorable cases have been (i) a patient with renal failure who had multiple Staph. albus abscesses of the costal cartilages, and (ii) a dentist with an enterobacter infection of a costal cartilage preceded by osteomyelitis of the dorsal spine - both secondary to a chronic dental abscess under a prized self-inserted gold filling! - Illus. **COSTAL CART INFECTION, Pt. 1a-c.**

Costal cartilage calcification is common, but is usually of no clinical importance.
  The first costal cartilages usually calcify first, commonly after age 20, and their prominent lower margins may give rise to the '**idiot tumour**' - see p. 6.27 and Illus. **IDIOT TUMOUR.**

Two joints may be present:
 (i) between the cartilage and the calcified rib (a synostosis) and
 (ii) the cartilage and the sternum (often synovial). **Both may be subject to osteophyte formation**, especially the latter.

  About 50% of costal cartilages eventually become calcified, and their pattern of calcification is of some interest. The type of calcification often seems to be related to a person's sex, although there is some overlap and mixed types may be found. Calcification usually becomes more marked over the age of 40, and is then more often seen in males. Occasionally excessive early calcification may be seen in prominent costal cartilages, which are the site of mild discomfort in young people (especially females - Fig. 12.19). Females also sometimes show precocious costal cartilage calcification, particularly if they have hyperthyroidism, but such findings are virtually unknown in males. An easy way of remembering which types occur in which sex, is to consider that men like vaginas and females phalluses i.e. the appearance is the opposite to the appearance of a person's own sex organs!
  Rarely increased calcification may be seen with a sclerotic secondary deposit within a costal cartilage.

(a) & (b) Peripheral or upper and lower marginal
    calcification first, followed by central,
    is usually **male.**

(a)

(b)

(c)   'Nipple' or tongue' type, and

(c)

(d)   Parallel linear shadows situated
    centrally are usually **female** types.

(d)

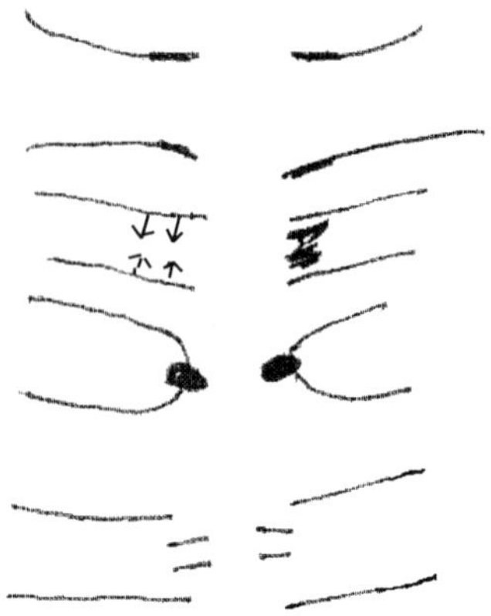

Fig. 12.19.   Patterns of costal cartilage calcification (after Sanders, 1966 - reproduced with permission from British Journal of Radiology).

See also Illus. **RIB-TONGUE** and Illus. **COSTAL CARTILAGE**, dep Pt. 1, inf Pt. 2, etc.

References.
King (1939) : Calcification of costal cartilages.
Sanders (1966) : Sexing by costal cartilage calcification.
Navani et al. (1970) : Studied 1,000 cases at Boston City Hospital.
Felson (1973)
Senac et al. (1985) : Early costo-chondral calcification in adolescent hyperthyroidism.

The manubrio-sternal joints may sometimes be more prominent than normal. About 50% of these joints are synovial and may be involved by granulomatous disease, such as rheumatoid, etc. They may also be involved by infection, secondary neoplasm or trauma. A joint affected by rheumatoid arthritis is more prone to dislocation, which may happen spontaneously, and if this happens the upper border of the body of the manubrium may give rise to a horizontal line projected over the upper sternum, which may sometimes mimic an air/fluid interface on frontal radiographs. However a lateral view will readily show the dislocation.

References.
Rivington et al. (1874) : Remarks on dislocation of the first and second pieces of the sternum.
Fowler (1957) : Flexion compression injury to the sternum.
Sevitt (1968) : Dislocation of the manubrio-sternal joint - detection on frontal radiographs - 3 cases with kyphosis - 2 had rheumatoid (study in causes of death in 250 road accidents).
Rapoport et al. (1979) : Manubrio-sternal joint subluxation in rheumatoid arthritis.
Holt and Rooney (1980) : Manubrio-sternal subluxation in rheumatoid arthritis.
Park et al. (1980) : Cervico-dorsal injury presenting as a sternal fracture.
Wiseman (1981) : Dislocation of the manubriosternal joint in rheumatoid arthritis.
Khong and Rooney (1982) : Manubriosternal joint subluxation in rheumatoid arthritis.
Kelly et al. (1986) : Manubriosternal joint dislocation in rheumatoid arthritis - the role of thoracic kyphosis.

The sterno-clavicular joints - may be affected by the following (* = may give a positive bone scan)

Trauma* - subluxation, fracture, etc.
Occasionally the medial end of the clavicle may be dislocated retro-sternally when the neurovascular structures may be damaged and the trachea compressed. Such an injury is best demonstrated by CT, so that early reduction can be performed. In severe cases serious damage to upper mediastinal structures, serious disability or even death may ensue. (See Buckerfield & Castle, 1984, Selesnick et al., 1984 - 4 cases, Djerf et al 1998 - retrosternal clavicular dislocation in a 52 year old female who fell off her bicycle onto her right shoulder).

Infection* - is uncommon, but may occur with tuberculosis or be secondary to a lung abscess. Infection from these joints may spread up into the neck or into the anterior mediastinum.

Osteoarthritis* or degenerative arthritis - gas may be present in these as with other degenerative or sprained joints or cartilages (pulled out of solution by the excessive mobility).

Condensing osteitis* of the medial end of the clavicle - well defined bony sclerosis involving the inferior aspect with slight expansion and a small hook-like osteophyte. It is probably degenerative in origin (see Brower et al., 1974 and Cone et al., 1983). It may also follow osteomyelitis (Mollan et al., 1984).

Stress induced osteolysis* of the medial end of the clavicle (Kaplan and Resnick, 1986) - (similar to post-traumatic osteolysis * of the outer end of the clavicle - Levine et al., 1976).

Rheumatoid arthritis* - erosions and cyst formation, etc.

Polymyalgia rheumatica* - among other joints, the sterno-clavicular joints are commonly affected with overlying swelling and small bone erosions, which as they heal produce small sclerotic lesions in the manubrium and inner ends of the clavicles (Paice et al., 1983 and Wright and Paice, 1983). This is probably the cause of several other illustrated cases of sterno-clavicular disease in the literature. See also note re probable prodromal effect of neoplasm - p. 23.5 and Illus. **BRAIN, Pt. 3a-d.**

Freidrich's disease* (osteo-chondritis of the medial end of the clavicle - Friedrich, 1924) - is seen mainly in females. It affects the inner ends of the clavicles and is usually bilateral, and may lead to secondary degenerative disease (Drewes and Gunther, 1982 and Jurik et al., 1985 - see also Fischel and Bernstein, 1975 and Levy et al., 1981).

Sterno-costo-clavicular hyperostosis* - a benign ossifying diathesis possibly related to ankylosing spondylitis, mainly affects the soft tissues between the clavicles. It may also involve the posterior parts of the upper ribs and adjacent vertebrae and the sacro-iliac joints. It may be associated with relapsing pustular erosions of the hands and feet. Sonozaki et al. (1978 unilateral cases, in 1979 - 22 cases, and in 1981 - 53 cases) graded the condition into three categories : (i) ossification of the costo-clavicular ligaments, (ii) progressive ossification of soft tissues and (iii) extensive soft tissue ossification with hyperostosis of the inner ends of the clavicles, adjacent ribs and sternum. The condition has been reviewed by Resnick (1980), Sartoris et al. (1986 who reported 11 cases), by Colhoun et al. (1987) and by Economou et al., 1993 who studied four cases with CT, three having positive bone scans. Another case, with a positive bone scan, was reported by Ipinyomi and Watt (1989).

Acromegaly may also cause hypertrophy of the inner ends of the clavicles and thickening of the first ribs, as well as generalised bone porosis.

Ankylosing spondylitis may cause fusion of these joints which may be a pointer to this condition. A former air-line pilot, with severe pulmonary fibrosis, on whom the author was performing chest CT, had this as the feature which suggested the diagnosis, which was confirmed - see also p. 19.90 and Illus. **ANKYLOSING SPONDYLITIS**. (He has also since seen a second pilot with a similar disability and findings).

Illustrations of the sterno-clavicular joints are shown in Illus. **STERNO-CLAV JOINTS**.

Further references.
Golden et al. (1973) : Sternoclavicular septic arthritis in heroin users.
Bayer et al. (1977) : Sternoclavicular pyoarthritis due to Gram-negative bacilli - 8 cases.
Destouet et al. (1981) : CT of the sternoclavicular joint and sternum.
Hatfield et al. (1984) : CT of the sternum and its articulations.
Hamilton-Wood et al. (1985) from Bristol divided diseases of the sterno-clavicular joints into three groups :
(i) those with a history of < 6 weeks, who either had a pyoarthrosis or malignant disease,
(ii) osteitis condensans, and
(iii) degenerative arthritis. They reported 13 patients with pain and/or swelling of these joints.
Muir et al. (1985) : Infectious arthritis of the sternoclavicular joint.
Alexander and Shin (1990) : CT manifestations of sternoclavicular pyoarthritis in pts. with intravenous drug abuse.
Pollack (1990) : Staphylococcal mediastinitis due to sternoclavicular pyoarthritis - CT appearance.
Wilson and Evans (1996) : Described sterno-costo-clavicular hyperostosis presenting with thoracic sinus formation.
Kelly (1997) and Brandsen (1993) : Pointed out that painful hyperostosis of the sternoclavicular joints and planto/palmar pustule formation are the hallmarks of an identical condition (SAPHO - synovitis, acne, planto-palmar pustulosis, hyperostosis & osteomyelitis).
Davies et al. (1998) : Dislocation of the sternoclavicular joints - review of 6 cases (4 posterior and 2 anterior). Plain radiographic findings can be subtle - CT is the investigation of choice. Delay in diagnosis is associated with morbidity and difficulty in obtaining a stable reduction. In one case of posterior dislocation, the clavicle was displaced superiorly.
Patten et al. (1999) : Gas in the sternoclavicular joints of patients with blunt chest trauma.

The clavicles.
   Clavicular disease may be secondary to a number of causes : -
Absence - (congenital) cranio-cleido-dysostosis - (acquired) secondary deposit or surgery) - Illus. **CLAVICLE ABSENT.**

Fracture - occasionally with persistent non-union or osteolysis - Illus. **CLAVICLE FRACTURE.**

Infection - rare (used to be not uncommon with syphilis - membrane bones - skull and clavicle were not uncommonly affected by gummata - used to be typical radiology exam. cases.)

Paget's disease - (of whole or either end and giving rise to symptoms in the active phase and warm to the touch) **-** Illus. **CLAVICLE PAGET'S.**

Chronic sclerosing osteitis - a rare but frequently misdiagnosed condition mainly in 4th and 5th decades (Greenspan et al., 1991) - sclerosis is also seen with polyarteritis nodosa (see refs. p.19.81) and Takayasu's disease (see also p. 10.17).

Degenerative - following trauma (Sudeck's atrophy after immobilisation) or following radiotherapy (with stress fractures which poorly heal).

Benign tumour - Illus. **CLAVICLE OSTEOMA.**

Secondary neoplasm (e.g. bronchus, breast, prostate, etc.) Illus. **CLAVICLE DEPOSIT.**

Primary tumour - sarcoma - (esp. after radiotherapy) - Illus. **CLAVICLE SARCOMA.**

Fractures of the clavicles (like those of the first ribs) may occasionally lead to severe complications such as damage to the subclavian vessels. According to one account King Rufus (the successor to William the Conqueror) died after falling from his horse and breaking a clavicle. (Another account says that he was hit by an arrow in the New Forest - possibly both occurred). He probably died from a traumatic rupture of the subclavian artery. Another famous case was Sir Robert Peel (Prime Minister from 1841) who in June 1850 fell off a newly acquired rogue horse in

Constitution Hill, after visiting Buckingham Palace, and sustained a comminuted fracture of his left clavicle and fractures of the upper left ribs. He developed a palpable adjacent pulsatile swelling and died three days later (for further details see The Times - 4 July 1850, Lancet - 6 July 1950 and Gash, 1972).

For potential and actual injuries to the subclavian vessels - see Illus. **CLAVICLE FRACTURE, Pts. 2a-b, 3a-c & 4.**

Acromio-clavicular joints and erosion of the outer end of the clavicle (as well as the inner) may follow trauma (e.g. injury playing Rugby football - dislocation or fracture of outer end of clavicle), occur with renal osteodystrophy, hyperparathyroidism or follow infection or the injection of steroids into the acromio clavicular joint. The joints may be eroded with some adjacent tumours, or be hypoplastic as in achondroplasia (see Illus. **ACROMIO-CLAV JOINT**).

Note also the **rhomboid fossa** in the lower inferior aspect of the inner end of the clavicle, caused by the origin of costo-clavicular (or rhomboid) ligament (Illus. **CLAVICLE, Rhomboid fossa 1 -3**) - see also p. 12.10.

Ultrasound of rib and costal cartilage lesions (see also p. 20.33).

Ribs usually cause dense acoustic shadows, which prevent structures behind them being identified. However decalcified ribs (from lytic secondary deposits or myeloma) do allow penetration by ultrasound, and this may assist in biopsies. Costal cartilages tend to reflect ultrasound less and destruction within them may occasionally be seen. In costo-chondritis surrounding soft tissue swelling is often seen (Illus. **COSTAL CARTILAGES, Cos cart inf Pt. 1a** and **Costal cart chond Pt. 6**).

Chapter 13 : **The Thoracic Lymphatic System and Lymph Nodes, and the Spread of Tumours within the Lungs, the Tracheobronchial Tree and the Mediastinum.**

Historical.

Because of their minute size and unrecognised function, lymph vessels were not observed until 1563, when Eustachius discovered the thoracic duct in a horse, and termed it the 'Vena Alba Thoracis', from its milk-like content. In 1653, Thomas Bartholinus published his book 'Vasa Lymphatica'. John Hunter (1759) wrote: "the lymphatics, though long known were not in the least suspected of performing the operation of absorbtions" - they were supposed to be a continuation of the extreme ends of the arteries, which were not large enough to carry red blood, but only lymph or serum. William Cruickshank (1786) distinguished 'superficial absorbents' in the lungs from those which were 'deeper seated', both sets of vessels draining into the 'glands' at the roots of the lungs. A year later, Mascagni (1787), in a book illustrating the lymphatics of the whole body in life-size woodcuts, demonstrated the sub-pleural and deeper lymphatics by the injection of mercury in cadavers, and noted the positions of the major lymph nodes in the angles of the bifurcations of the major arteries and bronchi. He also observed that crossed connections into the left or right side of the mediastinum could occur from the contralateral lung or hilar nodes. Illus. **LYMPHATICS, Mascagni** is a reproduction of his drawing of the nodes and vessels draining the lungs.

Becker (1826) classified the thoracic lymph nodes into parietal and visceral, distinguishing three groups: (i) lying close to the trachea, (ii) at the bifurcation of the trachea, and (iii) at the hila of the lungs. Parrot (1876) noted 'Les ganglions bronchiques sont comme le miroir du poumon'. Küss (1898) studied pulmonary tuberculosis in childhood and gave the first description of the 'primary focus' - ('le foyer pulmonaire primitif'), which was also studied by Ghon (1912) - the latter's name being more commonly associated with it - the '**Ghon focus**' - Illus. **GHON FOCUS**.

At the end of the 19th century, many publications appeared describing the anatomy of thoracic nodes in relation to pulmonary tuberculosis. Leaf (1898) noted the relationship of the left sub-aortic nodes to the left recurrent laryngeal nerve. Sukiennikow (1903) studied the topographic anatomy of the bronchial and tracheal nodes. He described spaces alongside the trachea and nodes below the carina, and observed the gradual lateral deviation of the node chains as they pass upwards towards the thoracic inlet. He thought that nodes were mainly of two types : (i) at the bifurcations of the trachea or bronchi, and (ii) interconnecting nodes. A different view was given by Engel (1926) who considered that nodes were usually associated with the pulmonary artery and its branches. Steinert (1928) believed that hilar nodes were related to both vessels and bronchi. He also noted anastomotic vessels linking the para-tracheal chains. Rouvière (1932) published a detailed study of the lymphatic system, including a chapter on the lung and mediastinum. This was further studied by some of his pupils - Cordier et al. (1958).

The thoracic and accessory thoracic ducts.

The thoracic duct arises in the upper abdomen from the cisterna chyli and enters the thorax behind and to the right of the aorta through the aortic opening in the diaphragm. In the lower mediastinum it lies posteriorly between the aorta and the azygos vein. At the level of D4 it inclines to the left and ascends behind the arch of the aorta on the left side of the oesophagus. It then passes behind the first part of the subclavian artery, before turning outwards and curving downwards over the subclavian artery and in front of scalenus anterior to form an arch, and finally terminating in the left subclavian vein, at its junction with the left internal jugular vein. In the mid thorax it may divide into two or more channels which soon reunite. Multiple valves may be present throughout its course. Within the chest it is joined by the lymph vessels from the left lung and left half of the mediastinum, and just before its termination the vessels from the left side of the head and neck and left arm.

The right (or accessory) thoracic duct is only about an inch long and receives lymph vessels from the right side of the thorax, the right side of the head and neck, and from the right upper limb. It enters the venous system by several small channels into the right jugular, subclavian and innominate veins. Occasionally it forms a right sided branch from a mid-thoracic division of the thoracic duct, and may enter the right subclavian vein, similarly to the entry of the thoracic duct on the left side.

Neoplasms which cause obstruction to the thoracic duct include reticuloses, and lung carcinomas, particularly those causing SVC obstruction. It may also be blocked by some parasites e.g. loa loa or filariasis.

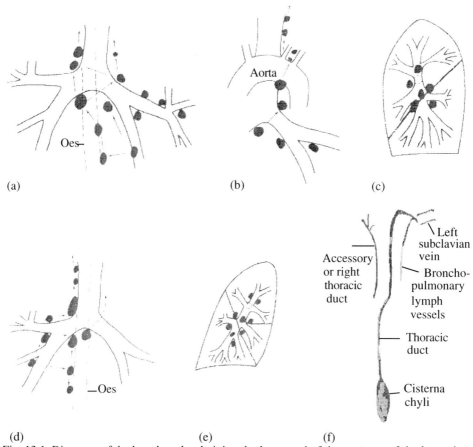

(a)   (b)   (c)

(d)   (e)   (f)

Fig. 13.1 Diagrams of the lymph nodes draining the lungs and of the anatomy of the larger intra-thoracic lymph vessels:
    (a to c) - AP and lateral views - left lung,   (d) and (e) - AP and lateral views - right lung,
            (f) larger thoracic lymph vessels - note that the right (or accessory) lymph duct enters the venous system by several small channels into the right jugular, subclavian and innominate veins.
(a - e after McCort and Robbins, 1951, reproduced from Radiology, **57**, 339 - 360 with permission, see also Nohl, 1962).

Lymphography of the thoracic ducts, nodes, etc.
    The duct may be demonstrated by lymphography (Illus. **THORACIC DUCT**), via the feet and in some cases by CT after drinking an emulsion of Lipiodol. When obstruction of the thoracic duct is present, lymphography will tend to opacify the mediastinal nodes, but this can happen in some patients without any evidence of obstruction, and probably because the lymphatic system is subject to considerable anatomical variation, with some vessels draining into the mediastinal and hilar nodes. It was not uncommon when lymphangiograms were more commonly carried out patients with lymphoma or seminoma to find several opacified mediastinal nodes on subsequent CT examinations. In some cases developmental abnormalities may cause the pulmonary, including subpleural, lymphatics to be visualised. A case is illustrated in Illus. **LYMPHATICS, Pt. 12a-e**, in which the patient developed chylothoraces secondary to lymphatic malformations and trauma.

Malformations of the lymphatic system may result in the thoracic duct draining directly into a pleural cavity (see Illus. **LYMPHATICS, Pt. 13**); lymphpcoeles may also be opacified by lymphography (Illus. **LYMPHATICS, Pt. 3a -b**).

Further references.
Van Pernis (1949) : Variations of the thoracic duct.
Watne, W. et al. (1960) : Clinical and autopsy study of tumour cells in thoracic duct lymph.
Pomerantz et al. (1963) : Functional anatomy of thoracic duct shown by lymphangiography.
White and Urquart (1966) : The demonstration of pulmonary lymphatics by lymphography in a pt. with chylothorax.
Baltaxe and Constable (1968) : Mediastinal lymph node visualisation in the absence of intra-thoracic disease.
Weidner and Steiner (1971) : Demonstration of intrapulmonary and pleural lymphatics during lymphography (including a case of chylothorax).
Rosenberger et al. (1972) : The thoracic duct - structural function and radiology - also noted reflux into mediastinal nodes at lymphography in 5 to 15%.
Grant and Levin (1974) : Lymphangiographic visualisation of pleural and pulmonary lymphatics via the inferior pulmonary ligaments.
Sachs et al. (1991) : Diagnosis and localisation of laceration of the thoracic duct - usefulness of lymphangiography and CT (12 cases - CT was of little additional value - 5 had leaks from the thoracic duct).
Lee and Cassar-Pullicino (2000) : Giant cisterna chyli shown by MR with Gd-DTPA enhancement.

Pulmonary lymphatics.

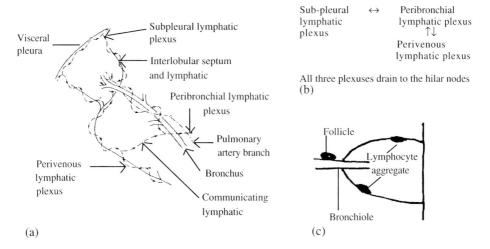

Fig. 13. 2   Lymphatic anatomy of the lung and visceral pleura.

(a) Lymphatics within the lung. (b) Drainage of lung and sub-pleural plexus to hilar lymph nodes.
   Spread of lung and bronchial tumours may take place via the peribronchial, perivenous and sub-pleural lymphatics, and their interconnections. (c) Lymphoid follicles and BALT at small bronchial and bronchiolar bifurcations and in septa of secondary lobules.

Notes : 1. The flow of fluid through the pulmonary lymphatics depends on the pumping action associated with respiration - see also Fig. 1.57, p. 1.44.
      2. The parietal pleural lymphatics drain by two routes :
          (i) posteriorly to the posterior intercostal and posterior mediastinal nodes, and
          (ii) anteriorly to the internal mammary nodes.
        3. Efferent vessels from the above, pass alongside the trachea, and into the posterior mediastinum (the 'broncho-mediastinal vessels') to join the thoracic and accessory thoracic ducts.

Pulmonary lymphatics have been studied by many authors, including Miller, W. (1937 & 1947) and Trapnell (1963, 1967 & 1970). They confirmed the view that there are two groups of lymphatics in the lungs, one in the sub-pleural space, and the second deep in the lungs in relation to the bronchi and blood vessels. The most comprehensive modern study was made by Nagaishi (1972) from Japan. He confirmed the presence of both deep and superficial pulmonary lymphatic systems in both men and animals, and divided the deep system into peribronchial and perivenous lymphatics. He also noted a marked anastomosis of the **peribronchial lymphatics with those in the bronchial walls**, particularly the larger bronchi. Many pulmonary lymphatics start in the region of the alveolar ducts and respiratory bronchioles (i.e. close to the alveolar walls) in the centre of secondary lobules, and run in the interlobular, pleural, peribronchial and perivascular connective tissue sheaths. Others drain the periphery of the lobules, starting in the interlobular septa, and run with the pulmonary veins. Anastomotic vessels link the perivenous and peribronchial vessels.

Subpleural lymphatics drain into a subpleural network, which in turn drains over the surface of the lung to the hilar nodes. Willis (1679) first showed the presence of valves in the subpleural lymphatics. Councilman (1900) reported that valves were present in the interlobular vessels and thought that they pointed towards the pleura, though Trapnell felt that they mainly point in the opposite direction, i.e. towards the hilum. According to Spencer (1984) communication between the deep and subpleural lymphatics takes place just deep to the pleural surface of the lungs. The author has carried out a few pulmonary lymphangiograms, injecting the Lipiodol directly into subpleural lymphatics of an excised lung (after a preliminary minute injection of patent blue, as soon as the chest has been opened, to allow them to be visualised) and has shown that the contrast medium passes readily into the peribronchial and intrabronchial plexuses, as well as the subpleural plexus, thus showing a good anastomosis (Illus. **LYMPHATICS 20a-c**).

Intrapulmonary lymphoid tissue and intra-pulmonary lymph nodes.

Aggregates of lymphoid tissue or 'follicles' of bronchus-associated lymphoid tissue (**BALT**) are present near the origins of lymph channels at the respiratory bronchioles. BALT follicles also occur at the bifurcations of distal bronchi and bronchioles. These are part of the '**pulmonary lymphatic sump**' and are analagous to mucosa-associated lymphoid tissue (**MALT**) such as Peyer's patches in the gut. They appear to play a part in the immune response to inhaled antigens and may enlarge in inflammatory, antigenic or hypersensitivity conditions (including rheumatoid, Sjögren's syndrome and eosinophilia) and when enlarged cause 'follicular bronchiolitis' (p. 3.28). Sometimes they may produce a miliary or mottled appearance on radiographs (e.g. with TB, mycoplasma, and rickettsial infections). They are often visible to the naked eye within some excised lungs and vary in size up to 0.5 cm in diameter. On CT sections they often appear as small nodules in immunocompromised patients - Illus. **HYPOGLOBULIN, Pt. 2e-f** show an example of hypoglobulinaemia. Such are also seen in AIDS patients with lymphoproliferative disorders, which are often stimulated by the Epstein-Barr virus - see p. 19.30.

In addition definite lymph nodes within a capsule may be found far out into some lungs and even peripherally close to the pleura. These nodes are not often demonstrated radiologically, but may become visible when enlarged with tumour metastases, sarcoidosis, lymphoma, leukaemia or pneumoconiosis, or in infectious mononucleosis (glandular fever or EB virus).
Illus. **INTRA PULM NODES** show examples - in lymphoma, and sarcoidosis. Unless occurring with such a likely cause, surgical excision may be the only route to a certain diagnosis.

Some notes on lymphocytes.

Lymphocytes are the basic cells of the lymphoid system and are of three main types - B, T and Null (i.e. not B or T). B lymphocytes when stimulated by antigens differentiate into plasma-cells which in turn produce antibodies. T lymphocytes are of several types: - (i) T-helper cells which produce cytokines and assist B lymphocytes, macrophages and granulocytes, (ii) T-cytoxic cells which destroy cells infected with viruses and tumour cells, and (iii) T-suppressor cells which turn down an immune response. Null cells destroy cells coated with antibodies. T cells are particularly produced in the thymus. Lymphocytes circulate in the blood, rapidly detect antigens (many are specific to certain antigens) and stimulate the production of more lymphocytes in nodes etc. to cause the immune response.

Table 13.1 - <u>Some lymphoproliferative diseases involving the chest.</u>

lymphoid hyperplasia -	Follicular bronchitis/ bronchiolitis - see p. 3.28
	Diffuse lymphoid hyperplasia - p. 19.119
	LIP - see ps. 5.33 & 19.119

        Pseudolymphoma (p. 5.29)
        Plasma cell granuloma or pseudotumour (p. 5.33)
        Angio -immunoblastic lymphadenopathy (p. 5.35)

(see also **Table 13.3** - p. 13.17 re nodes and Chapters 17 & 18 re the spleen and thymus).

<u>References.</u>
Liebow and Carrington (1973) : Diffuse lymphoreticular infiltrations associated with dysproteinaemia.
Heitzman et al. (1975b) : Lymphoproliferative disorders of the chest.
Feigin et al. (1977) : Non-malignant lymphoid disorders of the chest.
Kradin and Mark (1983) : Benign lymphoid disorders of the lung.
Bienstock (1984) : BALT.,   Roitt et al. (1989) : Immunology.
Herbert et al. (1985) : LIP identified as lymphoma of MALT.
Glickstein et al. (1986) : Non-lymphomatous lymphoid disorders of the chest.
Richmond et al. (1993) : BALT in the human lung, its distribution in smokers and non-smokers.
Bragg et al. (1994) : Lymphoproliferative disorders of the lung.
Koch et al. (1997) : Bronchus associated lymphoid tissue hyperplasia of the lung., Oh et al. (1999) : Air trapping.
Gibson and Hansell (1998) : Lymphocytic disorders of the chest.

Miller, W. (1911) : Felt that subpleural nodes only occurred in abnormal lungs, and that they developed from normal masses of lymphoid tissue.
Rouvière (1932) and von Hayek (1960) : Describing the anatomy of thoracic nodes referred to examples in the literature, but stated that they had not seen any definite intrapulmonary nodes.
Macklin (1955) : Pulmonary sumps, dust accumulations, alveolar fluid and lymph vessels.
Greenberg, H. (1961) : A hyperplastic right basal subpleural lymph node was demonstrated radiographically, surgically removed and examined histologically.
Trapnell (1964a) : Studied 92 lungs from 91 patients (age range 10-82 yrs.) - these were inflated and radiographed, but in only one case did plain radiographs reveal the presence of intrapulmonary nodes (three - each 0.5 cm in diameter). Following lymphography (injecting the subpleural lymphatics) intrapulmonary nodes were outlined in 5.
Greenfield and Jelaso (1965) : Tumour metastasis in a peripheral intrapulmonary node.
Spencer (1968) : Did not regard intrapulmonary nodes as uncommon on pathological examination.
Kradin (1985) : Enlargement of intrapulmonary nodes in ten patients with coal-miners pneumoconiosis. They were seen radiographically in almost all cases on lateral views, below carinal level, were under 2 cm in size and many were multiple.
Bankoff et al. (1996) : Prevalence of pathologically proven intrapulmonary lymph nodes and their appearance on CT.
Mikaye et al. (1999) : CT and pathology of intrapulmonary nodes in four patients.

<u>Congenital lymphatic malformations.</u>

Congenital pulmonary lymphangiectasis is found in infants and causes intercommunicating thin-walled, endothelium-lined, fluid-filled cysts of varying diameter in the subpleural, peribronchial and interlobular connective tissue. The affected infants develop respiratory distress with cyanosis soon after birth, most only surviving a few days. Chest radiographs may show the cystic lung masses or a mottled linear pattern throughout the lungs.

Mediastinal hygromas, lymphangiomas and lymphocoeles. Hygromas and lymphangiomas are developmental malformations of the lymphatic system. Most hygromas occur in infants and involve the neck and/or the (upper) mediastinum, and some consider them to be cystic lymphatic hamartomas (Illus. **LYMPHOCOELE, LYMPHATICS, Pt. 3a-b**). A few present in adults. They may be associated with chylous pleural effusions. A lymphocoele is similar but occurs following trauma, including surgical trauma.

Cystic dilatation of the thoracic duct per se may also occur (Tsuchiya et al., 1980 reviewed nine such cases). Kolbenstvedt and Aanesen (1986) reported a case causing a fluctuant mass in the left supraclavicular area and demonstrated by contrast medium injection.

Lymphangiomatosis causes lymphatic proliferation along normal lymphatic sites in the lung, with thickening of the septa, subpleural lymphatics and bronchovascular bundles (see also p. 1.55).

Lymphangiomyomatosis (characterised histologically by proliferation of atypical smooth muscle in the lungs and lymphatic system of the thorax and retroperitoneum) occurs in two types: (i) A mediastinal and pleural type, leading to mediastinal thickening with mediastinal lymphatic obstruction, the production of chylous effusions and occasionally pneumothoraces. It may also extend down into the retroperitoneum causing calcification or involving the renal tracts, and may lead to ascites; and (ii) a more localised form involving the lungs (see ps. 1.54 & 5.18). Both types occur almost exclusively in women - see Illus. **LAM**.

Further references.
Noonan et al. (1970) : Congenital pulmonary lymphangiectasis.
British Medical Journal (1972) : Congenital pulmonary lymphangiectasis.
Li et al. (1985) : Pulmonary lymphangiectasis.
Griffin et al. (1986) : Systemic lymphangioleiomyomatosis - a combined approach by lymphangiography and CT.
Levine (1989) : Primary disorders of the lymphatic vessels - a unified concept.

Emerson (1950), Ross (1961), Barlow & Gracey (1965) : Supradiaphragmatic thoracic duct cysts.
Moritten and Allen (1986) : Thoracic duct cyst - diagnosis with needle aspiration.
Gollub and Castellino (1996) : Cisterna chyli - potential mimic of retrocrural nodal enlargement at CT.
Ueda et al. (2000) : CT of dilated abdominal paraaortic lymphatic duct with 'stalk' to thoracic duct.

Touroff and Seley (1953) : Chronic chylothorax associated with hygroma of the mediastinum.
Higgins and Mulder (1970) : Mediastinal chyloma.
Pilla et al. (1982) : Two cases of mediastinal cystic duct hygroma in adults were well demonstrated by CT. They emphasised moulding of the masses to the mediastinum, and the envelopment of vessels.
Tatu et al. (1985) : CT of mediastinal cystic hygroma in an adult.
Korman et al. (1986) : Hygroma causing dyspnoea and stridor in a young woman.
Joseph et al. (1989) : Cystic hygroma + thoracic venous aneurysm (see also p. 9.9).
Gorenstein et al. (1992) : Cystic hygroma associated with venous aneurysm (see also p. 9.9).

Pardes et al. (1982) : Lymphangioma (predominantly cystic) causing a right upper anterior mediastinal mass with wave sign in a girl aged 12.
Brown, L. et al. (1986) : Intrathoracic lymphangioma.
Cohen et al. (1987) : Lymphangiectasia and cystic adenomatoid malformations shown by MR.
Shaffer et al. (1994) : Thoracic lymphangioma in adults (19 pts. - mostly female - 16 to 67 yrs. old) - CT and MR appearances. The most common was a smooth cystic mass in the anterior or superior mediastinum (less commonly in the pericardium, pulmonary hilum or lung). Unusual features included calcification, spiculated margins and homogeneous soft tissue density.
Mikaye et al. (1996) : Mediastinal lymphangiomas in adults - CT findings in 3 cases (i) 29 yr. old man with slowly enlarging well defined cystic mediastinal mass (19 HU) cont. small areas of calcification) since first detected age 16. It enveloped mediastinal structures but caused no compression. (ii) 67 yr. old man - homogeneous well defined cystic mass in R paratracheal region, and (iii) 17 yr. old man - haemorrhage into cysts, with increased size over 15 yrs.
Ellis et al. (1983) : Traumatic lymphocoele demonstrated with Tc^{99m} sulphur colloid lymphography.
Day and Warwick (1985) : Oral ultra fluid Lipiodol for the opacification of the thoracic duct prior to CT.
Shin et al. (1985) : Two hygromatous cysts shown by CT- (i) large right paratracheal cyst in a man aged 37, and (ii) an enlarging right upper mediastinal paravertebral cystic mass in a man of 72.
Sullivan and Wechsler (1985) : Lymphocoele after oesophagogastrectomy shown by CT following lymphography.

Collard et al. (1968) : Contribution of lymphangiography to the study of diffuse lymphangiomyomatosis.
Gray et al. (1975) : Lymphangiomyomatosis - case with ureteral involvement and chyluria.
Rumancik et al. (1984) : Atypical renal and pararenal hamartomas associated with lymphangiomyomatosis.
Bhatti et al. (1985) : Pleuropulmonary and skeletal lymphangiomyomatosis with chylothorax and chylopericardium.
Higgins et al. (1993) : CT of generalised lymphangiomyomatosis and chylothorax in an infant.
Peh et al. : (1994) Lymphangiomyomatosis with spontaneous peritoneal rupture.
(Further references are given on ps. 5.18 - 19).

Spread of tumours within the lungs and larger airways.

(a) **Hilic and lepidic growth of tumours** (see also ps. 5.38, 24.50 & App. p. 2)**.**

Peripheral lung tumours may enlarge by two methods. The first is **expansile** or 'hilic' growth, when the tumour enlarges concentrically to produce a solid mass, displacing the normal lung as it enlarges, and the second is **infiltrative** or 'lepidic' growth in which the tumour cells use the lung structures as a scaffolding, filling and covering the septa and alveoli with tumour cells and exudate, in a similar manner to inflammatory change with infections, etc. Thus **expansile** or 'hilic' tumours tend to have **well-defined outlines**, whilst **infiltrative** or 'lepidic' **are 'shaggy' or irregular**. Both types may expand centrally along tissue planes, or lymphatics. Not only may this lead to central metastases, but also to spread within the lung itself, leading to carcinomatous consolidation, neighbouring satellite tumour nodules, local fine areas of spread and tiny nodules (the **'galaxy'** or **'nebula   sign'** of bronchiolo-alveolar tumours - see ps. 5.1 et seq.), more remote tumour nodules in pulmonary septa, along the lymphatics centrally or peripherally with reversed lymph flow. Nordenström's **'corona maligna'** (Fig. 4.4b - 4.14) is very suggestive of tumour, and although some have suggested that it may occur with benign disease and preferring the term **'corona radiata'**, the author has not seen it with a benign process.

(b) **Lymphatic spread within the lung and larger airways and beyond.**

Tumour cells entering the lymphatics of the lung may travel centrally towards the hilar regions, or peripherally towards the sub-pleural plexus, depending on the direction of lymph flow. Centripetal spread takes place not only to the hilar lymph nodes, but also to the peribronchial and perivascular lymph plexuses. There are multiple submucosal lymphatics in the bronchial walls, which communicate with these, and in which tumour deposits may grow producing secondary tumours in the more central bronchial walls. These may become so large as to mimic primary tumours, and the author believes that many 'clinical' or 'bronchoscopic primary tumours' may in fact be secondaries from a small peripheral primary tumour, which may have been overlooked on plain radiographs. Spencer (1968 & 1984, in his Textbook of Pathology) noted that even in resected specimens and at autopsy, pathologists may mistake such proximal bronchial wall involvement for the primary tumour. It thus behoves the diagnostic radiologist to look carefully for small peripheral primary tumours. In fact with good tomographic studies, small peripheral tumours are not infrequently demonstrated.

Pathways of lymphatic spread of lung tumours are illustrated in Figs. 13.2a & b. Spread through these, within the lung, causing 'peri-bronchial infiltration', may give rise to 'peribronchial streaking' (Fig. 13.4), but this is not a certain sign of neoplasm, being seen also with some inflammatory processes passing towards the hilum.

Secondary involvement of the hilum and larger bronchi, in this way, will also tend to cause 'fixity' or 'rigidity' of the hilum, as determined at rigid-tube bronchoscopy. The possible presence of such spread is one of the reasons why bronchoscopy should **always** be carried out; in a high proportion of cases biopsy will be positive and will thus prove that the tumour is inoperable.

Tumour which has spread into the bronchial wall may enter the broncho-vascular connective tissue sheath, and grow along and through this and through the peri- and endobronchial lymphatic plexus to give rise to submucosal tumour spread, giving rise to one or more bronchial, carinal or tracheal mucosal or submucosal masses remote from the primary sites (see Fig. 13.3 below). Tracheal tumours (see p. 4.23) may also metastasise in the same way to give rise to 'seedling tumours' elsewhere in the trachea or larger bronchi. This type of spread is illustrated in the following diagrams:

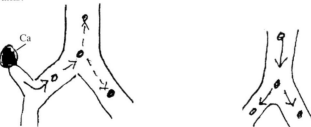

Fig. 13.3 (a) Bronchial ca spreading submucosally to trachea & (b) tracheal ca to main bronchi.

In the above diagram a bronchial tumour in the right upper lobe (a) is spreading through the submucosal lymphatics to the right main bronchus, carina, and on into the trachea and contra-lateral left main bronchus; and in (b) a tracheal tumour is spreading downwards through the submucosal lymphatics to the lower trachea and main bronchi.

When the central lymphatics become blocked by tumour deposits, the direction of lymph flow, which is usually controlled by valves, may be reversed producing congestion in the lung, and with retrograde flow towards the pleural surfaces, the valves becoming incompetent as occur with limb lymphoedema. Thus tumour involvement of the pleura (either 'dry' or with an effusion) may be produced not only by direct invasion of the pleura by the primary tumour, but also by the reversal of the greater normal centripetal lymph flow, carrying tumour cells peripherally, the blockage often occurring at a point remote from the primary tumour. This process also leads to lymphangitic tumour spread within the lung, and causing marked septal line engorgement with Kerley's A, B and C lines (see ps. 8.9 - 10).(Line shadows may also be present proximal or distal to a tumour and be due to linear collapse or pleural tags - see ps. 4.17 - 18. Unilateral lymphangitic spread of lung cancer is not uncommon, and may be the presenting feature. Illus. **LYMPHANGITIS, Pts. 1 & 4** and **CONGEST UNILAT, Congestion Pt. 17** show such unilateral 'lymphangitis carcinomatosa' - typical of diffuse spread, often with no primary tumour visible. The lymphatic type of spread also results in the small satellite tumours, particularly encountered with bronchiolo-alveolar tumours (see Illus. **GALAXY SIGN** and Fig. 4.3b).

The widespread nature of most tumours within the lung, shows how bad the prognosis is likely to be in many cases, but is of great importance in planning possible surgery or radiotherapy. The main point to emphasise is that lung tumours may diffusely spread through the lung, both centrally and peripherally. Both multifocal disease and satellite nodules may be found. As well as lymphatic spread, blood-borne metastasis to distal organs is very common, particularly to the liver, adrenals, brain and bone. This occurs because of the very vascular nature of the lung, and most commonly occurs with small-cell tumours.

Peri-bronchial and peri-arterial infiltration towards the hilum.

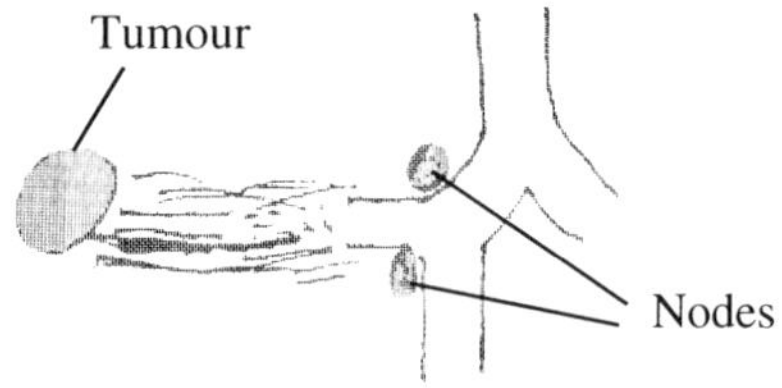

Tumour

Nodes

Less commonly perivenous infiltration to the lower mediastinum.

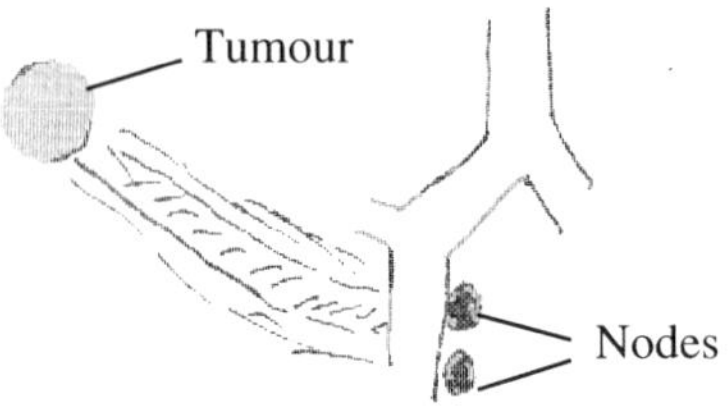

Tumour

Nodes

Spread of tumour to lymphatic plexus in the wall of a larger bronchus where it may mimic a primary tumour.

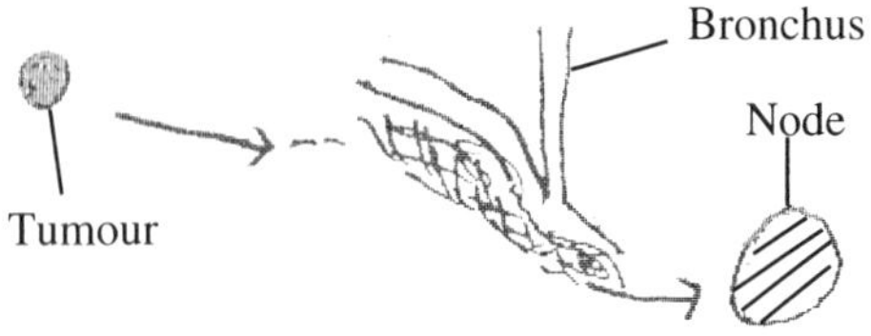

Bronchus

Node

Tumour

Fig. 13.4 Some patterns of tumour spread towards the hilum giving rise to peribronchial streaking.

Further references
Griess et al. (1945) : Proximal extension of lung cancer in the bronchial wall.
Liebow (1955) : Submucosal spread of bronchial tumours.   Cotton (1959) : Bronchial spread of lung cancer.
Nohl (1962) : Pointed out that a lung tumour may spread proximally through the submucosal vessels for several cms from its main bulk, thus allowing a positive biopsy at a more proximal site.
Baird (1965) : The pathways of lymphatic spread of carcinoma of the lung.
Willis (1960) : Expansile and infitrative growth of tumours. Spencer (1977&1985) : Hilic & lepidic tumour growth.
Theros (1977) : Varying manifestations of peripheral pulmonary neoplasms.
Schwartz and Levine (1978) : "The fact that bronchogenic carcinoma frequently spreads to distant areas within the lung is well known to pathologists; unfortunately it is not as widely appreciated by clinicians and radiologists."
Heitzman et al. (1982) : Pathways of tumour spread through the lung - also noted that 'long line shadows' i.e. longer than 1 cm in length and occurring proximal to a peripheral tumour, and without hilar lymph node enlargement, rarely represented tumour infiltration.
Watanabe et al. (1990) : Studied the mediastinal spread of bronchogenic carcinoma to mediastinal lymph nodes in a large series of patients who had undergone thoracotomies in Japan, and found that nodal metastases to the lower mediastinum from upper lobe cancer were frequently seen, as were often 'skip' metastases to the non-regional parts of the mediastinum, without regional node involvement.

Lymphatic spread of tumours within the mediastinum and crossed lymphatic drainage.
McCort and Robbins (1951), discussing the 'Roentgen diagnosis of intrathoracic lymph node metastases in carcinoma of the lung' reported a study of the sites of metastasis in 103 patients who had undergone thoracotomy for bronchial carcinoma. They found that several tumours showed contra-lateral mediastinal node involvement, and postulated that when a node becomes filled with tumour, it can no longer function as a filtering organ, the lymph flow being forced into other channels. They wrote : "Since it is unlikely that the valve system of the lymphatics can remain competent in the presence of blockage and dilatation, adjacent anastomotic channels take up the load. For this reason, the **lymph nodes which will become involved by carcinoma in any given anatomic unit cannot be predicted with certainty, no matter how thoroughly normal lymphatic pathways are understood**" (present author's italics).

Nohl (1956 & 1962) - later known as Nohl-Oser (1972), studied the pattern of lymph node spread of lung tumours, by noting the nodes involved at operation, with tumours of the various lobes. He also studied and quoted Mascagni's book. In the **right lung** he confirmed the presence of Borrie's '**lymphatic sump**' (1952), as a collection of lymph nodes grouped around the intermediate bronchus, which showed invasion from both upper and lower lobe tumours. He found that right upper lobe tumours rarely spread below hilar level, whereas right lower lobe tumours commonly spread to the subcarinal nodes. In the **left lung** tumours of the upper lobe mainly involved nodes in the area of the left main interlobar fissure (the '**left lymphatic sump**'), whereas tumours in the lower lobe spread into the lower part of this '**sump**' and into the subcarinal nodes. (The author however prefers to term the subcarinal nodes - the 'lymphatic sump' - see p. 13.27). Nohl-Oser also found that **crossed lymphatic spread** to the contralateral side was more common with left-sided tumours than those on the right. He found about 25% with tumours of the left lung, compared with about 4% on the right. His findings suggested that spread from left lower lobe tumours to the right upper mediastinum was commoner than to the same side. It was about equal to both sides with left upper lobe tumours, but was four times more common from those in the left lower lobe.

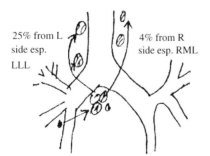

25% from L
side esp.
LLL

4% from R
side esp. RML

(b) Lymph trunks by-passing nodes and draining into more distal nodes. Some may even miss all nodes and drain into the

Fig. 13.5 (a) Diagram - crossed lymphatic drainage. thoracic or accessory thoracic ducts directly.

Crossed lymphatic drainage explains how contralateral scalene and other cervical node biopsies may be positive, and the common clinical finding of bilaterally enlarged cervical lymph nodes with advanced bronchial tumours (see also Onuigbo, 1962). Baird (1965) found crossed spread to scalene nodes to be about equal from either lung and Brantigan et al. (1973) also found a considerable incidence of contralateral spread to the scalene nodes.

The author has noted many examples of crossed lymphatic drainage and contralateral lymph node enlargement with lung tumours; this is most common with small-cell tumours, but may be seen with other types. He has also noted that it is not uncommon with tumours arising in the right middle lobe.

On both sides the lower lobe lymphatics also drain into nodes alongside the inferior pulmonary ligaments into paraoesophageal nodes and pulmonary ligament nodes - see Table 13.3.

Tumours of the left upper lobe commonly metastasise to nodes in the aorto-pulmonary window, and unlike tumours of the right upper lobe spread to the subcarinal nodes as well as the left upper mediastinum. Metastases from cancer of the left upper lobe tend to cross over to the right mediastinal nodes via the subcarinal nodes.

Because lymph trunks often 'by-pass' proximal nodes - Fig. 13.5b - both in the chest and other parts of the body, lymphatic tumour metastases often 'skip' past one or more nodes. Thus proximal nodes may be unaffected, whilst more distal nodes are involved - '**skipping metastases**'.

References.

Ishida et al. (1990) : Almost 30% of pts. with regional lymph node deposits from lung cancer had 'skip' metastases.

Stevens (1994) : Skip metastases to mediastinum from testicular seminoma which did not involve the retroperitoneal lymph nodes.

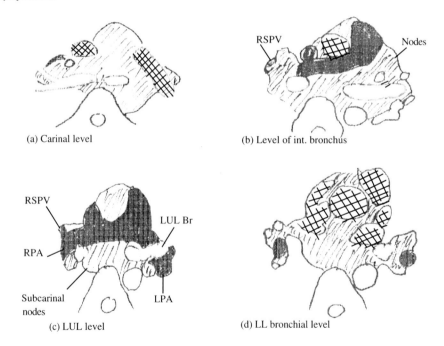

(a) Carinal level   (b) Level of int. bronchus

(c) LUL level   (d) LL bronchial level

Fig. 13.6. Diagrams showing generalised mediastinal enlargement (as seen in sarcoidosis): **Contrast enhancement of the pulmonary vessels is usually necessary for differentiation.** (Nodes = single hatching, pulmonary arteries = black, after Sone et al., 1983).

CT of hilar areas.
The Abnormal Hilum - CT.
Pulmonary vascular enlargements, especially of the arteries with emphysema, or other chronic lung disease, are very common and are usually readily recognised on CT studies as on plain radiographs. Arterial enlargement can usually be followed from the main pulmonary arteries into the lobar branches. Such enlargements are mainly 'smooth' in outline.

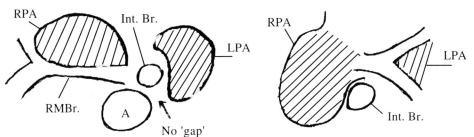

A small pulmonary artery, as with the Swyer James (Macleod) syndrome, etc. (see p. 7.9 - 10) is also readily recognised.

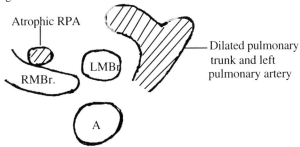

Fig. 13.7   Diagrams showing enlarged pulmonary arteries.
However for the recognition of nodal and other masses a detailed knowledge of anatomy is required.

The right hilum - Figs. 13.8 a - t..
In the **upper right hilum**, the apical segmental bronchus and its accompanying vessels are normally seen in cross sections. Masses in this region will tend to obscure these or produce larger opacities than the normal vessels (a).

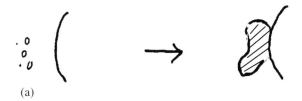

(a)

At the level of the **right upper lobe bronchus**, the right pulmonary artery normally produces a small convex shadow anterior to the bronchus. This may vary somewhat in size, but a distinct lateral bulge is not normally seen, and when present is usually due to a mass (b). Anterior nodal enlargement here may occur between the artery and the bronchus. A mass here may also press on, distort or obstruct the anterior segmental bronchus (c).

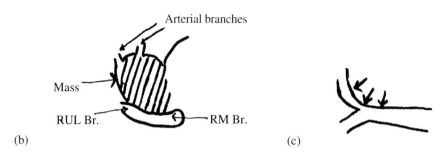

(b)   (c)

Enlargement of nodes in the region of the **right superior pulmonary vein** may apparently enlarge its shadow, or displace it antero-laterally (d).

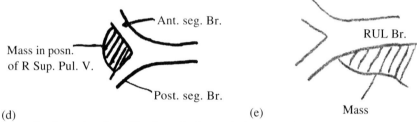

(d)   (e)   Mass

Laterally situated nodes will enlarge in the angle between the anterior and posterior segmental bronchi, whilst posterior nodes enlarge behind the wall of the upper lobe bronchus, where there are no mimicking vessels. Here the lung normally contacts the posterior aspect of the right upper lobe bronchus, and if it is obscured, or tissue is present behind it, this is a good sign of enlarged nodes or a mass (e).

A mass in the azygo-oesophageal recess (i.e. more medial to 'b' above) may cause a loss of the **'right retro-bronchial stripe'** (f).

(f) Mass behind RMB pressing into the azygo-oesophageal recess and causing a loss of the right retro-bronchial stripe. (Normal appearance is shown in Fig. 1.38).

At the level of the **intermediate bronchus**, the right superior pulmonary vein lies anterior to the descending part of the right pulmonary artery, and produces a large lobulated vascular shadow in the anterior aspect of the right hilum - the 'elephant head and trunk' or 'claw hammer' appearance (see Fig. 1.50, p. 1.37).

There are also other vessels to the right upper lobe and apex of the right lower lobe, and small abnormalities in this situation are not easily seen. however pressure deformity on the intermediate bronchus or thickening of its posterior aspect are usually good signs of adjacent tumour, as lung normally contacts its posterior wall (g) - see also Fig. 1.36, p. 1.24 re thickening due to heart failure, nodes, neoplasm or infection.

| (g) | Normal | Thickened posterior wall | Pressure deformity. |

Occasionally an anomalous vein may pass behind the intermediate bronchus and may simulate a hilar mass (Webb et al., 1984d) - Fig. 1.37, p. 1.25.
Nodal enlargement may be seen between the bronchi and/or vessels at the origins of their segmental branches.

Subcarinal node enlargement is discussed further on ps. 13.27 - 28; this may obliterate, or partly obliterate, the azygo-oesophageal recess (h). These nodes may also be seen between the pulmonary trunk and the posterior aspect of the left atrium and the spine.

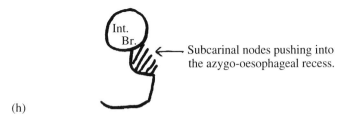

Subcarinal nodes pushing into the azygo-oesophageal recess.

(h)

At the level of the **right middle lobe bronchus**, the descending pulmonary artery produces an elliptical shadow behind the middle lobe bronchus. Lobulation of this strongly suggests the presence of enlarged nodes (i). The middle lobe bronchus should normally be seen with a distinct 'spur' (j).

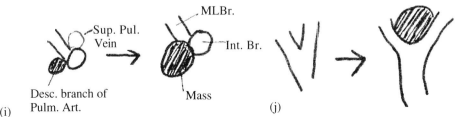

(i) Desc. branch of Pulm. Art.   Mass   (j)

Separation or obliteration of the middle lobe branches is very suggestive of a mass or consolidation. However, because of its orientation, only part of it may be seen on a single section.

Below the middle lobe bronchus, the pulmonary artery may be normally lobulated (where it branches), but a pronounced localised apparent enlargement may all indicate an enlarged node (k).

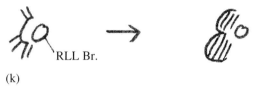

(k)

At the **level of the inferior pulmonary vein**, this obscures the posterior wall of the lower lobe bronchus, but the anterior wall is in contact with lung. Should a mass be present in this area, the anterior wall may become obscured (l).

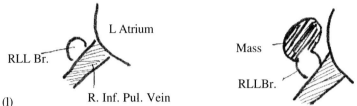

(l)

Normal : the posterior wall of the right lower lobe bronchus is obscured.

Abnormal : a mass obscures the anterior wall of the right lower lobe bronchus in addition.

Left hilum

In the superior part of the left hilum, the apico-posterior segmental bronchus is seen in cross section with its attendant vessels. A mass may be recognised as on the right side (m).

(m)

A little lower down, several branches arise from the pulmonary artery. Only small vessels are seen lateral to the upper lobe bronchus, which divides into its segments at the '**upper lobe spur**'. An opaque shadow lateral to this is usually due to disease (n).

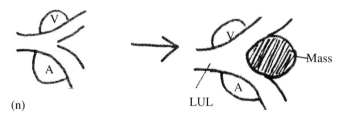

(n)

At the level of the origin of the **left main bronchus**, the left pulmonary artery lies posteriorly and should be distinguished from a tumour mass (o).

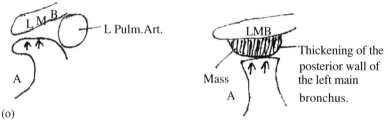

(o)

Tumour masses and nodes alongside the left main bronchus may cause '**stretching**' and '**straightening**' of the left main bronchus - the '**elongated and stiff bronchus sign**' (p) see also Illus. **BRONCHUS STRETCHED.**

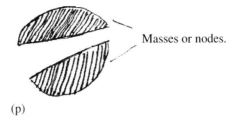

Masses or nodes.

(p)

The '**left retrobronchial stripe**' - the posterior wall of the left main bronchus is outlined in CT sections by air-filled lung. Thickening of this wall or 'stripe', or nodularity of it may indicate tumour infiltration of the bronchial wall or adjacent lymph node enlargement. Adjacent lung consolidation will also obliterate the 'stripe', but because the pleural space does not usually extend posterior to the bronchial wall, a pleural effusion will not usually affect it. The normal appearance of this is shown in Fig. 1.38, p. 1.25.

Behind the **medial** part of the left main bronchus and the origin of the lower lobe bronchus, the lung normally makes contact with the bronchi, so that tissue between the lung and the bronchi will usually signify disease, particularly tumour (q & r).

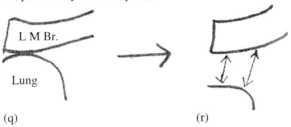

(q)   (r)

However, in about 10% of patients, the left lung fails to contact the posterior wall of the left main or lower lobe bronchi. When this happens the descending aorta is prominent and comes in contact with the medial aspect of the descending pulmonary artery (s). The 'stripe' may also be obliterated by a dilated descending aorta.

Interlobar nodal enlargement may be seen between the descending aorta and the descending part of the left pulmonary artery (t), and lower down, between the lower lobe bronchus and its corresponding artery.

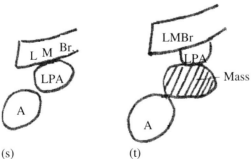

(s)   (t)

The effect of masses at the level of the left inferior pulmonary vein is similar to that seen on the right.

Lymph Node Mapping System.

Several systems have been developed for mapping nodes, both before and after surgery. The one illustrated below is based on one which has been used in Oxford, itself based on the Thoracic Society and American Thoracic Society recommendations - see Glazer, G et al., 1985. Mountain and Dresler's 1997 modifications in nomenclature are given in brackets. A further CT pictorial study of the revised regional nodal stations for lung cancer staging is given by Ko et al (2000).

[The 1985 American recommendations tended to place most intra-pulmonary nodes in group 11, and a modification of their recommendation (Glazer, H. et al., 1986) numbered the superior diaphragmatic nodes - 14, instead of 15 as below.]

Groups

X   Supraclavicular nodes

1   Highest mediastinal nodes

2   (Upper) paratracheal nodes

3   Pretracheal nodes
    (prevascular & retrotracheal)

4   Tracheo-Bronchial or lower
    paratracheal nodes including
    azygos nodes
    (N_2= single digit, ipsilateral
    N_3= single digit, contralateral
    or supraclavicular)

5   Aorto-pulmonary or
    subaortic nodes

6   Para-aortic or anterior
    mediastinal nodes
    (asc. aorta or phrenic nodes)

7   Subcarinal nodes

8   Para-oesophageal nodes
    (below carinal level)

9   Pulmonary ligament nodes

10 Hilar nodes

11 Inter-lobar nodes

12 Lobar nodes

13 Segmental nodes

14 Subsegmental nodes

15 Superior diaphragmatic nodes

    (a) internal mammary

    (b) para-cardiac

16 Posterior diaphragmatic nodes

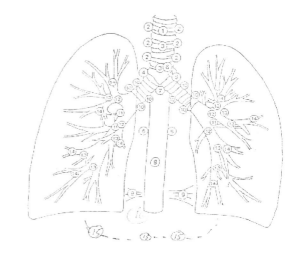

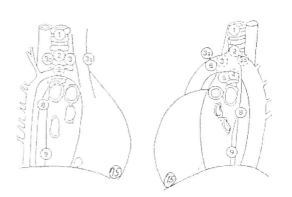

Fig. 13.9   Lymph node station chart.

<u>Hilar Lymph Nodes</u> may be divided into three groups :
(a) **Tracheo-bronchial   nodes** (groups 4 and 10) on mapping system - p. 13.16) - these are closely associated with three other groups of nodes :
    (i) **Subcarinal nodes** (group 7).
    (ii) **Lower paratracheal nodes** (groups 2 and 4) - these lie inferior to the carina, within its fascial envelope - the pretracheal fascia).
    (iii) **Pretracheal nodes** (group 3) - these lie in front of the lowest part of the trachea and the right main bronchus, bridging the subcarinal and right superior tracheobronchial nodes.
(b) **Broncho-pulmonary   nodes**   (interlobar and lobar nodes - groups 11 and 12) are situated alongside the lower portions of the main bronchi, or in the angles formed by their bifurcations into lobar bronchi.
(c) **Segmental and subsegmental nodes** (groups 13 and 14) are related to the divisions of the segmental or smaller bronchi or lie in the bifurcations of the corresponding branches of the pulmonary artery.

<u>Causes of hilar and mediastinal lymphadenopathy.</u>
  There are many possible causes, besides enlargement as a result of infiltration by tumours or reticuloses. Many of these are listed in Table 13.2. Tumours may cause reactive hyperplasia (see below) or a sarcoid-like reaction, which may precede its overt presentation (ps. 19.74 - 75). Besides tumours arising in the chest spreading to these nodes, others may spread up from the abdomen (see Chapter 17).
Some acute or chronic infections may give rise to lymphadenopathy in the hilar and mediastinal areas, especially tuberculosis and fungal diseases (ps. 19.16 et seq. & 19.38 - 43). Several times the author has seen a middle aged patient with a lobar or segmental collapse, a blocked bronchus on tomography and enlarged homolateral hilar nodes (an appearance immediately suggesting bronchial neoplasm), only to see the whole picture resolve spontaneously or with antibiotics in a few weeks - a fairly typical appearance of acute infection with **aspergillosis**, always something to think of in non-smokers! Acute pneumonia may also produce enlarged nodes which may be recognised on tomograms. Other infections which may produce lymphadenopathy include **infectious mononucleosis**, and the author has seen one patient with nodes so enlarged as to cause innominate vein compression and thrombosis.

Table 13.2 - <u>Structures which may be confused with lymphadenopathy.</u>
Overlying lung mass.
Dilated main pulmonary arteries or veins.
Right sided aortic arch or aberrant right subclavian artery (the author has seen several patients with right sided aortic erroneously treated for tuberculosis).
Dilated innominate vein, SVC, azygos or hemiazygos vein anomaly, including 'aortic nipple'.
Thyroid, thymic or other mediastinal masses, including neurofibromata.
Large superior or transverse pericardial recesses.

Table 13.3 - <u>Causes of enlarged hilar and mediastinal lymph nodes.</u>

    (a) Metastases from intrathoracic tumours, especially lung cancer, but also from mesotheliomas and some mediastinal tumours, breast carcinomas and extra-thoracic tumours, including melanomas, tumours arising in the GI and GU tracts (particularly tumours of the kidneys, prostate, bladder, cervix, ovaries and testes).
    (Note that nodal metastases from oesophageal tumours are usually small and rarely cause nodal enlargements that are visible on plain chest radiographs or tomograms until very late).

    (b) Reticuloses including Hodgkin's disease, non-Hodgkin's lymphoma, Castleman's disease, lymphoid granuloma, etc.

    (c) Infection - some bacterial pneumonias, especially aspergillosis and tuberculosis. Infection complicating lung cancer - 'reactive' or 'hyperplastic' nodes.
      Fungus infections.
      Viral - infectious mononucleosis, etc.

(d) Non-infective granulomas and sensitivity reactions :
   Sarcoidosis
   Sarcoid reactions to tumours
   Pneumoconiosis and Caplan's syndrome
   Amyloid
   Rheumatoid
   Hypersensitivity pneumonitis
   Sensitivity to some drugs and other agents.

(e) Blood dyscrasias
   Leukaemia
   Myeloma
   Extramedullary haemopoiesis
   Macroglobulinaemia.

(f) Complications of immunosuppression
   AIDS
   Kaposi's sarcoma, etc.

Some references.
Brincker (1972) : Sarcoid reactions in lymphomas.
Khouri et al. (1978) : Angioimmunoblastic lymphadenopathy.
Rohlfing et al. (1978) : Hilar and mediastinal adenopathy caused by bacterial lung abscess.
Webb (1979) : Hilar and mediastinal enlargement with **melanoma**.
Kaplan et al. (1980) : Mediastinal adenopathy in **myeloma.**
Gumbs and McCauley (1982) : Hilar and mediastinal adenopathy in **septic pulmonary embolic disease**.
Glazer, H. et al. (1985a) : Pitfalls in the CT recognition of mediastinal lymphadenopathy.
Mirvis et al. (1986) : Hilar adenopathy due to bacterial endocarditis.
Daly et al. (1988) : Granulomatous presentation of Hodgkin's disease.
Parr and Williams (1988) : Sarcoidosis mimicking metastatic testicular tumour.

Radiology of hilar and hilar node enlargement (see also ps. 1.33 to 1.38 re pulmonary vessels).
   McLeod et al. (1976) wrote that the detection and evaluation of hilar abnormalities is difficult. The appearance of the normal hilum varies considerably and PA and lateral radiographs are not always accurate in their evaluation.
   In the hila, one should always look for alterations or additions superimposed on the normal anatomy. Normal anatomy includes the main, lobar and segmental bronchi, the pulmonary arteries (the 'horizontal V' on the right, and the 'shepherd's crook' on the left - see Fig. 1.47), the pulmonary veins (which lie at a lower level than the arteries as they approach the left atrium), and the azygos vein (in the angle between the lower trachea and the right main bronchus).
   Enlarged hilar nodes usually are superimposed on the normal anatomy, but distort it when they are considerably enlarged. A big problem is in distinguishing dilated vessels from enlarged nodes and vice versa. Problems particularly occur where the right or left interlobar arteries are crossed by the inferior pulmonary veins, and in the upper left hilum where the pulmonary artery curves laterally and dorsally.
   Very often enlarged nodes are obvious on plain radiographs, especially when **previous radiographs are available for comparison**. In other cases tomograms are helpful for evaluating the size and extent of enlarged nodes, showing whether this is unilateral or bilateral, and in demonstrating calcification. Enlarged neoplastic nodes tend to cause considerable distortion of neighbouring structures (particularly the bronchi), whilst sarcoid (and some other inflammatory type) nodes are softer, and cause little distortion, even when the enlargement is massive.

Conventional tomography.
   Various methods of tomography have been employed for the hilar regions. A longitudinal blurring motion is not ideal, as detail of the mediastinum is often underexposed, and is distorted by ghost shadows from the heart and spine. In some centres 55° posterior oblique tomograms have been

employed (p. 20.13). Much better were inclined frontal tomograms, with a horizontal cross-wise blurring motion (p. 20.14).

The Valsalva* experiment and Müller manoeuvre** (forced expiration after a maximum inspiration, and attempted inspiration after a maximum expiration respectively, with the glottis closed - changing the intra-thoracic pressures by up to 80 to 100 cm of water) were sometimes used to demonstrate changes in sizes of e.g. the size of the azygos or other large veins during tomography, and hence differentiate them from nodes, or other solid structures. Another was the more simple expedient of taking similar sections in both the erect and supine positions.

Reference.
Whithley and Martin (1964) : The Valsalva manoeuvre in Roentgenologic diagnosis.

* Antonio Maria Valsalva (1666 - 1723) - Illus. **FAMOUS   PEOPLE, Valsalva's   monument** shows his monument just outside the anatomy theatre in Padua.
** Johannes Müller (1801 - 1858).

Lateral tomograms were often taken in addition, or as an alternative, if masses on plain radiographs appeared to lie in front of or behind the hila or major airways. Tomograms in one plane could often be misleading and **AP and lateral** were often carried out. **For best results lateral tomograms should be taken with the patient in the erect position, and the x-ray table upright**, since mediastinal distortion may occur if a patient with a normally mobile mediastinum lies on his side.

CT in many centres has replaced most of the tomographic work, but the author believes that conventional tomograms still have a place, particularly when CT is not available, at the time of the patient's attendance.

CT of the hila.
   In the recognition of nodal enlargement a good knowledge of anatomy is required to differentiate nodes from vascular structures, which mostly lie in close proximity, and various points are discussed in the following pages. One also has to realise that considerable anatomical variation occurs, and contrast enhancement, often with a bolus technique, may be required in some cases, as well as close 'interrogation' of the display by varying the window level. Some nodes may partially enhance with contrast and thus mimic vascular structures.
   Besides noting that enlarged nodes are present one also needs to be able to assess the likelihood of them being involved by tumour. Size alone may often be a good guide, especially if multiple lymph node areas are involved, and a fairly certain or certain corresponding primary tumour is present. Massive enlargement may be seen with small cell tumours and lymphoma, but considerably enlarged nodes (up to 4 cm or more in length) may be found as a result of **reactive hyperplasia**, present usually when chronic lung infection is present with a bronchogenic tumour. Other nodes may contain tumour deposits, and **not be enlarged, due to tiny tumour deposits.**   It therefore follows that lymph node size alone should not be the sole guide to inoperability, as this is subject to considerable error. Nevertheless pooled experience from various centres has given the following useful guide :
   Nodes (in cross section)   1 cm or less   -   probably normal
   - shorter axis   1 to 1.5 cm   -   probably affected
                              1 to 2 cm (or more) - very likely to be involved with tumour.
Notes of several series are given at the end of this chapter.
Even large nodes, feeling 'rubbery' to palpation may be reactive and not neoplastic, and 'hard' ones may or may not contain tumour - '**reactive hyperplasia**'.

Some references.
Naidich et al. (1981a) : CT of the normal pulmonary hilum. (1981b) : CT of the abnormal pulmonary hilum.
Webb et al. (1981a) : CT of the normal pulmonary hilum. (1981b) : CT of the abnormal pulmonary hilum.
Sone et al. (1983) : CT anatomy of hilar lymphadenopathy.
Webb and Gamsu (1983) : CT of the left retro-bronchial stripe.
Webb et al. (1983c) : Thickening of the posterior wall of the RUL bronchus as a sign of tumour - studied 30 patients and all had abnormal plain radiographs.

CT findings - (a) local alteration in hilar contour.
               (b) **thickening of posterior wall**
                     of RUL bronchus.

               (c) narrowing, displacement or
                     obstruction of bronchi.

(b)

Table 13.4 - Groupings of mediastinal nodes.

Anterior and middle mediastinal nodes
(a) Superior intercostal and internal mammary nodes (groups 1 & 15a on mapping system).
(b) Thymic nodes, lying within the thymic fat - these are most commonly enlarged with reticuloses.
(c) Paratracheal and azygos nodes (group 2) and pretracheal nodes (group 3).
(d) Tracheobronchial nodes (group 4).
(e) Aorto-pulmonary (or subaortic) nodes (group 5).
(f) Para-aortic nodes (group 6).
(g) Subcarinal nodes (group 7).
(h) Superior diaphragmatic nodes (group 15b).

Posterior mediastinal nodes.
(i) Para-oesophageal nodes (group 8).
(j) Nodes alongside the inferior pulmonary veins, and in the inferior pulmonary ligaments
    (draining the perivenous lymphatics in the lungs, and communication with the para-aortic nodes).
(j) Superior diaphragmatic nodes (group 16) and posterior parietal nodes.

Internal mammary and superior diaphragmatic nodes.
These nodes occur in various positions :
(i) Internal mammary nodes alongside the internal mammary vessels, just lateral to the posterior surface of the sternum and behind the medial ends of the costal cartilages.
(ii) Paracardiac nodes around the phrenic nerve insertions, adjacent to the pericardium and on the superior aspect of the diaphragm.

    These nodes may be seen on plain radiographs and/or tomograms if they become very large, in the cardiophrenic angles, or as parasternal masses displacing the adjacent lung. They are more easily shown by CT if moderately enlarged. Normally they do not exceed 1 cm in diameter. Rarely their enlargement may be enormous, when they may mimic cardiomegaly or a pericardial effusion.

    Tumours involving these nodes include: breast, mesothelioma, recurrent reticulosis and melanoma. They may also become enlarged due to tumours spreading cranially from the abdomen (e.g. ovarian). Occasionally they may be enlarged with florid sarcoidosis.

Ultrasound via the intercostal spaces may allow enlarged internal mammary nodes to be visualised Illus. **NODES-INTMAMM, Mesothel Pt. 43d, e & g**.

Isotope   scintigraphy has also been used to show them - a labelled colloid as used for liver scans) is injected into the upper part of the rectus sheath, and images are taken on a gamma camera two or more hours later. The position of the nodes is well shown and noted for radiotherapy planning especially with breast carcinoma or reticulosis, but defects within them are difficult to detect unless very large.

    Examples of enlarged internal mammary nodes and enlarged lower mediastinal nodes are shown in Illus. **NODES-INTMAMM** and Illus. **NODES-PARACARDIAC.** Diagrams showing the positions of internal mammary and superior diaphragmatic nodes are reproduced below.

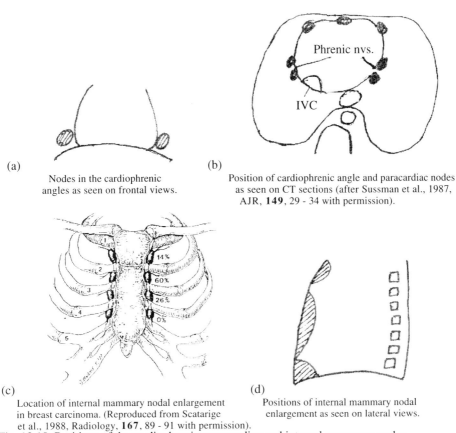

(a) Nodes in the cardiophrenic angles as seen on frontal views.

(b) Position of cardiophrenic angle and paracardiac nodes as seen on CT sections (after Sussman et al., 1987, AJR, **149**, 29 - 34 with permission).

(c) Location of internal mammary nodal enlargement in breast carcinoma. (Reproduced from Scatarige et al., 1988, Radiology, **167**, 89 - 91 with permission).

(d) Positions of internal mammary nodal enlargement as seen on lateral views.

Fig. 13.10 Positions of the cardiophrenic, paracardiac and internal mammary nodes.

Interpectoral nodes are discussed on p. 12.19 - see also Illus. **ROTTER'S NODE**.

Some references.

Massoud et al. (1964) : The radiological investigation of internal mammary lymph node metastases in breast cancer in 65 cases - tomography of the anterior mediastinum with and without pneumomediastinum.

Urban and Marjani (1971) : Internal mammary node metastases in breast cancer.

Castellino and Blank (1972) : Adenopathy of cardiophrenic or diaphragmatic nodes, especially on lateral films.

Ege (1976), Ege and Clarke (1985) and Smedley and Wraight (1982) : Internal mammary lymphoscintigraphy, particularly in patients with breast carcinoma and as a guide to radiotherapy treatment.

Bledin et al. (1980) : Cardiophrenic angle nodes - an unusual CT finding of advanced metastatic disease.

Meyer and Munzenrider (1981) : CT of internal mammary node metastases in pts. with locally recurrent breast ca.

Ege (1982) : CT demonstration of internal mammary lymph node metastasis in breast carcinoma.

Jochelson et al. (1983) : Peri and paracardial involvement in lymphoma.

Cho et al. (1984) : CT evaluation of cardiophrenic angle nodes in malignant lymphoma.

Meyer et al. (1985) : CT of cardiophrenic lymphadenopathy in Hodgkin's disease.

Aronberg et al. (1986) : Superior diaphragmatic lymph nodes - CT assessment.

Vock and Hodler (1986) : Cardiophrenic angle adenopathy - update of causes and significance.

Castellino et al. (1986) : CT finding of enlarged cardiophrenic angle nodes in lymphoma modified treatment in 18%.

Sussman et al. (1987) : CT of normal and abnormal para-cardiac nodes - normal nodes did not exceed 0.35 cm in diameter and usually no more than two were seen in normal subjects. Abnormal nodes were seen in lymphoma, abdominal neoplasms, breast carcinoma, sarcoma and in aspergillosis and histoplasmosis.

Karayalcin et al. (1988) : Parasternal lymphoscintigraphy using Tc^{99m} dextran in 24 patients with breast carcinoma and 10 volunteers - noted crossed drainage in 20%.

Scatarige et al. (1988) : Estimated that internal mammary nodes are involved in about 20% of patients with clinically operable breast cancer (45 of 219 examined by CT).
Scatarige et al. (1989) : Parasternal sonography of internal mammary nodes (used supine position, whilst author's practice is to examine them erect).
Ferretti et al. (1997) : CT demonstration of supra-diaphragmatic calcified nodes from **ovarian carcinoma**.
Holloway et al. (1997) : The significance of paracardiac lymph node enlargement in **ovarian cancer**.

Thymic nodes. (see also ps. 5.21 & 18.16 - 17).
  These are found within the thymus and the thymic fat, and overlie the upper part of the pericardium. They may become very enlarged with reticuloses (Illus. **NODES-THYMIC, Thymus Pt. 17a-c, 18, Hodgkin's disease 15a-b, 28, 31a-b, 32, 34, 39, 49a-c, & 58a-e and Lymphoma Pt. 1a-b**), and may deform and compress the trachea, and sometimes the oesophagus as well. Often their enormous size is out of proportion to the patient's symptoms, which may be mild with some general disability, slight loss of weight, etc.
  In **Hodgkin's disease**, nodal masses may sometimes extend across the chest anteriorly, sometimes almost from side to side, and be accompanied by pleural effusions and/or lung metastases. The tracheal deformity may result in severe respiratory obstruction, especially following anaesthesia, because of the tendency of the trachea to collapse.
  Degenerate areas may be visualised within the large nodal masses by ultrasound or CT. On CT sections, sometimes only the outer rims enhance with contrast media (Illus. **NODES-THYMIC, Hodgkin's disease. 58c**), indicating that the centres may be degenerate. In other cases there may be uniform or patchy enhancement.
  Sometimes these nodes are massively enlarged due to inflammatory disease. In the UK this is usually due to **tuberculosis**, but the author has also seen it with fungus disease, in patients returning from a visit to the USA. Illus. **NODES-THYMIC, TB nodes Pt. 2a-b** shows such enlargement in a 19 year old female Mexican student, who presented with coughing when leaning forwards (a not uncommon symptom with such nodes due to pressure on the trachea), and with slight generalised debility. Tubercle bacilli were obtained in material obtained by mediastinoscopy, and the nodes rapidly regressed with anti-TB chemotherapy.
  Both thymic and thoracic para-aortic nodes may also be enlarged with lung tumours, particularly oat-cell tumours, and sometimes with other neoplasms secondarily involving the chest. Small nodes may be seen with bronchial tumours which are invading the mediastinum, and these should always be distinguished from the normal '**left superior intercostal vein**' or '**hemiazygos arch**' - see also ps. 9.13 - 14.

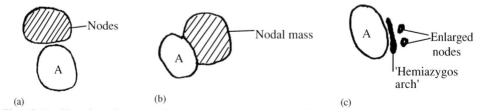

(a)   (b)   (c)

Fig. 13.11 Thymic and para-aortic nodes in the upper mediastinum.

Thymic nodal enlargements also have to be distinguished from thymomas (which are much less common and are usually smaller - see also ps. 18.20 - 23, and from goitres, etc. (see p. 18.8 - 9).
  Calcification is very rare in untreated enlarged thymic nodes due to reticulosis but may be seen following treatment (Illus. **CALC IN NODES, Hodgkin's disease, 5a-b**), in some thymic cysts, thymomas and in intrathoracic goitres.

Paratracheal and tracheobronchial nodes - (Illus. **PARATRACHEAL**).
  These nodes lie on either side of the trachea, and in the adjacent angles (or bays) produced by the main bronchi. Their enlargement may widen the upper mediastinum (to be differentiated from venous engorgement, fat, enlarged thymus or aorta, etc.).

On the **left** these nodes lie close to the pulmonary trunk and the ligamentum arteriosum. They extend upwards close to the phrenic nerve and up to the left innominate vein. Nodal enlargement in these areas is commonly associated with nodal enlargement in the aorto-pulmonary window and a left recurrent laryngeal nerve palsy (see ps. 15.1 - 2). The **right** sided nodes tend to be more numerous, and may become larger than on the left. The right sided nodes lie within a niche between the SVC and the trachea, parallel and anterior to the right phrenic nerve and inferior and lateral to the innominate artery. Their enlargement prevents lung tucking into the supra-azygos recess and the right paratracheal line is often displaced to the right - Fig. 1.16, p. 1.12.. They are particularly well seen in patients with deep recesses, but may be 'hidden' in those who have these less marked.

The lower right sided nodes, which lie close to the azygos vein, are termed the **'azygos nodes'** (see below). Enlargement of these will cause partial or complete obliteration of the mediastinal recess above the azygos arch, giving rise to a bulge or irregular interface between the mediastinal pleura, over the enlarged nodes, and the right main bronchus and lung.

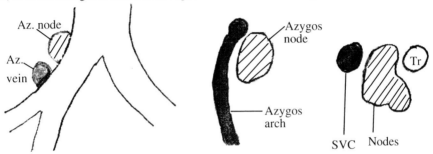

Fig. 13.12 Relative positions of the azygos vein and node(s) as seen on (a) frontal views, and (b & c) on axial views. On axial views, an enlarged azygos node lies **medial** to the azygos arch. Enlarged azygos and right paratracheal nodes also displace the SVC laterally. (See also Fig. 1.14 and p. 1.31 for the relative positions of these structures as seen on lateral views).

Azygos node enlargement is a common finding with bronchial neoplasms, particularly small cell and anaplastic tumours. It may also appear as a **'sentinel sign'** of abdominal disease, which has spread up to the thorax (.e.g. from prostate, pancreas, etc., rather like the clinically palpable Virchow node in the left supraclavicular fossa, or an enlarged retrocrural node seen on a lower thoracic CT section).

Azygos node enlargement is also common with reticuloses and in sarcoidosis (ps. 19.65 et seq.).With tumours, azygos node enlargement may be isolated (as a **'sentinel node'**), but as with the first mentioned conditions is more commonly associated with other nodal enlargements. It may also be caused by 'reactive hyperplasia' or by 'sarcoid reaction' in relation to a tumour.

Azygos and paratracheal nodal enlargement was not uncommon when tuberculosis was more common, and may still be seen in children with the disease. In them it is a sign which should **never** be ignored, as the proximity of the nodes to the great veins not uncommonly allowed caseous material to enter them and give rise to miliary TB.

Enlarged azygos nodes stretch the azygos arch as it passes over them (Illus. **NODES AZYGOS, Fib alv Pt. 35b, Pretracheal node Pt. 9**); sometimes it passes below them and may be compressed, as may the SVC. Many examples of azygos node enlargement are recognised on plain radiographs, but they have to be distinguished from azygos vein distension (cardiac failure, liver disease, pregnancy, venous obstruction, etc.). Valsalva and Müller manoeuvres were sometimes used for differentiation (see above p. 13.19), but an azygos vein may normally increase in size from about 0.7 cm using these to 1 (or sometimes 1.5 cm) with the patient supine. The position of an enlarged azygos node is usually more anterior to the shadow of a dilated azygos vein on lateral radiographs - see Fig. 1.14. Azygos node enlargement may also be mimicked by fluid in the transverse recess of the pericardium (see Fig. 15.26, p. 15.24). Rarely the author has seen patients in whom an enlarged (and presumably mobile) node became visible when lying down, and was not seen on erect views. In such circumstances, and in other difficult cases, contrast enhanced CT may be necessary for differentiation.

See Illus. **NODES AZYGOS and NODES AZPRETR.**

Some references.
Morgan and Ellis (1974) : Superior mediastinal masses secondary to tuberculosis.
McLeod et al. (1976) : Multiple tomographic cuts may show the azygos vein as a density sweeping posteriorly and inferiorly (see also Fig. 1.44a, p. 1.31 & Fig. 9.8, p. 9.12).
Tiech et al. (1984) : Azygos node enlargement as the initial manifestation of underlying disease.
Müller et al. (1985b) : Compared the signs of para-tracheal lymphadenopathy on plain radiographs and CT in 98 pts.
Whithley and Martin (1964) : The Valsalva manoeuvre in Roentgenologic diagnosis.

The pretracheal retrocaval space is bounded by the anterior aspect of the trachea, the medial wall of the aortic arch, the posterior aspect of the ascending aorta, the posterior aspect of the SVC and the medial border of the azygos arch. CT is the only practical method for showing this space, which is not an uncommon site for enlarged metastatic nodes from bronchial tumours, etc. Examples are shown in Illus. **NODES PRETRACHEAL**.

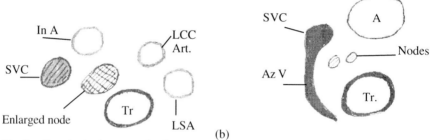

(a)   (b)

Fig. 13.13 Small nodes in the pretracheal space are not uncommonly seen on CT sections, and are often multiple. When enlarged (over 0.8 to 1 cm in short-axis diameter), this is commonly due to secondary neoplasm, but may also be caused by reactive hyperplasia. When nodes are very large, fat normally present within the space may be completely obliterated. Note that the azygos vein lies slightly inferior and lateral to the nodes.

Some references.
Schnyder and Gamsu (1981) : CT of the pretracheal, retrocaval space - studied 127 Swiss subjects, not expected to have disease involving the chest, and found (a) that the space was larger with adiposity and advancing age, (b) that nodes up to 1 cm in size were not uncommon, and (c) that nodes **over 1cm** in size were suggestive of **disease**.
Osborne et al. (1982) : Found a number of pretracheal nodes which were considerably enlarged (up to 19 mm) due to reactive hyperplasia.
Choi et al. (2000) : A 'high riding' superior pericardial recess may be confused with a pretracheal node - see p. 15.24.

The 'aorto-pulmonary window' (or **'sub-aortic fossa'**) - Illus. **AP WINDOW** and **AP WINDOW NODES.**
    The 'clear space' between the aortic arch and the pulmonary artery is usually termed the 'aorto-pulmonary window' by radiologists and corresponds to the surgical 'subaortic fossa', and nodes within the 'window' are often termed 'subaortic' or 'ductus nodes' by surgeons. The window is normally filled with areolar tissue and fat, but also contains nodes related to the ligamentum arteriosum, and some of the lower left tracheo-bronchial nodes. It is traversed by the left vagal and **recurrent laryngeal nerves**, the ligamentum arteriosum and the upper branch of the left bronchial artery. Laterally it is bounded by mediastinal pleura (reflected down from the aortic arch), medially by the left lateral wall of the trachea, anteriorly by the left main bronchus and posteriorly by the oesophagus. The 'window' is closed anteriorly by the mediastinal pleura. On tomograms a '**bow tie**' appearance may be produced in obese subjects by fat filling the 'window'.

transgressed by soft tissue extension until late - see p. 5.43) / myeloma/ leukaemia.
Reticulosarcoma / Paget's sarcoma,
Clear cell sarcoma, angiosarcoma,
Giant cell tumour,
Lymphoma.

(Note : About 5% of primary bone tumours occur in the ribs or sternum.)

Bone sarcomas - both Ewing's sarcomas and osteogenic sarcomas may occur in the ribs, sternum, scapulae or dorsal spine of children or young adults, but osteogenic sarcomas may also occur in older adults, particularly those who have had radiotherapy (see ps. 11.21 - 22).

Osteogenic sarcomas (including chondro- and fibro-sarcomas and mixed types) - the precise type of cell from which these tumours is radiologically less important than the diagnosis of malignancy. Malignant cells are often pleomorphic, with cartilaginous, osteogenic or fibroblastic cells predominating. Osteochondrosarcomas and chondrosarcomas may arise on pre-existing chondromas, and often contain areas of calcification (Illus. **OSTEOCHONDROSARCOMA**), but when they arise from a costal cartilage this may be minimal (Illus. **OSTEOCHONDROSARCOMA, Costal cart sarcoma, Pt. 1a-b**). When an osteogenic sarcoma arises in a rib, it may spread from end to end and be surrounded by a soft tissue swelling (Illus. **OSTEOGENIC SARCOMA, Rib tumour, Pt. 3a-b**). A **mesenchymal sarcoma** is a rare subtype which may involve the ribs and tends to occur in the 2nd and 3rd decades of life.

Ewing's sarcoma was described by Ewing in 1926 and 1928, but its cell of origin is still uncertain. It may arise in many bones, and probably about 5% arise in the ribs, others in the dorsal spine, etc. (Illus. **EWING'S SARCOMA**). As the tumour often metastasises to other bones, an isotope scan may be invaluable for showing these as well as the extent of the primary tumour, which is often very vascular (Illus. **EWING'S SARCOMA, 1e, 2e & 5e**). Affected patients (usually aged 10 to 20 and 70% male) may give a history of trauma or present with signs suggesting osteomyelitis, reticulosis or eosinophilic granuloma. Radiographic signs are variable and include lytic lesions, mottled destruction of the medulla, cortical erosion and periosteal new bone formation. Rib lesions may show an increased width of the medullary cavity and coarseness, leading to cortical destruction and bone expansion, with new periosteal bone deposited in layers, like **'onion skin'**. The boundary between normal and abnormal bone is often poorly defined, and there is usually a surrounding or adjacent soft tissue mass, which may become very large (see Illus. **EWING'S SARCOMA, Pt. 2a-f**). Some lesions, including deposits in other bones, and the lung are sclerotic or calcified. Not all cases have a hopeless prognosis, and chemotherapy with multiple drugs is becoming more effective. A patient is illustrated in Illus. **EWING'S SARCOMA, Pt. 1a-g** who had a large Ewing's tumour which arose in the left lower ribs, she had the diagnosis confirmed by 'radiological biopsy, followed by radiotherapy, when the tumour shrunk down; it was then removed surgically - she has since had two successful pregnancies and remains well.

MR is being used increasingly for the assessment of operability (Illus. **EWING'S SARCOMA, Pt. 2f**), but periosteal new bone and reactive sclerosis are more difficult to show with this technique.

Two variants of Ewing's sarcoma are:
(i) '**Extraskeletal Ewing's sarcomas**' and (ii) '**Askin tumours**' (Illus. **ASKIN TUMOUR**).
The first tends to occur in a slightly older age group (4 to 50) years, and may arise in the limbs, abdomen, or chest, especially in the chest wall or para-vertebral regions. They often have a pseudo-capsule and thus appear to be well-circumscribed on CT, ultrasound or MR, being hypoechoic and of low density, although spontaneous haemorrhage may change their features. Askin (or small cell) tumours of the chest wall were first described by Askin (1979) and are primitive neuro-ectodermal tumours of children and young adults, which may produce a large chest wall or intrathoracic mass (especially paravertebrally), rib destruction or a pleural effusion. They

Variations in the shape of the 'window' occur between different individuals and the pleural reflections also vary. The 'window' is larger in some people than others, particularly in those who are emphysematous, and in these the normal tongue of aerated lung in front of the aorta may be enlarged, and tuck between it and the left main bronchus. A similar appearance may be seen with a deficient left side of the pericardium. A **'closed'** window is not uncommonly due to a collapsed left upper lobe, or a left upper lobectomy.

(a) PA   (b) CT

Masses pushing the window outwards   Tongue of lung tucking between the LMB and the aorta.
Fig. 13.16   Bulged or closed AP window.

Some references.
Heitzman et al. (1975a) : Radiological evaluation of the aorto-pulmonary window.
Heitzman (1977 & 1988) : The mediastinum.
Swartz and Marmorstein (1975) : Radiographic sign of left sided mediastinal node enlargement.
Levett et al. (1986) : Bronchogenic carcinoma located in the aortic window.
Ferguson et al. (1986) : CT was less accurate in the evaluation of nodes in the aorto-pulmonary window than in other parts of the mediastinum.
Jolles et al. (1986) : Studied 80 patients with aorto-pulmonary window masses by CT. They measured these with horizontal and vertical (X and Y coordinate) lines, drawn parallel to the posterior and lateral aspects of the descending aorta, and found that when a mass was visible on plain radiographs it extended at least 1 cm beyond the 'Y line', and when not seen it did not extend so far. They also found that the position of a mass was more important than size alone in making it visible; thus more laterally placed lesions are more readily noted on plain radiographs, whilst those lying more medially will tend to be hidden by the descending aorta.

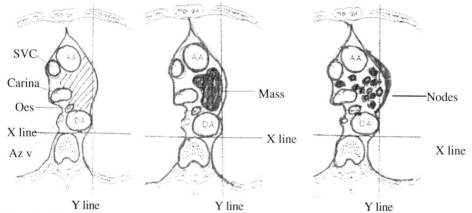

(a) Fat in the AP window.   (b) Mass within the AP window.   (c) Enlarged nodes causing a bulged window.
(Reproduced from Jolles et al. (1986), Radiology, **159**, 647 - 651 with permission.)

Shin and Jolles (1987) : Further studied the normal anatomy and pathology of the aorto-pulmonary window and illustrated : a large calcified lymph node, nodal enlargement in AIDS, neoplasm simulating an aortic aneurysm, localised pleural thickening and fibrosis in recurrent Hodgkin's disease, a persistent left SVC passing through the 'window' and an elevated left pulmonary artery due to previous resection of the left upper lobe.

The subcarinal area and nodes - Illus. **SUBCARINAL NODES.**

The subcarinal is an important area, which has often been neglected radiologically. This is because it is situated between the heart and the spine, and is mostly **poorly visualised on low KV** chest radiographs or AP conventional linear tomograms (and even **huge** nodal masses may be completely missed - Illus. **SUBCARINAL NODES, Pts. 6a-b, 13a-b, Mediastinal nodes, Pt. 11a-c, Sarcoid+ca Pt. 8a-c**). This space is bounded superiorly by the carina, laterally by the right main and intermediate bronchi, the left main bronchus and the right and left mediastinal pleurae, anteriorly by the ascending aorta and right pulmonary artery, and posteriorly by the oesophagus. Whilst enlarged nodes are the main masses which fill this space, other structures which may fill it include an enlarged left atrium, pericardial distension from a pericardial effusion or an enlarged pulmonary venous confluence (p. 1.27). Large hiatal hernias may extend up into this area (Illus. **HIATUS HERNIA, Pts. 17** & **18a**), and it may occasionally be filled by a bronchogenic cyst (Illus. **BRONCHOGENIC CYST, Pt. 10**). Primary oesophageal tumours and associated nodes may also become very large and fill the subcarinal space.

The **subcarinal nodes** are a group three, five or more nodes (sometimes termed the '**lymphatic sump**' e.g. by Nohl, 1962) enveloped in a connective tissue sheath lying below the tracheal carina. They are well illustrated in the reproduction of Mascagni's woodcut (Illus. **MASCAGNI**), which also shows the lymph vessels draining them passing up on **either** side of the midline, and accounting for the not uncommon **contra-lateral lymph node enlargements** which may be seen with lung tumours, especially those originating in the lower lobes, lingula and middle lobes.

The author agrees that it is more logical to term the subcarinal nodes the '**lymphatic sump**', rather than nodes in the right or left hilum - see also p. 13.9.

Two or three normal nodes up to 1.5 cm in diameter are often shown by CT. When they enlarge, they often widen the carinal angle, distort or compress the main bronchi (Illus. **SUBCARINAL NODES**) and when much of their bulk lies posteriorly, push the main bronchi and carina forwards and displace the oesophagus to the left and posteriorly (a point easily determined by a some barium in the oesophagus as seen on fluoroscopy or radiographs - Illus. **CA LUNG+OES INVOLVEMENT, Pts. 3, 7a-b, 8 & 9**). They may also protrude into the azygo-oesophageal recess, displacing the lung out of the recess and to the right. Enlargement may also obliterate the stripes of the medial walls of the main bronchi (especially right) and intermediate bronchi (see ps. 1.24 - 25).

Their enlargement is usually apparent on plain high KV radiographs see diagrams (Fig. 13.1). Barium in the oesophagus may show that this is deviated or compressed by enlargement of these nodes. Lateral and inclined frontal tomograms may also readily show enlargements, which are often 'pear-shaped' (Illus. **SUBCARINAL NODES, Sarcoid+ca Pt. 2a-c, Ca oat Pt. 24a-c**). CT also shows them, but on the cross-section cuts, they have been not infrequently missed by less experienced observers (perhaps surprising but true!).

When the nodes are enlarged as a result of sarcoidosis (Illus. **SUBCARINAL NODES, Sarcoid**), reticulosis or leukaemia, the nodes tend to be 'softer' than with carcinoma, and there is less bronchial deformity and no direct invasion. Amyloid and rheumatoid infiltration may also affect these nodes and cause gross pressure deformity of the main bronchi and lower trachea. The infiltration may also extend into them. (Illus. **SUBCARINAL NODES, Amyloid Pt. 3a-e**). Subcarinal nodal enlargement may occur with tumours arising in either lung, even upper lobe tumours. Massive enlargement is most common with small-cell tumours. These nodes may also become enlarged due to secondary tumours spreading up from the abdomen (renal, bladder, teratoma, etc.).

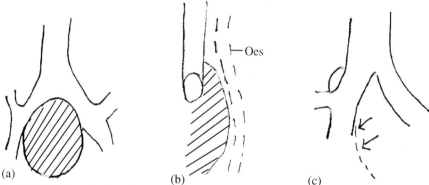

Fig. 13.17 Enlarged subcarinal nodes - (a) frontal view, (b) lateral view - oval shaped mass pressing backwards and also pressing on the oesophagus and (c) displacement of the para-oesophageal line with concavity to the left and obliteration of the azygo-oesophageal recess (arrowed).

Further references.
Chest with barium.
Lodge (1950) and Fleischner and Schasse (1963) : Took PA and lateral views with barium.
Middlemass (1953);   Lenk (1954) : Preferred the left oblique view.

Littleton et al. (1976) : Reproduced three tomograms of the mediastinum in patients with sarcoidosis, but omitted to comment on the subcarinal enlargement which seemed massive.
McLeod et al. (1976) : In discussing hilar masses, etc., only once mentioned the subcarinal area in a woman with undifferentiated carcinoma, but not with bronchial carcinoma in general, nor with sarcoidosis.

Blank and Castellino (1977) : Noted that subcarinal nodes are amongst the most difficult to detect on chest radiographs.
Gale and Pugatch (1982) : "Although standard sequential images at 10 mm intervals (on CT) are usually diagnostic for subcarinal lymph node enlargement, reconstruction may be helpful."
Müller et al. (1985a) : Made the same point and assessed 90 patients by high KV radiographs and CT; 60 had normal and 30 enlarged nodes on CT. Increased subcarinal density was seen in 40%, but they only saw an altered contour of the azygo-oesophageal recess in 25% of patients with lymphadenopathy. The outer borders of the medial walls of the right main and intermediate bronchi were visible in about 90% of patients with enlarged nodes, but only in about a third of patients with enlarged nodes. In normal cases CT showed that the exterior of the main and intermediate bronchi is delineated by air filled lung or mediastinal fat.
Platt et al. (1988) : Noted that subcarinal nodes are commonly involved by metastases from **either lung.**
Roberts et al. (2000) : **Transoesophageal US** for guided biopsy of subcarinal lymph nodes.

Paraoesophageal masses (including lymphatic spread alongside the pulmonary veins).
   The subcarinal area extends downwards and posteriorly into the paraoesophageal and para-aortic areas. In these, oesophageal tumours or enlarged nodes may displace the para-oesophageal line to the right and the preaortic or para-aortic lines to the left (see ps. 1.16 to 1.20). Nodes in this situation are not uncommonly enlarged with lung tumours, either via lymphatics passing to the mediastinum with the pulmonary veins (Fig. 13.4, p. 13.8 & Illus. **CA   LUNG+OES INVOLVEMENT, Pt. 10d**) or via retrograde spread from the subcarinal nodes.

Prespinal nodes may be enlarged, due to spread from oesophageal or other tumours, or in some patients with reticulosis. If very large, they may also displace the para-oesophageal line. Nodes in this situation may be mimicked by other masses such as large varices (see p. 18.31) or neurinomas - see also Tables 18.1 - 3, ps. 18.2 - 3.

Superior diaphragmatic nodes occur in relationship to the pericardium, the openings through the diaphragm and paravertebrally.

Posterior parietal nodes occur posteriorly in relation to the posterior aspects of the thoracic vertebral bodies and cost-vertebral joints, and merge with the retro-crural nodes at the dorsi-lumbar junction. Enlarged nodes in this group are seen in patients with lymphoma and other neoplasms spreading through this area e.g. renal, prostate, etc.

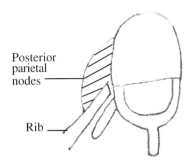

Fig. 13.18 Diagram showing position of posterior parietal nodes.

Studies of the number and size of **normal lymph nodes** in the various nodal groups have been made by :

Généreux and Howie (1983) : Studied mediastinal nodes by CT in 39 patients and by dissection in 12 cadavers. 99% of 225 nodes measured 16 mm in largest diameter (average size 12.6 x 8.3 mm). Nodes in the upper mediastinum tended to be smaller (0.5 cm) than those in the region of the carina.

Glazer G. et al. (1985) : Normal mediastinal lymph nodes - number and size according to the American Thoracic Society Mapping System (see p. 13.16).

Kiyotno et al. (1988) from Japan : Studied the number and size of thoracic nodes in 40 cadavers, and mapped them according to the above system. They found the largest normal nodes in the subcarinal area (up to 12 x 26 mm). The next largest were the right tracheo-bronchial nodes (11 x 20 mm), followed by the paratracheal, aorto-pulmonary and left tracheo-bronchial nodes (up to 9 x 15 mm). 10% of cadavers contained one or more bodies that exceeded these sizes.

Ingram et al. (1989) from London : Studied the size and number of normal mediastinal lymph nodes shown by CT in 140 young men with testicular tumours. Nodes were shown in 81% of normal chests, in the pretracheal retrocaval space in 46%, and in the right upper mediastinum in 28%. Nearly all of these nodes measured 5 to 10 mm or less in transverse diameter, and only one calcified node measured > 10 mm. One to three nodes were seen in the different areas of the mediastinum, fewer being visualised when there was little mediastinal fat. They concluded that the majority of normal nodes measured 0.5 cm in diameter, and that almost all normal nodes measure 10 mm or less.

Ikezoe et al. (1990) : Suggested that CT staging of mediastinal nodes is more accurate when group size criteria for nodes are employed.

Problems with 'normal' node sizes and CT assessment of nodal involvement by tumour.
The main problem with published node sizes is that many nodes have at some time been affected by granulomatous, etc. diseases, previous lung sepsis, chronic bronchitis, etc. series from the USA almost certainly have patients whose nodes have been affected by granuloma formation, which one would expect to make the nodes larger. Older patients often have larger nodes.
In the author's experience, older people, particularly smokers, often have larger nodes up to 1.5 to 2 cm in diameter, particularly in the pretracheal and subcarinal areas.
As discussed further on p. 13.18, CT can only show if nodes are enlarged, and not if they are necessarily enlarged by tumour. The supposition that a node with a short-axis diameter greater than 1.5 cm is necessarily involved by tumour is invalid, since even larger nodes up to 4 cm or more in diameter may sometimes be enlarged from reactive hyperplasia, sarcoid-like reaction to tumour (see above p. 13.17), etc.
Even small nodes < 1 cm in diameter may be involved by tiny tumour deposits, but this is less common with bronchial than oesophageal tumours, since bronchial tumour deposits often produce some reaction within the affected nodes.

Further references.

Mutzenbach (1967) : AP and lateral tomograms to study intrathoracic lymph node metastases in > 500 patients with bronchial carcinoma who underwent surgery. Good correlation in 70%. Nodes > 3 cm in diameter always contained tumour, > 2.5 cm likely to be due to neoplasm, but 1 to 1.5 cm were likely to be due to inflammation. **Calcification did not rule out metastatic involvement.**

Jost et al. (1978) : CT gives a new perspective in assessing the extent of bronchogenic carcinoma.

McLoud et al. (1979) : CT was invaluable for directing mediastinal and pleural extension, and by detecting additional lesions and calcification.

Miller, E. and Norman (1979), Shapeero et al. (1983) and Glazer, G. et al. (1983a) : Nodal metastases occasionally enhance with contrast media.

Underwood et al. (1979) : CT in the staging of bronchial carcinoma.

Ekholm et al. (1980) : 35 Patients with non-oat cell tumours and showed nodes in 31 patients. 17 were > 1 cm, but malignant in only 2. 5 nodes , 1 cm were involved with tumour. 9 were correctly thought to be inoperable, but 5 were incorrectly thought to be inoperable.

Faling et al. (1981 & 1982) : CT of the hila is insufficiently accurate, but is better for the mediastinum with about 90% sensitivity.

Rea et al. (1981) : CT was good at **excluding** malignant mediastinal involvement.

Schnyder and Gamsu (1981) : (i) lymph node enlargement does not always signify tumour and (ii) nodes infiltrated by tumour are not always enlarged.

Baron et al. (1982c) : 192 patients - guide - < 1 cm = normal, 1 to 1.5 cm = suspicious, and > 1.5 cm = involved with tumour, but I node of 1.7 cm was enlarged by reactive hyperplasia and 3 < 1 cm contained tumour deposits.

Lewis et al. (1982) : CT correctly predicted nodes in > 90%, whilst conventional tomograms were only 60% accurate. Some nodes < 1 cm contained tumour.

Moak (1982) : 'No radiological method should replace surgical staging, but CT and conventional tomograms can direct attention to areas of suspected nodal involvement.

Osborne et al. (1982) : CT was best for the mediastinum, but for the hilum CT and conventional tomograms were about equally good.

Spiro et al. (1982) : CT is not tissue specific and caution must be exercised in staging. Massive nodal enlargement did not invariably mean malignancy; conversely any visible lymph node in the mediastinum cannot be assumed to be free of tumour.

Cohen et al. (1983) : In 4 of 18 patients MR showed a greater extent of disease than CT.

Glazer, G. et al. (1983a) : CT with contrast enhancement opacified hilar vascular structures.

Konig et al. (1983) : 'Of all the mediastinal lymph nodes, the retrocaval and pretracheal groups can be most frequently demonstrated by CT.'

Breyer et al. (1984) : 32 patients - considered nodes to be involved if > 1.5 cm. No false positives but 3 false negative.

Epstein et al. (1984) : CT appeared to show nodes better than MR.

Glazer et al. (1984 & 1985) : Negative CT makes mediastinoscopy unnecessary, whilst positive CT should led to biopsy of the enlarged node.

Libshitz et al. (1984) and Libshitz and McKenna (1984) : Nodes > 1 cm were a poor prediction of tumour spread. Many did not contain tumour.

Richey et al. (1984) : Third generation CT is sensitive for recognising enlarged nodes, but is not specific for malignant disease.

Webb et al. (1984a, b & c) : MR more readily distinguished mediastinal structures from nodes. (1985) : MR better demonstrated nodes from vascular structures, but CT better for bronchial abnormalities.

Khan et al. (1985) : 50 cases - using > 1 cm as abnormal, 15 out of 18 considered enlarged on CT contained tumour and 3 out of 32 considered negative were positive at histology.

Black and Armstrong (1985) : ? different underlying diseases enlarge nodes in different areas.

Glazer et al. (1985) : Both CT and MR will routinely detect nodes 1 cm or more in diameter. Also noted the low accuracy of CT for assessing hilar node enlargement compared with the assessment of the hilum for a primary tumour mass.

Heelan et al. (1985) : MR detected more enlarged nodes in the mediastinum but in several cases these did not contain tumour.

Levitt et al. (1985) : MR had some disadvantages by not showing calcification, also adjacent lymph nodes shown by CT may appear to be a single enlarged node on MR. CT remained the radiological procedure of choice in the assessment of patients with bronchogenic carcinoma and other hilar and mediastinal masses.

Martini et al. (1985) : 34 patients with 'operable' tumours studied by CT and MR - 23 were completely resected. Both methods correctly assessed the hilum and mediastinal nodes, but neither correlated well for mediastinal invasion. Neither could differentiate hyperplastic from neoplastic nodes.

Müller et al. (1985b) : Assessed the signs of para-tracheal lymphadenopathy on plain chest radiographs andconfirmed these with CT. Plain film signs were widening of the right para-tracheal stripe, enlargement of the azygos node, convex lateral border of the SVC or increased density in the region of the SVC. CT showed that most of the enlarged nodes were either antero-lateral, rather than directly lateral to the trachea, or lay behind the SVC. Plain films were positive in 90%.

Pearlberg et al. (1985) : 23 patients with no evidence of deposits on plain radiographs or clinically - only one had nodes > 1 cm (confirmed histologically after mediastinoscopy).

Quint et al. (1986) : Assessed 5 cadavers by CT and found that the **short axis diameter of nodes was the best predictor of their volumes** - good correlation for right sided nodes, but poorer on the left, particularly in the peribronchial region.

Ferguson et al. (1986) : CT least accurate in the aorto-pulmonary window.

Musset et al. (1986) : No difference between CT and MR for evaluation of tumour extent or node involvement, but MR may be better for chest wall invasion.

Platt et al. (1987) : "Despite previous evidence that left-sided mediastinal nodes are less well evaluated by CT than right sided nodes, we found no statistically significant difference in the accuracy of mediastinal staging for cancer of the right vs left lung ... CT had high sensitivity (86%) and overall accuracy (86%) in assessment of metastasis to the mediastinal lymph nodes".

Poon et al. (1987) : "As long as nodal size remains the sole criterion in the detection of metastatic lymphadenopathy, MR imaging is unlikely to enable better interpretation than CT scanning".

Buy et al. (1988) : 97 patients with non-small cell lung cancer - considered nodes abnormal when the short axis of the largest node was 1 cm, and the difference between this and the largest in other areas was >5 mm. Claimed this gave greater accuracy. Also noted contra-lateral spread, especially from the left lower lobe, which they considered gives rise to contra-lateral as commonly as ipsilateral nodal enlargement. In nodes showing < 5 mm difference in size, as compared with those in other areas, the likelihood was of an inflammatory node.

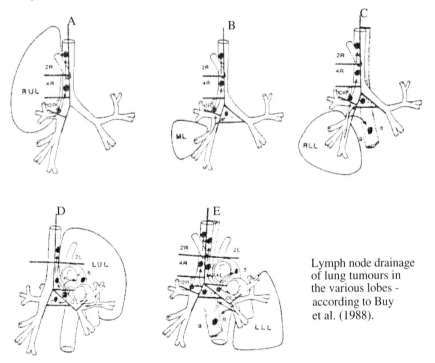

Lymph node drainage of lung tumours in the various lobes - according to Buy et al. (1988).

(Drawings reproduced from Buy et al., 1988, 'CT of mediastinal lymph nodes in non-cell lung cancer: A new approach based on the lymphatic pathway of tumor spread.' JCAT, **12**, 545 - 552, with permission from Lippincott - Raven.)

Gross et al. (1988) : Bronchogenic carcinoma metastatic to **normal-sized lymph nodes** ; frequency and significance.
Cybulsky et al. (1992) : Prognostic significance of CT in resected N2 lung cancer.
McLoud et al. (1992) : 143 patients - CT examinations with correlative lymph node mapping and sampling - the likelihood of metastases increased with lymph node size, however 7 of 19 lymph nodes that measured 2 to 4 cm in short-axis diameter were hyperplastic and did not contain metastases. 42 of their patients had nodal metastases confirmed at either mediastinoscopy or thoracotomy and the CT sensitivity for nodes on a per patient basis was 64% with a specificity of 62%.
Arita et al. (1995) : Metastases to normal sized mediastinal lymph nodes in bronchogenic carcinoma are a major problem in staging - hilar node enlargement also did not help to reliably predict the presence or absence of deposits in the mediastinal nodes.
Murray et al. (1995) : Studied the sizes of lymph nodes in Asians from the Indian subcontinent who were living in West London and found that "the generally accepted size criteria for mediastinal lymph node enlargement (greater than 10 mm) can reasonably be applied to all Asian patients when staging lymphoma or bronchogenic carcinoma."
Macis et al. (1996) : Are studying CT signs of extra-nodal infiltration in pts. with lung cancer - to test whether this CT sign can better predict survival than mere size alone (where there is 80% accuracy, with 20% false positives and 20% false negatives.) They cited Berg's findings (1965) that after surgical excision there was a marked difference in 5 yr survival of pts. with intra-nodal involvement (43%) as compared to those with extracapsular lymph node spread.

Shimoyama et al. (1997) : The normal hilar interstitium
(a) has margins that are concave or straight whilst the interstitium that contains metastatic nodes
(b) has margins that are convex to the lung parenchyma because
nodes that contain tumour deposits are enlarged and have changed shape.

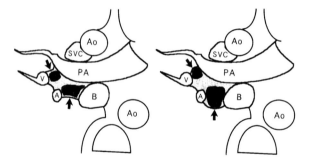

(Drawings reproduced from Shimoyama et al., 1997, 'Pulmonary hilar lymph node metastases from lymph node cancer: evaluation based on morphology at thin-section, incremental, dynamic CT.' - Radiology, **203**, 187 - 197 with permission).

See also [18]FDG PET scanning - ps. 22.9 & 22.11.

Lymph node imaging - review.
Metreweli (1999) : US, CT, MR and scintigraphy can show normal and abnormal nodes by their morphological features - size, shape, number, necrosis, calcification and surrounding oedema. Metabolic activity can be demonstrated by several different isotopes and by changes in vascularity - demonstrated by colour Doppler or US.

Chapter 14 : **The Extra-Pleural and Pleural Spaces, including Plombages, Pleural Tumours and the Effects of Asbestos.**

The Extra-pleural (or Semb's*) Space.   (* Semb - Former Professor of Surgery, Oslo.)
    This potential space, between the parietal pleura and the chest wall, is commonly involved by tumours of the chest wall, particularly those arising in the ribs and pressing inwards into the chest. Haematomas and other fluid collections may form in this space, particularly after surgery, paracentesis, insertion of pacemakers, etc. Empyemas in this space usually result from some similar procedures, but may complicate old TB (see Illus. **EXTRAPLEURAL SPACE**). Fluid collections may spread within it because the parietal pleura is easily stripped from the chest wall. Air may be present within it after operation, particularly after a thoracoplasty, surgery for the removal of bullae (p. 6.10) or e.g. gas tracking alongside a drainage tube. Extrapleural fat may be displaced medially by extrapleural tumour, oedema or haemorrhage.
    Masses arising outside the lung and invaginating the pleura (visceral or both visceral and parietal) cause such a mass to have a clearly marginated outline - sometimes referred to as 'pleural based'. However such a term is **erroneous** since such masses mostly arise outside the pleura, in the chest wall and project into the extra-pleural space, before invaginating both layers of the pleura.
    Felson (1977) wrote 'the intact parietal pleura and tumefaction in this space presents an extremely sharp convex contour facing the lung'. Rémy and Mabille (1977) termed a mass projecting into this space the **'pleural coiffe'** (i.e. head-dress or cap). Ellis (1977) noted that masses may have an incomplete border where they arise from the chest wall - the **'incomplete border sign'**. Völk et al. (2000) illustrated a resolving small extrapleural nodule with this sign by CT. Hammerman et al. (1990) studied the **extrapleural fat sign** by CT.

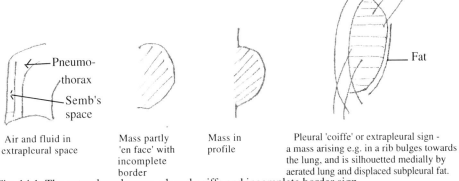

| Air and fluid in extrapleural space | Mass partly 'en face' with incomplete border | Mass in profile | Pleural 'coiffe' or extrapleural sign - a mass arising e.g. in a rib bulges towards the lung, and is silhouetted medially by aerated lung and displaced subpleural fat. |

Fig. 14.1 The extrapleural space, pleural coiffe and incomplete border sign.

Note the similarity of the fat line to the pleural 'white line' seen with ultra-sound - see p. 14.13.
A similar sign to the pleural coiffe is given by masses pressing into a pleural cavity from the mediastinum on CT. Masses pressing into the lung tend to give an obtuse angle from the pleura, in contrast to acute angles produced by masses arising in the lung (see also Fig. 14.11, p. 14.17). Intrapulmonary masses are commonly fully outlined by air (see ps. 4.12-13) as are nipples and skin papillomas (ps. 6.26-27).

Common causes :	Metastasis in rib bulging into or in extra-pleural soft tissues
	Rib fracture, chondroma, neurofibroma, other rib masses
	Mediastinal mass in central part of space
	Subphrenic mass
	Following surgical procedures
Uncommon causes :	Haematoma, loculated pleural reaction
	Chest wall infection e.g. TB rib
	Lobar agenesis pulling the chest wall inwards.
Tumours:	Lipoma, desmoid tumour, pl. fibroma, mesothelioma

Chronic sub-pleural thickening in this space may be caused by repeated trauma, as in boxers. The author has collected several cases. Such thickening elevates the parietal pleura from the ribs, and in time becomes replaced by fatty deposits (see also pseudo plaques - p. 14.39 and Illus. **BOXER**).

PA   Lateral projection

Fig. 14.2   Subpleural thickening.

Iatrogenic Pleural and Extra-Pleural Masses - especially 'Plombages'.
   These were commonly inserted into the extra-pleural space for the treatment of tuberculosis in the pre-chemotherapeutic era, as an alternative to artificial pneumothorax treatment or thoracoplasty (p. 11.15). Various substances were used, such as sponges, small plastic balls (like table tennis or small billiard balls), or bags containing fat or oil, and many older patients still retain them. Occasionally these may cause trouble years later by becoming secondarily infected, mainly by pyogenic infections, but also occasionally by recurrent tuberculosis, and air-filled cavities may then be found adjacent to them if the inflammatory process tracks into the adjacent lung and establishes a communication with it. Mostly however air in plombages is innocent - a 'sponge' becoming 'speckled', balls becoming fully or partly air-filled, all being manifestations of simple connections developing with the adjacent aerated lung - Illus. **PLOMBAGE, Pts. 2a-b, 6 & 10a-b**. Difficulty arises if a tumour develops close to a plombage.
   Sometimes plombages or their rims may become calcified and this may be seen on plain radiographs or tomograms. Illus. **PLOMBAGE, TB & plombage Pt. 1a-b** show a marginally calcified oleothorax, together with recrudescent tuberculosis in the contralateral lung.

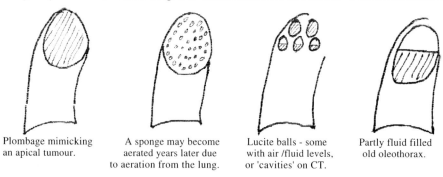

| Plombage mimicking an apical tumour. | A sponge may become aerated years later due to aeration from the lung. | Lucite balls - some with air /fluid levels, or 'cavities' on CT. | Partly fluid filled old oleothorax. |

Fig. 14.3   Types of plombage.

Chronic fluid collections   due to past TB, oleothoraces (paraffin and mineral oil), and some plombages may expand years later, due to fluid diffusing into them and cause not only enlargement on radiographs but genuine respiratory distress. They may be aspirated and the pleural surfaces examined by tomography after replacement with air (Illus. **PL-EFF GAS REPLACEMENT, TB pleural Pt. 5**).

Some references.
Hutton (1984) : Oleothorax - an expanding pleural lesion - enlarged many years later due to fluid ingress, with no sinister import, but led to respiratory distress.
Horowitz et al.(1992) : Late complications of plombage due to infection and/or migration of Lucite spheres - four cases: (i) bilateral plombage - infection L apex + fistula to oesophagus, through which one ball passed and caused

intestinal obstruction. (ii) Haemoptysis and infection caused by erosion of sphere into lung. (iii) Fistula draining into axilla. (iv) Extrusion of fluid into chest wall. All the patients recovered following removal of the material.
Kirschenbaum et al. (1995) : Pleurocutaneous fistula as a complication of oleothorax in three pts. - CT demonstration of inflammation and swelling surrounding an oleothorax rupture can be grounds for surgical intervention. The authors also remind us of Hippocrates' use of a pig bladder to achieve pulmonary collapse.
Chew et al. (1999) : Late tracheal compression complicating plombage.

Pleural disease.

This is commonly recognised on plain radiographs as fluid, thickening, gas, calcification, etc. Fluoroscopy and radiographs in different postures (e.g. decubitus views) may show movement of fluid. As discussed more fully below, fluid spreads around the lung by capillary attraction, unless a coincident pneumothorax is present, and may produce pleural thickening over the lung apex and adjacent to the mediastinum. It may also collect under the lung as a subpulmonary effusion (see also below). Many subpulmonary effusions have been shown by conventional tomography, but ultra-sound is now the main method of confirming pleural fluid.

The cause of pleural disease may be surmised in many patients by knowing the presence of metastases, heart failure, rib fractures, primary lung neoplasm, etc. However, aspiration of some fluid, which is now most conveniently carried out under ultra-sound control, is invaluable in many cases, and will immediately show if the fluid is 'clear', blood-stained, frank blood, pus, chyle, etc. The aspirate may be sent for cytology and/ or bacteriology.

The main problems are in distinguishing:
    (a) Pleural masses or fluid from non-aerated lung
    (b) Sub-pulmonary effusions
    (c) Pleural plaques
    (d) Tumours in the pleura
    (e) Pleural pus collections with pleural thickening, i.e. sub-acute or chronic empyemas.

Pleural masses, dry pleurisy and 'knobbly pleura'.

Most simple pleural masses are well demarcated by showing against the displaced aerated lung, which is often compressed. They differ from 'extra-pleural' masses, by not elevating sub-pleural fat. The real problem is when the adjacent lung is not fully aerated, or a pleural effusion is present, because then the pleural mass will be masked. Pleural masses may be single or multiple, the latter occurring particularly with malignant disease. When there are multiple 'knobs' present, this may indicate a **malignant dry pleurisy** (Illus. **PL-KNOBBLY**). This is commonly associated with severe pain, and may be caused by primary pleural tumours, or more commonly a bronchial tumour which has spread into the pleura and has not stimulated the production of any fluid. However it may also be seen with secondary tumour from other sites e.g. breast, abdomen, reticulosis, etc. Tumours pressing in from the chest wall (e.g. myeloma) may give an almost identical appearance. When pleural fluid is present the 'knobbly pleura' may be masked, unless it is aspirated or becomes absorbed. Air entering the pleura at paracentesis may also allow 'knobs' or 'mushrooms' to be seen.

A **pleural mouse** (Illus. **PL-MOUSE**) is a pleural nodule, usually oval in shape which may move or stay fixed in position. It may become calcified, sometimes enlarge, and like other pleural nodules may mimic an intra-pulmonary mass. Such 'mice' were more common when TB was more common, and was treated by artificial pneumothorax. Pleural 'mice' are still occasionally seen following other inflammatory diseases or a haemothorax (see ps. 14.8 & 14.28).

Pleural effusions - effect of posture, subpulmonary effusions, etc.

The pleural space normally contains only a few ml of fluid, which is formed by the parietal pleura, and is absorbed by capillaries and lymphatics in the visceral pleura (Black, 1972). Transudate effusions occur when systemic or pulmonary venous hypertension is present, when the plasma colloid osmotic pressure is reduced, when the intra-pleural pressure becomes excessively negative or when fluid crosses the diaphragm from the peritoneum.

In the absence of air in the pleural space, large pleural effusions tend to creep up around the aerated lung, rather like fluid surrounding an air-filled balloon pushed into a bucket of water (**'Balloon-in-the-bucket' sign** - Blank, 1989). In ambulant erect patients fluid behaves similarly, extending around the lung laterally, posteriorly and anteriorly, and being greater in amount at the base of the pleural cavity.

Small pleural effusions are often described as producing a small basal meniscus, with 'blunting' of the costo-phrenic angle - this may be seen on PA views, but is most commonly present posteriorly on lateral views. However 'displacement' of a costo-phrenic angle is also a frequent sign.

Blunting of costo-phrenic angle.

Displacement of costo-phrenic angle or 'lamellar pleuritis'.

Fig. 14.4   Small pleural effusion.

On changing posture, from erect to recumbent, supine to prone, or on turning into the decubitus position, free fluid can be shown to flow into the most dependent part of the affected pleural cavity or cavities. This was commonly done to prove the presence of pleural effusions with decubitus views, but with ultrasound and CT this technique is now only used occasionally. However turning the patient prone or onto his side may be valuable with CT, to show that the fluid is mobile and not just thickening, and also to remove the fluid from a particular area to show the underlying lung or pleura.

Pleural fluid may also often lie within or extend into the oblique or lesser fissures, apparently thickening them, or as larger collections - see below.

Sub-pulmonary effusions - (Illus. **PL-EFFUS SUBPULM**).

Despite the common text-book description of Ellis's 'S' shaped line, with fluid arising as a curved and almost triangular shadow, from the base of a pleural cavity (especially posteriorly and laterally) in the part of the pleural cavity adjacent to the chest wall, many effusions (about 25 to 50%) lie in the sub-pulmonary position, between the inferior aspect of the lung, and the superior surface of the diaphragm. These may often be inferred on the left by noting the position of the stomach gas bubble, and the distance between it and the lower part of the lung on both PA and lateral views.

A sub-pulmonary effusion may be readily confirmed by real-time ultra-sound. This is easier on the right, both sides may be examined via the lower inter-costal spaces (especially posteriorly) or via the liver (through which one can readily see the right sub-pulmonary space, and often also the left). Such an examination will also readily differentiate such a fluid collection from a mass within the liver - the former sometimes appearing as an hepatic 'pseudo-tumour'. Subpulmonary tumours also not uncommonly cause '**inversion**' of the **affected side of the diaphragm** (see also p. 15.4).

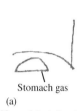

Stomach gas

(a)

Normal (< 1.5 cm)

(b)

Sub-pulmonary fluid
(> 1.5 cm)

(c)

Beware of a false sign of sub-pulmonary fluid due to an anterior hump of the left side of the diaphragm (after Rémy et al, 1981, with permission).

Fig. 14.5   Sub-pulmonary fluid

Pleural effusions tend to be homogeneous in density, unless air or calcification in present. They also tend to have tapering margins and sharp interfaces with the adjacent lung and chest wall.

Loculation is not uncommon, particularly behind the apex of a lower lobe, or within an interlobar fissure.

Large effusions may displace the mediastinum towards the contra-lateral side, and a failure of such movement may be a pointer to a fixed mediastinum, most often caused by tumour infiltration. Large effusions may cause anterior or posterior herniation, particularly the latter in the azygo-oesophageal recess (see also p. 2.40 and Illus. **MESOTHELIOMA, Pt. 23** and **PL-FIBROMA, Pt. 1c**), or lead to collapse, particularly of the lower lobes, which may often be seen floating within the fluid on CT or ultra-sound examinations - see also Fig. 2.33a, p. 2.33 & Illus. **PL-EFFUSION, Pts. 13 & 17**. See also Fig. 2.35a-b, p. 2.35 re the triangular shadow due to the pulmonary ligament, and tethering of the lower lobe by the ligament.

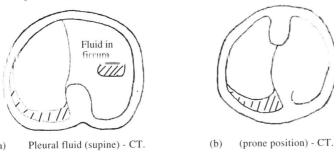

Fluid in fissure

(a)   Pleural fluid (supine) - CT.   (b)   (prone position) - CT.

Fig. 14.6 Free pleural fluid moving under gravity.

Further references.

Fleischner (1927) : Lamellar pleuritis (displacement of the lung medially from the costal pleura).
          (1963) : Atypical arrangement of free pleural effusion.
Rigler (1936) : Atypical distribution of pleural effusions (sub-pulmonary fluid).
Rothstein and Landis (1950) : Infrapulmonary pleural effusions.
Hessen (1951) : Roentgen-examination of pleural fluid - a study of the localisation of free effusions, etc.
Friedman (1954) : Infrapulmonary pleural effusions.
Dunbar and Favreau (1959) : Infrapulmonary pleural effusion - esp. in nephrosis - signs -
(i) Reversed meniscus,
(ii) Change in contour of lung base - curve reached maximum height at approx. junction of middle and lateral thirds,
(iii) Posterior fluid collection,
(iv) Separation of stomach bubble from the left leaf of the diaphragm,
(v) Shift of fluid with posture change,
(vi) Mediastinal effusion - esp. lower triangular fluid collection,
(vii) Anterior costophrenic sinus (lateral views),
(viii) Fluid in fissures.
Petersen (1960) : Recognition of infrapulmonary effusion.
Davis et al. (1963) : The shape of a pleural effusion.
Trackler and Brinker (1966) : Widening of the left paravertebral pleural line on supine chest Roentgenograms in free pleural effusions (see also paravertebral line - p.18.28).
Collins et al. (1972) : Minimal detectable pleural effusions - a Roentgen pathway model.
Vix (1974) : Radiological recognition of pleural effusion.
Schwarz et al. (1975) : A new radiological sign of subpulmonary fluid - absence of the normally visualised lower lobe vessels as they course posteriorly below the anterior hump of the diaphragm.
Bryk (1976) : Infrapulmonary effusion - effect of expiration in exaggerating the lateral displacement of an apparent diaphragmatic 'hump'.
Sukumaran and Berger (1979) : **Mediastinal herniation** of the pleural sac in massive pleural effusion curvilinear opacity extending beyond the midline (R→L in 10 cases and L→R in 6.)
Rudikoff (1980) : Early detection of pleural fluid.
Lams and Jolles (1982) : Any atypical configuration of pleural effusion or pneumothorax should direct attention to disease in the underlying lung parenchyma.
Marks et al. (1982) : Real-time evaluation of pleural lesions - new observations regarding the probability of obtaining free fluid.
Weiss, I. and Spodick (1983) : Association of left pleural effusion with pericardial disease.
          (1984) : Laterality of pleural effusions in chronic congestive heart failure.
Godwin (1984), Heitzman (1984), & Blank (1989) : Monographs on the chest.

Pistolesi et al. (1989) : The parietal pleura secretes about 10 ml fluid/ day and the normal visceral pleura contributes little to pleural fluid formation or absorption.

Davies and Turner (1990) : Enhancement of collapsed lung - a potential pitfall in CT interpretation - this may give rise to a fine rim of enhancing lung on CT sections.

Stark and Leung (1996) : Effects of lobar collapse on the distribution of pleural effusion and pneumothorax. The pleural space is under the effect of two opposing forces, exerted on the pleural membranes - the outward pull of the chest cage and the inward recoil of the lung. Average pleural pressure is -5 cm water at functional residual opacity. The pleural pressure gradient is about 0.2 cm water/ cm vertical distance with about 7.5 cm difference between lung apex and base.

Interlobar effusions (PL-EFFUSION FISS).

Localised collections of fluid in a fissure may be well outlined and appear as apparent lung masses. They may be seen on frontal or lateral views, or both. Sometimes within a greater fissure they may give rise to a 'dumb-bell' type of appearance due to the tangency of the fluid collection to the x-ray beam. They are commonly biconvex. On the right they have to be distinguished from a collapsed middle lobe, if necessary by tomography, bronchography or bronchoscopy. Most clear with resolution of the underlying cause of the effusion - the '**vanishing**' or '**pseudo-tumour**' - see also p. 6.30. Occasionally an empyema will be interlobar, and may be aspirated under TV fluoroscopic control (Illus. **EMPYEMA, Pts. 15 & 29a-c**).

In the lesser fissure fluid may give an elliptical shadow on the PA view, or only be evident on a lateral view (as for middle lobe collapse - p. 2.20). As well as loculated effusions being mistaken for tumours, tumours may be mistaken for interlobar effusions. A special case is a biconvex middle lobe tumour (Illus. **CA RML, Pt. 20a-b**).

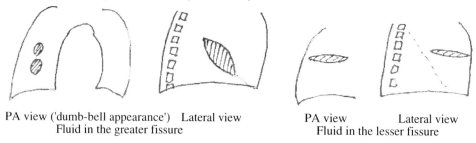

PA view ('dumb-bell appearance')   Lateral view
        Fluid in the greater fissure

PA view   Lateral view
    Fluid in the lesser fissure

Fig. 14.7   Interlobar pleural effusions - diagrammatic representations.

Fig. 14.8 The '**thorn sign**' - small pleural reactions in the lesser fissure, accessory fissures, or a little fluid extending up from larger basal effusions may give rise to this sign (Oestreich and Haley, 1981 - not a rare finding!). Compare this with the 'pleural tag' - see Fig. 4.6, p. 4.17.

Thorn sign.

Fluid in accessory fissures may also give rise to confusing shadows (Illus. **PL EFFUSION, Pt. 12a**).

References.

Feldman (1951) : Localised interlobar pleural effusion in heart failure.

Weiss, W. et al. (1953) : Localised interlobar pleural effusion due to congestive heart failure.

Higgins et al. (1955) : Localised interlobar pleural effusion due to congestive heart failure.

Feder and Wilk (1956) : Localised interlobar effusion in heart failure - '**phantom lung tumour**'.

Carvalho and Kerr (1991) : Pulmonary neoplasms simulating interlobar pleural effusions.

Van Gelderen (1994) : Vanishing pleural fluid collections in cardiac failure simulating lung tumours.

The recognition of pleural effusions on supine radiographs.

The recognition of fluid on plain radiographs is often very difficult, even when these are quite large. The reason is that in the supine patient, pleural fluid tends to lie as a flat pool deep to the air-filled lung, and often will not be seen lateral to the lung. It tends to 'creep' up to the apex, to form an '**apical cap**', and at the bases may mask the posterior and medial aspects of the diaphragmatic silhouette. Because of the concavity of the posterior aspect of the pleural cavity, fluid will tend to lie more medially than laterally, and with a short focus-film-distance, as used for most such examinations, the more lateral parts of the lungs will be projected clear of the fluid - Fig. 14.9a.

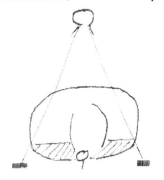
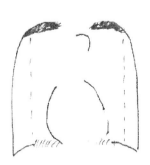
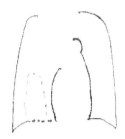

(a) No fluid is traversed by the more lateral divergent x-rays.

(b) Main features of a supine effusion - apical caps, loss of medial parts of diaphragm silhouettes , and the desc. aorta. Often there is only a moderate increased density due to the fluid. The costo-phrenic angles may be preserved.

(c) Sometimes a more loculated collection of fluid may be seen as an area of increased density through the overlying lung.

Fig. 14.9   Pleural fluid on supine radiographs.

Even large effusions are not infrequently overlooked particularly if they are accompanied by pulmonary congestion, therefore one should look for distended veins, particularly at the bases, engorged septal lines, etc. Supine effusions may be shown with decubitus views, real-time ultra-sound and may also be shown by CT (Illus. **PL-EFFUSION, Pt. 1a-b**).

References.
Møller (1984) : Use of the semi-supine position for radiographic detection of pleural effusions.
Onik et al. (1984) : Hydropneumothorax - detection on supine radiographs.
Woodring (1984) : How much pleural fluid is required for its recognition on supine radiographs?
Ruskin et al. (1987) : Supine radiographs are only moderately successful for diagnosing pleural effusions - only 24 out of 36 were so detected.

Pleural effusions - exudate or transudate?

As already noted, needle aspiration may show if the fluid is clear, blood-stained, frank blood, pus, chyle, etc. Although clear or straw coloured fluid collections are often classified as '**exudates**' (due to pleural inflammation and with a protein content > 3 g%, in the presence of inflammatory cells) or '**transudates**' (due to loss of fluid from the pleural capillary bed with pulmonary oedema, etc. - see Light et al., 1972 & Light, 1990), this distinction is often not very helpful as the two frequently overlap.

Common causes

Cardiac failure, renal failure, (chronic ambulatory peritoneal dialysis), overloaded circulation, cirrhosis, etc.

Lung infection - common with or following lobar pneumonia (para or post-pneumonic - may become purulent or lead to a frank empyema). May be the presenting feature with tuberculosis (often lymphocytic).

Pulmonary embolism or infarction - may be haemorrhagic and contain neutrophils or eosinophils.

Primary or secondary tumours of various types - mesothelioma, lymphoma, lung or oesophageal tumour, etc. (breast, bowel, renal, ovary, prostate, etc.).

Asbestosis, rheumatoid disease, DLE, etc.

A sympathetic effusion may occur in association with trauma (see p. 11.7), subdiaphragmatic disease - subphrenic abscess, liver or renal abscess, pancreatitis, ovarian disease, Meigs' syndrome, etc.

Less common or rare causes.

Chylothorax, pleural or thoracic ascites and urinothorax (see below).

Also : sarcoidosis, glandular fever, myeloma, drug reactions, yellow nail syndrome, etc.

Eosinophilic effusions - see p. 19.59 - may be due to adenocarcinoma.

Some special points.

(i) An effusion may be **eosinophilic** with collagen diseases, infarction, tropical pneumonias, allergic states, lymphoma, other tumours (including adenocarcinoma of lung - Illus. **PL-EFFUS EOS**) and mesothelioma.

(ii) **Spontaneous hydropneumothoraces** - small amounts of fluid are not uncommon with pneumothorax, but massive effusions are rare, but when they occur may be of serious emergency importance.

Haemothorax and haemopneumothoraces.

Haemothoraces and blood stained effusions may follow trauma (including medical trauma), or in association with tumours (e.g. lung tumours or pancreatic tumours causing low platelet counts, etc.), infarction or infection, or occasionally be spontaneous in origin. The case shown in Illus. **HAEMOTHORAX Pt. 1a-c** with bilateral haemothoraces had minor trauma, but was receiving anticoagulant treatment. Haemothoraces may follow the insertion of subclavian lines, with damage to the subclavian vessels, fractured ribs, lacerated lung, torn adhesions, etc. The author has seen some cases secondary to damage to intercostal vessels at paracentesis or the insertion of drainage tubes (see note p. 11.3). Other cases have complicated tuberculosis, renal failure, a lung or pleural malignancy, or a benign rib or chest wall tumour, especially a costal exostosis. A case the author has seen showed such a lesion complicating a left sided costal exostosis jutting into the pericardium and invaginating the left ventricle.

A spontaneous haemopneumothorax is a type of spontaneous pneumothoraces, adhesions being torn by the sudden lung collapse.   Clotting of blood in the pleural cavity has been studied by several authors, but in the absence of anticoagulants, it appears to occur normally, though not as solidly as blood within soft tissues. Blood which clots rapidly after aspiration almost certainly has come from a vessel in the chest wall or lung, etc. as respiratory movement tends to remove fibrin from clots and effusions. This fibrin becomes deposited as pleural thickening, or as a more localised mass, and may lead to a fibro-thorax, a fibrinous pleural body or a '**pleural   mouse**'- see also ps. 14.3 & 14.28 and Illus. **PL-MOUSE**.

Some authors have advocated fibrinolytic treatment to liquefy intra-blood and allow it to be more easily aspirated, whilst others have carried out surgical debridement. Infection may cause large haemothoraces to progress to empyemata.

Some general references.

Smyrnios et al. (1990) : Pleural effusion in an asymptomatic patient - those secondary to congestive heart failure, abdominal surgery and childbirth only need to be observed. Pleural nodularity needs biopsy re neoplasm. Other causes should be determined.

Leung et al. (1990) : CT in the differential diagnosis of diffuse pleural disease. The pleural response to a variety of diseases is limited largely to **three** radiologically detectable **manifestations - effusions, thickening and calcification**. When malignant disease has spread diffusely in the pleura, CT signs include, loss of volume of the affected hemi-thorax, circumferential and/or nodular pleural thickening, which may involve both the costal and mediastinal pleura.

Gawne-Cain et al. (1993) : Patients with bilateral (but not unilateral) effusions due to breast carcinoma had a poor prognosis with median survival times of three months.

Aquino et al. (1994) : Pleural exudates and transudates - diagnosis with contrast enhanced CT -
(i) Parietal pleural thickening almost always indicates the presence of an exudate. (ii) Transudative pleural effusions and a large percentage of malignant exudates do not show parietal pleural thickening or enhancement.
(iii) Thickening and increased density of extrapleural fat is suggestive of pleural inflammation or infection, and may be found with empyema but also malignancy and asbestos exposure.
Eibenberger et al. (1994) : In the quantification of pleural effusions, sonographic measurement is preferable to radiographic measurement.

Haemothoraces
Le Blanc and Trousseau (1834) : Performed experiments on horses and showed that blood coagulates normally in the pleural cavity.
Denny and Minot (1915) : The coagulation of blood in the pleural cavity.
Elliott and Henry (1916) : The morbid anatomy of wounds of the thorax.
Melick and Spooner (1945) : Experimental haemothorax - showed that a haemothorax may be followed within about five days of its onset by fibroblastic proliferation, which in turn leads to organisation and the production of a 'peel' on the contracted lung surface.
Calvert and Smith (1955) : Analytical review of spontaneous haemothorax, with report of three massive effusions.
Solomon et al. (1971) : Fibromyomata of the uterus with haemothorax - Meigs' syndrome?
Butchart et al. (1975) : Spontaneous rupture of intercostal artery in a patient with neurofibromatosis and scoliosis.
Propper et al. (1980) : Haemothorax as a complication of costal cartilaginous exostosis.
Larrieu et al. (1982) : Spontaneous massive haemothorax in von Recklinghausen's disease.
Sulis and Floris (1985) : Heamothorax due to extramedullary erythropoiesis in thalassaemia intermedia.
Smith, P. et al. (1988) : Massive haemothorax due to intrathoracic extramedullary haematopoiesis in a patient with thalassaemia intermedia.
Reynolds and Morgan (1990) : Haemothorax caused by a solitary costal exostosis.
Castells et al. (1993) : Haemothorax in hereditary multiple exostosis.
Chou et al. (1993) : Spontaneous haemothorax as an unusual presentation of lung cancer.
Kravis and Hutton (1993) : Solitary plasma cell tumour of the pleura presenting with a massive haemothorax.
Harrison et al. (1994) : Osteochondroma of a rib - an unusual cause of haemothorax.
Walsh et al. (2001) : Giant coronary bypass graft pseudoaneurysm presenting as a haemothorax.

Pleural or thoracic ascites (including Meigs' syndrome - Illus. MEIGS' SYNDROME) and the spread of metastatic disease from the abdomen to the chest through the diaphragmatic domes.

 This type of fluid and tumour spread takes place when fluid and /or tumour cells from the abdominal cavity pass into one or both pleural cavities, through 'pores' in the diaphragm. More commonly this occurs on the right (probably due to a 'blocking' action by the heart on the left), but it can also occur on the left, or on both sides simultaneously.

 Causes include ovarian tumours (giving rise to Meigs' syndrome, malignant effusions and pleural tumour deposits - see below), endometriosis (ps. 5.19 - 20), cirrhosis (with perihepatic adhesions, if no frank ascitic fluid is present), etc. The phenomenon may also be seen following the use of 'fertility pills' giving rise to the **'oestrogen hyperstimulation syndrome'**.

 The mechanism is explained by the observations of Lemon and Higgins (1929) and later Barer in Oxford (1961) that particles and fluid can pass through the diaphragm through tiny **'pores'**.These seem akin to a network of small lymphatic trunks, or tiny outpouchings of peritoneum, which are sucked up into the chest, and which 'pop' or burst when ascitic fluid is present. The negative pressure in the chest can even suck up virtually all the abdominal fluid produced with an ovarian swelling, so that only a typically right pleural effusion is clinically evident and no abdominal fluid.

 Small colloid particles labelled with a radioactive isotope have to be shown to pass in normal people from the peritoneum, through the diaphragm and into the pleural cavities, and thence to the mediastinum. The same occurs with patent blue dye injected into patients having peritoneal dialysis, which passes into the pleural cavities, and may be found in aspirated pleural fluid a few hours later (see Illus. **MEIGS' SYNDROME, Pl eff - perit dialysis**). It would appear that this is one of the normal pathways for fluid to be absorbed, being sucked up from the abdomen, as well as moving upwards by capillary attraction.

 With 'early' (supposed stage I) ovarian tumours, small tumour deposits may be present on the under aspect of the diaphragm, and these may cause blockage of the 'pores', leading to abdominal ascites, and sometimes causing this without tumour cells being found in the fluid following aspiration. The 'pores' also explain how malignant cells may pass into the pleural cavities, causing pleural deposits (with or without pleural fluid) in patients with ovarian tumours (Illus. **PL-EFFUSION, Pl effus Pt. 16a-d, Pl effus myx Pt. 1a-c, 2a-b**).

Localised subdiaphragmatic disease, e.g. renal, biliary, hepatic or subphrenic, commonly gives rise to localised basal pleural reaction and fluid, and this mechanism undoubtedly accounts in part for the pleural fluid and the tracking of subdiaphragmatic infection. A reversed flow of gas or fluid may also occur from the chest to the abdomen (Lieberman & Peters, 1970, & Fataar et al., 1981).

Further references.
Salmon (1934) : Benign pelvic tumours associated with ascites and pleural effusion.
Meigs and Cass (1937) : Ovarian fibroma with ascites and hydrothorax - report of 7 cases.
Rubin et al. (1944) : Ovarian fibromas and theca cell tumours - 78 cases with ascites and hydrothorax.
Williams (1950) : Pleural effusion produced by abdomino-pleural communication in a patient with Laennec's cirrhosis of the liver and ascites.
Meigs (1954) : Other ovarian tumours with ascites and hydrothorax - reviewed 84 cases of ovarian fibroma causing pleural effusions, and found these on the right side alone in 52, bilateral in 20 and 9 were on the left (the record of which side being lost in 3). He also pointed out that Demons (1887 - 1903 in Paris - see 1903 reference) had first described the condition, and noted that Funck-Brentano (1949) termed it "the '**Demons-Meigs' syndrome**...".
Cron (1954) from Milwaukee : Commented on Meigs' paper and said that he had seen only one case of Meigs' syndrome associated with an ovarian fibroma, but felt that the condition was more common with other ovarian and uterine tumours. He was prompted by Meigs' observation of the passage of particulate matter (Indian ink) into pleural fluid when introduced into the abdomen in such patients. He injected 150 ml of Au^{198} in 200 ml saline intraperitoneally in a patient with an ovarian liposarcoma, and found that it appeared in the right pleural cavity as early as two hours after administration. He estimated that 3.5% of the gold was recovered by repeated aspirations from the right pleural cavity by 46.5 hours.
Emerson and Davies (1955) : Hydrothorax complicating ascites.
Mokrohisky (1958) : So called 'Meigs' syndrome' associated with benign and malignant ovarian tumours.
Johnston and Loo (1964) : Hepatic hydrothorax.
Majzlin and Stevens (1964) : Meigs' syndrome - case report and literature review.
Lieberman et al. (1966) : Pathogenesis and treatment of hydrothorax complicating cirrhosis and ascites.
Lieberman and Peters (1970) : Cirrhotic hydrothorax - due to acquired diaphragmatic defect.
Solomon et al. (1971) : Fibromyomata of the uterus with haemothorax - Meigs' syndrome?
Hurlow et al. (1976) : Ascites and hydrothorax in association with struma ovarii.
Hartstein et al. (1980) : Pseudo-Meigs' syndrome with papillary adenocarcinomas of the ovary & fallopian tubes.
Fataar et al. (1981) : Recurrent non-surgical pneumoperitoneum due to spontaneous pneumothorax - showing how gas may occasionally track from the chest to the abdomen via the 'pores'.
Handler et al. (1982) : Atypical Meigs' syndrome.
Nassberger (1982) : Left sided pleural effusion secondary to continuous ambulatory peritoneal dialysis.
O'Flanagan et al. (1987) : Meigs' syndrome and pseudo-Meigs' syndrome.
Teshima et al. (1989) : A variant of Meigs' syndrome without ovarian neoplasm.
Bazot et al. (1993) : Fibrothecomas of the ovary - CT and US findings.
Troiano et al. (1997) : Fibroma and fibrothecoma of the ovary - MR findings.

Rare causes of a pleural effusion - (Illus. **PL-EFFUS CHYLOUS**).
Chylothorax. - this can arise in several ways:
(a) Trauma, including surgical trauma, to the thoracic duct, but there is often a delay of a few weeks before a chylothorax develops.
(b) Obstruction of the thoracic duct, or thoracic lymphatic malformations, lymphangiectasis, lymphangioleiomyomatosis, hygromas, lymphocoeles or the 'yellow nail syndrome' (with leaky lymphatics). Neoplasm is an uncommon cause, except with lymphomas, probably because of the large number of collateral pathways in the mediastinum, and also from its tendency to cause more obstruction to the lymphatic drainage to the lungs, than to the thoracic duct. Obstruction to this is seen with parasites (loa loa and filariasis) or from lymphomas, and these may also cause chyluria.

Schulman et al. (1978) suggested that a chylothorax can only occur after laceration or obstruction to the thoracic duct. After leakage of chyle into the mediastinum, it may then pass into a pleural cavity. Injury to the upper part of the thoracic duct, as it lies on the left side of the mediastinum, most commonly causes a left sided chylothorax, whilst one on the right side usually follows damage to the lower part of the thoracic duct or the right sided accessory duct (see also p. 13.1). Traumatic rupture of the lower part of the thoracic duct may be caused by a hyperextension injury (Brown, 1937) or follow child abuse (Green, 1980).

Lymphography may locate the site of an injury, and ligation of the duct proximally may cure the chylothorax, anastomoses allowing the contents of the thoracic duct to pass into the venous system. Leakage of Lipiodol into a pleural cavity is illustrated in Illus. **LYMPHATICS, Pts. 12, 13 & 14.**

(c) Venous obstruction may also lead to secondary lymphatic obstruction. A chylothorax may also lead to secondary lymphatic obstruction. A chylothorax has been found to be a complication of SVC thrombosis in both clinical and experimental studies (see references below). It may also occur as a complication of thrombosis around central venous catheters. The mechanism of a chylothorax being caused by venous obstruction appears to be mediastinal swelling, as ligation of the SVC in animals causes the mediastinal tissues and lymph nodes to become considerably congested with chylous fluid.

Possible treatments include :

Ligation of the cisterna chyli allowing anastomoses to develop;

Pleural repair, low fat diet, pleurodesis or pleuroperitoneal shunt.

Further references.

Blalock et al. (1936) : Experimental production of chylothorax by occlusion of the SVC caused a chylothorax in 60% of cats and dogs.

Loe (1946) : Injuries of the thoracic duct.

Goorwitch (1955) : Traumatic chylothorax treated by ligation of the thoracic duct.

Heilman and Collins (1963) : Identification of laceration of the thoracic duct by lymphangiography.

White, W. and Urquhart (1966) : Chylothorax following a fall from a bicycle - congenitally abnormal mediastinal lymphatics were injured in the lower mediastinum. Leakage from these and visualisation of the pulmonary lymphatics was shown by lymphography. Repair of a tear in the lower mediastinal pleura resulted in a cure.

Weidner and Steiner (1971) : Leakage of contrast medium into the pleura at lymphography.

Macfarlane and Holman (1972) : Chylothorax.

Diaconis et al. (1976) : Primary subclavian vein thrombosis + bilateral chylothorax shown by lymphangiography and venography.

Thurer et al. (1976), Kramer et al. (1981) and Seibert et al. (1982) : Leakage of contrast medium into the pleura, secondary to SVC obstruction in infants.

Azizkhan et al. (1983) : Pleuroperitoneal shunts in the management of neonatal chylothorax.

Sullivan et al. (1984) : CT diagnosis, with demonstration of fatty content of fluid.

Milsom et al. (1985) : Chylothorax - an assessment of current medical practice.

Warren et al. (1990) : Chylothorax secondary to obstruction of the SVC - a complication of the le Veen shunt.

Kitchen et al. (1991) : Denver pleuroperitoneal shunt for treatment of chylothorax caused by **filariasis** (p.19.52).

Yeoman et al. (1990) : **Fat-fluid level in pleural effusion** as a complication of a mediastinal dermoid - CT.

Song et al. (2000) : Pseudochylous pl. effusions with fat-fluid levels on CT - 6 cases - are usually due to TB or rheumatoid.

Urinothorax

Urine is an uncommon cause of pleural fluid. It may occur following injury to a kidney, be associated with a ruptured hemidiaphragm, or track into the thorax with a 'leaking pyelonephritis' or hydronephrosis. The author has also seen it track to the left main bronchus in a patient with renal tuberculosis to give rise to 'urinoptysis'. An unusual cause of urinary induced pleurisy occurred in a nurse, who injected her own urine into her chest with a syringe, so as to ask for 'help' after an aborted pregnancy, which she claimed was fathered by her priest following a confession!

Two mechanisms for urine making its way into a pleural cavity were postulated by Friedland et al. (1971) - direct leakage into the mediastinum and thence into the pleura, or drainage via the lymphatics. Corriere et al. (1968) considered that the latter was the more probable mechanism in their cases, and they noted that when a ureter is occluded, lymphatic drainage of the affected kidney increases. Barek and Cigtay (1975) reported a 49 year old woman who had a hysterectomy for fibroids, followed by an obstructed left ureter leading to a left pleural effusion. They noted that 'in adults as well as neonates, urinary ascites has been well described with obstructive uropathy'. Leung et al. (1981) however noted that although pleural effusions can be associated with urinary tract obstruction, the different chemical composition of the pleural fluid from extravasated urine may indicate a different mechanism.

Urine may also leak through the diaphragmatic 'pores' (see under Meigs' syndrome - above) from urine leaking under the diaphragm, and the author thinks this is usually the most likely route.

Further references.
Friedland et al. (1971) : Neonatal 'urinothorax' associated with posterior urethral valves.
Laforet and Kornitzer (1977) : Nephrogenic pleural effusion.
Lahiry et al. (1978) : Urinothorax following blunt trauma to the kidney.
Baron et al. (1981) : Intrathoracic extension of retroperitoneal urine collections.
Redman et al. (1982) : Hypertension and urinothorax following attempted percutaneous nephrostomy.
Stark, P. et al. (1982) : Biochemical features of **urinothorax**.
Shanes et al. (1982) : Pleural effusion associated with urinary tract obstruction.
Ralston and Wilkinson (1986) : Bilateral urinothorax shown by Tc^{99m} renal imaging.
Sahn and Miller (1986) : Obscure pleural effusion - look to the kidney.
Salcedo (1986) : Urinothorax - four cases and review.

The 'yellow nail syndrome' - (Illus. YELLOW NAIL SYNDROME).
   In this condition, the finger and toe nails become yellowish-brown in colour; they are also slow growing and have an increased transverse curvature. Vitamin E (Tocopherol - concerned with fat metabolism and as an integral structural component of membranes, maintaining their stability and metabolic integrity) may help alleviate the condition. Radiographically the patients present mainly with recurrent pleural effusions, and some have underlying malignancies, so that the pleural effusion may erroneously be ascribed to this cause. The patients may have lymphoedema of the lower limbs, and impaired lymph drainage. In carrying out lymphangiograms on such patients, the author (in the mid 1960's) noted that there is excessive permeability of the lymphatic trunk walls, with considerable leakage of contrast medium, even at low injection pressures and flow rates (**YELLOW NAIL SYNDROME, Pt. 2b**). He assumed that lymph vessels in the chest (including the thoracic duct) were hypoplastic and probably leaked similarly, leading to the formation of a pleural effusion which may be chylous.
   When examined by CT the patients may show pleural plaques, pulmonary fibrosis and bronchiectasis - Illus. **YELLOW NAIL SYNDROME, Pt. 1b**.
   The condition may be distinguished from tobacco staining, and yellowish nails may be seen in other conditions such as rheumatoid arthritis, myxoedema, the nephrotic syndrome, immunodeficiencies and Raynaud's disease.

References.
Samman and White (1964) : The yellow nail syndrome - 13 cases.
Wells (1966) : Yellow nail syndrome with familial primary hypoplasia of lymphatics - may manifest late in life.
Zerfas (1966) : Yellow nail syndrome with bilateral bronchiectasis. (Followed by note from Samman that since the syndrome was described, some patients have recurrent pleural effusions probably due to impaired lymph drainage.)
Emerson (1966) : Yellow nails, lymphoedema and pleural effusions.
Siegelman et al. (1969) : Lymphoedema, pleural effusions and yellow nails - associated immunological deficiency.
BMJ (1972) : Yellow nails and oedema.
Hiller et al. (1972) : Pulmonary manifestations - pleural effusions, chronic cough and bronchiectasis.
Nakielna et al. (1976) : Yellow nail syndrome - 3 cases.
Beer et al. (1978) : Pleural effusion associated with primary lymphoedema - perspective of the yellow nail syndrome.
Guin and Elleman (1979) : Possible association with malignancy.
Mattingly and Bossingham (1979) : Yellow nail syndrome in **rheumatoid arthritis**.
Muller et al. (1979) : Roentgenological and clinical signs in yellow nail syndrome.
Solal-Celigny et al. (1983) : The yellow nail syndrome.
Pavlidakey et al. (1984) : Yellow nail syndrome.
Venecie and Dicken (1984) : Five cases.
Norkild et al. (1986) : Yellow nail syndrome - the triad of yellow nails, lymphoedema and pleural effusions.
Wiggins et al. (1991) : Detection of bronchiectasis by HRCT in the yellow nail syndrome.

Pleural effusion - secondary to leakage from a silicone breast implant.
Taupmann and Adler (1993) : Silicone pleural effusion due to rupture of breast implant following chest drain inserted 1 yr. previously (see also p. 12.18).

Post-partum and post-operative effusions.

Hughson et al. (1982), and also the present author (when working at the Henry Ford Hospital in 1965) found that high KV chest radiographs, taken within 24 hours of delivery, not infrequently showed small basal effusions and congestion, presumably because the larger blood volume in late pregnancy had not decreased so soon after delivery. Udeshi et al. (1988) from Birmingham have however suggested that puerperal effusions may not be as common as supposed - they studied 50 'normal' women up to two days after delivery using real-time ultra-sound in the erect position and only found a basal effusion in one who had unknowingly had mild eclampsia.

A similar finding with early post-operative patients is not uncommon, presumably because of sodium and fluid retention and some IV over-infusion of fluids during surgery. The author has seen this most commonly in patients following renal transplantation, because both pre- and post-operative chest radiographs are regularly taken.

Further references.

Nielsen et al. (1989) : Post-operative effusion following upper abdominal surgery.
Fidler et al. (1993) : Cardiopulmonary complications of pregnancy - radiographic findings included oedema due to peripartum cardiomyopathy, the effects of ß-blockers (used to stop preterm labour), thromboembolic disease, amniotic embolism, aspiration or bacterial pneumonia.

Ultrasound of the pleura and pleural drainage.(see also ps. 12.20 - 21 & 20.33).

This is the easiest method of further examining the pleura following plain radiography. In the 1960s one only had 'A' scans, but even then one could recognise pleural and pericardial fluid collections. With compound 'B' scanning the patient lay flat with the detector above. This made the recognition of fluid in the pleura difficult, as it would tend to pass posteriorly. Now it is very easy, using real-time probes, to examine the patient in the **erect position,** either sitting or standing, and both pleural and pericardial effusions are readily detected, also loculations and in many cases inter-lobar effusions as well. A mass abutting the parietal pleural is also usually readily visualised, with a small curvi-linear probe pressed into the rib space overlying it. Localisation in this way makes drainage of fluid a very easy matter, and also biopsy of an underlying mass much easier and more convenient than CT! However, in some cases ultrasound and CT are complementary, the author having done CT using ultrasound for interventional guidance.

The 'white line' or hyperechoic pleural-lung interface line should always be noted as its integrity suggests an intact pleural surface. It may be displaced by benign masses, but loss or interruption of this line suggests extension of disease (especially a lung tumour) spreading into the chest wall (see also Fig. 12 12. and Illus. **PL-WHITE LINE ON US**). The normal thickness of the parietal pleura is < 3 mm - see also refs. on p. 20.35.

Other 'windows' for ultrasound examination of the pleura are provided by the liver or an enlarged spleen i.e. to examine the subpulmonary part of the pleura. This area may also be seen from a posterior approach above the kidneys. It is also often possible to examine high upper mediastinal masses via the supraclavicular areas in nonemphysematous patients, or the anterior mediastinum and the internal mammary areas, via the anterior intercostal spaces.

When fluid has been found by ultra-sound, it is often possible to determine whether it contains '**particulate-looking**' matter, usually indicating blood or pus (a 'complex effusion'), fibrous looking septa or 'protein strands' (usually with an empyema, but sometimes also with infected fluid, blood or malignancies). Tumour masses may also be seen within the pleura or the adjacent lung. Clotted blood or chyle may give a semi-solid appearance, like that found with a fibrothorax.

When particles are free to move within the fluid, this may give rise to a swirling movement, but when dense or clotted movement is not possible. Coarse particulate matter strongly favours an empyema, and in many cases this is immediately confirmed by aspiration. Occasionally gas bubbles may be seen in an empyema with loculi - Illus. **EMPYEMA, Pt. 5a-f, 25a-d.**

Following initial ultra-sound localisation, the author's practice, with all undiagnosed effusions, has been to aspirate a small or larger amount of fluid - a very simple procedure for a radiologist these days! **Tiny fluid collections are most readily aspirated (in a sitting patient) in expiration and often 2 - 3 ml will suffice for cytological and/or bacteriological examination,** and if positive will save a great deal of time and expense). It is also much easier to do in the radiology department, if it has real-time apparatus, than '**blindly**' in a chest department or ward. In difficult cases when CT has been carried out, it is best to return the patient to the real-time apparatus for the drainage to be carried out. Only when there is very thick pus or clotted blood will the technique fail, and then surgical decortication may be required. Even then this may be liquefied by injecting **streptokinase or ionic contrast medium**, both of which will tend to liquefy the pleural thickening (and the contrast medium also acts as a mild antibiotic). If one waits a few days, both empyemas and haemothoraces may be able to be fully aspirated.

Tube drainage* is also best carried out using ultra-sound control, but may not be necessary if the pleural collection is very large. Ultrasound is also invaluable for assessing the pleural space prior to medical pleurodesis, using autologous blood, talc, tetracycline (500 mg in 50 ml normal saline), bleomycin or Corynebacterium parvum, i.e. determining whether the pleural shadow on radiographs is fluid or solid.

If large pleural effusions are aspirated rapidly, sudden mediastinal movement may cause distress, and it is usually wise to stop when the patient starts to cough. A few patients may develop **re-expansion pulmonary oedema** if the aspiration is too quick (see p. 8.7), and if this occurs it should be treated with fluid by mouth (or IV) and **not** by diuretics which will only worsen the condition.

A simple but very effective aspiration 'set' consists of a No.1 (1.1 mm or 19 g. needle), a plastic extension tube (about 18 ins or 50 cm long) and a 50 ml syringe. These cost well under £1. Clamping of the tube with an artery forceps, when the syringe is being emptied will avoid entry of air up the tube, and this is a much more reliable method of preventing this than with a 3-way tap which almost invariably leaks. Such equipment should be readily available in every radiology department.

The method may also be used for assessing tumour nodules in the pleura e.g. in the post-pneumonectomy space when this contains persistent fluid.

Note that the lower tip of a collapsed lower lobe may 'dangle' in the fluid - see ps. 2.33 & 15.12-13.

*A recent commercial set for tube drainage and using a vacuum bottle is shown in Illus. **PL. DRAINAGE.**

References.

Doust et al. (1975) : Ultra-sound evaluation of pleural opacities.
Sample (1977) : Ultra-sound and CT of the pleura.
Lipscomb and Flower (1980) and Lipscomb et al. (1981) : 'A' scans in 24 patients.
Hirsch et al. (1981) : Real-time sonography of pleural opacities.
Connell et al. (1982) : Subpulmonary pleural effusion - US.
Marks, W. et al. (1982) : Real-time evaluation of pleural lesions - the probability of obtaining free fluid.
Felletti and Ravazzoni (1983) : Intrapleural Corynebacterium parvum for malignant pleural effusions (decrease or disappearance of malignant cells - best responders were those with mesotheliomas).
Kurtz and Schmitt (1983) : Ultra-sound compared with CT.
Rosenberg (1983) : Ultra-sound in the assessment of pleural disease.
Van Sonnenberg et al. (1984) : CT and ultra-sound guided catheter drainage of empyemas after chest tube failure.
Westcott (1985) : Percutaneous catheter drainage of pleural effusion and empyema.
Dorne (1986) : Differentiation of pulmonary parenchymal consolidation from pleural disease using the **sonographic bronchogram**.
O'Moore et al. (1987) : Sonographic guidance in diagnostic and therapeutic interventions in the pleural space - 187 procedures in 170 patients - fluid or empyema drainage, pleurodesis, biopsy or treatment of pneumothorax.
Henschke et al. (1989) : The pathogenesis, radiologic evaluation and therapy of pleural effusions.
Moulton et al. (1989) : Urokinase is a safe and effective method of facilitating drainage of loculated fibrinous or haemorrhagic pleural fluid collections.
Silverman et al. (1989) : Pleural interventions - indications, techniques and clinical applications.
Davis et al. (1990) : MR imaging of pleural effusions in 22 patients - heterogenicity, loculation and size of effusions were well evaluated, but MR was not specific for the aetiology.
Grogan et al. (1990) and Raptopoulos et al. (1991) : Sonography-guided thorocenteses were associated with fewer complications, including pneumothorax
Lomas and Flower (1990) : Real-time US signs in pleural fluid collections.
McLoud, T. and Flower (1991) : Comparison of sonography, CT and MR for the pleura - sonography allows easy identification of pleural fluid, loculation and differentiation from pleural masses. CT is best for characterising location and composition of pleural mass, whilst MR is somewhat limited, but is best for imaging superior sulcus tumours.
Nkere et al. (1991) : Pleural abrasion at thoracotomy, using a domestic scouring pad, combined with blebs or bullae being stapled or excised - 60 cases.
Yang et al. (1992) : Value of sonography in determining the nature of pleural effusion - analysis of 320 cases.

Lomas (1992 & 1993) : The sonographic appearances of pleural fluid - aspiration in 90 collections in 86 patients (54 anechoic unrestricted space within the pleura, 16 diffuse internal echoes, 12 primary loculations, 13 with internal septa and debris attached to the wall of the collection).

Morrison et al. (1992) : Sclerotherapy of malignant pleural effusion through sonographically placed small bore catheters - used tetracycline and also bleomycin.

Boland et al. (1995, from Boston, Mass.) : Also advised the use of US guidance in diagnostic thoracentesis and wrote "Sonographic guidance offers many advantages over CT guidance, namely speed, cost and the ability to perform the procedure at the bedside" - it thus appears that the Americans are now at last learning to use US for this purpose, but the present author notes that their paper was published in a British Journal (Clinical Radiology). As noted on p. 20.41 US is not used by all thoracic radiologists, particularly in the USA, and any trend to correct this can only be of advantage to the patients!

Klein et al. (1995) : Image-guided percutaneous drainage of pleural effusions, lung abscess, and pneumothorax.

Seaton et al. (1995) : Palliative treatment of malignant pleural effusions - value of small-bore catheter thoracostomy and deoxycycline sclerotherapy.

Wu et al. (1995) : 'Fluid colour' sign for discrimination between pleural thickening and pleural effusion.

Wernecke (1997) : Sonographic features of pleural disease - pictorial essay. **Pneumothorax** - absence of pl. movement & comet tail artefacts from aerated alveoli, **effusions** - transudates are usually anechoic, exudates often show septa or echogenic patterns esp. if RBC, WBC or fat droplets present, **pl. based mass** - ? extrapleural, pleural or parenchymal, **plaques** - iso or hyperechoic esp. along inferior costal margins, **fibromas** - lipomas, spread of lung cancer. pl. metastases, **mesotheliomas** and fibrosis.

Tattersall et al. (2000) : Chest drains - does size matter?

(See also ps. 20.33 - 34 and Illus. **ULTRASOUND**).

Tomography of the pleura.

(a) **Conventional tomography** is still useful for showing some pleural abnormalities. It will often well delineate rounded pleural masses, pleural thickening extending over an upper lobe or adjacent to the spine or loculated pleural fluid collections. Often the latter are best demonstrated with the patient sitting up for lateral tomography (see p. 20.13). Such a position often allows one to determine whether the shadowing is pleural, parenchymal or both, and often demonstrates its cause in the underlying lung.

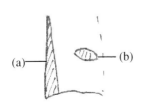

Pleural thickening or fluid
(a) behind RLL, and (b)
in lesser fissure.

Pleural thickening or fluid
and unresolved consolidation
in the underlying lung.

Pleural thickening or fluid with
small tumour in the apex of the
adjacent lower lobe.

Fig. 14.10   pleural thickening or fluid on conventional tomograms.

(b) **CT of the pleura** is often valuable for showing the extent or amount of fluid (especially if it lies posteriorly), pleural plaques or thickening, tumour masses within the pleura (and the shape and extent of these), the presence of calcification that is otherwise difficult to see, and the condition of the adjacent lung and chest wall.

(i) **CT of pleural fluid.**

Although ultra-sound in the upright position is likely to be the best method of confirming pleural fluid, CT will also demonstrate its presence, and by turning the patient from the supine position, or onto his side, will show that it is freely mobile, or loculated. It will also demonstrate fluid collections within the fissures, or adjacent to the mediastinum. It will help distinguish between pleural fluid and thickening.

Attempting to differentiate the cause of pleural fluid from density measurements is difficult. An acute haemothorax may have a slightly increased density (e.g. 30 to 40 HU), but when it becomes chronic it tends to reduce in density. A chylothorax, if it contains much fat, may give a mildly negative density e.g. -10 to -20 HU). Mostly however the type of fluid will be determined by paracentesis.

(ii) CT of pleural secondary deposits and other masses.

These may be lenticular, rounded, 'knobbly' or diffuse in shape. Sometimes the last will spread around a pleural cavity to give rise to a **'cancer en cuirasse'** type of appearance (Illus. **MESOTHELIOMA, Pt. 44b**). Tumours including mesotheliomas and secondary pleural tumours from lung, breast, etc. may cause a **'dry pleurisy'** i.e. diffusely spread pleural nodules and thickening, with little or no accompanying fluid (Illus. **DRY PLEURISY**). Secondary deposits may also give rise to **flat** or **mushroomed shaped mounds** within the pleura, and these may be separated by considerable distances within the pleural cavity (Illus. **PL-MUSHROOMS**); occasionally these may point outwards into the chest wall. When very small (1 to 3 mm) they may be too small to be visualised by CT, and only be seen by ultrasound, at thoracoscopy or at exploratory surgery. Because of possible **'seeding'** within the pleura, especially to a more dependent part, tumour nodules may sometimes be found above or close to the diaphragm, even with an upper lobe tumour. Most times, however, pleural extension of tumours, or frank deposits are accompanied by localised or free collections of pleural fluid.

Mesotheliomas are mainly discussed on ps. 14.44 et seq. These tumours often present with smaller or larger pleural effusions, but sometimes form discrete masses within the pleural space. They may push into the visceral pleura, deforming the adjacent lung, but more often spread around the pleural locally, forming a mass with a convex inner border and having tapering margins. There is often a sharp interface with the chest wall, and the underlying lung. Most are homogeneous in density, but some show slight contrast within them due to degeneration, haemorrhage or a slight fat content. Occasionally IV contrast may reveal an enhancing rim, particularly if the tumour encloses some fluid (a sign which may also be seen with some empyemas).

Several papers have attempted to differentiate pulmonary parenchymal lesions from pleural disease by their shapes as seen on CT sections. A lung mass tends to produce an acute angle with the pleura, whilst pleural disease usually gives rise to an obtuse or tapering angle. An empyema tends to have a thickened irregular wall and compresses the underlying lung. A zone of reduced density may be found at the pleuro-pulmonary interface, particularly with an abscess or lung mass. When the pleura is traversed, either pleural involvement may be seen, or direct extension into the chest wall with soft tissue and bony erosion.

Pugatch et al. (1978) wrote - "pleural lesions often have a convex border with tapering margins and a sharp interface. With lung abscesses or a parenchymal mass, there is often a zone of reduced density at the pleuro-pulmonary interface".

However, Naidich et al. (1984) in their book on 'CT of the Thorax', pointed out that there is considerable variation and overlap in the CT appearance of lung and pleural lesions. This depends on (i) the amount of spread of a mass within the lung, and (ii) the amount of invagination produced by a pleural mass (tumour, thickening or fluid), which will in turn depend on its consistency (solid, jelly-like or fluid) and adhesions and/or fibrosis in the pleura.

Aquino (1994) - exudate vs transudate - thick parietal pleura + increased attenuation of extrapleural fat & contrast enhancement of pleura is suggestive of exudate.

Flower (1999) pointed out that intralobar masses in the fissures are usually secondary deposits or mesotheliomas. A fibrothorax may be mimicked by a mesothelioma or adenocarcinoma, and such thickening is usually malignant if 1cm or more thick, is nodular or is circumferential and extends to the mediastinal aspect of the chest. Adenocarcinomas may produce a desmoplastic response to small 'nests' of malignant cells.

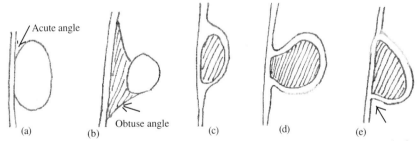

(a) A lung mass tends to produce an acute angle with the pleura when there is little spread of tumour into the surrounding lung.
(b) Considerable subpleural spread of a tumour in the lung giving rise to an obtuse angle.
(c) A pleural (or mediastinal) mass only slightly deforms the adjacent lung and tends to have a convex border with tapering margins and to make an obtuse angle with the visceral pleura and the air-filled lung.
(d) Localised pleural mass pressing into the lung.
(e) Pleural mass or fluid collection limited by an adhesion (arrowed).

Fig. 14.11 CT appearances of pleural and juxta-pleural lesions (after Naidich et al., 1984).

Some advantages and limitations of imaging procedures in pleural disease.

(i) Compared with ultra-sound, CT and MR are carried out with the patient lying down, so pleural fluid (unless loculated) tends to collect posteriorly in the supine position. It is therefore better to aspirate it under US control following CT or MR.
(ii) When there is extensive lung or pleural disease, there may be no well-defined CT interface between the lung and the pleura.
(iii) There may be little differentiation of tissues by CT with a chronic fibro-thorax.
(iv) With some empyemas, it may be very difficult to determine by CT whether the pleural disease is solid or fluid, or contains multiple septa producing loculation - US is better for drainage, but CT and MR give a better pictorial display.
(v) In many cases both lung consolidation and pleural disease may be present together - in these cases CT may readily show the extent of each.
(vi) It may sometimes be difficult to distinguish between pleural fluid and sub-phrenic collections by CT (see also p. 15.12 & Fig. 15.12).
(vii) Some tumour seedlings may give a 'mushroom appearance' on CT, but smaller ones may not be visualised.
(viii) US is usually best for the diagnosis of fluid, it also allows one to study the diaphragm, its movement or fixity with respiration.
(ix) CT may be superior for showing residual fluid collections, in the presence of a fibrothorax - also for showing calcification and apparent or true pleural thickening.

Further references.
Meyer (1966) : Metastatic carcinoma of the pleura.
Rigler (1977b) : An overview of disease of the pleura.
Raasch et al. (1982) : Explanation of some typical appearances of pleural effusion.
Vock and Fuchs (1983) : CT of the pleura and chest wall.
Bressler et al. (1987) : Bolus contrast enhancement for distinguishing pleural from lung disease - CT features.
Zinn et al. (1987) : Fluid with pre-existing pulmonary air spaces - a potential pitfall in the CT differentiation of pleural from parenchymal disease.
Henschke et al. (1989) : The pathogenesis, radiological evaluation and theory of pleural effusions.
Davis, S. et al. (1990) : MR imaging of pleural effusions in 22 patients - heterogenicity, loculation and size of effusions were well evaluated, but MR was not specific for the aetiology.
Morrison et al. (1992) : Sclerotherapy of malignant pleural effusion through sonographically placed small-bore catheters - used tetracycline and also bleomycin.
Gleeson et al. (1996a) : Compared the ability of CT to detect pleural disease in the presence of pleural effusion compared to thoracoscopy and found CT to be less sensitive in detecting subtle signs of malignant pleural disease.
Wu et al. (1995) : US Doppler gives rise to a 'fluid colour' sign, whilst pl. thickening results only in a clear space + pleural blood vessels.

Empyemas - (Illus. **EMPYEMA**).

Hippocrates (460-357 BC) recognised finger clubbing with empyemas (see also ps. 23.2 - 3) and that patients could recover if the empyema drained itself externally - indeed at one time patients were placed in sea water to encourage this to happen! Later localised posterior rib resections were carried out to allow the pus to drain. Empyemas are still common and although patients now unusually die from an empyema in Oxford, the condition still has an annual incidence in the UK of about 4,000 cases with up to 20% mortality. Their recognition is very important as they may be misdiagnosed by the unwary, and drainage usually causes a dramatic improvement of the patient's condition. There is still considerable truth in the old Latin tag - "Ubi pura - ibi evacua". The author saw several cases each year, several of which were misdiagnosed, as inoperable tumour, etc. Most cases follow or occur together with pneumonia, sometimes complicated by a lung abscess, whilst others are insidious in onset. Other are secondary to oesophageal perforation, trauma, or follow abdominal sepsis.

Illus. **EMPYEMA, Pt. 13a-d** show the images of a doctor who had been told he was dying from inoperable lung cancer, but without biopsy proof. He had considerable loss of weight and was cachectic. His fingers were grossly clubbed. A few seconds examination with ultrasound showed that much fluid and debris was present in the left pleural cavity. CT failed to show any tumour, and his liver and bones were normal. Seven pints of pus were drained, growing streptococci. He had bad teeth and was a smoker. During his convalescence the 'clubbed' finger nails grew out and were replaced by normal nails (Illus. **EMPYEMA, Pt. 13d**).

A famous case of an empyema was that of King George V, who in late 1928 had a right basal pneumonia and pleurisy. A rib drainage procedure was carried out, and in Jan. 1929 the King went to Bognor to 'take the sea air' and recuperate - hence 'Bognor Regis'. Extracts from the medical bulletins are given in Appendix 4 (ps. 7-9) and give a good insight into the seriousness of pneumonia and empyema in the pre-antibiotic era.

A loculated empyema commonly occurs behind a lower lobe, and especially its apex, and not uncommonly spreads down to the subpulmonary position. Any patient who is ill, with a pleural shadow in this position should have this considered. Loculated anterior or interlobar empyemas may also be seen (Illus. **EMPYEMA, Pts. 6, 15, 16a-d, 26, 28 & 29a-c**).

As well as clubbing, HPOA may be present, and may also resolve after drainage. Rarely now do we see an empyema pointing through the chest wall to the skin (i.e. an **empyema necessitatis**). Illus. **EMPYEMA, Pt. 1a-b** shows a pyonephrosis giving a similar picture. The author has seen tuberculous empyemas so presenting before CT was available, and cases examined by CT were reported by Bhatt and Austin (1985) and Peterson et al. (1987).

The easiest and most convenient method of confirming an empyema is to use ultrasound, to note the presence of fluid, multiple tiny 'bright' echoes within it, fibrin threads or loculi and pleural thickening. Aspiration will confirm the presence of pus. Not only may a sample be removed, but in many cases the empyema may be aspirated. A wide bore needle should be used for this as a thin one easily becomes blocked. It may be necessary to wash out the needle or cavity with saline, if it becomes blocked or to help aspirate all the pus, which because of its high protein content, tends to 'clot' and become very thick at its base. Traditionally large bore (28 F) drainage tubes have been employed for the drainage of thick empyemas, but many radiologists are now using much smaller tubes (e.g. 12 F) for drainage. This is often combined with the use of streptokinase, urokinase or ionic contrast media (see p. 14.14) to thin the empyema and allow easier drainage or repeated aspiration. Some cases with very thick empyemas may still require large tube or surgical decortication.

Radiological appearances reflect the stage of the disease - pleural fluid progressing to pleural thickening, inspissation, loculation, etc. Large effusions may cause contralateral mediastinal displacement and inversion of the diaphragm.

CT appearance and differentiation from lung abscess.

In its early stages an empyema often has an elongated or flattened contour, which conforms to the shape of the pleural space. As organisation occurs, the collection may become more rounded. As it lies within the pleural cavity and outside the lung, it tends to displace and deform the adjacent lung, and unless it extends within a fissure or indents the lung, it does not lie within the confines of the vessels and bronchi.

Pleural thickening occurs, initially more on the visceral pleura, but later on the parietal pleura, which may eventually be grossly thickened. The internal structure of an empyema tends to follow the viscosity of the pus; thus if thin it will behave as a simple effusion and will move readily with gravity; movement however also depends on the amount of loculation or developing adhesions. Gas and gas /fluid levels, often limited by loculation or strands may be present if it has tracked from an adjacent lung abscess, with some gas forming infections (Illus. **EMPYEMA, Pt. 5a-e, 12a-c, 25a-d & Gas gang Pt. 1a-e**) or following paracentesis. An enhancing rim (or **pleural rind**) on the visceral or parietal pleura may be seen with IV contrast agents (see below), and this may mimic a mesothelioma (see ps. 14. 44 et seq.).

Quite often the picture is complicated by underlying consolidation or abscess formation.

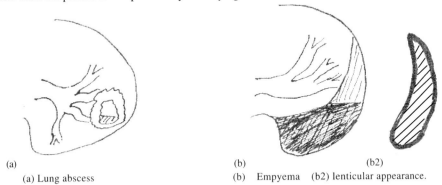

(a) (b) (b2)

(a) Lung abscess (b) Empyema (b2) lenticular appearance.

Fig. 14.12 Diagrams - differentiation of lung abscess from tumour - some distinguishing features.

A **lung abscess** is usually spherical in shape and has thick irregular walls. It is often surrounded by some consolidation and does not cross the inter-lobar fissures. It is most often not related to the pleura, though peripheral lung abscesses are not uncommonly accompanied by local pleural fluid or a frank empyema. The pulmonary vessels and bronchi extend up to it, but without being significantly displaced.

An **empyema** tends to be lenticular in shape. It often makes an obtuse angle with the chest wall. The bronchi and pulmonary vessels tend to be displaced inwards. When gas is present within the empyema, a smooth or slightly lumpy wall may be seen in the presence of thin pus, but when the pus is very thick, the wall of the empyema may be frankly nodular.

Contrast enhancement of its rim or margin is not uncommon, due to the presence of vascular granulation tissue (Illus. **PLEURAL RIND, Empyema Pts. 17 & 23**).

An interesting point with chronic empyemas or infection (esp. TB) is that there may be enlargement of adjacent ribs - the '**big rib sign**' - see also p. 12.22.

Several cases of malignancy complicating a long-standing pyothorax have been reported (principally from Japan - see refs. below).

Further note re empyemas and parapneumonic effusions

Light et al. (1972, 1980), Light (1981, 1985, 1990) and Hamm and Light (1997) have pointed out that as parapneumonic effusions (which are common - stage 1) progress through a fibrinopurulent stage (stage 2) to empyemas certain biochemical changes occur - the fluid becomes acidotic (pH <7.3), glucose content falls and lactate dehydrogenase level rises. Although some authors now advocate that any aspirated fluid should be tested for these changes, and that ultrasound is not infallible in differentiating infection from clear fluid, the author never used such tests as he felt that it was always best to aspirate **all** such effusions, whether frankly purulent (sometimes smelly) or not, and as well as having cultures done, check the patient again in two or three days. He used ionic contrast media* + antibiotics in those with obviously infected pleural fluid. Repeated aspiration (rather than tube drainage) usually sufficed when the pleural collection was still fluid (see Illus. **EMPYEMA**).

Many of the patients were treated as out-patients, only those with frankly purulent fluid being admitted to hospital (Wright and Charig, 1989).

* ionic contrast media released some free iodine thus having an antibiotic effect, and also acted as a liquefying agent; streptokinase (250K units in 100ml saline installed into the pleura for 4 hours) is now more popular but only has the latter effect. The most dramatic patient treated with ionic contrast medium was a lady who had had a chronically draining empyema through a sinus for three years. Several attempts by surgery had failed to cure it. The author (at the request of a thoracic surgeon) blocked the fistula with an inflatable enema balloon-catheter & filled the cavity with diluted contrast medium. Some hours later, the catheter and fluid dropped out, but the empyema was cured!

(See also US of pleura and pleural drainage - ps. 14.13 - 15.)

Further references.
Mayo and McElvein (1966) : Early thoracotomy for pyogenic empyema.
Baber et al. (1980) : 'Differentiating empyemas from peripheral pulmonary abscesses' - noted that **abscesses** had irregular shapes and relatively thick walls without discrete boundaries between them and the lung parenchyma, whereas **empyemas** had regularly shaped lumina, with smooth inner surfaces and sharply defined borders between them and the lungs. (Difficult cases were examined in both prone and supine positions).
Van Sonnenberg et al. (1982) : Percutaneous drainage of abscessses and fluid collections.
Shin and Ho (1983c) : CT of pleural empyema - wrote - "a typical empyema is characterised by lower thorax location, oblong or round contour in cross section, homogeneous content with or without air spaces or air-fluid levels, regularly thin wall opposing the chest wall (a rim sign), irregularly thick-wall opposing the lung parenchyma and smooth inner and outer margins. By application of such CT criteria, a pleural empyema can be readily distinguished from a peripheral lung abscess".
Stark, D. et al. (1983) : Differentiating lung abscess from empyema - radiography & CT - the '**split pleura sign**'.
Williford and Godwin (1983) and Williford et al. (1983) : Peripheral lung abscesses tend to have **acute angles**. and empyemas **obtuse angles** with the pleura. Similarly lung tumours with acute angles indicate a mass is confined to the lung, whilst an obtuse or less acute angle tends to indicate involvement or reaction of the adjacent pleura.
Jess et al. (1984) : Study of 259 cases of empyema - mortality 61% when there was underlying malignancy, and 25 % with benign pathology. In the elderly it was often a serious complication of underlying disease, particularly lung infection. Staph. aureus was most commonly found in the fatal cases.
van Sonnenberg et al. (1984) : CT and ultrasound guided catheter drainage of empyemas after chest tube drainage.
Lemmer et al. (1985) : Modern management of adult thoracic empyema.
Westcott (1985) : Percutaneous catheter drainage of pleural effusion and empyema.
Shapiro et al. (1988) : Open-window thoracostomy (or Eloesser procedure) for semi-permanent drainage of a chronic empyema - radiographic and CT appearance.
Hunnam and Flower (1988) : Radiologically guided fine tube catheters for draining 20 empyemas.
Silverman et al. (1988) : US and/or CT image-guided 12F catheter drainage in 43 patients.
           (1989) : Pleural interventions - indications, techniques and clinical applications.
Moulton et al. (1989): Treatment of loculated pleural effusions with transcatheter intracavitary urokinase - may fail if the catheter is poorly placed, or if the fluid is haemorrhagic or fibrinous.
Reinhold et al. (1989) : Treatment of pleural effusions, including empyemas, and pneumothoraces with small bore catheters placed percutaneously under radiological guidance.
Forty et al. (1990) : Review of 53 empyemas requiring surgical treatment in Cambridge. 47 had a thoracotomy and decortication, whilst 6 had rib resections. 20 had previous tube drainage. 27 followed pneumonia, 5 spontaneous rupture of the oesophagus and 3 followed oesophagoscopy. 8 followed an infected pneumothorax and 3 were tuberculous. There were 5 deaths, all in patients with other severe debilitating illnesses.
Neff et al. (1990) : CT follow up of empyemas - '**pleural peels**' resolve after percutaneous catheter drainage.
Waite et al. (1990) : Parietal pleural changes in empyemas shown by CT - enhancement of the parietal pleura with IV contrast agents plus parietal pleural thickening, thickening of the extrapleural subcostal tissues and increased density in the extrapleural fat. Similar findings were also found with malignant effusions (which had been treated by pleurodesis), mesotheliomas, pleural TB, 'reactive mesothelial hyperplasia', and in pleural effusions secondary to rheumatoid disease. Patients with resolved empyemas often showed persistent thickening of the extrapleural tissues, but with a return to normality of the extrapleural fat.
Cummin et al. (1991) : Used suction drainage in 13 patients with empyemas. A catheter was inserted into the empyema cavity under US guidance and strong suction was applied to try to obliterate the cavity.
Nigam (1991) : Used the same method to drain large pleural effusions.
Takasugi et al. (1991) : Pointed out that an empyema commonly produces inflammation in the overlying chest wall. Thus thickening and high attenuation in this on CT may indicate an underlying empyema. Simple pleural effusions do not cause this reaction.
Van Sonnenberg et al. (1991) : CT guided drainage of lung abscesses in 19 cases. in 17 drainage was through adjacent abnormal pleura. In 18 resolution of fever and relief of sepsis occurred within 48 hours.

Aquino et al. (1994) : Pleural exudates and transudates - diagnosis with contrast-enhanced CT.
Boland et al. (1995) : Interventional radiology of the pleural space - advocated image-guided drainage using indwelling 16-24F catheters.
Joseph et al. (1995) : Interventional radiology of the pleural space - advocated catheter (20-28F) suction drainage without an indwelling catheter.
Moulton et al. (1995) : Treatment of complicated pleural fluid collections (empyemas) with image-guided drainage.
Ferguson et al. (1996) : The clinical course and management of thoracic empyema.
Park, C. et al (1996) : Trans-catheter instillation of urokinase into loculated pleural effusion was effective in most patients, but not if pleural fluid had a honeycomb appearance on US or if pleural thickening >5mm on CT scans.
Gleeson et al. (1996b) : Randomised controlled trial of **intrapleural   streptokinase** in para-pneumonic pleural effusion and empyema - improved the success of tube drainage - no systemic effects. All Oxford patients with empyemata or infected effusions are treated with it (if septa are shown in the fluid on US). Streptokinase increases the output of pleural fluid. (See also Davies et al., 1997, Deegan & MacFarlane, 1997 & Gleeson & Davies, 1998).
Donnelly and Klosterman (1997) : CT of parapneumonic effusions in children is not specific for empyema.
Kuhlman (1997) : Complex disease of the pleura - new answers with CT and MRI.
Wait et al. (1997) : Used VATS for loculated complex fibrinopurulent empyemas - lower cost than fibrinolysis!
Kearney et al. (1998 & 2000) : Nodal enlargement in empyema - 18 of 50 pts. (28 R& 21 L, 1 bilat) - had nodes > 1 cm in shortest axis & mainly in line of lymph drainage - most were in para-tracheal or subcarinal groups - 62% ipsilateral, 29% bilateral & 9% contralateral (present author's comment - i.e. **in line of lymphatic drainage**).
Kearney et al. (1999) : CT, US & clinical history in pts. with parapneumonic effusions/empyemas.
Arenas-Jiminez et al. (1999) : CT illuminates causes of pleural effusions.

Cuttaneo and Klassen (1973) : Carcinoma of the chest wall complicating chronically draining empyema.
Hillerdal and Berg (1985) : Malignant mesothelioma secondary to chronic inflammation and old scar - two new cases and literature review.
Iuchi et al. (1987) : Non-Hodgkin's lymphoma of the pleural cavity developing from long-standing pyothorax.
Minami et al. (1991) : Radiological assessment of malignancy associated with chronic empyema.
Aozasa, et al. (1994) : Angiosarcoma developing from chronic pyothorax.
Fujiwara et al. (1995) : Fast spin-echo MR of non-Hodgkin's lymphoma arising from chronic tuberculous empyema.
Tong et al. (1997) : Imaging features of pleural lymphoma complicating a long-standing pyothorax.

Pneumothoraces - (Illus. **PNEUMOTHORAX**).

Radiography.

Although many books recommend chest radiographs both in inspiration and expiration for the detection of a pneumothorax in the ambulant patient, the author has for many years believed this is unnecessary and at times almost 'frightening', since the expiratory view may erroneously suggest that drainage may be required. It is true that an inspiratory view usually underestimates the size of a pneumothorax, as shown by CT studies, but the author has never seen a significant pneumothorax in ambulant adult patients which was not seen on an inspiratory view! Some authors recommend a decubitus view, with the suspected side of the pneumothorax upper-most, in order to detect small pneumothoraces, but if it is that small, no treatment will be required, and the extra view will in most cases be worthless! More difficulties occur with the supine patient (see below).

The only time when it may be necessary to diagnose a small pneumothorax in the ambulant patient, is prior to air travel. At normal cabin pressures (equivalent to 8,000 to 10,000 feet) the atmospheric pressure will be halved, and therefore a pneumothorax will be doubled in volume. The extra respiratory effort may also promote further leakage of air from the lung. Only for this reason has the author allowed an expiratory view!

Further references.

Kircher and Swartzel (1954) : The percentage of a pneumothorax is derived by subtracting the area of the collapsed lung from the area of the hemithorax on a frontal view.
Axel (1981) : A simple way to estimate the size of a pneumothorax - change in the volume of the lung is equal to the cube of the change in linear dimensions.
Lams and Jolles (1982) : The effect of lobar collapse on the distribution of free intrapleural air.
Rhea et al. (1982) : Whilst noting that the distribution of air in a pleural cavity may be affected by pleural adhesions and/or by disease of the underlying lung, produced a nomogram for calculating the percentage of a pneumothorax in cases not so affected (see nomogram - Fig. 14.13 below).
Bradley et al.(1991) : Value of routine expiratory films in diagnosis of pneumothorax - studied 79 patients with paired films, and found that all pneumothoraces could be seen on both inspiratory and expiratory films. They

concluded that **all pneumothoraces could be reasonably diagnosed on an inspiratory film alone** - a similar view was reached by Squance (1995) and Seow (1996) below.

Engdahl et al. (1993) : Chest radiography is **not** a satisfactory method for determining the size of a pneumothorax - CT sections show that it is often **markedly underestimated**.

Collins et al. (1995, from Christie Hosp., Manchester) : Quantification of pneumothorax size on chest radiographs using interpleural distances - regression analysis based on volume measurements from helical CT (See also nomogram below).

Seow et al. (1996) : Compared the effectiveness of expiratory and inspiratory chest radiographs for detecting pneumothoraces and found **no difference** with either technique for diagnosis - the extra view merely doubling the radiation dose and cost.

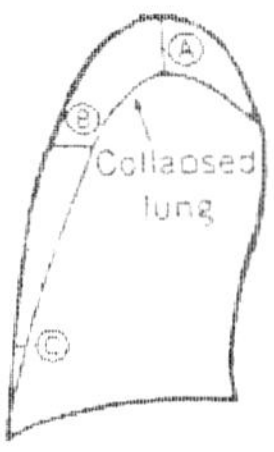

Average interpleural distance (mm)	Pneumothorax - size (%)	Sum of interpleural distances (cm)	Pneumothorax size (%)
$\dfrac{A+B+C}{3}$			
5	5	2.0	13.6
10	10	4.0	23.0
15	15	6.0	32.4
20	20	8.0	41.8
25	25	10.0	51.2
30	30	12.0	60.6
35	35	14.0	70.0
40	40	16.0	79.4
45	45	18.0	88.8
50	50	20.0	98.2

Average interpleural distance

$$= \dfrac{A+B+C}{3}$$

Rhea et al. (1982)
Radiology, **144**, 733 - 736
- reproduced with permission.

Collins et al. (1995)
AJR, **165**, 1127- 1130
- reproduced with permission.

Fig. 14.13 Nomograms showing how the size of a pneumothorax may be estimated. However the author agrees with Gross (Editor of Chest Chapter of Year Book of Diagnostic Radiology, 1997) that for most purposes 'small, moderate or large' suffices for most clinical purposes.

Pneumothoraces on supine radiographs.

When a patient is supine, free gas in a pleural cavity will tend to rise to the highest point in that pleural cavity. Commonly this will be anterior and over the lower parts of the lung. Localised hyperlucency and accentuation of mediastinal and diaphragmatic contours, without deviation of the lateral lung border, may be all that is visible. Not uncommonly pneumothoraces after trauma may be bilateral (Illus. **PNEUMOTHORAX BILATERAL, Aorta trauma Pt. 2a**) - these are often accompanied by air in the mediastinum and/ or chest wall.

If the patient is tilted head up, the air may rise towards the lung apex, pass laterally or medially if he is turned towards one side, or pass towards the base of the chest, if he is fully supine or head down. Adhesions or concomitant pleural fluid may somewhat modify the picture. Decubitus or lateral views have often been given considerable prominence in the American literature, but are often impracticable or of little help and CT is now often used for diagnosis in major US (and some UK) trauma centres, as only about 50% of pneumothoraces are recognised on plain films.

Giuffre (1984) reviewed the literature and gave the signs of pneumothoraces in supine patients as follows:

(a) fairly common (but occasionally mimicked) signs - lower zone lucency, visible anterior costo-phrenic sulcus, a deep lateral sulcus ('**deep sulcus sign**'), and sharp mediastinal or diaphragmatic contours, and

(b) uncommon (but specific) signs - lobulated epicardial fat pads (owing to the lack of air-filled lung pressing on the fat) and inter-lobar air. All these are due to adjacent pleural air accentuating these anatomical borders. He suggested that in difficult cases one should take coned views of a suspicious area, or use an oblique x-ray beam with the patient in expiration as suggested by Galanski et al. (1981) - see Fig. 14.14c.

One should always beware of the visceral pleural line of the lung in association with a pneumothorax being confused with a soft-tissue fold. Such folds are usually wide and ill-defined, compared with the well-defined visceral pleura having air-filled lung on its medial aspect.

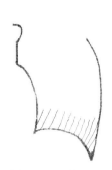  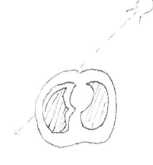

(a) Lower zone lucency with opened out costo-phrenic sulcus and well outlined lower heart border due to antero-medial gas - **deep sulcus sign**.

(b) Triangular lucencies due to inter-lobar or fissural gas.

(c) Supine oblique technique for the demonstration of a pneumothorax.

Fig. 14.14   Pneumothoraces in supine patients.

Further references.

Kurlander and Helmen (1966) : Subpulmonary pneumothorax.

Christensen and Dietz (1976) : Subpulmonary pneumothorax in patients with chronic obstructive pulmonary disease.

Adams (1979) : Tension pneumothorax in supine patients may be modified by pleural adhesions.

Gordon, R. (1980) : The **deep sulcus sign**.

Ziter and Westcott (1981) : Supine subpulmonary pneumothorax.

Tocino et al. (1985) : Distribution of pneumothorax in the supine and semirecumbent critically ill adult - studied 88 critically ill patients with 112 pneumothoraces. The antero-medial (38%) and subpulmonary (26%) recesses were most commonly filled with air in the supine and semi-recumbent positions. 30% of pneumothoraces were not initially detected by clinician or radiologist - half of these progressed to tension pneumothoraces. Diagnosis was particularly important in ARDS (see ps. 8.13 - 16) - CT may be of help in doubtful cases.

Spizarny and Goodman (1986) : Air in the minor fissure.

Cummin et al. (1987) : Pneumothorax in the supine patient.

Morgan et al (1993) : Detection of pneumothorax in supine patients with lateral shoot-through digital radiography.

Lichtenstein and Menu (1995) : Use of **US in the critically ill supine patient to exclude an anteriorly situated pneumothorax** - normally there is a to-and-fro movement with respiration at the lung-chest wall interface - the **lung sliding sign**' Its absence indicates a pneumothorax.

Sistrom et al. (1996) : Also used US, but found a low sensitivity and specificity - it could confirm a known pneumothorax, but not exclude one nor determine its size.

Wernecke (1997) : Also uses US for the detection of a pneumothorax - noting the absence of pleural movements and **comet tail artefacts** from aerated alveoli (see also ps. 14.13 - 14).

Easty et al. (1997) : From the London Hosp. to which the Helicopter Emergency Medical Service takes injured pts. from anywhere within the M25 motorway area - 1560 pts. were admitted over 6 yrs & 202 pts. had pneumothoraces, diagnosed on supine chest radiographs - almost certainly an underestimate. Special attention should be paid to pts. with density changes, rib fractures and chest wall haematomas. A lung edge was seen in 27%, other signs included hypertranslucency, anterior sulcus, & para-mediastinal gas. CT could show that up to 70% were occult and some were bilateral.

Goodman et al. (1999) : Ultrasound detection of pneumothorax.

Bilateral pneumothorax - Illus. BILATERAL PNEUMOTHORAX.

This may occasionally occur spontaneously on both sides e.g. with asthma, but more commonly after trauma, or with (degenerating) tumours or deposits. In most cases the second side is small. The condition may also be seen with a '**mediastinal window**' (connecting the two sides); either developmental or post-operative - '**Buffalo chest**' (see also ps. 7.7 & 11.15).

The author also had a case - on the left following a percutaneous needle lung biopsy and on the right due to asthma (accentuated by that on the left). Despite bilateral drainage she died. No mediastinal window was found at autopsy (see also p. 21.8).

References.
Pettersson et al. (1983) : Total bilateral spontaneous pneumothorax in a 29 year old man, with only moderate respiratory distress - treated with bilateral chest tubes.
Junoven et al. (1992) : Mediastinal window - a cause of bilateral simultaneous pneumothorax in a woman aged 19 - a chest radiograph showed a mediastinal air-bridge in the upper mediastinum communicating the two sides.

Loculated pneumothorax.
This may occur when pleural adhesions are present, the air appearing in any part of the pleural space, either peripherally, at the apex, adjacent to the mediastinum or above the diaphragm.

A 'central pneumothorax' tends to occur adjacent to the heart, and on the left it may apprear as a crescent-shaped shadow adjacent to the left ventricle - Fig 14.15 and Illus. **PNEUMOTHORAX CENTRAL, Pneumothorax Pt. 10** (in this case in a new-born baby and it became much larger following efforts at resuscitation).

'Central pneumothorax'
   adjacent to the heart.
Fig. 14.15

References.
Wright, J.(1965) : Radiological sign of '**clicking** pneumothorax' - systolic click on auscultation caused by a small L pneumothorax, with gas adjacent to the pericardium.
Moskowitz and Griscom (1976) : The medial pneumothorax.
Fletcher (1978) : Medial herniation of the parietal pleura - a useful sign of pneumothorax in neonates.
Cohen, A. (1981) : 'Occult pneumothorax'.
Nashef and Ferguson (1985) : 'Occult central pneumothorax' shown by tomography in a woman aged 33 - caused severe respiratory embarrassment. It followed previous generalised pneumothoraces treated with tube drainage and open lung biopsy for lung fibrosis.

'Pneumothorax ex vacuo' - adjacent to a collapsed lobe (especially the RUL).
In a few cases bronchial obstruction can lead to a localised pneumothorax adjacent to the periphery of a collapsed lobe, which clears after the bronchial obstruction has been relieved. This is seen mostly in children, and appears to be caused by traction on the collapsed lobe (from the hilum) pulling gas out of solution as in a 'vacuum disc' or joint and is termed 'pneumothorax ex vacuo'. (see Berdon et al., 1984 and Stark and Leung, 1996).

Lung peel sign - apparent lung cortical thickening due to unaerated and collapsed lung cortex - mimicking a pleural rind (a sign seen with empyemas and mesotheliomas - ps. 14.19, 14.41 & 14.45) - see Illus. **PNX LUNG PEEL SIGN.**

Causes of pneumothoraces.
These are protean; ruptured lung bleb, cyst or bulla, trauma (including medical trauma - surgery, needle lung biopsy - p. 21.4 et seq., chest aspiration, subclavian cannulation, supraclavicular or intercostal nerve block, breast biopsy, etc.), pneumonia (especially staphylococcal - but may be seen occasionally with other bacteria - see ps. 19.1 & 19.3), tuberculosis, hydatid disease, chronic lung disease producing honeycombing (see p. 6.6 re histiocytosis X and tuberose sclerosis, Marfan's syndrome, endometriosis, fibrosing alveolitis), rheumatoid lung disease, etc.

Pneumothorax as a presenting feature of neoplasm or complicating it (Illus. **PNX & TUMOUR**).

Occasionally a lung tumour may present with a spontaneous pneumothorax. This may be free or loculated from adhesions, and is occasionally loculated within an interlobar fissure. Such pneumothoraces probably arise as a result of air-trapping - a similar mechanism to that occurring with some infections and the production of acute bullae or pneumatocoeles (see ps. 19.1 & 19.3) and Fig. 6.13. Pneumothoraces may also complicate cavitating secondary deposits (which tend to be peripheral in position - see p. 1.45) or cavitating or peripheral cavitating primary tumours, and with these a tiny broncho-pleural fistula from the cavitating lesion to the pleura is the probable mechanism. In the latter type the pneumothoraces (which may be bilateral) may be persistent and difficult to treat.

Other tumours etc. producing pneumothoraces include - carcinoids, pulmonary endometriosis (ps. 5.19 - 20), cavitating infarcts, pneumoconiotic nodules and endo-bronchial foreign bodies. Secondary deposits the author has noted producing pneumothoraces include - renal tumours, cervix, breast, reticuloses, sarcomas, and endo-bronchial secondaries from various tumours.

The last is similar to the example shown in Illus. **PNX & TUMOUR, Oeser sign Pt. 3a-d**, where a small endo-bronchial tumour in the left main bronchus was associated with reduced vascularity of the left lung and obstructive emphysema. The mechanism in such cases would appear to be similar to that with bronchial trauma and asthma i.e. bronchial air leak, $\rightarrow$ subpleural air leak $\rightarrow$ pleural air (see also p. 6.31).

Treatment of pneumothoraces

This is mainly by observation when small, by aspiration or tube drainage with larger pneumothoraces (esp. if tension after trauma). The recurrence rate after tube drainage for a first pneumothorax is about 25 - 50%. Recurrent pneumothoraces (like persistent effusions) may be treated with autologous blood, tetracycline or talc 'poudrage'. References to the use of Heimlich valves in relation to biopsy complications are given on ps. 21.12 - 13. Note also re-expansion pulmonary oedema - p. 8.7.

An important point in draining apparent tension pneumothoraces is not to inadvertently drain a huge bulla, or pneumatocoele, as this is easily converted into a rapidly air-filling tension pneumothorax, which may be difficult to treat.

References.

General
Krasnik et al. (1987) : Tetracycline pleurodesis in spontaneous pneumothorax.
Conces, D. et al. (1988) : Treatment of pneumothoraces using small calibre chest tubes.
Milanez et al. (1994) : Intrapleural talc instilled at thoracoscopy for the prevention of recurrent pneumothorax.
Miller, A. and Harvey (1993) : Guidelines for the management of spontaneous pneumothorax.
Berger et al. (1996) : A fish induced pneumothorax - dilemma in the remote management of a sucking chest wound.
Tschopp et al. (1997) : Thorascopic talc pleurodesis under local anaesthesia is a safe & effective treatment for complicated spontaneous pneumothorax.
Murray, J. et al. (1997a) : CT of the pleural space after talc pleurodesis - the talc lies in clusters posteriorly.
Murray, J. et al. (1997b) : Talc pleurodesis simulating pleural metastases with [18]FDG PET.

Pneumothorax and tumours
Heimlich and Rubin (1955) : Pneumothorax as a presenting feature of lung cancer.
Citron (1959) : Spontaneous pneumothorax complicating bronchial carcinoma.
D'Angio and Iannaccone (1961) : Spontaneous pneumothorax as a complication of pulmonary metastases in childhood malignancies (esp. Wilm's tumours).
Janetos and Ochsner (1963) : Bilateral pneumothorax in metastatic osteogenic sarcoma.
Evans et al. (1965) : Five cases with pneumothorax, out of 66 patients with malignant trophoblastic disease.
Rose, M. et al. (1967) : One pneumothorax directly resulting from perforated bronchial carcinoma.
Spittle et al. (1968) : Spontaneous pneumothorax with pulmonary metastases in childhood malignancies.
Williams, H. and Kinder, (1971) : **Alveolar cell carcinoma** presenting as a pneumothorax.
Laucius et al. (1972) : Spontaneous pneumothorax and pneumomediastinum as complications of sarcoma.
Dines et al. (1973) : Malignant pulmonary neoplasms predisposing to spontaneous pneumothorax.
Khan and Seriff (1973) : Pneumothorax - a rare presenting manifestation of lung cancer.
Libshitz and Banner (1974) : Spontaneous pneumothorax as a complications of radiation therapy to the thorax.

Mahajan et al. (1975) : Pneumothorax - a rare manifestation of primary lung cancer.
Wright, F. (1976) : Spontaneous pneumothorax and pulmonary malignant disease - a not uncommon association with primary and secondary tumours.
Singh et al. (1977) : Bilateral spontaneous pneumothorax with pulmonary metastases from synovial cell sarcoma.
Yeung and Bonnet (1977) : Bronchogenic carcinoma presenting as spontaneous pneumothorax.
Cordier, J. et al. (1979) : Reviewed 72 cases of spontaneous pneumothorax complicating bronchial carcinoma of varying cell types (50% squamous) and reported 5 new cases.
Schulman et al. (1979) : Spontaneous pneumothorax as a result of intensive cytotoxic chemotherapy in young pts. - ovarian granulosa cell and carcinosarcoma testis.
Ayres (1980) : Pneumothorax associated with primary bronchial carcinoma.
Lote et al. (1981) : Pneumothorax during combination chemotherapy.
Helmkamp et al. (1982) : Spontaneous pneumothorax in gynaecological malignancies.
Laurens (1983) : Spontaneous pneumothorax in primary cavitating lung carcinoma.
Rammohan et al. (1986) : Pleurodesis in metastatic pneumothorax.
Berdon et al. (1984) : Localised pneumothorax within an interlobar fissure is association with bronchial obstruction.
Steinhauslin and Cuttat (1985) : Spontaneous pneumothorax - a complication of lung cancer.
Kader et al. (1987) : Pneumothorax in association with lung secondaries from angiosarcoma of the breast.
Bearn and Lau (1988) : Spontaneous pneumothorax due to metastatic carcinoma of the rectum.
Chippindale et al. (1989) : Spontaneous pneumothorax with metastatic seminoma.
Kryger-Baggesen (1990) : Spontaneous pneumothorax following regression of pulmonary metastases.
Lawton et al. (1990) : Bilateral pneumothorax as a presenting feature of metastatic angiosarcoma of the scalp.
Santosh-Kumar et al. : (1991) Spontaneous pneumothorax in metastatic chorioncarcinoma.
Sheard et al. (1991) : Five patients with malignant mesothelioma presented with a spontaneous pneumothorax.
Fenlon et al. (1996) : Bilateral recurrent tension pneumothorax complicating combination chemotherapy for pulmonary metastatic uterine leiomyosarcoma.
Okada et al. (1998) : Ipsilateral spontaneous pneumothorax after rapid development of large thin-walled cavities in two patients who had undergone radiation therapy for lung cancer.'

Artificial pneumothorax (see also p. 12.6).

Isaacs (1925) pointed out that the introduction of 400 - 600 ml of air into the pleural cavity might give valuable information, particularly in obscure cases where one cannot differentiate an interlobar empyema from a lung tumour, or to show the exact anatomical location of a lesion - i.e. whether it was in the mediastinum, the pleura, ribs or chest wall. He wrote that a bronchial carcinoma leading to collapse of a lobe, may be confused with an interlobar empyema, especially if there is concomitant pleural thickening, but the injection of a few hundred ml of air into the pleural cavity, readily differentiated the two.

The method has been used several times by the author. Particularly when aspirating fluid, it is very easy to instil some air into the pleural cavity. CT interpretation of chest wall or pleural involvement by tumours may be very difficult, and even a small amount of air may demonstrate separation of the lung from neighbouring structures, and that the tumour or other disease process does not extend into the chest wall (Illus. **PNEUMOTHORAX, Biopsy Pt. 13**). It may also show nodular pleural masses with pleural carcinomatosis, or with a mesothelioma. Illus. **PNEUMOTHORAX, Neurofibroma Pt. 18a-b** demonstrates a large sympathetic chain neurofibroma, following aspiration of a large pleural effusion and the installation of air.

As an alternative to air, oxygen or carbon-dioxide may be used - these are more soluble and are more quickly absorbed.

Further references.
Møller (1950) : Gave an example of the use of the technique in excluding neoplasm.
Rockoff (1982) : Showed the value of an accidental pneumothorax in differentiating an intra-pulmonary apical lung tumour, from a Pancoast tumour extending outside the lung into the pleural apex - in this case it had not, although there was brachial plexus irritation. (The author has had a similar case).
Watanabe et al. (1991) : Chest CT combined with artificial pneumothorax in determining the origin and extent of a tumour - studied 12 patients with intrathoracic tumours abutting the chest wall or mediastinum.
Yokoi et al. (1991) : CT after pneumothorax was especially helpful for assessing tumour invasion of the chest wall and mediastinum in lung cancer - study of 43 cases.
Takasugi et al. (1994) : CT after inadvertent pneumothorax at CT-guided percutaneous biopsy - showed that a LLL mass fell away from the descending aorta, and therefore was not invading the mediastinum and was resectable.

Gateley et al. (1991) : Pneumothorax - a complication of fine needle aspiration of the **breast** - **7 cases** (We have also seen cases in Oxford - produced by surgeons, not radiologists!).

Broncho-pleural fistula - (Illus. **BRON-PL FISTULA**).

This term signifies a communication between the bronchi and the pleura. This may happen spontaneously or follow trauma or surgery. Spontaneous cases may present with a pneumothorax or hydropneumothorax, from simple rupture of a bulla or bleb, or be due to larger fistulae from the bronchi (see Illus. **BRON-PL FISTULA, Pts. 2a-b & 4a-c**). Larger fistulae may complicate infection, infarction, cavitating tumours, etc. In traumatic and post-surgical cases there may be a large hole between a main bronchus and the pleura, particularly if a suture line has broken down. If this happens after the pleural cavity has filled with fluid, this may be aspirated into the contralateral lung, giving rise to a bronchopneumonic picture. Also loss of fluid, without tube drainage, may suggest that a fistula has occurred. With tube drainage rapid bubbling of air from the tube into the drainage system is a good indication of its presence.

A simple clinical test to prove the presence of a fistula is to inject methylene blue into the pleural cavity, and to note if it becomes coughed up. Large fistulae may be confirmed by bronchoscopy or be demonstrated by tomography, including CT. CT may also be useful in some cases for studying the position of a drainage tube and its track after removal. This latter may sometimes mimic an air-filled lung cavity - up to three to four weeks after removal.

Maier and Haight (1940) noted that loculated broncho-pleural fistulae tend to conform in shape to the adjacent chest wall. This point was also stressed by Friedman and Hellekant (1977) who noted that the three-dimensional shape of an air /fluid pocket as demonstrated on plain radiographs, may suggest its differentiation from an abscess or partially fluid-filled bulla. With the most common posterior costophrenic angle location of a loculated fistula, there is usually a fairly wide air /fluid collection as seen on the frontal view, whilst it appears more narrow on lateral views. By contrast abscess cavities tend to be more spherical.

References - broncho-pleural and other fistulae to the tracheo-bronchial tree.

Carmichael and Franklyn (1963) : Broncho-pleuro-colonic fistula - 2 cases (one had a colonic hernia into the chest).
Hines et al. (1966) : Colo-pleuro-bronchial fistula due to ca colon.
Gimes (1970) : Gastro-bronchial fistula.
Stark, P. (1981) : Bronchoenteric fistulae in lymphoma.
Clarke et al. (1984) : Enterobronchial fistula.
Richterman et al. (1987) : Enterobronchial fistula.
Ashley et al. (1988) : Colo-bronchial fistula - a late complication of appendicitis.
Irwin et al. (1988) : Gastro-pleuro-bronchial fistula mimicking bronchiectasis.
Chong and Constant (1990) : Gastrobronchial fistula from peptic ulcer in a hiatus hernia following fundoplication - quoted other cases from the literature following trauma, gastric or oesophageal surgery, subphrenic abscess, gastric ulcer, lymphoma or pancreatic neoplasm.
Cammarata et al. (1991) : Elevated right hemidiaphragm with yellow sputum due to a broncho-biliary fistula.
Richardson et al. (1992) : Gastrobronchial fistula - non-malignant causes.
Finkelstein and Small (1994) : Jejuno-bronchial fistula.
Singh et al. (1994) : Colo-bronchial fistula secondary to Crohn's disease.
Westcott and Volpe (1995) : CT evaluation of 20 pts. with peripheral broncho-pleural fistulae due to pneumonia, empyema or post-operative air-leak.
Smith, D. et al. (1995) : Broncho-pleural-subarachnoid fistula following surgical resection of a Pancoast tumour manifesting as intra-cranial gas (like an air-encephalogram filling the cerebral ventricles) on CT scans. (The author has only seen one respiratory-cerebral fistula in a young chicken farmer who filled his cerebral ventricles with air when he sneezed - see Illus. **BRAIN Pt. 22**).
Karmy-Jones et al. (1995) : Colobronchial fistula due to Crohn's disease.
Cameron et al. (1996) : Gastrobronchial fistula in untreated β cell lymphoma of stomach fundus invading LLL & spleen - quoted 38 other cases - mostly occurring postoperatively.
Stern et al. (1996) : Peripheral broncho-pleural fistulas - CT imaging features.
Baxter et al. (1998) : Ileo-bronchial fistula.   Gee and Wood (2000) : Transdiaphragmatic fistula - see p. 15.15.

Brennan et al. (1972) : Veno-bronchial fistula - a rare complication of central venous catheterisation for parenteral hyperalimentation.
Demeter and Cordasco (1980) : Key to successful management of aorto-bronchial fistula - the eventual untreated mortality rate is 100%.
Graber et al. (1980) : Successful management of fistulae between the aorta and the tracheo-bronchial tree.
Coblentz et al. (1988) : Aorto-bronchopulmonary fistula complicating aortic surgery - diagnosis in 4 cases.
Paull and Keagy (1990) : Management of aorto-bronchial fistula with graft replacement and omentopexy.

Hynes and Whitehouse (1997) : Haemoptysis due to aorto-bronchial fistula (with anterior segment bronchus RUL) caused by mycotic aneurysm of the ascending aorta associated with chronic osteomyelitis of the sternum two years after coronary by-pass and aortic valve replacement. This patient refused surgery and lived in comfort for 2 yrs.

See also tracheo bronchial fistulae with oesophagus - see ps. 16.10 - 12.

<u>Benign pleural tumours and masses,</u>
   These include :

   Fibromas (benign localised mesothelioma or solitary fibrous pleural tumour),
   Desmoid tumours (or aggressive fibrosis - see ps. 18.4 - 5),
   Lipomas and fibro-lipomas,
   'Whorled' or **'rounded'** nodules - really localised areas of chronic pleural thickening (see ps. 14. 42 - 44),
   Pleural plaques, localised pleural debris collections and **'mice'** - the last two used to follow tuberculous pleurisy, and when mobile such a mass often altered in position between one chest radiograph and another (hence the term **'mouse'** - see also ps. 14.3 & 14.6 & Illus. **PL-MOUSE** and under TB p. 19.17).

   Pleural fibromas (Illus. **PL-FIBROMA**), like extra-pleural masses, usually have very clear-cut and well-defined margins, due to their impression on the intact visceral pleura and air-filled lung, i.e. the 'pleural coiffe' sign - see p. 14.1. Fibromas may give rise to hormonal effects, including HPOA, finger clubbing, hyperinsulinism, hyponatraemia, etc (see also p. 23.1 - other non-islet cell tumours causing severe hypoglycaemia include leiomyosarcoma and fibrosarcoma - see ref. to Kishi et al., 1997 below). One case the author followed for over 25 years, recurred several times, the first few times with attacks of unconsciousness associated with hyperinsulinism. This case is illustrated in Illus. **PL-FIBROMA, Pt. 1a-c**, and was earlier partially reported by Spry et al. (1968). A number of similar cases have also been reported in the literature. These tumours usually arise in the visceral pleura, occasionally within a fissure, and are mostly well-encapsulated, non-calcified, firm and lobulated. Many have recurred following surgical resection. They may also eventually become malignant, and give rise to sclerotic metastases. On enhanced CT they are typically highly vascular.

<u>Further references.</u>
Maximow (1927) : Tissue culture of mesothelioma - fibroblasts and collagen fibres.
Doege (1930) : First report of tumour induced hypoglycaemia - especially tumours involving fibrous proliferation.
Klemperer and Rabin (1931) : A more diffuse type.
Stout and Murray (1942) : Thought that a pleural fibroma was a localised form of mesothelioma.
Clagett and Hausmann (1944) : Huge intrathoracic fibroma.
Fawcett (1945) : Large fibroma arising from pleura of right lower lobe.
Hawthorne and Frobese (1950) : Benign fibroma of the pleura.
Clagett et al. (1952) : Pleural fibroma - 24 cases.
Price Thomas and Drew (1953) : Fibroma of the visceral pleura - six cases - may be large and also cause HPOA.
Kerr and Nohl (1961) : Recurrence of benign intrathoracic fibromas - a not uncommon phenomenon and the pathological pattern may be one of progression towards greater malignancy.
Berne and Heitzman (1962) : The Roentgenological signs of pedunculated pleural fibromas - two cases. Pedunculation was shown by change in position of the mass with posture.
Shabanah and Sayegh (1971) : Solitary (localised) pleural mesothelioma (two cases) and review of 152 cases from the literature. Small tumours are usually asymptomatic, but some have HPOA, etc. Large tumours usually give rise to pain and a wide spectrum of pressure symptoms, increasing dyspnoea - collapse, pneumonia and SVC obstruction.
Okike et al. (1978) : 60 localised mesotheliomas of the pleura - 52 benign (11 with HPOA) & 8 malignant variants.
Dalton et al. (1979) : Localised primary tumours of the pleura - analysis of 40 cases.
Kniznik et al. (1979), Mandal et al. (1983), Touyz et al. (1986) : Hypoglycaemia associated with pleural fibroma.
Perks et al. (1979) : Hyponatraemia and mesothelioma.
Briselli et al. (1981) : Reviewed 368 cases of pleural fibroma - 360 from the literature + 8 new ones - 4% incidence of spontaneous hypoglycaemia & 35% HPOA - 12% had extensive local recurrences, often years after surgery.
Weisbrod and Yee (1983) : CT diagnosis of pedunculated fibrous mesothelioma.
Williford et al. (1983) : Benign pleural tumours showed localised oval soft-tissue masses - sharply delineated from adjacent lung and extra-pleural soft tissues.
Weilbaccher and Sarma (1984) : Localised fibrous mesothelioma.

Dedrick et al. (1985) : Studied six cases of fibrous mesothelioma by CT - well-delineated, often lobulated, non-calcified soft-tissue masses in close relationship to a pleural surface. Some were inhomogeneous and quite large, having associated pleural thickening, but showing no chest wall invasion. Some had smooth tapering margins.

England et al. (1989) : Localised benign and malignant fibrous tumours of the pleura - review of 223 cases.

Masson et al. (1991) : Spontaneous hypoglycaemia due to a pleural fibroma - note of insulin like growth factors. (64 year old woman with a long history of 'drop attacks' and dizzy spells was found to have spontaneous hypoglycaemia. She had had a right basal slowly enlarging pleural shadow for about five years).

Moat et al. (1991) : Spontaneous hypoglycaemia and pleural fibroma - role of insulin like growth factors (male 57).

Lee, K. et al. (1992) : CT findings in benign fibrous mesothelioma of the pleura - pathological correlation in nine patients. The tumours showed **intense contrast enhancement due to the vascularity of the tumours.** Areas of low attenuation within the tumours were due to foci of myxoid or cystic degeneration and haemorrhage. Pathologically these tumours are usually rounded, firm, white and scar-like in gross appearance. They are often highly vascular with prominent veins over the surface.

Saifuddin et al. (1992) : Preferred the term 'primary malignant localised fibrous tumours of the pleura' as 20% may be malignant- 5 cases - all presented with CT features suggesting malignancy. Four had local symptoms, and one HPOA at presentation and had large necrotic tumour masses (900 to 4,000 gms.), and one case was a recurrence of a pleural fibroma resected 7 years previously. They noted that these tumours can exhibit a great diversity of pathological patterns and hence have been termed fibroma, fibrosarcoma, fibrous histiocytoma, haemangiopericytoma, nerve sheath tumour, etc. The histological grading of malignancy did not correlate always with the final outcome, adequacy of resection being the most important factor.

Harris (1995) : **MR of benign fibrous mesothelioma of the pleura - low or intermediate signal on both T1 & T2 - most other pleural tumours having high signal on T2.**

Ferretti et al. (1997) : Range in size from 1 to 39 cm in diameter.

Kishi et al. (1997) : Reported hypoglycaemia in a 72 yr. old male with a large recurrent retroperitoneal leiomyosarcoma with pulmonary metastases.

Desser and Stark (1998) : 9 cases - small or large pleural masses, which may arise in the peripheral or mediastinal pleura + 1 in R greater fissure which grossly recurred 9 yrs. after surgery. Angiography in 2 cases showed vascular masses and MR intermediate signal intensity.

Karabulut and Goodman (1999) : Pedunculated solitary fibrous tumour of the interlobular fissure - a '**wandering**' chest mass.

Tuong et al. (2000) : Man aged 32 with localised lobulated mass containing calcification.

Malignant pleural disease (mesotheliomas are discussed on ps. 14.44 - 46).

Most cases of malignant pleural disease are due to the secondary spread of tumours. This may occur from lung tumours, which have spread into the pleura, or from other primary sites, including stomach, kidney, ovary, cervix - particularly adenocarcinomas. It may also be seen with reticulosis, leukaemia or multiple myeloma. Primary pleural tumours (mainly malignant mesotheliomas) have been less common, but with the increase in number of mesotheliomas the author has seen several such cases each year. Most lead to an effusion, but in others there is a malignant 'dry' pleurisy, with 'knobs' (often looking like '**mushrooms**' - see Illus. **PL-MUSHROOMS**) pleural thickening and loss of volume ('**cancer en cuirasse**' or '**encasing pleural mass**' - Illus. **MESOTHELIOMA, Pt. 44b**), or a mixed picture; these changes can be seen both with primary and secondary pleural malignant disease, including reticulosis.

Circumferential visceral pleural thickening is often referred to as a '**pleural rind**'. This is often due to a mesothelioma, but may also be seen with other types of tumour involving the pleura and also with empyemas, it frequently shows **enhancement** with contrast media

Malignant pleural effusions are frequently blood-stained, and often contain 'reactive cells' - polymorphs, histiocytes and 'reactive mesothelial cells'. Occasionally a frank eosinophilic effusion is produced (see p. 14.8).

Sometimes the affected pleural cavity is filled with tumour material, 'jelly' and granulation tissue, with very little fluid or only tiny scattered pockets within the 'organised pleura', and on ultrasound this may mimic the appearance of an empyema (see also ps. 14.18 - 19). This appearance is particularly seen with **pseudomyxoma**, which may spread up into the chest (and chest wall) from the abdomen, and is often a manifestation of mucin producing adenocarcinomas especially of the ovary - Illus. **PSEUDOMYXOMA**. The author has also seen it in some patients with chronic renal failure and no evidence of malignancy. It may also occur with an appendix mucocoele, abscess or chronic infection.

With bronchial tumours, a concomitant pleural effusion does not necessarily imply that the pleura has been invaded, as an effusion may be caused by secondary infection, infarction, pleural irritation or be secondary to lymph node blockage (see also staging - ps. 24.22 et seq.).

Malignancy may be confirmed by examination of pleural fluid (p. 21.13), pleural biopsy or thoracoscopy and biopsy. Imaging with FDG-PET seems promising for distinguishing malignant from benign pleural disease.

Malignancy complicating a chronic empyema is noted on p. 14.21.

Some references.

Le Roux (1962) : Pleural tumours.
Samuel (1969) : Radiology of serosal malignancy - thought that more mesotheliomas had been diagnosed as bronchial carcinoma than vice versa.
Heller et al. (1970) : Malignant pleural mesothelioma.
Ellis and Wolff (1977) : Mesotheliomas and secondary tumours of the pleura.
Suzuki (1980) : Pathology of human malignant mesothelioma.
Antman et al. (1981) : Clinical presentation and natural history of benign and malignant mesothelioma.
Antman and Corson (1985) : Benign and malignant pleural mesothelioma.'
Brenner et al. (1982) : Malignant mesothelioma of the pleura - review of 123 patients.
Campbell and Greenberg (1981) : Calcified liver metastases from mesothelioma.
Steiner et al. (1982) : Rib destruction with mesothelioma - a neglected finding.
Bhatt et al. (1984) : **Mesothelioma in an azygos fissure**.
Adams and Unni (1984) : Diffuse malignant mesothelioma of the pleura - criteria based on an autopsy study.
Yousem and Hochholzer (1987) : Malignant mesotheliomas with osseous and cartilaginous differentiation.
Lee, M. et al. (1991) : Described the CT characteristics of pleural granulocytic sarcoma - diffuse circumferential pleural thickening, multiple pleural fluid loculi and mediastinal adenopathy i.e. similar to mesothelioma and metastatic pleural disease.
Sheard et al. (1991) : Five patients (> age 40) with malignant pleural mesothelioma presented with a spontaneous pneumothorax in a period of five years.
Moran et al. (1992) : Thymomas presenting as pleural tumours.
Krishna and Haqqani (1993) : Liposarcomatous differentiation in diffuse pleural mesothelioma.
Radosavljevic et al. (1993) : **Pseudomyxoma** of the pleural and peritoneal cavities.
Richards and Robertson (1994) : Review of 45 cases of malignant pleural rind.
Frola et al. (1995) : Exudative effusions associated with mesothelioma show a significant enforcement of signal intensity after GdDTPA.
Hynes et al. (1996) : Pleural encasement secondary to acinar adenocarcinoma of the submandibular gland.
Bury et al. (1997) : 25 pts. examined with FDG-PET - of 16 with malignant disease, 14 had uptake & 2 moderate uptake. 7 benign cases showed no uptake & 2 with infectious pleural disease showed a moderate localised uptake.
Crotty et al. (1994) : Localised malignant mesothelioma - 6 cases - 4 were sessile tumours having a broad pleural attachment and were pedunculated - 3 were purely epithelioid lesions. All were resected - 3 had recurrences 4 - 18 months later & died 1 - 2 yrs. later, the others were well at follow up.

Ronnett et al. (1995) : Disseminated peritoneal adenomucinosis and peritoneal mucinous carcinomatosis - 109 cases.
Mor et al. (1996) : Pseudomyxoma extraperitonei.
Tsai (1998) : Ultra-sound features of disseminated adenonomucinosis (pseudomyxoma).

Bury et al. (1997) : Clear cell sarcoma of the pleura in a woman aged 30 - irregular circumferential pleural thickening, also around the mediastinum shown by CT - she had RT + radical surgery.
Jawahar et al. (1997) : Primary biphasic (both epithelial and spindle cells at microscopy) synovial sarcoma of the pleura - a rare tumour similar synoviomas of joints. Female aged 18 with large mass in R pleural cavity - CT showed it to be heterogenous. It was resected, but she had a recurrence at 5 months which was also removed.

Pleural encasement due to benign causes.

This may also be due to benign causes especially TB, empyema, fungus infections, asbestos, talc, fibrosing lung conditions (DLE, rheumatoid, ankylosing spondylitis), polyserositis, sarcoid and uraemic.

Reference.

Buchanan et al. (1988) : Cryptogenic bilateral fibrosing pleuritis.

Pleural (and chest wall) invasion by lung tumours (see also ps. 12.5 - 6 & 14.26 and Illus. **CA EXT CX WALL**).

Once the pleura has become involved, a pleural effusion is likely to develop, especially if there is venous or lymphatic obstruction to the underlying lung. However pleural effusions are not always due to tumours per se, and may arise as a result of secondary infection, infarction, pleural irritation or lymphatic obstruction. Sometimes little or no fluid is formed, and a 'dry pleurisy' results. Only a small amount of fluid is necessary for diagnostic aspiration to be carried out, and with only a few ml a small sample is easily obtained under ultrasound control (**in   expiration**) for cytology. This only takes a few moments, and in the author's view such sampling should be mandatory if fluid is present as it saves much time and effort, because if positive the patient is clearly inoperable. Blood staining of the fluid is itself suggestive of malignant involvement.

Whilst locating fluid with ultrasound, it is also worthwhile to check for fixity of the lung to the chest wall by noting respiratory movement - this can also be noted with insp/exp. films (p. 12.20).

Moving pleural surfaces pose a natural partial barrier to tumour crossing into the chest wall or adjacent lobe. However, when the pleura has become obliterated or adherent, a tumour may spread into the chest wall, an adjacent lobe or the mediastinum, without any significant pleural reaction. When the chest wall is invaded, or there is a 'dry pleurisy' the patient often experiences severe pain. Rib destruction, adjacent to a lung mass or from metastases, may be obvious on plain radiographs or Bucky views, and masses due to secondary deposits may give rise to the 'pleural coiffe' (see p. 14.1). In less clear-cut cases, isotope bone scans may show positive lesions (but always beware of non-malignant causes - cough or other fractures, Paget's disease, etc).

CT may be invaluable for demonstrating soft tissue masses in the chest wall, but bone erosion may sometimes be less readily seen than on plain radiographs. CT suffers from the disadvantage that only a part of a rib may be imaged on a given section, and erosion be either mimicked or not demonstrated. Ribs curve and are therefore only partly imaged on a given section, but the spine (and sternum) are more completely sectioned, and erosions of these are more easily noted. Soft tissue masses, surrounded by fat, are usually readily apparent, but tumour invasion of fat is less readily appreciated - it sometimes has a '**dirty fat**' appearance (see below). Simply noting that a '**fat-plane**' is less obvious, or is partly obliterated, is not a specific sign of tumour invasion. Other signs, which have been suggested, e.g. the **angle formed between a tumour and the pleura**, the **length of contact of a tumour with adjacent pleural surfaces**, **pleural thickening per se**, or the **integrity of extra-pleural fat** are **suggestive** signs of pleural or trans-pleural spread, but are in themselves uncertain and non-specific.

Glazer et al. (1985) studied 45 patients with peripheral bronchogenic tumours which extended to the pleural surface of the lung by CT. They analysed the angle and amount of contact the tumour had with the adjacent pleural surface, associated pleural thickening, the presence of a fat plane between the tumour and the chest wall, rib destruction and the presence of a mass in the chest wall. They found that CT was of limited value in separating those patients who had parietal pleural and possible extension into the chest wall, from those who did not. Helpful signs were an obtuse angle, > 3 cm of pleural contact and associated pleural thickening. A clear fat plane in the chest wall was a useful indicator of non-involvement, whilst bone erosion clearly showed it. Chest wall pain was about 95% specific, but not all bony deposits caused it.

The author has noted that tumours not uncommonly spread into the chest wall without causing rib erosion; often the spread appears to take place **around the ribs.** This may often be demonstrated by CT, as invaded thickened '**dirty fat**' (see above) together with soft tissue swelling , which may displace the adjacent pleura inwards. When tumour surrounds ribs in this way, there is often sufficient periosteal infiltration to give rise to a positive bone scan (Illus. **CA EXT CX WALL, Pt. 4a-b**), though in other cases it may be negative. In other cases frank bone erosion will lead to obviously positive bone scans (Illus. **CA EXT CX WALL**, **Bone scan Pt. 20**), and sometimes negative areas when the bone has been totally destroyed within that area. These signs may be seen with lung tumours, mesotheliomas and secondary tumours which have spread into the chest wall. Sclerotic, as well as lytic bony lesions, may occasionally be found with lung tumours. Adenocarcinomas, bronchiolo-alveolar cell carcinomas, and metastasising carcinoids may give rise to **sclerotic bony deposits**.

In differentiating a metastatic tuberculous or other chest wall abscess from a tumour deposit, a useful point to remember is that such abscesses are often painless, whereas tumour deposits most commonly cause severe pain. Occasionally TB abscesses are still seen particularly in immigrants, and these may mimic rib tumours, breast tumours, etc.

Further references.
Harwood et al. (1975) : Pseudo-mesotheliomatous carcinoma of the lung - a variant of peripheral lung cancer.
Chernow and Sahn (1977) : Carcinomatous involvement of the pleura - 96 patients.
Rigler (1977b) : Overview of diseases of the pleura.
Glazer H. et al. (1985b) : CT of pleural and chest wall invasion.
Pennes et al. (1985) : Limitations of CT evaluation of chest wall by lung cancer - studied 35 tumours adjacent to the pleura and found about a 40% accuracy for assessing chest wall invasion. The angle formed between a mass and the pleura was of low predictive value in assessing invasion, possibly because of previous benign pleural thickening. When pleural invasion was present, CT could not distinguish between visceral and parietal pleural invasion because these were often adherent.
Musset et al. (1986) : 5 patients with chest wall involvement studied by CT and MR.
Pearlberg et al. (1987) : Limitations of CT in chest wall invasion.
Haggar et al. (1987) : 19 patients studied with CT and MR - felt that MR could detect chest-wall invasion when CT findings were equivocal. Agreed that without the demonstration of bony erosion, CT findings were unreliable. They found MR to be particularly helpful at the lung apex.
Murata et al.(1994) : Chest wall and mediastinal invasion by lung cancer : evaluation with multisection expiratory dynamic CT - 15 cases - free movement of tumour along the peripheral or mediastinal pleura in 10, in 5 no movement or **fixed.**

Asbestos and asbestos related diseases.
   Asbestos is the generic name for hydrated fibrous inorganic silicates (particularly of magnesium). They are of two main groups :
(i) **Serpentines** (wavy or curled fibres); chrysotile (white) - $3MgO,2SiO,2H_2O$ (95% of world usage).
(ii) **Amphiboles** (straight needle-like fibres -especially iron silicates) -
crocidolite (blue - $Na_2O_2,Fe_2O_3, 3FeO,8SiO_2, H_2O$),
amosite (brown - $5.5FeO, 1.5MgO, 8SiO_2$),
anthophyllite ($7MgO, 8SiO_2, H_2O$),
tremolite ($2CaO, 5MgO,8SiO_2, H_2O$), and
actinolite ($2caO,4MgO,FeO,8SiO_2,H_2O$) with shorter fibres.
   Many patients are exposed to mixtures of different types of asbestos but the type of disease may to some extent be related to the types of fibre inhaled. Short thin chrysotile and anthophyllite fibres appear to show preferential drainage to the pleura, entering lymphatics and causing pleural fibroblastic proliferation, whilst crocidolite fibres tend to be retained in the lung producing fibrosis and asbestos bodies. Crocidolite also appears to be the principle fibre type which produces mesothelioma. Probably more than 99% of asbestos particles are expectorated and only the finest ($< 3\mu m$) pass down to the alveoli.
   Because asbestos is incombustible, heat, electrical and sound resistant, and has a high degree of flexibility, it has been extensively used in many industries - building construction, insulation of heat, electricity or sound, brake linings, ship building, moulded plastics, and some fire resistant textiles and paints. Exposure to asbestos fibres may occur not only in those actually engaged in the mining, transport, manufacture and application of asbestos, but also in those who come into contact with it later. These include people serving in the Royal Navy, shipbuilders and dockyard workers (warships used to contain much asbestos), RAF radar operators, pipe and boiler laggers, railway engineering workshop and carriage manufacturers and dismantlers, lab. workers using asbestos filters in pipettes, theatre stage workers (as a result of fire curtains, etc.), and paint and fire resistant clothing operatives and users - the list of occupations is almost protean. In addition workers in asbestos factories, or laggers, etc. have often taken much asbestos home, on their clothing or in their hair, and this has affected their spouses or families. Even workers in the neighbourhood of factories or quarries have been affected - to leeward of the prevailing wind in London and Liverpool - many more so in South Africa, Turkey and the USA, etc.
   Two well reported instances in the UK have been in the East End of London, and in Leeds. In the former, Newhouse and Thompson (1965) and Doniach et al. (1975) found exposure and mesotheliomas downwind from the factory not far from the London Hospital (see also p. 14.48). The author has also seen several people from that area who had lung fibrosis and/or marked calcified pleural plaque formations (e.g. Illus. **ASB LUNG FIBROSIS, Pt. 13**). A TV programme ('Alice - a fight for life' - BBC, 6 Dec. 1988) highlighted problems occurring around

an asbestos factory at Armley, near Leeds, where 29 deaths from mesothelioma were recorded in local residents, people passing through the area, etc. Several others were also affected. This instance was very distressing, as the firm concerned, a large well-known enterprise, apparently suppressed information regarding the development of mesothelioma and cancer for commercial reasons. They apparently had information that the death rate in their workers was ten times that in the general population, and also that 80% of mice inhaling asbestos fibres developed cancer. These figures were later reported by Doll (1955). Sider et al. (1987) found that 10% of spouses had pleural plaques or calcification.

The author found that even in Oxford hardly a month passed without a new case of mesothelioma presenting. Sometimes two or three cases are seen within a few days.

Davies, D. (1984) posed the question 'are all mesotheliomas due to asbestos?' He pointed out that in most cases exposure has been heavy, but in others light. Most lungs contain asbestos fibres, and in Liverpool 30% of controls contained > 20,000 fibres/g. of dried lung (the same number as in most mesothelioma patients), and very few contained none.

Although commercial exploitation of asbestos began in 1880, some mesotheliomas were diagnosed before that time. The interval between exposure and the development of mesothelioma is long. In gas mask workers, who had well defined exposure between 1939 and 1944, the first tumours appeared in 1963, with an interval range from 20 to > 30 years. In South Africa, in areas where pollution with crocidolite has been heavy, mesothelioma rarely develops before adult life.

Rogers et al. (1991) studied mesotheliomas and asbestos exposure in Australia, which has a high incidence. About two thirds of the victims were exposed to blue asbestos (crocidolite) in mining, manufacturing, ship building, power stations and railways. Some had been exposed only to chrysotile (white asbestos), but many lung samples contained fibres of blue, white and brown asbestos. They concluded that the risk of developing mesothelioma is related to the degree of exposure, and for each ten-fold increase in fibre concentration in the lung, the risk increases approximately 30 for blue asbestos, 16 times for white and twice for brown. They also noted that white asbestos (chrysotile) is cleared more quickly from the lungs.

Kamp and Weitzman (1999) - the molecular basis of asbestos induced lung injury - genotoxic agent which can induce DNA damage, gene transcription and protein expression in modulating cell proliferation, cell death and inflammation - free radicals especially iron-catalysed reactive oxygen species may play an important role.

Table 14.1   Main Effects of Asbestos.

Time : most effects are delayed, but **pleural effusions** may occur soon after inhalation or be recurrent and may lead to **diffuse pleural thickening**.

Fibres : sharp glass-like jagged fibres (like '**javelins**') are inhaled - most are expectorated, but some are phagocytosed in the lungs, whilst other travel through the bronchi, small air-passages and alveoli, under the influence of repeated inspirations, to reach the pleura and chest wall (see also p. 14.38). Where they hit bone or thick fibrous tissue, **pleural plaques** may be produced, but when they pass into the soft tissues of the chest wall (muscle, etc. they disappear).

Pleural effusions may be **acute, or delayed and recurrent**. Traction on the visceral pleura, and fibrous thickening leads to '**rounded collapse**' or '**whorled nodules**' in the underlying lung.

Lung changes include the '**white line**' between the lung cortex and medulla, fibrosis, honeycombing and tiny nodules, as well as '**rounded collapse**' or '**whorled nodules**'.

Parenchymal (or **trans-pulmonary peripheral 'radiating bands'**) may be due to pleural thickening in accessory fissures.

Development of neoplasm - lung cancer, or
                                           - malignant mesothelioma (usually after a latent period of 20 - 30 years - most die within a year of diagnosis).

Potentiation by smoking - lung nodules and lung cancer.

Whilst many people who develop **mesotheliomas** have other stigmata of asbestos exposure e.g. plaques, **some have only minimal changes**, even on HRCT examinations.

Pericardial disease is much less common than pleural, but is analogous to pleural disease with effusions, thickening, calcification, constrictive pericarditis and mesothelioma.

Peritoneal thickening with mesothelioma may also occur.

Lung changes due to the inhalation of asbestos fibres - (Illus. **ASB LUNG FIBROSIS**).

Lung changes start with an intra-alveolar reaction to entrapped asbestos particles. Within the alveoli, the particles become surrounded by macrophages. They are coated by protein, some of which becomes impregnated with haemosiderin (perhaps due to minute haemorrhages) to form **ferruginous bodies**, which stain with Prussian blue. There is also an inflammatory reaction with giant cells, histiocytes and fibrosis, which not only destroys the inhaled particles, but also damages the lungs. Some of the changes may in part be due to a hypersensitivity phenomenon. Small fibrotic intra-pulmonary nodules may be produced (either solitary, or multiple) as well as fine linear shadows, thickened inter-lobular septa and honeycombing. Progression to a coarser fibrosis, bronchiectasis and cystic change may be seen. Lung neoplasm may occur, but may be difficult to detect if the lung is very fibrotic. Occasionally small asbestos fibres are seen.

(a)   (b)

Fig. 14.16 Asbestos fibres - (a) **Particles** looking like minute javelins - 3μ to 100μ long.
(b) **Asbestos bodies** are often coated with protein and iron deposits, before being phagocytosed. The coated bodies are often termed 'ferritin granules', and when they become fibrotic 'ferruginous bodies' - similar bodies may also be produced by other fibres such as silicon carbide, talc and glass fibre (Dunnill, 1982).

The earliest radiological lung changes are increased peripheral density, and thickened septa in the lung cortex. This is followed by the development of incomplete and slightly irregular '**white lines**' antero-laterally or postero-laterally in the subpleural part of the lung, just deep to the cortex (see Illus. **ASB WHITE LINE** and refs. to Goddard, Yoshimura, Pilate & Rémy-Jardin - ps. 14.39 - 40). These lines are often denser than the subpleural bands and lines seen in rheumatoid lung disease (Fig. 19.11, p. 19.84), scleroderma and fibrosing alveolitis and (Fig. 19.15, p. 19.117). They are frequently accompanied by honeycombs (usually much smaller than those seen in fibrosing alveolitis) which are most common in the lung cortex or deep to it. Thickening of the peripheral interlobular septa may give rise to parenchymal lines or bands, short linear densities, radiating inwards from the pleural surface. In addition thicker and longer radiating and more widely spaced lines may be seen (mainly posteriorly) which probably represent pleural thickening in small accessory fissures - '**trans-pulmonary bands**'. In addition 'whorled nodules' may occur.

High and low density lines within the lung appear to be related to the concept of the 'cortex' and 'medulla' (see ps. 1.43 - 46). The **white** or high density line lies 0.5 to 1 cm from the outer edge of the lung. It is often accompanied by small bullae or honeycombing, either within the outermost secondary lobules and /or deep to these.

A big problem is that lung changes are often obscured by pleural fluid, even on CT sections in the supine position; it is thus important to take others in the prone position as well, after resting in this position for a few minutes for the pleural fluid to be drained anteriorly.

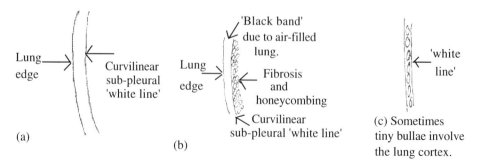

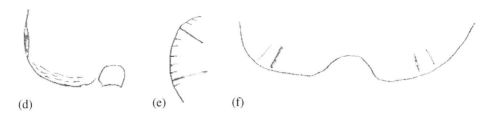

(d)   (e)   (f)

| subpleural increased pleural density | radiating 'parenchymal' or 'trans-pulmonary' bands - fibrotic bands in the lungs and ? thickening in accessory fissures - giving rise to the 'crows' feet' appearance - see also Fig. 14.23d (p.14.43). |

Fig. 14.17   Diagram showing some of the CT findings in asbestosis.
('Crow's foot' appearance is seen in Illus. **PARENCHYMAL BANDS, Plq-diaph Pt. 5b.**)

Some references.
Pooley (1975) : The identification of asbestos dust with an electron microscope microprobe analyser.
Morgan, A. and Homes (1980) : Concentrations and dimensions of coated and uncoated asbestos fibres in the human lung - the propensity for fibres to become coated to asbestos bodies varies with the dimension of the fibres and between individuals.

Pleural plaques - (Illus. **ASB PLEURAL PLQS**).
   Plaques are mainly **not** pleural but **subpleural** in relation to the parietal pleura. They are usually multiple and bilateral, but may be multiple and unilateral, or occasionally single. They are discontinuous fibrous or calcified patches, which mainly occur close to the more rigid parts of the chest wall, over the inner aspect of the ribs, spine, costal cartilages and adjacent sternum (for appearances see Fig. 14.18) and over the central tendinous parts of the dome of the diaphragm, where when they are calcified may produce an appearance like '**sugar icing on a cake**' (see p. 14.36). They may also be found anteriorly in the upper part of the chest, and overlying the aorta or the pericardium, but are virtually never found at the lung apices nor in the costo-phrenic angles. They may **occasionally be found within pleural fissures**, where they may mimic intra-fissural fat and may calcify (Illus. **PL-PLQ FISS ASB**). The **postero-lateral aspect of the pleura in the middle portion of the thorax and over the diaphragm appear to be the commonest places to find plaques**. Occasionally real (or apparent) periosteal reaction on the inner and lower aspect of the adjacent ribs may be seen.
   If a patient with plaques develops a spontaneous pneumothorax, the parietal pleural distribution may well be demonstrated (Illus. **ASB LUNG FIBROSIS, Pt. 10a**). The parietal distribution is also well seen at thoracotomy and autopsy.
   Pleural plaques are usually asymptomatic. Many are hyaline in consistency, whilst others are partially or more completely calcified; many have strips of adjacent pleural thickening. They occur mainly antero- and postero-laterally.
   Other causes of pleural thickening mostly involve the costo-phrenic angles, which are usually spared in asbestosis.

Pathology and radiology of pleural plaques.
   These largely consist of fibro-hyaline connective tissue. Some are densely calcified, especially in their central portions. Microscopically they are mainly cellular, with thick bundles of collagen separated by pseudo-lacunae. They are often covered by small nodules of collagen in which fibres are arranged concentrically like onion rings. The few cells present within them are largely fibroblasts. Asbestos bodies within them are difficult to detect, but according to Le Bouffant et al. (1973) may be found in large numbers, particularly in the calcified zones, if calcium deposits and collagen have been largely dissolved away. (They quote 30 - 40 x 10^6 in calcified areas, compared with 3 - 6 x 10^6 in the fibrous zones).

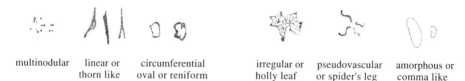

| multinodular | linear or thorn like | circumferential oval or reniform | | irregular or holly leaf | pseudovascular or spider's leg | amorphous or comma like |

Fig. 14.18   Patterns of pleural plaque calcification - after Fletcher and Edge (1970) with permission from Clinical Radiology.   Note that the circumferential type may simulate pulmonary nodules (see also Illus. **ASB PLEURAL PLQS, Pt. 24a-e**).

Slightly oblique views may sometimes be better than straight PA views for showing plaques, since a little obliquity will tend to make rather invisible plaques more 'end on' and thus be more readily seen. Such views will also help to differentiate plaques from the origins of the serratus anterior and external oblique muscles (see p. 12.16), fatty masses, intra-pulmonary nodules and other structures noted below. They may also avoid the necessity for CT.

On oblique views and CT sections, the dense calcification is often shown to be more patchy.

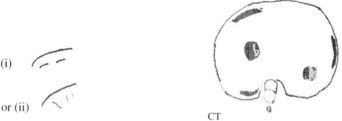

(i)

or (ii)

CT

Also with oblique views [(i) or (ii)] or on CT sections the superimposition of various plaques is removed, some being anterior, some central and others posterior or lateral.

Occasionally pleural plaques may fuse or become confluent to form calcified sheets and parietal pleural thickening, or give rise to an exudative reaction with pain and/or dyspnoea, but mainly they are asymptomatic.

In gross cases calcification in pleural plaques on the superior surface of the diaphragm may give rise to the '**sugar icing sign**' (like icing on a wedding, Christmas or birthday cake) as seen on plain chest radiographs (Illus. **ASB PLEURAL PLQS, Plq.-diaph Pt. 1** and **DIAPHRAGM-PLAQUES**). Pericardial plaques may also become calcified.

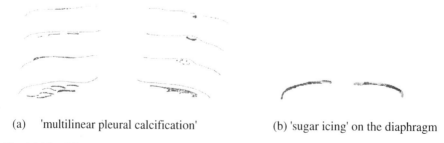

(a)   'multilinear pleural calcification'   (b) 'sugar icing' on the diaphragm

Fig. 14.19   Linear patterns of pleural and diaphragmatic calcification.
(a) after Fletcher and Edge (1970) which they considered to be 'very characteristic'.

Plaques should be distinguished from :
(a) subpleural fat, which tends to be more diffuse and less localised; thin fat collections are found even in thin subjects!,
(b) the transverse thoracic muscle anteriorly, serratus anterior and trapezius laterally,
(c) rib, pleural or muscular companion shadows, joining ribs or muscles, and seen mainly when ribs are sectioned obliquely on CT sections. The central part of a rib is most likely to be 'bare' and only covered by the thin 'pleural line' - such appearances usually being bilateral and symmetrical.
(d) intercostal veins, especially posteriorly,
(e) old healed rib fractures and spinal osteophytes,
(f) pseudoplaques.

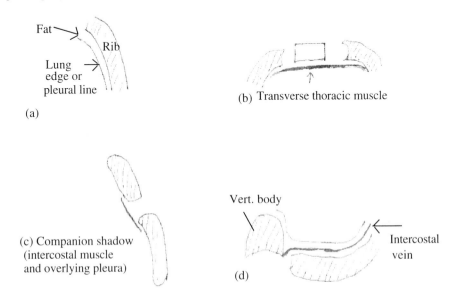

Fig. 14.20 Differential diagnosis of pleural plaques.

Pleural plaques, fat and 'hairy plaques'.
Often there is a thin layer of fat over the outermost surfaces of plaques, and this is seen by HRCT as a less dense line overlying the plaque.
Both high and low density lines may be found - the former ('white') due to the plaque itself, and a low (or black) density line immediately peripheral to this, and due to a thin layer of fatty tissue, perhaps enhanced by the Mach effect (see Appendices, p. 5), or in some cases just due to this.

Pleural plaques arise in or deep to the parietal pleura, often with a thin layer of fat deep to them. They may also push the adjacent outer lung border inwards and may cause a local reaction giving rise to the 'hairy plaque' appearance - see also Illus. **HAIRY PLAQUE**.

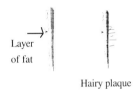

Fig. 14.21 Pleural plaque, fat and
'**HAIRY PLAQUE**' appearance.

CT of pleural plaques.

CT is excellent for demonstrating pleural plaques, in the parietal pleura, para-vertebrally and overlying the diaphragm, etc. They commonly indent the underlying lung and often have a thin layer of overlying fat, more adjacent to the chest wall. This layer may be visually enhanced by the Mach effect (Appendices, p. 5). Plaques may shown as tissue density (hyaline), or with varying amounts of calcification. In axial sections the calcified /noncalcified or fatty areas not uncommonly give rise to high density /low density lines. For their ideal demonstration, a good grey scale is required ('wide window') which will demonstrate both the chest wall and lung; this may also show adjacent "fuzziness" in the overlying lung (probably due to fibrosis) and causing the so-called **"hairy plaque"** - as shown in e.g. Illus. **ASB PLEURAL PLQS, Pl plqs Pt. 19b**.

CT also helps to distinguish plaques from the other structures noted above & in Fig. 14.20.

Im et al. (1989) used HRCT to study the posterior costal pleura in normal subjects, cadavers and persons who may have been exposed to asbestos. They found in normal subjects, a 1 to 2 mm thick line of soft tissue (the **'pleural line'**) at the point of contact between the lung and chest wall, representing the visceral and parietal pleura, pleural contents, endothoracic fascia and the innermost part of the intercostal muscle. They pointed out that paravertebrally there is no intercostal muscle, and the thin line here represents pleura and endothoracic fascia. Transverse muscle slips lie anteriorly, subcostal muscle slips inferiorly, and extrapleural fat pads posteriorly, where a thin layer of fat is usually thicker posteriorly than anteriorly - this lies internal to the ribs. When mild pleural thickening is present, the pleura is normally separated from the muscle by a thin layer of extra-pleural fat.

Normally intercostal muscle fibres do not extend in front of the paravertebral parts of a rib, but a thin layer of fat (a) or slips of the subcostal muscles (b) may do so in relation to the lowest ribs. These findings are usually symmetrical on either side.
(c) If only the edge of a rib (appearing thinner because of this) is sectioned, the muscle and pleura may appear to pass in front of the rib and mimic pleural thickening.
(d) Thickened pleura extends in front of the rib and is often separated from it by the thin layer of fat (and subcostal muscles at lowest levels).This is symmetrical on the two sides of the chest.

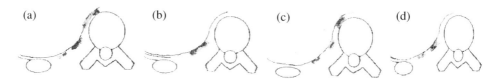

Fig. 14.22   Appearances of the costal pleura (reproduced from Im et al., 1989, Radiology, **171**, 125 - 131 with permission).

Why is the parietal pleura the seat of pleural disease in asbestosis?

The position of pleural plaques, which nearly always appear to lie on or in the parietal pleura, seems rather curious. Similarly, is the occasional case of asbestos pericarditis or pericardial mesothelioma. One might have expected both plaques and pleural tumours to arise on the visceral pleura, but this is very rare, except in the inter-lobar fissures. The reason for this paradox probably lies with the morphology and behaviour of asbestos particles, which on electron microscopy look like very fine javelins or wasp-stings (Fig. 14.16, p. 14.34). Inhaled particles, which are not expectorated or destroyed in the lungs appear to slowly progress with respiration through the lung towards the pleura, where they are eventually 'ground up', or 'stick' in the parietal pleura and adjacent chest wall, and stimulate the reaction. Radiography of autopsy specimens has shown that plaques may "originate against the inner surface of the rib, and extend with growth onto intercostal muscle" and pleura (Preger, 1978). He also noted the ease with which plaques may be stripped from ribs, despite their consistency akin to that of cartilage.

Such a mechanism (first postulated by Thomson, 1970) explains a number of phenomena (a) transitory pleural effusions, (b) the site of pleural plaque formation and thickening, and (c) the difficulty of finding asbestos particles in the plaques. A similar process seems likely with ingested asbestos particles, which pass through the intestinal wall to the peritoneum. A confirmatory study was by Hillerdal (1980) who found that radio-active labelled particles show a diffuse distribution in the lungs several days after administration, but after 100 days these are located subpleurally. Similar studies in rats by Brody et al. (1981) showed that the initial sites for the deposition of asbestos fibres were the respiratory bronchioles and the alveolar ducts. An earlier study with rats by Morgan et al. (1978) showed that asbestos fibres tend to concentrate subpleurally with time.

Others e.g. Rudd (1996) postulate that fibres may pass via the lymphatic system from the lung, through the lymphatic circulation to the intercostal and diaphragmatic lymph vessels to stimulate plaques - an exceptionally complicated and round-about route! Boutin et al. (1996) felt that asbestos fibres are taken up by Wang's stomas ('black spots' which absorb pleural fluid) on the parietal pleura.

At any rate plaques appear to be dose related and take 10-20 years to fully develop.

Other causes of pleural plaques and pseudoplaques.
These include the following :

> Previous **TB** or **fungus** infection.
> **Renal failure** and hyperparathyroidism.
> **Bird fancier's** and other fibrotic lung diseases e.g. **fibrosing alveolitis**.
> **Talc, arc-welders, carborundum, graphite, mica, erionite & glass-wool** (see also ps. 19.94 - 95).
> **Boxing** (see next section).
> Previous **radiotherapy** esp. for breast tumours or **lung infarction**.

The author has collected examples of plaques due to some of these causes (see Illus. **PL-PLQ NOT ASBESTOS**).

Pseudo-plaques.
These may be due to extrapleural fat, rib companion shadows, or secondary deposits in the chest wall or pleura. As already noted on p. 14.2 boxers may develop localised areas of extra-pleural thickening in relation to the ribs - especially in the mid-zones - presumably as a result of repeated chest wall trauma (haemorrhages into fat, etc) - the author collected several cases in the mid 1960s (together with Dr. I.M. Phalke, later in Swindon), and has subsequently examined some cases with CT (Illus. **BOXER**). A similar case has been shown to the Association of Chest Radiologists by Dr. John Latham of Norwich. (Both Drs. Phalke and Latham were formerly Senior Registrars to the author).

Some references.
Hourihane et al. (1966) : Tuberculous pleural plaques identical to asbestos.
Bydder and Kreel (1981) : Pancreatitis causing pleural plaques.
Akira (1995) : Uncommon pneumoconioses - arc welders & graphite (see also ps. 19.94 - 95).

Ultrasound of asbestos related pleural plaques.
Morgan et al. (1991) noted that pleural plaques can often be imaged with ultrasound. Working in Plymouth, Devon, they encounter many people who have been exposed to asbestos in the Royal Naval Dockyards, and not uncommonly find pleural plaques with ultrasound when examining the chest. liver and spleen. They found non-calcified plaques to be hypoechogenic, well-defined, and elliptical in shape with lengths of 2 to 18 cm in length and 5 to 12 mm thick. Calcified plaques had echogenic and irregular anterior margins with acoustic shadowing beyond, and were associated with a characteristic 'comet tail' and 'straight line' artefact. (A 3 MHZ probe was used for examining diaphragmatic plaques and a 5 MHZ probe for costal areas via the intercostal spaces).

Plaques and malignancy.
Although plaques themselves do not appear to be pre-malignant, they are signs of previous asbestos exposure (in most cases) and hence the patients may have an increased risk of developing bronchial carcinoma (see p. 24.2) and mesotheliomas. Plaques are found on CT in many patients with mesotheliomas, or with pleural effusions associated with asbestosis, but about 10 to 30% of those with mesotheliomas have none or only minimal plaque formations. This has led some to

wonder if gross plaque formation, or a generally thickened pleura protects against the development of a mesothelioma. However it seems that the likelihood of developing a tumour is probably related to the amount of asbestos inhaled rather than the presence of plaques.

Pleural effusions and diffuse pleural thickening due to asbestos.
  Pleural effusions due to asbestos exposure may occur:
(a) **Soon after the exposure** - these are usually transitory, but may lead to pleural thickening, calcification and plaque formation.
(b) **Months or years after the exposure**, waxing or waning or being recurrent. They may be unilateral or bilateral, and are usually exudative, and can be blood-stained. The author has investigated patients with effusions which have only become evident clinically eight to fifteen or more years after exposure to asbestos- e.g. Illus. **ASB PLEURISY, whorled nods Pt. 4a-e**.
  The recurrent cases seem particularly prone to cause **pleural   thickening** and 'rounded nodules'. The thickening may cause the lung on the affected side to become encased within a thick pleural coat, which in some cases may only relieved by surgical decortication. This severe reaction may develop over a period of a few months, and lead to **severe   disability   and   pain**. Such an exudative reaction involves both the parietal and visceral pleura, and also the cortex of the lung. It may occur after an effusion on one side, to be followed later by contralateral involvement. The condition can lead to compensation - see p. 14.46.
McLoud et al. (1985) felt that such a reaction is most likely caused by residues of past asbestos induced pleural effusions, rather than the more commonly held explanation of pulmonary fibrosis extending into the pleura.
(c) In response to the development of a **mesothelioma**. Such an effusion may become very thick and 'jelly-like' and be difficult to aspirate. Nodules or masses are often present within the fluid (see further discussion of mesotheliomas on ps. 14.44 et seq.).

Further references.
Paul Goddard (from Bristol) appears to have been the first to note the **subpleural   white   line**. He spoke about it in Bristol in 1979, and at the Thoracic Society in 1980. His MD thesis on 'CT of the Lung' (1982) noted this finding in three cases as "a narrow band of increased density around the outer part of the lung, but just in the lung field, being separated from the thoracic wall by a line of low density pixels of the same EMI value as the lung parenchyma." He illustrated a case, in which it was constant on re-examination, and thought that it probably represented subpleural fibrosis. It was also seen in patients with a central pattern of emphysema. He felt that the line was a very genuine phenomenon, with a darker line peripheral to it (Goddard, 1987b).

Craighead (1982) : Found that the subpleural parenchyma of the lower lobes to be the initial site of industrial fibrosis in asbestosis.
Yoshimura et al. (1986) : Studied 19 patients with asbestosis using thin section CT (1.5 mm thick with bone detail reconstruction using an IGE 8800 apparatus) and noted a pulmonary subpleural thin curvilinear shadow in 15, extending from the mid to the lower lung. It appeared to be a planar shadow and was about 0.5 cm from the outer aspect of the lung, occasionally deeper, but never more than 1 cm. It was seen particularly laterally and posteriorly. In one case which had post-mortem correlation they thought that the white line was associated with   the initial change of fibrosing bronchiolo-alveolitis, characteristic of pulmonary asbestosis.
Pilate et al. (1987) : CT study of subpleural curvilinear shadow in pulmonary asbestosis.
Friedman et al. (1988) : Comparison of CT and chest radiography in the recognition of asbestos-related pleural disease and asbestosis - CT shows subtle changes more readily and also differentiates subpleural fat from asbestos-related pleural disease.
Lynch et al. (1988) : Studied 260 asbestos-exposed individuals by conventional and HRCT and found 43 unsuspected asbestos-related focal lung masses in 27. These included fissural pleural plaques, dense fibrotic bands, rounded nodules, and other benign masses. Three carcinomas were also found. They felt that with most lesions, close surveillance could obviate the need for biopsy.
Aberle et al. (1988 & 1989) : Used HRCT to study benign asbestos-related diseases. They examined patients in both supine and prone positions to avoid dependent oedema and vascularity alterations with gravity and found :
(i) **Curvilinear subpleural lines** - linear densities within 1 cm of the pleural surface and parallel to it,
(ii) **Parenchymal bands** - linear densities, 2 to 5 cm long - these usually contacted the pleural surface and were distinguishable from pulmonary blood vessels in that they were thicker, did not taper peripherally, and often were oriented in a direction incompatible with normal vessels,
(iii) **Thickened   interstitial   short   lines** in the subpleural parenchyma, which represent thickened septa and interstitial lines,

(iv) **Subpleural dependent density** - bands 2 to 30 mm thick of poorly marginated increased lung density, paralleling the dependent pleura, and obscuring the underlying lung pathology,

(v) **Honeycombing** - cyst-like spaces - 1 cm in diameter with thickened walls,

(vi) **Pleural plaques**.

Akira et al. (1990) : HRCT - pathological correlation changes of asbestosis - studied 7 lungs removed at autopsy and inflated , fixed and air-dried. They described:

(a) **Thickened intra-lobular lines** (histologically peribronchial fibrosis),

(b) **Thickened inter-lobular lines** (due to inter-lobular fibrotic thickening or oedema),

(c) **Pleural based opacities** } (due to peribronchial fibrosis, most severe in the subpleural areas and extend-

(d) **Parenchymal fibrous bands**} ing proximally along the bronchovascular sheath to create band-like lesions).

(e) **Subpleural curvilinear shadows**,

(f) **A ground-glass appearance** (due to mild alveolar wall and intra-lobular septal thickening due to fibrosis or oedema).

(g) **Traction bronchiectasis**, and

(h) **Honeycombing**.

Their studies suggested that the early parenchymal changes seen on HRCT sections are 'subpleural dot-like structures connected to the most peripheral branch of the pulmonary artery, and that these dots increase in number to create a reticulonodular appearance on serial HRCT scans'.

Akira et al. (1991) : Serial CT studies showed progression of disease in 50% of studied cases. The subpleural curvilinear opacity probably represents an early stage of asbestosis and precedes honeycombing.

Gamsu et al. (1995) : The likelihood of interstitial disease being detected by HRCT and having functional significance is often related to the severity of the disease. HRCT studies are usually assessed subjectively. These authors used (a) a semiquantitative scoring method and (b) a cumulation of the HRCT abnormalities found (interstitial lines, parenchymal bands, **architectural distortion of the secondary pulmonary lobules**, subpleural lines and honeycombing). They found that a combination of the cumulative number of the different findings and an assessment of the extent and severity of the abnormalities could be complementary, and that asbestosis can be present histologically with a normal or near normal HRCT scan.

Rémy-Jardin (1998) : Considered that subpleural white lines may be due to compression on the lung.

Peacock et al. (2000) : Asbestos related benign pleural disease - review.

Interlobar plaques, etc.

Hillerdal (1981) : Non-malignant asbestos pleural disease.

Sargent et al. (1981) : Calcified interlobar pleural plaques - visceral involvement due to asbestos.

Webb et al. (1983) : Interlobar pleural plaque mimicking a lung nodule.

Rockoff (1987) : CT demonstration of interlobar calcification due to asbestos exposure.

Armstrong et al. (1990) : Illustration of interlobar plaque.

Gale and Grief (1986) : Intrafissural fat - CT correlation with chest radiography.

Plaques and malignancy.

Edge (1979) : Incidence of bronchial carcinoma in shipyard workers with pleural plaques.

Lilis et al. (1987) : Non-malignant chest x-ray changes in asbestos insulation workers with mesothelioma.

Weiss (1993) : Asbestos-related pleural plaques and lung cancer.

Rudd (1996) : New developments in asbestos-related pleural disease.

Wilkinson et al. (1995) : Is lung cancer associated with asbestos exposure when there are no small opacities on the chest radiograph? - **yes!**

Asbestos pleural effusions

Gaensler and Kaplan (1971) : Asbestos pleural effusion.

Epler et al. (1982) : Prevalence and incidence of benign asbestos pleural effusion in a working population.

Hillerdal and Ozesmi (1987) : Benign asbestos pleural effusion - 73 exudates in 60 patients.

Lilis et al. (1988) : Symptomatic benign pleural effusions among insulation workers.

Friedman et al. (1990) : Benign effusions usually may be observed during exposure or with the first 10 years after exposure has ceased, however latency may be as long as 30 to 58 years, overlapping that of mesothelioma'.

Leung et al. (1990) : CT in the differential diagnosis of diffuse pleural disease - review of 74 cases - 39 malignant and 35 benign. Helpful features were : **Circumferential pleural thickening** or **'RIND'** (see ps. 14.20, 14.24 & 14.44), **nodular pleural thickening**, parietal **pleural thickening** > 1 cm. and **mediastinal pleural involvement**. Not helpful : Loss of volume.

Miller, A. (1990) : Chronic pleural pain in four patients with asbestos induced pleural fibrosis.

Rudd (1996) : Diffuse pleural thickening is a more serious consequence of exposure to asbestos than benign pleural plaques, and often first appears as a sequel to benign pleural effusion.

Specificity of findings due to asbestos.

Gaensler et al. (1991) : Idiopathic pulmonary fibrosis in asbestos exposed workers is not always due to this cause! A problem is that at histology asbestos bodies may be few in number and are only present when exposure has been reasonably high.

Bergin et al. (1994) : Specificity of HRCT findings in pulmonary asbestosis - do patients scanned for other indications have similar findings? Found that subpleural curvilinear densities, subpleural density in dependent locations, parenchymal bands and thickened septal lines occur with conditions other than asbestosis and do not necessarily indicate the presence of asbestosis, even in the presence of plaques.

Lynch (1995) : Commented on the study by Gamsu et al. (above) and noted that for the asbestos-exposed person, CT is less sensitive and specific than pathological evaluation. It is also useful for the evaluation of masses, pleural plaques, emphysema, and for confirming unequivocal asbestosis, but the borderline between normal and abnormal is not always sharply defined.

Hansell (1995) : Specificity of imaging in asbestos exposure - experience has shown that some HRCT features, originally described as being specific for asbestosis are seen in other conditions and in a few normal individuals.

'Whorled nodule' (also termed 'rounded collapse', 'folded lung syndrome', 'pulmonary pseudo-tumour' or 'trapped lung' - Illus. **ASB WHORLED NODS** and Illus. **WHORLED NODULES**).

Sometimes following chest infection, localised pleurisy (especially associated with asbestos, but occasionally after injury leading to a haemothorax, or following an empyema), the pleura may become infolded into the adjacent lung to give a '**whorled nodule**' appearance. This occurs particularly at the base of the chest posteriorly, in the posterior basic segment or the apex of a lower lobe, and gives rise to a mass which at first sight may resemble a lung neoplasm. The whorled appearance of the nodule on tomography (including CT) and the **curling** around it of the peripheral bronchi and vessels are characteristic and give rise to the '**comet tail sign**' (Schneider et al., 1980).

The condition is not rare, but has been recognised as a localised pleurisy, or mistaken for neoplasm. It may also be mistaken for a mesothelioma, or vice versa. Occasionally it is bilateral, and may occur in the right middle lobe, the lingula or on the inferior surface of a lower lobe (Illus. **ASB WHORLED NODS, Pts. 1, 4a-d**). The whorled nodules may well start with pleural thickening in small accessory fissures, with a much more dense reaction than occurs with '**trans-pulmonary bands**' (see p. 14.35).

The phenomenon is not new, having previously been seen with tuberculous pleural effusions, empyemas, calcified pleural thickening, pneumothoraces, etc. It was first noted by Loeschke in 1928. Galy (1955) from Belgium, Roche et al. (1956), and Roche and Rousselin (1957) from France, and Amschler (1958) from Germany found the appearance in patients having artificial pneumothorax treatment for tuberculosis. Blesovsky (1966) in the UK described three cases, probably due to asbestos. Hanke (1971) described 50 cases and suggested that '**rounded collapse**' starts with a pleural effusion, leading to an area of collapse, within a part of the compressed lobe. The collapsed lung tissue floats within the effusion and is tilted upwards or downwards when the fluid diminishes. This tilted and collapsed lung tissue becomes engulfed by the surrounding visceral pleura of the remainder of the re-expanded lobe producing a mass folded around thickened pleural indentations, the folding causing the vessels and bronchi to curve.

The author has seen many cases due to asbestos exposure, whilst others have followed **trauma**, **cardiac or lung infarction** or **infection**. Some also occur postoperatively with Dressler's syndrome (p. 15.24), coronary artery by-pass surgery, heart transplantation, uraemia, etc. i.e. some form of pleuritis with visceral pleural fibrosis leads to the appearance.

CT is particularly useful for showing the pleural-based masses, with circling or converging bronchi and vessels (Illus. **ASB WHORLED NODS, Pt. 17c & 18b**), thus helping to differentiate them from neoplasm, loculated fluid or a pleural fibrin ball. Sinner (1980) termed this the '**vacuum cleaner sign**'. Adjacent lung disease, such as bullae, emphysema or scarring are not uncommon. Pleural plaques and other areas of pleural thickening are common in those cases secondary to asbestos.

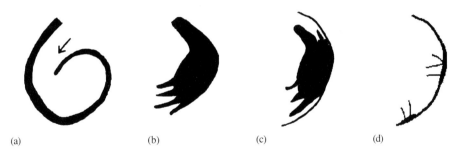

(a)   (b)   (c)   (d)

Fig. 14.23   Methods of formation and appearances of a 'whorled nodule' and 'crows' feet'.
(a) Infolding or curved invagination of the pleura.
(b) A curved 'whorled nodule' within the periphery of the lung.
(c) 'Crab on its side' appearance + localised pleural thickening (after Glass et al., 1983).
(d) 'Crows' feet' - localised pleural thickening and thickened intrapulmonary bands (see p. 14.35).

Whorled nodules should be kept under review, since they may occasionally be associated with neoplasm. Coleman et al. (1985) reported an 80 year old man who developed a lung tumour (nonenhancing with IV contrast at CT), within a whorled nodule. The author has also seen a whorled nodule in the early stage of a mesothelioma. Other associations with neoplasm have been noted by Greyson-Fleg (1985), Leone et al. (1986), Munden and Libshitz (1998) and Ng et al, (1999).

When whorled nodules are resected fibrous tissue is usually found. Further studies after surgery often show that the radiographic picture is similar to that seen preoperatively, i.e. the results of the fibrotic process are still present, and the rounded nodule may be replaced by an organising haematoma.

Occasionally whorled nodules contain small areas of calcification.

Whorled nodules may appear on the posterior or inferior surfaces of the lungs, or occasionally adjacent to an inter-lobar fissure, when they may become centrally retracted. They are almost always associated with some pleural thickening and some adjacent fibrosis.

Examples of non-asbestos round or '**whorled   nodules**' are shown in Illus. **WHORLED NODULES, Pts. 21 - 27.** Illus. **WHORLED NODULES, Pt. 21a-d** shows a 'whorled nodule' secondary to a chronic empyema, Illus. **WHORLED NODULES, Pt. 22** a whorled nodule secondary to an eosinophilic effusion, Illus. **WHORLED NODULES, Pt. 23a-c** one secondary to trauma (a prison officer who had been beaten up), Illus. **WHORLED   NODULES, Pt. 25** a whorled nodule secondary to pneumonia and Illus. **WHORLED   NODULES, Pts. 24, 26 & 27** whorled nodules following pulmonary infarction.

Further references.
Bénard et al. (1973), Brune et al. (1974), Kretzschmar (1975) : 5 cases, Choffel et al. (1977), Hanke and Kretzschmar (1980) : 80 cases, Schneider et al. (1980) : 5 cases, Hillerdal and Hemmingson (1980) : 10 cases.
Payne et al. (1980) : Lung folding simulating peripheral pulmonary neoplasm.
Sinner (1980) : 55 cases, Cho et al. (1981), Hillerdal (1981) : 6 cases, Mintzer et al. (1981) : 11 cases.
Dernevik et al. (1982) : Shrinking pleuritis with collapse., Mintzer and Cugill (1982)
Stark (1982b) : Termed the nodules 'pseudotumours'.
Tylén and Nilsson (1982) : 12 cases., Glass et al. (1983), Grabowski (1983), Yamazaki (1982)
Doyle and Lawler (1984) : 3 cases demonstrated by CT, described eight major CT signs -
    (i) Rounded peripheral mass, incompletely surrounded by air-filled lung.
    (ii) A mass most dense at its periphery.
    (iii) Acute angle with the pleura.
    (iv) Pleural thickening.
    (v) Vessels and bronchi curving towards the mass.
    (vi) At least two sharp margins.
    (vii) Blurred centrally directed edge.
    (viii) Air-bronchogram.
Gefter et al. (1984) : Three cases.

Geremia and Mintzer (1984) : One case with two rounded nodules and associated with a pleural effusion - eventually cleared spontaneously - stated that a 'comet tail sign is a sine qua non'.

Glazer et al. (1984) ; 2 cases , Scott et al. (1984) : 6 cases (asbestos related pleural disease).

Smith, L. and Schillaci (1984) : Rounded collapse due to acute exudative effusion.

Greyson-Fleg (1985) : Lung biopsy.

Verschakelen et al. (1986) : Diagnosis on conventional radiology and CT., Woodring (1987)

Buchanan et al. (1988) : Cryptogenic bilateral fibrosing pleuritis.

Lynch et al. (1988) : Asbestos related focal lung masses - HRCT findings.

Ren et al. (1988) : 2.5 cm mass in man aged 68. Thought that these masses usually present as incidental findings.

Taylor (1988) : Dynamic contrast enhancement of asbestos-related pulmonary pseudotumours.

Hillerdal (1989) from Uppsala : 74 patients between 1970 and 1986 with rounded collapse - 64 had been exposed to asbestos. In 13 the rounded collapse was associated with slowly increasing pleural fibrosis, but in 39 it was a 'sudden finding', with earlier radiographs showing only plaques or being normal. Of the 10 not exposed to asbestos, 2 occurred after trauma and 4 following pleural effusions.

McHugh and Blaquiere (1989) from Southampton : Condition diagnosed in 12 men between 1981 and 1988. CT in 9. 4 had bilateral whorled nodules. Listed three criteria -

(i) a rounded or oval mass (3.5 to 7 cm in diameter) abutting a pleural surface in lung periphery,

(ii) vessels and bronchi curving into the mass and blurring the central margin, and

(iii) associated pleural thickening with or without calcification.

Verschakelen et al. (1989) : MR appearance - T₁ signal intensity similar to liver. Density higher than the density of adjacent pleural fluid, possibly caused by low-signal lines in the nodule, which were probably caused by thickened indentations of the visceral pleura.

Carvalho and Carr (1990) : CT of folded lung - 22 examples in 9 patients. Supported Buchanan et al. ? fibrosing pleuritis with contracture. Also calcification can occur within the nodules & they may abut calcified pleural plaques.

Stancato-Pasik et al. (1990) : Rounded collapse caused by histoplasmosis.

Szydlowski et al. (1992) : Rounded atelectasis - a pulmonary pseudotumour.

Cantoni et al. (1995) : MR showed curvature of vasculature and bronchi towards and into a whorled nodule in a similar fashion to that shown by CT + a **'kidney-like'** pattern with hypointense lines coverging towards the centre of the nodule, due to thickened indentations of visceral pleural enveloped within it.

Marchbank et al. (1995 & 1996) : US of 'folded lung' - "mass" adjacent to thickening of the pleural and extrapleural fat layers with a central echogenic line.

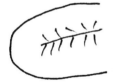

(a) MR - kidney-like pattern - hypointense lines converging to centre of mass.

(b) US - echogenic line ? due to infolded visceral pleura + hypoechoic centre of mass.

Batra et al. (1996) : Rounded collapse (review).

O'Donovan et al. (1997) : The presence of converging bronchovascular markings + localised pleural thickening, a pleural based mass, an indistinct central margin & indications of volume loss is strongly suggestive of rounded collapse.

Yamaguchi et al. (1997) : MR of rounded collapse.

Partrap (2000) : Comet tail sign.

Mesotheliomas - (Illus. **MESOTHELIOMA**).

Malignant pleural mesotheliomas are being seen much more frequently in the UK now, compared with 10 to 20 years ago. The increased incidence is also found in many other countries, and in some local areas (parts of South Africa, and Turkey) the incidence has almost reached epidemic proportions, carcinoma of the oesophagus apparently also occurring as a result of ingested asbestos. The Institute of Cancer Research in London estimates that the death rate for mesothelioma will soar from 1,010 in 1991 to almost 3,000 in 30 years time, i.e. the equivalent of one male death in every hundred (Times, 7 Jan. 1994).

Patients often present with pleural or chest wall pain, dyspnoea, cough, weight loss, pleural fluid or a mass. A pleural effusion and /or thickening, particularly with a **'knobbly'** outline (Illus.

MESOTHEL, Pts. 6b, 11, 16b & 25b), is very suggestive of a mesothelioma, but may also be seen with other malignant disease. Most patients have had exposure to asbestos and show other evidence of this with pleural plaques, chronic pleural thickening, lung fibrosis, etc. However in many cases pleural plaques are small and sparse, and are paradoxically often less marked than in those with severe benign disease. Pathological diagnosis may be difficult, but pleural fluid cytology or needle pleural biopsy may be positive. Some patients may need larger Tru-cut biopsies for certain diagnosis, but if possible open biopsy should be avoided, as this may allow tumour to spread into the chest wall, giving rise to a painful subcutaneous mass (**MESOTHEL, Pts. 6a-c, 9b, 42d &47c**).

Radiologically, a pleural mass, localised or more generalised thickening of these together with pleural fluid are found. The mass or pleural thickening may be extensive or small, diffuse or membranous surrounding a collection of fluid. Commonly the underlying lung is compressed, and the hemithorax reduced in size. The mediastinum often remains central, due to fixation by the disease process. Early in the clinical disease multiple tumour nodules may be found in the same pleural cavity, and with coalescence, these tend to become a thick irregular '**pleural rind**' (**MESOTHEL, Pts. 18b, 28, 32b, 45, 46 & 47b**) with contraction of the hemithorax (often a striking feature).

Invasion of the overlying or adjacent chest wall, including the ribs and sternum, is not uncommon, and may be shown by plain radiographs, CT or bone scans (**MESOTHEL, Pts. 2, 6, 9, 26 & 33**). Spread into the paravertebral gutter is also not uncommon, and adjacent bone involvement (sometimes on both sides) is often readily shown by bone scans (**MESOTHEL, Pt. 22e**). As already noted, spread into biopsy or thoracotomy tracks is not uncommon. Nodal enlargement, particularly of the internal mammary (**MESOTHEL, Pts. 17, 37 & 43**), cervical, supradiaphragmatic and retro-crural groups may be found, and sometimes also various mediastinal groups, where the enlargement may be massive. Nodal enlargement may also be mimicked by tumour masses abutting the mediastinum or extending into it. Tumour may encase the pericardium or extend through it to produce a malignant pericardial effusion. It may traverse the mediastinum and involve the contralateral pleural cavity. Both SVC and oesophageal obstruction may occur.

Occasionally small secondary deposits are seen in the ipsilateral or contralateral lung (**MESOTHEL, Pts. 27a-b**) - see also Uri et al., 1988) : this probably occurs via lymphatic permeation. Trans-diaphragmatic spread may also occur (**MESOTHEL, Pt. 16c**). Blood-borne metastases are uncommonly found during life, but are not uncommon at autopsy. They may be found in the liver (**MESOTHEL, Pt. 16e**), spleen, brain (**MESOTHEL, Pt. 16f**), lungs (**MESOTHEL, Pt. 27**) or bones (**MESOTHEL, Pts. 5c, 16g, 19k,l&m, 26a**). Deposits in the liver may contain calcification, and bone deposits may mimic myelomatosis (**MESOTHEL, Pts. 5 & 19**) or be sclerotic. Occasionally patients have HPOA (see p. 23.3).

Although others have suggested that plaques may be unusual in patients with mesotheliomas, the author usually finds one or two in virtually all cases. They should be carefully sought for, as they almost 'clinch' the diagnosis in patients presenting with an undiagnosed pleural effusion (see **MESOTHEL, Pts. 22, 26, 38, 40 & 46** - Pt. 22a-e shows a loculated mesothelioma + fluid at the left base, with collapse of the left lower lobe, containing a large mucocoele, and a calcified plaque on the upper surface of the diaphragm).

Ultrasound is invaluable for demonstrating the presence of fluid, pleural thickening, a pleural mass or masses, an irregular pleural border underlying the fluid, or nodules within it. It will also show the ideal site for paracentesis or biopsy. It can be used to detect enlarged internal mammary nodes (**MESOTHEL, Pts. 43d & e**).

CT is very useful for showing the extent of the tumour, its morphology, co-existing pleural plaques, calcification and lung changes associated with asbestosis. The affected hemithorax is often smaller, particularly when the tumour extends around and encases the underlying lung, giving rise to '**cancer en cuirasse**'. The fluid may be very viscous or loculated by adhesions, and then will not readily move with posture. A membranous type of tumour or one that is thicker (like orange peel) and may show '**rim enhancement**' with IV contrast medium (**MESOTHEL, Pt. 22**), similar to that seen with some empyemas. Occasionally calcification may be found within tumour masses (**MESOTHEL, Pts. 22 & 47c**). CT not uncommonly demonstrates multiple nodular pleural masses, internal mammary, retrocrural or hilar node enlargement, spread into the chest wall (and upper abdomen), with erosion of the ribs, sternum or spine. It may also show miliary spread in the lungs, contralateral hilar node enlargement, or more distal deposits in the liver, brain or skeleton (see **MESOTHEL, Pts. 16, 19, 37 & 43**).   Illus. **MESOTHEL, Pt. 42** shows a mesothelioma which has extended through the chest wall to produce a large mammary-mass.

CT may also demonstrate mesotheliomas within a pleural fissure (**MESOTHEL, Pts. 29 & 34**). Bhatt et al. (1984) reported one in an azygos fissure.

Mesotheliomas may also occur in other serous cavities - the pericardium and the abdomen, including the tunica vaginalis in males (see references and Illus. **MESOTHEL, Pt. 5** - a peritoneal mesothelioma). Illus. **MESOTHEL, Pericardium Pt. 28** - shows a pericardial mesothelioma - also under Illus. **MESOTHEL-PERITONEAL** or **-PERICARDIUM**.

Treatment.

Neither surgery, nor chemotherapy has much to offer. Radiotherapy and/chemotherapy are only marginally effective, but help to relieve pain, as may nerve blockage. Median survival time is 12 to 18 months from the onset of symptoms, but a few live longer.
Aspiration of fluid, which may be quite viscous and pleurodesis may relieve dyspnoea. Repeated aspiration of fluid may help to keep many patients active for many months (with the thickening that occurs, this is best carried out with ultrasound control, and the author has done very many of these aspirations, sometimes having to use a wide bore 'old-fashioned' trans-lumbar needle because of the very viscid fluid).

Pleuro-pneumonectomy (including removal of the ipsilateral hemidiaphragm) has been tried for 'early tumours' in some centres, but has been abandoned in most as impracticable as one cannot in practice remove the whole of the tumour in a block. Disability from the operation is considerable, and post-operative spread into the mediastinum, chest wall and abdomen is common, the last often occurring as a result of removal of the hemidiaphragm. Illus. **MESOTHELIOMA, Pericardium Pt. 29** shows a postoperative cardiac hernia in a young man following a left pleuro-pneumonectomy.

Pathology.

Mesotheliomas typically are **white**, well-defined firm or '**rubbery**' masses conforming to the shape of the pleural cavity. They may form localised pleural masses, be multiple or form a white knobbly 'rind' around the lung. They are typically avascular. Their consistency accounts for the difficulty of radiological biopsy.

Deposits may be found in the mediastinum, contra-lateral pleura, nodes (especially the internal mammary nodes), the lungs, liver, adrenals, bone marrow, etc. Intra-cranially, deposits occur in the brain and meninges, and may resemble meningeomas (see Illus. **MESOTHEL, Pt. 16f**).

A **staging** system was proposed by Butchart et al. (1976) - see reference under surgery below.

Compensation.

Patients (or their relatives after the patient's decease) may be able to claim compensation, either from the Government (under Industrial Injuries Benefit), or from employers or former employers (under civil litigation), and radiographs and CT studies may be important features in such claims.
The British Government's, Dept. of Social Security and Pneumoconiosis Board, recognises four 'conditions' to be caused by asbestos : (i) asbestos pneumoconiosis, (ii) bilateral diffuse pleural thickening, (iii) mesothelioma and (iv) carcinoma of the bronchus associated with (i) or (ii). 1988 figures were (i) 224, (ii) 117, (iii) 479 and (iv) 59.

Pleural plaques alone, being regarded as harmless and non-disabling are not a 'prescribed disease'. However many firms will pay a lump sum (often £1,000) in '**full and final settlement**' if plaques are found.

(A big problem that the author has encountered is that the Medical Officers of the DSS, have not seemed to have become conversant with CT, etc. findings, and tended to ignore these, preferring to rely on a 17 x 14 in PA film, with 'the patient's name recorded on it with white ink' !)

Further references.
Effects of asbestos.

Bridge and Henry (1928) : Industrial cancers.
Gloyne (1933) : Anatomy and histology of asbestosis plus first two reports of pleural and peritoneal mesotheliomas complicating asbestosis.
Gloyne (1936) : Oat cell cancer in asbestosis.
Smith, A. (1952): Pleural calcification resulting from exposure to certain dusts.
Jacob and Bohlig (1955) : First reported plaques of pleural calcification in an asbestos worker.
Kiviluto (1960) : Environmental exposure to asbestos - plaques in people living near two asbestos mines in Finland.
Wagner et al. (1960) : Diffuse pleural mesothelioma and asbestos exposure in North West Cape Province.
Doll (1955) : Mortality from ca lung in asbestos workers. Cordova et al (1962) : Asbestos & ca of the lung.
Newhouse and Thompson. (1965) : 56 pleural and 27 peritoneal mesotheliomas following exposure to asbestos in the London area.(see below p. 14. 48).
Hourihane et al. (1966) : Calcified and hyaline pleural plaques as an index of exposure to asbestos.
Anton (1967) : Multiple pleural plaques.
Collins (1968) : Pleural reaction associated with asbestos exposure.
Wagner et al. (1971) : Epidemiology of asbestos cancers.
Lawther (1971) : Asbestosis and allied diseases.
Whitwell and Rawcliffe (1971) : Diffuse pleural mesothelioma and asbestos exposure.
Fletcher (1972), Edge (1977 & 1979) and Edge and Choudhury (1978) : Found an increased incidence of lung cancer and mesothelioma in shipyard workers with pleural plaques in Barrow in Furness, Cumberland, compared with shipyard workers, without plaques.
Sargent et al. (1972) : Diaphragmatic pleural calcification after short exposure.
   (1977) : Pleural plaques - a signpost of asbestos dust inhalation.
   (1978) : Bilateral pleural thickening or plaques - manifestation of asbestos dust exposure.
   (1981) : Calcified inter-lobar pleural plaques.
Le Bouffant et al. (1973) : Structure and composition of pleural plaques.
Green and Dimcheff (1974) : Massive bilateral upper lobe fibrosis secondary to asbestos exposure.
Theros and Feigin (1977) : Pleural and pulmonary tumours - differential diagnosis,
Vix (1977) : Roentgenographic manifestations of pleural disease.
Hillerdal (1978) from Uppsala, Sweden : Frequency and development of pleural plaques and exposure to asbestos.
   (1981) : Studied 891 cases of non-malignant pleural disease and found - parietal pleural plaques, exudative pleurisy (22 cases), thickening of visceral pleura (in fissures) - a small group had asymptomatic pulmonary fibrosis.
   (1982) : Asbestos exposure and upper lobe involvement.
   (1983) : Malignant mesotheliomas - **review of 4,710 published** cases - three histological types - **epithelial, mesenchymal (or sarcomatoid) and mixed types**.
   (1990) : 1,600 people with pleural plaques seen in Uppsala over 15 years - 40 developed lesions mainly affecting the upper lobes - part of a diffuse pleural and parenchymal fibrosis involving the rest of the lung.
Rossiter et al. (1980) : Nine year follow up study of men exposed to asbestos in Devonport Royal Dockyard - the progression was greater in smokers than non-smokers - 30% had pulmonary fibrosis and 50% pleural plaques.
Craighead et al. (1982) : The pathology of asbestos-associated diseases of the lungs and pleural cavities - diagnostic criteria and proposed grading scheme.
Adams and Unni (1984) : Diffuse malignant pleural mesothelioma.
Adams et al. (1986) : Diagnosis of mesothelioma and survival in 92 cases.
Finkelstein and Vingilis (1984) from USA : Studied workers exposed to asbestos cement & found small irregular opacities & bilateral pleural thickening in 181. Men with abnormal radiographs had higher mortality rates.
McLoud et al. (1985) : Studied pleural disease in about 2,000 asbestos-exposed people - hyaline or calcified pleural plaques, and diffuse pleural thickening occurred with almost equal frequency (approx. 16.5 & 13.5% respectively).
Murphy (1986) : The diagnosis of non-malignant disease related to asbestos.
Oliver and Neville (1988) : Progressive apical pleural fibrosis - a "constrictive" ventilatory defect.
Friedman, A. et al. (1989) : Roentgenographic underestimation of early asbestosis.
Schwartz et al. (1990) : Asbestos-induced pleural fibrosis and impaired lung function.
Sheridan et al. (1990) : Mesothelioma - what relevance the contra-lateral pleura? The pleural changes of asbestos exposure are **uncommon** in patients with pleural mesotheliomas, half having a normal contra-lateral pleura. The low incidence of plaques may suggest that patients with typical bilateral plaques are less likely to develop mesothelioma than other asbestos exposed workers.
Solomon (1991) : Radiological features of asbestos-related visceral pleural changes.
Wilkinson et al. (1995) : Is lung cancer associated with asbestos exposure when there are no small opacities on the chest radiograph? The results suggest that asbestos is associated with lung cancer even in the absence of radiologically apparent pulmonary fibrosis.

McLoud (1992) : Conventional radiography in the diagnosis of asbestos-related disease.
Staples (1992) : CT in the evaluation of benign asbestos-related disorders.

CT & MR

Kreel (1976), Katz and Kreel (1979) : CT in pulmonary asbestosis.
    (1981) : CT in mesothelioma.
Law et al. (1982) : CT in malignant mesothelioma.
Law (1984) : Clinical aspects and symptomatic treatment.
Alexander et al. (1981) : CT of malignant mesothelioma - 5 cases, extensive irregular pleural mass surrounding the lung and spreading into fissures and mediastinum, - 2 cases with spread to contralateral side, 1 case to abdomen and chest wall.
Mikhael et al. (1982) : CT of mesothelioma with spinal canal invasion.
Rabinowitz et al. (1982) : Plain film and CT - 27 patients with mesothelioma and 13 with advanced asbestosis. Ga^{67} positive in 7 out of 9 patients with mesothelioma, but only 1 of 7 with asbestosis.
Grant et al. (1983) : CT appearances in 14 patients - all had pleural thickening on the side of the tumour - this was nodular and circumferential, plaque-like or nodular. Other findings included - decreased size of the affected hemithorax, contralateral pleural plaques, pleural calcification, pleural fluid, lung parenchymal, hilar or mediastinal involvement, pericardial thickening, rib erosion or liver deposits.
Mirvis et al. (1983) : CT of malignant pleural mesothelioma - showed local spread into the mediastinum, pericardium, diaphragm, contra-lateral hemithorax or abdomen, and found repeat examinations useful for monitoring progress. A pneumothorax would demonstrate the thickened visceral pleura.
Nichols and Johnson (1983) : Extensive calcification in a rapidly growing pleural mesothelioma (patient with renal failure).
Raithel and Valentin (1983) : CT of asbestosis and silicosis.
Shin and Bailey (1983) : CT of invasive pleural mesothelioma.
Wechsler et al. (1983) : Radiological review of 26 thoracic malignant mesotheliomas.
Williford et al. (1983b) : Mesotheliomas on CT appeared as extensive soft tissue masses encasing the lung (often with an irregular interface with the adjacent lung) - they may spread into the fissures or the mediastinum.
Gefter et al. (1984) : Radiographic evaluation of asbestos-related disorders.
Libshitz (1984) : CT permits a better interpretation of the extent of a mesothelioma and aids in the distinction of a tumour from rounded collapse, asbestos pleural changes, and pleural involvement by lymphoma, thymomas and metastases to the pleura.
Shin et al. (1984) : Seroma of subscapular region of chest wall following extrapleural pleurectomy for mesothelioma.
Coleman et al. (1985) : CT features of unusual hypervascular lung carcinoma complicating asbestos pleural disease.
Blaquiere and English (1987) : CT in pleural mesothelioma.
Rockoff (1987) : CT demonstration of inter-lobar fissure calcification due to asbestos exposure.
McLoud (1988) : The use of CT in examination of asbestos-exposed persons.
Rusch et al. (1988) : CT in the initial assessment and follow up of malignant pleural mesotheliomas - 20 cases - 18 had thoracotomy (8 extrapleural). **Limitations** included (i) chest wall involvement, (ii) mediastinal nodes, (iii) trans-diaphragmatic extension & (iv) peritoneal 'studding' and organ metastasis. It was also helpful in showing recurrence following operation.
Gamsu et al. (1989) : CT in the diagnosis of asbestos-related thoracic disease.
Lorigan and Libshitz (1989) : MR of malignant mesothelioma - three cases with circumferential pleural masses surrounding the lung on the affected side. The extent of the tumours and their effects on adjacent structures were well demonstrated on coronal views.
Lozewicz et al. (1989) : Role of CT in evaluating asbestos related lung disease.
Staples et al. (1989) : HRCT and lung function in asbestos-exposed workers with normal chest radiographs.
Akira et al. (1990) : Asbestosis - HRCT- pathological correlation.
Akira et al. (1991) : Evaluation of early asbestosis with HRCT.
Friedman, A. et al. (1990) : CT of benign pleural and pulmonary abnormalities related to asbestos exposure.
Kawashima and Libshitz (1990) : Malignant pleural mesothelioma - CT manifestations in 50 cases -
    Pleural thickening (46)
    Interlobar pleural thickening (43)
    Contraction of involved hemithorax (21)
    Chest wall involvement (9)
    Contralateral mediastinal shift (7)
    Mediastinum
    Pericardium (3)
    Anterior diaphragmatic, internal mammary and retrocrural nodes (13)
    Diaphragmatic thickening - common
    Contralateral haemothorax (2)
    Hepatic and lung deposits.
Sampson and Hansell (1992) : The prevalence of enlarged mediastinal lymph nodes in asbestos-exposed individuals - a CT study - all 14 patients examined had at least one enlarged lymph node.

General refs. - continued.

BBC - 'Face The Facts' (2 June 1993) : Inquiry into railway workshops and asbestosis. Safety measures were ignored as the Asbestos Industry Regulations (which required breathing apparatus in 1978), only applied to asbestos industries, not industries using asbestos! Many works had a day long 'blue haze', and the floors were often covered with a 2 inch thick layer of asbestos, with no extraction fans etc. Blue asbestos was mainly used. It has been estimated that 10% will develop a mesothelioma, and that up to 20,000 workers have been affected. In York 80 have had mesotheliomas, and it is expected that another 120 will develop them (The author has seen several such cases from the former Swindon, etc. railway works, and some from the railway carriage breakers yard at Milton Keynes). Another paradox is that British Rail employees sprayed **wet   asbestos**, onto the insides of railway carriages under construction using breathing apparatus (when there was no real hazard), whilst those who drilled the carriages afterwards (for pipes, electrical fittings, etc.) wore no protective apparatus - again probably because the latter were **not** considered to be asbestos workers! It is reported that 30 of these developed mesotheliomas.   Illus. **ASB PLEURISY+PL THICKENING, Whorled nods Pt. 4a-b** shows chronic pleurisy in a railway carriage dismantler. (A similar situation occurred in dockyards where some designated workers wore masks, whilst others working alongside them did not).

BBC - 'Face The Facts' (3 March 1995) : Evil effects of asbestos dust were recognised in 1898 - workers (paid 12s for a 56 hr week) were dying at about age 30 from pulmonary fibrosis (similar to knife grinders, etc.).
Wagner from Dorset first studied the effects of asbestos in South Africa (90 miles west of Kimberley, where some were exposed in childhood and developed tumours as young adults), and after returning to the UK collected 550 cases of mesothelioma from hospital records, coroners records, etc.
Asbestos regulations were introduced in 1931, but were largely flouted, and only applied to factories, and exceptions included 'workers who were only occasionally exposed to dust'.

Barking Council in East London petitioned the Home Secretary re the problems in East London, highlighted by **Newhouse   and   Thompson** (1965) who studied the records of 83 cases of mesothelioma (56 pleural and 27 peritoneal - see above) some of whom had died up to 30 yrs. previously. They interviewed surviving relatives, and obtained occupational histories.
Doniach et al. (1975) investigated the incidence of asbestos bodies in a necropsy series at the London Hospital - from a map showing the location of domicile of the cases (Illus. **ASBESTOS, Doniach et al.**) one can easily deduce the source of the pollution (a factory chimney close to the London Hospital, at Whitechapel) and from the direction of the prevailing south-west wind.

Asbestos was used extensively in ships (the Royal Navy stopped its use in 1967), and in buildings (660 tons were used in the Chase Manhattan skyscraper), particularly war-time buildings (aircraft-hangars, military buildings, etc.), lagging around pipes in the basements of large buildings, etc. In dockyards some designated workers wore masks, whilst others working alongside them did not. Many shipyard workers and sailors have pleural plaques, and several (of all ranks from seamen up to admirals) have developed mesotheliomas (e.g. Illus. **MESOTHEL, Pts. 10 & 27**).

Peto et al. (1995) : **Continuing increase in mesothelioma mortality in Britain** - analysed mesothelioma mortality since 1968 to assess the current state of the mesothelioma epidemic, and to predict its future course. Their data indicated that mesothelioma deaths will continue to increase for at least 15 and more likely 25 years, with "a peak of annual male mesothelioma deaths in about the year 2020 of between 2700 and 3300 deaths", and about 1% of all deaths for the worst affected cohorts (men born in the 1940s). There were approx. 1,000 deaths from mesothelioma in 1991. They also wrote "The eventual magnitude of the British mesothelioma epidemic is likely to be greater than in the USA". In 1999 he stated that between now and 2035, 250,000 in Europe would develop a mesothelioma, whilst an equal number would develop lung cancer from inhaling asbestos fibres decades previously.
   The annual import of asbestos to the UK reached over 150,000 tons in the 1960s and 1970s, **mainly chrysotile**. Figures suggested that 'brown asbestos' (**amosite**) produced equal numbers of pleural and peritoneal tumours in some groups of workers.

Stenton (1997) : Asbestos, Simian virus 40 and malignant mesothelioma - suggested that Simian virus 40 (which contaminated polio vaccines between 1958 & 1961) may act as a cofactor in inducing human mesotheliomas.
Munden and Libshitz (1998) : Round atelectasis and mesothelioma.
Miller, B. et al. (1996) : Malignant pleural mesothelioma - radiological/pathological correlation - treatment options remain generally disappointing.
Ng etal (1999) : CT study of 70 cases - felt that CT remains the dominant method for assessment, including treatment response, but it has some limitations re chest wall involvement, spread to mediastinal nodes, trans-diaphragmatic extension and peritoneal tumour seeding.

Cyprus and Turkey.

Yazicioglu (1976) : Pleural calcification associated with exposure to Chrysotile asbestos in SE Turkey.

Artvinli and Baris (1979) : Malignant mesotheliomas in a small village in the Anatolian region of Turkey (the villagers often live in caves as well as buildings).

Hillerdal and Baris (1983) : Radiological study of pleural changes in relation to mesothelioma in Turkey.

McConnochie et al. (1987) : Mesothelioma in Cyprus - the role of tremolite - one chrysotile mine in the island, but tremolite is found in domestic and environmental dust and may be more important for the development of mesothelioma.

Stein et al. (1989) : Pleural mesothelioma resulting from amosite asbestos used as insulating material in the construction of an office building.

Erzen et al. (1991) : CT findings in malignant pleural mesothelioma related to non-occupational exposure to asbestos and fibrous zeolite (erionite) - in Turkey mesothelioma is related to two mineral fibres - tremolite asbestos (nodular in 55%) and fibrous zeolite (flat and smooth tumours in 70%). In stage IV disease, calcified pleural plaques and chronic fibrosing pleuritis were more common with the erionite related mesotheliomas making differentiation difficult.

Sahin et al. (1994) : Malignant pleural mesothelioma caused by environmental exposure to asbestos or erionite in rural Turkey - CT findings in 84 patients - most common findings were unilateral pleural thickening or pleural nodules/masses with or without effusion. Other included pleural effusions, calcifications, involvement of fissures and volume contraction, esp. with chest wall involvement.

Surgery for pleural mesothelioma.

Butchart et al. (1976) : After assessing their experience with pleuro-pneumonectomy in 29 patients - proposed the following **staging system for mesotheliomas -**

Stage	I	Tumour confined to ipsilateral pleura and lung,
	II	Tumour involving the chest wall, mediastinum, pericardium or contra-lateral pleura,
	III	Tumour involving both thorax and abdomen or lymph nodes outside the chest,
	IV	Distant blood-borne metastases.

Shin et al. (1984) : Seroma of subscapular region of chest wall following extrapleural pneumonectomy for mesothelioma.

Sugarbaker et al. (1991) : Extrapleural pneumonectomy, chemotherapy and radiotherapy in the treatment of diffuse malignant pleural mesothelioma.

Patz et al. (1992) : Malignant pleural mesothelioma - value of CT and MR imaging in predicting resectability. For resectable tumours, CT and MR showed preservation of normal mediastinal fat without tumour infiltration of soft tissues (diaphragm, chest wall or mediastinum). Tumour was often contiguous with and inseparable from mediastinal structures with displacement, not encasement of the mediastinum. The most reliable feature of unresectable tumours on either CT or MR was infiltration of soft tissue with loss of normal fat planes, also tumour surrounding > 50% of mediastinal structure.

Heelan et al. (1999) : Staging of malignant pleural mesothelioma: comparison of CT and MR imaging.

Peritoneal mesothelioma.

Keal et al. (1960) : Asbestos and abdominal neoplasms.

Selikoff et al. (1964) : GI tract tumours due to asbestos.

Newhouse and Thompson. (1965) : 56 pleural and 27 peritoneal mesotheliomas following exposure to asbestos in the London area.

Young and Reddy (1980) : Peritoneal mesotheliomas - 4 cases with industrial exposure to asbestos in Gateshead - mucoid masses enveloping the bowel and filling the peritoneal cavities.

Dach et al. (1980) : CT, sonography and Ga^{67} scan of peritoneal neoplasms.

Brenner et al. (1981) : Malignant locally invasive peritoneal mesotheliomas in 25 patients - none had exposure to asbestos.

Wolk (1978) : Ga^{67} scanning of mesotheliomas.

Whitley et al. (1982) : CT of peritoneal mesothelioma (8 cases).

Raptopoulos (1985) : Peritoneal mesothelioma.

Guest et al. (1990) : The role of CT in the diagnosis and follow up of peritoneal mesothelioma in 15 patients - a discrete and measurable mass is unusual in comparison with the common occurrence of ascites. Omental and mesenteric infiltration was also studied.

Gupta et al. (1992) : Peritoneal mesothelioma simulating pseudomyxoma peritonei on CT and sonography.

Tunica vaginalis mesothelioma.

Fields et al. (1992) : Ultrasound appearance of a malignant mesothelioma of the tunica vaginalis testis (gives reference to several other cases - 33 reported up to 1989).

Amin (1995) : Malignant mesothelioma of tunica vaginalis - indolent course with several recurrences despite radical surgery and radiotherapy.

Mathew et al. (1996) : Malignant mesothelioma of tunica vaginalis 2 cases presenting with spinal deposit.

Pericardial asbestosis and mesothelioma.

Lund et al. (1987) : Primary malignant pericardial mesothelioma with intracardial extension, mimicking a left atrial myxoma in a 32 year old man.

Fischbein et al. (1988) : Chronic constrictive pericarditis associated with asbestos.

Pope et al. (1989) : Surgery for case of possible fibrous pericarditis due to asbestos.

Davies, D et al. (1991) : Asbestos induced pericardial effusion and constrictive pericarditis.

Cooper et al. (1996) : Asbestos related pericardial disease may follow relatively light exposure - poor prognosis of both fibrous and calcific pericarditis if untreated - recommended that the pericardium is inspected on all HRCT scans performed for the assessment of asbestos-related lung disease. Case report - 55yr. old retired builder's labourer died of congestive cardiac failure - CT showed pericardial calcification, pleural thickening and infolded lung.

Trogrlic et al. (1997) : Pericardial effusion associated with asbestos exposure.

Isotopes in the diagnosis of mesothelioma

Wolk (1978) : Ga^{67} scanning in the evaluation of mesothelioma.

Seo et al. (1980) : Demonstration of pleural mesothelioma by gallium scan.

Rabinowitz et al. (1982) : Ga^{67} positive in 7 out of 9 patients with mesothelioma, but only 1 of 7 with asbestosis (see also p. 14.48).

Armas and Goldsmith (1985) : Gallium scanning in peritoneal mesothelioma.

Nishikimi et al. (1987) : Primary pericardial mesothelioma detected by Ga^{67} scintigraphy.

Watanabe et al. (1999) : Th^{201} - marked uptake in an extensive L sided pleural mesothelioma.

Compensation

Seaton (1990) : Asbestos diseases and compensation - be wary of advising patients to sue.

Yates (1990) : Asbestos diseases and compensation.

De Vos Irvine et al. (1993) : Asbestos and lung cancer in Glasgow and the west of Scotland - deduced that a considerable proportion of cases of lung cancer in men were asbestos related - about two for every case of mesothelioma - but that many were not recognised for compensation purposes.(They also noted that the UK imported more crocidolite and amosite from South Africa than did any other country between 1945 and 1963, and that the highest rates were found in Clydebank which was a major shipbuilding area for over 200 years).

Mayall (1993) : Commented on the above paper and noted that by law deaths due to suspected occupational lung disease should be referred to a coroner and a coroner's post-mortem will usually be performed. Lung tissue can be taken at this time and an electron mineral fibre count be done, and the type of fibre identified. Lung biopsies in terminally ill patients are unnecessary and may be misleading.

Daily Telegraph (28 Oct. 1995) : One lady with mesothelioma and another whose husband died from mesothelioma won damages of £65,000 and £50,000 respectively against Turner and Newell, the owners of the notorious Armley asbestos factory in Leeds, which closed in 1958, and where the surrounding streets and houses were covered in asbestos dust, and children used to make "snow-balls" of asbestos.

Daily Telegraph (1 Sept. 1998) : A lady whose husband had died from a mesothelioma, also developed a mesothelioma as a result of asbestos dust he brought home on his overalls and was awarded £110,000 compensation. He had worked in an aluminium smelting plant in North Oxfordshire which had used asbestos.

Williams et al. (1998) : Lump sum compensation for asbestos related lung disease.

Peacock et al. (2000) : Asbestos related benign pleural disease also give an account of the present UK position re compensation for benign asbestos related disease.

Chapter 15 : **The Phrenic Nerves, Diaphragm and Pericardium.**

Phrenic nerves - **anatomy**.
   The phrenic nerves arise from C3 to C5 nerve roots and run in the lower neck obliquely in front of the scalenus anterior muscles (and deep to the sterno-mastoids) where they used to be crushed for the treatment of pulmonary tuberculosis. They can sometimes be demonstrated in this part of the neck by ultra-sound.
   They then pass over the first part of the subclavian arteries, between these and the subclavian veins, and cross the internal mammary arteries close to their origins. After coursing over the apex of the pleura, they run anterior to the lung hila, lateral to the pericardium, between it and the mediastinal pleura, until they reach the diaphragm, where they divide into their terminal branches (Figs. 15.1a - d). The right nerve lies on the lateral aspect of the right innominate vein, and crosses in front of the vagus and the aortic arch, before crossing the root of the lung.

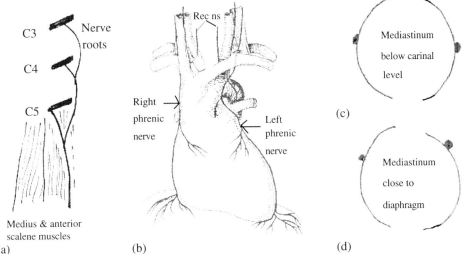

Fig. 15.1   Phrenic nerves in: (a) Neck, (b) Chest (frontal projection - after Lee et al, 1991, with permission from Clinical Radiology), (c) Below carinal level & (d) close to the diaphragm. (c and d = positions of phrenic nerves on CT).

   Where the phrenic nerves lie anterior to the hilum, they are usually too small to be visualised by CT, but as they approach the diaphragm, they may sometimes be seen as small 'nodules' on the pericardium or lines on the surface of the diaphragm, where they elevate a small sleeve of parietal pleura (Fig. 15.1d & Illus. **PHRENIC NERVE & PALSY, Anatomy Pt. 25**). These may be accompanied by supradiaphragmatic branches of the inferior phrenic vessels which have penetrated the diaphragm.

References.
Taylor et al. (1983) : CT demonstration of the phrenic nerve.
Berkmen et al. (1989) : R phrenic nerve - anatomy, CT appearance and differentiation from pulmonary ligament.
Lee et al. (1991) : Tumours involving intrathoracic vagus and phrenic nerves.
Ujita et al. (1993) : Appearance of the inferior phrenic artery and vein on CT - on helical CT scans, linear densities extending laterally from the mid-part of the right side of the IVC and from the posterior margin of the left ventricle on both sides of the chest.

Nerve palsies - recurrent laryngeal and phrenic nerves.
   Both the recurrent laryngeal and phrenic nerves may be involved by primary or secondary tumours within the thorax, either singly or in combination, and usually on the same side.
(a) **Recurrent laryngeal nerve palsy** (Illus. **RECURRENT NERVE PALSY**) due to neoplasm is much more common on the left than the right, because of the lower anatomical course

of the left recurrent laryngeal nerve, which passes around the aortic arch, where malignant enlargement is common. This is particularly true of bronchial carcinoma, which not uncommonly presents with hoarseness, the patient often visiting the ENT department first. Such a finding is nearly always a contraindication to surgery, as it implies that nodes in the sub-aortic fossa (or aorto-pulmonary window) are involved by tumour.

A **right recurrent nerve palsy** is rare. The right recurrent laryngeal nerve passes around the right subclavian artery, close to the lung apex, where it may sometimes be involved by a right-sided primary or secondary Pancoast tumour, a subclavian artery aneurysm or a tumour arising from the subclavian artery (see also ps. 12.5 - 6).

Extension of malignant pleurisy (e.g. of breast, bronchus or mesothelioma) to the lung apex may give rise to a left or right recurrent laryngeal nerve palsy - rarely is this caused by post-radiation fibrosis. Even when no tumour can be demonstrated radiologically, suspicion of recurrence of tumour should always be considered.

Benign nodal enlargement (due to tuberculosis, sarcoidosis and pneumoconiosis) usually does not cause a recurrent laryngeal nerve palsy, but may occasionally do so - see refs. p. 19.73 re recurrent nerve palsy and sarcoidosis.

Other causes of recurrent laryngeal nerve palsy include:

Aortic aneurysm (luetic used to be common, but is now rarely encountered); traumatic and dissecting aneurysms may causes a left recurrent laryngeal palsy.

Left atrial enlargement and pericardial effusions are often listed as causes, but have not been encountered by the author.

Malignant goitres in the neck or mediastinum may cause recurrent nerve palsies on one or both sides, as may surgical trauma in removing **large benign goitres.** (The author has seen three or four cases due to this - all 10 to 20 years ago, including one woman who remained in a mental hospital for over 20 years with a diagnosis of '**hysterical aphonia and stridor**', due to **undiagnosed surgical trauma** to both recurrent laryngeal nerves at thyroidectomy! - damage may also occur with an aberrant branch at parathyroidectomy).

(b) **Phrenic palsy** (Illus. **PHRENIC N & PALSY**) may be due to a number of causes -
(i) In the **neck** due to: Previous surgery, including previous phrenic crush which used to be carried out for the treatment of tuberculosis.
Stretching of a phrenic nerve, due to a sudden or unusual neck movement or posture e.g. turning the head quickly when swimming to avoid a suddenly observed underwater obstacle, carrying abnormal loads on the shoulder with the neck twisted, birth injury with stretching of the neck with a breech delivery, and difficulty in delivering the after-coming head (this last may be accompanied by a Horner's syndrome, adrenal calcifications due to past haemorrhages or haematomas due to the pressure of the obstetricians thumbs), etc.
CVP line insertion - local anaesthetic, haematoma or venous thrombosis & swelling (see p. 11.13).

(ii) In the **thorax** there are many causes including: - direct involvement by lung tumours arising in the lingula or middle lobe; secondary involvement by tumour deposits in anteriorly situated hilar or upper mediastinal nodes and surgical damage due to tumour resection, crushing, diathermy, ligature, excessive **cooling** (including use of the **cryoprobe** - Illus. **PHRENIC N & PALSY, Elevated diaph Pt. 4**), etc.

(iii) **Viral infections**, such as herpes, poliomyelitis, influenza, etc.

(iv) **Neurological disease** - paraneoplastic syndrome and toxic causes (see under bilateral phrenic palsy - below).

(v) **Fibrosis and radiotherapy** may also lead to a phrenic nerve palsy.

Recovery from injuries to the cervical parts of the phrenic nerves or damage following **viral infections**, may be slow and may not be complete for up to 12 or 18 months. When the phrenic palsy first occurs, patients are often quite disabled by breathlessness on exercise until they learn how to 'fix' the mediastinum, presumably by using the remaining partial intercostal nerve supply to the ipsilateral crus, plus the innervated opposite crus to do this. In patients with lung cancer, this is not often a presenting feature, as the mediastinum will tend to be fixed by the tumour, and the palsy will occur more gradually, thus allowing more time for accommodation.

Problems in the diagnosis of a phrenic nerve palsy.

Whilst gross cases are usually readily recognised by a markedly elevated hemidiaphragm on plain radiographs, and confirmed by paradoxical movement on deep inspiration or sniffing, as seen by TV fluoroscopy and /or ultra-sound, incomplete cases may be less obvious. Most cases may be recognised in the erect position, but in debilitated patients or with incomplete palsies, the paradoxical movement may only be noted in the recumbent position.

In addition eventrations, previous diaphragmatic injuries and partial degrees of impaired movement, as well as masses below the diaphragm due to subphrenic abscesses, an enlarged liver, etc. also have to be considered, and nowadays are usually ruled out by ultrasound. Reduced diaphragmatic movement may also be seen with diaphragmatic herniae, or with the Chilaiditidi (or Béclère) syndrome, when the transverse colon rises up in front of the liver to lie above it, although still under the right side of the diaphragm. (This syndrome is particularly seen in children and the elderly, or in other patients who have excessive gas in the bowel; in children it is commonly due to air swallowing whilst crying and in the elderly is usually secondary to constipation - see also p. 15.8).

Alexander (1966) discussed some of the difficulties in the diagnosis of phrenic palsy. He found that one side of the diaphragm was usually dominant, left dominance being twice as common as right, and that the sniffing test was not always a reliable guide. Young and Simon (1972) showed that inequality in movement of the two domes of the diaphragm is frequently present and in young adult males, a greater range of movement is found more often on the right.

Nodal enlargements causing nerve palsies may be secondary to tumours other than bronchial neoplasms, e.g. of the oesophagus, breast, etc. Nodal masses caused by lymphoma, do not so commonly cause nerve palsies, probably because the nerves are displaced and are not usually invaded by tumour. Sarcoid nodes likewise only rarely cause a phrenic palsy.

As with other nerve lesions, an understanding of anatomy is of great importance - Figs. 15.1a-d.

Bilateral phrenic palsy is an uncommon but well recognised cause of breathlessness, typically presenting with orthopnoea, less commonly breathlessness on exercise or immersion. It is a more difficult diagnostic problem than unilateral, and may be secondary to a 'toxic' or nervous system disease, including a paraneoplastic syndrome (e.g. from renal cell or other neoplasm), diphtheria, polyneuritis, polymyositis, brachial neuritis, syringomyelia, motor neurone disease, lead poisoning, myasthenia gravis, muscular dystrophy, hypothyroidism, tetanus antitoxin, dystrophia myotonica, and acid maltase deficiency. Another cause is SLE (see p. 19.8) in which typically a young adult female may complain of orthopnoea made worse by lying down - the '**shrinking lung syndrome**' - commonly they have bilateral basal linear collapse, poor diaphragmatic movement, and in long standing cases **paradoxical abdominal wall movement**. In rare cases bilateral weakness may follow influenza or other viral disease.

Caveat : One should always consider the possibility of a large abdominal swelling as a possible cause of abnormal diaphragmatic movement, e.g. a large ovarian cyst in a young woman. All of us can be caught in attributing breathlessness to a thoracic or diaphragmatic cause, when this may not be correct. A quick ultrasound examination may give the true answer!

Another rare cause - the author has seen two patients diagnosed as having long-standing 'hysterical aphonia' and mild stridor - each had had surgical damage to the recurrent nerves at thyroidectomy several years before. (See also references below re other cases).

Further references.

Comroe et al. (1951) : Motor neuritis after tetanus antiserum.
Sherman and Phillips (1968) from the Memorial Hospital New York : Recommended that radiologists should study the movement of both the diaphragm and the vocal cords by fluoroscopy in cases of chest disease.
Spitzer et al. (1973) : Transient bilateral diaphragmatic weakness.
Haas et al. (1981) : Diaphragm paralysis and respiratory failure in chronic proximal spinal muscular atrophy.

Benjamin et al. (1982) : LLL collapse/consolidation following cardiac surgery - effect of topical cooling of the phrenic nerve.

Fowler and Hetzel (1983) : TB mediastinal lymphadenopathy can cause L vocal cord paralysis.

Frija et al. (1984) : Studied 22 cases of recurrent laryngeal paralysis (18 left sided and 4 right) by CT and found 9 were causes by nodes, 9 by the tumour mass per se, 3 by a vascular cause and one undetermined.

Sherani et al. (1984) : Vocal cord paralysis associated with coal miners pneumoconiosis and PMF.

Thomas et al. (1984) : Bilateral phrenic palsy as a possible paraneoplastic syndrome caused by renal cell carcinoma.

Graham et al. (1985) : Neuralgic amyotropathy with bilateral diaphragmatic palsy.

Solbiati et al. (1985) : Used HRCT to study the recurrent laryngeal and phrenic nerves.

Hamilton et al. (1986) : Tuberculous left vocal cord palsy.

Stradling and Warley (1988) : Bilateral diaphragm paralysis and sleep apnoea with diurnal respiratory failure.

Wilcox et al. (1988) : Phrenic nerve function and its relationship to collapse after coronary artery by-pass surgery.

Gibson (1989) : Diaphragmatic paresis, pathophysiology, clinical features and investigations - supported the hypothesis that the 'shrinking lung syndrome' of SLE is due to diaphragmatic weakness.

Laroche et al. (1988) : Hypothyroidism presenting with respiratory muscle weakness.

Laroche et al.(1989) : Diaphragm strength in 'shrinking lung syndrome' of SLE.

Laroche and Green (1990) : Diaphragmatic paresis, pathophysiology, clinical features and investigation.

Glew et al. (1990) : Pleurisy and hepatic cysts - 3 patients who presented with pleuritic chest and shoulder tip pain, due to spontaneous bleeding into benign liver cysts.

Nisbet et al. (1991) : Bilateral diaphragmatic paralysis presenting with orthopnoea and apparent radiological evidence of pulmonary embolism - 2 cases, both 50 year old miners who on lying flat became dyspnoeic with pronounced paradoxical movement of the abdominal wall.

Houston et al. (1992) : Quantitative assessment of diaphragmatic movement using ultrasound.

Ch'en and Armstrong (1993) : Value of fluoroscopy in patients with suspected bilateral hemidiaphragm paralysis - used decubitus or oblique position.

Harker et al. (1994) : CT diagnosis of hemidiaphragm paralysis in a pt. with ca. R lung, invading the mediastinum, who could not breath hold during CT. Motion artefacts were only seen on the left, indicating a right phrenic palsy.

Tiede et al. (1994) : R phrenic palsy after cutting down a Christmas tree lying on his R side (man aged 58).

Houston et al. (1995) : US has technical, qualitative and quantitative advantages over fluoroscopy and should be the method of choice in the investigation of suspected hemidiaphragmatic movement abnormality.

Slater et al. (1999) : Hoarse voice due to aortic aneurysm in aorto-pulmonary window - ba swallow, CT & MR.

Inversion of the diaphragm - (Illus. **DIAPHRAGM INVERTED**).

The diaphragm may become inverted due to pressure from above, due to a large supradiaphragmatic mass, e.g. in a lower or middle lobe, a 'drowned' lower lobe (see ps. 4.19-20), severe emphysema, a large pleural or pericardial effusion , a cardiac aneurysm, a phrenic palsy or subpulmonary effusion, or a combination of these.

Inversion is more commonly seen on the left, as the liver tends to prevent it on the right side. Its presence on the left is usually noted on plain radiographs, by the fundal gas bubble being depressed, and having a concave upper border (see Illus. **DIAPHRAGM INVERTED, Pt. 1a-b**). On the right it is often only recognised by real-time ultrasound examinations. Occasionally severe emphysema will invert the diaphragm on both sides, and this may be noted on a lateral radiograph (Illus. **DIAPHRAGM INVERTED, Pt. 1b**). With large pericardial effusions, inversion may be a significant factor in the production of respiratory problems. The inverted hemidiaphragm may move paradoxically upwards in inspiration, reducing the aeration of the lung on the affected side.

References.

Sir William Osler (1892) : Noted that pericardial effusions depressed the left side of the diaphragm and left lobe of the liver, producing a prominence in the upper abdomen.

Williamson (1920) : In an experimental study with cadavers, found that pericardial effusions tend to accumulate along the inferior margins of the heart, depressing the left side of the diaphragm.

Mulvey (1965) : Effect of pleural fluid on the diaphragm.

Swingle et al. (1969) : Inversion of left hemidiaphragm.

Rogers and Meredith (1977) : Inversion of the left hemidiaphragm caused by a large pericardial effusion, which followed cardiac surgery. It was relieved by pericardiocentesis.

Katzen et al. (1978) : Pseudomass of the liver due to a subpulmonary effusion and inversion of the diaphragm.

Lowe et al. (1981) : Inversion of the right hemidiaphragm shown by ultrasound.

Subramanyam et al. (1981) : Sonography of the inverted right hemidiaphragm.

Dallemand (1982) : CT of pseudomass of the L upper quadrant, caused by inversion of the L hemidiaphragm.

Demos and Pieters (1984) : Abdominal pseudotumour due to inverted hemidiaphragm.

The Diaphragm - anatomically consists of two parts :

(a) The **dome** which attaches to the lowest parts of the lower ribs, the sternum and spine, and fascial bands and ligaments attached to these. The dome contains but little muscle and is mainly fibrotendinous. Normally it is only 2 to 3 mm thick. '**Pseudo-thickening**' is most commonly caused by a **subpulmonary pleural effusion**.

(b) The lumbar part, mainly the **crura**, passes down antero-laterally to the upper lumbar vertebrae and attaches to them. The rest of the lumbar part attaches to the medial and lateral arcuate ligaments - thickenings of the lumbar fascia overlying the anterior aspects of the psoas and quadratus lumborum muscles and attaching to the L1 vertebral body and the 12th ribs. The crura contain considerable amounts of muscle.

Muscle is also present where the diaphragm attaches to the chest wall. Each side is innervated by its respective phrenic nerve and the lower intercostal nerves.

Embryologically the diaphragm is derived from four portions - the central tendon, the pericardiaco-peritoneal membranes (forming the dome), the body wall or muscular component and the crura. (For accessory diaphragm - see p. 7.8).

Fig. 15.2   Normal anatomy of the diaphragm.
(Note that a foramen of Bochdalek properly refers to where the quadratus lumborum passes behind it, but the term is often used to refer to any posteriorly situated hernia, including those affecting the crura.)

M = Foramina of Morgagni (or 'sterno-costal triangles') through which the internal mammary vessels and lymphatics pass.
O = Oesophagus
A = Aorta
Arches over quadratus lumborum and psoas muscles shown.
Boch = Foramina of Bochdalek
C = crura

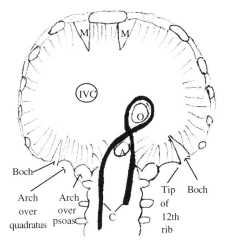

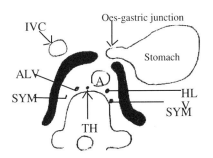

Fig. 15.3   The crura and central tendon.

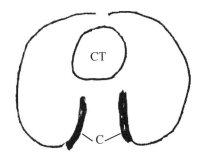

Note that the right crus is normally thicker than the left. (CT = central tendon, C = crura, ALV and HLV = azygo- and hemiazygo-lumbar veins. SYM = sympathetic trunks, TH = thoracic duct.)

Most commonly in younger patients, the right dome of the diaphragm is higher than the left by about 1.5 - 2.5 cm, but with increasing age, emphysema etc., the height difference on the two sides may be less marked and sometimes the left side is higher, especially if the stomach or hepatic flexure of the colon is distended with gas (see also refs. below). It is commonly thought that the **normal** right-sided elevation is due to the position of the liver, but as it is also commonly raised in patients with 'abdominal situs inversus' (but not thoracic - Illus. **SITUS INVERSUS, Pt. 7**) with the liver on the left and the stomach on the right, this is not the whole truth.

Diaphragmatic humps are very common, particularly on the right. Most are due to minor weaknesses, thinning of the diaphragm or to the arrangement of its muscle fibres. Many may be recognised as such by reference to previous radiographs, ultrasound or by fluoroscopy. The problem is in differentiating them from adjacent pleural or hepatic, etc. masses deforming the phrenic outline. Khan and Gould (1984) studied 22 successive patients having localised right sided humps with ultrasound, and found this usually sorted out the problem. A larger eventration or 'cupola' may involve most of one side as a 'complete eventration', which most often occurs on the left.

Eventrations of the diaphragm are shown in Illus. **DIAPHRAGM-EVENTRATED** - some of these may mimic diaphragmatic herniae, particularly Morgagni herniae.

The normal range of diaphragmatic movement is 2 to 3 cms during quiet respiration, and is grater with sniffing and in deep inspiration. Some paradox may be seen in about 5%. Its position may be altered by disease both above and below it. A large liver not uncommonly raises the right side of the diaphragm. Similarly a large renal or adrenal mass may elevate it, and loculated fluid collections above or below the diaphragm may alter its position.

On CT sections the position of the diaphragm often has to be inferred, because it itself is invisible when it abuts structures of similar density and there is no intervening fat, etc. In obese individuals fat may provide sufficient contrast to delineate one or both hemidiaphragms.

References.
Carlson et al. (1962) : Some observations on the relative influence of the heart and liver on the position of the diaphragm.
Wittenborg and Aviad (1963) : Organ influence on the normal posture of the diaphragm - a radiological study of inversions and heterotaxies - studied 60 children with anomalous organ positions - most had heart disease and the anomalous position of the organs was an accidental finding -'the more normally the heart is developed into a right and left side, the more likely will there be a clearly defined and constant disparity in the height of the diaphragm.'
Lennon and Simon (1965) : The height of the diaphragm in the chest radiograph of normal adults - 'the lower hemidiaphragm is primarily dependent on the mass and activity of the heart which depresses it and the posture of the diaphragm gives no reliable guide to the presence or absence of situs inversus'.
Simon et al. (1969) : Observations on the range of diaphragmatic movement - in 188 factory workers. It moved asynchronously in 77%, but the inequality of movement was usually less than 1 cm. In 23% the diaphragm moved less than 3 cm, but this was not an indicator of emphysema, and could be increased by instruction in what to do.
Simon (1975) : R dome is 1 - 2.5cm higher in 94% of normal subjects - in a few it may be higher. The L dome may be at the same level as the R or higher in about 5%.
Panicek et al. (1988) : The diaphragm, anatomical, pathological and radiological considerations.
Heitzman (1990) : Kerley Pergamon Lecture - The diaphragm. Radiologic correlations with anatomy and pathology.
Houston et al. (1992) : Assessment of diaphragmatic movement with ultrasound.
Houston (1995) : see note on staging of lung tumours ps. 24. 16 - 17 & 24. 23 - 25.

Diaphragmatic movement in decubitus and recumbent positions.

As is noted in the section on lateral tomography (p. 20.13), the decubitus position i.e. lying on one side, somewhat distorts the normal anatomy - the unfixed mediastinum flopping towards the dependent side, and the **lowermost side of the diaphragm becoming raised** - this position is maintained in both inspiration and expiration, and in addition the lower side normally has a greater excursion of movement with respiration. Perhaps the increased movement on the dependent side is to make greater use of the increased perfusion of the dependent lung, and to compensate for the decreased perfusion of the uppermost lung.

When recumbent, the lowermost part of the diaphragm (on both sides) is also usually higher in position than the upper, i.e. like the 'downside' in the decubitus position. This situation is maintained both in inspiration and expiration. Failure of the dependent hemidiaphragm to adopt a higher position may indicate air-trapping or emphysema (see also below).

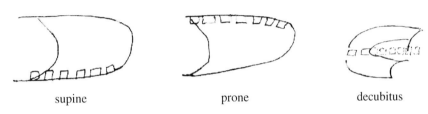

supine   prone   decubitus

Fig. 15.4 Position of diaphragm in recumbent and decubitus positions.

Lordotic and reversed lordotic projections.
   As is discussed on p. 14.7, there are problems with the diagnosis of pleural effusions, etc. on supine radiographs. It is often easy for a non-tangential x-ray beam to be used with a patient in bed, and lordotic or reversed lordotic central rays are not uncommon. These also have an effect upon the appearance of the diaphragm. With a reversed lordotic view (i.e. the x-ray beam being angled towards the abdomen) the diaphragm will not be properly in profile - this will tend to distort the lung bases and give the diaphragm a poor definition, not uncommonly simulating basal lung disease.

25° lordotic view -   25° reversed lordotic view -
diaphragm projected high   diaphragm poorly delineated

   A lateral view or a repeat PA with a tangential beam will usually elucidate the problem. Similarly a right basal fat-pad may simulate a basal lung mass or consolidation with a lordotic tilt, but it will be relatively invisible with a reversed lordotic tilt.

   Fluoroscopy (or ultra-sound) will usually allow one to differentiate normal physiology from basal lung disease e.g. partial collapse with infarction, infection or obstructive emphysema due to a partially blocked bronchus by a foreign body or tumour (Illus. **OBSTRUCTIVE EMPHYSEMA**).

Reference.
Capitanio and Kirkpatrick (1972) : Used the lack of a raised hemidiaphragm on the affected side of a foreign body, on a lateral decubitus view, as an indication of possible air-trapping from such a cause.

Diaphragmatic crura - (Illus. **DIAPHRAGM-CRURA**).
   The diaphragmatic crura envelop the aorta, as they pass downwards to their attachments with the upper lumbar vertebrae. Usually the right crus is larger and thicker than the left (but occasionally this may be reversed), and it blends with the anterior longitudinal ligament in front of the first three lumbar vertebrae. The (usually) smaller left crus arises from the first two lumbar vertebrae. Laterally and inferiorly the crura are continuous with the lumbo-sacral arches - tendinous bands covering the upper part of the psoas muscles - superiorly they may merge gradually into the

dome, but there is sometimes an abrupt transition. Superiorly they envelop the oesophagus and merge with the central fibro-tendinous dome.

The crura are often well seen on plain radiographs, particularly on the left, because more fat lies medial to the left crus, and it also has a more antero-posterior course. The retro-crural space lies postero-medially. Deviation of the crura or the para-spinal lines in the chest (see p. 18.27) should make one consider the possibility of retro-crural disease, particularly when there is a divergence extending downwards - the 'iceberg sign' (p. 18.31 and Illus. ICEBERG SIGN).

Left crus outlined by fat (AP view)   Gradual merger of crura with dome   More abrupt transition

Fig. 15.5   Diaphragmatic crura.

The posterior pleural recess is a potential space between the diaphragmatic pleura and the lateral parietal pleura, below the inferior tongue of the lung and may be seen on CT.

With pleural effusions, this recess will often appear widened. It may also be filled with a small portion of the lung - the 'retro-crural lung hernia' - see Fig. 15.10.

Fig. 15.6 Posterior pleural recess.

Parietal pleura
Diaphragmatic pleura
← 1mm
CT

Diaphragm
AP view

Variations in the diaphragmatic anatomy anteriorly.

Kleinman and Raptopoulos (1985) and Gale (1986 - see below) studied variations in the anatomy of the anterior part of the diaphragm as shown by CT, particularly in relation to Morgagni herniae. From the dome arises the middle leaflet of the central tendon, which lies below the inferior surface of the heart and blends partially with the parietal pericardium. This leaflet is attached by muscle fibres to the costal cartilages and the xiphoid process of the sternum. It is commonly seen as a smooth or slightly undulating soft tissue curve, continuous across the midline and concave posteriorly. It may have a gap in its middle portion, or appear as a broad band with irregular or ill-defined anterior margins. The normal position of the middle part is above the level of the xiphoid process. A 'curtain of muscle' anteriorly bounds gas or fluid collections within the peritoneal cavity and will also bound loops of large (or small) bowel which have risen in front of the liver (the 'Béclère or Chilaiditi's syndrome' - Illus. CHILIADITI'S SYNDROME). This is common in children and some elderly patients who are 'full of wind'. It may also occur in pregnancy, with emphysema, ascites, a pneumoperitoneum or an atrophic liver.

On CT sections a 'curtain of diaphragmatic muscle' lies **anterior** to normally placed abdominal structures, but **posterior** to a Morgagni hernia.

Diaphragm

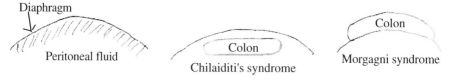

Peritoneal fluid   Colon
Chilaiditi's syndrome

Colon
Morgagni syndrome

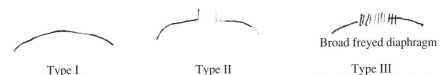

Type I   Type II   Type III

Normal appearance of anterior diaphragmatic muscle in cross section. The variation is due to the anterior fibres which pass downwards to connect with the base of the body of the sternum or to the xiphoid process.

Fig. 15.7   Variations in anterior diaphragmatic anatomy.

References.
Béclère (1899), Chilaiditi (1910 - 1911)
Linsman and Chalek (1950) : Hepatodiaphragmatic interposition of the small intestine.
Jackson and Hodson (1957) : Interposition of the colon between liver and diaphragm.
Vessal and Borhanmanesh (1976) : Hepatodiaphragmatic interposition of the intestine.
Kleinman et al. (1978) : Anterior pathway for transdiaphragmatic extension of pneumomediastinum.
Patterson and Taetes (1985) : CT measurements of the anterior portions of the diaphragm.
Heitzman (1990) : The diaphragm - radiological correlations with anatomy and pathology.

Diaphragmatic 'pseudo-tumours'.
   These are common and are of four main types:
(a) **Anterior pseudo-tumours**, mimicking enlarged internal mammary nodes. A distinguishing feature is that the pseudo-tumours are not fully rounded and merge with the diaphragm anteriorly.
(b) **Part of the dome** of the diaphragm, especially on the right, where it overlies the liver as seen on basal cross-sections.

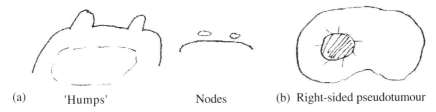

(a)   'Humps'   Nodes   (b) Right-sided pseudotumour

(c) **Peripheral or lateral pseudo-tumours** may simulate peripheral 'nodules' within or indenting the liver or the lumina of the transverse colon or stomach or appear as 'radiating fingers' from the left side of the dome - they are all due to muscle bands which connect the central tendon to the inner aspect of the thoracic cage.

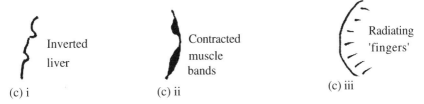

Inverted liver   Contracted muscle bands   Radiating 'fingers'

(c) i   (c) ii   (c) iii

(d) '**Lumpy crura**' due to muscular contractions of the crura in inspiration. These should be distinguished from enlarged lymph nodes and nodular secondary deposits.
   Occasionally the crura are formed of 'small knots of muscle' and are 'knobbly' both in inspiration and expiration. A 'lumpy crus' (particularly on the left) is more common in older people. (Retro-crural nodes are discussed in the next section).

(d) i   Expiration   (d) ii   Inspiration - 'lumpy crura' -   (d) iii 'lumpy crus'
                                      contracted muscle nodules
                                      usually extend up and down
                                      on adjacent CT sections.

Fig. 15.8   Diaphragmatic pseudo-tumours.

N.B. : Most diaphragmatic pseudo-tumours, due to contracted muscle, decrease in size and number in expiration.

References.

Naidich et al. (1983d) : CT of the diaphragm - normal anatomy and variants.
Rosen et al. (1983) : CT appearance of diaphragmatic pseudotumours.
Nightingale and Dixon (1984) : Crural change with respiration - a potential mimic of disease.
Anda et al. (1986) : CT appearance of the diaphragm, varying with respiratory phase and muscular tension.
Williamson et al. (1987) : Variations in the thickness of the diaphragmatic crura with respiration.
Hawkins and Hine (1991) : Diaphragmatic muscular bundles (slips) - US evaluation of incidence and appearance.
Caskey et al. (1989) : Ageing of the diaphragm.
Silverman et al. (1992) : Lateral arcuate ligaments of the diaphragm - may produce postero-lateral nodules.

The retro-crural space and nodes.

The normal retro-crural space contains fat, the aorta, azygos and hemiazygos veins, the thoracic duct and nerves (see Fig. 15.9). As noted in Figs. 15.6 & 10, lung may herniate behind the crura in a few individuals and this should be differentiated from gas in abscesses, etc., which may track downwards from chest infections or upwards from the abdomen as with pancreatitis.

Nodes may be enlarged in the retro-crural space, and should be distinguished from 'lumpy crura' or veins, see Fig. 15.8 & Illus. **RETROCRURAL NODES**. Such nodes are readily recognised on CT sections and sometimes may be seen via the liver with ultra-sound. They may become enlarged when involved by secondary tumours, from primary tumours in the chest or abdomen (e.g. lung, oesophagus, pancreas, kidney, prostate, testis, bowel, etc.) or with reticuloses. Only rarely are they enlarged due to sarcoidosis. They are sometimes termed 'posterior diaphragmatic nodes'.

When enlarged these nodes may cause splaying of the crura like a 'croquet-hoop' (Illus. **RETROCRURAL NODES, Hodgkin's disease, Pt. 56a & b**) and tumour extension from them may cause a large soft tissue mass silhouetting out the retro-crural nodes themselves.

Extension of disease inferiorly from the retro-crural nodes may sometimes occur from lung tumours, to involve the abdominal para-aortic node chains (and posterior para-renal spaces), leading in some cases to IVC obstruction, ascites and gross oedema of the lower limbs - often a very distressing complication (Illus. **ABDOMINAL NODES, Pt. 4**).

An enlarged node adjacent to the aorta or IVC in the may give rise to an apparent 'three vessel sign'.

A large cisterna chyli or a large paraaortic lymphatic duct may occasionally cause confusion with lymphadenopathy, with the latter there is usually a neck or stalk communicating with the thoracic duct (see also p. 13.6).

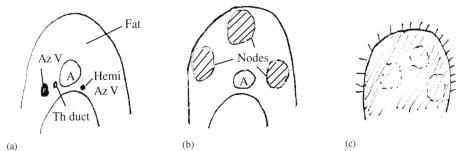

(a)   (b)   (c)

(a) Normal appearance of the retro-crural area - inferiorly this connects with the para-renal space.

(b) Enlarged retro-crural nodes producing the 'croquet-hoop' appearance smaller nodes should be distinguished from crural muscle (Fig. 15.8), azygos or hemi-azygos veins (a - above). Enlarged retro-crural nodes may occur with abdominal pelvic and genital tumours, chest tumours spreading downwards and reticulosis.

(c) Tumour extending out through the 'croquet-hoop' make the crura less well outlined With large masses the individual retro-crural nodes may be indistinguishable, i.e. tumour will completely replace the intervening fat.

Fig. 15.9 The retrocrural space.

When tumours involve both the aortic hiatus and the retro-crural space, CT sections may show a bilobed mass both in front of and behind the crura.

Large retro-crural nodes may also produce the **'ice-berg   sign'** -   Fig. 18.13, (p. 18.31) & Illus. **ICEBERG SIGN**.

Small lung herniae may occur into the retrocrural space :

Fig. 15.10 Air in **small lung herniae in the retro-crural space** (retro-crural air) - the postero-medial inferior tip of a lower lobe becomes 'tucked' behind a 'folded' or 'ridged' crus - may be found in 3% of normal people - distinguish it from fat.

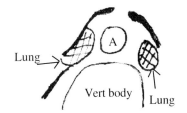

Defects in the crura may allow hiatal or Bochdalek herniae to occur :

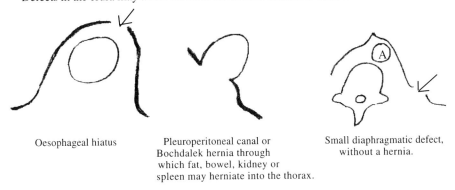

Oesophageal hiatus   Pleuroperitoneal canal or   Small diaphragmatic defect,
                              Bochdalek hernia through   without a hernia.
                              which fat, bowel, kidney or
                              spleen may herniate into the thorax.

Fig. 15.11 Crural defects + Bochdalek herniae - see also Fig. 15.19 (p. 15.17).

Distinguishing pleural from peritoneal fluid (including subphrenic abscesses) on CT examinations.
   The main key to localisation of fluid to the thorax or abdomen on CT sections, is to recognise the position of the diaphragm. The two sides are usually visible as thin stripes, but can be difficult to visualise where they curve and are not cut across tangentially. Fat, if present, may produce a thin radiolucent line. The crura lying posteriorly are almost always visible. Dwyer (1978) described '**the displaced crus**' sign for distinguishing between pleural fluid and ascites - pleural fluid tends to displace the upper muscular portions of the crura anteriorly and laterally, filling the postero-medial space between the crura and the spine. By contrast ascitic fluid lies anteriorly.

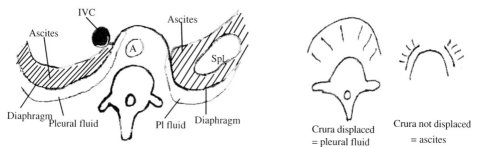

Fig. 15.12   Pleural fluid lies postero-medially to the diaphragm, whereas ascites collects antero-laterally to the crura, and extends around the liver and spleen.

When only pleural fluid is present and no ascites, the fluid interface with the spleen is imprecise - the '**imprecise spleen sign**' - Fig. 15.13.

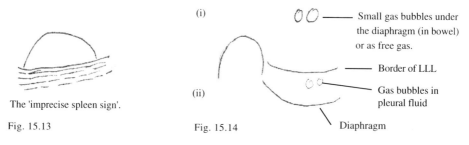

The 'imprecise spleen sign'.

Fig. 15.13   Fig. 15.14

Fig. 15.14 - a section through the lung base may show the lower lobe, pleural fluid and/or gas under the diaphragm. Gas may also sometimes be seen within the pleural fluid with gas-forming organisms and/or following infection.

   When there is a subpulmonary effusion, the secondarily collapsed lung base may mimic the diaphragm, by appearing as a curvi-linear band density. Such a lower lobe margin tends to taper laterally and be discontinuous. A lower CT section will readily confirm this or a complementary ultra-sound examination.

   A **potential pitfall** is the tip of a lower lobe 'dangling' in the fluid - see also ps. 2.33 & 14.14 - tethering of the pulmonary ligaments to the lower lobes which may be seen within pleural effusions and can be seen both with CT and US.

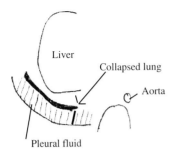

Fig. 15.15 Note that a collapsed portion of lung may mimic the diaphragm on CT sections (see also Silverman et al., 1985).

Fig. 15.16 On real-time US a collapsed lower lobe may 'dance' within the fluid with each resp. movt. (When the bronchi within such a lobe are full of fluid, then mucocoeles may be seen as well).

Ascitic fluid extends laterally around the liver and spleen. On the right it is restricted from contact with the bare area of the liver by the coronary ligaments. Loculated or large left subphrenic fluid collections may however be difficult to differentiate, particularly on the left, when it is often wise to opacify the stomach as well (Fig. 15.17). Combined pleural effusions and abdominal fluid collections, such as subphrenic abscesses may also cause problems in differentiation.

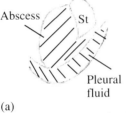

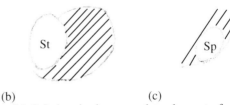

(a)

Fig. 15.17. (a) Left subphrenic abscess, on medial aspect of stomach, and accompanied by a pleural effusion.

(b)   (c)

(b) Subphrenic abscess on lateral aspect of stomach, extending around the spleen on a more caudal section (c).

Subphrenic and psoas abscesses and psoas infection - (Illus. **PSOAS**).

These abscesses used to cause great difficulty in diagnosis, unless a large gas collection was present within them, either as a result of a bowel perforation, or due to gas-forming organisms (most commonly B coli). Soft tissue masses due to the abscesses may cause elevation of the diaphragm, depression of the liver, displacement of a kidney, the stomach, etc. They are now, however, usually readily recognised by ultrasound and/or CT, and many may be drained percutaneously.

Subphrenic abscesses often provoke pleural reaction and/or fluid above the diaphragm.

Psoas abscesses may extend up to the diaphragmatic crura, and may be seen with CT or ultrasound (via the loin or close to the spine). They commonly follow inflammatory disease of the lower dorsal or upper lumbar spine, renal (e.g. infected hydronephrosis), bowel (e.g. ca, Crohn's disease) or lower posterior thoracic disease. Historically these abscesses were common with TB and TB psoas abscess are still commonly seen in India etc. - most being secondary to spinal or renal TB. They may also complicate spread of reticulosis, or a haematoma in the psoas muscle sheath - Illus. **PSOAS ABSCESS** and **HAEMATOMA**. Primary inflammatory cases (without frank pus) commonly occurs due to Staph. aureus infection.

Abscesses may be imaged with US and/or CT and drained. MR however is better for showing primary inflammatory disease which usually responds to antibiotics.

Psoas Deposits.
These may occur not only with renal tumours, but also from lung tumours (Illus. **PSOAS DEPOSIT, Pts. 6 & 7a-b**).
Clinical suspicion should be aroused by severe pain in the lumbar region, with inability to fully extend the lower limb. CT may show masses in the muscles and/or malignant fluid collections.

Tumours of the diaphragm are rare, but fatty masses arising on or adjacent to the diaphragm are common. The latter are readily confirmed by CT (see discussion on fat-pads - p. 6.15, & Figs. 6.8 & 6.9). Fluid collections or cysts are also not uncommon (e.g. pericardial cysts - see p. 15.27) and these may be confirmed with ultrasound and/or CT, and may be drained percutaneously. Cysts may be developmental (mesothelial, bronchogenic), follow trauma and haematomas, or rarely be due to hydatid disease.
   Besides lipomas, liposarcomas (Illus. **DIAPHRAGM   TUMOUR**), fibromas, fibrosarcomas, angiofibromas, neural tumours, teratomas, etc. may occasionally be found arising from the diaphragm. In addition tumours of ectopic tissues, **bronchogenic**   cysts (see ps. 3.13 - 14) **endometriomas** (see ps. 5.19 - 20), **liver**, etc. may occasionally be found (see references). Mesotheliomas may produce local masses overlying the diaphragm, and secondary tumours in the pleura, may all cause masses immediately above the diaphragm. HPOA may be present.
   A few cystic teratomas have been reported arising from the diaphragm. Müller (1986) reported one in a 65 year old woman with right upper quadrant pain and nausea. Plain chest radiographs showed a localised bulge of the right side of the diaphragm and CT demonstrated a mass containing fat, a small amount of soft tissue, localised calcification and a tooth. Five other cases were quoted from the literature.

Diaphragmatic irritation and shoulder tip pain.
   This is a well known association with biliary disease, superior subscapular hepatic secondary tumours and with abscesses within or above the liver, etc. It is transmitted by sensory fibres within the phrenic and intercostal nerves. Sometimes it is stated that the phrenic nerves are entirely motor, but if this were so it would be very difficult to understand how shoulder tip pain would occur in these situations. It would seem unlikely to occur via sensory pathways in the intercostal nerves. Some authors (e.g. Fraser and Paré, 1979) state that the phrenic nerves **do** contain sensory fibres, but neither they nor do standard anatomy text-books give references on this subject - nevertheless it seems the only rational explanation.

Further references.
General.
Campbell, J.(1963) : The diaphragm in Roentgenology of the chest.
Whalen and Shaheen (1971) : Visualisation of the subdiaphragmatic fat in the localisation of the diaphragm.
Callen et al. (1978) : CT of the diaphragmatic crura.
Borlaza et al. (1979) : Posterior para-renal space - escape route for retrocrural masses.
Rubinstein and Solomon (1981) : Partial eventration of the right hemidiaphragm.
Naidich et al. (1983d) : Normal anatomy and variants.
Stewart et al. (1983) : Radiology of the diaphragm as two muscles.
Tarver et al. (1984) : The diaphragm
             (1989) : Imaging the diaphragm and its disorders.
Panicek et al. (1988) : Anatomy, physiology and radiology of the diaphragm.
Caskey et al. (1989) : Ageing of the diaphragm - CT study - diaphragmatic defects and pseudotumours, nonexistent in the third and fourth decades, increased in number and size in the seventh and eighth decades. Also 84% of those with emphysema had diaphragmatic defects - these were also more common in women. The oesophageal hiatus width increased with age, but neither the status of the skeletal muscle nor the presence of obesity correlated with age or with the presence of diaphragmatic defects.

Retrocrural space.
Callen et al. (1977) : CT of the retro-crural, pre-vertebral space.
Donovan et al. (1981) : CT of psoas compartment of the retroperitoneum.
Silverman et al. (1982) : CT of retro-crural air - may be seen in about 3% of normal subjects.
Shapir et al. (1984) : Plain film findings of retro-crural disease.

Shin and Berland (1985) : CT of retrocrural space.   Heitzman (1990) : The diaphragm.

Distinguishing pleural fluid from ascites.
Teplick et al. (1982) : The interface sign.
Alexander et al. (1983) : Differentiation of subphrenic abscess and pleural effusion.
Naidich et al. (1983c) : Peridiaphragmatic fluid localisation - CT.
Griffin et al. (1984) : Differentiation of pleural and peritoneal fluid.
Federle et al. (1986) : Differentiating subpulmonary effusions from subphrenic fluid.
Schmitt et al. (1983) : Pleural calcification with persistent effusion.
Halvorsen et al. (1982) : Anterior left subphrenic abscess.
Roa and Woodlief (1981) : Excessive right subdiaphragmatic fat - a potential diagnostic pitfall.

Diaphragmatic tumours.
Weiner and Chou (1965) : Tumour of L hemidiaphragm in man aged 21 (angiofibroma) + review of 79 other cases.
Olafsson et al. (1971);
Anderson and Forrest (1973) : Primary tumours of the diaphragm.
Müller, N. (1986) : Teratoma of the diaphragm - CT features.
Schwartz and Wechsler (1989) : Diaphragmatic tumours and pseudotumours.
Takayusu et al. (1994) : Ectopic hepatocellular carcinoma arising from the left hemidiaphragm.

Psoas abscesses and deposits.
Ralls et al. (1980) : CT of inflammatory disease of the psoas muscle.
Clark, R. and Towbin (1983) : Abscess drainage under CT & US guidance.
Williams, M. (1986) : Non-tuberculous psoas abscess.
Avery (1988) : Metastatic adenoca masquerading as a psoas abscess.
Daly et al. (1992) : US, CT and MR in the investigation of ileopsoas compartment disease.
Pombo et al. (1993) : Percutaneous catheter drainage of TB psoas abscess.
Nash et al. (1996) : Adenoca of the lung metastatic to the psoas muscle.
Gupta et al. (1997) : Ileo-psoas abscess - percutaneous drainage under image guidance.
Yang et al. (1999) : Imaging of iliopsoas metastasis.

Subphrenic abscess.
Ochsner & De Bakey (1938) : Subphrenic abscess - collective review of 3,608 collected and personal cases - 10.5% developed a broncho-pleural fistula.
Gee and Wood (2000) : Transdiaphragmatic fistula linking a R subdiaphragmatic collection to the bronchial tree.
Van Gansbeke et al. (1989) : Percutaneous drainage of subphrenic abscess.

Domjan et al. (1997) : 'Bare-area' abscess (of liver i.e. the upper part not covered by peritoneum) - imaging findings and potential communication with the mediastinum - "the relatively central position of the collection should help to differentiate a 'bare-area' abscess from the more usual subphrenic collection." The 'bare-area' space normally contains some fat and fibrous tissue. (Diagram reproduced with permission from British Journal of Radiology).

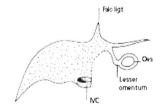

Thickness of the diaphragm.
de Bruin et al. (1997) : Resting diaphragm thickness is increased in young pts. with Duchenne muscular dystrophy with impaired respiratory muscle force - "pseudo-hypertrophy" - as measured by US (1.74 compared with 1.48 cm).

Transdiaphragmatic herniae.
(a) A **hiatal hernia** (Illus. **HIATUS   HERNIA**) occurs through the oesophageal hiatus of the diaphragm, as a rolling, sliding or para-oesophageal type of hernia. Commonly the stomach herniates, but the transverse colon, omentum or small bowel may also pass up into the hernial sac, either with the stomach or alone. Illus. **HIATUS HERNIA, Diaph HH Pts. 12 & 14** shows such herniae of the colon. Ascites may also extend up into a hiatal hernial sac, as may peritoneal secondary deposits, and these may surround and press on or lie to the left of the lower oesophagus. Such may mimic a foregut cyst, mediastinal abscess, necrotic tumour or a collection of fluid secondary to pancreatitis (Godwin and MacGregor, 1987).

Mostly hiatal herniae are chance findings, but serious problems may occur with severe gastro-oesophageal reflux, gastric etc. ulcers especially at the neck of the sac, or rarely as a result of a **gastric volvulus** within the hernial sac, leading to obstruction and necrosis of the stomach.

When there is an acute gastric obstruction. a **large**-**bore** drainage tube should be passed orally to relieve pressure, prior to emergency surgery, which may be life-saving, the radiologist often initiating the life-saving treatment. If gastric necrosis occurs then the outlook is grave.

The author has seen two patients who had necrosis of the stomach in a large hiatal hernia, one acute and very toxic (with black stomach contents) and the second which had become chronic with a large 'walled-off' cavity in the mediastinum communicating both with the oesophagus and the pylorus - both died despite surgery. Other cases without gastric necrosis have survived, with immediate drainage and subsequent surgery, and this important complication should not be forgotten.

(b) **Morgagni* herniae** (Illus. **MORGAGNI HERNIA**) most commonly present in infancy or childhood with gastro-intestinal or respiratory symptoms resulting from visceral herniation into the thorax. They arise through the Morgagni foramina between the sternal and costal origins of the diaphragm (Fig. 15.2), or Larrey's space (through which the superficial epigastric artery passes), and may contain bowel (especially colon), omentum or liver. With bowel, intraluminal gas may give the diagnosis, but barium by mouth or enema may be necessary for differentiation in some cases (Illus. **MORGAGNI HERNIA, Pts. 2 & 3**). The omentum or liver may simulate an intrathoracic mass. Liver herniation , as with an eventration (see p. 15.6), may be confirmed by ultra-sound, isotope scan (Illus. **DIAPHRAGM-EVENTRATED, Pt. 9**), or CT (Illus. **MORGAGNI HERNIA, Pts. 4 & 9**).

Omental fat (which can be mimicked by excess subdiaphragmatic fat - Rao and Woodlief, 1981) is readily confirmed by CT (Illus. **MORGAGNI HERNIA, Pts. 4 & 9**).

Gas may pass through the foramina from the mediastinum to the abdomen and vice versa.

The '**sign of the cane**' may be seen on **lateral** views, with small Morgagni herniae, when the parietal-properitoneal line is visible above its normal position within the thoracic cavity.

Properitoneal fat line raised above its normal position, with a loop of gas-filled bowel passing into the chest.
<u>Reference</u> : Lanuza (1971).

Fig. 15.18 'Sign of the cane' with a small Morgagni hernia (diagram reproduced with permission from Radiology, **101**, 293 - 296).

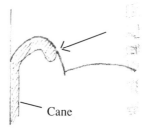

Cane

---

*Giovanni Battista Morgagni (1682 - 1771) - Professor of Pathological Anatomy, Padua.

(c) A **Bochdalek hernia** properly occurs posteriorly through an unobliterated pleuro-peritoneal canal (Illus. **BOCHDALEK HERNIA**), but the term is often used to describe any posteriorly situated diaphragmatic hernia. Mostly fat plugs the canal, but stomach, transverse colon or small bowel may pass up into such herniae, and be recognised by their gas content, fluid levels or faecal contents.

With a left-sided hernia, herniation of the spleen may occur, and this can usually be recognised by ultrasound or CT (it used to be confirmed by isotope scanning, using colloid or damaged and labelled RBCs).

Rarely a Bochdalek hernia may contain an **intra-thoracic kidney**, which may give rise to a 'bean-shaped' smooth mass lying posteriorly in the lower thorax, usually on the left. The author has only personally seen one case - on the left side - courtesy of the late Dr. George Burfield of Reading (1913-1988) who diagnosed the chest mass correctly.

Gale (1985) : Reviewed 940 CT examinations and found Bochdalek herniae in 52 patients - an incidence of 6% - left sided being about twice as common as on the right.
Criteria for diagnosis were -
(a) Soft tissue or fatty mass abutting the upper surface of the diaphragm in the characteristic postero-medial position.
(b) Interruption of the adjacent diaphragmatic musculature, and
(c) Continuity of sub- and supra-diaphragmatic densities through the defect in the diaphragm.

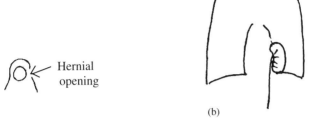

Hernial
opening

(a)   (b)

Fig. 15.19 Diagrams (a) CT of Bochdalek hernia. (b) Intra-thoracic kidney (IVP - Burfield's case).

Morgagni and Bochdalek herniae in children may present soon after birth if they are very large. Most however are clinically silent, whilst in others the hernia may be mistaken for other conditions if the child is ill, and has a chest radiograph taken. Problems may follow paracentesis due the diagnostic error. As in adults, incarcerated bowel may become inflamed, infarcted or obstructed within the hernial sac. Berman et al. (1988) : Reviewed delayed presentations of Bochdalek and Morgagni herniae in children and found that misdiagnoses were common. Bochdalek herniae were often misdiagnosed as 'infection with pneumatocoeles', tension pneumatocoeles', 'lung cysts' or 'gastric volvuli' and Morgagni herniae as 'middle lobe pneumonia'. Bochdalek herniae may also occur in pregnancy, and a trapped loop of bowel with a fluid-level may simulate an abscess; the bowel loop may also infarct; MR views may resolve the problem.
Neonates with left sided diaphragmatic herniae often have enlarged spleens. When the lung(s) have been considerably collapsed, the babies may do well for 1-2 days after the hernia repair until the respiratory distress syndrome (RDS) supervenes due to the poorly developed lung(s).

(d) **Aortic or 'retro-crural herniae'** are rare, when a tongue of lung tissue may protrude into the retrocrural areas', but pancreatic inflammatory fluid can track through these spaces and other orifices into the mediastinum. Tumours may also spread through the retrocrural area - see below.

(e) **Parasternal herniae** are the rarest herniae - a bilateral case was reported by Brown, R. (1952).

(f) **Traumatic** or other herniae (Illus. **DIAPHRAGM-TRAUMA**) may occur through the dome or central part of the diaphragm, either through a large congenital defect (not uncommon in the newborn as an extension of a large Bochdalek hernia) or be due to a traumatic rupture which may follow blunt or penetrating injury (see also p. 11.4). The latter may be acute or not become evident until a considerable time after the injury. Acutely herniation of viscera may be accompanied by attacks of hypotension, cyanosis and dyspnoea. Most, however, are asymptomatic or give rise to non-specific signs. There is commonly basal lung collapse and pleural fluid, an abnormal diaphragmatic contour, contra-lateral mediastinal shift, elevated fundal or colonic gas, air-filled viscera in the chest, etc. About 80% of cases occur on the left.
Many have a **delayed** clinical presentation, particularly those caused by non-penetrating or blunt trauma, which gives rise to an explosive rise in pressure from the abdomen to the chest. Tears caused in this way often do not heal spontaneously, because of the negative pressure within the chest which tends to suck up abdominal viscera, thus enlarging the defect. Basal shadows caused by traumatic herniae may be confused with tumours, other herniae, lung disease or cysts.
Symptoms may eventually occur due to incarceration and partial obstruction of viscera. If strangulation occurs, mortality rates are high despite surgical treatment, with sloughing of the stomach, etc. Diagnosis, even at surgery, may be missed.

The diagnosis of diaphragmatic rupture (in the absence of bowel in the chest) is one of the most difficult in chest radiology. With penetrating injuries causing these herniae (e.g. stab wounds), the entry wound is often in the abdomen. With injuries due to blunt trauma, more appear to occur on the left, as the liver tends to absorb the force on the right, and often plugs the tear (see below).

CT   Tear plugged by the liver   or   The liver may be eccentric and posterior
Fig. 15.20 Diaphragmatic tears and liver position.

The diaphragmatic tear may be small or large, and this injury often occurs with other multiple injuries, e.g. aorta, limbs, pelvis, etc. Damage to the hepatic veins may occur with a right sided rupture. Quite often the tear is only discovered at exploratory surgery or surgery performed for another injury. Some ruptures involve the pericardium, and viscera may herniate into this.

Some presentations are bizarre - such as a British army officer who was run over by a tank in the North African Desert in 1944, being squashed into the sand - forty five years later he presented with a large left sided diaphragmatic hernia! - Illus. **DIAPHRAGM-TRAUMA, Pt. 8a-b.**

'Bergquist's triad' refers to (i) multiple rib fractures, (ii) pelvic and /or spinal fractures and (iii) a ruptured diaphragm - all his patients were wearing seat belts!

Intubation and positive pressure mechanical respiration reduces herniation through a diaphragmatic rupture, which may **only become apparent when a patient is extubated** and repeat chest radiograph or CT may then be required.

Plain chest radiographs may show fluid at the base of a pleural cavity, or that gas-filled viscera have passed into the chest. On the left, contrast media (gas, iodine or barium) have been used to show the position of the stomach, etc. Similarly isotope liver scans have been used to show a 'notched' liver, where it passes through a tear in the diaphragm. An artificialpneumoperitoneum has sometimes been used to show the passage of gas from the abdomen to the chest.

On ultrasound the normal diaphragmatic 'white-line' - (Illus. **DIAPHRAGM-WHITE LINE, Mesothel. Pt. 19c**) may be recognised on either side particularly if a little pleural fluid is present, to give an acoustic window. An abrupt loss of it may indicate a rupture (especially if transgressed by fluid or abdominal contents - see Illus. **DIAPHRAGM-WHITE LINE, Diaphragm-trauma Pt. 3d**). Left sided tears are more prone to complications from strangulated bowel, etc., but right sided tears are also important to diagnose, if only to prevent a chest drain being inserted into the liver! Many left sided tears, and some right sided ones need surgical repair.

CT may be useful for showing the abnormal positions of the viscera, e.g. bowel herniated into the chest, or that the liver lies eccentrically and posteriorly with a right sided tear. Discontinuity of the diaphragm may be shown, but because of its thinness and curvature, the diaphragm is not always identifiable on CT sections, and this method may not be able to distinguish between a rupture and a phrenic palsy. However local thickening may indicate blunt trauma injury (Leung et al., 1999). When MR is available this may give the clearest demonstration of a diaphragmatic tear.

Some useful points :

Gas bubble - stomach or localised gas in the pleural cavity? - note position of naso-gastric tube, if present; or give the patient contrast (Ba or I) to opacify the stomach.

Tear readily shown by lateral MR.

A 'notched stomach' may
indicate where it passes
through the neck of a hernial
sac ('**collar sign**').

'**Notched liver**' on
isotope scan.

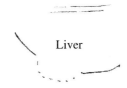

On the R side US is often the easiest
way to see if the diaphragm is intact
- it may also be possible to visualise
it on the left.

Fig. 15.21a   Some useful signs in the diagnosis of diaphragmatic rupture:

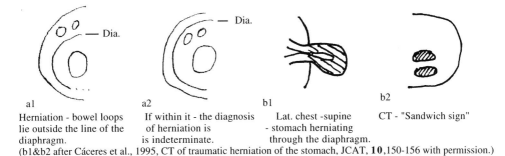

a1

Herniation - bowel loops
lie outside the line of the
diaphragm.

a2

If within it - the diagnosis
of herniation is
is indeterminate.

b1

Lat. chest -supine
- stomach herniating
through the diaphragm.

b2

CT - "Sandwich sign"

(b1&b2 after Cáceres et al., 1995, CT of traumatic herniation of the stomach, JCAT, **10**,150-156 with permission.)

Fig. 15.21b   Some CT signs in the diagnosis of diaphragmatic rupture:

Alpern (1996) suggested that using the position of the spleen may be a way of distinguishing
between rupture of the diaphragm and eventration.

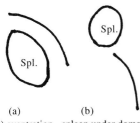

(a)   (b)

(a) eventration - spleen under dome
(b) rupture - spleen above dome.

Fig. 15.22 The position of the spleen.

Rarely a traumatic diaphragmatic hernia may extend
into the pericardium (see also Fagan, 1979).

Fig. 15.23 Hernia into pericardium.

(g) **Pregnancy**   with increased abdominal content and relaxation of ligaments, etc. may be
complicated by diaphragmatic herniae of various types - see references below.

Further references - **Diaphragmatic herniae.**
(a) **Congenital or developmental herniae.**
Harrington (1945 & 1951) : Reviewed 34 cases of diaphragmatic herniation, 14 - Morgagni in type and 7 bilateral.
Brown (1952) : Morgagni herniae account for under 3% of all diaphragmatic herniations. His series included one
bilateral case discovered at autopsy
Rickham (1955) : Strangulated diaphragmatic hernia in the neonatal period.
Hunter (1959) : ? a higher incidence of Morgagni herniae as the majority of cases are symptomless.

Kirkland (1959) : Congenital posterolateral diaphragmatic herniae in the adult.

Patton and Harris (1961) : Morgagni herniae are more common on the right as the heart and pericardium act as a protection on the left side of the anterior aspect of the diaphragm. Bilateral cases are very rare.

Snyder and Greaney (1965) : 77 consecutive cases of congenital diaphragmatic herniae.

Raichoudury et al. (1973) : Bochdalek herniae in adults.

Rennell (1973) : Foramen of Morgagni hernia with volvulus of the stomach.

de Martini and House (1980) : Partial Bochdalek's hernia - CT evaluation.

Robinson et al. (1980) : Bilateral antero-mediastinal defect of the diaphragm in children.

Siegel et al. (1981) : Delayed presentation of left sided congenital diaphragmatic herniae.

Schneidau et al. (1982) : A case of intermittent chest pain due to a Morgagni hernia.

Gaisie et al. (1983) : Late onset Bochdalek hernia with obstruction.

Appelquist and Høier-Madsen (1986) : Cribriform diaphragm - a variant of congenital diaphragmatic herniation.

Shin et al. (1987) : Bochdalek hernia in the adult - diagnosis by CT.

Berman et al. (1988) : Childhood diaphragmatic hernias presenting after the neonatal period.

Caskey (1989) : Found that these herniae were present more often in older people.

Brooks et al. (1990) : Bochdalek diaphragmatic hernias simulating pulmonary metastases on CT - 3 cases - 2 on left and one on right of small amounts of fat in herniae simulating chest masses.

Cloutier et al. (1993) : Lung hypoplasia with congenital diaphragmatic hernia in infants.

Saifuddin and Arthur (1993) : Congenital diaphragmatic hernia - a review of pre and postoperative chest radiology.

Collie et al. (1996) : MR of L sided Morgagni hernia in woman aged 69 - defect in diaphragm well shown.

Karamanoukian et al. (1997) : New insights into congenital diaphragmatic hernia gives an incidence of between 1 in 2,000 to 1 in 5,000 live births. A postero-lateral diaphragmatic defect allows abdominal viscera to herniate into the thoracic cavity early in gestation, inhibiting normal foetal lung growth and development. Pulmonary hypertension, surfactant deficiency and L vent. hypoplasia may act synergistically to produce a mortality > 60%. New treatment strategies were discussed. - see also Losty (1999) : Tracheal plugging in utero to encourage lung growth and also hormone or steroid treatment to stimulate lung maturation.

Dillon et al. (2000) : The overall survival of babies with cong. diaph. herniae is poor - 50% at 1 year due to pulm. hypoplasia - antenatal US + chromosome analysis may help in showing which have an isolated diaph. abnormality.

(b) Ectopic kidneys.

Campbell (1930) : Renal ectopia.

Fleischner et al. (1950) ; Franciskovic and Martinic (1959) : Intrathoracic kidney.

Fulsonie and Molnar (1966) : Intrathoracic kidney with Bochdalek hernia and pulmonary hypoplasia.

Malter and Stanley (1972), Leite de Noronha et al. (1974), Lundius (1975)

Nishitani et al. (1979) : Intrathoracic kidney shown by IVP and CT (also quoted six other cases).

Curley et al. (1984) : Bilateral intrathoracic kidneys.

Baillet and Escure (1988) : CT diagnosis of intrathoracic kidney.

Donat and Donat (1988) : Case report and literature review.

Greco et al. (1988) : CT of intrathoracic kidney.

Hawass et al. (1988) : Report of six cases.

Hulks et al. (1990) : Right sided intra-thoracic kidney associated with ipsilateral pulmonary hypoplasia and Bochdalek hernia in a 13 year old girl - shown by CT.

(c) Hiatal herniae.

Gerson and Lewicki (1970) : Intrathoracic stomach - when does it obstruct?

Lee and Bretnach (1990) : MR findings in paraoesophageal omental herniation.

Jewell et al. (1994) : Diaphragmatic herniation of the large bowel - 19 cases found on barium enema.

(d) Traumatic herniae.

Carter et al. (1951) : Traumatic diaphragmatic herniae - used barium meals and enemas in diagnosis and emphasised the danger of strangulation.

Clay and Hanlon (1951) : Pneumoperitoneum in the differential diagnosis of diaphragmatic herniae.

Peck (1957) : Right-sided diaphragmatic liver hernia following trauma.

Bernatz et al. (1958) : Problems of the ruptured diaphragm.

Strode and Vance (1958) : Rupture of the left side is far more common than on the right, as the liver tends to protect the right side. (104 on left and 8 on right).

Moore (1959) : Traumatic pericardial diaphragmatic herniae - 5 cases reviewed.

Probert and Havard (1961) : Where rupture of the right side occurs, the liver may protrude like a mushroom through the defect and give rise to bizarre symptoms.

Efron and Hyde (1967) : Non-penetrating traumatic rupture of the diaphragm - 3 cases plus a 4th due to eventration.

Bekassy et al. (1973) : 'Spontaneous' and traumatic rupture of the diaphragm - 14 traumatic and 5 spontaneous cases - 4 after sudden exertion - one lifting a wardrobe, one with a severe twisting movement, two after heavy work in a mine and one after a severe bout of coughing following a pneumonectomy.

Bisgaard et al. (1985) : Spontaneous rupture of the left side of diaphragm, presented 4 months after severe exercise.

Christiansen et al. (1974) : Rupture of the diaphragm (use of pnemoperitoneum in diagnosis).

Gourin and Garzow (1974) : Diagnostic problems in traumatic diaphragmatic hernia.

Grimes (1974) : Traumatic injuries of the diaphragm.

Hegarty et al. (1978) : Delayed presentation of traumatic diaphragmatic hernia - 25 cases, 24 on left (stabbing in 22, blunt trauma in 3).

Estrera et al. (1979) : Traumatic injuries to the diaphragm - two types : (a) due to penetrating wounds (41 cases) and (b) blunt trauma (23 cases) - also two iatrogenic at surgery - difficult pleurectomies following TB). They reviewed 307 autopsies following trauma and found diaphragmatic ruptures in 5.6%

Fagan et al. (1979) : CT demonstration of post-traumatic herniation of omentum and colon into the pericardial sac, with the herniated omentum lying in front of the heart. (Also quoted 10 other cases from the literature).

Fataar and Schulman (1979) : Diagnosis of diaphragmatic tears.

Heiberg et al. (1980) : CT recognition of traumatic rupture of the diaphragm

Rao and Woodlief (1980) : Grey scale ultra-sonic demonstration of ruptured right hemidiaphragm.

Ball et al. (1982) : Traumatic diaphragmatic hernia - errors in diagnosis (used liver scintigraphy for right sided tears).

Amman et al. (1983) : Real-time ultrasound in the diagnosis of traumatic rupture of the diaphragm.

Perlman et al. (1984) : Abnormal course of nasogastric tube in traumatic rupture of left side.

Gurney et al. (1985) : Omental fat simulating pleural fluid in traumatic diaphragmatic hernia - CT.

Rodriguez - Morales et al. (1986) : Acute rupture of the diaphragm - analysis of 60 patients.

Tocino and Miller (1987) : Computed tomography in blunt chest trauma.

Aronchick et al. (1988) : A pleural effusion overlying a traumatic hernia may indicate complications in herniated bowel - obstruction or infarction (five cases with air and fluid in the chest).

Baker et al. (1988) : CT of a traumatic diaphragmatic, Richter's hernia, mimicking an abscess.

Feliciano et al. (1988) : Delayed diagnosis of injuries to the diaphragm after penetrating wounds. Over 9 years collected 16 patients - 15 left sided. There was often a delay in diagnosis varying from 16 hours to 14 years. Often there was a misdiagnosis of plain chest radiography, or none was taken.

Mirvis et al. (1988) : MR imaging of traumatic diaphragmatic rupture.

Nilsson et al. (1988) : Radiological diagnosis in traumatic rupture of the diaphragm.

Demos et al. (1989) : CT in traumatic defects of the diaphragm showed examples of tears.

Broderick and Whyte (1990) : A diaphragmatic nick (patient presented with left sided severe **transdiaphragmatic hernia** of viscera four years after a knife wound to the left side of the chest).

Flower (1990) : Rupture of the diaphragm - the use of ultrasound in 7 cases.

Somers et al. (1990) : Rupture of the right hemi-diaphragm following blunt trauma - use of ultrasound in four cases.

Gelman et al. (1991) : Diaphragmatic rupture due to blunt trauma - sensitivity of plain chest radiographs - previous reports suggested that a preoperative diagnosis is made on the basis of chest radiographs in only one third of patients, but their experience was that chest radiographs were valuable particularly with left-sided tears. In 50 cases, chest radiographs were diagnostic in 20 and suspicious in 8; 5 were diagnostic on delayed radiographs. Of 6 with right sided injury, only one had a diagnostic chest radiograph.

Holland and Quint (1991) : Post-traumatic left-sided diaphragmatic rent shown by CT without visceral herniation.

McHugh et al. (1991) : Delayed presentation of traumatic diaphragmatic herniae. Nine cases secondary to blunt trauma - delay in diagnosis varied from 1 to 16 years. Found barium studies to be the most useful confirmatory investigations, but the diagnosis could usually be suspected on the plain chest radiograph.

Warren (1991) : Agreed with McHugh et al. but advised water soluble GI contrast medium in case the bowel wall was damaged.

Meyers and McCabe (1993) : Traumatic diaphragmatic hernia - occult marker of serious injury.

Cruz and Minagi (1994) : Large bowel obstruction resulting from previous traumatic diaphragmatic hernia - imaging findings in four cases.

Worthy et al. (1995) : CT findings - positive in 9/11 pts. (8 on L & 1 on R) - included **discontinuity of diaphragm**, herniation of abdominal contents to chest and constriction of stomach.

Carter et al. (1996) : Ciné loop MR in the diagnosis of a ruptured right hemidiaphragm.

Israel et al. (1996) : Use of helical CT with multiplanar reformatting in the demonstration of diaphragmatic rupture.

Shapiro et al. (1996) : The unreliability of CT scans and initial chest radiographs in evaluating blunt trauma induced diaphragmatic rupture.

(e) **Surgery.**

McCaig et al. (1996) : Transdiaphragmatic retrosternal distal gastric herniation following coronary arterial by-pass graft using the right gastroepiploic artery (fluid level lying in front of the heart on plain chest radiographs).

(f) **In pregnancy.**

Diddle and Tidrick (1941) : Diaphragmatic hernia associated with pregnancy.

Osborne and Foster (1953) :   ibid.

Bernhardt and Lawton (1966) : Pregnancy complicated by traumatic rupture of the diaphragm

Wolfe and Peterson (1988) : An unusual cause of massive pleural effusion in pregnancy.

Ultrasound of the diaphragm (see also p. 15.4 and Illus. **DIAPHRAGM-WHITE LINE**).

The right side of the diaphragm is usually readily seen as a strong echogenic 'white' line superior and adjacent to the liver. Movement with respiration and fixity or paradoxical movement with phrenic paralysis are easily studied, as are fluid collections above or below it, consolidation at the right lung base or adjacent masses, deposits or abscesses in the liver, etc. Disruption of the line may be caused by tumour invasion, from the chest or liver, or diaphragmatic rupture (see also ps. 15.18 & 20.34). Infection or tumour (e.g. mesothelioma) may make the line appear thicker. Fatty infiltration or adjacent fluid are common and may also cause apparent thickening as may diaphragmatic pleural plaques, but are usually readily distinguished. Tumour masses (as from mesothelioma) may also be recognised adjacent to the diaphragm (see Illus. **MESOTHELIOMA 16d & 19b**).

Sometimes the ultrasound beam may 'catch' the dome of the diaphragm twice, particularly if it undulates or is partially 'eventrated' or 'inverted', and it may then appear 'double'. A double echo may also be given by the diaphragm and the base of the lung, when there is a thin intervening subpulmonary effusion. This is usually readily differentiated, as is a subdiaphragmatic fluid collection, but some difficulty may be experienced if fluid or an abscess lies above the 'bare area of the liver'.

The right side may be seen in the supine patient but the author often prefers to examine the patient in the erect position, as this allows the liver to 'drop' lower and be more accessible. It is also then easier to examine both the liver and the diaphragm from anterior, lateral and posterior approaches. With a small curved probe, the left side and upper parts of the crura, as well as the right side, may usually be examined through the lower intercostal spaces.

References.
Callen et al. (1979) : Ultrasonography of the diaphragmatic crura.
Worthen and Worthen (1982) : Disruption of the diaphragmatic echoes - a sign of diaphragmatic disease.
Ammann et al. (1983) : Real-time ultra-sound in the diagnosis of traumatic rupture of the diaphragm.
Lewandrowski and Winsberg (1983) : Echographic appearance of the right hemidiaphragm.

The pericardium (see Illus. **PERICARDIUM**).

The pericardium has been recognised as an anatomical structure since the time of Homer in ancient Greece. In the Iliad he referred to the '**shaggy haired heart**' - an allusion to pericarditis. Galen (129 - 200 AD) observed the pericardium in injured Roman gladiators and noted that it could be resected for infection without affecting the action of the heart.

The pericardial sac consists of a double layer - the outer parietal pericardium and the inner visceral. The visceral is separated from the myocardium by a thin layer of fat which is usually visible as a thin (or sometimes thicker) lucent line over the apex and left side of the heart - the 'epicardial fat'. Anteriorly, lung (superiorly) and mediastinal fat (more inferiorly) separates the pericardium from the chest wall and sternum (important points when carrying out a paracentesis, mediastinal or sternal biopsy).

The thin line of pericardium can often be recognised between the anterior mediastinal fat and the epicardial fat on chest radiographs or tomograms. It may be thickened (> 2 to 3 mm) by pericardial fluid or thickening.

Epicardial fat also shows the position of the left ventricle, which may help in the diagnosis or exclusion of pericardial masses. It is often well demonstrated on CT sections, but care should be exercised in not mistaking it for extrapericardial fat, which may be displaced from the pericardium by a haematoma, cyst or cardiac rotation. Noting its position may aid in the recognition of a left pleural effusion.

References.
Kremens (1955), Torrance (1955) : Subepicardial fat as a new sign of pericardial fluid or thickening.
Lane and Carsky (1968) : Lateral film analysis.
Frolich et al. (1975) : Epicardial fat and left pleural effusion.
Carsky et al. (1980) : Epicardial fat - A reliable sign.
Demos et al. (1983) : Epicardial fat sign due to extrapericardial disease.
Isner et al. (1983) : Subepicardial fat producing echocardiographic appearance of pericardial effusion.
Stark et al. (1984) : MR imaging of the pericardium.
Hirji et al. (1986) : Epicardial fat pad sign due to cardiac laevorotation.

Paling and Williamson (1987) : Epicardial fat pad - CT findings.
Bull et al. (1998) : CT dimensions of the normal pericardial thickness (thinnest portion is 1.2 mm on 10 mm slices, and 0.7 mm on 1 mm slices).

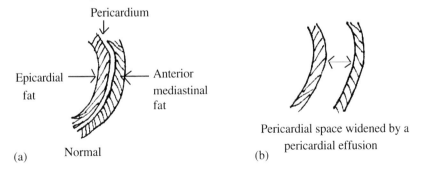

(a) Normal   (b) Pericardial space widened by a pericardial effusion

Fig. 15.24   Separation of epicardial and mediastinal fat by a pericardial effusion (may be seen in both frontal and lateral projections).

Pericardial recesses or sinuses.

It is important to know of these, since fluid can collect in them, and may be confused with mediastinal masses or enlarged lymph nodes. On CT sections fluid in the recesses may mimic nodal enlargements, bronchogenic cysts or thymic masses. Pericardial cysts may occasionally be found within a recess. Contrast enhanced CT or real-time ultrasound will usually differentiate.
The recesses include :
superior pericardial recess - between the thymus and the ascending aorta,
transverse   recess - behind the ascending aorta and the pulmonary trunk - fluid in this may sometimes mimic a pre-tracheal or azygos node - see p. 13.23.
oblique recess - behind the left atrium.
left pulmonary recess - between the left pulmonary artery and the left superior pulmonary vein
pulmonary   venous   recesses   on   either   side - between the superior and inferior pulmonary veins.
post caval recess - postero-lateral to the SVC.

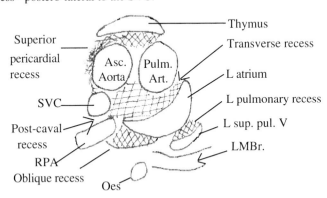

Fig. 15.25   Diagram of pericardial recesses.

References.
Aronberg et al. (1984) : CT appearance of the superior pericardial recess.
Levy-Ravetch et al. (1985) : CT of the pericardial recesses.
McMurdo et al. (1985) : Magnetic resonance imaging of the superior pericardial recesses.

Chiles et al. (1986) : Superior pericardial recesses simulating aortic dissection on CT - it may produce a swelling on the R just posterior to the ascending aorta or on the L anteriorly and above the L or main pulmonary artery.
Choe et al. (1987) : CT of the pericardial recesses.
Shin et al. (1987) : CT of distended pericardial recess presenting as a mediastinal mass.
Im et al. (1988) : MR of transverse sinus.
Winer-Muram and Gold (1990) : Effusion in the superior pericardial recess simulating a mediastinal mass.
Black et al. (1993) : The superior pericardial sinus - normal appearance on gradient-echo MR images.
Choi et al. (2000) : A 'high riding' superior pericardial recess may mimic a pretracheal node - see also p. 13.24.

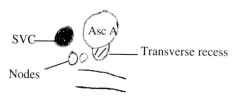

Fig. 15.26   A prominent transverse recess of the pericardium - filled with fluid - may be confused with azygos nodal enlargement. This recess lies behind the ascending aorta and may have fat extending behind it.

Illus. **PERICARDIAL RECESSES**   show haemorrhage into the transverse recess of the pericardium from a ruptured aneurysm of the ascending aorta.

Pericardial disease.
   This may be due to various non-malignant causes; viral or bacterial infection, post-myocardial infarction (**Dressler's   syndrome**), uraemia, myxoedema, trauma, aneurysm of the heart or intra-pericardial parts of the great vessels (such as the aortic root), post-irradiation or post-pericardiotomy syndrome, trauma, etc. Pericardial tuberculosis used to be not uncommon in hospital practice in the UK, but is now rarely seen (but did not stop a case occurring with organisms resistant to therapy in 1992 in a patient from Africa).
   A viral pericarditis may 'blow up' quite quickly, and give rise to a very large pericardial shadow on radiographs, with little disability in the patient. Effusions due to this cause are commonly blood-stained, and after aspiration, the raw surfaces of the pericardium rubbing together may give rise to an obvious rub and cause pain.
   Pericardial effusions are sometimes 'sympathetic' to lung infection or mediastinal tumours e.g. teratomas of the thymus, without any frank invasion of the pericardium.
   Frank invasion by tumours occurs with lung tumours, mesotheliomas, thymomas, lymphomas, etc. Pericardial involvement may also occur with secondary tumours of the breast, tumours spreading up from the abdomen, etc.
   Pericardial involvement by lung tumours may be difficult to recognise radiologically, but can often be surmised from the presence of a large adjacent mass and phrenic palsy, a large obstructed and occluded inferior pulmonary vein (Illus. **PULM VEINS, Ca lg & pul vein Pts. 1 to 9**) or by the presence of a pericardial effusion containing tumour masses or cells. Invasion of the heart is very difficult to determine, particularly with CT, due to movement artefacts, but gated MR shows this more accurately. Even direct extension of tumour from the subcarinal area into the left atrium, through the 'bare area of the pericardium' is very difficult to demonstrate. Pericardial effusions in patients with lung cancer are uncommon, except in those terminally ill.

Pericardial effusion - The pericardium normally contains 20 - 50 ml of fluid. Under 1 cm of thickening usually is of no clinical importance, and the sac can often be distended with 150 - 250 ml of fluid before any tamponade occurs.
   The development of a pericardial effusion may be suspected from an enlarging cardiac shadow - often 'pear-shaped' (and associated with a raised left main bronchus) and is usually confirmed by **ultrasound** (Illus. **PERICARDIAL EFFUSION, Pericardium Pts. 1c. 2b-c,   10c, Thymus Pts. 30e & 34e**). Effusions commonly produce enlargement of the 'apparent cardiac outline' on radiography (only when gas is present will the true outline be seen). Tumours, cardiac

aneurysms, and post-surgical defects may produce localised bulgings of the apparent cardiac outline.

A pericardial effusion (or a large heart) may compress the left lower lobe bronchus, leading to collapse of the lingula or left lower lobe (**Ewart's sign** - Illus. **SICKLE CELL DISEASE Pt. 1a-b**). In the presence of a pericardial effusion, the lungs are commonly free from oedema, although the pulmonary veins may be rather full.

Fluoroscopy has been used to show dampened cardiac pulsations, due to the fluid and the effect of gravity on this, i.e. movement over the cardiac apex obscured with the patient erect, and upper cardiac pulsations with the patient supine or head-down.

A big clinical problem is in differentiating constrictive pericarditis from restrictive cardiomyopathy, but differentiation is usually readily made with ultrasound.

Intravenous CO_2, or angiocardiography was sometimes used to demonstrate pericardial effusions (Illus. **PERICARDIAL EFFUSION, Pericardium Pts. 8a-b & 9a-d**), also the use of two isotope preparations, one demonstrating the lungs and the second the blood pool within the heart (Illus. **PERICARDIAL EFFUSION, Pericardium Pts. 11 & 15**).

<u>Further references.</u>   (see also p. 14.51 for pericardial disease due to asbestos).
Dressler (1959) : The post-myocardial infarction syndrome.
Siegel (1970) : Galen on surgery of the pericardium.
Spodick (1970) : Medical history of pericarditis - the '**hairy hearts of hoary heroes**'.
Wright (1972) : Ultrasound of free and loculated pericardial effusions in dialysis patients.
Houang et al. (1979) : Demonstration of pericardium and pericardial effusion by CT.
Rankin et al. (1980) : Primary chylopericardium - combined lymphographic and CT diagnosis.
Gouliamos et al. (1982) : Detection of pericardial heart disease by CT.
Gross et al. (1983) : CT of intracardiac and intrapericardial masses.
Higgins et al. (1983) : Post-operative pericardial effusion - CT guided aspiration.
Serlo and Heikkinen (1983) : Cardiac tamponade caused by a mediastinal teratoma.
Silverman and Harell (1983) : CT of normal pericardium.
Silverman et al. (1983) : CT of abnormal pericardium.
Glazer et al. (1984) : CT is better than echocardiography for showing masses posteriorly within the pericardium.
Hackney et al. (1984) : Experimental pericardial effusion evaluated by CT.
Millward et al. (1985) : Pericardial varices demonstrated by CT - woman of 64 with portal hypertension.
Moncada et al. (1985) : CT of congenital pericardial abscess shown by ultrasound and CT.
Sechtem et al. (1986a) : MR of the normal pericardium.
          (1986b) : MR of the abnormal pericardium.
Johnson, M. et al. (1986) : Two cases on intra-pericardial abscess shown by ultrasound and CT.
Clarke and Cosgrove (1987) : Real-time ultrasound for pericardiocentesis (24 cases in 2 years).
Gale et al. (1987) : Pericardial fluid distribution - CT analysis.
Miller, S (1989) : Imaging pericardial disease.
Olson et al. (1989) : CT and MR imaging of the pericardium.
Gallant and Studley (1990) : Delayed cardiac tamponade following accidental injection of non-ionic contrast medium into the pericardium.
Mikaye et al. (1991) : Delayed appearance of localised pericardial effusion after cardiac surgery - a localised bulge on the left heart border usually appears within a month after cardiac surgery but may be delayed.

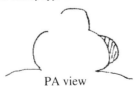
PA view

CT

Sarosi et al. (1991) : '**Milk of calcium**' pericardial **effusion** in patients previously treated with radiotherapy for Hodgkin's disease.
Stern and Frank (1994) : **Acute traumatic haemopericardium** may result from pericardial or myocardial contusion or aortic root rupture. In the absence of tamponade, arrhythmias or cardiac failure, most resolve spontaneously. Constriction may occur months later.
Hartnell et al. (1996) : MR of pericardial disease.

Lee, S et al. (1994) : US-guided pericardial drainage and intrapericardial instillation of Mitocin-C for malignant pericardial effusion.

Hingorani and Bloomberg (1995) : US-guided pigtail catheter drainage of malignant pericardial effusions - 9 cases with severe dyspnoea.

Clifford et al. (1993) : **TB pericarditis** with rapid progression to **constriction** - prompt diagnosis and treatment are needed.

Hayashi et al. (1998) : TB pericarditis - MR features with contrast enhancement.

Harries et al. (1998) : Azygos reflux: a CT sign of cardiac tamponade.

Pericardial thickening, calcification and constriction - (Illus. **PERICARDIAL CALCIFICATION** and **PERICARDIAL CONSTRICTION**).

This may follow an inflammatory pericarditis, e.g. tuberculous, pyogenic, rheumatoid, asbestos induced, etc.; it may also follow trauma. Fibrosis and/ or calcification may follow (in about 3%) leading to constriction, if the cardiac contraction is compromised, either with a small pericardial sac constricting a normal sized heart, or a normal sized sac constricting a failing heart. Asbestos may also lead to the rare **pericardial mesothelioma.** (For asbestos induced pericarditis and mesothelioma see p. 14.51).

Difficulty may be experienced in differentiating pericardial from cardiac calcification. Coronary artery calcification is readily distinguished by its movement and parallel line appearance, also its position in the left or right coronary artery. However myocardial calcification in the wall of a left ventricular aneurysm may be difficult to distinguish. McGregor et al. (1987) studied the radiographic distinction between pericardial and myocardial calcifications and noted that pericardial calcification principally occurs over the right cardiac chambers, in the A/V grooves, but infrequently over the left ventricle. When there is calcification over the left ventricle, there is usually more extensive calcification elsewhere in the pericardium.

Further references.

Gotsman et al. (1974) : The ciné angiocardiogram in constrictive pericarditis.

Shawdon and Dinsmore (1967) : Studied the radiological features and clinical significance in 26 patients - 18 had clinical evidence of constrictive pericarditis. The majority had calcification overlying the left heart chambers.

Jeffrey and Webb (1980) : CT of rheumatoid pericarditis - grossly thickened pericardium.

Doppman et al. (1981) : CT in constrictive pericardial disease.

Soulen et al. (1985) : MR of constrictive pericardial disease.

Masui et al.. (1992) : MR evaluation of constrictive pericarditis and restrictive cardiomyopathy.

Suchet and Horwitz (1992) : CT in tuberculous constrictive pericarditis.

Hartnell et al. (1996) : MR of pericardial constriction (comparison of ciné MR angiography and spin-echo).

Pneumopericardium - (Illus. **PERICARDIAL GAS**).

This is a rare spontaneous finding, and usually is seen after penetrating injuries or paracentesis. Occasionally it may be found with a perforation of the oesophagus or stomach. Illus. **PERICARDIUM, Pt. 21a-b** shows a spontaneous pneumopericardium due to a perforation from a stomach remnant, in a patient who had had a recurrence of tumour many years after a partial oesophago-gastrectomy. Other causes include partial absence of the pericardium, allowing a pneumothorax or pneumomediastinum to extend into it. Illus. **PERICARDIUM, Pt. 19** shows a pneumopericardium following aspiration of a tuberculous pericardial effusion.

References.

Dassel and Kirsch (1954) : Two cases of spontaneous pneumopericardium - one after surgery and radiotherapy for oesophageal carcinoma.

Romhilt and Alexander (1965) : Pyopneumopericardium secondary to perforation of benign gastric ulcer.

Beaugie et al. (1966) : Pneumopericardium complicating carcinoma of the stomach.

Cramm and Robinson (1971) : Pneumopericardium associated with gastric cancer.

Toledo (1972) : Spontaneous pneumopericardium in acute asthma.

Strong (1974) : Oesophago-cardiac fistula complicating achalasia.

Westaby (1977) : Pneumopericardium and tension pneumopericardium after closed chest injury.

Robson (1979) : Hydropneumopericardium and oesophagitis - a non-fatal case.

Burt and Lester (1982) : Neonatal pneumopericardium giving a characteristic **halo sign**.

Cyrlak et al. (1983) : Oesopago-pericardial fistula - causes and radiographic features.

Stridbeck and Samuelson (1983) : Pneumopyopericardium.
Cummings et al. (1984) : Pneumopericardium resulting in cardiac tamponade.
Johnson et al. (1986) : CT and ultrasound to detect a pericardial abscess.
Mirvis et al. (1986) : Post-traumatic tension pneumopericardium - the 'small heart' sign - 4 cases - sudden decrease in heart size until surgical release of gas.
Lehmann et al. (1987) : Right atrial-oesophageal fistula and hydropneumoperitoneum after oesophageal dilatation.
Müller, N. et al. (1987) : Tension pneumopericardium caused by invasive pulmonary aspergillosis.
Nair (1987) : Instrumental perforation of the oesophagus into the pericardial cavity.
Johnston and Oliver (1988) : Cardiac tamponade due to pneumopericardium - 20 year old asthmatic patient who had assisted respiration.
West et al. (1988) : Benign peptic ulcers penetrating pericardium and heart.
Katzir et al. (1989) : Spontaneous pneumopericardium - case report (84 year old man with a RLL carcinoma perforating into the pericardium) and literature review.
Cousins and Manhire (1991) : Duodenal ulcer causing duodenal-pericardial fistula.
Vennos and Templeton (1992) : Pneumopericardium secondary to oesophageal carcinoma in a 55 year old alcoholic man.
Van Gelderen (1993) : Two new signs of pneumopericardium due to stab wounds of the heart - (i) **Transverse band of air**' sign on frontal radiographs due to air in the transverse sinus, and (ii) 'triangle of air' sign - gas lying retrosternally on lateral radiographs with superior extension.

Pleuro-pericardial cysts (see also ps. 3.13 - 15, 6.15 - 16 & 18.3).
   These are thin-walled cysts lined by endothelium. Mostly they occur adjacent to the lower right side of the pericardium, and appear to arise as a diverticulum of its parietal component. Similar cysts may arise from the parietal pleura, particularly where it covers the pericardium, the upper mediastinum or paravertebral areas. They may also occur rarely in the posterior mediastinum.
   Usually these cysts cause no symptoms and increase in size only slowly. Most are found by chance, and the number in the population has been estimated as 1 per 10,000. These cysts are thin-walled and usually contain clear colourless fluid, hence the alternative name - '**spring-water cysts**'. In most cases the fluid content may be confirmed with ultra-sound, particularly with those in the anterior cardio-phrenic angles. The cysts are usually ovoid or spherical in shape, though this may change with respiration or posture. Rarely a small portion of fat may be present between the cyst and the pericardium. On CT the contents mostly show Hounsfield numbers of 5 to 25, but occasionally they contain more viscid fluid up to 40 HU. CT is also useful for differentiating these cysts from thymic tissue in the upper anterior mediastinum. Malignant change within them has not to the author's knowledge been recorded. The cysts may be aspirated under fluoroscopic, ultra-sound or CT control.   Examples are shown in Illus. **PERICARDIAL CYST.**

References.
Lillie et al. (1950) : Reviewed 29 cases (23 of their own), 15 being discovered on routine examination and having no symptoms. All were in the anterior mediastinum, 5 in the middle or superior mediastinum.
Bates and Leaver (1951) : Five cases in anterior mediastinum.
Loehr (1952) : Five cases in lower anterior mediastinum.
Rogers and Leigh (1953) : Differential diagnosis of right cardiophrenic angle masses.
Clough and Bernie (1955) : Benign mesothelial cyst of the diaphragm.
Ringertz and Lidholm (1956) : Pericardial cysts generally occur in the anterior mediastinum adjacent to the diaphragm - six cases in anterior mediastinum or on the diaphragm.
LeRoux (1959) : Pericardial coelomic cysts.
Mills (1959) : Pericardial cyst in the superior mediastinum (pericardial cysts, other than those adjacent to the diaphragm are rare) - reviewed 5 others in the superior or mid-mediastinum from the literature.
Ochsner and Ochsner (1966) : Congenital cysts of the mediastinum - 20 year experience with 42 cases.
Klatte and Yune (1972) : The diagnosis and treatment of pericardial cysts.
Edwards and Ahmad (1972) : Epicardial cyst.
Uflacker and Duarte (1977) : Right para-cardiac mass ten years after heart surgery, due to a granuloma arising on a piece of sponge, which simulated a pericardial cyst.
Pugatch et al. (1978) : CT of pericardial cysts - change in shape with gravity on prone and supine views.
Patel , B. et al. (1978) : Pericardial cyst simulating intracardiac mass.
Modic and Janicki (1980) : CT of mass lesions of the right cardio-phrenic angle, diagnosis on density - cyst, fat, etc.
Rogers et al. (1980) : CT for showing pericardial cysts in atypical positions.
Engle et al. (1983) : Right sided heart failure misdiagnosed as pericardial cyst.
Hynes et al. (1983) : Two-dimensional echocardiographic diagnosis of pericardial cyst.

Brunner and Whitley (1984) : A pericardial cyst with high CT numbers.
Walker (1985) : Fine needle aspiration of a pericardial cyst - CT before and afterwards.
Stoller et al. (1986) : Two pericardial cysts, shown to be of water-density by CT, enlarged in size over several months. One was in the upper mediastinum at the level of the aortic arch and the other was at carinal level.
Tung and Chan (1991) : Misdiagnosis of an atypical pericardial cyst presenting in a patient with chest trauma.
Warren and Kay (1991) : Large left mid and lower mediastinal pericardial cyst with consolidation in left lower lobe, presenting with acute chest pain.
Satur et al. (1996) from Guy's Hosp. : Two giant pericardial cysts containing 2 & 2.5 l. of fluid were resected at video-assisted thoracoscopy.

Bulges of the pericardium.
   Daves (1970) - 'skiagraphing the mediastinal moguls' likened the bulges or protruberances on the cardiac outline to '**moguls**' i.e. packed snow on a mountainside sculptured by turning skis.
   On the right side of the heart, the right atrium is the only normal bulge. On the left, the aortic knuckle is the 'first', the pulmonary artery - the 'second', and the cardiac apex - the 'fourth'. If a 'third' is present, it lies below the left main bronchus, and may be due to an enlarged left atrium (or its appendage), an enlarged sinus of Valsalva, an enlarged right ventricular infundibulum, a left ventricular aneurysm or a cardiac herniation.
   Both true aneurysms of the left ventricular wall (usually following myocardial infarction), and 'false aneurysms' may deform the left pericardial outline. The former are usually situated lower down. Higher ones may be true aneurysms, or be false aneurysms i.e. haematomas from partial rupture of the left ventricular wall following mitral valve replacement (Alfdridge et al., 1988). Even an aneurysm of a saphenous vein graft has produced a left mediastinal or pericardial bulge on a chest radiograph (Webster et al., 1993). Occasionally a right ventricular aneurysm, following previous surgery for Fallot's tetralogy, may bulge out from the left cardiac outline.
   On the right side the most common bulge or double shadow is due to a dilated left atrium.

Further references.
Sorrell et al. (1994) : Left ventricular pseudoaneurysm (loculated rupture) following infarction - US diagnosis.
Steiner et al. (1995) : Value of plain chest radiography in congenital heart disease in adult patients.

Defects in the pericardium and cardiac volvulus or herniation.
   These may be developmental, traumatic or post-surgical in origin. Congenital herniation occurs more often on the left side, and both left and right sided herniae may be found causing a mediastinal mass or local bulge.
   A pericardial defect is shown radiographically by the abnormal passage of gas and/or fluid between the pleural and pericardial cavities, or by an abnormal contour caused by herniation of part or all of the heart.
   Surgical defects may be large or small. Large ones result from pericardial resection for the treatment of constrictive pericarditis or intrapericardial lung tumour resections, whilst others follow cardiac operations. Coronary by-pass operations usually involve vertical incisions, and these usually heal well. **Cardiac herniae** only usually occur if the lung has also been removed. Many cause no problems, but a few may lead to myocardial ischaemia, resulting from strangulation of the ventricles, and torsion of the great vessels leading to hypotension. Right sided herniation may lead to SVC compression. Most acute cases occur within 24 hours of operation.

   When a **defect is present on the left side**, the heart may move further towards the left, and its left border will tend to be elongated with **three   convexities**; the **aortic   knuckle**, a **long main pulmonary artery** and the **herniated left   ventricle**. There may also be lung translucencies between (i) the aortic arch and the pulmonary artery and (ii) the left ventricle and the diaphragm (see following figure).

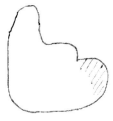

Fig. 15.27 Left sided herniation may mimic a
ventricular aneurysm, but can be readily
distinguished by fluoroscopy or ultrasound.

On the **right a volvulus or herniation** may follow an intrapericardial pneumonectomy, but
this is rare and often fatal. Radiological signs which may assist in recognition include :
(i) displacement of the **heart to the right**, (ii) **rotation of the heart on the great vessels**,
producing a '**notch**' between the rounded right heart border and the great vessels, probably due to
the thymus being seen 'side-on', (iii) **displacement and twisting of vascular lines**, (naso-
gastric tubes or cardiac catheters), but particularly venous catheters at the junction of the subclavian
and innominate veins, and (iv) herniation producing a mass due to the heart projecting out of the
pericardium laterally the '**snow-cone**' **sign.**
  A right cardiac hernia is shown in Illus. **PERICARDIUM, Pt. 29.**

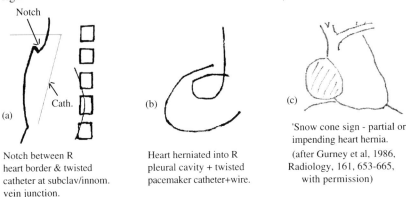

Notch between R heart border & twisted catheter at subclav/innom. vein junction.	Heart herniated into R pleural cavity + twisted pacemaker catheter+wire.	'Snow cone sign - partial or impending heart hernia. (after Gurney et al, 1986, Radiology, 161, 653-665, with permission)

Fig. 15.28 (a) Right-sided cardiac volvulus, (b) cardiac herniation and (c) impending herniation.

  Rarely a portion of the lung may herniate through a congenital pericardial defect into the
pericardial cavity (see also sections on lung herniation and lung torsion - ps. 2.37 - 2.40).

References.
Ellis et al. (1959) : Congenital deficiencies of the parietal pericardium.
Takasugi and Godwin (1989b) : Surgical defects of the pericardium.
Wright,M. et al. (1970) : Herniation of the heart.
Dieraniya (1974) : Cardiac herniation following intrapericardial pneumonectomy.
Tseherisch et al. (1976) : Acute cardiac herniation following pneumonectomy.
Cassorla and Katz (1984) : Management of cardiac herniation after intrapericardial pericardial pneumonectomy -
temporary measures include positioning of the pt. with the non-surgical side down, avoiding hyperinflation of the
remaining lung and injection of air into the surgical hemithorax.

Left side.
Mukergee (1964) : Congenital partial left pericardial defect with **bronchogenic cyst**.
Tabakin et al. (1965), Glover et al. (1969), Morgan et al. (1971) : Congenital absence of pericardium.
Yacoub et al. (1968) : Strangulation of the heart following intrapericardial pneumonectomy.
Dippel and Ehrenhaft (1973) : Herniation of the heart after pneumonectomy.
Hidvegi et al. (1981) : Herniation of the heart following left pneumonectomy.
Rothschild et al. (1987) : MR diagnosis of herniation of the left ventricle through a pericardial window.

Right side.

Hipona and Crummy (1964) : Congenital defect associated with Fallot's tetralogy - lung herniation into pericardium.

Castillo and Oldham (1985) : Cardiac herniation following right pneumonectomy for bronchial haemangioma.

Brady and Brogdon (1986) : Cardiac herniation following right pneumonectomy after trauma.

Gurney et al. (1986) : Cardiac herniation following surgery, two cases, one for trauma, the second a thymoma.

Brogdon and Gregory (1998) : Cardiac herniation to R following a RL lobectomy for gun-shot trauma - twisted CV catheter and heart in R pleural cavity.

Pericardial and cardiac tumours.

Pericardial tumours are rare, except perhaps for excess fat within the pericardium, which may mimic a lipoma. A true lipoma or liposarcoma may occur.

References to mesotheliomas involving the pericardium are noted on p. 14.51. Lymphomas, teratomas, chemodectomas (see ps. 18.37 - 38), neurofibromas, connective tissue tumours and cysts may also occur within the pericardium.

Cardiac tumours include myxomas (the most common and usually situated within the left atrium), hamartomas, myomas and myosarcomas (usually in association with tuberose sclerosis - see also ps. 5.14 - 15), fibrosarcomas (malignant fibrous histiocytomas) or intra-cavity angiosarcomas (the most common primary malignant heart tumour) or lymphomas. Tumours originating within the atria may extend retrogradely into the cava or pulmonary veins. A case involving the SVC is shown in Illus. **HEART, Pt. 27a-g**. Secondary tumours of the heart are rare (e.g. from the breast, etc. also a few have been recorded with osteosarcomas which tend to exhibit calcification and may be demonstrated by bone scintigraphy as well as CT), but are more common within the pericardium, particularly with reticulosis, bronchial neoplasm or thymomas.

Cardiac hamartomas are discussed on p. 5.16 and hydatids & heart-worms are noted on p. 19.52.

Illus. **PERICARDIAL DEPOSITS** show examples of breast and lung tumours involving the pericardium.

Illus. **PERICARDIAL TUMOUR, Pericardium Pt. 28** shows a pericardial mesothelioma.

Illus. **HEART TUMOUR** show examples of a right atrial tumour and a left ventricular fibroma.

References.

Silverman (1980) : Primary cardiac tumours.

Sumner et al. (1980), Whitton et al. (1980) : Intra-pericardial teratoma.

Grote et al (1982), Zingas et al. (1983) : Cardiac lipoma.

Andreou et al. (1983) : CT for the assessment of cardiac masses, esp, of left atrium.

Cornalba and Dore (1985) : Cardiac tumour associated with **tuberose sclerosis** - CT diagnosis.

Conces et al. (1985) : MR of left atrial myxomas.

Higgins et al. (1985) : MR of the heart - experience in 172 subjects.

Winkler and Higgins (1986) : Demonstration of peri-valvular infectious pseudoaneurysms.

        (1987) : Studied 34 patients who were suspected of having intracardiac masses by echocardiography. MR confirmed masses in 15 (rhabdomyomas, myxomas, thrombi, etc.), anatomical variants accounting for the abnormalities in 7 and found no abnormality in 12.

Conces et al. (1989) : Diagnosis of a myocardial lipoma using CT.

Gomes et al. (1987) : Studied 30 patients by MR. 14 had soft tissue tumours and 4 thrombi.

Kim, E. et al. (1989) : Two malignant fibrous histiocytomas and three angiosarcomas - MR features.

Lionarons et al. (1990) : Constrictive pericarditis caused by primary liposarcoma.

Bortolotti et al. (1992) : Giant intrapericardial solitary fibrous tumour.

Masui et al. (1995) : Cardiac myxoma - internal haemorrhage and surface thrombus calcification on MR.

Hayashi et al. (1996) : Ultrafast CT of epicardial lipoma in the pericardial sac - the **'split pericardium'** sign.

Heenan et al. (1996) : Percutaneous biopsy of a right atrial angiosarcoma under US guidance.

Ditchfield and Tung (1998) : 2 cases of primary cardiac lymphoma presenting with pericardial effusions and containing lymphoma cells + 3rd case with relapse of NHL involving the heart, pericardium and mediastinal nodes.

Daneman et al. (1983) : Cardiac metastasis from osteosarcoma - 2 cases.

Burke, A. et al. (1992) : Primary sarcomas of the heart.

Atra et al. (1998) : Metastatic cardiac osteosarcoma - from sarcoma of femur.

Burn et al. (1999) : R atrial metastatic melanoma detected by dynamic contrast enhanced spiral CT - gave references to 14 other cases of cardiac melanoma metastasis.

Collelly et al. (1999) : Cardiac metastasis from breast carcinoma.

Zissin et al. (1999) : L hilar metastasis from colonic cancer invading L atrium + tamponade - CT diagnosis.

Cardiac aneurysms and false aneurysms

Cardiac aneurysms may arise in the atrial or ventricular walls.

Left atrial aneurysms mostly occur with mitral valve disease, and right atrial aneurysms with tricuspid incompetence - see Illus. **HEART MITRAL VALVE** and **HEART TRICUSPID VALVE.**

About 80% of ventricular aneurysms occur anterolaterally near the cardiac apex and follow occlusion of the anterior descending branch of the left coronary artery leading to myocardial infarction, thinning and scarring. Typically they produce convex rounded bulges of the left cardiac contour, which often show paradoxical enlargement with each cardiac contraction, as seen with fluoroscopy or on ultrasound. Some may be calcified. Thrombosis within them may cause systemic emboli. Haemodynamic function may be improved by surgical resection. Some aneurysms may become false aneurysms with localised leakage of blood. Both true and false large cardiac aneurysms may cause pressure effects on the oesophagus or chest wall.

For illustrations - see Illus. **HEART L VENT ANEURYSM.**

False aneurysms may occur spontaneously or at the sites of previous surgery, including coronary bypass surgery, or cannulation sites for bypass circulation (see p. 12.31 for false aneurysms of chest wall).

Some references.

Davies, M. (1988) : Ischaemic ventricular aneurysms true or false?

McIlmoyle et al. (1973) : Massive false aneurysm of the L ventricle with dysphagia.

Charig and Partridge (1999) : Atypical chest pain from a L ventricular false aneurysm, causing pressure erosion of the overlying ribs as shown by isotope bone scan and CT; this patient had had a previous surgical repair of an ASD.

Walsh et al. (2001) : Giant coronary bypass graft pseudoaneurysm presenting as a haemothorax

Cardiac and vascular calcification (see Illus. **HEART CALCIFICATION** and **AORTIC CALCIFICATION**).

Vascular (particularly aortic and coronary) and valvular calcification is common in the elderly, but may be present as a result of disease, aneurysm, aortitis, rheumatic disease, luetic, trauma, etc. Heart wall (mainly ventricular) calcification is particularly seen following infarction, other types of myocarditis, and may be associated with a cardiac aneurysm; atrial calcification may follow rheumatic carditis.

Prostheses in vessels, or valves, old haematomas, surgical or traumatic scars may also calcify; also the occasional foreign body.

Calcification may also be associated with diabetes, renal failure or amyloid.

Some references.

Jefferson and Rees (1973 & 1980) : Clinical Cardiac Radiology.

Stanford et al. (1993) : Coronary artery calcification - detection and significance.

Lee V. et al. (1994) : Atypical and unusual calcifications of the heart and great vessels.

Lippert et al. (1995) : Calcification of aortic valve seen on CT scans - is common and usually clinically insignificant. In younger people it may be a pointer to underlying aortic stenosis.

Callaway et al. (1997) : Incidence of coronary artery calcification on standard thoracic CT scans.

Callaway et al. (1999) : Incidence of coronary artery calcification on conv. & spiral thoracic CT scans in 900 consecutive exams. - calcification increases with age and calcification is more prevalent in males than females.

Edwards, M. (1998) : Prosthetic Heart Valves.

For other cardiac and pericardial abnormalities see under:

Ebstein's anomaly (p. 7.4)
ASD, VSD, Fallot (p. 7.5)
Tricuspid incompetence (p. 17.2)
PDA (ps. 7.4 - 5)
MR angiography (p. 20.29 et seq.)

also Illus.

CARDIAC HERNIA
CORONARY ARTERY

CORONARY SINUS
HEART
HEART ADDISON'S DISEASE & ANOREXIA NERVOSA (small heart)
HEART ALCOHOL
HEART AORTIC VALVE
HEART ASD
HEART CALCIFICATION
HEART DEXTROROTATION
HEART EPSTEIN ANOMALY
HEART FAILURE
HEART FALLOT
HEART FALLOT+BLALOCK
HEART FOLDER
HEART HOCM
HEART L ATRIUM
HEART L VENT
HEART L VENT ANEURYSM
HEART MITRAL STENOSIS
HEART MITRAL VALVE
HEART TRANSPOSITION
HEART TRICUSPID VALVE
HEART TRUNCUS
HEART TUMOUR
HEART VALVE CALC
HEART VALVE PROSTHESIS
HEART VSD
HEART WEINBERG OPERATION (Internal mammary artery implantation into heart).
KYMOGRAM

PERICARDIAL CALCIFICATION
PERICARDIAL CONSTRICTION
PERICARDIAL CYST
PERICARDIAL DEPOSITS
PERICARDIAL EFFUSION
PERICARDIAL GAS
PERICARDIAL RECESSES
PERICARDIAL TUMOUR
PERICARDIUM

PACEMAKER

Re pacemakers, wires and prosthetic valves - noting the presence of a pacemaker (which the patient may have forgotten) or a prosthetic heart valve with a metal ball (very few have such now) may preclude an MR examination, as the pacemaker wires may become displaced, form loops, etc, or metallic balls become fixed during the MR examination - even epicardial wire tips may be pulled out of the myocardium.

Contrariwise **fixed metallic objects** e.g. arterial, oesophageal, bronchial etc. stents (and orthopaedic metal-wear) have no safety problems, but may cause artefacts on adjacent structures.

Fractures of pacemaker wires, misplacement or the formation of loops should be noted on chest radiographs. Loops may be associated with subacute bacterial endocarditis, as well as mechanical problems - see p. 9.18 re pacemaker wires in the coronary sinus.

PDA and ASD occlusion devices may give rise to 'collar-stud' opacities - such devices are now being commonly used in preference to open surgery.

(For references to IV catheters - see p. 11.12).

Chapter 16 : **The oesophagus.**

<u>The thoracic oesophagus and upper stomach.</u>

   Normal anatomy - the oesophagus lies centrally at the thoracic inlet and passes slightly to the right at the level of the aortic arch. It then returns almost to the midline, before passing to the left below carinal level. It is often deviated by a dilated or tortuous lower ascending aorta but may also be deviated by other structures, lie centrally within the posterior mediastinum (see Fig. 16.1, below) or to the right with situs inversus etc.

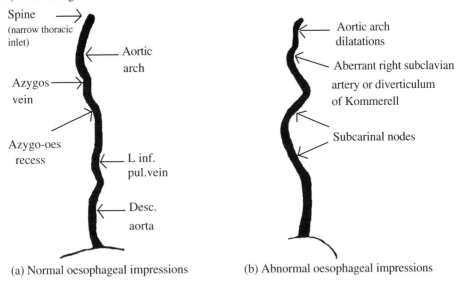

(a) Normal oesophageal impressions   (b) Abnormal oesophageal impressions

Fig. 16.1   Diagram of various structures which may press on the barium-filled oesophagus.

Normal impressions on the oesophagus include:
            The lower cervical &/or upper cervical spine esp. on R with narrow thoracic inlet.
            The aortic arch.
            The posterior part of the azygos arch (ps. 9.11 - 12).
            The azygo-oesophageal recess, containing the right lower lobe.
            The left inferior pulmonary vein.
Abnormal impressions or displacements include :
            Dilatations or aneurysms of the arch, and
            An atheromatous descending aorta (Illus. **OES-AORTA**).
            An aberrant right subclavian artery and/or diverticulum of Kommerell (p.10.2-3
                see also Illus. **OES-ABER SUB A**).
            Pulmonary arterial, pseudovascular rings or slings (ps. 7.5 - 6).
            Goitres,
            Nodal masses or other mediastinal tumours (Illus. **OES-DISPLACED & OES-
                PRESSURE**).

<u>References</u>
Chasen et al. (1984) : Mediastinal impressions on the dilated oesophagus.
Kendall et al. (1962) : Half shadow defect in the barium filled gullet between C7 & D3 on R due to trachea.
Serotopoulos et al. (1979) : Pectus excavatum deformities simulating mediastinal masses.
Bhadelia et al. (1996) : Oesophageal pseudomass at thoracic inlet on barium swallow.
Kirby et al. (2000) : Narrow thoracic inlet causing oesophageal pseudomass - 3 cases.

   When the oesophagus is in the resting phase, its lower end is normally intra-abdominal. On swallowing, this part ascends, and together with the adjacent upper stomach becomes intrathoracic. Normally after swallowing, and the passage of a food bolus, these are returned to the abdomen by the elastic fibres of the phreno-oesophageal ligaments (see Fig. 16.2 and discussion below). These parts also become intra-thoracic with hiatal herniae or abdominal distension including considerable obesity. With hiatal herniae a small sac of peritoneum envelops the cardia, and may be seen on CT sections, particularly if filled with ascitic fluid or gas.

Normally the oesophageal mucosa is squamous, but columnar cells line the mucus glands in its wall, and patches of gastric type mucosa may be found with a Barrett's oesophagus (see below).

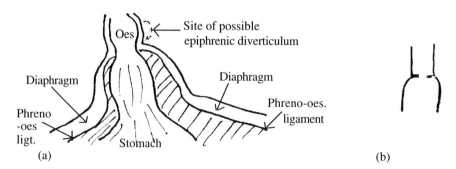

Fig. 16.2   (a) A portion of the peritoneum (hatched) may extend up into a hiatal hernial sac; and this may be involved by tumour, ascites, etc. (after Godwin and MacGregor, 1987, AJR, **148**, 31 - 32 with permission).

(b) Schatzki or mucosal ring at or close to the squamo-columnar junction - may be potentiated by reflux - see also p. 16.6-7 and Illus. **OES-SCHATZKI RING**.

Friedland (1978) reviewed the changing concepts of lower oesophageal anatomy (from the time of Hippocrates) and noted:

(i) The **cardia** denotes the point at which the oesophagus joins the stomach, but is not synonymous with where the squamous and columnar epithelia meet.

(ii) The phreno-oesophageal membranes (or 'ligaments' - first noted by Galen, 200 AD) are really double structures arising from fascia covering the upper and lower surfaces of the diaphragm. With advancing age, the upper part atrophies and the amount of elastic tissue in the lower part decreases. Excessive fat may prevent the downward pull of the elastic fibres returning the stomach to the abdomen following the swallowing of a bolus of food.

(iii) The '**vestibule**' (or '**cardiac antrum**') refers to the pouch which is often seen below the area of the sling fibres of the 'sphincter'; a diverticulum in this area (often very small) may slip between these fibres and provide localisation - the '**epiphrenic diverticulum**'.

(iv) Two rings may be seen - Wolf's 'A ring' (in the region of the sphincter), and the **Schatzki*** or 'B ring' - a muscular or mucosal ring occurring close to or at the squamo-columnar junction and which may be accentuated by reflux (Illus. **OES-SCHATZKI   RING**). When the author was at the Henry Ford Hospital in 1965 barium capsules were used to gauge the size of such rings (Illus. **OES-SWALLOWING, Pt. 1**) - similarly 13mm tablets have been used by van Westen and Ekberg (1993) for showing abnormalities not shown by liquid contrast medium.

* Described in a series of articles (with J.E. Gary between 1953 and 1963) - see Schatzki, S.C. (1988) : Richard Schatzki - a biography.

The oesophago-gastric junction.

In the absence of a hiatus hernia, this lies opposite the fissure in the liver for the ligamentum venosum (between the caudate and left lobes). It is surrounded by the upper part of the lesser omentum (gastro-hepatic ligament).

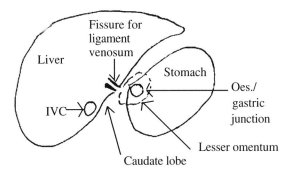

Fig. 16.3 Position of oesophago-gastric junction on CT section.

On plain radiographs, IVP's etc., fluid in the fundus of the stomach may produce a '**gastric pseudo-mass**', at or just below the level of the cardia (Illus. **ADRENAL FALSE TUMOUR**). The author has seen several examples diagnosed as adrenal tumours, and one patient from Dublin had even had two exploratory operations for this spurious adrenal tumour and was referred to Oxford for a third! A similar appearance is also commonly seen with fluid within a hiatus hernia. Difficulty may occur when a tumour and the pseudo-mass occur together, but they may be readily differentiated by filling the stomach fundus with gas or opaque contrast medium.

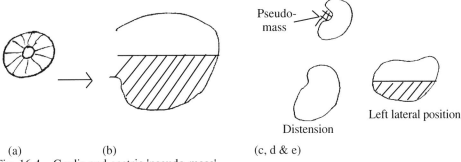

(a)   (b)   (c, d & e)

Fig. 16.4   Cardia and gastric 'pseudo-mass'.
(a) Normal cardia.
(b) No mass with gaseous and fluid distension of stomach.
(c, d & e) Gastric pseudo-mass.

Turning the patient into the left lateral decubitus position may cause a 'pseudo-mass' to disappear, i.e. by distension of that part of the mucosa. Halvorsen and Thompson (1984) considered this to be the best position for CT examination of this area. Others have turned the patient prone or into the left posterior oblique position. The author, however, usually uses standard supine and prone positions.

Further references.
Ingelfinger and Kramer (1953) : Dysphagia produced by contractile ring in lower oesophagus.
Ingelfinger (1971) : The sphincter that is a Sphinx.
Schatzki and Gary (1953 & 1956) : The lower oesophageal ring.
MacMahon et al. (1958) : The lower oesophageal ring.
Creamer et al. (1959) : Further observations on the gastro-oesophageal junction - a short segment of the gullet lies within the abdominal cavity. The junction has the properties of a valve i.e. a small resistance to forward passage and the ability to resist retrograde flow in the face of large inverse pressures. The sphincteric area and pressure barrier do not have synonymous positions.
Berridge (1961) : The mechanism of the cardia - reflux is prevented by bunching of the mucosal folds which are pressed into the form of a cone.

Johnson et al. (1961) : Hiatus hernia and hiatal disorder - 18 radiological signs.
Mendl and Evans (1962) : Incomplete lower oesophageal diaphragm.
Thompson et al. (1984) : Anatomy.
Marks et al. (1981) : The oesophago-gastric region - source of confusion on CT.
Lindell and Bernadino (1981) : Diagnosis of hiatus hernia by CT.
Pupols and Ruzicka (1984) : Hiatus hernia pseudomass.
Benacci et al. (1993), Orringer (1993) : Epiphrenic diverticulum - results of surgical treatment.

Gas in the oesophagus (dilated air-filled oesophagus or 'gas oesophagogram' - Illus. **OES-GAS**)

As noted in Chapter 1, small amounts of gas in the oesophagus are not uncommonly seen on high KV radiographs or tomograms. A partially gas-filled oesophagus may often be seen on a chest radiograph in patients with achalasia (Illus. **OES-ACHALASIA**). It may be more fully gas-filled in scleroderma (Illus. **OES-SCLERODERMA**), if a patient is about to belch, and with an adult type of non-malignant chronic type of tracheo-oesophageal fistula (p. 16.10). In the last, the oesophagus may be seen to fill with air in inspiration, due to the negative pressure in the chest pulling the oesophagus open.

An atonic oesophagus may also fill with air - such may be seen in patients with Parkinson's disease, pseudo-bulbar palsy or dystrophia myotonica (Illus. **OES-ATONIC, OES-PARKINSON** and **DYSTROPHIA MYOTONICA**). **Chaga's disease** (p. 19.56) although common in South America is rarely seen in the UK. A dilated gas-filled oesophagus may sometimes be seen above a stricture caused by caustic fluids or thermal burns (see p. 16.15 - 16). Other causes include chronic mediastinal disease, the post-operative state and those practising 'oesophageal speech' following laryngectomy.

Slowly growing tumours may give rise to a gas-filled oesophagus but rapidly growing tumours usually cause little dilatation, because the oesophagus usually takes several months to dilate, also patients with tumours tend to have blockage for food and fluid and tend to eructate any contents.

An air-filled and dilated oesophagus may cause apparent 'thickening' of the posterior tracheal and tracheo-oesophageal stripes (see ps. 1.23-24). It may also distort the azygo-oesophageal recess and paraoesophageal lines, and in the upper mediastinum the posterior junction line (see diagrams - Figs. 1.25 & 1.38).

Examples are shown in Illus. **OES-GAS**.

Achalasia of the cardia - (Illus. **OES-ACHALASIA**).

In this condition the oesophagus is commonly dilated like a fluid-filled cucumber, seen through the heart in the posterior mediastinum, and displacing the para-oesophageal line. The stomach fundal gas bubble is commonly absent, due to the fluid trap in the lower oesophagus. On a contrast swallow, a smooth **'bird's-beak' like narrowing of the cardia**, as well as poor peristalsis, may be seen. Differentiation from a smooth-looking neoplasm is often readily made by giving a hot drink, when the cardia will be seen to relax (Wright, 1984 & 1998). The **hot drink** (often hot water) is preferable to a relaxant drug (probanthine or buscopan), as it will **not** affect the eyes, nor make the patient feel faint (as with amyl nitrite), or upset bowel motility; many patients will have learnt this trick themselves - hot drink before or during a meal, and no old lady refuses a cup of tea! Many patients with achalasia also have a poor belching mechanism. (The author has seen cut chins from patients falling to the floor after inhaling amyl nitrite [given by registrars] and intestinal obstruction from inspissated oesophageal contents following bowel paralysis after e.g. much orange pith had suddenly passed on from the oesophagus to the stomach and duodenum following the IV injection of a relaxant drug.)

In some centres manometry is performed to show decreased motility, but this is time consuming and the author prefers fluoroscopic observation. In a few cases, which do not relax with a hot drink, endoscopy may be needed to exclude a smooth or short length neoplasm of the cardia simulating achalasia - **"pseudo-achalasia"**. Endoscopy may also be combined with balloon dilatation of the cardia. The traditional surgical approach is to perform a Heller's operation - a myotomy of the lower oesophageal muscle. Transoesophageal ultra-sound may show thickening of the circular and longitudinal muscle of the inferior oesophageal sphincter.

A very large oesophagus may extend to the right of the heart outline and simulate a mediastinal tumour; occasionally it may drape itself over the aortic arch, or even cause obstruction to the trachea or great veins. It may also be mistaken for a dilated trachea!

About 5% of cases of achalasia may be complicated by neoplasm, and a tracheo-oesophageal fistula may result. Such tumours occur most commonly in the mid or upper oesophagus, where the fluid level is most common. Examples are shown in Illus. **OES-ACHAL+NEOPLASM.**

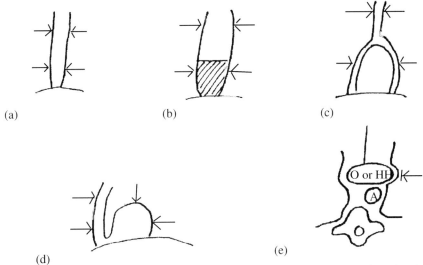

(a) (b) (c)

(d) (e)

Fig. 16.5   (a - d) Left and right - paraoesophageal lines with achalasia or a hiatus hernia. (e) A dilated oesophagus or a hiatus hernia will also produce a pleural reflection on the left.

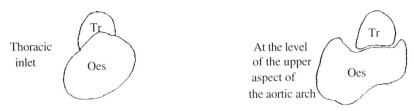

Thoracic inlet

At the level of the upper aspect of the aortic arch

Fig. 16.6   Diagram of the findings in a young woman who presented with severe dyspnoea, caused by pressure of a very dilated oesophagus on the trachea. At times she had to put her arms above her head, and put her head back in order to breathe.

Illus. **OES-ACHALASIA, Pt. 18** shows a slow-K tablet stuck in an old lady's narrowed oesophagus from achalasia - it was released by a hot drink! She had not been able to swallow for two days.

Illus. **OES-SPASM** shows a case of spasm in the lower oesophagus following a road traffic accident - this spasm also responded to a hot drink.

Further references.

Plummer and Vinson (1921) : Cardiospasm - a report of 301 cases.
Vinson (1927) : Cardiospasm complicated by pulmonary abscess (see also p. 19.3).
Johnstone (1960) : Diffuse spasm and diffuse muscle hypertrophy of the lower oesophagus.
Blomquist and Mahoney (1961) : Air-filled oesophagus on post-operative films in chronic inflammatory disease.
Wright, J. (1961) : 'The demonstration of response to Buscopan in a case with a dilated gullet is a confirmation of a diagnosis of uncomplicated achalasia. The absence of a response should raise a strong suspicion of neoplasm.'
Cimmino (1965) : Air in the mid-oesophagus - a normal finding, but a potential source of diagnostic error.

Harper and Jackson (1965), Martinez (1974) : Scleroderma as a cause of air-filled oesophagus.
Dinsmore et al. (1966) : Air filled oesophagus in scleroderma and with oesophageal speech.
Ellis, F. and Olsen (1969) : Achalasia.
Martel (1972) : Air filled oesophagus following caustic agents.
Wingfield and Karkowski (1972) : The treatment of achalasia by cardiomyotomy.
Dittrich and Bautz (1974) : Infants with functional abnormalities of the cardia.
Keats and Smith (1974) : Poor respiration in the neonate.
Castell (1976) : Achalasia and diffuse oesophageal spasm.
House and Griffiths (1977) : Air-filled oesophagus in scleroderma and achalasia.
Proto and Lane (1977) : Air in the oesophagus - a normal finding.
Meredith et al. (1981) : Oesophageal gas is not uncommon in the presence of a tumour.
Dodds et al. (1986) : Radiological amyl nitrite test for distinguishing pseudo-achalasia from idiopathic achalasia.
Foster, P. et al. (1987) : Achalasia like disorders in Von Recklinghausen's disease.
Ott et al. (1987) : Oesophageal radiography and manometry - correlation in 172 pts. with dysphagia.
Ziegler et al. (1990) : Endosonographic appearances of the oesophagus in achalasia.
Tuck et al. (1991) : Achalasia of the cardia in childhood.
Howard et al. (1992) : Five yr. study of the incidence, clinical features and diagnosis of achalasia in Edinburgh.
Mason and Wright (1992) : Childhood achalasia.
Meshkinopour et al. (1992) : Monometric and radiological correlations in achalasia.
Schima et al. (1992) : Oesophageal motor disorders - study of 88 pts. with fluoroscopy and manometry.
Parkman and Cohen (1993) : Malignancy-induced secondary achalasia.
Katz (1994) : Achalasia two effective treatment options - let the patient decide.
Tasker (1995) : Two cases of massively dilated air filled oesophagus causing respiratory compromise and stridor - both subsided spontaneously.
Spence and Fitzgerald (1996) : Transabdominal ultrasound detection of achalasia.
Schima et al. (1998) : Diagnostic accuracy of video-fluoroscopy in the detection of achalasia.
Woodfield et al. (2000) : Diagnosis of primary v. secondary achalasia - clinical & radiographic criteria (but no mention of a hot drink!).

(For pulmonary complications of achalasia - see ps. 19.2 - 3).

Idiopathic muscular hypertrophy of the oesophagus is a rare benign oesophageal disease, characterised by hyperplasia of all layers of the oesophageal wall, including the muscle layers. It produces chronic dysphagia, dilatation of the oesophagus and narrowing of the cardia. It is probably a variant of achalasia. CT shows gross thickening of the oesophageal muscle. Dilatation is usually of little use, but an extensive myotomy may be of help. About 100 cases have been reported.

Fig. 16.7 Muscle hypertrophy in
the oesophageal wall (diagram).

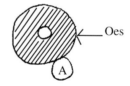

References.
Wood (1932), Sloper (1954), Ellis et al. (1960),
Johnstone (1960), Agostini et al. (1988).

Radiological changes of reflux oesophagitis (including webs and stricture formation).
Gastro-oesophageal reflux is extremely common. It may occur as a complication of a hiatal hernia, but in many it has no such relationship. The easiest method for its detection is to use the water-swallowing 'de Carvalho' test after swallowing the barium - the patient lies a few degrees head-down and a little turned to the right, whilst he drinks water via a straw from a cup, and it is a very easy matter to note reflux of barium back up the oesophagus. Clearance of refluxed fluid is probably of more importance than reflux itself, as it may indicate that gastric type fluid may lie in the oesophagus much of the night, and lead to ulceration and stricture formation. These may occur in any part of the oesophagus, but particularly where refluxed acid fluid tends to remain. It may be in the mid-oesophagus in those who are bed-bound and paralysed, in the lower oesophagus, above the cardia or a hiatus hernia, and the Schatzki ring (at or close to the oesophago-gastric mucosal junction) may be potentiated by reflux. Webs or strictures of the lower

pharynx or upper oesophagus are probably also caused by reflux, passing up to these areas at night; they may be associated with iron deficiency anaemia, presumably due to bleeding from oesophagitis. Severe cases may mimic varices or neoplasm, but most benign strictures are smooth in outline.

An important technical point is that motility and peristaltic studies (including tests for reflux) must be carried out **without** the use of relaxant drugs in order to be meaningful! Most patients find that symptoms are relieved by drinking a cup of water, whilst others find help from acid antagonists, etc. Surgical treatment in most cases is best avoided (except for dilating strictures) as it only usually starts the patient on a slippery slide to more and more surgery, the end result often being much worse than the patient had ever imagined!

In babies and young children, gastro-oesophageal reflux may be shown with transabdominal ultrasound.

Examples are shown in Illus. **OES-REFLUX, OES-STRICTURE** and **OES-WEB** or **PHARYNGEAL WEB.**

Frank vomiting may sometimes be observed during a barium enema examination if the patient retches and this proceeds to actual vomiting. Both increased abdominal pressure and gastric (± oesophageal) peristalsis may propel the stomach contents up to the throat and mouth. An example is shown in Illus. **OES-VOMITING.** See also reference to Lumsden and Holden (1969) - p. 16.14.

References.

Brown Kelly (1919) : Spasm at the entrance to the oesophagus causing a web.

Paterson (1919) : A clinical type of dysphagia.

Vinson (1922) : Hysterical dysphagia.   Slater (1991) : Plummer **never** wrote about oes. dysphagia.

Waldenström and Kjellberg (1939) : Radiological features of cricopharyngeal web - 'with the hypopharynx and the upper oesophagus filled with barium, a sharp horizontal translucent shelf is seen extending from the anterior wall into the barium column just below the cricoid cartilage'.

de Carvalho (1951) : **'Test du siphonage'** - used 100 - 200 ml. water with the patient in the Trendelenberg (head-down) position.

Shamma'a and Benedict (1958) : Oesophageal webs - 58 cases - an attempt at classification - upper oes. webs (with & without anaemia), mid oes. webs., lower oes. webs and benign mucous-membrane pemphigus.

Smiley et al. (1963) : Two thirds of patients with webs had hiatus hernias.

Sim (1964) : An evaluation of tests for hiatus hernia.

Blendis et al. (1965) : The aetiology of sideropenic web ("the presence of a crico-pharyngeal web only indicates atrophy and degeneration of the upper oesophagus which may or may not be associated with iron deficiency").

Pitman and Fraser (1965) : The postcricoid impression of the oesophagus.

Elswood and Pitman (1966) : Observer error in the radiological diagnosis of Paterson-Kelly webs - one should note the normal 'post-cricoid impression'.

Wright, F. (1975) : Diagnosis of reflux oesophagitis.

Rabin and Schmaman (1979) : Radiological changes of reflux oesophagitis.

Richter et al. (1987) : **'Nutcracker oesophagus'** - high pressure transit.

Sellar et al. (1987) : A sensitive test for gastro-oesophageal reflux - used compression method with double contrast.

Stevenson (1989) : Radiological examination for reflux was useful if it included answers to the questions :

(i) Is the reflux (a) free, repeated and spontaneous, (b) massive with provocation or (c) minimal or absent, even with water-siphon provocation?

(ii) Is there a hiatus hernia present with the patient supine and at rest?

(iii) Is primary peristalsis abnormal, and is non-peristaltic muscle activity present?

(iv) Can the oesophagus clear refluxed acid and barium?, with how many swallows?

(v) Are cricopharyngeal abnormalities of reflux disease present?

(vi) Are complications present, moderate or severe oesophagitis, Barrett's oesophagus, rings and strictures?

Ranjit Rajah (1990) : Concluded that even though Buscopan is known to reduce the lower oesophageal sphincter pressure, it does not induce reflux or interfere with detection of a hiatus hernia to any clinically significant degree.

Marks and Richter (1993) : Peptic strictures of the oesophagus.

Thompson et al. (1994) : Value of Ba studies compared with 24 hr pH monitoring - Ba with water-siphon test is useful for screening pts. suspected of having reflux - monitoring oes. pH is considered the most sensitive but is costly and often not available.

Huynh et al. (1995) : Treatment of symptomatic webs of upper oesophagus with fluoroscopically guided balloon dilatation.

Karasick and Lev-Toaff (1995) : Oesophageal strictures - findings on barium radiographs -
Webs - usually single and occur along anterior wall of cervical oes. as 'shelf-like' defects 1 or 2 mm thick, but can be circumferential, with severe luminal narrowing.
      - a few follow laryngectomy and/ or radiotherapy for ca larynx.
      - skin diseases (with blisters) - pemphigus vulgaris, bullosa dystrophica, and pemphigus.
      - eosinophilic oesophagitis (proximal oes.).
      - graft v host disease after bone marrow transplantation (late complication).
Infection - candida, herpes, TB.
Drugs - doxycline (vibramycin), tetracycline, aspirin, slow release KCl (contact with oes. mucosa esp in mid oes.), and quinidine.
Neoplasms (oes., bronchus, thyroid, breast, lymphoma, etc.) / **Radiation.**
Reflux (acid or alkaline), **Barrett's oes.**
Trauma - caustic injury, naso-gastric tubes, post sclerotherapy for varices.
Crohn's disease (may affect lower oes. causing long lower oes. ulcers).

Schima et al. (1996) : Video-fluoroscopy of the pharynx and oesophagus in globus sensation - most patients had significant abnormalities - hyperplastic tonsils, Zenker diverticula, webs, cervical osteophytes, dysfunctions of the pharyngo-oesophageal sphincter, pharyngeal or oesophageal carcinoma, oesophageal motor disorders, gastro-oesophageal reflux and hiatus hernia.
Foster (1997) : Pts. having endoscopic oeesophageal dilatation for benign peptic strictures - perforation in about 1% - water soluble contrast study should be performed - chest radiography is less valuable.

Columnar-lined or Barrett' s oesophagus   (see also p. 16.18).
   Barrett (1950) a surgeon at St. Thomas' Hospital noted that chronic peptic oesophageal ulcers tended to develop in gastric type, rather than squamous epithelium and thought that they should be distinguished from reflux oesophagitis. Heading (1987) felt that it occurs when the whole circumference of the squamo-columnar junction lies 3 cm or more above the lower end of the oesophagus. This may occasionally be congenital, but gastric type mucosa may develop as a metaplastic change in relation to reflux, as a result of repair occurring from glands in the oesophageal wall. In some series this type of mucosa appears to be more prone to the development of neoplasm.

Further references.
Allison and Johnstone (1953) : Oesophagus lined with gastric mucous membrane.
Pierce and Creamer (1963) : Diagnosis of columnar lined esophagus.
Levine et al. (1983) : Reticular mucosal pattern in Barrett's oesophagus.
Agha (1985) : Review of 34 cases of Barrett type adenocarcinoma of the lower oesophagus - suggested when a patient with long-standing gastro-oesophageal reflux develops a long vertical infiltrating or varicoid looking neoplasm.
Chen et al. (1985) : Radiological signs of Barrett's oesophagus - mid-oesophageal stricture, oesophageal ulceration and distal oesophageal widening were particularly indicative. Reflux, hiatal hernia and thickened irregular folds with a granular mucosal pattern were common.
Shapir et al. (1985) : 19 cases - felt that the diagnosis should only be made by histology, and that a reticular mucosal pattern was only rarely seen.
Gilchrist et al. (1987) : 200 examined by double contrast barium studies and oesophagoscopy - categorised into high, moderate or low risk, but correlation with endoscopy except in the gross cases was poor.
Kweka et al. (1987) : Determined the presence of gastric mucosa with Tc^{99m} pertechnetate in 8 cases - the same test for gastric mucosa in a Meckle's diverticulum (see also - Wright and Neale, 1980).
van der Veen et al. (1989) : Adenocarcinoma in Barrett's oesophagus - an over rated risk.
Glick et al. (1991) : Radiological diagnosis of Barrett oesophagus mucosal surface abnormalities on double contrast studies - reticular or villous pattern.
Cary et al. (1993): Combined oesophageal adenocarcinoma and carcinoid in Barrett's oesophagitis.
Little (1993) : Barrett's oesophagus - another oesophageal Sphinx - all pts. have gastro-oes. reflux even in the absence of symptoms also increased tendency towards malignancy as a result of the unstable mucosa.

Oesophageal diverticula and pseudodiverticula - (Illus. **OES-DIVERTICULA, OES-PSEUDODIVERTICULA** and **PHARYNGEAL POUCH**).
   Oesophageal (including pharyngeal) diverticula are not uncommon and may occur from the neck down to the lower mediastinum, and may be multiple. They may sometimes give rise to mediastinal masses, which may contain air /fluid levels. The best known is Zenker's diverticulum,

arising in the neck in Killian's* dehiscence, i.e. the potential space posteriorly below the oblique fibres of the crico-pharyngeus. These are usually small, but occasionally can fill the lower neck and track down into the mediastinum. Sometimes the patients present with repeated chest infections due to the inhalation of food from the pouch. Rarely a neoplasm may develop within a pouch (Illus. **PHARYNGEAL POUCH+CA**).

Mid oesophageal diverticula mainly arise at carinal level and probably arise by traction from a residual band attaching the oesophagus at this point to the trachea and left main bronchus - a residuum of the track which may also persist as a congenital tracheo-oesophageal fistula. As noted on p. 16.1, the oesophagus moves upwards on swallowing a solid bolus (watch a snake swallowing!), thus the band being pulled by the oesophagus during swallowing causes tension on the band and an outpouching of the oesophageal wall. Alteration in size of these diverticula can also be seen on a barium swallow if they are not large. The supposition that they are connected with tuberculous scarring seems erroneous (Wright, 1973 - below).

An epiphrenic diverticulum (see also p. 16.2) denotes the position of the 'sling' fibres of the lower oesophageal sphincter. It is usually tiny and of no clinical importance, but only rarely may become enlarged.

Multiple pseudodiverticula may occur as a result of **oesophageal dysfunction or spasm**, a milder form appearing as the '**corkscrew oesophagus**', which may be associated with bulbar or pseudo-bulbar palsy, but mostly occurs as a local phenomenon, sometimes stimulated by certain foods (e.g. some cheeses) or by acid reflux - Illus. **OES-CORKSCREW** - see also Illus. **OES-SPASM**.

* Justav Killian (1860 - 1921), Professor of Otolaryngology, Berlin.

References.
Turner (1963) : Carcinoma as a complication of pharyngeal pouch (two cases).
Wright, F. (1973) : On the nature of the mid oesophageal diverticulum - no cases where calcified nodes were present on tomography.
Kim et al. (1988) : CT diagnosis of giant epiphrenic diverticulum.
Etherington and Clements (1990) : Giant mid oesophageal diverticulum - a rare cause of dysphagia.
Hadley et al. (1997) : The radiological appearances after Dohlman's procedure - endoscopic crico-pharyngeal myotomy - a reduced height of the partition wall, ease of passage of barium and reduced content of the pouch indicate success of the procedure.

Benign tumours of the oesophagus, foreign bodies and bezoars.
Benign tumours account for about one fifth of oesophageal neoplasms.
Leiomyomas are the most common - they are smooth in outline, and being mainly in the oesophageal wall, appear as rounded or oval masses on one side of the lumen, rather than true intra-luminal masses. Many are found incidentally and most give rise to no or minimal clinical symptoms. Occasionally they may push out from the oesophageal wall into the mediastinum and indent one pleural cavity to give rise to a rounded mass on chest radiographs. There is usually no obstruction to the passage of barium, normal motility and distensibility of the oesophagus. Most cases proceed to thoracotomy, but some have wondered if this is necessary as malignant change is rare. Illus. **OES-LEIOMYOMA**.
Hamartomas (some of which undergo malignant change) may sometimes be seen in the oesophagus of a few children or adults with Down's syndrome.
Neurofibromas (a type of vagal neurofibroma) may occur in the oesophageal wall and radiologically be similar to leiomyomas.
Polyps - of fibrovascular, lipomatous or hamartomatous types - may be found in the oesophagus. As they tend to hang from a stalk, they often move up and down with swallowing, and also keep the oesophagus locally distended. A long stalk may allow a polyp to be vomited up into the pharynx and mouth, or even be inhaled with respiratory obstruction. Illus. **OES-POLYP**.
Bezoars and foreign bodies - some of these may mimic benign tumours. Radio-opaque masses may be seen on plain radiographs, but non-opaque ones may not always be suspected unless there is dysphagia or signs suggesting perforation. These may include swallowed dentures which are often non-opaque, or impacted food masses above a stricture (piece of meat, raw carrot, etc.) - Illus. **OES-FOREIGN BODY**.

Haematomas of the oesophageal wall may follow vomiting or eating hard food, particularly in women. They may resemble tumours, but resolve after a few days. The author has seen a few cases, one in a woman (having chronic dialysis treatment) was combined with a Mallory-Weiss tear, and others in haemophiliacs resembling gastric wall haematomas (see Wright, F. and Matthews, 1971). Cases have been reported by Kerr, W. (1980), Shay et al. (1981 - 4 cases), and by Herbetko and Brunton (1988 - 3 cases). Freeman and Dickinson (1988) described six females and one male and pointed out that blood strips off the mucosa like an - 'oesophageal dissection' - one of their cases had achalasia. Other pre-existing conditions (e.g. leukaemia and uraemia) may also be associated (Chen et al., 1971, Ashmin et al., 1978 and Atefi et al., 1978). Herbetko et al (1991) demonstrated two cases by CT.

Further references
Johnston et al. (1953) : Smooth muscle tumours of the oesophagus.
Arnorsson et al. (1984) : Benign tumours and cysts.

Leiomyoma - Glanville (1965), Griff and Cooper (1967), Deverall (1968), Dillow et al. (1970).
Gutman (1972) : A leiomyoma causing posterior mediastinal calcification.
Godard and McCranie (1973) : Multiple leiomyomas.
Glanz and Grünebaum (1977) : The radiological approach to oesophageal leiomyomas with a long-term follow-up.
Cohen, A. and Cunat (1981) : Giant oesophageal leiomyoma presenting as a mediastinal mass.
Rendina et al. (1990) : Leiomyoma of the oesophagus.
Jarosz et al. (1998) : Diffuse leiomyomatosis in the gastro-oesophageal region simulating malignancy.
Roviaro et al. (1998) : Video-thoracosopic treatment of oes. leiomyoma - 7 cases - only one needing thoracotomy.
Neurofibroma - Myers et al. (1951) : 2 girls aged 14 & 19 - also quoted two other cases.
Ogilvie (1988)
Fibrovascular polyps - Jang et al. (1969), Barki et al. (1981), Patel et al. (1984) - giant case, Walters and Coral (1988) - polyp demonstrated by barium swallow and CT.
Lipomatous polyps - Liliequist and Winberg (1974) - two cases,
Radin (1988) : Giant fibroadipose polyp of the oesophagus with corrugated appearance.
Halfhide et al. (1995) : Hamartoma presenting as a giant oesophageal polyp in a man of 41.
Bezoars and foreign bodies.
Wright, F. and Ramsden (1974) : Chronic localised lower oesophageal perforation due to a swallowed upper denture.
Ford and Turner (1984) : Intrathoracic bezoar visible on plain chest radiograph.

Tracheo-oesophageal fistulae.
Most of these are **malignant** and most occur secondary to bronchial tumours, a smaller number being due to tumours arising in the oesophagus. Most malignant cases occur between the carina or the left main bronchus and the adjacent oesophagus. The development of a fistula in such cases has often been close to a terminal event, as the size of the fistula often tends to increase, and also because pressure on the oesophagus or its obstruction, directs increasing amounts of fluid and food into the airway. Radiotherapy may cause or enlarge such an opening, and plastic or rubber endo-bronchial or endo-oesophageal tubes only give short palliation, but indwelling covered expandable metallic oesophageal (and/or airway) stents may be better in that they block the fistulous track in about 70 - 100% of cases (see also p. 16.20). Before these became available many considered that strong pain killing drugs, such as opiates, should be given, as they help to relieve the severe mental distress, and in many cases bring a merciful release from the hopeless and severely distressing complaint, but the newer stents have clearly revolutionised and provided useful palliation treatment.

Benign cases are uncommon in adults, but the author has seen a few. Chest trauma may produce fistulae, usually at or just above the carina; these appear to be produced by direct compression of the trachea and oesophagus between the sternum and vertebral bodies. A cuffed endo-tracheal tube may produce a high fistula; others may follow instrumentation or arise from perforation by an inhaled or swallowed foreign body. Other cases follow mediastinal sepsis (TB or fungal) or result from perforation of oesophageal or pharyngeal diverticula.

About 25% of **congenital fistulae** (to the lower trachea or main bronchi) may present in adolescence or in adult life The author has encountered a man aged 21 at first presentation - he only complained of a slight cough on drinking fluids! Five similar cases were reported by Im et al. (1991). Blackburn and Armoury (1966) analysed 260 patients in whom the mean age at diagnosis was 33 years. Other cases are referred to in the references below.

Another non-malignant case the author has seen was a man of 35, who was referred with apparent 'enormous dilatation of the trachea' as seen on plain radiographs - it was in fact the **oesophagus, which filled with air on inspiration and deflated with expiration.** This fistula had followed endo-tracheal intubation, following a road accident 25 years previously. He denied any swallowing or coughing problems!

In benign cases, the patients often have long histories. They may have recurrent pneumonias, bronchiectasis or lung abscesses as a result of inhalation. Many however learn to avoid this, and some swallow in the supine position to make it less likely (**'Ono's sign'**).

Clinical cases of tracheo-oesophageal fistula are shown in Illus. **TRACHEO-OES FISTULA.**

Further references.

Negus (1929) : Congenital oesophago-tracheal fistula in an adult.
Braimbridge and Keith (1965) : Congenital oesophago-bronchial fistula in adults (3 cases) and review of 20 cases from the literature.
Moscarella and Wylie (1968) : Congenital communication between the oesophagus and isolated ectopic pulmonary tissue.
Smith, D. (1970) : Congenital broncho-oesophageal fistula presenting in an adult without lung infection.
Yacoub et al. (1973) : Non-malignant tracheo-oesophageal fistula in an adult associated with **broncholithiasis.**
Acosta and Battersby (1974) : Congenital tracheo-oesophageal fistula in the adult.
Chu and Mullen (1978) : Congenital broncho-oesophageal fistula in the adult.
Black (1982) : Congenital atresia tracheo-oesophageal fistula in the adult.
Stanbridge (1982) : Tracheo-oesophageal fistula and bilateral laryngeal nerve palsies after blunt chest trauma.
Dunn et al. (1983) : Scintigraphic demonstration of tracheo-oesophageal fistula.
Osinowo et al. (1983) : Congenital broncho-oesophageal fistula in the adult.
Kameya et al. (1984) : Congenital oesophagobronchial fistula in the adult.
Yiengpruksawan et al. (1984) : Tracheo-oesophageal fistula as a result of bronchial artery infusion therapy.
Berkmen and Auh (1985) : CT diagnosis of acquired tracheo-oesophageal fistula in adults due to carcinoma of the lung or oesophagus.
Vaid and Shin (1986) : CT evaluation of tracheo-oesophageal fistula (four cases).
Smith, D. et al. (1987) : Congenital broncho-oesophageal fistula in the adult.
Vasquez et al. (1988) : Benign oesophago-respiratory fistulae in adults (four cases seen in 1 year - 3 due to TB or atypical mycobacteria and a 4th non-resolving pneumonia). Extensive literature review.
Peat et al. (1989) : Congenital tracheo-oesophageal fistula in an adult.
Parry et al. (1993) : 72 year old patient with 10 years of intractable cough, following the ingestion of fluids due to a congenital oesophageal-bronchial fistula (oesophagus to intermediate bronchus) - treated by painting with 10% NaOH solution, followed by 30% acetic acid.
Moreno Azcoita et al. (1994) : Congenital oesophagobronchial fistula to LMB in a 48 year old man.
Gudovsky et al. (1993, Moscow) : Tracheo-oesophageal fistulae - 41 cases - 11 malignant (ca oes. 5, ca tracheo-bron. tree 4, thyroid 1, Hodgkin 1), 15 traumatic (inc. surgery & FB), 5 corrosive burn, 4 perforation of oes. diverticulum, 1 lung abscess, and 1 mechanical ventilation.
Conces et al. (1995) : Tracheo-oesophageal fistula due to Wegener's granulomatosis.
Losty (1999) : Survival after surgery for neonatal oesophageal repair (1 in 5,000 live births) is now about 97%.

Recent advances in the treatment of oesophageal perforation or fistulae.
Watkinson et al.(1995) : Plastic-covered metallic endoprostheses in the management of oesophageal perforation in patients with oesophageal carcinoma - a quick, safe and cost-effective method particularly in patients with perforation following endo-oesophageal laser therapy.
Drury and Grundy (1995) : Management of oesophageal fistula by radiologically-guided installation of tissue adhesive.
Mohammed and Moss (1996) : Palliation of malignant tracheo-oesophageal fistula using covered metal stents.
Tan et al. (1996) : Review -minimally invasive therapy for advanced oesophageal malignancy - see also p. 16.20.

See also refs. under ca oes. - ps. 16.22 - 25.

Other fistulae.
Oesophago-subarachnoid fistulae may complicate an oesophageal carcinoma.
Wippold et al. (1982) : Showed intra-pulmonary Myodil, following a myelogram.
Cornwell et al. (1986) : Demonstrated a fistula between an oesophageal carcinoma and the spinal canal by CT.

Aorto-oesophageal fistulae may occur secondary to thoracic aortic aneurysms, oesophageal tumours, foreign bodies, the ingestion of corrosives, or follow surgery or trauma.

Ctercteko and Mok (1980) : Aorto-oesophageal fistula induced by FB - first recorded survival.
Carter et al. (1978); Baron et al. (1981) : Clinical and radiographic manifestations of aorto-oesophageal fistulae.
Hirakata et al. (1991) : Arterioenteric fistulae - diagnosis & treatment by angiography.
Longo et al. (1987) : CT demonstration of an aorto-oesophageal fistula.
Hollander and Quick (1991) : Aorto-oesophageal fistulae - a comprehensive review of the literature.
Maher et al. (1998) : Aorto-oesophageal fistula presenting as a submucosal oesophageal haematoma.
Lim et al. (2000) : Spiral CT demonstration of aorto-oesophageal fistula from fish bone - 18 yr old girl swallowed a fish bone two weeks previously and presented with syncope + a sentinal haemorrhage - successful surgery.

Oesophageal duplication cysts are similar to 'bronchogenic' and 'neurenteric' cysts - see p. 3.13 - 14. Most do not present until adulthood, and the majority are incidental findings. Symptomatic cases may have dysphagia, epigastric discomfort, retrosternal pain or a cough; ulceration, haemorrhage, infection and/ or rupture may occur leading to mediastinitis, empyema or pyopericardium.

Some further references.

Kirwan et al. (1973) : Cystic intrathoracic derivatives of the foregut and their complications.
Salo and Ala-Kolju (1987) : Congenital oesophageal cysts in adults.
Winslow et al. (1984) : Duplication of cervical oesophagus - an unrecognised cause of respiratory distress in infants.
Rafal and Markisz (1991) : Magnetic resonance of an oesophageal duplication cyst.
Holemans and Rankin (1995) : Oesophageal duplication cyst causing left lung collapse, hypoperfusion, oesophageal displacement and compression in a 6 month old child - CT showed a large cystic mass in front of the vertebral column, compressing the carina and main pulmonary artery anteriorly - the cyst was removed surgically and arose from the mid oesophagus.

Perforation of the oesophagus - (Illus. **OES-PERFORATION**).

Instrumentation is a common cause of oesophageal perforation and probably accounts for about 75% of cases. The most common site is in the lower third and particularly follows dilatation of strictures, biopsies or the removal of foreign bodies. Injury may be caused both by the rigid oesophagoscope and the more flexible gastroscope but is much less common with the latter. Perforation may also occur with vomiting - the 'Boerhaave syndrome' (see below - ps. 6.13-15).

Perforation also occurs at higher levels, including the neck (e.g. from a swallowed fish bone, following instrumentation or from a Zenker's diverticulum). It may also be intra-abdominal from the lowest part of the oesophagus, where it lies retroperitoneally and before it angles anteriorly and to the left to enter the stomach, and a perforation here may enter the lesser sac.

The type of treatment used to treat oesophageal perforation often provokes considerable debate, since with major tears there can be an 80 to almost 100% mortality. With early cases (i.e. under 12 hours) primary surgical debridement and suture may be the treatment of choice, after localising the site of the tear. However some feel that a more conservative approach is preferable and that this leads to a much reduced mortality, particularly with small tears. The object is to prevent leakage, especially of regurgitated fluid via the perforation by endo-oesophageal suction, nil given by mouth and the use of IV fluids and feeding.

Usually with this treatment the hole in the oesophagus rapidly becomes smaller. This may be checked by contrast swallow examination, and its rims may be cauterised with 10% sodium hydroxide or 30% acetic acid a few times. Abscesses and pleural effusions are drained if they form, but small ones tend to drain back into the oesophagus and spontaneously heal. Abscesses which occur in the neck are usually produced by small tears and should be drained. A technique now being developed of endoscopic suture may be of considerable help in the future as it will obviate a thoracotomy in what is already a very ill patient. Some surgeons have been performing an emergency oesophagectomy, but this produces a high mortality in an already shocked patient, and a less drastic approach seems more appropriate.

Stab and gun-shot wounds may also cause oesophageal perforation, but these are best treated by surgical repair and wide drainage.

As noted on p. 16.10 under tracheo-oesophageal fistula, malignant perforations, particularly into the trachea or left main bronchus are usually hopeless, but some useful palliation is being achieved with indwelling airway stents (see p. 16.20).

Boerhaave's syndrome. In 1724 Hermann Boerhaave* wrote about the Dutch Admiral Baron John Van Wassaner, who engorged himself with veal soup, cabbage boiled with sheep, spinach, calf sweetbreads (pancreas), duck, two larks, apple compote and bread, dessert of pears, grapes and sweetmeats, together with beer and wine. Following this he went horse riding. He then took tepid water with Carduus Benedictine, because something **irritated 'the opening to his stomach'** and he had often found this helpful. Shortly afterwards he vomited, but only a little and not easily. Then he drank more bitter Benedictine, and sitting on a chair trying to vomit, with his finger down his throat, suddenly gave forth a horrifying cry and complained that something near the upper part of his stomach was ruptured. He thought that death was inevitable. Over the next few hours he took some olive oil, beef broth, and various remedies but died. At autopsy there was much subcutaneous emphysema. Both pleural cavities contained much fluid - largely the fluid he had drunk and duck flesh. The lower oesophagus was ruptured and the stomach was grossly gas-distended with a narrowed pylorus (see reference to Derbes and Mitchell - below).

This syndrome particularly refers to rupture of the lower oesophagus caused by a sudden rise of intra-abdominal pressure **against a closed glottis** whilst vomiting or belching. Other acts causing it include being slapped on the back whilst shaving and /or belching, labour, defecation, etc., but most commonly it follows an alcoholic and gastronomic debauch. Most times the rupture occurs just above the gastro-oesophageal junction on the left, with perforation into the left pleural cavity. The mid oesophagus may also rupture, with perforation to the right or into both pleural cavities - (Illus. **OES-PERFORATION, Boerhaave's syndrome Pt. 3a-d** this patient recovered). Even a **'malignant Boerhaave's syndrome'** may occur, with the patient perforating a 'silent' tumour (Illus. **OES-PERFORATION, Boerhaave's syndrome 2a-e**).

*The Dutchman - Hermann Boerhaave (1668 - 1738) was termed "The Common Teacher of Europe" and the greatest physician of his time. His teaching was largely Hippocratic and his aim was to cure the sick, the doctor at the bedside setting aside many academic preconceptions and assessing the situation calmly for himself. When a patient died he conducted an autopsy with his pupils. (See also Booth, 1989 a & b & Illus. **Boerhaave**).

The **Mallory-Weiss syndrome (OES-PERFORATION, Mallory-Weiss syndrome)** is produced similarly, but the mucosal tear usually only results in a brisk haemorrhage, which soon settles down, or a mild lower chest discomfort with gas in the mediastinum (**Pt. 4**). **Pts. 4, 5 & 6** healed spontaneously. **Pt. 7** who had a similar lesion as shown radiologically, instead of having entirely conservative management, a gastroscope was passed, and the lower oesophagus was perforated with a fatal result. Clearly in this less marked syndrome, expectant treatment should be the by-word!

References.
Froggatt and Gunning (1966) : Reviewed 33 cases of oesophageal perforation in Oxford and advocated primary suture of the tear if diagnosed within 6 to 12 hours. After this period they recommended a conservative approach with drip, suction and drainage. more than one drain might be needed, also a gastrostomy and jejunostomy with large leaks.

In addition to a radiographic contrast examination, they also had the anaesthetist blow air down an oesophageal tube and noted the position of escaping air bubbles into the opened pleural cavity which was partly filled with saline.

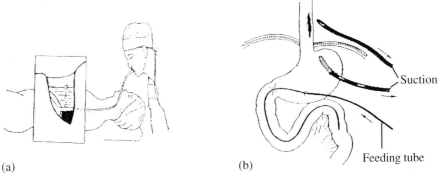

(a)   (b)

Fig. 16. 8   Detecting the site of an oesophageal perforation.   More than one drainage tube may be required.
(Diagrams reproduced from Thorax, 1960, **21**, 524 - 528 with permission from the BMJ Publishers Group).

Sealy (1963) : Rupture of the oesophagus.

Berry and Oschner (1973) : Oesophageal perforation - 30 year review.

Parkin (1973) : The radiology of perforated oesophagus - initial radiographs may be normal and soft tissue emphysema, mediastinal widening and abscess formation may not be seen for 24 hours. If pleural integrity is maintained, mediastinal changes develop rapidly and a pleural effusion appears late.

Cameron et al. (1974), Brown, R. & Cohen (1978), Lyons et al. (1978) : Conservative approach in selected cases.

Love and Berkow (1978) : Trauma to the oesophagus.

Appleton et al. (1979) : Perforated oesophagus - review of 28 consecutive cases.

Finley et al. (1980) : Management of non-malignant intrathoracic perforation - 8 cases, 7 post emetic.

Westaby (1980) : Primary repair of a lower oesophageal tear using a diaphragmatic pedicle.

Michel et al. (1981) : Oesophageal perforation - collective review.

Dodds et al. (1982) : Appropriate contrast media for diagnosis.

Goldstein and Thompson (1982) : Oesophageal perforation - 15 year experience.

Wechsler et al. (1982) : Iatrogenic oesophago-pleural fistula - subtlety of diagnosis in the absence of mediastinitis.

Phillips and Cunningham (1984) : Oesophageal perforation - radiological review.

Han et al. (1985) : Perforation of the oesophagus - correlation of the site and cause with plain film findings.

Rohmann and Acheson (1985) : Oesophageal perforation during double contrast examination of a patient with a lower oesophageal stricture : Spontaneous recovery.

Bladergroen et al. (1986) : Diagnosis and recommended management of oesophageal perforation and rupture.

Hine and Atkinson (1986) : Diagnosis and management of perforations of the oesophagus and pharynx sustained during intubation of neoplastic oesophageal strictures.

Wechsler (1986) : CT of oesophageal-pleural fistulae - 7 cases. CT may demonstrate that air or swallowed contrast medium has passed into the pleural cavity, usually into a fluid collection.

Nair (1987) : Instrumental perforation of the oesophagus into the pericardial cavity.

Adams et al. (1989) : Oesophageal tears during pneumatic balloon dilatation for the treatment of achalasia. nine out of 58 patients had tears, two of which were complete. One had a linear mucosal tear and six localised outpouchings or diverticula. - compare with : Grundy and Bellini (1988) : Balloon dilatation of upper GI tract strictures - no complications in 30 pts.

Stewart et al. (1979) : Desirability of Roentgen examination of the oesophagus after pneumatic dilatation for achalasia.

Maynar et al. (1988) : Balloon dilatation of oesophageal strictures - radial dilatation is superior to old fashioned bag dilatation (170 dilatations).

Set et al. (1992) : Delayed presentation of oesophageal perforation simulating intrathoracic malignancy - two cases - one due to a pork chop fragment, 4 months before, which caused paraspinal swelling, the second had a similar CT appearance.

Boerhaave's and Mallory-Weiss syndromes, and 'vomiting in man'.

Mallory and Weiss (1929) : Haemorrhages from lacerations of the cardiac orifice of the stomach due to vomiting - 15 cases who 'after long and intensive alcoholic debauch developed massive gastric haemorrhage with haematemesis'.

Derbes and Mitchell (1955) : English translation of Boerhaave's article.

Christoforidis and Nelson (1957) : Spontaneous rupture of the oesophagus - Radiological review.

Härmä et al. (1968) : Spontaneous rupture of the oesophagus - endoscopic treatment in the primary stage.

Lumsden and Holden (1969, from Oxford) : **The act of vomiting in man**. No peristalsis occurs during nausea, there is then a sudden drop of the lower part of the stomach due to loss of tone Retching starts with a series of spasmodic and abortive respiratory movements with the glottis closed, and culminates in a powerful sustained contraction of the abdominal muscles accompanied by descent of the diaphragm. They felt that this raised the intragastric pressure sufficiently not only to lift the gastric contents against gravity to the mouth but also to accelerate them to a considerable speed; when the cardia opens, the gastric contents are shot upwards into the gullet. (Note - they did not mention **retroperistalsis** starting in the duodenal cap and gastric antrum and spreading to the whole stomach, which the author has seen a few times whilst carrying out a barium meal - most times this has allowed him to get out of the way and avoid being covered in vomited barium!). It is only if the glottis fails to relax that an oesophageal tear will occur.

Bobo et al. (1970) : Boerhaave's syndrome - six cases.

McVay (1970) : Treatment of a case of combined Mallory-Weiss and Boerhaave's syndrome.

Rogers et al. (1971) : Mediastinal emphysema in Boerhaave's syndrome.

Carr (1973) : The Mallory-Weiss syndrome - 3 cases demonstrated by barium swallow with subsequent spontaneous recovery plus review of the literature.

Symbas et al. (1978) : Spontaneous rupture of the oesophagus.

Phillips et al. (1982) : Barogenic rupture of the oesophagus (Boerhaave's syndr.): Successful treatment of a late case.

Neff and Lawson (1985) : Boerhaave syndrome - interventional radiological management.

Sabanathan et al. (1990) : Boerhaave's syndrome complicating acute myocardial infarction - conservative management with parenteral and late jejunostomy treatment was successful. (Quoted two other similar cases from the literature).

Pezzulli et al. (1989) : CT demonstration of a mediastinal haematoma secondary to Boerhaave's syndrome - it pushed the heart forwards.

Heart
Oes mass
Aorta
Spine

Foreign bodies - (Illus. **OES-FOREIGN BODY**).

A variety of foreign bodies may be found in the oesophagus. Many pass on without causing any problem, but sharp objects may stick in the oesophageal wall or perforate it, and larger objects may block the oesophagus. These last may be food, especially in those with impaired oesophageal contractions or an existing stricture. Common items include lumps of meat, potatoes, whole carrots, meat bones, plastic objects, dentures or coins. Some uncommon objects the author has seen include pens, toothbrushes, bed springs, razor blades and cutlery (many of these being in mentally disturbed patients or prisoners in jail).

Metal objects are usually obvious on plain radiographs, but beware that they may be hidden behind the heart on low KV views, and both PA and lateral chest radiographs should be taken in adults. Aluminium, plastic objects and bones (including fish bones) may cause considerable difficulty in diagnosis. Gas in the oesophagus may be helpful, by helping to outline the foreign body, or by the presence of excessive gas above a fluid-level.

Sword   swallowers put their heads back, straighten out the pharynx and oesophagus and relax the cardia, with the tip passing down into a low lying body of stomach to allow the hilt to touch the teeth. They rarely harm themselves. Fluoroscopy of the procedure has occasionally been carried out, and has been done in Oxford!

Some references.

Wright, F. and Ramsden (1974) : Chronic foreign body in the oesophagus - a denture. A man of 37 had a chicken meal and several alcoholic drinks, following which he vomited several times in the street. The following day he found that he had lost his upper dental plate which contained a single incisor tooth. He had a dull central chest pain and walked to hospital. A chest radiograph was taken, but a little gas in the supraclavicular regions was not noted. Two weeks later he had a barium swallow examination, and a 'small outpouching' of the lower oesophaus was noted. A non-urgent oesophagoscopy was arranged, but in the meantime he was admitted to the Churchill Hospital for a rhinoplasty. He was still having some dysphagia, and a further swallow examination showed the filling defect in the lower oesophagus and a chronic local perforation (Illus. **OES-FOREIGN BODY, Pt. 4a-c**).

Aluminium

Levick et al. (1977) : The "invisible" can top - an 18 month old child had 'failed to thrive' from the age of ten months and was underweight. He was admitted to hospital with respiratory distress having choked on a piece of sausage. Barium swallow showed a stricture in the upper thoracic oesophagus; this was initially dilated endoscopically, but later explored and a 'diverticulum' was removed containing the can top ring.

Bradburn et al. (1994) : Radiographs and aluminium - a pitfall for the unwary.

NB. An electronic metal detector is being used in some centres to overcome this problem.

Fish bones

Record and de Lacey (1990) : Radiographic atlas of fish bones. Easy to see - cod, halibut, red mullet, sea bass, telapia, turbot, brill, grey mullet, sole and plaice bones.

Ell and Sprigg (1991) : Radio-opacity of fish-bones - only cod, haddock, cole fish, gurnard, lemon sole, monk fish, grey mullet and red snapper can be well seen on soft tissue radiographs.

Evans et al. (1992) from Hong Kong : felt that the patient's symptoms and signs were more sensitive and specific than radiography in predicting the presence of impacted fish bones.

Abdullah et al. (1996) : 2 film-screen combinations for detecting impacted fish bones; single film-screen was best.

Lim et al. (2000) : Spiral CT demonstration of aorto-oesophageal fistula from fish bone - see p. 16.12.

Food impaction

Robbins and Shortsleeve (1994) : Treatment of acute oesophageal food impaction with glucagon, an effervescent agent and water - lower oesophageal ring was the commonest cause.

Other oesophageal injuries.

Caustic fluids may be acids or alkalis, more commonly the latter and particularly caustic soda (NaOH) used for cleaning grease off cookers, etc. In some countries caustic soda is still sold in liquid form for this purpose. The danger is that this is often placed in used soft drinks bottles, and may be drunk mistakenly by children. The author has seen a few cases in the UK (many years ago) but when he visited a hospital in Spain 15 years ago there was almost a ward full of such children suffering from oesophageal burns and stricturing. Almost all had come from poor country villages. An example is shown in Illus. **OES-CAUSTIC SODA**.

Thermal burns may occur from eating hot coals, barbecue charcoal, etc., but these are rare, as the victim is likely to burn only his mouth and lips before spitting out the offending object.

An unusual burn of the oesophagus was reported by Flisak and Berman (1988) who described an electric burn in the upper oesophagus, due to a patient swallowing the cut end of an electric cord and then plugging it into an electric socket, in an attempt to commit suicide. It produced a stricture needing resection.

Drugs, particularly tablets, which stick in the oesophagus, may cause ulceration - slow K, NSAIDS (non-steroidals), fluorouracil, flucloxacillin - particularly in patients with poor oesophageal motility, strictures, webs, diverticula, or partial obstruction at the cardia (HH or achalasia, etc. - see Illus. **OES-FOREIGN BODY, Oes-achalasia Pt. 18**). Haematomas may also occur in patients on anticoagulants (see p. 16.10).

Some references on contrast media, and other diseases of the oesophagus.

General
Huepscher (1988) : 'Radiology of the Oesophagus' - contains much helpful technical and clinical advice.
Levine (1989) : 'Radiology of the Esophagus' - fine ulcers are well shown with double contrast - also polyps and tumours - scarring, sacculation, mucosal nodularity and thickened folds are well demonstrated in oesophagitis - good illustrations of fine ulcers in **candida** oesophagitis and **herpes (discrete superficial ulcers on a background of normal mucosa).**

Alcohol
O'Riordan et al. (1986) : Acute alcoholic oesophagitis.

Contrast media
James, A. et al. (1975) : Barium or Gastrografin for the diagnosis of oesophageal tears.
Dodds (1982) : Appropriate contrast media for evaluation of oesophageal disruption (preferred barium).
Foley (1982) : Reappraisal of contrast media for detection of upper GI perforation.
de Lange et al. (1987) : Barium leads to fewer complications when aspirated and provides better anatomical detail than water-soluble contrast agents.
Ginai et al. (1985) : Review of contrast media available for use in expected perforation.
Ginai (1987) : Hexabrix for radiographic evaluation of leakage of upper GI tract.
Mohammed and Hedegus (1986) : Dislodgement of impacted foreign bodies with carbonated beverages.
Cayea and Seltzer (1985), Conces et al. (1988) : 3% barium paste for the opacification of the oesophagus in CT of the thorax. (The author has usually found this more helpful than Gastrografin).

Eosinophilia
Vitellas et al. (1993) : Idiopathic eosinophilic oesophagitis.

Graft vs host disease
McDonald et al. (1984) : Radiographic features of oesophageal involvement in chronic graft-vs.-host disease.'

Monilia ('shaggy oesophageal mucosa' - seen in patients with diabetes, leukaemia, reticuloses, immune deficiency e.g. AIDS, general debility or having chemotherapy).
Andren and Theander (1956) : Two cases of monilia oesophagitis in which the thoracic part showed an irregular and ragged outline, made up of numerous small indentations and protrusions.
Eban and Symmers (1959) : In monilia oesophagitis, the outline of the oesophagus was irregular and 'shaggy', with numerous indentations and apparent filling defects, the longitudinal folds being almost completely obscured.
Kaufman et al. (1960) : 'A strikingly irregular and jagged outline of the mucosal pattern.'

Buckle and Nicol (1964) : Two cases - 'the outline of the oesophagus becomes shaggy and irregular and the mucosal pattern is lost. Small circular protrusions or filling defects due to pseudo-membrane appear.'
Grieve (1964) : Case report and review of 12 other cases.
Gibson, M. and Harris (1967) : One case with abrupt narrowing of the lumen at the level of the aortic arch, with large filling defects and shoulder formation resembling carcinoma.
Holt (1968) : Candida of the oesophagus.
Gefter, W. et al. (1981) : Four cases of candida complicating achalasia, scleroderma and fundoplication.

Examples of monilia oesophagitis are shown in Illus. **OES-MONILIA.**

Pemphigus
Al-Kutoubi and Eliot (1984) : Bullous lesions and scarring due to benign mucous pemphigoid.
Naylor et al. (1995) : Barium studies in oesophageal cicatricial pemphigoid.

Radiation
Lepke and Libshitz (1983) : Radiation-induced injury of the oesophagus.

Spasm
Gonzalez (1973) : Diffuse oesophageal spasm.

TB
Williford (1983) Oesophageal TB - findings on barium swallow and CT.
McNamara et al. (1987) : TB affecting the oesophagus.
Im et al. (1990) : CT of oesophago-mediastinal-fistula in TB mediastinal lymphadenitis.
Kaur et al. (1993) : Oesophageal TB mimicking a tumour during treatment for nodal TB.
(see also under - TB - Chapter 19).

Intrathoracic varices (Illus. **OES-VARICES**)
These are discussed in the chapters on systemic veins (see ps. 9.9 - 10) and the mediastinum (p. 18.31). They may be found both inside and outside the oesophagus; those inside sometimes being just the 'tip of the ice-berg'. Para-oesophageal masses due to varices are shown in Illus. **OES-VARICES, Pt. 6a-c & OES-VARICES, Syph varices Pt. 11a-h**. They may be further demonstrated by splenoportography or angiography. A simple method is to inject 10 ml of isotope labelled fine colloid into the spleen and to follow its passage through the portal venous system on a gamma camera.
Within the oesophagus varices may be demonstrated with barium or barium and gas, and are often best seen after a bolus has passed through it. They often appear like worms protruding into the lumen. They may extend into the stomach or duodenum.
If haemorrhage occurs it may be torrential. Surgery with port-caval shunts (etc.) may be carried out, the varices may be injected with sclerosants (like varicose leg veins) or endoscopic band ligation carried out.

Some references.
Wolf (1928) : First demonstrated varices radiologically.
Schatzki (1931, 1940) : Also found an increase in the size of varices in the supine position - described how varices may disappear with oesophageal contraction.
Bediczka and Taschakert (1932) : Described the radiographic appearances, which still hold.
Berg (1935) : Referring to the amount of barium necessary to demonstrate varices stated 'the less you use, the more you will see' he also found the supine position preferable.
Templeton (1944) : Barium swallow a year before death failed to outline varices in 6 of 10 patients with oesophageal varices at autopsy.
Brick and Palmer (1953) : 92 of 147 patients had varices, but only 18 had them shown radiologically.
Allcock and Berridge (1956) : Some aspects of cinematography to the radiology of the oesophagus.
Brombart (1956) : Clinical radiology of the oesophagus.
Nelson (1957) : Stressed the value of the Valsalva experiment in the demonstration of oesophageal varices.
Evans (1959) : Oesophageal and gastric varices. Valsalva or Müller manoeuvres sometimes helped, but simple inspiration could be just as effective. The earliest change was slight widening and minimal scalloping of the mucosal folds, later there was marked distortion of the mucosal pattern and globular or worm-like filling defects, which commonly extended up the oesophagus to the level of the azygos arch. Gastric varices were sometimes found on the lesser curve, as cardiac defects or over the gastric fundus.

Waldram et al. (1977) : Detection and grading of oesophageal varices by fibre-optic endoscopy and barium swallow with and without Buscopan (study of 56 patients).
Tihansky et al. (1984) : The oesophagus after injection sclerotherapy of varices.
Ginai et al. (1993) : Oesophageal varices - how reliable is a barium swallow? In 119 patients with liver disease it was found to be reliable, non-invasive and cheaper than endoscopy - used radiographs taken immediately after a swallow in horizontal prone with 20 to 20° Trendelenberg, as well as supine and both oblique positions. Double contrast, Buscopan and contrast-filled views were avoided as they tended to efface varices.
Hayes (1996) : The coming of age of band ligation for oesophageal varices - has a better record for preventing recurrent haemorrhage than injection sclerotherapy.

Non-specific motility disorders.
These include:
Achalasia - see ps. 16.4 - 6.
Corkscrew oesophagus - see p. 16.9 and Illus. **OES-CORKSCREW.**
Nutcracker (reflux) oesophagus - see p. 16.7.
Diffuse oesophageal spasm - (sometimes with frequent simultaneous non-peristaltic contractions - Illus. **OES-SPASM**).
Hypertensive lower oesophageal sphincter.

Reference.
Aly (2000) : Digital radiography in the evaluation of oesophageal motility disorders.

Malignant tumours   (see also Barrett's oesophagus p. 16.8).
Aetiology   - environmental factors seem to play a part in the causation of these tumours, which are common in parts of China, parts of the Middle East, Northern Italy, black townships in South Africa, etc. In China, nitrosamines in partly decayed cabbage or other vegetables, steeped in water, have been suggested as the likely cause. In the East Indies, a specific carcinogen has been found in the leaves of a shrub used for brewing tea., Fungus infected ground nuts and swallowed asbestos fibres have been implicated in South Africa. The ancient 'silk route' across the Middle East and Asia is a particularly well known tract for finding oesophageal carcinoma (as well as thalassaemia, syphilis, etc.) and strong tea, opium smoking and silicon fibres have been suggested as the cause.
    Chronic   obstruction   as   with   achalasia,   is   a   well   known   precursor   (Illus. **ACHALASIA+NEO**), and chronic reflux (as with a Barrett's oesophagus) also appears to be another factor (now probably more common as a result of long-term treatment of duodenal ulcers and acid reflux with H-antagonists); diverticula are sometimes associated with tumours (Illus. **PHAYYNGEAL   POUCH+CA**). In 1987 the DHSS listed smoking as the main cause of tumours (Hansard, 21 Nov. 1987), but this may be potentiated by alcohol (as with bladder carcinoma) - see also ps. 24.5 & 24.11 re smoking + alcohol. About 3,500 patients in the UK die from oesophageal carcinoma per year and it is the seventh most common malignancy world-wide.

Tumour types.
    Primary carcinoma of the oesophagus is usually squamous, but may be adenocarcinoma, especially in the lower third. The latter may occur from gastric carcinomas spreading up from the fundus of the stomach, or arise in mucous glands of the oesophagus, gastric rests or in a Barrett type oesophagus. Adenocarcinomas tend to be associated with greater submucosal invasion and also tend to metastasise earlier. The UK incidence of both types may be declining. Other primary oesophageal tumours include melanomas (Illus. **OES-MELANOMA**), reticulosis, sarcomas (leiomyosarcomas, neurofibrosarcomas, and plasmacytomas) and oat cell tumours. The author has encountered two examples of **oesophageal oat (or small) cell tumours** - both in female smokers in their 50s, and about 140 cases of such tumours have been reported in the World literature; they have a similar behaviour to small cell lung tumours; some respond to chemotherapy, but most patients with them are dead within three to nine months from the time of presentation. In the case illustrated in Illus. **OES-OAT CELL CA, Oes-ca Pt. 42a-f.** the patient had three separate tumours in the oesophagus (two were presumably 'skip lesions'); there was a marked tumour regression with chemotherapy but tumour necrosis resulted in a wide tracheo-oesophageal fistula, bronchopneumonia and death five months after first presentation.

Metastatic tumours may occur in the oesophageal wall e.g. from breast, bowel, melanoma, etc.

Prognosis in most patients with oesophageal carcinoma remains poor - often only 3 to 6 months from the time of diagnosis, because of obstruction or spread of the tumour, which tends to present late - 75% already having nodal metastases. Early tumours limited to the inner part of the oesophageal wall may have a better survival - particularly squamous types, and some have claimed a 40% survival at 5 years. In a few cases long survival is seen even with metastases, presumably due to slow growth of the tumour. Attempted curative surgery. however, is often disappointing, as spread to lymph nodes and into the mediastinum has often occurred. Another problem is that nodes involved with oesophageal carcinoma are often **not** enlarged.

Diagnosis of oesophageal carcinoma.

This is usually made by barium swallow, followed by endoscopy or by endoscopy and biopsy. An irregular stricture, ulceration associated with irregular narrowing or concentric narrowing extending up from the stomach are always suggestive. Most tumours are found relatively late, since dysphagia does not become much of a feature until the oesophageal lumen is considerably narrowed.

In 1957 Bruinisma described the use of abrasive balloons for obtaining cytological specimens of the oesophagus and stomach. This method has been used in some US jails, but has mainly been used in China as a cheap and accurate method for screening in susceptible areas, utilising partly inflated balloons (or condoms) covered with gauze swabs as abrasives. These are swallowed to approx. 30 cms, and withdrawn using an attached cord, then washed in saline to obtain cytological material. If positive, confirmatory oesophagoscopy is carried out, followed by surgery. With 'in situ' carcinoma, a cure rate of 92% has been claimed! (see also Li and Shiang, 1979 - 62,000 Chinese, Yang , 1980, Shu, 1983 - further use in China, Korsten et al., 1985 - alcoholics in jails in USA).

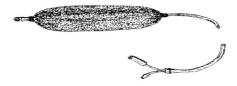

Fig. 16.9   Bruinisma's oesophageal balloon.

Staging of oesophageal tumours.

The following CT staging system is often used.

      Stage 0 = carcinoma in situ
          I = intraluminal mass
        II = mass and wall thickening
       III = spread to adjacent structure(s)

In staging oesophageal carcinomas, the object is to try to determine whether the tumour is limited to the oesophageal wall, or if it has extended into the surrounding tissues, nodes, etc. Although some authors (e.g. Halber et al., 1979 and Moss et al., 1981) consider that the oesophagus is clearly delineated by fat and therefore should be well outlined by CT, and that blurring of the fat planes or 'dirty fat' (with raised CT numbers) should be a good indication of extra-oesophageal extension of disease, nevertheless the oesophageal outline may be difficult to define. This particularly happens in patients who have lost weight, and there is little fat, thus poor delineation of the oesophageal outline may not necessarily indicate spread of disease. Picus (1983) pointed out that the mid oesophagus is most likely to be affected in this way, and that CT often understages the tumour and that nodal metastases may not cause enlargement. In many cases gross mediastinal metastases may be found a few months following surgery.

In the UK many centres have abandoned CT assessment of these tumours, because of the poor correlation that has been found with surgery and pathology, and that tumour spread has been greater than suggested by radiology. Many use a positive CT as a good indication of inoperability, but view the opposite with considerable suspicion. However up to 20% of false positives involving the aorta and tracheo-bronchial tree have been found in some series (Takashima et al., 1991). Doyle and Simpson (1994) and Doyle et al. (1995) point out that performing **CT with the patient prone helps to 'stretch' the mid and posterior mediastinum**, with the heart falling forwards, and thus allowing a better determination of aortic, peri-aortic fat and pericardial involvement.

CT signs suggesting inoperability include:

Thickening of oesophageal wall (normally < 3 mm - use 2% barium or Gastrografin to show the lumen) - often asymmetrical both around the circumference and lengthwise'.

Moderately enlarged nodes in the mediastinum, the retrocrural area or in the upper abdomen (especially coeliac nodes).

Infiltration of fat and neighbouring tissues, especially into nodes and tracheo-bronchial tree, with indentation or obliteration of the outline of the posterior wall of the trachea or main bronchus (especially left) and the intervening fat.

Metastases to lungs, liver, adrenals, etc.

Some further useful guides are:

(i) length of tumour (most readily seen on barium swallow or CT 'scout' view - CT alone tends to overestimate its length),

(ii) spread to the stomach or coeliac nodes.

(iii) spread to vertebrae and adjacent fascia.

(iv) spread around the aorta and pericardium.

Note that the multiplicity of inter-connecting lymphatic vessels allows early spread even before narrowing of the oesophagus and dysphagia have occurred. Lower oesophageal tumours give rise to subdiaphragmatic nodal metastases in about 60% of cases, whilst mid and even upper oesophageal tumours may give rise to such nodal deposits in about 30%. Enlarged nodes may be easy to see in some situations such as the pretracheal or retrocrural spaces (nodes in the latter do not normally exceed 6 mm in diameter) or in the anterior mediastinum, but in other situations are very difficult to define.

MR - produces similar results to CT, both with regard to oesophageal wall thickening and spread into adjacent soft tissues. It also tends to miss metastases in normal sized lymph nodes, but may show smaller hepatic deposits.

Treatment methods.

These depend on the stage of the disease, the general well-being of the patient, the number of such patients presenting, the degree of obstruction, tissue type, the medical opinions or 'fashions' at the time, etc. They are essentially of four types - surgical removal, an indwelling tube or stent (Illus. **OES-STENT/TUBE**) and/or endoscopic laser resection (see p. 24.45) or radiotherapy. Often a combination of treatments is employed.

Except in the very elderly (who may be treated by radiotherapy 'on spec.') it is important to try to differentiate between adeno- and squamous tumours of the lower oesophagus, because they have different natural histories and responses to radiotherapy, squamous usually responding (and perhaps allowing later surgery), whereas adenocarcinoma does not respond so well, and an indwelling tube may be required for palliation.

Surgery may be curative in a few instances, but in many the patients re-present with extensive tumour recurrence not many months after resection due to the tumour permeation of the lymphatic system and /or surgery having 'spread the tumour around'. A total oesophago-partial gastrectomy, via a thoraco-abdominal approach is a very time consuming procedure, and many surgeons will not attempt it without a 'clear mediastinum' on CT, even then finding some cases inoperable on exploration. As an alternative a **trans-hiatal** approach has been used in some centres, particularly in the USA. In this approach, blunt hand dissection from the abdomen, via the hiatus upwards, allows the oesophagus to be examined manually, and to be separated from the rest of the mediastinum. A second incision is made in the neck and the remainder of the lower oesophagus, following removal of the tumour, is passed upwards and anastomosed to the upper oesophagus or pharynx. Its advantages include speed, smaller wounds, good assessment of 'fixity' of the oesophagus, local spread, etc. The method has also been used for the treatment of some benign conditions. The main disadvantage is from intra- or post-operative bleeding which may be difficult to control. Other complications include (a) early - anastomotic leakage, abscess formation, gastric outlet obstruction and gastric necrosis, and (b) late - malignancy, aspiration reflux and broncho-oesophageal fistula.

Examples of oesophageal tumours are shown in Illus. **OES-TUMOUR**.

Radiological examination of the oesophagus.
   Most contrast studies of the oesophagus are carried out under fluoroscopic control.

Radiography - for most the author preferred 100 mm film, as this was readily and automatically changed between exposures, could be programmed for single or multiple views (as seemed appropriate), was cheap and could be readily processed; nowadays digital imaging is available in most centres. Larger spot views may also be taken - also full sized chest views with the oesophagus outlined with barium for radiotherapy planning.

Contrast medium - for most purposes barium is preferable, including when a leakage or fistula is suspected, but only **small amounts** are then given. Barium gives good radiographic contrast, and if it passes into the tracheo-bronchial tree is far less irritant than water-soluble media. Most of the latter are also less dense, and will often fail to demonstrate fistulous tracks or leaks. They are also hygroscopic and can pull quite large amounts of fluid into the bronchi. Deaths from their use for this purpose, have been reported (e.g. Reich 1969, and Chiu and Gambach, 1974).
   Barium is readily expectorated - usually completely, and if it passes into the alveoli is phagocytosed; however **large** amounts in the mediastinum may produce fibrosis and mediastinitis.

Reference.
Gollub and Bains (1997) : Diagnosis of postoperative oesophageal leaks - barium can be used safely to rule out an anastomotic leak.

Some use a little water soluble medium first when looking for leaks or fistulae, and if the examination is negative, follow with barium. Others have used non-ionic media, but these are very expensive for swallow examinations.
   Acid barium (pH 1.6 to 1.7) is sometimes used to provoke spasm in the detection of oesophagitis.

Plain film changes - include :
(a) widening of the mediastinum due to tumour mass, nodes or an accompanying abscess,
(b) dilated oesophagus - air or air /fluid filled,
(c) thickening or displacement of paraoesophageal line or obliteration of azygo-oesophageal recess,
(d) tracheal deviation on PA or lateral views or thickening of posterior tracheal line on lateral view,
(e) inhalation changes in the lungs from over-spill via the larynx, or an oesophago-tracheal fistula,
(f) absent or distorted gastric fundal gas bubble
(g) gas in the soft tissues of the neck, supraclavicular areas or mediastinum as a result of perforation.

Thickening of the oesophageal wall may be seen in inflammatory states e.g. oesophagitis, monilia infection (Illus. **OES-MONILIA**), fibrous stricture, etc. - also with varices. None of these will exhibit any evidence of fat infiltration or be associated with nodal enlargement.

Isotope studies of the oesophagus are usually unhelpful, because only small amounts of fluid are employed, and hence normal peristalsis is neither stimulated nor studied. There are however some exceptions gastric mucosa with a Barrett's oesophagus or high pressure transit ('nutcracker oesophagus' - Richter et al., 1987).

Ultrasound of the oesophagus and transoesophageal ultrasonography - endoscopic ultrasonography is now being carried out in an increasing number of centres, using a side-viewing probe fixed to a dedicated endoscope. The oesophageal wall can be well visualised, and adjacent lymphadenopathy noted. Infiltration of the oesophageal wall distorts its layers - usually five are visible (see Fig. 16.10 below) and effacement or masses within them may be recognised. 'Early oesophageal cancers' (i.e. limited to the oesophageal wall or mucosa) have been studied, particularly in Japan, where they are more commonly found. In the UK most tumours are found at diagnosis to have already broken through the boundaries of the different layers, and many will have spread laterally. Whether enlarged nodes are involved by tumour, or from 'reaction' to the tumour is difficult to distinguish (as with lung cancer), though well-defined, bean-shaped nodes are more likely to be reactive, whilst those with an altered echo-pattern and an irregular shape are more likely to have metastatic involvement.

Other oesophageal lesions may also be examined by this method - e.g. inflammatory conditions, lymphoma (which infiltrates the layers without destroying their boundaries), varices and recurrent tumour.

The instrument may also be used for studying adjacent mediastinal structures, such as the pericardium and heart, the aorta, adjacent mediastinal cysts, etc., and even the pulmonary arteries for emboli (see p. 7.27), but mediastinal examinations are limited, as the probe (7.5, 10 or 12 MHZ) only has a range of two to three cms. It may also be used for controlling laser treatment of oesophageal tumours, examinations of the adjacent descending aorta and the heart and pericardium.

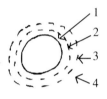

(a)   Normal

1 - Mucosa & inner part of
    submucosa
2 - Outer part of submucosa
3 - Muscularis propria
4 - Adventitia and perioesophageal fat

(b)

   Tumour extending into
surrounding tissue with loss
  of definition of layers of the
    oesophageal wall.

(c)

   Nodes - those with a
heterogenous pattern and
  which have lost their normal
'bean-shape' are likely to be
  filled with tumour tissue.

Fig. 16.10 Ultrasound patterns of the oesophageal wall.

Further references.

Day (1984) : The geographic pathology of cancer of the oesophagus.
McCort (1952) : Radiographic identification of lymph node metastases from carcinoma of the oesophagus.
Daffner (1978) : Retrotracheal abnormalities in oesophageal carcinoma - prognostic implications.
Daffner et al. (1979) : CT of oesophageal neoplasm.
Halber et al. (1979) : CT of the normal oesophagus.
Goldstein et al. (1981) : Benign and malignant tumours of the adult oesophagus.
Owen et al. (1983) : Radiological evaluation of complications after oesophagogastrectomy.
Picus et al. (1983) : CT in the staging of oesophageal carcinoma.
Halvorsen et al. (1984) : CT of the oesophagus. (1986) : CT staging of oesophageal ca. - long term follow-up.
Halvorsen and Thompson (1984) : CT of the gastro-oesophageal junction.
              (1987) : Critical review of oesophageal carcinoma. (1989) : CT of oesophageal neoplasms.
Samuelsson et al. (1984) : CT staging of oesophageal carcinoma.
Agha and Orringer (1984) : Colonic interposition.
Agha et al. (1985) : Gastric interposition following transhiatal oesophagectomy.
Quint et al. (1985a) : Oesophageal carcinoma - CT findings.
Quint et al. (1985b) : Oesophageal imaging by MR and CT - normal anatomy and neoplasms.
Levine et al. (1986) : Early oesophageal cancer.
Orringer and Sloan (1978) : Oesophagectomy without thoracotomy.
Orringer and Orringer (1983) : Oesophagectomy without thoracotomy - a dangerous operation?
Orringer (1985) : 65 cases of transhiatal oesophagectomy for benign oesophageal disease causing dysphagia - several with previous surgery.
Becker et al. (1986) : CT of 50 patients prior to transhiatal oesophagectomy for carcinoma - found this to be accurate and useful with tumours of the upper oesophagus in identifying those who were unsuitable owing to involvement of

the larger airways or the aorta. It was of less value with tumours of the middle and lower oesophagus, and was of low sensitivity in detecting abdominal lymph node metastases.

de Lange et al. (1987) : Used balloon dilatation for post-operative narrowing of the anastomotic site, associated with fistulae to the skin wound, following cervical anastomosis after oesophagectomy.

Brenøe et al. (1988) : Transhiatal oesophagectomy without thoracotomy (20 patients).

Brooks et al. (1988) : Two cases of large pneumoperitoneum following laser therapy for inoperable oesophageal tumours - these caused no constitutional upset and no perforation could be found - probably due to high pressure CO_2 (used to keep the tip of the laser clean) passing through the tumour and tracking into the peritoneum.

Hennessy (1988) : Choice of treatment in carcinoma of the oesophagus.

Recht et al. (1989) : CT demonstration of recurrent oesophageal carcinoma at the sites of thoracotomy incisions.

Slavin and Stout (1989) : 108 patients treated by radiotherapy at Christie Hospital, Manchester over a 10 year period. Crude 5 yr. survival was 8.3 %, but long-term survival was better in those > 65 years, in females and with tumours of the upper oesophagus - in the last the 5 yr. survival was 15.6 % and this was probably the treatment of choice.

Mantell (1990), Paterson (1990) : Advantage of radiotherapy over surgery for the treatment of cancer of oesophagus.

Kronthal et al. (1991) : Mediastinal seroma after oesophagogastrectomy (2 cases resolved with conservative management) - fluid masses compressing the stomach brought up into the oesophageal bed.

Takashima et al. (1991) : CT vs MR imaging in determining resectability.

Watson (1991) : Oesophageal adenocarcinomas are increasing in number (about 40)% tend to be more advanced with nodal involvement in 85%, compared with 54% for squamous. (Also cases of Barrett's oesophagus increasing with alkaline reflux - ? due to treatment of DU and acid reflux with H antagonists.)

Rankin (1990) and Rankin and Mason (1992) : CT and staging of oesophageal carcinoma.

I - An intraluminal polypoid mass without thickening of the oesophageal wall and no local invasion.

II - Thickening of the oesophageal wall > 5 mm without local invasion.

III - Thickening of the oesophageal wall with local invasion.

IV - Distant metastasis regardless of oesophageal stage.

Unfortunately approx. 75% of cases have nodal metastases at presentation. Tumours restricted to the oesophageal wall and no involved nodes have a better survival (40% at 5 yrs.) compared with those who have local or nodal spread (3 - 4% at 5 yrs.).

Unger et al. (1992) : CT staging in patients treated by radiation therapy and chemotherapy.

Anbari et al. (1993) : Evaluation of delayed leaks and fistulas after oesophagogastrectomy - from early anastomotic leaks that eventually seal; gastro-pleural and bronchial fistulae may occur even in pts. who do not have recurrent tumour or who have not had radiotherapy. Early (1st 4 wks) anastomotic breakdown is the most important complication in up to 30% of pts. and are associated with a high morbidity and mortality.

Carlisle et al. (1993) : Recurrent oesophageal carcinoma: CT evaluation of recurrent oesophageal carcinoma after oesophagectomy - tumour recurrence was seen most commonly as some combination of local or regional disease, distant metastasis and abdominal lymph node enlargement.

Van Overhagen et al. (1993, from Holland) : In their study CT was accurate in diagnosing tracheo-bronchial invasion, but was limited in diagnosing the invasion of other structures.

O'Reilly and Forastiere (1994) : New approaches to treating oesophageal cancer, combining chemotherapy, radiotherapy and surgery to improve survival. Noted that most cases have already metastasised by the time symptoms develop. Incidence is rising in Britain and USA. Best results have been obtained at Univ. of Michigan using a trans-hiatal approach, following chemotherapy and radiotherapy with 5 yr. survival rates of 34% for adeno. and 31% for squamous types. In those patients who had no visible tumour at surgery, a survival rate of 60% was obtained.

Foster, D. (1994) : Strecker oesophageal stent in 98 year old female with a benign oesophageal stricture.

Grundy (1994) : The Stricker oesophageal stent in the management of oesophageal strictures.

Nicholson et al. (1995) : Palliation of malignant oesophageal perforation and proximal oesophageal malignant dysphagia with covered metal stents.

Liang et al. (1996) : Oesophageal tumour measurement using supine CT in the prone position with gas distension of the oesophagus.

Watkinson et al. (1995) : Plastic covered metallic endoprostheses in the management of oesophageal perforation in patients with oesophageal carcinoma.

Watkinson (1996) : Metallic endoprostheses in oesophageal carcinoma - it is important that each inoperable case is addressed individually and an appropriate treatment plan chosen. The goal must be immediate and complete relief of swallowing problems with a short hospital stay, low morbidity and mortality and a dysphagia free survival period. Further improvements in stent design are awaited.

Tan et al. (1996) : **Review of minimally invasive therapy for advanced oesophageal malignancy** - the prognosis of oesophageal ca. is very poor, with approx. half the pts. unsuitable for curative resection at presentation.

Laser therapy - needs to be repeated on a 4 to 8 weekly basis.

R/T - gives sustained response rates of about 50%, but is complicated by fibrotic strictures in about 30%.

R/T + chemotherapy - results better but higher toxicity.

Intracavitary   brachytherapy (either alone or with external R/T) - more promising response rates but troublesome oesophagitis in up to 80% of cases.

Plastic stents - about 20% become dislodged.

Metallic expansile mesh stents - covered or uncovered (with delivery device of smaller diameter) - Wallstent or Gianturco stents appear to achieve better palliation than laser therapy in advanced oesophageal carcinoma. Early stents tended to cause fatal late haemorrhage in 3 to 15% (particularly if pts. had previous R/T). About 5% develop an oes./ respiratory fistula. Two disadvantages - (i) cost, (ii) permanent nature due to hooks and/or incorporation in oes. wall - are very difficult to remove and extreme care must be taken to ensure that optimal placement is achieved.

Concluded: "Based on currently available data, our approach is to treat patients with tumour involvement of the gastro-oesophageal junction with either laser therapy or uncovered stents. For tumours not involving the cardia, stenting (either with covered or uncovered endoprostheses) achieves the best palliation. Fistulae are best sealed by covered stents. Laser therapy is excellent for dealing with intaluminal tumours and for tackling subsequent tumour ingrowth or overgrowth. Both these modalities can be further combined with radiotherapy or chemotherapy...".

Grundy and Glees (1997) : Aorto-oesophageal fistula - a fatal complication of oesophageal stenting.

Laasch et al. (1998) : Gianturco stents provided effective palliation of malignant oesophageal obstruction.

Nicholson (1998) : Tracheal and oesophageal stenting for **carcinoma of the upper oesophagus invading the tracheobronchial tree** - two cases.

Rankin et al. (1998) : CT & PET in the pre-operative staging of oesophageal carcinoma - both are effective for showing the primary tumour and about equally sensitive for showing peri-oesophageal nodes. PET is more sensitive for showing distant metastases.

Haemangiopericytoma

Smith, R. et al. (1995) : Causing a large intraluminal mass in a 78 year old male.

Liposarcoma

Mansour et al. (1983) : Pedunculated liposarcoma.

Yates and Collins (1990) : Liposarcoma of the oesophagus - huge intraluminal mass - recurrent after six years.

Lymphoma

Levine et al. (1985) : Diffuse nodularity in oesophageal lymphoma.

Melanoma

Isaacs and Quirke (1988) : Two cases of primary malignant melanoma of the oesophagus.

Sabanathan and Eng (1990) : Three cases.

Chello et al. (1993) : Primary malignant melanoma of the oesophagus with left atrial metastasis - also noted that myocardial and pericardial metastases were common.

Myoblastoma

Cadotte (1974) : Malignant granular-cell myoblastoma.

Howe and Postlethwait (1981) : Granular myoblastoma of the oesophagus.

Hjelms and Thomsen (1986) : Large granular-cell myoblastoma of the oesophagus.

Oat cell tumours

McKeown (1952) : One case.,   Kelsen et al. (1980) : One case.

Briggs and Ibrahim (1993) : Clinicopathological study of 23 cases.

Doherty et al. (1984) : 6 cases.,   Beyer et al. (1991) : 11 cases.

Hartubise and Paquin (1986) : 2 cases.,   Hunter et al. (1994)

McCullen et al. (1994) : Long term survival in case treated by chemotherapy, autologous bone marrow transplantation and radiotherapy.

Fenlon et al. (1995) : 4 cases - 2 men and 2 women - extensive tumours with thoracic and abdominal lymphadenopathy - two has remissions following chemotherapy.

Plasmacytoma

Davies, R. and Boxer (1988) : Primary plasmacytoma of the oesophagus.

Plain film changes.

Kendall et al. (1962), Stark et al. (1990) Manifestations of oesophageal disease on plain chest radiographs.

Ultrasound

Rifkin (1984) : Used the method to examine the mediastinum, pancreas and liver.

Gussenhoven et al. (1986) : Transoesophageal two-dimensional echocardiography.

Murata (1987) : Performed histology on 705 nodes from 78 patients who had oesophageal resections for carcinoma and claimed 87% sensitivity and 90% specificity for assessing spread.

Shorvon et al. (1987), Shorvon and Hine (1988), Shorvon (1990).

Sutherland and Roelandt (1988) : Oesophageal echocardiography.

Page et al. (1989) : Trans-oesophageal ultrasound for examining and the control of aspiration of mediastinal cysts.

Vilgrain et al. (1990) : Staging of oesophageal carcinoma - comparison with endoscopic sonography and CT. When the echo-endoscope can be manoeuvred past the tumour, sonography can be used accurately to define extension through the layers of the oesophagus, extension to adjacent organs and involvement of lymph nodes. When this is not possible, CT is superior for showing mediastinal extension.

Das et al. (1992) : US-guided fine needle aspiration cytology of carcinoma involving intra-abdominal oesophagus.

Van Overhagen et al. (1993) : US and CT of supraclavicular and abdominal metastases in oesophageal and gastro-oesophageal junction carcinoma - both should be used and abnormalities confirmed by image-guided biopsy.

McLean and Fairclough (1996) : Reviewed endoscopic ultrasound and wrote "On EUS oesophageal cancer presents as an area of localised or, more often circumferential thickening of the oesophageal wall, with a hypoechoic or mixed echopattern. With increasing tumour penetration, the normal stratification of the wall is destroyed, with loss of the smooth outer margin, and with tumour pseudopodia extending into the surrounding echogenic paraoesophageal fat. In advanced disease, tumour may be seen to encase the aorta, azygos vein or trachea...Unfortunately, oesophageal cancer often presents late and the patient may not experience dysphagia until 50% of the luminal diameter is compromised...EUS is more accurate than CT in predicting nonresectability of oesophageal cancer - 91% for EUS versus 31% for CT. However, prediction of resectability is higher for adenocarcinoma (89%) than for squamous cell cancer because of the difficulty in recognising microscopic sub-mucosal spread of disease in the latter."

Chen et al. (1997) : Demonstration of the distal oesophagus (abdominal part) by transabdominal US via a L subcostal approach in supine and 45° right side up oblique positions - the latter showing a larger portion of it.

An oddity - an anti-reflux prosthesis.

Kennedy et al. (1999) : reported the CT appearances of a surgical collar placed around the gastro-oesophageal junction - an Angelchik prosthesis - which had migrated to the pelvis - about 25,000 were inserted world-wide and many are still in situ. If the Dacron fastening strap breaks they may migrate into the abdomen, chest or become intraluminal and cause small bowel obstruction. Most contain an opaque linear marker.

See also:

Angelchik and Cohen (1979) : A new surgical procedure for the treatment of gastro-oesophageal reflux and hiatus hernia.

Chapter 17 : **The Spread of Chest Tumours to the Abdomen, and some Abdominal Tumours to the Chest - also a consideration of some relevant abdominal conditions in differential diagnosis, particularly of the Liver, Spleen and Pancreas**.

Lung and thoracic tumours may spread to the abdomen in three ways (i) via the **blood stream**, (ii) via the **lymphatics** and (iii) by **direct extension** - either through the diaphragm or openings within it.

Blood stream spread is very common, particularly to the liver (which should be examined by ultra-sound in every case at presentation). Metastases also occur to the adrenals, spleen, pancreas, mesentery or omentum, bowel wall, etc.

Nodal and lymphatic spread occurs retrogradely, mainly via the retro-crural space, and may lead to para-aortic node enlargement, which in turn may lead to IVC compression, ascites and severe oedema of the lower limbs.

Direct extension may involve the para-spinal space (thence also spreading into the spine, etc.), and upper abdominal organs, which may be encased in tumour.

Many abdominal deposits may be clinically 'silent', whilst others may be the presenting feature, e.g. tender liver, jaundice, abdominal or back pain, ascites and /or lower limb swelling, or haemorrhage from an adrenal, renal or splenic deposit, bowel obstruction, renal or adrenal failure, etc. Some patients may present with secondary abdominal paraneoplastic syndromes (see Chapter 23), or stress related conditions e.g. duodenal ulcer. The author's practice has always been to take chest radiographs of patients with abdominal problems, and **every week** found patients with significant abnormalities.

Lymphatic connections of the chest with the abdomen. These are well illustrated in Figs. 17.1 & 17.5 also Illus. **MASCAGNI.**

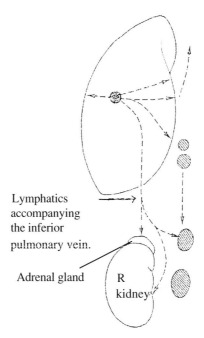

Fig. 17.1   The spread of metastases from lung tumours to the abdomen via the lymphatic system.
Note two main routes :
(i) via the hilar and mediastinal nodes and lymphatics, and
(ii) via the lymphatics in the inferior pulmonary ligaments.
As well as spread to the para-aortic nodes, this may also occur to the kidneys, adrenals, etc.

Lymphatics accompanying the inferior pulmonary vein.

Adrenal gland

R kidney

Retrograde lymphatic flow may occur not only into the cisterna chyli from the thoracic duct, but also via retrocrural and peridiaphragmatic vessels and nodes. In addition lymphatics may pass through the diaphragm at other points. Lymphatics in the inferior pulmonary ligaments may pass to the abdomen without necessarily passing through any intrathoracic lymph nodes. (They may be filled with tumour cells in patients with lymphangitis carcinomatosa - see Trapnell, 1973 - and these vessels have sometimes been demonstrated by lymphography). Not only may bronchial tumours spread to the abdomen via this route, but these vessels also explain how renal tumours sometimes give rise to a hilar node metastasis (usually right sided) mimicking an intra-thoracic tumour (see p. 13.1 et seq. & Fig. 17.1). This route for spread was also noted by Spencer (1985).

Renal metastases from bronchial tumours.

   Occasionally patients may have large renal metastases from bronchial tumours. These may be bilateral, and cause presentation with renal failure - examples are shown in Illus. **LUNG CA/RENAL DEP.**
Note also the nephrotic syndrome caused by lung tumours - see p. 23.1.

References to some reported series of abdominal deposits from lung tumours.
Onuigbo (1958 and 1962) : Studied post-mortem findings in 6,000 patients with bronchial neoplasms and found that 40% had hepatic metastases, 32% adrenal and 18% renal deposits. Less frequent were deposits in the bowel wall or pancreas. Abdominal nodes were involved in about 20%.
Sinclair and Gravelle (1967) : Noted various presentations of bronchogenic carcinoma, and found metastases in the para-aortic nodes, liver, retroperitoneal tissues, tail of pancreas, kidneys, adrenals, and in the wall of the colon, simulating primary bowel cancer.
Le Roux (1968) : Found that in 4,000 cases of bronchial carcinoma, 21 presented with dyspepsia and nine with abdominal masses (adrenal, renal, bowel wall, ovarian and omental).

Imaging of liver disease and hepatic secondary deposits - (Illus. **LIVER** and **LIVER DEPOSITS**).
Historical.   In the 1950s, when most liver disease was unrecognisable radiologically, all one could do was to recognise a large liver, (palpate its edge, note **pulsation** **with** **severe tricuspid** **incompetence**), or occasionally note intra-hepatic calcification.   Lumsden and Truelove (1957) in Oxford were able to visualise the surface of the liver and note masses deforming its surface following an induced **pneumoperitoneum**   (mostly with CO_2). **Coeliac and hepatic angiography** also showed some tumour masses (or a cirrhotic pattern) due to their abnormal circulation. **Thorotrast** (also used for angiography in the 1930s and 1940s - see Illus. **THOROTRAST**) was taken up in the reticulo-endothelial cells of the liver and spleen, and could be used to image the liver particularly with tomography, demonstrating large secondary deposits as negative defects. (Its long half-life of 1.4×10^{10} years in those who had gross metastatic disease, and the possibility of inducing tumours of the spleen and liver 20 or more years later was irrelevant). **Hepatography** using emulsified Lipiodol (injected into the portal venous system, via the unobliterated umbilical vein, usually found in the upper part of the umbilicus under local anaesthesia) was used in the 1960s, particularly in France; an advantage was that, as with lymphography, the liver remained opacified for up to 18 months. It is being used again now for CT enhancement of the liver (see references).
   Isotopic liver scans (mainly using a Tc^{99m} labelled colloid - see Illus. **LIVER COLLOID SCAN**) were the mainstay of liver examinations from 1965 until **real-time** **ultrasound** became available in the late 1970s. This was a great advance as it allowed one to determine whether a defect seen on isotope studies was solid or cystic. Real-time, particularly with small curved probes, allows one to examine nearly all of the liver, with the patient in the erect or lying positions, and to detect most secondary deposits, as well as dilated ducts, dilated hepatic or portal veins, etc.
Often there is a 'halo' of oedema around deposits (e.g. Illus. **LIVER** **Pt.** **23**) and sometimes degenerate centres, and rarely even abscesses within them (see Illus. **LIVER DEPOSITS**).
Isotope scans still have some place in determining if the liver is 'dead' (i.e. no uptake at all - Illus. **LIVER Pt. 41**), or if considerably damaged (as from radiotherapy) - Illus. **LIVER Pt. 50**.
   CT is invaluable for examining the liver, and may be carried out both with and without contrast enhancement, but the author believes that it should always be carried out with ultrasound, unless the CT findings are in themselves non-equivocal. This is for a number of reasons : (i) CT cannot always distinguish between solid lesions and cysts, (ii) CT may miss some lesions, either because

of their tiny size, or because there may be little density change between a lesion and the surrounding liver (as occurs with some secondary deposits, but mainly with hepatomas), (iii) artefacts due to streaking from gas in the bowel, or from the overlying ribs may produce density changes suggesting disease when none is present, and (iv) lesions outside the liver may appear to invade it, rather than just deform it from pressure, when ultrasound will usually show a definite separation.

A **small subscapular fluid collection** may sometimes be a 'clue' to tiny hepatic secondary deposits.

Fig. 17.2 Small anterior subcapsular haematoma providing a 'clue' to an otherwise invisible metastasis on CT - such may be confirmed easily with ultrasound.

MR has many advantages, being able to visualise the liver in several planes, and also allow of considerable tissue characterisation - particularly valuable with hepatomas, and excessive deposition of iron, fat, etc.

Treatment of hepatic deposits.
In a few patients (e.g. with breast secondary deposits, lymphoma, or small cell lung cancer) considerable resolution of hepatic deposits may take place in response to hormone and/or chemotherapeutic treatment - see Illus. **HEPATIC DEPOSITS, Liver Pt. 21** & ps. 24.41-42.

Sometimes deposits have degenerate cystic centres, which may look 'cloudy' on ultrasound examinations, and in a toxic or febrile patient infection of these may be present, or a patient with a lung lesion may also have a liver abscess. Such lesions should be aspirated and if infected the patient given antibiotics. The author has had several patients with infected liver deposits who recovered well from these and had several useful months of life.

Percutaneous radio-frequency ablation is being tried in some centres. Good results have recently been reported by Solbiati et al. (1997) - from Boston, Mass. and Vimercate, Italy - using a cooled-tip RF electrode which could coagulate 2-3 cm lesions, with complete necrosis of 66% of metastases as shown by CT or MR and with good survival rates. A similar technique using lasers is being used by Adam at St. Thomas' Hospital (2000).

Differential diagnosis of hepatic deposits.
Benign hepatic **haemangiomas** (Illus. **LIVER HAEMANGIOMA**) are quite common and should be differentiated from both cysts and tumour deposits. These on ultrasound are usually bright, echogenic and well-defined, and have **no** surrounding oedema or capsule. They only increase in size slowly over several years - the author has noted some increase in size in some cases over five to 10 years. Some may become invisible within a fatty liver. Some may degenerate, or exhibit internal haemorrhage, or rupture. They may enlarge in pregnancy or in response to oestrogen therapy.

Liver abscesses (as noted above) may mimic secondary deposits - more than one famous doctor has diagnosed secondaries in his own liver, and at autopsy was found to be suffering from amoebic lung abscesses as a result of a foreign visit. See also ps. 19.48-49.

Abscesses are usually well recognised by US and/or CT. US will often show 'clear fluid' or fluid containing debris or pus, and is of inestimable value in directing aspiration or drainage. Despite the clinical impression that all liver abscesses are tender to palpation, this is untrue and **many are not** (especially amoebic abscesses). Increasing numbers of liver abscesses are being seen due to Strep. milleri infection. Examples are shown in Illus. **LIVER ABSCESS**.

For 'bare-area' abscess see p. 15.15.

Inhomogeneity of the liver on CT examinations may be produced by cardiac failure and venous congestion, cirrhosis, or focal nodular hyperplasia.

Liver calcification occurs mainly in focal lesions and has several causes - past-infection (abscess [including amoebic] or granuloma), a haematoma, hamartoma, haemangioma, aneurysm, metastases (bowel, ovary, carcinoid, phaeochromocytoma, etc.), a hepatoma or other primary tumour, parasitic (esp. hydatid) or non-parasitic cyst) - see Illus. **LIVER CALCIFICATION.**

Liver cysts are not uncommon and are usually readily diagnosed with ultrasound and/or CT (Illus. **LIVER CYSTS**). They are most common in patients with polycystic kidneys, and like the renal cysts can become infected (Illus. **LIVER ABSCESS, Liver Pt. 8a-d**). Sometimes large simple cysts can become symptomatic causing abdominal pain or an uncomfortable mass. Aspiration + the use of sclerosants such as the antibiotic minocycline hydrochloride or alcohol to prevent recurrence has been reported by Cellier et al. (1998) and Larssen et al (1997) respectively - see also Year Book of Diagnostic Radiology, 1998, ps. 119 - 121.

Hepatomas are uncommon in the UK, but are more common in the Far East. Some examples are shown in Illus. **HEPATOMA**.

Nodular hyperplasia or **fibrotic nodules** may be seen in a cirrhotic or fibrotic liver - see refs. to Ohtomo et al. (1993), Mathieu et al. (1986) and Vilgrain et al. (1992) below.

Extramedullary haemopoiesis may also give rise to **liver masses** - see Illus. **EXTRAMED HAEMOPOIESIS 3** and ps. 18.33-35.

Pseudomasses within the liver also have to be considered. These may be due to a variety of causes e.g. subpulmonary effusion indenting it from above, a subphrenic abscess, enlarged right kidney or adrenal, large aortic aneurysm, etc. Even a large breast may mimic a liver lesion on an isotope scan carried out in the supine position, as may the effect of previous radiotherapy to the lung base (see also p. 11.21 and Illus. **LIVER ARTEFACT, Pts. 42 & 50** [+ its info sheet]).

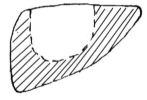

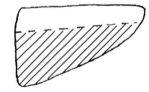

Pseudomass of the liver due to an overlying large female breast - elevation causes it to disappear!

Pseudomass, with straight lower border, due to a recent radiotherapy field for treating a RLL tumour.

Fig. 17.3 Pseudomasses of the liver on isotope liver scans.

Other conditions.
Examples are shown in Illus. **LIVER FATTY, LIVER CIRRHOSIS** and **LIVER TRAUMA** - see also **HYDATID CYSTS** and **LIVER** [under 'list view'].

Some references.
Yamamoto et al. (1988) : CT of congenital absence of the left lobe of the liver.
Gaines et al. (1990) : Lipiodol assisted ultrasound guided liver biopsies - may be seen with ultrasound and besides being taken up in hepatomas, it also accumulates in haemangiomas and regenerating nodules.
Ignotus et al. (1990) : Echo enhancement behind solid intra-hepatic metastases esp. in the presence of a fatty liver (a potential pitfall in diagnosis).
Ngan (1990) from Hong Kong : Lipiodol CT - how sensitive and specific is the technique in the diagnosis of hepatocellular carcinoma?
Turnbull et al. (1990 a & b) : Evaluation of iodised oil emulsion in the CT-detection of tumours.
Wernecke et al. (1991) : Comparative sensitivities of US, CT and MR for the detection of hepatic deposits - CT had a higher overall sensitivity but its size threshold is about 1 cm.
Fairlee and Adam (1991) : Persistence of Lipiodol for 13 months in metastatic deposits in the liver on CT.
Khan et al. (1992) : Liver adenomatosis presenting as **multiple calcified masses**.

Scatarige et al. (1983) : CT of **calcified liver masses**.

Gibney et al. (1987) : Followed 47 patients with 68 hepatic haemangiomas for up to six years. 56 showed no change in their appearance or size, but 12 changed; 3 could not be found, 7 were less echogenic, 1 was larger and 1 smaller.
Whitehouse (1990) : The use of CT attenuation values to assist in characterisation of **hepatic   haemangioma** - the commonest benign hepatic tumour. About 60% are hypodense compared with surrounding liver, and show peripheral enhancement on dynamic contrast enhanced CT. On delayed post-contrast CT they become isodense with liver. In a study of 21 cases all the haemangiomas had attenuations within 7 HU of caval blood.
Moody and Wilson (1993) : Atypical hepatic haemangioma:- a suggestive sonographic morphology. Just as a haemangioma may appear hypodense compared with a fatty liver on an unenhanced CT scan, it may appear hypoechoic on US. Large haemangiomas often have central necrosis or fibrosis and may have a reticular pattern or a thick echogenic 'rind'.
Mungovan et al. (1994) : Hepatic cavernous haemangiomas: lack of enlargement over time in 21 cases.
Chong and Fan (1994) : US hepatic pseudo lesion - normal parenchyma mimicking mass lesions in fatty liver.
Halavaara et al. (1995) : Spin lock MR imaging in the differentiation of hepatic haemangiomas and metastases.
Baudouin et al. (1996) : A comparison of T_2 weighted spin-echo sequences in the detection of focal liver lesions at 1.0 T - fast spin echo T_2 weighted sequences showed fewer lesions than a conventional T_2 weighted sequence.
McNicholas et al. (1996) : T_2 relaxation times of hypovascular and non-hypervascular liver lesions are similar and are significantly shorter than those of haemangiomas; therefore hypervascular lesions should not mimic haemangiomas on heavily weighted T_2-weighted images.
Ward et al. (1996) : Dynamic contrast enhanced MR imaging of the hepatic vasculature in liver transplants - typical patchy parenchymal enhancement of Budd-Chiari shown by spin echo and IVC thrombosis by DCEMR.
Brown, J. et al. (1997) : Imaging of hepatic cirrhosis.
Ernst et al. (1997) : Diagnosis and quantification of hepatic iron overload in **haemochromatosis**.
Hoe et al. (1997) : Dual-phase helical CT of the liver - value of early phase acquisition in the differential diagnosis of non-cystic focal lesions - improved the differentiation of hepatoma from other tumours.
Soyer et al. (1997) : Gd chelate-enhanced spoiled GRE imaging is more sensitive than T_2 weighted MR imaging obtained with a breath-hold or a non-breath-hold technique.
Callaway et al. (1998) : A large infarcted liver deposit from a ca head of pancreas.
Hale et al. (1998) : CT of **calcified liver deposits** in colorectal carcinoma.
Robinson (2000) : **Review - most commonly imaged deposits   are   1-2cm   in   size,** a few being 3-4mm in diameter. For improved **chemotherapy imaging of lesions 1-2mm in diameter will be necessary**.
Sica et al. (2000) : CT & MR imaging of hepatic metastases.

Imaoka et al. (1993) : MR imaging of a **carcinoid** tumour of the liver.
Kehagias et al. (1999) : Primary liver carcinoid with cystic and solid components on US, CT & MR.

Roberts, J. et al. (1986) : Lipomatous tumours of the liver - CT and US.
Blumgart et al. (1987) : Angiomyolipomas of the liver.
Cheung et al. (1993) : Liver hamartomas in **tuberose sclerosis**.
Carmody et al. (1993) : Hepatic lesions in tuberose sclerosis represent angiolipomas and a conservative approach may be adopted even with a lesion of entirely soft-tissue density.
Itai et al. (1996) : Hyperattenuating rim on non-contrast liver CT - a thin rim of hyperattenuation around tumour (1° or 2°) in liver, on non-contrast CT - suggests tumour in a fatty liver - probably due to peritumoral sparing of fatty infiltration.
Kane et al. (1996) : Pseudotumours of hepatic imaging - particularly when fatty masses or infiltration are present in cirrhosis, alcoholism, Gaucher's disease, Niemann-Pick syndrome, etc. - also 'nodular masses' may enhance in α_1 anti-trypsin deficiency, Budd-Chiari syndrome, etc.
Garibella et al. (1997) : Focal fatty liver infiltration causing mass effect.
Chen et al. (1998) : CO_2 enhanced US of hepatic haemangiomas.
Wachsberg and Jilani (1999) : Duplex Doppler sonography of small (<3 cm diameter) liver tumours; intralesional arterial flow does not exclude cavernous haemangioma.

Ohtomo et al. (1993) : Confluent hepatic fibrosis in advanced cirrhosis - MR imaging.
Mathieu et al. (1986) : Hepatic adenomas and focal nodular hyperplasia - dynamic CT study.
Vilgrain et al. (1992) : Focal nodular hyperplasia - MR in 37 patients.

Hensch (1964) : TB of the liver - study of 200 cases.
Hulnick et al. (1985) : Abdominal TB - CT evaluation.
Moskovic (1990) : Macronodular TB in a child - CT appearances.
Kawamori et al. (1992) : CT & MR of macronodular tuberculoma of the liver.

Bankier et al. (1995) : Abdominal tuberculosis - unusual findings on CT in 12 pts. - characteristic findings included solitary and multiple pelvic, adrenal, splenic and hepatic lesions, in 6 the findings mimicked malignancy.
Tan et al. (1998) : Tuberculoma of the liver presenting as a hyperechoic mass on US.

Dalla Palma (1998) : Review - diagnostic imaging and interventional therapy of hepatocellular carcinoma.
Ngan et al. (1998) : Hepatic arterial embolisation in the treatment of spontaneous rupture of hepatocellular ca.
Moulton et al. (1988) : CT abnormalities due to passive hepatic congestion in heart failure.
Holley et al. (1989) : Inhomogeneous enhancement of liver parenchyma due to passive congestion on enhanced CT.
Connor and Guest (1999) : Conversion of solid testicular teratoma deposits to fatty & cystic masses with therapy.
Note that ectopic liver 'rests' may occasionally give rise to a tumour. (see p. 15.14).

Adrenals - masses and metastases - (Illus. **ADRENALS** - see also p. 21.17 re biopsy).
Anatomy : the adrenals lie in the retroperitoneal fat, above and anterior to the kidneys. The right lies behind the IVC, whilst the left is adjacent to the left crus of the diaphragm. Both have '**tails**' - see Illus. **ADRENAL, Pts. 1, 4 & 12**. Rarely the adrenals may be joined - '**horse-shoe adrenals**'.
    Adrenal metastases from lung tumours are commonly found at autopsy, but during life were rarely diagnosed before the availability of CT. Engelman and McNamara (1954) reported 30% or more with adrenal metastases at autopsy, but this figure is probably too high in relation to the general population of lung cancer patients, as those autopsied will tend to have been the most ill cases and to have died in hospital. Probably a more correct figure is 5 to 10%. Many adrenal deposits or tumours are asymptomatic, but occasionally they may become so large as to mimic a renal mass or cause localised pain, particularly if haemorrhage has occurred into them (Illus. **ADRENAL, Pt. 5a-b**). Adrenal failure is uncommon from metastases, but may be masked in severely ill or dying patients with widespread metastases.
    Not all adrenal masses, even in patients with bronchial tumours, are due to secondary deposits. Some are due to benign causes such as cysts or adenomas, myelolipomas, haematomas or occasionally a phaeochromocytoma (see Illus. **ADRENAL TUMOUR, Adrenal Pt. 31-b**). Indeed it has been estimated that incidental adrenal masses may be found in up to about 10% of the adult population. The majority of these are adenomas, but it is difficult to differentiate them from metastases by CT, though a small smooth nodule is nearly always an adenoma. A CT number lower than zero on unenhanced scans implies some fat content, and a benign aetiology, contrariwise a HU >20 or enhancement is most likely an indication of malignancy.
    On MR studies, signals from an adrenal secondary deposit may be similar to those from the primary tumour, appear 'white' on STIR sequence, or show degenerative changes. Newer MR sequences my permit a chemical shift to be determined - signal drop-off on out-of-phase images also indicate a benign aetiology - see also ps. 20.30 - 31.
    Huge masses in patients are mostly due to secondary deposits, and in many patients with adrenal masses, the problem is often solved by finding other secondary tumours, e.g. in the liver, mediastinal nodes, etc. In a few biopsy may be important for confirmation and this may be carried out under ultra-sound or CT guidance - see p. 21.17.
    Examples of adrenal deposits are shown in Illus. **ADRENAL DEPOSIT.**

Ultrasound examination is easily carried out after examining the liver and kidneys, and may be done with the patient lying in the prone position, or erect slightly leaning forwards, with the patient seated, or standing. Nodules (or cysts) > 1 cm in diameter are frequently recognised.
Large adrenal masses may often be seen in the supine patient via the liver.

CT examination is readily carried out as part of the examination of the upper abdomen, a procedure which should always be **routine** in examining a patient with an intrathoracic tumour (the author usually continues this down to below the level of the kidneys).

Isotope studies - FDG/PET is usually positive with deposits and labelled norcholesterol or **MIBG** may be used to detect phaeochromocytomas (see ps. 22.12 - 13).

Retroperitoneal gas insufflation was used to demonstrate the adrenals in the pre US and CT era. Two examples are shown in Illus. **ADRENAL, Pt. 17** (a large right sided phaeochromocytoma) and **Pt. 18** (normal adrenals).

Adrenal hyperplasia may be secondary to excessive ACTH, as in Cushing's syndrome, or with some tumours (including lung tumours - see also p. 23.1 and Illus. **CUSHING'S SYNDROME**). Others include Conn's syndrome and the adreno-genital syndrome.

Adrenal cysts may be simple cysts, parasitic (e.g. hydatid), neoplastic (often showing loculi, resembling dilated renal calyces) or pseudocysts (with no epithelial lining).

Phaeochromocytomas are shown in Illus. **PHAEOCHROMOCYTOMA, Adrenal Pt. 3a-b, Pt. 17** and **Liver pt. 17.**

Adrenal neuroblastomas are discussed on p. 18.37 and examples are shown in Illus. **NEUROBLASTOMA.**

Adrenal calcification may be due to past tuberculosis, previous adrenal haemorrhage (either spontaneous, or from the obstetricians fingers at breech delivery), or within a tumour e.g. a phaeochromocytoma (Illus. **ADRENAL CALCIFICATION**). In severe cases it may be associated with Addison's* disease (Illus. **ADDISON'S DISEASE**).
* Thomas Addison, Physician, Guy's Hospital described a wasting disease, with 'smoky' brown skin pigmentation & pearly sclera associated with adrenal disease in 1855 - he produced a small book of drawings still used by students until recent years.

Adrenal pseudo-masses may be due to (a) fluid in the fundus of the stomach (Illus. **ADRENAL FALSE TUMOUR, Adrenals Pt. 15a**), (b) prominent splenic lobulations, splenunculi or tortuous splenic vessels, (c) renal vessels, (d) pancreatic masses, (e) diaphragmatic crura, and (f) varices (via the left inferior phrenic vein, which passes anterior to the left adrenal gland).

Further references.
Hill and Wheeler (1965) : Insufficiency due to deposits.
Hedeland et al. (1968) : The prevalence of adrenal adenomas at autopsy.
Wright, F. (1974a) : Demonstration of adrenal deposits by angiography.
Brownlie and Kreel (1978) : CT of normal adrenals. Korobkin et al. (1979) : CT in the diagnosis of adrenal disease.
Buck et al. (1982) : CT of adrenals - hypo and hyperplasia and neoplasms - primary and secondary.
Glazer, H. et al. (1982) : Incidental discovery of non-functioning adrenal masses by CT.
Lewis et al. (1982) : Examined the adrenals in 60 lung cancer patients having CT, and found one gross deposit (confirmed at laparotomy, 4 with abnormal adrenals (3 confirmed by biopsy and 1 by PM) and 3 doubtful (with no change on subsequent CT).
Nielsen et al. (1982) : CT demonstration and biopsy of adrenal deposits in non-small cell bronchial carcinoma .
Sandler et al. (1982) : Of 110 patients with bronchial carcinoma having CT, 11 patients had adrenal deposits (five were bilateral), six had other deposits or were medically inoperable, but five had no other evidence of inoperability.
Twomey et al. (1982) : Successful treatment of metastasis from large cell carcinoma of lung.
Gross et al. (1983) : CT demonstration and biopsy of unusual adrenal deposits.
Jafri et al. (1983) : CT detection of adrenal **lymphoma**.
Pagani (1983) : Normal adrenal glands in small cell lung carcinoma - CT & percutaneous biopsy.
Pagani (1984) : Non-small cell lung carcinoma adrenal metastases - CT & percutaneous needle biopsy.
Bernadino et al. (1985) : CT guided adrenal biopsy - 58 biopsies in 53 patients - successful in 44 at first attempt. Six complications - haemorrhage or hypertension.
Fink et al. (1985) : MR imaging of **phaeochromocytomas**.
Hussain (1985) : Differentiation of malignant from benign adrenal masses on CT.
Johnson et al. (1985) : CT demonstration of adrenal **pseudocyst**.
Reinig et al. (1985) : Distinction between adrenal adenomas and metastases using MR imaging.
            (1986) : MR of indeterminate adrenal masses. (1986) : Adrenal masses differentiated by MR.
Falke et al. (1986) : Comparison of MR and CT imaging of adrenals - complementary roles.
Glazer, G. et al. (1986) : Adrenal tissue characterisation using MR imaging.
Schwartz, A. et al. (1986) : Gastric diverticulum simulating an adrenal mass - CT demonstration.
Chang et al. (1987) : MR imaging of adrenal glands.
Gillams et al. (1990) : Adrenal biopsy & CT in staging bronchogenic ca. (24 masses in 22 patients) - concluded that low density, well defined masses < 2 cm in diameter, with a smooth high attenuating rim or involving only part of the gland were considered to be benign adenomas, but the majority had an indeterminate picture

(1992) The CT appearances of many adrenal lesions were insufficiently distinctive to exclude malignancy, and these had a biopsy. Low density lesions without a 'rim' were considered malignant.

Lee, M.J. et al. (1991) : Benign and malignant adrenal masses - CT distinction with attenuating coefficients, size and observer analysis.

Lee, S.H. et al. (1991) : Unusual appearance of a giant right adrenal pseudocyst (i.e. no epithelioid or endothelial lining) - tripled its volume over four years.

Dunnick et al. (1993) : Adrenal hyperplasia and adenomas - CT diagnosis - 29 pts. with primary aldosteronism.

Tsushima et al. (1993) : Adrenal masses - differentiation with chemical shift, fast low-angle shot MR imaging.

Welch et al. (1994) : Review of 10 yrs. experience of adrenal biopsy (277 biopsies in 270 pts.) - 90% accuracy - major complication in 8 was haemorrhage, in one case needing an adrenalectomy.

Boland et al. (1995) : Indeterminate adrenal mass in patients with cancer evaluation at PET with FDP.

Wong et al. (1996) : Rupture and growth of adrenal myelolipoma in two pts.

Erasmus et al. (1997) : Positron emission tomography using ^{18}F-flurodeoxyglucose is an accurate noninvasive way to differentiate benign lesions from malignant deposits from bronchial carcinoma (see also p. 22.11).

Varghese et al. (1997) : MR differentiation of **phaeochromocytoma** from other adrenal lesions based on qualitative analysis of T2 relaxation times.

Zammit-Maemfel (1997) : Interval (18 months) growth of adrenal myelolipomas on CT.

Pender et al. (1998) : The incidental nonhyperfunctioning adrenal mass - an imaging algorithm for chacterization.

Rao and Silver (1976) : Normal pancreas and splenic variants simulating suprarenal and renal tumours.

Berliner et al. (1982) : Adrenal pseudotumours on CT.

Mitty et al. (1983) : Adrenal pseudotumours due to porto-systemic veins.

Brady et al. (1985) : Adrenal pseudomasses due to varices - angiographic, CT and MRI pathological correlations.

Pancreatic disease and the thorax - (Illus. **PANCREAS**).
Pancreatic diseases which may affect the thorax include :

(i) **Fibrocystic disease** (see ps. 3.22 - 23).

(ii) **Diabetes mellitus** - diabetics are more prone to infections, including lung infections (pneumonia and tuberculosis). One still sees patients with TB complicating diabetes, the association sometimes being forgotten by some clinical colleagues. (The author has even had a registrar from the Indian subcontinent, who had diabetes and had been pronounced fit elsewhere, but died from active TB and coronary heart disease).

(iii) **Pancreatitis and pseudocysts** - patients with pancreatitis may have an acute and florid mediastinitis, as a result of pancreatic enzymes spreading up into the thorax through the larger openings in the diaphragm (alongside the cardia, the aorta or through the foramina of Morgagni or Bochdalek) or passing through the tiny pores in the diaphragm (see ps. 14.9 - 10).

Pleural effusions and pericarditis may also be present, and these may be haemorrhagic. Whilst much of this inflammatory reaction may resolve spontaneously, pseudocysts may form, as in the abdomen. These occur mainly in the lower mediastinum, or in relation to the diaphragmatic crura, and may become chronic. Occasionally secondary infection and/or fistulous communications with the viscera or bronchi occur.

Fig. 17.4 A pseudocyst lying in front of the diaphragmatic crura.

(iv) **Pancreatitis** may be complicated by **venous thrombosis** leading to IVC or portal vein thrombosis and pulmonary embolism.
Illustrations of pseudocysts etc. are shown in Illus. **PANCREATITIS**.

(v) **Pancreatic neoplasm** - patients with pancreatic neoplasms may present with multiple and diffuse lung nodules due to secondary deposits, lymphangitis carcinomatosa, or mediastinal or retro-crural node enlargement. They may also present with thrombo-embolism. Illus. **PANCREAS CA.**
(vi) **Pancreatic deposit** - rarely a bronchial neoplasm may give rise to a pancreatic deposit (Illus. **PANCREAS DEP FROM LUNG**).

References.

Trousseau (1865) : Association of venous thrombosis with obscure and asymptomatic cancer.
Sproul (1938) : Among 4,200 autopsies found 125 cases of body & tail pancreas ca., 70 having venous thromboses.
Duff (1939), Leach (1950) : Body and tail neoplasms more often metastasise.
Roseman et al. (1960) and Fishbein et al. (1962) : Pulmonary and pleuro-pulmonary manifestations of pancreatitis.
Mitchell et al. (1964) : Recurrent pericardial and pleural effusions with relapsing pancreatitis.
Ward, P. (1964) : Pulmonary and oesophageal presentations of pancreatic carcinoma (SVC or oesophageal obstruction, bronchopneumonia, pleural effusion or pulmonary infarct).
McClintock et al. (1965) : Large pancreatic pseudocyst extending into the mediastinum from the abdomen through the oesophageal hiatus.
Kaye et al. (1968) : Pleural effusions in pancreatitis - 60% left sided, 30% right and 10% bilateral.
Miridjanian et al. (1969) : Massive bilateral **haemorrhagic pleural effusions** in chronic relapsing pancreatitis.
Bell (1972) : Pancreatico-bronchial fistula in a patients with chronic relapsing pancreatitis and a Roux loop.
Tombroff et al. (1973) : Pleural effusion with pancreatico-pleural fistula.
Kirchner et al. (1977) : Pancreatic pseudocyst of the mediastinum.
Murphy et al. (1977) : The 'negative chest radiograph in acute pancreatitis.
Cameron (1978) : Chronic pancreatic ascites and pancreatic pleural effusions.
Pistolesi et al. (1978) : Mediastinitis due to pancreatitis - CT demonstration.
Weinfeld and Kaplan (1979) : Mediastinal pancreatic pseudocyst.
Owens et al. (1980) : CT evaluation of mediastinal pseudocyst.
Siegelman et al. (1980) : CT of fluid collections associated with pancreatitis.
Bydder and Kreel (1981) : Pleural calcification in pancreatitis demonstrated by CT.
Millward et al. (1983) : Do plain films of the chest and abdomen have a role in the diagnosis of acute pancreatitis ?
Faling et al. (1984) : Treatment of chronic pancreatic pleural effusion by catheter drainage of abdominal pseudocyst.
Gedgaudas-McClees et al. (1984) : Thoracic findings in GI tract pathology.
Godwin (1984) : Mediastinal pseudocyst.
Basran et al. (1987) : Amylase-rich pleural effusions are well recognised complications of acute pancreatitis.
Winsett et al. (1988) : MR imaging of pancreatic pseudocyst.
Wittich et al. (1988) : Percutaneous drainage of mediastinal pseudocysts.
Van Sonnenberg et al. (1989) : Percutaneous drainage of infected and non-infected pseudocysts - 101 cases.
Wilkinson et al. (1989) : Pleural complications - autopsy study of 19 cases - 8 had bilateral effusions and two unilateral right sided effusions. Those with large pleural effusions had subdiaphragmatic effusions.
Girbes et al. (1990) : Massive pleural effusion due to pancreatic pseudocyst.
Zeilinder et al. (1990) : Mediastinal pseudocyst associated with chronic pleural effusions.
Edwards, R. et al. (1992) : Pancreatic mediastinal pseudocyst - an unusual cause of palpitations.
Reznek and Stephens (1993) : The staging of pancreatic adenocarcinoma.
Saifuddin et al. (1993) : Comparison of MR and CT in severe acute pancreatitis.
Coley et al. (1997) : Spiral CT in the preoperative assessment of pancreatic ca.
Paciorek and Ross (1998) : MR imaging of primary pancreatic leiomyosarcoma.
Scott et al. (2000) : Mucinous cystic neoplasms of the pancreas.

Jones, A. et al. (1988) : IVC filter in the management of IVC thrombosis complicating acute pancreatitis.
Stringer et al. (1988) : IVC thrombosis complicating acute pancreatitis.
Peillon et al. (1991) : IVC thrombosis to chronic pancreatitis & pseudocyst.
Antony et al. (1994) : IVC thrombosis associated with acute pancreatitis.
Goerka et al. (1994) : Acute pancreatitis + pulmonary thrombo-embolism secondary to IVC thrombosis.

Whittington et al. (1982) : Tumour metastases to the pancreas (including sq. ca lung).
Rumancik et al. (1984) : CT - metastatic disease to the pancreas.
Wernecke et al. (1986) : US evaluation of pancreatic metastases.
Friedman, A. and Edmonds (1989) : Rare pancreatic malignancies.

Roland and van Heerden (1989) : Tumour metastases to the pancreas.
Glass et al. (1996) : Osteosarcoma metastatic to the pancreas.
Merkle et al. (1998) : Metastases to the pancreas.

Lambert et al. (1998) : Pancreatic cancer as a second tumour - 9 yrs. after R/T for Hodgkin's disease.

Patel et al. (1998) : Imaging of pancreatic trauma (these authors noted that it occurs in traffic accidents and less commonly with motor and pedal cyclists, due to trauma from the handlebars. It also occurs in horse-jockeys, particularly in association with flexion fractures of the lower dorsal and upper lumbar spine, which is why Jockey Club M.O.s visit jockeys (who have such injuries - usually after steeple-chasing) following admission to hospital to help ensure that pancreatic etc. is not missed. An excellent exposition on this subject was given by Michael Allen at a R.C.R. meeting in York.

Thoracic metastases from renal and other abdominal tumours.
   Renal and other abdominal tumours and those arising in the testes not uncommonly spread to the thorax. With renal tumours, this may be direct through the diaphragm to the pleura (particularly with an upper pole tumour), via the blood stream causing 'cannon ball' or miliary type deposits, rib and other bony deposits, or via the lymphatics to cause enlarged hilar and mediastinal nodes and 'lymphangitis carcinomatosa'. Occasionally deposits may be found endobronchially, presumably having spread retrogradely into the submucosal plexus. Renal tumours commonly involve the renal veins and a tumour-thrombus may extend into the IVC and right atrium, or become detached and cause pulmonary emboli.

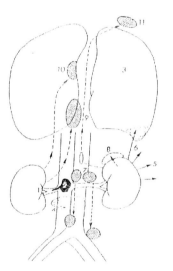

1 and 2	to renal veins and IVC
3	to lungs
4	to bone
5	to perirenal fat, etc.
6	via diaphragm to chest
7	to para-aortic nodes
8	to adrenals
9 & 10	to mediastinal & hilar (esp. R) nodes
11	to L supra-clavicular nodes.

Fig. 17.5   Patterns of spread of renal tumours
           - note how this may take place to
           the pleura, hilar and mediastinal
           lymph nodes.

   Rib deposits may give rise to the coiffe or incomplete border signs - see p. 14.1.

   The author (1975 & 1977) published two series of hilar and mediastinal nodal enlargements from renal tubular carcinomas. A surprising finding was the frequency of right hilar node enlargement, with both right and left sided renal tumours. Such should always be considered in the differential diagnosis of hilar and mediastinal masses; lower right hilar deposits from renal tumours are often well-defined in outline, and may mimic localised primary tumours. The reason for these is the pathway from the kidneys to the hilar and mediastinal nodes shown in Fig. 17.5 - one may also occasionally see these vessels (on TV fluoroscopy) when injecting water soluble contrast medium into a pyonephrosis, prior to percutaneous nephrostomy. Other patients with renal (and other GU tract) tumours may have a generalised hilar and mediastinal lymphadenopathy. Occasionally the nodal enlargement may extend from the groins to the neck. Enlarged 'sentinel' nodes may be palpated in the left supraclavicular fossa or noted radiologically in the azygos and retrocrural regions (see also ps. 13.23 & 15.10 - 11 and Illus. **SENTINEL NODES**). In some patients such nodal enlargement may be due to a sarcoid reaction (see ps. 19.74 - 75 and Illus. **SARCOID+CA**). See also Illus. **RENAL CA&DEPOSITS.**

Other lung nodules in association with renal disease.

   Pulmonary masses caused by fibrosis may be seen occasionally in patients with retroperitoneal fibrosis (Wright and Sanders, 1971), and in association with malakoplakia (an inflammatory disorder producing a renal mass) - see Crouch et al. (1984). Infected infarcts may be found in patients with infected A/V fistulae for treating renal failure (Illus. **INFARCT INFECTED, Emb/infarcts Pt. 22a-e**, and **Lung abscess Pt. 27**). Patients with chronic renal failure or having transplants may have lung nodules due to opportunistic infections (e.g. aspergillosis) or develop tumours e.g. lymphomas or bronchial neoplasm. Lymphoma may also be present coincidentally in the lung and kidney (see Illus. **LYMPHOMA, Pt. 21a-b**). Patients with renal failure may also develop primary bronchial tumours. Wegener's granuloma may produce lung and renal lesions (see ps. 19.76 - 79), as may some collagen diseases e.g. polyarteritis nodosa, with lung nodules and microaneurysms in the small arteries of the kidneys or intestine (Illus. **VASCULITIS, Pts. 1 & 3**).

Thoracic prostatic deposits.

   These may be of many types:

Lung : miliary deposits
        lymphangitis carcinomatosa
        masses in lungs
        endobronchial deposits leading to lung collapse.

Mediastinum : Nodes due to tumour per se or sarcoid type reaction (see also ps. 19.74 - 75).
               'Sentinel nodes' (ps. 12.3, 15.10-11 & 17.10).

Pleura : effusions/ nodules' pneumothorax.

Bones : Sclerotic, lytic or mixed deposits - occasionally expansive lesions in bones - see Illus. **PROSTATE CA, Pts. 3a-b & 9.**

(cf. pelvis and femora).

                    Examples are shown in Illus. **PROSTATE CA**.

Note also that deposits from the testes (lung masses, nodes, endobronchial deposits, rarely ribs - may also give rise to sarcoid like reaction). As has been shown by lymphography in the past, testicular seminomas tend to spread into the chest most commonly via the lymphatic pathway. They may also occasionally give rise to blood borne metastases to the lungs, bones etc. (see Illus. **TESTES DEPS**). Contrariwise teratomas more commonly have a haematogenous type of spread, or tend to 'skip' lower lymph nodes (see also Fig. 13.5b, p.13.9).

Also note deposits from cervix, uterus and ovaries (see also ps. 5.39 - 40 and 14.9 - 10).

References.

Caplan (1959) : Solitary endobronchial metastasis from renal tumour.
Arkless (1965) : Renal tumour - how it metastasises.
Winterbauer et al. (1973) : A clinical interpretation of bilateral hilar adenopathy.
Wright (1975) : Spread of renal tumour metastases to hilar and mediastinal nodes.
Wright (1977) : Enlarged hilar and mediastinal nodes (especially lower right hilar nodes) as a sign of metastasis of a renal tumour.
Reinke et al. (1976) : Bilateral hilar lymphadenopathy - unusual manifestation of metastatic renal cell carcinoma.
Latour and Schulman (1976) : Thoracic manifestations of renal cell carcinoma.
Lang (1977) : Renal cell carcinoma presenting with metastatic hilar nodes.
McLoud, T. et al. (1978) : Studied the spread of extra-thoracic neoplasms to intra-thoracic lymph nodes in over 1,000 patients, and found enlarged nodes in 25, with 12 from genito-urinary tumours. Nodes principally affected were the right paratracheal, anterior mediastinal and hilar with a preponderance to the right side.
Berman et al. (1979) : Hilar enlargement 20 years following resection of a renal cell tumour.
King, T. et al. (1982) : Bilateral hilar adenopathy - an unusual presentation of renal cell carcinoma.
Magill et al. (1982) : Wilm's tumour giving rise to right hilar and mediastinal nodes.
Gibson et al. (1990) : Intracardiac extension of Wilm's tumour - MR demonstration.

Kutty and Varkey (1984) : Intrathoracic metastases from renal cell carcinoma - 25 of 46 patients had spread to the chest, 14 to the lungs and 13 to hilar or mediastinal nodes.
Merine and Fishman (1988) : Mediastinal adenopathy and endobronchial involvement in metastatic renal cell ca.

Onuigbo (1958) : The spread of lung cancer to the kidneys.
Olsson et al. (1971) : 20% of patients dying from bronchial carcinoma had renal metastases.
Mitnick et al. (1985) : Bilateral metastasis to the kidneys from lung tumours 8 cases - US & CT.
Amin and Pagliero (1986), Bailey, M. et al. (1986) : Renal metastases from lung tumours.
Chippindale et al. (1989) : Squamous lung carcinoma with renal deposits - 2 pts.
Bhatt et al (1983) : Metastases in the kidneys are usually hypovascular (the author does not think this is correct).

Bolton (1965) : Pulmonary metastases from prostatic carcinoma.
Scheidemandel et al. (1972) : Pleural effusion - unusual presentation of prostatic carcinoma.
Lome and John (1973) : Pulmonary manifestations of prostatic carcinoma.
Falkowski and O'Conor (1981) : Long-term survivor of prostatic cancer with lung metastases.
Heffner et al. (1982) : Massive pleural effusions from prostatic lymphangitis carcinomatosa - resolution and endocrine therapy.
Lindell et al. (1982) : Mediastinal metastasis from prostatic carcinoma.
Shepherd, M. (1982) : Endobronchial metastatic disease may be the presenting feature in 5%.
Knox-Macaulay and Dahniya (1983) : Cor pulmonale in disseminated prostatic carcinoma.
Lalli et al. (1983) : Multiple endobronchial metastases from carcinoma of prostate.
Simpson et al. (1984) : Metastatic prostatic carcinoma presenting with respiratory symptoms.
Apple et al. (1985) Pulmonary manifestations of advanced prostatic carcinoma.
Mestitz et al. (1989) : Intrathoracic manifestations of disseminated prostatic adenocarcinoma - 4 cases - diffuse reticulo-nodular infiltrate and small pleural effusions, right pleural effusion. right hilar and paratracheal nodes, and pulmonary secondary deposits.
Taylor H. and Braude (1990) : Lobar collapse due to endobronchial metastatic prostatic carcinoma - re-expansion with anti-androgen treatment.

Scott, I. et al. (1986) : Mediastinal nodal enlargement from cervix uteri.
Williams, M. et al. (1987) : Testicular seminomas tend to give rise to nodal deposits, as compared with teratomas which tend to give rise to pulmonary deposits.
Scatarige et al. (1983), Yousen et al. (1986) : Nodal deposits from testicular tumours are usually echolucent on ultrasound, and may show low attenuation on CT sections.
Lien et al. (1987) : CT & conv. radiography in intrathoracic metastases from non-seminomatous testicular tumour.
Ferreti et al. (1997) : Supradiaphragmatic calcified nodes from ovarian carcinoma shown by CT.
Patel et al. (1999) : Supradiaphragmatic manifestations of ovarian papillary serous adenocarcinoma.

(Intrathoracic primary seminomas & teratomas are discussed on ps. 18.14 - 16).

The spleen - (Illus. **SPLEEN**).

Splenic tumours including lymphomas and deposits from thoracic tumours.

Primary splenic tumours are uncommon, but include lymphomas and sarcomas. Secondary are much less common than in the liver. A few scattered small deposits are not uncommonly found in the spleen, at autopsy, in patients dying from lung cancer. They may also be found in vivo by ultrasound or CT, particularly when the liver is grossly involved. Most commonly they are clinically unimportant as the patients have advanced disease. Occasionally patients with lung tumours may present with huge splenic deposits. An example is shown in Illus. **SPLENIC DEPOSIT, Spleen Pt. 11a-b**; this patient presented with upper abdominal pain and collapsed from bleeding which occurred into a large degenerate splenic deposit, which was secondary to a tiny squamous lung tumour.

Other tumours giving rise to splenic deposits include lymphomas, sarcomas, breast and ovarian tumours, etc. Until real-time US and CT became widely available it was common to perform a staging laparotomy and splenectomy with lymphomas, especially Hodgkin's disease, but this is now rarely done. Splenic masses may also be seen with extramedullary haemopoiesis - see ps. 18.33 - 35.

For illustrations of lymphomas affecting the spleen see Illus. **SPLENIC LYMPHOMA, Spleen Pts. 9 & 10.**

Splenic masses may also be seen with **extramedullary haemopoiesis** (p. 17.4).

Splenic trauma - a **ruptured spleen** does not always manifest immediately, and it is not uncommon for traumatised spleens to present with basal pleural reaction, basal 'pneumonia', or after a considerable interval (months or years) with a large post-traumatic splenic cyst. In cases of delayed presentation, the author has used ultra-sound and colloid isotope scans (Illus. **SPLEEN SCAN**) to demonstrate a large defect within the spleen, or that the splenic tissue is in two parts. CT may also demonstrate a ruptured spleen and a perisplenic haematoma (Illus. **SPLENIC HAEMATOMA & SPLENIC TRAUMA**).

As Roy (1984) and others (see references under splenic trauma) pointed out, the spleen should be preserved if possible, as it protects against infection, particularly in children. Regeneration, both by splenosis and the enlargement of splenunculi is probably a protective phenomenon. Following splenectomy, increased numbers of Howell-Jolly bodies are found in polymorphs in the peripheral blood, i.e. the number of aged cells is increased.

Splenic artery aneurysms - small ones are not uncommon, and small "ring calcifications" due to these are not uncommon on plain abdominal radiographs. They probably account for about 60% of visceral arterial aneurysms. Most are harmless, but larger ones may rupture and give rise to a large retroperitoneal haemorrhage - several such cases have been reported in pregnancy. (See Illus. **SPL+COEL ART AN+CALC**).

Splenic cysts (Illus. **SPLENIC CYST**) are of three main types - (i) degenerative (pseudocysts) following trauma, haemorrhage or infarcts, (ii) epidermoid cysts (with an epithelial lining), and (iii) due to hydatid disease (see ps. 19.50 et seq.). Others are due to dermoids, lymphangiomas or polycystic disease.

Splenosis refers to the metastatic spread of splenic tissue following trauma. It was first described by Buchbinder and Lipkoff (1939). Most commonly it is seen in the abdomen, but it may also occur in the chest, particularly if the spleen ruptures into the chest through a traumatic diaphragmatic rupture. Pearson et al. (1978) found recurrent splenic function in 13 out of 22 children who had their spleens removed.

Splenunculi are accessory spleens, which are sometimes present as well as a normal spleen, should be distinguished from tumours or tumour deposits. They commonly enlarge following splenectomy. They may also enlarge with reticuloses, and sometimes are found in normal people with an intact normal spleen. They should always be distinguished from tumour deposits. They are particularly important in patients with recurrent thrombocytopaenic purpura, since their removal may again cure the condition (Illus. **SPLENUNCULI**).

Polysplenia - sometimes multiple or accessory spleens are found in association with heterotaxic syndromes and anomalies of the IVC, such as azygos continuation (Illus. **IVC AZYGOS CONTINUATION**), a left sided IVC or a dilated hemiazygos system (see p. 9.3). The author has also seen polysplenia in associated with a hugely dilated left renal vein draining a large kidney containing multiple tumours, and with a large vascular shunt through it (see also Illus. **IVC THROMBOSIS, Pt. 4**).

Haemangiomas of the spleen are less common than in the liver. They may be cystic in type and should be distinguished from other splenic masses (Illus. **SPLENIC HAEMANGIOMA**).

Splenic lymphangiomas may be seen both in children and adults.

Splenic imaging.
The spleen, splenunculi, splenosis and polysplenia may be demonstrated by ultrasound, Doppler US, CT, MR or isotope studies using e.g. $Tc^{99m}Sn$ colloid or labelled damaged red cells.

Examples of splenic calcification are shown in Illus. **SPLENIC CALC.**

Further references.

Ayers et al. (1976) : The microvasculature of the spleen.

Rowland Hill and Wilson (1989) from St. Thomas' Hospital : Reviewed the US and CT examinations performed during one year to assess the incidence of splenic metastases in patients with non-lymphomatous malignancies. In most cases with splenic deposits, hepatic deposits were also present, but 4 (two adenoca's, one ca lung and one melanoma) had splenic deposits with clear livers - the one with lung cancer being shown by U/S alone.

Görg et al. (1997) : Studied the sonographic patterns of malignant splenic lymphomas over a 10 yr. period. 101 (out of 688) pts. had an abnormal splenic pattern - diffuse in 37, focal small nodular lesions in 39, focal large nodular lesions in 23, and bulky in 2. All the high-grade lymphomas showed either large or small nodular lesions, whilst the diffuse or small nodular pattern was seen mainly in low-grade lymphomas.

Wafula (1985) : US & CT demonstration of primary angiosarcoma of the spleen.

Bader et al. (1998) : Lymphangioma of the spleen in a 70 yr. old woman - US showed diffuse, irregular inhomogeneities & CT - hypodense centre with only slight enhancement.

Dachman et al. (1998) : Primary splenic lymphoma usually presents as a mass or masses rather than with splenomegaly alone. Splenectomy may be required for diagnosis.

Spencer et al. (1998) : Splenic metastasis in ovarian cancer.

Denneen (1942) : Haemorrhagic **cyst** of the spleen.

McClure and Altemier (1942) : Classification of splenic cysts.

Forde and Finby (1961) : Splenic cysts - 7 cases.

Wright, F. and Williams (1974) : Late post-traumatic splenic cyst diagnosed by isotope scan and US.

Bhaskara et al. (1981) : Cystic lymphangiomatosis of the spleen.

Pistoia & Markowitz (1988) : Splenic lymphangiomatosis - CT diagnosis.

Duddy and Calder (1989) : Cystic haemangioma of the spleen - US and CT findings.

Younger and Hall (1990) : Epidermoid cyst of the spleen and literature review.

Ito et al. (1995) : MR of cystic lymphangioma of the spleen.

Wright, F. et al. (1976) : Late **splenic rupture** in a haemophilic child.

Krivit et al. (1979) : Overwhelming postsplenectomy infection.

Leonard et al. (1980) : The overwhelming postsplenectomy sepsis problem.

Shapiro and Wright (1988) : Late diagnosis of splenic rupture in a young woman who fell from the wall of an Oxford college.

Jeffrey (1989) : **Dangerous to rely on CT alone** re conservative treatment of blunt hepatic and splenic injuries.

Mirvis et al. (1989) : Blunt splenic trauma in adults - CT classification.

Scatamacchia et al. (1989) : Impact of CT grading on management of splenic trauma.

Editorial, Clin. Rad.(1991) : Diagnosing splenic trauma - US v. CT - CT appeared to be better.

Siniluoto et al. (1992) : Ultrasonography in traumatic splenic rupture.

Dalton et al. (1971) : Intrathoracic **splenosis**.

Gentry et al. (1982) : Splenosis - CT demonstration.

Mendelson et al. (1982) : CT appearance of splenosis.

Scales and Lee (1983) : Non-operative diagnosis of intrathoracic splenosis.

Nelson et al. (1982) : Implantation of autologous splenic tissue after splenectomy for trauma.

Moncada et al. (1985b) : Case of thoracic splenosis and reference to 9 other cases.

Deren et al. (1987) : 11 cases of splenosis in 19 patients who had a splenectomy for trauma (used autologous heat damaged RBCs labelled with stannous chloride).

Logan et al. (1988) : Compared Tc^{99m}Sn colloid scanning with CT for the detection of splenosis in ten patients, and found small single foci of activity in five, two to three areas in one and widespread multiple areas of activity within and below the splenic bed in two. CT detected one of the latter cases, and two small areas of splenic tissue in other cases; it did not show any abnormality in the grossest and most widespread case as shown by colloid scanning.

Normand et al. (1993a) : Thoracic splenosis occurs not infrequently after combined splenic and diaphragmatic injury. The CT appearance is that of pleural masses or nodules; the MR appearance is relatively similar to normal spleen.

Normand et al. (1993b) : US features of abdominal ectopic splenic tissue.

Gunes et al. (1994) : Superiority of tomographic selective spleen scintigraphy in the detection of splenosis.

Madjar and Weissberg (1994) : Thoracic splenosis - two cases, one with excision of a pulmonary nodule. The presence of a pulmonary nodule in a patient with a history of injury to the diaphragm and spleen should arouse suspicion of splenosis.

Bondlee et al. (1995) : MR demonstration of thoracic splenosis.

Clark et al. (1972) : Angiography of **accessory spleens**.

Beahrs and Stephens (1980) : CT appearance of enlarged accessory spleens in postsplenectomy patients.

Holloway et al. (1997) : Portal hypertension causing massive enlargement of an accessory spleen - a rare cause of splenic pseudotumour.

Bertolotto et al. (1998) : US and Doppler features of accessory spleens & splenic grafts - could be distinguished as accessory spleens are typically round with smooth echogenic margins with a vascular hilum arising from the splenic vessels and splenic grafts have multiple feeding vessels.

Henderson (1998) : Enlarged accessory splenic tissue can even present as a scrotal mass.

Winer-Muram and Tonkin (1989) : Spectrum of heterotaxic syndromes, from isolated anomalies to the complex syndromes such as **polysplenia/aplasia syndromes**.

Baddeley (1993) : **Splenectomy** (or functional hypoplasia due to haemoglobinopathies, coeliac disease, autoimmune disorders, malignant splenic infiltration or amyloid) **and prevention of overwhelming infection** - recommended vaccination against S. pneumoniae, H. influenzae, and N. meningitidis or antibiotic prophylaxis.

Swischuk et al. (1993) : Torsion of the '**wandering spleen**'- whorled appearance of the splenic pedicle on CT.

Winer-Muram (1995) : Adult presentation of heterotaxic syndromes - polysplenia may present in adults, but asplenia is associated with almost universal severe cardiac anomalies that manifest in the neonatal period. Polysplenia may also be associated with Kartagener's syndrome (ps. 3.15 - 16).

Keane et al. (1995) : A histological basis for the '**sonographic snowstorm**' in opportunistic infection of the liver and spleen - 3 cases of 'miliary' snowstorm highly echogenic foci in liver, spleen, and other organs including bowel and pleura - in Candida albicans, aspergillus and pneumocystis infection - probably with fine fibrosis, fibrinous exudate and possibly early calcification.

Kehagias et al. (1998) : MR of a giant (12 cm) **splenic artery aneurysm** (mixed echogenicity on US).

Parmar et al. (2000) : Peliosis of the spleen - blood+gelatinous material - filling cystic lesions in a large spleen causing laft hypochondrial pain in an Indian woman. ? an immune-complex disease. It may cause spontaneous splenic rupture. The name refers to the blue/black colour of the blood within the cysts.

[For calcified '**snowstorm**' or miliary lesions in the spleen - see Illus. **SPLEEN, Pt. 3a & b.**]

Chapter 18 : **The Mediastinum (including pre-and para-spinal lines, neural tumours, and pneumomediastinum).**

The mediastinum is divided into superior and inferior parts by a plane through the manubriosternal joint and the 5th dorsal vertebra (roughly corresponding with the levels of the aortic and azygos arches), and into anterior, middle and posterior portions.

Anatomists term the anterior portion as that part which lies in front of the great vessels and pericardium, and the posterior behind the pericardium, but clinically and radiologically it seems better to use the definitions of Felson (1969) and Rémy et al. (1981) as shown in the following diagrams:

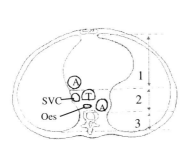
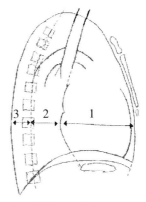

Fig. 18.1 Divisions of the mediastinum (1 = anterior, 2 = middle and 3 = posterior) - diagrams reproduced from Felson, B (1989) 'The mediastinum', Seminars in Roentgenology, **24**, 41 - 58 by permission from W.B. Saunders Company.

However, others have divided it differently, e.g. :

Sone et al. (1982) : Following pneumographic studies divided it into pre-cardiovascular and retro-cardiovascular compartments, and

Heitzman (1977 & 1988) : Used the azygos vein on the right, and the aortic arch on the left as dividing lines.

Dividing the mediastinum into its constituent parts is of considerable importance, as the position of a lesion often gives a considerable guide to its nature. However overlap occurs, and some lesions may be found in unusual positions.

MEDIASTINAL MASSES

Mediastinal masses may arise from any of the various types of tissue within the mediastinum. They may be tumours per se, cystic swellings or dilated vascular structures, herniae, a dilated oesophagus, an abscess or other fluid collection, or be enlarged lymph nodes or other tumour masses secondary to neoplasms seen in a particular centre will depend on the types of cases referred to it. Excluding nodal enlargements, the commonest masses are oesophageal, neural, thymic and dermoid type tumours, cysts of various types and fatty masses.

Nodal enlargement may take place in any part of the mediastinum, but is particularly likely to be found anteriorly and in the middle part of the mediastinum. These may be due to secondary neoplasm, reticulosis, sarcoid, infection (especially tuberculosis, but also aspergillosis, some pyogenic infections, etc.), amyloid, reactive hyperplasia, etc. Enlarged nodes in the posterior mediastinum often have a rather bizarre appearance, often being much larger than they at first appear.

Haematomas are discussed on p. 18.6.

Abscesses may occur with mediastinitis, follow surgery, perforation of the oesophagus, occur as a result of infected cysts or haematomas, be produced by caseous pus draining from an infected tuberculous node, spine, rib, etc. (Illus. **MEDIAST ABSCESS**).

Mediastinal masses are classified in Table 18.1, according to their positions in the mediastinum. Others include fibromas, fibrosarcomas, vascular tumours such as angiomas, haemangiomas and endotheliomas; thoracic duct cysts, lymphangiomas or hygromas. Fatty masses and lipomas are common and are discussed on ps. 6.12 to 6.13.

Some references.
Leigh (1963), Leigh and Weens (1959), 1969), Hochholzer et al. (1969) : Unusual lesions of the mediastinum. Grainger and Pierce (1969), Hallgrimsson (1972), Grainger and Allison (1986).
Ikezoe et al. (1989) : Studied the CT appearances in 147 patients with mediastinal tumours (113 benign and 34 malignant). Ten of the benign lesions showed atypical localisation or extension. Two lymphangiomas and one bronchogenic cyst spread over both compartments and a thymic cyst, a pericardial cyst and a thymic hypertrophy were located posteriorly. A Schwannoma was found anteriorly and oesophageal leiomyomas and reduplication cysts extended upwards and backwards beyond the azygos and aortic arches.

Table 18.1   Common masses and tumours of the mediastinum.

Divisions	Lesions
Anterior Mediastinum	
Superior	Sternal tumours
	Retrosternal thyroid (1/3rd extend into mid or post mediastinum)
	Parathyroid tumour
	Thymic tumour (thymoma, cyst, fat, reticulosis, etc.)
	Bronchogenic cyst, germ cell tumour, liposarcoma
	Aneurysm of ascending aorta, internal mammary arteries, etc.
	Hygroma/ lymphocoele (see p. 13.5)
	Lymphoma
Inferior	Fat pad, etc.
	Pericardial cyst, tumour or effusion
	Morgagni hernia
	Pancreatic pseudocyst
Middle mediastinum	Periaortic fat, etc.
	Aneurysm of aorta, chemodectoma
	Tumour of trachea or main bronchi
	Bronchogenic cyst, germ cell tumour, lymphoma.
	Oesophageal tumour, dilatation or hiatus hernia.
	Oesophageal diverticulum or reduplication cyst
	Mediastinal abscess, blood or fluid collection (chyloma, etc.)
	Pancreatitis/ pancreatic pseudo-cyst.
	Vagal, etc. neuromas
Posterior mediastinum	Mass arising from spine - tumour, abscess, haematoma, osteophytes, etc.
	Neurogenic tumour - intercostal nerves, sympathetic chain, Phaeochromocytoma, etc.
	Lateral thoracic meningocoele
	Fat (particularly in patients on steroids)
	Extramedullary haemopoiesis
	Oesophageal abscess, tumour, diverticulum, achalasia, etc.
	Bochdalek hernia
	Bronchogenic cyst (5 to 10% arise in the posterior mediastinum)
	Germ cell tumour, lymphoma.

Table 18.2 <u>Low density mediastinal masses as seen on CT sections.</u>
   (a)   Fat   (approx. minus 100 HU), fatty tumours (lipomas, thymolipomas,
                          liposarcomas), fat within hamartomas, degenerating tumours,
etc.

   (b)   Densities between fat and muscle (plus 50 to 55 HU)
                  cysts - bronchogenic, enteric, pericardial, thymic, etc.
                  lymphangioma (see p. 13.5)
                  neoplasms containing necrosis
                                        old haemorrhage
                                        inhomogeneous mass with thick walls
                  goitre or thyroid carcinoma, may also contain high densities - table 18.5, p. 18.28
                  lymphoma or thymoma containing degenerate areas or cysts
                  lymph nodes - involved by testicular, thyroid tumours, leukaemia, reticulosis, etc.
                               - following radiotherapy or chemotherapy
                               - Whipple's disease
                  neural tumours - Schwannomas or neurofibromas
                                     lateral thoracic meningocoele.
                  inflammatory - mediastinal abscess
                                  - tuberculous nodes
                  haematomas
                  venous thrombosis
                  loculated pleural fluid
                  dilated oesophagus
                  pericardial fluid

   (c)   Gas - with perforation, asthma, etc.
                       - in abscess cavities, diverticula, etc.

Table 18.3 <u>High density masses on unenhanced CT sections.</u>
   (a)   Calcification   -   lymph nodes   -   previous TB, sarcoid, fungus infection,
                                                        rheumatoid, amyloid, treated reticulosis,
                                                        Castleman's disease, etc.
                                      goitres (esp. in areas of previous haemorrhage)
                                      thymic cysts and tumour masses (esp. post. treatment)
                                      some neoplasms - esp. adenocarcinomas, histiocytomas,
                                                        phaeochromocytomas, etc.
                                      hamartomas, bronchial adenomas
                                      cyst wall or contents (including 'milk of calcium')
                                           - bronchogenic cyst or teratoma
                  High iodine content   -   goitres
                  High iron content   -   recent haemorrhage

Table 18.4 <u>Enhancing mediastinal and lung masses.</u>
            Thyroid masses
            Ectopic parathyroid adenomas
            Chemodectomas and phaeochromocytomas
            Carcinoids and some hamartomas
            Castleman's disease
            A/V malformations and haemangiomas
            Some lymph nodes
            Haemangiopericytoma
            Pleural fibroma ('benign mesothelioma)
            Liposarcoma (also high signal on T2 MR), hibernomas.

            (see Illus. **TUMOUR ENHANCEMENT**)

Mediastinitis (including systemic idiopathic fibrosis, and associated hilar and pulmonary fibrosis).

Both acute and chronic mediastinitis may result in mediastinal widening.

Acute infection of the mediastinum may follow perforation of the pharynx or oesophagus (see ps. 16.11 - 14), inflammatory disease in the lungs or airways, an infected tracheostomy stoma, an infected cyst or haematoma, extension of nodal or bony infection, etc. Gas may be present (usually from perforation) and may be present in the tissue planes; it may also be seen in an abscess cavity.

Chronic mediastinitis may lead to mediastinal fibrosis and a **fixed   mediastinum** (see also ps. 2.7 - 8 & 2.27 - 29), venous, including SVC, obstruction (ps. 9.6 - 7), pulmonary and arterial and venous obstruction, tracheal and bronchial narrowing, enlarged mediastinal nodes which may become calcified, and pleural effusions. Sometimes the fibrosis may extend to involve the oesophagus or the coronary vessels. Fibrosis may extend into or predominate in the hilar regions where it may be bilateral or unilateral.

Mediastinal fibrosis may be associated with prior radiotherapy, sarcoidosis, tuberculosis, chronic fungus infection (especially histoplasmosis which is more common in the USA - see p.19.45), other fibrosing conditions such as Riedel's thyroiditis, retroperitoneal fibrosis (involving the ureters and/or aorta and pelvis), biliary cirrhosis (or fibrosis of the common bile duct), fibrosis of the pancreas or salivary glands, pseudo-tumour of the orbit, lymphoid granuloma, pulmonary hyalinising granuloma, or as part of a widespread disease complex such as rheumatoid or amyloid. In some cases it may be associated with drugs such as methysergide or practalol. In others there is an abnormal immune response as shown by a raised IGg. Sometimes it follows an auto-immune or inflammatory response in adipose tissue - **Weber   Christian   disease** (see Mitchinson, 1965 & 1970). It may also follow repeated trauma (Goodwin, 1972) or past syphilis (see Illus. **SYPHILIS MEDIASTINITIS** & ps. 19.49 - 50) and may be stimulated by foreign materials e.g. silicone gel. Some cases appear to be idiopathic.

Aggressive fibromatosis produces the 'desmoid tumour' (see next section).

Desmoid tumours,

The '**desmoid   tumour**' (also known as 'infiltrative' or 'aggressive fibromatosis') is an invasive fibroblastic condition, which tends to spread along tissue planes, and often recurs after surgery - hence some regard it as slow-grade non-metastasising fibrosarcoma. It behaves like a keloid and was given its name (∂εσμοζ = flesh) by Müller (1882). Sir James Paget (1856) described a case in which the condition had been in the anterior abdominal wall for 14 years before being removed.

The fibrosis usually starts at muscular aponeurotic insertions, and occurs mainly in the limb girdles of the shoulder and hips. It may also occur within the chest and abdominal walls, and in the pleura, mediastinum and abdomen. It may be associated with **Gardner's   syndrome** (Gardner, 1951 and Gardner, et al., 1953 - bowel polyps and mesodermal tumours, osteomas of the skull and jaw, sebaceous cysts and skin tumours). It may follow trauma, pregnancy or oestrogen treatment.

The aggressive fibrosis shows extensive local growth, but is non-metastasising. In about 10% it occurs at multiple sites. Chest wall disease may spread into the pleura, mediastinum or base of neck. Recurrence rates of 20 to 60% have been reported despite wide resections. In a few cases ablation of the ovaries, the use of androgens or anti-oestrogens (e.g. Tamoxifen) has been beneficial. Radiotherapy has also been used.

Radiological findings.

Plain radiographs may show masses pressing into the pleura; ultrasound - low or mixed echogenicity; CT a discrete lesion (Illus. **DESMOID** or one spreading diffusely through the tissue planes. The CT density is usually homogeneous, but may contain small cystic areas or calcification, including plaque-like calcification (Fig 18.2). The abnormal tissue does not enhance. MR may give low or high density signals.

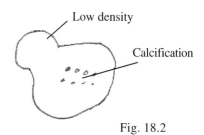

Low density

Calcification

Fig. 18.2

Following wide resection and the implantation of prosthetic material, secondary infection may mimic recurrence. A case in Oxford recurred three times in three years, despite wide resections, including ribs, much of the adjacent chest wall and the affected hemi-diaphragm.
It was subsequently complicated by gross sepsis (Illus. **DESMOID, Pt. 1a-f**).

Further references.
Mackenzie et al. (1983) : The fibromatoses - a clinicopathological concept.
de Graff et al. (1981) : Male aged 49 with large mediastinal abscess secondary to peri-tonsillar abscess - CT showed this spreading down to the pericardium with air/fluid levels 1,500 ml of foul-smelling fluid was aspirated.
Marsh, M. et al. (1984) : Young man with salmonella mediastinitis, secondary to a Racoon bite.
Breatnach et al. (1986) : CT showed the extent of infection and abscesses needing drainage - 14 cases of mediastinitis including oesophageal rupture, recent thoracic surgery, spread of lung infection (actinomycosis, histoplasmosis or staphylococcal) or following analgesic injection into the costo-chondral joints.
Carrol et al. (1987) : CT of mediastinal infections - 3 groups - (i) diffuse soft tissue infiltration with or without gas (i.e. mediastinitis), (ii) focal mediastinal abscess, (iii) mediastinal infection associated with empyema or sub-phrenic abscess: concluded - difficult to distinguish post-operative change from abscesses without the presence of gas.
Baker, A. et al. (1990) : Life-threatening peripharyngeal sepsis with mediastinitis.
Van der Brempt et al. (1990) : Ludwig's angina and mediastinitis complicating retropharyngeal abscess.
Watanabe et al. (1994) : Empyema and mediastinitis complicating retropharyngeal abscess.
Corsten et al. (1997) : Descending necrotising mediastinitis needed both cervical and chest drainage + broad spectrum IV antibiotics in 7 cases. The rapid spread is aided by the absence of barriers in the contiguous fascial planes of neck and mediastinum. Review of 7 cases with CT studies and review of literature.

Benfield et al. (1962) : Female pt. aged 51 with bilateral pulmonary fibrous nodules and retroperitoneal fibrosis - she had bilateral nephrostomy tubes in situ for 16 months as she was thought to be suffering from disseminated neoplasm. A lung biopsy then suggested the true diagnosis, nephrostograms showed that the uteteric obstruction had spontaneously resolved and the nephrostomy tubes were removed. 18 months later she was well.
Nelson et al. (1965) : Pulmonary artery obstruction and cor pulmonale due to fibrous mediastinitis.
Comings et al. (1967) : Familial multifocal fibrosclerosis - retroperitoneal fibrosis, mediastinal fibrosis, sclerosing cholangitis, Riedel's thyroiditis and pseudotumour of the orbit may be different manifestations of a single disease.
Wright, F. and Sanders (1971) : Is retroperitoneal fibrosis a self-limiting disease?
Yacoub and Thompson (1971) : **Chronic idiopathic pulmonary hilar fibrosis** is a condition related to mediastinal fibrosis, but limited to one or both pulmonary hila, causing pulmonary artery obstruction or pulmonary venous congestion with repeated haemoptyses, etc. Like retroperitoneal fibrosis the condition tends to be self-limiting, but may cause severe disability.

Goodwin et al. (1972) : Mediastinal fibrosis complicating healed primary histoplasmosis and TB.
Wieder and Rabinowitz (1977) : Fibrous mediastinitis - late manifestation of histoplasmosis.
Dines et al. (1979) : Pulmonary vascular occlusion and fibrosing mediastinitis.
Feigin et al. (1979) : Multiple manifestations of sclerosing mediastinitis.
Park et al. (1981) : Pulmonary scintigraphy in fibrosing mediastinitis due to histoplasmosis.
Paling and Hyams (1982) : CT in 'malignant fibrosis' or 'histiocytoma' - 11 cases showed poorly marginated masses with central necrosis spreading into the chest and pleura - similar appearances to abdominal retroperitoneal fibrosis.
Wieder et al. (1982) : Pulmonary artery occlusion due to histoplasmosis.
Weinstein et al. (1983) : In mediastinal fibrosis secondary to histoplasmosis, plain film findings may be non-specific. CT may allow the demonstration of hilar enlargement, para-tracheal thickening (often with calcification), narrowing of the trachea or larger bronchi.
Farmer et al. (1984) : Calcific fibrosing mediastinitis - pulmonary vascular obstruction - MR.
Rholl et al. (1985) : Seven cases of fibrosing mediastinitis - comparison of CT and MR - both showed associated adenopathy. CT was better for showing calcification, whilst MR predicted the benign nature of the disease by showing a relatively low signal intensity.
Berry et al. (1986) : Pulmonary vascular occlusion and fibrosing mediastinitis.
Kuramochi et al. (1991) : Multiple pulmonary hyalinising granulomas associated with systemic idiopathic fibrosis.
Kountz et al. (1989) : Fibrosing mediastinitis in the posterior thorax - probably due to histoplasmosis - one case.
Mallin, W. et al. (1993) : Fibrosing mediastinitis causing non-visualisation of one lung on pulmonary scintigram.
Sherrick (1994) : The radiographic findings of fibrosing mediastinitis.
Mole et al. (1995 - Brompton Hosp.) : Sclerosing mediastinitis is a slowly progressive condition associated with previous TB (or histoplasmosis), mediastinal malignancy and auto-immune disease - good prognosis in non-malignant cases - review of 18 cases.
Nakamura et al. (1997) : Systemic idiopathic fibrosis with inflammatory pulmonary lesions - man aged 74 - cough & weight loss - CXR + CT showed pulm. nodules, areas of pl. thickening, masses around the aortic arch & a mass

around the abd. aorta. Trans-bronchial biopsy of R lung lesion showed a few histiocytes accompanying inflammatory & fibrotic change. Following steroids the lesions regressed as shown by repeat CT.

Beaconsfield et al. (1998) : TB pulmonary arteritis - an unusual cause of pulmonary artery stenosis.
Rodríguez et al. (1998) : Fibrosing mediastinitis - CT and MR findings.

Sacks et al. (1978) : Isolated mesenteric desmoids.
Baron and Lee (1981) : Mesenteric desmoid tumours - two cases - US and CT appearance.
Campbell et al. (1983) : Aggressive fibromatosis in children.
Mackenzie et al. (1983) : The fibromatoses - a clinicopathological concept.
Greenberg et al. (1981), Leibel et al. (1983) and Kiel and Suit (1984) : Radiotherapy treatment of aggressive fibromatosis (desmoid tumour).
Harell (1983) : MR of desmoid tumours - extent difficult to define on CT - MR gives high tissue characterisation, multiplanar format - after radiotherapy 'dehydrated fibrous tissue'.
Klein et al. (1977), Dashiell et al. (1978) : Desmoid tumours of the chest wall.
Hudson (1984) : Aggressive fibromatosis - evaluation by CT and angiography.
Krause et al. (1985) : Child with intra-thoracic desmoid - ? stimulated by previous surgery.
Ashby et al. (1986) : Male student aged 25 - desmoid in right upper mediastinum, displacing the trachea and oes. - recurred two years after partial resection, causing a fatal haemorrhage from the right subclavian artery.
Hamlin et al. (1986) : MR of an abdominal desmoid tumour (T$_1$ and T$_2$ showed low density + low contrast difference from surrounding tissues).   Kaplan and Davidson (1986) : Intrathoracic desmoids - two cases.
Black et al. (1987) : CT of aggressive fibromatosis in the posterior mediastinum.
Chui (1989) : Fibromatosis of the brachial plexus and shoulder girdle.
Page et al. (1989) : Cross-sectional appearances of desmoid tumours.
O'Keefe et al. (1990) : MR in aggressive fibromatosis.
Einstein et al. (1991) : Abdominal desmoids - CT findings in 25 patients - many had Gardner's syndrome - several mesenteric and abdominal wall masses, especially following surgery.
Brodsky et al. (1992) : Desmoid tumours of the chest wall - a locally recurrent problem.
Ackman et al. (1994) : Aggressive fibromatosis of right lateral chest wall in a 19 year old man.
Ahn et al. (2000) : MR of fibromatosis in childhood. Shah et al. (2000) : Intrathoracic extension of fibromatosis.

<u>Mediastinal haematomas, haemangiomas and spontaneous rupture of thymic cysts.</u>
    Bleeding may occur from various mediastinal structures, follow trauma to vessels (aorta - see p.11.6 - 7, great veins, internal mammary vessels, etc.), or occur in patients on steroids, haemophiliacs, those having anticoagulant or haemodialysis treatment, etc.
    Haematomas may occur spontaneously in association with tumours (Illus. **MEDIAST HAEMATOMA**), dissecting or leaking aneurysms, following accidental or surgical trauma, in patients on anticoagulants, etc. A not uncommon present-day cause is following the insertion of central venous lines, etc. (Illus. **MEDIAST HAEMATOMA, Tube complication Pts. 1-3**). Such haematomas may spread up into the neck (Illus. **MEDIAST HAEMATOMA, Tube complication Pt. 1a-c**). Seltzer et al. (1984) noted that layering within a haematoma with a fluid /fluid level can be seen when cellular elements have separated and settled.

    Thymic masses (including cysts which may rupture spontaneously) seem particularly prone to haemorrhage, and patients with this may have severe dyspnoea, chest pain and a rapidly enlarging mediastinal mass. A large fatal spontaneous haematoma of the anterior and middle mediastinum demonstrated in life by transverse axial tomography was reported by Raphael (1963), from the author's hospital. He also studied the spread of haematomas within the anterior mediastinum by injecting barium into a cadaver, and found that haematomas were confined laterally by the mediastinal pleura, anteriorly by the retrosternal fascia and posteriorly by the perivisceral fascia. The blood and/or fluid may also pass into the pleural cavities, or up into the neck.

Seltzer et al. (1984) noted that layering within a resolving haematoma with a fluid/fluid level can be seen when cellular elements have separated and settled.

Fig. 18.3 Denser dependent blood elements in resolving haematoma- (edges may enhance with IV contrast agents).

Haemangiomas (about 0.5% of mediastinal masses) may also lead to mediastinal haematomas and be diagnosed from the dilated vessels and phleboliths (present in 30 to 50%) seen on CT and MR. An important point is that they may extend into the spinal canal and cause cord compression.

Haemangioendotheliomas may exhibit malignant behaviour, as more commonly do **haemangiopericytomas** (see ps. 5.10 -11).

Mediastinal haematoma secondary to **Boerhaave's syndrome** is discussed on p. 16.13.

Other fluid collections include ruptured cysts (of other origins), hygromas (p. 13.5) and lymphangiomas. Abscesses may occur with mediastinitis, follow surgery, perforation of the oesophagus, occur as a result of infected cysts or haematomas, be produced by pus draining from a tuberculous or otherwise infected node, the spine, rib, etc. They may also occur as a result of inflammatory disease tracking up from the abdomen, e.g. with pancreatitis (see p. 17.8).

Further references.
Ellison et al. (1981) : Spontaneous mediastinal haemorrhage in patients having chronic haemodialysis treatment.
Stilwell et al. (1981) : Spontaneous mediastinal haematoma,
Bethancourt et al. (1984) : Mediastinal haematoma simulating Hodgkin's disease during systemic chemotherapy.
Leibman (1984) : Spontaneous rupture of a thymic cyst in an adolescent.
Siefkin et al. (1984) : Unsuspected mediastinal haematoma in a haemophilic.
Suddes and Thomas (1988) : Mediastinal haemorrhage accompanying haemorrhagic pericarditis in a man aged 48 - at first treated with heparin and a plasminogen activator - it resolved spontaneously.
Adams and Bloch (1944) : Haemangioma of the mediastinum.
Feinberg (1957) : Posterior mediastinal haemangioma.
Toch et al. (1965) : Haemangioma of the mediastinum.
Tarr et al. (1986) : CT findings in benign haemangioendothelioma involving the posterior mediastinum (four cases plus 81 from the literature).
Davis et al. (1978) : Benign blood vascular tumours of the mediastinum - review of 85 cases.
Cohen et al. (1987) : Mediastinal haemangiomas.
Seline et al. (1990) : CT and MR imaging of mediastinal haemangioma - two cases - felt that MR appearance was nor specific, but 'puddles' of contrast medium within a mass (like a hepatic haemangioma) on a dynamic-enhanced CT using a bolus technique is probably diagnostic.
Schurawitzki et al. (1991) : CT and MRI in benign mediastinal haemangioma - two cases -
(i) male aged 52 - mediastinal widening following chest trauma; barium swallow showed an appearance like varices.
(ii) Female aged 16 - dysphagia for several months.
Felt that resection should not be attempted in asymptomatic patients who have no signs of malignancy, but subtotal resection following symptoms may produce an acceptable result.

Maze et al. (1983) : A huge mediastinal abscess shown by CT had 'masqueraded as cardiomegaly' on plain radiographs (20 year old man with previous sacral osteomyelitis and staphylococcal pneumonia).

McAdams et al. (1994) : Haemangiomas should be considered in the differential diagnosis of well marginated mediastinal masses which have heterogenous attenuation on CT scans, show central enhancement after IV contrast or contain punctate calcification (phleboliths). 14 pts. examined.
Worthy et al. (1995) : Multiple thoracic haemangiomas - a rare cause of spinal cord compression.

Joseph et al. (1989) : Neck & thorax venous aneurysms - association with cystic hygromas (see also ps. 9.10-11).

Mediastinal arteriovenous fistulae (see also ps. 7.12-16 & 12.9).
     Congenital arteriovenous fistulae within the mediastinum are rare and usually present in infancy with a continuous murmur and /or congestive cardiac failure. Adult cases may also be congenital or may follow procedures such as central venous cannulation, sternotomy or trauma.

References.
Martinez et a. (1981) : AV fistula of the thoracic aorta presenting with **SVC obstruction**.
Soler et. al. (1981) : Congenital systemic arteriovenous fistula between the descending aorta, azygos vein and SVC.
Gutierez et al. (1987) : Congenital AV malformation between brachiocephalic arteries and systemic veins.
Evans, A. et al. (1992) : Congenital mediastinal AV fistula in an adult diagnosed by digital subtraction angiography.
Ching et al. (2000) : CT & DSA of ruptured congenital AV malformation of posterior mediastinal aorta.

The Anterior Mediastinum

Anatomically this lies behind the sternum in front of the great vessels and pericardium, but radiologically it is better to consider that it includes the pericardium and its contents (see **Fig. 18.1**). It extends from the level of the top of the manubrium sterni superiorly to the diaphragm inferiorly. Masses within it are often better seen on lateral radiographs or tomograms, but large ones may be readily visible on frontal radiographs. Smaller ones may be recognised by deviating or deforming the anterior junction line or its recesses (see ps. 1.10 - 12).

Large anterior mediastinal masses may blur the definition of the heart and pericardium, displace, distort, or bow the trachea, or even the sternum.

Some of the main causes of an anterior mediastinal mass are listed in **Table 18.1** (p. 18.2). Thyroid masses are very common, as is enlargement due to fat, particularly in obese subjects and in those having prolonged steroid treatment. Thymic and pericardial cysts tend to be well defined and can often be visualised as such with ultrasound. Thymomas and teratomas tend to spread within and alongside the mediastinum. Haematomas may follow trauma, whilst others occur spontaneously. Abscesses may occur following infections, within cysts, haematomas, etc. Nodal enlargements are not uncommon with reticuloses, secondary neoplasm (e.g. breast, mesothelioma, melanoma, lung tumours, leukaemia), or with infections (especially tuberculous or fungus, or following surgical exploration via sternotomy). Sarcoidosis may sometimes enlarge these nodes.

Occasionally aneurysms of the aortic arch may enlarge forwards into this space. Syphilitic aneurysms even used to extend forwards and erode the sternum (Illus. **SYPHILIS, Pt. 2**).

Calcification may be seen within goitres, thymomas and teratomas, but is most commonly found within nodes (previous TB, fungus infection, past radiotherapy, etc.). It may also be found in the walls of some bronchogenic and thymic cysts, particularly dermoids.

References.
Chiu et al. (1986) : CT Angiography of the Mediastinum.
Brown and Aughenbaugh (1991) : CT and MR imaging of masses of the anterior mediastinum. CT is the main technique distinguishing between solid, fatty, cystic, calcified and vascular structures and **eliminating** the problem of superimposition of mediastinal structures. MR helps in patients who cannot tolerate IV contrast, and can give sagittal and coronal as well as axial images.

Thyroid masses and intrathoracic goitres.

These are common in the lower neck (e.g. in Leonardo da Vinci's famous Mona Lisa painting). They often extend down into the thoracic inlet and upper mediastinum. Mediastinal goitres are most often found with a normal or almost normal thyroid in the neck. Like cervical goitres, those in the mediastinum are three or four times more common in women than men.

Intrathoracic goitres descend from the isthmus of the thyroid (Illus. **THYROID LINGUAL, Thyroid Pts. 40 & 52**), in front of the great veins. They may lie anywhere between the posterior part of the tongue and the aortic arch or sometimes even lower (Illus. **THYROID, Pt. 39a-b**). About a third of mediastinal goitre become displaced behind the trachea and great vessels, and may even extend around and behind the oesophagus. Displacement usually occurs on the right, and these goitres are probably derived from the posterior and lateral aspects of the thyroid and may mimic an intrapulmonary mass (Illus. **THYROID, Pts. 31-37**). When not fixed (usually because of their size) goitres tend to move upwards on swallowing. A band between the goitre and the normal thyroid may sometimes be demonstrated by CT or more commonly an isotope scan. **Calcification** within a goitre is very common and is usually nodular or ring-like in type.

It appears to result from previous local haemorrhages and is best seen on tomograms. On CT sections a goitre is often a little denser than muscle, it also shows **marked persisting contrast enhancement.** Hypervascularity may be shown on angiograms. Most intrathoracic goitres are only minimally hormonally active, and an isotope scan using I^{131}, I^{123} or Tc^{99m} pertechnetate (which behaves as a halogen) tends to reflect this, and in most cases only a little of the isotope is taken up, but it is usually enough for diagnosis.

Bashist et al. (1983) listed helpful **CT** findings for the diagnosis of **intra-thoracic goitres** -
(i) continuity with cervical gland in nearly all cases,
(ii) well-defined borders,
(iii) punctate, coarse or ring like calcifications,
(iv) inhomogeneity, often with minimal or non-enhancing low-density areas,

(v) attenuation values at least 15HU greater than adjacent musculature pre- & 25HU post-contrast,
(vi) 'cradling' of the goitre by the innominate vessels and extension behind the great vessels to the para-tracheal or retro-tracheal regions.

As in the neck the trachea may be displaced or squashed by a goitre and a scabbard like appearance (see also p. 3.3) may be produced. A goitre which has slipped behind the trachea often bows it anteriorly (Illus. **THYROID, Pt. 38**) - the 'anterior tracheal displacement sign'. A cyst may have acute haemorrhage into it causing an acute tracheal compression (Illus. **THYROID MEDIAST CYST, Thyroid Pt. 41a-b**).

Rarely a thyroid swelling at the thoracic inlet in children or adolescents may be due to hereditary defects in enzyme synthesis of iodine into thyroglobulin ('**Pendred's   syndrome**' - the full syndrome includes deafness and is due to a defect in chromosome 7). Most of these will be inactive on isotope studies, but in a few cases there is an excessive TSH drive, and a highly active uptake (Illus. **PENDRED'S SYNDROME, Thyroid Pt. 2a-b**). The perchlorate challenge test causes 10% to 80% release of iodine from the thyroid. (See Pendred, 1896, Fraser et al., 1965, and Phelps et al, 1998).

Thyroid cysts are some of the most common thyroid masses, and haemorrhage causing additional swelling not uncommonly causes their presentation. They are most readily examined with **ultrasound**, usually differentiated from tumours and may be aspirated and the contents examined cytologically (see Illus. **THYROID, Pts. 53 & 54**). Malignancy in a cyst is rare, the author only having seen one in 30 years - in a young woman.

Malignant thyroid tumours arising in the thorax are rare, and most that involve the thorax spread down from the neck. They may encircle, compress and/or invade the trachea and the oesophagus, give rise to nodal and pulmonary deposits or invade the veins in the neck and upper thorax, causing secondary venous thrombosis; a patient presenting with this last manifestation is illustrated in Illus. **THYROID CA, SVC obst., Pt. 11a-g**.

Medullary thyroid carcinomas (MTCs) may present with a mass in the neck, and may contain calcification. They may invade locally into the larynx, trachea or the oesophagus. Nodes may be present in the neck or the mediastinum. They may give rise to lung and bone metastases, diarrhoea and intestinal hurry. They may occur per se, or in association with other endocrine tumours, giving rise to one of the multiglandular syndromes or '**multiple endocrine neoplasia type 2**' (MTC, phaeochromocytoma and parathyroid hyperplasia or adenoma) which is linked to chromosome 10 abnormalities (Ponder, 1990). Some are familial, and family screening may be valuable. For MEN 1 - see p. 18.12.

MTCs are also linked to APUD cells (see p. 24.13) and may mimic carcinoid tumours and contain amyloid. Patients with these may have high blood calcitonin and VMA. They may be imaged with Tc(V) DMSA (see p. 22.9) and this affinity may be linked to the calcitonin production. Their metastases may also be shown by DMSA or MIBG (see ps. 22.9 & 22.12 - 13).

Patients with metastases may have indolent disease and live in symbiosis with these for several years.

Thyroid metastases to the lungs. As noted on p. 5.39, pulmonary metastases from thyroid carcinomas may sometimes be indolent and spontaneously calcify. Rarely small deposits may calcify, resembling past chicken pox pneumonia. The author followed a female patient with such deposits which had been present for over 20 years, and others are noted on ps. 6.20 - 21.

Thyroid carcinoma deposits in the lungs may sometimes be shown first by nuclear medicine studies. Bonté and McConnell (1973) reported three examples of micro-metastases which were only shown by I[131] imaging and quoted two others from the literature. Němec et al. (1979) also studied the radiological characteristics of pulmonary thyroid deposits.

Other tumours occurring in the thyroid. Besides thyroid carcinoma per se, other malignant disease may arise in the thyroid e.g. lymphoma. This may spread down into the chest, causing mediastinal widening, pleural effusion, etc.

Tumour deposits from lung (particularly small cell tumours) or other tumours (e.g. breast or melanoma) may sometimes occur within the thyroid. They are mostly inactive on isotope studies but may occasionally be active and appear as 'hot' nodules, and give rise to thyrotoxicosis.

Ultrasound of the thyroid. Being very superficial, the thyroid is readily imaged by ultra-sound, especially with 7.5 & 10 MHZ probes (but see also the use of a water bag - p. 20.33). Cysts may be distinguished easily from more solid tissues and cysts aspirated. Such examinations should also be done in association with isotope thyroid function studies, particularly when an inactive nodule is found. Fine needle aspiration biopsies are readily obtained.

Multi-nodularity may be confirmed as nodules or cysts, or a mixture of both. In patients with thyrotoxicosis or thyroditis, the thyroid may develop a coarse 'fibrotic-looking' pattern, or become 'spotty'. Low density areas may be a pointer to the presence of a tumour, with a 'gelatinous' appearance similar to some breast tumours on ultra-sound. Fine moving 'granularity' is often seen with recent haemorrhage, but may also be seen with pus (as with an infected adjacent node) or debris within a branchial cyst.

Examples of thyroid examinations are shown in Illus. **THYROID** and **THYROID ECTOPIC**. Isotope examinations are shown in Illus. **THYROID SCAN**.

Further references.

Ansell and Rotblat (1948) : Radioactive iodine as a diagnostic aid for intrathoracic goitre.
Sweet (1949) : Intrathoracic goitre located in the posterior mediastinum.
Holt and Powers (1958) : Calcification in papillary carcinoma of the thyroid.
Shapiro et al. (1958) : Posterior mediastinal goitre (five cases).
Margolin et al. (1967) : Patterns of thyroid calcification - Radiological + histological study of excised specimens.
Fui et al. (1978) : Posterior intrathoracic goitre and thyrotoxicosis.
Irwin et al. (1978) : I^{131} scanning in preoperative diagnosis of mediastinal goitre.
Machida and Yoshikawa (1979) : Aberrant thyroid demonstrated by CT.
Binder et al. (1980) : Diagnosis of posterior mediastinal goitre by CT.
Som et al. (1981) : Some CT findings in occult thyroid disease.
Morris et al. (1982) : CT demonstration of intrathoracic thyroid tissue.
Glazer, G. et al. (1982) : Enhancement of goitres with IV contrast media.
Baron et al. (1983) : Standard for normal thickness of the thyroid gland.
Lin (1983) : Mediastinal uptake in isotopic thyroid imaging.
Perez and Brown (1984) : Goitre extending into IVC.
Sussman et al. (1986) : CT demonstration of isolated mediastinal goitre.
Makepeace et al. (1987) : Non-Hodgkin's lymphoma of the thyroid.
Park et al. (1987) : Found some uptake of isotope in intrathoracic goitre in 54 cases examined with thyroid scans.
Hall et al. (1988) : Substernal goitre versus intra-thoracic aberrant thyroid - a critical difference is that a substernal goitre is usually removed through a cervical incision, but this may be a disaster if the tumour arises in the chest. However only about 1% of thoracic goitres have a blood supply from intra-thoracic vessels.
Higgins and Auffermann (1988) : MR imaging of thyroid and parathyroid glands.
Vorne and Jarvi (1988) : Metastatic deposits detected as 'cold' nodules on the thyroid scan.

Park et al. (1976) : Unusual calcification in mixed papillary and follicular carcinoma of the thyroid gland.
Kowalafe (1981) : Radiological patterns and significance of **thyroid calcification**.

Hazard et al. (1959) : Medullary thyroid carcinoma is an entity (i) with a destructive cellular morphology, (ii) an intermediate grade of malignancy between the favourable papillary and follicular types and the highly malignant anaplastic tumours, and (iii) is associated with a high incidence of early regional lymph node metastases.
Gorlin et al. (1968) : Syndrome - multiple mucosal neuromas, phaeochromocytoma & medullary thyroid carcinoma.
Steiner, A. et al. (1968) : Multiple endocrine neoplasia - phaeochromocytoma, medullary thyroid carcinoma, hyperparathyroidism and **Cushing's disease**.
Wallace et al. (1970) : The radiological aspects of medullary (solid) thyroid carcinoma (review of 70 cases).
Saad et al. (1984) : Clinical features and prognostic factors in 161 patients with medullary carcinoma of thyroid.
Heron et al. (1990) : CT as an adjunct to screening for medullary carcinoma of the thyroid.
Clague et al. (1991) : Medullary carcinoma of thyroid presenting as multifocal bronchial carcinoma.

Strickland and Lavender (1991) : Spontaneous radiographic 'resolution' of retrosternal goitre, due to the retrosternal component moving up into the neck, thus giving the spurious impression of it having been surgically removed.

Kasagi et al. (1991) : Lymphoproliferative disorders of the thyroid gland - radiological appearances - lymphoma, plasmacytoma, ultra-sound, CT and Ga[67] in 8 patients.
Henshaw (1996) : Excess cases of thyroid cancer in children in Chernobyl 10 years on (accident 26 4 1986 - see also p. 11.22).

Naik and Bury (1998) : Imaging the thyroid. Buckley and Stark (1999) : Imaging mediastinal thyroid goitre.

The parathyroids and parathyroid tumours (including mediastinal parathyroid tumours)
   The parathyroids are normally four in number, and lie in upper and lower retro-thyroid positions, but extra ones may occur and be in an ectopic position, often in the mediastinum. Mediastinal parathyroid tumours are rare, and only rarely produce a mass large enough to be seen on a plain chest radiograph, but when present it may resemble a mediastinal goitre (Illus. **PARATHYROID, Pt. 8**). Small tumours may be found at the thoracic inlet alongside the trachea, or within the thymic tissue anterior to the aortic arch (Illus. **PARATHYROID, Pt. 3**). The 'tracheal overlap' sign of a posteriorly situated parathyroid adenoma may be helpful, and may be confirmed angiographically or by enhancement.
   Because the posterior superior mediastinum extends to the upper margin of the first rib, a parathyroid adenoma may be tucked far posteriorly in the mediastinum and mimic a neurofibroma. Posterior superior parathyroid mediastinal masses rarely descend deeply into the mediastinum. They are usually supplied by the inferior thyroid artery, and can often be removed surgically from the neck. About 80% of ectopic parathyroids are situated anteriorly and 20% posteriorly.

Investigation of parathyroid masses.
   Thirty years ago only plain radiographs, conventional tomograms, angiography and barium swallow (with large adenomas pressing on the oesophagus) were available, other than exploratory surgery. Fortunately experienced surgeons can find over 95% of parathyroid adenomas in the neck by careful dissection in both primary and secondary hyperparathyroidism. Surgical recognition can be aided by the use of **methylene (or patent) blue**. If the dye is injected IV immediately preoperatively, the parathyroids tend to 'stain' more than the surrounding tissues and become more easily recognised, and this method was used for many years at the author's hospital (see Dudley, 1971). Toluidine blue should **not** be used because of possible cardiac toxicity. Radioisotope labelled methylene (and toluidine) blue have been tried in some centres (see references).

   The main problem for radiologists is to locate recurrent, 'missed' or mediastinal adenomas, in patients with recurrent or persisting hyperparathyroidism following surgery.

Ultra-sound - now that short-focus probes (e.g. 7.5 MHZ) are becoming more readily available, ultrasound of the parathyroids is now becoming more of a practical reality. With a careful technique, most adenomas > about 8 mm in diameter can be visualised, also 10 to 20% of normal glands. Problems occur in that some adenomas are intra-thyroid, retro-sternal or mediastinal. Some glands are isoechoic with surrounding tissues, but others are cystic (about 5%) and some are easily confused with **thyroid nodules** or lymph nodes.

CT with contrast enhancement may be invaluable for detecting ectopic para-thyroid adenoma, particularly those in the mediastinum, where they are found mostly as 2 to 3 cm nodules in or near the **thymus**, and in relation to the trachea and the anterior aspect of the aortic arch. CT is more likely to be of help in patients over 40, because below this age small nodules may not be distinguishable from normal thymic tissue, as it may not have been replaced by fat though IV contrast enhancement will often help. (See Illus. **PARATHYROID, Pt. 2** - a patient who had recurrent renal calculi).

MR may also demonstrate ectopic parathyroids, particularly if haemorrhage has occurred into this vascular type of tumour. Fat suppression may allow small adenomas to be visualised (Wright, A. et al., 1992).

Selective angiography (especially with digital subtraction) may also be used for diagnosis, confirmation or ablation therapy (with alcohol) as an alternative to surgery.

Fig. 18.4   Typical positions of mediastinal parathyroid tumours.

Other methods which have been used include :
Thallium ^{201} (or Se^{75} methionine) studies combined with Tc^{99m}O$_4$ subtraction (first described by Ferlin, 1983). Adenomas > 50 mg. may be shown, with a sensitivity of about 70%; normal glands are not usually visualised (see Illus. **PARATHYROID, Pt. 7**). False positives may occur with thyroid adenomas or carcinomas, other neck masses including inflamed lymph nodes. Oral phosphate (1 g. per day for three days may improve the uptake of thallium in the parathyroids. (Se^{75} methionine studies are inferior as only glands > 2 cms in diameter are likely to be shown up.) Another isotopic compound is Tc^{99m} sestamibi (methoxy isobutyl isonitrile or 'Cardiolite' - also used for studying the myocardium as an alternative to thallium), but it is very expensive (see Coakley et al., 1989).

Venography with sampling of blood for parathormone levels - this method is very time-consuming and may be difficult to interpret because of the inconsistency of small veins in the mediastinum, and the presence of numerous collaterals. A case is shown in Illus. **PARATHYROID, Pt. 1a-f**).

Thrermography has been used for the neck, and may show a large vascular parathyroid mass, but it is often falsely negative and non-specific.

NB. **Multiple endocrine neoplasia 1** (MEN 1) = pituitary, parathyroid & pancreatic neoplasms (including gastrin tumours) - see also p. 18.9.

Further references.
Angiography - Seldinger (1954), Doppman, et al. (1969 & 1978), Rossi et al. (1971).
Krudy et al. (1984a) : Showed 2 out of 9 tumours with a selective technique and one with nonselective.
Lacombe et al. (1987) : Selective DSA for residual mediastinal glands after cervical parathyroidectomy.
Miller, D. et al. (1987) : Ten year experience of ablating parathyroid adenomas, including those in the mediastinum and especially supplied by the internal mammary artery, using high concentrations of ionic contrast media, following selective catheterisation of the feeding vessel. They claimed an almost 90% success rate (70 to 80% overall) in patients in whom contrast enhancement persisted in the adenoma on CT examinations carried out 24 hours later. (All the patients had persisting hyperparathyroidism following previous surgery).
Reidy et al. (1993) : Ablation of mediastinal parathyroid adenomas by embolisation with alcohol via the internal mammary artery.(See also comment by Miller, 1993).

CT
Adams et al. (1981) : Large gland - 2.5 cm in diameter.
Whitley et al. (1981), Sommer (1982).
College and Rohatgi (1983) : CT + ultra-sound - mediastinal parathyroid cyst.
Wolverson et al. (1981) : Diagnosis of parathyroid adenoma by CT.
Doppman et al. (1982) : Studied enlarged parathyroids in the posterior superior mediastinum by CT and were able to demonstrate rounded dense masses in the tracheo-oesophageal groove in five out of six cases.
Cates et al. (1988) : A parathyroid adenoma on CT usually appears as a round or oval mass posterior or just inferior to the thyroid with variable contrast enhancement. An adenoma must be distinguished from the oesophagus, tortuous vessels or thyroid nodules. Occasionally parathyroid nodules may contain calcification.
Hauet et al. (1997) : Compression of the trachea by a mediastinal parathyroid cyst.

Ultrasound (mainly of the neck)
Krudy et al. (1984b) : esp. in previously operated cases.
Graif et al. (1987) : 145 cases.
Edmunson et al. (1986) : Suggested that gross invasion of surrounding structures by tumour is the only reliable feature that can distinguish a parathyroid carcinoma from a large adenoma.
Daly et al. (1989) : Found more subtle signs of tumour invasion - irregularity of tumour margin, particularly if the tumour is > 2 cm in diameter.
Karstrup et al. (1989) : Ultrasound guided biopsy of suspected parathyroid tumours.
Murchison et al. (1991) : Ultrasonic detection of parathyroid adenomas.

Isotopes
Blower and Carter (1990) : Rapid preparation of I^{123} labelled methylene and toluidine blue - potential new agents for parathyroid scintigraphy.
Coakley (1991) : Parathyroid localisation - how and when?
Tsukamoto et al. (1995) : When positive, thallium-technetium subtraction scintigraphy will accurately predict the site of a solitary parathyroid adenoma in a high proportion of patients. The usefulness of the technique is limited by its low sensitivity for small tumours.

Thermography
Samuels et al. (1972)

Venography
Shimkin et al. (1972), Manhire et al. (1984).

Combined techniques
Krudy et al (1981) : CT, angiography and venous sampling.

General references
Nathaniels et al. (1970) : Review of 84 mediastinal parathyroid tumours.
Hargreaves and Wright (1981) : 190 g. parathyroid lipoadenoma.
Russell et al. (1981) : Surgery.
Lloyd (1989, from the Middlesex Hospital) : Found that the most valuable aid in finding residual or recurrent parathyroid enlargement was a detailed knowledge of the previous surgery. Neck lesions were well demonstrated by ultrasound plus parathyroid venography with sampling, and mediastinal lesions by arteriography.
Lloyd et al. (1990) : Preoperative localisation in primary hyperparathyroidism - ultrasound found 63% of glands > 3 cms in their normal situations, whilst parathyroid venography with sampling detected 79%.
Carlson and Farndon (1990) : Investigation of primary hyperparathyroidism.
Lossef et al. (1993) : Three discrete hyperplastic parathyroid glands in the anterior mediastinum (as well as the normal complement in the neck) shown by scintigraphy and arteriography.
Fayet et al. (1997) : The combination of MRI, sestamibi scintigraphy and venous blood sampling improved accuracy in detecting abnormal parathyroid glands before reoperation.
Ishibashi et al. (1999) : Localisation of ectopic parathyroid glands using 3-D CT, sestamibi & tetrofosmin in 2 pts.

Guvendik et al. (1993) : Parathyroid R mediastinal cyst causing hyperparathyroidism and tracheal obstruction.
Doppman et al. (1994) : Parathyroid adenoma within the vagus nerve.

N.B. Hyperparathyroidism affecting the hands, skull, spine, pelvis and ribs is discussed on p.12.23.

Cystic mediastinal masses and germ cell tumours.
    The neck and mediastinum (especially the former) are common sites for cystic masses. Those in the neck develop from anomalies of pharyngeal pouches and branchial clefts, to give rise to branchial, thyroglossal, thyroid, parathyroid, thymic, dermoid and hygromic cysts. Some of these can extend into or be found in the mediastinum e.g. thymic cysts which can occur from the angle of the jaw down to the level of the lower pericardium. Those in the neck and behind the manubrium sterni are readily demonstrated by ultra-sound, and can be readily drained, thus proving the diagnosis.
    In the mediastinum, besides neck cysts extending down during development or later life, others may arise from the bronchi, the oesophagus or spine (bronchogenic, enteric, neuro-enteric,

paraoesophageal cysts, etc. - see ps. 3.13 - 14), or from the pleura or pericardium. Others are degenerative (e.g. from degenerating tumour or reticulosis), or parasitic (e.g. hydatid, etc.) or may be post-inflammatory. Rarely digestive enzymes may track up from the pancreas to give rise to inflammation and pseudo-cysts (see p. 17.8).

As with cysts in the neck, those with an acoustic window to the chest wall (e.g. pleuro-pericardial cysts - see p. 15.27), are most readily examined and drained under ultra-sound control; others can be studied by tomograms including CT. Most cysts have a watery content, but in others there is more viscid fluid, cellular debris or fat, hair and bone (in dermoids). CT may suggest increased density in bronchogenic cysts, or they may develop a bronchial communication and fill with air (Illus. **MEDIAST CYST, Broncog cyst Pts. 3, 5, 6 & 8**). Marvasti et al. (1981) found some misleading densities in mediastinal cysts at CT and Tasson et al. (1984) considered that CT cannot be considered conclusive for diagnosis. Nevertheless the majority will be so diagnosed. Other examples are shown in Illus. **MEDIAST CYST.**

Thymic cysts   occur not only in the thymus, but also anywhere along the course of the embryological descent of thymus, from a mandible to the anterior pericardium or even as low down as the diaphragm. A cervical thymus may more commonly contain cysts, than the normally positioned organ, and these may cause tracheal or oesophageal compression (Arnheim and Gemson, 1950). Thymic cysts may also appear following radiotherapy treatment for reticulosis. Lindfors et al. (1985) reported three cases in which thymic masses and nodes in Hodgkin's disease regressed with irradiation and chemotherapy, and cysts occurred. A similar case of a girl of 16 which occurred three weeks after treatment was reported by Veeze-Kuijpers et al. (1987). Other may occur after thoracic surgery (see references and Brown, L. and Aughenbach, 1991). They may also present in association with calcification and a thymoma. Examples are shown under Illus. **THYMIC CYST.** Other references are given below.

Dysgerminomas - teratomas (including dermoid cysts) and seminomas - (Illus. **GERM CELL TUMOUR**).

These tumours should be considered as a group, as they are derived from multipotential embryonic cells. They are usually sex related i.e. more dermoids occur in females and more seminomas and atypical teratomas are seen in men, but all types may occur in either sex. Many patients are asymptomatic on presentation, which is often fortuitous, but pressure effects and hormonal problems may occur particularly with 'atypical teratomas'. Most of these occur in or in close relationship to the thymus, but some occur in other parts of the mediastinum.

In **dermoids** (cystic teratomas - Illus. **DERMOID**), ectodermal tissues predominate, but mesodermal tissues may also be present. Dermoids tend to be well demarcated and sometimes have a dense peripheral ring or denser central calcification (Illus. **DERMOID, Germ cell tumour Pts. 1a-b, 4a-b, 11a-d & 13a-e**) which may be seen on plain films or tomograms. On CT dermoids may be shown to contain bone elements and rarely teeth, or be relatively radiolucent due to their fat or cholesterol content - (findings more commonly seen with ovarian dermoids). Occasionally mixed cystic and solid tumours may be found, and these may show malignant extension on CT, particularly in males (up to 30%). When excised, dermoids may be found to contain hair and keratinaceous material. Their walls are composed of fibrous tissue and are relatively **thick**; this can be readily demonstrated by CT, and helps to differentiate them from thymic and pericardial cysts which have thin walls. However a thymoma or a reticulosis mass which is degenerating may give a similar appearance. Dermoids are apparently common in Japanese people (and are often termed by them '**mature cystic dermoids**'), but only half have a fatty content and many appear solid. Whilst most dermoids occur in the anterior and middle mediastinum, and often adjacent to the ascending aorta, a few (3 to 5 %) are found in the posterior mediastinum. Rarely they may be found on the diaphragm (see p.15.14) or within the pericardium. Occasionally malignant degeneration may occur within a dermoid, and the tumour may burst through its wall (Blomlie et al., 1988).

Mediastinal   **seminomas** tend to be well defined homogeneous masses when found before any spread has occurred. They may become quite large, and produce pressure effects including phrenic nerve palsies. Most are quite sensitive to radiotherapy, and like testicular seminomas also respond to chemotherapy. On CT sections it is important to study the fat planes between the tumour and the adjacent organs, as spread into other parts of the mediastinum may be inferred if the fat planes are lost. With spread the primary tumour masses also tend to become irregular in outline. Calcification is not a feature, and they only slightly enhance with iodine contrast agents. They tend to not be encapsulated. A few contain cystic spaces. Most occur in young men, and a few in young women. An example is shown in Illus. **GERM CELL TUMOUR, Pt. 2a-b**).

Teratomas (and chorioncarcinomas) are similar to those occurring in the testes i.e. they are highly malignant. Those with feminising and embryonic hormone effects occur particularly in young men and have been termed 'atypical teratomas' or 'yolk sac tumours'. These tend to produce 'fleshy' masses in the anterior mediastinum. They usually give rise to raised 'markers' such as α-feto-protein and β-human-gonadotrophin and placental alkaline phosphatase. Like similar testicular tumours, they are often sensitive to chemotherapy with cis-platinum, etc. Mixed seminomas/ teratomas also occur. On CT sections teratomas tend to have a non-homogeneous appearance, with low density areas, infiltration of surrounding fat planes and may be accompanied by pericardial and/or pleural effusions (Illus. **GERM CELL TUMOUR, Pt. 7a-c**).

The clinical question, have these tumours metastasised from the testes or ovaries, is often asked, but primary germ cell tumours not uncommonly occur in several extra-gonadal sites, including the anterior mediastinum, the retroperitoneal and pre-sacral areas, and the pineal and suprasellar regions. They probably arise from germ cells which have migrated to these areas during development, or occur by metaplasia within these tissues. (The author had several requests to perform lymphangiograms to look for possible lymph node metastases from genital organ primary tumours, or to look at the gonads with ultrasound, etc. but never found a positive case.)

Nevertheless secondary deposits from gonadal germ cell tumours often occur in the chest. Such testicular (seminoma and teratoma) deposits usually manifest with lung metastases, retro-cardiac or other lymph node enlargements (Illus. **TESTES DEPS**). Teratoma deposits may give rise to a huge liver, pleural effusions, etc. Bone metastases are rare, but Illus. **TESTES DEPS, Pt. 1a-f** shows a sclerotic rib metastasis with accompanying soft tissue swelling from a seminoma. This was confirmed by needle aspiration biopsy, and it responded well to radiotherapy and chemotherapy. Occasionally huge secondary tumour masses may be found in the mediastinum or lung (Illus. **TESTES DEPS, Pt. 5, 6, 8 & 13**). Large nodal masses may have low attenuation on CT, and appear almost 'jelly-like' on ultra-sound if a suitable 'window' is available to examine them (Illus. **TESTES DEPS, Pt. 11a-b**). They may also give rise to the '**iceberg sign**' (Illus. **TESTES DEPS, Pt. 12a-d** - see also p. 18.31). Ovarian tumours may also metastasise in a bizarre fashion via the diaphragm (ps. 14.9 - 10), giving rise to thoracic ascites. Illus. **PSEUDOMYXOMA, Pts. 1 & 2** show pseudomyxoma peritonei et pleurae due to this cause.

References.
Cystic teratomas or dermoids.
Saruk (1980) : Benign intra-pulmonary cystic teratoma.
Sumner et al. (1980) : Intrapericardial teratoma in infancy.
Weinberg et al. (1980) : Posterior mediastinal cystic teratoma.
Zarella and Halpe (1980) : Intrapericardial teratoma.
Friedman et al. (1982) : CT of dermoid in retrocrural space - contained fat/ water levels and a septum with a tooth.
Lewis et al. (1983) : Benign teratomas of the mediastinum.
Serlo and Heikkinen (1983) : Cardiac tamponade caused by a mediastinal teratoma.
Suzuki et al. (1983) : CT of six cases - fat in three, calcification on two but no teeth. Three had a thick capsule - 'thick walled cyst' of fibrous tissue containing yellowish fluid, hair and keratinaceous material.
Tasson (1984) : CT in cystic mediastinal lesions.
Karl and Dunn (1985) : Posterior mediastinal teratomas.
Billmine and Grossfeld (1986) : Teratomas in childhood - analysis of 142 cases.
Müller, N. (1986) : Teratoma of the diaphragm - CT features.
Brown et al. (1987) : CT of benign mature teratomas of the mediastinum.
Dobranowski et al. (1987) : CT demonstration of posterior mediastinal teratoma.
El Kalla et al. (1990) : Posterior mediastinal teratoma with abdominal extension in an infant.
Fulcher et al. (1990) : CT and plain film demonstration of fat/fluid level in a cystic teratoma of the mediastinum.
Yeoman et al. (1990) : Fat-fluid level in pleural effusion complicating a mediastinal dermoid - CT characteristics.
Hession and Simpson (1996) : Mobile fatty globules in benign cystic teratoma of the mediastinum.

Germ Cell Tumours.

Cox (1975) : Primary malignant germ cell tumours of the mediastinum.

Knapp et al. (1985) : Malignant germ cell tumours of the mediastinum.

Blomlie et al. (1988) : CT in primary non-seminomatous germ cell tumours of the mediastinum.

Lee et al. (1989) : Malignant primary germ cell tumours of the mediastinum.

Nichols (1991) : Mediastinal germ cell tumours - clinical features and biological correlations.

Rohlman et al. (1993) : Germ cell tumour in upper mediastinum - an unusual tumour in a patient with AIDS.

Moran and Suster (1997, I) : Primary germ cell tumours of the mediastinum - analysis of 322 cases.

(1997, III) : Yolk sac tumour, embryonal ca, **chorioncarcinoma** & combined non-teratomatous germ cell tumours of the mediastinum - study of 64 cases.

El-Khalib and Chew (1998) : Embryonal carcinoma of the anterior mediastinum - male aged 21 with huge mass.

Atypical teratoma syndrome.

Fox , R. et al. (1979) and Fox, M. and Vix (1980) : 12 patients with yolk sac tumours of the anterior mediastinum - flat topped masses - feto-protein and chorionic gonadotrophin positive,

Levitt et al. (1984) : : Four young men with large posterior mediastinal germ cell tumours.

Rusch et al. (1984) : Two cases with response to chemotherapy and surgery.

Metcalfe and Jones (1986) : B5 marker on erythrocytes.

Seminoma.

Sterchi and Cordell (1975) : Some are cystic.

Polanski et al. (1979) : Four new cases - quoted 103 from the literature.

Shin and Ho (1983b) : Reviewed 170 cases from the literature + two new cases, (i) female of 52 (? coarctation + aneurysm) and (ii) male of 39 with left phrenic palsy. CT showed massive tumours with sharply demarcated borders, loss of fat planes and extension into middle and posterior mediastinum.

Aygun et al. (1984) : Primary mediastinal seminoma.

(For thoracic deposits from abdominal and genito-urinary tract tumours - see ps. 17.9 - 11).

Note: chorioncarcinoma and germ cell tumours typically cause an increased blood ß human chorion gonadotropin (normal = < 5U/100ml); this can be assessed by blood assay - they may also be imaged by PET using FDG (see p. 22.11).

The Thymus.

(a) **General points.**

The thymus is an organ in the upper anterior mediastinum, which is relatively large in infants. It develops from the third branchial pouch as two lateral lobes which fuse centrally. It becomes relatively smaller (i.e. does not grow much with the rest of the child) during childhood, and atrophies in adolescence, leaving a largely fatty mass of tissue in adults. This latter shows up but little on plain chest radiographs or conventional tomograms. It is however readily seen on CT sections of the upper mediastinum, as a fatty structure resembling the prow of a boat in shape.

Rarely the thymus lies in the neck, where it may form cysts (see p. 18.13). Thymic tissue may also be found in abnormal sites in the mediastinum e.g. posteriorly or in the hilar areas as separate masses, or even down to the level of the diaphragm (i.e. such ectopic masses may occur anywhere along the line of the **thyropharyngeal   duct.** All of these should be distinguished from a single enlarged thymus.

The thymus appears to control or take part in many immune responses, by producing T-lymphocytes, which stimulate other cells to fight infections. Occasionally the thymus is aplastic or hypoplastic, and in children this may give rise to immunodeficiency syndromes, T-cell and B-cell defects, agammaglobulinaemia or lymphohypoplasia. Aplasia and hypoplasia may be associated with hypoplastic parathyroids (sometimes known as the **'Di George syndrome'** - Di George, 1965, Kirkpatrick and Di George, 1968), dyschondroplasia, ulcerative colitis, cerebellar disorders, telangiectasia or aortic arch abnormalities.

Primary tumours (thymomas, germ-cell tumours, etc.) may develop within it, but in young people swellings are more likely to be lymphatic tissue masses due to reticulosis (**'thymic**

lymphoma or **Hodgkin's**', etc.- see p. 5.21). Other swellings may be due to hyperplasia, fat (especially in those taking prolonged courses of steroids), cysts, thymolipomas or secondary carcinoma (e.g. oat cell lung tumour). The thymic fat may be directly invaded by thymomas or adjacent tumours, particularly those arising in the left upper lobe. Tumour extension from the abdomen to the pleura, or other pleural deposits, may also extend into the thymus. Lymphatic enlargement due to reticulosis may be massive, and extend widely into one or both pleural cavities, this usually being more marked on the right; these masses may also invade the lung (Illus. **THYMIC LYMPHOMA**). The thymic lymphatic tissue may also become enlarged with inflammatory disease, particularly tuberculosis (Illus. **THYMIC TB**).

Many thymic cysts and tumours are found fortuitously, whilst others present with local or more generalised symptoms. **Cysts** are discussed on p.18.13. Patients with thymic masses due to lymph node or tumour enlargements (including lymphoma and TB nodes) may experience **choking symptoms when lying down or leaning backwards,** presumably from pressure on the trachea. Others may have a cough or symptoms from SVC obstruction. With reticulosis, patients may have general debility, alcohol induced pain, etc. **Thymomas** may present with pleural and/or pericardial effusions, or may exhibit autoimmune problems, such as myasthenia gravis (see below). Other patients may have antibodies blocking the maturation of red cells, white cells or platelets, or a combination of these. Others may have a severe hypoglobulinaemia leading to severe respiratory infection (with rapidly progressive bronchiectasis and pansinusitis - see Illus. **THYMUS, Pt. 29a-g**), opportunistic infections (e.g. candida), and severe and intractable diarrhoea; these may not recover following removal of the thymoma and the patients may need continuing gamma-globulin treatment. Rarely patients may have polymyositis, arthritis, or skin lesions such as pemphigus, lichen planus or alopecia.

Myasthenia gravis (see Illus. **MYASTHENIA GRAVIS**) is an auto-immune condition characterised by muscular weakness and **fatiguability** (in contrast to the Eaton Lambert syndrome see p. 23.6). It may occur 'early' with a hyperplastic thymus or 'late' with an atrophic thymus. Ocular myasthenia is the most common manifestation, but in most patients other muscle groups become affected. The antibody causes the loss of response of the acetylcholine receptors at the neuro-muscular junctions. In some patients (even those with thymomas) the myasthenia may be a transient phenomenon. Medical control is largely with cholinesterase inhibitors or steroids - the latter probably protecting the acetylcholine receptors from immunological attack. Azathiaprine may also produce a remission and plasma exchange may be used in some severely affected patients.

The association of myasthenia with a thymic tumour appears to have been first noted by Laquer and Weigert (1901) and the first reports of improvement following removal of a thymic tumour were by Blalock at al. (1939, in the USA), Blalock (1944) and Keynes (1949, 1954, in the UK). Good (1947, from the Mayo Clinic) reported the radiological finding of a thymic tumour associated with myasthenia gravis, and Null et al. (1977) noted that 'thymic Hodgkin's disease may also be associated with myasthenia gravis, and in their case it was cured by thymectomy.

In many patients with myasthenia, particularly the younger ones, the thymus may be of normal size or be hypertrophied. Thymomas occur in about 10 to 15%, and these are found mainly in patients over the age of 40. Some patients respond to thymectomy, whether or not they have thymomas, and in a few only a degenerate thymus is found at surgery. Many patients are well controlled medically, and surgery is often reserved for those who do not so respond. Those most likely to respond to surgery are young females with short histories. Following the introduction of thymectomy, the mortality amongst patients without a thymoma was halved. Some claim that the reason for thymectomy is to try to obviate the potential risk of 'invasion', but 'extended thymectomy' (i.e. a clearance of the anterior mediastinal fat to remove 'thymic rests') may give a lower recurrence rate for myasthenia (Moore, 1989).

Fonseca and Havard (1990) wrote that the judicious use of thymectomy, cortiocosteroids and, if necessary, immunosuppressive drugs, offers patients a combination of reduced mortality, which now should be negligible, and a high rate of remission.

Ansell (1989) pointed out that contrast agents used with CT (both ionic and non-ionic) may provoke a myasthenic crisis or unmask myasthenia in patients with thymic abnormalities. He recommended that adequate provision for treatment of a crisis should always be available when such contrast studies are performed. (The author has, however, never encountered such a case).

Illus. **THYMUS, Pt. 21** is of a small anteriorly situated thymoma in a patient with myasthenia gravis. Illus. **THYMUS, Pt. 32** shows a thymoma extending into the right pleural cavity with nodules and a small right pleural effusion; he originally presented with myasthenia, but this responded to steroids and did not recur. Illus. **THYMUS, Pts. 25 & 30** also show thymomas in patients with myasthenia gravis, whilst Illus. **THYMUS, Pt. 15** is of a patient with myasthenia gravis and no radiological thymic abnormality.

(b) **The thymus in children.**

The infant thymus, which contains much of the body's immune response tissue, is relatively large and tucks itself into most of the available space in the anterior upper chest. Its radiographic appearance is variable - 'sail-like' (Kemp et al., 1948), having a 'wavy outline' due to indentations of the soft thymic tissue by the costo-chondral junctions (Mulvey, 1963), or giving rise to an 'angel's wing' or 'rocker bottom' appearance, the last two being seen with a pneumothorax (Moseley, 1960) or a pneumo-mediastinum (Kogutt, 1981).

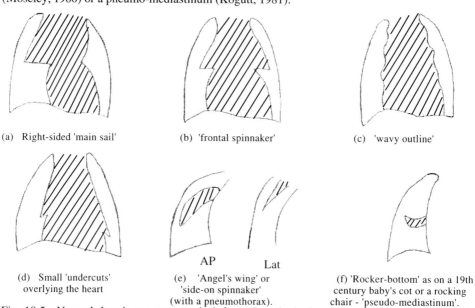

(a) Right-sided 'main sail'   (b) 'frontal spinnaker'   (c) 'wavy outline'

AP   Lat

(d) Small 'undercuts'   (e) 'Angel's wing' or   (f) 'Rocker-bottom' as on a 19th
     overlying the heart   'side-on spinnaker'   century baby's cot or a rocking
                               (with a pneumothorax).   chair - 'pseudo-mediastinum'.

Fig. 18.5   Normal thymic appearances in infants (b, c & d after Coussement, et al., 1984, by permission).

The infant thymus also tends to appear larger in expiration, with some rotation of the child or on a lordotic view. It may also be mistaken for a consolidated or collapsed right upper lobe, and in one case that came to the author for an opinion, the child had had a bronchogram which was normal! Harris et al. (1980) reported five cases where the infant thymus mimicked lung or mediastinal disease, and noted that a large thymus could compress the right upper lobe bronchus. Oh et al. (1971) reported three similar cases in adolescents. Meaney et al. (1993) described the use of ultrasound for diagnosing the thymus as the cause of an apparent mediastinal mass in an infant, and illustrated a large thymus extending posteriorly in the right upper mediastinum.

The relative size of the thymus in children is inversely related to their age. This relative size continues to decrease until adulthood, involution being complete at about age 40. Involution is also accompanied by fatty replacement (see Baron et al., 1982a).

When a pneumo-mediastinum is present, either spontaneously e.g. with an asthmatic attack, or induced deliberately (see p. 6.34), the thymus may be well demonstrated on plain radiographs, particularly lateral views (Illus. **THYMUS, Pts. 2, 3, 4, 5, & 27** and **Pneumomediastinum Pts. 5 & 9**).

Thirty to forty years ago, particularly in the USA, some infants with a large looking (but normal) thymus were thought to have **'status thymo-lymphaticus'**, and many had radiotherapy to the upper chest. Pifer et al. (1963) studied 2809 such individuals who were so treated in upstate New York between 1926 and 1957. These had the treatment performed with their heads turned, and were irradiated from sella to diaphragm, including the whole chest, neck and jaw areas. Several developed leukaemia, thyroid and salivary gland tumours, neurilemmomas and osteochondromas, etc. The author has seen three such cases, one in a US serviceman.

Rarely true tumours occur in the thymus in children e.g. lymphoma, thymoma, sarcoma and liposarcoma.

Further references.
Adam and Ignotus (1993) : Sonography of the thymus in 50 healthy children - easily visualised in children 2-8 yrs. of age - margins smooth and sharply defined.
Linegar et al. (1993) : Massive thymic hyperplasia in infants and children.
Mandell et al. (1994) : Cervical herniation of the normal thymus causing compression of the trachea by the innominate artery in infants leading to stridor, wheezing, cyanosis and apnoea; recurrent pneumonia and even death may ensue.
Iyer et al. (1998) : Thymic sarcoma in a 9 yr. old girl.

(c) The thymus in teenagers and adults.

In teenagers, although the thymus is much smaller than in young children, it is still a sizeable organ and may still at times be mistaken for a tumour. It is of water density (i.e. not fat) so nodules within it may not be readily apparent on CT sections. As noted above, the thymus is gradually involuted and replaced by fat, so that over age 25 to 30 fat predominates, but in young adults small islands of residual lymphatic tissue may still be seen on CT sections. The weight of the thymus is about 15 g. at birth and increases to a maximum of about 35 g. at puberty. Its size is usually constant throughout adult life.

The adult thymus is typically triangular or pyramidal in shape; it is a slightly bilobed structure, rather like the 'bow of a boat' or an 'arrow-head'. It has a concave base, and lies in front of the aortic arch and between the left innominate vein superiorly and the great vessels inferiorly. Sometimes it is present as two lobes, in contact with one another in the midline superiorly and diverging inferiorly. The upper poles are closely related to the trachea, and are attached to the corresponding lobes of the thyroid via the thyro-thymic ligaments. Occasionally only one thymic lobe is present (Baron et al., 1982b).

Unlike goitres, thymic enlargements only usually slightly deform the trachea, because they tend to be soft in texture like fat.

Francis et al. (1985) examined the thymus in 309 normal people by CT and found that over age 40, 50% showed total fatty involution. When present residual thymic tissue was usually small, of linear, oval or round shape and did not produce focal alterations in the lateral mediastinal contour. Multilobularity was not a feature of normal glands at any age and was seen only with thymic abnormality (see also Moore et al., 1983).

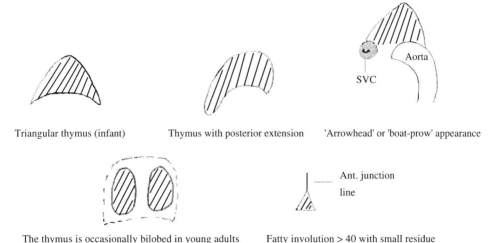

Triangular thymus (infant)   Thymus with posterior extension   'Arrowhead' or 'boat-prow' appearance

The thymus is occasionally bilobed in young adults   Fatty involution > 40 with small residue

Fig. 18.6.   Diagrams of cross sectional appearances of the thymus.

(NB - Until involution has occurred, the anterior junction line -ps. 1.11-12 - is poorly developed).

Thymic hyperplasia.
(a) <u>Infants</u>: as noted above the thymus may be huge and still normal - is uniform in texture with ultra-sound. (In the UK most cases are ignored, but may be biopsied in the USA).
(b) <u>Adults</u>: as noted by Williams, M. (1989), this may be of two types - (i) follicular (or lymphoid) hyperplasia, involving only the medulla, and (ii) true hyperplasia, involving both cortex and medulla. The first occurs in patients with myasthenia gravis, DLE and in some types of autoimmune haemolytic anaemia, and as this causes little or no change in the size of the thymus, it can seldom be recognised by CT. True hyperplasia with enlargement may be associated with thyrotoxicosis, parathyroid or other hormone disorders (the 'pleuri-glandular syndrome'), and may also be found in association with chronic adrenal insufficiency. Brown, L. and Aughenbach (1991) noted thymic enlargement with acromegaly and with Grave's disease.

'Stress' and 'Rebound' changes.
   The thymus may become smaller following stress. This is presumably steroid induced and can happen within 24 hours of the onset of an acute illness (Weaver et al., 1985), following steroid treatment (Caffey and di Liberty, 1959) and following thymic irradiation; it may also follow chemotherapy. Recovery may be associated with thymic regrowth to its original size or to an enlargement greater than this - the '**rebound phenomenon**' - seen mainly in children, adolescents and young adults. It has been seen after recovery from severe burns (Gelfand et al., 1972), major surgery, acute infections, the stopping of steroid treatment (Caffey and Sibley, 1960) and following the treatment of childhood tumours (Cohen et al., 1980 and Woodhead, 1984). It has also been seen following treatment for hypothyroidism (Yulish and Owens, 1980). Doppman et al. (1986) reported 'rebound thymic hyperplasia' after treatment of Cushing's syndrome in three patients (a boy of 15 following resection of an ACTH producing pituitary adenoma, a woman of 27 with a lung carcinoid and hilar node micro-metastases, and a man of 35 who was given a gluco-corticoid antagonist for an unlocalised ACTH source).
   Choyke et al. (1987) found thymic atrophy during cancer chemotherapy and regrowth afterwards in 90% of patients studied, and rebound hyperplasia in 25%. Kissin et al. (1987) also found CT evidence of benign enlargement in adults following chemotherapy. Foulner (1991) noted transient thymic calcification in association with rebound enlargement.
   In patients with lymphomas which have involved the thymus, rebound enlargement following the cessation of treatment (radiotherapy, chemotherapy or both) may mimic recurrence. However, when there is no other evidence of disease, this may be a cautious pointer to rebound, and a careful watch of the patient be maintained (see also p. 5.23). As well as CT, MR or gallium scanning (with tomography) has also been used to try to determine if viable tumour is still present (see also p. 22.10).

<u>Further references.</u>
Keller and Castleman (1974) : Hodgkin's disease of the thymus gland.
Federle and Callen (1979) : CT of cystic Hodgkins's lymphoma of the thymus.
Cohen et al. (1980) : Thymic rebound after treatment of childhood tumours.
Baron, R. et al. (1981b) : Thymic cysts following radiotherapy for Hodgkin's disease.
Lindfors et al. (1985) : Thymic cysts in mediastinal Hodgkin's disease.
Bode and Scheidt (1988) : Change of thymic size during and following cytotoxic therapy in young patients.
Heron et al. (1988) : CT of the thymus in Hodgkin's disease.
Wernecke et al. (1991) : Thymic involvement in Hodgkin's disease - CT and US.
Wenger et al. (1994) : Thymic rebound in a 25 year old man 22 months following surgery (and without chemotherapy or R/T for scrotal mesothelioma - the hypertrophied thymus was excised.
Wong-You-Chong and Radford (1995) : Enlargement of a mediastinal mass during treatment for Hodgkin's disease may be due to accumulation of fluid within thymic cysts.
Obaro (1996), Green and Rickett (1995) : True thymic hyperplasia in infants.

Plain radiographic and fluoroscopic appearances of thymic masses.
   Thymic masses may arise from the level of the aortic arch, down to the level of the diaphragm. Most are spherical or oval in shape, but others are lobulated, triangular or plaque-like. They are within the thymic fat and in most cases produce a bulge on the outline of the overlying mediastinal pleura. Large tumours may be readily seen on frontal plain radiographs, but smaller ones may not

be visible. Lateral views, especially with the arms behind the back ('Mary Queen of Scots view' - p. 20.9) may be valuable as they make the anterior mediastinum stick out well and on these most sizeable thymic masses may be seen pressing into the air-filled lung above and anterior to the heart.

Oblique views and /or fluoroscopy have also been used for showing thymic masses. Rosenthal et al. (1974 - from Israel) termed the projecting mass, as seen on oblique views, the 'Semitic or Jewish nose sign' (Illus. JEWISH NOSE SIGN). They also noted that during fluoroscopy, the apparent size of thymic masses could alter, being smaller in deep inspiration. Like Good (1947), they described two types of tumour, one being oval or lobulated and often showing calcification, whilst the second (and more difficult to detect) was plaque-like and tended to be closely applied to the pericardium and large blood vessels. Calcification occurs in about 30% (Harper and Guyer, 1965), but is mostly seen on tomograms, including CT. This may be linear, nodular or circular and is often faint (see Illus. THYMUS, Pts. 22, 23, 28, 34, 37 & 58). Dense ring-type calcification is more often seen with goitres and desmoids.

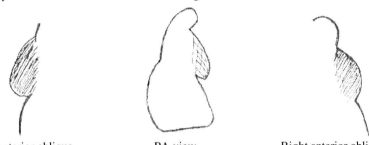

Left anterior oblique   PA view   Right anterior oblique

Fig. 18.7 The 'Semitic (or Jewish) Nose Sign' of a thymic mass, (after Rosenthal et al., 1974, 'Thymoma: clinical & additional radiologic signs', Chest, **65**, 428 - 430 with permission).

CT of the thymus and thymic masses.

CT has undoubtedly made the demonstration of thymic masses easier and more certain. It shows small masses that are invisible on plain radiographs, and also the extent and spread of thymic tumours. This is often local spread into the mediastinum or pleura, and especially into the adjacent mediastinal fat, but more widespread dissemination may occur (see Illus. THYMOMA). Difficulties may however occur as spread into the fat may not be obvious, and there are few tissue planes other than the overlying parietal mediastinal pleura which may be made indistinct by tumour spread. It may also be difficult to differentiate a thymoma from hyperplasia, and the latter may be present in 60 to 70% of patients with myasthenia. In patients under the age of 25, the thymus is still often quite large and it may be difficult to distinguish abnormalities from normal appearances.

<u>Some references.</u>
Day and Geduadas (1984) : Up to 35% of thymomas detected by CT may not be visible on plain chest radiographs.
Batra et al. (1987) : Compared plain chest radiographs, CT and MR with surgical findings in 16 patients with myasthenia gravis. CT showed better definition of the thymus than MR. In only two patients was a thymic mass shown on plain radiographs. Five had thymic hyperplasia - only found at surgery and not apparent on CT.
Ellis et al. (1988) : Concluded that in young patients (**under age 20**) with myasthenia (in whom the thymus is normally cellular and often relatively large) a thymoma may be undetected on chest radiographs or CT unless it is very large, produces a contour abnormality of the mediastinum, or contains calcification - CT is only of minimal advantage over chest radiographs. Between the **ages of 21 and 45**, cellular thymic remnants can mimic a thymoma, but **over the age of 45**, CT is better as fatty replacement has occurred (35% of patients with myasthenia in this age group have thymomas).
Williams, M. (1989) : Discussed problems in CT assessment of the thymus -
(i) Thymic shape rather than complex measurement is the key to recognition of an abnormal thymus. A multilobular appearance is abnormal at any age, as is a thymus which causes a focal alteration in mediastinal contour.
(ii) CT cannot replace histology, but invasion of the chest wall or vascular invasion are reliable indications of malignancy. These can occur with malignant thymoma, germ cell tumours and lymphoma. Fat densities within a thymic mass usually indicate a benign teratoma or a thymolipoma. Water-dense areas may be seen in necrotic parts of a tumour, within haemangiomas and lymphangiomas and in cysts, either occurring de novo or after radiotherapy.
Brown and Aughenbaugh (1991) : CT differentiation between a large normal thymus and a thymic mass is sometimes difficult, particularly in younger patients with a large thymus. A thymic mass usually appears as a solid,

oval or rounded density, with the bulk of the mass lateral to the mid line. Obliteration of the normal tissue planes indicates an infiltrating or invasive tumour. Occasionally only one lobe of the thymus is visible, and if large, may be confused with a mass.

Thymic tumours.

Thymic reticuloses are the most common masses which arise in the thymic region. They may be found in adolescents, young or middle aged adults and occasionally in the elderly. They are further discussed on ps. 5.21-22 & 18.16-17. Sometimes they are very large and almost fill half of the chest. They may give rise to pleural effusions, pulmonary metastases, etc. Occasionally calcifications are present (Illus. **THYMUS, Pts. 22, 23, 28, 34, 37 & HODGKIN'S DISEASE, Pt. 58**). Thymomas may mimic sarcomas, which may also occur in the thymus (e.g. fibrosarcomas, lymphosarcomas and liposarcomas) and both sarcomas and reticuloses may give rise to pulmonary metastases, etc.

Thymomas usually comprise both epithelial cells and lymphocytes, and in those causing hormonal or auto-antibody effects (e.g. red cell aplasia, hypoglobulinaemia with sinusitis and rapidly developing **bronchiectasis** - see Illus. **THYMUS Pt. 29a-g**), spindle cells are usually predominant. Some thymomas may occur together with cysts (Illus. **THYMUS Pt. 14a-b**). About 7% of thymomas exhibit calcification which can be coarse, dense, irregular or ring-like in type.
    There is often considerable difficulty in differentiating benign from more malignant thymomas. Thymomas rarely produce distant metastases and mainly spread through the thymic fat, up and down the tissue planes of the mediastinum, and into the sub-pleural or pleural spaces. When they extend down to the upper surface of the diaphragm, they may cause an appearance reminiscent of 'candle-wax dripping down the side of a burning candle and spreading onto the upper surface of the candle-stick base' (**'drop   metastases'**). They may also extend through the diaphragmatic openings into the abdomen, or up into the neck (Illus. **THYMUS, Pt. 34a-j**). Pleural effusions may be present, and may be transient; pleural deposits may also be seen, sometimes in an inter-lobar fissure (Illus. **THYMUS, Pt. 32a-g**).
    Because of their mode of spread, Zerhouni et al. (1982) suggested the term **'invasive thymoma'**. They examined ten such cases by plain radiography and CT, and found CT to be especially helpful for showing pleural deposits above the diaphragm, on the pericardium and invasion of the lung (see Fig. 18.8 and Illus. **THYMUS, Pts. 32, 34, 38 & 39**).

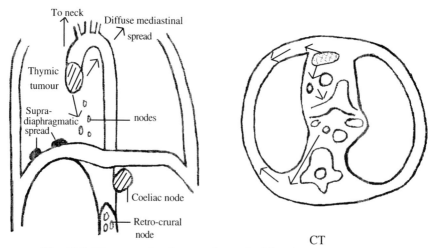

Fig. 18.8 Diagrams of pathways of spread of thymic tumours.
(Adapted from Zerhouni et al., 1982, 'Invasive thymomas', JCAT, **6**, 92 - 100 with permission from Lippincott - Raven).

Naidich et al. (1984) classified thymomas into three stages :

I : Confined within the capsule.
II : Pericapsular spread into the mediastinal fat ('infiltrating thymoma').
III : Spread into surrounding organs and subpleural tissues, thence into the lower mediastinum, the crural regions of the diaphragm and through the diaphragmatic orifices into the abdomen ('**metastasising thymoma**').

It is thus important to try to determine if the capsule has been breached, for if it has then surgical cure is much less likely. However thymomas may be slow to enlarge, and repeat examinations may be required to be sure about this point.

Moore et al. (1983) stated that usually a thymic tumour in a patient over 40 years of age is a neoplasm (but more 'malignant' or 'invasive' types seem to be reported from the USA than are found in the UK).

Histology may not differentiate between benign and malignant thymic tumours, and only their appearance at surgery, i.e. spreading into other tissues or their subsequent behaviour after removal may give a guide to prognosis. Even CT assessment showing a discrete mass may not be entirely reliable. Brown et al. (1983) reported two cases in which the masses appeared discrete, but showed adherence or infiltration on pathology.

CT assessment is also very difficult if little fat is present. On MR thymomas may show inhomogeneity and multinodularlty particularly with invasive types.

Thymic carcinoids - these tumours, like other neuro-endocrine tumours such as bronchial carcinoids, contain neuro-secretory granules and may produce similar hormonal effects. They may also be difficult to distinguish from medullary carcinomas of the thyroid. As with bronchial carcinoids, not all patients with these tumours have syndromes related to these hormones. These tumours may give a similar radiological appearance to thymomas - they may be locally invasive, cause SVC obstruction or produce extra-thoracic deposits (up to 50% - Wick et al., 1980). Occasionally they may contain calcification (Brown et al., 1982, Freundlich and McGavran, 1996). An example is shown in Illus. **THYMUS, Pt. 34a-j**; in this patient, the tumour slowly spread over a period of 14 years through the mediastinum, up into the thyroid area and down into the cardia and upper abdomen - all without causing any symptoms, except for a small swelling in the right side of the thyroid (in which he later developed a medullary carcinoma of the thyroid, which was resected) - all presumably part of a '**pleuri-glandular syndrome**'. Another patient had a mass which mimicked a mediastinal goitre on CT, but the thyroid was normal on an isotope scan - this tumour spread fairly widely in the upper mediastinum and was hormonally active giving rise to the carcinoid syndrome.

Similar tumours may occur in other parts of the mediastinum, and may mimic parathyroid tumours. Bony deposits are uncommon, but may give rise to sclerotic deposits.

Thymic carcinoma - is an uncommon tumour of the thymic epithelium; it is aggressive with both local spread and distant metastases, and has a poor prognosis. It may contain areas of necrosis, haemorrhage calcification and cyst formation. Paraneoplastic syndromes are uncommon. One case the author saw was of a young black West Indian athlete with a large irregular anterior mediastinal mass and multiple lung deposits (he was sent by his GP for chest radiography as persistent cough following 'flu).

Thymolipoma - this is a rare tumour. If small it will be indistinguishable from the fat normally present in the thymus. The thymic fat not uncommonly hypertrophies, especially in renal failure, etc. (see p. 6.13). Like fat elsewhere, it may behave like a lipoma. When very large it may drape itself around the heart, with a pendulous elongated 'tear drop' shape, simulating cardiomegaly on plain radiographs. CT may then show huge fatty masses on either side of the heart, arising from the area of the thymus, like large 'intrathoracic breasts'. Contrast enhancement may show 'streaky' opacification. Ultrasound may also suggest their fatty nature. Rarely such masses may prove to be liposarcomas and exhibit mixed attenuation (see also p. 6.13 and refs. p. 18.27).

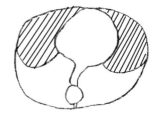

Fig. 18.9.   Thymolipoma mimicking
pendulous or 'intra-thoracic breasts'
or an 'elongated tear-drop' appearance.

Secondary deposits may also be found in the thymus.
Middleton (1966) : Involvement of the thymus by metastatic neoplasms.
Phillips (1994) : Metastatic malignant testicular teratoma of the thymus in a 23 year old man.

Thymic dermoids and teratomas - are discussed on ps. 18.13 - 15.

Thymic calcification.
This may be seen with cysts, following TB or fungus infection, lymphomas (esp. after radiation treatment) and thymomas. Sumner et al. (1993) noted thymic calcification in histiocytosis X in an infant.

Other methods for examining the thymus.
Ultrasound via the intercostal spaces may allow some thymic masses to be visualised. Cysts may be identified, and some fatty and partly degenerate masses of mixed density. Cystic masses may be drained percutaneously. The normal infant thymus is easily examined - see also ps. 18 18 - 19.
Kenny and Carty (1988) : illustrated three cases of anterior mediastinal teratomas in infants causing respiratory distress - ultrasound demonstrated mixed echogenicity.

Angiography was used in some cases before the advent of CT to define thymic tumours.
Gothlin et al. (1977) : performed angiography via the internal mammary artery in 30 patients. In thymomas there was an increase in the size of the thymic artery and the branches were localised in the periphery or cortex of the visualised mass, rather than in their centres. With carcinomas, there tended to be several feeding vessels from the internal mammary artery, and the increased vascularity spread into the tumour.

Thymic venography - was popularised by Kreel (1967 & 1968) and by Young, D. et al. (1970), but is now rarely used. It was a very time consuming procedure, but had many successes. Venous blood samples could also be taken for biochemical studies.

Gas mediastinography - combined with tomography - was often used before the advent of CT, and is still occasionally used in some centres (see Illus. **PNEUMOMEDIASTINUM**).

Isotopes - both Se^{75}methionine and Ga^{67} have been tried for the imaging of thymic masses, but neither have been found generally acceptable as they lack specificity. However Testa and Angelini (1979) in a series of 12 surgically proven cases of thymic hyperplasia (in 53 patients with myasthenia gravis), 8 had positive Se^{75}methionine scans.
Thomas and Gupta (1988) : pointed out that even unilobar enlargement of a normal thymus may cause some pressure on the trachea and cause matched decreased ventilation and perfusion on isotope lung studies.

Further references.
(a) **General.**
Goldstein and Mackay (1969) : The Human Thymus.
Kendall (1981) : The Thymus.
Baron et al. (1982a) : CT of normal thymus.,   Baron et al. (1982b) : CT of abnormal thymus.
Heiberg et al. (1982) : Normal thymic CT appearances under age 20.
Lee et al. (1983) : Thymic anatomy.
Day and Geduadas (1984) : Review of the thymus and radiology of its abnormalities.

de Geer et al. (1986) : Normal thymus - assessment by MR and CT.
Dixon et al. (1981) : CT of the thymic remnant.
Sone et al. (1980) : Normal anatomy and pneumomediastinography.
Arnheim and Gemson (1950): Cervical thymus gland.
Oh et al. (1971) : Three cases of large normal thymus in late childhood.
Ebel (1980) : Thymus in children.
Cohen, M. et al (1983) and Bar Ziv et al. (1984) : Posterior mediastinal or accessory thymus (thymic tissue extending posteriorly in children).
Cory et al. (1987) : Thymus in superior mediastinum simulating adenopathy - CT appearance.
St. Amour et al. (1987) : CT of normal and abnormal thymus in childhood.
Rollins and Currarino (1988) : MR imaging of the posterior mediastinal thymus.
Thomas, N. and Gupta (1988) : Unilobar enlargement of the normal thymus gland causing mass effect.
Siegel et al. (1989) : Normal and abnormal thymus in childhood - MR findings.
Molina et al. (1990) : Thymic masses on MR imaging.
Boothroyd et al. (1992) : MR appearances of the normal thymus in children.
Walter et al. (1992) : The Thymus : Diagnostic Imaging, Functions and Pathologic Anatomy.
Freundlich and McGavran (1996) : Abnormalities of the thymus.

Ansell (1989) : Problems in radiology - CT assessment of the thymus and imaging in myasthenia gravis. Contrast enhanced CT may precipitate a myasthenic crisis or unmask myasthenia in patients with myasthenia gravis, particularly in patients with a thymoma. Adequate provision for the treatment of a crisis should be available.

(b) Hyperplasia.
Franken (1968) : Thymic enlargement in Graves disease.
Lee, Y. et al. (1979) : Massive hyperplastic thymus in a 22 month old infant.
Rose and Lam (1982) : Thymic hyperplasia in association with hyperparathyroidism.
Sandler et al. (1983) : Micronodular enlargement.
Goldberg et al. (1987) : Serial CT scans in thymic hyperplasia.
Wortsman et al. (1988) : Immunoglobulins that cause thymocyte proliferation from a patient with Grave's disease and an enlarged thymus.
Obaro (1996) : True massive thymic hyperplasia in an infant- excised & weighed 3.66 kg!
Green and Rickett (1996, Leicester) : Hyperplasia in an **infant** - ? rebound following hyaline membrane disease & bronchiolitis - 2 CTs showed stretching of R innominate vein, a large posterior extension on the R, but normal airways on CT - it was excised & weighed 54g.
McHugh (1997, Oxford) : Questioned the need for surgery in Green & Rickett's case and felt that only US was required for studying it, and it could have been treated conservatively - Green & Rickett replied - posterior extension was the reason for surgery.

(c) Thymic cysts.
Podolsky et al. (1962) : Congenital thymic cyst attached to the pericardium.
Dyer (1967) : Cystic thymomas and thymic cysts.
Seltzer et al. (1968) : Mediastinal thymic cyst.
Mikal (1974) : Cervical thymic cyst.
Hurley (1977) : Cervical-mediastinal thymic cyst - cyst puncture and contrast demonstration (boy aged six).
Federle and Callen (1979) : Cystic Hodgkin's lymphoma of the thymus - CT appearance.
Baron et al. (1981) : Thymic cysts following radiotherapy for Hodgkin's disease.
Gouliamos et al. (1982) : CT demonstration of thymic cysts.
Dunne and Weksberg (1983) : Thymic cysts - usefulness of **ultrasound** in showing fluid in a cyst, if it lies in contact with the chest wall.
Graeber et al. (1984) : 46 patients with thymic cystic lesions. 40 were asymptomatic and nine were large enough to extend up into the neck. 39 were true cysts, but five were thymomas (two malignant), one was a seminoma and another a lymphoblastoma. They advised a combination of ultra-sound and CT for diagnosis, but also pointed out that a cystic lesion may be malignant.
Veeze-Kuijpers et al. (1987) : Benign thymic cyst following mantle radiotherapy for Hodgkin's disease.
Levine, C. (1988) : CT of large thymic cyst which extended from the right side of the neck to the tracheal bifurcation - it presented in the neck.
Merine et al. (1988) : CT and MR diagnosis of thymic cyst.

Cuassay et al. (1976) : Mediastinal thymic cyst after open heart surgery.
Krongrad et al. (1970) : Mediastinal thymic cyst after surgery for congenital heart disease.
Webb, W. and Gamsu (1980) : Postoperative anterior mediastinal masses (a) thymic cyst and (b) a **talc granuloma** (densely calcified within the thymus).
Jaramillo et al. (1989) : Apparent association between thymic cysts and prior thoracotomy.

(d) **Thymomas.**

Harper (1951) : The investigation of thymic tumours in myasthenia gravis - tumours occur in approx. 13% of pts. with myasthenia. The tumours may be rounded, lobulated or plaque-like and they vary considerably in position within the anterior mediastinum.

Harper and Guyer (1965) : Radiological features of thymic tumours - review of 65 cases.

Brown, L. et al. (1980) : Radiographic detection of thymoma.

Smith, S. et al. (1983) : CT of invasive thymoma.

Scatarige et al. (1985) : Transdiaphragmatic extension of thymomas - in 6 out of 19 cases - to right lateral liver surface, posterior para-renal space, left para-aortic region, peri-gastric soft tissue and spinal canal.

Magee and Stout (1986) : Malignant epithelial tumours of the thymus - survival after radiotherapy.

Peterson et al. (1965) : Pathogenesis of immune deficiency diseases - reviewed 10 cases of thymoma and agammaglobulinaemia.

Möffat (1976) : Radiologic changes in the thymoma - hypogammmaglobulinaemia syndrome.

Asherson and Webster (1980) : Immunodeficiency effects of thymomas.

Hirst and Robertson (1967) : Thymoma and erythroblastopenic anaemia.

Goldman et al. (1975) : Myasthenia gravis and invasive thymoma - 20 year experience.

Mink et al. (1978) : CT of anterior mediastinum in patients with myasthenia gravis and suspected thymoma.

Fon et al. (1982) : CT of anterior mediastinum in myasthenia gravis (57 patients).

Gurtler et al. (1982) : CT of 45 patients with myasthenia - four thymomas, one thymolipoma, eight thymic hyperplasia and one normal in 14 operated cases. They concluded that **CT cannot distinguish between normal thymus and hyperplasia.**

McCrea and Maslar (1982) : Thymoma with myasthenia and three distant localised areas of spread to pleura on the same side shown by CT.

Moore et al. (1982) : Thymomas shown by CT in patients with myasthenia gravis.

Brown, L. et al. (1983) : Compared CT and surgical findings in 19 patients with myasthenia gravis. CT showed nine thymomas, but they could not differentiate them from thymic cysts, hyperplasia or nodes. They also found that CT was inaccurate in predicting invasion or adherence of a thymoma, and that a thymus with histological hyperplasia is not necessarily enlarged. In their experience, thymomas did not occur under age 20.

Kaye et al. (1983) : CT of 119 patients with myasthenia - 36 had a subsequent thymectomy. CT showed all tumours and hyperplastic glands. Half were shown on plain radiographs, and 90% on linear tomograms. CT could not distinguish between a thymoma and hyperplasia.

Gupta et al. (1985) : Watery diarrhoea in a patient with myasthenia gravis, thymoma and immunodeficiency.

Soppi et al. (1985) : Thymoma with immunodeficiency (Good's syndrome) associated with myasthenia gravis and benign IgG gammopathy

Verley and Hollman (1985) : 200 cases of thymoma - comparative study of clinical stage, histology and survival.

Keen and Libshitz (1987) : CT in 24 patients with thymic lesions - the presence or absence of intervening fat planes was a good indicator of vascular or pericardial invasion by tumours.

Dobson et al. (1988) : Used MR to study 12 patients with myasthenia and found thymomas in two.

Ellis and Austin (1988) : Radiologic detection of thymoma in patients with myasthenia gravis.

Kaplan et al. (1988) : CT of 'ectopic' thymoma - large mass at left lung base, containing areas of necrosis with a mediastinal pedicle.

Korobkin and Casano (1989) : CT demonstration of SVC and intracardiac extension of a malignant thymoma.

Fox et al. (1992) : Spindle-cell thymoma with hypoglobulinaemia (Good's syndrome) - an unusual cause of bronchiectasis - does not respond to thymectomy.

Miller, W. et al. (1992) : Thymoma mimicking a thyroid mass.

Sakai et al. (1992) : MR imaging of thymoma - 17 patients - malignant type had an inhomogeneous signal.

(e) **Thymic carcinoids.**

Rosai and Higa (1972) : Thymic carcinoids (eight cases).

Brown, L. et al. (1982) : Primary corticotropin producing carcinoid tumours of the mediastinum - almost invariably thymic carcinoids (six cases).

Felson et al. (1982) : **Cushing's syndrome** associated with a mediastinal mass.

Fitzgerald et al. (1982) : ACTH secreting thymic carcinoid causing adrenal hyperplasia - both thymic and adrenal masses shown by CT.

Birnberg et al. (1982) : Thymic carcinoids with hyperparathyroidism.

Wang, D. et al. (1994) : Carcinoid tumours of the thymus.

Georgy et al. (1995) : Thymic carcinoids with bone metastases - report of two cases - if osteoblastic and diffuse in nature - can be confused with diffuse bone marrow disease on MRI.

Gross (1996) : Case of mediastinal widening due to lipomatosis + ant. med. mass (**thymic carcinoid**), sclerotic bone lesions & plump adrenals (as a result of ACTH produced by the tumour) - after resection of the carcinoid, the adrenals returned to normal size (see also Chapter 23).

Hanson et al. (1998) : CT of the thymus and anterior mediastinum in active **Cushing's syndrome** - study of 85 pts. - (i) fat replacement, (ii) linear strands of soft tissue, (iii) small nodules, (iv) larger nodules & (v) triangular bilobed thymus gland. 29 showed nodular or triangular soft tissue structure in ant. med. - these did not necessarily imply a thymic carcinoid, although their presence in older pts. should be viewed with suspicion.

(f) Thymic carcinomas.
Snover et al. (1982) : Five different histological variants.
Carlson et al. (1990) : Successful treatment of metastatic thymic carcinoma with cisplatin, vinblastine, bleomycin and etoposide.
Hartman et al. (1990) : Thymic carcinoma : report of five cases and review of the literature.
Suster and Rosai (1991) : Review of 60 cases - classified into low-grade (squamous, mucoepidermoid and basal cell) and high grade (lymphoepithelioma-like, small-cell, clear-cell, sarcomatoid and undifferentiated) groups.
Quagliano et al. (1996) : Three cases presenting with large invasive anterior mediastinal masses and extrathoracic metastases.

(g) Thymolipomas and thymoliposarcomas.
Teplick et al. (1973), Yeh et al. (1983), Shirkhoda et al. (1987) , Chew and Weissleder (1991)
Le Marc'hadur et al. (1991) : Thymolipoma in association with **myasthenia gravis** - 9 cases have been reported - ? a true thymoma that is so well differentiated as to remain encapsulated and to undergo adipose involution. It may also be associated with hyperthyroidism and Hodgkin's disease.
Rosado-de-Christenson et al. (1994) : Analysis of 27 cases - thymolipomas are anterior mediastinal masses which may conform to the shape of adjacent structures - diagnosis is supported by studies which demonstrate fat and soft tissue within the tumour. 12 cases simulated cardiomegaly on frontal radiographs, whilst 12 others were draped above the diaphragm and simulated hemidiaphragmatic elevation on lateral radiographs.
McManus et al. (1994) : Lipothymoma with red cell aplasia, hypogammaglobulinaemia and lichen planus.
Klimstra et al. (1995) : Liposarcoma of the anterior mediastinum and thymus.
Howling et al. (1999) : Lipolymphosarcoma - CT and pathologic findings.

(h) Gas mediastinography.
Sone et al. (1980) : Pneumediastinography - normal anatomy of the thymus and anterior mediastinum (34 cases with **myasthenia gravis**).
Mitsuoka et al. (1981) : CT of the mediastinum with gas contrast.
Sone et al. (1982) : CT pneumomediastinography.

(i) Angiography
Göthlin et al. (1977) : Angiographic appearance of thymic tumours - internal mammary angiography in 30 patients.

The Middle Mediastinum
The most frequent abnormal masses in this part of the mediastinum are enlarged lymph nodes, from many causes - inflammatory, granulomatous (esp. sarcoid) or neoplastic, including those spreading up from the abdomen. Other masses include tumours extending out from the trachea or larger bronchi, bronchogenic (or other cysts), oesophageal dilatations or masses, hiatal herniae, fluid collections (from mediastinitis or pancreatitis), haematomas, aneurysms, neural tumours (of vagi), chemodectomas, etc. (see also Table 18.1).

Nodal enlargements may occur in several nodal areas, e.g.. subcarinal, paratracheal, azygos, etc. (see Chapter 13), and the enlargement often extends into the hilar areas or superior mediastinum.

Radiological recognition is often by displacement of the paraoesophageal line, or from other manifestations of mediastinal, bronchial, etc. distortion (see Chapters 1 - 3). Subcarinal nodes may widen the carina or produce a 'pear-shaped' mass below the air-filled 'rings' of the main bronchi as seen on lateral views (see ps. 13.27 - 28). Frequently tomography (including CT) is required for confirmation and the extent of the abnormality.

For discussion of aortic abnormalities see Chapter 10.

The posterior mediastinum.

The pre-spinal line or stripe is seen on lateral chest or dorsal spine radiographs, lying in front of the vertebral column. It is usually about 2 to 3 mm thick, but may be displaced forwards by osteophytes, haematomas (with fractures), secondary tumours extending out of the vertebrae or running alongside them, or by enlargement of pre-spinal nodes. Other causes include spinal abscesses, neurofibromas, varices, etc. (see Table 18.5).

Table 18.5 Distortion or effacement of the thoracic pre- and para-spinal lines - usually indicates para-vertebral disease: -

(a) **Distortion and/or displacement.**
> Spinal disease:
>> Tumour with para-spinal spread
>>> Primary - plasmacytoma / sarcoma
>>> Secondary tumours, including bronchial and oesophageal tumours,
>>>> reticulosis, myeloma, etc.
>> Infection with abscess formation
>>> Tuberculosis
>>> Staph., strep., salmonella, typhoid, brucella, actinomycosis, proteus,
>>>> E. coli, enterobacter, etc.
>> Vertebral fracture with haematoma
>> Other spinal swelling - Scheuermann's disease, scoliosis, large osteophytes,
>>> Paget's disease, etc.
>> Para-spinal soft tissue enlargement
>>> fat
>>> lymph nodes - reticulosis, secondary tumour, etc.
>>> extramedullary haemopoiesis
> Vascular
>> Aortic abnormalities - coarctation, aneurysms, etc.
>> Azygos and /or hemiazygos vein dilatations or varices
>> Haematomas arising from the above
> Neural
>> Tumour - neurofibroma, etc.
>> Cyst, meningocoele
> Oesophagus
>> Tumour, dilatation, rupture.

(b) **Effacement**
> Adjacent lung collapse or consolidation - especially of lower lobes
> Pleural fluid, thickening or tumour in the pleural cavity.

(c) **Pneumomediastinum** - this may displace and enhance the line (Illus. **ANATOMY, Pnmed. Pt. 10**).

(d) **Calcification** - due to previous tuberculosis may have a similar effect (Illus. **ANATOMY, Pt. 6**).

The line depends upon the interface between the air-filled lung (mainly right) and the pleura lying in front of the spine, where on each side it contacts the posterior junction line (see ps. 1.14 to 1.16). It may be accentuated in patients with emphysema (older people, and with a left sided collapse which deviates the azygo-oesophageal recess to the left). It is lost with adjacent lung consolidation or pleural fluid. At the level of the azygos vein (T4 or T5) the line is interrupted, unless there is an azygos lobe, or the left lung continues the line.

Air in the oesophagus may mimic a widened stripe, and this is usually the cause if air is seen to pass through the level of the aortic and azygos arches, rather than only being present below and above.

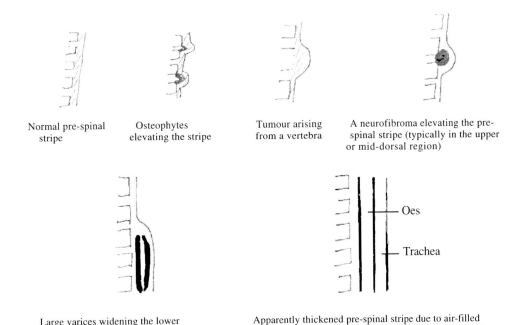

Normal pre-spinal stripe	Osteophytes elevating the stripe	Tumour arising from a vertebra	A neurofibroma elevating the pre-spinal stripe (typically in the upper or mid-dorsal region)

Large varices widening the lower part of the pre-spinal stripe

Apparently thickened pre-spinal stripe due to air-filled oesophagus (will often be a tracheo-oes. stripe as well).

Fig. 18.10   Prespinal stripes and some abnormalities.

Posterior para-spinal lines, para-spinal swellings and vertebral disease (see also p. 13.29).

   The posterior para-spinal lines   (spinal or para-vertebral lines) are present on both sides, but the left is usually more easily seen, especially between the level of the arch and the diaphragm. Like other mediastinal lines, their visualisation depends on aerated lung adjacent to the pleura; thus adjacent consolidation in the upper or lower lobes will obliterate part or all of the line on that side.

   These lines were first studied anatomically by Lachman (1942). Subsequent authors (Garland, 1942 & 1943, Brailsford, 1943, Billing, 1946, Dalton and Schwartz, 1956, Fraser and Paré, 1977 and Gupta and Mohan, 1979) thought that the lines were produced by the tangential projection of the lung/pleural borders overlying the mediastinal fat, spine, etc. Other (e.g. Heitzman, 1977 and Généreux, (1983a) wondered if they were Mach bands (see Appx. 3) i.e. optical edge enhancing phenomena formed by the lung-mediastinal interface, and produced in the viewing eye by strong differences in transmitted illumination. In support of this it was argued that a pleural effusion, adjacent to the spine on a supine view, should make the line thicker (but to the author this view seems illogical, as the line would tend to move this laterally and not efface it). Also Mach band formation is optimal when differences in transmitted light are made by structures whose surfaces are orientated at angles of less than 90⁰ (namely convex and concave surfaces). Such may happen in the posterior mediastinum, where the lung-mediastinal interface is usually concave, so that the eye may enhance it by forming a positive (white) Mach band, whilst the lung-descending aortic interface (the para-aortic line) tends to form a negative (black) Mach band. Heitzman (1988) pointed out their loss or partial loss, will indicate the presence of disease.

   Doyle et al. (1961) studying the 'left paravertebral shadow' concluded that it seemed to be formed by the pleural reflection between the descending aorta and the vertebral column. They noted that it may be displaced laterally by osteophytes, dilated azygos and hemi-azygos veins or by thoracic kyphosis.

   Probably the most common posterior mediastinal swelling is a **tortuous** and/or **dilated descending aorta**. Such may displace and distort the para-aortic, para-oesophageal and para-spinal lines (Chapter 1). (Note also that spinal bony spurs appear to be more common on the right, it being suggested that pulsations from a normal or dilated aorta will tend to prevent their development on the left - Goldberg and Carter, 1978) - see also Illus. **SPINE LIPPING**.

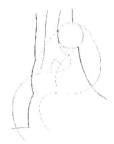

Fig. 18.11 A very tortuous aorta may displace the mediastinal lines (after Rémy et al, 1981. Le Poumon Pathologique, by permission) - see also Ohara and Tanno, 1958 and p. 10.6.

The left para-spinal line turns medially in its upper part at the level of the aortic arch, sometimes with quite a sharp angle, where it crosses the left superior intercostal vein.

The spine.

Brailsford (1943) noted that lateral displacement of the lines was commonly caused by an abscess or tumour originating in the vertebrae. He also noted that with infection the cartilaginous intervertebral disc (between the affected vertebrae) was usually reduced in height, and therefore severely damaged, whereas with tumours discs showed considerable resistance to tumour invasion. Erosion of discs does not always occur with infection, and in Asians TB not uncommonly leaves the discs intact, the infection 'creeping' around them into adjacent vertebrae and/or producing para-spinal abscesses. Secondary tumour deposits tend to affect multiple vertebrae, and partial collapse of a vertebra on one side may simulate disc narrowing (or cause squashing) as seen on lateral views.

Paus (1973) found almost as many discs were reduced in height with tumours as with infection and stressed that clinical history and laboratory tests were important plus needle or larger biopsy.

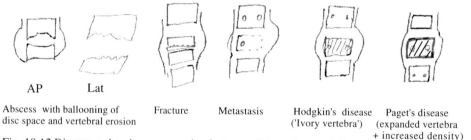

AP	Lat			
Abscess with ballooning of disc space and vertebral erosion		Fracture	Metastasis	Hodgkin's disease ('Ivory vertebra')	Paget's disease (expanded vertebra + increased density)

Fig. 18.12 Diagrams showing some major features of thoracic spinal disease.

Tumour seems very likely if a pedicle is destroyed and inflammatory disease if there is an acute change in the vertebral axis, para-spinal bulging and reduction in disc height. In the 1990s metastatic tumour is much more frequently seen than infection, and with common tumours such as the breast, prostate or oat cell lung cancer, multiple deposits may be found, often grouped together in the dorsal spine and adjacent ribs, being especially demonstrated by isotope lung scans, CT or MR studies. There may be extra-vertebral extension with some tumours, particularly myelomatosis (which may only show a 'rim' uptake with isotopes). MR of vertebral body plasmacytomas may show a 'mini-brain' appearance (Major et al., 2000).

A haematoma e.g. from a fractured vertebra or a leaking traumatic or other aortic aneurysm (see Brailsford, 1943 and Peters and Gamsu, 1980) may also produce a para-vertebral swelling (Illus. **SPINE TRAUMA, Pt. 2f & g**). Dennis and Rogers (1989) also noted that superior mediastinal widening may occur from spinal fractures mimicking aortic rupture on chest radiographs (lower cervical and upper dorsal spine in 54 patients). Similar findings may occur with a leak tracking from the oesophagus. Less marked swellings may sometimes be seen with non-tuberculous abscesses (e.g. typhoid, salmonella, brucella, etc.) osteomyelitis or even osteochondritis (Scheuermann's disease) in the acute phase. Even Paget's disease with enlargement of the dorsal vertebrae may displace the posterior spinal lines laterally.

A big problem remains in differentiating an osteoporotic fracture, with a haematoma, from a secondary deposit. Usually time suffices by symptoms subsiding, but a quicker result may be a reducing signal on serial T2 MR studies, which will support a resolving haematoma.

Occasionally one may still find long-standing or more acute cases of vertebral tuberculosis and the author has encountered several cases, initially considered to be tumour deposits. CT has aided the diagnosis by demonstrating destruction, calcification and abscess (including psoas abscess) formation. Cases are shown in Illus. **SPINE TB** - see especially **TB bone, Pt. 8a-c** (an old lady with TB spine who was referred from another hospital for radiotherapy), **TB Asian, Pt. 1a-f** (an Arab medical student with a gross para-spinal abscess) and **TB bone Pt. 10a-e,** (a young Asian female with spinal TB). Non-tuberculous vertebral osteomyelitis may also present with an insidious onset, and show para-spinal swellings, pulmonary infiltrates and/or pleural effusions, often accompanied by back pain and vertebral tenderness.

Lateral displacement of the para-spinal lines, as by an intra-thoracic para-spinal abscess, is often recognised by its **'plumber's joint'** appearance (Fig. 18.13a - see also Illus. **PLUMBER'S JOINT SIGN**). When the main part of the disease is low down, in the lower chest or upper abdomen, only the upper part of it will displace the para-spinal lines producing the **'iceberg sign'** (Fig. 18.13b - see also Illus. **ICEBERG SIGN**).

Whalen et al. (1983) reviewed nine cases of spinal TB and, in 1985, 16 cases of non-tuberculous spinal infection (S. aureus, proteus, E. coli and actinomycosis), 15 had epidural abscesses, 10 bone destruction involving a vertebral body or lamina and 5 paraspinal collections. Other findings included pleural effusions, sinuses or fistulae to the oesophagus.

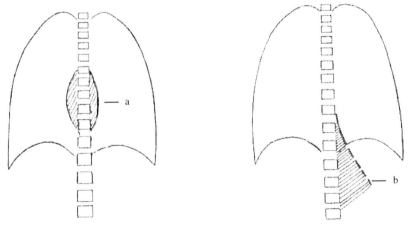

(a) The **'Plumber's joint sign'** (like a 'wiped' lead-pipe joint) indicates an intra-thoracic para-spinal mass. (Note the inferior tapering as well as that seen superiorly). This sign may be present on one, or both sides depending on the extent of the lesion.

(b) **'Iceberg sign'** implies a para-vertebral mass (tumour, nodes or abscess) extending down into the abdomen, where it is not so visible, as there is no air-filled lung to outline it there. It may also be seen with thoraco-abdominal aneurysms, and be simulated by azygos continuation of the IVC. (Note also retro-crural space and nodes p. 15.10).

Fig. 18.13 'Plumber's joint' and 'iceberg' signs of para-spinal masses, (b) after Rémy et al., 1981, Le Poumon Pathologique, by permission.

References - **'iceberg sign'**.
Rémy et al (1981) : Only the 'tip of the iceberg' is seen, the ballooned-out and larger part being intra-abdominal.
Felson (1973) : Termed this 'the thoraco-abdominal sign'.

Eklöf and Gooding (1967) : It may be a sign of upward extension of childhood neuroblastoma (see also p. 18.36)

Intervertebral discs.

These may be secondarily affected by local disease in the adjacent vertebrae, especially fractures and infection (TB or other infections - infection may also arise in discs). Neoplasms in the vertebrae usually spare the intevening disc. Degenerative conditions are common and may be very severe in rheumatoid, secondary amyloid or haemochromatosis. Calcification may be generalised as in ochronosis (porphyria) or be localised - with the latter beware of the possibility of a prolapsed dorsal disc with posteriorly displaced calcification causing cord compression and progressing to paraplegia. In ankylosing spondylitis fractures tend to pass through the disc space (see p. 19.90) and pseudarthroses may develop.

Examples of disc disease are shown under Illus. **INTERVERT DISCS.**

Nodal enlargements.

Pre-and para-vertebral nodal enlargements not uncommonly displace the para-spinal lines (as noted by Dalton and Schwartz, 1956, Witten et al., 1965, Gupta and Mohan, 1979, Efremedis et al., 1981), sometimes producing the signs noted above, but also others. A rather bizarre one appears to show the origins of the psoas muscles arising in the lower dorsal regions, rather than in the lumbar. Illus. **ICEBERG SIGN, Hodgkin's dis Pt. 21a & b** illustrate these points.

Neural tumours and meningocoeles.

These may also displace the para-spinal (and pre-spinal) lines. They are commonly associated with pressure erosions on the adjacent vertebrae or with bony defects due to connections with the theca (see also ps. 18.35 - and Illus. **PARASPINAL LINES, Meningocoele lat thor** and **Neurofibroma Pts. 9, 10, 19, 26, 33, 34, 36 & 41**).

Fat, oedema, haematomas and extramedullary haemopoiesis.

These can also displace the lines, the history (or lack of anything relevant) often suggesting the correct cause.

Extramedullary haemopoiesis occurs mainly with thalassaemia*, but can also occur with sickle cell disease, polycythaemia, myelofibrosis, pernicious anaemia, bone marrow transplantation, rickets, hepatic failure, severe Paget's disease (if the bone cortex bursts), lymphoma, leukaemia myeloid metaplasia, hereditary lipocytosis (with fatty replacement of erythropoietic tissue), tumour deposits severely and chronically involving the bone marrow, and following septicaemia. The erythrocyte producing masses commonly occur in the **posterior mediastinum**, but may also be found in other tissues, including the liver, spleen and lymph nodes, where they may mimic secondary tumour deposits, and the kidneys, adrenals, brain, lung, breast, thymus, presacral area, etc. where they may mimic primary tumours. Mostly they are incidental findings, but in confined spaces such as the spinal canal, they are of considerable diagnostic and clinical importance. Carbimazole and/or radiotherapy may readily cause their shrinkage.

In many cases, CT will show medullary tissue extending out of the ribs or vertebrae (see also ps. 12.27 - 28). The extra-medullary tissue may also be imaged by colloid isotope scans (Bronn et al., 1980), or MR (Savader et al., 1988). Such soft tissue masses may be associated with haemothoraces (Smith, P. et al., 1988, Kupferschmid et al., 1993, & Chu et al., 1999).

* 'Mediterranean anaemia' (the commonest group of inherited haemoglobinopathies) in which foetal type haemoglobins persist, which carry less oxygen. This leads to increased haemopoiesis and marrow hypertrophy, causing bone changes (Illus. **THALASSAEMIA**). Some have a trait, but those with the full syndrome do not live beyond childhood, and a number die from hepatic haemosiderosis as a result of iron overload from repeated red cell transfusions. A chelating agent is now being used to help reduce this. Iron overload may be detected by MR of the liver (see Ooi et al., 1999).

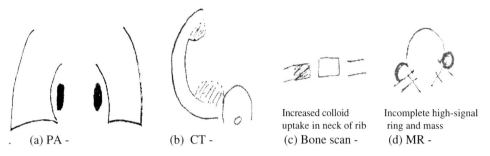

Increased colloid
uptake in neck of rib

Incomplete high-signal
ring and mass

. (a) PA -   (b) CT -   (c) Bone scan -   (d) MR -

Fig. 18.14   Extra-medullary haemopoietic masses arising from the inner anterior and posterior aspects of the ribs in thalassaemia (or fibro-fatty tissue in lipocytosis - see p. 6.14) - see also Illus. **EXTRAMED HAEMOPOIESIS**. Such masses may also be replaced by fat (Yamato and Furhman, 1987).

Dilated veins and varices in the posterior mediastinum.

The para-spinal lines may also be displaced by dilatations of the azygos and hemiazygos veins and their tributaries, which often extend around the lateral aspects of the spine. Garland (1942) noted that 'in a significant number of persons the azygos vein is small and the hemiazygos vein assumes a portion of its function in venous drainage. In this group the enlarged and elongated hemiazygos vein may cast its shadow to the left of the spine to produce the vertical linear shadow' of the left para-spinal line. Venous dilatations may also occur following vena caval thrombosis or ligation, or in pregnancy. (Castellino et al., 1968 noted that such dilatations may present as paravertebral intrathoracic masses). Such venous dilatations may be associated with varices (see also **'downhill varices'** p. 9.10). Examples are shown in Illus. **VARICES, Syph. varic Pt. 11a-h** and **Oes varices Pt. 6a-c**.

Ishikawa et al. (1980 & 1985) studied over 350 cases of portal hypertension and noted that such masses due to varices may be seen on plain radiographs in the mediastinum, alongside the descending aorta (obliterating its outline) and in the inferior pulmonary ligament. They also performed CT or vascular studies, and found that CT confirmed enhancing venous structures in the lower mediastinum, inferior pulmonary ligament, the oesophageal or gastric walls, the gastro-hepatic ligament, and the retroperitoneal or para-umbilical regions.

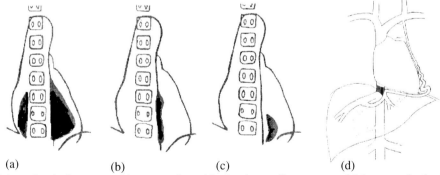

(a)   (b)   (c)   (d)

(a) mediastinal masses, (b) masses alongside the descending aorta, and (c) masses in the inferior phrenic ligament.   (d) para-cardiac mass caused by a dilated paracardiophrenic vein.

Fig.18.15   Plain film findings of para-oesophageal and para-cardiac varices:
(a to c - reproduced from Ishikawa et al., 1985, AJR, **144**, 701 - 704, and d reproduced from Chung et al., 1993, AJR, **160**, 25 - 28 with permission).

Further references.

General
Proto and Speckman (1979 & 1980) : Left lateral radiograph of the chest.
Heitzman (1981, 1984 & 1993) : The Mediastinum.
Lund and Lein (1982 & 1983) : Abnormalities of the azygo-oesophageal recess.
Rémy et al. (1975) : The retrocardiac mediastinum on the frontal chest radiograph.
Schulman et al. (1982) : Mediastinal gas will accentuate the para-spinal lines.
Gaisie and Oh (1983) : Para-spinal lines in children studied by CT.
Lien and Kolbenstvedt (1982) and Lien et al. (1984) : Normal and abnormal thoracic para-spinal shadows.

Spine
Allen et al. (1978) : Radiological changes in infections of the spine and their diagnostic value.
Horn and Byrd (1978) : Simulation of pleural disease by disc space infection.
Bloom et al. (1980) : Pleuro-pulmonary complications of thoracic vertebral osteomyelitis. In the pre-antibiotic era this was often complicated by mediastinal abscesses, empyema, necrotising empyema, etc.
Jain et al. (1993) : CT of vertebral TB - four patterns of bone destruction - fragmentary, osteolytic, and well-defined lytic with sclerotic margins.

Varices
Doyle et al. (1961) : The mediastinum in portal hypertension.
Moult et al. (1975) : Posterior mediastinal masses in patients with portal hypertension.
Clark et al. (1980) : CT of oesophageal and abdominal varices.
Balthazar et al. (1984) : CT recognition of gastric varices.
Millward, S. et al. (1985) : Pericardial varices shown by CT.
Ahn et al. (1997) : Venographic appearance of porto-systemic collateral pathways.

Fat   (see also p. 6.12 - 18)
Streiter et al. (1982) : Para-spinal fat.
Williams et al. (1993) : Intraosseous lipomas - 3 cases in vertebral bodies and 1 in pelvis - well defined expansile lesions - may be partly sclerotic - negative on isotope bone scan - asymptomatic.

Extramedullary haemopoiesis
Knoblich (1960) : Presentation with intrathoracic tumours - case report of case with thalassaemia minor.
Lowman et al. (1963) : Thoracic Roentgen manifestations
Sorsdahl et al. (1964) : Extramed. haemopoiesis causing mediastinal masses + spinal cord compression in 2 brothers.
Condon et al. (1965) : Exctramedullary haemopoiesis simulating intrathoracic tumour.
Papavasiliou (1965) : Tumour simulating extramedullary haemopoiesis.
Ross and Logan (1969) : Roentgen findings in extramedullary haemopoiesis.
Da Costa et al. (1974) : Extramedullary haemopoiesis with multiple tumour-stimulating mediastinal masses in haemoglobin E-thalassaemia disease.
Heitzman (1977) : Extramedullary haemopoiesis.
Cromwell and Kerber (1978) : Spinal cord compression by extramedullary haemopoiesis in agnogenic myeloid metaplasia. Contrary to previous reports in the literature (Ross and Logan) a lobulated, well-rounded, well-demarcated soft-tissue density in the posterior mediastinum is not necessary for the radiographic diagnosis.
Long et al. (1980) : CT of thoracic extramedullary haemopoiesis.
Faloppa et al. (1981) : Evaluation of thoracic extramedullary haemopoiesis by conventional radiography and CT.
Lawson et al. (1981) : The ribs in thalassaemia.
Shaver and Clore (1981) : Extramedullary haemopoiesis in myeloid metaplasia.
Danza et al. (1982) : Extramedullary hematopoiesis.
Heffez et al. (1982) : Spinal epidural extramedullary haemopoiesis with spinal cord compression in a patient with refractory sideroblastic anaemia.
Crawford et al. (1984) : Spinal cord compression by extramedullary haematopoiesis.
Sulis and Floris (1985) : Haemothorax due to extramedullary erythropoiesis in thalassaemia intermedia.
Gumbs et al. (1987) : Extramedullary haemopoiesis in sickle cell disease.
King et al. (1987) : Extramedullary haematopoiesis in the adrenal glands - CT characteristics.
Mann et al. (1987) : Paraplegia due to extramedullary haematopoiesis in thalassaemia.
Savader et al. (1988) : MR imaging of intra-thoracic extramedullary haematopoiesis.
Smith et al. (1988) : Massive haemothorax due to extramedullary haematopoiesis in a patient with thalassaemia,
Jackson and Burton (1989) : Spinal cord compression with extramedullary haemopoiesis in polycythaemia rubra vera.
Muthuswamy et al. (1989) : Extramedullary haematopoiesis simulating post-traumatic intrathoracic haemorrhage.

Singcharoen (1989) : Unusual long bone changes in thalassaemia, findings on plain radiography and CT (gives good illustration of intra-thoracic masses arising from the ribs).
Martin et al. (1990) : Fatty transformation of thoracic extramedullary haematopoiesis following splenectomy.
Papavasiliou et al. (1990) : CT and MRI of symptomatic spinal involvement by extramedullary haemopoiesis (5 cases - 4 with thalassaemia and 1 sickle disease).
Wright, R. (1991) : Pararenal extramedullary haematopoietic tissue - an unusual form of **myelofibrosis**.
Zonderland et al. (1991) : Extramedullary haematopoiesis of the breast.
Adams et al. (1995) : Fe^{52} imaging of intrathoracic extramedullary haematopoiesis in β-thalassaemia. [NB Fe^{52} is superior to In^{111} & sulphur colloid in that it accumulates in erythropoietically active tissue - it may be imaged with a high energy collimator or PET].
Wong et al. (1999) : Imaging features of focal intrahepatic extramedullary haematopoiesis - noted 'stellate' structures within the masses - also gave references to another 9 cases of focal liver lesions.

Neural tumours.
   Neural tumours account for about 80% of posterior mediastinal masses and may occur per se or as part of a more generalised condition. They are not uncommonly found as chance findings in young or middle aged adult females, on chest or spinal radiographs. Those arising on the sympathetic chains or intercostal nerves are usually asymptomatic. Those arising within the spinal canal or a neural foramen may be difficult to recognise, but are very important as they may lead to spinal cord compression.
   Neurofibromatosis (often termed von Recklinghausen's disease after his original description in 1882) is an hereditary autosomal dominant condition, in which patients have café au lait spots (brown macules with sharp borders, in contrast with those in fibrous dysplasia, which are irregular), freckling of the axillae, Lisch nodules (pigmented iris hamartomata - visible with the slit lamp in many cases), skin lesions such as fibrosum molluscum or cutaneous neurofibromas (which may be sessile or pedunculated, vary considerably in size, at times grow quickly and may be sarcomatous) , as well as neuromas on multiple nerves. Some patients have bone lesions, with porotic, hypoplastic or lytic areas, thinned bones ('**twisted   ribbon   ribs**'), kyphoscoliosis, hemivertebrae, pseudarthrosis, bowing, cyst formation, spontaneous fractures or an appearance similar to fibrous dysplasia (see Illus. **RIB   FIBROUS   DYSPLASIA**). In addition cortical or intra-medullary sclerosis may be found. Some develop optic nerve gliomas, cerebral and cerebellar astrocytomas, meningocoeles, meningeomas, gliomas of the brain and spinal cord, or sarcomas of the peripheral nerves. Acoustic neuromata, previously thought to be related, now appear to be a separate and unrelated entity controlled by a different gene (Huson, 1987). The lungs may be affected by an **interstitial   fibrosis** resembling fibrosing alveolitis (see also Massaro, 1966, Patechefsky et al. , 1973, Webb and Goodman, 1977).
   Some patients with neurofibromatosis may have phaeochromocytomas (up to 5% - see below) or renal artery stenosis, both a cause of hypertension and hyperparathyroidism - '**Sipple's syndrome**' (Sipple, 1961). Phaeochromocytomas associated with medullary carcinoma of the thyroid may also be associated with multiple mucosal neuromas (Gorlin et al., 1968) or with neurofibromatosis (Schimke et al. , 1968). Non-ossifying fibromas may also occur.
   When skin or subcutaneous nodules overlie the thorax, they may cast soft tissue shadows over the lungs, simulating pulmonary metastases -sometimes termed the '**button   sign**' (Miller et al., 1957 who painted them with barium for confirmation). Illus. **NEUROFIBROMA,   Pt.   31** shows subcutaneous neurofibromata especially overlying the left lung base, whilst Illus. **NEUROFIBROMA,   Pts.   1a-c** & **38a-b** show neurofibromata in the chest wall, the lungs and subcutaneously.
   The **plexiform   neuroma** is an important entity because it is often disfiguring and may cause severe symptoms and pain. It may involve the face, mouth, limbs, neck and trunk. A bizarrely arranged network of enlarged nerves infiltrates adjacent fat and muscle. When the enlargement is great it is sometimes referred to as '**elephantiasis   neuromatosa**', which particularly affects the lower limbs with complicating bony and skin involvement. A similar condition may affect the mediastinum (see Illus. **NEUROFIBROMA,   Pt.   11a-c**). Chalmers and Armstrong (1977) reported two such cases in children causing marked lobulated and mainly superior mediastinal swellings. Bourgouin et al. (1988) studied four patients with plexiform neurofibromatosis of the mediastinum by CT and showed the infiltrative processes and masses that involved the mediastinum along the distribution of the sympathetic chains, phrenic and vagus nerves. The

lesions were less dense than muscle (due to their lipid content or cystic degeneration). Peripheral contrast enhancement was seen in one case. Illus. **NEUROFIBROMA, Pt. 20a-b** shows a non-enhancing neurofibroma with an angioma and slight enhancement on CT is shown in Illus. **NEUROFIBROMA, Pt. 36.**

The **benign neuromas** include **neurofibromas** (which diffusely expand the parent nerve), **schwannomas** (or **neurilemmomas** - tumours of the nerve sheaths, which may occasionally become malignant, and which form lateral masses on the parent nerves), and **ganglioneuromas** (particularly of the sympathetic chains). Such neuromas may arise on any of the nerves which pass into or through the thorax, but most commonly are found on the sympathetic chains and intercostal nerves. The vagi (including the recurrent laryngeal nerves) may produce single or multiple neuromas (see below), but the phrenic nerves are rarely so affected.

When neuromas arise on the intercostal nerves, they tend to produce pressure erosions or notchings on the rib above (the nerve lies just below the rib - see Illus. **NEUROFIBROMA, Pts. 3, 19, 26, 28, 30 & 33** and p. 12.20). With neurofibromatosis the ribs may exhibit multiple notches. Like other tumours arising in the chest wall, they tend to push into the thorax, more than outwards, presumably as a result of the negative intrathoracic pressure with respiration.

Tumours arising on nerve roots may cause distortion of a vertebral pedicle, widening of an inter-vertebral foramen, scalloping of the posterior aspect of a vertebral body, or spinal cord compression (Illus. **NEUROFIBROMA, Pts. 17, 27 & 29**). 'Dumb-bell tumours' may be present if a neuroma lies partly within the spinal canal, and partly within the thoracic cavity. Rarely they may be mimicked by a **lateral thoracic meningocoele** (see below).

Most **neuromas** are spherical or ovoid in shape and most have smooth outlines. Calcification within them in uncommon, but when present tends to be patchy in type. An accompanying pleural effusion may suggest malignancy, but may also be seen accompanying some large tumours (Illus. **NEUROFIBROMA, Pt. 18a-b**).

Frequency of the various types - In a series reported by Reed et al. (1978) who collected 160 cases in the US armed forces, the distribution was as follow, 25% ganglioneuromas, 10% neurofibromas, 15% neuroblastomas, and 2% paragangliomas.

CT of neural tumours.

Although most neural tumours are less dense than muscle on CT sections, a few are denser, and some show some enhancement with contrast media (Illus. **NEUROFIBROMA, Pt. 36a-d**). CT does not really distinguish between **neurofibromas** and **schwannomas.** Both cause masses which are usually of lower density than muscle (due to fluid or fat within them and sometimes with cystic spaces or necrosis) , but some **neurofibromas** (because of their collagen content) may have a similar density to muscle. When they are of particularly low density, differentiation from a cyst or a meningocoele may be difficult (see also section below). The low attenuation in **plexiform neurofibromatosis** is related to the presence of lipid-containing Schwann cells and the entrapment of perineural adipose tissue.

Neurofibromas of the vagi are not very rare, and the vagi are probably the third most common site for neurofibromas to arise in the chest (after intercostal nerves and the sympathetic chains). Some appear as masses in the aorto-pulmonary window or just lateral to the aortic arch.

The author has seen several cases, four of which are illustrated (i) Illus. **NEUROFIB-VAGI, Pt. 45**) multiple neurofibromata causing widening of the upper mediastinum, (ii) Illus. **NEUROFIB-VAGI, Pt. 46** arising from the left recurrent laryngeal nerve in the aorto-pulmonary window, and (iii) Illus. **NEUROFIB-VAGI, Pt. 47** involving the intrathoracic vagi only and extending down into the mesentery (in a young man in whom it mimicked Hodgkin's disease, (iv) Illus. **NEUROFIBROMA, Pt. 11a-b** multiple neurofibromatosis of the intercostal nerves and vagi (in a middle aged man - one in the right upper chest later became malignant). Other reported cases are given in the references below.

Malignant types - (Illus. **NEUROFIB-MALIG**).

Neurosarcomas may arise independently, or in neuromas, especially in patients with neurofibromatosis. They may also arise in cutaneous **plexiform neuromas.** The latter are often very painful, and the tumours may recur locally after resection, and metastasise particularly to the lungs. Probably about 5% become malignant in these conditions. Clinical suspicion should be aroused with pain or progressive enlargement. Illus. **NEUROFIBROMA, Pt. 11a-c** shows a patient with multiple neuromata causing mediastinal widening in a patient with neurofibromatosis of the upper chest; these later caused SVC and oesophageal obstruction due to malignant change. A case with secondary deposits from a lower limb neurinoma, which had undergone sarcomatous change, is shown in Illus. **NEUROFIBROMA, Pt. 48a-c**.

Patel and Morehouse (1982) stressed the value of both angiography and CT to study neurofibrosarcomas, with fine capillary 'neovascularity' giving a well-defined blush in the capillary phase of an angiogram or with contrast enhanced CT.

Neuroblastomas are malignant tumours of the **sympathetic nervous system, adrenals**, the mediastinum or the retroperitoneum down to the pelvis. They occur mainly in young children and these are now potentially curable. A few occur in young adults, but these have a poorer prognosis. A similar tumour is the **ganglioneuroblastoma**. Both may produce paraspinal, posterior or middle mediastinal, retroperitoneal, adrenal or pelvic masses, which may be confused with lymphomas. Radiologically these tumours mimic neurofibromas, but the masses can be quite large. The most common primary site is in the mediastinum or the retro-crural area, but a multi-focal presentation is not uncommon. The tumours may contain patchy calcification as may their metastases. Malignant **schwannomas** are occasionally found.

Pulmonary neurogenic tumours.

These are rare and the author has only seen a single case of one occurring within a lingula bronchus. It recurred twice following local surgery - Illus. **NEUROFIB-ENDOBRON, Neurofib Pt. 7.** Pulmonary neurofibromas are shown in Illus. **NEUROFIBROMA, 1a-c.** Roviaro et al. (1983) from Italy found four cases (in a series of 1664 neurogenic tumours); three were neurilemmomas, and one a malignant schwannoma (the patient dying from metastases four months after surgery). See also under references below.

Lateral thoracic meningocoeles

Lateral thoracic meningocoeles may mimic neural tumours or be associated with them in patients with neurofibromatosis. Although benign they tend to recur following surgery, They present as discrete masses in the intra-thoracic paravertebral region. They are often accompanied by scoliosis, with the concavity on the side of the mass. They may show transmitted pulsation on fluoroscopy. Myelography with gas or water soluble contrast has been used to show the communication with the CSF. CT has shown that small meningocoeles are not uncommon in the lumbar regions of patients with neurofibromatosis; these are often bilateral and are usually asymptomatic.

An example of a recurring lateral thoracic meningocoele is shown in Illus. **MENINGOCOELE LAT THORACIC.**

Paragangliomas and chemodectomas of the thorax.

Chemodectomas (or ectopic phaeochromocytomas) may arise not only in the head and neck (in the jugular fossae or carotid bodies) but also in the thorax. These are uncommon tumours and may arise in a number of sites, the sympathetic chains (usually the upper parts), in the aortic or pulmonary bodies, or similar pressure receptors in the walls of these vessels or in the walls of the subclavian or coronary arteries or the inter-atrial ganglia. They may produce quite large masses, which are very vascular and tend to bleed after biopsy. Hypertension may be a clinical feature, particularly in young adults.

Their vascular nature may be demonstrated by angiography or dynamic CT. When they occur in a sympathetic chain or the vagi, they may resemble a neurofibroma, and an 'apparent neurofibroma' associated with sustained or paroxysmal hypertension in e.g. a young man should always make one think of this possible cause. (The author has seen such a case in a 19 year old with a clearly defined small mass at the left apex). Neural tumours and phaeochromocytomas may occur together, and be a part of a multiglandular syndrome in association with adrenal abnormalities (the 'type one' syndrome - 'type two' is associated with medullary thyroid tumours - see p. 18.9).

Only about 2% of phaeochromocytomas arise in the chest, 90% arising in the adrenals, and the remaining 8% being ectopic in the abdomen (mostly in sympathetic nerve tissue). Some may have a multicentric origin (Haber, 1964).

The use of isotopes for diagnosis and treatment of these tumours is discussed on ps. 22.12-13.

The Carney syndrome is discussed on p. 5.17.

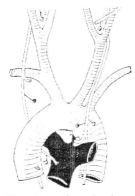

Neurofibromas or gangliomas of the sympathetic trunk

Fig. 18.16. (a) Aortic and pulmonary bodies. (after Berk, 1961, with permission from Clinical Radiology).

(b) These tumours arise as smooth rounded soft-tissue masses on the antero-lateral aspect of a vertebral body and occasionally contain calcification.

Illus. **CHEMODECTOMA, Pt. 3a-e** shows a chemodectoma arising in an aortic body, and Illus. **CHEMODECTOMA, Pt. 4a-c** a chemodectoma arising in a pulmonary body - see also Illus. **PHAEOCHROMOCYTOMA**.

Further references.
(a) **Neurofibromatosis** (general).
Westcott, R. and Ackerman (1947) : Elephantiasis neuromatosa.
Holt and Wright (1948) : Radiologic features of neurofibromatosis.
Levin (1958) : Neurofibromatosis - clinical and Roentgen manifestations.
Carey et al. (1960) : Neurogenic tumours of the mediastinum.
Barrett and Toye (1960) : Neurogenic tumours of the mediastinum.
Hunt and Pugh (1961) : Skeletal lesions in neurofibromatosis.
Bloor and Williams (1963) : Neurofibromatosis and coarctation of the abdominal aorta with renal artery involvement.
Loop et al. (1965) : Acquired thoracic abnormalities in neurofibromatosis.
Meszaros (1966) : Neurofibromatosis.
Perez et al. (1967) : Tumours of the sympathetic nervous system in children.
Sane et al. (1971) : Subperiosteal or cortical cyst and intramedullary neurofibromatosis.
Neiman et al. (1974) : Neurofibromatosis and congenital heart disease.
Itzchak et al. (1974) : Angiographic features of arterial lesions in neurofibromatosis - renal artery stenosis, abdominal aortic coarctation or multiple arterial stenoses.
Butchart et al. (1975) : Spontaneous rupture of an intercostal artery complicating neurofibromatosis and scoliosis.
Klatte et al. (1976) : Radiographic spectrum of neurofibromatosis.
Casselman et al. (1977) : von Recklinghausen's disease - incidence of Roentgen findings.
Beggs et al. (1981) : Neurofibromatosis, cystic bone lesions and aortic coarctation - case report (also quote 2nd case).
Francis and Glazer (1983) : Peripheral neurofibromatosis.
Kittredge et al. (1983) : CT of thoracic prevertebral and paravertebral spaces.
Aughenbaugh (1984) : Thoracic manifestations of neurocutaneous diseases.
Sampson et al. (1991) : Painless thoracic scoliosis due to dumb-bell ganglioneuroma - CT and MR appearances.
Jones et al. (1993) : Painful transthoracic needle biopsy - a sign of neurogenic tumour - two cases.
Beall and Kolk (1997) : Giant dorsal neurofibroma in a 26 yr. old male spreading across his back - MR study.
Peh et al. (1997) : MR imaging of subcutaneous diffuse neurofibroma.
Rossi et al. (1999) : Thoracic manifestations of neurofibromatosis.

Herron et al. (2000) : Intracranial manifestations of the neurocutaneous syndromes - neurofibromatosis and other phakomatoses.
Curtis and Lewis-Jones (2000) : Bilateral acoustic schwannomas and multiple ependymomas of the spinal canal.

(b) Neurofibromatosis (of vagi, lung and bronchi).

Strickland and Wolverson (1974) : Studied 24 patients with neurofibromas of the vagi (3 of their own and 21 from the literature - 12 L sided and 6 R sided) - most were located in the superior mediastinum, especially on the left. One patient had bilateral tumours. Pathological confirmation was obtained in 21 - 14 had neurofibromas (8 patients having neurofibromatosis) and 7 schwannomas but all but one of the left sided tumours (18) had a close relationship to the aortic arch, the exception being one which encircled the oesophagus just above the diaphragm. Those arising from the right vagus (6) largely made a localised bulge in the mediastinum.
Whalen et al. (1975) : Noted that a neurinoma of the vagus occurring in the upper mediastinum lies between the innominate vein and the trachea and does not displace the retrosternal line (see p. 1.27 - 29).

Strauss and Guckien (1951) : Schwannoma of the tracheobronchial tree - case report and review of the literature.
Bartley and Arean (1965) : Intrapulmonary neurogenic tumours.
Newman and So (1971) : Bilateral neurofibroma of vagi associated with neurofibromatosis.
Strickland and Wolverson (1974) : 3 pts. with vagal tumours and a review of others.
Ross et al. (1982) : Neurofibromatosis of vagi compressing the bronchi - CT (pt. with generalised disease).
Foster, P. et al. (1987) : Achalasia like disorders in Von Recklinghausen's disease.
Malik et al. (1987) : Intrabronchial Schwannoma.
Ikezoe et al. (1989) : CT revealed the atypical localisation of a benign mediastinal tumour - a vagal nerve neuroma.
Dabir et al. (1990) : Intrathoracic tumours of the vagus nerve.
Lee et al. (1991) : Described four patients with mediastinal tumours involving the intrathoracic vagus and phrenic nerves, one having plexiform neurofibromata involving both vagi and phrenic nerves. The other three had neurofibromata appearing as (i) a round mass in the right upper mediastinum in the retrocaval paratracheal area with multiple low attenuation areas, (ii) an ovoid mixed density on the lateral aspect of the aortic arch and (iii) a large round mass with low attenuation areas in the right mid mediastinum abutting the oesophagus (this was a large round mass with low attenuation areas within it).
Chow et al. (1993) : Intrathoracic vagus nerve neurofibroma and sudden death in a patient with neurofibromatosis.

(c) Neurofibromatosis and lung disease.

Massaro et al. (1965) , Massaro and Katz (1966) : Fibrosing alveolitis in neurofibromatosis.
Davison (1967) : Neurofibromatosis with diffuse interstitial pulmonary fibrosis and phaeochromocytoma.
Patchefsky et al. (1973) : Interstitial pulmonary fibrosis and von Recklinghausen's disease
Webb and Goodman (1977) : Fibrosing alveolitis in patients with neurofibromatosis.
Feldhaus et al. (1989) : A rare endobronchial neurilemmoma.

(d) Neurofibromatosis and vertebral scalloping.

Mitchell et al. (1967) : The various causes of scalloped vertebrae with notes on their pathogenesis.
Salerno and Edeiken (1970) : Vertebral scalloping in neurofibromatosis.
Casselman and Mandell (1979) : Vertebral scalloping and neurofibromatosis.

(e) Neurofibromatosis and meningocoeles (esp. lateral thoracic meningocoeles).

Pohl (1933) : First description of intrathoracic meningocoele - patient has neurofibromatosis and kyphoscoliosis.
Nanson (1957) : Thoracic meningocoele associated with neurofibromatosis - reviewed 27 cases and emphasised the bony changes in the vertebrae (scalloping of bodies) and pressure changes on adjacent ribs.
LaVielle and Campbell (1958) : Neurofibromatosis and intrathoracic meningocoele.
Bunner (1959) : Lateral intrathoracic meningocoele.
Heard and Payne (1962) : Six patients with neurofibromatosis and scalloping of the posterior vertebrae who had neither meningocoele nor intraspinal tumour. They regarded the vertebral abnormalities as developmental.
Chandler and Herzberger (1963) : Lateral thoracic meningocoele.
Robinson, R. (1964) : Intrathoracic meningocoele and neurofibromatosis.
Ya Deau (1965) : 3 cases of intrathoracic meningocoeles, none of which had neurofibromatosis or kyphoscoliosis.
Edeiken et al. (1969) : Intrathoracic meningocoele.
Miles et al. (1969) : Intrathoracic meningocoele and association with neurofibromatosis.
Blewett and Szpulkski (1974) : Double unilateral intrathoracic meningocoele.
Sickles and Winestock (1974) Bilateral intrathoracic meningocoeles.
Kornberg et al. (1984) : Thoracic vertebral erosion with meningocoele in a patient with neurofibromatosis.
Weinreb et al. (1984) : CT metrizamide myelography in multiple bilateral intrathoracic meningocoeles.
Sarkar and Fagan (1991) Intrathoracic meningocoele with LUZ mass & severe bony changes in a patient with neurofibromatosis.

(f) **Chemodectomas.**
Boyd (1937) : 4 sites for aortic bodies - (i) between ductus arteriosus and descending part of aortic arch, (ii) on the R side and upper surface of pulmonary artery, (iii) lateral to innominate artery root, and (iv) on L above aortic root.
Monro (1950) : Pulmonary glomerula and their tumours, with a case of aorto-pulmonary glomus tumour.
Glushein et al. (1953) : Phaeochromocytoma - its relationship to neurocutaneous syndromes.
Barrie (1961) : Intrathoracic tumours of carotid body type.
Berk (1961) : Chemodectoma of the glomus intervagale - case report and review.
Phillips (1963) : Mediastinal chemodectoma - thoracic angiography.
Haber (1964) : Retroperitoneal and mediastinal chemodectoma - case report and review of the literature. Also pointed out that they may have a multicentric origin.
Holsti (1964) : Malignant extra-adrenal phaeochromocytoma - 5 cases, 2 metastasising and one widely infiltrating.
Davison (1967) : Neurofibromatosis with diffuse interstitial pulmonary fibrosis and phaeochromocytoma.
Grainger et al. (1967) : Egg-shall calcification as a sign of phaeochromocytoma.
Gorlin et al. (1968) : Syndrome of multiple mucosal neuromas (lips, anterior tongue, conjunctivae, nasal and laryngeal mucosa), phaeochromocytomata and medullary carcinoma of thyroid (17 cases).
Schimke et al. (1968) : Bilateral phaeochromocytomata, medullary thyroid carcinoma and multiple neuromas.
Mapp et al. (1969) : Chemodectoma of the anterior mediastinum.
Wilkinson and Forgan-Smith (1969) : Chemodectoma in relation to the aortic arch (aortic body tumour).
McNeill et al. (1970) : Intrathoracic phaeochromocytomata.
James et al. (1972) : Radiological aspects of phaeochromocytomas - 117 patients - 16 had metastatic disease to bone, lymph nodes, liver and lung.
Victor et al. (1975) : Malignant mediastinal phaeochromocytoma.
Manger and Gifford (1977) : Phaeochromocytomas.
Olson and Salyer (1978) : Four aortic body tumours.
Ogawa et al. (1982) : Functioning paraganglioma in the posterior mediastinum.
Francis et al. (1983) : CT and ^{131}I MIBG scintigraphy in diagnosing phaeochromocytomata.
Shapiro, B. et al. (1984) : The location of middle mediastinal phaeochromocytomas.
Shirkoda and Wallace (1984) : CT of juxtacardiac phaeochromocytoma.
Fisher et al. (1985) : Intrapericardial phaeochromocytoma shown by MR, ^{131}I MIBG and CT.
Sheps and Brown (1985) : Localisation of mediastinal paragangliomas.
Dunn et al. (1986) : Functioning middle mediastinal paraganglioma (phaeochromocytoma) associated with intracarotid paragangliomas.
Gerrard et al. (1987) : Imaging and treatment of disseminated neuroblastoma using ^{123}I MIBG.
Drucker et al. (1987) : CT showed a vascular mediastinal paraganglioma in a woman aged 30 - gave as differential diagnosis - **Castleman's disease, haemangioma or goitre.**
Spizarny et al. (1987) : Five chemodectomas which enhanced with IV contrast at CT - 3 intrapericardial, 1 aortic arch and 1 supra-aortic.
Bomagni et al. (1988) : Compared ^{123}I MIBG and CT in studying 27 patients with neural crest tumours, and found MIBG to be slightly more accurate in showing spread and metastatic disease.
Evora et al. (1988) : Nonfunctioning paraganglioma of the posterior mediastinum.
Flickinger et al. (1988) : Magnetic resonance imaging of mediastinal paraganglioma.
Odze and Begin (1990) : Malignant paraganglioma of the posterior mediastinum - case report and literature review.
Cornford et al. (1992) : Malignant paraganglioma of the mediastinum - diagnostic and therapeutic use of radioMIBG.
Tanaka et al. (1992) : Paraganglioma of the posterior mediastinum - value of magnetic resonance imaging.
Buckley et al. (1995) : Diaphragmatic phaeochromocytoma.
Avila et al. (1999) : Multiple extraadrenal phaeochromocytoma.

(g) **Malignant neural and other associated tumours, and CT & MR of neural tumours.**
Bar-Ziv and Norgrady (1975) : Mediastinal neuroblastoma and ganglioneuroma.
Hope and Mulvihill (1981) : Malignancy in neurofibromatosis.
Armstrong et al. (1982) : CT of neuroblastoma and ganglioneuromas in children.
Patel and Morehouse (1982) : Neurofibrosarcomas in neurofibromatosis - role of CT and angiography.
Biondetti et al. (1983) : Examined two patients with neurofibromatosis by CT, and showed in both solid and water dense lesions, the latter probably representing meningocoeles. One patient also had an acoustic neuroma. They wrote that neurofibromas appeared CT as clearly outlined rounded soft tissue masses with largely homogeneous density (30 to 40 HU) and a poorly enhancing outer rim. Sarcomas could be dense or lucent. (see also above)
Coleman et al. (1983) : Studied seven patients with neurofibrosarcomas by CT (among 24 with neurofibromatosis) and in six showed low density areas that appeared to be due to necrosis, haemorrhage and/or cystic degeneration. The density differences were enhanced by contrast agents.
Daneman et al. (1983) : CT appearance of thickened nerves in neurofibromatosis.
Kumar et al. (1983) : CT of 15 pts. with extracranial nerve sheath tumours, including 8 with neurofibromatosis, and 3 with neurofibrosarcomas. Schwannomas were less dense than muscle, neurofibromas or cysts.

Sharif and Tucker (1985) : Rare skeletal manifestations in neurofibromatosis complicated with sarcoma.

Birch and Davies (1988) : CT in elephantiasis neuromatosa (gross enlargement due to neurofibromatosis).

Bourgouin (1988) : Attenuation values of nerve sheath tumours may be isodense or hypodense compared with surrounding vasculature - the low attenuation of plexiform neurofibromatosis is related to the presence of lipid containing Schwann cells and entrapment of perineural adipose tissue.

Lee et al. (1991) : Tumours involving the vagus and phrenic nerves demonstrated by CT - see p. 18.39.

Sakai et al. (1992) : Intrathoracic neurogenic tumours - MR-pathological correlation.

Gossios and Guy (1993) : Widespread neurofibromatosis of skin, mediastinum, liver, mesentery and psoas muscles.

Ko et al. (1998) : CT findings in 36 pts. with thoracic neurilemomas - 10 tumours were isodense, & 22 slightly hyposense compared with chest wall muscle. 1 tumour in T8 vertebral body mimicked a bone metastasis. 20 tumours had diffuse but inhomogeneous enhancement, 17 having multiple hypodense or cystic areas.

Mahony et al. (1982) : Spontaneous rupture of hepatic and splenic angiosarcoma demonstrated by CT.

Brown, R. et al. (1992) : Angiosarcoma arising from malignant schwannoma in pt. with neurofibromatosis.

Varma et al. (1992) : MR imaging of extracranial nerve sheath tumours.

Pang et al. (1996) : Angiosarcoma in a patient with von Recklinghausen's disease.

Ichikawa et al. (1996) : Ganglioneuromas - CT & MR - typically show punctate calcification and low attenuation hyperintensity on T_2 with gradual increasing enhancement on dynamic MR images. If a ganglioneuroma has atypical CT & MR features coexistence of a malignant component should be considered.

Pang et al. (1996) : Angiosarcoma in a patient with von Recklinghausen's disease.

Chapter 19 : **Inflammatory, Hypersensitivity and Immune Lung Diseases, including Parasitic Diseases.**

Lung consolidation (especially pneumonia).
   Lung consolidation may be caused by infection, haemorrhage, infarction, organising severe oedema or tumour infiltration, but the term 'consolidation' is often equated clinically with pneumonia. With infection the radiographic pattern to a large extent depends on the pattern of its spread within the lung, and the reaction of the tissues to it. Spread may take place in two ways : -
(i) via the 'pores of Kohn' and 'canals of Lambert' (see ps. 2.8-2.9) to give a **segmental or lobar distribution** with an '**air bronchogram**' (see ps. 2.1-3). However part of a lobe may escape the consolidation (e.g. apex of a lower lobe, with consolidated basal segments).
(ii) Via the bronchi to give rise to a **bronchopneumonic pattern** of small disseminated areas of consolidation.
   Most infections start as a small focus and spread through the lung by one or both routes. In addition infection can pass to the lungs via the vascular system, with infected emboli, and this will cause multiple peripheral nodular areas of consolidation (which may cavitate and be large with most pathogenic emboli, but miliary in type with TB and bacterial endocarditis).
   Reaction to the infection, and the degree of dehydration of the patient, determines the amount of cellular reaction. The oedema fluid is often teeming with organisms. The tissue reaction may be variable, sometimes with but little reaction, but in others gross and leading to a '**drowned lung**' appearance with a larger than normal lobe (e.g. with staphylococcal or klebsiella pneumonia), but it can also be seen with some diffuse tumours (see ps. 4.19 - 20 and Illus. **DROWNED LUNG**). Mostly however a consolidated lobe or segment will have a smaller than normal appearance, as it will not be able to expand normally in inspiration. Also it typically contains an '**air bronchogram**' which may be seen on plain films or tomograms, because the bronchi remain patent, although the alveoli are filled with fluid, etc. (Illus. **AIR BRONCHOGRAM**). Sometimes an area of '**spherical consolidation**' or '**rounded pneumonia**' (see also p. 4.16) may occur and be confused at the time with neoplasm, but clearing usually occurs rapidly with antibiotics (Illus. **ROUND PNEU/CONS**).
   Necrosis or abscess formation may lead to cavitation. With some pneumonias (e.g. staphylococcal) **pneumatocoeles** may occur, probably as a result of a flap-valve type of mechanism within smaller distorted bronchi (Illus. **PNEUMATOCOELES**). Such pneumatocoeles may in turn lead to a generalised or loculated (e.g. inter-lobar) pneumothorax. Complicating pleural effusions and/or empyemata may follow either type of consolidation.
   Pneumonia may complicate other diseases, e.g. diabetes mellitus, cardiac failure, lung and other tumours. It may also occur post-operatively, complicate renal failure or occur in immunocompromised patients.
   Consolidation which spreads from one area to another after clearing in the first, may be due to spreading infection or be secondary to a mobile intra-bronchial foreign body (or broncholithiasis). This is often termed '**wandering pneumonia**'. This appearance may also be seen in some collagen disease, or with other conditions leading to eosinophilia (e.g. parasites or aspergillosis, etc. - see also ps. 3.8, 3.24, 19.39 and 19.59).

Aspiration and Inhalation Pneumonia and Secondary Lung Abscesses.
There are many causes:
(i) **Oro-nasal disease** (infected teeth, tonsils, sinuses, etc.). It is not uncommon for infected oro-nasal secretions to become aspirated into the bronchi, particularly during sleep. These may give rise to infections producing mucus, in turn causing lung collapse, bronchiectasis or occasionally lung abscesses. Thus if a patient has basal collapse (e.g. middle lobe collapse) and especially if chronic, the nasal sinuses should always be examined for the presence of antral fluid or opacity, etc.
   Inhalation of infected material not uncommonly occurs from the nasal sinuses. Such 'snot' emboli are still a common cause of lung infection, often basal, repeated and chronic, even in the 1990s (Illus. **BRONCHIAL EMBOLUS**). This differs from the common distribution of pneumonia caused by bacteria contained in droplets, which not being so large, or so affected by gravity, may settle anywhere in the lungs.
(ii) **Foreign bodies** (tooth fragments, plastic or metal objects, peanuts, apple cores or other food material) may be inhaled, particularly in children. Acutely they may produce **obstructive**

emphysema (see ps. 2.5 - 6), later absorption collapse and/or consolidation. If not cleared and bronchial obstruction continues, bronchiectasis may supervene (Illus. **BRONCHIAL FB**).

(iii) **Chronic inhalation** may also lead to pulmonary fibrosis. This may occur with gastro-oesophageal reflux, hiatal herniae, achalasia, a pharyngeal pouch, neurological disorders affecting the oesophagus, etc. - see Illus. **INHALAT. LUNG CHANGES & INH. PNEUMONIA.** Inhalation changes at the lung bases may even be seen in children on plain films or CT sections.

(iv) **Anaesthesia, alcohol, epilepsy**, etc. when stomach contents may be regurgitated and inhaled - Mendelson's syndrome (described during obstetric anaesthesia), due to the high pH of gastric HCl. (Note however that during anaesthesia with an endo-tracheal tube, respiratory distress may be caused by the tube. If this is too long the distal end may pass into a main, the intermediate or a lower lobe bronchus, with collapse of the lung or lobe(s) which are not aerated - e.g. left lung and right upper lobe, if the tube has passed into the intermediate bronchus. The problem occurs because the tube appears to be the correct length with the head extended during intubation, but if the head is raised and the neck flexed, then a tube end which was previously at the carina, will then pass more distally - Illus. **ENDOTRACHEAL TUBE, Tube comp Pts. 5 & 6a-c**) - see also p. 2. 37.

(v) **Drowning** - fresh water is worse than salt water in causing pulmonary oedema.

(The differentiation of lung abscesses from empyemas is discussed on ps 14.18 - 19. For illustrations of lung abscesses see Illus. **LUNG ABSCESS**).

Lipoid pneumonia is discussed on p. 6.14.

References.

Chandler (1932) : Bronchiectasis and lung abscess.

Lord Brock and colleagues (1942) : Showed that lung abscesses which needed surgical treatment were usually caused by **'bronchial emboli'**. These were more common in the upper lobes than the lower, with a preponderance for the right side. He used iodised oil to show where such 'emboli' might lodge, with differing posture when the embolism occurred (e.g. in a dental chair, lying drunk on the ground, etc).

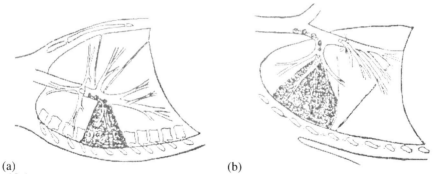

(a)   (b)

Fig. 19.1 Diagram showing the relationship between position and the site of a lung abscess. When the patient is lying supine (a) the apical part of the lower lobe is vulnerable and when lying on his side (b) the axillary and posterior parts of the upper lobe are dependent. (Reproduced from Dunnill, 1987 & Guy's Hospital Gazette).

Mendelson (1946) : Noted two types of aspiration pneumonitis:

(a) bland aspirates such as small food particles or blood which usually cause little respiratory embarrassment, and
(b) gastric contents with a pH of less than 2, tend to produce an immediate and intense chemical pneumonitis. This in turn causes rapid transudation of fluid into the alveoli, giving rise to an extensive and usually bilateral alveolar filling pattern of chest radiographs. Such a sudden post-operative appearance of extensive pulmonary oedema (with a normal preoperative examination) should alert the radiologist, clinician or an anaesthetist to this condition). It is usual to try to avoid this by having at least four hours starvation pre-operatively.

Wilkins et al. (1976) : Radiology in Mendelsohn's syndrome.

Landay et al. (1978) : Pulmonary manifestations of acute aspiration of gastric contents.

Kim et al. (1973) : Foreign body in the airway - a review of 202 cases.

Pochavesky et al. (1973) : Aspirated and ingested teeth in children.

Abulmajid et al. (1976) : Aspirated foreign bodies in the tracheo-bronchial tree (250 cases).

Ross, A. and McCormack (1980) : Foreign body inhalation.

BMJ, Editorial (1981) : Inhaled foreign bodies (**pea-nuts** causing **obstructive emphysema**).
Tarkka et al. (1988) : Bronchial stenosis after aspiration of an iron tablet.
Godden et al. (1991) : 'Iron lung' - following aspiration of an iron tablet (see also ps. 19.95-96).
Yung et al. (1994) : A bronchial 'butterfly' (part of a nose stud) which was inhaled and coughed up two months later.
Denholm and Goodwin (1995) : Aspiration of foreign bodies - the presence of food or other particles in the lung is all too easily overlooked in children, especially when the symptoms are confused with asthma.
Janoski et al. (2000) : Psyllium aspiration causing bronchiolitis.
Marom et al. (2000) : Lentil aspiration pneumonia may cause lung nodules mimicking metastases.

Vinson (1927) : Cardiospasm complicated by lung abscess.
Belcher (1949) : Pulmonary complications of dysphagia - reviewed 48 patients with dysphagia pneumonitis. Ten with achalasia had pulmonary fibrosis alone.
Anderson et al. (1953) : Reviewed 601 cases of achalasia, but only three had pulmonary fibrosis as the sole lesion.
Belsey (1960): Reviewed 1,308 patients with oesophageal disease. Many had pulmonary complications, including aspiration pneumonitis progressing to fibrosis or secondary bronchiectasis. Other complications included lung abscess, haemoptysis and collapse or progressive and collapse or progressive pulmonary fibrosis.
Pearson and Wilson (1971) : Diffuse pulmonary fibrosis and hiatus hernia.
Estrera et al. (1980) : Found a peak incidence of lung abscesses in the 4th and 5th decades and listed as main causes - poor oral and dental hygiene, alcohol abuse, cerebro-vascular accidents, post-pneumonic, epilepsy and dental surgery - used trans-bronchial angiographic catheters for drainage in suitable cases.
Johanson and Harris (1980) : Aspiration pneumonia, anaerobic infections and lung abscess.
Marom et al. (1999) : The many faces of pulmonary aspiration.

SOME ACUTE BACTERIAL PNEUMONIAS.

The majority of **community-acquired pneumonias** are bacterial in origin and most patients have a preponderance of one organism; a few having mixtures of Gram positive and negative organisms. Nosocomial (or **hospital-acquired   pneumonias**) occur particularly in those who cannot cough up secretions (e.g. post-operative), or who are ventilated.

Gram positive organisms.

Pneumococcus (also known as Strep. pneumoniae).
In the pre-antibiotic area, about 90% of pneumonias were attributed to this cause and probably about 50% still are. Before antibiotics the mortality rate was about 30%, with progression from exudation first to red, and later to grey 'hepatisation'. Death from uncomplicated pneumococcal pneumonia is now uncommon, except in the very elderly, or in those otherwise debilitated.
It more commonly gives rise to lobar pneumonia (with spread via the pores of Kohn - see ps. 2.8 - 9) than bronchopneumonia. More than one lobe may be involved, and sometimes only part of a lobe is affected. Cavitation is uncommon, but there is often an associated pleural reaction or effusion, which may be syn- or post-pneumonic. (Illus. **PNEUMOCOCCUS**).

Streptococcus is a common type of pneumonia in patients admitted to hospital. There are several types including ß haemolytic (usually giving rise to a bronchopneumonia, not uncommonly associated with pleurisy and/or an empyema) and S. faecalis (which may give rise to a cavitating pneumonia). S. milleri is becoming an increasing cause of pneumonia in patients admitted to hospital; it may also cause empyemas and liver abscesses (Illus. **MILLERI PNEUMONIA**).

Staphylococcal pneumonia is usually caused by **S. aureus** and may present in several ways :
(a) Before an immune response has developed (or with a poor immune response) patients may have a severe and rapidly progressive toxaemia causing sudden death. (Some have even died from this cause whilst driving on a motorway, or soon after admission to hospital with only a few hours of illness. Autopsy in such cases often shows the lungs to be filled with bacilli and some oedema fluid, but no polymorph response). A chest radiograph at this stage may only show poor expansion - it usually takes **12 hrs** for **consolidation** to become **apparent on a radiograph**.
(b) Segmental or lobar pneumonia - because of oedema the affected part of the lung may be larger than normal - giving rise to a 'drowned lung' type of appearance. More commonly the consolidated area appears smaller as it is unable to expand with air. There is often a marked 'air bronchogram'.
(c) Pneumatocoeles within the affected lung are common, especially in children. Although often regarded as a 'hall-mark' of this type of infection, they may also be seen with other pneumonias

(ps. 6.4 & 6.8). Rupture may give rise to a pneumothorax - may be localised within an interlobar fissure.

(d) Lung abscess formation is not uncommon, and it may rupture into the pleura to cause a pyo-pneumothorax.

(e) A 'sympathetic' pleural effusion or an empyema is not uncommon.

(f) A subclinical presentation may also occur, giving rise to dense consolidation with little systemic upset. Such consolidation may be very slow to clear, sometimes taking a few months.

(g) Nodular areas of pneumonia which progressively enlarge may be due to septic bronchial or vascular emboli; these may cavitate. (Septic emboli may also occur in the brain, bones, etc.).

In staphylococcus aureus pneumonia, the consolidated lobe or lung may have its vascularity severely reduced, and a lung perfusion scan may show an appearance similar to pulmonary embolism. Even after recovery the affected area of lung may continue to be poorly perfused, and if a large area of lung is affected the patient may have continuing dyspnoea. The damaged area may also become emphysematous or show varying degrees of fibrosis, and may become reinfected at a later date. Illus. **STAPH PNEUM+INF** show cases of Staph. pneumonia and spinal infection.

Staph. alba uncommonly causes pneumonia, which is usually much less virulent.

Gram negative organisms.

Many of these may give rise to pneumonia e.g. Haemophilus, B. coli, S. milleri (see above), Neisseria, Klebsiella, Proteus, Pseudomonas, Enterobacter, Actinobacter, etc. Many are transmitted to the lungs by droplet infection or by aspiration from the oro- or naso-pharynx, whilst others may reach the lungs by bacteraemic spread from an extra-thoracic source of infection e.g. in the renal tract. In diabetic patients B. coli infection may lead to gas formation - CO_2 - Illus. **B. COLI.**

Haemophilus   influenzae infection may complicate viral pneumonia, particularly influenza pneumonia (see also p. 19.29) and chronic lung or chest disease. In a pandemic it is particularly liable to cause severe bronchiectasis. For examples see Illus. **HAEMOPHILUS.**

Klebsiella (or **Friedlander's   bacillus** pneumonia is more common in the 'undeveloped world' and in the debilitated) and may cause a 'drowned lung' appearance (with a swollen lobe due to water retention and the affect of toxins - see also ps. 4.19 - 20) and also a destructive pneumonia (with pleurisy) giving rise to a high mortality and in both respects being similar to staphycoccal pneumonia (see above). It may occasionally cause a chronic broncho-pneumonia in e.g. 'refugees' who may be carriers of it. Occasionally it may cause 'hospital epidemics'. (See Illus. **KLEBSIELLA PNEUMONIA**).

Proteus mirabilis may give rise to segmental or lobar consolidation, which may cavitate and be accompanied by an empyema. It often complicates infection elsewhere, e.g. in an obstructed renal tract, and may occur after patients are convalescent from genito-urinary surgery.

Pseudomonas   pneumonia (Illus. **PSEUDOMONAS**) may complicate urinary tract infections, and the organism is commonly found in patients with **cystic fibrosis** (seee also ps. 3.22-24).

P. aeruginosa is an opportunistic pathogen which only causes disease in pts. with impaired host defences. In cystic fibrosis commensal flora may be killed by broad-spectrum antibiotics allowing P. aeruginosa and P. cepacia to colonise the lungs.

P. cepacia also causes soft rot in onions.

P. pseudomallei is found in the soil and water of rice paddy fields in SE Asia and causes meliodosis with pneumonia and septicaemia - a major cause of death in this area.

Salmonellae (of several types) may cause bronchopneumonia, lobar consolidation, miliary lesions or pleural effusions. It may follow infections of the gastro-intestinal tract (e.g. from infected poultry products) or from the inadvertent swallowing or inhalation of bird-guano. Salmonella osteomyelitis may also be seen (Illus. **SALMONELLA**).

Typhoid and para-typhoid also occasionally cause pneumonia.

Veilonella parvula (a normal mouth contaminant) may cause pneumonia and cavitation.

An important general point.
  Although some fairly specific radiological signs may suggest a particular infecting organism e.g. (i) TB - cavitation with surrounding inflammatory change and bronchopneumonic spread, or (ii) staphylococcal pneumonia - dense consolidation with pneumatocoeles and reduced lung perfusion, there is no absolutely certain radiographic pattern to indicate one organism - thus every effort should be made to isolate and culture it.

References.
General
Israel et al. (1956) : Delayed resolution of pneumonias.
Tillotson and Lerner (1966) : Pneumonias caused by Gram negative bacilli.
Recavarren et al. (1967) : The pathology of acute alveolar diseases of the lung.
Ziskind et al. (1967) : Acute isolated and diffuse alveolar pneumonias.
Rose and Ward (1973) : Spherical pneumonias in children simulating pulmonary and mediastinal masses.
Scanlon and Unger (1973) : Radiology of bacterial and viral pneumonias.
Tew et al. (1977) : Bacterial or nonbacterial pneumonia - accuracy of radiographic diagnosis.
Berkmen (1980b) : Uncommon acute bacterial pneumonias.
Généreux and Stilwell (1980) : Acute bacterial pneumonias.
Kirkpatrick (1980) : Pneumonia in children as it differs from adult pneumonia.
Hall and Simon (1987) : Occult pneumonia associated with dehydration - myth or legend?
Heitzman (1989) : The radiological diagnosis of pneumonia in the adult.
Goodman et al. (1980) : Radiographic evaluation of pulmonary infection.
Lynch and Armstrong (1991) : A pattern-orientated approach to chest radiographs in atypical pneumonia syndromes.
Johnson et al. (1996) : Causes of community acquired pneumonia in a study of 235 pts. needing intensive care -
no cause found 76, strep pneumonia (pneumococcus) 62, legionella 39, viruses (including varicella) 22, haemophilus influenzae 12, staph. aureus 12, mycoplasma or psittacosis 8, gram neg. enteric bacilli 4.
Sow et al. (1996) : The problems found in the management of community acquired pneumonia differ considerably between western and developing countries. Low doses of penicillin or amoxycillin can cure 90% of African pts. with pneumonia, compared with more aggressive treatments in European pts. who are both older and have greater co-morbidity.

Pneumococcus
Ziskind et al. (1970) : Incomplete consolidation in pneumococcal lobar pneumonia complicating emphysema.
Asmar et al. (1978) : Pneumococcal pneumonia with pneumatocoele formation.
Kantor et al. (1981) : The many radiological faces of pneumococcal pneumonia.
Boersma et al. (1991) : Pneumococcal capsular antigen detection and pneumococcal serology in patients with community acquired pneumonia - pneumococcal antigen detection in sputum or pleural fluid is of value in making a rapid diagnosis, especially in those receiving antibiotic treatment.
Codispoti et al. (1995) : Successful extracorporeal membrane oxygenation in fulminant pneumococcal pneumonia.

E. coli
Kohn and Lee (1973) : Pneumatocoeles with E. coli pneumonia in young babies.

Klebsiella or Friedlander's pneumonia
Felson et al. (1949) : Roentgen findings in acute Friedlander's pneumonia.
Hammond et al. (1990) : Intensive care of community-acquired Klebsiella pneumonia (18 cases - 1982 to 1987) - septicaemic shock, confusion and metabolic acidosis were the presenting features predicting a poor outcome.

Haemophilus
Quintiliani and Hymans (1971) : 29 cases were mainly associated with B strains, giving rise to lobular or segmental lung infection, especially on the right side.
Levin et al. (1977) : Bacteraemic Haemophilus in 24 adults.
Spencer (1977) : Haemophilus pneumonia in an influenza pandemic is esp. liable to cause severe bronchiectasis.
Tsou et al. (1978) : Two cases complicating long-standing oleothorax - noted that it used to be the predominant pathogen which infected artificial pneumothorax cavities.
Warner and Gordon (1981) : Two cases of pneumatocoeles in children with Haemophilus infection.
Pearlberg et al. (1984) : Haemophilus influenzae pneumonia in the adult.

Pertussis
Barnhard and Kniker (1960) : Roentgenographic findings in pertusssis esp. the '**shaggy heart outline**' sign.

Bellamy et al. (1987) : The chest radiograph in whooping cough.

Pseudomonas
Wilson and Dowling (1998) : P. aeruginosa and other related diseases.

Staphylococcus
Hendren and Haggerty (1958) : Staphylococcal pneumonia in infancy and childhood.
Watkins and Hering (1958) : Intracavitary suction tube drainage of staphylococcal tension pneumatocoeles.
Meyers and Jacobson (1959) : Staphylococcal pneumonia in children and adults.
Davidson (1960) : Conservative treatment of pneumatocoeles with staphylococcal pneumonia in infancy.
Olutola et al. (1983) : Multiple staphylococcal pneumatocoeles in a child.
Marchant and Brown (1987) : Toxic shock syndrome and staphylococcal pneumonia.
Davidson et al. (1990) : Staphylococcal pneumonia, pneumatocoeles and the toxic shock syndrome.

Other references to Pneumatocoeles and Pneumonia.
Boisset (1972) : Subpleural emphysema complicating staph. and other pneumonias.
Amitar et al. (1983) : Pneumatocoele in infants and children.
McGarry et al. (1987) : Pneumatocoele formation in adult pneumonia.
Quigley and Fraser (1988) : Pulmonary pneumatocoele - pathology and pathogenesis.

See also cysts under PCP (ps. 19.10 - 12), AIDS (ps. 19.32 - 33) and TB (ps. 19.16 -24).

Anaerobic lung (and pleural) infections and pulmonary gangrene.
   These often arise from aspiration of oro-pharyngeal seretions (bronchial emboli - see p. 19.1), but metastatic infections with septicaemia are another route. The infection often leads to lung necrosis, with cavitation and abscess formation (sometimes with a slough within a cavity - see also 'air crescent' or 'halo' sign - ps. 6.3 & 19.39 - 40). When lung necrosis is massive, the term 'gangrene' may be applied. Pleural effusions and empyemata are often also present.
   Anaerobic infections may complicate other debilitating disease, e.g. diabetes mellitus, the immunocompromised host, pulmonary infarction, or lungs damaged by bronchiectasis or bronchial obstruction (caused by tumour, foreign body, etc.).
   Organisms causing lung necrosis include Staph. aureus, Pneumococcus, Strep. milleri, Klebsiella, Pseudomonas, Bacteroides (of various types), Fusobacterium necrophorum, Clostridia (especially perfringens or welchii), Veilonella parvula, fungi such as Aspergillosis, Actinomycosis and Mucormycosis, and M. tuberculosis.
   An example of a large pulmonary embolus secondarily infected with Clostridium perfringens and giving rise to 'gas-gangrene of the lung' is shown in Illus. GAS GANGRENE and a huge gangrenous area in the left lung due to Mucormycosis in Illus. MUCORMYCOSIS. See also ps. 19.14 and 19.45.

References.
Banister (1575) in 'A Treatise of Chyurgerie' termed lung gangrene 'sphacelus' (σφακελος).
Bartlett and Finegold (1974) : Anaerobic infections of the lung and pleural space.
Bartlett (1979) : Anaerobic bacterial pneumonitis.
Landay et al. (1980) : Anaerobic pleural and pulmonary infections - lung necrosis was present in over 50% and pleurisy in 30% with many empyemata.

Humphreys (1945) : Spontaneous lobectomy i.e. lobar gangrene.
Danner et al. (1968) : Massive pulmonary gangrene.
Gutman et al. (1973) : Massive pulmonary gangrene.
O'Reilly et al. (1978) : Gangrene of the lung - successful medical management of three patients.
Khan et al. (1980) : Pulmonary gangrene occurring as a complication of pulmonary TB.
Knight et al. (1975) : Massive pulmonary gangrene complicating klebsiella pneumonia.
Zagoria et al. (1985) : Pulmonary gangrene as a complication of mucormycosis.
Phillips and Rao (1989) : Gangrene of the lung.
Reich et al. (1993) : Pulmonary gangrene and the air crescent sign - 5 cases - 2 aspergillosis (one in a previously irradiated area), and one each of TB, Pseudomonas, and inhalation.
Seetharaman and Saluga (1994) : Slough or 'iceberg' in a right hydropneumothorax due to S. pneumoniae.

Opportunistic Pneumonias (see also under AIDS ps. 19.32-36).

Poor resistance to infection occurs in a number of conditions such as diabetes, debilitated patients with tumours, those on steroids or receiving cyto-chemotherapy or radiotherapy for malignant disease, immuno-suppressive drugs, or those with other conditions damaging the immune system (reticuloses, leukaemia, collagen diseases, some thymomas, hypo-gammaglobulinaemia, chronic diabetes, renal failure, AIDS, etc.).

Pulmonary tuberculosis and infections of the feet, kidneys etc., are well known complications of diabetes. Diabetics may also develop other infections. The immunocompromised host may develop pneumonia not only from common pathogens, but also other organisms, which are not usually pathogenic to man.

Opportunistic pneumonias include infections due to Gram positive and negative cocci (including staph. and streptococci, enteric organisms, pseudomonas, mycoplasma, campylobacter), fungi (candida, aspergillosis, mucormycosis, etc.), protozoa (particularly pneumocystis or toxoplasmosis) and viruses (herpes simplex, cytomegalovirus, varicella-zoster and vaccinia). Not uncommonly multiple organisms are found, either following one another or at the same time.

The disease patterns on chest radiographs, due to opportunistic infections, are varied and include lobar and segmental consolidation, nodules with rapid growth and/ or cavitation (especially with fungal pneumonias or PCP), diffuse lung disease and miliary patterns (candida, herpes, TB, etc.) - see also under the various pneumonias including pneumocystis (ps. 19.10 - 12) and AIDS (ps. 19.32 - 33).

References. (see also under AIDS & lung transplantation p. 11.6)

Klatte et al. (1963) : Infections (fungi, etc.) complicating leukaemia.

Zornoza et al. (1970) : Radiology of Gram negative pneumonias in the neutropenic patient.

Bragg and Janis (1973) : Review of 49 patients with opportunistic lung disease including phycomycosis and staphylococcal infections.

Blank and Castellino (1975) : Pulmonary infection in patients with altered immunity.

Tucker et al. (1975) : Pulmonary fungal infection complicating treated malignant disease.

Greene (1980) : Opportunistic pneumonias.

Pagani and Libshitz (1981) : Studied 92 cases - Aspergillosis most commonly caused solitary or multiple areas of rounded pneumonia which slowly increased in size and/or number and ultimately haemorrhagic pulmonary infections. Candida mostly caused a non-specific bronchopneumonia. All could give rise to miliary patterns.

Brooks et al. (1985) : Infectious complications in heart-lung transplantation recipients.

Rosenow et al. (1985) : Pulmonary disease in the immunocompromised host,

Moore et al. (1988) : Multiple organism infections (including CMV) in renal transplant patients having treatment with cyclosporine often carried a poor prognosis (lower zone interstitial pattern).

Austin et al. (1989) : Pneumonia after cardiac transplantation - CMV, PCP and aspergillosis.

McLoud (1989) : Pulmonary infections in the immunocompromised host - general correlation between the type of radiographic pattern and the micro-organism causing the pneumonia.

Carlsen and Bergin (1990) : Reactivation of TB in a donor lung after heart-lung transplantation.

McLoud and Naidich (1992) : Thoracic disease in the immuno-compromised patient.

Janzen et al. (1993) : Acute pulmonary complications in immunocompromised non-AIDS patients - CT is superior to chest radiography in the differential diagnosis - both have comparable sensitivity in detecting complications - CT is superior for showing - ground glass shadowing with haemorrhage, PCP or CMV, - **nodules with irregular margins suggest invasive aspergillosis or candida.**

Brown, M. et al. (1994) : Acute lung disease in the immunocompromised host - CT & pathology.

Diedreich et al. (1994) : 31 lung transplant pts. with aspergillus infection - 5 had non-specific consolidation, 11 non-specific consolidation affecting mainly the ULs and 7 ill-defined nodules. Initially there was rapid progression, with much slower resolution on treatment.

Sharma et al. (1994) : 8 immunosuppressed patients developed invasive pulmonary aspergillosis in two wards adjacent to hospital building works - three also had other pathogens including TB.

Friedman, E. et al. (1995) : Interstitial infiltrates, ground glass & miliary shadowing, pleural effusion & nodes.

Logan et al. (1995) : Acute lung disease in the immunocompromised host - diagnostic accuracy of CXR.

Worthy et al. (1995) : Acute lung disease in the immunocompromised host - differential diagnosis at HRCT.

Herold (1996) : Pulmonary disease in the immunocompromised host - wide spectrum of pathogens - viruses, mycobacteria, fungi, PCP, etc. - considerable overlap in appearances - interstitial changes, nodules and micronodules.

Brown, M. et al. (1998) : Invasive aspergillosis in the immunocompromised host - CT and bronchovascular lavage.

Conces (1999): Endemic fungal pneumonia in immunocompromised patients (also Noninfectious lung disease).

McGuiness and Gruden (1999) : Viral and Pneumocystis carinii lung infections immunocompromised patients.

Pennington et al. (1999) : Pulmonary disease in the immunocompromised child.

Connolly et al. (1999) : Opportunistic fungal pneumonia.

Müller (2000) : HRCT in the immunocompromised host - **AIDS pts.** <u>ground-glass</u> - PCP, CMV, LIP; <u>consolidation</u>- bact. pn., TB, MAC, fungi, lymphoma; <u>nodules</u> - KS (peribronchovasc.), infection, septic emboli, TB (nodes may have central lower attenuation & rim enhancement), MAC, fungi, lymphoma.
Non-AIDS pts. ground-glass or consol. - <u>infection</u> - PCP, CMV, drug-induced disease, haemorrhage, oedema; <u>nodules</u> - infection, septic emboli, aspergillosis, nocardia, metastases, lymphoma, post-transplant lymphoproliferative disorder; nodule+ground-glass halo - invasive aspergillosis.
Leutner et al. (2000) : MR may show necrotising lesions better than CT.

Legionella Pneumonia.

This was so named when 221 veterans of the Pennsylvania Division of the American Legion attending the 1976 convention in Philadelphia developed this type of pneumonia and 34 died.

The organism is common in soil and natural water sources. It thrives in warm water, particularly in the pipe-work and wet (i.e. water-cooled) air conditioning systems of modern buildings which use recirculating water. The organism may be present in the water of cooling towers in vast numbers, particularly if they are poorly maintained and contain much sludge, scale, rust or algae. Droplets of water, containing the bacteria (which may become curved and hyphae-like when rapidly growing) may escape from the cooling towers as a mist or aerosol, and this may be inhaled by people (even passers-by) in the neighbourhood of the affected building. The towers are usually on the roofs of buildings, and a light wind can spread the infected droplets over an area of several hundred yards.

Two forms occur - (a) **Legionnaires' disease** - the pneumonic form and (b) **Pontiac fever** which is self-limiting, non-pneumonic and probably a sensitivity reaction. The incubation period is usually 3 to 6 days, but can vary from 2 to 10 days. About 100 sporadic cases occur per annum in the UK. Men are about three times more likely to develop the disease than women, and people between 40 and 60 years get it most commonly. It appears to mainly affect smokers, diabetics and those with chronic disease or who are immunocompromised. Most of those affected have high fever, rigors, headache, a dry cough, muscle pain and respiratory difficulty. One third have diarrhoea and/or vomiting, and half become confused. The fatality rate is about 10%.

Sporadic cases have been seen in Oxford (Illus. **LEGIONELLA PNEUMONIA**). A small outbreak occurred in the renal transplant unit at the Churchill Hospital, from infected shower water (see Tobin et al., 1981 and Kurtz et al, 1981).

The largest outbreak in the UK occurred in 1985, as a result of an infected cooling tower above the out-patient department of the South Staffordshire Hospital, with 101 cases and 28 deaths. Two outbreaks occurred in Central London, the first in 1988 due to infected cooling towers on the top of Broadcasting House, Portland Place, with 70 cases and three deaths, and the second in the Leicester Square area in early 1989, with 45 cases and 5 deaths. In the summer of 1990 the organism was found in some of London's fountains and in the air conditioning system of the Science Museum in South Kensington. Further small outbreaks occurred at a Nottingham Hospital in Aug. and in Portsmouth in Sept. 1992, and a third from droplet infection in Trafalgar Square, London in March/ April 1993. 16 deaths and 80 other cases were reported in an outbreak in Amsterdam in March 1999.

Cases are now being recognised more frequently and it is now thought that between 130 and 200 cases occur each year in England and Wales and result in up to 40 deaths.

In the pneumonic cases, chest radiographs show patchy alveolar infiltrates, which rapidly progress to frank consolidation, which may be lobar or rounded in type. Basal linear collapse is not infrequent. Multiple areas of the lungs may be affected. Cavitation is not uncommon. Small pleural effusions seem common but larger effusions seem to be related to concomitant cardiac failure. Complicating empyemas are rare. The radiographic extent of the disease seems to bear little relationship to eventual recovery. In mild cases spontaneous recovery often occurs. In others it may respond to erythromycin, sometimes with added rifampicin or deoxycycline, but these do not always prevent severe lung involvement or its spread to the lungs. More recently cipofloxacin has been used and has proved successful in outbreaks in France. Radiographic resolution tends to lag behind clinical improvement. In a few cases the disease may lead to pulmonary fibrosis.

Further references.
Fraser et al. (1977) : Legionnaires' disease - description of epidemic.
Dietrich et al. (1978) : Chest radiograph in Legionnaires' disease.
Jenkins et al. (1979) : Nottingham, England - 13 cases - all with lobar type pneumonia - two died.

Kirby et al. (1970) : Radiographic features of Legionnaires' disease.
Randolph and Beckman (1979) : Legionnaires' disease presenting with an empyema.
Roderick Smith (1979, Nottingham, UK) : 21 cases. Radiology showed unilateral consolidation at presentation in 15. The consolidation became denser and slowly resolved.
Swartz (1979) : Clinical aspects of Legionnaires' disease. Lake et al. (1979) : Legionnaires' disease & cavitation.
Tsai et al. (1979) : Legionnaires' disease - clinical features of the epidemic in Philadelphia.
Cordes and Fraser (1980, USA) : Legionellosis.
Evans et al. (1981, Liverpool, UK) : Analysis of the chest radiograph in Legionnaires' disease.
Tobin (1981, Oxford) : Isolation of Legionella pneumophilia from water systems.
Sato et al. (1985) : Bronchiolitis obliterans caused by Legionella pneumophilia.
Tobin (1987) : Legionnaires' disease.
Lo et al. (1983, Canada) : Radiographic analysis of the course of Legionella pneumonia.
Fairbank et al. (1983) : The chest radiograph in Legionnaires' disease - further observations.
Kroboth et al. (1983, Pittsburg, USA) : Clinicopathological correlation of the extent of the disease.
Meenhorst and Mulder (1983) : Chest radiograph in Legionella pneumonia.
Dobranowski and Stringer (1989) : Diagnosis of Legionella lung abscess by percutaneous needle aspiration - peripheral posterior cavitating nodular mass in right upper lobe.
Donald et al. (1989) : Study of radiographs of 17 cases from the epidemic centred around Broadcasting House, London in 1988. Five had normal chest radiographs initially, and three remained normal throughout the illness. Eight had unilateral lobar consolidation. Twelve had progressive disease, seven developing bilateral consolidation. Pleural effusions were present in six.

Legionnaires' Disease - House of Commons Employment Committee Report (1990) : Investigated outbreaks in Bolton, two in London, and a series of cases at University Hospital, Nottingham, and expressed deep concern at further outbreaks in 1988 and 1989. Because of the unknown aspects of the disease, the committee characterised it as "a moving target". Preconceptions that it attacks mainly the elderly had to be revised, and that old cooling towers were the most likely source - **new installations were implicated in the 1989 outbreak in central London.** The report cast doubt on Government health guidelines that checks are not necessary below a total micro biological level of 10^6/ml, as it appeared that a count of 10^4 could conceal a count of 10^9. (Hansard, 6 Feb. 1989).

Edelstein (1993) : It is impossible to differentiate Legionnaires' disease from common causes of pneumonia with clinical, nonspecific laboratory, or chest radiographic findings, which are often nonspecific, alveolar infiltrates being seen rather than interstitial ones. Concomitant infection with other organisms may occur in 5 to 10% of patients. The disease may be sporadic, endemic or epidemic, and whilst usually caused by L. pneumophilia aerosols, even unsterilised water for flushing nasogastric tubes may cause the infection.

Mycoplasma pneumonia.

This may present in a variety of ways, but particularly a 'flu-like illness. Most patients have pharyngitis and/ or bronchitis; many have considerable hypoxia. Concomitant viral infection is not uncommon. The mycoplasma titre is commonly raised, and **cold   agglutinins** may be present. Peaks of incidence tend to occur every four years, particularly in the winter and spring.

Some patients presenting with acute pneumonic disease (with chest pain, cough, weakness and fever) commonly have segmental or lobar consolidation associated with some volume loss, whilst others have a more insidious onset with malaise, lethargy and progressive breathlessness, increasing over two to three weeks. Lung infiltrates may be fluffy, fine nodular, nodular or diffuse, and may be accompanied by septal line engorgement or basal linear collapse. Concomitant pleural effusions, which may be haemorrhagic, are more common in those with frank consolidation. Such consolidation is often slow to clear, often taking four to eight weeks or even more. Occasionally an acute mycoplasma infiltration may progress to diffuse interstitial fibrosis. Relapsing or recurrent consolidation in the same or other areas of the lungs is also found. Sometimes, with a solely bronchitic type of infection, no abnormality may be seen on plain chest radiographs. HRCT may show an inflammatory type of bronchiolitis with ill-defined small shadows and branching lines - see also Fig. 1.60 & ps. 1.49-50 & 53 and 3.25.

Whilst many cases resolve spontaneously, treatment with erythromycin is usually effective.
Some cases are shown in Illus. **MYCOPLASMA PN.**

References.
Forsyth and Chanock (1966) : Mycoplasma pneumonia.
George et al. (1966) : Mycoplasma & adenovirus pn. compared with atypical pneumonias in a military population.
George et al. (1967) : Roentgenographic appearances of viral and mycoplasmal pneumonias.

Fine et al. (1970) : Frequency of pleural effusions in mycoplasma and viral pneumonias.
Stenström et al. (1972) : Mycoplasma pneumonias - review of 96 cases.
Foy et al. (1973) : Radiographic study of mycoplasma pneumonia.
Grix and Giammona (1974) : Mycoplasma pneumonitis with pleural effusion in children.
Murray et al. (1975) : Protean manifestations of Mycoplasma pneumonia infection in adults.
Putman et al. (1975) : Clinical and Roentgenological patterns.
Cameron et al. (1977) : Radiographic patterns of acute mycoplasmal pneumonitis.
Baltro (1979) : Radiological aspects of pulmonary lesions due to mycoplasma pneumonia - 70 cases.
Janower and Weiss (1980) : Mycoplasma, viral and rickettsial pneumonias.
Kaufman et al. (1980) : Progression to diffuse fibrosis.
Koletsky and Weinstein (1980) : Fulminant Mycoplasma pneumoniae infection.
Cockcroft and Stilwell (1981) : Lobar pneumonia caused by Mycoplasma pneumoniae.
Finnegan et al. (1981) : Radiographic appearances of mycoplasma pneumonia.
Demos et al. (1984) : Mycoplasma pneumonia presenting as a mediastinal mass.
Reittner et al. (2000) : Mycoplasma pneumonia - HRCT in 28 patients.

Necrobacillosis.

The anaerobe Fusobacterium necrophorum may occasionally give rise to a severe septicaemia, with lung consolidation, breakdown and cavitation. The condition should be considered in previously healthy adolescents and adults who develop a severe septicaemic illness with prominent symptoms after an initial sore throat. The presenting features are usually characteristic and were described in detail by Lémierre (1936), his name often being given to the condition. It can easily be confused with staphylococcal septicaemia, but the latter is not usually preceded by a sore throat. Affected patients may have painful submandibular lymphadenopathy. Untreated the illness is mostly fatal.

The organism is sensitive to many antibiotics in vitro, but metronidazole appears to be the best in vivo. Moore-Gillon et al. (1984) from St. Thomas' Hospital described five cases, and subsequent correspondence (Hudson et al., 1984 and Wardle et al., 1984) revealed three more, one with complicating meningitis.

Although almost forgotten, sporadic cases are still being seen and there have been several recent cases in Oxford. The first was a woman who had a complicating liver abscess. The second was a man of 22 who had a sore throat accompanied by enlarged cervical nodes suggesting infectious mononucleosis; infection spread to the chest and he had a two litre empyema with gas in the mediastinal tissue planes. Two others also had lung infection and pleurisy. A teenage boy had a sore throat, cervical nodes + L internal jugular thrombosis, R leg infection and bronchopneumonia with a small lung abscess. An obese woman had respiratory and adrenal failure with bronchopneumonia. Most recovered completely; the one fatal case had a rapidly progressive and toxic pneumonia affecting the RUL and was admitted with a hemiplegia secondary to cortical venous thrombosis. For illustrations see Illus. **NECROBACILLOSIS**.

The author has also been shown the radiographs of a London taxi driver, in whom there was bilateral cavitating consolidation, the cavities having an irregular outline, and with gas in the interstitial planes of the right lung.

Cases in the USA have been reported by Tynes and Utz (1960), Seidenfeld et al. (1982) and Kleinman and Flowers (1984). Forty three further cases have been noted by Eykyn (1989) and Moore-Gillon and Eykyn (1990). Ending a case report, Chippindale et al. (1990) wrote: "the characteristic syndrome of sore throat and painful lymphadenopathy followed by a septicaemic illness with metastatic abscess formation should alert the clinician to the possibility of this unusual infection".

Pneumocystis carinii pneumonia.

This protozoan infection is now commonly seen in patients who are immuno-compromised and is most common in patients with AIDS, but may also be found in transplanted organ recipients, and those having anti-tumour chemotherapy for lymphoma, leukaemia, etc.(see Jacobs et al., 1969 - needle biopsy in 6 cases). It used to be termed 'interstitial plasma cell pneumonia' when found in sickly children in orphanages after the Second World War. Probably most people develop immunity to the organism as a result of antibodies formed in childhood, and only develop the infection if immunity is suppressed, though sporadic cases occasionally occur in nonimmunocompromised people. The organism is fairly ubiquitous in temperate regions in rodents and other animals including pigs. Rats develop the disease if given tetracycline and steroids and this source is often used experimentally to study the condition.

The organism is found in two forms : (i) tiny cysts containing 2,4, or 8 dark staining bodies, 4 to 6μ in diameter, when stained with silver or polychrome e.g. Giemsa stain. The 'cysts' are often clumped together. (ii) Trophozoites which adhere to the host pneumocytes producing the typical **alveolar** inflammatory change. Collapsed sickle-shaped cysts are also seen.

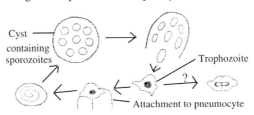

Fig. 19.2   Life cycle of Pneumocystis carinii (reproduced from Levine, SJ and White, DA, 1988, 'Pneumocystis carinii pneumonia' in Pulmonary Effects of AIDS. Clinics in Chest Medicine, **9**, 395 - 423 by permission WB Saunders Company).

Most patients with the disease do not have much sputum and transbronchial alveolar lavage or percutaneous lung biopsy may be used to recover the organism. This last has however produced some fatalities probably due to the puncturing of air cysts or bullae (see below). Bigby et al. (1986) used induced sputum (after the inhalation of a mist of 30% saline) to recover the organism. A DNA probe, using autoradiography, is being developed to detect traces of the organism in forcibly expectorated sputum (Wakefield et al., 1988 and 1990).

The disease may be difficult to detect on plain radiographs in its earlier stages. Commonly it causes a 'peri-hilar haze' which spreads out into the lungs within a few days to give a widespread diffuse infiltration, rather like a frank consolidation. As with other types of diffuse or atypical pneumonia, Kerley's 'B' lines are not uncommonly seen, and these may mimic or be mistaken as a sign of pulmonary oedema. Localised consolidation and pleural reaction may occasionally be found. It may also give rise to asymmetric or focal infiltrates which may produce local areas of emphysema, cavitate and give rise to pneumatocoeles and pneumothoraces (see below).

Levine and White (1988) found that the most common radiographic presentation of PCP is the development of diffuse, bilateral interstitial or alveolar infiltrates. During the early stages of pneumonia, ground glass perihilar interstitial infiltrates are often evident. As the infection progresses, these may either progress to a diffuse shadowing involving all of the lungs, or coalesce into a coarse pattern with homogeneous consolidation and air bronchograms. In some cases pulmonary oedema may be simulated. The peripheral parts of the lungs and apices may be spared in some cases.

CT studies of affected patients have shown a number of features :
(i) widely distributed or peripheral and sub-pleural shadowing and thickening,
(ii) peri-bronchial or bronchial wall thickening, (iii) air bronchograms in areas of consolidation, (iv) cavitation and (v) nodose patterns.

Associated nodal enlargement may sometimes be seen and nodes may calcify in the mediastinum and abdomen. Groskin et al. (1990) found rapidly enlarging and calcifying hilar and mediastinal nodes in a 15 year old girl. See also Radin et al.(1990).

Treatment with trimethoprim and sulphamethoxide (Septrin) is usually effective, and this is often used for prophylaxis.

Resolution in cases detected and treated early usually occurs within a few days. In chronic cases pulmonary fibrosis, nodules and ring shadows due to cavitation or lung cysts may be found and intractable pneumothoraces may occur. However all these last are rare in those with first attacks, and in those who have long-standing prophylactic chemotherapy to prevent a recurrence. Other coincident infections e.g. fungus (especially candida) or CMV may complicate the picture. In IV drug addicts pulmonary talcosis may also be a problem (see ps. 19.92 & 94).

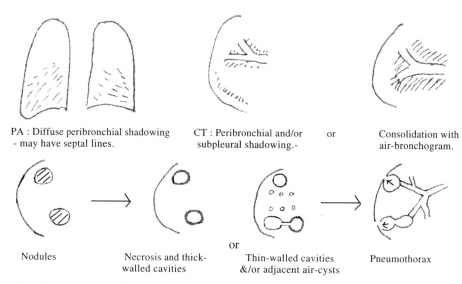

PA : Diffuse peribronchial shadowing - may have septal lines.

CT : Peribronchial and/or subpleural shadowing.-

or

Consolidation with air-bronchogram.

Nodules

Necrosis and thick-walled cavities

or

Thin-walled cavities &/or adjacent air-cysts

Pneumothorax

Fig. 19.3   Schematic drawing of the radiological appearances in pneumocystis pneumonia.

Examples of Pneumocystis pneumonia are shown in Illus. **PNEUMOCYSTIS PN.**

Further references.

Ahvenainen (1957) : 'Interstitial plasma cell pneumonia' in children.
Capitanio and Kirkpatrick (1966) : Pneumocystis carinii pneumonia.
Barnett et al. (1969) : Pneumocystis carinii in lymph nodes and spleen.
Forrest (1972), Siegel and Wolson (1977), Dee et al (1979) : Radiographic findings in PCP.
Le Golvan and Heidelberger (1973) : Disseminated granulomatous PCP.
Cross, A. and Steigbigel (1974) : PCP presenting as localised nodular densities.
Doppman et al. (1975) : Atypical radiographic features (one case with cavitation).
Gamsu et al. (1982), Vanley et al. (1982) : PCP in homosexual men.
Hopkin et al. (1983) : Diagnosis by alveolar lavage.
Young, L. (1983) : Monograph on PCP.
Gedroye and Reidy (1985) : 14 cases.
Hartz et al. (1985) : Solitary pulmonary nodule due to PCP.
Bier et al. (1986) : Single pulmonary nodule due to pneumocystis.
Milligan et al. (1985) : PCP radiographically resembling TB.
Barrio et al. (1986) : Cavitating and non-cavitating pulmonary nodules.
Bigby et al. (1986) : Induced sputum for the diagnosis of PCP in AIDS patients.
Goodman et al. (1986), Joe et al. (1986), Sherman et al. (1986) : Spontaneous pneumothorax with PCP.
Wright, F. (1986) : Peripheral distribution on CT in a renal transplant patient.
De Lorenzo et al. (1987) : Radiological patterns of PCP on 104 AIDS patients.
Eng et al. (1987) : Destruction of lung tissues due to PCP.
Abd et al. (1988) : Bilateral upper lobe PCP in a pt. having inhaled pentamidine prophylaxis.
Edelstein and McCabe. (1990) : Atypical presentations of PCP in pts. having inhaled pentamidine prophylaxis.
Afessa et al. (1988) : PCP complicated by lymphadenopathy and pneumothorax.
Baynes et al. (1989) : Pneumothorax in patients with AIDS - 10 cases with pneumocystis.
Bevan et al. (1989) : Bilateral pneumothoraces complicating AIDS related PCP.
Gurney and Bates (1989) : Comparison of PCP pneumatocoeles and bullous emphysema due to IV drug abuse.
Kuhlman et al. (1989) : Premature bullous pulmonary damage in AIDS patients shown by CT - may be due to IV drug abuse and previous infection.
Liu et al. (1989) : Necrotising pneumocystis carinii vasculitis.
Panicek (1989) : Cystic pulmonary lesions in patients with AIDS may lead to pneumothorax.
Sandhu and Goodman (1989) : Pulmonary cysts associated with PCP in AIDS patients.
Bergin et al. (1990) : CT and HRCT in 14 patients with PCP - diffuse bilateral perihilar air space disease was most common, with a 'ground-glass' mosaic-like shadowing in the lungs through which the vessels remained visible.

Feuerstein et al. (1990 a) : Thin-walled cavities, cysts and pneumothorax in PCP.
        (1990 b) : Widespread visceral and nodal calcifications in AIDS related PCP.
Groskin et al. (1990) : Calcified hilar & mediastinal lymph nodes in an AIDS patient with PC infection.
Kuhlman et al. (1990) : PCP - spectrum of parenchymal CT findings.
Moskovic et al. (1990) : HRCT of 11 cases of PCP suggested that changes often incompletely cleared despite clinical recovery, and that persisting cystic changes and fresh interstitial shadowing implied that the healing process may be complex. They noted the following radiological signs:
  (a) fine diffuse bilateral alveolar consolidation with bronchial wall thickening,
  (b) peripheral consolidation with sub-pleural sparing,
  (c) upper or lower zone predominance,
  (d) sometimes the disease is unilateral,
  (e) nodose and cystic patterns with bronchial dilatation.
Packe et al. (1990) : Bilateral pneumothoraces in PCP complicating AIDS.
Page and Wilson (1990) : Basal linear collapse as a feature of PCP - seen in about 40% of cases.
Radin et al. (1990) : Visceral and nodal calcification in patients with AIDS related PC infection.
Sanders et al. (1991) : Bilateral upper lobe PCP in a patient receiving aerosolised pentamidine.
Wakefield (1988) : Cloning DNA from pneumocytes in PC pneumonia.
        (1990) : Detection of pneumocystis by DNA amplification.
McCarty et al. (1992) : Disseminated Pneumocystis carinii infection in a patient with AIDS causing thyroid gland calcification and hypothyroidism.
Murray, C. and Schmidt (1992) : Tissue invasion by PC - a possible cause of cavitary pneumonia & pneumothorax.
Tung (1992) : Cystic pulmonary lesions in AIDS may occur during acute episodes of PCP or be due to sequelae of previous PCP or other causes including IV drug abuse. These may produce a wide spectrum of abnormalities.
Chow et al. (1993) : Cysts related to pneumocystis pneumonia are usually multiple, occur most often in the upper parts of the lungs, and tend to decrease in size or resolve after an acute infection.
Eagar et al. (1993) : Tumefactive Pneumocystis carinii infection in AIDS - three cases - hilar node enlargement, left apical mass, right psoas abscess.
Wasserman et al. (1993) : Chronic PCP in 3 pts. with AIDS causing extensive interstitial fibrosis, occasional giant cell reactions and honeycombing in upper lobes (esp. apices).
Blackmore et al. (1994) : Cystic pulmonary lesions in Pneumocystis carinii infection.
Mayor et al. (1994) : Mediastinal and hilar lymphadenopathy due to PC infections in AIDS patients - CT features.
Richards et al. (1995 & 1996) : HRCT showed ground glass shadowing in HIV patients with suspected PCP and a normal chest radiograph.
Armstrong (1995) : HRCT in 13 pts. with HIV & suspected PCP & a normal chest radiograph - patchy ground-glass shadowing in 3 + a 4th with interstitial thickening and denser peripheral shadowing (see also Richards et al., 1996).
Kuhlman (1996) : Pneumocystic infections - the radiologist's perspective.
Sinicco et al. ((1996) : PCP in a pt. with pulm. sarcoid and idiopathic CD4 + T cell lymphocytopenia.
Uwyged et al. (1996) : PCP presenting as a solitary cavitating lung lesion in non-HIV immunosuppressed pts.
Gruden et al. (1977) : HRCT in clinically suspected PCP in AIDS pts. with normal or equivocal chest radiographs.
Lundgren et al. (1997) : 40 staff (half exposed & half unexposed) had oropharyngeal washings tested for PCP RNA products - none were found.

Some uncommon acute bacterial pneumonias.

Anthrax

Inhalation anthrax (or 'woolsorter's disease') is now rare following the eradication of the disease in cattle, pigs and sheep in most Western countries. However occasional cases still occur resulting from the inhalation of spores from imported hides, etc. In endemic areas, cutaneous anthrax (the 'maligant pustule') with an untreated 25% mortality is far more prevalent. In thoracic anthrax, the spores enter the bronchi and alveoli, and most are expectorated, but some are phagocytosed and are carried to the hilar and mediastinal nodes via the lymphatics. They germinate in these, producing acute haemorrhage and tissue necrosis They also spread into the blood-stream giving rise to septicaemia and toxaemia. Haemorrhagic mediastinitis and lymphatic adenitis lead to blocked lymphatic drainage with secondary pulmonary oedema and secondary infection. Oedema of the chest wall develops - of gelatinous constituency. Death invariably follows in one to three days.

Some notes :
(i) Anthrax bombs were one of the 'secret weapons' of World War II, but were never dropped on Nazi Germany as intended. A test drop was made on sheep on the tiny Scottish island of Gruinard, off the Ross coastline in 1941 with

100% mortality. Landing on this island was forbidden until April 1990, when it was given the 'all clear'. For further details see Gordon, 1983, BMJ, **300**, 895 and Daily Telegraph 25 April 1990.

(ii) A leak of anthrax from a Soviet weapons factory at Sverdlovsk (close to the Ural mountains) in the 1980's killed 90 people.

(iii) On 30 June 1993 evidence was given to the Scott Inquiry into the Arms for Iraq etc. affair that the 'Super Gun' was intended to fire one ton bombs of anthrax into Israel.

Reference.
Vassal et al. (1975) from Iran : Two cases of anthrax pneumonia with radiological findings and literature survey.

Brucellosis.

In brucellosis pulmonary involvement is common. Other presenting features include fever, back and joint pains, excessive sweating and headache. Radiographic chest abnormalities include lung changes, peri-hilar and peri-bronchial infiltration, hilar and para-tracheal lymphadenopathy. Lung abscesses, pleural effusions, a pneumothorax and /or an empyema may also be found. The most typical is spinal infection with a para-spinal inflammatory mass, especially in the dorsal or lumbar region. Vertebral erosion may be central or marginal - these are often poorly defined and involve the anterior and/or superior margins of the vertebral bodies. Trabecular irregularities and disc space narrowing may follow i.e. a 'destructive arthritis'. Healing in the spine, and in lung nodules may be accompanied by marked calcification. An example of the disease in the cervical spine is shown in Illus. **BRUCELLOSIS**.

The disease commonly follows the ingestion of infected cow's or goat's milk. It is now uncommon in the UK, but is still common in the Middle East, etc. There it may occur from eating infected raw liver, etc. Veterinary surgeons and others may become infected delivering infected animals, and develop cutaneous lesions first. Several strains of the organism occur : abortus (in cows), suis (in pigs), melitensis (goats, etc.) and canis (dogs - usually with a brief and uncomplicated illness). Treatment is with streptomycin and deoxycycline.

References.
Patel et al. (1988) from Riyadh, Saudi Arabia : reviewed 165 cases.
Sharif et al. (1989) : Brucellar and tuberculous spondylitis: comparative imaging features.

Clostridium perfringens (welchii) or 'gas gangrene'.

This organism may infect infarcted lung and lead to gas collections within the lung and pleura, with thin pus in the latter. The infection gives rise to characteristic sickly musty smell, which once smelt is never forgotten - the author particularly remembers it in a boy aged 9 with gas gangrene of the brain + a sub-dural abscess as a result of a neglected penetrating injury by a fencing stake. Pulmonary infection is almost invariably fatal - a case is shown in Illus. **GAS GANGRENE Pt. 1a-e** and gas in subcutaneous tissues in Illus. **GAS GANGRENE Pt. 2**.

References.
Bayer et al. (1975) : Necrotising pneumonia and empyema due to Clostridium perfringens.
Spagnulo and Payne (1980) : Clostridial pleuro-pulmonary infection.
Misra and Hurst (1980) : Necrotising pneumonia and empyema due to Clostridium bifermentans.
Bashir and Benson (1990) : Necrotising pneumonia and empyema due to Clostridium perfringens complicating pulmonary embolus.

Corynebacterium (or Rhodococcus) equi is a soil organism which causes pneumonia in horses, cattle and pigs. It may also affect humans, particularly those who are immunocompromised, including AIDS patients.

References.
van Etta et al. (1985) : Review of 12 cases of c. equi pneumonia.
MacGregor et al. (1986): Opportunistic lung infection due to c. equi.
Samies et al. (1986) : Lung abscess due to c. equi.
Bishopric et al. (1988) : Pulmonary inflammatory pseudotumour in a patient with AIDS.
Wicky et al. (1995) : Radiological findings in 9 AIDS pts. with Rhodococcus equi pneumonia - cavitating nodules, dense consolidations & mediastinal lymphadenopathy.

Meliodosis.

This is caused by the Gram-negative bacillus Pseudomonas pseudomallei, which is endemic in the paddy field areas of South East Asia. It gives rise to a wide spectrum of clinical manifestations, including acute pneumonia or a more chronic or sub-acute form resembling cavitating tuberculosis.

References.

James et al. (1967) : Radiologic and pathologic findings.
Sweet et al. (1968) : Cavitating lung disease.
Everett and Nelson (1975) : 39 cases of pulmonary disease.
Dhiensiri et al. (1988) : 183 cases from Thailand - lung infiltration, nodular shadows or rapidly progressive consolidation. Some had breakdown or abscess formation.

Tularaemia is caused by Francisella tularensis - an anaerobic Gram-negative coccobacillus, named after Tulare County in California. The disease is endemic in several countries, including the USA, and may be acquired by humans from the infected skins of animals, from animal bites or insect vectors. Pneumonia is a common manifestation, and causes patchy consolidation, which may be accompanied by pericarditis and/or pleural effusions.

References.

Dennis and Bondreau (1957) : Pleuropulmonary tularaemia - its Roentgen manifestations.
Overholt and Tiggert (1960) : Roentgenographic manifestations of pulmonary tularaemia.
Miller, R. and Bates (1969) : Pleuropulmonary tularaemia - review of 29 patients.
Avery, F. and Barnett (1967) : Pulmonary tularaemia - report of five cases, pathogenesis and terminology.
Rubin (1978) : Radiographic spectrum of tularaemia.

Yersinia (Pasteurella) pestis - 'plague' or 'black death' (Illus. PLAGUE).

The organism is endemic in rodents, particularly rats, in many parts of the world, and is transmitted to man by rat fleas (their proventriculi becoming blocked by the bacilli). Sporadic cases of human infection occur, (e.g. in hunters etc.) in endemic areas. Although often considered a pestilence of the past, epidemics sometimes still occur in various parts of the world, as in India (and starting in Surat) in the autumn of 1994. The last major outbreak was in South Korea between 1965 and 1970 when 175,000 people died (including American servicemen). In southern USA plague infects prairie dogs (see National Geographic, April 1998).

Well known ancient epidemics include the plague of Athens in 430 BC (so vividly described by Thucydides). The first European pandemic started in AD 541 and the second, which killed over 50M people, lasted from 1347 to 1771, including the Black Death (1347 - 1351) and the Great Plague of London 1665, which is still referred to in the nursery rhyme 'Ring a ring a roses, a pocket full of poses, atishoo, atishoo, we all fall down' (i.e. ring of red spots, a bag of sweet-scented flowers - to try to ward off the infection - sneeze and die!). People could be well at breakfast time and be dead by evening - 50% of London's population died. If people had not become infected within 40 days they were safe from it - hence 'quarantine'.

Outbreaks of plague were particularly seen in cool autumns after hot summers (or cool periods after unusually hot winters), probably when rats entered buildings, and people tended to congregate in many with thatch roofs and straw covered floors which the rat fleas could infest, as they deserted dying or dead rats. In Europe the disease was spread from port to port by black rats in ships and then entered the local rodent population. The last UK outbreak was in Suffolk (mainly in farming people) from 1910 to 1918 and was probably due to infected rats in ships from the Far East reaching Ipswich). Fortunately the human flea (Pulex irritans) is a poor transmitter of plague. The virulence of the organism can also change, as happened in the late 17th century.

The disease usually starts with a blister at the site of the flea-bite; this may then become a 'black carbuncle'. Fresh carbuncles and spots may appear. Nodal disease then follows in the axillae or groins (**'bubonic plague'**), later becoming septicaemic with pneumonia (and occasionally also leading to plague meningitis). **When pneumonia occurs, with bacilli in the sputum ('pneumonic plague') air-borne transmission may occur from man to man.**

Pneumonic consolidation is usually massive and rapidly spreading; the affected lobe often being 'swollen' (i.e. larger than normal due to outward bowing of the adjacent fissures, as is also seen with Klebsiella, etc. pneumonia - see ps. 2.1, 2.3 & 4.19 - 20). Massive enlargement of the hilar and mediastinal lymph nodes often occurs.

Infection may also occur from post-mortem examinations, and from laboratory accidents (as at the UK Govt. Experimental Station at Porton Down, Wiltshire in 1962); it has also been used with homicidal intent!

Treatment with streptomycin or tetracycline is usually effective.

References.

Yersin (1894) : La Peste bubonique à Hong-Kong - internal parasite of rodents.
Reed et al. (1970) : Bubonic plague in SW USA - a review of recent experience.
Alsofrom et al. (1981) : Radiographic appearances in 42 cases in New Mexico (1975 - 1980).
Encyclopaedia Britannica (1971 - 200th Anniversary Edition) : Plague.
National Geographic (May 1988) : Good account of the pandemics.
Jardine (1994) : Never say it coudn't happen here.
Walsh (1994) : Return of the Black Death.

Tuberculosis

This is still a major health problem, particularly in undeveloped countries. The World Health Organisation estimates that over 1,700 million people (one third of the world's population) is infected with the tubercle bacillus, and that each year there are 10 million new cases and three million deaths from the disease.

In the U.K. the number of cases fell from about 50,000 per annum in 1960 to about 6,500 ten years ago, but recently the number has again been increasing and London now (in 1999) has 2,700 active cases, and 50 new cases each week. In Oxford about equal numbers present from the native (white) population as do immigrants (mainly from the Indian subcontinent and West Indies), which means that the incidence in the latter is larger. Whilst a few of the native population presenting with tuberculosis are young (e.g. medical students returning from 'electives' in the 'third world'), most are older and have a recrudescence of previous infection, in many cases as a complication of other debilitating disease such as malignancy (bronchial neoplasm, etc.), diabetes (see also p. 17.8) or immuno-suppression. Some are alcoholics or live in poor conditions, a few are tramps, whilst others the author has seen have been 'dons' (Oxford University tutors). Some have had underlying disease, diabetes, AIDS (see ps. 19.18 & 23 - 24), etc.

In older people, the condition can easily be confused with intrathoracic neoplasm or the two diseases may coexist (see Illus. **TB+CA LUNG**). Some with suspected neoplasm have returned from abroad (see Illus. **TB-CHEST, Pt. 65a-c**) and been delighted that they had a curable condition.

Immigrants with tuberculosis tend to be young and have acute primary disease affecting the mediastinal nodes, lung infiltration with acute bronchopneumonic spread, 'soft ' nodules and cavitation. Mediastinal enlargement, from nodes or abscess formation , may sometimes be massive and mimic lymphoma (see also p. 5.21 et seq. and Illus. **TB-ASIAN, Pt. 1a-f & TB-MEDIAST NODES, TB-Asian Pts. 14, 30 & Thymus, Pt. 16a-b**). Bone tuberculosis may also be present (spine, limb bones, etc.); abscesses may also arise from the ribs, sternoclavicular joints., etc. and give rise to **painless 'cold' abscesses** in the lower neck, chest wall or breasts (Illus. **TB-BONE, Pts. 16 & 19**). Coincident pelvic and abdominal tuberculosis is not uncommon, but it is unusual for it to affect the genito-urinary tracts in these people.

It is always a good working rule to consider the possibility of tuberculosis in people coming from undeveloped countries, particularly soon after their arrival , or following a visit 'home'. An English doctor who works in a mission type hospital in Pakistan recently told the author that over 95 % of her patients have this disease, and in most cases they do not have a chest radiograph carried out, as it is too expensive, but do sputum examinations for confirmation or just treat them empirically.

Choyke et al. (1983) wrote that even in the USA "more people die of tuberculosis than of all other reportable diseases combined". They also noted that in adults, as compared with children, there is a greater incidence of lower lobe disease, but infiltrates may involve the upper lobes or apices of the lower lobes. Adenopathy, cavitation and tuberculomas were also common.

In 1992 there was an epidemic of tuberculosis amongst the black population of New York (not just in those with AIDS). In the UK it is also being increasingly seen in people who sleep in 'homes' or 'shelters' for the homeless. There are now more strains, particularly in these groups, which are resistant to drugs. In many parts of Central and East Africa, TB is spreading rapidly especially in patients with AIDS, and it has been described as 'one of the greatest public health disasters since the bubonic plague' (Stanford et al., 1991). The WHO in 1995 reported that deaths from TB rose to 3M, more than at any time in history, and expects 18M cases in SE Asia by 2,000 and 0.5M in Western Europe. Many cases (including some in the UK) are now drug resistant, probably as a result of only partial drug therapy (including a failure to fully take or complete treatment, particularly in developing or poor countries) and in HIV patients.

Radiological signs.
Tuberculosis has often been classified as 'primary' or 'post-primary' infection, but 'acute' and 'chronic' connotations (as with other infections) are probably more appropriate. An acute primary chest infection, with a small peripheral lung lesion and an enlarged hilar or mediastinal node or nodes is often termed a '**Ghon focus**' (although first described by Küss, 1898 - see p. 13.1 - see also Illus. **TB-GHON FOCUS**). This may be seen particularly in teenagers or children on plain radiographs or tomograms. In children, nodes may be considerably enlarged and cause bronchial obstruction, first with 'obstructive emphysema' (Illus. **TB-CHILD, Pts. 8a-c & 10a-b**) and later collapse, especially of the middle lobe (Brock's syndrome - Brock, 1950). Nodal enlargement in children in the right upper mediastinum (Illus. **TB-CHILD, Pts. 3, 8 & 9**) used to cause considerable concern, as it was not uncommonly the precursor of miliary tuberculosis, presumably because of spread into the adjacent large veins, which could also become compressed. A case the author has seen in 1996 exemplified this point - a RUL abscess which partially calcified as shown by CT in a child with TB meningitis. As also noted by Im et al. (1987), Kuhlman et al. (1990) and Leahy et al. (1993) on CT studies, predominantly right paratracheal and subcarinal distribution of nodes is not unusual in TB.

The 'hallmarks' of tuberculosis are lung infiltration, or consolidation particularly of an upper lobe together with **cavitation** but it may also occur in the lower lobes. **Cavitation** may be thin or thick-walled, multiple or single (see **TB-CAVITATION**). When TB was more common cystic cavities often appeared following the clearing of consolidation and this part of the lung often contracted and showed scarring. Occasionally a pneumatocoele is seen. The infiltration tends to be multi-focal due to local spread; it is also often widely disseminated with 'broncho-pneumonic spread', due to the trans-bronchial dissemination of infected caseous material. Upper lobe infiltration, particularly lying posteriorly should always arouse suspicion as should infiltration and cavitation in the apex of a lower lobe, where the ratio of perfusion to ventilation is reduced, leading to a higher pH and a raised -HCO_3 (see also p. 1.47). On HRCT a '**tree in bud**' appearance may be seen with acute TB (see also refs. to Im et al., 1993, Walsh et al., 1996 & Loftus, 1997 - and Illus. **TREE IN BUD SIGN, TB Pt. 76 & TB Asian, Pt. 7**).

The demonstration of the disease pattern and its recognition usually gives the 'clue' to the diagnosis. After delayed hypersensitivity has developed a primary focus may undergo caseous necrosis, with the production of pasty material (cholesterol, phospholipids and unsaturated fatty acids), and this may be expectorated or be inhaled to give a bronchopneumonic type of dissemination to neighbouring and more distal parts of the lung(s).

A concomitant pleural effusion (or pneumothorax) together with an area of soft infiltration in the underlying lung, used to be a common presentation in young people and should still arouse considerable suspicion, as should an otherwise unexplained pericardial effusion. Localised pleural thickening may also be seen - see p. 14.28 and Ariyürek and Çil (2000).

All cases should have adequate radiography, including conventional tomograms or CT, to confirm the extent of the disease and possible cavitation - present in about 40 to 60 % of reactivated cases. These will also help to exclude the spurious cases - see below.

Tuberculous cavities tend to have moderately thickened walls, but not as irregular as with neoplasm, although some are difficult to differentiate radiologically even after tomography, and one may have to await sputum and or bronchial lavage cytology and bacteriology for confirmation. Occasionally percutaneous aspiration will be appropriate for a rapid answer (see Illus. **TB-CAVITATION, TB Pt. 19a-c**).

Endobronchial disease, lobar consolidation and mass-type lesions may also occur. Some patients may have a normal CXR with positive culture (Marceniuk et al.. 1999, reported 25 such cases).

Some tuberculous nodes may enhance with contrast media on CT sections, but as their centres are often necrotic, only the outer rims tend to opacify. This is not specific, as a similar finding may be seen with rapidly progressing lymphomas, and other neoplasms giving rise to enlarged nodes with necrotic centres.

Mediastinal, para-spinal or chest wall abscesses are sometimes seen on chest radiographs as the presenting features of the disease (particularly in Asians - see Illus. **TB-ASIAN**).

Spinal disease, especially in the elderly, should be differentiated from neoplasm, as radiotherapy or anti-cancer chemotherapy may cause a therapeutic disaster. Differentiation may be made by needle aspiration or biopsy - this is particularly important when other stigmata or neoplasm are not present, as tuberculosis may still be the cause - even in the 1990's! Both untreated spinal and chronic renal disease (e.g. an untreated tuberculous 'autonephrectomy') may lead to spread of infection, including miliary disease, later in life.

Miliary tuberculosis* is now uncommon but sporadic cases are still seen in immigrants, patients having dialysis, or in the elderly arising from a long standing quiescent focus in the spine or kidney. Its presentation may well be 'cryptic' with malaise, loss of weight, etc. The miliary shadows may also be delayed in presentation on chest radiographs.

As well as forming subcutaneous 'cold abscesses', which are usually **painless,** sinuses may occur, either externally or into the oesophagus, stomach, etc. The author has even seen a fistula from a tuberculous left kidney to the left main bronchus, but such an occurrence is very rare.

Occasionally even white patients still present with tuberculous laryngitis, skin, hepatic, splenic, bone or other manifestations, including miliary tuberculosis. Reactivation of old disease is also a not uncommon problem.

Sometimes a lung may become grossly diseased, with secondary loss of perfusion (as seen on a lung scan), and failure to respond to chemotherapy. In such a case surgical resection may still be required. Examples of miliary TB are shown in Illus. **TB-MILIARY.**

* We used to have a ward for such patients in Oxford in the 1950s & 1960s.

'Healed tuberculosis'.

Tuberculous scars or granulomas in elderly members of the white population are common, especially in the chest and are seen as scars or calcified foci in the lungs, pleura or lymph nodes; those in the abdominal and particularly the mesenteric nodes have usually arisen from milk-borne bovine tuberculosis. Pericardial calcification may indicate past pericardial tuberculosis - see also ps. 15.24 - 26.

Other causes of lung granulomas are given on p. 6.19.

Problems may arise in the chest with differentiation from tumour, tumour engulfment of old calcified tuberculous foci, or differentiation from other infections (especially aspergillosis) or other lung infiltrations. Old 'plombages' may become aerated (see p.14.2 and Illus. **PLOMBAGE**), and old tuberculous pleural collections may occasionally become reactivated (Illus. **PLOMBAGE, TB & plombage 1a-b**).

Spurious cases.

These include shadows from clothing ('bra' buttons), stains in linen, skin tags or warts, old fractures of ribs, neurofibromata, Indian women with low hanging hair-plaits, a right-sided descending aorta, an intra-thoracic goitre, Pakistani men with lung cancer or reticulosis treated as tuberculosis on clinical suspicion (see also Chapter 6). The author has seen examples of all of these, and several had been 'treated' as having 'resistant lesions'! Examples are shown under Illus. **TB-SPURIOUS.**

Patients with HIV infection.

Patients with HIV infection may develop florid tuberculosis and this may precede the onset of AIDS. This especially occurs in those at risk from their background environment, e.g. in Central Africa. In infected white people, drug addicts seem to be more at risk of developing pulmonary tuberculosis. Many white patients with AIDS, who also have tuberculosis, seem to manifest this mainly in the GI tract or liver, and may excrete the organism in the stools, or have it discovered by liver biopsy. Tuberculosis often occurs as a mixed infection with other organisms. Fistulae to the oesophagus or elsewhere may occasionally occur.

Treatment.
The diagnosis of tuberculosis is now almost always gratifying, as it is usually readily treatable. Most patients will nowadays not need admission to hospital, and collapse therapy or surgical resection is now rarely required (see below).

Some patients presenting with tuberculosis are very ill from other secondary bacterial infection, the acute respiratory distress syndrome (ARDS - see ps. 8.13 - 16) or intravascular coagulation. With these it may be more important to treat the secondary infection etc. first, before giving specific antituberculous chemotherapy, and to cover the patient against anaphylaxis with steroids.

Chemotherapy started with streptomycin in 1948, isoniazid in 1952 and PAS (sodium para-amino-salicylate), which delayed resistance to streptomycin, at about the same time. In many centres, only streptomycin and PAS were given, but Frank Ridehalgh in Oxford advocated triple-drug-therapy with streptomycin, isoniazid and PAS, and this appeared to be more effective and less prone to cause resistance. Even so it had to be given for 12 to 24 months to produce a 'cure'. The present treatment regimen usually lasts six months, two with rifampicin, isoniazid and pyrizinamide (to which ethambutol may also be added), followed by rifampicin and isoniazid for four months. Unfortunately resistance to standard drugs is reaching epidemic proportions in the Third World (see p. 19.17) and some parts of America (where BCG vaccine was abandoned over 30 years ago).

Historical.
Before drugs were available, treatment mainly depended on 'bed-rest' or ' resting' the affected lung by collapse therapy. Well-off patients found that a high altitude in the Alps helped to cure 'T.B.'; both this and bed-rest having a similar effect by correcting the normal poor perfusion of the lung apices in response to gravity in our upright position. An interesting finding was that patients with mitral valve disease, with well perfused apices, almost never developed tuberculosis. Collapse therapy was mainly by artificial pneumothorax (with refills as required), or occasionally a pneumoperitoneum. The former often led to a thickened or calcified pleura. Thoracoplasty (see also p. 11.15 and Illus. **THORACOPLASTY**), to reduce the volume of the affected upper hemithorax, was often employed as were less disfiguring 'plombages' - (bags of wax, sponges, ping-pong or table-tennis balls, etc. - see p. 14.2 & Illus. **PLOMBAGE**) - all were inserted extrapleurally between the ribs and the parietal pleura. Many of these are still seen in older people. As drug treatment was instituted, many had lobectomies to speed their recovery, but this is now rarely necessary.

The object of treatment was to (a) induce lung cavities to close, (b) to clear lung infiltration, and (c) to allow pleural effusions to become absorbed.

Radiological examination was often under their control of the chest physicians, who performed both plain radiography and fluoroscopy for the diagnosis and control of treatment. The Mass Miniature Radiography Service was set up during World War II (largely using photofluorography) and continued until the 1970s when the very small number of positive cases, plus the relatively high radiation dose, made it no longer worthwhile (see also p. 20.3 and Appendices p. 1).

A WHO report (BMJ 29 March 1997, **314**, 921) hailed as a 'break-through' at a conference in London to mark "World Tuberculosis Day" which advocated 'directly observed short course treatment' to prevent the development of drug resistance, seems like the re-invention of the wheel. It was long ago taught (e.g. by the late Sir William MacArthur) that people in some developing countries (particularly in Africa) should either have such essential medication given by injection or be observed actually swallowing it (and not just holding it in their mouths to later spit it out) to ensure that they actually took it.

Many illustrations of TB are shown under the following **KEYWORDS**:

TB GEN FOLDER	**TB-ASIAN**
TB&CROHNS	**TB-BONE**
TB&MYCETOMA/FUNGUS	**TB-CALC**
TB&SARCOID	**TB-CALC NODES**
TB+CA LUNG	**TB-CAVITATION**
TB-ADRENAL	**TB-CHEST**

TB-CHILD	TB-NODES CHILD
TB-CLAVICLE	TB-OLD
TB-CONGENITAL	TB-OMA
TB-FIBROSIS	TB-PERICARD EFFUSION
TB-FOOT	TB-PLEURAL
TB-GENERAL	TB-REN/AD
TB-GHON FOCUS	TB-RIB
TB-HANDS & WRISTS	TB-SACRO-ILIAC JOINT
TB-HILAR NODES	TB-SHOULDER
TB-HIP	TB-SKIN
TB-KIDNEY	TB-SPINE
TB-KNEE	TB-SPURIOUS
TB-MANTOUX	TB-THYMIC
TB-MEDIAST NODES	TB-TUBE/OVARY
TB-MILIARY	PLOMBAGE
TB-MIM CA LUNG	THORACOPLASTY
TB-NODES ADULT	EXTRAPLEURAL SPACE

Further references.

Sakula (1979) : Robert Koch (1843 -1910) - a study of his life and work. He isolated the anthrax bacillus in 1876 and shortly afterwards demonstrated staphylococci as the cause of wound infections. In 1887 he published his 'Die Aetiologie der Tuberkulose' which included his postulates : (i) the organism must be found in every case of the disease, (ii) it must not be found as an accidental or harmless parasite in other diseases, and (iii) after its isolation from the body and cultivation in pure culture, it must reproduce the same disease.

(Although these postulates are rarely capable of being fulfilled, they were an important discipline for the early study of bacteriology. In 1890 he discovered 'tuberculin', hailed at the time as a cure. It was unfortunately a failure in this respect, but became useful as a diagnostic test.)

Ryan, F. (1992) : Tuberculosis : The Greatest Story Never Told. Swift Publishers.

Rich (1951) : The Pathogenesis of Tuberculosis.

Adler, D. and Richards (1953) : Consolidation in primary pulmonary tuberculosis.

Clegg (1953) : Ulcerocaseous tuberculous bronchitis.

Tutelman and Drouillard (1953) : TB of the ribs.

Heaf (1957) : Symposium on Tuberculosis.

Lentino et al. (1957) : Segmental localisation of upper lobe TB - rarity of anterior involvement.

Joffe (1960) : Cavitating primary pulmonary TB in infancy - cavitation may be caused by:

(a) liquefaction occurring within the primary focus itself,

(b) liquefaction in caseous foci formed in other portions of the lung as a result of direct, bronchogenic or lymphatic spread from the primary focus, or

(c) erosion of a caseous lymph node into a bronchus with spread of infected caseous material and subsequent cavitation in resulting lung foci.

Jacobs (1964) : Studied 30 cases of osteo-articular TB in coloured immigrants. These had some unusual features :

(a) a tendency to a multiplicity of lesions,

(b) an unusual distribution, e.g. cervical spine, high dorsal spine and foot,

(c) rare sites e.g. ribs, vertebral appendages, pelvis, skull and shafts of long bones,

(d) florid or sclerotic reactions,

(e) exceptionally large associated abscesses, and

(f) lack of involvement of the intervertebral discs with spinal lesions.

Stead, W. et al. (1968) Clinical spectrum of TB in adults.

Weber et al. (1968) : Primary TB in childhood with emphasis on changes affecting the tracheo-bronchial tree.

Proudfoot et al. (1969) : Miliary TB in adults.

Jacques and Sloan (1970) : Changing pattern of miliary TB - incidence has fallen over previous 20 yrs., but now more common in adults than children.

Bell and Cochshott (1971) : TB of the vertebral pedicles.

LeRoux (1971) : Large TB abscesses in Asians & the Bantu in South Africa mimicking mediast. cysts & tumours.

Morgan and Ellis (1974) : Superior mediastinal masses secondary to TB - lymphadenitis in adults.

Wright, F. and Hamilton (1974) : Miliary TB twice - 2nd time from a chronically infected kidney (boy aged 16).

Albert and Petty (1976) : Endobronchial TB progressing to bronchial stenosis.

Khan, M. et al. (1977) : Clinical and Roentgenographic spectrum of pulmonary TB in the adult.

Amorosa et al. (1978) : Bilateral nodal lymphadenopathy esp. on the R in black people & Costa Ricans in the USA.

Liu et al. (1978) : TB mediastinal lymphadenopathy in adults - 3 cases simulating sarcoidosis.

Miller, W. and MacGregor (1978) : Frequency of unusual radiographic findings.

Geppert and Leff (1979) : The pathogenesis of pulmonary and miliary tuberculosis.

Palmer, P. (1979) : Usual and unusual presentations.

Brown (1980) : TB of the **ribs**.

Irving, H. and Brown (1980) : TB mediastinal lymphadenopathy in Bradford (18 cases - 16 in immigrants).

Bailey, C. and Windle-Taylor (1981) : TB laryngitis (37 cases).

Choyke et al. (1983) : Adult onset pulmonary TB.

Hulnick et al. (1983) : CT of 24 patients with active or inactive pleural TB. The most common finding was lung parenchymal disease with cavitation, and secondary pleural involvement.

National Survey of Tuberculosis Modifications in England and Wales (1983) ; Characteristics of Disease - **over one third of cases occurred in people from the Indian sub-continent.**

Williford et al.(1983) : Oesophageal TB - findings on barium swallow and CT.

Matthews et al. (1984) : Endobronchial TB simulating lung cancer.

Weaver and Lifeso (1984) : Radiological diagnosis of TB of the adult spine.

Davis, C. et al. (1985) from Houston, Texas : Reviewed 141 patients with active TB. At the time of death, 7 had overwhelming TB disease, 4 massive haemoptysis, 6 respiratory failure and 2 TB meningitis. 21 died from other causes including pulmonary embolism.

Barnett (1986) : CT findings in TB mediastinitis.

Hauser and Gurret (1986) : CT may reveal a micronodular pattern in the lung parenchyma before chest films are obviously abnormal. It also allows detection of adrenal enlargement.

Woodring, J. et al. (1986) : Radiographic features of pulmonary TB - update.

Coppola et al. (1987) : CT of 10 cases of musculoskeletal TB (6 affecting the dorsal spine, 2 the chest wall and two the sacrum or upper femur). CT showed destructive bone changes with adjacent soft tissue abscesses, most of which contained calcification, and with rim enhancement after IV contrast.

Im et al. (1987) : CT of TB mediastinal lymphadenitis.

Frew et al. (1987) : An outbreak of TB in an Oxfordshire school.

Mendelson, D. et al. (1987) : CT findings in five cases of TB mediastinitis - caused mediastinal masses with obliteration of the fat planes, and SVC obstruction in one case.

McNamara, M. et al. (1987) : TB of the oesophagus secondary to infected nodes. May lead to fistulae or empyemata - 3 cases. (Quoted eight other cases).

Smith, L. et al. (1987) : Endobronchial TB - serial optic bronchoscopy and natural history and endobronchial TB simulating lung cancer.

Pang, J. et al. (1989) : Tuberculostearic acid assay of bronchoscopic aspirate and lavage specimens for the diagnosis of pulmonary TB when sputum smear is negative - usual but nonspecific for the species of mycobacterium.

Ramakantan and Shah (1989) : Dysphagia due to **mediastinal fibrosis** in advanced lung TB.

Sharif et al. (1989) : Brucellar and tuberculous spondylitis - comparative imaging features.

Stead (1989) : TB in the elderly and in residents of nursing homes, correctional facilities, long-term care hospitals, mental hospitals, shelters for the homeless and jails.

Buckner and Walker (1990) : Radiologic manifestations of adult tuberculosis.

Carlsen and Bergin (1990) : Reactivation of TB in a donor lung after **heart-lung transplantation**.

Choe et al. (1990) : TB bronchial stenosis - CT findings in 28 cases - TB proven 18. In the other 10, the stenosis may have passed into the fibrotic stage. Stenosis may be caused by local infection or pressure from infected nodes.

Haque (1990) : The pathology and pathophysiology of mycobacterial infections.

Clarke (1990) : TB dactilitis in children - need for continued vigilance.

Im et al. (1990) : CT of oesophago-mediastinal-fistula in TB mediastinal lymphadenitis.

Morris (1990 from South Africa) : Pulmonary TB in the elderly - a different disease? Noted an increasing incidence in those aged over 65, the difficulty in making a diagnosis and the danger of spread in institutions, especially in those immunocompromised by age, drugs, other disease or malnutrition. He classified them into four groups :

Groups	**Chest radiographs**
Atypical (common)	Lower zone infiltrations, basal pleural effusions or thickening, few cavities in lung apices or lower zones.
'Classical' (unusual)	Apical interstitial fibrosis and pleural thickening, cavitation and lung opacities.
Disseminated (reactive)	Miliary TB
(cryptic)	Normal

Van den Brande et al. (1990) : Endobronchial TB in 11 elderly patients - not suspected on chest radiographs.

Moskovic (1990) : Macronodular hepatic TB in a child - CT appearance.

Ormerod (1990) : Chemotherapy and management of TB in the UK - recommendations of the Joint Tuberculosis Committee of the British Thoracic Society.

Reed et al. (1990) : Radiological diagnosis and management of a solitary **TB hepatic abscess**.

Bredin et al. (1991) : A school microepidemic of TB.

Finch et al. (1991) : Increased susceptibility of Hindus, especially women, to TB may be related to a culturally acquired immunodeficiency, caused by vegetarianism and associated vitamin deficiency (esp. vitamin D) in part due to lack of sunlight - 15 year study in South London.

Grzybowski (1991) : Tuberculosis in the third world - an extremely serious but soluble problem.

Kapoor et al. (1991) : US detection of tuberculomas of the **spleen**.

Lee et a. (1991) : Endobronchial TB - CT features.

Monaghan et al. (1991) : TB of the dorsal spine may manifest with destruction of the lateral aspects of the vertebral bodies resulting in an 'apple core' or 'cotton bobbin' appearance.

Destruction of the pedicles or spinous processes may also occur. There is commonly a surrounding soft tissue mass and the disc spaces are often well preserved.

Wright, F. (1991) : Tuberculosis past and present - a comparison of patients in Oxford between the 1950s and 1960s and the present time.

In the 1950s and 1960s acute TB principally affected young adults and children, with chronic cases (often 'carriers') in the older age groups. The disease affected all social classes, but was most prevalent in those who were malnourished or poorly housed. There were also the 'displaced persons' who came to the UK from Europe following World War II, many having been in concentration camps or severely starved. The number of cases nationally was about 50,000 per annum, with 5,000 deaths, most patients needing hospital treatment, at least initially. The 1991 figure is about 6,500 cases per annum, most of whom are treated as out patients.

Leung et al. (1992) : Radiographic manifestations of primary TB in childhood.

McGuiness et al. (1992) : HRCT findings in miliary lung disease.

Pombo et al. (1992) : Patterns of contrast enhancement of TB lymph nodes shown by CT. Unenhanced the nodes were of low attenuation (< 30 HU) in 18 cases and of soft tissue attenuation (> 35 HU) in 20 cases. Four patterns were found : (i) Peripheral rim enhancement (most common),

(ii & iii) Inhomogeneous or homogeneous enhancement, and (iv) Homogeneous non-enhancing nodes. In some the perinodal fat was obliterated.

Chan and Loveday (1992) : Widespread TB in sickle disease.

FitzGerald, R. and Hutchinson (1992) : TB of the ribs - CT findings.

Gaeta (1992) : **CT "halo sign"** in pulmonary tuberculoma.

Suchet and Horwitz (1992) : CT in tuberculous constrictive pericarditis.

Adler et al. (1993) : Tuberculosis of the chest wall : CT findings.

Denton and Hossain (1993) : Abdominal TB in a Saudi population esp. reference to US and CT.

Im et al. (1993) : CT findings in early active disease in 26 patients and sequential changes with therapy. They also studied 9 cadavers of patients who had died from the disease. On CT centrilobular lesions (nodular or branching linear structures - **'tree in bud appearance'**) were common and lesions in and around the small airways appeared to be the most characteristic feature of early acute TB. Most lesions cleared within five months.

Leahy et al. (1993 & 1994) : Mediastinal CT in a British Asian population - of 15 with active TB, 14 had mediastinal lymphadenopathy. In 9 this was the only positive radiological finding.

Lee, G. et al. (1993a) : Tuberculosis of the ribs - CT appearance.

Lee, L. et al. (1993b) : Adult-onset pulmonary TB - plain radiograph and CT findings.

Watson et al. (1993) : Tuberculosis in Britain today (plus subsequent correspondence).

Jain et al. (1993) : CT of vertebral TB in 30 patients (average age 38 yrs.) - patterns included fragmentary and osteolytic lesions associated with paraspinal masses.

Jamieson and Cremin (1993) : HRCT of lungs in acute disseminated TB in 5 children - nodules >2mm with a relatively uniform distribution, coalescence and large hidden cavity.

Cremin (1994) : From South Africa commented on the above (sees 30 cases/ year - average age 5 - 6 yrs.) and pointed out that the disease is indolent or painless. Early on there is a lytic circumscribed area of destruction in the vertebral body (as with other bones and as may be seen also with pyogenic infection, lymphoma and metastasis), disc narrowing may be subtle, the nucleus pulposus is compressed and driven into the vertebral body causing an internal implosion with vertebral body collapse (the 'fragmenting pattern'), and the paraspinal mass may contain calcification.

Ormerod (1994) : Tuberculosis in the 1990's at least 50% of new cases are linked to socio-economic deprivation, and in the homeless its incidence can be up to 100 times that for the normal population.

Bankier et al. (1995) : Abdominal tuberculosis - unusual findings on CT in 12 pts. - characteristic findings included solitary and multiple pelvic, adrenal, splenic and hepatic lesions, in 6 the findings mimicked malignancy.

Domjan et al. (1995) : The treatment of TB is not without side effects or complications. If their disease (not confirmed bacteriologically) is not responding to treatment, there may be a misdiagnosis - sarcoid, FA, mycetoma, primary or secondary tumour, infected cyst, etc.

Drobniewski (1995) : Tuberculosis in prisons - forgotten plague.

Enarson et al. (1995) : The challenge of tuberculosis - statements on global control & prevention.

Evans (1995) : Is TB taken seriously in the UK?

Freeman et al. (1995) : Studied Bristol's homeless population and found >9% of chest radiographs showed features of pulmonary TB with possible active disease.

Im et al. (1995) : CT of pulmonary tuberculosis.

Lee, S. and Im (1995) : CT in adults with chest TB : characteristic findings and management role.

McAdams, H. et al. (1995) : Radiological manifestations of pulmonary tuberculosis.

Peh et al. (1995) : Imaging features of TB of the extremities - 12 pts. with pain and/or swelling - the most useful radiographic pattern was progressive joint destruction. CT showed periarticular destruction, intramuscular abscesses and inflammatory masses. Synovial biopsy or needle aspiration was needed for certain diagnosis.

Set et al. (1995 from Hong Kong) : HRCT features of pulmonary TB in 35 patients - nodes (with peripheral enhancement), centri-lobular nodules (5 - 8 mm), thickened terminal bronchioles, bronchial wall thickening with bronchial stenosis or impaction, consolidation and cavities, pleural disease, esp. effusion (may be the only sign).

Sharma et al. (1995 from New Delhi) : Study of 100 cases of nonHIV associated miliary TB over an 11 yr. period - most common presenting feature was fever - 10 had meningitis. 12 died including 4/5 with ARDS.

Hatipoglu et al. (1996) : HRCT findings in pulmonary TB - centrilobular densities in and around the small airways and **"tree-in-bud"** appearances were the most characteristic CT features of disease activity. HRCT clearly differentiated fibrotic lesions from new lesions and demonstrated early bronchogenic spread.

Taylor. P. (1996) : Review of 90 cases in Manchester - collapse in 1/3, consolidation in 1/3, many with lower lobe disease. Some had small pl. effusions. One case with SVC obstruction. Disease esp. seen in young Asians.

Walsh et al. (1996) : CT for pulm. TB showed consolidation/cavitation - endobronchial disease, 'stable-state', chronic 'healed' cavities, **'tree-in-bud' appearance** - due to small airway disease of terminal & respiratory bronchioles indicating early endobronchial spread.

Drake et al (1997) : Pulmonary artery occlusion in two pts. caused by tuberculous mediastinal nodes.

Kim et al. (1997) : TB of the trachea and main bronchi - CT in 17 cases.

Ko et al. (1997) : Reversible cystic lung disease associated with pulmonary TB.

Loftus (1997, Hong Kong) : HRCT features of pulmonary tuberculosis - the typical findings in active TB are of 2-4 mm relatively well-defined centrilobular opacities which are either nodules or branching lesions giving a 'tree-in-bud' appearance, and corresponding pathologically with caseation in the bronchioles. Also seen are 5-8mm ill-defined, fuzzy nodules, probably representing the coalescence of centrilobular nodules. Post-treatment studies have shown that centrilobular tuberculous nodules can resolve to leave a central dot surrounded by emphysema; the central dot probably representing the fibrotic nodule which has caused post-obstructive distal emphysema.

Beaconsfield et al. (1998) : TB pulmonary arteritis - an unusual cause of R pulmonary artery stenosis.

Moon et al. (1998) : CT of mediastinal TB in 49 pts. - nodes with central low attenuation and peripheral enhancement suggested active disease, whilst homogeneous and calcified nodes suggested inactive disease. Low-attenuation areas within nodes pathologically corresponded to areas of caseation necrosis, suggesting active disease.

Suri et al. (1999) : Computed tomography in abdominal tuberculosis - pictorial review.

Leung (1999) : Pulmonary TB - the essentials.

TB and AIDS.

Pitchenik and Rubinson (1985) : The radiographic appearance of tuberculosis in patients with AIDS and pre-AIDS.

Rieder and Snider (1986), Chaisson et al. (1987), Goldman (1987) : TB in patients with AIDS.

Pitchenik et al. (1988) : Pulmonary effects of AIDS - mycobacterial disease - epidemiology, diagnosis, treatment and prevention - when TB occurs among patients with HIV infection, the radiographic picture is often atypical. Lower lobe infiltrates, diffuse or miliary infiltrates and/or hilar and paratracheal adenopathy are relatively common and resemble primary TB, even if reactivation of old disease has occurred. Fistulae of infected nodes to the oesophagus, TB brain abscess, GI involvement (with positive stool and blood cultures) may be found. Atypical bacteria, especially avium-intracellulare or other species may give a similar picture.

Goodman (1990) : Pulmonary tuberculosis in patients with acquired immunodeficiency syndrome.

Helbert et al. (1990) : Mycobacterial infection in patients with AIDS - 32 (out of 207 patients with AIDS at St. Mary's Hosp., London) had mycobacterial infection - TB in 15 (disseminated in 12), avium-intracellulare in 12, kansasii in 1 and ulcerans in 1. They found that subclinical carriage of avium-intracellulare was common. TB was sensitive to standard antibiotics, but avium intracellulare was often resistant & needing ansamycin and amikacin .

Perich et al. (1990) : Disseminated lymphatic TB in AIDS - CT finding.

Springett and Sutherland (1990) : Mycobacterial infection in patients with AIDS - "It is now generally accepted that the greatest incidence of TB in patients with AIDS than in the general population is due to breakdown of foci of TB infection acquired before infection with HIV. The incidence of TB in a group of patients will therefore depend mainly on the extent to which the group was infected with TB before acquiring HIV infection".

Allen et al. (1991) : TB broncho-oesophageal fistula in AIDS.

Buckner et al. (1991) : Changing epidemiology of TB and other mycobacterial infections in the USA - implications for the radiologist - the major factor accounting for the recent resurgence appears to be due to the HIV epidemic.

Saks and Posner (1992) : TB in HIV patients in South Africa - higher percentage of lymphadenopathy, pleural effusions, miliary or interstitial patterns - cavitation and collapse were less common.

Davies (1993) : HIV related TB appears to be as infectious as disease not related to HIV.

Pastores et al. (1993) : Intrathoracic adenopathy associated with pulmonary TB in patients with HIV infection.

Greenberg et al. (1994) : Active pulmonary TB in AIDS pts. - spectrum of radiographic findings (including normal).

Nunn et al. (1994) : Impact of HIV on tuberculosis in developing countries.

Lee, V. et al. (1994) : Pulm. mycobacterial infections in AIDS - Th (negative) - Ga (positive) mismatch pattern.

Neville et al. (1994) : Multidrug-resistant TB in AIDS pts. in large towns such as New York - the 'third epidemic'.

Small et al. (1994) : Evolution of chest radiographs in treated patients with pulmonary TB and HIV infection - 33 patients - 25 with TB only improved with treatment, worsening in 8 indicated a second pulmonary disease.
Goodman, P. (1995) : Tuberculosis and AIDS.
Leung et al. (1996) : HIV-seropositive patients had a lower prevalence of localised parenchymal disease and a higher prevalence of disseminated disease at CT.
Haramati et al. (1997, New York) : Chest radiographic and CT findings have shown that HIV-positive patients have more frequent atypical infiltrates and mediastinal lymphadenopathy and less frequent cavitation and infiltrates typical for reactivation TB than do HIV-negative patients.
Laissy et al. (1997) : Mycobacterium tuberculosis versus nontuberculosis mycobacterial infection of the lung in AIDS patients- CT and HRCT patterns.
Tshibwabwa-Tumba et al. (1997) : Radiological features of pulm. TB in 963 HIV-infected adults at 3 Central African Hospitals had more lymphadenopathy, effusions, miliary shadows and consolidation & less collapse or cavitation.
Lawn et al. (1999) : Pulm TB in West Africans coinfected with HIV - nodes & pl. effusions were most common.
A WHO report (BMJ 29.3.97 - **314**, 921) hailed as a "breakthrough" at a conference in London to mark "world tuberculosis day" which advocated "directly observed short course treatment" to prevent the development of resistant, seems like the re-invention of the wheel. (It was long ago taught that people in developing countries (particularly in Africa) should either have their medication via a needle, or be observed actually swallowing it - and not holding it in their mouths, to later spit it out - aphorism from the late Sir William MacArthur - specialist in Tropical Medicine).

TB in diabetics and immunocompromised patients.
Ikezoe et al. (1992) : Higher prevalence of multiple cavities with a given lesion and of nonsegmental distribution.

TB in cancer patients.
Hill (1984) : TB, atypical TB and BCGosis in a cancer treatment centre - mimicked ca in 64, coincident in 27 (including 7 with ca lung), & miliary disease in 6 following immunotherapy.
Libshitz et al. (1997) : TB and cancer pts. - update.

Atypical mycobacteria - (Illus. **ATYP MYCOBACT**).

There is a fairly large group of mycobacteria, but almost all (except for mycobacterium tuberculosis together with its bovine, etc. strains) only occur as saprophytes. Some are found in the soil, others in water and animals. A few give rise to human infections, principally in the lungs or cervical lymph nodes. Many infections occur in lungs already damaged by emphysema, industrial lung disease, etc. Previous tuberculosis produces no immunity to these mycobacteria, and old tuberculous scars may become secondarily infected. Pathologically and radiologically most infections resemble tuberculosis, but pleural involvement with atypical mycobacteria is uncommon. In cases we have seen in Oxford (mostly kansasii) the disease runs a milder course than tuberculosis. In some the infiltration clears spontaneously. Cavities may have thick walls, be of atypical shape (lozenge or diamond-like due to surrounding fibrosis and usually do not contain fluid). Bronchiectasis (which may be reversible) is often present.

M. kansasii - (Illus. **KANSASII INF**) - symptoms are usually minimal or absent. The disease

is frequently bilateral, and commonly occurs in the upper lobes (mainly the anterior or apical segments). Cavitation is common, and whilst most cavities are small, thin-walled and without fluid levels, other are thick and much larger (up to 2 cm or more). Some are not spherical and may be diamond or lozenge-shaped. Spread is usually by direct extension and by adjacent destruction, but tends to be very slow. Generalised pulmonary dissemination may also occur. Infection usually responds to anti-tuberculous drugs, but unlike present-day acute tuberculosis, healing often produces considerable scarring.

M   avium-intracellulare (also termed 'MAC' - Illus. **AVIUM-INTRACELLULARE**) -

these organisms are commonly found in food, soil and water. Infection due to this cause may occur on its own or complicate other underlying lung disease such as emphysema, pneumoconiosis or neoplasm. It is also not uncommonly seen in patients with AIDS. In these it may involve not only the chest, but also the GI tract and liver. Radiologically there are usually upper lobe infiltrates with multiple cavities. In AIDS patients enlarged nodes are common and may be necrotic with low density on CT and enhancing rims. Miliary disease may also be present. Treatment with rifampicin, ethambutol and isonoazid may cause clearing, but recurrence is not uncommon. Both AIDS and non-AIDS patients may develop resistance to the disease, which may become chronic.

M. fortuitum - rarely causes lung disease, despite its sporadic isolation in sputum or saliva. If pulmonary disease occurs it is usually indolent. Patients with a dilated oesophagus, as occurs with achalasia, and with stagnant contents may develop a saprophytic colonisation of these, which in turn can be inhaled. A few cases have been reported with multiple patchy areas of lung consolidation, accompanying pleural effusions or an empyema. The organism is not usually responsive to normal anti-TB treatment, but may respond to amikacin, doxycycline and sulphonamides.

M. scrofulaceum - occasionally causes pulmonary disease, but is more commonly associated with lymphadenopathy. It is often resistant to treatment.

M. xenopi - infection usually causes no symptoms, but produces lung nodules or upper lobe cavities. It is sensitive to the usual anti-TB drugs.

M. chelonei - may also complicate achalasia; it is also resistant to most anti-TB drugs, but may respond to erythromycin.

Other mycobacteria such as **M. asiaticum, M. flavescens, M. gordonae, M. malmoense** (Illus. **MALMOENSE**), **M. scrofulaceum, M. simiae and M. szulgai** may also give rise to human infections, especially in patients with AIDS. (The author has seen an elderly lady recently present with what appeared to be extensive TB in the RUL and a tumour at the left apex - both were due to **malmoense** - see Illus. **MALMOENSE, Mycobact Mal Pt. 2a-d**).

M. balnei (marinae) and M. phlei may cause skin granulomas. (One case of M. balnei skin infection the author has encountered occurred secondary to keeping tropical fish - see also Moss et al., 2000).

References.

General
Spitz and Wiot (1979), Tellis and Putnam (1980) : Non-tuberculous mycobacterial pulmonary disease.
Christensen et al. (1981) : Initial radiological appearances of TB, kansasii and intra-cellulare infections. Atypical mycobacterium tended to cause upper lobe cavity disease similar to TB.
Grebitz (1981) : Solitary pulmonary nodules caused by non-tuberculous mycobacteria.
Albelda et al. (1985) : Expanding spectrum of pulmonary disease caused by non-tuberculous mycobacteria. Noted that cavitation was less common than with TB. Many patients had lower zone disease. They also noted patchy nodularity associated with small cavities which resembled bronchiectasis.
Marinelli et al. (1986) : Nontuberculous bacterial infection in AIDS.
Woodring and Vandiviere (1990) : Emphasised fibroproductive disease with a potential for cavitation and a slow rate of change.
Conteras et al. (1988) : Nodules often cavitate.
Kuhlman et al. (1990) : CT features of thoracic mycobacterial disease.
Moore, E. (1993) : CT appearances in 40 patients. Common manifestations included air-space disease, nodules and screening - bronchiectasis was also present and appeared to progress as shown on serial studies.
Miller (1994) : Spectrum of pulmonary nontuberculous mycobacterial infection.
Primack et al. (1995) : Pulmonary TB and M. avium-intracellulare - comparison of CT findings - latter is a more potent cause of bronchiectasis than TB.
Torrens et al. (1998) : Non-tuberculous mycobacteria in **cystic fibrosis**.

Kansasii
Seibert and Tabrisky (1969) from Colorado : studied 91 cases. 8 had co-existent silicosis and had extremely large cavities in contrast to the usual conglomerate shadows usually seen with co-existent TB. Of the other 83, one-third had upper lobe cavities with well demarcated walls (large cavities for the amount of disease present, and with little surrounding infiltration), emphysema and no bronchogenic spread to the lung bases or basal pleural reaction. The remaining two-thirds had no specific pattern and were indistinguishable from TB or fungus infection.
Cook et al. (1971) from the Royal Brompton Hosp., London : described 'distinctive lesions', in some cases 'consisting of groups of 1 cm homogeneous shadows around translucent zones with line shadows radiating from each lesion', whilst other had 'small but thick-walled cavities' or 'shrunken upper lobes with only small cavities or dilated bronchi within them' - in others the appearances were non-specific.
Anderson et al. (1975) from Sheffield : studied 34 cases of 'opportunistic mycobacteria' including 30 with kansasii, 2 with intracellulare and one each with scrofulaceum and fortuitum. They found that pre-existing or associated pulmonary disease was common. In most cases the lesion was cavitary and spread to other parts of the lung was rare.

Healing took place by fibrosis with minimal pleural reaction or calcification. Cavities were most often single, about an inch in diameter and thin walled, but in a few cases several small cavities were grouped together. Surrounding infiltration was minimal.

Christensen et al. (1978) : Radiographic manifestations of pulmonary M. kansasii infections.

Zvetina et al. (1984 from Illinois) : Studied 263 cases of kansasii infection (49 previously untreated) and found four patterns of disease -

(i) a circumscribed opacity containing a cavity (40%), (ii) a circumscribed opacity containing multiple cavities (40%) (iii) multiple round or oval opacities containing cavities (5%), (iv) complex uncircumscribed opacity with cavities (15%)

Adjacent localised pleural thickening and 'tail signs' were common.

Crisp et al. (1992 from Nottingham) : Studied 28 patients and compared their presenting features with 56 patients with TB. They found that 10 to 30 % of infections with mycobacteria were non-tuberculous. M. kansasii tended to affect only the upper lobes. Thin-walled cavities were more common with kansasii, and the cavities tended to be smaller and to have no fluid levels. No pleural effusions were seen. Previous or coexistent lung disease was found equally with kansasii and TB.

Fishman et al. (1997) : Pulmonary M. kansasii in AIDS pts. often causes focal alveolar opacities which usually respond to therapy.

Avium-intracellulare.

Meissner and Anz (1977)

Nyberg et al. (1985) : Enlarged nodes with necrotic centres in AIDS patients.

Miller, R. et al. (1990) : Cavitation caused by avium-intracellulare in AIDS patients.

Benson, C. and Ellner (1993) : MAC complex infection and AIDS - advances in theory and practice.

Hartman et al. (1993) : Evaluation with CT in 62 patients - 40 had bronchiectasis and 60 infiltrates - usually of nodular type and with a preponderance of older women. 25 of 27 without small nodular infiltrates and bronchiectasis had underlying malignancy or were immunocompromised.

Siegler et al. (1996) : Bronchial artery aneurysms in association with Mycobacterium avium intracellulare complex in a 60 year old man with scleroderma.

Pantongrag-Brown et al. (1998) : Frequency of abdominal CT findings in AIDS patients with M. avium complex bacteraemia.

Chelonei

Burke and Ullian (1977) : Association with achalasia.

Hazleton et al. (2000) : CT in 14 pts. - resembled avium complex.

Fortuitum

Banergee et al. (1970), Aronchieck et al. (1986) : Association with achalasia.

Burns et al. (1990) : Disseminated M. fortuitum successfully treated with chemotherapy including ciprofloxacin.

Pacht (1990) : Lung abscess treated with trimethoprim and sulfamethoxazole.

Vadakekalam and Ward (1991) : M. fortuitum lung abscess treated with ciprofloxacin.

Malmoense

Evans et al. (1993) : Compared 16 patients with TB cases - cavities > 6 cm, thick-walled cavities, air fluid levels within cavities and coexistent and coexistent pneumoconiosis were more common features. Pleural effusions, pleural disease, cavitary disease and emphysema were seen with similar frequency in both groups.

Böllert et al. (1994) : Three patients with chronic obstructive lung disease developed coexisting M. malmoense and aspergillus infection - all suffered progressive lung destruction leading to early death despite prolonged antimycobacterial chemotherapy.

Meigh and Arnold (1994) : Not only may M. malmoense mimic a bronchial neoplasm, but also coexist with a bronchial neoplasm.

Crowe et al. (1997) : 18 cases seen in 3 yrs. - volume loss in 12, cavities in 10, emphysema in 6, opacity in 4, air space shadowing in 4, primary focus in 1.

'BCG-osis'.

Bacille Calmette-Guérin, as a live attenuated strain of M. bovis, is being increasingly used for the intra-vesical treatment of superficial bladder tumours, the bacillus inducing an immune stimulation which results in tumour necrosis. In under 5% of patients having treatment a systemic reaction may occur (in some leading to micronodules in the lungs) and in a few cases it may enter the blood-stream to cause miliary lung infections, pneumonia, empyema, hepatitis, etc. Anti-TB chemotherapy + steroids is usually given to treat this (as it is rare to obtain the organism from the lungs). Two cases of BCG-osis are shown in Illus. **BCG-OSIS.**

References.
Morales et al. (1973) : Intra-cavitary BCG in the treatment of superficial bladder tumours.
Hill (1984) : BCGosis in a cancer treatment centre - 2 cases following BCG immunotherapy - see also p. 19.24.
Lamm et al. (1985) : Complications of BCG immunotherapy in 1278 pts. - major side effects are unusual.
Steg et al. (1985) : Systemic complications of intravesical BCG for bladder cancer.
Brosman (1986) : BCG in the therapy of bladder carcinoma in situ.
Isreal-Biet et al. (1987) : Pulmonary complications of BCG for superficial bladder cancer.
Kesten et al. (1990) : Pulmonary disease following intravesical BCG treatment.
Wright (1991) : BCG-osis - Fig 11 in TB past and present.
Lamm et al. (1992) ; Incidence and treatment complications of BCG intravesical therapy in superficial bladder cancer.
McParland et al. (1992) : Miliary M. bovis introduced by intravesical BCG immunotherapy.
Kristjansson et al. (1993) : Molecular confirmation of BCG as the cause of pulmonary infection following urinary tract installation.
Smith, R. et al. (1993) : Pulmonary granulomata - complicating intravesical BCG for superficial bladder carcinoma.
Jasmer et al. (1996) : Miliary lung disease after intravesical BCG immunotherapy.
Foster, D. (1997), Rabe et al. (2000) : Miliary tuberculosis following intravesical BCG treatment.
Mooren et al. (2000) : Systemic granulomatous disease including chest after intravesical BCG treatment.

RICKETTSIAE

Psittacosis - (due to Chlamydia psittaci - an intracellular organism found in parrots, parakeets, macaws, cockatiels and to a lesser extent in budgerigars, pigeons and other birds, including poultry) may give rise to a wide spectrum of illness, ranging from a mild 'flu-like condition to a severe pneumonia with acute respiratory distress and multiple organ involvement. Patients typically have fever, headache, a dry cough and myalgia. Radiologically there are often 'soft' patchy lung infiltrates, but miliary changes and lobar pneumonia (sometimes without sparing of a segment, which is more often seen in bacterial types) may be found. Often the radiological changes are much greater than are suggested by physical signs, and they may take several weeks to clear.

In most patients the acute illness lasts only seven to ten days and symptoms then improve. Some have a more severe illness with pleurisy, myocarditis and endocarditis. Although mild cases recover without treatment, antibiotics help in the more severe cases, and have reduced the mortality to under 1%. Tetracycline, erythromycin and rifampicin have been used, and the first of these appears to be the most effective. The organism often quickly becomes resistant to penicillin.

Infectivity seems rather low, probably due to the low grade latent, rather than overt, infection in most affected birds. This may flare up, especially at breeding times, or when birds are kept in crowded insanitary conditions. Infectious discharges from their beaks and diarrhoea may cause contamination of their feathers, and the aviarist, poultry keeper or even neighbours may then inhale the organism. In some cases infection occurs with only passing contact with apparently healthy birds e.g. parrots, racing pigeons in transit, or in poultry processing plants. Even infected bird-droppings in church bell-towers has given rise to some human infections. In some outbreaks, infected birds have been given tetracycline to help eradicate the reservoir of the infection.

The organism cannot be cultured except in animals or embryonated eggs, and a rising antibody (or complement fixation) titre is usually required for certain diagnosis. This however does not occur for two weeks, and difficulties occur because of cross reference to other species of chlamydia. An immune assay using a monoclonal antibody against the lipopolysaccharide in the cell wall of chlamydia is now being developed for rapid diagnosis. The Communicable Disease Surveillance Centre receives about 300 notifications per year of respiratory infections due to chlamydia in England and Wales.

Two examples of psittacosis are shown in Illus. **PSITTACOSIS**, one with slight inflammatory change in the left lower lobe and the second with RUL consolidation.

Other pathogenic chlamydia.
C.   pneumoniae causes pneumonia via human to human spread without any avian contact, and may account for up to 10% of community acquired pneumonias admitted to hospital.

C. trachomatis, which more commonly causes genital and eye infections, may cause pneumonia in babies and adults. It may cause confusion with psittacosis, by cross reference to antibody and complement fixation tests.

'Q' (Queensland) fever with a 10 to 20 day incubation period, is caused by a rickettsia-like organism (**Coxiella burnetti**) which is carried by many insects, ticks and animals. The reservoir is commonly in sheep and cattle, in which it is subclinical. It may be transmitted to humans by airborne droplets or unpasturised milk, but many patients have no history of contact with farmyard animals, and domestic animals including cats may harbour the organism. Many animals release large numbers of the organism during parturition. The clinical features of the illness are protean and range from a subclinical infection, or influenza-like illness, to a not uncommonly fatal encephalitis or endocarditis. With the latter it particularly affects aortic valve or other arterial grafts.

On chest radiographs, many have a viral or mycoplasma-like patchy shadowing. This is often segmental (or lobar) in type and may be slow to clear. **'Rounded pneumonia'** with slow resolution may suggest the diagnosis. The organism is sensitive to tetracycline, clindamycin and chloramphenicol, but treatment may have to be continued for several weeks in resistant cases.

An example is shown in Illus. **Q FEVER**.

Rocky Mountain spotted fever, caused by a tick-borne rickettsia, is mainly found in the South-Eastern part of the USA. Cardiomegaly with pulmonary oedema, interstitial and alveolar infiltrates and pleural effusions may be seen on chest radiographs. The disease may also cause soft tissue necrosis e.g. of the finger tips. Pathologically it causes thrombosis of small vessels with capillary damage.

(Note : Rickettsiae or Bedsoniae both contain RNA and DNA as nucleic acids, whereas viruses only have one of these).

References.
(a) **Psittacosis and Chlamydia infections.**
Shaffner et al. (1967) : The clinical spectrum of endemic psittacosis.
British Medical Journal (1972) : Psittacosis.
Radkowski et al. (1981) : Chlamydia pneumonia in infants - chest radiographs in 125 cases.
Edelman et al. (1984) : Radiographic appearance of chlamydia trachomatis pneumonia in adults.
Riordan (1990) : Getting disease parrot-fashion.
Marrie (1993) : Chlamydia pneumoniae.
Grayston (1994) : Chlamydia pneumoniae infections in children - a common cause of pneumonia, bronchitis, sinusitis and pharyngitis in children aged 5 to 15. In adults - often a subacute pneumonia or bronchitis, with symptoms that are slow in onset and persist for days or weeks.
McConnell et al. (1994) : Radiographic appearances of Chlamydia pneumonia (formerly known as 'atypical pneumonia') - included alveolar consolidation (mostly unilateral), small to medium-sized pleural effusions, - progressing to bilateral mixed, interstitial and alveolar changes. Cavitation and lymphadenopathy were uncommon.
Johnson et al. (1996) : C psittaci infection causing pneumonia, myocarditis, encephalitis, and renal failure in a 32 yr old woman.

(b) **'Q' fever.**
Derrick (1937) : An acute undiagnosed illness among abattoir workers in Brisbane, Queensland, Australia, where the first cases were described.
Glucker and Munk (1952) : Radiological manifestations of 'Q' fever - review of 85 cases seen in Haifa - the main radiological feature was a circumscribed usually rounded lesion.
Millar (1978) : Chest film findings in 35 cases in N. Ireland - included multiple round segmental consolidations (esp. in lower lobes), linear collapse, lobar or partial lobar consolidation (esp. of RML). In many the pneumonitis occurred on the 3rd or 4th days.
Palmer and Young (1982) : 'Q' fever endocarditis in England and Wales.
Ellis et al. (1983) : Chronic or fatal 'Q' fever infection - 16 patients in NE Scotland.
Geddes (1983) : 'Q' fever - a review.
Gordon et al. (1984) : Radiographic features in 11 epidemic and 14 sporadic cases of 'Q' fever - higher incidence of rounded and multiple shadows in epidemic group.
Seggev et al. (1986) : Unusual manifestations - case with multiple cavitating nodules.
Pickworth et al. (1991) : Radiological appearances of 'Q' fever pneumonia.
Smith, D. et al. (1991) : Chest x-ray in 69 (out of 147) cases in West Midlands. The acute radiograph may be normal, even when respiratory symptoms are present; conversely radiographic abnormalities may be present without symptoms. Consolidation esp. occurred in the lower zones. Linear collapse and pleural reaction were rare. Deterioration may occur in the first two weeks and radiographic resolution may be delayed for six weeks or longer.
Voloudaki et al. (2000) : Q fever pneumonia in 10 pts. - mainly lobular airspace consolidation.

Chapter 19

(c) **Rocky Mountain spotted fever.**
Lees et al. (1978) Radiographic findings in 22 cases.
Martin et al. (1982) : The chest radiograph in Rocky Mountain spotted fever.

(d) **Scrub typhus** - Choi et al. (2000) : Mainly basal dependent ground-glass shadowing + centrilobular nodules.

VIRAL PNEUMONIA - (Illus. **VIRAL PNEUMONIA**).

There are several types - influenza, adenovirus, cytomegalovirus, herpes simplex, varicella, etc., and all may give rise to localised or more generalised nodular or diffuse lung consolidation. This may appear a few days after the onset of symptoms; it also tends to persist after clinical symptoms have resolved. With some viral pneumonias (particularly influenza) there is often much pulmonary oedema, which may lead to a '**drowned lung**' appearance (see also ps. 2.1, 4.20 & 6.6). Secondary bacterial infection often accompanies the viral inflammation, and Scadding (1937) pointed out that viral pneumonia is rarely fatal unless complicated by bacterial infection. A new exception to this is hantavirus (see ref. below).

Influenza pneumonia occurs mainly in epidemics and pandemics. Several pandemics have occurred with many deaths e.g. after the First World War (in 1918, when 20 M people died world-wide) and at intervals since, including 1957 - 1958. Two occurred in 1990 (in the spring and autumn). There are three common types of the virus - A which is highly unstable, constantly mutating in unexpected ways and giving rise to epidemics, B which is fairly stable and C a milder version like the common cold.

Those worst affected are usually the elderly and debilitated, in whom secondary bacterial infection and heart failure may be the principal causes of death. Radiologically there may be fine diffuse lung shadowing, particularly at the bases, probably at first due to bronchiolitis (ps. 3.25 - 30). This may progress to septal line engorgement ('B' lines - ps. 8.9 - 11 - indicating basal congestion) and consolidation. Some acute lung overexpansion is not uncommon. Some patients have accompanying cardiomegaly, with toxic myocarditis or pericarditis.

Long term effects include emphysema and diffuse lung scarring, fibrosing alveolitis (see ps. 19.116 - 119) and many years later bronchiolo-alveolar carcinoma (p. 5.1).

Secondary bacterial infection due to Haemophilus influenzae is noted on p. 19.4. Influenza may also be mimicked by bacterial infections such as Mycoplasma and Necrobacillosis (ps. 19.9 & 10).

Examples are shown in Illus. **INFLUENZA**.

Cytomegalovirus pneumonia is caused by a DNA virus which is similar to herpes simplex. It may occur on its own or in combination with other pathogens, particularly in immunocompromised patients (especially those with AIDS). Radiologically it often appears as a disseminated granular pattern or as small basal nodules. Oliff (formerly Wright) and Williams (1989) studied the radiological appearances of CMV infection in 35 patients, most of whom had had bone marrow transplantation for leukaemia. Chest radiographs showed mid and/or lower zone consolidation, interstitial or ground-glass shadowing, in which small nodules (2 - 4 mm in diameter) may be seen. Small pleural effusions were not uncommon, and a spontaneous mediastinum (or pneumothorax) were present in about a third. Bowel wall thickening and pneumatosis intestinalis may be seen below the diaphragm.

In other cases the appearance is similar to that of bronchiolitis or bronchiolitis obliterans (see ps. 3.25 - 30) with a widespread interstitial pattern. Scarring in children may lead to poor development, similar to that seen with adenovirus in the Swyer-James (Macleod) syndrome (ps. 7.9 - 10). Early diagnosis is of great importance for successful therapy, but no pattern is sufficiently characteristic to allow easy differentiation from other infections. (see also Waxman et. al. 1997).

The CT appearance is shown in Illus. **CMV PNEUMONIA**.

Varicella ('chicken pox') pneumonia - (also **smallpox**) may give rise to 'lung pocks' (see Illus. **VARICELLA**) - patchy small diffuse nodules. These are seen mainly in young adults or teenagers, who have a cough (usually mild) accompanying the infection. Rarely there is a segmental or lobar consolidation. The latter may be fatal (especially in pregnant women or in those who are immunocompromised - see refs. below) and it is estimated that about six to ten patients die each year from this cause in the UK. Most cases, however, recover completely, but about 10% develop miliary calcified scars. Lung scarring may rarely lead to finger clubbing (Greeves et al., 1971).

Pneumonia may also complicate herpes zoster, but this is usually due to secondary infection.

Calcified miliary lung shadows mostly occur as a result of chicken pox in teenagers or young adults. The credit for noting that such shadows may follow varicella pneumonia goes to Mackay and Cairney (1960) in New Zealand. Carstairs and Edmond (1963) noted that acute pulmonary fine nodular shadowing due to chicken pox tended to persist in some patients. Knyvett (1966) also studied patients with chicken pox pneumonia and three progressed from acute small shadows to miliary calcification. He also collected 88 cases with miliary calcification who had had chicken pox as young adults. Brunton and Moore (1969) in Southampton surveyed patients attending Mass Radiography Units in Wessex, and similarly found a number of cases. They found that most of the nodules were 1 - 3 mm in diameter, but occasionally were up to 7 mm. Lesions are usually numbered in thousands and tend to spare the apices. Such nodules are not uncommonly found on chest radiographs in Oxford, but may be present in addition to other disease. The acute lung disease is most commonly seen in young parents, or in patients with severe chicken pox in the infectious disease department and may progress onto bronchiolitis or ARDS (ps. 3.2 & 8.15).

The author has found that scattered lesions may be 'missed' on CT sections, as the lesions may lie outside given sections - but when seen they are typically tiny calcified ring shadows with less dense centres - they also often tend to be peripherally distributed (Illus. **VARICELLA, Varicella old Pt. 15a-d**).

One should be aware of the possibility that small peripheral lung nodules in patients having CT examinations for the staging or 'follow-up' of tumours (particularly young men with testicular tumours, may be due to chicken pox and not metastases (see also Levin, 1957 and Picken et al., 1994 - nodules on CT exam. at the time of a chicken pox rash).

Calcified lung 'pocks' may also be due to past **smallpox**, which sometimes followed a "'flu-like" illness after contact with small pox patients ("small pox handler's lung").

[NB. Queen Mary II (wife of William III) died from smallpox in 1694 - see Oxford Picts, **Radcliffe John**.]

(Other types of calcified miliary shadows are discussed in **Tables 5.6 & 6.5**, ps. 5.41 & 6.19.)

Infectious mononucleosis (glandular fever due to Epstein-Barr virus - Illus. **GLANDULAR FEVER)** is a disease which mainly affects young adults, typically presenting with malaise, fever, sore-throat, head-ache and cervical lymphadenopathy. It may give rise to patchy unilateral or bilateral lung infiltrates, particularly at the lung bases. Lymph nodes may become enlarged in the hilar areas or mediastinum, and the author has seen one case in which the nodes became so large as to cause left sided innominate vein compression and thrombosis, leading to pulmonary emboli (Illus. **GLANDULAR FEVER, Subclav vein Pt. 6a-c**). The spleen is not uncommonly enlarged (deforming or displacing the stomach gas bubble on chest radiographs); it may occasionally become very large, and be very active on an isotope scan (Illus. **GLANDULAR FEVER, Spleen Pt. 17**). The virus appears to selectively infect B lymphocytes which may proliferate in lymphoproliferative disorders in patients with immune deficiencies (congenital or acquired), post-transplant patients, etc. (see also p. 11.17). This may lead to a whole range of lymphoproliferative conditions from hyperplasia (with small lung nodules - see p. 13.4 - 5 and under AIDS below), LIP (p. 19.119), to frank lymphomas. It may also be the 'trigger' for neoplasm in some patients with AIDS (p. 19.33) and may also act as a trigger in Burkitt's lymphoma (p. 19.34), fibrosing alveolitis (p. 19.118) and for autoimmune hepatitis (see refs. below).

For inter-reaction with cyclosporine - see ps. 5.36 and 11.16 - 17.

Rubella - infection in utero may lead to both heart disease and lung scarring with calcification in infants - two examples are shown in Illus. **RUBELLA.**

Hantavirus - a zoonosis affected the southwestern USA in 1993, with high mortality. Those radiographed showed marked **pulmonary oedema,** presumably due to increased capillary permeability. (Ketai et al., 1994 & 1998).

Further references.
General
Conte et al. (1970) : Viral pneumonia - Roentgen pathological correlations.

Influenza pneumonia
Friedmann (1918) : 33 deaths mainly due to complicating Staph. aureus infection - severe congestion and consolidation.
Galloway and Miller (1959) : Lung changes in the 1957 influenza epidemic (406 patients admitted to Fazakerley Hospital, Liverpool - June to November). Many had broncho-pneumonic consolidation, which was especially basal. Others had lobar or segmental consolidation, particularly in the upper lobes. Some had complicating lung abscesses and/or pleural effusions. (Four had complicating tuberculosis).
Louria et al. (1959) : Studies on influenza in the pandemic of 1957 - 1958 - pulmonary complications.
Laraya-Cuassay et al. (1977) : Chronic pulmonary complications of early influenza virus in children.

Varicella
Levin (1957) : Chicken pox pneumonia with x-ray findings suggesting metastatic carcinoma.
Mermelstein and Freireich (1961) : Varicella pneumonia.
Bocles et al. (1964) : Abnormalities of respiratory function in varicella pneumonia.
Donnan (1965) : Varicella pneumonia in adults.
Weber and Pellechia (1965) : Varicella pneumonia in 110 US military men who had CXRs - 18 had fine nodules, some with areas of patchy confluence - follow up films showed clearing in 6-10 days.
Sargent et al. (1967 from California) : Six deaths from varicella pneumonia.
Nikki et al. (1982) : Severe bronchiolitis probably caused by varicella-zoster virus.
Meyer et al. (1986) : 41 year old man had persistent miliary shadows after recovery from varicella pneumonia. A year later an open lung biopsy showed necrotising granulomas with mononuclear infiltration and fibrous capsules.
Southard (1986) : Roentgen findings in chicken pox pneumonia - 5 cases + literature review.
Ellis et al. (1987) : Chicken pox pneumonia may be more common in adults who smoke. Seven cases were treated with acyclovir (an anti-viral agent). Sub-clinical cases may be detected by a reduced carbon monoxide transfer test.
Gilbert (1993) : Chicken pox during pregnancy - although only about 2% of reported cases of chicken pox occur in people > 20, these account for one quarter of all deaths, usually due to varicella pneumonia. Severe primary varicella also often occurs in immunocompromised patients, esp. those with cell mediated immune deficiency. The virus may cross the placenta causing severe congenital abnormalities. Prevention during pregnancy is clearly desirable - recommended zoster immune globulin for appreciable exposure and acyclovir for progressive infection.
Mann and Wyldes (1993) : Maternal death.   Nathwani (1993) : Is more severe in third trimester of pregnancy.
Oxford Journal (20 May 1993) : Girl aged 9 having steroid treatment for toxoplasmosis affecting her left eye died from disseminated varicella infection - this eventually cost Oxfordshire HA £100,000 in an out of court settlement (Oxford Mail 23 June 1997).
Daily Telegraph (26 June 1993) : Mother and new-born son both died from varicella.
Picken et al. (1994) : Pulmonary lesions of chicken pox pneumonia revisited.
Rice et al. (1994) : 27 year old woman taking 30mg prednisolone daily for idiopathic cytopenia had near fatal chicken pox, with severe back pain, rash, bilateral alveolar shadowing on CXR, DIC, renal and respiratory failure - good general recovery with acyclovir and intensive care treatment, but persistent retinal scotomas. The DOH now advises immunoglobulin prophylaxis for persons in contact with varicella who are taking steroids and who have not had chicken pox. An immunoassay is available for doubtful immunity.
Plotkin (1995) : Clinical and pathogenic aspects of varicella-zoster.
Daily Telegraph (10 Sept. 1997, p. 7) : Man aged 34 died from varicella pneumonia caught from his 4 yr. old son.
Ruehm et al. (1998) : CT appearances of hepatic involvement in systemic varicella-zoster - multiple hypodense nodular lesions 3-4 mm in diameter.
Kim et al. (1999) : HRCT in varicella-Zoster pneumonia - nodules ± ground-glass shadowing & some coalescence.

Smallpox
Howatt and Arnott (1944), Morris Evans and Foreman (1963) Ross et al. (1974), Foster (1994).

Infectious mononucleosis.
McCort (1949) : Infectious mononucleosis with special reference to Roentgenologic manifestations.
Hebert (1966) : The Roentgen features of Eaton agent pneumonia.
Ream and Giardina (1972) : SVC aneurysm in a 20 yr old student complicated by infectious mononucleosis leading to thrombophlebitis, pulmonary emboli, infarction and death (see also p. 9.10).
Landen and Palayew (1974) : Infectious mononucleosis - a review of chest Roentgenographic manifestations.
Andiman et al. (1981) : Clinical course, virology and serology of Epstein-Barr virus infection in association with childhood pneumonia.
Jones, J. et al. (1988) : T-cell lymphomas containing EB viral DNA in patients with chronic EB virus infections.
Weiss et al. (1989) : Detection of EB viral genomes in Reed-Sternberg cells of Hodgkin's disease.

Goddard et al. (1990) : Showed nodal and splenic enlargement in infectious mononucleosis by STIR sequence MR.

Nodes and spleen (where the disease is present appear white on STIR sequence).

Cohen (1991) : EB virus lymphoproliferative disease associated with acquired immunodeficiency.
Aceti et al. (1995) : A young woman with hepatitis after a sore throat.
Vento. et al. (1995) : Epstein-Barr virus as a trigger for autoimmune hepatitis in susceptible individuals.
Mikaye et al. (1986) : Infectious mononucleosis with pulmonary consolidation.
Collins et al. (1998) : Epstein-Barr-virus-associated lymphoproliferative disease of the lung - CT & histological findings - study of 24 pts. (5 with AIDS, 1 with immune deficiency & 18 having immunosuppressive therapy post organ transplantation or for vasculitis) - EBV lymphoproliferative disease ranges from benign lymphoid hyperplasia to high-grade lymphoma, the most common CT manifestation being multiple small lung nodules, with a predominantly peribronchovascular or subpleural distribution - see ps. 13.3 - 4 and 19.37. (These nodules follow the distribution of the lymphatic tissue in the lungs).

Acquired Immuno-Deficiency Syndrome (AIDS).

The causative agent is a retro-virus, one of the human T-cell lymphotrophic viruses - HTLV or HIV (human immunodeficiency virus). It particularly attacks the T_4 or 'helper' lymphocytes, which stimulate immunity, and also macrophages. It attaches itself first to the cell surface molecules CD4 before being incorporated into host genomes. There is a rapid turnover of virus (2.6 day/cycle) with many errors in replication and hence many mutants or strains.

The condition was first recognised in the UK and the USA in 1981, when previously healthy male homosexuals were found to have a severe and often fatal immunodeficiency associated with Pneumocystis pneumonia and/or an aggressive form of Kaposi's sarcoma. However cases (although unrecognised at the time) undoubtedly occurred several years before this. The first known British case was a 25 year old seaman based on a ship in Gibraltar. He had visited many North African ports, where 'he had been popular with a number of young ladies'. His health began to deteriorate in 1957, and he died from pneumonia and other complications after spending his last nine months in Manchester Royal Infirmary in 1959. At the time his death was ascribed to Wegener's granulomatosis, but tissue specimens were kept and later studies revealed HIV (Bell, 1990). It has been thought that the disease may have originated in Africa, possibly from monkeys infected with simian immunodeficiency virus (SIV). More recently it has been found that there are several HIV strains both in humans and monkeys. Gao et al. (1999) showed that the natural reservoir of HIV1 virus was probably in the Central chimpanzee (Pantroglodytes troglodytes) a native of Central Africa, where they have been used for food and in whom the virus is not so virulent. Passage to man has probably occurred from blood in killing or butchering the animals or through eating them. Spread in man has been hastened by 'opening up' the areas of habitat (particularly with logging and the use of 'bush-meat' to feed the loggers), civil unrest and promiscuity. Others (e.g. Kirk, 1999) noted that AIDS was first seen in Africa in 1957 and may have passed to humans by men copulating with 'little green monkeys' kept as pets in Central Africa, the condition then being termed 'green monkey disease'.

After infection there is often an apparent long latent period (when the immune system is able to 'neutralise' the production of virus), and the full blown syndrome occurs when the immune system starts to fail, and may be triggered by some intercurrent illness. Fortunately not all who are inoculated get the full disease. Transmission is usually by blood or through homo- or hetero-sexual contact. In Oxford many of the patients have been haemophiliacs who had non-heat or poorly treated Factor VIII produced from large blood pools collected in the USA between 1981 and 1985, in contrast to small batch NHS material with smaller risks.

Many patients develop or present with **Pneumocystis pneumonia** (which may be life-threatening), or other infections (mycobacterial - TB, etc - see ps. 19.16 et seq., fungi - aspergillosis, nocardia, histoplasmosis, etc., candida of the throat and oesophagus - see ps. 16.16 - 17, viruses - CMV (causing both lung infection and retinitis - leading to blindness), varicella, or protozoa - toxoplasma, etc.). Not uncommonly a mixture of infections is found (see also - opportunistic pneumonias - p. 19.7). Some patients produce drug reactions e.g. Stevens-Johnson syndrome. Non-specific pneumonitis, LIP (p. 19.119) may occur particularly in children, and congestive cardiomyopathy may also be present. Infections are often atypical and chronic and a fatal encephalopathy (particularly in patients with cryptococcal infection) is not uncommon. Sinusitis may also be an important clinical problem - see reference to Chong et al. (below). Secondary infections particularly occur when the T cell CD4 level drops below 200/ cu ml. (When the virus encounters a T cell, proteins on the virus bind to both CD4 and co-receptors and the virus enters the cell and its genetic material is integrated into the T cell's DNA to produce more viral protein which is released into new viruses).

April 1995 official figures reported that 24,502 people had the virus in the UK but this was probably an underestimate and 7,571 had died from the disease in the UK. According to figures from the 12th World Conference on AIDS, 1998, 20 M people were HIV infected world-wide (the largest number being in sub-Saharan Africa - 70% and Asia - 20%, compared with 2% in Europe and 4% in North America). The 1999/2000 estimate is that 38 M people (including 1.5 M children) are HIV positive, with 2.6 M AIDS related deaths in 1999, and probably total cumulative AIDS deaths of about 19 M world-wide. Half of those who are HIV positive progress to AIDS and death within 10 years and about 80% will have lung involvement at some stage.

Enlarged nodes may be due to AIDS per se or complicating Kaposi's sarcoma, lymphoma (especially non-Hodgkin's lymphoma), other tumours (see below) or infections, e.g. tuberculosis or atypical mycobacteria (see also references below). It is sometimes found that patients develop nodal enlargement and this resolves spontaneously, but it may be a bad sign that the immune system is completely failing, and that after a short period of well-being they will die - the T cells turn over very quickly in AIDS.

The drug **retrovir** (AZT or Zidovudine) has produced considerable amelioration of the condition, by postponing its grosser manifestations, but as yet there is no final cure. A recent study has suggested that giving both AZT and one of its "cousins" together may synergistically delay the onset of AIDS in those who are HIV positive. Some also give an anti-viral drug, e.g. a protease inhibitor or reverse transscriptase. Vaccines have also been tried but so far have been largely unsuccessful, probably because the virus is repeatedly changing its antigenicity. Possibly a live genetically altered and attenuated vaccine may be a way to produce immunity; a gene vaccine has been successful with the similar cat virus. A few individuals appear to already have or develop a natural immunity to the HIV virus (e.g. some Nairobi prostitutes who do not develop the condition) and this is promoting further study into using a booster live vaccine.

For illustrations see Illus. **AIDS** and **PNEUMOCYSTIS PN**.

Neoplasms and lymphoproliferative conditions in patients with AIDS.

These are being more commonly seen. The first noted were lymphomas (particularly non-Hodgkin's lymphomas) affecting the abdomen, chest or brain. Since then others have been reported, including rapidly progressive lung cancer (especially starting as an upper lobe mass), Kaposi sarcoma, non-Hodgkin's sarcoma, pulmonary, testicular and cervical tumours. Some of these appear to be triggered by concomitant viral infections (e.g. herpes → Kaposi sarcoma, EBV → lymphoid hyperplasia, LIP, lymphomas, including Burkitt's lymphoma and muscle tumours). The more benign conditions produce lung nodules or infiltration. Kaposi's sarcoma and lymphomas which complicate about 30 % of patients with AIDS are often aggressive multicentric tumours, producing nodular lung lesions, segmental consolidation or diffuse lung disease.

Illus. **AIDS Pt. 4** shows large axillary nodes in a patient with AIDS.

Kaposi's sarcoma.
Kaposi (1872) described an idiopathic sarcoma of the skin, with bluish, bluish-red or reddish-brown nodules and plaques which were tender and painful (Illus. **KAPOSI SARC, Pt. 2**). It appeared to have a multifocal origin. Before the onset of the AIDS epidemic, it was found in older men, especially of Eastern European, Italian or Jewish ancestry, and in children and young Negroes in Africa, it accounted for up to 10 % of all tumours. It was also found as a complicating tumour in patients with reticuloses, lymphosarcoma, leukaemia, myeloma, etc.

Since the advent of AIDS, it is being seen much more commonly in patients with HIV infection, but it is not seen in haemophiliac patients with AIDS (Rizza, 1995), or those with AIDS secondary to blood transfusions or drug addicts using 'dirty needles.'. This has suggested a second virus or precipitating factor in patients acquiring HIV through sexual transmission, and a herpes virus is now being implicated as a cause of Kaposi's sarcoma with similar DNA. Moore (1995) wrote that this virus occurred in up to 20% of AIDS patients, in cases of endemic Kaposi's sarcoma in Africa, in Kaposi's sarcoma of the elderly and in some lymphomas.

Clinical types of this sarcoma range from the indolent nodular type, with slowly progressive cutaneous lesions and late manifestations in the viscera, to the disseminated aggressive types involving many organ systems, including lymph nodes, with little or no skin involvement - the latter being the more usual type in AIDS patients. The chest radiograph may be normal, but nodal enlargement (small or large), pulmonary nodules, septal lines and pleural effusions may occur - (Illus. **KAPOSI SARC, Pt. 1**). Tiny nodules tend to be poorly defined or confluent (e.g. irregular flame-shaped nodules along the broncho-vascular bundles); they appear mainly in the mid and lower zones, and radiate from the hila. Tumour nodules may be complicated by haemorrhage.

Mean survival in AIDS patients is about 9 months or less and the tumour nodules may be rapidly progressive and double in size in three weeks.

Burkitt's lymphoma.

This lymphoma (a B cell type tumour with a rapid doubling time) is the most common neoplasm of children across a wide equatorial belt of Africa, typically causing jaw and abdominal tumours. Burkitt noted that its distribution was similar to the insect map of Africa and that a virus carried by an insect vector could be the cause. It was the only tumour that was cured by chemotherapy alone (see Denis Burkitt's obituaries - Daily Telegraph, 27 March and BMJ 10 April 1993). Epstein showed that it may be caused by the Epstein-Barr virus.

A second type (the non-African type) may be found in older patients, the most common presenting site being in the abdomen (with bowel or mesenteric masses). Some have head or neck swellings and others unilateral lymphadenopathy (see Illus. **AIDS, Pt. 4**). Disseminated disease is mostly found in immunocompromised patients, especially in those with AIDS.

Further references.

AIDS - general.

McCauley et al. (1982) : X-ray patterns of opportunistic lung infections & Kaposi sarcoma in homosexual men.

Cohen, B. et al. (1984) : Pulmonary complications of AIDS - radiological features.

Stern et al. (1984) : Intrathoracic adenopathy.

Acheson (1985) : Report by Chief Medical Officer, Dept. of Health.

Heron et al. (1985 from Middlesex Hospital) : Complications - pneumocystis pneumonia, other infections & KS.

Solal-Celigny et al. (1985) : Lymphoid interstitial pneumonitis in AIDS related complex.

Barter et al. (1986) from St. Mary's Hospital : 96 patients complicated by pneumocystis, pyogenic, mycobacterial and candida infections. (Many had neurological complications).

Suster et al. (1986) : Pulmonary manifestations of AIDS.

Corboy et al. (1987) : Congestive cardiomyopathy in association with AIDS.

Goodman, P. and Gamsu (1987) : Radiographic findings in AIDS.

Simmons et al. (1987) : Non-specific interstitial pneumonitis.

Federle et al. (1988) : Radiology of AIDS.

Fels et al. (1988) : Pulmonary effects of AIDS - multiple bacterial and fungal pneumonias.

Goodman, P. (1988) : Pulmonary manifestations of AIDS.

Hartelius et al. (1988) : CT of the lungs in AIDS.

Jacobson and Mills (1988) : Pulmonary cytomegalus infection.

Naidich, D. et al. (1988) : Pulmonary manifestations of AIDS.

Tierstein and Rosen (1988) : Pulmonary disease is the **major cause of death** in patients with AIDS - infection (PCP, avium-intracellulare, CMV, etc., non-specific interstitial pneumonitis, LIP or Kaposi sarcoma).

Kramer, M. and Sanger (1989) : Detection of thoracic infections by nuclear medicine techniques in AIDS (Gallium, labelled WBCs, etc.).

LeBoit et al. (1989) : **Epithelioid haemangioma-like vascular proliferation in AIDS** - ? manifestation of cat scratch bacillus infection.

Mitchell (1989) : Diagnostic problems in AIDS and the lung. The annual incidence of PCP amongst AIDS patients is about 35 %. Patients with pulmonary illness in AIDS usually present against a background of several weeks of ill health. A patient with PCP characteristically has a dry cough, fever with sweating, exertional dyspnoea and a feeling of difficulty with taking a deep breath.

Oldham et al. (1989) : Lymphocytic interstitial pneumonia complicating AIDS - 16 cases with a slow indolent interstitial infiltration esp. at the lung bases. Slow progression compared with infections or neoplasms.

Panicek (1989) : Cystic pulmonary lesions in patients with AIDS.

Similowski et al. (1989) : If an AIDS-related interstitial pneumonitis presents features that are not typical of PCP, one should consider **cryptococcosis.**
Amorosa et al. (1990) : Pyogenic pulmonary infections in patients with AIDS.
Baron, A. et al. (1990) : Bacillary angiomatosis in HIV infection - radiographic differentiation from Kaposi sarcoma - causes small osteolytic lesions in long bones.
Miller, W. et al. (1990) : Cryptococcal pulmonary infection in patients with AIDS.
Allen et al. (1991) : Tuberculous broncho-oesophageal fistula in AIDS.
Conces and Tarver (1991) : Noninfectious and nonmalignant pulmonary disease in AIDS.
Goodman, P. (1991a) : Mycobacterial disease in AIDS.
Radin (1991) : Disseminated histoplasmosis in AIDS.
Goodman, P. and Schnapp (1992) : Pulmonary toxoplasmosis in AIDS - 9 patients (bilateral symmetrical, coarse, poorly defined nodular opacities in 6, 3 were similar to PCP in having a diffuse fine fluffy nodular shadowing, and pleural effusions in 2. Treatment with sulphadiazine and pyrimethamine was effective).
McCarty et al. (1992) : Disseminated PC infections in AIDS pt. + thyroid gland calcification and hypothyroidism.
Tung (1992) : Cystic pulmonary lesions in AIDS.
Chong et al. (1993) : The prevalence of paranasal sinus disease in HIV infection and AIDS on cranial MR imaging.
Conces et al. (1993) : Disseminated histoplasmosis in AIDS.
McGuinness et al. (1993b) : Bronchiectasis associated with AIDS may be aggressive.
Makris et al. (1993) : Pulmonary strongyloidiasis - an unusual opportunistic pneumonia.
Pitkin et al (1993) : Changing patterns of respiratory disease in HIV positive patients in UK.
Trotman-Dickenson et al. (1993) : Bronchiectasis in late HIV disease (detected in 5 out of 6 patients who had been seropositive for between 5 and 10 years).
Banerjee (1994) : The Radiology of AIDS.
Banerjee and MacDonald (1994) : US of AIDS - widespread P carinii may be present in the spleen, kidneys and liver causing diffuse tiny echogenic foci throughout these organs (avium intracellulare may give a similar picture).
Hartman et al. (1994) : Accuracy of CT in the diagnosis of thoracic complications of AIDS - review of 102 patients. CT was most often accurate in the diagnosis of pneumocystis pneumonia and Kaposi's sarcoma. They gave the following guide -
Pneumocystis pneumonia - ground glass shadowing, interstitial infiltrates + thin-walled cysts.
Kaposi - Irregular nodules with perivascular distribution, interlobular septal thickening, lymphadenopathy, pleural effusions.
TB/atypical mycobacteria - Lymphadenopathy, necrotic non-enhancing nodes. Characteristic coarse reticulation and nodularity, focal consolidation, miliary shadows, pleural effusions.
Fungus - Nodules and masses, cavitation, pleural effusions, nodal enlargement.
Pyogenic infection - pneumonia/septic emboli.
Lymphoma - Large masses, lung nodules, lymphadenopathy, pleural effusions.
LIP/nonspecific interstitial pneumonitis - Reticular or alveolar infiltrates.
Kuhlman (1994) : Pulmonary manifestations of acquired immuno-deficiency syndrome.
Lessnau et al. (1994) : Radiographic findings in HIV positive pts. with TB - if repeat radiography (in the first two weeks of therapy) shows progressive disease, the likelihood of multi-drug-resistant TB is 95%.
McGuinness et al. (1994) : CMV complicating HIV - sputum findings in 21 patients.
Sider and Westcott (1994) : Cryptococcosis complicating HIV.
Coche et al. (1995) : Thoracic bacillary angiomatosis (infection caused by R quintana or henselae - the causes of trench foot or cat-scratch disease) in a patient with AIDS - hypervascular lesion in RLL extending into chest wall posteriorly demonstrated with MR - resected and treated with erythromycin.
Friedman, E. et al. (1995) : Cryptococcal pneumonia in patients with AIDS.
Kalayjian et al. (1995) : Pulmonary disease due to infection by M. avium complex in pts. with AIDS.
McGuinness et al. (1995) : Unusual lymphoproliferative disorders (LIP, mucosa-associated lymphoid tissue lymphoma or atypical lymphoproliferative disorder) in 9 adults with HIV or AIDS - **most had small lung nodules, either a few or multiple.**
Mayor et al. (1995) : Cavitating RUL pneumonia in 2 patients with Rhodococcus equi pneumonia.
Meyohas et al. (1995) : Localised and disseminated infections in 27 pts. with AIDS due to pulm. cryptococcosis.
Moore et al. (1995) : Bacillary angiomotosis in patients with AIDS - multiorgan imaging findings - should be considered particularly when KS is suspected clinically.
Staples et al.(1995) : Invasive pulmonary aspergillosis in AIDS : radiographic, CT and pathological findings.
Taylor et al. (1995) : Pulmonary complications of HIV disease : 10 year retrospective evaluation of yields from bronchoalveolar lavage, 1983-1993.
Armstrong (1996) : AIDS - the chest radiologist's perspective.
Allan et al. (1966) : Respiratory manifestations of **vertically acquired HIV infection** - **faster progress in children - 25% dead in 5 yrs**. Pentamidine drives PCP into extrapulmonary sites e.g. spleen - 1/400 may calcify. LIP is common, but lymphoma rare. Reticulonodular shadowing = LIP (5/6), consolidation & ground-glass shadowing = infection, retinal plaques in CMV, nodal enl. in both. Differential diagnosis included PCP, cryptococcus, viral, TB, atypical mycobacteria, pulm. haemorrhage, HIV related cardiomyopathy.

Diehl et al. (1996) : HRCT in 31 pts. with acute pulmonary conditions - in 24 a pathogen was identified, 19 having abnormal HRCT findings - PCP in 12, 3 avium intracellulare & 2 candida albicans. **Only in PCP cases were specific patterns seen. In some the HRCT was negative.**

Haramati et al. (1996) : Isolated lymphadenopathy on CXR of HIV-infected pts. - 18 cases - mycobacterial aetiology in 15 - TB in 9, avium in 4, TB+avium in 3, cryptococcus in 1, thymic hyperplasia in 1 and 1 with spontaneous resolution.

Owens et al. (1996) : The radiological spectrum of vertically-acquired HIV infection in 75 pts. in London - 15% vertical transmission rate of HIV, and 23% develop clinical manifestations <1 year of age. >50% present with resp. manifestations - 50% PCP, also CMV, para influenza and bacterial infections, TB, avium. EB virus may trigger lymphadenopathy, lymphoid hyperplasia, LIP and malignant lymphoma The children also had cerebral atrophy, basal ganglia and brain calcification and leucoencephalopathy, cardiomyopathy, GI disease, hepatomegaly, nephropathy and bacillary angiomatosis.

Pinching (1996) AIDS - continuing clinical challenges.

Traill et al. (1996) : **Pseudomonas** in 29 pts. with advanced AIDS - mimicked PCP - interstitial infiltrate in 20 (nodular in 9), consolidation in 7, ground-glass in 2, cavitation in 1 & 5 with pl. effusions. CXR may be normal.

Quinn (1996) : Global burden of the HIV pandemic.

Amin et al. (1997) : Lobar or segmental consolidation in pts. with HIV may be caused by a variety of causative agents, but the most common is bacterial infection, esp. PCP with upper lobe consolidation.

Beiser (1997) : Recent advances in aetiology, treatment & prophylaxis of opportunistic complications of HIV infection - the spectrum of opportunistic infections depends on geography. PCP is common in the developed world, but not in Africa where TB is the major problem. Other infections are seen elsewhere - Penicillium marneffei in N. Thailand, visceral leishmaniasis in parts of the Mediterranean and Latin America. With more advanced immunosuppression cytomegalus retinitis and Mycobacterium avium infections have become more common and these are more difficult to treat, these also occur with low CD4 counts. In 1995 the US Public Health guidelines established prophylaxis of PCP, TB as important measures that are cost effective and the standard of care.

Boiselle et al. (1997) : CXR interpretation of PCP, bacterial pneumonia and pulmonary TB in HIV-positive pts. - accuracy, distinguishing features and mimics.

McGuinness (1997) : Changing trends in the pulmonary manifestations of AIDS.

Marron et al. (1997) : Listeria monocytogenes empyema in an HIV infected patient.

Rottenberg et al. (1997) : Fulminant toxoplasma gondii pneumonia in a 35 yr. old Caucasian pt. with AIDS (contracted from her haemophilic husband) presenting with bilateral ground-glass lower zone shadowing, which was rapidly progressive causing extensive diffuse consolidation throughout the lungs.

Sansom et al. (1997) : With the exception of pts. presenting with PUO, abdominal CT remains an important investigation in the management of pts. with HIV infection.

Wood et al. (1997) : HIV and AIDS - average time from seroconversion to developing AIDS is 8-10 years, average survival after developing AIDS is 18-30 months, average prognosis with pulmonary Kaposi's sarc. is 3-9 months.

Logan. and Finnegan (1998) : Pictorial review: Pulmonary complications in AIDS - CT appearances.

Richards et al. (1998) : Review Chest imaging in AIDS.

Edinburgh et al. (2000) : Nodules at CT in pts. with AIDS, esp. those with a centrilobular distribution are typically infectious in origin. Those >1cm are often neoplastic. A peribronchovascular distribution suggests Kaposi's sarc.

(For refs. to TB and AIDS - see ps. 19.23 - 24, other mycobacteria, aspergillosis and AIDS ps. 19.26 & 19.43).

Neoplasms including Bronchogenic Ca (mostly adenocarcinoma) and **AIDS.**

Nyberg et al. (1986) : AIDS related lymphomas.

Nyberg and Federle (1987) : AIDS related Kaposi sarcoma and lymphoma.

Federle et al. (1988) : Malignant neoplasms, KS, lymphoma, etc. in pts. with AIDS.

Polish et al. (1989) : Pulmonary non-Hodgkin's lymphoma in AIDS.

Sider et al. (1989) : Varied appearance of AIDS-related lymphoma in the chest, causing pleural effusion, interstitial and alveolar lung disease, lung nodules, hilar and mediastinal lymphadenopathy.

Braun et al. (1990) : Six cases of lung cancer in patients seropositive for HIV (aged 30 - 48).

Heitzman (1990) : Pulmonary neoplastic and lymphoproliferative disease in AIDS - review.

Beral et al. (1991) : AIDS-associated non-Hodgkin lymphoma.

Goodman, P. (1991b) : Non-Hodgkin's lymphoma in AIDS.

Levine et al. (1991) : Human immunodeficiency virus-related lymphoma.

Banerjee et al. (1992) : The radiological appearances of bone lymphoma in AIDS.

Dodd (1992) : Thoracic and abdominal manifestations of lymphoma occurring in immunocompromised patients - those who are iatrogenically immune suppressed, as with organ transplantation, have the same strikingly increased incidence and peculiar manifestations of lymphoma as patients with AIDS.

Radin et al. (1993) : AIDS related non-Hodgkin's lymphoma - abd. findings in 112 patients affecting nodes, GI tract, liver, kidney and adrenals. Masses > 2 ins usually caused by lymphoma, but large nodes (esp. with central low density) may be due to mycobacterial disease. Smaller nodes may be caused by reactive hyperplasia or KS.

George et al.(1994) : The radiological features of adult T-cell leukaemia/lymphoma - six cases including one with mediastinal adenopathy.

Keys et al. (1994) : Endobronchial HIV associated lymphoma.

Blunt and Padley (1995) : AIDS related lymphomas - review of 116 cases - thoracic manifestations - pleural or intrapulmonary masses, frequently peripheral sometimes with cavitation pleural effusions and nodal enlargement.

McClain et al. (1995) : Association of EBV with leiomyosarcoma in young people with AIDS.

McGuinness et al. (1995) : Unusual lymphoproliferative disorders in 9 adults with HIV or AIDS.

Eisner et al. (1996) : The pulmonary manifestations of AIDS-related non-Hodgkin's lymphoma.

Kessar et al. (1996) : Multiple lytic lesions in HTLV1 associated adult T cell leukaemia/lymphoma in the absence of lymphadenopathy on peripheral blood changes.

Koch et al. (1997) : Bronchus associated lymphoid tissue hyperplasia of the lung.

Collins et al. (1998) : Epstein-Barr-virus-associated lymphoproliferative disease of the lung - see also p. 19.32.

Gibson and Hansell (1998) : Lymphocytic disorders of the chest.

Karp et al. (1993 from NY, USA) : 7 young patients with lung ca. mainly stage IV- median survival 4 weeks.

Fishman et al. (1995, from Miami) : Reviewed 30 pts. (mean age 48) and found that the bronchial ca. usually manifested as a peripheral UL mass in pts. who had had TB or PCP, whereas central masses were more common in those without a history of opportunistic infection.

White et al. (1995, from Baltimore and NY) : Studied 23 pts. (mean age 42) who had central or peripheral lung masses, or extensive malignant pleural disease.

Gruden et al. (1995, from SanFrancisco) : 13 patients - poorly differentiated, rapidly growing lung tumours in young smokers should raise the suspicion of coincident AIDS.

Benayoun et al. (1996, Paris) : 15 pts. (14 M - 29 to 71 yrs.) - all heavy smokers - all cell types - most were peripheral and very large. Enlarged nodes may be confused with lymphoma or TB - cavitation or abscess.

Canini et al. (1996, Bologna, Italy) : pulm. neoplasms in 411 HIV positive pts. - 7/49 with KS presented with pulm. lesions (linear & nodular infiltrates radiating from hila predominantly along bronchovascular bundles, pulm. nodules in 2, hilar nodes + small lung infiltrate in 1).

9/33 with non-Hodgkin's lymphoma presented with thoracic involvement - extra-nodal enlarging nodules or masses were most common ± pl. effusion or mediastinal adenopathy. 2 young pts. had adenocarcinomas - peripheral spiculated RUL nodules.

AIDS and the Radiology Department.

Wall et al. (1991) : AIDS risk and risk reduction in the radiology department -

(i) Do not recap needles (0.4 % for each needle-stick event).

(ii) Protective clothing, esp. for biopsy or angiographic procedures.

(iii) Puncture-resistant disposal containers for sharp instruments.

(iv) Closed flush systems for angiography or drainage procedures.

Kaposi's sarcoma.

Davies (1956) : Bone changes in Kaposi's sarcoma - analysis of 15 cases in Bantu Africans. It caused rarefaction, cyst formation, cortical erosions and destruction of limb bones. The lesions were very vascular at angiography.

Reynolds et al. (1965) : Kaposi's sarcoma - clinicopath. study of its relationship to the reticuloendothelial system.

Brown, R. et al. (1982) : Pulmonary features of Kaposi's sarcoma.

Misra et al. (1982) : Kaposi sarcoma of the lung - radiology and pathology.

McCaulay et al. (1982) : Kaposi sarcoma in homosexual men.

Greenberg et al. (1985) : Upper airway obstruction secondary to AIDS related Kaposi sarcoma.

Ognibene et al. (1985) : Kaposi sarcoma causing pulmonary infiltrations and respiratory failure in pts. with AIDS.

Pitchenik et al. (1985) : Kaposi's sarcoma of the tracheobronchial tree.

Au et al. (1986) : Kaposi's sarcoma presenting with endobronchial lesions.

Zibrak et al. (1986) : Bronchoscopic and radiological features of Kaposi's sarcoma involving the respiratory system.

Davis, S. et al. (1987) : Intrathoracic Kaposi sarcoma in AIDS patients - 24 patients (3 with lung nodules, but in 21 no abnormality was seen on CT).

Fouret et al. (1987) :Pulmonary Kaposi's sarcoma in patients with AIDS.

Garay et al. (1987) : Pulmonary manifestations of Kaposi's sarcoma.

Nyberg and Federle (1987) : AIDS related Kaposi sarcoma and lymphomas.

Sivit et al. (1987) : Kaposi's sarcoma of the lung in AIDS - radiologic-pathologic analyses - review of 9 cases.

Ognibene and Shelhamer (1988) : Pulmonary effects of AIDS related Kaposi's sarcoma.

Blank (1989) : CT may show **haemorrhage surrounding lung nodules** in patients with **Kaposi sarcoma**.

Naidich et al. (1989) : Kaposi's sarcoma - CT-radiographic correlation. On chest radiographs the predominant finding was a non-specific bilateral infiltrate (seen in 22 of 24 cases). CT showed abnormal hilar densities extending into the adjacent pulmonary parenchyma, along the perivascular and peribronchial pathways. Poorly marginated nodules were seen in the lungs in ten cases, but nodal enlargement was only seen in two.

Beral et al. (1990) : Kaposi's sarcoma among persons with AIDS - a sexually transmitted infection?

McCarty et al. (1990) from St, Mary's Hospital, London: Pulmonary Kaposi's sarcoma - review of the radiographic appearances in AIDS patients. Skin involvement is the most common, but the disease is systemic, particularly involving the lungs and GI tract. The chest may show nodular infiltrates in the lungs, pleural effusions or lymphadenopathy. Consolidation may complicate an endobronchial lesion.

Miller, R. et al. (1992) : Bronchopulmonary KS in pts. with AIDS (29 cases).

Wolff et al. (1993) : CT of thoracic KS in pts. with AIDS.

Beale et al. (1995 - St. Mary's Hosp., London) : Review of 44 AIDS pts. who had endobronchial KS and negative bronchoalveolar lavage for pathogenic organisms. The following chest radiographic features were seen - air trapping, reticulation, soft nodules, perihilar disease, septal lines, bilateral consolidation and pleural effusions. Lower lobe endobronchial lesions were particularly seen with CT.

Gruden et al. (1995) : AIDS-related Kaposi sarcoma of the lung - review of 76 pts. - compared bronchoscopic with radiographic staging and made two important points : (i) stage I disease may respond to chemotherapy, and
(ii) moderate or severe parenchymal KS may exist without submocosal extension and visible bronchoscopic lesions.

Ambroziak et al. (1995) : Herpes-like sequences in HIV-infected and uninfected Kaposi's sarcoma patients.

Howard et al. (1995) : Association of human herpes virus with pulmonary Kaposi's sarcoma.

Khali et al. (1995) : CT findings in intrathoracic Kaposi's sarcoma.

Lin et al. (1995) : Is KS associated with herpesvirus detectable in semen of HIV-infected homosexual men?

Whitby et al. (1995) : Detection of Kaposi's sarcoma associated herpes virus in peripheral blood of HIV infected pts. & progression to Kaposi's sarcoma.

Padley et al. (1996) : 111 of 886 pts. with AIDS had bronchopulmonary KS - confirmed that AIDS related KS occurs in advanced HIV disease where concurrent infections are frequent, CD4 counts are low and overall survival is poor.

Traill et al. (1996) : CT of 15 pts. with AIDS & KS - ill defined nodules were seen in all pts.; in 8 pts. > 20 nodules were present. Other signs included small areas of ground glass shadows, perihilar infiltrates extending into lung parenchyma along broncho-vascular bundles, interlobular septal thickening, fissural nodularity & small pleural effusions (often bilateral).

Burkitt's lymphoma.
Whittaker (1973) : Burkitt's lymphoma.
Cockshott (1975) : Radiological aspects of Burkitt's lymphoma.
Ferris et al. (1975) : Radiological manifestations of North American Burkitt's lymphoma.
Bennet et al. (1977) : Roentgenographic features of American Burkitt's lymphoma.
Dunnick et al. (1979) : Radiographic manifestations of Burkitt's lymphoma in American patients.
Krudy et al. (1981) : CT of American Burkitt's lymphoma.
Ziegler (1981) : Burkitt's lymphoma.
Ziegler et al. (1982) : Outbreak of Burkitt's lymphoma in homosexual men.
Strauss et al. (1986) : CT of American Burkitt's lymphoma.
Nzeh (1988) : Atypical intrathoracic manifestations of Burkitt's lymphoma.
Johnson, K. et al. (1995) : Imaging of Burkitt's lymphoma in 21 pts. - extra-nodal disease was the most common site at presentation in the abdomen.
Johnson, K. et al. (1998) : Imaging of Burkitt's and Burkitt-like lymphoma - review of 24 pts. aged 17 - 67 yrs. in Southampton.

FUNGUS DISEASE - (Illus. **FUNGUS**).

(a) Aspergillosis - (Illus. **ASPERGILLOSIS**).

Aspergillosis, due to Aspergillus fumigatus, a ubiquitous mould of decaying vegetation, is the most common fungal chest infection in the UK. Its spores are ubiquitous in the air and can release a **toxin** which can inhibit the activities of macrophages including phagocytosis. It causes a wide spectrum of disease, involving the bronchi, lungs and pleura. Bronchial infection may be minor and cause an 'allergic bronchitis' (ABPA) with **asthma** (which usually shows no chest radiographic abnormality), or more serious with the production of inspissated mucus, or thick mucus plugs, which may cause mucocoeles or 'bronchocoeles' ('**gloved fingers**' - dilated bronchi filled with fluid - see also ps. 2.10 - 12) or segmental or lobar collapse, which may mimic bronchial blockage due to a tumour (Illus. **ASPERGILLOSIS, Pt. 53**). The inspissated plugs may be expectorated, as slimy masses looking like '**garden slugs**' (sometimes grey and rubbery) or as **bronchial casts** (see Illus. **ASPERGILLOSIS, Pt. 45**). Long standing bronchial infection may cause localised bronchiectasis (often saccular and proximal in type - see ps 3.18 - 22), or thickening of the bronchial wall leading to 'bronchiectasis follicularis', with squamous metaplasia (Illus. **ASPERGILLOSIS** or **BRONCHIECTASIS FOLLICULARIS, Mucocoeles Pts. 3 & 5a-b**), or bronchocentric granuloma (see p. 19.60).

Pulmonary parenchymal involvement may produce several disease patterns.

(i) **An acute segmental or lobar pneumonia with marked hilar and/or mediastinal nodal enlargement, resembling neoplasm**. This may clear spontaneously or with antibiotics and steroids within a few weeks (Illus. **ASPERGILLOSIS, Pts. 8a-d & 14a-c**).

(ii) A 'wandering' or locally chronic **pneumonia** leading to **bronchiectasis**.

(iii) Miliary disease and **nodular lung masses** - particularly in immunocompromised patients with **invasive aspergillosis** - the latter may be confirmed by percutaneous biopsy (see also **opportunistic pneumonias** p. 19.7).

(iv) **Tissue necrosis** not uncommonly occurs via the Arthus type II and III reactions (see p. 19.54), and because the organism tends to invade blood vessels, and also releases toxins and proteolytic enzymes, it causes tissue necrosis and haemorrhagic infarction. Pathologically relatively early lung lesions appear to consist of central nodules of necrosis surrounded by zones of haemorrhage, the latter sometimes giving rise to a less dense outer rim as shown on CT sections (the '**CT halo sign**', which occurs much earlier than the 'air crescent'). Following necrosis sloughing and cavitation frequently occur. A central sequestrum may be found within a cavity, but is more commonly caused by a mycetoma.

(v) Aspergillosis is also commonly saphrophytic when it infects **pre-existing cavities or damaged lung** - apical or emphysematous bullae (including bullae secondary to ankylosing spondylitis), lung damaged by previous tuberculosis (Illus. **TB&MYCETOMA/FUNGUS**), sarcoid (Illus. **SARCOID+MYCETOMA**), pneumonia, or even a slowly growing cavitating squamous carcinoma (Illus. **CA+FUNGUS**). In these and in cavities formed by Aspergillus itself, a mycetoma may form, giving rise to the 'air crescent', 'meniscus' or 'target' signs, with a mycetomatous mass lying within a cavity (Illus. **AIR CRESCENT SIGN**). Sometimes several such lesions are present. They may be seen on plain films or tomograms, including CT sections. Such fungus balls may be shown to change position in response to gravity, by radiographing the patient in different positions (e.g. prone as well as supine with CT sections - Illus. **ASPERGILLOSIS, Pt. 22a-b**).

Pleural involvement is usually manifested by adjacent localised pleural thickening, rather than a pleural effusion, but local adjacent mycetomas may sometimes be seen if a localised pneumothorax is produced, Aspergillosis may also infect chronic pneumothoraces, or occur post-operatively around prostheses, or cause a fungus empyema if resection of a diseased area is attempted. Surgery is usually contraindicated, as resection of diseased lung often causes the diseased area to spread, and what was a relatively minor disability becomes a major one. Pleural disease is also notoriously resistant to treatment.

The '**air crescent**', '**meniscus**' and '**target**' signs (Illus. **AIR CRESCENT SIGN**) are produced by varying amounts of air separating a **mycetoma** or slough from an outer cavity wall. Whilst these appearances are usually due to an aspergilloma, similar appearances may sometimes be seen with actinomycosis, tuberculosis (e.g. haematoma within a TB cavity), septic pulmonary emboli, cavitating squamous or other carcinoma, sarcoma, a lung abscess or pulmonary gangrene, hamartoma within a cyst, leukaemic infiltrate (p. 5.48), a Rasmussen aneurysm (p. 7.12) or with hydatid disease (Fig. 19.7, p. 19.52).

The '**CT halo**' **sign** is produced by a nodule (usually due to invasive aspergillosis) surrounded by a rim of coagulative necrosis or haemorrhage causing ground-glass shadowing, and does not depend on air around a mass within a cavity for its detection. (It may also be seen with TB - Gaeta et al., 1992 - see also Fig 19.4, below).

A similar **MR 'target sign'** may be seen after Gd DTPA enhancement, or a later reversed target after 10 days. MR may also be able to haemorrhage - methaemoglobin with central degeneration within nodules.

| Cavity with a mycetoma in scarred or dense lung & overlying pl. thickening. | Gas above a non-moving ball - the 'air crescent' or 'meniscus sign'. | Target' or 'Halo' sign - mass within a cavity. | In the erect position or CT the mass drops to the bottom of the cavity. |

| CT halo sign - surrounding ground- glass shadowing due to coagulative necrosis or haemorrhage. | MR target sign with rim on T_1, after Gd enhancement. | Reversed target on T_2 (late sign). | Methaemoglobin with central degeneration in nodule. |

Fig. 19.4 Target or halo and air crescent signs.

Method of formation of a mycetoma - (see also Illus. **MYCETOMA**).

When a cavity is formed within an area of lung infected by aspergillosis, or the organism secondarily infects a pre-existing cavity, fronds of mycelial tissue may form and hang like stalactites from the inner lining of the cavity. These tend to fall into the cavity forming a sea-weed or sponge-like mass. CT may show small air-filled spaces within such a fungus ball, and occasionally calcified flecks may be seen within it. A fungus ball may also form when infected infarcted 'sponge-like' lung separates from its surroundings.

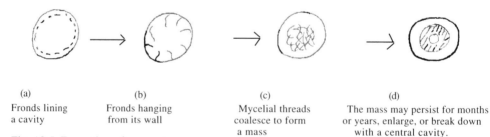

| (a) | (b) | (c) | (d) |
| Fronds lining a cavity | Fronds hanging from its wall | Mycelial threads coalesce to form a mass | The mass may persist for months or years, enlarge, or break down with a central cavity. |

Fig. 19.5 Formation of a mycetoma.

Treatment.

Acute infections may respond to penicillin or amoxycillin. Mucus plugs are best treated by physiotherapy and/or bronchial aspiration and lavage, if the former does not allow a collapsed lobe to re-expand. However, bronchoscopy is often required to exclude an endobronchial lesion, e.g. a slowly growing small tumour, but as noted above aspergillosis may itself cause bronchial wall thickening. Steroids may help with asthma, and with some acute infections.

Surgery has often been used to remove aspergillomata but it has a high morbidity and mortality (because of the often debilitated condition of the patients and severe adhesions) and may be complicated by a fungus empyema.

Theoretically anti-fungal agents should be of value, but in clinical practice, and although not infrequently given orally, they often do not seem to have any great effect. This is probably because by the time they are given, the condition is already chronic and the drugs (usually ketoconazole or itraconazole) do not penetrate into cavities and have no effect on mycetomas within them. However, Kuhlman et al. (1988) wrote that in immune-compromised patients, early lesions can be treated by high dose anti-fungal therapy, lesion development can be stopped, and they will then cavitate and heal with scarring.

Several authors (see references below) have installed anti-fungal agents into cavities by percutaneous catheter or needle.

Bronchial artery embolisation.

Some patients with chronic cavitating aspergillosis have intractable severe haemoptysis. In such people, the bronchial arteries may become dilated to the affected lung. In these bronchial artery embolisation has been of advantage (see also p. 7.21).

Other fungi which may give similar radiographic and clinical response to infection with Aspergillus fumigatus.

Occasionally patients are seen with allergic bronchopulmonary disease, due to other fungi. These include other species of Aspergillus, candida, stemphylia, helminthosporia, torulopsia and curvularia (see Halwig et al., 1985).

References
(a) General.
Hinson et al. (1952) : First description of broncho-pulmonary aspergillosis.

Goldberg, B. (1962) : Radiological appearances.

Ellis, R. (1965) : Total collapse of the lung in aspergillosis.

Irwin (1966) : Radiology of aspergilloma - three groups of reaction
(i) Saprophytic with the tissues not reacting to the fungus (aspergilloma),
(ii) Allergic with marked immunological response and exudate in the bronchi leading to asthma, eosinophilia, bronchial obstruction and secondary collapse or consolidation, and
(iii) Septicaemic or pyaemic with mycotic abscesses or granulomas.

Leggat and De Krester (1968) : Aspergillus pneumonia in association with an aspergilloma.

Henderson, A. (1968) : Allergic aspergillosis (review of 32 cases) - episodes of segmental shadowing occurred most frequently in the upper lobes and tended to recur in the same segment. Mucocoeles of large bronchi were seen in eight cases and saccular bronchiectasis in six. One developed aspergillomas and one died of invasive aspergillosis.

Henderson, A. et al. (1968) : Surveyed 107 consecutive patients attending hospital in Bristol with various chest diseases. Of 46 asthmatic patients, ten had probable or definite allergic aspergillosis. They concluded that "allergic aspergillosis is a more common condition and a more frequent cause of upper lobe damage than has been appreciated".

Davies, D. (1970) : Aspergilloma and residual tuberculous cavities.

McCarthy et al. (1970) : Radiological appearances in allergic bronchopulmonary aspergillosis (117 cases).

Young, R. et al. (1970) : Spectrum of disease in 98 patients -
(i) Necrotising bronchopneumonia (patchy haemorrhagic consolidation which may cavitate),
(ii) Haemorrhagic pulmonary infarction (fibrosis and exudates containing fungal hyphae),
(iii) Granulomatous disease resembling tuberculous bronchopneumonia,
(iv) Miliary abscesses,
(v) Lobar consolidation.

Zimmerman and Miller (1970) : Pulmonary aspergillosis.

Freundlich and Israel (1973) : Aspergillosis infection superimposed on other cystic or cavitating disease (18 out of 26 patients presented with haemoptysis and two died from it).

Meyer et al. (1973) : Aspergillosis complicating neoplastic disease.

Libshitz et al. (1974) : Pleural thickening as a manifestation of Aspergillus superinfection.

Karas et al. (1976) : Pulmonary aspergillosis - analysis of 41 patients.

Altman (1977) : Thoracic wall invasion secondary to pulmonary aspergillosis in childhood.

Blum et al. (1978) : Miliary aspergillosis associated with alcoholism.

Mintzer et al. (1978) : Spectrum of findings in ABPA.

Klein and Gamsu (1980) : Thoracic manifestations of aspergillosis.

Kruglik and Wayne (1980) : Occult lung cavity causing haemoptysis shown by CT.

Gefter et al. (1981a) : Allergic form - less common patterns - collapse and chronic consolidation, at times accompanied by cavitation.

Gefter et al. (1981b) : 'Semi-invasive' type.

Libshitz and Pagani (1981) : Aspergillosis and mucormycosis - two types of opportunistic pneumonia.

Greene, R. (1981) : Three types - allergic, invasive and mycetoma, with overlap between the different types. They may complicate other disease processes - mucoid impaction, eosinophilic pneumonia, bronchocentric granulomatosis, 'farmer's lung', or asthma.

Herbert and Bayer (1981) : Invasive pulmonary aspergillosis.   Ricketti et al. (1983) : ABPA.

Berken et al. (1982) : Lung consolidation caused by ABPA in non-asthmatic patients.

Binder et al. (1982) : Chronic necrotising pulmonary aspergillosis - a discrete clinical entity.

Jones, D. and Williams (1984) : Aspergilloma in irradiated lung following nodal irradiation for Hodgkin's disease.

Phelan and Kerr (1984) : Aspergillosis is not just a disease of upper zones, as it equally affects lower and mid zones. Perihilar consolidation - a striking feature. Persistent consolidation did not necessarily imply superimposed infection.

Mendelson et al. (1985) : Allergic aspergillosis - radiology is a good base line and for detecting bronchiectasis.

Costello and Rose (1985) : CT findings in pleural aspergillosis.

Simpson et al. (1986) : Pancoast's syndrome associated with **invasive aspergillosis**

Vail and Chiles (1987) : Invasive pulmonary aspergillosis - radiological evidence of tracheal involvement.

Sider and Davis (1987) : Nodular aspergillosis.

Currie et al. (1987) : Comparison of HRCT and plain chest radiography in chronic ABPA.

Greenberger (1988) : Allergic bronchopulmonary aspergillosis and fungoses.

Kuhlman et al. (1988) : CT of invasive pulmonary aspergillosis.

McConnochie et al. (1989) : Aspergillus colonisation of pulmonary rheumatoid nodule.

Palmer, L. and Schiff (1989) : Rapidly progressive pneumonia in a pt. with chronic obstructive pulmonary disease.

Neeld et al. (1990) : CT in the evaluation of allergic bronchopulmonary aspergillosis.

Clarke et al. (1991) : Fungal tracheobronchitis - 9 cases + literature review.

Palmer et al. (1991) : Corticosteroids as a risk factor for invasive pulmonary aspergillosis.

Davies, M. et al. (1992) : HRCT - ABPA tends to cause central bronchiectasis and bronchial wall thickening.

Gefter (1992) : Spectrum of pulm. aspergillosis. Aquino et al. (1994) : Imaging features with pathologic correlation.

Goyal et al. (1992) : High attenuation mucous plugs at CT in allergic bronchopulmonary aspergillosis.

Aquino et al. (1994) : Imaging features with pathological correlation.

Katz et al. (1994) : Invasive aspergillosis of LLL involving the descending aorta in a 14 year old boy with acute lymphoblastic leukaemia.

Logan et al. (1994) : Invasive aspergillosis of the airways - radiographic, CT and pathologic findings - peripheral consolidation or ill defined centrilobular nodules.

Purcell and Corris (1995) : Nebulised liposomal amphoteracin B in the successful treatment of aspergillus empyema.

Staples, C. et al. (1995) : Invasive pulm. aspergillosis in AIDS - plain film, CT & pathological findings.

Brown et al. (1998) : Invasive aspergillosis in the immunocompromised host - CT & bronchoalveolar lavage.

Ahn et al. (2000) : Pseudomembranous necrotizing bronchial aspergillosis in a pt. with acute myelocytic leukaemia - LUL collapse which reexpanded with amphoteracin B - died of **massive haemoptysis** 4 weeks later.

Kim et al. (2000) : Semiinvasive pulm. aspergillosis may cause persistent consolidation and masses in mildly immunocompromised pts.

Franquet et al. (2000) : Semiinvasive aspergillosis causing upper lobe consol or mult. nodules in pts. with COPD.

(b) Air crescent and mycetomas.

Levin (1956) : Pulmonary intracavitary fungus ball.

Watanabe (1979) : Mass in a pulmonary cavity ('**meniscus sign**').

Gross et al. (1982) : Mural nodule in cavitary opportunistic pulmonary aspergillosis.

Breuer et al. (1985) : Occult mycetoma shown by CT.

Curtis et al. (1979), Epling et al. (1984) : '**Air crescent sign**' in invasive aspergillosis.

Gefter et al. (1985) : '**Air crescent**' or '**halo sign**' in aspergillosis complicating leukaemia.

Kuhlman et al. (1985) : Invasive pulmonary aspergillosis and acute leukaemia - limitations and diagnostic ability of the '**air crescent sign**'.

Strickland (1986) : Method of formation of mycetoma. Roberts et al. (1987) : Method of formation of mycetoma and CT appearances.

Chintapalli et al. (1988) : Unusual '**cavity-in-cavity**' appearance of pulmonary aspergillosis.

Meziane (1988) : Sign may be seen with CT.

Morrison et al. (1993) : Cavitary aspergillosis as a complication of AIDS.

Fujimoto et al. (1994) : Aspergilloma within **cavitary lung cancer** - MR findings.

Hsieh et al. (1996) : Pulmonary actinomycosis appearing as a "ball-in-hole" on chest radiography and bronchoscopy.

Takahashi, N. et al. (1999) : Mycetoma in a lung cavity that followed a **gun-shot wound**.

(c) CT-Halo sign. (see also p. 6.3).

Hruban et al. (1987) : CT-halo sign in I PA (central fungal nodule surrounded by a rim of coagulative necrosis).

Kuhlman et al. (1988) : CT of invasive pulmonary aspergillosis.

Primack et al. (1994) : The **CT-halo sign** may also be associated with infections other than aspergillosis - other fungi, CMV or herpes simplex - also with Wegener's granuloma and metastatic angio- or Kaposi sarcoma.

Blum et al. (1996) : Invasive pulm. aspergillosis - MR, CT & plain films for diagnosis - 68 cases;

Blum et al. (1994) : 38 cases - wrote 'MRI findings are not as characteristic as the CT halo sign in the early course of the disease, but the MRI target sign with enhancement of the rim area & the "reverse target" on T_2 weighted images are strongly suggestive of IPA at a late stage of the disease.'

(d) Intracavitary treatment.
Stiksa et al. (1976) : Bilateral pulmonary aspergillomas in ankylosing spondylitis treated with transthoracic intracavitary installations of antifungal agents.
Hargis et al. (1980) : Intracavitary amphoteracin B in the treatment of symptomatic pulmonary aspergillomas.
Shapiro et al. (1988) : Severe **haemoptysis** in pulmonary aspergillosis - percutaneous intracavitary treatment.
Lee, K. et al. (1993) : Instilled Amphoteracin B into aspergilloma cavities in seven patients with haemoptysis. In all the haemoptysis ceased within five days, and the aspergillomata resolved or became smaller.
Jackson et al. (1993) : Catheterised four cases, two died and two improved.
Giron et al. (1993) : Injected glycerin and amphoteracin B paste in 15 cases - 12 regressed.
Jones, R. and Reynolds (1996) : 4 pts. amphoteracin 10 mg in 5% dextrose, increasing to 50mg/day for 9-12 /52.

(e) Aspergillosis and AIDS.
Keating et al. (1994) : 11 cases of pulm. aspergillosis in pts. with AIDS.
Miller et al. (1994); Höhler et al. (1995) : Pulmonary aspergillosis in patients with AIDS.
Shaunak (1995) : Aspergillosis is unusual in patients with AIDS but may manifest with cavitating upper lobe disease, focal opacities or bilateral interstitial disease.
Staples et al. (1995) : IPA in AIDS - thick-walled cavitating lesions are the commonest radiographic manifestations.

(f) Nasal aspergillosis.
Milosev et al. (1969) : Aspergilloma of nasal sinuses - 17 cases from the Sudan.
Zinreich et al. (1988) : Fungal sinusitis - CT & MR.   Coulthard et al. (1991) : Frontal sinus aspergilloma.
Patel et al. (1992) : CT findings in paranasal aspergillosis - high density masses or interlacing network pattern within a sinus. It typically has a radiolucent rim. The sinus wall may be expanded or eroded and a mass with calcification may extend into an orbit or intracranially.
DeShazo et al. (1997) : Current concepts of fungal sinusitis.
Dahniya et al. (1998) : CT of paranasal fungal sinusitis - a condition most common in the Sudan and Gulf states. It often presents as a chronic severe sinusitis which does not respond to antibiotics. CT shows a soft tissue mass ± erosion or expansion of bony margins. Intra-orbital and/or intracranial extension sometimes occurs.

See also references to eosinophilic pneumonia - ps. 19.59 - 61.

(b) Other fungus diseases.
These are more prevalent in e.g. North and South America than in the UK. In the UK they may occasionally be seen de novo, but are more often found in people who have visited America or other endemic areas e.g. the Far East and Africa. In the USA they are particularly prevalent in the arid areas of the southern states.

Actinomycosis   (Illus. **ACTINOMYCOSIS**) may cause chronic chest disease which may simulate tuberculosis, other fungal disease or neoplasm. Symptoms include chronic chest pain (which may be of several months duration), coughing (often accompanied by purulent sputum), weight loss and malaise. Early pulmonary disease may be accompanied by submucosal bronchial lesions. Later, abscess formation, nodal enlargement, tissue necrosis, cavities (including cavities containing a mass), pleurisy and an empyema may supervene, and penetration may occur through the chest wall to form external fistulae and sinuses. The infection may cause a chronic osteomyelitis of the ribs and spine, and may also spread into the pericardium. Considerable fibrosis is often present. Yellow-brown 'sulphur granules' may be seen with the naked eye in material draining from abscesses or sinuses, but diagnosis is hampered by the difficulty of isolating the organism from sputum, and biopsies and bronchial washings often provide the best method of diagnosis. Ultrasound and CT may demonstrate pleural and chest wall pus collections.
The most common species is Actinomyces israeli, but others including odontolyticus may give rise to clinical disease. The organisms are commonly found in tonsillar crypts and gingivo-dental tissues, and poor dental hygiene is usually present in those who develop chest infections. The organisms may cause infections in normal lungs, but tend to have a predilection for damaged or devitalised tissue, there being an increased incidence in patients with chest malignancy or in those who have had surgery. Infection may also occur in the abdomen, usually as chronic appendicitis and may present with a chronic fistula to the skin. In lung disease there is often a complicating

infection with pyogenic aerobic and anaerobic bacteria. Clinical cases in the UK are rare, and the author has only seen a few, one complicating an old pneumonectomy cavity (similar to aspergillosis in Illus. **MYCETOMA, Asperg Pt. 51**). Further references are given below (two from the UK - Frank and Strickland, 1974 and Bellingham, 1990).
Note : The author has found tuberculosis to be a more common cause of chest wall abscess and rib osteomyelitis (see Illus. **TB BONE, TB Pt. 21a-e**).

Blastomycosis   (due to Blastomyces dermatidis - see also Illus. **BLASTOMYCOSIS**) may give rise to miliary lung nodules, but more often causes a mass-like area of consolidation. This may cavitate and then lead to a diffuse bronchopneumonia. Skin and bones may also be affected. The condition occurs in the central and SE parts of the USA, Canada, Central and South America, and in Africa. The soil appears to be the natural habitat for the organism.

Botryomycosis infection closely mimics actinomycosis. About 90 cases of human infection have been recorded, most of which have been cutaneous. However abrominal and thoracic ceases have also been recorded, the latter particularly with long-standing foreign bodies.The condition is characterised by eosinophilic granules surrounded by proteinaceous material ? immunoglobulin.

Candida infections occur mainly in debilitated patients, in those with tumours having chemotherapy and/or radiotherapy, those suffering from other infections (including AIDS), diabetics, haemophiliacs, dialysis and renal transplant patients, etc. Candida may cause broncho-pneumonia, pharyngeal, tracheal and oesophageal infections - in the last giving rise to an irregular mucosa. Others may have a fungus pyelitis, endocarditis or skin infection.
(See also candida of the oesophagus - p. 16.16 and Illus. **OES MONILIA**).

Coccidioidomycosis (due to Coccidioides immitis - see Illus. **COCCIDIOIDOMYCOSIS**) is endemic in the arid regions of the south-western states of the USA (including California, Arizona and New Mexico). **Paracoccidioidomycosis** is found in Latin America and Brazil.
The fungi have two forms: (a) in living tissues as spherules or a sporangium within which several endospores form, break out and grow into further spherules, and (b) a mycelial form which grows in the soil, on pieces of wood, cactus, etc. to form myriads of minute spores. The spores may pass into the air, be distributed by wind and be inhaled. The primary site of immitis infection is usually in the lung, but about 10 to 20% of patients develop bone and joint lesions which are mostly lytic. Those worst affected are usually Negroes, Mexicans and American Indians. It also affects wild and domestic animals.
   In many people who become affected, no overt clinical disease is produced, and only a positive skin test will give an indication that they have had it. Symptomatic cases may have a mild chest infection, malaise, pleuritic chest pain, cough, toxic erythema, erythema nodosum and arthralgia. Names such as 'San Joaquin fever', 'Valley fever', or 'desert rheumatism' have been given to the disease. Patients may have segmental pneumonia, small infiltrates, miliary or larger pulmonary nodules, which may cavitate with thick or thin walled cavities, hilar and mediastinal lymphadenopathy and pleural effusions. The author has noted that the nodules may be grouped together in 'crops', and at CT are not as well circumscribed as most metastases (Illus. **COCCIDIOIDOMYCOSIS, Fungus Pt. 9**). Such disseminated nodules may be seen in chronic cases and acute florid disease, and may resemble metastatic neoplasm. In neonates it may cause a devastating and lethal illness.
   The chronic fibro-nodular form resembles tuberculosis, and may be found in US military personnel and tourists who have visited endemic areas. Calcification may occur with healing.

Cryptococcosis (European blastomycosis or torulosis - due to C. neoformans - a yeast - Illus. **CRYPTOCOCCOSIS**) may cause a potentially fatal pulmonary and meningeal infection which may be found in immunologically compromised patients, patients with malignant disease and others without obvious predisposing factors. The last tend to have peripheral pulmonary nodules, whereas the first two groups have nodules which progress to confluence or cavitation. Lobar, segmental or broncho-pneumonic consolidation may be present and be complicated by adenopathy and pleural effusion. Meningitis with a brain abscess associated with pneumonia may be a particular pointer towards the diagnosis, and it is worth making, since some patients will recover. The organism is found in the soil and in bird (especially pigeon) excreta.

The peripheral distribution of the nodules has allowed ultrasound guided percutaneous aspiration for diagnostic samples. Cryptococcosis may complicate AIDS and lead to ARDS.

Histoplasmosis (due to Histoplasma capsulatum - see Illus. **HISTOPLASMOSIS**) is found in many parts of the World, particularly in the Areas of the great river valleys of the south-eastern USA (Mississippi, lower Missouri and Ohio). It is found in bird and bat droppings* and is usually spread by dust-borne infectious mitochondria. It may give rise to acute or chronic pneumonia with fleeting infiltrates or larger areas of consolidation, small multiple or single lung nodules, or chronic cavities resembling tuberculosis. In some cases histoplasma nodules (and other fungus nodules) may progressively enlarge, simulating neoplasm (see Goodwin and Snell, 1969). Hilar and mediastinal node involvement is common. Nodes and lung nodules often become calcified, and fibrosis and calcification may also be found in the bronchi, giving rise to strictures or **broncholithiasis** (see ps. 3.24 - 25). It may also be found in the liver, pleura and pericardium. Myocardial involvement may lead to arrhythmias. Rarely large granulomatous masses, fibrosing mediastinitis or hilar fibrosis (with pulmonary artery narrowing) are caused by it (see p. 18.4). A few disseminated cases may end fatally, but in most there is only a mild or minimal clinical illness and healing occurs spontaneously.
Histoplasmosis and tuberculosis are the most common granulomatous calcifications in the USA. In endemic areas about 25% of patients with AIDS have histoplasmosis. As with tuberculosis, choroidal granulomata may be seen, especially with miliary disease.

Mucormycosis (Phocomycosis) is caused by fungi of Zygomycetes type which are inhaled as spores from moulds found in decaying vegetable matter. Most commonly immunosuppressed patients or those with diabetes, leukaemia or lymphoma are affected. The typical chest radiographic appearance is of a round area of pneumonia with poorly defined margins, but others have nodular or lobar infiltrates, activation, mediastinal widening, nodules or a miliary pattern. The main feature is of massive tissue invasion (Illus. **MUCORMYCOSIS**). Frequently pulmonary infection is complicated by haemorrhagic infarction, resulting in wedge-shaped infiltrates and gangrene. It may also lead to pulmonary aneurysm formation. Another important site of infection is in the sinuses (particularly the frontals) leading to orbital oedema and frontal lobe invasion.

Nocardia (Illus. **NOCARDIA**) may give rise to pulmonary or systemic infection. There are several species: asteroides, brasiliensis and caviae. They are world-wide in distribution but infections are most common in the USA and South America. Nodules, or an area of consolidation may be found, and haematogenous spread to brain or skin is not uncommon. Following chest surgery for such nodules, a fungus empyema is not uncommon. Nocardia caviae may lead to a mycetoma. The organism is found in soil, cattle dung, etc. and inhaled spores from the latter, on the under-sides of road or rail-road trucks that have been 'down south', have been postulated as the source of some cases found in the northern states. Its behaviour is similar to that of actinomyces with irregular interlacing hyphae, which break up into shorter forms. Infection may complicate renal, liver and heart transplantation - Raby et al. (1990) found the most common finding in some patients was a right pleural effusion.

Sporotrichosis (a yeast-like organism) may produce a chronic slowly progressive lung infiltration, and is found in some alcoholics and drug addicts.

General points.
  Whilst in some patients severe progressive disease may be produced by fungi, in the majority healing occurs spontaneously. In serious or resistant cases to spontaneous healing, anti-fungal agents e.g. amphoteracin-B, ketoconazole, micinazole or 5-fluorocytosine, etc. may be used. However these may in themselves be toxic, and in the case of ketoconazole, the Committee on the Safety of Medicines (1985), pointed out that it may cause irreversible liver damage, without any overt clinical evidence during the taking of the drug. A newer drug, itraconazole, is less hepato-toxic.
(see also opportunistic infections - p. 19.7).

* Bats can also carry rabies, and only slight contact is required (not necessarily a bite) for transmission to man to occur.

Further references.

General.

Schwarz and Baum (1970) : Common fungal diseases of the lungs.

Chick (1987) : Epidemiological aspects of the pulmonary mycoses.

Dismukes et al. (1983) : Treatment of systemic mycoses with ketoconazole - emphasis on toxicity with clinical response in 52 patients.

Thiele et al. (1983) : Failure of ketoconazole in two patients with blastomycosis.

Greene et al. (1988) : Failure of ketoconazole in an immunosuppressed patient with pulmonary blastomycosis - disease progressed during treatment.

Actinomycosis.

Cope (1938)

Blainey and Morris (1953) : Actinomycotic pyaemia.

Bates and Cruickshank (1957), Farrell (1981), James, R. et al. (1985) : Thoracic actinomycosis.

Batty (1958) : Actimomyces odontolyticus; a new actinomycete species regularly isolated from deep carious dentine.

Jepson et al. (1958) : Thoracic actinomycosis - two cases at the Westminster Hospital - one due to A. israeli causing right upper rib osteomyelitis and ending fatally after seven years, and the second caused by A. comitans with an upper mediastinal abscess from upper dorsal spine osteomyelitis.

Young, W. (1960) : Actinomycosis with involvement of the vertebral column.

Moore, W. and Scannell (1968) : Pulmonary actinomycosis **simulating cancer of the lung.**

Flynn and Felson (1970) : The Roentgen manifestations of thoracic actinomycosis.

Schwarz (1970) : Review.

Brown, J. (1973), Slade et al. (1973) : Human actinomycosis.

Frank and Strickland (1974) : 6 cases. One had the well-known 'triad' of **chronic pleural effusion,   underlying lung disease and periosteal rib involvement,** but the others had broncho-pulmonary changes with collapse simulating neoplasm.

Varkey et al. (1974) : Thoracic actinomycosis with dissemination to skin, subcutaneous tissue and muscle.

Smith, D. and Lockwood (1975) Disseminated actinomycosis.

Varkey (1975) : Pulmonary infiltrate with a chest wall mass.

Weese et al. (1975) : Study of 57 cases over a 36 year period.

Blum et al. (1978) : Miliary aspergillosis associated with alcoholism.

Balikian et al. (1978) Three cases of pulmonary actinomycosis.

Harrison, R. and Thomas (1979) : Acute actinomycotic empyema.

Fisher, M. (1980) : Miliary actinomycosis.

Rose, H. et al. (1982) : Thoracic actinomycosis caused by Actimomyces meyeri.

Webb and Sagel (1982) : CT demonstration of two cases involving the chest wall - showed consolidation, pleural and chest wall thickening and periostitis of a rib.

Fowler and Simpkins (1983) : Three abdominal cases.

Dershaw (1984) : Ultrasound findings in **empyema necessitans** due to actinomycosis.

Peloux et al. (1985) : Actinomycosis odontolyticus infections - review of six cases.

Roesler and Willis (1986) : CT features of hepatic actinomycosis.

Allen et al. (1987) : Actinomycosis : CT findings in six patients.

Shah et al. (1987) : CT findings in abdominal actinomycosis.

Aarnio et al. (1990) : Actinomycosis simulating pulmonary neoplasm.

Bellingham (1990) : Female aged 58 with a mass in the left chest wall spreading from the pleura, which subsequently metastasised to the muscle of the right calf and the cervical cord - all lesions recovered with high dose IV benzylpenicillin and oral metronidazole for six weeks. The organism, odontolyticus, was recovered by culture after Tru-Cut biopsy from the chest wall.

Morgan, D. et al. (1990) : Mediastinal actinomycosis presenting as mediastinal masses.

Turnbull and Cohen (1991) : Pelvic actinomycosis with retrosigmoid involvement.

Kwong et al. (1992) : Thoracic actinomycosis - CT findings in eight patients - air-space consolidation (lower lobe predominance) with adjacent pleural thickening and spread to adjacent tissues without regard to normal anatomical barriers- also may be multifocal, may cavitate and cause hilar node enlargement.

Conant and Wechsler (1992)

Lau (1992) : Endobronchial actinomycosis mimicking pulmonary neoplasm.

Hsieh et al. (1993) : Thoracic actinomycosis.

Hsieh et al. (1996) : Pulmonary actinomycosis appearing as a "ball-in-hole" on chest radiography and bronchoscopy.

Zeebrechts et al. (1996) : Transphrenic dissemination of actinomycosis - two cases with fistulae between the thoracic and abdominal cavities - treated with surgical drainage and high dose penicillin.

Blastomycosis.

Baum and Schwartz (1959) : North American blastomycosis.

Armstrong, J. (1973)   Rabinowitz et al. (1976)

Laskey and Sarosi (1978) : Radiological appearance of pulmonary blastomycosis.
Sarosi and Davies (1979) : Excellent review.   Halvorsen et al. (1984)
Stelling et al. (1984) : Miliary pattern in five cases.
Campbell and Chapman (1987)   Kaufman (1988) : Tracheal blastomycosis.
Batra (1992) : Pulmonary blastomycosis.
Winer-Muram et al. (1992) : Blastomycosis of the lung - CT features in 16 patients (8 acute, 6 chronic and 2 an exacerbation of chronic disease) - consolidation with air-bronchograms, nodules, satellite lesions, pleural thickening, small effusions and cavitation. (Two of the patients had lung resection for the presumptive diagnosis of neoplasm.)
Koen and Blumberg (1999) : North American blastomycosis in South Africa simulating TB - man aged 42 with infection in C3 and prevertebral abscess - initially treated as TB but needed drainage - developed miliary chest shadows - also wrist and knee infection.

Botryomycosis.
Tuggey et al. (2000) : Long standing cavitation in RLL, thought at first to be a cavitating tumour but unchanged after four years. Bronchoscopy + biopsy revealed infection with a chronic FB thought to be a peanut.

Candida.
Spear et al. (1976) : Tracheal obstruction caused by a fungus ball.
Buff et al. (1982) : Candida albicans pneumonia.

Coccidioidomycosis and paracoccidioidomycosis.
Birsner (1954) : Roentgen aspects of 500 cases., Greendyke et al. (1970), Sagel (1973)
Beller et al (1979) : Endobronchial obstruction causing large airway obstruction.
Kruglik and Wayne (1980) : Haemoptysis from occult lung cavity shown by CT.
Bayer (1981) : Pulmonary coccidioidal syndromes.   McGahan et al. (1981)
Moskowitz et al. (1982) : Tracheal infection causing upper airway obstruction in children.
Child et al. (1985) : Coccidioidomycosis in neonates and infants.
Stevens (1995) : Coccidioidomycosis - current concepts.
Williams, F. et al. (1998) : Reactivation of coccidioidomycosis in a fit American visitor aged 48 to the UK. He worked in California as a park ranger and 2 yrs. before had a 'flu-like illness + an abnormal CXR. It resolved spontaneously, and skin tests became positive. The UK illness was again initially 'flu-like + dyspnoea & a productive cough. He developed bilateral pneumonia, followed by pleural effusions. Despite amphoteracin B treatment he deteriorated but recovered with fluconazole. C immitis was grown from sputum and lavage fluid.
De Castro et al. (1999) : MRI of head & neck paracoccidioidomycosis- differentiation from TB, sq.ca. & lymphoma.
Funari et al. (1999) : Chronic pulmonary paracoccidiodomycosis - HRCT in 41 pts.

Cryptococcosis (see also under AIDS - ps. 19.34 - 36).
Bonmati et al. (1956), Donnan (1959) : Torulosis.   Kent (1972) : Massive pulmonary cryptocccosis.
Bahr et al. (1962) : RUL pneumonia., Long et al. (1972) : RUL consolidation with blocked RUL bronchus.
Meighan (1972), Feigin (1983) , Khoury et al. (1984) : 24 cases.
Balmes and Hawkins (1987), Patz and Goodman (1992)
Pantongrag-Brown (1991) : Pulmonary cryptococcoma - man of 38 with posteriorly situated LUL mass.
Carter et al. (1992) : Complete lung collapse - an unusual presentation of cryptococcosis.
Lee, L. et al. (1993) : Diagnosis of pulmonary cryptococcosis by ultrasound guided percutaneous aspiration.
Yoon et al. (1999) : Cervical and thoracic lymphadenopathy in a child shown by MR.
Awasthi et al. (2001) : Cerebral cryptococcosis - atypical appearances on CT.

Histoplasmosis.
Murray et al. (1957) : Benign pulmonary histoplasmosis (**'cave disease'**) in South Africa.
Babbit and Weisbren (1960) : Epidemic pulmonary histoplasmosis.
Baum and Schwartz (1962) : Chronic pulmonary histoplasmosis.
Schwartz (1962) : Roentgen manifestations.
Macleod et al. (1972) : Three cases in the UK.
Chick and Bauman (1974) : Acute cavitary histoplasmosis.
Baum (1975) : Cavitation in histoplasmosis - fact or fiction.
Connell and Muhm (1976) : Radiographic manifestations - 10 year review.
Goodwin and Des Prez (1978)
Christoforidis (1979) : Radiologic manifestations.
Loyd et al. (1988) : Mediastinal fibrosis complicating histoplasmosis.
Landay and Rollins (1989) : Mediastinal histoplasmosis granuloma - CT evaluation.
Radin (1991) : Disseminated histoplasmosis - abdominal CT findings in 16 pts. - 14 with AIDS.
Rubin and Winer-Muram (1992)
Cuncliffe and Denning (1993) : Histoplasmosis - of **bat caves** and AIDS.

Conces et al. (1993) : Disseminated histoplasmosis in AIDS - findings on chest radiographs were varied and nonspecific - nodular or linear irregular opacities in an AIDS patient in an endemic area should raise the possibility.
Kneale and Turton (1995) : Bronchial involvement in a case in the UK.
Conces (1996) : About 30 to 50% of those infected have normal chest radiographs.
Eyler (1999) : Calcifications in lungs of childern at a school in Michigan close to a wood - they became infected as a result of inhaling dust from bird droppings in the play-ground.

Mucormycosis (Phocomycosis).
Bartrum et al. (1973) : 6 fatal cases of mucormycosis.
Schwarz et al. (1982) : Upper airway obstruction due to tracheal disease.
Bigby et al. (1986) : Rapidly progressive pneumonia especially in diabetics.
Zagoria et al. (1985) : Causing pulmonary gangrene.
Loerner et al. (1992) : Multiple pulmonary artery aneurysms complicating invasive mucormycosis.
Rubin, S. et al. (1992) : Radiographic and clinical spectrum of pulmonary zygomycosis.
Terk et al. (1992) : Man aged 22 with insulin dependent diabetes and 3 wks. headache - MR - destructive lesion invading the base of skull from the sinuses with a hypointense signal on T_2.
McAdams et al. (1997) : Review of findings in 32 cases - mainly consolidation in immunocompromised or diabetic pts. with cavitation in 40%. CT showed unsuspected abnormalities in 30%. Definite diagnosis was usually from tissue examination, cultures rarely being positive.

Nocardia.
Baeman et al. (1976) : Nocardial infections in the USA (1972 - 1974).
Grossman et al. (1970), Balikian et al. (1978)
Brown et al. (1980) : Presentation as a bronchogenic tumour.
Curry (1980) , Feigin (1986) : 21 cases., Mitchell, R. (1987)
Raby et al. (1990) : Nocardia infection in patients with liver transplants or chronic liver disease.
Conant and Wechsler (1992)

Sporotrichosis.
Comstock and Wolson (1975), Jay et al. (1977)

PROTOZOA, SPIROCHAETES, PARASITES, ETC

Amoebic chest infection.
   Amoebic infection remains endemic in tropical and sub-tropical countries, and is still a common cause of morbidity in these areas. Thoracic involvement may be manifest by a sympathetic effusion or be due to direct extension of an amoebic liver abscess through the diaphragm. When this happens, there may be haziness and loss of definition of the diaphragmatic outline, progressing to basal collapse, consolidation and pleural reaction or effusion, followed by lung necrosis and/or an empyema. Amoebic liver abscesses (Illus. **AMOEBIC ABSCESS**) occur more commonly on the right, but may also be seen on the left (Illus. **AMOEBIC ABSCESS, Liver Pt. 7a-d**).
   Occasionally a pulmonary metastatic abscess from colonic infection may develop without hepatic involvement.
   The characteristic late clinical 'text-book' sign is the expectoration of '**anchovy   sauce**', when an abscess arising in the liver, ruptures through the diaphragm into the lung and bronchial tree.
   Aspirated pus from an abscess may not yield the organism, even when the specimen is kept warm and quickly examined, and one may have to rely on blood titres for proof of diagnosis.
Many cases are treated with Flagil on clinical suspicion, with rapid recovery.

References.
Manson-Bahr (1923) : Pulmonary amoebiasis.
Manson-Bahr and Low (1923) : Aspiration of liver abscess - 15 cases.
Campbell (1946) : Secondary amoebiasis of the right lung in an Indian stevedore, causing extensive abscess formation with large cavities. He presented to a British Military General Hospital with 'bronchitis'. It had extended into the chest from the liver.
DeBakey and Ochsner (1951) : Hepatic amoebiasis - 20 year experience and analysis of 263 cases.
Webster (1960) : Pleuropulmonary amoebiasis - a review with an analysis of 10 cases.
Stephen and Uragoda (1970) : Pleuro-pulmonary amoebiasis - a review of 40 cases.
Wilson, E. (1971) : Pleuro-pulmonary amoebiasis.
Kapoor and Shah (1972) : Pericardial amoebiasis secondary to amoebic abscess in left side of liver.

Ragheb et al. (1976, from Alexandria, Egypt) : Intrathoracic presentation of amoebic liver abscess (ten cases - 5 with right sided empyema, 3 with right lung abscess, one overlying the right lung and the tenth with amoebic pericarditis secondary to a an abscess in the left lobe of the liver). Early operative drainage was advised to drain thick pus and to avoid the serious complication of pleuro-pulmonary amoebiasis.
Ibarra-Pérez and Selman-Lama (1977) : Diagnosis and treatment of amoebic empyemata - 88 cases.
Nwafo and Egbue (1981) : Intrathoracic manifestations of amoebiasis.
Gupta et al. (1987) : Round mass at right base due to amoebic lung abscess was aspirated under fluoroscopic control; the patient also had a liver abscess.
Stables et al. (1991) : Hepato-bronchial fistula complicating amoebiasis - treated by percutaneous catheter drainage.
Saraswat et al. (1992) : Percutaneous catheter drainage of amoebic liver abscess - 15 patients.
De Villiers and Durra (1998) : Amoebic abscess of the brain.

Leptospirosis (leptospira icterohaemorrhagica - Weil's disease - Illus. **WEIL'S DISEASE**) may give rise to a haemorrhagic pneumonitis, with multiple small or larger lung nodules, areas of consolidation, especially basal consolidation with pleural effusions, etc.

The reservoir of this infection is mainly in rats (including water-rats or other rodents) which do not succumb to the infection, but continue to excrete the spirochaete in their urine, thus contaminating water (particularly slow-running river water at the end of a hot summer - several such cases occurred in Oxford some years ago after falling into the River Cherwell - a tributary of the Thames - at the end of a hot summer), food, etc. The leptospires may enter the body through the conjunctiva, skin abrasions, the nose, gut, vagina, etc. Once in the body multiplication is very rapid, and within 24 to 48 hours, most organs are infected. The clinical incubation period varies from two to twenty days. Many cases are mild with a self-limiting 'flu-like illness. During the first week (the 'septicaemic phase') patients have chills, myalgia (especially in the lower limbs and back), abdominal pain, headache and conjunctival injection, together with some hepatic and renal impairment. This is followed by the 'immune phase', when antibodies cause many of the leptospires to be killed, but in the more severe cases renal failure, jaundice, meningism and prostration occur. Some cases may be mistaken for pancreatitis or other serious intra-abdominal disease, and CT and ultra-sound may show the liver, spleen and kidneys to be swollen, with an undilated biliary tree and perhaps some local areas of haemorrhage in the pancreas. Despite dialysis, many severe cases still have a fatal outcome. A problem is that many cases in the UK, the 'appropriate history' is not often volunteered, and several patients presenting with renal failure have only given the appropriate history after direct and close questioning.

Chest findings have often been non-specific with basal effusions, collapse and consolidation, but CT had often shown the swollen kidneys, liver, etc.

Penicillin, tetracycline and deoxycycline may have beneficial effects, particularly when given early in the illness.

References.
Lee et al. (1981) : The chest radiograph in leptospirosis in Jamaica.
Sitprija (1987, from Thailand) : Leptospirosis.
Im et al. (1989, from Seoul) : Studied 58 patients with leptospirosis. 37 had pulmonary radiographic abnormalities (21 - small nodular densities, 6 - large confluent areas of consolidation and 10 diffuse ill defined ground-glass density suggesting multifocal areas of pulmonary haemorrhage). They believed that rapidly evolving, predominantly peripheral, diffuse nodular or confluent pulmonary lesions were typical of leptospirosis, and together with fever and an appropriate history, could reasonably suggest the diagnosis.

Pulmonary gumma and thoracic syphilis.

Rarely a round lung opacity may be due to a pulmonary gumma. The author has only seen one, about 25 years ago and in a member of a religious order! He had positive serology and the lung nodule cleared rapidly on treatment with penicillin and potassium iodide. Other cases have had the lung nodules removed as possible neoplasm. Fibrosis of the lung and/or mediastinum is also a manifestation. The author has also seen another clergyman who was clinically diagnosed as dying from lung cancer and SVC obstruction (see also ps. 9.6 - 7), but at autopsy was found to have been suffering from syphilitic fibrous mediastinitis. Gummata also used to be found in the clavicle and skull (both membrane bones) and were sometimes recognised as such on radiographs (the author was shown such a case, by the late Percy Whitaker, in a Liverpool sailor and correctly diagnosed it!). Schinz et al. (1953) listed three types of lues of the lungs - (i) fibrosis of the interstitial pulmonary tissue, (ii) large solitary gummas (especially of the apex of a lower lobe, or in the middle lobe), and (iii) chronic lobar pneumonia or 'carnification', with disseminated gummas.

Pathologically a gumma is a greyish-white firm mass, radiating into adjacent lung parenchyma. Central necrosis may be present, surrounded by a granulomatous reaction in which plasma cells predominate, but which also contains a few multinucleate giant cells, histiocytes and lymphocytes. Satellite or multiple lesions may be present. There is also a marked intimal fibrosis of involved arteries, with perivascular cuffing by plasma cells (Dunnill, 1982). Dunnill also refers to congenital lues of the lung or 'pneumonia alba' which used to be found in stillbirths or the newborn.

Aneurysms of the thoracic aorta are discussed on ps. 10.7 et seq. - see also Illus. **SYPHILIS-AORTA.**

Further references.

Conner (1903) : 129 cases of syphilitic stenosis of the trachea and bronchi.
Golden (1921) : Syphilis of the lungs., Lambie (1938) : Tracheal stenosis., Ingram (1950) : Bronchial stricture.
Dziadiw (1972) : Pulmonary gumma.
Geer et al. (1985) : Pulmonary gumma - a 37 year old homosexual (with a secondary syphilitic rash) had a lung nodule shown on CT to lie in the left lung behind the heart, close to the descending aorta and adjacent to the mediastinal pleura. On tetracycline treatment both the skin and chest lesions resolved. - also refs. to 8 other cases.

Fig. 19.6   (a) Sketch of author's case   (b) Sketch of Geer et al's case.

PARASITES.

Hydatid cysts - (Illus. **HYDATID CYSTS**).

These are mainly caused by **Echinococcus   granulosus** ('εχινοs = hedgehog). They are becoming rare in the UK, except for the Brecon area of S. Wales and the north of Scotland. The parasite is still relatively common in parts of the Eastern Mediterranean (Greece, Lebanon and Turkey). It is also found in India, New Zealand, Australia and South America.

The cystic or larval form normally occurs in sheep (also pigs, cattle, deer, horses and goats), whilst the adult tape-worm is found in the intestine of dogs, foxes, wolves and similar wild carnivores. Some dogs may harbour thousands of worms. Ova are passed with the dogs faeces and may contaminate the hair, paws and muzzle, and both children and adults, fondling contaminated dogs, may transmit the ova to their mouths, and infants crawling around a farmhouse floor may ingest dried dog faeces in mistake for biscuits. Vegetables and water may also become contaminated.

The Takara tribe in Kenya had a very high incidence of hydatid disease. Dogs fed on unburied human corpses which were infested with cysts; they also licked and were fondled by children, thus completing the cycle, in this case man to dog to man.

When swallowed, embryos escape from the eggs, penetrate the intestinal mucosa and enter the portal circulation. About 60 % pass to the liver, 25 % to the lungs, and the remainder to the spleen, kidneys, brain, bone, etc. Larvae which are not phagocytosed develop into cysts. Most patients harbour a single cyst, but about 20 % may have more, and these may occur in one or more organs.

Hydatid cysts have double walls, the outer or **pericyst** being formed by the host, and the inner or **endocyst** (also termed the 'germinal' or 'brood' layer) by the parasite. Sometimes there is a chitinous or avascular layer between these. The pericyst of liver hydatids is thickened with collagen and some inflammatory reaction, whilst in the lung it is much thinner.

In the thorax, cysts are usually single, but may be multiple. In the lungs they are usually spherical in shape, but being pliable may become umbilicated by vessels or deformed by bronchi (thus mimicking tumours). They may also alter in shape with respiration, becoming oval in deep inspiration (a point best seen with fluoroscopy). Hydatid cysts almost never calcify in the lungs, but may do so in the mediastinum, the chest wall and the abdomen.

Should the pericyst of a pulmonary hydatid cyst rupture, air may pass between it and the endocyst, giving rise to a **'crescent'**, **'halo'** or 'double arch sign' (Fig. 19.7). If the endocyst also ruptures, salty tasting fluid and daughter cysts may be coughed up. The cyst lining may fold up and give rise to the **'water lily appearance'** (also termed the **'sign of the Camalote'** - after a South African water plant - Fainsinger, 1949). Shihabi (1986) from Jordan stated that about half of his patients with pulmonary hydatids had the 'water lily appearance', but he regarded this as due to the folding and infolding of the collapsed cyst membrane, after the fluid had been coughed up, the daughter cysts being expectorated at the same time. A cavitated hydatid may become infected and simulate a lung abscess; it may also slowly contract in size to mimic a small neoplasm. Saksouk (1986) from the Lebanon studied 20 patients with 64 cysts by CT and found intact cysts, daughter cysts and detached or collapsed endo- or daughter cyst membranes. Consolidation around infected cysts could mask their presence. Surgical removal from the periphery of the lung may be relatively easy, since if the outer wall is incised through a small incision, the cyst may often be 'blown' out by forced inflation of the lung by the anaesthetist - this is how a former Oxford thoracic surgeon used to remove them when they were more common in the UK (Pile, 1960).

Pulmonary hydatid cysts may rupture into the pleura, allowing membrane, daughter cysts and 'hydatid sand' to enter it and produce the **'water lily' sign** there. Hadley (1985) reported an occult case presenting with a spontaneous pneumothorax, and Connellan et al. (1979) a tension pneumothorax. Rupture into the bronchial tree may give rise to transbronchial dissemination leading to multiple lung cysts (a point proved experimentally in sheep by Borrie et al., 1965, and reported following surgery by Kilani et al., 1992, see also references). Cysts within the chest wall may cause rib nodules, rib notching or separation (from pressure), erosion of the spine, or simulate a neurofibroma or a Pancoast tumour (see ps. 18.35 et seq., 12.7 & 19.4).

Most liver (and splenic) hydatids are discovered fortuitously on radiographs by calcification within their walls, or by ultrasound, CT or MR. Some within the upper part of the liver may give rise to pleural or shoulder tip pain. Some may rupture into the peritoneum or the biliary tree, with dissemination of daughter cysts in the abdomen. Retroperitoneal hydatids may erode the spine. Renal hydatids are rarely seen in the UK but in the 1960s and 1970s were said to be the most common renal cysts seen in Greece.

Several authors have studied the US and radiological appearances of hydatid cysts which may be grouped into a number of stages:
(i) a well defined cyst (young uncomplicated cyst),
(ii) the laminated membrane or endocyst floats inside the cyst after separation, with deposits of 'hydatid sand' (daughter cysts - or brood capsules and scolices, which can form new cysts if rupture occurs into the pleura or peritoneum, if they are inhaled into other parts of the lung [see above], or tapeworms if ingested by a primary host),
(iii) a multiloculated appearance due to a multivesicular cyst,
(iv) a heterogenous mass with more solid areas (or gelatinous matrix), due to accumulation of membranes or infection - this takes years to develop and mainly occurs in hepatic hydatids in older patients - this may also give rise to a pseudo-tumoral appearance on US or CT (and like degenerate squamous tumour - see Illus. **CA SQUAMOUS, Pt. 4**) may be confused with pus at surgery or on aspiration,
(v) a calcified or mummified cyst, but calcification of the pericyst does not indicate that a hydatid cyst has died.

Complications occur particularly after spontaneous rupture into serous cavities or the biliary tree, or following incomplete surgery. Franquet et al. (1999) reported hydatid pulmonary embolism from a ruptured mediastinal cyst with HRCT, angiographic and pathological findings.

'Crescent', 'double arch' or 'halo sign', caused by rupture of the pericyst (host layer) whilst the endocyst (parasitic layer) remains intact.

'Water lily' or 'Camalote' sign - with ruptured endocyst endocyst or floating membrane (erect view). Scolices and daughter cysts may give rise to 'hydatid sand' which may calcify to give rise to a dense lower part of a cyst.

Fig. 19.7   'Crescent' and 'water lily' signs of hydatid cysts.

Hydatid cysts rarely occur in the heart, but if they rupture may lead to vascular emboli and anaphylaxis. They may also cause arrhythmias and may be demonstrated by US or MR. An example in a Welsh sheep farmer was reported by Shields, O. (1990); others have been noted by Perez et al. (1973), Franquet et al. (1984), Trigano et al. (1985), Desnos et al. (1987) and Cantoni et al. (1993).

Other types of hydatid disease.
E. alveolaris (or multilocularis) with multiple honeycombed cysts is found in North America, Central Europe and Asia and Japan. It is spread to man by foxes (which deposit excrement on berries or other edible plants) or cats which eat rodents harbouring cysts. It gives rise to denser multi-loculated cysts, and in the liver may mimic malignant disease, because of the fibrous-inflammatory reaction surrounding external vesiculation. This slowly invades the liver (especially the portal spaces and hilum), the hepatic veins and IVC. Microcalcification and central necrosis occur commonly due to vascular involvement and ischaemia. Extra-hepatic extension may occur through the diaphragm, and also metastatic spread to the lungs, brain or bone.
Treugut et al (1980) studied 20 cases of pulmonary involvement by E. multilocularis and found two radiological types. The first showed multiple ill-defined irregular lesions (up to 3 cms) lying peripherally with some showing stippled calcification. The second was due to liver disease penetrating the diaphragm, giving rise to various changes at the right lung base.
Alltree (1979) from Saudi Arabia studied nine cases by CT and US, and pointed out that well-defined cysts are likely to be due to E. granulosus, whereas those due to E. multilocularis tend to be poorly marginated, are more aggressive in growth and are more likely to spread.
Claudon et al. (1990a) from Nancy, France studied 20 patients with hepatic E. alveolaris by serial CT examinations, and failed to confirm the usually reported poor prognosis. Only in four was there a progressive increase in size due to parasitic growth or necrosis. Imidazole treatment appeared to be efficacious in several cases.
Choji et al. (1992) used CT and US in 67 cases of alveolar hepatic hydatid disease and found the most significant radiological features to be metacestodal vesicles, predominantly around the periphery. Punctate calcification was present in about 90%.

Drug and aspiration treatment, and skin tests.
Hydatid cysts may respond to treatment with mebendazole or albendazole with reduction in the size of some cysts, clearing of daughter cysts and lessening of symptoms (if present).
Opperman et al. (1982) reported a case of mediastinal hydatids in a boy of 14 which disappeared on treatment with mebendazole, one rupturing during treatment and leading to a severe anaphylactic reaction.
Singcharoen et al. (1985) reported a liver cyst which responded to mebendazole and albendazole; the daughter cysts also became smaller but relapsed after stopping treatment.

Todorov et al. (1990) from Bulgaria studied 55 patients receiving mebendazole and albendazole for hydatid cysts in the liver, lungs, bone, brain, spleen, etc. Albendazole appeared to have the greater therapeutic effect. Response was noted by the development of echogenic foci, an increase in density of cyst fluid, thickening of the cyst wall, calcium deposition, detachment of membrane, a reduction in size or disappearance of the cyst. Enlargement was regarded as a failure of treatment. Aggarwal et al. (1991) from India treated 10 patients with albendazole for pulmonary echinococcosis and found no effect.

The author has also seen some hydatid cysts become smaller with treatment. Other reports on the effects of mebendazole and albendazole have been made by Heath and Chevis (1974), Saimot et al. (1983) and Morris et al. (1984 and 1987) - the last authors used MR in 12 cases to study the cysts.

Hepatic (and other) **hydatid cysts have been aspirated** and injected with a weak (10 to 15%) formalin solution, silver nitrate or alcohol to try to kill any daughter cysts, but sclerosing cholangitis has been reported as a complication of the use of formalin. Cetrimide may be a safer scolicidal agent (Schaefer and Khan, 1991, who reviewed 59 patients). There is always the possibility of spillage of scolices and also of anaphylaxis with cyst puncture, so it is probably best to treat hydatids first with mebendazole or albendazole (see above).

McCorkell (1984) reported a cyst-bronchial communication following aspiration, and Stampfel (1982) an anaphylactic reaction in a 21 year old woman. Clements (1986) felt that the risk of anaphylaxis is probably lower than commonly anticipated (see also reference to Saremi, 1992, below). Giorgio et al. (1992) treated 16 hydatid cysts in 14 patients with US guided fine-needle drainage followed by the injection of 95% alcohol and repeated the procedure three days later.(Other references to cyst puncture are given below).

The Casoni or intra-dermal skin test may not be positive unless the parasite has leaked and caused sensitivity. A similar serum test is now available. In S. Wales the drug Dronsil has reduced the incidence of tape worms in farm dogs , but some Brecon farmers still allow their dogs to scavenge for dead sheep, and some fox-hounds are still fed on uncooked sheep carcasses. Although the control programme in Powys, Wales has been largely successful, a reservoir remains in the older sheep and dogs. A coproantigen test indicates which dogs to treat. About 10% of sheep in Gwent still contain cysts at slaughter (Palmer et al., 1996).

Further references.
(a) **E. granulosus.**
Toole et al. (1953) : Intrapulmonary rupture of hydatid cysts of the liver.
Dévé (1960) : L'échinococcose primitive.
Rakower and Milswidsky (1960) : Primary mediastinal echinococcus.
Kegel and Fatemi (1961) : Ruptured pulmonary hydatid cyst.
Borrie (1962) from New Zealand (2.4M people and 48M sheep) : fifty thoracic hydatid cysts.
Catto (1964) : Multiple liver abscesses in hydatid disease (contained gas) - ? due to anaerobic secondary infection.
Bloomfield (1966) : Protean radiological manifestations of hydatid infestation.
Bonakdarpour (1967) : 112 cases from Iran and a review of 611 from the USA.
McPhail and Arora (1967) : Intrathoracic hydatid disease.
Sadrieh et al. (1967) : Review of 150 cases of hydatid cyst of the lung.
Xanthikis (1972) : Hydatids of the chest - 91 pts. - lung involvement in 88.
Bonakdarpour et al. (1973) : Six cases of costal echinococcosis.
Balikian and Mudarris (1974) : 50 lung hydatids.
Cuthbert (1974) : Sylvatic pulmonary hydatid disease.
Orueta et al. (1974) : Surgical treatment of hydatid cysts of lung.
Ramos (1975) : Radiological characteristics of perforated pulmonary hydatid cysts.
Aytaç et al. (1977) : 100 patients with pulmonary hydatid cysts.
Scherer et al. (1978) : CT in hepatic hydatid disease - 13 cases.
Connellan et al. (1979) : Hydatid disease presenting as tension pneumothorax.
Saksouk (1979) : Non-osseous hydatid of chest wall.
Saksouk (1986) : CT of pulmonary hydatids.
Ismail et al. (1980) : CT of 122 patients in Baghdad with cysts in chest, abdomen, head, etc.
Niron and Özer (1981) , Fulton et al. (1982) : US of hepatic hydatid disease.
Beggs (1983) : Radiology of hepatic hydatid disease.
Pandolfo et al. (1984) : CT findings in hydatid disease.

Beggs (1985) : Radiology of hydatid disease.

Gharbi et al. (1985) : Studied the US appearances of hydatid cysts and described five stages.

Hadley (1985) : Occult hydatid disease presenting as a spontaneous pneumothorax.

Rong and Nie (1985) from China : Bony hydatid disease - 20 cases including some affecting the thoracic vertebrae - these may invade the spinal canal causing cord compression. They may also involve the vertebral appendages and ribs, with cystic change or expansion with deformity and destruction but no periosteal or endosteal reaction.

Giordano et al. (1985) : Hydatid cysts of the spine.

Lewall and McCorkell (1985) : Hepatic echinococcal cysts - sonographic appearance and classification.

Lewall and McCorkell (1986) : Rupture of echinococcal cysts - diagnosis, classification and clinical implications.

Claudon et al. (1987) : Spinal involvement.

Heinze et al. (1987) : Anaphylactic shock during extirpation of an Echinococcus granulosus cyst of the thigh.

Morris et al. (1987) : MR in hydatid disease - 12 cases - also studied the effects of treatment.

Solak et al. (1988) : Surgery in hydatid disease of the chest - 460 cases.

Marani et al. (1990) : MR of hydatid disease.

Marti-Bonmati and Serrani (1990) : Complications of hepatic hydatid cysts - US, CT & MR.

Acunas et al. (1991) : Hydatid cyst in psoas muscle.

Behrns and van Heerden (1991) : Surgical management of hepatic hydatid disease.

Hendaoui et al. (1991) : Hydatid cyst of the aorta - a 13 cm cyst of the wall of the lower mediastinal part of the lower thoracic aorta, mimicking an aneurysm on plain chest films - also US and CT appearance.

Khuroo et al. (1991) : Management of hydatid cysts of the liver with percutaneous drainage.

Von Sinner (1991) : Radiography, US, CT & MR of hydatid disease related to pathology.

Filice et al. (1992) : Percutaneous drainage of hydatid liver cysts.

Saremi (1992) from Tehran : Use of trochar cutting device to remove daughter cysts and membrane percutaneously, together with 20 % hypertonic saline or 0.5 silver nitrate as a scolicidal agent.

Taourel et al. (1993) : Comparison of CT & MR with hydatid cyst of the liver.

Wen et al. (1993) : Diagnosis and treatment of human hydatidosis.

Guthrie et al. (1996) : MR of hydatid cyst of thigh - echo-poor daughter cysts within a coarse heterogeneous matrix.

Montero et al. (1996) & Beric and Blomley (1997) : A **fat-fluid level** may be seen in a hepatic hydatid cyst.

Imbracio et al. (1997) : Antero-mediastinal hydatid cyst with calcified wall shown by CT.

Khuroo et al. (1977) : Percutaneous drainage compared with surgery for hepatic hydatid cysts.

O'Donovan and Fitzgerald (1997) : CT demonstration of hydatid-enteric (colon) fistula - 79 yr. old man from S. Wales - died from overwhelming sepsis.

Lewall (1998) : Hydatid disease - Biology, pathology, imaging and classification.

Lewall and Nyak (1998) from Saudi Arabia : Reviewed 63 pts. with hydatid cysts of the liver. They felt that cysts with an exophytic component are probably unstable and unsuitable for treatment by percutaneous drainage or prolonged medical treatment. Also dilated pericystic ducts are a relative contraindication to non-surgical treatment because of the danger of complicating biliary obstruction. In both instances surgery should not be unduly delayed.

Men et al. (1999) : Percutaneous treatment of hepatic hydatid cysts.

Haddad et al. (1999) from Labanon and Saudi Arabia : Disagreed with Lewall and Nyak and felt that percutaneous drainage together with antihelminth chemotherapy is preferable to surgery in all types of hydatid cyst.

Bosanac and Lisanin (2000) : Review of 52 cases of percutaneous drainage of hydatid cysts in the liver using Betadine as a scolicidal agent.

Franquet et al. (1999) : Hydatid pulmonary embolism from a ruptured mediastinal cyst.

(b) E. alveolaris

Thompson et al. (1972) : Plain radiographic findings.

Scherer et al. (1978) : Hepatic cysts **mimicking malignant disease**.

Kasai et al. (1980) : Alveolar hydatids of the liver - 60 operated cases.

Claudon et al. (1985) : US in diagnosis and follow-up of alveolar hepatic disease.

Didier et al. (1985) : US and CT in hepatic alveolar disease - 24 cases.

Claudon et al. (1990b) : 19 cases studied by MR, but noted that CT is better for showing calcification within cysts.

(c) Hydatid disease causing the Pancoast syndrome (see also p. 12.7).

Stathatos et al. (1969); Aletras and Papaconstantinou (1982); Gotterer et al. (1990)

Parasites which may give rise to thoracic manifestations include:

Tape worm larvae which may become calcified.

Several types of tape worm larvae may migrate to and become calcified in the muscles of the chest wall, pelvis and limbs.

The best known are **cysticerci**, due to the larvae of **Taenia solium** (the pig tape worm) which look like 'date stones' within the muscles (Illus. **CYSTICERCI**). Note that in the brain (where there is no muscle to elongate them, the larvae form small fluid-filled cysts or 1 to 2 mm calcified rounded nodules on CT sections. In the UK cysticerci are largely found in people who have lived in the Far East (particularly amongst those who were imprisoned in very bad conditions by the Japanese in World War II) or Africa. Infection is caused by the ingestion of human faeces containing ova, either from the patient himself, if he harbours the tape worm, or from contaminated raw vegetables, etc. (Both Jews and Muslims consider pork to be 'unholy meat').

Ankylostoma affects the skin, but lung infiltration may occur as a result of antigens.

Armillifer armillatus is a parasite which lives in the trachea and lungs of pythons and some other snakes in Africa, the Far East and America. The males are 3 to 5 cm long and the females 3 to 12 cm. Their eggs, containing a developed larva, are passed out with air-way secretions and excretions of the snakes and may be ingested with contaminated food or water by rats, monkeys, various herbivores or man. The larvae pass to the liver or other soft tissues, and encyst as 'nymphs'. Most patients have no symptoms, the infestation only being found by radiography demonstrating the crescentic shaped calcified 'nymphs' (4 to 7 mm long).

Sarcocystis larvae may be present in man from the consumption of infected muscle (see Kremmydas, 1964, from Greece), similarly **Sparaginosis** larvae may be passed to man from frogs, chickens and snakes (especially in Indo-China).

Dirofilaria immitis (the dog heart worm) is a nematode conveyed by mosquito type vectors, the parasite being found in Canada, the USA (especially the Eastern states and on the Pacific coast), Australia, etc., its distribution presumably being related to the presence of wild foxes, dogs, etc. A subcutaneous infection precedes microfilaraemia. In man the worms die and produce small ischaemic lung infarcts, which may have calcified centres. A serological diagnostic test is available. The first human case was reported by Dashiell (1961). Leonardi et al. (1977) noted 61 cases, Levinson et al. (1979) four cases, Larrieu et al. (1979) 48 cases and Chesney et al. (1983) one case. Cholankeril et al. (1983) showed by CT that the nodules lie subpleurally in the lung. Kido et al. (1991) reported a case in Japan causing a small peripheral left lower lobe mass (which was resected) and a small pleural effusion.

Filariasis - three forms are of medical importance - Loa-Loa, Wucheria bancrofti and Onchcercosis. Worms in this group produce microfilariae, which undergo maturation in an insect (often the mosquito, especially Culix fatigans) and are thence transferred to man. Loa-Loa worms are transferred by horse-flies and may produce small calcified nodules 'Calabar swellings' (named after a town in Nigeria). The filarial worms tend to lodge in regional lymph nodes and cause lymphatic obstruction by mechanical means when they are present in large numbers, and by inflammatory reaction when they die and disintegrate. The affected nodes enlarge and contain dilated sinusoids, the nodal obstruction causing dilatation of more peripheral lymph vessels and lymphoedema and 'elephantiasis'. A novel way of diagnosing the condition is to use scrotal ultra-sound when dilated lymphatics (sometimes containing wriggling live worms) may be seen (Dreyer et al., 1994). Chylothoraces and thoracic duct obstruction are discussed on p. 14.10. Filariasis may also lead to endomyocardial fibrosis.
(See also reference to tropical eosinophilic lung ps. 19.59 - 60 and Illus. **FILARIASIS**.)

Guinea worm (Dracunculus medinensis) infestation, found in Pakistan, Africa, etc., is contracted through drinking unstrained water containing larvae, within small fresh-water crustacean cyclops. The adult worms may become calcified in the soft tissues of the chest wall, abdomen, pelvis and limbs. The male worms are small, and the females much larger (7.5 to 12 cm long) superficially resembling earthworms. In the chest wall and abdomen, the calcified worms tend to be convoluted, sometimes with surrounding dystrophic calcification, whereas in the lower limbs the calcified worms tend to be more extended - see Illus. **GUINEA WORMS.**

Paragonimiasis (due to P. westermanii) or 'lung fluke' is contracted by eating infected uncooked or improperly cooked crab or other crustacea. It is found particularly in China and other parts of the Far East, where it may give rise to 'epidemic haemoptysis'. As with ascaris, the larvae pass through the jejunal wall and migrate to the lungs and other organs, including the brain, liver, etc. Brownish sputum, containing ova, may be expectorated. The pulmonary lesions may resemble tuberculosis, with consolidation around the parasites. Later, nodules are formed, which in turn become thin-walled cysts, burrows or cavities, and finally the lesions may calcify often with 'target' or central calcification. CT may show small 'ring-shaped cysts' in the lungs, liver and brain. In the lungs they are mainly in the sub-pleural area and adjacent pleural reaction may be present.

Schistosomiasis (bilharziasis) is caused by trematode worms, mainly S. mansoni (in Africa, S. America, etc.), S. japonicum (in the Far East) which principally affect the small and large intestines and S. haematobium which mainly affects the ureteric and vesical venules. There are also many other species, many of which affect different animals. In their life-cycle worms excrete ova which hatch into free swimming miracidia which then infect fresh-water snails leading in turn to the production of cerceriae. Schistosomiasis begins with penetration of the skin by cerceriae - often followed by a hypersensitivity reaction - "swimmers' itch". About three weeks later and particularly with S. japonicum a generalised immune complex syndrome occurs - **'Katayama fever'** - with fever, anorexia, headache, diarrhoea and cough. It is often accompanied by eosinophilia.

Pulmonary involvement occurs early in the disease, when migration of the schistosomes produces a toxic reaction in the lungs with infiltrates, nodules, masses and consolidation. This usually clears. Occasionally nodules may calcify. Chronic infection allows ova to pass into the venous system, with hepato-splenomegaly, varices, pulmonary arterio-venous shunts (accompanied by finger and toe clubbing and cyanosis), cor pulmonale and cerebral schistosomiasis. The later lung changes appear to be related to embolised ova or worms.

Quite often acute schistosomiasis (or 'Katayama fever' - see above) in travellers to endemic regions who swim in rivers or lakes (e.g. the Nile or Lake Malawi, etc. in central Africa) is unrecognised, but chest radiographs and CT may show multiple lesions (Illus. **SCHISTOSOMIASIS**). Early treatment (with oxamniquine and praziquantel) is required to prevent chronic granulomata and fibrosis.
(see also under tropical eosinophilic lung - ps. 19.59 - 60).

Strongyloidiasis is an important cause of pulmonary infection leading to death in several countries, particularly in the tropics and subtropics. It is found in all parts of the USA. Man and dog are the common primary hosts. Infection occurs by filiform larvae in the soil penetrating bare skin. They migrate via the lymphatics and veins to the lungs. Some are coughed up and swallowed and become adults in the duodenum and upper small bowel. Ova are deposited in the interstitial mucosa; most are excreted but some pass into the circulation and also pass to the lungs, repeating the developmental cycle and giving rise to repeated autoinfection, which can persist for many years. Patients may have lung consolidation, pleural effusions, develop lung abscesses and pulmonary insufficiency.

Toxoplasmosis (due to T. gondii a protozoan infection of animals, particularly cats) as well as causing encephalitis, eye disease etc. in the foetus or infants - as a result of infection in pregnancy - may cause small lung nodules, hilar lymphadenopathy and interstitial pneumonia (see Prosmanne et al., 1984).

American Trypanosomiasis ('Chagas' disease' due to T. cruzi - common in Brazil and other parts of South America) may produce a mega-oesophagus and cardiomegaly. The dilated oesophagus resembles that of achalasia, as there is no obstruction to the cardia (see ps. 16.4 - 5). It may be accompanied by a megacolon. The concomitant cardiomegaly is caused by myocardial damage, which in turn may give rise to a cardiac aneurysm.

Falciparum (or malignant) malaria may also lead to pneumonia - (Illus. **MALARIA**).

Loeffler's syndrome (including ascaris worms) and tropical eosinophilic lung - see ps. 19.59 - 60.

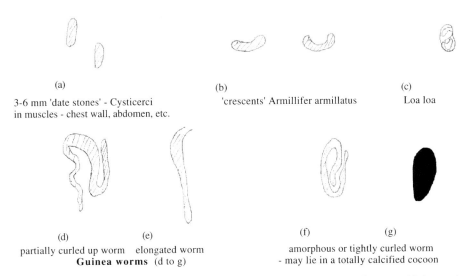

(a)

3-6 mm 'date stones' - Cysticerci
in muscles - chest wall, abdomen, etc.

(b)

'crescents' Armillifer armillatus

(c)

Loa loa

(d)   (e)

partially curled up worm   elongated worm
Guinea worms (d to g)

(f)   (g)

amorphous or tightly curled worm
- may lie in a totally calcified cocoon

Fig. 19.8 Diagrams showing appearances of some calcified worms or larvae, which may be seen
on chest radiographs.

Further references.

Chartres (1965) : Radiological manifestations of parasitism by the tongue worms, flat worms and the round worms
more commonly seen in the tropics.
Cochshott and Middlemiss (1979) : Clinical Radiology in the Tropics.
Middlemiss (1961) : Tropical Radiology.
Ardran (1948) : Armillifer armillatus - three cases.
Khajavi (1968) : Guinea worm calcification - a report of 83 cases.
Kanetkar et al. (1966) : Lymphographic patterns in filarial oedema of the lower limbs.
Andy et al. (1981) : Relation of severe eosinophilia and microfilariasis to chronic African endomyocardial fibrosis.
Makris et al. (1993) : Pulmonary strongyloidiasis - an unusual opportunistic pneumonia in a patient with ARDS.
Woodring et al. (1994) : Pulmonary strongyloidiasis - clinical and imaging features.
Jarratt (1995) : 62 yr. old man had inflammatory type shadowing in RUL + apex of RLL. 2 months later CT showed
a subpleural nodule in RLL - resection showed infarction with endarteritis and eosinophilic pneumonitis and a small
larva of D. immitis within a muscular pulmonary artery.

Ross et al. (1952) : The radiological diagnosis of **paragonimiasis** - advocated tomography for showing the cysts.
Muller, F. and Walker (1955) : Roentgen characteristics of pulmonary paragonimiasis - 85 % had abnormal chest
radiographs with small cysts in the periphery of the lung - often in a sub-pleural position.
Bahk (1962) : Pulmonary paragonimiasis as a cause of **Loeffler's syndrome**.
Ogakwu and Nwokolo (1973) : 100 cases in Nigeria.
Taylor and Swett (1982) : Pulmonary paragonimiasis in Laotian refugees.
Brown, R. et al. (1983)
Johnson, R. and Johnson (1983) Paragonimiasis in Indochinese refugees.
Singcharoen et al. (1988) : CT findings.
Im et al. (1992) : Pleuro-pulmonary paragonimiasis - CT and plain film findings in 71 patients.
Jawahiry and Karpas (1963) : Pulmonary **schistosomiasis**.
Thompson et al. (1979) : Pulmonary bilharzioma causing a mass in the RUL and adjacent hilar nodes, bilharzia ova
being found in the mass following resection. The patient also had **finger and toe clubbing**.
Cerri et al. (1984) : US manifestations of hepato-splenic schistosomiasis.
Cesmeli et al. (1997) : US & CT changes in the liver parenchyma in acute schistosomiasis - hypoechoic small
lesions on US & hypodense nodules on CT.
Mehta et al. (1997) : Cerebral schistosomiasis.
Gaur et al. (2000) : MR of intramedullary spinal **cysticercosis** - report of two cases.
Rahalkar et al. (2000) : The many faces of **cysticercosis**.

See Illus. **PARASITES.**

DISEASE DUE TO IMMUNOLOGICAL CAUSES.

Many conditions are due to these. Four types of common reaction occur, either singly or in combination - the 'Arthus reactions' :

Type I - Inhaled antigens produce an **immediate** response (within minutes) - asthma and bronchospasm. This is mediated by non-precipitating antibody, IgE - also known as 'reagin'. The reaction takes place on the surface of mast cells and leads to the release of histamine and histamine-like substances. Inhaled antigens are commonly bacteria, spores, fungi or bird protein, etc. (see also p. 19.101-105).

Type II - Antibodies are produced which are tissue specific and may lead to tissue damage and necrosis. They may be stimulated by viruses, whose surfaces may have similar antigenic properties to tissue cells - Goodpasture's syndrome (p. 19.98) is a variety of this. (The reaction time is variable).

Type III - Antigen and antibody complexes (IgG and IgM) plus complement unite causing inflammatory and necrotic changes in tissues - 'immune complex disease'. When antigen exceeds the amount of antibody (usually with soluble immune products), arthritis, proteinuria, vasculitis and serum sickness may occur. When insoluble products occur, with an excess of antibody, fibrinoid necrosis may be produced together with eosinophilic infiltration. This may be due to a lack of suppressor T cells, allowing B cells to produce excess antibody. Mucus plugs may be present with a Type III reaction leading to localised areas of collapse. They are commonly coughed up with the help of physiotherapy and most resolve spontaneously.

Examples include DLE, tissue necrosis with aspergillosis, extrinsic allergic alveolitis and fibrosing alveolitis. (The minimum reaction time is four to six hours).

Type IV - is a **delayed** reaction mediated by antigen and sensitised T lymphocytes leading to the formation of lymphocytic chemical mediators, which are cytotoxic and attract phagocytes. These in turn release lysosomal enzymes. It particularly produces a granulomatous type of reaction and is seen both with infectious and non-infectious granulomatous disease.

None of the **reactions** are mutually exclusive, and the development of one type does not exclude the simultaneous or subsequent development of another. Types I and II are often found together, and type IV may be associated with the other three. Immunodeficiency disease conditions may be either hormonal or cellular and are probably due to defects in the 'immune surveillance' system; a deficiency of T lymphocytes leading to impaired resistance to auto-antibodies or the enhancement of tumour growth.

References.
Pierce and Kerr (1978)
Paré and Fraser (1983)
Fraser et al. (1989)

Asthma is the most frequent allergic disease of the lung. It is a common functional condition characterised by dyspnoea, caused by spasm of the smaller and/or larger bronchi, which occurs for short or longer periods and resolves spontaneously or with treatment. Both intrinsic and extrinsic types are recognised (the former without recognisable allergic features), but there can be considerable overlap. Extrinsic types may be triggered by various allergens including pollen, dusts (house mites, etc), animal and vegetable proteins, bacterial infections, certain chemicals (including vehicle exhaust gases), smokes (including tobacco smoke), the presence of polyps in the nose or other airways, aspergillosis (ps. 19.38 - 43), etc.

The radiological appearance differs from emphysema, in that in asthma the lungs are hyperinflated, but without alveolar wall destruction and bullous formation. There may be some bronchial wall thickening and thinning of the intermediate sized lung vessels, but not a peripheral loss as with emphysema. The chest is often long and thin, and the posterior parts of the ribs may lie more horizontally than normal. The accessory muscles of respiration may be prominent in an asthmatic attack, but the heart is usually of normal size. Expiratory CT may show air trapping and bronchiolitis with bronchial wall thickening and narrowing, in others it only shows air trapping.

When the present author was performing many bronchograms particularly for bronchiectasis (see ps. 21.18 - 19) - views in expiration were almost routine and often showed contracted smaller bronchi and obstructive emphysema. For pneumomediastinum in asthma see p. 6.34.

Some examples are shown in Illus. **ASTHMA.**

References.
Lynch et al. (1993) : Comparison of CT appearance of the lungs in asthmatic and healthy subjects - leads to bronchial wall thickening.
Carr et al. (1996) : Correlation of lung function and CT-derived cross sectional lung area in asthmatics - compares with the degree of airway obstruction as measured by FEV_1 & RV/TLC - air trapping is a major component.
Grenier et al. (1996) : Abnormalities of the airways and lung parenchyma in asthmatics - CT observations in 50 pts.
Laurent et al. (1996) : In moderate asthma, air trapping on HRCT is correlated with obstruction but not with airway reversibility.
Mclean et al. (1998) : HRCT in asthma allows measurement of bronchial diameters in relation to bronchoconstriction, bronchial wall thickness, localised emphysema, mucoid impaction and collapse.

Pulmonary eosinophilia - (Illus. **PULM EOSINOPHILIA**).

Patients with asthma may have an increased blood eosinophilia. Other causes include reactions to **drugs** (see also ps. 19.110 to 19.112 the commonest now being non-steroidal analgesics), parasites, organic or other dusts, some bacteria (including pneumocystis) or **fungi** (particularly aspergillosis in the UK). Acutely there may an eosinophilic reaction with some pneumonias, Loeffler's syndrome, etc. Wheezing, areas of lung infiltration, consolidation or collapse and the expectoration of mucous plugs should raise the suspicion of aspergillosis (see p. 19.38 - 43); such infiltration may appear in one part of the lung (especially an upper lobe), clear and then appear elsewhere, giving rise to a '**wandering pneumonia**'. (A '**wandering pneumonia**' may also be seen with a mobile endobronchial foreign body - see ps. 3.8 and 19.1 and Illus. **WANDERING PNEUMONIA**, and with some collagen diseases such as DLE - see p. 19.80).

When eosinophilic consolidation persists, eventual clearing may reveal areas of particularly central bronchiectasis - almost a 'hall-mark' of resolving eosinophilic pneumonia due to aspergillosis; it may also cause upper lobe or peripheral fibrosis, as shown by CT. A variant is bronchocentric granuloma (see p. 19.74).

Pulmonary eosinophilia may also be associated with hypersensitivity or collagen diseases, such as rheumatoid, DLE or polyarteritis nodosa (see ps. 19.80 - 84), pleural eosinophilia (see below), some vasculitides e.g. Wegener's granuloma (ps. 19.76 - 79), Churg-Strauss syndrome (p. 19.79), or COP (p. 3.31). An eosinophilic pneumonia with pulmonary oedema may appear postoperatively. There is also a rare **eosinophilic leukaemia** - see p. 5.48.

Some patients with tumours affecting the lung (particularly lymphomas and adenocarcinomas) may have eosinophilia, or present with an eosinophilic pneumonia or an eosinophilic pleural effusion (Illus. **EOSINOPHIL EFFUSION**).

Loeffler's syndrome - (Illus. **LOEFFLER'S SYNDROME**).

This is characterised by patchy, fluffy or nodular areas of lung consolidation, which are usually transitory or self-limiting and are associated with eosinophilia. It was first described in young Swiss soldiers. Most cases are seen in young adults and most appear to be caused by ascaris or other larvae passing through the lungs. The ova are swallowed, 'hatch out' in the stomach or upper small bowel, migrate through the walls of these into the portal venous system, pass through the liver and enter the hepatic veins from which they pass to the lungs, where a sensitivity reaction occurs. (other pass into the alveoli, pass up the bronchi and trachea, to be swallowed and the adult worms live in the intestine, etc. - Illus. **ASCARIS**). Similar appearances may also be caused by the larval phases of strongyloides, paragonimiasis, hookworms, filariasis, toxacara (both canis and catis) and schistosomiasis (when the microfiliariae are released).

Tropical eosinophilic lung.

This condition appears to be largely due to the microfiliariae of filariasis, with the mosquito as the vector. It may occur within a few days or weeks of being bitten, or months later, when the microfilariae are being released into the circulation by adult worms. Pyrexia and attacks of coughing are common. The lungs may show a miliary pattern or fine, thicker or coarse strands, which are often peripherally placed. The shadows may progress to confluent opacities. The peripheral distribution with a cortico-medullary 'white-line' (Illus. FILARIASIS, Eos pn Pts. 3a-c & 4a-b - see also p. 1.45) appears to be due to the microfilariae lodging in the capillaries particularly at the cortico-medullary junction. In gross cases there may be a miliary pattern almost filling the lungs.

A similar condition may be caused by allergy to bat excrement or other allergens including other parasites, tiny mites, etc.

Chronic (or 'cryptogenic') eosinophilic pneumonia.

This has long been recognised as a more chronic and serious condition than Loeffler's syndrome. It may affect several organs, including the lungs and kidneys and give rise to systemic symptoms, similar to those seen with TB (night sweats, weight loss, etc.). It may be allied to polyarteritis nodosa (see p. 19.76). Spontaneous recovery is unusual but the condition often shows a good response to ACTH and/or steroids. Before these were available neo-arsphenamine (as used for syphilis) was used, sometimes with a good result.

Lung lesions may be single or multiple and appear as local areas of consolidation, which may be better shown on tomograms including CT. Hilar adenopathy is not unusual. The consolidation tends to be dense and if seen 'end-on' may give rise to the typical peripheral 'vertical bands' (Illus. FILARIASIS, Eos pn Pts. 3b & 4b). Lesions may recur either in similar or other sites in the lungs, and if present for a few months may lead to localised bronchiectasis. CT may show a similar appearance to that seen in tropical eosinophilia, COP or BOOP (see p. 3.31).

Bronchoalveolar lavage may reveal eosinophilia but open (surgical) or transbronchial lung biopsy may be necessary for certain diagnosis in many cases.

The 'eosinophilic myalgia syndrome' or 'eosinophilic hypersensitivity syndrome',

may give rise to radiographic chest abnormalities as well as muscle and nerve dysfunction including endo- and myo-carditis leading to mitral insufficiency, intracardiac thrombi and distal embolism.

Causes include analogues of L-tryptophane, toxic oil ingestion (impurities in cooking oil e.g. motor oil) and some viral infections - e.g. post viral/ influenza syndrome.

Williamson et al. (1991) reported chest x-ray findings in 18 patients: nine were normal, nine had fine irregular linear lung opacities especially at the lung bases with pleural effusions. Patients may also have skin abnormalities similar to those seen in scleroderma. Bronchoalveolar lavage may be helpful in some cases in recovering eosinophils but if negative lung biopsy may be necessary for certain diagnosis.

Further references.
Löffler (1932)
Crofton et al. (1952) : Pulmonary eosinophilia.
Khoo and Danaraj (1960) : Radiological appearance of eosinophilic lung (tropical eosinophilia).
Webb et al. (1960) : Demonstrated microfilariae in the lungs, liver and lymph nodes of patients with tropical pulmonary eosinophilia.
Christoforidis and Molnar (1961) : Eosinophilic pneumonia (2 cases).
Middlemiss (1961) : Miliary pattern.
Herlinger (1963) : Pulmonary changes in tropical eosinophilia.
Bean (1965) : Recognition of ascariasis by routine chest or abdominal radiographs.
Gelphi and Mustafa (1968) : Ascaris pneumonia.
Carrington et al. (1969) : Chronic eosinophilic pneumonia.
Liebow and Carrington (1969) : The eosinophilic pneumonias.
Gordon and Miller (1973) : Eosinophilic lung disease.
Healy (1974) : Eosinophilia in bronchogenic carcinoma.
Gaensler and Carrington (1977) : Peripheral opacities in chronic eosinophilic pneumonia - the photographic negative of pulmonary oedema.
B.M.J. (1977).- Pulmonary eosinophilia.
Neva and Ottesen (1978) : Tropical (filarial) eosinophilia., Reeder and Palmer (1980) : Acute Tropical Pneumonias.
Fox and Seed (1980) : Chronic eosinophilic pneumonia.
Lowe et al. (1981) : Tumour associated eosinophilia - a review.
Onitsuka et al. (1983) : CT of chronic eosinophilic pneumonia.

Geddes (1986) : Pulmonary eosinophilia.

Jederlinic et al. (1988) : Chronic eosinophilic pneumonia (19 cases).

Allen et al. (1989) : Acute eosinophilic pneumonia as a reversible cause of non-infectious respiratory failure.

Lee, T. (1989) : The eosinophil - its role in allergic respiratory disease is modulated by T-lymphocyte-derived factors. (It circulates in the peripheral blood for 3 to 8 hours and then migrates into peripheral tissues where it may contribute to tissue damage).

Mayo et al. (1989) : Chronic eosinophilic pneumonia - CT findings in six cases - peripheral air space consolidation plus mediastinal adenopathy in three.

Ricker et al. (1991) : Fatal pulmonary aspergillosis presenting as acute eos. pn. in a previously healthy child.

Goodwin and Glenny (1992) : Non-steroidal anti-inflammatory drug associated lung infiltrates with eosinophilia.

Roig et al. (1992) : Acute eosinophilic pneumonia due to **toxocara**.

Umeki (1992) : Re-evaluation of eosinophilic pneumonia and its diagnostic criteria.

Brander and Tukainen (1993) : Acute eosinophilic pneumonia in a heroin smoker.

Dupon et al. (1993) : Acute eosinophilic pneumonia induced by inhaled pentamidine.

Zaki et al. (1993) : Mediastinal lymphadenopathy in eosinophilic pneumonia.

Allen, J, and Davis (1994, USA) : Eosinophilic lung disease includes simple pulm. eosinophilia, chronic eos. pn., acute eos. pn., Churg-Strauss syndrome, asthma, allergic bronchopulmonary aspergillosis, bronchocentric granulomatosis, some parasitic infections and drug reactions.

Not all chronic cases have typical lung infiltrations, but about 90% have blood eosinophilia.

Hayakawa et al. (1994) : A clinical study of idiopathic eosinophilic pneumonia.

Wilson (1995, London) : Noted three subgroups where tissue and/or blood **eosinophils** are (i) pathogenically **important** - "classical" type; (ii) **inconstant**, "occasional" or of a mild nature - as with infection, neoplasm, Wegener, rheumatoid arthritis, sarcoid, etc.; (3) **coincident** to an extrapulmonary condition (bowel, etc). He also classified the causes into three groups (a) **airways disease**; (b) **eosinophilic pneumonias**; (c) **vasculitic/granulomatous disorders**, and pointed out that by combining radiological findings with the clinical investigations (degree of eosinophilia and serum IgE levels) it is often possible to limit the differential diagnosis to one or two possibilities.

Cheon et al. (1996) : Radiographic and CT findings in 6 pts. with acute eosinophilic pneumonia - bilateral reticular densities on CXRs & on CT ground-glass opacity with small septal thickening and pleural effusion with acute fever and dyspnoea may suggest the diagnosis.

Pope-Harman et al. (1996) : Acute eosinophilic pneumonia - 15 cases + literature review - rapid response to steroids.

Davies, C. et al. (1997) : Recurrent **postpartum pulmonary eosinophilia**.

King, M. et al. (1997) : Acute eosinophilic pneumonia should be considered a possible diagnosis when a previously healthy person presents with acute respiratory failure of unknown cause.

Martinez and Domingo (1997) : Acute eosinophilic pneumonia associated with 'tenidap' (a new NSAID) - painful interstitial infiltrates over both middle and lower lungs on chest radiographs & CT, with full recovery.

Johkoh et al. (2000) : Studied 111 cases and concluded that although eos. lung diseases often may be differentiated by HRCT, correlation with clinical features is required for a definitive diagnosis.

See also references under Churg-Strauss syndrome - p. 19.79, bronchocentric granuloma - p. 19.80, BOOP - p. 3.31, eosinophilic pleural effusion - p. 19.59, parasites - ps. 19.48 - 57 and aspergillosis - ps. 19.38 - 43.

Some 'storage' diseases.

Histiocytosis X (eosinophilic granuloma) - Illus. **HISTIOCYTOSIS and EOSINOPHIL GRANULOMA** - see also p. 1.54.

This is a granulomatous disorder of the mononuclear phagocytic cells, with the characteristic Langerhan's cell. The condition affects various organs, including the lungs, bones and posterior pituitary, which become infiltrated with histiocytes and eosinophils. The lungs may contain small nodules (2 to 10 mm in size) which progress to fibrosis and honeycombing with bullae (see also p. 6.6). Occasionally there are enlarged hilar and/or mediastinal nodes and pleural effusions. Many affected patients are teenagers or young adults (especially females aged 15 to 35), but some are older or younger. Patients may present with breathlessness, due to a spontaneous pneumothorax, diabetes insipidus or bone involvement, with small cyst-like formations or larger bone erosions like secondary tumour deposits (see also p. 12.28 & Illus. **HISTIOCYTOSIS, Pts. 6 & 7**). These may be complicated by fractures. When they occur in the jaws, the teeth may become loose and fall out. Cranial deposits may produce a 'geographic skull'. Rib lesions typically are found in the anterior or lateral ends of the lower ribs (Illus. **HISTIOCYTOSIS, Pt. 10c**). Other lesions may be found in the clavicles, the scapulae, spine, pelvis and long bones. Some also have involvement of the GI tract. Occasionally intra-thoracic lymph nodes are affected and may become enlarged, confluent and show amorphous calcification, e.g. in the thymus region.

Smoking should be discouraged as it can potentiate lung changes, but marked improvement may occur after stopping smoking. Asymptomatic minor bone cases may be left untreated; some may have a spontaneous resolution of the radiological changes: others may be given steroids, vincristine or localised small doses of radiotherapy. Those with single system disease appear to fare best, and those with lung involvement worst.

Formerly, lung disease was often fatal, but lung transplantation may be employed in suitable patients. However recurrent cases are now being reported in the donor lungs following transplantation with typical CT changes of nodules and cysts and response to cyclophosphamide.

HRCT studies have suggested that the sequence of changes in the lungs is firstly mainly nodular changes (with a few cysts), later the nodules become cavitated and form thick walled cysts, which in turn become thin walled or confluent cysts. The cysts do not show the peripheral preponderance seen in fibrosing alveolitis (ps. 19.116 et seq.), and are similar to those seen in lymphangioleiomyomatosis (ps. 5.18 - 19). A typical 'tennis racquet' appearance may be seen on electron microscopy of biopsy specimens (trans-bronchial is safest).

References.

Lichtenstein (1953) : Proposed the term Histiocytosis X to cover eosinophilic granuloma, Hand-Schuller-Christian and Letterer-Siwe diseases.

Nadeau et al. (1960) : Primary pulmonary histiocytosis X.

Melhem et al. (1964) : 15 paediatric cases - disseminated disease occurs predominantly in infants and young children, with localised forms in older children and adults. The presence of pulmonary involvement in disseminated cases was an omen of poor prognosis. Whilst this was usually asymptomatic, it occurred in the more severe forms of the disease. Those **with solitary lung involvement**, usually adults, had a **more favourable prognosis.**

Takahashi et al. (1966) : Pulmonary involvement is uncommon and presents difficulty in diagnosis because of the large number of diseases which may produce a similar radiographic appearance. The presence of diffuse nodular infiltration of the lung in a young otherwise healthy person should suggest the diagnosis, especially if characteristic bone lesions are present. They also pointed out that bone lesions may show spontaneous regression - an important point in evaluating a therapeutic agent!

Weber, W. et al. (1969) : Review of 18 cases.

Ennis et al. (1973) : Radiology of bone changes in histiocytosis X

Guardia et al. (1979) : Early pleural effusion in histiocytosis X.

Basset et al. (1976), Prophet (1982), Marcy and Reynolds (1985) : Pulmonary histiocytosis X.

Friedman et al. (1981) : Eosinophilic granuloma of the lung - clinical aspects of primary histiocytomas in adults.

Tittel and Winkler (1981) : Chronic recurrent pleural effusion in an adult with histiocytosis X

Lacronique et al. (1982) : Radiological features of 50 adult cases of pulmonary histiocytosis X.

Nakata et al. (1982) : Histiocytosis presenting with an anterior mediastinal mass in a child.

Eftekhari et al. (1986) : CT - cavitation in a mediastinal mass following chemotherapy for histiocytosis X.

Pomeranz and Proto (1986) : Unusual confusing features of eosinophilic granuloma.

Brauner et al. (1989) : HRCT of 18 patients with pulmonary histiocytosis - 17 had thin walled cysts of various sizes, bullae and micro-nodules (some of which had cavitated) which appeared to be due to interstitial granulomas or infiltrates in the walls of the bronchioles (when they become 1 to 3 mm or more in size, they may be seen on CT sections). Honeycombing appeared to correspond with conjoined and confluent cysts distributed throughout the lungs in advanced disease. Interstitial changes were also present.

Moore et al. (1989) : 17 patients - 11 had HRCT and showed cystic air spaces (usually <10 mm in diameter). In many nodules were also present (<5 mm in diameter) and appeared to lie in the centres of secondary lobules, and around small air-ways. Many showed preservation of intervening lung tissue. Serial scans in one case showed progression from nodules to cysts, and HRCT showed cystic changes which were invisible on plain radiographs.

Fichtenbaum et al. (1990) : Eosinophilic granuloma of the lung presenting as a solitary pulmonary nodule in a man of 58 (simulating a small neoplasm in a cigarette smoker).

Shanley et al. (1990) : Development of pulmonary histiocytosis X after chemotherapy for Hodgkin's disease.

Patel, B. et al. (1991) : Small bowel histiocytosis X.

Stern et al. (1992) : Expiratory scan in one case showed air trapping.

Gervais et al. (1993) : Pulmonary eosinophilic granuloma.

Lacronique et al. (1993) : La granulomatose pulmonaire à cellule de Langerhans.

Sumner et al. (1993) : Punctate thymic calcifications in histiocytosis X in an infant.

Unger et al. (1994) : Man age 46 with Hodgkin's disease developed miliary nodules due to eosinophilic granuloma whilst in remission. Noted the association of the two conditions in 18 patients quoted in the literature (six with lung involvement) - ? association related to T-cell deficits resulting in uncontrolled proliferation of Langerhans cells.

Mitchell et al. (1995) : It is not always possible to distinguish histiocytosis from lymphangioleiomyomatosis by HRCT, but in histiocytosis focal areas may be more severely affected.
Brauner et al. (1997) : Serial initial & final CT scans in 21 pts. allowed good assessment of the progression of histiocytosis - nodular lesions probably represent active disease and often undergo regression or transform into cysts.
Chan, Y. et al. (1997) : Sonographic appearance of hepatic Langerhans cell histiocytosis.
Habib et al. (1998) : Recurrent Langerhans cell histiocytosis.
Gabbay et al. (1998) : Recurrent histiocytosis following lung transplantation - responded to cyclophosphamide.
Parums (1998) : Langerhans cells are part of the system of "dendritic cells" which arise in the bone marrow - they are antigen presenting cells (usually for T cell mediated immunity) but also for mature eosinophils in histiocytosis - these latter have an abnormal phenotype & proliferate locally with mitoses, perhaps suggesting a neoplastic process.
Tazi et al. (2000) : Adult pulmonary Langerhans' cell histiocytosis (review).
Wittenberg et al. (2000) : Pulm. involvement in Erdheim-Chester disease (another similar lipoidosis).

Gaucher's disease may be complicated by severe pulmonary involvement, most patients with this rarely surviving longer than the second decade. Schneider et al. (1977) described diffuse bilateral pulmonary infiltrates in three adults spreading from the hila. Bone changes affecting the ribs are discussed on p. 12.28. Regression of lung and skeletal changes may occur after bone marrow transplantation (Starer et al., 1987). Patients tend to die from liver failure and monitoring its size by CT can be a useful guide to when liver transplantation may be required (Kolovos et al., 1995).

Further references.
Roberts and Friederickson (1967) : Pulm. Gaucher's disease causing pulmonary hypertension + recurrent pericarditis.
Wolson (1972) : Pulmonary fibrosis in Gaucher's disease.
Carson et al. (1994) : HRCT in a girl showed patchy irregular ground-glass shadowing (also bronchoalveolar lavage).
Aydin et al. (1997) : HRCT in a 54 yr. old man with Gaucher's disease, who had dyspnoea since age 10, showed ground-glass shadowing, interlobular and septal thickening and thickening and irregular interfaces along the costal pleura; also PA enlargement, hepato-splenomegaly, limb bone pains and easy bruising with minor trauma.
Karablut et al. (1997) : Obliteration of the maxillary and sphenoid sinuses in Gaucher's disease.

Whipple's disease of the chest may result in excess deposition of fat and fatty acids in the lungs leading to **basal infiltrates and involvement of the hilar and mediastinal lymph nodes, as well as the intestinal and mesenteric lymphatic tissue**. Patients may have a severe chronic cough, gastro-intestinal and neurological symptoms. CT of the chest may show low density tissue in the nodes. A recently isolated bacillus Tropheryma whippelii is the cause. Its DNA sequences have phylogenetic sequences similar to those seen with actinomyces; and a polymerase chain reaction amplification has formed the basis of a diagnostic test for the condition.

References.
Whipple (1907) : Described a missionary with weight loss, diarrhoea and abdominal pain with polyarthralgia and lymphadenopathy - argyrophilic rod shaped organisms were seen in mesentery lymph nodes at post mortem.
Winberg et al. (1978) : Whipple's disease of the lung.
Relman et al. (1992) : Identification of the uncultured bacillus of Whipple's disease.
Weeks et al. (1996) : Cerebral Whipple's disease.

Pulmonary alveolar proteinosis - (Illus. ALVEOLAR PROTEINOSIS).
    This a rare condition, which is characterised by the accumulation of surfactant materials in the alveoli; there is also an impaired clearance of alveolar macrophages. It probably represents a response by the lung to harmful stimuli, resulting in the overproduction of surfactant and a failure of the normal alveolar clearance mechanisms. Stimuli include infections, paints, fumes, solvents and dusts. The condition may also occur in immune-compromised subjects with lymphoma, leukaemia or following chemotherapy. Lavage of the phospho-lipoid-proteinaceous material with warm saline at bronchoscopy often results in recovery, but in some the condition may become chronic, and it may also be complicated by secondary infection with pneumocystis, fungi, etc.
    The condition was first reported by Rosen et al. (1958) - their patients had cough and dyspnoea with, 'fine, diffuse, perihilar, feathery or vaguely nodular, soft density, resembling in its butterfly distribution the pattern seen in severe pulmonary oedema'. They found the alveoli to be filled with

proteinaceous and lipid material, which they thought was derived from 'granuloma transformation of septal cells and their subsequent sloughing and necrosis'.

The age range is from infancy to old age. Characteristically it produces bilateral 'fluffy pulmonary infiltrates' radiating outwards from the hila, in a similar manner to pulmonary oedema. Kerley's B lines may be present. Patchy granular densities may appear in the lung and may be bilateral or unilateral. The superimposition of myriads of fluid-filled acini may give rise to the radiological appearance of large dense masses or to fluffy poorly defined nodules throughout the lungs, some containing 'air alveolograms'. A 'bat's wing' appearance may also occur.

As resolution occurs, areas of uneven aeration are often seen, within lung which is still consolidated. Clearing may be complete, particularly if no superimposed infection occurs.

Murch and Carr (1989) studied several patients by HRCT and showed not only alveolar filling within acini by opaque material, but also **thickened and oedematous   septa**, giving a CT appearance like '**crazy   paving**', with 3, 4 or 5 sided patterns. There were often normally air-filled segments between affected areas, or smaller air-filled areas or alveoli within the diseased areas (as seen both on CT and complementary biopsies) which caused the less dense or greyer areas within the boundaries of the thickened septa to be seen (see also p. 1.52).

Exudate filling some of the alveoli and secondary lobules, and looking like '**crazy paving**' on CT sections. The broncho-pneumonic distribution of the lesions and their angled and well-defined borders are characteristic. There is also thickening of the interlobular septa, which can just be seen with the naked eye on biopsy specimens.
In chronic cases thickening of the interlobular septa can give rise to honeycombing.

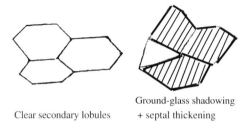

Clear secondary lobules

Ground-glass shadowing + septal thickening

Fig. 19.9 'Crazy paving' in alveolar proteinosis.

Note: a similar appearance may be seen with exogenous lipoid pneumonia, the mucinous type of bronchioloalveolar cell carcinoma and lymphangitis carcinomatosa (see also ps. 5.1 & 8.11 - 12).

Further references.

Carlson and Mason (1960) : Characteristic material in the sputum.   Plenk et al. (1960) : A new disease?
Ramirez (1964) : Roentgenological analysis.
Larson and Gordiner (1965) : Reviewed 85 cases, including 6 new ones, and noted that PAP may remit spontaneously, or be complicated by bacterial or fungus infection.
Ramirez et al. (1966) : Bronchial washings contained substances favouring the growth of organisms.
Anton and Gray (1967) : PAP presenting with a pneumothorax and honeycomb lung at autopsy. The radiological picture may show - a feathery appearance of individual lesions, a butterfly distribution, mainly basal opacities, homogeneous consolidation, diffuse nodulation, radiolucent cysts or a shifting pattern of the lesions.
Davidson and Macleod (1969) : PAP., Preger (1969) : PAP. British Medical Journal (1972) : Editorial - PAP.
Hudson et al. (1974) : Pulmonary **interstitial fibrosis** following alveolar proteinosis.
Carnovale et al. (1977) : Association with malignancy and lymphoma.
Selecky et al. (1977) : 10 year experience of whole lung lavage in PAP.
Rogers et al. (1978) : Physiological effects of bronchopulmonary lavage in PAP.
Rubin et al. (1981) : Relationship of PAP to silicosis and pulmonary infection.
McCook et al. (1981) : PAP in children - mottled or finely nodular pattern.
Miller, P. et al. (1981) : PAP with interstitial involvement.
Clague et al. (1983) : Pulmonary **interstitial fibrosis** associated with PAP.
Singh et al. (1983) : Staining for surfactant apoprotein in alveolar proteinosis and similar conditions. Air space filling is usually patchy, some patches being confluent.
Miller, R. et al. (1984) : PAP and aluminium dust exposure.
Newell et al. (1984) : CT of PAP in adults - noted minimal air bronchograms and preserved visibility of pulmonary vessels ? due to low density of material in the air spaces.

Gale, M. et al. (1986) : Bronchopulmonary lavage and chest radiographic observations.

Gonzalez-Rothi and Harris (1986) : Further evaluation of abnormal alveolar macrophages.

Grosser et al. (1986) : PAP. Prakash et al. (1987) : PAP - 34 cases + review.

Ruben and Talamo (1986) : Secondary PAP in two patients with AIDS.

Senac et al. (1986) : PAP with pulmonary interstitial thickening.

Godwin et al. (1988) : Nine cases studied by CT - findings ranged from ill-defined nodular shadows to patchy consolidation, sometimes confluent. The shadowing tended to be sharply demarcated from surrounding normal lung, giving rise to a geographic pattern. Air bronchograms were not a prominent feature. Thickened interlobular septa were also seen. Repeat examinations following lavage showed substantial clearing, but some patients still had residual patchy shadowing several months later.

Noma et al. (1990) : HRCT shows that the distribution of PAP may be centrilobular, perilobular and/or panlobular. Although usually considered to be an air-space disease, HRCT may show a dominant interstitial pattern, with perilobular distribution, and thickening of the interlobular septa - such a case was illustrated (see also Illus. **ALVEOLAR PROTEINOSIS, Pt. 3a-d**).

Hansell and Kerr (1991) : HRCT - thickening of interlobular septa in areas of air-space consolidation due to PAP.

Masuda et al. (1991) : Concentration of surfactant apoprotein-A in sputum for diagnosis.

Usui et al. (1992) : Interstitial lattice, enlarged mediast. nodes + elevated carcino-embryonic antigen in severe PAP.

Zimmer and Chew (1993) : PAP is a rare disease of unknown aetiology, which is characterised by the accumulation of surfactant materials and cellular debris in the alveoli, causing perihilar or 'bats-wing' shadowing. Impaired clearance of alveolar macrophages has been implicated. CT shows peripheral or central ill-defined nodular opacities or patchy consolidation. Occasionally superimposed septal oedema, infiltration or fibrosis results in an interstitial pattern. Definitive diagnosis is made by [open chest or trans-bronchial] biopsy, but detection of surfactant apoprotein A in sputum may allow a less invasive diagnosis.

Shah et al. (2000) : Clinical aspects and current concepts on pathogenesis.

Sarcoidosis - (Illus. **SARCOID**).

Historical review - The earliest reports were of skin eruptions. Besnier (1889 from France) described lupus pernio affecting the face, ears and fingers with non-caseating tuberculoid granulomas. Hutchinson (1889 in England) named the condition 'Mortimer's malady' after a patient of that name with similar but more widespread disease. Boeck (1899 from Norway) reported widespread skin changes with slightly elevated spots and yellow-brown patches accompanied by slight scaling on the limbs, trunk and face, but without ulceration. Groin, axillary and epi-trochlear nodes were enlarged. Boeck later described involvement of the lungs, nose, conjunctivae, spleen and bones of the hand and feet. Heerfordt (1909 from Denmark) noted 'sub-chronic uveo-parotid fever', i.e. irido-cyclitis, parotid gland enlargement and facial palsy. Löfgrens (1953 from Stockholm) found that bilateral hilar node enlargement with or without **erythema nodosum** (Illus. **ERYTHEMA NODOSUM**) was an early manifestation of sarcoidosis. (For further details of the history of sarcoidosis - see Scadding, 1987 & for Obituary to Scadding - see BMJ, **320**, 189 - 15 Jan. 2000).

Cause - The cause of sarcoidosis is still incompletely understood. It appears to be a non-caseating epithelioid granulomatous multi-system reaction, triggered by a response of the tissues to some substance or substances mostly unknown, but attributed in some cases to beryllium, pine needles, the tubercle bacillus or to tumour cells (see ps. 19.74 - 75).

The occasional transition to tuberculosis, with bacilli in the sputum, lead Scadding (1960) to write 'perhaps if I had the courage of my convictions, I would label my cases as non-caseating tuberculosis.' In 1987 he noted that in a few patients mycobacterial tuberculosis preceded or follows sarcoidosis, or mycobacteria may be isolated while the clinical picture has been that of sarcoidosis. The combination of sarcoidosis and tuberculosis is sometimes known as **'Scadding's disease'**. (See also references to sarcoid and tuberculosis below).

In some animals e.g. horses, sarcoid skin nodules may be found which mimic tumours, and these are usually thought to be due to a virus infection. In humans no transmissible agent has yet been identified, but Mitchell and Rees (1969) and Mitchell et al. (1976) found that they could transmit an agent to mice from patients with sarcoidosis or Crohn's disease, which gave rise to a positive Kveim test in the mice. It was inactivated by heat or irradiation. Both Crohn's disease and sarcoidosis give a similar micropathological appearance, and some have wondered if both of these conditions are manifestations of the same disease process. Several authors (including Mitchell and the present author) have seen a few patients in whom both conditions were present, either syn- or metachronously (Illus. **CROHN'S DISEASE**). One young man presented to the author with a severe milk intolerance - he also had marked splenic (and hepatic) involvement. Neilly et al. (1989) studied pulmonary abnormalities in 29 patients with Crohn's disease, and found that the lungs were relatively unaffected. In some cases mycobacteria may be found in old pathology specimens in pathology pots! Herman-Taylor (1996) found that M paratuberculosis may be responsible for most Crohn's disease cases in people with an inherited or acquired susceptibility. This bacterium is present in milk and it appears not to be completely destroyed at normal pasteurisation temperatures and may segregate in the cream. Kon and Du Bois (1997) wrote "there is accumulating evidence for the role of mycobacteria in patients with sarcoidosis" and quoted the work of Almenoff et al. (1996) in finding that acid fast cell wall deficient forms of bacteria (similar, if not identical to M. tuberculosis) may be grown from blood, bronchial washings, and anterior chamber eye fluid from patients with sarcoidosis.

As James, D. (1991a) noted, the pine pollen theory of sarcoidosis was all the rage in the 1960s. Its distribution in the USA correlated well with pine forests. Pine pollen contains similar acid fast staining qualities to M. tuberculosis, and contains long chain fatty acids and a substance similar to the 'wax' fraction in the tubercle bacillus. Pine pollen suspensions injected into guinea pigs produced sarcoid-like granulomas. He wrote "Following animal, etc. experiments it became apparent that granuloma formation could be induced by various agents, including bacteria, fungi, viruses, helminths, chemicals, BCG vaccine and even cancer." At the bedside, tuberculin and dinitrochlorobenzene skin tests highlighted the depression of delayed type hypersensitivity that was characteristic of sarcoidosis. Tuberculosis patients had normal delayed type hypersensitivity except for a small group of anergic subjects. The other distinguishing feature was the Kveim-Siltbach skin test. It would appear that antigenic invasion by micro-organisms, chemicals or cancer may be met by a granulomatous inflammatory response, which depends on close interplay between activated macrophages and T lymphocytes. T cells and macrophages tend to be abundant at the site of sarcoid inflammation, but are less evident away from the 'battlefield' and in the peripheral blood. Scadding (1996) wrote" a diagnosis of sarcoidosis claims no more than a granulomatous process about whose cellular and immunological pathogenesis we have some knowledge, underlies the symptoms and signs, but admits ignorance of the cause of this process".

Clinical course - Most patients with sarcoidosis are aged 20 to 55 (peak ages 20 to 35), and the condition is almost unknown before the mid teens. Female to male ration is about 2 : 1. As well as a peak in young women, there is a second peak incidence in older women, who are more likely to have symptoms. Few patients are very ill, but quite a number have a moderate malaise, with sweating, discomfort from uveitis, swelling of cervical lymph nodes, joint pains, etc. Some have transitory erythema nodosum (see p. 23.6 and Illus. **ERYTHEMA NODOSUM**). In a few the malaise can be quite marked, with considerable systemic upset, hypercalcaemia and altered calcium metabolism, a very painful arthropathy, etc. Rarely the patients may be very ill with intra-vascular coagulation and a gross systemic upset.

An epidemiological survey of sarcoidosis in 17 cities around the world was reported at the XIIth World Congress of Sarcoidosis and other Granulomatous Disorders in Kyoto (see James, D. 1991b) - 2,976 new intrathoracic cases were observed from 1981 to 1985. Women comprised 62% and 78% were aged 20 - 50. Racial differences were seen - the black population in the US and the West Indians in London often have severe, extensive and crippling disease, whereas in the Irish it is mild. In the same way that sarcoidosis occurs among London's migrants from the West Indies, so it is seen in Paris among individuals from Martinique and in New York City among those born in Puerto Rico.

Sweden is reported to have the highest incidence (64 per 100,000, according to Hillerdal et al., 1984, from Uppsala, who published a 15 year study). In the UK the incidence is similar to that in the white population in the USA (about 5 per 100,000, as compared with 40 per 100,000 in those of Negro ancestry). In the Black population in the USA and West Indians multiple nodules and a lobar type of consolidating infiltration seem to be not uncommon.

Granulomas are usually characteristic, but the initial lung lesion may be an alveolitis. In early disease there may be a predominance of inflammatory cells in the alveolar septa. Tiny granulomas may coalesce to form larger nodules with normal intervening lung parenchyma. Most granulomas resolve, but about 20% of patients develop varying degrees of pulmonary fibrosis and scarring.

Histological confirmation is obtained most frequently by fibreoptic bronchoscopy and transbronchial biopsy. Open lung biopsy, scalene node and mediastinoscopy are no longer as popular because they are more invasive.

The disease has been grouped radiologically as follows:

Group 0 : normal chest radiograph
1 enlarged nodes with normal lungs
2 enlarged nodes and lung changes (non-fibrotic)
3 non-fibrotic changes only
4 fibrotic lung disease.

Some cases may progress to end-stage lung (Illus. **SARCOID LUNGS, Pt. 32a-e**). In a few cases lung transplantation, either single or double has been carried out, and recurrence can occur in the transplanted lung. However most patients with sarcoidosis, particularly those with erythema nodosum and enlarged intra-thoracic nodes, will recover spontaneously, but in some symptomatic cases or in those with worsening lung disease, steroid treatment may be helpful. Relapses may occur following treatment, particularly after reducing steroids, and repeated courses or long-term therapy may be required. Other drugs, such as chloroquine, azathioprine, chlorambucil, or methotrexate have occasionally been used. In Oxford steroids are not routinely given, and tend to be reserved for those with increasing symptoms or worsening infiltration, other complications, etc.

Hepatic granulomas are common in acute sarcoidosis, and liver involvement may be found in up to 70% of cases having hepatic needle biopsies, but unless gross they rarely cause changes in hepatic function. Very rarely hepatic infiltration may lead to hepatic and/or biliary fibrosis (the 'cholestatic syndrome'). Splenic and abdominal node involvement is also not uncommon and may lead to calcification - see below.

Eye presentation with uveitis or lacrimal gland enlargement and exophthalmos (see Illus. **ORBIT**, **Sarcoid lac gl 1a**) is not uncommon.

Bone changes are rare despite the frequency with which hand radiographs showing small rounded erosions particularly in the phalanges are shown in higher medical examinations.

Pulmonary infiltration (Illus. **SARCOID-LUNGS**) is commonly more marked in the **mid zones,** and infiltrative disease in this position often suggests the diagnosis. Similarly, peri-broncho-vascular shadowing on CT also suggests sarcoid (see ps. 1.55 & 19.68). The lung infiltration may have a fine nodular or miliary pattern, become coalescent or give rise to larger nodules, occasionally mimicking secondary tumours, or becoming large areas of consolidation - the last mostly being seen in West Indians. Some have a fine linear and nodular appearance resembling pulmonary oedema or lymphangitis carcinomatosa. Pulmonary fibrosis may be accompanied by bullae, cystic bronchiectasis, thick walled cavities surrounded by a fibrotic mass, pleural thickening, hilar elevation and cor pulmonale. A few patients may have complicating aspergillosis. Some have severely '**shrinking lungs**' leading to '**destroyed lungs**' (p 19.123).

Nodal enlargement most commonly affects the **azygos** (or right paratracheal), **hilar** and **subcarinal nodes** - (Illus. **SARCOID-NODES**). The subcarinal enlargement is often not seen with 'poor' plain radiographs or linear tomograms, but is usually well demonstrated on high KV radiographs or inclined frontal tomograms. Such nodal masses are soft and do not compress bronchi as much as malignant nodes tend to do. Intra-pulmonary nodes may be affected (Illus. **INTRA PULM NODES, Pts. 1-3, Sarcoid unilat Pt. 2 & Sarcoid nodes Pt. 15a-b**). Both enlargement of the posterior mediastinal (or para-oesophageal) nodes and the sub-carinal nodes may cause dysphagia by their proximity to the oesophagus. Anterior mediastinal nodes are rarely markedly enlarged. Occasionally the nodal enlargement may be predominantly unilateral.

Nodal enlargement, like lung infiltration, usually resolves spontaneously, but it may sometimes persist for months or years. Occasionally chronically involved nodes may exhibit calcification, with a stippled, irregular, dense generalised, egg-shell, or ring type pattern - see also p. 6.24 and Illus. **NODES CALCIFICATION**.

Such nodal calcification may also extend down into the abdomen to the para-aortic nodes, etc. The author has seen this in some who had been treated in the acute phase many years ago with cod-liver oil. This may be accompanied by renal calcification and failure. Calcification may also occur in the spleen and be dense (as with patients with amyloid - see Illus. **AMYLOID, Pt. 6**). It may also occur in the liver, and is then often nodular in character.

Other signs - 'Peri-hilar haze' is sometimes seen when enlarged nodes are shrinking down, but may persist even after nodal enlargement is no longer apparent. **Ring shadows** are usually associated with generalised irreversible fibrosis. Occasionally they may also be seen early in the disease. Rohatgi and Schwab (1980) reported six cases occurring in areas of pre-existing lung shadowing and two disappeared after steroid therapy. Jones, D. et al. (1984) found three further cases. Such ring shadows may be caused by central necrosis in areas of coalescent granulomas or a check-valve mechanism in bronchi distal to endobronchial disease.

In severely fibrotic lungs, bullae are common and may be complicated by mycetomas. Rasmussen aneurysms may rarely be found, as in tuberculosis (see p. 7.12). They may lead to a fatal haemoptysis. Severely fibrotic lungs due to sarcoid may also lead to severe disability and cor pulmonale with a fatal outcome.

Unilateral disease is relatively uncommon, either with regard to lung infiltration or nodal enlargement. The author has however seen several such cases - (Illus. **SARCOID-UNILAT**).

Lung nodules vary in size from widespread miliary type nodules or small grouped nodules (2 to 5 mm) to larger nodules of 2 to 5 cm in diameter. The smaller ones may show central calcification, and may be similar to fungus etc. granulomata. The larger nodules may cavitate - see also Tellis and Putnam (1977) - (Illus. **SARCOID-NODULES**).

Pleural involvement and effusions are rare, but when present may lead to chronic pleural thickening or a fibrothorax - (Illus. **SARCOID-MISC, Sarcoid+pl eff**).

Bronchial involvement - endobronchial sarcoid may produce **bronchostenosis**, leading to a 'creeping bronchostenosis' (see p. 3.2 and Illus. **SARCOID-ENDOBRON**). This may lead to collapse and/or consolidation or bronchiectasis. Bronchography may be used to illustrate this and biopsies may be taken at bronchoscopy. Such bronchiectasis is often accompanied by severe fibrosis or nodal disease.

Prognosis and assessment of activity.

Patients with nodal enlargement and no lung infiltration, or other manifestations of the disease, appear to have the best prognosis. Over 80% will show complete resolution in under a year, and most within six months. Only a few will develop overt lung disease, and radiographic follow up to detect this after a few months is usually not warranted. In those who present with nodal enlargement and lung infiltration, this will mostly have resolved in two to three years, and usually without any treatment. A few will have disease which will wax and wane or show progressive or florid disease, whilst others will continue with asymptomatic lung infiltrates which may eventually clear. In only a very small percentage will infiltration progress to severe fibrosis, bullous disease and severe scarring, with the risk of severe respiratory impairment, cor pulmonale and death.

Some patients with acute disease may be ill, very rarely with a fulminating life-threatening condition. The author remembers a 17 year old youth who presented with rapidly progressive acute erythema nodosum, acutely progressive breathlessness and early infiltration on a chest radiograph. He came from his GP, but as he looked so unwell, the author kept him in the radiology department, and then had him admitted to hospital. Later that day he had to be transferred to ITU, developed disseminated intravascular coagulation, but eventually recovered.

In most patients assessment of activity on serial chest radiographs suffices, together with clinical assessment and spirometry. In some centres Ga^{67}, glucoheptonate, etc. scans (see Chapter 22) have also been used, as sarcoid granulomas may take up these agents.

CT in sarcoidosis.

CT gives a clearer representation of lung and nodal disease than plain radiographs. Fine sections show that the infiltration and granulomas tend to follow the bronchovascular bundles. They also show lung nodules when present and the predominantly upper and mid zone distribution of the disease. In problem cases, it may be used to show atypical appearances (e.g. dense consolidation), changing lung disease patterns or unusual node enlargement distributions. It will also illustrate more clearly gross scarring, bullous disease, bronchiectasis, proximal pulmonary artery dilatation with cor pulmonale, and mediastinal scarring. In a few cases **HRCT may show changes**

indistinguishable from CFA (see references below and Illus. **HRCT, Sarcoid lungs Pt. 49 & SARCOID+CA, Pt. 7b & c**).

Because the small granulomata in the lungs and bronchi may narrow and squash the airways air trapping may commonly be found in sarcoidosis with expiratory CT sections (see references).

In some long standing cases, nodal (both thoracic and abdominal) or splenic calcification may be demonstrated by CT (see illustrations).

Necrotising sarcoid granulomatosis.

This was first described by Liebow (1973) and further studied by Churg et al. (1979), but whether it is a variant of sarcoidosis or a separate entity remains uncertain. Neither a systemic nor glomeronephritis occur, and the only rare extrapulmonary feature is uveitis.

This vasculitis affects both arteries and veins. All reported cases have had abnormal chest radiographs, with solitary or multiple nodules or infiltrates; these may cavitate. Some nodules are very small and miliary in type, and may become confluent.

Histologically the lesions are sarcoid-like epithelioid giant cell granulomas, showing both necrosis and vasculitis, The vessel walls are infiltrated by inflammatory cells leading to vessel destruction and infarction.

Prognosis is good and many patients survive for several years untreated. Steroids may also be helpful.

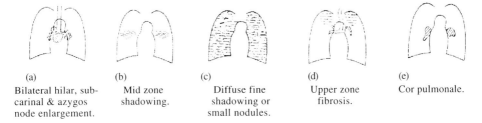

(a)	(b)	(c)	(d)	(e)
Bilateral hilar, sub-carinal & azygos node enlargement.	Mid zone shadowing.	Diffuse fine shadowing or small nodules.	Upper zone fibrosis.	Cor pulmonale.

Fig. 19.10. Sarcoidosis, pulmonary fibrosis and cor pulmonale.

Further references.

(a) **General and CT appearances**

Netter (1953) : Changes in the chest Roentgenogram in Boeck's sarcoid.

Smellie and Hoyle (1960) : Natural history of pulmonary sarcoidosis.

Ellis and Renthal (1962) : Roentgenographic observations on the course of the disease.

Siltbach (1961) : Kveim test in 750 patients.

Scadding (1967) : Monograph on sarcoidosis - revised by Scadding and Mitchell (1985).

Scadding (1970) : Late stages of pulmonary sarcoidosis.

Kirks and Greenspan (1973) : Review of radiological appearances.

Kirks et al. (1973) : Radiological features in 150 patients.

Mitchell and Scadding (1974) : Review.

Carrington et al. (1976) : Structure and function in sarcoidosis.

Putman et al. (1977) : Studied six cases by CT and demonstrated fine, diffuse or cavitary lung disease, and adenopathy in the para-tracheal and anterior mediastinal nodal groups.

Solomon et al. (1979) : CT in pulmonary sarcoid.

Williams, W.. & Davies (1980) : Eighth International Conference on Sarcoidosis and other Granulomatous Disease.

McLoud et al. (1982) : A radiographic classification with physiological correlation.

Fanburg (1983) : Sarcoid and Other Granulomatous Diseases (Multiple contributors).

De Remee (1983) : Roentgenological staging.

Gilman et al. (1983) : Used CT to study 'mean lung density' in sarcoid and other diffuse interstitial lung disease. They found it was increased to about 60 HU in sarcoidosis, compared with a normal mean of about 30 HU.

Keogh et al. (1983) : Considered pulmonary sarcoidosis to be a mononuclear cell alveolitis, with activated T-lymphocytes and alveolar macrophages, preceding the formation of granulomata and fibrosis. They assessed their patients with pulmonary function tests, broncho-alveolar lavage and gallium scanning. They noted that a high intensity alveolitis was followed by deterioration over the next six months, whereas a low intensity alveolitis was followed by functional deterioration only 8% of the time.

Berkmen (1985) : Radiologic aspects of intrathoracic sarcoidosis.

Freiman (1985) : Pathology of sarcoidosis.

Sharma (1985) : Clinical, laboratory and immunological aspects of sarcoidosis.

Thomas and Hunninghake (1987) : Current concepts of pathogenesis.

Conant et al. (1988) : Pulmonary sarcoidosis in the older patient - conventional radiographic features.

Bergin et al. (1989) : Correlated the appearances of the lungs on radiographs and CT sections with the degree of uptake on gallium scans and pulmonary function studies in 27 patients, They divided them into five categories on the CT findings : 1 = normal, 2 = segmental air-space disease, 3 = spherical (alveolar) mass-like opacities, 4 = multiple, discrete, small nodules, and 5 = distortion of parenchymal structures (fibrotic end-stage sarcoidosis). Patients in the first two categories had normal lung function, those in category 3 had mild functional impairment, whilst those in categories 4 and 5 showed moderate to severe dysfunction. In five patients CT showed extensive parenchymal disease, which had not been seen on plain radiographs. The CT grades correlated well with gallium uptake, or the percentage of lymphocytes recovered from broncho-alveolar lavage. They concluded that the CT patterns correlated well with pulmonary function tests and could be used to indicate respiratory impairment.

Brauner et al. (1989) : Examined 44 patients with biopsy proved sarcoidosis by HRCT and found nodules in every one (micro-nodules in 34, > 3 mm in 18 and confluent in 23, patchy areas with air bronchograms in 3 and cavitating nodules in 3). The nodules were isolated in 19 and associated with other lesions in 25. Other abnormalities were irregularity of interfaces, linear opacities (often organised in a network of large polygonal elements), overlying slight pleural reaction, ground-glass densities, lung distortion (in some cases associated with networks of air-filled cavities and traction bronchiectasis). New cases tended to show more ground-glass densities and a peripheral distribution, compared with long-standing cases who had fibrosis and distortion.

Lynch et al. (1989) : Correlated HRCT with chest radiographs, respiratory function tests, gallium scans and bronchial lavage in 15 patients.

Müller et al. (1989a) : Compared CT with chest radiography in the assessment of the severity of the disease in 27 patients. Those with predominantly irregular opacities had more severe dyspnoea and smaller lung volumes than patients with predominantly nodular opacities, but overall the radiographic and CT assessments showed similar correlation with clinical and functional impairment.

Müller (1989b) : Concluded that the characteristic CT appearances of sarcoid were **small nodules and irregular linear densities along the broncho-vascular bundles** (which corresponded with pathology) and to a lesser extent in the subpleural and septal lymphatics. They found HRCT to be superior to thick section CT for the assessment of sub-pleural nodules and irregular linear densities, but thick-section CT was better for the assessment of peribroncho-vascular nodules.

Austin (1989) : In an editorial 'pulmonary sarcoidosis: what are we learning from CT ?' commented on the papers by Bergin et al. (1989) and Müller et al. (1989a) and wrote that one might expect to find close correlations of CT findings with the degree of functional impairment in diffuse lung disease such as sarcoidosis, but the clinical situation is not so simple. It has long been recognised that chest radiographs of about half the patients with sarcoidosis are normal, or only show enlarged nodes at presentation, and that only a few of these will eventually show parenchymal lung disease. CT however appears to reveal focal pulmonary parenchymal abnormalities in many patients.

The manifestations of sarcoidosis at presentation are often typical and clinical management is seemingly straightforward. However atypical manifestations occur in about 25% of patients, and in about 60% of those over 50 years of age. These include solitary pulmonary nodules, multiple nodules, cavitation with or without mycetomas, isolated intra-pulmonary or mediastinal nodal enlargement, bronchostenosis, pulmonary arterial hypertension and pleural reaction. CT appears to be particularly helpful for assessing the atypical manifestations that alter the calibre of tubular structures, including bronchiectasis, bronchostenosis, post-obstructive collapse (e.g. the right middle lobe), nodes pressing on segmental or larger bronchi, the SVC or a pulmonary artery branch.

Baumann et al. (1990) : Serial chest radiographs detected the deterioration of sarcoidosis during corticosteroid withdrawal in most patients and could do so before changes in respiratory function became apparent.

Dawson and Müller (1990) : HRCT in pulmonary sarcoidosis - 60 to 70% of patients have a characteristic radiological appearance, but in the remainder CT may be helpful. The most typical appearances were tiny irregular nodules (1 to 5 mm in diameter) along the broncho-vascular bundles, major fissures and in the sub-pleural spaces (particularly in the mid and upper zones of the lungs) - these represent **granulomas along the lymphatics** - the '**hall-mark**' of the disease.

Popp and Watchler (1991) : Silver staining may be a sensitive tool for the investigation of biological cell activity of alveolar macrophages in sarcoidosis and other non-malignant conditions characterised by immunological activation.

James (1991b) : Kyoto - Aspects of sarcoidosis.

Murdoch and Müller (1992) : Pulmonary sarcoidosis - changes on follow-up CT examination.

Brauner et al. (1992) : CT assessment of lesion reversibility.

Murdoch and Müller (1992) : Changes in pulmonary sarcoidosis in follow-up CT examinations - ground-glass, nodular and irregular linear opacities and irregular septal thickening represent potentially reversible disease, while cystic air spaces and architectural distortion (including traction bronchiectasis) are irreversible findings.

Müller and Miller (1993) : Ground glass attenuation, nodules, alveolitis and sarcoid granulomas.

Nishimura et al. (1993) : Correlation of CT and histology in 8 patients - 7 had irregularly thickened bronchovascular bundles and 4 nodules along vessels; one had a complicating lung adenocarcinoma.

Rémy-Jardin et al. (1994) : Neither the appearance nor the extent of disease at CT can be considered a good predictor of functional impairment in any individual patient.

Berkmen (1995) : Radiological aspects of intrathoracic sarcoidosis.

Maña et al. (1995) : Excessive thoracic CT scanning in sarcoidosis. CT of the chest does not add clinically useful information to standard chest radiographs in patients presenting with typical radiological patterns. CT is only indicated with proven or suspected sarcoid when plain radiographs are normal or atypical, there is clinical suspicion of upper airway obstruction, haemoptysis, a suspected complicating second intrathoracic disease or is a candidate for lung transplantation.

Gleeson et al. (1996) : Evidence on expiratory CT scans of small air-way obstruction in sarcoid.

Tasker et al. (1997) : CT sections in expiration show that air-trapping is a common finding in sarcoidosis and correlates with physiological parameters of small airways disease.

Traill et al. (1997) : HRCT of pulmonary sarcoidosis - scattered & subpleural nodules with nodular scarring of interlobular septa - may aggregate to form larger nodules, tiny granules producing ground-glass shadowing, consolidation with air bronchograms, septal lines and thickening, fibrosis, destruction, cystic air space and traction bronchiectasis and air-trapping in expiration and occasional mycetoma.

Hansell (1997) : In sarcoidosis there is infiltration alongside the small bronchi as well as nodules causing air trapping in expiration in early disease, at pulmonary lobule level. Thus a reticular pattern is the major determinant of airflow obstruction. (see also under small airways disease - ps. 3.25-31.)

Davies et al. (2000) : Air trapping on CT & correlation with lung function.

(b) Typical and atypical manifestations.

Freundlich et al. (1970): Typical and atypical manifestations in 300 cases.

Rabinowitz et al. (1974) : Usual, unusual manifestations and 'hilar haze'.

Felson (1977) : Uncommon Roentgen patterns of pulmonary sarcoidosis.

Sharma (1977) : Unusual pulmonary manifestations.

Symmons and Woods (1980) : Recurrent sarcoidosis.

Mesbahi and Davis (1981) : Unilateral or segmental pulmonary involvement is rare.

Demicco and Fanburg (1982) : Sarcoidosis presenting as a lobar or unilateral lung infiltrate.

Rockoff and Rohatgi (1985) : Unusual manifestations - cavitation, unilateral lung disease, solitary pulmonary nodule, pleural effusion of pneumothorax, unusual nodal enlargement, bronchial narrowing, pulmonary vascular obstruction, heart enlargement, lobes - rib involvement is very rare.

Hamper et al. (1986) : Typical and atypical manifestations of pulmonary sarcoidosis - used CT in 36 patients with sarcoid, who had atypical presentations or no proven diagnosis, and found it to be superior to plain radiography for showing nodal enlargements and lung infiltrates. The latter were sometimes mass-simulating (with or without air-bronchograms), patchy, vague, diffuse or micronodular. In some cases the nodules coalesced to resemble pneumoconiotic masses. Complications included bullous disease, bronchiectasis, pleural reaction, aspergillosis and squamous carcinoma. Affected nodes were in the anterior mediastinum, the para-tracheal, hilar or sub-carinal areas, and in a few cases were calcified. In some the lungs showed areas of increased density, rather than frank calcification.

Conant et al. (1988) : Studied 29 patients presenting with pulmonary sarcoidosis over age 50. Half had atypical radiological appearances - localised or unilateral mediastinal and/or hilar adenopathy, solitary or multiple lung nodules or collapse. Five had extra-thoracic malignancies.

(c) Nodal involvement.

Hodgson et al. (1955) : Bilateral hilar adenopathy (6 of 90 pts. had tracheobronchial or pulmonary calcification).

Wigh and Montague (1955) : Evaluation of intrapulmonary adenopathy in sarcoidosis.

Smellie and Hoyle (1957) : Hilar lymph nodes with special reference to prognosis.

Kent (1965) : Recurrent unilateral hilar lymphadenopathy.

Spann et al. (1971) : 38 cases - unilateral hilar or mediastinal adenopathy.

Berkmen and Javors (1976) : Anterior mediastinal lymphadenopathy.

Bein et al. (1978 - from Yale) : Analysed the positions of enlarged nodes in 62 patients - 97% were bilateral hilar, 75% right paratracheal or aorto-pulmonary window, 20% subcarinal, 16% anterior mediastinal and 2% posterior mediastinal (25 had no lymphadenopathy).

Schabel et al. (1978) : Posterior lymphadenopathy in sarcoidosis.

Karasick (1979) : Atypical thoracic lymphadenopathy.

Tsou et al. (1980) : Sarcoidosis of anterior med. nodes, pancreas and uterine cervix - 3 unusual sites in same pt.

Kutty and Varkey (1982) : Sarcoidosis presenting with posterior mediastinal lymphadenopathy.

Steiger and Fanburg (1986) : Recurrence of thoracic lymphadenopathy in sarcoidosis.

Patil and Levin (1999) : Detection of thoracic lymphadenopathy in sarcoidosis using CT.

(d) **Calcification in nodes, etc.**
Israel et al. (1961) : The occurrence of intrathoracic calcification in sarcoidosis- 2 pts. (out of 447) had extensive thoracic node calcification.
Scadding (1961) : Calcification in sarcoidosis, (1968) : Further observations on calcification in sarcoidosis.
McLoud et al. (1974) : Egg-shell calcification with systemic sarcoidosis.
Israel et al. (1981) : Late development of mediastinal calcifications in sarcoidosis.
Gawne-Cain and Hansell (1996) : CT study of pattern and distribution of calcified mediastinal lymph nodes in sarcoid & TB - a focal pattern of calcification was more common in sarcoid & complete in TB.

(e) **Hypercalcaemia.**
Sandler et al. (1984) : Studies in hypercalcaemia in sarcoidosis.
(e) **Nodular pulmonary sarcoidosis.**
Chrisholm and Lang (1966) : Solitary circumscribed nodule - an unusual manifestation of sarcoidosis.
Sharma et al. (1973) : Nodular sarcoidosis.
Onal et al. (1977) : Clinical, Roentgenographic and physiological course in five patients.
Rosen et al. (1977a) : Occurrence of lung granulomas in stage I sarcoidosis.
Nutting et al. (1979) : Solitary pulmonary nodules due to sarcoidosis.
Rose et al. (1985) : Solitary pulmonary nodule.

(f) **Mimicking pulmonary tuberculosis or fibrosing alveolitis.**
Tierstein and Siltbach (1973) : Sarcoid of the upper lungs simulating TB.
Hafermann et al. (1978) : Sarcoidosis initially occurring as an apical infiltrate and pleural reaction.
Padhani et al. (1995) : Pulmonary sarcoidosis mimicking fibrosing alveolitis.
Padley et al. (1996) : Pulmonary sarcoidosis mimicking cryptogenic fibrosing alveolitis on CT.

(g) **Sarcoid and tuberculosis.**
Scadding (1960) : Myc. TB in the aetiology of sarcoid (2 cases).
Scadding (1969) : Further observations in sarcoidosis associated with M. tuberculosis infection.
Tierstein and Siltbach (1973) : Sarcoidosis of the upper lung fields simulating tuberculosis.
Knox et al. (1986) : Tuberculous pleural effusion occurring during corticosteroid treatment of sarcoidosis.
Mitchell, D. and Rees (1969) : A transmissible agent from sarcoid tissue.
Mitchell, D. et al. (1976) : Transmissible agents from human sarcoid & Crohn's disease.
Mitchell, D. (1996) : Mycobacteria and sarcoidosis.
Graham et al. (1992) : Mycobacterial aetiology of sarcoidosis.
Fidler et al. (1993) : Mycobacterial tuberculosis DNA in tissue affected by sarcoidosis.
Wong et al. (1998) : Concomitant TB and sarcoid with mycobacterial DNA present in the sarcoid lesion.
Wilsher et al. (1999) : Absence of TB DNA in lymph node and lung biopsy samples in pts. with sarcoidosis

(h) **Bronchial and/or tracheal narrowing.**
Citron and Scadding (1957) : Stenosis of the bronchi.
Honey and Jepson (1957) : Multiple bronchostenoses due to sarcoidosis - two cases.
Kalbian (1957) : Bronchial involvement.
Goldenberg and Greenspan (1960) : Middle lobe collapse (with hypercalcaemia and renal impairment).
Munt (1973) : Middle lobe collapse - prompt resolution with steroids.
Westcott and Noehren (1973) : Bronchial stenosis in chronic sarcoidosis.
Sharma (1978) : Airway obstruction in sarcoidosis.
Olsson et al. (1979) : Bronchostenosis - 8 cases out of 99.
Weisman et al. (1980) : Laryngeal sarcoidosis with airway obstruction.
Brandstetter et al. (1981) : Tracheal stenosis.,   Henry and Cho. (1983) : Tracheal stenosis.
Priestley and Delaney (1981) : Familial sarcoidosis presenting with stridor.
Hadfield et al. (1982) : Localised airway narrowing.
Corsello et al. (1983) : Endobronchial mass lesion due to sarcoidosis - complete resolution with corticosteroids.
Mendelsohn et al. (1983) : Bronchial compression - unusual manifestation.
Brown, K. et al. (1988) : Balloon dilatation of the left main bronchus in sarcoidosis.
Udwadia et al. (1990) : Bronchoscopic and bronchographic findings in 12 pts. with sarcoidosis and severe or progressive airways obstruction.
McCann and Harrison (1991) : Bronchial narrowing and occlusion in sarcoidosis causing airways obstruction.
Dorman et al. (1995) : Man aged 30 with cough and progressive dyspnoea - chest radiograph showed collapse of RM&LLs; conv. tomograms demonstrated stenosis of RMB. Pneumonectomy performed - sarcoidosis on histology.
Lenique et al. (1995) : CT assessment of bronchi in sarcoidosis - abnormalities found in 39 out of 60 cases (65%).

(i) **Bullae and cavitation.**
Scadding and Lennox (1950)
Bistrong et al. (1970) : Asymptomatic cavitary sarcoidosis.
Plit and Miller (1983)
Packe et al. (1986) : Large lung bullae in sarcoidosis. Judson and Strange (1998) : Bullous sarcoidisis - 3 cases.

(j) **Fungal infection and mycetoma.**
Freundlich et al. (1970) : 40% of patients with bullae had mycetomas.
Gorske and Fleming (1970) : Mycetoma formation in cavitary pulmonary sarcoidosis.
Kaplan and Johns (1979) : Mycetomas in pulmonary sarcoidosis - non-surgical management.
Breuer et al. (1982) : Used CT to show an '**occult mycetoma**'.
Israel et al. (1982) : Sarcoidosis and aspergillomata - role of surgery.
Johns (1982) : Management of haemoptysis with pulmonary fungus balls in sarcoidosis.
Wollschlager and Khan (1984) : Aspergillomas complicating sarcoidosis - prospective study in 100 patients.
Rubinstein et al. (1985) : Fungal infection complicating pulmonary sarcoidosis.

(k) **Pulmonary vascular disease and cor pulmonale.**
McCort and Paré (1954) : Pulmonary fibrosis and cor pulmonale.
Westcott and de Graff (1973) : Sarcoidosis causing hilar adenopathy and pulmonary artery narrowing.
Faunce at al. (1976) : Protracted yet variable major pulmonary artery compression in sarcoidosis.
Hietala et al. (1977) : Pulmonary arterial narrowing in sarcoidosis.
Rosen et al. (1977a) : Granulomatous pulmonary angiitis in sarcoidosis.
Battesti et al. (1978) : Chronic cor pulmonale in pulmonary sarcoidosis.
Damuth et al. (1980) : Major pulmonary artery stenosis causing pulmonary hypertension.
Smith et al. (1983) : Vascular sarcoidosis - a rare cause of pulmonary hypertension.
Edelman et al. (1985) : Rasmussen aneurysm with a fatal haemoptysis.
Hoffstein et al. (1986) : Sarcoidosis simulating pulmonary veno-occlusive disease.

(l) **Nerve palsy and neurological complications.**
Waldenström (1937) : Presentation with right-sided facial palsy in two patients and a right hypoglossal nerve palsy or bilateral optic neuritis in patients with sarcoidosis - they also had uveoparotitis (See also Smith and James, 1992).
Chijmatsu et al. (1980) : Hoarseness as an initial manifestation of sarcoidosis.
Swinburn et al. (1986) : Left recurrent laryngeal nerve palsy as the presenting feature of sarcoidosis.
El-Kassimi et al. (1990) : Sarcoidosis presenting as recurrent left laryngeal nerve palsy.
Grand et al. (1996) : Pseudotumoral brain lesions as the presenting feature of sarcoidosis.
Jarman et al. (1996) : Imaging of CNS sarcoidosis with Ga[67] single photon emission CT.
Oki et al. (1997) : MR findings in VIII th cranial nerve involvement in sarcoidosis.

(m) **SVC and innominate vein obstruction.**
Gordonson et al (1973) : SVC obstruction.
Javaheri and Hales (1980) : Innominate vein obstruction and massive pleural effusion.
Morgans et al. (1980) : SVC obstruction.
Radke et al. (1980) : SVC obstruction.
Brandstetter et al. (1981) : SVC syndrome as the initial clinical manifestation of sarcoidosis.

(n) **Pleural involvement.**
Berte and Pfotenhauer (1962) : Massive pleural effusion in sarcoidosis.
Chusid and Siltbach (1974) : Sarcoidosis of the pleura.
Wilen et al. (1974) : Pleural involvement.
Sharma and Gordonson (1975) : Six cases with pleural effusion.
Beekman et al. (1976) : Spectrum of pleural involvement in sarcoidosis.
Mikhail et al. (1976) : Sarcoidosis presenting with a pleural effusion.
Selroos (1977) : Exudative pleurisy and sarcoidosis.
Gardiner and Uff (1978) : Acute pleurisy in sarcoidosis - a study of two ethnic groups.
Vuyst et al. (1979) : Bloody pleural effusion in a patient with sarcoidosis.
Kanada et al. (1980) : Unusual presentations of pleural sarcoidosis.
Nicholls et al. (1980) : Sarcoid pleural effusion - three cases and literature review.
Johnson et al. (1982) : Presentation with massive pleural effusion.
Ravichander (1989) : Hydropneumothorax.
Jarman et al. (1995) : Sarcoidosis presenting with chylothorax.
Loughney and Higgins (1997) : Sarcoidosis presenting as a discrete pleural mass in a 29 yr. old woman.

Van der Werf and Vennik (1997) : Rare presentation or lead time bias in pleural sarcoidosis (2 women aged 48 & 49 presented with pleural pain caused by sarcoidosis without apparent lung involvement - 1st with a large R pl. effusion & contralateral hilar lymphadenopathy, the 2nd with a slight pl. effusion and mild eosinophilia).

(o) **Shrinking lungs.**
Miller (1981) : The vanishing lung syndrome.

(p) **Ethnic differences.**
Siltbach et al. (1974) : Course and prognosis of sarcoidosis around the world.
Sartwell (1976) : Racial differences in sarcoidosis.
Honeybourne (1980) : Ethnic differences in sarcoidosis in SE London.
Edmonstone and Wilson (1985) : Sarcoidosis in Caucasians, Blacks and Asians in London.
McNichol and Luce (1985) : Sarcoid in a racially mixed community.

(q) **Biopsy.**
Mitchell et al. (1980) : Transbronchial biopsy for the diagnosis of sarcoidosis.

(r) **Abdominal involvement.**
Mathieu et al. (1986) : CT of splenic sarcoidosis.
Britt et al. (1991) : Abdominal manifestations on CT.

(s) **Bone involvement.**
Stein, G. et al. (1956) : A Roentgenographic study of skeletal lesions in sarcoidosis.
Mather (1957) : Calcium metabolism and bone changes in sarcoidosis.
Bloch et al. (1968) : Punched out defects in some of the phalanges - also erosions of the pelvis and spine.
Neville et al. (1977) : Sarcoidosis of bone.

(t) **Gallium scanning.**
Lauver and Gooneratne (1979) : Lacrimal, parotid and mediastinal uptake in sarcoidosis.
Beaumont et al. (1982) : Ga^{67} in the evaluation of sarcoidosis.
Klech et al. (1983)
Fajman et al. (1984)
Bergin et al. (1989) : see under (a) above.

(u) **Transplanted lungs.**
Kazerooni et al. (1994) : recurrence of sarcoidosis in transplanted lungs - 2 cases - 1 after 3 months had biopsy and the second after 15 months - miliary nodules on CT which resolved after steroid therapy.
Walker, S. et al. (1998) : Harefield Hospital, London : Medium term results of lung transplantation for end-stage pulm. sarcoid - 12 cases - 3 developed sarcoid granulomas in the donor lungs, one needing retransplantation.

(v) **Nasal sarcoid.**
Gordon et al. (1997)
Jones and Zammat-Maempel (1997)

(vi) **Sarcoid & obstructive sleep apnoea.**
Shah et al. (1998).

(vii) **Familial sarcoid.**
Elford et al. (2000) : Five cases in one family.

Note - there is also a journal devoted to sarcoidosis.

Sarcoidosis and Neoplasm - (Illus. SARCOID+CA).

Some tumours including lung tumours may induce a sarcoid-like reaction in nodes draining areas where tumours are present. This is most commonly seen at necropsy and in surgical specimens. Clinically, a more florid type of reaction may occur, with markedly enlarged hilar and mediastinal nodes, and this may precede the presentation of the tumours by several months or even a few years. This sarcoid-like reaction may persist or wane spontaneously, or in response to steroid treatment. Nodes which have shrunk down may enlarge again later due to overt metastases.

The author has noted this type of sarcoid-like reaction particularly in response to genito-urinary tumours (renal, prostate, bladder and testes), where it may simulate nodal metastases or be a prodromal manifestation of a tumour. It may occur with bronchial tumours, carcinoids, the reticuloses (especially Hodgkin's disease) and with other tumours e.g. breast.

This type of reaction appears to be an immune type of reaction to microscopic secondary deposits. It must however be remembered that the more common form of sarcoidosis may occur in patients who have or have had various types of tumour (e.g. breast carcinoma) and that the two conditions in a given individual may be related or unrelated and that differentiation may be very difficult unless clearly overt metastases develop.

References.

Nadel and Ackerman (1950) : Lesions resembling Boeck's sarcoid in lymph nodes draining an area containing a malignant neoplasm.
Symmers (1951) : Localised tuberculoid granulomas associated with carcinoma - their relationship to sarcoidosis.
Goodbody and Taylor (1957) : Sarcoid and bronchial ca - case report.
Gorton and Linell (1957) : Malignant tumours and sarcoid reactions in regional lymph nodes.
Ellman and Hanson (1958) : Coexistence of bronchial carcinoma and sarcoidosis.
Gregorie et al. (1962) : Significance of sarcoid-like lesions in association with malignant lesions.
Brincker (1972) : Sarcoid reactions and sarcoidosis in Hodgkin's disease and other malignant lymphomata.
Brincker and Wilbek (1974) : The incidence of malignant tumours in patients with respiratory sarcoidosis.
Brincker (1986a) : Sarcoid reactions in malignant tumours., (1986b) : The sarcoidosis-lymphoma syndrome.
Brincker (1992) : Interpretation of granulomatous lesions in malignancy.
Laurberg (1975) : Sarcoid reactions in pulmonary neoplasms.
Israel (1978) : Sarcoid, malignancy and immunosuppressive treatment.
Sachs et al. (1978) : Epithelioid granulomas associated with Hodgkin's disease - 55 untreated patients.
Sybert and Butler (1978) : Sarcoidosis following methotrexate treatment for osteosarcoma.
Romer et al. (1980), Romer (1982) : Sarcoidosis and cancer., (1990) : Is there a causal relationship between sarcoidosis & malignancy?
Trump et al. (1981) : Sarcoidosis and sarcoid like lesions following treatment of testicular cancer.
Gefter et al. (1982) : Sarcoid causing intra-thoracic lymphadenopathy after treatment of testicular carcinoma.
Scully et al. (1982) : Young man with a diagnosis of sarcoidosis and a pulmonary mass.
Brennan et al. (1983) : Sarcoidosis and lymphoma in the same patient.
Fossa et al. (1985) : Sarcoid reaction of hilar and paratracheal lymph nodes in patients treated for testicular cancer.
Heffner and Milam (1987) : Sarcoid-like hilar and mediastinal lymphadenopathy in a patient with metastatic testicular cancer.
Daly et al. (1988) : Hodgkin's disease with a granulomatous presentation mimicking sarcoidosis. They suggested that a low serum angiotensin-converting enzyme activity and negative Kveim-Siltbach test may help in distinguishing pulmonary granulomatous reaction related to Hodgkin's disease from active sarcoidosis.
Conant et al. (1988) : Studied 29 pts. presenting with pulmonary sarcoidosis over the age of 50. Half had atypical appearances and **five had extra-thoracic malignancies.**
Parr and Williams (1988) : Sarcoidosis mimicking metastatic testicular tumour.
Morcos (1989) : Commented on Parr and Williams' paper and pointed out that in their two cases, the apparent sarcoidosis could have represented a sarcoid-like granulomatous reaction to the testicular tumour.
Moder et al. (1990) : Renal cell carcinoma associated with sarcoid-like tissue reaction.
James (1991b) : Kyoto - aspects of sarcoidosis.
Kirk et al. (1992) : Enlarging lymph nodes in patients with sarcoidosis - beware lymphoma - four cases - non-Hodgkin's lymphoma, nodular sclerosing Hodgkin, lymphoblastic lymphoma and mediastinal node Hodgkin.
Reich et al. (1995) : Linkage analysis of malignancy associated sarcoidosis.
Hunsaker et al (1996) : Sarcoidlike reaction in patients with malignancy - 10 cases (4 breast, 4 lymphoma, 2 bronchogenic ca).
Ryan et al. (1996) : Co-existing conjunctival non-Hodgkin's lymphoma and pulmonary sarcoidosis.
Gleeson (1999) : Sarcoidosis and malignancy (8 cases including testicular, lung, breast, lymphoma & colo-rectal) - see also Haggett (1999) - 9 cases reviewed.
Wright (1999) : Prodromal syndromes suggesting neoplasm including sarcoid (see cases in Illus. **SARCOID + CA** & Illus. **HORMONES/PARANEO**).

PULMONARY COLLAGEN DISEASES AND VASCULITIS.

These include a range of conditions, including sarcoid-like illnesses which progress in some cases to a severe vasculitis, with intra-vascular coagulation, lung nodules, consolidation, etc. Arthritis and erythema nodosum are often present at some stage of the disease process, and represent further manifestations of the immune response. Classification of these conditions is not entirely satisfactory, since there is some overlap with lymphoma (as with lymphomatoid granuloma), sarcoidosis (necrotising sarcoid granuloma), and with eosinophilic lung diseases (such as Loeffler's syndrome, etc.). Even in individual cases, there may be features common to more than one condition.

The following table lists the main conditions:

(a) **Granulomatous vasculitis**
Wegener's granuloma (both limited and generalised forms).
Allergic granulomatosis and angiitis (Churg-Strauss syndrome).
Necrotising sarcoid granuloma.
Bronchocentric granuloma.
Lymphomatoid granuloma (see under lymphomas - p. 5.29).

(b) **Pulmonary vasculitis associated with connective tissue disease.**
Systemic (or disseminated) lupus erythematosus.   Poly- (or peri-) arteritis nodosa.
Rheumatoid disease.   Scleroderma and dermatomyositis.
Sjögren's syndrome.   Takayasu's arteritis (see p. 10.17)
Behçet's disease.   Mixed connective tissue disease.

(c) **Hypersensitivity vasculitis + systemic illnesses producing autoantibodies.**
Goodpasture's syndrome.

General references.
Garland and Sisson (1954) : Roentgen findings in the 'collagen' diseases.
Thompson (1963) : Pulmonary changes in collagen diseases - wrote "Connective tissue consists of three elements - cellular, fibrillar and ground substance. The predominant cell is the fibroblast which is probably responsible for the formation of the fibrillary elements - elastic, reticular and collagenous within the ground substance. Mast cells are also present and liberate a polysaccharide into the ground substance which forms a complex within the collagen fibres. Mast cells are also correlated with sulphate metabolism and the formation of chondroitin sulphate, which gives cartilage its hard character. Mast cells also appear to store heparin and secrete hyaluronic acid which is responsible for the gel-like consistency of connective tissue and synovial fluid. Ground substance changes appear to be responsible for collagen diseases."
Liebow (1973) : Classified pulmonary angiitis and vasculitis into five groups, two being generalised and limited Wegener's granuloma. He omitted allergic granulomatosis and angiitis from his groupings.
Fauci (1977) : Granulomatous vasculitides - distinct but related.
Edwards (1982) : Vasculitis and granulomatosis of the respiratory tract.
Leavitt and Fauci (1986) : Pulmonary vasculitis.   Lane and Geddes (1987) : Classification.
Weisbrod (1989) : Pulmonary angiitis and granulomatosis - a review.
Gamsu (1992): Radiographic manifestations of thoracic involvement by collagen vascular diseases.
Tanoue (1992) : Pulmonary involvement in collagen vascular disease.   Burns (1998) : Pulmonary vasculitis.
Schwarz & Brown (2000) : Review - small vessel vasculitis of the lung (pulm. capillaritis) - CXR is non-specific and indicates air space disease that can be either patchy or diffuse - usually with no septal engorgement - CT offers little advantage over CXR in determining the aetiology of **diffuse alveolar haemorrhage**.
Seo et al. (2000) : Pictorial review of the radiological findings in pulmonary vasculitis.

Wegener's Granuloma - (Illus. WEGENER'S GRANULOMA).

This is a hypersensitivity or auto-immune multi-system disorder (mainly affecting the 40 to 60 age groups), which produces a necrotising granulomatous vasculitis especially of the upper and lower respiratory tracts and kidneys. It may also affect the eyes, ears, joints, heart, CNS, GI tract (including the small intestine, where gross ulceration may be produced, the mesenteric lymph nodes, the gall bladder and spleen), the adrenals, skin and muscle. Cardiac involvement also occurs in up to 30% of cases.

Nasal disease (Illus. **WEGENER'S GRANULOMA, Vasculitis Pt. 21d**) produces discharge, ulceration and severe crusting of the nares. Considerable bony necrosis may also occur, which may lead to collapse of the nasal bones mimicking malignant granuloma. The patients may also have oral and pharyngeal ulceration, and these may be the presenting feature. Ear disease is usually otitis media, and this may lead to deafness. Ocular complications include conjunctivitis, scleritis, uveitis and corneal ulceration. General symptoms such as fever, malaise and weight loss may be severe.

Lung manifestations are commonly **nodules** which may be single or multiple (Illus. **WEGENER'S GRANULOMA, Vasculitis Pt. 13, 14a, 15a, c-d, 16a-b, 17a-d, 18a-c, 19a-b, 20a-c & 21a-c**). When multiple they are commonly bilateral and widely distributed with no predilection for any lung area and vary in size from a few up to 10 cm in diameter. They may be well or poorly demarcated and **frequently cavitate producing thick or thin walled cavities**. Apical nodules, especially if cavitating, are not uncommonly mistaken for tuberculosis. Fluid may be seen within the cavities. The pattern of lung disease frequently changes. Patients may also present with pulmonary oedema, lung collapse, consolidation or frank clinical pneumonia. In some cases the picture is complicated by pulmonary haemorrhage (giving rise to low density infiltrates which clear). **CT may be helpful in showing the nodular or broncho-pneumonic pattern of the disease** (as shown in the illustrations quoted above); some long-term cases may show evidence of an interstitial fibrosis and evidence of tracheo-bronchial wall damage with narrowing and/or bronchiectasis, the fibrosis perhaps in some cases being related to cyclophosphamide treatment.

Laryngeal and/or tracheo- or broncho-stenosis may lead to hoarseness, stridor, obstructive emphysema or collapse. Hilar or mediastinal node enlargement is rare. Pleural fluid or thickening is uncommon, but may be gross. Occasionally a pneumothorax or a hydro-pneumothorax may result from rupture of a cavitating lung nodule.

Renal lesions are usually due to glomerulonephritis, but occasionally mass lesions have been demonstrated in the kidneys by angiography or CT. Renal and visceral angiography has also been used to show small aneurysms as with polyarteritis nodosa (Illus. **POLYART NODOSA, Vasculitis Pt. 3a-b**). The patient in Illus. **WEGENER'S GRANULOMA, Vasculitis Pt. 21a-e** had swollen kidneys, lung nodules and nasal involvement. It is rare for patients to present with renal failure in the absence of significant disease of the upper or lower respiratory tract. Occasionally haematuria may be the presenting feature due to prostatic involvement, and should be considered as a possibility when haematuria is present in association with a prostatic mass, particularly if it is cavitating, or with epididymitis.

The rheumatoid factor and anti-nuclear cytoplasm antibody ('ANCA') may be positive, but in 5% of cases these tests are negative. Needle biopsy may sometimes suffice for diagnosis (Illus. **WEGENER'S GRANULOMA, Vasculitis Pt. 16a**), but more commonly open lung biopsy is required, the typical histological picture being necrotising granulomata with vasculitis.

Prognosis seems to be most related to renal or bowel disease and the median survival time without treatment is commonly five to six months. Long term remission may be produced by cyclophosphamide, azathiaprine, vincristine and/or steroids, but in a few cases the drugs may show little or no effect. Local radiotherapy to the nose has sometimes been beneficial. **Patients with limited or localised disease, and with no demonstrable renal lesions seem to have a better prognosis**. ANCA titres tend to correlate with disease activity and a rising titre is often a predictor of relapse in patients with a clinical remission. Pulmonary relapses and damage due to cyclophosphamide may be seen on serial chest radiographs or serial CT examinations.

As noted above lung infection and/or pulmonary haemorrhage commonly complicate the radiographic picture, and the patients may present with a fairly typical bronchopneumonia, with large areas of consolidation, fever and the sputum positive for bacterial infection. De Remee et al. (1985) reported successfully treating 11 out of 12 patients with antibiotics, particularly co-trimoxazole (Septrin), which led them to speculate whether the condition may be triggered by infection in a susceptible host. Relapses are also often associated with intercurrent infections, probably via reactivation of circulating immune complexes.

Leukaemia, lymphoma or bladder cancer may occur during immunosuppressive therapy.

Further references.

Klinger (1931) : Probably the first clinical description - a granulomatous disease affecting the kidneys with vascular lesions - it also involved the spleen and lungs - ? related to polyarteritis nodosa.

Wegener (1936 & 1939) : Defined the syndrome, characterised by destructive rhinitis, pulmonary lesions and glomerulonephritis. He suggested that the early respiratory tract lesions were due to infection, this in turn resulting in a hypersensitivity reaction which also affected many other organs.

Leggat and Walton (1956) : Wegener's granulomatosis.

Felson and Braunstein (1958) : Non-infectious necrotising granulomatosis.

Bishoff (1960) : Non-infectious narcotising granulomatosis - pulmonary Roentgen signs (4 cases).

McGregor and Sandler (1964) : Clinical and radiological review - reported three cases; two severely affecting the nose; all three had lung lesions (two with cavitation). They noted that similar granulomatous lesions may be seen with drug reactions, in serum sickness and in other hypersensitivity states.

Lynch et al. (1964) : Pulmonary cavitation in Wegener's granuloma is usually thick-walled, but in their case (a man aged 51) the cavities in both lungs were thin-walled.

Carrington and Liebow (1966) : 16 cases - limited form without evidence of renal disease.

Gorlin and Sedano (1968) : Syndromes involving the sinuses - congenital and acquired.

Roghair and Ross (1970) : Reported a 70 year old woman, with nasal discharge, progressive deafness and corneal ulceration. She subsequently developed RML consolidation which did not clear. The lobe was resected.

Thomas, K. (1970) : Laryngeal manifestations of Wegener's granulomatosis.

Talerman and Wright (1972) : Laryngeal obstruction due to Wegener's granulomatosis.

Gohel et al. (1973) : Radiological manifestations.

Gonzalez and van Orstrand (1973) : 11 cases.

Landman and Burgener (1974) : Pulmonary manifestations.

Duke-Elder (1976) : Eye involvement.

Hsu (1976) : Limited form of the condition.

Maguire et al. (1978) : Unusual radiographic features.

Hensley et al. (1979) : Diffuse pulmonary haemorrhage & rapidly progressive renal failure in Wegener's granuloma.

Thomas, G. and Lewis (1979) : Death due to adrenal infarction and retroperitoneal haemorrhage following a good response to cyclophosphamide. Patient had cavitating apical lung disease.

Epstein et al. (1980) : Spontaneous pneumothorax - an uncommon presentation of Wegener's granulomatosis.

Farelly and Foster (1980) : Atypical presentation.

Pinching et al. (1980) : Relapses - the role of infection.

Arauz and Fonseca (1982) : Wegener's granulomatosis appearing initially in the trachea.

Farrelly (1982) : Review of pulmonary manifestations at initial presentation and during relapse (14 cases) - ? a variant of lymphoid granuloma.

Jaspan et al. (1982) : Spontaneous pneumothorax in Wegener's granulomatosis.

McDonald et al. (1982) : Involvement of the larynx and trachea.

Stokes et al. (1982) : Acute fulminating intrapulmonary haemorrhage in Wegener's granuloma.

Fauci et al. (1983) : Review of 85 cases.

Nichols (1983) : Cough, haemoptysis and bilateral adenopathy due to Wegener's granuloma.

Cohen et al. (1984) Tracheal and bronchial stenosis plus mediastinal adenopathy - CT findings.

Perry and Shevland (1984) : Limited disease - 6 cases.

Wechsler et al. (1984) : Comparison with lymphoid granuloma.

Haworth et al. (1985) : Pulmonary haemorrhage with Wegener's granuloma and microscopic granulomatosis.

Wolffenbuttel et al. (1985) : Pyopneumothorax - a rare complication of Wegener's granuloma.

Stein et al. (1986) : CT of diffuse tracheal stenosis in Wegener's granuloma.

Hellmann et al. (1987) : Wegener's granulomatosis - isolated involvement of the trachea and larynx.

Savage et al. (1987) : Prospective study of radioimmunassay for antibodies against neutrophil cytoplasm in the diagnosis of systemic vasculitis.

Sawicka (1987) : The necrotising vasculitides.

Socias et al. (1987) : Wegener and Wegener's granulomatosis.

Travis et al. (1987) : Diffuse pulmonary haemorrhage - an uncommon manifestation.

Carder and Harrison (1989) : ANCA is valuable in diagnosis, allowing early therapy. Patients may also develop opportunistic infections, especially whilst under treatment, and this may mimic recurrence. Infection may be mixed and include pneumocystis, aspergillus, herpes simplex and legionella.

Nolle et al. (1989) : ANCA antibodies in Wegener's granuloma.

Aberle et al. (1990) : Thoracic manifestations - diagnosis and course (19 patients).

Cordier et al. (1990) : Clinical and imaging study of 77 cases.

Foo et al. (1990) : Presentation on CT with tissue thickening surrounding the bronchovascular bundles.

Oliver et al. (1990) : Widespread and severe inflammation of bronchial mucosa (4 cases).

Singer et al. (1990) : Wegener's granuloma in children (two cases plus review of 37) - may have pulmonary nodules (often with cavitation), sinusitis with nasal bone erosion, renal vasculitis, orbital pseudo-tumours, and skin and joint involvement. Diagnosis is often delayed or obscured because of its rarity in children, and the slow evaluation of lesions in the respiratory tract and kidneys.

Kuhlman et al. (1991) : CT features of parenchymal lung disease in 8 patients. In addition to showing nodules, cavities, scarring and spiculation, CT identified the vasculitic nature of the illness; **blood vessels   leading   to**

nodules and cavities ('feeding vessels') and small peripheral wedge shaped densities suggesting pulmonary microinfarction.

Yousem (1991) : Bronchocentric injury in Wegener's granulomatosis.

Hoffman et al. (1992) : Analysis of 158 patients at NIH (Washington) with Wegener's granulomatosis - treated with cyclophosphamide (2 - 5 mg/kg/day) + prednisolone with considerable control of the condition (many patients having variability and an aggressive illness before diagnosis). Lung disease eventually recurred in 85%.

Papiris et al. (1992) : CT appearances of thoracic Wegener's granulomatosis.

Dreisin et al. (1993) : New perspectives in Wegener's granulomatosis - a rising ANCA titre may herald a clinical relapse which may occur soon after or up to two years later.

Maskell et al. (1993) : Wegener's granuloma - CT in 30 pts. - many showed bronchial damage and bronchiectasis.

Conces et al. (1995) : Tracheo-oesophageal fistula due to Wegener's granulomatosis.

Daum et al. (1995) : Tracheobronchial involvement in Wegener's granulomatosis.

Herridge et al (1996) : Subglottic stenosis complicating Wegener's granulomatosis + surgical repair.

Delany (1997) : Fatal case showing bilateral apical shadowing (like bilateral Pancoast tumours) + necrotic shadowing in lower lobes and necrotic bowel.   Burns (1998) : Pulmonary vasculitis.

Screaton et al. (1998) : Spiral CT evaluation of tracheal involvement in Wegener's granulomatosis.

Langford and Hoffman (1999) : Wegener's granulomatosis - review from USA.

Connor and Olliff (2000) : Asymmetrical hemithorax volume loss in three long standing cases.

Bicknell and Mason (2000) : Wegener's granuloma presenting as cryptogenic fibrosing alveolitis on CT.

Allergic granulomatosis and angiitis or 'Churg-Strauss syndrome'.

This condition mat start as an atypical allergic diathesis leading on to a necrotising vasculitis giving some appearances similar to periarteritis nodosa. Most affected patients have a history of allergy, including asthma, allergic rhinitis with polyposis and **eosinophilia**. Pulmonary infiltrates are found in about 70%; nodules are common, but cavitation is rare. Nodal enlargement and pleural effusions may occur. Some patients may also have glomerulonephritis, heart failure, myocardial infarction, pericarditis, cerebral haemorrhage or gastro-intestinal tract perforation or bleeding. (Small aneurysms have been seen in some cases on visceral angiography).

Clinically the condition resembles **Wegener's   granuloma**, but when left untreated 50% of cases die within three months. Steroids are usually effective, but cytotoxic drugs may also be required. In a case which presented to the author no therapy proved effective. This patient, a woman aged 35 (with young children) had increasing severe abdominal pain due to mesenteric involvement, and had a duodenal ulcer as well as small lung nodules which rapidly increased in size and number over three weeks before she died.

References.

Rachemann and Greene (1939) : Association of asthma, allergic disease and polyarteritis.

Churg and Strauss (1951) - two pathologists: Described 14 young adults with disseminated necrotising eosinophilic vasculitis and extravascular granulomas, with severe asthma, eosinophilia and fever. Most had died from the disease.

Sokolov et al. (1962) : Allergic granulomatosis - a nodular type of vasculitis.

Chumbley et al. (1977) : Allergic granulomatosis and angiitis - 30 cases.

Olsen et al. (1980) : Nasal manifestations.

Lanham et al. (1984) : Systemic vasculitis with asthma and eosinophilia, and the Churg-Strauss syndrome (16 pts.).

Clutterbuck and Pusey (1987) : Severe alveolar haemorrhage in Churg-Strauss syndrome.

Morgan et al. (1989) : Cardiac involvement shown by echocardiography.

Buschman et al. (1990) : HRCT and pathologic findings in Churg-Strauss pulmonary vasculitis - **enlarged irregular and stellate-shaped arteries and small patchy opacities were present in the   pulmonary parenchyma.** Histologically the arteries were enlarged due to eosinophilic infiltration in the vessel walls and the adjacent lymphatics were dilated.

Tervaert et al. (1991) : Antimyeloperoxidase antibodies - present in the serum of three patients.

Lanham et al. (1992) : The Churg-Strauss syndrome often has a phasic picture. The mean age of onset of the vasculitic phase is 38 years - often beginning with malaise, weight loss and fever - patients also commonly get leg cramps, especially in the calves. The diagnosis should be made by tissue biopsy (eosinophilic infiltration, granuloma formation and necrotising granulitis) and the ANCA test, but both may be negative. Damage to peripheral nerves often dominates the clinical picture and causes major disability.

Worthy (1997) : HRCT showed parenchymal opacifications; nodules may cavitate, bronchial dilatation or wall thickening (? related to asthma), also pulm. oedema & septal thickening; 25 - 50% died from cardiac failure.

Worthy et al. (1998) : Spectrum of pulmonary CT findings in 17 pts. - most common findings were random or peripheral areas of parenchymal opacification, but they were non-specific.

Scott and Harrison (1998) : 23 pts. - 2 young pts. died as a result of active disease with cardiac involvement & 3 out of 4 aged 70+ because of superadded infection.
D'Cruz et al. (1999) : Difficult asthma or Churg-Strauss syndome? Steroids may mask the latter.

Bronchocentric granuloma.

This necrosing granulomatous inflammatory condition involves the walls of bronchi. The bronchial lumina become filled with inspissated mucus. Frequently the disease is unilateral, and the upper lobes tend to be involved more often than the lower. Mucocoeles, obstructive pneumonitis, collapse, abscesses and areas of bronchiectasis may be seen. In many cases the condition appears to be an atypical reaction to aspergillus infection (see ps. 19.38 - 43).

References.
Liebow (1973) : Pulmonary angiitis and granulomatosis.
Katzenstein et al. (1975) : Bronchocentric granulomatosis, mucoid impaction and hypersensitivity reactions to fungi.
Goodman, D. and Sacca (1977) : Bronchocentric granulomatosis - a complication of allergic BP aspergillosis.
Robinson et al. (1982) : Radiological manifestations.
Berendsen et al. (1985) : Bronchocentric granulomatosis associated with seropositive arthritis.
Bonafelde and Benator (1987) : Bronchocentric granulomatosis and rheumatoid arthritis.
Ward et al. (2000) : Bronchocentric granulomatosis - CT findings in 5 pts.

Systemic (or disseminated) lupus erythematosus - (Illus. SLE).

SLE (or DLE) may affect either sex as adults or teenagers, but is most common in women of childbearing age. It may affect the connective tissues of any organ, giving rise to skin (butterfly rash, lupus and photosensitivity), oral, joint renal, cardiac, pleural, CNS and blood disturbances. In the kidneys the glomeruli may show a 'wire loop' appearance, due to fibrinoid thickening of the basement membrane.

Lung changes may acutely be due to lupus or secondary pneumonia, congestion, alveolar haemorrhage, etc. Breakdown or cavitation in nodules seems to be due to local infection or embolism, rather than vasculitis per se. **Pleuritis and pleural fibrosis are common**. Lung changes often cause the title '**mixed connective tissue disease**' (MCTD) to be applied.

In chronic cases, basal linear collapse is common (see p. 2.16) as well as **changes similar to those seen in fibrosing   alveolitis**, with thickening of interlobular septa, honeycombing and intralobular interstitial thickening or ground-glass shadowing on CT. **Dyspnoea may be due to poor diaphragmatic movement, or 'shrinking lungs'**. The poor diaphragmatic movement may be suggested by **paradoxical abdominal movement with respiration** (abdominal recession, instead of distension with inspiration); this may be confirmed with fluoroscopy or ultrasound. The reduced diaphragmatic movement is further discussed on p. 15.3.

A few cases are drug induced, due to sulphonamides, isoniazid, methyldopa or chlorpromazine. These are usually reversible with cessation of the drug. Pleural and pericardial effusions may be the initial manifestation of the disease.

References.
Libman and Sachs (1924) : Atypical 'verrucal' endocarditis.,   Israel (1953) : Pulmonary manifestations.
Gould and Daves (1957) : A review of Roentgen findings in SLE.
Taylor and Ostrum (1959) : Roentgen evaluation of DLE., Bulgrin et al. (1960) : Chest Roentgen changes in SLE.
Hoffbrand and Beck (1965) : Unexplained dyspnoea and shrinking lungs in DLE.
Thompson, W. (1963) : The disseminated form of LE is an acute, sub-acute or chronic degeneration of the collagen tissues throughout the body. It is more common in females and the greatest incidence occurs between 10 and 40 years of age. Pericardial and pleural effusions are the most common lesions in the chest - these may be small and persistent. Lung lesions, often basal and segmental, may be indistinguishable from bronchopneumonia or infarcts.
Hare and Mackay (1969) : Thymic involution in SLE.
Sawkar and Easom (1971) : Recurrent spontaneous pneumothoraces in SLE.
Levin (1971) : Proper interpretation of pulmonary Roentgen changes in SLE.
Bryd and Trunk (1973) : SLE presenting as pulmonary haemosiderosis.
Eisenberg et al. (1973) Diffuse interstitial lung disease in SLE.
Gibson, G. et al. (1977) : Diaphragm function and lung involvement in SLE
Gamsu and Webb (1978) : Pulmonary haemorrhage in SLE.
Yum et al. (1979) : Pseudolymphoma of the lung in a patient with SLE.

Castaneda-Zuniga et al. (1976), Webb and Gamsu (1981) : Cavitating pulmonary nodules in DLE.
Haupt et al. (1981) : The lung in SLE., Kinney and Angelillo (1982) : Bronchiolitis in SLE.
Turner-Stokes and Turner Warwick (1982) : Intrathoracic manifestations of SLE.
Asherson et al. (1983) : Pulmonary hypertension in SLE.
Carette et al. (1984) : Severe acute pulmonary disease in patients with SLE - 10 yrs experience at NIH, Washington.
Heiberg et al. (1988) : Body CT findings in SLE.
Laroche et al. (1989) : Diaphragm strength in the shrinking lung syndrome of SLE.
Prendergast et al. (1990) : Pulmonary involvement in SLE - evaluation with CT. In over 80% there was basal disease, either thickening or small effusions. Peripheral and basal, band-like opacities were the most common. Small areas of consolidation and poorly defined areas of increased parenchymal density were visible in about 60% of pts.
Gomez-Benites et al. (1992) : Survey of 104 pts. with lupus induced pulmonary haemorrhage and its pathogenesis.
Miller, W. (1991) : Drug related pleural and mediastinal disorders.
Gammon et al. (1992) : BOOP associated with SLE. Wiedemann and Matthay (1992) : Pulm. manifestations of SLE
Hsu et al. (1992) : Pulmonary haemorrhage complicating SLE - MR imaging.
Bankier et al. (1995) : CT assessment of discrete lung involvement in SLE in 48 pts. Of 45 with normal CXRs, 17 had abnormal CT findings - basal changes similar to those in fibrosing alveolitis, focal areas of consolidation, etc.
Fenlon et al. (1995 & 1996) : HRCT as a predictor of pulmonary involvement in SLE - interstitial disease is more common than previously documented (50% of cases showed pulmonary abnormalities), and often is seen in the absence of cigarette smoking. Pleural disease is less common than expected and mediastinal and axillary nodal enlargement is frequently found. HRCT findings include subpleural bands, basal bronchiectasis, septal thickening, parenchymal bands and ground-glass shadowing.
Ooi et al. (1997) : HRCT in 10 pts. with SLE & persistent respiratory symptoms showed a high incidence of chronic lung destruction with honeycombing, architectural distortion, parenchymal bands, pleural irregularity & a lower zone predominance.
Si-Hoe et al. (1997) : Abdominal CT in SLE - venous thrombosis (esp. renal), acute abscess, bladder involvement with hydronephrosis, enlarged or small kidneys, subcortical renal haematomas, serositis, bowel wall thickening, splenic, hepatic, pancreatic and/or lymph node enlargement.
Keane and Lynch (2000) : Review - pleuropulmonary complications of SLE.

Polyarteritis nodosa (Illus. **POLYART NODOSA**).

This collagen disease manifests as an inflammatory and necrotising reaction affecting the medium and smaller arteries, with inflammation spreading out into the peri-vascular tissues. Many organ systems are involved, and there may be an overlap with Wegener's granuloma and eosinophilic pneumonia. In the thorax, cardiac enlargement, pleural effusion, pulmonary oedema, patchy consolidation or parenchymal lung nodules may occur. There are often transient local shadows due to eosinophilia, which appear and disappear in various areas of the lung, and may give rise to a picture of 'wandering pneumonia'. Occasionally spherical or fine nodules are produced mimicking secondary tumour deposits, but more often irregular or streaky opacities are produced.

Other systems commonly involved are the GI tract, the kidneys and the CNS. The angiographic demonstration of micro-aneurysms in the small renal or intestinal vessels (Illus. **POLYART NODOSA, Vasculitis Pt. 3a-b**), infarctions and haemorrhages and multiple small infarcts.

References.

Kussmaul and Maier (1866) : Periarteritis nodosa - a vasculitic syndrome in which palpable nodules are found along the course of medium sized muscular arteries.
Garland and Sisson (1954) : Pulmonary changes in collagen diseases.
Rose, G. and Spencer (1957) : Pulmonary lesions were the first manifestation in 32 out of 111 cases.
Bron et al. (1965) : Diagnostic value of arteriography in polyarteritis nodosa.
Hunninghake and Fauci (1979) : Thought that lung involvement occurred rarely in polyarteritis nodosa.
Hekali et al. (1985) : CT of renal complications of polyarteritis nodosa.
Woodward et al. (1974) : Periosteal new bone formation in polyarteritis nodosa.
Meijers et al. (1995) : Periteritis nodosa and subperiosteal new bone formation.

Rheumatoid lung and thoracic disease - (Illus. **RHEUMATOID**).

Rheumatoid disease is an immune-complex condition, with excess antibody, leading to granulomatous lesions in the affected bones.

Rheumatoid lung infiltration starts as a proteinaceous exudate, which is followed by fibrosis and severe scarring. Intimal fibrosis takes place in muscular arteries which may lead to pulmonary hypertension, and may contribute to the formation of lung nodules.

Lung disease associated with rheumatoid arthritis was first noted by Ellman and Ball (1948). Patients may have non-specific pneumonitis, bronchiolitis (which may occur per se or be associated with treatment including gold - see p. 3.26), pleural disease (effusions - which may appear and disappear fairly rapidly, or be recurrent, pneumothoraces, and loculated or generalised empyemas), pulmonary fibrosis, honeycombing (see p. 6.6), necrobiotic nodules (see below under Caplan's syndrome), and pulmonary arteritis with hypertension.

When **fibrosis** occurs it is often described as being predominantly basal, but there is sometimes an upper lobe predominance, similar to that seen in ankylosing spondylitis - see p.19.90; and one wonders if poor rib movement with respiration may in part account for this. Poor rib movement and/or fibrosis from bronchiolitis may give rise to small volume lungs. Some patients develop a severe fibrosis spreading into the lungs from the periphery, as with fibrosing alveolitis and other fibrosing lung conditions (Illus. **RHEUMATOID, Pts. 1, 11, 12, 14a-c & Lung fibrosis 14a-b**). This may follow the disappearance of nodules or be due to associated bronchiolitis (see also p. 3.25 and the reference to Geddes et al., 1977). Illus. **RHEUMATOID, Pt. 16a-c** shows improvement in lung infiltration following steroid treatment.

Secondary infection of the lung and/or pleura is not uncommon, and may be bacterial or fungal (especially aspergillosis). Some pulmonary infiltrative changes may also be related to drugs such as gold or methotrexate (see ps. 19.111 - 112 and Illus. **RHEUMATOID, Drug reaction Pts. 8 - 12**).

Pleurisy may be uni- or bilateral. A rheumatoid effusion typically has a low glucose and high protein content and may be yellow in colour. The fluid may contain many lymphocytes and eosinophils. Rheumatoid effusions are often slow to clear (small ones may remain for years), and may leave a fibrous reaction; they are also prone to secondary infection, and localised empyemas are not uncommon and may be recurrent (Illus. **RHEUMATOID, Empyema 29a-c**). Pleural disease appears to be more common in men. Spontaneous pneumothoraces may also occur - see Illus. **RHEUMATOID, Pt. 20a-b**.

Rheumatoid disease may also cause acute or chronic hilar and/or mediastinal nodal enlargement. Such nodes may show central calcification, or become densely calcified with healing (Illus. **RHEUMATOID, Pt. 4a-d**).

Superior rib notches due to cystic bursae are described on p. 12.29.

Shoulder changes are more common - erosions and destructive changes in the humeral heads with upward migration of these - also tapering and erosion of the outer ends of the clavicles and widening of the acromio-clavicular joints (Illus. **RHEUMATOID, lung fibrosis Pt. 14b**).

Cervical spine - destructive changes involving the disc spaces and C1/2 arteritis and subluxation are not uncommon.

Temporo-mandibular joints - Redlund-Johnell (1988) pointed out the important association of rheumatoid arthritis of the TM joints and upper air way obstruction. Not only may upper airway narrowing be present, but this can be worse (especially with the patient supine) if the lower border of the mandible becomes more vertical, due to erosion of the mandibular heads and neck. (The author has encountered such a severe problem several years ago when he had to perform an emergency crico-thyroidostomy to relieve acute respiratory obstruction following direct puncture carotid angiography).

Hand changes are well known - some examples are shown in Illus. **RHEUMATOID, Pts. 5, 21-23**.

Necrobiotic nodules (Caplan's syndrome) and Rheumatoid Nodules.

Caplan (1953) described rapidly enlarging nodules in coal-miners, which could precede overt rheumatoid arthritis, and with only a slight or absent or absent background picture of pneumoconiosis. Radiographically there were multiple, well-defined round opacities (0.5 to 5 cm in diameter) distributed throughout the lungs (Fig. 19.11a); cavitation and calcification also occurred. The nodules tended to appear suddenly, and before, coincident-with or after the onset of arthritis. Some patients had a few nodules, others more. In some the nodules coalesced and became indistinguishable from progressive massive fibrosis (PMF). In 1959 Caplan noted that pulmonary nodules could antedate the onset of arthritis by up to 10 years, and in 1962 noted the presence of smaller nodules (0.3 to 1 cm in diameter) in rheumatoid arthritis.

Caplan type nodules may also be found with other dust diseases - asbestosis (Rickards and Barrett, 1958, Morgan, 1961, Telletson, 1961, Mattson, 1971, Greaves, 1979), iron foundry workers (Caplan et al., 1958), boiler scalers (Campbell, 1958), tile makers (Hayes and Posner, 1960), the making of grinding wheels (Posner, 1960), soap abrasive manufacture (Morgan and Wolfel, 1966), workers with china clay, talc, dolomite (Antilla, 1984), etc.

Other patients with rheumatoid arthritis and no industrial exposure may have similar nodules, which appear, cavitate with clefts and disappear, leaving small scars in the lungs, which in turn may calcify. New lesions may appear after others have cleared, and varying stages may be present at the same time, although they often tend to appear in crops, corresponding to generalised clinical exacerbations of the disease, often at the same time as subcutaneous nodules around the elbows or elsewhere. Clearing may be aided by steroids. In a few patients rheumatoid nodules may be found in the lungs, and the patients have a positive rheumatoid factor in the absence of arthritis (Burke et al., 1977). The patient in Illus. **RHEUMATOID, Pt. 14a-c** showed severe fibrosis before the onset of arthritis. Some nodules appear following other 'insults' e.g. intercurrent disease, local radiotherapy (for breast cancer, etc.).

CT may show the typical **sub-pleural** location of many of the nodules (Illus. **RHEUMATOID, 9b & 13b**), their grouping into clusters, with progression to cavitation and scar formation. It may also demonstrate other rheumatoid lung changes, such as inflammation, fibrosis, bullae, honeycombing and pleural disease. Other nodules are shown in Illus. **RHEUMATOID, Pts. 7a-b & 15-19.**

On gross pathology the nodules often appear to be encapsulated, and histologically they are similar to subcutaneous rheumatoid nodules, with a central zone of necrotic collagen, surrounded by a granulomatous reaction. Their central parts are usually filled with necrotic eosinophilic yellow or greenish-yellow material, surrounded by histiocytes and epithelial cells, the whole being enclosed within a rim of collagen. As Dunnill (1982) stated "the formation of subpleural nodules is perhaps not surprising when one considers that this is one of the areas of lung most plentifully endowed with collagen". Adjacent vascular intimal fibrosis is often found.

Occasionally nodules may be mistaken for peripheral lung tumours and be removed surgically. Occasionally cavitating nodules may be associated with a spontaneous pneumothorax. Nodules may also be involved with secondary infection, particularly fungal, if they are cavitating. Necrobiotic nodules may be found in association with retroperitoneal fibrosis, biliary fibrosis, etc.

These nodules often cavitate before they disappear to leave a scar (see also Fig. 6.3, p. 6.5).

Complications and associations of necrobiotic nodules.

Occasionally cavitating nodules may be associated with a spontaneous pneumothorax. Nodules may also be involved with secondary infection, particularly fungal, if they are cavitating. Necrobiotic nodules may be found in association with retroperitoneal fibrosis, biliary fibrosis, etc.

Confusion with other lung nodules.

Occasionally necrobiotic nodules have been mistaken for peripheral lung tumours, and have been removed surgically. Conversely metastatic deposits in patients with rheumatoid arthritis have been mistaken for rheumatoid nodules. Jolles et al. (1989) described seven such patients and suggested that biopsies should be obtained in patients with 'new rheumatoid nodules' so that a potentially curable malignancy is not misdiagnosed as benign disease. Illus. **RHEUMATOID, Pt. 6** shows a patient with rheumatoid arthritis and ca lung + a lung deposit both in the left lung.

(a)   Plain radiograph -
'Rheumatoid nodules'
- reproduced from Caplan (1953)
Thorax, **8**, 29 - 37 by permission from the
BMJ Publishing Group.

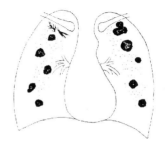

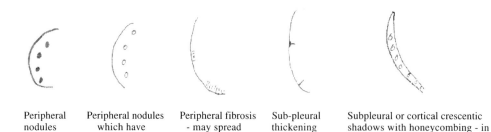

| Peripheral nodules | Peripheral nodules which have cavitated. | Peripheral fibrosis - may spread centrally. | Sub-pleural thickening ? in small accessory fissures | Subpleural or cortical crescentic shadows with honeycombing - in more advanced cases honeycombing +fibrosis may extend more centrally |

(b) CT

Fig. 19.11 Diagrams of the radiological appearances which may be seen in the lungs of patients with rheumatoid arthritis - note that the fibrosis & honeycombing is similar to that seen with other fibrosing lung conditions - see Fig. 19.15, p. 19.117.

Further references.

(a) **General**

Ellman and Ball (1948) : Joint and pulmonary manifestation.

Christie (1954) : Rheumatoid inflammation is 'disseminated, focal, non-suppurative, persistent and prone to result in dense hyaline scars which may undergo secondary changes.'

Cruickshank (1954) : The arteritis of rheumatoid arthritis.

Ellman and Cudkowicz (1954) : Rheumatoid lung syndrome.

Price and Skelton (1956) : Rheumatoid arthritis with lung lesions.

Sinclair and Cruickshank (1956) : Rheumatoid arthritis and visceral involvement.

Bagratuni (1956) : Anarthritic rheumatoid arthritis.

Emerson (1956) : Pleural effusion complicating rheumatoid arthritis.

Dixon and Ball (1957) : Honeycomb lung and chronic and chronic rheumatic arthritis - described as 'chronic pneumonitis' - a diffuse interstitial fibrosis which may rarely progress to 'honeycomb lung'.

Edge and Rickards (1957) : Rheumatoid arthritis with lung lesions.

Flatley (1959) : Rheumatoid pulmonary disease.

Horler and Thompson (1959) : Pleural and pulmonary complications of rheumatoid arthritis - noted that effusions could antedate the onset of arthritis.

Ward, R. (1961) ; Pleural effusion as the presenting feature of rheumatoid esp. in males.

Lee and Brain (1962) : three patients with chronic pulmonary interstitial fibrosis who later developed rheumatoid arthritis - the lung changes may be present without overt arthritis.

Locke (1963) : Rheumatoid lung - diffuse lung lesions, esp. basal, also nodules and unsuspected pleural effusions.

Thompson, W. (1963) : Areas of fibrinous pneumonia may occur - segmental and remaining unchanged for long periods of time. Also persisting and recurring pleural effusions - after aspiration and air replacement, nodular pleural lesions may be demonstrated.

Stretton and Leeming (1964) : Two cases of diffuse fibrotic lung disease in women aged 45 & 61 - rheumatoid disease without arthritis.

Hingle and Yates (1965) : Pyopneumothorax complicating rheumatoid disease.

Davies, D. (1966) : Pyopneumothorax in rheumatoid lung disease.

Ferguson (1966) : Cholesterol pleural effusion in rheumatoid lung disease.

Morgan and Wolfel (1966) : Pulmonary nodules in rheumatoid diseases.

Ramirez and Campbell (1966) : Rheumatoid disease of the lung with cavitation.

Burrows (1967) : Pulmonary nodules in rheumatoid diseases.

Walker, W. (1967) : Pulmonary infections and rheumatoid arthritis.

Martel et al. (1968) : Pulmonary and pleural lesions in rheumatoid disease.

Jones, F. and Blodgett (1971) : Empyema in rheumatoid pleuropulmonary disease.

Popper et al. (1972) : Interstitial rheumatoid lung disease.

Dieppe (1975) : Empyema in rheumatoid arthritis.

Ayzenberg et al. (1983) : Bilateral pneumothoraces and pleural effusions complicating rheumatoid disease.

Schechter et al. (1976) : HPOA and rheumatoid arthritis - simultaneous with diffuse interstitial fibrosis.

Burke et al. (1977) : Pulmonary nodules and rheumatoid factor in the absence of arthritis.

Geddes et al (1977) : Progressive airway obliteration in adults and its association with rheumatoid disease.

Turner-Warwick and Evans (1977) : Pulmonary manifestations of rheumatoid disease.

Torrington (1978) : Rapid appearance of rheumatoid pleural effusion.

Brennan and Daly (1979) : Pleural effusions in rheumatoid arthritis may become large and may be infected.

Herzog et al. (1979 & 1981) : Bronchiolitis and rheumatoid arthritis.
Strohl et al. (1979) : Apical fibrobullous disease with rheumatoid arthritis.
Petrie et al. (1980) : Upper lobe fibrosis and cavitation in rheumatoid disease.
Cooke et al. (1981) : Rheumatoid arthritis and chronic suppurative lung disease.
Armstrong, J. and Steele (1982) : Localised pulmonary arteritis in rheumatoid disease.
Ayzenberg et al. (1983) : Bilateral pneumothoraces and pleural effusions complicating rheumatoid lung disease.
Jurik and Grundal (1983) : Pleurisy in rheumatoid arthritis.
McCann et al. (1983) : Obliterative bronchiolitis and upper zone pulmonary consolidation in rheumatoid arthritis.
Steinberg and Webb (1984) : CT appearances - (i) the subpleural location of the nodules, which commonly appear in clusters and (ii) honeycombing, bullae and cavitation - better seen on CT than on plain radiographs.
Payne (1985) : Pulmonary complications of rheumatoid arthritis include pleural disease (effusion, friction, empyema, broncho-pleural fistula), pulmonary fibrosis (fibrosing alveolitis), rheumatoid nodules, increased susceptibility to infection, airways disease, eosinophilic pneumonia, Sjögren's syndrome, drug effects, shrinking lung, pulmonary vascular disease, amyloid, laryngeal disease and combined lesions.
Yue et al. (1986) : Apical fibro-cavitating lesions of the lung in rheumatoid arthritis (two cases).
McGowan et al. (1989) : HRCT in 18 patients with rheumatoid arthritis. Four with normal chest radiographs and pulmonary function tests had normal CT exams. In the rest (who all had abnormal pulmonary function tests) abnormalities were found including inflammatory changes, peripheral fibrosis, local areas of pleural thickening, emphysema, bronchiectasis and nodules.
McConnochie et al. (1989) : Aspergillus colonisation of pulmonary rheumatoid nodule.
Shannon and Gale (1992) : Noncardiac manifestations of rheumatoid arthritis in the thorax.
Aquino et al. (1994) : BO associated with rheumatoid arthritis, findings on HRCT and dynamic expiratory CT.
Rémy-Jardin et al. (1994) : CT findings in the lungs in 38 abnormal cases of RA - (a) bronchiectasis or bronchiolectasis, (b) rounded nodules, (c) ground-glass shadowing and (d) honeycombing.
Millar (1996) : Pleural rheumatoid may give rise to intense contrast enhancement.

(b) Caplan's syndrome
Gough et al. (1955) : Pathological studies of modified pneumoconiosis in coal-miners with rheumatoid arthritis.
Kantor and Morrow (1958) : Caplan's syndrome - a perplexing pneumonitis with rheumatoid arthritis.
Flatley (1959) : A rheumatoid nodule in the LLL was excised in mistake for a lung tumour - quoted nine other cases from the literature.
Ramirez et al. (1964) : Caplan's syndrome - a clinicopathological study.
Lindars and Davies (1967) : Rheumatoid pneumoconiosis - a study in colliery populations in the East Midlands coalfield.
Jolles et al. (1989) : Nodular pulmonary opacities in patients with rheumatoid arthritis - a diagnostic dilemma.

(c) Rheumatoid and drugs (gold, methotrexate, penicillamine, etc. - see under bronchiolitis obliterans [including penicillamine] - ps. 3.25-28, and under gold and methotrexate - ps. 19.111 - 112).

Scleroderma or diffuse systemic sclerosis - (Illus. SCLERODERMA).
There are two broad forms of scleroderma based on clinical findings : (i) a limited form and (ii) a diffuse form. About 60% of patients have limited disease usually manifested by the 'CREST' syndrome - which is an Americanism of the initial letters of: 'calcinosis of skin, Raynaud's phenomenon, esophageal dysfunction, sclerodactyly and telangectasia'.

Scleroderma affects the lungs in about 10 to 20 % of cases causing basal or more extensive fibrosis with fine honeycombing (see also ps. 1.55 & 6.6). Such fine basal honeycombs are sometimes termed 'sclerocystic changes'; and these may be seen better on plain films in females if the breasts are elevated (Illus. SCLERODERMA, Pt. 3). Larger cysts or bullae may occur, particularly when the lung disease progresses to a severe fibrosis, which may be accompanied by pulmonary vascular disease, pleural thickening and calcification. Some have thought that the lung changes may be related to oesophageal dysfunction, but the pulmonary fibrosis and honeycombing may occur without any oesophageal abnormality. The author when working in Detroit (at the Henry Ford Hospital in 1965) studied about 20 patients with severe lung disease, several of whom had no oesophageal disease (Illus. SCLERODERMA, Pts. 9 - 13). He has since seen many other cases, but none with such severe lung disease.

Ritchie (1964) studied pulmonary function in 22 patients with scleroderma and wrote that it is essentially a generalised disease, the extent of the visceral involvement being unrelated to the extent of the cutaneous malformations. Most of those with radiological changes (reticular and nodular shadows leading to cor pulmonale) had severe defects in pulmonary function, 'suggesting that the radiograph detects only the more severe pathological changes'. A lung biopsy in one case with small basal shadows on chest radiography showed small cystic spaces lined with ciliated columnar epithelium, increased interstitial fibrosis and smooth muscle tissue. In another case, autopsy showed replacement of normal alveolar architecture by cystic spaces and compact areas of fibrous tissue.

   CT of patients with acute chest symptoms may show nodularity or a fairly extensive patchy alveolar reaction in the mid or lower parts of the lungs ('ground-glass' shadowing), progressing to fibrosis with traction bronchiectasis and finally peripheral crescentic shadowing, honeycombing and cyst formation, similar to that seen in fibrosing alveolitis, and some term it '**the   fibrosing alveolitis of systemic sclerosis**'. It particularly affects the lower lobes and posterior aspects of the lungs.

   Some patients with pulmonary fibrosis later develop lung tumours - usually alveolar cell or adeno-carcinoma (see p.24.4 and Illus. **SCLERODERMA, Pt. 8a-c**).

   See also a rare association with Castleman's disease (ps. 5.30 - 31).

Other findings etc.

Female preponderance (3 females to 1 male) - 50% overall mortality at 7 years, pulmonary complications being the major cause of death.

Patients may have pulmonary vascular disease without interstitial lung disease. D-penicillamine and cyclophosphamide may help with interstitial lung disease and nifedipine may help with vasculitis.

Gastro-intestinal tract : oesophagus - loss of peristalsis, dilatation, sometimes with narrowing or
shortening (see also p. 16.4 and Illus. **OES-SCLERODERMA.**)
: stomach - decreased peristalsis, hiatus hernia, 'wide open cardia'
(distinguishing the oesophageal change from achalasia).
: small intestine - decreased peristalsis and pseudodiverticula.
: colon - decreased peristalsis, dilatation, localised narrowing.
(GI tract complications are shown in Illus. **SCLERODERMA,
Pts. 4, 7b, 8d, 15a-d, & 17 to 19.)**

Heart and kidneys   : decreased contraction of myocardium, progressive renal failure.

Phalanges : absorbtion of tufts of distal phalanges esp. of fingers, calcinosis, etc.- Illus.
SCLERODERMA, Pts. 14b, 15e-f & 20-24.

Teeth : widening of periodontal spaces.

Lymph nodes : sometimes enlarged mediastinal nodes may be found - see refs.

Subcutaneous calcification may be seen in patients with scleroderma and dermatomyositis - Illus. **SCLERODERMA, Pts. 15e-f, 16a-b, & 22.**

Facial appearances are shown in Illus. **SCLERODERMA, Pts. 8a & 24a.**

Note: there may an adverse interaction between scleroderma and radiotherapy (see Chapter 19).

Further references.

Harper (1953) : Radiological manifestations of diffuse systemic sclerosis.

Garland and Sisson (1954) : Radiological changes classified as diffuse or localised fibrosis or nodulation, sub-pleural (basal) cystic disease and calcification.

Opie (1955) : The pulmonary manifestations of generalised scleroderma.

Israel, M. and Harley (1956) : Spontaneous pneumothorax in scleroderma.

Richards and Milne (1958) : Cancer of the lung in progressive systemic sclerosis.

Gondos (1960) : Roentgen manifestations in progressive systemic sclerosis.

Schimke et al. (1964) : Calcinosis, Raynaud's phenomenon, sclerodactyly and telangiectasia.

Winterbauer (1964) : Multiple telangiectasia, Raynaud's phenomenon, and subcutaneous calcinosis.

Ashba and Ghanem (1965) : The lungs in systemic sclerosis.

Harper and Jackson (1965) : Progressive systemic sclerosis (review of 52 cases).

Weaver et al. (1967) : The lung in scleroderma.,   (1968) : Pulmonary scleroderma.

Twersky et al. (1976) : Scleroderma and carcinoma of the lung (two cases + 16 reviewed from the literature).

Kallenbach et al. (1977) : Progressive systemic sclerosis complicated by diffuse pulmonary haemorrhage.

Bettma and Kantrowitz (1979) : Rapid onset of lung involvement in progressive systemic sclerosis.

Owens et al. (1983) : Pulmonary function in progressive systemic sclerosis.

Blom-Bülow et al. (1985) : Lung function in progressive systemic sclerosis is dominated by poorly compliant lungs and stiff airways.

Konig et al. (1984) : Lung involvement in scleroderma.

Harrison, N. et al. (1987, Royal Brompton Hosp., London) : CT of the thorax in progressive systemic sclerosis.

(1989) : Used CT, bronchoalveolar lavage and ^{99m}Tc DTPA clearance studies in patients with systemic sclerosis - all were frequently abnormal in asymptomatic patients suggesting that fibrosing alveolitis is an early abnormality and may be present in those with normal chest radiographs.

(1990) : Evidence for protein oedema, neutrophil influx and enhanced collagen production in lungs of patients with systemic sclerosis.

(1991) : Studied 49 open lung biopsies from 34 pts. with interstitial lung disease and systemic sclerosis. The earliest changes included patchy lymphocyte and plasma cell infiltration of the alveolar walls; interstitial fibrosis and increased macrophages, but only occasional polymorphs and lymphocytes in the alveolar spaces. Alveolitis was not observed without fibrosis. The findings appeared to be **indistinguishable   from fibrosing alveolitis per se.**

Owens, G. and Follansbee (1987) : Cardiopulmonary manifestations of systemic sclerosis.

Pistelli et al. (1987) : Pulmonary involvement in progressive systemic sclerosis - a multidisciplinary approach.

Cooper and Denham (1990) : Progressive systemic sclerosis (diffuse scleroderma) and radiotherapy.

Garber et al. (1992a) : Enlarged mediastinal lymph nodes in the fibrosing alveolitis of systemic sclerosis - retrospective study of 78 pts - 66 had lung involvement on CT and many had at least one node > 12 mm in diameter.

(1992b) : Mediastinal lymphadenopathy in the fibrosing alveolitis of systemic sclerosis.

Griffin et al. (1990) : Diffuse alveolar haemorrhage with progressive systemic sclerosis.

Miller et al. (1990) : Lung disease associated with progressive systemic sclerosis.

Schurawitski et al. (1990) : HRCT was much more sensitive than chest radiography for assessing minimal lung involvement - subpleural lines, honeycombing and parenchymal bands.

Arroliga et al. (1992) : Pulmonary manifestations of scleroderma.

Bhalla et al. (1993) : Chest CT in 25 patients with scleroderma - prevalence of asymptomatic oesophageal dilatation (in 20) and mediastinal lymphadenopathy (in 25).

Hernández-Rodríguez et al. (1995) : Role of thrombin in pulmonary fibrosis - bronchoalveolar lavage fluid (BALF) thrombin concentrations were higher in patients with scleroderma than in controls and stimulated fibroblast proliferation (BALF from pts. with CFA and sarcoid also stimulated fibroblast proliferation but thrombin concentrations were low and thrombin inhibitors had no significant effect).

Neuwirth et al. (1995) : HRCT was superior to radiography in showing minimal evidence of disease especially at the apices - the most frequent signs were ill defined opacities, subpleural lines and bronchiectasis.

Aref et al. (1996) : Severe fibrosis in a pt. with scleroderma and previous radiotherapy - exaggerated fibrosis was seen in the treatment area (ca. breast).

Wechsler et al. (1996) : CT - lymphadenopathy is prevalent in pts. with syst. sclerosis & interstitial lung disease.

Chan et al. (1997) : CT of CFA and the FA of systemic sclerosis - impression has been that CFA is characterised by a coarser pattern of fibrosis but pts. present later in the course of their disease (?related to smoking related damage).

Hansell (1997) : Pts. with systemic sclerosis and pulmonary hypertension tend to die quickly - on CT are seen to lose the normal superior - inferior density gradient.

Mino et al. (1997) : Pulmonary involvement in polymyositis & dermatomyositis - sequential evaluation with CT - consolidation with patchy or subpleural distribution, parenchymal bands & irregular peribronchovascular thickening were characteristic and reversible.

Kirsch et al. (1997) : Multicentric Castleman's disease and POEMS syndrome (extensive mediastinal node enlargement + calcification, splenomegaly, pleural effusion, & skin thickening typical of scleroderma) in a woman aged 53.

Behçet's disease.

This multi-system connective tissue and vascular disorder occurs mainly in the second to fourth decades, and is rarely seen in children and patients over 50. It is somewhat more common in males than females (1.5 up to eight to one in different series). Most commonly it causes aphthous stomatitis, less commonly genital and cutaneous ulcers, uveitis and joint lesions (both polyarthralgia and polyarthritis). Skin papules may be found at the sites of minor injuries e.g. due to previous venepunctures. Most patients have only mild abnormalities such as the mouth ulcers, which wax and wane and most eventually stop recurring. Some may have erythema nodosum, thrombophlebitis of large veins (such as the SVC or IVC), intestinal or CNS involvement. Arterial lesions tend to carry a poor prognosis with thrombosis or aneurysm formation.

Chest involvement is unusual and occurs in about 5% of cases, and mainly in young men. It may progress to cavitation. A few have pleural reactions or effusions. Some patients have subpleural nodules or more central pulmonary artery aneurysms which may be demonstrated by plain radiography, tomography (including CT) and/or pulmonary angiography. Lung shadowing may be due to infarcts or haemorrhage, and in some patients there may be both infarcts and aneurysms. Both may cause haemoptysis, which may be a formidable clinical problem, especially if the patient is given anticoagulants and bleeds from a pulmonary artery aneurysm. Coronary artery aneurysms, or arterial thrombosis, mimicking Takayasu's disease (see p. 10.17) may also occur.

Renal involvement appears to be due to secondary amyloidosis.

The condition may be seen especially in its milder form in young men (e.g. undergraduates) in the UK, but is more common in the Far East (Japan, Korea and China) and parts of the Middle East (including Turkey, Israel, Lebanon, Iran and Egypt). In Turkey it affects about 0.3 % of the population.

Some of the more serious complications may resolve spontaneously, whilst others may progress despite treatment and be life-threatening. Lung complications may be acute with eosinophilic pneumonia or vasculitis (leading to infarction, haemorrhage and collapse - see above) and may respond to steroids. Azothiaprine, cyclophosphamide, cyclosporin, thalidomide or colchicine have also been used. Pulmonary artery aneurysms may be embolised or be removed surgically. Embolisation requires a patent peripheral vein and a patent IVC or SVC, which may not be present. Coronary artery or aortic disease may need surgical treatment.

The **Hughes-Stovin** **syndrome,** in which young males develop major vessel venous thromboses, as well as pulmonary artery aneurysms, is very similar to Behçet's syndrome, and may be a variant of it. It is also a vasculitis and clinical features include pyrexia, erythematous skin lesions, arthralgia, optic neuritis, cerebral thrombophlebitis and scrotal ulcers.

References.

Behçet (1937) : A Turkish dermatologist described a patient with recurrent oral and genital ulceration and relapsing ocular inflammation.
Dowling (1961) : 121 cases.
Kansu et al. (1972) : Behçet's syndrome with obstruction of the venae cavae in 7 cases.
Davies (1973) : Behçet's syndrome with haemoptyis and pulmonary lesions.
Chajek et al. (1975) : Review of 41 new cases + literature review.
Cadman et al. (1976) : Pulmonary manifestations in Behçet syndrome.
Petty et al. (1977) : Recurrent pneumonia in Behçet syndrome.
Williams, B. and Lehner (1977) : Immune complexes in Behçet's syndrome and recurrent oral ulceration.
Lehner (1987), Lehner and Barnes (1979 & 1986) : Reviews.
Ahonen et al. (1978) : Obstructive lung disease in Behçet syndrome.
Gamble et al. (1979) : Immune complex of glomerulonephritis and pulmonary vasculitis in Behçet disease.
Charlier et al. (1981) : Malady of Behçet with pulmonary artery aneurysm.
Grenier et al. (1981) : Three cases with pulmonary artery aneurysms.
Slavin and Degroot (1981) : Pathology of the lung in Behçet disease.
Gibson et al. (1982) : Bronchial obstruction in a patient with Behçet's disease.
Park et al. (1984) : Arterial manifestations of Behçet disease.
Ayoub et al. (1985) : Endothoracic manifestations.
Gibson et al. (1985) : Pulmonary artery aneurysms in Behçet's disease - one case had a massive and fatal haemorrhage. The aneurysm had been demonstrated by tomography (including CT) and angiography.
Lacombe et al. (1985) : Transcatheter embolisation of multiple pulmonary artery aneurysms in Behçet's syndrome.
Efthimiou et al. (1986) : Pulmonary disease in Behçet's syndrome - five cases (with two deaths) and 25 reviewed from the literature.
Salamon et al. (1988) : Massive haemoptysis complicating Behçet's syndrome.
Winer Muram and Gavant (1989) : Pulm. artery aneurysm in LUL containing thrombus - CT and angiography.
Raz et al. (1989) : Pulmonary manifestations.
Stricker and Malinverni (1989) : Multiple lung aneurysms of pulmonary arteries in Behçet's disease.
Do et al. (1990) : Pulmonary artery aneurysms in Behçet's disease treated with vaso-occlusion.
Erkan and Cavdar (1992) : Pulmonary vasculitis in Behçet's disease.
Puckette et al. (1994) : MR confirmation of pulmonary artery aneurysm in Behçet's disease.
Winer-Muram et al. (1994) : Thoracic vascular Behçet's disease in African-American men.
Ahn et al. (1995) : Radiographic and CT findings in 9 pts. - variable and non-specific - mediastinal widening due to SVC thrombosis, consolidation due to pulmonary haemorrhage or thrombosis or lung masses due to aneurysms.
Tunaci et al. (1995, from Instabul) : Review also noted that arteriography and venography should be avoided if possible in pts. with Behçet's disease, as aneurysms and thromboses may occur at puncture sites.
Tunaci et al. (1999) : CT findings of pulm. artery aneurysms during treatment for Behçet's disease.

Hughes and Stovin (1959) : Segmental pulmonary artery aneurysms with peripheral venous thrombosis.
Kopp and Green (1962) : Pulmonary artery aneurysms with recurrent thrombophlebitis.
Frater et al. (1965) : Pulmonary artery aneurysms, pulmonary artery thrombi and peripheral venous thrombi.

Wolpert et al. (1971) : The radiology of the Hughes-Stovin syndrome.
Teplick et al. (1974) : The Hughes Stovin syndrome.
Durieux et al. (1981) : Multiple pulmonary arterial aneurysms in Behçet's disease and Hughes-Stovin syndrome.
Roberts et al. (1982) : Multiple pulmonary artery aneurysms and peripheral venous thrombosis in the Hughes-Stovin syndrome.

Sjögren's syndrome.

Sjögren (1933) described the syndrome of keratoconjunctivitis sicca, xerostomia and parotid disease, occurring predominantly in menopausal women. Some have minor symptoms only, whilst others may develop other types of collagen or auto-immune disease, particularly myositis, interstitial nephritis and vasculitis. Some may progress to pseudolymphoma, Castleman's disease (lymphoid hyperplasia), Waldenström's macroglobulinaemia, or frank lymphoma. Lymphoid infiltrates may be present in many mucous secretory glands, including those of the trachea and bronchi; these may in turn become infiltrated with amyloid, calcify or cavitate. The lung alveoli may also be affected by inflammatory infiltration and fibrosis. HRCT may show a 'V & Y' appearance with follicular bronchiolitis, others in turn may lead to cyst formation. Recurrent pneumonia is common, and may progress to lymphoid interstitial pneumonia (LIP - see p. 19.119). Enlarged hilar and mediastinal nodes may be found, but are not specific to the condition (Andonopoulos et al., 1988).

The syndrome is consequent upon lymphocytic destruction of exocrine glands, which can occur alone (the '**primary**' type), or in association with other autoimmune diseases, most commonly rheumatoid arthritis (the '**secondary**' type). Those with the primary syndrome often have recurrent parotitis, but may have other autoimmune phenomena in the skin, GI tract, orbit, breast, thyroid, larynx, kidneys and meninges. The risk of developing lymphoma is estimated as about 45 times the risk in the general population.

Further references.
Block et al. (1965) : 62 cases.
Karlish (1969) : Lung changes in Sjögren's syndrome.
Fairfax et al. (1981) : Pulmonary disorders associated with Sjögren's syndrome.
Gumpel (1982) : Sjögren's syndrome.
Bariffi et al. (1984) : Pulmonary involvement.
Constantopoulos et al. (1984) : Xerotrachea and interstitial lung disease., (1985) : Respiratory manifestations.
Fox et al. (1984) : Clinical and immunopathological features of primary Sjögren syndrome.
Kobayashi et al. (1988) : Sjögren's syndrome with multiple bullae and pulmomary nodular amyloidosis.
Oyen et al. (1995) : Renal infiltration in primary Sjögren syndrome causing renal pseudotumours.
Desai and Hansell (1996) : Lymphocytic infiltration with amyloid - two pts. with Sjögren's syndrome.
Oxholm and Asmussen (1996) : Primary Sjögren's syndrome - the challenge for classification of disease manifestations.
Meyer et al. (1997) : Insp. & exp. HRCT in a pt. with Sjögren's syndrome & cystic lung disease caused by bronchiolitis - female aged 26 - preceded by SLE.
Desai et al. (1997) : HRCT in 3 pts. with Sjögren's syndrome with co-existing LIP and pulmonary amyloid showed an unusual combination of thin-walled cystic air-spaces and irregular opacities.

Mixed connective tissue disease.

This has overlapping features with rheumatoid arthritis, DLE, scleroderma, dermatomyositis and positive anti-nuclear factor serology. It may be accompanied by nephritis, arterial hypertension and mediastinal lymphadenopathy. Recurrent aspiration pneumonia may result from pharyngeal involvement.

References.
Schwarz, M. et al. (1975) : Interstitial lung disease in polymyositis & dermatomyositis - six cases and literature review.
Epler et al. (1979) : Bronchiolitis and bronchitis in connective tissue disease.
Guit et al. (1985) : Mediastinal lymphadenopathy and pulmonary hypertension in mixed connective tissue disease.
Prakash (1992) : Lungs in mixed connective tissue disease.
Schwarz, M. (1992) : Pulmonary and cardiac manifestations of polymyositis-dermatomyositis.

Ankylosing spondylitis - (Illus. **ANKYLOSING SPONDYLITIS**).

Patients with this condition commonly have breathlessness. Many have a deformed thorax, with a **dorsal kyphosis**, a narrow long AP diameter of the chest and fixity of the costo-vertebral, many intervertebral and sacro-iliac joints. The kyphosis often results in the chin being projected over the thoracic inlet on chest radiographs or in front of it on CT sections. It can rarely be so severe that the patient has to walk backwards with a mirror in his hand in order to see where he is going! **Fractures of the spine** in patients with this disease are often unstable and heal poorly because they tend to occur in the calcified interspinous ligaments, through the laminae and pedicles and through the disc, and usually do **not** involve the vertebral bodies per se. When muscle spasm has passed off severe dislocations or Charcot's type **pseudarthroses** may occur, and may easily cause nerve root or spinal cord damage (Illus. **ANKYLOSING SPONDYLITIS, Pt. 2a-d**) or even cord transection. It is thus very important to recognise spinal fractures in such patients, so that the area of the spine can be fixed to prevent the complications occurring - see also the fractured cervical spine in Illus. **ANKYLOSING SPONDYLITIS, Pt. 5**. Degenerative changes with calcification may also occur in the discs.

Patients with ankylosing spondylitis may have apical lung fibrosis, bullae or more extensive fibrosis resembling fibrosing alveolitis (Illus. **ANKYLOSING SPONDYLITIS, Pts. 1 & 4**). These, like the changes in the axial skeletal joints, may be caused by an autoimmune type of process, caused by the inherited gene abnormality. The lung changes appear to be accentuated by poor chest expansion due to the rigid rib cage, the pumping action of the diaphragm and our upright posture for most of the day (see p.1.47). They may also be colonised by aspergillosis giving rise to mycetomas within the bullae (Stiksa et al., 1976). Some patients may also have other fibrotic conditions e.g. sclerosing cholangitis. Others may develop renal failure, as a result of taking analgesics, and in these long-standing cases the author estimates that the incidence of apical fibrosis and bullous formation is about 10 to 20%, but others put the incidence at 1 to 2% (see references below).

Lung tumours may occur in these patients (Illus. **ANKYLOSING SPONDYLITIS, Pts. 1, 3 & 6**) - and the author has seen another such cases (see also references below). About 5% of those who had radiotherapy to the spine and pelvis years before may develop **leukaemia** (see p. 11.23).

A bone scan may demonstrate the active phase in the dorsal spine, the costo-vertebral joints and the sternoclavicular joints (see also p. 12.39) but old burnt-out disease will be negative, unless a fracture, pseudarthrosis, secondary infection or cancer deposit is present.

The condition may give rise to a positive HLAB 27 test, B 60 having a weaker effect. Many patients do not know they have the condition and only present in later life as a result of the condition, or have it found fortuitously.

References.
Hamilton (1949) : Pulmonary disease manifestations of ankylosing spondylitis.
Romanus and Yden (1952) : Erosions at disco-vertebral junction heal with sclerosis leading to the 'shiny-corner' sign
Graham and Smythe (1958) : The carditis and aortitis of ankylosing spondylitis.
Campbell, A. and MacDonald (1965) : Upper lobe fibrosis associated with ankylosing spondylitis.
Jessamine (1968) : Upper lobe fibrosis in ankylosing spondylitis.
Davies (1972) : Ankylosing spondylitis and lung fibrosis.
Brewerton (1974) : HLAB molecules trigger an immune response.
Chakera et al. (1975) : 42 patients with upper lobe fibrosis in six - also quoted other cases from the literature.
Wolson and Rohwedder (1975) : Upper lobe fibrosis and ankylosing spondylitis.
Rosenow et al. (1977) : Reviewed the records of over 2,000 patients with ankylosing spondylitis. 28 had upper lobe bullae, apical pleural thickening or fibrosis adjacent to the bullae (fibro-bullous disease). Many had fusion of the costo-vertebral joints.
Stika, S. et al. (1976) : Aspergillus colonisation causing mycetomas within the bullae in ank. spondylitis.
Ahern et al. (1982) : Ankylosing spondylitis and adenocarcinoma of the lung.
Parkin et al. (1982) : Regional lung ventilation in ankylosing spondylitis.
Hillerdal (1983) : Ankylosing spondylitis lung disease - an underestimated entity?
Rumancik et al. (1984) : CT of fibro-bullous disease of upper lobes - extra-skeletal feature of ank. spondylitis.
Kinnear and Shneerson (1985) : Acute pleural effusions in inactive ankylosing spondylitis.
Padley et al. (1991) : Tracheobronchomegaly in association with ankylosing spondylitis.
Collie et al. (1993) : ^{99m}Tc-MDP scintigraphy in ankylosing spondylitis.

Peh et al. (1993) : Pseudarthrosis at the thoraco-lumbar junction complicating a fracture in ankylosing spondylitis - appearances on MRI.
Hassan (1995) : Cauda equina syndrome (with csf diverticula) in ankylosing spondylitis.
Macpherson et al. (1995) : HRCT of the chest in ankylosing spondylitis - unexplained pleural or parenchymal abnormalities were found in 13 of 55 AS pts.- upper lobe fibrosis, bullae, honeycombing, emphysema in apex of LL, ground glass shadowing or patchy pleural thickening.
Tyrrell et al. (1995) : Signal changes in thoraco-lumbar intervertebral discs in ank. spon. on MR.
Fenlon et al. (1997) from Dublin : HRCT showed a spectrum of abnormalities including apical fibrosis, non-apical infiltrative lung disease, bronchiectasis, paraseptal emphysema and tracheobronchomegaly.
Remedios et al. (1998) : MR equivalent of Romanus sign in early ankylosing spondylitis.
Wordsworth (1998) : About 8% of people in the UK have HLAB 27, but not all develop ank. spondylitis. Other HLABs e.g. B60 have a weaker effect. Many present late - with the condition burnt out - as a fortuitous finding.
Turetschek et al. (2000) : Pts. with ank. spon. & a normal CXR frequently have lung abns. on HRCT.

Pneumoconioses - (Illus. **PNEUMOCONIOSIS**).

These are due to the inhalation of dusts (κονο = dust), mainly silicon, which is often combined with other substances, e.g. carbon, iron, tin, etc. Not only may silicosis occur with mining, but also as a complication of the manufacture of various products, boiler cleaning, in iron and steel works, the making of scouring powders, lens polishing, pottery manufacture, sand-blasting, grinding, quarry workers, etc.
Small particles become deposited in the lungs, and are phagocytosed (mostly within 48 hours) by macrophages which die and alveolitis and a fibroblastic reaction is stimulated. Small nodules may be formed, together with a fine fibrosis. Some septal line engorgement and lymph node enlargement may occur. As the disease progresses the nodules tend to coalesce, and in some cases large masses of **progressive massive fibrosis** ('potato-like pseudo-tumours' or PMF - Illus. **PMF**) may be present. CT shows that these often have a 'cake-like' appearance with surrounding smaller nodules, in which calcification may occur (Bégin et al., 1990). These large masses may later cavitate (Illus. **PMF+CAVITY**), the patients coughing up black ink-like sputum ('**anthracoptysis**'), easily identified by the patient coughing onto a white handkerchief. Considerable emphysema and elevation of the hilar regions, from upper lobe fibrosis, often occurs. 'Egg-shell' or patchy calcification of the lymph nodes may be seen (p. 6.24); other calcification may have resulted from past tuberculosis. Other nodules may result from Caplan's syndrome, in miner's etc. with rheumatoid arthritis (see ps. 19.82 - 83). Other patients may have pneumoconiosis and neoplasm (Illus. **PNEUMOCON+CA LUNG**).
Fewer cases are being seen in the UK, following precautions at work. In the last century for example, knife and scissor-grinders in Sheffield tended to die in their 20s, 30s and 40s.
from silicosis (as a result of inhaling dust from millstone-grit grinding wheels - Illus. **PNEUMOCONIOSIS, Pt. 38**).

Classification of nodules.

This is usually done according to the scheme drawn up by the International Labour Organisation:
Nodules - punctiform (p = < 1.5 mm), micronodular (q = 1.5 to 3 mm) or nodular (r = 3 to 10 mm), their profusion being graded 0 to 3 (1 having few nodules and 3 filling the lungs).To these were added symbols (s, t and u) for linear irregular shadows (particularly with asbestosis), and a combination of these were termed 'x, y and z' by McLoud et al. (1983) - see Fig. 19.12 (below).
Larger shadows (whether made up from several smaller lesions, or a single large one) are recorded by summation - A (total mass 1 to 5 cm in diameter), B (covering one-third of lung fields, e.g. right upper zone) and C (even more extensive lesions).
Pleural thickening, calcification and **diaphragmatic movement** may also be graded.
(For further details see ILO - 1971, 1980 & 1981 - also McLoud et al., 1983).

Pathologically lesions are typically found in the respiratory bronchioles, and often surround the small muscular pulmonary arteries; they may also be seen in relation to fluid and septal tissues. The small nodules may contain three fairly distinct zones - (i) a central hyaline zone (often containing a carbon pigment), (ii) a surrounding zone of concentrically arranged fibroblasts (but with few silica particles), and (iii) an outer zone of cellular fibrous tissue and macrophages with numerous silicon particles (Dunnill, 1982).

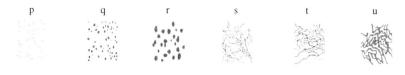

p to r - small rounded nodules   s to u - small irregular or linear shadows

Fig. 19.12   Small nodular and linear shadows due to pneumoconiosis (ILO classification).
(Reproduced from Medical Radiography and Photography (1972) - **48**, 67 - 76 with permission Kodak Ltd.)

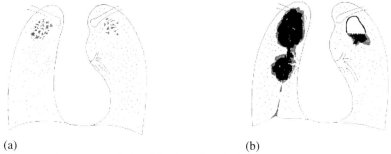

          (a)   (b)

(a) Early stage - tiny pneumoconiotic nodules throughout the lungs.
(b) PMF with 'potato-like' lung masses; cavitation and fluid level in breaking down large nodule in LUL - 'angel's wing appearance' (see also p. 6.4 and Illus. **ANGEL WINGS, Pneumocon Pts. 7 & 29**).

Fig. 19.13   Pneumoconiotic nodules and progressive massive fibrosis - diagrams reproduced from Caplan (1953), Thorax, **8**, 29 - 37 by permission from the BMJ Publishing Group.

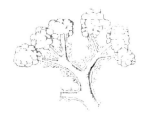

Fig. 19.14   The position of the tiny pneumoconiotic
opacities in relation to the smaller bronchi as shown
by reconstruction of serial CT sections
(reproduced from Akira et al., 1989, Radiology, **171**,
by permission).

Kaolinosis - kaolin or china clay deposits are found in the South West of England (in Devon and Cornwall) in the USA, etc. Kaolin is a non-fibrous aluminium silicate; it is inactive chemically and is insoluble in water. When washed free from granite (in which it occurs) a wet fat-like substance is produced, which may be used for making pottery, in cement, paint, glossy paper and for some pharmaceuticals. Inhalation may occur with transporting, bagging or the milling of dried kaolin, as well as in china clay and pottery workers.
    When deposited in the lungs, kaolin causes a nodular fibrosis, similar to that seen in coal miners, but progression of the condition is much slower, and only rarely can symptoms be attributed to it. Small rounded nodules (1.5 to 3 mm in diameter) may be seen radiographically, particularly in the lower zones, and larger irregular masses may also be present (like PMF). Fine fibrosis may also occur, as well as Caplan's syndrome in patients with rheumatoid arthritis.

Talc is also a magnesium silicate, and may cause lung scarring, nodular shadows (which may coalesce), pleural plaques and thickening. Acutely it gives rise to a diffuse lung haziness. Talc bodies (similar to asbestos bodies - Fig. 14.16, p. 14.34) may be found pathologically. It may be inhaled during talcum-powder manufacture, the powdering of surgical rubber-ware (including surgical gloves), and sometimes when used as baby-powder. It may also be injected IV in drug-addicts, if used by 'pushers' to dilute **cocaine, heroin**, etc. Talc has also been used for pleurodesis (see also p. 14.25).

Carborundum (silicon carbide) is produced by fusion of high-grade silica and finely ground carbon in an electric furnace at 2,400° C. It is used as an artificial abrasive with a hardness slightly less than diamond. It has been used for many years in abrasive wheels, as a grinding paste, and as a refractory in the manufacture of boilers and foundry furnaces. The question of its pathogenicity has been debated for several years.

Clark, W. and Simmons (1925), Clark (1929 and 1931) and Brunsgaard (1949) reported that it gave rise to pneumoconiotic changes on chest radiographs. Gardner (1935) and Holt (1967 - see refs. below) found that in sheep exposed to high concentrations of SiC dust, it did not give rise to lung fibrosis and was biologically inert. Because of this the Pneumoconiosis Board of the Department of Health has not regarded carborundum as a hazard. This view is probably incorrect, as the dust was fine and not in a fibrous form. The author has seen some toolmakers, who presented with severe fibrosis in the lungs or a mesothelioma, none having admitted to any significant exposure (Wright, F, 1990). With tungsten carbide it may cause granulomatous pneumonitis. (See Illus. **TOOL-MAKER**).

Funahashi et al. (1984) studied two men exposed to silicon carbide for many years, in a factory making refractory bricks. They developed reticulonodular densities in the lungs and dyspnoea. A biopsy in one showed a large amount of black material in fibroid alveolar septa and ferruginous bodies. Six different carbides were present and a trace of tungsten. They concluded "it is possible that some silicon carbides are more fibrogenic than others and that the previous negative animal study was due to this factor. At any rate it is important to be aware that workers who are exposed only to silicon carbide for prolonged periods may develop pneumoconiosis."

Birchall et al. (1988), using cell studies, compared commercially available man-made silicon-carbide 'whiskers' with fibres of blue asbestos and found a similar response to both. They felt that the geometry of particles, rather than their chemical composition, caused the particular response.

Bégin et al. (1989) found that carborundum particles are usually inert, but when in a fibrous form, carborundum behaves as other fibrous materials of comparable dimension in the lung tissue, causing inflammatory changes and fibrosis. Long fibres are retained in the tissue and cause a sustained accumulation of inflammatory cells (mainly macrophages) which produce an excessive amount of fibrous reaction and other fibroblast growth factors.

Pooley (1975 & 1990 from Cardiff) used electron microscopy to study dust particles in the lungs and noted that '**the shape of a microscopic particle of dust can be as important as its chemical composition when deciding if it can cause lung disease.**'

Other non-metallic pneumoconioses.

Mica, Fuller's earth, graphite and cement are among other substances which may produce pneumoconiosis, although the incidence of disease among workers in industries using these substances is low.

Further references.

General

Pendergrass (1958) : Silicosis and some other pneumoconioses - emphasis on radiologist's role.

Garusi et al. (1964) : Histo-radiographic studies of lung structures - good for demonstrating silicosis etc., pulmonary calcinosis and emphysema.

Greening and Heslep (1967) : The exact duration of exposure necessary to yield an objective clinical diagnosis is unknown, but is dependent upon the size of the particles, the concentration at the breathing level and the sensitivity of the subject exposed to the dust. Thus whilst one person may develop silicosis after 3 to 5 years, others exposed in the same way may never develop any detectable disability.

Kleinerman (1967) : The pathology of some familiar pneumoconioses.

Tepper (1967) : The work history in industrial dust disease.

Dee et al. (1978) : Four cases of acute silicosis due to sandblast etching of tombstones - alveolar involvement was more extensive than in chronic silicosis. In two an alveolar exudate, similar to that in alveolar proteinosis was seen.

Parkes (1982) : Diseases Due to Free Silica in Occupational Lung Disorders.

Bergin et al. (1986) : CT in silicosis - correlation with plain films and pulmonary function tests.

Bégin et al. (1987 and 1988) : Used CT to assess the amount of silicosis in exposed workers, and found that although CT showed more coalescence and opacities, it did not identify more patients with minimal parenchymal disease. They noted (1990) that only particles < 5 mm in diameter will reach the distal lung, where they are deposited in the small airways and alveoli. In a further paper (1991) they compared CT and HRCT findings. Standard thickness CT showed abnormalities in 90%, whilst HRCT showed abnormalities in a further 10%, and also showed pathology more clearly. They felt that **diffuse emphysema, detected by CT, was unrelated to silicon exposure, but was related to smoking habits.**

Kinsella et al. (1990) : Also carried out CT studies and felt that emphysema with pneumoconiosis (in the absence of PMF) was related to smoking.

Mannino et al. (1993) : Pneumoconiosis : Comparison of digitised and conventional radiographs.

Akira et al. (1989) : HRCT on 90 patients with pneumoconiosis (coal-miners, welders, graphite and talc workers, etc. - all had small rounded opacities on radiographs). Punctiform (or 'p' nodules) were seen as tiny binary branching structures, or a gathering of a few dots, representing fibrosis around and along the respiratory bronchioles. In some patients, non-peripheral small areas of low attenuation with a central dot were found, due to dust-induced focal emphysema.

Coal-workers

Two papers in the 1st issue of the Journal of the Faculty of Radiologists (the forerunner of Clinical Radiology) :

Gough et al. (1949) : Compared radiological appearances on chest radiographs with formalin-fixed autopsy lung slices in patients with coal-workers pneumoconiosis and noted "The radiographic patterns of 'reticulation' and 'granularity' seen in coal-workers are due to focal dust lesions ('coal nodules'). A distinctive form of emphysema ('focal emphysema') develops in relation to the coal nodules. The degree of this could not in general be assessed accurately by radiology, but a sharply defined net-like appearance in radiographs corresponded with severe focal emphysema. Except for occasional confusion with neoplasms, massive fibrosis due to infected pneumoconiosis could be diagnosed radiologically."

Fletcher et al. (1949) : Reviewed the radiological classifications of coal-miners pneumoconiosis and proposed a new one based on the size of nodules (similar to that given above) with small nodules in **simple pneumoconiosis** and much larger aggregates (of renal, cricket ball or angels-wing shape) in **complicated pneumoconiosis.** They also noted that it was emphysema and pulmonary hypertension which mainly caused the breathlessness.

Fletcher (1948) : Pneumoconiosis of coal-workers.

Rivers et al. (1957) : The prevalence of TB at necropsy in PMF of coal workers.

Williams and Moler (1973) : Solitary mass in the lungs of coal miners.

Collins et al. (1988) : Irregularly shaped small shadows on chest radiographs, dust exposure & lung function in coal-workers pneumoconiosis.

Rémy-Jardin et al. (1990) : Coal-worker's pneumoconiosis - CT assessment in exposed workers and correlation with radiographic findings.

Rémy-Jardin et al. (1992) : CT evaluation of silicosis and coal-worker's pneumoconiosis.

Matsumoto et al. (1998) : MR signal characteristics of PMF in silicosis - the most common appearance was isointensity on T1 and hypointensity on T2 when compared with skeletal muscle, with internal high signal areas on T2 and either rim enhancement or non-enhancement.

Rudd (1998) : Coal miners' respiratory disease litigation - Mr. Justice Turner in an action by miners in the High Court against British Coal considered that the preponderance of evidence supported the proposition that there is variability in the response to dust as well as to smoking and that the effect of dust is not a small effect evenly distributed across most of the population of miners, but an effect which can lead to disabling disease in some men.

Kaolin

Cunningham and Hugh (1973, Stoke on Trent, UK) : Pneumoconiosis in women in the pottery industry. They noted pulmonary mottling, occasionally PMF, Caplan's syndrome and egg-shell calcification in hilar lymph nodes (TB and neoplasm were also found in some workers).

Kennedy, T. et al. (1983), Lapenas et al. (1984) : Reviewed workers in Georgia, USA.

Oldham (1983) : Pneumoconiosis in Cornish china clay workers.

Wells, I. et al. (1985, UK) : Reviewed 68 kaolin workers.

Talc

Siegel, W. et al. (1943) : The dust hazard in tremolite talc mining.

Hopkins and Taylor (1970) : Pulmonary talc granulomatosis - complication of drug abuse.

Gould, S. and Barnardo (1972) : Respiratory distress after talc inhalation.

Brouillette and Weber (1978) : Massive aspiration of talcum powder by an infant.

Motomatsu et al. (1979) : Two infant deaths after inhaling baby powder.

Paré et al (1979) : Pulmonary 'main-line' granulomatosis (talcosis of IV methadone abuse).

Wells, I. et al. (1979) : Pulmonary disease caused by the inhalation of cosmetic talcum powder.

Mariani-Constantini et al. (1982) : Systemic visceral talc granulomatosis + miliary TB in a drug addict.
Crouch and Chart (1983) : Progressive massive fibrosis secondary to IV talc.
Feigin (1986) : Talc - understanding its manifestations in the chest.
Schwartz and Basken (1986) : Pulmonary vascular talc granulomatosis.
Ben-Haim et al. (1988) : Presenting as pulmonary infiltrates in an HIV positive heroin addict.
Pairaudeau et al. (1991) : Inhalation of baby powder - an unappreciated hazard.
Padley et al. (1993) : CT in 3 cases of pulmonary talcosis - 2 PMF and 1 ground glass shadowing.
Stern et al. (1994) : Basal pulmonary emphysema caused by Ritalin (an amphetamine which acts as a stimulant for children with attention-deficit hyperactivity syndrome - the tablets also contain talc).
Ward et al. (2000) : CT of talcosis - 12 cases - fine micronodular pattern, ground-glass attenuation & emphysema.

Carborundum
Coates and Watson (1971 from Henry Ford Hosp.) : 11 men & 1 woman - all tungsten carbide workers with diffuse pulm. disease - gradually progressive bilat., nodular & linear densities + cystic spaces in advanced cases.
Peters et al. (1984) : 35% prevalence of radiological abnormalities in carborundum industry in Quebec, Canada.
Gauthier et al. (1985) : Silicon carbide exposure caused interstitial linear lung infiltrates.
Hayashi and Kajita (1988) : Examined the dust content in lung tissue from a worker in the abrasive industry. Total dust, expressed as a percentage of dried lung was 12%, a value corresponding to that in coal miners with PMF.
Holt (1967) : Exteriorised the right upper lobe bronchi of sheep so that carborundum (or other foreign material) could be blown into them. They found that high concentrations of silicon carbide dust did not induce lung fibrosis, and concluded that the dust was inert.
Massé et al. (1988) : Pathology of silicon carbide pneumoconiosis.

Graphite
Dunner and Bagnall (1946) : Graphite pneumoconiosis complicated by cavitation due to necrosis.
Watson, A. et al. (1959) : Pneumoconiosis in carbon electrode makers.
Akira (1995) : Uncommon pneumoconioses - arc welders & graphite (see also p. 14.39).

Mica
Smith, A. (1952) : Pleural calcification in workers exposed to mica dust.
Landas and Schwartz (1991) : Mica-associated pulmonary interstitial fibrosis presented after initial exposure to mica whilst working in the rubber industry. Chest radiographs and CT showed diffuse fibrosis and honeycombing involving the upper and lower parts of the lungs peripherally. An open biopsy exhibited extrinsic fibrosis and consistent with MICA on spectroscopy and electron diffraction.

Glass wool   (see also p. 14.39).
Bjure et al. (1964) : Asbestos and glass wool.
Kilburn et al. (1992) : Reported pl. plaques or thickening in 20 of 284 workers with 20 yrs. or more exposure to fibre glass - some also had irregular lung opacities and small airways obstruction.
Hughes et al. (1993) : Follow up studies of workers found no adverse effects in seven man-made mineral plants, but made no specific comments on pleural abnormalities.

Desert lung syndrome.
Hirsch et al. (1974) : Simple siliceous pneumoconiosis of Bedouin females in the Negev desert - 18 cases - also gives references to other desert pneumoconiosis cases.
Nouh et al. (1989) : Is the desert lung syndrome (non-occupational dust pneumoconiosis) a variant of pulmonary alveolar microlithiasis? - see also p. 6.23.

Polyvinylchloride pneumoconiosis.
Arnauld et al. (1978)
White and Ehrlich (1997) : HRCT showed small regular nodules in both lower lobes - man aged 35 - plastics factory employee - regressed when removed from exposure.

Pneumoconiosis due to metals
(a) **Iron**
As noted in the following section on **haemosiderosis**, iron may be deposited in the lungs in various workers, such as iron ore workers, **welders** (almost a pure iron deposition - Illus. **WELDER**) and fettlers (boiler scalers, furnace and ferrous castings cleaners). Most have a degree of fibrosis due to the silicon inhaled with the iron, the iron itself being relatively inert and non-pathogenic. Similarly knife, scissor and razor grinders, e.g. working in Sheffield, used to have a

severe pneumoconiosis from the silicon in the 'millstone-grit' grinding wheels, and often died quite young (often in their 20's or 30's - Illus. **PNEUMOCONIOSIS, Pt. 38**). Silver polishers used to inhale some silver (which could be deposited in the lungs as small metallic densities), but much more ferric oxide from the 'rouge' used for polishing. This caused a fine stippled high-density pattern. Similar findings were found in lens polishers who also used 'rouge'.

(b) Other metals

Aluminium particularly as oxide in the inhalation of bauxite ore, may give rise to a severe fibrosis ('**Shaver's disease**'). It may also give rise to a sarcoid-like granulomatosis.

Beryllium may produce a hypersensitivity reaction similar to sarcoidosis (see also p. 19.65). This may be acute but it does not give rise to uveo-parotid fever. Chronic berylliosis may cause lung fibrosis and hilar and mediastinal lymphadenopathy.

Copper as used in fungicidal sprays may give rise to a granulomatous pneumonitis.

'**Hard metal disease**' is caused by **tungsten** carbide (which may give rise to a granulomatous interstitial pneumonitis - see below), **cobalt** (sometimes combined with **titanium**) or alloys of these + **tantalum**; it may give rise to lung fibrosis, and may be complicated by **carborundum**, particularly in tool maker's (see above).

Mercury may be inhaled, ingested or injected IV (either accidentally or deliberately - Illus. **MERCURY IV**). It is poorly absorbed from the intestine, unless in ionic form. Inhaled mercury may produce a localised bronchogram. IV mercury is relatively insoluble in blood and remains in droplet form for a long time. The droplets may be visible as small punctate shadows in the lung vessels and as a small pool in the right ventricle. Peripheral arterial emboli may cause localised gangrene. Damage to the kidneys and nervous system may occur from mercuric ions attacking the -SH groups on enzymes. (For mercury fumes see ps. 19.108 - 19.110).

Bismuth (injected IV) may give a similar appearance (see references below) - it has also been used in intramuscular injections for syphilis (Illus. **BISMUTH DEPOSITS**) and in large amounts orally for duodenal ulcers and dyspepsia, and by injection into abscesses (e.g. of the brain) for defining their extent and response to therapy.

Photocopier toner contains silicon, also metals such as Cu, Fe and Al. A few cases of apparent pneumoconiosis + lymphadenopathy have been reported as probably being due to this cause. It is suggested that the condition may be rare because it may not be the metals themselves which cause the reaction, but antigenicity after binding to proteins leading to the cellular immune response.

(c) Largely non-pathogenic metal pneumoconioses include :
'**Stannosis**' found in tin miners in Cornwall, '**baritosis**' from the inhalation of barium; also antimony and rare earths - the dense metals produce scattered densities (often very dense) on chest radiographs, but cause little (if any) fibrosis.

References.
McLaughlin et al. (1945) : Iron oxide and the lungs of silver polishers.
Doig and McLaughlin (1948) : Clearing of x-ray shadows in welders' siderosis.
Sferlazza and Bekett (1991) : The respiratory health of welders.

Akira (1995) : Uncommon pneumoconioses- CT and pathological features:
Arc welders (21 cases) : typical chest radiograph showed micronodules - most prominent in middle third in perihilar regions - may be reversible. CT - ill defined, diffusely distributed micronodules - some appeared as fine branching structures. In less affected lung, micronodules showed centrilobular distribution, ? due to minute Fe oxide particles along perivascular and peribronchial lymphatics. In more affected lung they coalesced to form a fine network

pattern or area of ground-glass attenuation, resembling CFA; emphysema was also present in smokers. Some had bronchiectasis and 1 of 3 with pleural irregularity had pleural plaques.

Graphite (19 cases) : small nodular densities, interlobular septal thickening, PMF and bullae - similar to coal workers. Pseudoplaques were present in 8.

Aluminium polishers and smelters (6 cases) : 3 forms - predominantly nodular, reticular or upper lobe fibrosis - differs from CFA by being more marked in both central and peripheral parts of the lung.

Hard metal workers (2 cases) : bilateral air space or ground-glass attenuation - mainly panlobular and multilobular in character with parenchymal distortion, traction bronchiectasis and dilated air bronchograms, more evident in the consolidation.

Shaver and Riddell (1947) : Lung changes associated with the manufacture of aluminium abrasives.
Mitchell, J. et al. (1961) : Pulmonary fibrosis in workers exposed to finely powdered aluminium.
Herbert et al. (1982) : **DIP** in an aluminium welder.
Miller et al. (1984) : Aluminium dust exposure and **pulmonary alveolar proteinosis**.
DeVuyst et al. (1987) : Sarcoid-like granulomatosis induced by aluminium dusts.
Jederlinic et al. (1990) : Pulmonary fibrosis in aluminium oxide workers.

Van Orstrand et al. (1945) : Beryllium poisoning.
Tepper et al. (1961) : Toxicity of beryllium compounds.
Weber et al. (1965) : Roentgenological patterns in long-standing beryllium disease.
Bost and Newman (1993) : Metal-induced interstitial lung disease.

Addrizzo-Harris et al. (1997) : Metallic punctate lung opacities + accumulation of metallic particles at the base of the R ventricle following IV injection of 'health tonic' containing bismuth two years earlier.

Villar (1974) : Vineyard sprayer's lung.

Bech et al. (1962) : Hard metal disease.
Coates and Watson (1967) : Diffuse interstitial lung disease in tungsten carbide workers.
Forrest et al. (1978) : Hard metal pneumoconiosis.
Davison et al. (1983) : Hard metal pneumoconiosis.

Ambre et al. (1977), and Wensel et al. (1980) : IV self administration of metallic mercury.
Spizarni and Renzi (1987) : Metallic mercury causing pulmonary emboli.
Cowan et al. (1992) : Metallic mercury embolism arising from deliberate self-injection.
Maniatis et al. (1997) : Self injected mercury - CT imaging.

Gallardo et al. (1994) : Woman aged 44 who worked in a photocopier shop for 6 yrs., developed shortness of breath. A chest radiograph showed diffuse interstitial micronodular shadowing which increased. A thoracoscopic lung biopsy showed pigment-containing macrophages. Silicon was detected in both lung biopsy cells and toner dust. Clinical symptoms were improved with steroids, but the radiographic appearances and the impaired lung function tests persisted.

Armbruster et al. (1996) : Man aged 39, who had worked for 18 months in a newspaper agency on computer based data collection, presented with a bilateral interstitial micronodular pattern and enlargement of hilar and mediastinal nodes. x-ray spectometry confirmed Si, Fe & Cu in transbronchial lung and mediastinal node biopsy specimens.

Sander (1967) : The nonfibrogenic (benign) pneumoconioses.

Pulmonary haemosiderosis (and haemochromotosis) - (Illus. **HAEMOSIDEROSIS** and Illus. **HAEMOCHROMOTOSIS**).

Pulmonary haemosiderosis may be due to a variety of causes including inhaled iron, especially in those handling iron-ore dust. It may also be found in welders, fettlers (cleaners of the insides of foundries, boilers and furnaces, who often had to do the work with hammer and chisel). It may also result from chronic episodes of pulmonary haemorrhage in Goodpasture's syndrome and related conditions (see next section), be associated with some heart conditions such as mitral stenosis, complicate a haemolytic anaemia or be **idiopathic** (sometimes termed 'Ceelen's disease'). Patients with the idiopathic type often have eosinophilia, cold agglutinins, lymphadenopathy of other signs suggesting an immunological cause.

Haemochromatosis is an inherited disorder of iron metabolism, in which excessive absorbtion leads to excessive iron deposition in the tissues in turn leading a severe degenerative type of multi-arthropathy (of hands and weight bearing joints, including spinal intervertebral discs, particularly in athletes and former athletes), cirrhosis, liver fibrosis and failure - Illus. **HAEMOCHROMATOSIS**). It may also affect the heart, pancreas (with diabetes) and spleen. Treatment is by repeated venesection to reduce the body's iron stores, chelating agents and P^{32} to reduce iron absorbtion and storage.

Many patients with idiopathic haemosiderosis are anaemic and therapeutic removal of blood is therefore impracticable; patients with this tend to have a slow relentless downhill course with increasing breathlessness lasting 12 to 24 months.

Radiological appearances.

Acutely in haemosiderosis there may be confluent diffuse lung shadowing. Chronic changes give rise to very tiny and widely dispersed multiple dense nodules and a fine honeycomb type of fibrosis throughout the lungs (Illus. **HAEMOSIDEROSIS Pt. 2b-c**). The chronic changes appear to be due to alveolar wall fibrosis together with iron-laden macrophages filling the alveoli.

The condition may be suspected when widespread fine shadows are found in the presence of iron-laden macrophages in the sputum or on alveolar lavage. In some cases surgical lung biopsy will demonstrate both the iron and the fibrosis.

References.
Ceelen (1931)
Ledrum (1950) and Ledrum et al. (1950) : Pulmonary haemosiderosis of cardiac origin.
Wynn-Williams and Young (1956) : Idiopathic haemosiderosis in an adult.
Bruwer et al. (1956) : Recurrent pulmonary haemorrhage with haemosiderosis (so-called idiopathic pulmonary haemosiderosis).
Bronson (1960) : Idiopathic pulmonary haemosiderosis in adults.
Grill et al. (1962) : Fulminant idiopathic pulmonary haemosiderosis.
Green, R. (1964) : Three patients with carcinoma of lung and recurrent haemorrhage - developed a nodular aspiration pulmonary haemosiderosis.
Lane and Hamilton (1971) : Idiopathic pulmonary haemosiderosis associated with steatorrhoea.
Bailey, D. and Groden (1979) : Idiopathic pulmonary haemosiderosis - report of two cases and literature review.
Turner-Warwick and Dewar (1982) : Last as causes - Goodpasture's syndrome, other renal disease (with or without immune complexes, including diabetes), chemicals and drugs (penicillamine, trimetallic anhydride, etc.), vasculitis (SLE, haemolytic anaemia, pulmonary vasculitis, etc.), lymphangioleiomyomatosis and small bowel disease.
Ernst et al. (1997) : MR diagnosis and quantification of hepatic iron overload in haemochromatosis.
McCurdie and Perry (1999) : Haemochromatosis and exercise related joint pains.

Diffuse intrapulmonary haemorrhage (including **Goodpasture's syndrome** or anti-glomerular basement membrane disease).

Intra-pulmonary haemorrhage may occur from a variety of causes including lung injury (caused by trauma, toxic gases, drug reactions, etc.), inhaled blood (from the tracheo-bronchial tree or above, A/V malformations, aspergillosis, TB. or other infections, etc.), bleeding disorders (e.g. SLE), various forms of vasculitis, with infections, uraemia and immune complex diseases affecting the kidneys and lungs. These last may be stimulated by various causes including infection by bacteria, viruses, fungi or blood borne parasites (e.g. malaria), drugs and chemicals, Goodpasture's syndrome and Wegener's granuloma. In Goodpasture's syndrome the same antibody attacks both the alveoli and the glomeruli, and is similar to the effects of severe serum sickness. Males appear to be more commonly affected.

In considering the underlying cause of pulmonary haemorrhage one should distinguish between localised (due to infection, tumours, injury, etc.) and diffuse (DPH) causes, and also note that the latter may be mimicked by inhaled blood, from the mouth, tracheo-bronchial tree, lung, etc. As the causes are so different, they should always be distinguished from DPH.

Many patients with acute renal failure have fluid overload, inflammatory lung changes and cardiac decompensation. Pulmonary haemorrhage and Goodpasture's syndrome may be suggested by haemoptysis or if the patient has a known or suspected disease that may be associated with diffuse intrapulmonary haemorrhage. Bleeding mainly occurs into the peripheral alveoli. Following an initial presentation with fluffy opacities or more extensive consolidation, transition occurs into a fine network pattern after the intra-alveolar blood has been transported by macrophages into the interstitial spaces and lymphatics. Repeated haemorrhages leading to increasing deposition are not uncommon and may result in larger areas of consolidation of consolidation or even breakdown and cavitation (Illus. **GOODPASTURE**).

Haemoptysis may be the presenting symptom but some patients do not have this, even with massive diffuse haemorrhage. Anaemia is common and occurs in nearly all patients with Goodpasture's syndrome. Cough and dyspnoea are also prominent features. As noted above the radiological changes are similar to those given by pulmonary oedema or diffuse infection or inhalation of blood. In some acute cases no abnormality may be seen on plain radiographs, and in others alveolar infiltrates may be transitory or migratory. Resolution often occurs within one or two weeks. CT is almost always positive.

Repeated bleeding into the lungs may lead to pulmonary haemosiderosis (see previous section).

References.

Goodpasture (1919) : Fatal illness with bouts of pulmonary haemorrhage, followed by glomerulonephritis and renal failure, complicating influenza in a male aged 18.

Bruwer et al. (1956) : Recurrent pulmonary haemorrhage with haemosiderosis (so-called 'idiopathic pulmonary haemosiderosis').

Brannan et al. (1963) : Roentgenographic appearance of pulmonary haemorrhage associated with glomerulonephritis.

Glay and Rona (1964) : The pulmonary renal syndrome of Goodpasture.

Sybers et al. (1965) : Roentgenographic aspects of Goodpasture's syndrome.

Beirne et al. (1973) : Goodpasture's syndrome - dissociation from antibodies to glomerular basement membrane.

Turner-Warwick (1974) : Basement membrane antibody in Goodpasture's syndrome - immunological aspects of systemic diseases of the lungs.

Golde et al. (1975) : Occult pulmonary haemorrhage in leukaemia.

Malina (1976) : Bronchopulmonary immunopathology.

Schwartz et al. (1977) : Pulmonary haemorrhage in renal disease - Goodpasture's syndrome, etc. - hilar shadowing or diffuse opacity.

Ewan et al. (1978) : Detection of intrapulmonary haemorrhage with carbon monoxide uptake.

Palmer et al. (1978) : Occult pulmonary haemorrhage in patients with disseminated intra-vascular coagulation, anti-coagulant therapy, etc.

Ahmad et al. (1979) : Pulmonary haemorrhage + haemolytic anaemia due to trimetallic anhydride.

Bowley et al. (1979) : The chest radiograph in pulmonary capillary haemorrhage - correlation with carbon monoxide uptake - reviewed 25 patients with Goodpasture's syndrome. 23 had pulmonary haemorrhage at some time during their disease and several had relapses. In seven episodes the chest radiograph was normal. Relapses were never isolated and were usually associated with infection (not necessarily in the chest) or occasionally with fluid overload. They used $C^{15}O$ to demonstrate excess haemoglobin in the lungs (but this technique is not readily available without a neighbouring cyclotron, as the half-life of C^{15} is only 2.5 secs. C^{11} has a half-life of 20.4 mins - N.B. - C^{14} used for historical dating has a half-life of 5730 years).

Bradley (1982) : The pulmonary haemorrhage syndromes.

Colebunders et al. (1983) : Pulmonary haematoma caused by oral anti-coagulant treatment.

Leatherman et al. (1984) : Diffuse microvascular lung haemorrhage in immune and idiopathic disorders.

Albelda et al. (1985) : Diffuse pulmonary haemorrhage - a review and classification.

Briggs et al. (1985) : Antiglomerular basement antibody mediated glomerulonephritis and Goodpasture's syndrome.

Williams, D. and Peters (1987) : Causes of glomerulonephritis and pulmonary haemorrhage.

Benditt et al. (1988) : Pulmonary haemorrhage with diffuse alveolar infiltrates in men with high volume chorioncarcinoma - haemorrhage at the site of metastasis - the so-called '**chorioncarcinoma syndrome**' (see also ps. 7. 19-20 & 8. 15-16).

Griffin et al. (1990) : Diffuse alveolar haemorrhage associated with progressive systemic sclerosis.

Tobler et al. (1991) : Anti-basement membrane disease with severe pulmonary haemorrhage and normal renal function.

Witte et al. (1991) : Diffuse pulmonary alveolar haemorrhage after bone marrow transplantation - study of 39 patients - similar appearances to pulmonary oedema or infection - the clinical course after haemorrhage is short often resulting in death.

Hsu et al. (1992) : Pulmonary haemorrhage complicating SLE - MR showed preferential T2 shortening due to the paramagnetic effects of ferric iron within the extravasated blood.

Cheah et al. (1993) : Computed tomography of diffuse pulmonary haemorrhage with pathological correlation. All six patients studied had diffuse nodular opacities (1 - 3 mm in diameter) and with no zonal predominance -were of uniform size in each patient. Recent haemorrhage produced 'ground glass' opacification which made the segmental bronchi appear prominent and obscured the background nodularity.

Wood< A. et al. (1994) : Lymphadenopathy in diffuse pulmonary haemorrhage - male aged 24 with recurrent haemoptyses, iron deficiency anaemia and dyspnoea over two years. Sputum contained many iron-laden macrophages. He was considered as to have idiopathic haemosiderosis. CT showed widespread ground-glass appearance, with sparing of periphery of the lung, and lymphadenopathy in the right para-tracheal area, the azygo-oesophageal recess and lateral to the aorta. They felt that the lymphadenopathy is likely to arise in an acute episode connected with clearing of haemosiderin-laden macrophages.

Primack et al. (1995) : Classified the causes of DPH into:

(a) immunocompetent host - Goodpasture's syndrome, collagen vascular and autoimmune diseases (SLE, Wegener's syndrome, etc.) and

(b) immunocompromised host - idiopathic diseases, disease associated with infection, tumours.

Sickle cell disease - (Illus. **SICKLE CELL DISEASE**).

Sickle cells result from an abnormal haemoglobin HbS, which is present in about 10% of the British black population. The disease results from a substitution of the hydrophilic acid valine for glutamic acid at position 6 of the Hb chain. This alters the solubility of the Hb molecule so that on deoxygenation spindle-shaped liquid crystals are formed. After repeated episodes, the RBCs remain sickled, and being less deformable aggregate in capillaries, causing vaso-occlusion. Such cells are constantly cleared from the circulation, and their life span is reduced, the patients having haemolytic anaemia, and increased marrow activity and expansion. Sickle cell disease occurs in the homozygous state, those who are heterozygote are usually healthy with the 'trait'.

Chest infections in patients with the sickle cell abnormality may cause serious problems. They may develop severe pneumonias with secondary cardiac problems. In addition sickle cell crises may give rise to severe pulmonary changes, although these are often difficult to recognise in the early stages. Patients with sickle cell disease are about 100 times more susceptible to pneumonia than the general population, and in many the pneumonia may recur.

The patients may experience pain in the chest, spine and/or abdomen and breathlessness (**acute chest syndrome**). The clinical condition may rapidly become worse and prompt treatment is essential. Radiologically there may be increased volume of the lungs and cardiomegaly, diminished size of peripheral pulmonary vessels particularly in the lower lobes with unilateral or bilateral congestion and/or consolidation (due to non-embolic infection and/or infarction). The infiltrates are best shown by HRCT (often a 'ground-glass appearance') and may be present with a normal chest radiograph. Signs of heart failure or scarring from past infection may be present. The consolidated lung contains much polysaccharide which may alter blood opsonins, in turn making the sickling worse. There is commonly a marked leukocytosis. Treatment is by hydration, antibiotics, oxygen, exchange transfusion or extracorporeal membrane oxygenation. However infections rather than crises are the commonest cause of death, which may occur in early childhood or as young adults.

Chronic lung changes include pleural tags and subpleural lines with lung fibrosis and architectural destruction, pulmonary arterial hypertension and a hyperkinetic circulation related to severe anaemia.

Patients may also develop **bone infarcts** (in the **ribs** and the upper femora, which may be shown as negative areas due to poor perfusion by **bone scintigraphy**), auto-splenectomy, the nephrotic syndrome, priapism or neurological symptoms.

Thoracic **extra-medullary haematopoiesis** may be seen (as in thalassaemia - see ps. 12.27-28 & 18.32 - 33 and Illus. **EXTRAMED HAEMOPOIESIS**).

Bone marrow transfusions may prevent further complications.

References.

Barrett-Connor (1971) : Acute pulmonary disease and sickle cell anaemia.
　　　　　(1973) : Pneumonia and pulmonary infection in sickle cell disease.
Oppenheimer and Esterly (1971) : Pulmonary changes in sickle cell disease.
Bromberg (1974) : Pulmonary aspects of sickle cell disease.
Haupt et al. (1982) : The lung in sickle cell disease - alveolar wall necrosis is a feature.
Davies and Hewitt (1984) : Sickle cell disease.
Davies et al. (1984) : Acute chest syndrome in sickle cell disease.
Bohrer (1987) : Bone changes in the extremities.
Gillet et al. (1987) : Life threatening sickle chest syndrome treated with extracorporeal membrane oxygenation.
Gumbs et al. (1987) : Thoracic extramedullary haematopoiesis in sickle cell disease.
Smith, J. (1987) : Cardiopulmonary manifestations of sickle cell disease in childhood.
Sebes (1989) : Bone and joint abnormalities associated with sickle cell haemoglobinopathies.
Chan, O. and Loveday (1992) : Widespread tuberculosis in sickle cell disease - TB is no more common with sickle cell disease than in other people.

Cockshott (1992) : Rib infarcts in sickling disease.

Harrison and Davies (1992) : Acute problems in sickle cell disease.

Bhalla et al. (1993) : CT evidence of microvascular occlusion in acute chest syndrome in sickle disease - 10 pts.- absence of arterioles, ground-glass attenuation or focal consolidation.

Gelfand et al. (1993) : Simultaneous rib infarcts and pulmonary infiltrates in sickle cell disease with acute chest syndrome.

Aquino et al. (1994) : HRCT showed interstitial lung abnormalities in 12 of 29 patients who had acute chest disease and showed scarring consistent with past infarction or infection.

Wetton and Tran (1995) : Splenic infarct in sickle cell disease.

Lee, A. et al. (1995) : Early diagnosis and simple prophylactic measures (penicillin to prevent pneumococcal septicaemia, parental education in early diagnosis of acute splenic sequestration and close monitoring) significantly reduce deaths associated with homozygous sickle disease.

A report from St Thomas's hospital, London (quoted in the BMJ 8.2.97 - **314**, 396) estimates that 9,000 people in London have the disease and that 2/3rds of the UK affected population live in London. Pts. felt that health authorities concentrated on the management of the acute painful episodes but neglected problems caused by the chronic nature of the illness.

Grubnic and Wilson (1997) : HRCT in 16 pts. - scarring manifested by pl. tags, subpleural lines, architectural distortion and mosaic perfusion. Many acute cases may completely resolve.

Selvedge and Gevant (1999) : Idiopathic pulmonary vein thrombosis shown by CT and MR imaging.

HYPERSENSITIVITY LUNG CONDITIONS CAUSED BY OTHER AGENTS.

Extrinsic allergic alveolitis ('hypersensitivity pneumonitis' in the USA - Illus. **ALLERGIC ALVEOLITIS**) - see also p. 1.54.

   This is an allergic lung disease caused by the inhalation of antigens contained in a variety of organic dusts. After sensitisation, there is a type IV immune reaction (see p. 19.58). In the acute stage, dyspnoea may occur a few hours after exposure to the allergen. Whilst variations may occur with some different allergens, the following changes are seen on chest radiographs:

(a) Acute heavy exposure causes diffuse air-space opacification.

(b) This resolves within a few days, leaving a fine nodular or reticulo-nodular appearance - the **sub-acute phase.**

(c) The **chronic** phase is characterised by fibrosis, which may occur months to years later.

(d) **Repeated   exposure** leads to acute and sub-acute changes, superimposed on progressive chronic fibrosis, causing lung destruction, bullous disease, elevation of the hila and cor pulmonale.

   The three stages may show some overlap, particularly in those exposed to repeated doses of antigen e.g. in bird fancier's disease. The author has encountered a few patients with acute large nodules due to allergy to anti-haemophilic globulin (AHG) - see Kernoff et al., 1972, and to other agents - an appearance which is more typically seen in Loeffler's syndrome (see p. 19.59).

CT and HRCT

   These give a much clearer picture of the lung changes. Hansell and Moskovic (1991) described the following changes:

(i) Increased parenchymal density plus a prominence of the bronchial walls.

(ii) A nodular pattern - nodules 4 mm in diameter, poorly defined, and distributed mainly in the mid and lower zones.

(iii) Patchy air-space opacification.

(iv) Focal air-trapping - esp. in expiration - with mosaic pattern.

(v) In chronic cases there is also pulmonary fibrosis and traction dilatation of the bronchi, as well as pleural scarring.

(vi) Focal pleural thickening.

(vii) No nodal enlargement.

   The most striking and constant CT finding in 11 patients with radiological abnormalities in the sub-acute phase was a uniform generalised increase in lung density with abnormal prominence of the bronchial walls, and a marked contrast between the density of the lung parenchyma and air in the major airways.

Value of expiratory HRCT

This can show a mosaic pattern and areas of air-trapping - (Illus. **MOSAIC PATTERN** and **AIR TRAPPING** - see also ps. 2.4 & 3.25-27).

<u>References.</u>

Small et al. (1996) : Showed air-trapping in about 50% of 20 patients with external allergic alveolitis, particularly within areas of ground-glass change.

Hansell (1997) : Extrinsic allergic alveolitis is really an allergic bronchiolitis - the nodules are organising pneumonia in and cellular reaction around small airways - often lymphocytic and leading to ground-glass shadowing, faint nodules and areas of decreased attenuation on CT in expiration. (See also under small airways disease - ps. 3.25 - 27).

Farmer's lung - (Illus. **FARMER'S LUNG**).

In this condition, allergens besides causing asthma, may cause lung infiltrates, which with repeated exposure may give rise to severe progressive parenchymal lung damage. In severe cases gross fibrosis and bullous formation may be present, with enlargement of the main pulmonary arteries and cor pulmonale.

The first description appears to have been by Bardino Ramazzini da Carpa (1700) in his 'De Morbis Artificium' which included a chapter on 'Diseases of sifters, measurers and handlers of grain' (quoted by Molina, 1976). Campbell, J. (1932) described 'farmers lung' occurring in response to mouldy hay. It occurs principally as a result of the inhalation of the spores of micropolyspora faeni, but other spores e.g. thermoactinomyces may be involved. Damp hay, grain or other vegetable matter promotes the growth of these and other thermophilic organisms. In the UK it is seen particularly in Devon and the Lake District and other areas where cattle are kept in a 'byre' during the winter. Compensation may be paid for severe disability. The disease is also seen in other countries.

Some farmers or grain dealers may develop - '**wheat weevil** lung' due to Sitophilus granarius.

<u>Other similar conditions</u> include **mushroom picker's lung**, **bagassosis** (due to mouldy overheated sugar cane infected with thermoactimomycetes sacchari), **cork worker's lung** (suberosis), **wood pulp worker's disease**, **cheese washer's disease**, **maple bark disease**, **coffee worker's lung**, **air conditioner lung**, **malt worker's lung**, **coptic lung** (due to infected cloth wrappings of mummies), **thatched roof lung** in New Guinea, etc. Like farmer's lung, most are due to an allergy developing in relation to inhaled fungus spores. A newer condition is **humidifier or air-conditioner lung**. It is interesting that with farmer's lung, even animals may be affected. The cattle themselves may develop symptoms, and zoo animals e.g. lions, have been killed by lung fibrosis secondary to spores in damp bedding.

In **byssinosis** the raw **cotton** may be directly adrenergic or the symptoms may be caused by bacteria in the cotton. Characteristically it affects workers after the week-end break - hence the term 'Monday fever'. It causes dyspnoea, fatigue and cough. (Cotton can also cause embolism in drug addicts and from wiping angiographic guide wires with cotton gauze - see Adams et al, 1965).

Synthetic resins in hair sprays may cause an allergic pneumonitis - '**thesaurosis**'.

Animal proteins which cause allergy include bird protein (e.g. budgerigar and pigeon protein), **pituitary snuff** (containing pig and/or cattle protein which used to be used for the treatment of diabetes insipidus, its use sometimes causing fibrotic lung changes - Illus. **PITUITARY SNUFF**, or DIABETES INSIPIDUS, **Drug reaction Pt. 15a-d**), furs (furrier's lung), etc.

Bird fancier's lung - (Illus. **BIRD ALLERGY**).

This is not uncommon in the UK, and unless considered in the differential diagnosis of miliary or fine nodular shadowing, fibrosis, etc., a potentially largely reversible condition may be missed. It is not uncommonly caused by sensitivity to budgerigar, pigeon or parrot protein, from their feathers or droppings. Elderly females most commonly have sensitivity to budgerigar or parrot protein, whilst 'pigeon fancier's lung' is largely confined to men.

In the early stages no radiological abnormality may be seen on plain chest radiographs, but later on fine diffuse or miliary changes occur, and these may progress to more confluent areas of shadowing or fibrosis resembling pneumonia. Occasionally nodal enlargement is found. Confusion may occur with other fibrotic lung diseases, particularly sarcoidosis and fibrosing alveolitis.

The author has studied a number of cases with HRCT (**BIRD ALLERGY, Pts. 2a-d, 3, 5a-b, 7a-c, 8a-c, 9b-c, 14b, 15b-f** and in gross cases has found similar appearances to those seen in fibrosing alveolitis, honeycombing, white lines and pleural plaques (Illus. **BIRD ALLERGY, Pt, 15a-f and Plaque bird fan Pt. 2a-b**). In acute cases with normal chest radiographs HRCT may be very valuable in showing diffuse acute disease - with ground-glass shadowing and air-trapping (mosaic pattern in expiration).

An unusual case of 'allergy' to bird protein is shown in Illus. **BIRD ALLERGY, Brain Pt. 22** - a young chicken farmer who developed a minor and transient hemiplegia each time he sneezed on entering chicken sheds.

References.

General
Friedman (1980) : Hypersensitivity pneumonias.
Coleman and Colby (1988) : Histological diagnosis of extrinsic allergic alveolitis.
Silver et al. (1989) : CT of 12 cases of hypersensitivity pneumonia.
Hansell and Moscovic (1991) : HRCT in external allergic alveolitis.
Adler et al. (1992) : HRCT in chronic hypersensitivity pneumonitis in 16 patients. Fibrosis is situated predominantly in mid and lower zones (the lung apices and bases were relatively spared). Distribution in transverse plane - random in 7, subpleural in 6 and peribronchovascular in three.
Akira et al. (1992) : CT of Japanese summer-type hypersensitivity pneumonitis - diffusely spread increased lung density (of ground-glass type), micronodules (which tended to persist after the increased density had cleared) and air-space consolidation, esp. at the lung bases.
Buschman et al. (1992) : HRCT in chronic hypersensitivity pneumonitis - centrilobular, peribronchiolar, indistinct nodular opacities in all cases (4 ground glass densities, 3 lobular areas of hyperlucency, 1 pulmonary fibrosis and honeycombing).
Hansell et al. (1996) : Correlation of individual CT patterns of hypersensitivity pneumonitis with functional abnormalities.
Kauczor et al. (1996) : HRCT can show signs of pulmonary immunostimulation with a ventilation dependent distribution after aerosolized interlukin-2 therapy for metastases of renal cell carcinoma.
Matar et al. (2000) : Hypersensitivity pneumonitis.

Bagassosis.
Sodeman (1949), Buchener (1962), Hearn (1968) , Hargreave et al. (1968)

Bird fancier's lung.
Plessner (1960) : Ducks and geese (une maladie des itreurs de plumes).
Reed et al. (1968) : Pigeon-breeder's lung.
Hargreave et al. (1966) : Pigeon breeder's (fancier's) lung.
Korn et al. (1968) : Sensitivity to hen litter.
Unger et al. (1968) : Pigeon breeder's disease - review of Roentgen appearances.
Avila (1971) : Extrinsic allergic alveolitis in workers exposed to fish meal and poultry.
Fink et al. (1972) : Clinical survey of pigeon breeders.
Hargreave and Pepys (1972)
Hargreave et al. (1972) : Radiological appearances in 41 cases tended to relate to the type of exposure. If massive and intermittent, it tended to result in nodular shadows, but if due to more continuous dust this tended to produce fibrosis of the alveoli, lobar contracture and honeycombing.
Bowey (1974) : Bird fancier's lung.
Zylak et al. (1975) : Hypersensitivity lung disease due to avian antigens.
Hendrick et al. (1978) : Budgerigar fancier's lung - the commonest variety of allergic alveolitis in Britain.
Harries et al. (1984) : Extrinsic allergic bronchiolitis in a bird fancier.
Rémy-Jardin et al. (1993) : Sequential CT of 27 patients. Acute cases had diffuse micronodules, ground-glass shadowing, focal air trapping or emphysema and mild fibrotic changes - all these dramatically improved after the cessation of exposure.. Chronic cases were assessed on the presence or absence of honeycombing.

Bourke and Boyd (1997) : Treating patients with pigeon fanciers lung requires an appreciation of both the fascination of the sport to fanciers and the complexity of the disease. Antigen avoidance and respiratory protection are the main aspects of treatment and corticosteroids have only a small role in the long term. It may not be necessary for the fancier to give up his pigeons, but ongoing supervision of symptoms, lung function and chest radiography is advisable.

Byssinosis.
Schilling (1950), Arnoldson et al. (1963)

Coffee worker's lung.
van Thoorn (1970)

Cork worker's lung (suberosis).
Pimental and Avila (1973).

Farmer's lung.
Pepys et al. (1962) & Pepys* and Jenkins (1965) : Precipitins against M. faeni.
Rankin et al. (1962)
Barrowcliffe and Arblaster (1968) : Study of a fatal early acute case in a boy of 17. The lungs at necropsy showed miliary nodules with an acute bronchiolitis, alveolar exudates and haemorrhage.
Hapke et al. (1968) : Clinical, radiographic, functional and serological correlation of acute and chronic stages.
Seal et al. (1968) : Pathology of acute and chronic stages - biopsied 5 patients in the acute phase and found interstitial pneumonia, sarcoid-like granulomata, bronchiolitis and vasculitis. Six patients in the chronic stage showed interstitial pulmonary fibrosis, cystic and pulmonary hypertensive changes.
Mindell (1970) : Roentgen findings.
Grant et al. (1972) : Prevalence of farmer's lung in Scotland., Smyth et al. (1975) : The disease in Devon.
Wenzel et al. (1974) : Serologic studies.
Braun et al. (1979) : Long term clinical and physiological outcome.
Hogg (1982) : Histological appearance., Reyes et al. (1982) : Pathology.
Dickey and Myers (1984) : An acute granulomatous interstitial pneumonitis occurring in agricultural workers.
Mönkäre et al. (1985) from Finland : ? country with greatest incidence - treatment with steroids did not affect the outcome of lung function or the appearance of chronic changes, but did hasten the disappearance of diffuse lung opacities and 55 cases at the end of treatment had clear chest radiographs.
Arshad et al. (1987) : Severe hypoxaemia in farmer's lung with normal chest x-rays.
Cook et al. (1988 from Devon): Acutely there is an upper and mid zone prominence of fluffy consolidation, whereas in the sub-acute stage the predominant feature is a fine shadowing in the middle and lower zones.

(* For obituary to Jacob Pepys, Professor of Clinical Immunology, Brompton Hospital (1967 - 79) see BMJ, **313,** 1077 - 26 Oct. 1996).

Furrier's lung.
Pimentel (1970)

Grain and seeds.
Dunner et al. (1946) : Pneumoconiosis in dockers dealing with grain and seeds.
Lunn and Hughes (1967) : Wheat weevil disease.

Malt worker's lung.
Riddle et al. (1968), Channell et al. (1969) : Allergic alveolitis in malt workers.

Maple bark disease.
Emanuel et al. (1966)

Mushroom worker's lung.
Bringhurst et al. (1959), Sakula (1967), Jackson and Welch (1970), Stoltz et al. (1976)
Olliff et al. (1990) : Illustrated a case with multiple ill-defined and diffusely spread out nodules which persisted unchanged for two years (shown by 2 mm CT section).

Hypersensitivity pneumonitis in a pearl nucleus worker.
Mitani et al. (1995)

Pituitary snuff taker's lung.
Pepys (1966) : Immunological responses to pituitary snuff in patients with diabetes insipidus.

Mahon et al. (1967) : Hypersensitivity to pituitary snuff causing miliary lung shadows.
Wright and Hamilton (1976) : Mild pulmonary fibrosis caused by pituitary snuff.
The author (then a medical house officer) started the snuff treatment of a 32 year old female with panhypopituitarism (secondary to a large Rathke pouch tumour) in 1955. It caused her open epiphyses to close, but three years later she started to develop the pulmonary fibrosis (Illus. **PITUITARY SNUFF, Drug reaction Pt. 15a-d**), which caused no disability for ordinary activity.

Sequiosis (Giant redwood trees).
Cohen et al. (1967)

Silo-filler's disease (see p. 19.109)

Thesaurosis.
Bergmann et al. (1958) : Following inhalation of hair spray.
Lancet, Editorial (1964) : Hair sprays.
Felson (1967) : Disseminated pulmonary alveolar diseases.

Wood-pulp worker's disease. (see also Illus. **SINUSES, Ca antrum**).
Shlueter et al. (1972) : Hypersensitivity pneumonitis caused by Alternaria.

Inhalation (or I /V) drug abuse.

The inhalation of nitrogen oxide, solvents or the smoking of drugs such as cannabis or cocaine may produce harmful effects on the lungs. Both acute and chronic changes may occur. Deep inspiration, followed by a prolonged Valsalva manoeuvre and violent coughing may lead to gas leaking from the alveoli and a pneumomediastinum and/or pneumothorax (see also ps. 6.34 - 35). A pneumomediastinum may also result from the rupture of sub-pleural blebs or bullae. In addition free-base cocaine (or 'crack') may cause chest pain and shortness of breath with radiographic findings of localised collapse or lung parenchymal opacification (similar to that seen in Loeffler's syndrome - p. 19.59), **acute pulmonary oedema** (which can resolve in 24 hours) or barotrauma. Inhaled cocaine may also lead to alveolar damage with haemoptyses and intra-pulmonary haemorrhage; the nares may also be inflamed leading to epistaxis and septal perforation. (See further details under Benson and Bentley below).

Further harm may be caused by talc or starch used for diluting (or as 'fillers') with powdered drugs (for talc - see ps. 19.92 - 93).

References.
Frand et al. (1972) : Heroin induced pulmonary oedema.
Saba et al. (1974) : Pulmonary complications of narcotic abuse - studied 45 patients. In 24 who had overdoses of barbiturates, tranquillisers, etc., 21 had normal radiographs and three pneumonia which cleared in a few days. In 21 with overdosage of heroin or pethidine (methadone), eight had pulmonary oedema on chest radiographs.
Wilen et al. (1975) : Roentgenographic manifestations of methadone-induced pulmonary oedema.
Merhar et al. (1981) : Cervico-thoracic complications of IV drug abuse.
LiPuma et al. (1982) : Nitrous oxide abuse.
Goldberg et al. (1987) : Pneumomediastinum associated with cocaine abuse - review.
Eurman et al. (1989) : Chest radiography in patients with chest pain and dyspnoea related to 'crack' cocaine smoking.
Hoffman and Goodman (1989) : Pulmonary oedema in cocaine smokers.
Forrester et al. (1990) : 'Crack lung' - four cases with an acute pulmonary syndrome.
McCarroll and Roszler (1991) : Lung disorders due to drug abuse.
Brander and Tukainen (1993) : Acute eosinophilic pneumonia in a heroin smoker.
Benson and Bentley (1995) : Lung disease caused by drug addiction - may be inhaled as powder (**cocaine** into the nose, where it may cause ischaemia and necrosis of the nasal mucosa) in smoke or fumes, ingested or taken parenterally - the last being the most dangerous from transmitted infection - HIV and hepatitis. **Crack** (free base cocaine) is a waxy substance and can be smoked. A hypersensitivity reaction may occur with diffuse alveolar or interstitial infiltrates, pulmonary oedema, barotrauma (with pneumomediastinum or pneumothorax). Many recover spontaneously, but others only after steroid treatment. Inhaled **cannabis** (marijuana) produces some dilatation of small airways, which may be of some benefit in asthma. After chronic use it impairs gas exchange to a similar degree to that seen with tobacco smoking. Smoking both together in a cannabis cigarette results in a fivefold increase in CO than with tobacco alone, also an increased tar inhalation. Squamous metaplasia of the bronchial mucosa occurs. **Opiates** (heroin, morphine, pethidine, etc.) lead to impaired consciousness and respiratory

depression, pulmonary congestion and bronchospasm or an acute eosinophilic pneumonia. IV they may lead to bullous degeneration esp. in the LLs, and talcosis with diffuse lung infiltrates.

Smith, G. et al. (1995) : Crack cocaine causing basal air trapping and basal perfusion defects on V/Q scan and mimicking pulmonary embolism.

Sullivan and Pierson (1997) : Pneumediastinum after freebase cocaine.

Johnson et al. (2000) : **Large lung bullae in marijuana (cannabis) smokers**.

Oxygen alveolopathy and bronchopulmonary dysplasia (hyaline membrane disease).

Even oxygen can be harmful in high concentrations and it becomes toxic to the lungs when the alveolar pressure exceeds half an atmosphere. It also harms the nervous system when the alveolar and arterial pressures exceed two atmospheres. High inhaled oxygen concentrations have two effects on the lungs - (i) promoting collapse by replacing the relatively insoluble nitrogen in the alveoli, and this may lead to hypoxia due to the collapsed areas not being oxygenated, and (ii) by free oxygen radicals irritating the endothelial and epithelial surfaces. At first oedema fluid is exuded, with macrophage proliferation. This is reversible, but if exposure is prolonged, fibrosis occurs and the lung may become permanently scarred.

Liebow et al. (1965) studying interstitial lung disease found that oxygen in high concentrations damages both the endothelium and the alveolar lining cells, particularly membranous pneumocytes (type I cells - p.24.14). Following the damage, hyperplasia of type II (granular) pneumocytes occurs and hyaline membranes give rise to fibroblastic proliferation, accompanied by interstitial infiltration and atypical hyperplasia. He found that a 'chronic' looking appearance (similar to fibrosing alveolitis) could occur in two weeks.

In young babies who have a reduced amount of pulmonary **surfactant** (phospholipids and surfactant proteins), excess oxygen may lead to hyaline membrane disease. In adults having prolonged assisted respiration, it may have a similar effect, but this is often associated with pressure effects giving rise to ARDS (see p. 8.13).

Northway et al. (1967) described chronic lung disease following ventilation of pre-term infants with severe idiopathic respiratory distress and Northway and Rosan (1968) termed it 'broncho-pulmonary dysplasia'. Northway et al. (1990) reported late pulmonary sequelae.

Tudor et al. (1976) termed it the 'idiopathic respiratory distress syndrome' and described three stages - (i) a fine miliary mottling throughout the lungs, (ii) coarser and more coalescent opacities, often with a clear demarcation of the bronchial tree, and (iii) more confluent shadowing as a result of lobar or lobular consolidation.

Fitzgerald et al. (1990) studied 20 infants with bronchopulmonary dysplasia and found that only half had the idiopathic respiratory distress syndrome (IRDS), with chest radiographs showing underaeration and homogeneous opacification of the lungs and 'air-bronchograms', before developing broncho-pulmonary dysplasia with hyperinflated lungs with multiple fine 'lace-like densities' throughout the lungs. They felt that IRDS is but one of the many radiological and clinical entities which precedes broncho-pulmonary dysplasia.

Cameron (1992) found that in infants under 1,500 g and ventilated for RDS, 15 to 45 % will develop broncho-pulmonary dysplasia. Chest radiographs often show progression from RDS, through interstitial emphysema to established BPD, which typically shows strands of opacification alternating with cystic emphysematous areas in a hyperinflated chest. BPD may also occur in term infants following meconium aspiration, congenital pneumonia and persistent foetal circulation.

Pressure effects (or barotrauma) also plays a part. In surfactant deficient lungs, positive pressure ventilation leads to overdistension of the distal airways, so that shearing forces are applied to the epithelium. Air leak may occur into the surrounding tissues manifesting as interstitial emphysema impairing gas exchange, the pulmonary circulation and pulmonary lymphatic drainage. Ventilatory support may need to be increased and pneumothoraces may follow. Lau and Lam (1991) noted that systemic air embolism could complicate ventilator therapy in hyaline membrane disease.

Respiratory infections (both bacterial or viral) may occur especially while the child is still intubated, and may lead to areas of consolidation. Pulmonary hypertension and cor pulmonale may supervene. Brain damage may occur from haemorrhage or ischaemia.

Most cases recover eventually showing the remarkable growth potential and regenerative power of the lungs, but some have some pulmonary insufficiency. Steroids have often been used in treatment. Animal surfactant products or synthetic surfactants (e.g. coloscleril palmitate - 'exosurf') are starting to be used, particularly as their use may improve oxygenation in a steady manner over a few hours, thus allowing the optimum adjustment of oxygen concentrations and ventilation settings - they are however very expensive.

<u>Further references.</u>
Pratt (1958) : Pulmonary capillary proliferation induced by oxygen inhalation.
Northway (1979) : Observations on bronchopulmonary dysplasia.
Joffe and Simon (1969) : Pulmonary oxygen toxicity in the adult.
Hall and Margolin (1972) : Oxygen alveolopathy in adults (six cases).
Burrows and Edwards (1970) : 7 children - pulmonary oedema of alveolar pattern or fine miliary or granular appearance with air bronchogram - similar to hyaline membrane disease.
Siegle et al. (1976) : Air embolus following pulmonary interstitial emphysema in hyaline membrane disease (two cases - mediastinal, intravascular and intracardiac spread plus literature review).
Tudor et al. (1976) : The value of radiology in IRDS (337 cases with 116 autopsies).
Mortenson et al. (1983) : Chest radiography and pulmonary mechanics in ventilator treated low birth weight infants.
Jackson (1985) : Pulmonary oxygen toxicity review.   Denison (1987) : The effect of oxygen on the lungs.
Sinclair and Bracken (1992) : Effective Care of the Newborn Infant.
Wilsher et al. (1990) : Pulmonary **surfactant** appears to suppress lymphocyte responses to mitogens rather than antigen presenting monocytes.   **Surfactant** - Hospital Update - Dec. 1992.
Abman and Groothius (1994) : Pathophysiology and treatment of bronchopulmonary dysplasia. Barotrauma is an important contributor to acute lung injury - high peak pressures and large tidal volumes are particularly harmful to developing lungs. High concentrations of inspired oxygen lead to pulmonary oedema and protein leakage in turn inhibiting the surface tension-lowering properties of surfactant, decreased lung compliance, collapse, etc. The resultant ischaemia also stimulates the production of toxic oxygen metabolites, leading to worse lung disease. The acute phase is followed by a marked proliferative response.
Cochran et al. (1994) : Pulmonary interstitial emphysema and type of chronic lung disease.
Oppenheim et al. (1994) : Value of CT in identifying pulmonary sequelae in survivors - multifocal areas of hyperaeration (with thinned vessels) numerous linear opacities facing triangular subpleural opacities on consecutive sections and **no** bronchiectasis.
Owens et al. (1995) : HRCT of BPD in long-term survivors - all showed some abnormalities including reticular densities, subpleural linear strands, areas of increased transradiancy (BO), small airways disease and bronchiectasis.
Howling et al. (2000) : HRCT of pulm. sequelae in adult survivors - multifocal areas of reduced lung attenuation & perfusion, bronchial wall thickening & decreased bronchus to pulm. artery diameter ratios.

Smoke inhalation.
   This is becoming a major cause of death in aircraft and other disasters (e.g. Manchester airport, 1986 and Kings Cross Underground station in Nov. 1987 - 31 deaths), factory, hotel and house fires, etc. Fortunately the fire in the Channel Tunnel in Nov. 1996, produced no fatalities.
   Thermal injury may occur to the oropharynx and tracheobronchial tree, leading to burns in these organs and the loss of mucociliary clearance. The lungs are affected mainly as a result of inhalation of the products of combustion (including organic acids, aldehydes, etc) causing: (i) airways obstruction as a result of acute spasm or tracheo-bronchitis, (ii) damage to the lung parenchyma, leading to pulmonary oedema, lung consolidation, etc., (iii) carbon monoxide poisoning and (iv) inflammatory metabolites released from surface or other wounds. Respiratory insufficiency may occur early or late. Secondary infection, ARDS (see p.8.31) and pulmonary emboli not uncommonly complicate the more severe injuries. Dyspnoea may also lead to a pneumothorax or pneumomediastinum. Some patients may be asymptomatic for up to 24 hours, before cyanosis and dyspnoea becomes apparent.
   It is important to note that chest radiographs may be **normal** in the acutely injured - **only about 50% showing signs of oedema or linear collapse on acute admission radiographs** (see references below).
   Much of the increased incidence in lung damage is due to the increasing use of plastics for wall tiles, floor coverings, aircraft cabin linings and fittings, plastic foam in cushions and upholstery, etc.; these quickly produce toxic smoke and gases when they ignite. To help combat the problem the British Government in Jan. 1988 (following pressure from Chief Fire Officers) banned the use of highly inflammable foam filling for upholstery. The Consumers Association also showed just how quickly foam filled upholstery fires can get out of control, often in 60 to 90 seconds, the polyurethane liquefying and burning fiercely with the production of dense acrid smoke - they also showed the necessity of **getting as close to the floor or ground as possible**, when escaping from a fire, to avoid toxic inhalation.

Blast injury - the effects of an explosive positive pressure wave may be conducted by air or water, but the lethal radius is **three times greater in immersion** than in an air blast. Many without evidence of an external injury may be found dead within the vicinity of an explosion and often have frothy blood-tinged mucus around the mouth or nose. In those surviving, pathological findings range from localised intra-pulmonary bleeding to widespread haemorrhage with ulceration of the lungs or bronchi and the production of interstitial emphysema, a pneumomediastinum, pneumo- and/or haemothorax. Radiologically emphysema, pleural changes, lung consolidation (patchy opacities, or larger areas), congestion and cavitation may be found. Cardiac, diaphragmatic and abdominal damage may also be present.

Other toxic gases and fumes.

Many gases and fumes may damage the lungs. These include NO_2, O_3, NH_4, Cl, H_2S, SO_2, (see also references below) strong acid or metal fumes - HCl, H_2SO_4, HnO_3, nitrous fumes, Zn, Cd, Hg or Be fumes, organic solvents such as toluene, war gases, including phosgene, chloropicrin, mustard gases (e.g. bis 2-chloro-ethyl sulphide) and lewesite (2 chlorovinyl dichlorarsine). Some towns in Eastern Europe have been particularly badly affected by smoke and fume emissions (e.g. Copsa Mica in Romania, where the whole town was covered in 'black powder from the sky', as well as its air filled with hydrogen sulphide fumes).

Other gases such as CO, arsine, 'nerve gases' (mainly organo-phosphorus cholinesterase inhibitors) and dioxin (ethylene dioxide) produce their effects by absorption.

When inhaled, each gas produces a different pathological result. Phosgene acts chiefly on the alveolar walls producing oedema, whilst mustard gas and lewesite cause rapid acute inflammation involving the large as well as the smaller bronchi. The oedema may be very severe, so that the victims 'drown' in their own pulmonary oedema fluid. In less severe cases, the damage caused by the gas may lead to secondary pneumonia (bacterial or viral or a mixture) and this may be slow to clear, and may in turn lead to bronchiolitis obliterans (ps. 3.25 - 27) or emphysema.

Lewesite has never been used in warfare, but some accidental cases of poisoning have occurred. An antidote 'British anti-lewesite' (a chelating agent was developed in 1944 by Sir Rudolf Peters - (later Professor of Biochemistry in Oxford).

With nerve gases, prostigmine and atropine at the time of the injury may help to mitigate their effects.

Some examples of serious gas poisoning have been: -

(i) **First World War** - the Germans started gas warfare with **chlorine** at Ypres in 1915. It was later used by the British at Loos. In 1917 the Germans used **mustard gas, cyanide and phosgene** in artillery shells. Poison gas produced 168,000 casualties by the end of the war.

(ii) **Vietnam War - dioxin** (ethylene dioxide) used by the USA largely as a defoliant.

(iii) **Seveso (Italy)** - accidental discharge of **dioxin**.

(iv) **Flixborough, Lincs.** (June 1974) - explosion & **chlorine** leak from a plant - 29 deaths.

(v) **Bhopal, India** (Dec. 1984) - over 500,000 were exposed to a leak of a cloud of **methyl-isocyanate** gas from the Union Carbide pesticide plant in the town. 2,500 to 3,000 were killed, some dying suddenly before the onset of pulmonary oedema, probably due to the concomitant production of H_2S. 50,000 were blinded and up to 400,000 still suffer from memory impairment, motor function disabilities, chest pain, breathlessness, eye problems or chronic depression. $ (US) 470M was paid in compensation in 1989. (For later reports see BMJ, 1994, Cullinan et al., 1997 and Beckett, 1998 - "persistent small airways obstruction among survivors ...may be attributed to gas exposure.").

(vi) **Iran/Iraq War** (1982 - 1988) - many thousands were killed or maimed by **mustard gas**, particularly in Iran and among the Kurds. Skin burns may occur from droplets, particularly in areas of increased heat or moisture. Blistering occurs but is often delayed for up to 48 hours, and is most marked at about seven to ten days. Gas and droplets may be inhaled, leading to damage to the tracheal and bronchial mucosa, often with severe narrowing of the major airways and secondary pneumonia. Endobronchial and endotracheal splinting was used in some cases to treat this - see p. 24.45. It is fortunate that this gas was not used in the 1991 Gulf War.

Silo-filler's disease is caused by nitrogen dioxide (from the reduction of nitrates in fresh ensilage) can lead to acute bronchiolitis and pulmonary oedema; bronchiolitis obliterans may be a late complication (see also p. 3.30 and Illus. **SILO-FILLERS DISEASE**).

Air pollution and health (see also Thames Valley Chest - p. 3.26).

Winters in London and other large towns in the UK used to be marked by fogs, contaminated with smoke and SO_2. These caused many deaths in the elderly, the debilitated and babies. Following smoke control under the 1956 Clean Air Act and the reduced use of coal for household heating, these problems have largely abated. However pollution problems associated with NO_2 and CO have increased. Both are produced during combustion and fermentation processes. In 1991 motor vehicle emissions accounted for >50% and power stations >25% of total UK NO_2 production. Many towns (both in the UK and elsewhere e.g. Athens) are attempting to reduce such pollution by restricting access to motor vehicles.

Both SO_2 and NO_2 as gases and microparticulates from diesel engines appear to be triggering asthmatic attacks and some estimate that over 20,000 people may die annually in the UK as a result of vehicle emissions. NO_2 is also a key contributor to the formation of ozone, of particular concern on warm windless sunny days (see also Cameron and Maynard, 1992).

Further references.

Smoke inhalation

Schatzki (1943) : Fleischner's lines, consolidation pattern of pulmonary oedema, and miliary shadows in lung injuries following the Coconut Grove nightclub fire of 1942.

Achauer et al. (1973) : Pulmonary complications of **severe burns** - (i) **acute respiratory distress**, due to smoke inhalation, carbon monoxide poisoning or from airway obstruction,

(ii) **asymptomatic for 24 hours**, followed by tachypnoea, cyanosis and hypoxia lasting up to five days. Chest radiographs may show fluffy infiltrates, which may progress to **bronchopneumonia and ARDS**, which in turn may need assisted respiration, and (iii) **pneumonia and pulmonary emboli as late complications**.

Kangarloo et al. (1977) : The radiographic spectrum of pulmonary complications in burn victims.

Putnam et al. (1977) : Radiographic manifestations of acute smoke inhalation.

Teixidor et al. (1983a) : Pulmonary complications in burn patients.

(1983b) : Reviewed 62 cases of smoke inhalation and noted that in many there may be a normal chest radiograph at first, proceeding to alveolar fluid, peribronchial cuffing and peri-vascular fuzziness.

Lee, M. and O'Connell (1988) : Studied 45 cases of smoke inhalation following a fire at a discotheque in Dublin and found peri-bronchial thickening and sub-glottic oedema (shown by endo-tracheal swelling below the larynx), followed by pulmonary oedema and patchy consolidation especially in the peri-hilar regions and upper zones. Pneumonia may follow as may an empyema, etc.

Fogarty et al. (1991) : Long-term effects of smoke inhalation in survivors of the King's Cross Underground station fire. They studied 14 patients who had inhaled considerable quantities of smoke and concluded that smoke inhalation may be associated with injury to the small airways.

Wittram and Kenny (1994a) : Studied the chest radiographs of 29 patients admitted with acute inhalation injury and burns, who required ventilatory support. 13 had signs of inhalation injury which included **oedema of nodular, consolidatory and interstitial pattern and linear collapse**, but concluded that in most of the remainder **significant lung damage may be present even with a normal chest radiograph.**

Hirsch and Bazani (1969) : **Blast injury of the chest**.

Whitaker (1946) studied the **effects of toxic gases on the lungs and their radiographic appearances**. He found that lethal gases may be divided into two groups - (i) those which have a general effect, and which (although they area absorbed through the lungs) do **not** produce any change in the lung parenchyma (e.g. the war gas arsine), and (ii) those whose maximum effect is on the skin and respiratory tract.

NO_2 and Silo-filler's disease.

Lowry and Schuman (1956) : A syndrome caused by nitrogen dioxide.

Cornelius and Betlach (1960) : Silo-fillers disease.

Ramirez and Dowell (1971) : Silo-fillers disease - nitrogen dioxide induced lung injury.

Scott and Hunt (1973), Morrisey et al. (1975), Horvath et al. (1978) - 23 pts. reviewed.

Department of Health (1993) : Advisory Group on the Medical Aspects of Air Pollution Episodes. Third report: oxides of nitrogen. London, HMSO.

Sulphur Dioxide.
Charan et al. (1979) : Pulmonary injuries associated with acute sulphur dioxide inhalation.
Advisory Group in the Medical Aspects of Air Pollution Episodes (1992) : SO_2, etc. - may trigger asthma.

Metal fumes.
Langham Brown (1988) : **Zinc fume fever** - widespread small nodules in the lungs, becoming confluent and ill defined in some areas - similar to allergic alveolitis or acute fungus infection.
Hashimoto et al. (2001) : Pulmonary CT findings in acute **mercury vapour** exposure - all resolved.

Polymer fume fever.
Harris (1951)
Robbins, J. and Ware (1964) : Pulmonary oedema from Teflon fumes.
Evans (1973) : Pulmonary oedema from PTFE fumes.   Williams et al. (1974) : Not so benign!
Blandford et al. (1976) : PTFE fumes from overheated non-stick frying pan affecting owner and cockatiel.
Purser (1989) : Toxicity of PTFE thermal decomposition products.
Zanen and Rietveld (1993) : Fumes from overheated PTFE component in a microwave oven. caused the death of two parakeets and acute dyspnoea with changes lasting over a month in their owner. (10% CaCl aerosol, O_2 and steroids may be helpful in treatment).

See also references to bronchiolitis obliterans ps. 3.25 - 28.

THORACIC DISEASE PRODUCED BY SOME DRUGS AND CHEMICALS.

(a) Drugs.   Several drugs (probably more than 200) may produce lung changes.
In some patients there may be a clear temporal relationship between taking the drug and the onset of symptoms, whilst in others there may be a time-lag of several years. Some drugs are intrinsically toxic (e.g. cancer chemotherapeutic agents) and their effects may be dose-related or cumulative. Other drugs appear to cause pulmonary abnormalities in a few patients due to hypersensivity or an idiosyncratic response. As the lung can only respond to insult in a few ways, most drug reactions can be classified according to their pathological response e.g.: -
> pulmonary fibrosis
> eosinophilia/ hypersensitivity reaction with bilateral air-space or ground-ground glass shadowing- clearing can be rapid with cessation of treatment.
> ARDS
> COP/BOOP - see ps. 3.31-33
> SLE - type reaction, and
> non-cardiogenic pulmonary oedema.

Those causing a **hypersensitivity** type of reaction (e.g. azathioprine, bleomycin, methotrexate, procarbazine, carmustine & nitrofurantoin) tend to produce oedema or ground-glass shadowing first, followed by alveolar consolidation, fibrosis and pleural reaction. With these many of the changes are reversible, in the early stages, by stopping the drug and the use of steroids. Clearance is often rapid.
A **bronchiolitis obliterans** type of picture is given by e.g. **penicillamine** and **sulphasalazine** which cause severe air-flow impairment and on HRCT dilatation of the smaller bronchi, bronchial wall thickening, attenuation of vessels and mosaic oligaemia.
Further details of some of the drug effects are given below.
In addition drugs that cause immunosuppression may lead to opportunistic infections and induce neoplasms.

Adriamycin (used for cancer chemotherapy) - cardiomyopathy. It may also cause the reactivation of radiation pneumonitis - see ps. 6.6 & 11.22.

Amiodarone (an antiarrhythmic) is concentrated in pulmonary parenchymal cells, deranging lipid metabolism and producing 'foamy macrophages' in 5 to 10% of pts. (esp. if >400mg/day). It causes infiltrates or high-density nodular shadows (on CT due to iodine deposition), especially in the upper zones. The upper zone preponderance may be due to the more alkaline environment of the lungs (see p. 1.47 and Gurney and Schroeder, 1988). In other cases an appearance similar to fibrosing alveolitis may be seen, and this may be generalised or basal in distribution. It may also cause neuropathy. The liver and lymph nodes may also show increased density (due to the iodine content) after prolonged treatment. Illus. **AMIODARONE, Drug reaction Pt. 2a-b** shows two CT views of high-density posterior lung infiltrates due to amiodarone.

Nicholson and Hayward (1989) performed HRCT on 9 cases and showed (a) areas of avascularity or air trapping anteriorly in the upper lobes, and (b) non-dependent basal peripheral high density pleuro-parenchymal linear shadowing.

Supine   Prone

Anticoagulants - haematoma of lung, mediastinum, oesophagus, haemothorax, etc. - also tracheo-bronchial calcification in children - see ps. 3.6 - 7.

Anti-haemophilic globulin (factor VIII) - nodular pulmonary oedema (see p. 8.7).

Azathioprine - an acute lung reaction to this is shown in Illus. **AZATHIOPRINE, Drug reaction 3a-c.**

BCNU (or **Carmustine**) - used for treating brain tumours, myeloma, lymphomas and melanoma) may cause acute pulmonary shadowing as well as its main effects on the bone marrow, GI tract and liver. Lung fibrosis may be found several years after the treatment has been given.
Taylor (1989) found six patients with the peripheral shadowing running parallel to the outer pleural surface, i.e. in the cortical and sub-cortical parts of the upper part of the lung and looking like 'acute fibrosis'.

Bleomycin (used in cancer chemotherapy with neuroblastomas, testicular tumours, etc.) has an advantage in not producing myelosuppression. Lung changes occur in 2 to 20% of patients treated, with 1% being fatal. The drug causes swelling of capillary and endothelial cells leading to oedema of the interstitium, together with necrosis of type I pneumocytes and proliferation of type II. Eventually widespread fibrosis occurs in the interlobular septa, the alveoli, perivascular and peribronchial spaces. Radiographically, shadowing is seen particularly peripherally in the costo-phrenic angles, and at the lung bases, but it may spread upwards. On CT sections, the shadowing appears mainly subpleurally, and is peripheral, basal and posterior. It varies from strands or ill-defined nodules to more extensive shadowing and fibrosis. Confluent shadows may mimic tumour recurrence.
   Provided the drug is withdrawn before severe damage has occurred, bleomycin toxicity may be reversible. In most cases, with minor or moderate shadowing, complete resolution occurs in about nine months, whilst residual changes tend to persist in those with more severe damage. For examples see Illus. **BLEOMYCIN.**
   Prior radiotherapy may potentiate its effect.

Busulphan (used for treating some types of leukaemia) - diffuse progressive pulmonary fibrosis (Illus. **BUSULPHAN**) - also neoplasm. May have an additive effect with **melphalan** (see references).

Cyclophosphamide (used in cancer chemotherapy and for treating or preventing rejection of e.g. renal transplant) may cause lung fibrosis with hilar elevation. It may also predispose to opportunistic pneumonia (and severe cystitis) - Illus. **CYCLOPHOSPHAMIDE, Lymphogranuloma Pt. 1c.**

Cytosine-arabinoside (used for treating leukaemia and reticuloses) - may cause lung infiltrates, pneumonitis or fibrosis spreading up from the lung bases and pleural effusions. (see Tham et al., 1987).

Ergotamine (used for treating migraine) - pleuro-pulmonary fibrosis.

Gold compounds - used for treating rheumatoid arthritis may cause or potentiate pulmonary oedema and fibrosis, and may partially clear after cessation of the gold treatment (also Au[198] for treating malignant pleural effusions) - Illus. **GOLD.**

Hexamethonium - pulmonary oedema.

Methotrexate (used for cancer chemotherapy, in rheumatoid arthritis, temporal arteritis and some skin conditions e.g. psoriasis) may cause a reversible hypersensitivity reaction, producing patchy or more generalised lung infiltrates. Resolution may be aided by steroids, and is usually rapid. The author has encountered a few such cases with lung infiltrates (Illus. **METHOTREXATE, Drug reaction Pts. 11-13**). Its use may also lead to the development of multiple primary neoplasms (Illus. **METHOTREXATE, Renal ca deps Pt. 39a-c**).

Methysergide (used for treating migraine) - mediastinal and retroperitoneal fibrosis (**DRUG REACTION, Methysergide Pt. 1a-b**).

Nitrofurantoin (used as a urinary tract antibiotic) - may cause pulmonary oedema and diffuse pulmonary interstitial thickening - and may clear with cessation of treatment. Sparing of clusters of secondary lobules may be seen on CT. (Cameron et al., 2000, two cases producing BOOP - considerable clearing of CT changes following steroids - see also Ellis, 2000, - below - BOOP - like nodules; Fawcett and Ibrahim, 2001 - further case. NB - COP/BOOP is discussed on ps. 3.31-34).

Penicillamine - BO type of reaction with severe air-flow impairment - see above.

Phenytoin - pleural effusion.

Prozac (fluoxetine - used for treating depression of obsessive compulsive disorders) may occasionally cause lung fibrosis or bronchiolitis obliterans. Shadowing with small areas of fibrosis may be seen in the midzones.

Steroids - excessive mediastinal, etc. fat deposition, osteoporosis, also bone decalcification, fractures & infarcts Illus. **STEROID HIP**.

Sulphomamides (including sulphasalazine - see above - used for treating ulcerative colitis).

Tocainide - an anti-arrhythmic.

Trimethoprim - nodular oedema (see Higgins and Niklasson, 1990).

Others which may harm the lungs include include :
Aminorex (see p. 7.18), **Chlorambucil, Cyclosporine** (see p. 5.36), **Diphenylhydantoin, Isoniazid, Nitrosoureas, Pentolinium, Procarbazine, Ritalin** (p. 19.95), **Tricyclic agents and Vincristine.** For IV drug abuse (**cannabis, cocaine, heroin**, etc.) see p. 19.105.

(b) Chemicals affecting the lungs include :

Bordeaux mixture (copper sulphate and lime), **household cleaners, insecticides, etc.**

Paraquat (gramoxone) poisoning - patients may die acutely from local corrosive effects on the throat or oesophagus, sometimes leading to perforation (see Ackrill et al., 1978) or from lung and/or renal damage. Davidson and Macpherson (1972) reported three cases in the UK and two with lung changes died. Lung disease is due to a progressive fibroblastic reaction, which in most cases is fatal. The renal disease may recover if the patient in maintained on dialysis. The toxic effects are thought to be the result of oxygen radicals (superoxide ions) which destroy cell membranes.

Im et al. (1991, from Korea) studied 42 cases of paraquat ingestion with abnormal chest radiographs. Common findings included diffuse consolidation during the first week, pneumomediastinum with or without pneumothorax and cardiomegaly. Small cystic and linear shadows occurred after 1 to 4 weeks, leading to focal honeycombing. HRCT after nine months revealed localised fibrosis containing small cysts.

There was a suggestion that vitamin C in high dosage, prednisolone, cyclophosphamide and radiotherapy to the lungs might all help to reverse the lung changes (see Webb, D. et al, 1984 and Talbot et al., 1988, from Changhua Christian Hospital, Taiwan where there were 321 cases from 1977 to 1985), but a case treated in Oxford with radiotherapy, steroids and cyclophosphamide showed no response (Bloodworth et al., 1986).

The author has studied a few cases who also had renal failure - one is shown in Illus. **PARAQUAT**).

Some patients have been treated with single or bilateral lung transplantation (Herman et al., 1989 a & b).

Further references,
General
Ansell (1969) & Ansell et al. (1996) : Radiological manifestations of drug-induced disease.
Aronchick and Gefter (1991) : Drug-induced pulmonary disease, an update.
Ansell et al. (1997) : Imaging Drug Reactions and Toxic Hazards.
Morrison and Goldman (1979) : Radiographic patterns of drug induced lung disease.
Gockerman (1982) : Drug induced interstitial lung changes.
Sostman et al. (1981) : Diagnosis of chemotherapy lung.
Cooper et al. (1986) and Cooper (1990) : Drug-induced pulmonary disease.
Collis (1991) : Chemotherapy - related morbidity to the lungs.
Kuhlman, J.E. (1991) : The role of chest CT in the diagnosis of drug-related conditions.
Padley et al. (1992) : HRCT of drug induced lung disease - more sensitive than plain radiography.
Padley and Flower (1996) : Complications of percutaneous intervention in the thorax.
Padley (1997) : Imaging drug induced lung disease. >200 drugs can cause lung problems - are often unrecognised.
Patterns = chronic pneumonitis ± fibrosis, hypersensitivity, ARDS including capillary permeability, BO.

(See also under eosinophilic pneumonia ps. 19.59-60).

Adriamycin
McInerney and Bullimore (1977) : Reactivation of radiation pneumonitis by adriamycin.

Amiodarone
Meier et al. (1979) : Neuropathy during chronic amiodarone treatment.
Gefter et al. (1983) : Lung disease caused by amiodarone - a new antiarrhythmic agent.
Rakita et al. (1983) : Amiodarone pulmonary toxicity.
Olson et al. (1984) : Pneumonitis after amiodarone therapy.
Butler and Smathers (1985) : CT showed localised areas of consolidation with air bronchograms - these were bilateral and affected the posterior and apical segments of the upper lobes.
Martin and Howard (1985) : Amiodarone induced lung toxicity.
Standerskjold-Nordenstam et al. (1985) : Amiodarone pulmonary toxicity - chest radiography and CT in asymptomatic patients.
Pellissier et al. (1984) : Peripheral neuropathy induced by amiodarone.
Wood, D. et al. (1985) : Amiodarone pulmonary toxicity - two fatal cases following pulmonary angiography.
Kennedy et al. (1987) : Amiodarone pulmonary toxicity - radiology and pathology.
Kuhlman et al. (1987) : CT showed high-density pleuro-parenchymal changes.
Arnon et al. (1988) : Rounded RUL mass with irregular borders - cleared after stopping drug.
Miller et al. (1988) : Respiratory failure following amiodarone neuropathy and severe procaine amide intoxication.
Parra et al. (1989) : Patient with pulmonary infiltrates - dramatic improvement with steroids and stopping amiodarone, but recurred on steroid withdrawal and without restarting amiodarone.
Kuhlman et al. (1990) : CT in 11 symptomatic patients - high-density parenchymal-pleural lesions in 8, also wedge-shaped consolidations or collapse with associated pleural reaction at periphery and at bases. Increased liver and/or spleen attenuation in 10 and in cardiac muscle in two.
Ren et al. (1990) : HRCT of 11 lungs removed at autopsy showed intralobular septal and visceral pleural thickening - directly associated with mural and intra-alveolar foam cells.
Delany, S. et al. (1995) : Radiological features of amiodarone pulmonary toxicity.
Nicholson et al. (1994) : Measurement of tissue-bound amiodarone (contains iodine) and its metabolites by CT.
Millar (1996) : Amiodarone may cause iodine deposition at pleural bases posteriorly - can be detected on HRCT.
Jessurun and Crijns (1997) : Early diagnosis is crucial as the pulmonary toxicity is reversible, esp. as BO or BOOP.

Azathioprine
Weisenburger (1978) : Interstitial pneumonitis.

BCNU
Aronin et al. (1980) : Prediction of BCNU pulmonary toxicity in patients with gliomas.
Hasleton et al. (1990) : BCNU pulmonary fibrosis (drug can continue to cause alveolar wall damage for years).
Taylor, P. et al. (1991) : Chronic lung fibrosis following BCNU.

Bleomycin
Fleischman et al. (1971) : Bleomycin induced pneumonia in dogs.
Horowitz et al. (1973) : 5 cases with diffuse bilateral interstitial infiltration which developed six to 12 weeks after starting bleomycin treatment. Four were linear in type and one stippled. Three resolved and two persisted.
Einhorn et al. (1976) : Enhanced pulmonary toxicity with bleomycin and radiotherapy in oat cell lung cancer.
Jones, A. (1978) : Bleomycin lung damage: the pathology and nature of the lesion.

Glasier and Siegel (1981) : Multiple pulmonary nodules due to bleomycin toxicity.

McCrea et al. (1981) : Bleomycin toxicity simulating metastatic nodules to the lungs.

Nachman et al. (1981) : CT - bleomycin induced pulmonary fibrosis mimicking recurrent metastatic disease.

Balikian et al. (1982) : CT observations.

Vogelzang and Stenlund (1983) : Residual pulmonary nodules after combination chemotherapy of testicular cancer.

Bellamy et al. (1985) : CT evidence of lung damage (100 cases).

Doll, D. (1986) : Fatal pneumothorax associated with bleomycin induced pulmonary fibrosis.

Bellamy et al. (1987) : Qualitative assessment of lung damage using CT.

Rimmer et al. (1985) : CT observations.

Yousem et al. (1985) : Chemotherapy induced eosinophilic pneumonia - reaction to bleomycin.

Morcos et al. (1986) : The posterior distribution of lung changes may be due to the patient lying down during the IV injections, when the posterior aspects would be better perfused.

Santrach et al. (1989) : Nodules (histologically like BOOP) developed in three adult patients given chemotherapy for osteogenic sarcomas - patients may also develop a hypersensitivity reaction with prominent eosinophilic infiltrates.

Mills and Husband (1990) : CT of pulmonary bleomycin toxicity.

Oliff et al. (1990) : Mimics of metastases from testicular tumours.

Zissin (1992) : Other mimics of lung metastases - a reminder.

Oliff (1992) : Serum markers may help in differentiation, and if doubt persists an early CT scan can be useful.

Maher and Daly (1993) : Severe bleomycin lung toxicity - reversal with high dose corticosteroids.

Sikdar et al. (1998) : Pneumediastinum complicating bleomycin related lung damage - two cases.

Bromocriptine (for treatment of Parkinson's disease and similar to methysergide used for migraine).

McElvaney et al. (1988) : Posterior basal pleuro-pulmonary changes.

Busulphan and Melphalan.

Oliner et al. (1961) : Interstitial pulmonary fibrosis due to busulphan.

Heard and Cooke (1968) : Six of 14 cases of chronic granulocytic leukaemia treated with busulphan had alveoli containing fibrinous oedema which was converting to fibrous tissue.

Littler and Ogilvie (1970) : Detection of fibrosing alveolitis due to busulphan.

Schallier et al. (1983) : Additive pulmonary toxicity.

Dapsone

Jaffuel et al. (1998) : Eosinophilic pneumonia induced by dapsone.

Ergotamine and Methysergide (for headaches).

Graham et al. (1966) : Fibrotic disorders associated with methysergide therapy for headache.

Taal et al. (1983) : Pleuro-pulmonary fibrosis after chronic excess intake of ergotamine.

Gold salts (see also bronchiolitis - p. 3.25)

Weaver and Law (1978) : Lung changes after gold salts.

Halla et al. (1982) : Sequential gold and penicillamine therapy in rheumatoid arthritis.

Cooke and Bamji (1983) : Gold and pulmonary function in rheumatoid arthritis.

Household cleaners

Reisz and Gammon (1986) : Toxic pneumonitis from mixing different types.

Isoniazid

Miyai et al. (1989) : Isoniazid induced interstitial pneumonia.

Methotrexate

Everts et al. (1973) : Methotrexate therapy and pulmonary disease.

Sostman et al. (1976) : Methotrexate induced pneumonitis.

Urban et al. (1983) : Chemical pleuritis as a cause of acute chest pain following high dose methotrexate treatment.

Wright (1991) : Methotrexate etc. lung in patients with rheumatoid arthritis (7 cases shown by HRCT).

Hassan et al. (1993) : Acute pneumonitis associated with low dose methotrexate treatment for rheumatoid arthritis.

Trotman-Dickenson et al. (1993 - author's cases) : Acute pneumonitis with low dose methotrexate treatment for rheumatoid arthritis.

McKendry and Dale (1993) : Life-threatening pneumonitis occurs in about 3% of Pts. with RA.

Carroll et al. (1994) : Pneumonitis is more likely in pts. with pre-existing lung disease.

Mulherin et al. (1992) : Methotrexate pneumonitis in RA - dramatic response to corticosteroid e.g. 60mg prednisolone daily, but if diagnosis in doubt do bronchial lavage to exclude opportunistic infection.

Nitrofurantoin
Heap and Roebuck (1972) : Chronic looking changes which may be reversible.
Holmberg and Boman (1981) : Pulmonary reactions to nitrofurantoin in 447 cases.

Paraquat
Bullivant (1966) : Two cases of accidental poisoning in man.
Bier and Osborne (1978); Levin et al. (1979) : Pulmonary changes in paraquat poisoning.
Lee, S. et al. (1995 from Korea) : Studied 23 pts. (15 survived) with CXR's and HRCT if the CXR was abnormal. 7 had normal CXR's (with 1 death from renal failure). In the 16 with chest abnormalities, these began with ground-glass shadowing, leading to consolidation with bronchiectasis or irregular lines.
Lheureux et al (1995) : Survival in a case of massive paraquat ingestion - early administration of antioxidant therapy (deferoxamine & acetylcysteine) is useful combined with measures preventing digestive absorbtion or increasing elimination. CT at 6 days confirmed the presence of condensed infiltrates mainly posteriorly at the lung bases.
Satoh et al. (1996) : Two young men having chronic positive pressure respiration following attempted suicide with paraquat, developed a pneumediastinum and subcutaneous emphysema, and one a pneumothorax - both showed interstitial pulmonary emphysema on CT.
Licker et al. (1998) : Single lung transplantation for ARDS after paraquat poisoning.

Penicillamine - see under BO - ps. 3.25 - 27.

Pyrimethamine
Pang (1989) : Non-cardiogenic pulmonary oedema associated with pyrimethamine.

Sulphasalazine
Moss, S. and Ind (1991) : Pneumonitis - time recovery of lung function.

Tocainide (an antiarrhythmic)
Stein et al. (1988) : CT in lung disease due to tocainide.

INTERSTITIAL PNEUMONIA.

A number of conditions have been grouped under the heading 'interstitial pneumonia', which is used more commonly in North America. These include :

Usual interstitial pneumonia (**UIP**) more commonly termed **fibrosing   alveolitis** (or cryptogenic fibrosing alveolitis - **CFA**) in the UK. The Americans are now using new terms - '**idiopathic pulmonary fibrosis**', '**acute**' and '**non-specific interstitial pneumonia**'.

Desquamative interstitial pneumonia (**DIP**) which is considered to be a variant of fibrosing alveolitis in the UK (with a more cellular response).

Lymphocytic interstitial pneumonia (**LIP**) }   Both LIP and GIP probably represent the
Giant cell interstitial pneumonia (**GIP**)   }   result of unrelated immunological disorders.
[For bronchiolitis obliterans (**BO**) and cryptogenic organising pneumonia (**COP** in the UK) or bronchiolitis obliterans organising pneumonia (**BOOP** in the USA) see ps. 3.31-33].

The term '**interstitial   pneumonia**' implies a disease process in the lung which takes place predominantly in the supporting tissues, rather than within the alveoli. Liebow (1975) wrote 'while exudation into the alveoli occurs, this is a relatively minor component of the total response, and when healing takes place, either by restitution to the initial state (resolution), or by fibrosis, the lumina of the distal air spaces remain essentially patent'. He also felt that the term 'fibrosing alveolitis' stressed only one possible end result of earlier injury, ignored the possibility of resolution, neglected the fact that extra-alveolar interstitial tissues such as those of the bronchioles, septa and pleura are often involved, and paid no heed to the initial diversity in morphology, probable pathogenesis, natural history, and in associated laboratory and clinical manifestations, of conditions that can all terminate in interstitial fibrosis.

Liebow also noted that some acute diffuse interstitial pneumonias e.g. those caused by viral or mycoplasmal agents may give rise to pulmonary manifestations such as fever - these usually resolve. A few with an acute onset may continue into a chronic phase. However most chronic interstitial pneumonias begin insidiously, with increasing breathlessness (sometimes accompanied by a cough) and clubbing of the fingers and toes. In the idiopathic syndrome described by Hamman and Rich (1935 & 1944) these manifestations were present and patients died within a year. Many are less fulminant in their progression, and some patients survive for several years.

Several disease processes can eventually lead to **severe   pulmonary   fibrosis**. These include sarcoid, rheumatoid, scleroderma, DLE, asbestosis, the pneumoconioses, viral infections, drugs, fumes and toxic gases, chronic inhalation , radiation exposure, etc. In addition a diffuse fibrosis may occur without any overt stimulus. All of these and some infiltrations including eosinophilic lung, lymphangiomyomatosis and some neoplastic processes may progress to 'end stage' or 'honeycomb lung' (see also ps. 19.123 & 6.6).

In scleroderma which produces a similar radiological picture to fibrosing alveolitis, the fibrosis tends to be finer in character, compared with the coarser features seen in CFA, but this may be because the latter usually presents late.

Fibrosing alveolitis - (Illus. **FIBROSING ALVEOLITIS**).

The incidence of this disease appears to be increasing with over 1,500 deaths/ year in the UK. It is also often misdiagnosed during life and unreported at death. Most patients are in the age group between 40 and 60 and present with a dry cough and breathlessness, and many have a poor prognosis (50% dying in under five years from diagnosis - see also below). The histological findings are essentially those seen in the Hamman-Rich syndrome (see note above). Some cases have a known cause - inflammatory (virus or mycoplasma), chemical (oxygen in high concentration, ozone, high concentrations of CO_2, ARDS, drugs, chemicals, paraffin, paraquat, antibodies as in Goodpasture's syndrome, rheumatoid factor, DLE, scleroderma, neurofibromatosis, ankylosing spondylitis, dermatomyositis (Fergusson et al., 1983), a familial aetiology, etc., but in the **majority** the cause is unknown, although it may possibly be related to a previous **viral infection**. It also appears to be **made worse by smoking**.

Fibrosing alveolitis appears to be a type of **response of the lung to injury, with a spectrum ranging from fibrotic to a cellular or mixed picture**. The initial insult is one of diffuse alveolar damage, in which both lining cells and endothelium are damaged in varying degrees, while the integrity of the alveolar basement membrane is largely retained. Capillary endothelial cells and the type I alveolar cells are the most vulnerable to injury; damage altering their permeability and the ground-glass appearance shown on CT. Resolution commonly occurs following minor degrees of this type of injury, but the condition may become chronic and progress to fibrosis with honeycombing (particularly of the lung cortex) and multiple small 'cysts'. This results in a focal or more generalised loss of many alveoli, with atypical epithelium, smooth muscle proliferation in the interstitium and some proliferation of the pulmonary lymphatics.

The whole process is often non-uniform, with 'acute' changes in one area, and 'chronic' changes in others - likened to **"fires and glowing embers"**. The maintenance of lung function depends on the quality and quantity of relatively intact lung, which may be relatively small but just adequate, and patients with extensive damage on chest radiographs may have almost normal function tests if some normal lung is still present. Contrariwise fine diffuse fibrosis, well demonstrated by HRCT, may be associated with marked function test impairment, with marked loss of diffusing capacity. The patients may develop severe dyspnoea, hypoxia and cor pulmonale. Fibrosis tends to be more marked at the lung bases, and this is often accompanied by crepitations (or crackles) heard at the lung bases with a stethoscope, probably **corresponding with the ground-glass shadowing** (which is not always due to an alveolitic process and can be caused by thickened interstitium or fine fibrosis). These findings compare with the 'dry' lung bases found in patients with sarcoidosis and in most cases of external allergic alveolitis. Some patients have periods of **accelerated   deterioration**, whilst others go slowly downhill with '**smouldering disease**'. Ground-glass shadowing may resolve, but patients with fibrosis and lung destruction have a poor prognosis. Only in a few is the apparent '**burnt-out**' appearance really static.

Liebow found that oxygen in high concentration could lead to a rapidly progressive pulmonary fibrosis in experimental animals. This could take place in two weeks, whereas the Hamman-Rich changes took longer to develop. He also noted that mercury vapour may give rise to a similar picture, in which extensive interstitial fibrosis developed after three weeks. Scadding (1964) noted that fibrosing alveolitis is characterised by the presence of connective tissue matrix proteins, within the acinar regions of the lung, in association with a variable cellular infiltrate within the alveoli and interstitium. Yenokida and Crystal (1985) suggested that immune complexes may be generated as a result of an immune response to some extrinsic agent such as a virus. This has been further studied by Matsui et al. (1994) who studied collagen formation by rat type II alveolar cells immortalised by viral gene products. Jiminez (1994) felt that this work strongly supported the hypothesis that viral proteins may be involved in the development of certain forms of human interstitial lung fibrosis.

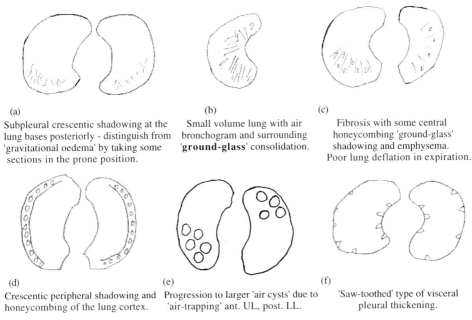

(a) Subpleural crescentic shadowing at the lung bases posteriorly - distinguish from 'gravitational oedema' by taking some sections in the prone position.

(b) Small volume lung with air bronchogram and surrounding **'ground-glass'** consolidation.

(c) Fibrosis with some central honeycombing 'ground-glass' shadowing and emphysema. Poor lung deflation in expiration.

(d) Crescentic peripheral shadowing and honeycombing of the lung cortex.

(e) Progression to larger 'air cysts' due to 'air-trapping' ant. UL, post. LL.

(f) 'Saw-toothed' type of visceral pleural thickening.

Fig. 19.15   Diagrams showing main CT appearances in fibrosing alveolitis.

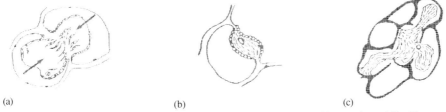

(a)   (b)   (c)

(a) Fibrin (arrowed) overgrowth from the alveolar epithelium is being invaded by round mural fibroblasts.
(b) Organisation has resulted in mural fibrous plaques.
(c) Simultaneous organisation in many alveoli has resulted in partial alveolar dissolution (After Spencer, 1977).

Fig. 19.16   Stages in the organisation of intra-alveolar exudate.

Radiological appearances.

     Plain radiographs often show that the lung volumes are reduced, together with a fine fibrosis, particularly at the lung bases, but in more severe cases spreading up into the mid and upper zones. The affected areas show a mixture of fine reticular, nodular and striate shadows throughout the affected parts of the lungs. Changes are usually symmetrical on the two sides, but the distribution in the vertical plane may be asymmetrical. Early changes may only be shown by CT.

     CT and HRCT are very useful for showing the distribution and extent of the disease, an indication of its activity and that not uncommonly considerable changes are present before they become visible on plain radiographs. In the early stages one may find shadowing similar to gravity orientated 'oedema' at the bases, together with sub-cortical crescentic shadowing. Later the sub-cortical shadowing becomes more marked, with fibrosis spreading into the underlying lung. The cortical acini become **cystic or honeycombed**, and show **'air-trapping'** in expiration with traction bronchiolectasis. As the condition gets worse, fibrosis (with thickening of the interstitium), honeycombing, cyst formation and emphysema, spreads more diffusely throughout the lungs, and the cysts tend to enlarge with worsening dyspnoea. Accompanying '**ground-glass**' shadowing is often a good indication of **continuing   activity** and that therapy with steroids and anti-inflammatory drugs may be helpful - see below. However those with both ground-glass shadowing and fibrosis are unlikely to show clearing. The pattern of disease although usually bilateral, is often asymmetrical. It is also usually more marked at the bases posteriorly, and in the anterior segments of the upper lobes.

The **pleural surfaces of the lungs often become** 'saw-toothed' particularly adjacent to the mediastinum. Dilatation of the smaller airways, bronchiolectasis and traction bronchiectasis may occur. **Moderately enlarged lymph nodes are not uncommon**, and appear to be enlarged from reactive hyperplasia (Illus. **FIBROSING   ALVEOLITIS, Pt.   35b**). Rarely patients may develop HPOA.

Prognosis and treatment.

    As noted above about 0.2 to 0.5 % of the population die from the disease each year in the UK, **most being cigarette smokers**, and the **5 year survival** of those with a predominantly fibrotic picture **is about 50%,** even with treatment - i.e. not much better than for lung cancer. Those with a more cellular type of reaction (on biopsy or HRCT) appear to have a better prognosis, some having reversible disease or disease with a reduced speed of progression. The mixed type also tend to fare badly. Therapy in the active or symptomatic cellular type cases tend to respond to high dose steroids and anti-inflammatory drugs (e.g. cyclophosphamide or azathioprine). Both HRCT (by showing the **ground-glass   shadowing**) and increased inhaled Tc^{99m} DTPA clearances (see p. 22.9) may be useful in indicating when active disease is present. Bronchoalveolar lavage for abnormal inflammatory cells may also be helpful as increased neutrophils may be seen in both early cases and those with late extensive and fibrotic disease. Eosinophils may also be seen in those with earlier and aggressive disease. **Smoking should be greatly discouraged**.

    However as Coker and Laurent (1997) noted "Recognition of the poor prognosis and long-term ineffectiveness of treatment with potentially serious side-effects has led many respiratory physicians to adopt conservative approaches to management." These authors studied the effect of cytokines (polypeptide mediators) in the pathogenesis of pulmonary fibrosis and concluded that there are compelling reasons to explore **anticytokine   therapeutic   approaches**. They quoted a current hypothesis that cytokines are released by resident lung cells (alveolar, epithelial and/or capillary cells) and recruited circulating inflammatory cells (monocytes, neutrophils, lymphocytes and eosinophils) in response to injury. These in turn stimulate the synthesis of increased amounts of collagen leading to pulmonary fibrosis.

    Patients with fibrosing alveolitis type changes in association with collagen diseases (e.g. systemic sclerosis) appear to have a better prognosis, and although they may look pathologically and radiologically similar, they have a different biological behaviour, with only about a quarter of the mortality seen with fibrosing alveolitis per se. However patients with systemic sclerosis + pulmonary hypertension tend to die more quickly (these also tend to lose their normal anterior/posterior density gradient on CT).

Cryptogenic Fibrosing Alveolitis and the Epstein-Barr Virus.

    Following reports that the E-B virus may give rise to lymphoproliferative disease and tumours in patients with AIDS (e.g. Burkitt's lymphoma and leiomyosarcoma - see p. 19.34), Egan et al. (1995) have suggested that the same virus may be an immune trigger or contribute to lung injury in CFA. They found that EBV replication may take place within type II alveolar cells, obtained by lung biopsy from immunocompetent patients with CFA. Hogg (1995) commented "If EBV infection can transform smooth muscle cells and allow them to proliferate, it is also possible that it might transform fibroblasts and produce the connective tissue changes that characterise FA. The virus presumably infects epithelial cells first, producing replicating infection, and then lymphocytes become infected as they circulate through the epithelium. Just how an infected epithelial cell or a lymphocyte might then infect and transform a smooth muscle cell or a fibroblast remains to be determined." Tsukamoto et al. (2000) concluded that EBV latent membrane protein 1 positivity may be associated with more rapid disease progression in idiopathic pulmonary fibrosis.

Desquamative interstitial pneumonia (more cellular than CFA and rare).
This was first described by Liebow et al. (1965). They studied 18 patients who had a condition somewhat resembling alveolar proteinosis, with an extensive desquamation of many large pneumocytes which appeared to be actively proliferating, both on the margins of and within the alveoli. There was no necrosis and relatively slight thickening of the alveolar walls.
Although DIP appears to be mainly consolidative, it contains a marked interstitial component, with an infiltrate of lymphocytes, plasma cells and some eosinophils. Interalveolar septa may be thickened, with oedema and varying amounts of fibrosis. The fissures and pleura may also be thickened. Alveolar lining cells are prominent, and desquamate into the lumina of alveoli or bronchioles, where they may be found in large numbers together with phagocytic pneumocytes. DIP differs from CFA and UIP by being essentially non-destructive and in some cases by being homogeneous throughout the affected parts of the lungs. It may progress to fibrosis, and is probably a different type of reaction to harmful agents or mechanisms.
As in CFA most cases have an insidious presentation, but some may have a mild fever or be associated with influenza. Many cases respond to steroid treatment.
Radiologically it gives rise to an area (or areas) of consolidation, which is often basal and may mimic infective pneumonia.
In accordance with the British view that DIP is a subdivision of CFA, Grant (1987) divided CFA into 'mural' (UIP) and 'desquamative' (DIP) types, if one or other of the histological patterns predominated, as the distinction may have some bearing on the nature of the radiographic abnormalities and perhaps on the response to steroid therapy. He also felt that all forms of fibrosing alveolitis may have an immunological basis, involving some form of autoimmune process. Many patients have non-specific auto-antibodies in the blood, although lung auto-antibodies have not been detected in the serum.
For alveolar cell carcinoma complicating DIP - see p. 5.1.

Lymphoid interstitial pneumonia.
Patients with LIP are usually symptomatic with cough, dyspnoea, weight loss, fever, etc. It is usually a benign, possibly allergic, lymphoid dysplasia which causes widespread lung infiltrates, similar to those seen with pseudo-lymphoma (see p. 5.29) or accentuate the normal broncho-vascular branches and inter-lobular septa to simulate lymphangitis carcinomatosa (ps. 8.11 - 13) i.e. interstitial and alveolar densities of varying severity with occasional nodular shadows. It may be related to lymphoma, be a precursor of this, or mask its presence. It may be found in patients with AIDS particularly children (ps. 19.32 - 33) and some autoimmune conditions e.g. Sjogren's syndrome (see p. 19.89 - about 25% are so affected), scleroderma, thyroiditis, myasthenia gravis, chronic active hepatitis, autoimmune haemolytic anaemia, DLE, pernicious anaemia, diffuse lymphoid hyperplasia, hypo- or macro-globulinaemia (ps. 5.46 - 48). Several workers have found evidence for a connection with both the Epstein Barr and AIDS viruses. It may be complicated by pulmonary amyloid (p. 5.43). Like other lymphoid lung diseases, it may originate anywhere in the extensive pulmonary lymphatic network. Aggregates of lymphoid tissue are present near the origins of lymphatic channels close to the respiratory bronchioles, and these are often affected (see also ps. 13.3 - 4) and may produce lung nodules. Nodules or infiltrates may be found in any part of the lung, especially the bases. Enlarged nodes or pleural effusions are rare. CT findings are non-specific and overlap lymphoid hyperplasia, atypical lymphoproliferative disease and some lymphomas.

Giant cell interstitial pneumonia.
This gives rise to an interstitial infiltrate like that seen with CFA (or UIP), but with many mononuclear cells within the alveoli, including many large multinucleated cells. Radiologically it may give rise to a severe mid zone bilateral fibrosis or infiltration. In some cases it appears to be related to tungsten carbide or cobalt dust ('**hard metal disease**' - see also p. 19.96).

Associated malignancy - (Illus. **FIBROSING ALV+NEO**).

Interstitial pneumonia may be associated with malignancy. In fibrosing alveolitis, tumourlets (see p. 24.18) are not uncommonly found, and may look like tiny squamous or other tumours. Some of these may progress to frank malignancy, the risk in smokers being increased about 20 to 30 times compared with that in non-smokers. The author has seen several such cases - seven cases are illustrated. Most had fairly obvious tumours; however, one had squamous cell carcinoma found submucosally on biopsy of the main bronchi, without any radiologically visible tumour, even on CT (Illus. **FIBROSING ALV+CA, Pt. 5a-b**). Another with an intractable pneumothorax complicating CFA, had an open lung biopsy at the time of a surgical pleurectomy, and this revealed several tumourlets (Illus. **FIBROSING ALV, Pt. 16a-b**). For references to other cases see below.

Several cases of adenocarcinoma or alveolar cell carcinoma have been reported in patients with fibrosing alveolitis complicating scleroderma (see also ps. 19.85 - 87). Such a case is illustrated in Illus. **SCLERODERMA, Pt. 8a-c**.

Further references.

(a) Fibrosing alveolitis.

Hamman and Rich (1944) : Acute diffuse pulmonary fibrosis in four patients.

Scadding (1964) : Termed the condition 'pulmonary fibrosis', but noted it was part of a group of disorders characterised by a progressive alveolar wall fibrosis and with variable intra alveolar and extrinsic exudate.

Carrington (1968) : The condition causes a cellular exudate in the interstitium, protein exudates in the air spaces and proliferation of the lining epithelium, gradually progressing to fibrosis and honeycombing.

Carrington et al. (1978) : Natural history and treated course of UIP and DIP.

Turner Warwick (1968) : Fibrosing alveolitis and chronic liver disease.

Turner Warwick et al. (1980) : Clinical features and their influence on survival - **a cellular type of reaction was the best prognostic factor**.

Fergusson et al. (1983) : **Dermatomyositis** may be associated with FA and may be classified into two groups :

(i) those in which the pulmonary disease runs an acute course, and in whom histologically there is an acute inflammatory infiltrate in the alveolar wall, which resolves with steroid treatment leaving minimal fibrosis, and

(ii) those who follow a chronic progressive course with a poor response to corticosteroids.

Wright, P. et al. (1984) : Cryptogenic fibrosing alveolitis - pattern of disease in the lung.

Bergin and Müller (1985) : CT of interstitial lung disease.

Müller et al. (1986) : CT of fibrosing alveolitis with pathological correlation.

Müller et al. (1987) : Found that reliable assessment of activity could only be shown by HRCT **which could also predict the findings on microscopy of biopsy material**.

Reticular densities were thought to represent fibrosis, and air-space opacification disease activity, and when the latter was present steroids usually resulted in clinical improvement or stabilisation.

Staples et al. (1987) : Usual interstitial pneumonia. CT, clinical and radiological findings.

Strickland and Strickland (1988) : HRCT study of 50 patients - views in expiration showed air-trapping, and prone views confirmed gravity orientated oedema. Lung disease was graded :

(a) minimal posterior basal crescentic shadowing.

(b) small peripheral cysts, sub-cortical shadowing and fibrosis with air trapping in the cortical alveoli and acini.

(c) widespread honeycombing and diffuse fibrosis.

The appearances differed from sarcoid and external allergic alveolitis, in that the pattern in these tended to be nodular and less peripheral. Also in sarcoid crescentic shadows are rare, and fine honeycomb pattern is not a feature. Peribronchial thickening is more prominent in sarcoid and external allergic aspergillosis, but not in fibrosing alveolitis. Pleural disease is uncommon, but has a distinctive appearance with tiny peaks, giving a '**saw-toothed**' appearance; this is most often seen peripherally, but may be seen adjacent to the mediastinum. Bilateral loss of lung volume and a consolidation-like picture may occasionally be seen.

Bergin and Castellino (1990) : **Moderate enlargement of mediastinal lymph nodes is common**, and is presumably related to the chronic inflammatory process. It may occur without superimposed infection and does **not** suggest that the patients necessarily have complicating lung cancer.

Hansell et al. (1990) : Disease activity in fibrosing alveolitis - HRCT grading ranged from parenchymal opacification alone (taken to reflect increased cellularity and therefore inflammatory infiltrate) through to a reticular pattern (representing fibrosis).

Hansell et al. (1991) : HRCT and broncho-alveolar lavage (BAL) cell profiles in fibrosing alveolitis - BAL neutrophilia is independently associated with extensive and fibrotic disease on CT.

Wiggins et al. (1990) : Combined fibrosing alveolitis and emphysema - value of HRCT in assessment.

Davies et al. (1991) : Atypical manifestations of fibrosing alveolitis on HRCT - usually a predominantly sub-pleural reticular pattern at the lung bases in the early stages, progressing to a widespread honeycomb pattern denoting end-stage disease. 21 (out of 142 patients seen over 6 years) had atypical features - focal disease or an asymmetrical or upper lobe distribution, pleural thickening, air bronchograms, or hyperinflation due to coexisting pulmonary emphysema.

Nishimura et al. (1992) : UIP - histological correlation with HRCT - studied 46 cases :
  (a) an accumulation of small cystic spaces with thick walls,
  (b) air bronchograms with areas of intense lung attenuation,
  (c) ragged pleural surfaces,
  (d) irregularly thickened pulmonary vessels,
  (e) bronchial wall thickening, and
  (f) slightly increased lung attenuation.

Air bronchograms in the areas of intense lung attenuation (i.e. microscopic honeycombing) corresponded to dilated bronchioles (> 1 mm in diameter) with fibrosis.

Irregularly thickened vessels and bronchial walls and irregular pleural surfaces were the result of fibrosis in the periphery of the secondary pulmonary lobules.

Areas of slightly increased lung attenuation seen on HRCT, correlated with patchy alveolar septal fibrosis or inflammation.

Tung et al. (1992) : Is open biopsy still necessary in fibrosing alveolitis ? - concluded that HRCT is highly accurate in showing the **ground-glass**, reticular and cystic air spaces in CFA, and suggested that the need for open lung biopsy in fibrosing alveolitis will diminish.

du Bois (1992) : Management of fibrosing alveolitis.

Hansell et al. (1992) : Studied the **predictive value of HRCT in CFA**, and pointed out that **prognosis is better** if there are no symptoms, a minor chest radiograph abnormality, a normal pO_2 and a **cellular type of lung biopsy**, but **when fibrosis is present it is no better than with lung cancer**. They also noted that although the pathology in patients with CFA and systemic sclerosis is similar, patients with the latter often have a better prognosis.

Wells et al. (1993) : Serial CT in 56 patients with fibrosing alveolitis (idiopathic or due to systemic sclerosis) - 'A **ground-glass** pattern **almost always regressed with treatment** when it was the **predominant abnormality seen at initial scanning**. However, when a ground-glass pattern coexisted with an equally extensive reticular abnormality, (the) extent of disease diminished with antiinflammatory treatment in fewer than half of the patients and increased despite treatment in a third of the patients. Thus in many instances a ground-glass pattern was apparently fixed or progressed in spite of therapy.' They concluded that the '**findings indicate that the prognostic significance of a ground-glass pattern depends on the extent of an associated reticular pattern and is independent of the extent and distribution of disease.**'

Akira et al. (1993) : Studied 29 patients by serial HRCT and found that **low dose steroids do not suppress alveolitis sufficiently to prevent continued deterioration of the alveolar structures due to honeycombing.** These were preceded by areas of ground-glass shadowing.

Lynch et al. (1995) : Studied 36 patients with idiopathic pulmonary fibrosis (IPF) and 27 with hypersensitivity pneumonitis (HP) - all diagnoses being confirmed or supported by open lung biopsy. Those with **IPF and UIP (CFA) were more likely to have honeycombing and peripheral or lower lung predominance** of disease and less likely to have micronodules, than were patients with chronic hypersensitivity pneumonitis. 3 patients with IPF and DIP had widespread ground-glass opacity indistinguishable from some cases of acute or subacute HP.

Mino et al. (1995) : Studied the enlargement of cystic spaces and honeycombing (in 16 pts. with FA) both with serial CT (6 to 43 months apart) and with microscopy of autopsy specimens (showing slit-like structures which could act as check-valves - between bronchioles and the cysts).

Gavelli et al. (1996 from Balogna, Italy) : HRCT of 29 pts. with UIP with follow up at 1 yr. Findings: poor accuracy of CXR in assessing the type of disease and global severity. 38% had enlarged nodes, also high incidence of pulmonary arterial hypertension and emphysema. Patients with ground-glass shadowing only were uncommon, but may respond to treatment with steroids and cyclophosphamide.

Hansell (1996) : **CXRs about 75% accurate for diagnosis - CT 90% with a better degree of confidence.**

Akira et al (1997) : CT findings during a phase of **accelerated deterioration** in pts. with idiopathic fibrosis may allow prediction of progress and response to treatment with steroids. Those with a peripheral parenchymal opacification corresponded to active fibroblastic foci. Pts. with supposed ARDS superimposed on FA are probably misdiagnosed and are really an acute flare-up of FA.

Franquet et al. (1998) : Pts. with CFA on steroid therapy had a significantly lower prevalence of mediastinal adenopathy than pts. who had not taken steroids.
Lee, J. et al. (1998) : The progression of honeycombing in UIP was faster in pts. with severe disease activity as measured by pathological score and the area of ground-glass activity.
Akira (1999) : CT & pathological findings in 19 pts. with fulminant forms of idiopathic interstitial pneumonia. All had progressive ground-glass shadowing, consolidation or both. Those with an acute exacerbation also had subpleural honeycombing. Follow up at 7 days showed a change from ground-glass shadowing to consolidation with distortion and a month later cystic lesions.

Hansell (1999) : (i) Theory of progression from a cellular type to a fibrotic appears to now be discarded;
(ii) Large lymph nodes seem to be related to the extent of the disease and not its activity;
(iii) Does the HRCT pattern predict the response to treatment?
(iv) Patients with ground-glass + fibrosis appear to fare just as badly as those with fibrosis, and the CT appearances do not alter with treatment;
(v) Ground- glass shadowing alone clears.

Reynolds and Hansell (2000) : **The interstitial pneumonias - understanding the acronyms**. Four categories of interstitial pneumonia are currently recognised:
1. **Usual interstitial pneumonia** - UIP.
2. **Non-specific interstitial pneumonia** - NSIP*
3. **Desquamative interstitial pneumonitis** and **respiratory bronchiolitis** with interstitial lung disease - DIP/BILD.*
4. **Acute interstitial pneumonitis** - AIP.*

* 2, 3 & 4 show a good response to steroids.
UIP is fibrotic from the outset with the fibroblast focus being central to the pathogenesis, and there is no early cellular phase - the pathogenesis is poor with little or no response to treatment.

Katzenstein and Fiorelli (1994) : **Nonspecific interstitial pneumonia** as a diagnosis in pathological specimens which did not conform to the typical findings seen in UIP, DIP, AIP or BOOP.
Park et al. (1995) :CT findings in 7 cases. & Kim et al. (1988) HRCT & pathological findings - ? characteristic CT appearance of bilateral patchy areas of subpleural ground-glass shadowing ± bilateral areas of consolidation with a predominance in inferior parts of lungs.
Cottin et al. (1998) : NSIP in a series of 12 patients.
Hartman et al. (2000) : Study of HRCT in 50 cases - variable appearance - 11 as above, 11 more consistent with UIP & 23 more consistent with other types of chronic infiltrative lung disease.
Coche et al. (2001) : NSIP showing a crazy paving pattern on HRCT.

(b) **Desquamative interstitial pneumonia.**
Tubbs et al. (1977) : DIP - cellular phase of fibrosing alveolitis.
Carrington et al. (1978) : Natural history and treated course of UIP and DIP.
Hartman et al. (1993) : HRCT in 22 patients with DIP - the predominant finding was the presence of ground-glass attenuation that particularly involved the middle and lower lung zones and was peripherally distributed in about half of the patients. About 30% showed a reticular and honeycomb pattern.
Herbert et al. (1982) : DIP in an aluminium welder.

(c) **Lymphoid interstitial pneumonia** (see also refs. under AIDS).
Halpin et al. (1972) : LIP.
DeCoteau et al. (1974) : LIP and erythrocyte sensitisation syndrome - deposition of immunoglobulins on the alveolar basement membrane.
Strimian et al. (1978) : LIP - review of 13 cases.
Herbert et al. (1985) : LIP identified as lymphoma of MALT (see also ps. 13.3 - 4).
Solal-Celigny et al. (1985) : LIP in AIDS.
Koss et al. (1987) : LIP - clinicopathological and immunopathological findings in 18 cases.
Teirstein and Rosen (1988) : Lymphoid interstitial pneumonia.
Oldham et al. (1989) : HIV associated LIP - radiological and pathological correlation.
Heitzman (1990) : Pulmonary neoplastic and lymphoproliferative disease in AIDS: A review.
Conces and Tarver (1991) : Non-infectious and non-malignant pulmonary disease in AIDS.
Amorosa et al. (1992) : Bronchiectasis in children with LIP and AIDS. Plain film and CT observation.
Travis et al. (1992) : LIP in 50 adults with AIDS.

Ichikawa et al (1994) : Lung cyst formation in LIP shown by CT.
Carignan et al. (1995) : HRCT appearances may be similar to post-transplantation lymphoproliferative disorders, but the most frequent finding was ground-glass shadowing.
McGuinness et al. (1995) : Ill defined 2 - 4 mm nodules were the predominant finding in HIV positive patients.
Johkoh et al. (1999) : LIP - HRCT in 22 pts. - predominant abnormalities were areas of ground-glass attenuation, poorly defined centrilobular nodules, subpleural small nodules, thickening of bronchovascular bundles, interlobular septal thickening, cystic air spaces and lymph node enlargement.

(d) CFA and malignancy.
Turner-Warwick (1980) : CFA and lung cancer (any cell type may be present).
Grant, I. (1987) : Up to 10% of patients with CFA may develop malignancy.
Blank (1989) : Illustrated squamous cell carcinoma complicating UIP.

Destroyed or end-stage lung - (Illus. DESTROYED LUNG or Illus. END STAGE LUNG).

(a) Unilateral.
When one lung is affected, the other is often normal or near normal. The diseased lung is usually small and may have a gross unilateral cystic bronchiectasis and/or fibrosis and loss of volume. It often results from a severe necrotising infection e.g. TB, other scarring pneumonia and may be a severe form of Swyer James (Macleod) syndrome (ps. 7.9 - 10). It may also follow infection following bronchial blockage by TB, etc. or radiotherapy (ps. 11.18 et seq.). In some cases (in developing countries and the under-privileged in developed countries) it may be related to the poor social conditions under which the affected people live. Secondary infection e.g. with aspergillosis may be found. A lung perfusion scan will show virtually absent perfusion in the affected lung.

(b) Bilateral
The term 'end-stage lung' is often applied to the sequelae of disease processes which destroy the lungs, and is characterised by the presence of honeycombing, extensive cystic changes or fibrosis. Such conditions include pneumoconiosis, other silicoses, asbestosis, fibrosing or allergic alveolitis and sarcoidosis. Small lung biopsies may not be specific as to aetiology, but CT can often give about a 90% accuracy as to cause.

(c) Ossification may take place in chronically damaged lung from many causes (see also discussion on calcification - ps. 6.19 et seq.).

Some references.
(i) Unilateral disease.
Gravesen (1961) : Two cases of 'destroyed lung'.
Steinberg and Lyons (1967) : Ipsilateral hypoplasia of a pulmonary artery in advanced bronchiectasis.
Lang et al. (1969) : Post-infective bronchiectasis of Polynesian children living in New Zealand.
Bateson and Woo-Ming (1976) : 12 cases in West Indians and Australian aborigines.

(ii) Bilateral disease.
Primack et al. (1993) : CT findings in 61 patients with end-stage lung disease - observers made a correct first-choice diagnosis in an average of 87% of cases.

(iii) General.
Gevenois et al. (1994) : CT demonstration of disseminated pulmonary ossification in end-stage pulmonary fibrosis.
Kazerooni et al. (1995) : Preoperative CT to check for unsuspected lung cancers in pre-lung transplant patients.
Erasmus et al. (1997) : Radiological issues in lung transplantation for end-stage disease.

Chapter 20 : **Techniques for Chest Radiography, Fluoroscopy, Tomography (including CT and MR) and Ultrasound.**

Chest radiography - High KV radiographic technique - (see also p. 1.1).
Historical - Kjellberg, in 1960 in Gothenberg, installed 190 KV, three phase, 150 HZ units in most of the radiographic rooms of the then new Salhgrenska Hospital. For chest work, 4 mm Al filters, stationary high ratio grids and automatic exposure timing were employed. Other Swedish centres used similar techniques (e.g. Nordenström, 1969a). The object was to show more of the lungs, particularly those areas hidden by the ribs, dome of the diaphragm and the mediastinum. The Swedish centres usually used a fine high ratio grid (see Illus. **HIGH & LOW KV - Heart 13a & b and APPTE02c - 200KV+ grid**).

Author's technique - From 1962 the author used 150 KV, 50 HZ, three phase generators, with high speed (10,000 rev/min) rotating anode tubes and small foci (0.6 mm^2). Copper filtration (using a thin - 0.32 mm brass sheet in front of the collimator) was added to remove the less penetrating radiation and hence render the x-ray beam relatively monochromatic and homogeneous. Scatter from the brass (effectively copper) was absorbed in the nine feet of air before the x-rays reached the patient. This heavy filtration resulted in an extremely low incident skin dose to the patient, of about one week's natural background for each PA view (see Appendix 1).
    Instead of using a grid between the patient and the cassette, scattered radiation was removed by an 'air gap' of 18 cm (7 ins). This avoided 'scatter-fogging' of aerated lung adjacent to opaque areas, as well as 'greying' of these, which happened when no scatter removing device is used. It was better than a stationary grid, in that no grid lines were present on the radiograph, and better than a moving grid because the 'air-gap' technique avoided the increased radiation that this would dictate. The exposure time was very short - approx. 3 msec. No automatic exposure control was needed, since only slight variation in time was needed for very thick or thin patients, the majority having a standard exposure time. The x-ray tube was dedicated to this work, and both it and the cassette holder were fixed in position, the patient's height being adjusted by the height of a round wooden seat affixed to an old dental-chair base with a hydraulic lift - Fig. 20.1.
    For best results it was essential that the central ray be carefully aligned to the centre of the cassette, and that the central part of the x-ray beam 'fired' horizontally. **No** attempt was made to centre over D4 or D 6 vertebrae (as is often advised in radiography books), and no adjustment of tube alignment was permitted once the initial accurate setting up had been carried out. Accurate alignment of the central ray was carried out by trigonometry, using a steel rule and triangulation with taut equal length pieces of cotton thread from (a) the x-ray tube ends vertically and (b) from a horizontally placed piece of wood (e.g. a metre rule) behind and at right angles to the vertical axis of the tube; and with equal length side markers on it (and placed parallel to the tube face) to the central point of the cassette holder, the position of the focal spot being noted on the anode disc by the observer's 'eye' in 'prep' - see Fig. 20.1 (b).
(Illus. **APPARATUS 21** shows a patient seated for a PA view).

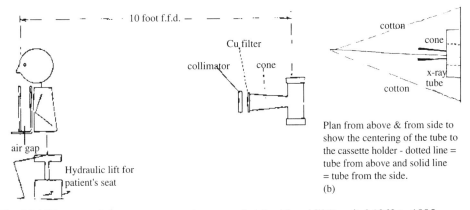

Fig. 20.1 Diagram of chest x-ray apparatus as used at the Churchill Hospital 1963 to 1995.

PA (AP), lateral and oblique views could be taken. For children, an extra cassette holder was used for direct chest contact with the cassette (a lower KV usually 90 being employed).

Extra lead-sheeting shielded the abdomen, but was really unnecessary owing to the high collimation of the beam with a long cone.

Further references.

Watson (1958) : First used an air gap technique and 120 KV.

Ardran and Crookes (1964) : Used only 90 KV for their 'high KV' radiographs, almost a misnomer as it was too low to adequately show the trachea or mediastinal anatomy, so their results were not really comparable. They surveyed largely fit Government employees, and not many patients with serious disease (particularly cancer) as in a hospital environment. They reduced the incident skin dosage by 25%.

Trout et al. (1975) : Studied various chest radiographic installations in the USA and found a 10 ft focus-film distance (f.f.d.) using an air gap gave only half the radiation exposure needed for a grid technique at 6 ft.

Herman et al. (1980) : Radiographed **lung**   **specimens** at 90, 140 and 350 KV (at the latter KV using condenser discharge equipment) and found that nodules < 3 mm in diameter and linear shadows < 0.3 mm thick were poorly or not seen at 350 KV. Larger nodules were well seen at all three KVs, the linear interfaces were clearer at 90 and 140 KV. **140 KV had the added advantage of superior penetration of overlying structures in vivo**.

In a further paper (1982) they also preferred 140 KV and an air gap to 350 KV.

Rossi et al. (1982) : Used a copper filter and reduced incident exposures by 30 to 40%.

Kelsey et al. (1982) : Noted better nodule detection at 120 KV than at 70 KV.

Coussement et al. (1984) : Used a 20 cm air gap technique and 3 to 4 metres f.f.d. for in-bed radiography, when the patients were wheeled to the x-ray department.

Manninen et al. (1984) : Wrote ' the results show clearly the superiority of the air-gap technique compared with the conventional grid technique, even with one third the radiation dose.'

Wandtke et al. (1985) : Wrote 'the use of rare-earth film-screen combinations and the application of **moderately high KV techniques (120 - 140 KVp)** are now standard practice, but several technical problems remain that undoubtedly account for some of the inaccuracy in chest radiographic diagnosis'.

Perry et al. (1985) : Questioned a distorted heart size on high KV radiographs, but the present author (Wright, 1986) thought this to be more accurate in relation to the whole chest.

Others who have used similar techniques include : Osborne (1982), Godwin (1984), Heelan et al. (1984), Fraser (quoted by Goddard, 1986) and Jolles et al. (1986).

Leitz et al. (1993) : In search of optimum chest radiography techniques.

Other methods which have been used for improving chest radiography.

Several other methods have been used or tried for improving chest radiography:

(a) Use of **linear accelerator** - Rigler (1965a) having moved from Minneapolis to Los Angeles, took some experimental radiographs with a 2 MeV linear accelerator to give an even greater high KV effect (see Illus. **HIGH & LOW KV - APPTE01 - 2MEV chest radiograph**).

Because even a thin lead sheet used as an 'intensifying screen' was not very efficient at this energy level, the method resulted in a heavy radiation dose to the patient - 75 Gy (0.75 Rad) per exposure. Lung detail was poor, but the lung outlines, bronchi and mediastinal shadows were well shown.

(b) **Condenser discharge 350 KV radiography** - this apparatus with a beryllium window was mainly designed for bedside radiography. Unfortunately the commercially designed machines were not very reliable. It also became apparent that at this KV, smaller lung nodules and line shadows were poorly seen (see references to Herman et al., 1980 & 1982 above).

(c) **Anatomical trough or compensatory filters** of varying shapes were made from aluminium, acrylic lead, cerium, etc. to try to produce more uniform chest radiographs, with limited success due to adverse scatter.

Some references.

Wieder and Adams (1981) : Trough filters improved visualisation of the tracheo-bronchial tree, retro-cardiac areas of the lungs and pleuro-mediastinal interfaces.

Gray et al. (1983) : Shaped lead loaded acrylic filters.

Kelsey et al. (1986) : Compared the detection of nodules or infiltrates on radiographs using shaped trough filters which shielded the lungs, with the results of conventional radiography. Exposures in both cases were made at 120 KV. They found no improvement in nodule or infiltrate detection and rib detail was adversely affected by scatter.

Manninen et al. (1986) from Finland : Used an anatomical compensation filter made of plastic impregnated with lead to prevent over-exposure of the lungs and to allow better exposure of the mediastinum. However it considerably increased the radiation dose to the mediastinum, compared with the high KV air-gap technique.
Guilbeau et al. (1988) : Use of a shaped filter had no overall diagnostic advantage.

(d) **Greater film latitude and film masking**, etc.

Kodak Ltd.(1983) tried using a film with greater exposure latitude to allow more detail to be seen in areas subjected to poor exposure and in 1993 produced their **Insight Thoracic Imaging System** using a dual emulsion zero-crossover film with different screen speeds on either side - one slow and the other six times faster. One side has constant contrast and is designed to optimise the lungs; the other has high contrast for the mediastinum and sub-diaphragmatic structures.

The Insight System was tried at the Churchill Hospital, Oxford, but did not appear to be as good as the high KV technique per se. It appeared to work best at up to 100 KV, but needed a 12 to 1 grid to avoid a rather flat film and was not as good at a f.f.d. of over 6 ft. It thus appears to have an advantage in departments with only conventional apparatus, but is inferior to a dedicated high KV technique. A different opinion was however given by Swensen et al. (1993), who felt that this system showed more clinically useful detail in the mediastinum and in the lung projected over the diaphragm and heart; in addition the radiation dose was about 30% reduced.

Further references.
Sorenson et al. (1981a & b) : Used a masking film in the cassette, to even out the exposure.
Logan et al. (1994) : Studying patients with sarcoidosis did not feel that the advantages of the Insight system compensated for the significant loss of parenchymal detail resulting from its use.
Kessel et al. (1994) : Insight resulted in improved quality of ITU chest radiography with reduced repeat rates.
Rottenberg et al. (1996) : Compared conventional radiography with the Insight system (in combination with a cassette incorporating a flexible grid) in 50 pts. in an intensive care unit. Insight provided better visualisation of lung parenchyma, mediastinal detail and position of endotracheal tubes, whilst CV catheters were generally better seen on conventional radiographs.
Sorenson and Mitchell (1987) : Used a tantalum air-interspace grid, wide latitude x-ray film and a LogEctronic printer for optical unsharp masking and contrast enhancement of the recorded image, and claimed improved contrast and detail across the entire range. The image was reversed (i.e. positive instead of negative) and nodules in poorly exposed areas were visualised, although poorly detected, in part due to the reversed image.

(e) **Photofluorography and image intensification** - 'Mass miniature radiographs' taken with an Odelca camera, via an intensifying screen, a curved mirror and a miniature camera (35, 70 or 100 mm) were commonly used in the 1940s to early 1960s when TB was more prevalent. It gave a high radiation dose (see Appendix 1) and because of this and the falling incidence of TB its use in mobile vans was phased out.

Philips have modernised this system using a horizontally orientated slit-shaped x-ray beam, which scans down the chest from an x-ray tube which nutates downwards in an arc during an exposure of 0.7 secs. The tube is manually coupled to a 2.4 x 40 cm linear caesium iodide intensifier, light from which is focused optically onto 100 mm film. No movement artefact is visible on the films. The incident skin exposure is approx. 0.05 mGy per exposure at 150 KV. Automatic exposure control over the whole of the film is made by measuring and modulating the emergent brightness of the intensifier, during an initial 2 msec 'flash' in the central position of the detectors. 2 mm Al or 0.5 mm Cu filtration may be employed.

Reference.   Eckelbrecht : (1987).

The x-ray tube nutates during the exposure - the central fan beam 'firing' at the linear intensifier, which moves downwards to cover the whole of the chest.

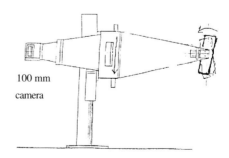

100 mm
camera

Fig.20.2   Philips 100 mm scanning camera for chest radiography -
(see also Illus. **ANATOMY Pt. 1a**).

Another approach has been to use a large size image intensifier, coupled to a 100 mm film camera and one has been used at London Airport, Heathrow for radiographing immigrants.

Powell (1987) from Sheffield described the use of a Siemens 57 cm diameter caesium iodide intensifier with two zoom magnifications, giving an incident skin dose of 0.004 mGy (0.4 mR). Manninen et al. (1988) from Finland described its use for routine chest radiography, especially for the detection of lung tumours and metastases.

This system can also be coupled to a TV camera and digitiser for digital radiography.

According to Fraser et al. (1989) digital images obtained by this technique are slightly better than high KV chest radiographs for the hilar and mediastinum, and also for lung masses, but interstitial lung disease is not quite so well seen as on conventional radiographs.

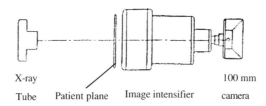

X-ray
Tube   Patient plane   Image intensifier   camera   100 mm

Fig. 20.3   Schematic diagram of image-intensifier photofluorography.

Digital Radiography.

Digitisation of radiographic images is being increasingly employed with CT, MR, nuclear medicine and ultrasound. Both digital fluoroscopy and radiography are employed with digital vascular imaging (DVI), which also allows subtraction. Digital recording and displays are also now becoming available for conventional radiographic procedures, including barium studies and chest radiography. Some companies are producing systems for storing all radiographic images in a central storage and retrieval system. In digitisation, the image is converted into a matrix of small pixels, rather like ancient Roman mosaic patterns. These can be processed using a computer to alter the density, contrast or polarity. Picture clarity depends on the number of pixels (or picture elements) within it, and the resolution of the system. The density of each pixel in the display can be represented according to the number of 'bits' (commonly eight, giving about 256 different levels).

Advantages of digitising chest radiographs include being able to alter the contrast and density, making each part optimum, and thus allowing one to study the lungs, mediastinum and bones separately. One may also optimise under- or over-exposed radiographs, produce masks and subtract these or another image from the display so as view only the bones, lungs or mediastinum, or form reversed images. There are however some disadvantages - cost of the computer, access only via a monitor terminal connected to the available memory, etc. Probably digitised records will never be as convenient as film, and it should be noted that for most medical purposes even CT etc. images are converted to 'hard copy', mainly on film. For routine use, film has great advantages - speed in reading (of great advantage to the radiologist who has to read a large number of radiographs in a short period of time between other duties), portability, a long storage life, the only real problem with film being storage space for large numbers of x-ray packets.

Chest radiographs may be digitised by a number of methods. In the simplest, conventional radiographs are made, and than scanned by a suitable detector and digitised. A storage phosphor plate may replace the cassette (see Figs. 20.4 & 5); the exposed plate is scanned by a laser beam, processing is carried out by a computer, and the displays are printed onto film, either as single views or as a multiple display (e.g. '4 up'), with images of different density plus a reversed polarity image. As noted above an intensifier system may be adapted for digitisation, by replacing the 100 mm camera with a TV tube and processor. The Philips system may also be adapted and Sashin et al. (1982) used a similar system employing a linear intensifier array of 160 diodes, for digital radiography. The technique gave good visualisation of the lung parenchyma, the trachea and larger bronchi, the mediastinum, ribs, spine, etc. IV contrast enhancement, as with CT can also be employed, and the Philips system has the advantage of less scatter that results from fan or pencil shaped beams - see below.

Following conversion of an image to a digitised system, all methods employ image processing and viewing. Initially there are two types of image geometry: (a) the conventional large field of view and (b) scanning using a narrow beam. The former images the whole field of view, has rapid image acquisition, but suffers from limited scatter control, even with an air gap or grid. Spot or slit scanning irradiates portions of the area of interest sequentially (i.e. not instantaneously) which may lead to some distortion from rapid motion, but the fine beam achieves greater scatter control; x-ray tube loading may also be a problem. In the systems employing a TV camera and /or lenses, these may be the cause of some loss of definition. Storage phosphor plates give good spatial resolution, with little 'noise', but only have a limited detection efficiency. Linear detector arrays improve x-ray detection and usually cause little 'noise', but may give poorer spatial resolution.

Photocunductivity

- (a) selenium drum system Instead of using x-ray luminescence to convert x-radiation into visible light followed by the production of electrical signals which can be digitised and stored, a one step process is achieved by photocunductivity, which avoids the additional noise sources that are associated with multi-stage conversions. In a commercially available apparatus - 'Thoravision' (Philips) a 0.5 mm thick selenium layer on a 50 cm diameter aluminium drum acts as an x-ray converter. An electrical surface charge distribution develops under irradiation, which is then scanned by microelectrometer probes and digitised. An improved signal-to-noise ratio can be reached with this system compared with screen-film or digital storage phosphor imaging, resulting in better detectability of small, low-contrast details and better visibility of lesions in chest images (Neitzel, 1995) - see Illus. **THORAVISION** - Eyler (1999) considers it the best high KV system available.

- (b) flat-panel detectors These are now starting to appear - they consist of a sandwich of (i) an x-ray sensitive layer (Se or CsI), (ii) an active layer of amorphous hydrogenated silicon - a-Si:H photodiodes and (iii) a matrix of signal and control lines and circuits for line scanning sequence, prior to amplification and multiplexing.

Both drum and flat-panel systems allow direct acquisition and presentation of the images without the use of cassettes, films or their transport.

A great advantage of the digital detector is the greater exposure latitude, as compared with screen-film combinations in cassettes as used in conventional radiography, often using one third or half of the radiation needed with intensifying screens and films. However a certain minimum of radiation is still required for adequate radiography, and if this is not employed the images may lack diagnostic quality and miss clinically important information.

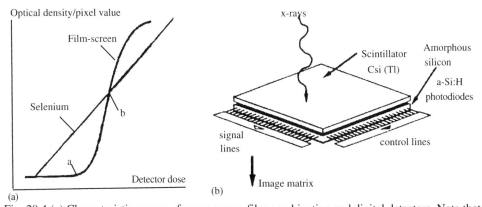

Fig. 20.4 (a) Characteristic curves of x-ray screen-film combination and digital detectors. Note that the curve for screen-film is 'S' shaped, and the useful part is shown between a and b; the curve for the selenium digital detector is a straight-line.   (b) Diagram of a flat panel x-ray detector.

(Reproduced from Kamm, 1997, with permission from British J. Radiology - see also p. 20.9).

In Fig. 20.4 (b) an image receptor ('**storage phosphor**' or '**photostimulable**') plate replaces a conventional cassette. The image is read by a laser beam, digitised and can be presented via a computer with more than one display e.g. (i) wide latitude with edge enhancement and (ii) with subtraction of bones, etc., if a dual energy system is used or 'four up' images i.e. with different densities and reversed polarity. The radiographic system uses a conventional generator and x-ray tube, but the reading system and computer are rather expensive compared with a film developing apparatus. The processing time is also rather slow. Images can be stored on magnetic tape, optical discs or CD. Great advantages are the increased latitude, that inadequate exposures can be enhanced and a high KV effect can be produced with lower KV.

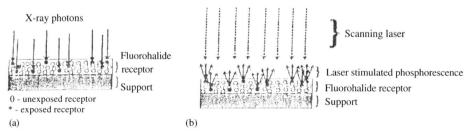

Fig. 20.5   Diagram of the photostimulable phosphor system. During the x-ray exposure (a) the fluorohalide phosphor stores the latent radiographic image. When the receptor is scanned with a laser (b) the stored energy is released. (Diagrams reproduced from Fraser et al., 1989, Radiology, **171**, 297 - 307 with permission).

Characteristics of Digital Systems for Chest Radiography.

	Film digitisation	Image intensifier	Photostimulable phosphor	Scanned projection
Geometry	Conventional	Conventional	Conventional	Fan beam
Detector	Large area	Large area	Large area	Limited area
x-ray detection	Fair	Fair	Fair	Fair
Spatial resolution	Good*	Poor-fair	Good	Fair
Scatter control	Poor-fair	Poor-fair	Poor-fair	Good
Electric noise	Good	Fair-good	Good	Good
Dual energy	No**	No**	Yes	Yes
Portable use	Yes	No	Yes	No

* Depends on type of digitiser
** Possible but not practical with existing equipment

Table 20.1   Characteristics of digital systems for chest radiography (after Fraser et al., 1989, Radiology, **171**, 297 - 307 with permission).

'**AMBER**' ('**Advanced multiple-beam equalisation radiography**') uses 20 detectors in front of the film cassette, coupled electronically to 20 modulators linked to feed-back circuits in front of the x-ray tube to alter the exposure during a horizontally oriented scan, with a slit x-ray beam, similar to the Philips scanning system (see Fig. 20.2), but using larger or full size films. The time taken to cover the chest is 0.8 sec, with a point exposure time of 50 msec, and pixel size 2 mm or less.

The method is especially good for portraying lung pathology normally obscured by the heart and diaphragm. About twice as many nodules are seen as on conventionally taken chest radiographs. Borders of the heart, etc. tend to be outlined with a black band, giving a 'big **MACH**' effect (see Appendix 3). One drawback is that hemi-thoracic alterations in density (e.g. due to a mastectomy, Macleod syndrome, etc.) tend to be evened out in exposure, with loss of contrast if large areas are affected. Fine shadowing due to diffuse lung disease (e.g. with fibrosing alveolitis and sarcoidosis) is readily detected. Also pathologically affected anatomy e.g. focal lung consolidation is readily portrayed and the certainty of normality or otherwise is greater than with most other techniques.

One of these machines, marketed in the UK by Kodak, has been in use at the Royal Brompton Hospital, London for several years (see Hansell, 1990 and Hansell et al., 1990 & 1991). Another such apparatus has been at the Churchill Hospital, Oxford since 1995, and some radiographs using it are shown in Illus. **AMBER**.

Further references.
Vasbloem and Schultze Kool (1988) & Schultze Kool et al. (1988).
Chotas et al. (1993) : Image quality was higher, most notably in dense phantom regions on radiographs of the chest with AMBER, than with new asymmetric screen-film combinations.
Nichols et al. (1993) : Alveolar consolidation detection with AMBER vs conventional chest radiography.

The 'scout' or preliminary view of a CT examination (taken by moving the patient through a narrow fan beam of x-rays with the tube and detectors stationary) also gives a digitised chest radiograph (Illus. **CT-SCOUT VIEW**), and can be used rather like a high KV chest radiograph. However fine detail within the lungs is not as good as with conventional radiographs. On most machines the contrast and density can be readily adjusted on the display unit to show the various anatomical features; magnification is also readily carried out. These views are especially good for displaying the mediastinal lines, shadows behind the heart, etc. A drawback is that the heart outline becomes stepped from the cardiac pulsations which take place whilst the patient is being driven through the x-ray beam. Some CT machines have been modified to optimise the scout view for digital chest radiography (Brody et al., 1981 and Effman, 1983).

Further notes and references.
Brody et al. (1981) : Modified a GE 8800 CT scanner for dual energy imaging and produced 'scout' type chest images with alternate lines generated by low (85) and high (135) KV. By using interpolation and subtraction it was possible to show (a) the bony structures alone, or (b) the soft tissues of the lung, the airways and the mediastinum.
Sorenson et al. (1981 a & b) and Sorenson and Mitchell (1987) : Unsharp masking improved nodule detection on chest radiographs.
Armstrong J. et al. (1983) : Suggested that both unsharp masking and slit-scanning in chest radiography may improve nodule detection, but found that only unsharp masking helped.
Effman et al. (1983) : CT localisation radiography compared with conventional high KV radiography.
Fraser et al. (1983 & 1986) and Fraser (1984) : Vertical-slit fan beam chest radiography, using 1024 detectors and an exposure time of 4.5 secs. Entrant skin dosage was 0.25 mGy (25 mR) as compared with the normal in their department of 0.1 to 0.12 mGy. Line pairs per mm were 1.0 compared with 3.5 to 4 with a conventional film-screen combination. They used four monitors for the display (one for communicating with the computer) and used half-sized imagers as compared with normal sized radiographs. Visualisation of mediastinal structures was consistently better on digital images, than on conventional radiographs, because of the ability to vary the 'window'. Edge enhancement of mediastinal lines and bronchi were well seen, but lung detail was poorer and it was difficult to see lung shadows that were faint. Kerley's lines were almost invisible. By altering the contrast, nodules in the lungs were better seen by digital radiography. Calcification could be more readily recognised, particularly with dual-energy subtraction, and could be measured in μg per gram of tissue. (Fraser et al. found calcification in one tumour).
Heubener (1983) : Compared scanned projection with standard chest radiography in 250 cases - it was **superior** for detecting extended objects with slight contrast differences and for assessing the mediastinal contours and juxta-pleural lesions, but was **inferior** for the detection of small pulmonary lesions.
Sonada et al. (1983) : Laser simulated luminescence for computed radiography - exposure times and tube loading were comparable to conventional radiography.
Barnes et al. (1985) : Linear detector array with 1024 elements for dual energy digital radiography.
Moore, C. and Eddlestone (1985) : Can current technology provide a reliable digital diagnostic radiology department?
Smathers and Brody (1985) : Digital radiography, current and future trends.
Sommer et al. (1985) : Digital processing of radiographs allows review and the alteration of contrast, with light films being increased in density and dark ones reduced, so that lost information is regained.
Wandtke and Plewes (1985) and Wandtke et al. (1985) performed 'scanned equalisation' radiography of the chest, using a rotating collimator and a stationary detector behind it, to allow a computer to adjust the exposure to each area of the chest, thus evening out the wide variation in absorption by the dense mediastinum and the air-filled lung. Despite a scan time of 4.5 secs, motion problems were minimal, detail in the lungs, retro-diaphragmatic and retro-cardiac areas was greatly improved making the recognition of nodules much easier.
Cowen et al. (1988) : Preliminary investigation of dual energy fluorography of the thorax.

Kundel et al. (1987) : Readers preferred the **simplicity of the viewing-box** to viewing a digital CRT display - **'this simplicity is undoubtedly the most difficult hurdle for anyone who aspires to compete against a viewing-box with a CRT'.**

Wandtke et al. (1988) and Wandtke and Plewes (1989) : Scanning equalisation radiography showed more abnormalities and nodules.

Goodman, L. et al. (1986) : Digital and conventional chest images - observer performance with film digital system.

   (1988) : Digital chest images improved the detection of hilar and mediastinal masses, but were inferior to conventional radiographs in the detection of pneumothorax and emphysema.

Lams and Cocklin (1986) : Spatial resolution requirements for digital chest radiographs.

McMahon et al. (1986) : Digital radiography of subtle pulmonary abnormalities - found that the diagnostic accuracy of observers increased as the pixel size was reduced to 0.1 mm but above this size there was some inaccuracy.

Fuhrman et al. (1988) : Found physicians (mainly radiologists) were willing to try reading storage phosphor radiographs, including '4 ups' - four minified images of the same radiograph - (a) normal, (b) unsharp masked image, (c) contrast-enhanced unsharp masked image and (d) reversed polarity image.

Ishigaki et al. (1988) : Clinical evaluation of one-shot, dual-energy subtraction with computed radiography - clinical evaluation - improved nodule assessment and calcification,. new information in 21 out of 140 patients.

Oestmann et al. (1988) : Found that edge enhancement and reversed polarity can **impair** the detectability of subtle lung cancers on digitised radiographs of medium resolution.

Yarwood and Moores (1988) : Image processing of digital chest ionograms.

Fajardo et al. (1989) and Goodman (1990) : A major problem with digital radiography is with the recognition of a **pneumothorax.** However Elam et al. (1992) found that radiologists detected pneumothoraces equally well on conventional screen radiographs and digital images printed on film, but less well on electronic viewing consoles. Similar findings were made in experimental pneumothoraces induced in cadavers by Carr et al. (1992) who also felt that the lateral decubitus view was the most sensitive.

Cox et al. (1990) : Comparison of high resolution digital displays with conventional and digital film - found that detectable differences in observer performance could be found even with 2,084 x 2,084 x 12 bits in the detection of obstructive and interstitial lung disease, pneumothorax and parenchymal masses.

Dawood (1990) : Digital radiology - a realistic prospect ?

Hansell (1990) : Digital chest radiography - current status.

McMahon et al. (1991) : Significant image deterioration can occur with high data compression ratios since digital chest radiography requires high-resolution images of the order of 2,048 x 2,048 pixels with 1,024 or more grey levels, and hundreds of these are produced each day in large radiology departments.

Schaefer et al. (1991) : Detection of mediastinal abnormalities with storage phosphor digital radiography. Whilst this may improve the detection of mediastinal abnormalities, they were **inferior to conventional high-KV chest radiography for the detection of pulmonary lesions.**

Saito et al. (1988) : Digital radiography in an intensive care unit.

Hansell (1991) : Phosphor storage plate computed radiography preferred for portable chest radiography, particularly in intensive care - advantages are greater exposure latitude and hence consistent images, and a 50% reduction in radiation dose - the disadvantage being the considerably increased cost.

Dobbins et al. (1992) : **Computed radiography necessitates about 75 to 100% more exposure to optimally match screen-film radiography.**

Jennings et al. (1992) : Computed images in intensive care allowed greater confidence in the identification of courses and tips of lines - best seen with edge enhanced images.

Goodman et al. (1993) Computed equalisation radiography optimises the image by obtaining two 1 sec fan beam scans, an initial low-dose prescan determining the location of the lungs by means of a stationary krypton detector.

Kido et al. (1993) Interpretation of subtle interstitial lung abnormalities: conventional versus storage phosphor radiography (SR). Although the advantages of SR (wide dynamic range, automatic density optimisation, flexible image processing) are quite effective in the detection of mediastinal lesions and lung nodules, the inferior spatial resolution of SR makes it difficult to detect more subtle lung abnormalities because the lost ? perceptual accuracy was achieved by experienced radiologists who read conventional screen-film radiographs, it can be assumed that critically important diagnostic information can be lost with SR images.

Kelcz et al. (1994) : Dual energy CT improved the detection and characterisation of pulmonary nodules.

Kano et al. (1994) : Digital image subtraction of temporally sequential chest images for detection of interval change.

McMahon and Vyborny (1994) : Technical advances in chest radiography.

Thaete et al. (1994) : Diagnostic performance and efficiency attainable with high-quality conventional radiographs is difficult to achieve or improve on with available digital radiography. Radiologists as a group did not perform as well with digitally acquired images displayed on a CRT as they did with conventional radiographs or computer-generated laser-printed radiographs when the abnormalities required the detection of high frequency components (such as interstitial disease or pneumothorax) - the combination of higher image noise, lower spatial resolution and reduced contrast discrimination may not be adequate for the recognition of such abnormalities.

Floyd et al. (1995) : Selenium-based chest digital radiography compared with film-screen radiographs - the former were preferred - they could be processed to meet the needs of individual radiologists, and being stored in a digital format can be reprinted (if mislaid) or to **enhance the appearance for different anatomical regions**.

Kido et al. (1995) : Clinical evaluation of pulmonary nodules with single-exposure dual-energy subtraction chest radiography with an iterative noise-reduction algorithm.

Kimme-Smith et al. (1995) : Underexposure of computed radiographs decreases the detection of low-contrast objects such as lung nodules, thus reducing diagnostic quality.

van Heesewijk et al. (1995) : Digital chest imaging with a selenium detector : comparison with conventional radiography for visualisation of specific anatomic regions of the chest - the digital selenium chest radiography system performs well in a clinical setting, providing visualisation of anatomical structures is better than or at least equal to that provided by standard screen film images.

Müller, R. et al. (1996) : Frequency of filtered image post-processing of digital luminescence radiographs in pulmonary nodule imaging - low dosage storage phosphor radiography - is not associated with a loss of diagnostic information. Image post-processing with large filter kernels even permits a gain in diagnostic performance coupled with an analogue screen-film system with equivalent information - thus there may be scope for further dosage reduction in digital storage phosphor radiography.

Schaefer-Prokop (1996) : The selenium detector improves detection of simulated fine linear and low-contrast micronodular details and appears to be superior to other detector systems for chest radiography.

Woodward et al. (1997) : Subjective visibility of pathology and normal anatomy was improved by selenium based digital radiography compared with conventional screen-film radiography.

Kamm (1997) : The future of digital imaging.

Hansell (1997) : Thoracic imaging - then and now.

Points of detail on chest radiographs.

PA Views - as well as having adequate penetration to see through the heart, PA views must be taken in **full** inspiration. If this is not done, the bases will not be fully expanded. Normally the diaphragm descends to the tenth or eleventh ribs. Poor inspiration may lead to crowding of basal vessels, simulating congestion or basal fibrosis, and small effusions will be masked. Similarly, distortion will be produced if the patient is not 'straight', with his arms and scapulae rotated antero-laterally, and the hands just touching the iliac crests. Centreing should be to the middle of the cassette (not the D4 vertebra!) and the x-ray beam should be **horizontal.**

Occasionally in large females with huge breasts, it is helpful to take a supplementary view to show the bases (if basal disease is suspected) with the patient holding up her breasts with her hands (that the fingers then obscure the upper zones does not matter - Illus. **BREASTS ELEVATED, Scleroderma 3b & 7a**).

Views in expiration may be useful for showing obstructive emphysema (see Illus. **OBSTRUCTIVE EMPHYSEMA** & ps. 2.5 - 6 & 19.2), but although often taken in the diagnosis of a pneumothorax, often add little to the diagnosis (p. 14.21). They may however assist in diagnosing fixity of the lung or a tumour to the chest wall - see ps. 12.20 - 21 & 24.24.

Lateral views - although it is often customary to place the diseased side of the chest adjacent to the cassette, it is really of little importance if a long focus-film distance (f.f.d.) and an air-gap are used, as lesions on both sides will be about equally visible. It might even be argued that if the lesion is on the far side from the cassette, magnification might render it more visible, and the contra-lateral side will tend to absorb scattered radiation. What is important is that the patient again fully inspires, and that he is in good position with his arms folded above his head (preferably holding his **elbows** with his hands), to get the shoulders well out of the way. He should also lean a little forwards, keeping his chin up, so as to bring the lung apex to the centre of the film - otherwise he will appear to be falling backwards.

When the anterior and upper part of the chest or the sternum is being studied, a lateral with the arms extended posteriorly (i.e. straight and oriented at about 45º from the vertical downwards and backwards) may help as it will tend to throw the sternum anteriorly and get the retrosternal part of the chest to be well expanded. The author terms this the '**Mary Queen of Scots view**' (as the position of the arms mimics that of people in Elizabeth I's time signifying that they were ready to be beheaded, with their chins lying on the 'block'). A similar effect may be produced with the arms hyper-extended and the hands touching the elbows behind the back.

An AP view - sitting in a wheel chair, in bed, etc. is usually made in infirm patients who are moderately sick, invalids, etc. who cannot easily move. It is really 'second best' as there is often a short f.f.d. and hence apparent enlargement of the heart and mediastinum.

A **supine AP** is usually done in the very sick, or those who cannot sit up at all. It is 'third best'. Vessels in the lungs may look 'congested' by physiological redistribution of blood from the bases towards the apices. It may be very difficult to recognise pleural fluid or air (see also ps. 14.13 - 14 & 14.23).

It is sometimes useful as a supplementary view to determine alteration in size or shape of vascular or fatty structures with posture.

Oblique views were commonly employed in cardiac studies when x-ray generators and tubes were limited in output in the 1920's and 1930's, but are now rarely taken, except with a Bucky diaphragm for rib lesions, pleural plaques or small effusions, lingula or middle lobe bullae, etc. Routinely they are largely valueless. Young et al. (1984) had a similar view after reviewing the results in 300 consecutive cases.

Lordotic and apical views also used to have some vogue, and are still used in some departments, but the author believes they are also largely useless, and not infrequently misleading. If a patient has strong clinical or radiological suggestion of an apical lesion, Bucky views may show the rib destruction, otherwise tomograms, including CT, are required. It is very easy to say from an apical or lordotic view that all is well, when **it is not**. Similarly lordotic views, taken for e.g. the middle lobe, may miss its collapse and a lateral is preferable.

The diaphragm and lordotic or reversed lordotic projections are discussed on p. 15.7. The calcified anterior end of a first rib, producing an '**idiot tumour**' may be confirmed with a lordotic view (Illus. **ARTEFACT, Pt. 13** - see also p. 6.27).

A point made by Rundle et al. (1959) is of historical interest; they used lordotic views to differentiate cervical from thoracic tumours, cervical being projected above the line of the thoracic inlet, whilst thoracic tumours were below it.

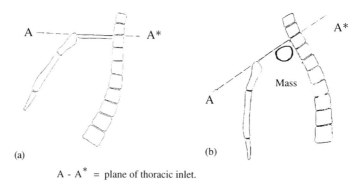

A - A* = plane of thoracic inlet.

Fig. 20.6 Lordotic view in (a) the plane of the thoracic inlet lies horizontally, whilst in (b) - a mass lying posteriorly in the upper thorax may appear to be above sternal level (reproduced from AJR, **81**, 316 - 321 with permission).

Further references.

Louw (1965) : Tilted the x-ray tube 10° upwards to throw the apices above the clavicles.
Hollman and Adams (1989) : Wrote that the lordotic projection produces considerable distortion and artefacts of thoracic structures and can lead to diagnostic errors. They compared 14 pairs of lordotic and standard chest radiographs; artefacts included - apparent elevation of the diaphragm, poor visualisation of the lung bases, loss of definition of the aortic knuckle, simulation of apical caps, apparent widening of the superior mediastinum, exaggerated pulmonary artery size and a bizarre cardiac outline. Such artefacts were greatly exaggerated when lordosis existed with pathology, the patient was rotated or took an inadequate inspiration.
Jacobson and Sargent (1968) : also discussed apical views and Zinn and Monroe (1986) : the lordotic position.

Bucky   views are invaluable for the demonstration of bone lesions (spine, arms, ribs, etc.). When a Pancoast type lesion is suspected (see ps. 12.5 - 6), an 'apical Bucky view' may demonstrate the bony destruction which is otherwise not apparent. The author often took 'spot views' of suspicious ribs under TV fluoroscopic control, using a fine focus (0.3 or 0.6 mm^2) and a moving grid (Illus. **RIB SPOT VIEW**).

Sternum - a lateral view (especially the Mary Queen of Scot's view (see above) is useful for fractures, gross secondary deposits or tumours. This may be supplemented by tomography, in the lateral, slightly oblique AP, inclined frontal or axial planes. The more usual oblique view of the sternum, so often done by radiographers appears to the author to be almost **useless !**

   Morris and Bailey (1970) described a simple method for demonstrating the ribs and sternum. They 'fixed' the thoracic cage with a Bucky band, the lungs being blurred by slight respiration during a long exposure and low mA. The patient was placed slightly obliquely, supine for the posterior parts of the ribs and prone for the anterior parts of the ribs and sternum.

TV fluoroscopy of the chest may still be useful as summarised in the following table :
1.   Is there maximum inspiration of both lungs ? Obstructive emphysema (in expiration) due to foreign bodies, endobronchial tumours, etc. ?
2.   Noting the patency of the trachea, carina and main bronchi (differentiating nodes from vessels is very difficult).
3.   Noting changes in shape and/or size of structures with respiration, posture, Valsalva or Müller manoeuvres - e.g. azygos vein, pulmonary varix or A /V malformation, fatty mass, diaphragmatic hump, etc.
4.   Determining the position of nodules prior to tomography (anterior, posterior, or in the chest wall, etc).
5.   Assessment of diaphragmatic and mediastinal movement with a phrenic palsy, etc.
6.   Examination of the oesophagus and stomach, etc.
7.   Noting calcification in the heart, pericardium, coronary vessels, pleura or lung.
8.   Monitoring of biopsy, bronchoscopy, bronchography, etc. Note - it is often easier to perform biopsies under fluoroscopy (particularly with a 'C arm') or ultrasound control after CT localisation.
9.   For taking 'spot views' of ribs - to show difficult fractures, deposits, lung nodules containing calcium, etc. (For this purpose low KV may be preferable.)

Value of PA and lateral radiographs.
   A national study by the Royal College of Radiologists (see RCR, 1979) - use of pre-operative chest x-rays among patients admitted for elective non-cardiopulmonary surgery recommended: -
" 'routine' pre-operative chest radiography is no longer justified. However pre-operative chest radiography may be clinically desirable in certain patients in the following categories:
(i) those with acute respiratory symptoms,
(ii) those with possible metastases,
(iii) those with suspected or established cardio-respiratory disease who have not had a chest radiograph in the previous 12 months,
(iv) recent immigrants from countries where TB is still endemic who have not had a chest radiograph within the previous 12 months.
   It should be noted that none of the above categories is routine and the reasons for examination should, therefore, always be given in the usual way."

   Author's comment : These recommendations seem dangerous in patients who are sick or who are to undergo any major surgery. All sick patients should have chest radiographs to exclude chest disease, and in those having major operations, this is particularly important for excluding chest disease which merits pre-operative attention, and for ensuring that abnormalities which may appear later were not present pre-operatively. The only exception might be in young people.
   Omission of chest radiography on the grounds of radiation dosage is really irrelevant with the high KV technique.- see Appendix 1, and the cost is not great. Indeed it may be less than possible damages for neglect in not carrying it out!

Some studies and references.

Sagel et al. (1974) : Studied the efficacy of routine screening PA and lateral chest radiographs in hospital patients and found that routine chest radiographs were not warranted in patients under 20 years of age, a lateral view was only required in patients over 40 with chest disease, or a reasonable probability of it, and in screening people over 40 years of age.

Forrest and Sagel (1979) : Reviewed high KV radiographs of over 10,000 patients, including 105 with bronchogenic carcinoma, and found that in no instance (even retrospectively with initially unrecognised cases) was a lesion detected on a lateral view only.

Mendelson et al. (1987) : Found that pre-operative chest radiography was very important as a base line for comparison - in 9% they were essential for deciding new or old abnormalities.

Stitik and Tockman (1978) : In discussing radiographic screening in early detection of lung cancer found that 3% of lesions could only be seen on a lateral view and that a further 5% were better seen on a lateral.

Sagel et al. (1974 see above) : Also found cases where **only** the lateral view showed the tumour.

Eyler et al. (1959) : The importance of the lateral view in the evaluation of left ventricular enlargement in rheumatic heart disease.

Hoffman and Rigler (1965) : Evaluation of left ventricular enlargement on lateral radiographs.

Chang (1969) : Value of lateral chest radiograph in pulmonary venous hypertension.

Figley (1969) : Mediastinal minutiae.

Nelson and Coggs (1973) : Lateral views were useful for showing gas in abdominal surgical wounds which indicated infection (4 patients).

Simon (1975) : The anterior chest radiograph - criteria for normality.

Riggs and Parvey (1976) : Differences between right and left lateral radiographs.

Naidich et al. (1979) : The **'big rib' sign** - localisation of basal pulmonary pathology in the lateral projection by differential magnification - used 6 ft. f.f.d. (**note also another 'big rib' sign - see p. 12.22**).

Proto and Speckman (1979 & 1980) : The left lateral radiograph of the chest.

Bachman et al. (1978) : The effects of minor degrees of obliquity on the lateral chest radiograph.

Austin (1984) : Lateral radiograph in the assessment of non-pulmonary health and disease.

Dunn et al. (1991) : The yield from follow up chest radiographs in men with germ cell tumours is very low.

Collins et al. (1993) : PA and lateral radiographs as part of routine staging and follow up of 227 patients with malignant melanoma - in only one was an abnormality evident only on the lateral view.

Brandstetter et al. (1994) : The benefit of lateral radiographs in an intensive care unit - these were taken with the patient turned onto the side and the x-ray beam directed from above to a cassette under the patient - they were helpful in several patients. [Note: in Oxford the bed is turned sideways on to the wall and the x-ray beam directed horizontally across the bed towards the wall, the patient still sitting up.]

Gibson, A. and Steiner (1997) : Imaging the neonatal chest - including discussion on tubes, defects of lung development, lobar emphysema, pleural effusions, lymphangiectasis, meconium inhalation, PDA, immature lung, RDS and surfactant deficiency.

Kurihara et al. (1999) : The vertical displacement sign - a technique for differentiating L & R ribs on lateral chest radiographs - used only L lateral views with 200 cm f.f.d. (6ft 7ins) - divergence of the radiographic beam projected the anterior ribs more cephalad and more caudal in position than the posterior ribs; thus the anterior ribs are the right ribs.

Conventional tomography
(a) **Historical**

Several workers (Bocage, 1922, Portes and Chausse, 1922, Pohl, 1927, Kieffer, 1929, Ziedses des Plantes, 1931, Bartelink, 1932 and Andrews, 1936) independently described techniques whereby a particular body section might be portrayed, whilst the layers above and below it were effaced. In these systems the x-ray tube and the film moved during an exposure in parallel planes and in opposite directions, following a linear or a more complex (cruciform, circular or spiral) path. In each case the ratio of focus-film distance remained constant, although the focus-film distance was varied (Fig. 20.7). Grossman (1935 a&b) described a modification in which the x-ray tube and film moved in an arc centred on the object plane. Twining (1937 from Manchester) devised a simple attachment to couple the x-ray tube to the cassette tray of a Potter-Bucky couch, and popularised tomography for investigating chest disease in the UK.

Tomography is often known as laminagraphy in the USA. Kieffer (1938) studied its various early forms.

(b) Clinical usage

A Siemens Planigraph was in use at the Churchill Hospital from 1952 to 1992 and was rewired rather than replaced in 1986, as no modern machines produced as good results. Its construction was rigid, with no tube wobble and the patient couch could be turned into the upright position, so necessary for good lateral chest tomography. In the vertical position there was no distortion of the mediastinum due to mediastinal movement towards the dependent side, as occurs when a patient with a normally mobile mediastinum lies on his side. The tilting couch also allowed tomography to be carried out in a semierect position. An exposure angle of 40^0 (20^0 on either side of the midline) was used with an exposure time of 1,75 sec. for thin sections and an angle of 20^0 with an exposure time of 0.9 sec. for thicker sections. It seems a great pity that most modern machines do not allow the couch to be tilted!

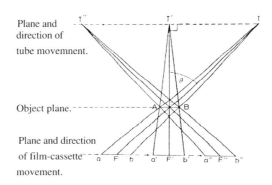

Fig. 20.7 The Planigraph.
With this apparatus the focus-object
and object-film distance vary continuously,
but their ratios remain constant
$(TO \; OF = T'O \; OF' = T''O \; OF'')$.
The x-ray tube and film-cassette
move on parallel paths.

Rotational tomography

Grossman's system can be altered so that the x-ray tube is stationary and the central ray fixed, whilst the object plane and the film rotate about parallel axes in line with the focus. Watson (an English radiographer) discovered the principle of rotational tomography in 1936 during experiments with a model using a stationary light source, with the object and projection screen rotating synchronously on separate parallel axes. He found that this held true for a stationary x-ray beam and a fluorescent screen or film, and built an apparatus, the Sectograph, which allowed a rotational movement of 360^0 (see Watson, W. 1937, 1939 & 1940). He published results of its use in 1943, but in 1962 noted that the usual British conservatism regarding new inventions (even British ones) resulted in the apparatus not finding much favour. The results of further work with the Sectograph were published by Stevenson (1950). Other workers produced similar machines e.g. the Zuder system (see Amisano, 1946, Amisano et al., 1950; and Vallebona. 1950) and the Transversotom (Hammer 1953). Frain et al. (1950 & 1955) and Frain and Duquesne (1962) demonstrated the Radiotome (Illus. **APPARATUS/TECHNIQUE, Radiotome**) on which the patient and film rotate, while the x-ray tube remains stationary; the author has used a similar apparatus since 1960, initially for transverse axial tomography and later inclined frontal tomography.

Transverse axial tomography

In this technique a cross section similar to modern axial CT was produced photographically, by rotating the patient and film cassette which was placed horizontally (or close to this) on a turntable during the x-ray exposure centred to the centres of rotation, the beam being angled downwards at about 30^0, it was able to demonstrate lung masses, larger structures in the mediastinum or hilar regions etc., but its detail was not as good as with modern CT. Our apparatus, the Radiotome was installed in 1964, but we found the results with transverse axial tomography rather poor (Illus. **TRANS AXIAL TOMO**), though it was **excellent for inclined frontal tomography** (see below). We also tried its use for determining tissue in homogeneity for radiotherapy planning but the photographic enlargement was a severe problem except with small patients.

Stevenson (1950 at the Royal Marsden Hospital) showed examples of aortic anomalies, a retrosternal goitre, bronchogenic carcinoma and tuberculosis. Drevvatne and Frimann Dahl (1961 in Oslo) used transverse axial (as well as AP and lateral) tomograms to study the morphology of lung tumours and their spread towards the hilum (see also p. 4.3). Blair Hartley (1960 & 1961 in Manchester) thought that the method gave a good assessment of the 'retrocarinal space' (i.e. the normally clear area behind the main bronchi and the carina) and in 1965 wrote "the traditional tomograms will provide most of the information regarding the type of lesion....., whilst transverse axial tomograms provide......information regarding mediastinal and particularly postcarinal spread"; and an atlas of the normal anatomy of the thorax shown by this method was produced (Farr et al., 1964). Other books were written by Bonté et al. (1955 from France), Gebauer and Schanen (1955 from Germany) and Takahashi (1969 from Japan). The last author used an apparatus in which the patient lay horizontally (instead of sitting up); he also produced a well illustrated atlas of normal anatomy from the head to the ankles, some pathological abnormalities and the use of the technique in the planning of radiotherapy.

Inclined frontal tomography.
In this technique the x-ray beam is horizontal. Films placed vertically (or inclined to the vertical) in front of or behind the axis of rotation will 'select' a parallel plane in the patient. A series of films are used at 1 or 1.5 cm spacing to cover the hilar regions and the mediastinum, after a preliminary lateral film with superimposed wire grid is taken for determining the angle the trachea and carina make with vertical and the AP positions of the pathology and the hila. A 90° angle of 'cut' (a quarter turn) is employed, and with a 1 sec exposure, the rotation speed of the patient (one rotation in 4 sec.) is not upsetting. The blurring motion is transverse, ideal for showing the hilar regions and the mediastinum, but with ghost shadows of these and the ribs and spine overlying the lungs. The larger airways, the aorta, pulmonary artery and veins, the subcarinal area, the oesophagus (with air in it) and the azygo-oesophageal line etc. are well demonstrated as well as enlarged nodes, other masses and adjacent lung pathology - see Illus. **INCL FRONT TOMO**.

Before CT became available the author took many thousands of these tomograms, and for several years found them complementary to CT for showing coronal views of the major airways (views which are now being made in some centres by reformatting spiral CT in this way - see p. 20.22 and Illus. **SPIRAL CT**).

Some references.
Frain et al. (1950, 1955 & 1962)
Greenwell and Wright (1965) : Rotational tomography.
McKinlay and Wright (1967) : Inclined frontal tomography of the sternum.
Wright et al. (1972) : Rotational tomography of hilar and mediastinal masses.
Wright (1973) : Radiology of Lung and Mediastinal Tumours.

55° Posterior oblique tomography.
This has been used in Canada, the USA and Europe to show the hilar regions and main bronchi, but its use has declined as CT has become available. An example is shown in Illus. **CA RLL, Pt. 18c**, but note that in this case lateral tomograms showed the bronchial block in the apex of the right lower lobe, which was not shown by this technique, and the CT views were clearly superior.
Some references.
Brown, L. and De Remee (1976), McLeod et al. (1976), Chasen and Yrizarry (1983)
Stiggson and Tylén (1983), Glazer, G. (1985b), Khan, A. et al. (1984 & 1985).

Computed tomography (formerly termed tomodensitometry in France).
a. **Historical**
The first CT system was developed by Sir Godfrey Hounsfield at EMI Research Laboratories in the late 1960s and early 1970s, but the principle was foreshadowed by Allan M. Cormack (Cormack 1963 & 1964) who shared the 1979 Nobel Prize for Physiology and Medicine with Hounsfield. Like others (including some of us in Oxford who were using rotational tomography), Cormack considered that corrections for body inhomogeneities, in patients undergoing radiotherapy, could be made by measuring x-ray transmission at many angles and projections through the body. He experimented with an aluminium and wood phantom, examined by a Co 60 source and a Geiger-Müller detector. (He also worked out the Fourier principle of edge

enhancement - see Appendices p. 5). He received the McRobert Award (the highest UK award for technical innovation), the FRS and many honorary degrees and gold medals.

Hounsfield, however, independently devised CT and used sodium iodide crystal detectors to measure the emergent x-ray beam, feeding the information into a computer for analysis. He first experimented with perspex and other plastic blocks which were slowly rotated on a modified lathe bed. Using an Am^{41} source, he found that he could reconstruct crude images. With a grant from the Dept. of Health, and using an x-ray tube and with the help of a young neuro-radiologist, James Ambrose from Atkinson Morley's Hospital, Wimbledon, he was able to image phantoms and lesions in post-mortem human and cattle brains. His first clinical apparatus was tried in Oct. 1971. Despite its rather crude pictures, it was an instant success, allowing brain lesions, only marginally different in density from normal brain, to be made visible. IV contrast enhancement was also tried, increasing the density of many lesions and making others visible. It avoided the necessity of air-encephalograms and many cerebral angiograms. The first presentation of the method and early clinical results was given at the 1972 British Institute of Radiology Congress in London, when only a small audience turned up. A short report appeared in the Times the following day (21 April 1972), and the first papers by Hounsfield and by Ambrose in 1973.

Webb, S. (1993 & 1995) reviewed the pre-1972 history and invention of CT and noted that although others had worked on the principles of reconstruction from as early as 1917, 'none of these led to the ability to routinely achieve section imaging in a hospital setting'.

Hounsfield studied a pig's body and with Kreel produced the first whole body apparatus at Northwick Park Hospital (see Kreel 1977a & b). EMI's patents were copied by several companies and EMI withdrew from the CT business in 1980 - the early development of CT in relation to EMI's patents and legal actions was reviewed by Strong and Hurst (1994) - see also reply by Cormack (1994).

The computer aspect has since been applied to MR (see p. 20.29 et seq.), ultra-sound and other applications. The basic principle is the reconstruction of the internal structure of an object from multiple projections. With Hounsfield's first apparatus, the x-ray tube and detectors moved laterally across the object (Fig. 20.8a). He improved this by repeating the traverse, after turning the tube and detectors through an angle of 10° at a time, with multiple projections up to 180° or 360°. Circular rotation of the combined x-ray tube and detector assembly (Fig. 20.8b) or of the tube within a circle of detectors were the next logical developments.

As well as the work done by Hounsfield, others also developed CT machines. Ledley et al. (1974) started to develop a combined body and head scanner (the ACTA Scanner) which was installed at the University of Minnesota in 1973, and the prototype of the Ohio Nuclear Scanner (using a fan-shaped array of multiple x-ray beams) was evaluated by Alfidi et al. (1975). IGE started to develop their third generation scanner a year later.

The first generation machine was essentially Hounsfield's research apparatus. Second generation machines were relatively slow with scan times of 20 secs up to a few minutes, depending on the number of traverses made (and were mainly used for brain examinations, with the patients head in a 'bolus' bag of water in order to obtain good quality images). They were also the basis of the first body scanners, but until the advent of the third and fourth generation machines, body scanning was not really practicable. In the UK, although the DHSS had greatly supported the development of head scanners, it was not convinced about the value of body apparatus; thus in many centres they had to be purchased privately, with local enthusiasm raising the necessary finance. However over the last seventeen years the situation has changed and the great value of CT for the neck, thorax, abdomen, pelvis, etc. has become paramount.

Improvements have occurred with more reliable detector systems, faster processing (with much smaller computers), better x-ray tubes (the first were therapy type tubes with stationary anodes), optical disc storage (rather than magnetic tape), a greater number of pixels, HR and spiral CT (see below) and laser film printers.

Recently greater efficiency has been achieved with continuous (non-pulsed) x-ray production using a 'cascade' type of mini-generator within the gantry. CT-fluoroscopy, using the detector array as an image-intensifier and a battery operated 'mobile' system allowing sufficient power to complete a study of up to 25 slices (with recharge from a standard wall-socket providing 2kW of power AC or DC) are now possible (see Illus. **APPARATUS, 19**).

As well as producing transverse sections, reconstructions using multiple adjacent slices, allow sections to be reconstructed in other directions, e.g. coronal, sagittal, etc, the clarity of these depending on the closeness of the original cross-sections. Using a 'tracker ball' a moving '3D' display can be achieved (as with some MR displays).

Very fast scan times (e.g. of 50 msec) allowing 'ciné CT' can be achieved with CT machines with no major mechanical moving parts. In these, focused electrons are rotated around a peripheral tungsten anode ring within a vacuum envelope, thus producing a 30° fan beam of x-rays which pass through the patient and collimators to a detector ring. (For references to this use see under ciné CT below).

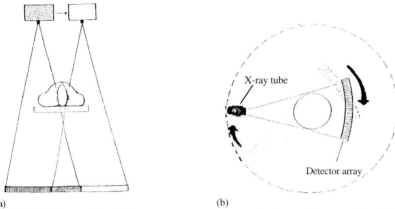

(a)   (b)

Fig. 20.8 (a) **1st Generation CT** - transverse movement of tube and detector(s) - EMI (1972). (b) **3rd Generation CT** - rotation of tube and detector system - continuously-rotating fan beam (based on EMIs Diamond Project, 1944).

Collimators are placed both in the primary beam to adjust the slice thickness and in front of the detectors to remove scatter.

Magnification of the display can be achieved in several ways :
(a) electronic magnification of the display (using a cursor box to pick out the area of interest),
(b) moving the x-ray tube-detector array, so that the detector was moved further from the patient - the 'geometric enlargement' in the earlier Philips systems.

(a) Normal sized image.   (b) Enlarged image.

(c) '**targeting**' - instead of an area being simply magnified, the portion examined (i.e. smaller than normal whole-body section) is reconstructed over the full number of pixels, thus giving a much more detailed enlarged picture (with a 512^2 matrix, the size of each pixel will be approx. 0.5 mm^2). This is especially valuable for research purposes.

The 8800 apparatus, which the author first used, had scan times of 5.7, 6.8 and 11.5 secs (using 50 Hz AC), whilst the later IGE Pace apparatus can give speeds down to 2 secs and 1.5 mm thickness.

CT scattering, absorption densities and Hounsfield Numbers or Units (HUs).

In CT most of the scattering in soft tissues is by the Compton effect, in which x-rays interact with the orbiting electrons in the atoms of the tissues, particularly hydrogen (one electron and one proton), but also with carbon, oxygen and nitrogen. In bone and with iodine contrast agents, photo-electric absorption takes place, and in this an inner electron of an atom absorbs the energy of an x-ray photon, emitting it as light.

CT differs from conventional tomography by using only a thin beam of x-rays, and does not only rely on blurring to eliminate unwanted information. All that is transversed by the beam should be depicted in the display (only scattered rays being removed by the collimator closer to the patient).

CT shows the density of tissues as mass per unit volume. Because it can differentiate small differences in the body, this is often sufficient for tissue differentiation, but it may be enhanced by iodine contrast media. Apparent density may be altered by the **partial volume effect** if a lesion, or area, does not entirely fill a 'pixel'. This is particularly seen with air and the difficulty of determining the density of small lung lesions. Most tumours will distort normal anatomy, and as well as having a different density, are often surrounded by oedema, contain necrosis or be accompanied by cyst formation.

The presence of fat or air gives rise to reduced density, whilst increased density may be due to haemoconcentration (in a haematoma), calcification or iodine contrast agents.

Absorption coefficients - Ambrose (1973) wrote 'The values of the absorption coefficients are calculated on a standard scale, adopting zero as the value for water.... Since the absorption coefficients are measured to an accuracy of 0.5 %, the method is able to detect and register small differences in tissue density.' Originally a scale from minus 500 for air to plus 500 for compact bone was used by Hounsfield (1973). He found that at 120 KV, fat had an absorption coefficient which was 10% less than water, whilst tissues on average gave a value approximately 3% greater than water. The 'print out scale' was doubled to extend from minus 1,000 (air density) to plus 1,000, the figures commonly being referred to as Hounsfield units. Water is 0, fat being about -80 to -100, CSF +2, blood +50, white and grey matter in brain +24 and + 36, kidneys +40, muscle +55, liver + 60 and haematomas and extravasated blood +80 to +90 (when blood clots, haemoconcentration recurs due to retraction of fibrin and this results in **increased density** on CT - this can last for 7 to 30 days, until liquefaction occurs). CT machines can detect iodine in contrast agents at a concentration of 1 in 1,000. Both air collections and surgical clips or other metal collections (e.g. prostheses or amalgam tooth fillings) may cause considerable artefact formation.

Whilst figures may not be entirely constant on the same apparatus or between one and another and are affected by partial volume sampling (i.e. including part of a different density within individual pixels) the figures give a useful guide to tissue characterisation. In the chest fat is readily differentiated from other tissues (usually -100 to -140 HU), pulmonary haemorrhage (+60 to +80) pulmonary calcinosis (+80 to +120), and calcification or frank bone (+150 to 1,000).

Some further historical references.
Cormack (1980) : Early two-dimensional reconstruction (CT scanning) and recent topics stemming from it - Nobel Lecture 8 Dec. 1979.
Hounsfield (1980) : Computed medical imaging - Nobel Lecture 8 Dec. 1979.
Friedland and Thurber (1997) : The birth of CT - reviewed not only the work of Cormack and Hounsfield, but also that of others who had worked with experimental reconstructions, including back projections, now used with most CT apparatus.

Clinical usage of chest CT.

The use of thoracic CT initially developed more slowly than that of the abdomen. Partly this was because plain radiographs and conventional tomograms were already good diagnostic tools, and the paucity of suitable CT apparatus in the UK and other countries. Detail of anatomy and pathology was less clear with earlier machines, due to fewer pixels, a slow scan speed and movement artefacts. Now about 40% of CT examinations may be of the chest, and many fewer conventional tomograms are carried out; indeed in some hospitals they are only used now for renal and bone work.

CT sections give a clarity of definition of intra-thoracic structures, that was not previously thought possible. **Definition at the periphery is as good as at the centre**. Ghost shadows are uncommon, as the patient usually places his arms above his head. Contrast resolution can be increased by a factor of 10 and with fine sections greater detail may be portrayed. Most patients are examined in the supine position, but to show movement with posture, or for biopsy control they may be examined in the prone position or lying on the side. Inspiration should be as full as possible, unless one is looking for 'air-trapping' as in bronchiolitis, when expiration is employed. Sections are taken at spacings suitable for the clinical problem being investigated, and with slice thicknesses commonly of 1, 2, 5 or 10 mm etc.

The cross-section display allows not only good evaluation of disease processes within the lungs, but also of the mediastinum, its various parts and recesses, where these are filled with fat or indented with air-filled lung. The mediastinum on early machines was difficult to assess by CT; however with newer apparatus this is no longer true. Pleural and chest wall disease is also well shown. Problems occur where there is opaque lung adjacent to the mediastinum, so that lung disease may spuriously appear to extend into it, or where there are no separating planes of different CT densities i.e., fat between adjacent soft tissues. Another major problem is often with differentiating nodes from vessels. With small lesions one always has to beware that these may be 'lost' between adjacent sequential sections, but spiral CT obviates this problem.

Early CT studies suggested that small calcified scars were usually equally well seen on plain radiographs as on CT. Edwards, S. and Kelsey Fry (1982) studied 100 patients with no known malignant disease, and found no calcified nodule was shown by CT which was not visible on plain radiographs. Kelsey Fry (1985) also found that **CT allowed lesions 2 to 3 mm in diameter to be seen, in comparison with 5 to 6 mm on conventional whole lung tomograms**.

In making a diagnosis and for studying the extent of a disease process by CT, considerable attention to detail is required. The practice of only reading small images on films taken by the technical staff is to be deprecated, since one **must** view and 'interrogate' the sections oneself on a viewing console and monitor, in order to gain the maximum information. This should preferably be done on an independent console, so as not to interfere with continuing work on the work-station console. In doing this one will examine sections at varying window settings, enlarging areas of particular interest, so as to portray pathology as clearly as possible, particularly for others (especially clinical colleagues) to view subsequently. (One should also note that several minute views on a single sheet of film may be almost meaningless to other medical colleagues, especially if detailed pathology is portrayed.)

When sections are taken at similar section levels within the patient, both before and after contrast medium, it is important to check enhancement of pathological structures at identical window levels and settings, and when there is doubt, to make density measurements and comparisons of HUs. If two monitors are available, this may be of advantage for simultaneous viewing of the complementary CT sections.

The author (like some others e.g. Webb et al, 1992) feels that the commonly used displays with the lungs partly '**whited out**' and with no detail of the chest wall or the mediastinum on them, are often unhelpful to viewers who have not seen the console display. The same is true of non-magnified views of mediastinal pathology with the lungs totally blacked out. Although it is true that many lesions will only be fully displayed at a single window level, every attempt should be made to show neighbouring structures as clearly as possible. Often 'artistry' on the part of the viewer will be required in adjusting window, etc. levels to produce the optimum portrayal of pathology, rather than standardised figures. However a general guide to standard settings is : lung parenchyma = -1,000 (window) and -700 (level); mediastinum = - 300 (window) and - 20 (level).

Some displays have an extended scale feature which shows the chest with grey scales in the manner of a conventional chest radiograph. This is of particular value for showing the lung cortex, the outermost part of which is often poorly portrayed on 'lung settings' alone. Other displays have double windows, but they may produce undesirable discontinuities in the image and are only a partial solution. 'Contour mapping' of densities is a common feature that is available on many machines.

Technique for CT of the chest.
   The technique used depends upon the clinical problem encountered in the individual patient. This should always be determined after perusal of recent plain radiographs. Closer sections are usually required through diseased areas than through normal areas. With tumours sections should be taken at 1 cm intervals through the area of the tumour, and areas of likely spread, whilst sections at 1.5 (or 2) cm may suffice in the remainder of the chest and upper abdomen.
   The author's practice is to routinely use IV contrast in such cases. A weak Gastrografin and 3% barium mixture is also given to opacify the oesophagus with oesophageal abnormalities. He does not give Gastrografin routinely, as opacified small bowel tends to obscure the kidneys etc., and adds very little in chest cases.
   With other lung disease, sections are taken through representative areas to sort out the clinical problem. The same is true for the pleura and the bones of the thorax, though when bone disease is suspected it is often of considerable help to perform a bone scan just prior to the CT examination so as to highlight suspicious areas for detailed study.
   In most cases the examination is carried out in the supine position, but sometimes the patient's condition dictates a decubitus or prone examination. In some cases, when a biopsy is to be carried out, it may be preferable to start in the prone position, if the lesion lies posteriorly. In other cases the patient may first be examined in the prone position, and then be turned into the prone position to remove fluid from masking the area of interest, or to remove gravity dependent oedema. It may also allow the previously dependent and poorly expanded lung to expand and be better examined. Sections taken in **expiration** may show air-trapping, in bullae or in lung which has a damaged bronchial supply, or lies behind a partial bronchial blockage with a valve effect.

The author also feels that the 'factory method' of conducting CT examinations - i.e. doing all examinations according to a fixed protocol, and only viewing the images later, does not obtain the optimum results - and it may also lead to increased radiation dosage to the patient by taking unnecessary views. Only personal attendance of the radiologist at the time of the examination, and individual tailoring of it to the patients clinical condition and the findings as they appear gives the best results.
(This does not of course prevent one having useful guide-lines, but they have to be modified in relation to the individual problems of the patient - even with the use of spiral CT.)

IV contrast medium.
   The precise technique will depend on the clinical problem involved. In some cases 50 ml of contrast medium will suffice, but if fine detail or fuller opacification of vessels e.g. the aorta with possible dissection, the SVC with possible compression or thrombosis, contrast enhancement of tumour or the thyroid, or the differentiation of vascular structures from nodes particularly in the hilar regions, then a **dynamic study** using 100 ml (or more) of rapidly injected medium just before the definitive sections are taken, may be required (and despite its cost non-ionic medium is preferable for this because of the infrequency of any adverse symptoms which might delay the taking of the appropriate sections). Some use a bolus, followed by an IV drip, to maintain the opacity of e.g. the thoracic veins or the aorta.
   The slight delay which occurs before the upper abdomen (liver, kidneys and adrenals) is imaged in a patient with a chest tumour is usually beneficial, but a long delay as should happen with pelvic tumours to allow the lower ureters and bladder to fill, is not usually necessary in patients with mainly thoracic pathology.

Section thickness and high-resolution CT (**HRCT**).
   Frequently and particularly for general purpose work 0.5 or 1 cm thick sections are taken, but for increased detail, narrower sections (2, 1.5 or 1 mm thickness) should be employed, and be taken with short scan times to remove movement artefact - the thinner sections often being termed **HRCT**. A 512 x 512 matrix (or greater) should be employed to increase detail.

5 mm sections are often adequate for many clinical purposes, and they also do not require a higher radiation dose, an important point in non-malignant disease.

A 'high spatial' (or bone algorithm) reconstruction is often employed for the fine sections, and they are frequently 'targeted' (see above) so as to produce the clearest magnification. However a soft tissue algorithm for thin lung sections may still be preferable in some cases, as this will give a less coarse contrast, a better grey scale, and will avoid most of the **artefacts and aliasing**, which sometimes can give gross Mach type effects, most pronounced at air /soft tissue interfaces (see Appendices p.5, Appx. 3). This artefact may also lead to erroneously high attenuation values at the periphery of lung nodules; thus HRCT should **not** be used for densitometry (see also Swensen et al., 1992).

Motion artefacts may cause a pleural fissure to appear double (see Fig. 1.12, p.1.7) and may make smaller bronchi appear enlarged - a form of **'pseudobronchiectasis'** (see also Tarver et al., 1988). A geometric phenomenon termed '**aliasing**' (which is more apparent with 'high spatial' reconstruction) results in fine streak artefacts radiating from the edges of sharply defined, high-contrast structures, such as ribs or vertebral bodies, and is most evident in the para-vertebral regions. It causes 'noise' overlying the lung parenchyma, mimicking a fine linear or network interstitial pattern, but the densities produced by 'noise' are finer than those due to pathology, and they are usually parallel with the posterior pleural surfaces (see also Brooks et al., 1979, Stockman et al., 1979 and Mayo et al., 1987).

Artefacts may be reduced by practising breathing with the patient so as to ensure similar depths of inspiration with each breath, and by **increasing the mA and kV in obese or large patients**, when the tissue thickness may severely reduce x-ray quanta reaching the detectors. However, **some movement artefacts are nearly always present in the lingula, due to cardiac movement.**

In many cases a number of thicker (often 1 or 0.5 cm) and thin (e.g. 0.2 cm) sections are taken at the initial examination, with fewer being taken on 'follow-up'. Some individual small nodules (e.g. tiny secondary deposits, old calcified chicken pox nodules, etc.) may be 'missed' on thin section examinations if they are out of the plane of the sections taken, but in most cases other representative lesions will be seen.

Radiation dosage - the radiation burden to the population at large is receiving increased attention, and great strides are being made in the design of apparatus to try to minimise this. In patients with advanced disease, and particularly malignant disease, the radiation dosage from CT is of little importance. It however becomes a problem in young people (e.g. with possible bronchiectasis), and in those with chronic disease, in whom repeat examinations may be carried out. When greater collimation and the same tube current is used, as compared with lesser collimation with thicker sections, then the overall chest dosage will be reduced. The same is true if fewer sections are taken. However, increasing the KV from 120 to 140 will double the incident skin dosage, and increasing the mA will also proportionately increase the x-ray dosage given. As noted above and in Appx. 1 the dosage from CT is much higher than from high KV or digital radiography, and with HRCT the dose at each slice position will be of the order of a few cGy (or rads). Because of this high radiation exposure, the author has always limited the number of slices in young people.

References.
Naidich et al. (1990) used a low mA (e.g. 10) and only half a scan rotation and claimed to be able achieve similar clinical results - see also reference to Zwirewich et al. (1991b) below.

The value of CT and HRCT for the chest.
Disease processes may be shown by CT which are not appreciated on plain radiographs e.g. emphysema, sarcoidosis, PCP, etc. CT may also show small nodules (e.g. secondary deposits, micro-metastases, second primary tumours etc.) that are 'hidden' (e.g. in sub-pleural areas or at extreme lung bases, in the costo-phrenic sulci, etc.).

Nodules or masses are usually readily differentiated from normal or abnormal vessels in the lung from their anatomical appearances, but more difficulty can be experienced with the differentiation of vessels from nodes in the hila (Just beginning to understand anatomy - Dixon, 1983 - Body CT). Further help is given by contrast enhancement (sometimes with dynamic injection, or spiral

CT). With longer scan times, vessel pulsation may cause the '**twinkling   star**' sign (with radial artefacts), whereas nodules are usually more clear-cut (see also Kuhns and Borlaza, 1980).

CT has produced almost a revolution in the amount of information which can be gained about possible mediastinal masses and disease, especially lymph node enlargement, in a non-invasive manner, rather than relying on contour abnormalities on plain radiographs. 'Hidden masses' such as in some nodal groups (e.g. enlarged internal mammary nodes), thymomas, and carcinoids may be found. Masses and their relationships to other structures may be studied, particularly because of contrast differences due to mediastinal fat, the neighbouring lung or by the use of IV contrast agents. The latter will not only enhance the density within vessels, but also show a '**blush'   in vascular   tumours,** such as goitres, teratomas, sarcomas, haemangiopericytomas, chemodectomas, carcinoids, Castleman's disease, some lymph nodes, or other mediastinal masses including liposarcomas, etc. It may also be seen on the edge of empyemas and mesotheliomas ('**rind**'). Note that lymph nodes are usually sectioned along their shorter (and not their longer) axes.

It is frequently used for guidance in the drainage of abscesses, fluid collections, etc. or for biopsy procedures.

In assessing **lung tumours** (see also Chapter 4. and the numerous illustrations in the Illus. files) CT shows well:

(a) the shape, density, internal structure and bronchi entering lung masses, whether these are -
   (i) spherical, etc. in shape, (ii) more diffuse or irregular, or (iii) carcinomatous consolidation,

(b) the orientation and spread of tumours within the lung, in relation to the curved thoracic and pleural surface of the lungs. It may also show spread into adjacent structures, particularly the muscle and fat of the chest wall, bone erosion (ribs, sternum or adjacent vertebrae), mediastinal nodes, spread around the aorta, SVC or the oesophagus. Nodes are best demonstrated when surrounded by fat.

(c) pulmonary deposits or second primary tumours.

(d) a big problem is when collapsed or opaque lung lies adjacent to the mediastinum, as this obscures the pleuro-mediastinal interface, a may give rise to spurious diagnosis of transgression. A method of differentiation is to induce a pneumothorax (see p. 14.26).

(e) another is that although many lymph nodes > 1 cm in diameter are often involved by tumour, these and much larger nodes may be enlarged from reactive hyperplasia. Also tiny nodal deposits are invisible at CT - see also p. 13.29.

Baron et al. (1981b) defined CT demonstration of direct mediastinal invasion by a lung tumour if the tumour replaces part of the adipose tissue or encircles the mediastinal vessels or the main bronchi.

HRCT will usually resolve pulmonary anatomy down to secondary lobule level. As noted on p. 1.40, the secondary lobules are mostly 1 to 1.5 cm in diameter and contain the acini, and in turn the primary lobules and alveoli. Within secondary lobules, the arterioles have a central position (together with their accompanying bronchioles and lymphatics, which form the broncho-vascular bundles) and they may be seen as small '**dots**' or branching structures. The venules and their accompanying lymphatics lie peripherally within the septa, which except in the cortical part of the lung are often incomplete. Those which are complete (especially posteriorly and subpleurally and overlying the diaphragm) when thickened give rise to the honeycombs or polygons seen on CT sections. In the more central parts of the lungs, where the septa are less well developed, linear opacities represent obliquely oriented septa. The alveoli, capillaries and supporting connective tissue lie between the broncho-vascular bundles and the perilobular septa.

Details of the extent and morphology of lung and bronchial disease may be readily demonstrated, especially with HRCT for parenchymal disease:

e.g.   consolidation with an 'air bronchogram'
      bullae and emphysema
      pattern of fibrosis, lung shadowing, etc. - whether peripheral, central, and affecting upper,
         middle or lower lung zones
      collapsed lobes or segments
      physiological or true pulmonary oedema, perivenous cuffing, etc.
      accompanying pleural disease, effusion, thickening, nodularity, etc.
      cavitation within inflammatory disease, tumours, etc.

Air-space diseases, such as infection, oedema or alveolar proteinosis tend to opacify the acini (often with some remaining air-filled), whilst centri-lobular emphysema enlarges them. Some conditions such as sarcoidosis tend to mainly affect the tissues around the broncho-vascular bundles, whilst others such as pneumoconiosis affect the interstitium; there is however often a considerable overlap. Lymphangitis carcinomatosa not only distends the lymphatics of the broncho-vascular bundle, but also those within the septa, giving rise to both enlarged dots and septal engorgement. Fibrotic diseases, like fibrosing alveolitis also affect both the alveoli and the interstitium.

As noted above HRCT may be abnormal, when plain radiographs show no abnormality. Whilst some appearances overlap, others are more clear cut. The technique also helps in planning the best route and site for biopsy, and is particularly valuable for planning the transbronchial route. It is a good research tool, for documenting the progress and structural changes in many lung diseases. It is also of value for documenting the degree of damage for compensation purposes, particularly when this is challenged by an employer or a Government agency (e.g. the Pneumoconiosis Board). In this context the author has seen the grossest disease from asbestosis challenged, until HRCT pictures were forwarded (together with an explanation of their meaning)!

Brief notes on some HRCT appearances are given on ps. 1.50 to 1.56, other details are given with the various sections describing particular conditions.

Spiral volumetric (or helical) CT (including 3D reconstruction).

The first spiral CT of an aneurysm was done in Switzerland in 1989, and the technique was described by Kalendar in 1990. The alternative name - 'helical scanning' - derives from its screw-like tube rotation in relation to the patient who moves in the Z-axis.

During a single breath hold, the patient is fed slowly through the gantry during continuous x-ray tube exposure and rotation. An entire volume of tissue is therefore scanned and the data can be reconstructed into sections of appropriate thickness (with 180 or 360° tube arc) for viewing. The technique is of considerable value in the detection of small lung nodules, as these may fall in or out of a slice plane on conventional CT (see diagram), but not on spiral CT, which will also more easily separate adjacent structures, give better shape reproduction and optimal contrast. The radiation dose is continuous slice by slice, and may be reduced by lowering the ma and increasing the pitch (speed of z axis as this determines the separation of tube arcs - pitch 1 = 10mm/ sec, and pitch 2 = 20mm/ sec.) but increased speed may increase artefacts. The technique is very useful for biopsy procedures, especially the demonstration of needle tips in relation to nodules, showing longitudinal and especially vascular structures such as the aorta, demonstrating dissections, and 'flaps' due to dissection, the pulmonary arteries, pulmonary emboli (see below), and contrast enhancement of nodules, tumours, etc. It also aids in the examination of the adrenals (avoiding missing nodules), or in the search for a small thymoma, etc.

nodule within a slice plane.   nodule outside a slice plane.

Fig. 20.9 Diagram - how a lesion may be missed between sections on chest CT.

New machines are now available for routine volumetric examinations, which can obtain all data for the complete examination in a single breath-hold (12 sec. suffices for most purposes). This almost eliminates respiratory artefacts, and with careful timing allows the systemic and/or pulmonary vessels to be visualised during maximum contrast opacification. Reconstruction (as with MR) can be made in any plane, which may be planar, curved or slab in type. 3D, ciné visualisations, and virtual reality imaging may be made and **CT   'bronchoscopy'** are becoming practical methods of studying the bronchi.

Spiral CT angiography has the advantage over conventional angiography that both intra- and extra-vascular abnormalities are readily visualised It is gradually replacing formal CT angiography, and only minimal experience appears to be necessary to obtain uniform and nearly constant opacification of intrathoracic vessels down to 2 - 3 mm in diameter with smaller volumes of contrast medium than are needed for conventional or digital angiography. The technique is clearly one that may be used routinely in the future for the diagnosis of **pulmonary embolism** (see references below and ps. 7.28-29).

Rémy Jardin (1997) recommended spiral CT angiography as the method of choice for studying bronchial tumours (e.g. veno-atrial invasion, differentiation of nodes from vessels), pulmonary emboli, the diagnosis of the cause of haemoptysis, AVMs and anomalies of pulmonary venous return (scimitar veins, etc.).

Some of the latest CT machines have the facility to perform not only spiral CT, but also multislice techniques using multirow detector systems (see Kalender, 1999 and Kalender et al., 1999) **and 'CT fluoroscopy' with digital storage of a series of images - the last being invaluable for biopsy and some interventional techniques.** (Multislice gives greater speed with more images and scope for different reconstructions - for radiation dosage etc. - see Appendix 1 ps. 1-3.)

CT references (see also ps. 1.56 - 1.58).

General
Stanley et al. (1976) : CT of the body - early trends in application and accuracy.
Heitzman (1977) : Analysis of the mediastinum using CT.
Kollins (1977) : CT of the pulmonary parenchyma and chest wall.
Kreel (1977a) : EMI general purpose scanner., (1978b) : CT of the thorax., (1978a) : CT of interstitial lung disease.
Crowe et al. (1978) : CT of the mediastinum.
Emani et al. (1978) : Value of CT in **radiotherapy** of lung cancer.
Robbins et al. (1978) : Observations on the medical efficacy of CT in the chest and abdomen.
Shevland et al. (1978) : Conventional tomography and CT in assessing the resectability of primary lung cancer.
Brooks et al. (1979) : Aliasing - a source of streaks on CT.
Siegelman (1979) : CT has become a valuable technique offering significant advantages over standard chest radiography in evaluating the pulmonary parenchyma, the mediastinum, pleura, chest wall and diaphragm.
Stockman (1979) : Simulation study of aliasing in CT.
Mintzer et al. (1979b) : Comparing CT & conventional tomograms of primary & secondary lung tumours.
Komaiko et al. (1980) : Para-vascular neoplasm which **enhances with IV contrast medium**.
Pugatch et al. (1980) : CT of benign mediastinal abnormalities.
Heitzman (1981) : CT of the thorax - current perspectives.
Kono et al. (1981) : Value of CT in the follow up of lung cancer and mediastinal tumours.
Husband and Fry (1981) : CT of the Body.
Pugatch and Faling (1981) : Value of CT in the follow up of lung cancer (CT of thorax - progress report).
Coddington (1982) : Pathological evaluation of CT images of the lungs.
Fram et al. (1982) : Three dimensional display of the heart, aorta, lungs and airways using CT.
Levi et al. (1982) : The unreliability of CT numbers as absolute values.
van Waes and Zonneveld (1982) : Direct coronal body CT.
Yee et al. (1982) : Technical accuracy and clinical efficacy of thoracic CT.
Brown, L. and Muhm (1983) : CT of the Thorax: current perspectives.
Dixon (1983) : Body CT - a Handbook.
Moss, Gamsu and Genant (1983) : CT of the Body.
Webb, W. (1983) : Advances in CT of the thorax.
McCullough and Morin (1983) : CT number, variability and thoracic geometry.
Généreux (1984) : CT of acute and chronic distal air space (alveolar) disease - 'Distal air space disease implies an acute or chronic increase in the radiographic density of the lung due to an abnormal accumulation of fluid, cells or other tissue elements within the smaller air spaces.'
Godwin (1984) : CT of the Chest.
Moore, A. et al. (1984) : CT of mediastinal and hilar masses.
Naidich et al. (1984) : CT of the Thorax.
Pizer et al. (1984) : Devised a method of showing most of the different types of tissue on a given slice, on a single image. They automatically adjusted the grey scale levels smoothly across the image by (i) allowing the grey scale assignment for each pixel to depend directly on a region of a specified size and shape surrounding it, or (ii) computing the desired grey level assignment at a coarsely selected group of image points and interpolating between these sample points - in this way lung and mediastinum may be displayed in each chest image.

Putman et al. (1984) : CT images and standard window settings.
Siegelman (1984) : CT of the Chest.,   Fry (1985) : Beyond the chest x-ray - CT of the lung.
Généreux (1985) : CT and the lung - review of anatomic and dosimetric features.
Zerhouni et al. (1985) : CT of the pulmonary parenchyma.
Chiu et al. (1986) : CT Angiography of the Mediastinum.
Shephard et al. (1986) : Flow-rate injector for dynamic CT - 20 g intra-cath attached to injector - 100 ml contrast
medium injected at 2 ml/sec, with an initial delay of 13 secs - sections taken at 6 sec intervals.
Mirvis, S. et al. (1987) : Thoracic CT to detect occult disease in 56 critically ill patients to search for sepsis, fever
or unexplained clinical deterioration. They found fluid collections, including empyemas, in several patients, which
had not been found by portable radiography. Other findings included consolidation or collapse, a chest wall abscess,
herniation of the lung through defects in the chest wall, traumatic lung cysts, cavitating lung haematomas, and
haematomas of the mediastinum.
Rémy (1987) : Tomodensitométrie du Thorax.,   Senac and Giron (1987) : Tomodensitométrie Thoracique.
Spizarny et al. (1987) : **Enhancing   mediastinal   masses** - five phaeochromocytomas (aortic arch, one supra-
aortic and three intrapericardial), four goitres, and one Castleman's disease.
Galluzzi et al. (1988) : Computed Tomography of the Lung - An Approach Based on Signs.
Littleton et al. (1990) : Pulmonary masses - Contrast enhancement.

Complication.
Corrigan and Vallance (1997) : Shoulder redislocation as a complication of CT scanning (due to arms being elevated
above the head).

Ciné and ultrafast CT.
Ell et al. (1985) : Ciné CT technique for dynamic airway studies - movement of the cervical airway with respiration.
Ell et al. (1986) : Ciné CT demonstration of non-fixed upper airway obstruction.
Brasch et al. (1987) : Upper airway obstruction in infants and children - evaluation with ultrafast CT.
Garrett et al. (1986) : Ciné CT of Ebstein anomaly.
Stein et al. (1987) : The upper trachea and pharynx in **sleep apnoea**.
Brody et al. (1991) : Airway evaluation in 20 children with use of ultrafast CT (Imatron C-100 using electron gun
technology to produce CT sections in 50 msec and HRCT in 100 msec) - Pitfalls and recommendations.

HRCT references.
Todo et al. (1982) : HRCT of the lung.
McLoud et al. (1983) : Diffuse infiltrative lung disease - a new scheme for description.
Bergin and Müller (1985) : CT in the diagnosis of interstitial lung disease.
Bergin and Müller (1987) : CT of interstitial lung disease.
Nakata et al. (1985) : HRCT of diffuse peripheral lung disease.
Zerhouni et al. (1985) : CT of the pulmonary parenchyma.
Murata et al. (1986) : HRCT of centrilobular lesions of the lung with pathological correlation.
Hruban et al. (1987) : HRCT of inflation fixed lungs and centrilobular emphysema.
Mayo et al. (1987) : HRCT of the lungs - an optimal approach.
Aberle et al. (1988 & 1989) : HRCT in asbestosis.
Itoh et al. (1988) : Imaging of diffuse lung disease - special interest in the secondary lobule.
Meziane et al. (1988) : HRCT of the lung parenchyma with pathological correlation - described a CT sign showing
connection of a nodule to a pulmonary branch - seen with secondary deposits and emboli (Illus. **MASS   VESSEL
SIGN** - see also p. 5.28).
Murata et al. (1988) : Optimisation of CT technique to demonstrate the fine structure of the lung.
Webb et al. (1988) : HRCT of normal and diseased isolated fresh autopsy lungs. In 6 (considered normal) they were
able to visualise normal interlobular septa and small pulmonary artery branches in the lobular cores, but lobular
bronchioles were not visible. In pathological lungs, oedema caused thickening and increased visibility of the
interlobular septa. In three emphysematous lungs, its degree and centrilobular nature were demonstrated. In two with
honeycombing, cysts lined by fibrosis were easily recognised, but tiny cysts under 1 mm in diameter were invisible.
Bergin et al. (1989) : Chronic lung diseases - specific diagnosis by using CT.
Evans, S. et al. (1989) : Radiation dosage to the breast in two scanning chest protocols.
Gamsu and Klein (1989) and Klein and Gamsu (1989) : HRCT of diffuse lung disease (two almost identical review
articles, the second having more illustrations.) covering lymphangitis, emphysema, bronchiectasis, fibrosis and
asbestosis. Both papers discussed technique and anatomy. Both papers noted that air space disease has a similar
appearance to that seen on plain chest radiographs, and that conditions which affect the interstitium (such as
lymphangitis and diffuse pulmonary fibrosis) primarily involve the interlobular septa, especially in the subpleural
and juxta-diaphragmatic regions where septa are best developed. More centrally linear opacities representing obliquely
septa may be seen. Irregularity of lung interfaces along the broncho-vascular structures reflects involvement of the
axial and peripheral interstitium. They also noted subpleural lines, parenchymal bands, honeycombing, hazy
increased density and architectural distortions.

Graves et al. (1989) : Gave a rather **contrary** view of the value of HRCT. They considered that HRCT offers no new diagnostic information compared with conventional CT. They wrote that it may some day be useful in distinguishing between the various forms of bronchiectasis, and that 'considering the lack of specificity, increased radiation exposure, and increased expense to the patient, the use of HRCT is difficult to justify in other than an experimental capacity'.

Hansell and Strickland (1989) : CT of diffuse lung disease.

Mathieson et al. (1989) : Chronic diffuse lung disease - compared diagnostic accuracy of CT and chest radiography.

Murata et al. (1989) : HRCT of pulmonary parenchymal parenchymal disease (review of 71 patients).

Naidich et al. (1989) : Pulmonary parenchymal HRCT - to be or not to be.

Staples et al. (1989) : HRCT and lung function in asbestos exposed workers with normal chest radiographs.

Strickland (1989) : HRCT in parenchymal lung disease - pointed out the importance of distribution and pattern of abnormal areas - discussed air trapping and the need for extra sections taken in expiration to demonstrate this. He discussed pneumocystis, fibrosing alveolitis, lymphangitis carcinomatosa, asbestosis, emphysema, bronchiectasis (including cystic fibrosis), alveolar proteinosis, aspergillosis (bilateral apical aspergillomas) complicating ankylosing spondylitis.

Swensen et al. (1989) : HRCT of the lung - good clinical emphasis & useful table of distribution of appearances in different diseases. (1992) : HRCT of the lungs - findings in venous pulmonary diseases.

Webb (1989) : HRCT of the pulmonary parenchyma.

Zwirewich et al. (1989) : High spatial frequency algorithm improves the quality of standard CT of the thorax.

Charig (1990 - Churchill Hospital, Oxford) : HRCT of the lungs - discussion of technique, indications and appearances with good clinical emphasis in fibrosing alveolitis, sarcoid, asbestos, bronchiectasis, lymphangitis carcinomatosa, pulmonary oedema, alveolar proteinosis, histiocytosis X and drug induced pneumonitis.

Huang et al. (1990) : Advances in medical imaging, including review of HRCT.

Müller and Miller (1990) : CT of chronic diffuse infiltrative lung disease.

Müller (1991) : Clinical value of HRCT in diffuse lung disease.

Miller (1992) : HRCT can (i) detect gross pathology not apparent by less sensitive means, (ii) delineate its characteristics, (iii) determine activity, be a guide to (iv) biopsy and (v) follow up.

Noma et al. (1990) : HRCT of the pulmonary parenchyma.

Naidich et al. (1990) : Low dose CT of the lungs.

Raymond (1990) : HRCT of the lung - chest radiographs can be notoriously insensitive in the detection of early disease, and seriously deficient in their specificity. Indeed, it can occasionally even be difficult to categorise pulmonary patterns as alveolar, interstitial or mixed.

Rémy-Jardin et al. (1990) : Subpleural micronodules in diffuse infiltrative lung diseases - evaluation with thin section CT in 244 patients and 29 healthy controls. Subpleural micronodules were found in lymphangitis, pneumoconiosis, sarcoidosis and some normal controls.

Adams et al. (1991) : Advised caution in using CT pulmonary density mapping for the study of emphysema, as normal individuals can show considerable variability in such mapping.

Grenier et al. (1991) : Value of chest radiography and HRCT in diagnosis of chronic diffuse interstitial lung disease - study of 163 patients.

Hansell and Kerr (1991) : HRCT in the diagnosis of interstitial lung disease. 10% of chest radiographs in patients with diffuse lung disease may appear normal, conversely chest radiographs of obese patients may erroneously suggest interstitial disease.

Leung et al. (1991) : Comparison of the diagnostic accuracy of HR and conventional CT. They studied 75 patients with 1.5 mm collimation and high spatial resolution, and found that in most of those with chronic infiltrative lung disease, a specific diagnosis can be made by obtaining a **limited** number of HRCT sections - e.g. at the level of the aortic arch, the tracheal carina and above the right hemidiaphragm.

Mayo (1991) : HRCT - technical aspects.

Padley et al. (1991) : Comparative accuracy of HRCT and chest radiography in the diagnosis of chronic infiltrative lung disease - studied 100 patients - 86 with chronic diffuse lung disease and 14 normals - were able to give a confident diagnosis with HRCT in 49% and with chest radiography in 41%, and were correct in 82% and 69% respectively. Concluded that diagnostic accuracy is increased by the use of HRCT, but that i**ts superiority to plain radiography may not be as great as has been suggested.**

Rémy-Jardin et al. (1991) : Assessment of diffuse infiltrative lung disease - comparison of conventional CT and HRCT in 150 patients - CT was superior to HRCT in the diagnosis of micronodules and infiltrates, but 15% of micronodules were recognised only with HRCT because of their small size and low density. Fine bronchial and parenchymal lesions were best seen with HRCT - it was also the only method for showing 'ground-glass' attenuation and a confident evaluation of diffuse infiltrative lung disease.

Webb (1991) : HRCT - normal and anatomical pathological findings.

Younger and Hansell (1992) : HRCT is diagnostically valuable in patients with normal chest radiographs who are suspected of having interstitial lung disease.

Zwirewich et al. (1991b) : Low dose HRCT of the lung parenchyma. Clinical information was almost as good - using 1/10 the dosage (but did not show ground glass opacity or emphysema as well). Normal HRCT skin dosage is 12 to 14 rads per slice (see also appendix 1).

Roddie et al. (1992) : Recommended the use of high resolution algorithm for routine chest CT, with improved lung detail (though no increased diagnostic yield), but felt that thin (2 mm) sections may be required to fully evaluate lung pathology, although moderate to severe degradation of the mediastinal image quality occurred.

Webb et al. (1992) : In their book High-Resolution CT of the Lung - noted that **large images are easier to read** e.g. **6 on 1 format**, using 17 x 14" film. On **smaller images subtle findings may be missed.** There is **no correct protocol that should be used.**

Grenier et al. (1993) : HRCT of the airways - to evaluate bronchial tumours 4 or 5 mm thick sections are best, but for bronchiectasis use 1.5 mm thick sections at 10 mm intervals (thus avoiding blurring of bronchial margins resulting from adjacent pulmonary arterial branches).

Lee, K. et al. (1994) : Low dose HRCT (80 mAs) for chronic infiltrative lung disease - at three levels (aortic arch, carina and lung base) gave satisfactory diagnostic accuracy, but conventional dose may be required in large patients - Mayo et al. (1995) : used 140 mAs.

Padley et al. (1993 & 1995) : Current indications for HRCT scanning of the lungs - many types of diffuse lung disease are now sufficiently well characterised on HRCT for lung biopsy to be avoided - this is particularly the case in patients with fibrosing alveolitis, sarcoidosis and lymphangitis carcinomatosa. In other cases HRCT is helpful in determining the type and site for lung biopsy. In patients with idiopathic pulmonary fibrosis, some have potentially reversible disease, manifested by ground-glass shadowing which may respond to steroid treatment, if fibrosis has not yet occurred. In patients with asbestos related disease, silicosis and pneumoconiosis the specificity of the changes is clearer than on plain radiographs, and changes due to smoking or PMF can often be made. In bullous emphysema, HRCT can assess when bullectomy may be of benefit with compressed but otherwise normal lung.

With airway disease, HRCT has replaced bronchography for the assessment of bronchiectasis; it may also show endobronchial tumours; and in BO a mosaic pattern may be seen, with areas of reduced attenuation that are relatively underperfused. HRCT may also reveal abnormalities in PCP, drug induced disease, external allergic alveolitis, eosinophilic pneumonia and COP. HRCT (at 10 mm intervals) delivers a dose about 15 times greater than a single PA radiograph.

Bankier et al. (1996) : Bronchial wall thickness - appropriate window settings for thin-section CT and radiologic-anatomic correlation.

Turner (1997) : Measuring the clinical impact of CT scanning - greatest impact would be expected in clinical situations where there is significant uncertainty about diagnosis, extent of disease, or prognosis.

Yang et al. (1998) : Enhancement of subtle density differences of the lung parenchyma on CT.

See also refs on ps. 1.56 to 1.58.

Paediatric HRCT (See also under Ciné and ultrafast CT, p. 20.24).

Lynch et al. (1990) : Assessment of paediatric pulmonary disease with ultrafast HRCT.

Helton et al. (1992) : BOOP in children with malignant disease.

Kuhn (1993) : HRCT of paediatric pulmonary parenchymal disorders.

Seely et al. (1997) : HRCT of paediatric lung disease - the appearances are similar to those seen in adults, however idiopathic lung fibrosis, fibrosis associated with scleroderma and histiocytosis may have different presentations and a more rapid progression in children - they illustrated TB, aspergillosis, IPF, systemic sclerosis, histiocytosis, extrinsic allergic alveolitis, pulmonary haemorrhage in Wegener's granulomatosis, BO, bronchiectasis, graft v host disease and Swyer James syndrome.

Wadsworth and Hansell (1999) : Aspects of HRCT in paediatric diffuse disease - PAP, idiopathic haemosiderosis, Gaucher (ground-glass shadowing), LAM, NSIP (upper zone honeycombing) - UIP is rare in children, but some have sarcoid-like changes.

Koh and Hansell (2000) : CT of diffuse interstitial lung disease in children.

Expiratory CT

Sweatman et al. (1990) : Examined patients with bronchiolitis obliterans both in inspiration and expiration - the changes were more marked in expiration.

Knudson et al. (1991) : Expiratory CT for assessment of suspected pulmonary emphysema.

Stern and Webb (1993) : Dynamic imaging of lung morphology with ultrafast HRCT - with air trapping, the air is not expelled in expiration and the involved lung remains more lucent than the surrounding normal lung.

Webb et al. (1993) : Dynamic pulmonary CT in 10 healthy adult men - **during exhalation the lung normally increases in density** because the amount of air in the lung is reduced, but in 4 with normal pulmonary function tests there were regions of inhomogeneity in lung density during rapid exhalation indicative of air trapping.

Stern and Frank (1994) : Findings at expiratory CT in small-airway diseases of the lungs - also noted that some non-diseased isolated secondary pulmonary lobules may not deflate with expiration.

Aquino et al. (1994) : BO associated with rheumatoid arthritis, findings on HRCT and dynamic expiratory CT.

Mitchell and Hansell (1995) and Mitchell et al. (1995) : Superimposing exp. on insp. scans showed a 55 to 57% volume change. Not all pts. with BO have an inhomogeneous pattern on expiratory scans.

Murata et al.(1994) : Chest wall and mediastinal invasion by lung cancer - evaluation with multisection expiratory dynamic CT - 15 cases - free movement of tumour along the peripheral or mediastinal pleura in 10, in 5 no movement or **fixed.**

Gruden et al. (1995) : Pitfalls in HRCT of the chest - **Technique**:

Airways disease - 1.5mm thick sections every 1 cm, patient supine. Expiratory scans as needed - window 700, width 1,000.

Diffuse lung disease - 1.5mm thick sections, every 2cm in both prone and supine positions. Special points to note: clearing of abnormality (e.g. subpleural line) in prone position; mucoid impaction of airways - small airways disease; dilatation of bronchi - bronchiectasis or LAM (lymphangioleiomyomatosis); L ventricular motion artefacts.

Gleeson et al. (1996) : Evidence on expiratory CT scans of small air-way obstruction in sarcoid.

Desai and Hansell (1997) : Small airways disease - expiratory CT comes of age.

Park et al. (1997) : Airway obstruction in asthmatic & healthy individuals - insp. & exp. thin-section CT.

Tasker et al. (1997) : CT sections in expiration show that air-trapping is a common finding in sarcoidosis and correlates with physiological parameters of small airways disease.

Bhalla et al. (1996): 'Diffuse lung disease: Assessment with helical CT - Preliminary observations of the role of maximum and minimum intensity projection images.

Wittram and Rappaport (1998) : Expiratory helical CT minimum intensity projection imaging in cystic fibrosis.

Chen et al. (1998) : Assessment of air trapping using post-expiratory HRCT was found in 7 out of 13 healthy volunteers and all of 14 pts. with obstructive lung disease.

Franquet et al. (2000) : Lateral decubitus position for insp./ exp. CT for showing air trapping.

Mosaic pattern of lung attenuation (see p. 2.4).

Extrinsic allergic alveolitis.

Kauczor et al. (1996) : HRCT can show signs of pulmonary immunostimulation with a ventilation dependent distribution after aerosolised interlukin-2 therapy for metastases of renal cell carcinoma.

Diederich et al. (1996) : Use of an experimental model with post-mortem specimens - fixed inflated lungs (polyethylene glycol, ethyl alcohol and formalin - allowed study of CT protocols with irradiation of living subject (CT accounts for 40% of medical radiation).

Spiral CT.

Kalender et al. (1990) : Technique of spiral volumetric CT with single breath-hold, continuous transport and continuous scanner rotation.

Kalender et al. (1995) : Comparison of conventional and spiral CT in the detection of spherical lesions (experimental study).

Kalender and Polacin (1991) : Physical performance characteristics of spiral CT scanning.

Vock et al. (1990) : Spiral CT with single breath-hold - 24 cases.

Costello et al. (1991) : Evaluation of pulmonary nodule with spiral volumetric CT.

Costello et al. (1992) : Spiral CT of the thorax with increased table speed.

Costello (1992) : Reduced volume of contrast medium needed for mediastinal diagnosis (24 sec breath hold).

Hacking and Dixon (1992) : Spiral versus conventional CT in soft tissue diagnosis.

Heiken et al. (1993) : Spiral (helical) CT.

Napel et al. (1992) : CT angiography with spiral CT and maximum intensity projection.

Polacin et al. (1992) : Evaluation of section sensitivity profiles and image noise in spiral CT.

Rubin et al. (1993) : Three-dimensional spiral CT angiography of the abdomen.

Dillon et al. (1993) : Spiral CT angiography.

Rémy-Jardin et al. (1993) : Detection of pulmonary nodules with thick-section spiral CT, compared with conventional CT.

Tello et al. (1993) : Subclavian vein thrombosis detected with spiral CT and three-dimensional reconstruction.

Vock and Soucek (1993) : Spiral CT in the assessment of focal and diffuse lung disease.

Brink et al. (1994) : Abnormalities of the diaphragm and adjacent structures have been difficult to image with conventional CT, but spiral CT (with multiplanar reconstruction - coronal and axial) now gives similar sensitivity to multiplanar MR.

Collie et al. (1994) : Comparison of spiral-acquisition and conventional CT in the assessment of pulmonary metastatic disease - found the spiral technique to be superior and with a similar radiation dose. 5mm reconstruction increments had no advantage over 10mm. Increasing the pitch could give a reduced radiation dose.

Engeler et al. (1994) : Spiral HRCT increased the diagnostic accuracy, particularly for bronchiectasis at lung bases.

Newmark et al. (1994) : Spiral CT evaluation of the trachea and bronchi.

Paranjpe and Bergin (1994) : CT lung scans using spiral and conventional CT at 5 & 8 mm collimation showed no differences in resolution, but at 1 & 3 mm curved structures such as the walls of bullae and fissures were somewhat indistinct.

Rémy (1994) : Three main indications for spiral CT : (i) Lung disease - continuous images, reduced motion artefacts, better definition of nodules and better densitometry.   (ii) Vascular structures are better visualised with a smaller amount of contrast medium; acute thromboembolic disease may also be detected. (iii) 3D imaging allows reconstruction in coronal, sagittal and other planes and makes CT angiography possible.

Rémy et al. (1994) : Unenhanced 3D helical CT - a reliable tool for evaluation of pulmonary AV malformations.

Kalender (1995) : The image quality of spiral CT can be considered equivalent to that of conventional CT in every respect; there are only very subtle differences. It also offers distinct advantages with respect to 3D spatial resolution.

Dixon (1995) : In the chest, exactly contiguous images can be obtained, leading to better delineation of pulmonary nodules, and hilar and mediastinal structures; it also aids the diagnosis of pulmonary embolism and aortic dissection.

Miszkeil and Shaw (1995) : Helical CT contrast studies for the diagnosis of pulmonary embolism showed complete obstruction or 'rail track' signs, including 'saddle emboli', particularly in the lower lobe vessels.

Quint et al. (1995) : Helical CT with multiplanar reconstructions may be more accurate than HRCT in showing mild stenoses of central airways, their lengths and horizontal webs. (Like IFTs - Year Book Diag. Rad., 1996, p.51).

Seltzer et al. (1995) : Ciné viewing of spiral CT of the chest improved the detection of nodules.

Buckley et al. (1995) : Narrow interscan spacing (4 - 5mm) improved the detection rate and confidence in diagnosis of pulmonary nodules.

Croiselle et al. (1995) : Improved detection of pulmonary nodules with spiral CT:

Lacrosse et al. (1995) : Spiral CT of the tracheobronchial tree.

Rémy-Jardin et al. (1995) : Spiral CT accurately depicts normal hilar lymph nodes and their major anatomical relationships.

Rémy Jardin and Rémy (1996) : Spiral CT of the Chest.   Brink et al. (1997) : review of helical/spiral CT.

Toma and Breatnach (1995) : Image artefacts associated with helical thoracic CT - more marked with a pitch of 2 (20mm/sec table speed) compared with a pitch of 1 (10mm/sec) - mainly pseudolucencies due to cardiac movement.

McWilliams and Chalmers (1995) : Pseudo-thrombosis of the infra-renal IVC during helical CT.

Zeman et al. (1995) : Helical/Spiral CT - a Practical Approach.

Fox et al. (1996) : Pseudothrombosis of intra-renal IVC during helical CT - ? cause (see also p. 9.4)

Kaneko et al. (1996) : Screening and detection of peripheral lung cancer with low-dose spiral CT vs radiography.

Wright, A. et al. (1996) : Pulm. nodules & effect of pitch - increasing from 1.0 to 1.2 to 1.5 to 2.0 leads to a slight tendency to undercount lesions; it is recommended that the pitch should not exceed 1.5 for staging malignant disease.

Rémy-Jardin et al. (1997a) : Optimisation of spiral CT acquisition protocol for peripheral pulm. arteries - 2mm collimation at 0.75 per revolution enables marked improvement in the analysis of segmental and subsegmental pulm. arteries.

Kalender (1999) : **Computed Tomography**; Kalender et al. (1999) : **Multislice CT builds on spiral CT**.

Silverman et al. (1995) : Normal and abnormal findings on 3D reconstructed images of upper airway on helical CT

Sinnatamby et al. (1995) : Spiral CT with 3D reconstruction of the major airways - an adjunct to bronchoscopy?

Zeman et al. (1995) : Value of helical CT with multiplanar reformation and 3D rendering to show aortic dissection and the extent of the intimal flap.

Ferretti et al. (1996) : Tracheo-bronchial CT - 3D spiral CT with bronchoscopic perspective.

Kauczor et al. (1996) : 3D spiral CT of the tracheobronchial tree.

Sagy et al. (1996) : Spiral 3D CT in the management of paediatric intrathoracic airway assessment.

Rémy (1996) : Multiplanar 3D and reconstruction techniques in CT of the chest - surface rendering techniques (shaded surface display) and volume rendering techniques (percentage of a given density). Useful for showing the trachea and bronchi (esp. for the extent and exterior extension of tracheal tumours) and stenosis (most commonly anterior); vessels, AVMs and hilar lymph nodes (upper lobes - lateral to PA; ML, lingula and LLs - lateral to bronchi & medial and anterior to PA).

Rémy Jardin and Rémy (1997) : Clinical indications of 3D reconstructions in chest diseases applied to central airways - a combination of multiplanar and 3D rendering of thin-section airway data can be useful to evaluate stenoses and the extent of bronchial lesions. Instead of analysing hundreds of axial images, a selection of shaded-surface-displays and volume-rendering-techniques enables the radiologist to produce a single view of complex anatomy. These also help in the delineation of thoracic outlet lesions.

Summers (1997) : Navigational aids for real-time virtual bronchoscopy.

Curtin et al. (1998) : Thin section volumetric CT for the assessment of lobar and segmental bronchial stenoses.

Richenberg and Hansell (1998) : Image processing and spiral CT of the thorax - review of multiplanar reconstruction, three-dimensional rendering and sliding-thin slab reconstruction.

Scheck et al. (1998) : Radiation dose and image quality in spiral CT - guidelines on optimal tube current for clinical protocols is desirable.

McAdams et al.(1998) : Virtual bronchoscopy for directing transbronchial needle aspiration of hilar and mediastinal lymph nodes.

Rémy-Jardin et al.. (1998) : Volume rendering of the tracheobronchial tree and clinical evaluation - improved the recognition of mild changes in airway calibre and the understanding of complex tracheobronchial anomalies.

Magnetic Resonance Imaging.

This imaging method depends on the nuclei of atoms resonating under certain conditions in response to applied magnetic fields. Protons and neutrons rotate about their central axes giving rise to angular momentum or 'spin'. Atomic nuclei with even numbers of protons have no 'net spin', because pairs of particles mutually cancel this out, whereas nuclei with odd numbers of protons or neutrons have a net spin and also a net charge and behave as tiny bar magnets. With most clinical MR work, the abundant hydrogen atoms (each with a single proton) are the main source of the diagnostic signal. Hydrogen atoms giving rise to a MR signal are mainly those in fat and water. Protons in larger molecules, such as protein (e.g. DNA) or in bone, do not usually contribute significantly to the MR signal, and with tissues most of the signal comes from intracellular water.

When placed in a very strong magnetic field, the individual magnetic fields of the protons become aligned (either parallel or at 180°) to the applied magnetic field. At equilibrium slightly more protons are aligned parallel than in the opposite direction, there then being a slight magnetic vector towards the applied field. The spinning motion of the protons about their axes is not exactly aligned with the main magnetic field, thus a 'wobbling motion' like a spinning top is produced ('**precessing**').

The protons already in equilibrium-orientation can be tipped as a group away from this by radiofrequency pulsation (RF) having the same frequency as the wobble of the protons. When the RF is turned off, the precessing nuclei return to their previous orientation, and in so doing release energy, also in the form of a RF signal.

The time taken to return to equilibrium is termed the 'T_1 (or spin-lattice) **relaxation time**' (or magnetic property), whilst the T_2 (or spin-spin) **relaxation time**' refers to the rate at which the emitted RF signal decays, this in turn depending on interference or relaxation between neighbouring spinning protons (proton density). Fat has short T_1 and T_2 relaxation times, whereas those for water are long.

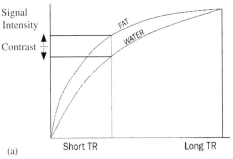 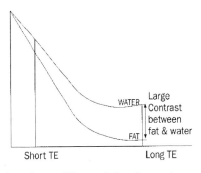

Fig. 20.10.   (a) T_1 weighting depends on the T_1 times between fat and water. TR controls how long each vector can recover before the next RF pulse. (b) T_2 weighting depends upon T_2 differences between fat and water, and this is determined by TE. (Reproduced from Silver, D., 1995, A reintroduction to MRI physics, Clinical MRI, **5**, 170 - 171, by permission).

T_1 weighting refers to a short time between each of the applied pulses, whilst T_2 weighting has longer time intervals. T_1 shows mediastinal and hilar masses surrounded by mediastinal fat, giving rise to low intensity nodes, although one may not always be able to distinguish them from fat. Most lesions in the lung and mediastinum have long T_1 and T_2 relaxation times, and thus give rise to low signal intensities on T_1 weighted images. A few give rise to high signal intensities - e.g. ganglioneuroma, phaeochromocytoma, bronchogenic cyst and lymphangioma. It is possible that the latter may be due to interactions between high molecular weight macromolecules and water.

On some MR images (especially spin-echo), **blood** passing through larger blood vessels appears **dark or black**, because the stimulated protons in flowing blood move out of the area being examined before signal acquisition takes place - 'flow void' (or there is rapid diphasing caused by motion). The 'flow void can be emphasised by using a thin section or long echo time (TE). In a fast spin-echo sequence, a long train of echoes is acquired using a series of RF pulses giving rise to enhanced 'wash-out' effects. Flow-voids may also be produced by presaturation, dephasing gradients and preinversion pulses. **Bright blood** is produced by 'time-of-flight' and phase contrast techniques such as gradient-echo pulse sequences, flow compensation, short echo time, Gd chelate, spiral scan pulses and turboFLASH sequences - these are particularly used for MR angiography.

Resistive, permanent or cryogenic magnets may be used (the latter being made e.g. by Oxford Instruments). With a cryogenic magnet, liquid helium and nitrogen keep the applied electric current constantly circulating in the surrounding wire coils which are in a superconducting state. Saddle and surface coils lie within the cavity of the magnet, and around the patient, in order to apply the RF, to determine the position of slices and to detect the responses.

Low field strength magnets give greater contrast, but the spatial resolution improves with higher field strengths. The ideal is difficult to judge, because in some situations, one or other may be preferable, and a compromise has to be reached for most machines.

A great advantage of MR over CT, is that any plane may be portrayed by MR in **the same detail**, whereas with most CT reconstructions, in any but the axial plane, are less detailed. The axial plane is comparable to CT for the mediastinum, though poor for the lungs, whilst the coronal corresponds to plain chest radiographs or AP tomograms. The sagittal plane is excellent for the spine and spinal cord.

Soft tissue contrast and spatial resolution with MR are often better than with CT, but when movement is a problem, as in the thorax, CT gives better detail. In order to overcome movement, both cardiac and respiratory and gating may be employed. In the chest, MR can give better contrast resolution than CT (though poorer tissue differentiation), particularly where pathology is adjacent to or within major vessels, and there is compression or involvement of vascular structures or the heart. It may show disease in areas where CT is equivocal, such as the subcarinal, hilar and aorto-pulmonary window areas, where differentiation from fat and vascular structures are important. MR will often clearly demonstrate invasion of adjacent structures, such as the trachea, blood vessels or spine. At present CT is superior to MR for showing endobronchial lesions. Within the lungs, the low proton density suffers from poorer spatial resolution as well as from movement artefacts. It will also **not** usually show **calcification within nodules, nor** some lesions under about 1 cm in diameter. However newer sequences are showing the lungs much more clearly, and b**ecause of the lack of signal from normal tissues, nodules tend to stand out clearly against a black background, and are readily differentiated from vessels.**

Coronal images often clearly show the trachea, the main bronchi, the main vessels (and subdiaphragmatic areas, including the adrenals) and may be better for the lung apices. Sagittal sections are particularly valuable for disease adjacent to the spine. Chest wall invasion is often difficult to assess both by MR and CT. CT has the advantage that bone destruction is usually well demonstrated, but the axial and coronal views taken with MR may often be more helpful, particularly with superior sulcus tumours. Inflammatory disease will often give a similar picture with both MR and CT.

Gated studies can be used to provide moving images, allowing diaphragmatic movement etc. to be studied; these can also assess 'fixity' of the mediastinum (see also ps. 2.7 - 8 & 15.2).

Techniques.

Spin echo - an RF pulse sufficient to 'flip' precessing protons 90° from their parallel alignment is followed by a second pulse which turns them through 180°. The results are predominantly T_2 weighted, but T_1 weighted images are provided by altering the times for repetition and to echo.

Inversion recovery - an initial 180° pulse is followed by a 90° pulse. The images are T_1 dependent and give a good demonstration of anatomy.

Saturation recovery - an this simple sequence, there is a single 90° pulse and a long repetition time between pulses. The emitted signal following the pulse depends on the proton density - T_2.

Partial saturation recovery - when the signal is repeated rapidly, there will be only a partial relaxation and the resulting signal will depend on proton density and T_1.

STIR or TurboSTIR ('short tau inversion recovery' sequence) - suppresses the signal from normal fat and may allow disease within or adjacent to fat to be highlighted and appear 'white'. T_1 and T_2 values are summated and structures (or lesions) with a **high extra-cellular water content appear bright**. It is very good for demonstrating abnormal hilar and para-aortic nodes (e.g. from lung cancer), also for showing pericardial and chest wall invasion, spinal deposits and abscesses. Malignancy and infection may appear similar, because of their aggressive nature and the propensity of both to cause tissue oedema. (This technique was devised at the Hammersmith Hospital, and has been popularised in the UK by Dr. Paul Goddard of Bristol). It is particularly valuable for showing tumour masses, recurrences of **lymphoma** and **malignant**, **sarcoid** and **inflammatory nodes** within the mediastinum (see Illus. **MR**). A preliminary T_1 coronal study is made for demonstrating the anatomy.

Turbo FLASH - breath-hold T_1-weighted rapid gradient echo sequence for ill patients or repeated images for ciné loop technique.

MAST (T_2 weighted - motion artefact suppression technique) - will also highlight pathology, producing a similar effect to a myelogram, enabling cord displacement or compression to be seen.

Flow sensitive (or phase contrast) techniques (including **GRASS** - gradient-recalled acquisition in the steady state) are useful for demonstrating vascular and cardiac abnormalities, including atrial myxomas and valvular insufficiencies, particularly with '3 D' video-displays.

Vascular contrast media for MR - the only really useful one at present is Gadolinium DTPA. It is strongly paramagnetic, and is chemically stable, as well as being quickly detoxicated and excreted. Gd DTPA may aid the demonstration of vascular tumour infiltration in the soft tissues of the neck, the chest wall or mediastinum. It may also enhance other very vascular lesions in the chest (e.g. adenomas) or vascular deposits in the liver or adrenals. Within areas of collapsed lung, malignant masses may enhance, with a slow 'wash-out'. Gd however does not appear to be of value for distinguishing benign and malignant lymph node enlargement, as heterogeneous enhancement may occur with an aggressive cause of nodal enlargement - malignancy, TB, histoplasmosis, and in some reactive nodes. However enlarged nodes of unusual shape, high signal on STIR and abnormal enhancement are all factors consistent with malignancy. Gd may also help distinguish malignant tissue from scar and fibrous tissue.

A basic chest examination protocol may be :
(i) T_1 weighted transverse.
(ii) STIR or TurboSTIR transverse.
(iii) Multicoronal.
Other sequences may be added : (iv) Ciné angiography, (v) TurboFLASH, (vi) Gd. enhancement.
Examples of MR studies are shown in Illus. **MR.**

In summary: - **The problems of imaging the lungs by MR** are low proton spin density (low signal to noise), cardiac and respiratory motion and considerable susceptibility gradients arising from the multiple air-tissue interfaces.

See also ps. 7.34 & 7.35 re MR and pulmonary emboli.

Note also that biopsy needle tips (non-magnetic metal) are usually poorly imaged with MR, and localisation is better with CT, fluoroscopy and US.

References.
General
Damadian et al. (1977) : First images in live human body - heart, etc.
Hinshaw et al. (1978) : Display of cross scetional anatomy of rabbit's head by nuclear magnetic imaging.
Alfidi et al. (1982) : Experimental results in humans and animals.
Pykett et al. (1982) : Principles of MR imaging.
Littleton and Durizch (1983) : Sectional imaging methods - a comparison.
Steiner (1983) : Early clinical experience at Hammersmith Hospital, London.
        (1987) : 600 MR machines in use worldwide.
Bydder and Young (1985) : Use of the inversion recovery sequence to increase the contrast between tissues with a high water content and surrounded by normal tissues.
Smith, M. (1985) : Physics and method.
Foster and Hutchinson (1987) : Practical MR imaging.
Weinreb and Redman (1987) : Magnetic Resonance of the Body.
Brown, J. et al. (1988) : MR imaging of low signal intensity lesions using flow sensitive techniques.
Bydder (1988) : Review - present status and future prospects of MR (24 machines in UK - half around London - compared with 150 CT scanners.
Gerhardt and Frommhold (1988) : Atlas of Anatomic Correlations in CT and MR.
Stark and Bradley (1988) : Magnetic Resonance Imaging.

Young (1988) : Magnetic Resonance Imaging.
    (1990) : MR resonance - boundless possibilities or possible boundaries.

MR of the thorax.
Gamsu et al. (1983) : MR of the thorax.
Kundel (1983) : Potential role of MR in thoracic disease.
Brasch et al. (1984) : MR imaging of the thorax in childhood.
Steiner (1984 & 1987) : MR of the heart and mediastinum.
Webb et al. (1984b) : Evaluation of MR sequences in imaging mediastinal tumours - studied 7 bronchial carcinomas and 3 benign lesions - readily showed vascular structures, and distinguished most soft tissue masses from fat - also detected fluid collections but considerable attention to detail was required. Lung lesions were poorly displayed.
    (1984e) : Coronal MR imaging of the chest - normal and abnormal appearances. (1985) : Sagittal MR of the chest.
Barter (1985) : MR of aortic aneurysm.
Dooms et al. (1985a) : Characteristics of lymphadenopathy by MR., (1985b) : MR of fatty masses.
Schmidt et al. (1985) : MR image contrast and relaxation times of solid tumours in the chest, abdomen and pelvis.
Westcott et al. (1985) : MR of the hilum and mediastinum using cardiac gating (20 patients).
McMurdo et al. (1985) : With MR the marked contrast between the signal void of normal vascular structures, the moderate signal intensity of tumour and the high signal intensity of a thrombus or slowly flowing blood allows ready detection of venous occlusion and its cause.
Von Schulthless et al. (1986a) : MR of coarctation of aorta., (1986b) : MR imaging of mediastinal masses.
Bauer et al. (1987) : Atlas of MR Tomography (Part 3, Heart and Thorax).
Cohen, M. et al. (1987) : MR of 38 children with lung disorders (including cystic adenomatoid malformation, lobar emphysema, lymphangiectasis, sequestration, A /V malformation, infection, congestive failure, infarction, tumour, collapse and haematoma) showed all lesions, but was not as sensitive as CT.
Mayr et al. (1987) : CT superior to MR for showing endobronchial abnormalities due to tumours.
Glazer et al. (1988) : Overlap of relaxation times within benign and malignant nodes.
Goddard (1988) : STIR sequence in ungated studies gives 'white' contrast in abnormal nodes.
Goddard et al. (1989) : MR has better contrast resolution than CT, particularly where pathology is adjacent to major vessels. It may show disease in areas where CT is equivocal, esp. in the subcarinal and hilar regions, the aorto-pulmonary window and chest wall, and show mediastinal, spinal, liver and adrenal deposits from lung cancer. It is also valuable for differentiating tumour recurrence from fibrosis and in the follow-up of patients with lymphoma.
Barakos et al. (1989) : High signal intensity lesions of the chest.
Hatabu et al. (1989) : MR imaging has usually been considered inferior to CT for demonstrating the bronchial tree and vessels owing to its poor spatial resolution and negative blood flow effect. However the application of a high signal technique in the lung may have the potential to depict not only small intrapulmonary structures, but also pulmonary blood flow. Preliminary results indicated that small pulmonary vessels may be imaged by MR with a combination of high-resolution techniques and ECG gating in diastole.
Templeton and Zerhouni (1989) : MR in the management of thoracic malignancies - can be used as a problem solving tool when CT findings are equivocal - in the assessment of vascular /mass relationships (SVC or aortic involvement), thrombosis (using GRASS), pericardial disease, assessment of an opacified hemithorax, chest wall, Pancoast tumour, reticuloses, adrenal metastases, etc.
Gefter et al. (1990) : Pulmonary vascular ciné MR imaging - a non-invasive approach to dynamic imaging of the pulmonary circulation (three with pulmonary emboli).
Lee, J. and Glazer (1990) : MR appearance of fibrosis - most studies have shown that mature fibrosis, regardless of cause, has low signal intensity on T_2 weighted images, whereas early fibrosis has a higher signal intensity.
Nagendank et al. (1990) : Lymphomas with dense fibrosis had higher signal intensity than those with little or no fibrosis (? new fibrosis).
Naidich et al. (1990) : MR compared with CT in evaluating cadaveric lung specimens.
Revel et al. (1990) : Haemorrhagic lung lesions had a characteristic high signal intensity on T_1 weighted images.
Goddard et al. (1992) : MR of respiratory movement using turbo-flash sequence - movements of diaphragm, chest wall, heart and abdominal organs were clearly shown.
Mayo et al. (1992) : Improved lung visualisation with short TE spin-echo.

Müller et al. (1992) : MR compared with CT in chronic infiltrative lung disease - although MR imaging is **inferior** to HRCT, it may play a role in the assessment and follow-up of patients with 'ground-glass' shadowing, and be preferable in young people as it will avoid the high radiation dose of HRCT.
Webb and Sostman (1992) : MR imaging of thoracic disease - clinical uses.
Kono (1993) : Clinical utility of Gd-DTPA-enhanced magnetic imaging in lung cancer.
Roobottom et al. (1994) : Use of turbo-flash allows 10 separate images over a 19s period. These can be viewed as a ciné loop to assess phrenic nerve palsy, large pleural effusions and large bullae.
Edelman (1993) : MR angiography - present and future.

Kanth et al. (1994) : Gd non-ionic MR contrast agents appear to enhance thoracic masses on T_1.

Freundlich et al. (1996) : MR imaging of pulmonary apical tumours.

Ng et al. (1996) : MR of normal lung anatomy comparing three sequences - remains a considerable technical challenge - further refinements are needed before MR imaging of the lung parenchyma becomes clinically applicable.

Schima et al. (1996) : Contrast enhanced MR imaging - review.

Shellock and Kanal (1994) : MR Bioeffects; and Shellock (1996) : Procedures and Metallic Objects - Update.

Vock et al. (1996) : HR-MRI of the lung using strong gradients and phased array coils - vasculitis, invasive aspergillosis, PMF, malignant nodes.

Hartnell et al. (1996) : MR angiography demonstration of congenital heart disease in adults.

Graves. (1997) : Magnetic resonance angiography - review article.

Callaway et al. (1998) : MR in the assessment of chronic cavitating lung conditions was used in cases needing follow-up, in view of the high radiation dosage from repeated CT! Cases where it was suitable included viral papillomatosis, bronchiectasis, aspergillosis, atypical mycobacteria (malmoense) and systemic fibrosis. It was a successful means at follow-up for assessing the cavitating lung and for showing reaction in the surrounding lung.

Hyperpolarised gases - He^3 and Xe^{129}

These gases may be inhaled or given IV. They allow much higher MR signals to be obtained as up to 60% hyperpolarisation can be obtained. This with helium compensates for grossly lower density (2,500 times) compared with hydrogen concentrates in tissue. Reduced aeration of areas of lung have been shown in relation to tumours, areas of emphysema, bronchiolitis, etc. The pulmonary vessels are demonstrated as areas without signal. The problem is cost as the gases are very expensive.

Some references.
Ebert et al (1996)
Kauczor et al. (1996)
Kauczor (1998)
Leach et al. (1999)

Ultrasound

The various methods and approaches to the use of ultrasound to examine the thorax are discussed in the various sections of this book. Most times a short-curved real-time 3.5 or 5 mHz transducer has been used by the author. This is ideal for the sub-costal approach to the liver and diaphragm, via the intercostal spaces for the pleura (with fluid, collapsed lobes or masses may be imaged), and masses within the lung may be seen if they are adjacent to the pleura, thus making biopsy easy and safe, since no air-filled lung will be traversed. A 7.5 or 10 MHz transducer is preferable for superficial lesions in the chest wall, superficial lymph nodes or the thyroid (see also ps. 12.40 and 18.9). However a useful ploy, when 7.5 or 10MHZ probe is not available for examining the chest wall, neck, thyroid (or breast) is to use a water-bag with a 3.5 or 5MHZ probe. An infusion bag is commonly available in most radiology departments and this can be covered with a coupling jelly. Using this the probe is 'stood-off' from the skin surface, the tissues show more contrast and are somewhat magnified. A lead-pencil tip, under the bag or probe can be used as a suitable pointer or marker.

When pleural fluid is present, or a cyst or solid tissue abuts the chest wall, an acoustic window may be present via the intercostal spaces, thus allowing not only the demonstration of fluid, but also a possible concomitant tumour (see Illus. **ULTRASOUND, Ca lg&cx wall 15b & 25d**). In addition ultrasound may easily be able to demonstrate the presence of an empyema, pleural haematoma, a pleural or adjacent lung tumour or demonstrate peripheral lung consolidation. It may also demonstrate a collapsed lower lobe within an effusion (see Illus. **ULTRASOUND, Mucocoeles Pt. 9 & Mesothel Pt. 22d**). This often moves with respiration or cardiac motion in a wave-like manner (sometimes termed '**flapping**'). When a bronchial block is present, fluid or mucous filled bronchi may give rise to a '**fluid bronchogram**'; an '**air bronchogram**' with bright echoes from the bronchi being due to residual air in the bronchi, e.g. in pneumonia.

Consolidation typically gives rise to a wedge-shaped hypoechoic area in the lung parenchyma containing the 'air bronchogram' and a lung abscess a hypoechoic area within the consolidated lung. A tumour may give rise to a hypo- or echogenic mass within the lung.

Interruption or displacement of the pleural 'white line' (Illus. ULTRASOUND, Ca lg+pleura Pt. 2) may indicate that a lung tumour is invading the chest wall; similarly loss of the 'diaphragmatic white line' and transgression of it by adjacent organs or fluid (Illus. ULTRASOUND, Diaph trauma 3d) may indicate a ruptured diaphragm (see ps. 15.18&22).

The author's practice is to always examine the chest with ultrasound prior to any attempted aspiration, as this will not only confirm the presence of fluid (not always easy by clinical methods of auscultation and percussion), but also show the best site for puncture. It will in addition obviate placing the aspiration needle or cannula into the liver, spleen or stomach!

Except in very emphysematous patients 'para-sternal' windows are present, which allow the heart and mid-mediastinum to be examined. This may be done with the patient in the erect position or lying on his side in a decubitus position. The right upper mediastinal nodes, and sometimes even nodes down to the subcarinal area may be examined by a suprasternal approach. Cysts of the mediastinum, or large bronchogenic cysts, often may be imaged via an overlying intercostal, etc. space, and percutaneous drainage may be used to remove the fluid.

For most ultrasound examinations of the thorax, the patient is best examined in the upright position (e.g. on a stool). A most convenient position (particularly when carrying out a paracentesis posteriorly) is for the patient to sit on a chair facing its back, with a pillow in front of his chest for support - like sitting on an antique 'library chair' - for the reader to fall asleep on (? & !), whilst the doctor sits on a stool.

A trans oesophageal route with a special probe attached to an endoscope may be used to examine the oesophageal wall, the upper part of the stomach and adjacent structures such as the aorta, pericardium, etc. and a similar one is being developed for the bronchi.

Doppler ultrasound is often useful in differentiating vascular from non-vascular structures in the chest wall, liver, etc. It may also be used with colour displays for detecting neovascularity in the chest wall e.g. by tumours of the lung or pleura invading it or for the demonstration of increased vascularity in enlarged axillary nodes. Within the lung (if the lesion is adjacent to the chest wall) increased vascularity may be seen not only with tumours (see also ps. 4.8 - 9) but also with consolidation, organising infarcts, etc.

Contrast agents (such as microbubbles of a few microns in diameter) are now being used, particularly to display vessels and vascularity. These resonate in 3 - 10 MHz ultrasound beams, as are typically used for diagnosis. Some only have a half life of a few seconds (particularly those that are hand-shaken) whilst others have stabilisers added, but rapidly become diluted in the circulation, and require a more sensitive technique such as Doppler to visualise them. Increased reflectivity of 3rd generation agents may allow clearer demonstrations of normal and pathological anatomy. See references below.

General comment.

The author has been amazed at the under usage of ultrasound in chest disease in many centres. Gross, B.H. (from the Henry Ford Hospital, Detroit) wrote in the 1993 Year Book of Radiology "Although I did 6 months of ultrasonography during my fellowship, I have never used it as a chest radiologist". Such a statement helps to explain the advised continued use of decubitus views etc. for pleural effusions in Blank's book 'Chest Radiographic Analysis' (1989), when ultrasound would have been better in most cases, and would have avoided much unnecessary radiation. Some other authors in the USA, have used ultrasound for the chest, and most of the major radiology and chest journals published in Europe and the USA contain many excellent articles on the use of ultrasound for the chest.

Gross* however reviewed several ultrasound papers in the 1994 Year Book of Radiology, and noted that percutaneous lung biopsies using ultrasound rarely lead to a pneumothorax as the needle rarely traverses aerated lung! In the 1995 Year Book he wrote (p 75) "I did my residency at a hospital where ultrasound was never considered an initial tool for excluding an abdominal abscess.: CT was the prime modality. To my surprise, ultrasound was used far more extensively where I did my fellowship. In two subsequent institutions we have returned to CT. I think the difference from place to place relates to the level of aggressiveness and invasiveness of the ultrasonographers."

The rush to CT and MR (more expensive techniques, as also noted by Gross) is not just confined to the USA, for some centres in the UK still use ultrasound infrequently. In part this probably stems from a lack of available apparatus and the idea that ultrasound needs a separate appointment or be carried out by a different radiologist, whilst **the author believes ultrasound should be akin to a 'stethoscope in a radiology department'!** He also agrees with the sentiment expressed at Imaging, Oncology , Science (2000) that it is no longer appropriate for a radiologist to mark a patient's back with an X but should **carry out the intervention himself**.

* Now Professor of Radiology at Ann Arbor, Michigan.

The author also ('tongue in cheek') cannot help remembering in a conference discussion that practitioners from another ancient UK university examined their patients **only** in the recumbent position, and did not believe that blood and pus often (but not always) gave a different picture from clear pleural fluid!

As noted above, for chest ultrasound, the author usually has the patient seated on a stool or in the reversed position on a chair.

Failure to examine the patient in the erect position (i.e. **standing**) as well as supine also seems to explain how quite a number of liver, splenic adrenal lesions and concomitant hydronephroses, etc. are missed. In the erect position the liver drops down and is more accessible - it is also very easy to quickly examine the upper abdomen in the erect position after (or before) an upper gastro-intestinal examination. The author found many important lesions in this way (not just gallstones - which drop into the fundus of the gall bladder or float half way up if small and non-opaque).

Some references.

Doust et al. (1975) : Ultrasonic evaluation of pleural opacities.

Hirsch, J. et al. (1981) : Real time sonography of pleural opacities.

Marks et al. (1982) : Real time US of pleural lesions - new observations regarding the probability of obtaining fluid.

Dorne (1986) : **Sonographic fluid bronchogram** to differentiate pulmonary consolidation from pleural disease.

O'Moore et al. (1987) : Sonographic guidance in diagnostic and therapeutic intervention in the pleural space.

Fataar (1988) : Ultrasound in chest disease.

Saito et al. (1988) : US of chest wall lesions - **pleural   white   line - displacement   by   benign   & disruption by malignant tumours**.

Acunas et al. (1989) : Chest sonography - differentiation of pulmonary consolidation from pleural disease.

Bradley (1989) : The uses of ultrasound in the diagnosis of the peripheral lung mass - imaging and biopsy.

Rasmussen and Boris (1989) : Ultrasound guided puncture of pleural fluid collections and superficial thoracic masses.

Wernecke et al. (1990) : Mediastinal tumours - sensitivity of detection with sonography compared with CT and radiography. In certain mediastinal regions (supra-aortic, pericardial, prevascular and paratracheal) sonography is so sensitive that CT and MR examinations may be obviated in patients with equivocal radiographic findings.

Margli et al. (1991) : Mediastinal sonography in the post treatment evaluation of patients with lymphoma.

McLoud and Flower (1991) : Imaging of the pleura by US, CT and MR.

Flower et al. (1993) : US of the chest.

Yang et al. (1985) : Peripheral pulmonary lesions - US and US guided aspiration biopsy.

Yang et al. (1990) : Lung tumours associated with obstructive pneumonitis : US studies.

Yang et al. (1991) : Transthoracic aspiration of lung abscess under US control.

Yang et al. (1992) : Value of sonography in determining the nature of pleural effusion - 320 cases.

Yang et al. (1992) : US guided core biopsy of thoracic tumours. Yang et al. (1992) : US of pulm. consolidation.

Yang et al. (1992) : Ultrasound guided biopsy of mediastinal malignancy through the supraclavicular approach.

Yuan et al. (1992) : US guided aspiration biopsy of small peripheral pulmonary nodules - mostly 1 to 3 cm in size.

Bradley and Metreweli (1991) : US in the diagnosis of the juxta-pleural lesion - **pleural   line   disruption**   with poor respiratory movement is a sign of **chest wall invasion.**

Hsu et al. (1992) : Detection of mass lesions in the collapsed lung by US.

Targhetta et al. (1992) : Diagnosis of pneumothorax by US immediately after US guided aspiration biopsy by noting the disappearance of the nodule from the US monitor screen.

Lee, L. et al. (1989) : US of thoracic lesions - 251 cases.

Lee, L. et al. (1993) : Diagnosis of pulmonary cryptococcosis by US guided percutaneous aspiration.

Lomas et al. (1993) : The sonographic appearances of pleural fluid.

Yu et al. (1992) : Diagnostic and therapeutic use of chest sonography in critically ill patients.

Yu et al. (1993) : US in unilateral hemithorax opacification - first line study.

Yuan et al. (1993) : US guided aspiration biopsy for pulmonary TB.

Wiersema et al. (1994) : Transoesophageal US guided fine-needle aspiration biopsy of mediastinal lymph nodes in the preoperative staging of non-small cell lung cancer.

Wernecke and Diederich (1995) : Sonographic features of mediastinal tumours - noted that 'although mediastinal sonography, thus far, is used rarely in the United States, it might play a role as an adjunctive examination technique to other imaging studies...'. It is particularly valuable for supra-aortic, pericardial and prevascular lesions - lymphoma, thymoma, goitre, cysts, liposarcoma, fatty masses, etc.

Bearcroft et al. (1995) : Use of US-guided cutting needle biopsy in the neck.

Civardi et al. (1993) : Vascular signals from pleural-based lung lesions studied with pulsed Doppler US.

and Gleeson (1994) : Colour Doppler sonography in the evaluation of pulmonary lesions abutting the pleura. Two categories of vessels were seen - (i) normally branching in pneumonia or lung collapse and (ii) randomly orientated vascular patterns with tumours or sarcoidosis.

Yuan et al. (1994) : Colour Doppler sonography of benign and malignant pulmonary masses - evaluated 50 lung cancers (in 46 pts.) and 28 with benign lesions. Only peripheral masses could be examined - most adenocarcinomas and oat cell tumours showed detectable flow signals, but under 50% of squamous cancers gave rise to a signal - presumably due to lower vascularity. Concluded that colour Doppler is useful for showing vascularity in pulmonary masses and may be helpful for differentiating malignant from benign lung tumours.

Köksoy et al. (1995) : Value of colour Doppler US in central venous catheter related thrombosis.

Wu et al. (1995) : 'Fluid colour' sign for discrimination between pleural thickening and pleural effusion.

Wang et al. (1995) : Transthoracic needle biopsy of thoracic tumours by a colour Doppler ultrasound puncture guiding device. Concluded: ' By using the colour Doppler ultrasound puncture device, vascular structures surrounding or within the target tumour can be verified. Visualisation of the needle shaft or tip is also better. Biopsy routes can be selected to avoid puncturing vessels. This approach should be particularly helpful for guiding biopsies of mediastinal tumours, where puncturing the heart or great vessels is a potential complication.'

MacSweeney et al. (1996) : Colour Doppler energy (power) mode ultrasound is better than conservative colour Doppler for detecting flow at low velocities in the microvasculature or in pathological vessels.

Cosgrove (1996a) : Why do we need contrast agents for ultrasound?

(1996b) : Ultrasound contrast enhancement of tumours - the demonstration of neovascularity etc. in tumours is an exciting and rapidly developing field, and may improve the sensitivity of US both in the detection of tumours and its specificity in separating benign from malignant processes.

Schlief (1996) : Developments in echo-enhancing agents.

Correas and Quay (1996) : EchoGen emulsion - a new ultrasound contrast agent based on phase shift colloids.

Leen and McArdle (1996) : Ultrasound contrast agents in liver imaging.

Burns (1996) : Harmonic imaging with ultrasound contrast agents.

Fritzsch and Schlief (1996) : Future prospects for echo-enhancing agents.

Tano et al. (1997) : Colour Doppler US - possibility of differentiating small hypoechoic liver tumours.

Gleeson (2000) : Review of thoracic US - identify pleural fluid & control of drainage;
- identification of pneumothoraces;
- pleural & chest wall invasion by lung tumours;
- identification & biopsy of pleural masses & masses abutting the pleura, lung masses infiltrating the pleura; mediastinal masses and rib lesions;
- pleural thickening and loss of pleural stripe/white line;
- diaphragm thickness and movement.

Other references to the usage of ultrasound are to be found throughout the volume e.g.:

p. 3.19 - sequestration.
p. 7.27 & 16.22 - pulmonary embolism (leg veins 7.35).
p. 12.3 - nodes in the neck.
p. 12.20 - 21 - chest wall, including ribs and costal cartilages,
p. 12.37 - Tietze's syndrome - costo-chondritis.
ps. 13.20-21 - internal mammary nodes and ant. mediastinum.
ps. 14.13 & 31 - pleural white line & fluid drainage etc.
ps 15.18, 24 & 26 - diaphragm, pericardium & pericardial cyst.
p. 16.22 - oesophagus and trans-oesophageal U/S for heart (e.g. diagnosis of atrial myxoma) adjacent mediastinum etc..
p. 17.2 - liver, 17.6, adrenals, 17.12-13 spleen.
p. 18.8, 10, 11 & 24 - thyroid and parathyroid.
p. 12.21 & 14.30 - juxta-pleural lesions.
p. 21.9, 13 & 16 - biopsy procedures.

Chapter 21 : **Biopsy etc. Procedures and Bronchography.**

Sputum Cytology.
   This is the simplest method for obtaining cytological diagnosis and is always worth trying, even with peripheral tumours. Its results depend largely on the specimens obtained. An **early morning** specimen, or one obtained after **physiotherapy**   (even simple physiotherapy in the doctor's or radiologist's examination room) is more likely to yield a positive result, which can be as high as 80%, although random samples only give about a 20% success. Frequently specimens from three successive days are obtained.
   The method was introduced by Dudgeon and Wrigley (1935) almost in the present form. Oswald et al. (1971) from St. Bartholomew's and the Royal Brompton Hospitals found 41% of first sputum samples positive for early carcinoma in 2,545 cases.

Needle Biopsy of Masses Abutting the Chest Wall and Fluid Aspiration.
   Quite often this is extremely easy and quick, with masses or fluid abutting the chest wall. Following plain radiography and using ultra-sound control, it is readily carried out with the patient sitting-up on a stool. In many cases all that is needed is a simple hypodermic syringe and needle. Following preliminary local anaesthesia, either a simple needle aspiration is carried out or a diagnostic aspiration of fluid obtained. When only a few ml of fluid is seen in a pleural cavity with ultrasound, even this can usually be sampled if the aspiration is carried out in **expiration.** Short bevelled needles should be used to avoid damaging the underlying lung.
   For larger aspirations, some flexible tubing may be employed, with artery forceps for clamping it whilst the syringe is emptied. Short bevelled needles should be used. (Further details are given below).

Bronchoscopy and Transbronchial Biopsy or Brushing.
   Fibre-optic bronchosopy was first introduced in Japan in 1967 (see Ikeda et al., 1979) and has now largely superseded rigid bronchoscopy, except in surgical departments. With this method both the larger air passages and the segmental bronchi including those of the upper lobes may be examined. Biopsies and brushings of suspicious lesions (Fennessy, 1966 & 1967) and suction of secretions may be carried out. It now possible to possible to insert a fine fibreoptic probe through the biopsy channel of the instrument and through this to visualise peripheral bronchi down to 2 mm in diameter (Tanaka et al. , 1988).

   Broncho-alveolar   lavage using saline washings passed down the small tube within the bronchoscope may be useful with distal tumours of the bronchial tree and for diffuse disease including alveolar cell neoplasm, alveolar proteinosis and opportunistic and other infections. It may also be of value in other conditions e.g. asbestosis and fibrosing alveolitis and in monitoring the activity of the latter.
   Few endobronchial masses will fail to yield a cytological diagnosis, not only for malignancy, but also for cell type, hence greatly helping to assess the prognosis. Endoscopic operability is also assessed at the same time. The complication rate is minimal. Minor haemoptysis is not unusual, but major complications are rare (see below).
   With more peripheral lesions, the tip of the bronchoscope may be directed under TV fluoroscopic control (e.g. using an intensifier/TV system on a 'C' arm as for percutaneous biopsy) towards the lesion, for closer study and biopsy.

Trans-bronchial biopsy of more peripheral lung disease or neighbouring mediastinal masses (including enlarged nodes) may also be carried out, usually under topical anaesthesia.
   This method is now commonly employed as it greatly lessens the risk of complications, such as pneumothoraces. It is also convenient as it combines the procedure with the almost routine bronchoscopy, and in many cases renders an external biopsy unnecessary.
   Tsuboi (1967 & 1970, and Wang et al, 1984a) beautifully illustrated the technique and its value. Tsuboi also pointed out the importance of the relationship of the bronchus running towards the lesion or nodule being biopsied.

(i) Bronchus leading directly into a tumour mass

(ii) Bronchus engulfed or narrowed by the tumour.

(iii) Extrinsic mass pushing into bronchus.

(iv) Submucosal or extrinsic compression narrowing the bronchus.

Fig. 21.1   CT 'bronchus   sign' (reproduced from Wang et al, 1984a, 'Transbronchial needle aspiration of peripheral pulmonary nodules.' Chest, **86**, 819 - 823 with permission.) - see also p. 4.10.

Types (i) and (ii) are easily biopsied. With type (iii) the mass is difficult to biopsy, as the bronchus tends to 'run away' from the lesion. With type (iv) brushing is not so good, nor local biopsy unless the mucosa is affected, but a needle can be passed through the narrowed area into the mass (as was noted by Wang et al., 1984a).

Radke et al. (1979, from the Henry Ford Hospital, Detroit) found that 2 cm (or larger) peripheral lung lesions can be accurately diagnosed by biplane, fluoroscopically guided flexible bronchoscopy and biopsy.

In teaching centres, in particular, **TV   video   recordings   of   bronchoscopies** are of considerable value, as are **colour photographs** of lesions - Illus. **BRONCHOSCOPY**.

An important feature is to note that **with   transbronchial   biopsies   there   is   a   ten   fold reduction of pneumothoraces**, as compared with the percutaneous approach.

Localised bronchography can also be carried out (using water-based contrast medium e.g. the myelographic medium Iotrolan, owing to the fine calibre of the tubing incorporated within the instrument).

Endobronchial   sonography is now being carried out in a few centres, by inserting a fine ultrasound probe through the bronchoscope into the bronchi to help visualise intra-mural tumours, tumour alongside the bronchi and para-bronchial nodes. The technique shows a tri-laminar pattern in the bronchial walls (Fig. 21.2).

Fig. 21.2   Diagram of an endobronchial sonogram. Note the tri-laminar pattern.

Rigid   bronchoscopy (which is usually carried out under general anaesthesia) still has some advantages. It can allow thicker secretions to be aspirated, and is better for sucking up a brisk haemorrhage after biopsy. (With severe bleeding, the only real method of control is to keep sucking until bleeding stops, but fortunately such bleeding is rare.) It also allows larger biopsies to be taken, small benign tumours to be excised, others coagulated, distortion of the tracheo-bronchial tree determined, dilatation to be carried out, and stents or tubes inserted. **'Fixity   of   the mediastinum'**, from fibrosis or tumour extension, may be gauged by moving the instrument as a lever, and in patients with neoplasm will usually be a good rough guide to inoperability.

It may also be preferable in patients with severely impaired respiratory reserve, in whom oxygen can be supplied via the instrument, at intervals during the procedure.

Complications of bronchoscopy

Simpson et al. (1986) surveyed complications of fibreoptic bronchoscopy in chest departments in the UK.   They found that in 1983, 40,000 bronchoscopies had been performed (87% with the fibreoptic instrument), compared with about 15,000 in 1974. Mortality for fibreoptic bronchoscopy alone was 0.04%, with major complications in 0.12%, and for transbronchial biopsy 0.12% and 2.7% respectively. The two major complications were (i) haemorrhage (see above) and (ii) respiratory distress due to a complicating pneumothorax (rare), or from partial obstruction due to the instrument. The last could lead on to myocardial infarction.

We have seen a bizarre complication illustrated in Illus. **CHEST WALL HAEMATOMA, Pt. 1a-c**, due to a ruptured superior superficial epigastric artery in a highly strung individual. Others have reported the occasional gas embolism or carcinoid crisis - the latter with an adenoma (see refs. below).

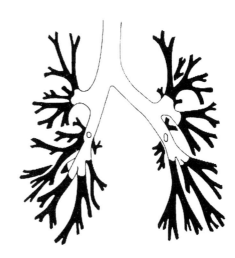

Fig. 21.3   The tracheo-bronchial tree -
the part which may be examined with the
rigid bronchoscope is shown in white;
whilst that which can be examined with
flexible (fibre-optic) bronchoscopy
(or by bronchography) is shown in black.

Further references.
Nordenström and Carlens (1964) : Bronchial biopsy in combination with bronchoscopy.
Stradling (1968 & 1976) : Diagnostic Bronchoscopy.
Bagg (1986) : Fibreoptic Bronchoscopy.

Knight and Clarke (1979) : Analysis of the first 300 fibreoptic bronchoscopies at the Royal Brompton Hospital - suggested that it would be an invaluable method for physicians.
Flower and Shneerson (1984) : Bronchography via the fibreoptic bronchoscope.

Greening (1982), Studdy et al. (1984) : Bronchoalveolar lavage.
Hopkin et al. (1983) : Rapid diagnosis of obscure pneumonia in immunosuppressed renal patients by cytology of alveolar lavage fluid.
Morrison and Stockley (1988) : The many uses of bronchoalveolar lavage.

Colice et al. (1985) : Compared CT with fibreoptic bronchoscopy in the identification of endobronchial abnormalities in patients with known or suspected lung cancer. They found bronchoscopy to be better for determining the presence of endobronchial involvement. They felt that CT was moderately accurate in defining the type of abnormality seen at bronchoscopy viz. localised mucosal change, endobronchial mass or extrinsic compression, and that CT should not be relied upon for the identification of endobronchial abnormalities in patients with known or suspected lung cancer.

Naidich et al. (1987) : Compared CT with fibreoptic bronchoscopy and wrote " In no case was malignancy missed by CT. CT was accurate for focal lesions, but inaccurate in predicting whether a given abnormality was endobronchial, submucosal or extrinsic."

Wang et al. (1978, 1983 and 1984 a & b) : Transbronchial needle biopsy.

Hürter et al. (1990) : Endobronchial sonography in the diagnosis of pulmonary and mediastinal tumours. - is a good addition to fibre-optic bronchoscopy. It readily shows the 'trilaminar' structures of the bronchial wall and adjacent vessels and masses, including nodes.

Tanaka et al. (1990) : Diagnosis of peripheral lung cancer using a new type of endoscope - the BF 2.2 T instrument is designed to pass through the 2.6 mm channel of the conventional fibreoptic bronchoscope, and allows small bronchi to be examined.

Erickson et al. (1979) : Cerebral air embolism complicating trans-bronchoscopic lung biopsy.
Sukumaran et al. (1982) : Acute carcinoid crisis following flexible fibreoptic bronchoscopy.
Grant (1986) : Hazards of bronchoscopy.
Strange et al. (1987) : Pulmonary haemorrhage and air embolism complicating transbronchial biopsy in pulmonary amyloidosis.

Goldberg et al. (1994) : US-assisted bronchoscopy with use of miniature transducer contained catheters.
George (1999) : Fluorescence bronchoscopy for the early detection of lung cancer.

Percutaneous or Transthoracic Biopsy of Lung Lesions.

(a) **Historical**

Leyden (1883) performed the first needle biopsy of the lung, when he aspirated organisms causing pneumonia. Menetrier (1886) diagnosed a lung carcinoma by needle aspiration and Horder et al. (1909) independently described the method - 'lung puncture as a new application of clinical pathology.' However the method was not often practised until the advent of cytological diagnosis of tissue fluids and needle aspirates in the 1940's and 1950's, when it was used particularly by radiotherapists. One of those who led in this field was my former Radiotherapy colleague in Oxford, Frank Ellis, who in 1947 published a paper on needle biopsies of tumours. He needle-biopsied not only superficial tumours but also deeper ones in the pleura, lung, etc. using a rotating drill, after localisation by plain radiography or by direct fluoroscopy (i.e. without image intensification). Nordenström (1965a & 1969a) and Dahlgren and Nordenström (1966) from Stockholm described percutaneous biopsy of lung lesions under TV fluoroscopic control, a technique also advocated by Stein and Evans (1966) from the USA and now the standard procedure. Nordenström also described the use of a metal stilette, covered with a thin plastic tube, through which cell samples could be obtained with different boring instruments, and in his first 2,000 cases obtained a positive diagnosis in over 90% (see also ps. 4.14 & 24.46 re electrocoagulation of lung lesions via the tube and the recording of electric potentials from pulmonary lesions).

The method was reviewed in the UK by Pierce (1973) and by Dick et al. (1974) who used single plane fluoroscopy in 227 cases and by Sargent et al. (1974) in the USA in 350 patients.
Flower and Verney (1979) in Cambridge diagnosed 180 tumours with 300 needle aspirations of peripheral lung masses, 102 cases were interpreted as non-malignant, but in 23 this interpretation proved to be incorrect.

(b) **Present practice.**

This varies to some extent from centre to centre, depending on experience and surgical preference. Some important questions always have to be answered:

(i) **Is the biopsy going to influence the management?**

If the patient has what appears to be an operable small neoplasm, why not just remove it surgically and carry out an 'excision biopsy' ? Also if no treatment is going to be given, because of age, probable metastases or other disease, what will be its value?
A knowledge of the cell type, the possibility of metastasis or recurrence, may affect surgery, radiotherapy or chemotherapy, and the indications in the individual patient should be carefully considered in each case.

Charig (1991, from the Churchill Hospital, Oxford) & Charig et al. (1991) in discussing the value of a negative fine-needle biopsy in suspected operable lung cancer wrote "it can be concluded that if a solitary pulmonary nodule has a high clinical suspicion of malignancy and the patient is a candidate for surgery, then fine-needle biopsy has little value in the management of the patient."

(ii) **Is a negative biopsy for neoplasm really negative?**
Small lesions within the lung are difficult to biopsy, and if the lesion looks like neoplasm and it and the patient are potentially operable, a negative report must be treated with caution, the biopsy repeated or the lesion excised.

With benign disease the specificity for precise diagnosis is only found in about 40%. Tubercle bacilli (and other organisms) may be recovered in appropriate cases (Illus. **BIOPSY, TB Pts. 19 & 23**).

Inflammatory disease can often be present adjacent to or within a tumour. Also a tumour may stimulate an immune reaction, and only a few cancer cells may be present (see below).

(iii) **Can the patient survive a pneumothorax?**
The procedure should not be carried out in the presence of severe emphysema, respiratory insufficiency, or if the patient has already had a pneumonectomy.

(iv) **Is the lesion more easily biopsied by the endobronchial route?**
This is best if there is likely to be an endobronchial component and is usually considered safer.

(v) **Is the lesion abutting the outer pleural surface of the lung, and is it visible with ultrasound?**
If it is visible with ultrasound, it means that aerated lung is **not** present between the lesion and the chest wall, and there is no reason for a pneumothorax to be produced. The author has biopsied most of these at first presentation and as out patients.

(vi) **Does the lesion contain calcification?**
This often points to a benign cause but a few tumours also contain calcification (see ps. 6.19 - 21).

(vii) **Is the lesion intrapulmonary, how deep in the lung, what size is it, where are the pleural surfaces (including fissures) in relation to it ?**
The radiologist should work out the best approach, and decide on whether to perform the biopsy under CT or fluoroscopic control. He will usually perform a diagnostic CT as an out patient and carry out the biopsy as an in-patient or day case.

(viii) **Are metastases present?**
If so, are any of these more readily biopsied - bone (e.g. rib), liver, adrenal, etc.?

(ix) **Likelihood of bleeding?**
Screening tests are usually a waste of time, but does the patient have leukaemia, severe alcoholism with cirrhosis, pulmonary hypertension etc.? Is the lesion likely to be vascular (aneurysm or varix), or very vascular and highly enhancing on CT?

(x) **Is this the correct procedure and if I were the patient would I have it done?**

(xi) Remember that even in the best hands **there are likely to be 15% false negative and about 0.8% false positive rates.**

Technique for percutaneous lung biopsy
It is necessary to localise the lesion to be biopsied before carrying out the procedure. This may be done by plain films, CT, fluoroscopy or ultrasound. One should determine the best approach (usually the shortest distance, but avoiding the scapula, ribs, etc.), and **try to avoid more than one pleural pass** and avoiding if possible the transgression of an interlobar fissure. CT is particularly valuable for localisation and determining the approach, but some lesions are then biopsied under fluoroscopic or ultrasound control, using the CT images as a guide.

If CT control is employed further sections are often taken to show the position of the needle tip in relation to the tumour (see also section below - p. 21.7).

The needles commonly used include :
(a) simple fine needles - e.g. of lumbar puncture type,
(b) rough spiral tipped trochar (to fix the lesion) within a biopsy cannula (Rotex needle - slide the sheath over the end of the screw for taking the biopsy), and

(c) various cutting needles (e.g. TruCut, Biopty and Temno type needles) to obtain a slice or 'core' of tissue - these are particularly valuable with diffuse lung diseases and also a 'core' may allow a more certain diagnosis of the type of tumour - e.g. small cell, type of lymphoma etc.

Other needles which have been used include Vim-Silverman (Silverman, 1938 - a new biopsy needle- cannula with inner split needle), Turner (see Lieberman et al., 1982), Menghini (see Tørp-Pedersen et al, 1984), Franseen, etc.

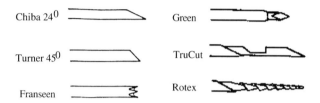

Fig. 21.4   Some needles which may be used for CT guided biopsy (adapted from Lieberman et al., 1982, AJR, **138**, 561 with permission).

Fine needle aspiration biopsy (FNAB).
   A 22 G lumbar puncture needle is suitable for many biopsies, and a short (6-7 cm long) child's LP needle is ideal for peripheral lesions and some pleural lesions. For deeper lesions a thin (trans-hepatic Chiba type) needle may be used. Quite often the resistance of the lesion can be 'felt'. With simple needles standard 10 or 20 ml. disposable plastic syringes are used, and suction is made by hand, or using a syringe holder. The aim of the negative pressure is **not** to tear cells from the tissue but to **hold** the tissue against the sharp cutting edge of the needle. Softer tissue in the lesion protrudes over its edge, is cut or scraped off and accumulates in the needle as it is advanced or moved a few times a little up and down. With friable lesions only one pass may be required before the negative pressure is released and the needle withdrawn. If no aspirate is obtained by simple suction, a little fluid may be injected quickly down the needle to disturb a few cells, and aspiration remade. The aspirate is immediately ejected onto glass slides and fixed (e.g. with a spray fixative or 70% alcohol) or dried. As fluid or blood are often unhelpful in the sample, the negative pressure is usually reduced before the needle is withdrawn. The ideal aspirate has many cells with a 'creamy' consistency. If very 'wet', smearing with the smearing slide almost vertical will often collect the cells at the far end of the slide, when they can then be flat smeared. An alternative is to place them within a suitable transport medium. Usually several slides are prepared. It cannot be over-emphasised that **good   cooperation with the   cytologist** is required. Often the fixed slides are stained by Papanicolau's method, whilst air dried slides are usually Giemsa stained.
   If a sheathed needle is used (such as the **plastic sheathed Temno needle**) the needle may be removed leaving the sheath in situ, and the sample (core or aspirate) be inspected and placed onto a slide or into fluid fixative, and if inadequate the needle may be reinserted and a further specimen obtained. A similar reinsertion may be made with a Rotex type trochar, but a problem with this is that the lung may be caught by the tip and torn.

   Larger diameter needles - 20 gauge - are about twice as likely to produce pneumothoraces than needles of 18 gauge which usually suffice.

   Sometimes the author has 'fixed' the lesion with one Rotex screw needle, before biopsying with a second needle (Illus. **BIOPSY, Pt. 7**), this allows a second specimen to be taken should a small pneumothorax occur.

   Difficulty may be found particularly with necrotic and cavitating tumours, if the sample only contains necrotic tissue. With large and cavitating lesions, samples should if possible be taken from the periphery. Contrariwise with inflammatory lesions positive bacteriology is more likely to be obtained from within cavities or the centre of abscesses.

Needles should if possible be inserted just **above a rib, in order to avoid damage to an intercostal vessel** (see Fig. 12.15, p. 12.29)**, and not too close to the sternum where they may damage an internal mammary artery**.

Core biopsy.

The **Biopty Gun** has detachable needles which fit into a 'gun' using 16 or 20 cm long needles of 18 or 20 G. On pressing the firing button, the inner trochar (containing the cutting needle and sample notch) is thrust forwards, followed almost instantaneously by a forward thrust of the outer cannula, which shears off the tissue sample. The apparatus is very good for the biopsy of solid masses which are readily palpable (e.g. a transplanted kidney), or easily localised (e.g. **within the chest wall, or lying within or adjacent to the pleura**). When **CT is used for localisation**, the biopsy gun is rather **awkward** to use, as the needle and cannula have to be fitted together, and the needle correctly positioned. An aid may be to use a short piece of plastic as a splint to hold the two parts together, or to use a thin needle as a guide and then place the Biopty needle alongside it. The apparatus can also be used to biopsy a destructive lesion arising within a rib, but the needles tend to bend if much residual bony tissue is present. When using ultrasound for control (and also with some CT machines) it is preferable for a second person to perform the localisation as two hands are really necessary to operate the Biopty gun and in the author's opinion its best use is for core biopsies of the pleura. (Illus. **BIOPSY/ASPIRATION, Biopty gun**) - see also note on p. 21.9 and refs. - p. 21.11. For rib biopsy the author prefers a needle with a guard - see p. 21.17.

Some points re CT control for biopsy

This may be more time consuming than using other methods (some have reported 1 to 3 hours, but 15 to 20 mins should normally be adequate). Repeat CT sections, a short spiral run (with e.g. 2 mm reconstruction slices) or direct vision using CT-fluoroscopy (if available) may help to localise the needle tip if the tumour is not felt with the needle.

Ideally the needle track should be vertical, and angling of the needle (if needed e.g. to avoid a rib or the scapula) should only be in one direction (as more may be too confusing), and the needle point should face the lesion to avoid it glancing off a solid mass ('bevel steering' - the bevel facing away from the lesion).

Patient respiration should be as constant as possible, so as to give as constant a position as possible of the lesion with respiration in relation to the marked CT section.

The space in the CT gantry around the needle is often rather limited, particularly with large patients, and it may be necessary to withdraw the couch from the centre of the aperture for the specimen to be taken.

Sedation should be avoided as the patient should be able to cough if a haemoptysis is produced.

Some people take an immediate post biopsy CT section to show the size of any consequent pneumothorax, but this was not the author's usual practice. Others turn the patient so that the biopsy site becomes dependent, reducing ventilation in this area, and also allowing any small haemorrhage to form a small haematoma and block the needle track - the **'turn-over technique'**. Probably the most important factor is to allow the patient to rest undisturbed on the CT couch for about 5 mins after a biopsy to allow the track time to 'seal'.

The "bottom line" of course lies in cooperation with and the skill of the cytologist. Without a good pathologist or cytologist, and good cooperation, there is little use in carrying out such biopsies. It is usually impracticable for the cytologist to be present during procedures, therefore the radiologist must become proficient in preserving specimens or making and fixing smears on glass slides.

Complications of lung biopsy.

The most common complication is a **pneumothorax**, the incidence following percutaneous biopsy being higher (up to 30% in some series) compared with 5% or less with a transbronchial approach; however only about 5 - 10% need tube drainage (and suitable drainage catheters - such a suprapubic 'banana' type catheter to be attached to underwater drainage or a Heimlich flutter valve - should be available). Using fine needles up to 18 gauge the complication rate for pneumothoraces needing treatment is low. Pneumothoraces are more likely to occur if there are no pleural adhesions overlying the lesion, more than one pleural surface is traversed and when there is aerated lung between the lesion and the puncture site, or the patient has emphysema, lung cysts or bullae.

Haemorrhage may occur with either percutaneous or transbronchial biopsies, either as haemoptysis (usually minor) or manifested by some immediate apparent enlargement in the size of the lesion. A significant haemothorax is very rare.
Haemorrhage is more likely with a Tru-cut type needle.

Significant complications can usually be avoided if thin needles are used and the patient stays still and avoids coughing for a few minutes after the procedure. This allows a small clot to form, and as noted above some use the '**turn-over   technique**' to assist its formation - see also note below.
Although most **hamartomas** are 'like rubber in texture' and difficult to puncture with a needle, a few are **vascular** and are likely to bleed, down the needle or around the lesion (sometimes causing a sudden apparent increase in size on a post-biopsy CT section or chest radiograph).
Biopsy of lung lesions in **AIDS patients** may also induce haemorrhage, or a broncho-vascular fistula with gross air embolism. Reference to such a case is given in the references below; the author also knows of other similar cases that have occurred - leading to sudden death in 4 to 5 mins post-biopsy.

With increasing experience, very few complications will occur, and only small or moderate pneumothoraces, needing no active treatment, are likely to be encountered. Most patients can have the procedure carried out as day cases, but remaining in hospital overnight, if more than a small pneumothorax occurs.

Further notes re needle-track blockage.
To try to minimise the effects of lung punctures, and to 'seal' the needle tracks some authors (e.g. McCartney, 1974) have injected some of the patient's own blood (or Gelfoam) down the needle (or plastic) sheath to try to seal it off. They also noted that "in patients who show a '**bloom**' of the biopsied pulmonary nodule secondary to intrapulmonary haemorrhage, pneumothorax is rare, the haemorrhage apparently preventing air leak. This self-sealing mechanism probably explains the fact that cutting and drill biopsies using the much larger needle and producing a higher incidence of bleeding, show little increase in the occurrence or severity of pneumothorax." Vine et al. (1982) carried out 100 biopsies using a 17 G Lee needle and used track obliteration using autologous blood clot but had the same complication rate for pneumothoraces as with aspiration biopsies using thinner needles. Others e.g. Bourgouin et al. (1988) and Hall and Simon (1988) doubted the value of trying to obliterate needle tracks in this way, or have found no difference in the pneumothorax rates in those in whom the blood patch was used or not used (Herman and Weisbrod, 1990).
Moore et al. (1990) performed 310 needle lung aspiration biopsies, and immediately afterwards placed the patients with the biopsy site dependent for at least half an hour, or until leakage stopped - the '**turn-over technique**', and claimed that this reduced complicating air leaks - see above but 10 mins usually suffices.
Engeler et al. (1992a) prevented pneumothoraces after lung biopsy by transpleural placement of compressed collagen foam plugs, which expanded on rehydration.

Pneumothorax.
If a pneumothorax develops it may be seen at once by fluoroscopy, or by taking a further CT section. In most cases a chest radiograph at one hour will suffice, and rarely does it develop later. The author's practice has been to take a radiograph at one hour with a superficial lesion, if covered by aerated lung, and at one and three to four hours if the lesion was much deeper, or in the hilum or mediastinum and the pleura has been transgressed more than once. If possible an extrapleural approach is used for mediastinal of hilar lesions.

Gas embolism.
This may rarely follow a percutaneous lung biopsy, the patients suddenly collapsing or having signs of cerebral gas embolism. Sudden collapse is best treated by lying the patient on his **right** side in the head down position so as to trap the air in the **left** atrium from where it will gradually be absorbed (i.e. **the opposite side from injected IV gas**). Cerebral symptoms often readily subside, but if they persist the patient should be transferred to a compression chamber. Such gas may be demonstrated in cerebral vessels by CT, but as pointed out by Hirabucki et al. (1988) initial

examinations may be negative, and later examinations in the absence of compression treatment may show evidence of brain swelling and infarction.

Intravascular gas and gas embolism is further discussed on p. 6.31.

Needle track metastasis.

Rarely a **needle track metastasis** may be caused. A few cases have been reported (see references) but the author has not encountered a single case following a fine needle aspiration; but has seen a few instances following repeated drainage of malignant pleural effusions (particularly mesotheliomas) or ascites.

Other complications

These include strokes, myocardial infarction, vaso-vagal attacks, pericardial effusion, mediastinal haematomas, lobar or lung torsion.

Conclusions.

A good rule is to avoid a needle biopsy of an intrapulmonary mass that is not adjacent to the outer pleural surface if it is going to be surgically removed, whatever the biopsy result - i.e. '**an excision biopsy' should be carried out**, and to reserve the procedure for doubtful and inoperable cases in whom cytological proof of neoplasm and its type may be necessary e.g. prior to radiotherapy.

If a lung mass is adjacent to the peripheral visceral pleura, and can be visualised with ultrasound, then it is usually safe to biopsy this without fear of any possible complication.

In patients with secondary deposits, it is often better (both safer and easier) to biopsy one of these (e.g. neck node, rib or liver).

If a percutaneous biopsy of a deeply lying lung lesion is to be carried out, it is important to: -
(a) use as short a needle track through the lung as possible,
(b) avoid traversing bullae,
(c) avoid traversing the pleura, adjacent to air filled lung more than necessary i.e.
(i) if a lesion abuts the pleura - enter it at this position if at all possible;
(ii) avoid crossing an inter-lobar fissure, or
(iii) the visceral pleura on the medial aspect of the lung (may not be possible with some mediastinal biopsies);
(d) avoid problems with needle tip positioning due to parallax, etc. by using a thin CT section for checking the position of the tip, or better CT fluoroscopy (if available),
(e) use a needle sheath (if possible) to avoid having to reinsert an unsheathed needle and reposition it de novo. If a good cytology specimen is obtained, a core biopsy may be unnecessary.
(f) a biopsy gun (e.g. Biopty gun - see above - p. 21.6) is really too cumbersome for a CT lung biopsy, biopsy but can be used for biopsying thickened pleura, where it can be inserted parallel to the lung/pleura interface.

Guidance - Ultra-sound is best if the lesion can be visualised in this way - it means that no aerated lung lies between the lesion and the chest wall and that therefore no pneumothorax should occur (Illus. **BIOPSY/ASPIRATION, Ca lg&cx wall 15a&b**) and no post-procedure chest film is required.

CT or fluoroscopy are used for other lesions including those in the mediastinum. Fluoroscopy is often quicker, and a 'C' arm is very helpful for biplanar localisation.

CT and **CT fluoroscopy** tends to be used more for the more difficult lung lesions and those in the mediastinum.

Fatalities.

The author had two fatalities after performing lung biopsies. The first occurred in an asthmatic with a large tumour of the right upper lobe. She developed bilateral pneumothoraces during an asthmatic attack an hour after the procedure. (No communication between the two pleural cavities was found at autopsy - see also p. 14.23). The second (with a large cavitating breast deposit) had a vaso-vagal attack (which did not respond to any therapy) following the sight of a moderate haemoptysis after fine-needle biopsy (she had been having such haemoptyses at home, but neither she nor her husband told her medical advisers about them before the procedure).

Other fatalities are noted in the references below.

Notes on some biopsy studies.

Westcott (1980) : Direct percutaneous needle aspiration of localised pulmonary lesions - results in 422 patients.

Adler et al. (1983 from Israel) : Performed 136 biopsies of mediastinal masses using 22 G needles with fluoroscopic or CT guidance. CT was advantageous at the thoracic inlet, in the hilum and middle mediastinum, with small masses and the SVC syndrome. They approached from above the upper border of a rib and felt the mass with the needle. A 20 ml syringe was used for suction, and the needle tip was gently rocked up and down 3 to 4 times along a track of 1 to 2.5 cm. Negative pressure was released before removing the needle.

Gobien et al. (1983) : Pointed out that 'thin needle aspiration' biopsy could considerably reduce hospital costs and stay in hospital; it obviated many thoracotomies.

Pinstein et al. (1983) : Used contrast enhanced CT to help avoid negative percutaneous biopsies.

Ikezoe, J. et al. (1984) : Used ultrasound guidance for lung masses adjacent to the chest wall, nodules in the apical or juxta-diaphragmatic regions or those overlain by a pleural effusion.

Cinti and Hawkins (1984) : Also used ultrasound guidance where possible.

Stevens and Jackman (1984) : Performed almost 500 biopsies in 348 out-patients using only **one pleural pass.** If this failed another attempt was made on a subsequent day. 40% had small pneumothoraces, but only 10% needed tube drainage. Rotex and Cook needles were preferred for tiny lesions or those having indistinct margins, where the chance of missing the lesion was greater. Discrete lesions, such as hamartomas and granulomas, were biopsied using relatively small calibre needles, but they sometimes used a Rotex needle first, fixing the lesion with the screw obturator before biopsy.

Khouri et al. (1985) : From Johns Hopkins Hosp., reported biopsy results in 650 benign and malignant lung lesions. They had 95% accuracy with cancer and 88% with benign and malignant lung lesions. 22% of noncalcified lesions were benign. They used mainly needles with 18 or 20 G tips and with 45° bevels. Needles larger than 20 G were not used if the outer edge of the lesion was > 3 cm from the lung surface. They used TV control following CT.

Lees et al. (1985) from Middlesex Hospital : 5 yr. experience of fine needle aspiration biopsies in 454 consecutive cases, mainly using 22 G spinal type needles and using fluoroscopic or US guidance. Specimens were obtained by vigorous agitation of the needle within the mass, whilst applying suction with a 20 ml syringe. The aspirate was immediately ejected onto a glass slide and smeared before fixation or air drying. Usually three biopsies were taken of various parts of the tumour mass, and with large tumours where the centre was likely to be necrotic, samples were taken from the periphery. They had a 70% specificity.

Pedersen et al. (1986) : 45 cases guided by real-time ultrasound - noted that US will localise masses adjacent to the diaphragm or chest wall provided that no bony structures or aerated tissue are interposed.

Stanley et al. (1987) : Aspirated 458 lung masses using 22 or 23 gauge needles mainly under biplane fluoroscopic guidance, but used CT for hilar lesions or for those that were difficult to visualise fluoroscopically. Found it to be a 'safe, reliable and accurate' procedure.

Fornage (1988) : Fine needle biopsy using a vacuum tube allow one to hold the ultrasound probe in one hand and the needle with an attached vacuum tube in the other.

Van Sonnenberg et al. (1988) : CT guided biopsy of difficult thoracic lesions in 150 cases.

Westcott (1988) : Concerns re reliability of percutaneous transthoracic biopsy include (a) cell type discrimination of carcinoma and (b) non-specific benign or negative results.

Armstrong (1989) : (i) about 30% of fine needle biopsies may be falsely negative for neoplasm, (ii) if clinical and radiological suspicions are high it is often better to proceed straight to surgery,
(iii) True-cut biopsies have about 30 times the complication rate compared with fine needles, but gives a higher confidence of a benign diagnosis, (iv) some reserve percutaneous biopsies for inoperable cases.

Reyes (1990) : A guidance device for CT-guided procedures.

Yankelevitz et al. (1993) : Percutaneous CT biopsy of chest lesions -its accuracy can be improved by choosing a long needle, the shortest distance to the lesion and the thinnest CT collimation (ideally no more than one third the diameter of the lesion). The sections on either side of the one localising the needle tip should also contain a portion of the lesion.

Yankelevitz et al. (1995) : Variability in lesion depth on prone and supine CT scans of the chest : Implications for the accuracy of transthoracic needle aspiration biopsy - nodules above the carina showed minimal change in depth, whilst those below the carina showed considerable variability, with depth changes ≤ 4.0 cm.

Goh et al. (1995 from Liverpool) : Used 20G spinal needles for FNAB of lung lesions (mainly under fluoroscopic control) in 27 cases and confirmed malignancy in 21 when the specimen was immediately studied by a cytopathologist. There was one false negative.

Padhani et al. (1995 from Johns Hopkin's Hosp.) : Studied 70 pts., 44 with the pathologist present and 26 when absent. They found that the number of needle passes tended to increase with the pathologist present, but that immediate cytology assessment does not alter the accuracy or complication rate.

Morgan et al (1995 from Galveston, Texas) : Had success with 68 out of 96 pts. with benign lesions using a coaxial needle system (included 29 fungal infections) 39% had pneumothoraces.

Mason et al. (1996) : Whilst absolute proof can only be obtained by a large trial, our impression and that of others is that immediate cytological evaluation in CT-guided needle biopsy is a safe and cost-effective practice, as it reduces the need for multiple passes when the first pass is determined to be diagnostic, therefore reducing patient risk.

Ghaye et al. (1996) : Comparison between conventional and spiral CT for guidance in percutaneous CT-guided transthoracic needle biopsy - **spiral CT neither improved results nor reduced complication rates and procedure time was not reduced.**

Müller-Leisse et al. (1996) : Fixation techniques for lung specimens - for CT-pathologic correlations, dried specimens which have been fixed with polyethylene glycol are most favourable.

Charig (1996, Wexham Park, Slough) : Outpatient percutaneous cutting needle biopsy of pulmonary parenchyma lesions with CT - 119 patients - 82% true positives, 8 negatives due to necrotic mass or "missed" -uses Temno-Cook needle - average procedure time = 16 mins.

Brown and Kanthapillai (1998) : TNB is a safe and reliable procedure in elderly pts. (> 70 yrs.) with suspected chest malignancy and is well tolerated.

Phillips, S. et al. (1998) : Percutaneous transthoracic needle biopsy - survey of thoracic radiologists in the UK - access to immediate cytology may influence needle choice (fine or cutting needle) and the number of passes made. Many used cutting needles for mediastinal biopsy - this is contrary to the 1989 guidelines of the American Thoracic Society, which may need revision.

Laurent et al. (2000) : CT guided automated 20 G coaxial cutting needle for nodules <2cm.

Further references.

Jennings and Shaw (1953) : Value of sputum cytology in the diagnosis of carcinoma of the bronchus.

Spriggs and Boddington (1957) : The Cytology of Effusions.

British Medical Journal (1972) : Malignant cells in sputum.

Grunze and Spriggs (1980) : History of Clinical Cytology (2nd Edn.).

Orell et al. (1986) : Manual and Atlas of Fine Needle Aspiration Cytology.

Letourneau et al. (1987) : Percutaneous Biopsy, Aspiration and Drainage.

Lane (1985), Macfarlane (1985), Goddard et al. (1986) : Biopsy of thoracic lesions - reviews.

Dick et al. (1974) - 227 cases., Flower and Verney (1979) - 300 cases, Coleman et al. (1982) - 54 cases, Sinner (1982) - 2726 cases., Johnson et al. (1983) - 200 cases : Percutaneous needle biopsy of thoracic lesions.

Sargent and Turner (1970) : Developed a needle holder for biopsy work to avoid irradiating the operator's hands,

Birnbaum et al. (1971) : Used a stainless steel spring on the plunger of the syringe to provide automatic suction during needle lung aspiration biopsy.

Zavala et al. (1971) : Used a high speed trephine (driven by a dental drill) to obtain rather larger biopsy specimens.

Janower and Land (1971) : Lung biopsy.

Sagel and Forrest (1976) : Fluoroscopically assisted lung biopsy.

Grech and Clarke (1978) : Used arterial needles fitted with a tap (the 'Oslo' needle).

Wang, K. et al. (1978, 1983 and 1984a & b) : Transbronchial needle biopsy.

Bergquist et al. (1980) : Transthoracic needle biopsy - accuracy & complications related to location & type of lesion.

Allison and Hemingway (1981) : Percutaneous needle biopsy of the lung.

Gobien et al. (1981) : CT assisted, fluoroscopically guided aspiration biopsy of central, hilar and mediastinal masses.

Westcott (1981) : "When resistance to the needle is encountered at the edge of the lesion, the stylet is withdrawn 2 - 3 cm and the needle advanced into the mass with a short thrust. The stylet is then removed, a 20 ml syringe attached to the needle hub, and **during continued hard suction, the needle is jiggled up and down several times, and then slowly withdrawn during continued suction**. Two or three passes are made if necessary. With large lesions it is important to obtain a sample from the periphery, because their centres are often necrotic."

Costello et al. (1982) : CT assisted biopsy using a grid reference system and light lasers.

Fink et al. (1982) : CT guided biopsy of mediastinum when too difficult for conventional fluoroscopy.

Sinner (1983) : Fine needle biopsy of tuberculosis coexistent with carcinoma of the lung.

Van Sonnenberg (1983) : CT guided biopsy of difficult mediastinal hilar and pulmonary lesions using a modified coaxial approach.

Cohan et al. (1984) : CT assistance for fluoroscopically guided aspiration biopsy.

Gatenby et al. (1984) : CT guided biopsy of small apical and peripheral upper lobe mass.

Orell et al. (1986) : Manual and Atlas of Fine Needle Aspiration Cytology,

Skupin et al. (1987) : Cytological diagnosis of lung lesions by fine-needle biopsy.

Conces et al. (1989) : Value of needle biopsy in the diagnosis of pulmonary infection.

Jennings et al. (1989) : Ultrasound guided core biopsy.

Wernecke et al. (1989) : Biopsy of mediastinal tumours under ultra-sound guidance.

Glynn (1990) : Transthoracic needle-biopsy - screwing a 20G. Westcott needle through the overlapping bone.

Macaulay et al. (1990) : Actinomycosis and carcinoma on sequential CT-guided biopsies.

Ogilvie (1990) : 450 cases - 19G. Surecut needle for pleura, chest-wall and mediastinum - low complication rate (compared with fine-needle series).

Haramati and Austin (1991) : Complications after CT-guided biopsy through non-aerated lung were few, compared with the needle traversing aerated lung.

Tarver and Conces (1994) : FNAB has about 95% accuracy for malignant lesions.

Sawhney et al. (1991) : Tru-cut biopsy of mediastinal masses guided by real-tine sonography using ultrasound to avoid puncture of the lung and mediastinal vascular structures.

Sheppard (1991) : Percutaneous biopsy of mediastinal tumours under sonographic guidance - large cylinders of tissue obtained with wide bore needles can be sufficient to aid in the diagnosis of **germ cell tumours**.

Jones, H.M. et al. (1993) : **Painful** transthoracic needle biopsy - a sign of **neurogenic** tumour - two cases.

Li et al. (1996) : Diagnostic accuracy and safety of CT-guided percutaneous needle aspiration of the lung - was less accurate for small than large pulmonary nodules, but the complication rates for both were low.

Dodelinger (1999) : Uses several needle types + guidance with CT, CT fluoroscopy or US for most lung biopsies. He regards the Biopty gun as too cumbersome. For the mediastinum he uses a 'salinoma' to avoid traversing the lung, and always tries to avoid a fissure. Uses the 'turn-over' technique, with the patient remaining on the table for 10 mins after the procedure to try to seal the puncture hole in the lung. Nearly all pneumothoraces are detected at 1 hour, and many small ones on a post-biopsy section.

Core biopsy

Lindgren (1982), Parker et al. (1989), Gleeson et al. (1989) : Biopty gun.

Lees (1990) : Preferred the Biopty gun to fine needle aspiration for lung lesions 'when there is either no discrete target or a complex necrotic mass'. In such cases neoplastic cells may be few in number within fibroblastic tissue, and a histological sample is more likely to give a diagnosis. Over 100 sections may be obtained from a single 18 SWG Biopty core. Shock wave deformity on ultrasound shows the position of biopsy.

Allen and Hansell (1991) : Biopsy of intrapulmonary lesions with the Biopty gun - 33 cases with 18 G needle.

Haramati, L.B. (1995) : CT-guided automated needle biopsy of the chest.

Arakawa et al. (1996) : Comparison between biopsy gun (18G) and fine needle aspiration (20G) - a core biopsy can increase the accuracy with a higher histological predictive rate and no obvious risk of increased complications.

Grief et al. (1999) : Percutaneous core biopsy compared with FNAB in diagnosing **benign lung lesions**.

Charig and Phillips (2000) : CT-guided core needle biopsy of parenchymal lung lesions (using Temno & other needles) is a safe and accurate out-patient procedure - study of 185 consecutive biopsies in 183 pts. - 150 malignant, 23 benign + 12 false negative results. Pts. were allowed home after CXR at 1 hr unless they had a 30% or larger pnx. - 48 pts. had a pnx (26%), 4 + small haemoptyses. 7 pts. with sympyomatic pnx were admitted, 2 needing intercostal drainage & 1 aspiration only. 1 returned with a 50% pnx at 24hrs which required drainage and another 2 days later with a 30% pnx. 13 had haemoptyses without pnx - all resolving within 1 hr. Only 10 had post-biopsy admissions.

Abscess drainage

Connell et al. (1980) : Upper abdominal abscess - a continuing and deadly problem.

Bernadino et al. (1984) : Drainage of liver abscess.

Gobien et al. (1984) : Percutaneous catheter drainage of mediastinal abscess.

Martin, E. et al. (1984) : Percutaneous drainage of abscesses - report of 100 cases.

Weissberg et al. (1984) : Percutaneous drainage of lung abscess.

Complications

Ochsner and DeBakey (1942) : Condemned needle biopsy because of possible spread of malignant and inflammatory lesions, although they did not document a single case.

Wolinsky and Lischner (1969) : Needle track implantation of tumour after percutaneous biopsy.

Meyer et al. (1970) : Fatal complications of percutaneous lung biopsy.

Berger, R. et al. (1972) : Dissemination of cancer cells by needle biopsy of lung.

Sinner and Zailcek (1976) : Implantation metastasis after percutaneous transthoracic needle aspiration biopsy.

Grech and Clark (1978) : Continued suction during needle removal to try to minimise the possible seeding of a needle track metastasis (they used relatively thick Oslo-type needles with short bevels and taps for their biopsies).

Nordenström and Sinner (1978) : Reported only one definite case of implantation metastasis and one possible one in over 4,000 biopsies. They advised that the trochar should **always** be withdrawn into the cannula before removing it to try to avoid this happening.

Müller et al (1986) : Seeding of malignant cells into the needle track after lung or pleural biopsy.

Seyfer et al. (1989) : One case of chest wall implantation of lung cancer following a biopsy using a Vim-Silverman needle. The patient developed the deposit within the right anterior chest wall six months after a right upper lobectomy for adenocarcinoma, and had this resected with a flap reconstruction of the chest wall.

Ayar et al. (1998) : Needle track metastasis after transthoracic needle biopsy - report of N. American survey - 8 were reported amongst over 68,000 biopsies.

Perlmutt et al (1986 & 1987) : Optimum time to take chest radiographs to detect pneumothoraces after percutaneous lung biopsies - they had 160 pneumothoraces in 673 procedures, 78 needing chest drainage or aspiration. 142 were visible immediately, 15 at one hour and 3 at four hours. Of those needing treatment 69 were apparent immediately and 9 at one hour. (They used a 9F tube attached to a Heimlich valve - Heimlich, 1968).

Perlmutt (1989) : Review of percutaneous transthoracic needle aspiration.

Fish et al. (1988) : 160 patients - 46% of those with obstructive airways disease developed a pneumothorax, (20% needing drainage), compared with only 7% without airways obstruction.

Murphy et al. (1990) : CT and chest radiography are equally sensitive in the detection of pneumothorax after CT-guided pulmonary interventional procedures.

Molina et al. (1990) : One piece Heimlich type one way valve with an aspiration port for treatment of a pneumothorax complicating needle biopsy.

Spouge and Thomas (1992) : Tension pneumothorax (following a CT guided biopsy of a small pulmonary nodule) after reversal of a Heimlich valve, inadvertently reversed by the patient after an accidental disconnection.

Klose (1993) : Extrapleural injection of saline for safe transpleural access to pulmonary lesions > 8 mm from pleura.

Laoide et al. (1994) : Treatment of post-biopsy pneumothorax with a self-contained pneumothorax treatment device.

Ansell et al. (1996) : Complications in Diagnostic Imaging and Interventional Radiology.

Kazerooni et al. (1996) : Risk of pneumothorax in CT-guided percutaneous lung biopsy.

Padley and Flower (1996) : Complications of percutaneous intervention in the chest.

Yankelevitz et al. (1996) : Percutaneous catheter aspiration of a large biopsy-induced pneumothorax is safe and easy to perform and may obviate chest tube placement - almost completely aspirated pneumothorax in 17 pts. - 12 did not need drainage tube placement - positioned puncture site down (18G IV catheter + 3-way 50ml syringe).

Berger, J. et al. (1998) : The frequency of pneumothorax after CT and fluoroscopically guided biopsy is similar. CT is more sensitive than CXR for detecting small pneumothoraces. In the series of 88 pts. studied, no pneumothoraces needed tube drainage.

Kumaradavan et al. (1998) : CT-guided percutaneous needle biopsy of lung and chest lesions in 66 pts. - greater number of complications in pts. undergoing CT-guided biopsies, also core biopsies increased the yield of diagnostic tissue, but with a higher complication rate.

Miller, J. et al. (1998) : Studied 50 pts. who had CT guided percutaneous core-needle lung biopsies; 7 had a pneumothorax, but only 1 was symptomatic and required drainage. All who had a pneumothorax had CT evidence of emphysema or interstitial fibrosis and spiculated borders of masses.

Smith, S. et al. (1998) : All significant pneumothoraces were detected on inspiratory films at 1 hour post-procedure.

Norenberg et al. (1974) : Two fatal haemoptyses using Silverman type cutting needles - no damage to a large vessel was found at autopsy in either case - reviewed 11 other deaths from literature, endobronchial haemorrhage, air embolus or tension pneumothorax - felt that cutting needles should be avoided.

Pearce and Patt (1974) : Fatal pulmonary haemorrhage after percutaneous aspiration lung biopsy.

Milner et al. (1979) : Fatal intrathoracic haemorrhage after percutaneous aspiration lung biopsy.

Doyle and Mullerworth (1988) : Bleeding as a complication of fine-needle lung biopsy.

Glassberg and Sussman (1990) : Life-threatening haemorrhage due to percutaneous transthoracic intervention - importance of the **internal mammary artery**.

Hasan et al. (1993) : Coronary artery to pulmonary artery fistula after transbronchial biopsy (left anterior descending artery to left pulmonary artery shown by coronary arteriography) after heart lung transplantation for cystic fibrosis

Westcott (1973) : Air embolism complicating percutaneous aspiration lung biopsy.

Aberle et al. (1987) : Fatal air embolism following lung needle aspiration in a 60 year old man with Wegener's granuloma and previous asbestos exposure.

Tolly et al. (1988) : Air embolism with air/fluid level in the left atrium, after misplacement and replacement of a thin lumbar puncture needle into a pulmonary secondary deposit. He fully recovered after supportive treatment.

Baker and Awwad (1988) : CT of fatal cerebral air embolism following percutaneous aspiration lung biopsy in a patient with ARDS.

Yamaura et al. (2000) : Massive intrathoracic haemorrhage after CT lung biopsy due to torn adhesions with a complicating pneumothorax.

Comparison of bronchoscopy and of transbronchial and percutaneous biopsies with CT.

Clearly **central lung masses** which involve the lumina of the larger bronchi are most accessible to the **transbronchial route.** With a **peripheral nodule, percutaneous fine needle aspiration** is likely to make a positive diagnosis in more than 80% of malignant lesions, but with a risk of pneumothorax, whereas transbronchial biopsy will give a lower yield of positive diagnoses for malignancy - 60% or less, a complicating pneumothorax being uncommon. Although Lane (1985) stated that neither technique is however good at providing a specific cytological diagnosis for benign lesions, the diagnosis of **diffuse lung disease by the transbronchial route is becoming widely used and reliable**, particularly if CT is carried out first to show the distribution of the disease, and to ensure that a representative area is sampled.

Colice et al. (1985) compared CT with fibreoptic bronchoscopy in the identification of endobronchial abnormalities in patients with known or suspected lung cancer, and found bronchoscopy to be the best technique for determining the presence and extent of endobronchial involvement. It was moderately accurate in predicting the presence of airway abnormalities, but was inaccurate in defining the type of abnormality seen at bronchoscopy (localised mucosal change, endobronchial mass or extrinsic compression).

Naidich et al. (1987) compared CT and fibreoptic bronchoscopy and wrote "In no case was malignancy missed by CT. CT was accurate for focal lesions, but inaccurate in predicting whether a given abnormality was endobronchial, submucosal or extrinsic."

A question was asked at the 1998 Annual Meeting of the Royal College of Radiologists about the number of lung biopsies being carried out in the UK. It was felt that the number of percutaneous biopsies was declining, particularly in relation to the number of trans-bronchial biopsies.

A study of 37 cases of percutaneous cutting needle biopsy of non-malignant disease processes at the Churchill Hospital, Oxford has shown that it can be a safe method of diagnosis with examination of the specimens by histology and bacteriological culture (Bungay et al., 2000).

Pleural biopsy.
There are several ways of doing this:

(a) **Fluid   cytology** is the method of choice when fluid is present. It is very easily carried out under ultrasound control (see also ps. 14.13 - 14). As adenocarcinomas and small cell tumours tend to produce more effusions (often blood stained), these types are most frequently found. Not all effusions, present in association with tumours, contain malignant cells (see also Chapters 4 and 16). Even in cases with diffuse pleural malignancy, fluid cytology may only be positive in 30-50%. The author often found that a specimen at the end of an aspiration was more likely to be positive than one from the beginning, but often had both such samples examined. Spriggs and Boddington (1968) from Oxford produced what is still a good atlas of malignancy in body fluids.

(b) **Fine needle aspiration biopsies** may also be directed by ultrasound, fluoroscopy or CT, and will often give good results (Illus. **BIOPSY/ASPIRATION, Mesothel Pt. 47i & j**).

(c) **Punch biopsy** using the Abrams or similar needles, is commonly used by Chest Physicians, but seems unnecessarily large, and **most radiologists prefer the Biopty, Tru-Cut or similar needles**. The biopsy should be taken with these along the line of the mass - see also note (f) under 'Conclusions' re Biopty gun. The technique should avoid injury to the intercostal and internal mammary vessels (see Fig. 12.15, p. 12.29).

(d) Open biopsy at mini or more formal thoracotomy.

Some references.
Abrams (1958) : A pleural biopsy punch.
Salyer et al. (1975b) : Efficacy of pleural needle biopsy and fluid cytology in the diagnosis of malignant tumour involving the pleura - were positive in 90%.
Herbert and Gallagher (1982a & b) : With suspected mesotheliomas, close attention to morphology could help pick out malignant cases. The immunoperoxidase technique stained reactive mesothelial cells positively for α_1 anti-chymotrypsin, whereas reactive malignant cells were mostly negative.
Ghosh et al. (1983) : Detected tumour antigens on the surface of malignant pleural cells.
Lane (1985) : Thoracic physician colleague in Oxford : Reviewed biopsy techniques and noted that although punch type pleural biopsies are usually considered routine procedures in most hospitals, they should **not** be left to 'inexperienced beginners' and attention to detail is required. The punch hole should be pointed laterally and downwards in the line of the ribs and the biopsy should ideally be taken when there is still plenty of fluid in the pleural space. Pulling hard outwards after feeling the catch of the pleura is a sure way of only obtaining skeletal muscle. Multiple biopsies also improve the diagnostic rate.
Morone et al. (1987) : Pleural biopsy with Cope and Abrams needles.
Mueller, P. et al. (1988) : Image guided pleural biopsies for (a) pleural masses or thickening not seen on chest radiographs or only on one view, and (b) small or loculated pleural effusions with no visible mass. Used standard needles if a definite pleural mass or thickening was seen; but if only fluid was present, reversed bevel needles were used for biopsy.
Flower (1990) : Accurate localisation with ultrasound or CT is often required.
Scott et al. (1995) : Percutaneous CT-guided cutting needle biopsy for **diffuse pleural thickening**.

Thoracoscopy.(for thorascopic surgery - see p. 24.47).

This technique appears to be coming back into vogue; it was not uncommonly used in patients with tuberculosis to divide adhesions and hence allow the lung to collapse with a pneumothorax. It may be used to study the pleural surfaces of the lung, the inner aspect of the chest wall and the outer borders of the mediastinum, if the lung is allowed to partially collapse. A drainage tube may be necessary for a few hours afterwards to aspirate the pneumothorax. The advantage is that lung and node biopsies may be readily taken under direct vision, and small peripheral tumours may be removed or cauterised. The fibre-optic bronchoscope can be used for this purpose.

Reference.

Gleeson (1995) : Thoracoscopy & CT in the evaluation of pleural malignancy. Small nodules may not be shown by CT, esp. on the visceral pleura, but many patients show **other** signs of malignancy. Uses an antero - or postero-lateral approach in patients with pleural effusions.

Mediastinoscopy

This is carried out from the supra-sternal fossa, via a small incision. The term is almost a misnomer, as most of the dissection and examination is carried out by the operator's index finger, feeling his way gradually down to the aortic arch and pulmonary artery, and noting the presence of tumour masses or enlarged lymph nodes. When these are felt, they may be inspected via the instrument which is inserted into the track so formed and biopsied. Palpation is essential to avoid damage to the vascular structures.

Only on the right can one get down to the level of the pulmonary artery because on the left the aortic arch overshadows the all-important 'sub-aortic' fossa (the 'aorto-pulmonary window' of radiologists). On the right it is particularly important to avoid damage to the SVC, the azygos vein, the ascending aorta and right pulmonary artery.

Ultrasound is also best on the right side.

Readily accessible : right para-tracheal nodes.

Possible : sub-carinal and aorto-pulmonary window nodes.

Difficult or impossible : most left sided nodes.

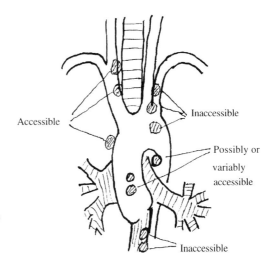

Fig. 21.5   Not all lymph node groups of the mediastinum are equally accessible to biopsy at mediastinoscopy.
(after Lunia et al., 1981, Cancer, **47**, 672 - 679, Fig. 3, copyright American Cancer Society, adapted by permission of Wiley Liss, Inc., a Subsidiary of John Wiley & sons Ltd.).

Mediastinal (including node) biopsy.

Surgery is often employed to obtain a small block of tissue for accurate histological diagnosis. This is still necessary with lymphomas, unless an affected and readily removable lymph node is available e.g. in the neck. However with many tumours and nodes a needle aspirate or a small core sample will often suffice, and with improvements in technique the indications for an open surgical approach have become much reduced.

However **radiologically controlled biopsies of the mediastinum nodes** (including hilar nodes) are being more commonly employed. This may be easy in the upper or anterior mediastinum using ultrasound guidance (see below). Paravertebral, parasternal, supraclavicular, transsternal, transoesophageal and transtracheo-bronchial routes are also available.

In 1972 Nordenström reported the use of a paravertebral route to biopsy mediastinal lesions, but the method did not find wide acceptance.

Williams (R.A.) et al. (1984) used a 20 g. disposable needle, introduced on the left adjacent to the spine, in the extra-pleural space, the needle being advanced under CT control, and bouncing it off the vertebral bodies as for trans-lumbar aortography. They preferred a left sided approach, medial to the descending aorta, so as to avoid traversing the lung in the azygo-oesophageal recess. Even lesions to the right of the oesophagus are accessible to a left sided approach, and it is particularly useful for oesophageal and para-oesophageal lesions.

Others have used gas-insufflation or saline injection to elevate the parietal pleura from adjacent structures, thus leaving a space in which a biopsy needle may safely be manipulated under CT control - an '**extra-pleural approach**'.

If aerated lung has to be traversed, then as with percutaneous lung biopsies, the needle should be as thin as possible, and one should ideally avoid traversing aerated vascular structures, or more than the minimum of aerated lung as possible, to try to minimise complications such as haemorrhage or pneumothoraces; one should also try to avoid puncturing the visceral pleura more than once unless absolutely necessary.

A trans-sternal route may avoid traversing lung, if the mass to be biopsied does not extend beyond the sternal edge, but this has to be done very carefully - see also sternal biopsy p. 21.17.

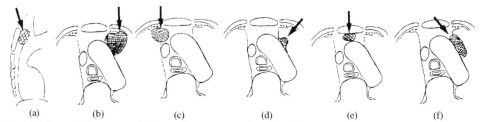

(a)   (b)   (c)   (d)   (e)   (f)

Fig. 21.6   Diagrams of the various approaches for biopsy to anterior mediastinal masses (reproduced from D'Agostino et al., 1993, Radiology, **189**, 703 - 705 with permission. In (b) & (c) the needle may run close to the **internal mammary artery** - normally 1.2 cm lateral to the sternal edge.)

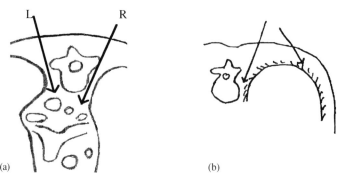

Fig. 21.7   Paravertebral approaches for biopsies (a) in the posterior mediastinum and (b) pleura.

In (a) note that because of pleural fixation the paravertebral mediastinum is more difficult to distend than the anterior mediastinum. In (b) the needle is angled along the line of the pleural thickening. The prone position is preferred as fluid tends to drain anteriorly, leaving the pleural thickening, which can then be biopsied.

Ultrasound is often invaluable, particularly following CT, since if the lesion is visualised by this method (e.g. parasternally), no intervening air-filled lung is likely to be in the line of the needle track. Parasternally it is important to note the position of the intercostal vessels, especially when larger needles are being employed. However in most patients there is about 0.5 cm of space between them and the sternal edge, and if the needle is angled medially it is unlikely to traverse these vessels. **Transoesophageal US** may be used to biopsy subcarinal nodes - see p. 13.28.

Sternal and rib biopsies.
These are important sites for biopsy. Localisation of the lesion or area to be biopsied is important, particularly with small lesions and this may be done by palpation (if a lump is present), 'spot view' taken under fluoroscopy control (Illus. **BIOPSY/ASPIRATION, bone deposits 32a-d** and Illus. **RIB SPOT VIEW**), isotope bone scans, CT, etc.

The lesions if soft may be aspirated with a short fine needle, but if still 'bony' really need a bone needle to penetrate the outer bone cortex. For this the author **always** used a special sternal aspiration needle attached in manufacture to a hand grip, similar to that of a screwdriver, and similar to many other medical trochars. This allows one to puncture the outer cortex with a screw-type motion. In addition this needle is fitted with an adjustable guard - a screw-clamp onto the outside to prevent it going in too deeply - and very important since the needle often suddenly slips into the medulla of the bone, and under the considerable pressure which is often needed, can easily transverse the deeper cortex or slip off the side of a rib or the sternum and enter underlying tissue - a needle with no guard being able to run in up to the base of the holder. If this happens then the needle can enter the lung, mediastinum, puncture the great vessels, or heart with serious or fatal results (for anatomy see ps. 1.30 & 1.33).

Such a needle can take both aspiration or small tissue samples. Using it the author never had any complications, but it was often advisable to introduce a little extra local anaesthetic when feeling the periosteum to avoid pain when screwing-in the needle, and at the same time adjust the guard and fix it to about 3mm from the skin surface to avoid it going deeper with penetration of the outer cortex. (This needle is also useful for intraosseous venography and a modification with 'wings' and a detachable handle was formerly used for infusion therapy.).

Tru-cut or similar needles with no guard should not be used for sternal biopsies (except on massive projecting lesions) as if they slip (and have not been inserted along the length of the sternum) serious complicating injuries may occur (Illus. **BIOPSY FOLDER, sternal biopsy**).

Fig. 21.8 Biopsy needle (trochar and cannula) with adjustable guard for sternal or rib biopsy (as advised by Hamilton Bailey, 1950). Illus. **BIOPSY FOLDER, sternal needle**. shows the modification used by the author.

Vertebral biopsy. (see also p. 22.6).
This may be carried out in the dorsal or lumbar region, either under CT control, as above, or with biplane, 'C arm' fluoroscopy or by using a single plane technique. With the last, the depth is determined by 'feel' as for trans-lumbar aortography, or by taking cross-table radiographs with a horizontal x-ray beam. An 'open-ended' trans-lumbar needle will often give a good aspiration biopsy result, but special needles or punches removing a core of material may be employed.

Further references.
Oakes et al. (1984) : Therapeutic **thoracoscopy.**
Carlens (1959) : **Mediastinoscopy** - a method for inspection and tissue biopsy in the superior mediastinum.

Van der Schaar and van Zanten (1965) : Experience with mediastinoscopy.

Palva et al. (1973) Mediastinoscopic observation of metastatic spread in pulmonary carcinoma.

Goldberg et al. (1974) : Mediastinoscopy for assessing mediastinal spread of lung cancer.

Whitcomb et al. (1976) : Indications for mediastinoscopy in bronchogenic carcinoma.

Pearson et al. (1982) : Significance of positive mediastinal nodes identified at mediastinoscopy in patients with resectable cancer of the lung.

Goldstraw et al. (1983) : Compared CT and mediastinoscopy in the preoperative staging of lung cancer. They found that the sensitivity and specificity of CT was inferior to mediastinoscopy for nodes, but was superior in predicting mediastinal invasion especially with lower lobe tumours.

Brion et al. (1985) : Examined 153 patients by CT and mediastinoscopy. Nodes >5mm were considered potentially metastatic and were correlated with surgery. They found that CT was more sensitive for detecting deposits than mediastinoscopy. 72% of nodes involved by tumour in nodes <5mm allowed them to omit mediastinoscopy with a negative CT.

Staples et al. (1988) : Compared CT and mediastinoscopy in the assessment of mediastinal nodes in 154 patients with bronchogenic carcinoma and found that CT could detect enlarged nodes as measured by long axis as well as by mediastinoscopy. Short axes were less reliable. In some of the patients with enlarged nodes, tumour was present not in these, but in other normal sized nodes.

Puhakka et al. (1990) : Mediastinoscopy in relation to clinical evaluation.

Astigarraga et al. (1994) : Post-mediastinoscopy changes in chest CT.

Herman et al. (1991) : Anterior mediastinal masses - utility of **transthoracic needle biopsy.**

D'Agostino et al. (1993) : Trans-sternal biopsy of anterior mediastinal masses with CT guidance.

Bressler and Kirkham (1994) : Alternative approaches for mediastinal biopsy - pleural space (via effusion or iatrogenic pneumothorax), lateral decubitus positioning or the suprasternal route.

Langen et al. (1995) : Distension of extrapleural spaces with dilute contrast medium or air - value in creating safe percutaneous access to the mediastinum in cadavers - allowing extrapleural access from R paravertebral, left retroaortic and parasternal directions for large-bore needles.

Williams, M.P. (1996) : Mediastinal node biopsy - uses a trans-saline elevation approach as much as possible - can even traverse the SVC without any serious problems to sample a node behind it. Tries to avoid the internal mammary vessels.

Grant et al. (1998) : Percutaneous needle biopsy of mediastinal masses using a CT guided extrapleural approach, using extrapleural fluid (saline + local anaesthetic) in 20 cases - diagnosis established in 18 - few complications.

Man et al. (1998) : Cardiac tamponade following fine needle aspiration of a right upper mediastinal mass due to Hodgkin's disease in a 37 year old female - the needle punctured the ascending aorta causing a haemopericardium - this was aspirated and the patient recovered.

McAdams et al.(1998) : Virtual bronchoscopy for directing transbronchial needle aspiration of hilar and mediastinal lymph nodes.

Stoker and Kissin (1985) : Performed 135 **vertebral** biopsies over a seven year period. They used a Jamshidi needle and had an accuracy of about 90%. To enter the posterior aspect of a vertebra, they inserted the needle through the skin, 8 cm from the midline in the lumbar and 5 - 6 cm in the dorsal region, advancing it at 30 to 45° to the sagittal plane. The needle cannula is advanced into the vertebra firmly and with alternate clockwise and counter-clockwise rotation. After it has gone in 1 cm the specimen core is severed by twisting the needle firmly several times in the same direction.

Gishen (1992) : **Bone biopsy** technique - used a **Jamshidi needle.**

Biopsy procedures of liver and pancreas.

These may be needle aspirations or core biopsies. For the diagnosis of malignant disease the former may be sufficient, but for cirrhosis or hepatitis the latter is usually required. US or CT control may be used, particularly the former. Liver biopsies are usually carried out with the patient supine and a subcostal approach **in inspiration**, but this may be varied for focal lesions in different positions. It is important to avoid puncturing the gall-bladder, colon etc., particularly when carrying out core biopsies. Biliary peritonitis may require drainage and cholecystectomy. Very vascular liver lesions, such as **haemangiomas,** may cause significant bleeding - the author has known such a lesion rapidly fill a syringe with blood via thin needle (Illus. **HAEMANGIOMA, Liver Pt. 31a-c**).

Reference.

Dodd et al. (1997) : Fine needle aspiration of the liver and pancreas - a cytological primer for radiologists.

Adrenal biopsy.
  This may be done under either CT or US control (see also ps. 17.6-7). The author usually preferred US control (as it gave a more accurate guide with changes in respiration to the position of the adrenal), with the patient lying prone, and with a pad under the abdomen to prevent the kidneys and adrenals dropping anteriorly. Others have used an antero-lateral approach (via the liver on the right), anterior or lateral approaches.

References.
Heiberg and Wolverson (1985) : Recommended an ipsilateral decubitus position using CT control.
Welch et al. (1994) : Review of 10-year experience of percutaneous adrenal biopsy (277 biopsies in 270 pts). concluded it is a safe and accuraate method (accuracy of 90%, lower on the left because of the more difficult approach); 8 had haematomas, only one needing an adrenalectomy - accuracy improves with 18 or 19g needles.
Clark, R.A. (Year Book of Diagnostic Radiology 1996, p. 157, commented on the above paper by Welch et al.) : Used US control with a lateral transhepatic approach for the right adrenal and a transabdominal route for the left.

Bronchography.
  Bronchography is now used much less than 10 years ago in the investigation of lung tumours, the decline being due to the more widespread use of CT and fibre-optic bronchoscopy, and the decline in the number of patients with bronchiectasis, but a short chapter is retained for reference purposes particularly as more interest is now being generated by multiplanar CT bronchography. Its value in the diagnosis of bronchiectasis is discussed on ps. 3.18.

Contrast media - historical.
  The earliest bronchograms were carried out accidentally, by the inhalation of bismuth or barium being used for swallow examinations, either via the larynx or a tracheo-oesophageal fistula (Illus. **INHALED BARIUM**). Much experimental work was done to produce acceptable media, at first using a fine powder of iodoform and bismuth salts in dogs, or introduced via a bronchoscope in humans.
  In 1921, Sicard and Forestier used iodised poppy-seed oil (Lipiodol) as a contrast agent for bronchography, and following their report bronchography with Lipiodol became fairly widely practised. Its drawbacks were 'alveolar' residues in the lungs which could persist on radiographs for many years, if the oil passed into the acini (Illus. **LIPIODOL, Bronchogram 14**), and diarrhoea and abdominal distress which ensued if much of the medium was swallowed. Allergies also occasionally occurred.
  Dionosil (propyliodone - the propyl ester of diodone) became available in 1952, either as a suspension in arachis oil or water. Its advantage was that if it passed peripherally into the bronchioles and alveoli, from which it cannot be expectorated, it was hydrolysed, absorbed and excreted. With the very small number of bronchograms carried out, as a result of CT and fibre-optic bronchoscopy, it was withdrawn from the market by Glaxo in 1990. The author never had a case of allergy to the arachis oil, although a few patients with asthma had some bronchospasm (usually relieved by IV aminophylline) - none were severe - but one carried out elsewhere showed severe spasm (Illus. **BRONCHOGRAM, Pt. 7b & c**).

Techniques for bronchography.
  Various techniques have been used, but the author mainly used the crico-thyroid route with local anaesthesia), performing about 8,000 such examinations over a 30 year period (the method being described in detail in Wright, 1974). Not only was the method useful for demonstrating bronchiectasis prior to surgical resection, which used to be widely practised, but also for the demonstration of deformities due to tumours, inflammatory etc. disease. Other methods have included a trans-nasal catheter, aspiration over the tongue, or via a bronchoscope.
  Some examples are shown in Illus. **BRONCHOGRAM**, and a chart of possible findings due to tumours in Fig. 21.8. Some of the examples (esp. Illus. **BRONCHOGRAM-BRCTSIS**) show how good the method was for showing bronchiectasis to surgeons, etc. With tumours a big problem was the poor portrayal of soft tissue abnormalities outside the bronchi.

Children have mainly been examined under general anaesthesia, with the contrast medium being injected via a catheter (with a previously marked length) being passed through the endotracheal tube. This method was also occasionally used in adults.

Some references.
Huizinga and Smelt (1950) : Bronchography.   Dijkstra (1958) : Bronchography.
Carmichael and Woodrow (1959) : Complete bronchial obstruction in asthma, an unusual bronchographic hazard - gross spasm of larger bronchi in left lung with complete block of left lower lobe bronchi following Neo-hydriol bronchogram.
Rinker et al. (1968) : Six signs of malignancy as found on bronchograms - amputation, sharp cut-off, a stretched or bent bronchus, symmetrical or 'rat-tail' narrowing of a bronchus or thumb-print indentation.
Laubenberger and de Brito-Paiva with Kodak-Pathé (1973) : Reference handbook of normal segmental bronchograms, performed by the catheter method.
Wright (1973) : Radiological Diagnosis of Lung and Mediastinal Tumours.
Lundgren et al. (1982), Flower and Shneerson (1984) : Bronchography via the fibre-optic bronchoscope.
Wright (1988) : Contrast media in bronchography.
Morcos et al. (1989) : Have used the myelographic contrast medium - Iotrolan (Schering) - 300 mg I /ml. slightly hyperosmolar and a dimer - for selective bronchography via the fibre-optic bronchoscope - 2 to 3 ml per lung segment (max. 15 ml/ patient). The low viscosity means that radiographs must be taken at once - ideally with the 100 mm camera. It is mostly cleared from the lungs by 24 hours.
Varkey and Morcos (1995) : Value of selective bronchography using Iotrolan in the diagnosis of the peripheral pulmonary nodule - was relatively accurate in diagnosing the malignant nodule but poor in identifying benign ones.
Ferretti et al. (2000) : Carried out CT bronchography for demonstrating benign abnormalities of central airways including carcinoid tumours but found no advantage over plain CT.

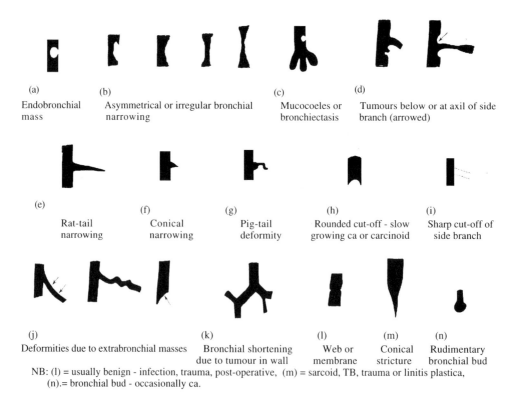

(a) Endobronchial mass

(b) Asymmetrical or irregular bronchial narrowing

(c) Mucocoeles or bronchiectasis

(d) Tumours below or at axil of side branch (arrowed)

(e) Rat-tail narrowing

(f) Conical narrowing

(g) Pig-tail deformity

(h) Rounded cut-off - slow growing ca or carcinoid

(i) Sharp cut-off of side branch

(j) Deformities due to extrabronchial masses

(k) Bronchial shortening due to tumour in wall

(l) Web or membrane

(m) Conical stricture

(n) Rudimentary bronchial bud

NB: (l) = usually benign - infection, trauma, post-operative, (m) = sarcoid, TB, trauma or linitis plastica, (n).= bronchial bud - occasionally ca.

Fig. 21.8   Bronchial deformities which may be produced by bronchogenic tumours (a - k) + bronchial blocks due to benign conditions - for comparison.

Chapter 22 : **Skeletal, Muscle, Brain, etc. Deposits and some Isotope Procedures.**

Secondary deposits in bone.

These are common in patients with lung cancer, and many patients present with pain or other symptoms due to their presence. They may occur in any bone, but are most common in the axial skeleton, shoulders, humeri, and upper femora. With small cell tumours, up to 60% of patients may have widespread dissemination into the skeleton at the time of diagnosis (as shown by radiography, isotope bone scans, MR or random marrow sampling). In patients with non-small cell tumours asymptomatic deposits are less common (about 1 to 5%) at the time of presentation, and a routine bone scan is not always carried out in the preoperative 'work up' (see also p. 24.26). When bone deposits occur in the latter group, they are often solitary or few in number, but their number increases with the duration and severity of the disease.

Most lung cancer deposits in bone are lytic in type (before radiation or other treatment is given), but a few are mixed or sclerotic. These latter are mostly deposits from adenocarcinomas, bronchiolo-alveolar carcinomas or metastasising carcinoids. In the differential diagnosis one should always consider other causes for sclerosis - healing fractures, Paget's disease, dense bone islands, osteomas or deposits from other tumours (prostate, breast, reticuloses, bowel, thyroid, kidney, chemodectoma, medulloblastoma, etc. The author has even seen a sclerotic rib deposit from a seminoma! - Illus. **BONE DEP SCLEROTIC, Test dep Pt. 1a-g**).

In many cases plain radiographs are adequate for the demonstration of deposits, but if the cortex has not been destroyed they may be invisible. Edelstyn et al. (1967) using an excised lumbar spine from a 57 year old woman, found that until 75% of the cancellous bone had been removed from a lumbar vertebra (with a defect 3 cm in diameter) or the cortex was breached, the defect was invisible on radiographs taken after both filling the defect with water and also immersing it.

In symptomatic cases, tomography (especially CT) will often demonstrate bony destruction (e.g. within a rib, the sternum, vertebral bodies or the pelvis - Illus. **BONE DEP-CT**). For rib lesions, localised 'spot' views taken under TV /fluoroscopic control are often invaluable for showing fine detail if e.g. a healing fracture or a rib deposit (Illus. **RIB SPOT VIEW**), and such views are **particularly helpful prior to biopsy** - indeed a needle rib biopsy is most often safer, easier, and less traumatic than one of the lung, unless the lung lesion abuts the pleural and chest wall and can be imaged with ultrasound. If the rib lesion is positive for cancer, the primary lung tumour is nearly always inoperable (a possible exception is when the lung lesion has extended into it, and the lung lesion and adjacent chest wall can be resected).

Some bones are difficult to demonstrate adequately by plain radiography e.g. the sternum (see p. 12.33) and the sacrum. A useful 'ploy' with the latter is to turn the patient into the prone position and to displace overlying bowel with an air-filled small plastic football or balloon (Fig. 22.1 below).The prone view will also allow a divergent x-ray beam to show more readily the sacro-iliac joints.

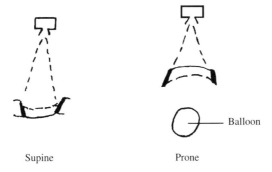

Supine	Prone

Fig. 22.1 Radiography of the sacrum and sacro-iliac joints.

In other cases, conventional tomography or CT will readily and more clearly show the bone destruction (Illus. **BONE DEP-CT**).

Within the spine, absent spinous processes or pedicles may indicate the presence of a deposit, but not uncommonly a spinous process is congenitally absent in the lower dorsal spine (most often at D 12 level). Adjacent soft tissue masses are common - see ps. 18.28 - 29. A point worth emphasising is that single views of the spine are inadequate for the diagnosis of metastases - gross lesions are easily missed (see also Davies, A. et al, 1993, Tyrrell et al., 1995, Whitehouse, 1995 and Blease, 1995).

Isotope bone scans.

These are used extensively for detecting bony deposits in patients with pain of possible bony origin and with doubtful or negative plain radiographs, in the 'work up' of possibly operable cases with lung, etc. tumours, and in those who may have disseminated disease (e.g. small cell and other anaplastic tumours). Even when some deposits have been recognised on plain radiographs, scans are often carried out to detect others, quite often many more being found than were suspected clinically. The scanning gamma camera is very useful for this, and even a single posterior scan (taking 10 to 15 mins of scanning time) may give all the clinical information required.

Occasionally a 'super-scan' (with a marked increased uptake generally throughout the skeleton) is seen with small cell, very anaplastic lung tumours and rapidly progressive bronchiolo-alveolar cell tumours (Illus. **BONE SCAN-SUPERSCAN**), but these are less common than with breast and prostatic primaries.

Not all bone deposits take up bone scanning agents avidly; some take up these only a little more than normal bone, but others much less i.e. they are 'negative lesions'. This particularly happens when there is gross bone destruction and little or no bony tissue remains (Illus. **BONE SCAN-NEG DEFECT**). Some patients show a mixture of both positive and negative lesions in different areas, or even within a single lesion (a negative area with a slightly positive adjoining portion or outer rim - like the 'dough-nut sign' described by Clarke et al., 1986 with myeloma deposits). Some deposits may not show up at all because :
(i) they are not stimulating osteogenesis in addition to bone destruction,
(ii) the affected bone has been completely destroyed,
(iii) the deposits are too small (with the 50 cm camera, deposits down to 0.5 cm in diameter could usually be detected), or
(iv) tumour infiltrating around or adjacent to bones (e.g. in the chest wall, adjacent to the scapulae, spine or iliac bones - see also below) has not stimulated sufficient periosteal reaction or bone destruction.

When the scan has been carried out, plain radiographs should always be taken of most possible areas visible on the bone scan, to confirm that these are due to secondary deposits and not to some other cause such as fracture(s) (particularly 'cough' or traumatic fractures of one or more ribs or the sternum, etc. - see also Chapter 12), areas of Paget's disease, osteoarthritic lipping or arthritis, oseomyelitis, etc. Ideally one should always see patients with their scans and complementary radiographs, and it is surprising how many lesions become visible on radiographs, when one knows where to look ! Their visibility may also be aided by a bright light or an electronic digitiser, especially if the radiographs have been overexposed.

Seeing the patient with both radiographs and scans also helps to avoid missing **clinically important lesions** which may not be obvious on either examination (e.g. in the cervical or upper dorsal spine, the shoulder regions, in and adjacent to the sacrum, etc.). In some, clinical symptoms and signs may prompt tomography (conventional or CT - the author abandoned SPECT (see p. 22.8) with bone scans as they are very time consuming and usually do not give a sufficiently specific demonstration of pathology). Also, as noted above, some tumour deposits spread alongside the spine, necks of the ribs and adjacent transverse processes and not give rise to a positive bone scan, whilst CT will often show more tumour present and not infrequently severe bone destruction. Such may be seen with mesotheliomas, some lung tumours and secondary deposits from other tumours (e.g. renal) spreading paraspinally. Also one has to remember other possible causes mimicking bronchial tumour deposits, e.g. TB (or other infection), trauma, or deposits from other primary tumours - remember also that what appears to be lung primary, may be a deposit from an occult primary elsewhere, and this may have also given rise to bony lesions. **Myeloma** (either a plasmacytoma or diffuse myelomatosis - see ps. 5.43 - 44) may sometimes be confused with deposits from lung tumours, although it usually causes a largely negative bone scan, the positive areas mainly being fractures of the overlying cortex.

When using bone scans for follow up purposes, and in particular when monitoring treatment, one has to be aware that activity may sometimes appear **increased** (compared with initial views) for a few weeks whilst bone repair is going on. Some deposits may show increased peripheral activity (around a negative centre), complementary radiographs showing generalised or edge sclerosis - Illus. **RIB DEPOSIT Pt. 4**.

Besides increased uptake in bone deposits, soft tissue uptake of bone scanning agents may sometimes be seen in a primary lung tumour (including carcinoids) but this usually only occurs when they contain calcification. Rarely an organising mediastinal or other haematoma will be the cause of intra-thoracic uptake.

The author has also occasionally seen increased uptake in large intramuscular secondary deposits (see p. 22.6). Increased uptake may also be seen with ganglioneuromas (p. 18.35 - 36), microlithiasis pulmonale (p. 6.23 & Illus. **MICROLITHIASIS**), tracheopathia osteoplastica (p. 3.6), Tietze's syndrome (p. 12.36), arthritic conditions of the sterno-clavicular joints (p. 12.38 - 39 & Illus. **STERNOCLAVICULAR JOINTS**), chronic renal failure, etc. HPOA is an important cause of increased periosteal and periarticular uptake in the limbs (p. 23.3 -4 & Illus. **BONE SCAN, HPOA Pts. 1, 2, 4, 9 & 10**).

As noted above not all bone deposits will give rise to areas of increased activity on a bone scan, some being due to nearly all of the bone being replaced, and no repair activity occurring - it is this last with the laying down of new bone in an attempt at replacing what is lost that gives rise to the increased activity. Negative areas besides being due to this cause, may be produced by **bone infarcts** as a result of long-term steroid therapy (e.g. with lymphoma etc. - Illus. **STEROID HIP, Hodgkin's disease Pt. 59**), or occur in patients with sickle cell disease (p. 19.100) or in those who have suffered bone infarction from the bends (ps. 6.32 - 33).

Because of problems with bone scan diagnosis the author's practice was often to book the patient with symptoms for a bone scan in the morning, followed by a CT in the afternoon. Thus even if bone deposits did not show up on the bone scan, they were nearly always diagnosed on the CT (Illus. **BONE SCAN Pts. 15a-d & 18a-b, Myeloma Pt. 1, Bone deposits Pts. 12a-b, 24a-c, 34a-b**). In other cases symptoms were due to soft tissue deposits alongside the bones, and these did not always stimulate periosteal activity.

Pseudo-deposits were sometimes seen due to excreted isotope in the urine being wiped across the clothing by a patient. A memorable case was a woman with a large cystocoele which needed manual reduction by herself in order to void - she wiped her wet fingers across her chest in order to dry them and to many observers the result looked like rib deposits!

Bone marrow imaging.
In addition to, or instead of, isotope bone imaging, the bone marrow may be demonstrated by ultra-fine colloids, which are taken up in the reticulo-endothelial cells. In the 1960's the author used to do this using Au^{198}, but the images were rather poor due to the apparatus then available and the limitation of the dose that was practicable. Recently fine colloids of human serum albumin (stabilised with stannous chloride) which are readily labelled with Tc^{99m} have become available.

The fine colloid particles (30 µm or smaller) are readily taken up in the bone marrow, and defects within the normal pattern may be seen. In some cases marrow scans will demonstrate bony deposits at an earlier stage than an isotope bone scan. They may also show extension of the disease into the more distal parts of the long bones of the limbs. The method has been superior to bone scans in small cell lung carcinoma and breast carcinoma, but has not shown as much improvement with other lung cancer deposits, perhaps because these more commonly affect and bind to bony trabeculae, thus tending to give a positive bone scan.

The method may also be used be used to demonstrate proliferation of bone marrow in polycythaemia and other conditions causing expansion of the marrow. Increased activity in the affected limb may be seen with osteomyelitis and bone sarcomas, presumably because of the increased vascularity.

Because of liver and spleen uptake these organs may be imaged.

The colloid may also be used to demonstrate lymph nodes if injected subcutaneously, etc. It has particularly been used for the axillary and internal mammary nodes (see also ps. 13.20-21).

MR of bone and bone marrow.

Protons in cortical bone are immobile in a crystalline lattice. Thus cortical bone appears as a black rim (signal void) around the marrow. The fat in bone marrow gives a high signal intensity on T_1 weighted images and appears near white. Cellular marrow in the ribs, sternum and vertebrae contains less fat and appears somewhat darker.

Because of the problems with bone scans, particularly some false negative scans, many now use a MR scan for the initial exclusion of bony deposits, with many tumours (e.g. lung and breast) and particularly when surgery is contemplated or as a baseline for studying the effects of chemotherapy. It gives rise to fewer errors in interpretation. Logistically, however, it cannot be carried out except in selected cases. It is particularly useful in showing spinal deposits with small cell lung tumours.

Isotopes for bone scanning.

The author started doing isotope bone scans in 1964, and thus has worked with almost the whole range of bone-seeking isotopes viz. : Sr^{85}, Sr^{87m}, F^{18}, Tc^{99m} stannous pyrophosphate, etc., but like others has almost exclusively used Tc^{99m} **methylene diphosphonate** from about 1980. For most scans 10 to 15 mCi (370 to 550 MBqs) of this is given IV, and the patient is examined about 1.5 to 2 hours later, having drunk up to 1.5 litres of water in the intervening period to help 'flush out' excreted isotope from the urinary tract. However the 'incidental IVP' may of itself be helpful and should not be neglected as it may show an obstructed or displaced kidney or ureter, bladder outlet obstruction, etc.

F^{18} scanning using its gamma emission needs a very thick collimator because of the high gamma energy (510 kev) and if this is not available the images are subject to considerable scatter degredation.

References

(a) **General**

Davies et al. (1988) : Parasymphyseal and associated insufficiency fractures of the pelvis and sacrum.
Peh et al. (1997) : Sacral insufficiency fractures masking malignancy - '**Honda or H sign**'.

Subramanian et al. (1972) : Tc^{99m} labelled pyrophosphate as a skeletal imaging agent.
Rosenthal et al. (1977) : Uptake of bone agents in areas of diffuse pulmonary metastatic calcification.
Brady and Croll (1979) : The role of bone scanning in the cancer patient.
Donato et al. (1979) : Bone scanning in the evaluation of patients with lung cancer.
Heck (1980) : Extra-osseous localisation of phosphate bone agents.
Pagani and Libshitz (1982) : Imaging bone metastases.
Wraight (1983) : Focal uptake of Tc^{99m} diphosphonate in pulmonary emboli associated with hypercalcaemia.
Brigg et al. (1984) : Uptake of Tc^{99m} diphosphonate in pulmonary focal metastatic calcification.
Brown, M et al. (1978), Shigeno et al. (1982) : Bone scintigraphy and pulmonary alveolar microlithiasis.
Garty et al. (1985) : Uptake in alveolar microlithiasis in siblings.
Merrick and Merrick (1986) : Prognostic significance of isotope bone scans in approx. 600 patients with lung cancer - pain and abnormal scans were both associated with reduced survival. Positive scans were found in a third of patients with mesotheliomas. False negative results were due to deposits which produced little or no osteoblastic reaction.
Merrick et al. (1992) : Evaluation and skeletal metastases.
McKillop et al. (1988) : Scintigraphy in lung cancer.
Easty and Garvie (1995) : Use of bone scintigraphy as a prognostic indicator in lung cancer staging - a positive bone scan at presentation shows poor prognosis for survival.
Pickuth and McCready (1996) : Focal areas of increased renal tracer uptake on bone scans can **mimic metastases in the lower ribs**.

Condon et al. (1981) : Assessment of progression of secondary bone lesions following ca breast or prostate using serial radionucleide imaging.
Janicek et al. (1994) : Healing flare in skeletal metastases from breast cancer.
Budd et al. (1989 a&b) : Uptake of Tc^{99m} MDP in bone is maximum during the active repair period of an experimental model using an injured and grafted mouse tail. It also is maximal in patients with prostatic cancer when maximum calcification is occurring in the deposits, and declines with either maximum calcification or remission of the disease.

(b) 'Cold' or inactive bone deposits, etc.

Charkes et al. (1968) : Negative scintiscan in 5% of patients with disseminated bone lesions, if there is a lack of bone repair at the time of examination.

Chafetz et al. (1978) : Decreased uptake may be seen in healed rib fractures.

Kim, E. et al. (1978),

Wright (1970), (1971a), (1987), Wright and Zambas (1984).

(c) Myeloma.

Leonard et al. (1981) : Radiology or bone scanning.

(d) Sclerotic deposits from lung tumours, etc.

Feld and Olivetti (1956) : Osteoblastic metastasis - one case.

Beer et al. (1964) : Five cases - one small cell, one anaplastic, three adenocarcinomas.

Napoli et al. (1973) : Nine cases - wrote ' Small cell and adenocarcinoma of the lung are commonly associated with diffuse bone marrow invasion, sometimes leading to radiographically visible osteoblastic metastases'.

Banna et al. (1970) : Sclerotic and mixed deposits from cerebellar medulloblastoma.

Bhushan et al. (1985) : Osteoblastic metastases from thyroid carcinoma.

Parnell and Dick (1988) : Female aged 19 - sclerotic deposits from a chemodectoma.

(Note the author has seen sclerotic bone deposits from adenocarcinoma, small cell tumour, alveolar cell carcinoma, carcinoids, pancreas, stomach and colon, ovary, medulloblastoma, seminoma, bladder as well as the common breast and prostatic deposits.)

Stabler (1995) : Ossifying metastases from ca colon shown by bone scans.

(e) Ivory vertebra (see also p.527 - lymphoma).

Sherazi et al. (1996) : Ivory vertebra due to osteoblastoma in children and young adults.

(f) Cortical bone deposits.

Coerkamp and Kroon (1988)

(g) Bone marrow scans.

Duncker et al. (1990)

Huggett et al. (1990)

(h) Magnetic resonance.

Daffner et al. (1986) : MR in the detection of malignant infiltration of bone marrow.

Hajek et al. (1987) : Focal fat deposition in axial bone marrow - MR characteristics.

Colman et al. (1988) : Early diagnosis of spinal deposits by CT and MR.

Mehta et al. (1989) : False-negative bone scan in extensive metastatic disease - CT and MR findings.

Stack et al. (1989) : Found diffuse bone marrow involvement in over half of the patients at the time of diagnosis.

Williams et al. (1989) : MR in suspected metastatic spinal cord compression.

Kattapuram et al. (1990) : Negative scintigraphy with positive MR imaging in bone metastases.

Ricci et al. (1990) : Normal age-related patterns of cellular and fatty bone marrow distribution in the axial skeleton as shown by MR.

Kerslake and Worthington (1991) : MR is the examination of choice for suspected metastatic spinal disease, and is more sensitive than bone scintigraphy. Osseous and paravertebral metastatic disease is reliably and readily demonstrated and spinal compression can be completely evaluated without the risks of myelography and the cranial and caudal extent of multiple levels may be identified.

Schweitzer et al. (1993) : The 'bull's eye sign' (a focus of high signal in the centre of an osseous lesion) was found to be a specific indicator of normal haemopoietic marrow, and the 'halo sign' and 'diffuse hypersensitivity' were a strong indicator of metastatic disease.

Brown, J. et al. (1998) : MR is a simple and effective method of detecting and sorting the response to treatment of spinal deposits in breast cancer - equally true for the lung.

Cross et al. (1998) : Imaging of vertebral haemangiomata causing spinal cord compression - vertebral fractures due to this cause have typical MR characteristics because of their high fat content - with very high T2 and a low or iso-intense signal on T1, but compressive haemangiomata may resemble metastases. Plain films and CT are usually characteristic.

Dickinson et al. (1998) : MR imaging of spinal metastatic and infiltrative disease - review of 120 scans showing malignant disease. No significant differences in signal characteristics were found between scans of different histologies. The majority of lesions had low T1 and mixed or high T2 signal, including those from prostate tumours where sclerotic lesions are expected to have low signal on both T1 and T2. Comparing with bone scans, MR had greater sensitivity in detecting more lesions in > 75%, and in 7 the bone scans were normal. However in 3 cases MR was normal when isotopes detected both spinal and peripheral lesions.

(i) **Percutaneous bone biopsy.**
Mink (1986) : ...in the patient with known or suspected osseous metastases.
Parsons and Hughes (1995) : CT guided biopsy of thoracic vertebral body using a trephine set - introduced via normal pedicle or costo-vertebral junction to obtain a 2mm diameter core biopsy specimen.

Tumour metastases in limb and extremity bones.
  These are uncommon, but examples in the first metatarsals and patella are shown in Illus. **BONE DEPS LIMBS**. When these occur they may be the only secondary deposits. They may occur in any of the long or small bones, and are rarely multiple, affecting many of the bones. Sometimes they occur in the cortices of these bones (e.g. tibiae) producing numerous small clear - cut defects in the bone cortex.

Some references.
Graham et al. (1973) : 43 cases - secondary deposits in the hand are rare, but when they occur they
often appear in the terminal phalanges.
Jacobs (1975) : Atlas of Hand Radiographs.
Libson et al. (1987) : Metastatic tumours of the hand and foot.
Jones, S. and Stoker (1988) : Secondary deposit from bronchial carcinoma in terminal phalanx of thumb.
Bloom et al. (1992) : Metastases to bones of the extremities.

Metastases in muscle and some other soft tissue metastases from lung tumours.
  Muscle involvement by tumour may occur in several ways : -
(a) direct extension e.g. into the chest wall (p. 12.20 - 21),
(b) direct extension from metastases - e.g. from the spine, bony pelvis, etc. into paraspinal tissues,
(c) extension from lymph node deposits into adjacent muscle,
(d) blood borne metastases directly to muscle - not uncommon following injury in patients with cancer. Dr. A Robb Smith (formerly head of clinical pathology in Oxford) used to say that a haematoma is good 'soil' for tumour growth. These are most common in the psoas muscles and glutei, but may occur in others e.g. around the scapula, limb muscles, etc.
(e) tumour implantation following biopsy or surgical procedures.
  Skin deposits are not uncommon terminally with lung tumours, but may be the presenting feature. The author has seen one on the tip of the nose (very distressing to its doctor owner!).
The author has also seen some in haematomas of the chest wall, back, buttock, or thigh, in bursae (e.g. subdeltoid, suprapatellar, etc). A few have presented as thyroid masses. In one memorable case a biopsy of a thyroid nodule in a 50 year old woman yielded jelly-like material - a secondary from an oat cell carcinoma. In another woman aged 30 an apparently autonomous hyperactive nodule (ten times normal) was caused by a bronchial adenocarcinoma deposit in the thyroid.
  See Illus. **DEP IN SOFT TISSUE**.

  Abdominal deposits are discussed in Chapter 17 and psoas deposits on p. 15.14.

References.
Avery (1988) : Metastatic adenoca masquerading as a psoas abscess.
Daly et al. (1992) : US, CT and MR in the investigation of ileopsoas compartment disease.
Mckeown et al. (1996) : Squamous cell carcinoma of the lung metastatic to pectoralis muscle.
Nash et al. (1996) : Adenoca of the lung metastatic to the psoas muscle.
Suto et al. (1997) : MR of skeletal muscle metastasis from lung carcinoma.
Yang et al. (1999) : Imaging of iliopsoas metastasis.

Ocular and orbital deposits.
  Choroidal deposits are more common than primary tumours, particularly melanomas. Most occur secondary to bronchial or breast tumours. Some may be seen with the ophthalmoscope, others with ultra-sound as low, undulating, broad-based lesions due to lateral tumour infiltration especially in the posterior pole.

Occasionally retro-orbital deposits (Illus. **ORBIT, Pts. 1a-d & 2a-b**) will cause a patient with a bronchial carcinoma to present with exophthalmos. This should be distinguished from an orbital pseudotumour, orbital sarcoidosis (Illus. **ORBIT, Sarcoid lac gl Pt. 1a-b**), Wegener's granuloma or a cavernous sinus thrombosis (Tolosa-Hunt syndrome). A myeloma deposit may give a similar picture.

References.
Downie et al. (1995) : A painful red eye.
Fielding (1996) : Ocular ultrasound.
Howling et al. (1998) : The CT features of orbital multiple myeloma.

Apparatus for bone etc. isotope scanning.

(a) **Rectilinear scanner** - A 'SELO double headed' scanner with two five inch crystal detectors (one above and one below the patient) was installed in the Churchill Hospital in 1964. The crystals could be used singly or in parallel to image the emergent gamma rays. Both crystals and collimators were thick and were primarily designed for use with high energy γ rays (such as I^{131} - 364 kev, or F^{18} - 532 kev). A thinner collimator (2 ins as compared with 4 ins) was available for Tc^{99m} (140 kev). Print out was on paper or film via a rate meter. The apparatus continued in use until 1989 for thyroid imaging.

(b) **Anger or gamma cameras** started to be produced in the mid 1960's, but the early machines suffered greatly from instability due to the use of electronic glass valves, and had to be recalibrated before each view was taken (the author visited Chicago at that time and was privileged to see such an early camera in use). Five cameras have been used at the Churchill Hospital since the late 1960's. The first four had 9, 17, 61 and 91 photo-multiplier (**PM**) tubes (the last of these was installed in 1989 - this was equipped with a motor drive to move the large camera head - 50 cm in diameter underneath or above the patient's couch to give skeletal 'body scans' and also takes localised 'static views' - both being of good quality until wear reduced the coincidence of the summated scanned images) - see Illus. **APPARATUS/TECHNIQUE, Gamma camera**. The latest apparatus installed in 1998 has dual detector heads for PET.

A gamma camera detects gamma rays passing normally to the collimator (and thus between its septa - γ rays passing in other directions being stopped by the lead septa). When the rays enter the large sodium iodide crystal (activated with thallium) most are converted to light. Light photons (which are partly reflected by the surface of the crystal, the supporting glass plate and the coupling medium) then pass into the adjacent photomultiplier (PM) tubes, which in modern cameras are tightly packed together, much as cells in a honeycomb. However in the PM tubes, only about a fifth are converted to electrons by the photocathodes. The current produced by the electrons is amplified and processed before being passed to the display modules.

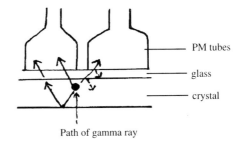

PM tubes

glass

crystal

Fig. 22.2   Diagram of gamma camera
- for photograph of camera see Illus.
**APPARATUS/TECHNIQUE,
Gamma camera**.

Path of gamma ray

Positional information is superior from photons striking the periphery of the PM tubes, whilst energy measurement is best in their centres. The greater the number of tubes in a camera (and hence per unit area) the better will be the definition, but this is largely dominated by the collimators, and to a lesser extent, digital corrections for energy and linearity. If too many photons hit the same area of the crystal too quickly, this may detract from the image, as 'after-glow' and 'pulse pile-up' may be produced, swamping or damping the effect of new light photons. There is thus an optimum range of count rates for each apparatus, and higher rates may give less information. Attempts are made to resolve two partially coincident events by means of electronic pulse shaping.

Two separate events   Overlap

Some cameras with large crystals have black paint on the supporting glass sheet to overcome linearity and positional problems, but this tends to reduce the amount of light entering the PM tubes; counts are then lost, and the dose to the patient may have to be increased.

Taking the best camera crystals which convert most of the gamma rays to light, only 80% of this will reach the photocathodes; in turn about 22% of this will be turned into electrons (i.e. of 5,000 incident gamma rays, only 900 will produce emergent electrons). 120,000, 250,000 or more counts are commonly collected for each static image.

Processing involves setting the energy level or 'window' required, the number of counts for a given picture, repeated rapid frames, looking at areas of interest within frames, smoothing, integrating frames or 'scans', etc.

SPECT = single photon emission computed tomograms - tomography using a rotating gamma camera coupled to a computer (This is much slower than taking planar views - up to 40 mins - coronal, sagittal and transverse sections may be taken).

Donaldson et al. (1982), Ell et al. (1982) : SPECT for showing defects in lung perfusion due to emboli.
McMillan et al. (1983) : SPECT plus CT demonstrated that some basal perfusion defects were due to bullae.

PET = Positron emission tomography needs two detectors i.e. a dual headed gamma camera.

Kubota et al. (1990) : Differential diagnosis of lung tumour with positron emission tomography - could distinguish most malignant tumours from benign ones.
  At the 1993 American Society of Nuclear Medicine meeting in Toronto, a main emphasis was on oncology. Otresan (Mallincrodt) fluordeoxyglucose scans were claimed to be detecting more lesions than CT or MR, and also appeared to be replacing MIBG.

Isotope studies for the localisation of tumours and their metastases.
  Many workers have tried to find an isotope which is selectively concentrated in tumour tissues. Sodee (1964) used Hg^{197} as 'neohydrin' or mercuric chloride and had some success.
Gallium.   Edwards and Hayes (1969) found an unexpected accumulation of Ga^{67} (half life 78 hours) in a patient with Hodgkin's disease, whilst performing a bone scan. This stimulated many others to try the method, as it appeared that Ga ions may be taken up by rapidly growing tumour cells, but whether by metabolism, diffusion or adhesion remains uncertain (they also adhere to glass surfaces). Hayes and Edwards (1972) published further results.
  Both primary tumours and their metastases may take up the isotope. This has been shown with some reticuloses, soft tissue and bone sarcomas, and some lung, thyroid, breast, gastro-intestinal and other abdominal tumours, etc. Poorly differentiated tumours appear to take up the isotope somewhat better than those that are well differentiated. It is also taken up by some inflammatory processes, such as lung abscess, pneumonia (including pneumocystis, TB and legionella) and in sarcoid granulomata, but not all cases show this. Some have used gallium studies to monitor the activity of chronic sarcoidosis or other inflammatory lung disease, but the author feels that this should not be done routinely, because of the high cost involved and the long half life of the

isotope. When tumours and inflammatory disease coexists, activity may be due to one or both entities.

Experience with the technique in the UK has been rather unpromising. Keeling (1970) found that the isotope was best accumulated in oesophageal tumours and reticuloses. Kay and McCready (1972) used it to study reticuloses. Lavender et al. (1971) found that the best uptake in a chest lesion, was in an abscess with no associated malignancy. The author's own experience was rather unpromising and too time-consuming for routine use - patients cannot be examined at once - only after a minimum of 8 hours, and often only usefully at 24 or 48 hours. Some large lung and mediastinal masses may give a positive scan, but others are negative, and many lymph node masses may be undetected. Uptake in the best reported cases varies from 60 to 90%, but the figures probably omit many small tumour masses. The isotope is also very expensive, and its gamma spectrum is not ideal - three peaks at 93, 184 and 296 KeV - but commonly more than one is summated, and resolution is inferior to that seen with Tc^{99m} products.

The author feels that the method is too unreliable for studying patients with lung cancer, and that it should be 'laid to rest' for this purpose - see also references below. It still has a role with inflammatory disease and may possibly have a role in assessing relapses or the effect of chemotherapy on oat-cell tumours. A few enthusiasts however give a contrary view (e.g. McKillop et al. - see reference below).

Other isotope preparations which have been tried or are being used in some centres include **Co^{57}bleomycin** (half life 270 days), **Tc^{99m}glucoheptonate** (half life 6 hours), **Th^{201}chloride** and **pentavalent Tc^{99m}DMSA** (used for studying medullary carcinomas of the thyroid and oat cell tumours, in which high calcitonin levels may be found), **In^{111}pentetreotide** and **F^{18} DGPET** (positron emission tomography - needing a dual headed gamma camera).

Table 22.1 - Some Nuclear Medicine Preparations and References.

Tc^{99m} is most commonly used as the radioactive label. It has a convenient half-life of 6 hrs, and a gamma energy of 140 keV, which is readily collimated by a 5cm thick lead collimator, as used with most gamma cameras. It is eluted as $Tc^{99m}O_4$ (pertechnetate) with sterile normal saline from a generator containing Mo^{99} (half-life 68 hrs giving a week's useful life).
Chemically $Tc^{99m}O_4$ behaves as a halogen.

Lung : (a) Perfusion - colloid particles 50 to 100μ (1 - 2 mCi)
(b) Ventilation - gases - Xe^{133} or Kr^{81}
- aerosols - e.g. Technegas (however these may be a problem as they tend to contaminate the apparatus, and quite a lot may be swallowed by the patient).
- ciliary activity and mucosal-ciliary escalator system in bronchi.
(c) Clearance of Tc^{99m} DTPA - enhanced clearance is often used in the assessment of lung epithelial permeability, and is believed to reflect inflammation. It has been used esp. in sarcoidosis, extrinsic allergic alveolitis and fibrosing alveolitis.
(d) Labelled leucocytes - Tc^{99m}HMPAO , I^{123} or In^{111} may be used for showing collections of pus, inflammatory disease, severe bronchiectasis, etc.
(e) Masses - see Chapter 25.
Liver : Tc^{99m} stannous colloid (1 - 5 mCi)
Bone : Tc^{99m} methylene diphosphonate (10 - 20 mCi)
Abscesses, bronchiectasis, etc. : Tc^{99m} or In^{111} labelled WBCs, Ga^{67} citrate.
Adrenals and chemodectomas : I^{131} or I^{123} meta-iodo-benzyl-guanidine (see also Chs. 17 &18).
Blood pool : $Tc^{99m}O_4$, Tc^{99m} methylene diphosphonate, DMSA or DTPA.
Kidneys : DMSA, DTPA, Hippuran
Spleen : Colloid (as for liver), heat damaged Tc^{99m} labelled RBCs.

Further references.

Alderson et al. (1986) : Scintigraphy of patients with lung cancer.

Fogelman and Maisey (1988) : Atlas of Clinical Nuclear Medicine.

Hughes (1990) : Radionucleides and the lung - past, present and future.

Britton and Granowska (1997) : Review - tumour identification using radiopharmaceuticals.

Ga^{67}

Savage et al. (1976) : Evaluation of Ga^{67} in the diagnosis of bronchial carcinoma - 4 treated with radiotherapy or chemotherapy no uptake was shown in the lesion. Neoplasm was accurately shown in 17 of the remaining 20 but it 'failed to indicate the extension of growth into the mediastinal glands'.

DeMeester et al. (1979) : Ga^{67} in staging of bronchial carcinoma.

King (1980) : Gallium scanning in lymphoma.

Lunia et al. (1981) Comparison of chest radiography and Ga^{67} scanning.

Libshitz et al. (1984) : Ga^{67} is unreliable in the mediastinal evaluation in lung cancer.

McLean et al. (1984) : Unexpected Ga uptake in benign pulmonary pathology.

Waxman et al. (1984) : Studied 51 patients - many false positive hilar deposits, also false negative mediastinal studies, besides true negatives and positives.

McKenna et al. (1985) : Studied 75 patients with Ga^{67} and by thoracotomy with 'total nodal dissection' - and found that Ga scans were **insensitive** in identifying **most** nodal deposits - they missed 77% of these, even when oblique views were taken to differentiate nodal uptake from that in the spine and sternum. Primary tumours had to be at least 2 cm in diameter to be detected. They concluded 'for the present nuclear medicine techniques using Ga^{67} **cannot be recommended** for preoperative staging of mediastinal metastases in patients with lung cancer.'

Hatfield et al. (1986) : 11 cases of recurrence of lung cancer were demonstrated in 111 patients, but there were 15 false positives.

Milroy et al. (1986) : Ga scans in small cell lung cancer were positive in 38 of 39 patients, plus suggestive spread in 31. 20 had repeat scans after chemotherapy showing a good correlation with clinical response to treatment - could also indicate a relapse.

Woolfenden et al. (1987) : Used Ga in patients with AIDS, showing positive scans with PCP, but they could be negative in Kaposi's sarcoma.

Dach et al. (1980), Armas and Goldsmith (1985) : Ga scanning for peritoneal mesothelioma.

Binstock et al. (1987) : Negative Ga scan in AIDS patient with PCP pneumonia.

McKillop et al. (1988) : Ga scanning has a place in the investigation of spread to mediastinal nodes if CT is not available. Intensive uptake of Ga is usual with small cell tumours and their deposits, but does not add anything to conventional methods of assessment of other tumours, except perhaps in the presence of post-radiation fibrosis.

Karimjee et al. (1989) : Compared Ga scanning using SPECT with CT in 30 patients with mediastinal Hodgkin's disease, and found that on follow up it showed nodes and diseased areas better than CT.

Fraser et al. (1989) : The frequency of false negative and false positive results in patients with lung cancer militates against the routine use of Ga^{67} and Co^{57}.

MacMahon et al. (1989) : Confirmed the utility of CT for staging lung cancer and results indicated the additional yield from gallium scintigraphy was relatively low.

Liang et al. (1985) : Demonstrated brachial plexus infiltration by non-Hodgkin's lymphoma.

Tumeh et al. (1987) : In 40 patients 55 (out of 57) sites of lymphoma in the chest were shown by Ga^{67} SPECT, as compared with 38 by planar imaging.

Co^{57}bleomycin.

Merrick et al. (1972), Niewig et al. (1983), Woolfenden et al. (1984), Slossman et al. (1985), Valdes Olmos et al. (1985), Polla and Slosman (1986).

Wathen et al. (1990) : Compared Co^{57} bleomycin with contrast enhanced CT for the assessment of the mediastinum in lung cancer and found **no clinical value** with the former (19 false negatives and only 5 true positives in 60 patients).

In^{111}pentetreotide.

O'Byrne et al. (1994) : Imaging of bronchial carcinoid tumours - 2 cases but both had been diagnosed previously - (i) by chest radiography + biopsy and (ii) an endobronchial lesion on CT & a 'cherry red' lesion on bronchoscopy.

Weiss et al. (1994) : In^{111}pentetreotide successfully localised an occult ACTH-secreting bronchial carcinoid.

Kirsch et al. (1994) : In^{111}pentetreotide in the diagnosis of pts. with bronchogenic carcinoma.

Tc^{99m}glucoheptonate.

Waxman et al. (1976), Vorne et al. (1982), Lieske et al. (1984), Langford et al. (1986), Apps et al. (1987),

Passamonte et al. (1983) : "We cannot recommend its use in detecting mediastinal spread of lung cancer due to its unacceptably high false-negative rate."

Tc^{99m}MIBI (methoxyisobutyl isonitrile).
Tirovola et al. (1996) : Use in multiple myeloma. Minai et al. (2000) : Solitary lung nodules esp. bronchial carcinoma - 18/21 tumours were positive, 1 adeno & 2 squamous ca were negative.

Th^{201}chloride
McKillop et al. (1988).
Tonami et al. (1991a) : Th^{201} SPECT showed a radiologically occult small cancer in the RMB, confirmed by bronchoscopy following positive cytology.
Tonami et al. (1991b) : Th^{201} SPECT showed lymph node metastases from lung cancer esp. at 3 hours.
Rusch et al. (1993) : NR-LU-10 monoclonal antibody scarring for non-small cell lung cancer.
Suga et al. (1993) : Difference in Th^{201} accumulation on single PET in benign and malignant thoracic lesions.
Yokoi et al. (1994) : Comparison of Th^{201} SPECT with CT for the examination of mediastinal lymph node metastasis in 113 pts. with lung cancer - cancerous nodes were present in a third and Th^{201} was particularly valuable with its high specificity in pts. with enlarged nodes shown by CT.

F^{18} Flurodeoxyglucose PET (greater activity in neoplastic and inflammatory cells).
Kubota et al. (1989) : Imaging of breast cancer with F^{18} Flurodeoxyglucose PET
Gupta et al. (1992) : Differentiation of benign from malignant solitary nodules in 20 cases (13 malignant) - was 100% accurate.
Lewis, P.et al. (1994) : Distinguishing benign from malignant nodules but false positives may occur with infection.
Wahl et al. (1994) : Use for determining operability of lung cancer - particularly of enlarged nodes in the mediastinum in pts. with non-small cell tumours.
Patz et al. (1994) : Detection of persistent or recurrent bronchogenic carcinoma with ^{18}FDGPET and distinction from **post-radiation fibrosis**.
Scott et al. (1994) : ^{18}FDGPET of lung tumours & mediastinal nodes - greater sensitivity + specificity than CT.
Patz et al. (1995) : ^{18}FDG imaging was 83% accurate & 82% specific for the detection of thoracic nodal metastases from bronchial ca, compared with CT - 43% & 85%.
Cook and Maisey (1996) : The current status of clinical PET imaging - it is possible to identify indeterminate pulmonary nodules as benign or malignant by using quantitative ^{18}FDG PET scanning, thus precluding the need for tissue biopsy in many cases. About 1/3 of pts. with non-small cell lung cancer (deemed operable by CT) had unsuspected lesions shown by PET. In others presenting with a lung lesion, PET showed this to be a metastasis from an unsuspected primary. It can also differentiate recurrent tumour from non-viable tumour or scar tissue following therapy, and is a more reliable method for assessing response to therapy than reduction in tumour volume.
Sazon et al. (1996) : FDGPET in the detection & staging of lung cancer - 100% sensitivity & 52% specificity.
Guhlmann et al. (1997) : F^{18} Flurodeoxyglucose PET is superior to CT scanning in the assessment of hilar and mediastinal nodal metastases from lung cancer.
Jones, H. et al. (1997) : Uptake of F^{18}FDG in lobar pneumonia, but not in bronchiectasis (which was associated with a prominent accumulation of labelled leucocytes).
Lamki (1997) : PET bronchogenic carcinoma and the adrenals. Noted that alternatives to PET FDG imaging are thallium, gallium and esp. sestambi imaging. The latter are more convenient in centres located far from a cyclotron.
Murray, J. et al. (1997b) : **Talc pleurodesis** simulating pleural metastases with ^{18}FDG PET.
Trübenbach et al. (1997) : Increased uptake of F^{18} FDG PET in chorioncarcinoma of the left pulmonary artery.
Worsley et al. (1997) : ^{18}FDG PET in the differential diagnosis of pulmonary nodules.
Erasmus et al. (1998) : Lower uptake of FDG/PET in primary pulm. carcinoid tumours than malignant tumours
Kim et al. (1998) : Lower uptake of FDG/PET in localised form of bronchoalveolar cell ca than other lung cancers.
Maisey et al. (1999) : Atlas of Clinical Positron Emission Tomography - esp. good for showing extent of untreated lymphomas, recurrences esp. in abdomen, bone marrow disease, pleural disease, lung ca. deposits, etc.
Erasmus et al. (2000) : Increased uptake of FDG PET of pl. effusions in non-small cell ca. usually = pl. deposits.
Pitman et al. (2000) : IV extension of lung ca to the L atrium shown by PET and CT (see also p. 7.16).
(See also ps. 5.23, 14.29. & 17.6 for use of F^{18} FDG PET with lymphoma, pleural and adrenal deposits.)

In^{111} and Tc^{99m} labelled leucocytes and HMPAO (hexa-methyl-propyleneamine oxine).
These are not-uncommonly used to identify foci of infection, collections of pus e.g. in lung, sub-phrenic, abdominal or mediastinal abscesses, areas of chronic infection with bronchiectasis, inflammatory bowel disease, etc. The labelled leucocytes, mainly neutrophils, migrate into the inflammatory lesions. Labelling can be very time consuming, and can be a potential source of

infection hazard to the laboratory technician and the patient. HMPAO is easier to use and is often better for acute chest lesions which it shows well, but it is not as good for chronic chest (and bowel) lesions with few lymphocytes, which may fail to be detected by this method.

In AIDS patients Ga^{67} is more convenient than using HMPAO. Focal pulmonary uptake is most commonly due to acute pneumonia, whilst diffuse uptake may indicate PCP, atypical mycobacterial infection, CMV, etc. Complicating Kaposi's sarcoma is usually negative and a negative Ga^{67}scan with increased disease on chest radiographs usually implies a poor prognosis.
See also 'the effects of polymorphs' on the lungs' p. 3.17.

References.

Roddie et al. (1988) : Imaging of inflammation with Tc^{99m} HMPAO-labelled leucocytes.

Reynolds et al. (1990) : Imaging inflammation with Tc^{99m} HMPAO-labelled leucocytes.

Bohdiewicz et al. (1993) : Unexpected pulmonary clumping of In^{111} leucocytes attributable to Indium oxine clumping - presented as multiple small foci of marked increased activity in the lungs.

Tudor et al. (1997) : The value of In^{111} labelled leucocyte imaging & ultrasonography in the investigation of PUO - review of 256 scans - in the cases where the leucocyte scan led to the diagnosis of infection, it was done within 4 wks. of the onset of symptoms, & was a guide to subsequent cross-sectional imaging.

Peters (1998) : The use of nuclear medicine in infections.

Labelled antibodies (particularly monoclonal antibodies) or 'Immunoscintigraphy'.

Considerable research has gone into the possibility of using radioactive labelled antibodies to demonstrate both primary and secondary tumours. Many such antibodies have been produced to various tumours, proteins, etc. Small particle epitopes may however show a greater affinity.

The author has tried imaging several primary and secondary lesions with monoclonal antibodies, but although some show up well, reliability has been poor, and many large lesions, even some fungating through the skin, have not been demonstrated at all.

To be active, the labelled antibody-protein must be able to 'latch' onto tumour cells. Degenerate or avascular cells are unlikely to be labelled, unless just dead. Initial experience with breast tumours was quite good, and it is also often good for histological preparations, but in vivo although many centres can find 'nice examples' in which the technique has worked, it is usually found wanting for routine clinical use. It has been thought that some of the problem may be due to normal as well as abnormal tissues combining with the reagent, and that blood background subtraction might enhance images of pathology; this helped a little, as has SPECT. Another ruse is to try to saturate the normal tissue receptors, and then to increase the dosage to the tumour tissue with more labelled antibody. A recent approach has been to use labelled antibody fragments, and this is proving more promising. Another factor is that cells may not be directly in contact with tissue fluids and blood, and as with chemotherapy are protected by a mucinous barrier (similar to the blood-brain barrier).

References.

Battifora and Trowbridge (1983) : Monoclonal antibody for differentiation between lymphoma and other neoplasms.

Keeling et al. (1986) : Radio-immuno-scintigraphy of patients with squamous cell tumours.

Morris et al. (1991) : Tc^{99m} monoclonal antibody fragment scintigraphy in the evaluation of small cell lung cancer.

Isotopes and neurogenic tumours.

Both I^{131} 6 iodomethyl 19 norcholesterol and more recently I^{131}MIBG- or I^{123}-meta-iodobenzyl-guanidine - which is structurally related to noradrenaline have been used for the detection of phaeochromocytomas, or for imaging recurrences after surgery or metastases of malignant tumours. I^{131} MIBG is particularly valuable for demonstrating ectopic tumours, or those which are bilateral and will give a very good indication of a pressor secretory tumour. I^{131} MIBG may also be concentrated in **neuroblastomas** or their metastases (as may also di-phosphonate bone scanning agents), **medullary carcinomas of the thyroid** (which may also give positive VMA's) and in metastases of **malignant carcinoid tumours** (about 50% take it up). It has also been used for studying the spread of oat cell tumours (and melanomas) but without much success.

MIBG   noradrenaline

These agents may also be used for therapy of such tumours.

Osteoscan and fluorodeoxyglucose are starting to be used for the demonstration of endocrine type and other tumours.

References.

Sisson et al. (1981) from Univ. of Michigan : Initially reported the use of I^{131}MIBG - found it to be superior to the cholesterol agent in being taken up both by malignant and benign phaeochromocytomas, whereas iodo-cholesterol was usually taken up by the benign tumours (later had experience of over 900 tumours).

Shih et al. (1982) : Found that a ganglioneuroblastoma in a two year old boy showed marked increased uptake with Tc^{99m} methylene-di-phosphonate, possibly related to fine calcification shown in the tumour specimen.

Geatti et al. (1985) : Ten cases of neuroblastoma examined with I^{131} MIBG.

Horne et al. (1985) : Uptake of a labelled monoclonal antibody as well as I^{123}MIBG in a neuroblastoma.

McEwan et al. (1985) : Diagnosis and treatment of adrenergic tumours using MIBG.

Mandell et al. (1985) : Examined 16 patients with neurofibromatosis using Tc^{99m}DTPA and found 28 sites of accumulation.

Ackery (1986) from Southampton : 80 cases - greatest value when the tumour is extra-adrenal or multifocal. Also treatment with high dosage for malignant phaeochromocytomata and neuroblastomata secondary deposits with symptomatic relief and reduction in the levels of catecholamine excretion.

Gerrard et al. (1987) : One case of disseminated neuroblastoma diagnosed and treated using I^{123}MIBG.

Shulkin et al. (1992) : I^{131} MIGB and bone scintigraphy for the detection of neuroblastoma - both show skeletal deps. but MIGB is better for extraskeletal disease.

Schwarz et al. (1997) : Positive MIBG scanning at the time of relapse in neuroblastoma which was MIBG negative at the time of diagnosis.

Kwekkenboom et al. (1991) : Radioiodinated somatostatin analogue scintigraphy in small-cell lung cancer - 11 pts. - deposits demonstrated in 5 of 8 pts.

King et al. (1993) : Imaging neuroendocrine tumours with radiolabelled somatostatin analogues and x-ray CT - a comparative study of 20 patients with 45 lesions (including carcinoids, insulinomas and gastrinomas). CT showed 42 and somatostatin receptor scanning 31. Three, missed by CT, were shown by scintigraphy. There were also six CT false positives.

McCready and Hicklish (1994) : Soamatostatin imaging function - octreotide scintigraphy shows promise for whole-body imaging, but the sensitivity is poor compared with other imaging methods. However it is more sensitive than other tests as a tumour marker.

Bomangi (1996) : Somatostatin receptor imaging with octreotide (In^{111}, I^{123} or Tc^{99m} labelled) is good for demonstrating widespread carcinoid (50% success rate same with MIBG), ? a good replacement for Ga^{67} in lymphoma, but can also accumulate in fibrous tissue, uptake also in oat cell tumours, neuroblastomas, gastro-entero-pancreatic tumours (gastrinomas, etc.) - 80% success, insulinomas(uptake in 50%, paragangliomas, medullary carcinoma of thyroid, parathyroids(60% success), phaeochromocytomas (MIBG better), granulomas, inflammatory bowel disease and rheumatoid arthritis.

Some references to lung scanning - see also Chapter 7.

Drew et al. (1978) : Endobronchial scintigraphy.

Buxton-Thomas and Wraight (1984) : Tc^{99m} DTPA aerosol ventilation scintigraphy in the diagnosis of pulmonary embolism.

Ashford et al. (1988) : Segmental ventilation defects following bronchography shown by DTPA aerosol.

Leigh, T. et al. (1994) : The use of inhaled radioisotopes for measuring the effect of sputum induction on tracheobronchial clearance rates.
Mackie et al. (1994) : Airborne radioactive contamination following aerosol ventilation studies. The aerosol may contaminate the hair, nasal passages and clothing of staff (therefore Technegas may be better).

Lymphatics.
Gibson et al. (1984) : Direct comparison between subcutaneous and intra-lymphatic injection for lymphoscintigraphy.

Brain metastases from lung and pleural tumours (Illus. **BRAIN DEPS**).
   As over 90% of patients with metastases from lung tumours have symptoms from the brain deposits, routine examinations for the exclusion of deposits seem largely unjustified in the absence of symptoms, except perhaps in those with small cell tumours.
   In the 1950's and early 1960's carotid angiography was used for this purpose, with tumours showing as 'vascular blushes', etc. Then followed isotope brain scintigraphy (with early peripheral vascular enhancement, and later diffusion into the deposits) or gross midline displacement shown by ultrasound 'A' scans. Most are now shown by CT (preferably with contrast enhancement) or by MR. Many are surrounded by considerable oedema, causing considerable displacement of adjacent brain tissue and the ventricular system. Cerebral secondary deposits on non-enhanced CT may be hypo-, iso- or hyper-dense, depending on cellular density, tumour neovascularity or necrosis. Some deposits may show 'bright' areas due to recent haemorrhage, or calcification (punctate, curvilinear, diffuse, or amorphous). A few cerebral deposits are difficult to detect, and may only appear as slightly reduced density areas which do not enhance. Some may show degenerate centres and appear like 'cysts' (enhancing rings with low density interiors - Fig. 22.2 and Illus. **BRAIN DEPS, Alv cell ca Pt. 43a, Brain Pt. 4b, & Brain 13**). Enhancement is related to neo-vascularity, or an impaired blood-brain barrier.

Fig. 22.3 'Doughnut sign' - active periphery of tumour tumour deposit with marked uptake and a negative centre.

(A similar appearance may be seen in myeloma and other bony deposits with a necrotic centre, or in the healing phase of deposits, when the periphery may be much more active than the centre).

   Cerebellar and brain stem deposits are sometimes seen with CT, but are usually better demonstrated by MR.
   Meningeal carcinomatosis is relatively uncommon, but may lead to head and back ache, raised intracranial pressure and increasing hydrocephalus (Illus. **BRAIN, Pt. 7a-b**). The CSF may contain malignant cells - in such cases paraventricular deposits may often be seen, as may others in the brain, the cerebral sulci (shown by intense enhancement and enlarged adjacent cisterns) and elsewhere in the body. A rapid enlargement of the ventricles on serial CT is often pathognomonic.

Some references.
Johnson, D. et al. (1983) : Limited clinical value of CT brain scans in staging of small cell lung cancer - in only one out of 84 cases did it affect staging.
Komaki et al. (1983) : Frequency of brain deposits in adeno- and large cell lung cancer and correlation with survival.
Pratt and Pearson (1995) : Routine brain scans did not significantly alter management in patients with large cell tumours with otherwise operable disease.
Collie et al. (1999) : Imaging features of **leptomeningeal metastases**.

Chapter 23 : **Hormonal and Para-Neoplastic Syndromes - also Skin Lesions.**

Para-Neoplastic, Endocrine and Metabolic Effects of Intrathoracic Tumours.

Some patients with lung, (some pleural and a few mediastinal tumours) appear to have an extraordinary ability to synthesise polypeptides, which often give rise to para-neoplastic (or endocrine) syndromes. These are most commonly seen with small (or oat) cell lung tumours, but can also occur with the other types, this probably being an expression of the heterogenicity of the tumours. Mostly these syndromes are seen with malignant tumours, but they may also occur with carcinoids of the lung or thymus, some benign pleural tumours, etc. The syndromes and effects are illustrated diagrammatically in Fig. 23.1.

Many of the patients also have a greater weight loss than might otherwise have been expected, and about 10 % show a degree of anaemia. Probably the best known para-neoplastic syndromes and effects are (i) **finger clubbing and HPOA**, and (ii) **increased anti-diuretic hormone production** (vasopressin) leading to water retention, nocturia, excessive excretion of sodium and hyponatraemia (with serum sodium < 130 m mol/litre), hypertension and elevated serotonin (sometimes with mental disturbance). This latter may occur with up to 30% of small cell undifferentiated tumours (Bondy and Gilbey, 1982). Some drugs e.g. cyclophosphamide may make this worse (Munro and Crompton, 1972), probably by stimulating the release of pituitary vasopressin. The condition is relieved by removing the tumour, or alleviated by restricted water intake and the use of demeclocycline.

Other patients experience general malaise, loss of weight, or **neurological manifestations** often preceding the discovery of neoplasm by several months and including (i) encephalopathy, (ii) cerebellar degeneration, (iii) myelopathy and (iv) motor and or sensory neuropathy affecting the spinal cord and/ or the peripheral nerves. Others may have a progressive myopathy or the Eaton Lambert syndrome (see below).

Gynaecomastia (often painful, and sometimes accompanied by testicular atrophy) is produced by an excess of human chorionic gonadotropin (Illus. **GYNAECOMASTIA**).

Cushing's syndrome (with excess ACTH production leading to hyperplasia of the adrenal cortex, but usually without the full blown clinical picture) is also fairly common and may lead to skin pigmentation, hypercalcaemia, nocturia, etc. Acromegaly, enteritis, or migratory thromboses may also be seen (Illus. **CUSHING'S SYNDROME**).

Thirst, polyuria, muscle weakness and skin pigmentation should always alert clinicians to the possibility of ectopic hormone production. **Hypertension** and quite profound **myopathy** are often found on examination. Biochemistry will often reveal **hypokalaemia** (< 3.0 mmol /litre) and an alkalosis with pH > 7.45. Blood and urinary corticosteroids are raised. Excessive hormone production may occur in the tumour, surrounding lung or by stimulation of the adrenals.

Nephropathy, leading to the nephrotic syndrome or renal impairment, encephalopathy, etc. may be caused by tumour anti-bodies, producing several types of auto-immune disease.

Thus these renal problems in association with bronchial tumours may be due to a number of causes : increased anti-diuretic hormone or serotonin production, the nephrotic syndrome, renal vein or IVC compression ± thrombosis due to enlarged para-aortic nodes or due to renal impairment secondary to metastases in the kidneys (Illus. **LUNG CA/RENAL DEP, 6a-b**).

Hormones produced by bronchial tumours esp. oat cell tumours include :
(a) adrenocorticotrophin - ACTH like substances - (10% of patients with **oat cell tumours** have hyperplasia of the adrenals),
(b) 5 hydroxytryptamine,
(c) anti-diuretic hormone like substance (arginine vasopressin),
(d) growth hormone like substances,

(e) β melanocyte stimulating hormone,
(f) insulin and insulin like growth factors (may also occur with pleural fibromas - see p. 14.28),
(g) cholecystokinin, glucagon, gastrin and bombesin (a gastrin releasing peptide),
(h) calcitonin and parathormone,
(i) female type hormones - chorionic gonadotropin (somato-mammotropin), FSH, oestradiol, prolactin and oxytocin,
(j) serotonin, somatostatin and vasopressin,
(k) lipotropin and transferrin.

Quite often more than one effect is present in a given patient and this is well illustrated in a report by Rees et al. (1974) of a 51 year old woman with an oat cell carcinoma who had features of Cushing's syndrome and where chemical examination of the tumour revealed significant amounts of ACTH, β-melanocyte stimulating hormone, arginine, vasopressin, neurophysin, insulin, prolactin, and corticotropin-intermediate-lobe peptide.

Excessive ACTH production and Cushing's syndrome - about 10 - 15 % of cases of Cushing's syndrome occur as a result of ACTH production by an extra-pituitary tumour. This can occur not only with lung tumours (usually small cell carcinomas), but also with bronchial adenomas (carcinoids), carcinoid tumours of the thymus, phaeochromocytomas, chemodectomas and medullary tumours of the thyroid. Patients typically have high peripheral blood levels of ACTH, a failure of urinary 17-hydroxy steroid excretion to suppress with high doses of injected steroids, and a radiographically normal pituitary fossa. They may have **hypertrophied adrenals with enhancing rims on contrast enhanced CT. The primary lung etc. tumour may be very small and difficult to find -** a good use for radioisotopes - Chapter 22.
Some of these effects may also be produced by **carcinoids** (see ps. 5.5 - 8) and **pleural tumours**, especially **benign mesotheliomas (or 'fibromas')** p. 14.28. The author has seen a pleural fibroma present with hyperinsulinism, and a local recurrence 10 years later also in the same way. It later became very large indeed (see Illus. **PL-FIBROMA, Pt. 1**). Insulin may also be produced by a variety of other intra-thoracic tumours, including bronchial carcinomas, sarcomas, etc.

References:
Williams and Azzopardi (1960) : Oat-cell bronchial carcinoma associated with carcinoid syndrome.
Parish et al (1964) : Excessive secretion of 5-hydroxytryptamine by a poorly differentiated oat-cell carcinoma arising within an area of squamous metaplasia in a man aged 51.
Azzopardi and Bellau (1965) : Carcinoid syndrome and oat-cell carcinoma.
Barden (1967), Azzopardi et al.(1970), Doyle (1970), Spencer (1984), and Dunnill (1987).
Azzopardi and Williams (1968) : Pathology of non-endocrine tumours associated with Cushing's disease - oat cell of bronchus, foregut endocrine tumours, phaeochromocytomas and some ovarian tumours.
Davies et al. (1982): Surgical management of the ectopic ACTH syndrome.
Chahal and O'Shea (1984) : Male aged 31 with Cushing/s syndrome - centripetal obesity, moon face and dark striae on the abdomen and lower limbs - also had conjunctival oedema and muscle weakness. CXR & CT showed a 1.5 cm tumour in the RLL - this was resected + 3 hilar nodes, 2 of which contained tumour, the adrenals were also enlarged.
Findling and Tyrrell (1986) : 10 cases - in 4 the source of the ectopic ACTH was not found for more than a year, and in 4 was never found .
Doppman et al. (1987) : 3 cases - two bronchial carcinoids and one in the thymus with nodal deposits. They identified the tumours by CT and needle aspiration with measurement of the raised ACTH levels by hormonal assay.
Marcus et al. (1990) : The radiological investigation of ectopic ACTH dependent Cushing's syndrome - review of 10 patients - small bronchial carcinoids in 6 (one had an adrenal deposit), 2 had pancreatic tumours, and a thymic carcinoid and one a medullary carcinoma of the thyroid.
Woll (1991) : Small cell lung cancers are characterised by the presence of cytoplasmic granules and their ability to synthesise a wide range of peptides - growth factors and hormones.
Vincent et al. (1993) : Radiological investigation of occult ectopic ACTH-dependent Cushing's syndrome.

α-fetoprotein and ß-human chorionic gonadotropin.
These hormones are produced by **dermoid** type tumours (p. 18.14), chorioncarcinomas - which may occur in the lungs and mediastinum (ps. 5.11, 5.40, 7.19-20 & 18.15-16), and some lung and pleural tumours.
Okunaka et al. (1992) : Primary lung cancer producing α-fetoprotein.

Finger (and toe) clubbing (Illus. **CLUBBING**).
Finger clubbing was first noted by Hippocrates, c . 460-357 BC, who wrote: " 'οι 'ονυχες των χειρων γτουπτουνται " (the finger nails become bent), a sign which he found in association with empyemata. Later such nails were considered to be pathognomonic for tuberculosis, but in the nineteenth century the specificity of 'Hippocratic nails' for tuberculosis was challenged, and it

became recognised that the phenomenon also occurred in patients with cachexia and with circulatory and respiratory disturbances.

Such nails are not uncommon with bronchial tumours, particularly those which are growing rapidly. They are seen in about 20% of patients with squamous tumours or adenocarcinomas, but less frequently in those with oat or small cell tumours, probably because these develop too rapidly for the effect to occur. Clubbing also occurs with carcinosarcomas, asbestosis and pleural tumours, chronic fibrotic and septic lung and pleural conditions, including empyemas, marked bronchiectasis, severe TB, cystic fibrosis, fibrosing alveolitis, alveolar proteinosis, severe fibrotic sarcoidosis - also pulmonary arterio-venous fistulae (the patient shown in Illus. **AV ANEURYSM/FISTULAE, Pt. 2a-b** was also severely clubbed), cardiac tumours, bacterial endocarditis, cyanotic heart disease, hepatic cirrhosis, etc. Rarely it is congenital and of no importance. The condition is often accompanied by a painful arthropathy, especially of the wrists or ankles which may be the presenting feature - Illus. **HPOA** - see also note on p. 5.5.

The curvature of the nails is caused by (usually) painless rather bulbous thickening and swelling of the soft tissues at the base of the nail, causing the angle between the skin and the nail bed to be lost. The adjacent soft tissues may also be swollen on the sides of the bases of the terminal phalanges, giving rise to '**drum stick fingers**' - Illus. **CLUBBING, Empyema Pt. 13d, HPOA Pt. 9a & b**. In doubtful cases it is best seen in the index fingers. It may also affect the toes.

Hypertrophic-pulmonary-osteoarthropathy (HPOA) was described by Pierre Marie in France in 1890 and by Bamberger in Germany in the same year, and in those countries is so eponymously known. Patients may have a painful polyarthritis, especially of the upper and lower limbs, often with local hyperaemia, and periosteal reaction (of 'onion-skin' or 'candle-wax' in type) may be seen along the shafts of the limb bones, particularly the lower ends of these, and along the shafts of the metacarpals and metatarsals.

In gross cases, there may be painful swelling of the upper or lower limbs, especially the latter, and particularly below the knees, but occasionally extending up to the groins.

Isotope bone scans may be used to demonstrate the condition, and in several cases these are more sensitive than plain radiographs (Illus. **HPOA, Pts. 1, 2b&c, 4d, 5, 9a & 10**). The use of isotope bone scans has also been noted by Terry et al. (1975), Donnelly and Johnson (1975), Freeman and Tonkin (1976) and Rosenthall and Kirsch (1976), for showing the periosteal reaction in the hands, wrists, thighs, legs and feet. In the long bones a '**double stripe sign**' may be seen with increased uptake on either side of the bones. Ali et al. (1980) studied the distribution of HPOA in 48 cases by isotope bone scans and found that the proximal and distal portions of each lung were involved with equal frequency. The condition also affected the mandible, maxilla, scapulae, clavicles and patellae in about 50 % of cases .

Craig (1937) pointed out that HPOA is often the first symptom of pulmonary neoplasm, and is often accompanied by finger and toe clubbing and may be present at a relatively early stage of tumour growth . A painful arthropathy is often also present and may be accompanied by painful gynaecomastia (Court et al., 1964) or by acromegalic features (Fried, 1948).

HPOA is most commonly seen with slow growing squamous tumours, but is also found with the other cell types. It occurs to a greater or lesser extent in about 10% of patients with lung cancer, and appears to be particularly associated with a 'corona maligna' (see ps. 4.13 - 14 and Illus. **CORONA MALIGNA, HPOA Pt. 4a -d**.

HPOA and clubbing may also occur with other intra-thoracic tumours or disease, etc. - fibrosing alveolitis, benign fibromas, mesotheliomas (p. 14.44), neurofibrosarcomas, tumours of the diaphragm, reticuloses and bilharzioma - p. 19.56. Hancock et al., 1976, reported such a case and quoted nine from the literature. There are several reports of their association with secondary tumours - renal tumours (Goldstraw and Walbaum, 1976), melanoma (Sonada and Krauss, 1975), osteogenic sarcoma (Howard et al., 1978), uterine cervix, breast, prostate (Serre et al., 1968) and ENT malignancies (Firooznia et al., 1975). HPOA has been found in a child with hypoglobulinaemia, (Beluffi et al., 1982) - see also references below.

For the association of clubbing or HPOA with alveolar cell carcinoma see Illus. **HPOA, Pt. 3**, and with carcinosarcoma - Illus. **HPOA, Sarcoma Pt. 2a-b**.

Empyemas (ps. 14.18 - 19), as well as causing finger clubbing, may also give rise to HPOA without there being any concomitant neoplasm. On the release of pus both conditions may subside.

Illus. **CLUBBING, Empyema Pt. 13d** shows the newly formed nail bases pushing out the abnormally curved portions in such an instance. The same may also be seen in patients with neoplasm following resection.

The cause of clubbing and HPOA remains uncertain. The main pathological change is widespread overgrowth of vascular connective tissue especially in the distal parts of the limbs. Turner Warwick (1963) showed an increased systemic vascular bed in the **unaffected** lung and the oesophagus. Blood flow in the limbs is also increased. (Beautiful pictures of increased circulation in the fingers may be seen in her paper). HPOA is also found in dogs, horses and lions, with both primary and secondary tumours, In dogs it is being found more commonly, possibly in part due to passive smoking and in relation to secondary tumours e.g. of the breast - it may be quite marked, extending up the limbs to produce ankylosis .

Holling and Brodey (1961) and Holling et al. (1961) demonstrated increased limb blood flow in dogs with HPOA associated with secondary lung neoplasms and found that vagotomy to the affected lung resulted in a sudden drop of limb circulation and permanent cure of the HPOA. Flavell (1956), Yacoub (1966) and also several other authors have found that vagotomy may also relieve the condition in some patients. Excision of tumours, radiotherapy (to tumour and/or affected bones), hypophysectomy, intercostal nerve section and α or β blockers can also relieve the condition, but the cause still remains an enigma - perhaps with both hormonal and neural components - see also Leading Article, BMJ (1977). Johnson et al. (1997) and Penson and Rudd (1997) reported that subcutaneous octreotide (a synthetic analogue of somatostatin - see also ps. 5.6-7 & 23.1) may relieve the pain - it is also effective in controlling the growth and secretions from pituitary adenomas, especially in acromegaly and neuroendocrine tumours, and also helps to control vomiting associated with intra-abdominal malignancies.

HPOA is similar to periosteal reaction and arthropathy in some other conditions:

(a) **thyroid acropachy**, in which patients may have clubbing of the fingers, exophthalmos and pre-tibial myxoedema. Periosteal reaction may be seen around the ankles, in the hands and feet, but it is usually of a lacework type or has a feather-like pattern and is not laminated as in normal HPOA, nor is it usually painful. It is often associated with increased thyroid stimulating hormone from the anterior pituitary. (Both pretibial myxoedema and HPOA can be very extensive and cause lower limb swelling which may even extend up the trunk - the author has seen examples with both signs extending above the waist !)

(b) **severely raised intra-cranial pressure** (with exophthalmos) due to a cerebral tumour can give rise to a syndrome like HPOA, but radiologically it is more like thyroid acropachy - see above.

(c) **venous and/or lymphatic stasis** - gravitational ulcers and lymphoedema commonly being associated.

(d) HPOA may also occur in an upper limb or in one or both lower limbs in association with an infected arterial graft (Angelena et al., 1987 and Ho et al., 1987 - upper limbs, and Stein and Little, 1978, Sorin et al., 1980, Walter and Resnik, 1981, and Fields et al., 1994 - lower limbs).

(e) **aluminium toxicity** in dialysis patients - this has been seen in some patients in Oxford - see also Chambers and Winney (1985).

(f) vinyl chloride.

(g) pachydermoperiostitis or '**pseudoacromegaly**' - thickened skin of face and hands (bulldog scalp and forehead) plus bone changes similar to HPOA and finger clubbing.

(h) **wine fluorosis** in its early stages.

(i) **idiopathic** and **familial** forms also occur.

Further references.

Benoit aand Ackerman (1952) : Osteoarthropathy associated with 3 fibrous mesotheliomas - resolution after surgery.

Ray and Fisher (1953) : Hypertrophic osteoarthropathies in pulmonary malignancies.

Wierman et al. (1954) : Articular manifestations in pulmonary disease.

Semple and McCluskie (1955): Generalised HPOA in association with bronchial carcinoma - it may precede the diagnosis of lung cancer by as much as 18 months.

Hammarsten and O'Leary (1957) : The features and significance of HPOA.

Baldry (1959) : Cavitation in pulmonary sarcomatous metastases with HPOA.

Coury (1960) : Hippocratic fingers and HPOA - a study of 350 cases.

Holman (1963) : Osteoarthropathy - disappearance after section of intercostal nerves.

Papavasiliou (1963) : Pulmonary metastases from cancer of the nasopharynx associated with HPOA.

Yacoub (1965) : Relation between histology of bronchial carcinoma and HPOA in 60 cases. He suggested that it occurs with most types of lung cancer except small cell . (However the author believes this is not correct, as with clubbing - he has seen both manifestations with small cell tumours; but both are most common with squamous tumours and adenocarcinomas, particularly those with a 'corona maligna' see above).

Yacoub et al. (1967) : HPOA in association with pulmonary metastases from extrathoracic tumours.

Greenfield (1967) : The various radiological appearances of HPOA.

Moule et al . (1970) and Torres-Reyes and Staple (1970) : Thyroid acropachy .

Caves and Jacques (1971) : HPOA in a patient with primary intrapulmonary neurogenic sarcoma and asbestosis.

Steinfeld and Munzenrider (1974) : The response of HPOA to radiotherapy .

Schechter and Bole (1976) : HPOA and rheumatoid arthritis - simultaneous occurrence in association with diffuse interstitial fibrosis.

Schumacher (1976) : Articular manifestations of HPOA.

Perkins (1977) : Delayed onset of secondary HPOA (bone scan) - presentation with severe clubbing of fingers and toes at the time of recurrence of a bronchial carcinoma three years after radiotherapy.

Benfield (1979) : Primary lymphosarcoma of the lung and HPOA.

Galks (1985) : HPOA in four patients with interstitial pulmonary disease.

Hansen-Flaschen and Nordberg (1987) : Clubbing and HPOA .

Saunders and Hanna (1988) : Unilateral clubbing of fingers associated with causalgia two years after a closed injury to the right forearm.

Wollner et al .(1989) : HPOA in a patient with **nasopharyngeal carcinoma**.

Davies, R. et al . (1991) : HPOA in pulmonary metastatic disease due to **breast carcinoma** - was present without finger clubbing - both the pulmonary deposits and finger clubbing remitted with chemotherapy for seven months and then recurred. (They also quoted several papers describing HPOA in relation to other pulmonary metastases, including bladder, osteogenic sarcoma, mesenchymal tumours and melanoma).

Emri et al . (1991) : HPOA in a patient with pulmonary alveolar microlithiasis.

Mattinez-Levin (1992) and Dickinson (1993) : HPOA may be due to the peripheral impaction of megakaryocytesand platelets.

Pitcher and Neale (1994) : Laxative abuse - unusual cause of clubbing.

Daly (1995) : Thoracic metastases from nasopharyngeal ca. presenting as HPOA - scintigraphic and CT findings.

Morgan et al. (1996) : HPOA found in staging skeletal scintigraphy for lung cancer has no prognostic significance, but a high index of suspicion for it as a cause of arthralgia may lead to earlier diagnosis of a potentially resectable lung cancer.

Ledson et al. (1999) : HPOA in a woman with haemangioendothelioma responded to indothemacid (see p. 5.5).

Capelastegui et al. (2000) : MR of knee and legs showing considerable soft tissue signal hyperintensity due to HPOA in a patient with lung cancer.

Polymyalgia and neoplasm.

In most patients polymyalgia rheumatica is a relatively minor self limiting disease. In its more severe forms it dramatically responds to steroids. However, like other reactions (see below) it sometimes appears as a prodromal manifestation of neoplasm (occurring in the lung or other sites) and usually preceding this by one to two years.

A memorable case was that of a man who helped the author in the Oxford Body Scanner Appeal. He had severe polymyalgia, forcing him to crawl around his flat on 'all fours', until given steroids which produced immediate relief. A year later whilst waiting for a lift home from the author, he had a grand-mal epileptic fit in the x-ray department. He had a tiny nodule in the right lung on plain chest radiographs and tomograms. Three months later he died from frontal lobe secondary deposits. This was presumably a bronchial tumour - he had been a heavy smoker (Illus. **BRAIN Pt. 3a-d**).

When a patient has a prodromal polymyalgia, treatment of the tumour by radiotherapy may exacerbate the polymyalgia, presumably as a result of release of metabolites into the circulation.

Polymyalgia rheumatica particularly affects the shoulder and pelvic girdle muscles and joints, the hands and wrists and temporo-mandibular joints. Tiny bone erosions may be seen on tomograms in the sub-articular regions, particularly of the sterno-clavicular joints (see also p.12.39). In the active phase of the condition, a positive isotope bone scan may be obtained, affecting the sternoclavicular, shoulder, elbow, wrist and finger joints. Such findings are not only obtained in patients known to have this condition, but also in some who are referred for possible metastases, as a result of high ESR and skeletal or limb girdle pain, and with no known primary neoplasm.

Examples are shown in Illus. **POLYMYALGRHEUM.**

References .
Paice et al. (1983) , Wright and Paice (1983)

Sarcoid type reaction to tumour cells in lymph nodes.

This is discussed more fully on ps. 19.74 - 75, and appears to be a sensitivity reaction to minute tumour deposits or possibly an immune reaction to the primary tumour. Enlarged nodes due to this cause may precede the clinical presentation of the tumour by months or a few years (Illus. **SARCOID+CA**).

Reactive hyperplasia is different and is usually a reaction to secondary infection.

The Eaton Lambert Syndrome.

This is caused by an auto-immune process which affects the release of acetyl-choline at the neuro-muscular junctions, and produces fatiguable weakness - weakness **decreased** by the use of the muscles, and the opposite to that seen in myasthenia gravis. Depressed or absent reflexes are enhanced by prior muscle contractions. Limb muscles are affected more than ocular, and the patient may not be able to rise from a chair to perform any simple function. Frequently the tumours, causing the syndrome, are small, and it is unfortunate that even after tumour resection, no recovery may occur, the patient slowly going down-hill until he dies from e.g. inhalation pneumonia. Recent cases in Oxford have been due to oat cell tumours, some with a considerable interval before the tumour became apparent. (Illus. **EATON LAMBERT**).

The failure of cure with surgery probably occurs because most of the tumours causing this syndrome are oat cell tumours, and have already spread into the bone marrow, etc., thus making surgery unlikely to be curative. However in a few cases remission may be produced by chemotherapy and/or radiotherapy, plasma exchange and immunosuppressive treatment.

References
Jenkyn et al. (1980) : Remission induced by chemotherapy and radiotherapy.
Newsom-Davies and Murray (1984) : Plasma exchange and immunosuppressive drug treatment.
Vincent (1994) : Pathogenic antibodies from small cell lung carcinoma tumour cross-react with Ca^2 channels expressed on the nerve terminals of the neuromuscular junction.

Disorders of haemostasis and distal or extremity ischaemia.

Thrombosis, migratory thromboses, diffuse intravascular coagulation, and digital or extremity ischaemia may occur in association with lung tumours and are usually due to platelet abnormalities or aggregation.

References.
Trousseau (1865)
Hawley et al. (1967) : Association between digital ischaemia and malignant disease.
Hagedorn et al . (1974) : Coagulation abnormalities in patients with inoperable lung cancer.
Field and Lane (1986) : Carcinoma of the lung presenting with digital ischaemia.
Milroy et al . (1988) : Abnormal haemostasis in small cell lung cancer.
Arrowsmith et al. (1991) : Finger tip gangrene caused by small cell lung cancer and platelet aggregation - dramatic improvement with aspirin.

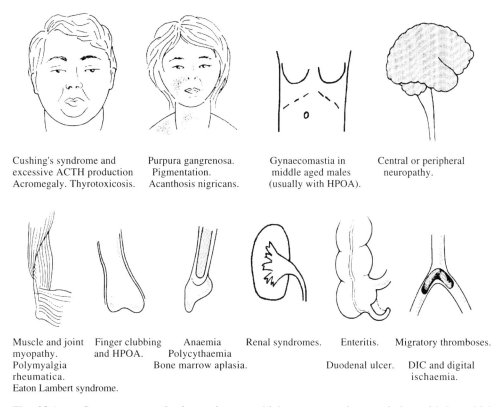

Cushing's syndrome and excessive ACTH production Acromegaly. Thyrotoxicosis.

Purpura gangrenosa. Pigmentation. Acanthosis nigricans.

Gynaecomastia in middle aged males (usually with HPOA).

Central or peripheral neuropathy.

Muscle and joint myopathy. Polymyalgia rheumatica. Eaton Lambert syndrome.

Finger clubbing and HPOA.

Anaemia Polycythaemia Bone marrow aplasia.

Renal syndromes.

Enteritis.

Duodenal ulcer.

Migratory thromboses.

DIC and digital ischaemia.

Fig. 23.1   Some para-neoplastic syndromes which may occur in association with bronchial tumours, particularly oat cell tumours (adapted from Barden, 1967, AJR, **100**, 626 - 630 with permission).

[For eosinophilia or eosinophilic effusion as a presenting feature of lung cancer - see p. 19.59.]

Skin lesions which may be associated with lung disease.

Some of these conditions are illustrated in Illus. **SKIN.** These include infections such as tuberculosis, tumours such as reticulosis with mycosis fungoides and Kaposi's sarcoma, skin thickening with breast cancer, scleroderma, purpura gangrenosa and pyoderma gangrenosum.
In addition illustrations of some skin lesions, particularly papillomata which may simulate lung lesions on plain chest radiographs are shown, as well as examples of erythema nodosum in sarcoidosis, acanthosis nigricans, progeria, telangiectases in Osler Weber syndrome, adenoma sebaceum and café au lait spots with tuberose sclerosis (see also p. 5.15), scleroderma (p. 19.85), skin thickening with ca breast and stretch-striae in Cushing's syndrome (in this case a **prodromal effect of Ca RUL**).

Other skin lesions which may be important in the diagnosis of lung lesions include scars (e.g. from drains or tubes about which the patient may have forgotten - important with foreign bodies, etc.), skin metastases with lung and other tumours (**much easier and safer to biopsy than small lung nodules**), telangiectasia and atrophy following radiotherapy, skin lesions with infestations (e.g. schistosomiasis), café au lait spots with neurofibromata & deformation of the skin contours (p. 18.35), etc.

Some notes.

Erythema nodosum is a manifestation of circulating immune complexes and can occur with several conditions. It gives rise to reddish blue, slightly raised, intra-dermal, patchy swellings about 1 cm. in diameter on the limbs (especially the lower limbs) and may be accompanied by some oedema of the limbs, larger areas of skin redness, arthralgia, etc. It is commonly seen in acute sarcoidosis (Illus. **ERYTHEMA NODOSUM**), tuberculosis, DLE, acute fungal infections, streptococcal infections, drug reactions, ulcerative colitis, Behçet's disease, disseminated intra-vascular thrombosis and may also occur in early pregnancy. It is not usually, but may be, a feature of tumour presentation.

Acanthosis nigricans (and other skin lesions) may occasionally precede the presentation of lung tumours by a few months or up to four or five years (Illus. **ACANTHOSIS NIGRICANS**).

Reference.
Menzies et al. (1988) : Acanthosis nigricans associated with alveolar cell carcinoma.

Purpura gangrenosa, pemphigus bullosa and pyoderma gangrenosum
These conditions may occasionally be associated with lung nodules which may cavitate before disappearing or leaving small lung scars. It has been suggested that the nodules in pyoderma gangrenosum may be similar to those in Wegener's granuloma, as they respond to steroids and immunosuppressive therapy. In purpura gangrenosa lung lesions would be expected to be small areas of haemorrhage and/or infarction, and this may be the same in the others as well. Similar lesions may cause bleeding into the gut and urinary tracts. Some type of antibody reaction is thought to be the cause.

References.
Taylor and Wright (1956) : Purpura gangrenosa (two cases - both recovered - one a young woman not given steroids had to have skin grafts and toes amputated, but the second - a woman aged 69 who was given steroids - then very scarce - by the present author fully recovered).
McCulloch et al. (1985) : Severe steroid-responsive pneumonitis associated with pyoderma gangrenosum and ulcerative colitis.
Wang et al. (1999) : Pyoderma gangrenosum with tracheal nodules, lung infiltration and pleural effusion.

Note also:
Davies et al. (2000) : **Xanthoma disseminatum** (a rare form of histiocytosis) with thickening of tracheo-bronchial mucosa and walls leading to respiratory failure. Skin lesions were smooth yellow papules in the axillae, submammary areas, the upper limbs and vulva.

Chapter 24 : **Lung Cancer** (a) **Diagnosis and Causes, Smoking Habits, etc.**

Difficulty of making an early diagnosis of lung cancer.

The suggestion that radiology only diagnoses lung cancer three to six months before a patient's death, is unfortunately true in some cases. Oat-cell and anaplastic tumours grow rapidly and most are unresectable from the onset of symptoms. Other patients may have sought advice late on in their clinical illness, or the tumour may have been missed due to poor techniques in radiography or interpretation. As Rigler (1966) noted, retrospective reviews of radiographs not uncommonly show that some tumours may produce recognisable abnormalities months (or in some cases years) before the tumours was discovered. This prompted a search for a better understanding of radiological abnormalities that may be encountered, so that these might be more readily recognised, particularly at a resectable stage. Poor quality (e.g. portable or under-exposed radiographs, etc) may be dangerous in causing quite gross lesions to be missed. All chest radiographs should be of good quality and show as much of the lungs and mediastinum as possible, which is why the author has used the high KV technique for over 30 years, at the Churchill Hospital, Oxford. More recently the Radiology Department has switched to AMBER - see ps. 20.6 - 7 and Illus. **AMBER**.

Low KV chest radiographs (often formerly employed for the demonstration of tuberculosis and other inflammatory diseases), and still unfortunately used in some centres, may show only 60% of the lungs, and will not show the areas behind the heart, the dome of the diaphragm, etc., and the hilar and mediastinal areas may be just a single "white shadow" with no detail seen within or through them.

An understanding of how disease processes show up in the lungs is of the greatest importance, since many tumours do not themselves give rise early on to opaque masses and the early signs may be subtle. These may be localised obstructive emphysema, localised collapse, a small and almost insignificant lung shadow, an endobronchial abnormality, a mucocoele or a localised area of pneumonia. These may be present before the clinical onset of disease, and may be found fortuitously on pre-operative radiographs or those done together with a GI examination, etc. Such often apparently insignificant abnormalities always warrant tomography for their confirmation, the studying of their morphology, or their rebuttal. Their small size and often atypical appearance makes the detection of lung tumours at a resectable stage potentially very difficult, as does the rapid spread of many of the tumours. As is also discussed on ps. 24.35 - 37, the clinical course of a tumour only accounts for 10% or less of its natural history.

A 'good radiograph' is not necessarily the type that radiographers may be taught to prefer during their training. Radiographs are not 'works of art', but are recordings of normal and pathological anatomy. A little over-exposure is usually better than under-exposure, since with a bright illuminator both lung and mediastinal details can mostly be readily seen. Under-exposure usually fails to record information which cannot be retrieved by any simple viewing method.

Unfortunately the number of patients with bronchial or lung tumours has continued to rise (though it may have reached a plateau in men in the UK), and is almost the most common severe chest disease seen in any radiology department. It is also the cause of many difficult medical diagnostic cases because of its protean manifestations and presentations.

Causes of lung cancer.

The cause of the disease in most cases has been ascribed to smoking (Doll* and Hill, 1952; Doll, 1953, 1954, 1956, 1966; Doll and Peto, 1976 and 1977, who particularly studied the death rates of British doctors in relation to smoking, and the Royal College of Physicians, 1962, 1971, 1977 and 1983). Similar conclusions have been made by the World Health Organisation (1960), the United States Surgeon General's Advisory Committee (Terry, 1964 and Kreyberg, 1969), etc. Mizell and Correa (1984) in their book "Lung Cancer: Causes and Prevention" wrote: approximately 90% of the deaths from lung cancer and almost one-third of the deaths from cancer of all kinds can be traced directly to cigarette smoking. Twenty-five per cent of all smoking healthy young adults today will die of lung cancer. In 1982 for the first time lung cancer was more prevalent than breast cancer (in women). * See Oxford Picts, **Sir Richard Doll**.

Air pollution from industry or diesel fumes may have some effect. Aromatic hydrocarbons in some industries - coal-tar, coal-gas, foundries, chimney-sweeps, etc. (see below) undoubtedly predispose to lung cancer. Myddleton (1964) incriminated carcinogens in diesel fumes, but there is little statistical evidence for these as a cause. In Venice, with no motor traffic and little industrial pollution, the lung cancer rate is as high as in the rest of Northern Italy (Wynder, 1961). Similar findings were made in Reykjavik, Iceland (Dungal, 1961). Also workers in London Transport and other bus garages do not show an overall increased incidence of lung cancer, only the smokers being affected. Other industrial factors predisposing to lung cancer include the inhalation of nickel, chromates (Baetjer, 1950), arsenic (Goldman, 1973), asbestos (see below and Chapter 14), chromethyl ethers, coal-tar distillates, mustard gas (12 widows whose husbands died from lung cancer induced by this as a by-product of a chemical manufacturing process won total damages of £1M at Cardiff Crown Court in March 1990), and the mining of radio-active materials, e.g. the cobalt mines of Saxony (Rostoski, 1926) and the uranium mines of Bohemia (Beyruther, 1924) - this has often been referred to as Schneeberger disease, referring to the district south of Leipzig and south-west of Dresden where many heavy mines (including for silver) were situated (Illus. **SCHNEEBERGER DISEASE**). Following World War II most of the uranium needed by the Soviet Union (some 200,000 tonnes) was mined in Saxony and Thuringia, and large densely populated areas were devastated. Over 5,000 cases of lung cancer have been officially recognised as occupational disease, but the numbers may rise to 20,000 (Burkart et al., 1996).

Other industries in which there may be some risk of lung cancer include haematite mining, isopropyl alcohol manufacture, iron and steel works and sandblasting (Raven, 1960 and Boyd et al., 1970). In rural Sussex lung cancer was known as the 'blacksmith's curse' (author - personal study). A Swedish study has shown that chimney sweeps may have a three-fold increase in lung cancer, plus a five-fold increase in throat and liver tumours (Daily Telegraph, 20 July 1988).

The higher lung cancer mortality in the UK and Germany, compared with France and Italy, has by some been ascribed in part to heavy industry, coal-burning and 'smog' (dense smoky fog) during the 40's, 50's and 60', (but this has now been largely eliminated by statutory smokeless zones). Analysis of death rates by counties in the USA has suggested an association between lung cancer deaths and chemical, petroleum, ship-building and paper industries. In Hong Kong there is a high incidence of lung cancer in women associated with smoking and the traditional kerosene stoves in poorly ventilated rooms. Holst et al. (1988) suggested that keeping pet birds in the home is an independent risk factor in lung cancer (6 - 7 times increased).

Industrial exposure may render the lungs more sensitive to the effects of tobacco and particularly cigarette smoke. In persons exposed to **asbestos**, smoking may make the development of lung cancer 50 to 100 times more likely (Berry et al., 1972). Horne and Spiro (1987) quoted the risk as 93 times that in non-smokers, whilst asbestos in non-smokers causes an increased risk of five to seven times. In Norway it is now illegal to employ a smoker in the asbestos industry. (See the discussion re retention of asbestos particles in the lungs of smokers - ps.14.38 - 39 & refs. p. 24.41).

Radon inhalation may also lead to lung cancer. Radon gas escapes from the ground as a result of the natural decay of uranium and radium. It may become trapped in houses with poor ventilation, due in part to greater insulation and energy efficiency. It is inhaled and may become entrapped in the lungs; it may also be ingested in water. A survey by the Institution of Health Officers (1988) showed that 50,000 homes in the UK may be affected with 400 Bq/m^3 of air, particularly in the 'granite areas' of the West Country, the Pennines, Deeside and other parts of Scotland. The National Radiological Protection Board (1990) halved the recommended permissible level for radon in houses to 200 Bq/m^3, thus implying that 90,000 houses in the UK needed remedial action. The average house contains air with 20 Bq/m^3 (i.e. 20 atomic disintegrations per second) giving an annual dose of approx. 10 mSv.

Fig. 24.1. Areas of the UK where houses are above the NRPB recommended radon limit. (Reproduced by permission from NRPB).

Black = worst areas

Grey = slightly above normal

The risk in houses can be reduced by the use of extractor fans, and under-floor ventilation. Sealing of floors is difficult as cracks soon develop. When radon has entered a building, it and its daughter products may attach to aerosols, which deposit on surfaces ('plateout'), rendering their removal more difficult, but less likely to be inhaled. Increased ventilation within a house may help to remove gaseous radon, but at the same time create a lower pressure within it, thus drawing more air into it, particularly with houses having basements. (A radon sump is probably the most effective counter measure where it can be used.)

This problem in the USA has been studied by Hart et al. (1989) and others where there are possibly 5,000 to 20,000 deaths per year from this cause, particularly in the North Eastern States. Because of radon, some nuclear industry workers have been found to have more radioactivity within them on entering work each day than when they go home!

The lung cancer risk from radon has been likened to the carcinogenic effect of 15 cigarettes per day, or 1,500 chest radiographs per annum. **After smoking it appears to be the next most important** cause of lung cancer, possibly causing 2,000 deaths in the UK per year. There appears also to be synergism with smoking, and smokers exposed to radon probably have ten times the risk of exposed non-smokers.

It has been suggested that ionised radon gas (or water droplets containing viruses) might account for an apparent increase in numbers of neoplasms (over what otherwise might be expected) occurring in persons, living or working close to strong electro-magnetic fields e.g. power lines and transformers, by being attracted towards them (Henshaw et al., 1996). However the NRPB made measurements in areas of high and lower electromagnetic fields at Didcot power station near Oxford and could not confirm any such effect (Miles, 1998). They also point out that radon in droplets is less likely to be inhaled as it will tend to adhere to surfaces - in buildings, on furniture, etc. The risk of skin tumours from this 'plateout' is much less than for lung cancer, as it is less sensitive than the lung to irradiation from radon also there is no evidence that radon causes other tumours (NRPB, 1996). A further study (NRPB, 2001) only found a possible weak link between power lines and childhood leukaemia and that any risk relates to about 0.5% UK homes.

Radon is also released by Thorotrast, which used to be used as a contrast agent, particularly for angiography. Ishikawa et al., 1992, studied 225 World War II veterans who had received Thorotrast (which produces Rn^{222} & Rn^{220}) - the incidence of lung cancer was 1.7 times that of the general Japanese population, with a predominance of the small cell type. [Thorotrast can also lead to tumours of the liver and spleen, leukaemia and soft tissue sarcomas mainly as a result of α particle irradiation (but also β radiation) following migration of the colloid to the lymph nodes, liver and spleen - see also Rundo, 1955, Mackenzie et al., 1962, Suckow et al, 1961, Boyd et al, 1968, Wright & Ardran, 1971, Janower et al., 1972, and Abbatt, 1979 and Illus. **THOROTRAST** - see also ps. 5.3 & 11.22. Vähäkangas et al. (1992) noted mutations of P 53 - a tumour suppressor gene in radon-associated lung cancer.

In South African mines the risk of lung cancer appears to be related to silicosis, smoking and uranium (Hnizdo et al, 1997).

Familial

Some **families** appear to have an increased incidence of lung cancer, and the author has personally investigated several such families, including one with four sons who all developed lung cancer under the age of 45, but all were smokers. Recent studies have also suggested a genetic background, on which smoking may potentiate the risk.

DNA aberrations, oncogenes, etc.

Certainly cigarette smoke appears to potentiate DNA aberrations, leading to lung cancer (Hopkin, 1981). Weber and McClure (1987) pointed out that many disparate factors may cause cancer - e.g. smoking, viral infections and U/V light - but all cancer may be reduced to fundamental mechanisms based on cancer risk genes or **oncogenes** within ourselves. These genes are derived from normal cellular genes expressed in an altered form and encode proteins that contribute to the malignant phenotype of the cell. They act synergistically and one alone cannot cause cancer. Hall (1993) in discussing 'the gene as a theme in the paradigm of cancer' pointed out that gene mutations (particularly in the concept of oncogenes) explain how agents, as diverse as viruses, radiations or chemicals, can all induce tumours that are essentially indistinguishable from one another; oncogenes also appear to act in a dominant manner.

Underlying lung disease complicated by lung cancer.

Among non-smokers (about a fifth of patients with lung cancer, according to Doll, 1953) and in females, the incidence of **adenocarcinoma** appears to be higher, and some (e.g. Kreyberg, 1962) have suggested that this type is not related to smoking. However this may only be partly true. This type may include some younger people, especially females, where it is not so related, and a larger group, which parallels the other cell types. Some adeno-carcinomas and **bronchiolo-alveolar cell carcinomas** (see ps. 5.1 - 3) may be induced by previous inflammation especially viral. '**Scar cancers**' (see also ps. 4.20 & 6.2) particularly occur in smokers in areas already damaged by bullae, fibrosis or previous inflammatory disease. Lung tumours may also arise within lungs damaged by severe scarring as with **fibrosing alveolitis** (ps. 19.116 - 120), **scleroderma, rheumatoid** and **ankylosing spondylitis** (ps. 19.81 - 87 & 90 - 91), or in relation to **cysts** or **bullae** (ps. 6.2 - 3), or the chronic inhalation of **medicinal paraffin** (see ps. 5.1 & 6.14). Very rarely bronchial carcinoma has been described as complicating bronchiectasis (ps. 3.18 - 20) although the reverse is true, and many patients with endobronchial tumours develop mucocoeles and bronchiectasis (ps. 2.10 - 12). Tumourlets are however associated with damaged lung (see ps. 24.18 - 19). The question of radiation induced lung tumours in patients who have had repeated chest radiography and fluoroscopy for tuberculosis has been considered, but the risks seem very slight (as also with the development of breast carcinoma - Hill et al., 1983), and in most cases coincident smoking has been the cause. The association of lung cancer with tuberculosis is discussed on p. 4.21 - see Illus. **CA+TB.**

History and Effects of Smoking,

Tobacco was introduced to England from the New World, where Red Indians had been smoking it for centuries, in about 1565. Sir Walter Raleigh (1550-1618), the country's first documented smoker, was imprisoned for treason soon after the accession of James 1st in 1603, and in the following year James 1st wrote and anonymously published "A Counter-Blaste to Tobacco". King James denounced smoking as "lothsome to the eye, harmful to the nose, harmful to the braine, dangerous to the lungs, and in the black stinking fume thereof nearest resembling the horrible Stigian smoke of the pit that is bottomless". He put up the tax on tobacco from 2d. to 6s. 8d. per lb. - an enormous sum in those days; it was later reduced with more income to the revenue through greater sales. (See Illus. **FAMOUS PEOPLE, Raleigh** & **OXFORD PICTS, James 1**).

Prince Albert (Queen Victoria's husband) tried to prevent women taking up smoking at the time of the Great Exhibition in Crystal Palace in London in 1851, see Illus. **ALBERT EXHIBITION** and in 1853 there were thriving Anti-Tobacco Leagues in London and Manchester. Wars, however, and particularly the two Great Wars, tended to spread the habit throughout the World.

Tobacco tar contains both 3:4 benzpyrene and 1:2 benzperylene - both well known carcinogens. The DHSS Froggatt Report (1988 - see also under passive smoking - below) listed 3,000 poisonous substances in cigarette smoke, of which 40 may be carcinogens. It is interesting that the Eastern 'Hubble Bubble' pipe greatly reduces the tar content of tobacco smoke and also the incidence of bronchial neoplasm in its devotees, but as these pipes are often shared, the incidence of tuberculosis is increased.

Not only is tobacco tar harmful, but also tobacco itself, which when used as snuff or sucked in the mouth ('Skoal Bandits' or chewing tobacco), produces nasal or oral cancer respectively. ('Skoal Bandits' targeted at adolescents were banned from sale in the UK in 1990).

Elson (1972) found a difference between the carcinogenic properties of air cured and fomented tobaccos (the latter is used in cigars) and that of kiln-dried tobacco. Air-cured tobacco produces an alkaline smoke which permits absorption of nicotine in the mouth. Kiln-dried tobacco produces more sugar and an acid smoke; this causes the smoker to inhale more smoke to obtain his nicotine. Kiln-cured tobacco, as used in the UK, would thus appear to be more dangerous than its American and Continental 'mild' counterparts, which are mainly air-dried. This may, in part, explain why Britain's lung cancer rate is about twice the American rate although Americans on average smoke more cigarettes. The British smoker also tends to smoke right down to the 'butt' and this may also increase the amount of tar inhaled.

A Government report was published in 1973 giving **tar-reading-figures** for all brands of cigarettes on sale in Britain, and has been updated each year since then. It grouped them into low, medium and high tar contents.

Tobacco smoke appears to provoke a state of chronic irritation in the lungs and bronchi, and this may predispose not only to chronic bronchitis, but also to parenchymal damage in both alveoli and bronchioles. Smoking also damages the cilia lining the bronchial epithelium and the normal muco-ciliary escalator which carries particles towards the trachea from where they may be expectorated. It also disorganises the mucus cells and stimulates squamous metaplasia and basal cell hyperplasia (Auerbach et al., 1956).

Jeffrey (1973) and Graham and Levin (1971) have shown that tobacco smoke inhaled by rats increases the cell turnover rate in the basal germinal layer of the bronchial mucosa. Damage to the ciliary and mucus producing cells in the larger bronchi may allow the more ready ingress of bacteria and viruses. Thus, if cigarette smoking is allied with breathing heavily polluted cold and damp air, the resulting bronchitis and parenchymal damage may become considerable. Damage and reformative changes probably play an important part in initiating lung cancer.

After stopping smoking for 2-3 months, some cell recovery occurs, but full recovery of bronchial mucosa takes 18-24 months. Cells with atypical nuclei do however remain for much longer and Auerbach (1962) noted that these decreased over many years. There is some evidence that if a person has given up smoking for five years or more, then his chances of developing carcinoma of the bronchus are considerably reduced, but it is surprising how many patients do still present with carcinoma, who gave up smoking 10-15 or more years previously. Certainly smoking in doctors is now very much less prevalent than 20 years ago and their death rate from bronchial carcinoma has plummeted in contrast to the trend in the general population.

The BMA and the Health Education Council published their booklet 'The Big Kill' (see Roberts and Graveling, 1985), which details the death rates from cancer of the lung in each district of the country. Almost 125 people then died per day from lung cancer in the UK, and more than twice as many from the effects of smoking. In Barnsley, Yorks., one in seven deaths have been due to lung cancer, and in Oxford we have had 2,000 per year. The World Health Organisation termed Glasgow the 'cancer capital of the world' with one in six dying from the disease and in some Glasgow hospitals it has been estimated that 25% of the patients are suffering from smoking related diseases. Glasgow City Council then aimed for a non-smoking city by the year 2,000.

It is depressing that whilst the scourge of young people dying from tuberculosis in their 20's and 30's had largely been eradicated, roughly similar numbers now die from the effects of lung cancer in their 40's, 50's and 60's, whilst others suffer from severe emphysema, certainly made worse, if not entirely caused by smoking - the latent period being 20-40 years.

It has been estimated that if nothing is done to reduce smoking, 250,000 of the children now at school will die from the disease.

Many smokers, it seems 'puff on' oblivious to, or ignoring the dangers of smoking, despite printed warnings on every cigarette packet and hoarding advertisements telling them that **smoking seriously damages their health**. They obviously believe that diseases of smoking will not individually affect them. Such diseases include not only bronchial and laryngeal carcinoma, chronic bronchitis and emphysema, coronary and peripheral vascular disease (especially the lower limbs) and duodenal ulcer. In addition, smoking has been incriminated in bladder and other urothelial neoplasms, carcinoma of pancreas, oesophagus, lower bowel, etc. (One of my former surgical colleagues, Kaisary, 1987 has found that smoking and alcohol appear to have a mutually potentiating effect in the development of bladder tumours). Barton et al. (1988) showed that the rising incidence of cervical cancer in young women may also be linked with smoking, smoking reducing the number of Langerhans cells which protect against viral infections of the cervix.

The author believes that whilst lower lobe emphysema may be due to α^1 anti-trypsin deficiency, upper lobe emphysema is more commonly due to smoking (Wright, 1983). Smoking appears to activate polymorph leukocytes in the lungs, causing them to release proteolytic enzymes and free oxygen radicals, which in turn damage the lungs, producing emphysema (see also p. 3.17).

'Passive smoking'

During recent years the effects of 'passive smoking', particularly on the spouses of heavy smokers has been shown to be not inconsiderable and account for about 1% of cases of lung cancer deaths. Hirayama (1981 & 1983 from Japan) showed that the non-smoking wives of heavy smokers have a higher risk of lung cancer. This, plus the now increased incidence of smoking in women, trailing behind men by about 25 yrs., accounts for the rising incidence in bronchial carcinoma in females (>10,000 per year in the UK). It was also not an uncommon occurrence to the author to investigate the extent of bronchial carcinoma in a man, and a few months or years later to have to investigate the same condition in his wife (or the reverse).

Shephard (1982) wrote a monograph on 'the risks of passive smoking'. Acute reactions include eye irritation, nasal irritation with excessive secretion and obstruction leading to mouth breathing, later effects being respiratory tract dryness, tumour formation, respiratory infections in children, and small airway disease in adults etc. He concluded "If the allegations are upheld, the passive smoker is likely to become a militant non-smoker, prepared to take much stronger action to gain protection against involuntary exposure to cigarette smoke. It is arguable that a smoker has the right to destroy his own health, so long as the resultant medical costs are not charged to the community. However, there are no grounds for allowing the smoker to endanger the health of family, friends and colleagues".

Wald et al. (1986) reviewed the available epidemiological studies of lung cancer and exposure to other people's smoke and found that non-smokers living with smokers have just over a 50% increased risk of developing lung cancer, compared with those not so doing, (0.007 p.a. compared with 0.005 risk per annum). The figures may be a little inaccurate, since some who describe themselves as non-smokers, may have been ex-smokers. However, even after making an allowance for this, it would appear that non-smokers have at least a 35% increased risk, when living with smokers.

Wells, A. (1988) estimated the increased risk for passive smoking in men as 100% and in women as 40% and Frank (1982) estimated that 30,000 to 50,000 victims die annually from the effects of passive smoking in the USA.

Repace and Lowrey (1985) reviewed deaths in the USA from lung cancer as a result of involuntary tobacco smoke inhalation. In 1980 there were 108,500 lung cancer deaths in the USA, roughly 15% of which (16,300) were in non-smokers. Of these Repace and Lowrey estimated that 4,700 (4%) developed these as a result of passive smoking.

Weiss (1986) reviewed the publications on the risks of passive smoking and pointed out that (i) side-stream smoke has the same carcinogens and co-carcinogens as mainstream smoke, mostly at significantly increased concentrations, (ii) mutagens and cotinine may be found in the urine of passive smokers and (iii) making some assumptions a study of Seventh Day Adventists (who have never smoked) suggested a figure of 7.4 lung cancer deaths/100,000 person-years i.e. close to the study by Hirayama (see above) which gave a figure of 6.8 deaths per 100,000 person-years.

In Sweden in 1982, a surviving spouse won a case for damages when her non-smoking husband died of oat-cell lung cancer, found at law as caused by inhaling his colleagues smoke.

The DHSS Froggatt Report on Smoking and Health (1988) concluded that passive smoking increased the risk of lung cancer among non-smokers by between 10% and 30% and that this could account for several hundred patients per year in the UK. Barry Smith from ASH (1990) gave a figure of 300 lung cancer deaths per year in passive smokers in the UK, and in the USA it was estimated that 4,000 'passive smokers' died from lung cancer during 1990, and 32,000 from heart disease (Conference on Lung Health, Boston, 1990).

In Jan. 1993, a Stockport Borough Council official won £15,000 compensation in an out of court settlement for the development of chronic bronchitis as a result of passive smoking. In August 1996 a Florida jury awarded $750,000 to a 66 year old man who developed lung cancer after smoking Lucky Strike cigarettes for 44 years, and this immediately depressed tobacco company shares. The AMA stated "This is a milestone case. It is the first time that a jury has seen internal documents of a tobacco company with evidence of their wrong doing over decades - documents were published one year ago by JAMA. It is also the first time a victim has lived long enough to see an award from the tobacco industry" (see BMJ, 14 8 96, **313**, 382).

Action against smoking.
The Royal College of Physicians (RCP) in 1971 set up a body - ASH (Action on Smoking and Health Ltd.), with an annual grant of £125,000 from the Department of Health and Social Security for the first few years, to **promote research projects and function as a 'pressure group' in preventing or reducing the smoking of cigarettes.** In 1977, the RCP publication **'Smoking or Health'** recommended: a rigorous public education programme, educating children not to smoke, limiting smoking in hospitals and public places, phasing out tobacco sales promotion, differential tar increases for tobacco products with heavier taxes on cigarettes with high tar or nicotine content (and the withdrawal of these as soon as possible) and an increase in research into smoking related diseases. A further RCP (l983) publication **'Health or Smoking'** pointed

out that the Government only put one briefly into effect, namely the 'Supplementary Tar Tax' and withdrew it in 1981. Also Health Ministers known to be favourable to the prevention programme were moved to other Ministries.

British Governments have unfortunately repeatedly fudged on smoking. According to Cabinet papers released in 1984, under the thirty year rule. Churchill's Government in 1954 was told of a definite link between smoking and lung cancer but no action was taken, despite the connection being termed '**causal**'. Similarly, Macmillan's cabinet in 1957 suppressed a Medical Research Council report attributing the big increase in lung cancer deaths in the previous 25 years to smoking.

The RCP Report (1983) also pointed out that tobacco accounted for about 15 - 20 % of all deaths and the loss of 50 million working days each year (four times the number then lost in strikes). This also cost the NHS £l81 M (lung cancer accounting for £120 M - the remainder on other smoking related disease), and now probably well over double this figure. The RCP report also noted that of 1,000 young male adult cigarette smokers, on average one will be murdered, six will die from road accidents, whilst **250 will be killed prematurely by tobacco** - i.e. **25 %.** Among **heavy smokers** it has been estimated that **40 % will not reach retirement age**.

It was also estimated that the total number of deaths caused by cigarette smoking in Britain was over 260,000 per year but this figure also included deaths due to chronic bronchitis, emphysema and cor pulmonale (the "English disease" with 30,000 deaths), aortic aneurysm, ischaemic heart disease and carcinoma of larynx, mouth and oesophagus (1986 figures - Hansard, 12 Nov. 1987).

The actual number of recorded deaths due to lung tumours is approximately 45,000 per annum, but some deaths due to lung tumours may well have been classified as pneumonia, and the number may well have been greater. Almost half of the lung cancer deaths occur in moderate smokers, smoking 15 cigarettes per day or less. It is disappointing that whilst the death rate in the UK from lung cancer has declined in men by 5% since 1980, it has increased by 20% in women and teenage girls are smoking more than boys. In men lung cancer is the most common fatal cancer and in women its incidence is second only to that of breast cancer and is continuing to rise in those aged over 55 years. Health of the Nation, Progress Report (1996) unfortunately notes that smoking by children (especially girls) is increasing in the UK. In the USA President Clinton introduced controls on advertising and vending machines to try to curb this trend.

The World Health Organisation stated in January 1986 that at least **one million people around the world died prematurely each year because of tobacco**, including 600,000 new cases of lung cancer, with smoking responsible for over 90% of these. It also accounted for 75% of cases of chronic bronchitis and 25% of cases of coronary heart disease, potentiated fibrosing alveolitis and some other lung diseases, and contributed or probably contributes to laryngeal, oral, throat, oesophageal, bladder, and even breast carcinoma. A further WHO conference in 1997 suggested that 3M world-wide will die from smoking each year and 30 M in ten years time unless something is done to curb the threat.

Prevention.

Around the world £70 billion per annum is spent on purchasing 4,000 billion cigarettes, more than 1,000 cigarettes for each man, woman and child, and it is estimated that a man taking up smoking at the age of 16, and smoking 20 cigarettes per day until age 57 will consume about 300,000 cigarettes - at a cost of about £30, 000 at today's prices. The WHO also denounced the massive exports of Cigarettes by European tobacco companies to famine stricken African countries, payment by them being made in hard currencies. Whilst tobacco consumption is decreasing in industrial countries at 1.1% per year, it is rising by 2.1% in the Third World.

Tobacco substitutes have been tried in cigarettes but despite some initial success (Freedman and Fletcher, 1976) have largely failed; they were not as acceptable to smokers and indeed their smoke also contained much tar. The WHO also noted that low-tar cigarettes are far from being safe and that 'most smokers will not tolerate for very long low nicotine-free cigarettes as substitutes for the real thing' - they compensate for lower levels of nicotine by inhaling more often or by smoking more cigarettes. It recommended the banning of tobacco advertisements and the sponsoring of sports and cultural events by the tobacco industry.

Young people still, too frequently take up the habit, perhaps because of advertising, the 'manly' image or just because they become 'hooked' on to the habit. This is particularly likely to happen when smoking is started in the early teens and it has been estimated that early smokers quadruple their chances of developing bronchial carcinoma compared with those starting after the age of 25 (RCP, 1983). It seems particularly important that children should be prevented from smoking, for there seems to be good evidence that if people do not smoke by the age of 25, they will not become addicted to the habit. Young people also seem to be able to return their bronchial linings to normal after giving up smoking.

A campaign 'Parents Against Tobacco' was waged in 1990 to try to prevent children taking up smoking. It is estimated that 300,000 teenagers under the age of 16 (the legal age for buying cigarettes in the UK) smoke and many retailers are breaking the law by selling cigarettes to them, particularly when packets of cigarettes are split and cigarettes are sold singly. It is estimated that such sales produce £60M profit annually in the UK. It also seems amazing that 90% of local authorities have never prosecuted for this offence', but the fine for this was increased to £1,000 in 1992.

The UK Government has largely relied on voluntary codes on advertising (agreed with the tobacco companies) but these have continually been flouted, with much indirect advertising on TV (even though direct advertising is prohibited) through sponsorship of sporting events. etc. The tobacco industry claims that advertising only influences the brands 'committed smokers' purchase, but the 'macho effect' probably still persuades many youngsters that it is 'grown-up' to smoke. They also probably feel like many adults that **"smoking cannot really be a danger or the Government would ban cigarette advertising"** (Marsh, 1985). Mrs Thatcher's speech, as Prime Minister (24 Jan. 1989) supporting 'Europe Against Cancer' promised £11 M towards the EEC campaign to stop teenagers, and **particularly girls from smoking** was a pointer that at last Government was beginning to understand the problem. It was felt that unless something was done to curb teenagers from starting the habit, they will become 'hooked' on it and it was estimated that 110,000 people will die each year as a result of having started the habit as teenagers.

The EEC (which ironically spends about £600 M per year on tobacco subsidies) in 1992 directed a ban on tobacco sponsorship advertising at the point of sale from 1993. The UK edged closer to banning tobacco advertising when the House of Commons Health Committee in Jan. 1993 endorsed the EEC proposals for a 'statutory ban', and stated that it could not afford to ignore the potential of a total ban on advertising, if the UK was to achieve its target of a 30% fall in smoking during the 1990s. The Government's White Paper - **'The Health of the Nation'** (1992) set a target to reduce the consumption by 40% and the prevalence of smoking to 20% by the year 2,000. Although a former Sec. of State for Health (Mrs V. Bottomley) proclaimed herself second to none in deploring the effects of smoking, she refused to ban TV advertising (now mainly carried out only in the form of sponsored sporting events, which prompt young people to wrongly believe that all sportsmen smoke!).

Many countries, including Australia, Canada, Finland, New Zealand and Norway, have made tobacco advertising illegal, with a reduction of smoking in young people. In Hong Kong as a result of government information and anti-smoking measures, between l982 and 1984, the number of people who smoked declined by 16%, and the number of teenage smokers was halved (Mackay and Barnes, 1986). Promotion in developing countries should also be curbed. How can a responsible society allow the promotion of a product which will kill about one half of its consumers?

London Transport in the summer of 1984 banned smoking on all Underground trains, and following the fires at Oxford Circus and King's Cross stations in 1985 and 1987, smoking has been totally banned on the Underground. Many air lines are prohibiting smoking; this is particularly important as air is recirculated in the cabins, and it is hoped that customer demand will hasten the trend to a world-wide agreement that smoking in an aircraft is as unacceptable as smoking in a church (T. Smith - Editor, BMJ, 2 Oct. 1988).

In the summer of 1987, smoking was banned in public places in Belgium, and similar legislation was introduced in France in 1992.

In 1985 the Government asked all District Health Authorities to draw up written policy statements for making non-smoking normal practice on Health Service premises, and for staff (see also Batten, 1988). This has slowly been implemented, with a **ban on smoking in all NHS hospitals from June 1993**. The Government also hoped to cut the number of England's 12 million smokers by a **third by the end of the century**.

Sir Donald Acheson, Chief Medical Officer, Dept. of Health (1985) wrote "...smokers underestimate both the damage smoking is doing them and the benefits they might gain by giving up." Marsh (1985) also stated "...whilst most smokers had accepted the message that smoking might damage their health, only the better educated and resourceful had responded to it...".

The medical lobby against smoking must continue, to try to prevent the all too frequent tumours and other diseases caused by smoking. Although the great number of lung tumours give radiologists and other doctors a vast experience of pathological anatomy, the untold misery that lies behind them should be avoided.

In the UK it is estimated that **only one-third of the adult population now smoke** (as compared with 70% of men and 50% of women in 1958), and it is becoming anti-social to do so. The real worry is with teenagers from "peer pressure", the generally "permissive society" or a natural teenager's " feeling of rebellion". It was hoped that those who do so will soon desist, but in 1997 among **15 yr olds, 28% of boys and 33% of girls had become regular smokers** (BMJ, **315**, 144). **Women also appear to be developing more oat cell tumours**.

The almost hysterical reaction of the public, including smokers, to the effects of asbestos exposure seems totally illogical in relation to the much more numerous cases of severe disability and death produced by cigarette smoking. Continuing education, as well as a total ban on advertising (except at the point of sale) seems needed to bring these points home to the population. Also legislation is needed to curb advertising further and to ban smoking in closed public places. The BMA has repeatedly urged Governments to raise the tax on tobacco, and it has done this to a modest degree 'in real terms'.

A WHO survey of 122 countries in 1988 showed that Britain had dropped from the highest cigarette-smoking nation to one of the lower (2,120 a year per head - about 50% of that in Cuba, Greece, Cyprus, Poland, USA and Japan). 32% were women (only 2 - 4% in Greece, India and Hong Kong). Western tobacco companies have since been targeting former Soviet countries, China and other developing countries for increased sales.

Since September 1992 smoking has been allowed as a contributory factor on death certificates.

Private member's Bills to ban tobacco advertising were introduced in Parliament in 1993 and 1994 - the second supported by members of all main parties, including some ministers, but the Government announced a new agreement with the tobacco industry to curb advertising just before its 'third reading' in May 1994 which then failed. This agreement provided for larger health warnings on advertisements including those for cigars and pipe tobacco as well as cigarettes + no advertisements to be permitted on buses, taxis, at bus stops, or within 200 m of school entrances. It also banned them on computer games and no humour was allowed in them and no free cigarette samples may be given to the under 18s. Lady Cumberledge (Under Sec. of State for Health) wrote in Dec. 1994 "It would have been extraordinary, at a time when smoking itself is still legal, to create a penalty of up to two years' imprisonment for someone who publishes, or causes to be published, an advertisement for a tobacco product." A £12M health education programme was launched to help parents and to encourage teenagers to give up smoking. The Govt. was also warning of the dangers of passive smoking to babies and children.

The new Labour Govt. proposed (in the Queen's speech) in May 1997 a concerted programme to reduce smoking in Britain, with a draft bill in the autumn, a ban on tobacco advertising, banning sales to young people under 18, and sports sponsorship by tobacco companies to be phased out. The Health Secretary, Frank Dobson said that sports would be given time to reduce their dependency on tobacco and rejected claims of the tobacco industry that advertising was not designed to promote sales and that the industry killed 120,000/yr. and had to recruit a like number to replace these (see BMJ, **314**, 1502).

A White Paper 'Smoking Kills' was published by the Government in Nov. 1998 to try to re-establish the downward trend in adult smoking, to result in 1.5M fewer smokers by 2010 and to save 3,000 lives a year. It proposes to implement the European Union (EU) directive and by 2,000 to end tobacco advertising on billboards and in printed media. Tobacco sponsorship of sports and arts will end in 2,000 but international football and Formula I motor racing can receive sponsorship until 2,006. Some curbs on children's access to vending machines and 'proof-of-age' cards are proposed, but as pointed out by Chambers (1999) for a country where female deaths are among the highest in the EU and more than three times the Union average, the time-scale is slow. Up to £110M is to be spent over the next 3 years in public education, targeted on young children, young people, pregnant women and working-class smokers (see BMJ, **316**, 1334 and **318**, 9).

In the USA smoking has been banned on public transport, in elevators, theatres, restaurants, etc. for a much longer time, but this has in part been a fear of fire in high buildings. In 1971 Congress banned tobacco advertising on TV and radio. Since 1988 smoking has been disallowed on air lines in the Continental USA following a law-suit by stewardesses over polluted air.

The US Forces banned smoking in working and living areas in 1986. They claim that smoking also produces a lack of concentration, poor vision in subdued lighting (necessary for working computers, etc.) and a generally reduced efficiency. Other studies in the USA have shown a diminished ability of the smoker to deploy processing operations selectively to capture those events which were central to the task. Smokers were involved in almost 2.5 times as many rear end automobile collisions as non-smokers.

The Jan. 1989 report of the US Surgeon General warned that tobacco is "the single most important preventable cause of death, responsible for 1 out of every 6 deaths in the USA", He pointed out that the toll from smoking is higher than previously thought and stated that it claimed 390,000 lives/year, two thirds dying from cardio-vascular disease, lung cancer and chronic bronchitis. He emphasised that the **average male smoker is 22 times as likely to die from lung cancer as is a non-smoker - double the previous risk estimate**. Only 29% of American adults then smoked, compared with 40% in 1965, the biggest decline being in men; one third compared with 50% in 1965; the problem areas being in blacks, blue-collar workers and in girls, who seem to be taking up tobacco at a younger age, the laws restricting its sale to children being largely ignored. The Surgeon General's goal is to make the US a "smoke free society by the year 2,000." In May 1996, Philip Morris proposed the withdrawal of cigarette vending machines to counter President Clinton's proposals for banning under age 18 smoking (Financial Times, 5 May - see also above).

The best-known and most effective anti-smoking campaign in the USA has been in California, which produced a 1.06% per year decline in smoking (almost double that in other states) but its influence declined following a reduction in financing (Pierce et al., 1998).

A BMJ Editorial (of 31 Jan. 1976) is still probably worth repeating. It stated that it is surprising how tobacco smoking became acceptable in public places and mixed company. Up to the First World War, smoking was mostly held to be impolite at best, and in many circles offensive. The smoker was mostly banned to a 'smoking room', the great outdoors, or to public bars liberally provided with spittoons. Following the War the 'obnoxious practice' became the 'norm' in many enclosed places, but not in London theatres; "smokers in general retaining a remarkable liberty to inflict their offence on people who resented it - a liberty taken often in public places, despite no smoking notices." The editorial suggested 'segregated smoking areas' in offices, restaurants, pubs, cinemas, public transport vehicles etc, as well as education to give some official encouragement to keep the smoker in his place.

A conference was held at the Royal Society in London in Feb. 1993 to celebrate Sir Richard Doll's 80th birthday. At this he said "These new results are much more extreme than had been suggested, where premature death was 'only' twice as common in smokers as in non-smokers. Our findings mean that those who start to smoke in their teenage years will be at particularly high risk... Doctors who abandoned the habit avoided most of their risk of tobacco. But the bad news is that **continuing to smoke is even more dangerous than was originally realised**."

Further references and notes.

Passive Smoking at Work - In 1988 an advisory body to Government, the Independent Scientific Committee on Smoking and Health, in its fourth report reviewed all the scientific evidence and concluded that it was consistent with passive smoking causing a small increase in the risk of lung cancer, and that it may be causing several hundred deaths a year in the UK. The Government accepted these findings. Later research suggested a possible connection with heart disease, and smaller babies in pregnant women. The Committee advised that non-smoking should be the norm in enclosed workplaces, and as a result in hospitals, on most forms of transport, places of public entertainment, etc. smoking has been restricted or banned. In the workplace more and more employers have introduced policies on smoking with the acceptance and agreement of their work-force surveys showing that most workers would prefer not to breathe air polluted by tobacco smoke when at work. In 1993 Regulations were made under the British Health and Safety at Work etc Act (1974) to ensure that from 1996 employers will have to ensure that there are arrangements to protect non-smokers from discomfort caused by tobacco smoke in rest rooms or rest areas. (Independent Scientific Committee on Smoking and Health. Fourth Report of the Independent Scientific Committee on Smoking and Health (1988). London, H.M.S.O.)

Crofton (1990) : Seventh World Conference on Tobacco and Health - children and especially girls are taking up the habit in the Third World.

Mackay (1991) : Tobacco - the third world war deprecates the increased promotion and selling of cigarettes to the Far East and developing countries.

United States Environmental Protection Agency. Respiratory health effects of passive smoking : lung cancer and other disorders (1992). Washington, DC.

Royal College of Physicians of London. Smoking and the Young (1992).

Alistair Cooke, Letter from America (BBC Radio 4, 20 March 1994) - the decline in smoking in the USA (from 50% down to 25%) now means that the tobacco industry is contracting and 400,000 people fear for their livelihoods.

Dye and Adler (1994) : Effects of cigarette smoke on epithelial cells of the respiratory tract.

Mainstream smoke is composed of a complex mixture of gases and condensed tar particles. Side-stream smoke (emitted from the burning tip of the cigarette - the major constituent of environmental tobacco smoke which may be different from mainstream smoke owing to prolonged time and cooling in the air) contains CO, ammonia, formaldehyde, benzene, nicotine, acrolein, other gases and particles, and an assessment of potentially genotoxic and/or carcinogenic organic compounds. Although studies of the smoke effects on individual cells of the epithelium are useful for eliciting underlying injury mechanisms, the overall respiratory system response depends on the integrated action of all effector cell populations with their corresponding target cells.

Richard Peto and **Jillian Boreham** from Oxford (Report of Imperial Cancer Research Fund, the WHO and American Cancer Society, 1994) : World-wide smoking-related diseases kill 3M people/year - a figure which is likely to rise to 10M by 2020. 50% of smokers will die as a result of their habit, one in four in middle age losing around 25 yrs. of life.

Peto at the 1998 meeting of the British Association for the Advancement of Science, stated "tobacco kills several million smokers a year around the world and the rate is increasing. Yet in Britain, deaths had been cut to half the level they were in the 1970s. No other country had seen such a drop. The fall could be correlated directly with the drop in cigarette sales, from 150 billion to 80 billion, and was a triumph for public education campaigns. In 1970, 80,000 people aged 35 - 69 died each year from tobacco use; now the rate is 40,000 a year. In 1970, British men had the worst death rates in the world from tobacco use, but half of the adults then stopped smoking. Since 1970 Britain had the world's biggest decrease in tobacco deaths, and journalists influenced public health more than doctors or scientists. However, tobacco was still the biggest killer in Britain and was now overwhelmingly a trouble of the lower social classes. The unemployed had five times the incidence of lung cancer than that of professionals. However people were classified - by income, education or social class - the lower group always smoked more.' (Daily Telegraph, 8 Sept., 1998).

Thatcher and Spiro (1996) New Perspectives in Lung Cancer - the illogical attitude towards the lack of regulation of tobacco promotion in Great Britain is highlighted and possible approaches to counteract the potentially disastrous effects of continued tobacco use in developing countries. Without the extinction of the tobacco plant one can expect only marginal improvements in survival through treatment of established disease.

BMJ 15 June 1996 (**312**, 1501) : Many teenagers say "Smoking can't be all that dangerous or the government would ban sports sponsorship by tobacco companies."

BMJ 4 Jan. 1997 (**314**, 11) : David Kessler - Commissioner of the US Food and Drug Administration 'Scourge of the tobacco industry' steps down. What's important he says "is that 400,000 Americans die each year of tobacco related disease. We focused on these things that would have the most public health benefit. As a paediatrician he is especially proud of the tobacco legislation, which is principally aimed at stopping children from becoming addicted. "If they don't start by age 19, they'll probably never start."

Iribarren et al. (1999) : Found in 1546 male **cigar** smokers that "independently of other risk factors regular cigar smoking can increase the risk of coronary heart disease, COPD, and cancer of the upper aerodigestive tract and lungs. Like McCoy et al. (1980) who found a synergistic effect of alcohol + cigarette smoking with such cancers, the same was true for cigar smoking.

Guernsey (one of the Channel Islands) in 1996 became the first part of the British Isles to impose a complete ban on tobacco advertising, including sponsorship of sports events. The minimum age for buying tobacco is also being raised from 16 to 18, and taxes are being increased.

In India smoking was banned in public buildings from Jan. 1997.

The BMA called for smoking to be banned in public places in the UK, as voluntary agreement will not work and are likely to be undermined. The BMA Chairman pointed out that "the evidence is now irrefutable and accepted by all but the tobacco industry that the health risks associated with passive smoking are sufficiently serious to warrant regulation and if necessary legislation" (BMJ 4.4.98, **316**, 1037).

In March 1997, the Liggett Group, the American maker of Chesterfield cigarettes was the first tobacco company to admit publicly that cigarettes are addictive and cause cancer. It agreed to settle all claims that it faced in 22 US states, which were suing the industry for the cost of smoking related illnesses and also agreed to hand over potentially damaging documents to the states to help them in their lawsuits. (Philip Morris however obtained a temporary restraining order against their release). The company's employees were promised to be released from constraints from testifying in support of the lawsuits. The deal gave the company immunity from further litigation and in return agreed to pay $25M + 25% of its pre-tax profits for the next 25 years to a fund that will share out the proceeds among the litigants (BMJ, 29. 3.97 - **314**, 919).

In June 97 this was followed by a much larger agreement with five other large US tobacco companies to pay $368.5 bn (£230M) over 25 yrs (starting at $10 bn/yr and rising to $15 bn) to compensate states for health care costs related to treating workers, pay individuals who sue finance health research and promote education programmes aimed at deterring young people from taking up smoking. The agreement also provides for bigger warning labels with harsher language on cigarette packets, and manufacturers may no longer use advertisements or cartoon characters, advertise on bill-boards, in stadia, or other outdoor sites, pay for product placement in cinemas or theatres and cigarette vending machines are doomed. The FDA will control the amount of nicotine and plans to lower the amount gradually over the next 12 years.

These agreements had to be ratified by the US Congress, but in June 1998, the Bill to implement them was rejected by the Senate. Tougher proposals emerged which the tobacco industry estimated would have cost at least $516 bn and with less legal protection. A huge industry campaign to paint the legislation as a tax increase helped to sink it (Time - 29 June 1998 - see also BMJ, **316**, 1185 - 'US tobacco companies pull out of deal'.)

Notes - BMJ - 5 August 2000 - several articles on tobacco and smoking.
        22 Jan. 2001 - Bill before Parliament to further limit tobacco advertising in the UK.

Chapter 24b : **Types of Lung Cancer, Clinical and Radiological Features of the Different Types. Cell types in the lungs.**

Presenting Clinical Features of Lung Tumours

These are protean , but most common are cough, haemoptysis, chest pain, dyspnoea, loss of weight and abdominal symptoms. In the author's view, every patient with chest symptoms should have a minimum of a high KV chest radiograph and further views if any abnormality is suspected on this or clinically. Likewise all patients over 40 with abdominal symptoms not otherwise explained should also have a chest radiograph. Several cases of bronchial carcinoma were thus found in the author's department each year and also the occasional case by pre-operative chest radiographs before other major surgery. The 'best case' to find is the asymptomatic one with no demonstrable spread and well differentiated histology, i.e. the 'chance-finding' of an early tumour.

Clinical features of lung cancer

(a) **General** The most disturbing feature in patients with lung cancer is its late presentation and in most there is a long latent period before the illness becomes manifest. This may well account for seven eighths, or **more** of the duration of the disease (Dunnill, 1987). Geddes (1979) suggested that it is usually diagnosed at least 10 years after malignant change has first occurred; Rigler (1957b) also pointed out that sometimes tiny lung abnormalities might be seen retrospectively on radiographs taken long before the clinical onset. Following the long latent period there is a relatively short clinical illness leading to death. A long latent period is most commonly seen in elderly patients with slowly growing squamous cell tumours, but the average expectation of life from when the patient first seeks advice is often no more than six months (as Brock noted in 1948).

(b) **Symptoms due to tumour**

Cough is common in all smokers, but one that has changed or becomes more persistent should alert one to the possibility of bronchial neoplasm.

Sputum too is common and may be secondarily infected.

Haemoptysis is alarming to the patient and frequently directs him to seek medical advice. Usually it is streaking of sputum, especially in the early morning, rather than a frank haemorrhage.

A localised **wheeze** or **stridor** may indicate narrowing of the trachea, the carina or a large bronchus, either by intrinsic tumour or pressure from nodes.

Dyspnoea may be due to infiltration of bronchial walls so that they cannot alter in diameter with respiration. Also major collapse, consolidation or pleural effusion, will limit the amount of lung which can be aerated. Concomitant emphysema is common and in the later stages of the disease, spread within the lung and mediastinum may render these more rigid. Even in advanced cases, it is surprising how much the stopping of smoking will relieve symptoms a point that many patients, find out for themselves. In fact many patients volunteer, as one of the presenting features of the disease, that they have given up smoking or lost the desire for it.

(c) **Spread of tumour in the chest**
Pain may be due to pleurisy, chest wall or mediastinal involvement, the effect of bony secondaries or even cough fractures.

Infection - pneumonia distal to a tumour is common and may lead to breakdown and abscess formation.

Hoarseness commonly follows involvement of the left recurrent laryngeal nerve as it hooks around the aorta. Right recurrent nerve involvement is much less common and usually accompanies a right aided Pancoast tumour.

Superior vena cava obstruction may give facial and neck oedema.

Dysphagia from compression of the oesophagus by mediastinal, and especially subcarinal nodes is not uncommon and may be the presenting feature, a barium swallow with the patient slightly turned to the left usually readily demonstrated oesophageal compression or displacement, but CT demonstration of nodes is now more common. Hepatic enlargement due to deposits may cause loss of appetite, etc. and this may direct the patient to be referred for a barium examination, when no stomach tumour may be found - the author always had a chest radiograph done as well and also examined the liver with ultrasound. Rarely involvement of the **heart** or **pericardium** will produce tamponade or cardiac arrhythmias.

(d) **Metastases**
Nodes are usually detected radiologically but in some cases, the presentation is with enlarged nodes in the neck - see Illus. **NODES-CERVICAL.**

Bone pain due to spinal or rib deposits is not uncommon, especially with oat cell tumours and is usually readily detected on isotope bone scans, quite often before a radiographic abnormalities have been found.

Liver deposits are not uncommon - even from a small lung primary, and may be shown with ultra-sound, isotope studies CT or a combination of these. There are often elevated levels of hepatic enzymes, particularly alkaline phosphatase.

Brain deposits give rise to presenting symptoms in about 5% of cases, either with epileptic fits or from neurological deficits. In terminal phases up to about 30% have neurological effects.

Adrenal deposits are not uncommon, but most are asymptomatic. Rarely they may lead to a sudden death from acute adrenal insufficiency. They should be distinguished from adrenal hypertrophy.

Skin, renal and splenic deposits are sometimes the presenting features; also pulmonary deposits, which may be so numerous as to mimic the clinical signs of pneumonia.

Lower limb oedema may be due to enlarged abdominal nodes, the nephrotic syndrome caused by the tumour (see p. 23.1), or be associated with HPOA.

Ascites is uncommon but may occur in association with diffuse spread of disease, particularly to most serosal cavities, e.g.. both pleural cavities and the peritoneum.

Cell types in the lungs, bronchi and pleura.

Bronchial mucosa
Normal bronchi are lined by, pseudo-stratified columnar, ciliated epithelium, lying on a basement membrane directly adjacent to the latter are the **basal** (or primitive stem) cells. In smokers the basal cells may be of a different type with numerous pleomorphic cytoplasmic granules (Sidhu, 1982). These cells proliferate and differentiate to form new columnar cells. Parocrine, 'K' (= Kulschitzsky), Feyrter (1951 and 1959) or 'APUD' (= amine precursor uptake decarboxylation system) cells lie between some of the basal cells. They are more numerous in the smaller bronchi and seromucinous glands, and are commoner in babies and young children. They contain round granules, and are thought to have both an endocrine and a chemoreceptor function, similar to APUD cells in the small intestine. They may be concerned with the response of the lung to hypoxia. Carcinoids or adenomas and oat-cell tumours are thought to arise from these cells.

Intermediate cells occupy a position midway between basal and ciliated cells and are capable of differentiation into mucous-secretory goblet cells or ciliated cells.

Columnar ciliated cells are found from the trachea down to the terminal bronchioles and play a vital role in pulmonary defence as the '**muco-ciliary escalator**' constituting the major method whereby particles are moved into the larger bronchi, prior to being expectorated. Each cell carries approximately 200 cilia.

Goblet or mucus secreting cells are less frequent in normal lung than ciliated cells.

Bronchial glands produce the major part of the mucus entering the bronchi. The glands mainly contain some ciliated cells and occasional K cells. Their openings become enlarged in chronic bronchitis (see also p.3.18). It has also been estimated that cells lining these glands produce forty times the volume of mucus that is produced by the goblet cells in the bronchial mucosa. (Dunnill, 1982).

Alveolar cells or pneumocytes are of two main types -
(a) Type I (membranous pneumocytes) or small alveolar cells which line most of the alveolar surfaces. They have little phagocytic activity.
(b) Type II (or granular pneumocytes) or large alveolar cells which contain numerous osmiophilic inclusion bodies and probably produce surfactant. Clara cells in the bronchioles have a similar appearance.
In addition there is the **alveolar macrophage** - the defence cell which together with ciliary action and expectoration removes over 90% of inhaled foreign material in less than one hour.

Regeneration and squamous metaplasia

Bronchial mucosa may be lost in a variety of conditions including infection etc. Regeneration follows a well recognised pattern, at first a simple stratified squamous type, which 3-4 weeks later differentiates into a columnar ciliated form. It seems probable that squamous metaplasia may result from attempts at regeneration. Commonly the cilia are lost or deformed and many atypical cells may be seen. When columnar cells are lost, basal cells promptly flatten out to cover the basement membrane (Erjefält et al. , 1997).

Metaplasia may lead to **'carcinoma in situ'.** Such is not an uncommon finding in the lungs of smokers - in areas remote from macroscopic neoplasms or in autopsy specimens of smokers not dying from neoplasm. It is often multi-focal and appears to develop secondarily to bronchial or basal cell hyperplasia, particularly when the bronchial epithelium loses its resemblance to normal ciliated or squamous epithelium and consists mainly of hyperchromatic cells, some of which become enlarged and contain more than one nucleus. The cells also become increased in number and may extend to as many as fifteen layers in the bronchial mucosa.

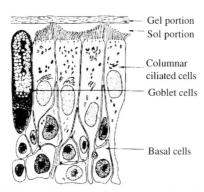

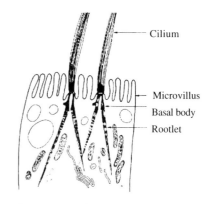

Fig. 24.2 (a) Diagrammatic representation of bronchial mucosa showing cilia lying in sol with their tips touching the gel portion of the fluid covering the respiratory tract.

(b) Diagram of luminal surface of ciliated cell.
(a & b reproduced from Dunnill, 1987 by permission from Churchill Livingstone).

Pleural lining cells.

The pleural surfaces are lined by a layer of mesothelial cells which lie on a framework of collagen and elastic fibres. These cells are variable in shape and width, although most are fairly thin. They exhibit considerable reaction to various stimuli, and may enlarge, become cuboid or columnar in shape and develop large nuclei with prominent nucleoli. Cytological differentiation of pleural reaction from neoplasm may be difficult.

Histological classification of lung and pleural tumours

Most lung tumours show considerable variability in their appearances and may contain more than one cell type although it is usual for one to be dominant. In 1967 the WHO published a classification of tumours by cell type, largely based on the work of Kreyberg. This was modified in 1981 with a table, summarised below, including benign and malignant conditions, and listing mesothelial, connective tissue and epithelial tumours.

Epithelial Tumours.
A. **Benign**
1. Papillomas - squamous or transitional.
2. Adenomas - pleomorphic (mixed tumours) or monomorphic (cystadenomas or solid masses).
B. **Dysplasia** (carcinoma in situ).
C. **Malignant** (or potentially malignant)
1. Squamous cell (epidermoid), including spindle cell.
2. Small cell including oat cell, intermediate and combined oat cell.
3. Adenocarcinoma, including acinar, papillary, bronchio-alveolar and solid carcinoma with mucus formation.
4. Large cell; including giant cell and clear carcinomas, with clear or foamy cytoplasm (like renal tubular cell carcinomas).
5. Adeno-squamous.
6. Carcinoids (adenomas) - have a low grade of malignancy and rarely cause the carcinoid syndrome.
7. Bronchial gland carcinomas - two types (a) adenocystic (cylindromas similar to salivary gland tumours) and (b) muco-epidermoid (resembling similar tumours of the larynx - usually have a better prognosis than other types of lung tumour).

Mesothelial (mainly pleural) tumours - epithelial, fibrous (spindle cell) and biphasic types.

Miscellaneous
A- Benign- - clear cell ('sugar') tumour paraganglioma (chemodectoma) and teratoma.
B. Malignant - carcino-sarcoma, blastoma, melanoma and lymphoma.
Tumour-like lesions include hamartomas (of chrondromatous or leiomyomatous types), lymphoproliferative lesions, pseudolymphomas (lymphoid interstitial pneumonia and lymphomatoid granuloma) tumourlets, eosinophilic granuloma 'sclerosing haemangioma' inflammatory pseudo-tumours, plasma cell granuloma, and pulmonary xanthomas.

Notes on the Pathological and Radiological appearances of the different types of lung cancer.

Squamous or epidermoid carcinoma (30 to 40% of all tumours).
Although there is no squamous epithelium in the normal bronchial tree, squamous metaplasia is often present (see p. 24.14), with many atypical forms. Squamous tumours are the commonest type in smokers. They are more common in men than women. The characteristic microscopic features are keratinisation, the presence of intercellular bridges, a fibrous stroma and multiple macrophages. Some tumours show clear-cut epithelial pearl formations, whereas others appear anaplastic. Necrosis and cavitation are common as the tumour enlarges.
Radiology : These tumours arise peripherally or centrally. Peripheral squamous tumours tend to grow more slowly than those of the other cell types and show a desmoplastic response or central scar formation. These masses frequently cavitate leaving an irregular and 'lumpy' inner wall (Illus. **CA SQUAMOUS, Ca cavitary**). The border is often well defined and lobulated, but with anaplastic squamous tumours may have an irregular outline. Such tumours often have earlier lymph node involvement. Large tumours may extend into the chest wall.

With centrally arising tumours, collapse, obstrucive pneumonitis, and pneumonitis - less common are frank infection, abscess formation or an empyema.

Examples are shown in Illus. **CA SQUAMOUS.**

Adenocarcinomas and bronchiolo-alveolar cell carcinomas (20 to 30% of all tumours).

Primary pulmonary adenocarcinomas are of several types (see above), and should be differentiated (if possible) from metastases (e.g. from pancreas, alimentary tract, ovary, etc.). Acinar tumours are probably derived from the mucus-secreting cells in the bronchial mucosa of small peripheral bronchi, and on microscopy acini, ducts and tubules may be found. Mucus formation is common, particularly with some bronchiolo-alveolar tumours, and this may lead to severe distress in about 5% of cases. Mixed adeno-squamous types are not uncommon. Some adenocarcinomas arise in pulmonary scars. **Bronchiolo-alveolar tumours** - ps. 5.1 - 5.4 - grow along existing alveolar walls before spreading out into the bronchioles, bronchi and surrounding tissues, then via the airways and lymphatics.

Radiology: Adenocarcinomas most often arise peripherally, and may present as spherical or lobulated masses with well-defined smooth borders. Some are accompanied by a desmoplastic response, causing retraction of the overlying pleura. Others may mimic small inflammatory lesions, look like small 'smudges' in the lungs on a CT section (see also p. 24.50), or occasionally look like an air cyst or cysts within the lung; some also complicate lung cysts - see also ps. 6.2 - 3. Many exhibit central fibrotic foci. The papillary histological subtype is most common. Accompanying pleural effusions are not uncommon and nodal enlargements often occur.

Examples are shown in Illus. **CA ADENO** and **ALV CELL CA.**

Note also : 'Scar cancer' (Illus. **SCAR CANCER**)   - see p. 4.20, 6.2
          'Intravascular bronchiolo-alveolar carcinoma'   - see p. 5.5
    Thin-walled cysts and adenocarcinoma (Illus. **CA+BULLAE, CYSTS ETC**) - see ps. 6.2 -3.

Large Cell (or undifferentiated) type of tumour (10 to 15% of all tumours).
These contain large or giant cells, which may be multi-nucleated (50 - 50μ in diameter) with intra-cellular mucin, tumour phagocytosis, etc. They are highly malignant, have a rapid local spread and show early metastases. Desmoplastic reaction to the tumour growth and cavitation are uncommon.
Radiology: The typical appearance is of a large peripheral mass, which may fill a lobe, and bulge out its inter-lobar fissures. Hilar and mediastinal nodal enlargement is common, but not as gross as with oat cell tumours. Deposits in the liver and bones are also common.

Reference.
Shin et al. (1986) : Giant cell carcinoma of the lung - clinical and radiological manifestations.

Small or Oat cell tumours (20 to 25% of all tumours).
Oat cell is the most distinctive variety (first described by Azzopardi, 1959) - small oval cells with darkly staining nuclei, and with extremely small amounts of cytoplasm. Mitoses are frequent and necrosis is often marked. There is usually little or no host response to the tumour, hence little fibrous stroma or lymphocyte infiltration. Spread is rapid, especially via the blood stream. Lymphatic and peribronchial tumour infiltration is often a notable feature. About 90% occur centrally.
These appear, like carcinoids or adenomas, to arise from the K or APUD cells and have also been termed 'Apudomas' by Arnold and Williams (1979). They are highly related to smoking. Many are associated with the production of ectopic hormones and electrolyte disturbances are common (see p. 23.1). The marked nodal enlargement may simulate lymphoma, but monoclonal antibody stains may be able differentiate them.

Staging of small or oat cell tumours.
Following the reviews by Hansen et al. (1978) in Denmark and Cohen and Matthews (1978) in the USA, on the sites and frequency of metastases with these tumours, staging is usually categorised as 'limited' (i.e. confined to one hemithorax) or 'extensive' (i.e. distant spread) - see also p. 24.25. Patients with limited disease tend to survive longer and to respond better to radiotherapy, chemotherapy or both (limited - median survival untreated is about nine months, and about 12 to 18 months with treatment, and with the extensive types about two months which may be extended to six or more months with treatment). In some cases more than one remission may be

produced by chemotherapy. In a few patients a 'cure' may be produced, and the author has studied such a patient who presented 15 years later with pneumonia! (Illus. **CA SURVIVAL Pt. 5a-b**).

Some long-term survivors may develop other tumours or CNS problems as a result of chemotherapy. It has even been suggested that relapses in the cases which respond well to treatment initially, may be due to new tumour clones developing.

Occasionally localised tumours may be operable, particularly in the cases where there is no pre-operative histology, and the tumour type is only found following excision.

Radiology

The presenting features may be collapse/consolidation ± a large mass of hilar and/or mediastinal nodes. In other cases there may well be a small or larger primary lung tumour (particularly in an upper lobe) + markedly enlarged nodes. The primary tumour may cavitate. exhibit e.g. the 'galaxy sign' (Fig. 4.3h) or only be found on tomograms, not being evident on plain radiographs. In some cases tomograms including IFT's and CT may show sub-carinal and other enlarged nodes more readily - this may be of importance in planning radiotherapy treatment, which may be of great urgency if the patient presents with gross dyspnoea (from pressure on the trachea or larger bronchi) or SVC obstruction. Pressure by enlarged nodes on the oesophagus is not uncommon, and when there is an admission of dysphagia by the patient, a chest-with-barium or a barium swallow should be carried out. Occasionally the primary tumour may show cavitation (Illus. **CA OAT, Pts. 2 & 22**). Bone involvement occurs in 50% or more of cases, and is often widespread throughout the axial skeleton, ribs and the long limb bones. Plain bone radiographs are often unimpressive because the deposits largely affect the medullary parts of the bones, and an isotope bone scan should always be carried out (Illus. **CA OAT, Bone scan**). MR studies have also demonstrated diffuse bone marrow involvement in over half of the patients examined at the time of diagnosis. Also random bone marrow aspirations not uncommonly reveal diffuse tumour infiltration.

Liver involvement is common (in 40 to 50 %, and may be massive; it is readily assessed with real-time ultra-sound. Other deposits may be found in the spleen, adrenals, thyroid, etc. Involved lower cervical nodes are important to find, either by palpation or with ultra-sound, as they may be readily biopsied for cytological confirmation of the diagnosis. Pleural effusions are common, but are usually not large, and are important as they may be tapped for cytological diagnosis. Pericardial effusions also occur, and in gross or terminal cases may produce tamponade. Brain deposits occur in about 10% of cases. Adrenal deposits are also common, and in some cases the adrenals may be hypertrophied (p. 17.6 & 23.1).

Aspiration biopsy of a primary oat cell tumour or one of its deposits (e.g. in neck nodes or thyroid) may yield 'jelly-like' material or degenerate material macroscopically looking like pus.

As well as occurring in the lung, **small cell tumours may also originate in the oesophagus** (p.16.18 & 24) or in the bladder (Blomjous et al., 1989 - 18 reported cases). Examples of oat cell tumours are shown in Illus. **CA OAT**.

Further references :
Oat or Small Cell Tumours.
Selby et al. (1963) : Studied 300 cases of oat cell tumours and described **four x-ray patterns at presentation.**
Group I: Para-mediastinal tumours inseparable radiologically, from the lung root or the mediastinum - frequently also enlarged hilar or mediastinal nodes (unilateral, bilateral and sometimes contra-lateral) - these may be massive in size.
Group II: as Group I but plus pleural effusion, collapse or both.
Group III: Peripheral type of tumour.
    (a) Rounded 'coin' lesion - 1 to 10 cm. in diameter (might be well marginated).
    (b) Inflammatory-like infiltrate - 1 to 5 cm. in diameter.
    (c) Apical mass or superior sulcus tumour.
Group IV: Miscellaneous - lung deposits.
Bensch et al. (1968) : Oat cell carcinoma - its origin and relation to bronchial carcinoid.

Sinner and Standstedt (1976), from Stockholm : Found that the usual radiological appearance of small cell carcinoma seems to be the '**hilar-mediastinal type**', i.e. central hilar lesions with mediastinal involvement (50%). When hilar changes are absent or slight it might mimic a mediastinal tumour. The second type is the '**peripheral   type**', i.e. a peripheral lesion with or without central involvement. Small peripheral lesions with relatively large hilar and/or mediastinal nodes are always suspicious of highly malignant undifferentiated tumours. In the third, the '**indirect or mixed type**' there was bronchial obstruction, obstructive emphysema, distal pneumonia, pleural effusion or phrenic palsy.

Weiss, R. (1977) : A notable characteristic is the rapidity of growth to mimic lymphomas, leukaemia.

Cohen and Matthews (1978) : Noted that small cell bronchogenic carcinoma presents with a central tumour mass, collapse, obstructive pneumonitis or a hilar mass in over 75% of cases.

Arnold and Williams (1979) : Small cell lung cancer, a curable disease? and review of its various presentations.

Dunnick et al. (1979) and Vas et al. (1981) : Abdominal CT in pre-treatment assessment of small cell lung cancer.

Ihde et al. (1982): Abdominal CT in small cell lung cancer.

Johnson et al. (1982): Limited value of brain CT scans in the staging of small cell lung cancer.

Lewis, E. et al. (1982) : Although CT showed the mediastinal involvement more clearly, this information was often of little clinical value, as the mediastinal involvement was already apparent from the plain films.

Poon et al. (1982) : CT of brain, liver and upper abdomen in the staging of small cell carcinoma of the lung.

Sorenson (1983) : Bronchoscopic findings in patients with complete radiographic remission.

Sorenson and Bake (1984) : Regional lung function in patients with a complete radiographic remission.

Whitley et al. (1984) : Studied 33 patients with small cell carcinoma and found that CT showed more mediastinal and hilar nodes than ordinary radiographs. Also after chemotherapy areas of residual or recurrent disease.

Meyer (1985) : The division of patients with small cell cancer into categories of 'limited' and 'extensive' is inadequate as it does not identify the few having a good prognosis for disease control - he preferred the TNM classification.

Cherryman et al. (1987) : Found that at presentation CT detected brain metastases in 11.6% of their patients with small cell carcinoma, and in follow up 13.6% at six months, 20% at nine and 16.6% at twelve months.

Mirvis et al. (1987) : Studied the abdomens of 87 patients with small cell tumours by CT; 44 had extensive disease i.e. beyond one hemithorax, etc. and 26 of these had metastatic abdominal disease. These patients seemed to have a worse prognosis than those without abdominal metastatic disease. They felt that "site specific staging within the classification of extensive disease, may be of greater prognostic value than the simple two-stage classification that is currently in use."

Pearlberg et al. (1988, from the Henry Ford Hospital) : Studied 37 patients with untreated small cell lung cancer by CT and found enlarged hilar and mediastinal nodes in 34 (96%). Pleural effusions and pericardial thickening were present in about 40%, tracheo-bronchial compression in about 70%, lung collapse in 30% and separate lung masses in 40%. They did not quote a figure for oesophageal involvement.

Jelinek et al. (1990) : Staging of small cell lung cancer by MR may give more information than other methods - studied 25 patients by MR, CT and isotope bone scans - MR showed all the metastatic sites shown by the other methods, and in addition more bone and liver deposits. A disadvantage was that MR took 2.5 hours.

Smit et al. (1994) : Retrospective study of 21 pts. who had a resection of small cell lung cancer (out of 500 referred) - 7 pts. with very limited disease were alive and disease free 19 - 116 months later.

Girling et al. (1994) : Expressed caution over the size of the above sample - others having similar results with chemotherapy and radiotherapy.

Urschel (1994) : Small cell tumours are sometimes seen as asymptomatic pulmonary nodules and these appear to have better prognosis for cure, with slower tumour growth properties - a subset of small cell tumour?

Yabuchi et al. (1999) : A homogeneous mass without necrosis is the most characteristic CT feature of peripheral small cell ca.

Carcinosarcoma.

This is a rare tumour in which both stromal and epithelial components are malignant. Squamous or adenocarcinoma cells grow in a stroma resembling a fibrosarcoma, occasionally bone and cartilage elements being included. They occur mainly as large tumour masses close to the lung hilum (Illus. **CARCINOSARCOMA**).

Some references.

Stackhouse et al. (1969) : Primary mixed malignancies of the lung - carcinosarcoma and blastoma.

Chaudhuri (1971) : Bronchial carcinosarcoma.

Davis et al. (1984, from the Mayo Clinic) : Reported 17 cases (0.2% of their cases of lung cancer between 1971 and 1982). Most were over the age of 60 and the median survival time was one year. Dexorabicin based chemotherapy produced a response in two of four patients treated.

Tumourlets - these are small round nodules of oat or spindle cells, filling alveoli and growing mostly from small bronchi and respective bronchioles. They are usually found in damaged and/or fibrotic lung and are frequently found in patients with fibrosing alveolitis (p. 19.120) bronchiolitis obliterans or bronchiectasis. They are often multi-focal. Most seem to have a benign course, though a few may metastasise.

References.
Whitwell (1955), Mikail and Sender (1962) : Tumourlets of the lung.

Combined carcinomas and heterogeneity in tumours.

Since the time of Virchow, pathologists have shown that tumours are often heterogeneous, with different cell types within a single tumour or its metastases and differing rates of growth in different parts of the tumour.

Most tumours appear to arise from basal cells, and then differentiate in one or more directions, the wide variation in histological type being due to the profound metaplastic potential of bronchial epithelium.

Heterogeneity is seen in all types of tumour. Small cell anaplastic tumours may show squamous or glandular differentiation; squamous and adenocarcinomatous cell types are also found in others. Some, producing endocrine effects are shown by immuno-cyto-chemical studies, metabolising 'markers' within some tumour cells but not in others. Tumour cell populations appear to be more unstable genetically than normal cells, either through further mutations or further differentiation.

References.
Dunnill (1982), Henson (1982)
Yesner and Carter (1982) : The polymorphism indicates that lung cancer should be regarded as a spectrum of differentiation that is capable of changing depending on changes in the cell environment, including treatment.

Overlapping morphology.

Despite generalisations, there is considerable overlap in the morphological appearance of the main types of bronchial tumour, which may in part be due to heterogeneity in the tumours. All types may also exhibit cavitation, though this is most common with squamous tumours. This may give rise to the irregular inner wall, which is often characteristic of squamous tumours (Illus. **CA SQUAMOUS, Ca cavitary**).

Lung cancer cell type and its relationship to smoking.

As already discussed on p.24.1, Doll et al. (1957) and Kreyberg (1962 and 1969) pointed out that squamous bronchial carcinomas were more frequent in males (at that time 35 : 1) and were more frequent in urban than rural populations, and were particularly related to cigarette smoking, whereas adeno-carcinoma was not so clearly related. However many adenocarcinomas are found in smokers, and **only** very few in true non-smokers, others being passive smokers e.g. spouses of heavy smokers. Bronchiolo-alveolar carcinoma does not appear to be related to smoking, although some have considered it contributory (see p. 5.1). Large cell and particularly oat cell tumours are also related to smoking.

Notes on some published studies of radiological appearances

Liebow (1955) studied the '**pathology of carcinoma of the lung as related to the Roentgen shadow**', particularly in relation to the **blood supply** and noted that **primary lung tumours received their main blood supply from the bronchial vessels**, pulmonary vessels usually being displaced by the tumours.

He classified the malignant bronchogenic tumours into epidermoid, anaplastic, adenocarcinoma, and mixed types. **Epidermoid tumours** were commoner in men and tended to occur at a later age than other tumours (60+). Transitions were seen from 'tumours composed of keratinized squamous epithelium' to 'undifferentiated forms'. Due to surrounding inflammation or collapse these were often pear or wedge shaped. They sometimes reached an enormous bulk by continuous growth without causing metastases, grew along bronchial walls and in some cases cavitated. **Anaplastic tumours (including oat cell)** occurred at about 40+ years of age, produced large nodal masses causing compression of the larger bronchi and in other cases a 'sunburst appearance' of lymphogenous spread. **Adenocarcinomas** involved the segmental bronchi and their immediate branches and tended to occur more peripherally than other tumours. In **bronchiolar cell carcinomas** the epithelium varied from case to case and from place to place within the same tumour. In some the cells were of a tall columnar mucus producing type in a single layer ('pulmonary adenomatosis') with only a few ciliated cells. In several cases the epithelial cells were more variable with scanty mucus and bizarre and irregular gigantic forms. The epithelium may become layered and even fill the distal air spaces whilst the stroma remains intact. Gradations between the two extremes were seen within a single tumour. He found calcification in the form of rounded lamellated psammoma bodies in about 50% of cases but this was not extensive and could not be demonstrated radiographically.

Further references. (non-small cell tumours).

Hukill and Stern (1962) : Histological factors affecting prognosis in **adenocarcinoma** of the lung. Patients with anaplastic tumours had a uniformly short survival and those with adenosquamous type had a relatively long survival. Other factors associated with a poor prognosis were (i) hilar node involvement (ii) involvement of lymphatic vessels, and (iii) the finding of exfoliative tumour cells on sputum cytology. Association of the tumour with an old parenchymal scar appeared to be associated with relatively long survival.

MAYO CLINIC SERIES - patients who had lung resections, (inoperable cases excluded):
(a) Lehar et al. (1967) : **Adenocarcinoma** - 126 patients. 75% had parenchymal masses and 18% hilar involvement - these were all potentially resectable cases - see Carr (1983).
(b) Byrd et al. (1968) : **Squamous cell carcinoma** - 263 patients. Most commonly presents (68%) as a hilar mass with ± obstructive pneumonitis or collapse distal to the lesions. Less commonly (24%) a circumscribed mass which may cavitate. No notching in Mayo series Eight of 263 = Normal chest radiograph due to central tumour. Eight were Pancoast tumours.
        Large cell carcinoma - 97 cases. 65% had peripheral or apical masses - 70% > 4 cm. in diameter. No notching but irregular margin. Cavitation occurred.
        Small cell - 114 cases. 87 (76%) had **hilar prominence** or a **hilar** or **peri-hilar** mass - 40% of these had bronchial obstruction, 16% mediastinal widening due to nodal masses. 32% had a peripheral or apical mass - only finding in 14% , 1 Pancoast. Notching of the tumour margin was **not** seen, nor cavitation.

Woodring and Stelling (1983a) : Studied 100 cases of **adenocarcinoma** presenting from 1976 to 1982 and noted that although these are generally accepted to occur as solitary, peripheral, subpleural or pulmonary masses with relatively infrequent hilar and rare mediastinal involvement, their cases showed hilar masses in 40% and mediastinal masses as well in 27% - in all 51% had central mediastinal involvement. They were more pleomorphic than is usually recognised and comprised 20-30% of all primary lung tumours. They felt that the biological behaviour of adenocarcinoma is more aggressive than squamous and the overall survival is considerably worse. At autopsy nodes were found to be involved in approximately 80%, the pleura 60% and the contralateral lung in 40%. 90% of men with this tumour were smokers and 80% women. The average length of survival is about eighteen months.
The difference in their findings from those of Lehar et al. is probably because Woodring and Stelling included inoperable cases in their study.
Woodring and Stelling (1983b) : Pointed out that (1) **adenocarcinoma** arising in or metastasising to a central location is not rare as is often thought and (2) the radiographic manifestations of any disease may change if the histopathological criteria used to diagnose that disease are changed. As further revisions occur in the criteria for the diagnosis of lung carcinoma further changes may be expected to occur in the radiographic manifestations of lung cancer.
Zwirewich et al. (1990) : Multiple adenocarcinoma of the lung - CT pathological correlation.

Theros (1977) : Studied 1,257 patients with lung tumours from the Archives of the US Armed Forces Institute of Pathology; average age was 53 years, ranging from 6 years (an adenoma) to 84 (squamous carcinoma). Peak incidence for carcinoma was seen in the sixth decade (with adenomas tending to be 20 years younger). 60% were on the right side with 60% involving the upper lobes, whilst 58% were central.
Lobulation was seen in 53% of peripheral masses. When well marginated or circumscribed, prognosis tended to be better and indicated well differentiated tumours. Those which showed no lobulation or had poorly defined margins were termed "smooth ball" (like 'tennis balls'), or "coin" lesions, depending on their size.
Cavitation was seen in 30% of squamous masses, the next commonest showing cavitation in this series being bronchiolo-alveolar carcinoma. Often a cavity was observed by being filled with fluid. Cavities were also caused by secondary infection but cavity size alone was a poor denominator as it may be filled with fluid or blood.
40% of all peripheral masses were adenocarcinomas and 5% of peripheral tumours arose from scar tissue. 22% were squamous and in this series 65% of squamous tumours arose in the larger or segmental bronchi (altered by metaplasia after chronic injury into a 'tougher protective integument like the skin when insulted by a harsh environment full of air pollutants. The smoker inhaling a great concentration of such pollutants ... may account for the more proximal location of most epidermoid carcinomas.') He also found that carcinoids and oat-cell tumours tended to arise in the proximal larger bronchi. Calcification was seen in only seven cases, four being due to engulfment of old granulomatous lesions.

Sider (1990) : Radiographic manifestations of primary bronchogenic carcinoma.

Kazerooni et al. (1994) : Adenosquamous carcinoma of the lung - radiological appearances - spectrum - typically a peripheral solitary nodule, less commonly a central hilar mass pr superior sulcus tumour. Scar or fibrosis within the lungs suggests that, like adenocarcinoma, it may arise in scarred lung parenchyma.

Kuriyama et al. (1999) : Ground-glass opacity on thin-section CT: Value in differentiating subtypes of adenocarcinoma of the lung.

Aoki et al. (2000) : There are two types of peripheral lung adenocarcinomas on CT sections (i) a localised ground-glass opacity with slow growth and (ii) a solid mass with rapid growth. The first type may cause a desmoplastic or scar type reaction.

Incidence of the different cell types of lung cancer.

Besides the figures given with the various headings above, some series have shown somewhat different incidences of the cell types, e.g.

Auerbach et al. (1975 - from New York) : In a series of 662 autopsies, found the following percentages - squamous in 35 %, adenocarcinoma in 25 %, small cell in 25 % and undifferentiated in 15 %.

Walter and Pryce (1955a - from Harefield Hospital, London) : In a consecutive series of 207 resected lung cancers found the following - squamous in 60 %, adenocarcinomas in 15.5 %, oat cell in 16 %, 'polygonal cell' tumours in 8 % and malignant 'adenomas' in 0.5 %.

Vincent et al. (1977) : Studied almost 1,700 cases of bronchial carcinoma and noted that in the period 1962 - 1975, adenocarcinoma increased from 17 to 30%, whilst squamous had dropped from approximately 50% to 25%, partly as a result of reclassification.

Capewell et al. (1991) : Lung cancer in life-long non-smokers - 74 /3070 patients with lung cancer (77% female and 26% male) - 42% adeno., 32% squamous and 15% small cell.

Rudd (1996) : Small cell (15 - 20%), squamous (40%), adeno (20%) and large cell undifferentiated (20%).

Sone et al. (1997) : Squamous 30 - 40%, adeno 25 - 30%, small cell 20% and large cell undifferentiated 10 - 15%.

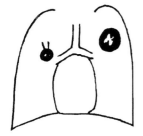 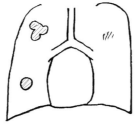 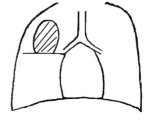

(a) **Squamous**
 (i) Tumour arising in a segmental bronchus. (ii) Cavitating peripheral mass, with irregular inner (and outer) wall (male preponderance).

(b) **Adenocarcinoma**
 (i) Lobulated peripheral mass.
 (ii) Ill-defined lesion or 'small area of consolidation'.
 (female preponderance).

(c) **Large cell anaplastic**
 Large rapidly growing peripheral mass.

(d) Oat or small-cell cancer - large or small peripheral mass (cavitation uncommon) Kerley's lines and lymphangitis. Large hilar, mediastinal and neck nodes (hilar and subcarinal nodes may be massive). Pressure on oesophagus and/ or SVC. Pleural and/ or pericardial effusions. Bone involvement in 50% (on isotope scan or MR). Liver deposits in 40 to 50% (may be massive). Adrenal deposits. Abdominal para-aortic nodes + lower limb oedema.

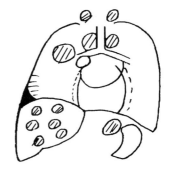

Fig. 24.3 Diagrams showing the typical radiographic appearances of the main cell types of bronchial carcinoma.

Chapter 24c : **The Radiologists' Role in the Investigation of Lung Cancer, TNM Staging, and the value of Radiological Surveys of Screening for the Detection of Lung Cancer.**

The radiologists' role in the investigation of lung cancer.

Not only should the modern radiologist try to detect lung or mediastinal tumours as early as possible, but when abnormalities are detected he should consider the possible causes, and when a tumour seems likely, show whether there is recognisable tumour metastasis or other serious disease. He should not just write a report giving his suspicions, but also use the many techniques at his disposal to show the full state of the disease. Only he is the expert on radiological techniques, and the author believes that he should instigate these, and not rely upon others to refer the patients back to him. Not only is valuable time lost, but it is more efficient and time saving to the radiologist to do all he can, often at one or two attendances, before referring the patient on to the most appropriate clinical colleague. In many cases the patient will have been first referred by his general practitioner, and sorting out the patients problems can often be done at his first attendance (including the taking of sputum, a simple needle biopsy or fluid aspiration for cytology). Clearly a radiologist cannot see all the patients coming through his department, but he can train his radiographers to consult him about problem cases so that he can study them further. The object should be to practice Clinical Radiology, and not just provide a radiographic and reporting service. Personal involvement with the patients besides being more efficient is also more rewarding, saves time and money, and makes the radiologist a true clinician.

In considering the differential diagnosis, inflammatory or other benign conditions must always be considered. Probably the most gratifying is to find a patient quite ill and with considerable loss of weight and finger clubbing who can be shown to have an empyema, from which he may fully recover after drainage (Illus. **EMPYEMA, Pt. 13**).

One should always try to exclude a non-neoplastic condition and if a tumour is present it should be confirmed by cytology or biopsy. Enlarged intra-thoracic nodes may not be due to lung cancer and can be inflammatory (especially acute aspergillosis - see p. 19.39 & Illus. **ASPERGILLOSIS, Pts. 4 & 29**), due to sarcoidosis, or lymphoma, and these may be amenable to treatment. Even when a neoplasm is present, nodes may be enlarged from reactive hyperplasia, but when patients have anaplastic and/or small cell tumours, enlarged nodes are most likely to be infiltrated by tumour. One also has to remember that normal sized nodes may contain tumour deposits, and that only a histological examination can with any certainty differentiate their nature.

Despite the fact that many patients at the presentation of their tumour will be inoperable, sparing the patient a useless thoracotomy is always of value. Also many may be symptomatic and in severe danger from metastases (e.g. massive nodes in the mediastinum, a severely narrowed trachea, SVC obstruction, or incipient spinal cord compression from spinal deposits) or have severe pain and the radiologist can often arrange that the patient receives appropriate urgent treatment.

Surgical inoperability (**Author's working guide**).
(i) Is the tumour really a primary tumour, and not a secondary deposit or a granuloma?
(ii) Patient's age - if over 70, the tumours may be slow growing and may cause little trouble, before the patient's death from some other cause. In many of these cases the tumour may itself be an incidental finding to other disease processes.
(iii) Emphysema and poor respiratory reserve, coronary or other severe arterial disease - will these allow surgery? Has he sufficient respiratory reserve for a lobectomy or pneumonectomy ? - A guide may be the FEV_1 (forced expiratory volume in litres/ 1 sec.) - most candidates for surgery should have a FEV_1 of 1.5, but a well motivated otherwise fit patient may tolerate lung resection with a lower FEV_1. Also one has to consider the slightly larger volume of the right lung, as compared with the left, and a low figure may well preclude a right pneumonectomy.

What is the state of the coronary, etc., circulation? Is he likely to die from myocardial infarction, during the anaesthetic or postoperatively? (Occasionally a coronary by-pass may be carried out at the same time as a lobectomy via an anterior approach.)
(iv) Has the patient stopped smoking? - our surgeons will not usually carry out chest surgery until the patient has given this up for a month, for fear of post-operative complications.

(v) Other severe disability - hepatic, GI, other tumour (e.g. prostate), etc.

(vi) A paralysed hemidiaphragm on the contralateral side to the tumour, which would upset postoperative respiration - the patient might not get off the ventilator!

(vii) A second lung tumour may be present. If on the same side, and especially if in the same lobe, it may be excised (see p. 4.18 and Illus. **MULTIPLE TUMOURS, Pt. 26a-b**), but if contralateral, surgery is often impractical.

(viii) Metastases or tumour spread:

(a) to bone, liver, brain, etc.;

(b) into neck or mediastinum, esp. nodes (thymic, azygos, para- and pre-tracheal, aorto-pulmonary window, subcarinal, pressure on the oesophagus, etc.);

(c) around great veins (SVC, azygos vein, etc., with or without SVC obstruction - Illus. **CA ADJ SVC/AZY VEIN** and **SVC OBSTRUCTION**) - these are usually impossible to resect (vein walls are quite thin!); - may be palliated by a SVC stent and/or RT - Illus. **SVC STENT.**

(d) chest wall involvement (Illus. **CA EXT CX WALL** and **CA ADJ CX WALL**) - except for possibly a single (etc.) adjacent rib;

(e) into para-aortic fat around the aorta - in some cases the tumour can be readily stripped off the aorta, but recurrence often occurs; Illus. **CA ADJ AORTA.**

(f) into inferior pulmonary vein (Illus. **CA ADJ PULM VEIN**) and pericardium (but the latter may be partially removed);

(g) Pancoast syndrome (Illus. **CA PANCOAST**) but note that a few cases may still be operable - see - ps. 12.5 & 6);

(h) recurrent laryngeal nerve palsy (with involvement of subaortic fossa), but note that an ipsilateral hemidiaphragm palsy is not an absolute contraindication to surgery - it depends on its cause - particularly if long standing;

(i) trans-mucosal /lymphatic spread in the tracheo-bronchial wall;

(j) airways or lymphatic spread (esp. with bronchiolo-alveolar carcinoma);

(k) secondary deposits in the lungs;

(l) lymphangitis carcinomatosa;

(m) diaphragmatic involvement (but in some cases this may be excised);

(n) spread to pleura, malignant effusion, 'knobbly pleura' (with trans-pleural spread), empyema;

(o) chest infection, pneumonia, TB, lung abscess, etc.

Staging system for lung tumours.

This is important in the assessment of lung (and other mediastinal) tumours but note:

(i) surgery in small cell tumours is usually regarded as unhelpful (unless they are small and peripheral), Most are treated by chemotherapy, steroids and/or radiotherapy.

(ii) The demonstration of metastases is important (lymph nodes, bone, liver, brain, etc). However it should be remembered that small metastases may not be demonstrated radiologically.

(iii) What is a small tumour radiologically may be large biologically and pathologically. When they become visible, they are really entering their later phases. The latent period may be months or years and depends on the rate of growth of the particular tumour. Some may produce hormonal or para-neoplastic syndromes when they are still otherwise undetectable (see also Chapter 23).

TNM Staging (1986 + further revision 1997).

T = Primary tumour.

T_{is} Pre-invasive carcinoma (carcinoma in situ).

T_0 No evidence of primary tumour.

T_x Tumour proven by the presence of malignant cells in bronchopulmonary secretions, but not visualised by imaging or bronchoscopy.

T_1 Tumour 3 cm or less in greatest diameter surrounded by lung or visceral pleura, without bronchoscopic evidence of invasion more proximal than the lobar bronchus.

T_2 Tumour with any of the following features of size or extent: > 3 cm in greatest diameter; involves main bronchus; $\geq$ 2 cm distal to the carina, invades the visceral pleura; or associated with collapse or obstructive pneumonitis that extends to the hilar region but does not involve the entire lung.

T_3 Tumour of any size that directly invades any of the following: chest wall (including superior sulcus tumours), diaphragm, mediastinal pleura, parietal pericardium; or tumour in the main bronchus < 2 cm distal to the carina , but without involvement of the carina or associated collapse or obstructive pneumonitis of the entire lung.

T4   Tumour of any size that invades any of the following: mediastinum, heart, great vessels, trachea, oesophagus, vertebral body, carina or tumour with a malignant pleural or pericardial effusion, or with a satellite tumour nodule(s) within the ipsilateral primary-tumour lobe of the lung.

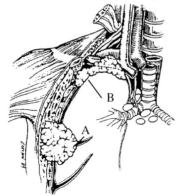

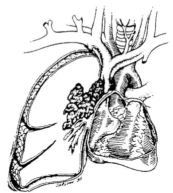

T3 a Localised adjacent chest wall invasion.
T3 b Superior sulcus tumour without
       vertebral invasion.

    T4   A tumour of any size with invasion of the
mediastinum (including the heart, great vessels,
trachea, carina or oesophagus), a vertebral body,
the carina, or the presence of a malignant pleural effusion.

Fig. 24.4 TNM staging (figures and tables reproduced or modified from Mountain, CF, 1986, 'New international staging system for lung cancer', Chest, **89**, 225S - 233S, and 1997, 'Revisions...', Chest, **111**, 1710 - 1717 with permission).

N = Regional lymph nodes.

N_x Regional lymph nodes cannot be accessed.
N_0 No metastasis to regional lymph nodes.
N_1 Metastasis to ipsilateral peribronchial and/or ipsilateral hilar lymph nodes, and intrapulmonary nodes involved by direct extension of the primary tumour.
N_2 Metastasis to ipsilateral mediastinal and/or subcarinal lymph node(s).
N_3 Metastasis to contralateral mediastinal, contralateral hilar, ipsilateral lymph or contralateral scalene or supraclavicular node(s).

M = Distant metastasis.

M_x Presence of distant metastasis cannot be assessed.
M_0 No distant metastasis.
M_1 Distant metastasis present (with site stated).

Notes: (i) A superficial bronchial tumour of any size with its invasive component limited to the bronchial wall and which may extend proximally to the main bronchus is classified as T_1.

(ii) Most pleural effusions associated with lung cancer are due to tumour. However there are a few patients in whom multiple cytopathological examinations of pleural fluid show no tumour. In these cases the fluid is not blood-stained and is not an exudate. With these provisos + clinical judgement dictate that the effusion is not related to the tumour, the effusion should be ignored for staging and classified T_1, T_2 or T_3 as appropriate.

(iii) Pericardial effusions are classified in the same way.

(iv) Separate metastatic tumour nodule(s) in the ipsilateral nonprimary-tumour lobe(s) of the lung are also classified M_1.

(v) Nodes are measured according to their short axes (as described in Chapter 13 - see Fig. 13.9, p. 13.16 for lymph node mapping system).

Stage groupings are:

0				Carcinoma in situ
Ia	T_1	N_0	M_0	Lobectomy/ pneumonectomy
1b	T_2	N_0	M_0	
IIa	T_1	N_1	M_0	Pneumonectomy (hilar node).
IIb	T_2	N_1	M_0	
	T_3	N_0	M_0	
IIIa	T_3	N_0 or $_1$	M_0	}
	T_{1-3}	N_2	M_0	}Mediastinal nodes involved

Possible operability ends here .... }   Poor overall prognosis.

IIIb	any T	N_3	M_0	}
	T_4	any N	M_0	}
IV	any T	any N	M_1	} Distant metastasis.

(A prefix 'p' may be added to denote surgical histopathology.)

61% of those with stage Ia disease and 38% of those with stage Ib are expected to survive $\geq$ 5 yrs.

The original system was first proposed by Denoix (1946) and was adapted by Mountain et al. (1974) and Carr and Mountain (1974 from the MD Anderson Hospital, Texas). It was adopted by the "American Joint Committee for Cancer Staging and End Result Reporting' (1979) and the 'International Union Against Cancer' (1980). The 1986 modifications were proposed by Mountain (see also Friedman, 1988). These ignored non-malignant effusions and distinguished between local invasion and spread to nodes which can be removed and non-resectable spread. The supraclavicular and scalene nodes were changed from distant metastases to N_3 as they are accessible to regional radiotherapy. The aim of the modifications was to help produce conformity between different centres, and to help assess patients for surgery or other treatment.
See also - Mountain (1990) - in refs. below - expanded possibilities for surgery in lung cancer - survival in stage IIIa disease; however others felt that Stage IIIa is little better than IIIb.
      Mountain (1997) - revisions in the international system for staging lung cancer - the azygos node was placed in station 4, classifying it as N_2 (see also Ko et al, 2000 & p. 13.16).

For **undifferentiated and small cell carcinomas**, a **'limited/extensive'** system is generally used instead of the TNM classification (see also ps. 24.16 - 17).
'Limited' means : confined to one hemithorax, including nodes, but excludes cytology positive pleural effusions.
'Extensive' means : extending beyond the confines of one hemithorax, plus or minus mediastinal or ipsilateral supraclavicular disease or ipsilateral pleural effusion.

Radiologically occult lung cancer - (see Illus. **CA T1 & TX**).
    Some tumours, which are invisible on plain radiographs, are discovered by sputum cytology, bronchoscopy, or tomography (including CT). Those only found by sputum cytology are classified as T_X lesions. Very careful bronchoscopy (with biopsy) may confirm their sites within the tracheo-bronchial tree. In a few cases these may be treated trans-bronchially, but review is necessary as recurrence may occur or new tumour nodules develop. Even some of these tumours may present with metastases.

Some references.
Tao et al. (1982) : Cytological diagnosis of radiologically occult squamous carcinoma - 20 cases - 5 'in situ', 3 microinvasive and 12 early invasive - four of the last group had positive nodes.
Cortese et al. (1983) : 54 cases in 10 years at Mayo Clinic - all were squamous. 11 patients developed a second primary squamous tumour, six of which were again occult.
Woolner et al. (1984) : Roentgenographically occult lung cancer - pathologic findings and frequency of multicentricity during a 10 year period.
Foster, W. et al. (1985) : Localised peri-bronchial thickening - a CT sign of occult bronchogenic carcinoma.

Shure et al. (1991) : 16% of patients with central bronchial tumours may have no signs of obstruction on **(inspiratory)** PA films. **These need expiratory views!**

Radiological 'WORK UP' of patients with lung cancer - as used by the author.
1. PA and lateral chest radiographs supplemented by rib, spinal, etc. views as indicated by clinical problem or plain chest radiographic appearance, etc.
2. Ultrasound of liver, renal and adrenal areas - also of chest to confirm pleural fluid or to find a small effusion and localise its position for immediate aspiration. Check lower neck/upper mediastinum by ultrasound, together with palpation for the possible presence of enlarged lymph nodes and if present, perform a needle biopsy.
3. Conventional AP and/or lateral tomograms may be taken to confirm the presence of a mass or its shape. Inclined frontal tomograms were used by the author for many years to demonstrate the trachea, the larger bronchi and subcarinal and hilar areas etc. (Illus. **INCL FRONT TOMO**).
4. CT (usually with IV contrast medium) is performed to examine the base of the neck, the thorax and upper abdomen (including liver, renal and adrenal areas). Sections are usually taken at 1 or 1.5 cm intervals. For areas of special interest, after noting the position of the tumour on plain radiographs - which should always be available at the time the CT is performed) the narrower intervals are used with a section thickness of 0.5 or 1 cm. In the suspected normal areas 1 cm thickness and 1.5 cm spacing usually suffices. Extra sections may be taken as felt necessary after inspection of the planned sections. (The brain is only examined in patients with neurological signs or symptoms).
5. Isotope bone scans are particularly important in patients with small cell tumours. They should be undertaken on patients with symptoms possibly referable to the skeleton, pain on the opposite of the chest from the tumour, etc, and in whom a simple plain radiograph of the ribs or spine, etc. has been negative or doubtful.
   It is always best to perform the isotope bone scan prior to CT, so that suspicious areas on the bone scan can be further carefully examined by CT - the author usually does this at the same attendance - bone scan first.
Note for the detection of recurrent cancer, or reticulosis, CT, MR, ultra-sound and isotope bone scans are often more accurate than plain radiography. MR may also more readily distinguish fibrosis from tumour.)
6. Cyto-histology is very important and should be obtained as soon as possible and by the easiest and least traumatic route.
(a) Sputum cytology - following some simple physiotherapy (easily given by the radiologist or a nurse) many patients are able to cough up useful sputum - most likely to be positive if slightly blood stained. An early morning specimen brought in if he is returning for CT etc, may also be positive.
(b) Pleural fluid - the diagnostic aspiration of a few ml may give positive cytology. This should be done under ultra-sound control, and when only a trace of fluid is present its aspiration in expiration may be more effective. Large effusions may be aspirated for symptomatic relief or prior to subsequent radiography or tomography to show the underlying lung pathology.
(c) Biopsy of a metastasis in bone (rib, pelvis, etc.), accessible lymph node or liver.
(d) Fibre-optic bronchoscopy, and endo-bronchial or trans-bronchial biopsy.
(e) Percutaneous lung and/or pleural biopsy. If the lesion is large and is situated adjacent to the parietal pleura and chest wall (with no intervening air-filled lung), a fine needle aspiration biopsy may be carried out at once on an out-patient basis.
   Smaller nodules will need more careful localisation (e.g. with CT).Those deep in the lung will need admission to hospital on a day or overnight basis).
(f) Mediastinoscopy may be necessary in a few cases.
(For further details of biopsy techniques see Chapter 21).

Two series from other centres in the UK.
   Delany (1990) from Southampton: 'Lung cancer - early detection and planning of further investigation' - wrote " Rapid detection, diagnosis and staging is largely in the hands of the diagnostic radiologist who should strive to maximise the chance of cure or quality of remaining life." He recommended the AMBER system for chest radiography (see ps. 20.6 - 7), thus flattening contrast and increasing its accuracy and always took lateral as well as PA views. Like the present author, he felt that a written radiological report is insufficient if a serious abnormality is detected - it is a doctor's duty to **personally inform a colleague of a serious abnormality in one of his patients**.
   He still uses <u>conventional tomography and fluoroscopy</u> to confirm or refute abnormalities. "When radiographic findings are strongly suggestive of tumour it is important to attempt to stage the disease and be responsible for

instigating the next imaging procedure which may be head, thorax or abdominal CT scan or liver and bone isotope imaging. The shortest, cheapest and most comfortable pathological definitive diagnosis and staging should be sought and where appropriate the radiologist should offer to perform intervention procedures with imaging guidance."

He also stressed the importance of looking behind the first ribs on plain radiographs for possible apical tumours and the commonness of second lung tumours - a point noted also by the present author (see p. 4.18).

Gomersall et al. (1992- from Aberdeen) reported their staging results in patients with bronchogenic carcinoma. They wrote 'Our local policy in those patients considered operable clinically, on CT of the chest and at bronchoscopy is to proceed with a radionucleide bone scan, ultrasound of the upper abdomen and CT head scan.' They reviewed a total of 1065 patients and found potentially resectable disease in 361. Ultrasound in 233 (of the 361) gave a 4.7% positive rate for metastatic disease, the bone scans (in 265) suggested skeletal involvement in 15.5% and CT head scans a 6.7% positive rate in 224 (reduced to 1.9% when used as a final screening procedure).

Some further references.

McLoud et al. (1979) : Used a prototype EMI CT 5000 Scanner to examine 109 patients. CT was of value in detecting **direct mediastinal and pleural extension** of lung cancer, and in patients with solitary or multiple nodules by detecting additional lesions and calcification.

Underwood et al. (1979) : CT of the thorax in the staging of bronchial carcinoma.

Ekholm et al. (1980) : CT in preoperative staging of bronchial carcinoma.

Hirleman et al. (1980) : Resectability of primary lung carcinoma - diagnostic staging review.

Faling et al. (1981) : CT of mediastinum in staging bronchial carcinoma.

Rea et al. (1981) : Accuracy of CT in the assessment of the mediastinum in bronchial carcinoma.

Baron et al. (1982c) : CT in preoperative assessment of bronchial carcinoma.

Modini et al. (1982) : CT in TNM staging of lung cancer.

Spiro et al. (1982) CT of the thorax in the diagnosis and management of malignant disease.

Shevland et al. (1983), from New Zealand : Assessed the mediastinum by CT in 57 patients with lung cancer. They felt that a negative CT scan made mediastinoscopy unnecessary, but **a positive CT scan needed tissue confirmation, as scanning techniques could not distinguish benign from malignant lymph nodes and false positive diagnosis of tumour infiltration could easily be made.**

Tisi et al. (1983) : Clinical staging of primary lung cancer.

Castellino et al. (1986b) : Contribution of chest CT in the initial staging evaluation.

Heavey et al. (1986) : CT in staging $T_1N_0M_0$ lung cancer.

Conces et al. (1989) : CT evaluation in $T_1N_0M_0$ lung cancer.

Duncan et al. (1993) : CT in $T_1N_0M_0$ non-small cell bronchial carcinoma - 9 of 63 patients (14%) had metastatic spread rendering them inoperable.

Armstrong (1990) : Cost effective analysis - an example using chest CT for $T_1N_0M_0$ lung cancer.

Seely et al. (1993) : T_1 lung cancer - studied 104 patients with CT prior to mediastinoscopy or surgery - nodal metastases were present in 22 (21%).

Quint et al. (1987) : CT in the assessment of pneumonectomy versus lobectomy - **CT gave a poor sensitivity for showing central bronchial and pulmonary artery involvement, with both false positives and negatives**. Thick (1 cm.) sections could suggest that tumours were crossing a major fissure, when no such spread had taken place, and when the fissure could be seen to be normal on thin sections.

Lewis et al. (1990): Can CT of the chest stage lung cancer? - The negative predictive accuracy for mediastinal lymph node metastasis remains high, but invasive staging can be deferred to definitive thoracotomy when no lymphadenopathy is seen on CT.

Mountain (1990) : Expanded possibilities for surgical treatment of lung cancer - survival in stage IIIa disease, esp. if the spread is to the hilar and peribronchial nodes. Peripheral tumours invading the chest wall, in the superior sulcus and with limited involvement of the pericardium or of the main bronchi were included. A 5 year cumulative survival rate of 28% was found in 198 consecutive patients with non-small cell cancer. A superior outcome was found with squamous cancers.

Salvattiera et al. (1990) from Spain : Extrathoracic staging of bronchogenic carcinoma - non-small bronchial cancer does **not** follow a set pattern of metastasis, but the rate with **adeno-carcinoma is significantly higher and dose not correlate with TNM staging**. 20% of brain deposits were asymptomatic and were recommended with adeno- and large cell carcinoma. 12% of patients with liver deposits did not have organ specific indicators to suspect this.

Stitik (1990) : Staging of lung cancer - CT demonstration of **enlarged lymph nodes** should only be a guide for further studies, as they **may only be reactive** (esp. true in patients with post. obstructive pneumonia). Continuity of a mass with the pleura does not indicate invasion, only when definite erosion, destruction or interdigitation is present can the CT findings be relied upon. MR may show the extent of chest wall invasion better than CT esp. in patients with superior sulcus tumours. A search for occult metastases in patients with non-small cell cancer, who do not have clinical or laboratory evidence to suggest metastatic disease should not be performed. If there is any suspicion of metastases, a CT scan of the brain as well as bone is indicated.

Bragg (1990) : The applications of imaging in lung cancer.
(i) Screening of high risk patients is not recommended.
(ii) Cross-sectional imaging should be tailored to the staging process with a large central primary or to confirm abnormalities seen on plain films.
(iii) Percutaneous biopsies were reserved for the patients at greater risk for surgery.
Woodring and Johnson (1991) : CT distinction of central thoracic masses. The most valuable CT feature in distinguishing central lung from mediastinal masses was the **poorly defined interface of over 90% of lung cancers with the lung**. Mediastinal masses tend to push in front of themselves a **smooth mediastinal connective tissue layer and the interface with the lung appears uniform.**

Stiglbauer et al. (1991) : Found **CT to be superior to MR for preoperative staging of bronchogenic carcinoma, as mediastinal invasion tended to be over diagnosed by MR.**
Webb et al. (1991) : CT and MR imaging in staging non-small cell bronchogenic carcinoma - report of the Radiologic Diagnostic Oncology Group - **MR should only be used for specific indications such as the extent of chest wall invasion or in patients with superior sulcus or peripheral carcinomas.**
Aitken and Armstrong (1992) : CT scanning in lung cancer.
(i) > 70% of lung cancer patients have metastases to regional lymph nodes at the time of diagnosis.
(ii) CT is not very sensitive in the early diagnosis of invasion of the diaphragm, pericardium or pleura - to be certain that a tumour has invaded the mediastinum there must be clear interdigitation of tumour with mediastinal fat.
(iii) nodes < 1 cm in short axis diameter are unlikely to contain tumour.
Izbacki et al. (1992) : CT and surgical assessment of nodes in lung carcinoma - strongly suggested that the node status depends on the tumour type and the node region studied. Adenocarcinoma gave rise to a high proportion of tumour-positive normal-sized nodes, whereas squamous showed a high proportion of enlarged tumour-free nodes.
Cybulsky et al. (1992) : Prognostic significance of CT in resected N_2 lung cancer - study of 124 pts. - 61 with mediastinal node metastases had negative CT - however despite this they had a better prognosis than those with enlarged nodes. Over half the negative exams. were in pts. with adenocarcinomas.
Miller et al. (1992) : Concluded that staging is best judged by bronchoscopy and at thoracotomy - CT has "fallen short in predicting direct invasion of the mediastinum and chest wall".
Daly, B. et al. (1993) : N2 lung cancer outcome in pts. with false-negative CT of the chest - of 681 consecutive patients, 37 (of 501 - 7.4%) had false negative CT results for mediastinal node involvement found at thoracotomy or mediastinoscopy. 25 with peripheral tumours had longer survival times than 12 with central tumours. There was no correlation in these with cell type, areas of the mediastinum involved or the extent of nodal involvement.
Padovani et al. (1993) : Showed that MR was superior to CT for the evaluation of chest wall invasion in 34 pts. T_1 weighted images were better than T_2 or Gd enhanced images. no false positive results occurred with the T_1 images, but the contrast enhanced images led to false positive results in two patients without chest wall invasion.
Seeley et al. (1993) : Compared CT and surgical findings in 104 patients with T_1 lesions and found a higher prevalence of lymph node metastases than previously reported (21%).
Suzuki et al. (1993) : Used **ultrasound to detect chest wall invasion** in 120 patients with lung cancer abutting the chest wall, 19 of whom proved to have invasion at surgery. These 19 were correctly identified by ultrasound. Two false positives were present, due to fibrous adhesions between the tumour and the chest wall. Ultrasound was considered positive when two of the following three findings were identified:
(i) disruption of the pleura,
(ii) extension through the chest wall, and
(iii) fixation of the tumour during breathing.
Webb et al. (1993) : Studied interobserver variability in CT and MR staging of lung cancer. 80 examinations on 40 pts. were read by four expert observers on one day. The greatest variations were in the evaluation of mediastinal lymph nodes.
Armstrong and Vincent (1993) : **Review of 'staging non-small cell lung cancer'** - concluded :
"Staging non-small cell lung cancer is a multidisciplinary process utilizing imaging, bronchoscopy and biopsy. Chest radiography and computed tomography are currently the routine imaging procedures for assessing intrathoracic spread and determining resectability.
MRI, ultrasound and radionucleide imaging are reserved for specific indications. The essential questions to be answered are: (a) has the tumour spread to hilar or mediastinal lymph nodes and, if so, which nodal groups are involved? (b) has the tumour involved the chest wall or mediastinum and, if so, is the tumour still potentially surgically curable?
If chest radiography and CT show no evidence of spread beyond the lung, other than to ipsilateral hilar nodes, in a patient who is fit for surgery, without evidence for extrathoracic metastases, and bronchoscopy shows that the tumour is resectable, then the patient should be offered surgical resection without further preoperative invasive procedures. Patients with ipsilateral hilar node involvement are managed similarly to patients whose tumours are totally confined to the lung, but in the realisation that the prognosis is poorer.

Spread to ipsilateral nodes, chest wall or mediastinum, whilst not necessarily precluding surgical resection, has a significant adverse effect on prognosis and if surgery is undertaken, it is performed with the understanding that the figures for 5-year survival are poor - up to 35% at best.

The poor specificity of computed tomography in determining nodal involvement must be appreciated. Nodal enlargement, whilst it may be due to metastatic carcinoma, may also be due to coincidental benign disease or to reactive hyperplasia directly connected to the presence of the tumour. Thus, biopsy confirmation of neoplastic involvement by mediastinoscopy, mediastinotomy or needle aspiration is usually essential before a patient is denied surgery."

Armstrong (1994) : Commented "Currently the only useful imaging sign of hilar/mediastinal lymph node metastases is enlargement. Neither CT density nor magnetic resonance imaging (MRI) signal density have proved reliable in determining or excluding metastatic involvement and gallium-67 radionucleide imaging is too insensitive and non-specific to be a routine staging test. Hope has been expressed recently that positron emission tomography with fluoro-deoxy-glucose may provide more reliable information than CT scanning, but whether this proves to be the case in the long run remains to be seen."

The **author of this book** largely concurs with the above comments, but has two important provisos: (i) that **all patients on first presentation at the radiology department with a probable carcinoma should have ultrasound of the liver carried   out.** If metastases are shown, then further investigation re possible surgery is out of the question. Ultrasound only takes a few moments, and should be done in the upright as well as the recumbent position (or lesions in the anterior upper aspect of the liver may be missed) - at the same time the other upper abdominal organs (kidneys, spleen and adrenals) can also be examined, and the diaphragmatic movement checked. (ii) **Chest wall pain should   always   suggest   chest   wall   invasion**, but this may be mimicked by an inflammatory response.

Primack et al. (1994) : Concluded that CT can be used to confirm or exclude the presence of a bronchogenic carcinoma and to obviate thoracotomy. CT's specificity is limited in its value for staging mediastinal lymph nodes.

In their study any nodules that were diffusely calcified were considered definitely benign. Solitary nodules ≤ 2 cm in diameter with smooth margins, and nodules with satellite lesions or localised areas of consolidation were considered probably benign. Non-calcified solitary nodules with spiculated margins or a diameter › 2 cm were considered to have bronchogenic carcinoma. Multiple nodules were considered to be due to metastatic disease.

Roobottom et al. (1994) : Studied 60 patients believed to have potentially curable treatable bronchial tumours by both CT and MR and found both methods were complementary in staging. All tumours were demonstrated by both methods, usually with the same efficacy. Of 16 with mediastinal invasion, MR was the only method to demonstrate it in 31%. MR was also better in showing pleural involvement, but CT was superior in showing bronchial involvement.

Shirakawa et al. (1994) : Used CT performed both in **inspiration and expiration** to note changes in the relative location between tumours of the chest wall and found it to be a reliable indicator of the lack of parietal pleural invasion of tumours in the middle and lower lobes.   (see also ps. 12.20 - 21).

White, P. et al. (1994) : In patients being considered for resection of lung cancer, CT used as the sole method of staging is of limited value in differentiating stage I or II and stage III tumours; thus patients should not be denied the opportunity for curative surgery on equivocal CT signs.

Houston et al. (1995) : US assessment of hemidiaphragmatic movement in 30 cases of non-small cell lung cancer as a sign of mediastinal invasion - no patient with an abnormal US examination had a resectable tumour.

Armstrong (1996) : Stage IIIa has little better prognosis than stage IIIb. CT staging is still adequate for surgery because any biopsy test will still be at random. MR is not routinely used - is no better and no worse than CT for residual nodes. MR is particularly good for studying Pancoast tumours particularly in coronal reconstructions.

Bakke et al. (1997)) : Felt that abdominal metastases were only found in pts. with clinical findings indicative of widespread disease (study of 279 consecutive patients).

Goddard et al. (1999) : Study of 50 pts. - MR was better at predicting the outcome than CT+surgery. **Squamous cell ca** gave rise to a heterogeneous signal in both primary tumour and nodes. MR was particularly good in defining chest wall and mediastinal invasion. Gd. opposed phase shift could distinguish between benign and malignant adrenal enlargements - malignant were often surrounded by soft tissue swelling. MR for biopsy control was less good than CT as the needle tip could not be defined.

How much reliability should be placed on radiological CT staging?

A problem with many of the published studies and series is that these evaluated the radiological appearances with surgical findings and surgical pathology and **not   with   survival** (shown in graph form in Fig. 24.7, p.24.37)**.** The latter is clearly the more important, the former apparently being more scientific, but unless these correlate, the results can be rather misleading. Many surgeons have found that heroic type surgery, particularly in patients with poorly differentiated tumours, is of little benefit to them, and only causes considerable morbidity, before severe recurrence occurs within a few months (see also notes on reported surgical series ps. 24.39 - 41). Many leave the follow up of such patients to physicians, oncologists and general practitioners, who probably find the above more frequently. Thus in many centres the tendency has developed not to refer patients for surgery if the bronchoscopic, radiological and/or cellular pathology appears bad. In Bristol (Goddard, 1994) a preliminary report on radiology, surgery, surgical pathology and survival has confirmed this impression.

Why should there be this discrepancy? This appears to be due to tumours spreading microscopically far further than most diagnostic methods show at the present time. Surgical pathology may be incomplete because (i) only a tiny number of tumour cells may be present in e.g. the chest wall or enlarged lymph nodes, (ii) they may already have passed more distally through the tissues (note the pathway for tumour spread through the submucosal lymphatic plexuses in the tracheo-bronchial tree - Fig. 13.2, ps. 13.3, and the diagrams showing lymphatics by-passing nodes - Figs. 13.3 &4, ps. 13.7 - 8 - both causing 'skip' metastases), (iii) not all reactive nodes are truly non-malignant, and may be enlarged from a 'sarcoid' type of reaction in relation to the tumour with only a very few metastasised cells causing this (ps. 19.74 - 75) and (iv) other organs may be involved at the time of surgery, the metastases being mostly too small to be detected by presently available methods.

The conclusion is that it appears that there is a lot of truth in the statement 'if the picture looks bad with lung cancer, it almost certainly   is', and simple inexpensive tests (Bucky view of ribs showing destruction, U/S of liver or diaphragm, etc.) may give a more reliable assessment than more complicated and expensive ones.* Also most oat cell tumours have metastasised widely at the time of diagnosis (to nodes, liver, bone marrow, etc.), and few if any patients with these are benefited by surgery, perhaps only those with small tumours which are resected without prior biopsy or knowledge of the cellular pathology. As explained in Chapter 14, the outlook is almost invariably bad with malignant pleural disease, especially mesothelioma, and patients with the latter usually have more spread than is radiologically detectable.

See also discussion re nodal metastases - Chapter 13.

* Gross, B.H. in 1995 Year Book of Diagnostic Radiology p.47 wrote "Once the cornerstone of noninvasive lung cancer staging, CT has come under attack. A number of articles have questioned whether CT's sensitivity for mediastinal lymph node metastases exceeds 60%..." However on p. 50 and commenting on Daly et al. (1993) : 'N2 lung cancer in patients with false negative chest CT scans' (see p. 24.28) - he pointed out that in their series of 501 pts. only 37 (7.4%) had false negative CTs.

Gross, B.H. in 1997 Year Book of Radiology p.88 commented on a paper by Lähle et al (1995) on the survival of pts. in relation to CT & surgical staging that the **real goal is to assess outcome** and that survival rates for CT & surgical staging were reasonably parallel

Value of Radiological Surveys for the Detection of Lung Tumours.
Results of Mass Surveys.

Although many 'mass' surveys have been carried out on various population groups, including those in certain occupations or industries, in an attempt to detect lung cancer earlier, the value of these surveys has not been overwhelming in comparison with the detection of tuberculosis by Mass Miniature Radiography (MMR) thirty or forty years ago. Quite often small tumours are very difficult to recognise, and the results of some surveys have shown that tumours have been missed even as close as one to six months of the clinical presentation of the disease. Sometimes this has been due to observer error, poor radiographic technique, or the difficulty of recognising that any abnormality is present (see discussion in Chapter 4 re the problems of early recognition, and also Appendix 4) : quite often, particularly with rapidly growing tumours, an abnormality on an earlier study may have been difficult or almost impossible to detect. Certainly the question of the value of miniature radiography in the absence of large numbers of patients with tuberculosis, the small pick-up rate of operable carcinoma and increasing costs has caused the cessation of this in the UK. In a few hospitals miniature chest radiographs are taken of asymptomatic medical out patients, etc using scanning techniques or a large size intensifier (see p. 20.3).

Nevertheless, when bronchial tumours are found fortuitously and the patients have no symptoms, the prognosis is often much better. Asymptomatic patients are usually detected on radiographs taken for other reasons e.g. attendance at hospital for IVP or GI tract examination, when it is useful to take a chest radiograph in people over 40 years of age, pre-surgical or pre-employment examinations, etc. Such people are more likely to benefit from surgery, the majority of symptomatic patients having incurable disease.

A number of surveys, both in the UK and elsewhere have been undertaken for the detection of lung cancer. These have been somewhat disappointing, particularly with regard to overall survival rates, nevertheless the detection rate is similar in heavy smokers to that with breast cancer (up to 6/1,000 examined). In the general population, the pick up rate is very much lower (under 1/1,000).

Notes on some surveys for the detection of lung cancer.

Garland (1955) : Estimated that not more than half of the lung cancers present in the examined population had been found by mass surveys.

Rigler (1957a) : Found that whilst much had been achieved by mass surveys in the detection of tuberculosis, there had been only a minor success with lung cancer. He felt that surveys were often improperly used and wrote 'The personnel is inadequate, rapidity of interpretation is far too great, and there is a lack of interest on the part of the examiners. The examination of 100 or even 200 chest films per hour is not an uncommon procedure*. Such work done hour after hour will invariably lead to a failure to observe the smaller lesions, the very ones that are most likely to be curable.'

The Philadelphia Neoplasm Research Project - Boucot et al. (1961 & 1964) and Weiss et al. (1966, 1969 & 1982) did a periodic survey, of over 6,000 men aged over 45 (of whom 86% were smokers or ex-smokers) who were studied with 70 mm radiographs on entering the project and these were repeated every six months for ten years. Eighty men were found to have lung cancer at their first visit and 121 had tumours found later. Although only 8% had a five year survival, some interesting points emerged. Of 830 non-smokers, none developed lung cancer. All three main types, squamous, adenocarcinoma and small cell (oat cell) had a dose-response relationship with smoking. Of those who developed lung cancer, it was noticeable that some had more severe symptoms than others, i.e. cough, sputum and dyspnoea. Unilateral wheeze, haemoptysis and worsening cough were late symptoms.

These authors noted that in the cases which presented later, a retrospective review showed that **the earliest abnormalities due to lung cancer were variable and often unimpressive**.

Bidstrup (1964) : From London in presenting the results of routine examinations including full-sized chest radiographs of men working in industries with special hazards associated with lung cancer, reported that in one industry 36% of cases failed to show any evidence of the tumour 1-5 months before the death of the patient. In a further 26% no evidence was seen 6-10 months before the patient's death. In another industry, Bidstrup found that in 40% of cases death occurred less than 6 months after the diagnosis had been made radiologically. (The radiographs seemed, however, to have been of rather poor quality and were probably interpreted poorly by present day standards).

Nash (1968) : In order to study whether six-monthly routine examinations could improve the prognosis of bronchial carcinoma, offered such a service by the mass x-ray units in South London to men aged 45 years or over. 67,400 men attended for a first examination, 75% of these returned at least once, and 197,500 repeat examinations were carried out. These revealed 147 patients with bronchial carcinoma, of whom 27% lived for 4 years or more. Of 83 men undergoing resection, 39 (47%) were alive 4 years later. Men aged 45-54 years, although having as great a proportion of growths resected as the older men, did badly, but the **experience with the 84 older men was encouraging**. The interval between the penultimate and the ultimate routine films was found to affect survival. Even more striking was the relationship of the interval between examinations to the prognosis after resection. Records revealed that six-monthly routine mass radiography picked up 56% of the bronchial carcinomas which developed, while 44% of the men became ill and were diagnosed clinically between the routine examinations. The overall four-year survival rate of the whole group was 18 per cent compared with 9% for all patients in the region, the difference being wholly in patients aged 55 years and over. Nash and his colleagues concluded that a mass x-ray unit concentrating on men aged 55 years and over who were smoking 15 cigarettes a day could salvage four-year survivors at a cost of only £300 each, every 1,000 films picking up one potential four-year survivor. Their figures showed a pick-up rate of 0.7 per 1,000 repeat examinations for men smoking 1-4 cigarettes a day, increasing to 2.8 per 1,000 in those who smoked more than 40 cigarettes daily.

Brett (1969) : Studied the relationship between earlier diagnosis and survival in lung cancer (that had been found at six-monthly examinations by the Mass Radiography Service) and noted considerably increased survival rates. He surveyed 29,416 men in a test group who were radiographed every six months for three years and compared the results with those in a control group of 25,311 men who had had radiographs only at the beginning and end of the three-year period. Excluding the cases of lung cancer discovered at the first x-ray examination, there were 101 cancer cases in the test series and 76 in the control series, giving an annual incidence of 1.1 and 1.0 per thousand respectively. Of the 101 test series cases, 65 were discovered by six-monthly x-ray examination and 36 by other means between surveys. In the test group as a whole, 43.6% of the patients underwent resection compared with 29% in the control group. Of the 65 patients detected by six-monthly surveys, 65% underwent resection. **The five-year survival rate in lung cancer cases discovered by six-monthly examination was 23% compared**

with 6% in the control series, the average expectation of life after diagnosis being 2.5 years in the test cases and 1.2 years in the controls. Of the patients with resected lung cancers, 32% in the test series and 23% in the control series survived for five years. The five-year survival rates for squamous carcinoma and adenocarcinoma in the test series were 28 and 25% respectively, compared with 15% and nil respectively in the control series. On the basis of these results, **Brett concluded that a modest improvement in the prognosis of lung cancer could be achieved through earlier radiological detection**. (Rimington, 1971, showed that in 21,579 male radiography volunteers that there was an increased incidence of lung cancer in those with chronic bronchitis).

Le Roux (1968) : Found that of 4,000 patients with bronchial carcinoma, 192 (4.8%) presented without symptoms and with an abnormal chest radiograph taken for an unrelated purpose. Such patients were more often suitable for surgical resection of the tumours than those who presented because of symptoms. Two thirds had peripheral tumours, and the proportion with undifferentiated tumours was lower in these. The operative mortality and the rate of non-resectability at exploratory thoracotomy (both 5%) were lower and the long-term survival rate for all resections (4%) was higher than in the rest of the series.

A survey by Heelan et al. (1984) : Reinforced these points. They used a similar technique for chest radiography to that described in Chapter 22 , viz., 140 KV, 3 metre f.f.d. and a 1.5 cm. air gap, and routinely took both P.A. and lateral views. Studying 10,040 male cigarette smokers over age 45, with annual radiography over a period of 48 years, supplemented by intercurrent examinations, they found 280 with lung tumours (2.8%). 53 were detected at their first examination and 227 subsequently. Of these latter, 42 had small cell tumours and 168 tumours of other types. Since both groups could possibly benefit from surgery, they were studied further. Approximately 60% of asymptomatic subjects had Stage I tumours, whereas only 26% of the symptomatic cases had these, with 5 year survival rates of 55% and 11% respectively.

73% of the tumours detected by routine radiography were adenocarcinomas, and were frequently peripheral tumours, i.e. more readily detectable on chest radiographs. Of the 168 non-small cell tumours, 102 were routinely detected and only 10% showed advanced disease, whilst 45% of the symptomatic patients had advanced disease. In the symptomatic cases, retrospective study of previous radiographs, revealed an abnormality in only 20%, compared with 65% in asymptomatic cases. The abnormalities were small infiltrates, nodules or line shadows and some had been present for up to 5 years, although initially very difficult to detect. **They concluded that slowly growing tumours found in the asymptomatic group were likely to be resectable with excellent prospects for the patients' survival, whilst those diagnosed as a result of symptoms, (after having had 'negative' radiographs, less than a year before) had rapidly developing cancers which did not respond well to any treatment and were associated with a very poor probability of survival.**

Goldman (1960) : Made a similar point and reported the detection of 161 new cases of lung neoplasm (and 1,045 with TB) in 9,158 people examined by miniature radiography in Liverpool - a rate of 0.35%. Of these, 87 had surgery, only 9 proving unresectable at thoracotomy.

Other centres have used both routine **sputum cytology and chest radiography**.

Melamed et al. (1963) in New York, found 12 patients who had positive cytology and normal radiography. Even so, in four the diagnosis was too late to allow operation, owing to difficulty in localising the lesion and only three patients at Johns Hopkins in Baltimore survived five years.

Baker et al. (1979) : Found 72 patients with Stage 0 or Stage 1 disease, of whom a third were alive after three years.

Fontana et al. (1975), at the Mayo Clinic : Concluded that there was no evidence that cytological screening resulted in decreased mortality.

The combined series of 31,360 male smokers over 45 radiographed at the Johns Hopkins, Sloane Kettering and Mayo Clinics (see references below) revealed 225 cases of lung cancer, i.e. 0.7%. **This figure however gave a comparable figure to the yield from mammography in post menopausal women, i.e. about 0.6% - a yield now considered worthwhile for wide-spread breast screening.**

CONCLUSION

The main outcome from all screening procedures for lung cancer is that as well as being time consuming and expensive, they have not done much to improve the detection of many tumours whilst they are at a 'curable' stage. However, a few patients have probably been saved.

Further references :

Gilbertsen (1964) : Chest x-ray examination - unsatisfactory method of detection of early lung cancer in asymptomatic individuals.

Stitik and Tockman (1978) : Radiographic screening in the early diagnosis of lung cancer.

Benaceraf et al. (1981) from Mass. General, and Peter Bent Brigham Hospitals, Boston, USA - assessed the value of routine chest radiography in symptomatic chest patients. They felt that in patients over 40, chest symptoms were a sufficient indication for chest radiography (47% were positive), but in those under 40, 96% had no physical signs or haemoptysis and no acute findings, i.e. omitting chest radiography in these would miss 2 to 3% of all lesions.

Amielle et al. (1982) - Paris : Reported that about 140,000 chest examinations in a large organisation revealed 54 cases of tuberculosis, 28 of sarcoid, 10 bronchial carcinomas and 26 miscellaneous conditions They felt that radiography should be reserved for high risk patients.

Williams and Cortese (1982) - Mayo Clinic : Thought that although screening seemed to find cases at an earlier stage of the disease, it did not seem to reduce mortality. They also found that of **surgically treated pts. 40% lived > 5yrs if they were symptomless at the time of operation and of the pts. who presented with clinical symptoms < 5% had resectable tumours at surgery and only 10% of these were alive after 5 yrs.**

Barclay and MacIntosh (1983) from Canada : 10 cases found in 23,000 men over 40 years - 9 with advanced disease.

Hayabuchi et al. (1983) from Japan : Slow growing lung cancer in a fixed population sample - biennial chest radiographs detected 50 out of 107 tumours. They wrote : "Among lung cancer patients, those with small asymptomatic lesions have the best prognosis. The size of the tumour and resection is especially important to survival".

Huhti et al. (1983) : 446 patients followed for 5 years until death - two groups. A - diagnosed on routine x-ray or for non-chest symptoms. B - Chest symptoms. Survival of Group A: 1 year - 50%, 5 years - 5%. B : 1 year - 24%, 5 years - 4%. Of those who had lesions seen retrospectively 6/12 before diagnosis, 9% were alive at 5 years. They concluded that screening does seem to improve the prognosis for lung cancer.

Muhm et al. (1983) : Mayo Clinic - 92 lung tumours were detected in patients having chest radiography every four months. 50 peripheral, 16 peri-hilar nodules, 20 hilar or mediastinal enlargement. 90% of peripheral tumours (which grew slowly) were visible retrospectively for months or years - however 705 were above Stage I.

Berlin et al. (1984) : The National Cancer Institute Cooperative early lung cancer detection programme. Results of initial screen (prevalence). Early lung cancer detection.

Flehinger et al. (1984) : Early lung cancer detection - results from Memorial Sloan-Kettering study.

Fontana et al. (1984) : Early lung cancer detection - results from Mayo Clinic study.

Melamed et al. (1984) : Screening for early lung cancer - results of Memorial Sloan-Kettering study in New York.

Heelan et al. (1984) : Non small cell lung cancers - results of the New York screening programme.

Teplick (1984) : In an Editorial considered the 'smoker's chest' to be a radiographic challenge and advocated that the radiographer note the smoking habits of every adult over 35, so that special attention might be made for early lesions. He wrote "virtually every radiologist and pulmonary physician can recall cases of bronchogenic carcinoma in which earlier films, even several years previously, were read as negative, but retrospectively shows an early or suspicious lesion at the site".

Batra et al (1987) : Considered what diagnostic imaging techniques should be used in patients with lung cancer. They felt that for the early detection of lung cancer (i.e. when localised and hence resectable), high risk persons should be screened periodically with sputum cytology and chest radiographs. PA and lateral radiographs should be followed by CT to study the hila, mediastinum, pleura, chest wall and upper abdomen. Distant deposits in the liver, brain or bones should also be sought, if clinical or biochemical findings suggested them.

Flehinger and Kimmel (1987) : The natural history of lung cancer in a periodically screened population.

Flehinger et al. (1988) : Natural history of adenocarcinoma - large cell carcinoma of the lung - conclusions from programmes in New York and Baltimore. Over half the cases were of these types, squamous tumours accounting for 30%. Very few undifferentiated or oat cell tumours were found early and their survival statistics were dismal. In both adenocarcinomas and large cell tumours, the mean duration of early stages of these tumours ranged upwards from four years, but the probability of detecting early disease by a single PA and lateral radiographic examination was poor. Long survival may be attributed in part to the slow course of early stage disease, rather than the favourable effects of treatment.

Sider and Horejs (1988) : Studied the frequency of extra-thoracic metastases from bronchogenic carcinoma in 95 patients with normal-sized hilar and mediastinal lymph nodes on CT. 24 had extra-thoracic deposits (16 adenos-, 5 squamous and 3 large cell) in brain (10), bone (8), liver (6), adrenals (6) and soft tissue (2).

Epstein (1990) : The role of radiologic screening in lung cancer. A review of the presently available data does not support the routine use of chest radiography or sputum cytology for the early detection of lung cancer. Although early asymptomatic cases may benefit from screening, **tumour biology is probably the most important factor affecting prognosis.**

Fontana et al. (1991) : Screening for lung cancer - a critique of the Mayo lung project. The Mayo Clinic trial compared offering chest radiography and sputum cytology every four months to offering advice that the two tests be obtained once a year. The trial showed increased lung cancer detection, resectability and survivorship in the group offered screening every four months. However there was no significant difference in lung cancer mortality rate in the two groups. As Gross noted in the 1992 Year Book of Radiology "there is apparently no pay-off in long-term survival" and "periodic screening cannot yet be endorsed".

Shure et al. (1991) : 16% of patients with central bronchial tumours may have no signs of obstruction on **(inspiratory)** PA films. **These need expiratory views!**

Soda et al. (1993, from Nagashi, Japan) : Screened 306,000 with 206 lung cancers detected (50% stage I). Also 19 false positives and 59 false negatives. There was a low detectability of stage I adenoca and late recognition of rapidly growing small and squamous cell cancers.

Latief et al. (1997) and Lynch (1997) : Search for a primary lung neoplasm in pts. with brain metastasis. Is the chest radiograph sufficient?

Strauss et al. (1997) : Screening may not decrease mortality, but may reduce morbidity with lower stage at detection.

Smith, I. (1999) and Henschke et al. (1999 from USA & Canada) : **Reappraisal of screening for lung cancer** - studied 1,000 heavy smokers > age 60 with CXRs & low dose CT - 27 small tumours were detected (over 5x the pick up rate for breast cancer). **See also notes on ps. 24.41 & 24.50.**

'Missed' lung cancer (see also Appx. 2 - ps. Appx. 3-5 and Illus. CA LUNG MISSED).

Rigler et al. (1953) : Many pts. had evidence of the disease months or yrs. before diagnosis - see p. 4.2.

Tala (1967) : from Finland studied 632 pts. suffering from lung cancer - 168 of these had previous serial radiographs and lesions subsequently diagnosed as cancer could be seen 1 yr. before in 71%, >2yrs in 35% & 3yrs in 15%. Only 4% were symptomless when the diagnosis was made.

Veese (1968) : from the Netherlands - radiological evidence of ca could be seen 6 months before diagnosis in 87%, 1 yr. in 54% & 3 yrs in 6%.

Austin et al. (1992) : Missed bronchogenic cancer is not uncommon - 12 to 30% of cases. 18 radiologists failed to detect tumours in 27 patients. The main cause was **failure to compare with previous radiographs**; others were missed in females and the upper lobes (esp. right).

Woodring (1990) : "The generally accepted error rate for detection of early lung cancer is between 20% & 50% and little improvement has been noted over the last few decades."

Potchen and Bisesi (1990 - from the USA) : Posed the question **'when is it malpractice to miss lung cancer on chest radiographs'**. They recognised that many suspected abnormalities seen on chest radiographs are not judged to be significant. Some will prove not to be on subsequent follow-up, whilst others will become obvious. Over-diagnosis may be hazardous to the patient. The problem is complicated because screening has not improved lung cancer survival, and has largely been abandoned.

Szamosi (1995) : A chest physician from the Karolinska Sjukhuset, Stockholm wrote a monograph 'Lung Cancer - the Art of Detection by Conventional Radiography'. - He asked how can symptomless tumours be detected? and noted that **surgically resectable carcinomas will be detected as a wholly unexpected result of a chest examination, initiated for some quite different reason**...if we are to detect potentially curable cases, we must not expect any hint of suspected lung cancer from the referring physician. He noted that size alone is not an indication of operability, this depends on metastases, which may already have occurred from a small tumour.

   He also noted that one of the most characteristic features of early lung cancers is their **unimpressive nature** and their lack of conspicuity - a complex phenomenon related to (i) the size, attenuation and borders of a tumour, (ii) their anatomical location, (iii) the radiographic projection, (iv) technical factors re exposure & development, and (v) experience and skill of the reviewer. Small peripheral tumours may mimic blood-vessels, be 'tube-like', be nebulous, etc. Tumours may also extend diffusely in the lung, diffusely spread along the thoracic wall, mimic broncho-pneumonia or be faint nebulous spots, cloud-like or punctate structures with an apparent concentration of minute vessels, or thin-walled cavities, which can fill up and empty again (these may be mistaken for TB). He felt that views with a slight obliquity could help sort out those difficult to diagnose - adjacent to scars, plaques or an apical cap, and also that it **is best if the stated smoking habits of the pt. do not influence scrutiny of a primary judgement on chest radiographs.**

Berlin (1994) : Reporting the 'missed' radiological diagnosis - the weight of legal opinion favours complete disclosure of all that is relevant to a pt's well-being, including iatrogenic errors, but the individual radiologist must decide how best to resolve this dilemma in each case.

Hendrix (1995) and Gross in 1996 (Year Book of Diagnostic Radiology, p. 26) : Liken a 'missed' lesion to Wally in Where's Wally? children's books (Waldo in the USA) - when found he is easy to spot, but before this he is often lost in a crowd! Gross also agrees that it is best to report the finding and to report that it was also present in retrospect. He says that this, in and of itself, doesn't establish a miss. Many times when something is present on a current radiograph, one can find evidence of its beginnings on a prior study even though it would not have been reasonable to have made the diagnosis of abnormality at the time of the earlier study.

Hendrix wrote "Unlike physical findings or the assessment of a patient's condition, which in retrospect can only be reconstructed inexactly from a patient's medical records, a radiographic image can be recalled at any time for review exactly as it appeared when first obtained. Hindsight can be 100% accurate. Therefore, when one testifies as an expert witness in defense of a subtle, missed lesion, it is difficult to convey to a plaintiff lawyer or to a jury how any radiologist could possibly miss a lesion that they, laymen, can see once it has been pointed out to them. Often it is even difficult to convince a clinician of this once they see the lesion. Obviously, the problem is not one of visual acuity but of perception.   In defense of a missed lesion, one can quote studies that have found that the error rate can be 30% or higher in the interpretation of certain radiologic studies. This is useful but the expert witness is put on the defensive and may appear lame or to be making excuses to cover up ineptitude.   Jurors and plaintiff lawyers are often skeptical even scandalized, when an expert witness suggests that a well-qualified, careful radiologist could under any circumstance miss a fracture, tumour, or other lesion that they, as laymen, presently see on a radiograph. To answer this skepticism, a suitable analogy is needed that is for a missed lesion - one that a layman can easily grasp. For this analogy, a situation is needed that is familiar to most people from daily experience. It needs to be a situation where they are looking for something diligently but are unable to find it even though they know that the object is clearly within their view." (He quoted several children's books by Handford, M - Where's Waldo etc.).

White et al. (1995) : **Missed lung cancer on chest CT scan** - reviewed 10 cases missed on initial CT interpretation. An endobronchial lesion was the most common type of missed lesion and the majority of these were in the lower lobes. Lack of clinical suspicion and the unanticipated nature of these cancers, or the presence of major unrelated pathology (including other tumours) were judged to have diverted the attention of the original observer in about 50%. (See also White et al. 1996; & 1999 noting that 45% of cases resulted in average $150,000 payments).

Berlin (1996) : Malpractice issues in radiology - (a) perceptual errors, (b) the importance of proper radiographic positioning & technique, (c) errors in judgement & (d) possessing ordinary knowledge.

Berlin (1997) : Countersuing plaintiffs & their lawyers who have sued for malpractice in **not** worth the effort.

Robinson (1997) : Radiology's Achilles' heel error & variation in the interpretation of the Roentgen image - "Errors arise from poor technique, failures of perception, lack of knowledge & misjudgements. Observer variation is substantial & should be taken into account when different diagnostic methods are compared; **in many cases the difference between observers outweighs the difference between techniques**. Strategies for reducing error include attention to viewing conditions, training of observers, availability of previous films and relevant clinical data, dual or multiple reporting, standardization of terminology and report format, and assistance from computers....."

Berlin (1999 & 2000) : Malpractice issues in radiology. Not comparing new radiographs with those obtained previously is negligent; Hindsight bias; Pitfalls of the vague radiology report.

Survival in relation to measurable tumour growth rates.

In 1935 Mottram noted that both benign and malignant warts produced by the application of tar to the skin of mice had constant growth rates from the time they become of macroscopic size. When size is plotted logarithmically against time, it is found to be exponential with a straight line relationship. The length of the invisible growth phase appears to be related to the growth measured during the visible phase, being longer with slower growth rates.

This concept has been applied to many human tumours, and in particular to bronchial carcinomas (Garland et al., 1963; Weiss et al., 1966). It is known as the '**doubling time hypothesis**'. It assumes that the origin of a tumour is unicellular or nearly so, and that the growth rate is geometric and constant. With these assumptions, the rate of growth can be measured by the time taken by a neoplasm to double its volume. It should be noted that when a tumour doubles in diameter, its volume is increased eight fold. This concept has been further developed by Collins et al. (1956), Nathan et al. (1962), Garland (1966) and Geddes (1979).

Such a hypothesis makes no allowance for cellular necrosis or for the shedding of cells into the lumen of a body passage from which they may be excreted (or expectorated in the case of bronchial tumours). Nor does it take into account any depressant effect on the tumour by endogenous or exogenous factors such as host resistance and hormone or other effects, including treatment. Nevertheless it is worth considerable study in relationship to the preclinical or invisible lifetime of tumours, since even if cancers could be detected when they had a diameter of 1 cm, two-thirds to three-quarters of their life-cycle would already have elapsed.

A single malignant cell 10μ in diameter will produce a nodule 1 mm. in diameter in 20 doublings and a nodule 1 cm. in diameter after ten more doublings. A further ten more doublings will create a mass of approximately 1 kg. and only a few more doublings would produce an insupportable amount of tumour tissue, so that death must occur after 40 doublings (Collins et al., 1956). These authors also made the following points:

(i) The inadequacy of the five-year cure period in common use may be explained by the fact that slowly growing neoplasms may require many years to reach a discernible size.

(ii) The long duration (often years) of invisible growth may explain the failure of 'early' radiographic detection to influence survival, since the diagnosis will not be early in terms of the many doublings which will have occurred by the time the tumour is visible.

(iii) Therapeutic measures are undertaken only during the final third or quarter of the cancer's course, and many therapeutic failures are due to metastases which are already present when therapy is instituted. The late appearance of metastases, even after years of survival without evidence of persistent disease at the treated primary site, does not necessarily require the concept of dormant cancer cells. A doubling time of 100 days, a not uncommon occurrence, means that a single cell metastasis would require 8 years to grow into a 1 cm nodule.

(iv) The impression of a sudden rapid increase in cancer size is an illusion. When volume increase is plotted arithmetically there appears to be an increasing rapidity of growth, but the rate of change is constant as given by the logarithmic straight line curve.

Weiss et al. (1966) found in their survey in Philadelphia, that out of 76 proven cases of bronchial carcinoma developing during an 8 to 10 year follow-up period among 6,137 men aged 45 years or over, 12 had had measurable peripheral tumours read as negative 5 to 7 months before the first radiograph on which the tumour was recognised. There was an inverse correlation between initial size and survival regardless of whether the tumour was resected - that is, the size of the tumour after a 'negative' chest radiograph reflected its rate of growth. This was confirmed in 8 cases by an inverse correlation between initial size and doubling time. The authors concluded that survival may be largely determined by the biological characteristics (such as growth rate) of each tumour, and that even if all other conditions are favourable for resection, such therapy may be effective only in patients, whose tumours grow so slowly that there is an opportunity to find them by serial chest radiography while they are still small and have not metastasized.' A tumour which is large when first seen on semi-annual chest Roentgenograms must be growing rapidly, but a tumour which is small may be growing rapidly or slowly.'

Such a concept, however, does not always explain the clinical course of a primary tumour or its metastases. A logarithmic curve plotted back to the origin of the tumour will sometimes suggest that a neoplasm which became clinically apparent in adult life originated in childhood, in foetal life, or even before conception! This is of course absurd, and in many cases the clinical impression is that tumours do have varying growth rates during their clinical course and that tumours may become more malignant and less differentiated as they progress (see also Gonpertz curve below).

Fig. 24.5 The Gonpertz curve largely explains the fallacy of extrapolating back a straight line curve to the beginning of a tumour. Early on few cells will be lost because of anoxia, voiding into a bronchus, etc. or through natural wastage -the first part of the curve should rise much more steeply.

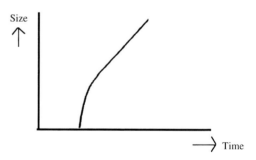

Lamerton (1972) pointed out that not all cells in a tumour are capable of dividing, and those which do divide may not do so at the same rate. As in normal intestinal epithelium or bone marrow, there are 'stem cells' from which are derived the 'intermediate cells' which rapidly divide, and 'adult cells' which may not undergo division. There are also dormant cells which may not divide without some external stimulus. This theory of a mixed population of cells in a tumour allows a much more rational understanding of a tumour's growth and of its response to treatment, either by radiotherapy or by chemotherapy, than does, the hypothesis of a constant rate of division. With treatment there is also an effect produced by the proximity of blood vessels to the cells, in that cells close to the vessels may survive while the more distant ones usually die.

Hall (1978) summarised the factors determining the growth rate of a tumour as (a) the cell cycle of the proliferative cells within the tumour, (b) the growth factor, i.e. that fraction of cells that are proliferating as opposed to being quiescent and (c) the rate of cell loss either by cell death or loss from the tumour. Some of the viable cells may be anoxic, many may outgrow their blood supply and cell loss can be up to 90%. He wrote : "The high cell loss in human tumours is illustrated by the large disparity between the cell cycle time of the individual dividing cells and the overall doubling time of the tumour". Thus whilst the doubling time may be 40 to 100 days, the cell cycle time may be relatively short at one to five days. "The cell loss from solid tumours is considerable and helps to explain why doubling times are on the average, 30 - 90 times longer than the duration of the cell cycle, but it cannot explain the differences between the mean duration of the doubling times in the different histological groups."

Geddes (1979) summarised published series from the literature and found the following doubling times in days - adenocarcinoma : 161, squamous : 88, undifferentiated : 86, and oat : 29. This gave rise to estimates of earliest diagnosis (1 cm. tumour) in 2.4 years for oat, 7.2 years for squamous and 15.4 years for adeno. Usual diagnosis (3 cm. tumours) occurred in estimated 2.8, 8.4 and 15.4 years and death in 3.2, 9.6 and 17.6 years.

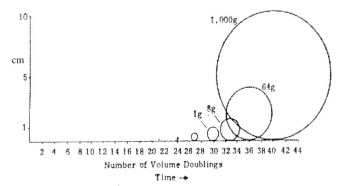

Fig. 24.6   The life of a solid tumour. Time is expressed as volume doublings. A tumour with a doubling time of one month takes 40 months to reach 10 cm, while another with a doubling time of 1 year takes 40 years. Doubling in volume increases the diameter by 1.25. (Reproduced from Geddes, DM, 1979, British Journal of Diseases of the Chest, **73**, 1-17 with permission from WB Saunders Company).

Toomes et al. (1983) observing 153 'coin' lesions for up to two years, found that 80 % had doubling times of six months or less.

Kerr and Lamb from Edinburgh (1984) measured the doubling time for 27 pulmonary neoplasms and found somewhat different figures with a wider range for squamous and large cell tumours and a narrower range for small cell and undifferentiated types. Mean times in days were squamous 146, large cell 111, adeno 72 and small cell 66 days Cell loss was estimated as: all tumours >70%, undifferentiated and poorly differentiated >90%.

Survival in relation to staging
Neglecting the cell types (except oat cell tumours, which are staged differently into limited and extensive types), expected survival rates for each stage group in the TMN system are as shown in the accompanying graph.

Fig. 24.7 Cumulative proportion of patients with bronchial tumours surviving five years by the clinical stage of the disease (reproduced from Mountain, CF, 1986, 'New international staging system for lung cancer', Chest, **89**, 225S - 233S with permission).

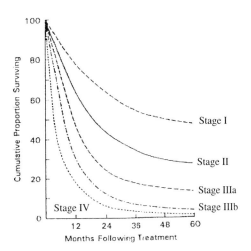

Nathan (1974) measured '**doubling times**' of lung masses from serial radiographs. This gave figures of 7 to 465 days for malignant lesions. He pointed out that lesions which doubled in size more quickly than 7 days or longer than 465 were usually benign. Theresa McLoud (1983) restated Good's advice (see p. 4.6 including important caveats) and wrote : 'it can be argued that every pulmonary mass which does not remain stable in size for two years, or is not a typical benign calcification, may be cancerous, regardless of any other radiographic or clinical feature indicating benignity and therefore should be biopsied.' (comment in a review of Freundlich, 1981 - 'Pulmonary Masses, Cysts and Cavities'). More commonly this is written : '**a nodule which remains unchanged in size for two years or more is almost certain to be benign**'. See also author's case - p. 4.6 - the exception to this rule.

It would appear that the most important prognostic factor with lung cancer (as with other tumour types e.g. breast) is the speed of growth - spread occurring most quickly with rapidly growing tumours. Thus patients with slowly growing tumours will tend to live longer than those with tumours with more rapid growth; they will also tend to have fewer metastases.

Delays in the management of lung cancer.

Billing and Wells (1996) from Leeds and Cambridge wrote "Patients admitted for resection of lung tumours frequently experience lengthy delays in diagnosis and preoperative investigations." They quoted a mean total delay from presentation to operation of 109 days, with surgery taking place after referral to a surgeon within a mean interval of 24 days.

Brown, J. et al. (1996) Age and the treatment of lung cancer - studied the pattern of investigation and care of 563 patients with lung cancer who presented to a single UK health district and found that fewer elderly patients present to, and are managed by specialist physicians; a decision to treat actively being strongly related to whether or not a patient had a histological diagnosis, with only 5% of patients over 75 without such diagnosis receiving active treatment.*

Muers and Haward (1996) in an Editorial comment in Thorax on the above two papers suggested that there is a need for the development and use of auditable standards.

George (1997) from the Middlesex Hosp., London wrote "There can be little doubt that the management of lung cancer in the UK is often suboptimal" and "Although there is no evidence to suggest that management delays adversely affect clinical outcomes, it seems likely that delays of four months, which approximate to one tumour volume doubling time for non-small cell carcinoma, will ensure that some patients will require more extensive resections while others with borderline operable tumours at presentation will become inoperable. Common sense therefore dictates that we should manage our patients more efficiently."

Laroche et al. (1998) : Improving surgical resection rate in lung cancer - quick access investigation, high histological confirmation rates, routine CT scanning and review of every pt. with confirmed lung cancer by a thoracic surgeon led to a substantial increase in the surgical resection rate.

How can radiologists affect the above?

As explained on p. 24.22 the author's view is that radiologists should not regard themselves as mere reporters of films, but must take a lead in investigating patients when they present to their departments. Referring back and forth to the GP or clinician wastes valuable time. The billing system of the NHS "Internal Market" since 1991 has also not helped - the author had all GPs agree to the author continuing his previous practice and to pay all his "bills" from their budgets.

Very often the radiographers will note the presence of a lung tumour. In the author's opinion it is their duty (if this is a new case, and not already under the care of a thoracic physician or surgeon) to bring this **immediately to the attention of the radiologists whilst the patient is still in the department, so that immediate further investigation can be started e.g. tomography, CT, US, sputum cytology, needle biopsy can be carried out immediately or an appointment arranged BEFORE referral to specialist clinical departments - thus cutting out considerable delay. Most GPs are very happy that this be done, and the appropriate referral suggested or made as a result particularly of CT.** As noted above it is particularly the asymptomatic patients, who are likely to come from their GPs (for other reasons) who are likely to be operable. The radiologist can also help by getting the patient to stop smoking at once, as many surgeons will not operate until they have ceased for a few weeks - the author found that a chest radiograph in front of a patient for him to see as well, and being told that his only chance was to give up smoking at once almost invariably succeeded.

An enthusiastic approach to sorting out patients' problems, using all the facilities available, gave him much pleasure in being able to help many of them, as well as clinical colleagues, and resulted in his department being voted by local GPs as the most efficient clinical department in Oxfordshire in the year of his retirement!

* Commenting on this Benson (1997 from the Churchill Hospital, Oxford) noted that some elderly patients do not wish to subject themselves to invasive investigations or treatment regimes which may be of uncertain benefit, and that whilst relief of symptoms is important, prolongation of life by a few months or even the prospect of a cure may be less important to the individual patient at the age of 80 than at the age of 50.

Chapter 24d : **Patient management - Possible treatment regimes and their effects. Possible surgery.**

The first question in management should always be the possibility of surgical cure. Staging and our own local criteria of inoperability were discussed in the last chapter.

Following the recognition of a lung nodule, the best decision should be made as to whether it is likely to be a neoplasm or not. Calcification within it often implies an old TB focus in the UK, but other possibilities have to be considered, including hamartomas, etc. It is also a great help to have a previous radiograph for comparison, and to note its possible presence previously. The problem of the nodule being a metastasis must also be considered.

All patients should first have ultrasound of the liver and upper abdomen (which only takes a few moments), followed by CT and bronchoscopy, as well as careful clinical assessment.

The position of pre-operative percutaneous biopsies is discussed in Chapter 21; briefly the feeling is that **biopsies should be carried out in likely inoperable cases** (for proof of neoplasm before radiotherapy and for planning chemotherapy), but that 'excision biopsies' should be carried out in the **potentially operable cases**. Knowing the cell types of tiny tumours will not usually affect the decision 'to operate or not', as even patients with tiny small cell tumours (and no demonstrable metastasis) may be cured by resection. Rapid enlargement of nodules on serial radiographs will perhaps suggest a very anaplastic tumour, but even these without demonstrable metastasis should probably have the chance of surgical cure.

Unless very elderly, patients with $T_1M_0N_0$ tumours are best treated by surgery, with an 85% expectation of cure, and those with an over 3 cm mass a 50% five year survival. A few may prefer radical radiotherapy, which may also be considered in those with other debilitating disease.

The real problem is with patients in whom local spread has occurred. Varying survival reports (up to 40%) with ipsilateral hilar and lower mediastinal node involvement have been reported. Much of this problem is due to 'skip lesions' or 'skipping metastases' (see p.13.10), which occur frequently in lung cancer.

Surgery of lung neoplasms in Oxford (1970 - 1983) was studied by Millar (1985). He found that the number of thoracotomies for lung neoplasm decreased markedly from about 200/year in 1974 to a low of 34 in 1983. Approximately equal numbers of lobectomies and pneumonectomies were carried out and in 10% of cases only a thoracotomy and no resection was performed. He estimated these numbers were out of a catchment number of 1,700 to 2,000 cases per annum.

To a large extent the figures reflected the greater pre-surgical work-up of patients, and the fact that 90% or more were inoperable at the time of presentation. He pointed out that a useless thoracotomy only produces greater morbidity for an already doomed patient (in the majority of cases) and this was particularly important in the elderly. He quoted Theodor Bilroth who stated "To operate without having any chance of success is to prostitute the art and science of surgery"!

The present policy is to try to sort out the operable from the inoperable cases as much as possible by radiological means (all available techniques being used as appropriate), + bronchoscopy and mediastinoscopy as required. An exploratory thoracotomy is only carried out in the younger patients, when spread of disease may not be as widespread as predicted e.g. due to reactive nodes.

In 1988, 108 patients had surgery for bronchial neoplasm, 53 had pneumonectomies and 53 lobectomies, two patients had thoracotomies only as they proved unresectable.
(The practice of 'debulking' lung tumours prior to chemotherapy is not commonly practised in Oxford).

Views on the value of surgery.

All centres have patients who have survived for many years following surgery. This is most likely to occur in those with small peripheral nodules and no nodal or distal involvement (stage 1 or $T_1N_0M_0$ - see ps. 24.23 to 24.25). In the majority of other cases a recurrence often occurs within the chest, liver, or bones, etc., within months or a few years, despite heroic efforts and careful surgery. Many feel that despite these unfortunate results, younger patients, with remotely possible surgical cure, should still be subjected to surgery, as this is their only real chance of prolonging their lives, despite the morbidity engendered in some cases by the surgery.

Some survivors develop a second primary tumour in the lungs years later (see also p. 4.18 and Illus. **CA MULT, Pts. 6, 17 & 24 and TRACHEA CA, Pt. 6**).

Controls of '**potentially operable   cases**' not treated by surgery are difficult to find, but a few who are treated by radiotherapy alone, also have long-term survivals (Illus. **CA SURVIVAL, Pts. 5** and 7). A few also have long term survival with no treatment (Illus. **CA SURVIVAL, Pt. 6**), and rarely '**spontaneous   regression**' or '**cures**' occur; the author has seen only one or two of the last, but was recently shown spontaneous regression in a proven right hilar small cell tumour. Some of these appear to occur in relation to an intercurrent severe infection or trauma.

Notes on some reported surgical series.

Christiansen and Smith (1962) : Found that of 462 patients referred for surgery, resection could be carried out in only 131 (35%). The five-year survival rate averaged 13%. All patients who had no resection died in the first twelve months. However, Overholt et al. (1955) found a 34% survival where the tumour was asymptomatic and confined to the lung.

Belcher and Anderson (1965) : Studied 1,134 patients with bronchial tumours who had surgery at the London Chest Hospital between 1949 and 1963. Operative mortality was 10%; 21% had a thoracotomy only and of those having a resection, 53% had a pneumonectomy and 47% a lobectomy. 26% of those who had a resection survived five years, and 16% ten years. Of those in whom resection was not possible, only 3% survived longer than two years; the average survival being nine months. Patients under 45 years had a similar prognosis to the whole series, whereas those over 70 fared extremely badly. They found that the incidence of the various types of tumour changed in the later years and that the proportion of undifferentiated and oat cell carcinomas rose at the expense of the squamous cell type. The proportion of adenocarcinomas did not alter despite the yearly increase in the total number of tumours.

Belcher continued this study and in 1983 reported results of 8,781 thoracotomies carried out in several centres He found a pneumonectomy, lobectomy and thoracotomy (only) ratio of 7:7:2. Operative mortality varied between 7 and 9.2% and survival rates were approximately 26% at 5 years, 17% at 10 years and 5% at 20 years. Death from carcinoma, in those dying under five years from operation, was approximately 90%, at 5-10 years 55%, and at 10-20 years 35%. Belcher's figures showed a great similarity to other published series, despite variations of geography, social customs, the patient's ages, indications for operation, resection and lobectomy rates, etc. He concluded that "**if improvement in operative mortality is excluded, there has been no improvement in the survival rates in the last thirty years**", and " **the disease process itself must be the dominant factor influencing the results.**"

Bignall et al. (1967) : Reviewed over 6,000 patients with bronchial carcinoma at the Royal Marsden and Royal Brompton Hospitals from 1944 to 1963. In 1,110 patients who had resections, the five year survival was 27%. There were also a few long-term survivors among those with inoperable tumours who had radiotherapy. Those who had a lobectomy fared better than those who had a pneumonectomy (73% and 54% at one year, and 35% and 22% at five years respectively).

Those having radiotherapy and surgery had a five-year survival close to 5%. They concluded that the prospects for a striking improvement in treatment or earlier diagnosis were not encouraging, and that more serious and energetic attempts at prevention were necessary.

Slack (1970) : Studied 2,291 patients and found that operative mortality was higher after pneumonectomy (17%), than after lobectomy (9%). Five year survival was better if the tumour was confined to the lung (44%), when the hilum or mediastinal nodes were involved and **all** visible tumour was resected it was 23%, and when residual tumour remained it was only 16%. He found that five year survivors as a group were not completely distinguishable from short term survivors, but more frequently had negative nodes and smaller tumours tending to be of the bronchiolar or squamous cell type, whereas short survivors more frequently had advanced disease and larger tumours tending to be of adenocarcinoma or anaplastic cell type. Factors with little influence on survival were age, race, sex, tumour location and vascular invasion.

Belcher and Rehahn (1979) : Studied 1,267 patients of whom 476 had a lobectomy, 473 a pneumonectomy and 304 only a thoracotomy and found a greater probability of survival with lobectomy, squamous tumours and the younger age group. They found an exponential risk in the survivors (as Bloom et al., 1962, found with breast carcinoma), suggesting that if the bulk of the tumour was removed, then the younger patients may have been able to inhibit metastases by natural means. (Author's note: On the other hand many young patients seem to have rapidly progressive tumours, related to the type of tumour or to hormone stimulation of growth).

Further references

Bloom et al. (1962) : Carried out a study of the natural history of breast cancer (1805 - 1933) and compared untreated and treated cases according to the histological grade of malignancy - one perhaps needs a similar long term study with lung cancer.

Boucot et al. (1967) and Weiss, W. and Boucot (1977) : Reported cases suggesting similar survival spans between operated and non-operated groups.

Borrie (1965) : Lung cancer - surgery and survival.

Steele et al. (1966) : Survival in males with bronchogenic carcinomas resected as asymptomatic pulmonary nodules.

Buell (1971) : The importance of tumour size in prognosis for bronchogenic carcinoma.

Kirsch et al. (1972) : The effect of cell type on prognosis of patients with bronchogenic carcinoma.

Steele and Buell (1973) : Asymptomatic solitary pulmonary nodules - host survival , tumour size and growth rate.

Hyde et al. (1973) : Studied the natural course of inoperable cancer in 7,500 pts. & found that oat cell tumours had the shortest prognosis and adenocas the longest, with squamous and undifferentiated having a middle position.

Overholt (1975) : Only 5% of 3,800 untreated patients lived more than five years.

Mittman and Brundeman (1977) : Lung cancer - to operate or not?

Shields et al. (1975) : Relationship of cell type & lymph node metastases to survival after resection of bronchial ca.

Rubinstein et al. (1979) : The influence of cell type and lymph node metastases on survival of patients with carcinoma of the lung undergoing thoracotomy.

Martini et al. (1980) : Prospective study of 455 lung carcinomas with mediastinal lymph node metastases.

Shields (1986) : Surgery of small cell tumours - may still be appropriate with small localised lesions.

Ishida et al. (1990) : Strategy for lymphadenectomy in lung cancer three cm or less in diameter in 221 patients : -

number of patients	size of tumour	nodes N_0	N_1	N_2	5 year survival
8	< 1 cm	100%	0%	0%	80%
84	1.1 - 2 cm	83%	5%	12%	74%
129	2.1 - 3 cm	62%	12%	25%	51%

In the 63 patients with nodal deposits, 'skip' metastases were present in 28.6%. 121 patients had a complete resection but during a 5 year follow up, 41% had a recurrence - 8% local and 33% distal metastases.

Spiro (1990) : **Management of lung cancer - remains surgery for cure of non-small & chemotherapy for small cell type.**

Roberts and Spiro (1990) : **80% of surgically treated pts. survived > 5 yrs if ca detected as stage I.**

Muscolino et al. (1997) : Stage III lung cancer classified as Pancoast tumour, is best treated by R/T, combined radio-surgical treatment being reserved for pts. with potentially resectable cancer without N_2 disease and/or malignant invasion of the first rib.

Smith (1999) and Henschke et al. (1999 from USA & Canada) : **Reappraisal of screening for lung cancer** - studied 1,000 heavy smokers > age 60 with CXRs & low dose CT - 27 small tumours were detected (over 5x the pick up rate for breast cancer). They felt that a reappraisal was required as the **5 year survival rates for stage I lung cancer can be as high as 70%, compared with a mere 12% in the absence of resection**. (In 1998 in the USA there were an estimated 160,000 deaths from lung cancer and an estimated 172,000 new cases). **See also note on p, 24.33.**

Blades and McCorkle (1954) : A case of spontaneous regression of an untreated bronchogenic carcinoma.

Nelson (1962) : Spontaneous regression of cancer.

Smithers (1962) : Spontaneous regression of tumours.

Bell et al. (1964) : Spontaneous regression of bronchogenic carcinoma with five year survival.

Everson and Cole (1966) : Spontaneous Regression of Cancer.

Sutton, M. and Pratt-Johnson (1970) : Spontaneous regression of carcinoma of the bronchus (woman aged 64).

Challis and Stam (1990) : Spontaneous regression of cancer - a review of cases from 1900 - 1987.

Charig (1999) : Spontaneous regression of a case of oat cell cancer involving the R hilum.
(See also p. 5.40).

Management of patients with lung cancer including radiotherapy and chemotherapy.

It follows from the previous section that 'treatment' is probably the wrong term for most patients with lung cancer, and that the term 'management' is better. As the majority of patients will have incurable disease at the time of presentation, the aim with these should be to relieve symptoms and to ensure that the remainder of the patient's lives will be as pleasant as possible. In only a few will life be able to be prolonged by intended curative surgery, 'radical radiotherapy' or chemotherapy. In those presenting with bone pain (due to direct invasion or bone metastases), SVC obstruction, cord compression, etc., radiotherapy is usually given palliatively at once, and often produces considerable alleviation. The same is true for disability due to large nodes pressing on the trachea or main bronchi, etc. Chemotherapy often combined with radiotherapy is particularly helpful with oat cell tumours - see p. 24.17.

Many patients with small cell tumours have a good initial response to treatment, particularly those with 'limited' as opposed to 'extensive' disease. This is seen both clinically and radiographically. The response may be to chemotherapy (e.g. six courses at three-weekly intervals of IV cisplatin + etoposide, alternating with cyclophosphamide, doxorubicin and vincristine), steroids alone, radiotherapy (especially for unilateral disease) or a combination of treatments. In most cases there are some side effects. Response tends to occur quickly and may persist for several months, in a few cases an 'apparent cure' being produced. Relapses may also respond, but many of these are more resistant, probably related to the development of new tumour clones, and such responses are variable. A memorable example has been the presentation of a patient with the liver full of small cell metastases. He had a very good initial response, with the disappearance of all secondary deposits on ultrasound; he later had four relapses which similarly responded, but the fifth showed very little improvement and he soon died.

Some patients will have inoperable disease due to the spread of tumour, whilst others will be inoperable from severe emphysema or other lung disease, coronary heart disease (though in a few cases both problems can be dealt with at the same thoracotomy), other serious disease, advanced age, etc. In all those with non-small cell tumours, unless the tumour is small and suitable for radical radiotherapy or the patient has symptoms due to the tumour, there is often little point in giving radiotherapy before these occur, as morbidity from the treatment is likely to cause more distress than a 'wait and see' policy. Usually radiotherapy can only be given once. Also in the elderly, growth of tumour may be quite slow, and the patient may live for months or a few years, without any major symptoms from the tumour and die from other intercurrent disease. In symptomatic patients a single dose of radiotherapy (e.g. 8 Gy) often gives as good pain relief as a more conventional ten day course of 30 Gy (radical treatment may require twice this dosage).

Antibiotics may be used to control secondary infections, the aspiration of pleural effusions or pleurodesis may make dyspnoea less, and pain can be aided by radiotherapy and/or drugs. Haemoptysis may need lung resection (despite tumour spread), radiotherapy or possible embolisation. Other severe symptoms e.g. HPOA (see ps. 23.1 - 7) may be alleviated by local resection of the tumour, but this responds but little to radiotherapy.

If possible one should determine the cell type at the time of presentation, and in those with symptoms or in whom curative surgery may be contemplated further investigation is required. One should also determine in the case of adenocarcinomas, that the primary tumour is in the lung and that it has not arisen elsewhere (e.g. Illus. **BREAST CA, COLON CA, OVARIAN CA, PROSTATE CA**), which might be amenable to other more appropriate treatment. Immunotherapy is unlikely to be of any practical value.

Chemotherapy has also been used in patients with non-small lung tumours, but the results have not often been as good. With a wider range of drugs e.g. mitomycin C, ifosfamide and cisplatinum about 50% of adenocarcinomas and squamous tumours may show some response, especially in the more anaplastic types, but the side effects tend to be greater.

Mode of action of chemotherapy.
     Chemotherapy may be effective for several reasons: - (i) It may block type 2 topoisomerase enzymes, which are dimers. These 'cut' and 'rejoin' the DNA strands which unravel during mitosis. Some tumour cells (especially teratoma cells) have a higher content of this enzyme, and are sensitive to drugs e.g. VP 10 and adriamycin, which block this enzyme.
(ii) It may interfere with other metabolic pathways - glucose, glycoprotein, calcium metabolism, etc., and affect the 'cytoplasmic protective factor'. Drugs which do this include - chlorambucil and glutathione.
(iii) An interesting concept is to 'block' normal cells first, e.g. with indomethacin and to follow this with the chemotherapeutic agent. Indomethacin fixes to 'binding sites' within many normal cells, thus allowing an effective dose of chemotherapy to be given without damage to the normal cells, but enough to stop DNA synthesis in the tumour cells. (A thymidine analogue - 5 iodo[131] 2 deoxyguanidine - may be used as a marker for this).
(iv) Drugs may promote apoptosis or cellular self-destruction by stimulating the attachment of regulating proteins (TNF) to specific cellular membrane receptors and leading through intracellular processes to the breakdown of DNA.

Some problems with chemotherapy
The drug(s) may not be effective for a number of reasons :
(i) Poor vascularity of the tumour, so that the drug cannot easily reach it. This may happen in areas of degeneration or where there is naturally little vascularity e.g. with mesotheliomas, but cells from the latter may be highly sensitive in 'vitro'.
(ii) Failure of the drug to penetrate the cell membranes - 'the cytoplasmic protective factor', or the inter-cellular matrix - mucin, keratin etc. (like an impermeable 'blood-brain barrier').
(iii) Chemotherapeutic agents may be removed rapidly from cells by a 'glucose/ATP pump', which normally acts to expel toxic materials. Nifedipine and verapmil can block this 'pump', but only at near toxic dosage.
(iv) The binding sites on enzymes to be attacked may be blocked.
(v) Some drugs may harm normal tissues e.g. bone marrow, renal tubular cells and intestinal mucosa as much as or more than tumour cells. Hair follicles are also particularly sensitive, and alopecia is a common problem in patients.
(vi) Tumour cells may behave differently in vitro from in vivo, e.g. small-cell bronchial tumour cells may form cell balls or loose branching phenotypes in vitro. Similarly cells from squamous tumours may grow attached to plastic sheets. Such changing morphology may give a false representation of what happens in vivo. Mesothelioma cell cultures are also very sensitive to chemotherapy in vitro, whereas they are insensitive in vivo (see also Chapter 14).

     Recent interest in the chemotherapy of tumours has centred on the **neovascularity** associated with tumours. Many have an increased blood supply (angiogenesis) around their peripheries (see also ps. 4.8 - 9) - a point most radiologists also know from the vascular rim shown with isotopes or contrast media, and also seen pathologically. This may be in part an inflammatory response initiated by the tumour or from necrosis metabolites (cf. the similar 'blush' around an abscess, empyema, and with mesotheliomas). The number of surrounding vessels also corresponds to nodal invasion, and is related to the presence of micrometastases in liver, bone marrow, etc.
     Attempts are being made to produce vessel antimetabolites to reduce the blood supply to tumours, as well as continuing a chemotherapeutic attack on the tumour cells with antibodies, genes and inhibitors to DNA manufacture. Thymidine produced by tissue necrosis, can itself stimulate an inflammatory response. Sumarin analogues may block heparin metabolism, which occurs in many tumours. The importance of 5FU (first used in the 1950s & 1960s) is continuing (but occasionally it can produce a toxic effect on mucosal surfaces).
     Radiation and drugs may have **synergistic   effects**. High oxygen saturation (e.g. given in a hyperbaric oxygen chamber) may potentiate the effect of radiotherapy, presumably by stimulating more cells into activity (partly through increasing vascularity) and rendering them more sensitive to radiation. Radiotherapy tends to reduce the likelihood of recurrence at the primary site, but in

disseminated cases it has little effect on survival if chemotherapy does not control disseminated disease adequately.

In some cases, steroids (particularly when started in large dosage) may produce a remission, and reduction in the size of the tumour and any secondary deposits. This is very useful with large tumours squashing the trachea and mediastinum (Illus. **CA RUL, Pt. 52a-b**) and with brain secondaries. The improvement is in part due to a reduction in the amount of oedema present (particularly with brain deposits using dexamethasone). Steroids are also often used in synergism with other drugs, and may make the patient feel better (but occasionally will produce a psychosis).

Tamoxifen (as used for treating breast carcinoma) may be used as an adjuvant if given in high dosage (e.g. 100 mg t.d.s. with Etoposide [VP16]). Provera is a progestogen, used first for the palliation of renal and some uterine tumours (see Paine et al, 1970).
Other agents may be used in a similar manner.

Pain killers
These are very valuable in cancer patients, and may be the mainstay of many treatment regimens.

Tumour recurrence is always a problem. Radical radiotherapy may only be given once, and repeat surgery is usually impractical. Chemotherapy may be given more than once with different treatment regimens, and at the present time more are being tried. Endo-bronchial laser and diathermy treatment has a place in a few cases. Sometimes an almost miraculous response may be seen following large dosage of steroids or progestogens (especially Provera). The patient illustrated in Illus. **CA RECURRENT, Pt. 1a-d** had had 'radical' radiotherapy to a right upper lobe adenocarcinoma, and two years later had a large local recurrence in the right upper lobe, with marked invasion of the adjacent trachea and gross stridor. She had a large dosage of prednisolone (100 mg daily for a month, then reducing to 30 mg), the recurrence rapidly reduced in size, and the stridor disappeared. She died a few months later.

Some references.
Shanks (1959) : "The treatment of cancer of the lung by irradiation is one of the least rewarding tasks of the radiotherapist".
Deeley (1967) : The treatment of carcinoma of the bronchus - patients referred for radiotherapy are usually inoperable because of advanced local disease, because the respiratory reserve is insufficient to allow lung resection to be performed or because of advanced age or poor general condition; there are in addition, a small number of operable cases who refuse operation.
Paine et al. (1970) from Oxford : The use of progestogen in the treatment of metastatic carcinoma of the kidney and uterine body.
Slack (1970) : Studied the effect of nitrogen mustard as an adjuvant to surgery in 1192 patients with bronchogenic carcinoma, but found no benefit.
Bakowski and Crouch (1983), Smith (1994) : Chemotherapy of non-small cell tumours.
Spiro (1985) and Livingston (1986) : Chemotherapy of small cell tumours.
Carney (1986) : Biology of small tumours and tumour markers.
Bleehen et al. (1989) : Survival, adverse reactions and quality of life during combination chemotherapy, compared with selective palliative treatment for small cell lung cancer - with immediate treatment, survival was longer, metastases were better controlled and the quality of life better (assessed intermittently by doctors) but worse from side effects by patients.
Spiro (1990) : **Management of lung cancer - remains surgery for cure of non-small cell type and chemotherapy for small cell type.**
Spiro and Souhami (1990) : Duration of chemotherapy in small cell lung cancer.
Woll (1991) : Despite intensive research into cytotoxic chemotherapy, the survival of patients with lung cancer has not improved in the past ten years. Small cell tumours are exquisitely chemosensitive and drug treatment can reduce a tumour mass dramatically but relapse due to development of resistance is almost invariable.
Macchiarini et al (1992) : **Neovascularity** in metastasis of non-small-cell lung cancer.
Burt et al. (1990) : Intraluminal irradiation (via a high-dose rate after loading device) of lung cancer.
Whitehouse, M. (1994) : Management of lung cancer, current clinical practices.
Non-Small Cell Lung Cancer Collaborative Group (1995) : chemotherapy - data from 52 randomised trials.
Rudd (1996) : Inoperable lung cancer.

Sheppard and Libshitz (1997) : Studied the patterns of recurrence in non-small cell cancer and found these to be different in surgical and non-surgical groups. **Local recrudescence is the most common presentation after R/T alone, whereas pleural nodularity is most common after surgery. Filling in of previously dilated or patent bronchi is an area of post-radiation fibrosis or bronchiectasis is highly suspect for recurrence.**
Armstrong, J.G. (1998) : Target volume definition for 3D conformal radiation therapy of lung cancer.

Other methods of treatment.
Endo-bronchial irradiation - may cure small tumours, but is mainly used for palliation, in combination with external beam radiotherapy or chemotherapy.

Some references.
Barber and Stout (1996) : High dose endobronchial brachytherapy for the treatment of lung cancer.
Stout (1996) : Over 800 pts. have been treated by endobronchial brachytherapy at the Christie Hospital, Manchester since 1988. It has been found to be a simple, safe and effective treatment.
Tredaniel et al. (1994) : Endobronchial curietherapy for relief of endobronchial tumour obstruction.

Endo-bronchial splinting - silicone rubber stents have been used to relieve extrinsic pressure from nodes, etc. This has been particularly valuable during radiotherapy for lesions compressing the carina, when post-irradiation oedema may make the obstruction worse. Splints have also been useful with endotracheal and endo-bronchial masses in the main bronchi, and in avoiding post-operative tracheal obstruction after the removal of large intra-thoracic goitres or nodal masses in lymphoma. Such splints may be double-ended or Y shaped for carinal lesions. Examples of such splinting are shown in Illus. **TRACH/BRON STENT.**
   More recently expanding metal splints, (spring or wire mesh similar to those used within vessels) have been employed, and in some cases have had a dramatic effect on lung function, allowing lobes or a lung to become reexpanded. These stents are very expensive (£250 to £700) per splint. They are inserted bronchoscopically under radiological control, and caution has to be exercised if the distal bronchi are full of pus, or spasm occurs when the guide wire is inserted. Gereral anaesthesia or considerable sedation is required. When the pulmonary vascular supply to the affected part of or the whole lung has been severely damaged (Oeser's sign - ps. 7.10 - 12) reaeration may be produced but without increased function.
   A caveat re splints - after initial enthusiasm, some late complications are now being seen (as with IVC filters), especially if a stent is too large. Continuing pressure and vibration from cardiac and respiratory movement may cause the wire stent to migrate through the bronchial wall, and extend into neighbouring organs e.g. the descending aorta and oesophagus with disastrous results. Probably **stents with springed points or clawed arms should never be used for benign lesions e.g. strictures following trauma or inflammatory disease**. A number of such stents were used in the treatment of tracheal and main bronchial strictures following mustard gas burns in the Iran/Iraqi war - see p. 19.108. The follow up of these has not been recorded (as far as the author has been able to ascertain).

Endoscopic bougie and balloon dilatation of bronchial stenoses have been used to dilate benign stenoses of the larger bronchi due to sarcoidosis, TB, amyloid, etc.

References
Westaby et al. (1982 - since 1987 senior consultant thoracic surgeon in Oxford): A bifurcated silicone rubber stent for tracheo-bronchial obstruction.
Cohen et al. (1984) : Balloon dilatation of tracheal and bronchial stenosis.
Wallace et al. (1986) : Tracheo-bronchial stents used in experimental and clinical applications.
Ball et al. (1991) : Endoscopic bougie and balloon dilatation of multiple bronchial stenoses - ten year follow up - four cases , 2 sarcoid, 1 berylliosis, 1 idiopathic.
Nakamura et al. (1991) : Tuberculous bronchial stenosis - treatment with balloon bronchoplasty.
De Souza et al. (1992) : The use of expandable metal stents for tracheobronchial obstruction.
Han et al. (1992) : TB bronchial stenosis treated with self-expanding metallic stent.

Bolliger et al. (1993) : Silicone stents in the management of inoperable tracheo-bronchial stenoses.

Rousseau et al. (1993) : Self expandable prostheses in the tracheo-bronchial tree - are of value in pts. with long stenoses or external compression who are not surgical candidates. Epithelialisation and incorporation of the prosthesis into the tracheo-bronchial wall occurs rapidly - more complications have been observed with the Gianturco than the Wallstent device.

Sawada et al. (1993a) : Treatment of tuberculous bronchial stenosis with expandable metal stents.

Sawada et al. (1993b) : Malignant tracheobronchial obstructive lesions treated with expandable metal stents.

Egan et al. (1994) : Expandable metal stents for tracheobronchial obstruction (18 cases - 12 malignant and 6 following lung or heart-lung transplantation).

Ferreti et al. (1995) : Treatment of benign non-inflammatory bronchial stenosis with balloon dilatation.

Reidy (1995) : Tracheo-bronchial stents - Wallstent experience - can get lobes or a lung to re-expand, in some cases with better respiratory function. Those that do not improve may have damaged or closed-off pulmonary vessels. Dramatic case of lady with collapse of residual R lung (previous RU lobectomy for ca.) Stents can be placed bilaterally.

Martinez-Ballarin et al. (1996) : Silicone stents in the management of benign tracheobronchial stenoses.

Müller-Hülsbeck et al. (1998) : Stenting of RMB & R pulmonary artery for malignant stenoses in a 75 year old woman with malignant nodes from squamous ca of mouth.

Wadsworth et al. (1999) : Massive fatal haemoptysis in a 55 yr. old woman caused by erosion of a Gianturco expandable bronchial wire stent used for treating a post-traumatic LMB stenosis which had followed reanastomosis of a bronchial tear sustained in falling off a horse. Plain films showed widening of the stent and CT migration into the oesophagus and a false aneurysm of the descending aorta. She died before any exploratory surgery could be carried out.

Laser treatment, cryotherapy and electro-surgery   - these are being used in many centres for the ablation of some endo-bronchial and oesophageal tumours. The object with endo-bronchial tumours is to attempt to restore the air-way. Mostly a NdYAG (neodymium yttrium aluminium garnet) laser is used, but some (particularly in Japan) have used an argon laser, with prior sensitisation of the tumour with haematoporphyrin. Laser treatment also helps to stop intractable bleeding.

A major problem is the time-factor. Both laser treatment and cryotherapy are slow to perform, and repeated treatments may be required, the patient coughing up necrotic tissue in the interim.

Many use a rigid bronchoscope, with a flexible one passed through it, so as to place the laser tip accurately and to allow adequate suction should bleeding occur. As general anaesthesia is often required, surgeons usually prefer rapid blunt dissection with the end of the rigid bronchoscope to clear airways e.g. the trachea, supplemented by diathermy and followed by rapid suction. This may be followed by endobronchial splinting and/or radiotherapy.

Laser induced fluorescence is also being used for the detection of some early and difficult-to-see tumours.

Electro-coagulation of tumours - Nordenström (1965b & 1971), besides studying the natural electro-potentials within tumours (see ps. 4.14 & 21.4), has used electric currents to damage tumours within the breast and lung. A similar method has been tried elsewhere (e.g. Watson at St. Bartholomew's Hospital, London, 1984). Such '**electro-coagulation**' is performed following the placement of a central electrode in the tumour under fluoroscopic control, and by checking the 'natural' potential difference (often positive) within the tumour. Only a few m amps (e.g. 10) and low voltage are required. In this way small tumours may be ablated, though affected nodes (if any) will be unaffected. With early tumours and in the elderly this may not be important.

Electro-cautery of pulmonary lesions (Perelman technique) - Perelman, a Russian surgeon, described this method of excising lung lesions - it may give rise to post-operative lung cavities like lacunae on radiographs! (see Stark et al., 1993).

Percutansous radiofrequency of lung tumours - Dupuy et al. (2000) have tried this in three patients (see also p. 17.3).

Cryotherapy (necrosis of tumour tissue by freezing) has been tried in the treatment of advanced tumours of the larger airways, particular to improve their patency. Some consider it easier than laser treatment, and it also may control bleeding. (Maiwand, 1986, used it in 75 patients).

References.
Dumon et al. (1984) : Yag laser.
Hayata et al. (1984) : Argon laser haematoporphyrin.
George and Hetzel (1965) : Laser in lung cancer.
Pearlberg et al. (1985) : CT and linear tomograms for assessing tracheo-bronchial lesions prior to laser treatment.
Joyner et al. (1980) : Repeated laser treatment (especially of sq. cas) via a flexible bronchoscope.
Hetzel et al. (1985) : Laser therapy in 100 tracheo-bronchial tumours.
Cortese (1986) : Endobronchial management of lung cancer.
Wolf et al.(1986) : Laser coagulation for the treatment of obstructing tumours of the oesophagus and stomach.
George et al. (1987) : Role of the neodymium YAG laser in the management of tracheal tumours.
Gerasin and Shafirovsky (1988): Endo-bronchial electro surgery.
Ross et al. (1988) : Pathogenesis of cerebral air embolism during neodymium - YAG laser photoresection of an endo-bronchial carcinoid tumour in a 27 year old man - probably occurred as a result of positive pressure ventilation during the laser photo-resection of the highly vascular tumour. He was successfully treated in a hyperbaric chamber.
Zwirewick et al.(1988) : In pre-laser treatment assessment, CT is superior to bronchoscopy for evaluating the extent of extrinsic compression by tumour, which often correlates with a poor response to laser treatment.
Miro et al. (1989) : Severe pulmonary **oedema** after laser relief of upper airway obstruction by a tracheal neoplasm.
Andersson-Engels (1990) : Laser induced fluorescence.
Walsh et al. (1990) : Bronchoscopic cryotherapy for advanced bronchial carcinoma.
George and Rudd (1990): Patients with tumours affecting the trachea and carina usually derive immediate and dramatic relief from laser treatment.
George et al. (1990) : Bronchography in the assessment of patients with lung collapse for endoscopic laser therapy.
Moghissi et al. (1997) : Combined Nd YG laser and endoscopic dynamic therapy may be an effective palliative treatment for pts. with inoperable endotracheo-bronchial cancer.

Thoracoscopic surgery. (see also ps. 6.10 & 6.12 and for thoracoscopy see p. 21.14).
   This is becoming increasingly popular for lung (or pleural) biopsy and/or wedge resection of small peripheral lung lesions. As with minimally invasive abdominal surgery, it may be controlled by TV/video visualisation. An important feature is the localisation of lesions prior to or during the procedure. For this methylene blue or hook wires (injected or inserted just before surgery), or intraoperative ultrasound may be employed.

References.
Landrenau et al. (1991) : Nd YAG laser **thorascopic surgery**.
Wakabayashi et al. (1991 & 1995) : Thoracoscopic CO_2 laser treatment of bullous emphysema (see also p. 6.12).
Kerrigan et al. (1992) : Methylene blue guidance for simplified resection of a lung lesion.
Lewis et al. (1992a) : Imaged thoracoscopic surgery - new technique for resection of mediastinal cysts.
Lewis et al. (1992b) : Video assisted resection of malignant lung lesions.
Plunkett et al. (1992) : Preoperative percutaneous localisation of peripheral pulmonary nodules with CT guidance.
Bensard et al. (1993) : Comparison of **video thoracoscopic lung biopsy to open lung biopsy in the diagnosis of interstitial lung disease**.
Mack et al. (1993a) : Thoracoscopy for the diagnosis of the indeterminate solitary pulmonary nodule.
Mack et al. (1993b) : Techniques for localisation of pulmonary nodules for thoracoscopic resection.
Peterson et al. (1993) : Chest radiographic and CT findings after laser-assisted thoracic surgery (being used increasingly for resection of peripheral nodules, biopsy of focal or diffuse lung disease or bullae). Transient small pneumothoraces or pleural effusions were common. A cavity or fluid filled area is often present at the site of the resected area and usually becomes smaller leaving a cavitary or linear scar.
Shah et al. (1993) : Localisation of peripheral pulmonary nodules using CT-guided hook-wire placement for thoracoscopic excision.
Shennib and Bret (1993) : Intra-operative US for the localisation of occult lung lesions.
Templeton and Krasna (1993) : Localisation of pulmonary nodules with needle/wire breast biopsy system for thoracoscopic resection.

Carnochan et al. (1994) : **Video assisted thoracoscopic lung biopsy** - compared with open lung biopsy - is as effective in providing histological diagnosis. Reduced postoperative disability in the video assisted group decreased hospital stay.

Mason et al. (1994a) : Needle wire localisation for thoracoscopic removal of small lung nodules.

Mason et al. (1994b) : About 11% of pts. having video assisted thoracoscopic surgery have complications.

Lenglinger et al. (1994) : Percutaneous staining of pulm. nodules with methylene blue before thoracoscopic surgery.

Wicky et al. (1994) : Hook wires or methylene blue for localising lung lesions prior to thoracoscopic resections.

Mason et al. (1995) : CT is neither sensitive nor specific for preoperative identification of pleural adhesions in patients undergoing VATS. Also pleural thickening on CT does not necessarily imply pleural adhesions are present.

Fry, W. et al. (1995) : Thoracoscopic implantation of cancer with a fatal outcome - man aged 34 had a small cavitating adeno-ca of LLL removed by VATS, followed by resection of the LLL. 5/12 later he had a recurrence in the chest wall which was resected but again recurred and he died 10 months after the initial resection.

Wait et al. (1997) : Used VATS for loculated complex fibrinopurulent empyemas - lower cost than fibrinolysis!

Thaete et al. (1999) : CT-guided wire localisation of pulmonary lesions before thoracoscopic resection is helpful.

Survival in patients with lung cancer and the effect of treatment.

Reported survival rates of patients with lung cancer differ to some extent from centre to centre, depending on the selection of patients before they are seen in particular clinics; they also depend on the type of tumour and the type of operation (if any) performed. Geddes (1979) pointed out that out of 100 patients with lung cancer, 80 will have inoperable disease at the time of diagnosis and most will die within three years, only one or two surviving for five years. Of the 20 (then considered potentially operable), only six survived for five years, despite surgery. Present studies with CT, etc. suggest that less than 10% are operable. Rudd (1996) gave the overall five year survival after apparently successful resection at about 25%, varying from 75% for a small tumour without nodal involvement (stage I) to 5% for tumours with nodal invasion (stage IIIa). He also quotes the long-term survival after radical radiotherapy as around 5% at five years.

In patients with small cell tumours who are untreated, survival is particularly poor, many dying within two to three months of diagnosis, but chemotherapy may help these patients (see ps. 24. 41-42) and although some initially have a good radiographic response and only rarely will a patient be cured of the disease (Illus. **CA SURVIVAL, Pt. 5**). Most will relapse due to the development of resistance to the drugs or the presence of new resistant cell clones.

Patients with squamous cell tumours tend to live the longest, and a few patients with well-differentiated slowly growing squamous tumours, who have no treatment may survive five years (or sometimes longer). The majority of patients with bronchial tumours however fare badly, with considerable morbidity, and an early death.

Radiotherapy may occasionally be curative and be given 'radically' for localised tumours, particularly in patients with other disease which contra-indicates surgery. Occasionally 'non-radically' planned treatment produces a 'cure' (Illus. **CA SURVIVAL, Pts. 1, 3 & 5**). Mostly, however, radiotherapy is used palliatively, to alleviate pain, haemoptysis, etc. Radiotherapy is not without its complications, with oesophagitis (often the most upsetting to the patient), radiation pneumonitis and fibrosis (see p. 11.19 - 21 and Illus. **POST-RAD LUNGS** and **POST-RAD CHS MEDIAST**), which may lead to severe and sometimes disabling dyspnoea. Recent trials have shown that two treatment fractions may be as effective as many more fractions given over 2 - 3 weeks - also much more convenient to the patient. Regarding non-small cell inoperable tumours, Durrant et al. (1971) from Oxford suggested that only patients with symptoms should have radiotherapy or chemotherapy, and that early treatment in the absence of symptoms does not alter the survival time in inoperable cases. In a further paper from Oxford, Laing et al. (1975), who also studied inoperable cases, pointed out that radiotherapy and chemotherapy both show little benefit, in terms of survival for most non-small cell tumours, and pointed out that untreated asymptomatic control patients may fare better than those who are treated, without having serious local symptoms. However some multidrug treatment regimens are now being tried to treat patients in relatively asymptomatic stages with some response. Percutaneous cryosurgery, electric or laser coagulation (see above) have also been tried for treating small primary tumours, but are not widely used. Such treatments will not have any effect on nodal involvement, but this may not matter, since if any spread has occurred, the chance of cure is small. As has repeatedly been shown, despite intensive research into cytotoxic chemotherapy, the survival of patients with most lung tumours which have spread has not much improved over the past fifteen years.

As is shown in Chapter 13, the lymphatic drainage from the lungs is diffuse and extends into the walls of the larger bronchi, the hilum and mediastinum, so that if any lymphatic spread of tumour has occurred it is very likely to be only incompletely resectable.

Bronchiolo-alveolar carcinomas, carinosarcomas, etc. are discussed separately under their various headings.

See also:

Royal College of Radiologists (1999) : Guidelines on the non-surgical treatment of lung cancer.

Simmonds (1999 - commenting on the above) : Managing patients with lung cancer - new guidelines should improve standards of care.

Clinical correlation.

1. **Radiographic evidence of disease existing before diagnosis.**
    Rigler et al. (1953) questioned the relatives and doctors of 50 patients with lung cancer, to trace previous radiographs. Reviewing these they found an abnormality in most cases. One patient had had a tumour for nine years before surgery, and another had a peripheral carcinoma for four years. In those still operable, the first radiographic abnormality preceded surgery by an average of three years.

    It is also not uncommon to find evidence of tumour on previous radiographs, months or even years before the time of initial diagnosis (Illus. **CA SURVIVAL, Pts. 6 & 9**) - see also ps 4.2 and 24.37.

2. **Age at onset.**
    The exponential doubling hypothesis suggests that lung cancer starts about 10 years before its presentation. This implies that the average age of onset is about 50, since the majority present at age 60. There appears to be a long latent period or loss of anti-tumour defence systems with advancing age. Thus young smokers who cease smoking before age 30 should have only a slightly increased risk and this is in accord with the findings of Doll and Peto (1976) who showed no increased risk in male doctors who ceased smoking by the age of 30.

    It is generally considered that younger patients tend to have tumours with shorter doubling times and have more aggressive disease compared with that in older patients. Our youngest was aged 18 and he started smoking at the age of seven. His disease progressed rapidly.

    However, Roviaro et al. (1985) from Milan, Italy carried out a retrospective survey of over 1,500 cases of lung cancer to assess whether the disease presents substantial differences in younger people (< 45 years) as compared with older patients, and in contrast to other studies they found no significant difference regarding sex, clinical picture, operability, histological type or prognosis.

Further references.
Buell (1971) : The importance of tumour size in prognosis for bronchogenic carcinoma.
Kirsch et al. (1972) : The effect of cell type on prognosis of patients with bronchogenic carcinoma.
Hyde et al. (1973) : Studied the natural course of inoperable cancer in 7,500 patients and found that oat cell tumours had the shortest prognosis and the longest was with squamous, the undifferentiated occupying a middle position.
Steele and Buell (1973) : Asymptomatic solitary pulmonary nodules - host survival, tumour size and growth rate.
Freise et al. (1978) : Bronchial carcinoma and long term survival.
DeCaro and Benfield (1982) : Lung cancer in young persons (35 pts.).
Huhti et al. (1983) : Does the location of lung carcinoma affect its prognosis?
Pemberton et al. (1983) : Bronchogenic carcinoma in patients younger than 40 years (112 pts.).
Athowiak et al. (1989) : Bronchogenic carcinoma in patients under age 40 (89 pts.).

Icard (1992) : Primary lung cancer in young patients (82 surgically treated pts.) - wrote "primary lung cancer seems to be related more to the extent of the disease than to a particularly aggressive behaviour pattern of the cancer."
McCambridge and Eliasson (1993) : Lung cancer in the young (23 pts.) - concluded "The fact that most lung cancers in young people present in late, inoperable stages of the disease argues for an aggressive behaviour pattern of the cancer." They also noted that lung cancers in young people often present in late, inoperable stages, and that 90% of young lung cancer pts. have symptoms at presentation (as in older pts.) but their duration is usually less (2 to 4 months).

Further notes on 'screening' for and prevention of lung cancer.

Dr. Henschke from Cornell Medical Center in New York in a TV programme on BBC 1 reported the use of spiral CT in studying 1,000 smokers or ex-smokers over age 60 (who had smoked at least 20 cigarettes a day for at least 20 years. She found six times as many lung tumours, compared with plain radiography. Small nodules were excised if they looked like tumours or if they increased in size on repeat examinations. She felt that 80 to 90% of patients with such small peripheral tumours could be cured by surgery. A further bonus was that any patients who were still smokers immediately gave up the habit after seeing the images with her straight after they had been taken.
  She plans a new trial of 10,000 smokers. They all pay $300 for the examination.

A similar trial may be set up in the UK (BMJ, 2000, **320**, 270). However, two problems in the UK would be the availability of the apparatus and the funding. As the majority of smokers are now in the lower income groups, would they pay privately for such examinations, if the NHS could not fund them?

A report - Nicotine addiction in Britain - states that nicotine addiction should be recognised as the central problem of smoking and urges the Government to set up a Nicotine Regulating Authority embracing tobacco products and nicotine therapies (BMJ, 2000, **320**, 391 - 392).

Canada is proposing stronger warnings on cigarette packets, including illustrations of cigarette induced disease (BMJ, 2000, **320**, 271).

It also appears that China is now consuming about a third of the world's production of tobacco, with most males smoking cigarettes and a rapidly rising lung cancer death rate.

Further references.
Henschke, C.I. (2000) 'Screening for lung cancer using spiral CT.' Watchdog Health Check, British Broadcasting Corporation, BBC 1, 10 Jan. 2000.
Early Lung Cancer Action Project in New York (Lancet, 1999, **354**, 99 - 105).
Yankelevitz et al. (1999) : Early repeat CT, 30 days after the first scan, can detect growth in most malignant tumours as small as 5 mm.
Sone et al. (2000), from Japan : Use of low-dose spiral CT for detecting lung tumours <2 cm in diameter; noted that small adenocas. were particularly of low-density and had ill-defined borders. Most of these small tumours were invisible on conventional chest radiographs. See also Hasegawa et al. (2000) - 82 tumours identified in 3 year mass screening programme - were mainly slowly growing adenocas.
Wang et al. (2000), from Japan : Retrospective study of 12 peripheral lung tumours of rapid growth - 7 (3 small cell, 3 adenocas. & 1 squam.) had a well defined homogenous soft tissue density of spicular or lobulated margin; 2 adenocas. had irregular edges & 1 adenoca an air bronchogram + a small cavity; 3 well diff. adenocas. had infiltrative (or lepidic) growth pattern with ground-glass densities.
Yang et al. (2001) : Visibility of small peripheral lung cancers on CXRs & CT screening - small adenocas with infiltrative (lepidic) growth were less well seen on CXRs compared with small cell and squamous tumours with expansile (or hilic growth).

Royal College of Physicians - Nicotine Addiction in Britain - Report of Tobacco Advisory Group, London, RCP, 2000.

Appendix 1 - **Radiation Dosage from Chest Radiography and Tomography, including CT.**

(a) <u>Radiography</u>

150 kV   11 ft. air-gap technique (3 phase, high-speed tubes - see p. 20.1).

	Screens	mAs	Radiation dose in mGy (1mGy = 0.01 mRad).		
			Incident	Exit	Gonad
PA view	Ca tungstate	12.5	0.15	0.015	0.008
	Rare earth*	3.2	0.02	0.002	0.001
Lat view		approx. double these figures			

* Kodak Lanex Regular screens.

70 kV 6 ft. distance (2 mm. Al filtration).

PA view	Ca tungstate	32.0	0.65	0.015	0.003
	Rare earth	6.4	0.13	0.002	0.001
AMBER 1 sec scan 150 kV		63	0.09	0.001	< 0.001

(When MMR photofluorography was used the incident dose per exposure was approx. 2.8 mGy, with 2 mm Al filter - AP views in females then not uncommonly gave a considerable dosage to the breasts).

The dose from a single high kV PA radiograph is thus much less than a weeks natural background exposure - 30 μSv (1.5 - 2 mSv or 150 mRem per year). It also corresponds to about one hours flight in Concorde - it is also interesting to note that airline crews have now become radiation workers! The RCR (April 1996) regarded the danger of a chest radiograph is roughly equivalent to that of smoking one cigarette.

(b) <u>Conventional tomography</u> (per section)

Linear - lung apex 70 kV, 75 mA		1.5 mGy
- hilum or mediastinum 100 kV, 75 mA		8.0 mGy
Radiotome - 90 kV, 75 mA		3.0 mGy

(c) <u>Computed tomography - axial and spiral</u> (a collimated x-ray beam and single slice detector arrays are used, some employing end array cells for calibration).

CT	- 120 kV, 160 mA	(342 pulses/scan)	10 - 15 mGy /slice
HRCT		approx.	12 to 15 mGy per slice.

(d) <u>Computed tomography - multislice</u> - may be used in both axial and spiral modes.
There are several differing geometric detector systems - principally adaptive arrays or matrix systems - the detectors (**not** the x-ray beam thickness per se) producing the separate images with the widths of reconstruction. In high speed spiral mode there may be a gap between the groups of spiral sections, but with high quality some end overlap of sections may occur with overlapping radiation exposure depending on the radiation and image slice widths employed. Radiation and image slice widths are very likely to be different. There are also thin septa between the detector elements.

Array scanner
(with some array scanners the detectors may not all be of similar size some being smaller at the the centre and larger at the periphery e.g. 1, 1.5, 2, 2.5 & 5mm)

Matrix scanner
(with matrix scanners the slice widths and number of sections are determined by the lines of elements used within the matrix.)

The terms   'beam pitch' = $\dfrac{\text{table feed per revolution}}{\text{x-ray beam collimation \& width}}$

            'detector pitch' = $\dfrac{\text{table feed per revolution}}{\text{data slice thickness}}$

may be employed and changing the detector pitch will change the beam pitch and dose e.g.

beam pitch = 1.5 with detector pitch = 6   (50% gap between each group of 4 slices)

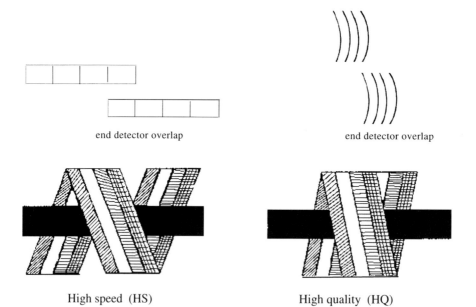

beam pitch = 0.75 with detector pitch = 3 (with end overlap).

High speed (HS)   High quality (HQ)

(Imagine a four coloured ribbon wrapped around a cardboard tube!)

Many manufacturers give an indication of CT radiation dose, either as $CTDI_w$ (weighted CT dose index) or mGy, but the author feels that the latter is much more informative to the operator and radiologist. The author also feels that dosage for CT fluoroscopy (when employed) should be indicated, as rather long times and high dosage may otherwise ensue.

Some references.

Faulkner et al. (1986) : 0.28 to 0.37 mGy for PA radiographs.
Shrimpton et al. (1986) : 0.23 mGy for PA, 0.30 for AP and 146 mGy for lateral (60 - 84 kV).
Powell (1987) : 0.0004 mGy using caesium iodide intensifier and Odelca camera.
Shope et al. (1982) : Doses outside the area of a CT slice are increased by multiple slices.
NRPB Report (Survey of CT Practice in the UK, 1992) : 'CT examinations...represent the most significant source of exposure to diagnostic X-rays for the UK population, providing approximately 20% of the revised annual collective dose from all medical and dental X-rays of about 20,000 man Sv.
Mayo et al. (1993) : Radiation dose of HRCT at 10 mm intervals was 4.5 mGy and at 20 mm was 2.5 mGy, compared with 36.3 mGy for 10 mm contiguous sections.
Shrimpton and Wall (1993) : CT - an increasingly important slice of the medical exposure of patients.
Czajka et al. (1994) : Measurement of computed tomography scanner slice widths.
Marshall et al. (1994) : Investigation into radiation dose associated with different imaging systems for chest radiography. The lowest entrance doses were obtained with scanning slit - AMBER (160), large field digital image intensifier (110), 100 mm camera (100), compared with film-screen and computed radiography (680) - figs in µGy.
Geleijns et al. (1994) : Two methods for assessing patient dose from CT - absorbed doses in the lung were approx. 35 - 50 mGy (120 kV, 100 mm slice thickness at 10 mm increment and 28 slices).
Warren-Forward et al. (1996) : Increasing the applied KV (to >90KV) and better film-screen combinations reduced the applied radiation dosage and improved the quality of the radiographs.
Diederich et al. (1996) : Use of an experimental model with post-mortem specimens - fixed inflated lungs (polyethylene glycol, ethyl alcohol and formalin - allowed study of CT protocols with irradiation of living subject (CT accounts for 40% of medical radiation).
Poletti (1996) : Dosimetry data showed a wide range of doses for similar examinations, due both to technical differences between scanners and to variations in clinical techniques e.g. for routine chest exams - 2.8 to 18.8 mSv.
Hart et al. (1994) : Estimation of effective dose in diagnostic radiology from entrance surface dose and dose area product measurements.
Wall and Hart (1997) : Typical effective* doses to standard adult pts. in the 1990s - chest PA 0.02 (range 0.008-0.03) mSv, lateral 0.04 (range 0.013-0.08) mSv, chest CT 8 (range 2.4 to 16) mSv.
  *"Effective dose" takes accord of the distribution of dose amongst the radiosensitive organs in the body by summing the individual organ doses, having weighted each one according to the relative sensitivity of the organ to radiation induced somatic or genetic effects.
Shrimpton and Edyvean (1998) : Relative dosage with different CT scanners in various body regions
Mutch, S. J. (2001 - medical physicist, Churchill Hospital, Oxford) - personal communication & poster at UK Radiological Congress, 2001.

Appendix 2 - **Threshold Visibilty of Pulmonary Shadows on Radiographs, and Perceptual Problems in Their Recognition.**

A major problem in viewing chest radiographs is that sometimes masses or infiltrates are present in the lungs which are invisible or only partly visible on the film. The author (1973) noted that in patients with widespread Hodgkin's disease who were radiographed close to their deaths, many areas of lung disease found at autopsy, were not recognised on the radiographs. Some of these measured 2 cm or more in diameter. Areas of consolidation due to infective processes are sometimes similarly invisible, whereas rounded secondary deposits are usually visible if they are > 0.5 cm in diameter.

Smaller shadows, such as linear (e.g. septal lines) or miliary shadows (e.g. TB or pneumoconiotic nodules) with a repetitive pattern visible, while much larger lesions up to the size of a collapsed lobe (for example, the right middle lobe) may be invisible on a single view, if a flat border of the collapsed portion of lung is not tangential to the radiographic beam.

Newell and Garneau (1951) radiographed Lucite objects of diverse shapes and sizes , and found that the visibility of a sharp shadow was unaffected by its size if > 0.5 cm, all simple shapes (circle, square, triangle, etc.) being equally visible. Fuzziness of the outline of an object lessened its visibility, and unsharpness made faint shadows less visible. If square or rounded lucite sheets had their edges **bevelled**, then as the bevelled edges became thinner the sheets became less visible on the radiographs, and almost disappeared, although the central thickness of the blocks remained the same. They considered that tiny shadows became visible because of their repetitive pattern and/or because of a summation of the shadows.

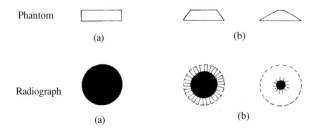

Fig. App. 2.1   Appearances on radiographs of phantoms simulating lung nodules made from Lucite sheets with (a) squared edges (like expansile or 'hilic' tumours) and (b) bevelled edges, like those of a mirror (simulating infiltrative or 'lepidic' tumours).

Coussement et al. (1984) noted similar phenomena and also pointed out the reason why the lower aspects of some ribs are indistinct, i.e. that well marked tangential borders are well demonstrated in contrast to poor tangential borders which are less well visualised.

Fig. App. 2.2 - A thinly formed tangential border makes a poorly defined edge on a radiograph.
Tuddenham (1957, 1962 & 1963) found that the perception of a lesion depends on the rate of change of illumination produced by that lesion on a radiograph when it is read, expressed as a function of distance across the viewer's retina. The 'visual stimulus' of such a shadow depends on the retinal illumination gradient that corresponds to its border, the gradient in turn being determined by the radiographic contrast across the shadow's border and by the width of the latter, or the unsharpness of the shadow expressed in terms of the visual angle it subtends at the observer's eye.
Under-exposure of radiographs is much more of a problem than over-exposure. Moderate over-exposure can be of benefit, in that the density of the lung fields will then be above unity, and mediastinal and otherwise hidden shadows may be revealed. **A chest radiograph is not a work of art**; it is merely a means of recording and recognising information. Under-exposed radiographs frequently fail to show abnormalities, which would otherwise have been recorded. With moderately over-exposed radiographs, often all that is required is a bright illuminator to bring out the information.
Minification (e.g. on digital radiographs, or photofluorograms, etc.) may not only help in reducing film costs, but also in the initial detection of disease, by simplifying the problems of visual search, in that the whole of the shadow can be appreciated in a single visual fixation. The reduced size of the image of an abnormality may also increase its apparent density. Minification can however be carried to excess on the often presented sheets of CT views, which are often too small for many observers, and really need to be enlarged to allow fine detail to be readily seen. (This applies particularly to clinicians, radiologists carrying out the examinations having the advantage of the viewing console.)

Magnification may be of considerable value in distinguishing between shadows in which the contrast difference is greater, such as those seen in studies employing positive contrast agents or on tomograms, where the contrast difference between soft tissues and gas is increased.

On chest radiographs, the contrast difference between abnormal shadows and the multiplicity of anatomical background structures is often poor, and much will depend on the viewer's method of scrutiny (see below), and his knowledge of normal anatomy, if disease abnormalities are to be appreciated. Paré and Fraser (1983) recommended viewing chest radiographs at a distance of 6 to 8 feet (or through diminishing lenses if closer).

Rigler (1969) wrote "It is common to see the statement that nodular lesions of the lung less than 1 cm in size are extremely difficult to detect and that those under 5 mm are practically never found." He radiographed patients with known primary tumours at monthly intervals to see how early he could detect a pulmonary metastasis, and on retrospectively reviewing the radiographs found that he was able to discern 1-2 mm lesions as beading along vessels.

The low density of a tumour makes its detection difficult if it is small, and even a 2 cm mass may be missed because of superposed rib shadows. High kV and a fine focal spot may permit better demonstration of small asymptomatic masses.

In order to demonstrate that the unsharpness of an object, and the presence of a well-defined edge tangential to the x-ray beam are of paramount importance in rendering an object visible on a chest radiograph, the author radiographed a loaf of bread (i.e. an air-filled cellular structure) into which three glycerine suppositories and also water-based-jelly had been inserted. It was clearly shown that the jelly which had partly diffused into the bread (and had an unsharp edge) had become almost invisible. The experiment was also repeated with CT, which was better able to resolve irregular and less well-defined borders (Illus. **APPARATUS/TECHNIQUE, Loaf of bread exp. a & b**).

The '**search patterns**' used in reading radiographs must also be considered. These are mainly of two types (a) **segmental** (or 'directed search') and (b) **global viewing** (or free search). Experienced readers commonly employ the latter, particularly when rapidly reading a series of films. They can do this quite quickly, and make very few mistakes. Some appear to have a 'photographic memory' or 'after-glow' of what they have just seen, so that they can still be noting abnormalities (e.g. to a secretary) whilst they are replacing the radiograph.

Students however need 'directed search', except for gross abnormalities, and should check every system, line etc. Success results from good training (noting at a glance if the lungs are fully expanded, all vessels, airways, ribs, etc. are present, and whether any abnormalities may be noted) **plus a great deal of experience and practice. Even experienced readers should always re-scrutinise problem areas, and areas relevant to the clinical problem.** Technical factors, such as the degree of inspiration (which should always be as maximal as possible), exposure factors, errors of positioning, processing, or due to clothing and other artefacts have also to be considered. **Double reading by two observers, also leads to greater accuracy** (but is often impracticable).

Patient's history - the author's practice is to ignore this until he has a first scrutiny of a chest radiograph. It may be misleading in some cases. He always however reviews them a second time having ascertained the history, including talking to, interrogating and clinically inspecting the patient if he is still present in the department.

(See also reference to Szamosi, 1995 - p. 24.34).

Further references.

Burger (1949) : Perceptibility of details in Roentgen examination of the lung.
Hemmingson et al. (1975) : Studied the detection of 2 cm disc phantoms superimposed on normal chest radiographs at different reading distances (0.3, 1.0 and 3 m) and found that objects with a tapered border were best seen at the longer distances.
Kundel and Nodine (1975) : Interpreting chest radiographs without visual search - chest radiographs seen for 0.2 sec., and reported an accuracy of 70%.
Revesz and Kundel (1977) : Competent observers miss about 30% of pulmonary nodules.
Carmody et al. (1980) : Nodules with sharper edges were identified quicker than those with less sharp edges, but segmental search did not increase the probability of nodule detection and resulted in more false-positives.

Szamosi (1980) : Studied the reproducibility of pulmonary structures on chest radiographs in relation to the degree of inspiration, pulmonary vessels, heart failure, etc.

Christensen et al. (1981) : Search time is important for the recognition of subtle changes; experienced readers conclude their search while they are still making positive observations.

Kundel (1981) : Although the visibility limit of soft tissue lung nodules is 3 mm, lung tumours are rarely detected until they are 8 - 10 mm in size - the size most observers can differentiate them from other shadows or artefacts, with a 90% chance of being correct.

Parker et al. (1982) : Nodule detection was more accurate with 'guided search'.

Brogden et al. (1983) : Factors affecting perception of pulmonary nodules.

Zylak et al. (1988) : Illusory consolidation of LLL - pitfall of portable radiography - **Law of Tangent** - the eye tends to join points and lines into expected patterns.

Berbaum et al. (1990) : 'Satisfaction of search' in diagnostic radiology - this occurs when other lesions remain undetected following the recognition of an initial lesion. They studied naturally occurring abnormalities as well as simulated added nodules on 70 chest radiographs, which were read by eight experienced observers, and found that detection of such nodules resulted in a diminished accuracy with regard to the pre-existing lesions.

Gale et al. (1990) : Reporting in a flash - compared 200 msec flash viewing with viewing for an unlimited time and found the importance of a well-developed schema in interpreting radiographs and the great significance of peripheral vision in preliminary assessment of a film and in directing subsequent fixations. The study also showed that earlier work has underestimated the amount of information which can be assimilated in a single fixation.

Good et al. (1990) : Does knowledge of the clinical history affect the accuracy of chest radiograph interpretation? The results suggested that this did not affect the accuracy in the detection of interstitial disease, nodules and pneumothoraces.

Kundel et al. (1990) : Computer-displayed eye position as a visual aid to pulmonary nodule interpretation. The time spent gazing at an area on a radiograph is significantly longer for false negative diagnoses than for true negative diagnoses. A second look at radiographs with areas of prolonged visual gaze highlighted resulted in improved detection.

Kundel et al. (1991) : Searching for lung nodules - the guidance of visual scanning. The time needed to scan the image and fixate a nodule was least for nodules that were accessible to the peripheral vision. Supported a model of visual search in which the first step is global analysis. Identified targets are checked by central vision and discovery scanning then begins.

Swensson and Theodore (1990) : Search and non-search protocols for radiographic consultation.

Bass and Chiles (1990) : Visual skill - correlation with detection of solitary pulmonary nodules - **training appears to mean more than innate visual ability.**

Geddes (1992) : Kerley Pergamon Lecture.

Looking at images - the ideal viewing distance is 90 cm for a 1 cm nodule.

Reporting does the history help? - it is inevitable that reports attempting a full diagnosis will be more accurate if the clinical history is given. Descriptions are almost always useful and are **best when brief.**

Pattern recognition - the demonstration of fine morphological detail continues to improve and the combination of better imaging techniques with increasing experience may well cause some disease patterns to be defined so well that a histopathological diagnosis can be predicted.

Eckstein and Whiting (1995) : Lesion detection in structural noise.

Kundel (1995) : Medical image perception.

Samuel et al (1995) : Obvious abnormalities capture visual attention and decrease vigilance for more subtle abnormalities.

Tudor et al. (1997) : An assessment of inter-observer agreement and accuracy when reporting plain radiographs - inter-observer agreement was greater for abnormal radiographs than for normal radiographs and the strength of agreement improved with a knowledge of the clinical history.

Krupinski et al. (1998) : The Medical Image Perception Society - key issues for image perception research.

Potchen (1998) : The process of radiology includes image generation, image perception, and communication of information.

Samei et al. (1999) : The detection of subtle lung nodules on CXRs is limited by anatomical noise.

Ethell and Manning (2000) : 30% of low contrast nodules are missed due to incomplete coverage of the image by the sensitive region of the retina.

30% of high contrast nodules stand out whilst low contrast ones merge into the background.

30% are rejected as a result of failure in decision making.

Appendix 3 - **Mach Bands.**

In 1865 Ernst Mach (an Austrian physicist) discovered the visual phenomenon in which bright and dark lines appear at the borders of structures of different optical density, producing a form of visual edge enhancement. These have since been termed 'Mach bands'. they need to be considered by radiologists and others looking at chest (and other) radiographs, since they not uncommonly explain what is seen.

The eyes tend to scan radiographs in relation to what the mind knows about anatomy and applied pathology. This may enhance certain true or spurious borders, apparent densities being subjectively altered and enhanced by background densities. The effect appears to be produced in the retina by lateral inhibition from adjacent receptors and the pattern of neural networks. Mach bands are similar to the Fourier enhancement of edges by processing in computers.

Spurious shadows are produced when discontinuous structures or lines become merged, because the eyes tend to merge contours that are oriented in a similar direction. Spurious Mach band formation is favoured where there are overlapping shadows of different radiographic density.

If a structure is bordered by a white halo, this is termed a 'positive Mach band' and a black halo is a 'negative Mach band'. Positive bands are produced when a convex surface of greater radiographic density meets a concave surface of lesser density e.g. the para-spinal line, and negative bands by the reverse e.g. the aortic arch and apparent heart outline (apparent as it is really the outline of the overlying air-filled lung which is seen - see also '**loss of silhouette   sign**' - p. 2.25).

The black line around the aortic arch and descending aorta, and a similar line on the left side of the heart can also be well visualised and accentuated by digitising radiographs (see ps. 20.4 - 6) and especially the **Big Mach** with the AMBER system (see ps. 20.6 - 7 and Illus. **AMBER**).

Examples of the phenomenon in the thorax are :
   (a) Enhancement of soft tissue/gas interfaces e.g.
      (i) The left lateral border of the descending aorta.
      (ii) The various mediastinal lines, especially the para-oesophageal line, the inner aspects of the trachea and major bronchi, etc.
      (iii) A cavity within a tumour.
      (iv) The clear outline of a mass pressing into the lung from the chest wall or pleura, and particularly when the pleural layers are intact.
      (v) Accentuation of a medial pneumothorax or pneumomediastinum.
      (vi) Para-pleural intra-pulmonary lines in asbestosis (see Fig. 14.15, p. 14.35).
      (vii) Enhancement of para-spinal lines (see p. 18.27).
   (b) Spurious chest lesions produced by :
      (viii) Vascular shadows in the lungs overlying ribs.
      (ix) Spurs on ribs or costal cartilages simulating lung lesions.
      (x) Spinal osteophytes.
      (xi) The contour of a fissure, in association with collapse, appearing to be continuous with the mediastinum or a pericardial fat pad, and simulating a tumour.
      (xii) Extrapulmonary structures causing bright density changes and simulating lung masses
         e.g. on the skin, etc.
      (xiii) Simulation of a medial pneumothorax (distinguish from a true one by shading the heart with cardboard, dark film, etc.).

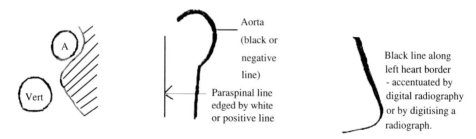

Fig. Appx. 3.1 Formation of Mach bands.

N.B. Brightness arising from outside the field of interest is a well known masking factor making lesions less readily visible.

References.
Ratcliff (1965) : Mach bands - quantitative studies on neural networks of the retina. (1972) : Contour and contrast.
Van der Plaats (1969) : 'The Mach effect is closely related to the physiological phenomenon of simultaneous contrast, which is to say that in a transition area of different brightness the eye sees the dark as darker and the bright as brighter than just outside that area...'
Steckel (1974) : The radiolucent kinetic border line in acute pulmonary oedema and pneumonia - suggested that a black line around the heart or the aortic arch, in patients with oedematous or consolidated lungs, ? due to pulsation.
Lane et al. (1976) : Mach bands and density perception.
Swischuk (1976) : Lesser known signs of **neonatal pneumothorax**.
Heitzman (1977 & 1988)
Daffner (1980) : Visual illusions in CT - related to Mach effect. (1983) : Visual illusions affecting Roentgen image.
Friedman et al. (1981) : Mach bands and pneumomediastinum.

Appendix 4 - **Some Royal Chest and Smoking Related Illnesses.**

These are interesting as they are well recorded and illustrate how four British sovereigns have severely suffered from chest disease or the effects of tobacco - (i) obesity and chronic bronchitis (ii) an empyema used to be very life-threatening, (iii) laryngeal carcinoma + an abdominal aortic aneurysm and (iv) lower limb ischaemia followed by an acute lung infection which heralded a much more serious underlying condition i.e. lung cancer.

Edward VII (King 1901 - 1910) had typhoid complicated by osteomyelitis at Sandringham in 1871. He later suffered from marked obesity and **chronic bronchitis**. He over-indulged in both food and tobacco, taking three to four meals daily, often with a dinner of twelve courses or more, and smoked twelve Havana cigars and twenty cigarettes daily. He died in 1910 following a trip to Biarritz to see if the sea air would improve his breathing (for further details see Whitfield, 1985).

George V (King 1910 - 1936) after recovering from **pleurisy and an empyema** in 1928, which almost proved fatal, died from myocardial failure in 1936 (for details of this illnesses see further notes below).

Edward VIII (King for 325 days in 1936 and subsequently Duke of Windsor) had an **abdominal aortic aneurysm** successfully resected and also a **laryngeal carcinoma**.

George VI (King 1936 - 1952) had lower limb ischaemia, for which he had a right sided sympathectomy in 1949.
In 1951 he had a **left pneumonectomy with hilar node and recurrent nerve resection*** for a lung carcinoma which was initially missed and treated with penicillin as **'pneumonitis'**.
He died four and a half months later, probably from myocardial infarction.
According to Sir Graham Hodgson (Royal Radiologist who wrote about the 1951 illness in 1972) **"the operation was six months too late"** and the King should have been investigated earlier.
A chest radiograph had been taken which had shown a 'shadow on his lung' (letter from KGVI to his mother, Queen Mary in late May - quoted by Wheeler-Bennett, 1958), but there was no follow-up.
Following treatment for the chest infection the King was advised to convalesce, which he did at Windsor and Sandringham. In August 1951 (as was usual) he went to Balmoral where the GP, Sir George Middleton (made CVO in 1951 & KCVO in 1962) felt the illness was **"more serious"** (see obituary, Daily Telegraph, 22 Oct. 1987). The King's physicians were called to Scotland, and the King returned to London. He was subsequently examined by Sir Peter Kerley (see p. 8.11), following the refusal by Graham Hodgson to use portable apparatus at Buckingham Palace, as the King ought to be examined in hospital. Kerley took a portable apparatus to Buckingham Palace, which he borrowed especially for the purpose, and later the same day the King had tomograms done at the Westminster Hospital. Bulletins of the King's illness are reproduced below.
* His Christmas 1951 broadcast had to be recorded in short bursts and was put together afterwards to try to conceal the laryngeal palsy (not so noticeable in ordinary conversation); the King also had a life-long severe stammer.

Smoking - none of the Royal Family now smokes and in 1999 Royal Warrants were withdrawn from tobacco companies by Buckingham Palace. Princess Margaret, who was almost a life-long smoker had a partial lung resection for a nodule reported as 'benign' at the Brompton Hospital in 1984, and 'pneumonia' in 1992. She has also had several more recent 'strokes'.

Further notes on the illness (empyema) of King George V (1928 - '29) and of his final illness in 1936.
    George V, following a visit to Goodwood races, caught a 'chill' which affected his right lung. In early December the nation was informed that his heart was weakening. The Prince of Wales (later Edward VIII) was summoned home from East Africa. The King became unconscious and there was a hush of a foreboding tragedy, but after a rib resection he began to recover slowly. Hopes revived, people prayed for him day and night, and gradually the carefully worded bulletins became less grave.

Royal Bulletins (+ notes from biography by Kenneth Rose, etc.).
Nov. 21 After a busy day at Buckingham Palace, the King felt too unwell to write his diary. Rather than break the habit of a lifetime, he dictated a brief entry to Queen Mary - "I was taken ill this evening. Feverish cold they called it, and returned to bed."
    22 Restless day owing to persistence of fever. Some congestion of one lung. Lord Dawson of Penn (his physician) called in Lionel Whitby (a pathologist) who found the King had a **streptococcal infection of the chest**.
    23 Quieter day - temperature lower 'no further extension of mischief in the lung'. **Portable chest x-ray by Dr. Graham Hodgson**.
    24 'The pleurisy which accompanies the type of congestion of the lung... continues to be a prominent feature.'
    25 Increase in fever. Lord Dawson later wrote "By the third or fourth day we had proved he had septicaemia, and just for public reasons were unable to say so. Not only is it an exceptionally big illness for any man to have and still more for a public person under modern conditions of Press and publicity, but this in itself presented a problem by itself occupying much time."
    26 Restless night and uncomfortable day (Temp. 101.6F).   27 Temp. lower.

28 Strength maintained. Lord Dawson, wrote 'The King was suffering from inflammation of the right lung with extensive plastic pleurisy ... Such an infection must be serious and the anxiety common to such illnesses must continue...'

29 The infective process was being held in check.

30 Some improvement but 'the time of possible exacerbation of the infection has not yet passed...'

Dec. 2 'The general strength...is...being taxed.'

3 Lord Dawson, Sir Stanley Hewitt and Sir Edward Farquhar Buzzard* (Regius Prof. of Medicine at Oxford) - 'Anxiety concerning the strength of the heart persists.'

8 **Portable chest radiography (Red Cross 'car outfit')** - neither percussion nor exploration by needle disclosed any appreciable effusion.

9 Fever persists.

10 Increased exhaustion.

12 The King had sunk into unconsciousness. 16 ounces (450 ml) of 'purulent fluid round the base of the right lung' were removed by needle puncture, followed by drainage of the right side of the chest by Sir Hugh Rigby (surgeon).

Following this and the return of the Prince of Wales from abroad, the King opened 'half an eye' and said "Damn you, what the devil are you doing here?" From then on he slowly got better but Dawson could not be certain of recovery and wrote "Safety, and still more convalescence are some distance away."

14 King's chest having 'ray treatment ' (? ultra-violet light).

[Dawson was subjected to considerable professional jealousy and Rose reports that the surgeon Lord Moynihan, after an angry exchange about the medical care of one of the royal children, taunted his adversary with this jingle: 'Lord Dawson of Penn, Has killed lots of men, So that's why we sing, God save the King.']

Jan. 22 'The time is approaching when his Majesty's removal to sea air will be advantageous.' Careful search was made for a residence not only suitable in itself but possessing the necessary attributes of close proximity to the sea, southern exposure, protection from wind, privacy and reasonable access to London.' Craigweil House, near Bognor was chosen.

Feb. 9 The King arrived in Bognor (not far from Goodwood) and the Bognor Post described the scene at Aldwick crossroads: Round the bend of the road came the ambulance at a speed not in excess of 10 mph. 'The blinds of the Royal vehicle were raised and the assembled multitude could see the long couch and the reclining figure against a billow of white pillows. For a brief moment there was sympathetic silence...then...the King waved back a greeting and the cheers would not be denied.'

Mar. 17 The King walked unaided for 50 yards, the first time since his illness began. (The Duke of York - later George VI - and his family came to stay with the King and Queen).

27 Audience with Prime Minister, Stanley Baldwin.

Apr. 19 The King gave accolade of Knighthood to Henry Seagrave (holder of the world's land and water speed records).

27 Was able to resume his personal diary.

May 15 The King returned to Windsor Castle, and on May 31st residual pus spontaneously burst out from the wound.

July 1 The King returned to Buckingham Palace and from there went to a service of thanksgiving on July 7th at Westminster Abbey. However he did not fail to remind his doctors of their shortcomings - **"Fancy a Thanksgiving Service with an open wound on your back."**

July 15 The residual empyema was further surgically drained, but the wound did not finally heal until 25 Sept., even then leaving the skin 'thin and sore.'

Nov. 19 Albert Mensdorf recorded the King's complete recovery, almost exactly a year after it's onset - "He was in a good mood and cursed as in earlier days."

* See Illus. **OXFORD PICTS, Buzzard, Sir Edward** (made Baronet following the King's recovery).

It is noteworthy that the King took almost twelve months to recover from pneumonia plus an empyema in the pre-antibiotic era. Many died from such conditions. He enjoyed his Silver Jubilee in 1935, but died from heart failure on 20th Jan. 1936 at the age of 70.

Special notes :

(i) Craigweil House was in Aldwick, an old-world Sussex village with quaint shops and winding streets - about a mile and a half to the west of Bognor - it was also in the Parish of Pagham and not in Bognor itself.

(ii) Following the king's recovery, the Bognor Urban District Council applied for the title 'Regis' to be added to the Town's name, and this was granted.

(iii) The King is also reported to have remembered Bognor on at least two occasions. In discussing his planned reprimand to the Prince of Wales (later Edward VIII & Duke of Windsor after his abdication) for his affair with Mrs. Wallace Simpson, he is reported to have said to Lord Dawson "Bugger Bognor, I'll do it here in London or not at all"; and when dying a year later in 1936, after being asked if he would like to return to Bognor to try to recover, again reputedly said "Bugger Bognor" (see Peffer, 1984). However the Times gave different final words, attributed to Queen Mary "How is the Empire".

(iv) Watson, F. (1986), Dawson's biographer, in an article describing the King's death, with extracts from Dawson's diary stated 'at about 11 a.m. the Private Secretary, having been suddenly summoned, found the King with copy of the Times...'He murmured something about the Empire...' Later that day he is reported to have said 'God damn you' to Sir Stanley Hewitt after he had given the King an injection of morphine. At 11 p.m. Dawson apparently 'decided to determine the end and injected morphine and shortly afterwards cocaine into the distended jugular vein. The King died 55 mins. later; death had apparently been brought forwards to allow its announcement to appear in the Times the following morning.

(v) Regarding the King's expletives, these had apparently been learned by the King when in the Royal Navy and when visiting troops in the trenches in Northern France in World War I. Rose reports that the King was injured when a horse suddenly reared up and threw him backwards when inspecting a detachment from the Royal Flying Corps in France in 1915. Rose also notes that 'bumping over *pavé* and shell-holed tracks for anything up to 100 miles a day, the King knew exactly what his troops expected of him.'

According to an apocryphal story from a relative of the author, the King one day became lost at the front, was blown or fell into a shell hole and was covered with mud; his rescuers asked him who he was but would not believe his claim to be the '....ing King' until they undid his greatcoat (revealing his insignia), after giving him a mugful of tea!

References.

The Times (1928 & 1929).
Young, G. (1983) : History of Bognor Regis.
Peffer (1984) : 20th Century Quotations.
Watson, F. (1986) : History Today.
Rose, K. (1983 with 1986 Postscript - reprinted 2000) : King George V.

Further notes on the final illness (bronchial carcinoma) of King George VI + Royal bulletins, 1951.

June 1   The King has been confined to his room for the past week with an attack of influenza. There is now a small area of catarrhal inflammation in the lung, but the constitutional disturbance is slight.

   4   The catarrhal inflammation ... has not entirely disappeared... he has reluctantly decided to cancel all his public engagements for at least four weeks.

  12   The temperature has been normal for the past week, and the inflammation in the lung has subsided. In view of the attacks of catarrhal infection his Majesty has suffered this year... a prolonged convalescence is essential (Daniel Davies, Horace Evans, Geoffrey Marshall, John Weir).

[The King took convalescence, but whilst at Balmoral (his normal residence for August) **Sir George Middleton, the Surgeon Apothecary or GP at Balmoral, diagnosed a much more serious condition, and a chest radiograph confirmed his suspicion of lung cancer** see Appendices p. 7. During mid September the King returned to London again and a bronchoscopy + biopsy confirmed malignancy.]

Sept. 18   During the King's recent illness a series of examinations has been carried out, including radiology and bronchoscopy. These investigations now show structural changes to have developed in the lung. His Majesty has been advised to stay in London for further treatment.

   21   The condition of the King's lung gives cause for concern. In view of the structural changes referred to in the last bulletin we have advised his Majesty to undergo an operation in the near future. This advice the King has accepted.

   23   The King underwent an operation for lung resection this morning.. (at Buckingham Palace by C. Price Thomas)....his Majesty's immediate post-operative condition is satisfactory.

   25   The King continues to gain strength. Further bronchoscopy for persistent cough in December.

1952 Feb. 6   The King, who retired last night in his usual health, passed peacefully away in his sleep at
          Sandringham early this morning.

References.
BMJ - 29 Sept. 1951.
London Gazette - 6 Feb. 1952.
Wheeler-Bennett (1958) : King George VI.
Graham Hodgson (1972).
Wright (1973).

Princess Diana died as a result of a torn pulmonary vein following a car crash in Paris on 30th
August 1997.

INDEX TO TEXT

Index

Index

Index

Index

9

INDEX TO SOME NAMES WITH ILLUSTRATIONS.